ODHAMS
CONCISE ENGLISH
DICTIONARY

ODHAMS
CONCISE ENGLISH
DICTIONARY

A COMPACT
GUIDE TO THE MEANING, PRONUNCIATION
AND USE OF WORDS AND PHRASES

EDITED BY

A. M. ALDEN, M.A. (Oxon)

ODHAMS BOOKS LIMITED
LONG ACRE, LONDON

PREFACE

THIS book, which is based on ODHAMS DICTIONARY OF THE ENGLISH LANGUAGE (edited by A. H. Smith, Ph.D., D.Lit. and J. L. N. O'Loughlin, M.A.), is more than a mere abridgment of a longer dictionary. In the first place, numerous additions and emendations to the original dictionary made by Norman Davis, M.B.E., M.A., Professor of English Language in the University of Glasgow, have been incorporated in the present work and add greatly to its value. Moreover, some modifications in procedure have been adopted, since it was desired to produce a dictionary which should be handy in size, easy of reference, and yet as complete as possible as regards both the range of words included and the information given under each entry.

The illustrations and appendices which formed an important feature of the longer work could not be accommodated in the CONCISE DICTIONARY. Also, a number of words clearly had to be omitted. In deciding which entries to delete it was considered best to leave out derivatives whose meaning was self-evident from the definitions given of the relevant root words. This permitted the retention of a large number of more unusual words which, in practice, are likely to necessitate reference to a dictionary more often than words in everyday use.

Several years have elapsed since the publication of ODHAMS DICTIONARY OF THE ENGLISH LANGUAGE, and during that period some new words have passed into use sufficiently widespread to justify their inclusion. In such cases the additions have been made.

A few hints on the most effective use of this dictionary are given below.

All headwords are printed in bold capitals, thus : **CHOP.** Permissible spelling variants are entered as headwords but are cross-referred to the headword with the preferred spelling thus : **CONNECTION,** see CONNEXION. Derivative phrases are entered in bold type and defined under the relevant headword thus : **EYE . . . to keep one's e. on,** to watch. Words which are compounded from the headword, where they do not require a separate entry, are given in small capitals under the relevant headword, thus : EYEBROW-PENCIL, cosmetic pencil. . . .

Some words of the same form have different derivations and entirely different meanings and these are listed separately; others have the same form and origin are used as different parts of speech, and these are generally grouped her under the part of speech of earliest origin. In all these cases the ntiation is shown plainly by means of a bracketed numeral, thus : **CARD** CARD (2), *n.* and **CARD** (3), *v.t.*

or an abbreviation in italic type within brackets, e.g. (*chem.*), preceding definition indicates a special sense of a word in general use. Where or abbreviation precedes the whole of the definition it indicates that ed only in relation to the subject mentioned. A complete list of the sed is given on p. vi.

onunciation on the facing page is important. It is thought that the e more readily understood and memorized than a complicated ols could be, and for practical purposes it will therefore be of t majority of users of ODHAMS CONCISE ENGLISH DICTIONARY.

A. M. A.

iv

KEY TO PRONUNCIATION

Symbol	Example	As in:	Symbol	Example	As in:
a (unstressed)	a-bet′	abet	n	nit, not	nit, knot
a	bat	bat	ng†	sing′er	singer
ā	ād	aid	ng-g	ling′ger	linger
āer	bāer	bear, bare	ngk	thingk	think
ah	pahst	past	o (unstressed)	pī′lon	pylon
ah(r)	kah(r)	car	o	a-to′mik	atomic
aw	aw′ther	author	ō	bōn	bone
aw(r)	waw(r)	war	oi	boi	boy, buoy
b	bad, kab	bad, cab	o͝o	sto͝od	stood
ch	chās	chase	o͞o	ro͞od	rude
d	dad	dad	ow	now	now
e (unstressed)	ā′jent	agent	p	po͝ot, nip	put, nip
e	bet	bet	r	rat, bēer	rat, beer
ē	dēd	deed	s	sit, si′ti	sit, city
ēer	rēer	rear	sh	shĭn, wosh	shine, wash
er*	be′ter	better	t	tīm, be′ter	time, better
f	fāer, lahf	fair, laugh	th	thingk, bahth	think, bath
g	gām, eg	game, egg	TH	THis, bāTH	this, bathe
h	hēer	hear	u (unstressed)	up-hē′val	upheaval
i (unstressed)	a′sid	acid	u	blud	blood
i	film	film	ur	slur	slur
ī	hī	high	v	ve′ri, luv	very, love
īer	fīer	fire	w	wāv	wave
j	ja′kit, rāj	jacket, rage	y	yung	young
k	kat	cat	yo͞o	yo͞o-ni′tid	united
ks	eks-klām′	exclaim	yo͞or	pyo͞or	pure
l	ba′tl, liv	battle, live	z	ri-zent′	resent
m	man, lam	man, lamb	zh	vi′zhn	vision

The stress mark (′) follows the syllable on which the stress falls.
* When this symbol precedes a vowel the r is to be sounded.
† This symbol in round brackets, thus (ng), is used to indicate the typical nasal vowels in French words or words of French origin which retain them.

LANGUAGES REFERRED TO IN DERIVATIONS

Afrik.	Afrikaans	FrCan.	French spoken in Canada	NFr.	Norman French
AmerInd.	American Indian	Fries.	Friesian	Norw.	Norwegian
Arab.	Arabic	Gael.	Gaelic	ON.	Old Norse
Ass.	Assyrian	Germ.	German	Pers.	Persian
Braz.	Brazilian	Gk.	Greek	Pol.	Polish
Bret.	Breton	Heb.	Hebrew	Portug.	Portuguese
Brit.	British	HighGerm.	High German	Provenc.	Provençal
Can.	Canadian	Hind.	Hindustani	Russ.	Russian
Celt.	Celtic	Icel.	Icelandic	Scand.	Scandinavian
Chin.	Chinese	IE.	Indo-European	Skr.	Sanskrit
Corn.	Cornish			Slav.	Slavonic
Dan.	Danish	Ir.	Irish	Span.	Spanish
Du.	Dutch	It.	Italian	Swed.	Swedish
E.	English	Jap.	Japanese	Turk.	Turkish
EcclesL.	Ecclesiastical Latin	L.	Latin	U.S.	United States
		LL.	Late Latin	Wel.	Welsh
Flem.	Flemish	Lith.	Lithuanian	WGerm.	West Germanic
Fr.	French	N.	North		

These abbreviations may be prefixed by the following : A, Anglo- ; M, Middle ; Md, Modern ; Med, Medieval ; O, Old ; Pr, Primitive.

(~) indicates indirect relationship ; (*) indicates a reconstructed or hypothetical form ; (-) before an auxiliary etymon indicates that it is a suffix ; following an auxiliary etymon, that it is a prefix. *Next* signifies that the derivation will be found under the headword following and *Prec.* that the derivation is given under the headword preceding.

ABBREVIATIONS USED IN THE DICTIONARY

abs.	absolute	*geol.*	geology	*philos.*	philosophy
acc.	accusative	*geom.*	geometry	*phon.*	phonetics
adj.	adjective	*ger.*	gerund(ive)	*phot.*	photography
adv.	adverb	*gram.*	grammar	*phr.*	phrase
aeron.	aeronautics			*phys.*	physics
agric.	agriculture	*her.*	heraldry	*physiol.*	physiology
alg.	algebra	*hist.*	history	*pl.*	plural
anat.	anatomy	*hort.*	horticulture	*poet.*	poetry
anthrop.	anthropology			*pol.*	politics
antiq.	antiquities	*i.*	intransitive	*pop.*	popular
arch.	architecture	*ichth.*	ichthyology	*pos.*	positive
archae.	archaeology	*imper.*	imperative	*p.pt.*	past participle
arith.	arithmetic	*impers.*	impersonal	*prec.*	preceding
art.	article	*ind.*	indicative	*pred.*	predicative
astrol.	astrology	*indef.*	indefinite	*pref.*	prefix
astron.	astronomy	*inf.*	infinitive	*prep.*	preposition
attrib.	attributive	*int.*	interjection	*pres.*	present
auxil.	auxiliary	*interrog.*	interrogative	*pret.*	past (preterite) tense
bacteriol.	bacteriology	*lang.*	language	*print.*	printing
bibl.	biblical	*leg.*	legal	*pron.*	pronoun
biochem.	biochemistry	*lit.*	literary	*pros.*	prosody
biol.	biology			*prot.*	protected trade-name
bot.	botany	*magn.*	magnetism		
		mas.	masonry	*prov.*	provincial
carp.	carpentry	*masc.*	masculine	*psych.*	psychology
cf.	compare	*math.*	mathematics	*pt.*	participle
chem.	chemistry	*mech.*	mechanics	*pyr.*	pyrotechny
chron.	chronology	*med.*	medicine		
class.	classical	*met.*	metaphysics	*R.C.*	Roman Catholic
coll.	colloquial	*metal.*	metallurgy	*reflex.*	reflexive
comm.	commerce	*meteor.*	meteorology	*rel.*	relative
comp.	comparative	*milit.*	military	*rhet.*	rhetoric
conj.	conjunction	*min.*	mineralogy	*Rom.*	Roman
crystal.	crystallography	*mus.*	music		
		myth.	mythology	*sci.*	science
dat.	dative			*sculp.*	sculpture
def.	definite	*n.*	noun	*sg.*	singular
dem.	demonstrative	*nat. hist.*	natural history	*specif.*	specific
dial.	dialect	*naut.*	nautical	*subj.*	subjunctive
dim.	diminutive	*nav.*	naval	*suff.*	suffix
dram.	dramatic	*neut.*	neuter	*superl.*	superlative
		nom.	nominative	*surg.*	surgical
eccles.	ecclesiastical	*N.T.*	New Testament		
econ.	economics	*numis.*	numismatics	*t.*	transitive
elect.	electricity			*teleg.*	telegraphy
eng.	engineering			*teleph.*	telephony
entom.	entomology	*obj.*	objective	*theol.*	theology
esp.	especially	*opt.*	optics	*transl.*	translation
eth.	ethics	*orig.*	originally	*typ.*	typography
ethn.	ethnology	*ornith.*	ornithology		
		O.T.	Old Testament	*uncert.*	uncertain
fem.	feminine			*unkn.*	unknown
fig.	figurative	*p.*	past	*usu.*	usually
fort.	fortification	*paint.*	painting		
fut.	future	*Parl.*	Parliamentary	*v.*	verb
		pass.	passive	*var.*	variant
gen.	genitive	*path.*	pathology	*vet.*	veterinary
geneal.	genealogy	*persp.*	perspective	*vulg.*	vulgar
geog.	geography	*philol.*	philology	*zool.*	zoology

The dagger sign (†) indicates an obsolete word, spelling or meaning.

A

A (1) [ā], first letter of the English alphabet; (mus.) sixth note in the natural diatonic scale of C major.

A (2), **AN** (before vowels and silent h) [a, an], indef. art. chiefly used to denote a noun in the singular and meaning "one," also precedes collective nouns. [OE.].

A- (3) [a], prep. compounded with verbal nouns to mean "in the act of," e.g., a-hunting; prefixed to words to form adverbial compounds, e.g., afoot. [OE.].

A- (4), pref. in Latin words, is equal to "away from," e.g., avulsion; in Greek words, is equal to "not" or "without," e.g., amoral. [Gk., L.].

A1 [ā-wun'], adj. sign used in Lloyd's marine insurance practice to place a ship in the first class as regards condition and seaworthiness; (fig.) excellent, first-rate; descriptive of the highest type of physique in military recruitment.

AARONIC(AL) [āer-o'nik(-al)], adj. connected with, pertaining to, Aaron or his priesthood. [Exodus iv. 14].

AARON'S BEARD [āer-onz-bēerd'], n. popular name for the large-flowered St. John's wort.

AARON'S ROD [āer-onz-rod'], n. the golden rod and the common mullein.

AB-, pref. from, away from. [L.].

ABACK [a-bak'], adv. to or towards the back; backwards; (naut.) blown backwards to the mast; **taken a.**, surprised. [OE.].

ABACUS (pl. **abaci**) [a'ba-kus, a'ba-sī], n. board covered with sand in which figures were traced for accounting purposes in ancient Greece; apparatus of parallel wires strung with beads, originally used by accountants, now chiefly for teaching arithmetic in kindergarten schools; (arch.) rectangular tablet functioning usually as the crowning unit of a column and its capital. [L.].

ABAFT [a-bahft'], adv. (naut.) at, on or towards the stern of a ship. [OE.].

ABANDON (1) [a-ban'don], v.t. to desert; give up; forsake. ABANDON (2), n. recklessness, unrestrained behaviour. ABANDONED, adj. deserted, left alone; continually yielding to vice, sexually unprincipled. ABANDONEDLY, adv. in an abandoned manner. [ME. from OFr.].

ABANDONEE [a-ban-do-nē'], n. one to whom something abandoned is assigned; (leg.) underwriter who accepts the work of salvaging a sunken ship.

ABANDONMENT [a-ban'don-ment], n. act of abandoning or state of being abandoned.

ABASE [a-bās'], v.t. to degrade, humble, lower in status. [OFr.].

ABASEMENT [a-bās'ment], n. condition of being abased.

ABASH [a-bash'], v.t. to put to shame by revealing guilt, discomfit, confound. [~OFr.].

ABASHMENT [a-bash'ment], n. state of being abashed.

ABATE [a-bāt'], v.t. to diminish, lessen; deduct; v.i. to become less, decrease; fail. [OFr. from L.].

ABATEMENT [a-bāt'ment], n. act of abating; sum subtracted from an account; (her.) mark of dishonour in a coat of arms; (leg.) defeat of a writ.

ABATTIS [a'ba-tis, a-ba'tis], n. (fort.) defensive structure, barricade, consisting of felled trees with the entangled branches facing the enemy. [Fr.].

ABATTOIR [a'ba-twah(r)], n. slaughterhouse; place in which cattle are killed. [Fr.].

ABB [ab], n. yarn for the woof or warp in a weaver's web. [OE.].

ABBA [a'bah], n. father; superior official in an ecclesiastical order. [Aramaic].

ABBACY [a'ba-si], n. tenure, rank and jurisdiction of an abbot.

ABBATIAL [a-bā'shal], adj. pertaining to an abbey or an abbot. [L.].

ABBÉ [a'bā], n. abbot; title of respect given to a French priest. [Fr.].

ABBESS [a'bes], n. mother superior of a nunnery. [OFr.].

ABBEY [a'bi], n. society of people of either sex, forgoing marriage, living in seclusion, and devoting their lives to religion; edifice in which such a group resides; church belonging, or formerly attached, to

such a society; private residence, once an abbey. [OFr.].

ABBOT [a'bot], n. male superior or head of an abbey or monastery. ABBOTSHIP, n. office and responsibilities of an a. [OE. from L.].

ABBREVIATE (1) [a-brē'vi-āt], v.t. to shorten; curtail; abridge. ABBREVIATE (2) [a-brē'vi-at], adj. (nat. hist.) short. ABBREVIATOR, n. person who abridges. [L.].

ABBREVIATION [a-brē-vi-ā'shn], n. act of shortening; one letter or a few used to denote a word or phrase; (math.) process of reducing fractions to their lowest terms; (mus.) one or more short strokes on the tail of a note to mark it as a quaver etc.

ABC [ā-bē-sē'], n. popular abbreviation for the alphabet, more particularly a book for children illustrating the alphabet; basic principles or essentials of a subject; railway time-table with the place-name entries in alphabetical order.

ABDICATE [ab'di-kāt], v.t. to resign from a position; renounce power; withdraw a claim or right; give up the right of exercising regal power. ABDICATIVE [ab'di-ka-tiv, ab-di'ka-tiv], adj. signifying or causing abdication. [L.].

ABDICATION [ab-di-kā'shn], n. act of abdicating.

ABDOMEN [ab-dō'men, ab'do-men], n. (anat.) the belly; lower part of a body, animal or human, including the intestines and stomach, liver and gall-bladder, pancreas and spleen; (entom.) posterior part of an insect. [L.].

ABDOMINAL [ab-do'mi-nal], adj. pertaining to, belonging to or placed in, the belly. ABDOMINALLY [ab-do'mi-na-li], adv. with reference to the abdomen.

ABDUCT [ab-dukt'], v.t. to lead away; kidnap; carry off by force or trickery.

ABDUCTION [ab-duk'shn], n. act of drawing or leading away; (leg.) forcible or fraudulent carrying off of a person, particularly of a child or ward or wife. [~L.].

ABDUCTOR [ab-duk'ter], n. person who abducts another; (anat.) any muscle which retracts a part of the body.

ABEAM [a-bēm'], adv. (naut.) at right angles to the ship's keel in the horizontal plane; facing the centre of the ship's hull; abreast of. [OE.].

ABECEDARIAN (1) [ā-bē-sē-dāer'i-an], adj. alphabetical; elementary. ABECEDARIAN (2), n. person learning or teaching the alphabet. [ABC].

ABED [a-bed'], adv. in one's bed. [OE.].

ABELE [a-bēl'], n. the white poplar. [LL.].

ABELMOSK [ā'bel-mosk], n. variety of the Syrian mallow. [Arab.].

ABERDEEN TERRIER [a-ber-dēn-te'ri-er], rough-haired variety of terrier, the Scotch terrier.

ABERDEVINE [a'ber-de-vīn], n. bird similar to the goldfinch. [Unkn.].

ABERDONIAN [a-ber-dō'ni-an], n. and adj. a native or inhabitant of, belonging or appertaining to, Aberdeen.

ABERRANCE [a-be'rans], n. deviation; mistake; moral lapse; (geom.) deviation of a line outside or inside its circular progression. [L.].

ABERRANT [a-be'rant], adj. straying from the right path, lapsing morally; (biol. and bot.) abnormal, materially deviating from type.

ABERRATION [a-be-rā'shn], n. act of departing from the normal or correct line or course; mental, emotional or moral lapse; intellectual deviation; (astron.) to an observer, a slight apparent movement of the fixed stars; (opt.) deviation of light rays not converging in one focus by refraction or reflection; (biol.) material deviation from type.

ABET (pres. pt. **abetting**, pret. and p.pt. **abetted**) [a-bet'], v.t. to help, encourage, incite illegal or immoral action; instigate. ABETTOR, -ER, n. person who abets; (leg.) confederate, accessory to a crime. [ME.].

ABEYANCE [a-bā'yans], n. remission, interruption, suspension; condition of temporary expectancy or suppression, esp. used of hereditary titles in legal practice. ABEYANT, adj. in a. [OFr.].

ABHOR [ab-haw(r)'], v.t. to feel intense loathing and hatred for; recoil in revulsion and horror from.

ABHORRER, *n.* one who loathes a person or object; (*pl.*) Tories who requested Charles II not to recall Parliament in 1679. [L.].

ABHORRENCE [ab-ho'rens], *n.* detestation; abomination.

ABHORRENT [ab-ho'rent], *adj.* repellent, loathsome, hateful. ABHORRENTLY, *adv.* with abhorrence; in a detestable manner.

ABIDE (*pret. and p.pt.* **abode, abided**) [a-bīd'], *v.t.* to endure; permit; await; be prepared for; *v.i.* to remain; live in a place for a time; **to a. by,** to accept, adhere to (a rule, decision etc.). ABIDER, *n.* person living in a place, or who remains in a place. [OE.].

ABIDING [a-bī'ding], *adj.* permanent; enduring. ABIDINGLY, *adv.* in an a. way.

ABIGAIL [a'bi-gāl], *n.* woman's name in the Bible; (*coll.*) lady's maid or lady-in-waiting. [Heb., 1 Samuel xxv].

ABILITY [a-bi'li-ti], *n.* power, physical or mental capability; faculty of understanding; skill or competence in performance; efficiency; **to the best of one's a.,** to the limit of one's capacity, as well as possible. [~OFr.].

ABIOGENESIS [a-bī-o-je'ni-sis], *n.* theory of spontaneous generation. ABIOGENETIC [a-bī-ō-je-ne'tik], *adj.* relating to spontaneous generation. ABIOGENIST [a-bī-o'je-nist], *n.* one believing in the doctrine of a. [Gk.].

ABJECT (1) [ab'jekt], *adj.* miserably reduced in means and condition; worthless; servile; vile; contemptible. ABJECT (2), *n.* an outcast; person accepting the most wretched and miserable conditions of life. ABJECTLY, *adv.* in an a. way. ABJECTNESS, *n.* condition of being a. [L.].

ABJECTION [ab-jek'shn], *n.* state of moral and emotional depression; degradation; low condition. [~L.].

ABJURATION [ab-jŏŏ-rā'shn], *n.* act of abjuring; denial on oath; **a. of the realm,** the taking of a solemn oath to leave one's country. [~L.].

ABJURE [ab-jŏŏr'], *v.t.* to renounce upon oath; relinquish one's sworn allegiance; disclaim, abandon, retract; recant a statement or belief. ABJUREMENT, *n.* renunciation; repudiation. [L.].

ABLATION [a-blā'shn], *n.* act of taking away or removing; (*geol.*) melting away of the surface of a glacier, or wearing away of rock through the action of water; (*surg.*) removal of part of the body by a surgical operation. [~L.].

ABLATIVE [ab'la-tiv], *n.* name given to the grammatical case in certain languages denoting *time* or *direction from.* [L.].

ABLAUT [ab'lowt], *n.* (*philol.*) vowel change, other than that caused by the influence of neighbouring sounds, occurring in certain words having the same base, e.g., ring, rang, rung. [Germ.].

ABLAZE [a-blāz'], *adj.* on fire, in a blaze; (*fig.*) shining with dazzling brilliance; in a state of extreme excitement, thoroughly roused.

ABLE [ā'bl], *adj.* having physical or mental power to do a thing, equipped with the means or ability, or in a position to do something (usually specified); competent, adept at, skilful, clever; (*leg.*) qualified by law for a position or office, legally entitled to. ABLY, *adv.* in a. fashion. [OFr. from L.].

ABLE-BODIED [ā-bl-bo'did], *adj.* physically fit and robust, well fitted for physical or manual labour, strong and vigorous; **a. seaman,** a naval rating.

ABLEGATE [ab'li-gāt], *n.* Papal envoy, *esp.* the bearer of the Red Hat to a newly appointed cardinal. [L.].

ABLET [ab'let], *n.* small river fish, the bleak. [Fr. from LL.].

ABLOOM [a-blŏŏm'], *adj. and adv.* in bloom, flowering. [ME.].

ABLUTION [a-blŏŏ'shn], *n.* act of cleansing; particularly a washing of the fingers before participating in a religious ceremony such as the celebration of the Eucharist; water used for such a cleansing; water and wine which the priest, after Communion, pours over the chalice and his fingers. ABLUTIONARY, *adj.* related to a. [L.].

ABNEGATE [ab'ni-gāt], *v.t.* to renounce; deny; relinquish; forbear. [L.].

ABNEGATION [ab-ni-gā'shn], *n.* renunciation; denial, disavowal.

ABNEURAL [ab-nyŏŏ'ral], *adj.* belonging or appertaining to the part of the system opposite to the main nerve ganglion. [AB- and NEURAL].

ABNORMAL [ab-naw'mal], *adj.* not conforming to type, rule or form; exceptional, peculiar; freakish. ABNORMALLY, *adv.* in an a. way. [L.].

ABNORMALITY [ab-naw-ma'li-ti], *n.* condition of being abnormal.

ABNORMITY [ab-naw'mi-ti], *n.* abnormality, monstrosity.

ABOARD (1) [a-bawd'], *adv.* (*naut.*) into or inside a ship; **hard a., close a.,** alongside; **to fall a.,** to collide with the side of a vessel; **to go a.,** to embark; **all a.,** command giving warning of immediate departure of a ship or vehicle. ABOARD (2), *prep.* (*naut.*) on board.

ABODE (1) [a-bōd'], *n.* permanent or temporary dwelling, residence; house; **to take up an a.,** to go to stay in. [ABIDE]. ABODE (2), *pret.* of ABIDE. [OE.].

ABOIL [a-boil'], *adv.* boiling; in a raging emotion.

ABOLISH [a-bo'lish], *v.t.* to destroy; annul; cancel; dissolve; repudiate; declare null and void; wipe out completely. ABOLISHABLE, *adj.* fit to be abolished. ABOLISHMENT, *n.* abolition. [~Fr.].

ABOLITION [a-bo-li'shn], *n.* act of abolishing; fact of being abolished; cancellation of the existence of laws, practices etc. ABOLITIONAL, *adj.* concerned with the a. of slavery. [~L.].

ABOLITIONIST [a-bo-li'shn-ist], *n.* (*hist.*) person who wished to abolish slavery. ABOLITIONISM, *n.* doctrine held by an a.

ABOMASUS [a-bo-mā'sus], *n.* fourth stomach of animals that chew the cud. [L.].

ABOMINABLE [a-bo'mi-na-bl], *adj.* foul, hateful, detestable. ABOMINABLENESS, *n.* quality or state of being a. ABOMINABLY, *adv.* in an a. way; excessively.

ABOMINATE [a-bo'mi-nāt], *v.t.* to detest, abhor, hate; dislike. [L.].

ABOMINATION [a-bo-mi-nā'shn], *n.* act of abominating, repugnance, antipathy; the thing loathed; a disgusting action.

ABORIGINAL (1) [a-bo-ri'ji-nal], *adj.* of the beginning; original; indigenous, applied to the native and natural plants, animals and inhabitants of a territory. ABORIGINAL (2) (*pl.* ABORIGINES) [a-bo-ri'ji-nal, 'nēz], *n.* an original and primitive native of a territory; applied to the flora and fauna native to the soil of a particular country. [AB- and ORIGINAL].

ABORT [a-bawt'], *v.i.* to miscarry, give birth to a child before the natural time; (*fig.*) of plans and processes, fail to come to the intended conclusion. [L.].

ABORTION [a-baw'shn], *n.* miscarriage, premature birth of a child; foetus delivered ill-formed and, perhaps, dead; whatever fails to mature, or is stunted in growth; monstrosity; (*leg.*) procuration of a deliberate miscarriage. ABORTIONIST, *n.* person procuring a.

ABORTIVE [a-baw'tiv], *adj.* unsuccessful, premature; (*biol.*) imperfectly developed. ABORTIVELY, *adv.* immaturely; prematurely; untimely; fruitlessly. ABORTIVENESS, *n.* condition of being a.

ABOULIA [a-bŏŏ'li-ah], *n.* (*path.*) loss of will-power. [Gk.].

ABOUND [a-bownd'], *v.i.* to have plenty, be plentiful, teem, possess a large quantity, used both of natural things and inherent qualities. ABOUNDING, *adj.* in abundance, plentiful. [OFr.].

ABOUT (1) [a-bowt'], *adv.* nearly, approximately, almost, thereabouts; here, there; around, in a circle; **a. turn,** (*milit.*) turn and face the opposite direction. ABOUT (2), *prep.* around; close to, on the verge of; with regard to, relating to, concerning. ABOUT (3), *v.t.* to place (a ship) on a different tack. [OE.].

ABOVE (1) [a-buv'], *adv.* in a higher place, overhead, on high, in heaven; higher in thought, power, motion or rank; before. ABOVE (2), *prep.* superior to or higher than; surpassing in number, quality or quantity; beyond, over all; **a. all,** before everything else; **to be a. oneself,** to be over-confident, conceited; **a. par,** larger or finer than normal. ABOVE (3), *adj.* preceding; previous. ABOVE (4), *n.* heaven; the aforesaid, aforementioned. [OE.].

ABOVEBOARD [a-buv'bawd], *adj.* fair, honest, frank.

ABRACADABRA [ab-ra-ka-dab'rah], *n.* spell, charm; meaningless incantation, mumbo-jumbo, used to charm away evil and disease. [Unkn.].

ABRADE [a-brād'], *v.t.* to wear away, rub off, by continual grazing, by friction; scrape away, file. ABRADANT, *n.* substance which will effect abrasion. [L.].

ABRASION [a-brā'zhn], *n.* friction, act of wearing

or rubbing away; a wound so caused. **ABRASIVE**, *adj.* tending to cause a.

ABREAST [a-brest'], *adv.* alongside, side by side, in a line; (*fig.*) up to date.

ABRIDGE [a-brij'], *v.t.* to lessen, reduce, shorten, compress, abbreviate; retrench; deprive. [ME. from OFr.].

ABRIDG(E)MENT [a-brij'ment], *n.* epitome, précis, synopsis, abbreviation.

ABROACH [a-brōch'], *adv.* opened up, broached, as of a cask; set at an angle to tap the cask of its liquor.

ABROAD [a-brawd'], *adv.* widely, at large over a wide area; distant, far away; beyond the bounds of, overseas, in foreign lands; current; (*fig.*) uncertain, confused. [ME.].

ABROGATE [ab'ro-gāt], *v.t.* to repeal by authority; annul, cancel. **ABROGABLE** [ab'ro-ga-bl], *adj.* capable of being abrogated. **ABROGATION** [ab-ro-gā'shn], *n.* act of abrogating. [L].

ABRUPT [a-brupt'], *adj.* steep, precipitous; sudden, unexpected, startling; uncivil, brusque, short; (*bot.*) terminated abruptly; (*geol.*) suddenly breaking out. **ABRUPTION** [a-brup'shn], *n.* sharp, sudden or violent separation. **ABRUPTLY**, *adv.* in an a. way. **ABRUPTNESS**, *n.* state of being a. [L.].

ABSCESS [ab'sis], *n.* inflamed gathering of pus in a part or organ of the body. [L.].

ABSCISSA (*pl.* **abscissae**) [ab-si'sah, 'sē], *n.* (*geom.*) a line cut off, more particularly, a part of the diameter or transverse axis of a conic section intercepted between any fixed point and a semi-ordinate. [L.].

ABSCISSION [ab-si'zhn], *n.* a cutting off; state of being cut off, severance; (*surg.*) amputation; (*rhet.*) sudden stop in the middle of a sentence. [~L.].

ABSCOND [ab-skond'], *v.i.* to leave a place abruptly and secretly, flee in order to evade the law. **ABSCONDENCE**, *n.* act of hiding; concealment. **ABSCONDER**, *n.* one who absconds. [L.].

ABSENCE [ab'sens], *n.* state of being absent, not present, state of being away; non-existence; period when some person or thing is away; distraction, inattention; (*leg.*) failure to attend court.

ABSENT (1) [ab'sent], *adj.* not present, away from a place, missing; non-existent; mentally distracted, inattentive. **ABSENT** (2) [ab-sent'], *v. reflex.* to keep (oneself) deliberately in another place. **ABSENTLY**, *adv.* absent-mindedly, forgetfully. [L.].

ABSENTEE [ab-sen-tē'], *n.* one who is not present, particularly when it is a duty to be present; person who does not live at home, or who resides apart from the position or district which is his source of income. **ABSENTEEISM**, *n.* residence apart from one's estate; practice of absenting oneself from work.

ABSENT-MINDED [ab-sent-min'did], *adj.* forgetful, preoccupied, not paying direct attention. **ABSENT-MINDEDLY**, *adv.* in an a. way, without paying attention. **ABSENT-MINDEDNESS**, *n.* state of being a.

ABSINTH [ab'sinth], *n.* wormwood, plant of bitter flavour with tonic properties; French liqueur having among its ingredients wormwood oils, anise and some aromatics. **ABSINTHIAL**, *adj.* similar to, or consisting of a. **ABSINTHIATED**, *adj.* impregnated with a. **ABSINTHIC**, *adj.* obtained from, or containing, a. [L.].

ABSINTHE [ab'sa(ng)t], *n.*, see ABSINTH. [Fr.].

ABSOLUTE (1) [ab'so-l(y)ōot], *adj.* unconditional, complete, unqualified, not governed, unlimited; complete in itself, unequivocal, not relative, self-existent; perfect, pure, unmixed; unlimited in power, supreme, despotic; positive, real, definite, certain. **ABSOLUTE** (2), *n.* that which is complete in itself; the self-dependent and self-existent being, force or cause of things; the infinite. **ABSOLUTELY**, *adv.* in an a. way; (*coll.*) very, entirely. [L.].

ABSOLUTION [ab-so-l(y)ōo'shn], *n.* remission of sin after confession and repentance by a Catholic; act of declaring such remission after repentance by a Protestant; (*leg.*) judge's declaration of acquittal. [L.].

ABSOLUTISM [ab'so-l(y)ōo-tizm], *n.* condition of being absolute; political doctrine the central principle of which is the necessity for an absolute ruler; (*theol.*) theory of predestination. **ABSOLUTIST** (1), *n.* person supporting or agreeing with the first principle of a.; (*philos.*) thinker who equates object with subject. **ABSOLUTIST** (2), *adj.* despotic, dictatorial or arbitrary.

ABSOLVE [ab-zolv'], *v.t.* to grant freedom from duty, oath, sin, guilt, obligation; (*eccles.*) grant absolution to. [L.].

ABSORB [ab-sawb'], *v.t.* to take in, eat or drink; suck up; swallow; (*fig.*) assimilate ideas, understand; occupy completely, take possession of the mind. **ABSORBED**, *adj.* deeply engaged in; engrossed. **ABSORBEDLY** [ab-saw'bid-li], *adv.* in absorbed fashion. [L.].

ABSORBABLE [ab-saw'ba-bl], *adj.* able to be absorbed. **ABSORBABILITY** [ab-saw-ba-bi'li-ti], *n.* quality of being a.

ABSORBEFACIENT (1) [ab-saw-bi-fa'shent], *adj.* inclined to cause absorption. **ABSORBEFACIENT** (2), *n.* (*med.*) agent which promotes absorption.

ABSORBENT (1) [ab-saw'bent], *adj.* imbibing, sucking in; able to absorb; spongy. **ABSORBENT** (2), *n.* that which absorbs liquid; (*chem.*) any substance which can take in moisture from the atmosphere; (*med.*) any substance capable of absorbing abdominal acids. [~L.].

ABSORBING [ab-saw'bing], *adj.* engrossing, fully occupying the attention, interesting. **ABSORBINGLY**, *adv.* in an a. way.

ABSORPTION [ab-sawp'shn], *n.* act of absorbing; condition of being absorbed; process of sucking in liquid; (*fig.*) mental preoccupation; (*physiol.*) assimilation through the blood, tissues or lymphatic matter of the body; (*chem.*) transformation, by fusion with another substance, of a gaseous liquid into a fluid or solid.

ABSORPTIVE [ab-sawp'tiv], *adj.* able to absorb.

ABSTAIN [ab-stān'], *v.i.* to forbear, avoid, hold back from, refrain, particularly from food or drink or strong desires, or from voting. **ABSTAINING** (1), *n.* abstention, *esp.* from alcohol. **ABSTAINING** (2), *adj.* abstemious; teetotal. [Fr.].

ABSTAINER [ab-stā'ner], *n.* person who abstains, particularly from intoxicants.

ABSTEMIOUS [ab-stē'mi-ōos], *adj.* temperate, strictly controlled in satisfying the desire for food, drink or pleasure, not self-indulgent. **ABSTEMIOUSLY**, *adv.* in an a. way. **ABSTEMIOUSNESS**, *n.* quality of being a. [L.].

ABSTENTION [ab-sten'shn], *n.* act of refraining; not exercising one's right to vote at an election; abstinence, self-restraint. [Fr.].

ABSTERGENT (1) [ab-stur'jent], *adj.* possessing a cleansing quality. **ABSTERGENT** (2), *n.* a detergent. [~L.].

ABSTERSION [ab-stur'shn], *n.* act of cleansing. **ABSTERSIVE**, *adj.* cleansing.

ABSTINENCE [ab'sti-nens], *n.* voluntary self-denial; a strict allowance, or complete refusal to partake, of food or strong drink, or pleasure. [L.].

ABSTINENT [ab'sti-nent], *adj.* refraining from indulgence, *esp.* in food and strong drink. **ABSTINENTLY**, *adv.* in an a. manner.

ABSTRACT (1) [ab'strakt], *adj.* separated in thought from material associations, abstruse, mental in quality; (*gram.*) titles of various classes, varieties or orders of things; **a. idea**, (*met.*) an idea considered as such, apart from material influences and relations. **ABSTRACTLY**, *adv.* in an a. way. **ABSTRACTNESS**, *n.* state of being a. **ABSTRACT** (2), *n.* whatever is taken out; extract, summary. **ABSTRACT** (3) [ab-strakt'], *v.t.* to remove, draw away, separate; take away illegally, steal; summarize. [L.].

ABSTRACTED [ab-strak'tid], *adj.* removed, separated; (*fig.*) mentally detached, absent-minded. **ABSTRACTEDLY**, *adv.* in an a. way, absently. **ABSTRACTEDNESS**, *n.* state of being a.

ABSTRACTION [ab-strak'shn], *n.* state of being abstracted, act of abstracting; withdrawal, removal; pilfering; act or process of thinking of a thing divorced from its substance, associations, or environment, of a substance apart from its attributes, or the converse; condition of withdrawal from the physical distractions of life; state of mental seclusion; object or vision existing only in the mind; absent-mindedness.

ABSTRUSE [ab-strōos'], *adj.* obscure, unintelligible, hard to understand. **ABSTRUSELY**, *adv.* in an a. fashion. [L.].

ABSURD [ab-surd'], *adj.* nonsensical, senseless, irrational; eccentric; ridiculous, laughable, comic. **ABSURDITY**, **ABSURDNESS**, *n.* quality of being a.; something which is a. **ABSURDLY**, *adv.* in an a. fashion. [L.].

ABUNDANCE [a-bun'dans], *n.* a great quantity; profusion, full measure; affluence. [L.].

ABUNDANT [a-bun'dant], *adj.* plentiful; fully

ōo is pronounced as in food; ŏŏ as in hood; th as in *think*, TH as in *that*; zh as in azure. ~ = related to.

DSE—A*

sufficient, ample, profuse. ABUNDANTLY, *adv.* in plenty.

ABUSE (1) [a-byōōz'], *v.t.* to misuse, use wrongly or badly; pervert, misapply; maltreat; insult, revile; violate; threaten, upbraid. ABUSE (2) [a-byōōs'], *n.* misuse, a wrong or bad use; misapplication, perversion; ill-treatment; violation; an evil or unjust action or practice; a succession of insults. [L.].

ABUSIVE [a-byōō'siv], *adj.* characterized by, or practising, abuse; perverted, improper. ABUSIVELY, *adv.* in an a. way. ABUSIVENESS, *n.* quality of being a.

ABUT [a-but'], *v.i.* to border upon, lean on; end at; put two planks end to end. ABUTMENT, *n.* anything which abuts. [OFr.].

ABUZZ [a-buz'], *adj. and adv.* full of buzzing noises.

ABYSM [a-bizm'], *n.* deep space, gulf; the bottomless pit of ancient cosmogony. [OFr.].

ABYSMAL [a-biz'mal], *adj.* bottomless or fathomless. ABYSMALLY, *adv.* in the manner of an abysm; (*fig.*) profoundly.

ABYSS [a-bis'], *n.* bottomless gulf or chasm; whatever is fathomless and immeasurable; the earth in its primeval state of chaos; the formless centre of the earth; hell. [L., Gk.].

ABYSSAL [a-bi'sal], *adj.* unfathomable, bottomless; (*biol.*) pertaining to the lowest depths of the ocean.

ACACIA [a-kā'shah], *n.* genus of mimosa trees having feather-shaped leaves. [Gk.].

ACADEMIC (1) [a-ka-de'mik], *adj.* academical; theoretical; pertaining to a university. ACADEMIC (2), *n.* follower of Plato's philosophy.

ACADEMICAL [a-ka-de'mi-kal], *adj.* belonging to an academy; related to the philosophy of Plato. ACADEMICALLY, *adv.* in an a. way.

ACADEMICIAN [a-ka-de-mi'shn], *n.* member of an academy or of a society for promoting the arts or sciences.

ACADEMY [a-ka'de-mi], *n.* association of scholars and specialists formed to promote the teaching and learning of the arts or sciences; building in which such a society meets; institution for the higher branches of education above university standard; originally, grove near Athens in which Plato taught his pupils; followers of Plato's philosophy; (*Scots*) secondary school. [Gk.].

ACADIAN [a-kā'di-an], *n. and adj.* a native of, pertaining to, Nova Scotia.

ACANTHA [a-kan'thah], *n.* (*bot.*) prickle of a plant; (*zool.*) fish's fin or spine shaped like a prickle. [Gk.].

ACANTHUS [a-kan'thus], *n.* a group of prickly plants; (*arch.*) formal leaf pattern copied from the foliage of the *A. spinosus.* [Gk.].

ACARPOUS [a-kah'pōōs], *adj.* unfruitful. [Gk.].

ACCEDE [ak-sēd'], *v.i.* to agree, consent, acquiesce; succeed to; adhere (to a party). [L.].

ACCELERANDO [ak-se-le-rahn'dō], *adv.* (*mus.*) gradually quicker. [It.].

ACCELERATE [ak-se'le-rāt], *v.t.* to hasten, increase the rate of movement; *v.i.* to become or travel faster. ACCELERATED, *adj.* increased in speed; **accelerated motion,** (*mech.*) a movement consistently changing its velocity; **accelerated force,** force acquired by a body as a result of the increased speed of its progression. ACCELERATIVE, *adj.* tending to increase velocity. [L.].

ACCELERATION [ak-se-le-rā'shn], *n.* act of accelerating; state or condition of being accelerated; increase of speed; (*mech.*) increase in a body's rate of movement per unit of time.

ACCELERATOR [ak-se'le-rā-ter], *n.* whatever accelerates or causes acceleration; (*eng.*) device used to control the speed of running of an internal-combustion engine.

ACCELEROGRAPH [ak-se'le-rō-grahf], *n.* (*phys.*) apparatus for measuring the pressure which is the result of an explosion taking place in a confined space. [L. and GRAPH].

ACCELEROMETER [ak-se-le-ro'mi-ter], *n.* instrument for measuring pressure of gas on any section of a gun; (*aeron.*) device for measuring the acceleration of an aircraft. [L. and METER].

ACCENT (1) [ak'sent], *n.* a style of speech, lingual expression, pronunciation; a particular pitch, tone or stress of speech, modulation of the voice expressive of emotion; (*phon. and mus.*) stress on a word or syllable or note; mark used to denote stress or vowel quality. ACCENT (2) [ak-sent'], *v.t.* to mark by a.; mark the beat; emphasize. ACCENTUAL [ak-sen'tyōō-al], *adj.* characterized by a. [L.].

ACCENTOR [ak-sen'ter], *n.* singer taking the leading part; (*ornith.*) hedge-warbler, hedge sparrow.

ACCENTUATE [ak-sen'tyōō-āt], *v.t.* to speak a word or syllable with emphasis; mark by accents; (*fig.*) give prominence to, lay stress on. [MedL.].

ACCENTUATION [ak-sen-tyōō-ā'shn], *n.* act of marking or pronouncing accents, of giving emphasis.

ACCEPT [ak-sept'], *v.t.* to assent, concur; admit; grant, concede, acquiesce, agree to permit; receive, agree to take; (*leg.*) acknowledge responsibility for; (*comm.*) agree to pay. ACCEPTED, *adj.* received, admitted, uncontested. [L.].

ACCEPTABLE [ak-sep'ta-bl], *adj.* worthy of acceptance, desirable; pleasing, welcome. ACCEPTABILITY, ACCEPTABLENESS [ak-sep-ta-bi'li-ti, ak-sep'ta-bl-nes], *n.* quality of being a. ACCEPTABLY, *adv.* in an a. way.

ACCEPTANCE [ak-sep'tans], *n.* the agreeing to take or receive; compliance with, agreement to, conditions of an offer; favourable reception; (*leg.*) acknowledgment of responsibility; (*comm.*) agreement to pay for; the record of such agreement.

ACCEPTATION [ak-sep-tā'shn], *n.* the normal and acknowledged sense or meaning of an expression or word. [LL.].

ACCEPTER, ACCEPTOR [ak-sep'ter, 'tor], *n.* one who accepts; (*comm.*) person who accepts a bill of exchange.

ACCESS [ak'ses], *n.* approach to a person or place; means of approach, opportunity of admission to; outburst (of emotion). ACCESSIBLE [ak-se'si-bl], *adj.* able to be approached; easy of approach. ACCESSIBILITY [ak-se-si-bi'li-ti], *n.* quality of being a. ACCESSIBLY, *adv.* so as to be a. [L.].

ACCESSARY [ak-se'sa-ri], *n. and adj.* (the usual form applied to persons) see ACCESSORY. ACCESSARILY, *adv.* in the fashion of an a. ACCESSARINESS, *n.* state of being accessory. [L.].

ACCESSION [ak-se'shn], *n.* act of coming, a coming to, approach, the attaining to an office, dignity, strength or state, *esp.* of a sovereign; whatever is added, an addition, augmentation; an acquisition; (*leg.*) increment in value of property on account of attendant development, growth or labour. ACCESSIONAL, *adj.* additional. [L.].

ACCESSORY (1) [ak-se'se-ri], *adj.* contributing, secondary; additional; subordinate to the main purpose or plan; helpful to the chief person as object. ACCESSORY (2), ACCESSARY, *n.* accomplice; secondary element contributing to a general effect; inessential, subordinate, but useful device or detail added to the main body or design; (*leg.*) person guilty of aiding and abetting a criminal or protecting him from the police; (*paint. and sculp.*) decorative additions to the main theme or composition. ACCESSORIAL [ak-se-saw'ri-al], *adj.* belonging to an a. [L.].

ACCIDENCE [ak'si-dens], *n.* (*gram.*) that part of grammar which is concerned with the various terminations in the declension or conjugation of words. [OFr.].

ACCIDENT [ak'si-dent], *n.* unexpected event or unintended action, unpremeditated act, apparently illogical occurrence, mishap, casualty, calamity; (*logic*) non-essential quality, property, power or attribute; (*her.*) unessential mark in a coat of arms. [L.].

ACCIDENTAL (1) [ak-si-den'tal], *adj.* happening unexpectedly or by chance; not essential, incidental, extrinsic. ACCIDENTAL (2), *n.* non-essential property or attribute; (*mus.*) incidental semitone not proper to the tonic key; sign used in musical notation before the note to be raised or lowered a semitone. ACCIDENTALLY, *adv.* in an a. way. ACCIDENTALNESS, *n.* quality of being a.

ACCIPITER [ak-si'pi-ter], *n.* (*zool.*) member of a group of birds of prey, including goshawks, eagles, falcons; (*surg.*) dressing for the nose, in the shape of a claw. ACCIPITRAL, ACCIPITRINE, *adj.* rapacious; belonging to birds of prey. [L.].

ACCLAIM (1) [a-klām'], *v.t.* to applaud loudly, signify joy or pleasure by cheering, show approval; shout, clap the hands. ACCLAIM (2), *n.* applause, acclamation. [L.].

ACCLAMATION [ak-la-mā'shn], *n.* applause, cheer of approval.

ACCLAMATORY [a-kla'ma-te-ri], *adj.* expressing approval or applause by cheering, shouts or clapping.

ACCLIMATATION [a-kli-ma-tā'shn], *n.* acclimatization.

ACCLIMATE [a-klī'mat], *v.t.* to acclimatize.

ACCLIMATION [ak-li-mā'shn], *n.* acclimatization.

ACCLIMATIZATION [a-kli-ma-tī-zā'shn], *n.* act

The accent ' after a syllable = stress (u-pon'). The mark ‾ over a vowel = length (ā in made; ō in bone).

or process of getting used to an unaccustomed climate.

ACCLIMATIZE [a-klī'ma-tīz], *v.t. and i.* to accustom any growing thing, plant or animal, to a climate foreign to its nature; to become so accustomed.

ACCLIVITY [a-klī'vi-ti], *n.* an ascending slope of ground. [L.].

ACCLIVOUS [a-klī'vŏŏs], *adj.* sloping upwards.

ACCOLADE [a'ko-lād], *n.* in the ceremony of conferring knighthood, the laying on the shoulder of a sword; (*mus.*) perpendicular line across the staves connecting them. [It.].

ACCOMMODATE [a-ko'mo-dāt], *v.t.* to adjust, adapt, modify, suit; reconcile, settle differences, set right; supply requisites, equip; lend; lodge. [L.].

ACCOMMODATING [a-ko'mo-dā-ting], *adj.* fitting in with, obliging, indulgent. ACCOMMODATINGLY, *adv.* in a. fashion.

ACCOMMODATION [a-ko-mo-dā'shn], *n.* adaptation, adjustment, modification to make correspond; reconciliation; provision of requisites; loan; lodging; **a. bill, note,** (*comm.*) bill exchanged authorizing a cash loan, and not for payment of goods received; **a. ladder,** light ladder let down at the side of a vessel; **a. train,** (*U.S.*) train comprising both passenger and goods carriages, and stopping at all stations. [~L.].

ACCOMPANIMENT [a-kum'pa-ni-ment], *n.* whatever is found alongside or together with something, adjunct; symmetrical adornment; (*mus.*) vocal or instrumental part or parts complementary to the melodic line. [Fr.].

ACCOMPANIST [a-kum'pa-nist], *n.* (*mus.*) person who plays the instrumental accompaniment.

ACCOMPANY [a-kum'pa-ni], *v.t.* to attend, go with as a friend, escort; be connected with; (*mus.*) play a supporting part subordinate to the main theme or leading singers or instruments. [Fr.].

ACCOMPLICE [a-kom'plis, a-kum'plis], *n.* associate in a crime. [Fr.].

ACCOMPLISH [a-kom'plish, a-kum'plish], *v.t.* to complete, carry out, succeed in finishing, realize in practice. ACCOMPLISHABLE, *adj.* capable of accomplishment. ACCOMPLISHED, *adj.* completed; talented, cultured, skilled. [OFr. from L.].

ACCOMPLISHMENT [a-kom'plish-ment, a-kum'-plish-ment], *n.* act of accomplishing; fulfilment, completion; quality belonging to a cultured or talented person.

ACCORD (1) [a-kawd'], *v.t.* to grant, confer, concede; *v.i.* to be in agreement, be in harmony, correspond with. ACCORD (2), *n.* agreement, assent, harmony of thoughts or sounds or actions; adjustment of differences; concurrence of factors. [OFr. from LL.].

ACCORDANCE [a-kaw'dans], *n.* agreement with a person; conformity with a thing; harmony.

ACCORDANT [a-kaw'dant], *adj.* corresponding, consonant. ACCORDANTLY, *adv.* in an a. way.

ACCORDING [a-kaw'ding], *adv. normally used in adverbial phrases;* **a. to,** in a manner agreeing with, consistent with, conforming to; on the authority of; **a. as,** to the extent that, in proportion as. ACCORDINGLY, *adv.* logically; agreeably to something said; consequently.

ACCORDION, ACCORDEON [a-kaw'di-on], *n.* (*mus.*) portable wind-instrument operated on the metallic-reed principle by the wind from bellows opened and closed by the hands. ACCORDIONIST, *n.* person who plays on the a. [Invented, from ACCORD (2).]

ACCOST [a-kost'], *v.t.* to approach and speak to a stranger familiarly, or with immoral intent, speak before being spoken to; salute. [L.].

ACCOUCHEMENT [a-kōōsh'mah(-ng), a-kōōsh'-ment], *n.* childbirth, delivery; period just previous to the act of delivery, confinement. [Fr.].

ACCOUCHEUR [a-kōō-shur'], *n.* male midwife; obstetrician. [Fr.].

ACCOUCHEUSE [a-kōō-shurz'], *n.* midwife. [Fr.].

ACCOUNT (1) [a-kownt'], *v.t.* to judge, estimate, assess; *v.i.* to explain, make a satisfactory statement. ACCOUNT (2), *n.* a list, reckoning, statement, calculation or record of money matters, services or goods; bill; recital, narrative or description, explanation or statement; the grounds, circumstances; sake, behalf, interest; estimation, opinion, judgment; **current a.,** a. with a bank from which money may be withdrawn on demand; **on a.,** in partial settlement of debt; **on a. of,** because of; **on no a.,** by no means,

certainly not; **on one's own a.,** at one's own responsibility; **to turn to a.,** to profit by; **to call to a.,** to reprimand; **to take into a.,** to consider; **to give a good a. of** oneself, to conduct oneself creditably. ACCOUNT-BOOK, book in which accounts are recorded. [OFr.].

ACCOUNTABLE [a-kown'ta-bl], *adj.* liable to be called to account; responsible. ACCOUNTABILITY [a-kown-ta-bi'li-ti], *n.* state of being a.; responsibility. ACCOUNTABLY, *adv.* in an a. way.

ACCOUNTANCY [a-kown'tan-si], *n.* profession or skill of an accountant.

ACCOUNTANT [a-kown'tant], *n.* person professionally engaged to keep accounts, or to examine and audit them; person trained in keeping accounts, book-keeper. ACCOUNTANTSHIP, *n.* position or duties of an a.

ACCOUTRE [a-kōō'ter], *v.t.* to equip with costume or uniform, to dress for military service. [Fr.].

ACCOUTREMENTS [a-kōō'tre-ments], *n.(pl.)* military equipment, except clothes and arms; (*fig.*) trappings. [Prec.].

ACCREDIT [a-kre'dit], *v.t.* to invest with authority, sanction, authorize; procure credit for; dispatch as an official ambassador or envoy, provide a messenger with credentials. ACCREDITED, *adj.* having credentials, *esp.* to negotiate; **accredited agent,** authorized agent; **accredited milk,** milk guaranteed to satisfy a minimum government standard. [L.].

ACCRETE (1) [a-krēt'], *v.t. and i.* to increase by growing; join to. ACCRETE (2), *adj.* (*bot.*) fastened to another body and growing with it. [L.].

ACCRETION [a-krē'shn], *n.* increase in size by additions from outside sources; that which is added in this way; (*leg.*) process by which possessions and property left to a legatee pass on to a co-legatee after the first claimant dies; (*med.*) growing together of parts normally growing apart, as fingers or toes. [L.].

ACCRUE [a-krōō'], *v.t. and i.* to become added to, be accumulated, be increased, as of possessions, profit or damages; (*leg.*) endow with a right. ACCRUEMENT, *n.* addition; act of increasing. [Fr.].

ACCUMBENT [a-kum'bent], *adj.* leaning or reclining. [L.].

ACCUMULATE [a-kyōō'myōō-lāt], *v.t. and i.* to increase in bulk, quantity or number; amass, store up, collect. [L.].

ACCUMULATION [a-kyōō-myōō-lā'shn], *n.* state of being accumulated; act of accumulating; mass; heap.

ACCUMULATIVE [a-kyōō'myōō-la-tiv], *adj.* tending towards accumulation, acquisitive; effected by increase. ACCUMULATIVELY, *adv.* in an a. way.

ACCUMULATOR [a-kyōō'myōō-lā-ter], *n.* person who piles up or stores up anything, specifically wealth; secondary cell or battery, which can store, and later release, electric energy; apparatus for transmitting water pumped up by pressure to another machine.

ACCURACY [a'kyōō-ra-si], *n.* correctness, precision, exactness.

ACCURATE [a'kyōō-rat], *adj.* correct, exact, precise; without mistakes. ACCURATELY, *adv.* in an a. fashion. ACCURATENESS, *n.* accuracy. [L.].

ACCURSED, ACCURST [a-kur'sid, a-kurst'], *adj.* under a curse, ill-fated, doomed to disaster; execrable, deserving of disaster.

ACCUSABLE [a-kyōō'za-bl], *adj.* able to be accused, chargeable with a crime; blamable. [L.].

ACCUSAL [a-kyōō'zal], *n.* an accusation.

ACCUSATION [a-kyōō-zā'shn], *n.* act of accusing; charge of a crime or offence brought against a person; (*leg.*) indictment. [L.].

ACCUSATIVE [a-kyōō'za-tiv], *adj.* (*gram.*) denoting the objective case. ACCUSATIVELY, *adv.* in an a. way; in the a. case. [L.].

ACCUSATORIAL [a-kyōō-za-taw'ri-al], *adj.* accusatory.

ACCUSATORY [a-kyōō'za-to-ri], *adj.* making an accusation. [L.].

ACCUSE [a-kyōōz'], *v.t.* to bring against a person a charge of a crime, fault or offence, indict, arraign, bring an action against, blame. ACCUSER, *n.* one who accuses. ACCUSINGLY, *adv.* in accusing fashion.

ACCUSTOM [a-kus'tom], *v.t.* to familiarize by habit or use, habituate, make familiar, inure. ACCUSTOMED, *adj.* habitual, usual, characteristic. ACCUSTOMEDNESS, *n.* state of being accustomed. [OFr.].

ACE [ās], *n.* a unit; card or side of a die with one spot; single spot or unit itself on a card or die side;

ŌŌ is pronounced as in food; ŏŏ as in hood; th as in *think*; TH as in *that*; zh as in azure. ~ = related to.

(*fig.*) the best, highest, most expert, winner; (*slang*) expert airman; (*tennis*) unreturnable service. [L.].

ACENTRIC (1) [a-sen′trik], *adj.* not centred, intentionally not centralized. ACENTRIC (2), *n.* (*aeron.*) type of aircraft whose propeller thrust is not aligned with the centre of gravity. [Gk.].

ACEPHALAN [a-se′fa-lan], *n.* (*zool.*) specimen of a group of molluscs characterized by having no head, e.g. an oyster. [Gk.].

ACEPHALIC [a-se-fa′lik], *adj.* headless. [Gk.].

ACEPHALOUS [a-se′fa-lŏos], *adj.* headless; (*bot.*) having no style to the seed-vessel. [~Gk.].

ACERA [a′se-rah], *n.*(*pl.*) (*entom.*) group of insects without wings or antennae; (*zool.*) group of molluscs without tentacles, e.g. snails. [Gk.].

ACERBATE (1) [a′ser-bāt], *v.t.* to make sour, embitter; exasperate, irritate. ACERBATE (2), *adj.* embittered, soured. [L.].

ACERBIC [a-sur′bik], *adj.* sour, harsh, sharp.

ACERBITY [a-sur′bi-ti], *n.* astringency, sourness, harshness to the taste; (*fig.*) severity, sharpness, harshness of nature, manner, speech. [L.].

ACERVATE [a-sur′vāt], *adj.* (*bot.*) growing in clusters, compact, compressed. [L.].

ACESCENT [a-se′sent], *adj.* turning sour; partly sour or acid. ACESCENCE, *n.* souring by fermentation; the attribute of sourness. [L.].

ACETABULUM [a-si-ta′byŏo-lum], *n.* (*anat.*) socket of a bone which fits the end of another bone. [L.].

ACETATE [a′si-tāt], *n.* a salt of acetic acid.

ACETATED [a′si-tā-tid], *adj.* mixed with acetic acid.

ACETIC [a-sē′tik], *adj.* pertaining to vinegar; sour; **a. acid,** pure acid of vinegar. [L.].

ACETIFY [a-se′ti-fī], *v.t.* and *i.* to change into acid or vinegar. ACETIFICATION [a-se-ti-fi-kā′shn], *n.* process of acetifying.

ACETONE [a′si-tōn], *n.* (*chem.*) a light inflammable liquid, used as a solvent. [ACETIC and Gk.].

ACETOSE [a′si-tōs], *adj.* resembling vinegar or acetic acid; sour.

ACETYLENE [a-se′ti-lēn], *n.* (*chem.*) a colourless, strong-smelling gas evolved from calcium carbide and water and used for lighting, welding etc.

ACHAEAN [a-kē′an], *n.* and *adj.* a native of, relating to, Achaia, a state of ancient Greece.

ACHE (1) [āk], *v.i.* to have a dull persistent pain, be persistently painful; (*fig.*) feel a strong and persistent desire for something. ACHE (2), *n.* a strongly persistent pain, physical, mental or emotional. [ME.].

ACHENE [a-kēn′], *n.* (*bot.*) dry fruit consisting of a single seed-cell and case. [Gk.].

ACHIEVE [a-chēv′], *v.t.* to finish, effect an end, to perform, bring to a desired conclusion. [Fr.].

ACHIEVEMENT [a-chēv′ment], *n.* act or fact of achieving, that which is successfully completed; exploit, heroic deed, skilful act or performance.

ACHROMATIC [ak-rō-ma′tik], *adj.* colourless; (*opt.*) transmitting light without splitting it up into its prismatic colour components. ACHROMATICALLY, *adv.* in an a. way. ACHROMATISM [a-krō′ma-tizm], *n.* condition of being a. ACHROMATIZE [a-krō′ma-tiz], *v.t.* to make a. ACHROMATOPSY [a-krō-ma-top′si], *n.* colour-blindness. [Gk.].

ACICULAE [a-si′kyŏo-lē], *n.*(*pl.*) (*nat. hist.*) prickly spikes. ACICULAR, *adj.* like a needle. [L.].

ACID (1) [a′sid], *adj.* sour, sharp to the taste; (*fig.*) bitter, sarcastic; (*chem.*) possessing the qualities of an acid; **a. drop,** acidulated boiled sweet; **a. test,** final criterion of value. ACID (2), *n.* sharp or sour matter or liquid; (*chem.*) substance containing hydrogen and combining with salifiable bases to form salts, recognized by its action of turning blue litmus paper red. ACIDLY, *adv.* in an a. manner. ACIDNESS, *n.* quality of being a. [L.].

ACIDIFY [a-si′di-fī], *v.t.* to make acid; change into acid. ACIDIFICATION [a-si-di-fi-kā′shn], *n.* act of acidifying. ACIDIFIER, *n.* that which can a.

ACIDITY [a-si′di-ti], *n.* acidness; acid condition of the stomach juices causing indigestion.

ACIDOSIS [a-si-dō′sis], *n.* (*path.*) poisoning of the blood due to a superfluity of fatty acids in the system. [ACID (1) and Gk.].

ACIDULATE [a-si′dyŏo-lāt], *v.t.* to make acidulous. [L.].

ACIDULOUS [a-si′dyŏo-lŏos], *adj.* slightly sour; caustic, sarcastic, petulant. [L.].

ACIERAGE [ā′si-er-ij], *n.* process of electrically plating a metal with a layer of steel. [Fr.].

ACINACEOUS [a-si-nā′shŏos], *adj.* having clusters of berries, like the blackberry; full of kernels.

ACINI [a′si-nī], *n.*(*pl.*) (*anat.*) granulations; (*bot.*) berries in clusters. ACINIFORM [a-si′ni-fawm], *adj.* (*bot.*) formed like the a.; (*anat.*) formed in grape-like clusters. [L.].

ACIPENSER [a-si-pen′ser], *n.* the sturgeon group of fishes. [L.].

ACK-ACK [ak-ak], *adj.* (*coll.*) anti-aircraft. [Army signallers' jargon for initial letters].

ACK-EMMA [ak-e′mah], *adv.* (*slang*) Army signallers' jargon for *a.m.*, before noon.

ACKNOWLEDGE [ak-no′lij], *v.t.* to admit, own, recognize; agree, assent; reward; report receipt of. ACKNOWLEDG(E)ABLE, *adj.* capable of being acknowledged. ACKNOWLEDG(E)ABLY, *adv.* in an acknowledgeable way. [~AD and KNOWLEDGE.].

ACKNOWLEDG(E)MENT [ak-no′lij-ment], *n.* act of acknowledging, confession; report of receipt; expression of appreciation in recognition of a service or duty.

ACLINIC [a-kli′nik], *adj.* (*magn.*) not dipping, descriptive of a magnetic needle; placed where a magnetic needle will not dip; **a. line,** the magnetic equator where the needle does not respond and dip. [Gk.].

ACME [ak′mi], *n.* the culminating point, highest stage, prime. [Gk.].

ACNE [ak′ni], *n.* a skin disease, eruption of inflamed pimples due to defective functioning of the sebaceous glands. [Uncert.].

ACOCK [a-kok′], *adv.* in a cocked position.

A-COCKBILL [a-kok′bil], *adv.* (*naut.*) (of an anchor) in position at the cathead prepared for dropping; dipped to denote mourning.

ACOLYTE [a′kō-līt], *n.* (*eccles.*) layman or person in minor orders belonging to the R.C. Church who attends to the lamps and prepares the accessories during Mass; (*fig.*) attendant, follower. [~Gk.].

ACONITE [a′kō-nīt], *n.* (*bot.*) the plant wolf's bane, monkshood; poisonous drug obtained from this. ACONITIC [a-kō-ni′tik], *adj.* belonging to a. ACONITINE [a-kō′ni-tēn], *n.* poisonous extract of a. [L.].

ACORN [ā′kawn], *n.* the oak tree fruit or nut. ACORN-CUP, capsule containing the a. ACORNED, *adj.* provided or fed with acorns; (*her.*) bearing acorns. [OE.].

ACORUS [ā′kō-rus], *n.* the plant sweet-flag. [Gk.].

ACOSMISM [a-koz′mizm], *n.* disbelief in the existence of a universal order or an external world. [Gk.].

ACOTYLEDON [a-kō-ti-lē′don], *n.* a cryptogam, plant bearing no seed-leaves, as ferns and mosses. ACOTYLEDONOUS, *adj.* without seed-leaves. [A (4) and COTYLEDON].

ACOUMETER [a-kow′mi-ter], *n.* apparatus for testing and measuring aural strength. [Gk.].

ACOUSTIC(AL) [a-kow′stik(-al), a-kŏo′stik(-al)], *adj.* belonging to the science of sound, or connected with hearing; **a. duct,** (*anat.*) passage of the ear leading to the aperture; **a. mine,** sea mine detonated by sound waves; **a. nerve,** (*anat.*) nerve responding to sound vibrations. [Gk.].

ACOUSTICS [a-kow′stiks, a-kŏo′stiks], *n.* science concerned with hearing and sound; the properties of a building which determine the audibility and quality of sounds made in it.

ACQUAINT [a-kwānt′], *v.t.* to inform, communicate, familiarize; introduce; **to a. oneself with,** to make oneself familiar with. [OFr.].

ACQUAINTANCE [a-kwān′tans], *n.* slight but direct knowledge of a person or fact; person known socially but not intimately. ACQUAINTANCESHIP, *n.* condition or state of being acquainted.

ACQUIESCE [a-kwi-es′], *v.i.* to agree to, accept, tolerate; continue satisfied with; consent to. [L.].

ACQUIESCENCE [a-kwi-e′sens], *n.* acceptance, submissive assent, tacit compliance.

ACQUIESCENT [a-kwi-e′sent], *adj.* remaining satisfied; acquiescing. ACQUIESCENTLY, *adv.* in an a. way.

ACQUIRABLE [a-kwier′a-bl], *adj.* capable of being acquired. ACQUIRABILITY [a-kwier-a-bi′li-ti], *n.* quality of being a.

ACQUIRE [a-kwier′], *v.t.* to gain or obtain, take possession of; come into possession of. ACQUIRED, *adj.* attained by artificial development, practice or environmental influence, not innately possessed or inherited. [L.].

ACQUIREMENT [a-kwier′ment], *n.* act of acquiring, thing which is acquired; attainment.

ACQUISITION [a-kwi-zi′shn], *n.* act of acquiring; that which is acquired.

ACQUISITIVE [a-kwi′zi-tiv], *adj.* greedy, grasping,

The accent ′ after a syllable = stress (u-pon′). The mark ‾ over a vowel = length (ā in made; ō in bone).

excessively desiring to acquire. ACQUISITIVELY, *adv.* in an a. way; by way of gain.

ACQUIT [a-kwit´], *v.t.* to judge not guilty of a fault, offence, charge or suspicion; *(leg.)* declare free from guilt; **to a. oneself,** to conduct oneself, behave. [OFr. from L.].

ACQUITTAL [a-kwi´tal], *n. (leg.)* act of acquitting; verdict which frees a person from a charge; legal discharge.

ACQUITTANCE [a-kwi´tans], *n.* discharge from liability or debt, release from obligation; document or receipt which is evidence of discharge and prevents further debt demands. [OFr.].

ACRE [ā´ker], *n.* measure of land containing 160 square rods or perches, or 4,840 square yards; **God's acre,** churchyard. ACREABLE, *adj.* per a. ACREAGE, *n.* number of acres in a piece of land. [OE.].

ACRID [ak´rid], *adj.* sharp, bitter, stinging, biting to the taste or smell; pungent; *(fig.)* acrimonious, sharp in speech, caustic. ACRIDLY, *adv.* in an a. way. ACRIDITY, ACRIDNESS [a-kri´di-ti, ak´rid-nes], *n.* a. quality. [L.].

ACRIMONIOUS [ak-ri-mō´ni-ŏŏs], *adj.* bitter, sharp in speech, nature or temper; discourteous. ACRIMONIOUSLY, *adv.* in an a. way.

ACRIMONY [ak´ri-mo-ni], *n.* sharpness, bitterness, severity of temper, speech, manner or nature. [L.].

ACRITA [ak´ri-tah], *n.(pl.)* plant-like animals without a definite nervous system. [Gk.].

ACRO-, *pref.* topmost, used in compound words, to denote growth to the highest degree or extreme. [Gk.].

ACROBAT [ak´rō-bat], *n.* gymnast performing skilful tricks, tumbler, tight-rope walker. [Gk.].

ACROBATIC [ak-rō-ba´tik], *adj.* agile, like an acrobat. ACROBATICALLY, *adv.* in the manner of an acrobat, with gymnastic skill.

ACROBATICS [ak-rō-ba´tiks], *n.* art or practice of balancing, tumbling, tight-rope walking etc.

ACROMEGALY [ak-rō-me´ga-li], *n. (path.)* abnormal and excessive development of the extremities of the body. [Gk.].

ACROPOLIS [a-kro´po-lis], *n.* citadel, *esp.* the one in Athens. [Gk.].

ACROSS (1) [a-kros´], *adv.* from side to side, cross-wise, in a counter direction, in a position crossing at an angle. ACROSS (2), *prep.* from side to side of, from one side to another, not lengthwise, at an angle with; making a cross with; in opposition to; **to put it a.,** *(slang)* impose on someone; act a part; **to get a.,** *(coll.)* to make an effective impression; **to get, put, (something) a.,** to succeed in making one's point about (something).

ACROSTIC (1) [a-kros´tik], *n.* poem etc. with the first letters of each line spelling a word which is the subject of the poem; puzzle, of which the solution is a number of words written one above another. ACROSTIC (2), *adj.* consisting of, pertaining to, an a. [Gk.].

ACT (1) [akt], *n.* action, something done, a specific movement, deed, performance; main division of a stage play; administrative principle, law, decree; document recording the principle; **a. of God,** *(leg.)* the workings of the forces of Nature causing unavoidable and disastrous effects, such as earthquakes, floods etc.; **a. of grace,** king's pardon for an offender; generous and voluntary action; **A. of Parliament,** bill framed, passed and authorized by Parliament, which has received the royal assent. ACT (2), *v.t.* to perform (a play); play (a part); simulate, imitate, personate; *v.i.* to be in motion, do things, operate; set in motion, bring power to bear upon, influence; perform, deputize for; behave, acquit oneself; *(theatre)* of plays, be suitable for performance (well, badly etc.). [L.].

ACTING (1) [ak´ting], *n.* action, practice of the dramatic art, representation of a character in a play. ACTING (2), *adj.* functioning, deputizing for, holding temporary office; of plays, specially edited for actors' use.

ACTINIC [ak-ti´nik], *adj. (phys.)* changing chemically by the action of light.

ACTINISM [ak´ti-nizm], *n. (phys.)* action of ultra-violet rays effecting chemical change, as distinct from heat or light changes; power inherent in such rays.

ACTINIUM [ak-ti´ni-um], *n.* a radio-active element in pitchblende.

ACTINO-, *pref. (phys.)* relating to actinic rays; *(nat. hist.)* having a radiated form. [Gk.].

ACTINOMYCOSIS [ak-ti-nō-mi-kō´sis], *n. (path.)*

an infective disease produced by ray-fungus, affecting cattle and, very rarely, human beings. [Gk.].

ACTINOTHERAPY [ak-ti-nō-the´ra-pi], *n. (med.)* treatment by rays of light. [Gk.].

ACTINOZOA [ak-ti-nō-zō´ah], *n.(pl.) (zool.)* class of polyps including sea-anemones and coral animals. [Gk.].

ACTION [ak´shn], *n.* state of acting, condition of being in motion, process of operating, production of energy; operation, function; deed, exploit; conduct, gesture; organic function; series of events and incidents embodied in a stage play, thematic progress of a play or film; *(leg.)* lawsuit attempting to establish a claim; *(milit.)* battle. [L.].

ACTIONABLE [ak´shn-a-bl], *adj. (leg.)* liable to an action, offering opportunity for action. ACTIONABLY, *adv.* in a way that calls for legal procedure.

ACTIVATE [ak´ti-vāt], *v.t.* to give cause for action, stir into action, make active; *(phys.)* convert so as to be capable of producing electrical or radio-active effects. ACTIVATION [ak-ti-vā´shn], *n.* act of activating; state of being activated.

ACTIVE [ak´tiv], *adj.* possessing the power to act, disposed to action, quick of movement; constantly busy, energetic, agile, alert; practical, as contrasted with meditative; involved in, occupied in; *(gram.)* implying action done to a person or thing; **a. service,** service in the armed forces in the field of war. ACTIVELY, *adv.* in an a. manner. ACTIVENESS, *n.* condition of being a. [L.].

ACTIVISM [ak´ti-vizm], *n.* philosophical theory which assumes that things have objective existence; policy of activity. ACTIVIST, *adj. and n.* (pertaining to) an advocate of a. (in either sense).

ACTIVITY [ak-ti´vi-ti], *n.* activeness; alertness, agility; movement, business.

ACTOR [ak´ter], *n.* person who acts; one who takes a part in a stage drama, professional stage player; *(fig.)* person participating in an event. [L.].

ACTRESS [ak´tres], *n.* female stage player.

ACTUAL [ak´tyŏō-al], *adj.* real, having existence at present, in contrast to what is potential, probable or possible.

ACTUALITY [ak-tyŏō-a´li-ti], *n.* condition of being actual; reality, realism; **a. programme,** broadcast programme or feature of a documentary nature. [LL.].

ACTUALIZE [ak´tyŏō-a-līz], *v.t.* to make actual, present in real form. ACTUALIZATION [ak-tyŏō-a-lī-zā´shn], *n.* making actual or real.

ACTUALLY [ak´tyŏō-a-li], *adv.* in truth, really; as a fact; at present.

ACTUARY [ak´tyŏō-a-ri], *n.* clerk of a court; registrar; statistician and calculator of premiums for an insurance company. ACTUARIAL [ak-tyŏō-āer´i-al], *adj.* belonging to an actuary or his profession. ACTUARIALLY, *adv.* in an a. way. [L.].

ACTUATE [ak´tyŏō-āt], *v.t.* to cause to act, influence, motivate. ACTUATION [ak-tyŏō-ā´shn], *n.* condition of being actuated or influenced. [MdL.].

ACUITY [a-kyŏō´i-ti], *n.* (of intelligence) keenness; (of a point) sharpness. [LL.].

ACULEUS [a-kyŏō´li-us], *n. (bot.)* prickle; *(zool.)* sting. [L.].

ACUMEN [a-kyŏō´men], *n.* mental acuteness, keenness and quickness of perception. ACUMINOUS, *adj.* having a.; quick in perception. [L.].

ACUMINATE (1) [a-kyŏō´mi-nāt], *adj. (bot.)* tapering to a point. ACUMINATE (2), *v.t.* to sharpen. [L.].

ACUSHLA [a-kŏŏsh´lah], *n.* sweetheart, darling. [Ir.].

ACUTE [a-kyŏōt´], *adj.* sharp, keen, needle-like; perspicacious, shrewd, sharp-witted, sensitive; *(math.)* less than ninety degrees; *(med.)* severely symptomatic, as contrasted with chronic; *(mus.)* high, shrill; **a. accent,** short line (´) marked over a letter. ACUTELY, *adv.* in an a. way. ACUTENESS, *n.* quality of being a.; state of being intense. [L.].

ACYCLIC [a-sī´klik], *adj. (chem.)* containing no ring of atoms; *(bot.)* not arranged in circles. [Gk.].

AD [ad], *n. (slang)* abbreviation for ADVERTISEMENT.

AD-, *pref.* to. [L.].

ADAGE [a´dij], *n.* proverb, old saying. [L.].

ADAGIO (1) [a-dah´ji-ō], *adv. (mus.)* slowly. ADAGIO (2), *n.* slow movement or piece of music. ADAGIO (3), *adj.* (of stage dancers) acrobatic. [It.].

ADAM (1) [a´dam], *n.* Biblical name of the first man; **the old A.,** sinful human nature; **A.'s apple,** thyroid cartilage of a man's larynx. [Heb.].

ADAM (2), *adj.* built by or **in** the style of the eighteenth-century architects, Robert and James *Adam.*

ŏŏ is pronounced as in food; ŏŏ as in hood; th as in *th*ink, TH as in *th*at; zh as in azure. ~ = related to.

ADAMANT [a′da-mant], *n.* an extremely hard substance. ADAMANTINE [a-da-man′tin], *adj.* composed of a.; (*fig.*) unbreakable, unyielding. [Gk.].

ADAPT [a-dapt′], *v.t.* to make to fit, modify, alter to suit, eliminate differences. [L.].

ADAPTABLE [a-dap′ta-bl], *adj.* able to be adapted; pliable, amenable, able to conform to varying circumstances. ADAPTABILITY [a-dap-ta-bi′li-ti], *n.* possession of the power of adapting.

ADAPTATION [a-dap-tā′shn], *n.* act of adapting, thing which is adapted.

ADAPTER, ADAPTOR [a-dap′ter], *n.* person who adapts something; (*chem.*) double-necked vessel; any means or instrument enabling two or more different instruments to work together; (*elect.*) fitting to a lamp-holder which carries an extension lead.

ADAPTIVE [a-dap′tiv], *adj.* capable of, or tending to, adaptation.

ADD [ad], *v.t.* to join one thing to another, combine one number or thing with another, augment, enlarge; *v.i.* **to a. up,** (*coll.*) to make the correct total, make sense. [L.].

ADDABLE, see ADDIBLE.

ADDENDUM (*pl.* **addenda**) [a-den′dum], *n.* appendix, that which is or is to be added. [L.].

ADDER (1) [a′der], *n.* person who adds. ADDER (2), *n.* poisonous snake of the viper species; **a.'s grass,** early purple orchis; **a.'s tongue,** fern with spiky reproductive fronds. [OE.].

ADDIBLE, ADDABLE [a′di-bl], *adj.* able to be added. ADDIBILITY [a-di-bi′li-ti], *n.* capacity of being a.

ADDICT (1) [a-dikt′], *v.t.* (with abnormality) to devote oneself to, accustom, practise a habit of. ADDICT (2) [a′dikt], *n.* person who is addicted to a habit almost beyond cure. ADDICTEDNESS, ADDICTION [a-dik′tid-nes, a-dik′shn], *n.* condition or quality of being addicted. [L.].

ADDITION [a-di′shn], *n.* process or act of adding, act of combining two or more numbers into one total; the final sum. ADDITIONAL, *adj.* supplementary, extra. ADDITIONALLY, *adv.* in a. [L.].

ADDLE [a′dl], *v.t.* to putrefy, make corrupt, confuse, muddle. ADDLED, *adj.* rotten; barren, descriptive of eggs that can produce no chicks; (*fig.*) confused, muddled. ADDLE-PATED [a-dl-pā′tid], *adj.* emptyheaded.

ADDOGRAPH [a′dō-grahf], *n.* machine that adds up numbers.

ADDRESS (1) [a-dres′], *v.t.* to direct; take aim at, as in golf; direct speech to; direct a letter, parcel etc. to; inscribe with an address; deliver a speech in public; concentrate one's energies or interests; woo. ADDRESS (2), *n.* description of a direction; residence of a person; public speech or lecture; bearing or behaviour of a person in public; message of respect, formal communication; (*pl.*) attentions of a lover. ADDRESSEE [ad-re-sē′], *n.* person to whom a letter is addressed. ADDRESSER, *n.* person who, or machine which, addresses. [Fr.].

ADDUCE [a-dyōōs′], *v.t.* to bring forward as evidence, allege as proof; cite. ADDUCEABLE, ADDUCIBLE, *adj.* able to be adduced. ADDUCENT, *adj.* (*anat.*) descriptive of muscles whose organic function is to draw close together the parts of the body which they control. [L.].

ADDUCTION [a-duk′shn], *n.* act of bringing forward. ADDUCTIVE, *adj.* tending to bring forward. [~L.].

ADDUCTOR [a-duk′ter], *n.* adducent muscle.

ADEMPTION [a-demp′shn], *n.* (*leg.*) revocation of a bequest or grant. [~L.].

ADEN-, *pref.* gland. [Gk.].

ADENOIDS [a′de-noidz], *n.* (*pl.*) (*med.*) enlarged growths of adenoidal tissue near the back of the throat which affect nasal breathing. ADENOIDAL, *adj.* glandiform, shaped like a nut; (of a voice) as if affected by a. [Gk.].

ADENOSE, ADENOUS [a′de-nōs, -nōōs], *adj.* similar to, or appertaining to, a gland.

ADEPT (1) [a′dept, a-dept′], *adj.* highly skilled, expert. ADEPT (2), *n.* person expert in any art or work. [L.].

ADEQUACY [a′di-kwa-si], *n.* state or quality of being adequate.

ADEQUATE [a′di-kwat], *adj.* enough, sufficient, equal to, proportionate to, commensurate with, satisfactory. ADEQUATELY, *adv.* in an a. way. [L.].

ADFECTED [ad-fek′tid], *adj.* (*alg.*) including different powers of an unknown quantity. [AFFECT].

ADHERE [ad-hēer′], *v.i.* to stick fast to, hold to, rest firmly attached to; persevere in. ADHERENCE, *n.* quality or state of adhering; steady attachment. [L.].

ADHERENT (1) [ad-hēer′ent], *adj.* sticking to; sticky, clinging; united with. ADHERENT (2), *n.* supporter, follower, disciple. ADHERENTLY, *adv.* in an a. way.

ADHESION [ad-hē′zhn], *n.* action of adhering, condition of sticking to, the fastening of two things together by a sticky substance; persistent attachment; (*path.*) abnormal joining of parts of the body to each other; (*phys.*) tendency of surfaces to form a contact. [L.].

ADHESIVE (1) [ad-hē′siv], *adj.* sticking, tenacious. ADHESIVE (2), *n.* an a. substance. ADHESIVELY, *adv.* in an a. fashion. ADHESIVENESS, *n.* state of being a.; tenacity; power to form attachments.

ADIABATIC [a-di-a-ba′tik], *adj.* (*phys.*) admitting no heat; referring to alterations in volume on account of pressure or volatility without loss or gain of heat. [Gk.].

ADIACTINIC [a-di-ak-ti′nik], *adj.* (*opt.*) not admitting actinic rays. [Gk.].

ADIANTUM [a-di-an′tum], *n.* maidenhair fern. [Gk.].

ADIAPHORISM [a-di-a′fo-rizm], *n.* religious indifference. [~Gk.].

ADIAPHOROUS [a-di-a′fo-rōōs], *adj.* indifferent, inessential; (*med.*) effecting neither good nor harm. [*Prec.*].

ADIATHERMIC [a-di-a-thur′mik], *adj.* (*phys.*) impervious to heat. [Gk.].

ADIEU (*pl.* **adieux**) [a-dyōō′], *n. and int.* farewell, good-bye. [Fr.].

ADIPOCERE [a-di-pō′sēer], *n.* waxy substance which dead animal tissue changes into when surrounded by dampness. ADIPOCEROUS [a-di-pō′se-rōōs], *adj.* containing a. [L.].

ADIPOSE, ADIPOUS [a′di-pōs, -pōōs], *adj.* fat; fatty; consisting of or including fat. ADIPOSITY [a-di-po′si-ti], *n.* fat, superfluous fatness. [L.].

ADIT [a′dit], *n.* entrance; (*mining*) horizontal opening or tunnel leading into a mine. [L.].

ADJACENCY [a-jā′sen-si], *n.* state of being adjacent. **ADJACENT** [a-jā′sent], *adj.* contiguous, neighbouring, lying near to. ADJACENTLY, *adv.* so as to be a., in a near-by place. [L.].

ADJECT [a-jekt′], *v.t.* to add or put to. ADJECTION, *n.* act of adding, addition. [L.].

ADJECTIVAL [a-jek-ti′val], *adj.* similar to or pertaining to an adjective. ADJECTIVALLY, *adv.* by means of an adjective; as an adjective.

ADJECTIVE (1) [a′jek-tiv], *adj.* belonging to an adjective; (*dyeing*) descriptive of colours that are impermanent unless they have a base. ADJECTIVE (2), *n.* (*gram.*) part of speech, word, which qualifies a noun, describing, defining, limiting the attributes of the noun. ADJECTIVELY, *adv.* adjectivally. [L.].

ADJOIN [a-join′], *v.t.* to be next to, join on to, be contiguous to. ADJOINING, *adj.* adjacent, neighbouring. [JOIN (1)].

ADJOURN [a-jurn′], *v.t.* to postpone, put off till another day or time, suspend proceedings. [L.].

ADJOURNMENT [a-jurn′ment], *n.* act of adjourning; duration of the postponement; suspension of proceedings.

ADJUDGE [a-juj′], *v.t.* to consider, decide and pronounce a judgment; make an award of judicial deliberation. ADJUDG(E)MENT, *n.* act of adjudging; decision; award. [JUDGE (2)].

ADJUDICATE [a-jōō′di-kāt], *v.t. and i.* to adjudge, make a judicial decision; act as a judge. ADJUDICATOR, *n.* person who adjudicates. [L.].

ADJUDICATION [a-jōō-di-kā′shn], *n.* act of adjudging; judgment or decision of a court, award or sentence. [L.].

ADJUNCT (1) [a′jungkt], *adj.* joined or added to; united, associated with. ADJUNCT (2), *n.* thing added or joined to another, an associate; (*met.*) a mental or physical quality, natural or acquired; (*gram.*) word added to qualify or extend the meaning of another. ADJUNCTIVE, *adj.* joining; possessing the qualities of an a. [L.].

ADJURATION [a-jōō-rā′shn], *n.* act of adjuring; solemn appeal, earnest affirmation; form of a solemn oath to be taken. [L.].

ADJURE [a-jōōr′], *v.t.* to urge with solemn emphasis; charge on solemn oath. ADJURATORY, *adj.* solemnly urging; including an adjuration. [L.].

ADJUST [a-just′], *v.t.* to settle differences, put in

order, set straight; adapt, fit, regulate, make correspond. ADJUSTABLE, *adj.* able to be adjusted. ADJUSTER, *n.* person who adjusts. [ML.].

ADJUSTMENT [a-just'ment], *n.* act of adjusting; arrangement; settlement.

ADJUTANT [a'jōō-tant], *n.* officer not above the rank of major who aids the commanding officer of a battalion in details of duty and discipline; a. bird, a species of stork. ADJUTANCY, *n.* office and duties of an a. [L.].

ADJUVANT (1) [a'jōō-vant], *adj.* assisting, helpful. ADJUVANT (2), *n.* assistant, aid; (*med.*) substance in a medicinal compound which facilitates the action of the principal ingredient. [L.].

ADMINISTER [ad-mi'nis-ter], *v.t.* to act as agent for, manage and look after affairs as an executor; direct or apply administratively rites, principles or laws; tender or offer, as an oath; give and/or bring supplies. [L.].

ADMINISTERIAL [ad-mi-nis-tēer'i-al], *adj.* connected with administration or the executive.

ADMINISTRATION [ad-mi-nis-trā'shn], *n.* act of administering, the organizing and conducting of public affairs; management of a business; the ministry, government or board of directors, any executive body; offices, duties or commission of an administrator. [L.].

ADMINISTRATIVE (1) [ad-mi'nis-tra-tiv], *adj.* concerned with administration, executive. ADMINISTRATIVE (2), *n.* department of a government etc. concerned with administration. ADMINISTRATIVELY, *adv.* as a matter of, or by, administration.

ADMINISTRATOR [ad-mi'nis-trā-ter], *n.* person who is in charge of the estate of one dying intestate; one who directs, manages or organizes as a deputy; one who has the power or faculty of organizing or administering. ADMINISTRATORSHIP, *n.* duties and office of an a. [L.].

ADMINISTRATRIX [ad-mi'nis-tra-triks], *n.* woman who administers.

ADMIRABLE [ad'mi-ra-bl], *adj.* possessing qualities to excite admiration; excellent, worth admiring. ADMIRABLENESS, *n.* quality of being a. ADMIRABLY, *adv.* in an a. way. [L.].

ADMIRAL [ad'mi-ral], *n.* the naval officer in command of a fleet; the admiral's ship; A. of the Fleet, highest rank in the navy, senior to a who is senior to VICE-ADMIRAL, who is senior to REAR-ADMIRAL; title customarily allowed to the senior captain of a fishing fleet; (*entom.*) a species of butterfly; (*zool.*) shell-fish of the genus *Conus*. [Arab.].

ADMIRALTY [ad'mi-ral-ti], *n.* the Lords of the Admiralty, a board of commissioners granted power to conduct naval affairs; buildings in which this board transacts its business; Court of A., (*leg.*) the supreme court sitting in judgment of maritime cases.

ADMIRATION [ad-mi-rā'shn], *n.* act of admiring; that which excites wonder. [L.].

ADMIRE [ad-mier'], *v.t.* to look at a person or object with wonder and delight; have mixed feelings of pleasure, awe and sympathy for something or someone; have a high opinion of. [L.].

ADMIRER [ad-mier'er], *n.* one who admires; lover.

ADMIRING [ad-mier'ing], *adj.* thinking highly of, wondering at. ADMIRINGLY, *adv.* with admiration.

ADMISSIBLE [ad-mi'si-bl], *adj.* that may be admitted, entitled to be accepted and considered. ADMISSIBILITY [ad-mi-si-bi'li-ti], *n.* quality of being a. ADMISSIBLY, *adv.* so as to be admitted. [LL.].

ADMISSION [ad-mi'shn], *n.* act of admitting; permission to enter; right of entry; confession, agreement as to truth or fact, acknowledgment; price of entry. ADMISSIVE, *adj.* of the character of an a.

ADMIT [ad-mit'], *v.t.* to permit to enter, give access to, grant entrance into, allow; confess, acknowledge as true or false. [L.].

ADMITTABLE [ad-mi'ta-bl], *adj.* capable of being admitted. ADMITTABLY, *adv.* admittedly.

ADMITTANCE [ad-mi'tans], *n.* act of admitting; admission, permission to enter.

ADMITTEDLY [ad-mi'tid-li], *adv.* accepted as correct, in agreement.

ADMIXTURE [ad-miks'tyōōr], *n.* act of mixing; addition of another ingredient to a mixture; the mixture or compound itself formed by such an addition.

ADMONISH [ad-mo'nish], *v.t.* to exhort; warn, advise; reprove mildly. [L.].

ADMONISHMENT [ad-mo'nish-ment], *n.* admonition, act of admonishing, reproof.

ADMONITION [ad-mo-ni'shn], *n.* mild reproof; friendly counsel; caution.

ADMONITORY [ad-mo'ni-te-ri], *adj.* serving as admonishment.

ADMORTIZATION [ad-maw-ti-zā'shn], *n.* amortization.

ADNATE [ad'nāt], *adj.* (*anat.* and *bot.*) organically attached by the whole surface. [L.].

ADNOMINAL [ad-no'mi-nal], *adj.* adjectival; connected with a noun.

ADNOUN [ad'nown], *n.* adjective; attribute of a noun.

ADO [a-dōō'], *n.* to-do, fuss, bustle; trouble. [ME.].

ADOBE (1) [a-dō'bi], *n.* brick baked by the sun; house or building made of these bricks. ADOBE (2), *adj.* built of sun-baked bricks. [Span.].

ADOLESCENCE [a-dō-le'sens], *n.* state of growing up; period of youth between puberty and maturity. [Fr. from L.].

ADOLESCENCY [a-dō-le'sen-si], *n.* adolescence.

ADOLESCENT (1) [a-dō-le'sent], *adj.* in the process of growing from puberty to maturity. ADOLESCENT (2), *n.* boy or girl becoming adult, youth. [Fr. from L.].

ADONIS [a-dō'nis], *n.* (*myth.*) handsome young man whom Venus loved; handsome man.

ADOPT [a-dopt'], *v.t.* to treat as one's own, appropriate; choose; take another's child, and treat and consider it as one's own; give formal approval to (a report etc.). ADOPTEDLY, *adv.* by adoption. [L.].

ADOPTION [a-dop'shn], *n.* act of adopting; acceptance of child not one's own into one's family, according it full privileges and rights; acceptance of another's plan, belief, resolution etc.

ADOPTIVE [a-dop'tiv], *adj.* that adopts, or that is adopted. ADOPTIVELY, *adv.* by adoption.

ADORABLE [a-daw'ra-bl], *adj.* worthy of being adored; calling for devoted love. ADORABLENESS, *n.* quality of being a. ADORABLY, *adv.* in a manner worthy of adoration.

ADORATION [a-do-rā'shn], *n.* act of worshipping; homage to that which is held sacred; devoted and intense affection. [L.].

ADORE [a-daw(r)'], *v.t.* to worship with deep and intense reverence, venerate; pay ardent homage to, love beyond everything else, idolize. [L.].

ADORN [a-dawn'], *v.t.* to decorate, embellish, add things of beauty to. [L.].

ADORNMENT [a-dawn'ment], *n.* decoration, ornament; embellishment.

ADOWN [a-down'], *prep.* and *adv.* down; towards the ground. [OE.].

ADRENAL [a-drē'nal], *adj.* close to the kidneys; a. glands, two small glands embedded in the face of the kidneys, the suprarenal capsules. [AD and RENAL].

ADRENALIN [a-dre'na-lin], *n.* hormone secreted by the suprarenal glands. [*Prec.*].

ADRIFT [a-drift'], *adv.* and *adj.* without moorings, floating haphazardly.

ADROIT [a-droit'], *adj.* skilful with the hands, dexterous; having expert resource and ability. ADROITLY, *adv.* in an a. way. [Fr.].

ADSCITITIOUS [ad-si-ti'shōōs], *adj.* adopted by way of supplement, supplemental, additional. [~L.].

ADSORB [ad-sawb'], *v.t.* to collect by adsorption.

ADSORPTION [ad-zawp'shn], *n.* (*chem.*) removal of dissolved substances from solution by the action of a colloid. [L.].

ADULATE [a'dyōō-lāt], *v.t.* to give extreme praise; flatter for a purpose. ADULATOR, *n.* flatterer. [L.].

ADULATION [a-dyōō-lā'shn], *n.* servile over-praise, excessive flattery. [L.].

ADULT (1) [a-dult'], *adj.* grown up, mature as a person. ADULT (2) [a-dult', a'dult], *n.* any living thing or creature which is full-grown. [L.].

ADULTERANT [a-dul'te-rant], *n.* person who, or substance which, adulterates.

ADULTERATE (1) [a-dul'te-rāt], *v.t.* to debase the quality of a substance or mixture by adding inferior ingredients. ADULTERATE (2), *adj.* spurious, debased, contaminated. [L.].

ADULTERATION [a-dul-te-rā'shn], *n.* act of adulterating; state of being adulterated.

ADULTERER [a-dul'te-rer], *n.* man guilty of adultery. [L.].

ADULTERESS [a-dul'te-res], *n.* woman guilty of adultery.

ADULTERINE [a-dul'te-rin], *adj.* proceeding from adulterous intercourse; spurious. [L.].

ADULTEROUS [a-dul'te-rōōs], *adj.* guilty of

ōō is pronounced as in foo*d*; ŏŏ as in hoo*d*; th as in *th*ink; TH as in *th*at; zh as in a*z*ure. ~ = related to.

adultery; illicit. ADULTEROUSLY, *adv.* in an a. way.

ADULTERY [a-dul'te-ri], *n.* sexual intercourse breaking the marriage vow of faithfulness.

ADUMBRATE [a'dum-brāt], *v.t.* to make a sketch of, outline, indicate briefly, to forecast. ADUMBRATIVE [a-dum'bra-tiv], *adj.* faintly representing, characterized by adumbration. [L.].

ADUMBRATION [a-dum-brā'shn], *n.* act of adumbrating; faint or imperfect representation, brief indication, incomplete forecast. [*Prec.*].

ADUST [a-dust'], *adj.* scorched, parched. [L.].

ADVANCE (1) [ad-vahns'], *v.t.* to move, lead or propel forward; promote; propose; improve; arrange an earlier time for; lend or pay money on security; *v.i.* to move forward; be promoted; make progress; (*milit.*) attack; (*comm.*) raise in price. ADVANCE (2), *n.* act of moving forward, progression; (*fig.*) promotion; progress; rise in wages or offer of money; loan of money; a move towards someone with friendliness; **in a.**, beforehand, in front, before. ADVANCE (3), *adj.* coming before, preliminary; (of books etc.) supplied before publication. ADVANCER, *n.* one who advances, promoter; second branch of a buck's horn. [OFr.].

ADVANCED [ad-vahnst'], *adj.* in the van of progress, modern in ideas, beliefs and behaviour; well on in years, aged.

ADVANCEMENT [ad-vahns'ment], *n.* act of advancing; state of being advanced; progress, promotion.

ADVANTAGE (1) [ad-vahn'tij], *n.* any condition, event, circumstance or source of benefit and favourable effect, means of gaining an end, conducive to happiness, success or beneficial effects; gain, benefit; superior position; (*tennis*) point scored after both sides have drawn level at "deuce"; **to take a. of,** to deceive, betray. ADVANTAGE (2), *v.t.* to promote the interest of; be beneficial to; create an a. for; benefit. [Fr.].

ADVANTAGEOUS [ad-van-tā'jōos], *adj.* useful, being of advantage; profitable; beneficial. ADVANTAGEOUSLY, *adv.* in an a. way. ADVANTAGEOUSNESS, *n.* quality or state of being a.

ADVENT [ad'vent], *n.* arrival, approach; the coming of Christ into the world; (*eccles.*) period of four weeks previous to the festival of the Nativity. ADVENTIST, *n.* member of one of the religious sects believing in the imminence of Christ's second coming. [OFr. from L.].

ADVENTITIOUS [ad-ven-ti'shōos], *adj.* accidental; casual; not inherent; out of the ordinary. ADVENTITIOUSLY, *adv.* in an a. way. ADVENTITIOUSNESS, *n.* state of being a. [L.].

ADVENTURE (1) [ad-ven'tyōor], *n.* enterprise full of risk and danger; experience of unforeseen events endangering the participants' lives or persons; unexpected and remarkable incident; a speculation. ADVENTURE (2), *v.t.* to risk, take a chance, gamble on failure or success. [L.].

ADVENTURER [ad-ven'tyōor-er], *n.* person who risks his life in difficult and extraordinary enterprises; person who lives by his wits, speculator.

ADVENTURESOME [ad-ven'tyōor-sum], *adj.* adventurous, fond of adventure. ADVENTURESOMENESS, *n.* quality of being a.

ADVENTURESS [ad-ven'tyōor-es], *n.* female adventurer.

ADVENTUROUS [ad-ven'tyōor-ōos], *adj.* venturesome, inclined to adventure; enterprising; risky. ADVENTUROUSLY, *adv.* in an a. way. ADVENTUROUSNESS, *n.* act or quality of being a.

ADVERB [ad'verb], *n.* word qualifying the meaning of a verb, adjective, participle or other adverb in terms of place, time, manner etc. ADVERBIAL [ad-vur'bi-al], *adj.* relating to an a. ADVERBIALLY, *adv.* with an a.'s function, in the manner of an a. [L.].

ADVERSARY [ad'ver-sa-ri], *n.* person or organized group hostile to one, opponent; enemy. [L.].

ADVERSATIVE [ad-vur'sa-tiv], *adj.* (*gram.*) denoting antithesis or contrast.

ADVERSE [ad'vers], *adj.* acting in a contrary direction; hostile; opposing; unprosperous, injurious; situated opposite. ADVERSELY, *adv.* in an a. way. ADVERSENESS, *n.* state of being a. [L.].

ADVERSITY [ad-vur'si-ti], *n.* adverse state of affairs, distress, calamity; misfortune. [L.].

ADVERT [ad-vurt'], *v.i.* to turn attention to; allude to. ADVERTENCE, ADVERTENCY, *n.* attention; regard. [L.].

ADVERTISE [ad'ver-tīz], *v.t. and i.* to announce to

the public; display a public notice; communicate merits and claims to the public by any means. ADVERTISER, *n.* person who advertises, publicist. [Fr.].

ADVERTISEMENT [ad-vur'tiz-ment], *n.* announcement, brought to the notice of the public, of products and prices; legal notification; notice of arrangements for public events.

ADVICE [ad-vīs'], *n.* counsel, considered judgment, recommended opinion, professional information; notification; (*pl.*) diplomatic report; (*comm.*) detailed information concerning bills, drafts etc. passed between business firms. [ME. from OFr.].

ADVISABLE [ad-vī'za-bl], *adj.* prudent, proper to be advised; expedient. ADVISABILITY [ad-vī-za-bi'li-ti], *n.* quality of being a. ADVISABLY, *adv.* with advice, wisely, prudently, advisedly.

ADVISE [ad-vīz'], *v.t. and i.* to counsel, give advice to; inform, give notice to; consult with. ADVISER, *n.* one who gives advice. [~Fr. from LL.].

ADVISED [ad-vīzd'], *adj.* performed on advice or with deliberation; intended. ADVISEDLY [ad-vī'zid-li], *adv.* in an a. way. ADVISEDNESS [ad-vī'zid-nes], *n.* caution, deliberate consideration; prudent procedure.

ADVISORY [ad-vī'ze-ri], *adj.* possessing power to advise; constituted to advise, containing advice.

ADVOCACY [ad'vo-ka-si], *n.* a pleading for; intercessional or judicial pleading. [MedL.].

ADVOCATE (1) [ad'vo-kāt], *n.* person who pleads another's cause, professional representative in a legal case, barrister; person who recommends or vindicates a cause; supporter of a proposal or plan; **Faculty of Advocates,** association of barristers allowed to plead in the Scottish Supreme Court; **judge a.,** officer in a court-martial appointed to conduct the prosecution; **Devil's a.,** in the R.C. Church, elected opposer obliged to argue against canonization of the person it is proposed to canonize. ADVOCATE (2) [ad'vō-kāt], *v.t.* to plead on behalf of, argue in favour of, recommend. ADVOCATESHIP, *n.* office, rank or duty of an a. [OFr. and L.].

ADVOWEE [ad-vow-ē'], *n.* one who owns the right of advowson. [OFr.].

ADVOWSON [ad-vow'son], *n.* right of presenting a cleric with or nominating him for a vacant benefice in the Church of England. [ME.].

ADYNAMIA [a-di-nā'mi-ah], *n.* (*med.*) weakness brought on by disease; diminution of the vital powers. ADYNAMIC [a-di-na'mik], *adj.* weak. [Gk.].

ADYTUM (*pl.* **adyta**) [a'di-tum], *n.* innermost and most sacred part of the shrine of a temple; (*fig.*) inner, private room. [L. from Gk.].

ADZE [adz], *n.* tool with a curved steel blade whose cutting edge is set at right angles to the handle. [OE.].

AEDILE [ē'dīl], *n.* Roman magistrate whose duty it was to supervise public works, games etc. [L.].

AEGER [ē'jer], *n.* sick leave in English universities, excusing attendance. [L.].

AEGIS [ē'jis], *n.* protecting shield, *esp.* the legendary shield of Minerva; any protecting influence. [Gk.].

AEGROTAT [ē'grō-tat], *n.* certificate of exemption from a part or the whole of an examination on account of illness; **a. degree,** degree awarded to a candidate who has been absent for part or the whole of the final degree examination, and in which no classification is made. [L.].

AEOLIAN [ē-ō'li-an], *adj.* pertaining to or caused by the wind; **A. harp,** stringed musical instrument operated by the action of the wind blowing across the strings. [L. from Gk.].

AEON [ē'on], *n.* immeasurably long indefinite period of time, eternity. [Gk.].

AERATE [āer'āt], *v.t.* to allow air to act upon a substance, charge with carbonic acid gas; (*med.*) impregnate the blood with oxygen by respiration; **aerated waters,** sparkling beverages of water charged with carbonic acid gas and sometimes flavoured. AERATION [āer-ā'shn], *n.* process of aerating or exposing to the action of air or carbonic acid gas.

AERIAL (1) [āer'i-al], *adj.* belonging to or resembling the air, consisting of or produced by air, existing or moving in the air; (*fig.*) light and delicate, unsubstantial, ethereal, at a great height. AERIAL (2), *n.* wire or wires supported in the air and used with radio receiving sets to collect the electrical waves, or with transmitting sets or stations to send out the electrical waves. AERIALLY, *adv.* in an a. fashion. [Gk.].

AERIE [āer'i], *n.* nest or brood of a bird of prey;

(*fig.*) dwelling place situated at a great height. [MedL.].

AERIFICATION [āer-i-fi-kā'shn], *n.* act of aerifying; condition of being aerified; act of becoming air, gas or vapour; state of being aeriform. [L.].

AERIFORM [āer'i-fawm], *adj.* having the form or nature of air or gas; (*fig.*) ethereal. [L.].

AERIFY [āer'i-fi], *v.t.* to infuse air into; fill with air. [L.].

AERO-, *pref.* air, pertaining to the air. [Gk.].

AEROBATICS [āer-ō-ba'tiks], *n.* stunting in aeroplanes, performance of spectacular, daring evolutions by aircraft. [AERO and ACROBATICS].

AEROBE [āer'ōb], *n.* one of the aerobia.

AEROBIA [āer-ō'bi-ah], *n.* bacteria which can live only in the presence of oxygen. AEROBIC, *adj.* relating to a. [Gk.].

AERODART [aer-ō-daht'], *n.* steel weapon or missile which can be released from aircraft.

AERODONETICS [āer-ō-dō-ne'tiks], *n.* (*aeron.*) science of gliding.

AERODROME [āer'ō-drōm], *n.* aircraft-station consisting usually of a large open flat area of land, at which aircraft may land or from which they may depart, and the buildings associated therewith. [Gk.].

AERODYNAMIC [āer-ō-dī-na'mik], *adj.* pertaining to aerodynamics. AERODYNAMICALLY, *adv.* as regards aerodynamics.

AERODYNAMICS [āer-ō-dī-na'miks], *n.* science dealing with the mechanical effects of air in motion, air resistance and pressure upon moving bodies in air etc. [Gk.].

AERODYNE [āer'ō-dīn], *n.* any aircraft heavier than air.

AERO-ENGINE [āer'ō-en-jin], *n.* aeroplane engine.

AEROFOIL [āer'ō-foil], *n.* (*aeron.*) an object, such as the wing of an aeroplane, the section of which is so shaped as to produce lift at right angles to the direction in which it is moving through the air.

AEROLITE, AEROLITH [āer'ō-lit, -lith], *n.* meteorite. [Gk.].

AEROLOGY [āer-o'lo-ji], *n.* science which deals with the air. [Gk.].

AEROMETER [āer-o'mi-ter], *n.* instrument used to measure the weight or the density of air and gases.

AEROMETRY [āer-o'mi-tri], *n.* science of measuring and weighing the air. AEROMETRIC [āer-ō-met'rik], *adj.* relating to the measurement of the air. [Gk.].

AERONAUT [āer'ō-nawt], *n.* one who navigates any lighter-than-air flying-machine, one who makes ascents in a balloon, air navigator. AERONAUTIC(AL) [āer-ō-naw'tik(-al)], *adj.* pertaining to the science of navigating the air. [Gk.].

AERONAUTICS [āer-ō-naw'tiks], *n.* science of navigating the air in aircraft of any description.

AEROPLANE [āer'ō-plān], *n.* mechanically propelled heavier-than-air flying-machine.

AEROSTATIC(AL) [āer-ō-sta'tik(-al)], *adj.* belonging to, concerning, weight, pressure and equilibrium of air and gases.

AEROSTATICS [āer-ō-sta'tiks], *n.* science of the pressure, weight and equilibrium of the air and gases, or the equilibrium of bodies which move or are sustained in them; aeronautics.

AEROTHERAPEUTICS [āer-ō-the-ra-pyōō'tiks], *n.* treatment of disease by air and sunshine.

AERTEX [āer'teks], *n.* (*prot.*) loosely woven fabric designed to act as a kind of insulating material against cold or heat.

AERY [āer'i], *adj.* ethereal; visionary. [Gk.].

AESCULAPIAN [ēs-kyōō-lā'pi-an], *adj.* pertaining to the art of healing. [L.].

AESTHETE [ēs'thēt], *n.* one professing a keen sense of the beautiful. [Gk.].

AESTHETIC [ēs-the'tik], *adj.* pertaining to the science and perception of the beautiful in art, able to appreciate beauty. AESTHETICALLY, *adv.* in an a. fashion. [Gk.].

AESTHETICISM [ēs-the'ti-sizm], *n.* zeal for or devotion to the study of the beautiful.

AESTHETICS [ēs-the'tiks], *n.* philosophy or science of the beautiful.

AESTIVAL [ēs-ti'val], *adj.* relating to summer. [L.].

AESTIVATE [ēs'ti-vāt], *v.i.* to spend the summer; (*zool.*) spend the summer in a state of rest and sleep. AESTIVATION [ēs-ti-vā'shn], *n.* (*zool.*) state of dormancy or extreme inactivity during the summer; (*bot.*) arrangement of the petals within the bud. [L.].

AETHER, see ETHER.

AETIOLOGY [ē-ti-o'lo-ji], *n.* philosophy or science of causes; (*med.*) study of origins or causes of disease or of pathological conditions. [Gk.].

AFAR [a-fah(r)'], *adv.* (*poet.*) a long distance away. [OE.].

AFEARD [a-fēerd'], *adj.* (*poet.*) frightened; afraid.

AFFABILITY [a-fa-bi'li-ti], *n.* cheerful good-naturedness, pleasant friendliness.

AFFABLE [a'fa-bl], *adj.* friendly, pleasant, courteous, easily approachable, cheerful and polite. AFFABLY, *adv.* in an a. way. [L.].

AFFAIR [a-fāer'], *n.* concern, business matter; vague reference to a happening or adventure; romantic intrigue; (*pl.*) public or private transactions or business; (*coll.*) thing, object or spectacle. [Fr.].

AFFECT (1) [a-fekt'], *v.t.* to pretend, lay claim to; show a fondness for, like, assume, assume a pose or artificial manner. [L.].

AFFECT (2), *v.t.* to concern, produce a change in, influence, stir the feelings of, produce an effect upon; attack (of a disease). [L.].

AFFECTATION [a-fek-tā'shn], *n.* pretence, artificially adopted mannerism; assumed air or character. [L.].

AFFECTED [a-fek'tid], *adj.* unnatural, artificially assumed, full of affectation, fond of adopting an artificial pose; influenced, emotionally stirred, exhibiting the effects of, inclined or disposed. AFFECTEDLY, *adv.* in an a. way. AFFECTEDNESS, *n.* affectation.

AFFECTING [a-fek'ting], *adj.* capable of stirring the emotions, touching, pathetic. AFFECTINGLY, *adv.* in an a. way.

AFFECTION [a-fek'shn], *n.* feeling, warm attachment, fondness, love, kindly disposition; (*pl.*) emotions, feelings of love for, inclinations; (*med.*) disease, disorder. AFFECTIONAL, *adj.* inferring a. [L.].

AFFECTIONATE [a-fek'shn-at], *adj.* full of or displaying affection, fond, loving, possessing an emotional attachment. AFFECTIONATELY, *adv.* in an a. manner. AFFECTIONATENESS, *n.* fondness, quality of being a.

AFFECTIVE [a-fek'tiv], *adj.* pertaining to the emotions, relating or belonging to the affections. AFFECTIVELY, *adv.* in an a. way.

AFFETTUOSO [a-fe-tyōō-ō'sō], *adv.* (*mus.*) with feeling. [It.].

AFFIANCE (1) [a-fi'ans], *n.* faith, trust in. AFFIANCE (2), *v.t.* to betroth or promise solemnly in marriage. [LL.].

AFFIDAVIT [a-fi-dā'vit], *n.* (*leg.*) written statement of facts signed upon oath before a person qualified to witness oaths, and generally used in presenting evidence before a judge or court. [LL.].

AFFILIABLE [a-fi'li-a-bl], *adj.* able to be affiliated.

AFFILIATE [a-fi'li-āt], *v.t.* to merge with or become a branch of, attach oneself to, be connected with a larger similar organization; establish the paternity of an illegitimate child in order that the putative father may contribute towards maintenance costs; (*pass.*) (*fig.*) be connected with on grounds of common origin (*esp.* of languages). [LL.].

AFFILIATION [a-fi-li-ā'shn], *n.* act of affiliating; the determining of the paternity of a bastard child; connexion with. [*Prec.*].

AFFINED [a-find'], *adj.* related.

AFFINITY [a-fi'ni-ti], *n.* close relation or points of similarity between two objects; resemblance in structure between plants, animals, languages, inferring an ultimate common origin; similarity of character, natural inclination or attraction, likeness serving as a connecting link; (*leg.*) relationship between one of two persons married to each other and the blood relations of the other; (*chem.*) tendency of certain bodies to combine with each other. [L.].

AFFIRM [a-furm'], *v.t.* to declare positively or formally, state a thing to be true; (*leg.*) confirm or ratify; *v.i.* (*leg.*) confirm testimony by solemn declaration instead of taking an oath. AFFIRMABLE, *adj.* able to be affirmed. AFFIRMABLY, *adv.* so as to be capable of affirmation. AFFIRMANT, *n.* one who affirms. [L.].

AFFIRMATION [a-fer-mā'shn], *n.* positive assertion, declaration that something is so, statement, confirmation; (*logic*) positive assertion, inferring the mutual concernment of the terms of a proposition; (*leg.*) solemn declaration made in a court of law as an alternative to the taking of an oath, and equally binding legally. [L.].

AFFIRMATIVE (1) [a-fur'ma-tiv], *adj.* stating that something is correct or true, or is a fact, opposed to

---

ōō is pronounced as in food; ŏŏ as in hood; th as in *th*ink; TH as in *th*at; zh as in azure. ～ = related to.

negative. AFFIRMATIVE (2), *n.* statement or expression which affirms the correctness or truth of something. AFFIRMATIVELY, *adv.* in an a. way. [L.].

AFFIRMATORY [a-fur'ma-te-ri], *adj.* confirmatory, that which affirms.

AFFIX (1) [a-fiks'], *v.t.* to attach, fasten to, append, put at the end of a document. AFFIX (2) [a'fiks], *n.* that which is added or attached to; (*gram.*) prefix or suffix added to a stem or base of a word. [L.].

AFFLATUS [a-flā'tus], *n.* breathing or blowing upon; divine inspiration. [L.].

AFFLICT [a-flikt'], *v.t.* to attack, harass, oppress, cause pain or grief. AFFLICTED, *adj.* harassed, stricken with, oppressed or grieved with a calamity; (*med.*) diseased, injured. AFFLICTING, *adj.* causing sorrow or pain, distressing. AFFLICTINGLY, *adv.* in an afflicting way. [L.].

AFFLICTION [a-flik'shn], *n.* condition of being afflicted, distress, adversity, calamity; (*med.*) a disorder, disease; (*pl.*) troubles. [L.].

AFFLICTIVE [a-flik'tiv], *adj.* producing affliction. AFFLICTIVELY, *adv.* in an a. way.

AFFLUENCE [a'floo-ens], *n.* profusion, abundance; prosperity, opulence. [L.].

AFFLUENT (1) [a'floo-ent], *adj.* wealthy, prosperous; freely flowing, profuse, ample. AFFLUENT (2), *n.* tributary stream or river. AFFLUENTLY, *adv.* in an a. way. [L.].

AFFLUX [a'fluks], *n.* a flowing to, gathering; (*med.*) rush of blood. [L.].

AFFORD [a-fawd'], *v.t.* to give, be able to concede; have the necessary means, be able to spare the money for, be able to allow a person to do something or a thing to happen; **cannot a. to,** dare not. [OE.].

AFFOREST [a-fo'rest], *v.t.* to turn into forest, plant with trees. AFFORESTATION [a-fo-res-tā'shn], *n.* process of converting ground into forest. [MedL.].

AFFRAY [a-frā'], *n.* a fight, brawl, riot; (*fig.*) struggle, dispute. [OFr.].

AFFRIGHT (1) [a-frīt'], *v.t.* (*poet.*) to terrify, alarm. AFFRIGHT (2), *n.* (*poet.*) sudden fear, terror.

AFFRONT (1) [a-frunt'], *v.t.* to insult openly, offend, speak insolently of a person to his face; face boldly, confront. AFFRONT (2), *n.* an insult, contemptuous or offensive treatment. [LL.].

AFFUSION [a-fyoo'zhn], *n.* sprinkling with water, *esp.* in baptism or to allay fever. [L.].

AFIELD [a-fēld'], *adj.* and *adv.* in the field; at some distance away from home; **to go too far a.,** to wander away from one's path. [OE.].

AFIRE [a-fīer'], *adj.* and *adv.* (*lit.* and *fig.*) on fire. [OE.].

AFLAME [a-flām'], *adj.* and *adv.* ablaze, lit up; (*fig.*) eagerly excited, glowing.

AFLOAT [a-flōt'], *adj.* and *adv.* at sea, floating, on board ship, awash; (*fig.*) out of debt; being circulated, current; adrift. [OE.].

AFOOT [a-foot'], *adj.* and *adv.* on foot; on the move, in prospect, being prepared. [ME.].

AFORE [a-faw(r)'], *adv.* and *prep.* in front; before; in or towards the front part of a ship. [OE.].

AFOREGOING [a-faw-gō'ing], *n.* and *adj.* (something) going before, preceding.

AFOREMENTIONED [a-faw-men'shnd], *adj.* mentioned before.

AFORENAMED [a-faw-nāmd'], *adj.* cited before.

AFORESAID [a-faw-sed'], *adj.* mentioned before.

AFORETHOUGHT [a-faw'thawt], *adj.* premeditated, thought out previously or in advance.

AFORETIME [a-faw'tīm], *adv.* in a previous time.

AFRAID [a-frād'], *adj.* frightened, scared; (*coll.*) **I am a.,** *phrase preceding some unpleasant news, or as a form of apology or excuse, or implying unwillingness.* [~AFFRAY]

AFRESH [a-fresh'], *adv.* anew, again.

AFRIKAANS (1) [af-ri-kahnz'], *n.* form of Dutch spoken in South Africa, the language of the Boers. AFRIKAANS (2), *adj.* in, of or pertaining to A. [Du.].

AFRIKANER [af-ri-kah'ner], *n.* and *adj.* member of, pertaining to, the Afrikaans-speaking population of South Africa, of Dutch descent. [Afrik.].

AFT [ahft], *adv.* (*naut.*) towards the stern or hinder part of a ship; **fore and a.,** (*naut.*) along the length of a ship, rigged with sails set lengthwise; **right a.,** in a direct line with the stern. [OE.].

AFTER (1) [ahf'ter], *adj.* and *adv.* later, following; (*naut.*) near to or pertaining to the stern; in the rear, behind, later. AFTER (2), *prep., adv. and conj.* immediately following, in pursuit of; about; at the end of, following upon; having affinity with, in imitation of; later than; in view of, in accordance with; **to take a.,** to resemble; **to look a.,** to attend to, take care of; **to shout a.,** to attract a person's attention by shouting; **to name a.,** to denote by the name of a specified person or thing; **a. all,** when all has been considered, in spite of everything said or done; **a. a manner, fashion,** imperfectly, half-heartedly; **man a. one's own heart,** person one admires, and with whom one has much in common; (*slang*) **a. you with,** when you have finished with (a request for an article); **a. hours,** after business hours; (*coll.*) after the period allowed for the sale of intoxicating drinks. [OE.].

AFTERBIRTH [ahf'ter-berth], *n.* (*obstet.*) placenta and membranes of the foetus expelled after parturition.

AFTER-CARE [ahf'ter-käer], *n.* attention given after the end of a course of treatment.

AFTERDAMP [ahf'ter-damp], *n.* poisonous gases remaining after an explosion of fire-damp in mines.

AFTERGLOW [ahf'ter-glō], *n.* glow remaining in the sky after sunset; also (*fig.*) in a metal becoming cool from white-heat.

AFTER-GRASS [ahf'ter-grahs], *n.* new crop of grass growing after the mowing of the first crop.

AFTERGROWTH [ahf'ter-grōth], *n.* second and succeeding growth.

AFTERGUARD [ahf'ter-gahd], *n.* (*naut.*) seamen stationed aft whose duty it was to attend to the aftersails.

AFTER-HOLD [ahf'ter-hōld], *n.* (*naut.*) that part of a vessel's hold to the rear of the mainmast.

AFTER-IMAGE [ahf'ter-i-mij], *n.* impression of an object or sensation remaining and perceptible to the senses after the external object or cause has been removed.

AFTERINGS [ahf'te-ringz], *n.*(*pl.*) the last drops of milk drawn from a cow.

AFTER-LIFE [ahf'ter-lif], *n.* future life here on earth or hereafter.

AFTERMATH [ahf'ter-mahth], *n.* a second crop of grass in a season; (*fig.*) consequences or results of some calamity. [OE.].

AFTERMOST [ahf'ter-mōst], *adj.* (*naut.*) furthest aft. [OE.].

AFTERNOON [ahf-ter-noon'], *n.* time between noon and evening.

AFTERPAINS [ahf'ter-pānz], *n.*(*pl.*) pains following upon childbirth.

AFTER PART [ahf'ter-paht], *n.* latter part; (*naut.*) the part of a ship towards the stern.

AFTERPIECE [ahf'ter-pēs], *n.* short dramatic piece performed after an important play.

AFTER-RAKE [ahf'ter-rāk], *n.* (*naut.*) the angle at which the hull projects at the stern beyond the keel; stern-rake.

AFTERSAILS [ahf'ter-sālz], *n.*(*pl.*) the sails on the mizenmast and stays, between the main and mizenmasts.

AFTERTASTE [ahf'ter-tāst], *n.* taste which remains in the mouth after eating or drinking.

AFTERTHOUGHT [ahf'ter-thawt], *n.* reflection upon a past act or happening, something thought of by way of an explanation or amplification.

AFTERWARD(S) [ahf'ter-wawd(z)], *adv.* in a later or subsequent time. [OE.].

AFTWARD [ahft'wawd], *adj.* towards the stern.

AGA [ah'gah], *n.* formerly a military title of rank in the Turkish army, now used also as a civil title and applied to men holding high positions and men of great wealth and influence; **A. Khan,** hereditary chief of the Ismailite sect of Moslems.

AGAIN [a-gān', a-gen'], *adv.* back to the original or former place; anew, repeatedly, once more, in return, a second time; expressing a quantity equal to a stated quantity; besides; on the other hand; **now and a.,** occasionally; **time and a.,** repeatedly; **as much a.,** twice as much. [OE.].

AGAINST [a-gänst', a-genst'], *prep. and adv.* opposite, close to, in contrast with, in contact with, contrary to, in an opposite direction, in opposition to, in competition with, alongside, facing, in preparation for, in collision with; **to run up a.,** to encounter unexpectedly. [OE.].

AGALACTIA, AGALAXY [a-ga-lak'ti-ah, a-ga-lak'si], *n.* (*med.*) absence of milk for suckling in mothers after childbirth. AGALACTOUS [a-ga-lak'-tōos], *adj.* destitute of milk for suckling purposes. [Gk.].

AGALAXY, see AGALACTIA.

AGALMATOLITE [a-gal-ma'tō-līt], *n.* kind of

clayey stone used in China for carving images. [Gk.].

AGAMA [a'ga-mah], *n.* (*zool.*) kind of lizard allied to the iguana family. [Caribbean].

AGAMI [a'ga-mi], *n.* trumpeter bird found in tropical America. [Fr. from Guiana name].

AGAMOGENESIS [a-ga-mo-je'ne-sis], *n.* reproduction asexually. [Gk.].

AGAPE (1) [a-gāp'], *adj. and adv.* staring with wide-open mouth in astonishment, bewilderment, expectation etc.

AGAPE (2) [a'ga-pi], *n.* (*eccles. hist.*) primitive Christian love-feast of charity held in connexion with Communion. [Gk.].

AGAR-AGAR [ā-gah(r)-ā'gah(r)], *n.* gelatinous substance obtained from dried seaweed, used for cultivating bacteria, in the manufacture of certain kinds of paper and silk, and soups and jellies in the East. [Malayan].

AGARIC [a'ga-rik], *n.* (*bot.*) genus of fungi having a fleshy cap; **a. mineral**, (*min.*) a deposit of carbonate of lime, resembling a fungus; a Tuscan stone, from which bricks can be made so light that they float in water. [Gk.].

AGASTRIC [a-gas'trik], *adj.* (*zool.*) lacking a distinct alimentary canal.

AGATE [a'gat], *n.* a very hard stone, being a semitransparent variegated compound variety of chalcedony; instrument used by gold-wire drawers for burnishing; (*print.*) an American size of type, about 5-point or 14 lines per in. AGATIFEROUS [a-ga-ti'fe-rŏŏs], *adj.* (*min.*) producing or containing a. AGATINE [a'ga-tīn], *adj.* resembling a. AGATIZE, *v.t.* to form into a. AGATIZED, *adj.* (*min.*) with coloured lines like a. [Gk.].

AGAVE [a-gā'vi], *n.* (*bot.*) genus of plant popularly and erroneously known as American aloes or century plant. [Gk.].

AGE (1) [āj], *n.* number of years or period of time during which anything has lived or been in existence, a period of life, maturity, the latter part of life when a person becomes old; an historical, archaeological or geological era; the people living at a certain period; a long, indefinite period of time; (*leg.*) period of life at which certain legal rights and responsibilities are obtained; (*pl.*) (*slang*) an unreasonably long time; **over/under a.**, too old/young; **to come of a.**, to become twenty-one years old; **to be of a.**, to be over twenty-one years old. AGE (2), *v.t. and i.* to grow old, seem to have grown old, cause to grow old; mature by keeping. [LL.].

AGED [ājd' (AGE 1), ā'jid (AGE 2)], *adj.* of a certain age; advanced in years, old; *n.*(*pl.*) old persons.

AGELESS [āj'les], *adj.* never appearing to become old.

AGENCY [ā'jen-si], *n.* the occupation of an agent; business or office of an agent; power, instrumentality, means of action. [MedL.].

AGENDA [a-jen'dah], *n.* statement of the business to be dealt with at a meeting, things to be done or considered. [L.].

AGENDUM [a-jen'dum], *n.* item of business to be considered at a meeting. [L.].

AGENESIS [a-je'-ni-sis], *n.* (*physiol.*) imperfect physical development. [Gk.].

AGENT [ā'jent], *n.* one who performs an action or causes something to occur, business representative, one appointed to act on behalf of or to look after the interests of another; a spy; the cause of certain effects or phenomena; (*science*) a force acting on matter and bringing about certain results; **army a.**, kind of authorized military banker who conducts the financial affairs of a regiment; **crown a.**, commercial or financial representative in Britain of a Dominion or Colony; **A. General**, crown agent appointed by certain self-governing colonies; **a. provocateur** [a-zhah(ng)-pro-vo-ka-tur'], one employed in inciting suspected offenders to commit some crime or offence in order that the offenders may be caught in the act. [~L.].

AGENTIAL [ā-jen'shal], *adj.* pertaining to agency.

AGGLOMERATE (1) [a-glo'me-rat], *n.* an agglomeration of articles; (*min.*) masses of volcanic fragments of rock fused together. AGGLOMERATE (2), *adj.* gathered into a heap, ball or mass. AGGLOMERATE (3) [a-glo'me-rāt], *v.t.* to gather together haphazardly into a pile, mass or heap. [L.].

AGGLOMERATION [a-glo-me-rā'shn], *n.* act of gathering into a mass; confused heap of articles loosely thrown together in a mass. [L.].

AGGLOMERATIVE [a-glo'me-ra-tiv], *adj.* apt to collect together into a mass.

AGGLUTINANT (1) [a-glŏŏ'ti-nant], *n.* any viscous

substance which produces or strengthens adhesion. AGGLUTINANT (2), *adj.* uniting as glue. [L.].

AGGLUTINATE (1) [a-glŏŏ'ti-nāt], *v.t. and i.* to glue together, fasten together by adhesion; form into a glue-like substance; combine words into compounds; become glued together; be made into a glue. AGGLUTINATE (2), *adj.* fastened together as with glue. [L.].

AGGLUTINATION [a-glŏŏ-ti-nā'shn], *n.* act of sticking together as with glue, state of being fastened together as with glue; (*philol.*) a method of joining together two or more distinct elements so that the union does not appear to be so perfect or close as with inflexion, but with the same purpose. AGGLUTINATIVE [a-glŏŏ'ti-na-tiv], *adj.* tending to cause a.; formed by or exhibiting a. [L.].

AGGLUTININ [a-glŏŏ'ti-nin], *n.* (*biol.*) substance found in animal organisms and bringing about agglutination.

AGGRANDIZE [a-gran'dīz], *v.t.* to make a person or state greater in power, rank or honour, enlarge, make more important. [Fr.].

AGGRANDIZEMENT [a-gran'diz-ment], *n.* increase in power, importance or wealth of a person or state, enlargement of the size of a state. [Fr.].

AGGRAVATE [ag'ra-vāt], *v.t.* to make worse, increase or intensify the gravity of anything; (*coll.*) annoy, exasperate.

AGGRAVATING [ag'ra-vā-ting], *adj.* making worse; (*coll.*) provoking, exasperating. AGGRAVATINGLY, *adv.* in an a. way.

AGGRAVATION [ag-ra-vā'shn], *n.* act or circumstance which increases the gravity or seriousness of anything; anything which aggravates; act of aggravating; (*coll.*) exasperation; annoyance.

AGGRAVATOR [ag'ra-vā-ter], *n.* person arousing aggravation.

AGGREGATE (1) [ag'ri-gat], *n.* the sum total; a collected mass, an amount; (*geol.*) rock consisting of a compound of minerals; (*building*) material mixed with lime to make concrete; (*phys.*) a whole formed by the union of homogeneous particles. AGGREGATE (2), *adj.* united into one body and capable of being regarded as a whole, collective; (*geol.*) of rocks composed of a compound of different minerals; (*bot.*) applied to flowers composed of florets united at the base in a common undivided receptacle; (*leg.*) consisting of two or more persons in association. AGGREGATE (3) [ag'ri-gāt], *v.t.* to collect together into a sum or mass, add up to, amount to. AGGREGATELY [ag'ri-gat-li], *adv.* collectively, as a whole. AGGREGATION [ag-ri-gā'shn], *n.* an aggregate, collective body of persons or things, act of aggregating, state of being aggregated. AGGREGATIVE [ag'ri-ga-tiv], *adj.* considered together. [L.].

AGGRESS [a-gres'], *v.i.* to be the first to attack; start the quarrel. [L.].

AGGRESSION [a-gre'shn], *n.* unprovoked attack upon a person or state. [L.].

AGGRESSIVE [a-gre'siv], *adj.* hostile, threatening, fiercely pugnacious, always ready or disposed to attack. AGGRESSIVELY, *adv.* in an a. way. [L.].

AGGRESSOR [a-gre'ser], *n.* state or individual that makes an unprovoked attack upon another, or first commences hostilities against another. [L.].

AGGRIEVE [a-grēv'], *v.t.* to oppress; injure the feelings of. AGGRIEVED, *adj.* suffering from injustice, having a grievance. [Fr.].

AGHAST [a-gahst'], *adj.* terrified, horror-stricken, awe-struck. [~OE.].

AGILE [a'jil], *adj.* nimble, active, quick in movement, quick-witted. AGILELY, *adv.* in an a. way. [Fr. from L.].

AGILITY [a-ji'li-ti], *n.* nimbleness, activity, quickness of movement (used also of the mind).

AGIO [a'jō, ā'jō], *n.* difference in value between paper money and actual coin, difference between two currencies in the same country or in different countries, premium or discount to be paid in exchanging one currency into another. AGIOTAGE [a'jo-tij], *n.* business of money exchange. [It.].

AGITATE [a'ji-tāt], *v.t.* to shake, stir violently; (*fig.*) disturb, upset, disquiet, excite (used of the mind and feelings); *v.i.* to cause public unrest, arouse public attention in order to bring about something, demand, often in a demonstrative fashion. [L.].

AGITATED [a'ji-tā-tid], *adj.* aroused, upset, in a state of mental disturbance or excitement due to fear.

AGITATION [a-ji-tā'shn], *n.* disturbance, mental

ŏŏ is pronounced as in food; ŏŏ as in hood; th as in *think*; TH as in *that*; zh as in azure. ~ = related to.

and emotional disquietude, perturbation, public excitement or unrest, movement arousing public attention to gain some end.

AGITATO [a-ji-tah′tō], *adv.* (*mus.*) in a quick, excited manner. [It.].

AGITATOR [a′ji-tā-ter], *n.* one who produces an agitation, one who excites or causes a disturbance for party or private interest, one who is persistently stirring up public unrest by his actions and speeches; (*mech.*) machine with a rotary beater for breaking up wood-pulp etc.

AGLET [ag′let], *n.* metal tag at the end of a lace; metallic dress ornament; gold braid, cord or pendant hanging from the shoulder in certain uniforms; a catkin. [Fr.].

AGLIMMER [a-gli′mer], *adv.* in a glimmering way.

AGLOW [a-glō′], *adj. and adv.* glowing; (*fig.*) eagerly excited. [L.].

AGLUTITION [ag-lōō-ti′shn], *n.* inability to swallow. [L.].

AGMATOLOGY [ag-ma-to′lo-ji], *n.* the part of science that deals with fractures. [Gk.].

AGNAME [ag′nām], *n.* nickname; cognomen added to the name and surname. [L.].

AGNATE (1) [ag′nāt], *n.* male relation on the father's side. AGNATE (2), *adj.* related on the father's side by descent from a common male ancestor. AGNATIC [ag-na′tik], *adj.* relating to descent by the male line. AGNATION [ag-nā′shn], *n.* (*leg.*) descent in a direct male line. [L.].

AGNOMEN [ag-nō′men], *n.* nickname, name in addition to the surname; (*hist.*) fourth name adopted by certain Romans. [L.].

AGNOSTIC (1) [ag-nos′tik], *n.* person who recognizes knowledge only of material phenomena, and who believes that nothing is known or can be known about the infinite, God, life hereafter etc. AGNOSTIC (2), *adj.* holding the belief of an a., sceptical of non-material phenomena. AGNOSTICISM [ag-nos′ti-sizm], *n.* doctrine and teaching of the agnostics. [Gk.].

AGNUS [ag′nus], *n.* lamb; **A. castus,** Mediterranean shrub with white flowers; **A. Dei,** (*R.C.*) prayer beginning with these words, part of the Mass; consecrated disk stamped with the figure of a lamb supporting a cross or flag. [L.].

AGO [a-gō′], *adv.* past, gone, in the past.

AGOG [a-gog′], *adj. and adv.* in a state of eager expectation or readiness. [Fr.].

AGONIC [a-gō′nik], *adj.* angle-less; **a. line,** line on the surface of the earth on which a magnetic needle points due north and south; line without magnetic declination.

AGONISTIC(AL) [a-go-nis′tik(-al)], *adj.* pertaining to athletic contests or to intellectual argument. [Gk.].

AGONIZE [a′go-nīz], *v.t. and i.* to be in extreme pain, suffer great anguish; put forth strenuous efforts; torture. [LL.].

AGONIZING [a′go-nī-zing], *adj.* causing great suffering to the mind or body. AGONIZINGLY, *adv.* in an a. way.

AGONY [a′go-ni], *n.* intense physical pain, extreme anguish or mental suffering; pangs of death; the sufferings of Christ in Gethsemane; **a. column,** column in a newspaper devoted to appeals for missing relatives and friends, personal messages etc. [Gk.].

AGORAPHOBIA [a-go-ra-fō′bi-ah], *n.* (*path.*) morbid fear of open places. [Gk.].

AGOUTI [a-gōō′ti], *n.* rodent found in South America and the West Indies. [Span.].

AGRAFFE [a-graf′], *n.* kind of ornamental buckle or clasp; (*med.*) instrument for keeping together the edges of a wound. [Fr.].

AGRAPHIA [a-gra′fi-ah], *n.* (*path.*) inability to express oneself in writing, due to mental illness. [Gk.].

AGRARIAN (1) [a-grāer′i-an], *n.* person or politician advocating better conditions for land workers, often including redistribution of estates. AGRARIAN (2), *adj.* pertaining to cultivated land, or landed property, or the apportionment of land; (*bot.*) growing wild in the fields; **a. laws,** laws passed in ancient Rome relating to the division of public and conquered lands. AGRARIANISM [a-grāer′i-a-nizm], *n.* principle of an equal division of lands, unrest caused by discontent with existing system of land tenure; policy favouring peasants. AGRARIANIZE [a-grāer′i-a-nīz], *v.t.* to share out land equally; infect with ideas of agrarianism. [L.].

AGREE [a-grē′], *v.i.* to consent to, accept, be content with a proposition; hold the same views as, be of the same opinion as (usually with *with*); tally with, be the same as; harmonize, live in concord; resolve to; come to terms; be suitable for one's constitution; (*gram.*) correspond in number, gender, case or person; *v.t.* to approve (the text of a document). AGREEABILITY [a-grē-a-bi′li-ti], *n.* agreeableness.

AGREEABLE [a-grē′a-bl], *adj.* pleasant, delightful, favourable to, willing, conformable to; **I am a.,** I am ready to do what has been suggested. AGREEABLENESS, *n.* condition or quality of being a. AGREEABLY, *adv.* pleasantly, in an a. manner. [Fr.].

AGREEMENT [a-grē′ment], *n.* correspondence of sympathies, sentiments, feelings, tastes etc., state of having the same opinions as, being of one mind with; a bargain, understanding; (*leg.*) written undertaking to perform a certain thing, which though not a contract is subject to the law of contract; (*gram.*) correspondence of number, gender, case or person. [OFr.].

AGRESTIC(AL) [a-gres′tik(-al)], *adj.* rustic, uncouth. [L.].

AGRICULTURAL [a-gri-kul′tyōōr-al], *adj.* pertaining to agriculture; **a. show,** exhibition of farm produce, livestock, implements etc.

AGRICULTUR(AL)IST [a-gri-kul′tyōōr(-al)-ist], *n.* one who obtains his living by, or who has made a special study of, agriculture, a farmer.

AGRICULTURE [ag′ri-kul-tyōōr], *n.* art or practice of cultivating the ground for the purpose of raising crops, and including the sowing of seed, gathering of crops and raising of livestock; theory and practice of farming. [L.].

AGRIMONY [ag′ri-mu-ni], *n.* (*bot.*) genus of plants of the order *Rosaceae,* esp. *Agrimonia eupatoria.* [L. from Gk.].

AGRIOLOGY [a-gri-o′lo-ji], *n.* comparative study of man in his primitive condition. AGRIOLOGIST, *n.* one who studies a. [Gk.].

AGRONOMICS [a-gro-no′miks], *n.* science of the management of land and production of crops. AGRONOMIC(AL), *adj.* pertaining to a.

AGRONOMY [a-gro′no-mi], *n.* study of the management of land and scientific cultivation of crops. [Gk.].

AGROSTOGRAPHY [a-gros-to′gra-fi], *n.* description of the species of grasses. [Gk.].

AGROSTOLOGY [a-gros-to′lo-ji], *n.* that branch of botany which treats of the grasses. [Gk.].

AGROUND [a-grownd′], *adv.* on the ground; (*naut.*) resting on the bottom in shallow water, no longer floating, stranded.

AGUE [ā′gyōō], *n.* kind of recurring malarial fever, characterized by fits of shivering. AGUED, *adj.* having a fit of a.; suffering from a. [OFr. from L.].

AGUE-CAKE [ā′gyōō-kāk], *n.* enlargement of the spleen.

AGUISH [ā′gyōō-ish], *adj.* characterized by shivering like an ague, causing an ague, prone to shivering fits and ague. AGUISHNESS, *n.* condition of being a.

AH [ah], *int.* exclamation used to convey almost any emotion according to the manner of utterance. [OFr.].

AHA [a-hah′, ah-hah′], *int.* exclamation expressing triumph, surprise, contempt etc. according to the way in which it is uttered. [Pers.].

AHEAD [a-hed′], *adv.* further in advance, in front; forward; before (often with *of*); **to go a.** (*coll.*) to start, begin; keep on, continue.

AHEM [a-hem′], *int.* exclamation or interjection used to call attention, indicate embarrassment, gain time in speaking etc.

AHOY [a-hoi′], *int.* (*naut.*) a sea term, used in hailing.

AHRIMAN [ah-ri-mahn′], *n.* the personification or source of all evil, according to the teaching of Zoroaster. [Pers.].

AHULL [a-hul′], *adv.* (*naut.*) applied to a ship with all sails furled and her helm lashed on the lee side on account of a storm.

AI [ä′ē], *n.* the three-toed sloth. [Echoic].

AID (1) [ād], *n.* assistance, help; means of help; (*leg.*) legal help claimed by a defendant in the defence of an action; **first a.** medical assistance rendered on the spot to a sick or injured person. AID (2), *v.t.* to help, succour, give assistance to. [L.].

AIDE-DE-CAMP (*pl.* **aides-de-camp**) [ā-de-kah(ng)′], *n.* (*milit.*) officer acting as secretary or agent to a king or general, and assisting him in the carrying out of his duties. [Fr.].

AIDE-MÉMOIRE [äd-me′mwah(r)], *n.* official intimation or declaration of policy or attitude upon a

---

The accent ′ after a syllable = stress (u-pon′). The mark ⁻ over a vowel = length (ā in made; ō in bone).

point in question sent by one government or state to another. [Fr.].

AIGRET, AIGRETTE [ā-gret'], *n.* the egret, plume of an egret, feathery plume attached to the seeds of several plants such as the thistle etc., head-dress in the form of a plume of feathers or a spray of jewels, rays of light visible from the edge of the moon during a solar eclipse. [Fr.].

AIGUILLE [ā-gwē'], *n.* one of the needle-like points of certain rocks and mountain peaks. [Fr.].

AIGUILLETTE, AIGULET [ā-gwē-yet', ā'gyōō-let], *n.* an aglet. [Fr.].

AIL [āl], *v.t.* to trouble with physical or mental pain, be the matter with, afflict; *v.i.* to be ill, in a state of continued ill health. [OE.].

AILANTHUS [ā-lan'thus], *n.* (*bot.*) tree, originally a native of China, on whose leaves a species of silkworm feeds.

AILERON [ā'le-ron], *n.* (*arch.*) side wall used to conceal a church aisle or a half-gable; (*aeron.*) hinged flap on the outer portion of the trailing edge of an aeroplane wing by which lateral balance may be maintained. [Fr.].

AILMENT [āl'ment], *n.* disease, indisposition.

AIM (1) [ām], *n.* the pointing or levelling of a weapon, or the directing of a missile or blow towards an object to be hit; estimation of direction, elevation etc. necessary in order to hit an object; purpose, goal, end to be sought after. AIM (2), *v.t. and i.* to train a weapon upon, direct a blow or missile towards an object; establish a goal or end to be striven after, try to achieve some object (usually with *at*, sometimes, *esp.* U.S., fold. by infin.); (*fig.*) make a remark intended to affect some particular person; direct, level at; take aim; **to a. high,** to be ambitious. [ME.].

AIMLESS [ām'les], *adj.* without aim, fixed direction, purpose or plan of action. AIMLESSLY, *adv.* in an a. fashion, haphazardly.

AIR (1) [āer], *n.* the gaseous substance forming the atmosphere which envelops the earth, state of the atmosphere at a particular time or place; (*fig.*) space immediately above the earth, the sky, light breeze or current of air; outward appearance, mien, demeanour, a particular expression on a person's countenance, affected manner, assumed bearing or look implying superiority (generally in the *pl.*); a continuous musical melody, composition for a solo voice or instrument with other voices or instruments providing an accompaniment, the tune, the principal melody part in a work for a number of instruments or voices, principal vocal part providing the tune; **in the a.,** current (of rumours); vague, unsettled (of projects); **castles in the a.,** fanciful dreams, imaginary schemes or projects; **fresh a.,** non-vitiated air containing its full complement of oxygen; **on the a.,** broadcast by wireless; **over the a.,** by means of wireless; **hot a.,** pointless and unbusinesslike or irrelevant talk; **to tread upon a.,** to be in a state of continued delight and exhilaration; **to beat the a.,** to expend one's energy needlessly in futile endeavour; **to give a person the a.,** (*U.S. slang*) to shun, dismiss. OPEN-AIR, *adj.* held outside a building, out of doors. AIR (2), *v.t. and i.* to ventilate, warm and dry before a fire etc., expose to the air in order to freshen; (*fig.*) express publicly, show off; become ventilated, warmed or freshened. [Fr. from Gk.].

AIR-BALLOON [āer'ba-lōōn], *n.* inflated toy-balloon filled with air or gas.

AIR-BASE [āer'bās], *n.* (*milit.*) aerodrome or place used as a base of operations by military or naval aircraft.

AIR-BED [āer'bed], *n.* airtight mattress inflated by air and used by the sick.

AIR-BLADDER [āer'bla-der], *n.* small sac containing air, the swimming bladder of a fish.

AIRBORNE [āer'bawn], *adj.* carried by aircraft, (of troops) carried by air to the battle zone and dropped by parachute or glider; (of aircraft) off the ground.

AIR-BRAKE [āer'brāk], *n.* brake worked by compression of air or by the action of air on a vacuum.

AIR-BUMP [āer'bump], *n.* (*aeron.*) sudden, uncontrolled movement of an aircraft caused by a change in the density of the air.

AIRCELLS [āer'selz], *n.* (*pl.*) (*bot. and anat.*) cavities or cells filled with air in plants, cavity in the body containing air.

AIR-CHIEF-MARSHAL [āer-chēf-mah'shal], *n.* second highest rank in the Royal Air Force.

AIR-COMMODORE [āer-ko'mo-daw(r)], *n.* rank in

the Royal Air Force corresponding to commodore in the Navy.

AIR-CONDENSER [āer'kon-den-ser], *n.* apparatus used to condense air; (*elect.*) condenser in which air acts as dielectric between the plates.

AIR-CONDITION [āer'kon-di-shn], *v.t.* to keep the air in a building clean, fresh and at predetermined temperature and humidity by mechanical means. AIR-CONDITIONER, *n.* air-conditioning plant. AIR-CONDITIONING, *n.* mechanical ventilation and temperature control.

AIR-COOLING [āer'kōō-ling], *n.* system of cooling a motor by currents of air.

AIRCRAFT [āer'krahft], *n.* flying machine; flying machines in general.

AIRCRAFT CARRIER [āer'krahft-ka-ri-er], *n.* warship carrying aircraft and having a specially constructed deck where aircraft may land or take off.

AIRCRAFTMAN [āer'krahft-man], *n.* lowest rank in the Royal Air Force.

AIR-DRAIN [āer'drān], *n.* cavity round the external walls of a building to keep off the earth and prevent dampness.

AIREDALE [āer'dāl], *n.* the largest kind of terrier, originally bred for otter hunting in the river Aire. [District in the West Riding of Yorkshire].

AIR-ENGINE [āer'en-jin], *n.* engine worked by heated air.

AIRER [āer'er], *n.* one who airs, framework on which clothes are hung in order to be aired.

AIRFIELD [āer'fēld], *n.* flat open space where aircraft can land and take off.

AIR-FILTER [āer'fil-ter], *n.* apparatus for purifying air; device for removing grit and dust from air before it enters the carburettor of a motor engine.

AIR FORCE [āer'faws], *n.* branch of the armed forces which is concerned with attack or defence from the air.

AIRGRAPH [āer'grahf], *n.* (*prot.*) letter photographed on a small scale for transmission by air.

AIR-GUN [āer'gun], *n.* gun which fires bullets etc. by means of compressed air.

AIR GUNNER [āer'gu-ner], *n.* one who operates a gun in military aircraft.

AIR-HOLE [āer'hōl], *n.* opening for the passage of air, hole in the ice of a frozen sea, river etc., hole in cast metal caused by bubbles of air escaping from the metal in its molten state.

AIRILY [āer'i-li], *adv.* in an airy manner, lightly, flippantly.

AIRING [āer'ing], *n.* exposure to the air or a fire, to ventilate or warm; exercise in the open air.

AIR-INTAKE [āer'in-tāk], *n.* passage admitting air in a coal mine; aperture which allows air to enter an internal combustion engine.

AIR-JACKET [āer'ja-kit], *n.* swimming jacket inflated with air to keep a person afloat in water; covering for pipes or boilers filled with air.

AIRLESS [āer'les], *n.* not well ventilated, not open to a free current of air.

AIR-LETTER [āer'le-ter], *n.* folding form of light paper for short letters to be sent by air-mail.

AIR-LIFT [āer'lift], *n.* regular system of goods transport by air.

AIR-LINE [āer'līn], *n.* (*aeron.*) a service of aeroplanes plying for hire; (*teleph.*) line above ground level.

AIR-LINER [āer'lī-ner], *n.* large passenger aeroplane.

AIR-LOCK [āer'lok], *n.* obstruction in the flow of fluid in a pipe caused by the presence of a bubble of air in the pipe.

AIR-MAIL [āer'māl], *n.* mails carried by aircraft.

AIRMAN [āer'man], *n.* aviator; official description, within the R.A.F., of all personnel of the rank of Warrant Officer and below.

AIR-MARSHAL [āer'mah-shal], *n.* third highest rank in the Royal Air Force.

AIR-PASSAGE [āer'pa-sij], *n.* (*bot.*) extended air-space between cells of certain plants; (*aeron.*) accommodation in an air-liner.

AIRPLANE [āer'plān], *n.* aeroplane (orig. U.S., now also form used in some English newspapers).

AIR-PLANT [āer'plahnt], *n.* non-parasitic plant which grows on another plant but obtains its nourishment and moisture from the air.

AIR-POCKET [āer'po-kit], *n.* localized atmospheric condition caused by irregular air currents and affecting an aeroplane so that it drops suddenly as into a cavity while flying.

AIRPOISE [āer'poiz], *n.* instrument used to measure the weight of air.

AIRPORT [āer'pawt], *n.* aerodrome provided with

ōō is pronounced as in *food*; ŏŏ as in *hood*; th as in *think*; TH as in *that*; zh as in a**z**ure.   ~ = related to.

accommodation for customs and immigration officials, and used as a landing place for aeroplanes coming from abroad.

AIR-PUMP [āer'pump], *n.* apparatus for pumping air or gas into or out of a vessel; (*motoring*) pressure pump which forces petrol to the carburettor.

AIR-RAID (1) [āer'rād], *n.* attack by aircraft dropping bombs. AIR-RAID (2), *adj.* of, concerned with, air-raids or defence against them of a passive nature.

AIR-SCOOP [āer'skōōp], *n.* (*aeron.*) projecting cowl which helps to keep up air pressure in the envelope of an airship.

AIRSCREW [āer'skrōō], *n.* propeller on an aircraft.

AIRSHAFT [āer'shahft], *n.* shaft for ventilation purposes.

AIRSHIP [āer'ship], *n.* aircraft of the lighter-than-air type sustained in the air by gas.

AIR-SICKNESS [āer'sik-nes], *n.* sickness caused by the motion of aircraft in flight.

AIR-SPACE [āer'spās], *n.* the amount of space containing air in a room or building, intervening space between two parallel walls, cavity in a bird's body containing air.

AIRSTREAM [āer'strēm], *n.* current of air cooling an aero-engine.

AIR-STRIP [āer'strip], *n.* landing ground, *esp.* temporary or emergency.

AIR-THERMOMETER [āer-ther-mo'mi-ter], *n.* instrument for measuring temperature by the expansion or contraction of air.

AIR-THREADS [āer'thredz], *n.(pl.)* fine threads of cobweb floating in the air, gossamer.

AIRTIGHT [āer'tīt], *adj.* not admitting air.

AIR-TRAP [āer'trap], *n.* contrivance for preventing the escape of foul air from drains.

AIR-TRUCK [āer'truk], *n.* (*aeron.*) aeroplane specially constructed for carrying freights.

AIR-VESSEL [āer've-sel], *n.* (*zool.*) vessel which contains air, breathing tube in insects, spiral vessel on the leaves of plants; (*hydraulics*) an air chamber.

AIR-VICE-MARSHAL [āer-vis-mah'shal], *n.* rank in the Royal Air Force corresponding to rear-admiral in the Navy and major-general in the Army.

AIRWAY [āer'wā], *n.* ventilation shaft in a mine; an air route.

AIRWOMAN [āer'wŏŏ-man], *n.* woman who flies aircraft.

AIRWORTHY [āer'wer-тні], *adj.* in a fit state for flying, applied to machines.

AIRY [āer'i], *adj.* resembling or belonging to the air, open to a current of air, well ventilated, unsubstantial, unpractical, light, sprightly, flippant, jaunty.

AISLE [īl], *n.* (*arch.*) one of the lateral divisions of a church, separated from the nave by pillars or piers, a passage between two blocks of pews in a church. [L.].

AIT [āt], *n.* small island in a river or lake. [OE.].

AITCH-BONE [āch'bōn], *n.* the buttock bone, the beef cut from over this bone. [OFr.].

AJAR [a-jah(r)'], *adv.* slightly open, as of a door. [OE.].

AKIMBO [a-kim'bō], *adv.* only in the phrase **arms a.**, with hands on hips and elbows bent outwards. [ME.].

AKIN [a-kin'], *adj.* related, resembling in nature, connected with.

ALABASTER (1) [a'la-bah-ster], *n.* a variety of gypsum, usually of a pure white colour and very soft. ALABASTER (2), *adj.* made of a., resembling a. ALABASTRIAN, ALABASTRINE [a-la-bah'stri-an, a-la-bah'strīn], *adj.* relating to, like, a. [Gk.].

ALACK [a-lak'], *int.* expression of sorrow, dismay, regret etc.

ALACK-A-DAY [a-lak-a-dā'], *int.* alas the day! an expression of sorrow.

ALACRITY [a-lak'ri-ti], *n.* willing and eager quickness and readiness, brisk promptitude. [L.].

ALALIA [a-la'li-ah], *n.* (*path.*) loss of speech. [Gk.].

ALAMEDA [a-la-mā'dah], *n.* promenade lined with trees. [Span.].

ALANTIN [a-lan'tin], *n.* starch manufactured from the elecampane. [Germ.].

ALAR [ā'lah(r)], *adj.* pertaining to or having wings, resembling wings; (*anat.*) axillary. [L.].

ALARM (1) [a-lahm'], *n.* call to arms, warning of danger usually sounded on a bell; bell or apparatus used to give the signal of sudden danger; (*fig.*) a warning; state of sudden terror, excitement or apprehension aroused by a threat of unexpected danger, catastrophe etc.; (*fencing*) a stamp on the ground with the advanced foot. ALARM (2), *v.t.* to

arouse to a feeling of danger, disturb with terror, excite with sudden fear, perturb, frighten. ALARM-BELL, bell rung to sound an alarm. ALARM-CLOCK, clock provided with an alarm-bell which can be set to be rung by clockwork mechanism or by electricity at a given time. ALARM-GAUGE, appliance fastened to a steam-engine to indicate excessive steam pressure or deficiency of water in a boiler. ALARMING, perturbing, exciting alarm or apprehension. ALARMINGLY, *adv.* in an alarming way. [It.].

ALARMIST (1) [a-lah'mist], *n.* one who is always starting scares or attempting to cause panic, one who is always apprehensive of real or imaginary danger. ALARMIST (2), *adj.* of a nature to cause alarm.

ALARUM [a-lah'rum], *n.* (*poet.*) alarm; ringing mechanism on an alarm-clock, ringing sound made by the bell on an alarm-clock.

ALAS [a-lahs', a-las'], *int.* exclamation expressing sorrow, pity, concern etc. [OFr.].

ALATE [ā'lāt], *adj.* provided with wings or wing-like appendages. [L.].

ALB [alb], *n.* long robe of white linen worn by priests officiating at the celebration of Mass. [L.].

ALBACORE, ALBICORE [al'ba-kaw(r)], *n.* kind of tunny-fish. [Arab.].

ALBATROSS [al'ba-tros], *n.* largest known sea-bird, found in the southern seas and the Behring Straits. [~Portug.].

ALBEIT [awl-bē'it], *conj.* (*poet.*) although, notwithstanding. [AL (though) IT BE (that)].

ALBERT [al'bert], *n.* kind of watch-chain. [ALBERT, Prince Consort].

ALBICORE, see ALBACORE.

ALBIGENSES [al-bi-jen'sēz], *n.(pl.)* sect of twelfth-century religious reformers in Albi and its neighbourhood.

ALBINISM [al'bi-nizm], *n.* state or condition of being an albino.

ALBINO [al-bē'nō], *n.* person or animal suffering from congenital deficiency of colouring pigment in the skin, hair and eyes, having thus a pale skin, white hair and pink eyes, unable to bear strong light. ALBINOTIC [al-bi-no'tik], *adj.* pertaining to albinism. [Span.].

ALBION [al'bi-on], *n.* ancient and now poetic name for Great Britain; **a. metal**, compound of tin and lead used in the manufacture of toys, cheap jewellery etc. [Celt.].

ALBITE [al'bīt], *n.* (*min.*) kind of felspar usually white in colour. [~L.].

ALBUGINEA [al-byōō-ji'ni-ah], *n.* (*anat.*) fibrous white substance covering the eye, testicle and certain other organs.

ALBUGO [al-byōō'gō], *n.* eye disease in which a white opaque spot forms in the cornea and affects vision. ALBUGINEOUS [al-byōō-ji'ni-ōōs], *adj.* resembling the white of an eye or of an egg. [L.].

ALBUM [al'bum], *n.* book with blank leaves on which may be affixed autographs, photographs, stamps, newspaper cuttings etc., a scrap book. [L.].

ALBUMEN, ALBUMIN [al'byōō-men], *n.* type of protein compound, a complicated substance forming a chemical constituent of most organic matter including the white of an egg, the serum of blood, the juice of flesh, lymph etc.; (*bot.*) farinaceous matter enclosing the embryo such as the flour of cereals etc. ALBUMENIZE [al-byōō'me-nīz], *v.t.* to impregnate with a., treat or coat with a solution of a. [L.].

ALBUMIN, see ALBUMEN.

ALBUMINATE [al-byōō'mi-nāt], *n.* a compound of albumen with certain bases.

ALBUMINOID (1) [al-byōō'mi-noid], *n.* one of the proteins forming the chief part of organic matter. ALBUMINOID (2), *adj.* resembling albumen.

ALBUMINOSE [al-byōō'mi-nōs], *n.* substance obtained from albumen by the action of dilute acid upon pepsin. ALBUMINOSE (2), *adj.* albuminous. [MdL.].

ALBUMINOSIS [al-byōō-mi-nō'sis], *n.* (*path.*) morbid condition in which too much albumen is in the blood.

ALBUMINOUS [al-byōō'mi-nōōs], *adj.* possessing the qualities of albumen. [L.].

ALBUMINURIA [al-byōō-mi-nyōō'ri-ah], *n.* condition in which albumen is present in the urine.

ALBURNUM [al-bur'num], *n.* (*bot.*) wood newly formed under the bark, sapwood. ALBURNOUS [al-bur'nōōs], *adj.* relating to or consisting of a.

ALCAIC [al-kā'ik], *adj.* belonging to the Greek poet

Alcaeus, pertaining to or written in the metre invented by him. ALCAICS, n.(pl.) verses written in A. metre. [Gk.].

ALCAZAR [al-ka-zah(r)'], n. Moorish or Spanish royal palace, fortress. [Arab.].

ALCHEMIC [al-ke'mik], adj. pertaining to alchemy. ALCHEMICALLY, adv. by alchemy. [MedL.].

ALCHEMIST [al'kem-ist], n. student of alchemy, one who practises alchemy. ALCHEMISTIC(AL) [al-ke-mis'tik(-al)], adj. practising or pertaining to alchemy. [MedL.].

ALCHEMIZE (alchemizes, alchemized, alchemizing) [al'ke-mīz], v.t. to change, as by alchemy.

ALCHEMY, ALCHYMY [al'ke-mi], n. study which aimed to prolong life indefinitely, to find the philosopher's stone which would change all base metals into gold, and to find a universal solvent. [OFr.].

ALCLAD [al'klad], n. alloy of aluminium used in building aeroplanes.

ALCOHOL [al'kō-hol], n. intoxicating product of fermentation from the juice of the grape and other substances, found in wine, beer, spirit and other fermented liquors; intoxicating liquors containing a certain amount of alcohol; (chem.) large group of compounds having chemical properties analogous to ethyl alcohol; **absolute a.**, alcohol with the water removed and containing more than 96 per cent pure alcohol. [Arab.].

ALCOHOLATE [al'kō-ho-lāt], n. (chem.) compound formed by a mixture of a metal and an alcohol, compound in which alcohol takes the place of the water of crystallization.

ALCOHOLIC (1) [al-kō-ho'lik], n. person whose health is impaired by excessive consumption of intoxicating beverages. ALCOHOLIC (2), adj. pertaining to, caused by, containing a certain amount of alcohol.

ALCOHOLIMETER, ALCOHOLOMETER [al-kō-ho-li'mi-ter, al-kō-ho-lo'mi-ter], n. apparatus used to calculate the percentage of alcohol in spirits.

ALCOHOLISM [al'kō-ho-lizm], n. habitual taking of alcoholic drinks and its effect upon the system.

ALCOHOLIZE [al'kō-ho-līz], v.t. to soak in alcohol, cause someone or something to come under the influence of alcohol. ALCOHOLIZATION [al-kō-ho-lī-zā'shn], n. process of subjection to the influence of alcohol.

ALCOHOLOMETER, see ALCOHOLIMETER.

ALCOVE [al'kōv], n. vaulted recess in a room often separated off by curtains, columns etc.; summerhouse. [Arab.].

ALDEHYDE [al'di-hīd], n. (chem.) generic name of compounds of alcohol intermediate between the alcohols and the acids, colourless volatile inflammable liquid with a suffocating smell, formed by oxidation of alcohol. ALDEHYDIC, adj. containing, characterized by, a.

ALDER [awl'der], n. plant of the order Betulaceae, growing in damp places.

ALDERMAN [awl'der-man], n. senior member of a county or municipal council who is concerned with the administration of local government and usually holds office for a longer term than ordinary members or councillors. ALDERMANCY [awl'der-man-si], n. position of an a. ALDERMANIC [awl-der-ma'nik], adj. relating to an a. ALDERMANLIKE, ALDERMANLY [awl'der-man-lik, awl'der-man-li], adj. like an a. ALDERMANRY [awl'der-man-ri], n. office or rank of alderman; district or ward whose representative is an alderman.

ALDERNEY [awl'der-ni], n. breed of cattle originating in Alderney.

ALDINE [awl'dīn], adj. produced by the press of Aldus Manutius and family between 1494 and 1570 at Venice, Rome and Bologna; one of the kinds of type used by Aldus in printing his editions.

ALE [āl], n. beverage consisting of fermented malt liquor generally flavoured with hops or other bitters, beer. [OE.].

ALEE [a-lē'], adv. (naut.) on or to the lee side. [OIcel.].

ALEMBIC [a-lem'bik], n. apparatus formerly used in distillation; (fig.) refining and distilling influence. [ME.].

ALERT (1) [a-lurt'], n. state of being alert; signal to be alert, esp. an air-raid warning; the period from this until the all-clear signal is given. ALERT (2), adj. watchful, ready to act immediately, lively, quick-witted. ALERTLY, adv. in an a. manner, smartly, briskly. ALERTNESS, n. condition of being a. [Fr.].

ALEUROMETER [a-lyoo-ro'mi-ter], n. instrument

for determining the bread-making qualities of wheaten flour. [Gk.].

ALEURONE [a-lyoo'rōn], n. albuminoid substance found in the ripening seeds of cereals and other plants. [Gk.].

ALEVIN [a'le-vin], n. young salmon. [Fr.].

ALEWIFE [āl'wīf], n. woman who keeps an alehouse; North American fish related to the shad.

ALEXANDERS [a-lek-zahn'derz], n. umbelliferous plant formerly used for salads. [Fr.].

ALEXANDRIAN [a-lek-zahn'dri-an], n. and adj. member of, pertaining to, the school of Greek literature which had its centre at Alexandria under the Ptolemies; (hence) artificial, derivative.

ALEXANDRINE [a-lek-zahn'drin], n. (pros.) line of six stresses or twelve syllables, usually having a pause after the sixth syllable. [Fr.].

ALEXIN [a-lek'sin], n. defensive protein; substance in the body which kills germs. [Gk.].

ALEXIPHARMIC (1) [a-lek-si-fah'mik], n. antidote to counteract the effects of poison. ALEXIPHARMIC (2), adj. acting as an antidote. [Gk.].

ALEXIPYRETIC [a-lek-si-pī-re'tik], n. remedy for fever. [Gk.].

ALFA [al'fah], n. esparto grass.

ALFALFA [al-fal'fah], n. the plant, Medicago sativa, grown chiefly in Argentina and the U.S.A. [Span.].

ALFRESCO [al-fres'kō], adj. and adv. in the fresh air, under the open sky; **a. meal**, picnic meal. [It.].

ALGAE (sg. **alga**) [al'jē, sg. al'gah], n.(pl.) order of plants, forming one of the divisions of cryptogamic plants, including the seaweeds, found in the sea and in fresh water or in damp places, and taking in nourishment through the whole of their surface. ALGAL [al'gal], adj. of, or pertaining to, alga or the algae. [L.].

ALGEBRA [al'ji-brah], n. kind of generalized arithmetic in which numbers, quantities, operations and often the results of operations are represented by symbols. ALGEBRAIC(AL) [al-ji-brā'ik(-al)], adj. relating to a. ALGEBRAICALLY, adv. by algebraic process, in accordance with a. [Arab.].

ALGEBRAIST [al-ji-brā'ist], n. one who studies algebra, an expert in algebra.

ALGEBRAIZE [al'ji-brā-īz], v.t. to reduce to algebraic form, solve by means of algebra.

ALGERINE [al'je-rin], n. inhabitant, usually a native, of Algiers.

ALGID [al'jid], adj. (med.) cold. ALGIDITY [al-ji'di-ti], n. chilliness. [L.].

ALGOID [al'goid], adj. like algae.

ALGOLOGY [al-go'lo-ji], n. (bot.) branch of botany concerned with the algae.

ALGOR [al'gaw(r)], n. (med.) chilliness at the onset of fever. [L.].

ALGORISM [al'go-rizm], n. Arabic system of notation of numerals, an arrangement or method of numeration. [Arab.].

ALGOUS [al'gōos], adj. relating to seaweed.

ALGUAZIL [ahl-gwah-thēl'], n. Spanish officer appointed to carry out the decrees of a judge. [Arab.].

ALGUM [al'gum], n. tree mentioned in the Bible in the Books of Kings and Chronicles, thought to be red sandalwood of India. [Heb.].

ALIAS (1) [ā'li-as], n. assumed name, false name. ALIAS (2), adv. otherwise known as. [L.].

ALIBI [a'li-bī], n. (leg.) plea by the defence by which the accused endeavours to establish that he was at a different place when the offence alleged was committed; (U.S. slang) excuse. [L.].

ALICANTE [ah-li-kahn'ti], n. a red, sweet Spanish wine.

ALICYCLIC [a-li-sī'klik], adj. (chem.) having the properties of both aliphatic and cyclic compounds.

ALIDADE [a'li-dād], n. movable arm of an instrument for measuring altitudes and distances, and carrying the sights and indicator. [Arab.].

ALIEN (1) [ā'li-en], n. person living in a different country from that of his birth, and who has not obtained the full rights of citizenship of that country, a foreigner. ALIEN (2), adj. strange, foreign, belonging to a different country, pertaining to aliens; of a different character from, not in sympathy with. [L.].

ALIENABLE [ā'li-e-na-bl], adj. able to be alienated. ALIENABILITY [ā-li-e-na-bi'li-ti], n. quality of being alienated.

ALIENATE [ā'li-e-nāt], v.t. to make a person out of sympathy with, turn against, estrange, lose the sympathy or support of, transfer property or rights

---

ŌŌ is pronounced as in food; ŎŎ as in hood; th as in think; TH as in that; zh as in azure. ~ = related to.

to the ownership of another. ALIENATOR, ALIENER [ā'li-e-nā-ter, ā'li-e-ner], n. person who alienates anything. [L.].

ALIENATION [ā-li-e-nā'shn], n. act of alienating, condition of being alienated, estrangement; insanity, mental derangement; (leg.) transference of rights or property to the ownership of another. [L.].

ALIENEE [ā-li-en-ē'], n. (leg.) one to whom rights or property are conveyed or transferred.

ALIENISM [ā'li-en-izm], n. state or condition of being an alien; (med.) study and treatment of mental diseases.

ALIENIST [ā'li-en-ist], n. (med.) specialist in the study and treatment of mental diseases.

ALIFORM [ā'li-fawm], adj. shaped like a wing. [L.].

ALIGHT (1) [a-līt'], adj. lighted, illumined; on fire.

ALIGHT (2), v.i. to dismount, end one's journey (by vehicle) at, get out at, descend and come to rest upon, land upon; fall on, come upon unexpectedly. [O.E.].

ALIGN, ALINE [a-līn'], v.t. and i. to bring, form or draw up into a line, bring the sights of a gun into line with the target; form up, fall into line with. [Fr.].

ALIGNMENT, ALINEMENT [a-līn'ment], n. arrangement or formation into a line; (milit.) act of adjusting or being adjusted to a straight line or lines (of soldiers); ground plan of a railway or road.

ALIKE (1) [a-līk'], adj. similar, having the same characteristics, appearance or effects. ALIKE (2), adv. equally, similarly, in the same manner, form or degree. ALIKENESS, n. resemblance, similarity. [O.E.].

ALIMENT (1) [a'li-ment], n. food, nourishment, sustenance; method of support; (Scots leg.) alimony. ALIMENT (2), v.t. and i. to keep up, maintain; (Scots leg.) provide for the support of a person. [L.].

ALIMENTAL [a-li-men'tal], adj. providing food; nourishing. ALIMENTALLY, adv. so as to provide nourishment.

ALIMENTARY [a-li-men'ta-ri], adj. nourishing, providing support, furnishing a means of sustenance, connected with the process, or with the organs, of nutrition; a. canal, passage through the body along which food travels, extending from the mouth to the anus. [L.].

ALIMENTATION [a-li-men-tā'shn], n. nourishment, act of affording nutriment, condition of being nourished. [Med.L.].

ALIMENTATIVENESS, ALIMENTIVENESS [a-li-men'ta-tiv-nes, al-i-men'tiv-nes], n. food-seeking instinct.

ALIMONY [a'li-mu-ni], n. provision for maintenance; (leg.) allowance paid by a husband to his wife during or pending a matrimonial suit, or after a legal separation not brought about by adultery or elopement of the wife. [L.].

ALINE, see ALIGN.

ALINEMENT, see ALIGNMENT.

ALIPHATIC [a-li-fa'tik], adj. relating to fat; (chem.) pertaining to certain organic compounds, such as the methane derivatives, which have a chain structure like the fatty acids. [Gk.].

ALIQUANT [a'li-kwont], adj. (of a number) not dividing exactly into another number. [L.].

ALIQUOT [a'li-kwot], adj. (of a number) dividing without remainder into another number. [L.].

ALIVE [a-līv'], adj. and adv. living, in a live state, in force, action or operation, active; wide awake, alert, aware of, ready for; crowded with, swarming with; look a., be quick!; sakes a., (coll.) an expletive. [O.E.].

ALIZARIN [a-li'za-rin], n. substance found in the root of the madder and used in dyeing to obtain shades of red, now synthetically prepared. [Fr.].

ALKALESCENT [al-ka-le'sent], adj. having to a certain degree the properties of an alkali. ALKALESCENCE, ALKALESCENCY, n. tendency or capacity to become alkaline.

ALKALI (pl. alkalis) [al'ka-lī], n. (chem.) a base or compound which is soluble in water, neutralizes acids and combines with them to form salts, corrodes animal and vegetable matter and changes the colour of many vegetable colouring matters, as turning reds to blue, yellows to brown, and purples to green. ALKALIGENOUS [al-ka-li'je-nŏŏs], adj. producing a. [Arab.].

ALKALIFY [al'ka-li-fī], v.t. to change into an alkali; v.i. to become an alkali. ALKALIFIABLE [al-ka-li-fī'a-bl], adj. able to be made alkaline.

ALKALIMETRY [al-ka-li'mit-ri], n. calculation of

the strength of alkaline solutions or the amount of free alkali in an alkaline substance. ALKALIMETRIC [al-ka-li-met'rik], adj. pertaining to a.

ALKALINE [al'ka-līn], adj. having the properties or characteristics of an alkali. ALKALINITY [al-ka-li'-ni-ti], n. condition or quality of being a., the characteristics of an a. substance or solution.

ALKALIZE [al'ka-līz], v.t. to make alkaline; v.i. to become an alkali. ALKALIZATION [al-ka-li-zā'shn], n. act of making alkaline by impregnating with an alkali.

ALKALOID [al'ka-loid], n. (chem.) one of a class of nitrogenous compounds having the properties of a base or alkali, found in living plants which are usually poisonous, and used as medicinal drugs. ALKALOIDAL, adj. like an a.

ALKANET [al'ka-net], n. a plant of the natural order Boraginaceae, the bark of whose root provides a deep red dye; the dye obtained from this plant. [Arab.].

ALL (1) [awl], n. the whole, everything, everybody, the whole quantity, amount, quality, number; (fig.) the whole of one's property, anything; after a., considering everything; a. in a., most precious thing; all's one, it is just the same; in a., altogether, all told; at a., in any way; a. my eye, (slang) totally wrong, untrue, absurd. [O.E.].

ALL (2), adj. the entire extent, amount or quantity of, every, any, the greatest possible; for good and a., for ever; once for a., for the last time, finally; at a. events, in any case; one and a., everybody, singly and collectively. [O.E.].

ALL (3), adv. entirely, wholly, completely, full of, so much; a. one, immaterial; a. at once, suddenly; a. but, almost; a. the same, immaterial, yet, nevertheless; a. over, (coll.) just like; a. right, in order, satisfactory, well; (coll. inter.) very well, agreed; a. there, (coll.) perfectly sane, very shrewd; a. along, throughout; a. out, (coll.) with the throttle wide open, straining every nerve; a. on, (cards) set to make the remaining tricks; a. for, (coll.) enthusiastically supporting; to be a. over, or up, with, (coll.) to be finished, beaten, ruined. [O.E.].

ALLA [a'lah], prep. (mus.) in the manner of. [It.].

ALLA-BREVE [a-lah-brā'vā], n. musical direction, originally indicating four minims to the measure, now indicating two minims to the measure and virtually amounting to a quick common time. [It.].

ALLA-CAPELLA [a-lah-ka-pe'lah], n. alla-breve. [It.].

ALLAH [a'lah], n. the name for God in Arabic, the Moslem word for the Supreme Deity. [Arab.].

ALLANTOIN [a-lan'tō-in], n. substance found in allantoic fluid and synthetically produced by boiling uric acid and lead dioxide.

ALLANTOIS [a-lan'tō-is], n. (anat.) thin membranous sac in the foetus of reptiles, birds and mammals, largely made up of blood vessels. ALLANTOIC [a-lan-tō'ik], adj. contained in the a. ALLANTOID(AL) [a-lan'toid(-al)], adj. relating to the a.; sausage-shaped. [Gk.].

ALLAY [a-lā'], v.t. to soothe, calm, appease, repress; calm, mitigate, assuage, abate, diminish. [O.E.].

ALL CLEAR [awl-klēer'], n. signal that raiding aircraft have passed out of the area.

ALLEGATION [a-li-gā'shn], n. statement, assertion (often unsupported by proof); (leg.) statement claimed to be true, but which has not been proved in a court of law.

ALLEGE [a-lej'], v.t. to state as a fact, assert, claim as true, advance as an excuse, plea, argument or evidence. ALLEGEABLE, adj. able to be alleged. [ME.].

ALLEGED [a-lejd'], adj. stated to be true, asserted, levelled (of charges), ascribed.

ALLEGIANCE [a-lē'jans], n. obedience or loyalty which every subject owes to the state or to the sovereign; fidelity, loyalty or devotion to a cause or group.

ALLEGORIC(AL) [a-li-go'rik(-al)], adj. relating to allegory, symbolical, figurative. ALLEGORICALLY, adv. in a figurative or symbolical way. [Gk.].

ALLEGORIST [a'li-go-rist], n. one who writes in allegory, one who treats a subject in an allegorical way.

ALLEGORIZE [a'li-go-rīz], v.t. to treat or interpret by means of allegory; v.i. to use allegory.

ALLEGORY [a'li-go-ri], n. figurative or symbolical description or story commenting upon or suggesting some real situation, yet placed in the realm of the imaginary, and in which the words and characters have another significance in addition to their literal meaning, figurative story in the form of a fable or parable generally having a moral import. [Gk.].

ALLEGRETTO [a-le-gret'tō], *adj. and adv. (mus.)* fairly fast, brisk and lively, not quite so quick as allegro. [It.].

ALLEGRISSIMO [a-le-gris'si-mō], *adj. (mus.)* very lively. [It.].

ALLEGRO [a-lā'grō], *adj. and adv.* brisk, lively; *(mus.)* with a quick lively rate of movement or time; at a quick lively rate. [It.].

ALLELOMORPH [a-lē'lo-mawf], *n. (biol.)* one of a pair of contrasting genes through which alternative pairs of Mendelian characteristics are inherited. [Gk.].

ALLELUIA, see HALLELUJAH.

ALLEMANDE [a-le-mahnd'], *n.* dance invented in France during the reign of Louis XVI; the music for this. [Fr.].

ALLERGIC [a-lur'jik], *adj.* affected by allergy; *(coll.)* antipathetic, feeling intense dislike (to).

ALLERGY [a'ler-ji], *n.* pathological condition peculiar to certain individuals of extreme sensitivity to particular substances. [Gk.].

ALLEVIATE [a-lē'vi-āt], *v.t.* to lessen, mitigate, afford relief, assuage. [L.].

ALLEVIATION [a-lē-vi-ā'shn], *n.* act or process of alleviating, that which provides relief, mitigation.

ALLEY [a'li], *n.* narrow passage between buildings, narrow squalid street; avenue or walk bordered by trees or bushes, bordered path in a garden; long narrow enclosed space in which bowls, skittles etc. are played; passage separating rows of pews; **blind a.,** one that is open at one end only; *(fig.)* situation or project that leads nowhere. ALLEYWAY, *n.* narrow passage. [OFr.].

ALL FOOLS' DAY [awl-fōōlz'dā], *n.* first of April.

ALL-FOURS [awl-fawz'], *n.* legs of a quadruped animal, arms and legs of a human being; card game so called from its four points; **on a.,** (of a person) on legs and arms; *(fig.)* on terms of equality, exactly similar.

ALL HALLOWE'EN [awl-ha-lō-ēn'], *n.* 31 October.

ALL-HALLOWMASS [awl-ha'lō-mas], *n.* All Saints' Day, the first day of November; festival of All Saints.

ALL-HALLOWS [awl-ha'lōz], *n.* all the saints; All Saints' Day.

ALLIACEOUS [a-li-ā'shōōs], *adj. (bot.)* pertaining to plants of the genus *Allium,* including onions, garlic etc.; having the pungent smell and taste of the plants of this genus. [L.].

ALLIANCE [a-lī'ans], *n.* relationship or union by marriage; league or treaty between two or more powers for mutual offence and defence against a common enemy, union between parties (usually political) or sections, to help bring about a common aim or object. [ME.].

ALLIGATOR [a'li-gā-ter], *n.* genus of reptiles of the crocodile family, found in swamps and marshes in America and China. [Span.].

ALLIGATOR-PEAR [a-li-gā-ter-pāer'], *n. (bot.)* tree of the order *Lauraceae* bearing a fruit similar to a large pear, known also as avocado pear.

ALL-IN [awl-in'], *adj.* all-embracing, comprehensive; **a. wrestling,** form of wrestling in which no tactics except biting and gouging are barred. ALL-IN (2), *adv.* completely exhausted, dead-beat.

ALLITERATE [a-li'te-rāt], *v.i.* to begin several words in a phrase, sentence or verse with the same initial consonant or make sentences or verses in which the words have the same initial consonant sound. [L.].

ALLITERATION [a-li-te-rā'shn], *n.* repetition of the same initial consonantal sound or of initial vowel sounds in a group of words forming a phrase, sentence or line of verse. [Prec.].

ALLITERATIVE [a-li'te-ra-tiv], *adj.* characterized by alliteration; **a. verse,** verse in which alliteration marks the stress, and together with it forms the essential part of the structure. ALLITERATIVELY, *adv.* by means of alliteration, so as to alliterate.

ALLOCATE [a'lo-kāt], *v.t.* to assign, allot, fix. [L.].

ALLOCATION [a-lo-kā'shn], *n.* allotment, distribution, apportionment, allowance on account, arrangement. [MedL.].

ALLOCATUR [a-lo-kā'ter], *n. (leg.)* certificate of allowance of costs. [MedL.].

ALLOCHROUS [a'lok-rōōs], *adj.* changing colour (as a symptom of illness). [Gk.].

ALLODIUM [a-lō'di-um], *n.* ancient system of land

tenure, whereby land was the absolute property of the owner who held it, as opposed to feudal tenure. ALLODIAL [a-lō'di-al], *adj.* (of land) held in absolute ownership. [MedL.].

ALLOGAMY [a-lo'ga-mi], *n.* cross-fertilization. [Gk.]

ALLOGRAPH [a'lo-grahf], *n.* writing or signature made by a person on behalf of the interested party. [Gk.].

ALLOMEROUS [a-lo'me-rōōs], *adj. (min. and chem).* retaining the same form, yet varying in chemical composition. [Gk.].

ALLOMORPH [a'lo-mawf], *n. (min.)* a distinct crystalline form with the same chemical composition. [Gk.].

ALLOMORPHISM [a-lō-maw'fizm], *n.* ability in substances to change their shape while they remain in other respects the same. [Gk.].

ALLOPATHY [a-lō'pa-thi], *n. (med.)* the usual method of treatment of disease, in contrast to homoeopathy. ALLOPATHIC [a-lō-pa'thik], *adj.* relating to a. ALLOPATHICALLY, *adv.* in an allopathic way. [Gk.].

ALLOPHYLIAN (1) [a-lō-fi'li-an], *n.* member of another race; *(specif.)* member of a non-Aryan or Semitic race dwelling in Europe or Asia. ALLOPHYLIAN (2), *adj.* pertaining to the non-Aryan or Semitic peoples or languages of Europe or Asia. [Gk.].

ALLOT [a-lot'], *v.t.* to apportion, assign, share out; appoint, determine; set apart for a special purpose. [OFr.].

ALLOTMENT [a-lot'ment], *n.* act of allotting; share, portion or distribution, small plot of land assigned or let out for cultivation; apportionment of shares; allowance from pay made by personnel in the armed forces to their dependants. ALLOTTEE [a-lo-tē'], *n.* one to whom an a. is made.

ALLOTROPY [a-lot'ro-pi], *n. (chem.)* existence of the same element in different forms, often with dissimilar external physical properties or characteristics. ALLOTROPIC [a-lo-tro'pik], *adj.* relating to a.

ALLOW [a-low'], *v.t. and i.* to permit, agree to, give consent to; acknowledge, admit, concede; render possible, bring about; grant, give a certain amount of money; deduct. [ME.].

ALLOWANCE [a-low'ans], *n.* fixed sum of money or quantity of a substance periodically granted; share, portion; deduction, discount; something taken into consideration, permission; **make allowances for,** regard indulgently. [OFr.].

ALLOY (1) [a'loi], *n.* substance produced by melting together two or more metals; the relative purity of gold and silver, a mixture of a base metal with a precious one; *(fig.)* mixture of good and bad, an impairing element. ALLOY (2) [a-loi'], *v.t.* to mix metals, lower the standard of purity in a metal by mixing with a base metal; *(fig.)* debase, impair. [Fr.].

ALL-RED [awl-red'], *adj.* (of routes) lying completely within British Commonwealth territory.

ALL-ROUND [awl-rownd'], *adj.* competent in all branches of any activity, *esp.* in sport, or in a wide variety of activities. ALL-ROUNDER, *n. (coll.)* one who is a.

ALL SAINTS' DAY [awl-sānts'dā], *n.* first day of November, on which day is held a festival in honour of all the saints.

ALL SOULS' DAY [awl-sōlz'dā], *n.* day of prayer which is held on 2 November for the souls of the faithful dead.

ALLSPICE [awl'spīs], *n.* dried, ground berry of a West Indian species of myrtle, having a flavour resembling a mixture of cinnamon, nutmegs and cloves.

ALLUDE [a-lyōōd'], *v.t.* to refer to, often in a vague, indirect manner, hint at, make a passing reference to. [L.].

ALLURE (1) [a-lyōōr'], *n.* charm, fascination; *(coll.)* sex-appeal, attractiveness. [Fr.]. ALLURE (2), *v.t.* to entice, tempt, charm, often implying a bad motive. [OFr.].

ALLUREMENT [a-lyōōr'ment], *n.* enticement, fascination, attractive temptation.

ALLURING [a-lyōōr'ing], *adj.* attractive and fascinating, tempting, possessing great charm. ALLURINGLY, *adv.* in an a. way.

ALLUSION [a-lyōō'zhn], *n.* reference either direct or vague, hint. [L.].

ALLUSIVE [a-lyōō'siv], *adj.* full of, containing,

ōō is pronounced as in food; ŏŏ as in hood; th as in *think*; TH as in *that*; zh as in azure. ~ = related to.

allusions. **ALLUSIVELY,** *adv.* in an a. manner. **ALLUSIVENESS,** *n.* condition of being a.

ALLUVIAL [a-lyōō'vi-al], *adj.* relating to soil which has been washed away by running water and later deposited.

ALLUVION [a-lyōō'vi-on], *n.* (*leg.*) gradual increase of land on a shore by the action of water; land thus deposited; mass of substances so collected. [Fr. from L.].

ALLUVIUM [a-lyōō'vi-um], *n.* (*geol.*) deposits of soil washed down by flowing water from rocks etc. and usually found in valleys, plains and deltas. [L.].

ALLY (1) [a'li], *n.* large prize marble used in the game of marbles. (Shortened form of ALABASTER).

ALLY (2) [a-li'], *v.t.* to unite or combine with, league together by marriage, treaty or agreement; (*fig.*) be connected by virtue of similar characteristics or affinities.

ALLY (3) [a'li, a-li'], *n.* friend, confederate, person who co-operates with another in an attempt to achieve some common aim; state leagued to another by treaty or agreement for political, defensive or offensive purposes. [OFr. from L.].

ALLYL [a'lil], *n.* (*chem.*) the isolated radical of a series of organic compounds.

ALMA [al'mah], *adj.* nourishing; **A. Mater,** the university, college or school at which a person received his education. [L.].

ALMACANTAR, ALMUCANTAR [al-myōō-kan'-tah(r)], *n.* a circle of the sphere parallel to the horizon; a circle of altitude. [Arab.].

ALMAGEST [al'ma-gest], *n.* celebrated astronomical treatise written by Ptolemy of Alexandria; later applied to other treatises on astronomy or astrology. [Arab.].

ALMAGRA [al-mag'rah], *n.* a deep-red ochre. [Span.].

ALMANAC [awl'ma-nak], *n.* document containing a list of days and months, data about the movements of the sun and moon, indication of feasts, holidays etc. and other miscellaneous information; **nautical a.,** one containing astronomical information, used by sailors in determining their longitude at sea. [MedL.].

ALMANDINE [al'man-din], *n.* violet-coloured garnet. [L.].

ALMIGHTY [awl-mi'ti], *adj.* all-powerful, omnipotent; (*coll.*) great; **the A.,** God. **ALMIGHTILY,** *adv.* omnipotently. [OE.].

ALMOND [ah'mond], *n.* tree related to the peach, with pinkish blossom; the edible nut-kernel enclosed in the stone of the fruit of this tree. [L.].

ALMOND-CAKE [ah'mond-kāk], *n.* solid residue left behind after the oil has been pressed out of almonds.

ALMOND-EYED [ah-mond-id'], *adj.* having long, almond-shaped eyes.

ALMOND-ICING [ah-mond-i'sing], *n.* layer of paste made with ground almonds spread under a coating of icing on a cake.

ALMOND-OIL [ah'mond-oil], *n.* oil expressed from the kernels of bitter and sweet almonds.

ALMONER [ah'mo-ner], *n.* official distributor of alms in a religious establishment; one who administers social service work for the benefit of patients at a hospital. [OFr.].

ALMOST [awl'mōst], *adv.* nearly; all but. [OE.].

ALMS [ahmz], *n.* (*sg. and pl.*) money or other charitable gifts given for the relief of the poor, donation for a religious or charitable purpose. [OE. from L.].

ALMSGIVING [ahmz'gi-ving], *n.* charitable gift of money or alms.

ALMSHOUSE [ahmz'hows], *n.* home maintained by private endowment or public support where certain aged poor people are housed and provided for.

ALMSMAN [ahmz'man], *n.* person maintained by alms.

ALMUCANTAR, see ALMACANTAR.

ALOE [a'lō], *n.* (*bot.*) genus of plants of the order *Liliaceae,* the juice of certain varieties of which possesses medicinal value; (*pl.*) (*med.*) the bitter juice of aloe leaves thickened by boiling and used as a purgative. [Gk.].

ALOETIC (1) [a-lō-e'tik], *n.* medicine composed chiefly of aloes. **ALOETIC** (2), *adj.* containing aloes; **a. acid,** acid obtained by the action of nitric acid upon aloes.

ALOFT [a-loft'], *adv.* high up, up above; (*naut.*) to a more elevated part of the ship. [OIcel.].

ALOIN [a'lō-in], *n.* the bitter element in aloes which acts as a purgative.

ALONE [a-lōn'], *adj. and adv.* unaccompanied, on

one's own, by oneself; unaided, single, solely; **to leave a., let a.,** (*coll.*) not to interfere with. [ME.].

ALONG (1) [a-long'], *adv.* lengthwise, extending in a lengthwise direction; onward, forward; **all a.,** from the commencement, all the time, the whole length of; **a. with,** together with. **ALONG** (2), *prep.* in a line with or parallel to the length, in a lengthwise direction advancing towards one end; **a. shore,** (*naut.*) by the shore. [OE.].

ALONGSIDE [a-long-sid'], *adv. and prep.* by the side of, close to the side of, side by side with.

ALOOF [a-lōōf'], *adv. and pred. adj.* at a distance away, away from, apart from (often implying absence of sympathy or approval); **to stand a.,** to take no part in voluntarily; **to hold oneself a.,** not to mix with, implying an attitude of reserve or disapproval. **ALOOFNESS,** *n.* condition or state of holding a. [Du.].

ALOPECIA [a-lō-pē'shah], *n.* (*med.*) baldness, falling out of the hair. [Gk.].

ALOUD [a-lowd'], *adv.* in an audible manner, with a loud voice. [ME.].

ALP [alp], *n.* a high mountain, mountain pasture in Switzerland; **the Alps,** mountain ranges in Switzerland, northern Italy and south-eastern France. [L.].

ALPACA [al-pa'kah], *n.* animal of the camel tribe found in the Andes; the wool of this animal; cloth made from a. wool and generally mixed with cotton or silk. [Peruvian].

ALPENSTOCK [al'pen-stok], *n.* long, pointed iron-shod stick used in mountaineering. [Germ.].

ALPHA [al'fah], *n.* first letter in the Greek alphabet; (*fig.*) the first or beginning, the first of a series (in scientific terminology); (*astron.*) the brightest star in a constellation; **the a. and omega,** the beginning and end; **a. particles,** positively charged particles given off by radio-active substances; **a. rays,** streams of alpha particles. [Gk.].

ALPHABET [al'fa-bet], *n.* the whole series of characters used in writing a language, and arranged in a certain fixed order; (*fig.*) elements of a study. **ALPHABETARIAN** [al-fa-be-tāer'i-an], *n.* one who is learning his a.; (*fig.*) a beginner. **ALPHABETIC**(AL) [al-fa-be'tik(-al)], *adj.* pertaining to an alphabet, arranged according to the alphabet. **ALPHABETIC-ALLY,** *adv.* in an alphabetic order or fashion. [Gk.].

ALPHENIC [al-fe'nik], *n.* white barley-sugar. [Fr.].

ALPHOS [al'fus], *n.* a variety of psoriasis. [Gk.].

ALPINE (1) [al'pin], *adj.* pertaining to the Alps or other high mountainous range; (*fig.*) lofty, belonging to or produced in high regions; **a. plants,** plants which grow in the region of the snow line in mountainous districts. **ALPINE** (2), *n.* an a. plant. [L.].

ALPINIST [al'pi-nist], *n.* climber in the Alps or other high mountains, mountaineer.

ALREADY [awl-re'di], *adv.* by or before a specified time, by this time, previously. [ME.].

ALSATIA [al-sā'shah], *n.* frontier region between France and Germany; name given to Whitefriars, a London district which was formerly a recognized retreat for criminals and debtors. [LL.].

ALSATIAN (1) [al-sā'shn], *n.* large kind of wolf-hound, used as a sheep-dog, watch-dog, police dog etc.; a native of Alsace. **ALSATIAN** (2), *adj.* pertaining to Alsace or the people of Alsace. [LL.].

ALSO [awl'sō], *adv. and conj.* in addition, besides, as well, furthermore, likewise; **a. ran,** racehorse which fails to attain a "place"; (*fig.*) an unsuccessful or inferior person or thing. [OE.].

ALT [alt], *n.* (*mus.*) the high notes in the scale, the octave above the treble stave commencing on the top note of the treble stave G. [Provenc. from L.].

ALTAR [awl'ter], *n.* flat-topped raised structure at which religious sacrifices were received or performed; the communion table, the table on which Mass is celebrated; **to lead to the a.,** to marry. [OE. from L.].

ALTAR-BREAD [awl'ter-bred], *n.* the bread used in the sacrament of Communion.

ALTAR-CLOTH [awl'ter-kloth], *n.* richly embroidered, ornamental cloth hanging down from the top of an altar and draping its front.

ALTAR-PIECE [awl'ter-pēs], *n.* a painting or sculpture in a frame over the altar; the reredos.

ALTAR RAILS [awl'ter-rālz], *n.* railing separating the raised platform on which stands an altar from the body of the church.

ALTER [awl'ter], *v.t. and i.* to change, make different, modify; become different, change (in appearance or character). [LL.].

ALTERABLE [awl'te-ra-bl], *adj.* capable of being

altered. ALTERABILITY [awl-te-ra-bi'li-ti], n. degree to which a thing is capable of altering or being altered. ALTERABLY, adv. so as to be capable of alteration. [Fr.].

ALTERATION [awl-te-rā'shn], n. change, state of being changed, act of altering, a correction, modification. [MedL.].

ALTERATIVE (1) [awl'te-ra-tiv], n. (med.) medicine which gradually brings about a change in the processes of nutrition and restores the healthy functions of the system. ALTERATIVE (2), adj. bringing about, susceptible to, alteration.

ALTERCATE [awl'ter-kāt], v.i. to engage in violent argument with, dispute hotly. [L.].

ALTERCATION [awl-ter-kā'shn], n. violent dispute, heated argument.

ALTER EGO [al-ter-e'gō], n. a second self, bosom friend. [L.].

ALTERNANT [awl-tur'nant], adj. (geol.) consisting of alternating layers.

ALTERNATE (1) [awl-tur'nat], adj. of two things occurring in regular succession one behind the other as regards time or position; every other, every second; (bot.) occurring on opposite sides of an axis in regular succession at different levels; (math.) occurring on opposite sides of a line in regular succession; **a. generation**, (biol.) of young, reproduced after the manner in which their grandparents were reproduced, but in a different way from that in which their parents were reproduced. ALTERNATE (2) [awl'ter-nat], n. person who shares alternatively with someone else in the execution of certain duties, offices etc.; (leg.) right to precedence in succession; precedence by rotation among persons of equal rank; (U.S.) substitute for a delegate. ALTERNATE (3) [awl'ter-nāt], v.t. to perform, arrange or interchange two things in succession one after the other; (of two things) cause to succeed in turn; v.i. to succeed or occur one after the other, vary between two things occurring in alternate succession; (elect.) of a current which reverses direction regularly at certain intervals. [L.].

ALTERNATELY [awl-tur'nat-li], adv. in alternate succession, first one then another in turn.

ALTERNATING CURRENT [awl-ter-nā-ting-ku'-rent], n. (elect.) electric current reversing its direction regularly at certain intervals.

ALTERNATION [awl-ter-nā'shn], n. act of alternating, state of being alternate, regular succession of one thing after another. [L.].

ALTERNATIVE (1) [awl-tur'na-tiv], n. choice of one of two things, courses of action etc.; choice of several methods of approach, courses of action etc.; (pl.) several courses of action, possibilities etc. differing from the one suggested. ALTERNATIVE (2), adj. offering a choice of two, differing from the one suggested. ALTERNATIVELY, adv. in an a. way, as an a., with a choice of. [MedL.].

ALTERNATOR [awl'ter-nā-ter], n. a dynamo, or generator, that produces alternating electric current.

ALTHAEA [al-thē'ah], n. genus of plants including the marsh-mallow and hollyhock. [Gk.].

ALTHOUGH [awl-THŌ'], conj. though, in spite of the fact that, even though. [ME.].

ALTIMETER [al'ti-mē-ter], n. (aeron.) kind of aneroid barometer, used in aircraft, to show the height above ground at which one is flying.

ALTITUDE [al'ti-tyōod], n. height of very tall objects measuring from bottom to top; height above horizon or sea-level; (esp. in pl.) high places or regions; (astron.) height of a heavenly body measured by its angular distance above the horizon; (geom.) perpendicular distance from the base of a triangle to its apex; **a. control**, (aeron.) device fitted to the carburettor or other part of the induction system to obtain a suitable mixture of fuel gas at high altitudes. ALTITUDINAL [al-ti-tyōo'di-nal], adj. pertaining to a. [L.].

ALTO [al'tō], n. (mus.) originally the highest male voice or counter-tenor, now the lowest female or boy's voice, the contralto; part taken by this voice in a score; person who sings the alto part; viola; (pop.) tenor violin. [It.].

ALTO CLEF [al'tō-klef], n. (mus.) the C clef placed on the third line of the stave.

ALTOGETHER [awl-to-ge'THer], adv. in all respects, wholly, entirely; **the a.**, (coll.) the nude.

ALTOMETER [al-to'mi-ter], n. barometer for recording altitudes.

ALTO-RELIEVO, ALTO-RILIEVO [ahl-tō-re-li-ā'vō], n. (sculp.) high relief; figures that project

half or more of their thickness from a flat surface. [It.].

ALTRUISM [al'trōō-izm], n. doctrine or principle which inculcates sacrifice of self for the interests of others. ALTRUIST [al'trōō-ist], n. one who practises **a.** ALTRUISTIC [al-trōō-is'tik], adj. unselfish, in accordance with a. ALTRUISTICALLY, adv. in an altruistic way. [Fr.].

ALUM (1) [a'lum], n. a mineral salt, double sulphate of aluminium and potassium. ALUM (2), v.t. to impregnate with a. [L.].

ALUMINA [a-lyōo'mi-nah], n. oxide of aluminium.

ALUMINIFEROUS [a-lyōo-mi-ni'fe-rŏŏs], adj. containing quantities of alum or alumina. [L.].

ALUMINITE [a-lyōo'mi-nīt], n. sulphate of alumina.

ALUMINIUM [a-lyōo-mi'ni-um], n. soft light white metal much used for household utensils and as an alloy, also used in the manufacture of aeroplanes, the chemical element Al.

ALUMINOUS [a-lyōo'mi-nŏŏs], adj. relating to or containing alum.

ALUMINUM [a-lyōo'mi-num], n. (U.S.) aluminium.

ALUMNA [a-lum'nah], n. woman graduate or former pupil or student. [L.].

ALUMNUS (pl. **alumni**), [a-lum'nus, 'nī], n. graduate, or former pupil or student of a given school or university. [L.].

ALUNITE [a'lyōo-nīt], n. (min.) hydrated sulphate of potassium and aluminium. [Fr.].

ALUNOGEN [a-lyōo'no-jen], n. (min.) fibrous aluminium sulphate.

ALVEOLAR [al-vē'o-lah(r)], adj. containing or relating to sockets, and esp. to the ridge just behind the upper teeth.

ALVEOLATE [al-vē'ō-lāt], adj. pitted, so as to resemble a honeycomb.

ALVEOLUS (pl. **alveoli**) [al-vē'ō-lus, al-vē'ō-li], n. cell in a honeycomb or shell; socket of a tooth. [L.].

ALVINE [al'vin], adj. pertaining to the intestines. [L.].

ALWAYS [awl'wāz], adv. on every occasion, at all times; continually, perpetually; in any circumstances, whatever happens. [OE.].

AM [am], 1st person sg. pres. ind. of BE. [OE.].

AMACRATIC [a-ma-kra'tik], adj. applied to a lens so photographically perfect as to unite all the actinic rays into one focus. [Gk.].

AMAIN [a-mān'], adv. with full force, with all one's might, violently, in full force of numbers, at full speed, at once, greatly. [OE.].

AMALGAM [a-mal'gam], n. alloy of mercury; mixture or compound of different substances. [Fr.].

AMALGAMATE (1) [a-mal'ga-māt], adj. alloyed (of mercury and another metal); combined, coalesced. AMALGAMATE (2), v.t. to combine mercury with another metal; (fig.) unite together, combine (used of business houses, firms, societies etc.); v.i. to combine in an amalgam; (fig.) mix; unite, blend; agree (of classes, races, ideas etc.).

AMALGAMATION [a-mal-ga-mā'shn], n. act or process of amalgamating; blending of different things; (comm.) a merger; union of two or more companies of the same nature into one concern.

AMALGAMATOR [a-mal'ga-mā-ter], n. one who amalgamates; machine used in mining to mix mercury with the ore in order to extract free metal.

AMANITIN [a-ma'ni-tin], n. poisonous principle contained in certain mushrooms. [Gk.].

AMANUENSIS [a-ma-nyōo-en'sis], n. one who writes to another's dictation, or copies what has been written. [L.].

AMARANTH [a'ma-ranth], n. the plant called love-lies-bleeding; an imaginary flower that never fades; colour inclining to purple. AMARANTHINE [a-ma-ran'thin], adj. pertaining to a.; unfading; of a purple colour. [Gk.].

AMARYLLIS [a-ma-ri'lis], n. group of bulbous plants; (poet.) country sweetheart or rustic maiden. [Gk.].

AMASS [a-mas'], v.t. to heap together, accumulate. AMASSMENT, n. heap or pile, accumulation. [Fr.].

AMASTHENIC [a-mas-the'nik], adj. amacratic. [Gk.].

AMATEUR (1) [a'ma-tyŏŏr, a-ma-tur'], n. one who pursues an art, sport or study from a love of it and not to make money; a non-professional (artist etc.); one who has incomplete knowledge of or is unskilful and clumsy in a subject. AMATEUR (2), adj. performed or done by an a. AMATEURISH [a-ma-tur'ish], adj. like an amateur, betraying lack of training

---

ōō is pronounced as in food; ŏŏ as in hood; th as in *th*ink; TH as in *th*at; zh as in azure. ~ = related to.

or skill; clumsily executed. AMATEURISHLY, *adv.* in unskilful fashion. AMATEURISHNESS, *n.* lack of practice or skill, clumsiness of execution. [Fr.].

AMATIVE [a'ma-tiv], *adj.* pertaining to love, *esp.* sexual love; amorous. AMATIVENESS, *n.* propensity to sexual love; faculty supposed by phrenologists to govern this propensity.

AMATOL [a'ma-tol], *n.* high explosive consisting of trinitrotoluene and ammonium nitrate.

AMATORY [a'ma-te-ri], *adj.* relating to love for the opposite sex. [L.].

AMAUROSIS [a-maw-rō'sis], *n.* (*path.*) decay or loss of sight due to disease of the optic nerve. AMAUROTIC [a-maw-ro'tik], *adj.* afflicted with a. [Gk.].

AMAZE (1) [a-māz'], *v.t.* to fill with awe or wonder, astonish. AMAZE (2), *n.* (*poet.*) amazement. AMAZEMENT [a-māz'ment], *n.* state or condition of being amazed, astonishment. AMAZING [a-mā'zing], *adj.* causing amazement. AMAZINGLY, *adv.* in an amazing way. [OE.].

AMAZON [a'ma-zon], *n.* one of a fabled race of female warriors in Scythia; a masculine woman. AMAZONIAN [a-ma-zō'ni-an], *adj.* pertaining to or like an a.

AMBASSADOR [am-ba'sa-der], *n.* messenger; minister of highest rank who represents the supreme power of his state abroad, *esp.* at a foreign court, and whose duty it is to transact the diplomatic business between his own and the foreign country. AMBASSADORIAL [am-ba-sa-daw'ri-al], *adj.* relating to an a. [Fr.].

AMBASSADRESS [am-ba'sa-dres], *n.* wife of an ambassador; woman ambassador.

AMBER (1) [am'ber], *n.* yellow semi-transparent fossil resin which when rubbed becomes electrified. AMBER (2), *adj.* consisting of or like a. [Fr. from Arab.].

AMBERGRIS [am'ber-grēs], *n.* wax-like substance used in perfumery, procured from the alimentary canal of the spermaceti whale and found floating in the seas it frequents. [Fr.].

AMBERITE [am'be-rit, *n.* a smokeless explosive.

AMBIDEXTER [am-bi-deks'ter], *n.* person who uses both hands with equal facility; a double-dealer; (*leg.*) juror who takes money from both parties. AMBIDEXTERITY [am-bi-deks-te'ri-ti], *n.* faculty or quality of being ambidextrous. [L.].

AMBIDEXTROUS [am-bi-deks'trōōs], *adj.* capable of using both hands equally; double-dealing. AMBIDEXTROUSLY, *adv.* in an a. way.

AMBIENT [am'bi-ent], *adj.* encompassing; surrounding. [L.].

AMBIGUITY [am-bi-gyōō'i-ti], *n.* state or quality of being ambiguous, double significance, lack of clarity. [L.].

AMBIGUOUS [am-bi'gyōō-ōōs], *adj.* liable to be interpreted in more than one way; doubtful; obscure; equivocal. AMBIGUOUSLY, *adv.* in an a. way. [L.].

AMBIT [am'bit], *n.* extent, scope, compass; precinct, circuit. [L.].

AMBITION [am-bi'shn], *n.* strong desire of success and superiority, of prosperity, admiration, advancement etc.; wish to achieve aspirations and ideals; the object of such aspirations and wishes. [L.].

AMBITIOUS [am-bi'shōōs], *adj.* having ambition, desirous of attaining fame, power, wealth etc.; (often) excessively desirous of attaining these; showing ambition, aspiring on a grand scale. AMBITIOUSLY, *adv.* in an a. way.

AMBIVALENCE [am-bi'va-lens], *n.* (*psych.*) simultaneous operation in the mind of two irreconcilable wishes.

AMBIVALENT [am-bi'va-lent], *adj.* (*psych.*) operating simultaneously (of two irreconcilable wishes).

AMBLE (1) [am'bl], *n.* an easy, unhurried pace. AMBLE (2), *v.i.* to move at an a., move easily without hurry or jolts. [L.].

AMBLING [am'bling], *adj.* with an easy, rolling pace.

AMBLYOPIA [am-bli-ō'pi-ah], *n.* incipient stage of amaurosis; defective vision. AMBLYOPIC [am-bli-o'pik], *adj.* weak-sighted. [Gk.].

AMBREIN [am'brē-in], *n.* fatty substance obtained from ambergris. [Fr.].

AMBROSIA [am-brō'zi-ah], *n.* (*myth.*) the food of the gods which rendered immortal anyone who tasted it; (*fig.*) anything having a very pleasing taste. AMBROSIAL, *adj.* having the qualities of a.; fragrant; delicious. [Gk.].

AMBROSIAN [am-brō'zi-an], *adj.* ambrosial; pertaining to St. Ambrose.

AMBRY, AUMBRY [am'bri, awm'bri], *n.* niche with

a door in a church near the altar, for the sacred vessels; cupboard. [OFr.].

AMBULANCE [am'byōō-lans], *n.* movable hospital for the wounded attached to an army in the field; vehicle which carries the wounded, sick and injured to hospital. [Fr.].

AMBULANT [am'byōō-lant], *adj.* that moves from place to place; (*med.*) of a disease, allowing the patient to walk about.

AMBULATOR [am'byōō-lā-ter], *n.* surveyor's wheel used for measuring distances traversed; odometer; walker. [L.].

AMBULATORY (1) [am'byōō-lā-te-ri], *adj.* having the power of walking, moving from place to place. AMBULATORY (2), *n.* space in which to walk, generally within a religious building. [L.].

AMBUSCADE (1) [am-bus-kād'], *n.* ambush. AMBUSCADE (2), *v.t.* to set an ambush for. [Fr. from Span.].

AMBUSH (1) [am'bōōsh], *n.* a lying in wait in a concealed position in order to attack an enemy by surprise; the place of concealment; the attack itself; the troops lying in wait. AMBUSH (2), *v.t.* and *i.* to arrange troops in hiding for a surprise attack, lie in wait for an enemy, attack suddenly from a hidden position. [ME. from L.].

AMEER, AMIR [a-mēer'], *n.* prince or ruler; an emir, the title borne by the Afghan kings. [Arab.].

AMELIORATE [a-mē'lyo-rāt], *v.t.* to render better; improve; *v.i.* to grow better. AMELIORABLE [a-mē'lyo-ra-bl], *adj.* improvable. AMELIORATIVE [a-mē'lyo-ra-tiv], *adj.* conducing to make better.

AMELIORATION [a-mē-lyo-rā'shn], *n.* act or process of making or becoming better; improvement.

AMEN [ā-men', ah-men'], *n.* the word itself sung or said at the end of a prayer, hymn etc.; *int.* so be it; a word used to ratify prayers or expressions of faith; **to say a. to,** to agree with. [Gk. from Heb.].

AMENABLE [a-mē'na-bl], *adj.* answerable, liable to be called to account; submissive, tractable. AMENABILITY [a-mē-na-bi'li-ti], *n.* quality of being a. AMENABLENESS [a-mē'na-bl-nes], *n.* state or quality of being a. AMENABLY, *adv.* in an a. way.

AMEND [a-mend'], *v.t.* to change for the better; improve; *v.i.* to grow or become better. AMENDABLE, *adj.* that can be amended. AMENDATORY [a-men'da-te-ri], *adj.* tending to amend; corrective. [OFr.].

AMENDE [a-mah(ng)d'], *n.* compensation, reparation; **a. honorable,** public apology for an insult offered or an injury done. [Fr.].

AMENDMENT [a-mend'ment], *n.* a change for the better; reformation; a word, clause or paragraph added, or proposed to be added, to a bill or motion; (*leg.*) the correction of an error in a writ or process.

AMENDS [a-mendz'], *n.* (*pl.*) compensation, reparation for an injury (chiefly in phrase **to make a.**).

AMENITY [a-mē'ni-ti, a-me'ni-ti], *n.* delightfulness, pleasantness; (of places) due to agreeable climate, convenient situation etc.; (of persons) to polished manners, gentle disposition etc. [L.].

AMENORRHOEA [ā-me-no-rē'ah], *n.* absence or abnormal suppression of the menses. [Gk.].

AMERCE [a-murs'], *v.t.* to punish with a fine. AMERCEMENT, AMERCIAMENT [a-murs'ment, a-mur'si-a-ment], *n.* fine or penalty inflicted at the discretion of the court.

AMERICAN [a-me'ri-kan], *n. and adj.* inhabitant of, pertaining to, the continent of America, *esp.* the United States; **A. Beauty,** variety of rose; **A. cloth,** kind of enamelled oilcloth; **A. tournament,** one in which each entrant plays each other entrant.

AMERICANISM [a-me'ri-ka-nizm], *n.* an American peculiarity or idiom; peculiar meaning given to an English word or phrase in the U.S.A.

AMERICANIZE [a-me'ri-ka-nīz], *v.t. and i.* to make American in character; naturalize in America. AMERICANIZATION [a-me-ri-ka-nī-zā'shn], *n.* the making or becoming American in character.

AMETABOLIAN [a-me-ta-bō'li-an], *n.* a division of insects not subject to metamorphosis. AMETABOLIC [a-me-ta-bo'lik], *adj.* not subject to metamorphosis. [Gk.].

AMETHYST [a'me-thist], *n.* precious stone, usually violet and of a crystalline nature; a purple colour. AMETHYSTINE [a-me-this'tin], *adj.* pertaining to, like or composed of, a. [Gk.].

AMHARIC [am-hah'rik], *n.* language of the Abyssinian nobility, official language of the country.

AMIABILITY [ā-mi-a-bi'li-ti], *n.* state or quality of being amiable.

AMIABLE [ā'mi-a-bl], *adj.* possessing kindly qualities;

lovable, worthy of affection. AMIABLENESS, *n.* quality of being a. AMIABLY, *adv.* in an a. way. [OFr. from L.].

AMIANTHUS [a-mi-an'thus], *n.* fine fibrous variety of asbestos. AMIANTHIFORM [a-mi-an'thi-fawm], *adj.* in the form of a. [Gk.].

AMIC [a'mik], *adj.* relating to or obtained from ammonia.

AMICABLE [a'mi-ka-bl], *adj.* friendly, peaceable. AMICABLY, *adv.* in an a. way. [L.].

AMICE, AMICT [a'mis, a'mikt], *n.* square piece of white linen worn round the shoulders by a priest when officiating at Mass. [OFr. from L.].

AMICT, see AMICE.

AMID (1), **AMIDE** [a'mid], *n.* substance derived from ammonia by substituting univalent acid radicals for hydrogen atoms.

AMID (2) [a-mid'], *prep.* in the midst or middle of; among, surrounded by. [OE.].

AMIDE, see AMID (1).

AMIDSHIPS [a-mid'ships], *adv.* (*naut.*) in the middle of a ship.

AMIDST [a-midst'], *prep.* amid (2). [ME.].

AMINE [a'min], *n.* substance derived from ammonia by substituting hydrocarbon radicals for the hydrogen atoms.

AMIR, see AMEER.

AMISS (1) [a-mis'], *adj.* (only as predicate) wrong, inopportune, undesirable. AMISS (2), *adv.* badly, ill, wrongly; (in negative constructions only) inopportunely, undesirably; **to take something a.,** take offence at something; **it will not come a.,** it will not be unwelcome, distasteful.

AMITY [a'mi-ti], *n.* harmonious relationship, friendship. [Fr.].

AMMETER [a'mi-ter], *n.* instrument for measuring the flow in ampères of an electric current.

AMMONAL [a'mo-nal], *n.* class of high explosive made by combining nitrate of ammonia with powdered aluminium.

AMMONIA [a-mō'ni-ah], *n.* compound of one part of nitrogen with three parts of hydrogen; pungent volatile alkaline gas obtained from hartshorn. AMMONIAC [a-mō'ni-ak], *adj.* like or containing ammonia; **sal a.,** hard salt used for medicinal purposes.

AMMONIACAL [a-mō-ni'a-kal], *adj.* containing ammonia or possessing its properties.

AMMONIATED [a-mō'ni-ā-tid], *adj.* united or impregnated with ammonia.

AMMONITE [a'mo-nīt], *n.* extinct mollusc, with flat, spiral shell.

AMMONIUM [a-mō'ni-um], *n.* alkaline radical ammonia with one more atom of hydrogen.

AMMUNITION (1) [a-myōō-ni'shn], *n.* formerly applied to military stores in general; collective name for projectiles and articles used to charge firearms and ordnance of all kinds, such as shells, explosives, cartridges etc. AMMUNITION (2), *adj.* formerly applied to articles made for use *esp.* for use by soldiers, as boots; **a. wagon,** one used to carry a. [Fr. from L.].

AMNESIA [am-nē'zi-ah], *n.* (*med.*) inability to remember, loss of memory. [Gk.].

AMNESTY [am'nes-ti], *n.* pardon granted to political offenders. [Fr.].

AMNION [am'ni-on], *n.* (*anat.*) the innermost membrane enclosing the foetus in the womb. AMNIOTIC [am-ni-o'tik], *adj.* relating to or contained in the a. [Gk.].

AMOEBA [a-mē'bah], *n.* (*zool.*) a protozoon which, as a consequence of its habit of absorbing its food at every point all over its body, is constantly changing its shape. AMOEBIFORM [a-mē'bi-fawm], *adj.* shaped like an a. AMOEBOID [a-mē'boid], *adj.* like the a. AMOEBOUS [a-mē'bōōs], *adj.* relating to the a. [Gk.].

AMOK, AMUCK [a-muk'], *adv.* (only in phrase **to run a.**) (to rush about) in a frenzied manner with the intent to kill every person encountered; (*fig.*) (get) out of control, (become) violent. [Malay].

AMONG [a-mung'], *prep.* mingled with, surrounded by, in the midst of, between. [OE.].

AMONGST [a-mungst'], *prep.* among, in the midst of. [ME.].

AMONTILLADO [a-mon-ti-lyah'dō], *n.* kind of pale sherry. [Span.].

AMORAL [a-mo'ral], *adj.* non-moral, neither moral nor immoral.

AMORIST [a'mo-rist], *n.* one who practises and cultivates love; philanderer. [L.].

AMOROUS [a'mo-rōōs], *adj.* easily inclined to love;

fondly in love; inspired by love; pertaining to love. AMOROUSLY, *adv.* in an a. way. AMOROUSNESS, *n.* state or quality of being a.

AMORPHOUS [a-maw'fōōs], *adj.* having no determinate shape; uncrystallized. AMORPHOUSNESS, *n.* lack of form. [Gk.].

AMORPHOZOA [a-maw-fō-zō'ah], *n.*(*pl.*) group of shapeless animals like sponges. [Gk.].

AMORTIZE [a-maw'tiz], *v.t.* (*leg.*) to alienate property in mortmain, that is, to transfer in perpetuity to a corporation or fraternity; (*comm.*) redeem by a sinking fund. AMORTIZATION [a-maw-ti-zā'shn], *n.* provision for paying off a debt by a sinking fund; act or right of amortizing. [L.].

AMOUNT (1) [a-mownt'], *n.* sum total, quantity, substance, result. AMOUNT (2), *v.t.* to rise (to) or reach a certain sum; come (to), be equivalent (to). [OFr.].

AMOUR [a-mōōr'], *n.* love intrigue, usually of an illicit or discreditable nature. [L.].

AMP [amp], *n.* shortened colloquial form of AMPERE.

AMPELOPSIS [am-pe-lop'sis], *n.* old family of climbing plants, now united with *Vitis.* [Gk.].

AMPERAGE [am'pe-rij], *n.* electric current, in a circuit, or given out by a generator or accumulator, measured in ampères.

AMPERE, ampère [am'pāer], *n.* unit of force in an electric current, the current sent by one volt through one ohm.

AMPERSAND [am-per-sand'], *n.* name given to the symbol & which is a monogram of *et* and.

AMPHI-, *pref.* both, about, around, on both sides. [Gk.].

AMPHIBIA [am-fi'bi-ah], *n.*(*pl.*) (*zool.*) creatures capable of living both in water and on land, the class of vertebrates intermediate between fishes and reptiles. [Gk.].

AMPHIBIAN [am-fi'bi-an], *n. and adj.* member of the Amphibia; (*aeron.*) aeroplane which can rise from and descend on to either land or water; (*milit.*) assault craft able to cross land or water.

AMPHIBIOUS [am-fi'bi-ōōs], *adj.* capable of living in air and water; (*milit.*) (of operations) conducted by land and water. AMPHIBIOUSLY, *adv.* in the manner of an amphibian.

AMPHIBOLOGY [am-fi-bo'lo-ji], *n.* (*logic*) phrase or sentence which may be interpreted in more than one way, ambiguous statement, obscure expression. AMPHIBOLOGICAL [am-fi-bo-lo'ji-kal], *adj.* ambiguous. [Gk.].

AMPHIBOLOUS [am-fi'bo-lōōs], *adj.* uncertain, ambiguous; (*path.*) of doubtful prognosis. [Gk.].

AMPHIBRACH [am'fi-brak], *n.* (*pros.*) metrical foot of three syllables, the middle long, the first and last short. [Gk.].

AMPHICARPIC [am-fi-kah'pik], *adj.* (*bot.*) having two kinds of fruit or seasons of ripening. [Gk.].

AMPHICARPOUS [am-fi-kah'pōōs], *adj.* amphicarpic.

AMPHIMACER [am-fi'ma-ser], *n.* (*pros.*) metrical foot of three syllables, the middle short, and the others long. [L.].

AMPHIMIXIS [am-fi-mik'sis], *n.* (*biol.*) union of germ cells from the male and female in sexual reproduction. [Gk.].

AMPHIPODA [am-fi'po-dah], *n.*(*pl.*) a sub-order of Crustaceans. [Gk.].

AMPHISBAENA [am-fis-bē'nah], *n.* a species of lizards, supposed by the ancients to have a head at either end. [Gk.].

AMPHITHEATRE [am'fi-thē-a-ter], *n.* oval or circular arena with seats round it raised in tiers; lower gallery of a modern theatre. AMPHITHEATRICAL [am-fi-thē-at'ri-kal], *adj.* pertaining to, performed in, an a. [Gk.].

AMPHITRYON [am-fit'ri-on], *n.* (*myth.*) king of Thebes whom Jupiter impersonated, and in whose person the god gave a feast; (*fig.*) host, entertainer. [Gk.].

AMPHORA [am-faw'rah], *n.* ancient two-handled vessel for wine or oil. AMPHORAL, *adj.* pertaining to or like an a. [Gk.].

AMPHORIC [am-fo'rik], *adj.* (*med.*) emitting a sound similar to that yielded by blowing into an empty decanter; produced by an empty lung cavity.

AMPLE [am'pl], *adj.* large, spacious, abundant; sufficient; liberal; full. [L.].

AMPLEXICAUL [am-plek'si-kawl], *adj.* (*bot.*) clasping the stem, used of sessile leaves. [L.].

AMPLIFICATION [am-pli-fi-kā'shn], *n.* extension, enlargement; act of amplifying; (*radio*) increasing

---

ōō is pronounced as in food; ŏŏ as in hood; th as in *think*; TH as in *that*; zh as in azure.   ~ = related to.

of electrical signals (oscillations); **a. factor,** maximum voltage amplification, also called μ(mu). [L.].

AMPLIFIER [am'pli-fī-er], *n.* something that enlarges; *(opt.)* magnifying lens; *(radio)* device for increasing power of radio waves, thereby magnifying the loudness of the sound.

AMPLIFY [am'pli-fī], *v.t. and i.* to increase, enlarge (upon), magnify, describe or discuss in greater detail, state more fully.

AMPLITUDE [am'pli-tyōōd], *n.* largeness, spaciousness, sufficiency, extent; *(astron.)* the arc of the horizon intercepted between the east or west point and the centre of the sun, or a star at its rising or setting during an alternation; *(elect.)* maximum value attained by an alternating quantity; **magnetical a.,** the arc of the horizon between the sun or a star at rising or setting, and the east or west point of the horizon by the compass; **a. of the range,** the line measuring the horizontal distance moved by a projectile. [L.].

AMPOULE [am-pōōl'], *n.* small container for a hypodermic dose. [Fr.].

AMPULLA [am-pōō'lah], *n.* narrow-necked globular vessel used by the Romans for anointing the body after bathing, cruet for the wine and water of the Eucharist; *(anat.)* dilated part of the semicircular canals of the ear. AMPULLACEOUS [am-pŏō-lā'shōōs], *adj.* resembling a bottle; swelling. [L.].

AMPUTATE [am'pyōō-tāt], *v.t.* to cut off a limb or portion of a limb. AMPUTATOR [am'pyōō-tā-ter], *n.* person who amputates. [L.].

AMPUTATION [am-pyōō-tā'shn], *n.* act or operation of amputating.' [L.].

AMUCK, see AMOK.

AMULET [a'myōō-let], *n.* ornament worn about the person as a charm against evil or disease; charm; talisman. [Fr.].

AMUSE [a-myōōz'], *v.t.* to occupy the attention agreeably, keep the mind pleasantly diverted, arouse laughter or interest, afford recreation or entertainment. AMUSEDLY [a-myōō'zid-li], *adv.* in an amused way, with amusement. [Fr.].

AMUSEMENT [a-myōōz'ment], *n.* state of being amused, mirth; that which causes one to be amused, recreation, entertainment, pastime; **a. park,** fairground containing swings, roundabouts and other forms of popular entertainment. [Fr.].

AMUSING [a-myōō'zing], *adj.* capable of causing amusement. AMUSINGLY, *adv.* in an a. way.

AMYGDALATE (1) [a-mig'da-lāt], *adj.* relating to or made of almonds. AMYGDALATE (2), *n. (chem.)* a salt of amygdalic acid. [L.].

AMYGDALIC [a-mig-da'lik], *adj.* obtained from or belonging to bitter almonds; **a. acid,** one obtained from amygdalin.

AMYGDALIN [a-mig'da-lin], *n.* glucoside prepared from the kernel of the bitter almond and other stone fruit. [L.].

AMYL [a'mil], *n.* starch; *(chem.)* supposed radical of such compounds as **a. alcohol** and **a. nitrite.** AMYLACEOUS [a-mi-lā'shōōs], *adj.* relating to starch. [L. from Gk.].

AMYLOID (1) [a'mi-loid], *n.* starchy substance found in some seeds. AMYLOID (2), *adj.* starchy, like starch.

AMYLOPSIN [a-mi-lop'sin], *n.* the fermenting substance of the pancreatic juice in converting starch into sugar.

AN (1) [an], form of the indefinite article before a word beginning with a vowel or silent *h.* [OE.].

AN (2) *conj.* † if, and if. [OE.].

AN- (3), *pref.* not, showing negation. [Gk.].

ANA- (1), *pref.* up, towards, up to, again, back. [Gk.].

ANA (2) [ā'nah, ah'nah], *n.* collection of personal reminiscences, literary anecdotes etc. usually associated with the name of some celebrity. [L.].

ANA (3) [a'nah], *adv.* an equal quantity of each in a medical prescription, usually shortened thus, āā. [Gk.].

ANABAPTIST [a-na-bap'tist], *n.* member of a sect which believed that those baptized in infancy should be baptized again when adults; one who believes that baptism should be administered to adults, and by total immersion. ANABAPTISM, *n.* the doctrine of the Anabaptists. ANABAPTISTIC [a-na-bap-tis'tik], *adj.* pertaining to the Anabaptists or Anabaptism.

ANABAS [a'na-bas], *n.* a freshwater fish, the Indian or climbing perch. [Gk.].

ANABASIS [a-na'ba-sis], *n.* a military advance; so

called from the march of Cyrus the Younger into Asia, recounted by Xenophon in his *Anabasis.* [Gk.].

ANABATIC [a-na-ba'tik], *adj. (meteor.)* term applied to winds caused by air flowing upwards.

ANABOLISM [a-na'bo-lizm], *n. (biol.)* building up nutritive substances into living protoplasm, constructive metabolism. [Gk.].

ANACATHARTIC [a-na-ka-thah'tik], *n. and adj. (med.)* (a substance) having the property of cleansing by exciting vomiting or expectoration.

ANACHRONISM [a-na'kro-nizm], *n.* a mistake in dating a historical event; (the representation of) an event or thing which is too early or too late for the period in which it is supposed to have happened or existed, or which appears out of keeping with the time at which it happens or exists. ANACHRONISTIC [a-na-kro-nis'tik], *adj.* wrongly dated, out of its correct period, relating to an a. [Fr. from Gk.].

ANACLASTIC [a-na-klas'tik], *adj.* due to or connected with refraction. [Gk.].

ANACOLUTHON *(pl.* **anacolutha)** [a-na-ko-lyōō'thon], *n.* a break in the structure or grammatical sequence of a sentence. ANACOLUTHIC, *adj.* pertaining or relating to a. ANACOLUTHICALLY, *adv.* in a disjointed way. [Gk.].

ANACONDA [a-na-kon'dah], *n.* large South American snake. [Unkn.].

ANACREONTIC (1) [a-na-krē-on'tik], *n.* poem in the manner of the Greek poet *Anacreon;* praising love and wine. ANACREONTIC (2), *adj.* in the style of *Anacreon;* in praise of love and wine; convivial; amatory.

ANACRUSIS [a-na-krōō'sis], *n. (pros.)* unstressed syllable preceding the first stressed syllable in a verse normally beginning with a stress; *(mus.)* introductory passage in a score. [Gk.].

ANADROMOUS [a-nad'ro-mōōs], *adj. (ichth.)* passing from the sea into rivers to spawn. [Gk.].

ANAEMIA [a-nē'mi-ah], *n.* deficiency of blood involving a lack of red corpuscles. [Gk.].

ANAEMIC [a-nē'mik], *adj.* pertaining to or suffering from anaemia; *(fig.)* feeble, colourless.

ANAEMOTROPHY [a-nē-mo'tro-fi], *n. (med.)* deficiency in nourishment of the blood. [Gk.].

ANAEROBE [a-nāer'ōb], *n.* one of the anaerobia.

ANAEROBIA [a-nāer-ō'bi-ah], *n.(pl.) (biol.)* bacteria able to exist without oxygen. ANAEROBIC [a-nāer-ō'bik], *adj.* able to live without free oxygen. [Gk.].

ANAESTHESIA [a-nes-thē'zi-ah], *n. (med.)* loss, due to disease, drugs or anaesthetics, of the sense of touch or feeling.

ANAESTHETIC (1) [a-nes-the'tik], *n.* an agent to deaden sensibility, commonly used during surgical operations etc. ANAESTHETIC (2), *adj.* deadening the sensibility, producing insensibility. [Gk.].

ANAESTHETIST [a-nēs'the-tist], *n.* an expert in the administration of anaesthetics.

ANAESTHETIZE [a-nēs'the-tīz], *v.t.* to render insensible by administering an anaesthetic. ANAESTHETIZATION [a-nēs-the-tī-zā'shn], *n.* process of administering anaesthetics; state of being anaesthetized.

ANAGLYPH [a'na-glif], *n.* ornament embossed or sculptured in relief. ANAGLYPHIC, ANAGLYPTIC [a-na-glif'tik, a-na-glip'tik], *adj.* connected with anaglyphs. [Gk.].

ANAGOGE, see ANAGOGY.

ANAGOGY, ANAGOGE [a'na-gō-ji], *n.* an allegorical or mystical interpretation of the Bible, particularly the Old Testament. ANAGOGICAL [a-na-go'ji-kal], *adj.* allegorical, mystical. ANAGOGICALLY, *adv.* in an anagogical sense or manner. [Gk.].

ANAGRAM [a'na-gram], *n.* word or phrase formed by transposing the letters it contains. ANAGRAMMATIC(AL) [a-na-gra-ma'tik(-al)], *adj.* containing an' a. ANAGRAMMATICALLY, *adv.* after the manner of an a. [Gk.].

ANAGRAMMATIZE [a-na-gra'ma-tīz], *v.i.* to compose anagrams.

ANAL [ā'nal], *adj.* relating to or near the anus. [MedL.].

ANALECT *(pl.* **analecta)** [a'na-lekt], *n.* selection of extracts from different authors. [Gk.].

ANALGESIA [a-nal-jē'si-ah], *n.* absence of, or local insensibility to, pain. [Gk.].

ANALGESIC (1) [a-nal-jē'sik], *n. (med.)* substance tending to produce analgesia. ANALGESIC (2), *adj.* tending to produce analgesia.

ANALOGIC(AL) [a-na-lo'jik(-al)], *adj.* pertaining

to or implying analogy. ANALOGICALLY, *adv.* in an a. way. [Gk.].

ANALOGIZE [a-na′lo-jīz], *v.t.* to explain or reason by analogy; treat analogically. ANALOGIST [a-na′lo-jist], *n.* one who reasons by analogy.

ANALOGOUS [a-na′lo-gŏŏs], *adj.* having analogy, corresponding to, similar. ANALOGOUSLY, *adv.* in an a. way. ANALOGOUSNESS, *n.* quality or state of being a. [Gk.].

ANALOGUE [a′na-log], *n.* a word or object of any kind which bears resemblance or analogy to another; something which acts similarly, or has the same function; a corresponding part. [Gk.].

ANALOGY [a-na′lo-ji], *n.* partial similitude or agreement between things; (*philol.*) process by which words and grammatical forms are constructed on the model of others with which they have some points of resemblance, or by which some forms are rebuilt in order to make them conform to the general rules and structure of a language; (*log.*) process of reasoning which concludes that if things are similar in certain respects they are probably similar in others as well; (*math.*) similitude of ratio, proportion; (*zool.*) resemblance in different species between organs which are essentially different. [Fr. from Gk.].

ANALYSE [a′na-līz], *v.t.* to resolve into its component elements; (*fig.*) examine minutely and critically; (*chem.*) split up a compound into its constituent parts; (*gram.*) examine closely the structure of a phrase or sentence, observing the exact function of every word. [Fr.].

ANALYSIS [*pl.* **analyses**] [a-na′li-sis, a-na′li-sēz], *n.* the resolution or splitting up of a compound into its constituent elements; (*fig.*) critical and detailed examination (of a statement etc.), classification (of the items of an account, chief points of a discussion etc.); (*gram.*) arrangement or description of a sentence indicating the grammatical function of each word and its relation to the rest of the sentence; (*math.*) resolving of problems by reduction to equations; (*mus.*) detailed study of a piece of music; psycho-analysis. [Gk.].

ANALYST [a′na-list], *n.* one who performs analysis, *esp.* chemical or pathological analysis.

ANALYTIC(AL) [a-na-li′tik(-al)], *adj.* relating to analysis; resolving a compound into its constituents; obtained by analysis; reasoning from particulars to principles, inductive; (of languages) expressing grammatical relations by separate words instead of inflexions. ANALYTICALLY, *adv.* after the manner of analysis. ANALYTICS, *n.(pl.)* science or study of analysis. [Gk.].

ANAMNESIS [a-nam-nē′sis], *n.* remembrance, recollection (*esp.* of events in a previous existence); (*med.*) the patient's account of his history and symptoms. [Gk.].

ANAMORPHOSIS [a-na-maw′fo-sis], *n.* distorted representation of an object which appears in correct proportion when looked at from a certain angle or when reflected from a convex or concave mirror; (*biol.*) an evolutionary change in form; (*bot.*) abnormal development in the form of a plant. [Gk.].

ANANDROUS [a-nan′drŏŏs], *adj.* (*bot.*) having no stamen. [Gk.].

ANANTHEROUS [a-nan′the-rŏŏs], *adj.* (*bot.*) having no anthers. [Gk.].

ANANTHOUS [a-nan′thŏŏs], *adj.* (*bot.*) having no flower. [Gk.].

ANAPAEST [a′na-pēst], *n.* (*pros.*) metrical foot consisting of two short syllables followed by one long, a dactyl reversed. ANAPAESTIC [a-na-pēs′tik], *n. and adj.* (poetic measure) composed of anapaests. [Gk.].

ANAPHRODISIAC [a-na-fro-di′zi-ak], *n. and adj.* (agent) reducing sexual desire. [Gk.].

ANAPHYLACTIC [a-na-fi-lak′tik], *adj.* relating to anaphylaxis.

ANAPHYLAXIS [a-na-fi-lak′sis], *n.* (*med.*) an increasing responsiveness to small doses of a serum. [Gk.].

ANAPLASTY [a′na-plas-ti], *n.* (*surg.*) operation of restoring a part of the body by the transfer of tissue. [Gk.].

ANAPLEROSIS [a-na-plē-rō′sis], *n.* (*med.*) renewal of destroyed or lost tissue, as in healing of wounds. [Gk.].

ANAPLEROTIC [a-na-plē-ro′tik], *n. and adj.* (substance) capable of renewing flesh. [*Prec.*].

ANARCH [a′nahk], *n.* (*poet.*) an anarchist, revolutionary. [Gk.].

ANARCHIC(AL) [a-nah′kik(-al)], *adj.* having no

civic rule; in a state of lawless confusion. ANARCHICALLY, *adv.* in a fashion tending to anarchy.

ANARCHISM [a′nah-kizm], *n.* political theory which regards any organized system of government as undesirable.

ANARCHIST [a′nah-kist], *n.* one who follows the tenets of anarchism or promotes anarchy.

ANARCHY [a′nah-ki], *n.* condition of society in which there is no governing body; (*fig.*) political and social chaos, lack of order, lawlessness and confusion in anything. [Gk.].

ANASARCA [a-na-sah′kah], *n.* (*med.*) general dropsy. ANASARCOUS, *adj.* relating to a.; dropsical. [Gk.].

ANASTIGMATIC [a-na-stig-ma′tik], *adj.* free from astigmatism, applied to a lens constructed to correct astigmatic aberration. ANASTIGMAT [a-na-stig′mat], *n.* (*phot.*) an a. lens.

ANASTOMOSIS [a-na-sto-mō′sis], *n.* intercommunication of a network of lines or streams; (*anat.* and *bot.*) the opening of one artery or vein into another. ANASTOMOSE [a-nas′to-mōs], *v.i.* to unite by a., join. ANASTOMOTIC [a-na-sto-mo′tik], *adj.* relating to a.; tending to open or remove obstructions. [Gk.].

ANATHEMA [a-na′the-mah], *n.* a curse solemnly pronounced by ecclesiastical authority, and accompanied by excommunication; person or thing accursed; curse or ban generally, person or thing thoroughly disliked. ANATHEMATIZE [a-na′the-ma-tiz], *v.t.* to utter an a. against. ANATHEMATIZATION [a-na-the-ma-ti-zā′shn], *n.* process of anathematizing. [L. from Gk.].

ANATOMICAL [a-na-to′mi-kal], *adj.* pertaining to anatomy. ANATOMICALLY, *adv.* in an a. way.

ANATOMIST [a-na′to-mist], *n.* one versed in anatomy.

ANATOMIZE [a-na′to-miz], *v.t.* to dissect, *esp.* animal bodies; analyse; discriminate. ANATOMIZATION [a-na-to-mi-zā′shn], *n.* process of anatomizing. [MedL.].

ANATOMY [a-na′to-mi], *n.* (*orig.*) the dissection of bodies, human and animal, in order to study the structure and distribution of their parts; art of dissecting; science learnt from dissection; the parts and details with which the science deals; a treatise upon the science, or upon the structure of animals; (*fig.*) the art of examining anything; the examination itself, or a treatise on it. [Fr. from L.].

ANATRIPSIS [a-na-trip′sis], *n.* (*med.*) massage. ANATRIPTIC, *n.* medicine applied by rubbing. [Gk.].

ANBURY, AMBURY [an′be-ri], *n.* soft tumour found on necks of horses and oxen; disease affecting roots of turnips and other plants.

ANCESTOR [an′ses-ter], *n.* one from whom a person is descended; a forebear. [OFr.].

ANCESTRAL [an-ses′tral], *adj.* pertaining to ancestors; descending from ancestors.

ANCESTRESS [an′ses-tres], *n.* woman ancestor.

ANCESTRY [an′ses-tri], *n.* ancestral lineage, persons composing the line of natural descent. [OFr.].

ANCHOR (1) [ang′ker], *n.* heavy iron or steel bar having at one end curved arms with hooks at each extremity so that when attached to a cable and thrown over the side of the ship it becomes firmly embedded in the sea- or river-bottom, and moors the ship securely; (*fig.*) anything fixed and steady, giving a sense of security; **to cast a.,** to drop the anchor overboard; **to weigh a.,** to draw up the anchor from the sea; (*fig.*) begin a voyage; **to come to a.,** to let down the anchor, stop sailing; **sheet a.,** largest type of anchor; (*fig.*) chief support or security. ANCHOR (2), *v.t.* to make fast by casting anchor, fix securely; *v.i.* to cast or come to anchor, come to a stop. [OE. from L.].

ANCHORAGE [ang′ke-rij], *n.* place suitable for anchoring; duty imposed on ships for anchoring in a harbour; (*motoring*) point at which a component is secured to the chassis-frame.

ANCHORET, ANCHORITE [ang′ke-ret, -rit], *n.* hermit; religious recluse. [L.].

ANCHOR-GAP [ang′ker-gap], *n.* (*radio*) small safety spark-gap, between the lead-in of the receiving aerial and earth, to protect the receiver from overpowerful oscillations.

ANCHORITE, see ANCHORET.

ANCHOVY [an′chŏ-vi, an-chŏ′vi], *n.* small herring-like fish, eaten salted. [Span.].

ANCHUSA [an-chŏŏ′zah, ang-kyŏŏ′zah], *n.* varieties of hairy-stemmed plants. [L.].

ANCHYLOSIS [ang-ki-lō′sis], *n.* (*med.*) stiffening of

ŏŏ is pronounced as in *food*; ŏŏ as in *hood*; th as in *th*ink; ᴛʜ as in *th*at; zh as in azure.   ~ = related to.

the joints. ANCHYLOSE [ang'ki-lōs], *v.t.* to become stiff by a. ANCHYLOTIC [ang-ki-lo'tik], *adj.* pertaining to or afflicted by a. [Gk.].

ANCIENT (1) [ān'shnt], *adj.* old, former, that happened or existed in the past or in antiquity, that has existed from past times to the present day; **a. lights,** window which is protected by law whereby no one may erect a building which will keep the light from it; **A. of Days,** God. ANCIENTS, *n.* (*pl. only*) those who lived in the times of the Greek and Roman empires, the classical writers of antiquity. [Fr.].

ANCILLARY [an'si-la-ri], *adj.* subordinate, auxiliary. [L.].

ANCONEAL [an-kō'ni-al], *adj.* pertaining to the elbow. [Gk.].

AND [and], *conj.* having the sense of adding something to what has gone before, used as a link between words and sentences; (*coll.*) in order to (after TRY, COME and GO). [O.E.].

ANDANTE (1) [an-dahn'tā], *n.* (*mus.*) a movement in slow time. ANDANTE (2), *adv.* (*mus.*) slowly. [It.].

ANDANTINO [an-dahn-tē'nō], *adv.* (*mus.*) moderately slowly but quicker than andante. [It.].

ANDIRON, ENDIRON [an'diern], *n.* horizontal iron bar inserted at each end of a hearth, to hold the logs of a wood fire; firedog; movable fire-irons. [OFr.].

ANDRO-, *pref.* man. [Gk.].

ANDROECIUM [an-drē'si-um], *n.* (*bot.*) the stamens of a flower. [Gk.].

ANDROGYNOUS [an-dro'ji-nŏŏs], *adj.* having the characteristics of both sexes, at once male and female, hermaphrodite; (*bot.*) having male and female organs on the same flower or plant. [Gk.].

ANDROMEDA [an-dro'mi-dah], *n.* (*astron.*) name of a northern constellation; (*bot.*) genus of shrubs of the heath family. [Gk.].

ANDROPHAGI [an-dro'fa-gī], *n.*(*pl.*) man-eaters, cannibals. ANDROPHAGOUS, *adj.* man-eating. [Gk.].

ANDROPHOBIA [an-dro-fō'bi-ah], *n.* abnormal fear or hatred of the male sex. [Gk.].

ANEAR [a-nēer'], *prep. and adv.* near.

ANECDOTE [a'nek-dōt], *n.* short, vivid narrative concerning a single striking event or witty phrase, usually conversational and personal in tone; story. ANECDOTAL [a-nek-dō'tal], *adj.* relating to or full of anecdotes. ANECDOTIC(AL) [a-nek-dō'tik(-al)], *adj.* addicted to or pertaining to anecdotes. ANECDOTIST [a'nek-dō-tist], *n.* one who collects or tells anecdotes. [Gk.].

ANELE [a-nēl'], *v.t.* to give Extreme Unction to. [O.E.].

ANELECTRODE [a-ne-lek'trōd], *n.* the positive pole of a galvanic battery. [Gk.].

ANEMO-, *pref.* wind. [Gk.].

ANEMOGRAPH [a-ne'mō-grahf], *n.* apparatus which registers the amount and variation of the force of the wind. ANEMOGRAM [a-ne'mō-gram], *n.* the register made by an a. ANEMOGRAPHY [a-ni-mo'gra-fi], *n.* study of the winds. [Gk.].

ANEMOLOGY [a-ni-mo'lo-ji], *n.* the science of the winds. [Gk.].

ANEMOMETER [a-ni-mo'mi-ter], *n.* instrument which measures the direction, force and velocity of the wind. ANEMOMETRY [a-ni-mo'met-ri], *n.* the determination of the force, velocity and direction of the winds. [Gk.].

ANEMONE [a-ne'mo-ni], *n.* the wind-flower, a genus of plant of the natural order *Ranunculaceae.* [Gk.].

ANEMOSCOPE [a-ne'mo-skōp], *n.* machine which shows the direction of the wind. [Gk.].

ANENT [a-nent'], *prep.* in reference to, concerning, about. [O.E.].

ANEROID [a'ne-roid], *adj.* describing that type of barometer which employs no fluid, but measures the pressure of the atmosphere on the lid of a metal box exhausted of air. [Gk.].

ANEURISM, ANEURYSM [a'nyŏŏ-rizm], *n.* (*med.*) hollow swelling filled with blood, in the diseased coat of an artery. ANEURISMAL [a-nyŏŏ-riz'mal], *adj.* of or pertaining to an a. [Gk.].

ANEURYSM, see ANEURISM.

ANEW [a-nyŏŏ'], *adv.* over again, once more, in a new form.

ANFRACTUOUS [an-frak'tyŏŏ-ŏŏs], *adj.* full of windings; (*fig.*) circumlocutory in speech. ANFRACTUOSITY [an-frak-tyŏŏ-o'si-ti], ANFRACTUOUSNESS [an-frak'tyŏŏ-ŏŏs-nes], *n.* condition of being a.

ANGARIA [an-gāer'i-ah], *n.* term used in international law denoting the seizure or destruction by a belligerent state of property belonging to neutral states within its frontiers for which it pays an indemnity. [Gk.].

ANGARY [ang'ga-ri], *n.* angaria.

ANGEL [ān'jel], *n.* spiritual being of powers greater than human and endowed with immortality who is the attendant and messenger of God; (*fig.*) human being of great goodness and beauty; one who ministers unselfishly to the needs of others; (*hist.*) old English coin, an angel noble, bearing the figure of the archangel Michael; **guardian a.,** spiritual protector; **his good** *or* **evil a.,** person who has a marked influence for good or evil on another; **to entertain an a. unawares,** to be unappreciative of the merits of one's company; **to rush in where angels fear to tread,** to interfere rashly where even those of great judgment would hesitate to intervene. [L. from Gk.].

ANGEL-FISH [ān'jel-fish], *n.* kind of shark, the monk fish.

ANGELIC [an-je'lik], *adj.* of or pertaining to angels; like an angel, having the qualities of an angel; looking supremely good or beautiful. [L.].

ANGELICA [an-je'li-kah], *n.* umbelliferous plant the preserved leaf-stalks of which are used as a confection; sweet Californian wine. [MedL.].

ANGELICAL [an-je'li-kal], *adj.* like or of the nature of an angel. ANGELICALLY, *adv.* in the manner of an angel.

ANGELOLOGY [ān-je-lo'lo-ji], *n.* the doctrine of angelic beings; a treatise on angels. [Gk.].

ANGELUS [an'je-lus], *n.* short form of prayer in the Roman Catholic Church in commemoration of the Incarnation, said in the morning, at noon and in the evening, when the Angelus bell rings.

ANGER (1) [ang'ger], *n.* a passion of the mind prompted by a sense of wrong; resentment, indignation, resentful sorrow, hot displeasure. ANGER (2), *v.t.* to excite anger, rouse resentment and indignation in a person, provoke. [ME. from OIcel.].

ANGEVIN [an'je-vin], *adj.* (*hist.*) of or pertaining to Anjou, relating to the Plantagenet House that reigned in England from 1154 to 1399. [Fr.].

ANGINA [an-jī'nah], *n.* (*med.*) affection of the throat, as tonsillitis or quinsy, accompanied by spasmodic fits of suffocation; **a. pectoris,** acutely painful constriction in the chest usually associated with the heart or great blood-vessels. [L.].

ANGIO- [an'ji-ō], *pref.* vessel, receptacle, hence contained in a seed-pod or blood-vessel. [Gk.].

ANGIOLOGY [an-ji-o'lo-ji], *n.* (*anat.*) the science of the blood-vessels and lymphatics of the human body.

ANGIONEUROSIS [an-ji-ō-nyŏŏ-rō'sis], *n.* (*med.*) neurosis of the blood-vessels. ANGIONEUROTIC [an-ji-ō-nyŏŏ-ro'tik], *adj.* caused by or of the nature of an a.

ANGLE (1) [ang'gl], *n.* (*geom.*) the inclination of one line to another which it meets; the space included between two meeting lines or surfaces; narrowing space (as a corner in a room); projecting corner resembling an a. in shape (as of a building etc.); (*fig.*) position, point of view; (*U.S.*) an approach to or light on a subject. [Fr. from L.].

ANGLE (2), *n.* member of a Low German tribe who settled in Britain and ultimately gave their name to the people of the whole country. [L.].

ANGLE (3), *n.* fish-hook, fishing-tackle. ANGLE (4), *v.i.* to use an a. for fishing, to fish; (*fig.*) seek to obtain something by indirect means. [O.E.].

ANGLE-IRON [ang'gl-iern], *n.* L-shaped piece of iron used to fasten or strengthen framework.

ANGLER (1) [ang'gler], *n.* one who fishes with an angle.

ANGLER (2), *n.* (*ichth.*) a sea-fish, *Lophius piscatorius.*

ANGLICAN (1) [ang'gli-kan], *n.* member of the Church of England, *esp.* of the High Church party. ANGLICAN (2), *adj.* connected with the Church of England; (*U.S.*) English. [MedL.].

ANGLICANISM [ang'gli-ka-nizm], *n.* the principles and practice of the English Church.

ANGLICE [ang'gli-sē], *adv.* in the English language or in an English style. [MedL.].

ANGLICISM [ang'gli-sizm], *n.* English idiom.

ANGLICIZE [ang'gli-sīz], *v.t.* to give an English form to, make English.

ANGLING [ang'gling], *n.* fishing with a rod and line; the art of the fisherman.

ANGLO- [ang'glō], *pref.* pertaining to the English. [L.].

ANGLO-AMERICAN (1) [ang-glō-a-me'ri-kan], *n.*

The accent ' after a syllable = stress (u-pon'). The mark ‾ over a vowel = length (ā in made; ō in bone).

American who is of English descent; Englishman whose home is in the U.S. ANGLO-AMERICAN (2), *adj.* of or pertaining to Anglo-Americans.

ANGLO-CATHOLIC [ang-glō-ka'tho-lik]. *n. and adj.* (a person) belonging to the Church of England and embracing High Church principles and ritual.

ANGLO-CATHOLICISM [ang-glō-ka-tho'li-sizm]. *n.* the beliefs of the High Church party in the Church of England.

ANGLO-EIRE [ang-glō-āer'e]. *adj.* Anglo-Irish.

ANGLO-FRENCH (1) [ang-glō-frensh']. *n.* the French language used in England after the Norman Conquest. ANGLO-FRENCH (2), *adj.* of or pertaining to England and France or to Anglo-French.

ANGLO-INDIAN [ang-glō-in'di-an]. *n.* an Englishman born or living in India; a Eurasian. ANGLO-INDIAN (2), *adj.* of or pertaining to England and India or to Anglo-Indians.

ANGLO-IRISH (1) [ang-glō-īer'ish]. *n.(pl.)* the descendants of the original settlers within the Pale; the offspring of marriages between the Irish and the English; English persons born or long resident in Ireland. ANGLO-IRISH (2), *adj.* of or pertaining to England and Ireland.

ANGLOMANIA [ang-glō-mā'ni-ah]. *n.* excessive admiration for everything English.

ANGLO-NORMAN (1) [ang-glō-naw'man]. *n.* a Norman living in England after the Conquest; Norman-French as spoken in England after the Conquest. ANGLO-NORMAN (2), *adj.* pertaining to Anglo-Norman.

ANGLOPHIL(E) [ang'glō-fīl]. *n. and adj.* (a person) friendly to England and things English.

ANGLOPHOBE [ang'glō-fōb]. *n. and adj.* (a person) hating England and things English.

ANGLOPHOBIA [ang-glō-fō'bi-ah]. *n.* hatred of everything English.

ANGLO-SAXON (1) [ang-glō-sak'son]. *n.* a native of England before the Norman Conquest; the language of England before the 12th century; *(pop.)* person of British or American nationality descended from English stock. ANGLO-SAXON (2), *adj.* pertaining to Anglo-Saxons. ANGLO-SAXONISM, *n.* anything peculiarly Anglo-Saxon; belief in the superiority of the English-speaking races.

ANGOLA [ahng-gō'lah]. *n.* cloth of Angora wool; **A. cat,** silky-haired cat. [Corruption of ANGORA].

ANGORA [an-gaw'rah]. *n.* Anatolian city, also called Ankara; **a. wool,** hair of the A. goat, mohair; **a. rabbit,** rabbit with fine white hair.

ANGOSTURA [ahng-gō-stōō'rah]. *n.* place in Venezuela; **A. bark,** pungent bark of *Cusparia*; **A. bitters,** flavouring made from A. bark.

ANGRY [ang'gri]. *adj.* full of anger, enraged; *(fig.)* inflamed (of a sore). ANGRILY, *adv.* in a. manner. ANGRINESS, *n.* state of being a.

ANGSTROM UNIT, ångström unit [ahng'strom-, ong'-strerm-yōō-nit]. *n. (phys.)* a minute unit of measurement, the ten-millionth part of a millimetre.

ANGUISH (1) [ang'gwish]. *n.* keen pain of body or mind, any intensely painful feeling. ANGUISH (2), *v.t.* to distress with acute pain or grief. [OFr. from L.].

ANGULAR [ang'gyōo-lah(r)]. *adj.* having angles or corners; *(fig.)* (of people) thin and bony; stiff, overformal in manner; difficult to get on with. ANGULARITY [ang-gyōo-la'ri-ti], *n.* state of being a. ANGULARLY [ang'gyōo-lah-li], *adv.* with angles or corners, in an a. manner. [L.].

ANGULATE(D) [ang'gyōo-lāt(-id)], *adj.* with angles, angled.

ANGUSTIFOLIATE [ang-gus-ti-fō'li-at], *adj. (bot.)* with narrow leaves. [L.].

ANHARMONIC [an-hah-mo'nik], *adj. (math.)* not harmonic.

ANHEDRAL [an-hē'dral], *adj. (aeron.)* of the angle at which the wing of an aircraft is inclined to the lateral axis. [Gk.].

ANHELATION [an-he-lā'shn], *n.* shortness of breath, panting; *(fig.)* desire or aspiration.

ANHIMA [an'hi-mah], *n. (zool.)* a South American bird, the horned screamer. [Brazilian].

ANHYDRITE [an-hī'drīt], *n. (min.)* anhydrous calcium sulphate.

ANHYDROUS [an-hī'drōos], *adj. (chem.)* (of substances) without water of crystallization. [Gk.].

ANIGH [a-nī'], *adv. (poet.)* near.

ANIL [a'nil], *n. (bot.)* kind of indigo plant. [Arab. from Skr.].

ANILINE (1) [a'ni-lēn], *n.* chemical obtained by the distillation of coal-tar, and used in the manufacture of numerous dyes. ANILINE (2), *adj.* pertaining to anil or aniline. [ANIL].

ANIMADVERSION [a-ni-mad-vur'shn], *n.* criticism of a hostile nature, censure; *(leg.)* judicial criticism of an offence or of evidence given. [~L.].

ANIMADVERT [a-ni-mad-vurt'], *v.i.* to observe, refer to, direct attention to; remark upon, in criticism or censure. [L.].

ANIMAL (1) [a'ni-mal], *n.* an animate creature; living being characterized by sensation and voluntary motion, as distinct from the other series of organized beings such as the vegetables; the lower animals as distinct from man; used contemptuously of a man little better than a beast, a brutish, sensual creature. ANIMAL (2), *adj.* pertaining to living beings; physical, belonging to the animal or sensual part as opposed to the spiritual; **a. heat,** the even temperature maintained within the bodies of living creatures; **a. magnetism,** mesmerism, the hypnotizing of one person by another; **a. spirits,** natural exuberance and vitality. [L.].

ANIMALCULA [a-ni-mal'kyōo-lah], *n.(pl.) (zool.)* minute animals, generally discernible only through a microscope. ANIMALCULAR, *adj.* pertaining to a. [L.].

ANIMALCULE [a-ni-mal'kyōol], *n. (zool.)* minute animal, one of the animalcula.

ANIMALISM [a'ni-ma-lizm], *n.* conduct motivated by animal instincts; the doctrine that man is merely an animal.

ANIMALITY [a-ni-ma'li-ti], *n.* the qualities characteristic of an animal.

ANIMALIZE [a'ni-ma-līz], *v.t.* to give animal life or qualities to; turn into an animal; lower, abase; brutalize. ANIMALIZATION [a-ni-ma-lī-zā'shn], *n.* act of animalizing.

ANIMATE (1) [a'ni-mat], *adj.* living. ANIMATE (2) [a'ni-māt], *v.t.* to give life to, give spirit to; inspire. [~L.].

ANIMATED [a'ni-mā-tid], *adj.* having life or spirit; vivacious, brisk; **a. cartoon,** series of drawings so photographed as to appear in motion when projected on a cinema screen. ANIMATEDLY, *adv.* in a lively manner.

ANIMATION [a-ni-mā'shn], *n.* act of animating, imparting vitality; state of being animated; vivacity. [~L.].

ANIMATOR [a'ni-mā-ter], *n.* person who or thing which animates; draughtsman who adapts drawings for animated cartoons.

ANIMISM [a'ni-mizm], *n.* doctrine which regards the soul as the source of all forms of life; attribution of a soul to inanimate objects; belief in the existence of soul or spirit apart from matter. ANIMIST, *n.* one who believes in a. ANIMISTIC [a-ni-mis'tik], *adj.* pertaining to a. [L.].

ANIMOSITY [a-ni-mo'si-ti], *n.* active hostility of mind, bitter hatred, violent prejudice. [~L.].

ANIMUS [a'ni-mus], *n.* animosity, hostility; soul, mind, purpose, spirit. [L.].

ANISE [a'nis], *n.* Levantine plant with aromatic and medicinal seeds. [Fr. from Gk.].

ANISEED [a'ni-sēd], *n.* seed of anise.

ANISETTE [a-ni-zet'], *n.* liqueur flavoured with aniseed. [Fr.].

ANISO-, *pref.* unequal, unsymmetrical. [Gk.].

ANISODYNAMOUS [a-ni-sō-di'na-moōs], *adj. (bot.)* growing more on one side of the axis than on the other. [Gk.].

ANISOMERIC [a-ni-sō-me'rik], *adj.* unsymmetrical. [Gk.].

ANITROGENOUS [a-ni-tro'je-noōs], *adj. (chem.)* non-nitrogenous.

ANKLE [ang'kl], *n.* the joint in human beings which connects the foot and the leg; slender part of the leg between the ankle joint and the calf.

ANKLET [ang'klet], *n.* ring-shaped ornament or fetter for the ankle.

ANKYLOSIS, see ANCHYLOSIS.

ANNA [a'nah], *n.* small copper coin, value one-sixteenth of a rupee. [Hind.].

ANNAL [a'nal], *n.* narrative of the events of a year; Roman Catholic anniversary Mass; *sg.* of annals. ANNALIST [a'na-list], *n.* one who writes annals. [L.].

ANNALS [a'nalz], *n.(pl.)* historical narrative that records events year by year; chronicle. [L.].

ANNEAL [a-nēl'], *v.t.* to temper glass or metals by subjecting them to intense heat and then letting them cool slowly; heat glass and earthenware so as to fix colours; temper by heat; bake, as of tiles.

ōō is pronounced as in *food*; ŏŏ as in *hood*; th as in *think*; TH as in *that*; zh as in azure ~ = related to.

DSE—B

ANNEALING, *n.* process of tempering metal etc. [O.E.].

ANNELIDA [a-ne′li-dah], *n.(pl.)* (*zool.*) animals like the earthworms, whose bodies are formed by a succession of rings. [~L.].

ANNEX (1), **ANNEXE** [a′neks], *n.* something annexed, an addition; additional, subsidiary building designed to supply extra accommodation. [Fr.].

ANNEX (2) [a-neks′], *v.t.* to add, attach; (of a state) take over additional territory. ANNEXATION [a-nek-sā′shn], *n.* act of annexing. ANNEXURE [a-nek′shŏŏr], *n.* something annexed. [L.].

ANNEXE, see ANNEX (1).

ANNIHILATE [a-nī′i-lāt], *v.t.* to reduce to nothing, completely destroy; (*fig.*) reduce to defeated silence. ANNIHILABLE [a-nī′i-la-bl], *adj.* able to be annihilated. ANNIHILATOR [a-nī′i-lā-ter], *n.* one who or that which annihilates. [~L.].

ANNIHILATION [a-nī-i-lā′shn], *n.* act of annihilating; condition of being annihilated. [Fr.].

ANNIVERSARY (1) [a-ni-vur′sa-ri], *n.* the return in subsequent years of the date on which a certain event took place; celebration taking place on an annually recurring date. ANNIVERSARY (2), *adj.* pertaining to an a. [L.].

ANNO DOMINI [a-nō-do′mi-nī], *adv.* in the year since the birth of Christ, usually written A.D.; (*slang*) advancing age. [L.].

ANNOTATE [a′nō-tāt], *v.t. and i.* to comment upon by means of notes, write explanatory notes to any text or document. ANNOTATED, *adj.* with explanatory notes. [~L.].

ANNOTATION [a-nō-tā′shn], *n.* act of annotating; explanatory note. [~L.].

ANNOTATOR [a′nō-tā-ter], *n.* one who annotates. ANNOTATORY [a-nō-tā′te-ri], *adj.* pertaining to an a. or annotation.

ANNOUNCE [a-nowns′], *v.t.* to make known, declare; pronounce or declare judicially; make known the approach or presence of. [Fr. from L.].

ANNOUNCEMENT [a-nowns′ment], *n.* act of announcing.

ANNOUNCER [a-nown′ser], *n.* one who announces, used *esp.* of the officials who introduce programmes and broadcast news by wireless.

ANNOY [a-noi′], *v.t.* to irritate, harass, plague, vex. [OFr.].

ANNOYANCE [a-noi′ans], *n.* action of annoying; vexation, trouble.

ANNOYING [a-noi′ing], *adj.* causing annoyance. ANNOYINGLY, *adv.* in an a. manner. ANNOYINGNESS, *n.* quality of being a.; vexation.

ANNUAL (1) [a′nyŏŏ-al], *n.* that which appears yearly, *esp.* a publication; plant which lives only one year or season; **hardy a.,** a hardy a. plant; (*fig.*) event which recurs with tiresome monotony each year or at intervals. ANNUAL (2), *adj.* returning every year, lasting only one year or season. ANNUALLY, *adv.* every year. [LL.].

ANNUITY [a-nyŏŏ′i-ti], *n.* sum of money paid every year for the lifetime of the recipient. ANNUITANT [a-nyŏŏ′i-tant], *n.* person in receipt of an a. [Fr.].

ANNUL (*pres.pt.* **annulling,** *pret. and p.pt.* **annulled**) [a-nul′], *v.t.* to render void or null, reduce to nothing, cancel, declare invalid. [Fr. from L.].

ANNULAR [a′nyŏŏ-ler], *adj.* in the form of a ring, round; **a. eclipse of the sun,** (*astron.*) eclipse in which the moon so covers the disk of the sun that only a bright ring is seen round the border; **a. ligament,** (*med.*) strong muscular band ringing the wrist and ankle; **a. space,** (*math.*) space between an inner and outer cylinder. ANNULARLY [a′nyŏŏ-ler-li], *adv.* in an a. manner. ANNULARY, *adj.* having a ring-like form. [L.].

ANNULATE(D) [a′nyŏŏ-lāt(-id)], *adj.* ringed, marked with ring-like grooves. ANNULATION [a-nyŏŏ-lā′shn], *n.* ring-like formation. [L.].

ANNULMENT [a-nul′ment], *n.* act of annulling, of rendering null and void.

ANNULOSE [a′nyŏŏ-lōs], *adj.* (*zool.*) furnished with rings, formed of ring-like segments. [L.].

ANNUNCIATE [a-nun′si-āt], *v.t.* to announce officially, proclaim, bring tidings of. [~L.].

ANNUNCIATION [a-nun-si-ā′shn], *n.* act of announcing; (*eccles.*) the announcing of the Incarnation by the Angel Gabriel to the Virgin Mary; **A. Day,** church festival on 25 March in commemoration of the A. [~L.].

ANNUNCIATOR [a-nun′si-ā-ter], *n.* one who announces; mechanism connected with a bell to indicate the room in which attendance is required.

ANODE [a′nōd], *n.* (*elect.*) point at which an electric current passes from a source of electrical energy into an external circuit; a positive electrode; (*radio*) metal plate or cylinder in a thermionic valve which attracts some of the electrons emitted by the filament. ANODAL [a′nō-dal], *adj.* pertaining to the a. ANODIC [a-no′dik], *adj.* (*physiology*) proceeding towards a nerve-centre; (*elect.*) anodal. [Gk.].

ANODYNE (1) [a′nō-dīn], *n.* medicine to alleviate pain; (*fig.*) anything which soothes wounded feelings or softens the sense of misfortune. ANODYNE (2), *adj.* soothing, assuaging bodily or mental pain. [Gk.].

ANOESIS [a-nō′i-sis], *n.* (*psych.*) consciousness with sensation but without thought. [~Gk.].

ANOINT [a-noint′], *v.t.* to pour oil upon, smear with oil or unctuous substance; (*eccles.*) consecrate with oil; (*fig.*) **to a. the palm,** to bribe. ANOINTING, *n.* act of applying oil or ointment, consecration with oil. [OFr. ~L.].

ANOINTED (1) [a-noin′tid], *n.* a consecrated being; **the Lord's A.,** Christ; the sovereign after anointing. ANOINTED (2), *adj.* smeared with oil; **an a. king,** king by divine right.

ANOMALISTIC [a-no-ma-lis′tik], *adj.* irregular, departing from established rule; **a. month,** time taken by the moon to pass from perigee to perigee; **a. year,** time taken by a planet to pass from perihelion to perihelion.

ANOMALOUS [a-no′ma-lŏŏs], *adj.* incongruous; deviating from rule, irregular. ANOMALOUSLY, *adv.* in an irregular manner. ANOMALOUSNESS, *n.* quality of being a., irregularity. [Gk.].

ANOMALY [a-no′ma-li], *n.* irregularity, deviation from rule, inconsistency (in human action); (*astron.*) the angular distance of a planet from its perihelion, irregularity in a planet's motion. [L., Gk.].

ANON (1) [a-non′], *adv.* soon, in a short time, directly; **ever and a.,** every now and then. [OE.].

ANON (2), *adj.* anonymous. [Abbrev.].

ANONA [a-nō′nah], *n.* genus of plants including the pineapple. ANONACEOUS [a-nō-nā′shŏŏs], *adj.* pertaining to the a. [L.].

ANONYM [a′no-nim], *n.* nameless person; assumed name. [Fr.].

ANONYMITY [a-no-ni′mi-ti], *n.* state of being anonymous.

ANONYMOUS [a-no′ni-mŏŏs], *adj.* lacking a name, without any name acknowledged; of unknown or undeclared authorship. ANONYMOUSLY, *adv.* without a name, in an a. manner.

ANOREXIA [a-nō-rek′si-ah], *n.* (*med.*) lack of appetite. [Gk.].

ANORTHIC [a-naw′thik], *adj.* without right angles; (*geol.*) irregular in crystallization. [Gk.].

ANOSMIA [a-noz′mi-ah], *n.* (*med.*) loss of the sense of smell. [Gk.].

ANOTHER [a-nu′THer], *adj. and pron.* not the same, a second, further, additional, any other; a second similar. [OE.].

ANSERINE [an′se-rīn], *adj.* pertaining to the goose; stupid. [L.].

ANSWER (1) [ahn′ser], *n.* a reply, response, statement made in reply to a question; argument, defence, resulting action; (*math.*) solution of a problem; (*leg.*) reply made to a charge, counterstatement of facts in a course of pleadings. ANSWER (2), *v.t.* to speak, write or act in consequence of another's words or actions; reply to, speak or write in return to, say or do in reply, refute, serve; *v.i.* to reply, speak or reply by way of return, rebut a charge, defend oneself; (of a plan) succeed; **to a. for,** to be responsible for; **to a. to** (such a description, name), to be known by, correspond to. [OE.].

ANSWERABLE [ahn′se-ra-bl], *adj.* capable of being answered; liable; **a. for,** responsible for; **a. to,** obliged to give an account to. ANSWERABLY, *adv.* correspondingly, in due proportion.

ANT (1) [ant], *n.* small gregarious insect of the genus *Formica.* [OE.].

ANT- (2), see ANTE-.

ANT- (3), see ANTI-.

ANTACID (1), **ANTIACID** [an-ta′sid], *n.* substance which counteracts or neutralizes an acid; alkali; medicine for correcting stomach acidity. ANTACID (2), *adj.* counteracting an acid.

ANTAGONISM [an-ta′go-nizm], *n.* condition of being opposed; mutual resistance of two forces. [Gk.].

ANTAGONIST [an-ta′go-nist], *n.* one who is opposed to or contends with another; adversary.

---

opponent; (anat.) muscle counteracting the action of another. [Gk.].

ANTAGONISTIC(AL) [an-ta-go-nis'tik(-al)], adj. opposed to, unsympathetic, hostile. ANTAGONISTICALLY [an-ta-go-nis'ti-ka-li], adv. in an a. manner.

ANTAGONIZE [an-ta'go-niz], v.t. to contend with, dispute the mastery with; make antagonistic to, render hostile. [Gk.].

ANTALGIC [an-tal'jik], n. medicine which relieves pain. [Gk.].

ANTALKALI [an-tal'ka-li], n. (chem.) substance which neutralizes the effect of alkalis. ANTALKALINE, adj. pertaining to an a.

ANTAPHRODISIAC [an-taf-rō-di'zi-ak], adj. and n. (drug or medicine) counteracting sexual desire.

ANTARCTIC [an-tahk'tik], adj. and n. (pertaining to) the zone round the South Pole.

ANTASTHMATIC, ANTIASTHMATIC [an-tas-ma'tik], adj. and n. (med.) (medicine) tending to alleviate asthma.

ANTE- (1), **ANT-** (2), pref. before, in front of, earlier than. [L.].

ANTE (2) [an'ti], n. in the game of poker, a stake laid before new cards are drawn. ANTE (3), v.t. and i. in poker, to put up a preliminary stake; (slang, esp. U.S.) to pay (up).

ANT-EATER [ant'ē-ter], n. South American quadruped of the order Myrmecophaga which feeds on ants; similar Australian quadruped of the Monotremata.

ANTECEDENCE [an-ti-sē'dens], n. act or state of going before in place, time or rank; precedence; (astron.) apparent motion of a planet towards the west, or contrary to the order of the signs. [L.].

ANTECEDENT (1) [an-ti-sē'dent], n. that which goes before in time, place or rank; (gram.) the noun or pronoun to which a relative pronoun refers; (log.) the conditional clause of a hypothetical proposition; (math.) the former of two terms of ratio; (pl.) prior conduct; one's previous record, circumstances of ancestry, birth, education, past experience. ANTECEDENT (2), adj. going before in time, place or rank; prior, previous. ANTECEDENCY, n. condition of being a. ANTECEDENTLY, adv. previously, before.

ANTECHAMBER [an'ti-chām-ber], n. an entrance room, room leading to the chief apartment.

ANTE-CHAPEL [an'ti-cha-pel], n. (arch.) anteroom to a chapel.

ANTEDATE [an-ti-dāt'], v.t. to date before the actual time, to anticipate, precede in time.

ANTEDILUVIAN (1) [an-ti-di-lōō'vi-an], adj. existing before the Deluge; (fig.) antiquated. ANTEDILUVIAN (2), n. a very old-fashioned person. [L.].

ANT-EGGS [ant'egz], n.(pl.) the ant's pupae.

ANTELOPE [an'ti-lōp], n. a ruminant akin to the deer and goat. [OFr.].

ANTEMERIDIAN [an-ti-me-ri'di-an], adj. before noon.

ANTENATAL [an-ti-nā'tal], adj. existing or taking place before birth; **a. clinic,** clinic where medical attention is given to pregnant women.

ANTENNA (pl. **antennae**) [an-te'nah, -nē], n. sensory organ or feeler on an insect's head; (radio) an aerial. ANTENNAL, adj. pertaining to an a. ANTENNIFEROUS [an-te-ni'fe-rōōs], adj. bearing or having antennae. ANTENNIFORM [an-te'ni-fawm], adj. having the form of antennae. [L.].

ANTEPAST [an'ti-pahst], n. a foretaste, appetizer, hors d'oeuvre. [L.].

ANTEPENULT [an-ti-pe-nult'], n. the last but two.

ANTEPENULTIMATE [an-ti-pe-nul'ti-mat], adj. pertaining to the antepenult.

ANTEPRANDIAL [an-ti-pran'di-al], adj. pertaining to the time before dinner.

ANTERIOR [an-tēer'i-er], adj. before in time or place; preceding, earlier, prior. ANTERIORITY [an-tēer-i-o'ri-ti], n. state of being a. in time or position. ANTERIORLY [an-tēer'i-er-li], adv. before, previously. [L.].

ANTEROOM [an'ti-rōōm], n. antechamber.

ANTHELION (pl. **anthelia**) [ant-hē'li-on], n. halo surrounding the shadow of an observer's head on a bank of fog or cloud opposite the sun. [Gk.].

ANTHELIX, see ANTIHELIX.

ANTHELMINTIC [ant-hel-min'tik], adj and n. (medicine) destroying intestinal worms. [Gk.].

ANTHEM [an'them], n. musical composition, usually from the Scriptures or Liturgy, sung antiphonally or by two voices or choirs responsively; any triumphant song of praise or gladness. [OE.].

ANTHER [an'ther], n. (bot.) the part of the stamen

of a flowering plant containing the pollen. ANTHERAL adj. pertaining to an a. ANTHER-DUST, n. pollen.

ANTHERIDIUM [an-the-ri'di-um], n. the male organ of cryptogams.

ANTHESIS [an-thē'sis], n. (bot.) the period of full bloom. [Gk.].

ANT-HILL [ant'hil], n. small mound thrown up by ants in making their nest.

ANTHO-, pref. flower. [Gk.].

ANTHOBIAN [an-thō'bi-an], n. beetle which lives on flowers. [Gk.].

ANTHOCARPOUS [an-thō-kah'pōōs], adj. (bot.) bearing fruit formed by masses of flowers adhering together, as in the pineapple. [Gk.].

ANTHOID [an'thoid], adj. flower-like. [Gk.].

ANTHOLOGIST [an-tho'lo-jist], n. one who compiles an anthology.

ANTHOLOGY [an-tho'lo-ji], n. collection of choice specimens of verse, esp. applied to Greek verse; any collection of choice passages from the works of an author or different authors. ANTHOLOGICAL [an-tho-lo'ji-kal], adj. pertaining to an a. [Gk.].

ANTHOPHYLLITE [an-tho'fi-līt], n. (min.) variety of hornblende. [MdL.].

ANTHOZOA [an-thō-zō'ah], n.(pl.) (zool.) order of marine polyps, the corals. [Gk.].

ANTHRACENE [an'thra-sēn], n. a hydrocarbon dyestuff; **a. oil,** thick green oil distilled from coaltar; **a. red,** artificial alizarin. [~Gk.].

ANTHRACITE [an'thra-sīt], n. (min.) hard slow-burning non-bituminous coal. ANTHRACIFEROUS [an-thra-si'fe-rōōs], adj. bearing a. ANTHRACITIC [an-thra-si'tik], adj. pertaining to, resembling, a. [Gk.].

ANTHRAX [an'thraks], n. carbuncle; malignant disease common to sheep and cattle, occurring also in man. [L.].

ANTHROPO-, pref. man. [Gk.].

ANTHROPOCENTRIC [an-thrō-pō-sen'trik], adj. with man as the pivot of the universe. [Gk.].

ANTHROPOGENY [an-thrō-po'je-ni], n. science which investigates the evolution of man. [Gk.].

ANTHROPOGRAPHY [an-thrō-po'gra-fi], n. ethnography. [Gk.].

ANTHROPOID (1) [an'thrō-poid], n. species of the Anthropoidea, highest order of the primates which are nearest to man in structure, as the gorilla and other apes. ANTHROPOID (2), adj. (zool.) of human form, resembling man. [Gk.].

ANTHROPOLOGY [an-thrō-po'lo-ji], n. that branch of science which investigates the position of mankind zoologically, studying its evolution, history, physiology and psychology and their mutual bearing; study of primitive customs, myths and religions of mankind. ANTHROPOLOGICAL [an-thrō-pō-lo'ji-kal], adj. pertaining to a. ANTHROPOLOGIST [an-thro-po'lo-jist], n. one who studies or is skilled in a. [Gk.].

ANTHROPOMETRY [an-thrō-po'mi-tri], n. measurement of the human body for scientific purposes. ANTHROPOMETRIC(AL) [an-thrō-pō-met'rik(-al)], adj. pertaining to a. ANTHROPOMETRIST [an-thro-po'met-rist], n. one skilled in a. [Gk.].

ANTHROPOMORPHISM [an-thrō-pō-maw'fizm], n. the attribution of the human form or human qualities and affections to the Deity, or of human faculties to the lower animals or inanimate things. ANTHROPOMORPHIC, adj. relating to or characterized by a.; resembling man. ANTHROPOMORPHIST, ANTHROPOMORPHITE [an-thrō-pō-maw'fist, an-thrō-pō-maw'fīt], n. one who attributes a human personality to God or to animals. ANTHROPOMORPHIZE, v.t. to attribute to the Deity human form and qualities. [Gk.].

ANTHROPOPATHY [an-thrō-po'pa-thi], n. the ascription of human passions and emotions to the Deity. ANTHROPOPATHICAL [an-thrō-pō-pa'thi-kal], adj. pertaining to a.

ANTHROPOPHAGI [an-thrō-po'fa-ji], n.(pl.) man-eaters, cannibals. ANTHROPOPHAGOUS [an-thrō-po'fa-gōōs], adj. man-eating. ANTHROPOPHAGY [an-thrō-po'fa-ji], n. cannibalism. [Gk.].

ANTHROPOTOMY [an-thrō-po'ta-mi], n. anatomy of the human body. [Gk.].

ANTI-, ANT- (3), pref. against, opposite, in hostility to. [Gk.].

ANTIACID, see ANTACID.

ANTI-AIRCRAFT [an-ti-āer'krahft], adj. opposed to aircraft, used in defence against an attack by hostile aircraft.

ANTIAR [an'tyah(r)], n. upas tree of Java; poison

obtained from it. ANTIARIN [an'tya-rin], *n.* virulent principle in a. [Javanese].

ANTIASTHMATIC, see ANTASTHMATIC.

ANTIATTRITION [an-ti-a-tri'shn], *n.* a counter-active of friction; (*mech.*) substance applied to moving parts of machinery to eliminate friction.

ANTIBIOTIC [an-ti-bi-o'tik], *n. and adj.* (substance) which inhibits the growth of (harmful) organisms; *esp.* applied to organic substances such as penicillin. [Gk.].

ANTIBODY [an'ti-bo-di], *n.* (*path.*) substance in the blood which is a natural antidote to infection.

ANTIC (1) [an'tik], *n.* act of buffoonery. ANTIC (2), *adj.* grotesque, ludicrous, whimsical, fantastic. [It. from L.].

ANTICARDIUM [an-ti-kah'di-um], *n.* (*anat.*) pit of the stomach. [Gk.].

ANTICATARRHAL [an-ti-ka-tah'ral], *n. and adj.* (a substance) remedying catarrh.

ANTICHRIST [an'ti-krist], *n.* the opponent of Christ, name given to great opponent of Christ and His Kingdom expected by the early Church to appear before the second coming of Christ.

ANTICHRISTIAN [an-ti-kris'ti-an], *adj.* opposed to Christ and Christianity. ANTICHRISTIANISM, *n.* opposition to the Christian religion.

ANTICIPANT (1) [an-ti'si-pant], *n.* one who antici-pates. ANTICIPANT (2), *adj.* expectant, anticipating. [~L.].

ANTICIPATE [an-ti'si-pāt], *v.t.* to be beforehand in acting or seeing, forestall, foresee, look forward to, be prepared for. [~L.].

ANTICIPATION [an-ti-si-pā'shn], *n.* act of antici-pating, forestalling, foreseeing or being prepared for; foretaste; (*leg.*) assignment of income derived from a trust estate before it is actually due; (*mus.*) beginning one chord before the preceding one has ceased to sound. [~L.].

ANTICIPATIVE [an-ti'si-pa-tiv], *adj.* anticipatory.

ANTICIPATOR [an-ti'si-pā-ter], *n.* one who antici-pates. ANTICIPATORY [an-ti'si-pā-te-ri], *adj.* being in anticipation of, in advance of.

ANTICLERICALISM [an-ti-kle'ri-ka-lizm], *n.* move-ment opposed to the sacerdotal claims of the clergy or directed against the influence of the clergy; movement against the intrusion of the clergy into politics. ANTICLERICAL, *adj.* pertaining to a.

ANTICLIMAX [an-ti-kli'maks], *n.* the opposite of climax; (*rhet.*) sudden change from dignity to triviality of expression.

ANTICLINAL [an-ti-kli'nal], *adj.* dipping or sloping down in opposite directions; **a. axis,** (*geol.*) line from which strata dip on either side. [Gk.].

ANTI-CLOCKWISE [an-ti-klok'wiz], *adj. and adv.* counter-clockwise.

ANTICOMMUNIST [an-ti-ko'myōō-nist], *n. and adj.* (person) opposed to communism.

ANTICYCLONE [an-ti-si'klōn], *n.* an atmospheric condition opposite to that of a cyclone; the central area of this condition, where winds blow spirally outwards, tending to produce improved weather conditions.

ANTI-DAZZLE [an-ti-da'zl], *adj.* designed to prevent visual glare (*esp.* from motor-car headlights).

ANTIDEMOCRATIC(AL) [an-ti-de-mo-kra'tik(-al)], *adj.* opposing democracy.

ANTIDISESTABLISHMENTARIANISM [an-ti-di-ses-tab-lish-men-tāer'i-a-nizm], *n.* opposition to the disestablishment of the Church.

ANTIDOTE [an'ti-dōt], *n.* medicine to counteract poison or diseased condition; (*fig.*) remedy. ANTIDOTAL [an-ti-dō'tal], *adj.* pertaining to, serving as, an a. ANTIDOTALLY, *adv.* as an a. [Gk.].

ANTIEPISCOPAL [an-ti-e-pis'kō-pal], *adj.* opposed to episcopacy.

ANTIEVANGELICAL [an-ti-ē-van-je'li-kal], *adj.* antagonistic to evangelicalism.

ANTIFOULING [an-ti-fow'ling], *n.* substance for preventing the growth of barnacles and weeds on ships' hulls.

ANTI-FREEZE [an-ti-frēz'], *n.* substance, usually ethylene glycol, added to the water in the cooling system of motors to prevent freezing.

ANTIFRICTION (1) [an-ti-frik'shn], *n.* antiattrition. ANTIFRICTION (2), *adj.* decreasing or eliminating friction.

ANTI-GAS [an-ti-gas'], *adj.* giving protection against poison gas.

ANTIGEN [an'ti-jen], *n.* (*med.*) substance which forms antibodies in the blood. [Gk.].

ANTIHELIX, ANTHELIX [ant-(i-)hē'liks], *n.*

(*anat.*) the semicircular prominence of the ear in front of and within the helix.

ANTI-JACOBIN (1) [an-ti-ja'kō-bin], *n.* member of a French political party opposed to the French Revolution of 1789. ANTI-JACOBIN (2), *adj.* per-taining to the anti-Jacobins.

ANTILOG [an'ti-log], *n.* antilogarithm.

ANTILOGARITHM [an-ti-lo'ga-riᴛʜm], *n.* (*math.* the number represented by a logarithm.

ANTILOGOUS (1) [an-ti'lō-gŏŏs], *n.* (*elect.*) that pole of a crystal which, when heating, is negative, and when cooling, positive. ANTILOGOUS (2), *adj.* contradictory. [Gk.].

ANTIMACASSAR [an-ti-ma-ka'ser], *n.* loose cover-ing on the backs of chairs to keep them from being soiled by oil on the hair.

ANTIMASONIC [an-ti-ma-so'nik], *adj.* opposed to freemasonry.

ANTIMASQUE [an'ti-mahsk], *n.* grotesque inter-lude introduced into a masque.

ANTIMONARCHIC(AL) [an-ti-mo-nah'kik(-al)], *adj.* opposed to monarchy.

ANTIMONARCHIST [an-ti-mo'na-kist], *n.* person opposed to monarchy.

ANTIMONIAL [an-ti-mŏ'ni-al], *adj.* pertaining to, composed of, antimony.

ANTIMONIATE [an-ti-mŏ'ni-āt], *n.* a salt of antimonic acid.

ANTIMONIATED [an-ti-mŏ'ni-ā-tid], *adj.* prepared with or containing antimony.

ANTIMONIC [an-ti-mŏ'nik], *adj.* pertaining to antimony; (*chem.*) pertaining to compounds of antimony in which it combines as a pentad.

ANTIMONIOUS [an-ti-mŏ'ni-ōŏs], *adj.* containing antimony; (*chem.*) pertaining to compounds of antimony in which it combines as a triad.

ANTIMONITE [an-ti'mŏ-nīt], *n.* (*chem.*) a salt of antimonious acid.

ANTIMONY [an'ti-mo-ni], *n.* chemical element designated Sb; brittle, bluish-white metal of flake-like crystals; **a. tartrate,** tartar emetic. [LL. from Arab.].

ANTINATIONAL [an-ti-na'shn-al], *adj.* hostile to one's nation, opposed to a national party or policy.

ANTINOMIAN [an-ti-nŏ'mi-an], *n.* one of a sect who maintained that moral law is superseded and set aside by the Gospel. ANTINOMIANISM [an-ti-nŏ'mi-a-nizm], *n.* the doctrine of the Antinomians. [Gk.].

ANTINOMY [an-ti'no-mi], *n.* contradiction between two laws or two parts of a law; (*met.*) contradiction between apparently equally logical conclusions. [Gk.].

ANTIPAPAL [an-ti-pā'pal], *adj.* opposed to the Pope or popery.

ANTIPAPISTIC(AL) [an-ti-pa-pis'tik(-al)], *adj.* antipapal.

ANTIPATHETIC(AL) [an-ti-pa-the'tik(-al)], *adj.* having an antipathy to.

ANTIPATHIC [an-ti-pa'thik], *adj.* opposed to, of contrary nature or character.

ANTIPATHY [an-ti'pa-thi], *n.* hostile feeling, natural aversion or dislike; essential difference between substances (as oil and water) which prevents their uniting. [Gk.].

ANTIPERISTALTIC [an-ti-pe-ri-stal'tik], *adj.* (*physiol.*) contrary to peristaltic motion.

ANTIPERISTASIS [an-ti-pe-ris'ta-sis], *n.* the oppo-sition of a contrary quality, resistance to an action; (*rhet.*) conceding a point, but drawing a different conclusion. ANTIPERISTATIC [an-ti-pe-ri-sta'tik], *adj.* pertaining to a. [Gk.].

ANTI-PERSONNEL [an-ti-per-so-nel'], *adj.* of a bomb, intended to injure or destroy persons rather than material.

ANTIPHLOGISTIC [an-ti-flo-jis'tik], *adj.* (*med.*) counteracting inflammation. ANTIPHLOGISTINE [an-ti-flo-jis'tēn], *n.* (*prot.*) registered trade name for a plaster. [Gk.].

ANTIPHON [an'ti-fon], *n.* composition in prose or verse consisting of passages or verses sung alter-nately by two church choirs; an anthem. ANTI-PHONAL (1) [an-ti'fo-nal], *n.* book of antiphons. ANTIPHONAL (2), *adj.* (*mus.*) pertaining to an a.; sung alternately. ANTIPHONALLY [an-ti'fo-na-li], *adv.* (*mus.*) in antiphonal fashion. [LL.].

ANTIPHONARY [an-ti'fo-na-ri], *n.* (*R.C.*, *eccles.*) service-book which contains antiphons.

ANTIPHONIC [an-ti'fo-nik], *adj.* antiphonal.

ANTIPHONY [an-ti'fo-ni], *n.* antiphon.

ANTIPHRASIS [an-ti'fra-sis], *n.* (*rhet.*) use of a

The accent ' after a syllable = stress (u-pon'). The mark ⁻ over a vowel = length (ā in made; ō in bone)

word in a sense opposite to its usual meaning.
ANTIPHRASTIC(AL) [an-ti-fras'tik(-al)], *adj.* of the
nature of a.; ironical. ANTIPHRASTICALLY, *adv.* in
an a. manner. [Gk.].
ANTIPODAL [an-ti'pō-dal], *adj.* pertaining to the
antipodes; (*fig.*) diametrically opposed to.
ANTIPODEAN [an-ti-po-dē'an], *adj.* pertaining to
the opposite side of the world.
ANTIPODES [an-ti'pō-dēz], *n.(pl.)* those regions
lying on the exact opposite side of the globe from
any given point; (*fig.*) anything diametrically
opposed to something else. [Gk.].
ANTIPOPE [an'ti-pōp], *n.* pope elected as rival to a
properly elected pope.
ANTIPRELATICAL [an-ti-pre-la'ti-kal], *adj.* opposed
to the prelacy.
ANTIPYRETIC [an-ti-pī-re'tik], *adj.* (*med.*) preventing or curing fever.
ANTIQUARIAN (1) [an-ti-kwāer'i-an], *n.* an
antiquary; a standard size of drawing paper, 53 by
31 inches. ANTIQUARIAN (2), *adj.* pertaining to an
antiquary or to antiquity; **a. bookseller,** seller of
second-hand books. ANTIQUARIANISM, *n.* the work
of an a.; interest in antiquities. [L.].
ANTIQUARY [an'ti-kwa-ri], *n.* one devoted to the
study of antiquity or antiquities. [~L.].
ANTIQUATE [an'ti-kwāt], *v.t.* to render obsolete,
put out of date. [~L.].
ANTIQUATED [an'ti-kwā-tid], *adj.* old, out of
date, old-fashioned; (of persons) advanced in age
and outlook. [*Prec.*].
ANTIQUE (1) [an-tēk'], *n.* a relic, artistic object of
considerable age; (*typ.*) bold type-face in which all
the strokes are of equal thickness. ANTIQUE (2),
adj. pertaining to olden times, ancient, old-fashioned;
pertaining to or in the style of an antique. [L.].
ANTIQUITY [an-ti'kwi-ti], *n.* great age, the remote
past, ancient times; (*pl.*) relics of ancient civilizations.
[~L.].
ANTIRACHITIC [an-ti-ra-ki'tik], *n. and adj.*
(substance) preventive or curative of rickets.
ANTIRRHINUM [an-ti-rī'num], *n.* (*bot.*) the genus
of the snapdragon. [L. from Gk.].
ANTISABBATARIAN [an-ti-sa-ba-tāer'i-an], *n.*
opponent of the strict observance of the Sabbath.
ANTISCORBUTIC [an-ti-skaw-byōō'tik], *n. and
adj.* (substance) efficacious against scurvy.
ANTI-SEMITE [an-ti-se'mīt], *n.* one opposed to the
Jews. ANTI-SEMITIC [an-ti-se-mi'tik], *adj.* opposed
to the Jews. ANTI-SEMITISM [an-ti-se'mi-tizm], *n.*
hostility to the Jews.
ANTISEPTIC [an-ti-sep'tik], *n. and adj.* (any
substance) resisting the growth of septic bacteria
which cause putrefaction.
ANTISLAVERY [an-ti-slā've-ri], *adj.* opposed to
slavery.
ANTISOCIAL [an-ti-sō'shal], *adj.* averse to society
and social intercourse, opposed to the principles
underlying society.
ANTISPASMODIC [an-ti-spaz-mo'dik], *n. and adj.*
(substance) efficacious in counteracting spasms.
ANTISTROPHE [an-tis'trō-fi], *n.* (*dram.*) the
return to the right of the chorus in Greek drama in
answer to a previous move to the left; the stanza
or lines sung during this movement. ANTISTROPHIC
[an-ti-stro'fik], *adj.* pertaining to an a. [Gk.].
ANTITHESIS (*pl.* **antitheses**) [an-ti'thi-sis, an-ti'
thi-sēz], *n.* (*rhet.*) an emphatic contrast of ideas,
usually attained by using two contrasting words
with equivalent grammatical function in two
adjacent clauses; strong contrast. ANTITHETIC(AL)
[an-ti-the'tik(-al)], *adj.* pertaining to a.; opposing,
contrasting. ANTITHETICALLY, *adv.* by a. [Gk.].
ANTI-TOTALITARIAN [an-ti-tō-ta-li-tāer'i-an], *n.
and adj.* (person) opposed to totalitarianism.
ANTITOXIN [an-ti-tok'sin], *n.* (*physiol.*) one of
several soluble chemical compounds in the blood,
neutralizing specific poisons or toxins. ANTITOXIC,
adj. pertaining to a. [Gk.].
ANTITRADE [an-ti-trād'], *n.* upper tropical wind
which blows in a direction contrary to and above
the trade wind.
ANTITRINITARIAN [an-ti-tri-ni-taer'i-an], *n. and
adj.* (person) rejecting the doctrine of the Trinity.
ANTITRINITARIANISM, *n.* (*theol.*) doctrine which
denies the Trinity.
ANTITYPE [an'ti-tīp], *n.* that which is represented
by a type or symbol. ANTITYPICAL [an-ti-ti'pi-kal],
adj. pertaining to an a., explaining the type.
ANTITYPICALLY, *adv.* in the manner of an a.
ANTI-VIVISECTION [an-ti-vi-vi-sek'shn], *adj.*

opposed to vivisection. ANTI-VIVISECTIONIST, *n.* one
who opposes vivisection.
ANTLER [ant'ler], *n.* lowest branch of a stag's horn;
the whole or any part of the horn. ANTLERED, *adj.*
bearing antlers. [OFr.].
ANTLIKE [ant'līk], *adj.* resembling ants.
ANTONOMASIA [an-to-no-mā'zi-ah], *n.* (*rhet.*)
figure of speech in which a common noun is used
for a proper noun or a proper noun for a common
noun. [Gk.].
ANTONYM [an'to-nim], *n.* the opposite of a
synonym, a word which is opposite in meaning to
another. [Gk.].
ANTRUM [an'trum], *n.* (*anat.*) cavity, *esp.* one within
a bone; large cavity in the upper maxillary bone
connected with the nose, the maxillary sinus. [L.].
ANURA [a-nyōō'rah], *n.* the order of tailless amphibia,
such as frogs. [MdL.].
ANUS [ā'nus], *n.* (*anat.*) lower orifice of the alimentary canal. [L.].
ANVIL [an'vil], *n.* heavy iron block on which a
smith hammers and shapes his work; anything on
which blows are struck. [OE.].
ANXIETY [ang-zī'e-ti], *n.* state of being anxious;
intense solicitude, concern, uneasiness about some
future event; keen desire (to effect some end).
[~L.].
ANXIOUS [ang'shŏŏs, angk'shŏŏs], *adj.* greatly
concerned about something, *esp.* in the future or the
unknown; state of being intensely solicitous, full of
concern, earnestly desirous (to effect some purpose).
ANXIOUSLY, *adv.* in an a. manner, with painful
uncertainty, solicitously. [L.].
ANY [e'ni], *adj., pron. and adv.* one, one out of many,
some, in interrogative or negative context; an
indefinite number or quantity; one or more unspecified in a group; a small quantity. [OE.].
ANYBODY [e'ni-bo-di], *n.* one person out of many,
any person, someone; (*fig.*) person of importance.
ANYHOW [e'ni-how], *adv.* by any means, in any
possible way, in any case; (*fig.*) carelessly, in disorder.
ANYTHING [e'ni-thing], *n.* something of any kind,
a single thing; unspecified object or notion.
ANYWHERE [e'ni-wāer], *adv. and pron.* in any
place.
ANZAC [an'zak], *n.* Australian-New Zealand Army
Corps which fought in Gallipoli in 1915; member of
that corps. [Initial letters of the corps].
AORIST [ā'aw-rist], *n.* (*gram.*) indefinite past tense
in a verb. AORISTIC, *adj.* pertaining to the a.;
indefinite. [Gk.].
AORTA [ā-aw'tah], *n.* (*anat.*) the great artery,
proceeding from the left ventricle of the heart to the
two iliac arteries. AORTAL, AORTIC, *adj.* of or pertaining to the a. [Gk.].
APACE [a-pās'], *adv.* at a pace, quickly, step by step,
with steady speed.
APACHE [ah-pah'che], *n.* tribe of North American
Indians; [a-pahsh'] Parisian thief or cut-throat.
[AmerInd.].
APANAGE, see APPANAGE.
APART [a-paht'], *adv.* (of space) on one side, separately, at a distance from; (of purpose, thought)
separately, independently, individually; **to set a.,**
to set aside for a special purpose, separate, devote,
consecrate. [Fr.].
APARTMENT [a-paht'ment], *n.* single room in a
house; (*U.S.*) a flat; (*pl.*) lodgings, set of rooms set
aside for the use of one person or family. APART-
MENT-HOUSE, *n.* house divided into separate rooms
or suites for letting. [Fr.].
APATHETIC [a-pa-the'tik], *adj.* of or pertaining to
apathy; insensible, indifferent. APATHETICALLY, *adv.*
in a. fashion, listlessly.
APATHY [a'pa-thi], *n.* want of feeling, insensibility
to passion or emotion, indifference, indolence of
mind.
APATITE [a'pa-tīt], *n.* (*min.*) native crystallized
phosphate of lime. [Gk.].
APE (1) [āp], *n.* monkey, *esp.* of the tailless species
more closely related to man; (*fig.*) servile or silly
imitator. APE (2), *v.t.* to imitate servilely another's
manners, speech etc.; mimic; pretend to have. [OE.].
APEAK [a-pēk'], *adv.* on the point; (*naut.*) perpendicularly, in a vertical line. [Fr.].
APERIENT (1) [a-pēer'i-ent], *n.* (*med.*) laxative
medicine. APERIENT (2), *adj.* laxative. [~L.].
APERITIF [a-pe'ri-tēf], *n.* alcoholic drink taken as an
appetizer before meals.
APERITIVE [a-pe'ri-tiv], *n.* aperient; aperitif. [Fr.].

APERTURE [a'per-tyōōr], *n.* opening, gap; opening in a telescope or other optical instrument through which light passes; *(phot.)* adjustable circular hole in a plate fitted to a lens to control the amount of light admitted to a camera. [L.].

APETALOUS [a-pe'ta-lŏŏs], *adj.* *(bot.)* without petals.

APEX *(pl.* **apices)** [ā'peks, ā'pi-sĕs], *n.* tip, point, summit, peak, pointed end; *(geom.)* top point of a triangle or cone. [L.].

APHANITE [a'fa-nīt], *n.* *(min.)* a dark hornblende. [Gk.].

APHASIA [a-fā'zi-ah], *n.* *(med.)* loss of the power of speech through a lesion of the brain. [Gk.].

APHELION *(pl.* **aphelia)** [a-fē'li-on], *n.* *(astron.)* point of a planet's or comet's orbit most distant from the sun. [Gk.].

APHELIOTROPISM [a-fē'li-ō-tro-pizm], *n.* *(bot.)* power of plants to turn away from the sun. APHELIOTROPIC [a-fē-li-ō-tro'pik], *adj.* pertaining to a. [Gk.].

APHEMIA [a-fē'mi-ah], *n.* *(med.)* form of aphasia marked by difficulty in articulation. [Gk.].

APHESIS [a'fi-sis], *n.* *(philol.)* occasional loss of an unstressed vowel at the beginning of a word. [Gk.].

APHIS *(pl.* **aphides)** [a'fis, ā'fis, ā'fi-dēz, ā'fi-dĕz], *n.* *(zool.)* plant-louse, greenfly. APHIDIAN [a-fi'di-an], *adj.* of or pertaining to the aphides. [MdL.].

APHONIA, APHONY [a-fō'ni-ah], *n.* complete loss of the voice. APHONOUS [a'fo-nŏŏs], *adj.* voiceless. [Gk.].

APHONY, see APHONIA.

APHORISM [a'faw-rizm], *n.* concise statement of a principle; maxim, precept. APHORIST, *n.* one who makes aphorisms. APHORISTIC [a-faw-ris'tik], *adj.* pertaining to an a., full of aphorisms. APHORISTICALLY, *adv.* in an aphoristic manner, pithily.

APHRISITE [af'ri-zīt], *n.* *(min.)* black Norwegian tourmaline.

APHRITE [af'rīt], *n.* *(min.)* variety of calcite or carbonate of lime. [Gk.].

APHRODISIAC (1) [af-rō-di'zi-ak], *n.* drug which tends to produce sexual desire. APHRODISIAC (2), *adj.* tending to excite sexual desires, venereal. [Gk.].

APHRODISIAN [af-rō-di'zi-an], *adj.* pertaining to sexual love. [Gk.].

APHTHA [af'thah], *n.* *(path.)* a disease of the mouth, thrush. APHTHOUS [af'thŏŏs], *adj.* pertaining to a. [Gk.].

APHTHAE [af'thē], *n.(pl.)* *(path.)* small white specks or ulcers in the mouth symptomatic of thrush. [Gk.].

APHYLLOUS [a'fil-lŏŏs], *adj.* *(bot.)* without leaves. [Gk.].

APIAN [ā'pi-an], *adj.* of or pertaining to bees. [L.].

APIARY [ā'pi-a-ri], *n.* place where bees or beehives are kept. APIARIAN [ā-pi-āer'i-an], *adj.* relating to bee-keeping. APIARIST [ā'pi-a-rist], *n.* one who keeps bees. [L.].

APICAL [a'pi-kal], *adj.* pertaining to an apex. [L.].

APICES [ā'pi-sĕz], *n.(pl.)* of APEX.

APICULTURE [ā'pi-kul-tyōōr], *n.* bee-keeping. [L.].

APIECE [a-pēs'], *adv.* for each piece, article or person; each severally or by itself.

APITPAT [a-pit'-pat], *adv.* in quick palpitations.

APLACENTAL [a-pla-sen'tal], *adj.* *(bot.)* without a placenta.

APLANATIC [a-pla-na'tik], *adj.* *(opt.)* totally free from aberration of the rays of light. [Gk.].

APLASTIC [a-plas'tik], *adj.* not plastic or easily moulded, tending to irregularity of organic structure. [Gk.].

APLOMB [a-plom'], *n.* self-possession, poise, assurance of manner. [Fr.].

APNOEA [ap-nē'ah], *n.* *(med.)* temporary cessation of breathing. [Gk.].

APO-, *pref.* from, derived from, asunder, away, back again; *(chem.)* origin, derivation from. [Gk.].

APOCALYPSE [a-po'ka-lips], *n.* a revelation; the revelation of the future to St. John; the New Testament book recording this; revelation of an unusual kind. APOCALYPTIC [a-po-ka-lip'tik (-al)], *adj.* pertaining to the Apocalypse; revealing. APOCALYPTICALLY, *adv.* in the manner of the A. [Gk.].

APOCARPOUS [a-pō-kah'pŏŏs], *adj.* *(bot.)* with carpels entirely or partially distinct. [Gk.].

APOCOPE [a-po'kō-pi], *n.* the cutting off or loss of the last letter or syllable of a word. [Gk.].

APOCRYPHA [a-pok'ri-fah], *n.(pl.)* those books

appended to the Old Testament which are regarded as canonical by the Roman Catholic Church, but uncanonical by the Greek and Protestant Churches. APOCRYPHAL [a-pok'ri-fal], *adj.* of or pertaining to the A., not canonical; of uncertain authorship or intent; fictitious. APOCRYPHALLY, *adv.* in apocryphal fashion; falsely. [Gk.].

APOD *(pl.* **apodes)** [a'pod, a'po-dēz], *n.* *(ichth.)* fish which has no ventral fins. APODAL [a'po-dal], *adj.* footless, without ventral fins. [Gk.].

APODEICTIC, APODICTIC [a-pō-dīk'tik], *adj.* clearly demonstrative of absolute certainty. APODEICTICALLY, *adv.* in a. fashion. [Gk.].

APODICTIC, see APODEICTIC.

APODOSIS [a-po'do-sis], *n.* *(gram.)* the consequent clause in conditional propositions. [Gk.].

APOGEE [a'pō-jē], *n.* *(astron.)* the point in the moon's or a planet's orbit most distant from the earth; *(fig.)* topmost point. APOGEAN [a-pō-jē'an], *adj.* of or belonging to the a. [Fr. from Gk.].

APOLAUSTIC [a-pō-laws'tik], *adj.* self-indulgent. [Gk.].

APOLLYON [a-po'li-on], *n.* the destroying angel, the devil. [Gk.].

APOLOGETIC [a-po-lō-je'tik], *adj.* excusing with regret; (of manner) deferential, conciliatory; (of an opinion etc.) defending without admitting wrong. APOLOGETICALLY, *adv.* in an a. manner. [Gk.].

APOLOGETICS [a-po-lō-je'tiks], *n.(pl.)* *(theol.)* branch of theology which sets out to defend the Christian religion.

APOLOGIA [a-po-lō'jah], *n.* defence in word or writing. [L.].

APOLOGIST [a-po'lo-jist], *n.* one who pleads in authority or defence; one who defends a cause or opinion.

APOLOGIZE [a-po'lō-jīz], *v.i.* to speak in excuse or defence; make an excuse; own to and express regret for an indefensible action. APOLOGIZER, *n.* person who apologizes. [Gk.].

APOLOGUE [a'po-lŏg], *n.* allegorical story, moral fable. [Fr. from Gk.].

APOLOGY [a-po'lō-ji], *n.* expression of regret for injury inflicted, explanation that no injury or offence was intended; *(fig.)* bad attempt, makeshift, poor substitute. [Gk.].

APONEUROSIS *(pl.* **aponeuroses)** [a-pō-nyōō-rō'sis], *n.* *(anat.)* white, shining membrane of interlaced fibre in the form of an extension of a tendon or the envelope of a muscle. APONEUROTIC [a-pō-nyōō-ro'tik], *adj.* pertaining to a. [Gk.].

APOPHTHEGM [a'pō-them], *n.* terse, pithy saying, brief sententious maxim. APOPHTHEGMATIC(AL) [a-pō-the-ma'tik(-al)], *adj.* of the character of an a., in the habit of using apophthegms; sententious. APOPHTHEGMATIST [a-pō-the'ma-tist], *n.* collector or inventor of apophthegms. APOPHTHEGMATIZE, *v.i.* to use or make apophthegms. [Gk.].

APOPHYSIS *(pl.* **apophyses)** [a-po'fi-sis], *n.* *(anat.)* protuberance or offshoot of a bone; swelling beneath the spore-case in mosses. [Gk.].

APOPLECTIC (1) [a-po-plek'tik], *n.* one predisposed to apoplexy. APOPLECTIC (2), *adj.* having the character of, predisposed to, apoplexy. [Gk.].

APOPLEXY [a-po-plek-si], *n.* sudden deprivation of sense and movement usually caused by some effusion of blood in the brain. [Gk.].

APORT [a-pawt'], *adv.* on or towards the port or left side of the ship.

APOSIOPESIS [a-pō-si-ō-pē'sis], *n.* *(rhet.)* abrupt halt in a discourse, from a real or pretended disinclination to proceed further. [Gk.].

APOSTASY [a-pos'ta-si], *n.* abandonment or renunciation of beliefs or principles once professed; desertion from a religious sect or political party. [Gk.].

APOSTATE [a-pos'tāt], *n.* person who has apostatized, deserter, renegade. APOSTATIC(AL) [a-pos-ta'tik (-al)], *adj.* in the manner of an a. APOSTATIZE [a-pos'ta-tīz], *v.i.* to forsake religious or political principles. [Gk.].

APOSTLE [a-po'sl], *n.* one chosen by Christ to preach the Gospel, one sent on or dedicated to some high mission; early missionary; messenger; **Apostles' Creed,** the earliest form of confession of Christian faith; **a. spoon,** antique silver spoon whose handle is fashioned in the form of one of the Apostles. APOSTLESHIP, *n.* status or condition of an a. APOSTOLATE [a-pos'tō-lāt], *n.* office or rank of an a.; mission. [OE. from Gk.].

APOSTOLIC [a-pos-to'lik], *adj.* of or pertaining to

the Apostles; **A. Fathers,** Christian teachers contemporary with Christ's Apostles; **A. See,** see of Rome; **A. succession,** doctrine of the lineal transmission from the Apostles of spiritual power and authority. APOSTOLICAL, *adj.* a. APOSTOLICALLY, *adv.* in the manner of the Apostles, according to the Apostles; through the Apostles. [Fr.].

APOSTROPHE [a-pos'trō-fi], *n.* (*rhet.*) digression or interruption of an exclamatory or hortatory nature in the course of a speech or literary work, often one where an appeal is made to someone absent or dead as if he were present; (*gram.*) contraction of a word by the omission of a letter or letters, and the insertion of a punctuation sign; (*gram.*) the sign (') denoting the possessive case. APOSTROPHIC [a-pos-tro'fik], *adj.* pertaining to an a. APOSTROPHIZE [a-pos'trō-fīz], *v.t.* to address an a. to; omit a letter of a word and insert an a. [Gk.].

APOTHECARY [a-po'thi-ka-ri], *n.* one who prepares medicines and sells drugs, a chemist. [LL.].

APOTHEM [a'pō-them], *n.* (*math.*) a perpendicular from the centre of a regular polygon to one of its sides.

APOTHEOSIS [a-po-thē-ō'sis], *n.* deification, raising of a mortal to rank among the gods, supreme deification of a person or thing. APOTHEOSIZE [a-po'thē-ō-sīz], *v.t.* to deify.

APOTOMY [a-po'to-mi], *n.* (*math.*) the difference between two quantities which are commensurate, or commensurable only in power; (*mus.*) a major semi-tone. [Gk.].

APPAL (appalling, appalled) [a-pawl'], *v.t.* to depress with fear, dismay, terrify. APPALLING, *adj.* calculated to dismay or shock. APPALLINGLY, *adv.* to a shocking extent, in an appalling way. [OFr.].

APPANAGE, APANAGE [a'pa-nij], *n.* lands and revenue assigned to a younger son of a royal house; perquisite; a dependency; natural attribute or endowment. [OFr.].

APPARATUS [a-pa-rā'tus], *n.* a collection of instruments or utensils for performing an operation or experiment, or for practising an art. [L.].

APPAREL (1) [a-pa'rel], *n.* clothes, dress; ornament embroidered on an alb or amice. APPAREL (2) (APPARELLING, APPARELLED), *v.t.* to clothe, adorn, furnish. [OFr.].

APPARENT [a-pa'rent], *adj.* visible, easily seen, obvious, conspicuous; clear to the understanding, evident; appearing to be a fact, seeming; **heir a.,** next rightful heir to a throne or estate. APPARENTLY, *adv.* in an a. manner; evidently, seemingly. [OFr.].

APPARITION [a-pa-ri'shn], *n.* act of appearing, appearance; appearance of supernatural things, ghost, spectre; (*astron.*) first appearance of a star after having been obscured. APPARITIONAL, *adj.* of or pertaining to an a. [~L.].

APPARITOR [a-pa'ri-taw(r)], *n.* (*leg.*) officer of ancient Rome who attended magistrates; (*eccles.*) officer who serves the process of a spiritual court; beadle in a university. [L.].

APPEAL (1) [a-pēl'], *n.* urgent demand for aid, entreaty; call to an authority for a decision in one's favour; attraction; (*leg.*) action by which a case is brought from a lower to a higher court in the hope of obtaining a favourable judgment; **court of a.,** court of law which investigates and confirms or reverses decisions of lower courts. [OFr.].

APPEAL (2), *v.i.* to call upon another to decide an issue; refer to another as witness, invoke aid, pity or mercy, have recourse to; (*leg.*) demand the judgment of a higher tribunal; (*fig.*) move the feelings, attract, appear pleasing; *v.t.* to remove a case from an inferior to a superior court. [OFr.].

APPEALING [a-pē'ling], *adj.* which appeals; (*leg.*) pertaining to a higher court; (*fig.*) imploring, affecting, moving. APPEALINGLY, *adv.* in an a. manner.

APPEAR [a-pēer'], *v.i.* to come into view, become visible, be manifest; come into public notice, go into society; be obvious to the mind, manifest; seem, convey the impression of; (*leg.*) go before a court. [OFr.].

APPEARANCE [a-pēer'ans], *n.* act of appearing, act of coming before the public in some prominent rôle or of coming into society; thing seen, phenomenon; outward semblance, look; strange phenomenon as a ghost, phantom; (*leg.*) act of appearing in court; **to enter an a.,** to appear in court; **to put in an a.,** to come, appear; **to all appearances,** as far as may be seen; **to keep up appearances,** to maintain a good outward show. [OFr.].

APPEASE [a-pēz'], *v.t.* to pacify, allay; soothe the feelings of; satisfy the physical needs of. APPEASABLE, *adj.* able to be appeased. APPEASER, *n.* one who appeases; pacifier, peace-maker. [OFr.].

APPEASEMENT [a-pēz'ment], *n.* action of appeasing; peaceful condition; policy of making concessions to win over potential enemies.

APPELLANT [a-pe'lant], *n.* one who asks for aid or justification; (*leg.*) one who appeals to a higher court. [OFr.].

APPELLATION [a-pe-lā'shn], *n.* name, title or designation of a person or thing; specific name. [~L.].

APPELLATIVE (1) [a-pe'la-tiv], *n.* distinctive name, appellation; general name; (*gram.*) name for a class of things or any specimen in that class; common noun. APPELLATIVE (2), *adj.* serving to name or mark out; (*gram.*) pertaining to a common noun. APPELLATIVELY, *adv.* in an a. manner. [L.].

APPEND [a-pend'], *v.t.* to hang something on, attach as a pendant; add something in writing to furnish additional matter. [L.].

APPENDAGE [a-pen'dij], *n.* something hung on, attached to, hanging on; (*fig.*) person closely attached to another, often as a dependant.

APPENDANT (1) [a-pen'dant], *n.* something which is attached as an adjunct. APPENDANT (2), *adj.* hanging attached; (*leg.*) attached by right to a landed estate or property. [Fr.].

APPENDICITIS [a-pen-di-sī'tis], *n.* (*med.*) acute inflammation of the vermiform appendix.

APPENDIX (*pl.* **appendices, appendixes**) [a-pen'-diks, a-pen'di-sēz], *n.* something hung on or appended; matter added at the end of a book but not essential to its main argument; very short, thin tube with closed end leading off the large intestine. [L.].

APPERCEPTION [a-per-sep'shn], *n.* recognition by the mind of its own quality and power. [Fr.].

APPERTAIN [a-per-tān'], *v.i.* to belong to as parts to the whole; be related; pertain; be appropriate or suitable. APPERTINENT [a-pur'ti-nent], *adj.* appertaining or belonging to; suitable for. [OFr.].

APPETITE [a'pi-tīt], *n.* desire or inclination to obtain gratification, *esp.* for the natural activities and functions of the body; hunger, craving. APPETITIVE [a-pe'ti-tiv], *adj.* having the quality of desiring, desiring gratification. [OFr.].

APPETIZER [a'pi-ti-zer], *n.* something which creates an appetite for food; aperitif.

APPETIZING [a'pi-ti-zing], *adj.* creating a desire or appetite, stimulating the appetite. APPETIZINGLY, *adv.* in a manner likely to stimulate the appetite.

APPLAUD [a-plawd'], *v.t. and i.* to express approval by clapping the hands or in any other noisy way; approve of, praise. APPLAUSIVE [a-plaw'ziv] *adj.* applauding. [L.].

APPLAUSE [a-plawz'], *n.* action of applauding; loud praise; clapping. [L.].

APPLE [a'pl], *n.* the round, firm, fleshy fruit of *Pyrus malus*, cultivated in many varieties; fruit of similar structure or appearance; **a. of the eye,** the pupil; (*fig.*) very precious object; **a. of discord,** one contended for by the three goddesses, Juno, Minerva and Venus, hence any subject or matter of acrimonious dispute; **Adam's a.,** prominent part of the throat formed by the thyroid cartilage. [OE.].

APPLE-CART [a'pl-kaht], *n. only fig. in phr.* **to upset the a.,** to spoil one's plans, wreck an enterprise.

APPLE-FACED [a-pl-fāst'], *adj.* with a round bright-complexioned face, chubby-faced.

APPLE-JACK [a'pl-jak], *n. (U.S.)* spirit distilled from apple juice.

APPLE-PIE [a-pl-pī'], *n.* apples covered with pastry and baked in a dish; **a. order,** perfect order; **a. bed,** bed with the sheets folded so as to prevent a person from lying in it.

APPLE-SAUCE [a-pl-saws'], *n.* sauce made of stewed apples.

APPLE-TREE [a'pl-trē], *n.* tree which bears apples.

APPLIANCE [a-plī'ans], *n.* act of applying, putting into practice; thing applied to achieve any purpose; piece of apparatus, utensil.

APPLICABLE [ap'li-ka-bl], *adj.* able to be applied, appropriate, fitting. APPLICABILITY [ap-li-ka-bi'-li-ti], *n.* quality of being a.; suitability. APPLICABLY [ap-li'ka-bli], *adv.* in such a manner that it can readily be applied.

APPLICANT [ap'li-kant], *n.* one who applies, one who asks for something; candidate for a post. [~L.].

APPLICATION [ap-li-kā'shn], *n.* act of applying

of placing a thing in juxtaposition to another; the thing applied; act of making a request or petition; letter of request; the putting on of a remedy; the remedy so applied; close attention to study; the testing of something theoretical by applying it in practice. [~L.].

APPLICATIVE [ap'li-ka-tiv], *adj.* which may be applied; practical.

APPLIQUE, appliqué [a-plē'kā], *n.* needlework of a material laid over and secured to another material. [Fr.].

APPLY [a-plī'], *v.t.* to lay or put on; put a thing in contact with another; put into practice; use or mention a word in reference to some person or thing; direct the mind or attention to; bring to bear on; *v.i.* to fit, be relevant; make an application in order to obtain something. [OFr. from L.].

APPOGGIATURA [a-po-jya-tōō'rah], *n.* (*mus.*) grace-note which precedes a full note in a melody. [It.].

APPOINT [a-point'], *v.t.* to fix, designate, set apart; decree, settle, determine authoritatively; ordain or nominate a person to a certain office or to perform certain duties; (*leg.*) determine the disposition of an estate. APPOINTED [a-poin'tid], *adj.* fixed, previously arranged or agreed upon; equipped, furnished. [OFr.].

APPOINTMENT [a-point'ment], *n.* act of appointing to an office; situation or office; arrangement to meet, assignation; that which is decreed or appointed; command or order; (*leg.*) grant to a person of the power to dispose of a property; (*pl.*) equipment, furnishings, fittings. [OFr.].

APPORTION [a-paw'shn], *v.t.* to divide and assign in due portions, distribute. APPORTIONMENT, *n.* act of apportioning, division into fair shares. [OFr.].

APPOSITE [a'po-zit], *adj.* suitable, entirely applicable. APPOSITELY, *adv.* in an a. manner, appropriately, to the point. APPOSITENESS, *n.* quality of being a. [L.].

APPOSITION [a-pō-zi'shn], *n.* action of adding to, application, addition; (*gram.*) the placing of a word parallel with another of the same function to explain and illustrate or modify it. APPOSITIONAL, *adj.* of or relating to a. APPOSITIVE [a-po'zi-tiv], *adj.* (*gram.*) pertaining to a. [~L.].

APPRAISAL [a-prā'zal], *n.* valuation by authority, the fixing of a price; (*fig.*) estimate of worth.

APPRAISE [a-prāz'], *v.t.* to set a price on, evaluate; value as a professional appraiser; (*fig.*) estimate the spiritual worth of. APPRAISEMENT, *n.* action of appraising. [OFr.].

APPRAISER [a-prā'zer], *n.* one who values property, one licensed and sworn to estimate and fix the value of property.

APPRECIABLE [a-prē'sha-bl], *adj.* able to be estimated or recognized; perceptible; large enough to be perceived. APPRECIABLY, *adv.* to an a. extent.

APPRECIATE [a-prē'shi-āt], *v.t.* to judge correctly, set a just value on; perceive slight differences; set a high value on, be grateful for; be alive to the merits of, enjoy discriminatingly; *v.i.* to rise in value. [~L.].

APPRECIATION [a-prē-shi-ā'shn], *n.* act of appreciating or estimating; written or spoken estimate of a person, thing or situation; perception or recognition of merit; power of distinguishing slight variations; rise in value.

APPRECIATIVE [a-prē'sha-tiv], *adj.* having appreciation; recognizing merit; grateful. APPRECIATIVELY, *adv.* with appreciation.

APPRECIATOR [a-prē'shi-ā-ter], *n.* one who appreciates. APPRECIATORY, *adj.* capable of justly appreciating.

APPREHEND [ap-ri-hend'], *v.t.* to take hold of, seize, arrest, grasp with the mind, understand; think with fear; *v.i.* to form a conception, think. [L.].

APPREHENSIBLE [ap-ri-hen'si-bl], *adj.* capable of being apprehended.

APPREHENSION [ap-ri-hen'shn], *n.* act of apprehending or seizing; act of arresting; faculty of conception, opinion; fear or dread of future evil, gloomy foreboding. [L.].

APPREHENSIVE [ap-ri-hen'siv], *adj.* capable of apprehending, understanding; fearful, suspicious. APPREHENSIVELY, *adv.* in an a. fashion. APPREHENSIVENESS, *n.* condition of being a.

APPRENTICE (1) [a-pren'tis], *n.* young person bound for a term of years to serve some craft or trade under a master who in turn binds himself to instruct

him. APPRENTICE (2), *v.t.* to bind under a master to learn a craft or trade. APPRENTICESHIP, *n.* state of being an a.; term during which the service must last. [OFr.].

APPRISE [a-prīz'] *v.t.* to give notice to, inform. [Fr.].

APPRO [ap'rō], *n.* (*coll.*) approval; **on a.**, on approval.

APPROACH (1) [a-prōch'], *n.* act of coming near or nearer; means or way of coming near, passage; attempt to establish personal relationships; (*golf*) stroke to place the ball on the green. [Next].

APPROACH (2), *v.t.* to advance to, come near or nearer; (*fig.*) come near so as to be compared with, approximate to; make advances or overtures to a person; *v.i.* to come nearer (of time), draw nearer. [Fr.].

APPROACHABLE [a-prō'cha-bl], *adj.* able to be approached, accessible.

APPROACHING (1) [a-prō'ching], *n.* (*golf*) that stage in the game where the ball is played on to the putting green; (*hort.*) the ingrafting of a shoot of one tree on to another without severing it from the parent stock. APPROACHING (2), *adj.* advancing towards, drawing nearer.

APPROBATION [ap-rō-bā'shn], *n.* act of approving, approval, commendation, formal sanction. APPROBATIVE [a-prō'ba-tiv], APPROBATORY [ap-rō-bā'te-ri, ap-rō'ba-te-ri], *adj.* tending to approve. [~L.].

APPROPRIATE (1) [a-prō'pri-at], *adj.* set apart for a particular person or purpose, belonging to some person or thing; suitable, fitting. APPROPRIATELY, *adv.* in an a. fashion, fittingly. [L.].

APPROPRIATE (2) [a-prō'pri-āt], *v.t.* to make over to a person; grant, take over; set apart for a particular purpose; (*leg.*) alienate a benefice. APPROPRIATIVE [a-prō'pri-a-tiv], *adj.* which appropriates, having a tendency to appropriation. APPROPRIATOR, *n.* person who appropriates.

APPROPRIATION [a-prō-pri-ā'shn], *n.* action of appropriating to one's own use or to some special purpose; sum of money so appropriated; (*leg.*) sequestering of a benefice to the perpetual use of a spiritual corporation; **a. clause,** clause in a money bill by which Parliament assigns revenue for a special purpose. [~L.].

APPROVAL [a-prōō'val], *n.* approbation, sanction; **on a.** (*comm.*) of goods, sent for inspection without obligation to buy.

APPROVE [a-prōōv'], *v.t. also v.i., with* of, to be pleased with, think favourably of, sanction formally, ratify, commend; (*reflex.*) prove one's qualities. [OFr.].

APPROVED [a-prōōvd'], *adj.* proved, tried, worthy of approbation; **a. course,** course of action or study prescribed by regulations as suitable for a specified purpose; **a. school,** state school to which convicted juvenile delinquents may be sent; **a. society,** trade union or insurance company formerly operating National Health Insurance with State approval.

APPROVER [a-prōō'ver], *n.* one who approves; (*leg.*) one who, originally an accomplice, turns Queen's evidence.

APPROXIMATE (1) [a-prok'si-mat], *adj.* approaching, nearly correct, nearly resembling or corresponding with. APPROXIMATE (2) [a-prok'si-māt], *v.t.* to bring near, cause to be near; *v.i.* to come near, approach, agree nearly in quantity, character etc. APPROXIMATELY [a-prok'si-mat-li], *adv.* in an a. manner, nearly, almost. [L.].

APPROXIMATION [a-prok-si-mā'shn], *n.* act of approximating, approach; (*math.*) continual approach nearer and nearer to a quantity which is sought, when no process is known for arriving at it exactly.

APPUI [a-pwē'], *n.* prop or stay; (*milit.*) defensive support; **point d'appui,** (*milit.*) predetermined position on which troops form into line. [Fr.].

APPURTENANCE [a-pur'ti-nans], *n.* that which appertains to something else larger or of more consequence; adjunct; appendage. [AFr.].

APPURTENANT [a-pur'ti-nant], *adj.* belonging or pertaining to as of legal right; proper, appropriate to. [*Prec.*].

APRICOT [ā'pri-kot], *n.* orange-coloured, oval, soft stone fruit allied to the plum. [Fr.].

APRIL [ā'pril], *n.* fourth month of the Christian year; **A. fool,** one who has a trick played on him on 1 April. [L.].

APRON [ā'prun], *n.* piece of cloth or baize worn over the front of the body to keep the clothes clean or protect them from injury; similar garment worn by bishops, deans etc.; (*mech.*) guard on the slide-rest of a lathe to protect the lead-screw from

---

The accent ' after a syllable = stress (u-pon'). The mark ‾ over a vowel = length (ā in made; ō in bone).

shavings; (*theatre*) part of the stage projecting in front of the curtain, also **a.-stage; to be tied to the a.-strings,** to be greatly influenced by a female. APRONED, *adj.* wearing an a. [ME. from OFr.].

APROPOS (1) [a-pro-pō´], *adj.* to the point or purpose; pertinent to the place, time or subject; opportune. APROPOS (2), *adv.* with *of*, in regard to or with reference to. [Fr.].

APSE [aps], *n.* (*arch.*) arched semicircular or polygonal recess at the end of a church. APSIDAL [ap´si-dal], *adj.* in the shape of an a. [L.].

APSIS (*pl.* **apsides**) [ap´sis, ap´si-dēz], *n.* apse; (*astron.*) one of the two points in the orbit of a satellite, one nearest to, the other farthest from, its primary body. [L.].

APT [apt], *adj.* fit, suitable, pertinent; skilled, promising; liable to, having a tendency to. [L.].

APTERAL [ap´te-ral], *adj.* (*entom.*) wingless; (*arch.*) with no columns along the sides.

APTEROUS [ap´te-roŏs], *adj.* wingless.

APTERYX [ap´te-riks], *n.* New Zealand bird, the kiwi. [Gk.].

APTITUDE [ap´ti-tyoŏd], *n.* fitness, natural capacity, readiness in learning. [Fr.].

APTNESS [apt´nes], *n.* quality of being apt; fitness for a purpose.

APTOTE [ap´tōt], *n.* (*gram.*) indeclinable noun. APTOTIC [ap-tō´tik], *adj.* uninflected. [Gk.].

APYRETIC [a-pi-re´tik], *adj.* (*med.*) without fever. [Gk.].

AQUA-, *pref.* water. [L.].

AQUA FORTIS [a-kwah-faw´tis], *n.* (*pop.*) nitric acid. [L.].

AQUAMARINE (1) [a-kwah-ma-rēn´], *n.* (*min.*) blue-green beryl. AQUAMARINE (2), *adj.* bluish-green. [L.].

AQUA REGIA [a-kwah-rē´jah], *n.* (*chem.*) mixture of hydrochloric and nitric acids capable of dissolving the "royal" metals, gold and platinum. [L.].

AQUARIUM [a-kwāer´i-um], *n.* tank or building containing tanks for aquatic plants and creatures. [L.].

AQUARIUS [a-kwāer´i-us], *n.* the water-bearer, eleventh sign of the Zodiac. [L.].

AQUATIC (1) [a-kwa´tik], *n.* plant which grows in water; (*pl.*) exercises or games in or on the water. AQUATIC (2), *adj.* pertaining to water. [L.].

AQUATINT [a´kwah-tint], *n.* form of engraving and etching produced by aqua fortis on copper.

AQUEDUCT [a´kwi-dukt], *n.* artificial conduit or structure for conveying water; (*anat.*) small passage connecting different organs of the body or separate parts of the same organ. [L.].

AQUEOUS [ā´kwi-oŏs], *adj.* consisting of, containing or deposited in, water; **a. humour,** transparent limpid fluid which fills the space between the cornea and the crystalline lens; **a. rocks,** rocks formed by deposition of sand in water. [AQUA].

AQUILEGIA [a-kwi-lē´jah], *n.* (*bot.*) columbine. [LL.].

AQUILINE [a´kwi-līn], *adj.* pertaining to an eagle; hooked, curved like an eagle's beak. [L.].

ARAB [a´rab], *n.* a native of Arabia; Arab horse; **street a.,** homeless urchin who wanders about the streets. [Fr.].

ARABESQUE (1) [a-ra-besk´], *n.* style of decoration derived from the Moors and Arabs, with fantastic patterns of formalized foliage and flowers and of geometrical forms. ARABESQUE (2), *adj.* in the style of ornament in favour among the Moors and Arabs, exhibiting arabesque. [Fr.].

ARABIAN (1) [a-rā´bi-an], *n.* native of Arabia; Arabian horse; the language of Arabia. ARABIAN (2), *adj.* pertaining to Arabia; **A. Nights,** famous collection of oriental tales; fabulous stories. [~L.].

ARABIC (1) [a´ra-bik], *n.* Semitic language spoken by Arabs. ARABIC (2), *adj.* of or pertaining to Arabia and its language; **A. numerals,** the figures 1, 2, 3 etc.; **gum a.,** gum derived from the *Acacia.*

ARABIN [a´ra-bin], *n.* chief soluble substance in gum arabic.

ARABIST [a´ra-bist], *n.* student of Arabic language, literature or medicine.

ARABLE [a´ra-bl], *adj. and n.* (land) suitable for ploughing. [L.].

ARACHIS [a´ra-kis], *n.* (*bot.*) genus of leguminous plants including the groundnut. [Gk.].

ARACHNID (*pl.* **arachnida**) [a-rak´nid], *n.* spider, mite or scorpion. [Gk.].

ARACHNOID [a-rak´noid], *adj.* resembling a spider's

web, appertaining to arachnida; **a. tunic,** (*anat.*) thin membrane spread over the brain and spinal cord. [Gk.].

ARAMAIC (1) [a-ra-mā´ik], *n.* northern Semitic language anciently spoken in Palestine and Syria. ARAMAIC (2), *adj.* pertaining to Syria and Chaldaea.

ARAMEAN [a-ra-mē´an], *adj.* Aramaic. [Gk.].

ARANEIDAE [a-ra-nē´i-dē], *n.*(*pl.*) (*zool.*) the spiders. ARANEIDAN, *adj.* pertaining to the a. [L.].

ARAUCARIA [a-raw-kāer´i-ah], *n.* genus of trees including the monkey-puzzle.

ARBALEST [ah´ba-lest], *n.* ancient military engine, working on the principle of the crossbow. [L.].

ARBITER [ah´bi-ter], *n.* judge of a dispute, one given power by contending parties to decide their dispute; one having control. [L.].

ARBITRAGE [ah´bit-rij], *n.* (*comm.*) simultaneous buying and selling in different markets so as to profit by the difference in price; traffic in bills of exchange, stocks and shares etc. [OFr.].

ARBITRAMENT [ah-bit´ra-ment], *n.* control; decision, award by an arbiter. [OFr.].

ARBITRARY [ah´bi-tra-ri], *adj.* determined solely by personal judgment or by individual chance, dependent upon a person's caprice and discretion, uncertain; hastily decisive, tyrannical, beyond external control. ARBITRARILY [ah´bi-tra-ri-li], *n.* in a. fashion. ARBITRARINESS, *n.* state of being a. or capricious. [L.].

ARBITRATE [ah´bi-trāt], *v.t.* to hear and decide as an arbitrator; *v.i.* to decide, judge between parties, settle disputes by discussion. ARBITRATIVE [ah´bi-trā-tiv], *adj.* having the power to a.; pertaining to arbitration. [L.].

ARBITRATION [ah-bi-trā´shn], *n.* the hearing and decision of a dispute by a person or persons chosen by the disputants jointly; **Permanent Court of A.,** the Hague Tribunal.

ARBITRATOR [ah´bi-trā-ter], *n.* arbiter, one who arbitrates. [L.].

ARBITRESS [ah´bi-tres], *n.* female arbitrator. [OF.].

ARBOR [ah´ber], *n.* (*bot.*) a tree, as distinct from a shrub; arbour; axis of a wheel. ARBORACEOUS [ah-be-rā´shoŏs], *adj.* wooded; tree-like. [L.].

ARBOREAL [ah-baw´ri-al], *adj.* pertaining to, living in, trees; (*fig.*) rustic, leafy. [~L.].

ARBOREOUS [ah-baw´ri-oŏs], *adj.* wooded; arbored.

ARBORESCENT [ah-be-re´sent], *adj.* resembling or growing like a tree. ARBORESCENCE, *n.* condition of being a. [~L.].

ARBORICULTURE [ah-bo-ri-kul´tyoŏr], *n.* cultivation of trees. ARBORICULTURAL, *adj.* of. or pertaining to, a. ARBORICULTURIST, *n.* cultivator of trees. [L.].

ARBORIZATION [ah-be-ri-zā´shn], *n.* tree-like figures in certain minerals; (*med.*) similar phenomenon caused by distension of the blood-vessels in inflammation.

ARBOUR [ah´ber], *n.* seat shaded by trees; bower. ARBOURED, *adj.* having an a.; shady. [~OFr. from L.].

ARBUTUS [ah-byoō´tus], *n.* genus of evergreen trees and shrubs. ARBUTEAN, *adj.* of or pertaining to the A. [L.].

ARC [ahk], *n.* segment of a circle, apparent path of a heavenly body; **a. light,** very bright lamp in which the current passes as a flame between two electrodes. [L.].

ARCADE [ah-kād´], *n.* row of arches supported on columns; arched walk; long arched building or gallery lined with shops. [Fr.].

ARCADIA [ah-kā´di-ah], *n.* region in the Peloponnesus whose inhabitants were supposed to be simple, rustic and contented; hence a rural paradise, the restful innocence supposed to exist in such circumstances. ARCADIAN, *adj.* pastoral, ideally simple, rustic. [Gk.].

ARCANUM (*pl.* **arcana**) [ah-kā´num], *n.* a secret. [L.].

ARCH (1) [ahch], *n.* arc, curve, bow; curved overhead structure; any place covered with an arch; **Court of Arches,** court of appeal in ecclesiastical causes lying within the province of Canterbury. ARCH (2), *v.t.* to cover with an arch; form into a curve; *v.i.* to make an a. or arches. [Fr. from L.].

ARCH (3), *adj.* coy, waggish, roguish. [*Next*].

ARCH- (4), *pref.* chief, principal, pre-eminent. [Gk.].

ARCHAEO-, *pref.* old, primitive. [Gk.].

ARCHAEOLOGY [ah-ki-o´lo-ji], *n.* study of ancient history and culture by means of material remains. ARCHAEOLOGICAL [ah-ki-o-lo´ji-kal], *adj.* pertaining

---

oō is pronounced as in food; oŏ as in hood; th as in *think*; TH as in *that*; zh as in *azure*. ~ = related to.

DSE—B*

to a. ARCHAEOLOGICALLY, *adv.* in archaeological fashion. ARCHAEOLOGIST [ah-ki-o'lo-jist], *n.* one expert in a. [Gk.].

ARCHAIC [ah-kā'ik], *adj.* ancient, very obsolete, primitive; (*philol.*) displaying an older form. ARCHAICALLY, *adv.* primitively.

ARCHAISM [ah'kā-izm], *n.* archaic word or expression; literary affectation of an obsolete form or idiom. ARCHAIST, *n.* one given to a. ARCHAISTIC [ah-kā-is'tik], *adj.* pertaining to, characterized by, a. ARCHAIZE [ah'kā-īz], *v.t. and i.* to use archaisms, make archaic.

ARCHANGEL [ah'kān-jel], *n.* angel of a superior order. ARCHANGELIC [ah-kan-je'lik], *adj.* in the manner of, pertaining to, an a.

ARCHBISHOP [ahch-bi'shop], *n.* chief bishop, chief bishop of a province, a metropolitan. ARCHBISHOPRIC, *n.* a.'s jurisdiction or see.

ARCHDEACON [ahch-dē'kun], *n.* (*eccles.*) dignitary with temporal jurisdiction over part of a diocese with control of rural deans. ARCHDEACONATE, *n.* office of an a. ARCHDEACONRY, *n.* position, jurisdiction or residence of an a.

ARCHDIOCESE [ahch-dī'o-sis], *n.* jurisdiction or see of an archbishop.

ARCHDRUID [ahch-drōō'id], *n.* chief druid.

ARCHDUCAL [ahch-dyōō'kal], *adj.* pertaining to an archduke.

ARCHDUCHESS [ahch-du'ches] consort of an archduke; princess of the former Austrian Royal Family.

ARCHDUCHY [ahch-du'chi], *n.* land ruled by an archduke.

ARCHDUKE [ahch-dyōōk'], *n.* chief duke; prince of the former Austrian Royal Family.

ARCHEGONIUM [ah-ki-gō'ni-um], *n.* ovary of cryptogams. [~Gk.].

ARCH-ENEMY [ahch-e'ne-mi], *n.* the greatest enemy; Satan.

ARCHER [ah'cher], *n.* one who shoots arrows with the bow; ninth sign of the Zodiac; **a. fish**, species of fish which drown insects with drops of water. ARCHERESS, *n.* female archer. [L.].

ARCHERY [ah'che-ri], *n.* art of shooting with bow and arrow. [OFr.].

ARCHETYPE [ah'ki-tīp], *n.* original model from which things are made, prototype; (*numis.*) standard coin on which others are modelled; (*anat.*) assumed original pattern for each great division of living creatures. ARCHETYPAL, *adj.* pertaining to an a.; original, primitive.

ARCH-FIEND [ahch-fēnd'], *n.* chief fiend; Satan.

ARCH-FOE [ahch-fō'], *n.* chief foe; Satan.

ARCH-HYPOCRITE [ahch-hi'pō-krit], *n.* great hypocrite.

ARCHIDIACONAL [ah-ki-dī-a'ko-nal], *adj.* of or pertaining to an archdeacon.

ARCHIEPISCOPAL [ah-ki-e-pis'ko-pal], *adj.* pertaining to an archbishop.

ARCHIEPISCOPATE [ah-ki-e-pis'ko-pāt], *n.* archbishop's office or tenure of office.

ARCHIL, ORCHIL [ah'kil], *n.* species of lichen producing violet dye, litmus etc. [OFr.].

ARCHIMANDRITE [ah-ki-man'drīt], *n.* head or abbot of a Greek Orthodox monastery or monastic order. [Late Gk.].

ARCHIMEDEAN [ah-ki-mē'di-an], *adj.* relating to Archimedes.

ARCHIMEDES' PRINCIPLE [ah-ki-mē'dēz-prin-si-pal], Archimedes' discovery that a body immersed in fluid loses weight to the extent of the weight of fluid which it displaces. [Gk.].

ARCHING (1) [ah'ching], *n.* arch, system of arches. ARCHING (2), *adj.* curving like an arch.

ARCHIPELAGO [ah-ki-pe'la-gō], *n.* the Aegean Sea; sea containing many islands; group of islands. ARCHIPELAGIC [ah-ki-pe-la'jik], *adj.* pertaining to an a. [Gk.].

ARCHITECT [ah'ki-tekt], *n.* one who draws plans for, and superintends the erection of, a building; (*fig.*) one who frames a complex plan; one making a broad and detailed plan for a desired end, constructor; **the Great A.**, God. [Gk.].

ARCHITECTONIC [ah-ki-tek-to'nik], *adj.* pertaining to, suited for, architecture; having a controlling function; (*met.*) relating to the co-ordination of knowledge. ARCHITECTONICS, *n.(pl.)* science of architecture; (*met.*) systematic arrangement of observed knowledge.

ARCHITECTURAL [ah-ki-tek'tyō-ral], *adj.* relating to or concerning the rules and science of architecture;

harmonious and impressive structure or conception. ARCHITECTURALLY, *adv.* in an a. manner.

ARCHITECTURE [ah'ki-tek-tyōōr], *n.* art and skill of building an edifice; style in which a thing is built; construction, framework; study of building methods and fashions; **naval a.**, art of building water craft.

ARCHITRAVE [ah'ki-trāv], *n.* the part of an entablature resting immediately on the column; ornamental mouldings round a door or window. [It.].

ARCHIVE(S) (usually *pl.*) [ah'kiv(z)], *n.* place of security for ancient documents; historical document or record. ARCHIVAL [ah-kī'val] *adj.* relating to archives. ARCHIVIST [ah'ki-vist], *n.* keeper of archives; one expert in the methods of preserving archives. [LL.].

ARCHNESS [ahch'nes], *n.* arch behaviour, coyness.

ARCHON [ah'kon], *n.* one of the nine chief magistrates of Athens; ruler or chief magistrate. ARCHONSHIP, *n.* an a.'s office or tenure of office. [Gk.].

ARCHWAY [ahch'wā], *n.* passage going under an arch.

ARCTATION [ahk-tā'shn], *n.* (*med.*) construction, compression as of an artery. [~Fr.].

ARCTIC (1) [ahk'tik], *n.* the North Polar region. ARCTIC (2), *adj.* pertaining to the Polar regions; (*fig.*) very cold; **A. Circle**, lesser circle parallel to equator 23 degrees 28 minutes from the North Pole. [L. from Gk.].

ARCTURUS [ahk-tyōō'rus], *n.* star of the first magnitude in the constellation Boötes; (*pop.*) constellation, the Great Bear. [Gk.].

ARDENT [ah'dent], *adj.* (*fig.*) fiercely hot, glowing, intense, passionate, eager, hotly loyal. ARDENCY, *n.* intense heat; (*fig.*) passion, lust, burning enthusiasm. ARDENTLY, *adv.* in a. fashion. [~L.].

ARDOUR [ah'der], *n.* heat; (*fig.*) warmth, violence of emotions, zeal, earnestness. [L.].

ARDUOUS [ah'dyōō-ōōs], *adj.* steep, difficult to climb; (*fig.*) difficult to accomplish, laborious. ARDUOUSLY, *adv.* in a. fashion, laboriously. ARDUOUSNESS, *n.* condition of being a. [L.].

ARE (1) [ah(r)], *n.* metric unit of surface-area equal to 100 square metres. [Fr. from L.].

ARE (2), *pres. ind. pl.* of BE. [OE.].

AREA [āer'i-ah], *n.* piece of open or vacant land; measure of the extent of a plane surface; region, particular district; sunken courtyard before the basement of a town house; (*fig.*) range, scope; (*geom.*) superficial content of a figure; (*comm.*) district allotted to travelling salesman. AREAL [āer'i-al], *adj.* relating to an a. [~L.].

ARECA [a-rē'kah], *n.* species of Asiatic palm, its fruit being chewed with the betel leaf. [Canarese].

ARENA [a-rē'nah], *n.* open space in the middle of an amphitheatre where combats and contests were held; place where public contests are held; (*fig.*) scene of any active conflict. [L.].

ARENILITIC [a-re-ni-li'tik], *adj.* pertaining to sandstone. [L. and Gk.].

ARENOSE [a're-nōs], *adj.* very sandy. [L.].

AREOLA (*pl.* **areolae**) [a-rē'o-lah], *n.* (*anat.*) the red circle round the nipple; inflamed ring round a pustule; (*bot.* and *anat.*) interstitial space in tissues. AREOLAR, *adj.* pertaining to an a.; **a. tissue**, cellular tissue. [L.].

AREOLATE [a-rē'o-lāt], *adj.* separated into areolations. AREOLATION [a-rē-o-lā'shn], *n.* separation into small areas by different colours, textures etc.

AREOMETRY [a-ri-o'mi-tri], *n.* science of measuring the specific gravity of fluids. AREOMETRICAL [a-ri-ō-me'tri-kal], *adj.* relating to a. [Gk.].

AREOPAGUS [a-ri-o'pa-gus], *n.* hill in Athens where the ancient council was held; highest judicial court of Athens. AREOPAGITE [a-ri-o'pa-gīt], *n.* member of the A. AREOPAGITIC [a-ri-o-pa-gi'tik], *adj.* pertaining to the A. [Gk.].

ARETE, arête [a-rāt'], *n.* sharp rising ridge on a mountain, knife-edge. [Swiss Fr.].

ARGAL, ARGOL, ORGAL [ah'gal], *n.* hard tartar crust found on the sides of wine-casks.

ARGENT (1) [ah'jent], *n.* (*poet.*) silver; (*her.*) silver. ARGENT (2), *adj.* silvery, bright. ARGENTAL [ah-jen'tal], *adj.* resembling or pertaining to silver. ARGENTIC [ah-jen'tic], *adj.* (*chem.*) containing silver as a monad. ARGENTIFEROUS [ah-jen-ti'fe-rōōs], *adj.* bearing or producing silver. ARGENTOUS, *adj.* (*chem.*) containing silver as a dyad. [L.].

ARGENTAN [ah-jen'tan], *n.* alloy of nickel, zinc and copper, German silver. [L.].

ARGENTINE (1) [ah'jen-tin], *n.* small fish with

brilliant silver scales; variety of porcelain coated with metal; (bot.) silverweed; native of the Republic of Argentina; **The A.**, Argentina. ARGENTINE (2), adj. silvery; pertaining to the Republic of Argentina. [L.].

ARGENTUM [ah-jen'tum], n. silver; (chem.) white metallic element (Ag). [L.].

ARGIL [ah'jil], n. potter's clay. ARGILLACEOUS [ah-ji-la'shoōs], adj. pertaining to clay, clayey. ARGILLIFEROUS [ah-ji-li'fe-roōs], adj. containing clay. ARGILLITE [ah'ji-lit], n. clay-slate. [Fr., L., Gk.].

ARGIVE (1) [ah'giv], n. inhabitant of Argos in Greece; Greek, generally an heroic one. ARGIVE (2), adj. pertaining to Argos; Greek; (fig.) hardily virtuous and noble. [L.].

ARGOL, see ARGAL.

ARGON [ah'gon], n. chemical element (Ar), inert gas, found in the atmosphere in very small quantities. [Gk.].

ARGONAUT [ah'gō-nawt], n. one who sailed in Jason's ship Argo in search of the golden fleece; (fig.) daring sailor; (zool.) genus of molluscs. ARGONAUTIC [ah-gō-naw'tik], adj. relating to the Argonauts. [Gk.].

ARGOSY [ah'go-si], n. originally a ship from the Dalmatian port of Ragusa; richly laden merchant ship. [It.].

ARGOT [ah'gō], n. low Parisian slang; thieves' slang, low jargon. [Fr.].

ARGUE [ah'gyōō], v.t. and i. to maintain one opinion against another by stating reasons, give reasons in a dispute, dispute; discuss in the light of reason, debate keenly, persuade by discussion. ARGUABLE, adj. able to be argued, possibly justifiable, reasonable. ARGUER, n. one who argues. [L.].

ARGUMENT [ah'gyōō-ment], n. disputation, discussion; line of reasoning put forward in support of conclusions; synopsis of the plot or subject of a play, book or poem. [L.].

ARGUMENTATION [ah-gyōō-men-tā'shn], n. process of reasoning; debate. [~L.].

ARGUMENTATIVE [ah-gyōō-men'ta-tiv], adj. given to argument or dispute; disputatious; controversial. ARGUMENTATIVELY, adv. in a. fashion. ARGUMENTATIVENESS, n. disputatious behaviour or habit of mind.

ARGUS [ah'gus], n. wakeful mythological creature with a hundred eyes; **a. eyed**, keen-sighted, vigilant; **a. pheasant**, East-Indian bird allied to the peacock; **a. shell**, a porcelain-shell. [Gk.].

ARIA [ah'ri-ah], n. (mus.) air, melody; elaborate air sung solo in an oratorio or opera. [It.].

ARIAN (1) [āer'i-an], n. follower of the fourth-century heresy of Arius, who denied that Christ was of one substance with God. ARIAN (2), adj. pertaining to Arius or his heresy.

ARID [a'rid], adj. dry, parched with heat; infertile; (fig.) barren, incapable of feeling or imparting interest. ARIDITY, ARIDNESS [a-ri'di-ti, a'rid-nes], n. condition of being a. [L.].

ARIEL (1) [āer'i-el], n. (zool.) Arabian gazelle; flying phalanger of Australia. [Arab.].

ARIEL (2), n. the spirit of the air; inmost satellite of Uranus. [Heb.].

ARIES [āer'i-ēz], n. (astron.) the Ram, first sign of the Zodiac; the constellation. [L.].

ARIETTA [a-ri-et'tah], n. (mus.) short air. [It.].

ARIGHT [a-rit'], adv. rightly, correctly. [OE.].

ARIOSO [a-ri-ō'sō], adv. (mus.) in a melodious fashion. [It.].

ARISE (pret. **arose**, p.pt. **arisen**) [a-riz'], v.i. to rise up, appear; (fig.) develop, come about. [OE.].

ARISTOCRACY [a-ris-tok'ra-si], n. government of a state by its best citizens, state governed by such citizens; the nobles, those distinguished in lineage and inheritance; (fig.) the best people, in any sphere. [Gk.].

ARISTOCRAT [a'ris-tō-krat], n. member of the aristocracy, a noble. ARISTOCRATIC [a-ris-tō-kra'-tik], adj. being or behaving like an a. ARISTOCRATICALLY, adv. in the manner of an a. or aristocracy. [Fr.].

ARISTOPHANIC [a-ris-tō-fa'nik], adj. relating to the Greek comic dramatist Aristophanes.

ARISTOTELIAN [a-ris-to-tē'li-an], adj. relating to the teachings of Aristotle. ARISTOTELIANISM, n. the theories and doctrines of Aristotle.

ARITHMETIC [a-rith'me-tik], n. science of numbers; art of counting, computing or calculating. [Gk.].

ARITHMETICAL [a-rith-me'ti-kal], adj. pertaining

to arithmetic; **a. progression**, series of numbers increasing or decreasing by equal quantities, as 4, 7, 10, 13, 16, etc. ARITHMETICALLY, adv. in a. fashion.

ARITHMETICIAN [a-rith-me-ti'shn], n. one learned in arithmetic.

ARK [ahk], n. chest, box, coffer; vessel in which Noah and his family rode safe from the Flood; **A. of the Covenant**, sacred chest containing the tablets of Moses' Law; **Noah's A.**, child's toy in the shape of an ark and containing animals; **out of the A.**, very antiquated. [L.].

ARM (1) [ahm], n. each of the human limbs attached to the body at the shoulder; part of a garment covering this limb, sleeve; part of a chair or seat supporting the arm; branching-out of the sea, trees etc.; part of a lever from the fulcrum to the point where the force is applied; **to keep at arm's length**, to hold aloof from; **to make a long a.**, to reach; **children in arms**, infants too young to walk. [OE.].

ARM (2), n. instrument for fighting, weapon; power, authority; branch of the fighting services; (pl.) military equipment; (her.) (pl.) heraldic devices; **coat of arms**, heraldic device; **small arms**, pistols, revolvers; **to be up in arms**, to be roused to activity in indignation. SERGEANT-AT-ARMS, mace-bearer who carries out disciplinary measures in the British Houses of Parliament. [Fr.].

ARM (3), v.t. to furnish with arms; provide with equipment suitable for a task or situation; be possessed of some mental, moral or psychological advantage; v.i. to take up arms for oneself, prepare oneself with the means of war. [L.].

ARMADA [ah-mah'dah], n. great fleet, esp. that of Philip II of Spain; great fleet of aircraft. [Span.].

ARMADILLO [ah-ma-di'lō], n. (zool.) South American edentate protected by hard bony plates. [Span.].

ARMAGEDDON [ah-ma-ge'don], n. place of the last battle at the Day of Judgment, according to Rev. xvi. 16; (fig.) a great and ruinous conflict. [Heb.].

ARMAGNAC [ah-mah-nyahk'], n. brandy made in the French district formerly so called.

ARMAMENT [ah'ma-ment], n. force equipped for war, equipment and materials of war; (pl.) weapons of war owned by the state. [Fr.].

ARMATURE [ah'ma-tyōōr], n. armour; piece of iron connecting the two poles of a magnet; rotating part of a dynamo or electric motor. [Fr. from L.].

ARM-CHAIR [ahm-chāer'], n. chair with side supports for the arms; easy chair; (fig.) used as adj. to describe critics who take no part in the things they criticize.

ARMED [ahmd], adj. provided with weapons, armoured; (her.) having the talons coloured differently from the rest of the body, having claws, talons etc.

ARMFUL [ahm'fōōl], n. quantity the arms can hold; (fig.) difficult or unwieldy burden, large quantity.

ARM-HOLE [ahm'hōl], n. hole in a garment for the arm to pass through.

ARMIGER [ah'mi-jer], n. esquire, person entitled to bear heraldic arms. [L.].

ARMINIAN (1) [ah-mi'ni-an], n. follower of the sixteenth-century Dutch theologian Arminius, believer in free will. ARMINIAN (2), adj. pertaining to Arminius or his doctrines. ARMINIANISM, n. theology and teachings of Arminius.

ARMISTICE [ah'mis-tis], n. temporary suspension of hostilities by agreement; truce between armies. [L.].

ARMLET [ahm'let], n. ornament for the arm; brassard.

ARMORIAL (1) [ah-maw'ri-al], n. book of armorial bearings. ARMORIAL (2), adj. (her.) pertaining to arms or to the bearing of arms; **a. bearings**, heraldic device or insignia.

ARMOUR [ah'mer], n. covering for the body, of iron or other material, to protect it in fighting; steel plates for the protection of warships and other war machines against hostile ammunition; any protective covering; supporting fighting vehicles collectively; ARMOUR-PIERCING, adj. of bombs, shells etc. designed to pierce armour-plate before exploding. [OFr.].

ARMOURED [ah'merd], adj. provided with armour; **a. cable**, electric wire with an outer protective covering of metal tape; **a. car**, motor vehicle employed in warfare and protected by armour-plate; **a. cruiser**, heavily protected cruiser; **a. division**, division operating tanks and armoured cars; **a. fighting vehicles**, tanks, a. cars and similarly protected military vehicles.

ARMOURER [ah'me-rer], n. person who makes or

looks after armour or arms; (*milit.*, *nav.*) one who has charge of a store of small arms.

ARMOUR-PLATE [ah-mer-plāt'], *n.* steel plates protecting warships, forts or military machines.

ARMOURY [ah'me-ri], *n.* place where arms are stored or repaired. [OFr.].

ARMPIT [ahm'pit], *n.* the axilla; hollow underneath the arm at the junction with the trunk.

ARMY [ah'mi], *n.* body of armed men organized under one supreme commander for warlike purposes on land; an armed force; any large body of people organized for a particular purpose; crowd of people, multitude; **a. corps** (*milit.*, *Brit.*), section of an army consisting of two or more divisions complete with auxiliary services; **a. list,** official list of commissioned officers in the army; **standing a.,** military force in service in time of peace. [Fr.].

ARNICA [ah'ni-kah], *n.* genus of plants including mountain tobacco; drug or liniment made from this plant.

AROMA [a-rō'mah], *n.* fragrance, perfume, pleasant odour; fragrance of plants; (*fig.*) characteristic atmosphere of something. [Gk.].

AROMATIC (1) [a-rō-ma'tik], *n.* plant or drug having a. qualities. AROMATIC (2), *adj.* spicy, fragrant, having a warm, pungent taste or smell. [Fr. from Gk.].

AROMATIZE [a-rō'ma-tīz], *v.t.* to make aromatic, impregnate with an aroma. AROMATIZATION [a-rō-ma-ti-zā'shn], *n.* act or state of aromatizing. [Gk.].

AROSE [a-rōz'], *pret.* of ARISE. [OE.].

AROUND (1) [a-rownd'], *adv.* round about, in circles, in the neighbourhood. AROUND (2), *prep.* about, surrounding, in the neighbourhood of.

AROUSE [a-rowz'], *v.t.* to rouse up, stir, excite; awaken from sleep or lethargy, incite to activity.

AROW [a-rō'], *adv.* in a row; in order.

ARPEGGIO [ah-pe'ji-o], *n.* (*mus.*) the sounding of the notes in a chord in quick succession from below upwards as if on a harp; the distinct sound of the notes in an instrumental chord. [It.].

ARQUEBUS [ah'kwi-bus], *n.* primitive type of hand-gun. ARQUEBUSIER [ah-kwi-bu-sēer'], *n.* man armed with an a.

ARRACK [a'rak], *n.* Eastern spirit distilled from rice and molasses. [Arab.].

ARRAIGN [a-rān'], *v.t.* (*leg.*) to accuse or indict on a criminal charge; call to account, charge, call in question. ARRAIGNER, *n.* one who arraigns. ARRAIGNMENT, *n.* action of indicting, process of being arraigned; charge, accusation. [ME. from AFr.].

ARRANGE [a-rānj'], *v.t.* to set in order for a purpose, sort, adjust, settle, classify; make preparations for a thing; fix the course of some event in advance; (*mus.*) adapt; *v.i.* to come to agreement, adjust matters in advance. [OFr.].

ARRANGEMENT [a-rānj'ment], *n.* act of arranging, order, state of things put in order; preparations for carrying out a thing, agreement, compromise or understanding; (*mus.*) adaptation of a musical score.

ARRANT [a'rant], *adj.* erring, notorious; complete, thorough. ARRANTLY, *adv.* in an a. manner. [ERRANT].

ARRAS [a'ras], *n.* tapestry, wall hangings of tapestry or similar material.

ARRAY (1) [a-rā'], *n.* line of battle, mass of troops, large body set in order, organized splendour for show or pageantry; rich dress, splendid ornaments; (*leg.*) empanelled jury. ARRAY (2), *v.t.* to set out in order, draw up a body of troops in formation; deck out, dress splendidly; (*leg.*) empanel a jury. [ME. from OFr.].

ARREAR [a-rēer'], *n.* (of obligations) that which remains to be done; overdue payment of a regular series; **in arrears,** in debt; behindhand. ARREARAGE, *n.* money overdue. [OFr. from LL.].

ARREST (1) [a-rest'], *n.* retardation or stoppage of motion, check; (*leg.*) seizure and detention of a person on a criminal or other charge; **under a.,** detained by a legal authority; **a. of judgment,** stopping of legal proceedings. ARREST (2), *v.t.* to stop, check; (*leg.*) seize and detain on legal grounds, apprehend; (*fig.*) seize, attract. ARRESTING, ARRESTIVE, *adj.* striking, drawing the attention. [OFr.].

ARRIS [a'ris], *n.* line at which two planes meet to form an exterior angle; sharp edge. ARRISWISE, *adv.* in a sharp edge, like a ridge. [OFr. from L.].

ARRIVAL [a-rī'val], *n.* act of arriving; the coming to its destination of a ship, train or other means of conveyance; person who arrives. [AFr.].

ARRIVE [a-rīv'], *v.i.* to come to a destination, place,

conclusion; (*coll.*) achieve success. [OFr. from LL.].

ARROGANCE [a'ro-gans], *n.* insolent pride or conceit, haughty bearing of authority, display of superiority. [L.].

ARROGANT [a'ro-gant], *adj.* insolently superior, proud, overbearing, haughtily self-assertive. ARROGANTLY, *adv.* in an a. manner. [∼L.].

ARROGATE [a'ro-gāt], *v.t.* to make undue or excessive claims to power, place or importance, usurp an undeserved superiority; attribute. ARROGATION [a-ro-gā'shn], *n.* act of arrogating. [∼L.].

ARROW [a'rō], *n.* straight, sharp-pointed stick made to be shot from a bow; object resembling this; sign indicating direction; **broad a.,** mark shaped like the head of an arrow and used to signify ownership by the British Government. [OE.].

ARROW-HEAD [a'rō-hed], *n.* metal, bone or flint head of an arrow; anything resembling this in shape; (*bot.*) aquatic plant with arrow-shaped leaves. ARROW-HEADED, *adj.* shaped like an a., like any ancient characters resembling cuneiform.

ARROWROOT [a'rō-rōōt], *n.* edible farinaceous substance, made from the roots of various species of *Maranta*.

ARROWY [a'rō-i], *adj.* moving, shaped like an arrow, pertaining to arrows; piercing, keen.

ARSE [ahs], *n.* (*vulg.*) buttocks. [OE.].

ARSENAL [ah'se-nal], *n.* government factory and store for arms; **the A.,** famous London football club. [It. from Arab.].

ARSENATE, ARSENIATE [ah'se-n(i)āt], *n.* salt formed by arsenic acid combined with a chemical base.

ARSENIC [ah'se-nik], *n.* (*chem.*) greyish brittle metal, the chemical element As; (*pop.*) arsenious oxide, also called white arsenic. ARSENICAL [ah-se'ni-kal], *adj.* containing a. ARSENICATE [ah-se'ni-kāt], *v.t.* to compound with a. [L. from Gk.].

ARSENIOUS [ah-sē'ni-ōōs], *adj.* (*chem.*) containing arsenic as a triad in chemical compounds; **a. acid,** white arsenic.

ARSIS (*pl.* **arses**) [ah'sis, ah'sēz], *n.* (*pros.*) the stressed syllable in English verse. [Gk.].

ARSON [ah'son], *n.* wilful and malicious burning of property. [OFr. from LL.].

ART (1) [aht], *n.* craft or skill employed by man to do or make a thing; skill or aptitude in aesthetics or in certain crafts; a branch of aesthetics itself; organized general principles of many crafts and activities; cunning, skill in deception, subtlety; (*pl.*) occupations requiring sensibility, ingenuity or intellect, primarily the fine arts such as poetry, painting, music etc.; secondarily the useful arts as of manufacture or the household etc.; thirdly the purely intellectual arts such as mathematics etc.; (*fig.*) wiles, tricks; academic term for all courses of study except the sciences and economics; **black arts,** black magic, alchemy; **Bachelor of Arts, Master of Arts,** graduates of British universities qualified in humanistic branches of learning. [∼L.].

ART (2), (*archaic*) *2nd person sg. pres. ind.* of BE.

ARTEFACT, ARTIFACT [ah'ti-fakt], *n.* (*esp. archae.*) object made by man, as distinct from natural objects. [L.].

ARTEMISIA [ah-ti-mi'si-ah], *n.* (*bot.*) genus of plants including wormwood. [Gk.].

ARTERIAL [ah-tēer'i-al], *adj.* pertaining to the arteries; **a. road,** main road between important centres. ARTERIALIZE, *v.t.* to change venous into a. blood by its contact with oxygen. ARTERIALIZATION, *n.* the making of a. roads; (*med.*) process of arterializing.

ARTERIO-SCLEROSIS [ah-tēer-i-ō-skle-rō'sis], *n.* disease of the arteries in which the walls are hardened and thickened. [Gk.].

ARTERY [ah'te-ri], *n.* one of the vascular tubes carrying blood from the heart to all parts of the body; (*fig.*) important channel of communication. [Gk.].

ARTESIAN [ah-tē'zi-an], *adj.* pertaining to Artois; **a. well,** well bored to a point in a stratum lower than the point at which it outcrops, so as to obtain a continual upward flow. [OFr.].

ARTFUL [aht'fŏŏl], *adj.* cunning, crafty in a petty fashion, full of tricks, ingenious.

ARTHRITIC [ah-thri'tik], *adj.* pertaining to or suffering from arthritis. [Gk.].

ARTHRITIS [ah-thri'tis], *n.* inflammation of the joints. [Gk.].

ARTHROPODA [ah-thro'po-dah], *n.*(*pl.*) animals

The accent ' after a syllable = stress (u-pon'). The mark ‾ over a vowel = length (ā in made; ō in bone).

having jointed feet, including insects, spiders and crustaceans. ARTHROPODOUS, *adj.* pertaining to, having the characteristics of, a. [Gk.].

ARTHURIAN [ah-thyōō'ri-an], *adj.* concerning the legendary British King Arthur.

ARTICHOKE [ah'ti-chōk], *n.* species of vegetable akin to the thistle; **Jerusalem a.**, species of sunflower with edible roots. [It. from Arab.].

ARTICLE (1) [ah'ti-kl], *n.* object distinct from others of a class, an item; commodity of merchandise; prose contribution, on a particular subject, published in a periodical; tenet of belief; (*leg.*) item in a legal document or contract; (*gram.*) definite or indefinite demonstrative adjective; **articles of association.** (*leg.*) statement of the conditions under which a legally constituted association operates; **leading a.**, principal article in a newspaper, expressing editorial opinion or policy; **Thirty-nine Articles**, tenets of the Church of England set out as an appendix to the Book of Common Prayer. [L.].

ARTICLE (2), *v.t.* to draw up into separate details; (of apprentices, solicitors' clerks etc.) bind by articles of agreement to learn a trade or profession; enumerate charges in articles.

ARTICULAR [ah-ti'kyōō-ler], *adj.* pertaining to the joints; jointed. ARTICULARLY, *adv.* in an a. or articulate fashion. [L.].

ARTICULATE (1) [ah-ti'kyōō-lat], *adj.* having joints; composed of distinguishable syllables and words; (*fig.*) having the power of speech, fluent. ARTICULATELY, *adv.* in a. fashion. [L.].

ARTICULATE (2) [ah-ti'kyōō-lāt], to unite by a joint; utter a sound clearly and distinctly; form into separate and distinct sounds; speak clearly and with good enunciation. [*Prec.*].

ARTICULATION [ah-ti-kyōō-lā'shn], *n.* act or method of jointing; manner of speaking, speech; clear enunciation, distinct utterance; (*anat.*) joint between two bones; (*bot.*) junction of separate parts of plants. [—L.].

ARTICULATOR [ah-ti'kyōō-lā-ter], *n.* one who articulates, prosector; dental instrument for ensuring proper connexion between artificial teeth.

ARTIFACT, see ARTEFACT.

ARTIFICE [ah'ti-fis], *n.* ingenious device, trick; cunning or deceptive contrivance. [L.].

ARTIFICER [ah-ti'fi-ser], *n.* skilled workman, mechanic; inventor; (*nav.*) engineer with petty officer's rating. [*Prec.*].

ARTIFICIAL [ah-ti-fi'shl], *adj.* made by art, not natural; contrived as a substitute for something real or genuine, imitation; (of persons) unnatural, constrained, shallow; false; **a. respiration**, inducement by force of breathing in suffocated persons. ARTIFICIALIZE, *v.t.* to render a. ARTIFICIALLY, *adv.* in a. fashion. [L.]

ARTIFICIALITY [ah-ti-fi-shi-a'li-ti], *n.* condition of being artificial; artificial behaviour or appearance; (*fig.*) unnaturalness; insincerity.

ARTILLERY [ah-ti'le-ri], *n.* missile-throwing weapons larger than can be carried and fired by a single soldier; ordnance, the equipment required for its transport and discharge; troops by whom the weapons are worked; science of gunnery; (*fig.*) arguments of an overwhelming sort; **field a.**, light guns attached to the forward troops; **a. train**, a. grouped and ordered for transport; **a. wheel**, heavy motor-car wheel of the same design as the wheels of gun-carriages. ARTILLERIST, *n.* artilleryman. [OFr.].

ARTILLERYMAN [ah-ti'le-ri-man] *n.* soldier serving in the artillery.

ARTINESS [ah'ti-nes], *n.* quality of being arty.

ARTISAN [ah-ti-zan'], *n.* one skilled in a trade; handicraftsman, manual worker. [Fr.].

ARTIST [ah'tist], *n.* one skilled in a fine art, such as painting or drawing; performer in an entertainment; one following an aesthetic pursuit; one taking intense and precise care over a thing for its own sake; one having aesthetic sensibility. [Fr.].

ARTISTE [ah-tēst'], *n.* (*coll.*) music-hall or radio performer etc. [Fr.].

ARTISTIC [ah-tis'tik], *adj.* having aesthetic sensibility; skilful in one of the fine arts; (*coll.*) (of an object) pleasing or tasteful in appearance. ARTISTICALLY, *adv.* in a. fashion. [Fr.].

ARTISTRY [ah'tis-tri], *n.* artistic skill; (of conduct or action) attention to the smallest details so as to make an artistic whole.

ARTLESS [aht'les], *adj.* lacking art, guileless; natural,

sincere; simple, unsophisticated. ARTLESSLY, *adv.* in a. fashion. ARTLESSNESS, *n.* state of being a.

ARTOCARPAD [ah-to-kah'pad], *n.* (*bot.*) breadfruit tree. [Gk.].

ART PAPER [aht'pā-per], *n.* thick glossy paper suitable for book illustrations.

ART SILK [aht'silk], *n.* silk-like material made from cellulose; rayon.

ARTY [ah'ti], *adj.* (*coll.*) affecting singularities in dress or behaviour such as are popularly attributed to artists; **a. crafty**, showing artiness *esp.* in handicrafts.

ARUM [āer'um], *n.* genus of plants including the wake-robin; **a. lily**, the white lily. [Gk.].

ARYAN (1) [āer'i-an], *n.* an Indo-European; (*pop.*) a non-Jewish North European; virile, fair-haired person; hypothetical prototype of the Indo-European languages. ARYAN (2), *adj.* belonging to the Indo-European family of languages; (*pop.*) nobly Germanic; Nordic. [Skr.].

AS [az], *adv.*, *conj.* and *rel. pron.* like to, equal to; in the capacity of; in the aspect or having the appearance of, in the circumstances, since; because of; for instance; resembling; in relation to; though, when, while; **a. for, a. to**, concerning; **a. yet**, so far; **a. well**, also; **a. it were**, so to speak. [OE.].

ASAFOETIDA, ASSAFETIDA [a-sa-fē'ti-dah], *n.* gum derived from the plant *Ferula asafoetida* and used as an antispasmodic. [Pers. and L.].

ASBESTOS [as-bes'tos], *n.* incombustible greyish-white fibrous mineral, used in making fire-proof material or articles. ASBESTIC, ASBESTOUS, *adj.* pertaining to a. ASBESTIFORM [as-bes'ti-fawm], *adj.* resembling a. in structure. ASBESTINE [as-bes'tin], *adj.* like a., non-inflammable. ASBESTOID, *adj.* resembling a. [Gk.].

ASCARIDES [as-ka'ri-dēz], *n.(pl.)* intestinal threadworms. [Gk.].

ASCEND [a-send'], *v.t.* to climb, get up or up to something; *v.i.* to move upwards, go up, rise come to a higher level; rise in rank; (*mus.*) rise in pitch. [L.].

ASCENDANCY, ASCENDENCY [a-sen'dan-si], *n.* power, controlling influence, domination.

ASCENDANT (1) [a-sen'dant], *n.* (*astrol.*) the sign of the Zodiac that is just above the eastern horizon at any particular time; **in the a.**, becoming more important or influential. ASCENDANT (2), *adj.* ascending, rising; dominating, having superiority; rising; (*astrol.*) having influence; (*astron.*) above the horizon. [—L.].

ASCENSION [a-sen'shn], *n.* action of moving upwards, an ascending; Christ's ascent to Heaven; **A. Day**, festival commemorating this on the sixth Thursday after Easter. [—L.].

ASCENSIONTIDE [a-sen'shn-tīd], *n.* the ten days between Ascension Day and Whitsun.

ASCENT [a-sent'], *n.* act of ascending; slope of a hill; upward way or path. [ASCEND].

ASCERTAIN [a-ser-tān'], *v.t.* to find out, determine, discover accurately. [OFr.].

ASCETIC (1) [a-se'tik], *n.* one who pursues a life of asceticism. ASCETIC (2), *adj.* pertaining to asceticism or an ascetic, self-denying as to the more carnal pleasures. ASCETICAL, *adj.* relating to asceticism. ASCETICALLY, *adv.* in a. fashion. [Gk.].

ASCETICISM [a-se'ti-sizm], *n.* denial or suppression of bodily pleasures and appetites, voluntary pursuit of an austere, frugal life; mortification of the flesh.

ASCIDIANS [a-si'di-anz], *n.(pl.)* (*zool.*) group of partially vertebrate molluscs. [Gk.].

ASCIDIUM (*pl.* ascidia) [a-si'di-um], *n.* (*zool.*) one of the group of Ascidians; (*bot.*) bag-shaped appendage on the leaves of certain plants.

ASCITES [a-si'tēz], *n.* (*med.*) morbid fluid accumulation in the perineum. ASCITIC [a-si'tik], *adj.* pertaining to or having a. [Gk.].

ASCRIBE [a-skrib'], *v.t.* to impute, attribute, assign. ASCRIBABLE, *adj.* capable of being attributed, due. [L.].

ASCRIPTION [a-skrip'shn], *n.* act of ascribing; statement or declaration that ascribes. [—L.].

ASDIC [az'dik], *n.* (*nav.*) apparatus used for the detection of submarines.

ASEPSIS [ā-sep'sis, a-sep'sis], *n.* state of wounds in which there is no pus. [Gk.].

ASEPTIC [a-sep'tik], *adj.* free from pus. [*Prec.*].

ASEXUAL [ā-sek'shōō-al], *adj.* without sex or sexual organs; (*fig.*) frigid. ASEXUALITY [ā-sek-shōō-a'li-ti], *n.* state or quality of having no sex.

ASH (1) [ash], *n.* the tree, *Fraxinus excelsior*; wood

ōō is pronounced as in f*oo*d; ŏŏ as in h*oo*d; th as in *th*ink; TH as in *th*at; zh as in a*z*ure. ~ = related to.

of the ash tree; **mountain a.**, the rowan tree. ASH (2), *adj.* made from a. wood. [OE.].

ASH (3), *n.* (usually in *pl.*) greyish powdery material left after combustion; **A. Wednesday**, the first day of Lent; (*pl.*) residue of something burnt; remains of a cremated corpse; **the Ashes**, said to be held by the winners of each series of cricket Test matches between England and Australia; in **sackcloth and ashes**, in repentant abasement; **to turn to dust and ashes**, to destroy, thwart. [OE.].

ASHAMED [a-shāmd'], *adj.* moved by shame, abashed, feeling moral embarrassment, disconcerted by some emotion, usually guilty. ASHAMEDLY [a-shā'med-li], *adv.* in an a. manner. [OE.].

ASHEN (1) [a'shen], *adj.* pertaining to or made of ash. [ASH (1)]

ASHEN (2), *adj.* pertaining to ash; having the colour of ashes; pale, grey. [ASH (3)].

ASHIVER [a-shi'ver], *adv.* in a shiver, cold.

ASHLAR [ash'ler], *n.* hewn stones used for facing walls; (*arch.*) facing of wrought and squared stones. ASHLARING, *n.* low wall of timbering in a roof to close off the angle between the floor and the rafters; a. stonework. [OFr. ~L.].

ASHORE [a-shaw(r)'], *adv.* on shore, towards the shore.

ASH-PAN [ash'pan], *n.* pan beneath a fire-grate to receive ashes.

ASH-PIT [ash'pit], *n.* place for receiving ashes, bottom of a furnace.

ASIAN [ā'shn], *n.* and *adj.* Asiatic.

ASIATIC [ā-shi-a'tik], *n.* and *adj.* native of, pertaining to, Asia. [Gk.].

ASIDE (1) [a-sīd'], *n.* confidential remark slipped in between open statements, particularly a personal remark exchanged by actors or public speakers during the performance. ASIDE (2), *adv.* on or to one side, out of mind, apart, away from the direct course, away from immediate use.

ASININE [a'si-nīn], *n.* pertaining to the ass; (*fig.*) stupid, silly. ASININITY [a-si-ni'ni-ti], *n.* state or quality of being a. [L.].

ASK [ahsk], *v.t.* and *i.* to beg or entreat for; request, inquire; seek information from; claim, demand; invite; demand as a price. [OE.].

ASKANCE [a-skahns'], *adj.* sideways, obliquely, from the corner of the eye; **to look a. at**, to regard dubiously or with suspicion. [Unkn.].

ASKARI [as-kah'ri], *n.* native African mercenary in the service of his European overlords, *esp.* a Somali in the British or Italian forces. [Arab.].

ASKEW [a-skyōō'], *adj.* awry, disordered, unbalanced; crooked. [Uncert.].

ASLANT [a-slahnt'], *adv.* askew, obliquely.

ASLEEP [a-slēp'], *adj.* and *adv.* sleeping, unawakened; dull, unaroused. [OE.].

ASLOPE [a-slōp'], *adj.* and *adv.* sloping, leaning, tilted.

ASP (1) [asp], *n.* small venomous Egyptian viper, the horned adder; any small poisonous snake.

ASP (2), see ASPEN (1).

ASPARAGIN [as-pa'ra-jin], *n.* crystallizable substance found in asparagus.

ASPARAGUS [as-pa'ra-gus], *n.* liliaceous plant, the young shoots of which are edible. [Gk.].

ASPECT [as'pekt], *n.* a look; outward appearance; view, direction faced, outlook; side of an opinion, partial view of a subject or idea; (*astron.*) situation of a planet in respect of another; (*gram.*) verbal form, *esp.* in Slavonic languages, expressing certain qualities of action, particularly completion or continuity; **a. ratio**, (*aeron.*) the ratio of the span to the mean chord of the wing or tailplane of an aeroplane. [L.].

ASPEN (1), **ASP** [as'pen], *n.* variety of poplar tree. ASPEN (2), *adj.* pertaining to the a., made of a. wood. [OE.].

ASPERGES [as-pur'jēz], *n.* Roman Catholic ceremony of sprinkling altar, clergy and congregation with holy water. [L.].

ASPERGILLUM [as-per-ji'lum], *n.* small brush used in Roman Catholic churches to scatter holy water over the congregation.

ASPERIFOLIATE, ASPERIFOLIOUS [as-pe-ri-fō'li-at, -ōōs], *adj.* having rough leaves. [L.].

ASPERITY [as-pe'ri-ti], *n.* roughness, sharpness, harshness, severity. [L.].

ASPERMOUS [as-pur'mōōs], *adj.* (*bot.*) having no seed. [Gk.].

ASPERSE [as-purs'], *v.t.* to besprinkle; cast aspersions upon, disparage. [L.].

ASPERSION [as-pur'shn], *n.* spray; (*eccles.*) sprinkling; (*fig.*) slanderous remark or charge, disparagement, calumny. [L.].

ASPHALT (1) [as'falt], *n.* mineral pitch, a hard, brittle, bituminous substance; bituminous pitch mixed with sand, gravel etc. and used for surfacing roads and pavements. ASPHALT (2), *v.t.* to surface with a. [Gk.].

ASPHODEL [as'fō-del], *n.* flower similar to the lily; (*myth.*) flower said to cover the Elysian fields. [Gk.].

ASPHYXIA [as-fik'si-ah], *n.* suffocation caused by lack of oxygen in the blood; suspended animation, insensibility. ASPHYXIAL, *adj.* indicating, relating to, a. [Gk.].

ASPHYXIATE [as-fik'si-āt], *v.t.* to kill by asphyxia.

ASPIC [as'pik], *n.* meat jelly in which certain foods are suspended. [Fr.].

ASPIDISTRA [as-pi-dis'trah], *n.* flowering plant of the lily family. [Gk.].

ASPIRANT [as'pi-rant], *n.* one who aspires, candidate, ambitious novice. [~L.].

ASPIRATE (1) [as'pi-rat], *n.* voiceless sound formed by friction of expired breath on the lining of the throat and mouth, represented by H. ASPIRATE (2) [as'pi-rāt], *v.t.* to pronounce with an audible breathing; (*sci.*) draw away gas or fluid by means of an aspirator. [L.].

ASPIRATION [as-pi-rā'shn], *n.* aspiring ambition, desire for some high attainment, eager and noble seeking; act of aspirating.

ASPIRATOR [as'pi-rā-ter], *n.* (*med.*) apparatus for removing gases or liquids by suction.

ASPIRE [a-spīer'], *v.i.* to desire highly, have ambitions towards, rise up or strive to rise up, attempt some high purpose. [L.].

ASPIRIN [as'pi-rin], *n.* compound of salicylic acid used for the relief of pain. [Germ.].

ASPIRING [a-spīer'ing], *adj.* ambitious, having aspirations. ASPIRINGLY, *adv.* in an a. manner.

ASPRAWL [a-sprawl'], *adv.* sprawling.

ASS [as], *n.* long-eared quadruped related to the horse; (*fig.*) stupid person, fool. [OE. from L.].

ASSAFETIDA, see ASAFOETIDA.

ASSAGAI, ASSEGAI [a'sa-gī], *n.* Kaffir stabbing spear. [OFr., Portug. from Berber].

ASSAI [a-sī'], *adv.* (*mus.*) sufficiently. [It.].

ASSAIL [a-sāl'], *v.t.* to attack violently, assault; attack with criticism; beset with questions, doubts etc. ASSAILABLE, *adj.* able to be assailed. [ME. from OFr., L.].

ASSAILANT [a-sā'lant], *n.* one who assails, attacker.

ASSASSIN [a-sa'sin], *n.* political murderer, secret killer. [It. from Arab.].

ASSASSINATE [a-sa'si-nāt], *v.t.* to kill for political motives, murder a person of political importance. ASSASSINATOR, *n.* assassin. [*Prec.*].

ASSASSINATION [a-sa-si-nā'shn], *n.* act of assassinating, political murder.

ASSAULT (1) [a-sawlt'], *n.* violent or sudden attack, attack made on a fortress or town, violent physical onslaught; (*leg.*) attempt or threat to injure another bodily; **a. craft**, small naval vessels specially constructed for landing troops to attack shore positions. ASSAULT (2), *v.t.* and *i.* to make an a. upon, attack. [OFr.].

ASSAY (1) [a-sā'], *n.* test, examination; estimation by test of the amount and value of precious metals in alloys or ores. ASSAY (2), *v.t.* and *i.* to test, determine the quality of precious metals in an alloy or ore; try, attempt. ASSAYABLE, *adj.* able to be assayed. ASSAYING, *n.* act of making an a. [OFr. from L.].

ASSAYER [a-sā'yer], *n.* metallurgist or mint official who assays bullion and coin.

ASSEGAI, see ASSAGAI.

ASSEMBLAGE [a-sem'blij], *n.* a gathering of persons or things; act of making an assembly; the putting together of the components of a machine; machine put together. [Fr.].

ASSEMBLE [a-sem'bl], *v.t.* and *i.* to bring together (a number of persons or things) in one place; come together, congregate; fit together (the component parts of a machine). [Fr., L.].

ASSEMBLY [a-sem'bli], *n.* act or state of being assembled; a meeting for a specific purpose; (*milit.*) signal and act of coming to general parade; **a. room**, room for social functions; **a. line**, that part of a factory where components are assembled into the completed product. [OFr.].

ASSENT (1) [a-sent'] *n.* act of agreeing, agreement,

The accent ' after a syllable = stress (u-pon'). The mark ‾ over a vowel = length (ā in made; ō in bone).

approval, consent; agreement of the sovereign to the bills presented to him by Parliament. ASSENT (2), *v.i.* to agree, consent. ASSENTER, *n.* one who agrees. ASSENTIENT [a-sen'ti-ent], *n. and adj.* (person) assenting. [OFr.].

ASSENTOR [a-sen'ter], *n.* (*leg.*) one who, not being proposer or seconder, adds his name in support at the nomination of a candidate in an election.

ASSERT [a-surt'], *v.t.* to affirm, declare; maintain and uphold (a right or claim); **to a. oneself,** to put oneself forward in an aggressive manner. ASSERTABLE, *adj.* that may be asserted. ASSERTER, *n.* one who asserts. [~L.].

ASSERTION [a-sur'shn], *n.* act of asserting; positive declaration, statement or claim not yet tested. [~L.].

ASSERTIVE [a-sur'tiv], *adj.* positive, asserting strongly, insolently forward. ASSERTIVELY, *adv.* in a. fashion. ASSERTIVENESS, *n.* quality of being insistently a. [ASSERT].

ASSERTOR [a-sur'ter], *n.* one who asserts, defender of a cause. ASSERTORY [a-sur'te-ri], *adj.* asserting.

ASSESS [a-ses'], *v.t. and i.* to determine the value of; set an official value on property, income etc. for the purpose of taxation; estimate the liability of a person for damage or injury done to another. ASSESSABLE, *adj.* able or liable to be assessed. [OFr.].

ASSESSMENT [a-ses'ment], *n.* act of assessing; valuation of property or income for taxation; amount at which anything is assessed; judicial determination of the extent of a loss or damage. [AFr.].

ASSESSOR [a-se'ser], *n.* one who assesses property for taxation; adviser assisting a judge or chairman upon technical matters. [OFr.].

ASSET [a'set], *n.* possession, advantageous quality, factor or position, a gain; (*pl.*) possessions, property; (*leg.*) property as security against debts. [OFr.].

ASSEVERATE [a-se've-rāt], *v.t.* to affirm positively or solemnly. [~L.].

ASSEVERATION [a-se-ve-rā'shn], *n.* solemn and considered statement. [~L.].

ASSIBILATE [a-si'bi-lāt], *v.t.* to pronounce with a hissing sound. ASSIBILATION, *n.* action of assibilating. [~L.].

ASSIDUITY [a-si-dyōō'i-ti], *n.* constant, close and careful application to an enterprise, diligence. [L.].

ASSIDUOUS [a-si'dyōō-ōos], *adj.* attentive, persistent, diligent. ASSIDUOUSLY, *adv.* in a. fashion. ASSIDUOUSNESS, *n.* assiduity. [L.].

ASSIGN (1) [a-sīn'], *v.t.* to apportion, allot to someone; determine, fix or order (a military duty etc.); place, ascribe to a cause, attribute to a period (work of art etc.), ascribe a particular reason for a thing; (*leg.*) transfer property to another. ASSIGN (2), *n.* (*leg.*) one to whom property or rights are transferred. ASSIGNABLE [a-sī'na-bl], *adj.* capable of being assigned. [L.].

ASSIGNATION [a-sig-nā'shn], *n.* engagement to meet at a specified place and time, usually for a furtive, erotic or dishonest purpose; assignment. [~L.].

ASSIGNEE [a-sī-nē'], (*leg.*) person authorized to act for another, person to whom some right or charge is assigned. [OFr.].

ASSIGNMENT [a-sīn'ment], *n.* act of assigning; (*U.S.*) allotment of work; (*leg.*) transference of a right or property, document in which such a transfer is made, right or property transferred.

ASSIGNOR [a-sī'ner], *n.* (*leg.*) one who assigns. [AFr.].

ASSIMILABLE [a-si'mi-la-bl], *adj.* capable of being assimilated. ASSIMILABILITY, *n.* state or quality of being a.

ASSIMILATE [a-si'mi-lāt], *v.t.* to make similar; convert into a substance similar to that of another organism; absorb mentally with understanding; *v.i.* to become absorbed, become amalgamated. ASSIMILATIVE, ASSIMILATORY [a-si'mi-la-tiv, a-si-mi-lā'te-ri], *adj.* tending to a. [L.].

ASSIMILATION [a-si-mi-lā'shn], *n.* action of assimilating, state of being assimilated. [~L.].

ASSIST [a-sist'], *v.t.* to aid, help; (*coll.*) lend money to; *v.i.* to help; take part in, have a secondary position in; be present at an event. [L.].

ASSISTANCE [a-sis'tans], *n.* help, aid.

ASSISTANT (1) [a-sis'tant], *n.* one who assists, an auxiliary, junior co-worker; shop-assistant. ASSISTANT (2), *adj.* aiding, subordinate.

ASSIZE [a-sīz'], *n.* trial by a judge and jury; (*pl.*) periodical sitting of judges of the High Court in each

English county to deal with criminal and civil actions. [OFr. from L.].

ASSOCIABLE [a-sō'shi-a-bl], *adj.* capable of being associated in thought; (*med.*) liable to be affected sympathetically. ASSOCIABILITY [a-sō-shi-a-bi'li-ti], *n.* condition of being a. [Fr.].

ASSOCIATE (1) [a-sō'shi-āt], *n.* person connected with another by common activities, companion, colleague, partner; inferior or subordinate partner in a work; one who has passed certain examinations below degree standard at certain universities; junior member of certain academies. ASSOCIATE (2), *adj.* in close connexion; co-operating in an office without full power. [L.].

ASSOCIATE (3) [a-sō'shi-āt], *v.t. and i.* to join, unite with; keep company with, frequent the society of; join as a partner or co-worker; (*reflex.*) express agreement with a policy etc.; connect ideas by thought; give free play to irrational connexions, *esp.* in psychological treatment. ASSOCIATED, *adj.* allied, connected. ASSOCIATIVE, *adj.* pertaining to association. [~L.].

ASSOCIATION [a-sō-shi-ā'shn], *n.* act of associating, state of being associated; group of people acting in co-operation for a common purpose; intellectual or psychological connexion; **A. football,** football played under the rules of the Football Association. ASSOCIATIONAL, *adj.* pertaining to an a. ASSOCIATIONISM, *n.* theory that a. of ideas is the basic mental principle, and the fundamental explanation of intellectual processes. [~L.].

ASSONANCE [a'so-nans], *n.* similarity in sound between words or stressed syllables; use of this for rhymes. ASSONANT, *adj.* having the quality of assonance. [~L.].

ASSORT [a-sawt'], *v.t. and i.* to arrange or distribute into groups, classify roughly on grounds of similarity; sort out. ASSORTED, *adj.* of various sorts, mixed. [OFr.].

ASSORTMENT [a-sawt'ment], *n.* act of assorting; group or collection of assorted objects.

ASSUAGE [a-swāj'], *v.t.* to soften, soothe, relieve. ASSUAGEMENT, *n.* act of assuaging, that which assuages. ASSUASIVE [a-swā'siv], *adj.* tending to a. [OFr., L.].

ASSUME [a-syōōm'], *v.t.* to take, arrogate to oneself, seize, appropriate; become like, take on a quality or character; pretend, counterfeit something; take for granted, suppose without proof; take for granted in an argument; *v.i.* to be arrogant; (*leg.*) take on oneself an obligation. ASSUMED, *adj.* pretended, feigned; supposed. ASSUMING, *adj.* presumptuous. [L.].

ASSUMPTION [a-sump'shn], *n.* act of assuming, thing assumed; arbitrary taking over; pretence of possession of a quality; act of taking something as true and correct, supposition; thing so assumed; Church feast commemorating the admission of the Virgin Mary into Heaven. [~L.].

ASSUMPTIVE [a-sump'tiv], *adj.* capable of being assumed, overbearing; (*her.*) (of arms) assumed to mark a particular achievement.

ASSURANCE [a-shoor'ans], *n.* positive declaration, firm statement to allay anxiety; definite undertaking, guarantee; certainty, confidence, self-possession, firmness of mind; self-conceit, presumption; insurance. [OFr.].

ASSURE [a-shoor'], *v.t.* to make certain, ensure; assert confidently; allay the anxiety of; convince; undertake, promise confidently; insure. ASSURABLE, *adj.* capable of being assured or insured. ASSURANT, *n.* one taking out an assurance policy. ASSURER, *n.* one who assures. [OFr.].

ASSURED [a-shoord'], *adj.* made safe, certain; insured; confident, self-possessed. ASSUREDLY, *adv.* certainly, beyond all doubt. ASSUREDNESS, *n.* condition of being a.

ASSYRIOLOGY [a-si-ri-o'lo-ji], *n.* study of Assyrian history and culture. ASSYRIOLOGIST, *n.* expert in A.

ASTATIC [a-sta'tik], *adj.* (*elect.*) producing no external magnetic field; (*magn.*) without polarity, unaffected by terrestrial magnetism.

ASTER [as'ter], *n.* genus of herbaceous plants with bright flowers.

ASTERIAS (*pl.* **asteriae**) [a-stēer'i-as], *n.* the five-rayed and other starfish. [Gk.].

ASTERISK [as'te-risk], *n.* typographical sign (*). [Gk.].

ASTERN [a-sturn'], *adv.* in, at or towards the back of a ship; backwards.

ASTEROID [as'ter-oid], *n.* one of the minor planets

---

between the orbits of Mars and Jupiter. ASTEROIDAL, *adj.* pertaining to the asteroids. [Gk.].

ASTHENIA [as-thē'ni-ah, as-the-ni'ah], *n.* (*med.*) debility, loss of strength, emaciation. ASTHENIC [as-the'nik], *adj.* feeble, weak. [Gk.].

ASTHMA [as'thmah], *n.* (*med.*) chronic or acute spasm of the bronchial tubes. ASTHMATIC(AL) [as-thma'tik(-al)], *adj.* pertaining to, liable to, a. ASTHMATICALLY, *adv.* in an asthmatic manner. [Gk.].

ASTIGMATIC [as-tig-ma'tik], *adj.* suffering from, pertaining to, astigmatism; correcting astigmatism.

ASTIGMATISM [a-stig'ma-tizm], *n.* (*med.*) defect in the curvature of the eye which interferes with the focusing of images at a common point; blurred vision; (*opt.*) similar defect in a lens. [Gk.].

ASTIR [a-stur'], *adv.* on the move, stirring.

ASTOMATOUS [a-sto'ma-tŏŏs], *adj.* (*zool.*) astomous.

ASTOMOUS [as'to-mŏŏs], *adj.* (*bot.*) having no mouth. [Gk.].

ASTONISH [a-sto'nish], *v.t.* to excite with sudden surprise, surprise violently. ASTONISHING, *adj.* very surprising, amazing. ASTONISHINGLY, *adv.* in astonishing fashion. [~OFr.].

ASTONISHMENT [a-sto'nish-ment], *n.* condition of being astonished, amazement, violent surprise.

ASTOUND [a-stownd'], *v.t.* to overcome with amazement, overwhelm with surprise and shock. ASTOUNDED, *adj.* shocked with surprise. ASTOUNDING, *adj.* extremely astonishing, amazing. [OFr.].

ASTRADDLE [a-stra'dl], *adv.* astride, in a straddling position.

ASTRAGAL [as'tra-gal], *n.* (*arch.*) rounded moulding at the top or bottom of a column; ring moulding. [Gk.].

ASTRAGALUS [a-stra'ga-lus], *n.* (*anat.*) ball of the ankle joint; (*bot.*) genus of plants including the milkvetches. [L. from Gk.].

ASTRAKHAN [as-tra-kahn'], *n.* skin of very young lambs from Astrakhan; (*pop.*) any lambskin with curled fleece.

ASTRAL [as'tral], *adj.* pertaining to the stars; **a. body**, (*theosophy*) ethereal form believed to correspond to a human or animal body. [Fr.].

ASTRAY [a-stray'], *adv.* wanderingly, in the wrong direction, from the true and proper course.

ASTRIDE [a-strid'], *adv. and prep.* with legs apart, with a leg on either side of.

ASTRINGENT [a-strin'jent], *n. and adj.* (substance) having the property of binding or of drawing the tissues together; styptic; (*fig.*) severe, harsh, stimulating, piquant. ASTRINGENCY, *n.* quality of being a. ASTRINGENTLY, *adv.* in a fashion. [L.].

ASTRO- [as'trō], *pref.* relating to the stars.

ASTRO-HATCH [as'trō-hach], *n.* (*aeron.*) transparent cover of the cockpit in an aeroplane.

ASTROLABE [as'trō-lāb], *n.* instrument formerly used to ascertain the positions of the heavenly bodies. [ME., Gk.].

ASTROLOGER [a-stro'lo-jer], *n.* student of astrology, one foretelling the future by this means.

ASTROLOGY [a-stro'lo-ji], *n.* practical study of the stars and planets with the object of determining the future course of events by the position and relation of the heavenly bodies at a given moment. ASTROLOGICAL [as-trŏ-lo'ji-kal], *adj.* pertaining to a. ASTROLOGICALLY, *adv.* in astrological fashion. [Gk.].

ASTRONOMER [a-stro'no-mer], *n.* one skilled in astronomy. [~Gk.].

ASTRONOMY [a-stro'no-mi], *n.* scientific study of the heavenly bodies. ASTRONOMIC(AL) [as-tro-no'-mik(-al)], *adj.* pertaining to a.; (*fig.*) (of numbers) extraordinarily large. [OFr.].

ASTRO-PHYSICS [as-trō-fi'ziks], *n.(pl.)* that part of astronomy dealing with the physical characteristics of the stars.

ASTUTE [a-styōōt'], *adj.* shrewd, mentally quick, cunning, sharp. ASTUTELY, *adv.* in a fashion. [L.].

ASUNDER [a-sun'der], *adv.* in, into two or more separate parts or places; apart. [OE.].

ASYLUM [a-si'lum], *n.* place of safety, sanctuary, refuge; institution for the unfit, *esp.* the insane. [Gk.].

ASYMMETRY [ā-si'me-tri], *n.* lack of symmetry.

ASYMPTOTE [a'sim-tōt], *n.* (*math.*) line approaching a curve, but never meeting it. ASYMPTOTICAL [a-sim-tō'ti-kal], *adj.* pertaining to an a. [Gk.].

ASYNCHRONISM [a-sin'kro-nizm], *n.* noncoincidence in time.

ASYNDETON [a-sin'di-ton], *n.* (*gram.*) construction

in which the connectives are left out. ASYNDETIC [a-sin-de'tik], *adj.* pertaining to an a. [Gk.].

ASYSTOLE [a-sis'tō-li], *n.* (*med.*) stopping of the normal contractions of the heart.

AT [at], *prep.* *expressing presence or proximity*, by, near; *or motion towards*, to, near to, towards; *expressing state or condition*, in, with; *expressing the hour or season of occurrence*, during, in, on; *expressing and governing number, quantity etc.*; for, to be; **to be a.**, to be doing. [OE.].

ATAVISM [a'ta-vizm], *n.* tendency in offspring to revert to an ancestral type, appearance of physical and mental features more characteristic of earlier ancestors than of parents. ATAVISTIC [a-ta-vis'tik], *adj.* tending to, due to, pertaining to a. [Fr. from L.].

ATAXIA, see ATAXY.

ATAXY, ATAXIA [a-tak'si(-ah)], *n.* (*med.*) disease of the nerves and muscles resulting in faulty bodily co-ordination; **locomotor a.**, disease in which the sufferer is unable to control the voluntary movements. ATAXIC [a-tak'sik], *adj.* pertaining to a. [Gk].

ATE [et], *pret.* of EAT.

ATELIER [a-tel'yā], *n.* artist's studio. [Fr.].

ATHANASIAN (1) [a-tha-nā'si-an], *n.* follower of Athanasius, one believing in the Trinity. ATHANASIAN (2), *adj.* pertaining to Athanasius and his doctrines; **A. creed**, formula of the Christian faith formerly attributed to Athanasius.

ATHEISM [ā'thē-izm], *n.* disbelief in a supreme personal god; denial of the existence of God. [Gk.].

ATHEIST [ā'thē-ist], *n.* one who denies the existence of a God; (*fig.*) one who wilfully rejects and scoffs at any accepted belief. ATHEISTIC(AL) [ā-thē-is'tik(-al)], *adj.* pertaining to atheism. ATHEISTICALLY, *adv.* in an atheistical manner. [Gk.].

ATHELING [a'the-ling], *n.* (*hist.*) Anglo-Saxon prince or noble. [OE.].

ATHENAEUM [a-the-nē'um], *n.* temple of Athene; club or institution for the encouragement of science and the arts. [Gk.].

ATHEROMA [a-the-rō'mah], *n.* (*med.*) sebaceous cyst. ATHEROMATOUS [a-the-ro'ma-tŏŏs], *adj.* pertaining to an a. [Gk.].

ATHIRST [a-thurst'], *adj.* thirsty; (*fig.*) desperately eager.

ATHLETE [ath'lēt], *n.* an expert in athletics; (*fig.*) one possessing bodily vigour and strength. ATHLETIC, [ath-le'tik], *adj.* pertaining to athletics; strong and active, fit in body. ATHLETICALLY, *adv.* in athletic fashion. ATHLETISM, *n.* qualities of an a., physical poise of an a. [Gk.].

ATHLETICS [ath-le'tiks], *n.(pl.)* physical sports; the practice of skilful games and sports (running, jumping etc.) to develop and utilize the physical fitness of the body. ATHLETICISM [ath-le'ti-sizm], *n.* devotion to a.; doctrine that a. are highly important; insistence on a.

AT-HOME [at-hōm'], *n.* social function devoted to the general reception of visitors and guests at a stated time.

A-THROB [a-throb'], *adv.* throbbing palpitatingly.

ATHWART [a-thwawt'], *adv. and prep.* across, from side to side, against; (*naut.*) across the course.

A-TILT [a-tilt'], *adv.* tilted, tilting.

ATLANTEAN [at-lan-tē'an], *adj.* pertaining to Atlas; strong.

ATLANTIC [at-lan'tik], *n. and adj.* (relating to) the ocean dividing Europe and Africa from America. [Gk.].

ATLAS [at'las], *n.* (*myth.*) one of the older Greek gods who supports the sky on his shoulders; (*geog.*) bound collection of maps of all parts of the world; (*anat.*) first vertebra of the spine, supporting the head. [Gk.].

ATMOLOGY [at-mo'lo-ji], *n.* study of aqueous vapours and vaporization. ATMOLOGICAL [at-mo-lo'ji-kal], *adj.* relating to a. ATMOLOGIST [at-mo'lo-jist], *n.* one learned in a. [Gk.].

ATMOLYSIS [at-mo'li-sis], *n.* (*phys.*) separation of gases into their constituents, by passing them through porous substances. [Gk.].

ATMOMETER [at-mo'mi-ter], *n.* instrument for measuring the rate of evaporation from a humid surface. [Gk.].

ATMOSPHERE [at'mos-fēer], *n.* gaseous substance surrounding some of the planets, *esp.* the earth; the air; (*fig.*) mental or moral environment; psychological impression produced by a place; (*phys.*) pressure of approximately 15 lb. to the square inch. ATMOSPHERIC(AL) [at-mos-fe'rik(-al)], *adj.* pertaining to the a., relating to air. ATMOSPHERICALLY, adv. by means of, through, the air. [Gk.].

ATMOSPHERICS [at-mos-fe'riks], n.(pl.) interference with wireless reception due to electrical disturbances in the ether.

ATOLL [a-tol'], n. coral reef or island. [Malay].

ATOM [a'tum], n. (chem.) the minutest portion of a chemical element which can exist by itself or in combination with other elements (formerly thought to be indivisible); (fig.) a very minute particle; **a. bomb**, atomic bomb. [Gk.].

ATOMIC(AL) [a-to'mik(-al)], adj. pertaining to, consisting of, derived from atoms; **a. bomb**, bomb deriving explosive power from nuclear fission; **a. energy**, power obtained by nuclear fission; **a. number**, (chem.) number given to an element to mark its place in the series of elements arranged in order of their atomic weights; **a. philosophy**, belief of the Epicureans that atoms are endowed with motion, and formed the universe without supernatural agency; **a. theory**, theory that ultimate matter consists of uniform, indivisible particles in varying combinations; **a. weapons**, armaments deriving power from a. energy; **a. weight**, relative weight of an atom to that of hydrogen.

ATOMICITY [a-to-mi'si-ti], n. valency.

ATOMIZE [a'to-miz], v.t. to reduce to atoms; break up a liquid into a fine spray. ATOMIZATION, n. the breaking up of liquid into a fine spray. ATOMIZER, n. apparatus for breaking liquid up into a fine spray; hand spray.

ATOMY (1) [a'to-mi], n. (coll.) skeleton. [ANATOMY].

ATOMY (2), n. atom, tiny being. [Fr.].

ATONAL [a-to'nal], adj. (mus.) composed without specific reference to any scale.

ATONE [a-ton'], v.i. to make recompense for, expiate, repair a wrong, suffer for a crime. ATONABLE, adj. able to be atoned for. ATONEMENT, n. act or state of atoning. [AT and ONE].

ATONIC (1) [a-to'nik], n. (phon.) unaccented syllable. ATONIC (2), adj. (phon.) unaccented; (med.) in indifferent health, weak. [Gk.].

ATONY [a'to-ni], n. (med.) debility, weakness. [Gk.].

ATOP [a-top'], adv. on top of, at the top of.

ATRABILIAR(Y) [at-ra-bi'lyar(-i)], adj. having a melancholic humour, splenetic, hypochondriac. [L.].

ATRABILIOUS [at-ra-bi'li-ŏŏs], adj. melancholic. ATRABILIOUSNESS, n. condition of being a. [L.].

ATREMBLE [a-trem'bl], adv. tremblingly.

ATRIUM (pl. atria) [ā'tri-um], n. entrance hall and principal room in a Roman house; forecourt; (anat.) cavity of the heart receiving blood from the veins. [L.].

ATROCIOUS [a-trō'shŏŏs], adj. (of behaviour) extraordinarily cruel, wicked or infamous; (coll.) in very bad taste, abominable. ATROCIOUSLY, adv. in a. fashion. ATROCIOUSNESS, n. quality of being a. [L.].

ATROCITY [a-tro'si-ti], n. act of cruelty or wickedness; violence done to non-combatants and prisoners by the enemy; (coll.) very bad work of art. [L.].

ATROPHY (1) [at'ro-fi], n. wasting away due to lack of nourishment; (biol.) wasting or cessation of development of parts of plants or animals for which there is no longer biological necessity; (fig.) slow disappearance of some moral quality through lack of use. ATROPHY (2), v.t. and i. to waste away through a.; cause a. in. ATROPHIC [a-tro'fik], adj. pertaining to a. ATROPHIED [at'ro-fid], adj. suffering or resulting from a.; wasted, shrunken, starved. [Gk.].

ATROPINE [at'ro-pēn], n. poisonous vegetable alkaloid obtained from deadly nightshade. ATROPISM, n. poisoning caused by misuse of a.

ATTABOY [a'ta-boi], int. exclamation of enthusiastic congratulation on some feat and encouragement to further efforts. [U.S.].

ATTACH [a-tach'], v.t. to fasten to, join to, connect with; cause to adhere to, win over (support etc.); appoint to by authority; (reflex.) unite with, accompany; (fig.) attribute to, assign to; (pass.) be fond of, interested in; (leg.) arrest or seize (a person or property) under legal authority. ATTACHABLE, adj. able to be attached. [OFr.].

ATTACHÉ, attaché [a-ta'shā], n. military or other expert attached to an embassy or legation; **a. case**, small hand-case for carrying documents. [Fr.].

ATTACHMENT [a-tach'ment], n. state or condition of attaching or being attached; that by which a

thing is attached; something attached, a fitting; bond of affection, strong liking; (leg.) arrest of a person or legally authorized seizure of his property; writ authorizing this. [Fr.].

ATTACK (1) [a-tak'], n. state or condition of attacking or being attacked, violent assault or hostile onslaught; (fig.) method of approach to, or starting upon. [Fr.].

ATTACK (2), v.t. and i. to make an assault upon, make an onslaught on; (milit.) make an offensive against an enemy; advance and initiate (a conflict), strike the first blow; (fig.) open opposition with argument, blame or reproach bitterly; set to work on a task with furious energy; (of disease etc.) act violently or injuriously upon. ATTACKABLE, adj. able to be attacked. [Fr.].

ATTAIN [a-tān'], v.t. and i. to gain, accomplish, reach, achieve (a place, position or object); come to, arrive at. ATTAINABILITY [a-tā-na-bi'li-ti], n. possibility of attainment. ATTAINABLE, adj. able to be attained. [OFr. from L.].

ATTAINDER [a-tān'der], n. act or state of attainting or being attainted, deprivation of civil and legal rights on a sentence of death or outlawry; **Bill of A.**, legislation imposing the penalties of a. without legal trial. [ATTAINT].

ATTAINMENT [a-tān'ment], n. act or state of attaining, thing attained; acquirement, skill, knowledge or talent gained by effort.

ATTAINT [a-tānt'], v.t. to subject or sentence to attainder; dishonour; corrupt, taint. [OFr., L.].

ATTAR, OTTAR, OTTO [a'ter], n. perfume obtained from rose-petals. [Pers.].

ATTEMPER [a-tem'per], v.t. to mix in proportion, modify by mixing; temper; adapt, soothe. [L.].

ATTEMPT (1) [a-tempt'], n. an endeavour to do or obtain something (usually with difficulty or uncertainty); violent attack against someone or something. ATTEMPT (2), v.t. to strive after, endeavour, try to achieve or get something by force, attack. [L.].

ATTEND [a-tend'], v.i. to wait upon in order to serve, follow in attendance upon; listen carefully, give good heed to; v.t. to be present at; wait upon; visit to perform some service (esp. of a doctor); accompany inseparably; go to habitually (as school or church). [L.].

ATTENDANCE [a-ten'dans], n. act of attending; those who attend something; a waiting upon, attention. [OFr.].

ATTENDANT (1) [a-ten'dant], n. one who attends; member of a retinue; personal servant of a superior sort; usher. ATTENDANT (2), adj. attending; accompanying, consequential, connected. [OFr.].

ATTENTION [a-ten'shn], n. act or state of attending; state or act of mental application to the subject in hand, watchful notice; solicitous care; assiduous civility; (pl.) courtesies, such as those offered by a man to a woman; (milit.) basic position in drill, in which a person stands rigidly upright with feet together and arms to the side. [~L].

ATTENTIVE [a-ten'tiv], adj. paying attention; heedful. ATTENTIVELY, adv. in a. fashion. ATTENTIVENESS, n. condition of being a. [Fr.].

ATTENUATE [a-te'nyŏŏ-āt], v.t. and i. to thin, make slender, dilute, reduce the power of; become thin and wasted. ATTENUATE(D), adj. made thin or slender; diluted; tapering. ATTENUATION, n. act of attenuating or state of being attenuated. [~L.].

ATTEST [a-test'], v.t. and i. to bear witness to, certify; (leg.) witness (a signature etc.); offer proof of; (fig.) make manifest, show evidently; put (a person) on oath; testify to. ATTESTABLE, adj. able to be attested. ATTESTOR, ATTESTER, n. one who attests, witness. [L.].

ATTESTATION [a-tes-tā'shn], n. act of attesting, thing attested. [~L.].

ATTIC (1) [a'tik], n. top room of a house immediately below the roof; (fig.) any small and often sordid room at the top of a house, garret. [Fr.].

ATTIC (2), adj. pertaining to Attica, and hence to Greece generally; (fig.) artistic, noble, simple, austere; (arch.) characteristic base of Ionic and Corinthian columns; **A. base**; **A. salt**, wit. ATTICISM [a'ti-sizm], n. style of or idioms peculiar to Athenian Greek; elegant expression; partiality towards Athens. ATTICIZE [a'ti-sīz], v.i. to affect the manners of Athens or Greece. [Gk.].

ATTIRE (1) [a-tier'], n. clothes, dress; ceremonial or elaborate dress; (her.) antlers. ATTIRE (2), v.t. to dress, clothe, adorn. [OFr.].

ATTITUDE [a'ti-tyōōd], n. posture of body, bearing

ŏŏ is pronounced as in food; ŏŏ as in hood; th as in think; TH as in that; zh as in azure. ~ = related to.

of head and limbs; general mien; disposition of mind or opinion; position of a nation or class personified in relation to some circumstances. ATTITUDINAL [a-ti-tyōō'di-nal], *adj.* relating to a. ATTITUDINARIAN [a-ti-tyōō-di-nãer'i-an], *n.* person who affects attitudes. [Fr.].

ATTITUDINIZE [a-ti-tyōō'di-nīz], *v.i.* to strike an attitude, affect a pose, ape a deportment or mental disposition.

ATTORNEY [a-tur'ni], *n.* (*leg.*) one legally empowered to act for another, solicitor, legal practitioner; **by a.,** by legal deputy; **A. General,** officer appointed to act for the sovereign in all state cases; **power of a.,** legal warrant to act for another. [OFr.].

ATTRACT [a-trakt'], *v.t. and i.* to cause to approach, draw towards; (*fig.*) rouse feelings of interest and admiration in a person, charm, allure, entice by moral and non-material means; draw attention, provoke observation upon oneself; (*phys.*) draw towards itself. ATTRACTABLE, *adj.* capable of being attracted. ATTRACTOR, *n.* person who or thing which attracts. [~L.].

ATTRACTION [a-trak'shn], *n.* act or condition of attracting; influence of that which attracts; that which attracts; (*coll.*) public entertainment. [~L.].

ATTRACTIVE [a-trak'tiv], *adj.* having the power of attracting; (*fig.*) pleasing, engaging, alluring. ATTRACTIVELY, *adv.* in a. fashion. [Fr.].

ATTRIBUTE (1) [at'ri-byōōt], *n.* that which is attributed, characteristic, property, inherent quality; object or symbol, *esp.* associated with an office or position; (*gram.*) word denoting quality, adjective. [L.].

ATTRIBUTE (2) [a-tri'byōōt], *v.t.* to ascribe to, impute to, take as belonging to, assume as a property of, presume as a cause for; (*lit.*) assign to a particular time, place or authorship. ATTRIBUTABLE, *adj.* able to be attributed. [~L.].

ATTRIBUTION [at-ri-byōō'shn], *n.* act of attributing; quality attributed; statement or thing imputed. [~L.].

ATTRIBUTIVE [a-tri'byōō-tiv], *n.* thing attributed; (*gram.*) word denoting an attribute. ATTRIBUTIVE (2), *adj.* pertaining to an attribute or attribution; (*gram.*) denoting an attribute. ATTRIBUTIVELY, *adv.* in an a. manner.

ATTRITION [a-tri'shn], *n.* act, state or process of wearing away by abrasion; (*milit.*) tactic to exhaust the enemy in men and material before attempting a decisive onslaught. [L.].

ATTUNE [a-tyōōn'], *v.t.* to tune, adjust one sound to another; (*fig.*) bring into physical, spiritual or psychological harmony.

ATYPICAL [a-ti'pi-kal], *adj.* not conforming to type.

AUBADE [ō-bahd'], *n.* song at dawn, musical composition for morning performance, morning concert. [Fr. from Span.].

AUBERGINE [ō-bãer-zhēn'], *n.* (*bot.*) fruit of the egg-plant. [Fr.].

AUBRIETIA [aw-brē'shah], *n.* genus of plants of the order *Cruciferae.* [Claude *Aubriet*].

AUBURN [aw'bern], *adj.* brownish red. [OFr. from L.].

AUCTION (1) [awk'shn], *n.* public sale in which the goods go to the highest of competing bids; **Dutch a.,** the offering of goods at high value, reducing the price until a purchaser is found; **a. bridge,** variety of bridge in which overtricks count towards game. AUCTION (2), *v.t.* to put up for sale by a. [~L.].

AUCTIONEER [awk-shn-ēer'], *n.* one who officiates at an auction, one licensed to auction property for sale.

AUDACIOUS [aw-dā'shŏŏs], *adj.* bold, daring, recklessly brave, impudent, insolently presuming, shameless. AUDACIOUSLY, *adv.* in a. fashion. [~L.].

AUDACITY [aw-da'si-ti], *n.* quality of being audacious.

AUDIBLE [aw'di-bl], *adj.* able to be heard, loud enough to be heard. AUDIBILITY [aw-di-bi'li-ti], *n.* state of being a. AUDIBLY, *adv.* in a. fashion. [MedL.].

AUDIENCE [aw'di-ens], *n.* act of hearing; formal interview given by a potentate to an inferior person; judicial session to hear cases; assemblage of persons to witness some spectacle, *esp.* dramatic entertainment. [L.].

AUDILE [aw'dīl], *adj.* perceived through the auditory nerves; (of persons) tending to remember and recollect aurally instead of visually or tactually. [L.].

AUDIT (1) [aw'dit], *n.* official examination of accounts

of a business or institution; settlement of accounts; **a. ale,** strong ale; **a. house,** annex to a cathedral, for the transaction of business; **commissioner of a.,** commissioner to overlook public accounts. AUDIT (2), *v.t.* to examine accounts, make an a.

AUDITION [aw-di'shn], *n.* act of hearing or listening, sense and capacity of hearing; preliminary test for wireless, film and stage aspirants. [~L.].

AUDITIVE [aw'di-tiv], *adj.* pertaining to hearing.

AUDITOR [aw'di-ter], *n.* person appointed to carry out an audit; listener. AUDITORIAL [aw-di-taw'ri-al], *adj.* pertaining to an audit or an auditor. AUDITORSHIP [aw'di-ter-ship], *n.* office or duty of an a. [L.].

AUDITORIUM [aw-di-taw'ri-um], *n.* the part of a public building in which the audience assembles.

AUDITORY (1) [aw'di-te-ri], *n.* audience; auditorium. AUDITORY (2), *adj.* pertaining to the sense of hearing.

AUGEAN [aw-jē'an], *adj.* filthy, unclean, filled with the accumulated dirt of years; **A. stables,** which contained three thousand oxen and remained uncleansed for thirty years. [Gk.].

AUGER [aw'ger], *n.* tool used by carpenters for boring large holes; tool for boring soil or rocks. [OE.].

AUGHT (1) [awt], *n.* anything. AUGHT (2), *adv.* at all, in any way. [OE.].

AUGITE [aw'jīt], *n.* (*min.*) variety of pyroxene, found in volcanic rocks. [Gk.].

AUGMENT (1) [awg'ment], *n.* (*gram.*) vowel prefixed to the verb in certain languages to denote the past tense. AUGMENT (2) [awg-ment'], *v.t.* to make larger, increase; (*gram.*) prefix an a. to; *v.i.* to grow bigger, increase. AUGMENTABLE, *adj.* able to be augmented. [L.].

AUGMENTATION [awg-men-tā'shn], *n.* process or act of augmenting; state of being increased; that which is added; (*her.*) addition to a coat-of-arms as a mark of honour; (*mus.*) repetition of a subject in notes of greater value. [~L.].

AUGMENTATIVE (1) [awg-men'ta-tiv], *n.* (*gram.*) affix used to enlarge or intensify the meaning of a root word. AUGMENTATIVE (2), *adj.* with the quality or power of augmenting; (*gram.*) enlarging the meaning. [Fr.].

AUGMENTED [awg-men'tid], *adj.* added to; (*mus.*) larger by a semitone than the normal or major interval.

AUGUR (1) [aw'ger], *n.* ancient Roman who foretold future events, soothsayer. AUGUR (2), *v.t.* to forebode, betoken, be a sign of; *v.i.* to conjecture from signs or happenings; promise. [L.].

AUGURY [aw'gyŏo-ri], *n.* practice of divination by an augur; omen, prediction. AUGURAL, AUGURIAL [aw'gyŏo-ral, aw-gyŏō'ri-al], *adj.* pertaining to augurs or a. [L.].

AUGUST (1) [aw'gust], *n.* eighth month of the year. [L. Emperor *Augustus*].

AUGUST (2) [aw-gust'], *adj.* grand, majestic, inspiring awe and reverence. AUGUSTLY, *adv.* in majestic manner. AUGUSTNESS, *n.* state of being a. [L.].

AUGUSTAN [aw-gus'tan], *adj.* pertaining to Augustus Caesar or his time, *esp.* to the highly developed Latin literature of that time; **A. Age,** period of a nation's history when its literary activity is marked by superlative refinement and finish.

AUGUSTINIANS [aw-gus-ti'ni-ans], *n.(pl.)* an order of friars. [St. *Augustine* of Hippo.].

AUK [awk], *n.* web-footed sea-bird. [OIcel.].

AULARIAN (1) [aw-lãer'i-an], *n.* member of a hall at a university. AULARIAN (2), *adj.* pertaining to a hall. [L.].

AUMBRY, see AMBRY.

AUNT [ahnt], *n.* sister of one's father or mother, or wife of an uncle; **A. Sally,** dummy figure in the form of a woman at which missiles are thrown as a pastime. [OFr. from L.].

AURA [aw'rah], *n.* aroma, effluvium; (*fig.*) atmosphere created by associations of words; (*elect.*) current of air caused by an electrical discharge; (*med.*) sensation which precedes an attack of epilepsy. AURAL (1), *adj.* pertaining to an a. [Gk.].

AURAL (2) [aw'ral], *adj.* belonging to or connected with the ear. [~L.].

AUREATE [aw'ri-at], *adj.* golden; gilded. [~L.].

AUREOLA, AUREOLE [aw-rē'ō-lah, aw'ri-ōl], *n.* halo or gold disk with which painters surround the head of Christ, the Virgin and the saints. [L.].

AURIC [aw'rik], *adj.* pertaining to or like gold. [~L.].

AURICLE [aw'ri-kl], *n.* (*anat.*) the outer ear; (*pl.*)

The accent ´ after a syllable = stress (u-pon´)   The mark ¯ over a vowel = length (ā in made; ō in bone) two muscular cavities in the heart above the ventricles. [L.].

AURICULA [aw-ri'kōō-lah], *n.* species of *Primula.* [L.].

AURICULAR [aw-ri'kyōō-lah(r)], *adj.* relating to the ear, or to the sense of hearing; confided to the ear, *esp.* of confession; pertaining to the auricles of the heart. AURICULARLY, *adv.* in a. fashion.

AURICULATE(D) [aw-ri'kyōō-lāt(-id)], *adj.* ear-shaped; having ear-like protuberances.

AURIFEROUS [aw-ri'fe-rōōs], *adj.* gold-bearing, containing gold. [L.].

AURIGNACIAN [aw-rig-nā'shn], *adj.* represented by remains discovered in the Aurignac cave.

AURISCOPE [aw'ri-skōp], *n.* instrument used to examine the ear, otoscope. [L. and Gk.].

AURIST [aw'rist], *n.* ear specialist.

AURORA [au-raw'rah], *n.* dawn; goddess of the dawn, sunrise; **a. borealis,** luminous electrical phenomenon seen in the sky of the northern hemisphere at night; **a. australis,** similar phenomenon in the southern hemisphere. AURORAL, *adj.* pertaining to the dawn or the northern lights. [L.].

AUROUS [aw'rōōs], *adj.* pertaining to or containing gold. [L.].

AURUM [aw'rum], *n.* Latin name for gold; the chemical element Au. [L.].

AUSCULTATE [aws'kul-tāt], *v.t. and i.* to sound a person's lungs and heart with a stethoscope. AUSCULTATOR, *n.* one who auscultates. [L.].

AUSCULTATION [aws-kul-tā'shn], *n.* listening; (*med.*) the art of diagnosis by sounding the lungs, heart etc. with a stethoscope or by the ear alone. AUSCULTATORY, *adj.* relating to a. [∼L.].

AUSPICE (*pl.* auspices) [aws'pis, 'pi-sez], *n.* omen, generally favourable; augury, prediction; (*pl.*) protection, patronage. [L.].

AUSPICIOUS [aws-pi'shŏŏs], *adj.* auguring well, giving high promise, fortunate, favourable, gracious. AUSPICIOUSLY, *adv.* in a. fashion. AUSPICIOUSNESS, *n.* condition of being a. [*Prec.*].

AUSSIE [o'zi, o'si], *n.* (*coll.*) Australia; an Australian.

AUSTERE [aws-tēer'], *adj.* severe, stern, strict; bare of decoration, severe in appearance. AUSTERELY, in a. fashion. AUSTERENESS, *n.* austerity. [L.].

AUSTERITY (1) [aws-te'ri-ti], *n.* severity in mode of life, manner or style. AUSTERITY (2), *adj.* showing simplicity and economy in life or style. [OFr.].

AUSTRAL [aws'tral], *adj.* southern. [L.].

AUSTRALIANISM [aws-trā'li-a-nizm], *n.* expression or idiom characteristic of Australian English.

AUTHENTIC [aw-then'tik], *adj.* having a known origin or authority, being what it claims to be, genuine; (*leg.*) properly attested with all due formalities. AUTHENTICALLY, *adv.* in a. fashion. [OFr. from Gk.].

AUTHENTICATE [aw-then'ti-kāt], *v.t.* to make authentic; attest formally; determine the origin or genuineness of; (*leg.*) make valid. AUTHENTICATION, *n.* act or process of authenticating. [*Prec.*].

AUTHENTICITY [aw-then-ti'si-ti], *n.* condition of being authentic, genuineness.

AUTHOR [aw'ther], *n.* one who creates or originates anything; one who creates or compiles a literary work; (*fig.*) the books or works of an author. [OFr., from Gk.].

AUTHORESS [aw'the-res], *n.* woman author.

AUTHORITARIAN [aw'tho-ri-tāer'i-an], *adj.* undemocratic, dictatorial, repressive. AUTHORITARIANISM, *n.* (the holding of) a. principles.

AUTHORITATIVE [aw-tho'ri-ta-tiv], *adj.* accustomed to command, peremptory, dictatorial; having the approval of authority, having authority. AUTHORITATIVELY, *adv.* in a. fashion. AUTHORITATIVENESS, *n.* condition of being a.

AUTHORITY [aw-tho'ri-ti], *n.* power or legal right to command and be obeyed; person or group of persons having such right or power; influence, power or weight derived from rank, knowledge, experience etc.; books giving accurate information and reliable judgments; person expert in a particular subject. [Fr., L.].

AUTHORIZE [aw'the-rīz], *v.t.* to give authority to; sanction, allow; approve or establish by authority. AUTHORIZABLE, *adj.* able to be authorized. AUTHORIZATION [aw-the-ri-zā'shn], *n.* act of authorizing; permission, sanction. AUTHORIZED, *adj.* having authority or permission; **Authorized Version,** English translation of the Bible officially approved and issued in 1611. [Fr.].

AUTHORSHIP [aw'ther-ship], *n.* state of being an author; identity of the author of a work; status of an author.

AUTO- [aw'tō], *pref.* done by or for oneself; spontaneous; without interference from others. [Gk.].

AUTOBIOGRAPHY [aw-tō-bī-o'gra-fi], *n.* account of a man's life written by himself. AUTOBIOGRAPHER, *n.* one who compiles an a. AUTOBIOGRAPHICAL [aw-tō-bī-o-gra'fi-kal], *adj.* relating to or containing an a.

AUTOCHTHON (*pl.* autochthones) [aw-tok'thon, aw-tok'tho-nēz], *n.* one of the original primitive inhabitants of a country, an aboriginal. AUTOCHTHONAL, AUTOCHTHONIC, AUTOCHTHONOUS, [aw-tok'-tho-nal, aw-tok-tho'nik, aw-tok'tho-nŏŏs], *adj.* aboriginal, pertaining to the earliest known inhabitants of a place. [Gk.].

AUTOCRACY [aw-tok'ra-si], *n.* government by a single all-powerful ruler; supreme and independent power in government. [Gk.].

AUTOCRAT [aw'tō-krat], *n.* absolute monarch or ruler; person who habitually behaves in a dictatorial and peremptory fashion. AUTOCRATIC(AL) [aw-to-kra'tik(-al)], *adj.* pertaining to or behaving like an a.; dictatorial and overbearing in manner. AUTOCRATICALLY, *adv.* in a. fashion. [Fr. from Gk.].

AUTO-CYCLE [aw'tō-sī-kl], *n.* a two-wheeled vehicle fitted with an inbuilt engine of low power and light weight and having, in addition, pedalling gear.

AUTO-DA-FE (*pl.* autos-da-fé) [ow-to-dah-fā'], *n.* solemn trial and sentence of a heretic by a Court of the Inquisition; execution of the sentence. [Portug.].

AUTOGRAPH (1) [aw'tō-grahf], *n. and adj.* (in) a person's own handwriting, *esp.* his signature, writer's own manuscript; **a. album,** album containing specimens of the handwriting of various people etc. AUTOGRAPH (2), *v.t.* to write one's name as a mark of favour in a book etc. AUTOGRAPHIC(AL) [aw-tō-gra'fik(-al)], *adj.* pertaining to an a. AUTOGRAPHY [aw-tog'ra-fi], *n.* study of autographs; transference of a subject to a lithographing stone.

AUTOGYRO [aw-tō-jī'rō], *n.* flying machine with horizontal wind-driven rotors which enable it to rise and descend vertically.

AUTO-INTOXICATION [aw-tō-in-tok-si-kā'shn], *n.* poisoning due to toxic matter produced by internal changes in the tissues of the body.

AUTOLYSIS [aw-to'li-sis], *n.* (*anat.*) destruction of cells in the body by its own serum. [Gk.].

AUTOMATIC (1) [aw-tō-ma'tik], *n.* quick-firing self-loading pistol or revolver. AUTOMATIC (2), *adj.* working by itself, self-acting, mechanically operated, involuntary. [Gk.].

AUTOMATION [aw-tō-mā'shn], *n.* system in factories etc. whereby the various processes are rendered more nearly automatic.

AUTOMATISM [aw-to'ma-tizm], *n.* mechanical or automatic action; theory that the behaviour of animals is automatic.

AUTOMATON (*pl.* automata, automatons) [aw-to'ma-ton], *n.* anything which moves of itself; machine or mechanical device which acts of itself; mechanical figure constructed so as to imitate the movements of a human being; human being who merely follows mechanically prescribed routine. AUTOMATOUS, *adj.* self-acting; acting without conscious stimulation. [Gk.].

AUTOMOBILE [aw-tō-mō-bēl'], *n.* (*mostly U.S.*) motor-car.

AUTONOMOUS [aw-to'no-mŏŏs], *adj.* self-governing; independent.

AUTONOMY [aw-to'no-mi], *n.* power or right of self-government; independence in conducting one's own affairs; a self-governing community. AUTONOMIAN [aw-tō-nō'mi-an], *adj.* relating to a. AUTONOMIC [aw-tō-no'mik], *adj.* autonomous. AUTONOMIST [aw-to'no-mist], *n.* supporter of a. [Gk.].

AUTOPLASTY [aw'tō-plas-ti], *n.* (*surg.*) the grafting of skin or other tissues from another part of a person's body. AUTOPLASTIC [aw-tō-plas'tik], *adj.* pertaining to a. [Gk.].

AUTOPSY [aw-top'si, aw'top-si], *n.* (*med.*) examination of a corpse by dissection.

AUTOPTIC(AL) [aw-top'tik(-al)], *adj.* observed or seen by oneself. AUTOPTICALLY, *adv.* from personal observation. [Gk.].

AUTO-RADIOGRAM [aw-tō-rā'di-ō-gram], *n.* radio-gramophone fitted with an automatic record-changing device.

AUTO-SUGGESTION [aw-tō-su-jes'tyun], *n.* suggestion by oneself to oneself.

AUTOTHERAPY [aw-tō-the'ra-pi], *n.* treatment of

ōō is pronounced as in f*oo*d; ŏŏ as in h*oo*d; th as in *th*ink; TH as in *th*at; zh as in azure. ∼= related to.

disease by use of pathological secretions of the patient.

AUTO-TOXIN [aw-tō-tok'sin], *n.* toxic matter produced by internal changes in the tissues in the body.

AUTO-TRANSFORMER [aw-tō-trans-faw'mer], *n.* (*radio*) transformer for a small change in voltage in which primary and secondary form a single winding.

AUTOTYPE [aw'tō-tīp], *n.* facsimile; (*phot.*) reproduction by a process of photographic printing. AUTOTYPOGRAPHY [aw-tō-tī-pog'ra-fi], *n.* (*print.*) process by which reproductions on a gelatine base are transferred to metal plates and printed therefrom.

AUTOVAC [aw'tō-vak], *n.* (*eng.*) vacuum device to raise petrol from a low tank to one from which it will run by gravity to the carburetter.

AUTUMN [aw'tum], *n.* third season of the year (21 September to 20 December), the fall; (*fig.*) maturity, late middle age, beginning of decline. AUTUMNAL [aw-tum'nal], *adj.* pertaining to a.; produced or gathered in a.; pertaining to the decline of life. [L.].

AUXESIS [awk-sē'sis], *n.* (*rhet.*) hyperbole. AUXETIC [awk-sē'tik], *adj.* pertaining to a., magnifying. [Gk.].

AUXILIARY (1) [awg-zi'lye-ri], *n.* helper, assistant; (*gram.*) auxiliary verb; (*pl.*) foreign troops, usually hired. AUXILIARY (2), *adj.* helping, assisting; **a. verb**, verb which helps to form the moods and tenses of other verbs. [L.].

AVA [ah'vah], *n.* intoxicating Hawaiian beverage. [Native].

AVAIL (1) [a-vāl'], *n.* profit, advantage, use, benefit. AVAIL (2), *v.t.* to benefit, profit, be of use; *v.i.* to be of use, value, service; (*reflex.*) take advantage of, make use of, profit by. [Fr.].

AVAILABLE [a-vā'la-bl], *adj.* able to be made use of; close at hand, easy to get at; legally usable or valid. AVAILABILITY, AVAILABLENESS [a-vā-la-bi'-li-ti, a-vā'la-bl-nes], *n.* condition of being a. AVAILABLY, *adv.* in a. fashion.

AVALANCHE [a'va-lahnsh], *n.* mass of loosened ice and snow hurtling down a mountain side; (*fig.*) that which comes suddenly and with overwhelming force or in huge quantities. [Fr. dialect].

AVANT-COURIER [a-vah(n)-kōō'ri-er], *n.* herald. [Fr.].

AVANT-GARDE [a-vah(n)-gahd'], *n.* vanguard of an army. [Fr.].

AVARICE [a'va-ris], *n.* immoderate greed for wealth; miserliness, covetousness. [L.].

AVARICIOUS [a-ve-ri'shŏŏs], *adj.* afflicted with avarice; covetous, miserly, grasping. AVARICIOUSLY, *adv.* in a. fashion. AVARICIOUSNESS, *n.* state or quality of being a. [Fr.].

AVAST [a-vahst'], *int.* (*naut.*) hold! stop! [Du.].

AVATAR [a'va-tah(r)], *n.* (*myth.*) descent to earth of a Hindu deity, and his incarnation as man or beast. [Skr.].

AVAUNT [a-vawnt'], *int.* †begone! depart! [Fr.].

AVE [ā'vē, ah'vā], *int.* prayer to the Virgin Mary, so called from the opening words, *Ave Maria*, Hail Mary! AVE (2), *int.* hail! [L.].

AVELLAN [a've-lan, a-ve'lan], *n.* filbert. [L.].

AVENACEOUS [a-ve-nā'shŏŏs], *adj.* pertaining to oats. [L.].

AVENGE [a-venj'], *v.t.* to exact satisfaction or retribution on behalf of (often *reflex.*); obtain vengeance for, inflict just punishment. AVENGEMENT, *n.* vengeance. AVENGER, *n.* person who avenges. [OFr.].

AVENUE [a've-nyŏŏ], *n.* broad and usually tree-lined roadway, *esp.* one forming the drive to a mansion; double line of trees or other objects between which one may walk; street or road; (*fig.*) way of approach. [Fr.].

AVER (*pres.pt.* averring, *pret. and p.pt.* averred) [a-vur'], *v.t.* (*leg.*) to declare to be true; affirm positively; establish as just and right. [Fr.].

AVERAGE (1) [a've-rij], *n.* mean quantity or value of any number of unequal quantities, obtained by adding these together and dividing the resultant amount by the number of quantities concerned; generalized estimate arrived at by this means; usual standard, common quantity or rate. AVERAGE (2), *adj.* constituting a mean proportion, obtained by a.; ordinary, of the usual standard. AVERAGE (3), *v.t. and i.* to find the a. of, reduce to a mean, distribute according to an a.; **a. out, at**, to give an a. of. AVERAGELY, *adv.* according to a. [L.].

AVERMENT [a-vur'ment], *n.* act of averring; posi-

tive affirmation; something averred; (*leg.*) offer to vindicate a plea advanced in a suit.

AVERRUNCATOR [a-ve-rung-kā'ter], *n.* pruning shears. [L.].

AVERSE [a-vurs'], *adj.* viewing with repugnance or disfavour; unwilling, disinclined. AVERSELY, *adv.* in a. fashion. AVERSENESS, *n.* state or quality of being a. [L.].

AVERSION [a-vur'shn], *n.* strong feeling of repugnance, dislike, loathing; disinclination; object of dislike. [L.].

AVERT [a-vurt'], *v.t.* to turn away from, turn aside; ward off; (*fig.*) prevent (a catastrophe etc.). AVERTABLE, *adj.* preventable, avoidable. AVERTED, *adj.* turned aside (*esp.* of the eyes) as though in shame or horror. [L.].

AVESTA. see ZEND-AVESTA.

AVIAN [ā'vi-an], *adj.* relating to birds. [L.].

AVIARY [ā'vi-a-ri], *n.* place for keeping or rearing birds. [L.].

AVIATION [ā-vi-ā'shn], *n.* art or science of flying aircraft.

AVIATOR [ā'vi-ā-ter], *n.* one who pilots aircraft. AVIATE, *v.i.* to fly (in aircraft).

AVIATRESS [ā'vi-ā-tres], *n.* woman flier.

AVIATRIX [ā'vi-ā-trix], *n.* aviatress.

AVICULTURE [ā'vi-kul-tyŏŏr], *n.* the breeding and keeping of birds. AVICULTURIST [ā-vi-kul'tyŏŏ-rist], *n.* bird-fancier. [L.].

AVID [a'vid], *adj.* eager for, keenly desirous of, greedy. AVIDLY, *adv.* greedily. [L.].

AVIDITY [a-vi'di-ti], *n.* vehement desire, eagerness, greed. [L.].

AVIETTE [ā-vi-et'], *n.* engineless flying-machine, glider. [Fr.].

AVIFAUNA [ā'vi-faw-nah], *n.* the birds of a given region. [L.].

AVIGATO. see AVOCADO.

AVOCADO, AVIGATO [a-vŏ-kah'dŏ], *n.* alligator pear. [Span. from Mexican].

AVOCATION [a-vŏ-kā'shn], *n.* a person's proper calling, business or occupation; minor, subsidiary employment.

AVOCET, AVOSET [a'vŏ-set], *n.* bird of the snipe group. [Fr.].

AVOID [a-void'], *v.t.* to keep away from, shun the company of; abstain from; evade, escape; (*leg.*) make void, annul. AVOIDABLE, *adj.* able to be avoided. AVOIDER, *n.* one who avoids. [AFr.].

AVOIDANCE [a-voi'dans], *n.* act of avoiding, shunning a person's company.

AVOIRDUPOIS [a-ver-dyŏŏ-poiz'], *n.* system ot weights used for common commodities. [OFr.].

AVOSET. see AVOCET.

AVOUCH [a-vowch'], *v.t. and i.* to affirm, attest; admit openly; vouch for, certify to. AVOUCHABLE, *adj.* able to be avouched. AVOUCHMENT, *n.* act of avouching.

AVOW [a-vow'], *v.t.* to confess openly, own up to, admit freely; (*leg.*) admit and be prepared to justify, vindicate. [Fr.].

AVOWAL [a-vow'al], *n.* frank admission, confession, open acknowledgment.

AVOWED [a-vowd'], *adj.* openly admitted, self-confessed. AVOWEDLY [a-vow'id-li], *adv.* in openly acknowledged fashion.

AVULSION [a-vul'shn], *n.* a pulling or rending from or asunder; forcible separation or removal. [L.].

AVUNCULAR [a-vung'kyŏŏ-ler], *adj.* pertaining to an uncle. [L.].

AWAIT [a-wāt'], *v.t.* to wait for, look for, expect; attend. [AFr.].

AWAKE (1) (*pret. and p.pt.* awoke, awaked) [a-wāk'], *v.t.* to cause to resume the power of mental and bodily activity after sleep or any state of inertia, come out of sleep; make aware of; stir up, revive; *v.i.* to cease sleeping, rouse oneself; become aware of. AWAKE (2), *adj.* not sleeping; aroused from sleep; (*fig.*) mentally alive, alert. [OE.].

AWAKEN [a-wā'ken], *v.t.* to awake, stir up; *v.i.* to become awake. AWAKENER, *n.* one who awakens. AWAKENING, *n.* act of awaking or being awaked. [OE.].

AWARD (1) [a-wawd'], *n.* judgment, decision or grant by judges; payment granted by arbitrators; prize, scholarship or distinction given. AWARD (2), *v.t.* to make an a.; give as a prize or special distinction for outstanding merit; grant, bestow. AWARDABLE, *adj.* able to be awarded. [AFr.].

AWARE [a-wāer'], *adj.* knowing, informed, conscious. AWARENESS, *n.* condition of being a. [OE.].

AWASH [a-wosh'], *adj.* on a level with the surface, so that water just washes over; washed about by the waves.

AWAY [a-wā'], *adv.* at or to some distance; not near; in the direction from; absent; also used as *adj.* denoting games played on a ground other than that of the team concerned; **a. with you!** go away!; **a. with it!** take it away!; **to explain (something) a.**, to excuse; **to pass a.**, to die; **to work a.**, to work without interruption. [OE.].

AWE (1) [aw], *n.* fear and wonder at, mingled with reverence for, dread, feeling of respect tinged with terror at something sublimely impressive. AWE (2), *v.t.* to strike with fear or dread, inspire with a. [OScand.].

AWEATHER [a-weTHer], *adv.* to the windward side, facing the wind.

AWEIGH [a-wā'], *adv.* (*naut.*) with the anchor raised clear of the ground.

AWESOME [aw'sum], *adj.* fearsome, terrible; awe-inspiring.

AWESTRUCK [aw'struk], *adj.* struck with fear.

AWFUL [aw'fŏŏl], *adj.* inspiring with awe or dread; solemn, worthy of reverence; terrible, dreadful, shocking; (*coll.*) very bad. AWFULLY, *adv.* in an a. way; (*coll.*) very, exceedingly.

AWHEEL [a-wēl'], *adv.* on a bicycle, cycling.

AWHILE [a-wil'], *adv.* for a short time.

AWKWARD [awk'werd], *adj.* difficult to use; clumsy, unskilful; inconvenient; inelegant; disconcerting, difficult to deal with. AWKWARDLY, *adv.* in a. fashion. [OScand.].

AWL [awl], *n.* small sharp tool for piercing small holes. [OE.].

AWN [awn], *n.* the beard or slender sharp hair at the end of the seed-cluster in grasses etc. AWNER, *n.* device by which the awns are separated from the grain. [OScand.].

AWNED [awnd], *adj.* bearded; (*bot.*) with awns; covered with an awning.

AWNING [aw'ning], *n.* cover, usually of canvas fastened to a framework, to protect from the sun; (*naut.*) part of the poop deck extending beyond the bulkhead of the cabin. [Uncert.].

AWOKE [a-wŏk'], *pret.* of AWAKE. [OE.].

AWRY [a-rī'], *adv.* unevenly, crookedly; wrongly, in the wrong way.

AXE (1), **AX** [aks], *n.* sharp-edged tool with a heavy head set at right angles to a long handle, for cutting down trees etc.; (*fig.*) execution by decapitation; drastic cutting down of public expenses; **to have an a. to grind**, to have an ulterior motive in adopting a line of action. AXE (2), *v.t.* to abolish, *esp.* for the sake of economy. [OE.].

AXIAL [ak'si-al], *adj.* relating to an axis. AXIALLY, *adv.* along an axis.

AXIL [ak'sil], *n.* (*bot.*) angle made on the upper side by a leaf with the stem, or by a branch with the trunk. [AXILLA].

AXILLA [ak-zi'lah], *n.* armpit; axil. AXILLARY, *adj.* relating to the armpit; developing from the axil of plants. [L.].

AXIOLOGY [ak-si-o'lo-ji], *n.* (*philos.*) study of values. [Gk.].

AXIOM [ak'si-om], *n.* generally accepted principle taken as the starting point of a science or process of reasoning, self-evident truth; (*math.*) proposition

so obvious that it requires no proof or demonstration. AXIOMATIC(AL) [ak-si-o-ma'tik(-al)], *adj.* self-evident. AXIOMATICALLY, *adv.* in a self-evident manner. [Gk.].

AXIS (*pl.* **axes**) [ak'sis, 'sēz], *n.* straight line round which a figure or body revolves or appears to revolve; axle; (*math.*) straight line in a plane figure which may revolve round it to produce a solid figure of circular section; line which divides a regular figure into two symmetrical parts; (*anat.*) second vertebra on which the head turns; (*bot.*) central line of a plant about which the organs are arranged; (*opt.*) central line of a ray of light which meets a lens at right angles; (*fig.*) line about which the world is supposed to revolve; **the A.**, former international anti-Communist bloc headed by Germany. [L.].

AXLE [ak'sl], *n.* spindle on which a wheel revolves. AXLED, *adj.* having an a. [OE.].

AXLE-BOX [ak'sl-boks], *n.* box accommodating the end of a revolving axle and containing lubricant.

AXLE-TREE [ak'sl-trē], *n.* bar of wood or metal the ends of which form or hold the spindles or axles of a pair of wheels. [ME.].

AXMINSTER [aks'min-ster], *n.* kind of carpet formerly made at *Axminster* in Devon.

AXOID [ak'soid], *n.* cycloid.

AXOTOMOUS [ak-so'to-mŏŏs], *adj.* (*min.*) with a cleavage perpendicular to the axis. [Gk.].

AXUNGE [ak'sunj], *n.* goose-grease, lard. [L.].

AY (1), see AYE (3).

AY (2), **AYE** [ā], *adv.* always, ever. [OScand.].

AYAH [i'yah], *n.* native Hindu waiting woman, children's nurse. [Indian from Portug.].

AYE (1) [i], *n.* affirmative answer; (*pl.*) those who vote in favour of a motion in Parliament. [Unkn.].

AYE (2), see AY (2).

AYE (3), **AY** [i], *int.* yes, indeed. [Unkn.].

AZALEA [a-zā'li-ah], *n.* genus of plants or shrubs with brightly coloured fragrant flowers. [Gk.].

AZIMUTH [a'zi-mŏŏth], *n.* angular horizontal direction point of the compass; quadrant of a great circle which passes through the nadir and zenith cutting the horizon at right angles; horizontal angular distance from an observer between a fixed point on the horizon and a point where the horizon is cut at right angles by a great circle which passes through a heavenly body; **a. compass**, mariner's compass with vertical sights for determining the a. of a star. AZIMUTHAL [a-zi-myŏŏ'thal], *adj.* pertaining to the a. [Fr., Arab.].

AZOIC [a-zō'ik], *adj.* without sign of life. [Gk.].

AZONIC [a-zo'nik], *adj.* not belonging to a particular region or zone.

AZTEC [az'tek], *n. and adj.* member of, pertaining to, an extinct Mexican race. [Native].

AZURE (1) [a'zhŏŏr, ä'zhŏŏr], *n.* blue colour of the sky; (*poet.*) the sky itself, when unclouded; (*her.*) blue. AZURE (2), *adj.* sky-blue; (*her.*) blue. AZURED, *adj.* blue-coloured. [OFr., Arab.].

AZURIN [a'zhyŏŏ-rin], *n.* bluish coal-tar dye.

AZURINE [a'zhyŏŏ-rin], *n.* the blue roach.

AZURITE [a'zhyŏŏ-rit], *n.* blue variety of malachite.

AZYME [a'zim], *n.* unleavened bread eaten by the Jews at the Feast of the Passover. AZYMOUS, *adj.* unleavened; not fermented. [Gk.].

AZYMITE [a'zi-mit], *n.* one who advocates the use of unleavened bread in celebrating the Eucharist. [Prec.].

B

B [bē], second letter of the English and related alphabets; (*mus.*) seventh note of the major scale beginning on C.

BAA (1) [bah], *n.* cry or bleat of a sheep. BAA (2), *v.i.* to cry or bleat.

BABA [bah'bah], *n.* sponge cake soaked in wine, rum or brandy. [Fr.].

BABBIT-METAL [ba-bit-me'tal], *n.* alloy, normally of tin, copper, lead and antimony, used in bearings. [*Babbit*, inventor].

BABBLE (1) [ba'bl], *n.* idle talk; incoherent speech; childish prattle; sound made by shallow water

flowing over stones. BABBLE (2), *v.t. and i.* to utter words indistinctly, as an infant; talk incoherently and rapidly; reveal secrets indiscreetly; make a gentle and incessant murmuring sound as of a flowing stream. BABBLER, *n.* person or thing that babbles; tropical species of long-legged thrush. BABBLING, *n.* empty or foolish talk. [Fr.].

BABE [bāb], *n.* young child, baby; (*fig.*) unsophisticated tyro. [ME.].

BABEL [bā'bel], *n.* (*bibl.*) tower in Shinar where human speech first became confused; (*fig.*) uproar, din caused by several people all talking loudly at

---

once; scene of disorder and tumult. [Heb. *Babel*, capital of Babylonia].

BABIRUSA, BABYROUSSA [ba-bi-rōō′sah], *n.* East Asiatic hog. [Malay].

BABOO, see BABU.

BABOON [ba-bōōn′], *n.* large monkey with long snout like that of a dog. [Fr.].

BABOUCHE [ba-bōōsh′], *n.* Eastern heelless slipper. [Pers.].

BABU, BABOO [bah′bōō], *n.* Hindu clerk; title of respect to a Hindu gentleman; term of contempt for a Hindu of imperfect education, cultivating English speech and manners. [Hind.].

BABUL [ba-bōōl′], *n.* thorny tree of the mimosa genus; gum-arabic tree. [Hind.].

BABY [bā′bi], *n.* very young child; person who behaves like a child; thing which is a small example of its kind; youngest member of a family or group; (*U.S. slang*) sweetheart, girl-friend; **to hold the b.**, (*slang*) to be left to handle a difficult problem, be the dupe. [ME.].

BABY-FARMER [bā′bi-fah-mer], *n.* one who makes money by looking after unwanted babies. BABY-FARMING, *n.* the boarding-out of unwanted newly born infants to nurses for payment.

BABY-GRAND [bā-bi-grand′], *n.* small grand piano.

BABYHOOD [bā′bi-hōōd], *n.* infancy.

BABYISH [bā′bi-ish], *adj.* like a baby; childish, foolish. BABYISHNESS, *n.* quality of being b.

BABYLON [ba′bi-lon], *n.* capital of Babylonia, notorious for the vice and luxury of its citizens, later used as a derogatory term for Rome or the papal power; (*fig.*) sinful city. [Heb.].

BABYLONIAN [ba-bi-lō′ni-an], *n. and adj.* inhabitant of, pertaining to, Babylon; luxurious, dissolute.

BABYLONIC [ba-bi-lō′nik], *adj.* Babylonian.

BABYLONISH [ba-bi-lō′nish], *adj.* Babylonian.

BABYROUSSA, see BABIRUSA.

BACCALAUREATE [ba-ka-lo′ri-at], *n.* lowest University degree, that of Bachelor. [MdL.].

BACCARAT, BACCARA [ba′ka-rah], *n.* French gambling card game.

BACCATE [ba′kāt], *adj.* berried, producing berries; like a berry. [L.].

BACCHANAL (1) [ba′ka-nal], *n.* one who indulges in noisy, drunken revels; priest or follower of Bacchus, god of wine; drunken orgy; (*pl.*) dances or songs performed in honour of Bacchus. BACCHANAL (2), *adj.* belonging to Bacchus; noisily intoxicated. [L.].

BACCHANALIA [ba-ka-nā′li-ah], *n.(pl.)* drunken and riotous feasts; feasts in honour of Bacchus. [L.].

BACCHANALIAN [ba-ka-nā′li-an], *n. and adj.* intoxicated reveller; riotously, rowdily drunken.

BACCHANT (1) [ba′kant], *n.* priest or follower of Bacchus; (*fig.*) a bacchanalian. BACCHANT (2), *adj.* fond of drunken orgy and revelry. BACCHANTIC [ba-kan′tik], *adj.* pertaining to the priests of Bacchus.

BACCHANTE [ba′kant, ba-kan′ti], *n.* priestess of Bacchus; (*fig.*) woman fond of wine and noisy revelry.

BACCHIC [ba′kik], *adj.* belonging to Bacchus; (*fig.*) rowdily drunken in a frenzy of intoxication. [Gk.].

BACCHUS [ba′kus], *n.* god of wine in Greek and Roman religion. [Gk.].

BACCIFEROUS [bak-si′fe-rōōs], *adj.* producing berries. [L.].

BACCIFORM [bak′si-fawm], *adj.* shaped like a berry.

BACCIVOROUS [bak-si′ve-rōōs], *adj.* living on berries. [L.].

BACCY [ba′ki], *n.* (*coll.*) tobacco.

BACHELOR [ba′che-ler], *n.* unmarried man; one who has taken his first degree at a University; member of the lowest degree of knighthood. BACHELORDOM, *n.* condition of being a b. [OFr.].

BACHELORHOOD [ba′che-ler-hōōd], *n.* condition of being a bachelor.

BACHELOR'S-BUTTON [ba-che-lerz-bu′ton], *n.* button which can be attached without sewing; (*bot.*) one of several species of button-shaped flowers.

BACHELORSHIP [ba′che-ler-ship], *n.* bachelorhood.

BACILLARY [ba-si′le-ri], *adj.* composed of small rods, shaped like rods, relating to bacilli. [L.].

BACILLIFORM [ba-si′li-fawm], *adj.* like bacilli in shape. [L.].

BACILLUS (*pl.* **bacilli**) [ba-si′lus, ba-si′lī], *n.* rod-shaped, minute vegetable organism causing decay in organic matter. [L.].

BACK (1) [bak], *n.* hinder part of the human or upper rear part of an animal's body from the lower end of the spine to the base of the neck; the spine; hinder part of anything, part of an object most distant from the observer; vertical support for the spine; part of the hand opposite the palm; non-cutting edge of a tool; that part of a brush to which the bristles are attached; (*football, hockey etc.*) player immediately in front of the goalkeeper; the rear line(s); upper surface of a wave; rear part of a house; ship's keel; thick well-tanned hide; covers of a book; upper edge of a non-vertical beam; (*fig.*) the body; **behind one's b.**, in an underhand, deceitful way; **to put one's b. into anything**, to work zealously at; **to put someone's b. up**, to offend or anger someone; **to make a b. for**, to bend down as at leap-frog; **to turn one's b. upon**, to desert, ignore; **to break one's b.**, to overburden oneself, make extremely strenuous efforts; **with one's b. to the wall**, hard-pressed, in difficult straits; **at the b. of one's mind**, dimly, half-remembered. [OE.].

BACK (2), *n.* shallow tray used in brewing, distilling and dyeing. [Fr.].

BACK (3), *adj.* situated in the rear, remote, inferior; overdue; no longer current, out of date; (*phon.*) made with the back of the tongue; **to take a b. seat**, to occupy an inconspicuous position.

BACK (4), *adv.* to the rear; to the place from which one has come; again, in return; away from, at a distance; towards the past, to a former condition or time; behind; **to go b. upon**, to withdraw one's support or promise; **to answer b.**, to reply, often with a rude retort; **to take b.**, to withdraw; **to pay someone b.**, to have one's revenge on someone.

BACK (5), *v.t.* to provide with a back; give moral, legal or material support to; mount or get upon the back of; bet or gamble in favour of a competitor in a contest; cause to go backwards, reverse; sign one's name on the back of (a financial or legal document), thus assuming responsibility; (*phot.*) coat a plate or film with non-actinic material to prevent halation; *v.i.* to move or go backward or away from; move in an opposite direction; **to b. up**, to support; **to b. down, b. out of**, to withdraw from, abandon; **to b. sail**, to lay the sail so that it faces the wind; **to b. water**, to reverse the movement of a boat by pushing oars forward instead of pulling.

BACK-BAND [bak′band], *n.* strap fastened over the saddle of a horse to support the shafts of a cart.

BACK BENCH [bak-bench′], *n.* (*usu.pl.*) (*pol.*) one of the benches in the House of Commons where the less prominent members of a parliamentary party sit.

BACK-BENCHER [bak-ben′cher], *n.* member of parliament who sits on one of the back benches.

BACKBITE (*pret.* **backbit**, *p.pt.* **backbitten**) [bak′bit], *v.i.* to speak evil of persons absent.

BACKBITING [bak′bi-ting], *n.* maligning of absent persons, slander.

BACKBOARD [bak′bawd], *n.* board placed at the back, or forming the back of a cart, boat or picture-frame; board fastened across the back of a person to correct a stoop.

BACKBONE [bak′bōn], *n.* the spinal column; (*fig.*) steadiness of purpose, firmness of character, strength of will-power, determination; chief support, prop, foundation or main constituent of anything. [ME.].

BACKBOXES [bak′bok-sez], *n.(pl.)* (*print.*) boxes on the top of the upper case for small capitals or peculiars.

BACK-BREAKER [bak′brā-ker], *n.* (*coll.*) extremely arduous task; hard master, slave-driver.

BACK-CASING [bak′kā-sing], *n.* (*mining*) temporary lining in a shaft, inside which the permanent lining is constructed.

BACK-CHAT [bak′chat], *n.* humorous cross-talk or repartee, exchange of facetious observations (often personal); impudent retort.

BACK-CLOTH [bak′kloth], *n.* painted cloth hung across the back of a stage in a theatre as part of the scenery and to provide a background.

BACK COUNTRY [bak′kun-tri], *n.* (*esp. U.S.*) sparsely populated land lying behind settled districts; hinterland.

BACKED [bakt], *adj.* furnished with a back; having a back; on which bets have been placed.

BACKER [ba′ker], *n.* one who gives material or moral help, supporter; one who bets in favour of a competitor in a sporting event.

BACK-FALL [bak′fawl], *n.* a fall in wrestling in which one is thrown on the back; part of the coupling mechanism of an organ.

BACK-FIRE (1) [bak-fier′], *n.* premature explosion in the cylinder of an internal combustion engine, tending to reverse the motion; (*coll.*) explosion in

---

The accent ′ after a syllable = stress (u-pon′). The mark ‾ over a vowel = length (ā in made; ō in bone).

the silencer of a motor vehicle; ignited discharge from the breech of a gun. BACK-FIRE (2), *v.i.* to experience a b.; (*fig.*) to undergo a sudden violent paroxysm of suppressed emotion.

BACK-FORMATION [bak'faw-mā-shun], *n.* (*philol.*) grammatical form which, though derived analogically from a second form, would appear to be its base.

BACKGAMMON [bak'ga-mun], *n.* game played by two persons on a board, on which the movements of the pieces are decided by the throwing of dice.

BACKGROUND [bak'grownd], *n.* (*paint.*) the pictorial representation of more distant or obscurely defined objects less significant, against which the principal figures stand out; back part of a stage or scene; obscure position from which one is not easily noticed; (*fig.*) cultural environment, wide general knowledge of a subject.

BACKHAND (1) [bak'hand], *n.* writing that slopes upwards to the left; (*tennis etc.*) a backhand stroke or repertory of strokes. BACKHAND (2), *adj.* (*tennis etc.*) executed with the arm across the front of the body and the back of the hand facing forward.

BACKHANDED [bak-han'did], *adj.* with the back of the hand; with a backhand stroke (*also adv.*); (*of writing*) in which the letters slope upwards to the left; (*fig.*) unfair; ambiguous, doubtful.

BACKHANDER [bak-han'der], *n.* stroke delivered with the back of the hand; (*fig.*) unexpected news, generally of an unpleasant nature; an extra glass of wine out of one's turn.

BACK-HEEL [bak-hēl'], *n.* movement with the foot in wrestling to bring about a throw; kick or flick at football made with the heel.

BACKING [ba'king], *n.* action of supporting; act of putting or going back; process of providing with a back; the mounting of a horse; material for making a back; assets to support an issue of paper-money; moral or material support; (*phot.*) a coating to prevent halation.

BACKING-UP [ba-king-up'], *n.* support, help, readiness to help.

BACKLASH [bak'lash] *n.* irregular jerky rotary movement of gear wheels not in perfect mesh, play; (*radio*) defect in a system which causes it to go into oscillation at a different setting from that at which oscillation ceases.

BACKLOG [bak'log], *n.* arrears of work, or of orders on a tradesman's or manufacturer's books.

BACK-MARKER [bak'mah-ker], *n.* competitor with the largest handicap in a handicap sporting event.

BACK NUMBER [bak-num'ber], *n.* out-of-date copy of a periodical; (*fig.*) person who is old-fashioned, past his prime and no longer of any account; (*coll.*) nonentity.

BACK-PEDAL [bak-pe'dal], *v.i.* to reverse the normal direction of rotation of the pedals on a bicycle by which a braking mechanism may be made to operate; (*coll.*) retreat.

BACKPLATE [bak'plāt], *n.* (*aeron.*) steel plate in front of the fuselage to which the engine is fastened.

BACK-PRESSURE [bak'pre-sher], *n.* the resistance of the exhaust steam or the atmosphere to the stroke of a piston in a steam engine; resistance of burnt gas which has not escaped from the cylinder in an internal-combustion engine.

BACKREST [bak'rest], *n.* support or rest at the back or rear of anything; light frame attached to the back of certain typewriters to support the sheet of paper; contrivance fastened to the slide-rest of a lathe to support the work; contrivance to steady or ease the back of a person when seated or performing certain types of manual labour; (*weaving*) bar used to support the warp passing from the warp-beam.

BACK ROOM [bak'rŏŏm], *n.* room at the back of a house. BACK-ROOM BOYS, (*coll.*) scientists working secretly in wartime; experts whose work is not publicly known.

BACK-SCENE [bak-sēn'], *n.* (*stage*) background or rear part of a scene.

BACK-SCRATCHER [bak'skra-cher], *n.* instrument formerly used for scratching the back; (*fig., vulg.*) one given to back-scratching.

BACK-SCRATCHING [bak'skra-ching], *n.* (*vulg.*) mutual praise, reciprocal flattery.

BACK SEAT [bak-sēt'], *n.* seat at the back of a theatre or vehicle; **to take a b.,** to be relegated to an inferior position.

BACKSET [bak'set], *n.* check, temporary reverse; counter-current.

BACKSHEESH, BAKSHEESH, BAKSHISH

[bak'shēsh], *n.* a tip, oriental begging cry. [Pers., Hind.].

BACKSIDE [bak'sīd], *n.* back or rear portion of anything; (*vulg.*) buttocks.

BACKSIGHT [bak'sīt], *n.* sight facing the bench-mark with which the surveyor begins levelling; gun-sight nearest the eye of the marksman.

BACK-SLANG [bak'slang], *n.* form of slang in which words are spelt backwards and pronounced in accordance with the changed spelling.

BACKSLIDE [bak-slīd'], *v.i.* to relapse into sin; fall away from a previous high standard of moral virtue. BACKSLIDER, *n.* one who backslides. BACKSLIDING, *n.* a relapsing into sin or evil ways; a forsaking of one's principles.

BACK-SPACER [bak-spā'ser], *n.* device on a type-writer, operated by a key which, when depressed, causes the carriage to move backwards.

BACK-STAGE [bak-stāj'], *n., adj. and adv.* behind the scenes in a theatre.

BACKSTAIRS (1) [bak-stäerz'], *n.(pl.)* private stairs or steps at the back of a house, staircase for the use of servants. BACKSTAIRS (2), *adj.* (*fig.*) secret, underhand.

BACKSTAYS [bak-stāz'], *n.(pl.)* (*naut.*) ropes extending from the masthead to the sides of a ship.

BACK-STICKS [bak-stiks'], *n.* (*hockey*) foul stroke with the wrong side of the stick.

BACKSTITCH [bak'stich], *n.* stitch which is looped through the front of the preceding one.

BACK-STOP [bak'stop], *n.* (*baseball*) fence placed behind the home base to stop balls missed by the catcher.

BACK-STROKE [bak'strōk], *n.* stroke in swimming performed upon the back.

BACKSWORD [bak'sawd], *n.* sword having one sharp edge; single-stick.

BACKWARD (1) [bak'werd], *adj.* turned towards the back, or in a reverse or contrary direction; reluctant, not eager for action; of subnormal intelligence, mentally retarded; not properly developed; behind in time or progress. BACKWARD (2), *adv.* backwards, in b. fashion. BACKWARDLY, *adv.* in b. fashion. BACKWARDNESS, *n.* condition of being b. [ME.].

BACKWARDATION [bak-waw-dā'shn], *n.* (*comm.*) allowance paid by sellers of stocks and shares to buyers in return for an extension of time for delivery.

BACKWARDS [bak'werds], *adv.* towards the back, in a reverse or contrary direction or manner to normal, with the back foremost, on the back; from a better to a worse condition; from the end to the beginning; towards the past.

BACKWASH [bak'wosh], *n.* disturbance of waves behind a vessel as it moves through the water, water disturbed by oars at the end of the stroke; (*fig.*) disturbance consequent upon some action.

BACKWATER (1) [bak'waw-ter], *n.* pool or creek of still water, fed by or leading into a stream or river but cut off from the direct flow or course; water accumulated by an artificial obstruction; (*fig.*) con-dition of being isolated from new ideas and progress; place so isolated.

BACK-WATER (2) [bak-waw'ter], *v.i.* to reverse the normal direction of motion of the oars or paddles in a rowing boat, canoe etc., in order to check its progress or reverse its direction.

BACKWOODS [bak'wŏŏdz], *n.(pl.)* uncultivated forest land far from towns or settlements.

BACKWOODSMAN [bak-wŏŏdz'man], *n.* settler in the backwoods; (*slang*) uncultured, uncouth per-son; peer who seldom visits the House of Lords.

BACON [bā'kun], *n.* back and sides of a pig, cured for eating; **to save one's b.,** (*coll.*) to have a narrow escape; **to bring home the b.,** to achieve one's end. BACONER, *n.* pig suitable for making into b. [OFr.].

BACONIAN (1) [bā-kŏ'ni-an], *n.* follower or disciple of Bacon; person who thinks that Bacon wrote the plays usually ascribed to Shakespeare. BACONIAN (2), *adj.* belonging to the philosophy of Bacon, or to the theory that Bacon wrote Shakespeare's plays. [Sir Francis *Bacon*].

BACTERIA [bak-tēer'i-ah], *n.(pl.)* microscopic living things found on all organic matter and frequently acting deleteriously to their hosts. BACTERIAL, *adj.* of, or arising from, b. [Gk.].

BACTERICIDAL [bak-tēer-i-sī'dal], *adj.* causing bacteria to die.

BACTERIOLOGIST [bak-tēer-i-o'lo-jist], *n.* special-ist in bacteriology.

BACTERIOLOGY [bak-tēer-i-o'lo-ji], *n.* study of

---

bacteria. BACTERIOLOGICAL [bak-tĕer-i-o-lo'ji-kal], *adj.* relating to b. [Gk.].

BACTERIOLYSIS [bak-tĕer-i-o'li-sis], *n.* destruction of bacteria by dissolution in an anti-bacterial serum. BACTERIOLYTIC [bak-tĕer-i-o-li'tik], *adj.* having the power to destroy bacteria.

BAD (1) [bad], *adj.* lacking good or goodness; evil, wicked, immoral; worthless, corrupt, debased, not reaching the required standard; offensive; decayed, unsound; painful, diseased; severe; harmful; unfortunate; not liked; incorrect; profane; (*leg.*) not valid; **b. blood,** unpleasant or angry feeling; **b. debt,** debt which cannot be collected; **b. egg, b. hat, b. lot,** worthless, disreputable character. BAD (2), *n.* illfortune; evil ways; loss, deficit. BADDISH, *adj.* somewhat b. [ME.].

BADE [bad], pret. of BID. [OE.].

BADGE [baj], *n.* distinguishing mark or token of a particular rank or office or party. [ME.].

BADGER (1) [ba'jer], *n.* short-legged carnivorous animal with long coarse hair; paint brush with its bristles made of badger's hair. [Unkn.].

BADGER (2), *v.t.* to annoy, tease, pester; worry by questioning.

BADIGEON [ba-di'jon], *n.* mixture of plaster and freestone used by sculptors to fill up small holes in statues and other defects; mixture of sawdust and glue used by joiners to hide faults in wood. [Fr.].

BADINAGE [ba'di-nahzh], *n.* light, playful talk or gentle banter. [Fr.].

BADLY [bad'li], *adv.* in bad fashion; in an unsatisfactory, imperfect or bad manner; hopelessly; strongly, very much. [ME.].

BADMINTON [bad'min-tun], *n.* game in which a shuttlecock is hit to and fro across a net with light rackets; drink made with claret, soda-water and sugar. [*Badminton,* the Duke of Beaufort's seat].

BADNESS [bad'nes], *n.* condition of being bad.

BAEDEKER [bä'de-ker], *n.* one of a series of guidebooks for travellers; **B. raids,** air-raids on cities famous for historical associations. [K. *Baedeker,* the original publisher].

BAFFING-SPOON, see BAFFY.

BAFFLE (1) [ba'fl], *n.* plate in a furnace to deflect the course of the air or burning gases; (*radio*) screen of non-resonant material placed in loud-speakers in order that low frequencies may be reproduced; large board on which a loud-speaker is mounted.

BAFFLE (2), *v.t.* to puzzle, frustrate, disconcert, delude; check, perplex. [OFr.].

BAFFLING [baf'ling], *adj.* puzzling, perplexing. BAFFLINGLY, *adv.* in a b. fashion. BAFFLINGNESS, *n.* tendency or quality of b.

BAFFY, BAFFING-SPOON [ba'fi], *n.* (*Scots*) wooden golf club with a sharply lofted face. [Scots].

BAG (1) [bag], *n.* receptacle for the conveyance of small or light articles, having an opening which can be closed; sac or pouch in an animal's body containing some secretion; the number of game animals shot on a single outing; diplomatic mail bag, immune from customs and censorship; (*comm.*) a determinate quantity of a commodity; (*pl.*) pair of trousers; (*slang*) prostitute; (*pl.*) (*slang*) heaps, great amount, large number; **blue b.,** small bag filled with blue powder, used in laundry work; **the whole b. of tricks,** every possible device or feature, all the lot; **b. and baggage,** with everything belonging to one; **to let the cat out of the b.,** to reveal a secret carelessly; **in the b.,** acquired and securely held. [ME.].

BAG (2) (*pres.pt.* **bagging,** *pret.* and *p.pt.* **bagged**), *v.i.* and *i.* to put into a bag, collect; (*sport*) kill during a day's shooting; acquire, obtain; (*slang*) take without permission, steal; take on the grounds of priority of claim, *esp.* in phr. **Bags I**; swell, bulge out.

BAGATELLE [ba-ga-tel'], *n.* game resembling billiards, played on a nine-holed board; thing of no importance, trifle; piece of music of light character. [It.].

BAGFUL [bag'fool], *n.* amount contained in a bag.

BAGGAGE [ba'gij], *n.* tents, utensils and other portable equipment of an army; traveller's luggage; (*coll.*) prostitute; impudent young girl. [OFr.].

BAGGAGE-CHECK [ba'gij-chek], *n.* label attached to the luggage of passengers travelling on American railways.

BAGGING (1) [ba'ging], *n.* material from which bags are made. BAGGING (2), *adj.* bulging, distended.

BAGGY [ba'gi], *adj.* bulging out like a bag; shapeless. BAGGINESS, *n.* b. nature or appearance.

BAGMAN [bag'man], *n.* commercial traveller.

BAGNIO [bah'nyō], *n.* brothel; Turkish gaol. [It. from L.].

BAGPIPE [bag'pīp], *n.* musical wind instrument. BAGPIPER, *n.* one who performs upon the bagpipes. [ME.].

BAHADUR [bah-hah'der], *n.* word added as a title of honour in India; title of respect used by orientals in speaking ceremoniously of European officers; (*slang*) pompous person. [Hind.].

BAIL (1) [bāl], *n.* sum of money paid to secure the release of a prisoner awaiting trial on condition that he will present himself for trial when required; surety of a prisoner on bail; **to surrender one's b.,** to appear for trial at the prescribed time; **to forfeit one's b.,** to fail to appear for trial. [OFr.].

BAIL (2), *n.* bar which separates two horses in an open stable; (*cricket*) one of the two rods laid across the tops of the stumps to complete the wicket; (*milit.*) outer line of fortifications made of stakes, wall of a castle court; (*Australian and N.Z.*) frame which holds up a cow's head during milking; half-hoop used to secure the covering canvas over a wagon. [L.].

BAIL (3), *n.* shallow vessel used in bailing. [Fr.].

BAIL (4), *v.t.* to secure the release of a prisoner awaiting trial by paying the sum demanded as a guarantee of his appearance at the appointed time; (*comm.*) deliver goods in trust upon a contract. [BAIL (1)].

BAIL (5), *v.t.* to throw water out of a boat by means of hand-vessels or cupped hands. [BAIL (3)].

BAIL (6), *v.t.* (*cricket*) to bowl out a batsman with a ball which removes the bails but does not disturb the stumps; **to b. up,** to fasten a cow's head during milking; (*Australian*) to make a person hold up his arms above his head, preparatory to robbing him; *v.i.* to put the hands up.

BAILABLE [bā'la-bl], *adj.* entitled to be released on bail; (of lighter offences) admitting of bail.

BAILBOND [bāl'bond], *n.* bond deposited by a prisoner and his surety as bail.

BAILEE [bā-lē'], *n.* (*leg.*) person with whom goods are deposited in trust.

BAILER [bā'ler], *n.* one who bails or stands bail.

BAILEY [bā'li], *n.* outer walls round a castle; space enclosed by such walls; **the Old B.,** the Central Criminal Court in London.

BAILEY BRIDGE [bā-li-brij'], *n.* easily-erected bridge of steel girders designed for military engineering. [D. C. *Bailey,* the designer].

BAILIE, BAILLIE [bā'li], *n.* municipal official in Scotland corresponding to an English alderman.

BAILIFF [bā'lif], *n.* officer of a sheriff who serves writs, makes arrests and distrains goods; land steward; **water b.,** officer who protects rivers from poachers. [OFr.].

BAILIWICK [bā'li-wik], *n.* jurisdiction of, or territory under, a bailiff. [*Prec.* and OE.].

BAILLIE, see BAILIE.

BAILMENT [bāl'ment], *n.* (*leg.*) delivery of goods in trust under an agreement for their return after they have fulfilled their purpose; bailing out of a prisoner.

BAILOR [bā'law(r)], *n.* one who commits goods to another (the *bailee*) under a contract of bailment.

BAILPIECE [bāl'pēs], *n.* (*leg.*) document which contains a recognizance of bail.

BAILSMAN [bālz'man], *n.* bailer.

BAIRAM [bī'rahm], *n.* name of two Moslem festivals.

BAIRN [bāern], *n.* (*northern dial.*) infant. [OE.].

BAIT (1) [bāt], *n.* real or imitation food used to entice animals into traps or fish on to the hook; food for horses; (*fig.*) trap, enticement, snare.

BAIT (2), *v.t.* and *i.* to provide with bait in order to catch fish or animals; give food and refreshment to horses on a journey; worry or harass (bulls, bears etc.) with dogs; (*fig.*) entice, allure, provoke, tease. [OScand.].

BAITING [bā'ting], *n.* that which is used as bait; act of using bait; harassing of animals, often with dogs.

BAIZE, BAYZE [bāz], *n.* coarse woollen cloth chiefly used for linings. [Fr.].

BAKE [bāk], *v.t.* and *i.* to dry and harden by cooking in a closed chamber or on a hot surface; harden and dry by the heat of the sun's rays; become dry or hardened in heat; (*slang*) become excessively hot by exposure to the sun's rays. HALF-BAKED, (*coll.*) undeveloped; dull, stupid. [OE.].

BAKEHOUSE [bāk'hows], *n.* building in which bread, cake etc. is baked. [ME.].

BAKELITE [bā'ke-līt], *n.* (*prot.*) insulating material readily moulded and hardened by heating. [H. *Baekeland,* the inventor].

BAKER [bā'ker], *n.* one who bakes or sells bread,

---

cakes etc.; small oven; **baker's dozen,** thirteen. [OE.].

BAKERY [bā'ke-ri], n. establishment where baking is carried on, business or premises of a baker.

BAKING (1) [bā'king], n. cooking of bread, cakes etc., esp. by a baker; quantity baked at one time. BAKING (2), adj. extremely hot.

BAKING-POWDER [bā'king-pow-der], n. mixture of bicarbonate of soda and tartaric acid used to leaven bread, cakes etc.

BAKSHEESH, BAKSHISH, see BACKSHEESH.

BALAAM [bā'lam], n. old newspaper matter kept for filling up gaps in a newspaper. [Balaam, the prophet].

BALACLAVA-HELMET [ba-lak-lah-vah-hel'met], n. (milit.) woollen headgear protecting the head and neck.

BALALAIKA [ba-lah-lī'kah], n. Russian musical instrument resembling a guitar; concert of popular Russian music and traditional songs. [Russ.].

BALANCE (1) [ba'lans], n. condition of equilibrium between two opposing forces, weights, quantities etc.; equality of weight or quantity; method of determining this state of equality; weighing apparatus actuated by levers or springs for determining the weight of an object by comparison with known weights; amount required to make two different weights or quantities equal to each other; sum of money required to equalize a credit and debit account; amount of money required to complete a payment; sum standing to one's credit in a bank; (fig.) position of steadiness, equality and harmony of proportion; (gymnastics) exercise performed on the parallel or horizontal bar; (astron.) seventh sign of the Zodiac; **b. of trade,** difference in value between exports and imports; **to hold the b.,** to have power to determine something; **to lose one's b.,** to fall, lose one's grip mentally; **to strike a b.,** to make out a balance-sheet; **b. in hand,** sum of money left over after equalizing profit and loss, income and expenditure; **on b.,** on the whole, taking everything into account. [Fr. from L.].

BALANCE (2), v.t. to bring to, or keep in, a state of equilibrium; compare in one's mind in order to decide the relative worth; adjust (accounts) in order to equalize the debit and credit side of the accounts; have equal weight with; pay the outstanding deficit on an account; v.i. to be in a state of equilibrium or equality; be adjusted so as to be equal; hesitate, waver.

BALANCE-SHEET [ba'lans-shēt], n. (comm.) document which gives a summary of assets and liabilities of a person or company.

BALANCE WHEEL [ba'lans-wēl], n. small wheel which regulates the beat in a watch.

BALANCING (1) [ba'lan-sing], n. state of balance or equilibrium, poise; act of bringing or coming to a state of balance. BALANCING (2), adj. having balance, equalizing; **b. act,** theatrical performance displaying skill in balancing.

BALCONY [bal'ko-ni], n. platform-like structure provided with a railing or parapet, and projecting from the external wall of a house; tier of seats immediately below the gallery in a theatre. [It.].

BALD [bawld], adj. without hair on the head, esp. the top or back; bare, without vegetation; simple, unadorned (of style); dull; unconcealed; (zool.) (of certain animals or birds), having a white spot on their heads. BALDLY, adv. in b. fashion. BALDNESS, n. state of being b.

BALDACHIN, BALDAQUIN [bal'da-kin], n. silken canopy held over the Pope's head and in processions, also over the Blessed Sacrament; canopy of stone placed over bishops' thrones and over altars. [It.].

BALDERDASH [bawl'der-dash], n. words jumbled together without meaning or sense; nonsense. [Uncert.].

BALD-HEADED [bawld-he'did], adj. having a bald head; **to go b. (at),** (coll.) to act without restraint or thought for the consequences.

BALDRICK [bawl'drik], n. belt hanging from the shoulder across the body and from which was slung a sword or bugle. [OFr.].

BALE (1) [bāl], n. large bundle of goods, wrapped usually in canvas and corded or fastened with a metal band; woolpack; (pl.) goods, merchandise. BALE (2), v.t. to make into a b.; pack in bales. [OFr.].

BALE (3), n. calamity, dire misfortune. [OE.].

BALE (4), v.i. to ladle with buckets; **b. out,** (aeron.)

drop from an aeroplane by parachute. [BAIL (5)].

BALEEN [ba-lēn'], n. and adj. whalebone. [L.].

BALE-FIRE [bāl'fier], n. large fire, bonfire; signal fire. [OE.].

BALEFUL [bāl'fŏŏl], adj. harmful, bringing evil and misery, malicious. BALEFULLY, adj. in b. fashion.

BALER [bā'ler], n. bucket or bowl used in baling water out of a boat.

BALISTIC, see BALLISTIC.

BALK, BAULK (1) [bawk], n. unploughed ridge of land between furrows; large rough beam of timber; (fig.) frustration, hindrance; (billiards) area at the bottom of a billiard-table, marked out by a line drawn parallel to the bottom cushion, the middle portion of the line forming the base of a semicircle from which play begins. BAULK (2), v.t. and i. to impede the progress of, obstruct; thwart, check, frustrate; omit; stop suddenly, jib. [OE.].

BALKER [baw'ker], n. (fishing), man on shore who signals by shouting the movements of shoals of herrings.

BALL (1) [bawl], n. spherical or roundish object, solid or hollow, of any substance or size; solid missile fired by a cannon, rifle etc.; round or oval-shaped object used in playing games; (fig.) the earth; any celestial body; material formed or wound into a round mass; (cricket) a delivery of the ball by the bowler; (pl.) (vulg.) testicles; nonsense, rubbish; **b. of foot,** rounded part of the foot below the joint of the big toe; **b. of eye,** eye within the lids; **b. and socket,** form of joint in which a ball can turn in any direction within the close-fitting socket enclosing it; **to keep the b. rolling,** to take one's share in conversation, to keep anything going; **no b.,** (cricket) ball which is unfairly delivered; **on the b.,** (football) up with the game; (fig.) alert, energetic. BALL-BEARINGS, series of small steel balls placed in a groove between revolving parts and axles to reduce friction. [Fr.].

BALL (2), n. assembly or social gathering for dancing, a dance; **to open the b.,** to start the first dance; (fig.) to commence operations. [L.].

BALL (3), v.t. and i. to form into a ball or spherical mass; **balled up,** (esp. U.S.) confused, muddled.

BALLAD [ba'lad], n. popular, traditional story of adventure told in a simple metre; (mus.) short song of simple construction, generally of a sentimental character. [OFr.].

BALLADE [ba-lahd'], n. poem consisting of three stanzas of eight lines each together with a stanza of four lines called an envoy, each verse and the envoy ending with the same line or refrain; musical composition of a romantic nature. [OFr.].

BALLADMONGER [ba'lad-mung-ger], n. maker or seller of ballads; (coll.) inferior poet.

BALLADRY [ba'lad-ri], n. subject or manner of writing ballads.

BALLAST (1) [ba'last], n. heavy material placed in the hold of a ship or in a balloon to keep it stable; that which is used to make anything steady; earth or gravel laid between the rails and sleepers on a railway line; (fig.) elements making for steadiness and stability of character. BALLAST (2), v.t. to provide with b.; keep steady by means of b. BALLASTAGE [ba'las-tij], n. duty paid for permission to take b.

BALL-COCK [bawl'kok], n. valve or cock controlling the supply of water to a cistern and actuated by a floating ball attached to it by a lever.

BALLERINA [ba-le-rē'nah], n. ballet girl, female ballet-dancer. [It.].

BALLET [ba'lā], n. scenic representation of actions, characters etc., by means of a series of dances performed to music. [Fr.].

BALLETOMANIA [ba-le-to-mā'ni-ah], n. inordinate enthusiasm for attending ballet performances. BALLETOMANE [ba'le-tō-mān], n. one who has b.

BALL-FLOWER [bawl'flow-er], n. architectural ornament resembling a ball placed in a circular flower.

BALLISTIC, BALISTIC [ba-lis'tik], adj. concerning the throwing of missiles or shooting projectiles; **b. curve,** path of a projectile. BALLISTICS, n.(pl.) science of projectiles.

BALLISTITE [ba'lis-tīt], n. a smokeless explosive.

BALLOON (1) [ba-loon'], n. inflated ball of airtight material; large spherical bag which rises and floats when filled with gas lighter than air; small inflated sphere of thin rubber; inflated bag which keeps an airship up in the air; (chem.) hollow glass receiver used in distilling; **b. barrage,** system of captive balloons employed as a defence against low-flying aircraft; **observation b.,** captive b. from which an observer can watch the progress of a battle. BALLOON (2), *v.t. and i. (of sails etc.)* to bulge out like a b.; make an ascent in a b.; *(football)* to kick the ball aimlessly high into the air. BALLOONING, *n.* construction and management of balloons. BALLOONIST, *n.* one who builds or makes ascents in a b. [It.].

BALLOON-TYRE [ba-lōon-tīer'], *n.* large pneumatic tyre used on motor vehicles and aircraft.

BALLOT (1) [ba'lot], *n.* ball, ticket or paper used to record a secret vote; act or practice of voting secretly, any voting by paper or ticket; total number of votes cast. BALLOT (2), *v.i.* to vote by b., vote secretly; make a choice by b.; **to b. for,** to elect by secret vote. BALLOTING, *n.* action of voting by b. [It.].

BALLOT-BOX [ba'lot-boks], *n.* box in which the voting papers are deposited at an election.

BALLROOM (1) [bawl'rōom], *n.* room or hall for dancing. BALLROOM (2), *adj.* (of dancing) of a kind suited to a b., as distinguished from ballet, folk-dancing etc.

BALLYHOO [ba-li-hōo'], *n.* advance publicity of an exaggerated nature; *(fig.)* empty bombast, grossly deceitful talk. [U.S. slang].

BALM [bahm], *n.* sap, juice or gum resin obtained from various aromatic or fragrant shrubs and trees; fragrant or valuable healing ointment; *(fig.)* anything soothing mental or physical pain; *(bot.)* aromatic plants or garden herbs of the genus *Melissa*; **B. of Gilead,** resin of the tree, *Commiphora Opobalsamum*; resin of a North American tree, *Abies balsamea.* [OFr., L.].

BALMY [bah'mi], *adj.* like balm; fragrant, soothing. BALMILY, *adv.* in b. fashion.

BALNEOLOGY [bal-ni-o'lo-ji], *n.* study or science of the use of natural and medicinal baths and waters in healing. BALNEOLOGIST, *n.* an expert in b. [L. and Gk.].

BALSAM [bawl'sam], *n.* aromatic resinous substance obtained from certain plants or trees; artificial, oily or resinous ointment made by dissolving various substances in oil or turpentine; flowering plant; *(fig.)* substance which heals or soothes; *(chem.)* compounds made from resins and volatile oils and insoluble in water; **Canada b.,** type of b. used in mounting microscopic objects. BALSAMIFEROUS [bawl-sa-mi'fe-rōos], *adj.* yielding b. [L.].

BALSAMIC (1) [bawl'sa-mik], *n.* soothing oily medicine. BALSAMIC (2), BALSAMICAL, *adj.* having the qualities of balsam; soothing. BALSAMICALLY [bawl-sa'mi-ka-li], *adv.* soothingly.

BALUSTER [ba'lus-ter], *n.* small pillar usually slender at its top and base but swelling out in the middle, used to support a handrail. [It.].

BALUSTRADE [ba-lus-trād'], *n.* row of balusters together with a coping supported by them, serving as an ornamental parapet to a balcony etc. [Fr.].

BAMBINO [bam-bē'nō], *n.* Italian baby; representation of the infant Christ. [It.].

BAMBOO [bam-bōo'], *n.* genus of tropical giant grasses with round jointed stalks; stalk of this plant used for innumerable purposes.

BAMBOOZLE [bam-boo'zl], *v.t.* to hoax, deceive, mystify. [Fr.].

BAN (1) [ban], *n.* prohibition, proscription; sentence of excommunication passed by ecclesiastical authority; method of showing public disapproval. BAN (2), *v.t. and i.* to forbid, prohibit. [OE.].

BANAL [bā'nal, ba-nal'], *adj.* commonplace, obvious; vulgar. [Fr.].

BANALITY [ba-na'li-ti], *n.* condition of being banal; a commonplace, vulgarity, something which is obvious.

BANANA [ba-nah'nah], *n.* tropical fruit tree; long curved edible fruit of this tree.

BANBURY CAKE [ban'be-ri-kāk], *n.* kind of pastry turnover originating in *Banbury,* Oxfordshire.

BAND (1) [band], *n.* thin strip of material fastened round a number of objects or a mass of loose material to make a compact package or to fasten the objects together; narrow flat strip of cloth forming part of a garment; belt or stripe of material on an object, distinguishable in appearance from the remainder of the object; *(pl.)* pair of white strips of cloth hanging down from the collar in front and worn by barristers, certain clergymen, and with certain academic robes; *(mech.)* belt for the transmission of power in a machine. [OE.].

BAND (2), *n.* a gathering of people; company of persons brought together for a common purpose;

(mus.) company of instrumentalists gathered together to perform a musical composition; **B. of Hope,** association of persons pledged to total abstinence from intoxicating liquors.

BAND (3), *v.t. and i.* to make a band, secure or adorn with a band; join together in a company, associate. BANDED, *adj.* united, joined together in a band; furnished or decorated with coloured bands.

BANDAGE (1) [ban'dij], *n.* strip of woven fabric used to dress and bind up wounds and injuries; that which is bound over something else. BANDAGE (2), *v.t.* to bind with a b. BANDAGING, *n.* bandages; material for bandages. [Fr.].

BANDANNA [ban-da'nah], *n.* coloured Indian silk handkerchief spotted with white or yellow; method of calico-printing or dyeing. [Hind.].

BANDBOX [band'boks], *n.* light box of cardboard or thin wood for hats and other light articles; **to have come out of a b.,** to be spruce and neat in appearance.

BANDEAU [ban-dō'], *n.* ribbon tied round a woman's head to bind her hair; flat ring inside a woman's hat. [Fr.].

BANDERILLA [ban-de-rē'lyah], *n.* barbed dart used to excite the bull in bull-fighting. [Span.].

BANDEROL(E) [ban'de-rol], *n.* long, narrow streamer flown at the masthead; ornamental pennant fastened to the end of a knight's lance; *(arch.)* ribbon-like band with an inscription. [Fr.].

BANDICOOT [ban'di-kōot], *n.* huge Indian rat; Australian marsupial insect-eater. [Telugu].

BANDINESS [ban'di-nes], *n.* state or quality of having bandy legs.

BANDIT *(pl.* **bandits, banditti)** [ban'dit], *n.* outlaw, armed robber, lawless or desperate person. MOTOR-BANDIT, *(coll.)* thief who uses a motor-car to make a swift raid and escape. [It.].

BANDITRY [ban'di-tri], *n.* the activities of bandits.

BANDMASTER [band'mah-ster], *n.* conductor of a musical band.

BANDOG [ban'dog], *n.* large dog which is kept chained-up on account of its ferocious nature; bloodhound or mastiff.

BANDOLEER, BANDOLIER [ban-dō-lēer'], *n.* leather belt formerly worn by musketeers over the shoulder to secure their firearms; shoulder belt with small pockets for holding cartridges. [Fr. from It.].

BANDOLIER, see BANDOLEER.

BAND-PASS [band'pahs], *adj. (radio)* constructed so as to pass only a particular band of frequencies.

BANDSAW [band'saw], *n.* thin saw stretched on a frame; endless saw running over two pulleys.

BANDSMAN [bandz'man], *n.* performer in or member of a musical band.

BANDSTAND [band'stand], *n.* raised roofed outdoor platform on which a musical band gives performances.

BAND-WAGON [band'wa-gon], *n. (U.S.)* wagon carrying a band leading a procession; **to climb on the b.,** *(slang)* to make sure of a prominent position by joining a promising movement.

BANDY (1) [ban'di], *n.* kind of hockey played on the ice. [Unkn.].

BANDY (2), *adj.* of legs, having an outward curve at the knee; bow-legged.

BANDY (3), *v.t. and i.* to beat to and fro, toss about; exchange, give and take; **to b. words,** to engage in violent and rapid discussion with someone. [BANDY (1)].

BANDY-LEGGED [ban-di-legd', ban-di-le'gid], *adj.* having curved or bowed legs.

BANE [bān], *n.* source of death or injury; cause of vexation, worry or ruin; poison; destruction, death; sheep-rot. [OE.].

BANEFUL [bān'fŏol], *adj.* destructive, deadly, evil.

BANEWORT [bān'wurt], *n.* deadly nightshade; lesser spearwort. [OE.].

BANG (1) [bang], *n.* sudden loud noise; loud report of a firearm; a hard violent blow. [BANG (4)].

BANG (2), *n. (U.S.)* hair cut straight across in a fringe. [Uncert.].

BANG (3), *adv.* in the manner of a bang; *(coll.)* precisely and abruptly, exactly; completely. [Next].

BANG (4), *v.t. and i.* to make a sudden loud noise, cause something to make a bang; beat in a noisy manner, thump; bring or come into violent contact with; handle in a rough manner. [OScand.].

BANG (5), see BHANG.

BANGLE [bang'gl], *n.* ornament in the form of a ring or bracelet encircling the arm. [Hind.].

BANGUE, see BHANG.

BANIAN, BANYAN [ban'yan], *n.* Hindu trader;

kind of dressing-gown; kind of jacket of wool, silk or flannel; Indian fig-tree. [Portug. from Skr.].

BANISH [ba'nish], *v.t.* to condemn to exile; drive or force away; dismiss from one's thoughts. [OFr.].

BANISHMENT [ba'nish-ment], *n.* act of banishing; condition of being banished; exile.

BANISTER [ba'nis-ter], *n.* handrail together with the supporting railings of a staircase. [Form of BALUSTER].

BANJO (*pl.* **banjoes, banjos**) [ban'jō], *n.* stringed instrument having a body like a tambourine and neck like a guitar, played with the fingers; casing of the differential gear of a motor-car. **BANJOIST** [ban'jō-ist], *n.* one who plays the b.

BANJULELE, BANJO- [ban-ju-lā'li], *n.* stringed instrument combining the characteristics of banjo and ukulele.

BANK (1) [bangk], *n.* heaped-up mound of earth, snow or sand; raised shelf of ground on the bed of a river or sea; sloping ground forming the edge of a river, lake or cutting; artificial slope or gradient built round a curve of a road to allow a vehicle to maintain speed round the curve; piled-up mass of clouds. [ODan., OIcel.].

BANK (2), *n.* establishment which trades in, receives, lends or exchanges money; building occupied by such an establishment; company engaged in this business; fund; pool in a gambling game; **B. of England**, London bank which manages the public debt, receives revenue, issues notes which are legal tender etc.; **B. Holiday**, public holiday declared by Act of Parliament; **b. rate**, rate at which the Bank of England discounts bills of exchange. [LL.].

BANK (3), *v.t.* and *i.* to form a bank, make into a bank, heap, become heaped; raise a heap of earth or stones about, strengthen with a bank, confine with banks; (*aeron.*) tilt an aeroplane at an angle in turning, travel with one side higher than the other; **to b. a fire**, to heap a fire with fuel and reduce the draught so that it may burn slowly; **to b. on**, (*coll.*) to rely upon, count on. [BANK (1)].

BANK (4), *v.t.* and *i.* to deposit money in a bank, change into money; carry on the business of banking, trade in money; (*gaming*) hold the sum of money from which losses are paid. [BANK (2)].

BANKABLE [bang'ka-bl], *adj.* able to be accepted at a bank.

BANK-BILL [bangk'bil], *n.* bill of exchange drawn by one bank upon another.

BANK-BOOK [bangk'book], *n.* pass-book containing a statement of a customer's account at a bank.

BANKER (1) [bang'ker], *n.* one who keeps a bank or carries on the business of banking; group of persons engaged in banker; gambling card game; (*gaming*) person who holds the pool in a gambling game.

BANKER (2), *n.* vessel in the cod-fishery on the banks of Newfoundland; bench on which masons cut and square their work; horse trained to jump banks.

BANKET [bang'ket], *n.* conglomerate rock forming the gold reef of the Transvaal. [Du.].

BANKING (1) [bang'king], *n.* act of erecting a bank; artificially constructed bank of a motor-racing track; fishing on a sea-bank; (*aeron.*) the tilting of an aeroplane at an angle when turning.

BANKING (2), *n.* business of a banker, act of carrying on this business; the depositing of money in a bank.

BANKING (3), *adj.* pertaining to or conducted by a bank; **b. house**, commercial firm transacting banking.

BANKNOTE [bangk'nōt], *n.* promissory note payable on demand, issued by a bank.

BANKRUPT (1) [bangk'rupt], *n.* person who on becoming insolvent has come under the jurisdiction of a court which administers and distributes his assets for the benefit of his creditors; person legally declared to be unable to pay his debts; insolvent person. **BANKRUPT** (2), *adj.* unable to pay one's debts, insolvent; (*fig.*) destitute of; totally unsuccessful. **BANKRUPT** (3), *v.t.* to make or declare b. [It.].

BANKRUPTCY [bangk'rupt-si], *n.* state of being legally declared bankrupt, act of becoming a bankrupt; (*fig.*) absolute loss, state of being morally or intellectually destitute; **Act of B.**, act by which a debtor renders himself liable to be declared a bankrupt; **B. Court**, court of law which deals with this.

BANKSIA [bangk'si-ah], *n.* (*bot.*) genus of evergreen Australian shrubs. [Sir J. *Banks*, botanist].

BANK-STOCK [bangk'stok], *n.* shares held in the capital stock of a bank.

BANNER [ba'ner], *n.* flag or ensign supported on a pole; rectangular piece of cloth, suitably inscribed,

fastened to and carried on one or two poles in a procession or demonstration; (*fig.*) flag or cause of a country; anything used as a symbol of opinions or a cause; **to unfurl one's b.**, to announce one's cause or principles; **b. headline**, newspaper headline put prominently across the page; **b. screen**, fire-screen suspended from a pole or mantelpiece. **BANNERED**, *adj.* provided with banners. [OFr.].

BANNERET [ba'ne-ret], *n.* knight having his own vassals accompanying his banner in war. [OFr.].

BANNERETTE [ba-ne-ret'], *n.* small banner. [OFr.].

BANNEROLE [ba'ne-rōl], *n.* banner carried at the funerals of great men and placed over their tombs. [BANDEROLE].

BANNOCK [ba'nok], *n.* cake of oatmeal baked on an iron plate over the fire. [OE. from Gael.].

BANNS [banz], *n.*(*pl.*) notice of intention of marriage given in church on three successive Sundays. [BAN (1)].

BANQUET (1) [bang'kwet], *n.* sumptuous feast generally of a formal or official nature; dinner with speeches in celebration of some occasion; (*pop.*) very good meal. **BANQUET** (2), *v.t.* and *i.* to treat with a feast or rich entertainment; feast sumptuously, regale oneself with rich fare. **BANQUETER**, *n.* one who attends a b. [It.].

BANQUETING [bang'kwe-ting], *n.* act of feasting sumptuously, luxurious living; **b. hall**, large luxurious dining-room.

BANQUETTE [bang-ket'], *n.* (*milit.*) raised step behind a parapet from which to fire; footpath of a bridge raised above the roadway. [Fr.].

BANSHEE [ban'shē], *n.* Irish female spirit whose wail is said to give warning of death in the family to which she is attached; (*coll.*) air-raid siren. [OIr.].

BANSTICKLE [ban'sti-kl], *n.* the stickleback. [Unkn.].

BANT [bant], *v.i.* to follow a special diet to reduce weight. [Back-formation from BANTING].

BANTAM [ban'tam], *n.* small spirited breed of domestic fowl; small highly spirited person; boxer of bantam weight; **b. weight**, boxer whose fighting weight lies between eight stone and eight stone six pounds; **b. battalions**, special battalions formed during the war of 1914-18 of small but strong men. [*Bantam*, place in Java.].

BANTER (1) [ban'ter], *n.* joking or jesting; pleasant chaffing or ridicule. **BANTER** (2), *v.i.* to rail humorously. [Unkn.].

BANTING [ban'ting], *n.* diet for reducing weight by avoiding sugar, starch and fat; act of reducing corpulence. [William *Banting*, originator].

BANTLING [bant'ling], *n.* an infant. [Germ.].

BANTU (1) [ban-tōō'], *n.* group of South and Central African native languages; African native belonging to a race whose native language is B. **BANTU** (2), *adj.* pertaining to B. [Native].

BANXRING [bangks'ring], *n.* quadruped with a long pointed snout, found in the Indian Archipelago. [Javanese].

BANYAN, see BANIAN.

BANZAI [bahn-zah'ē], *n.* Japanese shout of joy. [Jap.].

BAOBAB [bā'o-bab], *n.* African tree. [Unkn.].

BAP [bap], *n.* (*Scots*) small variously shaped loaf of bread with a thin soft crust. [Unkn.].

BAPTISM [bap'tizm], *n.* initiation into membership of the Christian Church by sprinkling with or immersion in water as a sign of purification, usually accompanied by name-giving; **b. of fire**, soldier's first battle; (*fig.*) severe initiatory test or ordeal. **BAPTISMAL** [bap-tiz'mal], *adj.* pertaining to b. [OFr.; Gk.].

BAPTIST [bap'tist], *n.* one who administers baptism, *esp.* John the Baptist; member of a religious sect who believe in baptism of adults only and total immersion at the ceremony of baptism. [Gk.].

BAPTISTRY [bap'tis-tri], *n.* place where baptism is administered; receptacle in which the immersion takes place. [Gk.].

BAPTIZE [bap-tīz'], *v.t.* and *i.* to administer baptism; initiate into membership of the Christian Church by baptism; (*fig.*) give a name to. [Gk.].

BAR (1) [bah(r)], *n.* long narrow piece of wood, metal or other rigid material, used for the purposes of support or of obstruction or restriction; anything resembling this; bank of sand or gravel heaped up at the mouth of a river or harbour partially blocking up the entrance; place in a court of justice at which prisoners stand when on trial, part of the court where the judges sit; railing enclosing the space occupied by barristers in a court of law; enclosed space in a public-house, hotel or place of refreshment from which drinks are served; room in a public-house or hotel containing a bar; † (leg.) barriers in the Inns of Court separating the unqualified students from the barristers and other members of the governing body; the whole body of qualified barristers; railing in the House of Commons to which persons are brought for the purpose of examination or censure by Members of Parliament; (fig.) moral or intellectual restriction, barrier or obstacle to progress; tribunal of public opinion; (mus.) vertical line drawn across the stave in a musical score; (pop.) a measure; (her.) space enclosed by two straight lines drawn horizontally across the escutcheon; (eng.) an ingot, moulded but unwrought piece of metal; (meteor.) unit of atmospheric pressure; (milit.) strip of metal added below the clasp of a medal to denote that the decoration has been won a second time; **b. sinister**, (pop.) bend sinister, an implication or sign of illegitimacy; **trial at b.**, (leg.) trial in the Queen's Bench division; **to practise at the B.**, to follow the profession of a barrister; **to be called to the B.**, **be at the B.**, **go to the B.**, to become a barrister; to be called within the B., to be appointed Queen's Counsel. [ME.].

BAR (2) (pres.pt. **barring**, pret. and p.pt. **barred**), v.t. to fasten by means of a bar, obstruct, hinder, impede; except or exclude; prevent, forbid; take exception to; mark with stripes of a different colour; (leg.) stay by legal objection. [Prec.].

BAR (3), prep. with the exception of; **b. none**, unreservedly, without exception. [Prec.].

BARB (1) [bahb], n. curved point projecting outwards below the point of an arrow, spear or fish-hook to prevent withdrawal; one of the pointed projections on barbed wire; filament of a feather springing from the quill; tuft of hair like a beard; anything resembling this, as the feelers of a barbel. BARB (2), v.t. to provide with a b. [L.].

BARB (3), n. Barbary horse; pigeon. [Fr.].

BARBACON, see BARBICAN.

BARBARIAN (1) [bah-bãer'i-an], n. member of a rough uncivilized community; uncouth, wild, savage-like person, deficient in humanity and uncivilized; uneducated, uncultured person. BARBARIAN (2), adj. rude, uncivilized, cruel, pitiless, inhuman. [Gk.].

BARBARIC [bah-ba'rik], adj. pertaining to a barbarian; uncultured, wild, savage. [Gk.].

BARBARISM [bah'ba-rizm], n. state of being barbaric or uncivilized; brutality, cruelty; form of speech in which foreign or vulgar idioms are used. [Gk.].

BARBARITY [bah-ba'ri-ti], n. state of being barbarous; cruelty; fierceness.

BARBARIZE [bah'ba-rīz], v.t. to make barbarous. BARBARIZATION [bah-ba-ri-zā'shn], n. action of making or becoming barbarous. [Gk.].

BARBAROUS [bah'ba-roōs], adj. barbaric, uncivilized; unidiomatic. BARBAROUSLY, adv. in b. fashion. BARBAROUSNESS, n. condition of being b. [Gk.].

BARBECUE (1) [bah'bi-kyoō], n. wooden framework on which meat is smoked or dried; hog, ox or any large animal broiled or roasted whole; hence, a function in the open air, at which animals are cooked whole; terrace, platform on which coffee-beans are spread to dry in the sun. BARBECUE (2), v.i. to smoke or cure meat. [Span.].

BARBED [bahbd], adj. bearded; furnished with barbs; **b. wire**, galvanized wire having two twisted strands which hold projecting spikes placed a few inches apart.

BARBEL [bah'bel], n. freshwater fish of the carp family; beard-like filaments of such fishes. [OFr.].

BARBER (1) [bah'ber], n. one who shaves or trims beards and cuts hair, man's hairdresser; **barber's itch**, sycosis thought to be contracted from a barber's brush; **barber's pole**, pole spirally striped in red, white and blue, and used as a sign outside a barber's shop. BARBER-SURGEON, one who practised both shaving and bleeding. BARBER (2), v.t. to trim a beard, shave, cut the hair of. [OFr. from L.].

BARBER(R)Y, **BERBER(R)Y** [bah'be-ri], n. (bot.) kind of shrub with spiny shoots, hanging clusters of yellow flowers and small orange-red berries. [Md L.].

BARBETTE [bah-bet'], n. (fort.) terrace inside a parapet so raised as to allow cannon to be fired over the top; armoured turret of a warship. [Fr.].

BARBICAN, **BARBACON** [bah'bi-kan], n. (fort.) fortification erected to guard the entrance to a town or castle; opening in a fortified wall through which guns are fired. [OFr.].

BARBITONE [bah'bi-tōn], n. hypnotic drug, veronal. [Fr.].

BARBITURATE [bah-bi'tyoō-rāt], n. one of the salts of barbituric acid, some of which are used as narcotics.

BARBITURIC [bah-bi-tyoō'rik], adj. **b. acid**, compound obtained by heating alloxantin with sulphuric acid. [Fr.].

BARBOLA [bah-bō'lah], n. the decoration of small articles with modelled plaster work painted. [Unkn.].

BARCAROLLE, **BARCAROLE** [bah'ka-rōl], n. melody sung by Venetian gondoliers; boating song. [It.].

BARD [bahd], n. wandering minstrel, ancient Celtic minstrel-poet; Welsh poet who has been recognized at the Eisteddfod; poet or singer. BARDIC, adj. pertaining to a b. or his poetry. [Ir.].

BARE (1) [bãer], adj. naked, without its normal covering, uncovered, stripped, without ornament, empty; poor, meagre; slight, without further proof, plain, without concealment; **to lay b.**, to disclose, expose. BARE (2), v.t. to strip, make b.; uncover, reveal, make a confession. [OE.].

BARE (3)†, pret. of BEAR. [OE.].

BAREBACK [bãer'bak], adj. and adv. without a saddle.

BAREFACED [bãer-fāst'], adj. with the face uncovered; (fig.) without attempt at concealment; brazen, shameless.

BARELEGGED [bãer-le'gid], adj. having the legs bare; with the knees and upper part of the calf uncovered.

BARELY [bãer'li], adv. in a bare or naked fashion; openly; scarcely, hardly, only just. [OE.].

BARESARK, see BERSERK.

BARETTER, see BARRETTER.

BARGAIN (1) [bah'gan], n. agreement between two persons usually concerning the selling and buying of a thing on terms mutually advantageous or acceptable; thing obtained by this means; article offered on advantageous terms to the purchaser; something offered at a reduced price; **to make or strike a b.**, to come to terms with; **to make the best of a bad b.**, to face misfortune or trouble cheerfully and optimistically; **into the b.**, over and above, in addition to; **a Dutch, wet, b.**, b. sealed with a drink; **a b. sale**, seasonal sale at which the price of articles is reduced. BARGAINEE, n. one who accepts a b. BARGAINER, n. one who makes a b. [OFr.].

BARGAIN (2), v.t. and i. to argue about the purchase or sale of an article with a view to obtaining the most favourable terms; **to b. for**, to expect, allow for, be prepared for. [OFr.].

BARGAIN-BASEMENT [bah'gan-bās-ment], n. lowest storey, below street level, of a large store, where goods are sold cheaply.

BARGE (1) [bahj], n. large flat-bottomed boat for transporting heavy burdens on canals or rivers, or used in loading and unloading ships; boat for the use of the chief officers of a man-of-war; boat of state propelled by oars and used on ceremonial occasions; college house-boat. [Var. of BARQUE.].

BARGE (2), v.i. to transport by barge; collide heavily with; (slang) make an abrupt and unannounced entry; **to b. about**, to plunge about in a rough, clumsy manner. [Prec.].

BARGE-BOARD [bahj'bawd], n. (arch.) board hanging down from the outer edge of a gable. [MedL. and BOARD].

BARGE-COUPLE [bahj'ku-pl], n. (arch.) pair of gable-beams mortised one into the other.

BARGE-COURSE [bahj'kaws], n. that part of the tiling of a roof which juts out beyond the gable; the coping of a wall formed by a course of bricks placed edgeways.

BARGEE [bah-jē'], n. person in charge of a barge; (fig.) tough, pugnacious individual; **to swear like a b.**, to swear fluently and forcefully.

BARGEMASTER [bahj'mahs-ter], n. person who owns a barge.

BARGEPOLE [bahj'pōl], n. pole for propelling a barge.

BARIA, see BARYTA.

BARIC (1) [bah'rik], adj. barometric. [Gk.].

BARIC (2) [bã'rik], adj. pertaining to or containing barium.

BARITONE (1), **BARYTONE** [ba'ri-tōn], n. male

The accent ' after a syllable = stress (u-pon'). The mark ‾ over a vowel = length (ā in made; ō in bone).

voice whose compass lies between the bass and tenor; singer possessing such a voice; (Gk. *gram.*, in this sense spelt **bary-**) word whose final syllable does not bear the acute accent. BARITONE (2), *adj.* (*mus.*) lying between bass and tenor, suitable for a baritone voice. [It. from Gk.].

BARIUM [bāer'i-um], *n.* metal found in baryta, the chemical element symbolized by Ba.

BARK (1), see BARQUE.

BARK (2) [bahk], *n.* outer protective covering of the trunk and branches of a tree; kind of bark used medicinally, *esp.* Peruvian bark; bark used in tanning leather. [OScand.].

BARK (3), *n.* cry of certain animals such as the dog, fox or wolf; (*slang*) sound made by a person coughing; report of a firearm; **his b. is worse than his bite**, he is not so severe in his actions as in his words. [BARK (5)].

BARK (4), *v.t.* to peel the bark from; (*slang*) graze the skin. [BARK (2)].

BARK (5), *v.i.* to utter a bark; (*slang*) cough loudly; speak sharply and loudly; make a loud report; **to b. up the wrong tree**, to be on a false scent, be mistaken. [OE.].

BARK-BOUND [bahk'bownd], *adj.* (*hort.*) not growing at a normal rate on account of its bark being too close and firm.

BARKER [bah'ker], *n.* one who barks; one who barks trees; (*coll.*) one who touts for customers at a shop-door, auction etc.; (*slang*) revolver.

BARLEY [bah'li], *n.* cereal plant whose grain is used for making malt in brewing and distilling, and also as a food; **Scotch b.**, barley grain which has had the husk stripped off; **pearl b.**, barley which has been polished, rounded and dressed; **patent b.**, flour obtained by grinding pearl barley. [OE.].

BARLEY-BREAK [bah'li-brāk], *n.* old rustic game.

BARLEY-BREE [bah'li-brē], *n.* strong beer.

BARLEY-BROTH [bah-li-broth'], *n.* broth made by boiling barley and flesh with certain vegetables; strong ale.

BARLEYCORN [bah'li-kawn], *n.* grain of barley; **John B.**, malt liquor.

BARLEYMOW [bah'li-mō], *n.* store for reaped barley; stack of barley.

BARLEY-SUGAR [bah-li-shoō'ger], *n.* sweetmeat made from boiled sugar.

BARLEY-WATER [bah'li-waw-ter], *n.* drink made by boiling pearl barley in water.

BARM [bahm], *n.* yeast; froth which forms upon malt liquor when fermenting, used as leaven. [OE.].

BARMAID [bah'mād], *n.* female attendant serving drinks in the bar of a public-house or hotel.

BARMAN [bah'man], *n.* man who serves drinks in an hotel or public-house.

BARMASTER [bah'mah-ster], *n.* arbitrator for miners. [Germ.].

BARMECIDE [bah'mi-sīd], *adj.* (*fig.*) unreal, disappointing. [The *Barmecide* who, in *Arabian Nights*, gave a feast with rich but empty dishes].

BARMY [bah'mi], *adj.* containing barm, frothy; (*slang*) mad, insane, foolish.

BARN [bahn], *n.* building in which hay, straw, grain etc. is stored; (*fig.*) large, bare, unadorned room or building. [OE.].

BARNACLE [bah'na-kl], *n.* genus of marine crustaceous animals which cling by long stalks to ship hulls, rocks etc. covered by the sea; (*fig.*) one who cannot be shaken off; kind of wild goose. [OFr.].

BARN-DANCE [bahn'dahns], *n.* a rustic dance.

BARNDOOR (1) [bahn-daw(r)'], *n.* large door of a barn; very large target. BARNDOOR (2), *adj.* reared in the farmyard; **b. fowls**, cross-bred domestic fowls.

BARN-OWL [bahn'owl], *n.* the screech-owl.

BARNSTORMER [bahn'staw-mer], *n.* itinerant actor playing in barns and similar places; (*fig.*) crude, boisterous player.

BARO-, *pref.* pertaining to atmospheric pressure.

BAROGRAPH [ba'rō-grahf], *n.* kind of aneroid barometer which records on paper successive variations of atmospheric pressure; record of atmospheric changes drawn on a graph in this way.

BAROLOGY [ba-ro-lō-ji], *n.* science of weight. [Gk.].

BAROMETER [ba-ro'mi-ter], *n.* instrument which indicates variations of atmospheric pressure and relates them to variable weather conditions; (*fig.*) anything which indicates changes in public opinion.

BAROMETRIC(AL) [ba-rō-met'rik(-al)], *adj.* per-

taining to a barometer or atmospheric pressure. BAROMETRICALLY, *adv.* by means of a barometer.

BARON [ba'ron], *n.*, lowest title or rank in the British peerage; foreign title of nobility; (*hist.*) tenant of the king whose lands were obtained in return for military service; **b. of beef**, two undivided sirloins of beef. [OFr.].

BARONAGE [ba'ro-nij], *n.* the collective body of barons; the peerage; book containing a list of, and information about, barons and their families. [OFr.].

BARONESS [ba'ro-nes], *n.* baron's wife or widow; woman holding a barony in her own right. [OFr.].

BARONET [ba'ro-net], *n.* lowest British hereditary title or rank, in order of precedence between a knight and a baron. [Dim. of BARON].

BARONETAGE [ba'ro-ne-tij], *n.* the collective body of baronets; book containing a list of, and information about, baronets and their families.

BARONETCY [ba'ro-net-si], *n.* dignity and title of a baronet.

BARONIAL [ba-rō'ni-al], *adj.* pertaining to or belonging to a baron; sumptuous, suitable for a baron; (*arch.*) resembling a castle in style.

BARONY [ba'ro-ni], *n.* lands or estate of a baron; rank or title of a baron; division of an Irish county. [OFr.].

BAROQUE (1) [ba-rōk'], *n.* the baroque style in architecture, art etc. BAROQUE (2), *adj.* elaborately grotesque, floridly irregular, fancifully ornamental; *esp.* of a style of architecture and decoration characteristic of late Renaissance Italy and of Europe in general in the 18th century. [Fr., Portug.].

BAROUCHE [ba-roōsh'], *n.* old-fashioned, four-wheeled horse-drawn carriage. [Germ. from It., L.].

BARQUE, BARK [bahk], *n.* sailing-ship with three masts and having the foremast and mainmast square rigged and the mizzenmast fore-and-aft rigged. [Fr.].

BARQUENTINE [bah'ken-tēn], *n.* three-masted vessel, square rigged on the foremast and fore-and-aft rigged on the mainmast and mizzenmast. [Prec.].

BARRACK (1) [ba'rak], *n.* (*usu. pl.*) large building in which military troops are quartered; temporary hut or shelter; (*fig.*) large bare gaunt building. [Fr., It.].

BARRACK (2), *v.t. and i.* to accommodate in barracks; (*sport*) shout derisive remarks at, cheer or applaud ironically. BARRACKING, *n.* (*sport*) ironical cheering or applause, cries of derision directed towards a player.

BARRACOUTA, BARRACUDA [ba-ra-koō'tah], *n.* large fish of the genus *Sphyraena*. [Unkn.].

BARRAGE [ba'rahzh], *n.* act of barring; artificial embankment across the bed of a river to raise the water-level; (*milit.*) violent concentration of artillery fire over a given area; **b. balloon**, one forming part of a balloon b. [Fr.].

BARRATRY [ba'ra-tri], *n.* practice of exciting or encouraging lawsuits; dishonest or careless action by the captain or crew of a ship whereby loss is suffered by the owners and others. BARRATOR [ba'ra-ter], *n.* one who commits b. BARRATROUS, *adj.* guilty of or given to b. [OFr.].

BARREL (1) [ba'rel], *n.* long cylindrical vessel, usually made of curved staves or bars of wood secured by hoops at the ends and in the middle, and having its maximum girth in the middle; the quantity contained in a barrel; hollow metal tube in a firearm through which the shot is fired; revolving cylinder on which a chain, rope or spring is wound; cylindrical object forming the trunk or body of something; belly and loins of a horse etc.; reservoir of a fountain-pen; **b. of the ear**, hollow space in the ear behind the tympanum. BARREL-BULK, *n.* (*naut.*) five cubic feet. BARREL-VAULTED, *adj.* with a semi-cylindrical roof. BARREL (2), *v.t.* to put or pack in a b. [OFr.].

BARREL-ORGAN [ba'rel-aw-gan], *n.* large musical instrument played by street musicians and automatically producing a series of tunes when a driving handle is turned.

BARREN [ba'ren], *adj.* sterile, incapable of producing offspring; not producing fruit or seed; with little or no vegetation; (*fig.*) unfruitful, unprofitable; lacking ideas; **b. of**, totally deficient in. BARREN (2), *n.* barren region; (*pl.*) prairie land in Western America. BARRENNESS, *n.* state of being b., sterility [OFr.].

BARRETTER, BARETTER [ba-re'ter], *n.* (*elect.*) device for maintaining a constant flow of current in a circuit in spite of a possible change of voltage.

BARRICADE (1) [ba-ri-kād'], *n.* hastily and roughly improvised barrier for obstruction, protection or shelter. BARRICADE (2), *v.t.* to make or use a b. [Fr.].

BARRIER [ba'ri-er], *n.* obstacle or obstruction, generally to bar an approach; limit or boundary; erection designed to keep people from a particular place; (*fig.*) hindrance, obstacle preventing progress, restriction; **b. reef,** coral b. encircling islands or running parallel to a shore and enclosing a lagoon. [OFr.].

BARRING [bah'ring], *prep.* excepting, excluding. [BAR (1)].

BARRISTER [ba'ris-ter], *n.* person who has been called to the Bar by one of the Inns of Court, and who is entitled to plead as counsel in the higher courts. [BAR (1)].

BARROW (1) [ba'rō], *n.* small hand-cart with one or two wheels and legs, usually having handles by which it is raised or pushed; the amount contained in a barrow. [ME.].

BARROW (2), *n.* mound of earth or stone anciently built over a grave. [OE.].

BARRY [bah'ri], *adj.* (*her.*) divided across by an equal number of horizontal bars of two alternately recurring colours. [Fr.].

BARSAC [bah'sak], *n.* white wine made in Barsac, near Bordeaux.

BARTER (1) [bah'ter], *v.t.* to exchange goods of approximately equal value; (*fig.*) exchange; give away for an unworthy reward; bargain; *v.i.* to trade by exchanging goods. BARTER (2), *n.* trade carried on by exchange of goods instead of by money; that which is bartered. [OFr.].

BARTIZAN [bah-ti-zan'], *n.* turret overhanging the corner of an ancient fortification.

BARTON [bah'ton], *n.* farmyard. [OE.].

BARUKHZY [bah-ruk'zi], *n.* Afghan hound.

BARWOOD [bah'wood], *n.* red African dye-wood.

BARY-, *pref.* heavy. [Gk.].

BARYTA, BARIA [ba-ri'tah, bäer'i-ah], *n.* (*chem.*) barium monoxide.

BARYTES [ba-ri'téz], *n.* (*min.*) barium sulphate, occurring as a mineral deposit. BARYTIC [ba-ri'tik], *adj.* relating to or containing baryta or barium. [BARIUM].

BARYTONE, see BARITONE.

BASAL [bā'sal], *adj.* belonging to or forming the base; fundamental.

BASALT [ba'sawlt], *n.* (*geol.*) dark, crystalline, igneous rock, generally found in natural columns; black porcelain first made by Wedgwood. BASALTIC [ba-sawl'tik], *adj.* relating to or containing b. [L.].

BASANITE [ba'sa-nīt], *n.* (*min.*) black, compact, flinty slate. [Gk.].

BASCULE [bas'kyōōl], *n.* balanced lever centrally pivoted, one end rising when the other is lowered; **b. bridge,** bridge with a counterpoise operating in this way. [Fr.].

BASE (1) [bās], *n.* foundation on which an object rests, bottom or lowest part of anything; pedestal on which a statue stands; (*fig.*) chief element or constituent; groundwork, starting-point; (*arch.*) part of a column at the bottom of the shaft; (*milit.*) headquarters from which military operations proceed; (*bot.*) point of junction of an organ to a trunk; (*geom.*) lowest line or side of a plane or solid figure; (*chem.*) substance combining with an acid to form a salt; (*surveying*) line of which the length and position are accurately known, and which is used as starting-point for trigonometrical calculations; (*math.*) number used as a starting-point for logarithms; (*philol.*) root form of a word from which cognate forms in different languages are derived; (*baseball*) stations at the four points of the diamond over which the batsman must cross to score a run; **b. on balls,** (*baseball*) b. allowed to the batsman after receiving four legitimate balls; **b. hit,** hit by which a batsman is able to reach a b.; **b. hospital,** military hospital behind the field of battle. [Fr. from Gk.].

BASE (2), *adj.* low-lying; low in rank or condition, of humble origin; cowardly; of poor spirit; impure, worthless; (*leg.*) not free; **b. metals,** metals of low worth. [Fr.].

BASE (3), *v.t.* to place upon a foundation; *esp.* (*fig.*) place (ideas) upon a logical basis or starting-point; (*reflex.*) rely. [BASE (1) and (2)].

BASEBALL [bās'bawl], *n.* ball game resembling rounders, played by two teams of nine players on a field marked out as a diamond.

BASEBORN [bās-bawn'], *adj.* of humble parentage; illegitimate.

BASELESS [bās'les], *adj.* without foundation, unwarranted. BASELESSNESS, *n.* state or quality of being b., *esp.* of an accusation or charge.

BASELINE [bās'līn], *n.* line from which surveying and military operations begin; (*tennis*) one of the parallel lines marking the ends of a tennis-court; (*baseball*) the space a yard wide reaching from base to base.

BASELY [bās'li], *adv.* in base fashion.

BASEMENT [bās'ment], *n.* lowest inhabited room of a house, usually below ground level.

BASENESS [bās'nes], *n.* quality of being base.

BASH (1) [bash], *v.t.* (*coll.*) to strike violently; beat, thrash. BASH (2), *n.* (*coll.*) a blow. BASHER, *n.* (*coll.*) one who strikes heavy blows, *esp.* of a boxer. [~Dan.].

BASHFUL [bash'fōōl], *adj.* shy, timid, modest, shamefaced. BASHFULLY, *adv.* in a b. fashion. BASHFULNESS, *n.* state of being b. [ABASH].

BASHI-BAZOUKS [bah-shi-bah-zōōks'], *n.*(*pl.*) irregular volunteers in the Turkish army infamous for committing atrocities. [Turk.].

BASIC [bā'sik], *adj.* fundamental; forming the base; constituting a standard starting-point in scales of pay, rations etc.; (*chem.*) having the base in excess of the acid; **B. English,** simplified variety of English, with a vocabulary of about 850 words, apart from technical and scientific words. BASICALLY, *adv.* fundamentally, essentially. [BASE (1)].

BASICITY [ba-si'si-ti], *n.* (*chem.*) the capacity of an acid to combine with a base.

BASIC-SLAG [bā-sik-slag'], *n.* fertilizer obtained as a by-product of steel-smelting.

BASIL [ba'zil], *n.* aromatic herb. [OFr., Gk.].

BASILIAN [ba-zi'li-an], *n.* monk belonging to the order of St. Basil.

BASILICA [ba-si'li-kah], *n.* (*hist.*) royal palace; Roman public hall, oblong, with an apse at one end; Christian church resembling this. BASILIC(AL) [ba'si-lik, ba-si'li-kal], BASILICAN [ba-si'li-kan], *adj.* (*arch.*) pertaining to a b. [L. from Gk.].

BASILICON [ba-si'li-kon], *n.* resinous ointment supposed to act as a sovereign remedy. [Gk.].

BASILISK (1) [ba'si-lisk], *n.* fabulous African creature, said to be hatched by a snake from a cock's egg, whose look or breath was fatal; species of lizard having a crest which can be erected at will. BASILISK (2), *adj.* cold, relentless, deadly, full of venom. [Gk.].

BASIN [bā'sin], *n.* broad, shallow, hollow vessel with curved smooth sides sloping inwards towards a flat circular base; the amount contained in such a vessel; large hollow opening or depression in land containing water; harbour or bay enclosed by land; that area of a country drained by a river; a hollow; (*geol.*) trough or hollow formation in which the strata dip everywhere towards a common centre; shallow valley circular or oval in shape. BASINED, *adj.* contained in a b. [OFr.].

BASIS (*pl.* **bases**) [bā'sis], *n.* foundation, base, essential principle on which a thing is built up, chief constituent; (*milit.*) region from which military operations are originated. [Gk.].

BASK [bahsk], *v.i.* to enjoy oneself; expose oneself pleasurably to the sun's rays; revel in. [OIcel.].

BASKET [bahs'kit], *n.* hollow open receptacle made of cane, rushes etc.; receptacle resembling this; the contents of a basket; guard for the hand on a single-stick; **b. stitch,** one in which the stitches are taken into openings made by previous stitches; **pick of the b.,** the best, choicest. [ME.].

BASKET-BALL [bahs'kit-bawl], *n.* game played with a large ball, in which a goal is scored by dropping the ball into a basket-like receptacle suspended from the top of a pole.

BASKET-CHAIR [bahs'kit-chāer], *n.* chair made of wickerwork.

BASKET-FISH [bahs'kit-fish], *n.* species of starfish.

BASKET-HILT [bahs-kit-hilt'], *n.* hilt of basket-work used as a hand-guard on a fencing-stick or sword.

BASKETRY [bahs'kit-ri], *n.* wickerwork.

BASKETWORK [bahs'kit-werk], *n.* wickerwork.

BASKING-SHARK [bahs'king-shahk], *n.* species of shark; the sun-fish.

BASQUE (1) [bahsk], *n.* one of a race of people dwelling in the Western Pyrenees, having their own unrelated language; language spoken by the Basques; extension of a bodice below the waist. BASQUE (2), *adj.* pertaining to the Basques or to their language. [Fr., L.].

BAS-RELIEF, BASS-RELIEF [bas-ri-lēf'], *n.* method

The accent ′ after a syllable = stress (u-pon′). The mark ‾ over a vowel = length (ā in made; ō in bone).

of sculpture or carving in which the figures stand out slightly above the surface upon which they are carved; carving in this style. [It.].

BASS (1) [bas], *n.* (*zool.*) the common perch; allied N. American species; the sea perch and allied species. [OE.].

BASS (2), *n.* (*bot.*) the American linden-tree; inner bark of this tree; matting made from its bark; fibre obtained from the leaves of certain palms, used in making brooms, ropes etc. [Corruption of BAST].

BASS (3), *n.* proprietary brand of bitter ale. [*Bass*, the brewers].

BASS (4) [bās], *n.* (*mus.*) lowest range of notes in a vocal or instrumental composition; deepest male voice; one who sings the lowest part in the harmony; singer with a deep voice; lowest-sounding string of certain musical instruments. BASS (5), *adj.* very low and sonorous, deep sounding; indicating an instrument whose compass lies in the lowest register; suitable for a bass singer; **b. clef,** the F clef in the bottom stave. [Fr., It.].

BASS-BAR [bās'bah(r)], *n.* strip of wood inserted lengthwise in the body of string instruments, to resist the pressure of the bridge.

BASSET (1) [ba'sit], *n.* short-legged dog used in hunting. [Fr.].

BASSET (2), *n.* (*geol.*) portion of rock or stratum showing at the surface of the ground.

BASSET-HORN [ba'sit-hawn], *n.* tenor clarinet.

BASSETTE [ba-set'], *n.* small bass-viol. [It.].

BASS-HORN [bās-hawn'], *n.* bassoon with a deep tone.

BASSINETTE, BASSINET [ba-si-net'], *n.* wicker-work cradle with a hood; perambulator (shaped like this). [Fr.].

BASSO [ba'sō], *n.* singer with a bass voice. [It.].

BASSOON [ba-sōōn'], *n.* musical instrument of the wood-wind class, having a double reed and a deep bass tone. BASSOONIST, *n.* b. player. [Fr.].

BASS-RELIEF, see BAS-RELIEF.

BASS-VIOL [bās-vi'ol], *n.* violoncello.

BAST [bast], *n.* (*hort.*) inner bark of lime and other trees cut into strips and made into cords, mats etc., used by gardeners for tying. [OE.].

BASTA [bas'tah], *int.* stop! cease! [It.].

BASTARD (1) [bas'terd, bahs'terd], *n.* an illegitimate offspring. BASTARD (2) [bas'terd], *adj.* illegitimate; spurious, counterfeit; deviating from the normal in shape or size; **b. slip,** (*bot.*) sucker springing in an unexpected place from a tree; **b. bar,** (*her.*) heraldic sign of illegitimate descent. [OFr.].

BASTARDIZE [bas'ter-dīz], *v.t.* to pronounce or make illegitimate. BASTARDIZATION [bas-ter-dī-zā'shn], *n.* act of bastardizing.

BASTE (1) [bāst], *v.t.* to thrash or beat violently; put fat upon meat while roasting to moisten it. [Unkn.].

BASTE (2), *v.t.* to tack, sew with long loose stitches. [OFr.].

BASTILLE, BASTILE [bah-stēl'], *n.* (*milit.*) small fortress; huts used as dwelling places for besieging soldiers; old castle in Paris, used as a state prison and demolished by the Revolutionary mob in 1789. [Fr.].

BASTINADO (1), **BASTINADE** [bas-ti-nah'dō, bas-ti-nād'], *n.* Eastern form of punishment or torture, in which the soles of the victim's feet were beaten with a bamboo cane; a beating with a stick. BASTINADO (2), BASTINADE, *v.t.* to punish or torture by the b. [Span.].

BASTION [bas'ti-on], *n.* (*fort.*) advanced work with two flanks and two faces projecting from the angles of a rampart, as a salient angle. BASTIONED, *adj.* furnished with bastions. [Fr., It.].

BASUTO [ba-sōō'tō], *n.* member of a South African tribe of the Bantu group.

BAT (1) [bat], *n.* flying mammal with a body shaped like that of a mouse and a pair of large membranes attached to the forelegs and body to form wings. [ME., OScand.].

BAT (2), *n.* one of various kinds of clubs or implements used in striking the ball in various ball-games; sheet of cotton prepared for quilting; layer of fur or hair and wool used in making hats; a blow; (*coll.*, *cricket*) batsman; **to carry one's b.,** (*cricket*) to remain undefeated from the commencement until the close of one's side's innings; **off one's own b.,** (*coll.*) entirely unaided, without instruction. BAT (3), *v.t. and i.* to beat, wield a bat at cricket or baseball; (*cricket*) have an innings; beat with a stick or beater; move the eyelid quickly, wink. [OE.].

BATCH [bach], *n.* the quantity of bread made at a single baking; a quantity of similar things, group of things made at one time or arriving together. [ME., ~BAKE].

BATE (1) [bāt], *n.* alkaline solution used in tanning to soften hides. BATE (2), *v.t.* to steep hides in b. [Uncert.].

BATE (3), *n.* (*slang*) rage, temper, fury. [Unkn.].

BATE (4), *v.t. and i.* to lessen, reduce, diminish. BATED, *adj.* held back by conscious effort; **with b. breath,** in a state of awe or tense apprehension. [Fr.].

BATH (1) [bahth], *n.* vessel containing sufficient water for a person to be immersed in so as to wash the whole body; act of washing or soaking the body completely; quantity of liquid in which the whole or part of the body of persons may be soaked for remedial or medicinal purposes; swimming-pool; (*usu. pl.*) building in which baths of various kinds may be taken or swimming indulged in; (*phot.*) solution in which prints or plates are steeped; **Order of the B.,** a British order of chivalry; **B. bun,** spiced and sugared fruit bun originating from Bath; **B. Oliver,** kind of biscuit. BATH-BRICK, siliceous earth in the form of a brick, for cleaning stone and metal. BATH-METAL, alloy of zinc and copper. BATH (2), *v.t. and i.* to give a b. to; take a b. [OE.].

BATH-CHAIR [bahth-chãer'], *n.* chair in which invalids may be wheeled, first used at Bath.

BATHE (1) [bāth], *v.i.* to immerse the body in water in a bath, the sea, a river etc., either to cleanse it or for enjoyment and recreation; expose the body to the sun's rays; *v.t.* to pour liquid over (part of the body), soak in liquid; flow by, wash (of a river or sea); suffuse, saturate; (*fig.*) steep in or soak; **to b. in blood,** to cause bloodshed to. BATHE (2), *n.* act of bathing and swimming; immersion of the body in the sea, pools etc. for pleasure. BATHER [bã'THer], *n.* one who bathes. [OE.].

BATHETIC [ba-thet'ik], *adj.* relating to bathos.

BATHING [bã'THing], *n.* act of immersion of the body in water for recreation and enjoyment or for remedial purposes; **b. machine,** hut on wheels where bathers may undress. [BATHE (1)].

BATHOS [bã'thos], *n.* (*rhet.*) anti-climax, sudden passing from the sublime to the ridiculous, unexpected descent from the elevated and dignified to the commonplace and mean. [Gk.].

BATHYSCAPHE [ba'thi-skãf], *n.* a free-floating vessel in which men can descend to great depths in the sea for scientific observation. [Gk.].

BATHYSPHERE [ba'thi-sfēer], *n.* hollow metal sphere in which men can be lowered to a great depth in the sea. [Gk.].

BATIK [bah-tēk'], *n.* (*print.*) method used in printing coloured designs upon textiles. [Javanese].

BATING [bã'ting], *prep.* excepting. [BATE (4)].

BATISTE [ba-tēst'], *n.* kind of cambric.

BATMAN [baht'man], *n.* (*milit.*) officer's servant.

BATON [ba'ton], *n.* short staff or truncheon carried as a badge of office; wand used by conductors of orchestras; police officer's truncheon; (*her.*) truncheon in a shield; **b. sinister,** (*her.*) sign of illegitimacy. [Fr.].

BATRACHIA [ba-trã'ki-ah], *n.*(*pl.*) (*zool.*) order of amphibians, comprising frogs, toads and newts. BATRACHIAN (1), *n.* one of the b. BATRACHIAN (2), *adj.* pertaining to a batrachian. [Gk.].

BATS [bats], *adj.* crazy, having "b. in the belfry." [BAT (1)].

BATSMAN [bats'man], *n.* one who bats at cricket or baseball; one notable for his batting ability. BATSMANSHIP, *n.* art of batting.

BATTALION [ba-ta'li-on], *n.* (*milit.*) body of troops generally consisting of five companies; (*fig.*) legion or great number. BATTALIONED, *adj.* divided into battalions. [It.].

BATTELS [ba'telz], *n.*(*pl.*) provisions obtained from the buttery in an Oxford college; charge made for these. BATTEL, *v.i.* to obtain one's food as b. [Uncert.].

BATTEN (1), **BATTON** [ba'ten], *n.* long narrow board used for making floors, strengthening laths etc.; long narrow wooden bar nailed across a door as a clamp or support, or used to fasten down hatches on hatchways. BATTEN (2), *v.t.* to fasten or strengthen with battens. BATTENING, *n.* act of fastening battens; battens thus secured. [BATON].

BATTEN (3), *v.t. and i.* to become fat, thrive or become prosperous, feed luxuriously and parasitically. [OScand.].

BATTER (1) [ba'ter], *n.* mixture of flour, milk and

ōō is pronounced as in f*oo*d; ŏŏ as in h*oo*d; th as in *th*ink; TH as in *th*at; zh as in azure. ~ = related to.

eggs whipped together to a thick consistency for cooking; (print.) defective type or stereotype-plate. [Next].

BATTER (2), v.t. to strike with a succession of violent blows; disfigure by beating; (milit.) attack heavily with artillery or bombs; beat down or demolish. [OFr.].

BATTERED [ba'terd], adj. beaten; disfigured, dilapidated.

BATTERING-RAM [ba'te-ring-ram], n. (milit.) ancient military engine used for demolishing walls.

BATTERY [ba'te-ri], n. an attack with blows; (leg.) unlawful attack on the body of another; (milit.) number of guns grouped for action, unit of artillery with men and equipment; similar unit of search-lights; (elect.) cell or series of cells, each made of two electrodes in contact with certain chemicals to produce electricity on completing the external circuit; storage apparatus for electricity; (opt.) series of lenses in combination; (fig.) full resources at one's command. [Fr.].

BATTING [ba'ting], n. the wielding of a bat in cricket or baseball; cotton or wool in sheets, ready to be used to make quilts.

BATTLE (1) [ba'tl], n. fight or combat between large opposing bodies of armed men; contest, struggle, strife; **b. royal**, fight of the greatest vigour; cockfight with several birds taking part; **pitched b.**, one fought on specified or limited ground; **line of b.**, troops or ships drawn up in readiness for fighting. BATTLE (2), v.t. and i. to fight, contend, strive against. [OFr.].

BATTLE-AXE [ba'tl-aks], n. axe anciently used as a fighting weapon.

BATTLE-CRUISER [ba'tl-krōō-zer], n. large heavily armed and armoured cruiser comparable in size with a battleship.

BATTLE-CRY [ba'tl-kri], n. war-cry, martial slogan, rallying cry.

BATTLEDORE [ba'tl-daw(r)], n. light bat used in the game of battledore and shuttlecock; wooden instrument used in laundry work. [Uncert.].

BATTLE-DRESS [ba'tl-dres], n. modern uniform of the British Army, as opposed to parade or ceremonial wear.

BATTLEFIELD [ba'tl-fēld], n. place where a battle is fought.

BATTLEGROUND [ba'tl-grownd], n. place of conflict; (fig.) subject of dispute.

BATTLEMENT [ba'tl-ment], n. (arch.) indented parapet. BATTLEMENTED, adj. provided with battlements. [OFr.].

BATTLE-PLANE [ba'tl-plān], n. (aeron.) aeroplane equipped with guns and bomb-dropping apparatus.

BATTLE-SCHOOL [ba'tl-skōōl], n. establishment for training troops to become accustomed to the conditions of battle.

BATTLER [bat'ler], n. one who battles, fighter; (boxing) boxer remarkable for his vigour and pluck.

BATTLESHIP [ba'tl-ship], n. largest and most heavily armed type of warship; **pocket b.**, small warship of considerable power, yet of relatively light tonnage and armament.

BATTON, see BATTEN.

BATTUE [ba-tyōō'], n. method of killing game by surrounding a game-preserve with beaters who drive the game towards the sportsmen; game beaten up from cover in this way; wanton massacre. [Fr.].

BAUBEE, see BAWBEE.

BAUBLE [baw'bl], n. thing of little intrinsic value with an attractive exterior, trifle; (fig.) symbol of the transitoriness of human greatness. [OFr.].

BAULK, see BALK.

BAUXITE [bawk'sīt], n. rock from which aluminium is obtained. [Les Baux, in France, where mined].

BAWBEE, BAUBEE [baw'bē], n. Scots halfpenny. [Unkn.].

BAWD [bawd], n. procurer or procuress; prostitute; keeper of a brothel.

BAWDY (1) [baw'di], adj. unchaste, obscene. BAWDY (2), n. b. conversation or writing. BAWDILY, adv. in b. fashion. BAWDINESS, n. obscenity, lewdness. [ME.].

BAWDY-HOUSE [baw'di-hows], n. brothel.

BAWL (1) [bawl], v.t. and i. to shout loudly in a rough, rude manner; speak or sing in an unusually loud voice; **b. out**, (U.S.) to reprimand. BAWL (2), n. loud shout or cry.

BAWLING [baw'ling], n. act of shouting in a loud, rough voice.

BAY (1) [bā], n. opening or recess in a wall, often

between buttresses; space provided in a room by the outward projection of a window beyond the wall-line; horse's stall; forepart of a ship between decks used as a hospital; subordinate terminus line in a railway station. [OFr.].

BAY (2), n. large opening into the land, of a sea or lake; recess in a mountain range. [Fr.].

BAY (3), n. bay-tree; (pl.) wreath of laurels or bay leaves awarded for a noteworthy achievement; (fig.) honour, fame. [OFr. from L.].

BAY (4), adj. (only of horses) of a reddish colour, darker than chestnut. BAY (5), n. a b. horse. [Fr. from L.].

BAY (6), v.t. and i. to bark continuously (as hounds in pursuit of their quarry); bark at, pursue with barking. [OFr.].

BAY (7), n. the bark of a hound or pack of hounds; noise made by a pack of hounds as they come upon the hunted animal; **at b.**, (of a hunted animal) forced to halt and face its pursuers; (fig.) cornered, in dire straits; **to keep at b.**, to ward off. [Prec.].

BAYARD [bā'yahd], n. chivalrous person. [Chevalier Bayard, famous French knight].

BAYBERRY [bā'be-ri], n. wax-myrtle, the berry of which is used in making bay-rum.

BAYONET [bā'yo-net], n. short, sword-shaped blade which can be rapidly attached to the muzzle of a rifle; **b. cap, b. catch, b. fitting, b. joint**, cap etc., in which one member with small projections is secured to another with corresponding grooves. BAYONET, v.t. to transfix with a b. [Fr.].

BAYOU [bi'yōō], n. (U.S.) marshy creek or outlet in a river or lake in the southern states. [Uncert.].

BAY-RUM [bā-rum'], n. fragrant spirit obtained by distillation from the West Indian bayberry.

BAYSALT [bā'sawlt], n. salt formed in pits by evaporating sea-water. [BAY (2).].

BAY-TREE [bā'trē], n. laurel.

BAY WINDOW [bā-win'dō], n. large window built as a projection from a room.

BAZAAR [ba-zah(r)'], n. Eastern market-place; large store fitted up with stalls containing fancy goods; social function at which goods are sold, usually for charity, a sale of work. [Pers.].

BAZOOKA [ba-zōō'kah], n. American light anti-tank weapon, firing an explosive projectile through a tube. [Invented].

BDELLIUM [de'li-um], n. aromatic gum-resin from certain trees. [Gk.].

BE (1) (**am, is, are, was, were, been, being**), v. auxil. (a) used with the past participle of verbs to denote the passive voice, (b) with the past participles of certain intransitive verbs to form the perfect tense, (c) to express continuous action (with the present participle); used also as a link joining subject and predicate; v.i. to exist, have an existence, live, occur; stay, remain; be worth, cost; be made to be; be established; become; be the cause of; amount to; have to; be the same as; occupy the position or status of; **for the time being**, temporarily; **maybe**, perhaps; **to-b.**, future, intended; **b.-all**, the essential thing; **to be. off**, to depart; **to b. for**, to intend to go; support; **to b. in on**, (coll.) to take part in, know about. WOULD-BE, adj. desirous of being. [OE.].

BE- (2), pref. used to intensify, to form transitive verbs, to form verbs from nouns and adjectives; also with sense round, alongside. [OE.].

BEACH (1) [bēch], n. edge of a sea, lake or other large tract of water, usually a narrow strip of land covered with sand and pebbles; shore; strip of land at the edge of the sea exposed at low tide and inun-dated at high tide. BEACH (2), v.t. to drag up on to the b., run aground on a b.

BEACHCOMBER [bēch'kō-mer], n. long rolling wave; idle longshoreman, one who searches the beach for goods washed up by the sea.

BEACHHEAD [bēch'hed], n. fortified position established by an invading force on a shore held by the enemy.

BEACH-LA-MAR [bēch'la-mah(r)], n. kind of pidgin English used in the Western Pacific. [Portug.].

BEACHMASTER [bēch'mah-ster], n. officer respon-sible for the disembarkation of attacking troops.

BEACON (1) [bē'kon], n. fire lighted on a prominent hill as a signal of danger or of national rejoicing; lighthouse or prominent object used as a signal of warning of danger; hill forming a landmark; traffic-sign marking a place at which pedestrians have priority in crossing the road. BEACON (2), v.t. and i. to act as a b.; guide, warn or give a signal. [OE.].

BEAD (1) [bēd], n. small perforated piece of precious

stone, glass etc., threaded with many others on to a string, generally to form a necklace; small globular drop of liquid or moisture; (*arch.*) small rounded moulding or ornament; (*pl.*) collection of beads on a string forming a necklace or rosary; a prayer; small metal rounded protuberance forming the front-sight of a gun; flange of a pneumatic tyre; **to tell one's beads,** to say one's prayers; **to draw a b. on,** to take aim with a firearm. BEAD (2), *v.t. and i.* to furnish with beads, make into a string of beads, form into beads. BEADED, *adj.* covered or decorated with beads or beading; shaped like a b.; (of edges, as of tyres) thickened and rounded. [O.E.].

BEAD-FRAME [bēd′frām], *n.* abacus.

BEADING [bē′ding], *n.* narrow moulding.

BEADLE, BEDEL(L) [bē′dl], *n.* †parish officer appointed to supervise poor relief, act as constable etc.; court official or judicial servant of a trade guild or company; macebearer at certain universities, senior porter or attendant at a university; doorkeeper at a synagogue. BEADLEDOM, *n.* stupid officiousness. BEADLESHIP, *n.* position or rank of a b. [O.E.].

BEAD-PROOF [bēd′prŏŏf], *n.* rough method of determining the strength of spirituous liquors by observing the time the bubbles remain after shaking.

BEADSMAN, BEDESMAN [bēdz′man], *n.* one who prays for another; person endowed to pray for the souls of his benefactors; inmate of an almshouse; (*Scots*) licensed beggar. [M.E.].

BEADY [bē′di], *adj.* of the shape or appearance of beads; covered with beads; protruding and shining.

BEAGLE (1) [bē′gl], *n.* small hound for hunting hares, and followed on foot by the field. BEAGLE (2), *v.i.* to hunt with beagles, follow on foot after beagles. [M.E.].

BEAK [bēk], *n.* hooked, sharp-pointed termination of the jaws of birds; pointed, horny, mandible ends of animals such as the turtle; curved sharp-pointed peak or projection; projection at the prow of ancient warships; (*chem.*) spout of a retort; (*slang*) prominent, curved nose; magistrate or judge, headmaster. [Fr.].

BEAKER [bē′ker], *n.* drinking-cup; cylindrical glass vessel for laboratory use. [OScand.].

BEAM (1) [bēm], *n.* long straight heavy piece of timber or metal, often one of the main supports of a building or ship; wooden roller in a loom; chief timber or bar in a plough; bar forming the top pivoted member of a balance and from the extremities of which the scales are suspended; greatest width of a ship; pivoted bar transmitting the reciprocating motion of the piston-rod of a steam-engine to the crank end; crank of the wheel shaft; ray or column of light emitted by the sun, moon or other luminous body; concentrated stream of wireless waves directed to a specific place; (*fig.*) cheerful happy smile; expression of good-natured pleasure in a person's countenance; **on the b.,** (*naut.*) at right angles to the keel of a ship; **on her b. ends,** (*naut.*) (of a ship) keeled over and lying on her side; **to be on one's b. ends,** (*coll.*) to be hard pressed for money, be out of work; be at one's wits' end; **broad in the b.,** stout, thick-set; **to turn the b.,** to weigh; **b. sea,** a sea broadside on to the ship. BEAM (2), *v.i.* to shine, emit rays of light; (*fig.*) smile in a kindly fashion, radiate good-natured cheerfulness; *v.t.* to concentrate and direct (wireless waves); (*coll.*) send by b. wireless. [O.E.].

BEAM-COMPASS [bēm′kum-pas], *n.* instrument for drawing large circles.

BEAMING (1) [bē′ming], *n.* emission of rays of light. BEAMING (2), *adj.* radiant with happiness, smiling broadly.

BEAM-TREE [bēm′trē], *n.* tree related to the apple and pear. [WHITEBEAM.]

BEAM WIRELESS [bēm-wier′les], *n.* (*radio*) system for emitting short waves in a beam which does not disperse in all directions.

BEAMY [bē′mi], *adj.* like a beam; emitting rays of light; radiant; (of a stag) having antlers; broad.

BEAN [bēn], *n.* one of several kinds of comestible leguminous seeds grown in pods; plant which produces these seeds; **old b.,** (*slang*) old fellow; **full of beans,** in high spirits; **to give a person beans,** to punish severely; **not to have a b.,** to be penniless. [O.E.].

BEANFEAST [bēn′fēst], *n.* dinner or excursion of celebration; (*slang*) jolly outing. [Gael.].

BEAN-GOOSE [bēn′gōōs], *n.* wild goose.

BEANO [bē′nō], *n.* (*slang*) beanfeast.

BEAR (1) [bāer], *n.* powerfully built, large mammal

with a thick shaggy coat and strong claws; (*fig.*) clumsy ill-mannered person; (*Stock Exchange*) one who sells stock to be delivered on a specified future date, in the hope that by that time the price will have fallen, and he will be able to buy at a lower rate than that at which he has sold; **Great B. and Little B.,** two constellations in the northern hemisphere. BEAR (2), *v.i.* (*comm.*) to cause the depreciation of stocks and shares. [O.E.].

BEAR (3) (*pret.* **bore, bare†,** *p.pt.* **borne**), *v.t.* to support, carry; push; suffer, endure; wear, exhibit, admit of, be suitable for, stand the test of; possess and use, wield; have written on; (*pass.*) have one's name on the books of; cherish; tolerate, submit to; bring forth, give birth to, yield; (*reflex.*) comport, behave; *v.i.* to suffer; have or take effect; be situated in a certain direction with respect to something else; make one's way in a certain direction, turn; have relation to, concern (with *on*); rest, lean; be strong enough to sustain a weight; **to b. away,** (*naut.*) to change the course of a ship so that it runs before the wind; **to b. down,** to overthrow, force to the ground; (*naut.*) drive towards; **to b. down upon,** to approach; (*naut.*) crowd on all sail in order to come near; **to b. in,** (*naut.*) to run or sail towards; **to b. out,** to support, confirm, justify; **to b. up,** to keep up one's courage, cheer up; **to b. with,** to tolerate, allow for; be patient with; **to b. a hand,** to help; **to b. in mind,** to remember, take into consideration; **to b. witness,** to testify to, give proof of; **to bring to b.,** to bring into effective operation (upon); **borne in upon,** impressed upon. [O.E.].

BEARABLE [bāer′a-bl], *adj.* able to be endured. BEARABLY, *adv.* in b. fashion.

BEAR-BAITING [bāer′bā-ting], *n.* ancient amusement of baiting bears with dogs.

BEARD (1) [bēerd], *n.* hair growing on a man's face, *esp.* on the cheeks, chin and adjacent parts; tuft on the chin of a goat, lion etc.; (*zool.*) gills of the oyster and other bivalves; (*bot.*) awn of grasses; web of a feather; (*print.*) front part of type extending beyond the face, allowing for proper spacing between the lines; horizontal additions to the letters. BEARD (2), *v.t.* to pull the b. of; tackle boldly, discuss frankly some delicate question. BEARDED, *adj.* possessing a b. [O.E.].

BEARDLESS [bēerd′les], *adj.* lacking a beard; (*fig.*) youthful. BEARDLESSNESS, *n.* condition of being b.

BEARD-MOSS [bēerd′mos], *n.* the grey lichen.

BEARER [bāer′er], *n.* one who bears something; porter; member of a medical corps whose duty is to carry the wounded from the field; one on whose shoulders the coffin is borne at a funeral; one who holds or walks beside the pall spread over the coffin at a funeral; (*bot.*) fruit-yielding tree or plant; one who delivers a letter; one who presents a cheque or banknote payable on demand; (*eng., carp.* etc.) device for sustaining the weight of something; **b. bonds,** securities on which the owner's name is not inscribed, and which can be transferred without formality. [M.E.].

BEAR-GARDEN [bāer′gah-den], *n.* place where bears were baited; noisy assembly; scene of great disorder.

BEARING [bāer′ing], *n.* connexion, relation; aspect, mien, behaviour; suffering, endurance; direction with respect to a meridian, direction in which a point lies, situation of a point with regard to a fixed point in terms of the compass points; action of producing or giving birth to; (*her.*) charge or device on a shield; (*mech.*) surface upon which a machine shaft rotates, or which takes the end thrust of a shaft; **to take one's bearings,** to find out one's position and establish one's course (mentally or physically); **to lose one's bearings,** to lose one's sense of location, direction or proportion.

BEARING-REIN [bāer′ing-rān], *n.* rein fixed from the bit to the saddle to keep a horse's head lifted; (*fig.*) restraining influence.

BEARISH [bāer′ish], *adj.* like a bear; rough-mannered, surly; (of a stock-market) showing a tendency for prices to fall.

BEARLEADER [bāer′lē-der], *n.* keeper of a bear; (*coll.*) tutor who travels around with his pupil.

BEAR-PIT [bāer′pit], *n.* shallow pit where bears are kept.

BEAR'S GREASE [bāerz′grēs], *n.* fat of bears made into a pomade.

BEARSKIN [bāer′skin], *n.* skin of a bear; tall fur cap worn by the Brigade of Guards.

BEAST [bēst], *n.* animal, animal of lower order than

ŏŏ is pronounced as in food; ōō as in hood; th as in *think*; TH as in *that*; zh as in azure. ~ = related to.

DSE—C

man, mammal as distinct from birds, fishes etc.; domestic bovine animal, animal used for carrying burdens; (fig.) human being with the unpleasant characteristics or behaviour of an animal; coarser or lower nature in man; (coll.) exceptionally difficult thing or person; **the B.**, Antichrist. [OFr., L.].

BEASTLY (1) [bēst′li], adj. like a beast in behaviour; brutal, filthy, coarse; unpleasant, very bad; obscene, disgusting. BEASTLY (2), adv. in the manner of a beast; (coll.) used in an intensifying sense. BEAST-LINESS, n. quality of being b. [ME.].

BEAT (1) [bēt], n. stroke or blow; regularly recurring stroke, pulsation or throb; path or course habitually patrolled; (mus.) movement of the hand used to indicate rhythm and time in music; main stresses in a measure of music or of poetry; (acoustics, mus.) pulsation arising from the joint vibrations of two sounds of slightly different pitch sounding simultaneously; (radio) pulsation caused by two wavemotions of slightly different frequency being superimposed. [Next].

BEAT (2) [pret. **beat**, p.pt. **beaten**], v.t. to strike or hit repeatedly or continuously, chastise by repeated blows, thrash; conquer, defeat, surpass; shape by hammering; prove too difficult for, baffle; reduce to a powder by pounding; stir up rapidly; dash or strike against, knock; tread down; force out of; v.i. to throb, pulsate; strike down with force; **to b. about**, to run in all directions in an endeavour to escape; (naut.) sail against the wind by tacking; **to b. about the bush**, to evade the point at issue; **to b. down**, to force a person to reduce his price by bargaining; **to b. the air**, to work at something which can have no result; **to b. the band**, to be very remarkable or surprising; **to b. the bounds**, to traverse the boundaries of a district or parish and strike the principal boundary marks with rods as a method of indicating them; **to b. time**, to indicate the accents and time of a piece of music by regular motions of the hand or foot; **to b. up**, to thrash soundly; (naut.) sail against the wind by tacking; **to b. up and down**, (hunting) to double on one's tracks; **to b. the tattoo**, to call to quarters; **to b. a retreat**, to run away; **to b. it**, (slang) to run away. [OE.].

BEAT (3), adj. in a state of extreme fatigue, esp. **dead b.**; (coll.) exhausted. [Prec.].

BEATEN [bē′ten], adj. vanquished; fatigued; wrought or hammered out; thrashed; trodden down. [BEAT (2)].

BEATER [bē′ter], n. one who strikes or beats; instrument for pounding, hammering or whisking substances; one employed in beating up game.

BEATIFIC(AL) [bē-a-ti′fik(-al)], adj. making happy; blessed, radiant. BEATIFICALLY, adv. in b. fashion. [L.].

BEATIFY [bē-a′ti-fī], v.t. to make happy; bless with heavenly enjoyment; (R.C.) declare publicly and officially that a person is received into heaven, and is to be reverenced as blessed. BEATIFICATION [bē-a-ti-fi-kā′shn], n. (R.C.) act of beatifying. [LL.].

BEATING [bē′ting], n. act of a person or thing that beats; punishment by infliction of repeated blows; defeat. [ME.].

BEATITUDE [bē-a′ti-tyōōd], n. happiness of the highest order, extreme felicity; a saying ascribing particular blessedness; (pl.) heavenly joys enunciated in the Sermon on the Mount. [L.].

BEAU (pl. **beaux**) [bō, bōz], n. foppish, dandified, faultlessly attired, affected man; lady's man; (slang) young woman's boy friend. [Fr.].

BEAU-GESTE [bō-zhest′], n. act of kindness or graciousness, good deed. [Fr.].

BEAU-IDEAL [bō-i-dēal′], n. the ideal, conception of perfection.

BEAUJOLAIS [bō-zho′lā], n. a red Burgundy wine. [Fr.].

BEAU-MONDE [bō-mond′], n. the fashionable world, society. [Fr.].

BEAUNE [bōn], n. a red Burgundy wine. [Fr.].

BEAUTEOUS [byōō′ti-ōōs], adj. beautiful.

BEAUTIFUL (1) [byōō′ti-fōōl], adj. endowed with beauty, pleasing and delighting the senses (esp. the ear and eye); approaching perfection of its kind, excellent, admirable, lovely. BEAUTIFUL (2), n. that which constitutes or has beauty. BEAUTIFULLY, adv. in a b. fashion; perfectly, admirably.

BEAUTIFY [byōō′ti-fī], v.t. to make beautiful; ornament, adorn. BEAUTIFIER, n. person who or thing which beautifies, decorator. [BEAUTY].

BEAUTY [byōō′ti], n. a combination of qualities or attributes arousing a sense of aesthetic satisfaction or affording keen pleasure and delight to the senses; material and spiritual feature giving charm or satisfaction; beautiful lady; excellent example of its kind; used ironically as the reverse of its true meaning; term of affection. BEAUTY-CULTURE, art of acquiring or maintaining personal b. by artificial methods. BEAUTY-PARLOUR, establishment where personal b. may be attained by artificial methods. BEAUTY-SLEEP, sleep obtained before midnight. BEAUTY-SPOT, small patch or spot placed on the face to heighten b.; beautiful place amid pleasant surroundings. [Fr.].

BEAVER (1) [bē′ver], n. large rodent, living by rivers and lakes; fur of the beaver; hat made of beaver fur; (slang) person with a beard. [OE.].

BEAVER (2), n. front lower guard of a helmet.

BECALM [bi-kahm′], v.t. and i. to calm, appease; (naut.) come to rest through the absence of wind (of a sailing ship). BECALMED, adj. (naut.) unable to proceed through lack of wind.

BECAME [bi-kām′], pret. of BECOME. [ME.].

BECAUSE [bi-koz′], conj. and adv. for this reason; on account of this; since, seeing that; inasmuch as. [ME.].

BECCAFICO [be-ka-fē′kō], n. (ornith.) small migratory bird eaten in Italy as a delicacy. [It.].

BECHAMEL, **béchamel** [be′sha-mel], n. white sauce of butter, flour and milk. [Marquis de Béchamel, inventor.].

BECHANCE [bi-chahns′], v.t. to befall, happen.

BECHE-DE-MER, **bêche-de-mer** [bāsh-de-māer′], n. a sea-slug; South Sea trading dialect of Melanesia. [Fr.].

BECK (1) [bek], n. a stream. [OScand.].

BECK (2), v.t. and i. to beckon. BECK (3), n. silent signal or gesture made by a slight movement of the hand, finger or head; a nod; **at one's b. and call**, in continual and subservient attendance. [Short form of BECKON].

BECKET [be′kit], n. device in ships to secure loose ropes, tackles etc. [Unkn.].

BECKON [be′kon], v.t. and i. to call someone by means of a slight movement of the hand, finger or head; greet by a gesture of acknowledgment. [OE.].

BECLOUD [bi-klowd′], v.t. to cloud, obscure.

BECOME [pret. **became**, p.pt. **become**] [bi-kum′], v.t. to suit, be in agreement with; enhance one's personal appearance; be suitable for; **to b. of**, to happen to; v.i. to come to be; develop into, acquire the characteristics, rank or position of. [OE.].

BECOMING [bi-ku′ming], adj. suitable, fit; charming. BECOMINGLY, adv. in a b. fashion. BECOMINGNESS, n. condition of being b.

BED (1) [bed], n. that on which something rests; something on which a person or animal may rest or sleep; framework, supported on four legs, on which is placed a mattress and coverings, and designed for purposes of resting or sleeping; (fig.) sexual relations; plot of ground in which plants are cultivated; bottom of a river, sea, lake etc.; stratum of rock or other mineral; solid, level surface forming a foundation upon which a structure, machine etc. lies; **b. and board**, lodging and food; **bring to b.**, to be delivered of a child; **to die in one's b.**, to die from natural causes; **to keep one's b.**, **take to one's b.**, to become ill; **to make a b.**, to straighten and rearrange the coverings, mattress and pillow; **to get out of b. on the wrong side**, to be bad-tempered and irritable. [OE.].

BED (2) [pres.pt. **bedding**, pret. and p.pt. **bedded**], v.t. and i. to place in a bed; plant (flowers or vegetables) in a bed; lay flat on a bed or solid foundation. [Prec.].

BEDABBLE [bi-da′bl], v.t. to sprinkle, moisten; splash, stain.

BEDAZZLE [bi-da′zl], v.t. to confuse or cloud the sight by its brilliance, dazzle completely.

BED-BUG [bed′bug], n. parasitic insect.

BEDCHAMBER [bed′chăm-ber], n. room to sleep in; **Ladies of the B.**, certain ladies appointed to wait upon the queen; **Gentlemen and Grooms of the B.**, certain officers of the royal household, whose duty it is to wait upon the sovereign.

BEDCLOTHES [bed′klōthz], n.(pl.) sheets, blankets, coverlets etc. for a bed.

BEDDER [be′der], n. one who attends to the repose of animals; plant suitable for cultivation in a flower-bed; (slang) woman who makes the beds of students in some universities; bedroom.

BEDDING [be′ding], n. blankets, covers, sheets,

mattress etc. which form a bed when placed on the framework; straw, hay etc. used to make a bed for animals; foundation; formation of rocks in strata; process of setting plants in beds. [BED (1)].

BEDECK [bi-dek′], v.t. to deck out, adorn.

BEDEL(L), see BEADLE.

BEDESMAN, see BEADSMAN.

BEDEVIL (pres.pt. **bedevilling,** pret. and p.pt. **bedevilled**) [bi-de′vil], v.t. to throw into confusion and disorder, upset thoroughly; exasperate, bewitch. BEDEVILMENT, n. state of being bedevilled, exasperation.

BEDEW [bi-dyōō′], v.t. to moisten with dew; suffuse or sprinkle with.

BEDFELLOW [bed′fe-lō], n. one who occupies a bed with another; (fig.) associate, companion.

BEDIM (pres.pt. **bedimming,** pret. and p.pt. **bedimmed**) [bi-dim′], v.t. to make dim, obscure.

BEDIZEN [bi-di′zen, bi-di′zen], v.t. to deck out in garish fashion.

BEDLAM (1) [bed′lam], n. priory of St. Mary of Bethlehem, in London, later turned into a hospital for lunatics; madhouse, asylum; (fig.) uproarious assembly, pandemonium. BEDLAM (2), adj. fit for a madhouse, resembling a madhouse. BEDLAMITE, n. a patient of Bethlehem Hospital; lunatic. [Late ME.].

BEDLINEN [bed′li-nin], n. linen for beds.

BEDLINGTON [bed′ling-ton], n. kind of terrier. [Bedlingtonshire, place in Northumberland].

BEDMAKER [bed′mā-ker], n. one who makes beds; bedder.

BEDOUIN (1), **BEDUIN** [be′dōō-in], n. (sg. and pl.) nomadic race of Arabs; member of such a tribe. BEDOUIN (2), BEDUIN, adj. pertaining to the Bedouin. [Arab.].

BED-PAN [bed′pan], n. chamber-pot for use in bed.

BEDPLATE [bed′plāt], n. plate forming the bed of a machine.

BEDPOST [bed′pōst], n. one of the four posts at the corner of a bed to which the frame is fastened.

BEDRAGGLE [bi-dra′gl], v.t. to soil by trailing through mud and dirt in walking; cause to hang down limply through being wet.

BED-REST [bed′rest], n. piece of furniture for supporting the back when sitting up in bed.

BEDRIDDEN [bed′ri-den, bed′rid], adj. confined to bed by age or infirmity. [OE.].

BED-ROCK (1) [bed′rok], n. solid rock existing beneath alluvial or other loose formations; (fig.) essential facts or foundations. BED-ROCK (2), adj. lowest, fundamental.

BEDSIDE (1) [bed′sīd], n. side or immediate vicinity of a bed. BEDSIDE (2), adj. for use beside the bed; **b. manner,** (fig.) (of a doctor) manner calculated to win confidence or inspire cheerfulness.

BED-SITTING-ROOM [bed-si′ting-rōōm], n. room combining the functions of bedroom and sitting-room.

BED-SOCKS [bed′soks], n.(pl.) knitted woollen socks worn in bed.

BEDSORE [bed′saw(r)], n. sore on the skin, caused through continued lying in bed in one position.

BEDSPREAD [bed′spred], n. cover spread upon the top of a bed in the daytime to keep out dust etc.

BEDSTEAD [bed′sted], n. frame supporting a mattress and other bedding.

BEDSTRAW [bed′straw], n. plant of the genus Galium. [ME.].

BED-TABLE [bed′tā-bl], n. small short-legged table, which can be put on a bed, for the use of an invalid etc.

BEDTICK [bed′tik], n. covering for a mattress etc.

BEDTIME [bed′tīm], n. hour for going to bed.

BEDUIN, see BEDOUIN.

BEE [bē], n. genus of hymenopterous insects, esp. the honey-bee; number of persons gathered together for some charitable purpose, competition etc.; (fig.) busy worker; **spelling b.,** spelling game or contest; **to have a b. in one's bonnet,** to be obsessed with an idea to an unreasonable extent. BEE-BREAD, pollen gathered by bees as food for their young. BEE-GLUE, propolis. BEE-ORCHIS, plant with flower in part resembling a b. [OE.].

BEECH [bēch], n. tree with a smooth bark and oval-shaped leaves. BEECH-MARTEN, stone-marten. BEECH-MAST, fruit or nut of the b. BEECH-OIL, oil obtained from beech-mast. [OE.].

BEECHEN [bē′chen], adj. consisting of beechwood or beech bark. [OE.].

BEECHWOOD [bēch′wood], n. wood of the beech.

BEEF (1) (pl. **beeves**†) [bēf, bēvz], n. name formerly given to an ox; now the flesh of an ox, bull or cow when killed; (fig.) flesh and muscle; power, vigour. BEEF (2), v.i. (slang) to complain loudly. [Fr.].

BEEFEATER [bē′fē-ter], n. Yeoman of the Guard, warder of the Tower of London; genus of African birds.

BEEFINESS [bē′fi-nes], n. state of being beefy.

BEEFSTEAK [bēf′stāk], n. thick slice of beef.

BEEF-TEA [bēf-tē′], n. broth made from stewed beef, often given to invalids.

BEEF-WOOD [bēf′wood], n. reddish timber obtained from certain Australian trees.

BEEFY [bē′fi], adj. resembling beef; resembling an ox in physical characteristics.

BEE-HAWK [bē′hawk], n. (zool.) the honey-buzzard.

BEEHIVE [bē′hīv], n. structure in which bees are kept and in which they store up honey. [ME.].

BEELINE [bē′līn], n. undeviating direct line; **to make a b. for,** to rush straight towards, along the shortest path of approach.

BELZEBUB [bē-el′zi-bub], n. the prince of devils, Satan. [Heb.].

BEEN [bēn], p.pt. of the verb BE.

BEER [bēer], n. alcoholic beverage usually made from fermented malted barley flavoured with hops; **small b.,** weak inferior b.; (fig.) of little account or value. BEER-BARREL, barrel in which b. is kept. BEER-ENGINE, -PUMP, hand-pump for drawing beer from barrels in a cellar to the bar. BEER-MONEY, allowance made to hired labourers instead of beer. BEER-PULL, handle of a beer-pump. BEERSHOP, licensed house at which beer may be sold. [OE.].

BEERY [bēer′i], adj. having the taste or smell of beer; slightly intoxicated; showing signs of having consumed beer, or of fondness for beer.

BEESTINGS [bē′stingz], n.(pl.) first milk yielded by a cow after calving. [OE.].

BEESWAX (1) [bēz′waks], n. solid substance secreted by bees, with which they construct their combs. BEESWAX (2), v.t. to polish with beeswax.

BEESWING [bēz′wing], n. film of tartar which forms on old port wine.

BEET [bēt], n. plant having two species: one with crimson roots, used as a vegetable, the other with white, used for the production of sugar. [OE.].

BEETLE (1) [bē′tl], n. kind of insect whose wings are covered and protected by hard outer wing-cases; (pop.) the large black variety, the cockroach. [OE.].

BEETLE (2), n. heavy, solid piece of wood furnished with a small projecting handle, and used for hammering in paving-blocks etc. BEETLE (3), v.t. to hammer or crush with a b. [OE.].

BEETLE (4), v.i. to project, jut out over. BEETLE (5), adj. overhanging; (of eyebrows) bushy. [Unkn.].

BEETLE-BROW [bē-tl-brow′], n. prominent, overhanging brow. BEETLE-BROWED, adj. having a b.

BEETLING [bēt′ling], adj. overhanging, projecting.

BEETROOT [bēt′root], n. crimson root of the beet, used as a vegetable.

BEET SUGAR [bēt-shōō′ger], n. sugar extracted from beet.

BEEVES†, n.pl. of BEEF.

BEFALL (pret. **befell,** p.pt. **befallen**) [bi-fawl′], v.t. and i. to happen, occur, take place; happen to. [OE.].

BEFIT (pres.pt. **befitting,** pret. and p.pt. **befitted**) [bi-fit′], v.t. to suit, be fitting for, become.

BEFLOWER [bi-flow′er], v.t. to adorn with flowers.

BEFOG (pres.pt. **befogging,** pret. and p.pt. **befogged**) [bi-fog′], v.t. to envelop completely in fog, cloud over with fog; (fig.) obscure, perplex.

BEFOOL [bi-fōōl′], v.t. to delude, fool completely, deceive. [ME.].

BEFORE (1) [bi-faw(r)′], adv. in front, farther on ahead; preceding, earlier; previously, ago; already. BEFORE (2), prep. and conj. in front of; in the presence or sight of; ahead of; in preference to, sooner than; earlier than, in less time than; confronting; rather than, previous to, **to be b. the mast,** (naut.) to be a common sailor; in the same direction as, and driven by, the wind. [OE.].

BEFOREHAND [bi-faw′hand], adv. in advance, in anticipation of; in front, ahead of schedule; **to be b. with,** to foresee, be prepared in advance for. [ME.].

BEFOUL [bi-fowl′], v.t. to soil, make dirty, pollute.

BEFRIEND [bi-frend′], v.t. to make friends with; act kindly towards.

BEG (pres.pt. **begging,** pret. and p.pt. **begged**)

ōō is pronounced as in food; ŏŏ as in hood; th as in think, TH as in that; zh as in azure.   ~ = related to.

[beg], *v.t. and i.* to make known to another a desire so that it may be effected; ask for charity, request as a gift; ask a favour, implore, beseech; (of animals) sit up with the forepaws outstretched; ask humbly, politely or formally; **to b. to,** to take the liberty of, presume; **to b. the question,** to avoid the point at issue; **to go a-begging,** to be not taken advantage of. [Uncert.].

BEGAD [bi-gad'], *int.* exclamation or polite oath.
BEGAN [bi-gan'], *pret.* of BEGIN.
BEGET (*pres.pt.* **begetting,** *pret.* **begot,** *p.pt.* **begotten**) [bi-get'], *v.t.* to get, procreate; (*fig.*) cause, bring about. BEGETTER, *n.* person who begets. [OE.].
BEGGAR (1) [be'ger], *n.* one who begs, one who obtains his living by soliciting alms; person living in a state of extreme poverty; (*coll.*) rogue, fellow. BEGGAR (2), *v.t.* to reduce to poverty, ruin; (*fig.*) upset, make useless, spoil; **b. my neighbour,** card game in which the aim is to acquire the whole of an opponent's cards. [ME.].
BEGGARLY (1) [be'ger-li], *adj.* poor, mean, trifling, meagre, squalid. BEGGARLY (2), *adv.* in a poor manner. BEGGARLINESS, *n.* condition of being b.
BEGGARY [be'ga-ri], *n.* extreme poverty, destitution. [ME.].
BEGGING (1) [be'ging], *n.* the practice of asking for alms or gifts. BEGGING (2), *adj.* asking for something; mendicant.
BEGIN (*pres.pt.* **beginning,** *pret.* **began,** *p.pt.* **begun**) [bi-gin'], *v.t. and i.* to start, commence, perform the initial act of; enter upon; originate; have an original existence; **to b. with,** first of all. [OE.].
BEGINNER [bi-gi'ner], *n.* one who begins; (*fig.*) learner, novice.
BEGINNING [bi-gi'ning], *n.* the start, origin, sources; (*pl.*) the rudiments, elements.
BEGIRD (*pret. and p.pt.* **begirt**) [bi-gurd'], *v.t.* to fasten with a girdle; surround, enclose, bind. [OE.].
BEGONE [bi-gon'], *int.* go away! depart! [ME.].
BEGONIA [bi-gō'ni-ah], *n.* genus of tropical plants with gaily coloured flowers. [Michel *Begon,* French botanist].
BEGOT [bi-got'], *pret.* of BEGET.
BEGRIME [bi-grim'], *v.t.* to blacken with dirt, soil, make dirty.
BEGRUDGE [bi-gruj'], *v.t.* to be reluctant to allow, envy for having something, give unwillingly, grudge. [ME.].
BEGUILE [bi-gil'], *v.t.* to deceive, cheat; deprive of under false pretences; charm, divert; pass (the time etc.) in pleasant manner; (*reflex.*) amuse oneself. BEGUILEMENT, *n.* act of beguiling; that which beguiles; state of being beguiled. BEGUILER, *n.* person who or thing that beguiles. BEGUILING, *adj.* deluding; charming. BEGUILINGLY, *adv.* in a beguiling way. [ME.].
BEGUINE [be'gēn], *n.* member of a twelfth-century Netherlands order of women who, without taking a monastic vow, spent their time in devotion and charity. [Lambert le *Bègue,* founder].
BEGUM [bē'gum], *n.* Indian title for a Moslem princess or lady of rank. [Turk.].
BEGUN [bi-gun'], *p.pt.* of BEGIN.
BEHALF [bi-hahf'], *n.* **on b. of,** *prep.* instead of, in place of, as representative of. [BY and HALF].
BEHAVE [bi-hāv'], *v.i. and reflex.* to act, conduct oneself, acquit oneself (in a particular way); conduct oneself properly, exhibit good manners; (*fig.*) (of a machine) function; **well-, ill-behaved,** having good (bad) manners. [OE.].
BEHAVIOUR [bi-hāv'yer], *n.* way in which a person or thing acts; conduct, manners, mode of behaving; reaction under a set of imposed conditions.
BEHAVIOURISM [bi-hāv'ye-rizm], *n.* psychological method of observing conduct in response to externally applied mental or physical stimuli; theory that reactions to particular external stimuli will always be the same.
BEHEAD [bi-hed'], *v.t.* to decapitate, cut off the head of. BEHEADING, *n.* act of cutting off the head. [OE.].
BEHELD [bi-held'], *pret. and p.pt.* of BEHOLD.
BEHEST [bi-hest'], *n.* command, request, order. [OE.].
BEHIND (1) [bi-hīnd'], *adv.* in the rear, backwards; remaining after a departure; past; in arrears; on the further side and invisible to an observer; not apparent, held in reserve; **to fall b.,** to be in arrears. BEHIND (2), *prep.* at the back of, to the rear of, on the remote side of; after; inferior to; in support of;

b. one's back, without one's knowledge, in an underhand, deceitful way; **b. the scenes,** (*fig.*) not disclosed or known to the public, secret; **b. time,** late; **to put b. oneself,** to dismiss from one's consideration. BEHIND (3), *n.* (*coll.*) the buttocks. [OE.].
BEHINDHAND [bi-hīnd'hand], *adj. and adv.* late, slow, backward; in arrears, slightly antiquated.
BEHOLD (*pret. and p.pt.* **beheld**) [bi-hōld'], *v.t. and i.* to see, witness, look carefully at, fix one's eyes upon; (*imper.*) look! consider! [OE.].
BEHOLDEN† [bi-hōl'den], *pred. adj.* grateful, deeply obliged; indebted. [BEHOLD].
BEHOOF [bi-hōōf'], *n.* advantage, profit, benefit. [ME.].
BEHOVE [bi-hōv'], *v. impers.†* to be necessary; be incumbent upon. [OE.].
BEIGE [bāzh], *n.* an undyed, unbleached woollen fabric; pinkish shade of buff. [Fr. from LL.].
BEING [bē'ing], *n.* existence, life; person who is alive; essential nature; **the Supreme B.,** God.
BEJEWELLED [bi-jōō'eld], *adj.* adorned with jewels.
BEKNOWN [bi-nōn'], *adj.* known.
BEL [bel], *n.* unit of measurement of intensity of sound. [BELL (1)].
BELABOUR [bi-lā'ber], *v.t.* to thrash soundly; (*fig.*) exert strenuous efforts upon.
BELATE [bi-lāt'], *v.t.* to cause to be late, delay.
BELATED [bi-lā'tid], *adj.* arriving late, coming too late, overdue. BELATEDNESS, *n.* condition of being b.
BELAUD [bi-lawd'], *v.t.* to praise excessively.
BELAY [bi-lā'], *v.t.* (*naut.*) to secure (a running rope) by winding it round a fixed pin or cleat. BELAYING-CLEAT, -PIN [bi-lā'ing-klēt, -pin], *n.* (*naut.*) horizontal piece of wood or iron with projecting ends, to which a rope may be temporarily fastened. [~OE.].
BEL CANTO [bel-can'tō], *n.* (*mus.*) style of singing which pays special attention to a smooth, musical (as distinct from dramatic) interpretation of a piece. [It.].
BELCH (1) [belch, belsh], *n.* noisy expulsion of wind upwards from the stomach, eructation; (*fig.*) sudden eruption of smoke, flames etc. BELCH (2), *v.t. and i.* to make a b.; (*fig.*) spurt forth, emit suddenly in large quantities. [OE.].
BELCHER [bel'cher], *n.* coloured neckerchief. [J. *Belcher,* famous pugilist].
BELDAM(E) [bel'dam], *n.* old woman; violent, obscene hag. [OFr.].
BELEAGUER [bi-lē'ger], *v.t.* to besiege, blockade. BELEAGUERMENT, *n.* act of beleaguering, state of being beleaguered. [Du.].
BELFRY [bel'fri], *n.* that part of a church tower or steeple in which the bells are hung; **to have bats in the b.,** to be crazy, mad or eccentric. [OFr.].
BELGA [bel'gah], *n.* Belgian unit of money, equivalent to five francs. [L.].
BELGIAN (1) [bel'jan], *n.* native of Belgium. BELGIAN (2), *adj.* pertaining to or belonging to Belgium.
BELGIC [bel'jik], *adj.* pertaining to the Belgae; Belgian. [L.].
BELGRAVIAN (1) [bel-grā'vi-an], *n.* one of the upper classes. BELGRAVIAN (2), *adj.* belonging to Belgravia or to fashionable society. [*Belgravia,* London district].
BELIAL [bē'li-al], *n.* Satan; the spirit of wickedness; **sons of B.,** worthless wicked persons.
BELIE [bi-lī'], *v.t.* to contradict by implication, misrepresent, give the lie to, fail to conform with. [OE.].
BELIEF [bi-lēf'], *n.* something regarded by a person as true; firm conviction, considered opinion; faith in the truth of a body of religious doctrines, a creed; confidence, trust; a formula or exposition of doctrine; **The B.,** Apostles' Creed. [OE.].
BELIEVABLE [bi-lē'va-bl], *adj.* capable of being believed. BELIEVABILITY [bi-lē-va-bi'li-ti], BELIEVABLENESS, *n.* quality of being b.
BELIEVE [bi-lēv'], *v.t.* to regard personally as true, have faith in, feel convinced of the truth of the remarks of (a person); conceive, imagine; be under the impression, think; *v.i.* (with *in*) to hold a conviction or opinion; place one's trust in; set store by; regard as advantageous; profess faith in Christianity. MAKE-BELIEVE, to imagine, pretend. BELIEVING, *adj.* having complete faith in, accepting as true. BELIEVINGLY, *adv.* in a believing way. [ME. from OE.].
BELIEVER [bi-lē'ver], *n.* one who believes, one who adheres to the Christian religion.
BELIKE [bi-līk'], *adv.* probably, perhaps.
BELITTLE [bi-li'tl], *v.t.* to make light of, minimize

---

the importance of, disparage. BELITTLEMENT, *n.* act of belittling, state of being belittled.

BELL (1) [bel], *n.* hollow bowl-shaped vessel which emits a clear musical sound when struck with a clapper; anything resembling a bell in shape; hollow metal case in which divers may work under the sea; (*pl.*) (*naut.*) strokes of a ship's bell indicating half-hours of a watch, even numbers of strokes always denoting the hours; **to bear the b.,** to be the leader; **to ring the b.,** (*coll.*) to win the prize, be exactly right. BELL (2), *v.t. and i.* to provide with, or to adorn with bells; open and grow like a b. in shape; **to b. the cat,** to approach an exceptionally formidable person on a matter expected to be unwelcome to him. [O.E.].

BELL (3), *v.i.* to bellow as a deer at rutting time. [O.E.].

BELLADONNA [be-la-do'nah], *n.* (*bot.*) poisonous British plant, deadly nightshade; (*med.*) medicine or drug prepared from this. [It.].

BELL-BIRD [bel'berd], *n.* (*zool.*) South American bird with a bell-like note; name also given to an Australian and to a New Zealand bird.

BELL-BOTTOMED [bel-bo'tumd], *adj.* of trousers, wider at the bottom of the leg than at the knee.

BELL-BUOY [bel'boi], *n.* buoy with a bell which gives warning of danger.

BELL-CRANK [bel'krangk], *n.* (*mech.*) L-shaped lever pivoted at its centre with its two arms set at an angle to change the direction of the motion transmitted in a machine.

BELLE [bel], *n.* a fashionable and beautiful lady; (*fig.*) the most beautiful or most admired lady in a group. [Fr.].

BELLES-LETTRES [bel-letr'], *n.* artistic and literary writings; light literature; the aesthetic of literature. BELLETRIST [bel-let'rist], *n.* one who writes b. [Fr.].

BELL-FLOWER [bel'flow-er], *n.* plant of the genus *Campanula.*

BELL-FOUNDER [bel'fown-der], *n.* one who casts large bells. BELL-FOUNDRY, *n.* place in which bells are cast.

BELL-GLASS [bel'glahs], *n.* bell-shaped protection for plants, or delicate ornaments and instruments.

BELL-HANGER [bel'hang-er], *n.* one who is employed in fixing or hanging large bells. BELL-HANGING, *n.* the trade of hanging bells.

BELLICOSE [bel'i-kōs], *adj.* warlike, aggressively hostile. BELLICOSITY [be-li-ko'si-ti], *n.* quality of being b. [L.].

BELLIED [be'lid], *adj.* (*bot.*) swollen out like a belly; bulging in the middle.

BELLIGERENT (1) [be-li'je-rent], *n.* nation, state or party engaged in war. BELLIGERENT (2), *adj.* engaged in war; pugnacious; **b. rights,** rights of a nation, state or party at war. BELLIGERENCE, BELLIGERENCY, *n.* state of being a b. [L.].

BELLMAN [bel'man], *n.* town-crier who rings a bell to attract attention.

BELL-METAL [bel'me-tal], *n.* alloy of copper and tin from which bells are founded.

BELLONA [be-lō'nah], *n.* Roman goddess of war; (*fig.*) tall majestic woman. [L.].

BELLOW (1) [be'lō], *v.i.* to roar as a bull or ox, utter a loud resonant cry; shout continuously, speak or sing in an unnecessarily loud manner; make a deep, loud roaring sound. BELLOW (2), *n.* a deep, loud roar. BELLOWING, *n.* loud hollow sound, loud roar or clamour. [O.E.].

BELLOWS [be'lōz], *n.(pl.)* bag or other receptacle which when compressed produces a strong current of air; (*phot.*) extending portion of a camera for varying the distance between lens and film or plate; **pair of b.,** two-handled, portable b. [O.E.].

BELL-PEPPER [bel'pe-per], *n.* a plant, a species of *Capsicum,* with bell-shaped fruit.

BELL-PULL [bel'pool], *n.* cord or handle, which when pulled causes a bell to ring.

BELL-PUNCH [bel'punch], *n.* metal case containing a ticket-perforator and bell.

BELL-PUSH [bel'poosh], *n.* button which is pushed to ring an electric bell.

BELL-RINGER [bel'ring-er], *n.* one who rings church or other bells, campanologist.

BELL-ROPE [bel'rōp], *n.* rope or cord by which a bell is rung.

BELL-TENT [bel'tent], *n.* large conical tent.

BELLWETHER [bel'we-THer], *n.* sheep which leads the flock and has a bell on its neck.

BELLWORT [bel'wert], *n.* the bell-flower.

BELLY (1) [be'li], *n.* lower part of the trunk extending

from the diaphragm to the thighs in mammals; stomach; that part of anything which swells out or forms a bulge-like protuberance, the thick part of a muscle, front curved part of a violin; (*fig.*) greed, gluttony, the inside or interior; hollow, enclosed space. POT-BELLY, protruding abdomen. BELLY (2), *v.i.* to swell out, bulge, become protuberant. [O.E.].

BELLY-BAND [be'li-band], *n.* band passing under a horse's belly in harness, a girth; (*naut.*) strengthening band of canvas on a sail.

BELLYFUL [be'li-fool], *n.* as much as satisfies the appetite, a sufficiency; (*coll.*) as much as one can tolerate, more than enough.

BELLYING [be'li-ing], *adj.* protuberant, swelling out, distended.

BELONG [bi-long'], *v.i.* to be the attribute of, pertain to, relate to; be the business, duty or concern of, be connected with; be a resident or native of; be the property of; have its right place, go with. BELONGINGS, *n.(pl.)* goods, possessions, luggage. [ME.].

BELOVED (1) [bi-lu'vid], *n.* person loved by someone, betrothed person, spouse. BELOVED (2) [bi-lu'vid, bi-luvd'], *adj.* dearly loved.

BELOW (1) [bi-lō'], *adv.* beneath, in a lower place from a specified position, further or lower down; (*naut.*) underneath the deck, in the cabins or holds; **place b.,** Hell; **here b.,** on earth. BELOW (2), *prep.* lower down than, lower in position than, not up to, beneath; inferior to (in merit, morals, rank etc.); too low to be affected by; unworthy of; **b. the ground,** dead and buried; **b. the mark,** not up to the usual standard; **b. par,** (*comm.*) not having their nominal value (of shares); (*fig.*) indisposed, unwell; **b. the surface,** not apparent, unrevealed. [ME.].

BELT (1) [belt], *n.* strap or girdle encircling the waist; girdle indicating the rank of earl or knight; leather strap or indiarubber band connecting wheels or shafts, and transmitting rotary motion, to drive machinery; broad strip of approximately uniform width; long, narrow region, a zone; band of distinguishable colour or material laid upon another; broad strip of armour-plating built along the water-line of a battleship; strap containing cartridges, which feeds a machine-gun; **cartridge b.,** belt containing cartridges, worn over one shoulder and under the other arm; **Sam Browne b.,** (*milit.*) officer's leather belt supported by a strap crossing one shoulder; **to hit below the b.,** (*boxing*) to hit too low; (*fig.*) take an unfair advantage of; **to tighten one's b.,** to live more frugally. BELT (2), *v.t.* to encircle or enclose with a b.; secure by means of a b.; distinguish with a b. of colour; (*coll.*) thrash soundly. BELTED, *adj.* wearing a b., provided with a b.; marked by a b.; bearing the distinctive b. of an earl or knight. [O.E.].

BELTANE [bel'tān], *n.* ancient Gaelic and Irish spring festival. [Ir., Gael.].

BELTING [bel'ting], *n.* system of belts driving machinery; material from which belts are made; (*coll.*) a thrashing with a belt.

BELUGA [be-lyōo'gah], *n.* species of dolphin. [Russ.].

BELVEDERE [bel've-dēer], *n.* small pavilion or turret on the top of a house; summer-house built on raised land and so having a wide prospect. [It.].

BEMIRE [bi-mier'], *v.t.* to soil or drag in the mud.

BEMOAN [bi-mōn'], *v.t.* to lament, bewail. [~OE.].

BEMUSED [bi-myōozd'], *adj.* absorbed in musing; stupefied, dazed; as if in a trance.

BEN [ben], *adv., adj. and n.* (*Scots and northern dial.*) within, inside; an inner room. [O.E.].

BENCH (1) [bensh], *n.* long wooden seat or form, often backless; stone seat; cross-seat in a boat; work-table used by persons engaged in various forms of handicrafts; seat where judges or magistrates sit in a court of justice; (*fig.*) the judge or magistrates in a court of law; court of law or of inquiry; dignity and rank of a judge or magistrate; **b. of bishops,** the bishops of the Anglican Church who sit in the House of Lords; **King's, Queen's B.,** a court anciently presided over by the king in person, now a division of the High Court of Justice. BENCH (2), *v.t. and i.* to provide with benches; sit on a b. or seat of justice. [O.E.].

BENCHER [ben'sher], *n.* senior member of an Inn of Court.

BENCH-MARK [bensh'mahk], *n.* (*surveying*) a surveyor's mark, used as a reference mark in determining altitudes.

BENCH-WARRANT [bensh'wo-rant], *n.* (*leg.*) warrant issued by a judge.

BEND (1) [bend], *n.* a curve, anything not forming a

---

straight line; slight change of direction in a road; (*naut.*) kind of knot used by sailors; (*her.*) diagonal band across a shield; **b. sinister**, (*her.*) diagonal band across a shield from upper left to right base to denote illegitimacy. [O.E.].

BEND (2) (*pret. and p.pt.* **bent**), *v.t.* to alter the existing curve or direction of, curve, make crooked (of rather rigid material); straighten something curved or crooked; stoop, arch (the eyebrows); lower, incline, abase; (*fig.*) direct one's thoughts to, apply oneself closely to; (*naut.*) fasten or bind a rope; *v.i.* to depart from an upright position; be curved, sag; (*pass. fig.*) be determined upon, have set one's mind upon; be submissive to, defer to. BENDED, *adj.* bent, *esp.* **on b. knees**, kneeling. BENDER, *n.* something that is used for bending; (*slang*) a sixpenny piece; a binge. [O.E.].

BEND-LEATHER [bend'le-ᴛʜᴇʀ], *n.* thickest kind of leather used for making soles.

BENE- [be'ni], *pref.* well. [L.].

BENEATH (1) [bi-nēth'], *adv.* below, at a lower place, lower down; (*bibl.*) on earth. BENEATH (2), *prep.* under, below, underneath; inferior to, lower than (in social position or merit); unworthy of, at the foot of. [O.E.].

BENEDICK [be'ni-dik], *n.* confirmed bachelor who suddenly marries, newly married man. [Shakespeare's *Much Ado About Nothing*].

BENEDICTINE (1) [be-ni-dik'tēn], *n.* monk of an order founded by St. Benedict; liqueur prepared by these monks. BENEDICTINE (2), *adj.* relating to the order of monks founded by St. Benedict.

BENEDICTION [be-ni-dik'shn], *n.* a blessing, act of blessing or giving thanks, pronouncement of a blessing at the close of a church service; (*R.C.*) service for the blessing of the people by the priest with the Blessed Sacrament; (*fig.*) advantages or benefits of blessing. BENEDICTIVE, BENEDICTORY, *adj.* expressing b. [L.].

BENEFACTION [be-ni-fak'shn], *n.* good action, generous deed, benefit rendered; gift to charity.

BENEFACTOR [be-ni-fak-ter], *n.* one who performs a beneficial act, one who gives help, money or service. BENEFACTORY [be-ni-fak'te-ri], *adj.* conferring benefits upon. [L.].

BENEFACTRESS [be-ni-fak-tres], *n.* female benefactor.

BENEFICE [be'ni-fis], *n.* an ecclesiastical living, church endowed with a revenue for the purpose of maintaining divine service. BENEFICED, *adj.* appointed to a b. [L.].

BENEFICENCE [be-ne'fi-sens], *n.* the practice of doing good, practical kindness, good and generous deeds. [L.].

BENEFICENT [be-ne'fi-sent], *adj.* charitable, doing good, kindly, munificent. [L.].

BENEFICIAL [be-ni-fi'shl], *adj.* doing good, helpful, useful, advantageous, providing benefits. [L.].

BENEFICIARY (1) [be-ni-fi'sha-ri], *n.* one who holds an ecclesiastical living, one who acquires benefits or material advantages by the terms of a will or trust; (*leg.*) one who receives as a gift. BENEFICIARY (2), *adj.* held in subordination to others, held as a gift or benefice. [L.].

BENEFIT (1) [be'ni-fit], *n.* a favour, generous action; advantage; public theatrical performance or sporting contest given for charity; pension or allowance due to a person under an insurance scheme; **b. of clergy**, right to be tried by the ecclesiastical courts of justice, claimed by clerical delinquents, and later extended to all who could read a verse of Psalm li; **b. society**, friendly society whose funds are used for the alleviation of sick, aged or poor members; **sick b.**, monetary allowance paid by the State to an insured person during absence from work through illness; **unemployment b.**, money paid weekly under certain conditions by the State to a person who is out of work. BENEFIT (2), *v.t. and i.* to do good to, improve, be advantageous to; profit from, be improved (by), derive advantage (from). [AFr. from L.].

BENELUX [be'ni-luks], *n.* customs union of Belgium, the Netherlands and Luxemburg, formed in 1947.

BENEVOLENCE [be-ne'vo-lens], *n.* disposition to do good, goodwill, kind-heartedness; act of kindness. [L.].

BENEVOLENT [be-ne'vo-lent], *adj.* kind-hearted, doing good to others, charitable; **b. society**, society whose funds are used for the relief of distressed members. BENEVOLENTLY, *adv.* in b. fashion.

BENGALI (1) [beng-gaw'li], *n.* language spoken in

Bengal; a native of Bengal. BENGALI (2), *adj.* pertaining to the people or language of Bengal.

BENGAL LIGHT [beng-gawl-lit'], *n.* firework giving a continuous brightly-coloured flame.

BENIGHT [bi-nit'], *v.i.* to overtake by night, envelop in darkness, obscure. BENIGHTED, *adj.* overtaken by night; ignorant, backward, uninformed.

BENIGN [bi-nin'], *adj.* gracious, gentle, good-natured, pleasant; (*med.*) non-virulent, not malignant. BENIGNLY, *adv.* in b. fashion. [L.].

BENIGNANT [bi-nig'nant], *adj.* gracious, favourable, good-natured. BENIGNANTLY, *adv.* in a b. way.

BENIGNITY [bi-nig'ni-ti], *n.* quality of being benignant.

BENISON [be'ni-son], *n.* blessing, benediction. [OFr. from L.].

BENJAMIN [ben'ja-min], *n.* youngest child. [*Genesis* xlii, 4].

BENT (1) [bent], *n.* a stiff, wiry, creeping grass; withered stalks of this; place covered with stiff, wiry grass, a heath. BENTY, *adj.* overgrown with b. [O.E.].

BENT (2), *n.* inclination, aptitude, inherent ability at and interest for; **to the top of one's b.**, to the utmost extent. [BEND (2)].

BENT (3), *adj.* curved, crooked, not straight. [BEND (2)].

BENTHAMISM [ben'tha-mizm], *n.* philosophy expounded by Jeremy Bentham which stressed mass satisfaction in preference to individual happiness. BENTHAMITE [ben'tha-mit], *n.* follower of Bentham.

BENUMB [bi-num'], *v.t.* to make numb, deprive of feeling; render (the mind) incapable of feeling.

BENZENE [ben'zēn], *n.* (*chem.*) colourless vaporizable liquid hydrocarbon, C_6H_6, distilled from coal-tar.

BENZINE [ben'zēn], *n.* colourless volatile liquid obtained from crude petroleum.

BENZOATE [ben'zō-āt], *n.* a salt of benzoic acid.

BENZOIC [ben-zō'ik], *adj.* relating to benzoin; **b. acid**, acid obtained from gum-benzoin and also prepared from the hydrocarbon, toluene.

BENZOIN [ben'zō-in], *n.* solid brittle resin, used as incense, as a cosmetic and in pharmacy.

BENZOL [ben'zol], *n.* benzene.

BENZOLINE [ben'zo-lēn], *n.* benzine.

BENZOYL [ben'zoil], *n.* the radical of benzoic acid.

BEQUEATH [bi-kwēth'], *v.t.* to leave (property or money) to a person by will, transmit or hand down to posterity. BEQUEATHABLE, *adj.* able to be bequeathed. BEQUEATHAL, BEQUEATHMENT, *n.* act of bequeathing, that which is bequeathed. [O.E.].

BEQUEST [bi-kwest'], *n.* something bequeathed, act of bequeathing.

BERATE [bi-rāt'], *v.t.* to chide vehemently, scold.

BERBER (1) [bur'ber], *n.* member of a tribe inhabiting North Africa; language of this people. BERBER (2), *adj.* relating to the Berbers or their language. [Arab.].

BERBERIN [bur'be-rin], *n.* bitter yellow substance obtained from the root of the barberry plant.

BERBERRY, see BARBERRY.

BEREAVE (*pret. and p.pt.* **bereaved, bereft**) [bi-rēv'], *v.t.* to deprive of, make destitute of, remove from; suffer the loss by death of a friend or relative. BEREAVED, *adj.* deprived by death of a relative or friend. BEREAVEMENT, *n.* state of being bereaved. [O.E.].

BEREFT [bi-reft'], *adj.* deprived of, suffering the loss of, destitute, devoid of. [BEREAVE].

BERET [be'rā], *n.* flat, round, peakless cap. [Fr.].

BERG [burg], *n.* iceberg.

BERGAMASK, see BEGOMASK.

BERGAMOT (1), **BURGAMOT** [bur'ga-mot], *n.* kind of orange producing an aromatic oil; perfume or essence from this plant; species of mint plant. [*Bergamo*, in Italy].

BERGAMOT (2), *n.* kind of pear. [Turk].

BERGSCHRUND [bäerg'shroont], *n.* large crevasse running across a glacier. [Germ.].

BERGYLT [bur'gilt], *n.* the Norway haddock. [Unkn.].

BERHYME [bi-rim'], *v.t.* to write rhymes about, celebrate in rhymed verse.

BERI-BERI [be-ri-be'ri], *n.* (*med.*) disease due to lack of vitamin B. [Singhalese].

BERLIN BLACK [ber-lin-blak'], *n.* dull black carbon paint.

BERLIN IRON [ber-lin-iern'], *n.* easily moulded fusible iron containing phosphorus.

BERNACLE, see BARNACLE.

BERNARDINE (1) [bur'nah-dēn], *n.* monk of the

Cistercian order, founded by St. Bernard of Clairvaux; a Trappist. BERNARDINE (2), *adj.* relating to the order of monks founded in 1115 by St. Bernard.

BERRY (1) [be′ri], *n.* small spherical pulpy fruit of certain trees; (*bot.*) fleshy fruit containing no hard parts except the seed; eggs in the roe of certain fish. BERRY (2), *v.i.* to bear or produce berries. [OE.].

BERSAGLIERI [bäer-sah-lyäer′i], *n.(pl.)* troop of Italian light infantry or sharpshooters. [It.].

BERSERK (1), **BERSERKER, BARESARK** [ber′serk(-er), bäer′sahk(-er)], *n.* ancient Scandinavian warrior who in sudden fits of fury fought with terrific ferocity. BERSERK (2), *adj. and adv.* not wearing armour; furious, raging. [OIcel.].

BERTH (1) [burth], *n.* place in which a ship may be moored or swing at anchor; sufficient sea-room in which to manoeuvre; sleeping place in a ship or in other vehicles of transport; any lodging or sleeping place; employment on board ship; any post or situation of employment; **to give a wide b. to,** to avoid. BERTH (2), *v.t. and i.* to anchor, bring a ship into a b.; distribute berths or accommodate persons in berths; settle a person in employment. [Unkn.].

BERTHA [bur′thah], *n.* wide lace collar on a low-necked dress.

BERTHAGE [bur′thij], *n.* fees paid for berthing a ship, the berth provided.

BERTHING [bur′thing], *n.* (*naut.*) bulwark of a ship; place where ships are moored; arrangement of sleeping accommodation in ships etc.

BERTHOLLETIA [ber-to-lē′shah], *n.* (*bot.*) South American tree which yields the Brazil nut. [*Berthollet,* French chemist].

BERYL [be′ril], *n.* pale green precious stone. BERYLLINE, *adj.* like b. [Gk.].

BERYLLIUM [be-ri′li-um], *n.* metal found in beryl and certain other minerals, the element whose symbol is Be.

BESEECH [bi-sēch′], *v.t.* to beg, pray to, implore. BESEECHER, *n.* one who beseeches. BESEECHING, *adj.* that beseeches or implores. BESEECHINGLY, *adv.* in beseeching fashion. [ME.].

BESEEM [bi-sēm′], *v.t.* to become, suit, befit, be appropriate. BESEEMING, *adj.* becoming. BESEEMINGLY, *adv.* in a beseeming way. BESEEMLY, *adj.* beseeming. [ME.].

BESET (*pres.pt.* **besetting,** *pret. and p.pt.* **beset**) [bi-set′], *v.t.* to surround, encompass, press from all sides; harass, perplex; (*pass.*) be set round with, be adorned with; be fraught with, be assailed with. BESETMENT, *n.* condition of being beset; a personal failing. BESETTING, *adj.* that which besets, continually present and pressing. [OE.].

BESHREW† [bi-shrōō′], *v.t.* to abuse; **b. thee,** may evil befall you! [ME.].

BESIDE [bi-sīd′], *prep.* near by, close by, alongside, by the side of; equal with, on a level with; in addition to; apart from, irrelevant to, distinct from; **to be b. oneself,** to allow one's feelings to get out of hand.

BESIDES (1) [bi-sīdz′], *adv.* over and above, in addition; moreover, furthermore. BESIDES (2), *prep.* in addition to, except, other than. [ME.].

BESIEGE [bi-sēj′], *v.t.* (*milit.*) to lay siege to; (*fig.*) press upon, crowd round, hem in. BESIEGEMENT, *n.* act of besieging, state of being besieged. [ME.].

BESLAVER [bi-sla′ver], *v.t.* to slaver all over; (*fig.*) praise and flatter fulsomely.

BESLIME [bi-slim′], *v.t.* to daub with slime; befoul.

BESLOBBER [bi-slo′ber], *v.t.* to slaver over; (*fig.*) praise excessively, embrace effusively.

BESMEAR [bi-smēer′], *v.t.* to daub, smear over, soil; (*fig.*) defile. [OE.].

BESMIRCH [bi-smurch′], *v.t.* to discolour, soil, darken; (*fig.*) cast a stain upon, blot.

BESOM [be′zum, bē′zum], *n.* gardener's broom made of twigs bound to a long handle; (*coll.*) hag, worthless woman. [OE.].

BESOT (*pres.pt.* **besotting,** *pret. and p.pt.* **besotted**) [bi-sot′], *v.t.* to infatuate, make a fool of. BESOTTED, *adj.* infatuated, stupid; stupefied as with drink, in a state of continual intoxication. BESOTTEDLY, *adv.* in a besotted fashion.

BESOUGHT [bi-sawt′], *pret. and p.pt.* of BESEECH. [OE.].

BESPANGLE [bi-spang′gl], *v.t.* to adorn with spangles.

BESPATTER [bi-spa′ter], *v.t.* to cover or soil with splashes of mud, dirt etc.; (*fig.*) besmirch, abuse.

BESPEAK (*pret.* **bespoke,** *p.pt.* **bespoken, bespoke**)

[bi-spēk′], *v.t.* to speak for or engage beforehand, order or reserve in advance, claim; betoken. BESPEAKER, *n.* person who bespeaks. [OE.].

BESPECKLE [bi-spe′kl], *v.t.* to cover with speckles or spots.

BESPECTACLED [bi-spek′ta-kld], *adj.* wearing spectacles.

BESPOKE [bi-spōk′], *adj.* made to order. [BESPEAK.]

BESPREAD [bi-spred′], *v.t.* to spread over. [ME.].

BESPRENT [bi-sprent′], *adj.* (*poet.*) sprinkled over, scattered with. [ME.].

BESPRINKLE [bi-spring′kl], *v.t.* to sprinkle on, strew with, scatter over. [ME.].

BESSEMER [be′si-mer], *n. and adj.* process of making steel by passing air through molten iron. [Sir H. *Bessemer,* inventor].

BEST (1) [best], *n.* that which is of the highest quality; (*coll.*) the experts, acknowledged superiors; **all for the b.,** to one's ultimate advantage; **for the b.,** with the best intentions; **to have the b. of it,** to win, prove superior; **to make the b. of,** to derive as much benefit as possible from; **to the b. of,** to the utmost extent of; **to be at one's b.,** to excel oneself; **to come off second b.,** to lose; **to give someone b.,** to admit someone's superiority. BEST (2), *adj.* (*superl.* of GOOD and WELL), good or excellent in the highest degree, unsurpassed in quality, most advantageous, suitable or appropriate, greatest, of most value or merit, unequalled; largest; **b. man,** chief groomsman at a wedding. BEST (3), *adv.* to the highest degree, in the most excellent way or manner; to an unsurpassed extent, above all others; **we had b.,** it would be most advantageous for us to, we ought to. BEST (4), *v.t.* to get the better of, overcome. [OE.].

BESTED, BESTEAD [bi-sted′], *adj.* beset, treated, placed. [ME.].

BESTIAL [bes′ti-al], *adj.* like a beast; brutal, beastly, depraved; obscene, sexually unnatural. BESTIALITY [bes-ti-a′li-ti], *n.* quality of being b.; (*leg.*) unnatural sexual intercourse between a human being and an animal. BESTIALIZE, *v.t.* to make b. [L.].

BESTIARY [bes′ti-a-ri], *n.* medieval collection of animal stories with allegorical and religious explanations. [MedL.].

BESTIR (*pres.pt.* **bestirring,** *pret. and p.pt.* **bestirred**) [bi-stur′], *v. reflex.* to rouse oneself to activity. [OE.].

BESTOW [bi-stō′], *v.t.* to put in a certain place, deposit; give, confer ceremoniously, award. BESTOWAL, *n.* act or ceremony of bestowing. BESTOWER, *n.* person who bestows. BESTOWMENT, *n.* act of bestowing; that which is bestowed. [ME.].

BESTRADDLE [bi-stra′dl], *v.t.* to bestride.

BESTREW [bi-strōō′], *v.t.* to scatter, scatter over with, litter up with. [OE.].

BESTRIDE (*pret.* **bestrode, bestrid,** *p.pt.* **bestridden, bestrid**) [bi-strīd′], *v.t.* to stand or sit with the legs on either side of anything; mount (a horse); extend or stretch across, span; stride over. [OE.].

BEST-SELLER [best-se′ler], *n.* book which sells in abnormally large quantities.

BET (1) [bet], *n.* a wager, the supporting of one's opinion upon some past or future event against that of another, by depositing or staking a sum of money to be forfeited to the winner by the loser; amount wagered. BET (2), *v.t. and i.* to wager on an event, indulge in betting, make a bet; **I b., I'll b.,** (*coll.*) it is my opinion. [Unkn.].

BETAINE [bē′tān], *n.* alkaloid obtained from beet. [L.].

BETAKE (*pret.* **betook,** *p.pt.* **betaken**) [bi-tāk′], *v. reflex.* to depart, make one's way, go. [ME.].

BETA-RAYS [bē′tah-rāz], *n.(pl.)* a flow of electrons from radio-active substances such as radium. [Gk. *beta* (letter of the alphabet) and RAY].

BETATRON [bē′ta-tron], *n.* (*phys.*) electrical apparatus for accelerating the speed of electrons. [BETA (-RAYS) and (ELEC)TRON].

BETEL [bē′tel], *n.* (*bot.*) East Indian variety of pepper, the leaves of which are used to contain a piece of betel nut and lime, chewed by natives; **b. nut,** nut of the fruit of the areca palm, so named from being chewed with betel leaf. [Portug., Malayan].

BETE NOIRE, bête noire [bāt-nwah(r)′], *n.* bugbear, pet aversion, person or thing especially disliked. [Fr.].

BETHEL [be′thel], *n.* place for divine worship; Nonconformist chapel. [Heb.].

BETHINK (*pret. and p.pt.* **bethought**) [bi-thingk′],

v. reflex. to recall, recollect, remember; consider, reflect. [O.E.].

BETIDE [bi-tīd'], *v.t. and i.* to happen to, occur to, take place, come about. [M.E.].

BETIMES [bi-tīmz'], *adv.* in good time, early in the morning; soon, quickly. [M.E.].

BETISE, bêtise [be-tēz'], *n.* foolishness, foolish remark or action. [Fr.].

BETOKEN [bi-tō'ken], *v.t.* to signify, be a sign of, foreshadow, augur. [M.E.].

BETON [be'ton], *n.* a concrete made from sand, lime and gravel. [Fr.].

BETONY [be'to-ni], *n. (bot.)* plant with spiked purple flowers. [L.L.].

BETOOK [bi-toŏk'], *pret.* of BETAKE.

BETRAY [bi-trā'], *v.t.* to deliver treacherously or by breach of trust into the hands of an enemy; be unfaithful to, deal falsely with, reveal what has been entrusted as a secret; seduce, lead astray; reveal unconsciously or inadvertently; show signs of display. BETRAYAL, *n.* act of betraying, breach of trust or confidence, deceitful act. BETRAYER, *n.* traitor; person who betrays. [M.E.].

BETROTH [bi-trōth'], *v.t.* to affiance; promise to marry; *(pass.)* become engaged to be married. BETROTHAL, BETROTHMENT, *n.* act of being betrothed. BETROTHED, *n.* person engaged to be married. [M.E.].

BETTER (1) [be'ter], *n.* (usually *pl.*) one superior in quality, rank or merit; **to get the b. of,** to prove superior, defeat; **to think the b. of,** to have a higher opinion of. BETTER (2), *adj. (comp. of GOOD and WELL)*, good or excellent in a greater degree than another, superior to, more desirable, of higher merit, worth or rank; more efficient, useful, suitable, advantageous or appropriate; larger, chief, greater; improved in health, well again; **b. half,** *(coll.)* wife; **to have seen b. days,** to have become relatively poor, be old and shabby; **to be b. than one's word,** to do more than one has promised. BETTER (3), *adv. (comp. of WELL)* in a superior way, to a higher degree; again and again, frequently, repeatedly; **to know b. than to,** not to be so stupid as to; **to think b. of,** to change one's mind or intentions; **b. off,** in better circumstances, more favourably situated; **to go one b. than,** to surpass; **to feel b.,** to have recovered in some measure from an illness or indisposition; **I had b.,** I ought to. BETTER (4), *v.t. and i.* to improve. [O.E.].

BETTER (5), **BETTOR** [be'ter], *n.* person who bets. **BETTERMENT** [be'ter-ment], *n.* act of bettering, improvement.

BETTING [be'ting], *n.* the making of bets; allocation of money wagered as bets.

BETTONG [be'tong], *n.* species of kangaroo rat. [Maori].

BETTOR, see BETTER (5).

BETWEEN (1) [bi-twēn'], *adv.* somewhere in the space separating two objects or places. BETWEEN (2), *prep.* lying in an intermediary position in relation to, near to without the interposition of one of the objects specified; with something placed on either side of; *with a specified temporal or spatial unit or period,* occurring or situated on either side of a unit; *implying a choice of two or more alternatives; implying a condition related to two stated extremes within which it lies;* extending from one stated place to another, *implying communication from one stated place to another; expressing a relationship of two things whether of difference, similarity, separation or connexion;* restricted to and shared by, amongst; by the combined efforts of; **b. two fires,** torn by two opposing forces or desires; **b. the devil and the deep blue sea,** faced with no favourable alternative, vulnerable spot; **b. you and me,** in confidence. [O.E.].

BETWEEN-DECKS [bi-twēn-deks'], *adv.* between two decks; below deck.

BETWEEN-MAID [bi-twēn'mād], *n.* servant who helps other servants.

BETWEEN-TIMES [bi-twēn'tīmz], *adv.* between-whiles.

BETWEEN-WHILES [bi-twēn'wīlz], *adv.* during the intervals.

BETWIXT [bi-twikst'], *prep. and adv.* between; **b. and between,** *(coll.)* neither one thing nor the other.

BEUDANTITE [byoō'dan-tīt], *n. (min.)* crystalline mineral containing iron, lead and silica. [*Beudant,* French mineralogist].

BEVEL (1) [be'vel], *n.* an oblique or sloping edge, edge which does not form a right angle to the surface;

instrument consisting of a fixed arm with a movable tongue or square which can be set to form any angle with the fixed arm, used for marking out angles. BEVEL (2), BEVILE, *adj.* having a sloping edge which does not form a right angle; **b. angle,** angle other than a right angle; **b. wheel,** gear wheel whose teeth are set at an angle to the shaft; **b. edge,** sloping edge of a chisel or other similar cutting tool; **b. joint,** oblique joint formed by two bevelled edges of wood being fastened together. BEVEL (3) *(pres.pt.* BEVELLING, *pret. and p.pt.* BEVELLED), *v.t. and i.* to cut to a b. angle, provide with a b. edge; have an edge which does not form a right angle. [O.Fr.].

BEVEL-GEAR [be-vel-gēer'], *n.* system of engaging bevel wheels to transmit motion from one shaft to another set at an angle to the first shaft; bevel wheel.

BEVELLED [be'veld], *adj.* having a bevel edge.

BEVELLING [be've-ling], *n.* the cutting of the edge of timber or other material to an oblique or bevel angle; a bevelled edge.

BEVELMENT [be'vel-ment], *n. (min.)* the cutting away of the edge of a crystal, so that in place of the original edge there are two similar planes, each forming an equal angle with the adjacent faces.

BEVERAGE [be've-rij], *n.* a drink, liquid that can be drunk. [O.Fr.].

BEVILE, see BEVEL.

BEVY [be'vi], *n.* group of roes, quails or larks; company, assembly or gathering, *esp.* of girls; *(fig.)* a collection, group of objects. [Fr.].

BEWAIL [bi-wāl'], *v.t.* to bemoan, lament, express grief at. BEWAILABLE, *adj.* lamentable. BEWAILING, *adj.* lamenting, weeping. BEWAILINGLY, *adv.* in a bewailing way. BEWAILMENT, *n.* act of bewailing. [M.E.].

BEWARE [bi-wāer'], *v.t. and i. (now used only in imper., inf. and pres. subj.)* to guard against, take care about, regard with caution, be wary of. [O.E.].

BEWIGGED [bi-wigd'], *adj.* wearing a wig.

BEWILDER [bi-wil'der], *v.t.* to puzzle, baffle, perplex, confuse utterly. BEWILDERINGLY, *adv.* in bewildering fashion. [M.E.].

BEWILDERMENT [bi-wil'der-ment], *n.* condition of being bewildered; act of bewildering.

BEWITCH [bi-wich'], *v.t.* to lay under a spell of magic or witchcraft; *(fig.)* charm, allure. [M.E.].

BEWRAY [bi-rā'], *v.t.* to disclose, betray unintentionally; expose. BEWRAYER, *n.* revealer of secrets. BEWRAYINGLY, *adv.* in a bewraying fashion. BEWRAYMENT, *n.* act of bewraying. [M.E.].

BEWROUGHT [bi-rawt'], *adj.* worked round, adorned with embroidery or fancy work. [O.E.].

BEY [bā], *n.* Turkish governor; person of high rank. BEYLIK, *n.* province or district governed by a b. [Turk.].

BEYOND (1) [bi-yond'], *n.* the future life; the unknown or unexplored; **the back of b.,** a very remote place. BEYOND (2), *adv.* on the farther side, at a distance. BEYOND (3), *prep.* farther on than, past, on the far side of; later than; out of reach of, exceeding the range or limit of, surpassing; in addition to, more or greater than; except *(with negative)*; **to be b. someone,** *(coll.)* to be incomprehensible to someone; **b. one's depth,** *(fig.)* too difficult to grasp. [O.E.].

BEZANT, BESANT [be'zant], *n.* gold coin formerly current in Europe. [O.Fr.].

BEZBOZHNIK [bez-bozh'nik], *n.* member of the League of the Godless in Soviet Russia. [Russ.].

BEZEL, BEZIL [be'zel], *n.* the sloping cutting edge of a chisel or similar tool; the sloping facets of a cut gem; groove into which the glass of a watch fits. [O.Fr.].

BEZIL, see BEZEL.

BEZIQUE [be-zēk'], *n.* game of cards for two or four persons; a hand at b. containing the queen of spades and the knave of diamonds.

BHANG, BANG, BANGUE [bang], *n.* Indian hemp; the leaves and small stalks of this, dried and used as an intoxicant or a sweetmeat; hashish. [Hind.].

BI-, *pref.* two, twice, twofold; having two; lasting for or occurring every two; *(chem.)* having twice the quantity of acid or base. [L.].

BIACID [bi-a'sid], *adj. (chem.)* combining in two different proportions with an acid.

BIANGULAR [bi-ang'yoō-ler], *adj.* containing two angles.

BIARTICULATE [bi-ah-ti'kyoō-lat], *adj.* possessing two joints.

BIAS (1) [bi'as], *n.* wedge-shaped piece of cloth, cut

in a slanting direction across the texture; (*bowls*) weighted or slightly elongated side of a bowl, which causes it to depart from a straight course; (*fig.*) a leaning in a particular direction, partiality, strong preference, prejudice, influence; **on the b.**, cut in a diagonal direction to the texture of the fabric. BIAS (2), *v.t.* to provide with a b., cut with a b.; (*fig.*) cause to incline or lean in a particular direction, prejudice, influence in a particular way. BIASED, *adj.* partial, unfairly influenced, prejudiced. [Fr.].

BIB (1) [bib], *n.* small piece of linen fastened under the chin of an infant when feeding etc.; upper part of an apron; **best b. and tucker,** (*coll.*) best clothes. [*Next*].

BIB (2) (*pres.pt.* **bibbing,** *pret.* and *p.pt.* **bibbed**) [bib], *v.i.* to drink excessively, tipple. BIBBER, *n.* a tippler. [L.].

BIBASIC [bī-bā′sik], *adj.* (*chem.*) combining in two different proportions with a base.

BIBLE [bī′bl], *n.* the collection of sacred and historical writings forming the body of belief of the Christian religion; (*fig.*) any sacred book; book regarded as the ultimate authority on a subject; **B. oath,** solemn oath sworn on the Bible; **B. societies,** societies formed for the distribution of the Bible in various languages. BIBLE-CLERK, *n.* student at certain Oxford colleges, who reads the lessons in chapel. [Gk.].

BIBLICAL [bib′li-kal], *adj.* pertaining to, contained in, or authorized by the Bible. BIBLICALLY, *adv.* according to the Bible, in the manner of the Bible.

BIBLICISM [bib′li-sizm], *n.* adherence to the letter of the Bible. BIBLICIST, *n.* one who follows out literally the instruction of the Bible; student of the Bible.

BIBLIO- [bib′li-ō], *pref.* pertaining to or referring to books. [Gk.].

BIBLIOGRAPHER [bib-li-o′gra-fer], *n.* one skilled in bibliography.

BIBLIOGRAPHIC(AL) [bib-li-ō-gra′fik(-al)], *adj.* pertaining to bibliography. BIBLIOGRAPHICALLY, *adv.* with respect to bibliography.

BIBLIOGRAPHY [bib-li-o′gra-fi], *n.* the study of the history of books, their publication, printing etc., as distinct from their subject-matter; list of books or writings about a particular subject; list of an author's works. [Gk.].

BIBLIOLATRY [bib-li-o′la-tri], *n.* excessive respect for, or devotion to, the letter of the Holy Scriptures. BIBLIOLATER, *n.* a biblicist. [Gk.].

BIBLIOLOGY [bib-li-o′lo-ji], *n.* literature or doctrine relating to the Bible; bibliography. BIBLIOLOGICAL [bib-li-ō-lo′ji-kal], *adj.* pertaining to b. [Gk.].

BIBLIOMANCY [bib′li-ō-man-si], *n.* divination by interpretation of passages of Scripture opened at random. [Gk.].

BIBLIOMANIA [bib-li-ō-mā′ni-ah], *n.* extravagant zeal or love for book-collecting. BIBLIOMANIAC, *n.* rabid book-collector. BIBLIOMANIACAL [bib-li-ō-ma-nī′a-kal], *adj.* obsessed by a passion for books. [Gk.].

BIBLIOPHIL(E) [bib′li-ō-fil], *n.* lover or collector of books. BIBLIOPHILIA [bib-li-o′fi-lizm], *n.* love of bibliography or of books. BIBLIOPHILIST [bib-li-o′fi-list], *n.* a bibliophile. [Gk.].

BIBLIOPOLE [bib′li-ō-pōl], *n.* dealer in books, bookseller. BIBLIOPOLIC(AL) [bib-li-ō-po′lik(-al)], *adj.* pertaining to bookselling or booksellers. BIBLIOPOLIST [bib-li-o′po-list], *n.* bookseller. BIBLIOPOLY, *n.* bookselling.

BIBLIOTHECA [bib-li-ō-thē′kah], *n.* library; collection of books or writings. BIBLIOTHECARY [bib-li-ō-thē′ka-ri], *n.* librarian. [L.].

BIBLUS [bib′lus], *n.* papyrus. [Gk.].

BIBULOUS [bi′byōo-lŏos], *adj.* addicted to drink, slightly intoxicated; absorbent. BIBULOUSLY, *adv.* in a b. way. [L.].

BICAMERAL [bī-ka′me-ral], *adj.* (of legislative assemblies) composed of two chambers. [L.].

BICARBONATE [bī-kah′bo-nāt], *n.* (*chem.*) an acid salt of carbonic acid. [BI and CARBONATE].

BICE [bis], *n.* basic pigment used in painting. [Fr.].

BICENTENARY [bī-sen′te-na-ri], *n.* anniversary at the end of two hundred years. [BI and CENTENARY].

BICENTENNIAL [bī-sen-te′ni-al], *adj.* lasting two hundred years, happening every two hundred years.

BICEPHALOUS [bī-se′fa-lŏos], *adj.* having two heads. [Gk.].

BICEPS [bī′seps], *n.* a muscle having two heads; chief flexor muscle of the upper arm; corresponding

muscle in the leg. BICIPITAL [bī-si′pi-tal], *adj.* (*anat.*) with two heads (as a muscle). [L.].

BICHLORIDE [bī-klaw′rīd], *n.* (*chem.*) compound having two equivalents of chlorine to one of a base.

BICHROMATE [bī-krō′māt], *n.* (*chem.*) compound having two molecules of chromic acid to one of a base.

BICKER (1) [bi′ker], *v.i.* to quarrel, dispute petulantly, wrangle. BICKER (2), *n.* quarrel, skirmish. BICKERING, *n.* quarrelling, squabbling, petty dispute, altercation.

BICORN [bī′kawn], *adj.* two-horned. BICORNOUS, *adj.* (*bot.*) b. [L.].

BICRURAL [bī-krōo′ral], *adj.* two-legged. [L.].

BICUSPID (1) [bī-kus′pid], *n.* tooth with two fangs. BICUSPID (2), BICUSPIDATE, *adj.* having two fangs. [L.].

BICYCLE [bī′si-kl], *n.* vehicle with two wheels in series propelled by rotating two pedals with the feet. BICYCLIST, *n.* one who rides a b. [Gk.].

BID (1) (*pres.pt.* **bidding,** *pret.* **bade,** *p.pt.* **bidden**) [bid], *v.t.* and *i.* to command, order; ask pressingly, beg, invite; offer, make an offer of a price at a sale or auction; (*cards*) make a bid at certain card games; **to b. fair,** to appear likely. BID (2), *n.* an offer of a sum of money for an article, as at an auction; (*cards*) an undertaking at certain card games to obtain a specified number of tricks; (*coll.*) an attempt, effort. BIDDABLE, *adj.* obedient, willing; (*cards*) that can be bid successfully. [OE.].

BIDDING [bi′ding], *n.* command; request; offer; invitation; bids or offers of prices at an auction or at the opening of certain card games; **b. prayer,** exhortation in which the congregation are directed to pray for a certain thing, and ending with the Lord's Prayer.

BIDE [bid], *v.i.* (*archaic*) to remain, await; endure. [OE.].

BIDENT [bī′dent], *n.* implement having two prongs or forks. BIDENTAL [bī-den′tal], *adj.* having two prongs or teeth. BIDENTATE(D), *adj.* having two tooth-like projections. [L.].

BIDET [bi-det′, bi′dā], *n.* small horse; bathing vessel designed to be bestridden. [Fr.].

BIENNIAL (1) [bī-e′ni-al], *n.* plant which does not flower until the second year. BIENNIAL (2), *adj.* lasting for only two years; occurring once in two years. BIENNIALLY, *adv.* once in two years; at two-yearly periods. [L.].

BIER [bēer], *n.* carriage or framework for conveying a corpse to its grave; (*fig.*) grave, tomb. [OE.].

BIFEROUS [bi′fe-rŏos], *adj.* producing fruit or flowers twice a year. [L.].

BIFF (1) [bif], *n.* (*slang*) a heavy blow, violent smack. BIFF (2), *v.t.* (*slang*) to strike heavily, administer a violent blow to.

BIFFIN [bi′fin], *n.* red variety of cooking apple.

BIFID [bī′fid], *adj.* separated into two parts by a cleft. [L.].

BIFLOROUS [bī-flaw′rŏos], *adj.* producing two flowers on a stem. [L.].

BIFOCAL [bī-fō′kal], *adj.* (of spectacles) having two segments of different focus. [BI and FOCAL].

BIFOLIATE [bī-fō′li-at], *adj.* (*bot.*) two-leaved.

BIFURCATE (1) [bī′fer-kāt], *v.t.* and *i.* to divide into two branches, fork. BIFURCATE (2) [bī′fer-kat], *adj.* two-forked; having two prongs or branches. BIFURCATED [bī′fer-kā-tid], *adj.* divided into two branches or forks. BIFURCATION [bī-fer-kā′shn], *n.* a forking into two branches; point at which such forking takes place; the two branches produced by forking.

BIG [big], *adj.* and *adv.* large in size, power or quality, great in bulk, ample; tall, broad, capacious; (*fig.*) noble, generous, magnanimous, proud; (*coll.*) important, influential; grown up; **b. words,** words intended to intimidate or impress; **to talk b.,** (*coll.*) to boast; **to be too b. for one's boots,** to be conceited; *often used in compound words.* [ME.].

BIGAMY [bi′ga-mi], *n.* crime of marrying another while still legally married. BIGAMIST, *n.* person guilty of b. BIGAMOUS, *adj.* having committed b., involving b. BIGAMOUSLY, *adv.* in a bigamous way. [Gk.].

BIG-END [big′end], *n.* (*eng.*) that part of a connecting-rod bearing on a crankshaft.

BIGG [big], *n.* the four-rowed barley. [OIcel.].

BIGHT [bit], *n.* a bend, curve; loop or coil in a rope; break in the straightness of a coastline formed by a creek; small, shallow bay. [OE.].

BIGNONIA [big-nō′ni-ah], *n.* (*bot.*) genus of climbing shrubs. [Abbé *Bignon*, French scholar].

BIGOT [bi′got], *n.* narrow-minded person holding

ōō is pronounced as in food; ŏŏ as in hood; th as in *think*, TH as in *that*; zh as in azure. ∼ = related to.

stubbornly to a particular opinion or belief. BIG-
OTED, *adj.* prejudiced, narrow-minded. BIGOTEDLY,
adv. in a bigoted manner. BIGOTRY, *n.* quality of
being bigoted. [Uncert.].

BIGWIG [big′wig], *n.* (*coll.*) person of considerable
importance or influence.

BIJOU (1) (*pl.* **bijoux**) [bē′zhōō], *n.* jewel, trinket.
BIJOU (2), *adj.* small, neat. [Fr.].

BIJOUTERIE [bē-zhōō′te-rē], *n.* jewellery, trinkets.
[Fr.].

BIKE (1) [bik], *n.* (*coll.*) bicycle. BIKE (2), *v.i.* (*coll.*)
to cycle. [Abbreviation.].

BIKINI [bi-kē′nē], *n.* two-piece bathing costume.

BILATERAL [bī-la′te-ral], *adj.* two-sided; affecting
two parties; arranged upon or forming two sides.
BILATERALLY, *adv.* in b. fashion; from both sides.

BILBERRY [bil′be-ri], *n.* (*bot*) whortleberry, a hardy
shrub-like plant yielding a sweet-tasting purple berry.

BILE [bil], *n.* yellow, bitter secretion of the liver,
aiding in the digestion of fatty substances; unhealthy
condition arising from disorders of the bile; (*fig.*) ill-
humour, bitter feeling.

BILEDUCT [bil′dukt], *n.* (*anat.*) channel or duct for
conveying bile.

BILGE (1) [bilj], *n.* broadest and flattest part of a
ship's hull; filth, dirt and noisome material accumulating there; bulging part of a cask; (*fig.*) (*coll.*)
rubbish, stupid, nonsensical statements. BILGE-
WATER, *n.* water which collects in the b. of a ship,
having a strong offensive smell. BILGE (2), *v.t. and i.*
to split the bottom of a ship; spring a leak by a
fracture of the b. BILGED, *adj.* provided with a large
b.; springing a leak by a fracture of the b. [Uncert.].

BILHARZIA [bil-haht′zi-ah], *n.* liver-fluke found in
the veins and in the bladder of human beings.
BILHARZIOSIS, *n.* chronic internal disorder set up by
the b. [T. *Bilharz*, discoverer of the worm as a
disease-producing agent].

BILIARY [bi′li-a-ri], *adj.* pertaining to the bile.

BILINGUAL [bī-ling′gwal], *adj.* characterized by or
formed from two languages; speaking two languages
naturally; written in two languages. BILINGUALISM,
n. the habitual use of two languages. [L.].

BILIOUS [bi′li-ŏŏs], *adj.* caused by or relating to
disorder of the bile; liable to be afflicted by disorder
of the bile; (*fig.*) morose, peevish; (*coll.*) sick.
BILIOUSLY, *adv.* in b. fashion, irritably. [L.].

BILK (1) [bilk], *n.* person who cheats, bilker. BILK (2),
v.t. to defraud or swindle by non-payment, in a mean,
underhand way; escape from; cheat, deceive.
BILKER, *n.* person who bilks. [Unkn.].

BILL (1) [bil], *n.* beak of a bird; small, narrow promontory; point of the fluke of an anchor. BILL (2),
v.i. rub or stroke beak against beak; (*fig.*) caress, **to
b. and coo**, to make love like doves. [OE.].

BILL (3), *n.* obsolete infantry axe, halberd; tool used
for chopping hedges etc. with a long curved blade.

BILL (4), *n.* written list or statement of particulars;
legislative measure put before the Houses of Parliament for approval; account of money due for services
rendered or goods purchased; printed proclamation
or advertisement; (*leg.*) statement of a case in writing
formerly put before a grand jury; (*U.S.*) banknote;
b. of exchange, (*comm.*) promissory note, signed
written order authorizing the person to whom it is
addressed to pay to the bearer, on a specified date,
a certain sum of money for value received; **b. of
credit**, (*comm.*) document authorizing a person to
receive money from a third party; note issued on
the credit of the state and passed as money; **b. of
entry**, written account of goods entered at a customs
house; **b. of fare**, menu; **b. of health**, (*naut.*)
certificate issued by port authorities to masters of
ships certifying the state of health of the crew at the
time of departure; **b. of lading**, receipt given by a
shipmaster for goods consigned to him; **b. of sale**,
formal document authorizing the conveyance or
transfer of personal chattels, given as security to a
creditor; **a true b.**, formerly, declaration by a grand
jury that evidence furnished by a plaintiff warranted
a trial; **to fill the b.**, to be suitable. BILL (5), *v.t.*
to advertise or announce by means of a placard;
announce upon a bill of entertainment as playing
a certain rôle. [L.].

BILL-BROKER [bil′brō-ker], *n.* person who trades
in money bills.

BILL-DISCOUNTER [bil′dis-kown-ter], *n.* broker
who discounts bills of exchange.

BILLED [bild], *adj.* provided with a bill; advertised
on a placard.

BILLET (1) [bi′lit], *n.* a log of firewood; (*metal.*) gold

ingot or bar of steel; (*arch.*) ornamental moulding in
Norman architecture resembling a rounded wood b.
[Fr.].

BILLET (2), *n.* formal note; document demanding
the feeding and lodging of soldiers etc. in a town
by householders; accommodation of this type;
soldier's lodgings; apartments in general; (*coll.*)
position, employment. BILLET (3), *v.t.* to quarter
in billets, place in a b. [AFr.].

BILLET-DOUX [bi-lā-dōō′], *n.* love-letter, note.
[Fr.].

BILLHEAD [bil′hed], *n.* printed heading of a bill, bill
form.

BILLHOOK [bil′hŏŏk], *n.* knife with a hooked end,
used for chopping hedges etc.

BILLIARD [bi′li-erd], *adj.* relating to billiards.

BILLIARDS [bi′li-erdz], *n.*(*pl.*) indoor game played
with three small balls and a leather-tipped cue, on
an oblong flat table enclosed by raised rubber
cushions and fitted (in England) with six pockets.
[Fr.].

BILLING [bi′ling], *n.* act of caressing or fondling in
the manner of doves. [BILL (2)].

BILLINGSGATE [bi′lingz-gāt], *n.* bad or abusive
language of the type associated with the fish market
at *Billingsgate*.

BILLION [bi′yon], *n.* a million millions; in France
and America a thousand millions. [Fr.].

BILLON [bi′lon], *n.* alloy of copper and silver containing an excess of copper. [Fr.].

BILLOW (1) [bi′lō], *n.* large rolling wave of the sea
(*fig.*) (*pl.*) the sea; (*poet.*) sudden sweep, surge or
roll of flame, cloud, smoke etc. BILLOW (2), *v.i.* to
form into billows, surge or roll in sweeping waves.
BILLOWED, *adj.* like a b. BILLOWY *adj* like a b.,
full of billows, sweeping, surging or rolling like
billows. [OScand.].

BILL-POSTER [bil′pōs-ter], *n.* one who posts up
bills or employs others to do so.

BILL-STICKER [bil′sti-ker], *n.* one who pastes up
bills on hoardings.

BILLY [bi′li], *n.* (*coll. orig. Australian*) tin can used
for cooking. [Uncert.].

BILLYCOCK [bi′li-kok], *n.* (*coll.*) bowler hat.

BILLY-GOAT [bi′li-gŏt], *n.* male goat.

BILLY-O, BILLY-HO [bi′li-ō], (*coll.*) only in intensive phr. **like b.**, vigorously, fiercely, violently.

BILOBED [bi-lōbd′], *adj.* having two lobes.

BILOBULAR [bi-lŏ′byŏŏ-ler], *adj.* bilobed.

BILTONG [bil′tong], *n.* strips of lean meat dried in
the sun, and eaten as food in South Africa. [Du.].

BIMANOUS [bi′ma-nŏŏs], *adj.* having two hands.
BIMANAL, *adj.* (*zool.*) b. [L.].

BIMETALLIC [bi-me-ta′lik], *adj.* based on or consisting of two metals (of currency).

BIMETALLISM [bi-me′ta-lizm], *n.* the use of coins
of two metals as currency, at a fixed ratio of value
to each other. BIMETALLIST, *n.* advocate of b.

BIMONTHLY [bi-munth′li], *adj.* every two months;
twice a month.

BIN (1) [bin], *n.* large receptacle provided with a lid
in which bread, grain or corn may be stored; receptacle in which dust, ashes etc. are temporarily kept;
division or partition in a wine-cellar for storing; any
similar partition in a store; kind of basket used in
hop-picking. BIN (2) (*pres.pt.* BINNING, *pret. and
p.pt.* BINNED), *v.t.* to store in a b. [OE.].

BINARY [bi′na-ri], *adj.* characterized by, or composed
of, two; **b. form**, (*mus.*) music based on the interchange of two themes to a set pattern; **b. stars**,
(*astron.*) two stars revolving round a common centre,
or one which revolves round another. [L.].

BINATE [bi′nāt], *adj.* (*bot.*) growing or set out in
pairs.

BINAURAL [bi-naw′ral], *adj.* having two ears;
adapted to the two ears. [L.].

BIND (1) (*pret. and p.pt.* **bound**) [bind], *v.t.* to fasten
together or confine (a loose mass) by means of a
band, join objects together; wrap round firmly with
a band, bandage up; tie up or render incapable of
movement with fetters, chains, ropes etc.; fasten a
strip of material round an object or along the edge
of an object for strengthening purposes; cause to be
constipated; pledge oneself to, lay under an obligation; fasten together the leaves of a book in a cover;
conclude (an agreement); subject to a legal obligation;
apprentice; *v.i.* to form into a hard mass under
pressure; contract; **bound up in**, completely
absorbed in; **I'll be bound**, I am certain. BIND (2),
n. a stalk of hops; (*min.*) hardened clay occurring
between levels of coal; (*mus.*) curved mark denoting

a tied note; **measure of quantity** of eels or salmon. [O.E.].

BINDER [bin'der], *n.* person who binds; piece of material used for binding purposes; piece of material used to confine the body (*esp.* of a baby); machine that binds.

BINDERY [bin'de-ri], *n.* place where books are bound.

BINDING (1) [bin'ding], *n.* act of binding; anything that binds; strong material used to bind a book, manner of binding it; strong protective material fastened to the edges of carpet, fabric etc.; (*eng.*) excessive friction causing loss of power in machinery; bandage. **BINDING** (2), *adj.* that which binds, obligatory; tending to cause constipation. **BIND-INGLY,** *adv.* in b. fashion.

BINDWEED [bind'wed], *n.* (*bot.*) common name for plants of the genus *Convolvulus* and certain other climbing plants.

BINE [bin], *n.* (*bot.*) creeping, slender stem of various climbing plants, long pliant stem of the hop. [BIND (2)].

BINGE [binj], *n.* (*slang*) drinking bout or outing, hilarious jollification. [Uncert.].

BINNACLE [bi'na-kl], *n.* (*naut.*) box which contains the compass on a ship. [Span.].

BINOCULAR (1) [bi-no'kyoo-ler], *n.* field-glass, opera-glass or microscope through which an object may be seen with both eyes simultaneously. **BINOCULAR** (2), *adj.* suited for or employing both eyes simultaneously. [L.].

BINOMIAL (1) [bi-nō'mi-al], *n.* (*alg.*) expression containing two terms, connected by a plus or minus sign. **BINOMIAL** (2), *adj.* pertaining to binomials; consisting of two terms; binomial; **b. theorem,** formula for raising a binomial equation to any power, or for extracting any root of it without lengthy multiplication or division, by a converging infinite series. [L.].

BINOMINAL [bi-no'mi-nal], *adj.* (*bot. and zool.*) possessing two names. [L.].

BIO- [bi'ō], *pref.* life. [Gk.].

BIOBLAST [bi'ō-blahst], *n.* a minute mass of protoplasm, possessing formative power. [Gk.].

BIOCENTRIC [bi-ō-sen'trik], *adj.* considering life as central.

BIOCHEMISTRY [bi-ō-ke'mis-tri], *n.* study of the chemical composition of animal and plant structure.

BIODYNAMICS [bi-ō-di-na'miks], *n.*(*pl.*) study of vital forces.

BIOGENESIS [bi-ō-je'ni-sis], *n.* science of the origin and development of life or of new species. **BIO-GENETIC** [bi-ō-je-ne'tik], *adj.* relating to b.

BIOGRAPHER [bi-o'gra-fer], *n.* one who writes the life story of a person.

BIOGRAPHIC(AL) [bi-ō-gra'fik(-al)], *adj.* relating to, or containing, biography.

BIOGRAPHY [bi-o'gra-fi], *n.* an account of the life of a particular person; that section of literature concerned with accounts of the lives of individuals. [Gk.].

BIOLOGICAL [bi-ō-lo'ji-kal], *adj.* pertaining to biology.

BIOLOGIST [bi-o'lō-jist], *n.* one expert in biology.

BIOLOGY [bi-o'lō-ji], *n.* study of living plants and animals, their relationship, distribution, origin, structure, functions and manner of living. [Gk.].

BIOMAGNETISM [bi-ō-mag'ne-tizm], *n.* animal magnetism.

BIOMETRICS [bi-ō-met'riks], *n.*(*pl.*) study of the statistics and quantitative valuation of biological facts. [Gk.].

BIOMETRY [bi-o'me-tri], *n.* biometrics. **BIO-METRIC(AL)** [bi-ō-met'rik(-al)], *adj.* pertaining to b. **BIOMETRICIAN** [bi-ō-me-tri'shn], *n.* an expert in b. [Gk.].

BIONOMICS [bi-ō-no'miks], *n.*(*pl.*) study of biological phenomena according to the laws of physics.

BIOPLASM [bi'ō-plazm], *n.* protoplasm.

BIOPLAST [bi'ō-plast], *n.* a germ-plasm.

BIOSCOPE [bi'ō-skōp], *n.* early kind of cinematograph.

BIOSTATICS [bi-ō-sta'tiks], *n.*(*pl.*) study and science of living structure.

BIOTAXY [bi'ō-tak'si], *n.* branch of biology dealing with the classification of organisms according to likenesses and differences. [Gk.].

BIOTRON [bi'ō-tron], *n.* (*radio*) two thermionic valves coupled so as to give a very steep curve.

BIPAROUS [bi'pa-roos], *adj.* producing or yielding two at once. [L.].

BIPARTIENT (1) [bi-pah'shent], *n.* number which exactly divides another number into two equal parts. **BIPARTIENT** (2), *adj.* dividing into two parts. [L.].

BIPARTITE [bi-pah'tit], *adj.* set out in or consisting of two corresponding parts; shared by the two parties concerned; (*bot.*) divided into two parts to the base. **BIPARTITION** [bi-pah-ti'shn], *n.* act of making b. [L.].

BIPED (1) [bi'ped], *n.* animal having two feet. **BIPED** (2), *adj.* having two feet. **BIPEDAL** [bi'pe-dal], *adj.* b.; caused or made by two feet. [L.].

BIPLANE [bi'plan], *n.* aeroplane having two planes.

BIPOLAR [bi-pō'ler], *adj.* with two poles.

BIQUADRATE [bi-kwod'rāt], *n.* the fourth power in arithmetic or algebra, the square (root) of the square (root). **BIQUADRATIC** (1) [bi-kwod-ra'tik], *n.* (*math.*) the b. **BIQUADRATIC** (2), *adj.* (*math.*) relating to the b.

BIRCH (1) [burch], *n.* (*bot.*) genus of hardy trees with a smooth, shining, whitish bark; wood of this tree; bundle of twigs fastened together and used to inflict corporal punishment (especially upon schoolboys). **BIRCH** (2), *adj.* made of or consisting of b. **BIRCH** (3), *v.t.* to flog with a b. **BIRCHEN,** *adj.* made of b.; consisting of birch trees. [O.E.].

BIRD [burd], *n.* two-legged feathered vertebrate animal which lays eggs; (*slang*) physically attractive woman; person, fellow; bad reception; **birds of a feather,** persons with similar characters; **b. of passage,** migratory b.; (*fig.*) restless nomadic person; **b. of prey,** b. which preys on living birds and animals. [O.E.].

BIRDCAGE [burd'kāj], *n.* receptacle of wire or wicker in which captive birds may be kept.

BIRD-CALL [burd'kawl], *n.* pipe which can imitate the notes of birds and decoy them.

BIRD-EYE, see BIRD'S-EYE.

BIRD-FANCIER [burd'fan-si-er], *n.* one who rears and keeps birds as an expert.

BIRDIE [bur'di], *n.* (*golf*) holing-out in one stroke less than bogey.

BIRDLIME [burd'lim], *n.* viscous substance smeared on trees to entangle birds. **BIRDLIMED,** *adj.* smeared over with b.

BIRDSEED [burd'sēd], *n.* grain suitable for small cage-birds.

BIRD'S-EYE (1), **BIRD-EYE** [burd(z)'i], *n.* (*bot.*) one of various species of flowers having central spots or eyes; germander speedwell; kind of cut tobacco containing sections of stems like mottled stalks. **BIRD'S-EYE** (2), *adj.* seen from above; **b. view,** panoramic view seen from a height; (*fig.*) general survey.

BIRD'S-FOOT [burdz'foot], *n.* (*bot.*) one of several plants with cylindrical claw-like fruits.

BIRD'S-FOOT-TREFOIL [berdz-foot-trē'foil], *n.* (*bot.*) yellow leguminous pasture-plant.

BIRD'S-NEST (1) [burdz'nest], *n.* nest of a bird; nest of certain kinds of swift eaten as a delicacy by the Chinese; name given to various plants from the shape of their roots. **BIRD'S-NEST** (2), *v.i.* to search for bird's-nests, usually in order to take the eggs.

BIRD-WATCHING [burd'wo-ching], *n.* observation of the habits of wild birds, usually carried on as a hobby. **BIRD-WATCHER,** *n.* one who practises b.

BIRETTA [bi-re'tah], *n.* square-shaped, stiff-sided cap worn by Roman Catholic priests. [It.].

BIRR [bur], *n.* whirring, rattling noise; rush or force of a rapidly moving object; violent thrust; forceful energetic pronunciation; strongly trilled consonant *r.* [OScand.].

BIRTH [burth], *n.* process of being born; that which is born; family, lineage, environment into which a person is born; noble rank by birth; (*fig.*) origin, beginning. [O.E.].

BIRTH-CONTROL [burth'kon-trōl], *n.* regulation or prevention of conception by the use of chemical or mechanical contraceptives.

BIRTHDAY [burth'dā], *n.* day of one's birth; anniversary of that day; **in one's b. suit,** naked; **B. honours,** distinctions conferred according to custom to mark the Sovereign's birthday.

BIRTHMARK [burth'mahk], *n.* disfigurement in the form of a discoloured patch on the skin, naevus.

BIRTHPLACE [burth'plās], *n.* place where a person was born.

BIRTHRATE [burth'rāt], *n.* ratio of births to the population of a country.

BIRTHRIGHT [burth'rit], *n.* rights and privileges acquired at birth as a member of a family, nation etc.

BIS [bis], *adv.* (*mus.*) again, to be repeated; (in references) occurring twice. [L.].

BISCUIT [bis'kit], *n.* thin, hard, crisp, dry cake or

ōō is pronounced as in food; ŏŏ as in hood; th as in *think*; TH as in *that*; zh as in azure. ~ = related to.

bread, made of flour, water, eggs etc.; porous, unglazed porcelain or earthenware after the first firing; (army slang) a square brown mattress; **sea. ship's b.,** coarse, unfermented b. much used at sea instead of bread; **to take the b.,** to surpass (in impudence) everything. [Fr. from L.].

BISE [bēz], *n.* keen north-easterly wind frequently occurring in Switzerland. [Fr.].

BISECT [bi-sekt'], *v.t.* to divide into two portions; (*math.*) cut or divide into two equal parts. **BISECTION,** *n.* act of bisecting. **BISECTOR,** *n.* that which bisects. [L.].

BISEGMENT [bi-seg'ment], *n.* one half of a bisected line.

BISEXUAL [bi-sek'shoō-al], *adj.* of two sexes; containing both sexes in one body.

BISHOP [bi'shop], *n.* priest consecrated for the spiritual government of a diocese; piece in chess, often with a carved top in the form of a mitre; mulled wine. [OE. from Gk.].

BISHOPRIC [bi'shop-rik], *n.* the office of bishop; jurisdiction and diocese of a bishop. [OE.].

BISHOP-SLEEVE [bi'shop-slēv], *n.* sleeve of a lady's dress shaped like that worn by a bishop.

BISK [bisk], *n.* rich soup made from birds or crayfish. [Fr.].

BISMITE [biz'mit], *n.* (*min.*) bismuth oxide or bismuth ochre.

BISMUTH [biz'muth], *n.* brittle pale reddish-white metal, the chemical element whose symbol is Bi. **BISMUTHAL, BISMUTHIC** [biz'mu-thal, biz'mu-thik], *adj.* containing b., pertaining to b. **BISMUTHINE,** *n.* a compound of b. **BISMUTHITE,** *n.* a natural b. carbonate. [Germ.].

BISON (*pl.* **bison**) [bi'sun], *n.* European wild ox; American buffalo. [L.].

BISQUE (1) [bisk], *n.* bisk.

BISQUE (2), *n.* handicap allowance given to a player in a tennis or a golf tournament, to be used only at some stage of the match; extra turn allowed to a player at croquet. [Fr.].

BISQUE (3), *n.* kind of unglazed white porcelain used for ornaments. [BISCUIT].

BISSEXTILE (1) [bi-seks'til], *n.* a leap-year. **BISSEXTILE** (2), *adj.* containing the extra day added in a leap-year. [L.].

BISTORT [bis'tawt], *n.* (*bot.*) perennial plant of the buckwheat family. [LL.].

BISTOURY [bis-tōō'ri], *n.* a scalpel. [Fr.].

BISTRE [bis'ter], *n. and adj.* brown oily pigment obtained from the soot of wood. [Fr.].

BIT (1) [bit], *n.* the cutting edge of a tool; boring tool used with a drill, brace etc.; that part of a key which moves or grips the levers of a lock; the part of a bridle which is put in a horse's mouth. **BIT** (2), *n.* morsel, small portion or piece; a share; small amount; short interval of time; small silver coin; (*slang*) a young woman. **BIT** (3) (*pres.pt.* **BITTING,** *pret. and p.pt.* **BITTED),** *v.t.* to place a b. in a horse's mouth; (*fig.*) hold back, curb. **BIT** (4), *pret. and archaic p.pt.* of **BITE** (2). [OE.].

BITCH [bich], *n.* the female of dog, wolf or fox; (*vulgar*) term of reproach for a woman. [OE.].

BITE (1) [bit], *n.* small portion of food, mouthful; wound made by the teeth or a sting; a piercing with the teeth; sting; sharp taste; seizing or snap at bait by a fish; (*col.*) a fish; attractive, enticing offer; the gripping action of an edge upon another surface; (*print.*) part of the impression improperly printed, owing to the frisket not being sufficiently cut away. [OE.].

BITE (2) (*pret.* **bit,** *p.pt.* **bitten, bit†**), *v.t. and i.* to pierce, sever or wound with the teeth; cut into; snap at; grip, hold by friction; eat into so as to corrode; wound the feelings of; nip, damage; be liable to attack persons with the teeth; (*fig.*) cause sharp pain; possess a sharp taste; seize the bait with the teeth; pinch with cold; (*pass.*) be tempted by an attractive offer; (*coll.*) swindle, deceive; **to be bitten with,** (*coll.*) to be very enthusiastic about; **to b. the dust,** to be utterly defeated and humbled. [OE.].

BITER [bi'ter], *n.* person or thing that bites.

BITING [bi'ting], *adj.* sharp, severe, very cold, piercing; painfully sarcastic, bitter. **BITINGLY,** *adv.* in b. fashion.

BITTER (1) [bi'ter], *adj.* having an acrid, sharp, pungent taste, sour; (*fig.*) keen, piercing, harsh, malignant; cruel, stinging; distressing, lamentable; **b. beer,** light clear ale; **to the b. end,** to the very end, however unpleasant. **BITTER** (2), *n.* anything b.; **b. beer. BITTERISH,** *adj.* rather b. **BITTERLY,**

adv. in a b. manner. **BITTERNESS,** *n.* quality of being b., a b. taste. [OE.].

BITTERN (1) [bi'tern], *n.* marsh-haunting bird related to the heron. [OFr.].

BITTERN (2), *n.* product remaining from evaporated sea-water after the removal of the common salt; mixture used to adulterate beer. [BITTER (1)].

BITTERS [bi'terz], *n.* liquor brewed from bitter roots or herbs, used for flavouring drinks.

BITTER-SWEET (1) [bi'ter-swēt], *adj.* that which is partly bitter and partly sweet; (*fig.*) pleasant with some feeling of mental pain. **BITTER-SWEET** (2), *n.* woody nightshade; meadow-sweet.

BITTERWOOD [bi'ter-wōōd], *n.* quassia.

BITTERWORT [bi'ter-wert], *n.* the yellow gentian.

BITTS [bits], *n.(pl.)* (*naut.*) pairs of vertical posts fastened to the deck of a ship to secure ropes etc. **BITT,** *v.t.* (*naut.*) to put a cable, rope etc. round the b. [Uncert.].

BITUMEN [bi'tyoō-men], *n.* (*min.*) mineral pitch, asphalt; (*chem.*) general name for a group of inflammable mineral hydrocarbons. **BITUMINATE** [bi-tyoō'mi-nāt], *v.t.* to impregnate with b. **BITUMINIFEROUS** [bi-tyoō-mi-ni'fe-rŏŏs], *adj.* yielding b. **BITUMINIZE** [bi-tyoō'mi-niz], *v.t.* to turn into or impregnate with b. **BITUMINOUS** [bi-tyoō'mi-nŏŏs], *adj.* containing or like b. [L.].

BIVALENT [bi'va-lent], *adj.* (*chem.*) able to replace two atoms of hydrogen. [L.].

BIVALVE (1) [bi'valv], *n.* mollusc having a hinged shell of two halves, as an oyster etc.; (*bot.*) seed-vessel with two valves. **BIVALVE(D)** (2), *adj.* having a double, hinged shell; (*bot.*) having two valves. **BIVALVOUS** [bi-val'vŏŏs], *adj.* having b. shells. **BIVALVULAR** [bi-val'vyōō-ler], *adj.* with two small valves.

BIVOUAC (1) [bi'vŏŏ-ak], *n.* an encampment of soldiers in the open for the night; any one-night camp. **BIVOUAC** (2), *v.i.* to camp out for the night, *esp.* with little equipment. [Fr. from Germ.].

BI-WEEKLY [bi-wēk'li], *adj.* fortnightly; occurring twice in a week.

BIZARRE [bi-zah(r)'], *adj.* eccentric, odd, peculiar, fantastic, grotesque. [Fr.].

BIZONE [bi'zōn], *n.* zone formed by the amalgamation of two zones, and administered jointly by the authorities formerly responsible for the separate zones; *esp.* the jointly-administered British-American zone of Germany, after 1947. **BIZONAL** [bi-zō'nal], *adj.* pertaining to a b.

BLAB (1) [blab], *n.* one who blabs. **BLAB** (2) (*pres.pt.* **BLABBING,** *pret. and p.pt.* **BLABBED),** *v.i.* to reveal secrets unwisely, betray confidences. [Uncert.].

BLACK (1) [blak], *n.* the absence of light or visible colour; the colour, dye or pigment which absorbs all incident light; smut of soot; black clothing; negro; dirt; (*fig.*) mourning apparel; (*bot.*) dark fungus which injures wheat.

BLACK (2), *adj.* having no colour or light, absorbing all visible colours; of the darkest colour; pertaining to negroes, having dark features, swarthy-skinned; dirty; (*fig.*) unpropitious, gloomy, mournful; wicked, foul, infamous; sullen, cross; **b. art,** magic, necromancy; **b. cap,** cap worn by judges when passing sentence of death; **b. draught,** black-coloured purgative; **b. eye,** dark-coloured bruise around the eye; **in b. and white,** written down; **b. guard,** member of the former German protective guards; **b. market,** illegal dealing in Government-controlled commodities; **b. marketeer,** one who operates on the b. market; **B. Maria,** (*coll.*) police van for carrying prisoners; **B. Monks,** the Benedictines; **B. Rod,** the usher to the Lord Chamberlain and the House of Lords. [OE.].

BLACK (3), *v.t.* to make black; polish with blacking or black lead; soil; **to b. out,** to delete, obliterate; screen (lights) so as to prevent their being seen from outside, *esp.* from the air; *v.i.* to suffer from temporary unconsciousness.

BLACKAMOOR [bla'ka-mŏŏr], *n.* negro; black man.

BLACKBALL (1) [blak'bawl], *n.* small wooden or ivory black ball used to indicate an adverse vote in balloting; kind of boiled sweet. **BLACKBALL** (2), *v.t.* to vote against by putting a black ball into the voting box; vote against, reject, expel.

BLACK-BEETLE [blak-bē'tl], *n.* cockroach.

BLACKBERRY (1) [blak'be-ri], *n.* (*bot.*) the small black berry of the bramble; (*pop.*) the bramble. **BLACKBERRY** (2), *v.i.* to gather blackberries.

BLACKBIRD [blak'berd], *n.* dark-coloured species of thrush; species of American birds related to the starling and crow. **BLACKBIRDING**, *n.* kidnapping of negroes into slavery.

BLACKBOARD [blak'bawd], *n.* large board painted black, which is written upon with chalk.

BLACKBROWED [blak-browd'], *adj.* frowning, sullen.

BLACKCAP [blak'kap], *n.* (*zool.*) a European warbler bird; American species of titmouse.

BLACK-COAT [blak'kōt], *n.* (*coll.*) clergyman; **black-coated worker**, one engaged in non-manual labour, who receives weekly wages as distinct from a salary.

BLACK-COCK [blak'kok], *n.* the heath-cock.

BLACK CURRANT [blak-ku'rant], *n.* small black fruit.

BLACKDROP [blak'drop], *n.* drink made of opium mixed with vinegar and spices; (*astron.*) dark band or spot visible during the passage of the planets Venus and Mercury across the sun's disk.

BLACKEN [bla'ken], *v.t. and i.* to make black, darken; (*fig.*) defame, sully, disparage.

BLACKFELLOW [blak'fe-lō], *n.* an aboriginal of Australia.

BLACK-FISH [blak'fish], *n.* American edible sefish; Mediterranean fish allied to the mackerel; species of small pilot whale.

BLACK FLAG [blak-flag'], *n.* pirate flag; flag symbolizing death.

BLACKFRIAR [blak-frī'er], *n.* Dominican friar.

BLACK FROST [blak-frost'], *n.* frost with which no rime appears.

BLACK-GAME [blak'gām], *n.* black-grouse.

BLACKGUARD [bla'gahd], *n.* base, unprincipled, dishonourable scoundrel. **BLACKGUARD** (2), *v.t.* to revile in violent language, call a b. **BLACKGUARDISM**, *n.* behaviour or language of a b. **BLACKGUARDLY** (1), *adj.* like a b.; vile, dishonourable. **BLACKGUARDLY** (2), *adv.* in the manner of a b. [Uncert.].

BLACKHEAD [blak'hed], *n.* small black pimple.

BLACKHEARTED [blak-hah'tid], *adj.* having an evil, wicked character.

BLACK-HOLE [blak-hōl'], *n.* place of confinement for insubordinate prisoners.

BLACKING [bla'king], *n.* black liquid or paste used for cleaning and polishing footwear.

BLACK-JACK [blak'jak], *n.* a black draught; (*U.S.*) kind of bludgeon.

BLACK LEAD (1) [blak-led'], *n.* plumbago, graphite, used in making pencils, blackening fire-grates etc.; writing or drawing pencil. **BLACK LEAD** (2), *v.t.* to polish and blacken with b.

BLACKLEG [blak'leg], *n.* swindler, fraud; one who continues to work during an official strike; nonunion member who will work for less than union rates of pay; cattle disease.

BLACK-LETTER (1) [blak-le'ter], *n.* (*print.*) ornate form of type, Gothic, Old English type. **BLACK-LETTER** (2), *adj.* printed in b.

BLACK-LIST (1) [blak'list], *n.* official or private list of fraudulent or insolvent people; list of convicted, suspected or discredited persons. **BLACK-LIST** (2), *v.t.* to put down (a person's name) on a b.

BLACKMAIL (1) [blak'māl], *n.* (*hist.*) levy or tax of money, livestock etc. formerly paid on the Scottish Border to robbers to secure immunity from pillage; (*leg.*) the obtaining or attempt to exact money from a person under threat of exposure of some discreditable secret. **BLACKMAIL** (2), *v.t.* to obtain money from a person by b.

BLACK MARK [blak-mahk'], *n.* mark set down against the name of a person who does wrong.

BLACK-OUT [blak'owt], *n.* sudden cutting off of all stage lights to end a scene with effect; complete failure of a public supply of electricity at night; extinction or screening of all lights in a particular area; state of temporary unconsciousness, especially one due to a sudden turn or dive while navigating an aircraft.

BLACK PUDDING [blak-pŏŏ'ding], *n.* sausage made from suet, pig's blood etc.

BLACK-ROT [blak-rot'], *n.* destructive blight or fungus afflicting certain vegetables.

BLACK-RUST [blak-rust'], *n.* disease occurring in wheat.

BLACK SHEEP [blak-shēp'], *n.* person of bad character, scapegoat.

BLACKSMITH [blak'smith], *n.* smith who works in iron.

BLACKSNAKE [blak'snāk], *n.* one of various snakes of dark colour.

BLACKSTRAP [blak'strap], *n.* (*coll.*) strong inferior kind of port wine; mixture of rum and molasses.

BLACK-TAIL [blak'tāl], *n.* kind of perch.

BLACKTHORN [blak'thawn], *n.* the sloe, kind of thorn-tree with white flowers and black berries; staff made of the wood of this tree.

BLACK-WASH (1) [blak'wosh], *n.* solution used for blackening an object; (*med.*) lotion of calomel and lime-water. **BLACK-WASH** (2), *v.t.* to cover or treat with b.

BLACKWATER FEVER [blak-waw-ter-fē'ver], *n.* (*med.*) a tropical West African fever.

BLADDER [bla'der], *n.* (*anat.*) thin muscular bag, lined with mucous membrane, in the bodies of animals, serving as a receptacle for secreted fluids such as urine; thin membranous sac of an animal used as a windbag for bagpipes etc.; tough rubber or membranous bag inflated with air; (*bot.*) small baglike protuberance in certain plants. **BLADDERED**, *adj.* swollen out like a b. **BLADDERY**, *adj.* resembling a b.; containing bladders. [OE.].

BLADDER-KELP [bla'der-kelp], *n.* (*bot.*) seaweed with small bladder-like protuberances on its fronds.

BLADDER-WORT [bla'der-wert], *n.* (*bot.*) water plant with tiny bladders on the leaves.

BLADDER-WRACK [bla'der-rak], *n.* bladder-kelp.

BLADE [blād], *n.* narrow leaf of grass or corn; the broad part of any leaf; anything similar in shape to this; the cutting part of a tool or weapon; the broad part of an oar, propeller, paddle etc.; a flattened broad bone; front part of the tongue; (*fig.*) sword or similar weapon; (*coll.*) dashing young man. **BLADED**, *adj.* possessing a b. or blades; blade-like. [OE.].

BLADEBONE [blād'bōn], *n.* the shoulder-blade.

BLAEBERRY [blā'be-ri], *n.* (*bot.*) bilberry or whortleberry. [OScand. *bla* dark blue and BERRY].

BLAGUE [blahg], *n.* humbug, pretentious nonsense. [Fr.].

BLAH [blah], *n.* (*slang*) foolish, empty, exaggerated talk or writing.

BLAIN [blān], *n.* inflamed swelling, pustule, blister; growth on the root of the tongue in cattle. [OE.].

BLAMABLE [blā'ma-bl], *adj.* deserving blame.

BLAME (1) [blām], *n.* censure, reproof, disapproval, imputation of a fault; responsibility for failure or wrong action, guilt. **BLAME** (2), *v.t.* to censure, find fault with; hold responsible for an offence or fault, accuse. [OFr. from L.].

BLAMEFUL [blām'fŏŏl], *adj.* blamable.

BLAMELESS [blām'les], *adj.* free from guilt or blame, innocent. **BLAMELESSLY**, *adv.* in b. fashion. **BLAMELESSNESS**, *n.* quality of being b.

BLAMEWORTHY [blām'wer-тНi], *adj.* deserving reproof. **BLAMEWORTHINESS**, *n.* quality of being b.

BLANCH [blahnsh], *v.t. and i.* to make white, deprive of colour, bleach; remove the skin of (almonds); (*fig.*) gloss over, palliate; grow white; turn pale. **BLANCHED**, *adj.* whitened, bleached; skinned (of almonds). **BLANCHER**, *n.* one who blanches. **BLANCHING**, *adj.* whitening; **b. liquor**, bleaching solution of chloride of lime. [Fr.].

BLANCMANGE [bla-monzh'], *n.* opaque jelly pudding made from cornflour etc. [Fr.].

BLAND [bland], *adj.* gentle, affable, ingratiatingly polite; mild, balmy. **BLANDLY**, *adv.* in a b. manner. **BLANDNESS**, *n.* quality of being b. [L.].

BLANDISH [blan'dish], *v.t.* to flatter, coax, wheedle with soft, ingratiating words. **BLANDISHING**, **BLANDISHMENT**, *n.* flattering cajolery; alluring manner or thing. [~Fr. from L.].

BLANK (1) [blangk], *n.* an unmarked whiteness; piece of paper having nothing written or printed upon it; unsuccessful ticket in a lottery; emptiness, state of vacancy or emptiness; piece of metal ready for stamping or finishing; white point in the centre of a target; empty space in a document to be filled up later; unmarked half of a domino; **a double b.**, domino with no spots; **to draw a b.**, to be unsuccessful, fail.

BLANK (2), *adj.* appearing as a blank; white without mark; devoid of all writing or marks; vacant; destitute of interest or incident; abortive; unrelieved, pure; expressionless, nonplussed; (*poet.*) not rhyming; *also used coll. as the verbal equivalent of the dash used in printing in place of some profane expletive*; **a b. cheque**, signed cheque with the amount to be drawn left to be filled in by the possessor; (*fig.*) a free hand; **b. cartridge**, one without ball or bullet. **BLANK** (3), *v.t.* to make b. **BLANKLY**, *adv.* in a b. fashion; utterly, absolutely. [Fr.].

BLANKET (1) [blang'ket], *n.* thick, soft, looselywoven cloth used as a covering; (*print.*) piece of such

---

ŏŏ is pronounced as in food; ŏŏ as in hood; th as in *think*; TH as in *that*; zh as in azure. ~ = related to.

a fabric or of rubber inserted between paper and platen to absorb uneven pressure etc.; (fig.) thick bank of clouds, belt of fog; **a wet b.**, (fig.) one who spoils enjoyment for others. BLANKET (2), adj. (coll., orig. U.S.), inclusive, all-embracing. BLANKET (3), v.t. to cover with a b.; (naut.) take the wind out of a vessel's sails by drawing alongside to windward. BLANKETING, n. cloth or material for blankets; tossing in a b. [OFr.].

BLANKETY [blang'ke-ti], adj. (coll.) used as a humorous substitute for a profane expletive; also **b. blank.**

BLANQUETTE [blahng-ket'], n. a highly seasoned stew. [Fr.].

BLARE (1) [blãer], n. loud sonorous noise or blast as of a trumpet etc. BLARE (2), v.t. and i. to bellow, make a deafening sound. [Du.].

BLARNEY (1) [blah'ni], n. coarse flattery; grossly deceitful speech; crude cajolery. BLARNEY (2), v.t. and i. to flatter, coax. [Blarney, in Ireland, where a stone stands which if kissed is said to endow the person who kisses it with a flattering persuasive tongue].

BLASPHEME [blas-fēm'], v.t. and i. to curse, swear, use bad language; desecrate in speech, utter impious, profane remarks about; revile. BLASPHEMER, n. one who blasphemes. BLASPHEMING, n. the utterance of blasphemy. [Gk.].

BLASPHEMOUS [blas'fe-mŏŏs], adj. speaking or containing blasphemy. BLASPHEMOUSLY, adv. in a b. way.

BLASPHEMY [blas'fe-mi], n. impious, profane, contemptuous speech or behaviour with regard to things held sacred; foul abuse, bad language. [Gk.].

BLAST (1) [blahst], n. sudden strong current of air, natural as a gust of wind or artificially produced as in a current of air driven through a furnace or by an explosive; loud sound produced by blowing certain wind instruments, chiefly brass; explosion in splitting up rocks by dynamite etc.; amount of explosive used; pernicious, blighting disease attacking plants and animals; (fig.) withering destructive influence; **in full b.**, (fig.) in a state of great activity. BLAST-PROOF, impervious to, giving protection against, bomb b. BLAST (2), v.t. to shrivel up, wither, blight; break up or blow up by the use of explosives; (fig.) discredit, ruin, curse; indulge in profane abuse. BLAST (3), int. (a profane exclamation) confound. BLASTED, adj. blighted, withered; (coll.) confounded, infernal. [OE.].

BLASTEMA [blas-tē'mah], n. primary material out of which plants or animals are formed and developed. BLASTEMAL [blas-tē'mal], adj. pertaining to the b. [Gk.].

BLAST-FURNACE [blahst'fer-nis], n. smelting furnace in which heated air is driven through the molten metal.

BLASTING [blah'sting], n. the breaking up of rocks by explosion; shrivelling or withering, blighting; the blaring of certain wind instruments; (radio) distortion, esp. on loud notes.

BLASTOCARPOUS [blas-tō-kah'pŏŏs], adj. (bot.) germinating inside the pericarp. [Gk.].

BLASTOCOLLA [blas-tō-ko'lah], n. (bot.) sticky substance with which certain buds are coated. [Gk.].

BLASTODERM [blas'tō-derm], n. (biol.) the external layers of cells of an embryo in its earliest form. [Gk.].

BLASTOGENESIS [blas-tō-je'ni-sis], n. (biol.) theory that life originates from the germ plasma. [Gk.].

BLASTOSPHERE [blas'tō-sfēer], n. embryo having a blastoderm and a cavity. [Gk.].

BLAST-PIPE [blahst'pip], n. pipe in locomotives to convey waste steam up the chimney, creating a draught through the fire.

BLATANT [blã'tant], adj. noisily vulgar, loud-voiced, clamorous; gross, palpable. BLATANCY, n. condition of being b. BLATANTLY, adv. in b. fashion. [The Blatant Beast in Spenser's Faerie Queene].

BLATHER (1) and (2), see BLETHER (1) and (2).

BLAY [blã], n. a small river fish, the bleak. [OE.].

BLAZE (1) [blãz], n. burst or jet of flame, stream of light from a fire; a fire; dazzlingly brilliant glow; (fig.) sudden flaring up of emotion; white spot or mark on the forehead of a horse; white mark made by notching the bark of trees; **like blazes**, with great vigour. BLAZE (2), v.t. and i. to burst into flames, burn with a bright, strong light; shine brilliantly and powerfully; fire off ammunition continuously and rapidly; (fig.) show fierce anger; mark

trees by cutting away part of the bark; **to b. up, out,** to give way to a sudden burst of anger; **to b. a trail,** to mark out a path by blazing the trees; (fig.) engage in pioneer work. [OE.].

BLAZE (3), v.t. to proclaim far and wide, spread or publish abroad. [OScand.].

BLAZER [blã'zer], n. light, often brightly-coloured, flannel sports jacket. [BLAZE (2)].

BLAZING [blã'zing], adj. that blazes; (fig.) furiously angry; (of a fox's scent) very strong; glaring.

BLAZON (1) [blã'zon], n. shield or coat of arms together with its heraldic devices; description in heraldic terms, or drawing, of armorial bearings; (fig.) display of excellencies, titles etc. BLAZON (2), v.t. to depict or inscribe armorial bearings; describe coats of arms in proper terms; embellish; make known far and wide. BLAZONER, n. one who blazons, a herald. BLAZONMENT, n. act of blazoning. [OFr.].

BLAZONRY [blã'zon-ri], n. a collection of coats of arms or armorial bearings; art of describing coats of arms in proper heraldic terms.

BLEACH [blēch], v.t. and i. to whiten, pale, deprive of colour by chemical action or exposure to sunlight; become lighter in this way; **b. cream**, cream, ointment, containing bleaching powder, used as an antidote for mustard-gas. BLEACHER, n. person who or thing which bleaches. BLEACHERY, n. place where bleaching is carried out. BLEACHFIELD, n. field in which cloth is bleaching. BLEACHING, n. process of whitening or making lighter by chemical agents or exposure to sunlight. [OE.].

BLEAK (1) [blēk], small river fish allied to the carp. [Uncert.].

BLEAK (2), adj. cheerless, bare, unsheltered; dismal, uninviting. BLEAKLY, adv. in a b. way. BLEAKNESS, n. condition of being b. [OScand.].

BLEAR (1) [blēer], adj. (of the eyes) dim, watery. BLEAR (2), v.t. and i. (of the eyes) to dim, make indistinct, blur, dull or cloud; **to b. the eyes,** to deceive, hoax. BLEAREDNESS, n. condition of being bleared. [ME.].

BLEAR-EYED [blēer-īd'], adj. not able to see distinctly.

BLEARY [blēer'i], adj. blear.

BLEAT (1) [blēt], v.t. and i. to make the cry of a sheep; (fig.) babble, blurt out foolishly. BLEAT (2), the cry of a sheep; (fig.) a feeble wail. BLEATING, n. the crying of a sheep. [OE.].

BLEB [bleb], n. small blister or swelling. BLEBBY, adj. covered with blebs. [Unkn.].

BLEED (bled) [blēd], v.t. to take blood from a person surgically; (fig.) exact large amounts of money from a person wrongfully; (motoring) draw fluid from a hydraulic braking system; v.i. to lose blood, emit blood; (bot.) emit sap; **one's heart bleeds**, (fig.) one feels anguish. BLEEDER, n. person suffering from haemophilia. [OE.].

BLEEDING (1) [blē'ding], n. flow of blood from a wound; haemorrhage; the operation of letting blood; (bot.) flow of sap from cut stems. BLEEDING (2), adj. that bleeds; (fig.) full of anguish or pity.

BLEMISH (1) [ble'mish], v.t. to mar, impair; tarnish, sully; deface, spoil the perfection of. BLEMISH (2), n. fault or flaw marring anything, disfigurement, physical or moral defect. [OFr.].

BLENCH [blensh], v.t. to flinch, quail, shrink back. [OE.].

BLEND (1) [blend], v.t. and i. to mix together so as to form an agreeable compound or combination; mingle easily, mix well together; unite imperceptibly. BLEND (2), n. a mixture of wholly or slightly different substances to form a harmonious or pleasing whole. BLENDER, n. one who blends. [ME.].

BLENDE [blend], n. (min.) native sulphide of zinc. [Germ.].

BLENHEIM [ble'nem], n. breed of spaniel. **B. orange**, orange-red variety of eating apple. [Blenheim, near Oxford].

BLENNOGENOUS [ble-no'ji-nŏŏs], adj. (path.) yielding mucus. [Gk.].

BLENNORRHOEA [ble-no-rē'ah], n. excessive discharge of mucus.

BLENNY [ble'ni], n. small freshwater fish covered with mucus. [Gk.].

BLENT [blent], archaic p.pt. of BLEND (1).

BLESBOK [bles'bok], n. a South African antelope. [Du.].

BLESS [bles], v.t. to pronounce holy, consecrate; worship, adore, praise; thank, remember with gratitude; invoke God's favour upon; make happy or prosperous, be favoured with; **to b. oneself,** to make the sign of the Cross; **to b. one's stars,** to count oneself fortunate. [O.E.].

BLESSED (1), **BLEST** [ble'sid, blest], *n.* those who are beatified. BLESSED (2), BLEST, *adj.* prosperous, fortunate, consecrated, venerated; beatified, possessing or enjoying certain joys; eternally happy; *(coll.)* used ironically as expletive meaning "cursed," "confounded." BLESSEDLY, *adv.* in a b. way. BLESSEDNESS, *n.* state of being b.

BLESSING [ble'sing], *n.* prayer, invocation for divine favour or happiness; benediction, grace; divine gift, favour or benefit; cause of happiness; something to be remembered with gratitude.

BLEST, see BLESSED.

BLETHER (1) [ble'THer], *v.i.* to talk nonsense. BLETHER (2), *n.* foolish empty talk. [OScand.].

BLETONISM [ble'to-nizm], *n.* faculty of water-divining. BLETONIST, *n.* water-diviner. [M. *Bléton*].

BLEW [blōō], *pret.* of BLOW (3).

BLEWIT [blōō'it], *n.* a species of mushroom. [Uncert.].

BLIGHT (1) [blit], *n.* effect produced by disease, attacks of insects or parasitic fungi which cause plants to wither or decay; *(fig.)* anything which destroys hope. BLIGHT (2), *v.t.* to affect with b.; wither, cause to decay. [Uncert.].

BLIGHTER [bli'ter], *n. (slang)* utter cad; fellow.

BLIGHTING [bli'ting], *n.* action of affecting or being affected with blight. BLIGHTINGLY, *adv.* in a b. way.

BLIGHTY [bli'ti], *n. (coll.)* England; **a. b. one,** severe wound which led to the return of a soldier to England. [Hind.].

BLIMP [blimp], *n.* small non-rigid dirigible military airship; *(coll.)* person, usually of official rank, with exaggeratedly nationalist and imperialist ideas. [Unkn.].

BLIND (1) [blind], *adj.* unable to see, deprived of sight; *(fig.)* without understanding, judgment or appreciation; dark, obscure, admitting no light; having no outlet; pertaining to the blind; **to turn a b. eye to,** to pretend not to notice. BLIND (2), *v.t. and i.* to make b., obscure the perception, vision or judgment of; *(fig.)* deceive; *(coll.)* proceed without taking care where one is going. BLIND (3), *n.* screen of cloth or other material which can be lowered from a roller to cover a window; deception, something intended to produce a misleading impression; *(coll.)* drinking bout; **the b.,** b. people. [O.E.].

BLINDAGE [blin'dij], *n.* screen used for military purposes.

BLIND ALLEY (1) [blind-a'li], *n.* alley leading nowhere; *(fig.)* an occupation with no prospects. BLIND-ALLEY (2), *adj.* (of work) without prospects of advancement.

BLIND-COAL [blind'kōl], *n.* anthracite.

BLIND FLYING [blind-fli'ing], *n. (aeron.)* aerial navigation entirely by means of instruments.

BLINDFOLD [blind'fōld], *v.t.* to make a person unable to see by covering his eyes with a bandage. BLINDFOLD (2), *adj. and adv.* having the eyes covered over with a bandage; *(fig.)* lacking understanding or judgment; deceived.

BLIND-GUT [blind'gut], *n. (anat.)* the caecum.

BLINDLY [blind'li], *adv.* as if blind; *(fig.)* recklessly, without judgment, ignorantly; without question.

BLIND-MAN'S-BUFF [blind-manz-buf'], *n.* game in which one, who is blindfolded, tries to catch any other player and guess his identity.

BLINDNESS [blind'nes], *n.* state of being blind.

BLIND SIDE [blind'sid], *n.* the vulnerable side.

BLIND SPOT [blind'spot], *n.* part of the retina insensible to light.

BLIND TOOLING [blind-tōō'ling], *n. (bookbinding)* lettering or design impressed on covers without ink or gold leaf.

BLINDWORM [blind'werm], *n.* the slow-worm, a legless lizard with extremely small eyes.

BLINK (1) [blingk], *v.t. and i.* to open and shut the eyelids repeatedly and quickly, wink; glance, shine with fitful gleams; ignore, evade purposely, refuse to recognize or admit. BLINK (2), *n.* sudden flash of light; glimpse, glance, wink. [Du.].

BLINKERS [bling'kerz], *n.(pl.)* broad rectangular pieces of leather fastened on each side of a horse's head over the eyes. BLINKERED, *adj.* wearing b.; *(fig.)* short-sighted, having a narrow outlook.

BLINKING [bling'king], *adj. (coll. as a mild expletive)* confounded.

BLISS [blis], *n.* supreme happiness; perfect joy and

blessedness of souls in paradise; highest spiritual or physical delight. [O.E.].

BLISSFUL [blis'fōōl], *adj.* happy, enjoyable, full of bliss. BLISSFULLY, *adv.* in a b. manner.

BLISTER (1) [blis'ter], *n.* pustule or bladder-like protuberance on the skin containing serum or watery matter, and caused by a burn, injury etc.; similar swelling on a heated or painted surface; *(med.)* something applied to raise a blister. BLISTER (2), *v.t. and i.* to raise a b.; come out in blisters; *(fig.)* shrivel with scorn or sarcasm. [OFr.].

BLISTER-FLY [blis'ter-fli], *n.* Spanish fly, used medically to blister.

BLISTER-STEEL [blis'ter-stēl], *n.* steel whose surface is covered with blisters during conversion from iron.

BLITHE [blīTH], *adj.* merry, joyous, happy. BLITHELY, *adv.* in a b. way.

BLITHERING [bli'THe-ring], *adj.* drivelling, utter. [BLETHER (1)].

BLITHESOME [blīTH'sum], *adj.* gay, cheerful, jolly. BLITHESOMENESS, *n.* blitheness.

BLITZ (1) [blits], *n.* violent and sudden attack. BLITZ (2), *v.t.* to subject to a violent and sudden attack, *esp.* from the air. [Shortened form of *next*].

BLITZKRIEG [blits'krēg], *n.* form of warfare dependent on the very rapid movement of attacking forces, *esp.* of aeroplanes and tanks. [Germ.].

BLIZZARD [bli'zerd], *n.* violent snowstorm, accompanied by a heavy gale. [Imitative].

BLOAT [blōt], *v.t. and i.* to cure herrings by salting and smoking them over an oak-fire; cause to swell; become swollen. [~OScand.].

BLOATED [blō'tid], *adj.* swollen with self-indulgence, turgid, flabby, fat by gluttony; *(fig.)* swollen with pride; (of fish etc.) cured by salting and smoking.

BLOATER [blō'ter], *n.* herring which has been cured by salting and smoking.

BLOB [blob], *n.* a blot, globule of liquid or semi-liquid; *(coll. cricket)* nought, a duck.

BLOBBER-LIP [blo'ber-lip], *n.* a thick, protruding, loose lip. BLOBBER-LIPPED, *adj.* having thick, hanging lips.

BLOC [blok], *n.* group of parties supporting or opposing a government; group of nations acting in concert. [Fr.].

BLOCK (1) [blok], *n.* solid mass of stone, wood etc.; such a thing on which substances may be chopped or hammered, piece of wood on which persons laid their necks when about to be beheaded; continuous row or group of buildings without intervening spaces; large quantity of shares; frame casing on which are mounted one or more grooved pulleys; obstruction to the natural flow or free passage of anything, especially liquid, traffic etc.; small piece of hard wood on which an engraving is made, etched metal plate mounted on wood for printing illustrations; pad of sheets of paper attached at one edge; dull, stupid person; *(cricket)* that part of the popping-crease in which a batsman rests his bat in readiness for play; **b. system,** traffic system whereby a section of a railway line has to be reported clear before a train is allowed to enter it; *(coll.)* **a chip of the old b.,** child who strongly resembles his father in person, interests, character or ability. BLOCK (2), *adj.* inclusive in a group; **b. vote,** vote by a group of people given as a whole by a delegate. BLOCK (3), *v.t.* to obstruct; shut in, blockade; shape on a b.; cut out in blocks; support with blocks; prevent or delay anything; *(cricket)* stop a ball without attempting a scoring stroke; **to b. out,** to shape out roughly, make a rough draft; obstruct the line of vision etc. [Fr. from OHigh Germ.].

BLOCKADE (1) [blo-kād'], *n.* the surrounding of a port by enemy warships to prevent communication with, or receiving of supplies from, other places by sea; the besieging of a place by hostile forces, so as to cut it off from the outside world; **a paper b.,** an alleged but ineffective b.; **to raise a b.,** to end a b.; **b. runner,** ship which tries to get through a b. BLOCKADE (2), *v.t.* to subject hostile territory to a b. [BLOCK (3)].

BLOCKHEAD [blok'hed], *n.* stupid person.

BLOCK-BUSTER [blok'bus-ter], *n. (coll.)* aerial bomb powerful enough to destroy a whole block of buildings.

BLOCKHOUSE [blok'hows], *n. (milit.)* small fortified hut or similar military post.

BLOCKISH [blo'kish], *adj.* stupid, clumsy.

BLOCK LETTERS [blok-le'terz], *n.(pl.)* capital sanserif letters.

BLOCK-PLANE [blok'plān], *n.* plane having the

blade set so as to work across the grain of the wood.
BLOCK PRINTING [blok'prin-ting], *n.* method of printing from engraved blocks.
BLOCK-SHIP [blok'ship], *n.* ship moored or sunk so as to close the entrance to a harbour.
BLOKE [blōk], *n.* (*slang*), a fellow. [Unkn.].
BLOND (1) [blond], *n.* person with light hair and fair complexion. **BLOND** (2), *adj.* having light hair and fair complexion. [Fr.].
BLONDE [blond], *n.* woman with light hair and fair complexion; kind of silk lace with hexagonal meshes.
BLOOD (1) [blud], *n.* opaque red fluid circulating through the arteries and veins of the human body and of other animals; (*fig.*) temper, passion, character; carnal nature as opposed to spiritual; bloodshed; murder, guilt of murder; sacrifice; life or essence, vital being; connexion by descent, lineage, relationship by birth; noble birth; good pedigree; smart man about town, swell; (*slang*) sensational thriller or mystery story; **flesh and b.**, human nature; **in cold b.**, deliberately; **blue b.**, noble birth or lineage; an aristocratic strain; **base b.**, illegitimacy; illegitimate birth; **first b.**, first advantage in any contest; **fresh, new b.**, (*fig.*) new influences, members, ideas etc.; **to taste b.**, to kill and eat a hunted animal; (*fig.*) to have a first success calculated to make one eager for more; **to spill b.**, to commit murder; **to have a person's b. on one's head**, to be guilty of his death; **to make one's b. boil**, to make a person extremely angry or indignant; **to make one's b. run cold**, to terrify, horrify a person; **to make bad b.**, to arouse ill-feeling; **one's b. is up**, used of a person whose anger is aroused; **b. sports**, the hunting and killing of animals for pleasure. BLOOD (2), *v.t.* to cause to let b.; initiate a hound to the taste, scent etc. of b.; smear with b.; (*fig.*) initiate. BLOODED, *adj.* smeared with b., given the first taste of b. [OE.].
BLOOD-BROTHER [blud-bru'THer], *n.* male person born of the same parents as another.
BLOOD COUNT [blud'kownt], *n.* the determination of the number of corpuscles in a given quantity of blood.
BLOOD-DONOR [blud'dō-ner], *n.* one who contributes blood for transfusion.
BLOOD FEUD [blud'fyōōd], *n.* feud between two families arising out of the murder of a member of one by a member of the other.
BLOOD-GROUP [blud'grōōp], *n.* (*med.*) classification of the different types of blood; classification of all persons who have the same type of blood.
BLOOD-GUILTY [blud'gil-ti], *adj.* responsible for bloodshed or murder.
BLOOD-HEAT [blud'hēt], *n.* the temperature of the human blood, normally about 98·4° Fahrenheit.
BLOOD-HORSE [blud'haws], *n.* thoroughbred horse.
BLOODHOUND [blud'hownd], *n.* variety of dog with an acute sense of smell, used to pursue game or fugitives.
BLOODLESS [blud'les], *adj.* without bloodshed; lacking in blood; (*fig.*) devoid of energy or passion.
BLOODLETTING [blud'le-ting], *n.* (*surg.*) the drawing of blood from a vein.
BLOOD-MONEY [blud'mu-ni], *n.* reward paid for information leading to a conviction for murder; compensation paid to the heirs of a murdered man.
BLOOD-ORANGE [blud'o-rinj], *n.* variety of orange yielding a fruit streaked with red and having red juice.
BLOOD-POISONING [blud'poi-zo-ning], *n.* infected condition of the blood.
BLOOD-PRESSURE [blud'pre-sher], *n.* the pressure of the blood on the walls of the blood-vessels; (*pop.*) unhealthy condition arising when this pressure becomes abnormal.
BLOOD PUDDING [blud-pōō'ding], *n.* black pudding.
BLOOD-RED [blud'red], *adj.* red with blood, of the colour of blood.
BLOOD RELATION [blud-ri-lā'shn], *n.* one related by birth or descent.
BLOOD-ROOT [blud'rōōt], *n.* (*bot.*) plant related to the poppy family.
BLOODSHED [blud'shed], *n.* shedding of blood, slaughter, fierce fighting.
BLOODSHOT [blud'shot], *adj.* (of the eyeball) suffused with blood.
BLOOD SPAVIN [blud'spa-vin], *n.* dilatation of the vein along the inside of a horse's hock.
BLOODSTAIN [blud'stān], *n.* discoloration caused

by smearing with blood. BLOODSTAINED, *adj.* coloured or smeared with blood.
BLOOD-STOCK [blud'stok], *n.* thoroughbred or pedigree stock.
BLOODSTONE [blud'stōn], *n.* one of several precious stones streaked with red; heliotrope; haematite.
BLOODSUCKER [blud'su-ker], *n.* creature which sucks blood; (*fig.*) one who extorts money from another. BLOOD-SUCKING (1), *n.* act of sucking blood by leeches. BLOOD-SUCKING (2), *adj.* that sucks blood.
BLOODTHIRSTY [blud'thers-ti], *adj.* eager for slaughter, fierce, desirous of bloodshed. BLOODTHIRSTINESS, *n.* state of being b.
BLOOD-TRANSFUSION [blud'trans-fyōō-zhn], *n.* transference of blood from one person to another who suffers from loss or lack of blood.
BLOOD-VESSEL [blud've-sel], *n.* artery; vein; vessel through which blood circulates.
BLOODWORM [blud'werm], *n.* blood-red larva of a gnat found in water; blood-red worm used as bait by anglers.
BLOODY (1) [blu'di], *adj.* covered or stained with blood; (*fig.*) murderous; accompanied with bloodshed; of the same colour as blood; (*vulg.*) bad, disagreeable; *used also as a common vulgar expletive.* BLOODY (2), *v.t.* to stain with blood. BLOODYMINDED, *adj.* of a bloodthirsty disposition; (*vulg.*) ill-disposed. [OE.].
BLOOM (1) [blōōm], *n.* lump of puddled iron forming a rough mass after smelting, and not yet rolled out into shapes. [OE.].
BLOOM (2), *n.* blossom or flower of a plant; prime, time of life in which the nearest state to perfection is reached and enjoyed; rosy flush of health; fine dust found on certain fruits when newly gathered; yellowish powdery deposit on leather, new coins etc. BLOOM (3), *v.i.* to blossom, flower; (*fig.*) flourish, prosper, reach the prime of life. BLOOMY, *adj.* full of b., blossoming. [OScand.].
BLOOMER [blōō'mer], *n.* (*coll.*) a mistake. [Unkn.].
BLOOMERS [blōō'merz], *n.*(*pl.*) women's knickers; woman's garment (now obsolete) with long knickers fastened round the ankles. [Mrs. *Bloomer*, inventor].
BLOOMING (1) [blōō'ming], *n.* state of being in bloom; process of converting cast iron into a malleable form; clouded appearance sometimes assumed by varnish on the surface of a picture. BLOOMING (2), *adj.* in bloom, in a state of flower or blossom; in the full flush of health and beauty; (*coll.*) as a mild expletive. BLOOMINGLY, *adv.* in a b. fashion.
BLOSSOM (1) [blo'sum], *n.* flower on a tree preceding the fruit; mass of flowers on certain trees. BLOSSOM (2), *v.i.* to bloom, grow b.; (*fig.*) achieve success suddenly. BLOSSOMY, *adj.* full of blossoms. [OE.].
BLOT (1) [blot], *n.* a stain, spot, disfiguring mark; one caused by ink on paper; (*fig.*) disgrace, fault. BLOT (2) [*pres.pt.* BLOTTING, *pret. and p.pt.* BLOTTED], *v.t.* to make blots or disfiguring marks upon, dry up (ink) with blotting paper; obliterate; render completely obscure to the sight; (*fig.*) sully, blemish. [ME.].
BLOTCH (1) [bloch], *n.* eruption or pimple on the skin; spot or discoloured patch. BLOTCH (2), *v.t.* disfigure with blotches. BLOTCHY, *adj.* disfigured with blotches. [Unkn.].
BLOTTER [blo'ter], *n.* anything used to dry up ink, whether pad, book of blotting paper, or implement with base covered with blotting paper.
BLOTTING [blo'ting], *n.* the drying up of ink by paper; **b. paper**, unsized absorbent paper used for drying up ink quickly; **b. out**, total obliteration, complete effacement.
BLOTTO [blo'to], *adj.* (*slang*) drunk. [BLOT (2).].
BLOUSE, BLOWSE [blowz], *n.* light, loose upper outer garment or bodice. [Fr.].
BLOW (1) [blō], *n.* violent stroke, hard knock, sudden, violent impact; (*fig.*) unpleasant shock, sudden calamity, strong disappointment or set-back. [Uncert.].
BLOW (2), *n.* sudden forceful expulsion of breath through the nose or mouth; outing in a strong breeze or gale, walk in the fresh air; stream of water emitted by a whale through its blow-hole; egg deposited by a fly. BLOW-OUT, a tyre-burst; (*slang*) feast, beano. [*Next*].
BLOW (3) [*pret.* **blew**, *p.pt.* **blown**], *v.t.* to drive or direct a current of air from a bellows, or from the lungs through the mouth, upon or through (an

object); drive or carry by a current of air; clear or empty of matter by forcing a current of air through; direct a stream of air from the lungs through the mouth into (a musical wind-instrument); (of a fly) deposit (eggs); cause to get out of breath by undue exertion; (*coll.*) reveal, disclose; (*imper.*) mild expletive equivalent to confound, or damn; *v.i.* to cause a current of air or gust; expel air forcibly through the nose or mouth; pant, puff; (of a whale) eject a stream of water from its blow-hole; sound when blown, used of a wind-instrument; (*elect.*) (of fuses) melt when overloaded; **to b. over,** to pass away without effect, subside, be forgotten; **to b. out,** to extinguish by blowing upon; burst; **to b. out one's brains,** to kill oneself by firing a shot through the head; **to b. up,** to pump or force air into and cause to distend, inflate; explode; destroy by means of explosives; (*coll.*) fall into a sudden rage; rate soundly, scold; **to b. off steam,** (*coll.*) to give vent to one's feelings; **to b. in,** (*coll.*) to visit; **to b. hot and cold,** to vacillate, waver; **to b. one's own trumpet,** to boast, speak well of oneself. [O.E.].

BLOW (4), *v.i.* (*poet.*) to blossom, come in flower. [O.E.].

BLOW-BALL [blō'bawl], *n.* (*bot.*) fluffy head of a dandelion or similar plant when in seed.

BLOWER [blō'er], *n.* one who blows; whale; contrivance for producing a forced current of air through a fire; escape of fire-damp from fissures in the coal; (*coll. mech.*) supercharger.

BLOW-FLY [blō'flī], *n.* (*zool.*) fly which taints meat by laying eggs on it.

BLOW-GUN [blō'gun], *n.* tube from which darts are propelled by the breath.

BLOW-HOLE [blō'hōl], *n.* opening in a whale's head for ejecting a spout of water; hole for the escape of foul air, steam etc.

BLOWLAMP [blō'lamp], *n.* lamp with its fuel under pressure and vaporized by its own heat which produces an intensely hot beam of flame.

BLOWPIPE [blō'pīp], *n.* tube through which air is blown on a flame to concentrate it at a particular place and increase its heat; blow-gun.

BLOWSE, see BLOUSE.

BLOWZE [blowz], *n.* ruddy, fat-faced slattern. BLOWZED, *adj.* blowzy. [Uncert.].

BLOWZY [blow'zi], *adj.* dishevelled, fat, tawdry. [Prec.].

BLUBBER (1) [blu'ber], *n.* fat of whales and other large sea-animals; kind of jelly-fish. [M.E.].

BLUBBER (2), *v.t. and i.* to weep noisily; make cheeks red and swollen with weeping. [M.E.].

BLUDGEON (1) [blu'jon], *n.* short heavy stick, stout cudgel. BLUDGEON (2), *v.t.* to beat with a b.; (*fig.*) bully, hector. [Unkn.].

BLUE (1) [blōō], *n.* the colour of a cloudless sky; colour of an approximate wave-length of about ·00045 of a millimetre; colour of the visible spectrum between violet and green; pigment or dye of this colour; person who has taken part in an inter-university sporting or athletic contest between Oxford and Cambridge; preparation used in laundering linen; (*fig.*) sky; sea; **a bolt from the b.,** unexpected occurrence. BLUE (2), *adj.* having the colour b., livid colour of the skin when affected by intense cold, a bruise etc.; (*fig.*) depressed, in low spirits; (*coll.*) indecent, obscene; **true b.,** staunch, loyal, genuine; **B. cat,** species of Siberian cat; **a b. funk,** (*coll.*) extreme fear; **b. gum,** tree of the eucalyptus family; **once in a b. moon,** very rarely; **like b. murder,** (*slang*) at top speed; **B. Peter,** (*naut.*) b. flag with a white square in the centre used to indicate the departure of a ship; **b. ribbon,** Order of the Garter; ribbon worn by total abstainers; **the b. riband,** distinction of holding the fastest sea-crossing of the Atlantic; (*fig.*) highest honour or prize in certain sports, racing etc.; **b. rock,** rock dove; **b. vitriol,** copper sulphate. BLUE (3), *v.t.* to make b., launder with b.; (*coll.*) squander. [Fr. from OHigh Germ.].

BLUEBEARD [blōō'beerd], *n.* one who marries, and subsequently murders, more than one wife. [*Bluebeard,* character in fiction].

BLUEBELL [blōō'bel], *n.* the wild hyacinth; (*Scots and northern dial.*) the harebell.

BLUEBERRY [blōō'be-ri], *n.* (*bot.*) American species of whortleberry.

BLUEBIRD [blōō'berd], *n.* small singing bird.

BLUE-BLACK [blōō'blak'], *adj.* dark blue.

BLUE-BONNET [blōō-bo'nit], *n.* cornflower; flat cap worn by a Scottish peasant.

BLUE BOOK [blōō-book'], *n.* general name given to

official reports or publications published by order of Parliament.

BLUE BOTTLE [blōō'bo-tl], *n.* cornflower; large blue species of blow-fly.

BLUE-CAP [blōō'kap], *n.* the blue titmouse; blue-bonnet; salmon less than one year old.

BLUECOAT [blōō'kōt], *n. and adj.* pupil at, pertaining to, Christ's Hospital school.

BLUE-FISH [blōō'fish], *n.* species of fish related to the mackerel.

BLUEING [blōō'ing], *n.* the giving of a bluish tint to white clothes; heating of metals till blue; discoloration of lenses by condensation; (*coll.*) extravagant spending of money.

BLUEJACKET [blōō'ja-kit], *n.* seaman of the Royal Navy.

BLUENOSE [blōō'nōz], *n.* popular name for an inhabitant of Nova Scotia.

BLUE-OINTMENT [blōō-oint'ment], *n.* (*med.*) mercurial ointment.

BLUE-PENCIL [blōō-pen'sil], *v.t.* to strike out, *orig.* with a blue pencil; censor.

BLUE-PILL [blōō-pil'], *n.* (*med.*) a preparation of mercury.

BLUEPRINT [blōō'print], *n.* technical diagram or plan photographed on blue paper; (*fig.*) a detailed plan.

BLUES [blōōz], *n.* U.S. Negro folk songs *orig.* consisting of improvised three-line stanzas in jazz rhythm; (*coll.*) melancholy; **The B.,** name given to the Royal Horse Guards from the colour of their tunics.

BLUE-STOCKING [blōō'sto-king], *n.* literary or pedantic woman belonging, originally, to an eighteenth-century club which met to discuss literature, and at which men wore blue stockings. BLUE-STOCKINGISM, *n.* female pedantry.

BLUE-THROAT [blōō'thrōt], *n.* migratory bird with sky-blue markings on its breast.

BLUFF (1) [bluf], *adj.* steep and almost perpendicular, rising sheer; (*fig.*) rough, hearty, outspokenly honest. BLUFF (2), *n.* headland formed by the steep banks of a lake, stream etc. BLUFFNESS, *n.* steepness; blunt heartiness. BLUFFY, *adj.* abounding in prominent headlands. [Unkn.].

BLUFF (3), *v.i.* to disguise one's real intentions, give a misleading impression of one's strength. BLUFF (4), *n.* deliberate deception as to true motives or state of affairs; **to call one's b.,** (*poker*) to challenge a player to show his hand and so reveal his deception in staking; (*fig.*) challenge a person to show the sincerity of his statements by taking them at their face value. BLUFFER, *n.* person given to bluffing. [Unkn.].

BLUISH [blōō'ish], *adj.* tinged with blue.

BLUNDER (1) [blun'der], *v.t. and i.* to flounder about, proceed in a clumsy manner; make a careless mistake, commit a tactless, stupid action; mismanage by clumsy inefficiency. BLUNDER (2), *n.* stupid mistake, error; ill-advised or careless action. BLUNDERER, *n.* stupid, clumsy person continually committing blunders. [M.E.].

BLUNDERBUSS [blun'der-bus], *n.* old-fashioned short gun fired by a flint-lock. [Du.].

BLUNDERING [blun'de-ring], *adj.* that blunders, clumsy, erratic. BLUNDERINGLY, *adv.* in b. fashion.

BLUNT (1) [blunt], *adj.* having an edge or point that is not sharp; (*fig.*) dull, thick-headed; plain-spoken, abrupt, unpolished in manners. BLUNT (2), *n.* thick needle. BLUNT (3), *v.t.* to dull the edge or point of; (*fig.*) make less sensitive, (of feelings, sensibilities) make less acute or refined. BLUNTLY, *adv.* abruptly, unceremoniously, outspokenly. BLUNTNESS, *n.* condition of being b. [Unkn.].

BLUR (1) [blur], *n.* a smear, blot or stain; indistinct outline or appearance. BLUR (2) (*pres.pt.* BLURRING, *pret. and p.pt.* BLURRED), *v.t. and i.* to smear, smudge; make indistinct, obscure the outlines of; dim; weaken or confuse the impression of. [Unkn.].

BLURB [blurb], *n.* publisher's eulogistic description of a book, often printed on the jacket. [Invented].

BLURT [blurt], *v.t.* to reveal by means of a hasty and often inadvertent utterance. [Uncert.].

BLUSH (1) [blush], *v.i.* to grow red in the cheeks or face when moved by some strong emotion or feeling of modesty or embarrassment; (*fig.*) feel ashamed. BLUSH (2), *n.* redness suffusing the cheeks of a person when moved by some strong feeling of modesty, shame, confusion, indignation; rosy colour; **at the first b.,** at the first glance. BLUSHFUL, *adj.* prone to b. BLUSHFULLY, *adv.* in a blushful manner.

BLUSHING (1) [blu'shing], *n.* act of becoming red

in the face or cheeks under the stress of strong feeling, or through modesty. BLUSHING (2), adj. covered or suffused with blushes; (fig.) modest, embarrassed, bashful. BLUSHINGLY, adv. in a b. fashion.

BLUSTER (1) [blus'ter], v.i. to rage in boisterous fashion (of winds, waves); (fig.) threaten, scold, boast or rave in a noisy manner; bully in an empty, swaggering way. BLUSTER (2), n. loud, roaring noise of stormy waves or gusts of wind; (fig.) boisterous, empty boasting; excited commotion, noisy display of temper. BLUSTERER, n. one who blusters. BLUSTERING, adj. noisy, stormy, boisterous (of wind or waves); threatening, boasting or scolding in a loud manner. [Unkn.].

BO [bō], int. (word used to startle); **to say b. to a goose,** to perform an action requiring the minimum of courage. [Imitative].

BOA [baw'ah, bō'ah], n. genus of non-venomous snakes, found in South America, which crush their prey in their coils; (pop.) python or any similar serpent; boa-shaped fur worn by women round the neck. BOA-CONSTRICTOR, large snake of this genus. [S.Amer.].

BOANERGES [bō-a-nur'jēz], n. loud-voiced, vehement orator or preacher. [Gk. from Heb., Mark iii, 17].

BOAR [baw(r)], n. male uncastrated pig; European wild boar. [OE.].

BOARD (1) [bawd], n. long, narrow, prepared piece of timber more than 4 in. wide and not more than 2 in. thick; plank; table; vertical piece of wood on which notices are placed; food received at a table, meals taken regularly at a house in return for a specific charge; piece of wood or cardboard on which certain games are played; official body of persons having the management, control or superintendence of some public company, office or trust; strong pasteboard used as the outside cover of a book; (naut.) deck or side of a ship; line of a ship's course between two tacks; (pl.) the stage; **above b.,** openly, honestly, fairly; **to go by the b.,** (naut.) to be swept away (of masts); (fig.) be lost for good; **on b.,** aboard ship; **to sweep the b.,** to take all the prizes or rewards, be extremely successful. FLOOR-BOARD, a board usually from 6 to 7 in. wide and 1½ in. or less in thickness. BOARD (2), v.t. to cover with boards; supply with regular meals in return for a stipulated payment; go on board a ship, enter a vehicle of transport; (fig.) accost; v.i to receive meals at one's lodging in return for a specified payment; (naut.) tack; **to b. out,** to take one's meals out, put out in lodgings. [OE.].

BOARDER [baw'der], n. one who receives board and lodgings at the house of another in return for a stipulated payment; schoolboy or girl who lives at school during term-time; one who boards a ship.

BOARDING HOUSE [baw'ding-hows], n. lodging-house where persons board.

BOARDING-SCHOOL [baw'ding-skool], n. school where the pupils are housed and fed during term.

BOARD-SCHOOL [bawd'skool], n. elementary school under the management of one of the now obsolete school boards.

BOARD-WAGES [bawd-wā'jiz], n. wages together with money allowed to domestic servants to keep themselves in food when living away from their employers.

BOAST (1) [bōst], n. arrogant expression of self-conceit; proud assertion; cause for boasting. BOAST (2), v.t. and i. to make a statement of self-glorification, brag, glory in oneself or one's possessions; assert in an arrogant, conceited manner; be graced with, possess as an attraction. [ME.].

BOASTFUL [bōst'fool], adj. given to boasting; arrogant, containing boasts. BOASTFULLY, adv. in a b. fashion. BOASTFULNESS, n. condition of being b.

BOASTING (1) [bōs'ting], n. the making of boasts. BOASTING (2), adj. full of boasts. BOASTINGLY, adv. in a b. fashion.

BOAT (1) [bōt], n. long symmetrically shaped hollow vessel that floats upon water, is propelled by oars, the action of wind on sails, or by mechanical means, and which is used as a means of transport, esp. a ship's lifeboat; small dish in the shape of a boat; **to be in the same b.,** to be placed in like circumstances; **to burn one's boats,** to be irretrievably bound to a certain line of action. BOAT (2), v.t. and i. to travel or sail in a b., place in a b.

BOATBILL [bōt'bil], n. South American bird of the heron family.

BOAT-DRILL [bōt'dril], n. exercises held in ocean liners to accustom passengers to the procedure necessary in case of shipwreck.

BOATER [bō'ter], n. (coll.) hard round straw hat with a flat top and brim.

BOAT-FLY [bōt'fli], n. aquatic insect.

BOATFUL [bōt'fool], n. what one boat will hold.

BOATHOOK [bōt'hook], n. hook on a long pole, used to control the movements of a boat near land etc.

BOAT-HOUSE [bōt'hows], n. shed for storing small boats.

BOATING [bō'ting], n. act of rowing or sailing in boats.

BOATMAN [bōt'man], n. man who hires out or is in charge of a small boat.

BOAT-RACE [bōt'rās], n. race between crews of two or more boats rowing in craft usually specially adapted for such racing.

BOAT-SHAPED [bōt'shāpt], adj. possessing the shape of a boat.

BOATSWAIN, BOSUN† [bō'sn], n. warrant officer in the Royal Navy or a Mercantile Marine officer, who has charge of the boats, sails, rigging etc., and summons the men to duty. [OE.].

BOAT-TRAIN [bōt'trān], n. railway train whose arrival at or departure from a port is timed to approximate to the departure or arrival of a passenger steamer.

BOB (1) [bob], n. short, jerky, ducking motion, curtsey; weighted ball on a pendulum, plumb-line or kite; slight tap; method of dressing women's hair by cutting it short; horse's tail when docked; bunch or knot of ribbon-like tassels; bunch of worms used as eel-bait; wig of short hair; peal of several sets of changes in bell-ringing; (coll.) shilling. BOB (2) (pres.pt. BOBBING, pret. and p.pt. BOBBED), v.i. to move about or up and down, with a short jerking motion; make a rough curtsey; angle for eels; ride on a bob-sleigh; v.t. move with a sudden, sharp, jerking motion; cut short a horse's tail, cut a woman's hair so that it lies close and thick round the back of the neck; snatch with the mouth at a suspended object; **to b. up,** (coll.) to appear suddenly and unexpectedly. [Unkn.].

BOBBED [bobd], adj. (of women's hair) cut short.

BOBBIN [bo'bin], n. wooden cylinder on which thread, wire etc. is wound; **b. lace,** n. lace made by hand with bobbins.

BOBBISH [bo'bish], adj. (slang) lively, hearty.

BOBBLE [bo'bl], n. agitated movement of disturbed water; small spherical ornament on a dress or hat. [Onomatopoeic].

BOBBY [bo'bi], n. (coll.) policeman. [Sir Robert Peel, Home Secretary].

BOBBY-DAZZLER [bo'bi-daz-ler], n. (slang) brilliant object.

BOBBY-SOXER [bo'bi-sok-ser], n. (U.S. slang) adolescent girl, "teen-ager." [From their short socks].

BOBOLINK [bo'bo-lingk], n. North American songbird.

BOB-SLED [bob'sled], n. bob-sleigh.

BOB-SLEIGH [bob'slā], n. sleigh holding two or more persons and steered by a movable front part.

BOBSTAY [bob'stā], n. (naut.) rope which steadies the bowsprit.

BOBTAIL [bob'tāl], n. horse or dog with a docked tail. BOBTAILED, adj. with the tail cut short; **b.wig,** bobwig.

BOBWIG [bob'wig], n. wig of short hair.

BOCHE [bosh], n. (slang) German. [Fr.].

BOCK-BEER [bok'bēer], n. a German lager. [Germ.].

BODE [bōd], v.t. to portend, be an omen of. BODEFUL, adj. ominous, threatening. [OE.].

BODEGA [bo-dē'gah], n. wine shop. [Span. from Gk.].

BODICE [bo'dis], n. close-fitting woman's garment covering the body above the waist, upper part of a woman's dress. [BODY].

BODIED [bo'did], adj. having a body, embodied.

BODILESS [bo'di-les], adj. having no body.

BODILY (1) [bo'di-li], adj. pertaining to the body. BODILY (2), adv. in person, physically, in the flesh; (fig.) in a body, as a whole.

BODING (1) [bō'ding], n. omen, presentiment. BODING (2), adj. threatening, ominous.

BODKIN [bod'kin], n. large blunt needle for threading tape etc. through a hem or piercing holes. [ME.].

BODY (1) [bo'di], n. material, physical structure or organism of living creatures; trunk as distinct from the head and limbs; corpse; bodice; main portion of

---

The accent ' after a syllable = stress (u-pon'). The mark ‾ over a vowel = length (ā in made; ō in bone).

a structure or work as distinct from appendages; part of a vehicle which accommodates passengers or freight; material object or substance; group of persons united by a common purpose, majority of the people, number of individuals legally constituted or organized, and usually having some official function or position; strength, quality, consistency; (coll.) person, human being; (theol.) the bread in the sacrament of Communion; **heavenly bodies**, sun, moon and planets. BODY (2), v.t. to display in some external form, give shape to; be an example of. [OE.].

BODY-BUILDER [bo'di-bil-der], n. one who builds the bodies of vehicles; a strengthening food.

BODY-COLOUR [bo'di-ku-ler], n. pigment possessing consistence, body and colouring power as distinct from a wash; opaque colour containing a certain amount of white.

BODYGUARD [bo'di-gahd], n. group of soldiers guarding the person of a sovereign, ruler or high dignitary; protective escort.

BODY-LINE [bo'di-lin], n. (cricket) short-pitched, fast bowling deliberately aimed at the batsman.

BODY-SERVANT [bo'di-ser-vant], n. valet or other personal servant.

BODY-SNATCHER [bo'di-sna-cher], n. one who disinterred and sold bodies for dissection. BODY-SNATCHING, n. illegal exhumation of corpses for dissection.

BODYWORK [bo'di-werk], n. material and workmanship of vehicle bodies.

BOEOTIAN [bē-ō'shn], adj. pertaining to Boeotia; dull, stupid. [Boeotia, district in ancient Greece].

BOER [bō'er], n. inhabitant of the Transvaal of Dutch descent, Dutch colonist in South Africa. [Du.].

BOFFIN [bo'fin], n. (slang, orig. R.A.F.) scientist employed on special work in the armed forces. [Invented].

BOFORS GUN [bō'ferz-gun], n. kind of light anti-aircraft gun. [Bofors, town in Sweden].

BOG (1) [bog], n. marshy ground, quagmire; (vulg.) latrine, water-closet. BOG (2) (pres.pt. BOGGING, pret. and p.pt. BOGGED), v.t. and i. to sink or become entangled in a b.; (pass.) become fast or trapped in a b. [Ir.].

BOGEY (1), **BOGY** [bō'gi], n. ghost, evil spirit, the devil; bugbear, pet dislike. [Uncert.].

BOGEY (2), n. (golf) number of strokes in which a "scratch" golfer would hole out at each hole on a golf-course, bogey for the course being the sum total of these strokes. [Mythical Colonel Bogey].

BOGEY-MAN [bō'gi-man], n. a bogey.

BOGGLE [bo'gl], v.i. to falter, shrink from, raise scruples about; bungle. BOGGLER, n. over-scrupulous, timorous person, doubter. [BOGLE].

BOGGY [bo'gi], adj. full of bogs, marshy.

BOGIE [bō'gi], n. frame provided with wheels and pivoted below the frame of a railway carriage or locomotive to reduce the fixed wheel-base and enable the vehicle to take curves of small radius. [Unkn.].

BOGLE [bō'gl], n. goblin, bogey; bugbear; scarecrow. [Unkn.].

BOG-OAK [bog'ōk], n. black oak found in bogs and used for ornamental purposes.

BOG-SPAVIN [bog'spa-vin], n. encysted tumour on the inside of a horse's hock.

BOG-TROTTER [bog'tro-ter], n. Irishman.

BOGUS [bō'gus], adj. sham, counterfeit. [Unkn.].

BOHEA [bō-hē'], n. a variety of black tea. [Chin.].

BOHEMIAN (1) [bō-hē'mi-an], n. gipsy; one whose mode of living is free and unconventional. BOHEMIAN (2), adj. unconventional, gipsy-like. BOHEMIANISM, n. habits of a B. [Fr.].

BOIL (1) [boil], v.i. to be heated to such a temperature as to cause a liquid to bubble and be agitated; reach boiling point; be cooked by boiling; (of a river or sea) be violently stirred up by wind or strong currents; (fig.) be wildly aroused by passion; (coll.) be excessively hot; v.t. to heat (a liquid) to such a temperature as to cause it to bubble; heat (a liquid) to boiling point; cook by immersion in boiling water; subject to heat in a boiling liquid, for cleansing purposes etc.; **to b. away**, to evaporate by boiling; **to b. down**, to reduce by boiling; (fig.) abridge. BOIL (2), n. state of boiling. [OFr. from L.].

BOIL (3), n. inflamed swelling on the skin, containing pus. [OE.].

BOILER [boi'ler], n. person who boils; vessel in which anything is boiled; metallic vessel in which

water is heated or converted into steam for various domestic and industrial purposes etc.; **b. suit**, trousered outer garment covering the body and limbs and used for dirty work.

BOILING (1) [boi'ling], n. process of bringing a liquid to the boil; process of cooking by boiling; amount of material boiled at a time. BOILING (2), adj. in a state of boiling; (fig.) extremely hot, violently agitated by emotion; **b. point**, temperature at which a liquid turns to vapour.

BOISTEROUS [bois'te-roos], adj. rough, noisy, hearty. [ME.].

BOKO [bō'kō], n. (slang) nose. [Unkn.].

BOLAS [bō'las], n. native missile used in South America. [Span.].

BOLD [bōld], adj. daring, courageous; impudent; standing out, conspicuous; emphatic; steep. BOLDLY, adv. in b. fashion. BOLDNESS, n. courage, daring; impudence, lack of modesty. [OE.].

BOLD-FACE [bōld'fās], n. (typ.) letters made up of thick bold strokes. BOLD-FACED, adj. impudent, brazen; (typ.) having heavy thick strokes.

BOLE (1) [bōl], n. trunk of a tree. [OScand.].

BOLE (2), n. compact, red or yellowish clayey earth. [Gk.].

BOLERO [bo-lāer'ō], n. popular Spanish dance; [bo'le-rō], short jacket or blouse barely reaching the waist. [Span.].

BOLIDE [bō'lid], n. meteor which explodes in the air. [Gk.].

BOLIVAR [bo-lē'vah(r)], n. unit of currency in Venezuela. [Simon Bolivar].

BOLL (1) [bōl], n. globular seed vessel of flax or the cotton-plant. BOLL (2), v.i. to form into bolls. [OE.].

BOLL (3), n. measure of grain varying from two to six bushels. [OScand.].

BOLLARD [bo'lerd], n. strong post on the deck of a ship or quayside for securing ropes. [Uncert.].

BOLOGNA SAUSAGE [bo-lō-nyah-so'sij], n. polony. [Bologna in Italy].

BOLOMETER [bo-lo'mi-ter], n. apparatus for measuring radiant heat. [Gk.].

BOLONEY [bo-lō'ni], n. (U.S. slang) nonsense, rubbish. [Invented].

BOLSHEVIK (1) [bol'she-vik], n. member of that extremist, and majority, party at the split in the Russian Social Democratic Party in 1903, which seized power after the Russian Revolution of 1917; (pop.) Communist or extreme revolutionary. BOLSHEVIK (2), adj. pertaining to the Bolsheviks or Bolshevism. [Russ.].

BOLSHEVISM [bol'she-vizm], n. political principles and policy of the Bolsheviks.

BOLSHEVIST [bol'she-vist], n. and adj. Bolshevik.

BOLSHY [bol'shi], n. and adj. (coll.) Bolshevik.

BOLSTER (1) [bōl'ster], n. long under-pillow of a bed; base; strengthening in various pieces of mechanism. BOLSTER (2), v.t. to support with a b. or pad; **to b. up**, to give support to, prop up. BOLSTERER, n. one who bolsters, supporter. BOLSTERING, n. propping up, support. [OE.].

BOLSTER-CASE [bōl'ster-kās], n. cover for a bolster.

BOLT (1) [bōlt], n. short thick arrow shot from a crossbow; thick metal bar fastened to a door, and sliding out into a socket in the door-post to prevent the door from opening; window catch which prevents the window from being opened from the outside, sliding pin which locks a rifle breech; metal pin with a head and screwed shank; thunderbolt, lightning; rapid start or dart away, sudden dash; long roll of fabric; rapid gulp of unchewed food; **to shoot one's b.**, (coll.) to make a final effort. BOLT (2), v.t. to secure or fasten with a b.; swallow hastily and without proper mastication; fasten together by nut and bolt; v.i. to dart off, run away quickly and suddenly. [OE.].

BOLT (3), v.t. to sift; (fig.) investigate. [OFr.].

BOLT-AUGER [bōlt'aw-ger], n. large boring tool.

BOLT-HEAD [bōlt'hed], n. head of a bolt; (chem.) spherical distillation flask fitted with a long cylindrical neck.

BOLT-HOLE [bōlt'hōl], n. hole into which an animal runs for safety; (fig.) any place of refuge.

BOLTING [bōl'ting], n. act of fastening with a bolt; sudden dash or dart; act of gulping down food.

BOLT-SPRIT, see BOWSPRIT.

BOLT-UPRIGHT [bōlt-up'rit], adj. perfectly erect.

BOLUS [bō'lus], n. large pill. [L. from Gk.].

BOMB (1) [bom], n. metal case filled with explosive

---

oo is pronounced as in food; oo as in hood; th as in think; TH as in that; zh as in azure. ~ = related to.

etc. which detonates or catches fire; apparatus arranged to explode at a given time; **b. rack**, rack in which bombs are packed in an aeroplane, ready for release. BOMB (2), *v.t.* to attack with bombs; **to b. out**, to drive from a building by the effects of bombing; **to b. up**, to load (aircraft) with bombs. [Fr.].

BOMBARD [bom-bahd′], *v.t.* to attack with artillery; (*fig.*) fire or direct a continuous stream (of questions etc.) at. [Fr.].

BOMBARDIER [bom-ber-dēer′, bum-ber-dēer′], *n.* lowest grade of non-commissioned artillery officer; **b. beetle**, beetle which when assailed expels an acrid fluid. [Fr.].

BOMBARDMENT [bom-bahd′ment], *n.* an attack with bombs or artillery.

BOMBARDON [bom-bah′don], *n.* (*mus.*) brass wind-instrument; organ-stop producing a similar sound.

BOMBASINE, see BOMBAZINE.

BOMBAST [bom′bast], *n.* high-sounding, pompous language. BOMBASTIC [bom-bas′tik], *adj.* high-flown, pompous. [L. from Gk.].

BOMBAX [bom′baks], *n.* genus of large, soft-wooded tropical trees. [Gk.].

BOMBAY-DUCK [bom-bā-duk′], *n.* small Indian transparent fish which, salted and dried, is considered a great delicacy.

BOMBAZINE, BOMBASINE [bom-ba-zēn′], *n.* twilled fabric of silk or cotton and worsted. [OFr. from L.].

BOMB-BLAST [bom′blahst], *n.* violent rush of air accompanying the explosion of a bomb.

BOMBE [bawmb], *n.* sweet or iced pudding made in a cone-shaped mould.

BOMBER [bom′er], *n.* bomb-carrying aeroplane; soldier who throws bombs.

BOMBIC [bom′bik], *adj.* pertaining to the silkworm; **b. acid**, (*chem.*) acid obtained from the silkworm.

BOMB-PROOF [bom′prŏŏf], *adj.* affording protection against bombs.

BOMBSHELL [bom′shel], *n.* bomb; (*fig.*) violent surprise.

BOMB-SIGHT [bom′sīt], *n.* instrument for aiming bombs dropped from aircraft.

BOMB-SITE [bom′sīt], *n.* area in a city ruined by air-raids.

BOMBYX [bom′biks], *n.* silkworm, genus of moths to which the silkworm moth belongs. [L. from Gk.].

BONA FIDE [bō-nah-fī′dē], *adj. and adv.* genuine, without fraud or deception. [L.].

BONA FIDES [bō-nah-fī′dēz], *n.* (*leg.*) good faith.

BONANZA [bo-nan′zah], *n.* vein of rich ore in a mine; (*fig.*) windfall of good fortune, prosperity. [Span.].

BONBON [bon′bon], *n.* sweetmeat or confection. [Fr.].

BONBONNIERE, bonbonnière [bon-bo-ni-āer′], *n.* small dish or box for sweetmeats. [*Prec.*].

BOND (1) [bond], *n.* that which binds; chain, fetter; (*fig.*) connecting link, element which serves to join together; (*leg.*) written agreement or promise to perform a certain action or pay a certain sum of money; acknowledgment of money lent; method of arranging bricks in a wall so that they overlap and hold together; government custody of goods until duty has been paid; fine type of writing paper. BOND (2), *adj.* in a state of bondage. BOND (3), *v.t.* to connect (bricks in building) by means of a b.; change (a loan) into a b.; hold (imported goods) until the duties are paid. [OE.].

BONDAGE [bon′dij], *n.* lack of freedom, slavery, captivity; (*fig.*) subjugating influence of anything. [ME.].

BOND-CREDITOR [bond′kre-di-ter], *n.* creditor secured by a bond.

BOND-DEBT [bond′det], *n.* debt incurred under a bond.

BONDED [bon′did], *adj.* secured or held by a bond; **b. goods**, goods retained by the government until duty on them is paid; **b. warehouse**, store for goods so retained.

BONDHOLDER [bond′hōl-der], *n.* bond-creditor.

BONDING [bon′ding], *n.* the joining of bricks by a bond; (*aeron.*) gauze used to make a good electrical earth.

BONDSLAVE [bond′slāv], *n.* person in slavery.

BONDSMAN [bondz′man], *n.* surety; slave.

BOND(S)WOMAN [bond(z)′wŏŏ-man], *n.* female slave.

BONE (1) [bōn], *n.* hard substance forming the

skeleton or framework of mammals, birds, fishes and reptiles; each of the parts which are joined together to form the skeleton; other hard substances in the animal body resembling this; (*pl.*) corpse; pieces of bone held between the fingers and rattled together rhythmically; (*fig.*) system, nature; **a b. of contention**, cause of dispute; **to have a b. to pick**, to intend a dispute about a certain matter; **to make no bones**, (*coll.*) to have no hesitation. BONE (2), *v.t.* to remove the bones from; stiffen or manure with bones; (*slang*) steal; (*surveying*) test the level of with boning rods. BONED, *adj.* possessing bones; with the bones taken out. [OE.].

BONE-BLACK [bōn′blak], *n.* charcoal obtained from burnt bones.

BONE-BREAKER [bōn′brā-ker], *n.* the osprey.

BONE-DRY [bōn-drī′], *adj.* absolutely dry, like a weathered bone.

BONE-DUST [bōn′dust], *n.* manure made of crushed bones.

BONELESS [bōn′les], *adj.* without bones; (*fig.*) lacking spirit.

BONEMEAL [bōn′mēl], *n.* meal made from ground bones.

BONESETTER [bōn′se-ter], *n.* one who sets broken or dislocated bones.

BONESHAKER [bōn′shā-ker], *n.* old-fashioned bicycle; any decrepit rattling vehicle.

BONE-SPAVIN [bōn′spa-vin], *n.* bony growth on the inside of a horse's hock.

BONETTA, see BONITO.

BONFIRE [bon′fīer], *n.* fire in the open air lighted as a beacon at festivities, or to destroy rubbish.

BONGO [bong′gō], *n.* large striped antelope.

BONHOMIE [bo′no-mē], *n.* good-nature, geniality. [Fr.].

BONING [bō′ning], *n.* (*surveying*) act or method of judging a plane surface, or of setting objects on the level by looking along the top of a line of rods spaced out at intervals.

BONITO, BONETTA [bō-nē′tō], *n.* stripe-bellied tunny. [Span.].

BON MOT (*pl.* **bons mots**) [baw(ng)-mō′], *n.* a witty repartee. [Fr.].

BONNET (1) [bo′nit], *n.* soft, brimless head-covering fastened under the chin with strings and worn by women and babies, flat cap worn by Scotsmen; cowl on a chimney or locomotive, protective covering of thin metal sheets encasing the engine of a motor-car, protective cap over the works of certain kinds of machinery. BONNET (2), *v.t.* to put on a b.; pull down forcibly a person's hat over his eyes. BONNETED, *adj.* wearing a b.; having the hat crushed down over the eyes. [Fr.].

BONNY [bo′ni], *adj.* handsome, comely, naturally good looking. BONNILY, *adv.* in a b. fashion. BONNINESS, *n.* quality of being b. [ME.].

BONUS [bō′nus], *n.* extra remuneration, or money paid in excess of salary to workmen for services performed; extra dividend to shareholders, insurance policy-holders etc., paid out of profits made. [L.].

BON-VIVANT [baw(ng)-vē-vah(ng)′], *n.* epicure. [Fr.].

BONY [bō′ni], *adj.* resembling or pertaining to a bone, hard; full of or characterized by bones; having large prominent bones; (*coll.*) emaciated.

BONZE [bonz], *n.* Buddhist monk in China or Japan. [Jap.].

BONZER [bon′zer], *adj.* (*Australian slang*) excellent. [Uncert.].

BOO (1) [bŏŏ], *int.* verbal indication of disapproval. BOO (2) (BOOES, BOOED), *v.t. and i.* to express verbal disapproval by saying "boo," drive away an animal by this cry; greet with boos.

BOOB [bŏŏb], *n.* (*slang*) stupid fellow. [Germ.].

BOOBY [bŏŏ′bi], *n.* stupid blockhead, dunce; species of gannet. [Span.].

BOOBY-HATCH [bŏŏ′bi-hach], *n.* (*naut.*) the covering over the hatchway to the forepeak.

BOOBY-PRIZE [bŏŏ′bi-prīz], *n.* prize awarded as a jest to the least successful competitor.

BOOBY-TRAP [bŏŏ′bi-trap], *n.* trap in the form of an object arranged so as to fall on the head of a passer-by or to cause him to trip up; (*milit.*) similar trap operating an explosive charge.

BOODLE [bŏŏ′dl], *n.* (*slang*) a crowd; the whole lot; money for political bribery; a card game. [Unkn.].

BOOGIE-WOOGIE [bŏŏ-gi-wŏŏ′gi], *n.* (*U.S. coll.*) extempore jazz music; swing. [Imitative].

BOOK (1) [bŏŏk], *n.* collection of blank, printed or

---

written sheets bound together at the back, usually enclosed in protective covers and forming a compact whole; written or printed treatise sufficiently large to form a book; large section of a long literary work; words of an opera etc., as distinct from the music; financial records of a business or other undertaking; record of the bets made by a bookmaker on the result of a race or sporting contest; the Bible; (*fig.*) medium providing instruction; (*pl.*) studies; list of patients, clients, customers; **b. matches**, matches packed in the form of a booklet; **bring to b.**, to call to reckoning; **in one's good or bad books**, in or out of favour; **to take a leaf out of a person's b.**, to copy or imitate a person; **to suit one's b.**, to please, satisfy; **to make a b.**, to act as a bookmaker. BOOK (2), *v.t.* to enter or write down in a b.; order in advance, reserve a place or seat; buy a ticket; engage a person in advance to perform a certain action on a future specified occasion. [OE.].

BOOKABLE [bŏŏ′ka-bl], *adj.* able to be reserved.
BOOKBINDER [bŏŏk′bin-der], *n.* one who binds books. BOOKBINDERY, *n.* factory or workshop for binding books. BOOKBINDING, *n.* art or trade of binding books.
BOOKCASE [bŏŏk′kās], *n.* upright case fitted with shelves for holding books.
BOOK-DEBT [bŏŏk′det], *n.* debt charged in an account book.
BOOKED [bŏŏkt], *adj.* reserved, engaged, registered in a book, bound, engaged to perform a certain action, having an appointment fixed with; **b. up**, completely engaged or reserved.
BOOK-ENDS [bŏŏk′endz], *n.*(*pl.*) pair of heavy ornaments to keep unshelved books in a row erect.
BOOKIE [bŏŏ′ki], *n.* (*coll.*) bookmaker.
BOOKING [bŏŏ′king], *n.* act of entering or registering in a book, anything so entered or registered; (*pl.*) reservations; seats at a public entertainment, on a vehicle etc., engaged in advance; **b. clerk**, person who enters up or makes bookings, *esp.* a clerk who issues railway tickets, person who reserves seats at a theatre etc., or rooms at an hotel; **b. office**, office where tickets are obtained for a journey, public entertainment etc.
BOOKISH [bŏŏk′ish], *adj.* relating to books or studies; studious, fond of reading, based on or obtained from books. BOOKISHLY, *adv.* in the fashion of one who is b.
BOOK-KEEPER [bŏŏk′kē-per], *n.* person who keeps the accounts of a business or other undertaking.
BOOK-KEEPING [bŏŏk′kē-ping], *n.* art or method of recording financial transactions in an accurate and comprehensible manner.
BOOK-KNOWLEDGE [bŏŏk′no-lij], *n.* book-learning.
BOOK-LEARNING [bŏŏk′ler-ning], *n.* learning acquired by reading and study, as opposed to knowledge derived from personal experience or observation. BOOK-LEARNED [bŏŏk′ler-nid], *adj.* well-read.
BOOKLET [bŏŏk′let], *n.* small book, pamphlet.
BOOK-MAKER (1) [bŏŏk′mā-ker], *n.* one who makes or compiles books.
BOOKMAKER (2) *n.* person professionally engaged in making or taking bets on races or other sporting events. BOOKMAKING, *n.* profession or business of a b.
BOOKMAN [bŏŏk′man], *n.* scholar, learned man; one interested in books.
BOOKMARK [bŏŏk′mahk], *n.* thin strip of material such as paper, leather etc., placed in a book to enable a person to find a particular page easily.
BOOK-MUSLIN [bŏŏk′muz-lin], *n.* kind of fine muslin.
BOOK-OATH [bŏŏk′ōth], *n.* oath sworn on the Bible.
BOOKPLATE [bŏŏk′plāt], *n.* ornamental label pasted on the inside of a book-cover to indicate the owner's name.
BOOK-POST [bŏŏk′pōst], *n.* (rates and regulations governing) the sending of books through the post.
BOOKSELLER [bŏŏk′se-ler], *n.* person who trades in books. BOOKSELLING, *n.* business of a b.
BOOKSHELF [bŏŏk′shelf], *n.* shelf on which books are kept.
BOOKSHOP [bŏŏk′shop], *n.* shop selling books.
BOOKSTALL [bŏŏk′stawl], *n.* open stall where books are sold.
BOOKSTORE [bŏŏk′staw′r], *n.* bookseller's shop; section of a library where little-used books are stacked.
BOOKWORM [bŏŏk′werm], *n.* larva of several

genera of beetle which eat into the bindings and leaves of books; (*fig.*) person continually reading or poring over books.
BOOM (1) [bŏŏm], *n.* obstruction in the form of beams fastened together, iron chains etc., across the mouth of a harbour or river to prevent entry; (*naut.*) long pole or spar used to extend the bottom of certain sails; (*cinema*) movable arm from which a film-camera is suspended in photographing scenes from above. [Du.].
BOOM (2), *v.t. and i.* to make a deep, hollow, resonant or humming sound; prosper, increase rapidly in value or price, advance in popularity; come with a sudden violent rush; boost, make known by vigorous publicity. BOOM (3), *n.* deep, resonant hollow sound (as of thunder, the firing of cannon etc.); sudden rapid activity in a particular trade, commercial enterprise etc., sudden activity in financial speculation in a certain commodity or business concern, resulting in a rapid increase in the value of stocks and shares; vigorous advertising or electioneering campaign. [ME.].
BOOMERANG [bŏŏ′me-rang], *n.* curved flat missile of hard wood which returns to the thrower if it misses its objective, chiefly used by the aborigines of Australia; (*fig.*) action recoiling on the performer or instigator. [Native].
BOON (1) [bŏŏn], *n.* (*archaic, poet.*) a favour, request; blessing, gift. [OScand.].
BOON (2), *adj.* pleasant; genial, jovial. [ME. from L.].
BOOR [bŏŏr], *n.* a peasant, rustic; (*fig.*) coarse, ill-mannered, uneducated person. BOORISH, *adj.* ill-bred, rude in manner, uneducated. BOORISHLY, *adv.* in boorish fashion. BOORISHNESS, *n.* condition of being boorish. [Du.].
BOOST (1) [bŏŏst], *v.t.* to lift or raise by pushing; increase the popularity, value, or sale of an article, or the fame or popularity of a person, by a campaign of vigorous publicity. BOOST (2), *n.* a help-up, advance or increase in popularity, favour or value; helpful publicity. BOOSTER, *n.* one who, that which, boosts; (*eng.*) small additional steam engine fitted to one of the bogies of large locomotives; (*med.*) injection intended to reinforce the effect of an earlier dose. [Unkn.].
BOOT (1) [bŏŏt], *n.* a covering for the foot, generally of leather, and extending over the ankle; box or compartment for luggage on a coach; luggage compartment at the back of a motor-car; **the b.**, (*coll.*) the sack, dismissal. RIDING-BOOT, long boot covering the foot and calf of the leg. BOOT (2), *v.t. and i.* to put on boots; kick; **to b. out**, (*coll.*) to dismiss. [OFr.].
BOOT (3), *n.* advantage, profit; **to b.**, in addition. BOOT (4), *v.i.* (*impers.*) to profit, do good, be of use or advantage. [OE.].
BOOTBLACK [bŏŏt′blak], *n.* person who earns his living by cleaning boots, usually in the street.
BOOTEE [bŏŏt-tē′], *n.* knitted woollen boot worn by babies; kind of half-boot for ladies.
BOOTH [bŏŏтн], *n.* covered stall at a market, temporary shed or shelter, tent at a fairground; **polling b.**, building or temporary structure where voters register their votes at an election. [ODan.].
BOOTJACK [bŏŏt′jak], *n.* appliance for pulling off long boots.
BOOTLACE [bŏŏt′lās], *n.* thong or lace used for fastening boots.
BOOT-LAST [bŏŏt′lahst], *n.* model of the foot upon which a shoemaker makes or repairs boots, boot-tree.
BOOTLEG [bŏŏt′leg], *v.i.* (*U.S. slang*) to carry prohibited alcoholic liquor etc. hidden on one's person, indulge in wholesale smuggling of alcoholic liquor. BOOTLEGGER, *n.* person engaged in the wholesale smuggling of alcoholic liquor. [Liquor was originally hidden in the leg of a tall boot].
BOOTLESS [bŏŏt′les], *adj.* unavailing, useless, unprofitable. BOOTLESSLY, *adv.* in a b. manner. BOOTLESSNESS, *n.* condition of being b. [BOOT (3)].
BOOTS [bŏŏts], *n.* hotel servant who cleans the boots and performs other odd jobs.
BOOT-TREE [bŏŏt′trē], *n.* shaped block inserted into boots or shoes to stretch them or preserve their shape.
BOOTY [bŏŏ′ti], *n.* plunder, spoils of war captured from an enemy, goods or loot seized and distributed among the captors. [Uncert.].
BOOZE (1) [bŏŏz], *v.i.* (*coll.*) to drink large quantities of alcoholic liquor. BOOZE (2), *n.* (*coll.*) alcoholic

drink, a drinking party. BOOZY, *adj.* fond of excessive quantities of alcoholic liquor; partially intoxicated. [MDu.].

BORA [baw'rah], *n.* cold north wind of the Upper Adriatic. [It. from L.].

BORACIC [baw-ra'sik], *adj.* containing, derived from, or pertaining to, borax; **b. acid,** a compound of boron with hydrogen and oxygen forming white crystals, used as an antiseptic and food preservative.

BORAGE [bu'rij], *n.* genus of plants used in making cordials. [OFr.].

BORATE [baw'rāt], *n.* a salt of boracic acid.

BORAX [baw'raks], *n.* (*chem.*) white crystalline salt, sodium tetraborate, or the sodium salt of pyroboric acid. [L. from Arab.].

BORDEAUX [baw-dō'], *n.* white or red wine produced in the district of Bordeaux; claret.

BORDEAUX-MIXTURE [baw-dō-miks'tyōōr], *n.* a preparation of copper sulphate and lime for spraying plants.

BORDER (1) [baw'der], *n.* edge, margin, extremity, boundary, frontier; narrow strip running along the edge of anything, and distinguished in appearance, material etc., from the thing to which it is attached; strip of ground in a garden forming a fringe or margin to a portion of the garden; **The B.,** the frontier of England and Scotland. BORDER (2), *v.t. and i.* to furnish with a b., mark the limits of, be adjacent to; be situated on the b. of; (*fig.*) approach, verge on. [OFr.].

BORDERER [baw'de-rer], *n.* one who lives on the frontiers of a country.

BORDERLAND [baw'der-land], *n.* land adjoining the boundaries of two adjacent countries; (*fig.*) intervening region.

BORDERLINE (1) [baw'der-līn], *n.* the line of demarcation between two regions; (*fig.*) point of distinction between two categories. BORDERLINE (2), *adj.* (*fig.*) sharing some of the characteristics of two distinct categories; doubtful.

BORE (1) [baw(r)], *v.t.* to drill a hole into by means of a revolving sharp-pointed tool, furnish with a bore or hollow inside; (*racing*) impede by moving so closely to another horse or vehicle as to force it out of its course; (*fig.*) bring about a complete lack of interest in a thing, weary with repetition of what is dull and tedious; *v.i.* to make a hole, burrow through. BORE (2), *n.* instrument used for drilling holes; hole made by boring; hollow inside of a tube or barrel of a gun, diameter of the cavity of a tube or gun-barrel; (*fig.*) dull, uninteresting, monotonous work or method of passing one's time; person whose conversation or remarks are wearisome and tedious. [OE.].

BORE (3), *n.* high tidal wave on a river caused by the sudden, rapid influx of an unusually high tide in a narrow or funnel-shaped estuary. [OScand.].

BORE (4), *pret.* of BEAR.

BOREAL [baw'rē-al], *adj.* northerly, relating to the north or north wind.

BOREAS [baw'rē-as], *n.* (*poet.*) the north wind.

BOREDOM [baw'dom], *n.* state of being bored, tedium.

BORER [baw'rer], *n.* instrument for boring, a drill; larvae of certain insects which bore holes in wood.

BORIC [bo'rik], *adj.* pertaining to or containing boron or borax, boracic.

BORING (1) [baw'ring], *n.* process of piercing by means of drills or bores; hole made by boring. BORING (2), *adj.* dull, tedious, causing boredom; used for boring.

BORN [bawn], *p.pt.* of BEAR only in sense "give birth to" and only passive; **to be b.,** to be brought forth as offspring; *adj.* natural, perfect; destined or inheriting by birth. [OE.].

BORNE, *p.pt.* of BEAR.

BORON [baw'ron], *n.* (*chem.*) non-metallic substance found in borax and other compounds; chemical element denoted by B. [BORAX].

BOROUGH [bu'rer], *n.* a corporate town; **municipal b.,** town possessing an organized government with a mayor and corporation, and certain privileges granted by royal charter; **parliamentary b.,** town sending at least one representative to Parliament; **rotten or pocket b.,** (*hist.*) in which a wealthy or influential person controlled the election of a parliamentary representative. BOROUGH-ENGLISH, † custom found in certain English boroughs, by which lands descended to the youngest son. [OE.].

BORROW [bo'rō], *v.t. and i.* to accept something to be repaid or returned later; (*fig.*) make use of, obtain or copy from; obtain the loan of money or

articles. BORROWER, *n.* one who borrows. BORROWING, *n.* act of one who borrows; thing borrowed. [OE.].

BORSTAL [baw'stal], *n.* system whereby young offenders between the ages of sixteen and twenty-one are sent to an institution to acquire a trade or occupation instead of going to prison; institution for such a purpose. [*Borstal* in Kent, site of the original institute].

BORZOI [baw'zoi], *n.* Russian wolfhound, long-haired variety of greyhound with silky, white coat.

BOSCAGE, BOSKAGE [bos'kij], *n.* dense woody undergrowth. [OFr.].

BOSH [bosh], *n. and int.* (*coll.*) rubbish, nonsense, empty talk. [Turk.].

BOSHBOK, see BUSHBUCK.

BOSJESMANS [bōōsh'manz], *n.* aboriginal tribe dwelling in the western part of South Africa. [Du.].

BOSK(ET) [bosk'(it)], *n.* a thicket, woody grove. [ME. from L.].

BOSKAGE, see BOSCAGE.

BOSKY [bos'ki], *adj.* with much undergrowth, full of dense thickets, bushy.

BOSOM (1) [bōō'zum], *n.* the breast; the portion of a garment covering the breast; (*fig.*) the surface of the sea or earth, innermost part, the depths; emotions, feelings, affections or passions. BOSOM (2), *adj.* dear, intimate. BOSOM (3), *v.t.* to enclose or conceal in the bosom, cherish. [OE.].

BOSS (1) [bos], *n.* a protuberant part, knob, stud, central stud on a shield; (*arch.*) raised ornament or moulding placed at the intersection of arches or ribs in a roof. BOSS (2), *v.t.* to emboss, furnish with bosses. [Fr.].

BOSS (3), *n.* (*coll.*) master, supervisor, manager. BOSS (4), *v.t.* to supervise; (*coll.*) attempt to domineer. [Du.].

BOSS-EYED [bos-īd'], *adj.* (*coll.*) squinting, cross-eyed; (*fig.*) crooked, out of shape.

BOSSY (1) [bo'si], *adj.* containing a boss; ornamented with bosses.

BOSSY (2), *adj.* (*coll.*) masterful, arrogant. BOSSINESS, *n.* tendency to domineer.

BOSUN†, see BOATSWAIN.

BOSWELLIAN [boz-we'li-an], *adj.* after the manner of Boswell. [James *Boswell*, biographer of Dr. Johnson].

BOT, BOTT (*pl.* **botts**) [bot], *n.* larva of the bot-fly, which attacks the skin and intestines of horses, sheep and cattle; (*pl.*) disease or swelling set up by this fly. [Unkn.].

BOTANIC(AL) [bo-ta'nik(-al)], *adj.* pertaining to botany or to plant life. BOTANICALLY, *adv.* according to botany.

BOTANIST [bo'ta-nist], *n.* a student of botany.

BOTANIZE [bo'ta-nīz], *v.i.* to make a botanical investigation; gather plants. BOTANIZER, *n.* one who collects plants for purposes of botanical study.

BOTANY (1) [bo'ta-ni], *n.* the science of the structure, growth and function of plants. [Gk.].

BOTANY (2), *n.* fine Australian wool. [*Botany* Bay, New South Wales].

BOTCH (1) [boch], *v.t. and i.* to mend or patch clumsily, bungle, put together in an unskilful, rough way. BOTCH (2), *n.* clumsy, makeshift work; unskilful, ill-finished work. BOTCHER (1), *n.* person who does clumsy, ill-finished work. BOTCHILY, *adj.* in a botchy manner. BOTCHY, *adj.* full of bungling work. [ME.].

BOTCHER (2) [bo'cher], *n.* a grilse, young salmon.

BOT-FLY [bot'fli], *n.* fly of the genus *Gastrophilus* or bot.

BOTH [bōth], *adj.* the two together; *pron.* the one and the other; *adv.* as well as, not only . . . but also. [OScand.].

BOTHER (1) [boᴛʜ'er], *v.t. and i.* to worry, annoy, trouble, make anxious, worry about, be anxious or troubled; trouble oneself, take care; pay too much attention to; take the trouble to; *also used as a mild imprecation.* BOTHER (2), *n.* disturbance, fuss, trouble, worry; difficulty. [Unkn.].

BOTHERATION [boᴛʜe-rā'shn], *n.* bother, trouble, worry; *int.* confound it!

BOTHERSOME [boᴛʜer-sum], *adj.* tiresome, troublesome, annoying.

BOTHY, BOTHIE [bo'thi], *n.* hut or cottage; one-roomed building for housing workmen. [Uncert.].

BO-TREE [bō'trē], *n.* the pipal or sacred fig-tree of India and Ceylon, regarded as holy by Buddhists. [Singhalese].

BOTTLE (1) [bo'tl], *n.* vessel, usually of glass or

earthenware, having a narrow neck with a small opening at the top, and used for holding liquid; contents of such a vessel; (*fig.*) alcoholic beverage, drink; baby's feeding flask. BOTTLE (2), *v.t.* to put into bottles; (*fig.*) restrain, repress, keep in check. [OFr.].

BOTTLE (3), *n.* bundle or truss of hay. [OFr.].

BOTTLE-BRUSH [bo'tl-brush], *n.* brush adapted for cleaning bottles; (*bot.*) Australian plant.

BOTTLED [bo'tld], *adj.* (*coll.*) drunk.

BOTTLE-GLASS [bo'tl-glahs], *n.* coarse green glass used for making bottles.

BOTTLE-GREEN [bo-tl-grēn'], *n.* a dark green colour.

BOTTLE-HOLDER [bo'tl-hōl-der], *n.* a second at a prize-fight; (*fig.*) supporter, backer.

BOTTLENECK [bo'tl-nek], *n.* short strip of road narrowing suddenly so that it becomes congested or unsafe; stage in manufacture which holds up production.

BOTTLENOSE [bo'tl-nōz], *n.* variety of whale of the dolphin family.

BOTTLENOSED [bo'tl-nōzd], *adj.* having a swollen, red, bulbous nose.

BOTTLE-PARTY [bo'tl-pah-ti], *n.* social gathering to which each guest brings a bottle of some alcoholic drink; a night club.

BOTTLE-RACK [bo'tl-rak], *n.* rack on which bottles are placed in an inverted position to drain.

BOTTLE-TIT [bo'ti-tit], *n.* the long-tailed tit.

BOTTLE-WASHER [bo'tl-wo-sher], *n.* one who washes bottles; general drudge, hack; (*coll.*) **head cook and b.**, one in charge.

BOTTOM (1) [bo'tm], *n.* the lowest or deepest part, part most remote from the top, foot, base; end or surface on which an object rests; ground or bed underneath a mass of water; keel of a ship; seat of a chair; lowest part of a valley; (*coll.*) the buttocks; (*fig.*) a ship; foundation, basis, the depths of one's thoughts, feelings; endurance, stamina; (*motoring*) the lowest gear of a gear-box; **to touch b.**, to run aground, (*fig.*) reach the worst; **to be at the b. of**, to be the cause of; **to get to the b. of**, to sift or probe thoroughly; get a complete understanding of. BOTTOM (2), *adj.* lowest, last, at the b.; **b. heat**, heat supplied to certain plants by substances placed below their soil. BOTTOM (3), *v.t. and i.* to provide with a b.; reach or get to the b. of, understand thoroughly; found, base, start from, build upon. [OE.].

BOTTOMLESS [bo'tm-les], *adj.* having no bottom; (*fig.*) unfathomable, of immeasurable depth; groundless, unjustifiable.

BOTTOMMOST [bo'tm-mōst], *adj.* lowest down, at the extreme bottom.

BOTTOMRY [bo'tm-ri], *n.* (*leg.*) a form of contract in which a ship is pledged by the owner or master in order to raise money to enable her to complete her voyage. [Du.].

BOTULISM [bo'tyoo-lizm], *n.* form of food poisoning caused by eating preserved meat etc. infected with *Bacillus botulinus*. [L.].

BOUDOIR [bōō'dwah(r)], *n.* a lady's private sitting-room. [Fr.].

BOUGAINVILLEA [bōō-gān-vi'li-ah], *n.* genus of tropical South American spinous climbing shrubs. [*Bougainville*, French explorer].

BOUGH [bow], *n.* a large branch of a tree. [OE.].

BOUGHT [bawt], *pret. and p.pt.* of BUY.

BOUGIE [bōō'zhi], *n.* smooth cylindrical rod introduced into the rectum, urethra or oesophagus in order to distend these canals to remove obstructions. [Fr.].

BOUILLABAISSE [bōō-yah-bās'], *n.* French dish of fish-stew.

BOUILLI [bōō'yē], *n.* stewed meat; bully-beef. [Fr.].

BOUILLON [bōō'yo(ng)], *n.* broth; soup. [Fr.].

BOULDER [bōl'der], *n.* large detached rock with its edges smoothed and rounded by the effect of water; (*geol.*) large, weather-worn mass of stone detached from its original position and transported elsewhere by glacial action; **b. period**, the Ice Age. BOULDER-CLAY, clay containing boulders deposited by glaciers. [ME.].

BOULE, see BUHL.

BOULEVARD [bōō'le-vah(r)], *n.* street or promenade planted with trees. [Fr.].

BOUNCE (1) [bowns], *v.t. and i.* to strike against and rebound; rush about or move in a boisterous, violent manner; cause to bounce; cause a person to perform a hurried, unconsidered action. BOUNCE (2), *n.* the power of rebounding, elasticity, resilience; the rebound; (*fig.*) impudence. BOUNCER, *n.* a blusterer, boaster; brazen lie; (*fig.*) anything large or well-developed. [ME.].

BOUNCING [bown'sing], *adj.* that which bounces; (*fig.*) large, healthy, well-developed, bustling, boisterous. BOUNCINGLY, *adv.* in a b. manner.

BOUNCY [bown'si], *adj.* resilient; (*fig.*) with an ebullient manner, self-assertive.

BOUND (1) [bownd], *n.* the edge, limit, boundary; (*pl.*) a prescribed area; (*fig.*) limit, restraints; **out of bounds**, beyond the lawful or prescribed boundary, and therefore forbidden. BOUND (2), *v.t.* to mark the boundary of, confine, set limits to; (*fig.*) restrain, restrict. [OFr.].

BOUND (3), *v.i.* to leap, move forward with a series of rapid springs or leaps; rebound. BOUND (4), *n.* a vigorous upward spring or leap; sudden violent throb (of the heart). [OFr.].

BOUND (5), *adj.* prepared, destined, intended to go, journeying (*with* for). [OScand.].

BOUND (6), *pret. and p.pt.* of BIND.

BOUNDARY [bown'da-ri], *n.* that which marks the limits or extreme edge of anything; the bounds; (*cricket*) that which marks the limits of the field of play; a stroke which causes the ball to reach the boundary line, and which counts a certain number of runs to the batsman. [BOUND (1)].

BOUNDEN [bown'den], *adj.* morally binding, under compulsion or obligation. [OE.].

BOUNDER [bown'der], *n.* (*coll.*) vulgar, ill-mannered cad, rank outsider. [BOUND (3)].

BOUNDLESS [bownd'les], *adj.* without bound or limit. BOUNDLESSLY, *adv.* in a b. fashion. BOUNDLESSNESS, *n.* quality or state of being b. [BOUND (1)].

BOUNTEOUS [bown'ti-ŏŏs], *adj.* liberal, generous, full of goodness; freely given, munificent, plentiful. BOUNTEOUSLY, *adv.* in b. fashion. BOUNTEOUSNESS, *n.* quality or condition of being b. [BOUNTY].

BOUNTIFUL [bown'ti-fŏŏl], *adj.* generous, liberal; freely given, abundant. BOUNTIFULLY, *adv.* in b. fashion. BOUNTIFULNESS, *n.* quality or state of being b.

BOUNTY [bown'ti], *n.* generosity, open-handedness, liberality, munificence; gratuity, reward; premium given to encourage enlistment in the Services, or a branch of industry; **Queen Anne's B.**, provision formerly made for supplementing poor church livings; **Queen's b.**, gift or grant made to the parents of triplets. [OFr. from L.].

BOUQUET [bōō-kā'], *n.* a bunch of flowers; the aromatic perfume of wine.

BOUQUETIN [bōō'ke-tin], *n.* the ibex. [Fr.].

BOURBON [bōōr-baw(ng)'], *n.* whisky manufactured from Indian corn and rye. [*Bourbon*, U.S.A.].

BOURDON [bōōr'don], *n.* bass stop in an organ or harmonium; drone of a bagpipe. [Fr.].

BOURGEOIS (1) [ber-jois'], *n.* printing type which provides approx. 8½ lines to an inch. [*Bourgeois*, French typographer].

BOURGEOIS (2) [bōōr'zhwah], *n.* member of the (upper) middle classes. BOURGEOIS (3), *adj.* pertaining to the (upper) middle classes. [Fr.].

BOURGEOISIE [bōōr-zhwah-zē'], *n.* the middle classes; **petite b.**, lower middle classes.

BOURGEON, see BURGEON.

BOURN (1) [bawn], *n.* a stream. [OE.].

BOURN(E) (2), *n.* a boundary, limit; destination. [Fr.].

BOURRÉE, bourrée [bōō-rā'], *n.* lively Spanish or French dance, music written for this. [Fr.].

BOURSE [bōōrs], *n.* continental exchange where financial business is transacted. [Fr., Gk.].

BOUT [bowt], *n.* a spell of more or less continuous activity, a round, amount done at one time; contest, fight; attack of illness or indisposition. [Uncert.].

BOUTS-RIMES, bouts-rimés [bōō-rē'mā], *n.* list of rhyming words, form of verse-making in which verses are written to fit given rhymes. [Fr.].

BOVINE [bō'vīn], *adj.* pertaining to the ox; (*fig.*) dull, sluggish, heavy-witted. [LL.].

BOW (1) [bō], *n.* weapon from which arrows are shot, consisting of a piece of flexible wood, steel etc., slightly curved so that its ends are joined by a taut string, which when drawn back and released, propels the arrow; anything in the form of a bow, rainbow; (*mus.*) slender staff of slightly curved wood strung with horsehair, which produces the tone in some stringed instruments; double-looped slip-knot,

---

ōō is pronounced as in food; ŏŏ as in hood; th as in *think*; TH as in *that*; zh as in azure. **~** = related to.

necktie or piece of ribbon tied in such a way; **to have more than one string to one's b.**, (*fig.*) to have several resources or courses of action; **to draw the long b.**, (*coll.*) to exaggerate. BOW (2), *v.t. and i.* to use a b. in playing stringed musical instruments. [OE.].

BOW (3) [bow], *v.i.* to incline the head or bend the body as a respectful gesture of greeting, departure, polite acknowledgment etc.; express by a bow; incline the person or stoop in sign of reverence or submission; (*fig.*) submit to, acknowledge as superior, yield to; *v.t.* to bend, crush, subdue, oppress, depress; (*lit. and fig.*) usher in or out with bows; **to b. the knee to**, to worship, revere; **a bowing acquaintance**, slight acquaintance. BOW (4), *n.* a respectful inclination of the head or bending of the body as a sign of greeting or departure; **to make one's b.**, to arrive; retire. [OE.].

BOW (5) [bow], *n.* the fore-end of a ship or boat, consisting of the curving sides meeting at the prow; (*coll.*) the oarsman nearest the bow. [OE.].

BOW-COMPASSES [bō-kum′pa-siz], *n.(pl.)* pair of compasses having jointed legs which turn inwards.

BOWDLERIZE [bowd′le-rīz], *v.t.* to expurgate a book. BOWDLERISM, *n.* expurgation of what is thought obscene. [Dr. *Bowdler*, who published an expurgated edition of Shakespeare].

BOWEL (1) [bow′el], *n.(pl.)* the intestines of man or animals; (*fig.*) the interior, depths; feelings, emotions. BOWEL (2), *v.t.* to remove the bowels from. [OFr.].

BOWER [bow′er], *n.* a lady's chamber, private apartment; arbour, shady retreat, sheltered recess covered in with shrubs etc.; rustic dwelling. [OE.].

BOWER-BIRD [bow′er-berd], *n.* one of several species of Australian birds of the starling family.

BOWERY (1) [bow′e-ri], *n.* district of New York popularly supposed to be insalubrious. [Du.].

BOWERY (2), *adj.* like a bower, characterized by bowers.

BOW-HAND [bō′hand], *n.* the hand which holds a bow.

BOWIE-KNIFE [bō′i-nif], *n.* sheath knife or hunting dagger having a long blade double-edged at the point. [Colonel *Bowie*, American].

BOWING [bō′ing], *n.* (*mus.*) art of using a bow.

BOWL (1) [bōl], *n.* wide hollow vessel or rimless basin, drinking-vessel, rounded hollow part of a tobacco pipe in which the tobacco is placed, hollow bowl-shaped part of a utensil or implement. [OE.].

BOWL (2), *n.* heavy wooden ball provided with a bias, and rolled along a bowling green in the game of bowls. BOWL (3), *v.t. and i.* to trundle or roll a hoop; deliver a ball at cricket; deliver a ball which hits the batsman's wicket and dislodges a bail; roll a b.; play the game of bowls; **to b. over**, to nonplus, upset thoroughly; **to b. out**, defeat, disconcert. [Fr.].

BOW-LEG [bō-leg′], *n.* leg which bends outwards in the shape of a bow from the hip downwards; malformation arising from this condition. BOW-LEGGED, *adj.* having bow legs.

BOWLER (1) [bō′ler], *n.* person who plays bowls; person who delivers the ball to the batsman at cricket.

BOWLER (2), *n.* hard round felt hat with a curved brim. [BOWL (1)].

BOWLINE [bō′lin], *n.* (*naut.*) rope fastened by bridles to loops on the perpendicular edge of a square sail, and used to steady the weather edge of the sail forward when the ship is sailing close to the wind; **b. knot**, knot used for fastening the b. bridles to the cringles.

BOWLING [bō′ling], *n.* act or recreation of playing bowls; act of delivering the ball to the batsman at cricket, method or skill with which this is done; sport of playing skittles in a bowling alley; **b. alley**, long, narrow, enclosed alley in which the game of skittles is played; **b. crease**, (*cricket*) line from behind which the bowler delivers the ball; **b. green**, smooth prepared lawn upon which the game of bowls is played.

BOWLS [bōlz], *n.* game played on a bowling green with bowls.

BOWMAN [bō′man], *n.* one who uses a bow; archer.

BOW-NET [bō′net], *n.* kind of wicker basket used for catching lobsters etc.

BOW-OAR [bow′awr], *n.* oarsman nearest the bow.

BOW-SAW [bō′saw], *n.* saw with a narrow blade stretched across a strong frame in the manner of a bow-string.

BOW-SIDE [bow′sīd], *n. and adj.* (pertaining to) the

starboard side of a rowing boat, over which the oar nearest to the bow is placed.

BOWSPRIT, BOLT-SPRIT [bō′sprit], *n.* (*naut.*) the large spar projecting over the stem of a ship to which are fastened the foremast and fore-topmast stays and stay-sails. [OE.].

BOW-STRING (1) [bō′string], *n.* the string of a bow; cord formerly used by the Turks in strangling offenders. BOW-STRING (2), *v.t.* to strangle with a b.

BOW-WINDOW [bō-win′dō], *n.* curved window-frame projecting from a wall.

BOW-WOW [bow′wow], *n.* the bark of a dog; (*children's language*) a dog. [Imitative].

BOWYANGS [bō′yangz], *n.(pl.)* (*coll.*) straps or cords worn by labourers below the knees of trousers.

BOX (1) [boks], *n.* case, receptacle, or chest, usually with a lid, made of various hard materials; contents of a box; driver's seat on a coach; compartment in the auditorium of a theatre, with seats for several persons; square pew; small wooden hut or shelter; small country lodge; protective case over various kinds of machinery or mechanism; piston of a pump; axle-box; (*print.*) one of the cells of a type case; enclosed portion of a court of law for the jury, or for witnesses. CHRISTMAS-BOX, Christmas gift. BOX (2), *v.t.* to put into a b.; furnish with a b.; enclose or confine in an uncomfortably narrow space; make a cut in the trunk of a tree to obtain the sap; (*cards*) disarrange the cards in shuffling so that their backs do not all face the same way; **to b. the compass**, (*naut.*) to repeat all the points of the compass in their proper order; (*fig.*) make a complete turn; **to b. off**, (*naut.*) to turn the head of a vessel by altering the sails. [OE.].

BOX (3), *n.* evergreen tree or shrub having dark green leaves and a hard, close-grained wood; wood of this tree. [OE. from L.].

BOX (4), *n.* a blow with the open hand, usually on the side of the head; a cuff. BOX (5), *v.t. and i.* to strike the side of a person's head; fight with the closed fists protected by padded gloves. [ME.].

BOX-CALF [boks-kahf′], *n.* kind of leather treated with chromic oxide and having a double grain. [I. *Box*, bootmaker].

BOXER (1) [bok′ser], *n.* person trained in the art of fighting with the fists; professional pugilist.

BOXER (2), *n.* member of a Chinese secret society of an extremely nationalist and anti-foreign nature.

BOXHAUL [boks′hawl], *v.t.* to veer a ship suddenly round on her keel.

BOXING [bok′sing], *n.* art of fighting with the fists.

BOXING-DAY [bok′sing-dā], *n.* first weekday after Christmas Day, when Christmas-boxes are given.

BOX-KITE [boks-kīt′], *n.* kite made of two rectangular oblong boxes joined together.

BOX-OFFICE [boks′o-fis], *n.* office at a theatre etc., where seats may be booked.

BOX-PLEAT [boks′plēt], *n.* double pleat or fold in a cloth.

BOX-SPANNER [boks-spa′ner], *n.* spanner having a socket so shaped as to fit completely round the nut to be turned.

BOX-TREE [boks′trē], *n.* shrubby evergreen tree.

BOX-WOOD [boks′wood], *n.* wood of the box-tree.

BOY [boi], *n.* male child, often applied also to a young man; native personal servant. [ME. from AFr.].

BOYAR [boi′ah(r)], *n.* formerly a nobleman of Russia or Rumania. [Russ.].

BOYCOTT (1) [boi′kot], *v.t.* to combine together to have no dealings or intercourse with (a person); refrain deliberately from buying, using or dealing in an article or merchandise as a means of reprisal or injury; (*fig.*) ostracize, shun the company of. BOYCOTT (2), *n.* organized system of social or commercial ostracism. [Captain *Boycott*, Irish land-agent, against whom it was first employed].

BOYHOOD [boi′hood], *n.* the period of life of a male child from birth to puberty.

BOYISH [boi′ish], *adj.* like a boy; fresh, lively; inexperienced, puerile. BOYISHLY, *adv.* in a b. fashion. BOYISHNESS, *n.* quality of being b.

BRACE (1) [brās], *n.* anything used as a support, stay, steadying or stiffening influence; rope to adjust the sails of a ship; cord used to keep a drum taut; carpenter's drilling tool consisting of a handle in the form of a crank to rotate, with a socket into which a bit fits, the whole forming a **b. and bit**; (*print.*) bracket in the form { } connecting two or more words or lines of type; a pair, *esp.* of dogs or game animals and birds; (*pl.*) two adjustable straps passing over the shoulders and uniting on the back, fastened to

---

buttons on the trousers, both back and front, in order to support them. BRACE (2), *v.t.* to fasten together, bind or tie, strengthen, support or steady; tighten, make taut; fasten and support with braces; *(fig.)* prepare oneself for a special effort; freshen, stimulate, strengthen, invigorate; *v.i.* to b. up, *(slang, orig. U.S.)* to brace oneself. [OFr.].

BRACELET [brās'let], *n.* circular ornament worn by women round the wrist or arm; *(coll., pl.)* handcuffs. [Fr.].

BRACHIAL [brā'ki-al], *adj.* pertaining to the arm; resembling an arm. [L. from Gk.].

BRACHY-, *pref.* short. [Gk.].

BRACHYCEPHALIC [bra-ki-se-fa'lik], *adj.* short-headed, having a head whose lateral diameter is at least four-fifths of its longitudinal diameter. [Gk.].

BRACHYCEPHALOUS [bra-ki-se'fa-lŏŏs], *adj.* brachycephalic.

BRACING [brā'sing], *adj.* invigorating, freshening, stimulating. [BRACE (2)].

BRACKEN [bra'ken], *n.* species of coarse fern. [OE.].

BRACKET (1) [bra'kit], *n.* an angular piece of metal or wood projecting as a support from a wall; *(arch.)* flat-topped projecting support for an arch, statue, shelf etc.; short shelf fastened to a wall; gas pipe with burner, usually attached to a hinged fixture, and projecting from a wall; *(print.)* one of the marks [ ] used in printing to enclose or separate words, or a portion of a mathematical formula; a group. BRACKET (2), *v.t.* to enclose in brackets, join by means of a b.; associate or mention two persons together; provide with brackets; in artillery range-finding, fire one shot beyond the target and another short of it.

BRACKISH [bra'kish], *adj.* salty. [Du.].

BRACT [brakt], *n.* *(bot.)* leaf growing out beneath the calyx from the peduncle of a flower. BRACTEATE, *adj.* *(bot.)* having bracts. [L.].

BRAD [brad], *n.* thin wire nail with a small head. [ME.].

BRADAWL [bra'dawl], *n.* small hand boring tool for making holes for nails or screws.

BRAE [brā], *n.* *(Scots)* the side of a hill, slope. [OScand.].

BRAG (1) [brag], *n.* boast, boastful language; gambling card-game. BRAG (2) *(pres.pt.* BRAGGING, *pret.* and *p.pt.* BRAGGED), *v.i.* to boast, indulge in self-praise. [ME.].

BRAGGADOCIO [bra-ga-dō'shi-ō], *n.* one who brags; bragging. [Coined by Spenser, *Faerie Queene*].

BRAGGART [bra'gert], *n.* and *adj.* a boaster, boastful. [OFr.].

BRAHMIN, BRAHMAN [brah'min], *n.* member of the highest caste or hereditary priests of Hinduism. BRAHMINICAL [brah-mi'ni-kal], *adj.* pertaining to the Brahmins. [Skr.].

BRAID (1) [brād], *n.* plait of hair; narrow band of woven fabric used for trimming or binding the edges of cloth, woven band of gold etc.; thread used as ornamentation on uniforms. BRAID (2), *v.t.* to weave by intertwining strands, plait (hair), trim or bind with b. BRAIDING, *n.* a trimming of b. [OE.].

BRAIL (1), **BRAYLE** [brāl], *n.* *(naut.)* rope at the corner of a sail used to truss up the bottoms, corners and skirts of a sail before furling. BRAIL (2), *v.t.* *(naut.)* to haul in a fore-and-aft sail by means of a b. [OFr.].

BRAILLE [brāl], *n.* system of printing in relief for the blind by an alphabet of raised dots read by touch. [Louis *Braille*, inventor].

BRAIN (1) [brān], *n.* a convoluted mass of soft substance enclosed in the skull, the centre of the nervous system and of mental processes; the cephalic ganglion in invertebrates; *(fig.)* the mind, intelligence, understanding, thought, imagination; *(pl.)* the most intellectual, cleverest person of a group or organization; to have something on the b., to be obsessed by an idea; to pick a person's brains, to make use of the fruits of another's mental effort; to turn one's b., to cause to become mad. BRAIN (2), *v.t.* to dash out the brains of. [OE.].

BRAIN-FAG [brān'fag], *n.* nervous exhaustion due to continued mental strain.

BRAIN-FEVER [brān-fē'ver], *n.* inflammation of the brain; meningitis.

BRAINPAN [brān'pan], *n.* the skull containing the brain.

BRAINSTORM [brān'stawm], *n.* sudden mental derangement.

BRAINS TRUST [brānz'trust], *n.* committee of

experts appointed by a government or other body to aid in planning; *(coll.)* group of persons appointed to answer without previous preparation questions asked by an audience or the general public on subjects of current interest.

BRAINWAVE [brān'wāv], *n.* *(coll.)* sudden, brilliant idea or inspiration.

BRAINY [brā'ni], *n.* *(coll.)* clever, highly intelligent.

BRAISE [brāz], *v.t.* to cook by stewing in a covered pan. [Fr.].

BRAKE (1) [brāk], *n.* bracken; place overgrown with bracken etc.; a thicket. [ME.].

BRAKE (2), *n.* instrument used for pounding flax or hemp; baker's kneading-board; heavy wooden machine for breaking up clods of earth; machine for crushing hops in brewing. BRAKE (3), *v.t.* to crush or beat hemp; break up clods of earth; knead dough. [ODu.].

BRAKE (4), *n.* apparatus for slowing down or arresting the motion of a wheel by friction applied to the axle or wheel; *(fig.)* restraining influence. BRAKE (5), *v.i.* to apply the brake(s) to a revolving wheel. BRAKELESS, *adj.* having no brakes; *(fig.)* unchecked. [Uncert.].

BRAKE (6), **BREAK** [brāk], *n.* large open wagonette, heavy four-wheeled carriage used for breaking in horses. [Unkn.].

BRAKE(S)MAN [brāk(s)'man], *n.* man in charge of a brake.

BRAKE-VAN [brāk'van], *n.* compartment in a train from which a brake is controlled.

BRAMBLE [bram'bl], *n.* a coarse, wild shrub; wild blackberry. BRAMBLED, *adj.* covered with brambles. BRAMBLY, *adj.* thorny, covered with brambles. [OE.].

BRAMBLING [bramb'ling], *n.* the mountain finch.

BRAN [bran], *n.* the husk of ground oats, wheat etc., separated from the flour after grinding and used as meal, the coarsest part of the grain. [OFr.].

BRANCH (1) [brahnsh], *n.* the limb or arm of a tree, an off-shoot or outgrowth from anything; a subdivision or extension of anything; division or group of some subject of knowledge etc. BRANCH-PILOT, pilot possessing a Trinity House certificate. BRANCH (2), *v.i.* to grow branches, separate into divisions, extend at various angles; to b. out, to extend, expand, turn in new directions; display unexpected potentialities. [Fr.].

BRANCHIAE [brang'ki-ē], *n.(pl.)* fish gills. [Gk.].

BRANCHIAL [brang'ki-al], *adj.* relating to gills.

BRANCHIATE [brang'ki-at], *adj.* possessing gills.

BRANCHY [brahn'shi], *adj.* having branches, covered with branches.

BRAND (1) [brand], *n.* a burning piece of wood; mark made by burning, such a mark made on criminals as a punishment or on cattle or other property for identification; *(fig.)* a mark of infamy; trade-mark, used as an evidence of quality, the vintage date and shipper's name stamped on wine corks; *(poet.)* † a sword. BRAND (2), *v.t.* to mark with a b.; attach a stigma to; designate. BRANDED, *adj.* marked with a b. [OE.].

BRANDIED [bran'did], *adj.* strengthened, mixed with brandy.

BRANDING IRON [bran'ding-iern], *n.* iron for branding.

BRANDISH [bran'dish], *v.t.* to wave or flourish in threatening fashion. [OFr.].

BRAND-NEW [brand-nyŏŏ'], *adj.* absolutely new.

BRANDY [bran'di], *n.* a strong alcoholic spirit distilled from wine; b. ball, round brown sweet. [Du.].

BRANDY-PAWNEE [bran-di-paw'nē], *n.* brandy and water. [BRANDY and Hind.].

BRANDY-SNAP [bran'di-snap], *n.* thin, sticky, cylindrical gingerbread biscuit.

BRANNY [bra'ni], *adj.* containing bran.

BRANT-GOOSE [brant'gŏŏs], *n.* small wild goose, the brent-goose. [~Germ.].

BRASH (1) [brash], *n.* small fragments of broken rock, rubble. [Fr.].

BRASH (2), *n.* a belch of acidulous fluid from the stomach. [Uncert.].

BRASH (3), *adj.* impetuous, hasty; brittle. [Uncert.].

BRASIER, see BRAZIER.

BRASS (1) [brahs], *n.* an alloy of copper and zinc; a plate of this substance engraved with effigies etc., and set on a church wall or floor as a memorial; *(coll.)* coined money; *(coll.)* impudence, effrontery; *(mus.)* the metal wind-instruments of an orchestra. BRASS (2), *adj.* made of b. BRASS (3), *v.t.* and *i.* to cover with brass; brazen, put a bold face on. [OE.].

ŏŏ is pronounced as in *food*; ŏ̄ŏ as in *hood*; th as in *think*; TH as in *that*; zh as in *azure*.   ~ = related to.

BRASSARD, BRASSART [bra′sahd], *n.* armlet worn as a badge. [Fr.].

BRASS-BAND [brahs-band′], *n.* band consisting only of brass instruments; (*coll.*) military band.

BRASSERIE [bra′se-ri], *n.* beer hall and eating place. [Fr.].

BRASSFOUNDER [brahs′fown-der], *n.* worker in a brass foundry, one who casts brass.

BRASS-HAT [brahs-hat′], *n.* (*coll.*) high-ranking military staff officer. [From the gilt and metal embellishments formerly round his cap].

BRASSIE, BRASSY [brah′si, bra′si], *n.* golf club having a brass sole.

BRASSIERE, brassière [bra′si-āer], *n.* undergarment worn by women to shape and support the breasts. [Fr.].

BRASSY (1) [brah′si], *adj.* made of brass; (of sound) harsh, loudly metallic; glaringly hot; impudent.

BRASSY (2), see BRASSIE.

BRAT [brat], *n.* small, nasty, troublesome child; (*coll.*) child. [OE.].

BRAVADO [bra-vah′dō], *n.* arrogant challenging boast, ostentatious show of courage. [Span.].

BRAVE (1) [brāv], *adj.* courageous, valiant, gallantly bearing suffering or misfortune, unflinching in the face of danger; fine, attractive, gay. BRAVE (2), *n.* a b. man; Red Indian warrior. BRAVE (3), *v.t.* to face boldly, brazen out, venture; vaunt, swagger. BRAVELY, *adv.* in b. fashion.

BRAVERY [brā′ve-ri], *n.* courage, intrepidity; splendour of apparel. [Fr.].

BRAVO (1) [brah′vō], *n.* hired bully BRAVO (2), *int.* well done! [It.].

BRAVURA [bra-vōō′rah], *n.* a dashing display, show of spirit, something executed with a flourish; (*mus.*) spirited passage. [It.].

BRAWL (1) [brawl], *n.* noisy fight; vulgar, loud quarrel; uproar. BRAWL (2), *v.i.* to create or take part in a b. BRAWLING, *adj.* noisy, quarrelsome. BRAWLINGLY, *adv.* in brawling fashion. [ME.].

BRAWN [brawn], *n.* a compressed mould of pieces of spiced meat; muscle, muscular power. [OFr.].

BRAWNY [braw′ni], *adv.* muscular. BRAWNINESS, *n.* condition of being b.

BRAY (1) [brā], the cry of the ass; any loud noisy cry or similar sound. BRAY (2), *v.i.* to make a b. [OFr.].

BRAY (3), *v.t.* to crush, pound; (*coll.*) beat. [OFr. from OHigh Germ.].

BRAYLE, see BRAIL (1).

BRAZE [brāz], *v.t.* to join metals together by heating or fusing the joint with silver, brass or spelter. [OScand.].

BRAZEN (1) [brā′zen], *adj.* made from brass, relating to or resembling brass; (*fig.*) impudently bold; (of a sound) resembling that given out by a brass instrument. BRAZEN (2), *v.t.* **to b. a thing out,** to attempt to avoid or override criticism of something by acting brazenly. BRAZENLY, *adv.* in b. fashion. BRAZEN-NESS, *n.* impudence. [OE.].

BRAZIER (1) [brā′zi-er], *n.* open pan containing burning coals or charcoal. [Fr.].

BRAZIER (2), **BRASIER**, *n.* one who works in brass. [BRASS].

BRAZIL NUT [bra-zil′nut], *n.* three-sided edible nut from Brazil.

BRAZIL-WOOD [bra-zil′wood], *n.* red dye-wood from Brazil.

BREACH (1) [brēch], *n.* a breaking, infringement, violation, the dishonouring of an obligation; the thing broken; a material gap, hole made in something; (*milit.*) gap in fortifications made by bombardment or assault; **b. of the peace,** (*leg.*) riot, public disorder. BREACH (2), *v.t.* to make a b.; (*milit.*) break a way through walls or defences. [~BREAK].

BREAD [bred], *n.* man′s staple food, made of flour baked usually with yeast etc.; (*fig.*) food generally; means of livelihood. [OE.].

BREAD-BASKET [bred′bahs-kit], *n.* basket for bread; (*pop.*) the belly; type of bomb consisting of a number of small bombs which are scattered by impact and burst separately.

BREAD-FRUIT [bred′frōōt], *n.* fruit of a tree native to the Pacific Islands, resembling bread.

BREAD-LINE [bred′lin], *n.* (*U.S.*) a queue for bread; (*fig.*) economic distress.

BREAD-ROOM [bred′rōōm], *n.* that part of a ship′s hold in which the biscuit is stored.

BREADSTUFFS [bred′stufs], *n.*(*pl.*) flour, meal etc.; cereals used for making bread.

BREADTH [bredth], *n.* the shorter lineal dimension of surface, distance across from edge to edge at right angles to the length and depth; quality of being broad; (*fig.*) broad tolerance, wideness of interest or understanding. [OE.].

BREADTHWAYS [bredth′wāz], *adv.* from side to side, across.

BREADTHWISE [bredth′wīz], *adv.* breadthways.

BREAD-WINNER [bred′wi-ner], *n.* one who maintains a family by his or her earnings.

BREAK (1) (*pret.* **broke,** *p.xt.* **broken**) [brāk], *v.t. and i.* to divide forcibly into pieces; make or cause a break; ruin, make bankrupt; interrupt or disturb continuity; open ground for planting; come apart, be fractured; give way, collapse; disregard, ignore (the laws); deviate from the original direction (of a ball); become harsh and deep (of the male voice at puberty); **to b. down,** to crush down, destroy; analyse; **to b. in,** to tame (of horses); **to b. into,** to enter by force; begin to use (one′s resources etc.); **to b. off,** to discontinue; **to b. out,** to become violent; become infected as to the skin; **to b. the ice,** (*fig.*) to make first social advances; **to b. a record,** to surpass the previous best performance. BREAK (2), *n.* the forcible division of anything into (often irregular) parts; fracture, the thing broken; an interruption in time, interference in continuity; period for rest between the classes in a school; escape from prison; (*slang*) piece of good (or bad) fortune; (*billiards*) continuous score at one visit to the table, not necessarily during one period of play; change in the direction of the ball in cricket after pitching. [OE.].

BREAK (3), see BRAKE (6).

BREAKABLE [brā′ka-bl], *adj.* easily broken, fragile.

BREAKAGE [brā′kij], *n.* act of breaking, things broken; amount of damage by breaking.

BREAKAWAY (1) [brā′ka-wā], *n.* act of breaking away. BREAKAWAY (2), *adj.* detaching itself from a main body or group.

BREAKDOWN [brāk′down], *n.* a complete break; unforeseen cessation of action or work; accidental stoppage of a machine; nervous collapse; a statistical analysis; **b. gang,** workmen sent to repair damage to railway lines etc. caused by accident; **b. van,** van equipped to deal with mechanical breakdowns.

BREAKER [brā′ker], *n.* one who breaks; a wave breaking in foam.

BREAKFAST [brek′fast], *n.* the earliest meal of the day. BREAKFAST (2), *v.i.* to eat b. [BREAK (1) and FAST].

BREAKING [brā′king], *n.* (*phon.*) the diphthongization of certain vowels by the influence of following consonants, called also FRACTURE. [Germ.].

BREAK-JOINT [brāk′joint], *n.* the laying of stones or bricks so that the joints in an upper layer do not coincide with those of the layer immediately below.

BREAKNECK [brāk′nek], *adj.* dangerously fast.

BREAK-THROUGH [brāk′thrōō], *n.* act of breaking through an enemy line.

BREAKWATER [brāk′waw-ter], *n.* barrier or wall run at an angle into the sea to break the force of the waves.

BREAM [brēm], *n.* a broad, thin freshwater carp; a sea fish. [Fr. from OHigh Germ.].

BREAST (1) [brest], *n.* that part of the body between the throat and the navel; soft protuberance on the chest terminating in the nipple; mammary glands in women; (*fig.*) the heart, seat of the emotions and passions; **to make a clean b. of it,** to confess fully to some fault. BREAST (2), *v.t.* to face resolutely, oppose face to face; rise over the top of. [OE.].

BREASTBONE [brest′bōn], *n.* the sternum.

BREAST-FED [brest′fed], *adj.* (of infants) fed at the mother′s breast, not by a bottle.

BREAST-HIGH [brest-hi′], *adj. and adv.* as high as the breast.

BREASTPLATE [brest′plāt], *n.* plate of armour worn to protect the breast.

BREAST-STROKE [brest′strōk], *n.* (*swimming*) stroke in which a swimmer propels himself by froglike movements of arms and legs without raising them out of the water.

BREASTSUMMER, see BRESSUMMER.

BREAST-WHEEL [brest′wēl], *n.* waterwheel receiving the water at the level of the axle.

BREASTWORK [brest′werk], *n.* (*milit.*) rough parapet, low earthen rampart.

BREATH [breth], *n.* the air drawn into and exhaled from the lungs at a single respiration; (*poet.*) life; (*fig.*) a light breeze; **to take one′s b. away,** utterly to astound one. [OE.].

BREATHABLE [brē′THa-bl], *adj.* able to be breathed.

BREATHE [brēTH], *v.t. and i.* to inhale and exhale air, give vent to breath, blow gently and pleasantly; blow gently on, utter softly; *(fig.)* express a quality. BREATHED, *adj. (phon.)* uttered without voice; voiceless; *(philol.)* having a breathing. [OE.].

BREATHER [brē′THer], *n. (coll.)* mild open-air exercise as relief from a task, relaxation from violent effort; breathing-space.

BREATHING [brē′THing], *n.* respiration, action of inhaling and exhaling the breath continuously; gentle sound or movement; *(philol.)* aspiration, a stressed breath, mark indicating aspiration; **rough b.,** the strong aspiration of an initial vowel or *r* in Greek. BREATHING-SPACE, *n.* opportunity to get one's breath, short respite.

BREATHLESS [breth′les], *adj.* out of breath, breathing heavily and rapidly; scarcely able, or unable, to breathe, gasping; *(fig.)* tensely expectant, fearfully eager. BREATHLESSLY, *adv.* in b. fashion. BREATHLESSNESS, *n.* state or quality of being b.

BREATH-TAKING [breth′tā-king], *adj.* astonishing.

BRED [bred], *adj.* possessing inherited qualities.

BREECH (1) [brēch], *n.* the lower rear parts of the body, buttocks; part of the trousers covering the buttocks; hinder part of a gun, part of a gun which opens for loading. BREECH (2) [brich], *v.t.* to dress *(esp.* for the first time) in breeches. [OE.].

BREECH-BLOCK [brēch′blok], *n.* the part of a gun closing the breech after loading.

BREECHES [bri′chiz], *n.(pl.)* garments worn on the legs and lower part of the body, trousers; garment fitting tightly round the knees as worn for riding; **b. buoy,** canvas breeches slung along a rope to carry people from a sinking or wrecked ship. [*pl.* of BREECH].

BREECHING [bri′ching], *n.* the harness-strap passing round a horse's haunches; ropes lashing a gun to the sides of a ship.

BREECH-LOADER [brēch′lō-der], *n.* cannon or gun loaded at the breech.

BREED (1) [bred] [brēd], *v.t. and i.* to beget, bear, cause to arise; educate, develop, bring up; propagate desired types by ordered pairing of selected mates; reproduce, give birth; *(fig.)* grow and increase of itself. BREED (2), *n.* race or stock, racial variety, kind, group possessing common qualities; good breeding. [OE.].

BREEDER [brē′der], *n.* one who breeds, one who supervises the breeding of animals.

BREEDING [brē′ding], *n.* act or process of reproducing; descent, ancestry; aristocratic manners; education.

BREEKS [brēks], *n.(pl.) (Scots)* trousers. [BREECH].

BREEZE (1) [brēz], *n.* a light wind; *(fig.)* brief, sharp disturbance; sudden quarrel; **to have the b. up,** *(slang)* to be nervous, alarmed. [Fr.].

BREEZE (2), *n.* coal refuse, small cinders; **b. block,** a form of building unit made from cement and breeze. [OFr.].

BREEZY [brē′zi], *adj.* subject to breezes; *(fig.)* lively and jovial in manner. BREEZILY, *adv.* in b. fashion.

BREN CARRIER [bren′ka-ri-er], *n.* light armoured caterpillar vehicle armed with a Bren gun.

BREN GUN [bren′gun], *n.* type of machine gun *orig.* made at Brno in Czechoslovakia.

BRENT-GOOSE [brent′gōōs], *n.* the brant-goose.

BRESSOMER, see BRESSUMMER.

BRESSUMMER, BRESSOMER, BREASTSUMMER [bre′su-mer], *n. (arch.)* horizontal beam placed above a door or window to bear the weight of the wall above. [BREAST and Fr.].

BRETHREN [breTH′ren], *n.* † brothers, members of the same group. [*pl.* of BROTHER].

BRETON [bre′ton], *n. and adj.* a native of, pertaining to, Brittany; the Celtic language spoken in Brittany. [OFr.].

BREVE [brēv], *n. (mus.)* a note equal to two semibreves; mark (⌣) denoting a short syllable. [L.].

BREVET (1) [bre′vit], *n. (milit.)* document recording the appointment of an officer to a higher rank without extra pay. BREVET (2), *adj.* holding rank by b. [Fr.].

BREVIARY [brē′vi-e-ri], *n.* Roman Catholic book containing the daily services for the year. [L.].

BREVIER [bre-vēer′], *n. (print)* type of a size which prints approx. 9½ lines to an inch. [Prec.].

BREVITY [brē′vi-ti], *n.* quality of briefness, conciseness. [L.].

BREW (1) [brōō], *v.t. and i.* to make beer and similar liquor by boiling and fermenting from malt and hops; prepare any liquid by mingling and boiling; *(fig.)* cunningly to plot and contrive mischief; undergo the process of brewing; be in preparation, imminent. BREW (2), *n.* something brewed, a particular brewing of beer. [OE.].

BREWAGE [brōō′ij], *n.* a brewing, something brewed.

BREWERY [brōō′e-ri], *n.* factory where brewing is carried out.

BREWHOUSE [brōō′hows], *n.* a brewery.

BREWING [brōō′ing], *n.* act of making ale or beer, the liquor so brewed at any one time.

BREWSTER [brōō′ster], *n.* a brewer; **b. sessions,** a sitting of magistrates to grant licences to sell alcoholic liquor.

BRIAR (1) **BRIER** [bri′er], *n.* the wood of *Erica arborea*; a pipe made from this. [Fr.].

BRIAR (2), **BRIER**, *n.* the wild rose; any prickly bush or shrub; a thorn or prickle; *(fig.)* difficulties, troubles. BRIAR (3), BRIER, *adj.* made from b. [OE.].

BRIBE (1) [brib], *n.* a reward promised or given for an act contrary to right or duty. BRIBE (2), *v.t.* to seduce, influence by a b. BRIBABLE, *adj.* open to bribery. [OFr.].

BRIBERY [bri′be-ri], *n.* practice of giving and taking bribes.

BRIC-A-BRAC, bric-à-brac [brik′a-brak], *n.* a collection of miscellaneous, ornamental oddments or knick-knacks; curiosities of no great value or use. [Fr.].

BRICK (1) [brik], *n.* rectangular block of clay baked hard and used as a building stone; *(pl.)* blocks of wood used as children's toys; *(coll.)* person of sterling qualities; **to drop a b.,** to make a tactless and indiscreet blunder. BRICK (2), *adj.* made of b. BRICK (3), *v.t.* (usually **b. in** or **b. up**) to fill up, build up, with bricks. [OFr.].

BRICKBAT [brik′bat], *n.* a broken piece of brick; such a piece used as a missile.

BRICK-FIELD [brik′fēld], *n.* field where clay is obtained and baked into bricks.

BRICK-KILN [brik′kiln], *n.* kiln for baking bricks.

BRICKLAYER [brik′lā-er], *n.* workman skilled in building with bricks. BRICKLAYING, *n.* craft of building with bricks.

BRICK-NOGGING [brik′no-ging], *n. (arch.)* brickwork fitted in between timber framing.

BRICKWORK [brik′werk], *n.* building in brick, those parts of an edifice made with brick.

BRICKYARD [brik′yahd], *n.* place in which bricks are made.

BRICOLE [bri′kōl], *n.* a medieval siege-catapult; *(billiards)* a shot off the cushion; also an indirect stroke in tennis. [Fr.].

BRIDAL [bri′dal], *adj.* pertaining to a bride or wedding. [OE.].

BRIDE [brid], *n.* a woman about to be or just married, a newly married woman. [OE.].

BRIDE-CAKE [brid′kāk], *n.* very rich cake with white icing, eaten at a wedding feast.

BRIDE CHAMBER [brid′chām-ber], *n.* the bedroom shared by a couple on their wedding night.

BRIDEGROOM [brid′grōōm], *n.* a man about to be or just married.

BRIDESMAID [bridz′mād], *n.* an unmarried girl or woman attending the bride at a wedding.

BRIDEWELL [brid′wel], *n.* gaol; house of correction. [St. *Bride's Well*, London].

BRIDGE (1) [brij], *n.* structure carrying a road, railway etc. across a gap, river etc., linking the two sides; anything resembling this in shape or purpose; a way between two points passing above some intervening obstacle; raised deck from which a ship is navigated; a rest for a billiard cue; wooden support for the taut strings of a violin or similar instrument; hard upper structure of the nose; metal bar for keeping false teeth in place. BRIDGE (2), *v.t.* to build or erect a bridge; *(fig.)* surmount, overcome. [OE.].

BRIDGE (3), *n.* card game for four people, in which one of the two sets of partners undertakes to win so many tricks; **auction b.,** variety of the game in which the declarers undertake to score a certain minimum number of tricks; **contract b.,** variety in which only the tricks mentioned in the "contract" count towards "game." [Unkn.].

BRIDGE-HEAD [brij′hed], *n.* the land at the end of a bridge, leading to and dominating it; defences guarding the approach to a bridge; position which an attacking force has established across a river.

BRIDGE-TRAIN [brij′trān], *n. (milit.)* the engineers and equipment for building a military bridge.

BRIDLE (1) [bri′dl], *n.* the head-gear of a horse's

harness to which the controlling reins are attached; (*naut.*) a mooring cable; (*fig.*) a galling constraint. BRIDLE (2), *v.t. and i.* to control a horse with a b., put on a b.; (*fig.*) restrain; draw oneself up in haughty anger. [OE.].

BRIDLE-HAND [brī'dl-hand], *n.* the hand holding the reins; the left hand.

BRIDLE-PATH [brī'dl-pahth], *n.* a horse-track, path wide enough for a single mounted horse.

BRIDLE-REIN [brī'dl-rān], *n.* the thong of a bridle, attached to the bit.

BRIDLE-ROAD [brī'dl-rōd], *n.* bridle-path.

BRIDLE-WAY [brī'dl-wā], *n.* bridle-path.

BRIDOON [bri-dōōn'], *n.* snaffle and rein of a cavalry bridle. [Fr.].

BRIE [brē], *n.* soft cheese made in the French district of Brie.

BRIEF (1) [brēf], *n.* statement of a client's case given to the barrister who is to conduct it; the engagement of a barrister to argue a case; a papal letter. BRIEF (2), *v.t.* to instruct a barrister to conduct a case; instruct (troops) in a specific task to be undertaken. [OFr.].

BRIEF (3), *adj.* short, concise; abrupt (of conversation). BRIEFLY, *adv.* shortly, in brief. [OFr. from L.].

BRIEFING [brē'fing], *n.* detailed instruction for an approaching task.

BRIEFLESS [brēf'les], *adj.* lacking a brief; (*fig.*) (of a barrister) unsuccessful.

BRIER, see BRIAR.

BRIERY [brī'e-ri], *adj.* abounding in briers, rough, prickly. [OE.].

BRIG [brig], *n.* vessel having two square-rigged masts. [BRIGANTINE].

BRIGADE (1) [bri-gād'], *n.* military unit subsidiary to a division, and under the command of a brigadier; organized semi-military body, usually uniformed, with some common purpose. BRIGADE (2), *v.t.* to join together into brigades; (*fig.*) press into service.

BRIGADE-MAJOR [bri-gād-mā'jer], *n.* the adjutant or staff officer of a brigade.

BRIGADIER [bri-ga-dēer'], *n.* the commander of a brigade, next in rank above colonel.

BRIGAND [bri'gand], *n.* a bandit, member of a band of robbers who waylay travellers in country districts. BRIGANDAGE [bri'gan-dij], *n.* occupation of a b., robbery by companies of bandits. [OFr.].

BRIGANTINE [bri'gan-tēn], *n.* a two-masted vessel, square-rigged on the foremast and fore-and-aft rigged on the mainmast. [Fr.].

BRIGHT [brīt], *adj.* reflecting light, giving out light, glittering; vivid, vividly coloured; cheerful; encouraging; quick in mind, lively; splendid, illustrious. BRIGHTEN, *v.t. and i.* to make b., become b. BRIGHTLY, *adv.* in b. fashion, brilliantly, gaily. BRIGHTNESS, *n.* quality of being b. [OE.].

BRIGHT'S DISEASE [brīts'di-zēz], *n.* (*med.*) a disease of the kidneys. [Dr. *Bright*, physician].

BRILL [bril], *n.* flatfish akin to the turbot. [Cornish].

BRILLANTE [bri-lan'tā], *adj.* (*mus.*) in gay and lively fashion. [It.].

BRILLIANCE [bril'yans], *n.* quality of being extremely bright; exceptional talent. BRILLIANCY, *n.* b.

BRILLIANT (1) [bril'yant], *n.* brightly sparkling jewel, fine diamond; a spangle. [Fr.].

BRILLIANT (2), *adj.* shining, sparkling, blazingly bright, exceptionally talented; splendid, fashionable. BRILLIANTLY, *adv.* in b. fashion. [Fr.].

BRILLIANTINE [bril-yan-tēn'], *n.* liquid or solid preparation of alcohol and oil for brightening, scenting and fixing the hair. [Fr.].

BRIM (1) [brim], *n.* the edge of the rim around the opening of a vessel; flattish rim round the crown of a hat; edge of the sea or a river, extreme edge of a chasm. BRIM (2), *v.i.* to be filled up to the b. BRIMFUL, *adj.* full to the top. BRIMLESS, *adj.* without a b. BRIMMED, *adj.* having a b.; brimming over. BRIMMER, *n.* vessel filled to the b. BRIMMING, *adj.* filled to the very top, overflowing. [ME.].

BRIMSTONE (1) [brim'stōn], *n.* sulphur; (*fig.*) hell-fire. BRIMSTONE (2), *adj.* made of or like b. [ME.].

BRINDLE, BRINDLED [brin'dl], *adj.* having tawny streaks on black.

BRINE [brīn], *n.* water saturated with salt; sea-water; salt water used in pickling. [OE.].

BRINEPAN [brīn'pan], *n.* pit in which brine is evaporated in order to extract the salt.

BRING (*pret. and p.pt.* **brought**) [bring], *v.t.* to cause

to come; carry along (to a place where the speaker is or will be), produce, cause to arise; (*leg.*) initiate an action; **to b. about**, to cause to arise; **to b. back**, to call to mind; **to b. down**, to shoot down; **to b. forth**, to give birth to; **to b. forward**, to carry on a total etc., to the following page in book-keeping; **to b. off**, to accomplish, usually by luck or exceptional skill or in face of difficulty; **to b. on**, to induce; **to b. over**, to convert; **to b. round**, to restore to consciousness, convert; **to b. up**, to educate, rear; vomit; raise a matter. [OE.].

BRINK [bringk], *n.* the extreme edge of a hilltop or precipice; (*fig.*) immediate neighbourhood of anything alarming. [ODan.].

BRINY (1) [brī'ni], *adj.* like brine, salty. BRINY (2), *n.* (*coll.*) the sea.

BRIO [brē'ō], *n.* (*mus.*) vivacity. [It.].

BRIOCHE [brē-osh'], *n.* kind of horseshoe-shaped bread or pastry. [Fr.].

BRIONY, see BRYONY.

BRIQUETTE [bri-ket'], *n.* brick-shaped cake of compressed material used in household fires; similarly shaped piece of ice-cream. [Fr.].

BRISE-BISE [brēz'bēz], *n.* short curtain in front of a window. [Fr.].

BRISK (1) [brisk], *adj.* active, spirited, quick and efficient in movement; (of fires) burning brightly; (of wind) sharp and fresh. BRISK (2), *v.t. and i.* to make or become b. BRISKLY, *adv.* in b. fashion. BRISKNESS, *n.* quality of being b. [Uncert.].

BRISKET [bris'kit], *n.* the breast of an animal; part of the beast nearest the ribs. [OFr.].

BRISLING [briz'ling], *n.* the sprat. [Norw.].

BRISTLE (1) [bris'l], *n.* the quills of a hedgehog, stiff hair of swine, any short, stiff, rough hair; the stiff hairs in a brush. BRISTLE (2), *v.i.* to raise the bristles from rage or fear; (*fig.*) bridle with anger; show or make a group of projecting points, display many weapons ominously; (*fig.*) be beset with. BRISTLING, *adj.* displaying, having bristles; rising in anger. [ME.].

BRISTLY [bris'li], *adj.* with bristles; rough, unshaven. BRISLINESS, *n.* condition of being b.

BRISTOL BOARD [bris'tol-bawd], *n.* fine smooth cardboard used by artists. [*Bristol*].

BRISTOL BRICK [bris'tol-brik], *n.* brick for cleaning cutlery.

BRISTOL CREAM [bris-tol-krēm'], *n.* (*prot.*) fine rich brand of sherry.

BRISTOL DIAMOND [bris-tol-dī'a-mond], *n.* rock-crystal found near Bristol.

BRISTOL-FASHION [bris'tol-fa-shn], *adj.* (*naut.*) in good order.

BRISTOL STONE [bris'tol-stōn], *n.* Bristol diamond.

BRITANNIA METAL [brī-ta-ni-ah-me'tal], *n.* white metal alloy used as a cheap substitute for silver.

BRITANNIC [bri-ta'nik], *adj.* pertaining to Britain or the inhabitants of Britain. [L.].

BRITISH [bri'tish], *adj.* pertaining to Britain or to the inhabitants of Britain, or to the British Empire and Commonwealth; **B. warm**, short overcoat worn by British Army officers. [OE.].

BRITISHER [bri'ti-sher], *n.* (*U.S.*) a Briton.

BRITON [bri'ton], *n.* a native of Great Britain; an ancient Brythonic inhabitant of England; (*fig.*) person of sterling qualities. [OFr.].

BRITTLE [bri'tl], *adj.* fragile, liable to break easily. BRITTLENESS, *n.* condition of being b. [ME.].

BROACH (1) [brōch], *n.* pointed hand tool for making small holes bodkin, awl, any boring bit tapered to an end; roasting spit. BROACH (2), *v.t.* to bore a hole in a cask of liquor, tap; enter upon, begin, approach a subject, mention a matter for discussion; (*naut.*) bring a ship broadside on to wind and sea. BROACHER, *n.* one who starts a new subject for discussion. BROACH-SPIRE, spire rising directly from a church-tower wall without resting on a parapet. [Fr. from L.].

BROAD (1) [brawd], *adj.* wide, extended, extensive, not narrow, of extensive measurement from side to side; general, comprehensive, widespread; liberal, unprejudiced; bold, distinct; indelicate, coarse, gross; **as b. as it is long**, the same either way; **B. Church**, Protestants who tend to regard dogma with indifference. BROAD (2), *n.* wide stretch of a river etc. [OE.].

BROAD ARROW [brawd-a'rō], *n.* mark in the shape of an arrow-head set upon government property, and formerly upon the uniform of convicts.

BROAD AWAKE [brawd-a-wāk'], *adj.* wide awake.

BROAD BEAN [brawd-bēn'], *n.* a large edible bean.

BROAD-BILL [brawd'bil], *n.* a variety of duck.

BROADCAST (1) [brawd'kahst], *n.* (*agr.*) a scattering of seed when sowing; (*radio*) speech, music or other sounds transmitted to the public over a network of wireless telephony. BROADCAST (2), *adj.* sown by scattering, scattered by hand; (*fig.*) widely disseminated; transmitted by wireless telephony. BROADCAST (3) (*pret. and p.pt.* BROADCAST), *v.t.* to transmit by wireless telephony; *v.i.* speak or perform before a transmitting microphone.

BROADCASTER [brawd'kahs-ter], *n.* one who broadcasts.

BROADCLOTH [brawd'kloth], *n.* a fine woollen cloth.

BROADEN [braw'den], *v.t. and i.* to grow broad; make broad.

BROAD-GAUGE [brawd'gāj], *n.* railway track with the rails set wider apart than the standard width of four feet eight and a half inches.

BROADLY [brawd'li], *adv.* in a broad manner; on the whole; approximately.

BROAD-MINDED [brawd-mīn'did], *adj.* tolerant. BROADMINDEDNESS, *n.* a tolerant and liberal attitude of mind.

BROADSHEET [brawd'shēt], *n.* sheet of paper printed only on the face; tract or ballad printed on one side of a sheet of paper and sold to the public, a broadside.

BROADSIDE (1) [brawd'sīd], *n.* a broadsheet; the whole length of one side of a ship; the simultaneous firing of all guns on one side of a ship aiming at the same objective; (*fig.*) concentrated attack against an individual. BROADSIDE (2), *adv.* on or facing the b.

BROADTAIL [brawd'tāl], *n.* kind of fur resembling astrakhan. [Germ.].

BROADSWORD [brawd'sawd], *n.* sword with a broad blade.

BROADWAYS [brawd'wāz], *adv.* broadwise.

BROADWISE [brawd'wīz], *adv.* towards the side, laterally, along the breadth.

BROBDINGNAGIAN [brob-ding-na'gi-an], *adj.* gigantic. [*Brobdingnag,* in Swift's *Gulliver's Travels*].

BROCADE (1) [brō-kād'], *n.* fabric usually of silk and embossed or decorated with silver and gold threads. BROCADE (2), *v.t. and i.* to make b.; stitch designs on cloth. BROCADED, *adj.* woven or worked with b.; dressed in b. [Span.].

BROCAGE, see BROKAGE.

BROCCOLI [bro'ko-li], *n.* hardy species of cauliflower bearing a number of small sproutings. [It.].

BROCHE, broché (1) [bro'shā], *n.* fabric, particularly of silk, on the surface of which an embossed pattern is woven. BROCHE (2), *adj.* woven like b. [Fr.].

BROCHURE [bro'shŏŏr, bro'shŏŏr], *n.* small descriptive pamphlet. [Fr.].

BROCK [brok], *n.* badger. [OE.].

BROCKET [bro'kit], *n.* two-year-old stag. [Fr.].

BROGUE (1) [brōg], *n.* coarse leather shoe; heavy leather shoe with hand-tooled reinforcements for hard wear. [Ir.].

BROGUE (2), *n.* the accent of an Irishman speaking English; English as spoken in Ireland. [Unkn.].

BROIDER [broi'der], *v.t.* (*poet.*) to embroider.

BROIL (1) [broil], *n.* turmoil; row, noisy quarrel. [Fr.].

BROIL (2), *v.t. and i.* to grill, cook in the flames of a fire, generally upon a gridiron; be heated; sweat with heat. BROILING, *adj.* being cooked by fire; extremely hot. [OFr.].

BROILER [broi'ler], *n.* person who enjoys or excites broils; person who cooks meat by broiling; gridiron; fowl suitable for broiling; (*coll.*) extremely hot day.

BROKAGE, BROCAGE [brō'kij], *n.* brokerage.

BROKE (1) [brōk], *pret.* of BREAK (1). BROKE (2), *adj.* (*coll.*) penniless, ruined, bankrupt. [BREAK (1)].

BROKEN [brō'ken], *adj.* (*p.pt.* of BREAK), being in fragments, crushed, dispirited, weak; interrupted; (*bot.*) variegated; (of land, ground) rough, uneven; (of water) choppy. [BREAK (1)].

BROKEN-BACKED [brō-ken-bakt'], *adj.* having the spine broken.

BROKEN-DOWN [brō-ken-down'], *adj.* worn out by illness or work, stopped through a breakdown.

BROKEN-HEARTED [brō-ken-hah'tid], *adj.* overcome by sorrow, inconsolable.

BROKENLY [brō'ken-li], *adv.* in a broken fashion; with breaks, intermittently.

BROKEN WIND [brō-ken-wind'], *n.* affection of the lungs of horses causing laboured and spasmodic breathing. BROKEN-WINDED, *adj.* affected by b.

BROKER [brō'ker], *n.* agent working on a commission basis who buys and sells stocks and shares or goods in bulk for clients; dealer in second-hand goods; one licensed to sell distrained property. [OFr.].

BROKERAGE [brō'ke-rij], *n.* business of a broker; commission charged by a broker.

BROKING [brō'king], *n.* business of a broker.

BROLLY [bro'li], *n.* (*slang*) umbrella.

BROMATE [brō'māt], *n.* (*chem.*) a salt of bromic acid.

BROMIC [brō'mik], *adj.* (*chem.*) containing bromine; **b. acid,** acid containing hydrogen, bromine and oxygen, $HBrO_3$.

BROMIDE [brō'mīd], *n.* a compound of bromine with a base, used medically as a sedative; (*fig.*) (*coll.*) uninteresting, conventional remark, having a sedative effect on the listener. BROMIDIC [brō-mi'dik], *adj.* containing b.

BROMIDE PAPER [brō'mīd-pā-per], *n.* (*phot.*) printing paper coated with a silver-bromide emulsion, used especially for enlargements.

BROMINE [brō'mēn], *n.* non-metallic poisonous liquid giving off a bad stench, the chemical element denoted by Br. [Gk.].

BRONCHI [brong'kī], *n.*(*pl.*) (*anat.*) the two branches of the windpipe entering the lungs. [Gk.].

BRONCHIAL [brong'ki-al], *adj.* pertaining to, affected in, the bronchi.

BRONCHITIS [brong-kī'tis], *n.* inflammation of the bronchial tubes. BRONCHITIC [brong-ki'tik], *adj.* pertaining to, affected with, b. [Gk.].

BRONCHO-, *pref.* appertaining to the windpipe. [Gk.].

BRONCHOCELE [brong'kō-sēl], *n.* (*med.*) goitre. [Gk.].

BRONCHOSCOPE [brong'kō-skōp], *n.* (*med.*) instrument for inspecting the interior of the bronchi. [Gk.].

BRONCHOTOMY [brong-ko'to-mi], *n.* (*surg.*) operation of cutting into the windpipe. [Gk.].

BRONCO [brong'kō], *n.* (*U.S.*) untamed horse. [Span.].

BRONTOSAURUS [bron-tō-saw'rus], *n.* (*geol.*) extinct giant lizard of the prehistoric age. [Gk.].

BRONX [brongks], *n.* (*U.S.*) district in New York lying north of Manhattan; kind of cocktail.

BRONZE (1) [bronz], *n.* alloy of copper and tin with or without other metals; ornament or cast statue of this metal; reddish colour of the alloy; **B. Age,** (*archae.*) historical period between 1800 and 1000 B.C. when most implements were made of b. BRONZE (2), *adj.* made of b.; of the colour of b. BRONZE (3), *v.t. and i.* to give or acquire the colour or appearance of b. [It. from L.].

BROOCH [brōch], *n.* a clasp, usually ornamented, fastened by a clip and catch to the clothes at the breast or throat. [Variant of BROACH].

BROOD (1) [brōōd], *n.* the number of young birds hatched at one sitting; all the offspring of one parent; (*fig.*) offspring, progeny, children. BROOD (2), *v.i.* to sit on eggs to hatch them; cover and guard with the wings and feathers; (*fig.*) sit quietly, be at rest; meditate, ponder for a long time. BROODING, *adj.* meditating deeply and for long. BROODINGLY, *adv.* meditatively. [OE.].

BROOD-MARE [brōōd'māer], *n.* mare kept for breeding purposes.

BROODY [brōō'di], *adj.* having a natural urge to brood.

BROOK (1) [brōōk], *n.* small stream. [OE.].

BROOK (2), *v.t.* to bear; endure; tolerate. [OE.].

BROOKLET [brōōk'let], *n.* small brook.

BROOKLIME [brōōk'līm], *n.* (*bot.*) the water-speedwell.

BROOM [brōōm], *n.* shrub bearing clusters of small yellow flowers and having short spiky leaves; besom, long handle with a short board bearing a bush of bristles attached to one end, used for sweeping; **new b.,** person new to a post and active in his duties or reorganizing. [OE.].

BROOMCORN [brōōm'kawn], *n.* the common millet.

BROOMRAPE [brōōm'rāp], *n.* (*bot.*) the strangle-weed.

BROOMSTICK [brōōm'stik], *n.* the handle of a broom.

BROSE [brōz], *n.* porridge; **Athole b.,** drink of honey, cream and whisky. [OFr.].

BROTH [broth], *n.* stock water in which meat has

been cooked or vegetables boiled; kind of soup with meat and vegetables. [OE.].

BROTHEL [bro'thel], *n.* establishment kept for prostitution. [ME.].

BROTHER (*pl.* **brothers**, †**brethren**) [bru'THer], *n.* male having the same father and mother as another person; person closely connected with another; member of the same society as another, associate; member of a religious order; person resembling another in any characteristic; fellow man. HALF-BROTHER, son having one parent in common with another person. BROTHER-GERMAN, full brother. BROTHER-UTERINE, son related to another by having the same mother. [OE.].

BROTHERHOOD [bru'THer-hŏŏd], *n.* state of being a brother; society, fraternity, association, any group of persons working towards a common end.

BROTHER-IN-LAW [bru'THer-in-law], *n.* brother of a husband or wife, or a sister's husband.

BROTHERLY [bru'THer-li], *adj.* like a brother, affectionate. BROTHERLINESS, *n.* state of being b., friendliness.

BROUGHAM† [brŏŏm], *n.* closed carriage with a light chassis and body on four wheels, drawn by one horse. [Lord *Brougham*, the designer].

BROUGHT [brawt], *pret. and p.pt.* of BRING.

BROW [brow], *n.* the forehead, part of the forehead above the eyes, ridge above each eye; slight crescent of hair that covers this ridge; top edge of a steep hill. [OE.].

BROWBEAT [brow'bēt], *v.t.* to act overbearingly towards, threaten arrogantly, intimidate, bully.

BROWN (1) [brown], *n.* colour which is a mixture of yellow, red and black in various shades. BROWN (2), *adj.* having the colour of b.; **b. study**, deep thought. BROWN-SHIRT, a Nazi. BROWN (3), *v.t. and i.* to make b.; cause to become b. in colour by applying heat, roast or grill; become b.; **browned off**, (*slang*) utterly disgruntled, fed up. [OE.].

BROWN COAL [brown-kōl'], *n.* lignite.

BROWNIAN [brown'ni-an], *adj.* (*phys.*); **B. movement**, the motion of finely divided particles suspended in a fluid, caused by the impact of molecules on one another. [Dr. R. *Brown*, who first described it].

BROWNIE [brow'ni], *n.* elf or fairy helpful to human beings; member of the Girl Guides under eleven years of age.

BROWNING (1) [brow'ning], *n.* process of imparting a brown colour to the surfaces of articles made of iron; liquid used in cookery as a colouring.

BROWNING (2), *n.* an automatic pistol. [*Browning*, inventor].

BROWNISH [brow'nish], *adj.* slightly brown.

BROWNIST [brow'nist], *n.* follower of the religious principles of Robert *Browne*, who seceded from the Established Church of England about 1580.

BROWNNESS [brown'nes], *n.* quality or state of being brown.

BROWSE (1) [browz], *n.* the tender shoots of herbage eaten by cattle. BROWSE (2), *v.i.* to feed on grass and young shoots while moving aimlessly from place to place; graze; (*fig.*) study or read fitfully. BROWSING, *n.* ground for browsing. [OFr.].

BRUIN [brŏŏ'in], *n.* a bear. [Du.].

BRUISE (1) [brŏŏz], *v.t. and i.* to injure the flesh without drawing blood, cause the flesh to discolour by a heavy blow, contuse; crush by squeezing or pounding; display the effects of a blow. BRUISE (2), *n.* injury to the flesh accompanied by discoloration due to a blow, contusion. BRUISER, *n.* person who bruises; concave tool for grinding the specula of telescopes; (*slang*) professional boxer. [OE.].

BRUIT [brŏŏt], *v.t.* to rumour.

BRUNCH [brunch], *n.* (*slang*) meal heavier than breakfast, lighter than lunch, at which dishes from both meals are eaten. [BR(EAKFAST) and (L)UNCH].

BRUNETTE (1) [brŏŏ-net'], *n.* woman or girl with a brown complexion and colouring, with dark eyes and hair. BRUNETTE (2), *adj.* dark-haired; of dark complexion. [Fr.].

BRUNSWICK-BLACK [brunz-wik-blak'], *n.* dull black paint.

BRUNSWICK-GREEN [brunz-wik-grēn'], *n.* pigment composed of copper carbonate and chalk.

BRUNT [brunt], *n.* the fiercest attack; heaviest shock; first blow. [Unkn.].

BRUSH (1) [brush], *n.* hand utensil made of a bunch of bristles, feathers or twigs set in a piece of wood or other material with a handle, used for sweeping, removing dirt, brushing hair or wearing apparel etc.; stick with a small bunch of fine hair or bristle used to apply paint; bushy tail of a fox; rough, wild shrubs growing close together, undergrowth; skirmish, insignificant encounter with opponents; (*elect.*) discharge of electricity with the sparks resembling the bristles of a brush; piece of copper gauze or carbon for conducting an electric current to or from the commutator of a dynamo or electric motor; **b. work**, painting. BRUSH (2), *v.t. and i.* to use a b.; graze against, rub lightly in passing; **to b. away**, **to b. off**, to remove with a quick movement; **to b. aside**, to ignore, summarily reject; **to b. up**, (*fig.*) to refresh the memory concerning. [OFr.].

BRUSHWOOD [brush'wŏŏd], *n.* undergrowth, scrub; a thicket.

BRUSHY [bru'shi], *adj.* rough or bushy, like a brush.

BRUSQUE [brŏŏsk], *adj.* curt, abrupt in manner. BRUSQUELY, *adv.* in b. fashion. BRUSQUENESS, *n.* quality of being b. [Fr.].

BRUSSELS CARPET [bru-selz-kah'pit], *n.* type of carpet originally imported from *Brussels*.

BRUSSELS SPROUTS [bru-selz-sprowts'], *n.(pl.)* vegetables resembling small cabbages which sprout from an upright stem or stalk.

BRUTAL [brŏŏ'tal], *adj.* characteristic of a brute; cruel, coarse, rough. BRUTALISM, *n.* brutality. BRUTALLY, *adv.* in b. fashion. [Fr.].

BRUTALITY [brŏŏ-ta'li-ti], *n.* state of being brutal; brutal act.

BRUTALIZE [brŏŏ'ta-līz], *v.t.* to make brutal, treat brutally. BRUTALIZATION [brŏŏ-ta-li-zā'shn], *n.* act of brutalizing; state of being made brutal.

BRUTE (1) [brŏŏt], *n.* a beast, mammal, as distinct from a man; brutal person, savage, uncivilized human being, crude and cruel person. BRUTE (2), *adj.* brutal, inhuman, irrational. [Fr. from L.].

BRUTISH [brŏŏ'tish], *adj.* like a brute, stupid, unfeeling; savage. BRUTISHLY, *adv.* in a b. fashion. BRUTISHNESS, *n.* state of being b.

BRYOLOGY [brī-o'lo-ji], *n.* study of mosses. BRYOLOGIST, *n.* one who studies mosses. [Gk.].

BRYONINE [brī'o-nin], *n.* bitter principle from the root of the white bryony.

BRYONY, BRIONY [brī'o-ni], *n.* (*bot.*) a wild climbing plant. [Gk.].

BRYOZOA [brī-o-zō'ah], *n.(pl.)* the polyzoa. BRYOZOAN, *n.* one of the b. [Gk.].

BRYTHONIC [bri-tho'nik], *adj.* pertaining to the Celtic races of southern Britain, British. [Wel.].

BUBAL [bŏŏ'bal], *n.* kind of North African antelope. [Gk.].

BUBBLE (1) [bu'bl], *n.* a thin globular or hemispherical skin of liquid inflated with air or gas; small round air- or gas-filled pocket in a liquid or solid; (*fig.*) anything lacking a solid or sound basis, any scheme in danger of being destroyed by the intrusion of the facts of reality; fraudulent plan. BUBBLE (2), *v.i.* to make or cause bubbles, effervesce, be in a state of activity due to the formation of bubbles, contain bubbles; flow with the noise of innumerable bubbles bursting. BUBBLING, *n.* process of forming bubbles, sound of boiling or flowing water. [~Du., Swed.].

BUBBLE-AND-SQUEAK [bu-bl-and-skwēk'], *n.* dish composed of potato, cabbage, minced meat etc., fried.

BUBBLY [bub'li], *adj.* full of bubbles; *n.* (*slang*) champagne.

BUBO [byŏŏ'bō], *n.* (*med.*) pus-emitting swelling in the groin or armpit due to an inflamed gland. BUBONIC [byŏŏ-bo'nik], *n.* (*med.*) affected with, characterized by, buboes; **b. plague**, plague, the Black Death. [L.].

BUBONOCELE [byŏŏ-bo'no-sēl], *n.* (*med.*) rupture in the groin. [Gk.].

BUCCAN (1) [bŏŏ-kan'], *n.* (*S. Amer.*) hurdle of sticks bound together. BUCCAN (2) [bŏŏ'kan], *v.i.* to smoke meat over a fire on a b. [Fr.].

BUCCANEER [bu-ka-nēer'], *n.* seventeenth-century pirate; originally a French settler in Haiti who buccaned meat. [Prec.].

BUCENTAUR [byŏŏ-sen'taw(r)], *n.* the state barge of a Venetian doge. [Gk.].

BUCEPHALUS [byŏŏ-se'fa-lus], *n.* horse celebrated as the favourite charger of Alexander the Great; a charger. [Gk.].

BUCHMANITE [buk'ma-nīt], *n.* member of the Oxford Group. [Frank *Buchman*, founder].

BUCK (1) [buk], *n.* male of the deer family, of rabbits and hares, antelope; (*fig.*) fop, dandy, beau; (*U.S.*) (*coll.*) dollar; (*poker*) any article of value put in the pool in place of chips; **to pass the b. to**, (*slang*) to transfer responsibility to. BUCK (2), v.t. and i. to swagger, strut; (of horses) jump up and down with all four feet leaving the ground; jump, kick the legs out; **to b. up**, (fig.) to cheer up, take confidence; increase efforts, make haste. BUCKED, p.pt. adj. elated. [OE.].

BUCKET (1) [bu'kit], n. cylindrical, often tapering, vessel for holdi ' water or waste matter; **to kick the b.**, (slang) to d ' BUCKET (2), v.t. to take it out of a horse by hara riding; (in rowing) to rush forward at the end of a stroke. [OFr.].

BUCKETFUL [bu'kit-fŏŏl], n. amount a bucket will hold.

BUCKET-SHOP [bu'kit-shop], n. the office of stock-brokers, not members of the Stock Exchange, dealing chiefly in trashy shares.

BUCKHOUND [buk'hownd], n. breed of dog for tracking down stags.

BUCKISH [bu'kish], adj. pertaining to a buck; foppish.

BUCK-JUMP [buk'jump], n. (of an unbroken horse) a leap with all four feet clear of the ground. BUCK-JUMPER, n. vicious or unbroken horse.

BUCKLE (1) [bu'kl], n. metal, bone etc. frame with a crossbar on which a hinged prong is often placed, usually attached to one end of a strap or strip of material to fasten it temporarily to the other end; clasp for adorning a shoe or handbag. BUCKLE (2), v.t. and i. to fasten with a b.; gird oneself with armour; curl up, bend under pressure, crumple; **to b. to**, to devote one's energy to, start work. [Fr.].

BUCKLER [buk'ler], n. round shield with a boss in the centre; (zool.) thick-skinned, shell or bone parts covering some animals, such as the armadillo.

BUCKO (1) [bu'ko], n. (naut. slang) swaggerer, boaster. BUCKO (2), adj. (naut. slang) boastful, swaggering.

BUCKRAM [buk'ram], n. coarse linen cloth stiffened with gum and used in bookbinding and tailoring. [OFr.].

BUCK RAREBIT [buk-rãer'bit], n. Welsh rabbit ("rarebit") with an egg added.

BUCKSHEE (1) [buk-shē'], n. (slang) extra army rations; anything given away or obtained free. BUCKSHEE (2), adj. (slang) free, gratis. [BACK-SHEESH].

BUCK'S HORN [buks'hawn], n. (bot.) one of several species of plants with leaves like the horns of a buck; a plantain.

BUCKSHOT [buk'shot], n. large-sized shot used with sporting guns.

BUCKSKIN (1) [buk'skin], n. the skin of a buck; soft yellow leather made from this; (pl.) breeches made from this leather. BUCKSKIN, adj. made of b.

BUCKTHORN [buk'thawn], n. (bot.) thorny shrub bearing berries which yield a powerful cathartic.

BUCK-TOOTH [buk'tōōth], n. prominent tooth.

BUCKWHEAT [buk'wēt], n. (bot.) species of Polygonum, bearing seeds like beech-nuts. [OE.].

BUCOLIC (1) [byŏŏ-ko'lik], n. poem having a pastoral subject matter. BUCOLIC (2), adj. pertaining to the countryside or to pastoral imagery. [Gk.].

BUD (1) [bud], n. (bot.) embryonic growth of compact leaves or flower breaking out of the main stem; half-opened flower; **to nip in the b.**, (fig.) to put an end to an action or idea by stopping it in its initial stages. BUD (2), v.t. and i. to graft (a b.) into another plant; to put out buds, grow buds. [ME.].

BUDDHISM [bŏŏ'dizm], n. great Asiatic religious system of Siddhartha, or Buddha. [Skr.].

BUDDHIST [bŏŏ'dist], n. one who believes in Buddhism. BUDDHISTIC, adj. pertaining to Buddhism.

BUDDING (1) [bu'ding], n. the growth of buds; (hort.) act of grafting a bud to another plant or tree. BUDDING (2), adj. opening out as a bud; (fig.) promising, likely to do well.

BUDDLEIA [bud'lē-ah], n. variety of shrub with purple or yellow flowers of many forms. [A. Buddle, botanist].

BUDDY [bu'di], n. (U.S. coll.) brother, comrade. [Uncert.].

BUDE-LIGHT [byŏŏd'lit], n. brilliant light produced by burning oxyhydrogen gas in the centre of an Argand burner. [Bude, where the inventor lived].

BUDGE [buj], v.t. and i. to cause to move slightly with difficulty, shift; to make a slight movement under pressure, shift.

BUDGERIGAR [bu'je-ri-gah(r)], n. the Australian green parakeet, a love-bird. [Native].

BUDGET (1) [bu'jit], n. † small bag, contents of such

a bag; annual statement made in the House of Commons by the Chancellor of the Exchequer summarizing the country's financial position; financial statement presented by official organizations; estimate of future financial expenditure. BUDGET (2), v.i. to estimate financial expenditure; **to b. for**, to make provision for. BUDGETARY, adj. of, or pertaining to, a b. [OFr.].

BUFF (1) [buf], n. leather prepared from the skin of the buffalo or ox; polisher made of leather; colour of buff leather, a pale muddy yellow. BUFF (2), adj. having the colour of b. BUFF (3), v.t. to polish with a b. [Fr.].

BUFFALO [bu'fa-lŏ], n. wild ox. [Portug.].

BUFFER (1) [bu'fer], n. shock-absorbing device consisting of spring-loaded flat metal plates so placed on a vehicle as to make contact with similar plates on other vehicles; such a contrivance fitted to the platform of a terminus functioning by hydraulic pressure; a polisher; **b. state**, small state situated between two larger and potentially hostile ones, which prevents their coming into immediate contact with each other.

BUFFER (2), n. (coll.) fellow (used contemptuously); foolish old man.

BUFFET (1) [bŏŏ'fā], n. sideboard; place for light refreshments. [Fr.].

BUFFET (2) [bu'fit], n. a blow struck with the hand, a cuff; (fig.) misfortune, calamity. BUFFET (3), v.t. and i. to strike with the hand or fist, to cuff; struggle, contend. BUFFETING, n. a beating with the hands or fists, series of slaps; the action of waves beating against a ship. [~OFr.].

BUFFO [bŏŏ'fŏ], n. comedian, comic actor. [It.].

BUFFOON [bu-fŏŏn'], n. person who amuses others with simple knockabout humour; clown, jester. [Fr., It.].

BUG [bug], n. verminous blood-sucking insect, often infesting old or dirty houses; **big b.**, (coll.) person considering himself important. [OScand.].

BUGABOO [bu'ga-bŏŏ], n. bugbear. [Uncert.].

BUGBEAR [bug'bãer], n. an object of dread, often spectral. [Uncert.].

BUGGER [bu'ger], n. † heretic (orig. from Bulgaria); (leg.) one guilty of buggery; (vulg.) term of abuse for a fellow. BUGGERY, n. (leg.) unnatural intercourse with another male, sodomy. [Fr.].

BUGGY (1) [bu'gi], n. light two- or four-wheeled carriage drawn by one horse; gig. [Uncert.].

BUGGY (2), adj. infested with bugs.

BUGLE (1) [byŏŏ'gl], n. small trumpet for sounding calls to troops. BUGLE (2), v.i. (milit., mus.) to play or blow a b. [OFr. from L.].

BUGLE (3), n. long glass bead, usually black, sewn on to a woman's dress as an ornament. [Uncert.].

BUGLE (4), n. (bot.) creeping plant of the genus Ajuga. [Fr.].

BUGLER [byŏŏ'gler], n. one who sounds a bugle.

BUGLOSS [byŏŏ'glos], n. (bot.) either of two plants, Echium vulgare and Lycopsis arvensis. [Fr.].

BUHL, BOULE [bŏŏl], n. style of inlaying wood with gold or brass and mother-of-pearl. [A. Boulle, French cabinet-maker].

BUILD (1) [bild], v.t. and i. to (built, builded†) construct by fixing securely together various component parts according to a plan, raise, rear; develop gradually, strengthen, improve; practise building; **to b. on**, to rely upon; **to b. up**, to increase, strengthen; (fig.) emphasize the worth or importance of. BUILD (2), n. shape, form, construction; proportions of the human body. [OE.].

BUILDING [bil'ding], n. occupation of a builder; edifice; **b. society**, co-operative loan society lending capital at interest to subscribers building or buying their own houses.

BUILD-UP [bild'up], n. (coll.) act or process of building up, assembling forces etc.

BUILT [bilt], adj. formed, composed of parts.

BUILT-UP [bilt-up'], adj. (of an area) closely covered with buildings.

BULB [bulb], n. enlarged, ovoid base of the stem of certain plants such as the daffodil; expanded section of a stem or tube of a similar shape; electric lamp. BULBED, adj. having a b.; round-headed. BULBI-FEROUS [bul-bi'fe-rŏŏs], adj. (bot.) bearing bulbs. BULBIFORM, adj. possessing the form of a b. [Gk.].

BULBOUS [bul'bŏŏs], adj. possessing a bulb; bulb-shaped; round, swollen.

BULBUL [bŏŏl'bŏŏl], n. genus of Asiatic singing-birds; the Persian nightingale. [Arab.].

BULGE (1) [bulj], n. a protuberant part, swelling;

irregular protuberance; projecting sector of the front of an army. BULGE (2), v.t. and i. to swell out, expand in an ungainly way. BULGING, adj. protuberant, swelling. [L.].

BULGER [bul'jer], n. golf-club with a wooden convex face. [Prec.].

BULK (1) [bulk], n. magnitude of mass, large volume; a large quantity; (naut.) cargo in a ship's hold; laden in b., left unbattened in the hold; to sell in b., to sell in large unpacked amounts. BULK (2), v.i. to appear important, loom large; v.t. to measure the b. of (a cargo); make a number of consignments into one. [OIcel.].

BULKHEAD [bulk'hed], n. main partition in a ship's hull.

BULKY [bul'ki], adj. large and clumsy in size. BULKINESS, n. condition of being b.

BULL (1) [bool], n. male of any species of the bovine group still able to propagate; male of other large animals such as the elephant; (fig.) person as powerful and crude as a bull; Stock Exchange speculator who has gambled on a rise of share prices; bull's-eye; the constellation Taurus; Taurus, one of the twelve Zodiac signs; (slang) policeman; (vulg.) nonsense; to take the b. by the horns, to take courage and grapple with danger without flinching; a b. in a china shop, an excessively clumsy or tactless person. BULL (2), v.t. and i. to deal as a b. with Stock Exchange shares. [OE.].

BULL (3), n. edict issued by the Pope. [L.].

BULL (4), n. ludicrous mistake in speech. [Fr. from L.].

BULLACE [bool'as], n. wild plum. [ME.].

BULL-BAITING [bool'bā-ting], n. sport of baiting bulls with dogs.

BULL-CALF [bool'kahf], n. male calf.

BULLDOG [bool'dog], n. squat, flat-faced English breed of dog, remarkable for its tenacity; formerly used in baiting bulls; university proctor's attendant.

BULLDOZE [bool'dōz], v.t. (U.S.) to crush into submission. [Uncert.].

BULLDOZER [bool'dō-zer], n. powerful excavating and lifting machine used in road-making; (fig.) person who gains his point by overbearing argument. [Prec.].

BULLET [bool'lit], n. lead pellet or short, solid, pointed rod of metal, fired from a rifle or revolver. [Fr.].

BULLETIN [bool'li-tin], n. official report or public announcement, often concerning the health of a distinguished invalid. [Fr.].

BULLET-PROOF [bool'lit-proof], adj. able to resist a bullet.

BULL-FIGHT [bool'fit], n. Spanish sport in which a bull is goaded, attacked and finally slain. BULL-FIGHTER, n. matador.

BULLFINCH (1) [bool'finch], n. high hedge with a ditch alongside. [Earlier bull-fence].

BULLFINCH (2), n. British singing-bird with short beak, large head, and thick neck.

BULL-FROG [bool'frog], n. species of large frog.

BULL-HEAD [bool'hed], n. small freshwater fish with a large head; (fig.) stupid man.

BULLION [bool'li-on], n. uncoined gold and silver; gold and silver money assessed for its raw material value. BULLIONIST, n. one who opposes the use of a paper currency.

BULLIRAG, BULLYRAG [bool'li-rag], v.t. to bully, badger.

BULL-NECKED [bool-nekt'], adj. having a thick neck.

BULLOCK [bool'lok], n. young bull; gelded bull. [OE.].

BULL-PUP [bool'pup], n. young bulldog.

BULLRING [bool'ring], n. bull-fight arena.

BULL'S-EYE [boolz'ī], n. small round window or opening; centre of a target; small sweetmeat ball.

BULL-TERRIER [bool-te'ri-er], n. breed of dog, a cross between a terrier and a bulldog.

BULL-TROUT [bool'trowt], n. large-headed trout resembling a small salmon.

BULLY (1) [bool'li], n. blustering, overbearing person; the putting of the ball into play by two opposing players in hockey. BULLY (2) (BULLIES, BULLIED), v.t. to attack with blustering menaces, tyrannize over, treat cruelly, esp. the young or weak. [Unkn.].

BULLY (3), adj. (slang) excellent.

BULLY BEEF [bool-li-bēf'], n. tinned corned beef.

BULLYRAG, see BULLIRAG.

BULRUSH [bool'rush], n. the rush Scirpus lacustris; now more commonly applied to the reed-mace.

BULWARK (1) [bool'wawk], n. (fort.) rampart; (naut.) ship's side above the deck; (fig.) any form of defence which gives security. BULWARK (2), v.t. to protect with a b. [Du.].

BUM (1) [bum], n. (slang) the buttocks. [Unkn.].

BUM (2), n. (U.S. slang) habitual loafer.

BUM (3), adj. (U.S. slang) of bad quality.

BUMBAILIFF [bum'bā-lif], n. (coll.) sheriff's officer; bailiff who apprehends debtors etc.

BUMBLE-BEE [bum'bl-bē], n. hairy wild bee with a loud hum.

BUMBLEDOM [bum'bl-dom], n. fussy pomposity of petty officialdom. [Mr. Bumble, in Dickens's Oliver Twist].

BUMBLEPUPPY [bum'bl-pu-pi], n. game played with racquets and a tennis ball slung to a tall post. [Unkn.].

BUMBOAT [bum'bōt], n. boat carrying provisions to, and refuse from, ships at some distance from shore. [Dan.].

BUMF [bumf], n. (slang) toilet paper; paper in general. [Short for bum-fodder].

BUMMALO [bu'ma-lō], n. small fish, the Bombay duck. [Hind.].

BUMMAREE [bu-ma-rē'], n. dealer in the fish trade; (slang) money-lender. [Unkn.].

BUMP (1) [bump], v.t. to strike dully against anything hard or solid; jolt along an uneven road in a vehicle; v.t. to cause a protuberance to rise on the skin by violent collision; (in a boat-race) come up with and touch the boat immediately in front; to b. off, (slang) to kill, murder. BUMP (2), n. heavy blow, dull thud caused by a collision; jolt in the movement of a vehicle or aircraft; irregularity in a road surface; protuberance on the head, sometimes believed to indicate character; swelling caused by a blow; (in boat racing) the overtaking of the boat ahead. [Echoic].

BUMPER (1) [bum'per], n. horizontal metal bar attached before or behind a motor-car to protect it in collisions.

BUMPER (2), n. glass or cup brimful.

BUMPER (3), adj. large, plentiful.

BUMPINESS [bum'pi-nes], n. irregularity of surface, unevenness.

BUMPKIN [bump'kin], n. rough, loutish countryman. [Du.].

BUMPTIOUS [bump'shoos], adj. conceited, arrogant. [Invented].

BUMPY [bum'pi], adj. uneven, abounding in bumps; jolting.

BUN [bun], n. small, round sweet cake; small round bunch (as of hair); (slang) to take the b., to be first or worst in anything, behave startlingly. [ME.].

BUNA [boo'nah], n. (prot.) a synthetic substitute for rubber. [Germ.].

BUNCE [buns], n. (slang) extra profit, something gained.

BUNCH (1) [bunsh], n. bundle, cluster or group of objects of a similar kind; knot, tuft, portion of any garment or material gathered closely together; (coll.) group of people; the best of the b., the pick of anything. BUNCH (2), v.t. and i. to gather up into a b. [Unkn.].

BUNCHY [bun'shi], adj. forming a bunch; growing in bunches. BUNCHINESS, n. state of being b.

BUNCOMBE, see BUNKUM.

BUNDLE (1) [bun'dl], n. a number of things gathered together loosely; anything wrapped in a form convenient for carrying; package. BUNDLE (2), v.t. to tie in, or make up into, a b.; collect, gather into a mass; v.i. to depart hurriedly with all one's encumbrances; sleep in one's clothes on the same bed with a person of the opposite sex. [ME.].

BUNG (1) [bung], n. a stopper for the hole in a cask. BUNG (2), v.t. to stop the hole of a cask with a b.; (fig.) stop; shut (up); close by the swelling of surrounding parts; (slang) throw (missiles). [ODu.].

BUNGALOID [bung'ga-loid], adj. consisting of, covered with, bungalows; b. growth, large area covered with bungalows and made hideous by them.

BUNGALOW [bung'ga-lō], n. one-storied house, usually detached. [Hind.].

BUNGHOLE [bung'hōl], n. the hole in a cask through which it is filled.

BUNGLE (1) [bung'gl], v.t. to perform clumsily; botch, spoil by inexpert handling. BUNGLE (2), n. clumsy performance, blunder. [Unkn.].

BUNGLER [bung'gler], n. one who bungles; unskilful workman; tactless negotiator.

BUNGLING [bung'gling], adj. clumsy, awkward,

The accent ' after a syllable = stress (u-pon').   The mark ⁻ over a vowel = length (ā in made; ō in bone)

unskilful. BUNGLINGLY, *adv.* in a b. manner, unskilfully.

BUNION [bun´yun], *n.* large inflamed swelling on the foot, *esp.* at the base of the big toe. [OFr.].

BUNK (1) [bungk], *n.* recessed shelf fitted with bedding in a ship's cabin, railway carriage etc.; sleeping berth; **to do a b.,** (*slang*) to disappear, run away hastily. BUNK (2), *v.i.* to lie down on one's b.; (*slang*) run away. [Unkn.].

BUNK (3), *n.* (*slang*) humbug, bunkum. [BUNKUM].

BUNKER (1) [bung´ker], *n.* large receptacle or storage for coal in a steamship; sandy hollow or other obstruction on a golf course; (*fig.*) any obstruction. BUNKER (2), *v.t.* to fill a ship's bunkers (with); *v.i.* (of a ship) to load coal for use on a voyage. BUN-KERED, *adj.* (*golf*) stopped by a b. or other obstruction; (*fig.*) in a difficult place, obstructed. [Uncert.].

BUNKER (3), *n.* (*milit.*) strongly fortified post (in the war of 1939-45). [Germ.].

BUNKUM, BUNCOMBE [bung´kum], *n.* nonsense; empty, futile talk spoken to impress. [*Buncombe,* constituency in North Carolina whose member in Congress spoke in this way.]

BUNNY [bun´ni], *n.* (*coll.*) a rabbit. [Unkn.].

BUNSEN BATTERY [bun-sen-ba´te-ri], *n.* (*elect.*) a voltaic battery. [*Bunsen,* German chemist].

BUNSEN BURNER [bun-sen-bur´ner], *n.* jet which burns gas and air to produce great heat. [*Prec.*].

BUNT (1) [bunt], *n.* parasitic fungoid which attacks wheat and turns the grain black. [Unkn.].

BUNT (2), *n.* the pouched part of a fishing-net; (*naut.*) middle part of a sail gathered to form a cavity. BUNT (3), *v.t.* to strike, knock, push; (*baseball*) stop the ball with the bat without swinging the latter; (*aeron.*) execute a bunt. BUNT (4), *n.* (*aeron.*) manoeuvre consisting of half an outside loop followed by a half roll to regain normal equilibrium. [Unkn.].

BUNTING (1) [bun´ting], *n.* group of birds of the genus *Emberiza,* including the yellow-hammer. [Unkn.].

BUNTING (2), *n.* open-mesh, coarse cloth used for flags and streamers, employed on ships and in the streets for decorative purposes. [Uncert.].

BUOY (1) [boi], *n.* (*naut.*) floating sphere or drum moored to indicate the presence of a shoal, rock etc., dangerous to shipping. BUOY (2), *v.t.* to keep afloat, bear up; (*fig.*) hold up, sustain. BUOYAGE, *n.* the placing of buoys. [OFr.].

BUOYANCY [boi´an-si], *n.* power of floating lightly; (*fig.*) lightness, gaiety.

BUOYANT [boi´ant], *adj.* floating, capable of rising to the surface if submerged; (*fig.*) light-hearted, not easily crushed; (of revenue) tending to rise. BUOY-ANTLY, *adv.* in b. fashion.

BUR (1), **BURR** [bur], *n.* prickly fruit or flowerhead, husk of the chestnut; kind of dentist's drill; rough ridge or edge left on metal or other material after cutting, filing etc.; (*fig.*) anything which clings like a bur; person hard to get rid of. [ME.].

BUR (2), **BURR**, *n.* the dialectal pronunciation of *r* with a uvular trill. BUR (3), BURR, *v.i.* to articulate with a b. [Echoic].

BURBLE [bur´bl], *v.i.* to flow with a bubbling sound; (*coll.*) talk indistinctly or incoherently. [Echoic].

BURBOT [bur´bot], *n.* a freshwater fish. [AFr.].

BURDEN (1), **BURTHEN** † [bur´den], *n.* something borne or carried, a load, weight; (*fig.*) anything which is wearisome or oppressive to bear; (*naut.*) freightage capacity of a ship; **beast of b.,** animal used for carrying loads; **b. of proof,** responsibility of proving. BURDEN (2), BURTHEN †, *v.t.* to load, encumber, impose a b. on, oppress. [OE.].

BURDEN (3), **BURTHEN** †, *n.* the chorus of a song; the main topic. [Fr.].

BURDENSOME [bur´den-sum], *adj.* heavy to bear; oppressive. BURDENSOMELY, *adv.* in b. fashion.

BURDOCK [bur´dok], *n.* plant with prickly flowers and dock-like leaves.

BUREAU (*pl.* bureaux) [byōō-rō´], *n.* desk with drawers and a movable flap for writing on; public office; government department. [Fr.].

BUREAUCRACY [byōō-ro´kra-si], *n.* system of government administration in departments each under the control of a chief; government officials; officials as a body. [BUREAU and Gk.].

BUREAUCRAT [byōō´ro-krat], *n.* advocate of bureaucracy; state official with an undue reverence for the letter rather than the spirit of the law. BUREAUCRATIC [byōō-rō-kra´tik], *adj.* having the nature of a b., relating to a bureaucracy.

BURETTE [byōō-ret´], *n.* graduated glass tube with

stopcock at the bottom, for measuring fluids. [Fr.].

BURGAMOT, see BERGAMOT (1).

BURGEE [ber-jē´], *n.* small swallow-tailed pennant or flag used by yachts as a distinguishing flag of their club. [Unkn.].

BURGEON [bur´jon], *v.i.* to sprout, come into bud. [Fr.].

BURGESS [bur´jes], *n.* citizen, borough freeman, one who has the full rights of citizenship. BURGESS-SHIP, *n.* citizenship, freedom of a borough. [OFr.].

BURGH [bu´rer], *n.* (*Scots*) borough; **royal b.,** corporate body erected by a charter from the Crown. BURGHAL [bur´gl], *adj.* pertaining to a borough.

BURGHER [bur´ger], *n.* inhabitant or freeman of a borough, citizen, *esp.* of Dutch and German towns. [Du.].

BURGLAR [bur´gler], *n.* one who commits burglary. [Uncert.].

BURGLARY [bur´gla-ri], *n.* act or crime of breaking into a house after sunset with intent to steal. BURGLARIOUS [ber-glāer´i-ōōs], *adj.* pertaining to b. BURGLARIOUSLY, *adv.* in the manner of a burglar.

BURGLE [bur´gl], *v.t. and i.* (*coll.*) to commit burglary; break into. [BURGLAR].

BURGOMASTER [bur´go-mah-ster], *n.* mayor of a Dutch or Flemish town. [Du.].

BURGUNDY [bur´gun-di], *n.* wine made in Burgundy.

BURIAL [be´ri-al], *n.* act of burying or placing in the ground, *esp.* a dead person; funeral; **b. board,** public authority controlling a cemetery. [OE.]. BURIAL-GROUND [be´ri-al-grownd], *n.* cemetery.

BURIN [byōō´rin], *n.* graver, tool for engraving. [Fr.].

BURKE [burk], *v.t.* to murder, particularly by suffocation; smother quietly and get rid of; (*fig.*) hush up, avoid any discussion of. [*Burke,* who committed such murders in Edinburgh].

BURL (1), [burl], *n.* matted lump in wool or cloth. BURL (2), *v.t.* to dress cloth by removing knots and matted lumps. BURLER, *n.* one who burls cloth. [OFr.].

BURLAP [bur´lap], *n.* coarse cloth of hemp or jute for packing. [Unkn.].

BURLESQUE (1) [ber-lesk´], *n.* ludicrous representation; parody of a serious work. BURLESQUE (2), *adj.* tending to excite laughter by b. BURLESQUE (3), *v.t.* to turn into ridicule by parody; caricature. [Fr.].

BURLY [bur´li], *adj.* stout, massively built, corpulent, robust. BURLINESS, *n.* condition of being b. [ME.].

BURN (1) [burn], *n.* brook, small stream. [BOURN].

BURN (2), *n.* injury or bodily hurt caused by fire or heat, or by a corrosive chemical.

BURN (3) (*pret. and p.pt.* **burnt, burned**), *v.t.* to destroy or injure by subjecting to fire or great heat, or the action of a corrosive chemical; put to death by burning; scorch; harden by treatment with fire; parch, crack by heat, dry up, shrivel up; **to b. down,** to destroy utterly by fire; **to b. one's fingers,** to suffer from interfering in dangerous enterprises; **to b. one's boats,** to act irrevocably. BURN (4), *v.i.* to be on fire, in a state of conflagration, glow; (*fig.*) feel excess of heat; be inflamed with passion or desire; suffer from the heat of fever. [OE.].

BURNER [bur´ner], *n.* device which permits gas etc. to burn for heat or illumination.

BURNET [bur´net], *n.* (*bot.*) a brown-leaved plant.

BURNING [bur´ning], *adj.* on fire, much heated; (*fig.*) vehement, excited, intense; **b. bush,** name of several shrubs which give off highly volatile oil; **b. glass,** lens which concentrates the sun's rays to produce intense heat.

BURNISH (1) [bur´nish], *v.t.* to polish by friction, make bright, give a lustre to by polishing; *v.i.* to take a polish. BURNISH (2), *n.* polish, brightness, lustre. BURNISHER, *n.* one who burnishes; implement used in polishing. [OFr.].

BURNOUS(E) [ber-nōōs´], *n.* hooded cloak worn by desert dwellers in Arabia. [Fr. from Arab.].

BURNT, BURNED [burnt], *adj.* acted on by fire; (*fig.*) hurt, injured by some intensity of suffering.

BURNT-EAR [burnt´eer], *n.* a disease in corn.

BURNT OFFERING [bernt-o´fe-ring], *n.* offering sacrificed by fire to a deity.

BURNT SACRIFICE [bernt-sak´ri-fīs], *n.* burnt offering.

BURNT-SIENNA [bernt-si-e´nah], *n.* orange-red pigment produced by burning sienna; the pigment sienna.

BURR, see BUR.

BURROW (1) [bu´rō], *n.* hole made in the ground by

ōō is pronounced as in *food*; ŏŏ as in *hood*; th as in *think*; TH as in *that*; zh as in *azure*.   ∼ = related to.

DSE—D

rabbits, foxes etc., as a lair. BURROW (2), v.t. to make a b., dig a way underground; (fig.) penetrate below the surface of a subject. BURROWER, n. one who burrows. [Uncert.].

BURR-PUMP [bur'pump], n. (naut.) large bilge-pump in which the piston is devised so as to eliminate check-valves.

BURSAR [bur'ser], n. treasurer, particularly in a college; student who holds a scholarship at a university. BURSARSHIP, n. office of a b. [MedL.].

BURSARY [bur'sa-ri], n. treasury of a college or monastery; grant to assist a scholar to continue his studies; a scholarship.

BURST (1) [burst], n. act of bursting; sudden explosion or tearing asunder; sudden activity; a brief vigorous effort, spurt. [OE.].

BURST (2), v.t. to break or tear open with violence; cause to break open, come apart; v.i. to break or fly open suddenly and with violence; disrupt violently; explode; break; (fig.) be plentifully endowed with, overflow with; appear suddenly and unexpectedly; **to b. with laughing**, to be helpless with excess of laughter; **to b. out**, begin to speak violently. [OE.].

BURTHEN [], see BURDEN.

BURTON (1) [bur'ton], n. (naut.) tackle formed by two blocks or pulleys used to tighten rigging.

BURTON (2), n. kind of beer brewed at Burton-on-Trent.

BURY [be'ri], v.t. to put a dead body into the earth; inter with funeral rites in the earth or at sea; put anything into the earth; hide, immerse; (fig.) forget and forgive; **to b. the hatchet**, to settle a quarrel. [OE.].

BUS [bus], n. omnibus; (coll.) motor-car or aeroplane; **to miss the b.**, to miss a good opportunity. [Short form of OMNIBUS].

BUSBY [buz'bi], n. tall fur cap, usually bearskin, worn by certain regiments of the British Army. [Unkn.].

BUSH (1) [boosh], n. a shrub with densely growing branches; wild uncultivated forest region with a thick undergrowth; in Australia, any wild land, not necessarily wooded; †b. hung outside a tavern as its sign; (fig.) anything thick or bushy, esp. the tail of a fox; **to beat about the b.**, to go indirectly to work; **good wine needs no b.**, a good article needs no advertisement. BUSH (2), v.i. to grow thick and bushy. [ME.].

BUSH (3), n. short length of tube forming the bearing of a rotating shaft. [MDu.].

BUSHBUCK, BOSHBOK [boosh'buk], n. antelope of the genus Tragelaphus.

BUSH-CAT [boosh'kat], n. the serval.

BUSHED [boosht], adj. (Australian) lost in the bush.

BUSHEL [boo'shel], n. a dry measure of eight gallons; **to hide one's light under a b.**, to conceal one's merits unnecessarily. [OFr.].

BUSH-HARROW [boosh'ha-rō], n. harrow in which bushes or bushy branches are interwoven to scour the land.

BUSHMAN [boosh'man], n. woodsman, settler in the bush; member of a South African native tribe.

BUSHRANGER [boosh'rān-jer], n. Australian outlaw, man who has taken to the bush and lives by robbery.

BUSH-WHACKER [boosh'wa-ker], n. (Australian and N.Z.) one employed in clearing forests, lumberman; (U.S.) bush-fighter; backwoodsman.

BUSHY [boo'shi], adj. overgrown with bushes, full of branches; thick and spreading. BUSHINESS, n. quality of being b.

BUSINESS [biz'nis], n. trade or profession followed for a livelihood; commercial enterprise, trading; that which has to be done, a special and necessary duty; affair, subject, concern; (theatre) actions of performers, as distinct from words; **to send a man about his b.**, to dismiss a man, snub him. [BUSY].

BUSINESS-LIKE [biz'nis-līk], adj. suitable for business; orderly, efficient.

BUSK (1) [busk], n. piece of steel or whalebone used to strengthen corsets. [~Fr.].

BUSK (2), v.t. to get ready, prepare oneself; improvise. BUSKER, n. itinerant musician or actor. [OScand.].

BUSKIN [bus'kin], n. high boot with a thick sole worn by Greek and Roman tragic actors; (fig.) tragedy. BUSKINED, adj. wearing buskins; of or pertaining to tragedy. [OFr.].

BUSKY [bus'ki], adj. bosky, wooded. [BOSKY].

BUSMAN [bus'man], n. driver or conductor of a bus; **busman's holiday**, holiday in name only.

BUSS (1) [bus], n. a kiss, esp. a loud, hearty one. [Wel.].

BUSS (2), n. (naut.) three-masted or two-masted herring lugger. [Du.].

BUST [bust], n. the head, neck, shoulders and chest of the human figure; representation of these in sculpture; the bosom. [Fr.].

BUSTARD [bus'terd], n. European bird related to cranes and plovers. [OFr.].

BUSTLE (1) [bu'sl], v.t. to move, stir up to activity; v.i. to stir about fussily, be actively busy, bestir oneself. BUSTLE (2), n. hurry; noisy, fussy activity; a great stir. [ME.].

BUSTLE (3), n. stuffed pad or framework to cause a skirt to project behind from the waist. [Unkn.].

BUSY (1) [bi'zi], adj. working hard, actively employed; diligent; full of activity or occupation; meddlesome, officious. BUSY (2), v.t. to cause to be b.; occupy. BUSY (3), n. (slang) a detective. [OE.].

BUSYBODY [bi'zi bo-di], n. one who meddles in others' business.

BUT (1) [but], prep. without, with the exception of, except, save. BUT (2), adv. only, not more than, without, outside; **all b.**, very nearly. BUT (3), conj. except that, unless, than, only. [OE.].

BUTCHER (1) [boo'cher], n. one who slaughters animals for meat; one who sells meat; one who kills others violently and unnecessarily; murderer. BUTCHER (2), v.t. to kill animals for food; murder with cruelty; slaughter human beings ruthlessly; massacre. [OFr.].

BUTCHER-BIRD [boo'cher-berd], n. one of various kinds of shrike.

BUTCHER'S BROOM [boo'cherz-broom], n. (bot.) the knee-holly.

BUTCHERY [boo'che-ri], n. occupation of a butcher; place where animals are killed; massacre. [Fr.].

BUTLER [but'ler], n. the principal man-servant in an establishment and the one who has charge of the plate and wines. [OFr. from L.].

BUTT (1) [but], n. large cask for beer or wine; barrel. [OFr.].

BUTT (2), n. object to aim at in shooting; mound behind a target; grouse-shooter's stand; thrust given by the head of an animal; (fig.) person or object of ridicule. [Fr.].

BUTT (3), n. the end of a thing, esp. the thick or handle end of a weapon or tool. [OScand.].

BUTT (4), v.t. and i. to strike, thrust, push violently with the head or the horns; **to b. in**, to interfere, intrude. [OFr.].

BUTT-END [but'end], n. a butt. [BUTT (3)].

BUTTER (1) [bu'ter], n. a firm fatty substance obtained from cream by churning; similar foodstuff obtained from other materials; (fig.) flattery. BUTTER (2), v.t. to cover or spread with b.; **to b. up**, to flatter; **to know which side one's bread is buttered**, to be aware of one's own best interests. [OE.].

BUTTER-BEAN [bu'ter-bēn], n. large dried haricot bean.

BUTTER-COOLER [bu'ter-koo-ler], n. water-vessel with an inner container to keep butter cool.

BUTTERCUP [bu'ter-kup], n. a variety of Ranunculus with bright yellow cup-shaped flowers.

BUTTER-DISH [bu'ter-dish], n. small dish in which butter is served at table.

BUTTER-FINGERED [bu'ter-fing-gerd], adj. having weak or nerveless fingers; not able to grasp firmly; clumsy. BUTTER-FINGERS, n. one who is b.

BUTTERFLY [bu'ter-flī], n. insect of the order Lepidoptera, having four wings and knobbed antennae, usually brightly coloured; (fig.) any gay, rather trivial person; an idler. [Uncert.].

BUTTER-KNIFE [bu'ter-nif], n. a blunt knife, often of silver, for cutting butter at table.

BUTTERMILK [bu'ter-milk], n. the liquid which remains when butter has been churned.

BUTTER-MUSLIN [bu'ter-muz-lin], n. thin, loosely-woven cloth with fine mesh, used primarily as a wrapping for butter.

BUTTERNUT [bu'ter-nut], n. nut of the genus Caryocar; oily edible nut of the American white walnut tree.

BUTTER-PRINT [bu'ter-print], n. carved or ridged piece of wood with handles for rolling pats of butter.

BUTTER-SCOTCH [bu'ter-skoch], n. hard toffee made of sugar and butter.

BUTTER-STAMP [bu'ter-stamp], n. carved piece of wood for stamping patterns on butter.

BUTTERWORT [bu'ter-wert], n. (bot.) a marsh

The accent ' after a syllable = stress (u-pon'). The mark ‾ over a vowel = length (ā in made; ō in bone).

plant with oil-secreting prickles which catch small insects.

BUTTERY (1) [bu'te-ri], *n.* room where provisions are stored, *esp.* in colleges. [OFr.].

BUTTERY (2), *adj.* of the nature of or containing butter; (*fig.*) oily, nauseatingly flattering.

BUTTOCK [bu'tok], *n.* one of the fleshy protuberances of the rump; (*pl.*) rump, posterior. [ME.].

BUTTON (1) [bu'tn], *n.* a knob or disk of metal or other material used for the purpose of fastening one part of the dress to another by being passed through a slit or loop in a corresponding place on the opposite side of a garment; similar small disk worn for ornament or as a badge; any small round object resembling this. BUTTON (2), *v.t. and i.* to fasten with a b. or buttons. [Fr.].

BUTTONHOLE (1) [bu'tn-hōl], *n.* hole, slit or loop through which a button slips and is fastened; flower or small nosegay worn in a buttonhole on the breast. BUTTONHOLE (2), *v.t. and i.* to make buttonholes; (*fig.*) detain a reluctant victim in conversation.

BUTTONHOOK [bu'tn-hŏŏk], *n.* small metal or bone hook fitted to a handle for drawing a button through a buttonhole.

BUTTON-MOULD [bu'tn-mōld], *n.* metal or wooden shape over which material is stretched to make a button.

BUTTONS [bu'tnz], *n.* uniformed boy attendant.

BUTTON-STICK [bu'tn-stik], *n.* soldier's instrument for keeping polish off the uniform when polishing buttons.

BUTTRESS (1) [but'res], *n.* (*arch.*) construction of wood, stone or brick against the outside of a wall to strengthen it by receiving part of the thrust; (*fig.*) a prop or support. BUTTRESS (2), *v.t.* to support by a b., prop; (*fig.*) support, give strength to. [OFr.].

BUTTS [buts], *n.*(*pl.*) place for archery; rifle-range. [BUTT (2)].

BUTTY [bu'ti], *n.* foreman; (*min.*) middleman who contracts to raise coal and pays workmen to do it. [Unkn.].

BUTTY-BOAT [bu'ti-bōt], *n.* barge towed by another.

BUTYRIC [byōō-ti'rik], *adj.* pertaining to, made of, butter; **b. acid**, colourless acid with a rancid smell, found in butter.

BUXINE [buk'sēn], *n.* bitter alkaloid extracted from the box-tree.

BUXOM [buk'sum], *adj.* plump and good-looking. BUXOMNESS, *n.* plump comeliness. [ME.].

BUY (1) (*pret. and p.pt.* **bought**) [bī], *v.t.* to acquire in exchange for payment in money or goods or services; purchase; obtain by bribery; **to b. in**, to buy for oneself what one has already set up for sale, purchase a stock of commodities; **to b. off**, to pay a price for release from some obligation; **to b. out**, to purchase the share of another person in any concern; obtain release from the army by a money payment; **to b. up**, to purchase the entire available amount of anything, *esp.* goods or stock. BUY (2), *n.* (*orig. U.S.*) a purchase. BUYABLE, *adj.* able to be bought. [OE.].

BUYER [bī'er], *n.* one who buys, purchaser; person in large stores who is responsible for the choosing and buying of goods from wholesalers.

BUZZ (1) [buz], *v.t. and i.* to make the humming sound of a bee etc.; whisper, spread abroad secretly; **b. off**, (*coll.*) to go away, depart. BUZZ (2), *n.* the hum of a bee or fly; confused murmuring hum made by a number of people talking together; **b. saw**, circular saw. [Echoic].

BUZZARD [bu'zerd], *n.* one of the various birds of the falcon family. [OFr.].

BUZZER [bu'zer], *n.* steam-whistle or hooter to summon people to work as in a factory; foghorn; (*elect.*) vibrating armature which produces a buzzing sound.

BY (1) [bī], *prep.* close to, near; through, with (*denoting the author, means etc.*); according to; by direction, authority or example of; to the amount or number of; during the course of, within the compass or period of; *used to introduce oaths*, as **b. Jove**; **b. all means**, certainly, without doubt; **b. no means**, not at all. BY (2), *adv.* near; in the same place; at hand; aside; so as to pass; **b. and b.**, in the near future, soon, presently; **to stand b.**, to support; (*naut.*) be in readiness; **b. the b.**, by the way, in passing; **b. and large**, in general. [OE.].

BY- (3), **BYE-**, *pref.* secondary, minor, subsidiary; indirect, secret, private. [OE.].

BY (4), **BYE**, *n.* something not the immediate object of regard; (*cricket*) run scored when ball has passed batsman without touching him and is neither a wide nor a no-ball; in games, the odd man or team who waits until the next round to compete; **leg b.**, (*cricket*) run scored when the ball has touched the batsman's person but not his bat or hand. [BY (1)].

BY-BLOW [bī'blō], *n.* a side blow; (*dial.*) illegitimate child.

BYE, see BY.

BY-ELECTION [bī'i-lek-shn], *n.* election held owing to a special vacancy and not at a General Election.

BY(E)-LAW [bī'law], *n.* special law made by a corporation, town council, or society. [ODan.].

BYGONE (1) [bī'gon], *n.* the past; a past incident; **let bygones be bygones**, forget past grievances. BYGONE (2), *adj.* over and past, belonging to the past.

BY-NAME [bī'nām], *n.* nickname, name of reproach or contempt.

BY-PASS (1) [bī'pahs], *n.* pipe or outlet used when the main supply or current is cut off; arterial road which passes by, without going through, a town. BY-PASS (2), *v.t.* to avoid by means of a b.

BY-PLAY [bī'plā], *n.* (*drama*) significant action taking place as an aside while the main action goes forward.

BY-PRODUCT [bī'pro-dukt], *n.* incidental product; (in manufactures) subsidiary article produced incidentally in the manufacture of some other article.

BYRE [bīer], *n.* cowhouse. [OE.].

BYRONIC [bī-ro'nik], *adj.* applied to poetry or conduct supposedly in the manner of Lord *Byron*; cynical, daring and picturesque.

BYSTANDER [bī'stan-der], *n.* one who stands by onlooker.

BY-WAY [bī'wā], *n.* side road; (*fig.*) **b. of learning**, line of study off the main track.

BY-WORD [bī'werd], *n.* † common saying, proverb; object of contempt or derision.

BYZANTINE [bi-zan'tin, bī-zan'tin], *adj.* pertaining to Byzantium (Constantinople), former capital of the Eastern Roman Empire.

C

C [sē], third letter of the English alphabet; (*mus.*) dominant or fifth note of the scale of F major; key of C major; (Roman numerals) 100.

CAB [kab], *n.* small horse-drawn or motor-driven carriage plying for public hire; covered part of a locomotive engine sheltering the driver and fireman; covered driving seat of a motor truck. [Fr.].

CABAL (1) [ka-bal'], *n.* small party of persons engaged in a secret state intrigue, the intrigue itself; (*hist.*) small committee of the Privy Council of 1671, the initials of the surnames of the members of which spelt *cabal*. CABAL (2) (CABALLING, CABALLED), *v.i.* to engage in intrigue, plot. [Fr. ~*Next*].

CABALA, CABBALA, KABBALA [ka'ba-lah], *n.* mystical interpretation of the Scriptures handed down orally through generations of Jewish Rabbis; any occult science. CABALISM, *n.* mystical interpretation of the Jewish Scriptures; occultism. [Heb.].

CABANA [ka-bah'nyah], *n.* a brand of cigars. [Span. surname].

CABANE [ka-bahn'], *n.* (*aeron.*) mast-like structure projecting above the body of early monoplanes, to which the upper strengthening wires of the wings were attached. [Fr.].

CABARET [ka'ba-rā], *n.* licensed restaurant where

singing and dancing shows are given at night; such a show; small tavern. [Fr.].

CABBAGE (1) [ka'bij], *n.* plant eaten as a green vegetable; white butterfly which, in the caterpillar stage, feeds on cabbages; **sea c.,** sea kale; **c. rose,** large coarse double red rose. [Fr.].

CABBAGE (2), *n.* clippings of cloth pilfered by tailors. CABBAGE (3) *v.i.* to filch. [Variant of GARBAGE].

CABBAGE-TREE [ka'bij-trē], *n.* (*bot.*) a palm of the genus *Oreodoxa.*

CABBALA, see CABALA.

CABBY [ka'bi], *n.* (*coll.*) the driver of a cab. [CAB].

CABER [kā'ber], *n.* roughly-trimmed tree-trunk used in Highland games for hurling as a trial of strength. [Gael.].

CABIN (1) [ka-bin], *n.* hut; poor man's house; room in a ship; building on a railway from which points and signals are worked. CABIN-BOY, junior servant in a ship, who waits on the officers. CABIN (2), *v.t.* to confine in a small space. [Fr.].

CABINET [ka'bi-net], *n.* small room, closet; piece of furniture for preserving or displaying valuable objects, china, glass etc.; (*pol.*) the group of ministers who hold the principal offices in the government; **c. pudding,** pudding made of bread, eggs, milk, raisins, and covered with a sauce; **shadow c.,** council formed from the opposition with a view to taking office on coming into power.

CABINET-MAKER [ka'bi-net-mā-ker], *n.* skilled wood-worker who designs and makes cabinets and other high-class furniture.

CABINET MINISTER [ka-bi-net-mi'nis-ter], *n.* member of the cabinet, who is also usually parliamentary head of a government department.

CABLE (1) [kā'bl], *n.* thick rope of twisted strands of hemp or wire; insulated wires for transmitting electricity; such a wire on the sea bottom or underground to transmit telegraphic messages etc.; message transmitted in this way; (*arch. and goldsmith's work*) moulding shaped like a rope; (*naut.*) rope or chain carrying the anchor; measure of depth equal to 100 fathoms. CABLE (2), *v.t. and i.* to secure or provide with a c.; transmit a message by submarine telegraphy; (*arch.*) ornament with c. moulding. [OFr.].

CABLE-CAR [kā'bl-kah(r)], *n.* tramcar moved by an endless cable.

CABLEGRAM [kā'bl-gram], *n.* message sent by cable.

CABLE-LAID [kā'bl-lād], *adj.* twisted like a cable with three strands.

CABLESE [kā-bl-ēz'], *n.* jargon in which words are joined and contracted for the sake of economy, much used by journalists in foreign cables.

CABLE-SHIP [kā'bl-ship], *n.* ship specially equipped to lay submarine cables.

CABLET [kā'blet], *n.* cable-laid rope less than ten inches in circumference.

CABLE-TIER [kā'bl-tēer], *n.* place where cables are stored; (*naut.*) heap of coiled cable.

CABOB (1) [kā'bob, ka-bob'], *n.* (*usu. pl.*) oriental dish of meat roasted in small pieces and spiced with ginger, garlic etc. CABOB (2), *v.t.* to prepare cabobs. [Arab.].

CABOCHON [ka'bo-sho(ng)], *n.* a jewel, polished but not cut. [Fr.].

CABOOSE [ka-bōōs'], *n.* (*naut.*) room on deck where food is cooked; (*U.S.*) van on a freight-train accommodating the men in charge. [Du.].

CABOTAGE [ka'bo-tahzh], *n.* coasting, carrying along the coast from port to port; the carriage of persons and goods for hire within the territory of a sovereign state. [Fr.].

CAB-RANK [kab'rangk], *n.* approved parking place for taxicabs in a street.

CABRIOLE (1) [kab'ri-ōl], *n.* curved leg typical of Queen Anne and Chippendale furniture. CABRIOLE (2), *adj.* (of furniture) having a c. [Fr.].

CABRIOLET [kab'ri-ō-lā], *n.* small covered carriage on two wheels drawn by a single horse. [Fr.].

CAB-STAND [kab'stand], *n.* a cab-rank.

CA'-CANNY [kaw-ka'ni], *n. and adj.* (*coll.*) (pertaining to) a policy of deliberately reducing the amount of work done; "go-slow." [Northern dial. CALL and CANNY].

CACAO [ka-kā'ō, ka-kah'ō], *n.* tropical American plant the seeds of which provide cocoa. [Span. from Mexican].

CACHALOT [ka'sha-lot, ka'sha-lō], *n.* sperm whale having teeth growing in its lower jaw. [Fr.].

CACHE (1) [kash], *n.* store or storehouse where things are hidden; illegal hoard of arms and ammunition; (*zool.*) hoard of food which some animals make ready for the winter. CACHE (2), *v.t.* to place in a c. [Fr.].

CACHECTIC(AL) [ka-kek'tik(-al)], *adj.* (*med.*) afflicted with or pertaining to cachexy.

CACHET [ka'shā], *n.* seal, stamp; (*fig.*) any mark or sign of excellence or authenticity; (*med.*) a capsule. [Fr.].

CACHEXY [ka-kek'si], *n.* (*med.*) low physical condition.

CACHOU [ka'shōō], *n.* small lozenge taken to sweeten the breath; any small scented sweet. [Fr.].

CACHUCHA [ka-chōō'chah], *n.* vigorous Spanish dance. [Span.].

CACIQUE [ka-sēk'], *n.* a West Indian, American Indian native chieftain; (*coll.*) Spanish political boss. [Span.].

CACKLE (1) [ka'kl], *v.i.* to make a cackle; (*fig.*) chatter and laugh in a loud silly fashion. CACKLE (2), *n.* the cry of a hen or goose; (*fig.*) loud silly talk or laughter. [ME.].

CACO- [ka'ko-], *pref.* badly, ill-, mis-. [Gk.].

CACODEMON, CACODAEMON [ka-kō-dē'mon], *n.* evil spirit, malignant person. [Gk.].

CACODYL, KAKODYL [ka'ko-dil], *n.* highly inflammable and evil-smelling compound of arsenic and methyl. [Gk.].

CACOETHES [ka-kō-ē'thēz], *n.* evil propensity of mind or body; constant desire to be doing something which it is not wise to do; recurrent bad health. [Gk.].

CACOGRAPHY [ka-ko'gra-fi], *n.* bad handwriting or spelling. [Gk.].

CACOPHONY [ka-ko'fo-ni], *n.* a discordant sound, unpleasantly sounding speech. CACOPHONIC, CACOPHONOUS, *adj.* discordant. [Gk.].

CACOTROPHY [ka-ko'tro-fi], *n.* malnutrition. [Gk.].

CACTUS (*pl.* **cactuses, cacti**) [kak'tus, kak'tu-siz, kak'tī], *n.* (*bot.*) family of plants distinguished by their fleshy and prickly stems, usually without leaves. CACTACEOUS [kak-tā'shōōs], *adj.* (*bot.*) pertaining to the c. family. [Gk.].

CACUMINAL [ka-kyōō'mi-nal], *adj.* (*phon.*) with the tip of the tongue turned upwards and pointing backwards to the hard palate. [L.].

CAD [kad], *n.* ill-bred person who is always ready to take a mean advantage. [Fr.].

CADASTRAL [ka-das'tral], *adj.* pertaining to a survey of landed property and its taxable value. [Fr.].

CADAVER [ka-dā'ver], *n.* a corpse. CADAVERIC [ka-da've-rik], *adj.* relating to corpses; resembling one. [L.].

CADAVEROUS [ka-da've-rōōs], *adj.* corpse-like, pale and emaciated like a corpse. CADAVEROUSLY, *adv.* in a c. fashion. CADAVEROUSNESS, *n.* quality of being c.

CADDICE, see CADDIS.

CADDIE, see CADDY (1).

CADDIS, CADDICE [ka'dis], *n.* larva of a caddis-fly. [Unkn.].

CADDIS FLY [ka'dis-flī], *n.* species of the *Trichoptera,* whose larvae live in fresh water and are used as bait for fish.

CADDISH [ka'dish], *adj.* in the manner of a cad.

CADDY (1), **CADDIE** [ka'di], *n.* attendant who accompanies a golfer round the course, chiefly to carry the clubs. [Fr.].

CADDY (2), *n.* container for tea. [Malay].

CADENCE [kā'dens], *n.* rhythm; the rhythm and tonal quality of speech, a falling intonation of voice; (*mus.*) a closing phrase or concluding chords. [Fr.].

CADENCY [kā'den-si], *n.* cadence; descent from a younger member of a family as distinct from the main branch. [*Prec.*].

CADENT [kā'dent], *adj.* falling, modulating. [L.].

CADENZA [ka-den'zah, ka-dent'sah], *n.* (*mus.*) elaborate ornamental passage outside the general structure, but bringing it to a conclusion. [It.].

CADET [ka-det'], *n.* younger son; member of a school which prepares men to hold commissions in the forces; member of a Cadet Corps; **C. Corps,** military body where boys are trained for the Officers' Training Corps. [Fr.].

CADGE [kaj], *v.t. and i.* to get by begging, beg. CADGER, *n.* person who cadges. [Uncert.].

CADI, KADI [kā'di], *n.* minor Arab or Turkish judge. [Arab.].

CADMEAN [kad-mē'an], *adj.* (*class. myth.*) pertaining

to Cadmus, who is supposed to have introduced the alphabet into Greece; **C. victory,** victory fatal in its consequences for the victor; doubtful praise or compliment. [Gk.]

CADMIUM [kad'mi-um], *n.* (*chem.*) bluish-white metal, chemical element denoted by Cd; **c. yellow,** brilliant yellow pigment containing c. [L.]

CADRE [kah'der], *n.* (*milit.*) the officers and men forming the permanent nucleus of a battalion; the officers of a battalion. [Fr.].

CADUCEUS (*pl.* **caducei**) [ka-dyoo'si-us, -i], *n.* (*antiq.*) herald's wand. [L.].

CADUCIBRANCHIATE [ka-dyoo-si-brang'ki-at], *adj.* (*zool.*) having gills which fall off before maturity is reached, as in frogs etc. [L. and Gk.].

CADUCITY [ka-dyoo'si-ti], *n.* fleetingness, perishableness; (*bot.*) tendency to fall very early. [Fr.].

CADUCOUS [ka-dyoo'koos], *adj.* (*bot.*) tending to fall at an early date. [L.].

CAECUM [sē'kum], *n.* (*anat.*) the blind gut or appendix, a sac in the large intestine with only one opening. **CAECAL,** *adj.* (*anat.*) of, or pertaining to, the c. [L.].

CAESAR [sē'zer], *n.* title taken by Augustus, first Roman emperor, and held by his successors; emperor. **CAESARISM,** *n.* system of autocratic government like that of the Roman emperors. [Family name of Julius *Caesar*].

CAESAREAN, CAESARIAN [sē-zāer'i-an], *adj.* pertaining to Caesar; **c. operation, c. section,** surgical operation to effect the birth of a child through the abdomen.

CAESIUM [sē'zi-um], *n.* silvery-coloured metal; chemical element denoted by Cs. [L.].

CAESURA [sē-zhōor'ah], *n.* (*pros.*) pause in the rhythm of a line of verse. **CAESURAL,** *adj.* (*pros.*) relating to c. [L.].

CAFE, café [ka'fā], *n.* coffee-house, restaurant where (non-alcoholic) drinks and other refreshments are served; **c. au lait,** coffee with milk. [Fr.].

CAFELITE [ka'fi-lit], *n.* plastic material made from coffee beans.

CAFETERIA [ka-fi-tēer'i-ah], *n.* restaurant where customers serve themselves. [Span.].

CAFFEIC [ka-fē'ik], *adj.* pertaining to coffee or caffeine.

CAFFEINE [ka'fēn, ka'fān], *n.* alkaloid present in coffee etc., sometimes used as a drug. [Fr.].

CAFFRE, see KAFFIR.

CAFTAN, KAFTAN [kaf-tahn'], *n.* long-sleeved garment with a girdle worn in the Near East. [Turk.].

CAGE (1) [kāj], *n.* room or edifice with bars, trellis, or other open work on at least one side, in which an animal may be kept; metal box with sides of wire trellis-work where birds or other small pets may be kept; anything resembling this; the lift in a mine. CAGE (2), *v.t.* to shut up in, or as if in, a c. [Fr.].

CAGOULARD [ka-gōo-lah(r)'], *n.* member of a former French anti-Communist organization. [Fr.].

CAIMAN, see CAYMAN.

CAIN [kān], *n.* a fratricide; **to raise C.,** to create a violent disturbance. [Gen. iv].

CAINOZOIC, KAINOZOIC [kā-nō-zō'ik], *adj.* tertiary; pertaining to the whole post-mesozoic age up to the present, including tertiary and quaternary eras. [Gk.].

CAIQUE [kah-ēk'], *n.* small boat common in the Bosphorus; Levantine sailing-vessel. [Turk.].

CAIRENE [ki'rēn], *n.* and *adj.* inhabitant of, pertaining to, Cairo.

CAIRN [kāern], *n.* heap of stones, *esp.* when erected as a memorial; cairn terrier. [Gael.].

CAIRN TERRIER [kāern-te'ri-er], *n.* breed of small Scots terrier with a shaggy coat.

CAISSON [kā'son], *n.* wooden framework or casing; chest containing bombs to be buried under the road of an enemy; (*milit.*) movable chest for holding ammunition; (*eng.*) water-tight chamber which can be lowered into water and supplied with air from pumps above, so that men can work in it; iron container filled with cement in which the supports of a bridge are sunk. [Fr.].

CAITIFF [kā'tif], *n.* and *adj.* (characteristic of) a low-spirited, despicable wretch, coward. [OFr. from L.].

CAJEPUT, CAJUPUT [ka'ji-poot], *n.* (*bot.*) tree which yields an aromatic oil. [Malay].

CAJOLE [ka-jōl'], *v.t.* to flatter (someone) so as to influence his actions, opinions, feelings as one wishes; seduce or persuade by blandishment.

CAJOLEMENT, *n.* act of cajoling. **CAJOLER,** *n.* person who cajoles. [Fr.].

CAJOLERY [ka-jō'le-ri], *n.* process of cajoling, arts of flattery and blandishment.

CAJUPUT, see CAJEPUT.

CAKE (1) [kāk], *n.* dough sweetened, flavoured and baked in a symmetrical form; the material itself or a piece of it; any other piece of food similar in appearance; any substance resembling this; **cakes and ale,** jollity and rejoicing; **to take the c.,** to be very excellent or remarkable. CAKE-WALK, grotesque dance among American negroes, the prize for which was a cake; Edwardian dance called after this. CAKE (2), *v.t.* and *i.* to form into a c.; dry hard. [Uncert.].

CALABAR BEAN [ka-la-ba-bēn'], *n.* seed of an African plant, from which a poisonous drug is extracted. [*Calabar,* West Africa].

CALABASH [ka'la-bash], *n.* South American tree bearing gourds; gourd from this tree; any kind of gourd, *esp.* one which has been dried. [Fr. from Arab.].

CALAMARY [ka'la-ma-ri], *n.* kind of cuttle-fish. [L.].

CALAMINE [ka'la-mēn], *n.* an ore of zinc used medicinally for soothing inflammation of the skin etc. [MdL. from L.].

CALAMINT [ka'la-mint], *n.* (*bot.*) an aromatic herb. [Gk.].

CALAMITOUS [ka-la'mi-tŏos], *adj.* disastrous, arising out of or producing calamity.

CALAMITY [ka-la'mi-ti], *n.* disaster, event causing terrible and often widespread misery; misfortune, often more acute on account of its suddenness. [Fr. from L.].

CALAMUS [ka'la-mus], *n.* (*bot.*) genus of palms whose stems provide rattan canes; wind instrument made of a reed. [L.].

CALANDO [ka-lan'dō], *adv.* (*mus.*) gradually dying away. [It.].

CALASH† [ka-lash'], *n.* light low-wheeled carriage. [Fr.].

CALC-, *pref.* lime, chalk. [L.].

CALCANEUM [kal-kā'ni-um], *n.* (*anat.*) the heel bone. **CALCANEAL,** *adj.* (*anat.*) pertaining to the c. [L.].

CALCAR (1) [kal'kah(r)], *n.* furnace used in making glass. [It.].

CALCAR (2), *n.* (*bot.*) spur-like formation in flowers. CALCARATE [kal'ka-rat], *adj.* (*bot.*) having a spur. [L.].

CALCAREOUS [kal-kāer'i-ŏos], *adj.* relating to or containing lime. [L.].

CALCAVELLA [kal-ka-ve'lah], *n.* Portuguese sweet wine. [*Carcavelhos* in Portugal].

CALCEDONIC, see CHALCEDONIC.

CALCEDONY, see CHALCEDONY.

CALCEOLARIA [kal-si-ō-lāer'i-ah], *n.* (*bot.*) genus of plants comprising the slipperworts. [L.].

CALCEOLATE [kal'si-ō-lāt], *adj.* (*bot.*) resembling a slipper in shape. [L.].

CALCIC [kal'sik], *adj.* (*chem.*) resembling or containing calcium.

CALCIFEROL [kal-si'fe-rol], *n.* vitamin D in pure crystalline form.

CALCIFEROUS [kal-si'fe-rŏos], *adj.* containing or producing lime or carbonate of lime. [L.].

CALCIFICATION [kal-si-fi-kā'shn], *n.* conversion into chalk with salts of lime. [L.].

CALCIFY [kal'si-fi], *v.t.* and *i.* to make or become stony by deposit of lime. [Fr.].

CALCIMINE (1), **KALSOMINE** [kal'si-mīn], *n.* white or slightly coloured wash for distempering walls and ceilings. CALCIMINE (2), KALSOMINE, *v.t.* to whitewash with c.

CALCINATION [kal-si-nā'shn], *n.* reduction to ashes by burning.

CALCINE [kal'sīn], *v.t.* and *i.* to reduce to lime by burning, reduce to ashes by burning. [Fr. from L.].

CALCITE [kal'sīt], *n.* a native carbonate of lime. [L.].

CALCIUM [kal'si-um], *n.* the metallic element in lime, found naturally in compounds only, the chemical element denoted by Ca. [~L.].

CALCOURANITE [kal-kō-yŏo'ra-nīt], *n.* hydrated phosphate of calcium and uranium.

CALC-SINTER [kalk'sin-ter], *n.* stalactitic calcium carbonate, calcareous tufa. [Germ.].

CALC-SPAR [kalk'spah(r)], *n.* calcite.

CALC-TUFF [kalk'tuf], *n.* carbonate of lime in alluvial deposit, calcareous tufa.

CALCULABLE [kal'kyŏo-la-bl], *adj.* able to be

calculated. CALCULABILITY [kal-kyōō-la-bi'li-ti], *n.* quality of being c.

CALCULATE [kal'kyōō-lāt], *v.t. and i.* to reckon by mathematics; compute or estimate. [L.].

CALCULATING [kal'kyōō-lā-ting], *adj.* that calculates; careful; designing, cunning.

CALCULATION [kal-kyōō-lā'shn], *n.* act or process of calculating; result of a mathematical computation; estimation, forecast of likely results. CALCULATIVE [kal'kyōō-lā-tiv], *adj.* relating to c. [L.].

CALCULATOR [kal'kyōō-lā-ter], *n.* one who calculates; calculating machine.

CALCULOUS [kal'kyōō-lōōs], *adj.* (*med.*) pertaining to calculus.,

CALCULUS (1) (*pl.* **calculi**) [kal'kyōō-lus, kal'kyōō-lī], *n.* (*med.*) a morbid hard or stony concretion formed in organs of the body. CALCULUS (2), *n.* a mathematical process, method of calculating. [L.].

CALDRON, see CAULDRON.

CALEDONIAN [ka-li-dō'ni-an], *n. and adj.* a native of, pertaining to, Caledonia or Scotland.

CALEFACIENT (1) [ka-li-fā'shnt], *n.* (*med.*) substance exciting or producing heat. CALEFACIENT (2), *adj.* (*med.*) generating heat. [L.].

CALEFACTORY [ka-li-fak'te-ri], *adj.* producing or imparting heat.

CALENDAR (1) [ka'lin-der], *n.* system by which the beginning and end and subdivisions of the year are fixed; list of days and months in a given year; almanac; list of days in the year of special interest to a particular class or group of persons; list of documents in a collection giving the date and a summary of each; register of cases up for trial before a criminal court. CALENDAR-LINE, imaginary line through the Pacific Ocean, to be east or west of which signifies a day's difference in time. CALENDAR (2), *v.t.* to enter on a c. [OFr. from L.].

CALENDER (1) [ka'lin-der], *n.* machine consisting of two hot rollers for pressing cloth, smoothing paper etc.; person who calenders. CALENDER (2), *v.t.* to press, smooth or polish in a c. [Fr. from Gk.].

CALENDER (3), *n.* a mendicant dervish. [Pers.].

CALENDS, KALENDS [ka'lendz], *n.(pl.)* the first day of every month, in the Roman year; **Greek c.,** date or occasion which never arrives. [L.].

CALENDULA [ka-len'dyōō-lah], *n.* (*bot.*) variety of marigold.

CALENDULIN [ka-len'dyōō-lin], *n.* a gum obtained from the marigold.

CALENTURE [ka'len-tyōōr], *n.* delirious fever due to exposure in a hot climate, sunstroke. [Fr. from L.].

CALF (1) (*pl.* **calves**) [kahf, kahvz], *n.* young bull or cow; also applied to other animals when young, such as the elephant, seal etc.; leather from the skin of a calf; stupid, clumsy youth; **to kill the fatted c.,** to prepare a hearty welcome for a prodigal. CALF-LOVE, an immature fondness in a girl or boy for one of the other sex. [OE.].

CALF (2) (*pl.* **calves**), *n.* the muscles of the back of the leg between ankle and knee. [OScand.].

CALFSKIN [kahf'skin], *n.* the hide of a calf from which leather is made.

CALIBAN [ka'li-ban], *n.* sub-human monster; ugly, brutal person. [*Caliban,* in Shakespeare's *Tempest*].

CALIBRATE [ka'li-brāt], *v.t.* to determine the calibre of; make marks of measurement on a gauge or measure. [CALIBRE].

CALIBRATION [ka-li-brā'shn], *n.* the measuring of the calibre of a gun; the marking of standard measurements on a gauge or other measure; the marks so made.

CALIBRE [ka'li-ber], *n.* the diameter of the bore of a gun; size of a bomb, bullet or shell; (*fig.*) mental or moral capacity or quality. CALIBRED [ka'li-berd], *adj.* possessing a c. [Fr.].

CALICO [ka'li-kō], *n.* fine cotton cloth; **c. printing,** process of printing figured patterns on c. CALICO-BALL, *n.* dance at which fancy dresses made of cotton are worn. CALICO-PRINTER, *n.* one who prints patterns on c. [*Calicut* in India].

CALIN [kā'lin], *n.* alloy of tin and lead used by the Chinese for making tea-canisters etc. [Fr. from Arab.].

CALIPASH [ka'li-pash], *n.* the dull green fat below a turtle's upper shell. [Uncert.].

CALIPEE [ka'li-pē], *n.* the pale yellow fat on a turtle's lower shell. [Uncert.].

CALIPERS, see CALLIPERS.

CALIPH, KALIF [ka'lif, kā'lif, ka(h)-lēf'], *n.* title

assumed by the successors of Mohammed as civil and religious rulers. [Arab.].

CALISAYA [ka-li-sā'yah], *n.* a bark found in Peru. CALISAYINE [ka-li-sā'yin], *n.* extract of c. used for making bitters. [Peruvian].

CALISTHENIC, see CALLISTHENIC.

CALIX (*pl.* **calices**) [ka'liks, ka'li-sēz], *n.* (*biol., bot.*) organ or part of the body shaped like a cup. [L.].

CALK (1) [kawk], *n.* piece of sharp-pointed iron fixed to shoe heels in America to prevent slipping; a calkin. CALK (2), *v.t.* to provide with a c. or calkin. [L.].

CALK (3), see CAULK.

CALK (4) [kawk, kalk], *v.t.* to take a copy of a drawing by chalking its back and tracing the design on other paper placed under the chalked back, by running a blunt point or pencil over the lines of the original drawing. CALKING (1), *n.* act of one who calks a drawing; a drawing so prepared. [Fr. from L.].

CALKER [kaw'ker], *n.* man who calks; calkin.

CALKIN [kaw'kin, kal'kin], *n.* projection at the ends of a horseshoe to make a grip. [OFr. from L.].

CALKING (2), see CAULKING.

CALL (1) [kawl], *n.* a shout or loud interjection to attract attention; cry of one bird or animal to another; note on a bugle or huntsman's horn; message over the telephone; a reading over of names to discover those present and those absent; summons of any sort; vocation; a feeling that one is fitted to take up certain work; attraction of a person, thing or idea; claim on one's generosity; short visit; message to one's partner at cards by playing one's hand in a particular way, a bid; **a port of c.,** port at which a ship calls regularly; **a house of c.,** public-house; **within c.,** nearby, within earshot; **to have no c. to,** to have no need to. [*Next*].

CALL (2), *v.t. and i.* to cry out, utter a call, shout for attention or help; summon, attract, draw; give a name to; waken, rouse from sleep; summon someone to take up a particular position or duty; consider to be, reckon; pay a visit; **to c. for,** to demand, deserve; **to c. forth,** to occasion; **to c. in,** to order the return of or payment of; send for, request services and opinion of; **to c. on,** to pay a short visit to; invoke (usually the Deity); request (a person, *esp.* for a speech); **to c. out,** to utter cries in a loud voice; summon to action; challenge to a duel; **to c. over,** to read out a list of names to find out if anyone is missing; **to c. up,** to summon for m'litary service; (*fig.*) evoke (a mental image); **to c. the banns,** to publish banns of a marriage in church; **to c. atten-tion to,** to bring to notice; **to c. into being,** to create, produce, give life to; **to c. to mind,** to (cause to) remember, recollect; **to c. in question,** to cast doubt upon; **to c. to order,** to make a demand for orderly conduct at a public meeting; **to c. (a person) names,** to abuse and insult (a person); **to c. off,** to cancel. [OE. from OScand.].

CALLA [ka'lah], *n.* (*bot.*) genus of floating water plants. [Invented].

CALL-BIRD [kawl'berd], *n.* bird trained to entice others.

CALL-BOX [kawl'boks], *n.* public telephone booth.

CALL-BOY [kawl'boi], *n.* boy who calls actors to be ready to appear on the stage; messenger boy at an hotel; captain's boy.

CALLER (1) [kaw'ler], *n.* visitor; one who makes a telephone call; card-player who calls.

CALLER (2) [ka'ler], *adj.* fresh, brisk, cool; **c. herring,** fresh herrings. [Scots].

CALLIGRAPHIST [ka-li'gra-fist], *n.* one who prac-tises calligraphy, skilled penman.

CALLIGRAPHY [ka-li'gra-fi], *n.* art of beautiful writing, skilful penmanship; handwriting. [Gk.].

CALLING [kaw'ling], *n.* trade, profession, vocation.

CALLIOPE [ka-lī'ō-pi], *n.* mechanical organ. [*Cal-liope,* Muse of Song].

CALLIPERS, CALIPERS [ka'li-perz], *n.(pl.)* instrument resembling compasses for measuring the internal or external diameters of round bodies. [CALIBRE].

CALLISTHENICS [ka-lis-the'niks], *n.(pl.)* exercises developing graceful carriage and physical strength. CALLISTHENIC, CALISTHENIC, *adj.* pertaining to c. [Gk.].

CALL-NOTE [kawl'nōt], *n.* the cry of a bird to its mate.

CALLOSITY [ka-lo'si-ti], *n.* a part of the skin hardened by friction. [Fr. from L.].

CALLOUS [ka'lōōs], *adj.* (of skin) hardened; (*fig.*) unfeeling, indifferent to other people's pain and sorrow. CALLOUSLY, *adv.* in a c. way. CALLOUS-NESS, *n.* condition of being c. [L.].

CALLOW [ka'lō], *adj.* (of birds) unfledged, bare of feathers; (*fig.*) (of boys and youths) immature, inexperienced. CALLOWNESS, *n.* condition of being c. [OE.].

CALL-SIGN [kawl'sīn], *n.* identification sign used by a wireless station when transmitting.

CALLUS [ka'lus], *n.* (*med.*) callosity, lump forming round a bone during healing after fracture. [L.].

CALM (1) [kahm], *n.* condition of the atmosphere or weather when there is no wind at all; (*fig.*) (of the mind or of a state of affairs) quiet, tranquillity. CALM (2), *adj.* windless; tranquil, not agitated, leisurely; (*coll.*) impudent, shameless. CALM (3), *v.t. and i.* to make or become c.; smooth, pacify, settle down; **to c. down,** to soothe, appease. CALMLY, *adv.* in a c. way. CALMNESS, *n.* condition of being c. [Fr.].

CALMATIVE (1) [kah'ma-tiv], *n.* (*med.*) sedative, drug which induces quiet in the patient. CALMATIVE (2), *adj.* having a calming or sedative effect.

CALOMEL [ka'lo-mel], *n.* (*med.*) a chloride of mercury, useful as a purgative. [Gk.].

CALORESCENCE [ka-lo-re'sens], *n.* (*phys.*) the changing of light rays into heat rays. [L.].

CALORIC (1) [ka-lo'rik], *n.* warmth, heat. CALORIC (2), *adj.* relating to heat. CALORICITY [ka-lo-ri'si-ti], *n.* power of producing heat.

CALORIE [ka'lo-ri], *n.* standard unit of heat, the amount required to raise the temperature of one gramme of water one degree centigrade, heat unit in the determination of nutrition values; **large c.,** unit of a thousand calories. [Fr. from L.].

CALORIFACIENT (1) [ka-lo-ri-fā'shnt], *n.* substance supplying animal heat. CALORIFACIENT (2), *adj.* heat-producing, supplying animal heat. [L.].

CALORIFIC [ka-lo-ri'fik], *adj.* producing heat; relating to heat; **c. rays,** invisible heat-giving rays of the sun. [Fr.].

CALORIFICATION [ka-lo-ri-fi-kā'shn], *n.* production of heat.

CALORIFIER [ka-lo'ri-fī-er], *n.* apparatus for heating water by contact with steampipes or hot-water pipes.

CALORIMETER [ka-lo-ri'mi-ter], *n.* apparatus for measuring heat.

CALOTTE [ka-lot'], *n.* skull-cap worn by Roman Catholic ecclesiastics; (*arch.*) small round cavity resembling a cap. [Fr.].

CALPAC [kal'pak], *n.* sheepskin hat worn in the Near East. [Turk.].

CALTHA [kal'thah], *n.* (*bot.*) kingcup, or marsh marigold.

CALTROP [kal'trop, kawl'trop], *n.* instrument with four iron spikes used in medieval warfare to lame enemy horses; (*bot.*) variety of spiny plant or thistle. [OE.].

CALUMBA [ka-lum'bah], *n.* East African climbing plant, the root of which is used as a bitter tonic. [*Colombo*, Ceylon].

CALUMET [ka'lyōō-met], *n.* ceremonial pipe used among the North American Indians. [Fr., L.].

CALUMNIATE [ka-lum'ni-āt], *v.t.* to spread evil reports concerning, slander, speak ill of. CALUMNIATION [ka-lum-ni-ā'shn], *n.* act of calumniating. CALUMNIATOR [ka-lum'ni-ā-ter], *n.* person who calumniates. CALUMNIATORY [ka-lum'ni-ā-te-ri], *adj.* slanderous, calumnious. [CALUMNY].

CALUMNIOUS [ka-lum'ni-ōos], *adj.* pertaining to calumny, slanderous.

CALUMNY [ka'lum-ni], *n.* a false charge, slander, injurious report about a person. [Fr. from L.].

CALVARY [kal'va-ri], *n.* place where the Crucifixion took place; model of the Crucifixion erected in the open air for devotional purposes. [L., translation of Heb.].

CALVE [kahv], *v.i.* to give birth to a calf; (of icebergs) cast off floes. [OE.].

CALVES-FOOT [kahvz'fŏŏt], *adj.* denoting a jelly for invalids made from the boiled foot of a calf.

CALVINISM [kal'vi-nizm], *n.* austere religious system evolved by *Calvin*, French Protestant reformer. CALVINIST, *n.* follower of Calvin and his doctrines. CALVINISTIC(AL) [kal-vi-nis'tik(-al)], *adj.* relating to C.; (*fig.*) stern, morally strict.

CALX [kalks], *n.* lime, chalk; residue of a substance after calcination. [L.].

CALYX [kā'liks], *n.* (*bot.*) cup-shaped whorl of sepals of a flower. CALYCINAL, CALYCINE [ka-li'si-nal, ka'li-sīn], *adj.* relating to a c. [Gk.].

CAM [kam], *n.* (*mech.*) projection on the edge of a wheel, for converting a rotary motion into a rapid reciprocal motion. [Du.].

CAMARADERIE [ka-me-rah'de-rē], *n.* loyalty and good fellowship. [Fr.].

CAMBER (1) [kam'ber], *n.* a slight convex curving of a road section or ship's deck; the gradual raising of the level of a curved road towards its outer radius; curvature of the wing sections of an aeroplane. CAMBER (2), *v.t. and i.* to curve or arch; make a c. [Fr.].

CAMBIST [kam'bist], *n.* banker; one expert in the science of exchanges. [Fr.].

CAMBIUM [kam'bi-um], *n.* (*bot.*) pith or soft tissue lying beneath the bark from which both new wood and bark are developed. [L.].

CAMBLET, see CAMLET.

CAMBREL [kam'brel], *n.* wooden or iron hook for hanging up meat. [Unkn.].

CAMBRIAN [kam'bri-an], *adj.* relating to Cambria, or Wales; (*geol.*) pertaining to the first period of the palaeozoic era. [L. from Wel.].

CAMBRIC [kām'brik], *n.* fine white linen. [*Kamerijk* or Cambrai].

CAME [kām], *pret.* of COME.

CAMEL [ka'mel], *n.* large ruminant ungulate quadruped, with a thick coarse coat, large flat feet and one (**Arabian c.** or dromedary) or two (**Bactrian c.**) humps, used in desert regions for transport; large floating device for carrying ships over bars into a port and for raising sunken ships. [OE., L.].

CAMEL CORPS [ka'mel-kaw(r)], *n.* body of soldiers mounted on camels.

CAMEL-HAIR [ka'mel-hāer], *n.* rough hair of the camel; fine hair from a squirrel's tail for making paint-brushes.

CAMELLIA [ka-mē'li-ah], *n.* Asiatic evergreen shrub. [Joseph *Kamel*, who brought it to Europe from China].

CAMELOPARD [ka-me'lo-pahd], *n.* † giraffe; (*fig.*) tall, ungainly woman. [L.].

CAMELRY [ka'mel-ri], *n.* body of soldiers mounted on camels.

CAMEMBERT [ka'mem-bāer], *n.* a rich cheese. [*Camembert*, in Normandy].

CAMEO [ka'mi-ō], *n.* piece of jewellery cut from a stone which has layers of different colours, e.g. agate, so that the design cut in one layer contrasts with the background formed by the next. [It.].

CAMERA [ka'me-rah], *n.* (*phot.*) light-tight box or other structure with a lens at one end throwing an inverted image of what stands before it upon a sensitized photographic plate or film placed at the other end; **c. lucida,** (*opt.*) prismatic apparatus which projects an image from a microscope eyepiece upon a piece of paper so that the image can be easily drawn; **c. obscura,** (*opt.*) dark room fitted with a lens to throw an image of things outside upon a screen; **in c.,** (*leg.*) in private, with the public excluded. [L.].

CAMERA-MAN [ka'me-rah-man], *n.* cinema photographer.

CAMERA-REPORTER [ka-me-rah-ri-paw'ter], *n.* press photographer.

CAMERONIAN [ka-me-rō'ni-an], *n.* follower of Richard Cameron, Scottish covenanter; adherent of the Reformed Presbyterian Church, which he founded, (*pl.*) First Battalion Scottish Rifles, formed originally from followers of Cameron.

CAMI-KNICKS, CAMI-KNICKERS [ka'mi-niks], *n.(pl.)* woman's undergarment, a bodice and knickers in one piece.

CAMISOLE [ka'mi-sōl], *n.* woman's under-bodice. [Fr.].

CAMLET, CAMBLET [kam'let], *n.* thin material originally made of camel's hair, now usually of wool or silk. [Fr.].

CAMOMILE, CHAMOMILE [ka'mo-mil], *n.* strong-scented bitter plant used medicinally and for toilet purposes. [Fr.].

CAMORRA [ka-mo'rah], *n.* Neapolitan secret society. [It.].

CAMOUFLAGE (1) [ka'mŏŏ-flahzh], *n.* (*milit.*) the disguising or hiding of objects from the enemy, practice of making an object or idea appear different from what it is. CAMOUFLAGE (2), *v.t.* to conceal or disguise by c. [Fr.].

CAMP (1) [kamp], *n.* tract of ground where tents or other shelters, often temporary, are erected for soldiers or others; persons inhabiting such a place; any structure erected for temporary shelter in open country; (*fig.*) the soldier's life; faction, party.

ŏŏ is pronounced as in food; ŏŏ as in hood; th as in *think*, TH as in *that*; zh as in azure. ∼ = related to.

CAMP (2), *v.t.* to pitch a c.; encamp; take up temporary quarters; **to c. out**, to live, sleep in a tent or the open air. [Fr. from L.].

CAMPAIGN (1) [kam-pān'], *n.* (*milit.*) a series of concerted military operations towards a single general objective; length of time that an army is in the field at a stretch; series of actions planned with a definite purpose. CAMPAIGN (2), *v.i.* to direct or work in a c. [Fr.].

CAMPAIGNER [kam-pā'ner], *n.* one who campaigns; one who has served in many campaigns, veteran soldier.

CAMPANILE [kam'pa-nīl, kam-pa-nē'lā], *n.* high detached bell-tower. [It.].

CAMPANOLOGY [kam-pa-no'lo-ji], *n.* art of bell-ringing. CAMPANOLOGIST, *n.* an exponent of c. [L. and Gk.].

CAMPANULA [kam-pa'nyōō-lah], *n.* (*bot.*) genus of plants, including the bell-flowers. [~L.].

CAMPANULATE [kam-pa'nyōō-lāt], *adj.* (*bot.*) shaped like a bell.

CAMP-BED [kamp-bed'], *n.* camp-bedstead.

CAMP-BEDSTEAD [kamp-bed'sted], *n.* narrow bedstead made to fold up so that it can be readily carried or packed away.

CAMPER [kam'per], *n.* one who camps in the open.

CAMP-FOLLOWER [kamp'fo-lō-er], *n.* a non-combatant, male or female, who follows an army on the march or hangs about a military camp.

CAMPHINE, CAMPHENE [kam'fēn], *n.* a hydro-carbon which crystallizes in white prisms.

CAMPHOR [kam'fer], *n.* volatile, strong-smelling, semi-transparent solid substance useful in medicine; **c. balls**, small balls of naphthalene placed among clothes to keep away moths. [MdL., Arab.].

CAMPHORACEOUS [kam-fo-rā'shoos], *adj.* resembling camphor.

CAMPHORATE (1) [kam'fo-rāt], *n.* salt formed from camphoric acid and a base. CAMPHORATE (2), *v.t.* to permeate or impregnate with camphor.

CAMPHORIC [kam-fo'rik], *adj.* containing or per-taining to camphor; **c. acid**, acid produced by successive distillations of camphor.

CAMPING [kam'ping], *n.* act of living in camp.

CAMPION [kam'pi-on], *n.* (*bot.*) one of the plants included in the genera *Lychnis* or *Silene*. [Uncert.].

CAMP-MEETING [kamp'mē-ting], *n.* open-air religious meeting.

CAMP-STOOL [kamp'stōōl], *n.* folding stool.

CAMPUS [kam'pus], *n.* (*U.S.*) the grounds of a school or university. [L.].

CAMSHAFT [kam'shahft], *n.* (*motoring*) rotating shaft to which cams are attached to lift the valves.

CAM-WHEEL [kam'wēl], *n.* wheel with a cam on its periphery.

CAMWOOD [kam'wŏŏd], *n.* a red dye-wood. [Unkn.].

CAN (1) [kan], *n.* small metal container. CAN (2), *v.t.* to put into, preserve in, an air-tight can; **c. it**, (*slang*) stop such talk. [OE.].

CAN (3) (*pret.* could), *v. aux.* to be able to; know how to, have the power to. [OE.].

CANAILLE [ka'nīl], *n.* the rabble. [Fr. from L.].

CANAL [ka-nal'], *n.* artificial watercourse made for navigation or irrigation; (*anat.*) duct in a living body; (*zool.*) flute or groove in structure of a shell to allow for the passage of the breathing tube; **c. rays**, (*phys.*) positive rays. [L.].

CANALICULATE(D) [ka-na-li'kyōō-lāt(-id)], *adj.* (*biol.*) finely channelled, furrowed, ridged.

CANALIZE [ka'na-līz], *v.t.* to make into a canal, provide with canals; (*fig.*) concentrate and lead in a specified direction. CANALIZATION [ka-na-lī-zā'shn], *n.* the making of canals; canal system of a district.

CANARD [ka'nah(r)], *n.* false or misleading report; (*aeron.*) aeroplane with the elevator in front of the main planes. [Fr.].

CANARY (1) [ka-nãer'i], *n.* yellow or greenish-yellow song-bird; † wine popular in England in the sixteenth and seventeenth centuries. CANARY (2), *adj.* like a c.; bright yellow.

CANARY-CREEPER [ka-nãer-i-krē'per], *n.* climbing plant with yellow flowers.

CANARY-GRASS [ka-nãer'i-grahs], *n.* plant which yields canary-seed, used as food for canaries.

CANASTER [ka-nas'ter], *n.* rush basket used for packing tobacco; kind of coarse tobacco. [Span.].

CAN-BUOY [kan'boi], *n.* (*naut.*) large buoy in the shape of a cone.

CAN-CAN [kan'kan], *n.* wild dance in which there is much high kicking. [Fr.].

CANCEL (1) [kan'sel], *v.t. and i.* to cross out, delete; wipe out; countermand, annul; neutralize, balance; (*math.*) take out the same factor on both sides of an equation or fraction; **c. out**, to balance, neutralize. CANCEL (2), *n.* something deleted; a punch for tickets; leaf in a book substituted for that originally printed; leaf so deleted. [L.].

CANCELLATED [kan'se-lā-tid], *adj.* (*bot.*) reticu-lated. [L.].

CANCELLATION [kan-se-lā'shn], *n.* act of can-celling, fact of being cancelled.

CANCER [kan'ser], *n.* constellation of the Crab, fourth sign of the Zodiac; (*med.*) malignant tumour which gradually consumes the tissues of the body; (*fig.*) any similar corruptive or destructive evil; **tropic of C.**, parallel of latitude 23° 27' north of the equator. [L.].

CANCEROUS [kan'se-rŏŏs], *adj.* pertaining to, or like, a cancer. CANCEROUSLY, *adv.* after the manner of a cancer.

CANCRIFORM [kang'kri-fawm], *adj.* shaped like a crab; (*path.*) like a cancer tumour.

CANCROID [kang'kroid], *adj.* resembling cancer; resembling a crab.

CANDELABRUM (*pl.* **candelabra**) [kan-di-la'-brum] (**candelabra** also used as *sg.* with new *pl.* **candelabras**), *n.* branched candlestick holding several candles; chandelier. [L.].

CANDID [kan'did], *adj.* frank, outspoken, sincere. CANDIDLY, *adv.* in c. fashion. [L.].

CANDIDATE [kan'di-dāt], *n.* one offering himself for appointment, election or examination. CAN-DIDACY, CANDIDATESHIP, CANDIDATURE, *n.* state of being a c. for any office, examination or prize. [L.].

CANDIED [kan'did], *adj.* sweet, covered with sugar; (*fig.*) suave, flattering. [CANDY (2).].

CANDLE [kan'dl], *n.* simple device for illumination consisting of a narrow cylinder of wax, tallow etc., surrounding a wick which is ignited; **Roman c.**, firework discharging coloured stars; **not fit to hold a c. to**, not to be compared with; **with bell, book and c.**, with the observance of due form and cere-mony (the objects named being used in excommuni-cation); **to burn the c. at both ends**, to exhaust one's energy by doing too many things at once, or for too long at a stretch. CANDLE-POWER, a unit of measurement of light, being the amount of light given by a c. of standard weight (2½ oz.), burning at the rate of 120 grains per hour. [OE. from L.].

CANDLEBERRY [kan'dl-be-ri], *n.* the wax-myrtle or its berry.

CANDLE-COAL, see CANNEL-COAL.

CANDLEMAS [kan'dl-mas], *n.* Feast of the Purifica-tion of the Blessed Virgin (2 Feb.). [OE.].

CANDLESTICK [kan'dl-stik], *n.* a stand for a candle. [OE.].

CANDLE-TREE [kan'dl-trē], *n.* the wax-myrtle.

CANDOUR [kan'der], *n.* impartiality, frankness and justice of speech or thought. [L.].

CANDY (1) [kan'di], *n.* a form of sugar obtained after repeated boiling and evaporation; (*U.S.*) a sweetmeat, sweets. CANDY (2), *v.t. and i.* to encrust (fruit etc.) with c. [Fr. from Arab.].

CANDYTUFT [kan'di-tuft], *n.* plant of the genus *Iberis*. [*Candia*, in Crete, and TUFT].

CANE (1) [kān], *n.* the hollow-jointed hard stem of large reeds, as bamboo, sugar-cane; walking-stick, stick for punishing schoolboys; canes prepared for use in making chairs etc.; stem of fruit-bushes such as the raspberry and loganberry. CANE (2), *v.t.* to punish by beating with a c.; make or repair the back or seat of a chair with strips of split c. [Gk.].

CANE CHAIR [kān-chãer'], *n.* chair made of, or with a seat of, woven cane.

CANE SUGAR [kān-shŏŏ'ger], *n.* sugar extracted from sugar cane.

CANICULAR [ka-ni'kyōō-ler], *adj.* relating to the dog-star; excessively hot, as in the dog-days.

CANINE [ka'nīn], *adj.* pertaining to a dog; **c. teeth**, two pairs of sharp, pointed teeth between the incisors and the premolars. [L.].

CANING [kā'ning], *n.* corporal punishment with a cane.

CANISTER [ka'nis-ter], *n.* small box or can, generally of metal, in which tea, sugar etc. are stored; **c. shot**, kind of old-fashioned ammunition. [L.].

CANKER (1) [kang'ker], *n.* ulcerous sore, small sore found in the mouth of children; disease in a horse's foot; ulcer affecting the ears of dogs and cats; disease which rots the bark and wood of trees; (*fig.*) any-thing which corrupts and destroys. CANKER (2), *v.t.* to corrupt or destroy by c.; *v.i.* to be afflicted with c. CANKERED, *adj.* disgruntled; ill-natured. [L.].

CANKEROUS [kang'ke-rŏŏs], *adj.* affected by, corroding like a, canker.

CANKER-WORM [kang'ker-werm], *n.* insect destructive to plants and fruit-trees.

CANNA [ka'nah], *n.* numerous genus of tropical plants. [L.].

CANNED [kand], *adj.* packed and sold in cans; (*coll.*) (of music) recorded; (*coll.*) intoxicated.

CANNEL-COAL, CANDLE-COAL [ka'nel-kōl], *n.* variety of hard bituminous smokeless coal.

CANNERY [ka'ne-ri], *n.* factory where foodstuffs are canned.

CANNIBAL (1) [ka'ni-bal], *n.* human being who eats the flesh of other human beings; animal which eats others of its own kind. CANNIBAL (2), *adj.* pertaining to cannibals or cannibalism. CANNIBALLY, *adv.* in c. fashion. [Span., form of *Carib.*].

CANNIBALISM [ka'ni-ba-lizm], *n.* act of being a cannibal; (*fig.*) monstrous, inhuman cruelty.

CANNIKIN [ka'ni-kin], *n.* small can.

CANNING [ka'ning], *n.* trade or process of preserving foodstuffs in sealed cans.

CANNON (1) [ka'non], *n.* large mounted gun for heavy ammunition. [It.].

CANNON (2), *n.* stroke in billiards in which the cue ball is made to strike the other two balls in succession. CANNON (3), *v.i.* to make a c. in billiards; **to c. into,** to bump heavily into. [Uncert.].

CANNONADE [ka-no-nād'], *n.* rapid and sustained discharge of artillery, bombardment, the noise of this.

CANNON-BALL [ka'non-bawl], *n.* ball of iron or stone discharged from a cannon.

CANNON-BIT, CANON-BIT [ka'non-bit], *n.* round smooth bit for a horse.

CANNON-BONE [ka'non-bōn], *n.* bone in a horse's leg between the hock and the fetlock.

CANNON-PROOF [ka'non-prŏŏf], *adj.* impenetrable by cannon-shot.

CANNON-SHELL [ka'non-shel], *n.* shell for use in a cannon, *esp.* one of small calibre.

CANNON-SHOT [ka'non-shot], *n.* ammunition for cannon, cannon-balls; the firing range of a cannon.

CANNOT [ka'not], *negative* of CAN.

CANNULA [ka'nyŏŏ-lah], *n.* surgical metal tube. CANNULAR, *adj.* tubular. [L.].

CANNY [ka'ni], *adj.* and *adv.* (*coll.*) shrewd; cautious; knowing; **to ca' c.** (= to call c.), to be cautious, go carefully; slack off work during working hours, limit output. [OScand.].

CANOE (1) [ka-nŏŏ'], *n.* light boat propelled by paddles. CANOE (2), *v.i.* to go in a c. CANOEIST, *n.* one skilled in propelling a c. [Span.].

CANON, cañon (1), see CANYON.

CANON (2) [ka'non], *n.* (*eccles.*) body of laws or rules set up by the Church to which doctrine and conduct etc. must conform; the collection of books of Holy Scripture recognized by the Christian Church as divinely inspired models of faith and conduct; general standard, rule or criterion for conduct, taste, or for sorting the genuine and spurious works of an author; those writings of an author which are accepted as authentic; (*mus.*) a continued fugue; (*typ.*) name of a large kind of type; **c. law,** ecclesiastical law. [OFr. from Gk.].

CANON (3), *n.* dignitary of the Church, member of a cathedral chapter; **minor c.,** canon who conducts services in a cathedral but who is not a member of the chapter. [OFr. from L.].

CANON-BIT, see CANNON-BIT.

CANONIC(AL) [ka-no'nik(-al)], *adj.* prescribed by, according to or pertaining to the canon; orthodox; regular; **c. hours,** official times for prayer.

CANONICALS [ka-no'ni-kalz], *n.*(*pl.*) the robes and vestments prescribed for any particular ecclesiastical or academic rank or office.

CANONICATE [ka-no'ni-kāt], *n.* canonry.

CANONIST [ka'no-nist], *n.* one expert in canon law. CANONISTIC [ka-no-nis'tik], *adj.* relating to a c.

CANONIZE [ka'no-nīz], *v.t.* (*R.C.*) to declare officially to be a saint. CANONIZATION [ka-no-ni-zā'shn], *n.* act or process of canonizing.

CANONRY [ka'non-ri], *n.* rank or office of a canon.

CANOODLE [ka-nŏŏ'dl], *v.t.* and *i.* (*coll.*) to caress, fondle, cuddle. [Unkn.].

CAN-OPENER [kan'ō-pe-ner], *n.* instrument for opening sealed cans of preserved food.

CANOPUS [ka-nō'pus], *n.* star in the constellation *Argo.* [Gk.].

CANOPY (1) [ka'no-pi], *n.* a covering forming a roof over a bed, throne etc.; covering supported by poles and held over the head of a distinguished person at state functions; (*arch.*) roof over a pulpit, statue etc. CANOPY (2), *v.t.* and *i.* to provide or cover with a c. CANOPIED, *adj.* provided with a c. [Gk.].

CANOROUS [ka-naw'rŏŏs], *adj.* tuneful, sonorous. [L.].

CANT (1) [kant], *n.* the plaintive whining of beggars; peculiar slang of beggars and thieves; clichés or catch phrases of any sect or group of people; insincere platitudes; hypocritical religious or political jargon. CANT (2), *v.i.* to utter platitudes or clichés, use c. [L.].

CANT (3), *n.* an inclining of anything, slope, slant. CANT (4), *v.t.* to cause to slope; *v.i.* to slope, incline to one side. [ODan.].

CAN'T [kahnt], (*coll.*) cannot.

CANTAB [kan'tab], *n.* member, past or present, of the University of Cambridge. [L.].

CANTABILE [kan-tah'bi-lā], *adj.* (*mus.*) in a tuneful singing style. [It.].

CANTALOUPE, CANTALOUP [kan'ta-lŏŏp], *n.* species of musk-melon. [*Cantalupo,* Italy].

CANTANKEROUS [kan-tang'ke-rŏŏs], *adj.* quarrelsome, surly, cross-grained. [Uncert.].

CANTATA [kan-tah'tah], *n.* (*mus.*) a dramatic choral work; musical setting of a narrative or dramatic poem. [It.].

CANTATRICE [kan'ta-trēs], *n.* female singer. [Fr.].

CANTEEN [kan-tēn'], *n.* refreshment bar and store, *esp.* in a camp, barracks, factory etc.; soldier's drinking-bottle; complete outfit of table cutlery. [Fr. from It.].

CANTER (1) [kan'ter], *n.* a light gentle gallop; **preliminary c.,** (*fig.*) trial outing. CANTER (2), *v.t.* to make to canter; *v.i.* to ride or move at a c. [*Canter(bury pace),* the easy pace of Canterbury pilgrims].

CANTERBURY [kan'ter-be-ri], *n.* a stand with rows of partitions for holding music, papers etc. [*Canterbury* in Kent].

CANTERBURY-BELL [kan-ter-be-ri-bel'], *n.* the flower *Campanula medium.*

CANTHARIDES [kan-tha'ri-dēz], *n.*(*pl.*) blister-beetles, the so-called Spanish flies, used for medicinal purposes when dried.

CANTHARIDIN [kan-tha'ri-din], *n.* the principle of cantharides, which causes blistering.

CANTHOOK [kant'hŏŏk], *n.* (*U.S.*) instrument for levering logs.

CANTHUS [kan'thus], *n.* the angle or corner of the eye. [Gk.].

CANTICLE [kan'ti-kl], *n.* short chant or hymn; one of the songs in the Prayer Book; (*pl.*) the Song of Solomon. [L.].

CANTILEVER [kan'ti-lē-ver], *n.* (*arch., eng.*) long beam projecting from a single support, usually arranged in pairs projecting from adjacent piers and joined by a centre girder, long projecting piece of wood, iron or stone giving support to a balcony, cornice etc. [CANT (3) and LEVER].

CANTING [kan'ting], *adj.* whining, hypocritical, insincere; (*her.*) allusive. CANTINGLY, *adv.* in c. fashion. [CANT (2)].

CANTLE [kan'tl], *n.* rear, upward, sloping part of a saddle; segment cut out of anything; thick slice [OFr.].

CANTO [kan'tō], *n.* one of the main divisions of a long poem; (*mus.*) the upper melody of a composition in several parts; **c. fermo,** (*mus.*) melody on which the counterpoint is based; plainsong. [It.].

CANTON (1) [kan-ton', kan'ton], *n.* small division of territory; one of the separate states of which Switzerland is composed; (*her.*) small square division in the upper corner of a shield or flag. CANTON (2), *v.t.* (*her.*) to place in the upper corner of a shield or standard; quarter troops. CANTONAL [kan'to-nal], *adj.* relating to a c.

CANTONMENT [kan-tŏŏn'ment], *n.* (usually *pl.*) quarters for soldiers.

CANTORIAL [kan-taw'ri-al], *adj.* belonging to the precentor's or northern side of a choir.

CANVAS (1) [kan'vas], *n.* strong coarse cloth made of hemp etc., used for sacks, tents, sails etc. and for painting on; **under c.,** (*milit.*) in tents; (*naut.*) under sail. CANVAS (2), *adj.* made of c. [Fr. from L.].

CANVAS-BACK [kan-vas'bak], *n.* species of mottled American duck.

CANVASS (1) [kan'vas], *v.t.* and *i.* to discuss, examine closely; solicit votes or orders systematically.

ŏŏ is pronounced as in food; ŏŏ as in hood; th as in *think*; TH as in *that*; zh as in azure. ~ = related to.

DSE—D*

CANVASS (2), *n.* act of canvassing. CANVASSER, *n.* one who canvasses. [CANVAS (1)].

CANYON, CAÑON, cañon [kan'yon], *n.* deep and precipitous ravine. [Span.].

CANZONE [kant-zō'nā], *n.* (*mus.*) two- or three-part-song. [It.].

CANZONET [kan-zo-net'], *n.* (*mus.*) a short air. [*Prec.*].

CAOUTCHINE [kow-chēn'], *n.* hydrocarbon found in oil of caoutchouc.

CAOUTCHOUC [kow'chŏŏk]. *n. and adj.* rubber in its raw state; india-rubber; made of rubber. [Fr.].

CAP (1) [kap], *n.* a covering for the head, usually of cloth or similar material, without a brim and often having a stiffened peak; (*sport*) coloured head-covering denoting membership of a representative team; covering over various objects; small casing containing explosive designed to fit over the nipple of a gun or pistol to detonate the charge; paper imitation of this for use in children's toy pistols; **c. in hand,** humbly, as a petitioner; **if the c. fits,** if the allusion is applicable; **to set one's c. at,** to try to attract the admiration and attention of. CAP (2) (*pres.pt.* CAPPING, *pret. and p.pt.* CAPPED), *v.t.* to put a c. on (a person's head); to cover or provide with a c.; (*Scots*) confer a university degree upon; (*fig.*) surpass, go one better than; reply to and complete (a quotation); award an official cap to at sport; raise one's cap by way of greeting. [OE.].

CAPABILITY [kā-pa-bi'li-ti], *n.* quality of being capable.

CAPABLE [kā'pa-bl], *adj.* possessing ability, competent, clever, skilful, qualified; susceptible of, liable to. CAPABLY, *adv.* in a c. fashion. [LL.].

CAPACIOUS [ka-pā'shŏŏs], *adj.* able to contain much; roomy, spacious. CAPACIOUSLY, *adv.* in a c. way. CAPACIOUSNESS, *n.* state of being c. [L.].

CAPACITATE [ka-pa'si-tāt], *v.t.* to make capable or eligible; qualify.

CAPACITOR [ka-pa'si-ter], *n.* (*elect.*) a condenser.

CAPACITY [ka-pa'si-ti], *n.* power of holding or containing; ability to grasp and retain; capability, talent; room; cubic content; (*elect.*) quantity of electricity which a condenser can store; number of ampère-hours a battery is capable of when charged. [Fr. from L.].

CAP-A-PIE, cap-à-pie [ka-pa-pi'], *adv.* from head to foot; all over; completely. [OFr.].

CAPARISON (1) [ka-pa'ri-son], *n.* harness, trappings (of a horse); equipment of an armed man. CAPARISON (2), *v.t.* to furnish with equipment or trappings.

CAPE (1) [kāp], *n.* short loose-fitting sleeveless cloak; loose covering for the neck and shoulders. [Fr. from Span.].

CAPE (2), *n.* headland, piece of coast projecting into the sea, promontory. [Fr. from L.].

CAPE GOOSEBERRY [kāp-gŏŏs'be-ri], *n.* the plant, *Physalis capensis,* or its bright orange fruit. [*Cape* of Good Hope].

CAPELINE [ka'pe-lēn], *n.* (*surg.*) hood-shaped bandage.

CAPER (1) [kā'per], *n.* the flower-bud of a species of shrub, *Capparis,* used in making sauces; the plant itself. [Gk.].

CAPER (2), *n.* a playful leap; lively frisking about; (*fig.*) pranks, giddy and irresponsible behaviour; **to cut capers,** to frisk about in a lively way; (*fig.*) play foolish tricks. CAPER (3), *v.i.* to jump about, frolic in sprightly fashion. [Uncert.].

CAPERCAILZIE [kā-per-kā'lye, kā-per-kāl'zi], *n.* wood grouse. [~Gael.].

CAPIAS [kā'pi-as], *n.* (*leg.*) writ to authorize seizure of person or goods. [L.].

CAPIBARA, see CAPYBARA.

CAPILLARITY [ka-pi-la'ri-ti], *n.* quality of being capillary, power of capillary attraction.

CAPILLARY (1) [ka-pi'le-ri], *n.* one of the minute hair-like blood vessels. CAPILLARY (2), *adj.* pertaining to hair; resembling a hair; **c. attraction,** physical attraction between a solid and a liquid, which determines the rise and fall of fluid in capillary vessels. [L.].

CAPITAL (1) [ka'pi-tal], *adj.* relating to life; punishable by the loss of life; of first importance; chief, principal; excellent; pertaining to or employed as capital; **c. ship,** a battleship or battle-cruiser. CAPITAL (2), *n.* the principal city of a state or country; wealth amassed by an individual or company and set apart to produce further wealth; money or stock used in starting and carrying on a business; the class of people who possess such wealth; (*print.*) capital letter; (*fig.*) that which is turned to one's account, personal advantage. [L.].

CAPITAL (3), *n.* (*arch.*) the head of a column. [L.].

CAPITALISM [ka'pi-ta-lizm], *n.* economic system under which capital or wealth may be owned by individuals.

CAPITALIST [ka'pi-ta-list], *n.* one who possesses capital, by which he may live; one who believes in and conforms to capitalism.

CAPITALIZE [ka'pi-ta-līz], *v.t.* to convert into capital; invest with capital; convert a periodical payment into a sum equivalent to the amount of capital that would produce it. CAPITALIZATION [ka-pi-ta-li-zā'shn], *n.* act of capitalizing.

CAPITALLY [ka'pi-ta-li], *adv.* in a first-rate or capital way.

CAPITATE [ka'pi-tāt], *adj.* (*bot.*) having a head (of flowers); growing in a head. [L.].

CAPITATION [ka-pi-tā'shn], *n.* tax upon each person; levy on each individual in a group. [L.].

CAPITOL [ka'pi-tol], *n.* large Roman temple; important public building, as the seat of the U.S. government at Washington. [L.].

CAPITOLIAN, CAPITOLINE [ka-pi-tō'li-an, ka'pi-tō-lin], *adj.* belonging or relating to the Capitol in Rome.

CAPITULAR [ka-pi'tyŏŏ-lah(r)], *adj.* pertaining to a cathedral chapter. CAPITULARY [ka-pi'tyŏŏ-la-ri], *n.* collection of ordinances or decrees of a chapter. [L.].

CAPITULATE [ka-pi'tyŏŏ-lāt], *v.i.* to yield, give in, surrender; (*milit.*) surrender on terms. [L.].

CAPITULATION [ka-pi-tyŏŏ-lā'shn], *n.* act of capitulating; terms of surrender; (*pl.*) certain special treaties between nations granting extra-territorial rights.

CAPITULUM [ka-pi'tyŏŏ-lum], *n.* (*bot.*) a little head; small compact cluster of flowers in a composite plant; (*anat.*) piece of bone protruding so as to fit into a hollow of another bone. [L.].

CAPNOMOR [kap'no-maw(r)], *n.* oily fluid obtained from the smoke of wood-tar and other organic matter. [Gk.].

CAPOC, KAPOK [kā'pok, ka-pok'], *n.* soft light fibre obtained from cotton-seeds. [Malay].

CAPON [kā'pon], *n.* castrated male fowl, *esp.* one fattened for eating. [Fr.].

CAPORAL [ka'po-rahl], *n.* kind of French tobacco. [Fr.].

CAPOT (1) [ka-pot'], *n.* the winning of all tricks at piquet. CAPOT (2), *v.t.* to make a c. against. [Fr.].

CAPPAGH-BROWN [ka-pa-brown'], *n.* colouring matter obtained from manganese and iron earth-deposits. [*Cappagh* in Ireland].

CAPRIC [kap'rik], *adj.* (*chem.*) related to capric acid; **c. acid,** acid found in butter etc., having a slight goat-like smell. CAPRATE [kap'rāt], *n.* (*chem.*) a salt of c. acid.

CAPRICCIO [ka-pri'ch(i)ō], *n.* (*mus.*) a free and often fanciful composition. [It.].

CAPRICCIOSO [ka-pri-ch(i)ō'sō], *adv.* (*mus.*) in a free and fanciful style. [It.].

CAPRICE [ka-prēs'], *n.* an irrational change of opinion or humour, whim. [Fr.].

CAPRICIOUS [ka-pri'shŏŏs], *adj.* acting by caprice, whimsical, irrational. CAPRICIOUSLY, *adv.* in a c. fashion. CAPRICIOUSNESS, *n.* state or quality of being c.

CAPRICORN [kap'ri-kawn], *n.* a constellation, the Goat, tenth sign of the Zodiac; **tropic of C.,** parallel of latitude 23° 27' south of the equator.

CAPRINE [kap'rin], *adj.* goat-like.

CAPRIOLE (1) [kap'ri-ōl], *n.* a leap, prance. CAPRIOLE (2), *v.i.* to leap about, caper, skip, prance. [It. from L.].

CAPROIC [ka-prō'ik], *adj.* like a goat; **c. acid,** acid with a goat-like odour obtained from butter and other oils. CAPROATE [kap'rō-āt], *n.* (*chem.*) a salt obtained from c. acid. [CAPRIC].

CAPSICUM [kap'si-kum], *n.* genus of American tropical plants whose fruits, chillies or red peppers, are ground to produce cayenne. [L.].

CAPSIZE [kap-sīz'], *v.t. and i.* to turn upside down, upset (*esp.* of boats). [Uncert.].

CAPSTAN [kap'stan], *n.* upright revolving drum turned by detachable projecting bars and round which a cable is wound in hoisting up an anchor or similar operations. [Fr.].

CAPSULE [kap'syōōl], *n.* small case or vessel; metal or rubber cap to enclose the neck of a bottle etc.;

The accent ' after a syllable = stress (u-pon'). The mark ‾ over a vowel = length (ā in made; ō in bone) (*anat.*) membranous sac, or protective covering; (*bot.*) seed-vessel; (*med.*) gelatinous sheath containing medicine. CAPSULAR, *adj.* relating to a c. [L.].

CAPTAIN (1) [kap'tin], *n.* naval officer immediately below a rear-admiral in rank; military officer immediately below a major; commanding officer of a merchant ship or aircraft or of certain trained bodies of men; leader of a sports team; (*fig.*) gifted commander and leader. CAPTAIN (2), *v.t.* to lead, command as c. CAPTAINCY, *n.* rank and status of a c. [OFr.].

CAPTION [kap'shn], *n.* a heading, short title of a film scene, section of a book etc.; title under a picture; (*leg.*) certificate appended to a legal document to show its authority. [L.].

CAPTIOUS [kap'shoos], *adj.* inclined to catch at faults; fault-finding, apt to cavil. [L.].

CAPTIVATE [kap'ti-vāt], *v.t.* to enthral, charm, fascinate; capture the fancy of. CAPTIVATING, *adj.* enchanting, charming, fascinating. CAPTIVATION, *n.* act of captivating. [L.].

CAPTIVE (1) [kap'tiv], *n.* prisoner, one who has been captured. CAPTIVE (2), *adj.* taken prisoner, captured; **c. balloon,** balloon secured to the ground. [L.].

CAPTIVITY [kap-ti'vi-ti], *n.* condition of being captive. [Fr. from L.].

CAPTOR [kap'ter], *n.* one who captures a prisoner or prize. [L.].

CAPTURE (1) [kap'tyoōr], *n.* act of seizing, taking prisoner; that which is seized or caught. CAPTURE (2), *v.t.* to catch, seize as prisoner, take as prize. [L.].

CAPUCHIN [ka'pyoō-chin], *n.* order of Franciscan friars wearing pointed cowls; **c. monkey,** South American hooded monkey; **c. pigeon,** pigeon with a crest of feathers like a cowl. [Fr. from It.].

CAPYBARA, CAPIBARA [ka-pi-bah'rah], *n.* (*zool.*) the largest extant rodent. [Brazil].

CAR [kah(r)], *n.* wheeled vehicle; mechanically propelled passenger vehicle; railway carriage; motor car; passenger section of an aeroplane or airship. [OFr. from L.].

CARABINEER [ka-ra-bi-nĕer'], *n.* mounted soldier armed with a carbine. [Fr.].

CARACAL [ka'ra-kal], *n.* the Persian lynx, or its fur. [Fr. from Pers.].

CARACK, CARRACK [ka'rak], *n.* large armed trading vessel. [Fr.].

CARACOLE (1) [ka'ra-kōl], *n.* half-turn or a series of these by a horse; (*arch.*) spiral staircase. CARACOLE (2), *v.i.* to make a c. [Fr.].

CARAFE [ka-rahf'], *n.* a glass bottle, usually for wine, water or perfume. [Fr.].

CARAMBOLA [ka-ram-bō'lah], *n.* tree or fruit of the Coromandel gooseberry. [Portug.].

CARAMBOLE [ka'ram-bōl], *n.* a cannon at billiards. [Fr.].

CARAMEL [ka'ra-mel], *n.* burnt sugar, used for colouring and flavouring; kind of toffee. [Fr. from L.].

CARAPACE [ka'ra-pās], *n.* hard upper shell of certain reptiles and crustaceans. [Span.].

CARAP-OIL [ka'rap-oil], *n.* oil obtained from the seeds of the crab-wood tree.

CARAT [ka'rat], *n.* measure of weight for diamonds and other gems; standard of purity of gold, reckoned in twenty-fourths. [Fr.].

CARAVAN (1) [ka'ra-van], *n.* a company of travellers journeying together, *esp.* in the desert; covered wagon used as a domicile by gipsies and holiday-makers; kind of small house on wheels; vehicles transporting a travelling circus. CARAVAN (2), *v.i.* to travel in a c., *esp.* of holiday campers. CARAVANEER, *n.* man in charge of the camels of a c. [Fr. from Pers.].

CARAVANSERAI [ka-ra-van'se-rā], *n.* Eastern inn with a large central courtyard, affording accommodation for the night to caravans. [Pers.].

CARAVEL [ka'ra-vel], *n.* lateen-rigged four-masted sailing vessel. [Fr.].

CARAWAY, CARRAWAY [ka'ra-wā], *n.* a plant with aromatic seeds. [Fr. from Arab.].

CARBIDE [kah'bīd], *n.* a combination of carbon with another element, usually a metal; calcium carbide used in the preparation of acetylene. [CARBON].

CARBINE [kah'bīn], *n.* † short rifle used by mounted soldiers. [Fr.].

CARBOHYDRATE [kah-bō-hī'drāt], *n.* an organic compound of carbon, oxygen and hydrogen. [CARBON and HYDRATE].

CARBOLIC (1) [kah-bo'lik], *adj.* derived from

carbon; **c. acid,** antiseptic prepared from coal-tar, phenol. CARBOLIC (2), *n.* c. acid. [L.].

CARBON (1) [kah'bon], *n.* non-metallic substance existing, other than in compounds, as charcoal, graphite and diamond; chemical element denoted by C; thin rod of this used in an electric arc-light; copy reproduced by carbon paper; **c. paper,** sheet of thin paper covered with a pigment on one side, used for producing duplicate copies of written work. CARBON (2), *v.i. and pass.* (of internal combustion engines) to become coated with c.; also **c. up.** [L.].

CARBONACEOUS [kah-bo-nā'shoōs], *adj.* belonging to, containing or composed of coal or carbon.

CARBONATE [kah'bo-nāt], *n.* (*chem.*) a salt of carbonic acid.

CARBONATED [kah'bo-nā-tid], *adj.* combined or impregnated with carbonic acid gas.

CARBONIC [kah-bo'nik], *adj.* pertaining to, coming from carbon; **c. acid gas,** carbon dioxide, gas produced in respiration etc.

CARBONIFEROUS [kah-bo-ni'fe-roōs], *adj.* yielding coal; relating to the middle period of the upper palaeozoic era. [L.].

CARBONIZE [kah'bo-nīz], *v.t.* to turn into carbon.

CARBORUNDUM [kah-bo-run'dum], *n.* compound of silicon and carbon formed under great heat, used as an abrasive for grinding. [CARBON and CORUNDUM].

CARBOY [kah'boi], *n.* globular glass bottle, usually encased in basket-work. [Pers.].

CARBUNCLE [kah'bung-kl], *n.* inflamed boil or tumour; brilliant deep red gem, *esp.* a garnet. CARBUNCLED, adorned with carbuncles; afflicted with carbuncles. CARBUNCULAR [kah-bung'kyoō-ler], *adj.* pertaining to a c.; like a c. [L.].

CARBURET (*pres.pt.* **carburetting**, *pret. and p.pt.* **carburetted**) [kah-byoō-ret'], *v.t.* to impregnate or cause to combine with carbon. CARBURETTED, *adj.* combined with carbon. [CARB(ON) and (SULPH)UR].

CARBURETTOR, CARBURETTER [kah-byoō-re'ter], *n.* device in an internal combustion engine in which petrol is vaporized and mixed with air to form an explosive mixture.

CARBURIZE [kah'byoō-rīz], *v.i.* to carburet.

CARCAJOU [kah'ka-zhoō], *n.* the wolverine. [Fr.].

CARCASE, CARCASS [kah'kas], *n.* dead body of an animal, *esp.* when dressed by a butcher; framework of a ship, building etc. [OFr.].

CARCINOLOGY [kah-si-no'lo-ji], *n.* the scientific study of crustaceans. [Gk.].

CARCINOMA [kah-si-nō'mah], *n.* (*med.*) kind of cancer affecting the organs or connective tissue. CARCINOMATOUS [kah-si-nō'ma-toōs], *adj.* (*med.*) affected by cancer, cancerous. [Gk.].

CARD (1) [kahd], *n.* piece of thin pasteboard bearing a person's name and address, invitation, expression of good wishes for a special occasion, postcard, programme of events or score sheet, or an advertisement; one of fifty-two pieces of thin pasteboard used in many games; (*coll.*) queer, peculiar person; **on the cards,** liable to occur, possible; **to put one's cards on the table,** to act openly and reveal one's intentions, plans etc.; **a house of cards,** impracticable scheme doomed to failure. [Fr. from L.].

CARD (2), *n.* machine for combing flax, hemp, wool etc. CARD (3), *v.t.* to comb flax, hemp and wool with a c. [Fr. from L.].

CARDAMOM [kah'da-mom], *n.* an aromatic pungent spice. [Gk.].

CARDAN [kah'dan], *adj.* (*eng.*) **c. joint,** universal joint; **c. shaft,** shaft with a c. joint at both ends. [*Cardano,* Italian mathematician].

CARDBOARD [kahd'bawd], *n.* stiff pasteboard.

CARD-CASE [kahd'kās], *n.* case for visiting cards.

CARDIA [kah'di-ah], *n.* (*anat.*) the opening where the gullet enters the stomach. [Gk.].

CARDIAC [kah'di-ak], *adj.* relating to, concerned with the heart and heart-disease. [Gk.].

CARDIALGY [kah'di-al-ji], *n.* heartburn. [Gk.].

CARDIGAN [kah'di-gan], *n.* knitted jacket. [Earl of *Cardigan*].

CARDINAL (1) [kah'di-nal], *adj.* of primary importance, fundamental; principal; chief; pertaining to a c.; deep scarlet; **c. numbers,** the numbers one, two, three etc. CARDINAL (2), *n.* (*R.C.*) one of the seventy members of the Pope's Council, next in rank to the Pope himself; the cardinal-bird. [L.].

CARDINAL-BIRD [kah'di-nal-berd], *n.* a North American song-bird with red plumage.

CARDINAL-FLOWER [kah'di-nal-flow-er], *n.* a plant with brilliant red flowers.

CARD-INDEX (1) [kahd-in'deks], *n.* index in which

each item is entered on a separate card for easy reference. CARD-INDEX (2), *v.t.* to make a c. of.

CARDING MACHINE [kah′ding-ma-shēn], *n.* machine for carding and cleansing flax and hemp.

CARDIOGRAPH [kah′di-ō-grahf], *n.* device for recording the beats of the heart. CARDIOGRAPHY [kah-di-o′gra-fi], *n.* the recording of the beats of the heart. [Gk.].

CARDIOID [kah′di-oid], *n.* curve shaped like a heart, traced by a point on the circumference of a circle rolling round the circumference of an equal circle. [Gk.].

CARDIOLOGY [kah-di-o′lo-ji], *n.* specialized study of the heart. [Gk.].

CARDIOMETRY [kah-di-o′mi-tri], *n.* measurement of the beats of the heart. [Gk.].

CARDITIS [kah-dī′tis], *n.* (*med.*) inflammation of the muscles of the heart. [Gk.].

CARDOON [kah-dōōn′], *n.* the globe artichoke. [OFr.].

CARD PLAYER [kahd′plā-er], *n.* one who plays card games.

CARDSHARPER [kahd′shah-per], *n.* a cheat at cards.

CARD-TABLE [kahd′ta-bl], *n.* small collapsible table with a green baize top for playing cards on.

CARE (1) [kāer], *n.* attention, solicitude; worry, anxiety; heed, regard; responsibility; (*poet.*) sorrow, grief; **c. of,** *in addressing letters, written before the name of the occupier of the house where the addressee is temporarily staying.* CARE (2), *v.i.* to feel anxious, sorrowful, display a strong interest, mind; be concerned; **to c. for,** to be fond of, like; look after. [OE.].

CAREEN [ka-rēn′], *v.t.* to lay a ship on her side for caulking or repairing; *v.i.* to heel over. CAREENAGE, *n.* place suitable for, or cost of, careening. [~L.].

CAREER (1) [ka-rēer′], *n.* rapid motion, a rushing onwards; gradual improvement of status through life, advance through life; profession or business providing means of personal advancement. CAREER (2), *v.i.* to rush madly, race. CAREERIST, *n.* person whose chief aim in life is personal advancement. [Fr. from LL.].

CAREFUL [kāer′fŏŏl], *adj.* full of care; anxious, solicitous; provident; heedful, cautious. CAREFULLY, *adv.* in a c. way.

CARELESS [kāer′les], *adj.* without care, carefree; indifferent, unconcerned; heedless; negligent, thoughtless, slovenly, inconsiderate. CARELESSLY, *adv.* in a c. fashion.

CARESS (1) [ka-res′], *n.* movement or act of endearment or affection; embrace. CARESS (2), *v.t.* to fondle, embrace, touch with affection; flatter; soothe. CARESSING, *adj.* loving, affectionate, soothing. CARESSINGLY, *adv.* in a caressing fashion. [Fr.].

CARET [ka′ret], *n.* a mark ⋏ placed below the line in writing or in proof-correcting to indicate that something has been omitted and must be added at that place. [L.].

CARETAKER [kāer′tā-ker], *n.* one employed to look after a building or other property, *esp.* in the owner's absence; **c. government,** ministry holding office temporarily until a properly-constituted administration can be appointed.

CARGO [kah′gō], *n.* freight, goods carried by a ship. [Span. from L.].

CAR-GOOSE [kah′gōōs], *n.* the crested grebe.

CARIATIDES, see CARYATIDES.

CARIBOU, CARIBOO [ka′ri-bōō], *n.* the North American reindeer. [AmerInd.].

CARICATURE (1) [ka′ri-ka-tyŏŏr], *n.* a ludicrous exaggerated imitation of someone's mannerisms, style or appearance; grotesque drawing of a person exaggerating his peculiarities; ill-formed or ugly person or thing. CARICATURE (2), *v.t.* to make a c. of. CARICATURIST [ka-ri-ka-tyŏŏr′ist], *n.* person who caricatures. [It.].

CARIES [kāer′i-ēz], *n.* decay of a bone or tooth. [L.].

CARILLON [kah-rē-yaw(ng)′], *n.* a chime of bells, usually operated by one person or by mechanism; tune played on a peal of bells. [Fr.].

CARIOUS [kāer′i-ŏŏs], *adj.* rotten, decayed. [CARIES.]

CARKING [kah′king], *adj.* harassing; worrying. [OFr.].

CARLINE [kah′lin], *n.* (*bot.*) genus of plants related to the thistle. [L.].

CARLINGUE [kah′ling], *n.* (*aeron.*) the foundation of a nacelle. [Fr.].

CARLISM [kah′lizm], *n.* the movement supporting the claims of Don Carlos and his heirs to the Spanish throne.

CARLOVINGIAN [kah-lō-vin′ji-an], *adj.* relating to Charlemagne or to the dynasty he founded.

CARMAGNOLE [kah-ma-nyōl′], *n.* boisterous dance, popular with the French revolutionaries; Jacobin soldier in the French Revolution. [Fr.].

CARMAN [kah′man], *n.* a carter, man who drives a cart or other vehicle carrying goods.

CARMELITE (1) [kah′me-lit], *n.* member of the religious order of White Friars. CARMELITE (2), *adj.* pertaining to the order of White Friars and its members. [Mount *Carmel*].

CARMINATIVE (1) [kah-mi′na-tiv], *n.* agent to relieve flatulence. CARMINATIVE (2), *adj.* relieving or curing flatulence. [L.].

CARMINE (1) [kah′min], *n.* crimson-red pigment obtained from cochineal. CARMINE (2), *adj.* crimson, carmine-coloured. [Fr.].

CARNAGE [kah′nij], *n.* heavy wanton slaughter of human beings; bloodshed. [Fr.].

CARNAL [kah′nal], *adj.* of the flesh; sexual, sensual; worldly; **c. knowledge,** sexual intercourse. CARNALIST, *n.* sensualist; materialist. CARNALLY, *adv.* in a c. way. [L.].

CARNALITY [kah-na′li-ti], *n.* worldliness; sensuality; lust.

CARNATION [kah-nā′shn], *n.* a pink colour; kind of clove-pink. [L.].

CARNELIAN, see CORNELIAN.

CARNIVAL [kah′ni-val], *n.* week of revelry and festivity just before Lent, *esp.* in Roman Catholic countries; revelry, organized jollification. [It.].

CARNIVORA [kah-ni′ve-rah], *n.(pl.)* (*zool.*) flesh-eating mammals. [L.].

CARNIVOROUS [kah-ni′ve-rŏŏs], *adj.* flesh-eating.

CAROB [ka′rob], *n.* the locust-tree or its fruit. [Fr. from Arab.].

CAROL (1) [ka′rol], *n.* song of gladness and rejoicing, *esp.* to celebrate Christmas; happy song. CAROL (2) (*pres. pt.* CAROLLING, *pret. and p.pt.* CAROLLED), *v.i.* to sing carols; sing joyfully. [OFr.].

CAROLINE [ka′rō-lin], *adj.* pertaining to Charles, *esp.* Charles I and II of England, and their period. [L.].

CAROLINGIAN [ka-rō-lin′ji-an], *adj.* Carlovingian. [Fr.].

CAROM [ka′rom], *n.* a cannon in French billiards. [Fr.].

CAROSS, see KAROSS.

CAROTID (1) [ka-ro′tid], *n.* one of the two main arteries in the neck which carry blood from the aorta to the head. CAROTID (2), *adj.* pertaining to or connected with either of the carotids. [Gk.].

CAROTIN [ka′ro-tin], *n.* the vitamin present in carrots. [L.].

CAROUSAL [ka-row′zal], *n.* a feast; merry, rowdy drinking bout.

CAROUSE (1) [ka-rowz′], *n.* carousal. CAROUSE (2), *v.i.* to drink and make merry; feast; revel. CAROUSER, *n.* person who carouses. [Fr. from Germ.].

CARP (1) [kahp], *n.* a freshwater fish. [OFr., L.].

CARP (2), *v.i.* to cavil; criticize sharply and persistently. [OScand.].

CARPAL [kah′pal], *adj.* pertaining to the carpus or wrist.

CARPEL [kah′pel], *n.* (*bot.*) single cell into which a compound fruit may be divided; simple fruit having only a single cell. CARPELLARY [kah-pe′la-ri], *adj.* pertaining to a c. [L. from Gk.].

CARPENTER (1) [kah′pen-ter], *n.* one who works in wood, wood-worker. CARPENTER (2), *v.i.* to work in wood, as a c. CARPENTERING, *n.* carpentry. [OFr.].

CARPENTRY [kah′pen-tri], *n.* art or work of a carpenter.

CARPET (1) [kah′pit], *n.* covering for floors and stairs usually of some heavy woven fabric; quantity or piece of this fabric; even natural covering for the ground; **on the c.,** being reproved, reprimanded; under discussion; **c. knight,** knight or soldier who has never seen service in the field. CARPET-BAGGER, candidate for parliament who does not live in his constituency and is a stranger to it. CARPET (2), *v.t.* to cover with or as with a carpet; (*coll.*) reprimand. [OFr.].

CARPET-BAG [kah′pit-bag], *n.* bag made of carpeting, often used to carry tools.

CARPETING [kah′pi-ting], *n.* material for carpets; carpets.

CARPHOLOGY [kah-fo′lo-ji], *n.* floccillation. [Gk.].

CARPING [kah′ping], *adj.* critical in a petty and

disagreeable way, cavilling, captious. CARPINGLY, *adv.* in a c. way. [CARP (2)].

CARPUS [kah'pus], *n.* (*anat.*) wrist. [L.].

CARRACK, see CARACK.

CARRAGEEN [ka'ra-gēn], *n.* edible Irish seaweed or moss. [*Carragheen*, Ireland].

CARRAWAY, see CARAWAY.

CARRIAGE [ka'rij], *n.* act of carrying or transporting; charge made for transport and delivery of goods; wheeled passenger vehicle, *esp.* one with four wheels and drawn by a horse or horses; passenger compartment on a railway train; device used to support and move heavy objects, as guns; the movable part of a typewriter which holds the paper; way of holding one's self, deportment, bearing; (*print.*) part of a press in which type formes are placed for printing; **c. forward**, indication that the fee for conveyance is to be paid by the addressee. [OFr.].

CARRICK BEND [ka'rik-bend], *n.* (*naut.*) kind of knot. [Uncert.].

CARRICK BITTS [ka'rik-bits], *n.*(*pl.*) (*naut.*) pair of bitts supporting the windlass.

CARRIER [ka'ri-er], *n.* one who conveys goods from one place to another, an out-porter; contrivance for carrying luggage attached to the back of a car or bicycle; any person or thing that transmits infection; (*mech.*) part of a machine which carries something from one position to another; paper shopping-bag. CARRIER-PIGEON, pigeon trained to carry messages.

CARRION (1) [ka'ri-on], *n.* dead and rotting flesh; bad meat. CARRION (2), *adj.* like, pertaining to, or feeding on, c. [OFr.].

CARRONADE [ka-ro-nād'], *n.* kind of ship's cannon with short barrel and large bore. [*Carron*, Scotland].

CARRON-OIL [ka'ron-oil], *n.* oil for treating scalds as used at *Carron* ironworks.

CARROT [ka'rot], *n.* yellowish-red edible root of *Daucus Carota*; (*pl.*) (*coll.*) (person with) red hair. CARROTINESS, *n.* state or quality of being carroty. CARROTY, *adj.* resembling a c. in colour; reddish-yellow. [Fr.].

CARRY (1) [ka'ri], *v.t.* to bear; transport, convey, lift and move from one place to another; support; extend; storm, take by force; retain (in the memory); succeed in passing; gain approval for; involve, imply; (*math.*) bring over from one column to another; (*naut.*) have (sail); *v.i.* to transport, lift and bear things from one place to another; reach to a certain distance; be audible; (of a hare) run over ground which sticks to the feet; (of a horse) hold the head in a particular way; **to c. one's bat**, (*cricket*) to bat from the opening of an innings until all the other ten batsmen are out; **to c. weight**, (*horse-racing*) be handicapped by extra weight; be reasonable and convincing, tend to influence; **to c. the day**, to win, gain one's point; **to be carried away**, to be wildly stirred; **to c. forward**, to proceed with; (*book-keeping*) transfer an entry to the next page; **to c. off**, to remove by force; kill; **to c. off well**, to handle with ease and equanimity, make the best of; **to c. on**, to continue; persevere; (*coll.*) behave in a foolish, excited and generally conspicuous manner; flirt; **to c. out**, to complete, accomplish, fulfil; **to c. over**, (*Stock Exchange*) to allow (a due account) to remain until next settling-day; **to c. through**, to complete, achieve; maintain, sustain. CARRY (2), *n.* position of gun or sword held ready for salute; range, length of flight, distance anything carries. [Northern OFr.].

CARRY-ALL [ka'ri-awl], *n.* (*orig. U.S.*) capacious vehicle (now motor-driven) for carrying both passengers and goods.

CARRYING [ka'ri-ing], *adj.* bearing, conveying, removing or transporting; **c. trade**, transport of goods, particularly by water.

CARRY-OVER [ka-ri-ō'ver], *n.* (*Stock Exchange*) postponement of payment until next settling-day; amount so held; anything remaining to be dealt with on a later occasion.

CART (1) [kaht], *n.* wheeled vehicle drawn by horses or oxen for transporting goods; **dog c.**, light two-wheeled horse-drawn passenger vehicle; **in the c.**, (*coll.*) in trouble, in a difficult situation. CART (2), *v.t. and i.* to transport in a c.; undertake the carrying of loads in a c. [OE.].

CARTAGE [kah'tij], *n.* act or cost of carting.

CARTE (1) [kaht], *n.* bill of fare, menu card; **à la c.,** selected from the items on the bill of fare. [Fr.].

CARTE (2), **QUARTE**, *n.* a position in fencing. [Fr.].

CARTE-BLANCHE [kaht-blahnsh'], *n.* blank piece of paper to be filled in as the possessor pleases; **to give a person c.**, to give him a free hand, *esp.* with regard to expenditure. [Fr.].

CARTE-DE-VISITE [kaht-de-vi-zēt'], *n.* particular size of small photograph. [Fr.].

CARTEL [kah'tel], *n.* written agreement between opposing parties in a war as to exchanging prisoners; unarmed vessel used for such an exchange; written challenge to a duel; a trust; working agreement between rival commercial concerns. [Fr.].

CARTESIAN (1) [kah-tē'zi-an], *n.* disciple of the French philosopher, Descartes, or his doctrines. CARTESIAN (2), *adj.* relating to Descartes and his philosophy. [*Descartes*].

CARTHORSE [kaht'haws], *n.* a heavy horse.

CARTHUSIAN (1) [kah-thyōō'zi-an], *n.* member of a religious order founded by St. Bruno at Chartreuse; pupil of Charterhouse School. CARTHUSIAN (2), *adj.* pertaining to a Carthusian or to Charterhouse School. [L.].

CARTILAGE [kah'ti-lij], *n.* gristle, elastic tissue from which bone is formed. CARTILAGINOUS [kah-ti-la'ji-nōōs], *adj.* connected with, or consisting of, c. [L.].

CARTOGRAPHIC(AL) [kah-tō-gra'fik(-al)], *adj.* pertaining to cartography. [Fr.].

CARTOGRAPHY [kah-to'gra-fi], *n.* art or science of map-making. CARTOGRAPHER, *n.* map-maker.

CARTOMANCY [kah'to-man-si], *n.* fortune-telling by playing-cards. [Fr. and Gk.].

CARTON [kah'ton], *n.* small cardboard box or container; white disk in the centre of a target. [Fr.].

CARTOON (1) [kah-tōōn'], *n.* design or sketch on strong paper, as for tapestry etc.; picture, usually of the nature of a caricature, illustrating and usually satirizing topical events; cartoon-film. CARTOON (2), *v.t. and i.* to draw, represent in a c.; draw a c. [Fr.].

CARTOON-FILM [kah-tōōn-film'], *n.* film, usually humorous, photographed from black-and-white or coloured drawings, with appropriate music and sound effects.

CARTOONIST [kah-tōō'nist], *n.* one who draws cartoons.

CARTOUCHE [kah-tōōsh'], *n.* oval-shaped device, containing titles and names, on ancient Egyptian monuments; (*arch.*) scroll forming the top of a column; ornamental device with an inscription inside. [Fr. from It.].

CARTRIDGE [kaht'rij], *n.* container in which a charge of explosive for a firearm etc. is packed; **ball c.**, c. charged with a bullet; **blank c.,** c. containing explosive but no shot. [*Prec.*].

CARTRIDGE-PAPER [kaht'rij-pā-per], *n.* strong paper used for making cartridge-cases and for artists' drawings.

CART-WHEEL [kaht'wēl], *n.* wheel of a cart; (*coll.*) sideways somersault.

CARTWRIGHT [kaht'rīt], *n.* man who makes carts.

CARUNCLE [ka'rung-kl], *n.* soft excrescence of flesh, as in a cock's comb. CARUNCULAR [ka-rung'-kyōō-ler], *adj.* in the shape of a c. CARUNCULATED [ka-rung'kyōō-lā-tid], *adj.* furnished with a c. [L.].

CARVE [kahv], *v.t. and i.* to cut, chisel or engrave a design or figure upon wood, stone etc.; cut or serve up in slices meat or fowl prepared for the table; (*fig.*) shape, make, mould. [OE.].

CARVEL-BUILT [kah'vel-bilt], *adj.* (*naut.*) with the edges of the planks flush instead of overlapping as in clinker-built. [CARAVEL].

CARVER [kah'ver], *n.* one who carves; knife used to carve meat at table.

CARVING [kah'ving], *n.* act of one who carves; figure carved in stone or wood.

CARYATID (*pl.* caryatides) [ka-ri-a'tid, ka-ri-a'ti-dēz], *n.* (*arch.*) carved stone figure of a woman serving to support an entablature. [Gk.].

CARYOPSIS (*pl.* caryopsides) [ka-ri-op'sis, ka-ri-op'si-dēz], *n.* (*bot.*) fruit in which seed and pericarp are one, as in grasses. [Gk.].

CASAL [kā'sal], *adj.* (*gram.*) pertaining to case.

CASCADE (1) [kas-kād'], *n.* waterfall; (*fig.*) something falling freely like a waterfall; **in c.**, (*elect.*) so connected that the output of the first constitutes the input for the second. CASCADE (2), *v.i.* to fall in a c. [Fr.].

CASCARA [kas-kah'rah], *n.* laxative extracted from the bark of the Californian buckthorn. [Span.].

CASCARILLA [kas-ka-ri'lah], *n.* acrid aromatic bark of *Croton Cascarilla*. [MdL.].

CASE (1) [kās], *n.* that which falls, or happens;

ŌŌ is pronounced as in food; ŌŌ as in hood; th as in *think*, TH as in *that*; zh as in azure. ⌣ = related to.

circumstances; special or actual state of affairs; event; predicament; instance, example; fact; (*leg.*) question to be settled, cause to be tried or which has been tried and decided; facts or evidence supporting one side; (*med.*) example of a particular disease in someone; person afflicted with a particular disease; (*gram.*) a change in the form of a noun, pronoun or adjective, to show its relation to other words in the sentence; grammatical relationship of a noun, pronoun or adjective; **in c.,** lest, in the event that; **in any c.,** whatever happens; **in that c.,** if that is so; **leading c.,** (*leg.*) one often quoted in subsequent actions. [OFr. from L.].

CASE (2), *n.* box or chest of various kinds in which things may be kept; leather bag for toilet articles, writing materials, travelling etc.; box with glass covering to exhibit and protect the contents; linen or cotton bag to hold pillow, bolster etc.; (*print.*) box divided up into compartments for holding type; **lower c.,** box for small letters; small letters themselves; **upper c.,** box for capital letters; capital letters themselves. CASE (3), *v.t.* to encase. [OFr.].

CASEHARDEN [kās′hah-den], *v.t.* to give a hard skin to steel or iron; (*fig.*) render insensitive, hard and unfeeling. [L.].

CASEIC [kā′si-ik], *adj.* pertaining to, obtained from, cheese. [L.].

CASEIN [kā′si-in], *n.* the coagulated cheesy substance in milk. [L.].

CASE-LAW [kās′law], *n.* (*leg.*) administration of justice on the basis of decisions made in previous cases.

CASEMATE [kās′māt], *n.* (*fort.*) strong armoured vault in fortification, with openings for guns; armoured covering surrounding guns in a warship.

CASEMENT [kās′ment], *n.* window opening outwards on side hinges. [Fr.].

CASEMENT-CLOTH [kās′ment-kloth], *n.* strong cotton cloth, used chiefly for curtains.

CASEOUS [kā′si-ōōs], *adj.* like cheese. [L.].

CASE-SHOT [kās′shot], *n.* shrapnel.

CASE-WORM [kās′werm], *n.* the caddis.

CASH (1) [kash], *n.* money in coin or notes, ready money; (*coll.*) money in any form; **c. down,** payment immediately on receiving goods; **c. on delivery (C.O.D.),** payment by the addressee on delivery of goods by a postman. CASH (2), *v.t.* to give or receive coins or notes in exchange for a cheque; convert into ready money; **to c. in on,** to take advantage of (an event or state of affairs). [Fr.].

CASH (3) (*pl.* **cash**), *n.* small Eastern coin, usually perforated so that it can be carried on a string. [Tamil].

CASH-ACCOUNT [kash′a-kownt], *n.* account of sales and purchases for cash.

CASHEW [ka-shōō′], *n.* tropical American tree. [Fr. from Braz.].

CASHIER (1) [ka-shēer′], *n.* one who pays out and receives cash, and who keeps an account of monetary transactions in a bank or other commercial institution. [Fr.].

CASHIER (2), *v.t.* to dismiss or discharge with ignominy from the fighting services, deprive of rank. [Du. from Fr.].

CASHMERE [kash′mēer], *n.* soft, silky hair of the Cashmere goat; material woven from this or resembling it. [*Kashmir*, India].

CASH-REGISTER [kash′re-jis-ter], *n.* machine which records the amount of money placed in it.

CASING [kā′sing], *n.* that which envelops or encases; framework of windows and doors.

CASINO [ka-sē′nō], *n.* place of public amusement at a pleasure resort, with facilities for gambling. [It.].

CASK [kahsk], *n.* kind of barrel; amount contained in a cask; measure of capacity. [Span.].

CASKET [kahs′kit], *n.* small case for jewels, trinkets etc.; (*U.S.*) coffin. [Uncert.].

CASLON [kaz′lon], *n.* type-face popularized by W. Caslon.

CASQUE [kahsk], *n.* (*archaic*) helmet. [Fr.].

CASSATION [ka-sā′shn], *n.* (*leg.*) reversal or annulment of a judgment. [Fr.].

CASSAVA [ka-sah′vah], *n.* plant with tuberous roots; starch or flour made from the roots. [Haiti].

CASSEROLE [ka′se-rōl], *n.* fireproof cooking dish with a lid; food cooked in such a utensil. [Fr.].

CASSIA [ka′si-ah], *n.* large genus of plants including the senna. [L.].

CASSITERITE [ka-si′te-rīt], *n.* the principal ore of tin. [Gk.].

CASSOCK [ka′sock], *n.* long, sleeved garment worn,

usually over ordinary secular attire, by clergymen, choristers etc. [Fr. from It.].

CASSOWARY [ka′sō-wāer-i], *n.* large bird resembling a small ostrich. [Malay].

CAST (1) (*pret. and p.pt.* **cast**) [kahst], *v.t.* to throw, hurl, fling; direct towards; shed, throw off; let fall, throw overboard; produce; reject; assign parts in a play to actors; record, give (votes); mould; work out, reckon up; *v.i.* to throw a fishing-line; mould iron or other metals, concrete etc.; **to c. the lead,** (*naut.*) to measure the depth of water, by letting down a plumb-line; **the die is c.,** there is no going back; **to c. about for,** to seek a way, devise a plan; **to c. down,** (*fig.*) to depress, fill with gloom; **to c. off,** to leave destitute, abandon; (in knitting) finish off a piece of work by slipping stitches off the needles and securing them; (*print.*) find how many printed pages a manuscript will make; **to c. on,** to knit the first row of stitches on to a needle. CAST (2), *n.* act of casting; a throw; something thrown or shed; the distance thrown; skin of a snake; little pile of earth left by earthworms; piece of gut to which a fish-hook and bait are fixed; plaster or other material moulded into a particular shape; a mould; the actors of a play; characteristic feature, expression or mien. [OScand.].

CASTALIAN [kas-tāl′yan], *adj.* belonging to Castalia, a spring on Mount Parnassus sacred to the Muses; (*fig.*) poetic. [Gk.].

CASTANETS [kas-ta-nets′], *n.(pl.)* pair of small concave clappers of hard wood or ivory, struck against each other to music. [Span.].

CASTAWAY [kahs′ta-wā], *n.* one wrecked on a desolate shore; (*fig.*) an outcast.

CASTE [kahst], *n.* hereditary social division among the Hindus; any exclusive social class; **to lose c.,** to lose respect and social prestige. [Portug.].

CASTELLATED [kas′te-lā-tid], *adj.* having turrets, parapets or battlements like a castle; **c. nut,** (*eng.*) nut with grooves in its top to accommodate a securing pin; **c. shaft,** (*eng.*) spliced shaft. [L.].

CASTER (1), **CASTOR** [kahs′ter], *n.* bottle or other receptacle with a perforated lid, for pepper, sugar etc.; small wheel on a swivel fixed to the legs of chairs etc.; **c. action,** (*motoring*) trailing action in steering which tends to keep the wheels on a straight course. CASTER (2), *n.* one who casts, a computer. [CAST (1)].

CASTER-SUGAR, CASTOR-SUGAR [kahs-ter-shōō′ger], *n.* finely powdered sugar.

CASTIGATE [kas′ti-gāt], *v.t.* to chastise; administer punishment to; scold; criticize severely; emend, correct. CASTIGATOR, *n.* one who castigates. CASTIGATORY, *adj.* corrective; punishing. [L.].

CASTIGATION [kas-ti-gā′shn], *n.* act of castigating. [L.].

CASTILE SOAP [kas-tēl-sōp′], *n.* fine white, hard soap. [*Castile*, Spain].

CASTING [kah′sting], *n.* act of throwing; act of shaping metal in moulds; piece of metal shaped in this way.

CASTING VOTE [kah′sting-vōt], *n.* vote of a president or chairman at a meeting, to decide the issue when the votes of each party are otherwise equal; decisive vote.

CAST IRON [kahst-iern′], *n.* iron melted in a furnace and poured into moulds. CAST-IRON, *adj.* made of c.; (*fig.*) unyielding, inelastic; unassailable.

CASTLE (1) [kah′sl], *n.* large building elaborately fortified, with battlements and often a moat, fortress; large house resembling this in architectural style; **c. in Spain,** impracticable ideal or plan. CASTLE (2), *v.i.* in the game of chess, to move simultaneously the king and rook, so as to bring them side by side. CASTLED, *adj.* possessing castles. [OE. from L.].

CAST-OFF [kahst′of], *n.* something put aside as useless; calculation of the number of printed pages a manuscript will make.

CASTOR (1) [kah′ster], *n.* genus of rodents, including the beaver. [Gk.].

CASTOR (2), *n.* twin brother of Pollux, commemorated with him in the sign of the Zodiac *Gemini*; (*meteor.*) corposant. [Gk.].

CASTOR (3), see CASTER (1).

CASTOR-OIL [kah-ster-oil′], *n.* a vegetable oil, with purgative action.

CASTOR-SUGAR, see CASTER-SUGAR.

CASTRATE [kas-trāt′], *v.t.* to make sexually impotent by excising the testicles, emasculate, geld; (*fig.*) expurgate. [L.].

CASTRATION [kas-trā′shn] *n.* process of castrating.

CAST STEEL [kahst-stĕl'], *n.* steel fused and poured into moulds.

CASUAL [ka'zyōōl], *adj.* accidental, occasional, resulting from chance, haphazard; unsettled, uncertain; incidental; unmethodical, slack; **c. labourer,** worker who lives by taking odd jobs; **c. ward,** ward for vagrants. CASUALLY, *adv.* in a c. fashion. CASUALNESS, *n.* condition of being c. [L.].

CASUALTY [ka'zyōōl-ti], *n.* accident involving physical injury; (*pl.*) those wounded or dead in a battle; **c. ward,** hospital ward for those hurt in accidents.

CASUARINA [ka-zyōō-a-ri'nah], *n.* large genus of Australian and Polynesian trees. [CASSOWARY].

CASUIST [ka'zhōō-ist], *n.* one skilled in casuistry. [Fr. from L.].

CASUISTRY [ka'zyōō-ist-ri], *n.* doctrine which professes to arrive at conclusive judgments on particular problems of conduct, by arguing from general principles of ethics; a quibbling line of argument, sophistry.

CASUS BELLI [kā-zus-be'lī], *n.* act considered a sufficient cause of war; (*fig.*) ground for a quarrel. [L.].

CAT (1) [kat], *n.* small carnivorous animal with short jaws, sharp teeth and soft fur, of which there are both wild and domesticated varieties; (*zool.*) any species of the genus *Felis*; (*fig.*) spiteful woman; (*naut.*) tackle for drawing up the anchor to the cathead; double tripod designed to stand upright on three of its six feet; cat-o'-nine-tails; **to let the c. out of the bag,** to divulge a secret. CAT (2) (*pres. pt.* CATTING, *pret. and p.pt.* CATTED), *v.t.* (*naut.*) to hoist to the cathead CAT (3), *v.i.* (*slang*) to vomit [OE.].

CATA-, *pref.* back, against, down to, along, over, thoroughly. [Gk.].

CATABOLISM [ka-ta'bo-lizm], *n.* (*biol.*) the breaking down of complex organic matter to a simpler form. [Gk.].

CATACAUSTIC (1) [ka-ta-kaw'stik], *n.* a curve produced by reflection. CATACAUSTIC (2), *adj.* (*opt.*) formed by reflection into curves. [Gk.].

CATACHRESIS [ka-ta-krē'sis], *n.* (*rhet.*) misapplication of a figure of speech. [Gk.].

CATACLYSM [ka'ta-klizm], *n.* a deluge, all-enveloping flood; (*geol.*) violent alteration in the face of the earth; (*fig.*) violent and radical shift of mental and emotional balance, revolutionary upheaval.

CATACOMB [ka'ta-kōm], *n.* underground vault or gallery, or series of these, in which the dead are buried. [Fr.].

CATACOUSTICS [ka-ta-kow'stiks], *n.* study of echoes or reflected sounds. [Gk.].

CATADIOPTRIC [ka-ta-di-op'trik], *adj.* (*opt.*) having the power of refracting and reflecting light. [Gk.].

CATADROMOUS [ka-ta'dro-mŏŏs], *adj.* (*zool.*) leaving a river to spawn in the sea, as salmon. [Gk.].

CATAFALQUE [ka'ta-falk], *n.* temporary structure upon which the coffin is placed during a lying-in-state. [Fr.].

CATALAN (1) [ka'ta-lan], *n.* a native or the language of Catalonia. CATALAN (2), *adj.* pertaining to Catalonia or its language. [*Catalonia*, Spain].

CATALECTIC [ka-ta-lek'tik], *adj.* (*pros.*) lacking a syllable. [Gk.].

CATALEPSY [ka'ta-lep-si], *n.* (*med.*) state of insensibility, suspension of sensation brought on suddenly as in a fit. CATALEPTIC [ka-ta-lep'tik], *adj.* of, or pertaining to, c. [Gk.].

CATALOGUE (1) [ka'ta-log], *n.* list or register systematically compiled and set out; list of goods offered for sale; **c. raisonné,** c. arranged in order of subjects with explanatory matter under each entry. CATALOGUE (2), *v.t.* to make a c. of. [Gk.].

CATALYSIS [ka-ta'li-sis], *n.* (*chem.*) chemical change effected in a substance by something which does not undergo any change itself. [Gk.].

CATALYST [ka'ta-list], *n.* (*chem.*) substance producing catalysis.

CATALYTIC (1) [ka-ta-li'tik], *n.* (*chem.*) catalyst; (*med.*) medicine which destroys toxins in the blood. CATALYTIC(AL) (2), *adj.* effecting or pertaining to catalysis.

CATAMARAN [ka-ta-ma-ran'], *n.* log raft; peevish woman. [Tamil].

CATAMENIA [ka-ta-mē'nyah], *n.(pl.)* the menses. CATAMENIAL, *adj.* relating to c. [Gk.].

CATAPHORESIS [ka-ta-fo-rē'sis], *n.* (*med.*) the passing of medicine through the pores of the skin by electricity.

CATAPLASM [ka'ta-plazm], *n.* (*med.*) a poultice.

CATAPLEXY [ka'ta-plek-si], *n.* actual or feigned hypnotic sleep brought on in an animal by extreme fear. [Gk.].

CATAPULT (1) [ka'ta-pult], *n.* small forked stick with a length of rubber fastened to both ends of the fork for shooting pebbles; ancient military device for hurling boulders, rocks etc.; mechanism for launching aircraft from the deck of a ship. CATAPULT (2), *v.t. and i.* to shoot with a c.; hurl, throw or propel as from a c. [Gk.].

CATARACT [ka'ta-rakt], *n.* great waterfall or series of waterfalls; (*med.*) disease of the eye affecting the crystalline lens. CATARACTOUS, *adj.* pertaining to c. [Gk.].

CATARRH [ka-tah(r)'], *n.* (*med.*) inflammation of the mucous membrane; a cold. CATARRHAL, *adj.* of, or infected with, c. [Gk.].

CATASTROPHE [ka-tas'tro-fi], *n.* disaster, calamity with irremediable effects, overwhelming upheaval in the accepted order of things; the decisive action in a play which produces the climax; (*geol.*) cataclysm. CATASTROPHIC [ka-ta-stro'fik], *adj.* having the characteristics of a c. [Gk.].

CAT-BURGLAR [kat-bur'gler], *n.* thief who enters a house by climbing drainpipes etc.

CATCALL [kat'kawl], *n.* squealing instrument used to express disapproval in public places, theatres etc.; a noise of disapproval intended to interrupt.

CATCH (1) (*pret. and p.pt.* **caught**) [kach], *v.t. and i.* to seize, get hold of, seize after pursuit, capture; ensnare, trap; draw level with; receive in communication; hear with difficulty; entangle; hold (one's breath); grasp; attract, engage; receive by contagion or infection; be in time for; detect, discover; intercept; lay hold of, fasten on to; become entangled, become fastened to; **to c. on,** (*slang*) to become popular, take the public fancy; understand; **to c. out,** (*cricket*) to put (a batsman) out by catching the ball he has struck before it falls to the ground; (*fig.*) detect in a mistake or misdemeanour; **to c. up,** to overtake; **to c. a crab,** to get the oar jammed under water while rowing; **to c. it,** (*coll.*) to be severely reprimanded. CATCH (2), *n.* act of seizing or grasping; sudden halt or break; thing which catches or holds; (*fig.*) a trick to deceive or trap; thing caught, haul of fish; (*coll.*) thing worth catching; (*mus.*) a round. CATCHER, *n.* one who, that which, catches. [OFr.].

CATCHFLY [kach'fli], *n.* one of the several genera of plants which catch flying insects by sticky secretions.

CATCHING [ka'ching], *adj.* taking; contagious, infectious.

CATCHMENT [kach'ment], *n.* stretch of land which may be drained of its water; drainage.

CATCHPENNY [kach'pe-ni], *adj.* worthless yet superficially attractive, showy.

CATCHWORD [kach'werd], *n.* word placed at the bottom of a page which is the same as the first on the succeeding page; word at the head of a page or column in reference books; word an encyclopaedia or dictionary explains or defines; actor's cue; popular cliché or slogan.

CATCHY [ka'chi], *adj.* appealing, attractive to the eye; deceptive, tricky; easy to remember (of a tune).

CATECHETIC(AL) [ka-ti-ke'tik(-al)], *adj.* having the form of a catechism. CATECHETICALLY, *adv.* in a c. form.

CATECHISM [ka'ti-kizm], *n.* instruction in the form of question and answer, *esp.* in religious doctrine; **the C.,** the formulae expressing the religious principles of the Church of England. [L.].

CATECHIST [ka'ti-kist], *n.* one who teaches by means of a catechism; church official who instructs in the principles and doctrines of religion. CATECHISTIC(AL), *adj.* having the form of a catechism. CATECHISTICALLY, *adv.* in a catechistical way.

CATECHIZE [ka'ti-kīz], *v.t.* to instruct by asking set questions in a definite order with the answers already formulated and supposed to have been learnt by heart; question thoroughly. CATECHIZATION [ka-ti-kī-zā'shn], *n.* procedure or act of catechizing. [Gk.].

CATECHU, CASHOO [ka'te-chŏŏ, ka'shŏŏ], *n.* astringent substance obtained from the *Acacia catechu*. CATECHUIC [ka-te-chŏŏ'ik], *adj.* consisting of, or pertaining to, c. [Malay].

CATECHUMEN [ka-ti-kyŏŏ'men], *n.* convert

ōō is pronounced as in food; ŏŏ as in hood; th as in think; TH as in that; zh as in azure. ∼ = related to.

obtaining religious education before being baptized; novice, beginner; person taught orally. [Gk.].

CATEGORICAL [ka-ti-go'rik(-al)], *adj.* belonging or pertaining to a category; absolute, positive, unqualified, not conditional. CATEGORICALLY, *adv.* in a c. way.

CATEGORY [ka'ti-ge-ri], *n.* class or group of which the individual members or elements share certain common characteristics; one of the ten basic forms of thought existing in the understanding independent of experience. [Gk.].

CATELECTRODE [ka-ti-lek'trŏd], *n.* the negative electrode of a battery. [Gk.].

CATENA [ka-tē'nah], *n.* a chain; series of arguments.

CATENARY (1) [ka-tē'na-ri], *n.* (geom.) the curve formed by a chain of uniform weight and strength hanging freely between two points of suspension placed at the same height. CATENARY (2), *adj.* having the form of a chain, like a chain.

CATER [kā'ter], *v.i.* to provide food or amusement. CATERER, *n.* person who caters. CATERING, *n.* business of providing food, *esp.* in public restaurants. [OFr.].

CATERPILLAR [ka'ter-pi-ler], *n.* larva of a moth or butterfly; endless jointed band of strong material, running over two or more wheels, to enable vehicles to traverse rough ground; **c. tractor,** motor vehicle driven by caterpillars for drawing very heavy loads over rough ground; **c. wheel,** large wheel with broad divided tread for use on rough ground. [OFr.].

CATERWAUL [ka'ter-wawl], *v.i.* to make a noise like a howling cat. [ME.].

CAT-FALL [kat'fawl], *n.* (naut.) a rope to draw up the anchor.

CAT-FISH [kat'fish], *n.* a fish with cat-like whiskers.

CATGUT [kat'gut], *n.* strong resilient cord made from the twisted intestines of animals, used as strings for musical instruments, for stitching wounds etc. [Uncert.].

CAT-HARPINGS [kat'hah-pingz], *n.(pl.)* (naut.) ropes used to tighten the shrouds.

CATHARSIS [ka-thah'sis], *n.* (med.) cleansing of the body by purging; (fig.) emotional and moral purgation. [Gk.].

CATHARTIC (1) [ka-thah'tik], *n.* a purgative.

CATHARTIC(AL) (2), *adj.* purgative. [Gk.].

CATHARTINE [ka-thah'tēn], *n* the bitter principle of senna.

CATHEAD (1) [kat'hed], *n.* (naut.) pair of bars projecting from the sides of a ship's bows and bearing pulley blocks at their outer extremities for weighing anchor. CATHEAD (2), *v.t.* (naut.) to secure to the c.

CATHEDRA [ka-thē'drah], *n.* bishop's throne; **ex c.,** with authority. [Gk.].

CATHEDRAL (1) [ka-thē'dral], *n.* the principal church in a diocese, in which the bishop's throne is set. CATHEDRAL (2), *adj.* pertaining to, possessing, regarded as, a c. [Prec.].

CATHERINE-WHEEL [ka'the-rin-wēl], *n.* (arch.) circular window with divisions radiating outwards from a common centre; (pyr.) firework which rotates like a wheel when set alight [St. Catherine, martyred on a wheel].

CATHETER [ka'thi-ter], *n.* (surg.) slender tubular instrument used to draw off urine or other fluid from the body. [Gk.].

CATHODE [ka'thŏd], *n.* (elect) the negative electrode; (radio) the filament of a thermionic valve which emits a stream of electrons to the anode. [Gk.].

CATHODE-RAY [ka-thŏd-rā'], *n.* (usu. pl.) (elect.) a negative emission at the cathode of a vacuum tube; **c. tube,** tube in which a minute beam of electrons is controlled by plates of various potentials and directed to a fluorescent screen at the end.

CATHOLIC (1) [ka'tho-lik], *n.* member of the Catholic Church; a Roman Catholic; **C. Church,** the Christian Church in all its sects; the Roman Catholic Church. CATHOLIC (2), *adj.* universal, applicable to all, embracing all people and all things, liberal, comprehensive, impartial, broad-minded; pertaining to the Catholic Church or to Roman Catholics. [Gk.].

CATHOLICISM [ka-tho'li-sizm], *n.* the religious doctrine, liturgy and observances of Catholics; state of being a Catholic.

CATKIN [kat'kin], *n.* long fluffy hanging flower of the willow or hazel etc. [Dim. of CAT].

CATLING [kat'ling], *n.* (surg.) small knife for delicate work in amputation.

CATMINT [kat'mint], *n.* scented plant like mint.

CAT-O'-NINE-TAILS [kat-o-nin'tālz], *n.* whip with nine thongs or knotted cords used for scourging prisoners.

CATOPTRIC [ka-top'trik], *adj.* pertaining to catoptrics.

CATOPTRICS [ka-top'triks], *n.* (opt.) study of reflected light. [Gk.].

CAT'S CRADLE [kats-krā'dl], *n.* game played with a length of string, its ends tied together, alternately lifted by each of two players from the fingers of the other on to his own, to form fresh and more intricate symmetrical designs.

CAT'S EYE [katz'ī], *n.* chrysoberyl, a semi-precious opalescent stone.

CATSMEAT [kats'mēt], *n.* meat, usually horseflesh, sold for feeding cats.

CAT'S PAW [kats'paw], *n.* a dupe, person tricked into acting on behalf of another in a dangerous or illegal undertaking; (naut.) slight breeze; hitch twisted in the bight of a rope for hooking on tackle.

CAT'S TAIL [kats'tāl], *n.* (bot.) one of several plants and grasses resembling the catkin, the horse-tail etc.

CAT'S WHISKER [kats'wis-ker], *n.* fine wire used in a crystal wireless receiving set.

CATTISH [ka'tish], *adj.* feline; (fig.) spiteful, vindictive.

CATTLE [ka'tl], *n.(pl.)* domesticated farm beasts such as cows, bulls, oxen. [OFr.].

CATTY [ka'ti], *adj.* cat-like; cattish; spiteful.

CAUCASIAN (1) [kaw-kā'zhn], *n.* one living in the Caucasus; member of the white races of man. CAUCASIAN (2), *adj.* of or pertaining to the Caucasus or to the white races of man.

CAUCUS [kaw'kus], *n.* small committee of people privately formed to decide policy and tactics for electoral purposes or for arranging administrative details. [Unkn.].

CAUDAL [kaw'dal], *adj.* relating to a tail; having a tail. [L.].

CAUDATE [kaw'dāt], *adj.* (bot.) having a tail or tail-like appendage. [L.].

CAUDILLO [kow-THē'lyo], *n.* the head of the Spanish government after the Civil War of 1936-9. [Span.].

CAUDLE [kaw'dl], *n.* hot spiced drink, warm gruel mixed with wine for invalids. [L.].

CAUGHT [kawt], *pret. and p.pt.* of CATCH.

CAUL [kawl], *n.* membrane covering the fœtus. [OFr.].

CAULDRON, CALDRON [kawl'dron], *n.* large bowl-shaped kettle or boiler of copper or iron. [OFr. from L.].

CAULIFLOWER [ko'li-flow-er], *n.* variety of cabbage, with a large white edible flower. [L.].

CAULK, CALK [kawlk], *v.t.* to make water-tight by filling in the seams of a ship's hull or deck with oakum, tow and pitch; stop a crack. CAULKING, CALKING, *n.* process of making a ship's seams watertight; a mixture of oakum, tow and pitch. [OFr., L.].

CAUSAL (1) [kaw'zal], *n.* (gram.) word introducing a phrase or clause expressing a reason or cause. CAUSAL (2), *adj.* expressing or pertaining to a cause. CAUSALLY, *adv.* in a c. sequence or manner.

CAUSALITY [kaw-za'li-ti], *n.* state of being a cause; operation of cause and effect.

CAUSATION [kaw-zā'shn], *n.* act of causing, progress from cause to effect. CAUSATIONAL, *adj.* pertaining to c. CAUSATIONIST, *n.* person who believes that every event occurs in causal sequence.

CAUSATIVE [kaw'za-tiv], *adj.* able to cause an effect, causing; (gram.) expressing cause. CAUSATIVELY, *adv.* in a c. fashion.

CAUSE (1) [kawz], *n.* the motivating force or inspiration of any act; the person or thing which produces, or contributes to, an effect; that which moves a person to action, a reason, motive; the principle, ideal or interest to which are devoted the energies, beliefs and fervour of a person or group; object of thought and action held as an end in itself; lawsuit, case, grounds for litigation; **c. célèbre,** famous lawsuit. CAUSE (2), *v.t.* to effect, bring about, produce, induce, actuate. [OFr. from L.].

CAUSERIE [kō-ze-rē'], *n.* gossip, light discussion, particularly in a newspaper; any short and informal essay or article. [Fr.].

CAUSEWAY [kawz'wā, kaw'zi], *n.* stone-paved roadway; highway; raised pavement at the side of a thoroughfare. [OFr. from L.].

CAUSTIC (1) [kaw'stik], *n.* substance which burns or corrodes. CAUSTIC (2), *adj.* corrosive, burning or eating away or into; (fig.) sharp, severe, sarcastic;

The accent ′ after a syllable = stress (u-pon′)   The mark ‾ over a vowel = length (ā in made; ō in bone)

c. curve, (*phys.*) curve of light rays which are reflections from a curved surface; **c. soda**, sodium hydroxide. CAUSTICITY, *n.* property of being c. [Gk.].

CAUTERIZE [kaw'te-rīz], *v.t.* to apply heat with a caustic or a hot iron, *esp.* to diseased tissue; sear. CAUTERIZATION [kaw-te-rī-zā'shn], *n.* (*med*) process of cauterizing. [Gk.].

CAUTERY [kaw'te-ri], *n.* process of cauterizing; hot iron used as a cauterizing instrument.

CAUTION (1) [kaw'shn], *n.* prudence, carefulness; deliberate care when expecting danger; warning, reproof, admonition; (*coll.*) mischievous child or person. CAUTION (2), *v.t.* to give a warning or c. to. CAUTIONER, *n.* one who cautions. [L.].

CAUTIONARY [kaw'shn-a-ri], *adj.* acting or designed to act as a warning, cautioning.

CAUTIOUS [kaw'shŏos], *adj.* exercising caution, careful, wary. CAUTIOUSLY, *adv.* in a c. fashion.

CAVALCADE [ka-val-kād'], *n.* official procession, procession on horseback; historical sequence. [Fr. from It.].

CAVALIER (1) [ka-va-lēer'], *n.* horseman; knight; gentleman escort, lady's man, dashing gallant; (*hist.*) follower of Charles I in the Civil War. CAVALIER (2), *adj.* gay, free and easy; disdainful, haughty, off-hand. [Fr.].

CAVALRY [ka'val-ri], *n.* (*milit.*) troops mounted on horseback. [Fr. from L.].

CAVATINA [ka-va-tē'nah], *n.* (*mus.*) short simple melody. [It.].

CAVE (1) [kāv], *n.* space hollowed out of the earth, subterranean den or chamber in a rock or cliff; anything resembling this; group of seceders from a political party. CAVE (2), *v.i.* †to hollow out; **to c. in**, to fall in; (*fig.*) give in. [Fr. from L.].

CAVE (3) [kā'vi], *int.* (*school slang*) have care; beware. [L.].

CAVEAT [kā'vi-at], *n.* a warning; (*leg.*) notice to bring about a temporary cessation of proceedings. CAVEATOR [kā'vi-ā-taw(r)], *n.* person who enters a c. [L.].

CAVEATING [kā'vi-ā-ting], *n.* (*fencing*) a disengaging of one's sword.

CAVE-MAN [kāv'man], *n.* prehistoric man dwelling in a cave; (*slang*) a boisterous, virile male.

CAVENDISH [ka'ven-dish], *n.* cake of tobacco mixed with molasses. [Uncert.].

CAVERN [ka'vern], *n.* deep hollow in the earth, underground cave. CAVERNED, *adj.* with caverns; cavernous. CAVERNOUS, *adj.* resembling a c., full of caverns, hollow. [L.].

CAVIAR, CAVIARE [ka'vi-ah(r)], *n.* roe of the sturgeon salted and prepared for eating; (*fig.*) that which is relished only by a highly developed taste. [Turk.].

CAVIL (1) [ka'vil], *n.* trivial objection, quibble, sophism. CAVIL (2), *v.i.* to quibble, carp, raise unnecessary objections. CAVILLER, *n.* person who cavils. CAVILLING, *adj.* quibbling, raising captious objections. CAVILLINGLY, *adv.* carpingly. [L.].

CAVITY [ka'vi-ti], *n.* hollow place or part. [Fr. from L.].

CAVORT [ka-vawt'], *v.i.* (*coll.*) to frisk about like a horse.

CAVY [kā'vi], *n.* small rodent, any species of *Cavia*, as the guinea-pig. [Fr. from Braz.].

CAW (1) [kaw], *n.* hoarse cry of a rook. CAW (2), *v.i.* to utter the cry of a rook. [Echoic].

CAXTON [kak'ston], *n.* book printed by Caxton; (*typ.*) type similar to that used by Caxton. [W. Caxton, first English printer].

CAYENNE PEPPER [kā-yen-pe'per], *n.* a red and very pungent pepper. [Braz.].

CAYMAN, CAIMAN [kā'man], *n.* variety of South American tropical alligator. [Carib.].

CEASE [sēs], *v.t. and i.* to stop, discontinue, leave off; cut short, pull up; desist; come to an end, finish. [L.].

CEASE-FIRE [sēs-fīer'], *n.* (*milit.*) command to stop hostilities.

CEASELESS [sēs'les], *adj.* continuous, unending. CEASELESSLY, *adv.*

CEDAR (1) [sē'der], *n.* coniferous evergreen tree having a fragrant wood. CEDAR (2), *adj.* made of c.; **c. bird**, American waxwing; **c. oil**, oil extracted from a species of juniper. CEDARED, *adj.* covered or planted with cedars. CEDARN, *adj.* belonging to, or made of, c. [Gk.].

CEDE [sēd], *v.t. and i.* to yield, surrender, submit; allow. [L.].

CEDILLA [si-di'lah], *n.* sign resembling a comma

sometimes placed under the letter *c* in French or Portuguese. [Span.].

CEIL [sēl], *v.t.* to cover over with a ceiling, plaster a ceiling. [~L.].

CEILING [sē'ling], *n.* the inside surface of a house roof, upper side of a room, layer of plaster spread under the timber which supports an overhead floor; (*aeron.*) altitude above which an aeroplane cannot fly; highest price which may be charged for an article. [*Prec.*].

CELANDINE [se'lan-dīn], *n.* **greater c.**, the swallow wort; **lesser c.**, the pilewort. [Gk.].

CELANESE [se-la-nēz'], *n.* (*prot.*) proprietary brand of artificial silk fabrics.

CELEBRANT [se'li-brant], *n.* person who celebrates; officiating priest. [L.].

CELEBRATE [se'li-brāt], *v.t.* to praise, honour publicly, commemorate by an official ceremony, commend; remember the past with joy and ritual; (*slang*) have a good time. CELEBRATED, *adj.* widely praised, well known, renowned.

CELEBRATION [se-li-brā'shn], *n.* act of celebrating, a festivity. [L.].

CELEBRITY [se-leb'ri-ti], *n.* status of being widely known for important achievements, fame, renown; a celebrated or greatly distinguished person. [Fr. from L.].

CELERIAC [se-le'ri-ak], *n.* turnip-rooted variety of celery, which sprouts biennially.

CELERITY [se-le'ri-ti], *n.* speed, swiftness. [L.].

CELERY [se'le-ri], *n.* a vegetable having edible stalks. [Gk.].

CELESTE [si-lest'], *n.* (*mus.*) name of an organ stop. [Fr.].

CELESTIAL (1) [si-les'ti-al], *n.* a Chinaman. CELESTIAL (2), *adj.* belonging to the heavens or sky, heavenly, divine; (*fig.*) excellent; having the colour of the sky; **C. Empire**, the former Chinese Empire. CELESTIALLY, *adv.* in a c. fashion. [OFr.].

CELESTINE [se'les-tēn], *n.* (*min.*) sulphate of strontium. [It.].

CELIAC [sē'li-ak], *adj.* belonging or referring to the lower abdomen. [COELIAC].

CELIBACY [se'li-ba-si], *n.* condition of being unmarried.

CELIBATARIAN (1) [se-li-ba-tāer'i-an], *n.* person who favours celibacy. CELIBATARIAN (2), *adj.* favouring celibacy.

CELIBATE (1) [se'li-bat], *n.* one who is unmarried. CELIBATE (2), *adj.* unmarried.

CELL [sel], *n.* small room in a prison; monk's or nun's small room; hut or small refuge of a hermit; single unit of a whole composed of similar units, particularly a unit of a honeycomb; subsidiary, often secret, unit of a political organization; (*biol.*) smallest unit of living tissue; (*elect.*) one complete unit in a battery, containing a single pair of metallic elements. [L.].

CELLAR [se'ler], *n.* storeroom beneath ground level, basement used for storage purposes, vault; a stock of wine. [L.].

CELLARAGE [se'la-rij], *n.* cellars; space for cellars, storage capacity of a cellar or cellars; charge for storage in a cellar.

CELLARER [se'la-rer], *n.* monk looking after the monastery cellars; any person detailed to look after a cellar; wine merchant.

CELLARET [se-la-ret'], *n.* case, or cupboard in a sideboard, fitted for storing wine etc.

CELLED [seld], *adj.* having cells, being in the form of cells.

CELLIFORM [se'li-fawm], *adj.* cell-shaped.

CELLIST [che'list], *n.* a violoncellist.

CELLO [che'lō], *n.* a violoncello.

CELLOPHANE [se'lō-fān], *n.* (*prot.*) transparent material made of wood pulp and used as a wrapping paper.

CELLULAR [se'lyŏo-ler], *adj.* containing or consisting of cells; porous; **c. tissue**, an organic mass of minute living cells. CELLULATED, *adj.* formed with or composed of cells.

CELLULE [se'lyŏol], *n.* a small cell. [L.].

CELLULOID (1) [se'lyŏo-loid], *n.* synthetic substance, consisting of cellulose treated with camphor, used as a substitute for bone, ivory etc., and as a base for photographic film. CELLULOID (2), *adj.* consisting of or pertaining to c.; **c. base**, (*phot.*) negative film before being treated with sensitized emulsion. [L. and Gk.].

CELLULOSE (1) [se'lyŏo-lōs], *n.* chemical substance obtained from the cell walls of vegetables or plants, extensively used in the manufacture of artificial silk, paints etc. CELLULOSE (2), *adj.* consisting of cells, cellular; pertaining to or containing c. CELLULOSE (3), *v.t.* to paint with a c. preparation.

CELSIUS (1) [sel'si-us], *n.* the scale of the Centigrade thermometer. CELSIUS (2), *adj.* Centigrade. [A. *Celsius*, inventor].

CELT (1), **KELT** [selt, kelt], *n.* member of those peoples whose languages include Welsh, Breton, Gaelic and Erse. [L., Gk.].

CELT (2) [selt], *n.* (*archae.*) prehistoric flint-cutting implement. [L.].

CELTIC [kel'tik, sel'tik], *n. and adj.* one of the languages of the Celts; pertaining to the Celts. CELTICISM [kel'ti-sizm, sel'ti-sizm], *n.* custom or idiom peculiar to the Celts.

CEMENT (1) [si-ment'], *n.* substance compounded of ground limestone and water which, when placed in thin layers between stones or bricks, hardens rapidly and binds them firmly together; any adhesive substance used for securing joints; (*fig.*) that which has the power of uniting people, groups or units. CEMENT (2), *v.t.* to join together, or cause to cohere, with c.; (*fig.*) unite firmly; effect a firmer or closer alliance, consolidate. [L.].

CEMENTATION [sē-men-tā'shn], *n.* process of cementing or of being cemented; (*chem.*) process of surrounding a solid body with another powdered substance or substances, and fusing them together by heat to produce a chemical change; conversion of iron into steel by covering the iron with powdered charcoal and heating.

CEMETERY [se'mi-te-ri], *n.* burying-place, piece of ground, having no parish church on it, consecrated for the burial of the dead. [Gk.].

CENOBITE [sē'nō-bīt], *n.* member of a religious order, living continually in a convent. CENO-BITIC(AL) [sē-nō-bi'tik(-al)], *adj.* living in community, participating in a communal life. [~Gk.].

CENOTAPH [se'nō-tahf], *n.* monument or tomb not containing the body of the person whose life and death it commemorates; the monument raised in Whitehall, London, commemorating British soldiers killed in the Wars of 1914-18 and 1939-45. [Gk.].

CENSE [sens], *v.t.* to burn incense. [CENSER].

CENSER [sen'ser], *n.* vessel designed for burning incense in. [OFr.].

CENSOR (1) [sen'ser], *n.* official authorized by a public body to ban books, plays, films or other material for publication, on the grounds of their containing matter injurious to morals or religion, libellous or seditious; one charged with suppressing news publication and examining private correspondence, *esp.* in wartime, to ensure that information is withheld from the enemy; officer appointed by the University of Oxford to supervise men students not attached to a college; (*hist.*) officer in ancient Rome with duties of tax-collecting, census-taking and protecting public morals. CENSOR (2), *v.t. and i.* to do the work of a c., examine material for the purpose of censorship; delete or suppress by authority. [L.].

CENSORIAL [sen-saw'ri-al], *adj.* belonging to a censor.

CENSORIOUS [sen-saw'ri-ŏŏs], *adj.* given to censure; severe in criticism; expressing censure.

CENSORSHIP [sen'ser-ship], *n.* act of censoring; office, duties or tenure of a censor.

CENSURE (1) [sen'shŏŏr], *n.* blame, condemnation, criticism, admonition, imputation of wrong. CEN-SURE (2), *v.t.* to blame, reproach; admonish, reprimand; stigmatize; find fault with; condemn after judgment. [L.].

CENSUS [sen'sus], *n.* official count of a country's population, hence, any official collection of statistics. [L.].

CENT [sent], *n.* abbreviation of L. *centum* one hundred; hundredth part of any unit, as of a U.S. dollar; name of an American coin of this value; **per c.**, rate by the hundred, rate of interest in units of a hundred; **hundred per c.**, (*slang*) wholly, completely. [L.].

CENTAL [sen'tal], *n.* hundred pounds weight, particularly of corn.

CENTAUR [sen'taw(r)], *n.* creature of mythological origin, half man and half horse. [Gk.].

CENTAURY [sen'taw-ri], *n.* (*bot.*) plant having medicinal properties. [Prec.].

CENTENARIAN [sen-te-nāer'i-an], *n.* person a hundred years of age or more.

CENTENARY (1) [sen-tē'na-ri], *n.* period of a

hundred years; commemoration after a hundred years. CENTENARY (2), *adj.* relating to a hundred or a c. [L.].

CENTENNIAL (1) [sen-te'ni-al], *n.* a centenary. CENTENNIAL (2), *adj.* lasting or having lived a hundred years; happening once every hundred years. [L.].

CENTERING [sen'te-ring], *n.* (*arch.*) temporary frame supporting an arch or vault while under construction.

CENTESIMAL [sen-te'si-mal], *n. and adj.* hundredth part; hundredth. [L.].

CENTI-, *pref.* one hundred; (*metric system*) one hundredth. [L.].

CENTIGRADE [sen'ti-grād], *adj.* graded into a hundred degrees; **c. thermometer**, thermometer having the interval between the freezing and the boiling points of water divided into 100 deg. [L.].

CENTIGRAM(ME) [sen'ti-gram], *n.* one-hundredth part of a gramme.

CENTILITRE [sen'ti-lē-ter], *n.* one-hundredth part of a litre.

CENTILLION [sen-til'yon], *n.* the one-hundredth power of one million.

CENTIME [sah(ng)'tēm], *n.* coin of the value of one-hundredth part of a franc. [Fr. from L.].

CENTIMETRE [sen'ti-mē-ter], *n.* one-hundredth part of a metre.

CENTIPEDE [sen'ti-pēd], *n.* many-legged wingless arthropod. [L.].

CENTNER [sent'ner], *n.* German measure of weight of 110·2 pounds avoirdupois. [L.].

CENTO (*pl.* **centos**) [sen'tō], *n.* form of composition in literature or music made up of selections from the works of various writers or musicians; anthology. [L.].

CENTRAL [sen'tral], *adj.* pertaining to or situated in or near the centre of anything; accessible, important, chief; **c. heating**, system of heating a building by a series of pipes heated from a single boiler. CENTRALISM, *n.* quality of being concentrated in a centre; centralization of government or control. CENTRALIST, *n.* one who advocates centralization in government. CENTRALITY [sen-tra'li-ti], *n.* quality or state of being c. CENTRALLY, *adv.* in a c. position, in the centre, accessibly.

CENTRALIZATION [sen-tra-li-zā'shn], *n.* act of centralizing, act of concentrating at one centre the government of a country or the administration and directorate of a large business firm.

CENTRALIZE [sen'tra-līz], *v.t.* to draw to a centre, concentrate in one place or at one point.

CENTRE (1) [sen'ter], *n.* (*geom.*) the point round which a circle is described, the point in a circle or sphere which is equidistant from all points on the circumference, a point equally distant from two extremities; (*fig.*) point or position round which persons or objects are grouped, person or object in the middle; important position in the middle of an environment in which a particular activity is carried on, the environment itself; (*phys.*) that point in a body acting as a pivot for some particular activity or phenomenon; (*pol.*) party standing for a moderate programme holding principles which are neither entirely reactionary nor entirely revolutionary; (*sport*) player in the middle of a line, *esp.* **c. forward**, player occupying the middle position of five forwards in association football; **c. of gravity**, (*phys.*) the point about which all the parts of the body exactly balance each other, whether in motion or at rest. CENTRE (2), *v.t.* to place on or in the c., determine the central point of, draw towards the middle, concentrate in the middle; (*association football*) kick the ball towards the middle of the field, *esp.* in front of goal; (*fig.*) concentrate; *v.i.* to be concentrated at a point, be moved towards the middle, be placed on or in the middle, converge. CENTRE (3), *adj.* central. [Gk.].

CENTRE-BIT [sen'ter-bit], *n.* boring tool worked with a brace, and rotating on a projecting central point.

CENTREBOARD [sen'ter-bawd], *n.* adaptable keel fitted to a boat, which can be raised or lowered as desired.

CENTRE-PIECE [sen'ter-pēs], *n.* ornament in the centre of a table.

CENTRIC [sen'trik], *adj.* central. CENTRICALLY, *adv.* in a central position, centrally. CENTRICITY [sen-tri'si-ti], *n.* quality or state of being c.

CENTRIFUGAL [sen-tri'fyŏŏ-gal], *adj.* tending to move away from the centre of a revolving body; (*bot.*) (of a plant's flowers) opening at the centre before those at the outside; **c. force.** (*phys.*) the force which impels a revolving body to fly outwards from the centre. [Gk. and L.].

CENTRING [sen'tring], *n.* a moving towards the centre.

CENTRIPETAL [sen-tri'pi-tal], *adj.* tending to move towards the centre; (*bot.*) (of a plant's flowers) opening first at the outside; (*biol.*) proceeding from the periphery to the nerve-centre. [Gk. and L.].

CENTROBARIC [sen-trō-ba'rik], *adj.* belonging to the centre of gravity. [L. and Gk.].

CENTUPLE (1) [sen'tyŏŏ-pl], *adj.* hundredfold. CENTUPLE (2), *v.t.* to multiply a hundredfold.

CENTURION [sen-tyŏŏ'ri-on], *n.* (*hist.*) officer in the Roman army having command of a century. [L.].

CENTURY [sen'tyŏŏ-ri], *n.* period of a hundred consecutive years; any period of a hundred years following on the conventionally accepted year of Christ's birth; a hundred things of the same kind, a collective hundred, particularly a hundred runs made by a batsman in an innings at cricket; (*hist.*) Roman company of infantry, originally numbering a hundred men; **c. plant,** American aloe or agave. [L.].

CEPHAL(O)-, *pref.* head. [Gk.].

CEPHALIC [se-fa'lik], *adj.* of, or relating to, the head; **c. index,** (*anthrop.*) the ratio of length to breadth in a skull. [Gk.].

CEPHALOPOD [se'fa-lō-pod], *n.* member of the class of molluscs having tentacles growing from the head, as octopus, squid etc. [Gk.].

CERACEOUS [se-rā'shŏŏs], *adj.* waxy, or resembling wax. [L.].

CERAMIC, KERAMIC [se-ra'mik, ke-ra'mik], *adj.* relating to pottery. CERAMICS, *n.* art of making objects with clay, pottery. [Gk.].

CERASIN [se'ra-sin], *n.* gum formed by the cherry and the plum. [L.].

CERASTES [se-ras'tēz], *n.* horned venomous snake, species of viper. [Gk.].

CERATE [sēer'āt], *n.* ointment composed of wax, oil etc. CERATED, *adj.* smeared or covered with wax. [L.].

CERBEREAN [ser-bēer'i-an], *adj.* (*myth.*) pertaining to Cerberus, the three-headed dog guarding the entrance to hell. [Gk.].

CEREAL (1) [sēer'i-al], *n.* plant which bears edible grain; the grain itself; breakfast food made from this. CEREAL (2), *adj.* pertaining to or made from edible grain. [L.].

CEREALIN [sēer'i-a-lin], *n.* (*chem.*) substance containing nitrogen found in bran.

CEREBELLAR [se-ri-be'ler], *adj.* pertaining to the cerebellum.

CEREBELLUM [se-ri-be'lum], *n.* (*anat.*) the tissue of nerves forming the hinder and lower part of the brain. [L.].

CEREBRAL [se'ri-bral], *adj.* relating to the brain; **c. hemispheres,** the two main sections of the brain. CEREBRALISM, *n.* theory that the mind works according to the actions of the brain. [L.].

CEREBRATION [se-ri-brā'shn], *n.* action of the brain. [L.].

CEREBRIN(E) [se'ri-brin], *n.* (*chem.*) a substance obtained from the brain.

CEREBRO-SPINAL [se-ri-brō-spī'nal], *adj.* (*anat.*) relating to or connected with both brain and spine; **c. meningitis,** an epidemic affection of the membranes surrounding the cerebrum and spine, spotted fever.

CEREBRUM [se'ri-brum], *n.* the higher nerve-centre of the brain. [L.].

CERECLOTH [sēer'kloth], *n.* cloth smeared with wax used for shrouding a corpse.

CEREMENT [sēer'ment], *n.* (*usu. pl.*) winding-sheet smeared with wax, grave-clothes. [Fr.].

CEREMONIAL (1) [se-ri-mō'ni-al], *n.* a sequence of customs and rites in formal order, observed on a solemn occasion, and expressing reverence; ritual. CEREMONIAL (2), *adj.* pertaining to ceremony. CEREMONIALISM, *n* ritualism. CEREMONIALLY, *adv.* in a c. fashion.

CEREMONIOUS [se-ri-mō'ni-ŏŏs], *adj.* characterized by ceremony, ritualistic, deferential, formal, courteous. CEREMONIOUSLY, *adv.* in a c. fashion. CEREMONIOUSNESS, *n.* condition of being c.

CEREMONY [se'ri-mu-ni], *n.* an act, or series of acts or rites in a formal order, observed in public for the expression of reverence in honour of a solemn event; formality of manners, courteousness; **master of**

ceremonies, person who superintends the order of events at a public function. [L.].

CEREOUS [sēer'i-ŏŏs], *adj.* waxen; resembling wax. [L.].

CERES [sēer'ēz], *n.* Roman goddess of nature, mother of the earth. [L.].

CERIPH. see SERIF.

CERISE (1) [se-rēs'], *n.* a tint of red with a tone of purple in it, the colour of a ripe cherry. CERISE (2), *adj.* having the colour of c. [Fr.].

CERIUM [sēer'i-um], *n.* (*chem.*) a greyish malleable metal, the chemical element denoted by Ce.

CERO-, *pref.* wax. [Gk.].

CEROGRAPHY [se-ro'gra-fi], *n.* art of engraving on wax; painting in coloured wax. [Gk.].

CERT [surt], *n.* (*slang*) a certainty, particularly a racehorse regarded as certain to win. [CERT(AINTY)].

CERTAIN [sur'ten], *adj.* sure, positive, unequivocal, beyond doubt, undisputed; inevitable, accurate; fixed, accepted; unspecified, some, more than one. [OFr. from L.].

CERTAINLY [sur'ten-li], *adv.* surely, without doubt, without fail.

CERTAINTY [sur'ten-ti], *n.* that which is certain; assurance, conviction; security.

CERTIFIABLE [sur'ti-fī-a-bl], *adj.* able or liable to be certified insane.

CERTIFICATE [ser-ti'fi-kat], *n.* a document which certifies a fact; written testimony bearing official recognition of achievement or fact; authorized statement. [CERTIFY].

CERTIFY [sur'ti-fī], *v.t. and i.* to make certain; give assurance, give a certificate; testify officially in writing; judge insane. CERTIFICATION [ser-ti-fi-kā'shn], *n.* act of certifying. [Fr. from LL.].

CERTITUDE [sur'ti-tyŏŏd], *n.* certainty; assurance. [LL.].

CERULEAN [si-rŏŏ'li-an], *adj.* a deep blue having a transparent quality, sky-blue. [L.].

CERULIN [sē'rŏŏ-lin], *n.* substance of intense blueness obtained from indigo.

CERUMEN [si-rŏŏ'men], *n.* the yellow wax secreted by the ear. [L.].

CERUSE [sē'rŏŏs], *n.* white lead, a carbonate of lead used as white paint.

CERUSSITE [se'ru-sīt], *n.* (*min.*) carbonate of lead, white lead ore.

CERVICAL [ser-vī'kal, sur'vi-kal], *adj.* of, or relating to, the neck. [L.].

CERVINE [sur'vin], *adj.* relating to a stag or deer. [L.].

CESAREWITCH [se-zah're-vich], *n.* the eldest son or successor of the Russian Tsar; horserace at Newmarket, run in late autumn. [~TSAR].

CESPITOSE [ses'pi-tōs], *adj.* (*bot.*) growing in tufts. [~L.].

CESSATION [se-sā'shn], *n.* a stoppage, ceasing; pause; rest. [L.].

CESSION [se'shn], *n.* (*leg.*) act of formal surrender. [L.].

CESSPIT [ses'pit], *n.* cesspool.

CESSPOOL [ses'pŏŏl], *n.* pit for the sewage from a house. [Uncert.].

CESTOID [ses'toid], *n.* tapeworm. [Gk.].

CETACEAN [si-tā'shn], *n.* whale, dolphin. CETACEOUS, *adj.* relating to the cetaceans. [Gk.].

CETIC [se'tik], *adj.* relating to the whale; obtained from spermaceti. [*Prec.*].

CETIN(E) [sē'tin], *n.* crystalline mass of spermaceti.

CETYL [sē'til], *n.* radical principle in spermaceti. [Gk.].

CHABLIS [shah-blē'], *n.* a white Burgundy wine. [*Chablis,* France].

CHACONNE [sha-kon'], *n.* stately Spanish dance; slow music for this dance. [Span.].

CHAFE [chāf], *v.i.* to rub against, fret, be made sore by rubbing; (*fig.*) fret, be goaded or fretted into impatience; *v.t.* to rub so as to make warm, abrade, rub till sore; (*fig.*) cause anger, goad. [OFr. from L.].

CHAFER [chā'fer], *n.* winged beetle which feeds on leaves. [OE.].

CHAFF (1) [chaf, chahf], *n.* the husk of grain; fodder of finely chopped straw; (*fig.*) worthless matter; banter. CHAFF (2), *v.t.* to banter. [OE.].

CHAFFER (1) [cha'fer], *n.* bargaining, haggling over prices. CHAFFER (2), *v.t. and i.* to bargain, haggle. [OE., ME.].

CHAFFINCH [cha'finch], *n.* small British bird. [OE.].

CHAFFY [cha'fi, chah'fi], *adj.* similar to or full of

---

chaff; light; spurious, worthless; full of jokes and banter.

CHAFING-DISH [chā′fing-dish], *n.* portable stove; dish heated at table.

CHAGRIN (1) [sha-grēn′], *n.* annoyance, vexation; ill-humour. **CHAGRIN** (2), *v.t.* to fret, vex. [Fr.].

CHAIN (1) [chān], *n.* a number of circular or oval metal links, each link passing through the next; a fetter; device for measuring land, consisting of 100 links, equal to 66 ft.; (*pl.*) bondage, imprisonment; (*fig.*) sequence of similar things or ideas connected in series. **CHAIN** (2), *v.t.* to secure or fasten with a c.; confine by chains, fetter; (*fig.*) bind, restrain, restrict the freedom of. [OFr. from L.].

CHAIN-BELT [chān′belt], *n.* a chain in the form of a driving belt running on sprockets in a machine.

CHAIN-BRIDGE [chān′brij], *n.* suspension bridge supported by chains from points higher than road level.

CHAIN-GANG [chān′gang], *n.* a number of prisoners, each secured to the next by a chain.

CHAINLESS [chān′les], *adj.* having no chains; out of bondage, free.

CHAIN-LETTER [chān-le′ter], *n.* letter intended to be forwarded by each recipient in turn.

CHAIN-LIGHTNING [chān-lit′ning], *n.* forked lightning flashing continuously

CHAIN-MAIL [chān′māl], *n.* armour of interwoven rings.

CHAIN-PUMP [chān′pump], *n.* pump in which the liquid is elevated by a series of small buckets secured at intervals on a rotating endless belt.

CHAIN-SHOT† [chān′shot], *n.* (*milit.*) two cannon-balls joined together by a length of chain.

CHAIN-SMOKER [chān′smō-ker], *n.* person who smokes cigarettes in unbroken succession.

CHAIN-STITCH [chān′stich], *n.* (*sewing*) an arrangement of stitches to form a chain; stitch made with two threads.

CHAIN-STORE [chān′staw(r)], *n.* one of a series of shops owned and operated by a single firm.

CHAIR (1) [chāer], *n.* movable seat made of various materials with a seat, usually four legs and a back-rest; block of steel which secures a railway line to a sleeper; (*fig.*) seat of authority, post of university professor, chairmanship of a meeting; (*U.S.*), the electric chair, execution. **CHAIR** (2), *v.t.* to carry a person on high throu,⅃ a public throng as a token of enthusiasm for an achievement. [OFr. from Gk.].

CHAIRMAN [chāer′man], *n.* person presiding over a meeting; principal director of a commercial company; sedan-chair or bath-chair attendant.

CHAIRMANSHIP [chāer′man-ship], *n.* status of a chairman.

CHAISE [shāz], *n.* light one-horsed four-wheeled carriage; **c. longue**, sofa or couch. [Fr.].

CHALCEDONY, CALCEDONY [kal-se′do-ni], *n.* one of various forms of translucent quartz valued as semi-precious. **CHALCEDONIC, CALCEDONIC** [kal-si-do′nik], *adj.* relating to c.

CHALCOGRAPHY [kal-ko′gra-fi], *n.* art of engraving on copper. [Gk.].

CHALDAIC [kal-dā′ik], *n. and adj.* pertaining to Chaldea or its inhabitants; their language.

CHALDRON [chawl′dron], *n.* a measure of coal of one ton and a quarter. [OFr.].

CHALET [sha′lā], *n.* a Swiss cottage, hut built on a mountain side; summer bungalow. [Swiss Fr.].

CHALICE [cha′lis], *n.* (*eccles.*) sacramental cup. **CHALICED**, *adj.* (*bot.*) possessing a cell or cup. [L.].

CHALK (1) [chawk], *n.* opaque, soft, earthy, white limestone; the geological rock strata in which this is found; material consisting of or similar to chalk for drawing or sketching purposes; a mark made with chalk; **french c.**, soapstone; **not to know c. from cheese**, not to recognize things obviously different; **better by a long c.**, being far more likely to win or score, thus finer by a considerable degree. **CHALK** (2), *v.t.* to make a mark with c.; (*fig.*) score, record the score in a game. [OE. from L.].

CHALKPIT [chawk′pit], *n.* pit from which chalk is obtained.

CHALKY [chaw′ki], *adj.* containing, or resembling, chalk. **CHALKINESS**, *n.* quality or state of being c.

CHALLENGE (1) [cha′lenj], *n.* a provocation or deliberate defiance; a call to account; invitation to a contest or athletic competition, incitement to prove one's skill or strength; sentry's call; objection to a person as a member of a jury. **CHALLENGE** (2), *v t.* to make a c. to; call in question; claim (attention etc.). **CHALLENGEABLE**, *adj.* liable or able to be

challenged. **CHALLENGER**, *n.* one who challenges. **CHALLENGINGLY**, *adv.* in such a manner as to convey a c. [OFr. from L.].

CHALYBEATE (1) [ka-li′bi-at], *n.* water or a liquor into which iron has entered. **CHALYBEATE** (2), *adj.* containing iron. [Gk.].

CHAM [kam], *n.* Oriental despot; literary dictator. [KHAN].

CHAMADE [sha-mahd′], *n.* (*milit.*) signal given by trumpet or drum to retreat or call a truce. [Portug. from L.].

CHAMBER (1) [chām′ber], *n.* apartment, room in a house or public building, room of a high official such as lawyer or judge; large room in which legislative bodies assemble; assembly of such bodies itself; apartment rented for lodging in; cavity, hollow space; chamber-pot; (*milit.*) the part of a gun's breech made to hold the projectile or charge. **CHAMBER** (2), *v.t. and i.* to make a hollow, hollow out; be residing in a c. **CHAMBERED**, *adj.* divided into compartments. [OFr. from L.].

CHAMBER-COUNSEL [chām′ber-kown-sel], *n.* (*leg.*) barrister giving his opinion in chambers, but not pleading in court.

CHAMBERLAIN [chām′ber-lin], *n.* the officer in charge of the private apartments of a king or noble; treasurer of a corporation or city; **Lord C.**, the head of the Royal Household. **CHAMBERLAINSHIP**, *n.* rank or office of a c. [OFr.].

CHAMBERMAID [chām′ber-mād], *n.* female servant whose task is to keep the bedrooms clean and tidy.

CHAMBER-MUSIC [chām′ber-myōō-zik], *n.* music to be played in a room by a few performers as distinct from music to be played by a full orchestra in a public hall.

CHAMBER-POT [chām′ber-pot], *n* bedroom utensil to receive urine.

CHAMBER-PRACTICE [chām′ber-prak-tis], *n.* the practice of a chamber-counsel.

CHAMBERS [chām′berz], *n.(pl.)* apartments situated in the Inns of Court; private rooms in the law courts for settling cases or details of routine.

CHAMBERTIN [shahm′bār-ta(ng)], *n.* a rich red Burgundy wine. [*Chambertin*, France].

CHAMELEON (1) [ka-mē′li-on], *n.* one of a genus of lizard with the power of changing its colour to match its surroundings. **CHAMELEON** (2), pertaining to the c ; (*fig.*) changeable, inconstant. [Gk.].

CHAMFER (1) [cham′fer], *n.* a bevel cut at the line of union of two planes. **CHAMFER** (2), *v.t.* to cut a bevel in. [OFr.].

CHAMOIS (1) [sha′mwah], *n.* agile horned animal of the antelope kind found in Europe. **CHAMOIS** (2) [sha′mi], *n.* soft leather made from the skin of the chamois. [Fr.].

CHAMOMILE, see **CAMOMILE**.

CHAMP [champ], *v.t. and i.* (of a horse) to keep biting with the teeth; (*fig.*) chew; crunch, munch. [Uncert.].

CHAMPAGNE [sham-pān′], *n.* a light and effervescent French wine. [*Champagne*, district in France].

CHAMPAIGN [cham′pān], *n.* a stretch of level open country. [OFr. from L.].

CHAMPERTY [cham′per-ti], *n.* (*leg.*) illegal bargain with one of the parties in a lawsuit to share what may be recovered in the suit in return for sharing the cost. [Fr. from L.].

CHAMPION (1) [cham′pi-on], *n.* defender of a cause, faith, title or another person; person proved as superior to all others in skill or strength; expert in skill or strength; expert in a form of athletics; animal winning the first prize in a show. **CHAMPION** (2), *adj.* (*dial.*) finest, best. **CHAMPION** (3), *v.t.* (*fig.*) to defend, support (a cause).

CHAMPIONSHIP [cham′pi-on-ship], *n.* rank or status of champion, position of a winner of a series of eliminating contests; a contest or series of contests held to find a champion at a particular sport.

CHANCE (1) [chahns], *n.* the result of untraced causes; course of events, occurrence; unforeseen circumstance; luck, fortune; opportunity, possibility, probability; **on the (off) c.**, acting on the (unlikely) possibility that something may happen; **the main c.**, personal interest. **CHANCE** (2), *adj.* fortuitous, happening by chance, accidental, unforeseen. **CHANCE** (3), *v.t. and i.* to happen; occur, experience by accident; (*coll.*) risk, dare, take a gamble on; **to c. upon**, to meet or find unexpectedly.

CHANCECOMER [chahns′ku-mer], *n.* person who comes by chance.

CHANCEL [chahn′sel], *n.* the eastern part of a church

---

in which the clergy and choir sit during service; that part of a church where the altar is, and usually railed off. [OFr., L.].

CHANCELLERY [chahn'se-le-ri], *n.* position or department of a chancellor; offices of an embassy; **the chancelleries of Europe**, diplomatic circles.

CHANCELLOR [chahn'se-ler], *n.* the title of certain high officials; **c. of a diocese**, legal adviser to a bishop; **C. of the Duchy of Lancaster**, minister of the Crown who exercises certain special duties in relation to Crown lands in the Duchy of Lancaster; **C. of the Exchequer**, the minister of finance; **Lord High C.**, keeper of the Great Seal, the principal judge presiding over the House of Lords. CHANCELLORSHIP, *n.* office and tenure of a c. [OFr. from L.].

CHANCERY [chahn'se-ri], *n.* division of the High Court of Justice, presided over by the Lord Chancellor; the offices of a diplomatic mission. [*Var.* of CHANCELLERY.]

CHANCRE [shang'ker], *n.* venereal ulcer. CHANCROUS, *adj.* (*med.*) ulcerous. [Fr.].

CHANCY [chahn'si], *adj.* (*coll.*) risky; uncertain.

CHANDELIER [shan-de-lêer'], *n.* a fitting usually in the form of symmetrical brackets or arms, hanging from the ceiling for holding a number of lights, formerly candles. [CANDLE].

CHANDLER [chahnd'ler], *n.* candlemaker; dealer in soap, candles etc.; **ship's c.**, seller of ship's provisions. CHANDLERY, *n.* articles sold by a c. [CANDLE].

CHANGE (1) [chānj], *n.* an alteration, variation or replacement of one thing for another; variety; a passing from one condition or state to another, transition; coins of low denomination given as equivalent in value for coins of higher denomination; money in excess of the purchase price returned by the seller to the buyer of a commodity; (*coll.*) the Exchange; the order in which a chime of bells is rung; (*fig.*) **to ring the changes on**, to repeat in different forms. [Fr. from LL.].

CHANGE (2), *v.t.* to make a change or modification; cause to become different; substitute or adopt one thing for another; alter the order or nature of a thing or person; exchange coins of lower denomination equivalent in value to higher; *v.i.* to undergo a c., become different, be in a state of transition, pass into a new phase; undress and put on different clothes; move from one train to another; **to c. over**, to move to a new position, adopt a new system etc.; **to c. with**, to exchange. [OFr.].

CHANGEABLE [chān'ja-bl], *adj.* liable to change; capable of being changed, variable, inconstant. CHANGEABILITY, CHANGEABLENESS [chān-ja-bi'li-ti, chān'ja-bl-nes], *n.* quality or condition of being c. CHANGEABLY, *adv.* in a c. fashion.

CHANGEFUL [chānj'fŏŏl], *adj.* constantly changing, full of change; inconstant, fickle. CHANGEFULLY, *adv.* in a c. fashion. CHANGEFULNESS, *n.* condition or quality of being c.

CHANGELESS [chānj'les], *adj.* unchanging, immutable.

CHANGELING [chānj'ling], *n.* child substituted for another; any substitute.

CHANGE-OVER [chānj'ō-ver], *n.* act of changing to a new position, system etc.

CHANGE-RINGING [chānj'ring-ing], *n.* practice of ringing peals of bells in varying order.

CHANNEL [cha'nel], *n.* watercourse, bed of a river; deep in a harbour or bay taking the main current; narrow sea between two land-masses and joining two seas; groove, passage or duct naturally or artificially formed to carry water; (*fig.*) path, means of communication. CHANNELLED, *adj.* grooved lengthwise, connected by means of channels. [OFr.].

CHANSON [shah(ng)-son(ng)'], *n.* song; **c. de geste**, medieval French narrative heroic poem. [Fr.].

CHANSONETTE [shah(ng)-so-net'], *n.* short song, ditty. [Fr.].

CHANT (1) [chahnt], *n.* song, melody, one which accompanies church canticles; words in a church service, half sung, half recited. CHANT (2), *v.t. and i.* to sing a song; recite poetry; repeat monotonously; intone. [Fr. from L.].

CHANTER [chahn'ter], *n.* person who chants; solo singer; tenor or treble pipe in a bagpipe.

CHANTICLEER [chahn'ti-klêer], *n.* a cock, especially one which crows lustily and clearly. [OFr.].

CHANTRY [chahn'tri], *n.* endowment of a chapel in which a priest is to chant Mass daily for the soul of the founder or other deceased person; chapel or part of a chapel so endowed. [OFr.].

CHANTY [shan'ti], *n.* a sailors' shanty.

CHAOS [kā'os], *n.* the formless confusion, the abyss, supposed to have existed before the creation of the universe; state of anything before it is put in order; disorder, muddle. [Gk.].

CHAOTIC [kā-o'tik], *adj.* having or resembling the nature of chaos; confused. CHAOTICALLY, *adv.* in c. fashion.

CHAP (1) [chap], *n.* (*coll.*) boy, man, fellow. [CHAPMAN].

CHAP (2), *n.* jaw; **Bath c.**, dressed pig's cheek. [Uncert.].

CHAP (3) (*pres.pt.* chapping, *pret. and p.pt.* chapped), *v.t. and i.* to cause a crack or cracks or soreness, particularly in the skin. CHAP (4), *n.* a crack, slit, particularly on the skin. [~CHOP].

CHAPBOOK [chap'bŏŏk], *n.* small book, pamphlet or tract of popular tales and verses sold by chapmen.

CHAPEL [cha'pel], *n.* small building for worship, generally belonging to or part of a church; part of a church with an altar; hall used for worship in a remote part of a parish; private place of worship; place of worship for Nonconformists; section of printers' or allied workers' trade-union, meeting held by these workers. [OFr., L.].

CHAPERON (1) [sha'pe-rŏn], *n.* responsible person, usually a married or elderly lady, in charge of a young unmarried girl in assemblies where men are present. CHAPERON (2), *v.t.* to act as a c. CHAPERONAGE, *n.* duty of a c. [Fr.].

CHAPFALLEN, CHOPFALLEN [chap'faw-len], *adj.* having the lower jaw drooping; dejected.

CHAPITER [cha'pi-ter], *n.* (*arch.*) a capital. [Fr.].

CHAPLAIN [chap'lin], *n.* clergyman appointed to serve official bodies such as the army. CHAPLAINCY, CHAPLAINSHIP, *n.* office or rank of a c. [OFr.].

CHAPLET [chap'let], *n.* wreath, garland or band worn round the crown of the head; rosary. [OFr.].

CHAPMAN [chap'man], *n.* hawker, pedlar. [OE.].

CHAPTER [chap'ter], *n.* one of the main sections of a book; heading, principal topic or aspect, episode; Act of Parliament; decretal epistle; governing body of a cathedral church presided over by the dean; meeting held by such a body; **c. of accidents**, series of misfortunes; **c. and verse**, exact authority. [OFr.].

CHAPTER-HOUSE [chap'ter-hows], *n.* building attached to a cathedral in which the chapter meets.

CHAR (1) [chah(r)], *n.* species of trout. [Gael.].

CHAR (2), *n.* charwoman.

CHAR (3) (*pres.pt.* charring, *pret. and p.pt.* charred), *v.i.* to do housework for payment by the hour. [OE.].

CHAR (4) (*pres.pt.* charring, *pret. and p.pt.* charred), *v.t.* to reduce to charcoal by burning; burn partially. [Uncert.].

CHAR-A-BANC, CHARABANC [sha'ra-bang], *n.* long open brake or motor car with seats for many people; motor coach. [Fr.].

CHARACTER (1) [ka'rak-ter], *n.* inscribed mark, letter or alphabetical symbol, symbol; style of letter forms; mark which distinguishes, peculiarity; qualities which give individuality to a person, expressive habits of a person in action and emotional reaction; good reputation; (*biol.*) the peculiarities typical of the species; written estimate of mental and physical abilities, testimonial; person well known for certain individual traits or achievements; odd individual, eccentric; person taking part in the action of a play or novel; the representation on the stage by an actor of a person; **c. actor**, one who plays highly individual or eccentric parts (as distinct from more commonplace rôles). CHARACTER (2), *v.t.* to characterize, describe a character; inscribe. [Gk.].

CHARACTERISTIC (1) [ka-rak-te-ris'tik], *n.* that which constitutes or exposes the character, an individual feature or peculiarity, mental or physical. CHARACTERISTIC (2), *adj.* pertaining to or revealing character; typical. CHARACTERISTICALLY, *adv.* in a c. fashion. [Gk.].

CHARACTERIZE [ka'rak-te-riz], *v.t.* to expose the character of, give character to; distinguish; describe the peculiar qualities of. CHARACTERIZATION [ka-rak-te-ri-zā'shn], *n.* act of characterizing, descriptive or dramatic portrayal of character. [Gk.].

CHARACTERLESS [ka'rak-ter-les], *adj.* possessing little distinctive character.

CHARADE [sha-rahd'], *n.* a riddle game, usually in

the form of extempore dramatizations of the syllables of a word. [Fr.].

CHARCOAL [chah′kōl], *n.* the residue of partially burnt wood etc., being an impure form of carbon. [CHAR (4) and COAL].

CHARGE (1) [chahj], *n.* a full loading, *esp.* of something meant to be emptied out, such as muskets or glasses; the thing loaded; the electricity contained in a battery; liability, tax, claim or debt; price demanded or extracted for a thing; a debit entry; injunction, exhortation, obligation; responsibility for something, control, jurisdiction over; that for which responsibility is assumed; judicial instruction and command; formal accusation of some crime; furious approach to attack; (*her.*) a bearing on an escutcheon. [OFr.].

CHARGE (2), *v.t. and i.* to load, fill with; fill with electricity; ask payment for something, make a claim, exhort, enjoin; entrust someone with something; (*leg.*) accuse, make a charge against, instruct a jury; run violently against, make a violent rush. [OFr.].

CHARGEABLE [chah′ja-bl], *adj.* able to be charged for; attributable.

CHARGE D'AFFAIRES, chargé d'affaires [shah-zhā-da-fāer′], *n.* ambassador's deputy in his absence; diplomatic representative to or from a minor state. [Fr.].

CHARGE-HAND [chahj′hand], *n.* in factories, a workman in charge of certain tasks, under the supervision of a foreman.

CHARGER (1) [chah′jer], *n.* battle horse. [CHARGE (2)].

CHARGER (2), *n.* large dish for carrying joints. [OFr.].

CHARGE-SHEET [chahj′shēt], *n.* list of offenders taken into custody by the police, with the charges against them.

CHARILY [chāer′i-li], *adv.* cautiously, warily.

CHARINESS [chāer′i-nes], *n.* quality of being chary, prudence.

CHARIOT [cha′ri-ot], *n.* two- or four-wheeled horse-drawn vehicle. [OFr.].

CHARIOTEER [cha-ri-ta-tēer′], *n.* one who drives a chariot.

CHARITABLE [cha′ri-ta-bl], *adj.* generous to the needy, benevolent; giving help of various kinds to the necessitous without asking payment, with a tendency to judge others favourably. CHARITABLE-NESS, *n.* condition of being c. CHARITABLY, *adv.* in c. fashion. [OFr.].

CHARITY [cha′ri-ti], *n.* the fact, act or quality of being charitable; liberality, generosity without expectation or call for repayment of any kind; Christian love of others; compassion, benevolence; an institution or trust with a charitable object. [L.].

CHARIVARI [shah-ri-vah′ri], *n.* mock serenade of discordant music; satirical journal. [Fr.].

CHARLATAN [shah′la-tan], *n.* quack, impostor, flaunter of sham learning and skill. CHARLATANIC-(AL) [shah-la-ta′nik(-al)], *adj.* pertaining to a c. [It.].

CHARLATANISM [shah′la-ta-nizm], *n.* quality of being a charlatan, quackery.

CHARLATANRY [shah′la-tan-ri], *n.* charlatanism.

CHARLES'S WAIN [chahl-ziz-wān′], *n.* (*astron.*) the Plough, seven stars in the constellation of the Great Bear. [OE.].

CHARLESTON [chahlz′ton], *n.* energetic ballroom dance popular in the nineteen-twenties. [*Charleston*, U.S.A.].

CHARLOCK [chah′lok], *n.* wild mustard. [OE.].

CHARLOTTE [shah′lot], *n.* a sweet, usually made with apples, consisting of the fruit, sugar and breadcrumbs baked together; **c. russe,** sweet having sponge-cake and cream as its basis. [Queen *Charlotte*].

CHARM (1) [chahm], *n.* incantation with supposed magical effect, magical or occult effect or influence; trinket or ornament believed to possess magical powers for aiding the wearer; (*fig.*) quality of attractiveness, indefinable fascination. CHARM (2), *v.t.* to bewitch, influence by magic, reduce to service and affection by magic or apparent magic; (*fig.*) enchant, fascinate. [Fr. from L.].

CHARMER [chah′mer], *n.* one who charms, fascinates; attractive young woman; one who tames snakes.

CHARMEUSE [shah-murz′], *n.* kind of rich dress material. [Fr.].

CHARMING [chah′ming], *adj.* delightful, attractive.

CHARNEL-HOUSE [chah′nel-hows], *n.* place where corpses are kept, any place reeking of death, or dismally morbid. [OFr. from L.].

CHARPIE [shah′pi], *n.* lint used for dressing wounds. [Fr.].

CHART (1) [chaht], *n.* a navigation map, recording features and dangers of the sea or coast; any detailed map or plan; graph. CHART (2), *v.t.* to make a c. of. [Fr. from L.].

CHARTER (1) [chah′ter], *n.* document granting or confirming rights, properties etc.; manifesto of rights and liberties claimed by the people for themselves. CHARTER (2), *v.t.* to hire a vessel, hire any vehicle; grant a c. to. CHARTERED, *adj.* holding some right or position by virtue of a c.; (*fig.*) acting as though under c. [OFr.].

CHARTER-PARTY [chah′ter-pah-ti], *n.* an agreement concerning the hire of a vessel and the freight. [Fr.].

CHARTISM [chah′tizm], *n.* early nineteenth-century radicalism whose supporters demanded universal suffrage and other democratic reforms. [The People's *Charter*, programme of the movement, published in 1838].

CHARTIST [chah′tist], *n.* follower of chartism.

CHARTREUSE [shah-trurz′], *n.* a Carthusian monastery; fine liqueur made by the Carthusians. [Fr.].

CHARTREUX [shah-trur′], *n.* a Carthusian.

CHARWOMAN [chah′wōō-man], *n.* woman who chars. [CHAR (3)].

CHARY [chāer′i], *adj.* doubtful, cautious, hesitating. [OE.].

CHASE (1) [chās], *v.t. and i.* to pursue (an animal) in order to catch and kill; hunt; drive away by pursuing in threatening fashion, drive out; rush about for some purpose. CHASE (2), *n.* act of chasing, *esp.* **the c.,** hunting; quarry pursued; land in which game is bred and hunted; liberty to hunt over certain land. [OFr.].

CHASE (3), *n.* the part of a cannon taking the charge; (*print.*) metal frame for holding type when it has been set up. [OFr.].

CHASE (4), *v.t.* to engrave on metal. [OFr.].

CHASER [chā′ser], *n.* one who chases; (*naut.*) gun at bow or stern; (*eng.*) flat tool with a serrated edge for cutting screw-threads in a lathe; (*coll.*) a drink immediately following another. [CHASE (1) and (4)].

CHASING [chā′sing], *n.* chased work on metal; patterns so engraved on the metal.

CHASM [kazm], *n.* deep cleft in the earth, deep and alarming gap; (*fig.*) irreconcilable division of outlook. [Gk.].

CHASSE, chassé [sha′sā], *n.* a gliding step in ballroom dancing. CHASSE, *v.i.* to make this step. [Fr.].

CHASSIS [sha′si], *n.* the frame or skeleton on which other components are mounted, as of a motor vehicle, radio set etc. [Fr.].

CHASTE [chāst], *adj.* continent, sexually pure, undefiled; (*fig.*) clean and simple in design. CHASTELY, *adv.* in c. fashion. [Fr. from L.].

CHASTEN [chā′sn], *v.t.* to punish for a just cause, particularly to humble pride and insolence; restrain. CHASTENED, *adj.* subdued in spirit as though punished. [OFr. from L.].

CHASTENING [chā′sn-ing], *adj.* humbling, punishing, restraining.

CHASTISE [chas-tīz′], *v.t.* to punish with justice, chasten and restrain erring or unruly inferiors as by beating; beat. [CHASTEN].

CHASTISEMENT [chas′tiz-ment], *n.* process of chastising, corporal punishment.

CHASTITY [chas′ti-ti], *n.* quality or condition of being chaste, virgin purity; (*fig.*) restraint. [OFr.].

CHASUBLE [cha′zyōō-bl], *n.* outer vestment worn over the alb by the priest officiating at Mass. [MedL.].

CHAT (1) [chat], *n.* bird of the thrush family. [CHATTER].

CHAT (2) (*pres.pt.* **chatting,** *pret. and p.pt.* **chatted**), *v.i.* to converse lightly and informally on casual subjects. CHAT (3), *n.* casual talk of a light, informal kind, idle conversation; chatter. BACK-CHAT, brightly offensive questions and answers. [CHATTER].

CHATEAU [shah′tō], *n.* French castle or large country house. [Fr.].

CHATELAINE [sha′te-lān], *n.* the lady of a house, hostess; lady's chain to hold keys etc. [Fr.].

CHAT-POTATOES [chat-po-tā′tōz], *n.*(*pl.*) small

The accent ′ after a syllable = stress (u-pon′). The mark ‾ over a vowel = length (ā in made; ō in bone).

potatoes unfit for the market; also CHATS. [Unkn.].
CHATTEL [cha′tel], *n.* a possession; (*leg.*) movable article of property. [OFr.].
CHATTER (1) [cha′ter], *v.i.* to talk rapidly and pointlessly, talk with careless indiscretion; click together rapidly and continuously; jabber rapidly, utter shrill inarticulate cries. CHATTER (2), *n.* rapid, casual talk; noise made by monkeys, magpies etc. [ME.].
CHATTERBOX [cha′ter-boks], *n.* chatterer.
CHATTERER [cha′te-rer], *n.* one who chatters, talkative person; (*ornith.*) bird related to the wax-wing.
CHATTY [cha′ti], *adj.* talkative.
CHAUCERIAN [chaw-sēer′i-an], *adj.* pertaining to or resembling Chaucer and his works. [*Chaucer*, English poet.].
CHAUFFEUR [shō-fur′], *n.* servant employed to drive a private motor-car. [Fr.].
CHAUFFEUSE [shō-furz′], *n.* woman chauffeur.
CHAUVINISM [shō′vi-nizm], *n.* nationalist militarism, jingoism. CHAUVINIST, *n.* devotee of c. [*Chauvin*, supporter of Napoleon].
CHEAP [chēp], *adj.* low in price, inexpensive; second-rate, in bad taste, vulgar, facile. CHEAPLY, *adv.* at a low price. CHEAPNESS, *n.* quality of being c. [OE.].
CHEAPEN [chē′pen], *v.t. and i.* to make cheap; degrade; become cheap, lessen in value.
CHEAP-JACK [chēp′jak], *n.* hawker of cheap articles.
CHEAT (1) [chēt], *v.t. and i.* to trick, deceive, swindle; escape from; break some rule in order to gain an unfair advantage. CHEAT (2), *n.* one who cheats, fraud, trickster; a deception, sham. CHEATING, *n.* being a c. at cards, unfair play. CHEATINGLY, *adv.* in cheating fashion. [ESCHEAT].
CHECK (1) [chek], *n.* an obstruction, rebuff, interference with progression, sudden slowing down or hesitation; control or supervision or the means of supervising; record of some event or action kept for purposes of comparison; token or pledge of identification, cloakroom ticket; bill, invoice; cheque; notification in chess that a piece threatens the opposing king, the situation when a king is so threatened; chessboard pattern, pattern of alternate dark and light coloured squares, fabric of such a pattern. CHECK (2), *adj.* with squares alternately light and dark. CHECK (3), *v.t. and i.* to obstruct, cause to slow down, interrupt, hinder, restrain; verify, test; threaten the king in chess; (*naut.*) ease off a rope; come to a stop, hesitate. [OFr. from Pers.].
CHECK-BOOK, see CHEQUE BOOK.
CHECKER (1) [che′ker], *n.* one who checks.
CHECKER (2), see CHEQUER.
CHECKER-WORK, see CHEQUER-WORK.
CHECKMATE (1) [chek-māt′], *n.* the winning position in chess, when a king is in such a situation that he would inevitably be taken at the next move; (*fig.*) move or situation by which someone's plans are brought to an impotent standstill. CHECKMATE (2), *v.t.* (*chess*) to bring one's opponent to c.; (*fig.*) frustrate. [Arab.].
CHECK-REIN [chek′rān], *n.* coupling strap between harness and bridle preventing the horse from lowering its head.
CHECK-ROLL [chek′rōl], *n.* list of employees in an office or works, used to check attendance, pay etc.
CHECKWEIGHER [chek′wā-er], *n.* colliery worker who represents the miners and checks the amount of coal mined.
CHEDDAR [che′der], *n.* variety of cheese. [*Cheddar*, Somerset].
CHEEK (1) [chēk], *n.* one of the two fleshy sides of the face, one of two corresponding sides; (*fig. and coll.*) insolence, pert rudeness. CHEEK (2), *v.t.* (*coll.*) to insult impertinently. [OE.].
CHEEK-BONE [chēk′bōn], *n.* bone supporting the cheek.
CHEEKY [chē′ki], *adj.* (*slang*) impertinent.
CHEEP (1) [chēp], *n.* shrill chirrup of a young bird. CHEEP (2), *v.i.* to utter a c. CHEEPER, *n.* young bird. [Imitative].
CHEER (1) [chēer], *n.* mood, state of mind; encouragement; shout of triumph and delight, roar of applause; entertainment, rich food. CHEER (2), *v.t. and i.* to encourage, make or be made cheerful; enliven; applaud. CHEERER, *n.* one who cheers. [OFr. from LL.].
CHEERFUL [chēer′fŏŏl], *adj.* full of cheer, brightly

happy, inspiriting, bright. CHEERFULLY, *adv.* in c. fashion. CHEERFULNESS, *n.* condition of being c.
CHEERILY [chēer′i-li], *adv.* in cheery fashion.
CHEERING (1) [chēer′ing], *n.* the sound of cheers, continuous cheers. CHEERING (2), *adj.* gladdening, encouraging, tending to make cheerful. CHEERINGLY, *adv.* in c. fashion.
CHEERIO [chēer-i-ō′], *int.* good-bye; *also used as an informal toast.*
CHEER-LEADER [chēer′lē-der], *n.* person whose duty it is to lead the cheers at a sports meeting.
CHEERLESS [chēer′les], *adj.* joyless, dreary, gloomy. CHEERLESSNESS, *n.* condition of being c.
CHEERY [chēer′i], *adj.* heartily cheerful, bright.
CHEESE (1) [chēz], *n.* milk-curd compressed into a solid mass; various substances resembling cheese; heavy wooden disk used in playing skittles. CHEESE (2), *v.t.* (*slang*) **to c. it,** to stop, desist. [OE.].
CHEESECAKE [chēz′kāk], *n.* cake made from curds, sugar and butter.
CHEESEPARING (1) [chēz′pāer-ing], *n.* thin piece of rind cut from a cheese; (*fig.*) stinginess. CHEESEPARING (2), *adj.* pettily mean, stingy.
CHEESY [chē′zi], *adj.* tasting, smelling or looking like cheese.
CHEETAH [chē′tah], *n.* Indian hunting leopard. [Skr.].
CHEF [shef], *n.* head male cook, chief cook in a restaurant. [Fr.].
CHEF-D′OEUVRE [shā-durvr′], *n.* masterpiece.
CHEIROPTERA [kīer-op′te-rah], *n.* the order of flying mammals. [Gk.].
CHEKA [chā′kah], *n.* Soviet Russian secret police. [Russ.].
CHELONIA [ke-lō′ni-ah], *n.(pl.)* class of reptiles including tortoises and turtles. CHELONIAN, *adj.* pertaining to the c. [Gk.].
CHELSEA [chel′sē], *n.* artists' quarter of London; **C. bun,** kind of rolled currant bun; **C. pensioner,** inmate of the C. Royal Hospital; **C. ware,** porcelain made in C. in the eighteenth century.
CHEMICAL [ke′mi-kal], *n. and adj.* (substance) used or made in chemistry; pertaining to chemistry. CHEMICALLY, *adv.* in accordance with the principles of chemistry, by chemical process.
CHEMIN DE FER [she-ma(ng)-de-fāer′], *n.* form of baccarat. [Fr.].
CHEMISE [she-mēz′], *n.* woman's undergarment. [Fr.].
CHEMIST, CHYMIST† [ke′mist], *n.* one practising or skilled in chemistry; trader in drugs. [ALCHEMIST].
CHEMISTRY, CHYMISTRY† [ke′mis-tri], *n.* science of the properties of elements and their combinations and of the behaviour and reactions of substances to each other.
CHENILLE [she-nēl′], *n.* tufted silk or cotton cord used in embroidery work. [Fr.].
CHEQUE [chek], *n.* bill of exchange or draft by which a bank is authorized by a client to make a payment to another person from funds held by the bank on his behalf; printed form on which this instruction is given. CHEQUE (1).].
CHEQUE-BOOK, CHECK-BOOK [chek′bŏŏk], *n.* blank cheques issued bound in convenient bookform.
CHEQUER (1), **CHECKER** [che′ker], *n.* check pattern, pattern of alternate squares of different colour. CHEQUER (2), CHECKER, *v.t.* to mark in check pattern; variegate, cause to alternate between opposites; **chequered career,** career marked by very varying fortune. [OFr. from L.].
CHERISH [che′rish], *v.t.* to hold very dear, protect, show great solicitude for; keep in mind. [OFr. from ~L.].
CHERISHING [che′ri-shing], *adj.* so as to cherish. CHERISHINGLY, *adv.* in c. fashion.
CHERMES, see KERMES.
CHEROOT [she-rōŏt′], *n.* small strong cigar, open at both ends. [Tamil].
CHERRY (1) [che′ri], *n.* fruit of the genus *Cerasus;* tree bearing this fruit. CHERRY (2), *adj.* relating to a c., or the wood of the c. tree; red. [OFr. from Gk.].
CHERRY-BRANDY [che-ri-bran′di], *n.* sweet liqueur made by steeping cherries in brandy.
CHERRY-PIE [che-ri-pī′], *n.* pie made with cherries; purple heliotrope.
CHERRY-PIT [che′ri-pit], *n.* children's game of throwing cherry-stones into a hole.
CHERUB (*pl.* **cherubs, cherubim**) [che′rub], *n.*

ōō is pronounced as in food; ŏŏ as in hood; th as in *think*, TH as in *that*; zh as in azure. ~ = related to.

angel next in order to the seraphim; beautiful, chubby childlike angel; (coll.) pretty, rosy-cheeked chubby child. [Heb.].

CHERUBIC(AL) [che-rōō'bik(-al)], adj. pertaining to or like a cherub, angelic; chubby and rosy-cheeked.

CHERVIL [chur'vil], n. herb used for flavouring. [OE. from Gk.].

CHESIL [che'zil], n. shingle. [OE.].

CHESS [ches], n. game of skill played with thirty-two pieces upon a board of sixty-four squares. [OFr.].

CHESSMAN [ches'man], n. a piece used in chess.

CHEST [chest], n. large heavy box with a lid for storage; financial office of an institution, treasury; (anat.) front part of the body between throat and abdomen, thorax; (coll.) the lungs; **c. of drawers**, series of drawers arranged above one another in a piece of furniture; **c. of tea**, 108 pounds of tea. CHESTED, adj. having a c.; kept in a c. [OE.].

CHESTERFIELD [ches'ter-fēld], n. long sofa with upright ends; kind of overcoat. [Earl of Chesterfield].

CHESTNUT (1) [chest'nut], n. edible nut of the Castanea vulgaris; bitter, inedible Aesculus hippocastanum or horse-chestnut; the trees bearing either of these; (slang) old, worn out joke; reddish-brown horse. CHESTNUT (2), adj. reddish-brown. [OFr. from Gk. and NUT].

CHEVAL [she-vahl'], n. frame; **c. glass**, tall narrow mirror swung on a frame. [Fr.].

CHEVALIER [she-va-lēer'], n. cavalier; a foreign title of honour; gallant young man. [Fr.].

CHEVIN [che'vin], n. the chub. [OFr.].

CHEVIOT [che'vi-ot], n. sheep bred on the Cheviots; cloth made from the wool of such sheep. [Cheviot Hills].

CHEVRON [she'vron], n. (her.) honourable ordinary representing two rafters of a house meeting at the top; (arch.) V-shaped device, ornament of zigzag work; (milit.) mark on the coat-sleeves of a non-commissioned officer. CHEVRONED, adj. having a c., decorated with chevrons. [OFr.].

CHEVY [che'vi], v.t. to chivy.

CHEW [chōō], v.t. and i. to bite and grind up with the teeth into small pieces, masticate, champ; (fig.) meditate deeply on some problem. [OE.].

CHEWING GUM [chōō'ing-gum], n. sweetened and flavoured preparation of chicle or similar gums, used for masticating.

CHIAN [kī'an], adj. pertaining to the Aegean island of Chios.

CHIANTI [kē-ahn'ti], n. light Italian red wine. [Chianti, Italy].

CHIAROSCURO [kyah-ro-skōō'rō], n. variation in light and shade. [It.].

CHIASM [kī'azm], n. (anat.) an x-shaped crossing of two portions of the optic nerve. [Gk.].

CHIASMUS [kī-az'mus], n. (rhet.) the inversion of word order in a repeated phrase. [Prec.].

CHIC (1) [shik, shēk], n. smartness. CHIC (2), adj. smartly dressed, just right, in good taste. [Fr.].

CHICANE (1) [shi-kān'], n. obstruction by quibble, deceit by verbal subterfuge; (bridge) small score allowed to players holding no trumps. CHICANE (2), v.t. and i. to employ c., cheat by c. [Fr.].

CHICANERY [shi-kā'ne-ri], n. quibbling, the method and employment of chicane, sophistry. [Fr.].

CHICK [chik], n. a very young chicken.

CHICKADEE [chi'ka-dē], n. American titmouse. [Imitative].

CHICKEN (1) [chi'ken], n. young domestic fowl; domestic fowl as a dish; very young, helpless person. CHICKEN (2), adj. made of chicken flesh. [OE.].

CHICKEN-FEED [chi'ken-fēd], n. food for chickens; (fig., coll.) something small and trivial.

CHICKEN-HEARTED [chi-ken-hah'tid], adj. cowardly, spiritless.

CHICKEN-POX [chi'ken-poks], n. pustulous contagious disease, Varicella.

CHICKLING [chik'ling], n. small chicken; vetch.

CHICK-PEA [chik'pē], n. an edible pea. [L.].

CHICKWEED [chik'wēd], n. a creeping plant.

CHICLE [chik'li], n. gum from which chewing gum is prepared. [Mexican].

CHICORY [chi'ke-ri], n. plant which has a root sometimes ground and mixed with coffee. [OFr. from Gk.].

CHIDE (pret. chid, chided; p.pt. chidden, chided) [chid], v.t. and i. to scold, rebuke. [OE.].

CHIDING [chi'ding], n. a scolding, rebuke.

CHIEF (1) [chēf], n. the head of a body of people,

leader of a tribe, head of a clan, native tribal ruler; (coll.) boss, active head of a business; (her.) upper third of an escutcheon. CHIEF (2), adj. principal, supreme, highest of its kind, primary, most important. [OFr. from L.].

CHIEFLY [chēf'li], adv. principally.

CHIEFTAIN [chēf'tan], n. leader and senior man of a clan or tribe, chief. CHIEFTAINCY, CHIEFTAINSHIP, n. rank and rule of a c. [OFr.].

CHIFF-CHAFF [chif'chaf], n. the British warbler. [Imitative].

CHIFFON [shi'fon], n. light gauzy material. [Fr.].

CHIFFONIER [shi-fo-nēer'], n. low sideboard with shelves for ornaments. [Fr.].

CHIGNON [shē'nyo(ng)], n. coil of hair worn by women at the back of the head. [Fr.].

CHILBLAIN [chil'blān], n. painful inflamed swelling on hands and feet, caused by cold and bad circulation of the blood.

CHILD (pl. **children**) [chīld, chil'dren], n. very young infant, unborn infant, young person before the age of puberty, a minor; simple, undeveloped person, very innocent and harmless person; descendant, offspring; disciple, follower; one produced by certain circumstances, one apparently having origin in some class; something produced by something, result of some process. [OE.].

CHILDBEARING [child'bāer-ing], n. childbirth.

CHILDBED [child'bed], n. parturition, state of labour.

CHILDBIRTH [child'berth], n. parturition, act of bringing forth a child.

CHILDERMAS [chil'der-mas], n. Feast of the Holy Innocents (28 December). [OE.].

CHILDHOOD [child'hōōd], n. state of being a child, period before adolescence; **second c.**, extreme senility inducing childishness of mind.

CHILDISH [chil'dish], adj. like a child, innocent, simple; pertaining to, fit for, a child; silly, foolish, ridiculous. CHILDISHLY, adv. in c. fashion. CHILDISHNESS, n. condition of being c.

CHILDLESS [child'les], adj. without children or descendants. CHILDLESSNESS, n. condition of being c.

CHILDLIKE [child'līk], adj. like a child in appearance or outlook; innocent, simple, gullible, unspoilt.

CHILD'S-PLAY [chīldz'plā], n. the play of children; an absurdly easy task.

CHILI, see CHILLI.

CHILL (1) [chil], n. sudden sensation of cold; internal inflammation or illness caused by cold, damp etc.; (fig.) depressing atmosphere. CHILL (2), adj. cold, chilly; dismal, unenthusiastic. CHILL (3), v.t. and i. to make or become c.; strike with a c., make cold internally; depress, make dismal; keep meat cold to preserve it; strengthen steel by suddenly cooling it. [OE.].

CHILLI, CHILI [chi'li], n. dried pod of the capsicum. [Mexican].

CHILLY [chi'li], adj. rather cold, suddenly cold.

CHILTERN [chil'tern], adj. relating to the Chilterns; **C. Hundreds**, nominal stewardship under the Crown, an office which a member of Parliament may accept to obtain his resignation from the House.

CHIME (1) [chīm], n. resonant musical sound of pure timbre, such as is produced by a bell; a bell itself, group of tuned bells set in a church tower, sound made by such bells, sound made by a clock striking the hours; harmony. CHIME (2), v.t. and i. to make, strike or sound chimes; harmonize; **to c. in**, to intervene suddenly in conversation. [L.].

CHIMERA, CHIMAERA [kī-mēer'ah], n. fabulous creature with a lion's head, goat's body and serpent's tail, furious and terrifying beast; imagined but non-existent thing. [Gk.].

CHIMERICAL [ki-me'ri-kal], adj. unfounded, unreasoned and imaginary. CHIMERICALLY, adv. in c. fashion. [Prec.].

CHIMNEY [chim'ni], n. hollow shaft or tube above a fire to carry away the fumes and gaseous products of combustion; vertical glass cylinder surrounding the flame of an oil-lamp; opening of a chimney; narrow cleft in a rock by which a climber can ascend. [OFr.].

CHIMNEY-BREAST [chim'ni-brest], n. projecting part built out of a wall to contain the fireplace in a house.

CHIMNEY-CORNER [chim'ni-kaw-ner], n. inglenook.

CHIMNEY-PIECE [chim'ni-pēs], n. ornamental border set into the wall round a fireplace.

CHIMNEY-POT [chim'ni-pot], n. earthenware tube

The accent ' after a syllable = stress (u-pon'). The mark ‾ over a vowel = length (ā in made; ō in bone).

set at the top end of a house chimney; (coll.) kind of tall silk hat worn by men in the late nineteenth century.

CHIMNEY-STACK [chim′ni-stak], n. tall factory chimney; masonry from which the chimney-pots of a house project.

CHIMNEY-SWEEP [chim′ni-swēp], n. one who clears soot from the insides of chimneys.

CHIMPANZEE [chim-pan-zē′], n. African anthropoid ape. [Native].

CHIN [chin], n. front extremity of the lower jaw. [OE.].

CHINA (1) [chi′nah], n. glazed porcelain ware; household crockery. CHINA (2), adj. made of c.; (fig.) fragile, delicate. [China, where originally made].

CHINA-CLAY [chi′nah-klā], n. kaolin, fine potters' clay.

CHINAMAN [chi′nah-man], n. a native of China.

CHINA-ORANGE [chi-nah-o′rinj], n. the sweet orange, originally imported from China.

CHINATOWN [chi′nah-town], n. Chinese quarter of a city.

CHINAWARE [chi′nah-wāer], n. articles made of china.

CHINCHILLA [chin-chi′lah], n. South American rodent prized for its fur. [Span.].

CHIN-CHIN [chin-chin′], n. (coll.) polite greeting before drinking. [Chin.].

CHINE (1) [chin], n. the back of an animal; a rock ridge. CHINE (2), v.t. to cut along or through the backbone, remove the backbone of a fish. [OFr.].

CHINE (3), n. deep, narrow ravine. [OE.].

CHINEE [chi-nē′], n. (coll.) a Chinese. [Supposed singular form].

CHINESE (1) (pl. **Chinese**) [chi-nēz′], n. a native of China, the language of China; (pl.) the race native to China. CHINESE (2) [chi′nēz], adj. pertaining to China or the Chinese; **C. lantern**, collapsible lantern made of coloured paper and used as a decoration; **C. white**, white oxide of zinc, used as a pigment.

CHINK (1) [chingk], n. long narrow opening, slit. [Unkn.].

CHINK (2), n. sound as of two coins or pieces of glass striking together; (coll.) money. CHINK (3), v.t. and i. to make a light metallic sound, cause (coins) to make this sound. [Imitative].

CHINK (4), n. (coll.) a Chinaman.

CHINOISERIE [shē-nwah′ze-rē], n. Chinese trinket.

CHINOOK [chi-nŏŏk′], n. North-west American Indian tribe; dialect used between the North American traders and the Indian tribes; warm dry wind along the western slope of the Rocky Mountains. [Amer Ind.].

CHINTZ [chints], n. cotton cloth or calico, printed with patterns in different colours. [Hind.].

CHIP (1) [chip], n. small thin strip or splinter of wood, small fragment of brittle substance broken away from a vessel or implement, rough crack or cut left by the breaking away of such a fragment; chip-basket; (pl.) thin slices of fried potato; (cards) counters used in a gambling game; (naut.) small block of wood at the end of a log-line; **a c. of the old block**, one who inherits certain paternal characteristics; **c. shot**, (golf) short lofted approach shot on to a green. CHIP (2) (pres.pt. CHIPPING, pret. and p.pt. CHIPPED), v.t. and i. to cut into chips; break off a c. from; fry slices of potato; (slang) tease, banter; break off in chips; **to c. in**, to intervene in a conversation. [Uncert.].

CHIP-BASKET [chip′bahs-kit], n. light basket of thin plaited strips of wood.

CHIP-HAT [chip-hat′], n. hat manufactured from thin strips of woody fibre or thick straw.

CHIPMUNK [chip′mungk], n. small American ground squirrel. [AmerInd.].

CHIPPENDALE [chi′pen-dāl], n. fine style of furniture made in the eighteenth century. [Thos. Chippendale, cabinet-maker].

CHIPPER [chi′per], adj. (U.S. coll.) lively, cheerful, nimble.

CHIPPING [chi′ping], n. act of cutting off in chips; a chip; the breaking off in chips or pieces from the edges of earthenware; banter.

CHIRO-, pref. hand. [Gk.].

CHIROGNOMY [ki-rog′no-mi], n. judgment of character from the hand. [Gk.].

CHIROGRAPH [ki′rō-grahf], n. (leg.) a formal document, engrossed and duly signed, indenture, charter. [Gk.].

CHIROMANCY [ki′rō-man-si], n. palmistry. [Gk.].

CHIROPODIST [ki-ro′po-dist], n. one skilled in treatment of diseases or disorders of the hands and feet. [Gk.].

CHIROPRACTIC [ki′rō-prak-tik], n. method of healing which relies upon the removal of nerve interference by manual adjustment of the spinal column. CHIROPRACTOR, n. one who practises c. [Gk.].

CHIRP (1) [churp], v.t. and i. to utter a series of short, shrill notes as a bird; speak in a thin, shrill, cheerful voice. CHIRP (2), n. the shrill cry of a bird. CHIRPER, n. chirping bird or insect. CHIRPINGLY, adv. in a chirping fashion. [Imitative].

CHIRPY [chur′pi], adj. (coll.) cheerful, lively.

CHIRR (1) [chur], v.i. to utter the monotonous chirp of the grasshopper or cricket. CHIRR (2), n. the sound itself. [Imitative].

CHIRRUP (1) [chi′rup], v.i. to chirp, twitter. CHIRRUP (2), n. a cheerful, lively chirp. [CHIRP].

CHIRURGEON† [ki-rur′jun], n. surgeon. [OFr. from Gk.].

CHISEL (1) [chi′zel], n. cutting tool having a long steel or iron blade with a bevelled cutting edge at the end. CHISEL (2) (pres.pt. CHISELLING, pret. and p.pt. CHISELLED), v.t. to cut, pare or shape with a c.; (slang) cheat, defraud.

CHISELLED [chi′zeld], adj. cut, as with a chisel, clear-cut, having a bold outline. [Imitative].

CHIT (1) [chit], n. child, inexperienced, immature young woman or girl. [OE.].

CHIT (2), n. short letter, memorandum, certificate. [Hind.].

CHIT-CHAT [chit′chat], n. gossip. [CHAT].

CHITIN [ki′tin], n. hard horny substance forming the protective shell of certain crustaceans and the wing cases of certain insects. [Fr. from Gk.].

CHITTERLINGS [chi′ter-lingz], n.(pl.) part of the smaller intestines, particularly of swine, used as food. [Uncert.].

CHIVALRIC [shi′val-rik, chi′val-rik], adj. pertaining to chivalry, chivalrous.

CHIVALROUS [shi′val-rŏŏs, chi′val-rŏŏs], adj. pertaining to chivalry; endowed with the qualities possessed by the ideal knight, courageous, courteous, noble, protective of the weak. CHIVALROUSLY, adv. in a c. fashion.

CHIVALRY [shi′val-ri, chi′val-ri], n. the organization, institution, aims and spirit of knighthood in the Middle Ages; the body or order of knights; military prowess, knightly skill, display of qualities of an ideal knight, courtesy, nobility, respect for weaker persons. [OFr.].

CHIVE [chiv], n. small onion related to the garlic. [Fr.].

CHIVY (1) [chi′vi], v.t. to chase, cause to run away; (fig.) harass, worry continually, tease persistently. CHIVY (2), n. playground game resembling prisoner's base. [Chevy Chase, ballad].

CHLOASMA [klō-az′mah], n. skin affection characterized by yellowish-brown or dark patches. [Gk.].

CHLOR-, **CHLORO-**, pref. green, containing chlorine. [Gk.].

CHLORAL [klaw′ral], n. (chem.) liquid prepared by passing dry chlorine gas through absolute alcohol; (pop.) white crystalline chloral hydrate used as a hypnotic and anaesthetic. CHLORALISM, n. diseased condition induced by excessive use of c.

CHLORATE [klaw′rāt], n. a salt of chloric acid.

CHLORIC [klaw′rik], adj. of or from chlorine; **c. acid**, an acid of chlorine and hydrogen, $HClO_3$.

CHLORID(E) [klaw′rid], n. a compound of chlorine with another element.

CHLORINATE [klo′ri-nāt], v.t. (chem.) to treat with chlorine. CHLORINATION [klo-ri-nā′shn], n. (chem.) act of chlorinating.

CHLORINE [klaw′rēn], n. heavy greenish gas with a suffocating odour, used as a disinfectant and bleaching agent, and as a poison gas in warfare; the chemical element denoted by Cl. [CHLOR.].

CHLORITE [klaw′rit], n. (geol.) group of soft green minerals consisting of magnesium, iron and aluminium silicates; (chem.) a salt of chlorous acid.

CHLOROFORM (1) [klo′rō-fawm], n. volatile, colourless liquid used as an anaesthetic. CHLOROFORM (2), v.t. to administer c. to in order to render insensible. [CHLORO and FORMIC].

CHLOROPHYLL [klo′rō-fil], n. (bot.) the green colouring matter of plants. [Gk.].

CHLOROSIS [klo-rō′sis], n. (med.) form of anaemia affecting young girls in which the skin assumes a yellowish-green colour, green-sickness; (bot.) disease

---

ŏŏ is pronounced as in food; ŏŏ as in hood; th as in 'hink; ᴛʜ as in that; zh as in azure.   ∼ = related to.

in plants in which the leaves turn yellow. CHLOROTIC [klo-ro'tik], *adj.* relating to, or affected by, c. [Gk.].

CHLOROUS [klaw'roŏs], *adj.* (*chem.*) similar to, pertaining to or containing chlorine; **c. acid,** the acid $HClO_2$.

CHOCK (1) [chok], *n.* small block of wood; (*naut.*) wooden block or wedge to support articles or prevent their rolling about on board ship; (*aeron.*) similar block to hold aircraft wheels. CHOCK (2), *v.t.* to support or secure with chocks. [OFr.].

CHOCK-A-BLOCK [chok-a-blok'], *adj.* (*naut.*) hoisted up so as to touch the blocks of the hoisting tackle; (*fig.*) crammed full, packed tightly.

CHOCK-FULL [chok-fool'], *adj.* quite full, full to capacity.

CHOCOLATE (1) [cho'kŏ-lāt], *n.* sweetmeat in the form of a paste composed of the kernels of the cacao tree, ground down, sweetened and combined with some flavouring substance; (*pl.*) small sweetmeats made of or coated with this; drink made by mixing this in boiling milk or water. CHOCOLATE (2), *adj.* of the colour of c., dark brown. [Span. from Mexican].

CHOCTAW [chok'taw], *n.* tribe of North American Indians; step in figure-skating. [*Choctaw,* Indian tribe].

CHOICE (1) [chois], *n.* act or process of selecting or discriminating; thing selected; opportunity for selection or preference; best or most preferable; number of things from which a selection may be made; **Hobson's c.,** a c. with no alternative. CHOICE (2), *adj.* selected with care, select, of special value. CHOICELY, *adv.* with care in choosing; carefully, in a c. manner. CHOICENESS, *n.* condition of being c., superiority. [OFr.].

CHOIR (1) [kwier], *n.* organized body of singers (*esp* those taking part in church services) trained to sing together under the guidance of a conductor; that part of a church extending eastward from the nave to the altar. CHOIR (2), *v.t. and i.* to sing together as a c. or in chorus. [OFr. from Gk.].

CHOIR-ORGAN [kwier'aw-gan], *n.* the softest of the three organs of which a large, multiple three-manual organ is built up.

CHOKE (1) [chōk], *v.t.* to block or compress the windpipe or introduce fumes into the lungs, so as to stop the passage of breath; impede a free passage partially or completely; stifle, smother through lack of air or light; apply the c. of a petrol engine; (*fig.*) suppress forcibly (one's feelings); *v.i.* to suffer a stoppage of breath; **to c. off,** to kill by choking, discourage, cause to abandon; **to c. down,** to swallow or repress with great difficulty. CHOKE (2), *n.* device for closing the air-inlet of a petrol engine; (*radio*) choking coil, coil offering, by self-induction, a high impedance to the flow of an alternating current; the narrow part of a gun; (*slang*) prison. [ME.].

CHOKE-BORE [chōk'baw(r)], *n.* sporting gun having a tapering bore.

CHOKE-CHERRY [chōk'che-ri], *n.* the fruit of *Prunus virginiana.*

CHOKE-DAMP [chōk'damp], *n.* poisonous gas found in disused wells, pits and in coal-mines after the explosion of firedamp.

CHOKER [chō'ker], *n.* anything that chokes; (*coll.*) large, high collar or scarf worn round the neck.

CHOKY (1) [chō'ki], *n.* (*slang*) gaol. [Hind.].

CHOKY (2), *adj.* causing, or producing a feeling of, choking.

CHOL-, *pref.* bile. [Gk.].

CHOLAGOGUE [ko'la-gog], *n.* a medicine to increase the flow of bile. [Gk.].

CHOLER [ko'ler], *n.* bile; anger, hot temper; † one of the four humours of medieval physiology, thought to produce irascibility of temper. [Gk.].

CHOLERA [ko'le-rah], *n.* a malignant disease, characterized by vomiting, diarrhoea and severe cramps, and generally fatal. CHOLERAIC [ko-le-rā'ik], *adj.* relating to c. [Gk.].

CHOLERIC [ko'le-rik], *adj.* hot-tempered, angry, quickly enraged.

CHOLESTERIN [ko-les'te-rin], *n.* a form of alcohol present in protoplasm, occurring in excess in bile. CHOLESTERIC, *adj.* obtained from c. [Gk.].

CHONDRIN(E) [kon'drin], *n.* gelatinous liquid obtained from cartilage.

CHONDRO-, *pref.* cartilage, grain. [Gk.].

CHOOSE (*pret.* **chose,** *p.pt.* **chosen**) [chooz], *v.t. and i.* to select, make a choice (of), discriminate in favour (of), pick out; elect; decide to, feel inclined

to, prefer. CHOOSY, *adj.* fussy, over-particular. [OE.].

CHOP (1) [chop], *v.t. and i.* to cut off by a quick downward blow from a sharp instrument such as an axe etc.; hew, hack, direct a chopping blow at; **to c. up,** to cut up into pieces, mince; **to c. down,** to fell; **to c. off,** to sever by means of a chopping blow. CHOP (2), *n.* act of cutting by striking with an axe or knife; something chopped off, a chopped-off piece of meat, usually with a rib; (*cricket*) stroke in which the bat cuts down smartly on the ball; (*tennis*) similar stroke in tennis, which causes the ball to rebound to a lesser height than usual. [Uncert.].

CHOP (3), *v.t. and i.* to exchange, barter; (*fig.*) exchange arguments with; (*naut.*) veer round (of the wind); **to c. and change,** to alter, be variable; **to c. logic,** to wrangle. CHOP (4), *n.* an exchange, change. [Uncert.].

CHOP (5), *n.* jaw; (*pl.*) side of the face, the jaws and mouth. [CHAP (2).].

CHOP (6), *n.* stamp, seal, official permit; **first c.,** of first rate quality. [Hind.].

CHOP-CHOP [chop-chop], *adv. and int.* (*Pidgin English*) quickly. [Chin.].

CHOPFALLEN, see CHAPFALLEN.

CHOP-HOUSE [chop'hows], *n.* eating-house.

CHOPPER [cho'per], *n.* axe.

CHOPPING (1) [cho'ping], *n.* the rough motion of waves caused by a sudden freshening of the wind; **c. and changing,** altering, vacillation. CHOPPING (2), *adj.* abrupt, jerky, interrupted, having a rough, jerky, agitated movement.

CHOPPY [cho'pi], *adj.* (of wind) constantly veering; (of the sea) rough, agitated by a sudden freshening of the breeze.

CHOPSTICKS [chop'stiks], *n.(pl.)* two smooth pieces of wood, ivory or bamboo, used by the Chinese and Japanese to convey food to the mouth. [CHOP-CHOP and STICK].

CHOP-SUEY [chop-soo'i], *n.* Chinese dish of fried meat, onions etc., accompanied with rice. [Chin.].

CHORAGUS, CHOREGUS [ko-rā'gus], *n.* (*antiq.*) leader of a chorus among the ancient Greeks; official in the University of Oxford who organizes the practice of music; choir-master. CHORAGIC [ko-ra'jik], *adj.* relating to a c. [Gk.].

CHORAL [kaw'ral], *adj.* pertaining to a choir, written or arranged for a choir, sung by a choir; **c. service,** a service in the Church of England with canticles, anthems etc. sung by the choir. CHORALLY, *adv.* in a c. manner. [CHORUS].

CHORALE [ko-rahl'], *n.* sacred hymn or psalm tune of the German Protestant churches sung in harmony or unison. [Prec.].

CHORD [kawd], *n.* the string of a musical instrument; anything resembling this in structure or function, *esp.* (*anat.*) certain string-like structures, as vocal chords; (*mus.*) combination of musical notes sounding simultaneously and arranged according to the rules of harmony; harmonious and unbroken feeling or emotion considered as a musical chord; harmonious combination of colours; (*geom.*) straight line connecting two points on the circumference of a circle; (*aeron.*) distance from the leading edge to the trailing edge of the wing of an aeroplane. [Gk.].

CHORE [chaw(r)], *n.* (*U.S.*) small task or job. [CHAR].

CHOREA [kaw-rē'ah], *n.* nervous disease characterized by convulsive muscular twitches; St. Vitus's dance. [Gk.].

CHOREGUS, see CHORAGUS.

CHOREOGRAPHY [ko-ri-o'gra-fi], *n.* art of representing a dance by signs; design of a ballet; art of ballet-dancing. CHOREOGRAPHER, *n.* an arranger of ballets. CHOREOGRAPHIC [ko-ri-o-gra'fik], *adj.* pertaining to c. [Gk.].

CHORIC [kaw'rik], *adj.* relating to a chorus. [Gk.].

CHORION [kaw'ri-on], *n.* (*anat.*) exterior membrane enclosing the foetus in the womb; (*bot.*) pulpy matter forming the nucleus of the seed. [Gk.].

CHORISTER [ko'ris-ter], *n.* singer in a choir, choir boy.

CHOROID (1) [kaw'roid], *adj.* (*anat.*) resembling the chorion, forming an enclosing membrane. CHOROID (2), *n.* vascular membrane forming a lining to the ball of the eye. [Gk.].

CHORTLE (1) [chaw'tl], *v.i.* to chuckle loudly. CHORTLE (2), *n.* a chuckle. [Invented by Lewis Carroll.]

CHORUS (1) [kaw'rus], *n.* group of actors or singers helping to interpret the action in a Greek drama, the words uttered by the chorus; in Elizabethan drama, a single prologue-speaker; organized group of singers who sing together the choral parts of a musical drama, parts of a musical drama sung by such a group; group of female performers distinguished rather by their physical charms and dancing ability than by their histrionic talent; recurring part of a song sung together by a number of persons as a refrain; a musical composition for a number of voices singing in harmony; (*fig.*) remarks, cries or shouts uttered simultaneously by a group of persons or animals. CHORUS (2) (*pres.pt.* CHORUSING, *pret.* and *p.pt.* CHORUSED), *v.t* and *i.* to sing or speak in chorus. [Gk.].

CHORUS-GIRL [kaw'rus-gerl], *n.* girl who sings and dances in the chorus of a variety show etc.

CHOSE (1) [shōz], *n.* (*leg.*) property; **c. in action**, money due for a bond or as a debt recoverable in law. [Fr.].

CHOSE (2) [chōz], *pret.* of CHOOSE.

CHOSEN [chō'zen], *adj.* specially selected, elect, distinguished by preference; **the C. Race**, the Jews. [ME. *p.pt.* of CHOOSE].

CHOUGH [chuf], *n.* bird of the crow family; (*pop.*) jackdaw; (*fig.*) chatterer, babbler. [ME.].

CHOW [chow], *n.* Chinese dog having a black tongue and a thick furry coat; (*Austral.*) Chinaman. [*Next*].

CHOW-CHOW [chow'chow], *n.* Chinese mixture of pickles or preserves; any mixture. [Uncert.].

CHOWDER [chow'der], *n.* American dish of fish or clams, stewed with salt pork, onions etc. [Fr.].

CHRISM [krizm], *n.* consecrated oil used in the Roman Catholic and Greek Churches in the sacraments. CHRISMAL, *adj.* relating to the c. [Gk.].

CHRISOM [kri'sum], *n.* white robe laid on a child at baptism; christening robe; one used as the shroud of a child dying before a month old; **c. child**, child in its first month, child dead within a month of baptism. [*Prec.*].

CHRIST [krist], *n.* the Jewish Messiah or Lord's Anointed One, name given to Jesus as the Messiah. [Gk.].

CHRISTADELPHIAN [kris-ta-del'fi-an], *n.* member of a religious sect who believe in Jesus, but not in the Trinity. [Gk.].

CHRISTEN [kri'sn], *v.t.* to baptize, admit into the Christian faith by the ceremony of baptism; give a name to. [OE.].

CHRISTENDOM [kri'sn-dum], *n.* the whole body of Christians, Christian countries.

CHRISTENING [kri'sn-ing], *n.* act or ceremony of baptism.

CHRISTIAN (1) [kris'ti-an], *n.* one who professes to follow Christ or his teaching, one whose life and conduct conform to the example and precepts given by Christ; (*coll.*) decent human being. CHRISTIAN (2), *adj.* pertaining to Christ or to his teaching, pertaining to a C.; **C. era**, period regarded as beginning with the year of the birth of Christ; **C. name**, name given to a person at baptism as distinct from the surname; **C. Science**, American religious organization which maintains that sin and disease are due solely to wrong thinking. [L.].

CHRISTIANITY [kris-ti-a'ni-ti], *n.* the religion and teaching of Christ, the Christian faith; the beliefs and conduct characteristic of a Christian. [L.].

CHRISTIANIZE [kris'ti-a-nīz], *v.t.* to make Christian, convert to Christianity. CHRISTIANIZATION [kris-ti-a-ni-zā'shn], *n.* process of conversion to Christianity.

CHRISTIANLIKE [kris'ti-an-līk], *adj.* as befits a Christian.

CHRISTIANLY [kris'ti-an-li], *adj. and adv.* befitting a Christian; in a Christian fashion.

CHRISTMAS [krist'mas], *n.* the church festival in memory of the birth of Christ, observed annually on 25 December; **C. card**, decorated card sent out as a greeting at Christmas; **C. Day**, 25 December; **C. Eve**, 24 December; **C. number**, special Christmas issue of a periodical; **C. rose**, the black hellebore. [OE.].

CHRISTMAS-BOX [krist'mas-boks], *n.* present or gift of money given at Christmas time.

CHRISTMASTIDE [krist'mas-tīd], *n.* the days about Christmas.

CHRISTMAS TIME [krist'mas-tim], *n.* the season of Christmas which officially lasts from 24 December to 6 January (Epiphany).

CHRISTMAS-TREE [krist'mas-trē], *n.* Christmas decoration consisting of a small tree, usually a fir, decorated with tinsel, ornaments and presents.

CHROMA-, CHROMATO-, CHROMO-, *pref.* colour. [Gk.].

CHROMAT-, see CHROMA.

CHROMATE [krō'māt], *n.* (*chem.*) a salt of chromic acid.

CHROMATIC [krō-ma'tik], *adj.* of or pertaining to colour, highly coloured; (*mus.*) including or referring to notes not included in a major or minor diatonic scale, foreign to the key in which a passage of music is written; (*biol.*) capable of taking a stain. CHROMATICALLY, *adv.* in a c. fashion. [Gk.].

CHROMATICS [krō-ma'tiks], *n.* (*opt.*) the branch of optics dealing with the science of colour; (*mus.*) chromatic notes.

CHROMATIN [krō'ma-tin], *n.* (*biol.*) that part of the nucleus of cells which can be stained by dyes.

CHROMATISM [krō'ma-tizm], *n.* (*opt.*) chromatic aberration; (*bot.*) abnormal coloration.

CHROMATO-, see CHROMA.

CHROMATYPE [krō'ma-tīp], *n.* method of obtaining photographs by using a paper sensitized by a salt of chromium, picture so obtained.

CHROME [krōm], *n.* yellow pigment obtained from lead chromate; yellow; **c. green**, oxide of chromium, dark green pigment used in enamelling; **c. steel**, alloy of steel and chromium. [CHROMA].

CHROMIC [krō'mik], *adj.* pertaining to, containing, or obtained from chromium.

CHROMIDIUM [krō-mi'di-um], *n.* alloy of chromium used in making brake-drums etc.

CHROMITE [krō'mīt], *n.* (*min.*) brownish-black metal, the chief ore of chromium.

CHROMIUM [krō'mi-um], *n.* (*chem.*) greyish-white metal used in giving hardness to alloys, the chemical element denoted by Cr. [CHROME].

CHROMIUM-PLATE [krō-mi-um-plāt'], *n.* coating of chromium electrically deposited on metal giving it a hard, lustrous and untarnishable surface.

CHROMOGEN(E) [krō'mo-jěn], *n.* vegetable colouring matter or compound which, when acted upon by an acid or alkali, is converted into a dye-stuff. [Gk.].

CHROMOGRAPH [krō'mō-grahf], *n.* apparatus for duplicating copies of written matter.

CHROMOLITHOGRAPH [krō-mō-li'tho-grahf], *n.* a coloured lithograph. CHROMOLITHOGRAPHY [krō-mō-li-tho'gra-fi], *n.* art of printing lithographs in colours.

CHROMOSOME [krō'mō-sōm], *n.* a minute body formed from chromatin and occurring in the germ cells of animals. [Gk.].

CHROMOTYPOGRAPHY [krō-mō-tī-po'gra-fi], *n.* colour-printing.

CHRONIC [kro'nik], *adj.* continuous, lingering (of a disease), long-lasting, slowly developing and of a rather mild nature; (*vulg.*) bad. CHRONICALLY, *adv.* in a c. manner. [Gk.].

CHRONICITY [kro-ni'si-ti], *n.* (*med.*) condition of being chronic.

CHRONICLE (1) [kro'ni-kl], *n.* a record of events, systematically arranged in order of time; a narrative, history; **The Chronicles**, two historical books in the Old Testament. CHRONICLE (2), *v.t.* to record in a c., record in order of occurrence. CHRONICLER, *n.* compiler of a c., historian. [ME. from Gk.].

CHRONO-, *pref.* time.

CHRONOGRAPH [kro'nō-grahf], *n.* instrument for measuring and registering minute portions of time with great precision, and for recording the time of an event with extreme accuracy. [Gk.].

CHRONOGRAPHER [kro-no'gra-fer], *n.* a chronologer.

CHRONOGRAPHY [kro-no'gra-fi], *n.* the chronological arrangement of past events. [Gk.].

CHRONOLOGICAL [kro-no-lo'ji-kal], *adj.* pertaining to chronology; arranged in order of time. CHRONOLOGICALLY, *adv.* in a c. fashion.

CHRONOLOGY [kro-no'lo-ji], *n.* art of reckoning time or periods of time and arranging events in the correct sequence of time; correct dating of events; register or table of dates. CHRONOLOGER, CHRONOLOGIST, *n.* one expert in c.

CHRONOMETER [kro-no'mi-ter], *n.* very accurate watch or clock used in determining longitude at sea. CHRONOMETRIC(AL) [kro-nō-met'rik(-al)], *adj.* relating to, or measured by, a c.

CHRONOMETRY [kro-no'mi-tri], *n.* science of measuring time with great precision and accuracy.

CHRONOPHER [kro'no-fer], *n.* electrical apparatus for transmitting time signals by radio. [Gk.].

CHRONOSCOPE [kro'no-skōp], *n.* instrument for

ōō is pronounced as in food; ŏŏ as in hood; th as in *think*; TH as in *that*; zh as in azure. ~ = related to.

measuring accurately extremely small intervals of time.

CHRYSALID (1) [kri′sa-lid], *n.* a chrysalis. CHRYSALID (2), *adj.* pertaining to a chrysalis.

CHRYSALIS (*pl.* **crysalides** or **chrysalises**) [kri′sa-lis, kri-sa′li-dēz, kri′sa-li-siz], *n.* the membranous sheath in which the larva of a moth etc. is enclosed when developing into its final winged state; torpid state of a larva when so enclosed. [Gk.].

CHRYSANTHEMUM [kri-zan′thi-mum], *n.* large genus of composite plants consisting of herbs with single flowers and with many small petals thickly set. [Gk.].

CHRYSO-, *pref.* gold. [Gk.].

CHRYSOBERYL [kri′sō-be-ril], *n.* (*min.*) a precious stone, yellowish-green in colour.

CHRYSOLITE [kri′sō-līt], *n.* the most transparent form of olivine, a hard yellowish-green semi-precious stone. [Gk.].

CHRYSOPRASE [kri′sō-prāz], *n.* a golden-green variety of chalcedony. [Gk.].

CHRYSOTYPE [kri′sō-tīp], *n.* photographic process in which gold chloride is used as a developer.

CHUB [chub], *n.* a thick, rounded freshwater fish of the carp family. [ME.].

CHUBBY [chu′bi], *adj.* fat, plump. CHUBBINESS, *n.* condition of being c. [Uncert.].

CHUCK (1) [chuk], *n.* a cluck, clicking sound made with the tongue against the hard palate. CHUCK (2), *v.i.* to make a click, cluck. [Echoic].

CHUCK (3), *n.* word of endearment, childish name for a chicken. [Corruption of CHICKEN.].

CHUCK (4), *n.* small block or lump; device for holding a piece of wood or metal on the revolving mandrel of a lathe. CHUCK (5), *v.i.* to secure in position in a c. [CHOCK].

CHUCK (6), *n.* (*slang*) food; **hard c.,** (*naut.*) ship's biscuit. [Unkn.].

CHUCK (7), *v.t.* to give a light, playful or amorous pat under the chin; throw, hurl, toss; (*coll.*) stop, break off relations with, give up; **to c. away,** to squander; **to c. out,** to throw out forcibly, cause to be withdrawn (of a bill, proposal); **to c. up,** to give up, abandon. CHUCK (8), *n.* a light, playful or amorous tap under the chin; **to give a person the c.,** (*slang*) to dismiss, sack; finish with. [Uncert.].

CHUCKER-OUT [chu-ker-owt′], *n.* attendant whose duty is to remove by force disorderly persons from a public assembly, public-house etc.

CHUCKLE (1) [chu′kl], *v.t.* and *i.* to cluck; laugh in a quiet half-suppressed manner; (*fig.*) have a feeling of inward triumph or exultation. CHUCKLE (2), *n.* a quiet laugh. [Imitative].

CHUCKLE-HEAD [chu′kl-hed], *n.* thick-headed stupid person. CHUCKLE-HEADED, *adj.* thick-headed. [CHUCK (4).].

CHUCKLING [chuk′ling], *n.* a series of chuckles, half-suppressed laughter.

CHUG [chug], *v.i.* to emit steady low explosive sounds. [Echoic].

CHUKKER [chu′ker], *n.* one of the periods of play in a game of polo. [Hind.].

CHUM (1) [chum], *n.* familiar friend, partner; pal, chap. CHUM (2) (*pres.pt.* CHUMMING, *pret. and p.pt.* CHUMMED), *v.i.* to share a room or dwelling with another; strike up an intimate friendship, *esp* **to c. up with.** CHUMMY, *adj.* friendly, intimate. [Unkn.].

CHUMP [chump], *n.* short, thick piece of wood, solid lump of meat; (*fig.*) the head; stupid person; **off one's c.,** (*coll.*) out of one's mind, crazy. [Uncert.].

CHUMP CHOP [chump-chop′], *n.* chop from the chump-end.

CHUMP-END [chump′end], *n.* thick end of a loin of mutton nearest the rump.

CHUNK [chungk], *n.* a thick roughly cut piece, rough, unhewn lump or block. CHUNKY, *adj.* (*coll.*) thick-set, stocky. [Uncert.].

CHURCH (1) [church], *n.* a building specially devoted to religion, one consecrated to the (Christian) worship of God; a religious sect; the Christian religion; a branch of this; the collective body of Christians; building in which Church of England services only are held (as distinct from a chapel); the clergy; **C. Army,** organization for work in the C. of England for mission and relief work amongst the poor; **Established C.,** the form of religion, doctrine and ritual recognized and supported by the State; **C. Militant,** the body of Christians, considered as warring against all spiritual evil; **to enter the C.,** to become a clergyman. CHURCH (2), *v.t.* to

bring into membership of the C.; bring a woman to church after childbirth for thankoffering for safe delivery. CHURCHING, *n.* (*eccles.*) ceremony of thankoffering of a woman safely delivered of a child. [OE. from Gk.].

CHURCH-BELL [church′bel], *n.* bell in or near a church, rung to summon worshippers.

CHURCH-GOER [church′gō-er], *n.* one who regularly attends church. CHURCH-GOING (1), *n.* habitual attendance at church. CHURCH-GOING (2), *adj.* regularly attending church.

CHURCHMAN [church′man], *n.* clergyman; member of the Established Church. CHURCHMANLY, *adj.* like a c. CHURCHMANSHIP, *n.* condition of being a c.

CHURCH-MEMBER [church-mem′ber], *n.* recognized member of a church, one entitled to receive Communion.

CHURCH MUSIC [church-myōō′zik], *n.* music written for or suitable for performance in church.

CHURCH OWL [church-owl′], *n.* the common barn-owl.

CHURCH RATE [church′rāt], *n.* ground-rent or house-rate collected for the upkeep of the parish church.

CHURCH-TEXT [church′tekst], *n.* (*print.*) Old English or black-letter type.

CHURCHWARDEN [church′waw-den], *n.* one of two honorary officials elected in every Anglican parish to look after the church fabric, enforce decorum in church and distribute gifts to the church; (*coll.*) long-stemmed clay pipe.

CHURCHWOMAN [church′wŏŏ-man], *n.* female member of the Established Church.

CHURCH-WORK [church′werk], *n.* work on behalf of a church.

CHURCHY [chur′chi], *adj.* (*coll.*) excessively devoted to the Church, and displaying this in an obtrusive manner; displaying an excessive preference for the Established Church as against the Nonconformist Churches.

CHURCHYARD [church′yahd], *n.* piece of consecrated ground surrounding a church and used for interments; **c. cough,** cough seeming to herald death.

CHURL [churl], *n.* peasant; rude, ill-bred person, niggard. [OE.].

CHURLISH [chur′lish], *adj.* boorish, rude, uncivil; niggardly. CHURLISHLY, *adv.* in a c. manner. CHURLISHNESS, *n.* state of being c. [OE.].

CHURN (1) [churn], *n.* rotating drum or other vessel in which cream is agitated for the production of butter; large milk can. CHURN (2), *v.t. and i.* to agitate in a c. in order to produce butter; (*fig.*) stir, agitate with continued violence (of liquids) so that a froth appears; make butter in a c. CHURNING, *n.* process of making butter in a c., quantity of butter so produced at one time; (*fig.*) violent agitation or disturbance (of liquids). [OE.].

CHUT [chut], *int.* exclamation of impatience.

CHUTE [shōōt], *n.* steeply sloping channel or enclosed passage down which heavy objects are slid to a lower level; steep channel which causes an abrupt descent to a lower level and along which water flows; steep cutting; (*coll.*) parachute; **water c.,** steep framework leading into water, down which specially constructed boats are shot so that they bump about after hitting the water. [Fr.].

CHUTNEY [chut′ni], *n.* East Indies spiced sauce made of fruit, vinegar etc. [Hind.].

CHYLE [kīl], *n.* (*physiol.*) milky fluid into which food is converted in the intestines by the process of digestion. CHYLIFACTIVE [kī-li-fak′tiv], *adj.* forming or turning into c.; having the power to make c. CHYLIFEROUS [ki-li′fe-rōōs], *adj.* containing or transmitting c. CHYLIFICATION [ki-li-fi-kā′shn], *n.* process of making c. CHYLOPOIETIC [kī-lō-poi-e′tik], *adj.* pertaining to the production of c. CHYLOUS, *adj.* relating to, or consisting of, c. [Gk.].

CHYME [kīm], *n.* pulpy mass into which food is converted in the stomach by the action of the gastric juices. CHYMIFICATION [kī-mi-fi-kā′shn], *n.* process of becoming, or being made into, c. CHYMIFY [kī′mi-fī], *v.t. and i.* to form, or be formed into, c. CHYMOUS, *adj.* pertaining to, or consisting of, c. [Gk.].

CHYMIST†, see CHEMIST.

CHYMISTRY†, see CHEMISTRY.

CICADA [si-kā′dah], *n.* one of a group of insects belonging to the order *Homoptera.* [L.].

CICALA [si-kah′lah], *n.* cicada. [It.].

CICATRICE [si′ka-tris], *n.* scar remaining on the

skin after a wound has healed; (*bot.*) scar left on the bark of a tree. [L.].

CICATRICLE [si-ka´tri-kl], *n.* scar-like germinating point in the embryo of a seed or the yolk of an egg; (*bot.*) scar formed when the leaf separates from its stem. [L.].

CICATRIX (*pl.* **cicatrices**) [si-kā´triks, si-ka-tri´sēz], *n.* cicatrice.

CICATRIZE [si´ka-trīz], *v.t. and i.* to heal a wound or to heal by the formation of new skin or a cicatrice. CICATRIZATION [si-ka-tri-zā´shn], *n.* formation of a scar in the healing of a wound.

CICELY [si´si-li], *n.* the plant *Myrrhis odorata* and similar umbelliferous plants. [Gk.].

CICERONE (*pl.* **ciceroni**) [chi-che-rō´ni], *n.* a guide, person who shows sightseers the historical curiosities or objects of interest of a place. [It. from L. *Cicero*, Roman orator].

CICERONIAN (1) [si-se-rō´ni-an], *n.* admirer or follower of the style of Cicero. CICERONIAN (2), *adj.* resembling Cicero in style, classical and eloquent. [*Cicero*, Roman orator].

CID [sid], *n.* chief, commander, *esp.* the eleventh-century Spanish hero Rodrigo Diaz; the epic of his life and deeds. [Arab.].

CIDER, CYDER [si´der], *n.* liquor made from the fermented juice of apples. [OFr., Heb.].

CIDER-PRESS [si´der-pres], *n.* machine which extracts the juice for cider from apples.

CI-DEVANT [sē-de-vah(ng)´], *adj.* late, former. [Fr.].

CIGAR [si-gah(r)´], *n.* small roll of tobacco-leaf for smoking. [Span.].

CIGARETTE [si-ga-ret´], *n.* small roll of finely cut tobacco-leaf enclosed in a thin paper cylinder for smoking. [*Dim.* of CIGAR].

CIGARETTE-HOLDER [si-ga-ret´hōl-der], *n.* small tube shaped so as to hold a cigarette at one end, the other end tapering to a slit-like aperture which is held in the mouth.

CIGAR-SHAPED [si-gah´shāpt], *adj.* cylindrical but tapering towards the ends.

CILIA [si´li-ah], *n.(pl.)* the eyelashes; (*bot.*) fine hairy appendages on plants; (*zool.*) microscopic filaments found on the surface of animal tissue. CILIARY [si´li-a-ri], *adj.* relating to the eyelids or to c. CILIATE(D), *adj.* provided with c. CILIFORM, *adj.* resembling c. [L.].

CIMBRIAN [sim´bri-an], *n. and adj.* Cimbric.

CIMBRIC (1) [sim´brik], *n.* the language of the Cimbri. CIMBRIC (2), *adj.* pertaining to the Cimbri, an ancient North Germanic tribe. [L.].

CIMEX (*pl.* **cimices**) [si´meks, si´mi-sēz], *n.* the genus of bed-bugs. CIMICIC [si´mi´sik], *adj.* (*chem.*) **c. acid,** acid obtained from the liquid secreted by bugs. [L.].

CIMMERIAN (1) [si-mēer´i-an], *n.* mythical race described by Homer as living in perpetual gloom. CIMMERIAN (2), pertaining to the Cimmerians; **C. darkness,** perpetual and profound darkness.

CINCH (1) [sinch], *n.* saddle-girth; (*slang.*) certainty, sure thing. CINCH (2), *v.t. and i.* to fix by means of a girth, tighten the saddle-girth; (*slang.*) have a hold upon. [Span.].

CINCHONA [sing-kō´nah], *n.* South American evergreen tree which yields quinine; bark of this species of tree; drug extracted from the bark. CINCHONACEOUS [sing-ko-nā´shōōs], *adj.* relating to c. CINCHONIC [sing-ko´nik], *adj.* obtained from c. bark [Countess of *Chinchon*, cured of fever by taking this bark].

CINCHONATE [sing´ko-nāt], *n.* a salt of cinchonic acid.

CINCHONINE [sing´ko-nēn], *n.* alkaloid obtained from several species of cinchona, used medicinally to alleviate fever.

CINCHONISM [sing´ko-nizm], disordered condition due to excessive use of cinchona.

CINCINNATUS [sin-si-nā´tus], retired statesman capable of aiding his nation in a crisis. [*Cincinnatus,* Roman statesman].

CINCTURE (1) [singk´tyōōr], *n.* belt, girdle, ring; (*arch.*) ring at the top and bottom of the shaft of a column; encircling band. CINCTURE (2), *v.t.* to encircle, encompass. CINCTURED, *adj.* provided with a c. or girdle. [L.].

CINDER [sin´der], *n.* the hard friable residue of coal after it has ceased to burn or flame, but before it has been reduced to ashes, refuse from smelting processes. [OE.].

CINDERELLA [sin-de-re´lah], *n.* any person (usually in humble surroundings) whose beauty or goodness escapes general notice; (*fig.*) that which is continually neglected or overlooked. [*Cinderella,* in the fairy tale.]

CINDERELLA-DANCE [sin-de-re´lah-dahns], *n.* informal dance ending at midnight. [*Prec.*].

CINDERPATH [sin´der-pahth], *n.* path or running track made of, or covered with, an even layer of cinders.

CINDERSIFTER [sin´der-sif-ter], *n.* sieve for sifting cinders from ashes.

CINDER TRACK [sin´der-trak], *n.* cinderpath.

CINDERY [sin´de-ri], *adj.* resembling or composed of cinders.

CINE-CAMERA [si-ni-ka´me-rah], *n.* camera which takes a continuous series of photographs at momentary intervals on a cinematograph film.

CINE-FILM [si´ni-film], *n.* film wound on a spool, and used with a cine-camera or a cinematograph.

CINEMA, KINEMA [si´ni-mah, ki´ni-mah], *n.* theatre in which moving pictures are projected upon a screen; (*fig.*) the showing of moving pictures as a medium of entertainment and instruction. [Abbreviation of CINEMATOGRAPH].

CINEMA-ORGAN [si´ni-mah-aw-gan], *n.* large organ containing many unusual stops from which a great variety of effects may be obtained, played in some large cinemas.

CINEMATOGRAPH, KINEMATOGRAPH [si-ni-ma´tō-grahf, ki-ni-ma´tō-grahf], *n.* apparatus by which a continuous succession of photographs are magnified and projected on to a screen in rapid sequence, so that an impression of steady movement is produced. CINEMATOGRAPHIC, KINEMATOGRAPHIC, *adj.* pertaining to, resembling, the c. or cinematography. [Gk.].

CINEMATOGRAPHY, KINEMATOGRAPHY [si-ni-ma-to´gra-fi, ki-ni-ma-to´gra-fi], *n.* art of making and exhibiting pictures by a cinematograph. [Gk.].

CINE-PROJECTOR [si´ni-prō-jek-ter], *n.* projector used in the showing of cinematograph films.

CINERARIA [si-ne-räer´i-ah], *n.* (*bot.*) South African genus of composite plants with small brightly-coloured flowers. [L.].

CINERARIUM [si-ne-räer´i-um], *n.* place where a cinerary urn is deposited.

CINERARY [si´ne-ra-ri], *adj.* pertaining to or containing ashes; **c. urn,** vase or urn in which the ashes of a cremated person are kept. [L.].

CINEREOUS [si-nēer´i-ōōs], *adj.* like ashes, having the colour of ashes, ashen-grey. [L.].

CINGALESE, see SINGHALESE.

CINNABAR [si´na-bah(r)], *n.* (*min.*) red mineral substance, the crystalline form of mercuric sulphide; red or vermilion pigment obtained from this.

CINNAMON [si´na-mon], *n.* inner bark of an East Indian species of laurel, used as a spice and for medicinal purposes; tree from which the bark is obtained; yellowish-brown colour of dried cinnamon. [Gk.].

CINQUE [singk], *n.* five, five at cards or dice; **C. Ports,** those English ports, originally five, Dover, Sandwich, Hastings, Romney and Hythe, which had special privileges in return for providing a navy. [Fr. from L.].

CINQUECENTIST [ching-kwe-chen´tist], *n.* artist or writer of the Italian sixteenth-century school, characterized by a reversion to classical models, one who models his style upon that school. [It.].

CINQUEFOIL [singk´foil], *n.* (*bot.*) one of several plants of the genus *Potentilla,* having leaves made up of five leaflets; (*arch.*) form of ornament used in circular windows etc., and consisting of five foliated divisions. [L.].

CIPHER, CYPHER (1) [si´fer], *n.* the arithmetical character 0 or zero, the Arabic numerals, any arithmetical number; a disguised or secret method of writing which can be understood only by those holding the key to it, the key by which such writing is made intelligible; monogram having several initials or letters interwoven to form a whole; organ note which sounds continuously, through an imperfect valve; (*fig.*) person of no importance, nonentity. CIPHER-CLERK, cipherer. CIPHER-KEY, key by which writing in c. is made intelligible. CIPHER, CYPHER (2), *v.t. and i.* to calculate by arithmetic; write in c. or secret writing; work out arithmetical problems; sound continuously (of an organ note). [OFr. from Arab.].

CIPHERER, CYPHERER [si´fe-rer], *n.* one employed in coding and decoding messages.

CIPHERING [si´fe-ring], *n.* calculating with

numerals; arithmetic; writing in cipher; sounding continuously (of an organ note).

CIRCA [sur'kah], *adv. and prep.* about, approximately. [L.].

CIRCASSIAN [ser-ka'si-an], *n.* kind of thin worsted cloth; native of Circassia.

CIRCE [sur'si], *n.* name of the mythical sorceress supposed to change men into swine by her magic potions; (*fig.*) enchantress, vamp. [Gk.].

CIRCEAN [ser-sē'an], *adj.* dangerously infatuating, fascinating but harmful.

CIRCLE (1) [sur'kl], *n.* (*geom.*) plane figure enclosed by a curved line, every point on which is equidistant from a point within called the centre; anything of this form, such as a ring, halo; lowest gallery of a theatre, usually semicircular in shape; system or series making a complete revolution and returning to the starting-point; recurring succession of events, cycle; (*logic*) fallacious method of argument by which the thing to be proved is stated as a major premise, a conclusion inferred from it, and the conclusion used to prove the major premise; number of persons associated together by affinity of interests; social class; (*fig.*) compass, limits; area of influence or action; **vicious c.**, argument in a circle, in which the thing to be proved is assumed; series of events intensifying one another; **to square the c.,** (*fig.*) to attempt the impossible. CIRCLE (2), *v.t. and i.* to surround as with a c., make a complete c. round, move in a c. [L.].

CIRCLET [sur'klet], *n.* small circle, small circular band.

CIRCLING [sur'kling], *adj.* encircling.

CIRCUIT (1) [sur'kit], *n.* a round, path or journey round an area, act of moving or going round in a circle, distance round, space enclosed in moving round an area; (*fig.*) periodical visitation of judges to different towns in a district to hold assizes; the barristers making this round; (*elect.*) the closed path traversed by an electric current; (*fig.*) roundabout method, detour; chain of cinemas owned by one distributing company and generally showing the same films at the same time. CIRCUIT (2), *v.t. and i.* to pass round, encircle; move round in a c. CIRCUITEER, *n.* one who travels on a c. [L.].

CIRCUITOUS [ser-kyōo'i-tŏŏs], *adj.* indirect, roundabout. CIRCUITOUSLY, *adv.* in a c. fashion.

CIRCUITY [ser-kyōo'i-ti], *n.* indirect proceeding.

CIRCULABLE [sur'kyōo-la-bl], *adj.* capable of being circulated.

CIRCULAR (1) [sur'kyōo-ler], *adj.* pertaining to, or in the shape of, a circle, forming part of a circle; moving in a circle, making a circle; sent to a number of persons; **c. ticket,** ticket for a tour which returns to the point of departure by a different route; **c. note,** letter of credit furnished by a banker to travellers, and exchangeable for cash at different places; **c. number,** (*math.*) number whose power terminates in the same digits as the root. CIRCULAR (2), *n.* letter, notice, advertisement etc., printed and sent to a large number of people. CIRCULARITY [ser-kyōo-la'ri-ti], *n.* condition of being c. [L.].

CIRCULARIZE [sur'kyōo-la-rīz], *v.t.* to send circulars to.

CIRCULATE [sur'kyōo-lāt], *v.i.* to move round and return to the point of departure; move around freely, pass through many hands or channels; be handed round; (*math.*) recur; *v.t.* to pass round, cause to move from person to person or from place to place, spread. CIRCULATIVE [sur'kyōo-la-tiv], *adj.* tending to c. or to cause to c. [L.].

CIRCULATING [sur'kyōo-lā-ting], *adj.* moving round or causing circulation; **c. decimal,** recurring decimal; **c. library,** institution which lends or hires out books to members or subscribers for a definite period of time; **c. medium,** currency, medium of exchange.

CIRCULATION [ser-kyōo-lā'shn], *n.* process or act of circulating; state of being circulated; (*anat.*) the flow of blood from the heart through the arteries and back by way of the veins; (*bot.*) flow of sap through the veins of a plant; extent to which a thing is circulated, number of copies sold or otherwise reaching the public; continual passage of water through pipes, so that it returns to its starting-point. CIRCULATORY [ser-kyōo-lā'te-ri], *adj.* pertaining to c. [L.].

CIRCULATOR [sur'kyōo-lā-ter], *n.* one who circulates; domestic hot-water boiler.

CIRCUM-, *pref.* round. [L.].

CIRCUMAMBIENT [ser-ku-mam'bi-ent], *adj.* going

round about, surrounding CIRCUMAMBIENCY, *n.* action of encompassing or surrounding.

CIRCUMAMBULATE [ser-ku-mam'byōo-lāt], *v.t. and i.* to walk or go round; (*fig.*) approach in an indirect fashion, avoid coming straight to the point. CIRCUMAMBULATION [ser-ku-mam-byōo-lā'shn], *n.* act of circumambulating. [L.].

CIRCUMAMBULATORY [ser-ku-mam'byōo-lā-te-ri], *adj.* indirect, round about.

CIRCUMBENDIBUS [ser-kum-ben'di-bus], *n.* circumlocution. [Humorous, from CIRCUM and BEND (1)].

CIRCUMCISE [sur'kum-sīz], *v.t.* to cut off the foreskin of; (*fig.*) purify, cleanse from sin. [L.].

CIRCUMCISION [ser-kum-si'zhn], *n.* act of circumcising; (*fig.*) purification, cleansing of the spirit; (*eccles.*) festival in celebration of the circumcision of Christ (1 January). [L.].

CIRCUMFERENCE [ser-kum'fe-rens], *n.* the curved line which marks or encloses a circle the length of this line. CIRCUMFERENTIAL [ser-kum-fe-ren'shal], *adj.* relating to the c. [L.].

CIRCUMFERENTOR [ser-kum-fe-ren'ter], *n.* a kind of theodolite.

CIRCUMFLECTION, see CIRCUMFLEXION.

CIRCUMFLEX (1) [sur'kum-fleks], *n.* (*gram.*) a mark or accent used in Greek ⌃ and in French ˄. CIRCUMFLEX (2), *v.t. and i.* to mark with a c. accent; bend round. CIRCUMFLEXION, CIRCUMFLECTION [ser-kum-flek'shn], *n.* a bending or curving round; the addition of a c. [L.].

CIRCUMFLUENT [ser-kum'flŏŏ-ent], *adj.* flowing around. [L.].

CIRCUMFUSE [sur'kum-fyōoz], *v.t.* to pour round, spread round. CIRCUMFUSION, *n.* act of pouring round. [L.].

CIRCUMJACENT [ser-kum-jā'sent], *adj.* lying round anything, lying on every side. [L.].

CIRCUMLOCUTION [ser-kum-lo-kyōo'shn], *n.* a talking around, indirect verbose mode of speech or writing, an example of this. CIRCUMLOCUTORY, [ser-kum-lo'kyōo-te-ri], *adj.* given to, characterized by, c., indirect, verbose. [L.].

CIRCUMNAVIGATE [ser-kum-na'vi-gāt], *v.t.* to sail round. CIRCUMNAVIGABLE [ser-kum-na'vi-ga-bl], *adj.* capable of being sailed round. CIRCUMNAVIGATION [ser-kum-na-vi-gā'shn], *n.* act of sailing round, *esp.* round the world. CIRCUMNAVIGATOR [ser-kum-na'vi-gā-ter], *n.* one who sails round, *esp.* the world. [L.].

CIRCUMPOLAR [ser-kum-pō'ler], *adj.* about the Poles; (*astron.*) (of stars) never disappearing below the horizon.

CIRCUMSCRIBE [sur'kum-skrīb], *v.t.* to draw a line round, hem in on all sides; (*fig.*) limit, restrict. CIRCUMSCRIBABLE, CIRCUMSCRIPTIBLE [ser-kum-skrī'ba-bl, ser-kum-skrip'ti-bl], *adj.* able to be circumscribed. CIRCUMSCRIBER, *n.* one who circumscribes. [L.].

CIRCUMSCRIPTION [ser-kum-skrip'shn], *n.* act of circumscribing; state of being circumscribed; that which circumscribes, a circular inscription. CIRCUMSCRIPTIVE, *adj.* pertaining to c. [L.].

CIRCUMSOLAR [ser-kum-sō'ler], *adj.* surrounding or round the sun.

CIRCUMSPECT [sur'kum-spekt], *adj.* careful, warily cautious, prudent; decorous, proper. CIRCUMSPECTION [ser-kum-spek'shn], *n.* quality of being c., c. behaviour. CIRCUMSPECTIVE, *adj.* c. CIRCUMSPECTLY, *adv.* in a c. fashion. [L.].

CIRCUMSTANCE [sur'kum-stans], *n.* the accidental accompaniments or unrelated factors of an event, the independent conditions in which something happens, a single event, detail, factor; (*pl.*) economic conditions, monetary situation; **pomp and c.,** gorgeous formalities, worldly glory. CIRCUMSTANCED, *adj.* in a specific situation, situated. [L.].

CIRCUMSTANTIAL [ser-kum-stan'shal], *adj.* very detailed, minutely describing the circumstances; incidental, indirect, unrelated to the essential events; **c. evidence,** presumptive evidence inferred from numerous circumstances attendant on an event but not directly linked to the event itself. CIRCUMSTANTIALITY [ser-kum-stan-shi-a'li-ti], *n.* quality or condition of being c. CIRCUMSTANTIALLY [ser-kum-stan'sha-li], *adj.* inferentially, by virtue of the c. details; in minute detail.

CIRCUMSTANTIATE [ser-kum-stan'shi-āt], *v.t.* to confirm, support circumstantially.

CIRCUMVENT [ser-kum-vent'], *v.t.* to outwit, overreach, prevent, out-manoeuvre. CIRCUMVENTION,

---

n. act of circumventing. CIRCUMVENTIVE, *adj.* circumventing, scheming to c. [L.].

CIRCUMVOLUTION [ser-kum-vo-lyōō'shn], *n.* act of rolling or winding round; something coiled up, a winding. [L.].

CIRCUS [sur'kus], *n.* (*Rom. antiq.*) circular sports arena built round with tiers of seats; show derived from this consisting of exhibitions of horsemanship and tricks with wild beasts, interspersed with clowning and acrobatic feats; open, circular space at the junction of several roads [L.].

CIRRHOSIS [si-rō'sis], *n.* morbid state of the liver. CIRRHOTIC [si-ro'tik], *adj.* suffering from or relating to c. [Gk.].

CIRRI-, CIRRO-, *pref.* curl, tuft, tendril. [L.].

CIRRIPEDE [si'ri-pēd], *n.* crustacean moving by means of curling legs. [L.].

CIRRO-, see CIRRI-.

CIRRO-CUMULUS [si-rō-kyōō'myōō-lus], *n.* type of cloud characterized by small, fleecy masses. [L.].

CIRRO-STRATUS [si-rō-strah'tus], *n.* type of cloud consisting of layers of fleecy cloud. [L.].

CIRRUS (*pl.* cirri) [si'rus], *n.* series of tufted fleecy clouds faintly resembling hair; (*bot.*) curling tendril; (*zool.*) tendril-like filament. [L.].

CIS-, *pref.* on this side, on the near side of. [L.].

CISALPINE [si-sal'pīn], *adj.* on the south or Italian side of the Alps. [L.].

CISSY, see SISSY.

CISTERCIAN (1) [sis-tur'shn], *n.* member of the monastic order founded by St. Bernard at Citeaux. CISTERCIAN (2). *adj.* relating to the C. Order and its members. [L.].

CISTERN [sis'tern], *n.* tank for storing water. [L.].

CISTUS [sis'tus], *n.* genus of shrubs related to the rock-rose. [L.].

CITADEL [si'ta-del], *n.* fortress commanding or protecting a city. [It.].

CITATION [si-tā'shn], *n.* reference, quotation; act of referring to or quoting; (*leg.*) order to appear before a court; (*milit.*) special mention of an individual or unit in dispatches.

CITE [sīt], *v.t.* to quote from an authority, instance as an example or precedent; (*leg.*) summon to appear before a court; name as a participant in a legal cause. [L.].

CITHARA [si'thah-rah], *n.* ancient triangular musical instrument. [Gk.].

CITHERN, CITTERN [si'thern, si'tern], *n.* medieval lute, sort of zither. [OE.].

CITIZEN [si'ti-zen], *n.* inhabitant of a city, one having rights and duties by virtue of belonging to a city; townsman; civilian, national. [ME. from OFr.].

CITIZENRY [si'ti-zen-ri], *n.* all the inhabitants of a city or town.

CITRATE [sit'rāt], *n.* (*chem.*) a salt of citric acid.

CITRIC [sit'rik], *n.* pertaining to citron; **c. acid,** acid to which oranges, lemons, limes etc. owe their peculiar flavour.

CITRINE (1) [sit'rēn], *n.* variety of yellowish quartz. CITRINE (2), *adj.* yellowish-green, lemon-coloured. [Fr.].

CITRON [sit'ron], *n.* large fruit of the lemon and lime family; tree producing this fruit; pale yellow-green colour. [Gk.].

CITRONELLA [si-tro-ne'lah], *n.* oil used to ward off mosquitoes. [*Prec.*].

CITROUS [sit'rŏŏs], *adj.* belonging to the genus Citrus.

CITRUS [sit'rus], *n.* and *adj.* genus of trees bearing such fruits as the lemon, lime, citron etc. [L.].

CITTERN, see CITHERN.

CITY [si'ti], *n.* great town, town having a Royal Charter, cathedral town; (*fig.*) seat or headquarters of some force; centre of London in a state, esp. the City of London; **in the C.,** in business; **C. company,** guild of merchants in a particular trade. CITYWARDS, *adv.* towards the c. [OFr. from L.].

CIVET [si'vit], *n.* small African and Asian carnivore; musk-like substance used in perfumery, extracted from glands in the anus of this creature. [Arab.].

CIVET-CAT [si'vit-kat], *n.* civet.

CIVIC [si'vik], *adj.* pertaining to a city, a citizen, or citizenship; **c. crown,** garland of oak leaves, the highest Roman award for valour; **c. virtues,** the qualities which make the state possible. [L.].

CIVIC CENTRE [si-vik-sen'ter], *n.* building or group of buildings housing the offices of a local authority, and some or all of the amenities run by it.

CIVICS [si'viks], *n.* study of civil administration.

CIVIL [si'vil], *adj.* pertaining to, based on, the social life of organized groups; pertaining to citizens, citizenship and the state; pertaining to the non-military members or organization of a community; courteous, polite, urbane, obediently respectful; **c. engineer,** one concerned with non-mechanical construction; **c. case,** (*leg.*) case concerned with the personal and private relations of the citizens and not with criminal charges; **c. law,** legal system regulating the obligations of society; **c. list,** annual parliamentary grant for Royal maintenance etc.; **C. Service,** the state departments of administration etc. as distinct from the armed forces; **c. war,** war between parties who are members of the same state; **c. defence,** defence of the civilian population by non-combatants; **c. disobedience,** mass refusal to pay taxes etc. for political reasons. [L.].

CIVILIAN (1) [si-vil'yan], *n.* one who is not a member of the armed forces. CIVILIAN (2), *adj.* pertaining to civil life, non-military. [L.].

CIVILITY [si-vi'li-ti], *n.* politeness, courtesy, quality of being civil; (*pl.*) conventional attentions. [OFr.].

CIVILIZATION [si-vi-li-zā'shn], *n.* process of civilizing and the achievement of this process; structure of organized society; a highly developed culture of mankind.

CIVILIZE [si'vi-līz], *v.t.* to instruct in the culture and organization of a more developed form of society, raise from barbarism; (*fig.*) educate out of ignorance and lack of breeding.

CIVILLY [si'vi-li], *adv.* in relation to civil life; in civil fashion.

CIVVIES [si'viz], *n.*(*pl.*) (*coll.*) mufti; plain clothes. [*Dim.* of CIVILIAN].

CLACK (1) [klack], *n.* loud click; sharp, abrupt sound, frequently repeated; that which clacks; continual talking; the tongue; hinged flap forming a valve in a pump. CLACK (2), *v.t.* and *i.* to make a c.; keep up a continual nagging talk. [ME.].

CLAD [klad], *adj.* clothed. [OE.].

CLAIM (1) [klām], *n.* the demanding of a right; the right demanded; mode in which the demand is made; legitimate right; piece of land acquired by a settler; **to stake one's c.,** to mark out a plot of new land with stakes; (*fig.*) establish oneself in a position. CLAIM (2), *v.t.* to make a c. for; seek to establish as fact; contend; state that lost property is one's own; require, need; ask for damages in a court of law in respect of an injury. CLAIMABLE, *adv.* able to be claimed. [OFr., L.].

CLAIMANT [klā'mant], *n.* one who claims. [OFr.].

CLAIR-AUDIENCE [klāer-aw'di-ens], *n.* alleged psychic faculty of hearing sounds normally inaudible. [Fr. and L.].

CLAIRVOYANCE [klāer-voi'ans], *n.* alleged psychic faculty of perceiving objects and events not normally perceptible to the senses. CLAIRVOYANT (1), *n.* one having the power of c. CLAIRVOYANT (2), *adj.* pertaining to c. [Fr.].

CLAM [klam], *n.* an edible mollusc; (*U.S. slang*) very reserved person; **as close as a c.,** secretive. [Uncert.].

CLAMANT [kla'mant], *adj.* clamorous, beseeching urgently, crying out for immediate attention. [L.].

CLAMBER (1) [klam'ber], *v.t.* to climb awkwardly, scramble up. CLAMBER (2), *n.* a rough climb. [ME.].

CLAMMY [kla'mi], *adj.* damp and cold. CLAMMINESS, *n.* quality of being c. [OE.].

CLAMOROUS [kla'me-rŏŏs], *adj.* vociferous, noisily insistent. CLAMOROUSLY, *adv.* in c. fashion. CLAMOROUSNESS, *n.* condition of being c.

CLAMOUR (1) [kla'mer], *n.* noisy, confused outbreak of voices, loud threatening and demanding outcry; insistent noisy complainings. CLAMOUR (2), *v.t.* and *i.* to raise a c., shout at. [L.].

CLAMP (1) [klamp], *n.* device, usually of wood or iron, for holding things together, esp. when being assembled; thick plank in a ship's side supporting the ends of the deck-beams. CLAMP (2), *v.t.* to hold together or fasten with a c.; (*fig.*) hold very firmly. [Du.].

CLAMP (3), *n.* pile of bricks; heap of potatoes covered with straw and earth for storage; dung heap. CLAMP (4), *v.t.* to store potatoes in a c. [MDu.].

CLAMP (5), *n.* heavy stamping tread, lumbering tramping. CLAMP (6), *v.i.* to tramp heavily with a c. [Onomatopoeic].

CLAMPER [klam'per], *n.* iron plate studded with points fitted to the shoe for walking on ice.

CLAMS [klamz], *n.*(*pl.*) pair of pincers for extracting nails; kind of vice or clamp; movable jaws of a vice used for holding delicate work. [OE.].

CLAN (1) [klan], *n.* tribal group, *esp.* in Scotland and Ireland, united by supposed descent from the same individual; (*fig.*) exclusive group of people having common interests, jealously self-sufficient set. CLAN (2), *v.i.* to join together in a c., unite in a clique. [Gael.].

CLANDESTINE [klan-des'tin], *adj.* secret, surreptitious, furtively hidden. CLANDESTINELY, *adv.* in c. fashion. [L.].

CLANG (1) [klang], *n.* resonant ringing sound made by the striking together of metal objects, as bells etc. CLANG (2), *v.t. and i.* to make or cause to make a c. [~OHighGerm.].

CLANGOUR [klang'er], *n.* continual loud clanging sound. CLANGOROUS, *adj.* loudly clanging.

CLANK (1) [klangk], *n.* dull, heavy, metallic sound, such as that made by iron chains. CLANK (2), *v.t. and i.* to make or cause to make a c. [Onomatopoeic].

CLANNISH [kla'nish], *adj.* pertaining to a clan; cliquish; regarding outsiders with suspicion and hostility, concerned solely with the welfare of one's own small group. CLANNISHLY, *adv.* in c. fashion.

CLANSHIP [klan'ship], *n.* state of belonging to a clan.

CLANSMAN [klanz'man], *n.* member of a clan; male member of a clan old enough to bear arms.

CLAP (1) [klap], *n.* sound made by the sudden forcible impact of two hard flat surfaces; sudden burst of thunder; noise made by striking together the palms of the hands; friendly slap; tongue of a bell; lower mandible of a hawk. CLAP (2) (*pres.pt.* CLAPPING, *pret. and p.pt.* CLAPPED), *v.t.* to make or cause to make a c.; applaud by claps; strike in friendly fashion with the palm of the hand; bring into contact in a rapid and forcible manner; **to c. into,** to confine forcibly and expeditiously. [OE.].

CLAP (3), *n.* (*vulg.*) gonorrhoea. [~OFr.].

CLAP-BOARD [klap'bawd], *n.* stave used in making barrels; plank thicker at one edge than the other, used for the outside walls of wooden buildings. [Uncert.].

CLAP-NET [klap'net], *n.* fowler's net which can be suddenly closed by bringing the two halves of the rim together.

CLAPPER [kla'per], *n.* person or thing that claps; tongue of a bell; striker of a mill-hopper which causes the corn to run on to the millstones; (*slang*) the tongue.

CLAP-TRAP [klap'trap], *n.* pretentious, plausible nonsense.

CLAQUE [klahk], *n.* organized group of bribed applauders, or noisy vehement supporters. [Fr.].

CLARABELLA [klah-rah-be'lah], *n.* organ-stop with a flute-like note. [L.].

CLARENCE [kla'rens], *n.* closed, four-wheeled carriage. [Duke of *Clarence*, afterwards William IV.].

CLARENCEUX [kla'ren-syōō], *n.* King-of-Arms of the district south of the Trent. [Duke of *Clarence*, son of Edward III.].

CLARENDON [kla'ren-don], *n.* (*typ.*) a bold-faced type. [*Clarendon* Press, Oxford].

CLARET (1) [kla'ret], *n.* red Bordeaux wine; a dark red colour. CLARET (2), *adj.* dark red in colour.

CLARET-CUP [kla'ret-kup], *n.* drink made of claret, lemon, spices etc.

CLARIFICATION [kla-ri-fi-kā'shn], *n.* process of clarifying, state of being clarified. [L.].

CLARIFY [kla'ri-fī], *v.t. and i.* to make clear, purify; render intelligible, clear up obscurities. CLARIFIER, *n.* that which clarifies; vessel for clarifying liquor. [L.].

CLARINET [kla'ri-net], *n.* wood-wind instrument having a single reed in the mouthpiece; organ-stop with a note similar to that of this instrument. [Fr. from L.].

CLARION (1) [kla'ri-on], *n.* shrill slender trumpet; organ-stop resembling the note produced by this; shrill ringing call. CLARION (2), *adj.* shrill; (*fig.*) nobly inspiring. [OFr. from L.].

CLARIONET [kla-ri-o-net'], *n.* clarinet. [*Dim.* of *prec.*].

CLARITY [kla'ri-ti], *n.* quality of being clear. [L.].

CLARKIA [klah'ki-ah], *n.* (*bot.*) brightly coloured flowering plant allied to the willow-herb. [W. *Clarke*, American explorer].

CLARY [klāer'i], *n.* sweet herb used as a seasoning. [ME.].

CLASH (1) [klash], *n.* harsh metallic sound produced by the violent impact of metals; (*fig.*) sudden violent conflict of opinions, hostile armed forces etc. CLASH (2), *v.t. and i.* to make or cause to make a c.; come into violent contact (with); (of events) take place at the same time and so interfere with each other; (of colours) be violently inharmonious. CLASHING, *adj.* making a c., conflicting, opposing. [Onomatopoeic].

CLASP (1) [klahsp], *n.* a secure grasp, hearty grip, strong encompassing embrace; catch or hook for fastening two ends together; metal bar attached to the ribbon of a medal to mark the stages of a campaign. CLASP (2), *v.t.* to embrace firmly, fold in the arms, hug; grip hands; secure with a c. [ME.].

CLASP-KNIFE [klahsp'nīf], *n.* knife in which the blade folds up into the handle.

CLASP-LOCK [klahsp'lok], *n.* spring-lock.

CLASP-NAIL [klahsp'nāl], *n.* nail with a flat, broad head.

CLASS (1) [klahs], *n.* category, type, kind, sort, a division of things according to some common characteristic; group of organisms, subordinate to a kingdom, but embracing orders and genera; an economic and social division of society; group of students studying the same subject at the same place and time, a form; division of candidates according to their success in an examination; distinction according to quality; distinction in the style and comfort of accommodation on a train or ship according to the price paid; standard of approximation to a fixed ideal of excellence; **no c.,** vulgar; **working c.,** industrial proletariat. CLASS (2), *adj.* relating to a c. or to c. in general. CLASS (3), *v.t.* to assign to a c., place in a group or category by some standard. CLASSABLE, *adj.* able to be classed. [L.].

CLASS-CONSCIOUS [klahs'kon-shŏŏs], *adj.* unduly sensitive about belonging to a particular social class, *usu.* the working class, and hostile to other classes. CLASS-CONSCIOUSNESS, *n.* state of being c.

CLASSIC (1) [kla'sik], *adj.* relating to Greece and Rome and their culture; alleged to be in accordance with the spirit of ancient Greece and Rome; (of art and literature) of accepted importance and merit; in the best taste; austerely balanced and restrained; uniquely perfect, constituting the best example of its kind; pertaining to one of the five great horse-races. [L.].

CLASSICAL [kla'si-kal], *adj.* relating to the classics or to Greek and Roman culture; pertaining to or expert in the study of the classics; (of literature, music etc.) the best and most balanced in taste. CLASSICALISM, *n.* devotion to the classics; aesthetic mode following the classics; a c. turn of phrase. CLASSICALITY [kla-si-ka'li-ti], *n.* quality of being c. or classic. CLASSICALLY, *adv.* in c. fashion.

CLASSICISM [kla'si-sizm], *n.* a classical turn of phrase; classic proportion of form; an affectation of the classics.

CLASSICIZE [kla'si-sīz], *v.t. and i.* to imitate the classic style; cause to conform to the classic.

CLASSIFIABLE [kla'si-fi-a-bl], *adj.* able to be classified.

CLASSIFICATION [kla-si-fi-kā'shn], *n.* act, method or result of classifying.

CLASSIFICATORY [kla'si-fi-kā-te-ri], *adj.* relating to classification.

CLASSIFY [kla'si-fī], *v.t.* to arrange, sort or allot into classes. CLASSIFIER, *n.* one who classifies. [Fr.].

CLASS-WAR [klahs'waw(r)], *n.* hostility of members of one social class towards those considered to be better off.

CLASSY [klah'si], *adj.* (*coll.*) of high class, superior.

CLATTER (1) [kla'ter], *n.* confused, repeated sharp rattling din, noisy babble of voices. CLATTER (2), *v.t. and i.* to make or cause to make a c.; walk about in a noisy manner. CLATTERER, *n.* one who clatters. [OE.].

CLAUSE [klawz], *n.* (*leg.*) a distinct and particular section or part of a contract, agreement etc.; (*gram.*) a division of a main sentence, grammatically complete in itself, but subordinate to a sentence; **a saving c.,** the solitary but decisive element of good in a person or situation. [~L.].

CLAUSTRAL [klaws'tral], *adj.* pertaining to or restrained by cloisters; living a monastic life. [L.].

CLAUSTROPHOBIA [klaws-tro-fō'bi-ah], *n.* neurotic fear of small or confined spaces. [L. and Gk.].

CLAUSTRUM [klaws'trum], *n.* grey matter in the cerebellum. [L.].

CLAVICHORD [kla'vi-kawd], *n.* (*mus.*) early type

---

of piano in which the strings were struck by small brass hammers. [MdL.].

CLAVICLE [kla'vi-kl], *n.* the collar-bone.

CLAVICULAR [cla-vi'kyoo-ler], *adj.* pertaining to the collar-bone. [L.].

CLAVIER [kla-veer', kla'vi-er], *n.* keyboard of an organ or piano. [Germ. from L.].

CLAW (1) [klaw], *n.* one of the sharp nails on the feet of birds and some animals; limb or pincer of certain crustaceans; anything resembling this; tool for extracting nails from wood; grappling-hook. CLAW (2), *v.t.* to scratch or pluck with a c.; (*fig.*) grab at ravenously; **to c. away**, (*naut.*) to turn to windward from a lee shore. CLAWED, *adj.* having claws; scratched. CLAW-HAMMER, *n.* hammer with one end of the head curved into two claws. [OE.].

CLAY (1) [klā], *n.* a plastic and sticky earth which, when mixed with water, can be moulded and baked hard; (*fig.*) corpse, human flesh. CLAY (2) (*pret. and p.pt.* CLAYED), *v.t.* to daub, cover with c. CLAYEY, *adj.* like c., sticky, clammily tenacious. CLAYISH, *adj.* like c. [OE.].

CLAYMORE [klā'maw(r)], *n.* double-edged ancient Highland broadsword. [Gael.].

CLAY-PIGEON [klā-pi'jun], *n.* small clay disk sent spinning into the air to be fired at.

CLEAN (1) [klēn], *adj.* free from dirt, infection or impurity; freshly washed; honest, free from guilt or vice; undefiled; smooth, sharp-edged, without jagged edges; new, unblemished; clear-cut; blank; **to make a c. breast of**, to confess completely; **to come c.**, (*U.S. slang*) to confess. CLEAN (2), *adv.* (*coll.*) completely; exactly. CLEAN (3), *v.t.* to make c., free from dirt or impurity, polish, brighten and smarten; **to c. out**, (*slang*) to drain completely of money; **to c. up**, to finish up arrears of work or remnants of difficulties; purge of vice or dishonesty. CLEAN (4), *n.* act or operation of cleaning; also CLEAN-OUT, CLEAN-UP. CLEANING, *n.* act of making c. [OE.].

CLEANER [klē'ner], *n.* one who, or that which, cleans; one who cleans a public building.

CLEAN-HANDED [klēn-han'did], *adj.* guiltless, free from blame.

CLEANLILY [klen'li-li], *adv.* in cleanly fashion.

CLEAN-LIMBED [klēn-limbd'], *adj.* well-proportioned and strong.

CLEANLINESS [klen'li-nes], *n.* quality of being and keeping clean.

CLEANLY (1) [klen'li], *adj.* clean in habits and in person. CLEANLY (2) [klēn'li], *adv.* in a clean manner.

CLEANNESS [klēn'nes], *n.* state of being clean.

CLEANSE [klenz], *v.t.* to make clean, purify. CLEANSABLE, CLEANSIBLE, *adj.* able to be cleansed. CLEANSER, *n.* one who, or that which, cleanses. [OE.].

CLEANSING (1) [klen'zing], *n.* act of making clean. CLEANSING (2), *adj.* making clean, tending to cleanse or purify; **c. station**, *n.* post or depot where persons who have been in contact with poison gas may be cleansed.

CLEAR (1) [klēer], *adj.* free from obscurity, plain, lucid; obvious, open; bright, free from cloud etc.; translucent, transparent; unobstructed; free; distinct; with a pure ringing sound; whole, entire; **a c. head**, sound judgment. CLEAR (2), *adv.* completely; unhindered. CLEAR (3), *v.t.* to make c.; make a space; make tidy; get rid of, disentangle; free from suspicion of guilt; surmount, pass an obstacle; get payment on (a cheque or bill); *v.i.* to become c.; (*naut.*) pay harbour dues etc.; become free of encumbrances; **to c. away**, to tidy up, remove debris of a meal; go away; **to c. out**, to go away; **to c. up**, to put into order, make tidy; solve; improve (*esp.* the weather).

CLEARAGE [klēer'ij], *n.* clearing, clearance.

CLEARANCE [klēer'ans], *n.* act or result of clearing; certificate that a ship has been cleared; a permit; room to pass clear; amount of space required to enable one thing to move past or in another without touching it; **c. sale**, sale at a shop, intended to get rid of stock at any price. [OFr. from L.].

CLEARCOLE [klēer'kōl], *n.* first coat of paint applied to woodwork. [Fr.].

CLEAR-CUT [klēer-kut'], *adj.* distinct, clear in outline, obvious.

CLEAR-EYED [klēer-īd'], *adj.* clear-sighted, honest.

CLEAR-HEADED [klēer-he'did], *adj.* acute, intelligent, sound in judgment.

CLEARING [klēer'ing], *n.* act of making clear; justification; tract of land cleared for cultivation;

(*comm.*) the exchanging of the drafts on banking houses, and settling of the differences.

CLEARING-HOUSE [klēer'ing-hows], *n.* central organization at which the cheques and bills payable to various banks are credited and exchanged.

CLEARING-STATION [klēer'ing-stā-shn], *n.* temporary front-line hospital for receiving casualties for immediate treatment before they are passed to the base.

CLEARLY [klēer'li], *adv.* in clear fashion, obviously.

CLEARNESS [klēer'nes], *n.* quality of being clear.

CLEAR-SIGHTED [klēer-sī'tid], *adj.* able to see distinctly; discerning.

CLEARSTARCH [klēer'stahch], *v.t.* to stiffen and launder with clear starch.

CLEARSTORY, see CLERESTORY.

CLEAT (1) [klēt], *n.* (*naut.*) small tapering piece of wood fastened sideways to a spar etc.; device for belaying ropes; narrow lateral strengthening piece of wood or metal in joinery; wedge-like projection. CLEAT (2), *v.t.* to belay, fasten by a c. [ME.].

CLEAVABLE [klē'va-bl], *adj.* able to be cloven or split.

CLEAVAGE [klē'vij], *n.* division, particularly by cutting or splitting; place where anything is split; condition of being split; (*min.*) natural line of division in a mineral or rock; (*fig.*) sharp division of opinion leading to a split. [CLEAVE (1)].

CLEAVE (1) (*pret.* clove, clave†, cleaved, cleft, *p.pt.* cloven, clove, cleaved, cleft) [klēv], *v.t. and i.* to divide forcibly by cutting, split, make a fissure; fall apart; **in a cleft stick**, in a hopeless position, in a dilemma; **the cloven hoof**, evil qualities. [OE.].

CLEAVE (2) (*pret.* cleaved, clave†, *pret. and p.pt.* cleaved), *v.i.* to adhere, stick; (*fig.*) join oneself with, stand by closely and loyally. [OE.].

CLEAVER [klē'ver], *n.* person or thing that cleaves; butcher's chopper.

CLEAVERS [klē'verz], *n.* goose-grass.

CLEEK [klēk], *n.* iron-faced golf club with a narrow head; large grappling-hook. [OE.].

CLEF [klef], *n.* (*mus.*) sign denoting the pitch of a stave. [Fr. from L.].

CLEFT (1) [kleft], *n.* split made by cleaving, natural fissure in rock, chasm. [ME.].

CLEFT (2), *pret. and p.pt.* of CLEAVE (1).

CLEFT-GRAFT [kleft'grahft], *v.t.* (*hort.*) to engraft by cleaving the stock and grafting on a scion.

CLEFT-PALATE [kleft-pa'lat], *n.* deformity of the roof of the mouth, in which the two halves are imperfectly joined.

CLEG [kleg], *n.* horse-fly, gadfly. [OScand.].

CLEM [klem], *v.t. and i.* to starve; be pinched with cold or hunger, be in dire want. [OE.].

CLEMATIS [kle-mā'tis, kle'ma-tis], *n.* genus of climbing plants bearing vividly coloured flowers. [Gk.].

CLEMENCY [kle'men-si], *n.* quality of being clement. [L.].

CLEMENT [kle'ment], *adj.* merciful, lenient, mild. CLEMENTLY, *adv.* in c. fashion. [L.].

CLENCH [klensh], *v.t. and i.* to grip tightly, hold firmly with the hand; secure (a rivet etc.) by hammering down the ends; double the hand; (*fig.*) conclude definitely. [ME.].

CLERESTORY, CLEARSTORY [klēer'staw-ri], *n.* upper row of windows above the nave in large churches. [CLEAR and STOREY].

CLERGY [klur'ji], *n.* people consecrated and professionally engaged in religion in any Christian denomination; **benefit of c.**, former right of clergy, and others able to read, to be tried before the ecclesiastical courts. [OFr.].

CLERGYMAN [klur'ji-man], *n.* minister of religion.

CLERIC [kle'rik], *n.* clergyman. [OE. from Gk.].

CLERICAL [kle'ri-kal], *adj.* relating to the clergy; pertaining to a clerk. CLERICALISM, *n.* belief in the domination and importance of the clergy. [Prec.].

CLERIHEW [kle'ri-hyoo], *n.* humorous composition in irregular verse, in four lines of variable length and rhythm, rhyming in pairs. [E. *Clerihew* Bentley, the deviser].

CLERK [klahk], *n.* religious, legal or political officer, whose duties formerly involved writing and recording; minor parish official; person employed to keep accounts, make written entries etc. in the offices of a business; one in holy orders; †scholar. CLERKLY, *adj.* pertaining to a c. CLERKSHIP, *n.* position and duty of a c. [CLERIC].

CLEVER [kle'ver], *adj.* intelligent, quick-witted; apt

ōō is pronounced as in food; ŏŏ as in hood; th as in *think*; TH as in *that*; zh as in azure. ~ = related to.

with the hands, skilful in devising, adroit; displaying powers of foresight, resource and good management; *also in derogatory sense*, superficially smart but shallow. CLEVERISH, *adj.* fairly clever. CLEVERLY, *adv.* in c. fashion. [Uncert.].

CLEW (1) [klōō], *n.* thread or yarn wound into a ball; (*naut.*) lower corner of a square sail; cords supporting a hammock. CLEW (2), *v.t.* to wind into a ball; (*naut.*) pull up to the yard-arm (a sail); *v.i.* (*naut.*) to complete some task. [OE.].

CLICHE, cliché [klē′shā], *n.* much used, hackneyed phrase, trite and cheap in form. [Fr.].

CLICK (1) [klik], *n.* short, sharp snapping sound. CLICK (2), *v.t. and i.* to make a c.; fasten or bring together with a clicking sound; (*slang*) succeed in attracting the amorous attention of a member of the opposite sex. [Fris.].

CLICK-BEETLE [klik′bē-tl], *n.* coleopterous insect of the family *Elateridae*, firefly.

CLICK-CLACK [klik′klak], *n.* repeated clicking noise.

CLICKER [kli′ker], *n.* (*print.*) head compositor; foreman who cuts out and distributes leather to shoemakers; (*slang*) shopkeeper's tout; tape-machine.

CLIENT [kli′ent], *n.* customer; one who employs members of a profession as his agents, as in legal affairs etc. [~L.].

CLIENTELE, clientèle [klē-ahn-tāl′], *n.* the clients or customers of a business collectively; customers or clients as a class. [Fr.].

CLIFF [klif], *n.* steep declivity, lofty wall of rock, high edge of land bordering the sea. CLIFFY, *adj.* having cliffs. [OE.].

CLIMACTERIC (1) [kli-mak′te-rik, kli-mak-te′rik], *n.* period of supposed great physical and mystical importance in human life associated with the failing of physical powers or the menopause; period of great importance; event of great importance; **grand c.**, sixty-third year. CLIMACTERIC(AL) (2) [kli-mak-te′rik(-al)], *adj.* pertaining to the c.; crucially important. [Gk.].

CLIMACTIC [kli-mak′tik], *adj.* pertaining to a climax.

CLIMATE [kli-mat], *n.* general weather conditions as affecting the atmosphere of a region. CLIMATIC(AL) [kli-ma′tik(-al)], *adj.* pertaining to c. CLIMATICALLY, *adj.* with regard to c. [Gk.].

CLIMATOGRAPHY [kli-ma-to′gra-fi], *n.* study of climate. CLIMATOGRAPHICAL [kli-ma-to-gra′fi-kal], *adj.* pertaining to c. [Gk.].

CLIMATOLOGY [kli-ma-to′lo-ji], *n.* science of climate and the factors governing it. CLIMATOLOGICAL [kli-ma-to-lo′ji-kal], *adj.* relating to c. [Gk.].

CLIMAX [kli′maks], *n.* the culminating event of a series, final stage of a happening; highest point; (*rhet.*) figure by which the phrases rise in dignity and importance to the end of a series; culminating point of a drama. [Gk.].

CLIMB (1) [klim], *v.t. and i.* to ascend, reach a higher position, mount; (*fig.*) rise socially; (*bot.*) creep upwards clinging by tendrils; **to c. down**, abandon a claim or position rather ignominiously in face of pressure. CLIMB (2), *n.* act or way of ascending; thing ascended; ascent, rise in status. CLIMBABLE, *adj.* able to be climbed. CLIMBING, *adj.* ascending, that climbs, relating to a climber. [OE.].

CLIMBER [kli′mer], *n.* one who climbs; one who seeks social advancement; (*bot.*) climbing plant.

CLIME [klim], *n.* (*poet.*) region of the earth with a characteristic climate. [L.].

CLINCH (1) [klinsh], *v.t. and i.* to hold fast, make fast; hold with a rivet, fall into a clinch in boxing; (*fig.*) conclude an agreement or argument definitely. CLINCH (2), *n.* firm grip, a hold; position in boxing in which one of the boxers closes and holds his opponent in his arms; rivet. CLINCHER, *n.* that which clinches, riveter, tool for clinching. [CLENCH].

CLING (*pret. and p.pt.* **clung**) [kling], *v.i.* to adhere, hold on to by clasping with the arms; (*fig.*) pervade, remain present by or associated with; keep close to; remain constant to; hold to for support. CLINGY, *adj.* tending to c. [OE.].

CLINGSTONE [kling′stŏn], *n.* kind of peach in which the pulp adheres closely to the stone.

CLINIC [kli′nik], *n.* institution for medical, hygienic or psychological treatment or instruction, usually specializing in a single method of treatment; the teaching of surgery and medicine by practical demonstration on actual cases or patients in hospitals; class of students receiving such instruction. [Fr.].

CLINICAL [kli′ni-kal], *adj.* relating to a clinic or its

methods; pertaining to practical instruction or demonstrations on patients in a hospital; taking place on the sick-bed; **c. thermometer,** instrument for taking the bodily temperature. CLINICALLY, *adv.* in c. fashion. [Gk.].

CLINK (1) [klingk], *n.* light resonant sound caused by the gentle impact of metals. CLINK (2), *v.t. and i.* to make or cause to make a c. [Du.].

CLINK (3), *n.* (*slang*) prison, gaol. [Uncert.].

CLINKER (1) [kling′ker], *n.* hard, fused cinders from a furnace. [LGerm.].

CLINKER (2), *adj.* having overlapping strakes. CLINKER-BUILT, (*naut.*) built of planks each overlapping the next and fastened together with clinched nails.

CLINKSTONE [klingk′stŏn], *n.* greyish-blue resonant felspathic rock.

CLINO-, *pref.* sloping. [Gk.].

CLINOMETER [kli-no′mi-ter], *n.* instrument for measuring angles of inclination. CLINOMETRIC(AL) [kli-no-met′rik(-al)], *adj.* pertaining to, ascertained by, a c.

CLINT [klint], *n.* a hard rock; stone first thrown in curling. [ODan.].

CLIP (1) (*pres.pt.* **clipping**, *pret. and p.pt.* **clipped**) [klip], *v.t. and i.* to fasten or be held by a clip; hold fast by squeezing. CLIP (2), *n.* device for holding a number of things together, usually two bars drawn together one on each side of the group of objects; metal holder for cartridges designed to be loaded bodily into the magazine of an automatic weapon. [OE.].

CLIP (3) (*pres.pt.* **clipping**, *pret. and p.pt.* **clipped**), *v.t. and i.* to snip off, cut off by nipping between two blades; punch (a ticket); cut short and trim; shear (a sheep); cut pieces from the rims of (coins); cut off sharp (words); strike with a sharp blow with the open hand; (*slang*) move fast; **to c. the wings of,** (*fig.*) to restrain from free activity. CLIP (4), *n.* a snip, the act of clipping off; thing clipped off; wool of a season's sheep-shearing; sharp, clicking sound made by snipping or clipping; neat, sharp blow with the open hand on the face or side of the head; (*coll.*) speed, pace. [Uncert.].

CLIPPER [kli′per], *n.* one who, that which, clips; (*naut.*) speedy sailing vessel with a forward-raking bow; transoceanic flying-boat.

CLIPPERS [kli′perz], *n.(pl.)* small shears.

CLIPPIE [kli′pi], *n.* (*coll.*) female bus-conductor. [CLIP (3)].

CLIPPING [kli′ping], *n.* piece cut off by clipping; cutting from a newspaper.

CLIQUE [klēk], *n.* group of persons united in an attitude of exclusiveness; self-conscious coterie. CLIQUISH, *adj.* tending to join in cliques. [Fr.].

CLITORIS [kli′te-ris], *n.* (*anat.*) rudimentary organ in females corresponding to the penis. [Gk.].

CLOACA (*pl.* **cloacae**) [klŏ-ā′kah], *n.* sewer; (*anat.*) cavity in birds, fishes etc. into which the alimentary canal and urinary ducts open. [L.].

CLOAK (1) [klŏk], *n.* long loose sleeveless outer garment wrapped round the body; disguise, concealment, pretext; **c. and dagger,** in the manner of melodramatic tales of intrigue, espionage etc. CLOAK (2), *v.t.* to wrap, conceal with a c.; (*fig.*) hide, cover up.

CLOAKING [klŏ′king], *n.* wrapping in a cloak; (*fig.*) concealment.

CLOAKROOM [klŏk′rōōm], *n.* place in stations, restaurants, hotels etc. where coats and luggage may be left till called for; a toilet.

CLOCHE [klosh], *n.* bell-shaped glass covering for forcing outdoor plants; woman's close-fitting hat. [Fr.].

CLOCK (1) [klok], *n.* device for telling the time of the day, employing sand, falling weights or metal springs etc. CLOCK (2), *v.t.* to time (as a runner); **to c. in, on, out, off,** to register the time of arrival or departure from work by means of some timing device; start or finish any work. [LL.].

CLOCK (3), *n.* pattern worked in silk as an ornament on the side of a stocking or sock. CLOCKED, *adj.* ornamented with clocks. [Unkn.].

CLOCK-GOLF [klok-golf′], *n.* form of putting played clockwise into holes set out as the numbers on a clock-face.

CLOCKWISE [klok′wiz], *adv.* moving in the same direction as the hands of a clock.

CLOCKWORK [klok′werk], *n.* machinery operating a clock; prime mover driven by a coiled spring unwinding and transmitting its rotary motion through gear-wheels; **like c., without hitch or** interruption.

CLOD (1) [klod], *n.* lump of earth or clay, mass of turf; the ground; (*fig.*) that which is earthy or base; (*fig.*) gross, stupid fellow. CLOD (2), (*pres.pt.* CLODDING, *pret. and p.pt.* CLODDED), *v.t. and i.* to clot; pelt with clods. CLODDISH, *adj.* stupid, doltish. [ME.].

CLODHOPPER [klod'ho-per], *n.* stupid rustic, heavy-witted farm-labourer; heavy clumsy shoe or boot.

CLOG (1) [klog], *n.* heavy shoe with a wooden sole with a protective iron; block of wood tied to the legs of animals to restrain them; impediment, *esp.* dirt in machinery; (*fig.*) anything which hinders. CLOG (2) (*pres.pt.* CLOGGING, *pret. and p.pt.* CLOGGED), *v.t. and i.* to hamper, hinder; slow up by encumbrances; choke up, block up; hamper free activity; become coagulated. [ME.].

CLOG-DANCE [klog'dahns], *n.* kind of tap dance in clogs.

CLOGGY [klo'gi], *adj.* that clogs, adhesively encumbering. CLOGGINESS, *n.* state of being c.

CLOISONNE, cloisonné (1) [klwah-zo'nā], *adj.* (of enamelled work) having the design in metal raised above the level of the enamelled surfaces. CLOISONNE (2), *n.* c. work. [Fr.].

CLOISTER [klois'ter], *n.* covered way running round an open court or quadrangle in a monastic or similar building; monastery, convent; retreat. CLOISTER (2), *v. reflex. and t.* to confine in a c.; withdraw from the world. CLOISTERED, *adj.* having a c.; living in a c.; secluded, sheltered. CLOISTRAL, *adj.* relating to, or resembling, a c.; retired. [OFr. from L.].

CLONE [klōn], *n.* (*bot.*) group of cultivated plants all derived by grafting etc. from a single original stock. CLONAL, *adj.* (*bot.*) pertaining to a c. [Gk.].

CLONUS [klō'nus], *n.* (*med.*) violent spasmodic muscular contractions and relaxations in rapid succession. CLONIC [klo'nik], *adj.* (*med.*) relating to, or resembling, c. [Gk.].

CLOP [klop], *n.* the sound of a horse's hoofs on hard ground. [Imitative].

CLOSE (1) [klōs], *adj.* near, next to; intimate; restricted; solid, compact, not porous; imprisoned; secluded; (*fig.*) reserved; reticent; stingy; nearly equal, almost exact or identical; thorough, careful, detailed; sultry, stuffy; (*philol.*) protected by or ending in a consonant; **c. vowel,** vowel uttered with the tongue near the roof of the mouth; **a c. call, c. shave,** narrow escape. CLOSE (2), *adv.* closely; at hand. CLOSE (3), *n.* piece of ground partly enclosed by walls or buildings, *esp.* precinct of a cathedral; blind passage leading only to an inner courtyard. [OFr. from L.].

CLOSE (4) [klōz], *v.t.* to bring to an end, finish; shut, shut up, enclose completely; make access to something impossible; (*milit.*) arrange in close formation; *v.i.* to come to an end, finish; cease speaking; become closed, shut; come to grips; **to c. down,** to stop, bring an enterprise or activity to an end; **to c. in,** to approach on several sides, often with hostile intention; (of days) become shorter; **to c. with,** to come to blows or grips; come to an agreement, accept an offer. CLOSE (5), *n.* conclusion, end; a coming to grips in fighting; (*mus.*) cadence. [L.].

CLOSED [klōzd], *adj.* restricted, limited to a few people (of professions, scholarships etc.); **c. shop,** factory or other employment to which only workers belonging to recognized trade unions are admitted.

CLOSE-FISTED [klōs-fis'tid], *adj.* mean, stingy.

CLOSE-HAULED [klōs-hawld'], *adj.* (*naut.*) with the corners of the sails drawn in tightly for sailing close to the wind.

CLOSELY [klōs'li], *adv.* in close fashion.

CLOSENESS [klōs'nes], *n.* condition of being close.

CLOSE QUARTERS [klōs-kwaw'terz], *n.(pl.)* barriers used for defence when a ship is boarded; **to come to c.,** to come to grips with an enemy.

CLOSER [klō'zer], *n.* speaker who sums up a debate; (*arch.*) brick ending the horizontal course of a wall.

CLOSE-REEFED [klōs-rēft'], *adj.* (*naut.*) with all reefs taken in.

CLOSE-SEASON [klōs'sē-zon], *n.* breeding season when it is illegal to catch certain fish or shoot certain game; any annual period when some sport does not take place.

CLOSE-STOOL [klōs'stōōl], *n.* chamber-pot with a wooden seat.

CLOSET (1) [klo'zit], *n.* small retiring room entered

from a large room, private chamber for undisturbed rest; lavatory, privy; large cupboard. CLOSET (2), *v.t.* to take into a private apartment for secret conclave, shut away; **to be closeted with,** to talk secretly with.

CLOSE-TONGUED [klōs-tungd'], *adj.* reticent, uncommunicative.

CLOSE-UP [klōs'up], *n.* photograph, *esp.* cinema, taken at close range; (*fig.*) detailed view.

CLOSING [klō'zing], *n.* conclusion, end.

CLOSING-TIME [klō'zing-tim], *n.* hour at which shops or public-houses close.

CLOSURE [klō'zyŏŏr], *n.* the taking of a vote in order to bring a debate to a close; (*elect.*) completion of a circuit; declaration at cricket; a bringing to an end; act of closing. [OFr.].

CLOT (1) [klot], *n.* a coagulation of fluid, small coagulated lump. CLOT (2) (*pres.pt.* CLOTTING, *pret. and p.pt.* CLOTTED), *v.t. and i.* to form or cause to form into clots. [OE.].

CLOTH (1) [kloth], *n.* pliable stuff woven from various fibrous materials, principally used for garments; piece of this material, *esp.* as used for cleaning or as a covering for anything; breadth of canvas in a sail; (*fig.*) the clergy; **C. of Estate,** canopy held above the sovereign. CLOTH (2), *adj.* made of c. [OE.].

CLOTHE [klōtH], *v.t.* to put garments on, dress, supply with clothes; deck out in; conceal; surround, endue with. [OE.].

CLOTHES [klōtHz], *n.* garments, articles of dress; bodily coverings; bed-coverings; **plain c.,** civilian dress. [OE.].

CLOTHES-BASKET [klōtHz'bahs-kit], *n.* basket in which soiled clothes are taken to be washed.

CLOTHES-BRUSH [klōtHz'brush], *n.* brush for coats and other heavy garments.

CLOTHES-HORSE [klōtHz'haws], *n.* frame to dry clothes on.

CLOTHES-LINE [klōtHz'lin], *n.* line on which clothes are hung out to dry.

CLOTHES MOTH [klōtHz'moth], *n.* moth whose larvae feed on woollen fabric.

CLOTHES-PEG [klōtHz'peg], *n.* forked peg for fastening clothes to a clothes-line.

CLOTHES-PRESS [klōtHz'pres], *n.* device for pressing clothes; chest for storing clothes.

CLOTH-HALL [kloth'hawl], *n.* medieval cloth exchange, building formerly used for this purpose.

CLOTHIER [klō'tHi-er], *n.* dealer in cloth or clothes; outfitter, tailor.

CLOTHING [klō'тHing], *n.* clothes or garments in general, attire, dress.

CLOTH-SHEARER [kloth'shēer-er], *n.* one who removes unnecessary nap on woollen cloth.

CLOTHWORKER [kloth'wer-ker], *n.* maker of cloth.

CLOTHYARD [kloth'yahd], *n.* former unit of measurement for cloth; rod used to determine such measurement; **c. shaft,** arrow of this length fired from the long bow.

CLOTTED [klo'tid], *adj.* coagulated, formed into clots.

CLOUD (1) [klowd], *n.* mass of thick vapour, mass of water-vapour suspended in the atmosphere; mass of suspended dust; (*fig.*) anything resembling this; vast mass of rapidly moving particles or objects; vast multitude; that which shadows, darkens or disgraces; that which threatens; dark or blurred colour in a stone or translucent body; (*pl.*) sky, heaven, great height; **under a c.,** in disgrace; **up in the clouds,** abstracted, not noticing ordinary happenings; very happy. CLOUD (2), *v.t. and i.* to cast a c. on; become dark, blurred; mark or cover with a c.; spoil, disparage; lour. [OE.].

CLOUDBERRY [klowd'be-ri], *n.* mountain bramble.

CLOUDBURST [klowd'berst], *n.* torrential rainstorm, deluge.

CLOUD-CAPT [klowd'kapt], *adj.* lost in the clouds, lofty.

CLOUD-CASTLE [klowd'kah-sl], *n.* day-dreamed ambition.

CLOUDED [klow'did], *adj.* covered with clouds, cloudy; blurred; spoilt; with the colours confusedly merging.

CLOUDLESS [klowd'les], *adj.* lacking clouds, clear, untroubled.

CLOUDLET [klowd'let], *n.* little cloud.

CLOUD-WRACK [klowd'rak], *n.* ragged and scattered clouds remaining after a storm.

CLOUDY [klow'di], *adj.* covered in, surrounded, by

clouds; (of the weather) dull, overcast; dim, indistinct, obscure; not clarified, thick, opaque; blurred. CLOUDILY, *adv.* in c. fashion.

CLOUGH [kluf], *n.* small deep valley. [OE.].

CLOUT (1) [klowt], *n.* heavy swinging blow with the hand; rough cloth, rag for cleaning; centre of the target in archery; iron plate fixed on the heel of a shoe or on an axle-tree to prevent wear. CLOUT (2), *v.t. and i.* to strike with a c.; mend with a patch; make fast with clout-nails. [OE.].

CLOUT-NAIL [klowt'nāl], *n.* short large-headed nail for securing the soles of shoes; copper nail formerly used in coating ships.

CLOVE (1) [klōv], *n.* aromatic Moluccan spice from the dried flower-bud of *Caryophyllus aromaticus*. [OFr. from L.].

CLOVE (2), *n.* small bulb growing separate from another.

CLOVE (3), *pret. of* CLEAVE (1).

CLOVE-GILLYFLOWER [klōv-ji'li-flow-er], *n.* species of *Dianthus*, the flower of which has a clove-like fragrance.

CLOVE-HITCH [klōv'hich], *n.* knot in the form of two half-hitches round a spar or rope.

CLOVEN [klō'ven], *adj.* split up into two parts; **to show the c. hoof,** to reveal evil characteristics. CLOVEN-FOOTED, CLOVEN-HOOFED, *adj.* having the hoof split up into two parts, as the ox.

CLOVE-PINK [klōv-pingk'], *n.* clove-gillyflower.

CLOVER [klō'ver], *n.* plant of the genus *Trifolium*, with fragrant pink or white flowers; **to be in c.,** to be in easy circumstances. [OE.].

CLOWN (1) [klown], *n.* buffoon, *esp.* an intentional one; buffoon in pantomime or a circus who amuses by tumbling, somersaulting etc.; (*archaic*) a rustic; bad-mannered oaf. CLOWN (2), *v.i.* to act the fool. CLOWNERY, *n.* behaviour like that of a c., buffoonery. [OScand.].

CLOWNISH [klow'nish], *adj.* like a clown; ill-mannered, clumsy. CLOWNISHLY, *adv.* in c. fashion.

CLOY [kloi], *v.t. and i.* to satiate, glut, sicken with sweetness or plenty, cloth with richness or abundance. [Fr.].

CLUB (1) [klub], *n.* heavy, thick-ended piece of wood used for striking blows; stick with a knobbed or heavy end for striking the ball in several games, as golf etc.; lowest valued suit in playing cards, bearing a trefoil emblem; number of persons meeting together for some common, generally social, purpose; building in which such an assembly is held; an organization for the pursuit of a common interest. CLUB (2) (*pres.pt.* CLUBBING, *pret. and p.pt* CLUBBED), *v.t. and i.* to strike with a c., use as a c. (some other weapon); join in a c.; **to c. together,** to pool resources to achieve some common object. [OScand.].

CLUBBABLE [klu'ba-bl], *adj.* sociable, disposed to club life.

CLUBBED [klubd], *adj.* used, held like a club; thickened at the end.

CLUB-FOOT [klub'fŏŏt], *n.* congenital deformity of the foot in which it is short, distorted and thickened. CLUB-FOOTED, *adj.* having a c.

CLUB-HAUL [klub'hawl], *n.* desperate method of tacking a ship about, by dropping the lee anchor, thus bringing her head to the wind, and then casting off the cable as soon as she pays off.

CLUB-HOUSE [klub'hows], *n.* building occupied by a club; sports pavilion for rest and refreshment.

CLUB-LAND [klub'land], *n.* district round St. James's and Pall Mall in London, where the leading clubs are found.

CLUB-LAW [klub'law], *n.* rule by brute force.

CLUBMAN [klub'man], *n.* one frequenting clubs.

CLUB-MOSS [klub'mos], *n.* (*bot.*) plant of the genus *Lycopodium*.

CLUB-ROOM [klub'rŏŏm], *n.* room reserved for social relaxation in some building.

CLUB-ROOT [klub'rŏŏt], *n.* (*bot.*) a plant disease.

CLUB-RUSH [klub'rush], *n.* (*bot.*) plant of the genus *Scirpus*.

CLUCK (1) [kluk], *n.* thick clicking sound made by the tongue against the back of the palate; call of the hen. CLUCK (2), *v.i.* to utter a series of clucks. [Imitative].

CLUE [klōō], *n.* fact helping to solve or throw light on some puzzle or mystery. CLUELESS, *adj.* (*coll.*) without a clue; stupid. [CLEW].

CLUMBER [klum'ber], *n.* species of spaniel bred at *Clumber*, Notts, formerly the Duke of Newcastle's seat.

CLUMP (1) [klump], *n.* small, solid group of people or objects (*esp.* trees) in an open place; shapeless lump, clod; clay in coal strata; thick slab of leather on the sole of a boot; (*coll.*) heavy blow, clout. CLUMP (2), *v.t. and i.* to gather, come together in a c.; fasten a c.; tread heavily; (*coll.*) clout heavily. CLUMPY, *adj.* consisting of clumps, in heavy clods.

CLUMSY [klum'zi], *adj.* awkward, apt to stumble and fumble; with the muscles and movements imperfectly co-ordinated; ungainly, heavy-handed, lacking in grace; slow, unskilful; inelegant, gauche. CLUMSILY, *adv.* in c. fashion. CLUMSINESS, *n.* state of being c.

CLUNG [klung], *pret. and p.pt.* of CLING.

CLUNIAC [klŏŏ'ni-ak], *n. and adj.* member of, pertaining to, a reformed Benedictine order of monks. [*Cluny*, Burgundy.].

CLUPEA [klŏŏ'pi-ah], *n.* genus of fishes of which the herring, sprat and pilchard are members. CLUPEOID, *adj.* pertaining to the genus *C.* [L.].

CLUSTER [klus'ter], *n.* small group of people or objects collected together in fairly close formation; bunch of flowers, fruit etc. growing together or from the same stem; mass of bees lumped together during swarming; mass of septic matter. CLUSTER (2), *v.i.* to grow in a c., crowd round in a c. or clusters. CLUSTERED, *adj.* grouped in a c.; **clustered column,** Gothic pillar resembling a mass of slender columns arranged in a single group. CLUSTERINGLY, *adv.* in clusters. [OE.].

CLUTCH (1) [kluch], *v.t. and i.* to grab at desperately, contract the fingers spasmodically, snatch, seize with the hand. CLUTCH (2), *n.* a gripping with the hands, sudden snatch, desperate grab at; firm, sudden grasp; mechanical device for connecting or disconnecting at will one rotating shaft with another in the same axis by means of a projecting tooth or a friction plate between the two. [OE.].

CLUTCH (3), *n.* the eggs laid by a bird at one sitting; the chickens hatched from these. [OScand.].

CLUTTER (1) [klut'er], *n.* mess of litter, confused, disorderly hustle. CLUTTER (2), *v.t.* to make untidy, choke up, clog up. [Uncert.].

CLYDESDALE [klīdz'dāl], *n.* heavy breed of draught horse. [*Clydesdale*, Scotland].

CLYPEATE [kli'pi-āt], *adj.* shaped like a buckler, shield-like. [L.].

CLYSMIC [kliz'mik], *adj.* purging, cleansing. [Gk.].

CLYSTER [klis'ter], *n.* an enema. [Gk.].

CO-, *pref.* together, together with, joint action, coincidence of some kind. [L.].

COACH (1) [kōch], *n.* large closed horse-drawn carriage with a box outside for the driver, one of several four-wheeled varieties of horse-drawn passenger conveyance; motor char-a-banc carrying passengers for long distances; passenger carriage of a railway train; a number of compartments; teacher, instructor, *esp.* one employed to train and prepare for a particular contest or examination; trainer to a team of athletes or to a sports club. COACH (2), *v.t. and i.* to travel by c.; give special instruction or training for an examination or athletic contest. [Hungarian].

COACHBOX [kōch'boks], *n.* the driver's seat on a coach.

COACHBUILDER [kōch'bil-der], *n.* one who makes coaches; one who makes the bodies of motor vehicles.

COACH-BUILT [kōch'bilt], *adj.* of a car, having the bodywork made by a coachbuilder.

COACH-DOG [kōch'dog], *n.* carriage-dog; Dalmatian hound.

COACH-HOUSE [kōch'hows], *n.* shed in which to keep a coach.

COACHING [kō'ching], *n.* travelling by coach; the driving of a coach; tutoring or training of a person for an examination or athletic contest.

COACHMAN [kōch'man], *n.* the driver of a coach; artificial fly used as a bait for trout. COACHMANSHIP, *n.* skill in driving a coach.

COACHMASTER [kōch'mahs-ter], *n.* proprietor of a coach or stable.

COACH-OFFICE [kōch'o-fis], *n.* booking office for a stage-coach or motor coach.

COACHWORK [kōch'werk], *n.* the material and workmanship of a motor-car body.

COACTIVE [kō-ak'tiv], *adj.* compulsive, concurrent. COACTIVELY, *adv.* in c. fashion.

COADJUTANT (1) [kō-aj'ŏŏ-tant], *adj.* assisting. COADJUTANT (2), *n.* an assistant.

COADJUTOR [kō-a'jŏŏ-ter], *n.* an assistant, bishop who assists another bishop. [L.].

COAGULABLE [kō-a'gyŏŏ-la-bl], *adj.* capable of

coagulation. COAGULABILITY [kō-a-gyōō-la-bi'li-ti], *n.* quality of being c.
COAGULANT [kō-a′gyōō-lant], *n.* substance producing coagulation.
COAGULATE [kō-a′gyōō-lāt], *v.t. and i.* to make partly solid, clot, curdle and semi-solidify; become clotted or curdled, congeal. COAGULATIVE [kō-a′gyōō-la-tiv], *adj.* producing, liable to, coagulation. COAGULATOR, *n.* that which produces coagulation. [L.].
COAGULATION [kō-a-gyōō-lā′shn], *n.* process or state of coagulating; substance coagulated. [L.].
COAL (1) [kōl], *n.* solid black combustible mineral, chiefly carbon, burnt as fuel; piece of this material; **to haul over the coals,** to rebuke, reprimand; **to heap coals of fire on,** to give good for evil; **to carry coals to Newcastle,** to take something where there is already plenty of it. COAL (2), *v.t. and i.* to load with, take on board, c. [OE.].
COALBED [kōl′bed], *n.* a coal stratum.
COALBOX [kōl′boks], *n.* coal-scuttle.
COAL-BUNKER [kōl′bung-ker], *n.* that part of a ship in which the coal is stored.
COAL-CELLAR [kōl′se-ler], *n.* cellar or shed in which coal is stored.
COALESCE [kō-a-les′], *v.i.* to grow together, fuse, unite completely and inseparably, intermingle; *(fig.)* unite, join together as one. COALESCENCE, *n.* process of coalescing, state of having coalesced. COALESCENT, *adj.* coalescing; tending to coalesce. [L.].
COAL FACE [kōl′fās], *n.* surface of a seam of coal on which miners work.
COALFIELD [kōl′fēld], *n.* seam of coal; region in which coal is mined.
COAL-FISH [kōl′fish], *n.* species of codfish.
COAL-GAS [kōl′gas], *n.* inflammable gas obtained from coal and used for illumination and heating.
COALHEAVER [kōl′hē-ver], *n.* one employed in carrying or loading coal.
COAL-HOLE [kōl′hōl], *n.* circular opening in the pavement through which coal may be tipped into the cellar of a house etc.; store for coal.
COAL-HOUSE [kōl′hows], *n.* small building by a house for keeping coals.
COALING [kō′ling], *n.* act of filling a ship's bunkers with coal.
COALITION [kō-a-li′shn], *n.* act of coalescing; alliance between two or more persons or organizations by which they temporarily co-operate while maintaining their individuality entirely; temporary union between two or more normally incompatible political parties to form a government. COALITIONIST, *n.* one supporting some political c. [COALESCE].
COALMASTER [kōl′mahs-ter], *n.* mineowner or lessee of a coal-mine.
COAL METER [kōl′mē-ter], *n.* one in charge of the measuring of coal.
COAL-MINE [kōl′mīn], *n.* underground workings from which coal is dug; **coal-miner,** *n.* worker in a c.
COAL-OWNER [kōl′ō-ner], *n.* mineowner.
COALPIT [kōl′pit], *n.* unit of a coal-mine, group of workings sharing and grouped round a common entrance and pithead.
COAL-SCREEN [kōl′skrēn], *n.* mechanical sieve for sorting coal.
COAL-SCUTTLE [kōl′sku-tl], *n.* container in which coals are stored for a domestic fire.
COAL-TAR [kōl′tah(r)], *n.* tar obtained by the destructive distillation of coal.
COAL-TIT [kōl′tit], *n.* small passerine bird.
COAL-TRIMMER [kōl′tri-mer], *n.* one employed in coaling ships.
COAL-WHIPPER [kōl′wi-per], *n.* one who unloads coal from ships.
COAMING [kō′ming], *n.* raised ledge round a ship's hatch to prevent water from entering.
COARSE [kaws], *adj.* rough, harsh; unpolished; unrefined; not finely finished; (of screws) having the threads widely spaced; made of, or having, large particles; *(fig.)* ill-mannered; lacking in sensibility, vulgar. COARSELY, *adv.* in c. fashion. COARSENESS, *n.* state of being c. [Uncert.].
COARSE-GRAINED [kaws-grānd′], *adj.* having a rough widely spaced grain (of wood); *(fig.)* crude, lacking in sensibility.
COARSEN [kaw′sen], *v.t. and i.* to make coarse, become coarse.
COAST (1) [kōst], *n.* the part of the land bordering

on the sea or on any large tract of water; **the c. is clear,** there is no one about whom you would wish to avoid. COAST (2), *v.t. and i.* to skirt the edge of anything; travel in a mechanical vehicle without help of engine or restraint of brakes, freewheel; *(U.S.)* toboggan. [OFr. from L.].
COASTAL [kōs′tal], *adj.* relating to, or near, the coast.
COASTER [kōs′ter], *n.* vessel employed in trading between ports in the same country; low round decanter-stand.
COASTGUARD [kōst′gahd], *n.* guard stationed on the coast to prevent and detect smuggling or illicit entry.
COASTING [kōs′ting], *adj.* that coasts; **c. vessel,** a coaster.
COASTLINE [kōst′līn], *n.* the coastal outline of a country; stretch of coast, *esp.* when viewed from the sea.
COASTWISE [kōst′wīz], *adv.* along the coast.
COAT (1) [kōt], *n.* (sleeved) outer garment fastening down the front; outer furry or hairy skin of an animal; *(anat.)* membranous layer enclosing an organ of the body; (layer) of any substance spread over a surface; *(her.)* background on which armorial bearings are portrayed; *(bot.)* outer layer of a bulb. COAT (2), *v.t.* to cover with a c. [OFr. from L.].
COAT ARMOUR [kōt′ah-mer], *n.* armorial bearings of a person or family.
COATEE [kō-tē′], *n.* short close-fitting coat.
COAT-HANGER [kōt′hang-er], *n.* curved piece of wood etc. on which clothes may be hung from the shoulder.
COATI [kō-ah′ti], *n.* long-nosed South American mammal related to the racoon.
COATING [kō′ting], *n.* coat, layer of something covering something else; material for making coats.
COAX [kōks], *v.t.* to persuade by flattery or fondling; humour into doing something, cajole. COAXER, *n.* one who coaxes. COAXING, *adj.* wheedling, cajoling. COAXINGLY, *adv.* in a coaxing way. [Uncert.].
CO-AXIAL [kō-ak′si-al], *adj. (maths. and phys.)* having a common axis.
COB (1) [kob], *n.* the spike of maize; compound of clay and straw used as a substitute for stone and brick for building walls etc.; small lump of coal; stocky, sturdy horse, in size between a horse and a pony; the male swan. [Unkn.].
COB (2), *n.* the greater black-backed gull. [~Fris.].
COB (3) *(pres.pt.* cobbing, *pret. and p.pt.* cobbed), *v.t.* to beat on the buttocks; hit over the head. [Unkn.].
COBALT [kō′bawlt], *n.* brittle, greyish or reddish-grey metal, the chemical element denoted by Co; pigment obtained from a compound of this metal; **c. blue,** deep blue pigment obtained from this compound. COBALTIC, *adj.* pertaining to, mixed with c. [Germ.].
COBBER [ko′ber], *n. (Australian)* friend, mate.
COBBLE (1) [ko′bl], *n.* small round stone, formerly used for paving streets; lump of coal of similar size. COBBLE (2), *v.t.* to pave with cobbles. COBBLY, *adj.* paved with cobbles; uneven. [Unkn.].
COBBLE (3), *see* COBLE.
COBBLE (4), *v.t.* to mend or make boots or shoes; sew or patch rudely; *v.i.* to work clumsily. [Unkn.].
COBBLER [ko′bler], *n.* boot and shoe repairer; clumsy mender, botcher; *(U.S.)* iced drink flavoured with lemon and sweetened; **cobbler's punch,** hot spiced beer. [Prec.].
COBBLESTONE [ko′bl-stōn], *n.* large rounded pebble, cobble.
CO-BELLIGERENT [kō-be-li′je-rent], *n. and adj.* (pertaining to) a nation actively engaged in war on the same side, but not admitted to full alliance.
COBLE, COBBLE [kō′bl], *n.* flat-bottomed fishing boat with a deep rudder, driven by one lugsail; flat-bottomed rowing boat. [Wel., Bret.].
COBNUT [kob′nut], *n.* variety of large hazelnut.
COB-PIPE [kob′pīp], *n.* pipe made of a corn-cob.
COBRA [kō′brah], *n.* venomous Asiatic snake with erectile hood-like folds of skin round its neck; similar African species; **king c.,** ring c, or hamadryad. [Portug. from L.].
COBWEB [kob′web], *n.* spider's network of gossamer threads for catching insects; *(fig.)* any thin transparent fabric; that which is fluffy or obscure. COBWEBBED, *adj.* thick with cobwebs; *(bot.)* covered with a thick interwoven pubescence. COBWEBBY, *adj.* covered with cobwebs, resembling cobwebs.
COCA, CUCA [kō′kah, kyōō′kah], *n.* South Ameri-

ōō is pronounced as in food; ŏŏ as in hood; th as in *think*; TH as in *that*; zh as in azure. ~ = related to.

can plant, the leaves of which have tonic properties. [Peruvian].

COCA-COLA [kō-ka-kō′lah], *n.* (*U.S.*) mildly stimulating beverage. [*Prot.*].

COCAINE [kō-kān′], *n.* alkaloid substance obtained from the coca plant, taken as a drug, and employed as a local anaesthetic. COCAINISM, *n.* c. poisoning; morbid craving for c. COCAINIST, *n.* habitual taker of c. [COCA].

COCAINIZE [kō-kā′nīz], *v.t.* to give cocaine to; drug with cocaine. COCAINIZATION [kō-kā-ni-zā′shn], *n.* state of being drugged with cocaine.

COCCIDIA [kok-si′di-ah], *n.*(*pl.*) parasitic organisms formed in the cell-tissues of animals. [Gk.].

COCCUS (*pl.* **cocci**) [ko′kus, kok′sī], *n.* spherical kind of bacteria producing disease; genus of four-winged insects harmful to plants; (*bot.*) capsule, single cell. [Gk.].

COCCYGEAL [kok-si′ji-al], *adj.* of, or relating to, the coccyx.

COCCYX [kok′siks], *n.* (*anat.*) the bone at the base of the spine. [L. from Gk.].

COCHIN [kō′chin], *n.* breed of domestic fowls originally imported from China. [*Cochin-China*].

COCHINEAL [ko′chi-nēl], *n.* base for scarlet dye formed from compounded bodies of a South American insect. [Span.].

COCHLEA [kok′li-ah], *n.* (*anat.*) part of the internal ear, shaped like a snail-shell. COCHLEAN, COCH-LEATED, *adj.* twisted in the form of a snail-shell, spiral.

COCK (1) [kok], *n.* male of the domestic fowl or other birds; weather-vane in the form of a cock; device for regulating the flow of water through a pipe; gnomon of a sundial; needle or pointer of a balance; small bracket in a clock which supports the pivot of the pendulum; (*fig.*) swaggering, osten-tacious man; smart curl or angle, particularly of a hat; part of a gun operated by the trigger to fire the cartridge; (*slang*) fellow, chap; (*vulg.*) penis. COCK (2),*v.i.* to lift up alertly; *v.t.* to set erect, place at an angle, as a hat; draw back the hammer of (a gun) ready for firing. [OE.].

COCK (3), *n.* heap of farm produce, hay or manure, piled in a cone. COCK (4), *v.t.* to heap up in a c. [OE.].

COCKADE [ko-kād′], *n.* ornamental rosette or badge of office fastened to the side of a hat. COCKADED, *adj.* wearing a c. [Fr.].

COCKAHOOP [ko-ka-hōōp′], *adj.* exultant. [Un-cert.].

COCK-A-LEEKIE, see COCKY-LEEKIE.

COCKALORUM [ko-ka-law′rum], *n.* (*coll.*) strut-ting conceited man of small stature.

COCK-AND-BULL [kok-and-bōōl′], *adj.* fantastic, incredible (story).

COCKATEEL [ko-ka-tēl′], *n.* Australian crested parrot of the cockatoo group. [Du. from Portug.].

COCKATOO [ko-ka-tōō′], *n.* one of several birds of the parrot family, characterized by a crest of feathers on the head; (*Australian*) small farmer. [Malay].

COCKATRICE [ko′ka-tris], *n.* mythical reptile supposed to be hatched from a cock's egg, a basilisk; (*her.*) fabulous creature with the head, wings and legs of a cock and a snake's body and tail. [OFr.].

COCKAYNE, COCKAIGNE [ko-kān′], *n.* country of the imagination offering idleness and luxury; London. [OFr.].

COCK-BOAT [kok′bōt], *n.* small boat towed behind a ship.

COCKCHAFER [kok′chā-fer], *n.* beetle which makes a whirring noise when flying.

COCK-CROW [kok′krō], *n.* dawn.

COCKED [kokt], *adj.* erect; ready for firing; **c. hat,** hat with brim permanently turned up, *esp.* three-cornered.

COCKER (1) [ko′ker], *n.* cock-fighter; kind of spaniel.

COCKER (2), *v.t.* to fondle, indulge. [~Dan.].

COCKEREL [ko′ke-rel], *n.* young cock not more than a year old. [*Dim.* of COCK].

COCKEYED [ko-kīd′], *adj.* having squinting eyes; (*slang*) slanted, crooked, topsy-turvy.

COCK-FIGHTING [kok′fī-ting], *n.* sport of matching two fighting gamecocks.

COCKHORSE [kok-haws′], *n.* hobby-horse; **a c.,** on horseback, astride.

COCKING [ko′king], *n.* action of drawing back the hammer of a gun ready to fire.

COCKLE (1) [ko′kl], *n.* plant growing among corn. [OE.].

COCKLE (2), *n.* edible bivalve mollusc; **to warm the**

cockles of one's heart, to cheer up, comfort and please.

COCKLE (3), *v.t. and i.* to contract into wrinkles, pucker. [*Prec.*].

COCKLE-SHELL [ko′kl-shel], *n.* one of the shells of the cockle; (*fig.*) fragile boat.

COCKLOFT [kok′loft], *n.* top loft immediately under the roof.

COCKNEY (1) [kok′ni], *n.* Londoner, person born within sound of Bow Bells; the vulgar London dialect. COCKNEY (2), *adj.* belonging to, or connected with, a c., belonging to London. COCKNEYDOM, *n.* City of London. COCKNEYFIED, *adj.* having acquired the characteristics of a c. COCKNEYISH, *adj.* per-taining to, or like, a c. COCKNEYISM, *n.* dialect of a c.; c. idiom. [ME.].

COCKPIT [kok′pit], *n.* enclosed space or pit in which fighting gamecocks are matched against each other; (*fig.*) battlefield; (*naut.*) temporary ward on the lower deck of a warship for the wounded; confined space in an aeroplane where the pilot sits.

COCKROACH [kok′rōch], *n.* large black creeping insect infesting kitchens. [~Span.].

COCKSCOMB [koks′kōm], *n.* the comb of a cock; plant of the genus *Celosia*.

COCK'S HEAD [koks′hed], *n.* (*bot.*) the common red clover.

COCK-SHY [kok′shī], *n.* (*coll.*) a shot or shy at an object for amusement; the object itself aimed at.

COCK-SPARROW [kok-spa′rō], *n.* male of the sparrow; (*fig.*) pert, self-important dapper little man.

COCKSURE [kok-syōōr′], *adj.* conceitedly sure of success, confidently certain.

COCKTAIL [kok′tāl], *n.* short iced drink of mixed ingredients, usually gin, bitters and a flavouring of some kind, well shaken up; a beetle, the Devil's Coach-horse, which erects the hind part of its body.

COCK-UP [kok′up], *n.* (*typ.*) superior letter used in abbreviations.

COCKY (1) [ko′ki], *n.* (*Australian*) a small farmer. [COCKATOO].

COCKY (2), *adj.* vain, conceited, confidently and aggressively certain of ability and importance.

COCKY-LEEKIE, COCK-A-LEEKIE [ko-ki-lē′ki], *n.* (*Scots*) a broth cooked with leeks. [COCK and LEEK].

COCOA [kō′kō], *n.* powder from the seeds of the cacao plant; drink of chocolate flavour made from this. [CACAO].

COCOA-BEAN [kō′kō-bēn], *n.* seed of the cacao plant.

COCOA-NIBS [kō′kō-nibz], *n.*(*pl.*) uncrushed cocoa-beans after husking.

COCOA-NUT [kō′kō-nut], *n.* coconut.

COCONUT [kō′kō-nut], *n.* fruit of a tropical palm, in the form of a white hollow kernel containing milk, and covered with a hard brown shell; **c. butter,** buttery substance obtained from the c. [Portug.].

COCOON [ko-kōōn′], *n.* small silken case spun by certain insects. [Fr.].

COD (1) [kod], *n.* pod, husk; bag; the scrotum; **pease c.,** pod of peas. [OE.].

COD (2), *n.* large sea-fish. [Unkn.].

COD (3) (*pres.pt.* **codding**, *pret. and p.pt.* **codded**), *v.t.* (*slang*) to play tricks on a person, hoax, fool. [Unkn.].

CODA [kō′dah], *n.* (*mus.*) short separate concluding section. [It. from L.].

CODDLE (1) [ko′dl], *v.t.* to nurse excessively, spoil. [Uncert.].

CODDLE (2), *v.t.* to boil, simmer. [Unkn.].

CODE (1) [kōd], *n.* accepted social customs; system of principles or laws, tacit or authorized; system of special symbols for conveying messages rapidly **or** secretly. CODE (2),*v.t.* to put in c. form (a message). [Fr., from CODEX].

CODEINE [kō′dēn], *n.* an alkaloid produced from opium. [Gk.].

CODEX (*pl.* **codices**) [kō′deks, kō′di-sēz], *n.* ancient manuscript volume, particularly of the Scriptures or of a system of laws; (*med.*) a collection of prescrip-tions. [L.].

COD-FISH [kod′fish], *n.* the cod.

CODGER [ko′jer], *n.* (*coll.*) old man with eccentric ways; miser. [CADGER].

CODICIL [kō′di-sil], *n.* supplement to a will, altering or explaining it further. CODICILLARY [ko-di-si′le-ri], *adj.* connected with, of the nature of, a c. [Fr. from L., *dim.* of CODEX].

CODIFY [kō′di-fī], *v.t.* to make into a code or system.

The accent ′ after a syllable = stress (u-pon′). The mark ‾ over a vowel = length (ā in made; ō in bone).

CODIFICATION [kō-di-fi-kā′shn], *n.* process of codifying. CODIFIER, *n.* one who codifies.

CODLING (1) [kod′ling], *n.* a cooking apple. CODLING-MOTH, a moth, the larva of which feeds on this and other apples. [Ir.].

CODLING (2), *n.* young cod.

CODLIVER-OIL [kod-li-ver-oil′], *n.* oil extracted from cod's liver, and employed medicinally.

CODPIECE† [kod′pēs], *n.* flap formerly used to cover the front of breeches. [COD (1).]

CO-ED [kō-ed′], *n.* (*U.S. coll.*) female student at a co-educational school or university. [Abbreviation of CO-EDUCATIONAL].

CO-EDUCATION [kō-e-dyōō-kā′shn], *n.* the education of boys and girls together. CO-EDUCATIONAL, *adj.* pertaining to, characterized by, c.

COEFFICIENT (1) [kō-i-fi′shent], *n.* that which is united with a unit to bring about a specific result; (*alg.*) number preceding other numbers or symbols which it multiplies; (*phys.*) number expressing the deviation of various substances from a standard unit. COEFFICIENT (2), *adj.* co-operating, combining, uniting. COEFFICIENTLY, *adv.* in a c. manner.

COELENTERATA [sē-len-te-rā′tah], *n.(pl.)* group of invertebrates comprising sea-anemones, jelly-fish etc. [Gk.].

COELIAC [sē′li-ak], *adj.* relating to the lower abdomen; c. disease, diarrhoeal disease of children, often accompanied by failure of growth. [Gk.].

COENAESTHESIS [sē-nas-thē′sis], *n.* (*psych.*) the amalgam of sensations constituting the consciousness of the whole body. [Gk.].

COENO- [sē′nō], *pref.* common, together. [Gk.].

COENOBITE [sē′nō-bīt], *n.* member of a religious order living in a convent or monastery, in community with others. [L. from Gk.].

COENURE [sē′nyōor], *n.* larva of the tapeworm. [Gk.].

COEQUAL (1) [kō-ē′kwal], *n.* person equal to another. COEQUAL (2), *adj.* having complete equality with another person or thing. COEQUALITY [kō-ē-kwo′li-ti], *n.* condition of being c. COEQUALLY, *adv.* in c. fashion.

COERCE [kō-urs′], *v.t.* to force, constrain, compel, restrain or keep in subjection by force. COERCIBLE, *adj.* able to be coerced. [L.].

COERCION [kō-ur′shn], *n.* act of coercing; state of being coerced.

COERCIVE [kō-ur′siv], *adj.* tending or intended to coerce. COERCIVELY, *adv.* in c. fashion.

CO-ESSENTIAL [kō-i-sen′shal], *adj.* possessing the same essence, being equally essential.

CO-ESTABLISHMENT [kō-es-tab′lish-ment], *n.* joint establishment.

COETANEOUS [kō-i-tā′ni-ōōs], *adj.* coeval. [L.].

CO-ETERNAL [kō-i-tur′nal], *adj.* equally eternal. CO-ETERNALLY, *adv.* in a c. way. CO-ETERNITY, *n.* joint eternity.

COEVAL (1) [kō-ē′val], *n.* one of the same age, contemporary object or person. COEVAL (2), *adj.* equally old, of contemporaneous origin. [L.].

CO-EXECUTOR [kō-eg-ze′kyōō-ter], *n.* executor acting with another.

COEXIST [kō-eg-zist′], *v.i.* to exist at the same time or together. COEXISTENCE, *n.* existence at the same time. COEXISTENT, *adj.* existing at the same time.

CO-EXPAND [kō-eks-pand′], *v.t. and i.* to expand equally.

CO-EXTEND [kō-eks-tend′], *v.t. and i.* to extend equally through the same space. CO-EXTENSION, *n.* act or state of co-extending.

CO-EXTENSIVE [kō-eks-ten′siv], *adj.* equally extensive, extending simultaneously. CO-EXTENSIVELY, *adv.* in c. fashion. CO-EXTENSIVENESS, *n.* equal extensiveness, simultaneous extension.

COFFEE [ko′fi], *n.* evergreen shrub bearing small berries possessing highly flavoured seeds; these berries ground and roasted; drink made from this. [Arab.].

COFFEE-BEAN [ko′fi-bēn], *n.* the seed of a coffee berry.

COFFEE-BUG [ko′fi-bug], *n.* one of the gall-insects.

COFFEE-HOUSE [ko′fi-hows], *n.* house where coffee and other refreshments can be taken.

COFFEE-MILL [ko′fi-mil], *n.* mill for grinding coffee beans.

COFFEE-POT [ko′fi-pot], *n.* pot in which coffee is brewed or contained.

COFFEE-ROOM [ko′fi-rōōm], *n.* public refreshment room in an hotel.

COFFER [ko′fer], *n.* box or chest for storing money,

jewellery etc., large cash-box; ornamental panel sunk in a ceiling or dome; (*hydraulics*) watertight box; lock in a canal. [OFr. from Gk.].

COFFER-DAM [ko′fer-dam], *n.* watertight enclosure on a sea- or river-bed, used to obtain a dry foundation for piers and similar structures; watertight attachment to a ship's side to enable under-water repairs to be made.

COFFIN (1) [ko′fin], *n.* wooden chest or case in which the dead are interred; anything resembling this in form or use; hoof of a horse below the coronet; wooden frame on the bed of a hand printing-press which holds the stone; c. block, wooden or metal block fitted with a brass frame to take electrotype or stereotype plates; c. bone, small pulpy bone inside a horse's hoof. COFFIN (2), *v.t.* to place in a c.; (*fig.*) enclose, entomb. [OFr. from Gk.].

COG (1) [kog], *n.* tooth-like projection repeated at regular intervals round the rim of a wheel as a means of communicating power and motion to a similar wheel. COG (2) (*pres.pt.* COGGING, *pret. and p.pt.* COGGED), *v.t.* to provide with cogs. [~Dan.].

COG (3) (*pres.pt.* cogging, *pret. and p.pt.* cogged), *v.t.* to cheat by using loaded dice. [Unkn.].

COGENCY [kō′jen-si], *n.* quality of being cogent.

COGENT [kō′jent], *adj.* compelling, forcible; convincing. COGENTLY, *adv.* in c. fashion. [L.].

COGITABLE [ko′ji-ta-bl], *adj.* conceivable. [L.].

COGITATE [ko′ji-tāt], *v.t. and i.* to reflect, think, meditate; think out. COGITATION [ko-ji-tā′shn], *n.* act of cogitating. COGITATIVE [ko′ji-tā-tiv], *adj.* meditative, reflective; capable of thinking, relating to reasoning. [L.].

COGNAC [ko′nyak], *n.* brandy of the highest quality distilled in France; brandy. [*Cognac*, French town].

COGNATE (1) [kog′nāt], *n.* (*philol.*) word in one language corresponding in form to, and derived from the same etymon as, a word in another language; (*Scots law*) male related to the mother's side of the family. COGNATE (2), *adj.* having blood relationship, akin; related in origin; resembling, similar in kind; (*philol.*) (of a word) mutually corresponding and derived from the same etymon; (of languages) having a common prototype; (*leg.*) descending from the same ancestor. [L.].

COGNATION [kog-nā′shn], *n.* kinship, affinity of origin or of nature.

COGNITION [kog-ni′shn], *n.* the fundamental faculty of the mind to know, recognize and conceive; knowledge acquired personally and empirically by the senses and retained by the mind in an abstract form. COGNITIVE [kog′ni-tiv], *adj.* of, or relating to, c., having the power to cognize. [L.].

COGNIZANCE [kog′ni-zans, ko′ni-zans], *n.* knowledge, recognition, conscious awareness; (*her.*) badge or mark of distinction; (*leg.*) official notice and trial of a case in court; judicial right of conducting a trial; acknowledgment of an alleged fact in evidence; defendant's plea substantiating the right of taking another's goods as his bailiff; to take c. of, to take notice of. [OFr.].

COGNIZANT [kog′ni-zant, ko′ni-zant], *adj.* knowing, having cognizance of; competent to judge.

COGNIZE [kog-nīz′], *v.t.* to perceive, become aware of, know consciously. COGNIZABLE [kog′ni-za-bl], *adj.* able to be known or apprehended; liable to come under judicial notice. [~L.].

COGNOMEN [kog-nō′men], *n.* surname, family name. COGNOMINAL [kog-no′mi-nal], *adj.* pertaining to a, c. COGNOMINATE [kog-no′mi-nāt], *v.t.* to give a surname to. [L.].

COGNOSCE [kog-nos′], *v.t.* (*leg.*) to investigate officially, inquire into judicially. COGNOSIBLE, *adj.* cognizable. [L.].

COGNOSCENTE (*pl.* cognoscenti) [ko-nyō-shen′ti], *n.* connoisseur, knowing person. [It.].

COGNOVIT [kog-nō′vit], *n.* (*leg.*) signed acknowledgment by a defendant of the plaintiff's claim, and agreement to judgment being entered against him. [L.].

COG-WHEEL [kog′wēl], *n.* wheel fitted with cogs.

COHABIT [kō-ha′bit], *v.i.* to live together, particularly as husband and wife without being married. COHABITANT, *n.* one who cohabits with another. [L.].

COHABITATION [kō-ha-bi-tā′shn], *n.* act or state of cohabiting.

CO-HEIR [kō-āer′], *n.* joint heir.

CO-HEIRESS [kō-āer′es], *n.* joint heiress.

COHERE [kō-hēer′], *v.i.* to stick together, adhere,

unite; (*fig.*) be logically connected or consistent. [L.].

COHERENT [kō-hēer'ent], *adj.* sticking together; (*fig.*) connected, consistent; clear and rational; logical. COHERENCE, COHERENCY, *n.* quality of being c. COHERENTLY, *adv.* in c. fashion.

COHERER [kō-hēer'er], *n.* person who or thing which coheres; (*radio*) device in early forms of receiver in which the cohering of metal filings indicated the presence of electro-magnetic waves.

COHESION [kō-hē'zhn], *n.* act and power of cohering; the force with which molecules of any substance hold together; (*fig.*) emotional or purposive unity. agreement. [L.].

COHESIVE [kō-hē'siv], *adj.* characterized by or producing cohesion. COHESIVELY, *adv.* in c. fashion. COHESIVENESS, *n.* quality of being c.

COHORT [kō'hawt], *n.* company of the Roman army comprising one-tenth of a legion; detachment or body of soldiers; a company in general; (*bot.*) allied group superior to a natural order. [L.].

COIF (1) [koif], *n.* head-dress or cap fitting close to the scalp; white cap, later becoming a black-centred white patch on the wig, distinguishing serjeants-at-law. COIF (2) *v.t.* to cover the head with a c. [OFr. from OHighGerm.].

COIFFEUR [kwah-fur'], *n.* hairdresser. [Fr.].

COIFFURE [kwah-fyōōr'], *n.* the style in which a woman's hair is dressed. [Fr.].

COIGN [koin], *n.* corner, corner-stone; (*arch.*) external angle of a wall; wedge; **a c. of vantage,** a splendid viewpoint. [OFr. from L.].

COIL (1) [koil], *n.* series of spiral rings or loops placed next to, or on top of, one another; single ring or fold of this nature; (*elect.*) device consisting of insulated wire wound round a former, creating a magnetic field when electricity is passed through it. COIL (2), *v.t. and i.* to gather, form or loop into a coil or coils. [OFr. from L.].

COIL† (3), *n.* noise, turmoil. [Unkn.].

COIN (1) [koin], *n.* piece of metal, embossed, stamped and authorized as money; unit of money made of metal; cash; die used in minting. COIN (2), *v.t.* to stamp (money) out of metal, mint; (*fig.*) invent, create; **to c. money,** (*coll.*) to be extremely prosperous. [OFr., L.].

COINAGE [koi'nij], *n.* practice or art of coining money; coins of a particular period or country; expense of coining; invention, fabrication of phrases or words; words or phrases so coined.

COINCIDE [kō-in-sīd'], *v.i.* to occupy the same position, correspond, or come together, in time or space; concur, be in agreement; be equivalent to.

COINCIDENCE [kō-in'si-dens], *n.* act or fact of coinciding; combination of events which happens purely by chance. [Fr.].

COINCIDENT(AL) [kō-in'si-dent, kō-in-si-den'tal], *adj.* coinciding. COINCIDENTLY [kō-in'si-dent-li], *adv.* by coincidence.

COINER [koi'ner], *n.* person who coins, one who makes counterfeit money.

CO-INTEREST [kō-in'te-rest], *n.* joint or mutual interest.

COIR [koir], *n.* coarse fibre made from coconut husks; cordage manufactured from this. [Malay].

COITION [kō-i'shn], *n.* sexual intercourse. [L.].

COKE (1) [kōk], *n.* dark-grey brittle fuel, which is the residue of coal from which most of the gas has been extracted by heating in a furnace. COKE (2), *v.t.* to transform into c. [Unkn.].

COKE (3), *n.* (*slang*) cocaine.

COKERNUT [kō'ker-nut], *n.* coconut.

COL (1) [kol], *n.* high pass through a mountain range. [Fr.].

COL- (2), *pref.* standing for CON or CUM before *l*.

COLA [kō'lah], *n.* West African tree. COLA-NUT, nut from this tree having tonic properties. [West African].

COLANDER, CULLENDER [ku'lin-der], *n.* vessel with a perforated bottom used as a strainer in cookery. [L.].

COLATITUDE [kō-la'ti-tyōōd], *n.* the complement of the latitude, 90 deg. minus the latitude.

COLCANNON [kōl-ka'non], *n.* dish of mashed cabbage and potatoes. [Uncert.].

COLCHICUM [kol'chi-kum], *n.* the meadow saffron or autumn crocus; narcotic preparation from the seeds of this. [Gk., pertaining to *Colchis*].

COLD (1) [kōld], *n.* sensation or state of being cold; cause of this sensation, low temperature, absence of heat; (*med.*) a chill, acute nasal catarrh. COLD (2),

adj. lacking in heat, having relatively little warmth, low in temperature, frigid; (*fig.*) having no passion, spiritless; indifferent, apathetic; unfriendly; chaste, virginal; lacking in brilliance of colour; **in c. blood,** deliberately, without the excuse of passion; **c. comfort,** poor consolation, small compensation; **c. feet,** fear; **c. steel,** hand-to-hand fighting with bayonets or similar weapons; **c. war,** conflict with no fighting in battle but with propaganda etc.; **to pour c. water on,** to discourage. [OE.].

COLD-BLOODED [kōld-blu'did], *adj.* having cold blood; readily feeling the cold; (*fig.*) unsympathetic, hard-hearted, pitiless.

COLD-CHISEL [kōld-chi'zel], *n.* chisel for working on cold metal.

COLD-CREAM [kōld-krēm'], *n.* cooling scented ointment for the skin.

COLD-HEARTED [kōld-hah'tid], *adj.* lacking in feeling, unfriendly, unsympathetic. COLD-HEARTEDLY, *adv.* in c. fashion. COLD-HEARTEDNESS, *n.* quality of being c.

COLDISH [kōl'dish], *adj.* rather cold, cool, chilly.

COLDLY [kōld'li], in a cold fashion.

COLDNESS [kōld'nes], *n.* condition of being cold.

COLD-SHOULDER (1) [kōld-shōl'der], *n.* studied neglect, snub. COLD-SHOULDER (2), *v.t.* to shun deliberately, snub.

COLD SNAP [kōld'snap], *n.* sudden spell of cold weather.

COLD STORAGE [kōld-staw'rij], *n.* the preservation of perishable foodstuffs in refrigerating chambers.

COLECTOMY [kō-lek'to-mi], *n.* (*surg.*) removal of part of the colon. [Gk.].

COLEOPTERA [kō-li-op'te-rah], *n.* (*zool.*) the beetle order of insects, having external protective wing-cases. COLEOPTERAL, COLEOPTEROUS, *adj.* relating to the c. COLEOPTERIST, *n.* student of beetles. [Gk.].

COLESEED [kōl'sēd], *n.* seed of *Brassica campestris* from which is obtained rape or sweet oil; the plant itself.

COLE SLAW [kōl'slaw], *n.* (*U.S.*) raw cabbage, shredded and dressed as a salad. [Du.].

COLIC (1) [ko'lik], *n.* abdominal gripe, severe pain in the bowels. COLIC (2), *adj.* pertaining to the colon or to c. COLICKY, *adj.* having or resembling c.

COLISEUM, see COLOSSEUM.

COLITIS [ko-li'tis], *n.* (*med.*) inflammation of the colon. [Gk.].

COLLABORATE [ko-la'bo-rāt], *v.i.* to work together with someone for some object; produce work jointly with another. COLLABORATION [ko-la-bo-rā'shn], *n.* act or process of collaborating. [L.].

COLLABORATIONIST [ko-la-bo-rā'shn-ist], *n.* one who collaborates with an enemy occupier of his country.

COLLABORATOR [ko-la'bo-rā-ter], *n.* one who collaborates; one who assists foreign occupiers of his country, *esp.* in the war of 1939-45.

COLLAGEN [ko'la-jen], *n.* chief constituent in cartilage and bone which turns into gelatine when boiled. [Gk.].

COLLAPSABLE [ko-lap'sa-bl], *adj.* collapsible.

COLLAPSE (1) [ko-laps'], *v.i.* to fall to pieces, break up, break down, crumble to ruin, disintegrate suddenly; (*fig.*) be suddenly prostrated, go to pieces, give way suddenly and completely under strain or opposition; fail completely. COLLAPSE (2), *n.* a sudden falling down, falling to pieces or breaking up, falling in, crumbling into a heap; (*fig.*) cessation of resistance; complete physical or nervous prostration, breakdown. [L.].

COLLAPSIBLE [ko-lap'si-bl], *adj.* made to collapse, able to fold up into a small space.

COLLAR (1) [ko'ler], *n.* something worn round the neck, article of masculine dress worn around the neck and attached to the shirt permanently or by studs; leather or metal harness put round the neck of a dog for control and identification, neck harness of a horse or similar animal; jewelled band worn round the throat by women; that part of the coat or upper garment fitting round the neck; part of the insignia of numerous orders worn round the neck; anything resembling these in form or function; (*mech.*) band joining two rods of a machine, encircling band strengthening the joints of a pipe; (*naut.*) upper part of a stay; (*zool.*) markings about the neck of an animal; (*bot.*) part of a plant next to, and above, the ground. COLLAR (2), *v.t.* to encircle, restrain with a c.; tackle successfully in Rugby football; (*coll.*)

The accent ' after a syllable = stress (u-pon'). The mark ˉ over a vowel = length (ā in made; ō in bone).

seize, grab; get hold of. COLLARED, *adj.* wearing a c.; (*coll.*) seized, caught and held fast. [L.].

COLLAR-BONE [ko'ler-bōn], *n.* the clavicle.

COLLARET, COLLARETTE [ko-la-ret'], *n.* small collar; piece of lace etc. worn round the neck. [Fr.].

COLLATE [ko-lāt'], *v.t.* to bring together for comparison, compare and contrast in detail one manuscript etc. with another; put together the sheets of a book in preparation for binding; present to a benefice. COLLATABLE, *adj.* capable of being collated.

COLLATERAL (1) [ko-la'te-ral], *adj.* running parallel or side by side; coexistent but subsidiary; derived from a common ancestor but through a different line; **c. security,** additional security given with the principal security. COLLATERAL (2), *n.* a c. relation; c. security. COLLATERALLY, *adv.* in a c. way. COLLATERALNESS, *n.* state of being c. [L.].

COLLATION [ko-lā'shn], *n.* act, process, or result of collating; light meal quickly brought together. [L.].

COLLATIVE [ko-lā'tiv], *adj.* (*eccles.*) in the patronage of the bishop of the diocese.

COLLATOR [ko-lā'ter], *n.* one who collates.

COLLEAGUE [ko'lēg], *n.* professional associate, co-worker, fellow worker appointed by the same authority. COLLEAGUESHIP, *n.* status of a c. [L.].

COLLECT (1) [ko'likt], *n.* short prayer used in church on appointed days or occasions. [L.].

COLLECT (2) [ko-lekt'], *v.t. and i.* to gather together scattered things or persons; accumulate specimens of some kind as a hobby; beg money for some cause from scattered sources by an appeal to charity; (*reflex.*) put the mind in order, pull oneself together; infer something; come together, accumulate. COLLECTABLE, *adj.* able to be collected. [L.].

COLLECTANEA [ko-lek-tā'ni-ah], *n.(pl.)* miscellany of selected literary work. [L.].

COLLECTED [ko-lek'tid], *adj.* cool, self-possessed, sensible; (works of an author) gathered together into one book or series of books. COLLECTEDLY, *adv.* in c. fashion. COLLECTEDNESS, *n.* c. state of mind.

COLLECTION [ko-lek'shn], *n.* act or process of collecting, sum of money obtained for charity or religion by collecting from individuals; the assemblage of objects collected; terminal examination in Oxford colleges. [L.].

COLLECTIVE [ko-lek'tiv], *adj.* regarded as a whole; belonging, or related, to the whole body, or to the sum of all the constituents of a group; operated by a group (as c. farming); **c. noun,** (*gram.*) noun singular in form but plural in meaning; **c. security,** security to be obtained by uniting a number of states to protect peace, justice and their own common interests. COLLECTIVELY, *adv.* as a whole, in c. fashion.

COLLECTIVISM [ko-lek'ti-vizm], *n.* doctrine of centralized state control of all the means of production and distribution; state capitalism. COLLECTIVIST, *n.* believer in c.

COLLECTIVIZE [ko-lek'ti-vīz], *v.t.* to transfer ownership of property from private persons to public or co-operative bodies. COLLECTIVIZATION [ko-lek-ti-vī-zā'shn], *n.* substitution of collective for private ownership.

COLLECTOR [ko-lek'ter], *n.* one who, or that which, collects; one who assembles specimens, *objets d'art* etc. as a hobby; one who gathers payments or taxes, or who collects tickets, passes etc.; formerly the chief administrator in a district of an Indian province. COLLECTORSHIP, *n.* position or office of a c.

COLLEEN [ko'lēn], *n.* a girl. [Ir.].

COLLEGE [ko'lij], *n.* self-governing group acting or living by common rules for a common purpose; semi-independent unit of a university; any school or educational establishment of a senior or superior sort; buildings in which a college is housed; **electoral c.,** body of electors to a certain office; **c. pudding,** pudding made with flour, suet and dried fruit. COLLEGIAL, *adj.* constituted as a c. COLLEGIAN, *n.* member of a c. [L.].

COLLEGER [ko'li-jer], *n.* foundation scholar at Eton College.

COLLEGIATE [ko-lē'ji-at], *adj.* constituted as or pertaining to a college; **c. church,** non-cathedral church governed by a dean and chapter. [L.].

COLLENCHYMA [ko-len'ki-mah], *n.* elastic cell tissue. [Gk.].

COLLET [ko'lit], *n.* ring or band; that part of a finger ring in which a jewel is set. [Fr., L.].

COLLIDE [ko-līd'], *v.i.* to run into violent impact

with; bump forcibly into something; (*fig.*) come into direct conflict, clash violently. [L.].

COLLIE [ko'li], *n.* long-haired Scottish sheepdog.

COLLIER [ko'li-er], *n.* coal-miner; dealer in coals; ship employed in the transportation of coal. [ME.].

COLLIERY [kol'ye-ri], *n.* coal-mine.

COLLIGATE [ko'li-gāt], *v.t.* to sort out and bring together under one head. COLLIGATION, *n.* act of colligating. [L.].

COLLIMATE [ko'li-māt], *v.t.* (*opt.*) to bring into line or render parallel, bring to the line of sight. COLLIMATING, *adj.* (*opt.*) correcting, or adjusting to the line of sight. COLLIMATOR, *n.* small auxiliary telescope fastened to a larger one to correct deviation from the line of sight. [L.].

COLLIMATION [ko-li-mā'shn], *n.* adjustment to the line of sight; **line of c.,** line of sight of a telescope. [L.].

COLLINEAR [ko-li'ni-er], *adj.* in the same straight line.

COLLINEATION [ko-li-ni-ā'shn], *n.* act or process of aligning.

COLLISION [ko-li'zhn], *n.* act or process of colliding, violent impact between objects, *esp.* between moving vehicles.

COLLOCATE [ko'lō-kāt], *v.t.* to arrange, station, put in order. COLLOCATION, *n.* act of collocating; disposition, arrangement; things arranged or grouped in association. [L.].

COLLODION [ko-lō'di-on], *n.* gummy solution of gun-cotton in ether and alcohol, used to produce thin films in surgery and photography. COLLODIONIZE, *v.t.* to treat with c. [Gk.].

COLLOGUE [ko-lōg'], *v.i.* to discuss together confidentially; plot, scheme together. [L.].

COLLOID (1) [ko'loid], *n.* (*chem.*) any non-crystalloid inert substance which, suspended in a liquid, does not pass through a membrane. COLLOID (2), *adj.* gluelike; pertaining to c. COLLOIDAL [ko-loi'dal], *adj.* like a c. COLLOIDALITY [ko-loi-da'li-ti], *n.* condition of being c. [Gk.].

COLLOP [ko'lop], *n.* (*Scots*) (*pl.*) minced meat; thick slice of meat. [Unkn.].

COLLOQUIAL [ko-lō'kwi-al], *adj.* pertaining to, found in, everyday speech; characteristic of ordinary conversation; unliterary in phrase. COLLOQUIALLY, *adv.* in c. fashion. [L.].

COLLOQUIALISM [ko-lō'kwi-a-lizm], *n.* a colloquial usage or expression.

COLLOQUY [ko'lo-kwi], *n.* conference, conversation, discussion. COLLOQUIST, *n.* one taking part in a c. COLLOQUIZE, *v.i.* to hold c. [L.].

COLLOTYPE [ko'lō-tīp], *n.* (*print.*) process of reproducing photographs from a sensitized gelatine plate suitably developed and inked.

COLLUDE [ko-lyōōd'], *v.i.* to work in collusion. [L.].

COLLUSION [ko-lyōō'zhn], *n.* a working together in secret for a dishonest purpose. [L.].

COLLUSIVE [ko-lyōō'siv], *adj.* in collusion. COLLUSIVELY, *adv.* in c. fashion. COLLUSIVENESS, *n.* quality of being c.

COLLYRIUM [ko-li'ri-um], *n.* eye lotion. [Gk.].

COLLY-WOBBLES [ko'li-wo-blz], *n.(pl.)* (*coll.*) internal digestive disturbances. [Echoic].

COLOCYNTH [ko'lo-sinth], *n.* (*bot.*) Asiatic or North African plant, the fruit having purgative properties; violent purgative. COLOCYNTHIN [ko-lo-sin'thin], *n.* purgative essence of c. [Gk.].

COLOGNE-EARTH [ko-lōn-urth'], *n.* lignite earth [*Cologne,* Germany].

COLOGNE-WATER [ko-lōn'waw-ter], *n.* eau de cologne.

COLOMBIER, see COLUMBIER.

COLON (1) [ko'lon], *n.* (*anat.*) the large intestine. [Gk.].

COLON (2), *n.* (*gram.*) the punctuation mark (:) used to denote the completion of the grammatical structure rather than of the sense of the sentence. [Gk.].

COLONEL [kur'nel], *n.* the rank immediately below that of brigadier in the British Army; the lieutenant-colonel of a battalion. COLONELCY, *n.* office or rank of a c. [It.].

COLONIAL (1) [ko-lō'ni-al], *adj.* pertaining to a colony; **C. Office,** state department responsible for the colonies. COLONIAL (2), *n.* inhabitant of a colony. COLONIALISM, *n.* c. characteristic.

COLONIST [ko'lo-nist], *n.* one who colonizes, pioneer settler in a colony.

COLONIZE [ko'lo-nīz], *v.t. and i.* to people with one's

ōō is pronounced as in food; ŏŏ as in hood; th as in *think,* TH as in *that,* zh as in azure. ~ = related to.

DSE—E*

own nation or race, provide with a settlement or colony; settle in a colony. COLONIZATION [ko-lo-nī-zā′shn], n. act of colonizing. COLONIZATIONIST, n. advocate of colonization.

COLONNADE [ko-lo-năd′], n. row of columns ranged at regular intervals; double row of columns forming a passage. [It.].

COLONY [ko′lo-ni], n. settlement established in a distant, and usually uncivilized and sparsely inhabited, country by people of another race, living together and preserving their national characteristics; people taking part in such a settlement; number of aliens of the same nationality living in a city or country; quarter where such aliens live; (biol.) body of organisms grouped closely together. [L.].

COLOPHON [ko′lo-fon], n. inscription or device at the beginning or end of a book. [Gk.].

COLOPHONY [ko′lo′fo-ni], n. dark resin obtained from coniferous trees. [L.].

COLOQUINTIDA [ko-lo-kwin′ti-dah], n. colocynth. [Gk.].

COLORADO BEETLE [ko-lo-rah-dō-bē′tl], n. a beetle, the larva of which is destructive to the potato. [Colorado, U.S.A.].

COLORATION, COLOURATION [ku-le-rā′shn], n. process or effect of colouring; disposition and blending of colours. [L.].

COLORATURA [ko-le-ra-tōō′rah], n. (mus.) highly ornate variations for embellishment. [It.].

COLORIFIC [ku-le-ri′fik], adj. able to colour; brightly coloured. [Fr.].

COLORIMETER [ku-le-ri′mi-ter], n. instrument for calculating the strength of dyes or colours.

COLOSSAL [ko-lo′sal], adj. gigantic, stupendous. [COLOSSUS].

COLOSSEUM, COLISEUM [ko-lo-sē′um], n. Vespasian's great amphitheatre at Rome; any large amphitheatre or place of public entertainment. [L.].

COLOSSUS [ko-lo′sus], n. gigantic statue; immense statue of Apollo which stood in the harbour at Rhodes; (fig.) man of great power or stature. [Gk.].

COLOSTOMY [ko-los′to-mi], n. (surg.) the formation of a permanent artificial anus into the colon. [Gk.].

COLOSTRUM [ko-los′trum], n. the first milk after parturition. [L.].

COLOTOMY [ko-lo′to-mi], n. (surg.) an incision in the colon. [Gk.].

COLOUR (1) [ku′ler], n. hue, tint; the different sensations of this produced on the retina by light waves of varying frequencies; variously tinted pigments and their use in painting; human complexion; (fig.) appearance, show; false show, pretence; kind, quality; (fig.) life, vividness, zest; (mus.) variety of tone; (pl.) military standard; distinguishing badges of jockeys, athletic teams etc.; **to see the c. of,** to test the reality of; **man of c.,** Indian, negro; **local c.,** vivid detail used as a literary background; **to come off with flying colours,** to emerge triumphantly from some test or ordeal; **off c.,** unwell, slightly indisposed. COLOUR (2), v.t. and i. to stain, paint, dye or tint with c.; (fig.) distort, exaggerate, tinge with one's own feelings or ideas; become coloured, flush. [L.].

COLOURABLE [ku′le-ra-bl], adj. specious, plausible. COLOURABLENESS, n. speciousness. COLOURABLY, adv. in c. fashion.

COLOURATION, see COLORATION.

COLOUR-BLIND [ku′ler-blīnd], adj. unable to distinguish colours. COLOUR-BLINDNESS, n. condition of being c.

COLOUR-BOX [ku′ler-boks], n. box of artist's paints.

COLOUR-COMPANY [ku′ler-kum-pa-ni], n. company which carries the colours of a battalion.

COLOURED [ku′lerd], adj. having a colour; not white-skinned.

COLOURFUL [ku′ler-fōōl], adj. full of colour, bright.

COLOURING [ku′le-ring], n. process, effect, manner or skill of laying on colour; colour so laid on; complexion.

COLOURIST [ku′le-rist], n. one who colours, one skilled in commercial colouring.

COLOURLESS [ku′ler-les], adj. having no colour; dull, drab; (fig.) lifeless, uninteresting. COLOUR-LESSLY, adv. in a c. manner; uninterestingly.

COLOURMAN [ku′ler-man], n. dealer in paints, oils, artists' materials etc.

COLOUR-SERGEANT [ku′ler-sah-jant], n. senior sergeant of the colour company.

COLPORTEUR [kol′paw-ter], n. one who hawks

Bibles or distributes religious tracts. COLPORTAGE, n. distribution of tracts by hawkers. [Fr.].

COLT (1) [kolt], n. young horse; young, inexperienced person. COLTISH, adj. like a c., frolicsome. [Uncert.].

COLT (2), n. early American revolver; automatic pistol. [S. Colt, inventor].

COLTER, see COULTER.

COLTSFOOT [kolts′fōōt], n. plant with yellow flowers, and leaves used medicinally.

COLUBRINE [ko′lyōō-brin], adj. relating to the snake; (fig.) cunning, subtle. [L.].

COLUMBARIUM [ko-lum-bāer′i-um], n. dovecote. [L.].

COLUMBIER, COLOMBIER [ko-lum′bēer], n. a size of drawing paper, generally $34\frac{1}{2} \times 23$ in. [Fr.].

COLUMBINE (1) [ko′lum-bīn], n. perennial plant of the genus Aquilegia. [Fr.].

COLUMBINE (2), n. Harlequin's partner in pantomime. [It.].

COLUMBINE (3), adj. dovelike, dove-coloured. [Fr.].

COLUMBITE [ko-lum′bīt], n. mineral composed of niobium, iron and manganese. [Next].

COLUMBIUM [ko-lum′bi-um], n. niobium. [Columbia, America].

COLUMN [ko′lum], n. pillar, upright shaft, lofty support to the arch or roof of a building, anything resembling this; any tall, slender, upright body; vertical division of a page of type; set of figures arranged vertically; body of troops arranged so that there are fewer abreast than there are deep; **to dodge the c.,** to shirk one's duty. COLUMNED, adj. having columns. [L.].

COLUMNAR [ko-lum′ner], adj. in the form of, pertaining to, a column. [L.].

COLUMNIST [ko′lu-mist], n. journalist who contributes a regular column of special material to a newspaper or periodical.

COLZA [kol′zah], n. rape oil. [Du.].

COMA (1) [kō′mah], n. trance-like stupor produced by disease or injury; (fig.) deep abstraction. [Gk.].

COMA (2), n. (astron.) nebulous covering round the nucleus of a comet; (bot.) tufted ends of certain seeds; leafy head of a tree. [Gk.].

CO-MATE [kō-māt′], n. companion.

COMATOSE [kō′ma-tōs], adj. suffering from coma, lethargic.

COMB (1) [kōm], n. instrument having many tooth-like projections in a row for cleaning, adjusting or holding the hair, similar article for separating and cleansing wool, flax etc.; crest of a cock; cellular store place built by bees for their honey. COMB (2), v.t. and i. to adjust and smooth with a c.; separate and cleanse with a c.; (fig.) search a place minutely; **to c. out,** to remove (selected workers) from one task and apply (them) to another, esp. the armed forces. [OE.].

COMBAT (1) [kom′bat, kum′bat], n. physical contest, fight, battle. COMBAT (2) (pres.pt. COM-BATING, pret. and p.pt. COMBATED) [kom-bat′], v.t. and i. to fight, strive against; struggle, be opposed to. [Fr.].

COMBATANT [kom′ba-tent, kum′ba-tent], n. one who fights or struggles; soldier etc. COMBATANT (2), adj. taking part in combat; **c. officer,** (milit.) leader of a unit actively engaged in fighting.

COMBATIVE [kom′ba-tiv, kum′ba-tiv], adj. pugnacious. COMBATIVENESS, n. quality of being c.

COMBE [kōōm], n. small valley. [COOMBE].

COMBER (1) [kō′mer], n. one who or that which combs, machine for combing flax; breaking wave.

COMBER (2) [kum′ber], n. the sea-perch.

COMBINABLE [kom-bī′na-bl], adj. that may be combined. COMBINABLENESS, n. quality of being c.

COMBINATION [kom-bi-nā′shn], n. act or process of combining; state of being combined; union, league, alliance; (of persons) league, partnership; (math.) various arrangements of common factors; (pl.) long undergarment reaching from neck to knee; **motor-cycle c.,** motor-cycle and sidecar. [L.].

COMBINATIVE [kom′bi-na-tiv], adj. tending to combine; occurring in combination.

COMBINE (1) [kom′bīn], n. combination; union of companies or trading organizations for business purposes; mechanical harvester combining the functions of reaper and thresher.

COMBINE (2) [kum-bīn′], v.t. and i. to cause to unite, amalgamate, fuse, join together; mix, come together, coalesce; **combined operations,** military

---

The accent ′ after a syllable = stress (u-pon′)   The mark ‾ over a vowel = length (ā in made; ō in bone).

operations carried out by air, sea and land forces under a single command. **COMBINER**, *n*. one who or that which combines. [LL.].

COMBING [kō'ming], *n*. treating with a comb; dead hair etc. removed by combing.

COMBUSTIBLE (1) [kom-bus'ti-bl], *adj*. inflammable; (*fig.*) easily excited. **COMBUSTIBLE** (2), *n*. inflammable material. **COMBUSTIBILITY** [kom-bus-ti-bi'li-ti], **COMBUSTIBLENESS** [kom-bus'ti-bl-nes], *n*. liability to combustion. [LL.].

COMBUSTION [kom-bust'shn], *n*. process or state of burning, sudden bursting into flame. [LL.].

COME (*pret*. **came**, *p.pt*. **come**) [kum], *v.i.* approach, be in motion towards, move towards something; arrive, reach; (*fig.*) appear; occur, take place, happen; originate in; **to c. about**, to happen; **to c. across**, (*slang*) to hand over under pressure; find by chance; **to c. at**, to attack furiously; **to c. back**, to return; **to c. down**, to decline economically, socially etc.; **to c. down on**, to blame strongly; **to c. in**, to prove useful; to be the fashion; **to c. in for**, to meet with, inherit; **to c. into**, to inherit; **to c. off**, to succeed, perhaps in some measure by luck; take place; **to c. on**, to improve; **to c. over**, to become (faint etc.); **to c. out**, to become apparent; go on strike; (of a girl) appear in society as a debutante; **to c. out with**, to blurt out; **to c. round**, to recover, become placated; **to c. through**, to survive; **to c. to**, to recover consciousness; **to c. under**, to be classed as; **c. off it!** (*slang*) stop, desist. [OE.].

COME-BACK [kum'bak], *n*. (*coll.*) a return to one's former state after a decline or retirement.

COMEDIAN [ko-mē'di-an], *n*. actor of comedy; buffoon. [Fr.].

COMÉDIENNE [ko-mē-di-en'], *n*. female comedian. [Fr.].

COMEDIETTA [ko-mē-di-e'tah], *n*. light comedy with music. [It.].

COMEDO [ko-mē'do], *n*. a blackhead. [L.].

COME-DOWN [kum'down], *n*. a fall in position, humiliation.

COMEDY [ko'mi-di], *n*. drama intended to arouse laughter rather than pity or terror, or in which the humour is obtained from normal behaviour in everyday life; play of this kind; amusing incident in real life arising from the combination of character and situation rather than farcical event. [Gk.].

COMELY [kum'li], *adj*. becoming, pleasing to the eye. **COMELINESS**, *n*. condition of being c. [OE.].

COMER [ku'mer], *n*. one who comes.

COMESTIBLE (1) [ku-mes'ti-bl], *n*. food. **COMESTIBLE** (2), *adj*. edible, relating to food. [L.].

COMET [ko'mit], *n*. heavenly body consisting of a solid nucleus and a gaseous, luminous tail. **COMETARY, COMETIC**, *adj*. pertaining to a c. [Gk.].

COMFIT [kum'fit], *n*. a sweetmeat. [Fr.].

COMFORT (1) [kum'fert], *n*. consolation; solace; encouragement in fear, trouble or anxiety; person who, or thing which, comforts; well-being, feeling of physical satisfaction and ease, freedom from or release from pain; freedom from physical want or unease. **COMFORT** (2), *v.t.* to provide c. for. [LL.].

COMFORTABLE [kum'fer-ta-bl], *adj*. providing or enjoying comfort; enough to satisfy one's needs or wants. **COMFORTABLY**, *adv*. in c. fashion. [OFr.].

COMFORTER [kum'fer-ter], *n*. one who or that which comforts; the Holy Ghost; thick woollen muffler; dummy teat for infants.

COMFORTLESS [kum'fert-les], *adj*. lacking all comfort; unable to be comforted. **COMFORTLESSLY**, *adv*. in c. fashion. **COMFORTLESSNESS**, *n*. quality of being c.

COMFREY [kum'fri], *n*. (*bot.*) plant formerly used as a remedy for wounds. [OFr.].

COMIC (1) [ko'mik], *adj*. relating to comedy, laughter-provoking. **COMIC** (2), *n*. (*coll.*) comedian; comic paper. [Gk.].

COMICAL [ko'mi-kal], *adj*. comic, extremely funny, amusing by ludicrous antics. **COMICALITY, COMICAL-NESS** [ko-mi-ka'li-ti, ko'mi-kal-nes], *n*. quality or condition of being c. **COMICALLY**, *adv*. in c. fashion.

COMIC-STRIP [ko-mik-strip'], *n*. humorous newspaper cartoon continued from day to day in which the amusing adventures of a group of stock characters are told in a series of drawings.

COMING (1) [ku'ming], *n*. approach, movement towards; **Second C.**, Christ's return to judge the world. **COMING** (2), *adj*. about to come, approaching, future, inevitable.

COMINFORM [ko'min-fawm], *n*. the *Communist Inform*ation Centre formed at Belgrade in 1947.

COMINTERN [ko'min-täern], *n*. former *Communist Intern*ational, ostensibly dissolved in 1943.

COMITADJI [ko-mi-ta'ji], *n*. member of an irregular armed band, *esp*. in the Balkans. [Turk.].

COMITY [ko'mi-ti], *n*. mutual courtesy, common civility, respect of manners; **c. of nations**, mutual respect and tolerance among nations. [L.].

COMMA [ko'mah], *n*. the mark of punctuation (,) used to mark off the phrases and clauses of a sentence; (*mus.*) an enharmonic interval; **c. butterfly**, butterfly so named from the mark on its wing; **inverted commas** (" "), commas placed above the line to enclose a quotation. [Gk.].

COMMAND (1) [ko-mahnd'], *v.t. and i.* to have command or authority over; compel, order, demand without questioning; (*milit.*) dominate a position; exact, be sold for; possess. **COMMAND** (2), *n*. complete power, rule or authority, control; order which must be obeyed; position of one holding such authority; body of troops or area under such control; words in which such orders are given; **the high c.**, the general staff of an army; **a c. performance**, theatrical performance given by royal c. **COMMAND-ABLE**, *adj*. capable of being commanded. [Fr.].

COMMANDANT [ko'man-dant], *n*. military officer commanding a post, fort or town. **COMMANDANT-SHIP**, *n*. position of a c. [Fr.].

COMMANDEER [ko-man-dēer'], *v.t.* to seize for military purposes; convert arbitrarily to one's own use; take by virtue of command; conscript. [Du.].

COMMANDER [ko-mahn'der], *n*. one who commands; (*milit.*) officer in command of any military division; (*nav.*) officer immediately below the rank of captain; member of one of the higher ranks of certain orders of knighthood; heavy wooden mallet. **COMMANDERSHIP**, *n*. rank or office of c. [OFr.].

COMMANDERY, COMMANDRY [ko-mahn'de-ri], *n*. (*hist.*) estate belonging to an order of knights and governed by one of them; the commandership in an order of knights. [MedL.].

COMMANDING [ko-mahn'ding], *adj*. having command over, chief; having a broad view; overlooking; dignified, nobly striking. **COMMANDINGLY**, *adv*. in c. fashion.

COMMANDMENT [ko-mahnd'ment], *n*. solemn command; holy law, one of the clauses in the Decalogue formulated by Moses. [OFr.].

COMMANDO [ko-mahn'dō], *n*. body of irregular troops, *esp*. of armed Boers in the South African War; small, mobile, independent body of special-service troops; member of such a body. [Portug.].

COMMANDRY, see COMMANDERY.

COMMEASURABLE [ko-me'zhe-ra-bl], *adj*. commensurable.

COMMEMORATE [ko-me'me-rāt], *v.t.* to call to remembrance some act or person by a memorial or a celebration; perpetuate, honour the memory of, something. **COMMEMORATIVE**, *adj*. serving to c. [L.].

COMMEMORATION [ko-me-me-rā'shn], *n*. act of commemorating, ceremony in honour and memory of something or someone. [L.].

COMMENCE [ko-mens'], *v.t. and i.* begin, initiate; start. [Fr.].

COMMENCEMENT [ko-mens'ment], *n*. beginning, start, origin; time of a beginning. [OFr.].

COMMEND [ko-mend'], *v.t.* to entrust, commit; recommend; praise, express appreciation of; (*archaic*) send one's good wishes to. **COMMENDATORY**, *adj*. commending. [L.].

COMMENDABLE [ko-men'da-bl], *adj*. able to be commended. **COMMENDABLY**, *adv*. in a c. fashion.

COMMENDATION [ko-men-dā'shn], *n*. act of commending; recommendation, praise. [L.].

COMMENSURABLE [ko-men'shyōō-ra-bl], *adj*. in proportion, able to be measured by the same standard. **COMMENSURABILITY, COMMENSURABLE-NESS** [ko-men-shyōō-ra-bi'li-ti, ko-men'shyōō-ra-bl-nes], *n*. quality of being c. **COMMENSURABLY**, *adv*. in c. fashion. [L.].

COMMENSURATE [ko-men'shyōō-rat], *adj*. in just accordance with, corresponding. **COMMENSURATELY**, *adv*. in c. fashion. **COMMENSURATENESS**, *n*. quality of being c. [L.].

COMMENT (1) [ko'ment], *n*. a critical remark, observation on something; editorial note explaining some difficulty or obscurity in a text. **COMMENT** (2), *v.i.* to make a c. on something; utter an observation, notice something. [L.].

COMMENTARY [ko'men-te-ri], *n*. critical comments on a text, often published as an independent work;

running c., continuous series of observations on some happening. [L.].

COMMENTATE [ko'men-tāt], *v.t. and i.* to make comments on, annotate; give a running commentary on. COMMENTATION [ko-men-tā'shn], *n.* the making of a commentary. [L.].

COMMENTATOR [ko'men-tā-ter], *n.* one who commentates. COMMENTATORIAL [ko-men-ta-taw'-ri-al], *adj.* relating to the functions of a c.

COMMERCE [ko'mers], *n.* trade (on a large scale), exchange of goods and its organization; intercourse; **Chamber of C.,** body set up to foster and organize trade in a district; **c. raider,** warship sent out to attack the merchant shipping of the enemy. [L.].

COMMERCIAL (1) [ko-mur'shl], *adj.* relating to, characteristic of, commerce or business, run on business lines; **c. traveller,** one employed in arranging the sale of a manufacturer's products to tradesmen. COMMERCIAL (2), *n.* (*coll.*) c. traveller. COMMERCIALISM, *n.* outlook based purely upon motives of commerce. COMMERCIALIST, *n.* one who is actuated by commercialism. COMMERCIALLY, *adv.* in commerce, from a c. standpoint.

COMMERCIALIZE [ko-mur'sha-līz], *v.t.* to make into a matter of business; make some uneconomic scheme or product a commercial possibility.

COMMINATION [ko-mi-nā'shn], *n.* a threatening of punishment, *esp.* of God's vengeance on the wicked; **c. service,** service held by the Church of England on Ash Wednesday, threatening Divine punishment of sinners. [L.].

COMMINATORY [ko-mi'na-te-ri], *adj.* threatening, denouncing.

COMMINGLE [ko-ming'gl], *v.t. and i.* to mix, mingle together; merge.

COMMINUTE [ko'mi-nyōōt], *v.t.* to reduce to powder, break into parts; **comminuted fracture,** fracture in which the bone is broken into fragments. COMMINUTION [ko-mi-nyōō'shn], *n.* act of comminuting. [L.].

COMMISERABLE [ko-mi'ze-ra-bl], *adj.* deserving pity.

COMMISERATE [ko-mi'ze-rāt], *v.t. and i.* to sympathize, express or feel pity or sorrow at, deplore. [L.].

COMMISERATION [ko-mi-ze-rā'shn], *n.* act of commiserating; pity, sympathy. COMMISERATIVE [ko-mi'ze-ra-tiv], *adj.* relating to c. COMMISERATIVELY, *adv.* in commiserative fashion. [L.].

COMMISSAR [ko-mi-sah(r)'], *n.* commissioner; Soviet state official. COMMISSARIAL [ko-mi-sāer'i-al], *adj.* relating to a c. or commissary.

COMMISSARIAT [ko-mi-sāer'i-at], *n.* (*milit.*) that section of an army in charge of the rations and food supplies; the supplies themselves. [Fr.].

COMMISSARY [ko'mi-sa-ri], *n.* commissioner, one to whom an office, duty or special responsibility has been delegated; (*eccles.*) bishop's delegate, having authority in his absence. COMMISSARYSHIP, *n.* office of a c. [LL.].

COMMISSION (1) [ko-mi'shn], *n.* act of committing; warrant, written authority permitting and enjoining the execution of some office, *esp.* that of an officer in the armed forces; rank of officers generally; body set up to conduct an inquiry and issue a report; authority to act on behalf of another, *esp.* to make purchases or conclude deals etc.; agreed percentage paid as recompense for such action; **to put into c.,** to make a naval vessel ready for sea; **c. agent,** bookmaker. COMMISSION (2), *v.t.* to grant a c. to, instruct someone to act on one's behalf; authorize the fitting out of a warship. [L.].

COMMISSIONAIRE [ko-mi-shn-āer'], *n.* uniformed doorkeeper; member of the corps of ex-soldiers organized for such duties. [Fr.].

COMMISSIONAL [ko-mi'shn-al], *adj.* appointing or appointed by commission.

COMMISSION-DAY [ko-mi'shn-dā], *n.* opening day of assizes, on which the judge's commission is read aloud.

COMMISSIONER [ko-mi'shn-er], *n.* person acting under a commission; local governor in certain colonies; high administrative official of the former Indian Civil Service; member of a commission; **High C.,** London representative of a member-state of the British Commonwealth, or of the British Government accredited to such a state. COMMISSIONERSHIP, *n.* office or tenure of a c. [MedL.].

COMMISSION-MERCHANT [ko-mi'shn-mer-chant], *n.* merchant who trades on commission.

COMMISSURE [ko'mi-syōōr], *n.* (*anat.*) the junction of two parts of the body, suture; line formed by the closing of the lips or eyelids, corner of the lips or eyelids when closed; (*bot.*) junction of the carpels in umbelliferous plants. COMMISSURAL [ko-mi-syōōr'al], *adj.* of, or pertaining to, a c. [L.].

COMMIT (*pres.pt.* **committing,** *pret. and p.pt.* **committed**) [ko-mit'], *v.t.* to entrust, give to someone's charge, commend to keeping; pledge, engage (oneself) irretrievably; do; perform (a bad action); send to prison; (*leg.*) send for trial before a superior court. [L.].

COMMITMENT [ko-mit'ment], *n.* act of committing; undertaking, pledge or monetary obligation to which one is committed, a responsibility.

COMMITABLE [ko-mi'ta-bl], *adj.* liable to be committed (to prison); (of an offence) rendering the one who commits it liable to trial.

COMMITTAL [ko-mi'tal], *n.* act of committing.

COMMITTEE [ko-mi'tē], *n.* body of persons set up to examine and report on some problem; governing body of a club, association or society. [Fr.].

COMMITTEE-MAN [ko-mi'tē-man], *n.* member of a committee, one addicted to committees.

COMMITTEE-ROOM [ko-mi'tē-rōōm], *n.* room where a committee meets.

COMMITTER [ko-mi'ter], *n.* one who commits.

COMMITTOR [ko-mi'ter], *n.* magistrate who commits a minor or insane person to the care of others.

COMMIXTURE [ko-miks'tyoor], *n.* act of mixing; state of being mixed; substance or solution formed by mixing. [L.].

COMMODE [ko-mōd'], *n.* chamber-pot; chest of drawers.

COMMODIOUS [ko-mō'di-ŏŏs], *adj.* roomy, ample in space. COMMODIOUSLY, *adv.* in c. fashion. COMMODIOUSNESS, *n.* condition of being c. [L.].

COMMODITY [ko-mo'di-ti], *n.* merchandise, something for sale; (*pl.*) (*econ.*) goods in which direct dealings can be made. [L.].

COMMODORE [ko'mo-daw(r)], *n.* naval courtesy title given to a captain performing special duties, or acting in seniority to others of the same rank; captain of a yacht squadron or a merchant fleet. [LL.].

COMMON (1) [ko'mun], *n.* piece of land open to all, and on which certain tenants have grazing rights; (*pl.*) the common people; the lower elective House in the British Parliament; (share of) common provisions, rations; **on short commons,** on a restricted diet.

COMMON (2), *adj.* shared by two or more, not private; open to or related to all; undertaken by, affecting the whole of a group; plentiful, widespread, regularly happening, familiar; ordinary, nondescript; of low birth; vulgar, ill-bred; cheap, shoddy; in bad taste; **a c. noun,** (*gram.*) name applicable to any single one of a group; **c. room,** living-room shared at a school or university; **c. sense,** good sense, normal understanding, sensible self-interest; **c. serjeant,** a judge in the City of London. [L.].

COMMONABLE [ko'mo-na-bl], *adj.* held in common; permitted to be pastured on common land.

COMMONAGE [ko'mo-nij], *n.* right of pasturing on a common; use of something in common; the common people.

COMMONALTY, COMMONALITY [ko'mo-nal-ti, ko-m(u)-na'li-ti], *n.* the common people. [MedL.].

COMMONER [ko'mo-ner], *n.* one of the common people, one without hereditary rank; one with a right in a common.

COMMONLY [ko'mon-li], *adv.* usually.

COMMONNESS [ko'mon-nes], *n.* quality of being common.

COMMONPLACE (1) [ko-mon-plās], *n.* a trite and platitudinous remark. COMMONPLACE (2), *adj.* ordinary, common, unremarkable, happening frequently, trite. COMMONPLACENESS, *n.* quality of being c.

COMMONPLACE-BOOK [ko-mon-plās'bŏŏk], *n.* notebook for recording other people's thoughts and observations.

COMMON PLEAS [ko-mon-plēz'], *n.* civil legal actions; **Court of c.,** former court for trying civil cases.

COMMONWEAL [ko'mon-wēl], *n.* the public good, the common profit.

COMMONWEALTH [ko'mon-welth], *n.* the state, a political community or union; protectorate under Cromwell; Federated States of Australia; **the British C. of Nations,** the political entity formed by the

United Kingdom and the self-governing territories overseas which acknowledge the sovereignty of the British Crown, together with the Republic of India.

COMMOTION [ko-mō'shn], *n.* agitation, disturbance, uproar, violent stir. [L.].

COMMUNAL [ko-myōō'nal], *adj.* relating to common ownership; shared by others; relating to a commune or communities; public. [LL.].

COMMUNALISM [ko-myōō'na-lizm], *n.* government by local communes. COMMUNALIST, *n.* supporter of c. COMMUNALISTIC [ko-myōō-na-lis'tik], *adj.* pertaining to c.

COMMUNE (1) [ko'myōōn], *n.* local French administrative division under the direction of a mayor and council; mob movement which controlled Paris for part of 1871. [L.].

COMMUNE (2) [ko-myōōn'], *v.i.* to talk quietly and intimately with a person, be in close spiritual contact (with). [L.].

COMMUNICABLE [ko-myōō'ni-ka-bl], *adj.* able to be communicated. COMMUNICABILITY [ko-myōō-ni-ka-bi'li-ti], *n.* quality of being c. COMMUNICABLY, *adv.* in c. fashion.

COMMUNICANT (1) [ko-myōō'ni-kant], *n.* (*eccles.*) one who receives Holy Communion; one who communicates. COMMUNICANT (2), *adj.* communicating, linking. [L.].

COMMUNICATE [ko-myōō'ni-kāt], *v.t. and i.* to impart, pass on or transmit a message, information etc.; exchange ideas or information with, be in touch with; have access to, be connected (with); take Holy Communion. [L.].

COMMUNICATION [ko-myōō-ni-kā'shn], *n.* act of communicating; thing communicated; means of communicating; (*pl.*) (*milit.*) means of connexion between an army and its base for the replenishment of supplies; **c. cord**, chain passing through all compartments of a railway train which, when pulled, operates the brake in an emergency. [L.].

COMMUNICATIVE [ko-myōō'ni-ka-tiv], *adj.* ready or eager to communicate. COMMUNICATIVENESS, *n.* quality of being c.

COMMUNICATOR [ko-myōō'ni-kā-ter], *n.* one who or that which communicates. COMMUNICATORY, *adj.* useful for the communication of information.

COMMUNION [ko-myōō'ni-on], *n.* mutual intercourse between two or more persons, fellowship, communication, mutual intercourse or spiritual contact in religious worship or doctrine; body of Christians who have one common belief and are members of a particular church; celebration of the Lord's Supper. COMMUNIONIST, *n.* one of the same c.; one holding strong views about the Holy Communion. [L.].

COMMUNIQUÉ, communiqué [ko-myōō'ni-kā], *n.* official bulletin or official statement on military operations. [Fr.].

COMMUNISM [ko'myōō-nizm], *n.* political theory that all property should be held in common or by the State; policy of those who hold that this objective demands the violent overthrow of capitalism and establishment of a "Dictatorship of the Proletariat," as ostensibly in the U.S.S.R. [Fr.].

COMMUNIST [ko'myōō-nist], *n.* believer in communism, militant socialist.

COMMUNIST(IC) [ko'myōō-nist, ko-myōō-nis'tik], *adj.* inclined or appertaining to communism.

COMMUNITY (1) [ko-myōō'ni-ti], *n.* a society; group living together and linked by national, economic or social relationships or under a common religious authority; the people of a state generally, the public; that which is held or shared in common. COMMUNITY (2), *adj.* pertaining to a c., common to a group.

COMMUNIZE [ko'myōō-nīz], *v.t.* to transfer to public ownership, convert to communism or impose communism upon. COMMUNIZATION [ko-myōō-ni-zā'shn], *n.* the liquidation of private ownership.

COMMUTABLE [ko-myōō'ta-bl], *adj.* able to be commuted. COMMUTABILITY [ko-myōō-ta-bi'li-ti], *n.* quality of being c.

COMMUTATION [ko-myōō-tā'shn], *n.* act of commuting.

COMMUTATIVE [ko-myōō'ta-tiv], *adj.* relating to commutation. COMMUTATIVELY, *adv.* by way of exchange or substitution.

COMMUTATOR [ko'myōō-tā-ter], *n.* device for changing the direction of a current in an electric circuit.

COMMUTE [ko-myōōt'], *v.t.* to substitute; change a mode of payment; (*leg.*) reduce a legal sentence;

(*elect.*) regulate the direction of a current; (*U.S.*) (*coll.*) travel to work daily by public conveyance. COMMUTER, *n.* (*U.S.*) one who commutes by public conveyance.

COMPACT (1) [kom'pakt], *n.* agreement, unwritten but binding understanding. [L.].

COMPACT (2) [kom-pakt'], *adj.* packed together, dense, firmly and neatly compressed; convenient to handle; concise, briefly comprehensive. COMPACT (3) [kom'pakt], *n.* pocket vanity case, face-powder enclosed in a small case. COMPACT (4) [kom-pakt'], *v.t.* to join firmly together; compress; compose. [L.].

COMPACTED [kom-pak'tid], *adj.* closely united, compressed together. COMPACTEDNESS, *n.* condition of being compact.

COMPACTION [kom-pak'shn], *n.* act of making a compact; state or quality of being compact.

COMPACTLY [kom-pakt'li], *adv.* in compact fashion.

COMPACTNESS [kom-pakt'nes], *n.* quality of being compact.

COMPAGINATE [kom-pa'ji-nāt], *v.t.* to unite firmly. COMPAGINATION [kom-pa-ji-nā'shn], *n.* structure, joining of parts; complex connexion. [L.].

COMPANION (1) [kom-pan'yun], *n.* one who accompanies, comrade, familiar friend, associate; person hired to attend, accompany and amuse an old, invalid, lonely or bored person; low rank in an order of knighthood; exact match, complement of one of a pair; handbook, guide. COMPANION (2), *adj.* matching, completing a pair or set of objects. COMPANION (3), *v.t.* to be c. to. COMPANIONLESS, *adj.* without a c. [OFr.].

COMPANION (4), *n.* the shelter over a stairway in a ship; **c. hatch**, opening leading from the deck to cabins below; **c. ladder**, ladder by which officers reach the quarterdeck; **c. way**, staircase descending to the cabins. [It.].

COMPANIONABLE [kom-pan'yu-na-bl], *adj.* sociable, friendly, making a good companion. COMPANIONABLY, *adv.* in c. fashion.

COMPANIONSHIP [kom-pan'yun-ship], *n.* fellowship, state of being companions, association; status of companion in an order of knighthood; (*print.*) group of compositors working together.

COMPANY [kum'pa-ni], *n.* group of people gathered together in companionship, gathering of persons with a common bond; qualities which make a person a (pleasant) companion; quality of being entertaining socially or to oneself personally; association of persons for business purposes; ship's crew; group of actors working together under common management; (*milit.*) subdivision of a battalion; **to keep c. with**, to associate habitually with. [LL.].

COMPARABLE [kom'pa-ra-bl], *adj.* able to be compared, having some affinity with, within measurable similarity. COMPARABLY, *adv.* in a c. manner. [L.].

COMPARATIVE [kum-pa'ra-tiv], *adj.* based on, related to, judged by, comparison; qualified from the point of comparisons, relative; that compares; **c. degree**, (*gram.*) the form of an adjective or adverb denoting a higher degree than the positive. COMPARATIVELY, *adv.* in a c. manner, relatively. [L.].

COMPARE (1) [kum-pāer'], *v.t. and i.* to examine things in relation to each other, examine things in respect of their similarities; note the resemblance between things; be similar, resemble; be worthy of comparison. COMPARE (2), *n.* comparison. [L.].

COMPARISON [kum-pa'ri-son], *n.* act of comparing; state of being compared; relative resemblance, closeness of degree between persons or objects; degree of similarity, possibility of comparing two objects; expression which compares two or more things. [L.].

COMPARTMENT [kum-paht'ment], *n.* a division or separate part partitioned off; one of the separate units which make up a railway-coach; the part of a Parliamentary Bill for which a limit of time is allowed. [LL.].

COMPASS (1) [kum'pas], *n.* circumference, encircling boundary; extent, range, reasonable or inevitable limit; instrument containing a needle sensitive to the magnetic pole and used to find direction; (*pl.*) instrument pivoting on a fixed leg, used for describing arcs and circles. [LL.].

COMPASS (2), *v.t.* to extend round, enclose, surround;

plot, devise (usually some wicked act); achieve, accomplish. COMPASSABLE, *adj.* that may be compassed. COMPASSING, *adj.* surrounding, encompassing; bringing about, causing to happen. [Fr.].

COMPASS-CARD [kum'pas-kahd], *n.* card on which the points of the compass are marked.

COMPASS-DIAL [kum'pas-di-al], *n.* pocket sundial fitted with a compass-needle.

COMPASSION [kom-pa'shn], *n.* pity mingled with kindness, sympathy and wish to alleviate suffering or distress. [L.].

COMPASSIONATE (1) [kom-pa'shn-at], *adj.* inclined to compassion, showing pity or mercy; granted without legal obligation, on grounds of compassion. COMPASSIONATE (2) [kom-pa'shn-āt], *v.t.* to take c. on. COMPASSIONATELY, *adv.* in c. fashion. COMPASSIONATENESS, *n.* quality of being c.

COMPASS-NEEDLE [kum'pas-nē-dl], *n.* the magnetized needle of a compass.

COMPASS-PLANE [kum'pas-plān], *n.* plane with a rounded bottom for planing concave surfaces.

COMPASS-SAW [kum'pas-saw], *n.* narrow saw designed for cutting curves.

COMPASS-SIGNAL [kum'pas-sig-nal], *n.* flag signal indicating the points of the compass.

COMPASS-TIMBER [kum'pas-tim-ber], *n.* curved beams.

COMPATIBLE [kum-pa'ti-bl], *adj.* congruous, suitable; agreeing with, circumstantially feasible or natural; able to live or get on with (someone). COMPATIBLY, *adv.* in c. fashion. [MedL.].

COMPATIBILITY [kum-pa-ti-bi'li-ti], *n.* quality of being compatible.

COMPATRIOT (1) [kum-pat'ri-ot], *n.* fellow countryman. COMPATRIOT (2), *adj.* of the same country. [Fr.].

COMPEER [kom-pēer', kom'pēer], *n.* an equal, associate, companion. [L.].

COMPEL (*pres.pt.* compelling, *pret.* and *p.pt.* compelled) [kom-pel'], *v.t.* to force, make someone do something, bring about by force. COMPELLINGLY, *adv.* in compelling fashion. [L.].

COMPENDIOUS [kom-pen'di-ŏŏs], *adj.* concisely comprehensive, containing a great volume of necessary information in extremely compact form. COMPENDIOUSLY, *adv.* in c. fashion. COMPENDIOUSNESS, *n.* state of being c. [L.].

COMPENDIUM (*pl.* compendiums or compendia) [kom-pen'di-um], *n.* comprehensive but compact summary of all relevant information. [L.].

COMPENSATE [kom'pen-sāt], *v.t. and i.* to recompense for a loss or injury, *esp.* by monetary payment, give something of equal value to make amends for some loss; (*mech.*) counterbalance a variation. COMPENSATIVE [kom-pen'sa-tiv], *adj.* compensatory. COMPENSATOR, *n.* one who or that which compensates. COMPENSATORY [kom-pen'sa-te-ri], *adj.* making compensation, in compensation. [L.].

COMPENSATION [kom-pen-sā'shn], *n.* act of compensating; thing given to make amends for some loss or injury; (*psych.*) development of a physical or mental condition to compensate for some psychological disability. [L.].

COMPERE, compère [kom'pāer], *n.* person introducing the turns in a cabaret or revue. [Fr.].

COMPETE [kom-pēt'], *v.i.* to strive against others for a common object, rival something in quality; take part in a contest of ability. [L.].

COMPETENCE [kom'pi-tens], *n.* quality of being competent; ability; means or money sufficient for life. [LL.].

COMPETENT [kom'pi-tent], *adj.* capable, efficient; satisfactory; fitted; of sound mind; (*leg.*) having legal authority, legally capable. COMPETENTLY, *adv.* in c. fashion. [L.].

COMPETITION [kom-pi-ti'shn], *n.* act of competing; struggle of two or more persons for a prize; organized contest, public test of skill for some prize or distinction; rivalry in trade. [L.].

COMPETITIVE [kom-pe'ti-tiv], *adj.* relating to, by means of, competition. COMPETITIVELY, *adv.* in c. fashion.

COMPETITOR [kom-pe'ti-ter], *n.* one engaging in competition, a rival. COMPETITORY, *adj.* engaging in competition. [L.].

COMPILATION [kom-pi-lā'shn], *n.* act or result of compiling; book made up from other works or sources. [L.].

COMPILE [kom-pīl'], *v.t.* to amass together material, *esp.* literary material, so as to produce a new work;

make out, draw up, compose, write, from various data or sources of information. COMPILER, *n.* one who compiles. [L.].

COMPLACENCY [kom-plā'sen-si], *n.* self-satisfied serenity, contented tranquillity. [MedL.].

COMPLACENT [kom-plā'sent], *adj.* unruffled, feeling or showing complacency. COMPLACENTLY, *adv.* in c. fashion. [L.].

COMPLAIN [kom-plān'], *v.i.* to express discontent at a circumstance; show this discontent by sounds of grief, grumble at, find fault with; bewail, state that one is suffering; make a formal accusation. COMPLAININGLY, *adv.* in complaining fashion. [LL.].

COMPLAINANT [kom-plā'nant], *n.* one who complains; (*leg.*) one who commences a legal action against an offender, plaintiff.

COMPLAINT [kom-plānt'], *n.* the expression of complaining; expression or cause of dissatisfaction; statement of injury or grievance; ailment, illness; formal accusation. [Fr.].

COMPLAISANCE [kom'pli-zans, kum-plā'zans], *n.* civility, conscious courtesy, desire to oblige or appear agreeable, over-readiness to defer or comply. [Fr.].

COMPLAISANT [kom'pli-zant, kum-plā'zant], *adj.* showing complaisance. COMPLAISANTLY, *adv.* in c. fashion. [Fr.].

COMPLEMENT (1) [kom'pli-ment], *n.* that which completes or is needed to complete; (*milit. and nav.*) the full number of men to a unit or ship; (*math.*) the number of degrees by which an acute angle is less than a right angle; (*gram.*) that part which completes the meaning; (*mus.*) the interval needed to make an octave with a given interval. COMPLEMENT (2), *v.t.* to make complete. COMPLEMENTAL [kom-pli-men'tal], *adj.* pertaining to or standing as a c. [L.].

COMPLEMENTARY [kom-pli-men'ta-ri], *adj.* completing; supplying a deficiency; c. angles, angles whose sum equals a right angle; c. colours, colours which, together with a specified colour, make up white.

COMPLETE (1) [kom-plēt'], *adj.* entire, whole, lacking nothing, finished; (*coll.*) absolute, utter. COMPLETE (2), *v.t.* to finish, bring to an end; make c. COMPLETELY, *adv.* entirely, wholly, in c. fashion. COMPLETENESS, *n.* condition of being c. [L.].

COMPLETION [kom-plē'shn], *n.* act of completing; state of being complete. [L.].

COMPLEX (1) [kom'pleks], *n.* a complexity, complex conclusion; (*psych.*) combination of repressed emotions producing a neurotic state; (*coll.*) a mental tendency. COMPLEX (2), *adj.* complicated, intricate, composed of many interlocking parts; (*fig.*) difficult, involved; c. sentence, (*gram.*) sentence containing subordinate clauses. COMPLEXLY, *adv.* in c. fashion. [L.].

COMPLEXION [kom-plek'shn], *n.* the colour of the face; (*fig.*) outlook, external prospect. COMPLEXIONAL, *adj.* depending on or relating to the c. [L.].

COMPLEXITY [kom-plek'si-ti], *n.* state of being complex.

COMPLIANCE [kom-plī'ans], *n.* state of being compliant; act of complying with.

COMPLIANT [kom-plī'ant], *adj.* complying, yielding, giving way, obliging. COMPLIANTLY, *adv.* in c. fashion.

COMPLICACY [kom'pli-ka-si], *n.* state of being complicated.

COMPLICATE (1) [kom'pli-kāt], *v.t.* to involve, make more complex, difficult or awkward. COMPLICATE (2), *adj.* complicated; (*bot.*) doubled over together lengthwise. [L.].

COMPLICATED [kom'pli-kā-tid], *adj.* complex, involved, difficult, intricate; c. fracture, fracture accompanied by adjacent injuries.

COMPLICATION [kom-pli-kā'shn], *n.* act of complicating, state of being complicated; that which complicates; (*med.*) fresh trouble arising during an illness, increasing the danger. [L.].

COMPLICITY [kom-plī'si-ti], *n.* state of being an accomplice in some wrong. [Fr.].

COMPLIMENT (1) [kom'pli-ment], *n.* an expression of praise or regard uttered with intention to please irrespective of its truth; a formal courtesy; (*pl.*) polite greeting, expression of good wishes. COMPLIMENT (2), *v.t.* to utter a c.; praise, congratulate. [Fr.].

COMPLIMENTARY [kom-pli-men'ta-ri], *adj.* pertaining to a compliment; containing compliments;

The accent ' after a syllable = stress (u·pon'). The mark ⁻ over a vowel = length (ā in made; ō in bone).

flattering, full of praise; given with the compliments of the donor; free of charge.

COMPLIN, COMPLINE [kom'plin], *n.* the last prayer or service of the day in the Roman Catholic Church. [OFr. from L.].

COMPLY [kom-plī'], *v.i.* to give way, yield (to a request), consent, oblige; **to c. with,** to observe, agree to. [L.].

COMPO [kom'pō], *n.* stucco, kind of concrete used by plasterers. [COMPO(SITION)].

COMPONENT (1) [kom-pō'nent], *adj.* constituting, forming part of a whole. COMPONENT (2), *n.* a constituent, one of the elements of which a thing is composed. [L.].

COMPORT [kum-pawt'], *v.t., refl. and i.* to bear, conduct oneself; be appropriate or suitable; be consistent with. COMPORTMENT, *n.* deportment, bearing. [L.].

COMPOSE [kom-pōz'], *v.t.* to make up, form from constituents, put together, constitute by combining parts; (*mus.*) create a work of music; create any work of art or literature; make calm; restore the bearing or features to calmness or repose; put in order, adjust, so as to suit the occasion; arrange properly; (*print.*) set up type in type. [L.].

COMPOSED [kom-pōzd'], *adj.* formed by composing; calm, undisturbed. COMPOSEDLY, *adv.* in c. fashion. COMPOSEDNESS, *n.* condition of being c.

COMPOSER [kom-pō'zer], *n.* one who composes, *esp.* music.

COMPOSING [kom-pō'zing], *adj.* putting together; fitted for composing; restoring to reposeful calm; **c. frame,** (*print.*) frame holding a printer's type cases; **c. stick,** (*print.*) receptacle of adjustable width in which type is set up in lines by the compositor.

COMPOSITAE [kom-po'zi-tē], *n.(pl.)* (*bot.*) the largest natural order of plants, in which many small flowers are closely grouped to form a single flower-head as in the dandelion etc. [L.].

COMPOSITE (1) [kom'po-zit], *adj.* made up of distinct parts; mixed; (*bot.*) of the order *Compositae*; (*math.*) capable of being divided into whole numbers other than one. COMPOSITE (2), *n.* that which is c.; (*bot.*) a c. flower. [L.].

COMPOSITION [kom-po-zi'shn], *n.* act of composing or of putting together; thing composed; the writing of music; the music composed, essay or other short piece of writing; the arrangement and proportion of a work of art; compound of various substances; settlement, agreement to settle a debt by the payment of a proportion of the amount due, a legal compromise; (*print.*) the setting up of type. [L.].

COMPOSITOR [kom-po'zi-ter], *n.* (*print.*) typesetter. [L.].

COMPOST (1) [kom'post], *n.* mixture of soil and various manures as a fertilizer; mixture for plastering the exterior of houses. COMPOST (2), *v.t.* to apply c. to; make into c. [OFr.].

COMPOSURE [kom-pō'zhoor], *n.* calmness, serenity, unruffled frame of mind.

COMPOT, see COMPOTE.

COMPOTE, COMPOT [kom'pōt], *n.* fruit stewed or preserved in syrup. [Fr.].

COMPOUND (1) [kom'pownd], *adj.* made up of several elements, not simple; **c. interest,** interest accumulating on to interest; **c. householder,** householder whose rent includes his rates; **c. quantity,** quantity composed of several simple quantities connected by a mathematical sign, as (a-b); **c. word,** word made up of two or more separate words. COMPOUND (2), *n.* a c. substance, something compounded; (*chem.*) substance containing chemically united elements.

COMPOUND (3) [kom-pownd'], *v.t. and i.* to bring together different elements to form a compound substance; make a mixture; settle by mutual agreement or composition; discharge a recurrent debt, subscription etc. by paying a lump sum; (*leg.*) overlook an offence for gain; come to a composition. COMPOUNDABLE, *adj.* able to be compounded. COMPOUNDER, *n.* one who compounds, *esp.* crime or debt. [L.].

COMPOUND (4) [kom'pownd], *n.* fenced-in ground round a dwelling place or factory in India, China etc. [Malay].

COMPREHEND [kom-pri-hend'], *v.t.* to include, contain within a bound or scope; understand. [L.].

COMPREHENSIBLE [kom-pri-hen'si-bl], *adj.* able to be comprehended. COMPREHENSIBLENESS, *n.*

quality of being c. COMPREHENSIBLY, *adv.* in c. fashion.

COMPREHENSION [kom-pri-hen'shn], *n.* act or power of comprehending, intellectual capacity. [L.].

COMPREHENSIVE [kom-pri-hen'siv], *adj.* covering a wide range, inclusive, extensive. COMPREHENSIVELY, *n.* in c. fashion. COMPREHENSIVENESS, *n.* quality of being c.

COMPRESS (1) [kom-pres'], *v.t.* to press together, bring pressure on to, constrict, crush into a small space, condense. COMPRESS (2) [kom'pres], *n.* (*surg.*) pad of wet material held down by a bandage. COMPRESSED [kom-prest'], *adj.* pressed together; (*fig.*) made concise, condensed. [L.].

COMPRESSIBLE [kom-pre'si-bl], *adj.* able to be compressed. COMPRESSIBILITY [kom-pre-si-bi'li-ti], *n.* quality of being c.

COMPRESSION [kom-pre'shn], *n.* act of compressing, state of being compressed; (*motoring*) condition of a petrol engine in regard to its efficiency in holding the explosive gas when compressed in the cylinder by the piston; (*fig.*) conciseness. COMPRESSION-TAP, tap in a motor engine by which the compressed gas can escape from the cylinder-head to reduce c.

COMPRESSIVE [kom-pre'sive], *adj.* tending to, able to compress.

COMPRESSOR [kom-pre'ser], *n.* apparatus for compressing air; anything used to compress.

COMPRISE [kom-prīz'], *v.t.* to contain, be made up of, consist of. [Fr. from L.].

COMPROMISE (1) [kom'pro-mīz], *n.* agreement in which the parties make mutual concessions for the sake of settlement, decision endeavouring to make the best of incompatibles. COMPROMISE (2), *v.t. and i.* to come to agreement by c.; throw into danger by careless folly; bring under suspicion, *esp.* of illicit sexual intercourse. [L.].

COMPTOMETER [komp-to'mi-ter], *n.* (*prot.*) calculating machine. [Fr.].

COMPTROLLER, see CONTROLLER.

COMPULSION [kom-pul'shn], *n.* act of compelling, force, constraint. [L.].

COMPULSIVE [kom-pul'siv], *adj.* compelling. COMPULSIVELY, *adv.* in c. fashion. COMPULSIVENESS, *n.* quality of being c.

COMPULSORY [kom-pul'se ri], *adj.* coercive, compelling; that must be made or performed, enforced by compulsion. COMPULSORILY, *adv.* in c. fashion.

COMPUNCTION [kom-pungk'shn], *n.* scruple; impulse to show mercy; moral qualm or hesitation in regard to a wrong; prick of conscience. COMPUNCTIONLESS, *adj.* without c. [L.].

COMPUNCTIOUS [kum-pungk'shoos], *adj.* feeling, inducing compunction. COMPUNCTIOUSLY, *adv.* with compunction.

COMPUTATION [kom-pyoo-tā'shn], *n.* process or result of computing, a reckoning.

COMPUTE [kom-pyoot'], *v.t. and i* to count, calculate, estimate. COMPUTABLE, *adj.* able to be computed. COMPUTER, COMPUTIST, *n.* one who computes.

COMRADE [kom'rād], *n.* companion, associate. [OFr.].

COMRADELY [kom'rād-li], *adj.* friendly, worthy of a comrade.

COMRADESHIP [kom'rād-ship], *n.* fellowship, friendly feeling.

COMTISM [kom'tizm], *n.* (*philos.*) positivism. COMTIST, *n.* (*philos.*) positivist. [G. *Comte*, French philosopher].

CON- (1), *pref.* with, together. [L.].

CON (2) (*pres.pt.* **conning,** *pret. and p.pt.* **conned**) [kon], *v.t.* to study carefully, scrutinize, learn by heart. [OE.].

CON (3) (*pres.pt.* **conning,** *pret. and p.pt.* **conned**), *v.t.* to direct a ship.

CONARIUM [ko-nãer'i-um], *n.* (*anat.*) the pineal gland. [L. from Gk.].

CONATION [kō-nā'shn], *n.* the faculty of will, volitional impulse. CONATIVE [kō'na-tiv], *adj.* pertaining to the exercise of will. [L.].

CONATUS [kō-nā'tus], *n.* natural impulse, desire to live. [L.].

CONCATENATE [kon-ka'ti-nāt], *v.t.* to link together in a series, join as in a chain. [L.].

CONCATENATION [kon-ka-ti-nā'shn], *n.* series of links united, series of interdependents; act of concatenating. [L.].

CONCAVE (1) [kon'kāv], *adj.* hollow, curving

ōō is pronounced as in f*oo*d; ŏŏ as in h*oo*d; th as in *th*ink; TH as in *th*at; zh as in a*z*ure.   ~ = related to.

inwards, forming a curved hollow; (opt.) with the surface of a lens ground to a hollow curved profile. CONCAVE (2), n. a concavity, a curving inwards. CONCAVELY, adv. in c. fashion. [L.].

CONCAVITY [kon-ka'vi-ti], n. hollowness; inside surface of a hollow spherical or vaulted body. [L.].

CONCAVO-CONCAVE [kon-kā-vō-kon'kāv], adj. (opt.) concave on both surfaces.

CONCAVO-CONVEX [kon-kā-vō-kon'veks], adj. (opt.) concave on one side and convex on the other.

CONCEAL [kon-sēl'], v.t. to hide, keep from sight or knowledge; keep secret. CONCEALABLE, adj. able to be concealed. CONCEALED, adj. hidden, secret. [L.].

CONCEALMENT [kon-sēl'ment], n. act of concealing; state of being concealed; hiding-place, disguise. [OFr.].

CONCEDE [kon-sēd'], v.t. and i. to yield, give way, admit, grant something previously denied; let go without resistance. [L.].

CONCEIT [kon-sēt'], n. state of being conceited; exaggerated self-admiration; a quaint intellectual fancy; witty and ingenious notion. [CONCEIVE].

CONCEITED [kon-sē'tid], adj. full of self-esteem, displaying petty personal pride. CONCEITEDLY, adv. in c. fashion.

CONCEIVABLE [kon-sē'va-bl], adj. imaginable, possible. CONCEIVABILITY, CONCEIVABLENESS [kon-sē-va-bi'li-ti, kon-sē'va-bl-nes], n. quality of being c.

CONCEIVABLY [kon-sē'va-bli], adv. in conceivable or intelligible fashion, possibly.

CONCEIVE [kon-sēv'], v.t. and i. to become pregnant; generate, form mentally; devise, plan, formulate; imagine, consider possible. [OFr.].

CONCENTRATE (1) [kon'sen-trāt], v.t. to bring together in a single place and body, esp. to mass troops in a place; fix one's attention, energy on a single object; (chem.) intensify the strength of a substance or liquid by evaporation or purification; v.i. to come together round a single centre, mass in a single place; exercise intense mental effort, focus all the intellect on one point; devote oneself entirely. CONCENTRATE (2), adj. produced by concentration, in a state of concentration. CONCENTRATE (3), n. substance in a state of concentration, esp. cattle food. [L.].

CONCENTRATION [kon-sen-trā'shn], n. act of concentrating; condition of being concentrated; that which is concentrated; c. camp, prison camp in which political prisoners are confined.

CONCENTRATIVE [kon-sen'tra-tiv], adj. relating to concentration, that concentrates. CONCENTRATIVENESS, n. faculty of concentration.

CONCENTRATOR [kon'sen-trā-ter], n. pneumatic machine used in mining to concentrate particles of ore; apparatus for producing a concentrated substance or solution.

CONCENTRE [kon-sen'ter], v.t. and i. to gather together in a common centre; come together for a common object. [Fr.].

CONCENTRIC(AL) [kon-sen'trik(-al)], adj. having a common centre; c. fire, (milit.) fire concentrated on one point. CONCENTRICALLY, adv. in c. fashion. CONCENTRICITY [kon-sen-tri'si-ti], n. condition of being c.

CONCEPT [kon'sept], n. idea, abstract or general notion. [L.].

CONCEPTION [kon-sep'shn], n. act of conceiving; thing conceived; (physiol.) the first forming of the embryo in the womb; the imaginative or creative intellectual faculty; idea, plan, notion. CONCEPTIONAL, CONCEPTIVE, CONCEPTUAL, adj. pertaining to c. or to concepts. [L.].

CONCEPTUALISM [kon-sep'tyōō-a-lizm], n. (philos.) medieval philosophical doctrine that universals have only subjective reality; epistemological doctrine that the mind is capable of creating an idea corresponding to the general term. CONCEPTUALIST, n. believer in c. CONCEPTUALIZE, v.t. to form a concept of.

CONCERN (1) [kon-surn'], v.t. to relate to, have to do with, affect, be connected with the interests of; disturb, cause anxiety in; be a responsibility to; (reflex.) take trouble (over), show a strong interest (in). CONCERN (2), n. that which concerns, that which affects or is related to; anxiety; responsibility; business; a commercial firm. [L.].

CONCERNED [kon-surnd'], adj. having concern with or for, interested, anxious. CONCERNEDLY [kon-ser'ned-li], adv. in c. fashion.

CONCERNING [kon-sur'ning], prep. relating to.

CONCERT (1) [kon'sert], n. concord, harmony, unison; agreement; (specif.) musical entertainment in which singers or instrumentalists take part. CONCERT (2) [kon-surt'], v.t. to join together in an operation, agree to undertake in common. [It.].

CONCERTANTE [kon-cher-tan'tā], n. (mus.) musical composition for solo instruments or voices with accompaniments. [It.].

CONCERTED [kon-sur'tid], adj. in harmony, by mutual effort, joint; (mus.) arranged in parts.

CONCERT-GRAND [kon'sert-grand], n. large grand piano for use at concerts.

CONCERTINA [kon-ser-tē'nah], n. (mus.) manual wind-instrument, the air-stream being provided by bellows and controlled by the note keys on the ends. [Invented].

CONCERTO (pl. concertos) [kon-chāer'tō], n. (mus.) composition usually for a single instrument with orchestral accompaniment. [It.].

CONCERT PITCH [kon'sert-pich], n. a musical tuning to a pitch slightly higher than normal; (fig.) at the top of condition.

CONCESSION [kon-se'shn], n. act of conceding, thing conceded; land or privilege granted by a government, esp. to a foreign commercial undertaking; grant of specially favourable terms to a customer. CONCESSIONIST, n. one advocating c. [L.].

CONCESSIONAIRE [kon-se-shn-āer'], n. person to whom a concession has been made. [Fr.].

CONCESSIONARY (1) [kon-se'-shn-a-ri], adj. pertaining to concessions. CONCESSIONARY (2), n. concessionaire.

CONCESSIVE [kon-se'siv], adj. relating to concession; (gram.) expressing concession. CONCESSIVELY, adv. by concession. [L.].

CONCH [kongk], n. large spiral shell of a marine mollusc, such a shell used as a trumpet in Hindu temples, or sounded by the Tritons; (arch.) vault of a semicircular apse; the apse itself. [Next].

CONCHA [kong'kah], n. a conch; (anat.) the larger cavity of the external ear. [L.].

CONCHIFEROUS [kong-ki'fe-rōōs], adj. having a shell; (geol.) containing shells.

CONCHOID [kong'koid], n. (math.) a curve for finding two mean proportionals. [Gk.].

CONCHOLOGY [kong-ko'lo-ji], n. scientific study of shells and molluscs. CONCHOLOGICAL [kong-ko-lo'ji-kal], adj. relating to c. CONCHOLOGIST, n. one expert in c. [Gk.].

CONCHYLIACEOUS [kong-ki-li-ā'shōōs], adj. relating to or resembling a shell. [Gk.].

CONCIERGE [kon'si-āerzh], n. hall porter, janitor. [Fr.].

CONCILIATE [kon-si'li-āt], v.t. to modify the hostility of, mollify, placate, make peace between; win the favour of. CONCILIATIVE, adj. conciliatory.

CONCILIATION [kon-si-li-ā'shn], n. act or result of conciliating; settlement of labour disputes by negotiation. [L.].

CONCILIATOR [kon-si'li-ā-ter], n. person who conciliates. [L.].

CONCILIATORY [kon-si'li-a-te-ri], adj. tending to conciliate; showing good will.

CONCISE [kon-sīs'], adj. briefly clear and comprehensive, terse, short and to the point. CONCISELY, adv. in c. fashion. CONCISENESS, n. quality of being c. [L.].

CONCISION [kon-si'zhn], n. conciseness; division, mutilation. [L.].

CONCLAVE [kon'klāv], n. (R.C.) assembly of cardinals for a Papal election; place in which this assembly meets; any secret meeting or discussion. [L.].

CONCLUDE [kon-klōōd'], v.t. and i. to bring or come to an end or a decision; finish, end; infer, form an opinion. [L.].

CONCLUDING [kon-klōō'ding], adj. finishing, completing, final. CONCLUDINGLY, adv. in conclusion.

CONCLUSION [kon-klōō'zhn], n. act of concluding; state of being concluded, an end, finish; that which is concluded, deduction. [L.].

CONCLUSIVE [kon-klōō'siv], adj. bringing to a conclusion; decisive, convincing. CONCLUSIVELY, adv. in c. fashion.

CONCOCT [kon-kokt'], v.t. to form or devise, by the mixture of various ingredients; (fig.) plan, scheme. CONCOCTER, -OR, n. person who concocts. [L.].

CONCOCTION [kon-kok'shn], n. act of concocting; that which is concocted, a mixture.

CONCOMITANCE [kon-ko'mi-tans], n. state of

---

being concomitant; (*theol.*) complete presence of the body and blood of Christ in each of the Eucharistic elements. [MedL.].

CONCOMITANCY [kon-ko'mi-tan-si], *n.* concomitance.

CONCOMITANT (1) [kon-ko'mi-tant], *adj.* accompanying. CONCOMITANT (2), *n.* attendant circumstance, accompaniment. CONCOMITANTLY, *adv.* as a c. [L.].

CONCORD [kon'kawd], *n.* agreement, personal harmony, *esp.* in opinions or ideas; (*gram.*) grammatical agreement in number, person and case; (*mus.*) harmonious combination of intervals. [L.].

CONCORDANCE [kon-kaw'dans], *n.* state of being concordant; index of the words in a book or author's works. [L.].

CONCORDANT [kon-kaw'dant], *adj.* harmonious, agreeing, in accord. CONCORDANTLY, *adv.* in c. fashion.

CONCORDAT [kon-kaw'dat], *n.* agreement between a temporal sovereign or government and the Pope; compact, agreement. [Fr.].

CONCOURSE [kon'kaws], *n.* great assembly, vast throng; a gathering or flowing together. [L.].

CONCRESCENCE [kon-kre'sens], *n.* a coalescence of organisms.

CONCRETE (1) [kon'krēt], *adj.* formed into a solid mass, possessing mass or matter; tangible, real; particular; made of concrete; (*gram.*) denoting a material object. CONCRETE (2), *n.* mixture of sand, gravel and cement used in building; concrete thing, real object; **reinforced c.**, c. strengthened with steel. CONCRETE (3) [kon-krēt'], *v.t. and i.* to form into a solid mass, cause to become c.; [kon'krēt] surface with c. CONCRETELY, *adv.* in c. fashion. CONCRETENESS, *n.* quality of being c. [L.].

CONCRETION [kon-kre'shn], *n.* act of becoming concrete; state of being concrete; a concreted mass; (*med.*) internal stone or calculus. CONCRETIONAL, CONCRETIONARY, *adj.* pertaining to a c.

CONCUBINE [kong'kyōō-bīn], *n.* woman cohabiting with a man without marriage. CONCUBINAGE [kong-kyōō'bi-nij], *n.* state of being a c. CONCUBINARY [kong-kyōō'bi-na-ri], *adj.* relating to, born in, concubinage. [L.].

CONCUPISCENCE [kong-kyōō'pi-sens], *n.* lust, continuous sexual desire. CONCUPISCIBLE [kong-kyōō'pi-si-bl], *adj.* libidinous. [L.].

CONCUPISCENT [kong-kyōō'pi-sent], *adj.* lustful. [L.].

CONCUR (*pres.pt.* **concurring**, *pret. and p.pt.* **concurred**) [kon-kur'], *v.i.* to agree, *esp.* to assent to another's opinion or decision; coincide, meet at a point. [L.].

CONCURRENCE [kon-ku'rens], *n.* act or state of concurring; agreement.

CONCURRENT (1) [kon-ku'rent], *adj.* agreeing, coinciding; taking place at the same time, contributory, converging. CONCURRENT (2), *n.* something concurring, a cause acting with another. CONCURRENTLY, *adv.* in c. fashion. CONCURRENTNESS, *n.* condition of being c. [L.].

CONCUSS [kon-kus'], *v.t.* to shake, strike heavily; cause concussion in. [L.].

CONCUSSION [kon-ku'shn], *n.* shock, violent impact; (*med.*) injury resulting from a heavy blow, collision etc., *esp.* to the brain. CONCUSSIVE, *adj.* tending to cause c.

CONCYCLIC [kon-sī'klik], *adj.* lying in the circumference of a circle.

CONDEMN [kon-dem'], *v.t.* to pronounce guilty; declare to be unfit for use; sentence to destruction; censure, deprecate; (*leg.*) pass sentence on. CONDEMNABLE [kon-dem'na-bl], *adj.* fit to be condemned. CONDEMNATORY [kon-dem'na-te-ri], *adj.* that condemns. [L.].

CONDEMNATION [kon-dem-nā'shn], *n.* act of condemning; state of being condemned; censure. [L.].

CONDEMNED [kon-demd'], *adj.* having suffered condemnation; **c. cell**, cell where a prisoner under sentence of death is kept.

CONDENSABLE [kon-den'sa-bl], *adj.* able to be condensed. CONDENSABILITY [kon-den-sa-bi'li-ti], *n.* capacity for being condensed.

CONDENSATION [kon-den-sā'shn], *n.* act of condensing, *esp.* the change from vapour to liquid; state of being condensed.

CONDENSE [kon-dens'], *v.t. and i.* to make dense, compact, to compress; (*phys.*) make more dense, change from vapour to liquid; (*fig.*) make concise,

reduce to a few words; (*opt.*) focus, concentrate; become denser or more compact. [L.].

CONDENSED [kon-denst'], *adj.* compressed, compact, terse, liquefied; **c. milk**, tinned evaporated milk.

CONDENSER [kon-den'ser], *n.* that which condenses; vessel in which vapour is reduced to liquid form; (*elect.*) device for storing an electric charge; (*opt.*) device for concentrating light rays on an object.

CONDESCEND [kon-di-send'], *v.i.* to lower one's actions or behaviour consciously and voluntarily below one's position of superiority; perform actions unworthy of, or beneath, one; descend socially and deliberately to the level of an inferior. CONDESCENDENCE, *n.* condescension. [L.].

CONDESCENDING [kon-di-sen'ding], *adj.* characterized by condescension; patronizing. CONDESCENDINGLY, *adv.* in c. fashion.

CONDESCENSION [kon-di-sen'shn], *n.* act of condescending; self-conscious display of familiarity to inferiors. [L.].

CONDIGN [kon-dīn'], *adj.* appropriate, just, merited. CONDIGNLY, *adv.* in c. fashion. CONDIGNNESS, *n.* quality of being c.

CONDIMENT [kon'di-ment], *n.* seasoning, highly flavoured spice. CONDIMENTAL [kon-di-men'tal], *adj.* pertaining to a c. [L.].

CONDITION (1) [kon-di'shn], *n.* state of being, existence; state of repair; health, physique; rank, social status; a qualification, stipulation, limitation; determining cause; (*pl.*) environment; (*psych.*) factor determining behaviour, cause producing a reflex. CONDITION (2), *v.t.* to make conditions; qualify, adapt or determine by conditions; bring to good health; (*psych.*) treat so that certain stimuli will produce determined reflexes. [L.].

CONDITIONAL [kon-di'shn-al], *adj.* depending upon conditions, qualified; (*gram.*) expressing a condition. CONDITIONALITY [kon-di-shn-a'li-ti], *n.* quality of being c. CONDITIONALLY, *adv.* upon conditions.

CONDITIONATE (1) [kon-di'shn-āt], *adj.* conditional. CONDITIONATE (2), *v.t.* to put under conditions.

CONDITIONED [kon-di'shnd], *adj.* limited by conditions; (*psych.*) done as an acquired reflex to certain causes; **well c.**, in good condition.

CONDOLE [kon-dōl'], *v.t.* to express sympathy with; share the grief of another in sympathy. CONDOLATORY, *adj.* expressing condolence. CONDOLE, *n.* condolence. [L.].

CONDOLENCE [kon-dō'lens], *n.* expression of sympathy and commiseration upon a cause of grief.

CONDOMINIUM [kon-dō-mi'ni-um], *n.* joint sovereignty. [L.].

CONDONATION [kon-dō-nā'shn], *n.* act of condoning. [L.].

CONDONE [kon-dōn'], *v.t.* to overlook or forgive an offence, *esp.* adultery. [L.].

CONDOR [kon'daw(r)], *n.* large South American vulture; Chilean gold coin. [Span.].

CONDOTTIERE (*pl.* **condottieri**) [kon-dot-tyäer'i], *n.* Italian leader of mercenaries of the Renaissance period. [It.].

CONDUCE [kon-dyōōs'], *v.i.* to tend to produce, promote, bring on.

CONDUCIVE [kon-dyōō'siv], *adj.* tending to bring about, inducing. CONDUCIVENESS, *n.* quality of being c.

CONDUCT (1) [kon'dukt], *n.* management, carrying out; behaviour, comportment. SAFE-CONDUCT, warrant granting safe passage through hostile territory.

CONDUCT (2) [kon-dukt'], *v.t.* to direct, manage, look after; lead, guide, escort; (*mus.*) direct and control the performance of an orchestra or choir; (*reflex.*) behave; (*phys.*) transmit, allow to pass through. [L.].

CONDUCTANCE [kon-duk'tans], *n.* (*elect.*) power of conducting, conductivity.

CONDUCTIBLE [kon-duk'ti-bl], *adj.* able to conduct or to be conducted. CONDUCTIBILITY [kon-duk-ti-bi'li-ti], *n.* (*phys.*) power of conducting electricity, heat etc.

CONDUCTION [kon-duk'shn], *n.* conductivity; act of conducting; (*phys.*) transmission of heat through adjacent bodies.

CONDUCTIVE [kon-duk'tiv], *adj.* able to conduct (heat etc.). CONDUCTIVITY [kon-duk-ti'vi-ti], *n.* ability to conduct heat, electricity etc.

CONDUCTOR [kon-duk'ter], *n.* guide, one who conducts, *esp.* a choir or orchestra; attendant who collects fares and issues tickets on a bus, tram etc.; substance or instrument able to conduct heat, electricity etc. CONDUCTORSHIP, *n.* position or quality of a c. [LL.].

CONDUIT [kun'dit, kon'dit], *n.* pipe or channel to convey water or other fluid; narrow connecting passage or channel. [Fr. from LL.].

CONDYLE [kon'dil], *n.* (*anat.*) protuberance at the end of a bone fitting into the socket of another. CONDYLOID, *adj.* (*anat.*) resembling a c. [Gk.].

CONE [kōn], *n.* solid body tapering regularly to a point from a circular base; anything having a similar shape; (*bot.*) roughly cone-shaped fruit of certain trees and shrubs, in which the seeds are covered by hard scales; (*geom.*) straight line always fixed at one point, any other point of which describes a fixed closed curve; univalve mollusc with an inversely conical shell. [Gk.].

CONEY, see CONY.

CONFAB [kon'fab], *n.* (*coll.*) confabulation.

CONFABULATE [kon-fa'byōō-lāt], *v.i.* to chat confidentially. CONFABULATORY [kon-fa'byōō-lā-te-ri], *adj.* relating to confabulation.

CONFABULATION [kon-fa-byōō-lā'shn], *n.* confidential chat.

CONFECTION [kon-fek'shn], *n.* a mixing into a compound preparation; sweetmeat; any fashionable article of women's dress. [L.].

CONFECTIONARY (1) [kon-fek'shn-a-ri], *n.* place where sweetmeats are made; a sweetmeat. CONFECTIONARY (2), *adj.* pertaining to confections.

CONFECTIONER [kon-fek'shn-er], *n.* maker of, or dealer in, confectionery.

CONFECTIONERY [kon-fek'shn-e-ri], *n.* sweetmeats, pastries, cakes and other confections; business or shop making and selling these.

CONFEDERACY [kon-fe'de-ra-si], *n.* a uniting in alliance; league, number of independent states united in close alliance for a common purpose; criminal conspiracy.

CONFEDERATE (1) [kon-fe'de-rat], *adj.* allied, in confederacy, leagued together. CONFEDERATE (2), *n.* member of a confederacy; accomplice. CONFEDERATE (3) [kon-fe'de-rāt], *v.t. and i.* to form into a confederacy. [L.].

CONFEDERATION [kon-fe-de-rā'shn], *n.* formation of a confederacy, close alliance between states. [LL.].

CONFEDERATIVE [kon-fe'de-ra-tiv], *adj.* pertaining to a confederacy.

CONFER (*pres.pt.* **conferring,** *pret. and p.pt.* **conferred**) [kon-fur'], *v.t. and i.* to bestow upon, award; consult with, discuss. CONFEREE [kon-fer-ē'], *n.* person with whom one confers; one on whom something is conferred. CONFERRABLE, *adj.* able to be conferred. [L.].

CONFERENCE [kon'fe-rens], *n.* consultation; formal gathering to discuss or examine a problem or situation and exchange views. CONFERENTIAL [kon-fe-ren'shal], *adj.* pertaining to a c. [Fr.].

CONFERMENT [kon-fur'ment], *n.* act of conferring.

CONFERRING [kon-fur'ing], *n.* deliberation, conference; bestowal.

CONFERVA (*pl.* **confervae**) [kon-fur'vah, 'vē], *n.* (*bot.*) green freshwater algae. CONFERVACEOUS [kon-fer-vā'shōōs], *adj.* relating to, or resembling, a c. CONFERVOID [kon-fur'void], *adj.* articulated like the confervae. [L.].

CONFESS [kon-fes'], *v.t. and i.* to admit, disclose, acknowledge (error or misdeed); (*eccles.*) hear a confession; declare one's sins to a priest. CONFESSANT, *n.* one who confesses to a priest. [L.].

CONFESSEDLY [kon-fe'sid-li], *adv.* admittedly.

CONFESSION [kon-fe'shn], *n.* act of confessing; thing confessed; declaration or avowal of faith or belief. [L.].

CONFESSIONAL (1) [kon-fe'shn-al], *n.* curtained box in which a priest hears confessions. CONFESSIONAL (2), *adj.* relating to, or based upon, a confession.

CONFESSIONARY (1) [kon-fe'shn-a-ri], *n.* a confessional. CONFESSIONARY (2), *adj.* relating to confession.

CONFESSOR [kon-fe'ser], *n.* †one who makes a declaration of his religious faith; priest who hears confession. [MedL.].

CONFETTI [kon-fe'ti], *n.*(*pl.*) small pieces of thin coloured paper thrown at a bridal pair. [It.].

CONFIDANT [kon-fi-dant'], *n.* one to whom something is confided, intimate friend.

CONFIDANTE [kon-fi-dant'], *n.* female confidant.

CONFIDE [kon-fid'], *v.t. and i.* to entrust to, tell a secret to; have trust or reliance in. [L.].

CONFIDENCE [kon'fi-dens], *n.* trust; steadfast reliance, assurance, self-assurance; that which is confided as a secret; **c. trick,** deception in which the victim's confidence is gained with a view to cheating him; **in c.,** in secrecy. [L.].

CONFIDENT [kon'fi-dent], *adj.* trusting; sure of oneself and one's powers, self-reliant; certain, convinced (of success). CONFIDENTLY, *adv.* in c. fashion. [L.].

CONFIDENTIAL [kon-fi-den'shal], *adj.* told in confidence, secret; intimate, familiar. CONFIDENTIALLY, *adv.* in confidence; privately.

CONFIDER [kon-fi'der], *n.* one who confides.

CONFIDING [kon-fi'ding], *adj.* tending to confide, trusting. CONFIDINGLY, *adv.* in a c. manner.

CONFIGURATION [kon-fi-gyōō-rā'shn], *n.* the figure or appearance formed by the arrangement and relation of parts; (*geog.*) variation in the surface elevation of a region; (*astron.*) relative position of the planets at a given time. [L.].

CONFINE (1) [kon'fin], *n.* boundary, frontier; (*pl.*) area. [Fr.].

CONFINE (2) [kon-fin'], *v.t.* to keep or restrict within limits; imprison, shut up. CONFINABLE, *adj.* able to be confined. CONFINED, *adj.* restricted, imprisoned, limited; giving, or having just given, birth to a child. [Fr.].

CONFINEMENT [kon-fin'ment], *n.* imprisonment, detention, restriction; childbearing, labour.

CONFIRM [kon-furm'], *v.t.* to make firm, strengthen, fortify; ratify; corroborate; (*eccles.*) admit to full membership of the Church. CONFIRMABLE, *adj.* able to be confirmed. CONFIRMEE [kon-fer-mē'], *n.* (*eccles.*) one about to be confirmed. CONFIRMER [kon-fur'mer], *n.* one who, or that which, confirms. [L.].

CONFIRMATION [kon-fer-mā'shn], *n.* act of confirming, state of being confirmed; supporting evidence, that which confirms; (*eccles.*) ceremony of admission to full membership of the Church. [L.].

CONFIRMATIVE [kon-fur'ma-tiv], *adj.* confirmatory. CONFIRMATIVELY, *adv.* in c. fashion.

CONFIRMATORY [kon-fur'ma-te-ri], *adj.* that confirms, corroborative.

CONFIRMED [kon-furmd'], *adj.* established, settled; inveterate.

CONFISCATE (1) [kon'fis-kāt], *v.t.* to seize by legal authority, appropriate legally without compensation, deem to be forfeited. CONFISCATE (2), *adj.* confiscated; deemed to be forfeited. CONFISCATOR, *n.* one who confiscates. CONFISCATORY [kon-fis'ka-te-ri], *adj.* pertaining to confiscation. [L.].

CONFISCATION [kon-fis-kā'shn], *n.* act of confiscating, legal appropriation as a forfeit. [L.].

CONFITEOR [kon-fi'ti-aw(r)], *n.* (*R.C.*) general form of confession of faith used at the beginning of Mass. [L.].

CONFLAGRATION [kon-fla-grā'shn], *n.* huge fire or blaze. [L.].

CONFLICT (1) [kon'flikt], *n.* fight, struggle; quarrel, strong difference of opinion; marked disagreement, incompatibility. [L.].

CONFLICT (2) [kon-flikt'], *v.i.* to strive, fight, contend; be in opposition, be contradictory or mutually incompatible, clash. [L.].

CONFLUENCE [kon'flōō-ens], *n.* a flowing together; place where streams join; (*fig.*) concourse, gathering.

CONFLUENT (1) [kon'flōō-ent], *adj.* flowing together, joining; (*bot.*) joined at some part; (*med.*) merging together, as of pustules. CONFLUENT (2), *n.* stream which joins another. [L.].

CONFLUX [kon'fluks], *n.* confluence of people or things.

CONFORM [kon-fawm'], *v.t.* to make similar to, cause to agree with; *v.i.* to correspond, be similar to in form; (*fig.*) agree or comply with, obey; observe the practices of the Established Church. [Fr. from L.].

CONFORMABLE [kon-faw'ma-bl], *adj.* alike in form, resembling; agreeable, compliant; (*geol.*) in parallel formation. CONFORMABILITY [kon-faw-ma-bi'li-ti], *n.* condition of being c. CONFORMABLY, *adv.* in c. fashion.

CONFORMATION [kon-faw-mā'shn], *n.* the manner of formation; agreement, shape, structure. [L.].

CONFORMIST [kon-faw'mist], *n.* one who conforms to the observances of the Established Church.

CONFORMITY [kon-faw'mi-ti], *n.* likeness in structure, shape, manner etc.; consistency; agreement;

The accent ′ after a syllable = stress (u-pon′). The mark ‾ over a vowel = length (ā in made; ō in bone).

(*eccles.*) observance of the forms of worship of the Established Church.

CONFOUND (1) [kon-fownd'], *v.t.* to confuse, perplex; mix up; put to shame; destroy. CONFOUND (2), *int.* (*coll.*) bother. [L.].

CONFOUNDED [kon-fown'did], *adj.* confused, abashed; (*coll.*) infernal, abominable. CONFOUNDEDLY, *adv.* (*coll.*) extremely, infernally, abominably. CONFOUNDEDNESS, *n.* condition of being c.

CONFRATERNITY [kon-fra-tur'ni-ti], *n.* brotherhood; brotherly friendship.

CONFRERE, confrère [kon'frãer], *n.* fellow member, associate, colleague. [Fr.].

CONFRONT [kon-frunt'], *v.t.* to face, stand facing and staring at; stand up boldly to; bring face to face with, set before. CONFRONTATION [kon-frun-tā'shn], *n.* act of confronting.

CONFUCIAN [kon-fyoo'shn], *adj.* pertaining to Confucius or his philosophy. CONFUCIANISM, *n.* religion or philosophy established by Confucius. [*Confucius*, Chinese philosopher].

CONFUSE [kon-fyooz], *v.t.* to mix up; muddle; mistake for; be unable to discriminate between; bewilder; perplex; embarrass. CONFUSABLE, *adj.* liable to be confused. [L.].

CONFUSED [kon-fyoozd'], *adj.* mixed together; muddled; perplexed; embarrassed. CONFUSEDLY, *adv.* in a c. fashion. CONFUSEDNESS, *n.* condition of being c.

CONFUSION [kon-fyoo'zhn], *n.* state of being confused, act of confusing. [L.].

CONFUTATION [kon-fyoo-tā'shn], *n.* act of confuting. [L.].

CONFUTE [kon-fyoot'], *v.t.* to disprove; prove to be false or wrong. CONFUTABLE, *adj.* able to be confuted. [L.].

CONGA [kong'gah], *n.* modern ballroom dance based on West Indian rhythms.

CONGÉ, congé [kon'zhã], *n.* dismissal, *esp.* from service or employment; leave; **c. d'élire** [kon-zhã-dã-lĕer'], authority to elect a bishop granted by the sovereign to a dean and chapter. [Fr.].

CONGEAL [kon-jĕl'], *v.t. and i.* to freeze; become solid through cold; coagulate. CONGEALABLE, *adj.* able to be congealed. CONGEALMENT, *n.* process of congealing. [Fr. from L.].

CONGELATION [kon-je-lā'shn], *n.* congealment. [L.].

CONGENER [kon'je-ner], *n.* person or thing of the same genus or nature. CONGENERIC [kon-je-ne'rik], *adj.* of the same genus or nature; akin. [L.].

CONGENIAL [kon-jē'ni-al], *adj.* having similar tastes or views; agreeable, suitable. CONGENIALITY [kon-jē-ni-a'li-ti], *n.* condition of being c. CONGENIALIZE, *v.t.* to render c. [L.].

CONGENITAL [kon-je'ni-tal], *adj.* inherited, present from birth; since birth. [L.].

CONGER [kong'ger], *n.* large variety of sea-eel. [L.].

CONGERIES [kon-je'ri-ēz], *n.* collection of several particles or small bodies in one mass. [L.].

CONGEST [kon-jest'], *v.t.* to crowd together in a dense mass; overcrowd, pack so tightly as to impede normal movement; (*med.*) accumulate abnormally in an organ (of blood). [L.].

CONGESTED [kon-jes'tid], *adj.* overcrowded, blocked; (*med.*) having too much blood accumulated in one place.

CONGESTION [kon-jest'shn], *n.* act of congesting; state of being congested; (*med.*) excess of blood in any organ.

CONGESTIVE [kon-jes'tiv], *adj.* inducing or indicating congestion.

CONGLOMERATE (1) [kon-glo'me-rat], *adj.* formed from a number of separate parts gathered securely together in one mass. CONGLOMERATE (2), *n.* quantity of objects piled up together; (*geol.*) rock composed of pebbles naturally cemented together. CONGLOMERATE (3) [kon-glo'me-rãt], *v.t. and i.* to collect together in one rounded mass. [L.].

CONGLOMERATION [kon-glo-me-rā'shn], *n.* act of conglomerating; state of being conglomerated; mixture.

CONGOU [kong'goo], *n.* kind of black China tea. [Chin.].

CONGRATULATE [kon-gra'tyoo-lãt], *v.t.* to express one's appreciation for the success of another, compliment; wish joy to. CONGRATULABLE [kon-gra'tyoo-la-bl], suitable for congratulation. CONGRATULATORY [kon-gra'tyoo-la-te-ri], *adj.* expressing congratulation.

CONGRATULATION [kon-gra-tyoo-lā'shn], *n.*

act of congratulating; words used in congratulating anyone.

CONGREGATE [kong'gri-gãt], *v.t. and i.* to collect; bring or come together; assemble, gather. [L.].

CONGREGATION [kong-gri-gā'shn], *n.* assembly of people, *esp.* in church; those attending worship at a church or chapel; name of various special assemblies or committees, as of Roman Catholic cardinals, members of a university etc. [L.].

CONGREGATIONAL [kong-gri-gā'shn-al], *adj.* relating to a congregation or to congregationalism.

CONGREGATIONALISM [kong-gri-gā'shn-a-lizm], *n.* system of church government among Nonconformists whereby each church and congregation is autonomous. CONGREGATIONALIST, *n.* one who believes in c.

CONGRESS [kong'gres], *n.* gathering, assembly, conference; federal governing body of the United States of America.

CONGRESSIONAL [kong-gre'shn-al], *adj.* relating to a congress, *esp.* the U.S. Congress.

CONGRESSMAN [kong'gres-man], *n.* member of the U.S. Congress.

CONGRUENCE [kong'groo-ens], *n.* quality of being congruent, agreement. [L.].

CONGRUENCY [kong'groo-en-si], *n.* congruence.

CONGRUENT [kong'groo-ent], *adj.* agreeing, according; corresponding exactly; (*math.*) (of two numbers) leaving the same remainder when divided by a third number. [L.].

CONGRUITY [kong-groo'i-ti], *n.* condition of being congruous.

CONGRUOUS [kong'groo-ōōs], *adj.* suitable; consistent, in keeping. CONGRUOUSLY, *adv.* in c. fashion. CONGRUOUSNESS, *n.* condition of being c. [L.].

CONIC [ko'nik], *adj.* relating to cones and their properties; in the shape of a cone; **c. sections**, curves formed by the intersection of the surface of a cone with planes which cut the cone in various directions.

CONICAL [ko'ni-kal], *adj.* conic. CONICALLY, *adv.* in the shape of a cone.

CONICS [ko'niks], *n.*(*pl.*) (*math.*) theory of cones.

CONIFER [kō'ni-fer], *n.* (*bot.*) cone-bearing shrub or tree. [L.].

CONIFEROUS [kō-ni'fe-rōōs], *adj.* cone-bearing.

CONIFORM [kō'ni-fawm], *adj.* having the form of a cone.

CONIN, CONINE (1) [kō'nēn], *n.* poisonous alkaloid found in hemlock. CONINE (2), *adj.* pertaining to, derived from, hemlock. [Gk.].

CONJECTURAL [kon-jek'tyoo-ral], *adj.* based on conjecture. CONJECTURALLY, *adv.* in c. fashion. [L.].

CONJECTURE (1) [kon-jek'tyōor], *n.* guess, supposition, inference with little proof. CONJECTURE (2), *v.t.* to guess, surmise, suppose, to judge as likely; *v.i.* to make a c. CONJECTURABLE, *adj.* able to be conjectured. CONJECTURER, *n.* person who conjectures. [L].

CONJOIN [kon-join'], *v.t. and i.* to unite, join, blend. [Fr. from L.].

CONJOINT (1) [kon-joint'], *adj.* united, joined, associated; in conjunction with. CONJOINT (2) [kon'joint], *n.* (*coll.*) final examination of the Conjoint Board of the Royal College of Physicians and that of Surgeons. CONJOINTLY [kon-joint'li], *adv.* in c. fashion. [Fr.].

CONJUGAL [kon'joo-gal], *adj.* pertaining to marriage. CONJUGALLY, *adv.* in a c. manner. [L.].

CONJUGATE (1) [kon'joo-gãt], *v.t. and i.* (*gram.*) to inflect, recite the parts of (a verb); have inflexions. CONJUGATE (2), *adj.* joined; united in pairs. [L.].

CONJUGATION [kon-joo-gā'shn], *n.* (*gram.*) act of conjugating; one of the classes into which verbs may be divided according to their terminations. CONJUGATIONAL, *adj.* pertaining to c.

CONJUNCT [kon-jungkt'], *adj.* conjoined, united. CONJUNCTLY, *adv.* in a c. way. [L.].

CONJUNCTION [kon-jungk'shn], *n.* act of conjoining; state of being conjoined; combination; (*astron.*) nearness to each other of two heavenly bodies; (*gram.*) indeclinable particle joining sentences or parts of them. CONJUNCTIONAL, *adj.* pertaining to a c. [L.].

CONJUNCTIVA [kon-jungk-tī'vah], *n.* (*anat.*) the membrane in contact with the eyeball.

CONJUNCTIVE [kon-jungk'tiv], *adj.* that connects or joins; (*gram.*) used as a conjunction; (of verbal mood) used only in conjunction with some other verb, or in hypothetical sentences; subjunctive. CON-JUNCTIVELY, *adv.* in a c. way. [L.].

CONJUNCTIVITIS [kon-jungk-ti-vī'tis], *n.* inflammation of the conjunctiva, pink-eye.

CONJUNCTURE [kon-jungk'tyoŏr], *n.* combination of events. [Fr. from L.].

CONJURATION [kon-joo-rā'shn], *n.* act of conjuring; spell or charm; earnest entreaty. [L.].

CONJURE (1) [kon-joŏr'], *v.t.* to entreat earnestly, implore solemnly. CONJURE (2) [kun'jer], *v.i.* to practise magic; perform tricks of sleight of hand or mystifying illusions; **name to c. with**, influential name; **to c. up**, to invoke, bring forth by magic and sorcery; (*fig.*) invoke an image in the mind. [Fr. from L.].

CONJURER, -OR [kun'je-rer], *n.* one skilled in conjuring.

CONJURING (1) [kun'je-ring], *n.* art of performing tricks of legerdemain or creating baffling illusions. CONJURING (2), *adj.* executed by legerdemain.

CONJURY [kun'je-ri], *n.* art of performing conjuring tricks.

CONK [kongk], *v.i.* (*coll.*) to fire badly or fail to fire; **to c. out**, (*coll.*) to cease to fire; break down. [Echoic].

CONKER [kong'ker], *n.* (*slang*) horse-chestnut; (*pl.*) game played with these.

CON MAN [kon'man], *n.* (*coll.*) confidence trickster.

CONNATE [ko'nāt], *adj.* congenital; (*bot.*) of the same origin. [L.].

CONNATURAL [ko-na'tyoŏ-ral], *adj.* inborn; of similar nature. CONNATURALITY, CONNATURALNESS [ko-na-tyoŏ-ra'li-ti, ko-na'tyoŏ-ral-nes], *n.* state of being c. CONNATURALIZE, *v.t.* to render c. CON-NATURALLY, *adv.* in c. manner. [Fr.].

CONNECT [ko-nekt'], *v.t.* to join, fasten together; show the relationship between events; associate; *v.i.* to unite, join on to, fix together; follow logically. CONNECTED, *adj.* joined, linked; associated with; related by family. CONNECTEDLY, *adv.* in a connected fashion. [L.].

CONNECTING-ROD [ko-nek'ting-rod], *n.* rod or bar which connects a piston to a crank.

CONNECTION, see CONNEXION.

CONNECTIVE [ko-nek'tiv], *adj.* connecting, able to connect; **c. tissue**, tissue which binds together the organs of the body. CONNECTIVELY, *adv.* in c. fashion.

CONNECTOR [ko-nek'ter], *n.* one who, or that which, connects.

CONNEXION, CONNECTION [ko-nek'shn], *n.* act of connecting; state of being connected; anything which connects; relation, close union; sexual intimacy; clientèle; the fitting in of hour of arrival of one train and the departure of another; train or boat timed to meet the arrival or departure of another; (*pl.*) influential friends; relatives; group of persons bound together in the pursuit of some common object. CONNEXIONAL, *adj.* having c.; relating to a c. [L.].

CONNING [ko'ning], *n.* (*naut.*) the directions of the helmsman. CONNING-TOWER, *n.* (*nav.*) armoured compartment in a warship or submarine, from which it is steered. [CON (3)].

CONNIVANCE [ko-nī'vans], *n.* act of conniving; intentional oversight, implying consent or help.

CONNIVE [ko-nīv'], *v.i.* to overlook and deliberately encourage wrongdoing, be a secret accessory to. [L.].

CONNOISSEUR [ko-ni-sur'], *n.* critical expert, *esp.* in matters of art. CONNOISSEURSHIP, *n.* skill or taste of a c. [Fr.].

CONNOTATION [ko-nō-tā'shn], *n.* act of connoting; that which is connoted; (*logic*) all that is comprehended by a term.

CONNOTE [ko-nōt'], *v.t.* to imply, infer, indicate; suggest beyond its original meaning; signify. CONNOTATIVE [ko-nō'ta-tiv], *adj.* having connotation; implying in addition. [L.].

CONNUBIAL [ko-nyoŏ'bi-al], *adj.* relating to the married state or to marriage. [L.].

CONOID (1) [kō'noid], *adj.* almost conical, like a cone in shape. CONOID (2), *n.* cone-shaped object; (*geom.*) solid figure formed by the revolution of a conic section about its axis; (*anat.*) pineal gland. CONOIDAL, CONOIDIC, *adj.* conoid. [Gk.].

CONQUER [kong'ker], *v.t.* to overcome by force, defeat; subjugate; (*fig.*) put down, vanquish; *v.i.* to overcome, win. [L.].

CONQUEROR [kong'ke-rer], *n.* one who conquers; **The C.**, (*hist.*) William I, King of England.

CONQUEST [kong'kwest], *n.* act of conquering;

that which is conquered; **The C.**, (*hist.*) conquest of England by William I, in 1066. [Fr.].

CONQUISTADOR [kon-kis'ta-daw(r)], *n.* one of the Spanish conquerors of Peru and Mexico. [Span.].

CON-ROD [kon'rod], *n.* (*motoring*) connecting-rod.

CONSANGUINEOUS [kon-sang-gwi'ni-oŏs], *adj.* of the same blood; connected by birth. [L.].

CONSANGUINITY [kon-sang-gwi'ni-ti], *n.* blood relationship.

CONSCIENCE [kon'shns], *n.* power of distinguishing right and wrong; moral feeling for this; **c. clause**, clause in law making allowance for possible conscientious scruples in religious matters; **c. money**, money paid to salve one's conscience; **in all c.**, certainly, by all reasonable standards. CONSCIENCELESS, *adj.* lacking a c. [Fr. from L.].

CONSCIENCE-SMITTEN [kon'shns-smi-ten], *adj.* struck with compunction or remorse.

CONSCIENTIOUS [kon-shi-en'shoŏs], *adj.* governed by conscience; scrupulous, taking one's duties and responsibilities seriously; **c. objector**, one who refuses to fight in wartime on grounds of conscience. CONSCIENTIOUSLY, *adv.* in a c. fashion. CONSCIEN-TIOUSNESS, *n.* quality of being c.

CONSCIOUS [kon'shoŏs], *adj.* having the faculty of thought; able to think, perceive and feel; aware, possessing knowledge (of); in control of one's mental powers; able to know and recognize what is happening; awake and sensible. CONSCIOUSLY, *adv.* wittingly; in c. fashion. CONSCIOUSNESS, *n.* quality or state of being c. [L.].

CONSCRIBE [kon-skrīb'], *v.t.* to enrol as a soldier etc. under compulsion. [L.].

CONSCRIPT (1) [kon'skript], *adj.* enlisted, enrolled under compulsion. CONSCRIPT (2), *n.* conscript soldier etc. CONSCRIPT (3) [kon-skript'], *v.t.* to enrol by conscription, conscribe. [L.].

CONSCRIPTION [kon-skrip'shn], *n.* compulsory enrolment for national service.

CONSECRATE (1) [kon'si-krāt], *adj.* consecrated, sanctified. CONSECRATE (2), *v.t.* to make holy, hallow; set aside for, or dedicate to, the service of the church. CONSECRATOR, *n.* person who consecrates. CONSECRATORY, *adj.* that consecrates. [L.].

CONSECRATION [kon-si-krā'shn], *n.* act or ceremony of consecrating.

CONSECUTION [kon-si-kyoŏ'shn], *n.* train of reasoning, natural sequence; (*gram.*) logical sequence of related tenses or words. [L.].

CONSECUTIVE [kon-se'kyoŏ-tiv], *adj.* following in correct, suitable or regular order; coming in uninterrupted succession; (*gram.*) expressing consequence; **c. chords**, (*mus.*) succession of similar intervals. CONSECUTIVELY, *adv.* in c. fashion. CONSECUTIVE-NESS, *n.* state of being c. [*Prec.*].

CONSENSUAL [kon-sen'shoŏ-al], *adj.* (*leg.*) arranged by consent of all parties; (*physiol.*) reacting in sympathy. [L.].

CONSENSUS [kon-sen'sus], *n.* agreement or unanimity in opinion or response. [L.].

CONSENT (1) [kon-sent'], *v.i.* to agree, accept, acquiesce in another's propositions; yield to another's demands. CONSENT (2), *n.* mutual agreement, concurrence; permission; assent. CONSENTER, *n.* person who consents. [OFr.].

CONSENTANEOUS [kon-sen-tā'ni-oŏs], *adj.* suited, consistent with, unanimous. [L.].

CONSENTIENT [kon-sen'shnt], *adj.* agreeing, unanimous, giving mutual consent. [L.].

CONSENTINGLY [kon-sen'ting-li], *adv.* with consent.

CONSEQUENCE [kon'si-kwens], *n.* fact or event dependent on an immediate cause, effect, result; logical conclusion or inference; importance, value. [L.].

CONSEQUENT (1) [kon'si-kwent], *n.* that which is given existence by a cause, an effect; that which follows on something else. CONSEQUENT (2), *adj.* existing as a result of what has previously occurred; following on logically as an effect or by inference. [L.].

CONSEQUENTIAL [kon-si-kwen'shal], *adj.* arising or resulting as a consequence; pretentiously claiming importance, pompous. CONSEQUENTIALLY, *adv.* in c. fashion. CONSEQUENTIALNESS, *n.* condition of being c.

CONSEQUENTLY [kon'si-kwent-li], *adv.* in consequence of something.

CONSERVABLE [kon-sur'va-bl], *adv.* able to be preserved.

CONSERVANCY [kon-sur'van-si], *n.* body of

The accent ' after a syllable = stress (u-pon'). The mark ⁻ over a vowel = length (ā in made; ō in bone).

officials appointed to safeguard **rivers or forests;** conservation of rivers or forests in this way.

CONSERVATION [kon-ser-vā'shn], *n.* act of conserving, preservation. CONSERVATIONAL, *adj.* relating to c., conserving.

CONSERVATISM [kon-sur'va-tizm], *n.* tendency to conserve what is established; (*pol.*) principles of the Conservative Party.

CONSERVATIVE (1) [kon-sur'va-tiv], *adj.* inclined or tending to conserve; disliking violent innovation; moderate, cautious; (*pol.*) wishing to retain what is best in existing institutions. CONSERVATIVE (2), *n.* person of c. temperament or conviction; preservative; (*pol.*) person who is cautious in abandoning the main features of the existing system of law and government; member of the Conservative Party.

CONSERVATOIRE [kon-sur'va-twah(r)], *n.* institution devoted to the study of music. [Fr.].

CONSERVATOR [kon'ser-vā-ter], *n.* person who preserves from harm, protector; official keeper or custodian of a museum or similar public building. [L.].

CONSERVATORY [kon-sur'va-te-ri], *n.* shed built of framed glass in which young or delicate plants are grown or kept, greenhouse.

CONSERVE (1) [kon-surv'], *v.t.* to keep unchanged or in a sound state, preserve, safeguard. CONSERVE (2), *n.* sweetmeat made of preserved fruit, jam. CONSERVER, *n.* one who conserves. [L.].

CONSHY [kon'shi], *n.* (*slang*) conscientious objector.

CONSIDER [kon-si'der], *v.t. and i.* to think, examine closely in the mind, meditate on, pay attention to; take into account; judge, hold; have regard for, respect; come to a conclusion. CONSIDERER, *n.* one who considers carefully. [L.].

CONSIDERABLE [kon-si'de-ra-bl], *adj.* worthy of note, worth considering, important; relatively large, much, great. CONSIDERABLY, *adv.* to a c. degree.

CONSIDERATE [kon-si'de-rat], *adj.* thoughtful, mindful of others. CONSIDERATELY, *adv.* in c. fashion. CONSIDERATENESS, *n.* quality of being c.

CONSIDERATION [kon-si-de-rā'shn], *n.* act of considering, thought; determining cause or reason; payment for a particular action or service, compensation; careful regard for the feelings of others; (*leg.*) stipulation governing a contract. [L.].

CONSIDERING [kon-si'de-ring], *prep.* in view of, taking into account. CONSIDERINGLY, *adv.* in a c. manner.

CONSIGN [kon-sīn'], *v.t. and i.* to deliver or give up into another's charge; (*comm.*) dispatch goods for delivery. CONSIGNABLE, *adj.* able to be consigned. CONSIGNATION [kon-sig-nā'shn], *n.* act of consigning. [L.].

CONSIGNEE [kon-sī-nē'], *n.* person to whom goods are consigned.

CONSIGNER, CONSIGNOR [kon-sī'ner, kon-sī-naw(r)'], *n.* person who consigns goods.

CONSIGNMENT [kon-sīn'ment], *n.* act of consigning; thing consigned, goods dispatched to a customer.

CONSIGNOR, see CONSIGNER.

CONSIST [kon-sist'], *v.i.* to be made up; **c. in,** to comprise, be derived from; **c. of,** be composed of, have as constituent parts. [L.].

CONSISTENCE [kon-sis'tens], *n.* state or quality of being consistent, degree of solidity, firmness, density.

CONSISTENCY [kon-sis'ten-si], *n.* consistence.

CONSISTENT [kon-sis'tent], *adj.* having a nature which is fixed; in keeping with, not contradictory, uniform; regular. CONSISTENTLY, *adv.* in a c. fashion.

CONSISTORY [kon-sis'te-ri], *n.* council, assembly; (*eccles.*) court under the jurisdiction of a bishop; College of Cardinals at Rome; assembly of Presbyterian elders. CONSISTORIAL [con-sis-taw'ri-al], *adj.* pertaining to a c. [LL.].

CONSOCIATION [kon-sō-shi-ā'shn], *n.* act of meeting or grouping together as associates; (*eccles.*) association of Christian churches. [L.].

CONSOLABLE [kon-sō'la-bl], *adj.* able to be comforted.

CONSOLATION [kon-so-lā'shn], *n.* act of consoling; that which consoles or is intended to console; **c. prize,** prize given to a runner up. [L.].

CONSOLATORY [kon-sō'la-te-ri], *adj.* tending to console or comfort.

CONSOLE (1) [kon'sōl], *n.* table with legs in the form of carved scrolls; keyboard of an organ; (*arch.*) ornamental bracket resembling a scroll, which supports a mantelpiece, shelf or cornice. [Fr.].

CONSOLE (2) [kon-sōl'], *v.t.* to comfort a person suffering grief or disappointment; compensate, afford solace. [L.].

CONSOLIDATE [kon-so'li-dāt], *v.t. and i.* to strengthen or make more secure, give greater solidarity to; combine or unite into a single strong unit; solidify, grow firm and hard. CONSOLIDATIVE, *adj.* having the power to consolidate. CONSOLIDATOR, *n.* one who, or that which, consolidates. [L.].

CONSOLIDATED [kon-so'li-dā-tid], *adj.* brought into a compact state, united; **c. fund,** fund for the payment of interest on the national debt controlled by the government.

CONSOLIDATION [kon-so-li-dā'shn], *n.* act of consolidating.

CONSOLS [kon-solz'], *n.*(*pl.*) (*comm.*) British Government stock. [CONSOL(IDATED)].

CONSOMME, consommé [kon-so'mā], *n.* clear meat soup. [Fr.].

CONSONANCE [kon'so-nans], *n.* quality of being consonant; agreement, harmony.

CONSONANCY [kon'so-nan-si], *n.* consonance.

CONSONANT (1) [kon'so-nant], *adj.* consistent, agreeing, in accordance. CONSONANTLY, *adv.* in a c. fashion. [L.].

CONSONANT (2), *n.* (*phon.*) speech sound in which the flow of air from the lungs is partially or completely impeded in its passage through the mouth; alphabetical letter or symbol denoting such a sound. CONSONANTAL, *adj.* consisting of, resembling, relating to a c.

CONSORT (1) [kon'sawt], *n.* intimate associate, spouse, *esp.* a royal spouse; ship accompanying another as an escort; **Prince C.,** husband of a reigning queen; **Queen C.,** wife of a king. [L.].

CONSORT (2) [kon-sawt'], *v.t. and i.* to associate with, be habitually in the company of; mix with, agree with.

CONSORTIUM [kon-saw'shi-um, kon-saw'ti-um], *n.* union of several powers or interests for the purpose of joint action. [L.].

CONSPECTUS [kon-spek'tus], *n.* general view; brief survey. [L.].

CONSPICUOUS [kon-spi'kyŏŏ-ŏŏs], *adj.* readily seen or noticed; commanding the attention, standing out well from a background; attracting notice because of unusual qualities. CONSPICUOUSLY, *adv.* in c. fashion. [L.].

CONSPIRACY [kon-spi'ra-si], *n.* act of conspiring; secret association of people planning to commit some illegal act, a plot; prearranged and secret determination or agreement. [L.].

CONSPIRATOR [kon-spi'ra-ter], *n.* person who conspires. CONSPIRATORIAL [kon-spi-ra-taw'ri-al], *adj.* pertaining to conspiracy, characteristic of conspirators.

CONSPIRE [kon-spier'], *v.i.* to plot, combine secretly for some unlawful purpose. CONSPIRER, *n.* conspirator. CONSPIRING, *adj.* plotting together. CONSPIRINGLY, *adv.* in a conspiring manner. [L.].

CONSTABLE [kun'sta-bl], *n.* policeman; **chief c.,** head of a city or county constabulary; **special c.,** civilian called upon to act as c. upon special occasions; **to outrun the c.,** to get into debt. CONSTABLESHIP, *n.* office or rank of a c. [OFr.].

CONSTABULARY (1) [kon-sta'byŏŏ-la-ri], *n.* police force of a city or district. CONSTABULARY (2), *adj.* pertaining to, or consisting of, constables. [L.].

CONSTANCY [kon'stan-si], *n.* quality of being constant. [L.].

CONSTANT (1) [kon'stant], *adj.* steadfast; faithful; unchanging; continual. CONSTANT (2), *n.* (*math.*) an unvarying quantity. CONSTANTLY, *adv.* in c. fashion. [L.].

CONSTANTIA [kon-stan'shi-ah], *n.* sweet wine from South Africa. [*Constantia*, near Cape Town].

CONSTELLATE (1) [kon'ste-lāt], *v.t. and i.* to group or form into a constellation. CONSTELLATE (2), *adj.* abounding in, adorned with, stars. [L.].

CONSTELLATION [kon-ste-lā'shn], *n.* cluster or group of stars; (*fig.*) gathering or collection of notabilities; (*astrol.*) relation of the planets to one another, *esp.* as influencing human affairs, and particularly at the time of one's birth. [L.].

CONSTERNATION [kon-ster-nā'shn], *n.* alarm, dismay. [L.].

CONSTIPATE [kon'sti-pāt], *v.t.* to bind, render the bowels inactive or irregular in functioning. [L.].

CONSTIPATION [kon-sti-pā'shn], *n.* state of being constipated. [L.].

CONSTITUENCY [kon-sti'tyŏŏ-en-si], *n.* electorate

of a parliamentary division; a parliamentary division.

CONSTITUENT (1) [kon-sti'tyōo-ent], *adj.* forming part of, making up a whole; having the right to elect; (of an assembly) having power to make a constitution. CONSTITUENT (2), *n.* component part; voter in a parliamentary constituency. [L.].

CONSTITUTE [kon'sti-tyōot], *v.t.* to set up, establish by authority; compose, make what it is; appoint or elect, create officially; be legally or officially regarded as. CONSTITUTED, *adj.* established; appointed; made up. [L.].

CONSTITUTION [kon-sti-tyōo'shn], *n.* act or manner of constituting; person's physical condition, qualities or capacities; principles according to which a state, society, institution etc. is organized and governed; (*hist.*) official decree. [L.].

CONSTITUTIONAL (1) [kon-sti-tyōo'shn-al], *adj.* connected with the bodily constitution; pertaining to the constitution of a state or society, restricted or limited by the constitution. CONSTITUTIONAL (2), *n.* a walk habitually taken for the sake of health.

CONSTITUTIONALISM [kon-sti-tyōo'shn-a-lizm], *n.* principles of the constitution, or of constitutional government; constitutional government.

CONSTITUTIONALIST [kon-sti-tyōo'shn-a-list], *n.* supporter of constitutional government or of a constitution.

CONSTITUTIONALLY [kon-sti-tyōo'shn-a-li], *adv.* according to the constitution; by nature.

CONSTITUTIVE [kon'sti-tyōo-tiv], *adj.* that constitutes; determinative.

CONSTRAIN [kon-strān'], *v.t.* to compel, force; effect by compulsion; bring pressure to bear upon. CONSTRAINED, *adj.* compelled; embarrassed. CONSTRAINEDLY [kon-strā'nid-li], *adv.* in a constrained manner. [OFr.].

CONSTRAINT [kon-strānt'], *n.* compulsion, force; self-consciousness, embarrassment; control. [OFr.].

CONSTRICT [kon-strikt'], *v.t.* to draw together, contract, bind close. CONSTRICTIVE, *adj.* that constricts or tends to c. [L.].

CONSTRICTION [kon-strik'shn], *n.* act of constricting; (in the chest etc.) feeling of tightness. [L.].

CONSTRICTOR [kon-strik'ter], *n.* (*anat.*) muscle which contracts or constricts a part; (*zool.*) large kind of South American snake which kills its victims by crushing them in its coils.

CONSTRINGENT [kon-strin'jent], *adj.* constricting; contracting. [L.].

CONSTRUCT [kon-strukt'], *v.t.* to build, fit together, form; compose, make up; (*geom.*) draw. [L.].

CONSTRUCTION [kon-struk'shn], *n.* act of constructing; that which is constructed; interpretation, meaning; (*gram.*) arrangement and connexion of words in a sentence. CONSTRUCTIONAL, *adj.* pertaining to c. [L.].

CONSTRUCTIVE [kon-struk'tiv], *adj.* possessing ability to construct; creative, formative; pertaining to construction; inferred from interpretation and not directly expressed. CONSTRUCTIVELY, *adv.* in a c. manner. CONSTRUCTIVENESS, *n.* ability to construct.

CONSTRUCTOR [kon-struk'ter], *n.* person who constructs; builder.

CONSTRUE [kon-strōo'], *v.t.* to discover the meaning or syntactical construction of a sentence by analysis; translate; (*fig.*) interpret, ascribe a particular meaning to; *v.i.* to analyse syntactically; be capable of syntactic analysis. [L.].

CONSUBSTANTIAL [kon-sub-stan'shal], *adj.* of the same substance, essence or nature. CONSUBSTANTIALITY, *n.* quality of being c.

CONSUBSTANTIATE [kon-sub-stan'shi-āt], *v.t.* and *i.* to unite; join together in one common substance.

CONSUBSTANTIATION [kon-sub-stan-shi-ā'shn], *n.* theological doctrine that the sacramental elements in the Eucharist are united with Christ's body and blood after consecration.

CONSUETUDE [kon'swi-tyōod], *n.* usage, habit, custom, *esp.* when enforceable by law. CONSUETUDINARY [kon-swi-tyōo'di-na-ri], *adj.* customary. [L.].

CONSUL [kon'sōol], *n.* official agent of a state in a foreign country, who looks after its nationals and commercial affairs there; (*hist.*) one of two chief magistrates of the Roman Republic; (*hist.*) one of the three chief magistrates of the French Republic from 1799–1804. [L.].

CONSULAR [kon'syōo-ler], *adj.* pertaining to a consul or his office.

CONSULATE [kon'syōo-lat], *n.* rank or office of a

consul; term of office of a consul; official residence of a consul. [L.].

CONSULSHIP [kon'sōol-ship], *n.* post of a consul; duration of his office.

CONSULT [kon-sult'], *v.t.* to ask or seek advice from or the opinion of, refer to for information; consider, have regard to; *v.t.* to take counsel with another. [L.].

CONSULTANT [kon-sul'tant], *n.* person who consults another; expert who may be consulted for professional advice for a fee. [L.].

CONSULTATION [kon-sul-tā'shn], *n.* act of consulting; conference. [L.].

CONSULTATIVE [kon-sul'ta-tiv], *adj.* pertaining to consultation; charged with giving advice when consulted.

CONSULTING [kon-sul'ting], *adj.* giving (expert) advice; **c. room**, room in which a doctor or lawyer sees his patients or clients professionally.

CONSUME [kon-syōom'], *v.t.* to destroy; waste; eat, devour; obsess. CONSUMABLE, *adj.* capable of being consumed.

CONSUMER [kon-syōo'mer], *n.* person or thing that consumes; one who buys for use or consumption; **c. goods**, articles needed for constant use in daily life, such as food, clothing etc.

CONSUMMATE (1) [kon-su'mat], *adj.* brought to perfection, complete, supreme. CONSUMMATELY, *adv.* to perfection; completely; perfectly. [L.].

CONSUMMATE (2) [kon'su-māt], *v.t.* to complete, perfect, finish; make a marriage legally complete by sexual intercourse. [*Prec.*].

CONSUMMATION [kon-su-mā'shn], *n.* act of consummating; sexual intercourse at marriage. [L.].

CONSUMPTION [kon-sump'shn], *n.* act of consuming; quantity consumed; (*econ.*) use or amount used of commercial or industrial products; (*med.*) tuberculosis of the lungs, phthisis. [L.].

CONSUMPTIVE (1) [kon-sump'tiv], *adj.* tending to consume; suffering from tuberculosis. CONSUMPTIVE (2), *n.* person suffering from consumption. CONSUMPTIVENESS, *n.* condition of being c.

CONTACT [kon'takt], *n.* state of touching; close sympathetic communication; clash, collision; (*elect.*) proximity to each other of two conductors so that the electric current can pass from one to the other; (*med.*) one who has been in contact with an infectious case; (*math.*) meeting of two curves, surfaces or straight line and curve; (*milit.*) communication; (*slang*) an acquaintance, *esp.* in underhand dealings. CONTACT (2) [kon-takt'], *v.t.* and *i.* to have personal dealings with, get in touch with. [L.].

CONTACT-BREAKER [kon'takt-brā-ker], *n.* device for interrupting an electric circuit.

CONTAGION [kon-tā'jn], *n.* communication of a disease by contact; disease communicated by contact; (*fig.*) evil influence communicated from one to another. [L.].

CONTAGIOUS [kon-tā'jōos], *adj.* (*med.*) communicated by contact, liable to spread disease by contact with others; (*fig.*) catching, affecting others by contact. CONTAGIOUSLY, *adv.* in c. fashion. CONTAGIOUSNESS, *n.* condition of being c. [L.].

CONTAGIUM [kon-tā'ji-um], *n.* agent which transmits a disease from one person to another.

CONTAIN [kon-tān'], *v.t.* to hold, have as a component part, comprise, include; have space for; (*arith.*) be divisible by; (*geom.*) enclose, bound; (*milit.*) hold an enemy force to a position; (*reflex.*) maintain self-control. CONTAINABLE, *adj.* able to be contained. CONTAINER, *n.* one who, or that which, contains; vessel, receptacle. [OFr. from L.].

CONTAMINATE [kon-ta'mi-nāt], *v.t.* to render impure or noxious, pollute, taint; (*fig.*) exert a bad influence upon. CONTAMINATIVE, *adj.* that contaminates. [L.].

CONTAMINATION [kon-ta-mi-nā'shn], *n.* act of contaminating; state or quality of being contaminated, *esp.* with poison-gas; corruption of a text. [L.].

CONTANGO [kon-tang'go], *n.* (*Stock Exchange*) percentage paid by the buyer to the seller of stock for the privilege of carrying over completion of purchase to a following account day. [MedL.].

CONTEMN [kon-tem'], *v.t.* to scorn, despise. CONTEMNER, *n.* one who contemns. [L.].

CONTEMPLATE [kon'tem-plāt], *v.t.* to observe, look at fixedly, gaze upon; meditate on, think closely about; intend; anticipate; *v.i.* to meditate, reflect. CONTEMPLATED, *adj.* deliberate, intended.

The accent ' after a syllable = stress (u-pon'). The mark ⁻ over a vowel = length (ā in made; ō in bone).

CONTEMPLATOR, *n.* one who contemplates. [L.].
CONTEMPLATION [kon-tem-plā'shn], *n.* act of contemplating.
CONTEMPLATIVE [kon-tem'pla-tiv], *adj.* given to contemplation or meditation; studious, thoughtful. CONTEMPLATIVELY, *adv.* in c. fashion. CONTEMPLATIVENESS, *n.* quality of being c.
CONTEMPORANEOUS [kon-tem-po-rā'ni-ŏŏs], *adj.* existing or happening at the same time. CONTEMPORANEOUSLY, *adv.* at the same time. CONTEMPORANEOUSNESS, *n.* state of being c. [L.].
CONTEMPORARY (1) [kon-tem'po-ra-ri], *adj.* living, existing at the time (of speaking or writing); contemporaneous; belonging to the same period of time. CONTEMPORARY (2), *n.* one who, or that which, is c. CONTEMPORIZE, *v.t.* to make c.; *v.i.* to be c. [L.].
CONTEMPT [kon-tempt'], *n.* scorn, disdain; disgrace, state of being despicable; **c. of court**, disrespect for, or disobedience to, a court of law. [L.].
CONTEMPTIBLE (1) [kon-temp'ti-bl], *adj.* despicable, provoking contempt. CONTEMPTIBLE (2), *n.* that which is c.; **Old C.**, member of the "contemptibly small" British Expeditionary Force of 1914. CONTEMPTIBILITY, CONTEMPTIBLENESS [kon-temp-ti-bi'li-ti, kon-temp'ti-bl-nes], *n.* state of being c. CONTEMPTIBLY, *adv.* in a c. fashion. [L.].
CONTEMPTUOUS [kon-temp'tyŏŏ-ŏŏs], *adj.* expressing contempt, scornful; disdainful. CONTEMPTUOUSLY, *adv.* in c. fashion. [L.].
CONTEND [kon-tend'], *v.i.* to strive, compete; dispute; maintain; face in opposition. CONTENDER, *n.* one who contends. CONTENDING, *adj.* striving, opposing. [L.].
CONTENT (1) [kon'tent, *also pl.* kon-tents'], *n.* that which is contained, essential part, true significance, material contained; capacity of a receptacle; (*philos.*) the substance of an idea; (*geom.*) area or volume contained within a certain space; (*pl.*) that which is contained in anything; that which makes up or comprises a book, treatise etc. [L.].
CONTENT (2) [kon-tent'], *n.* contentedness; (*pl.*) (*parl.*) those members of the House of Lords who vote in favour of a motion. CONTENT (3), *adj.* satisfied, easy in mind, happy. CONTENT (4), *v.t.* to make contented; (*reflex.*) satisfy oneself with, accept without demur, limit oneself to. [Fr., L.].
CONTENTED [kon-ten'tid], *adj.* content, easy in mind. CONTENTEDLY, *adv.* in a c. fashion.
CONTENTION [kon-ten'shn], *n.* conflict, contest of words, controversy; the point contended in argument; **bone of c.**, disputed point.
CONTENTIOUS [kon-ten'shŏŏs], *adj.* argumentative, quarrelsome; controversial. CONTENTIOUSLY, *adv.* in c. fashion. [L.].
CONTERMINOUS [kon-tur'mi-nŏŏs], *adj.* equally extensive in time or space; with two ends meeting; within the same bounds; neighbouring, approaching. [L.].
CONTEST (1) [kon-test'], *v.t.* to fight or struggle for; (*pol.*) offer oneself as a parliamentary candidate for (a constituency) in opposition to some other candidate; (*leg.*) take legal action about, defend at law; *v.i.* to vie, contend. CONTEST (2) [kon'test], *n.* fight, dispute; competition, struggle for victory or pre-eminence. CONTESTABLE [kon-tes'ta-bl], able to be disputed. CONTESTED, *adj.* disputed; settled by c.; opposed. [Fr. from L.].
CONTESTANT [kon-tes'tant], *n.* one who contests. [Fr.].
CONTESTATION [kon-tes-tā'shn], *n.* act of contesting. [L.].
CONTEXT [kon'tekst], *n.* the adjacent parts of a passage in a specimen of literature or other writing. [L.].
CONTEXTUAL [kon-teks'tyŏŏ-al], *adj.* pertaining to the context. CONTEXTUALLY, *adv.* by, or arising from, the context.
CONTEXTURE [kon-teks'tyŏŏr], *n.* interweaving of several parts into one; the way in which anything is constructed; something woven.
CONTIGUITY [kon-ti-gyŏŏ'i-ti], *n.* state of being contiguous. [L.].
CONTIGUOUS [kon-ti'gyŏŏ-ŏŏs], *adj.* touching, adjoining, in contact. CONTIGUOUSLY, *adv.* near. [L.].
CONTINENCE [kon'ti-nens], *n.* restraint, moderation in sexual indulgence, chastity. [L.].
CONTINENCY [kon'ti-nen-si], *n.* continence.
CONTINENT (1) [kon'ti-nent], *adj.* chaste; abstaining from indulgence in sexual intercourse; moderate,

temperate, showing self-restraint. CONTINENTLY, *adv.* in a c. fashion.
CONTINENT (2), *n.* one of the five main territorial divisions of the earth's surface; any very large unbroken stretch of land; the mainland, *esp.* of Europe.
CONTINENTAL (1) [kon-ti-nen'tal], *adj.* pertaining to a continent, *esp.* to that of Europe. CONTINENTAL (2), *n.* inhabitant of the mainland of Europe.
CONTINGENCE [kon-tin'jens], *n.* contingency. [Fr.].
CONTINGENCY [kon-tin'jen-si], *n.* liability to happen; that which may happen, a possibility; chance occurrence; resultant event. [Next].
CONTINGENT (1) [kon-tin'jent], *adj.* that may or may not happen, liable to occur, possible, conditional; (*leg.*) dependent upon a possibility. CONTINGENT (2), *n.* contingency; share, due proportion; predetermined number of soldiers, ships etc. CONTINGENTLY, *adv.* in c. fashion. [L.].
CONTINUAL [kon-ti'nyŏŏ-al], *adj.* unceasing, unremitting; persistent, recurring, often repeated. CONTINUALLY, *adv.* without ceasing; persistently.
CONTINUANCE [kon-ti'nyŏŏ-ans], *n.* persistence; duration; continuity.
CONTINUANT [kon-ti'nyŏŏ-ant], *n.* (*phon.*) consonantal sound produced by allowing the breath to escape in a continuous stream.
CONTINUATION [kon-ti-nyŏŏ-ā'shn], *n.* act or process of continuing; state of being continued; that which continues, an extension, prolongation, uninterrupted succession. [L.].
CONTINUATION-DAY [kon-ti-nyŏŏ-ā'shn-dā], *n.* (*Stock Exchange*) the day on which interest is paid.
CONTINUATIVE [kon-ti'nyŏŏ-a-tiv], *adj.* that continues. [L.].
CONTINUE [kon-ti'nyŏŏ], *v.t.* to extend, prolong; unite without a break; carry on after interruption; *v.i.* to go on, extend; go on doing something; remain. CONTINUATOR, CONTINUER, *n.* one who, that which, continues. [L.].
CONTINUED [kon-ti'nyŏŏd], *adj.* sustained; extended in length; proceeding without stop; continuous. CONTINUEDLY, *adv.* in a c. fashion.
CONTINUING [kon-ti'nyŏŏ-ing], *adj.* lasting, enduring.
CONTINUITY [kon-ti-nyŏŏ'i-ti], *n.* state or condition of being continuous; (*cinema*) fully detailed form of scenario; **c. writer**, one who prepares this.
CONTINUO [kon-ti'nyŏŏ-ŏ], *n.* (*mus.*) (formerly) an accompaniment for harpsichord or organ. [It.].
CONTINUOUS [kon-ti'nyŏŏ-ŏŏs], *adj.* joined in unbroken succession, uninterrupted; unceasing. CONTINUOUSLY, *adv.* in a c. fashion. [L.].
CONTINUUM [kon-ti'nyŏŏ-um], *n.* sequence; unbroken quantity, continuous entity. [L.].
CONTORT [kon-tawt'], *v.t.* to distort, twist out of shape; (*fig.*) twist the meaning of. [L.].
CONTORTION [kon-taw'shn], *n.* act of contorting; twisting, distorting; state of being contorted. [L.].
CONTORTIONIST [kon-taw'shn-ist], *n.* acrobat or dancer who twists his body into contortions.
CONTOUR (1) [kon'tŏŏr], *n.* outline of a figure or object; contour-line; **c. ploughing**, method of ploughing which follows land contours. CONTOUR-LINE, line drawn on a map to show relative elevation. CONTOUR-MAP, map with lines to show the surface of the country. CONTOUR (2), *v.t.* to show the c. of; indicate contour-lines on. [Fr.].
CONTRA- (1), *pref.* against; (*mus.*) opposite to, indicating an octave lower than the usual form. [L.].
CONTRA (2), *prep. and adv.* against, opposing; to the contrary, in opposition. CONTRA (3), *n.* a contrary vote; **pros and con(tra)s**, votes or points for and against. [L.].
CONTRABAND (1) [kon'tra-band], *n.* smuggling; goods smuggled and offered for sale illegally; **c. of war**, goods which may not be sold to a warring nation by neutrals. CONTRABAND (2), *adj.* prohibited by law, smuggled. CONTRABANDIST, *n.* smuggler. [Fr.].
CONTRABASS [kon'tra-bās], *n.* largest kind of bass-viol, double-bass.
CONTRACEPTION [kon-tra-sep'shn], *n.* prevention of conception, by drugs or mechanical means.
CONTRACEPTIVE [kon-tra-sep'tiv], *n. and adj.* (appliance or drug) preventing conception.
CONTRACT (1) [kon'trakt], *n.* a solemn agreement; bargain, compact; bond; betrothal; solemn and binding promise; document containing the terms of

an agreement; terms or conditions of an agreement or compact; **c. bridge,** form of bridge in which tricks won above those contracted for do not count towards game. [OFr.].

CONTRACT (2) [kon-trakt'], *v.t.* to draw up an agreement with another, arrange by contract; *v.i.* to enter into a contract to do something; **to c. in, out,** to make an agreement to participate or not to participate in certain activities, organizations etc. [L.].

CONTRACT (3), *v.t.* to draw together, tighten up; knit together, causing to wrinkle; shrink, narrow, shorten; incur; catch (a disease); *v.i.* to draw together; become tighter or shorter; shrink. [L.].

CONTRACTED [kon-trak'tid], *adj.* drawn up, knit together; shortened; *(fig.)* narrow, limited. CONTRACTEDLY, *adv.* in a c. fashion.

CONTRACTIBLE [kon-trak'ti-bl], *adj.* liable to contract. CONTRACTIBILITY, CONTRACTIBLENESS [kon-trak-ti-bi'li-ti, kon-trak'ti-bl-nes], *n.* condition of being c.

CONTRACTILE [kon-trak'til], *adj.* tending to contract; able to contract. CONTRACTILITY [kon-trak-ti'li-ti], *n.* power or capacity of contracting. [Fr.].

CONTRACTING [kon-trak'ting], *adj.* drawing together; shortening; able to contract; bound or engaged in contract.

CONTRACTION [kon-trak'shn], *n.* act or process of contracting; that which is contracted; abbreviated form of a word. [L.].

CONTRACTIVE [kon-trak'tiv], *adj.* tending to contract.

CONTRACTOR [kon-trak'ter], *n.* person who solemnly contracts to do work at an agreed price; builder and house repairer; *(anat.)* a contracting muscle.

CONTRACTUAL [kon-trak'tyōō-al], *adj.* pertaining to a contract.

CONTRADICT [kon-tra-dikt'], *v.t.* to deny emphatically; state the exact opposite of what someone says; be at variance with. CONTRADICTABLE, *adj.* that may be contradicted. CONTRADICTIOUS, *adj.* contradictory. [L.].

CONTRADICTIVE [kon-tra-dik'tiv], *adj.* contradictory. CONTRADICTIVELY, *adv.* contradictorily.

CONTRADICTORY (1) [kon-tra-dik'te-ri], *adj.* that contradicts. CONTRADICTORY (2), *n.* an assertion to the contrary; anything which contradicts something else. CONTRADICTORILY, *adv.* in c. fashion.

CONTRADISTINCTION [kon-tra-dis-tingk'shn], *n.* distinction by contrasting qualities.

CONTRADISTINCTIVE [kon-tra-dis-tingk'tiv], *adj.* distinguished by contrast.

CONTRADISTINGUISH [kon-tra-dis-ting'gwish], *v.t.* to distinguish by contrast.

CONTRA-INDICANT [kon-tra-in'di-kant], *n.* *(path.)* symptom discouraging the usual treatment.

CONTRA-INDICATE [kon-tra-in'di-kāt], *v.t.* *(path.)* to indicate a different treatment from usual. CONTRA-INDICATION [kon-tra-in-di-kā'shn], *n.* *(path.)* indication which discourages the usual treatment.

CONTRALTO (1) [kon-tral'tō], *n.* *(mus.)* part sung by the lowest-pitched female voice or, rarely, by the highest-pitched male voice; deep female voice; woman with such a voice. CONTRALTO (2), *adj.* *(mus.)* resembling or suitable for a c. [CONTRA and ALTO].

CONTRAPLEX [kon'tra-pleks], *adj.* having two telegraphic messages passing each other simultaneously in opposite directions.

CONTRAPOSITION [kon-tra-po-zi'shn], *n.* opposition, contrast; *(log.)* form of conversion.

CONTRAPTION [kon-trap'shn], *n.* a makeshift, contrivance, strange device. [Invented word].

CONTRAPUNTAL [kon-tra-pun'tal], *adj.* relating to counterpoint. CONTRAPUNTIST, *n.* *(mus.)* an expert in counterpoint. [It.].

CONTRARIETY [kon-tra-rī'e-ti], *n.* state or quality of being contrary; an inconsistency. [L.].

CONTRARILY [kon'tra-ri-li], *adv.* in contrary fashion.

CONTRARINESS [kon'tra-ri-nes], *n.* state of being contrary; [kon-trāer'i-nes], perverseness.

CONTRARIWISE [kon'tra-ri-wiz], *adv.* in contrary fashion; on the contrary; in reverse directions.

CONTRA-ROTATION [kon-tra-rō-tā'shn], *n.* reverse rotation.

CONTRARY (1) [kon'tra-ri], *adj.* opposed to, contradicted by, against, opposite; unfavourable; **c. propositions,** *(log.)* propositions which contradict each

other; **c. terms,** *(log.)* terms which express the exact opposites; *(coll.)* [kon-trāer'i] perverse, self-willed. CONTRARY (2) [kon'tra-ri], *n.* the very opposite; *(log.)* c. proposition or term; **on the c.,** on the other hand; **to the c.,** in opposition. [L.].

CONTRAST (1) [kon'trahst], *n.* act of contrasting; dissimilarity between things set in comparison; the things which show such unlikeness; unfavourable comparison; *(phot.)* degree of variation between the lightest and darkest parts of a photograph. CONTRASTY [kon-trahs'ti], *adj.* *(phot.)* showing marked difference of light and shade. [Fr.].

CONTRAST (2) [kon-trahst'], *v.t.* to compare objects so as to cause their differences to stand out clearly; compare; *v.i.* to show dissimilarity when set in comparison, stand out sharply. CONTRASTIVE, *adj.* that can be contrasted. [Fr.].

CONTRAVENE [kon-tra-vēn'], *v.t.* to oppose, violate, be at variance with; contradict. [L.].

CONTRAVENTION [kon-tra-ven'shn], *n.* act of contravening.

CONTRETEMPS [kon'tre-tah(ng)], *n.* unexpected and unfortunate accident; a hitch. [Fr.].

CONTRIBUTE [kon-tri'byōōt], *v.t. and i.* to give, subscribe along with others for a common end; supply (help); add (to knowledge); write articles, stories etc. for a publication. CONTRIBUTABLE [kon-tri'byōō-ta-bl], *adj.* that may be contributed. CONTRIBUTIVE, *adj.* that contributes. [L.].

CONTRIBUTION [kon-tri-byōō'shn], *n.* act of contributing; amount or thing contributed. [L.].

CONTRIBUTOR [kon-tri'byōō-ter], *n.* person who contributes.

CONTRIBUTORY [kon-tri'byōō-te-ri], *adj.* pertaining to, maintained by, contributions; that contributes.

CONTRITE [kon'trīt], *adj.* deeply penitent or repentant, stricken with remorse. CONTRITELY [kon'trīt-li, kon-trīt'li], *adv.* in c. fashion. CONTRITENESS, *n.* contrition.

CONTRITION [kon-tri'shn], *n.* penitence; remorse. [L.].

CONTRIVANCE [kon-trī'vans], *n.* act of contriving; that which is contrived; device.

CONTRIVE [kon-trīv'], *v.t.* to devise, plan; invent; *v.i.* to scheme or devise, manage. CONTRIVABLE, *adj.* able to be contrived. CONTRIVER, *n.* one who contrives. [OFr.].

CONTROL (1) [kon-trōl'], *n.* authority and guidance, restraint, supervision, the manual or mechanical management of machines etc.; the accepted standard for comparison; spirit alleged to direct the movements of a medium at spiritualistic seances; *(pl.)* instruments by which the movements of a machine are guided; regulations governing trade, work and other aspects of daily life. [Fr.].

CONTROL (2) *(pres.pt.* **controlling,** *pret. and p.pt.* **controlled),** *v.t.* to curb, restrain; regulate; guide, superintend; direct, supervise; verify by the aid of an accepted standard. CONTROLLABLE, *adj.* able to be controlled. [Fr.].

CONTROLLER, COMPTROLLER [kon-trō'ler], *n.* one who controls; official who supervises the expenditure of the services, the Queen's household etc.; mechanical device for controlling machines. CONTROLLERSHIP, *n.* office or rank of a c.

CONTROL ROOM [kon-trōl'rōōm], *n.* room from which (military) operations are directed.

CONTROVERSIAL [kon-tro-vur'shal], *adj.* pertaining to, or inducing, controversy. CONTROVERSIALIST, *n.* one skilled in, or fond of, controversy. CONTROVERSIALLY, *adv.* in c. fashion.

CONTROVERSY [kon'tro-ver-si], *n.* a dispute, argument, disputation, discussion. [L.].

CONTROVERT [kon'tro-vert], *v.t.* to debate, argue, dispute about; deny. CONTROVERTER, CONTROVERTIST, *n.* one who controverts. [L.].

CONTROVERTIBLE [kon-tro-vur'ti-bl], *adj.* able to be controverted. CONTROVERTIBLY, *adv.* in c. fashion.

CONTUMACIOUS [kon-tyōō-mā'shŏŏs], *adj.* disobedient, refractory, insubordinate; *(fig.)* showing contempt of court. CONTUMACIOUSLY, *adv.* in c. fashion. [L.].

CONTUMACY [kon'tyōō-ma-si], *n.* wilful disobedience, insubordination. [L.].

CONTUMELIOUS [kon-tyōō-mē'li-ŏŏs], *adj.* insolent, contemptuously abusive. CONTUMELIOUSLY, *adv.* in c. fashion. CONTUMELIOUSNESS, *n.* quality of being c.

CONTUMELY [kon-tyōōm'li, kon'tyōō-me-li], *n.*

The accent ' after a syllable = stress (u-pon'). The mark ‾ over a vowel = length (ā in made; ō in bone).

insolent language, behaviour or treatment; disgrace. [L.].

CONTUSE [kon-tyōōz´], *v.t.* to cause injury without breaking the skin, bruise. [L.].

CONTUSION [kon-tyōō´zhn], *n.* (*med.*) a bruise; act of contusing. CONTUSIVE, *adj.* causing a c. [L.].

CONUNDRUM [ko-nun´drum], *n.* a riddle, puzzling question. [Unkn.].

CONURBATION [ko-ner-bā´shn], *n.* group of neighbouring towns which have grown by a peripheral development into a single continuous built-up area. [L.].

CONVALESCE [kon-va-les´], *v.i.* to recover one's strength and normal health after illness. [L.].

CONVALESCENCE [kon-va-le´sens], *n.* process of convalescing; period necessary for this. [Fr.].

CONVALESCENT (1) [kon-va-le´sent], *adj.* regaining health after illness; pertaining to convalescence. CONVALESCENT (2), *n.* one who is convalescing.

CONVECTION [kon-vek´shn], *n.* the transmission of heat or electricity by the movement of a substance which is heated or electrified. [L.].

CONVECTIVE [kon-vek´tiv], *adj.* that conveys; pertaining to convection.

CONVENANCES [kaw(ng)´ve-nah(ng)s], *n.(pl.)* an accepted standard of conduct or behaviour; conventional propriety. [Fr.].

CONVENE [kon-vēn´], *v.t. and i.* to summon, cause to gather together, assemble, meet. CONVENABLE, *adj.* that may be convened. CONVENER, *n.* one who convenes. CONVENING, *n.* act of convening. [L.].

CONVENIENCE [kon-vē´ni-ens], *n.* quality of being convenient, that which is convenient; material comfort; useful contrivance or fitting, *esp.* in a house; lavatory, water-closet; **to make a c. of someone,** to take advantage of a person's good nature. [L.].

CONVENIENT [kon-vē´ni-ent], *adj.* suitable, fitting, commodious; not causing trouble; suiting one's personal comfort; (*coll.*) comfortably accessible, near at hand. CONVENIENTLY, *adv.* in a c. manner. [L.].

CONVENT [kon´vent], *n.* religious community, particularly of nuns, observing the rule of a religious order; building in which such a community lives. [L.].

CONVENTICLE [kon-ven´ti-kl], *n.* formerly a secret religious meeting of Dissenters; building where such meetings were held; small Nonconformist chapel. [L.].

CONVENTION [kon-ven´shn], *n.* act of convening; formal assembly convened to conduct business; an agreement; accepted mode of conduct or play. [L.].

CONVENTIONAL [kon-ven´shn-al], *adj.* according to convention or generally accepted practice; rigidly adhering to convention; traditional, stilted; unoriginal. CONVENTIONALISM, *n.* state of being c.; rigid acceptance of convention. CONVENTIONALIZE, *v.t.* to make c. CONVENTIONALLY, *adv.* in a c. fashion. [L.].

CONVENTIONALITY [kon-ven-shn-a´li-ti], *n.* quality of being conventional; that which is conventional.

CONVENTIONARY (1) [kon-ven´shn-a-ri], *adj.* on terms settled by a convention or special contract or agreement. CONVENTIONARY (2), *n.* a party to a convention; tenant on agreed terms.

CONVENTUAL (1) [kon-ven´tyōō-al], *adj.* pertaining to a convent; pertaining to the Conventuals. CONVENTUAL (2), *n.* inmate of a convent; member of the more lenient branch of the Franciscan order. [L.].

CONVERGE [kon-vurj´], *v.t.* to cause to converge; *v.i.* to approach and meet at a point; (*math.*) (of a series) approximate towards a definite limit in certain of its terms; (*fig.*) be focused on. CONVERGENCE, *n.* act of converging; tendency to c. CONVERGENT, *adj.* converging, inclined to c. [L.].

CONVERSABLE [kon-vur´sa-bl], *adj.* easy and ready in conversation, sociable. CONVERSABLENESS, *n.* quality of being c. CONVERSABLY, *adv.* in a c. manner.

CONVERSANT [kon´ver-sant], *adj.* familiar, acquainted; having intimate knowledge of, experienced in. CONVERSANCE [kon´ver-sans], *n.* quality of being c. CONVERSANTLY, *adv.* in a c. manner.

CONVERSATION [kon-ver-sā´shn], *n.* talk, as a form of social intercourse; **c. piece,** painting of a group of figures; **to make c.,** to talk merely to avoid a silence, without having anything special to say. CONVERSATIONALIST, CONVERSATIONIST, *n.* a good talker. [L.].

CONVERSATIONAL [kon-ver-sā´shn-al], *adj.* skilled in the art of conversation; relating or suited to conversation; chatty and informal.

CONVERSAZIONE [kon-ver-sat-si-ō´nā], *n.* a meeting for conversation, soirée given by a learned, scientific, or literary body. [It.].

CONVERSE (1) [kon-vurs´], *v.i.* to talk, have conversation with. CONVERSE (2) [kon´vers], *n.* conversation, social intercourse or friendly dealings. [L.].

CONVERSE (3) [kon´vers], *adj.* reverse opposite, contrary. CONVERSE (4), *n.* the exact opposite, antithesis. CONVERSELY [kon-vurs´li], *adv.* in c. fashion. [L.].

CONVERSION [kon-vur´shn], *n.* act of converting; state of being converted, *esp.* to another form of religion; spiritual awakening; (*log.*) interchanging of the terms of a proposition; **fraudulent c.,** misappropriation to one's own use of funds entrusted to one by a body or a number of individuals. [L.].

CONVERT (1) [kon-vurt´], *v.t.* to transform, change from one form or function to another; persuade to adopt some particular religious creed; awaken spiritually; (*comm.*) change one kind of stock to another of like value; (*econ.*) change a quantity of a certain currency into the equivalent in another; (*leg.*) misappropriate to one's own use; (*Rugby football*) complete a try by kicking a goal. CONVERT (2) [kon´vert], *n.* one who has been converted, *esp.* to a new religious creed. [L.].

CONVERTER [kon-vur´ter], *n.* one who, or that which, converts; receptacle in which molten iron is converted into steel; **rotary c.,** electric motor and dynamo for converting the applied current into another form.

CONVERTIBLE [kon-vur´ti-bl], *adj.* able to be converted. CONVERTIBILITY [kon-ver-ti-bi´li-ti], *n.* the capacity for, possibility of, being converted. CONVERTIBLY, *adv.* interchangeably.

CONVEX [kon´veks], *adj.* with the surface curving outwards. CONVEXED, *adj.* made c. in form. CONVEXLY, *adv.* in a c. shape. [L.].

CONVEXITY [kon-vek´si-ti], *n.* quality or state of being convex.

CONVEY [kon-vā´], *v.t.* to transport, take, carry from one place to another; lead, conduct; (*fig.*) communicate, make known; (*leg.*) transfer real property. CONVEYABLE, *adj.* able to be conveyed. [OFr.].

CONVEYANCE [kon-vā´ans], *n.* act or process of conveying; means by which something is conveyed; vehicle, carriage; (*leg.*) the making over of real property to different ownership; legal document embodying such a transfer.

CONVEYANCER [kon-vā´an-ser], *n.* (*leg.*) one employed in drawing up conveyances of property.

CONVEYANCING [kon-vā´an-sing], *n.* (*leg.*) the drawing up of conveyances of property; branch of law dealing with this.

CONVEYER, CONVEYOR [kon-vā´er], *n.* one who, or that which, conveys; mechanical apparatus for conveying goods.

CONVICT (1) [kon-vikt´], *v.t.* to find guilty of a crime after trial in a judicial court; (*fig.*) prove guilty of a fault. CONVICT (2) [kon´vict], *n.* person convicted after trial in a court of law; person serving a sentence of imprisonment. CONVICTED, *adj.* declared guilty. [L.].

CONVICTION [kon-vik´shn], *n.* act of convicting; fact of being convicted; state of being convinced; firm belief, convinced opinion; **to carry c.,** to sound convincing. [L.].

CONVICTIVE [kon-vik´tiv], *adj.* able to convince or convict.

CONVINCE [kon-vins´], *v.t.* to satisfy the mind, or compel belief by evidence; cause to feel certain that, persuade to believe something. CONVINCIBLE, *adj.* capable of being convinced. CONVINCINGLY, *adv.* in convincing fashion. CONVINCINGNESS, *n.* power of convincing. [L.].

CONVIVIAL [kon-vi´vi-al], *adj.* festive, jovial, social. CONVIVIALIST, *n.* one displaying conviviality. CONVIVIALLY, *adv.* in c. fashion. [L.].

CONVIVIALITY [kon-vi-vi-a´li-ti], *n.* festivity; good humour befitting a feast; good-fellowship.

CONVOCATION [kon-vō-kā´shn], *n.* act of convoking; formal assembly convoked for a particular purpose; (*eccles.*) synod of provincial clergy; legislative body in the Universities of Oxford and

Durham; collective body of registered graduates at certain universities. CONVOCATIONAL, *adj.* pertaining to a c. [L.].

CONVOKE [kon-vōk'], *v.t.* to call together, summon, assemble; convene. [L.].

CONVOLUTE [kon'vo-lyōōt], *adj.* (*bot.*) rolled together or upon itself; coiled. [L.].

CONVOLUTED [kon'vo-lyōō-tid], *adj.* (*zool.*) coiled, rolled up into a spiral.

CONVOLUTION [kon-vo-lyōō'shn], *n.* act of convolving; state of being convolved; a winding, fold, coil.

CONVOLVE [kon-volv'], *v.t. and i.* to roll together; roll one part on another; roll back upon itself. [L.].

CONVOLVULUS (*pl.* **convolvuluses**) [kon-vol'-vyōō-lus], *n.* (*bot.*) large genus of plants, including the bindweed. [L.].

CONVOY (1) [kon'voi], *v.t.* to agitate violently; poses of protection; escort non-combatant vessels in time of war. CONVOY (2), *n.* ships of war which c. merchant vessels; merchant ships so convoyed; group of ships or vehicles moving in company. [OFr.].

CONVULSE [kon-vuls'], *v.t.* to agitate violently; unsettle, upset deeply; set up a series of spasmodic muscular contractions; overcome with a paroxysm of emotion. [L.].

CONVULSION [kon-vul'shn], *n.* sudden, violent shaking or disturbance; strong social or political upset or upheaval; (*pl.*) fit characterized by a series of spasmodic, involuntary twitchings of the muscles; overpowering paroxysm of strong emotion. CONVULSIONARY, *adj.* connected with, relating to, c. [L.].

CONVULSIVE [kon-vul'siv], *adj.* producing or attended by convulsions. CONVULSIVELY, *adv.* in c. fashion. [Fr.].

CONY, CONEY [kō'ni], *n.* the rabbit. CONY-SKIN, *n.* skin of rabbits. [OFr. from L.].

COO (1) [kōō], *v.i.* to utter the soft cry of pigeons and doves; (of babies) utter gentle inarticulate sounds of content; speak gently and soothingly; **to bill and c.,** to make love by endearments and fondling. COO (2), *n.* the soft cry of doves or pigeons; soft, gentle sound resembling this. [Imitative].

COOEE [kōō'ē], *int.* call of the Australian bushmen; similar cry to attract attention.

COOK (1) [kōōk], *n.* one who cooks, *esp.* a domestic servant employed to prepare food for eating. COOK (2), *v.t.* to prepare food for eating by roasting, boiling, frying etc.; (*fig.*) subject to great heat; prepare something falsely, fake; *v.i.* to be prepared for eating by subjection to heat; **to c. one's goose,** to spoil one's scheme. [OE. from L.].

COOKER [kōō'ker], *n.* stove or other apparatus for cooking; fruit particularly fitted for cooking.

COOKERY [kōō'ke-ri], *n.* art and practice of cooking.

COOK-GENERAL [kōōk-je'ne-ral], *n.* domestic servant who does general housework as well as cooking.

COOK-HOUSE [kōōk'hows], *n.* camp-kitchen.

COOKIE [kōō'ki], *n.* (*Scots*) plain bun; (*U.S.*) small cake.

COOKING [kōō'king], *adj.* (of fruit) suitable mainly for cooking.

COOK-SHOP [kōōk'shop], *n.* eating-house, shop where cooked food is sold.

COOL (1) [kōōl], *adj.* pleasantly cold; chilly; fresh, not too warm; (*fig.*) clear-headed; deliberate, calm; lukewarm, apathetic; lacking in friendliness or warmth of feeling; off-hand, impudent; (*hunting*) (of scent) faint. COOL (2), *n.* coolness; that which is c. COOL (3), *v.t.* to make c.; *v.i.* to become c., grow c.; **to c. one's heels,** to be kept waiting; **to keep one's breath to c. one's porridge,** not to waste one's words. [OE.].

COOLER [kōō'ler], *n.* anything which abates heat or excitement; vessel in which things are cooled; (*slang*) a lock-up.

COOL-HEADED [kōōl-he'did], *adj.* not easily excited or alarmed.

COOLIE [kōō'li], *n.* hired native servant or porter in India, China and Malaya. [Native].

COOLNESS [kōōl'nes], *n.* state or quality of being cool; difference of opinion, disagreement.

COOMBE, COMBE [kōōm], *n.* deep, narrow valley, often wooded; hollow on the top of a hill. [OE.].

COON [kōōn], *n.* racoon; (*coll.*) negro; shrewd fellow. [(RA)COON].

COOP (1) [kōōp], *n.* cask or barrel; wooden cage for hens; wicker basket for catching fish. COOP (2), *v.t.* to put in a c.; confine; **to c. in, up,** to confine within a small space. [L.].

CO-OP [kō'op], *n.* (*coll.*) co-operative society or shop.

COOPER (1) [kōō'per], *n.* one who makes barrels and casks. COOPER (2), *v.t.* to repair barrels. [ME.].

COOPER (3), see COOPER (1).

COOPERAGE [kōō'pe-rij], *n.* price paid for work done by the cooper; cooper's work or workshop.

CO-OPERATE [kō-o'pe-rāt], *v.i.* to work or act together for a common end; aid one another in producing an effect.

CO-OPERATION [kō-o-pe-rā'shn], *n.* act of co-operating; group of people working together in the production or provision of goods for the common profit.

CO-OPERATIVE [kō-o'pe-ra-tiv], *adj.* working or acting together for the same end or a common purpose; willing to work with others; (of a trading concern) sharing some of the profits among its members; *also n.,* such a concern. CO-OPERATIVELY, *adv.* in c. fashion.

CO-OPERATOR [kō-o'pe-rā-ter], *n.* person who co-operates.

CO-OPT [kō-opt'], *v.t.* to elect to membership of a body by the votes of its existing members. CO-OPTION [kō-op'shn], *n.* election to a body by the votes of its existing members.

CO-ORDINATE (1) [kō-aw'di-nat], *adj.* in the same order; of equal rank or importance. CO-ORDINATE (2), *n.* that which is c.; (*math.*) any one of a system of magnitudes used to fix the position of a line or point. CO-ORDINATELY, *adv.* in the same order or in equal rank.

CO-ORDINATE (3) [kō-aw'di-nāt], *v.t.* to make co-ordinate; bring into proper order or relation. CO-ORDINATIVE, *adj.* that co-ordinates. CO-ORDINATOR, *n.* one who co-ordinates. [L.].

CO-ORDINATION [kō-aw-di-nā'shn], *n.* act of co-ordinating; condition of being co-ordinate.

COOT [kōōt], *n.* a water-fowl. [ME.].

COP (1) (*pres.pt.* **copping**, *pret. and p.pt.* **copped**) [kop], *v.t.* (*slang*) to catch, take in charge; detect, find in the act (of committing an offence); **to c. it,** (*slang*) to get into trouble. COP (2), *n.* (*slang*) act of catching or finding out; policeman; **no great c.,** not much of a haul, not much use. [Uncert.].

COPAIBA, COPAIVA [ko-pī'bah, 'vah], *n.* balsam made from juice from the copaiva tree. [Span. from Braz.].

COPAL [kō'pal], *n.* juice of certain tropical trees, used for varnishing. [Mexican].

COPARCENER [kō-pah'se-ner], *n.* co-heir, fellow partner. COPARCENARY, *n.* joint inheritance or heirship. [CO and PARCENER].

COPARTNER [kō-paht'ner], *n.* joint partner, fellow partner.

COPARTNERSHIP [kō-paht'ner-ship], *n.* joint business concern; persons who own or direct a joint concern; partnership between employers and employed.

COPARTNERY [kō-paht'ne-ri], *n.* copartnership.

COPE (1) [kōp], *n.* vestment in the form of a long ornamented cloak, worn by the clergy on special occasions; (*fig.*) anything which covers, envelops, like a cope; (*arch.*) coping. COPE (2), *v.t.* to array in a c.; (*arch.*) furnish with a coping. [MedL.].

COPE (3), *v.t.* to handle, deal with a difficult person or situation successfully. [OFr.].

COPECK, KOPECK [kō'pek], *n.* Russian copper coin. [Russ.].

COPER (1), **COOPER** (3) [kō'per], *n.* ship surreptitiously supplying grog to deep-sea fishermen in the North Sea. [Du.].

COPER (2), *n.* horse-dealer. [~Du.].

COPERNICAN [ko-pur'ni-kan], *adj.* relating to the astronomical theories of Copernicus. [*Copernicus,* astronomer].

COPIER [ko'pi-er], *n.* person who copies.

CO-PILOT [kō-pī'lot], *n.* fellow pilot (*esp.* of aircraft).

COPING [kō'ping], *n.* (*arch.*) top course of a wall; projecting edge running along the top of a wall. COPING-STONE, *n.* stone which forms a c. [COPE (1)].

COPIOUS [kō'pi-oos], *adj.* abundant; plentiful; prolific; diffuse. COPIOUSLY, *adv.* in a c. way; diffusely. COPIOUSNESS, *n.* plenteousness, abundance; diffusiveness of style in treating a subject. [L.].

COPPER (1) [ko'per], *n.* a malleable metal, reddish-brown in colour, and a good conductor; (*chem.*)

The accent ′ after a syllable = stress (u-pon′). The mark ‾ over a vowel = length (ā in made; ō in bone).

chemical element denoted by Cu; coin made of copper, penny or halfpenny; large vessel (formerly of copper) for boiling clothes in. COPPER (2), *v.t.* to cover with c.
COPPER (3), *n. (slang)* policeman. [COP (1).].
COPPERAS [ko'pe-ras], *n.* sulphate of iron, also called green vitriol. [Fr.].
COPPER-BEECH [ko-per-bēch'], *n.* beech-tree with copper-coloured leaves.
COPPER-BOTTOMED [ko-per-bo'tomd], *adj. (naut.)* plated with copper below the water-line.
COPPERHEAD [ko'per-hed], *n.* venomous North American snake.
COPPERPLATE (1) [ko'per-plāt], *n. (print.)* plate or sheet of polished copper with an engraving or etching upon it; print taken from the plate. COPPERPLATE (2), *adj.* like a print made from a c.; neat, beautifully and carefully formed with fine lines, *esp.* of handwriting.
COPPERSMITH [ko'per-smith], *n.* craftsman who works in copper.
COPPER-TOP [ko'per-top], *n. (slang)* red-headed person.
COPPERY [ko'pe-ri], *adj.* blended with copper, made of copper; like copper.
COPPICE [ko'pis], *n.* thicket of brushwood; small wood, cut periodically for fuel. [OFr.].
COPRA [kop'rah], *n.* dried coconut kernels, from which coconut oil is extracted. [Malayalam].
COPSE [kops], *n.* small wood, thicket of small trees and undergrowth; coppice.
COPT [kopt], *n.* a Christian Egyptian. [Gk.].
COPTIC (1) [kop'tik], *n.* language of the Copts, or Christian descendants of the Ancient Egyptians. COPTIC (2), *adj.* pertaining to the Copts.
COPULA [ko'pyōō-lah], *n. (anat.)* a joining, a connecting bone or cartilage; *(gram.)* word which links subject and predicate. [L.].
COPULATE [ko'pyōō-lāt], *v.i.* to join, unite in copulation.
COPULATION [ko-pyōō-lā'shn], *n.* union, binding together; the sexual act, coition.
COPULATIVE (1) [ko'pyōō-la-tiv], *adj.* pertaining to copulation; *(gram.)* serving to connect as a copula. COPULATIVE (2), *n.* a connecting word. [L.].
COPULATORY [ko'pyōō-la-te-ri], *adj.* pertaining to copulation.
COPY (1) [ko'pi], *n.* an imitation; transcript; reproduction; one of a number of similar examples of a book or other document; literary or other matter in manuscript ready to be printed; *(leg.)* record of the admission of tenants to land under copyhold. COPY (2), *v.t. and i.* to make a c., imitation or transcript of; imitate. [Fr. from L.].
COPY-BOOK [ko'pi-book], *n.* book in which specimens of handwriting are provided for the young to imitate in learning to write.
COPYHOLD [ko'pi-hōld], *n. (leg.)* tenure of land at the will of the lord of the manor; land held under this system.
COPYHOLDER [ko'pi-hōl-der], *n.* one who holds land in copyhold; proof-reader's assistant who reads the copy to him.
COPYING-PENCIL [ko'pi-ing-pen-sil], *n.* indelible pencil.
COPYING-PRESS [ko'pi-ing-pres], *n.* machine for taking an exact copy of handwritten documents.
COPYIST [ko'pi-ist], *n.* one who copies; transcriber; imitator.
COPYRIGHT (1) [ko'pi-rīt], *n.* the exclusive right of an author, artist etc. to reproduce his works over a fixed period. COPYRIGHT (2), *adj.* protected by c. COPYRIGHT (3), *v.t.* to protect by c.
COPYWRITER [ko'pi-rī-ter], *n.* one who devises the text of advertisements. COPYWRITING, *n.* the work of a c.
COQUET, COQUETTE [kō-ket'], *v.i.* to flirt, try to attract the admiration of the male sex; *(fig.)* play with an idea for a short time. [Fr.].
COQUETRY [kō'ke-tri], *n.* flirtatious behaviour; superficial prettiness. [Fr.].
COQUETTE [kō-ket'], *n.* woman who attempts to win the admiration of the other sex by coquetry; kind of crested humming-bird. [Fr.].
COQUETTISH [kō-ke'tish], *adj.* behaving like a coquette. COQUETTISHLY, *adv.* in c. fashion.
CORACLE [ko'ra-kl], *n.* small row-boat made of wickerwork covered with skin, leather or canvas, used by the ancient Britons and still occasionally used in Wales and Ireland. [~Wel.].
CORACOID (1) [ko'ra-koid], *adj.* like a crow's beak

in shape. CORACOID (2), *n. (anat.)* small bone helping to articulate the fore-limb. [Gk.].
CORAL (1) [ko'ral], *n.* sea-water zoophyte found in the tropical oceans; white or reddish hard substance left by coral organisms; bead or ornament made of this. CORAL (2), *adj.* made of c.; resembling c. in colour. CORALLIFEROUS [ko-ra-li'fe-roōs], *adj.* containing, producing c. CORALLIFORM [ko-ra'li-fawm], *adj.* like c. [OFr.].
CORALLINE (1) [ko'ra-līn], *n.* seaweed or animal like coral in appearance. CORALLINE (2), *adj.* made of, or like, coral.
CORALLITE [ko'ra-līt], *n.* a petrified coral; *(zool.)* skeleton of a single zoophyte.
CORALLOID(AL) [ko'ra-loid, ko-ra-loi'dal], *adj.* like coral; branching like coral.
CORAL-REEF [ko-ral-rēf'], *n.* series of marine ridges formed by the deposit of coral.
CORALWORT [ko'ral-wert], *n. (bot.)* toothwort.
CORANACH, see CORONACH.
COR ANGLAIS [kaw-ah(ng)-glā'], *n.* a wood-wind instrument, the tenor oboe. [Fr.].
CORANTO [ko-ran'tō], *n.* sprightly dance, courante; tune to which this could be danced. [Span.].
CORBAN [kaw'ban], *n.* offering dedicated exclusively to God. [Heb.].
CORBEL (1) [kaw'bel], *n. (arch.)* bracket or stone projection from the face of the wall used as a support; short beam set lengthwise under a girder. CORBEL (2) *(pres.pt.* CORBELLING, *pret. and p.pt.* CORBELLED), *v.t.* to support by a c. [OFr.].
CORBIE [kaw'bi], *n. (Scots)* a crow. [~OFr.].
CORD (1) [kawd], *n.* thin rope; thick, stout string; *(anat.)* parts of the body resembling this; ribbed cloth; unit of measurement of wood, 128 cu. ft.; *(pl.)* breeches made of ribbed cloth. CORD (2), *v.t.* to make fast or tie with a c. [Gk.].
CORDAGE [kaw'dij], *n.* ropes or cords in general; the series of cords forming the rigging of a ship; store of ropes. [Fr.].
CORDATE(D) [kaw'dāt(-id)], *adj. (bot.)* shaped like a heart. [~L.].
CORDED [kaw'did], *adj.* fastened with cords; made of cords; ribbed.
CORDIAL (1) [kaw'di-al], *adj.* connected with the heart; stimulating; hearty, sincere, cheerfully friendly; heartfelt. CORDIAL (2), *n.* medicinal drink to strengthen and encourage the action of the heart; warming or refreshing drink. CORDIALLY, *adv.* in c. fashion. [L.].
CORDIFORM [kaw'di-fawm], *adj.* heart-shaped. [L.].
CORDILLERA [kaw-di-lyāer'ah], *n.* ridge in a group of parallel mountain ranges, *esp.* in South America. [Span.].
CORDITE [kaw'dīt], *n.* smokeless explosive in the form of short lengths of cord.
CORDON (1) [kaw'don], *n.* ribbon worn as a badge of honour; *(fort.)* row of stones jutting before a rampart; *(milit.)* line of military posts; ring of people surrounding anything to cut it off from outside communication; *(hort.)* fruit-tree pruned to grow as a single stem; **c. bleu,** blue ribbon on which hung the insignia of the order of the Holy Ghost in France; *(fig.)* first-class distinction; excellent cook. CORDON (2), *v.t.* to surround with a c.; **to c. off,** to isolate by a c. [Fr.].
CORDOVAN [kaw'dō-van], *n.* leather from Cordova. [*Cordova,* Spain].
CORDUROY [kaw'dyōō-roi], *n. and adj.* (made of) a thick cotton material corded and ribbed with a velvety finish; *(pl.)* trousers made of this; *(U.S.)* roadway across swampy ground made by laying tree-trunks transversely side by side. [Fr.].
CORDWAINER [kawd'wā-ner], *n.* † shoemaker; member of the Cordwainers' Company in London. [OFr.].
CORE (1) [kaw(r)], *n.* the innermost part of anything, the heart; central dry radical part of certain fruits which contains the pips; *(elect.)* central soft iron bar in a magnetic coil; *(founding)* inner part of a mould; *(fig.)* inmost part, kernel, root, substance. CORE (2), *v.t.* to remove the c. of. [OFr.].
CO-RELATION, see CORRELATION.
CO-RELATIVE, see CORRELATIVE.
CO-RELIGIONIST, CORRELIGIONIST [kō-ri-li'jn-ist], *n.* person of the same religious faith as another.
COREOPSIS [ko-ri-op'sis], *n.* yellow daisy-like garden plant. [Gk.].
CO-RESPONDENT [kō-ri-spon'dent], *n. (leg.)* man

ōō is pronounced as in f*oo*d; ŏŏ as in h*oo*d; th as in *th*ink; TH as in *that*; zh as in azure. ~ = related to.

charged with adultery with the petitioner's wife in a divorce suit; **c. shoes,** shoes of white canvas and brown leather.

CORF (*pl.* **corves**) [kawf], *n.* basket for carrying minerals in mines; floating basket in which fish are kept alive. [Du.].

CORGI, CORGY [kaw'gi], *n.* breed of small dogs. [Wel.].

CORIACEOUS [ko-ri-ā'shŏŏs], *adj.* resembling leather; tough. [L.].

CORIANDER [ko-ri-an'der], *n.* plant whose seeds have aromatic and carminative properties. [L.].

CORINTHIAN (1) [ko-rin'thi-an], *adj.* pertaining to Corinth or to the Corinthians of the Regency; **C. column,** the most ornate of the three types of column in Greek architecture. CORINTHIAN (2), *n.* native of Corinth; fashionable amateur of sport.

CORIUM [kaw'ri-um], *n.* the innermost layer of the skin. [L.].

CO-RIVAL [kō-rī'val], *n.* fellow rival. CO-RIVALRY, CO-RIVALSHIP, *n.* joint rivalry.

CORK (1) [kawk], *n.* light, resilient bark of the cork oak; piece of this cut down and shaped to make a stopper for a bottle; (*bot.*) the bark, external covering of woody plants. CORK (2), *adj.* made of c. CORK (3), *v.t.* to stop up a bottle by fitting a c. in its neck; give wine the taste of the c. [Span.].

CORKAGE [kaw'kij], *n.* charge made at hotels for serving a guest's own wine; the corking or uncorking of bottles.

CORKED [kawkt], *adj.* stopped up or filled with cork; (of wine) tasting of cork.

CORK-JACKET [kawk-ja'kit], *n.* jacket lined with cork, worn as a support in swimming.

CORKSCREW (1) [kawk'skrōō], *n.* screw with a handle, to extract corks from bottles. CORKSCREW (2), *v.t. and i.* to move in a spiral course.

CORK-TREE [kawk'trē], *n.* western European species of oak, the bark of which is manufactured into corks.

CORKY [kaw'ki], *adj.* consisting of cork; like a cork in taste or appearance; (*slang*) lively or skittish.

CORM [kawm], *n.* (*bot.*) short solid bulb-like underground stem. [Gk.].

CORMORANT [kaw'mo-rant], *n.* a voracious seabird; (*fig.*) glutton. [Fr.].

CORN (1) [kawn], *n.* grain, seed of cereal plants; cereal plants which yield grain; wheat; (*U.S.*) maize; *also* **Indian c.** CORN (2), *v.i.* to form into grains; granulate, preserve meat by salting; feed with oats. [OE.].

CORN (3), *n.* small painful excrescence of hardened horny skin, usually on the foot; **to tread on a person's corns,** (*fig.*) to hurt his feelings. [OFr.].

CORN-BREAD [kawn'bred], *n.* bread made from maize.

CORN-CHANDLER [kawn'chahnd-ler], *n.* dealer in corn.

CORN-COB [kawn'kob], *n.* woody centre part of the stalk, or spike, on which the ears of maize grow; pipe having this for a bowl.

CORN-CRAKE [kawn'krāk], *n.* bird with a peculiarly harsh cry; the landrail.

CORNEA [kaw'nē-ah], *n.* strong transparent membrane protecting the ball of the eye. [L.].

CORNED BEEF [kawnd-bēf'], *n.* pickled and salted beef.

CORNEL [kaw'nel], *n.* cornelian-tree. [OFr.].

CORNELIAN, CARNELIAN [kaw-nē'li-an], *n.* a precious stone, a kind of red chalcedony. [Fr.].

CORNELIAN-TREE [kaw-nē'li-an-trē], *n.* (*bot.*) the dogwood, yielding a small edible fruit like a cherry. [L.].

CORNER (1) [kaw'ner], *n.* point or line where two lines or surfaces meet; angle, *esp.* one formed by two plane sides of any object; secluded place; region of the earth; (*comm.*) system by which the whole of the available supply of an article is bought up, so that the buyers can sell again at their own price; (*football*) corner-kick; **to turn the c.,** (*fig.*) to start to improve; **to drive into a c.,** (*fig.*) to bring to bay; **tight c.,** difficult position. CORNER (2), *v.t.* to drive into a c.; bring to bay, trap; (*comm.*) make a c. in some commodity; *v.i.* to round a c., *esp.* in motor-racing. CORNERED, *adj.* with corners or angles; (*fig.*) caught, trapped. [OFr.].

CORNER-KICK [kaw'ner-kik], *n.* (*Association football*) free kick taken from one of the opponents' corners of the field.

CORNER-STONE [kaw'ner-stōn], *n.* (*arch.*) the stone which joins two walls of a building at the corner; the principal stone; (*fig.*) foundation, prop.

CORNER-WISE [kaw'ner-wīz], *adv.* diagonally; with the corner forward.

CORNET [kaw'net], *n.* (*mus.*) brass instrument like a trumpet with pistons; player of this instrument in an orchestra; hollow cone-shaped wafer for holding ice-cream; † (*milit.*) officer in a cavalry troop who formerly carried the colours; white headdress of Sisters of Charity. CORNETIST, *n.* performer on the c. [OFr.].

CORNFLOUR [kawn'flow-er], *n.* finely ground flour of Indian corn or maize.

CORNFLOWER [kawn'flow-er], *n.* (*bot.*) plant growing in cornfields, having a deep blue flower.

CORNICE [kaw'nis], *n.* (*arch.*) ornate moulding capping a building; part of the entablature, above the frieze; plaster moulding running round the walls of a room, just below the ceiling. [Fr.].

CORNISH [kaw'nish], *n. and adj.* pertaining to, native of, Cornwall; the extinct Celtic language of Cornwall.

CORNLAND [kawn'land], *n.* land used for or suitable for the production of corn.

CORNLOFT [kawn'loft], *n.* granary.

CORNO [kaw'nō], *n.* (*mus.*) the French horn. [It.].

CORN-RENT [kawn'rent], *n.* rent paid in corn instead of money.

CORNUCOPIA [kaw-nyŏŏ-kō'pi-ah], *n.* (*myth.*) the horn of the goat which suckled Zeus, symbol of plenty; representation of this in sculpture, painting etc.; (*fig.*) plenty, abundance. [L.].

CORNUTE(D) [kaw-nyŏŏt'(-id)], *adj.* having horns; horn-shaped.

CORNY [kaw'ni], *adj.* producing, containing or extracted from corn; (*U.S. slang*) old-fashioned; hackneyed.

COROLLA [ko-ro'lah], *n.* (*bot.*) the inner whorl of a flower, comprising the petals. COROLLACEOUS [ko-ro-lā'shŏŏs], *adj.* relating to, or resembling, a c. COROLLATE(D) [ko'ro-lāt(-ed), *adj.* like a c.; ornamented with corollas. [L.].

COROLLARY [ko-ro'la-ri], *n.* a further inference from an established proposition; (*geom.*) proposition following naturally upon one which has been proved; natural result, logical consequences.

CORONA (1) [ko-rō'nah], *n.* (*astron.*) halo round the sun or moon; disk of light round the sun, seen beyond the moon's rim in a total eclipse of the sun; crown-shaped chandelier for holding the tapers in a church; (*anat.*) upper surface of a tooth; (*arch.*) large flat projecting part of a cornice; (*bot.*) appendage of the corolla in certain flowers; (*elect.*) blue discharge of electricity from a transmitting aerial using a high voltage. [L.].

CORONA (2), *n.* (*prot.*) brand of Havana cigar. [Span.].

CORONACH, CORANACH [ko'ro-nakh], *n.* funeral dirge in the Scottish Highlands; public lamentation by hired mourners at an Irish burial. [Gael.].

CORONAL (1) [ko'ro-nal], *n.* circlet of precious gems for the head; circular garland of flowers worn as a crown. CORONAL (2), *adj.* pertaining to the crown of the head; pertaining to or resembling a corona. [L.].

CORONARY [ko'ro-na-ri], *adj.* pertaining to a crown, resembling a crown; (*anat.*) placed like a crown (of vessels, ligaments etc.). [L.].

CORONATION [ko-ro-nā'shn], *n.* the solemn ceremony of crowning a sovereign. [OFr.].

CORONER [ko'ro-ner], *n.* officer appointed to hold an inquest or inquiry into the cause of death of persons killed or dying unexpectedly, or to determine the ownership of treasure-trove. [AFr.].

CORONET [ko'ro-net], *n.* small crown worn by princes and peers; ornamental gold head-dress worn by ladies of rank or position; wreath of flowers worn round the head. CORONETED, *adj.* wearing or entitled to wear a c. [OFr.].

COROZO-NUT [ko-rō'zō-nut], *n.* nut of a South American palm, used as vegetable ivory. [Native].

CORPORAL (1) [kaw'pe-ral], *adj.* pertaining to the human body; bodily; **c. punishment,** whipping or flogging. CORPORALLY, *adv.* bodily. [L.].

CORPORAL (2), *n.* non-commissioned officer ranking between a sergeant and a private; (*naut.*) petty officer dealing with disciplinary matters. CORPORALSHIP, *n.* office or position of c. [It.].

CORPORALITY [kaw-po-ra'li-ti], *n.* state of existing in bodily form.

CORPORATE [kaw'po-rat], *adj.* united into a corporation, pertaining to or belonging to a corporation;

The accent ´ after a syllable = stress (u-pon´). The mark ‾ over a vowel = length (ā in made; ō in bone).

c. state, system of government through officially sponsored trade and professional organizations. CORPORATELY, *adv.* in a c. way. [L.].

CORPORATION [kaw-po-rā'shn], *n.* group or body of persons constituting a single legal entity; body appointed by election to conduct civic business; (*U.S.*) joint-stock company; (*slang*) large belly. CORPORATIVE [kaw'po-ra-tiv], *adj.* pertaining to a c. CORPORATOR [kaw'po-rā-ter], *n.* member of a c. [L.].

CORPOREAL [kaw-paw'ri-al], *adj.* bodily, physical, material; (*leg.*) tangible, consisting of physical objects or substances. CORPOREALITY [kaw-pawri-a'li-ti], *n.* condition of being c. CORPOREALIZE [kaw-paw'ri-a-liz], *v.i.* to assume bodily or tangible form, materialize. CORPOREALLY [kaw-paw'ri-a-li], *adv.* in bodily form.

CORPOREITY [kaw-paw-rē'i-ti], *n.* material being, bodily substance or existence.

CORPOSANT [kaw'pō-sant], *n.* luminous electric flashes occasionally seen about the rigging and mastheads of a ship, St. Elmo's fire. [Portug.].

CORPS (*pl.* **corps**) [kaw(r)], *n.* one of the largest manoeuvrable subdivisions of an army; particular section or part of the army; organized group of trained persons; **c. de ballet,** the whole company of dancers in a ballet; **c. diplomatique,** the entire group of persons attached to the diplomatic service in a foreign country. [Fr.].

CORPSE [kawps], *n.* the dead body, generally of a human being. [L.].

CORPSE-CANDLE [kawps'kan-dl], *n.* will-o'-the-wisp; tall candle placed by a bier.

CORPULENCE [kaw'pyōō-lens], *n.* state of being corpulent. [L.].

CORPULENCY [kaw'pyōō-len-si], *n.* corpulence.

CORPULENT [kaw'pyōō-lent], *adj.* stout, fat, obese. CORPULENTLY, *adv.* in a c. fashion. [L.].

CORPUS [kaw'pus], *n.* corpse; the whole extant body of writings of a particular kind or age; the principal of a fund; one of the special structures of the body; (*leg.*) body of rules, precedents, examples etc. which establish the law; **C. Christi,** church festival in honour of the Eucharist.

CORPUSCLE [kaw'pu-sl, kaw-pu'sl], *n.* minute physical body; (*biol.*) small fragment of protoplasm; (*physiol.*) microscopic body forming part of the blood; (*phys.*) an electron. [L.].

CORPUSCULAR [kaw-pus'kyōō-ler], *adj.* pertaining to or consisting of corpuscles; **c. philosophy,** philosophy holding that the universe is produced by adjustments of corpuscles into various forms of matter; **c. theory,** (*phys.*) former theory that light consists of emanations of minute particles of matter from a luminous body. CORPUSCULARIAN [kaw-pus-kyōō-lāer'i-an], *n.* one who upholds the c. philosophy or theory.

CORRAL (1) [ko-ral'], *n.* enclosure or pen for cattle or for imprisoning wild animals; space within an enclosed defence of wagons and equipment. CORRAL (2) [pres.pt. CORRALLING, *pret.* and *p.pt.* CORRALLED], *v.t.* to enclose in a c. [Span.].

CORRECT (1) [ko-rekt'], *v.t.* to put right; make correct; reprove, censure, punish for misbehaviour; modify or adjust in order to make a thing conform with a required standard; nullify or cure malformity or disorder. CORRECT (2), *adj.* free from error, right, accurate, true; conforming to a recognized conventional standard or code, proper, fitting, in good taste. CORRECTLY, *adv.* in a c. fashion. CORRECTNESS, *n.* quality of being c. [L.].

CORRECTION [ko-rek'shn], *n.* act of correcting; corrected or amended version; **house of c.,** reformatory, prison. CORRECTIONAL, *adj.* pertaining to c., intended to correct. [L.].

CORRECTITUDE [ko-rek'-ti-tyōōd], *n.* correctness. [Fr.].

CORRECTIVE [ko-rek'tiv], *n.* and *adj.* (something) able, intended or tending to correct. [Fr.].

CORRECTOR [ko-rek'ter], *n.* one who, or that which, corrects; (*print.*) proof-reader; (*hist.*) governor or director. [L.].

CORRELATE [ko'ri-lāt], *v.t.* and *i.* to stand in mutual relationship; bring into relation with, show the proper connexion between. CORRELATE, *n.* either of two mutually connected things, so related that one forms the complement of the other. CORRELATABLE, *adj.* able to be correlated. [CO and RELATE].

CORRELATION, CO-RELATION [ko-ri-lā'shn], *n.* reciprocal relation; act of correlating.

CORRELATIVE (1), **CO-RELATIVE** [ko-re'la-tiv],

adj. so related that one implies or involves the other, mutually dependent; (*gram.*) corresponding or complementary to one another and regularly used together (as *either . . . or*). CORRELATIVE (2), CO-RELATIVE, *n.* that which stands in reciprocal relation to something else. CORRELATIVELY, *adv.* in a c. relation or manner. CORRELATIVENESS, *n.* quality of being c.

CORRELIGIONIST, see CO-RELIGIONIST.

CORRESPOND [ko-res-pond'], *v.i.* to agree, be in accordance with, suit, fit; be similar, conform to; be equivalent to; write letters, maintain connexion or communication with a person by the writing of letters. [MedL.].

CORRESPONDENCE [ko-res-pon'dens], *n.* act of corresponding, conformity, similarity; communication between persons by means of letters; letters so exchanged; **c. course,** course of study by postal tuition; **c. column,** portion of a newspaper devoted to letters from readers.

CORRESPONDENT (1) [ko-res-pon'dent], *n.* one who corresponds with another; special writer on a newspaper or magazine who contributes periodical articles, or who is sent abroad to report some special happening or news from a particular area; person who occasionally writes letters to a newspaper to air his views; (*comm.*) firm having regular business dealings with another; **foreign c.,** clerk who deals with a firm's foreign letters; expert writer on a newspaper who deals with foreign affairs. CORRESPONDENT (2), *adj.* corresponding, suitable, analogous to. [MedL.].

CORRESPONDING [ko-res-pon'ding], *adj.* that corresponds. CORRESPONDINGLY, *adv.* in a c. manner.

CORRIDOR [ko'ri-daw(r)], *n.* long narrow passage in a building connecting several rooms or sections on the same floor; narrow passage extending along the whole length of certain types of railway-coach; (*pol. geog.*) narrow strip of territory not under the control of the state through which it passes; **c. train,** train made up of coaches with corridors. [It.].

CORRIE [ko'ri], *n.* (*Scots*) valley on a mountain side. [Gael.].

CORRIGENDUM (*pl.* **corrigenda**) [ko-ri-jen'dum], *n.* something to be corrected; (*pl.*) list of corrections to be made in a book. [L.].

CORRIGIBLE [ko'ri-ji-bl], *adj.* capable of being corrected. [L.].

CORROBORANT (1) [ko-ro'be-rant], *adj.* strengthening, invigorating; corroborating. CORROBORANT (2), *n.* fact which corroborates. [L.].

CORROBORATE [ko-ro'be-rāt], *v.t.* to strengthen, confirm, support by additional information. CORROBORATOR, *n.* one who corroborates. CORROBORATORY, *adj.* corroborative. [L.].

CORROBORATION [ko-ro-be-rā'shn], *n.* act of corroborating; that which corroborates.

CORROBORATIVE [ko-ro'be-ra-tiv], *adj.* tending to confirm or corroborate.

CORROBOREE [ko-ro-be-rē'], *n.* traditional Australian festival, consisting largely of dances; (*coll.*) a celebration. [Native].

CORRODE [ko-rōd'], *v.t.* and *i.* to eat away or destroy by degrees, wear away gradually, rust; (*fig.*) gnaw, prey upon. CORRODENT, *n.* and *adj.* (substance) causing corrosion. CORRODIBILITY [ko-rō-di-bi'li-ti], *n.* corrosibility. CORRODIBLE, *adj.* corrosible. [L.].

CORROSIBLE [ko-rō'zi-bl], *adj.* capable of corrosion. CORROSIBILITY [ko-rō-zi-bi'li-ti], *n.* susceptibility to corrosion.

CORROSION [ko-rō'zhn], *n.* act or process of corroding. [L.].

CORROSIVE (1) [ko-rō'siv], *adj.* tending to set up corrosion; **c. sublimate,** mercuric chloride, a virulent poison. CORROSIVE (2), *n.* substance which corrodes. CORROSIVELY, *adv.* in c. fashion. CORROSIVENESS, *n.* power of corroding. [OFr.].

CORRUGATE [ko'ru-gāt], *v.t.* and *i.* to wrinkle, contract into wrinkles and folds; form into small rounded ridges and furrows. CORRUGATED, *adj.* wrinkled, contracted into folds and ridges, furrowed; **c. iron,** sheet iron formed into a series of rounded parallel ridges and hollows. [L.].

CORRUGATION [ko-ru-gā'shn], *n.* act of corrugating, state of being corrugated; a wrinkle, fold.

CORRUGATOR [ko'ru-gā-ter], *n.* (*anat.*) muscle which wrinkles or furrows the forehead in frowning.

CORRUPT (1) [ko-rupt'], *adj.* putrid; tainted; impure, depraved, perverted, morally evil; open to

---

ōō is pronounced as in food; ŏŏ as in hood; th as in *think*; TH as in *that*; zh as in azure ~ = related to bribery, venal; mixed (of languages); (of texts) not representing the original or correct version. COR-RUPT (2), *v.t. and i.* to make c.; consume, wear away; become c. CORRUPTER, *n.* one who or that which corrupts. [L.].

CORRUPTIBLE (1) [ko-rup′ti-bl], *adj.* capable of being corrupted. CORRUPTIBLE (2), *n. c.* substance, the body. CORRUPTIBILITY [ko-rup-ti-bi′li-ti], *n.* quality of being c. CORRUPTIBLY, *adv.* in a c. manner.

CORRUPTION [ko-rup′shn], *n.* act of corrupting; state of being corrupt; that which corrupts. [L.].

CORRUPTIVE [ko-rup′tiv], *adj.* causing corruption.

CORRUPTLY [ko-rupt′li], *adv.* in corrupt fashion.

CORRUPTNESS [ko-rupt′nes], *n.* condition of being corrupt.

CORSAGE [kaw′sij, kaw′sahzh], *n.* bodice of a dress; (*mostly U.S.*) posy worn on the bodice. [OFr.].

CORSAIR [kaw′sāer], *n.* pirate; Barbary privateer; pirate ship. [Fr. from LL.].

CORSE [kaws], *n.* (*archaic*) corpse. [OFr.].

CORSET [kaw′set], *n.* woman's close-fitting undergarment worn to give shape to the figure; stays. CORSETED, *adj.* wearing a c. CORSETING, CORSETRY, *n.* art of fitting or making corsets.

CORSETIERE [kaw-set-yāer′], *n.* woman who makes or sells corsets. [Fr.].

CORSLET, CORSELET [kaws′lit], *n.* close-fitting sleeveless armour covering the body; pliable form of corset; (*entom.*) thorax of an insect. [Fr.].

CORTEGE, cortège [kaw-tāzh′], *n.* accompanying train of attendants on official occasions; procession, funeral procession. [Fr. from It.].

CORTEX (*pl.* **cortices**) [kaw′teks, kaw′ti-sēz], *n.* (*bot.*) bark of a tree; (*anat.*) external layer or part of an organ; outer mass of grey matter of the brain. CORTICAL [kaw′ti-kal], *adj.* pertaining to or resembling the c. [L.].

CORTICATE(D) [kaw′ti-kāt(-id)], *adj.* resembling or covered with bark. [L.].

CORUNDUM [ko-run′dum], *n.* (*min.*) a mineral aluminium oxide of great hardness, known as emery when opaque, sapphire when transparent and blue, and ruby when transparent and red.

CORUSCANT [ko-rus′kant], *adj.* flashing, sparkling. [L.].

CORUSCATE [ko′rus-kāt], *v.i.* to sparkle, glitter, flash, gleam. [L.].

CORUSCATION [ko-rus-kā′shn], *n.* sudden gleam of light, sparkle.

CORVETTE [kaw-vet′], *n. orig.* a full-rigged warship having one row of guns and no quarterdeck; small anti-submarine escort vessel. [Fr. from L.].

CORVINE [kaw′vīn], *adj.* relating to the crow family. [L.].

CORYBANT [ko′ri-bant], *n.* one of the frenzied priests or attendants of Cybele. CORYBANTIC [ko-ri-ban′tik], *adj.* resembling the Corybantes; wild, unrestrained. [Gk.].

CORYDON [ko′ri-don], *n.* traditional shepherd of pastoral poetry; young rustic. [Gk.].

CORYMB [ko′rimb], *n.* (*bot.*) form of inflorescence having a broad, level cluster of flowers. CORYMBOSE [ko-rim′bōs], *adj.* (*bot.*) like, or relating to, a c. [Gk.].

CORYPHAEUS [ko-ri-fē′us], *n.* leader of a chorus; (*fig.*) chief, leader. [Gk.].

CORYPHEE, coryphée [ko′ri-fā], *n.* principal dancer in a ballet. [Fr.].

CORYZA [ko-rī′zah], *n.* (*med.*) inflammation of the mucous membrane of the nose; catarrh in the head. [Gk.].

COS [kos], *n.* long-leaved lettuce grown originally in the island of Cos. [*Kos*, one of the Aegean Islands].

COSECANT [kō-sē′kant], *n.* (*geom.*) the secant of the complement of an arc or angle.

CO-SEISMAL (1) [kō-sīz′mal], *n.* line or curve connecting places where simultaneous shocks from an earthquake wave are felt. CO-SEISMAL (2), *adj.* pertaining to a c.

CO-SEISMIC [kō-sīz′mik], *adj. and n.* co-seismal.

CO-SENTIENT [kō-sen′shnt], *adj.* feeling or perceiving together with.

COSEY, see COSY (2).

COSH (1) [kosh], *n.* (*slang*) heavy, thick truncheon, life-preserver. COSH (2), *v.t. and i.* (*slang*) to strike or fell with a c.; strike vigorously. [Unkn.].

CO-SIGNATORY [kō-sig′na-te-ri], *n.* one who takes part in the signing of an official document along with others.

COSILY [kō′zi-li], *adv.* snugly, comfortably.

COSINE [kō′sīn], *n.* (*geom.*) the sine of the complement of an arc or angle.

COSLETTIZE [koz′le-tiz], *v.t.* to render steel rustproof by a special process. [From the name of the inventor].

COSMETIC (1) [koz-me′tik], *adj.* intended to heighten the beauty of the skin or hair. COSMETIC (2), *n.* substance applied externally to the skin or hair to aid the complexion or appearance. [Gk.].

COSMIC [koz′mik], *adj.* pertaining to the universe as a systematized entity; harmonious, orderly; vast, enormous; **c. philosophy**, doctrine of the evolution of the universe; **c. rays**, rays of extremely high penetrative power, thought to originate above the atmosphere.

COSMICAL [koz′mi-kal], *adj.* cosmic. COSMICALLY, *adv.* in relation to the universe, coinciding with the rising of the sun.

COSMO-, *pref.* the universe. [Gk.].

COSMOGONY [koz-mo′go-ni], *n.* the evolution or origin of the universe, the study of this; theory about this. COSMOGONIC [koz-mo-go′nik], *adj.* pertaining to c. COSMOGONIST [koz-mo′go-nist], *n.* student of c. [Gk.].

COSMOGRAPHY [koz-mo′gra-fi], *n.* a description of the universe; science which deals with this. COSMOGRAPHER, *n.* one who studies c. COSMOGRAPHICAL [koz-mo-gra′fi-kal], *adj.* relating to c. [Gk.].

COSMOLOGY [koz-mo′lo-ji], *n.* the study of the universe as a system; branch of metaphysics which deals with the ideas underlying the universe. COSMOLOGICAL [koz-mo-lo′ji-kal], *adj.* relating to c. COSMOLOGIST, *n.* one who studies c. [Gk.].

COSMOPOLITAN (1) [koz-mo-po′li-tan], *adj.* without national prejudices or attachments; universal, belonging to or common to the whole world; (*nat. hist.*) found all over the world. COSMOPOLITAN (2), *n.* citizen of the world, much-travelled person who is at home anywhere and unprejudiced by national feeling. COSMOPOLITANISM, *n.* quality or state of being a c. [Gk.].

COSMOPOLITE [koz-mo′po-līt], *n.* a cosmopolitan. COSMOPOLITICAL [koz-mo-po-li′ti-kal], *adj.* pertaining to international politics. COSMOPOLITISM, *n.* cosmopolitanism, universal outlook. [Gk.].

COSMOS [koz′mos], *n.* the universe as a well-planned system; planned and regulated system; harmony, order. [Gk.].

COSSACK [ko′sak], *n.* member of a tribe inhabiting the south-eastern parts of Russia, famed for their horsemanship. [Turk.].

COSSET [ko′sit], *v.t.* to fondle, pamper, indulge. [Uncert.].

COST (1) (*pret. and p.pt.* **cost**) [kost], *v.t.* to be purchasable or accomplishable at (a certain price), require or involve (a stated expenditure of money, effort etc.); cause to forfeit or lose, bring about some painful or detrimental experience; (*comm.*) calculate or determine the cost of. COST (2), *n.* price charged for an article, expense of some undertaking; (*leg.*) (*pl.*) expenses incurred in a lawsuit; (*fig.*) expenditure or sacrifice involved in the accomplishment of an object; pain, suffering, detriment; **c. price**, the price which the seller paid; **at all costs**, whatever happens. [OFr.].

COSTAL [kos′tal], *adj.* pertaining to the ribs. [L.].

CO-STAR (*pres.pt.* **co-starring**, *pret. and p.pt.* **co-starred**) [kō-stah(r)′], *v.i.* to share the chief rôles or parts in a play or film.

COSTARD [kos′tahd], *n.* large variety of apple. [Uncert.].

COSTATE(D) [kos′tāt(-id)], *adj.* (*bot. and zool.*) ribbed. [L.].

COSTER [kos′ter], *n.* costermonger.

COSTERMONGER [kos′ter-mung-ger], *n.* person hawking fruit and vegetables through the streets on a handcart or barrow. [COSTARD and MONGER].

COSTING [kos′ting], *n.* scientific calculation of the cost of, or analysis of expenses to be incurred in, a business undertaking.

COSTIVE [kos′tiv], *adj.* constipated; (*fig.*) sluggish. COSTIVENESS, *n.* condition of being c. [OFr. from L.].

COSTLINESS [kost′li-nes], *n.* quality of being costly.

COSTLY [kost′li], *adj.* of a high price, expensive; sumptuous, precious.

COSTMARY [kost′māer-i], *n.* (*bot.*) aromatic plant formerly used for flavouring ale. [Gk.].

COSTUME (1) [kos′tyōōm], *n.* fashion or mode of

The accent ′ after a syllable = stress (u-pon′). The mark ‾ over a vowel = length (ā in made; ō in bone).

dress, outer clothes, *esp.* when characteristic of a people, period etc.; period dress worn by actors in an historical play; two-piece female attire consisting usually of a short coat and a skirt; **c. piece,** play etc. in which the actors wear clothes characteristic of an earlier period of history; **c. ball,** fancy-dress ball. COSTUME (2), *v.t.* to dress, clothe in a c. COSTUMER, *n.* dealer in or maker of period costumes or fancy dress. [OFr. from L.].

COSTUMIER [kos-tyōō´mi-er], *n.* one who makes, sells or deals in costumes; dressmaker. [Fr.].

CO-SURETY [kō-shōōr´ti], *n.* surety with another.

COSY (1) [kō´zi], *adj.* snug, comfortable. COSY (2), COSEY, *n.* thick cover put over a teapot to keep it hot when the tea has been brewed. [~Norw.].

COT (1) [kot], *n.* shelter or protective covering; small cottage. [OE.].

COT (2), *n.* small bed; child's crib; bed in a children's hospital; (*naut.*) hammock-like bed suspended from beams for officers and sick persons. COT-CASE, invalid too ill to walk. [Hind.].

COTANGENT [kō-tan´jent], *n.* (*geom.*) the tangent of the complement of an arc or angle.

COTE [kot], *n.* dwelling or shed for small farm animals or birds. [OE.].

COTEMPORARY [kō-tem´po-ra-ri], *n. and adj.* contemporary.

CO-TENANT [kō-te´nant], *n.* joint tenant.

COTERIE [kō´te-rē], *n.* group or circle of people bound together in association by similarity of interests, outlook etc.; exclusive social set, clique. [Fr.].

COTERMINOUS [kō-tur´mi-nōōs], *adj.* having a common border or boundary. [L.].

COTHURNUS [kō-thur´nus], *n.* the high buskin worn by actors in Greek and later Roman tragedies; (*fig.*) tragedy. COTHURNATE(D), *adj.* buskined; (*fig.*) pertaining to tragedy. [Gk.].

CO-TIDAL [kō-tī´dal], *adj.* pertaining to the simultaneous occurrence of a high tide at different places; **c. line,** line on a map connecting all places at which high tide occurs at approximately the same time.

COTILLION, COTILLON [ko-til´yon], *n.* dance for eight persons; music to which it is danced. [Fr.].

COTONEASTER [ko-tō-ni-as´ter], *n.* (*bot.*) genus of small trees or shrubs bearing orange-red berries. [L.].

CO-TRUSTEE [kō-trus-tē´], *n.* joint trustee.

COTSWOLD [kots´wold], *n.* long-haired sheep occurring on the Cotswolds. [*Cotswold* Hills, Gloucestershire].

COTTA [ko´tah], *n.* (*eccles.*) short ecclesiastical vestment in the form of a surplice. [LL.].

COTTAGE [ko´tij], *n.* small dwelling-house in a village or the country; **c. loaf,** round loaf of bread with a small rounded lump of dough on top; **c. piano,** small upright piano; **c. pie,** dish of minced meat covered with mashed potatoes and baked. COTTAGED, *adj.* containing cottages. COTTAGER, *n.* person who lives in a c. [ME.].

COTTAR, COTTER (1) [ko´ter], *n.* (*Scots*) peasant or farm-labourer dwelling in a cottage attached to a farm in return for farm service. [MedL.].

COTTER (2), *n.* thin wedge, bolt or pin, driven through a slot or hole to fasten machinery. [Unkn.].

COTTON (1) [ko´ton], *n.* (*bot.*) plant of the genus *Gossypium*; the soft downy hairs on the seeds of this plant used in the manufacture of cloth and thread; thread made from these hairs; cloth woven from this thread. COTTON (2), *adj.* made of c. COTTON (3), *v.i.* (*fig.*) to be attracted by; be on terms of friendship with; **to c. on to,** to like; gather (an idea) with; **to c. (up) to,** to make friends with. [Arab.].

COTTON-CAKE [ko´ton-kāk], *n.* compressed cotton-seed, with the oil expressed, used as a food for cattle.

COTTON-FIELD [ko´ton-fēld], *n.* field where cotton is grown.

COTTON-GIN [ko´ton-jin], *n.* machine for separating the seeds from cotton.

COTTON-GRASS [ko´ton-grahs], *n.* (*bot.*) sedge of the genus *Eriophorum*, having long cottony heads.

COTTONIAN [ko-tō´ni-an], *adj.* pertaining to the library of Sir Robert *Cotton*, now in the British Museum.

COTTON-PLANT [ko´ton-plahnt], *n.* (*bot.*) a species of *Gossypium*.

COTTON-PRESS [ko´ton-pres], *n.* machine in which cotton is compressed into bales.

COTTON-SEED [ko´ton-sēd], *n.* seed of the cotton.

COTTON-WASTE [ko´ton-wāst], *n.* refuse from the manufacture of cotton, used for cleaning machinery.

COTTON-WOOL [ko-ton-wōōl´], *n.* the thick fluffy mass of the hairs of the cotton-plant after cleansing and extraction of seeds, used as packing and for surgical purposes.

COTTONY [ko´to-ni], *adj.* soft, downy; resembling cotton.

COTYLEDON [ko-ti-lē´don], *n.* (*bot.*) the seed-leaves of the embryo plant. COTYLEDONAL, *adj.* (*bot.*) in the form of a seed-leaf. COTYLEDONOUS, *adj.* (*bot.*) relating to cotyledons; having a seed-leaf. [Gk.].

COUCH (1) [kowch], *n.* long piece of furniture on which a person may recline and rest, sofa; (*poet.*) bed; place for rest and sleep, lair; (*paint.*) first coat of colour covering the surface to be painted; (*malting*) framework on which a mass of grain germinates. COUCH (2), *v.t.* to lay down as in rest; hold a spear or lance ready for immediate use; bend, lower; express in speech or writing; (*surg.*) perform the operation for removal of a cataract from the eye; (*malting*) heap grain on the floor to germinate; *v.i.* to lie down, as on a c., recline; crouch down; stoop; lie hidden. [OFr.].

COUCHANT [kow´chant], *adj.* (*her.*) lying down with the head lifted up. [Fr.].

COUCH-GRASS [kowch´grahs], *n.* (*bot.*) a creeping weed. [~QUITCH].

COUCHING [kow´ching], *n.* act of one who couches; (in needlework) the laying down of one or more threads held by single transverse stitches at certain intervals.

COUGAR [kōō´gah(r)], *n.* large South American cat-like quadruped, the puma. [Native].

COUGH (1) [kof], *n.* a sudden and forcible expulsion of air from the lungs, accompanied by an abrupt harsh sound, and caused by temporary irritation of the windpipe, catarrh etc.; diseased or inflamed condition of the larynx or windpipe causing frequent bouts of coughing. COUGH (2), *v.i.* to utter a c., or a series of coughs periodically; clear the throat audibly; **to c. up,** to get rid of by coughing; (*coll.*) reveal, disclose information, pay up, under compulsion. [~OE.].

COUGH-DROP [kof´drop], *n.* medicinal lozenge sucked to alleviate a cough; (*slang*) a "character."

COULD [kōōd], *pret.* of CAN.

COULEUR-DE-ROSE [kōō-ler-de-rōz´], *adj.* rose-coloured; (*fig.*) pleasant. [Fr.].

COULISSE [kōō-lēs´], *n.* a slide along which the side-scenes of a stage run; the wings of a stage. [Fr.].

COULOIR [kōō´lwah(r)], *n.* deep cleft or gully in the side of a mountain. [Fr.].

COULOMB [kōō-lom´], *n.* (*elect.*) the unit of quantity at the rate of one ampère in one second. [C. A. de *Coulomb*, French physicist].

COULTER, COLTER [kōl´ter], *n.* the front vertical blade of a plough immediately before the share. [OE. from L.].

COUNCIL [kown´sil], *n.* assembly summoned together for deliberation and consultation, or to perform some executive or legislative function; group of men elected to carry on the local government of a borough, city etc.; (*fig.*) discussion of proposed action; **Privy C.,** select group of persons appointed to advise the Sovereign in the administration of the government upon certain occasions. [L.].

COUNCIL-BOARD [kown´sil-bawd], *n.* table round which a council meets.

COUNCIL-CHAMBER [kown´sil-chām-ber], *n.* room in which the members of a council officially and habitually meet.

COUNCIL HOUSE [kown´sil-hows], *n.* dwelling-house erected by a local authority.

COUNCILLOR [kown´sil-er], *n.* member of a council.

COUNCILMAN [kown´sil-man], *n.* member of a city or borough council.

COUNCIL SCHOOL [kown-sil-skōōl´], *n.* school supported by a local authority.

COUNSEL (1) [kown´sel], *n.* deliberation, consultation; advice, direction; legal adviser, barrister retained to plead his client's case in a court of law; the group of advocates or barristers who conduct the prosecution and defence in a law-suit; **Queen's C.,** English barrister acting as Counsel to the Crown, and thus taking precedence; **to keep one's c.,** to keep one's plans secret. COUNSEL (2) (*pres.pt.* COUNSELLING, *pret. and p.pt.* COUNSELLED), *v.t.* to advise, recommend a certain course of action. [L.].

COUNSELLOR [kown´se-ler], *n.* adviser; barrister, advocate or counsel; rank in the diplomatic service immediately below that of minister. COUNSELLOR-SHIP, n. the office of a c. [OFr. from L.].

COUNT (1) [kownt], n. a foreign title of nobility about equivalent to an English earl, but often merely honorary. [OFr. from L.].

COUNT (2), n. act of numbering or reckoning; the total counted; account, reckoning, consideration; (leg.) a charge in an indictment setting forth a cause for prosecution; (cotton spinning) number of hanks equal to a pound weight; (boxing) process of counting out; **on all counts**, in every respect. [AFr. from L.].

COUNT (3), v.t. to name the numerals in a correct sequence up to a stated number; reckon, sum up the total number of things; calculate; take into account, include; consider, value, esteem; v.i. to repeat the numerals in their correct order; enter into consideration in determining or reckoning something; be of value, be important, help; be of some consequence; keep the number or score of anything; **to c. for**, to be considered as; **to c. on**, to rely upon, expect; **to c. out**, (parl.) to adjourn a meeting after counting those present, and finding that there are not enough to constitute a quorum; (boxing) declare a boxer defeated upon his failure to stand up within ten seconds of the referee's beginning to count. [AFr. from L.].

COUNTENANCE (1) [kown'ti-nans], n. the face, facial expression, the features; composure, demeanour; encouragement; patronage; **to keep one's c.**, to appear unruffled by any expression of emotion; **out of c.**, disconcerted, confounded; **to put out of c.**, to abash; **to lose c.**, to show disappointment or dejection. COUNTENANCE (2), v.t. to favour, view with approval; stomach; tolerate, permit. [L.].

COUNTER (1) [kown'ter], n. small thin disk used as a stake or as a means of reckoning in card or other games; long, flat-topped table or desk behind which shopkeepers, bankers and others stand to carry on exchange of goods and money with the public; one who counts.

COUNTER (2), n. (naut.) the curved part of a ship's stern; the part of a horse lying between the shoulders and under the neck; stiff leather round the heel of a boot or shoe. [Unkn.].

COUNTER (3), n. (fencing) circular parry made without changing the position of the hand; (boxing) blow dealt in answer to, and at the same time as, that of an opponent; (coursing) the opposite direction to that taken by the game; (mus.) an under part in contrast to the principal voice part. COUNTER (4), adj. opposite, contrary, in opposition. COUNTER (5), adv. in the opposite direction to, contrary to, against, in antagonism to. COUNTER (6), v.t. and i. to give a return blow; oppose, reply in opposition to; (boxing) reply with a c. [L.].

COUNTERACT [kown-te-rakt'], v.t. to have a counter effect upon, neutralize, check, mitigate, hinder, defeat. COUNTERACTION, n. contrary action. COUNTERACTIVE (1), adj. tending to c. COUNTER-ACTIVE (2), n. anything which counteracts.

COUNTER-AGENT [kown'te-rā-jent], n. that which counteracts.

COUNTER-ATTACK (1) [kown'te-ra-tak], n. attack made in reply to an enemy advance, with the object of regaining lost ground. COUNTER-ATTACK (2), v.t. and i. to make a c.

COUNTER-ATTRACTION [kown'ter-a-trak-shn], n. rival or competing attraction.

COUNTERBALANCE (1) [kown-ter-ba'lans], n. weight used to balance another; (fig.) force or power neutralizing another. COUNTERBALANCE (2), v.t. to weigh against with an equal weight or power; neutralize the effect of, make up for.

COUNTERCHANGE [kown-ter-chānj'], v.t. and i. to interchange, transpose; (her.) reverse the colouring, chequer.

COUNTERCHARGE (1) [kown'ter-chahj], n. (milit.) charge made in retaliation; attack or accusation in which the attacker or accuser is charged in reply. COUNTERCHARGE (2), v.t. to make a c.

COUNTERCHECK [kown'ter-chek], n. a double check.

COUNTERCLAIM (1) [kown'ter-klām], n. (leg.) claim made by a defendant against a plaintiff. COUNTERCLAIM (2), v.t. to make a c.

COUNTER-CLOCKWISE [kown-ter-klok'wiz], adj. in a circular direction or motion opposite to that of the hands of a clock.

COUNTER-CURRENT [kown'ter-ku-rent], n. current running in an opposite direction to another.

COUNTER-DIE [kown'ter-di], n. the upper stamp of a die.

COUNTER-ESPIONAGE [kown-ter-es'pi-o-nahzh], n. system of spy-work designed to frustrate the activities of enemy spies.

COUNTER-EVIDENCE [kown-ter-e'vi-dens], n. evidence offered to offset other evidence.

COUNTERFEIT (1) [kown'ter-fēt], adj. forged, not genuine, made in skilful imitation in order to deceive; spurious, false. COUNTERFEIT (2), n. a forgery, anything made, usually dishonestly, in skilful imitation of another article; cheat, impostor, fraud. COUNTERFEIT (3), v.t. to feign, simulate, pretend; make in imitation of, with a view to passing it off as genuine. COUNTERFEITED, adj. forged, imitated, assumed. COUNTERFEITER, n. forger. [OFr.].

COUNTERFOIL [kown'ter-foil], n. the counterpart of a document such as a cheque, postal order etc., retained by the giver or issuer as a record.

COUNTER-IRRITANT [kown-ter-i'ri-tant], n. (med.) substance used to produce counter-irritation. COUNTER-IRRITATION, n. (med.) production of a slight secondary irritation in order to relieve the main irritation.

COUNTERJUMPER [kown'ter-jum-per], n. (coll.) shop assistant.

COUNTERMAND (1) [kown-ter-mahnd'], v.t. to reverse a command; prohibit, cancel or revoke by countermand. COUNTERMAND (2), n. order cancelling a previous order; (leg.) act which nullifies a previous act. [OFr.].

COUNTERMARCH (1) [kown'ter-mahch], n. (milit.) a marching back again; change of the wings or face of a battalion, so as to bring the right to the left, or the front to the rear. COUNTERMARCH (2), v.i. to march back again, perform a c.

COUNTERMARK (1) [kown'ter-mahk], n. additional mark placed on goods for greater security; hall-mark of the Goldsmiths' Company put on silver or gold articles in addition to that of the maker; artificial cavity made in the teeth of horses to disguise their age. COUNTERMARK (2), v.t. to mark with a c.

COUNTERMINE (1) [kown'ter-mīn], n. (milit.) mine constructed by the besieged to intercept and destroy one made by the attackers; (nav.) mine laid to blow up an enemy's mines; (fig.) plot to defeat another plot. COUNTERMINE (2), v.t. and i. to make or sink a c.; (fig.) frustrate by a counterplot.

COUNTER-MOVE [kown'ter-mōōv], n. move in reply to, or to check, another.

COUNTERPANE [kown'ter-pān], n. coverlet for a bed. [OFr.].

COUNTERPART [kown'ter-paht], n. part corresponding to another part; (leg.) the opposite and subsidiary part of an indenture; duplicate, copy; complementary part; (mus.) part written as an accompaniment to another part; person or thing resembling another.

COUNTERPLEA [kown'ter-plē], n. (leg.) reply to a plea or request.

COUNTERPLOT (1) [kown'ter-plot], n. plot to frustrate another, subsidiary plot of a play. COUNTERPLOT (2) (pres.pt. COUNTERPLOTTING, pret. and p.pt. COUNTERPLOTTED), v.t. and i. to defeat with a c.; devise a c.

COUNTERPOINT [kown'ter-point], n. style of musical composition with a melody or melodies written above or below a given melody so as to harmonize with it.

COUNTERPOISE (1) [kown'ter-poiz], n. weight or force sufficient to balance another; condition of equilibrium; (fig.) neutralizing or counterbalancing force; (radio) insulated wire(s) placed beneath an aerial. COUNTERPOISE (2), v.t. and i. to balance by a c.; bring into a state of equilibrium; act against with equal power or force. [OFr.].

COUNTER-PROOF [kown'ter-prōōf], n. (engraving) an impression taken from one newly printed. COUNTER-PROVE, v.t. to take a c. from.

COUNTER-REVOLUTION [kown-ter-re-vo-lōō'-shn], n. revolution, in opposition to one which has taken place, to restore a former state of affairs.

COUNTER-SECURITY [kown-ter-si-kyōō'ri-ti], n. a security given to one who is security for another.

COUNTERSIGN (1) [kown'ter-sin], n. soldier's password or watchword to be given when challenged by the guard; secret signal in reply to another; countermark. COUNTERSIGN (2), v.t. to sign a document already signed by another person; (fig.) confirm, attest.

COUNTERSIGNATURE [kown-ter-sig'na-tyōōr],

n. signature added to a signed document for confirmation or ratification.

COUNTERSINK (1) (*pret.* **countersank**, *p.pt.* **countersunk**) [kown′ter-singk], *v.t.* to bevel the edge of (a hole) to receive the head of a screw etc.; sink (a screw etc.) in such a bevelled depression. COUNTERSINK (2), *n.* drill or bit for countersinking.

COUNTER-TENOR [kown-ter-te′ner], *n.* (*mus.*) high tenor part sung by a male alto voice; male alto voice; singer possessing such a voice.

COUNTER-TURN [kown′ter-tern], *n.* a turn in the reverse direction; unexpected development in a plot of a play at the climax.

COUNTERVAIL (1) [kown-ter-vāl′], *v.t. and i.* to act against with equal effect or power; neutralize the effect of. COUNTERVAIL (2), *n.* an equivalent, counterbalance. COUNTERVAILING, *adj.* equalizing, counterbalancing.

COUNTESS [kown′tes], *n.* wife or widow of an earl or count, holder of an equivalent title in her own right; roofing slate 20 by 10 in. [AFr.].

COUNTING-HOUSE [kown′ting-hows], *n.* business office devoted to the keeping of accounts.

COUNTLESS [kown′les], *adj.* innumerable.

COUNT-OUT [kownt-owt′], *n.* premature close of a debate, meeting etc., when it is found that there are not enough members present to form a quorum.

COUNTRIFIED [kun′tri-fīd], *adj.* resembling or belonging to the country, rural, rustic.

COUNTRIFY [kun′tri-fī], *v.t.* to make rustic.

COUNTRY (1) [kun′tri], *n.* land or territory known by a particular name, possessing clearly established limits and inhabited by a particular nation; the nation, inhabitants of such a land; one's native land; the rural part of the land characterized by the absence of industrial settlement; the physical characteristics of an area of land; (*naut.*) a particular region of the sea; (*fig.*) fields of learning; (*cricket*) the outfield; **to go to the c.,** to resort to a General Election. COUNTRY (2), *adj.* rural, rustic, pertaining to, or peculiar to, a c. [OFr. from LL.].

COUNTRY CLUB [kun′tri-klub], *n.* club with premises and land in the country for the pursuit of sport.

COUNTRY DANCE [kun-tri-dahns′], *n.* dance in which the partners are arranged opposite to each other in lines at the start.

COUNTRY GENTLEMAN [kun-tri-jen′tl-man], *n.* formerly a man of the upper classes living upon his estate in the country.

COUNTRYMAN [kun′tri-man], *n.* a compatriot, member of the same nation; one who lives in the country, a rustic.

COUNTRY MEMBER [kun′tri-mem-ber], *n.* member of a social or sports club in town who, being resident in the country, is admitted at a reduced subscription.

COUNTRY PARTY [kun′tri-pah-ti], *n.* a political party representing agricultural interests.

COUNTRY SEAT [kun-tri-sēt′], *n.* a country house.

COUNTRYSIDE [kun′tri-sīd], *n.* rural district, expanse of country.

COUNTRYWOMAN [kun′tri-wŏŏ-man], *n.* a female compatriot, woman who dwells in the country.

COUNTY (1) [kown′ti], *n.* an administrative division of a country, a shire; the inhabitants of a county, landed gentry of a county; **c. borough,** borough whose local administration is independent of the county in which it lies; **c. palatine,** county whose lord formerly possessed royal privilege; **c. town,** the administrative centre of the county. COUNTY (2), *adj.* pertaining to a c. or to the landed gentry. [AFr. from L.].

COUNTY COURT [kown′ti-kawt], *n.* local civil court used chiefly for the recovery of small debts etc. COUNTY-COURT, *v.t.* (*coll.*) to sue in the c.

COUP [kŏŏ], *n.* a sudden and drastic action; strikingly successful business deal or gamble; **c. d'état,** (*pol.*) sudden forcible change of government by illegal methods; **c. de grâce,** finishing blow; **c. d'oeil,** rapid general survey and appreciation of a situation or scene; **c. de théâtre,** surprise turn of events or sensational action; theatrical success. [Fr.].

COUPE, coupé [kŏŏ′pā], *n.* short four-wheeled closed carriage for two; closed two-doored motor-car; end-compartment of a railway carriage with seats on one side only. [Fr.].

COUPEE, coupée [kŏŏ′pā], *n.* dance-step in which one leg is stationary while the other moves forward or backward. [Fr.].

COUPLE (1) [ku′pl], *n.* two similar things connected or related to each other; two of a kind; pair, brace; husband and wife; betrothed man and woman; two dance-partners; (*mech.*) two equal parallel forces acting in opposite directions upon a body; (*arch.*) principal rafter in a roof. COUPLE (2), *v.t. and i.* to fasten together, connect; associate, join; copulate; unite in marriage, mate. [OFr. from L.].

COUPLER [kup′ler], *n.* anything which couples; mechanical device for coupling two parts of machinery.

COUPLET [kup′let], *n.* two consecutive lines of verse of the same metre which rhyme and form a complete unit; (*music*) two notes introduced for cross-rhythm in a passage of triple rhythm and having the same time value as a triplet. [Fr.].

COUPLING [kup′ling], *n.* that which couples or connects; act of fastening together; apparatus for connecting together parts of systems of shafting of machinery; contrivance which joins one railway carriage to another; (*elect.*) connexion of two circuits so that a change of current in one affects the other inductively. COUPLING-BOX, metal box connecting the ends of two shafts. COUPLING-PIN, bolt used to couple together railway carriages and other machinery.

COUPON [kŏŏ′pon], *n.* detachable piece of a ticket or document; detachable certificate attached to bearer bonds to be presented for payment of interest due; detachable ticket which may be exchanged for goods etc.; ration ticket for clothing, food, petrol etc.; part of an advertisement in a periodical or newspaper, to be returned to the advertiser in exchange for a sample of goods advertised, or to be used as an entry form for a competition; entry form for a football pool. [Fr.].

COUPON-FREE [kŏŏ-pon-frē′], *adj.* requiring no coupons for purchase, unrationed.

COURAGE [ku′rij], *n.* strength of character to resist danger, hardship or suffering; bravery, pluck; **Dutch c.,** temporary c. acquired as a result of drink. [OFr.].

COURAGEOUS [ku-rā′jŏŏs], *adj.* displaying or requiring courage. COURAGEOUSLY, *adv.* in c. fashion. COURAGEOUSNESS, *n.* quality of being c.

COURANTE [kŏŏ-rahnt′], *n.* quick French dance in triple time with a regular flowing rhythm; music to which this was performed. [Fr.].

COURIER [kŏŏ′ri-er], *n.* express messenger, bearer of special dispatches; attendant who makes all arrangements on a conducted foreign tour. [Fr.].

COURSE (1) [kaws], *n.* continuous progress or trend; the route traversed (of a moving body), direction or path of motion; ground over which a race is run; specially prepared tract of land over which certain games (e.g. golf) are played; channel along which a moving body flows; the duration of a period of time; method of procedure, line of action; regular succession of related events, a sequence, progress; one of a succession of divisions of a meal; (*arch.*) a continuous layer of bricks at the same level throughout the whole length of a building; race between two greyhounds, both of which are chasing a hare; (*pl.*) (*naut.*) the lower squaresails, the staysails on the lower masts, the main staysails of brigs and schooners; a point of the compass to which a ship sails; (*pl.*) (*vulgar*) menstrual discharge; **in due c.,** at the proper time, in a natural succession; **as a matter of c.,** automatically. COURSE (2), *v.t. and i.* to hunt; hunt game with greyhounds; (*fig.*) pursue, traverse; race or move quickly through. [OFr. from L.].

COURSER [kaw′ser], *n.* swift horse; (*poet.*) horse; one who courses.

COURSING [kaw′sing], *n.* form of sport in which greyhounds hunt hares by sight.

COURT (1) [kawt], *n.* paved yard surrounded by houses and usually entered by a narrow passage; open space or quadrangle enclosed by buildings; large mansion or manor; enclosed area or building in which certain ball games may be played; lawn or hard, level surface on which lawn tennis may be played; residence of a sovereign and royal family; official function at which people formally meet the sovereign; place where judicial inquiries are held or cases heard; the judges, magistrates or officials assembled for administering justice; session of such an assembly; solicitous attention to gain favour, amorous attentions; **to put oneself out of c.,** (*fig.*) to behave in such a way as to forfeit favourable consideration. COURT (2), *v.t. and i.* to endeavour to please or gain the favour of, by assiduous attention or deference; pay amorous attentions to, woo;

ōō is pronounced as in f*oo*d; ŏŏ as in h*oo*d; th as in *th*ink; TH as in *th*at; zh as in a*z*ure.   ~ = related to.

(*fig.*) act in such a way as to merit, run the risk of. [OFr. from L.].

COURT CARD [kawt′kahd], *n.* king, queen or knave in playing cards.

COURT CIRCULAR [kawt-sur′kyōō-ler], *n.* daily bulletin describing the activities of the royal court.

COURT-CRAFT [kawt′krahft], *n.* skill in moving about a tennis-court.

COURT-DRESS [kawt′dres], *n.* formal dress prescribed for appearance at a royal court.

COURTEOUS [kur′ti-ŏŏs], *adj.* courtly; displaying courtesy; polite, well-mannered. COURTEOUSLY, *adv.* in c. fashion.

COURTESAN [kaw′ti-zan], *n.* woman of easy virtue, prostitute. [Span.].

COURTESY [kur′ti-si], *n.* politeness of manners and good breeding, accompanied by kindness, dignity and considerateness; favour; a respectful act; **c. title**, title given by social custom to certain persons not strictly entitled to it; **tenure by c.**, (*leg.*) tenure by which a man holds certain kinds of property inherited by his wife after her death. [OFr.].

COURT-FOOL [kawt′fŏŏl′], *n.* buffoon or jester formerly kept at a royal court for amusement.

COURT-GUIDE [kawt-gīd′], *n.* directory of persons presented at court, or of the upper classes.

COURT-HOUSE [kawt′hows], *n.* building in which courts of law are held.

COURTIER [kaw′ti-er], *n.* person attached to a royal court; exceedingly deferential person, flatterer. [OFr.].

COURTING [kaw′ting], *n.* courtship.

COURTLINESS [kawt′li-nes], *n.* quality of being courtly.

COURTLY [kawt′li], *adj.* pertaining to or characteristic of a court; dignified, well-bred, refined.

COURT-MARTIAL (1) (*pl.* courts-martial) [kawt-mah′shl], *n.* tribunal of naval or military officers legally authorized to conduct an inquiry into and to punish offences against naval or military law; trial of a sailor, soldier or airman by this means. COURT-MARTIAL (2) (*pres.pt.* COURT-MARTIALLING, *pret.* and *p.pt.* COURT-MARTIALLED), *v.t.* to try a person by c.

COURT-PLASTER [kawt′plahs-ter], *n.* sticking plaster consisting of coloured or transparent silk applied to cuts etc.

COURT-ROOM [kawt′rŏŏm], *n.* room in which a court is held.

COURTSHIP [kawt′ship], *n.* the period of wooing with a view to marriage.

COURTYARD [kawt′yahd], *n.* large paved court wholly or partially enclosed by a building or buildings entered from it.

COUSIN [ku′zn], *n.* the offspring of one's uncle or aunt; †kinsman or distant relative; formal royal title of address to another sovereign or to a peer of the realm; **c. german**, child of an uncle or aunt, (*fig.*) closely related thing. COUSINSHIP, *n.* the relationship of cousins. [Fr.].

COVE (1) [kōv], *n.* small creek or inlet; cavern; narrow gap in the side of a mountain; (*arch.*) concave moulding or vault. COVE (2), *v.t.* to arch over in concave form. [OE.].

COVE (3), *n.* (*slang*) a fellow. [Uncert.].

COVENANT (1) [ku′ve-nant], *n.* a mutual agreement, solemn undertaking; (*leg.*) signed agreement in writing between two parties with respect to a promise; clause of a legal document containing such a promise; **Solemn League and C.**, (*hist.*) a contract between the Church of Scotland and the English Parliament in 1643 recognizing Presbyterianism in Scotland in return for military help against the King. COVENANT (2), *v.t.* and *i.* to grant by a c.; bind oneself by a c. COVENANTED, *adj.* pledged or bound by c. [OFr. from L.].

COVENANTER [ku′ve-nan-ter], *n.* person who covenants; supporter of the National Covenant of Scotland or the Solemn League and Covenant.

COVENTRY [ku′ven-tri], *n.* **to send to C.**, to ostracize, ignore deliberately, refuse to talk to. [*Coventry*, Warwickshire].

COVER (1) [ku′ver], *v.t.* to place one thing over another so as to hide it; spread, lie over; clothe; lay down a sum of money equal to one offered or wagered; place something in front of or over an object to protect it, shield; protect against possibility of loss; allow for, be adequate for, provide for; stain or splash extensively, envelop; travel (a certain distance); (*fig.*) treat of, include; overwhelm; conceal, refrain from disclosing; level a firearm at; (of animals) mate with, incubate; (*coll.*) report (a meeting

etc.); **to remain covered**, to keep one's hat on one's head; **to c. in**, to fill in (a hole); **to c. up**, (*boxing*) to adopt a defensive attitude, and protect one's vulnerable parts. COVER (2), *n.* anything made to fit over and c. an object, lid, wrapper, case, screen; anything affording protection or hiding; (*pl.*) dining utensils laid for each person at a meal; outer boards of a book; (*comm.*) money deposited against loss which could be sustained by a fall in prices; (*cricket*) cover-point; (*fig.*) pretence, cloak; (*coll.*) press report of a public meeting or social function. [OFr. from L.].

COVERAGE [ku′ve-rij], *n.* (*orig. U.S.*) the risks covered by an insurance policy; the aggregate of press reports of a particular event.

COVER-CHARGE [ku′ver-chahj], *n.* basic charge made in a restaurant irrespective of what is consumed.

COVERED WAY, COVERT WAY [ku′verd-wā], *n.* roofed passage or corridor.

COVERING [ku′ve-ring], *n.* that which covers; case, cover.

COVERING LETTER [ku-ve-ring-le′ter], *n.* letter accompanying a document in explanation or amplification of it.

COVERLET [ku′ver-lit], *n.* outer cover or quilt of a bed; any cover.

COVER-POINT [ku′ver-point], *n.* (*cricket*) (the position of) the fieldsman behind and (for a right-handed batsman) to the right of point.

COVERT (1) [ku′vert], *adj.* disguised, surreptitious; **feme c.**, (*leg.*) married woman as being under the protection of her husband. COVERT (2) [ku′ver(t)], *n.* shelter, hiding-place (*esp.* for game); small feather covering parts of larger feathers in birds; **to draw a c.**, to search thickets etc. for game or for a fox. COVERTLY, *adv.* in c. fashion. COVERTNESS, *n.* condition of being c. [OFr.].

COVERT COAT [ku′vert-kōt], *n.* short, light, waterproof overcoat.

COVERTURE [ku′ver-tyŏŏr], *n.* covering, shelter; disguise, veil; state of a married woman. [OFr.].

COVERT WAY, see COVERED-WAY.

COVET [ku′vit], *v.t.* and *i.* to desire earnestly and unlawfully, to long for, hanker after. COVETABLE, *adj.* liable to be coveted.

COVETOUS [ku′vi-tŏŏs], *adj.* inordinately desirous of possessing, excessively eager to acquire, avaricious, grasping. COVETOUSLY, *adv.* in a c. manner. COVETOUSNESS, *n.* state of being c.

COVEY [ku′vi], *n.* group or brood of partridges; (*fig.*) company, party, family. [OFr.].

COVING [kō′ving], *n.* (*arch.*) arched part of a roof; curved part of a vault or ceiling; curved sides of a fireplace.

COW (1) [kow], *n.* female of the ox or other animals of the genus *Bos*, *esp.* when domesticated; female of certain other animals, as elephant, whale and seal; **c. gun**, (*slang*) large naval gun. SEA-COW, marine mammal of the order *Sirenia*. [OE.].

COW (2), *v.t.* to intimidate with threats or bullying; reduce to a state of perpetual fear and docility. [OIcel.].

COWARD (1) [kow′erd], *n.* person destitute of courage; one who is afraid to face danger or hardship. COWARD (2), *adj.* lacking courage, faint-hearted. [OFr.].

COWARDICE [kow′er-dis], *n.* want of courage, ignoble fear.

COWARDLY [kow′erd-li], *adj. and adv.* like a coward, faint-hearted, craven; in the manner of a coward. COWARDLINESS, *n.* condition of being c.

COW-BELL [kow′bel], *n.* bell fastened to a cow's neck to enable her to be found easily.

COWBOY [kow′boi], *n.* (*U.S.*) man employed in looking after cattle grazing on a ranch.

COWCATCHER [kow′ka-cher], *n.* (*U.S.*) strong framework or grating fitted to the front of a locomotive to clear obstructions from the rails, and as a safety-guard.

COWER [kowr], *v.i.* to crouch or gather oneself into a squat posture through fear, cold etc.; shrink back or cringe in fear. [OIcel.].

COW-HEEL [kow′hēl], *n.* the stewed edible foot of a cow.

COWHERD [kow′herd], *n.* one who looks after cows.

COW-HIDE (1) [kow′hīd], *n.* leather made of the hide of a cow; coarse riding-whip of this. COW-HIDE (2), *v.t.* to flog with a c.

COWHOUSE [kow′hows], *n.* cowshed.

COWL [kowl], *n.* hooded garment worn by monks;

The accent ′ after a syllable = stress (u-pon′)   The mark ⁻ over a vowel = length (ā in made; ō in bone).

the hood itself; hood-shaped contrivance attached to the top of a chimney-pot; wire cap of a locomotive funnel; hood-shaped ventilator on the deck of a large ship; the structure of shaped panelling in front of the radiator of a motor-car. COWLED, *adj.* provided with a c. [OE.].

COWLICK [kow′lik], *n.* tuft of hair straying over the forehead.

COWLING [kow′ling], *n.* (*aeron.*) the casing over radiators or air-cooled cylinders to direct the air-stream.

COWMAN [kow′man], *n.* cowherd.

COW-PUNCHER [kow′pun-cher], *n.* (*U.S.*) (*coll.*) cowboy.

CO-WORKER [kō-wur′ker], *n.* one who works along with another.

COW-PARSLEY [kow′pahs-li], *n.* (*bot.*) an umbelliferous plant, *Anthriscus sylvestris.*

COW-PARSNIP [kow′pahs-nip], *n.* (*bot.*) plant of the genus *Heracleum.*

COW-POX [kow′poks], *n.* vaccine disease in which pustules appear on the teats of a cow, the pus from these pustules formerly used for vaccination.

COWRY, COWRIE [kow′ri], *n.* small shell used as native money in parts of India and Africa. [Hind.].

COWSHED [kow′shed], *n.* building in which cows are housed.

COWSLIP [kow′slip], *n.* plant of the primrose family with fragrant yellow flowers. [OE.].

COX (1) [koks], *n.* steersman of an oar-propelled racing boat. COX (2), *v.t.* to act as c. to. [COXSWAIN].

COXA (*pl.* coxae) [kok′sah, kok′sē], *n.* (*anat.*) the hip-joint; (*entom.*) joint next to the body on an insect's leg. COXAL, *adj.* of, or pertaining to, the c. COXALGIA [kok-sal′ji-ah], *n.* disease of the hip-joint. [L.].

COXCOMB [koks′kōm], *n.* †cap resembling a cock's comb, formerly worn by jesters; conceited dandy, vain, swaggering fop. COXCOMBRY [koks′kōm-ri], *n.* the manners or behaviour of a c., conceited affectation. [COCK and COMB].

COXSWAIN [kok′sn], *n.* sailor in charge of the steering of a boat, leader and helmsman of a lifeboat; cox. COXSWAINLESS, *adj.* (*rowing*) having no cox. [COCK and SWAIN].

COY [koi], *adj.* modest, bashful, shy. COYLY, *adv.* in a c. fashion. COYNESS, *n.* condition of being c. [Ofr. from L.].

COYOTE [kō-yō′ti], *n.* the prairie wolf. [Mexican].

COZ [kuz], *n.* (*archaic*, as a term of address) cousin.

COZEN [ku′zn], *v.t. and i.* to cheat, defraud. COZEN-AGE, *n.* deceit, cheating. COZENER, *n.* one who cozens. [Uncert.].

CRAB (1) [krab], *n.* ten-footed crustacean having a shallow, rounded body and strong claws like nippers; one of the signs of the Zodiac; (*pl.*) crab-lice; kind of capstan, the drum of a portable winch; **to catch a c.,** to make a faulty rowing stroke so that the handle of the oar is forced against the rower, causing him to lose balance. CRAB (2), *v.t.* (*falconry*) to scratch, claw; find fault with unfairly, disparage, carp at. [OE.].

CRAB (3), *n.* the small sour fruit of the wild apple tree; the tree itself; (*fig.*) cross-tempered, embittered person. [ME.].

CRABBED [kra′bid], *adj.* sour, peevish, embittered; difficult to read, badly-formed; difficult to understand. CRABBEDLY, *adv.* in a c. fashion. CRABBED-NESS, *n.* condition of being c.

CRABBY [kra′bi], *adj* perplexing; peevish.

CRAB-LOUSE (*pl.* crab-lice) [krab′lows], *n.* the body louse.

CRAB-POT [krab′pot], *n.* wickerwork receptacle for catching crabs.

CRACK (1) [krak], *n.* sudden, loud report; sharp blow; chink, long narrow opening or slit; slight fissure or break in a brittle substance, usually marked by a thin line of fracture; an instant, very short interval of time; (*slang*) expert performer; (*slang*) an attempt, endeavour to accomplish something; (*slang*) wisecrack; **c. of dawn,** daybreak; **c. of doom,** judgment day. CRACK (2), *adj.* expert; champion; first-rate. CRACK (3), *v.t.* to fracture, break by pressure; cause a c. in; flick or let off with a c.; (*coll.*) tell (a joke); decompose (petroleum) by heat or pressure into lighter hydrocarbons; (*slang*) hit with a c.; **to c. up,** (*coll.*) boost, boast of; **to c. a crib,** (*slang*) to burgle a house; **to c. on,** (*naut.*) to crowd on all sail; *v.i.* to break into a c.; (of a male voice) undergo a lowering in tone at puberty;

(of a voice) become hoarse and broken; wilt, snap; (*pass.*) (*coll.*) be crazy. [OE.].

CRACK-BRAINED [krak′brānd], *adj.* crazy, senseless.

CRACKED [krakt], *adj.* containing cracks, split, broken; harsh, dissonant, untuneful; (*coll.*) slightly crazy, weak in the head; damaged, containing flaws.

CRACKER [kra′ker], *n.* small explosive firework emitting a series of loud reports when lit; firework enclosed in a cylinder of brightly coloured paper, which explodes with a crack when the ends are pulled; thin, dry, flaky biscuit; (*U.S.*) any biscuit; (*pl.*) tool for cracking nuts.

CRACKERJACK [kra′ker-jak], *n. and adj.* (*slang*) (person or thing) of unusual excellence.

CRACKERS [kra′kerz], *adj.* (*slang*) mad, crazy.

CRACKJAW [krak′jaw], *n.* (*coll.*) a tongue-twister; hard sort of toffee.

CRACKLE (1) [kra′kl], *v.i.* to make a crackling sound. CRACKLE (2), *n.* a series of faint crisp reports rapidly sounding; china, porcelain or glassware whose surface is ornamented with a tracery of small cracks. [*Dim.* of CRACK (3)].

CRACKLING [krak′ling], *n.* the making of frequently repeated crackles; crisp rind of roast pork.

CRACKNEL [krak′nel], *n.* variety of light, dry, flaky biscuit. [Fr.].

CRACKSMAN [kraks′man], *n.* (*slang*) burglar.

CRADLE (1) [krā′dl], *n.* little cot or crib, usually on rockers, for a baby; anything resembling this; (*fig.*) infancy; birthplace, place of origin; (*naut.*) rigid bedstead for a wounded seaman; basket suspended from a rope in which people are swung ashore from wrecks; supporting frame placed under a ship during construction or repairs; small movable framework slung from pulleys fastened to scaffolding, and used by steeplejacks etc.; (*surg.*) protective framework for a broken or injured limb; chisel with one bevelled side; rocking trough for washing gold free of earth. CRADLE (2), *v.t. and i.* to lay or rock in a c.; soothe or lull as in a c.; rear, nurse from birth; (*min.*) wash gold in a c. [OE.].

CRADLING [krād′ling], *n.* (*arch.*) a framework of wood; timber to support the lathing and plastering of vaulted ceilings.

CRAFT [krahft], *n.* art, skill, dexterity, workmanship; cunning, guile; a skilled trade or occupation requiring special manual training; the members of such a trade, especially when banded into a collective body; a boat (*pl.* unchanged); **the C.,** the collective body of Freemasons. [OE.].

CRAFTILY [krahf′ti-li], *adv.* in a crafty fashion.

CRAFTINESS [krahf′ti-nes], *n.* quality of being crafty.

CRAFTSMAN [krahfts′man], *n.* skilled artificer or other manual worker; (*fig.*) an artist; one skilled in the aesthetic arts. CRAFTSMANSHIP, *n.* highly skilled workmanship.

CRAFTY [krahf′ti], *adj.* skilful, cunning, full of guile. [OE.].

CRAG [krag], *n.* steep, jutting, rugged rock or point of rock.

CRAGGY [kra′gi], *adj.* full of crags, characterized by crags. CRAGGINESS, *n.* condition of being c.

CRAGSMAN [kragz′man], *n.* skilled rock climber.

CRAKE [krāk], *n.* the corn-crake; grating cry of this bird.

CRAM (1) [kram], *v.t.* to stuff, force or pack into a small space; thrust in by force; feed excessively in order to fatten; (*fig.*) coach intensively for a particular examination; *v.i.* to eat greedily and to excess; (*coll.*) tell an untruth; (*fig.*) undergo a period of intensive study in order to pass an examination. CRAM (2), *n.* information obtained by cramming; (*slang*) a lie. [OE.].

CRAMBO [kram′bō], *n.* game in which one person gives a word, to which another finds a rhyme; **dumb c.,** kind of charade in which a rhyme is to be found is given. [L.].

CRAMMER [kra′mer], *n.* one who crams, person who gives intensive coaching for examinations.

CRAMP (1) [kramp], *n.* sudden spasmodic and involuntary muscle contraction attended with great pain. [LGerm.].

CRAMP (2), *n.* piece of iron bent at the ends, to bind objects together; kind of screw-clamp; (*fig.*) restraining influence. [Du.].

CRAMP (3), *v.t.* to affect with cramp; bind with a cramp, clamp together; (*fig.*) restrain, hinder, hamper. [CRAMP (1) and (2)].

CRAMP-IRON [kramp′īern], *n.* piece of metal, bent

at right angles at each end, for fastening stonework together; crampon.

CRAMPON [kram'pon], *n.* grappling-iron, hooked bar of iron; tool in the form of two hooked bars of iron for raising stone or timber; spiked plate attached to the sole of the shoe in order to get a better foothold. [Fr.].

CRAN [kran], *n.* a measure for herrings containing 37½ gal. [Gael.].

CRANAGE [krā'nij], *n.* the right of using a crane at a wharf; price paid for this.

CRANBERRY [kran'be-ri], *n.* (bot.) small dark red berry, the fruit of a dwarf shrub.

CRANE (1) [krān], *n.* wading bird with long legs, slender neck and narrow bill; machine for raising or moving heavy loads; siphon for drawing liquid out of a vessel. CRANE (2), *v.t.* to stretch forward the neck as far as possible; hoist or lower with a c.

CRANE-FLY [krān'flī], *n.* insect of the genus *Tipula*, daddy-longlegs.

CRANE'S-BILL [krānz'bil], *n.* (bot.) any species of *Geranium*.

CRANIAL [krā'ni-al], *adj.* pertaining to the cranium; **c. index**, the ratio of the width of a skull to its length.

CRANIO-, *pref.* the cranium. [Gk.].

CRANIOLOGY [krā-ni-o'lo-ji], *n.* science of the structure of the skull as significant of race. CRANIOLOGICAL [krā-ni-o-lo'ji-kal], *adj.* relating to c. CRANIOLOGIST [krā-ni-o'lo-jist], *n.* one skilled in c. [Gk.].

CRANIOMETRY [krā-ni-o'mi-tri], *n.* measurement of the cranium. [Gk.].

CRANIOTOMY [krā-ni-o'to-mi], *n.* (surg.) the operation of opening the head of the foetus. [Gk.].

CRANIUM [krā'ni-um], *n.* the bones enclosing and forming a protective covering for the brain, the skull. [L. from Gk.].

CRANK (1) [krangk], *n.* a bent axle or handle to convert lineal into rotary motion or vice versa, or to impart motion to a wheel; starting handle of a motor vehicle; angular-shaped device used in bellhanging to change the direction of motion; (fig.) twist or strange turn of speech, verbal conceit; mental kink or caprice; person with a mental twist or kink, eccentric person. CRANK (2), *v.t.* to bend in the form of a c.; fasten with a c., impart motion by means of a c.; provide with a c.; **to c. up**, (coll.) to start up a motor-car engine by hand. [ME., ~OE.].

CRANK-CASE [krangk'kās], *n.* the casing in which the crankshaft of a motor engine works.

CRANKILY [krang'ki-li], *adv.* in cranky fashion.

CRANKINESS [krang'ki-nes], *n.* quality of being cranky.

CRANK-PIN [krangk'pin], *n.* (engin.) a pin, eccentric to a shaft, which rotates in the big-end bearing of a connecting-rod.

CRANKSHAFT [krangk'shahft], *n.* (engin.) a shaft fitted with cranks to which piston-rods are attached, so that the movement of the pistons rotates the shaft.

CRANKY [krang'ki], *adj.* out of order; unstable, shaky; ill-tempered; eccentric, crotchety; full of twists, tortuous.

CRANNIED [kra'nid], *adj.* full of chinks.

CRANNY [kra'ni], *n.* small aperture, chink, crack, cleft; secret hiding-place.

CRAPE [krāp], *n.* thin, light, transparent stuff, with wrinkled surface, usually dyed black, and used for mourning attire; band of this as a sign of mourning. [Fr.].

CRAPS [kraps], *n.* (U.S.) gambling dice game; **to shoot c.**, to play this game. [Fr.].

CRAPULENT [kra'pyōō-lent], *adj.* pertaining to, or suffering from, crapulence. CRAPULENCE, *n.* indisposition occasioned by excessive drinking; excessive drinking, debauchery. [L.].

CRAPULOUS [kra'pyōō-lōōs], *adj.* crapulent. [L.].

CRAPY [krā'pi], *adj.* resembling crape.

CRASH (1) [krash], *v.t. and i.* to fall and break with a crash; collide with something with a crash; (aeron.) fall suddenly to the ground with a heavy impact; (fig.) collapse, fall in ruins, fail hopelessly; (slang) gate-crash. CRASH (2), *n.* sudden loud explosive sound; the violent impact of a heavy fall or collision; aircraft accident involving a sudden fall to the ground; (fig.) ruin; failure, heavy financial loss. [Imitative].

CRASH (3), *n.* coarse linen cloth, chiefly used for towels. [Unkn.].

CRASH-DIVE (1) [krash'dīv], *n.* sudden rapid dive made by a submarine. CRASH-DIVE (2), *v.i.* to make a c.

CRASH-HELMET [krash'hel-mit], *n.* stout padded helmet worn by aviators and racing motorists, to protect the head in case of accident.

CRASHING (1) [kra'shing], *n.* the noise of a crash. CRASHING (2), *adj.* that crashes; (slang) utter and unmistakable (of a fool, bore etc.).

CRASIS [krā'sis], *n.* (gram.) the contraction of two vowels belonging to different syllables into one long vowel or diphthong. [Gk.].

CRASS [kras], *adj.* thick, coarse, gross; utter, unmistakable, complete. CRASSLY, *adv.* in c. fashion, impenetrably. [L.].

CRASSITUDE [kra'si-tyōōd], *n.* coarseness, grossness; utter stupidity or dullness. [L.].

CRATCH [krach], *n.* grated rack for fodder; wooden framework or grating. [Fr.].

CRATE [krāt], *n.* framework packing-case, or wickerwork basket in which fragile goods are transported. CRATE (2), *v.t.* to pack in a c. [L.].

CRATER [krā'ter], *n.* the mouth of a volcano; (milit.) rounded hole in the ground caused by an explosion. CRATERED, *adj.* pitted with craters. CRATERIFORM [krā-te'ri-fawm], *adj.* in the shape of a c. [Gk.].

CRAVAT [kra-vat'], *n.* old-fashioned necktie. CRAVATTED, *adj.* wearing a c. [Fr.].

CRAVE [krāv], *v.t.* to beg earnestly, entreat humbly, implore or demand, long for intensely. CRAVER, *n.* one who craves. [OE. from OScand.].

CRAVEN (1) [krā'ven], *adj.* cowardly. CRAVEN (2), *n.* a coward. [Unkn.].

CRAVING (1) [krā'ving], *n.* uncontrollable desire, persistent longing, yearning. CRAVING (2), *adj.* imploring, longing. CRAVINGLY, *adv.* in a c. fashion.

CRAW [kraw], *n.* the crop of birds. [ME.].

CRAWFISH, see CRAYFISH.

CRAWL (1) [krawl], *v.i.* to move slowly and laboriously on hands and knees; advance at a slow laboured pace; (fig.) humble oneself abjectly; be full of, or covered with, crawling objects. CRAWL (2), *n.* act of crawling; slow, laborious rate of progress; a racing stroke in swimming; (slang) leisurely tour of publichouses. CRAWLER, *n.* one who, or that which, crawls; (fig.) lazy or servile creature; (pl.) infant's garment in which it can c. without damaging its ordinary clothes. [OScand.].

CRAWL (3), *n.* pen or enclosure of stakes and hurdles for sea fish. [Du. from Span.].

CRAWLING [kraw'ling], *adj.* moving at a crawl; insinuating, fawning; full of, or covered with, crawling things. CRAWLINGLY, *adv.* in c. fashion.

CRAYFISH, CRAWFISH [krā'fish, kraw'fish], *n.* a freshwater crustacean; langouste or rock lobster, an edible salt-water crustacean. [OFr.].

CRAYON (1) [krā'on], *n.* thin stick of coloured chalk, wax-like pencil, charcoal used as a drawing implement; a drawing done by this means; the carbon point in an electric arc-lamp. CRAYON (2), *v.t.* to draw with crayons. [Fr.].

CRAZE (1) [krāz], *v.t.* to derange the mind, make insane, drive mad; crack; produce the effect of a network of small cracks on the glaze of pottery. CRAZE (2), *n.* an inordinate passion, exaggerated enthusiasm or fondness for; the attraction of the moment. CRAZED, *adj.* crazy; of pottery, glazed with a network of small cracks. [Swed.].

CRAZY [krā'zi], *adj.* mad, mentally deranged; wildly enthusiastic about; broken-down, decrepit; unreasonable, senseless, wild; **c. pavement, c. paving**, pavement constructed of flat stones of varying unsymmetrical shapes. [Fr.].

CREAK (1) [krēk], *v.t. and i.* to make a creak. CREAK (2), *n.* a sharp, harsh, grating sound. [Imitative].

CREAM (1) [krēm], *n.* a rich fatty substance forming on the surface of undisturbed milk; sauce or dressing resembling this; cosmetic ointment or hair fixative of the rich oily nature of this; whitish-yellow colour; (fig.) the choicest part, the flower; **cold c.**, a cosmetic ointment; **c. of tartar**, potassium bitartrate used medicinally and in cookery. CREAM (2), *v.t. and i.* to form into a c.; foam, form a frothy scum on its surface; skim the c. from; add c. to; cook with c. [Fr. from Gk.].

CREAM-CAKE [krēm'kāk], *n.* light puffy sponge cake containing cream.

CREAM-CHEESE [krēm-chēz'], *n.* soft white cheese made from cream and curdled milk.

CREAMER [krē'mer], *n.* instrument which separates the cream from the milk.

CREAMERY [krē'me-ri], *n.* place at which butter

---

and cheese are manufactured; shop where cream, milk, butter etc. are sold.

CREAM-LAID [krēm′lād], *adj.* (of laid paper) of a glossy cream colour.

CREAM-WOVE [krēm′wōv], *adj.* (of wove paper) of a cream colour.

CREASE (1) [krēs], *n.* the line at which the two surfaces of a fold meet; fold or continuous mark made on the surface of soft pliable material by pressure; the continuous straight fold down the back and front of trousers; (*cricket*) two parallel straight lines marked in white at each wicket, marking the limits of the position of the batsman and bowler. CREASE (2), *v.t. and i.* to make a c., wrinkle, furrow (the brow); press trousers in order to produce a straight c. in them; make irregular creases in cloth by careless folding or wear; acquire creases. [Unkn.].

CREATE [krē-āt′], *v.t.* to bring into being, cause the existence of, produce, give an independent existence to; produce or make something new or original; develop, cause to arise. [L.].

CREATIN(E) [krē′a-tin], *n.* a crystalline substance present in blood and urine. [Gk.].

CREATION [krē-ā′shn], *n.* act or process of creating, the bringing into existence of the world; that which is created, the universe; a strikingly original and fashionable garment; an original invention or production of the mind.

CREATIONISM [krē-ā′shn-izm], *n.* doctrine that the soul is specially created for each human being at birth; doctrine that the universe was created by God out of nothing; doctrine that all living species were simultaneously created by God.

CREATIVE [krē-ā′tiv], *adj.* that creates, original; pertaining to creation. CREATIVELY, *adv.* in c. fashion. CREATIVENESS, *n.* quality of being c.

CREATOR [krē-ā′ter], *n.* person who creates; God.

CREATURE [krē′tyōōr], *n.* anything created, a living being; dupe, puppet, dependant; (*fig.*) product or offspring of creation; (*coll.*) strong spirits, *esp.* whisky. CREATURELY, *adj.* pertaining to the c.; having the qualities of a c. [L.].

CRECHE, **crèche** [krāsh], *n.* day nursery where babies and small children may be left while their mothers are at work. [Fr.].

CREDENCE [krē′dens], *n.* belief, credit; (*eccles.*) small side-table on which the bread and wine are placed before consecration in the Eucharist; **letter of c.**, letter of introduction, reference. [MedL.].

CREDENTIAL [krē-den′shal], *n.* (*usu. pl.*) *and adj.* document or attestation of confidence and trust in a person entitling to credence or credit.

CREDIBILITY [kre-di-bi′li-ti], *n.* state of being credible.

CREDIBLE [kre′di-bl], *adj.* trustworthy, capable of being believed or of being accepted as true.

CREDIT (1) [kre′dit], *n.* belief, faith; anything which adds to a person's honour or merit; person or action of which one may be justly proud; personal honour, good name; reputation, prestige; just reward or recognition, acknowledgment of merit; (*comm.*) faith in a person's promise or ability to pay subsequently for goods received on trust; reputation for solvency, trustworthiness and honesty; (*banking*) sum standing to a person's account in a bank; (*book-keeping*) that part of an account in which are entered all sums received in payment; (*coll.*) a "pass-with-credit" awarded in some examinations to candidates who attain a certain standard in a subject; **letter of c.**, banker's letter sanctioning a payment to the holder; **line of c.**, form of loan enabling a country to purchase goods up to a certain value from the lending nation without immediate payment; **public c.**, confidence in the ability of a nation to fulfil its financial obligations; **c. title**, announcement at the beginning of a cinema film giving the names of various specialists concerned in its production. CREDIT (2), *v.t.* to believe, accept as true; allow a person c. for something, assign; (*book-keeping*) set to the c. of. [L.].

CREDITABLE [kre′di-ta-bl], *adj.* honourable, reputable; bringing c. to a person. CREDITABLY, *adv.* in c. fashion.

CREDITOR [kre′di-ter], *n.* person to whom a debt is owed; (*book-keeping*) credit side of an account. [OFr.].

CREDO [krē′dō], *n.* a creed, *esp.* the Apostles' Creed. [L.].

CREDULITY [kre-dyōō′li-ti], *n.* quality of being credulous. [L.].

CREDULOUS [kre′dyōō-lōōs], *adj.* readily believing

or accepting as true what one is told, without sufficient evidence or verification, gullible. CREDULOUSLY, *adv.* in c. fashion. [L.].

CREED [krēd], *n.* form of belief or body of beliefs held by the members of a particular religious faith; set of principles consistently followed; summary of the main points of the Christian faith. [OE. from L.].

CREEK [krēk], *n.* narrow opening in the coast; small, narrow harbour; small tributary river; narrow, winding passage. CREEKY, *adj.* full of creeks; winding. [OScand.].

CREEL [krēl], *n.* angler's wicker fishing-basket. [OFr.].

CREEP (1) (*pret. and p.pt.* **crept**) [krēp], *v.i.* to move stealthily and silently, *esp.* on hands and knees, in order to avoid attracting attention; (*bot.*) grow with branches and stem close to the ground or to a wall; (*fig.*) approach unobtrusively and imperceptibly; (*coll.*) worm one's way into favour; experience a sensation of living things creeping over the surface of the skin; (*naut.*) drag with a creeper; (*mech.*) increase in length under great pressure; (*phys.*) form crystals by evaporation along the sides of a receptacle. CREEP (2), *n.* action of creeping; (*mining*) a forcing up of the floor of a gallery by the downward pressure of the props; (*geol.*) the gradual movement of loose rock or earth; (*mech.*) the small increase in length in a bar of rigid material when subjected to heavy pressure; (*pl.*) nervous sensation of horror or fear. [OE.].

CREEPER [krē′per], *n.* person who, or thing which, creeps; family of birds which run along the stems of trees; (*bot.*) plant which grows along the ground or clings to the side of a wall by tendrils; iron-hooked instrument used for dragging; spiked plate fitted to the sole of a shoe for climbing etc.; grain-conveyor; conveyor-belt; (*slang*) one who is unduly deferential to his superiors. [OE.].

CREEPING [krē′ping], *adj.* moving very slowly; **c. barrage**, artillery barrage which gradually advances; **c. paralysis**, locomotor ataxia. CREEPINGLY, *adv.* in a c. manner.

CREEPY [krē′pi], *adj.* producing a tingling sensation of horror.

CREMATE [kri-māt′], *v.t.* to burn a corpse to ashes. CREMATOR, *n.* person employed in cremating; furnace used in cremation. [L.].

CREMATION [kri-mā′shn], *n.* act of cremating. CREMATIONIST, *n.* supporter of c.

CREMATORIUM [kre-ma-taw′ri-um], *n.* place where bodies are cremated; refuse destructor.

CREMATORY (1) [kre′ma-te-ri], *adj.* relating to cremation. CREMATORY (2), *n.* crematorium.

CREME-DE-MENTHE, **crème-de-menthe** [krăm-der-mah(ng)t′], *n.* green liqueur with a strong peppermint flavour. [Fr.].

CREMONA [kri-mō′nah], *n.* old and valuable make of violin. [*Cremona*, Italian town].

CRENATE(D) [kre-nāt′(-id)], *adj.* (*bot.*) having the edge indented with rounded notches; (*physiol.*) (of a blood corpuscle) with toothed edges. [L.].

CRENELLATED [kre′ne-lā-tid], *adj.* (*arch.*) (of the parapet of a battlement) having openings at regular intervals; having indented mouldings resembling these. [MedL.].

CREOLE [krē′ōl], *n. and adj.* (pertaining to) a native of the West Indies, parts of South America etc., of European ancestry; person of mixed European and native descent born in these regions. [Span.].

CREOSOTE [krē′ō-sōt], *n.* pungent antiseptic liquid used medicinally and as a protective coating for wood. [Gk.].

CREPE, **crêpe** [krăp], *n. and adj.* crape; **c. de Chine**, crape-like material made of silk; **c. paper**, crinkled or pleated paper; **c. rubber**, rubber rolled into sheets with a corrugated surface. [Fr. from L.].

CREPITATE [kre′pi-tāt], *v.i.* to crackle, rattle. CREPITATION, *n.* act of crepitating; crackling or rattling sound.

CREPON [kre′pon], *n.* crape-like material of worsted or silk. [Fr.].

CREPT [krept], *pret. and p.pt.* of CREEP.

CREPUSCULAR [kre-pus′kyōō-ler], *adj.* pertaining to, or resembling, twilight; (*fig.*) dim, obscure; (*zool.*) seen only at twilight. [L.].

CRESCENDO (1) [kre-shen′dō], *n.* (*mus.*) gradual increase in loudness, a direction signifying this, a passage of this character; (*fig.*) progressive heightening towards a climax. CRESCENDO (2), *adj. and adv.* (*mus.*) with, or characterized by, a c. [It.].

CRESCENT (1) [kre′sent], *n.* the moon as it waxes or wanes in the first or last quarter, when it appears as a convexo-concave area of light terminating in points; any figure resembling this shape; (her.) a half-moon; the national emblem of Turkey; (fig.) the Turkish power; the Mohammedan religion; a row of buildings built in the form of an arc. CRESCENT (2), adj. growing, increasing, developing; like the c. of the moon; in the shape of a c. CRESCENTED, adj. adorned with, or shaped like, a c. [L.].

CRESS [kres], n. any of several edible species of plants of the order Cruciferae, having a pungent taste. [OE.].

CRESSET [kre'sit], n. iron vessel containing fuel, suspended and lit as a torch, beacon or lamp. [Fr.].

CREST (1) [krest], n. tuft of hair or feathers on the top of the head of certain animals, birds, fishes or reptiles; distinguishing plume of feathers fastened to the top of a helmet as a badge; (her.) distinctive personal device placed over the shield and helmet on a coat of arms; such a device stamped on personal articles as a badge of ownership; (poet.) helmet; top or highest point of anything; line of the neck of a dog or horse; (anat.) ridge along the surface of a bone; (arch.) crown of a roof, topmost layer of a wall. CREST (2), v.t. and i. to provide or ornament with a c.; reach the topmost point of; crown as a c.; form into a c. [L.].

CRESTFALLEN [krest'faw-len], adj. having a drooping crest; (fig.) dejected, disheartened, chastened.

CRETACEOUS [kri-tā'shŏŏs], adj. chalky, composed of, or resembling, chalk; (geol.) belonging to the highest system or period of the Mesozoic group of strata. [L.].

CRETIN [kre'tin], n. person suffering from cretinism. CRETINOUS, adj. suffering from cretinism. [Swiss Fr. from L.].

CRETINISM [kre'ti-nizm], n. disease producing a form of idiocy, with physical deformity or stunted growth [Prec.].

CRETONNE [kre-ton'], n. strong, unglazed cotton cloth decorated with a printed, coloured pattern. [Creton, Normandy].

CREVASSE [kre-vas'], n. a deep crack in a glacier. [Fr.].

CREVICE [kre'vis], n. a crack, cleft, fissure. [OFr.].

CREW [krōō], n. group of sailors belonging to, and employed in sailing, a ship (often excluding the officers); gang of workmen; (coll.) body of people with similar interests. [OFr.].

CREWEL [krōō'el], n. thin worsted yarn for tapestry or embroidery. [Unkn.].

CRIB (1) [krib], n. child's cot; small room; hut; rack or manger for fodder; wickerwork fishing trap; (archaic) ox-stall; (mining) wooden framework for lining the sides of a shaft; (cards) cards discarded to the dealer at cribbage; (coll.) literary theft, plagiarism; translation of a foreign or classical work; (slang) building to be burgled. CRIB (2) (pres.pt. CRIBBING, pret. and p.pt. CRIBBED), v.t. and i. to provide with a c., copy from the works of another author, and misrepresent as one's own work; translate by copying from a c.; cheat in an examination; confine in a small space so as to cramp. [OE.].

CRIBBAGE [kri'bij], n. card game for two or more persons. [CRIB (1)].

CRIBBING [kri'bing], n. act of one who cribs; lining of a mine shaft.

CRIB-BITING [krib'bī-ting], n. bad habit among horses of biting the manger and noisily breathing in.

CRICK (1) [krik], n. painful spasmodic stiffness chiefly affecting the muscles of the neck or back. CRICK (2), v.t. to cause a c. in. [CREEK].

CRICKET (1) [kri'kit], n. small brown insect, characterized by the chirruping noise produced by the friction of its wing covers. [OFr.].

CRICKET (2), n. outdoor summer game played with bats, ball and wickets between two teams of eleven players; not c., (coll.) not sporting, unfair. [~OFr.].

CRICKETER [kri'ki-ter], n. one who plays cricket.

CRICOID [krī'koid], adj. ring-shaped; (anat.) c. cartilage, cartilage of the larynx. [Gk.].

CRIER [krī'er], n. one who cries; usher in a court of justice; person whose duty it is to proclaim public announcements. [CRY].

CRIM-CON [krim'kon], n. abbreviation of CRIMINAL CONVERSATION.

CRIME [krīm], n. an offence against public laws and social welfare, and punishable in a court of justice; (fig.) sin, wrongdoing, extremely ill-advised or unjust action.

CRIMINAL (1) [kri'mi-nal], adj. amounting to a

crime; guilty of a crime; pertaining to crime and its punishment; c. conversation, unlawful sexual intercourse. CRIMINAL (2), n. person guilty of a crime; (pop.) perpetual or grave offender against the law. CRIMINALLY, adv. in a c. fashion. [L.].

CRIMINALITY [kri-mi-na'li-ti], n. state or quality of being criminal, crime. [L.].

CRIMINATE [kri'mi-nāt], v.t. to accuse of a crime; find fault with, condemn. CRIMINATION [kri-mi-nā'shn], n. act of criminating, state of being criminated. CRIMINATORY [kri'mi-nā-te-ri], adj. criminating. [L.].

CRIMINOLOGY [kri-mi-no'lo-ji], n. the study of crime. [L.].

CRIMP (1) [krimp], n. one who decoys persons to complete the crew of a short-handed ship. CRIMP (2), v.t. to decoy as seamen to make up a ship's crew. [Unkn.].

CRIMP (3), v.t. to wrinkle, corrugate; curl (of hair); gash the flesh (of a fish) when caught so as to make it more firm and hard. CRIMP (4), n. a crease, wrinkle or fold. CRIMP (5), adj. crisp, friable, brittle. [OE.].

CRIMPING-IRON [krim'ping-iern], n. apparatus for curling hair, or for crimping material.

CRIMPY [krim'pi], adj. full of, or characterized by, short fuzzy curls (of hair), wavy.

CRIMSON (1) [krim'zon], n. deep red colour with a purplish tinge. CRIMSON (2), adj. of a deep, purplish-red colour; (fig.) bloody. CRIMSON (3), v.t. and i. to turn c.; (fig.) blush. [ME. from Arab.].

CRINGE (1) [krinj], v.i. to shrink back from, cower; bow or stoop in a servile or frightened manner, fawn in terror upon. CRINGE (2), n. fawning servility, act of cringing. CRINGING, adj. shrinking back in cowardice or servility, fawning. CRINGINGLY, adv. in a cringing fashion. [OE.].

CRINITE [krī'nīt], adj. hairy; (bot. and zool.) resembling tufts of hair. [L.].

CRINKLE (1) [kring'kl], v.t. and i. to twist or curl into crinkles; bend; rumple, crease, crush into innumerable irregular folds (of paper etc.). CRINKLE (2), n. wrinkle, a winding or turn. CRINKLY, adj. wavy, curly, wrinkled. [L.].

CRINOID (1) [krī'noid], adj. lily-shaped, applied to the crinoids. CRINOID (2), n. (zool.) one of the encrinites or sea-lilies. CRINOIDAL, adj. relating to the crinoids. [Gk.].

CRINOLINE [kri'no-lin], n. stout fabric made from horsehair and coarse thread; petticoat of this, stiffened with narrow steel hoops and worn to distend or support the skirt of a dress; torpedo-net fitted round the sides of a warship. CRINOLINED, adj. wearing a c. [L.].

CRIPES [krīps], int. (vulg.) a distortion of CHRIST.

CRIPPLE (1) [kri'pl], n. lame person, one who has a maimed limb. CRIPPLE (2), adj. lame, having a maimed limb; (fig.) ruined, impaired. CRIPPLE (3), v.t. to lame, disable, maim in a limb; (fig.) lessen, handicap severely, injure, weaken. [OE.].

CRISIS (pl. crises) [krī'sis, krī'sēz], n. the critical moment in any business or affair; (med.) the turning point; a dangerous climax; any difficult and dangerous situation in public affairs. [Gk.].

CRISP (1) [krisp], adj. (of hair) curly, frizzy, full of short curls; brittle, dry and firm; bracing, cold and dry; lively, clear-cut, brisk, sharp. CRISP (2), n. thin wafer of potato fried hard. CRISP (3), v.t. and i. to curl in short, firm curls; make c.; become c. [OE. from L.].

CRISPATE [kris'pāt], adj. crisp; (bot.) curled over at the edge. CRISPATION [kris-pā'shn], n. act of crisping or curling; state of being crisped.

CRISPED [krispt], adj. curled.

CRISPY [kris'pi], adj. frizzy, full of short curls (of hair); brittle, dry and hard.

CRISS-CROSS (1) [kris'kros], n. † child's alphabet at the beginning of which was a cross; the force resulting from the union of two forces moving at an angle to each other; network of intersecting lines. CRISS-CROSS (2), adj. arranged in, or marked with, intersecting lines. CRISS-CROSS (3), adv. in opposite directions, crosswise, at cross-purposes. CRISS-CROSS (4), v.t. to mark with intersecting lines; v.i. to form a network of crossing lines. CRISS-CROSS-ROW, n. the alphabet. [CHRIST CROSS].

CRISTATE(D) [kris'tāt(-id)], adj. crested, tufted. [L.].

CRITERION (pl. criteria) [kri-tēer'i-on, kri-tēer'i-ah], n. standard of quality by which a thing is judged, a guide. [Gk.].

CRITIC [kri'tik], n. person who criticizes, esp. literary

The accent ′ after a syllable = stress (u-pon′). The mark ‾ over a vowel = length (ā in made; ō in bone).

or artistic works; person employed in writing critical reviews of musical or dramatic performances, works of art, books etc.; one skilled in textual criticism; (pop.) fault-finder, severe judge. [Gk.].

CRITICAL [kri'ti-kal], adj. pertaining to a moment or point at which a great change may take place in the course of events; pertaining to a crisis; fateful, dangerous, involving risk; discriminating, expressing a reasoned judgment; (of an edition) containing textual criticism; fault-finding, judging harshly; (phys., math.) indicating or constituting a limit beyond which a change occurs; (zool., bot.) differing but slightly. CRITICALLY, adv. in a c. fashion or condition.

CRITICISM [kri'ti-sizm], n. the guiding principles of a critic; art or act of estimating the quality of literary or artistic work by an analysis of its merits and defects; analysis or review of anything; expression of adverse opinion about; (philos.) the philosophy of Kant; **textual c.**, scientific examination or analysis of manuscripts in order to establish the transmission of the original text.

CRITICIZE [kri'ti-siz], v.t. to give a critical estimate of, point out the merits and defects of; discuss in a critical manner; find fault with, point out defects in. CRITICIZABLE, adj. capable of being criticized. CRITICIZER, n. one who criticizes.

CRITIQUE [kri-tēk'], n. critical review of a literary, artistic or musical work; the critical art. [Fr.].

CROAK (1) [krōk], v.i. to utter the low, harsh, dissonant cry of a frog or raven; speak hoarsely; (fig.) grumble, talk or think as a pessimist; (slang) die; v.t. (slang) kill. CROAK (2), n. the low, harsh cry of a frog or raven; hoarse sound. [OE.].

CROAKER [krō'ker], n. fish or animal which croaks, fish of the genus Micropogon; person who croaks; person with a deep voice or cough.

CROAKING [krō'king], adj. that croaks; grumbling, pessimistic; foreboding evil.

CROAKY [krō'ki], adj. croaking.

CROATS [krō'ats], n.(pl.) the inhabitants of Croatia, now part of Yugoslavia; light irregular cavalry of the former Austro-Hungarian Empire in which many Croats served.

CROCHET (1) [krō'shā], n. form of knitting done with a small hook. CROCHET (2), v.t. and i. to work in c., work with a c. needle. [Fr.].

CROCK (1) [krok], n. earthenware or iron vessel; broken piece of earthenware. [OE.].

CROCK (2), n. an old ewe; old broken-down horse; (fig.) cripple or injured person; useless inefficient person. CROCK (3), v.t. and i. to become a c., break down in health; (coll.) be injured or lamed, suffer a breakdown in health; injure, lame. [Unkn.].

CROCKERY [krok'e-ri], n. domestic earthenware and china vessels; (coll.) china and porcelain ornaments or vessels.

CROCKET [krok'it], n. (arch.) an ornamentation of curved foliage along the end of a gable or spire. [AFr.].

CROCODILE [krok'ō-dīl], n. (zool.) large long-tailed aquatic reptile, having powerful jaws which can open to a great width; (coll.) group of schoolgirls walking out in double file; (fig.) person shedding false tears; **c. tears**, sham grief, false sorrow. CROCODILIAN [krō-kō-di'li-an], adj. of, or like, the c. [Gk.].

CROCUS [krō'kus], n. (bot.) genus of plants of the family Iridaceae, bearing brightly coloured flowers. [Gk.].

CROFT [kroft], n. small piece of land for pasture or tillage, usually adjoining a house; small farm-holding. CROFTER, n. one who rents and farms a c., esp. in the Scottish Highlands. [OE.].

CROIX-DE-FEU [krwah-de-fur'], n. a former political party in France.

CROMA [krō'ma], n. (mus.) a quaver or note held half the length of a crotchet. [It.].

CRO-MAGNON [krō-ma'nyo(ng)], n. (anthrop.) prehistoric European race dwelling in the late palaeolithic age. [Cro-Magnon, France].

CROMLECH [krom'lek], n. a prehistoric structure consisting of a large flat stone laid across two or more upright ones; a dolmen. [Wel.].

CRONE [krōn], n. decrepit old hag; old ewe. [ME. from ODu.].

CRONY [krō'ni], n. intimate companion, bosom friend. [Unkn.].

CROOK (1) [krook], n. stick bent at the top in the form of a hook; shepherd's staff bent in this way; crosier; anything bent or curved, a hook; (slang) dishonest person, swindler; (pl.) (mus.) curved metal

tubes attached to brass wind-instruments to change the pitch; **by hook or by c.**, by fair means or foul. CROOK (2), v.t. and i. to bend or curve into a c., bend, be turned from a direct line. [OScand.].

CROOKBACK [krook'bak], n. one who has a crooked back. CROOKBACKED, adj. hunchbacked.

CROOKED [krook'id], adj. bent, curved, twisted, winding; deformed; dishonest. CROOKEDLY, adv. in c. fashion. CROOKEDNESS, n. condition of being c.

CROOKES [krooks], adj. denoting various inventions or discoveries made by Sir William Crookes.

CROON [kroon], v.t. and i. to hum in a gentle undertone; sing in the soft, plaintive manner cultivated by vocalists in a dance band. CROONING, n. style of subdued singing into a microphone. [Du.].

CROONER [kroo'ner], n. person who croons, one engaged by a dance band to croon vocal numbers.

CROP (1) [krop], n. the stock or handle of a whip; short hunting-whip with a leather loop at the end; pouch-like swelling in the gullet of birds, the craw; produce yielded by cultivation of the earth; (pl.) grain, grass, fruit, vegetables etc. growing in a particular district at certain seasons; (fig.) group or mass of objects accumulated together; a whole tanned hide; (mining) an outcrop; hair-cut; **neck and c.**, completely and bodily. CROP (2) (pres.pt. CROPPING, pret. and p.pt. CROPPED), v.t. and i. to cut, lop or break off the tops of plants; (of animals) bite the tops (of grass etc.); cut short (the hair), cut off; (fig.) put a sudden end to; gather, mow, reap; produce crops; **to c. out, up**, (mining and geol.) to be exposed (of a stratum); **to c. up**, (fig.) to arise in an unforeseen manner. [OE.].

CROP-EARED [krop'ēerd], adj. with the ears cropped; (of Roundheads) with the hair cut short, allowing the ears to show.

CROPFUL [krop'fool], adj. having a full crop; satiated.

CROPPER [krop'er], n. person who, or thing which, crops; cloth-facing machine; plant producing a crop; pouter pigeon; (coll.) a heavy fall; **to come a c.**, to have a crashing fall; meet with sudden disaster.

CROPPING [krop'ing], n. act of cutting off; the raising of crops.

CROQUET (1) [krō'ki], n. game played on a lawn, with balls struck by long-handled mallets through hoops in succession. CROQUET (2) (pret. and p.pt. CROQUETED), v.t. and i. after having struck an opponent's ball with one's own and then having placed the two together, to strike one's own ball and so drive both away. [ONFr.].

CROQUETTE [kro-ket'], n. crisply-fried ball of minced meat, potato or rice etc.; rissole. [Fr.].

CROSIER, CROZIER [krō'zi-er], n. bishop's staff; (bot.) top of a young fern when curled. [OFr.].

CROSS (1) [kros], n. bar or line intersected with a transverse bar at right angles; the intersection of two bars; wooden instrument of this shape to which malefactors were nailed; structure of this shape upon which Christ suffered; the symbol of Christianity; (fig.) Christ's sufferings or passion; an affliction; anything (a mark, ornament etc.) fashioned with the intersection of two lines or bars; the intersection of two roads; that which crosses, thwarts or perplexes; a mixing of breeds in the production of plants or animals; plant or animal so produced; (her.) figure consisting of two intersecting bars; **C. of Calvary**, c. set up on three steps; **fiery c.**, wooden c. with its ends alight, used as a call to arms by Scottish Highlanders; **George C.**, c. awarded as a distinction for deeds of valour and available to British civilians; **Iron C.**, medal of iron awarded for distinguished service in the German Army; **C. of Jerusalem**, c. with a small crossbar at the end of each arm; **Latin c.**, vertical c. with the lower member longer than the three other members; **Maltese c.**, in which the four members gradually widen from the point of intersection so as to form a nearly complete square; **St. Andrew's c.**, c. shaped like X; **St. Anthony's c.**, shaped like T (also called **Tau c.**); **Southern C.**, constellation in the form of a c., visible in the southern hemisphere; **Victoria C.**, bronze c. awarded as the highest distinction in the British Services for personal valour in action; **to take up one's c.**, to suffer one's afflictions; **to cut on the c.**, to cut obliquely across the texture, grain etc. [L.].

CROSS (2), adj. and adv. lying or falling athwart, transverse, moving at an angle to the main direction, or from side to side; opposite; perverse, peevish, contrary; crossbred.

CROSS (3), v.t. and i. to make the sign of a cross on,

draw a line or place a thing across or athwart another; erase by lines passing from side to side; move athwart or from side to side, move over a line, river, sea etc.; pass; thwart, obstruct; interbreed; **to c. a cheque**, to draw two parallel lines on a cheque and write *& Co.* in between them; **to c. one's mind,** *(impers.)* to occur suddenly to one's mind; **to c. a person's hand with silver,** to give a silver coin to a person; **to c. the suit,** *(cards)* to change trumps from a red suit to a black at euchre.

CROSS-ACTION [kros′ak-shn], *n. (leg.)* legal case in which one person brings an action against a second person and the second person brings an action arising out of the same transaction against the first.

CROSSBANDED [kros-ban′did], *adj. (carp., arch.)* covered with a veneer of wood the grain of which runs in the direction of the shorter dimension.

CROSSBAR (1) [kros′bah(r)], *n.* a transverse bar, bar fixed between other bars, *esp.* the horizontal bar across or between goal-posts. CROSSBAR (2) *(pres.pt.* CROSSBARRING, *pret. and p.pt.* CROSSBARRED), *v.t.* to put bars across.

CROSSBEAM [kros′bēm], *n.* a transverse beam; beam running from side to side of a structure.

CROSSBEARER [kros′bāer-er], *n.* one who bears a cross in a procession; priest who bears an archbishop's cross.

CROSS-BEARINGS [kros-bāer′ingz], *n.(pl.)* the bearings of two known points or more from a fixed point, the position of the fixed point being determined from the angles so formed.

CROSS-BELT [kros′belt], *n.* belt worn over one shoulder and under the opposite arm.

CROSS-BENCH [kros′bensh], *n.* bench placed at right angles to the other benches in the House of Lords, on which independent members sit.

CROSSBILL (1) [kros′bil], *n.* a bird, the curved tips of whose beak cross when the bill is closed.

CROSS-BILL (2), *n. (leg.)* bill filed by a defendant against the plaintiff, to pray relief against the plaintiff.

CROSSBONES [kros′bōnz], *n.(pl.)* symbol of two human thigh-bones placed obliquely across each other, generally below a skull, as an emblem of piracy and death.

CROSSBOW [kros′bō], *n.* medieval weapon for shooting arrows, consisting of a grooved stock for the arrow, a bow fixed across the end of the stock, and a catch for releasing the bow-string.

CROSSBRED [kros′bred], *adj. and n.* hybrid, mongrel.

CROSSBREED (1) [kros′brēd], *n.* a mongrel breed. CROSSBREED (2) *(pret. and p.pt.* CROSSBRED), *v.t. and i.* to breed from plants or animals of different species or kinds.

CROSS-BUN [kros′bun], *n.* bun marked with a cross; **hot c.,** such a bun eaten hot on Good Friday.

CROSS-BUTTOCK [kros-bu′tok], *n. (wrestling)* a throw in which an opponent is pulled round the hip and hurled head first to the ground across the buttocks.

CROSS-CHANNEL [kros-cha′nel], *adj.* that crosses the English Channel.

CROSS-COUNTRY [kros-kun′tri], *adj. and adv.* across fields and open country between the roads.

CROSS-COURSE [kros′kaws], *n. (mining)* mineral vein lying at an angle across a main vein.

CROSSCUT (1) [kros′kut], *n.* a cut from side to side; path connecting two roads. CROSSCUT (2), *adj.* used for crosscutting; having crosscuts; **c. chisel,** chisel with a long narrow cutting edge for making grooves in metal; **c. file,** file whose teeth are formed by two sets of diagonal crosscuts; **c. saw,** large saw with a handle at each end for use by two men in sawing trees etc. CROSSCUT (3) *(pres.pt.* CROSSCUTTING, *pret. and p.pt.* CROSSCUT), *v.t.* to cut transversely, cut from side to side.

CROSSE [kros], *n.* racket with triangular head and long handle used in the game of lacrosse. [Fr.].

CROSSED [krost], *adj.* marked with a cross or the sign of a cross; with a line or lines drawn from side to side; *(fig.)* cancelled, thwarted.

CROSS-EXAMINATION [kros-ek-za-mi-nā′shn], *n.* process of cross-examining.

CROSS-EXAMINE [kros-ek-za′min], *v.t.* to examine carefully by questions to control the results of a previous examination; *(leg.)* subject a witness who has given evidence for one side to questioning by the opposing side.

CROSS-EYED [kros-īd′], *adj.* squinting, suffering from internal strabismus.

CROSS-FERTILIZE [kros-fur′ti-līz], *v.t.* to fertilize

by pollen brought from another plant. CROSS-FERTILIZATION [kros-fer-ti-li-zā′shn], *n.* process of cross-fertilizing.

CROSS-FIRE [kros′fīer], *n. (milit.)* lines of fire from different directions which cross each other.

CROSS-FROG [kros′frog], *n. (eng.)* the intersection of two rails grooved to allow the free passage of a flanged wheel on either rail.

CROSS-GARNET [kros-gah′nit], *n.* a T-hinge. [ME. from L.].

CROSS-GRAINED (1) [kros-grānd′], *adj.* (of wood etc.) with the grain running transversely from side to side or irregularly; *(fig.)* intractable, perverse, contrary. CROSS-GRAINED (2), *adv.* against or across the grain.

CROSS-HATCH [kros′hach], *v.i.* to hatch or engrave two sets of parallel lines at an angle to produce effects of shade (in an engraving). CROSS-HATCHING, *n.* process of engraving with two intersecting sets of parallel lines; shadow effect so produced.

CROSSHEAD [kros′hed], *n.* bar or rod stretching across the top of something; *(eng.)* bar or block fixed to the end of the piston-rod of a reciprocating steam-engine and moving to and fro to transmit the motion to the connecting rod; *(print.)* a heading across a page or column.

CROSSING [kro′sing], *n.* act of making a cross, marking or drawing a cross; process of crossbreeding; a moving across; place of crossing; pathway or track across a road or railway; **pedestrian c.,** track across a road marked by two parallel lines where pedestrians have a preferential right of way over traffic.

CROSS-LEGGED [kros-legd′], *adj.* having one leg lying across the other when sitting.

CROSSLY [kros′li], *adv.* in a cross manner.

CROSSNESS [kros′nes], *n.* state of being cross.

CROSS-OVER [kros′ō-ver], *n.* that which crosses from side to side; bodice with its two ends drawn across the front of the body and tied behind.

CROSSPATCH [kros′pach], *n.* cross, bad-tempered person.

CROSS-PIECE [kros′pēs], *n.* piece of anything lying at an angle over anything else.

CROSS-POLLINATION [kros-po-li-nā′shn], *n. (bot.)* cross-fertilization.

CROSS-PURPOSE [kros-pur′pus], *n.* a contrary, opposing purpose or intention; **to be at cross-purposes,** to deal with another person in a contrary manner through unintentional misunderstanding of each other's purpose.

CROSS-QUESTION (1) [kros-kwest′shn], *n.* question asked in a cross-examination; question asked in return by someone who has been questioned. CROSS-QUESTION (2), *v.t. and i.* to ask questions in cross-examination.

CROSS-REFERENCE [kros-re′fe-rens], *n.* a reference from one place in a book to another place in the same book.

CROSSROAD [kros′rōd], *n.* a road crossing another; minor road joining two main roads; *(pl. used as sg.)* place where two roads cross; *(fig.)* situation requiring a momentous decision.

CROSS-SECTION [kros′sek-shn], *n.* the cutting across of anything; plane exposed or visualized by cutting transversely across anything; a drawing of such a plane; *(fig.)* representative sample.

CROSS-STITCH [kros′stich], *n.* stitch made by two stitches crossing (X); needlework embroidered with such stitches.

CROSS-TALK [kros′tawk], *n. (coll.)* talking back at someone, back-chat.

CROSSTREES [kros′trēz], *n.(pl.) (naut.)* transverse horizontal timbers at the top ends of the upper and lower masts.

CROSSWAYS [kros′wāz], *adv.* transversely, crosswise.

CROSSWISE [kros′wīz], *adv.* in the form of a cross, across, athwart.

CROSS-WORD [kros′werd], *n.* a puzzle consisting of a square marked off in smaller squares some of which are blacked to form stops, the remaining squares being filled with letters which form words horizontally and vertically from clues provided.

CROTALID [krō′ta-lid], *n. (zool.)* rattlesnake.

CROTCH [kroch], *n.* stake with a forked top; fork of a tree or bough. CROTCHED, *adj.* having a c. bifurcated. [ONFr.].

CROTCHET (1) [kro′chit], *n.* hook, hook-shaped figure or symbol; *(typ.)* square bracket [ ]; *(mus.)* the representation of a note of half the time value of a minim, ♩; note represented in this way; *(fig.)*

The accent ′ after a syllable = stress (u-pon′). The mark ‾ over a vowel = length (ā in made; ō in bone).

fancy, whim, perverse idea. CROTCHET (2), *v.t. and i.* (*mus.*) play in regular crotchets. [Fr.].

CROTCHETY [kro'chi-ti], *adj.* having crotchets; (*fig.*) of fanciful, whimsical or perverse ideas. CROTCHETINESS, *n.* state of being c.

CROTON [krō'ton], *n.* (*bot.*) a euphorbiaceous plant, such as *Croton Cascarilla* and *Croton Tiglium*; (*pop.*) a plant, *Codiaeum Pictum*; **c. oil**, purgative oil obtained from the seeds of *Croton Tiglium*. CROTONIC [krō-to'nik], *adj.* (*chem.*) of or from c. oil; **crotonic acid**, acid derived from c. oil. [Gk.].

CROUCH (1) [krowch], *v.i.* to stoop with the whole body, bend down with the legs, with the trunk pressed against the thighs; (*fig.*) cringe, fawn. CROUCH (2), *n.* action of crouching. [OE. from L.].

CROUCH-WARE [krowch'wāer], *n.* finely glazed pottery formerly made in Staffordshire. [Unkn.].

CROUP (1) [krōop], *n.* inflammation, usually of the larynx, resulting in a hoarse cough and difficult breathing. CROUPINESS, *n.* condition of having c.; tendency towards c. CROUPY, *adj.* having, or like, c. [OScand.].

CROUP(E) (2), *n.* the hind-quarters or buttocks of a horse, ass etc. [Fr.].

CROUPIER [krōo'pi-er], *n.* one who presides at a gambling-table; vice-chairman at a banquet who sits at the lower end of the table. [Fr.].

CROUT, see SAUERKRAUT.

CROUTON, croûton [krōo'ton], *n.* small portion of fried bread eaten with soups. [Fr.].

CROW (1) [krō], *n.* large black bird of the genus *Corvus*; the cry of such a bird or of a cock; the joyful cry of an infant. CROW (2), *v.i.* to utter a c. or a succession of crows; (*fig.*) boast, swagger. [OE.].

CROW (3), *n.* a crowbar. [OE.].

CROWBAR [krō'bah(r)], *n.* iron bar with one end slightly flattened and bent, and used as a lever.

CROWBERRY [krō'be-ri], *n.* moorland plant producing a black berry; fruit of this plant. [Dan.].

CROWD (1) [krowd], *v.t. and i.* to throng, swarm, press round or on, confine; gather in crowds in or at (a place); press into too small a space; **to c. sail**, (*naut.*) to carry a press of sail. CROWD (2), *n.* large number of people gathered into a closely packed mass; large collection of things placed close together. CROWDED, *adj.* filled with a large number of people; closely packed. CROWDING, *n.* action of crowding, overcrowding. [OE.].

CROWFOOT [krō'fŏot], *n.* (*bot.*) kind of buttercup.

CROWN (1) [krown], *n.* a fillet, wreath or garland placed on the head as a mark of honour; headband or head-dress of precious metal, worn as an emblem of sovereignty; sovereignty, royalty, dignity; the wearer of a crown, the king's office, the king; the governing power of a monarchical state; the figure or shape of a crown; anything which bears such a mark; coin of the value of five shillings; size of paper (20 x 15 in.); the top of the head, the top of other things, the head; the exposed part of a tooth; the rounded top of a bell; crest of a bird; slightly arched centre of a road; (*arch.*) highest part of a cornice; (*naut.*) end of an anchor shank; (*fig.*) completion, perfection. [Scand. from L.].

CROWN (2), *adj.* pertaining to or belonging to the Crown, as a symbol of regal authority, belonging to the kingdom; **C. Agents**, government department having charge of the financial and commercial affairs of the Crown Colonies; **C. Colony**, colony governed direct by the Crown and not self-governing; **C. law**, the common law of England as applicable to criminal matters; **C. office**, a section of the High Court of Justice which deals with the administration of Crown law (criminal matters).

CROWN (3), *v.t. and i.* to place a crown upon the head; invest with a crown as a symbol of royal power and dignity, enthrone; honour, adorn in a dignified and splendid manner; reward; complete successfully; cover the head or crown of something; (*draughts*) put one draught upon another to make a king which can then move backwards. [L.].

CROWN-AND-ANCHOR [krown-and-ang'ker], *n.* gambling game played with dice marked with crowns and anchors and other symbols.

CROWN-COURT [krown'kawt], *n.* assize court in which criminal affairs are dealt with.

CROWNED [krownd], *adj.* adorned with, invested with a crown; crested; (*fig.*) perfect.

CROWNER [krow'ner], *n.* one who crowns; † a coroner.

CROWN-IMPERIAL [krown-im-pēer'i-al], *n.* (*bot.*)

a cultivated flowering plant, *Fritillaria imperialis*.

CROWNING (1) [krow'ning], *n.* action of crowning, coronation; that which crowns; the top of an arch. CROWNING (2), *adj.* finishing, perfecting, perfect.

CROWN LANDS [krown'landz], *n.(pl.)* lands belonging to the Crown or State.

CROWN-PIECE [krown-pēs'], *n.* silver coin worth five shillings, crown.

CROWN PRINCE [krown-prins'], *n.* prince who is heir to a throne.

CROWN-WHEEL [krown'wēl], *n.* gear-wheel with its teeth set on the periphery at right angles to the plane of the wheel; balance-wheel of a watch.

CROWN-WITNESS [krown-wit'nes], *n.* witness who gives evidence for the Crown in a criminal case.

CROW'S FEET [krōz'fēt], *n.(pl.)* (*coll.*) wrinkles at the outer corners of the eyes.

CROW'S NEST [krōz'nest], *n.* cylindrical look-out shelter fixed to a ship's mast.

CROZIER, see CROSIER.

CRUCIAL [krōo'shal], *adj.* (*anat., surg.*) in the form of a cross; (*fig.*) decisive, conclusive, critical. [Fr. ~L.].

CRUCIBLE [krōo'si-bl], *n.* small earthenware pot used for melting metals; hollow place at the bottom of a furnace where molten metal is received; (*fig.*) severe test; **c. steel**, hard cast-steel used in tool-making. [MedL.].

CRUCIFERAE [krōo-si'fe-rē], *n.* (*bot.*) family of plants whose flowers have four petals arranged in the form of a cross.

CRUCIFEROUS [krōo-si'fe-rōos], *adj.* adorned with a cross; (*bot.*) having four petals arranged in a cross.

CRUCIFIX [krōo'si-fiks], *n.* representation or image of Christ on the cross. [OFr., L.].

CRUCIFIXION [krōo-si-fik'shn], *n.* act of crucifying; punishment of being crucified; the death of Christ on a cross.

CRUCIFORM [krōo'si-fawm], *adj.* cross-shaped; (*bot.*) arranged in the form of a cross. [L.].

CRUCIFY [krōo'si-fi], *v.t. and i.* to nail a person to a cross by the hands and feet; put to death in this way; (*fig.*) mortify, torment, subject to severe pain. CRUCIFYING, *adj.* torturing, excruciating. [OFr., L.].

CRUDE [krōod], *adj.* raw, in the natural state, unripe; untreated by any artificial process; undigested; uncooked; (*fig.*) immature; ill-considered, unpolished; (of colours, music) gaudy, unrefined. CRUDELY, *adv.* in c. fashion. CRUDENESS, *n.* quality of being c. [L.].

CRUDITY [krōo'do-ti], *n.* crudeness; that which is crude. [L.].

CRUEL [krōo'el], *adj.* inflicting pain or sorrow upon others, unkind, unreasonably harsh; intended to produce distress or suffering, painful; (*vulg.*) very hard, severe. CRUELLY, *adv.* in a c. fashion. [Fr. from L.].

CRUELTY [krōo'el-ti], *n.* state of being cruel; cruel act; severity, harsh treatment causing pain or distress. [L.].

CRUET [krōo'it], *n.* small bottle for condiments; group of these placed in a stand; (*eccles.*) small vessel in which wine or water for the Eucharist is contained; **c. stand**, *n.* stand fitted with several compartments for cruets. [AFr.].

CRUISE (1) [krōoz], *v.i.* to sail about on a cruise; (of a taxi) drive slowly looking for a fare. CRUISE (2), *n.* leisurely sea-voyage with calls at various places; sea-voyage of a warship to patrol a wide area with no particular destination in view.

CRUISER [krōo'zer], *n.* a ship, particularly a warship, which cruises; lightly-armoured and speedy type of warship specially designed for cruising; boxer who fights at c.-weight. CRUISER-WEIGHT, (*boxing*) light-heavy-weight, a boxer weighing not more than 12 st. 7 lb.

CRUMB [krum], *n.* small fragment of bread broken from a loaf; the soft inner part of bread; (*fig.*) small portion or amount, scrap. CRUMB (2), *v.t.* to break into crumbs; spread over with crumbs. CRUMB-BRUSH, curved narrow brush for sweeping crumbs from a tablecloth. [OE.].

CRUMBLE [krum'bl], *v.t. and i.* to break into small pieces or crumbs; disintegrate. CRUMBLY, *adj.* easily crumbled, friable.

CRUMP [krump], *n.* (*slang*) heavy explosive shell; dull heavy explosion. [Echoic].

CRUMPET [krum'pit], *n.* soft thin sponge-like yeast-cake; (*slang*) the head. [Uncert.].

CRUMPLE [krum'pl], *v.t. and i.* to fold up or press

ōo is pronounced as in f*oo*d; ŏŏ as in h*oo*d; th as in *th*ink; TH as in *tha*t; zh as in a*z*ure. ~ = related to.

into creases in careless fashion, rumple; squeeze (paper) into a compact ball; (fig.) cause a person to collapse completely; become ruffled or full of creases; wilt and collapse completely, fall to pieces. [~OE.].

CRUNCH (1) [krunsh], v.t. and i. to crush or crumble noisily with the teeth, grind or crush with a harsh grating noise. CRUNCH (2), n. act or noise of crunching. CRUNCHY, adj. (coll.) of such a texture as to be liable to be crunched when eaten. [Imitative].

CRUPPER [kru'per], n. hindquarters of a horse; leather strap in harness extending from the back of a saddle under a horse's tail, to keep the saddle firmly fixed. [OFr.].

CRURAL [kroo'ral], adj. (anat.) pertaining to the leg. [L.].

CRUSADE (1) [kroo-sād'], n. one of the military expeditions undertaken in the Middle Ages by Christian rulers, to win back Palestine and the Holy Sepulchre from the Saracens; holy war against infidels, sanctioned by the Pope; (fig.) enthusiastic campaign against some alleged social evil or abuse. CRUSADE (2), v.i. to take part in a c. [MedL.].

CRUSADER [kroo-sā'der], n. one taking part in a crusade.

CRUSE [krooz], n. small earthenware receptacle, drinking-vessel. [OScand.].

CRUSH (1) [krush], v.t. and i. to press, squeeze forcibly, apply pressure so as to break, injure or destroy; press or squeeze tightly in order to express the contents, change the form or shape of; crease, rumple; grind or pound to small particles; squeeze into a restricted space; (fig.) subdue, suppress; overwhelm, destroy completely; abash; force one's way into an already crowded space; become creased or crumpled. CRUSH (2), n. closely packed mass of people collected or moving in a restricted space; violent pressure, act of crushing; **a c. on**, (slang) a passion for. CRUSH-HAT, collapsible opera-hat. [OFr.].

CRUST (1) [krust], n. the hard, crisp brown covering of a loaf or roll of bread; hard stale piece of bread; outer covering of pastry baked over a pie; any hard shell or protective covering; the solid exterior surface of the earth; a crystal-like film from wine collecting on the inside of the bottle. CRUST (2), v.t. and i. to cover with a c.; form or gather into a c. [L.].

CRUSTACEA [krus-tā'shi-ah], n.(pl.) (zool.) one of the classes of Arthropoda, comprising chiefly aquatic animals with a hard protective shell as lobsters, shrimps, crabs etc. [L.].

CRUSTACEAN [krus-tā'shi-an], n. and adj. one of, belonging to, the crustacea.

CRUSTACEOUS [krus-tā'shoos], adj. relating to a crust; of the nature of crust or shell; hard and brittle; crustacean. CRUSTACEOUSNESS, n. condition of being c.

CRUSTY [krus'ti], adj. like crust; hard; surly; morose. CRUSTILY, adv. in a c. fashion. CRUSTINESS, n. quality of being c.

CRUTCH (1) [kruch], n. long staff with a padded top which rests under the armpit, used by the crippled as a support in walking; (fig.) support, prop; fork-shaped contrivance in certain machinery; forked leg-rest in a side-saddle; the fork of the human body. CRUTCH (2), v.t. and i. to prop up with a c., support on crutches; walk on crutches. CRUTCHED (1), adj. supported on crutches. [OE.].

CRUTCHED (2) [krucht], adj. distinguished by a cross; **c. friars**, order of friars who wore or carried a cross. [OE. from L.].

CRUX [kruks], n. a difficult problem, troublesome point, difficult passage; the real issue. [L.].

CRY (1) (pl. **cries**) [krī], n. the distinguishing call of an animal; loud vocal sound, expressive of strong emotion, uttered by human beings; call for help; shout or call of excitement; shriek, scream, wail; act of weeping; popular rumour or report; party slogan or political catchword; prayer, audible entreaty; characteristic shout uttered by street hawkers etc. to attract attention to their wares; pack of hounds; **hue and c.**, pursuit, public agitation or clamour; **a far c.**, a long way removed; **within c.**, within earshot; **in full c.**, in hot pursuit. CRY (2), v.t. and i. to utter a c.; call loudly in order to attract notice; weep, shed tears; proclaim loudly and publicly; **to c. up**, to praise; **to c. down**, to disparage; **to c. off**, to withdraw from, ask to be excused; **to c. quits**, to declare matters equal; **to c. shame**, to protest against; **to c. for the**

moon, to want what is unreasonable to expect. [OFr. from L.].

CRYING (1) [krī'ing], n. outcry, clamour, act of crying. CRYING (2), adj. calling for immediate redress.

CRYOPHORUS [krī-o'fe-rus], n. instrument for freezing water by its own evaporation. [Gk.].

CRYPT [kript], n. subterranean vaulted cell or cave, esp. a burial-chamber under a church. [Gk.].

CRYPTIC(AL) [krip'tik(-al)], adj. secret, mysterious, occult; (zool.) hiding, concealing. CRYPTICALLY, adv. secretly, in a c. manner. [Gk.].

CRYPTO-, pref. hidden, secret. [Gk.].

CRYPTOGAMIA [krip-tō-gā'mi-ah], n.(pl.) (bot.) class of plants having no apparent flowers or seeds, as mosses, ferns etc. CRYPTOGAM [krip'tō-gam], n. (bot.) one of the c. CRYPTOGAMIC, CRYPTOGAMOUS [krip-to-ga'mik, krip-to'ga-moos], adj. relating to the c.

CRYPTOGRAM [krip'to-gram], n. anything written in cipher. [Gk.].

CRYPTOGRAPH [krip'tō-grahf], n. a cryptogram. CRYPTOGRAPHER [krip-to'gra-fer], n. one skilled in writing in cipher or in deciphering. CRYPTOGRAPHICAL [krip-to-gra'fi-kal], adj. written in cipher. [Gk.].

CRYPTOGRAPHY [krip-to'gra-fi], n. art of writing in secret characters. [Gk.].

CRYSTAL (1) [kris'tal], n. (min.) a clear transparent variety of quartz; (chem., min.) a body naturally bounded by plane surfaces in more or less symmetrical arrangement; any structure resembling a crystal in form; (fig.) anything clear and transparent; a spherical piece of rock crystal used in fortune-telling; fine cut-glassware of high transparency; (radio) a natural mineral deposit which passes an electric current in one direction only; **rock c.**, transparent or colourless quartz. CRYSTAL-GAZING, fortune-telling by means of a c. CRYSTAL (2), adj. made of c., resembling c., clear, transparent, limpid. [Gk.].

CRYSTALLINE [kris'ta-līn], adj. made of or like a crystal; clear, transparent; (min., chem.) having the structure of a crystal; **c. lens**, (anat.) the transparent body behind the iris of the eye, which focuses the rays of light on the retina. [Gk.].

CRYSTALLIZATION [kris-ta-lī-zā'shn], n. process of crystallizing; **water of c.**, the water contained in certain crystalline substances.

CRYSTALLIZE [kris'ta-līz], v.t. and i. to form into crystals; cover with sugar crystals; (fig.) give a definite form to; (fig.) become clearly defined and settled. CRYSTALLIZABLE, adj. able to be crystallized.

CRYSTALLOGRAPHY [kris-ta-lo'gra-fi], n. the scientific study of crystals. CRYSTALLOGRAPHER, n. one skilled in c. CRYSTALLOGRAPHIC(AL) [kris-ta-lo-gra'fik(-al)], adj. relating to c. CRYSTALLO-GRAPHICALLY [kris-ta-lo-gra'fi-ka-li], adv. in the manner of c. [Gk.].

CRYSTALLOID (1) [kris'ta-loid], n. a substance resembling a crystalline substance. CRYSTALLOID (2), adj. resembling a crystal, crystalline. [Gk.].

CRYSTAL-SET [kris'tal-set], n. (radio) simple form of wireless receiving apparatus in which a crystal is used to rectify the incoming waves.

CSARDAS [chah'dahsh], n. a Hungarian national dance. [Magyar].

CUB (1) [kub], n. the young of the fox, bear or other beast; (fig.) a rough-mannered inexperienced youth; (coll.) young person; junior member of the Boy Scouts. CUB (2) v.i. (pres.pt. CUBBING, pret. and p.pt. CUBBED), to give birth to cubs; hunt cubs. [Ir.].

CUBAGE [kyoo'bij], n. the cubic content of a solid; the calculation of this. [CUBE].

CUBATURE [kyoo'ba-tyoor], n. the calculation of the cubage.

CUBBING [ku'bing], n. the hunting of fox-cubs.

CUBBISH [ku'bish], adj. ill-mannered, rough.

CUBBY [ku'bi], n. a cosy retreat. CUBBY-HOLE, very small room. [Unkn.].

CUBE (1) [kyoob], n. a regular six-sided solid body, with all its sides square and identical; anything resembling this; (math.) the third power, the product of the square of a number multiplied by the number itself. CUBE (2), v.t. (math.) to raise to the third power, calculate the c. of. [Gk.].

CUBEB [kyoo'beb], n. small aromatic berry of the plant Piper Cubeba, used medicinally. CUBEBINE, n. vegetable substance extracted from the seeds of the c. [Arab.].

CUBIC [kyoo'bik], adj. resembling a cube; involving

The accent ' after a syllable = stress (u-pon'). The mark ˉ over a vowel = length (ā in made; ō in bone).

three dimensions; (*math.*) pertaining to the cube or third power. [Gk.].

CUBICLE [kyōō′bi-kl], *n.* one of the small, separate enclosed changing-rooms or sleeping-compartments in a school, hostel etc. [L.].

CUBISM [kyōō′bizm], *n.* style of painting in which only geometrical figures in three dimensions are employed. CUBIST (1), *n.* an exponent of c. CUBIST (2), *adj.* of, or pertaining to, c. or cubists.

CUBIT† [kyōō′bit], *n.* a measure of length, about 18 in.; (*anat.*) the forearm. [L.].

CUBITAL [kyōō′bi-tal], *adj.* of the length of a cubit; (*anat.*) relating to the elbow.

CUBOID (1) [kyōō′boid], *n.* anything shaped like a cube, but not strictly cubical. CUBOID (2), *adj.* resembling a cube. CUBOIDAL, *adj.* cuboid. [Gk.].

CUCA, see COCA.

CUCKING-STOOL [ku′king-stōōl], *n.* chair or stool in which scolds, rogues etc. were formerly fastened and publicly exhibited or ducked. [OScand.].

CUCKOLD (1) [ku′kold], *n.* man whose wife commits adultery. CUCKOLD (2), *v.t.* to make a husband a c. CUCKOLDOM, *n.* act of adultery; state of being a c. CUCKOLDRY, *n.* adultery. [ME.].

CUCKOO [kōō′kōō], *n.* the migratory bird *Cuculus canorus*; (*slang*) fool, stupid person; **cuckoo's meat**, wood-sorrel. CUCKOO-PINT, the plant, *Arum maculatum*. [Imitative].

CUCKOO-FLOWER [kōō′kōō-flow-er], *n.* (*bot.*) one of several plants including the lady's smock and the wild orchis.

CUCKOO-SPIT [kōō′kōō-spit], *n.* cuckoo-spittle.

CUCKOO-SPITTLE [kōō′kōō-spi-tl], *n.* spittle-like secretion deposited on plants by certain parasitic insects such as the froghopper.

CUCUMBER [kyōō′kum-ber], *n.* edible fruit of a plant of the gourd family; the plant itself. [L.].

CUCURBITA [kyōō-kur′bi-tah], *n.* gourd; genus of plants of which the gourd is a species. [L.].

CUD [kud], *n.* food which ruminating animals return to the mouth to chew at leisure; **to chew the c.,** (*fig.*) to ponder. [OE.].

CUDBEAR [kud′bāer], *n.* (*bot.*) a lichen, used in dyeing purple. [Dr. *Cuthbert* Gordon].

CUDDLE (1) [ku′dl], *v.t. and i.* to hug, embrace warmly, fondle; **to c. up,** to lie close together, curl up in sleeping. CUDDLE (2), *n.* a hug, embrace. CUDDLESOME, CUDDLY, *adj.* (*coll.*) of such a kind as to invite cuddling. [Unkn.].

CUDDY (1) [ku′di], *n.* (*naut.*) small cabin under the poop. [Unkn.].

CUDDY (2), *n.* a donkey; (*fig.*) fool. [Uncert.].

CUDGEL (1) [ku′jel], *n.* short thick heavy stick, stout club; **to take up the cudgels (for),** to defend vigorously. CUDGEL (2) (*pres.pt.* CUDGELLING, *pret. and p.pt.* CUDGELLED), *v.t.* to beat with a c.; **to c. one's brains,** to rack one's brains, puzzle over. [OE.].

CUE (1) [kyōō], *n.* the last words of a speech in a play, forming a guide or signal to an actor to enter or begin speaking; (*mus.*) a lead in, signal to begin playing or singing after a rest; (*fig.*) a hint, lead; guide to the attitude to adopt. [Uncert.].

CUE (2), *n.* pigtail, plait of hair attached to the back of a wig; long slender tapering rod used in billiards etc. [Fr. from L.].

CUFF (1) [kuf], *n.* the lower portion of the sleeve, often starched or ornamented; band at the end of a shirt-sleeve by which it is fastened round the wrist; (*pl.*) (*coll.*) handcuffs. [ME.].

CUFF (2), *v.t.* to give a blow or succession of blows with the open palm. CUFF (3), *n.* a blow so given. [Swed.].

CUFF-LINK [kuf′lingk], *n.* two small and often ornamental pieces of metal, joined by a short link, used to fasten the cuff of a shirt-sleeve round the wrist.

CUIRASS [kwi-ras′], *n.* piece of body-armour of leather or metal. [Fr.].

CUIRASSIER [kwi-ra-sēer′], *n.* cavalryman wearing a cuirass. [Fr.].

CUISINE [kwi-zēn′], *n.* the cooking department; cookery; style of cooking. [Fr.].

CUL-DE-SAC [kōōl-de-sak′], *n.* street or passage closed at one end; (*fig.*) situation offering no way of escape. [Fr.].

CULEX [kyōō′leks], *n.* (*entom.*) genus of insects including gnats and mosquitoes. [L.].

CULINARY [kyōō′li-na-ri], *adj.* pertaining to a kitchen or cookery; that may be cooked. [L.].

CULL (1) [kul], *v.t.* to pick out, gather; select, collect. CULL (2), *n.* anything selected, an animal weeded out from the flock. CULLING, *n.* act or process of selecting or gathering; the thing culled. [OFr.].

CULM (1) [kulm], *n.* (*bot.*) the jointed hollow stalk of grasses. [L.].

CULM (2), *n.* slack, coal-dust; slack from anthracite, inferior coal; (*geol.*) deposits of shale. [Unkn.].

CULMINANT [kul′mi-nant], *adj.* having reached its topmost point; (*astron.*) at the zenith. [L.].

CULMINATE [kul′mi-nāt], *v.i.* (*astron.*) to reach the zenith; (*fig.*) reach the highest point, attain the highest point of development; come to a head. [L.].

CULMINATION [kul-mi-nā′shn], *n.* the highest point attained; (*astron.*) highest altitude reached by a heavenly body.

CULPABLE [kul′pa-bl], *adj.* censurable, criminal, blameworthy. CULPABILITY [kul-pa-bi′li-ti], *n.* quality of being c. CULPABLY, *adv.* in c. fashion. [L.].

CULPRIT [kul′prit], *n.* guilty person, offender, one responsible for a crime; (*leg.*) prisoner brought to trial. [AFr. and OFr.].

CULT [kult], *n.* system of religious worship with its particular ritual or observances; devotion or homage paid to anything or anyone; adoration, worship; (*coll.*) popular fad or fashion. [L.].

CULTIVATE [kul′ti-vāt], *v.t.* to till, prepare land for the raising of crops; grow; (*fig.*) improve, develop by labour or study, foster. CULTIVABLE, CULTIVATABLE [kul′ti-va-bl, kul′ti-vā-ta-bl], *adj.* able to be cultivated. CULTIVATED, *adj.* tilled; (*fig.*) possessing culture, refined. [L.].

CULTIVATION [kul-ti-vā′shn], *n.* art or practice of cultivating, state of being cultivated; culture.

CULTIVATOR [kul′ti-vā-ter], *n.* one who cultivates; agricultural machine for tilling the land.

CULTURAL [kul′tyōo-ral], *adj.* of, or pertaining to, culture. CULTURALLY, *adv.* in respect of culture.

CULTURE [kul′tyōor], *n.* cultivation; artificial rearing of plants, micro-organisms etc.; set of micro-organisms so reared; (*fig.*) education of the mind for improvement and refinement; the result of such education; possession of a correct, sensitive taste, rational judgment, refinement of manner, and highly developed intellectual outlook; form of civilization or state of intellectual progress. CULTURELESS, *adj.* devoid of c. CULTURIST, *n.* a cultivator. [L.].

CULVER [kul′ver], *n.* pigeon, wood-pigeon. [OE.].

CULVERT [kul′vert], *n.* large pipe or enclosed drain for conveying water beneath a road, canal etc. [Uncert.].

CUMBER (1) [kum′ber], *v.t.* to burden, hinder, restrict and obstruct freedom of movement by unwieldiness. CUMBER (2), *n.* encumbrance. CUMBERLESS, *adj.* unhampered, unburdened. [OFr.].

CUMBERSOME [kum′ber-sum], *adj.* burdensome, difficult to manage on account of its weight or size. CUMBERSOMELY, *adv.* in a c. fashion. CUMBERSOMENESS, *n.* quality of being c.

CUMBRIAN [kum′bri-an], *adj.* pertaining to Cumberland. [L.].

CUMBROUS [kum′brŏŏs], *adj.* cumbersome. CUMBROUSLY, *adv.* in a c. fashion. CUMBROUSNESS, *n.* condition of being c. [CUMBER].

CUMIN [ku′min], *n.* (*bot.*) a plant with bitterish, pungent, carminative seeds. [Heb.].

CUMMERBUND, KAMARBAND [ku′mer-bund], *n.* sash worn round the waist. [Pers.].

CUMQUAT [kum′kwot], *n.* fruit like a small orange, with a sweet rind and bitter pulp. [Chin.].

CUMULATE [kyōō′myōo-lāt], *v.t. and i.* to accumulate. CUMULATION, *n.* accumulation. [L.].

CUMULATIVE [kyōō′myōo-la-tiv], *adj.* continually piling up or increasing; increasing in force by successive accumulations; **c. vote,** system of voting by which each voter may keep all his votes for only one candidate; **c. preference shares,** (*comm.*) shares entitling the holder to arrears of interest before other shareholders receive the current interest or dividend. CUMULATIVELY, *adv.* by accumulation.

CUMULUS [kyōō′myōo-lus], *n.* a heap, accumulation; cloud formation in which the clouds appear as heaped-up convex masses. [L.].

CUNEATE(D) [kyōō′ni-āt(-id)], *adj.* (*bot.*) wedge-shaped. [L.].

CUNEIFORM (1) [kyōō-nē′i-fawm], *adj.* wedge-shaped; **c. characters,** wedge-shaped characters in which some ancient Eastern inscriptions were written. CUNEIFORM (2), *n.* c. character. [L.].

CUNNING (1) [ku′ning], *n.* subtle craft, astuteness,

cleverness, artfulness; (*archaic*) skill, power. CUNNING (2), *adj.* skilful, dexterous; wily, crafty, astute, subtle; ingenious. CUNNINGLY, *adv.* in c. fashion. [ME.].

CUP (1) [kup], *n.* small drinking-vessel with a handle; contents of such a vessel; large ornamental vessel given as a prize in games etc.; (*eccles.*) vessel containing the wine used in the Communion Service; anything resembling these in shape; (*pl.*) indulgence in intoxicating liquor, drinking bout; any of the several drinks made from wine mixed with other ingredients; (*surg.*) cupping glass; **in one's cups**, in a state of intoxication. CUP (2) (*pres.pt.* CUPPING, *pret. and p.pt.* CUPPED), *v.t. and i.* (*surg.*) to apply a cupping glass to; form into the shape of a c.; hold as in a c. [OE. from LL.].

CUP-BEARER [kup'bāer-er], *n.* official wine server in a prince's household, person who performs a similar function at official banquets.

CUPBOARD [ku'berd], *n.* large cabinet fitted with shelves and doors, used for storing domestic crockery, provisions etc.; **c. love**, display of affection from motives of self-interest.

CUPEL [kyōō'pel], *n.* vessel used in refining and testing the purity of precious metals. [LL.].

CUPFUL [kup'fōōl], *n.* the measure of the contents of a cup when full.

CUPID [kyōō'pid], *n.* Roman god of love, representation in sculpture, painting etc. of Cupid; (*fig.*) beautiful young boy. [L.].

CUPIDITY [kyōō-pi'di-ti], *n.* inordinate desire to possess; covetousness. [L.].

CUPOLA [kyōō'po-lah], *n.* (*arch.*) small dome projecting above a roof; (*metal.*) furnace for melting; revolving gun-turret on a warship; (*anat.*) dome-shaped organ or process. [L.].

CUPPED [kupt], *adj.* bled by cupping, formed like a cup.

CUPPING [ku'ping], *n.* (*surg.*) application of a cupping glass to a part of the skin in order to draw an increased amount of blood to that part; **c. glass**, cup-shaped glass vessel heated and applied to a portion of the skin in cupping.

CUPPY [ku'pi], *adj.* like a cup, *esp.* (*golf*) **c. lie**, position of the ball when it lies in a small depression.

CUPREOUS [kyōō'pri-ōōs], *adj.* of or like copper. [L.].

CUPRIC [kyōō'prik], *adj.* (*chem.*) containing copper in its higher valency. [L.].

CUPRO-NICKEL [kyōō-prō-ni'kel], *n.* alloy of copper and nickel used in coinage and for sheathing bullets.

CUPRO-URANITE [kyōō-prō-yōō'ra-nīt], *n.* hydrated phosphate of uranium and copper.

CUPROUS [kyōō'prōōs], *adj.* (*chem.*) containing copper in its lower valency.

CUP-TIE [kup'ti], *n.* football match in a knock-out competition.

CUPULA, CUPULE [kyōō'pyōō-lah, kyōō'pyōōl], *n.* (*bot.*) cup-like receptacle holding the acorn, hazel-nut etc.; (*zool.*) a cup-like organ; small round cavity. CUPULIFEROUS [kyōō-pyōō-li'fe-rōōs], *adj.* bearing cupules. [L.].

CUR [kur], *n.* low-bred or mongrel dog; (*fig.*) cowardly wretch. [OIcel.].

CURABLE [kyōō'ra-bl], *adj.* able to be cured. CURABILITY [kyōō-ra-bi'li-ti], *n.* ability to be cured. [L.].

CURACAO, curaçao [kyōō-ra-sō'], *n.* liqueur flavoured with orange peel, cinnamon and mace. [*Curaçao*, Dutch island in the Caribbean Sea].

CURACY [kyōō'ra-si], *n.* office or post of a curate.

CURARE, CURARI [kyōō-rah'ri], *n.* poisonous extract from the bark of the tree *Strychnos toxifera*, used by South American natives for tipping arrows. CURARINE, *n.* alkaloid obtained from c. [Native].

CURASSOW [kyōō-ra'sō], *n.* South American bird resembling a turkey. [*Curaçao*, in the Caribbean Sea].

CURATE [kyōō'rat], *n.* clergyman appointed to assist the incumbent of a parish; priest who has the cure of souls. [LL.].

CURATIVE (1) [kyōō'ra-tiv], *adj.* remedial, intended to cure. CURATIVE (2), *n.* remedy, cure.

CURATOR [kyōō-rā'ter], *n.* one who is in charge of official property or possessions; official in charge of a museum, art-gallery, library etc.; (*Scots leg.*) guardian appointed to manage the affairs of a minor or a lunatic. CURATORSHIP, *n.* office or tenure of a c. [L.].

CURB (1) [kurb], *n.* chain or strap under the lower

jaw of a horse and attached to the bit, used as a check; (*fig.*) a check, framework or border round something (often spelt *kerb*), rim round a fireplace or round the top of a well or copper; long stone setts placed lengthwise along the edge of a pavement; **c. roof**, roof having two slopes of differing steepness on each side. CURB (2), *v.t.* to restrain, check, keep under control. [L.].

CURD (1) [kurd], *n.* the thickened substance which separates and coagulates when milk is left, or treated with acid, and from which cheese is made; any substance similar to this. CURD (2), *v.t. and i.* to curdle. CURDY, *adj.* like c.; full of c. [ME.].

CURDLE [kur'dl], *v.t. and i.* to thicken into curd; coagulate, congeal (of blood).

CURE (1) [kyōōr], *n.* act of curing; that which cures or is intended to cure, remedy for disease; term of residence at a health resort or spa, *esp.* **to take the c.**; (*eccles.*) the spiritual care of souls, office or parish of a priest; (*fig.*) alleviation, remedy; vulcanization of rubber. CURE (2), *v.t.* to heal, restore to normal health; remedy, banish; (*fig.*) put right, cause a person to give up that which is harmful or evil; preserve (foodstuffs) by salting, drying and pickling; vulcanize (rubber); prepare (tobacco) for smoking. CURELESS, *adj.* incurable. CURER, *n.* one who cures foodstuffs etc. [L.].

CURE, curé [kōō'rā], *n.* French parish priest. [Fr.].

CURETTE (1) [kyōō-ret'], *n.* (*surg.*) instrument shaped like a small scoop. CURETTE (2), *v.t. and i.* to scrape with a c. [Fr.].

CURFEW [kur'fyōō], *n.* (*hist.*) the ringing of a bell at a fixed hour in the evening as a signal that all fires and lights were to be put out; the bell so rung; the time at which it was rung; fixed time by which all persons must be within their houses. [AFr.].

CURIA [kyōō'ri-ah], *n.* one of the subdivisions into which the Roman tribes were divided; senate house or public place of worship; (*hist.*) medieval court of judicature of the king, being the supreme court; **The C.**, the Papal court. [L.].

CURIE [kyōō'ri], *n.* amount of radio-activity produced by one gramme of radium. [M. and Mme. *Curie*, discoverers of radium].

CURIO [kyōō'ri-ō], *n.* object having some unusual characteristics of value to collectors. [CURIO(SITY)].

CURIOSITY [kyōō-ri-o'si-ti], *n.* quality of being curious; that which is curious; a curio. [L.].

CURIOUS [kyōō'ri-ōōs], *adj.* of a rare or unusual nature, surprising, strange, remarkable; odd, peculiar; indecent; desirous of knowing or ascertaining, eager to obtain information about; inquisitive. CURIOUSLY, *adv.* in a c. manner. [L.].

CURL (1) [kurl], *v.t. and i.* to form into a c. or curls; ripple (of water); roll up at the edges; play at curling; **to c. up**, (*fig.*) to collapse suddenly; overwhelm. CURL (2), *n.* a lock of hair twisted into a spiral roll or ringlet; anything resembling this in shape; (*pl.*) curly hair. [Dan.].

CURLER [kur'ler], *n.* clip or other device round which a lock of hair is twisted to form a curl.

CURLEW [kur'lyōō], *n.* a wading bird. [OFr.].

CURLINESS [kur'li-nes], *n.* quality of being curly.

CURLING (1) [kur'ling], *n.* Scottish winter game resembling bowls, played on the ice with large, round, flat-bottomed stones, thrust with a curling movement of the arm. CURLING (2), *adj.* curly, that curls. CURLINGLY, *adv.* in a curly fashion. [CURL (1)].

CURLING-IRONS [kur'ling-īernz], *n.(pl.)* curling-tongs.

CURLING-TONGS [kur'ling-tongz], *n.(pl.)* a pair of tongs heated for curling the hair.

CURL-PAPER [kurl'pā-per], *n.* piece of paper into which a lock of hair is twisted and set to form a curl.

CURLY [kur'li], *adj.* having curls; tending to curl; full of ripples or small waves.

CURMUDGEON [ker-mu'jon], *n.* bad-tempered, surly, miserable misanthrope. CURMUDGEONLY, *adv.* churlish, like a c. [Unkn.].

CURRAGH (1) [ku'rah], *n.* a coracle. [Ir.].

CURRAGH (2), *n.* boggy waste land, marshy swamp; **The C.**, military camp and famous racecourse near Dublin. [Ir.].

CURRANT [ku'rant], *n.* small sweet dried Levantine grape; the juicy fruit of several species of *Ribes*. [*Corinth*, Greece, where grown].

CURRENCY [ku'ren-si], *n.* condition of being in current use; that which is current; the particular form or system of money in use in a state; prevalence. [L.].

CURRENT (1) [ku'rent], *adj.* running, flowing; in

The accent ' after a syllable = stress (u-pon'). The mark ¯ over a vowel = length (ā in made; ō in bone).

circulation; in general use at the present time; prevalent, generally accepted at the moment; present; of the latest issue. CURRENT (2), *n.* a continuous flow, generally in one direction, of air or water or of electricity; part of such a mass, moving at a more rapid rate than the main body; (*fig.*) course, trend, drift. CURRENTLY, *adv.* in c. fashion; generally. [L.].

CURRICLE [ku'ri-kl], *n.* two-wheeled carriage drawn by two horses abreast. [L.].

CURRICULUM [ku-ri'kyoo-lum], *n.* course of study or training given or prescribed. [L.].

CURRIER [ku'ri-er], *n.* one who curries and colours leather after tanning. [L.].

CURRISH [kur'rish], *adj.* like a cur; snarling, spiteful, snappish. CURRISHLY, *adv.* in a c. fashion. CURRISHNESS, *n.* a c. disposition, state of being c.

CURRY (1) [ku'ri], *n.* highly flavoured Indian dish, made from stewed meat, fish etc., seasoned with spices and turmeric; hash or stew flavoured with this or with curry-powder. CURRY-POWDER, compound of strong spices and turmeric used as a relish. CURRY (2), *v.t.* to season with c., make a c. from. [Tamil].

CURRY (3), *v.t.* to dress leather after it is tanned; rub down and clean (a horse's coat) with a comb; **to c. favour,** to try to win a person's favour by flattery and fawning. [OFr.].

CURRYCOMB [ku'ri-kōm], *n.* metal comb with a handle, used in currying horses' coats.

CURRYING [ku'ri-ing], *n.* art of dressing tanned skins; act of rubbing down a horse with a curry-comb.

CURSE (1) [kurs], *n.* utterance invoking evil or misfortune upon a person; profane oath, blasphemy; cause or source of evil or misfortune; (*eccles.*) censure, excommunication; **c. of Scotland,** the nine of diamonds. CURSE (2), *v.t. and i.* to lay under a c.; swear (at); regard with bitter regret; pursue with misfortune or calamity; (*eccles.*) excommunicate. [OE.].

CURSED, CURST [kurst], *adj.* blasted by a curse; deserving a curse; detestable, execrable; (*coll.*) confounded. CURSEDLY, *adv.* in a c. fashion.

CURSING [kur'sing], *n.* the utterance of a curse; blasphemy, swearing.

CURSIVE [kur'siv], *adj.* (of handwriting) flowing, in which the characters are formed and connected by curved strokes. [MedL.].

CURSORY [kur'se-ri], *adj.* hasty, hurried, superficial. CURSORILY, *adv.* in a c. fashion.

CURST, see CURSED.

CURT [kurt], *adj.* short, terse, rudely abrupt. [L.].

CURTAIL [ker-tāl'], *v.t.* to cut short, abridge, shorten; cut down. CURTAILMENT, *n.* act of curtailing; state of being curtailed. [Uncert.].

CURTAIL-STEP [kur'tāl-step], *n.* bottom step in a flight of stairs, ending at its outer edge in a scroll.

CURTAIN (1) [kur'tan], *n.* long piece of cloth hanging from a bed or window, which can be drawn to screen it completely; long piece of cloth drawn across a room to partition it; sheet of heavy material which can be lowered to conceal the stage in a theatre from the audience; the descent of this; protective barrier; (*fig.*) anything serving as a cover or screen; (*fort.*) part of a rampart between the flanks of two bastions; **to draw a c. over,** (*fig.*) to say nothing about; **to lift the c.,** (*fig.*) to reveal, disclose information. CURTAIN (2), *v.t.* to cover, screen or partition off by a c. [LL.].

CURTAIN-LECTURE [kur'tan-lek-tyōōr], *n.* reproof delivered by a wife to her husband in bed.

CURTAIN-RAISER [kur'tan-rā-zer], *n.* short dramatic piece performed before the play of the evening.

CURTAL-AXE [kur'tal-aks], *n.* short, broad, heavy sword. [*Var. of* CUTLASS].

CURTATE [kur'tāt], *adj.* cut short, reduced; **c. distance,** (*astron.*) the distance of a planet from the sun or earth reduced to the plane of the ecliptic. CURTATION [ker-tā'shn], *n.* (*astron.*) the difference between the actual and the c. distance of a planet from the sun. [L.].

CURTLY [kurt'li], *adv.* in curt fashion.

CURTSEY (1), **CURTSY** [kurt'si], *n.* a bending of the knees as a sign of respect or acknowledgment by women. CURTSEY (2), CURTSY, *v.i.* to make a c. [COURTESY].

CURVATION [ker-vā'shn], *n.* bending, curving. [L.].

CURVATURE [kur'va-tyōōr], *n.* act of curving;

state of being curved; amount of curve; a curve; (*geom.*) rate of change of direction of the tangent per unit length of arc. [L.].

CURVE (1) [kurv], *n.* line with a finite radius of curvature; rounded bend, bend not in the form of an angle; curved part of anything. CURVE (2), *v.t. and i.* to bend in a c., have the form of a c. [L.].

CURVET (1) [ker-vet'], *n.* leap of a horse in which the forelegs are raised together, and then, while these are still in mid air, the hind legs are raised. CURVET (2) (*pres.pt.* CURVETTING, *pret. and p.pt.* CURVETTED), *v.i.* to perform a c. [It.].

CURVI-, *pref.* curved. [L.].

CURVILINEAL [ker-vi-li'ni-al], *adj.* curvilinear.

CURVILINEAR [ker-vi-li'ni-er], *adj.* bounded by, or formed of, curved lines. CURVILINEARITY [ker-vi-li-ni-a'ri-ti], *n.* state of being c. CURVILINEARLY, *adv.* in a c. way.

CURVING [kur'ving], *n. and adj.* (in the form of) a curve.

CUSEC [kyōō-sek'], *n.* (*eng. coll.*) one cubic foot per second.

CUSHAT [ku'shat], *n.* ring-dove or wood-pigeon. [OE.].

CUSHION (1) [kōō'shn], *n.* large pad or case of cloth, silk etc., stuffed with soft, yielding material, and used for sitting or resting upon; anything resembling this and used to form a resilient support of anything; elastic lining round the raised inner sides of a billiard-table; steam left in a steam-engine, to resist the movement of the piston; fleshy frog of a horse's hoof; **lady's c.,** (*bot.*) a species of saxifrage; **sea c.,** the sea pink. CUSHION (2), *v.t.* to provide with or bolster up with a c. [AFr.].

CUSHY [kōō'shi], *adj.* (*slang*) comfortable, pleasant, easy. [Hind.].

CUSP [kusp], *n.* (*geom.*) the point in a curve at which its two branches have a common tangent; (*arch.*) projecting point from which two curves spring in Gothic tracery; (*astron.*) either horn of the crescent moon; pointed projection, sharp pointed end of anything. CUSPIDAL [kus'pi-dal], *adj.* pointed; terminating in a c. CUSPIDATE(D), *adj.* having a c. [L.].

CUSPID [kus'pid], *n.* tooth with a fang or fangs. [L.].

CUSPIDOR [kus'pi-daw(r)], *n.* spittoon. [Portug.].

CUSS [kus], *n.* (*vulg.*) curse; fellow, customer. [CURSE, CUS(TOMER)].

CUSSEDNESS [ku'sid-nes], *n.* obstinacy, perverseness. [CURSEDNESS].

CUSTARD [kus'terd], *n.* a mixture of milk and eggs, sweetened and baked or boiled to a thick consistency. [L.].

CUSTARD-APPLE [kus'terd-a-pl], *n.* the fruit of *Anona reticulata,* a West Indian plant with a soft pulp.

CUSTODIAN [kus-tō'di-an], *n.* one who looks after, or is in charge of, some public building etc.; guardian, keeper.

CUSTODY [kus'to-di], *n.* care, guardianship, responsibility for looking after; detention, by imprisonment; the safe-keeping of the police; **to take into c.,** to arrest. [L.].

CUSTOM [kus'tum], *n.* habit, usual practice, established usage having the status of authority or law; continual patronage of a trader by a customer; (*pl.*) duties imposed by law upon exported or imported goods; **customs union,** the adoption by a number of states of a common tariff policy; the states so associated. [OFr. from L.].

CUSTOMARY (1) [kus'tu-me-ri], *adj.* according to custom, usual, habitual, in common practice; originating in or founded on custom. CUSTOMARY (2), *n.* book of laws and usages established by custom. CUSTOMARILY, *adv.* habitually; commonly, usually. CUSTOMARINESS, *n.* quality of being c. [MedL.].

CUSTOMER [kus'tu-mer], *n.* one who makes or intends to make a purchase from a trader, dealer or seller; regular purchaser or patron at a particular shop or trading establishment; (*coll.*) person, fellow. [MedL.].

CUSTOM-HOUSE [kus'tum-hows], *n.* establishment where customs revenue is collected; place where customs duties are paid.

CUT (1) (*pres.pt.* **cutting,** *pret. and p.pt.* **cut**) [kut], *v.t.* to gash, wound or make an incision by means of a sharp-edged instrument, chisel, carve into shape; engrave or incise marks or characters upon a hard substance; grind, shape and polish (gems etc.) into facets; detach, separate into small portions; carve; mow, reap; (of land) yield as a crop; trim, crop in order to shorten (hair); pare; abridge, curtail; omit, delete; reduce in amount; (of teeth) appear in the gums; intersect; deliver a smart, sharp stroke; divide a pack of cards; castrate; construct (a road) by removing obstacles; perform, execute; (fig.) ignore; (cricket) hit the ball with a chopping stroke; (tennis) hit the underside of the ball so as to produce back-spin; (billiards) strike on its extreme edge with the cue-ball; (coll.) absent oneself unlawfully from; v.i. to gash, make an incision, sever; be sharp enough to gash or sever easily; (fig.) produce a painful smarting sensation; (slang) run away, be off; **to c. no ice,** to fail to impress; **to c. to the quick,** to offend or distress deeply; **to c. a dash,** to make a show; **to c. a poor figure,** to show up in an unfavourable light; **to c. in,** (motoring) to overtake a car in face of oncoming traffic which is dangerously near; interrupt; (cards) take the place of someone else; **to c. loose,** to cease to be connected with; behave in a frivolous, wild manner; **to c. off,** to discontinue supplies of, exclude from, deprive of; (of a telephone call) disconnect; (pass.) die suddenly; **to c. off with a shilling,** to disinherit; **to c. out,** (coll.) to desist from, esp. **c. it out;** (eng.) to disconnect; (of a motor) stop; **to c. up,** to criticize severely; review very unfavourably; become rough and uneven; distress sorely; **to c. up rough,** to become angry or insulting; **to c. both ways,** to have an opposite effect in addition to the one intended. [ME.].

CUT (2), n. act of cutting; a smart stroke, slash; the result of cutting or being cut, a wound, mark made by cutting; that which is cut or cut off; method or style in which anything is cut; (print.) engraved block from which prints are impressed, a print obtained in this way; **a c. above,** a class superior to; **a short c.,** a more direct method of approach.

CUT (3), adj. divided, gashed, wounded; shaped, ornamented or otherwise altered by cutting; detached, severed; shortened, reduced; shredded (of tobacco); **c. grass,** spear-grass; **c. and dried,** ready-made, straightforward, stereotyped.

CUTANEOUS [kyōō-tā'nī-ōōs], adj. pertaining to the skin. [MedL.].

CUT-AWAY [ku'ta-wā], n. and adj. (coat) cut so as to curve back from the waist.

CUT-BACK [kut'bak], n. (cinema) repetition of shots previously shown to heighten the dramatic effect.

CUTE [kyōōt], adj. sharp, cunning, clever, keen-witted; (U.S. slang) attractive, charming; quaint. CUTENESS, n. quality of being c. [(A)CUTE].

CUTICLE [kyōō'ti-kl], n. the epidermis, outer skin of animals, thin external covering of plants. CUTICULAR [kyōō-ti'kyōō-ler], adj. belonging to the c. [L.].

CUTIS [kyōō'tis], n. true skin beneath the cuticle. [L.].

CUTLASS [kut'las], n. short sword with a broad, slightly curving, single-edged blade. [Fr.].

CUTLER [kut'ler], n. one who makes, sells or repairs knives or cutting instruments. [ME.].

CUTLERY [kut'le-ri], n. business of a cutler; knives and other sharp-edged instruments. [OFr.].

CUTLET [kut'let], n. small chop or slice of meat cut off from the rib-bones. [Fr.].

CUT-OFF [kut'of], n. device in the valve-gear of a steam-engine by which the steam can be cut off from the cylinder in the course of the piston-stroke; device to prevent the flow of a liquid; device to prevent cartridges from moving from the magazine of a rifle into the breech chamber.

CUT-OUT [kut'owt], n. (elect.) device which automatically breaks the circuit of an electric current when it exceeds a fixed strength; (motoring) device for releasing exhaust gases without their passing through a silencer.

CUTPURSE [kut'pers], n. (archaic) thief, pickpocket.

CUTTER [ku'ter], n. one who, or that which, cuts; one who cuts out cloth to measure; small boat used by ships of war; single-masted vessel with a running bowsprit, fore-and-aft rigged, with gaff mainsail, foresail and jib; (U.S.) light sledge; (pl.) variety of brick; **revenue c.,** fast motor vessel, used for customs purposes.

CUT-THROAT (1) [kut'thrōt], n. murderer, fierce ruffian. CUT-THROAT (2), adj. murderous, cruel; (fig.) merciless; **c. bridge, whist,** three-handed bridge, whist etc.

CUTTING (1) [ku'ting], n. act of one who cuts; that which is cut out; excavation, passage cut through a hill for a railway, road etc.; printed extract cut out

of a publication; slip from a plant, cut off and replanted to form a new plant; reduction in prices. CUTTING (2), adj. that cuts or is used to cut; (of wind etc.) penetrating, bitter; (fig.) sarcastic, intended to hurt the feelings.

CUTTLE-BONE [ku'tl-bōn], n. internal shell of the cuttle-fish, used in polishing.

CUTTLE-FISH [ku'tl-fish], n. marine cephalopod animal, with long tentacles, and a sac from which it shoots out a black fluid when attacked. [OE.].

CUT-WATER [kut'waw-ter], n. (naut.) the forepart of a ship's prow; wedge-shaped end of a pier of a bridge against which the current flows and is divided; an American water-fowl.

CUT-WORM [kut'werm], n. caterpillar, grub or worm destructive to young cultivated plants.

CYANAMIDE [sī-a'na-mīd], n. (chem.) the amide of cyanogen; certain compounds of this, esp. calcium cyanamide, used as a fertilizer.

CYANIC [sī-a'nik], adj. blue; containing cyanogen. [Gk.].

CYANIDE (1) [sī'a-nīd], n. a salt of hydrocyanic acid, prussic acid. CYANIDE (2), v.t. (metal.) to treat (ores) with a c. in order to extract metals.

CYANINE [sī'a-nin], n. a blue colouring principle.

CYANITE [sī'a-nīt], n. an anorthic silicate of aluminium, a hard, infusible mineral. [Gk.].

CYANO-, pref. blue. [Gk.].

CYANOGEN [sī-a'nō-jen], n. (chem.) a compound radical of nitrogen and carbon, a colourless, poisonous gas. [Gk.].

CYANOSIS [sī-a-nō'sis], n. blueness of the skin because of the lack of the normal amount of oxygen in the blood. [Gk.].

CYCLAMEN [sik'la-men], n. (bot.) genus of plants with beautiful flowers and fleshy root-stocks; the colour of this flower. CYCLAMINE, n. poisonous substance obtained from the roots of the c. [Gk.].

CYCLE (1) [sī'kl], n. a succession of the same events regularly returning at uniform intervals of time; period of time taken for this recurrence; fixed period of time regularly recurring; (astron.) one of the heavenly circles; long indefinite period of time, an age; complete series, round or course; group of poems, songs or legends revolving round or associated with some theme; (elect.) one complete positive and negative wave of an alternating current; (coll.) bicycle. CYCLE (2), v.i. to recur or revolve through a c., ride a bicycle. [Gk.].

CYCLE-CAR [sī'kl-kah(r)], n. a form of light motor vehicle, often three-wheeled.

CYCLIC [sī'klik], adj. pertaining to, revolving or returning in, connected with, a cycle; **c. poets,** epic poets who wrote of the Trojan War; **c. arrangements,** (bot.) growth in which leaves etc. are attached at the same level. CYCLICAL, adj. c.

CYCLIST [sī'klist], n. one who rides a bicycle.

CYCLO-, pref. circle. [Gk.].

CYCLOID (1) [sī'kloid], n. geometrical curve described by a point in the circumference of a circle as it completes a single revolution in moving along a straight line. CYCLOID (2), adj. circular, resembling a circle in form. CYCLOIDAL, adj. relating to a c. [Gk.].

CYCLOMETER [sī-klo'mi-ter], n. instrument for measuring circles or circular arcs; instrument attached to the wheel of a vehicle to record the distance travelled. CYCLOMETRY [sī-klo'mi-tri], n. art of measuring circles. [Gk.].

CYCLONE [sī'klōn], n. system of winds blowing or rotating spirally inwards towards a centre of lower barometric pressure; hurricane, tornado, sudden violent whirling wind. CYCLONIC [sī-klo'nik], adj. pertaining to a c. [Gk.].

CYCLOPEAN [sī-klō-pē'an], adj. pertaining to, or resembling, the Cyclops; gigantic, vast; pertaining to an ancient style of architecture using huge blocks of unhewn stone. [Gk.].

CYCLOPEDIA [sī-klō-pē'di-ah], n. encyclopedia. [Gk.].

CYCLOPS [sī-klops], n. fabulous race of one-eyed giants, in Greek mythology; (zool.) small crustacean having only one eye; one-eyed person. CYCLOPIC [sī-klo'pik], adj. Cyclopean. [Gk.].

CYCLORAMA [sī-klō-rah'mah], n. series of pictures of a landscape or scene arranged to form a hollow cylinder round an observer; stage backcloth of similar form. [Gk.].

CYCLOSTOMATA [sī-klō-sto'ma-tah], n. (pl.) the lowest class of invertebrate animals. [Gk.].

CYCLOSTYLE (1) [sī'klō-stīl], n. apparatus in the

form of a pen fitted with a small toothed wheel which cuts a stencil in specially prepared paper, from which many copies of a written document may be printed; any duplicator. CYCLOSTYLE (2), *v.t.* to copy by means of a c. [CYCLO and STYLE].

CYCLOTRON [si′klō-tron], *n. (phys.)* electro-magnetic apparatus for accelerating the speed of ions. [CYCLO-(ELEC)TRON].

CYDER, see CIDER.

CYGNET [sig′net], *n.* a young swan. [L.].

CYLINDER [si′lin-der], *n.* the solid enclosed by a circle or other closed curve moving perpendicularly in one direction only; object of similar form to this, a roller; *(eng.)* cylindrical chamber in which the piston is driven; *(print.)* hollow metal roller inking or bearing the type or printing surface. CYLINDER-BLOCK, the main casting containing the group of cylinders of an engine. CYLINDER-HEAD, the top, usually detachable, of an engine's c. [Gk.].

CYLINDRIC(AL) [si-lin′drik(-al)], *adj.* having the shape of a cylinder.

CYLINDROID [si′lin-droid], *n.* a solid body like a cylinder, the ends of which form an ellipse. [Gk.].

CYMA, CIMA [si′mah], *n. (arch.)* the moulding of a cornice, the profile of which is formed of a convex curve joined to a concave curve. [Gk.].

CYMBAL [sim′bal], *n.* musical percussion instrument in the form of a thin, hollow plate of brass. [Gk.].

CYME [sim], *n. (bot.)* flowering process in which the principal single-flowered stem bears several single-flowered stems, which in turn bear similar stems, all the stems being of proportionate length so that a flat-topped or rounded mass of flowers is produced. CYMOID, *adj.* like a c. [Gk.].

CYMOGRAPH [si′mō-grahf], *n.* revolving cylinder covered with graph paper on which something is recorded. [Gk.].

CYMOMETER [si-mo′mi-ter], *n.* device used in wireless telegraphy to measure the wavelengths. [Gk.].

CYMOSCOPE [si′mō-skōp], *n.* wave detector in wireless telegraphy or telephony. [Gk.].

CYMOSE [si′mōs], *adj.* containing a cyme; in the shape of a cyme.

CYMRIC [kim′rik], *adj.* Welsh. [Wel.].

CYMRY [kim′ri], *n.* the Welsh people. [Wel.].

CYNANCHE [si-nang′ki], *n. (med.)* disease of the throat and tonsils. [Gk.].

CYNIC (1) [si′nik], *n.* member of a group of ancient Greek philosophers who believed in rigid self-control, self-denial and complete independence of external conditions; one tending to see the worst in things, a pessimistic realist. CYNIC (2), *adj.* pertaining to the Cynics or their philosophy; cynical. [Gk.].

CYNICAL [si′ni-kal] *adj.* resembling the Cynics in philosophy or opinions; having the frame of mind of a cynic. CYNICALLY, *adv.* in c. fashion.

CYNICISM [si′ni-sizm], *n.* the opinions, character or frame of mind of a cynic; an example of this.

CYNOSURE [si′nō-shoōr], *n. (astron.)* the northern constellation, the Little Bear; *(fig.)* a centre of attraction, object of immediate attention or interest. [Gk.].

CYPERUS [si′pe-rus], *n. (bot.)* genus of plants of the sedge family. [Gk.].

CYPHER, see CIPHER.

CY PRES [sē-prā′], *adj. and adv. (leg.)* near; to be applied to an object as near as possible to that specified by the benefactor. [AFr.].

CYPRESS [si′pres], *n.* genus of dark-coloured evergreen coniferous trees; the hard reddish wood of this tree; *(poet.)* the tree or its branches as the emblem of mourning. [Gk.].

CYPRIAN (1) [sip′ri-an], *n.* immoral woman. CYPRIAN (2), *adj.* belonging to the island of Cyprus. [L.].

CYPRIOT [sip′ri-ot], *n.* inhabitant or native of Cyprus. [L.].

CYRENAIC [si-re-nā′ik], *adj.* pertaining to the Hedonistic school of philosophy originated by Aristippus of Cyrene. [Gk.].

CYRILLIC [si-ri′lik], *adj.* pertaining to the Slavonic alphabet. [St. *Cyril*, its supposed inventor].

CYST [sist], *n.* a membranous cavity in the body containing fluid; closed sac containing pus or other morbid matter. [Gk.].

CYSTI-, CYSTO-, *pref.* a cyst or bladder. [Gk.].

CYSTIC [sis′tik], *adj.* pertaining to, resembling or containing, cysts; pertaining to the gall-bladder or urinary bladder.

CYSTITIS [sis-ti′tis], *n.* inflammation of the bladder. [Gk.].

CYSTOCELE [sis′tō-sēl], *n.* hernia of the urinary bladder. [Gk.].

CYSTOID [sis′toid], *adj.* like a cyst. [Gk.].

CYSTOMA [sis-tō′mah], *n.* tumour full of cysts. [Gk.].

CYSTOSCOPE [sis′tō-skōp], *n.* instrument used to examine the inside of the bladder. [Gk.].

CYSTOTOMY [sis-to′to-mi], *n.* operation of cutting into the bladder to remove a stone etc. [Gk.].

CYTHEREAN [si-the-rē′an], *adj.* belonging, or pertaining, to Venus. [Gk.].

CYTOBLAST [si′tō-blahst], *n.* the nucleus of a cell. [Gk.].

CYTOLOGY [si-to′lo-ji], *n.* study of cell-division in its bearing on heredity. [Gk.].

CYTOPLASM [si′tō-plazm], *n.* the protoplasm of a living cell. [Gk.].

CZAR, TSAR [zah(r)], *n.* king, chief, title of the former emperors of Russia. [Russ. from L.].

CZARDAS, *erroneous variant of* CSARDAS.

CZAREVITCH [zah′re-vich], *n.* title of the eldest son of the former emperors of Russia. [Russ.].

CZAREVNA [zah-rev′nah], *n.* a daughter of the former emperors of Russia. [Russ.].

CZARINA [zah-rē′nah], *n.* title of the former empress of Russia. [Russ.]

D

D [dē], fourth letter in the English alphabet; *(mus.)* second note of the scale of C major; *(Roman numerals)* 500.

DAB (1) [dab], *n.* a sea flat-fish. [Unkn.].

DAB (2), *n. (coll.)* an expert at anything. [Unkn.].

DAB (3), *v.t.* to apply by dabbing; *v.i.* to touch lightly, repeat this action for a time. DAB (4), *n.* light tap, gentle blow; that which is dabbed on; dabber. [ME.].

DABBER [da′ber], *n.* that which dabs; *(print.)* ball or pad for inking type.

DABBLE [da′bl], *v.t. and i.* to dip repeatedly in, play with, or splash about in, water; make wet with little splashes; *(fig.)* take a superficial interest in anything, meddle with. DABBLER, *n.* person who dabbles. DABBLINGLY, *adv.* in a dabbling fashion. [DAB].

DABCHICK [dab′chik], *n.* small species of grebe; moorhen.

DA CAPO [dah-kah′pō], *(mus.)* repeat from the beginning. [It.].

DACE [dās], *n.* a freshwater fish. [OFr.].

DACHSHUND [dahks′hoōnt], *n.* variety of dog, long in the body, with short, bandy legs. [Germ.].

DACOIT, DAKOIT [da-koit′], *n.* member of a gang of Burmese thieves; river pirate. DACOITY, DAKOITY, *n.* practices of a d. [Hind.].

DACTYL [dak′til], *n. (pros.)* foot of one long and two short syllables. DACTYLIC (1) [dak-ti′lik], *adj.* relating to a d. DACTYLIC (2), *n.* dactylic line of verse; poem in this metre. [Gk.].

DACTYLOGRAM [dak′ti-lō-gram], *n.* finger-print impression taken for identification. [Gk.].

DACTYLOLOGY [dak-ti-lo′lō-ji], *n.* study and use of the dumb alphabet; conversation by signs of the fingers. [Gk.].

DAD [dad], *n. (coll.)* father. [Unkn.].

DADDA [da′dah], *n. (childish)* father. [Prec.].

DADDY [da′di], *n.* father. [DAD].

DADDY-LONGLEGS [da-di-long′legz], *n.* a crane-fly of the genus *Tipula.*

DADO [dā′dō], *n. (arch.)* the square part between the cornice and base of a pedestal; wainscoting of a

---

oō is pronounced as in *food*; ŏ as in *hood*; th as in *think*; TH as in *that*; zh as in *azure*. ~ = related to.

wall; decorated part of a wall close to the floor. [It.].

DAEDAL [dē'dal], *adj.* skilful, intricate. [Gk. *Daidalos*, a mythical builder].

DAFFODIL [da'fo-dil], *n.* (*bot.*) yellow spring flower of the genus *Narcissus*; pale yellow colour. [Gk.].

DAFFY [da'fi], *adj.* (*slang*) daft.

DAFT [dahft], *adj.* foolish, idiotic. [OE.].

DAG [dag], *n.* shred; dag-lock. [Uncert.].

DAGGER [da'ger], *n.* short double-edged weapon for stabbing; (*fencing*) blunt blade having a basket-hilt; (*print.*) mark of reference shaped like a dagger (†) or a double dagger (‡); **at daggers drawn**, at bitter enmity. [Fr.].

DAGGLE [da'gl], *v.t.* to drag in wet grass and mud. [Uncert.].

DAG-LOCK [dag'lok], *n.* (*usu. pl.*) piece of dirty wool on the hinder parts of a sheep.

DAGO [dā'gō], *n.* (*slang*) person of dark complexion; half-breed. [Span.].

DAGUERREOTYPE (1) [dah-gāer'ō-tīp], *n.* early type of photograph on a glass or metal plate which had an emulsion developed in mercury vapour. DAGUERREOTYPE (2), *v.t.* to photograph by the d. process. [L. *Daguerre*, inventor].

DAHABIAH [dah-hah-bē'yah], *n.* passenger sailing boat plying on the Nile. [Arab.].

DAHLIA [dā'li-ah], *n.* (*bot.*) herbaceous plant with large bright flowers. [A. *Dahl*, Swedish botanist].

DAIL EIREANN [doil-ā'rahn], *n.* lower chamber of the Irish parliament. [Ir.].

DAILY (1) [dā'li], *adj.* happening, issued, every day; **d. bread**, one's livelihood. DAILY (2), *n.* newspaper published every weekday; maidservant who does not live in. DAILY (3), *adv.* on every day. [OE.].

DAINTY (1) [dān'ti], *n.* a delicacy, something very pleasant to the palate. DAINTY (2), *adj.* fastidious, delicate; affectedly refined. DAINTILY, *adv.* in a d. manner. DAINTINESS, *n.* condition of being d. [OFr. from L.].

DAIRY (1) [dāer'i], *n.* the building or room in a farm for making and storing butter and cheese; shop where milk, eggs etc. are sold. DAIRY (2), *adj.* relating to, or made in, a d. DAIRY-FARM, farm producing only or mainly d. produce. DAIRYING, *n.* business of running a d. [ME.].

DAIRYMAID [dāer'i-mād], *n.* woman employed in a dairy.

DAIRYMAN [dāer'i-man], *n.* man who keeps or works for a dairy.

DAIS [dā'is], *n.* raised platform placed usually at one end of a room. [OFr.].

DAISY (1) [dā'zi], *n.* (*bot.*) small, composite, wild plant, having white petals and a yellow centre; (*slang, chiefly U.S.*) something of unusual excellence. DAISIED, *adj.* full of, decorated with, daisies. [OE.].

DAISY-CHAIN [dā'zi-chān], *n.* a string of daisies fastened together by their stems.

DAISYCUTTER [dā'zi-ku-ter], *n.* (*cricket*) ball which comes along fast and close to the ground; horse which barely lifts its hooves.

DAK [dahk], *n.* a system of transmitting letters in the East. [Hind.].

DAKOIT, see DACOIT.

DAKOITY, see DACOITY.

DALAI-LAMA [dah-li-lah'mah], *n.* the ruler of Tibet. [Native].

DALE [dāl], *n.* valley. [OE., OScand.].

DALESMAN [dālz'man], *n.* person who lives in the northern dales.

DALLIANCE [da'li-ans], *n.* dallying. [OFr.].

DALLY [da'li], *v.i.* to waste time, trifle; play or flirt (with); (*fig.*) contemplate (a scheme or idea). DALLYING, *n.* act of one who dallies. [AFr.].

DALMATIAN [dal-mā'shn], *n.* breed of spotted dog, originally bred in Dalmatia.

DALMATIC [dal-ma'tik], *n.* robe worn by kings at their coronation, and by deacons and bishops. [L.].

DALTONISM [dawl'to-nizm], *n.* colour-blindness.

DAM (1) [dam], *n.* mother, *esp.* of animals. [DAME].

DAM (2), *n.* obstruction built across a river to control its flow. DAM (3) (*pres.pt.* DAMMING, *pret.* and *p.pt.* DAMMED), *v.t.* to obstruct with a d. [ME.].

DAMAGE (1) [da'mij], *n.* injury to an object, person or reputation; (*coll.*) the estimated cost of repair; (*pl.*) (*leg.*) amount of money claimed or awarded as compensation; **d. feasant**, (*leg.*) compensation claimed for d. to property by cattle. DAMAGE (2), *v.t.* to injure, reduce the value of. DAMAGEABLE, *adj.* liable to be damaged. [OFr.].

DAMASCENE (1) [da-ma-sēn'], *adj.* relating to

Damascus. DAMASCENE (2), *v.t.* to decorate (steel) with gold and silver patterns.

DAMASK (1) [da'mask], *n.* fabric of silk or linen with a raised pattern woven into it; the colour of the damask rose; steel made in Damascus. DAMASK (2), *adj.* of the colour of a d. rose. DAMASK (3), *v.t.* to weave a pattern on fabrics; decorate steel in the Damascene fashion. [*Damascus*, Syria].

DAMASK ROSE [da-mask-rōz'], *n.* a pink rose from Damascus.

DAMASK-STEEL [da-mask-stēl'], *n.* fine steel made in the Levant for sword blades.

DAME [dām], *n.* woman holding authority; wife of a baronet or knight; female knight of the Order of the British Empire; (*U.S. slang*) woman; in pantomime, the part of a farcical old woman, played by a man; **dame's school**, kindergarten school run by a woman. [OFr. from L.].

DAMN (1) [dam], *v.t.* to pass a sentence of eternal punishment on, condemn; swear, curse; ruin a reputation; criticize heavily. DAMN (2), *n.* (an oath); (*coll.*) a jot. [L.].

DAMNABLE [dam'na-bl], *adj.* worthy of damnation. DAMNABILITY, DAMNABLENESS [dam-na-bi'li-ti, dam'na-bl-nes], *n.* quality or condition of being d. DAMNABLY, *adv.* in a d. fashion.

DAMNATION [dam-nā'shn], *n.* act of damning; state of being damned. [L.].

DAMNATORY [dam'na-te-ri], *adj.* effecting condemnation, condemnatory. [L.].

DAMNIFY [dam'ni-fi], *v.t.* (*leg.*) to cause damage to. DAMNIFICATION [dam-ni-fi-kā'shn], *n.* (*leg.*) act of injuring. [L.].

DAMNING [da'ming], *adj.* causing or exposing to damnation; sufficient to convict.

DAMOCLEAN [da-mō-klē'an], *adj.* constantly menacing. [Gk. *Damokles*, over whose head a sword was hung on a thread].

DAMOSEL [da'mō-zel], *n.* maid, virgin. [~DAM-SEL].

DAMP (1) [damp], *n.* humidity, slight wetness; moist vapour, fog; gas accumulating in coal mines; (*fig.*) dejection. CHOKE-DAMP, carbonic acid gas. FIRE-DAMP, noxious explosive gas in coal mines. DAMP (2), *adj.* moist, humid. DAMP (3), *v.t.* to make d., slow the combustion of a boiler fire by checking the entry of air; (*fig.*) discourage; (*mus.*) stop the vibration of a string. [Du.].

DAMP-COURSE [damp'kaws], *n.* a layer, usually of slate or bitumen, inserted in brickwork or masonry to check the percolation of moisture.

DAMPEN [dam'pen], *v.t.* to make damp.

DAMPER [dam'per], *n.* person who, or thing which, damps; iron plate controlling the draught in a furnace; (*mus.*) felt pad checking the vibration of a piano string.

DAMPING [dam'ping], *n.* the rate at which radio oscillations lessen in intensity.

DAMPNESS [damp'nes], *n.* condition of being damp.

DAMP-PROOF [damp'prōof], *adj.* waterproof.

DAMSEL [dam'zel], *n.* maiden. [OFr.].

DAMSON [dam'zon], *n.* small sour plum; tree on which this grows. [OFr. from L.].

DANCE (1) [dahns], *v.t.* to perform (a dance); make to dance; *v.i.* to execute a dance; caper about; **to d. attendance upon**, to accompany constantly, fawn round. DANCE (2), *n.* a series of rhythmic, bodily movements usually performed to music; any special form of d.; party or gathering for a d.; **St. Vitus's d.**, convulsive nervous movements of muscles, chorea; **to lead a person a d.**, to distract or obstruct a person deliberately. [OFr.].

DANCER [dahn'ser], *n.* person who dances; ballet girl.

DANCING [dahn'sing], *n.* art of the dance. DANCING-MASTER, man who teaches dancing.

DANDELION [dan'di-li-on], *n.* (*bot.*) a wild plant with a bright yellow flower and a deeply indented leaf. [Fr.].

DANDER [dan'der], *n.* anger, temper. [Unkn.].

DANDIACAL [dan-dī'a-kal], *adj.* dandified.

DANDIE [dan'di], *n.* breed of Scottish terriers. [*Dandie* Dinmont, in Scott's *Guy Mannering*].

DANDIFY [dan'di-fi], *v.t.* to give the appearance of a dandy to. DANDIFIED, *adj.* having the dress or manners of a dandy.

DANDLE [dan'dl], *v.t.* to jiggle (a child) on the knee; fondle. [It.].

DANDRUFF, DANDRIFF [dan'druf, dan'drif], *n.* scurf of dry skin on the scalp. [Uncert.].

DANDY (1) [dan'di], *n.* fop, man of fashion; a yawl.

The accent ' after a syllable = stress (u-pon'). The mark ‾ over a vowe l= length (ā in made; ō in bone)

DANDY (2), *adj.* in the style of a d., foppish; (*coll.*), (*esp. U.S.*) fine, excellent. DANDYISH, *adj.* resembling a d. DANDYISM, *n.* foppishness, manners and dress of a d. [Uncert.].

DANDY-BRUSH [dan'di-brush], *n.* hard brush used in grooming horses.

DANE [dān], *n.* a native of Denmark; great d., breed of large dogs trained in Denmark for hunting boars. [OScand.].

DANEGELD [dān'geld], *n.* (*hist.*) tax levied in the tenth century to buy off the invading Danes.

DANGER [dān'jer], *n.* whatever produces risk of injury or death; condition or cause of peril; exposure to risk of injury or death; d. signal, signal denoting the presence of d. [OFr.].

DANGEROUS [dān'je-rŏŏs], *adj.* full of danger, unsafe, menacing. DANGEROUSLY, *adv.* in a d. fashion.

DANGLE [dang'gl], *v.t. and i.* to swing loosely; hang about. DANGLER, *n.* person who dangles. [OSwed.].

DANK [dangk], *adj.* moist, rotting. DANKISH, *adj.* somewhat damp. [ME.].

DANTESQUE [dahn-tesk'], *adj.* resembling the work of Dante.

DAP (*pres.pt.* dapping, *pret. and p.pt.* dapped) [dap], *v.t. and i.* to drop bait gently into the water; (of a ball) bounce. [Uncert.].

DAPHNE [daf'ni], *n.* genus of flowering shrubs. [Gk.].

DAPPER [da'per], *adj.* smart, neat, well-dressed; sprightly. [ME.].

DAPPLE (1) [da pl], *adj.* marked with spots of different colours or shades. DAPPLE (2), *v.t.* to speckle, variegate with spots. [Unkn.].

DARBIES [dah'biz], *n.(pl.)* (*slang*) handcuffs. [Unkn.].

DARBY [dah'bi], *n.* tool for levelling plaster on a ceiling. [Unkn.].

DARE (dared, †durst) [dāer], *v.t. and i.* to challenge or defy a person to do something by an implication of cowardice; venture upon, have sufficient courage for; I d. say, I believe it possible (often with irony). [OE.].

DAREDEVIL [dāer'de-vil], *n. and adj.* (characteristic of) a person who dares any danger.

DARING (1) [dāer'ing], *n.* reckless courage. DARING (2), *adj.* brave, fearless, audacious. DARINGLY, *adv.* in a d. fashion.

DARING-NET [dāer'ing-net], *n.* net for capturing birds.

DARK (1) [dahk], *adj.* completely without light, with very little light, almost black; gloomy, sombre; sallow complexioned; (*fig.*) without understanding or knowledge; hidden, obscure; secret; evil, sinister; d. ages, (*hist.*) period from the fifth to the eleventh centuries in Europe; d. blues, athletes representing Oxford University; d. horse, competitor whose form or potentialities are unknown; d. room, (*phot.*) light-proof room in which negatives are developed. DARK (2), *n.* darkness, obscurity, gloom; (*fig.*) ignorance, secrecy. [OE.].

DARKEN [dah'ken], *v.t. and i.* to make dark or darker, shut out light from; (*fig.*) render ignorant, immoral or foul; cause confusion; sadden; give a darker tone to; become dark or darker.

DARKLING (1) [dahk'ling], *adj.* gloomy, dim. DARKLING (2), *adv.* in the dark. [ME.].

DARKLY [dahk'li], *adv.* in the dark; not clearly, mysteriously.

DARKNESS [dahk'nes], *n.* condition or quality of being dark; (*fig.*) ignorance, wickedness.

DARKSOME [dahk'sum], *adj.* dark; dismal.

DARKY [dah'ki], *n.* (*coll.*) negro.

DARLING (1) [dah'ling], *n.* person dearly beloved, sweetheart. DARLING (2), *adj.* much loved; pretty. [OE.].

DARN (1) [dahn], *v.t.* to mend a hole or tear in a material by imitating the texture of the stuff with new threads. DARN (2), *n.* place mended by darning. [OE.].

DARN (3), *v.t.* (*coll.*) to confound. [~DAMN].

DARNEL [dah'nel], *n.* (*bot.*) a grass which grows among corn. [ME.].

DARNER [dah'ner], *n.* person who, or instrument which, darns.

DARNING [dah'ning], *n.* action of making a darn; articles to be darned. DARNING-NEEDLE, large needle used in d.

DART (1) [daht], *n.* light, pointed weapon usually fitted with guide feathers, thrown by hand, formerly used in close fighting and now in the game of darts;

a rapid movement forward; (*dressmaking*) small fold made in the cloth so that it fits more closely. DART (2), *v.t. and i.* to jerk rapidly forward, shoot out; play a game of darts; move suddenly and rapidly forward; (*fig.*) fly in the air like a swallow. [OFr.].

DARTBOARD [daht'bawd], *n.* marked board, usually circular in form, at which darts are thrown.

DARTS [dahts], *n.* game in which two or more persons compete in throwing darts at a suitably marked board.

DARWINIAN (1) [dah-wi'ni-an], *adj.* pertaining to Charles Darwin and his theories. DARWINIAN (2), *n.* believer in the Darwinian theory.

DARWINISM [dah'wi-nizm], *n.* the scientific theories of Darwin. [C. *Darwin*, scientist].

DASH (1) [dash], *v.t. and i.* to throw violently; smash, shatter; bespatter; rush with fury or violence; (*fig.*) abash, lower the spirits of; (*int.*) confound. DASH (2), *n.* sudden, short rapid run, a rush; a flavouring of one liquid in another; (*fig.*) resolute energetic action; swift stroke with pen, pencil or brush, *esp.* a horizontal line, as ——, to signify a pause or parenthesis; mild expletive; show, swagger, ostentation; to cut a d., to make a show, give a false impression of wealth or ability. [ME.].

DASHBOARD [dash'bawd], *n.* wooden screen to protect the driver of a horse-drawn vehicle from mud etc.; board in front of the driver in a motor-vehicle fitted with gauges, switches etc.

DASHER [da'sher], *n.* the plunger in a churn; (*coll.*) modish fellow.

DASHING [da'shing], *adj.* bold, energetic; showy.

DASTARD [das'tahd], *n.* contemptible coward; person who takes mean advantages. [ME.].

DASTARDLY [das'tahd-li], *adj.* cowardly, taking a mean advantage, brutal.

DATA [dā'tah], *n.(pl.)* facts assumed to be fixed or true, from which inferences are drawn and opinions formed. [DATUM].

DATE (1) [dāt], *n.* the day, month and year when something occurred; specified moment in time; numerical designation of a day; to make a d., to arrange an appointment; out of d., old-fashioned, obsolete; to d., up to the present; up to d., up-to-d., abreast of the times, modern, fashionable. DATE (2), *v.t. and i.* to assign a d. to; derive from a past period or point of time; become obsolete or old-fashioned. DATABLE, *adj.* able to be dated. DATELESS, *adj.* undated; immemorial. [L.].

DATE (3), *n.* oval, sweet, firm-fleshed fruit of the date-palm. [Fr. from Gk.].

DATE-LINE [dāt'līn], *n.* hypothetical line in the Pacific on the east of which time is a day ahead of time on the west side; the heading giving the origin of a press message.

DATE-PALM [dāt'pahm], *n.* palm-tree *Phoenix dactylifera*, yielding dates.

DATIVE [dā'tiv], *n.* (*gram.*) the case of a noun which denotes the indirect object of a verb, and is used after some prepositions in certain languages. DATIVAL [da-tī'val], *adj.* relating to the d. [L.].

DATUM (*pl.* data) [dā'tum], *n.* something ascertained or assumed; fact given or known and from which inferences are made; d. line, (*surveying*) line from which are reckoned all the heights along a section. [L.].

DATURA [da-tyŏŏ'rah], *n.* (*bot.*) genus of poisonous plants including the thorn-apple. DATURINE, *n.* poisonous alkaloid extracted from the thorn-apple. [Skr.].

DAUB (1) [dawb], *v.t. and i.* to smear with any sticky matter; paint badly. DAUB (2), *n.* paint of mixed colours applied widely; a poorly painted picture. DAUBER, DAUBSTER, *n.* person who daubs. [OFr. from L.].

DAUGHTER [daw'ter], *n.* female child or descendant; (*fig.*) woman deriving certain characteristics from a specified source. [OE.].

DAUGHTER-IN-LAW [daw'ter-in-law], *n.* a son's wife.

DAUGHTERLY (1) [daw'ter-li], *adj.* like, or appertaining to, a daughter. DAUGHTERLY, (2) *adv.* in a d. way. DAUGHTERLINESS, *n.* state of being d.

DAUNT [dawnt], *v.t.* to quell; intimidate. [OFr., L.].

DAUNTLESS [dawnt'les], *adj.* courageous, intrepid.

DAUPHIN † [daw'fin], *n.* title of the eldest son of the King of France. [Fr.].

DAVENPORT [da'ven-pawt], *n.* small writing-table. [Uncert.].

DAVITS [da'vits], *n.* (*pl.*) (*naut.*) metal uprights in

ŏŏ is pronounced as in food; ŏŏ as in hood; th as in *think*; TH as in *that*; zh as in azure. ~ = related to.

which a boat is slung on a ship's deck, ready to be lowered to the water; **fish d.**, small crane over the bows for hoisting up the anchor. [OFr.].

DAVY JONES [dā-vi-jōnz'], *n.* (*naut.*) the Devil; **Davy Jones's locker**, the sea as a grave. [Unkn.].

DAVY LAMP [dā'vi-lamp], *n.* safety-lamp lessening the risk of explosion in mines. [Sir Humphry *Davy*, inventor].

DAW [daw], *n.* the jackdaw. [ME.].

DAWDLE [daw'dl], *v.i.* to waste time, hang about, wander aimlessly. [Unkn.].

DAWN (1) [dawn], *v.i.* to begin to grow light; (*fig.*) begin to open or appear; **to d. upon,** (*coll.*) to enter the consciousness or mind of. DAWN (2), *n.* daybreak; (*fig.*) a beginning. DAWNING, *n.* d.; action of that which dawns. [ME.].

DAY [dā], *n.* the time from sunrise to sunset; a period of twenty-four hours; the part of this period devoted to work; a period of time, epoch (often *pl.*); daylight; an appointed time; **d. by d.,** daily, occurring on each successive d.; **d. of doom,** the d. of judgment; **d. of grace,** (*theol.*) the period during which mercy is granted to sinners; **D. of Judgment,** the time of the Last Judgment; **d. rule,** (*leg.*) licence granted to a prisoner to go beyond the bounds of prison; **day's work,** labour completed in one d.; **d. ticket,** return ticket available for both journeys on the d. of issue only; **days of grace,** (*leg.*) period of delay granted a defendant; period of delay after the stipulated d. of settlement of credit notes; **this d. week,** the corresponding d. of next week; **to win the d.,** to gain the victory; **to call it a d.,** to agree to finish; **civil d.,** period of twenty-four hours from midnight to midnight; **d. in, d. out,** every d. without intermission; **d. off,** holiday; **d. out,** excursion, servant's free d. TODAY, this day. [OE.].

DAY-BOOK [dā'book], *n.* (*comm.*) record of day-to-day sales or business transactions.

DAY-BOY [dā'boi], *n.* non-resident boy attending a secondary or public school.

DAYBREAK [dā'brāk], *n.* dawn.

DAYDREAM (1) [dā'drēm], *n.* a foolish fancy; reverie; visionary scheme offering little hope of materialization. DAYDREAM (2), *v.i.* to indulge in daydreams. DAYDREAMER, *n.* one who daydreams.

DAY-FLY [dā'fli], *n.* a May-fly, any species of *Ephemera.*

DAY-LABOUR [dā'lā-ber], *n.* work performed during the daytime. DAY-LABOURER, *n.* labourer engaged by the day.

DAYLIGHT [dā'līt], *n.* the light of the sun; natural light; **to see d.,** to see one's way out of a difficulty; **D. Saving Act,** Act passed by Parliament in 1916 whereby the clock is set forward in the summer months.

DAY-NURSERY [dā'ner-se-ri], *n.* institution looking after young children during the day while their mothers work.

DAY-SCHOOL [dā'skool], *n.* school where the pupils come daily to be taught, but are not boarded.

DAYSPRING [dā'spring], *n.* the dawn; (*fig.*) beginning.

DAY-STAR [dā'stah(r)], *n.* the morning star.

DAYTIME [dā'tīm], *n.* the period when there is daylight, from dawn to sunset.

DAZE (1) [dāz], *v.t.* to numb the brain, stupefy; dazzle. DAZE (2), *n.* state of stupefaction; (*min.*) a glittering stone. [OScand.].

DAZZLE (1) [da'zl], *v.t. and i.* to confuse or cause to be temporarily blinded by a powerful glaring light; camouflage by painting; (*fig.*) be agreeably overwhelmed by some quality in a person or object so that the power of judgment is affected. DAZZLE (2), *n.* that which dazzles. [~DAZE].

D-DAY [dē'dā], *n.* (*milit.*) the opening day of a major offensive, *esp.* of the invasion of the European continent from Britain in 1944.

DE-, *pref.* away, down; over; completely; also expressing negation, deprivation, deficiency. [L.].

DEACON [dē'kn], *n.* (*eccles.*) church official helping the priest; one who has been ordained to the ecclesiastical order next below the priesthood; person responsible for the secular management of a Presbyterian church; church official helping the minister and taking part in the secular administration of a Congregational church. DEACONRY, DEACONSHIP, *n.* office or status of a d. [OE. from Gk.].

DEACONESS [dē'ku-nes], *n.* female deacon; member of a Protestant religious and charitable organization for women.

DEAD (1) [ded], *adj.* deprived of life, no longer alive;

deathlike, resembling death; inorganic, inanimate; numbed; no longer operative; not now spoken as a language, inert; heavy, (of a sound) dull; useless, unprofitable; (*coll.*) absolute, certain; unresponsive; lustreless; (*sport*) out of play; (*leg.*) without rights of citizenship; **d. ropes,** (*naut.*) ropes uncontrolled by blocks or grooves; **d. set,** steady and unwavering concentration of activity upon; **d. shot,** marksman who does not miss; **d. water,** (*naut.*) eddying water closing in behind the stern of a moving ship. DEAD (2), *n.* (*pl.*) those who have died; **the d. of night,** the time of night characterized by the absence of all sound or activity. DEAD (3), *adv.* (*coll.*) thoroughly, completely. [OE.].

DEAD-AND-ALIVE [ded-and-a-līv'], *adj.* lethargic, dreary; monotonous, boring, exasperatingly quiet.

DEAD-BEAT (1) [ded-bēt'], *n* escapement in a watch by which the seconds hand halts at each second; (*U.S. slang*) an idler, tramp. DEAD-BEAT (2), *adj.* (*coll.*) utterly tired out, exhausted.

DEAD-CENTRE [ded-sen'ter], *n.* (*eng.*) one of the two points in a revolution of a cranked shaft when the piston, connecting-rod and crank are all in line.

DEAD-COLOURING [ded'ku-le-ring], *n.* the first layer of colours in a picture.

DEADEN [de'den], *v.t.* to lessen, diminish the force of, numb; blunt; make spiritless; dull the gloss or brilliancy of.

DEAD END [ded'end], *n.* the end of a road, railway etc.; a blind alley.

DEAD-EYE [ded'ī], *n.* (*naut.*) round, wooden block pierced with three holes to receive the lanyards.

DEAD-HEAD [ded'hed], *n.* the tail stock of a lathe; (*coll.*) person using a free ticket for a theatrical performance; fool.

DEAD HEAT [ded-hēt'], *n.* the result of a race in which two or more competitors arrive at the winning post simultaneously. DEAD-HEAT, *v.i. and t.* to run a d. with.

DEAD-HOUSE [ded'hows], *n.* a mortuary.

DEAD LETTER [ded-le'ter], *n.* letter which the post office has been unable to deliver; defunct, inoperative law.

DEADLIGHTS [ded'līts], *n.(pl.)* (*naut.*) coverings made exactly to fit over the cabin windows, and used during stormy weather.

DEAD-LINE [ded'līn], *n.* arbitrary line barring further progress; (*sport*) line which when crossed puts a ball out of play; (*print.*) time of going to press.

DEADLINESS [ded'li-nes], *n.* quality of being deadly.

DEADLOCK [ded'lok], *n.* a complete standstill of progress; impasse.

DEADLY (1) [ded'li], *adj.* having the power to cause death; fatal; relentless; like death; (*coll.*) unbearable. DEADLY (2), *adv.* in a manner like that of death; (*coll.*) excessively.

DEADLY NIGHTSHADE [ded-li-nīt'shād], *n.* (*bot.*) the poisonous plant, *Atropa Belladonna.*

DEAD MARCH [ded'mahch], *n.* a funeral march.

DEADNESS [ded'nes], *n.* condition of being dead.

DEAD-NETTLE [ded'ne-tl], *n.* (*bot.*) any species of the genus *Lamium.*

DEAD-POINT [ded'point], *n.* dead-centre.

DEAD RECKONING [ded-re'ko-ning], *n.* (*naut.*) calculation of a ship's position without the aid of the stars.

DEAD-WEIGHT [ded'wāt], *n.* heavy weight of an inanimate thing; useless encumbrance.

DEADWOOD [ded'wood], *n.* (*naut.*) supporting blocks of timber on the keel of a ship; the dead branches of trees; (*fig.*) useless material.

DEAF (1) [def], *adj.* unable to hear; able to hear only imperfectly; (*fig.*) disregarding, wilfully ignoring. DEAF (2), *n.* (*pl.*) those who are d. DEAFLY, *adv.* in a d. fashion. [OE.].

DEAFEN [de'fen], *v.t.* to make deaf; prevent from being heard by the interposition of a loud noise; (*arch.*) render sound-proof.

DEAF-MUTE [def-myoot'], *n.* one who is deaf and dumb.

DEAFNESS [def'nes], *n.* condition of being deaf.

DEAL (1) [dēl], *n.* pinewood, firwood; plank of firwood not more than 3 in. thick, 7 or more in. broad and 6 ft. or more long. DEAL (2), *adj.* made of d. wood. [LGerm.].

DEAL (3) (**dealt**) [dēl, delt], *v.t. and i.* to give, share out, distribute; distribute playing cards to the players; **to d. in,** to trade in; **to d. with,** to be concerned with; treat, behave; handle, settle, manage; trade or do business with. DEAL (4), *n.* a considerable number or amount. DEAL (5), *n.*

The accent' after a syllable = stress (u-pon'). The mark ¯ over a vowel = length (ā in made; ō in bone).

business transaction, successfully concluded negotiation; act or result of dealing out cards. [OE.].

DEALER [dē'ler], *n.* trader, merchant; one who deals the playing cards.

DEALING [dē'ling], *n.* conduct in relation to others; (*pl.*) transactions in buying and selling; traffic, trade.

DEAN [dēn], *n.* (*eccles.*) the head of a cathedral chapter; head of a university faculty; disciplinary official in certain colleges; **rural d.,** clergyman appointed to supervise a portion of a diocese. [OFr. from LL.].

DEANERY [dē'ne-ri], *n.* office, status or jurisdiction of a dean; official residence of a dean.

DEANSHIP [dēn'ship], *n.* office, status or tenure of a dean.

DEAR (1) [dēer], *adj.* beloved, lovable; costly, expensive; in excess of the normal or reasonable price; used as the conventional mode of address in letter-writing. DEAR (2), *n.* a darling, loved one, lovable person. DEAR (3), *int.* expressing surprise, regret etc.; often **d. me.** [OE.].

DEARLY [dēer'li], *adv.* at a high price; with great lovingness.

DEARNESS [dēer'nes], *n.* quality of being dear.

DEARTH [durth], *n.* lack, deficiency. [ME.].

DEARY, DEARIE [dēer'i], *n.* (*coll.*) dear.

DEATH [deth], *n.* act of dying, state or fact of being dead; cause of death; manner of dying; **Black D.,** bubonic plague which swept Europe in the fourteenth century; **civil d.,** the taking away of rights of citizenship; **at death's door,** apparently about to die; **d. duties,** taxes collected by the state on the estate owned by a person who has just died. [OE.].

DEATH-ADDER [deth'a-der], *n.* the most venomous of Australian snakes.

DEATHBED [deth'bed], *n.* the bed on which a person dies.

DEATH-BLOW [deth'blō], *n.* blow destroying life or hope.

DEATHFUL [deth'fool], *adj.* deadly, bringing death. DEATHFULNESS, *n.* quality of being d.

DEATHLESS [deth'les], *adj.* incapable of death, immortal, everlasting. DEATHLESSLY, *adv.* in d. fashion. DEATHLESSNESS, *n.* quality of being d., immortality.

DEATHLIKE [deth'līk], *adj.* resembling death.

DEATHLY (1) [deth'li], *adj.* like death. DEATHLY (2), *adv.* in a d. fashion.

DEATH-MASK [deth'mahsk], *n.* plaster cast of the face made shortly after death.

DEATH-RATE [deth'rāt], *n.* the proportion of deaths in a given district during a given period.

DEATH-RATTLE [deth'ra-tl], *n.* rattling sound in the throat, signifying approaching death.

DEATH-ROLL [deth'rōl], *n.* the record of the dead; the number of dead (in an accident etc.).

DEATH'S-HEAD [deths'hed], *n.* human skull; representation of this; the pirate flag decorated with a skull and crossbones; **d. moth,** a species of hawk-moth.

DEATH-THROES [deth'thrōz], *n.*(*pl.*) the pangs of death.

DEATH-TRAP [deth'trap], *n.* a source of potential death.

DEATH-WARRANT [deth'wo-rant], *n.* official order for the execution of a criminal.

DEATH-WATCH [deth'woch], *n.* small beetle which eats its way into woodwork, the male of which makes a call like the tick of a clock.

DEB [deb], *n.* (*slang*) débutante.

DEBACLE, débâcle [dā-bahkl'], *n.* (*geol.*) torrential flow of water sweeping along with it rocks, trees etc.; the breaking up of ice on a river; (*fig.*) crushing or unexpected overthrow. [Fr.].

DEBAG (*pres.pt.* debagging, *pret. and p.pt.* debagged) [dē-bag'], *v.t.* (*slang*) forcibly to remove the trousers from. [DE and BAG (1)].

DEBAR (*pres.pt.* debarring, *pret. and p.pt.* debarred) [di-bah(r)'], *v.t.* to forbid the privilege or enjoyment of, or approach or entry to, bar from.

DEBARK [dē-bahk'], *v.t. and i.* to disembark. DEBARKATION [dē-bah-kā'shn], *n.* act of debarking.

DEBASE [di-bās'], *v.t.* to lower in purity or value, adulterate, degrade, depreciate. DEBASEMENT, *n.* act of debasing; state of being debased. DEBASER, *n.* one who, or that which, debases. DEBASING, *adj.* tending to d., degrading. DEBASINGLY, *adv.* in a debasing manner. [DE and ABASE].

DEBATABLE [di-bā'ta-bl], *adj.* able to be disputed, of a contentious character; **d. land,** borderland.

DEBATE (1) [di-bāt'], *v.t. and i.* to take part in a d.; discuss a subject from all angles, argue; (*fig.*) endeavour to make up one's mind about, reflect, deliberate; **debating point,** argument which is intended to achieve an effect by logic or wit rather than truth. DEBATE (2), *n.* formal discussion of a motion, usually in public and according to recognized procedure; argument, disputation, controversy. DEBATER, *n.* one who debates. DEBATINGLY, *adv.* in a debating manner. [OFr.].

DEBAUCH (1) [di-bawch'], *v.t.* to corrupt or vitiate; seduce from duty or from virtue; plunge into an orgy of immorality. DEBAUCH (2), *n.* an occasion of drunken and immoral conduct, a drinking bout. DEBAUCHEDLY, *adv.* in a dissipated manner. DEBAUCHEDNESS, *n.* intemperance, dissipation. [OFr.].

DEBAUCHEE [de-baw-chē', de-bo-shē'], *n.* dissipated person; libertine, profligate.

DEBAUCHERY [di-baw'che-ri], *n.* indulgence in debauch.

DEBENTURE [di-ben'tyoor], *n.* (*comm.*) written acknowledgment issued by a public company in exchange for money subscribed, entitling the holder to a first claim on dividends as interest arising from profits; one bond of an issue of such bonds; certificate granted by the custom-house, entitling an exporter to an allowance on import duties previously paid on commodities which he re-exports. DEBENTURED, *adj.* entitled to an allowance as a drawback. [L.].

DEBILITATE [di-bi'li-tāt], *v.t.* to make feeble, impair the strength of, enervate. DEBILITATING, *adj.* that debilitates. DEBILITATION [di-bi-li-tā'shn], *n.* act of debilitating; state of being debilitated. [L.].

DEBILITY [di-bi'li-ti], *n.* functional weakness, absence of normal power, feebleness. [L.].

DEBIT (1) [de'bit], *n.* (*comm.*) an entry in an account-book of a debt; the left-hand side of a ledger devoted to such entries. DEBIT (2), *v.t.* to record a debt in an account-book, enter as a d. [L.].

DEBONAIR [de-bo-nāer'], *adj.* well-mannered and spruce; genial and well-bred, bright and cheerful. DEBONAIRLY, *adv.* in d. fashion. [OFr.].

DEBOUCH [di-bowch', di-bōōsh'], *v.i.* (*milit.*) to march out of a confined place into the open; flow out into a wider outlet. DEBOUCHMENT, *n.* act of debouching; embouchure of a river. [Fr.].

DEBRIS, débris [de'brē, dā'brē], *n.* confused and ruined remains left by a destructive force; accumulation of broken fragments; (*geol.*) loose, worn and crumbled rock heaped up. [Fr.].

DEBT [det], *n.* something owed or due to be paid to another; material or moral obligation or liability; **bad d.,** debt which will not be paid; **national d.,** the money owed to investors in state securities. [OFr., ~DEBIT].

DEBTOR [de'ter], *n.* person in debt to another person; (*comm.*) a debit.

DEBUNK [dē-bungk'], *v.t.* (*slang*) to remove the accumulated cant, hypocrisy and sentimentality which surrounds anything, expose. [DE and BUNK (3)].

DEBUS [dē-bus'], *v.i.* (*milit.*) to disembark from motor transport vehicles. [DE and BUS].

DEBUT, début [dā'bōō], *n.* first public or social appearance of a player, performer, society girl etc.; beginning, start. [Fr.].

DEBUTANTE, débutante [dā-byōō-tahnt'], *n.* lady making her début, lady who has been, or is to be, presented to the Sovereign at a recent or specified formal court reception. [Fr.].

DECA-, *pref.* ten, tenfold. [Gk.].

DECADE [de'kād], *n.* series or aggregate of ten, period of ten years. DECADAL [de'ka-dal], *adj.* relating to a d.; consisting of, counted in, series of tens.

DECADENCE [de'ka-dens], *n.* decay, deterioration in moral quality. [LL.].

DECADENCY [de'ka-den-si], *n.* decadence.

DECADENT (1) [de'ka-dent], *adj.* marked by decadence. DECADENT (2), *n.* a degenerate. DECADENTLY, *adv.* in d. fashion.

DECAGON [de'ka-gon], *n.* (*geom.*) plane figure of ten sides and angles. DECAGONAL [de-ka'go-nal], *adj.* pertaining to a d. [Gk.].

DECAGRAMME [de'ka-gram], *n.* metric weight of ten grammes.

DECAHEDRON [de-ka-hē'dron], *n.* (*geom.*) solid body possessing ten sides. DECAHEDRAL, *adj.* possessing ten sides. [Gk.].

DECALCIFY [dē-kal'si-fī], *v.t.* to extract the lime from.

DECALCIFICATION [dē-kal-si-fi-kā'shn], n. act of decalcifying. [DE and CALCIFY].

DECALITRE [de'ka-lē-ter], n. metric measure of capacity consisting of ten litres.

DECALOGUE [de'ka-log], n. the Ten Commandments. [Gk.].

DECAMETRE [de'ka-mē-ter], n. metric measure of length containing ten metres.

DECAMP [di-kamp'], v.i. to depart from a camp; run away secretly, escape. DECAMPMENT, n. act of decamping.

DECANAL [di-kā'nal, de'ka-nal], adj. relating to a deanery or to a dean. [~L.].

DECANDROUS [de-kan'drŏŏs], adj. (bot.) possessing ten stamens.

DECANT [di-kant'], v.t. to pour off gently; pour wine or other liquid from one vessel into another without disturbing the sediment; pour into a decanter from a bottle. DECANTATION [dē-kan-tā'shn], n. process of decanting. [L.].

DECANTER [di-kan'ter], n. glass bottle for holding decanted liquor.

DECAPITATE [di-ka'pi-tāt], v.t. to cut off the head of, behead. DECAPITATION [di-ka-pi-tā'shn], n. act of beheading. [L.].

DECAPOD (1) [de'ka-pod], n. crustacean having ten feet. DECAPOD (2), adj. possessing ten limbs, as a crustacean. [Gk.].

DECARBONIZE [dē-kah'bo-nīz], v.t. to deprive of carbonic acid or carbon; remove carbon accumulated on the pistons and cylinder-head of an internal-combustion engine. DECARBONIZATION [dē-kah-bo-nī-zā'shn], n. process of decarbonizing.

DECASUALIZE [dē-ca'zhŏŏ-a-līz], v.t. (of labour) to remove casual elements from, engage for an extended period instead of for temporary jobs. DECASUALIZA-TION [dē-ka-zhŏŏ-a-lī-zā'shn], n. process of decasualizing. [DE and CASUAL].

DECASYLLABIC [de-ka-si-la'bik], n. and adj. (pros.) (line of verse) containing ten syllables.

DECATHLON [de-kath'lon], n. contest in athletic skill consisting of ten events. [Gk.].

DECAY (1) [di-kā'], v.i. to suffer or undergo d. DECAY (2), n. a decline towards dissolution, decomposition, disintegration, rotting; gradual weakening. DECAYED, adj. rotten, decomposed; deteriorated. DECAYEDNESS, n. decayed state. DECAYER, that which induces d. [L.].

DECEASE (1) [di-sēs'], n. death. DECEASE (2), v.i. to die. [L.].

DECEASED (1) [di-sēst'], adj. dead. DECEASED (2), n. (leg.) a dead person.

DECEIT [di-sēt'], n. act of deceiving; deception, fraud; quality of being deceitful, duplicity; (leg.) any fraudulent practice. [OFr.].

DECEITFUL [di-sēt'fŏŏl], adj. tending or intended to deceive; given to deceiving; deceptive, misleading. DECEITFULLY, adv. in d. fashion. DECEITFULNESS, n. quality of being d.

DECEIVABLE [di-sē'va-bl], adj. able to be deceived.

DECEIVE [di-sēv'], v.t. to practise deceit on, mislead deliberately, impose on, delude; put under a delusion. DECEIVER, n. person who deceives. [L.].

DECELERATE [dē-se'le-rāt], v.t. to slow down, cause the rate of motion to diminish. DECELERA-TION [dē-se-le-rā'shn], n. act of decelerating. [L.].

DECEM-, pref. ten. [L.].

DECEMBER [di-sem'ber], n. the twelfth and last month of the year. [L.].

DECENCY [dē'sen-si], n. quality of being decent; modesty, decorum; (coll.) good manners. [L.].

DECENNIAL [de-se'ni-al], adj. consisting of, lasting for, ten years, or occurring every ten years.

DECENT [dē'sent], adj. becoming, fitting, seemly, chaste, proper, modest; (coll.) tolerable, satisfactory, likeable. DECENTISH, adj. (coll.) quite d. DECENT-LY, adv. in a d. fashion. [L.].

DECENTRALIZE [dē-sen'tra-līz], v.t. to remove from the centre; split up an administration among branches instead of concentrating in one central place or authority. DECENTRALIZATION [dē-sen-tra-lī-zā'shn], n. act of decentralizing.

DECEPTION [di-sep'shn], n. act of deceiving; state of being deceived; that which deceives or is intended to deceive. [L.].

DECEPTIVE [di-sep'tiv], adj. tending to deceive, misleading. DECEPTIVELY, adv. in a d. fashion. DECEPTIVENESS, DECEPTIVITY, n. [di-sep'tiv-nes, dē-sep-ti'vi-ti], n. quality of being d. [L.].

DECI- [de'si], pref. tenth. [L.].

DECIDE [di-sīd'], v.t. and i. to judge, select as best or right; settle; determine. DECIDER, n. a further race or contest to d. a tie; person who, or thing which, decides. [L.].

DECIDED [di-sī'did], adj. firm, resolute, determined; definite, unmistakable. DECIDEDLY, adv. in a d. way.

DECIDUOUS [di-si'dyŏŏ-ŏŏs], adj. (bot.) shedding its leaves annually; (of leaves etc.) falling off seasonally; (zool.) shedding horns, teeth etc. DECIDUOUS-NESS, n. (bot.) condition of being d. [L.].

DECIGRAMME [de'si-gram], n. metric measure of weight, one-tenth of a gramme.

DECILITRE [de'si-lē-ter], n. metric measure of cubic capacity equal to one-tenth of a litre.

DECILLION [di-sil'yun], n. the tenth power of a million. [DECI and (mi)llion].

DECIMAL (1) [de'si-mal], adj. numbered by tens, expressed or reckoned in tens or powers of ten, arranged in multiples of ten; d. fraction, fraction whose denominator is taken as ten or a power of ten; d. system, system of calculation of weights and measures based on powers of ten. DECIMAL (2), n. (math.) a fraction having some power of ten as its denominator; recurring d., fraction in which the final figure or group of figures repeats indefinitely. DECIMALISM, n. the principles of the d. system. DECIMALIST, n. an advocate of the d. system. DECIMALIZE, v.t. to reduce to terms of the d. system, convert into decimals. DECIMALLY, adv. by tens; by means of decimals. [L.].

DECIMATE [de'si-māt], v.t. to eliminate every tenth part; put to death every tenth man as reprisals; (fig.) destroy in great numbers. DECIMATION [de-si-mā'shn], n. act of decimating; condition of being decimated. DECIMATOR, n. person who, or thing which, decimates. [L.].

DECIMETRE [de'si-mē-ter], n. metric measure of length equal to the tenth of a metre.

DECIMO-SEXTO [de-si-mō-seks'to], n. book with its pages one-sixteenth of the size of a full sheet, usually written 16mo. [L.].

DECIPHER [di-sī'fer], v.t. to interpret a cipher in terms of a recognized language, decode; make out, read and understand, discover the meaning of. DECIPHERABLE, adj. able to be deciphered. DECIPHERMENT, n. act of deciphering.

DECISION [di-si'zhn], n. final judgment; settlement; firmness of purpose, resolution; (leg.) authoritative opinion or verdict of a judge. [L.].

DECISIVE [di-sī'siv], adj. that decides, conclusive; exhibiting decision; decided. DECISIVELY, adv. in a d. way. DECISIVENESS, n. quality of being d.

DECK (1) [dek], n. horizontal covering enclosing the top of a ship's hull, in large ships at several levels; floor of an omnibus or tramcar; pack of cards; to clear the decks, to prepare for action. DECK-CABIN, cabin on the level of the promenade or upper d. of a liner. DECK-CARGO, cargo carried on the d. of a ship instead of in the hold. DECK-HAND, man employed in doing work on d. DECK-HOUSE, cabin or shelter on d. [MDu.].

DECK (2), v.t. to adorn, decorate; provide with a deck. [MDu.].

DECK-CHAIR [dek-chāer'], n. portable, folding chair with a canvas support across a light wooden frame.

DECKER [de'ker], n. one who, or that which, decks or adorns; ship or omnibus with a specified number of decks.

DECKING [de'king], n. ornament; deck planking.

DECKLE [de'kl], n. adjustable apparatus which determines the size of a sheet of paper in manufacture or cutting. DECKLED, adj. (of paper) deckle-edged. [Germ.].

DECKLE EDGE [de-kl-ej'], n. the rough edge of untrimmed paper. DECKLE-EDGED, adj. (of paper) having untrimmed edges.

DECK-TENNIS [dek-te'nis], n. game adapted from lawn tennis, played on board ship.

DECLAIM [di-klām'], v.t. and i. to speak or recite to an audience with exaggerated gesture for effect, deliver poetry or a set speech to an audience in a rhetorical and dramatic manner; to d. against, to raise an outcry against. DECLAIMER, n. person who declaims. DECLAIMING, n. rhetorical harangue. [L.].

DECLAMATION [dek-la-mā'shn], n. act of declaiming; speech declaimed.

DECLAMATORY [di-kla'ma-te-ri], adj. characterized by, or suited to, declamation.

DECLARATION [dek-la-rā'shn], n. act of declaring; that which is declared; document recording this;

affidavit; (*leg.*) formal statement of a claim by a plaintiff.

DECLARATIVE [di-kla´ra-tiv], *adj.* having the nature of a declaration, explanatory. DECLARATIVELY, *adv.* in a d. manner.

DECLARATORY [di-kla´ra-te-ri], *adj.* making a declaration. DECLARATORILY, *adv.* by declaration.

DECLARE [di-klâer´], *v.t. and i.* to make known, announce; assert, affirm; state directly and explicitly; (*cards*) name a suit as trumps; (*leg.*) enumerate the grounds of complaint against the defendant; announce that one has certain dutiable goods in one's possession; (*cricket*) announce one's innings to have finished; **to d. oneself,** to admit one's intentions or sympathies. DECLARABLE, *adj.* liable to be declared; dutiable. DECLARANT, *n.* (*leg.*) person who makes a declaration. DECLAREDLY, *adv.* confessedly. [L.].

DECLENSION [di-klen´shn], *n.* act of declining; tendency towards a lower level of quality, power etc.; (*gram.*) changes in the endings of nouns, pronouns and adjectives according to the different cases; a particular type of inflexion. [L.].

DECLINABLE [di-kli´na-bl], *adj.* capable of declension.

DECLINATION [dek-li-nā´shn], *n.* a downward slope; (*astron.*) the distance, measured at an angle north or south, that a heavenly body is situated from the celestial equator; (*elect.*) the angular difference between the true north and south and the magnetic north and south.

DECLINATORY [di-klī´na-te-ri], *adj.* relating to declination; indicating a refusal.

DECLINE (1) [di-klīn´], *v.t. and i.* to slope downward; droop; degenerate, deteriorate; diminish; refuse, reject; (*gram.*) inflect; waste away; (*comm.*) fall in price. DECLINE (2), *n.* a gradual falling off in quality or strength; tendency towards a lower level of health; (*comm.*) slow fall in price; (*med.*) tuberculosis. [L.].

DECLIVITOUS [di-kli´vi-tŏŏs], *adj.* having a declivity, steeply sloping.

DECLIVITY [di-kli´vi-ti], *n.* the downward slope of the ground; a surface which slopes downward. [L.].

DECLUTCH [dē-kluch´], *v.i.* to disconnect the engine shaft from the transmission shaft in a motor-car by depressing the clutch.

DECOCT [di-kokt´], *v.t.* to prepare by boiling; extract substances by boiling.

DECOCTION [di-kok´shn], *n.* act of decocting; the essence decocted. [L.].

DECODE [dē-kōd´], *v.t.* to decipher.

DE-COKE [dē-kōk´], *v.i.* (*coll.*) to decarbonize.

DECOLLETAGE, décolletage [dā-ko´le-tahzh], *n.* the low neck of a dress; the wearing of a low-necked dress. [Fr.].

DECOLLETE, décolleté [dā-ko´le-tā], *adj.* low-necked; wearing a low-necked gown. [Fr.].

DECOLORATE [dē-ku´lo-rāt], *v.t.* to bleach. DECOLORATION [dē-ku-lo-rā´shn], *n.* act or result of decolorating. [L.].

DECOLOUR [dē-ku´ler], *v.t.* to decolorate. DECOLOURANT, *n.* substance which decolours.

DECOMPOSE [dē-kom-pōz´], *v.t. and i.* to break up into component parts or elements; disintegrate; decay, go bad. DECOMPOSABLE, *adj.* able to be decomposed. DECOMPOSITION, *n.* act of decomposing; state of becoming or being decomposed.

DECOMPOUND (1) [dē-kom´pownd], *adj.* composed of compound parts. DECOMPOUND (2), *n.* substance composed of compounded parts. DECOMPOUND (3) [dē-kom-pownd´], *v.t.* to decompose; combine into a fresh compound something already compounded.

DECOMPRESS [dē-kom-pres´], *v.t.* to reduce a high pressure to a more normal one.

DECONSECRATE [dē-kon´si-krāt], *v.t.* to deprive of sacred character, secularize.

DECONTAMINATE [dē-kon-ta´mi-nāt], *v.t.* to free from contamination, *esp.* gas-contamination.

DECONTAMINATION [dē-kon-ta-mi-nā´shn], *n.* act or process of decontaminating, *esp.* from poison gas.

DECONTROL (*pres.pt.* **decontrolling,** *pret. and p.pt.* **decontrolled**) [dē-kon-trōl´], *v.t.* to release from control, *esp.* from state control and management; abolish an official control of speed on a road. DECONTROLLED, *adj.* without control; (of a road) having no restriction of speed for vehicular traffic.

DECOR, décor [dā´kaw(r)], *n.* the stage-setting of a ballet, play or opera. [Fr.].

DECORATE [de´ke-rāt], *v.t.* to adorn, deck with ornament; embellish; confer an honour; award a badge or medal of honour to; paint and paper the interior of a room or house; **Decorated,** (*arch.*) period of English Gothic preceding Perpendicular. [L.].

DECORATION [de-ke-rā´shn], *n.* act or manner of decorating; state of being decorated; that which decorates; badge or medal of honour.

DECORATIVE [de´ke-ra-tiv], *adj.* that decorates; suitable as, or pertaining to, decoration, ornamental.

DECORATOR [de´ke-rā-ter], *n.* person who decorates; person employed in house painting and interior decoration.

DECOROUS [de´ke-rŏŏs, di-kaw´rŏŏs], *adj.* seemly, proper, suitable. DECOROUSLY, *adv.* in d. fashion. DECOROUSNESS, *n.* quality of being d. [L.].

DECORTICATE [di-kaw´ti-kāt], *v.t.* to strip off bark; peel, husk. [L.].

DECORUM [di-kaw´rum], *n.* propriety of speech or behaviour, decency, social convention. [L.].

DECOY (1) [di-koi´], *n.* tame bird or animal used to entice wild birds or animals into a snare; place in which wild birds may be easily ensnared; (*fig.*) a trap; person used to lead someone into a trap. DECOY (2), *v.t.* to entice into a trap, ensnare by means of a d. DECOY-DUCK, real or imitation duck used to decoy others into a snare; (*fig.*) person who decoys others. [Du.].

DECREASE (1) [di-krēs´], *v.t. and i.* to cause to become less or smaller, lessen, diminish; become less or smaller. DECREASE (2) [dē´krēs], *n.* act of decreasing; state of being decreased; a lessening, diminution. DECREASINGLY, *adv.* in a decreasing fashion. [L.].

DECREE (1) [di-krē´], *n.* an order or law authorized by a legislative body; established law; a judgment; an arbitrary law enforced by undemocratic means; (*fig.*) an inevitable principle; (*leg.*) a decision of a judge, court of law etc.; (*theol.*) the absolute principle of God; a law authorized by a church council; **d. nisi,** an order for divorce subject to ratification. DECREE (2), *v.t. and i.* to order, command, make or impose a d.; settle, appoint or fix by d. [L.].

DECREMENT [dek´ri-ment], *n.* process of decreasing; amount by which anything is decreased.

DECREPIT [di-kre´pit], *adj.* worn out, broken down and weakened by age, illness etc.; tumbledown, rickety. DECREPITUDE, *n.* state of being d. [L.].

DECRESCENT [di-kre´sent], *adj.* decreasing, waning.

DECRETAL (1) [di-krē´tal], *adj.* pertaining to a decree. DECRETAL (2), *n.* an authorized decree; (*eccles.*) decree issued by the Pope, establishing an ecclesiastical precedent; (*pl.*) a collection of these constituting canon law. [L.].

DECRY [di-krī´], *v.t.* to cry down the value of, disparage, depreciate. DECRIAL, *n.* act of decrying. DECRIER, *n.* one who decries.

DECUMBENT [di-kum´bent], *adj.* lying down, recumbent; (*bot.*) lying close to the ground. DECUMBENCE, DECUMBENCY, *n.* state or act of lying down.

DECUPLE (1) [de´kyŏŏ-pl], *adj.* tenfold. DECUPLE (2), *n.* a number ten times a specified number. DECUPLE (3), *v.t.* to increase tenfold. [L.].

DECUSSATE (1) [dē-ku´sāt], *v.t.* to grow, cross or intersect at right angles or in the form of an X. DECUSSATE(D) (2), *adj.* crossing or intersecting to form an X. [L.].

DEDENTITION [dē-den-ti´shn], *n.* (*physiol.*) the shedding of teeth, particularly of the milk-teeth.

DEDICATE [de´di-kāt], *v.t.* to consecrate solemnly to a holy purpose; assign to a special purpose by solemn ritual; devote exclusively to some specific cause; write an inscription in a book assigning it to a particular person. DEDICATEE [de-di-ka-tē´], *n.* one to whom something is dedicated. DEDICATOR [de´di-kā-ter], *n.* one who dedicates. DEDICATORY [de´di-kā-te-ri], *adj.* relating to, or serving as, a dedication. [L.].

DEDICATION [de-di-kā´shn], *n.* act of dedicating; inscription dedicating a book to someone. [L.].

DEDUCE [di-dyŏŏs´], *v.t.* to trace the steps in; reason from preceding facts or statements; infer. [L.].

DEDUCT [di-dukt´], *v.t.* to take away, subtract. [L.].

DEDUCTION [di-duk´shn], *n.* act of deducting; that which is subtracted; act of deducing; that which is deduced.

DEDUCTIVE [di-duk´tiv], *adj.* using or dependent upon deduction; **d. reasoning,** (*logic*) process of reasoning proceeding from the general to the particular. DEDUCTIVELY, *adv.* by way of deduction.

DEED [dēd], *n.* something done, an action, act; an

actual fact; (*leg.*) sealed document embodying the terms of an agreement, settlement etc.; document setting out a title to real estate. DEED-POLL, a d. made by one party only, recorded on polled (*i.e.* not indented) paper. DEEDFUL, *adj.* marked by effective deeds. DEEDLESS, *adj.* not performing any deeds. [OE.].

DEEM [dēm], *v.t.* to consider, judge. DEEMSTER, *n.* a judge in the Isle of Man. [OE.].

DEEP (1) [dēp], *adj.* extending far down, situated a long distance beneath a certain level; extending a long distance across a surface; penetrating far into a mass; profound, having the power to deal with abstruse ideas, problems etc.; thoroughly preoccupied by; difficult to comprehend; hidden; cunning, artful; having a powerful emotional effect; intense, dark, rich in tone; (*mus.*) low in pitch; (*milit.*) some distance behind the front line; (*tennis*) placed near the opponent's base-line; **to go (in) off the d. end,** to become temporarily mad; lose one's temper suddenly; become suddenly reckless. DEEP (2), *n.* that which is deep; the sea; (*cricket*) the outfield; (*naut.*) the distance between two depths on a loadline. DEEP (3), *adv.* far down, thoroughly, deeply. [OE.].

DEEPEN [dē'pen], *v.t. and i.* to make or become deeper.

DEEPLY [dēp'li], *adv.* to considerable depth; profoundly; with considerable emotion; gravely; thoroughly; considerably.

DEEP-MOUTHED [dēp-mowтнd'], *adj.* having a loud, hollow voice; possessing a deep bark.

DEEPNESS [dēp'nes], *n.* condition of being deep; depth.

DEEP-SEA [dēp'sē], *adj.* belonging to the sea at its deeper levels.

DEER (*pl. deer*) [dēer], *n.* family of ruminant horned ungulates with deciduous antlers. [OE.].

DEER-HOUND [dēer'hownd], *n.* large breed of dog employed originally for deer-hunting.

DEERSKIN [dēer'skin], *n.* the skin of the deer; soft supple leather made from it.

DEERSTALKER [dēer'staw-ker], *n.* person stalking deer to shoot them; cloth cap with peaks back and front. DEERSTALKING, *n.* act of stalking deer.

DEFACE [di-fās'], *v.t.* to destroy or spoil the face of anything, disfigure; (of writing) obliterate or make indistinct. DEFACEMENT, *n.* act of defacing; that which defaces; injury effected by defacing.

DE FACTO [dē-fak'tō], *adv.* in actual fact though not by legal right. [L.].

DEFALCATE [dē'-fal-kāt], *v.i.* to misappropriate or embezzle money. DEFALCATOR, *n.* one who defalcates. [L.].

DEFALCATION [dē-fal-kā'shn], *n.* act of defalcating; irregular deficit in funds left in the charge of a person.

DEFAMATION [dē-fa-mā'shn, de-fa-mā'shn], *n.* act of defaming; calumny; slander.

DEFAMATORY [di-fa'ma-te-ri], *adj.* defaming, slanderous.

DEFAME [di-fām'], *v.t.* to harm the reputation of by calumny, make slanderous or libellous remarks about, speak or write evilly and falsely about. DEFAMER, *n.* one who defames another. DEFAMING, *n.* defamation. DEFAMINGLY, *adv.* so as to d. [L.].

DEFAULT (1) [di-fawlt'], *n.* failure to fulfil an obligation, a neglect of duty; fault, deficiency; (*leg.*) failure to appear in court at the appointed time. DEFAULT (2), *v.t. and i.* to fail in fulfilling an obligation or in performing a duty; fail to complete a contract; (*leg.*) fail to appear in court at the appointed time; nominate a person as failing to appear in court when officially required. DEFAULTER, *n.* one, *esp.* a soldier, who defaults. [OFr.].

DEFEASANCE [di-fē'zans], *n.* a rendering null and void; (*leg.*) conditional clause in a document which, if taking effect, renders the whole null and void; document containing such a clause. [OFr.].

DEFEAT (1) [di-fēt'], *v.t.* to conquer, overthrow, vanquish; frustrate, nullify, destroy. DEFEAT (2), *n.* act of defeating, conquest; frustration, ruin, destruction. [OFr. from L.].

DEFEATISM [di-fē'tizm], *n.* advocacy of surrender, acceptance of defeat as inevitable.

DEFEATIST (1) [di-fē'tist], *n.* one who overrates the possibilities of defeat. DEFEATIST (2), *adj.* of, or pertaining to, a d. or his views.

DEFECATE [dē'fē-kāt], *v.t. and i.* to purify, clarify; (*physiol.*) empty the bowels. DEFECATION [dē-fē-kā'shn], *n.* act of defecating. [L.].

DEFECT [di-fekt'], *n.* want; imperfection, flaw, fault,

error. DEFECTIBLE, *adj.* defective, tending to fail. [L.].

DEFECTION [di-fek'shn], *n.* desertion from allegiance or duty; revolt; apostasy. [L.].

DEFECTIVE [di-fek'tiv], *n. and adj.* (one) having defects, lacking in something; imperfect, incomplete. DEFECTIVELY, *adv.* in d. fashion. DEFECTIVENESS, *n.* condition of being d.

DEFENCE [di-fens'], *n.* act of defending; that which defends, a fortification; (*leg.*) the case of a defendant in reply to charges made by the prosecution; (*pl.*) (*milit.*) series of fortified positions one behind the other; **d. area,** district in which civilian movements are restricted by military authorities in wartime. DEFENCED, *adj.* fortified, protected by defences. [OFr.].

DEFENCELESS [di-fens'les], *adj.* without defence, helpless. DEFENCELESSLY, *adv.* in d. fashion. DEFENCELESSNESS, *n.* state of being d.

DEFEND [di-fend'], *v.t.* to protect from, shield against assault, resist, repulse an enemy; assert a case in reply to an attack; support by a speech; vindicate, excuse; (*leg.*) plead not guilty in a court and attempt to establish one's innocence; seek to prove the innocence of (the accused). DEFENDER, *n.* person who defends. [L.].

DEFENDANT [di-fen'dant], *n.* one who defends; (*leg.*) person accused or prosecuted. [Fr.].

DEFENSIBLE [di-fens'si-bl], *adj.* offering a means of defence, capable of being defended; excusable. DEFENSIBLY, *adv.* in a d. way. [L.].

DEFENSIVE (1) [di-fen'siv], *adj.* prepared for defence; serving as a defence. DEFENSIVE (2), *n.* condition of expecting, and being ready to meet, attack; (*milit.*) the limitation of activities to those of defence. DEFENSIVELY, *adv.* in a d. fashion. DEFENSIVENESS, *n.* condition of being on the d.

DEFER (1) (*pres.pt.* **deferring,** *pret. and p.pt.* **deferred**) [di-fur'], *v.t. and i.* to delay, postpone, transfer from one date to a later one; put off; reserve for a subsequent occasion. [L.].

DEFER (2) (*pres.pt.* **deferring,** *pret. and p.pt.* **deferred**), *v.i.* to submit, yield to another's opinion. [L.].

DEFERENCE [de'fe-rens], *n.* act of deferring; regard, respect, consideration.

DEFERENT (1) [de'fe-rent], *adj.* deferential; (*anat.*) conveying away fluids. DEFERENT (2), *n.* (*anat.*) duct in the human body to carry off fluids. [L.].

DEFERENTIAL [de-fe-ren'shl], *adj.* showing deference. DEFERENTIALLY, *adv.* in a d. manner.

DEFERMENT [di-fur'ment], *n.* act of deferring, state of being deferred.

DEFERRED [di-furd'], *adj.* delayed, postponed, not for immediate delivery; having the right to a dividend after paying off prior charges; **d. annuity,** annuity becoming payable only after the lapse of a certain period of time or at death.

DEFIANCE [di-fī'ans], *n.* act of defying; **in d. of,** contrary to, disobeying. [OFr.].

DEFIANT [di-fī'ant], *adj.* expressive of defiance; insolent, agressively disobedient. DEFIANTLY, *adv.* in a d. way.

DEFICIENCY [di-fi'shn-si], *n.* state of being deficient; amount by which anything is deficient; **d. bills,** Bank of England loan to government facilitating payment of dividends on government stock; **d. disease,** disease caused by lack of protective foods.

DEFICIENT [di-fi'shnt], *adj.* lacking, wanting; not sufficient, inadequate; not having enough, defective; incomplete; **mentally d.,** slightly or completely imbecile. DEFICIENTLY, *adv.* in a d. manner. [L.].

DEFICIT [de'fi-sit], *n.* deficiency, the amount short; shortage; excess of debts over credit. [L.].

DEFILE (1) [di-fīl'], *v.i.* to march in single file. DEFILE (2) [dē'fīl], *n.* very narrow passage-way or pass in the hills. [Fr.].

DEFILE (3) [di-fīl'], *v.t.* to make dirty, soil, pollute; (*fig.*) corrupt, render morally unclean. DEFILEMENT, *n.* act of defiling; state of being defiled; that which defiles. DEFILER, *n.* one who, or that which, defiles.

DEFINABLE [di-fī'na-bl], *adj.* able to be defined. DEFINABLY, *adv.* in d. fashion.

DEFINE [di-fīn'], *v.t.* to mark clearly and fix the boundaries or limits of something; describe accurately and comprehensively; state in exact terms the meaning of a word, idiom or phrase; outline. DEFINER, *n.* person who defines. [L.].

DEFINITE [de'fi-nit], *adj.* having exact and fixed limits; settled; precise, exact; (*gram.*) limiting the

The accent ' after a syllable = stress (u-pon'). The mark ‾ over a vowel = length (ā in made; ō in bone).

application. DEFINITELY, *adv.* in a d. fashion. DEFINITENESS, *n.* quality of being d. [*Prec.*].

DEFINITION [de-fi-ni'shn], *n.* act of defining; process of being defined; exact description of the nature of a thing; concise explanation of the exact meaning of a word or phrase; (*phot.*) sharpness of detail, clearness; (*opt.*) power of a lens to form a sharp image.

DEFINITIVE [di-fi'ni-tiv], *adj.* conclusive, determinate, positive, final. DEFINITIVELY, *adv.* in a d. manner. DEFINITIVENESS, *n.* quality of being d.

DEFINITUDE [di-fi'ni-tyōōd], *n.* definiteness.

DEFLATE [di-flāt'], *v.t.* to release or let out air; reduce the amount of paper money in circulation. DEFLATABLE, *adj.* able to be deflated. [L.].

DEFLATION [di-flā'shn], *n.* act or result of deflating. DEFLATIONARY, *adj.* pertaining, tending, to d. DEFLATIONIST, *n.* advocate of a policy of d.

DEFLECT [di-flekt'], *v.t. and i.* to turn aside from a straight or direct line or course. DEFLECTED, *adj.* turned aside; (*bot.*) bending down archwise. DEFLECTIVE, *adj.* tending to d. [L.].

DEFLECTION, DEFLEXION [di-flek'shn], *n.* act of deflecting, state of being deflected. [L.].

DEFLECTOR [di-flek'ter], *n.* appliance for improving combustion, fitted to a lamp burning gas.

DEFLEXION, see DEFLECTION.

DEFLORATION [dē-flaw-rā'shn], *n.* act of deflowering. [L.].

DEFLOWER [di-flow'er], *v.t.* to deprive a woman of her virginity; (*fig.*) take from anything its original beauty and purity. DEFLOWERER, *n.* one who deflowers.

DEFOLIATE [di-fō'li-āt], *v.t.* to deprive of leaves. DEFOLIATION [di-fō-li-ā'shn], *n.* (*bot.*) the shedding of leaves; the time of shedding leaves.

DEFOREST [dē-fo'rist], *v.t.* to clear of trees; disafforest.

DEFORM [di-fawm'], *v.t.* to mar the form of, disfigure, make ugly or misshapen.

DEFORMATION [dē-faw-mā'shn], *n.* act of deforming; state of being deformed.

DEFORMED [di-fawmd'], *adj.* abnormally formed in limb or body, disfigured, misshapen. DEFORMEDLY, *adv.* in a d. manner.

DEFORMITY [di-faw'mi-ti], *n.* state of being deformed; malformation; a misshapen organ or limb; disfigurement, ugliness. [L.].

DEFRAUD [di-frawd'], *v.t.* to deprive of, withhold from wrongfully, by fraud; cheat, swindle. DEFRAUDER, *n.* person who defrauds.

DEFRAY [di-frā'], *v.t.* to pay the cost of. DEFRAYAL, DEFRAYMENT, *n.* act of defraying.

DEFROCK [dē-frok'], *v.t.* to remove from the office or status of priest.

DEFROST [di-frost'], *v.t.* to render unfrozen; unfreeze meat frozen for storage purposes; remove frost from.

DEFT [deft], *adj.* dexterous, manually skilful, handy. DEFTLY, *adv.* in a d. fashion. DEFTNESS, *n.* quality of being d. [OE.].

DEFUNCT (1) [di-fungkt'], *adj.* dead. DEFUNCT (2), *n.* a dead person. [L.].

DEFY [di-fi'], *v.t.* to challenge; resist; disobey; flout; baffle, frustrate. [Fr.].

DEGAUSS [dē-gows'], *v.t.* to make (iron etc.) incapable of affecting a magnet. [DE and GAUSS].

DEGENERACY [di-je'ne-ra-si], *n.* state of being degenerate.

DEGENERATE (1) [di-je'ne-rat], *adj.* being in a condition of development lower than a norm previously attained; fallen from a physical, mental or moral standard, depraved, defective, subnormal; having deteriorated. DEGENERATE (2), *n.* one who is d. DEGENERATELY, *adv.* in a d. fashion. DEGENERATIVE, *adj.* tending to degeneracy. DEGENERATE (3) [di-je'ne-rāt], *v.i.* to become degenerate; to worsen, deteriorate, to develop into something inferior. [L.].

DEGENERATION [di-je-ne-rā'shn], *n.* act of degenerating; state of being degenerate.

DEGLUTITION [dē-glōō-ti'shn], *n.* act or power of swallowing. [L.].

DEGRADATION [deg-ra-dā'shn], *n.* act of degrading; state of being degraded; condition of sordid poverty and misery; (*biol.*) degenerate state; (*chem.*) reduction.

DEGRADE [di-grād'], *v.t. and i.* to reduce or lower the moral or physical level; reduce in rank as a form of punishment; take away honours and official recognition; lower the dignity and self-respect of, dishonour; reduce the value of. DEGRADED, *adj.* having

suffered degradation, mean, debased. DEGRADING, *adj.* that degrades. DEGRADINGLY, *adv.* in a degrading manner. [LL.].

DEGREE [di-grē'], *n.* position, rank or grade relative to a line of development; extent, amount, measure in relation to a larger; rank, status; award conferred by a university as a mark of a certain proficiency in a branch of learning, or sometimes as an honour to one otherwise distinguished; (*alg.*) the rank of an equation as denoted by the highest power of the unknown quantity; (*phys.*) a unit of measurement of temperature; (*geom.*) one of the three hundred and sixty divisions of a circle, constituting a unit of measurement; (*gram.*) a form of qualification of adjectives; **by degrees,** step by step, gradually; **to a d.,** exceedingly; **third d.,** (*coll.*) severe examination often accompanied by direct or indirect physical and mental torture for the purpose of extracting or forcing a confession; **degrees of latitude,** hypothetical lines at equal distances from each other drawn round the globe parallel to the equator; **degrees of longitude,** hypothetical lines encircling the earth and passing through the poles. [Fr. from LL.].

DEGRESSION [di-gre'shn], *n.* lowering of the rate of taxation on sums below a certain level. [L.].

DEHISCE [dē-his'], *v.i.* (*bot.*) to burst asunder, as the capsules of plants, to release the ripened seeds or pollen. DEHISCENCE [dē-hi'sens], *n.* (*bot.*) act of dehiscing. DEHISCENT, *adj.* (*bot.*) characterized by dehiscence. [L.].

DEHUMANIZE [dē-hyōō'ma-nīz], *v.t.* to deprive of human qualities, render brutal or savage.

DEHYDRATE [dē-hi'drāt], *v.t.* (*chem.*) to extract or remove water from. DEHYDRATION [dē-hi-drā'shn], *n.* (*chem.*) act of dehydrating.

DEHYDROGENIZE [dē-hi'drō-je-nīz], *v.t.* (*chem.*) to extract the hydrogen from a chemical compound.

DE-ICE [dē-īs'], *v.t.* to prevent ice from forming on the surface of (an aeroplane). DE-ICER, *n.* apparatus for de-icing aircraft.

DEIFICATION [dē-i-fi-kā'shn], *n.* act of deifying; state of being deified.

DEIFY [dē'i-fi], *v.t.* to exalt to the rank of a god, worship as a god, make a god of. DEIFIED, *adj.* ranked with the gods. [LL.].

DEIGN [dān], *v.t. and i.* to condescend, lower one's dignity. [OFr. from L.].

DEISM [dē'izm], *n.* philosophical doctrine accepting a Divine Being existing apart from the world, but rejecting the manifestation of God in Christ. [L.].

DEIST [dē'ist], *n.* person believing in deism; freethinker. DEISTIC(AL) [dē-is'tik(-al)], *adj.* relating to deism or to deists. DEISTICALLY, *adv.* in the manner of deists.

DEITY [dē'i-ti], *n.* condition of being a god, divinity, the Supreme Being; a god or goddess. [L.].

DEJECT [di-jekt'], *v.t.* to depress; discourage, dishearten. [L.].

DEJECTED [di-jek'tid], *adj.* depressed, disheartened. DEJECTEDLY, *adv.* in a d. fashion. DEJECTEDNESS, *n.* condition of being d.

DEJECTION [di-jek'shn], *n.* state of being dejected; lowness of spirit; (*med.*) act of evacuating the bowels. [L.].

DE JURE [dē-jōō'ri], *adv.* by law, as lawful. [L.].

DEKKO [de'kō], *n.* (*slang*) a look, sight of. [Hind.].

DELAINE [de-lān'], *n.* a light dress-material, originally of wool. [Fr.].

DELAY (1) [di-lā'], *v.t. and i.* to defer, postpone; retard, detain; procrastinate, linger, waste time. DELAY (2), *n.* act of delaying; condition of being delayed, interval of waiting, a pause or retarding. [OFr. from L.].

DEL-CREDERE [del-krā'de-ri], *n.* (*comm.*) guarantee of the solvency of a purchaser. [It.].

DELE [dē'li], *v.t. imper.* (*print.*) omit, delete. [DELETE].

DELECTABLE [di-lek'ta-bl], *adj.* delightful, pleasant, charming. DELECTABLENESS, *n.* quality of being d. DELECTABLY, *adv.* in a d. manner. [L.].

DELECTATION [dē-lek-tā'shn], *n.* act of pleasing, delight. [L.].

DELEGACY [de'li-ga-si], *n.* system of representing by delegates; group of delegates, committee.

DELEGATE (1) [de'li-gat], *n.* person sent as a representative of a group or class of people. DELEGATE (2) [de'li-gāt], *v.t.* to elect or send as a d.; entrust to another as representative or deputy. [L.].

DELEGATION [de-li-gā'shn], *n.* act of delegating; group or body of delegates; group of delegates.

ōō is pronounced as in food; ŏŏ as in hood; th as in *think*, TH as in *that*; zh as in azure. ~ = related to.

appointed to represent a state in international negotiations.

DELENDA [di-len'dah], *n.(pl.)* things to be deleted. [L.].

DELETE [di-lēt'], *v.t.* to erase, expunge, take out. DELETORY, *adj.* effacing, deleting. [L.].

DELETERIOUS [de-li-tēer'i-ŏŏs], *adj.* harmful to life, injurious, noxious. [Gk.].

DELETION [di-lē'shn], *n.* act of deleting, state of being deleted; that which is deleted. [L.].

DELFT [delft], *n.* kind of glazed earthenware. [*Delft*, Holland].

DELIBERATE (1) [di-li'be-rat], *adj.* intentional; done with deliberation, studied; slow and decided in speech and movement. DELIBERATE (2) [di-li'be-rāt], *v.t. and i.* to reflect upon, consider; think over carefully, study closely; confer about, debate. DELIBERATELY, *adv.* in a d. fashion. DELIBERATE-NESS, *n.* quality of being d. [L.].

DELIBERATION [di-li-be-rā'shn], *n.* act of deliberating; deliberateness.

DELIBERATIVE [di-li'be-ra-tiv], *adj.* pertaining to, acting by, deliberation. DELIBERATIVELY, *adv.* by deliberation.

DELICACIES [de'li-ka-siz], *n.(pl.)* choice eatables, food delicate to the taste; luxuries.

DELICACY [de'li-ka-si], *n.* condition of being delicate; anything delicate to the palate.

DELICATE [de'li-kat], *adj.* fine in texture, material and form, of slight and shapely proportions; soft, slender, refined; subtle in sensibility, precisely adjusted; nice in perception; susceptible to illness or injury, fragile; (*of colours*) pale or subtly blended; difficult to deal with; complex and highly responsive in nature. DELICATELY, *adv.* in a d. manner. [L.].

DELICATESSEN [de-li-ka-te'sen], *n.* shop or store selling cooked savoury foodstuffs; the goods sold by such a shop. [Germ.].

DELICIOUS [di-li'shŏŏs], *adj.* very agreeable to the palate, highly pleasing to the taste or the senses; giving exquisite pleasure. DELICIOUSLY, *adv.* in d. fashion. DELICIOUSNESS, *n.* quality of being d. [L.].

DELIGHT (1) [di-līt'], *v.t. and i.* to please intensely, gladden, give d. to; be highly pleased, enjoy greatly. DELIGHT (2), *n.* intense pleasure or satisfaction; that which causes such pleasure or satisfaction. DELIGHTED, *adj.* full of d., very pleased, charmed. DELIGHTEDLY, *adv.* in delighted fashion. [OFr. from L.].

DELIGHTFUL [di-līt'fŏŏl], *adj.* giving delight, charming, pleasant. DELIGHTFULLY, *adv.* in a d. manner. DELIGHTFULNESS, *n.* quality of being d.

DELIGHTSOME [di-līt'sum], *adj.* delightful. DE-LIGHTSOMELY, *adv.* delightfully. DELIGHTSOMENESS, *n.* quality of being d.

DELIMIT [dē-li'mit], *v.t.* to fix the boundaries of; take off a specific restriction. DELIMITATION [dē-li-mi-tā'shn], *n.* act of delimiting; state of being delimited.

DELINEATE [di-li'ni-āt], *v.t.* to mark or sketch in outline, trace out, sketch; describe. DELINEATION [di-li-ni-ā'shn], *n.* act of delineating; that which is delineated, a sketch, outline. DELINEATOR, *n.* one who, or that which, delineates. [L.].

DELINQUENCY [di-ling'kwen-si], *n.* failure or omission of duty; fault, offence, a crime. [L.].

DELINQUENT (1) [di-ling'kwent], *adj.* guilty of delinquency. DELINQUENT (2), *n.* a criminal type, offender; one who fails in or neglects a duty.

DELIQUESCE [de-li-kwes'], *v.i.* (*chem.*) to melt or turn to liquid by absorption of moisture from the atmosphere. DELIQUESCENCE [de-li-kwe'sens], *n.* process or characteristic of deliquescing. DELIQUES-CENT, *adj.* that deliquesces. [L.].

DELIRIOUS [di-li'ri-ŏŏs], *adj.* suffering from delirium. DELIRIOUSLY, *adv.* in a d. fashion. DELIRIOUSNESS, *n.* state of being d.

DELIRIUM [di-li'ri-um], *n.* mental disorder in which the patient is unconscious of his surroundings, and suffers from hallucinations; **d. tremens**, state of d. induced by alcoholic excesses. [L.].

DELIVER [di-li'ver], *v.t.* to set free, save from something objectionable or injurious; send, forward; give up, hand over, transfer; help at childbirth; pronounce, utter, make (a speech); aim a blow; (*cricket*) bowl a ball; (*leg.*) hand over formally or officially. DELIVERABLE, *adj.* able or requiring to be delivered. [LL.].

DELIVERANCE [di-li've-rans], *n.* act of delivering; state of being delivered.

DELIVERER [di-li've-rer], *n.* person who delivers.

DELIVERY [di-li've-ri], *n.* act of delivering; a giving out or taking of postal matter to the addressee; style of speaking; ball bowled at cricket; style of a bowler at cricket; childbirth.

DELL [del], *n.* small wooded valley. [OE.].

DELLA-ROBBIA WARE [de-lah-ro'bi-ah-wäer], *n.* earthenware founded on terra-cotta enamelled and moulded. [*Della Robbia*, Italian originator].

DELOCALIZE [dē-lō'ka-līz], *v.t.* to centralize.

DELPHIAN [del'fi-an], *adj.* Delphic.

DELPHIC [del'fik], *adj.* relating to Delphi, or the oracle of Apollo there; resembling in ambiguity one of Apollo's oracular statements. [*Delphi*, ancient Greek temple of Apollo].

DELPHINIUM [del-fi'ni-um], *n.* (*bot.*) genus of plants to which the larkspur belongs. [L. from Gk.].

DELTA [del'tah], *n.* fourth letter in the Greek alphabet; flat triangular-shaped alluvial land through which some rivers, such as the Nile, find several outlets to the sea; **d. metal**, alloy of zinc, copper and ferro-manganese. DELTAIC [del-tā'ik], *adj.* relating to, or resembling, a d. [Gk.].

DELTOID (1) [del'toid], *adj.* (*anat.*) (of a muscle) triangular in shape; (*bot.*) shaped like a delta. DELTOID (2), *n.* (*anat.*) the large triangular muscle of the shoulder used to elevate or move the arm. [Gk.].

DELUDE [di-lyŏŏd'], *v.t.* to impose on, deceive, mislead deliberately; (*reflex.*) convince oneself by false hopes. [L.].

DELUGE (1) [de'lyŏŏj], *n.* an overwhelming flood of water; (*fig.*) spate of words; (*coll.*) cloudburst; **the D.**, Noah's flood DELUGE (2), *v.t.* to overwhelm with water; inundate; (*fig.*) overwhelm. [Fr.].

DELUSION [di-lyŏŏ-zhn], *n.* act of deluding; state of being deluded; mistaken belief, fallacy, deception; firm and absurd belief of a pathological nature. DELUSIONAL, *adj.* exhibiting delusions. [L.].

DELUSIVE [di-lyŏŏ'siv], *adj.* tending to delude. DELUSIVELY, *adv.* in a d. fashion.

DELUSORY [di-lyŏŏ'se-ri], *adj.* delusive.

DELVE [delv], *v.t. and i.* to dig with a spade; (*fig.*) make an active and exhaustive study of. DELVER, *n.* person who digs or delves. [OE.].

DEMAGNETIZE [dē-mag'ne-tiz], *v.t.* to eliminate magnetic qualities from; deprive of polarity.

DEMAGOGIC(AL) [de-ma-go'gik(-al)], *adj.* relating to, or resembling, a demagogue or demagogy.

DEMAGOGUE [de'ma-gog], *n.* person purporting to speak for the interests of the mass of the people, agitating on their behalf and leading them against the ruling classes; politician with principles of dubious sincerity playing on the emotions of the people. DEMAGOGISM, *n.* methods and practices of a d. [Gk.].

DEMAGOGY [de'ma-go-gi], *n.* principles and tactics of a demagogue.

DEMAND (1) [di-mahnd'], *n.* a claim by right of agreement, authorized request; urgent request, claim requiring immediate settlement; aggressive request; (*econ.*) the necessities or requirements of consumers. DEMAND (2), *v.t.* to make a d. for; require, need, ask for. DEMANDABLE, *adj.* able to be demanded. DEMANDANT, *n.* person who demands; (*leg.*) plaintiff. [L.].

DEMARCATE [dē'mah-kāt], *v.t.* to mark out and fix a boundary. DEMARCATION [dē-mah-kā'shn], *n.* act of demarcating; dividing line or boundary demarcated. [Fr.].

DEMARCHE, démarche [dā-mahsh'], *n.* diplomatic representations made to a foreign government; a step, proceeding. [Fr.].

DEMATERIALIZE [dē-ma-tēer'i-a-liz], *v.t.* to deprive of material aspect, spiritualize; *v.i.* to become spiritualized.

DEMEAN (1) [di-mēn'], *v.t. and refl.* to lower, degrade, humiliate. [MEAN (3), by confusion with *next*].

DEMEAN (2), *v.t. and refl.* to behave; conduct. [OFr.].

DEMEANOUR [di-mē'ner], *n.* behaviour, bearing, deportment. [ME.].

DEMENT [di-ment'], *v.t.* to render insane, drive mad. [L.].

DEMENTED [di-men'tid], *adj.* insane, crazy. [L.].

DEMENTI, démenti [dā-mah(ng)'ti], *n.* denial, official contradiction. [Fr.].

DEMENTIA [di-men'shi-ah], *n.* insanity. [L.].

DEMERARA [de-me-räer'ah], *n.* kind of brown sugar from D. in British Guiana.

DEMERIT [dē-me'rit], *n.* undesirable trait, defect; characteristic worthy of censure. [L.].

DEMESNE [di-mān', di-mēn'], *n.* land immediately

The accent ' after a syllable = stress (u-pon')   The mark ‾ over a vowel = length (ā in made; ō in bone).

surrounding a country house; land worked by the owner himself. DEMESNIAL, *adj.* of, or belonging to, a d. [AFr.].

DEMI-, *pref.* half, partial, [Fr.].

DEMITONE [de'mi-tōn], *n.* (*mus.*) a minor third.

DEMIGOD [de'mi-god], *n.* half divine being sprung from the union of a god and a mortal; (*fig.*) one possessing godlike qualities, or regarded as a god.

DEMIJOHN [de'mi-jon], *n.* glass or earthenware bottle with a large body and small neck, enclosed in wickerwork. [Fr.].

DEMI-MONDE [de-mi-mond'], *n.* class of women of doubtful character and uncertain social position. DEMI-MONDAINE [de-mi-mon'dān], *n.* member of the d. [Fr.].

DEMIREP [de-mi-rep'], *n.* woman of doubtful character. [DEMI and REP(UTE)].

DEMISE (1) [di-mīz'], *n.* action of conveying property; transmission of an estate or hereditary privilege by death, *esp.* on the death of the sovereign; death. DEMISE (2), *v.t.* to grant by deed, lease etc.; transmit by inheritance. DEMISABLE, *adj.* that may be transferred by lease or inheritance. [OFr.].

DEMISEMIQUAVER [de'mi-se-mi-kwā-ver], *n.* (*mus.*) note half the length of a semiquaver.

DEMITONE [de'mi-tōn], *n.* (*mus.*) a semitone.

DEMOB (1) [dē-mob'], *v.t.* (*coll.*) to demobilize. DEMOB (2), *n.* (*coll.*) demobilization. [*Next*].

DEMOBILIZE [dē-mō'bi-līz], *v.t.* to disband military forces; discharge a person from the fighting forces after a war. DEMOBILIZATION [dē-mō-bi-li-zā'shn], *n.* act of demobilizing. [DE and MOBILIZE].

DEMOCRACY [di-mok'ra-si], *n.* government by all classes for the benefit of all classes; a state having this form of government; the mass of people in such a state. [Gk.].

DEMOCRAT [de'mo-krat], *n.* person who believes in democracy; (*U.S.*) member or supporter of the Democratic Party. [Fr.].

DEMOCRATIC(AL) [de-mō-kra'tik(-al)], *adj.* pertaining to, in favour of, founded on, democracy. DEMOCRATICALLY, *adv.* in a d. fashion.

DEMOCRATIZE [di-mok'ra-tiz], *v.t.* to make democratic.

DEMODE, démodé [dā-mō'dā], *adj.* out of fashion, dated. [Fr.].

DEMOGRAPHY [di-mog'ra-fi], *n.* social study of a community as revealed by statistics of its births, deaths or diseases. DEMOGRAPHER, *n.* student of d. DEMOGRAPHIC [de-mō-gra'fik], *adj.* pertaining to d. [Gk.].

DEMOLISH [di-mo'lish], *v.t.* to pull down, destroy; (*coll.*) eat up completely. DEMOLISHER, *n.* one who demolishes. [Fr.].

DEMOLITION [dē-mo-li'shn], *n.* act of demolishing. [L.].

DEMON [dē'mon], *n.* a spirit, supernatural being; one's guiding genius; evil spirit or genius, devil; (*coll.*) naughty child; wicked or supremely evil person. DEMONESS, *n.* she-devil. [Gk.].

DEMONETIZE [dē-mu'ni-tiz], *v.t.* to deprive of standard value, as money; withdraw from use as currency. [Fr.].

DEMONIAC (1) [di-mō'ni-ak], *adj.* pertaining to demons; influenced or produced by demons or wicked spirits; frenzied. DEMONIAC (2), *n.* person possessed by a demon. [Fr.].

DEMONIACAL [dē-mo-ni'a-kal], *adj.* demoniac, diabolical; possessed of a demon. DEMONIACALLY, *adv.* in a d. fashion.

DEMONIC [di-mo'nik], *adj.* relating to a demon; possessed or inspired by a demon.

DEMONISM [dē'mo-nizm], *n.* belief in the existence and power over human beings of demons. DEMONIST, *n.* believer in demons.

DEMONIZE [dē'mo-niz], *v.t.* to turn into a demon; put under the power of a demon.

DEMONOLATRY [dē-mo-no'la-tri], *n.* demonworship. [Gk.].

DEMONOLOGY [dē-mo-no'lo-ji], *n.* study concerned with the belief in demons or evil spirits. DEMONOLOGIC(AL) [dē-mo-no-lo'jik(-al)], *adj.* pertaining to d. DEMONOLOGIST, *n.* person skilled in d. [Gk.].

DEMONSTRABLE [di-mon'stra-bl], *adj.* able to be demonstrated. DEMONSTRABLENESS, *n.* state of being d. DEMONSTRABLY, *adv.* in a d. fashion. [L.].

DEMONSTRATE [de'mon-strāt], *v.t. and i.* to offer logical proof of, set forth the arguments supporting, prove; give practical examples of the working of, use or make work for inspection; organize or take part in a public meeting in support of one's opinions; (*milit.*) show willingness for action. [L.].

DEMONSTRATION [de-mon-strā'shn], *n.* act of demonstrating; exhibition, practical illustration; public exhibition of feeling; active expression of public dissatisfaction; (*anat.*) the exhibiting of parts dissected; (*milit.*) movement of troops with a view to deceive; (*logic*) series of syllogisms all of whose premises are either definitions, self-evident truths, or propositions already established. [L.].

DEMONSTRATIVE [di-mon'stra-tiv], *adj.* logically conclusive; clearly demonstrating; frank, given to demonstration; (*gram.*) that points out emphatically a specific thing. DEMONSTRATIVELY, *adv.* in a d. fashion. DEMONSTRATIVENESS, *n.* quality of being d.

DEMONSTRATOR [de'mon-strā-ter], *n.* one who demonstrates; one who assists a professor of science in his practical demonstrations and experiments; practical teacher of science. DEMONSTRATORY [di-mon'stra-te-ri], *adj.* tending to demonstrate.

DEMORALIZATION [di-mo-ra-li-zā'shn], *n.* act of demoralizing; condition of being demoralized.

DEMORALIZE [di-mo'ra-liz], *v.t.* to undermine or corrupt the morals, courage or discipline of, destroy the moral fibre of. [Fr.].

DEMOS [dē'mos], *n.* the common people, *esp.* those of an ancient Greek state. [Gk.].

DEMOSTHENIC [dē-mos-the'nik], *adj.* pertaining to Demosthenes, the Greek orator; eloquent.

DEMOTE [dē-mōt'], *v.t.* (*coll.*) to degrade, reduce in rank. [DE and -MOTE as in PROMOTE].

DEMULCENT [di-mul'sent], *n. and adj.* (substance) having a soothing quality; softening. [L.].

DEMUR (1) [pres.pt. **demurring**, *pret. and p.pt.* **demurred**] [di-mur'], *v.i.* to hesitate from uncertainty, disapprove, feel scruples concerning; (*leg.*) raise an objection which stops proceedings until it is decided. DEMUR (2), *n.* objection, hesitation, questioning. [Fr.].

DEMURE [di-myōōr'], *adj.* serious, grave, quietly decorous, modest. DEMURELY, *adv.* in a d. fashion. DEMURENESS, *n.* state or quality of being d. [OFr.].

DEMURRAGE [di-mu'rij], *n.* detention of ship, railway trucks etc., longer than agreed; charge made in compensation for this; charge made by transport undertakings for storage of goods not removed in due time; Bank of England charge in exchanging notes for bullion. [OFr.].

DEMURRER [di-mu'rer], *n.* person who demurs; (*leg.*) pleading which, while it admits the truth of the facts as set out by the opponent, declares that he is not legally entitled to redress, and brings the action to a halt pending a decision on this question by the court. DEMURRABLE, *adj.* (*leg.*) of such a nature as to call for a d. [AFr.].

DEMY [di-mī'], *n.* a regulation size of paper, measuring 22¼ × 17½ in. for printing, and 20 × 15½ in. for writing on; foundation scholar at Magdalen College, Oxford. DEMYSHIP, *n.* foundation scholarship at Magdalen College, Oxford. [DEMI].

DEN [den], *n.* lair, home or hiding-place of a wild animal; cage for wild beasts in a menagerie etc.; (*fig.*) place of retreat or abode; hiding-place of thieves; small, dark, sordid room or dwelling, small private room for work or leisure. [OE.].

DENARIUS [de-nāer'i-us], *n.* ancient Roman silver coin; (in books on law) English penny. [L.].

DENARY [dē'na-ri], *adj.* pertaining to the number ten; decimal. [L.].

DENATIONALIZE [dē-na'shn-a-liz], *v.t.* to divest of national rights; deprive of the status of a nation; divest of its national character; to restore to private ownership properties or concerns which have been acquired by the state.

DENATURALIZATION [dē-na-tyōō-ra-li-zā'shn], *n.* act of denaturalizing; state of being denaturalized.

DENATURALIZE [dē-na'tyōō-ra-liz], *v.t.* to render unnatural; deprive of the rights and standing of a citizen.

DENATURE [dē-nā'tyōōr], *v.t.* to adulterate so as to change the essential quality of; make unsuitable for consumption. DENATURANT, *n.* that which changes the nature of a thing; an adulterative addition. DENATURATION [dē-nā-tyōō-rā'shn], *n.* process of denaturing. [Fr.].

DENDRO-, *pref.* of a tree or trees. [Gk.].

DENDROLOGY [den-dro'lo-ji], *n.* study of trees. DENDROLOGIST, *n.* one learned in d. [Gk.].

DENE [dēn], *n.* little hollow on a hillside or on downland. [OE.].

DENEHOLE [dēn'hōl], *n.* ancient, deep excavation,

ōō is pronounced as in food; ŏŏ as in hood; th as in *think*; TH as in *that*; zh as in azure. ~ = related to.

usually in chalk, widening into chambers or passages at the bottom.

DENGUE [deng′gā], *n.* (*med.*) tropical fever characterized by redness of the skin and severe rheumatic pains. [W. Indian Span.].

DENIABLE [di-nī′a-bl], *adj.* which may be denied.

DENIAL [di-nī′al], *n.* act of denying; statement which denies something.

DENIGRATE [de′ni-grāt], *v.t.* to blacken; (*fig.*) blacken the character of, slander. [L.].

DENIM [de′nim], *n.* coarse cotton drill used for making aprons and overalls. [Fr. (*serge*) *de Nîmes*].

DENIZEN (1) [de′ni-zen], *n.* inhabitant of a place, native or otherwise; naturalized alien; inhabitant, dweller. **DENIZEN** (2), *v.t.* to make a d. or subject; populate, settle a country. [OFr.].

DENOMINATE [di-no′mi-nāt], *v.t.* to give a name to; call. **DENOMINABLE,** *adj.* capable of being named. [L.].

DENOMINATION [di-no-mi-nā′shn], *n.* act of naming; name, title; group called by the same name; religious sect; (*arith.*) unit of measure. [L.].

DENOMINATIONAL [di-no-mi-nā′shn-al], *adj.* pertaining or belonging to a religious denomination; sectarian. **DENOMINATIONALISM,** *n.* spirit of exclusive devotion to the interests and tenets of a sect or party.

DENOMINATIVE [di-no′mi-na-tiv], *adj.* that gives a name to; (*gram.*) also *n.* (word) derived from a noun. **DENOMINATIVELY,** *adv.* by way of denomination. [L.].

DENOMINATOR [di-no′mi-nā-ter], *n.* person who or thing which names; (*arith.*) number placed below the line in a vulgar fraction. [L.].

DENOTATION [dē-nō-tā′shn], *n.* act of denoting; thing by which anything is denoted; (*log.*) the meaning of a word, extent of a term's application. [L.].

DENOTE [di-nōt′], *v.t.* to mark out; show; indicate; stand as a symbol for. **DENOTATIVE,** *adj.* having power to denote. [L.].

DENOUEMENT, dénouement [dā-nōō′mah(ng)], *n.* the last dramatic revelation in a plot, the unravelling of a plot or situation, climax. [Fr.].

DENOUNCE [di-nowns′], *v.t.* to censure openly and threateningly; accuse publicly; bring to an end. **DENOUNCEMENT,** *n.* denunciation. [OFr.].

DENSE [dens], *adj.* tightly packed together; crowded, thick; opaque, impenetrable; (*fig.*) stupid, dull of comprehension. **DENSELY,** *adv.* in a d. fashion. [L.].

DENSITY [den′si-ti], *n.* quality of being dense; (*phys.*) relation of mass to bulk; specific gravity. [L.].

DENT (1) [dent], *n.* depression or hollow mark made by pressure or a blow; indentation. **DENT** (2), *v.t.* to make a d. in. [OE.].

DENTAL [den′tal], *adj.* pertaining to the teeth or to dentistry; (of certain consonants) pronounced by putting the tip of the tongue to the upper teeth. [MedL.].

DENTATE(D) [den′tāt, den-tā′tid], *adj.* edged with teeth or tooth-like projections. [L.].

DENTED [den′tid], *adj.* with indentations; toothed.

DENTI-, *pref.* of, or relating to, teeth. [L.].

DENTIFORM [den′ti-fawm], *adj.* in the form of a tooth, tooth-shaped.

DENTIFRICE [den′ti-fris], *n.* powder or paste for cleaning the teeth. [L.].

DENTILINGUAL [den-ti-ling′gwal], *adj.* (*phon.*) (of certain consonants) pronounced by applying the tongue to the gum above the upper teeth.

DENTINE [den′tin], *n.* hard, bone-like ivory tissue forming the body of a tooth.

DENTIST [den′tist], *n.* person skilled, and professionally engaged, in the care of the teeth. [Fr.].

DENTISTRY [den′tis-tri], *n.* profession or skill of a dentist.

DENTITION [den-ti′shn], *n.* production of the teeth, teething; character and arrangement of the teeth; the teeth themselves. [L.].

DENTURE [den′tyōōr], *n.* set of false teeth. [Fr.].

DENUDATION [de-nyōō-dā′shn], *n.* act of denuding; (*geol.*) the uncovering of an underlying formation by the erosion of the outer layer of soil or soft rock. [L.].

DENUDE [di-nyōōd′], *v.t.* to make or lay bare; strip, divest. [L.].

DENUNCIATE [di-nun′si-āt], *v.t.* to denounce. [L.].

DENUNCIATION [di-nun-si-ā′shn], *n.* act of denouncing. [L.].

DENUNCIATOR [di-nun′si-ā-ter], *n.* one who

denounces, accuser. **DENUNCIATORY,** *adj.* characterized by denouncing, that denounces. [L.].

DENY [di-nī′], *v.t.* to say that a statement is untrue or untenable; disown, repudiate, refuse; cause to abstain from. [Fr.].

DEODAR [dē′ō-dah(r)], *n.* cedar of the Western Himalayas, Hindu sacred tree. [Hind.].

DEODORANT [dē-ō′de-rant], *n.* deodorizing agent.

DEODORIZE [dē-ō′de-rīz], *v.t.* to take away the smell of; disguise or remove unpleasant or unhealthy smells from an object by the use of chemicals. **DEODORIZATION** [dē-ō-de-ri-zā′shn], *n.* act of deodorizing. **DEODORIZER,** *n.* a deodorant.

DEOXIDIZE [dē-ok′si-dīz], *v.t.* to remove oxygen from; reduce from the state of an oxide. **DEOXIDIZATION** [dē-ok-si-di-zā′shn], *n.* act of deoxidizing.

DEOXYGENATE [dē-ok′si-je-nāt], *v.t.* to deoxidize. **DEOXYGENATION** [dē-ok-si-je-nā′shn], *n.* deoxidization.

DEPART [di-paht′], *v.i.* to go away, leave; die; start, set out; **to d. from,** to turn aside from an accustomed course; change. **DEPARTED,** *adj.* gone, vanished, dead; as *n.* (often *pl.*) dead person. **DEPARTER,** *n.* one who departs. **DEPARTING,** *n.* going away, separating; dying. [OFr.].

DEPARTMENT [di-paht′ment], *n.* a separate part, section, division or branch; an administrative division of territory in France; **d. store,** large shop supplying a great variety of goods. [Fr.].

DEPARTMENTAL [dē-paht-men′tal], *adj.* pertaining to a department of business or territory; concerned with, affecting, a particular department or departments. **DEPARTMENTALISM,** *n.* addiction to bureaucratic methods of administration; red tape.

DEPARTURE [di-pah′tyōōr], *n.* act of departing; (*naut.*) distance travelled east or west of a meridian; **a new d.,** a change in method. [OFr.].

DEPASTURE [di-pahs′tyōōr], *v.t.* to turn cattle out to pasture, graze upon; *v.i.* to graze. **DEPASTURAGE,** *n.* act or right of grazing or pasturing.

DEPEND [di-pend′], *v.i.* to be suspended; **to d. on,** to be waiting to be decided; rely on; look to for help, support, maintenance, sympathy; be a question of; follow as a result of; trust. [L.].

DEPENDABLE [di-pen′da-bl], *adj.* that may be depended upon; trustworthy. **DEPENDABILITY** [di-pen-da-bi′li-ti], *n.* quality of being d.

DEPENDANT, DEPENDENT (1) [di-pen′dant], *n.* one who is dependent on, or supported by, another; servant, retainer. [Fr.].

DEPENDENCE [di-pen′dens], *n.* condition of being dependent on another; reliance, trust, faith. [Fr.].

DEPENDENCY [di-pen′den-si], *n.* that which is attached but subordinate to something; state or dominion governed by another.

DEPENDENT (1), see **DEPENDANT.**

DEPENDENT (2) [di-pen′dent], *adj.* hanging down; subsisting or supported by; relying on for support, favour, benefit; that depends on something. **DEPENDENTLY,** *adv.* in a d. manner.

DEPENDING [di-pen′ding], *adj.* pendent, hanging down; dependent; (*leg.*) awaiting settlement.

DEPICT [di-pikt′], *v.t.* to delineate, draw, paint, sculpture; portray; draw a word-picture. **DEPICTION,** *n.* act of depicting. **DEPICTOR,** *n.* artist who depicts or describes. [L.].

DEPICTURE [di-pik′tyōōr], *v.t.* to depict.

DEPILATE [de′pi-lāt], *v.t.* to strip off, remove, pull out hair. **DEPILATION** [dē-pi-lā′shn], *n.* the removing of the hair. [L.].

DEPILATORY (1) [di-pi′la-te-ri], *adj.* able to remove hair. **DEPILATORY** (2), *n.* preparation which removes superfluous hair. [L.].

DEPLETE [di-plēt′], *v.t.* to let out contents of; empty out; exhaust; diminish considerably. **DEPLETIVE, DEPLETORY,** *adj.* inducing depletion. [L.].

DEPLETION [di-plē′shn], *n.* act of depleting; state of being depleted; (*med.*) blood-letting.

DEPLORABLE [di-plaw′ra-bl], *adj.* causing grief or pity; wretched; lamentable. **DEPLORABLENESS,** *n.* condition of being d. **DEPLORABLY,** *adv.* in d. fashion.

DEPLORE [di-plaw(r)′], *v.t.* to lament; express regret about. **DEPLORATION** [dē-plaw-rā′shn], *n.* act of deploring. **DEPLORINGLY,** *adv.* in a deploring manner. [L.].

DEPLOY [di-ploi′], *v.t.* (*milit.*) to open out for action; *v.i.* to spread out into open formation. **DEPLOYMENT,** *n.* act of deploying. [Fr.].

DEPLUME [dē-plōōm′], *v.t.* to pull out or pluck the feathers of. **DEPLUMATION** [dē-plōō-mā′shn], *n.* act

---

The accent ′ after a syllable = stress (u-pon′).   The mark ‾ over a vowel = length (ā in made; ō in bone).

of depluming; (*med.*) affection of the eyelids causing loss of eyelashes. [Fr.].

DEPOLARIZE [dē-pō'la-rīz], *v.t.* (*elect.*) to destroy the polarity of; (*fig.*) unsettle. DEPOLARIZATION [dē-pō-la-ri-zā'shn], *n.* act of depolarizing.

DEPONE [di-pōn'], *v.t.* (*leg.*) to make a statement upon oath; depose. [L.].

DEPONENT (1) [di-pō'nent], *n.* one who depones, a sworn witness; a deponent verb. DEPONENT (2), *adj.* laying down; **d. verb**, (in Latin and Greek grammar) a verb passive in form but otherwise active. [L.].

DEPOPULATE [dē-po'pyōō-lāt], *v.t.* to lessen or destroy population of an area; *v.i.* to become sparsely populated. DEPOPULATION [dē-po-pyōō-lā'shn], *n.* act of depopulating. DEPOPULATOR, *n.* one who depopulates. [L.].

DEPORT [di-pawt'], *v.t.* to expel; send back by force to one's own country; (*v. reflex.*) behave. DEPORTEE [dē-paw-tē'], *n.* one who is deported. [Fr. from L.].

DEPORTATION [dē-paw-tā'shn], *n.* act of deporting; state of being deported. [L.].

DEPORTMENT [di-pawt'ment], *n.* carriage, bearing, behaviour. [Fr.].

DEPOSE [di-pōz'], *v.t.* to remove from a throne or other high office or rank; (*leg.*) give evidence on oath. DEPOSABLE, *adj.* capable of being deposed. DEPOSAL, *n.* act of deposing. [Fr.].

DEPOSIT (1) [di-po'zit], *n.* that which is deposited; sediment from a liquid; money paid into a banking account; money paid on account to render a contract binding. DEPOSIT (2), *v.t.* to lay or drop down; leave as a sediment; entrust for safe keeping; pay money in advance to render a contract binding. DEPOSITARY, *n.* one to whom a d. is paid. [L.].

DEPOSITION [dē-po-zi'shn], *n.* act of deposing; sworn testimony; state of being deposed. [L.].

DEPOSITOR [di-po'si-ter], *n.* one who pays deposits into a bank; person or machine for laying a deposit. [L.].

DEPOSITORY [di-po'zi-te-ri], *n.* storehouse or place of safe-keeping. [MedL.].

DEPOT [de'pō], *n.* place of deposit for goods of any kind, *esp.* for military stores; (*milit.*) headquarters of a regiment or recruiting centre when the main body is abroad; railway terminus; place where transport vehicles are housed. [Fr.].

DEPRAVE [di-prāv'], *v.t.* to corrupt, morally abase, pervert. DEPRAVATION [dep-ra-vā'shn], *n.* act of depraving; moral debasement. DEPRAVEDLY, *adv.* in depraved fashion. [L.].

DEPRAVITY [di-pra'vi-ti], *n.* moral corruption; (*theol.*) man's inherent sinfulness.

DEPRECATE [de'pri-kāt], *v.t.* to feel and express regret or reluctance about; protest against, condemn. DEPRECATINGLY, *adv.* in a deprecating manner. DEPRECATION [de-pri-kā'shn], *n.* act of deprecating. DEPRECATIVE, DEPRECATORY [de'pri-ka-tiv, de'pri-kā-te-ri], *adj.* tending to d. DEPRECATOR, *n.* one who deprecates. [L.].

DEPRECIATE [di-prē'shi-āt], *v.t.* to bring down the value of; (*fig.*) disparage, belittle; *v.i.* to fall in value; become less valuable through wear and tear. DEPRECIATINGLY, *adv.* in depreciating fashion; so as to d. DEPRECIATIVE, DEPRECIATORY, *adj.* tending to d. or undervalue. DEPRECIATOR, *n.* person who depreciates. [L.].

DEPRECIATION [di-prē-shi-ā'shn], *n.* act of depreciating; condition of being depreciated; allowance for wear and tear in assessment; (*fig.*) disparagement.

DEPREDATE [dep'ri-dāt], *v.t.* to plunder or pillage; *v.i.* to make depredations. DEPREDATOR, *n.* person who or thing which makes depredations. DEPREDATORY [dep'ri-dā-te-ri], *adj.* plundering, laying waste. [L.].

DEPREDATION [de-pri-dā'shn], *n.* act of plundering or ravaging; robbery. [L.].

DEPRESS [di-pres'], *v.t.* to press down, lower; make dispirited, dreary; weaken in vigour or intensity; (*fig.*) render lower in rank or fortune. DEPRESSANT, *n.* (*med.*) a sedative. DEPRESSIBLE, *adj.* capable of being depressed. DEPRESSING, *adj.* tending to d. DEPRESSINGLY, *adv.* in depressing fashion. DEPRESSIVE, *adj.* apt to d. [OFr.].

DEPRESSED [di-prest'], *adj.* pressed down; flattened; (*fig.*) crippled in vitality and power for action; low, dejected; **the d. areas**, those parts of a country where poverty and unemployment are widespread.

DEPRESSION [di-pre'shn], *n.* act of depressing, state of being depressed; little valley, slight concavity on the surface of anything; (*fig.*) low spirits, lethargy, melancholy; (*comm.*) period of inactivity and slump; (*meteor.*) area in which there is a low barometric pressure.

DEPRESSOR [di-pre'ser], *n.* person who or thing which depresses; (*anat.*) muscle which pulls down a part of the body. [L.].

DEPRIVATION [de-pri-vā'shn], *n.* act of depriving; loss; (*leg.*) deposition from the clerical order or a church benefice. [MedL.].

DEPRIVE [di-prīv'], *v.t.* to divest (of), debar from use or enjoyment (of); dispossess; strip of ecclesiastical rank or office. DEPRIVABLE, *adj.* subject to deprivation. DEPRIVATIVE [di-pri'va-tiv], *adj.* depriving, that deprives. DEPRIVER, *n.* person who or thing which deprives. [Fr.].

DEPTH [depth], *n.* state or quality of being deep; the measure of anything downward or inward; extent of penetration or of distance from front to back; quality of being intellectually deep, learned or difficult; profundity, intensity of feeling; strength of colour; (*mus.*) quality of being rich and low in pitch; (*pl.*) that which is deep; (*fig.*) the heart; **out of one's d.**, too deep for the bottom to be touched with the feet; (*fig.*) confronted with something beyond one's power of comprehension; **defence in d.**, (*milit.*) defence system involving interlinked strong points spread over a wide area rather than one solid front line. DEPTHLESS, *adj.* unfathomable. [ME.].

DEPTH-CHARGE [depth'chahj], *n.* explosive weapon against submarines, which is designed to explode under water at a certain predetermined depth.

DEPTH-GAUGE [depth'gāj], *n.* instrument for measuring depth.

DEPUTATION [de-pyōō-tā'shn], *n.* act of deputing; body of representatives or delegates.

DEPUTE [di-pyōōt'], *v.t.* to appoint as proxy or proxies; delegate (duties) to others. [L.].

DEPUTIZE [de'pyōō-tīz], *v.i.* to act on behalf of someone else.

DEPUTY [de'pyōō-ti], *n.* one who deputizes; member of a deputation; coalminer who is in charge of the working conditions and output of a group of other miners; (in France and elsewhere) member of the lower house of the legislature. [Fr.].

DERACINATE [dē-ra'si-nāt], *v.t.* to uproot, destroy completely. [Fr.].

DERAIL [dē-rāl'], *v.t. and i.* to run off the rails; cause to run off the rails. DERAILMENT, *n.* act of derailing; condition of being derailed.

DERANGE [di-rānj'], *v.t.* to put out of order, throw into confusion; upset the normal function of; cause an abnormal state of mind in. DERANGEMENT, *n.* act of deranging; state of being deranged. [Fr.].

DERATE [dē-rāt'], *v.t.* to free from or reduce liability to rating; relieve industries from municipal taxation by Act of Parliament.

DERATION [dē-ra'shn], *v.t.* to free from the restrictions of a rationing system, take off the ration.

DERBY [dah'bi], *n.* horse race instituted by the twelfth Earl of Derby, and run at the Epsom Summer Meeting; (*U.S.* [dur'bi]), a hard felt hat; **Crown D.**, kind of porcelain first made at Derby in the eighteenth century.

DERELICT (1) [de'ri-likt], *adj.* abandoned by its owner; (*fig.*) (of a person) old and considered to be of no further use. DERELICT (2), *n.* a wreck adrift on the open sea; anything thrown away, relinquished or abandoned by its owner, *esp.* goods found at sea. [L.].

DERELICTION [de-ri-lik'shn], *n.* neglect of duty; permanent abandonment; condition of being abandoned. [L.].

DERESERVE [dē-ri-zurv'], *v.t.* to remove from a reserved status.

DERIDE [di-rīd'], *v.t.* to mock at with scorn; hold in contempt or ridicule. DERIDER, *n.* one who derides. DERIDINGLY, *adv.* in a deriding fashion.

DERISION [di-ri'zhn], *n.* act of deriding; state of being derided, mockery, ridicule. [L.].

DERISIVE [di-ri'siv], *adj.* expressing derision; worthy of derision. DERISIVELY, *adv.* in a d. fashion. DERISIVENESS, *n.* quality or state of being d.

DERISORY [di-ri'se-ri], *adj.* characterized by derision, mocking; ridiculous, negligible. [L.].

DERIVABLE [de-ri'va-bl], *adj.* that may be derived; deducible. DERIVABLY, *adv.* in a derivative fashion.

DERIVATION [de-ri-vā'shn], *n.* act of deriving; origin, source; original form or word from which the present form of a word is derived, the etymology. DERIVATIONAL, *adj.* of, or pertaining to, d. [L.].

ōō is pronounced as in food; ŏŏ as in hood; th as in *th*ink; TH as in *th*at; zh as in azure. ~ = related to.

DERIVATIVE (1) [di-ri'va-tiv], *adj.* derived; proceeding from another; secondary; **d. chord**, (*mus.*) chord derived from a fundamental combination; **d. conveyances**, (*leg.*) secondary deeds, such as releases, surrenders, consignments etc. DERIVATIVE (2), *n.* that which is derived from another word. DERIVATIVELY, *adv.* in a d. fashion. [L.].

DERIVE [di-riv'], *v.t.* to receive by regular transmission or conveyance; obtain, get as from a source; trace from; give the etymology as being; *v.i.* to come or proceed from. [L.].

DERM, DERMA [dur'mah], *n.* the true skin or layer of skin underneath the epidermis; the corium. DERMAL, DERMATIC [dur'mal, der-ma'tik], *adj.* pertaining to the skin. [Gk.].

DERMATITIS [der-ma-ti'tis], *n.* (*path.*) eruption of, or inflammation on, the true skin. [Gk.].

DERMATO-, *pref.* pertaining to the skin.

DERMATOLOGY [der-ma-to'lo-ji], *n.* study of the skin and its diseases. DERMATOLOGIST, *n.* student of d. [Gk.].

DERMOID [dur'moid], *adj.* like or resembling skin. [Gk.].

DERNIER [däer'ni-ā], *adj.* last, final; **d. cri** [krē], latest fashion. [Fr.].

DEROGATE [de'ro-gāt], *v.t.* to take away some part; detract from; disparage; invalidate some part of a law or established rule; *v.i.* to detract; lessen. DEROGATION [de-ro-gā'shn], *n.* act of derogating; detraction. [L.].

DEROGATORY [di-ro'ga-te-ri], *adj.* detracting from authority, honour, prestige; disparaging, disrespectful. DEROGATORILY, *adv.* in d. fashion. [L.].

DERRICK [de'rik], *n.* a contrivance, in various forms, for raising heavy weights; kind of crane; framework over an oil-well or similar boring. [*Derrick*, former hangman].

DERRING-DO [de-ring-dōō'], *n.* desperate courage, valiant action. [From *in dorryng don* in daring to do].

DERRINGER [de'rin-jer], *n.* (*U.S.*) short, rifled pistol of large bore, so named from the inventor.

DERRIS [de'ris], *n.* a plant, from the root of which insecticide preparations are made.

DERVISH [dur'vish], *n.* member of a Mohammedan religious sect or order, professing extreme poverty and austerity; **dancing d.**, member of one of the orders of dervishes who dance to attain religious ecstasy. [Pers.].

DESCANT (1) [des'kant], *n.* melody played or sung above an air as a variation or accompaniment to it; part-song; air or soprano in a part-song; long conversation or discussion; series of comments upon a theme. DESCANT (2) [des-kant'], *v.i.* (*mus.*) to sing or play a d.; converse at length on one theme or topic. DESCANTER [des-kan'ter], *n.* person who descants. [OFr.].

DESCEND [di-send'], *v.t.* to walk, move or pass downward upon or along; pass from the top to the bottom of; (*astron.*) move to the southward; (*mus.*) pass from sharp to flat; **to d. to**, (*fig.*) to stoop, lower oneself to; **to d. upon**, to attack unexpectedly. (*fig.*) visit without notice; *v.i.* to move in a downward course, proceed to a lower position; sink; proceed from a source or origin; be derived; pass from one heir to another; lower or degrade oneself. DESCENDABLE, DESCENDIBLE, *adj.* capable of being transmitted by inheritance. [L.].

DESCENDANT [di-sen'dant], *n.* person or animal descended from another; progeny. [Fr. from L.].

DESCENT [di-sent'], *n.* act of descending; declivity, downward slope; ancestry; hereditary transmission; sudden unexpected invasion. [OFr.].

DESCRIBE [di-skrib'], *v.t.* to give a detailed account of; delineate by word or pictorial representation; (*geom.*) mark out, draw. DESCRIBABLE, *adj.* capable of being described. DESCRIBENT, *n.* (*geom.*) point, line or surface which describes by its motion a line, surface or solid. [L.].

DESCRIED [di-skrid'], *adj.* observed, noticed. [DESCRY].

DESCRIPTION [di-skrip'shn], *n.* act of describing; that which describes, representation or account of anything by words and images; class, kind, variety. [L.].

DESCRIPTIVE [di-skrip'tiv], *adj.* that describes, fond of or skilled in description. DESCRIPTIVELY, *adv.* in d. fashion. [LL.].

DESCRY [di-skri'], *v.t.* to espy, discover by sight; see something in the distance. [OFr.].

DESECRATE [de'si-krāt], *v.t.* to divert from a sacred purpose or character; profane. DESECRATION [de-si-krā'shn], *n.* act of desecrating; condition of being desecrated. [L.].

DESENSITIZE [dē-sen'si-tiz], *v.t.* to make insensitive, *esp.* to light. DESENSITIZER, *n.* apparatus or agent which desensitizes.

DESERT (1) [de'zert], *n.* uninhabited tract of land; wilderness; vast sandy or stony expanse almost destitute of moisture or vegetation. DESERT (2), *adj.* barren, uninhabited, desolate. [OFr.].

DESERT (3) [di-zurt'], *n.* what one deserves as a reward or punishment; due return. [OFr.].

DESERT (4), *v.t. and i.* to forsake, leave without warning given or permission granted; (*milit.*) make an unauthorized departure from the fighting services, run away. [OFr., LL.].

DESERTER [di-zur'ter], *n.* one who deserts, *esp.* a soldier or sailor who leaves the service without permission.

DESERTION [di-zur'shn], *n.* act of deserting; condition of being deserted.

DESERVE [di-zurv'], *v.t. and i.* to merit, be worthy of; earn. DESERVEDLY [di-zur'vid-li], *adv.* according to desert. DESERVER, *n.* person who deserves. DESERVING, *adj.* worthy of reward, meritorious. DESERVINGLY, *adv.* in a deserving fashion. [L.].

DESHABILLE, see DISHABILLE.

DESICCATE [de'si-kāt], *v.t.* to dry up; draw all moisture from; (*chem.*) dry thoroughly so as to form a powder; *v.i.* to become dry. DESICCATION [de-si-kā'shn], *n.* act of desiccating; condition of being desiccated. DESICCATIVE [di-si'ka-tiv], *adj.* that dries up. DESICCATOR [de'si-kā-ter], *n.* agent or apparatus which desiccates. [L.].

DESIDERATE [di-si'de-rāt], *v.t.* to feel the want of, miss; wish to have. DESIDERATION [di-si-de-rā'shn], *n.* act of desiderating. [L.].

DESIDERATIVE [di-si'de-ra-tiv], *adj.* having or implying desire; (*gram.*) of or pertaining to a verb formed from another to denote desire to perform the action of the original verb. [L.].

DESIDERATUM (*pl.* **desiderata**) [di-si-de-rā'tum], *n.* a real or felt want; that which is greatly desired. [L.].

DESIGN (1) [di-zin'], *v.t.* to plan or delineate by drawing; draft a scheme for the construction of some object; project; plan in the mind; give, set apart for, in intention; intend, purpose. DESIGN (2), *n.* draft or scheme to serve as a guide in subsequent practical work; mental plan, intention, aim; the adapting of means to a preconceived end; a form of painting or drawing based on the harmony of line and colour rather than the representation of objects; art of making such paintings or drawings; qualities of grace and proportion in anything made. DESIGNABLE, *adj.* capable of being designed or marked out. [L.].

DESIGNATE (1) [de'zig-nāt], *v.t.* to indicate by visible lines, marks, descriptions; name and settle the identity of; assign for appointment. DESIGNATE (2), *adj.* nominated to an office. DESIGNATIVE, DESIGNATORY, *adj.* serving to d. DESIGNATOR, *n.* one who designates. [L.].

DESIGNATION [de-zig-nā'shn], *n.* act of designating; state of being designated; that which designates, a distinctive appellation or title.

DESIGNED [di-zind'], *adj.* delineated, planned, intended. DESIGNEDLY [di-zi'nid-li], *adv.* intentionally, on purpose.

DESIGNER [di-zi'ner], *n.* one who designs, *esp.* patterns, draughtsman; designing person.

DESIGNING (1) [di-zi'ning], *n.* art of drawing designs or patterns; act of planning. DESIGNING (2), *adj.* intriguing, given to crafty scheming.

DESILVERIZE [dē-sil've-riz], *v.t.* to extract silver from other metals.

DESIRABILITY [di-zier-a-bi'li-ti], *n.* condition of being desirable.

DESIRABLE [di-zier'a-bl], *adj.* worthy of desire, exciting a wish to possess; agreeable, choice. DESIRABLY, *adv.* in a d. fashion. [Fr.].

DESIRE (1) [di-zier'], *v.t.* to wish to possess or enjoy; long for, covet; utter a wish; ask, beg; request. DESIRE (2), *n.* strong wish to possess or enjoy some object; prayer or request; the object desired; lust, sexual passion. DESIRED, *adj.* wished for, coveted. [Fr. from L.].

DESIROUS [di-zier'ōōs], *adj.* having a wish or desire for; longing; covetous. DESIROUSLY, *adv.* in d. fashion.

DESIST [di-zist'], *v.i.* to cease to act, leave off, stop;

The accent ' after a syllable = stress (u-pon'). The mark ˉ over a vowel = length (ā in made: ō in bone).

forbear; discontinue. DESISTANCE, *n.* act of desisting. [L.].

DESK [desk], *n.* table, board or box for writing or reading from; similar flat-topped piece of furniture fitted with drawers at each side; place from which prayers are read; (*U.S.*) specialized department of a newspaper or similar office. [ME. from LL.].

DESMO-, *pref.* bond, fastening, chain, ligature. [Gk.].

DESMOLOGY [des-mo'lo-ji], *n.* (*anat.*) study of ligaments and sinews. [Gk.].

DESOLATE (1) [de'sō-lat], *adj.* destitute or deprived of inhabitants, desert, dismal, barren and dreary; neglected, lonely, extremely unhappy. DESOLATE (2), [de'sō-lāt] *v.t.* to strip of inhabitants, lay waste; ruin; ravage; make lonely; bereave. DESOLATELY, *adv.* in a d. manner. DESOLATING, *adj.* wasting, ravaging; saddening. [L.].

DESOLATION [de-so-lā'shn], *n.* act of desolating; devastation; state of being desolate; extreme sadness.

DESPAIR (1) [di-spāer'], *v.i.* to have no hope; abandon hope. DESPAIR (2), *n.* hopelessness, despondency, desperation. [L.].

DESPAIRING [di-spāer'ing], *adj.* that despairs, prone to despair; indicating despair. DESPAIRINGLY, *adv.* in a d. manner.

DESPATCH, see DISPATCH.

DESPERADO [des-pe-rah'dō], *n.* violent ruffian; desperate, lawless fellow. [OSpan.].

DESPERATE [des'pe-rat], *adj.* reckless of danger; furious, sticking at nothing; without hope, hopeless; beyond hope of recovery; done in despair. DESPERATELY, *adv.* in a d. fashion. [L.].

DESPERATION [des-pe-rā'shn], *n.* state of despair or of being desperate; desperate disregard of safety or danger; **to drive to d.**, to make violently angry, goad to extreme measures. [L.].

DESPICABLE [des'pi-ka-bl, di-spi'ka-bl], *adj.* deserving of being despised; contemptible; vile; mean. DESPICABLENESS [des'pi-ka-bl-nes, di-spi'ka-bl-nes], n. quality or state of being d. DESPICABLY [des'pi-ka-bli, di-spi'ka-bli], *adv.* in a d. fashion. [L.].

DESPISE [di-spiz'], *v.t.* to look down on; feel contempt for. DESPISAL, *n.* contempt, scorn. DESPISER, *n.* person who despises. DESPISINGLY, *adv.* with contempt. [ME. from OFr.].

DESPITE (1) [di-spit'], *n.* malice, spite; defiance with contempt; (*archaic*) injury. DESPITE (2), *prep.* notwithstanding, in spite of. [OFr.].

DESPITEFUL [di-spit'fōŏl], *adj.* spiteful, malignant. DESPITEFULLY, *adv.* spitefully, maliciously. DESPITEFULNESS, *n.* condition of being d.

DESPOIL [di-spoil'], *v.t.* to rob; strip by force. DESPOILER, *n.* person who despoils. DESPOILMENT, *n.* despoliation. [L.].

DESPOLIATION [di-spō-li-ā'shn], *n.* act of despoiling; condition of being despoiled. [OFr.].

DESPOND [di-spond'], *v.i.* to be in low spirits or dejected; despair. [L.].

DESPONDENCE [di-spon'dens], *n.* despondency.

DESPONDENCY [di-spon'den-si], *n.* desponding state of mind, dejection, low spirits.

DESPONDENT [di-spon'dent], *adj.* dejected in spirit, depressed, despairing. DESPONDENTLY, *adv.* in d. fashion.

DESPONDING [di-spon'ding], *adj.* yielding to despondency, depressed, dejected. DESPONDINGLY, *adv.* in a d. fashion.

DESPOT [des'pot], *n.* one who rules with absolute power or authority in a state; tyrant. [Gk.].

DESPOTIC(AL) [di-spo'tik(-al)], *adj.* pertaining to a despot or to despotism; having the power of a despot; arbitrary, tyrannical. DESPOTICALLY, *adv.* in d. fashion.

DESPOTISM [des'po-tizm], *n.* rule by a despot; state governed by a despot; tyrannical government.

DESQUAMATE [des'kwa-māt], *v.t.* to scale off, peel. DESQUAMATION [des-kwa-mā'shn], *n.* process of desquamating. DESQUAMATORY [di-skwa'ma-te-ri], *adj.* characterized by desquamation. [L.].

DESSERT [di-zurt'], *n.* a course of fruit and confections when the substantial part of a meal is completed; (*U.S.*) pies, puddings, sweets etc. [OFr.].

DESSERT-SPOON [di-zurt'spŏŏn], *n.* spoon intermediate in size between a tablespoon and a teaspoon. DESSERT-SPOONFUL, quarter of a liquid ounce.

DESTINATION [des-ti-nā'shn], *n.* the place for which one has set out, place to which anything is to be sent, goal.

DESTINE [des'tin], *v.t.* to ordain, appoint; fix or

predetermine unalterably; devote or doom; intend. [L.].

DESTINY [des'ti-ni], *n.* the fate to which a person or thing is preappointed; the inevitable power which governs and determines action; personification of this power. [OFr.].

DESTITUTE [des'ti-tyŏŏt], *adj.* not having or possessing, lacking; in a condition of great poverty; lacking means of support. [L.].

DESTITUTION [des-ti-tyŏŏ'shn], *n.* state of being abandoned or left destitute; lack of the necessaries of life. [L.].

DESTROY [di-stroi'], *v.t.* to reduce to nothing, ruin; pull down, demolish, lay waste; kill. [ME. from OFr.].

DESTROYER [di-stroi'er], *n.* one who, or that which, destroys; (*nav.*) small, lightly-armed, swift warship, capable of firing torpedoes.

DESTRUCTIBLE [di-struk'ti-bl], *adj.* able to be destroyed. DESTRUCTIBILITY [di-struk-ti-bi'li-ti], *n.* state of being d. [L.].

DESTRUCTION [di-struk'shn], *n.* act of destroying; state of being destroyed; ruin; that which destroys.

DESTRUCTIVE (1) [di-struk'tiv], *adj.* causing destruction; ruinous, injurious. DESTRUCTIVE (2), *n.* that which is d. DESTRUCTIVELY, *adv.* in a d. manner. [L.].

DESTRUCTOR [di-struk'ter], *n.* person who or thing which destroys; furnace where refuse is destroyed by burning.

DESUETUDE [dē'swi-tyŏŏd], *n.* state of being disused; discontinuance, disuse. [L.].

DESULTORY [de'sul-te-ri], *adj.* rambling from one thing to another without order or connexion; casual, spasmodic. DESULTORILY, *adv.* in d. fashion. DESULTORINESS, *n.* state of being d. [L.].

DETACH [di-tach'], *v.t.* to separate, unloosen; unfasten; (*milit.*) bring men from the main contingent for some special duty. DETACHABLE, *adj.* able to be detached. [Fr.].

DETACHED [di-tacht'], *adj.* separated, standing apart or separately; (*fig.*) impartial, free from personal bias.

DETACHMENT [di-tach'ment], *n.* act of detaching; condition of being detached; (*fig.*) freedom from personal concern; aloofness; (*milit.*) unit separated from the main body of troops for some special service.

DETAIL (1) [dē'tāl], *n.* one item; individual fact, circumstance or portion taken in conjunction with others; something of slight importance; **in d.**, item by item; thoroughly and exactly. DETAIL (2), *v.t.* to make a detailed report of, recount item by item; (*milit.*) appoint for certain work. DETAILED, *adj.* related item by item; exact, thorough and minute. DETAILER [di-tā'ler], *n.* person who details. [Fr.].

DETAIN [di-tān'], *v.t.* to hold or keep back; cause to be delayed, prevent from continuing, keep possession of; (*leg.*) retain in custody. [OFr.].

DETAINER [di-tā'ner], *n.* (*leg.*) one who unlawfully withholds or keeps property which belongs to another; **writ of d.**, writ issued against prisoners in custody in order that they may be detained on further charges.

DETECT [di-tekt'], *v.t.* to notice, perceive; become aware of the existence of; discover, apprehend. DETECTABLE, *adj.* able to be detected. [L.].

DETECTION [di-tek'shn], *n.* act of detecting; criminal investigation. [L.].

DETECTIVE (1) [di-tek'tiv], *adj.* of or pertaining to detection; employed in detecting; **d. story**, type of fiction dealing with crimes and the detection of those responsible for them. DETECTIVE (2), *n.* police officer who investigates cases of crime; private person who is engaged professionally in investigating cases of crime or irregular conduct.

DETECTOPHONE [di-tek'to-fōn], *n.* instrument for tapping telephone wires.

DETECTOR [di-tek'ter], *n.* discoverer; one who, or that which, detects; (*radio*) device for rectifying high-frequency oscillations. [L.].

DETENT [di-tent'], *n.* a catch in a machine; a stop in a clock, which controls the striking mechanism. [Fr.].

DÉTENTE, détente [dā-tah(ng)t'], *n.* relaxation of tension in the diplomatic relations of two states. [Fr.].

DETENTION [di-ten'shn], *n.* act of detaining; condition of being detained; custody; confinement; the punishment of being kept in school after hours; **d. barrack**, military prison.

DETER [di-tur'], *v.t.* to hold back or restrain; prevent.

ŏŏ is pronounced as in *food*; ŏŏ as in *wood*; th as in *think*; TH as in *that*; zh as in azure.   ~ = related to.

dissuade by describing the consequences of action. [L.].

DETERGENT (1) [di-tur′jent], *adj.* cleansing. DETER-GENT (2), *n.* cleansing agent. DETERGENCY, *n.* cleansing quality. [L.].

DETERIORATE [di-tēer′i-e-rāt], *v.t.* to lower the value of, make inferior or worse; *v.i.* to become worse; degenerate. DETERIORATIVE, *adj.* that deteriorates. [L.].

DETERIORATION [di-tēer-i-e-rā′shn], *n.* act of deteriorating; condition of having deteriorated.

DETERMENT [di-tur′ment], *n.* act of deterring; that which deters.

DETERMINABLE [di-tur′mi-na-bl], *adj.* that may be determined. DETERMINABILITY [di-ter-mi-na-bi′li-ti], *n.* state or quality of being d. [L.].

DETERMINANT (1) [di-tur′mi-nant], *adj.* having the power of determining; serving to determine or fix. DETERMINANT (2), *n.* that which determines. [L.].

DETERMINATE [di-tur′mi-nat], *adj.* limited, fixed, definitely settled; **d. problem**, (*math.*) problem having a limited number of solutions. DETER-MINATELY, *adv.* in a d. fashion.

DETERMINATION [di-ter-mi-nā′shn], *n.* act of determining; condition of being determined; firm resolution, decision of character; (*leg.*) judicial sentence; (*med.*) tendency of blood to flow to any part more copiously than is normal. [L.].

DETERMINATIVE (1) [di-tur′mi-na-tiv], *adj.* that determines anything. DETERMINATIVE (2), *n.* that which determines.

DETERMINE [di-tur′min], *v.t. and i.* to fix the size or range of; settle by mental or judicial decision; give a direction to influence the choice; resolve, settle (an issue); ascertain; decide, make up one's mind; (*leg.*) end. DETERMINATOR, *n.* one who determines. [L.].

DETERMINED [di-tur′mind], *adj.* having a firm or fixed purpose; resolute. DETERMINEDLY, *adv.* in a d. manner.

DETERMINISM [di-tur′mi-nizm], *n.* doctrine that man is not free to act as he wills, but is governed entirely by forces outside himself. DETERMINIST, *n.* person who maintains the doctrine of d. DETER-MINISTIC [di-ter-mi-nis′tik], *adj.* pertaining to d.

DETERRENCE [di-te′rens], *n.* act of deterring; something which deters

DETERRENT (1) [di-te′rent], *adj.* that deters or tends to deter. DETERRENT (2), *n.* something which deters.

DETERRING [di-tur′ring], *n.* action of hindering or dissuading through fear.

DETEST [di-test′], *v.t.* to feel a loathing of; hate deeply; abominate. DETESTED, *adj.* intensely hated; abhorred. [L.].

DETESTABLE [di-tes′ta-bl], *adj.* to be detested, loathsome, execrable.

DETESTATION [dē-tes-tā′shn], *n.* extreme hatred, intense dislike, abhorrence. [L.].

DETHRONE [di-thrōn′], *v.t.* to remove from the throne; strip of royal power; remove from a position of power or influence. DETHRONEMENT, *n.* act of dethroning. DETHRONER, *n.* person who dethrones.

DETONATE [de′to-nāt], *v.t.* to cause to explode; *v.i.* to explode with a sudden bang. DETONATING, *adj.* that detonates; exploding; containing explosive. DETONATIVE, *adj.* causing detonation or explosion. [L.].

DETONATION [de-to-nā′shn], *n.* act of detonating; sudden loud explosion; the noise of this.

DETONATOR [de′to-nā-ter], *n.* contrivance which explodes an explosive; percussion cap; fog signal which explodes on a railway line.

DETOUR, détour [dā-tōōr′], *n.* circuitous or indirect way; deviation from the shortest way of approach. [Fr.].

DETRACT [di-trakt′], *v.t.* to take away from the quality, excellence or standing of; derogate from; diminish. [~L.].

DETRACTION [di-trak′shn], *n.* act of detracting; calumny, depreciation. [L.].

DETRACTIVE [di-trak′tiv], *adj.* that detracts from anything. DETRACTIVENESS, *n.* quality of being d.

DETRACTOR [di-trak′ter], *n.* one who disparages the merits or reputation of a person or thing. DETRAC-TORY, *adj.* detractive. [L.].

DETRAIN [dē-trān′], *v.t. and i.* (*esp. milit.*) to remove from a railway train, alight from a railway train.

DETRIMENT [det′ri-ment], *n.* loss, damage, hurt, mischief, injury. [L.].

DETRIMENTAL (1) [det-ri-men′tal], *adj.* occasioning loss or damage, harmful. DETRIMENTAL (2), *n.* undesirable person. DETRIMENTALLY, *adv.* in d. fashion; so as to occasion detriment.

DETRITION [di-tri′shn], *n.* act of wearing down by continual rubbing. DETRITED [di-tri′tid], *adj.* worn down; produced through d.

DETRITUS [di-tri′tus], *n.* waste or disintegrated material; (*geol.*) mass of fragments produced by the wearing away of exposed surfaces of rocks etc. [L.].

DETRUNCATE [di-trung′kāt], *v.t.* to lop off a portion of; shorten by lopping off. DETRUNCATION [dē-trung-ka′shn], *n.* act of detruncating. [L.].

DETUMESCENCE [dē-tyōō-me′sens], *n.* the going down of swelling. [L.].

DEUCE [dyōōs], *n.* two, card or die marked with two pips; score of forty-all at lawn tennis; (*slang*) the devil. DEUCE-ACE, a throw of two dice in which two and one are scored respectively. [Fr.].

DEUCED [dyōō′sid, dyōōst], *adj.* (*slang*) confounded, devilish, extreme. DEUCEDLY [dyōō′sid-li], *adv.* (*slang*) confoundedly, extremely.

DEUT-, see DEUTO-.

DEUTERIUM [dyōō-tēer′i-um], *n.* (*chem.*) an isotope of hydrogen, denoted by D. [*Next*].

DEUTER(O)-, *pref.* second, secondary. [Gk.].

DEUTERONOMIST [dyōō-te-ro′no-mist], *n.* the writer of the book of Deuteronomy.

DEUTEROPATHY [dyōō-te-ro′pa-thi], *n.* (*med.*) sympathetic affection of one part of the body with another. [Gk.].

DEUTO-, DEUT-, *pre.* (*chem.*) of the second in any series; (*biol.*) second. [Gk.].

DEUTZIA [doit′si-ah], *n.* (*bot.*) Chinese and Japanese shrub. [*Deutz*, Dutch botanist].

DEVA [dā′vah], *n.* a god; beneficent spirit in Hindu mythology. [Skr.].

DEVALUATE [dē-va′lyōō-āt], *v.t.* to devalue.

DEVALUATION [dē-va-lyōō-ā′shn], *n.* act or process of devaluing.

DEVALUE [dē-va′lyōō], *v.t.* to reduce the value of (*esp.* currency).

DEVANAGARI [dā-vah-nah′gah-ri], *n.* the Sanskrit alphabet. [Skr.].

DEVASTATE [de′vas-tāt], *v.t.* to lay waste, ravage; (*slang*) captivate, fascinate. [L.].

DEVASTATION [de-vas-tā′shn], *n.* act of devastating; condition of being devastated.

DEVELOP [di-ve′lop], *v.t.* to unfold, bring out all that is contained within; expand; enable to evolve what is latent or in embryo; explain more fully, enlarge upon; prepare (land) for closer settlement, *esp.* by building; (*phot.*) cause the images to show up on a photographic negative by the use of certain chemical agents; *v.i.* to grow, enlarge, be more completely evolved; become more mature in appearance or character. DEVELOPABLE, *adj.* capable of being developed or of developing. [Fr.].

DEVELOPER [di-ve′lo-per], *n.* person who or thing which develops; (*phot.*) chemical solution employed in developing photographic negatives.

DEVELOPMENT [di-ve′lop-ment], *n.* act of developing; state of being developed; that which has developed from something; event or circumstance newly arising or becoming known; (*biol.*) evolution; (*mus.*) that part of a complex musical composition in which a certain theme is developed; **d. area**, district formerly afflicted with unemployment to which new industries are directed. DEVELOPMENTAL [di-ve-lop-men′tal], *adj.* pertaining to d. DEVELOP-MENTALLY, *adv.* in course of d.

DEVERBATIVE [dē-vur′ba-tiv], *n. and adj.* (*gram.*) (word) derived from a verb.

DEVIATE [dē′vi-āt], *v.i.* to turn aside, diverge; (*fig.*) stray or swerve from a certain moral course. [L.].

DEVIATION [dē-vi-ā′shn], *n.* act of deviating; deflection; **d. of the compass**, deflection of the needle from the magnetic meridian due to external causes. [MedL.].

DEVICE [di-vis′], *n.* act of devising; result of contriving; something devised; plan, scheme, trick; gadget, contrivance; (*her.*) emblematic figure, design adopted by some family or association of people, as a badge; **left to one's own devices**, left to do as one thinks fit. [OFr.].

DEVIL (1) [de′vil], *n.* the leader of the spirits of evil, Satan; any evil spirit, demon; false god or idol; (*fig.*) human being of fiendish wickedness; poor wretched creature; clever rogue, mischievous or reckless person; one doing subordinate work as a legal junior counsel under a leader; writer employed by another for hack work; (*coll.*) temper, spirit; (*cookery*) highly seasoned dish; **printer's d.**, (*print*.) errand-boy to a printer; **between the d. and the deep sea**, on the horns of a dilemma; **devil's advocate**, advocate who opposes a proposed canonization; one whose advocacy does more harm than good; **d. to pay**, trouble ahead; **to give the d. his due**, to be fair even to the undeserving; **to go to the d.**, to be on the road to ruin; **to play the d. with**, to ruin, injure; **the very d.**, source of great trouble. DEVIL (2) (*pres.pt.* DEVILLING, *pret. and p.pt.* DEVILLED), *v.t.* to cook by grilling with hot condiments, *esp.* mustard; *v.i.* to do hack work for another. [OE.].

DEVIL-FISH [de′vil-fish], *n.* one of several gigantic Atlantic rays.

DEVILISH (1) [de′vi-lish], *adj.* like the devil, extremely wicked or mischievous. DEVILISH (2), *adv.* (*coll.*) exceedingly. DEVILISHLY, *adv.* in a d. manner; excessively. DEVILISHNESS, *n.* condition of being d.

DEVILISM [de′vi-lizm], *n.* attributes or behaviour of a devil; devil worship.

DEVIL-MAY-CARE [de′vil-mā-kāer], *adj.* reckless, rollicking, happy-go-lucky.

DEVILMENT [de′vil-ment], *n.* action characteristic of a devil; mischief.

DEVILRY [de′vil-ri], *n.* devilment, devilish practices or conduct.

DEVIL'S COACH-HORSE [de-vilz-kŏch′haws], *n.* species of large black beetle.

DEVIL WORSHIP [de′vil-wer-ship], *n.* the propitiation by primitive tribes of the devil or spirit of evil.

DEVIOUS [dē′vi-ŏŏs], *adj.* off the common way, remote; departing from a straight course, circuitous; indirect; (*fig.*) erratic, crooked, deceitful. DEVIOUSLY, *adv.* in d. fashion. [L.].

DEVISE (1) [di-vīz′], *v.t.* to arrange, contrive, think out; plan out, invent, design; (*leg.*) assign real estate by will. DEVISE (2), *n.* (*leg.*) act of devising property; statement in a will concerned with such assignment. DEVISABLE, *adj.* that may be devised; (*leg.*) that can be bequeathed. DEVISEE, *n.* (*leg.*) person to whom property is devised. DEVISER, *n.* inventor, schemer. DEVISOR, *n.* (*leg.*) one who devises property. [OFr.].

DEVITALIZE [dē-vī′ta-līz], *v.t.* to deprive of vitality; drain of energy or vigour. DEVITALIZATION [dē-vī-ta-li-zā′shn], *n.* act of devitalizing.

DEVOIR [dev′wahr], *n.* duty, appointed task; (*pl.*) courteous attention, conventional civilities. [Fr.].

DEVOLUTION [dē-vō-lyŏŏ′shn], *n.* act of devolving; (*biol.*) degeneration, deterioration in course of descending.

DEVOLVE [di-volv′], *v.t.* to roll down; deliver over, pass on; hand down, transfer; delegate; *v.i.* to fall to the lot of; cause to be performed by; (*leg.*) descend by inheritance.

DEVONIAN [di-vō′ni-an], *adj.* (*geol.*) pertaining to the geological formation which lies above the Silurian and below the Carboniferous systems as found in Devonshire.

DEVOTE [di-vōt′], *v.t.* to set apart, dedicate; give oneself to, direct the attention wholly or chiefly to. [L.].

DEVOTED [di-vō′tid], *adj.* given up to, consecrated to; strongly attached to; zealous. DEVOTEDLY, *adv.* with devotion.

DEVOTEE [de-vō-tē′], *n.* one who is deeply devoted; enthusiastic supporter.

DEVOTION [di-vō′shn], *n.* state of being devoted to anything or anyone; devout yielding of the heart and affections to God; religious worship, act of respect; ardent love or affection; strong attachment; (*pl.*) prayers. DEVOTIONIST, *n.* one who formally practises or professes d. [L.].

DEVOTIONAL [di-vō′shn-al], *adj.* related or suited to devotion. DEVOTIONALISM, *n.* extreme devotions of a formal character. DEVOTIONALIST, *n.* person given to religious devotion. DEVOTIONALLY, *adv.* in a d. fashion.

DEVOUR [di-vowr′], *v.t.* to eat up greedily; consume, ravage, destroy; (*fig.*) look fiercely, intently at; read avidly, with consuming interest. DEVOURER, *n.* one who, or that which, devours. [L.].

DEVOURING [di-vowr′ring], *adj.* consuming, wasting, destroying; (*fig.*) overwhelming, intense. DEVOURINGLY, *adv.* in a d. manner.

DEVOUT [di-vowt′], *adj.* reverential, pious, religious; expressing devotion; (*fig.*) earnest, deep, heartfelt. DEVOUTLY, *adv.* in a d. fashion. DEVOUTNESS, *n.* state or quality of being d.

DEW (1) [dyŏŏ], *n.* aqueous vapour condensed on the cool surfaces of plants etc. during the night; (*fig.*)

anything soft, fresh and shining like this. DEW (2), *v.t. and i.* to wet with d.; bedew; fall as d.

DEW-BERRY [dyŏŏ′be-ri], *n.* a species of blackberry; the fruit of this tree.

DEW-CLAW [dyŏŏ′klaw], *n.* (*anat.*) rudimentary claw occurring in dogs and deer.

DEW-DROP [dyŏŏ′drop], *n.* one of the drops of moisture into which dew collects.

DEW-FALL [dyŏŏ′fawl], *n.* time when the dew begins to fall in the evening.

DEWLAP [dyŏŏ′lap], *n.* loose flesh which hangs from the throat of cattle and certain other animals. DEWLAPPED, *adj.* having a d.

DEW-POINT [dyŏŏ′point], *n.* temperature at which dew can be deposited.

DEW-POND [dyŏŏ′pond], *n.* shallow pool on chalk downs, often artificial, replenished by drainage of dew and condensed mist from neighbouring ground.

DEW-WORM [dyŏŏ′werm], *n.* the common earth-worm.

DEWY [dyŏŏ′i], *adj.* wet with dew; (*fig.*) like dew in its freshness and softness, glistening.

DEXTER [deks′ter], *adj.* on the right-hand side; (*her.*) on the right-hand side of a shield or coat of arms, i.e. the left-hand side of the drawing. [L.].

DEXTERITY [deks-te′ri-ti], *n.* quality of being dexterous, manipulative skill, adroitness. [L.].

DEXTEROUS, DEXTROUS [deks′te-rŏŏs], *adj.* right-handed; quick and expert in bodily or mental activity; adroit, skilful, deft. DEXTEROUSLY, DEXTROUSLY, *adv.* in d. fashion.

DEXTRAL [deks′tral], *adj.* situated on the right-hand side; running from left to right. DEXTRALITY [deks-tra′li-ti], *n.* right-handedness.

DEXTRIN [deks′trin], *n.* starch gum, soluble matter into which the interior substance of starch globules is convertible by acids, diastase or heating. [Fr.].

DEXTRO-, *pref.* turning towards the right; (*chem.*) causing the plane of a ray of polarized light to turn to the right. [L.].

DEXTRO-GLUCOSE [deks-trō-glŏŏ′kōs], *n.* (*chem.*) granular sugar, so named as being dextro-gyrate.

DEXTRO-GYRATE [deks-trō-jī′rāt], *adj.* (*min.*) revolving the plane of polarization to the right. [L.].

DEXTROSE [deks′trōs], *n.* dextro-glucose; ordinary glucose or grape-sugar.

DEXTROUS, see DEXTEROUS.

DEZYMOTIZE [di-zī′mo-tīz], *v.t.* to rid of disease-germs.

DHOBI(E) [dō′bi], *n.* native washerman in India. [Hind.].

DHOW [dow], *n.* Arab vessel, *esp.* one which has a lateen sail on one or two masts. [Unkn.].

DI- (1), *pref.* expressing separation. [L.].

DI- (2), *pref.* two, twice, double. [Gk.].

DIA-, DI- (3), *pref.* through the influence of, by means of; through, throughout. [Gk.].

DIABETES [dī-a-bē′tēz], *n.* (*med.*) disease characterized by an abnormal amount of sugar in the urine, which is passed excessively. [Gk.].

DIABETIC (1) [dī-a-bē′tik], *adj.* (*med.*) of, or pertaining to, diabetes. DIABETIC (2), *n.* (*med.*) person having diabetes.

DIABLERIE, DIABLERY [dē-ah′ble-rē], *n.* machinations of the devil, witchery, devilment. [Fr.].

DIABOLIC(AL) [dī-a-bo′lik(-al)], *adj.* devilish, fiendish, extremely wicked. DIABOLICALLY, *adv.* in d. fashion. [Gk.].

DIABOLISM [dī-a′bo-lizm], *n.* worship of the devil or demons; dealings with the devil, witchcraft; diabolical behaviour or nature.

DIABOLIZE [dī-a′bo-līz], *v.t.* to render diabolical. DIABOLIZATION [dī-a-bo-li-zā′shn], *n.* act of rendering diabolical.

DIABOLO [dī-a′bo-lō], *n.* game played with a top shaped like an hour-glass spun on and thrown from a string tied between two sticks. [Gk.].

DIACONAL [dī-a′ko-nal], *adj.* of or belonging to a deacon. [L.].

DIACONATE [dī-a′ko-nāt], *n.* rank or position of a deacon; period of tenure of a deacon's office; deacons generally. [L.].

DIACRITIC (1) [dī-a-kri′tik], *adj.* distinguishing, distinctive; (*gram.*) (of certain marks) used on letters to indicate a special sound or value. DIACRITIC (✗), *n.* a distinguishing sign; d. mark. [Gk.].

DIACRITICAL [dī-a-kri′ti-kal], *adj.* diacritic.

DIACTINIC [dī-ak-ti′nik], *adj.* capable of transmitting the actinic rays of light. [Gk.].

DIADEM [dī′a-dem], *n.* the arch on a crown; head-band or fillet worn as a badge of royalty or eminence;

ŏŏ is pronounced as in *food*; ŏŏ as in *hood*; th as in *think*; TH as in *that*; zh as in *azure*. ~ = related to.

crown; sovereign power; **d. spider,** the garden spider.
DIADEMED, *adj.* wearing a d., crowned. [L.].

DIAERESIS [dī-ēer'i-sis], *n.* the resolution of a diphthong or syllable into two parts; mark (¨) placed over the second of two successive vowels to signify that they are to be pronounced separately. [Gk.].

DIAGNOSE [dī'ag-nōz], *v.t.* to find out the nature of an illness from an investigation of its symptoms.

DIAGNOSIS (*pl.* **diagnoses**) [dī-ag-nō'sis], *n.* identification of an illness from an investigation of its symptoms; statement embodying this; (*fig.*) conclusions reached about any unsatisfactory condition by observation of its manifestations. [Gk.].

DIAGNOSTIC (1) [dī-ag-nos'tik], *adj.* indicating the nature of a disease or unsatisfactory state of affairs. DIAGNOSTIC (2), *n.* the symptom of a disease; (*pl.*) study of symptoms. DIAGNOSTICALLY, *adv.* by means of diagnosis.

DIAGNOSTICIAN [dī-ag-nos-ti'shn], *n.* an expert in diagnosis.

DIAGONAL (1) [dī-a'go-nal], *adj.* extending as a straight line between any two non-adjacent angles of a rectilineal figure; stretching from corner to corner; oblique; forming or crossed with oblique lines. DIAGONAL (2), *n.* (*geom.*) a d. line. DIAGONALLY, *adv.* in a d. fashion. [L.].

DIAGRAM [dī'a-gram], *n.* (*geom.*) figure drawn to help in demonstrating the proof of a proposition; explanatory sketch or drawing; pictorial summary of statistics. DIAGRAMMATIC [dī-a-gra-ma'tik], *adj.* involving a d.; resembling a d. DIAGRAMMATICALLY, *adv.* by means of a d. DIAGRAMMATIZE [dī-a-gra'ma-tiz], *v.t.* to put into the form of a d. [Gk.].

DIAGRAPH [dī'a-grahf], *n.* instrument for mechanical enlargement of diagrams, maps etc., or for the drawing of projections. DIAGRAPHIC(AL), *adj.* connected in drawings or figures. [DIA and GRAPH].

DIAL (1) [dīl], *n.* the graduated face of any instrument for telling the time of day; any scale resembling a clock-face with a movable index; (*teleph.*) movable disk marked with numbered and lettered fingerholes for operating an automatic telephone system; (*slang*) the human face. DIAL (2) [*pres.pt.* DIALLING, *pret.* and *p.pt.* DIALLED], *v.t.* and *i.* to measure by a d.; (*teleph.*) use the d. of an automatic telephone system to call a particular number. [LL.].

DIALECT [dī'a-lekt], *n.* a recognized local or personal variation in the pronunciation, grammar or vocabulary of a language. DIALECTAL [dī-a-lek'tal], *adj.* of, or belonging to, a d. DIALECTALLY, *adv.* in d. [Gk.].

DIALECTIC [dī-a-lek'tik], *n.* the investigation of truth by argument or by the logical examination of hypotheses and theories; (*philos.*) criticism emphasizing the contradictions of scientific principles. DIALECTICAL, *adj.* belonging to d.; **dialectical materialism,** a materialist doctrine based upon alleged contradictions in natural and social forces; Marxism. DIALECTICALLY, *adv.* by d.; in d. DIALECTICIAN [dī-a-lek-ti'shn], *n.* one skilled in d. DIALECTICS, *n.(pl.)* art of employing d. [Gk.].

DIALECTOLOGY [dī-a-lek-to'lo-ji], *n.* study of dialects. DIALECTOLOGIST, *n.* one who studies dialects. [Gk.].

DIALLING [dī'ling], *n.* art of making or using dials; **d. tone,** sound indicating that a telephone is ready for a number to be dialled.

DIALOGUE (1) [dī'a-log], *n.* conversation in speech or writing between two or more persons; the words spoken by the actors in a drama. DIALOGUE (2), *v.t.* and *i.* to put in the form of a d.; hold a conversation. DIALOGIZE [dī-a'lo-jīz], *v.t.* to put in d. form; *v.i.* to carry on a d. [Gk.].

DIALYSIS [dī-a'li-sis], *n.* (*chem.*) separation of substances by diffusion through a parchment membrane. DIALYTIC [dī-a-li'tik], *adj.* pertaining to d. [Gk.].

DIAMAGNETISM [dī-a-mag'ne-tizm], *n.* (*phys.*) property possessed by some substances of adopting a position at right angles to a magnetic current. DIAMAGNETIC (1) [dī-a-mag-ne'tik], *adj.* exhibiting d. DIAMAGNETIC (2), *n.* a diamagnetic substance. DIAMAGNETICALLY, *adv.* in a diamagnetic manner. [DIA and MAGNETISM].

DIAMANTE [dē-a-mah(ng)'tā], *n.* cloth to which shining particles of glass or other material are attached to make it sparkle. [Fr.].

DIAMANTIFEROUS [dī-a-man-ti'fe-roŏs], *adj.* bearing diamonds. [Fr.].

DIAMETER [dī-a'mi-ter], *n.* (*geom.*) a straight line, bounded by the circumference, passing through the centre of a circle or sphere which it bisects; a chord passing through the centre of a conic; the measurement from side to side, through the centre, the width and thickness of objects having a circular contour; (*opt.*) unit of measurement of the magnifying power of lenses. DIAMETRAL, *adj.* diametrical. [OFr. from Gk.].

DIAMETRICAL [dī-a-met'ri-kal], *adj.* pertaining to a diameter; exactly opposite. DIAMETRICALLY, *adv.* exactly, directly.

DIAMOND (1) [dī'a-mond], *n.* the hardest and most precious of all the precious stones, being a crystal of pure carbon; glazier's tool for cutting glass; (*typ.*) the second smallest type, intermediate between pearl and brilliant; (*geom.*) a rhomboidal figure stood on end; (*her.*) lozenge; playing card marked with red lozenge-shaped figures; suit at cards characterized in this way; **d. jubilee,** sixtieth anniversary; **d. wedding,** sixtieth anniversary of the wedding-day; **rough d.,** (*fig.*) good and intelligent but uncultured man; **d. cut d.,** cunning matched against equal cunning; **black d.,** coal. DIAMOND (2), *adj.* made of, or ornamented with, diamonds; having many diamonds, like a diamond in shape. DIAMOND (3), *v.t.* to set with diamonds.

DIAMONDIFEROUS [dī-a-mon-di'fe-roŏs], *adj.* producing diamonds.

DIAMOND-POINT [dī'a-mond-point], *n.* engraving tool whose point is a diamond; (*pl.*) diamond-shaped figure formed by the crossing of two sets of railway lines.

DIANA [dī-a'nah], *n.* (*myth.*) Roman virgin goddess of the moon and hunting; (*fig.*) a huntress, the moon. [L.].

DIANDROUS [dī-an'droŏs], *adj.* (*bot.*) two-stamened; (*zool.*) mating with two males.

DIANTHUS [dī-an'thus], *n.* (*bot.*) genus of plants of which the pinks and carnations are members. [Gk.].

DIAPASON [dī-a-pā'zon], *n.* (*mus.*) music written in harmony; musical passage containing a harmonious arrangement of parts; natural range of a voice or instrument; scale by which instruments are tuned; (*fig.*) rich, harmonious sound; **open d., closed d.,** two stops in an organ which open or close its whole compass. [Gk.].

DIAPER (1) [dī'a-per], *n.* cloth woven in a diamond or some other regular pattern; baby's napkin or towel; design based on a diamond-shaped pattern; (*her.*) pattern in diamonds forming the groundwork of a design. DIAPER (2), *v.t.* to decorate in a d. pattern. DIAPERING, *n.* decoration in a d. pattern. [OFr.].

DIAPHANOUS [dī-a'fa-noŏs], *adj.* transparent.

DIAPHORETIC [dī-a-fo-re'tik], *n.* and *adj.* (*med.*) (medicine) promoting perspiration. [Gk.].

DIAPHRAGM [dī'a-fram], *n.* (*anat.*) the midriff or large circular movable muscle separating the chest or thorax from the abdomen or lower belly; a dividing membrane; a partition; (*opt.*) plate with an opening through for cutting off superfluous rays of light; (*elect.*) thin vibrating plate in a microphone. DIAPHRAGMAL [dī-a-frag'mal], *adj.* belonging to a d. DIAPHRAGMATIC [dī-a-frag-ma'tik], *adj.* pertaining to, of the nature of, a d. [Gk.].

DIARCHY [dī'ah-ki], *n.* system of government in which two powers have sovereignty. DIARCHAL, DIARCHIC [dī-ah'kal, dī-ah'kik], *adj.* pertaining to a d. [Gk.].

DIARIST [dī'a-rist], *n.* one who writes a diary.

DIARRHOEA [dī-a-rē'ah], *n.* disorder consisting in fluid stools and frequent evacuations. [Gk.].

DIARY [dī'a-ri], *n.* a record of daily events; book in which this is recorded; small engagement-book with dated pages. [L.].

DIASTASE [dī'a-stās], *n.* (*chem.*) enzyme found in malt which changes starch into sugar. DIASTATIC [dī-a-sta'tik], *adj.* pertaining to, or of the nature of, d. [Gk.].

DIASTOLE [dī-as'to-li], *n.* (*med.*) the rhythmic dilatation of the heart, alternating with systole. DIASTOLIC [dī-a-sto'lik], *adj.* connected with or resembling d. [Gk.].

DIATHERMY [dī-a-thur'mi], *n.* (*med.*) theory or practice of administering electric currents to produce heat in parts of the body below the surface. DIATHERMIC, *adj.* able to transmit radiant heat.

DIATHESIS [dī-a'thi-sis], *n.* (*med.*) physical condition making the body particularly susceptible to a disease. [Gk.].

DIATOMIC [dī-a-to'mik], *adj.* (*chem.*) of two atoms.

DIATONIC [dī-a-to'nik], *adj.* (*mus.*) pertaining to

The accent ' after a syllable = stress (u-pon'). The mark ⁻ over a vowel = length (ā in made; ō in bone).

the natural scale of any key without chromatic intrusions; composed of the notes proper to the natural scale of a certain key. DIATONICALLY, adv. in accordance with the d. scale. [Gk.].

DIATRIBE [dī′a-trīb], n. a discourse; spirited and wordy attack on some person or work, piece of invective or abuse. DIATRIBIST, n. one who indulges in d. [Gk.].

DIB [dib], n. counter used in playing at cards; (pl.) (slang) money. [Uncert.].

DIBBER [dib′ber], n. a dibble.

DIBBLE (1) [di′bl], n. pointed tool used in gardening for making holes for planting. DIBBLE (2), v.t. to use a d. [DAB].

DICE (1) [dīs], n.(pl.) small cubes marked with a different number of pips on each surface and used for games of chance; dicing; (cookery) meat or vegetables cut into small cubes. DICE (2), v.i. to play with d.; cut into the shape of d. DICED, adj. cut into small cubes like d.; ornamented with figures made like d. DICER, n. person who plays with d. [pl. of DIE].

DICE-BOX [dīs′boks], n. small tubular box used for shaking dice in gambling.

DICHOTOMIC [dī-ko-tō-mik], adj. dichotomous.

DICHOTOMIZE [dī-ko-tō-mīz], v.t. and i. to divide in two.

DICHOTOMOUS [dī-ko-tō-mŏŏs], adj. dividing in two; (bot.) dividing regularly in pairs. DICHOTO-MOUSLY, adv. in d. fashion.

DICHOTOMY [dī-ko-tō-mi], n. (log.) continuous division by pairs into groups distinguished by contradictory qualities; (bot.) continuous forking into pairs; (coll.) a contradiction, conflict. [Gk.].

DICHROIC [dī-krō′ik], adj. showing different colours when viewed in different directions, esp. referring to fog on a photographic negative. [Gk.].

DICHROMATIC [dī-krō-ma′tik], adj. having two different colours. [DI (2) and CHROMATIC].

DICHROMIC [dī-krō′mik], adj. recognizing only two of the primary colours; showing a different colour when looked at, from the one seen when looked through. [DI (2) and CHROMIC].

DICING [dī′sing], n. act of playing or gambling with dice.

DICK [dik], n. fellow, man; (slang) detective. [Christian name Dick].

DICKENS [di′kinz], int. (slang) the devil! the deuce! [Uncert.].

DICKER (1) [di′ker], n. (comm.) a group of ten. DICKER (2), v.i. to haggle, bargain. [ME. from L.].

DICKEY [di′ki], n. the driving seat of a horse carriage; small seat usually folding in behind a car, coach or cab; (slang) false shirtfront.

DICKY (1), n. childish name for any bird. [Unkn.].

DICKY (2), adj. (slang) shaky, unsteady; liable to ill-health; financially unstable. [Unkn.].

DICOTYLEDON [dī-ko-ti-lē′don], n. (bot.) plant which bears two seed-leaves. DICOTYLEDONOUS, adj. (bot.) bearing two cotyledons.

DICTA [dik′tah], n.(pl.) proverbial sayings, authoritatively sounding or brilliant phrases. [pl. of DICTUM].

DICTAPHONE [dik′ta-fōn], n. (prot.) machine for the recording of dictations to be subsequently reproduced audibly.

DICTATE (1) [dik-tāt′], v.t. and i. to command, give orders for; tell another what to do, say or write; compose letters, speeches etc. orally for someone to write down; recite something to be copied down verbatim by others; override, play the despot. DICTATE (2) [dik′tāt], n. a command; precept. DICTATED, adj. commanded; spoken so as to be taken down verbatim. [L.].

DICTATION [dik-tā′shn], n. act or habit of dictating; material that is dictated; passage spoken slowly to be written down verbatim as a spelling exercise. [LL.].

DICTATOR [dik-tā′ter], n. one who dictates; despot, absolute ruler. [L.].

DICTATORIAL [dik-ta-taw′ri-al], adj. after the manner of a dictator; absolute, authoritative, overbearing; having an assertive tone of voice or manner. DICTATORIALLY, adv. in a d. fashion.

DICTATORSHIP [dik-tā′ter-ship], n. rule or status of a dictator in a state; period of a dictator's office; any position of absolute authority; **d. of the proletariat**, system in which all classes except the wage-earning class are deprived of political power.

DICTATORY [dik′ta-ter-i], adj. dictatorial. [L.].

DICTATRESS [dik-tāt′res], n. female dictator.

DICTION [dik′shn], n. style of speech or writing so

far as it concerns the choice of words and phrases; enunciation; **poetic d.**, specialized poetical vocabulary. [L.].

DICTIONARY [dik′shn-a-ri], n. lexicon, book consisting of an alphabetical list of the words of a language or of an author, showing their forms, meanings and sometimes their etymologies etc.; book of precise information on any subject, usually arranged under alphabetical headings. [MedL.].

DICTOGRAPH [dik′tō-grahf], n. (prot.) instrument for recording sounds, esp. speech sounds.

DICTUM (pl. dicta) [dik′tum], n. a saying; authoritative pronouncement; (leg.) personal opinion given by a judge, not having the force of an official pronouncement or decision. [L.].

DID [did], v.t. pret. of DO.

DIDACTIC [di-dak′tik], adj. designed to impart information and instruct, esp. morally; giving instruction out of season, unpleasantly superior. DIDACTICALLY, adv. in d. fashion. DIDACTICISM, n. quality of being d. DIDACTICS, n.(pl.) method or art of teaching. [Gk.].

DIDAPPER, DIEDAPPER [dī′da-per], n. the dabchick or little grebe. [ME.].

DIDDLE [di′dl], v.t. (coll.) to cheat, trick, dupe. DIDDLER, n. (coll.) person who diddles, swindler, cheat. [Unkn.].

DIE (1) (pl. dice, dies) [dī], n. (pl. dice), small solid cube having each of its faces marked with dots from one to six, and thrown from a box or the hand in games of chance (only used in the pl.); (pl. dies), piece of metal or stamp engraved with a design which can be impressed in reverse upon some softer material; specially shaped piece of metal with a screwed hole for cutting the thread on a rod; (arch.) the dado of a pedestal; **the d. is cast**, all is irretrievably settled and decided. [OFr.].

DIE (2), v.i. to depart from life, cease to exist, pass away; perish, be eternally lost, pass out of existence; wither; fade away; (coll.) **to be dying for**, to long for something; (fig., poet.) languish; **to d. away**, to become fainter, diminish in intensity; **to d. back**, (bot.) to wither from the branches down to the root; **to d. down**, to subside, lessen; **to d. out**, to become extinct. [OE.].

DIE-AWAY [dī′a-wā], adj. languishing.

DIEDAPPER, see DIDAPPER.

DIEHARD (1) [dī′hahd], adj. extreme, out-and-out. DIEHARD (2), n. one who resists to the end (particularly innovation or change).

DIELECTRIC (1) [dī-i-lek′trik], n. an insulating substance, non-conductor of electricity. DIELECTRIC (2), adj. insulating, non-conductive. [DI (1) and ELECTRIC].

DIESEL-ENGINE [dē′zel-en-jin], n. internal-combustion engine burning heavy oil ignited by compression. [R. Diesel, inventor].

DIE-SINKER [dī′sing′ker], n. engraver of dies. DIE-SINKING, n. process of engraving dies.

DIESIS [dī′e-sis], n. (print.) the double dagger reference mark (‡); (mus.) one of various intervals less than a tone, the difference between three major thirds and an octave. [Gk.].

DIES NON [dī-ēz-non′], n. (leg.) day on which no legal business may be done; a day which does not count. [L.].

DIESOLIUM [dē-sō′li-um], n. (prot.) a heavy crude oil fuel. [DIE(SEL) and L.].

DIET (1) [dī′et], n. international or national conference or congress; regular national assembly of elected representatives in certain European countries, for purposes of government. [MedL.].

DIET (2), n. specially prescribed course of food for medical purposes, as a punishment etc.; type of meals or food habitually eaten. DIET (3), v.t. and i. to follow out or keep to a d.; subject to, prescribe a d. for. DIETED, adj. fed according to a d. [Gk.].

DIETARY (1) [dī′e-ta-ri], n. a diet; allowance of food. DIETARY (2), adj. pertaining to a d.

DIETETIC(AL) [dī-e-te′tik(-al)], adj. pertaining to a diet.

DIETETICS [dī-e-te′tiks], n.(pl.) scientific study of foods and diets required for sound health. DIETETIST, n. one who seeks to cure disease by prescribing a diet.

DIETICIAN, DIETITIAN [dī-e-ti′shn], n. specialist in dietetics.

DIETIST [dī′e-tist], n. one who studies, undergoes, or prescribes a system of dieting.

DIF–, pref. form of the prefix DIS used before f.

DIFFER [di′fer], v.i. to be unlike, be dissimilar; disagree, hold a contrary opinion; be at variance;

ŏŏ is pronounced as in food; ōō as in hood; th as in think; TH as in that; zh as in azure. ~ = related to.

to d. from, to be distinguished from, disagree with. [L.].

DIFFERENCE [di'fe-rens], *n.* dissimilarity; act of differing; state or quality of being different; that by which things differ, that which makes anything different; amount by which anything differs; (*her.*) figure or device added to a coat of arms to distinguish a younger member or branch; **to split the d.,** to compromise. [L.].

DIFFERENT [di'fe-rent], *adj.* not the same, unlike; various, separate; changed, altered; distinct. [L.].

DIFFERENTIA (*pl.* **differentiae**) [di-fe-ren'shi-ah], *n.* mark of difference; (*log.*) distinguishing feature peculiar to a particular species. [L.].

DIFFERENTIAL (1) [di-fe-ren'shl], *adj.* pertaining to, causing or forming a difference, distinguishing; (*math.*) pertaining to infinitely small differences of quantity; (*econ.*) varying according to differing conditions; (*mech.*) pertaining to, showing, causing, or marked by, a difference of pressure, motion etc., or other physical attributes; **d. calculus,** (*math.*) method of calculation dealing with differentials and the determination of the relative rate of change in magnitude between the two interdependent variable quantities; **d. equation,** (*math.*) equation involving differentials; **d. gear,** combination of toothed gear wheels connecting two axles and allowing them to rotate at different speeds; **d. thermometer,** (*phys.*) thermometer consisting of two bulbs joined by a bent tube containing liquid which registers differences in temperature between the two bulbs. DIFFERENTIAL (2), *n.* (*math.*) an infinitely small difference between two consecutive states of a variable quantity; a d. gear. DIFFERENTIALLY, *adv.* by means of a differentia or d. [MedL.].

DIFFERENTIATE [di-fe-ren'shi-āt], *v.t. and i.* to discriminate between, recognize, form, or establish a difference between, distinguish; make different; (*math.*) find the differential of; become different. [MedL.].

DIFFERENTIATION [di-fe-ren-shi-ā'shn], *n.* act of differentiating; state of being differentiated.

DIFFERENTLY [di'fe-rent-li], *adv.* in a different way; variously.

DIFFICULT [di'fi-kult], *adj.* hard, not easy, causing trouble; involving strenuous mental or physical exertion; needing skill to perform; not easy to understand or appreciate; awkward, involving strain, worrying; hard to satisfy, troublesome to deal with, refractory, taking offence or bursting into fits of temper. DIFFICULTLY, *adv.* with difficulty. [L.].

DIFFICULTY [di'fi-kul-ti], *n.* quality of being difficult, trouble; that which is difficult, or which makes anything difficult, an obstacle; (*pl.*) financial trouble. [L.].

DIFFIDENCE [di'fi-dens], *n.* state or quality of being diffident. [L.].

DIFFIDENT [di'fi-dent], *adj.* shy, modest, retiring, bashful; wanting self-confidence; self-effacing. DIFFIDENTLY, *adv.* in d. fashion. [L.].

DIFFRACT [di-frakt'], *v.t.* to break into pieces; (*opt.*) break up rays of light into the coloured bands of the spectrum by passing close to the edge of, or through a slit in, an opaque substance; break up or deflect sound waves. DIFFRACTION, *n.* act of diffracting. DIFFRACTIVE, *adj.* causing diffraction. [L.].

DIFFUSE (1) [di-fyōōs'], *adj.* not concise, unnecessarily wordy, prolix; spread out, widely dispersed; (*path.*) attacking a large area of the body. DIFFUSE (2) [di-fyōōz'], *v.t. and i.* to spread over a large area, shed, disperse widely; send out, radiate; (*phys.*) mingle by diffusion. DIFFUSEDLY [di-fyōō'zid-li], *adv.* in a diffused fashion. DIFFUSEDNESS, *n.* condition of being diffused. DIFFUSELY, *adv.* in d. fashion. DIFFUSER, *n.* one who, or that which, diffuses. [L.].

DIFFUSIBLE [di-fyōō'zi-bl], *adj.* able to be diffused. DIFFUSIBILITY, DIFFUSIBLENESS [di-fyōō-zi-bi'li-ti, di-fyōō'zi-bl-nes], *n.* quality of being d.

DIFFUSION [di-fyōō'zhn], *n.* act or process of diffusing; state of being diffused; diffusiveness; (*phys.*) the gradual unaided mingling of gases, liquids or solids when brought into contact with each other; **d.-tube,** instrument for finding the rate of d. for different gases. [L.].

DIFFUSIVE [di-fyōō'siv], *adj.* tending to diffuse or be diffused; diffuse. DIFFUSIVELY, *adv.* in a d. fashion. DIFFUSIVENESS, *n.* quality of being d.

DIG (1) (*pret. and p.pt.* **dug**) [dig], *v.t. and i.* to break and turn up the earth with a spade or similar sharp-bladed instrument; break up the ground with paws,

claws etc.; hollow out or construct in the earth; (*coll.*) poke, nudge sharply prod; (*fig.*) unearth or discover by diligent research or investigation; (*slang*) lodge; **to d. in,** to mix with and cover over with soil by digging; (*milit.*) fortify a position with trenches; **to d. oneself in,** to establish oneself firmly in slow but sure fashion; **to d. out,** to unearth; (*coll.*) discover. DIG (2), *n.* (*coll.*) a nudge, poke, light smart blow; (*fig.*) sarcastic remark directed against anything or anyone; (*pl.*) (*slang*) lodgings. [OFr.].

DIGAMMA [di-ga'mah], *n.* a double gamma (F) pronounced like *w*. [Gk.].

DIGASTRIC (1) [di-gas'trik], *adj.* (*anat.*) having two belly-like protuberances separated by a thin portion; (*anat.*) pertaining to the digastric muscle, which is of this shape. DIGASTRIC (2), *n.* (*anat.*) muscle working the lower jaw. [Gk.].

DIGEST (1) [di-jest', di-jest'], *v.t. and i.* to convert food in the stomach and intestines into a liquid form which can be assimilated into the system; (*fig.*) study and master the details of, absorb into the mind as knowledge; stomach, endure; (*chem.*) dissolve by boiling or heating with a solvent; undergo the process of digestion; dissolve gradually in a slow heat. DIGEST (2), *n.* a systematic summary, condensed compilation, abstract; code of laws. DIGESTEDLY [di-jes'tid-li], *adv.* in a methodical and regular manner. DIGESTER, *n.* one who, or that which, digests; strong vessel in which bony substances are digested; apparatus in which carcases of animals are boiled down. [L.].

DIGESTIBLE [di-jes'ti-bl], *adj.* able to be digested. DIGESTIBILITY [di-jes-ti-bi'li-ti], *n.* quality of being d. DIGESTIBLY, *adv.* in a form capable of digestion.

DIGESTION [di-jest'shn], *n.* process of digesting, or of being digested; ability to digest food thoroughly and completely. [L.].

DIGESTIVE (1) [di-jes'tiv], *adj.* pertaining to digestion; encouraging or helping digestion; easily digested. DIGESTIVE (2), *n.* preparation which encourages or helps digestion. DIGESTIVELY, *adv.* so as to digest. [L.].

DIGGABLE [di'ga-bl], *adj.* capable of being dug.

DIGGER [di'ger], *n.* one who, or that which, digs; person who digs for gold; (*slang*) Australian.

DIGGING [di'ging], *n.* act of one who digs; (*pl.*) goldfield and mine where gold is dug; (*pl.*) (*coll.*) lodgings.

DIGHT† [dit], *adj.* arrayed, dressed, decked. [OE.].

DIGIT [di'jit], *n.* finger or toe; finger's breadth, three-quarters of an inch; any integer less than ten from 0 to 9; (*astron.*) the twelfth part of the diameter of the sun or moon. [L.].

DIGITAL (1) [di'ji-tal], *adj.* pertaining to the fingers, resembling a digit. DIGITAL (2), *n.* a key of a musical instrument, such as a pianoforte, struck with the finger; (*coll.*) finger. [L.].

DIGITALIN [di-ji-tā'lin], *n.* poisonous vegetable alkaloid obtained from the leaves of the foxglove, used medicinally.

DIGITALIS [di-ji-tā'lis], *n.* (*bot.*) genus of plants, including the foxglove; poisonous drug prepared from the foxglove or synthetically and used medicinally in cases of heart disease. [L.].

DIGITATE(D) [di'ji-tāt(-id)], *adj.* (*bot.*) branching into distinct leaflets or lobes like fingers; (*zool.*) having separate fingers or toes. DIGITATELY, *adv.* in d. fashion. DIGITATION [di-ji-tā'shn], *n.* state of being d.; (*zool.*, *bot.*) one of a series of finger-like processes. [L.].

DIGITIGRADE (1) [di'ji-ti-grād], *adj.* (*zool.*) walking on its toes. DIGITIGRADE (2), *n.* a d. animal. [L.].

DIGITOXIN [di-ji-tok'sin], *n.* poisonous substance obtained from the foxglove, used medicinally. [DIGIT(ALIS) and TOXIN].

DIGNIFIED [dig'ni-fid], *adj.* possessing and expressing dignity, stately, majestic, commanding respect.

DIGNIFY [dig'ni-fi], *v.t.* to invest with honour, confer distinction on; render exalted; give dignity to, represent as impressive. [LL.].

DIGNITARY [dig'ni-ta-ri], *n.* person with a high rank or official position.

DIGNITY [dig'ni-ti], *n.* sense of one's superior position; ability to command respect; unaffected stateliness of manner, natural air of distinction or nobility; high office, rank, title, position or honour; high estimation or reputation in which a thing is held; majesty or deference naturally associated with an institution; dignitary; (*astrol.*) increased influence of a planet on account of its particular position in the zodiac, or with respect to other planets. [L.].

DIGRAPH [di'grahf], *n.* two letters representing

---

only a single sound. DIGRAPHIC [dī-gra'fik], adj. relating to a d. [DI (2) and GRAPH].

DIGRESS [dī-gres'], v.i. to turn aside, wander from one's course; (fig.) stray or depart temporarily from the main topic, start to talk or write about something which is not strictly relevant to the main topic. [L.].

DIGRESSION [dī-gre'shn], n. act of digressing; that which digresses. DIGRESSIONAL, adj. digressive.

DIGRESSIVE [dī-gre'siv], adj. that forms a digression; habitually digressing. DIGRESSIVELY, adv. by way of digression. [L.].

DIHEDRAL [dī-hē'dral], adj. having two plane faces or sides; **d. angle**, angle between two planes; (aeron.) angle at which the wings of an aeroplane are inclined to each other from the horizontal to minimize rolling. [Gk.]

DIHEDRON [dī-hē'dron], n. figure with two sides or surfaces; (geom.) that part of two planes placed one on the other enclosed by a regular polygon.

DIK-DIK [dik'dik], n. a small antelope, the duikerbok. [Unkn.].

DIKE (1), **DYKE** [dīk], n. ditch, channel along which water flows; high bank of earth, stones, clay etc. constructed to safeguard low-lying country from the sea, rivers or streams; (fig.) barrier; (geol.) mass of igneous rock formed while molten in the fissures of stratified rocks. DIKE (2), v.t. and i. to protect or provide with dikes; make a d. DIKING, n. act of ditching or protecting by a d. [OScand.].

DILACERATE [dī-la'se-rāt], v.t. to tear up in pieces. DILACERATION [dī-la-se-rā'shn], n. act of dilacerating; (dental surg.) a shifting of a growing tooth on its base, and its subsequent misplaced development. [L.].

DILAPIDATE [dī-la'pi-dāt], v.t. and i. to allow to fall into a state of ruin or disrepair; (fig.) waste, squander; decay through neglect. DILAPIDATED, adj. in a state of ruin or decay, tumbledown; shabby, in great need of repair. [L.].

DILAPIDATION [dī-la-pi-dā'shn], n. state of being dilapidated; process of becoming or causing to be dilapidated; (leg.) act of permitting church property to become dilapidated while in the possession of an incumbent; (pl.) damage done to property by an occupier; the crumbling or wearing away of masses of rock by natural forces. [L.].

DILATABLE [dī-lā'ta-bl], adj. able to be dilated. DILATABILITY [dī-lā-ta-bi'li-ti], n. quality of being d.

DILATATION [dī-la-tā'shn], n. state of being dilated, act of dilating. [L.].

DILATE [dī-lāt'], v.t. and i. to become larger, expand, grow wider and bigger; (fig.) speak or expound at great length; make larger. DILATION, n. dilatation. DILATOR, DILATER, n. one who, or that which, dilates. [L.].

DILATORY [dī'la-te-ri], adj. slow, tardy, causing delay, dallying. DILATORILY, adv. in d. fashion. DILATORINESS, n. quality of being d. [L.].

DILEMMA [di-le'mah, dī-le'mah], n. perplexing situation in which all the possible courses of action are equally unfavourable, quandary; (log.) argument offering only a choice of two equally difficult alternatives. DILEMMATIC [dī-le-ma'tik], adj. belonging to dilemmas. [Gk.].

DILETTANTE (pl. **dilettanti**) [di-li-tan'ti], n. one who trifles in the fine arts in a superficial or casual way; amateur dabbler in anything. DILETTANTISH, adj. that becomes a d., amateurish. DILETTANTISM, n. casual and rather superficial cultivation of the fine arts, method of a d. [It. from L.].

DILIGENCE (1) [di'li-jens], n. careful steady application, constant industry, zealous and assiduous labour; (leg.) reasonable and careful attention demanded from persons under certain conditions. DILIGENCE (2), n. heavy, four-wheeled, horse-drawn stage-coach, with a hood, a deck and a dickey. [L.].

DILIGENT [di'li-jent], adj. exhibiting diligence, careful and industrious, assiduous; hard-working and steady, laboriously zealous. DILIGENTLY, adv. in a d. way. [L.].

DILL [dil], n. (bot.) umbelliferous Mediterranean medicinal plant; **d. water**, medicinal preparation obtained from the fruits or the oil of the d.; **d. oil**, yellow oil obtained from the seeds of d., used as a carminative. [OE.].

DILLY-DALLY [di'li-da-li], v.i. to waste time in indecision, delay continually in making up one's mind. [DALLY].

DILUTE (1) [di-lyōōt'], v.t. to weaken, thin down or reduce in strength, by adding more fluid to; (fig.)

lessen the force or effect of, tone down; of labour, use unskilled workers for tasks normally done by skilled men. DILUTE (2) [di'lyōōt, di-lyōōt'], adj. reduced in strength, weakened, watered down. DILUTEDLY, adv. in a diluted way. DILUTER, n. that which dilutes. [L.].

DILUTION [di-lyōō'shn], n. act of diluting; condition of being diluted; that which is diluted.

DILUVIAL [di-lōō'vi-al], adj. pertaining to a flood, esp. that recorded in the Old Testament; caused by a flood; (geol.) pertaining to the theory that certain geological phenomena are the result of floods. DILUVIALIST, n. one who believes that certain geological phenomena are the result of a world-wide flood. DILUVIAN, adj. pertaining to a flood, or the Great Flood.

DILUVIUM [di-lōō'vi-um], n. (geol.) comparatively recent and superficial deposits of loam, sand, gravel etc. produced by a flood or a sudden strong rush of water. [L.].

DIM (1) [dim], adj. faint, not bright or clear; indistinct, with the outlines not clearly defined; shadowy; dull; scarcely heard; not seeing clearly; (fig.) vague, (coll.) (of persons etc.) dull, stupid. DIM (2) (pres.pt. DIMMING, pret. and p.pt. DIMMED), v.t. and i. to make or become d. [OE.].

DIME (1) [dim], n. (U.S.) silver coin of the value of ten cents. DIME (2), adj. cheap, inferior, costing a d. [Fr.].

DIMENSION [di-men'shn], n. measurement or extent in space of length, breadth or depth or a combination of these; (pl.) size, magnitude, proportions; scope; (math.) spatial measurement in any direction or form; factors of a term of an algebraic expression. DIMENSIONAL, adj. pertaining to the number of dimensions involved, relating to d. DIMENSIONED, adj. having dimensions.

DIMETER [di'mi-ter], n. (pros.) verse made up of two measures. [Gk.].

DIMINISH [di-mi'nish], v.t. and i. to lessen, reduce, decrease; (mus.) reduce an interval by a semitone. DIMINISHABLE, adj. able to be diminished. DIMINISHED, adj. lessened, reduced, made smaller; (mus.) (of intervals) decreased by a semitone. DIMINISHER, n. one who, or that which, diminishes. DIMINISHINGLY, adv. in a diminishing manner. [Fr.].

DIMINUENDO [di-mi-nyōō-en'dō], n. (mus.) progressive lessening of the loudness of sound, sign > denoting this; passage in which the tone becomes gradually softer. [It.].

DIMINUTION [di-mi-nyōō'shn], n. act of diminishing, state of being diminished; (mus.) repetition of a contrapuntal theme in notes whose time value is half or a quarter that of the original; (her.) the disfiguring of an escutcheon; a difference; (leg.) omission of part of the record of a case sent up to a Court of Appeal; (arch.) tapering of a column shaft. [L.].

DIMINUTIVE (1) [di-mi'nyōō-tiv], adj. small; (gram.) conveying the idea of, or indicating, diminution. DIMINUTIVE (2), n. (gram.) word formed from another word by the addition of an affix denoting diminution. DIMINUTIVAL [di-mi-nyōō-ti'val], adj. relating to a d. DIMINUTIVELY [di-mi'nyōō-tiv-li], adv. in a d. fashion. DIMINUTIVENESS, n. state of being d. [L.].

DIMITY [di'mi-ti], n. stout cotton cloth, ornamented with raised stripes or decorative patterns. [Gk.].

DIMLY [dim'li], adv. in a dim fashion.

DIMMER [di'mer], n. (motoring) device to dim headlamps.

DIMMISH [di'mish], adj. rather dim.

DIMORPHISM [di-maw'fizm], n. property of crystallizing in two distinct forms; (biol.) existence of two different forms in the same plant, or in different plants or animals of the same species. DIMORPHIC, DIMORPHOUS, adj. exhibiting d. [Gk.].

DIMPLE (1) [dim'pl], n. small, natural rounded hollow in the cheek or other fleshy part of the body; shallow hollow in the ground. DIMPLE (2), v.t. and i. to form into dimples; cause dimples to appear. DIMPLED, adj. having dimples. DIMPLY, adj. full of dimples. [OE.].

DIN (1) [din], n. loud, continued noise, persistent clamour or uproar. DIN (2) (pres.pt. DINNING, pret. and p.pt. DINNED), v.t. and i. to impress with noisy persistence; create a d. [OE.].

DINAR [dē'nah(r)], n. Eastern gold coin; Yugoslavian coin formerly worth about twopence; unit of currency in Iraq. [Arab. and Serb. from L.].

DINARIC [di-nah'rik], adj. pertaining to a race of

people inhabiting the northern Adriatic coasts. [*Dinara*, Dalmatian mountain].

DINE [dīn], *v.t. and i.* to have dinner; give or provide dinner for. [Fr.].

DINER [dī'ner], *n.* one who dines; dining-car; **d.-out**, one who is fond of dining away from home.

DING-DONG (1) [ding'dong], *n.* loud continuous ringing noise, the sound produced by the striking of two differently toned bells. DING-DONG (2), *adj.* closely and fiercely contested. [Imitative].

DINGHY, DINGEY [ding'gi], *n.* small ship's boat, small pleasure-skiff or rowing-boat; collapsible rubber boat used by airmen in case of forced landings on water. [Hind.].

DINGINESS [din'ji-nes], *n.* state or quality of being dingy.

DINGLE [ding'gl], *n.* a wooded dell. [ME.].

DINGLE-DANGLE [ding'gl-dang-gl], *adj. and adv.* hanging loosely, dangling.

DINGO [ding'gō], *n.* native wild dog of Australia. [Native].

DINGY [din'ji], *adj.* dark, dull, lacking lustre; disreputable; dirty, drab, shabby. [Unkn.].

DINING-CAR [dī'ning-kah(r)], *n.* railway carriage in which meals are provided during a journey.

DINING-HALL [dī'ning-hawl], *n.* hall or large room used for dining.

DINING-ROOM [dī'ning-rŏŏm], *n.* room in which meals are taken.

DINING-TABLE [dī'ning-tā-bl], *n.* table on which meals are taken.

DINKUM [ding'kum], *adj.* (*Australian slang*) genuine, straightforward. [Unkn.].

DINKY [ding'ki], *adj.* (*coll.*) neat, attractive, dainty. [Scots].

DINNER [di'ner], *n.* principal meal of the day; formal, official banquet to mark some occasion; **d. jacket**, black dress coat without tails; **d. wagon**, set of shelves on wheels on which articles used at dinner are placed. DINNER-TABLE, dining-table. DINNER-TIME, usual time for dining. DINNERLESS, *adj.* without d. [Fr.].

DINOSAURIA [dī-nō-saw'ri-ah], *n.*(*pl.*) (*geol.*) group of large, prehistoric extinct reptiles. [Gk.].

DINOTHERE [dī'nō-thēer], *n.* one of a genus of extinct gigantic mammals. [Gk.].

DINT (1) [dint], *n.* blow, powerful stroke; effort, force, violence; large crease or hollow in something hard, made by a violent blow; **by d. of**, as a result of, after. DINT (2),*v.t.* to make a d. or dints in. [OE.].

DIOCESAN (1) [dī-o'si-zan], *adj.* pertaining to a diocese. DIOCESAN (2), *n.* a bishop; one of the members of a diocese.

DIOCESE [dī'ō-sēz], *n.* the ecclesiastical district over which a bishop holds authority. [Gk.].

DIODE [dī'ōd], *n.* thermionic valve having only two electrodes. [Gk.].

DIOPTER [dī-op'ter], *n.* index arm of a graduated circle; (*opt.*) a dioptre. [Gk.].

DIOPTRE [dī-op'ter], *n.* (*opt.*) unit of measurement of the refractive power of a lens. [*Var. of prec.*].

DIOPTRIC (1) [dī-op'trik], *adj.* pertaining to the refraction of light; aiding vision by refracting light through lenses. DIOPTRIC (2), *n.* (*opt.*) a dioptre; (*pl.*) that branch of optics concerned with the refraction of light by lenses. DIOPTRICAL, *adj.* d. [Gk.].

DIORAMA [dī-ō-rah'mah], *n.* pictorial representation of a natural scene, viewed through an aperture and illuminated by hidden and varied lighting; building in which such an exhibition takes place. DIORAMIC [dī-ō-ra'mik], *adj.* belonging to a d. [Gk.].

DIOSMOSIS [dī-os-mō'sis], *n.* osmosis. [Gk.].

DIOXIDE [dī-ok'sīd], *n.* (*chem.*) compound having two equivalents of oxygen to one of metal or metalloid. [DI (2) and OXIDE].

DIP (1) (*pres.pt.* DIPPING, *pret. and p.pt.* DIPPED) [dip], *v.t.* to immerse quickly in a liquid and take out again immediately; dye by plunging in a liquid dye for a brief time; wash (sheep) in an antiseptic solution; soak (a wick) in hot tallow to make a candle; move quickly down and up again; *v.i.* to submerge in liquid and quickly reappear; plunge into a receptacle or liquid in order to remove something from it; slope gently down; sink down and disappear; (*geol.*) (of strata) incline so as to form an angle with the horizontal; **to d. into**, to make a casual, incomplete examination of; read here and there (in a book). DIP (2), *n.* act of dipping, short rapid immersion; brief bathe; the liquid in which anything is plunged for washing or dyeing; tub of bran, sawdust etc., in which prizes are hidden, to be obtained by dipping

the hand into the tub; a candle, wick soaked in hot tallow and used as a candle; slope or depression; (*magn.*) inclination of a magnetic needle from the horizontal line; (*surveying*) apparent sloping of the horizon seen by an observer standing above sea-level; (*geol.*) downward slope of strata. [OE.].

DIPCHICK [dip'chik], *n.* the dabchick.

DIPHTHERIA [dif-thēer'i-ah], *n.* serious infectious disease attacking the throat and air-passages. DIPHTHERIAL, DIPHTHERIC, DIPHTHERITIC [dif-thēer'i-al, dif-thēer'ik, dif-the-ri'tik], *adj.* pertaining to, or caused by, d. DIPHTHEROID [dif'the-roid], *adj.* resembling d. [Gk.].

DIPHTHONG [dif'thong], *n.* (*phon.*) a sound of two vowels together dominated by a single accent or stress. DIPHTHONGAL [dif-thong'gal], *adj.* pertaining to a d. DIPHTHONGALLY, *adv.* in a dipthongal way. [Gk.].

DIPHTHONGIZE [dif'thong-gīz], *v.t. and i.* to form into a diphthong. DIPHTHONGIZATION [dif-thong-gī-zā'shn], *n.* process of diphthongizing.

DIPLEGIA [dī-plē'ji-ah], *n.* (*med.*) paralysis of corresponding parts on each side of the body. [Gk.].

DIPLOMA [di-plō'mah], *n.* official state document or charter; certificate or document awarded by a recognized authority as an honour, distinction, licence or privilege, *esp.* one granted by a university or other authority attesting the recipient's proficiency in some subject of study. [Gk.].

DIPLOMACY [di-plō'ma-si], *n.* art of conducting business between nation and nation; the forms and formalities of such business and the skill with which it is carried out; dexterity and tact in social or business relationships. [Fr.].

DIPLOMAT [dip'lo-mat], *n.* person employed professionally in international diplomacy, person of tact and social dexterity. [Fr.].

DIPLOMATIC [dip-lo-ma'tik], *adj.* pertaining to international diplomacy; skilled and adroit in managing people; tactful; **d. corps**, body of d. representatives accredited to a government. DIPLOMATICALLY, *adv.* in a d. manner. [Fr.].

DIPLOMATIC(S) [dip-lo-ma'tik(s)], *n.* science of deciphering and studying of old documents.

DIPLOMATIST [di-plō'ma-tist], *n.* a diplomat.

DIPLOPIA [di-plō'pi-ah], *n.* (*med.*) disease of the eye in which objects are seen double. [Gk.].

DIPPER [di'per], *n.* one who, or that which, dips; water-ouzel or other diving bird; a Baptist, *esp.* a member of an American group of Baptists; vessel for ladling water; (*motoring*) device which lowers and raises the headlamp beam of a motor vehicle.

DIPPING-NEEDLE [di'ping-nē-dl], *n.* (*magn.*) instrument which shows the angle of dip of a magnetic needle.

DIPPY [di'pi], *n.* (*slang*) mad, crazy.

DIPSAS [dip'sas], *n.* serpent whose bite was supposed to cause an unquenchable thirst; genus of nonvenomous tree snakes; genus of freshwater bivalves of the mussel family. [Gk.].

DIPSOMANIA [dip-sō-mā'ni-ah], *n.* (*med.*) nervous disease characterized by an uncontrollable desire for alcohol.

DIPSOMANIAC [dip-sō-mā'ni-ak], *n.* one suffering from dipsomania; confirmed drunkard.

DIPSTICK [dip'stik], *n.* (*motoring*) measuring rod inserted in the sump of a car engine to ascertain the amount of oil present.

DIPTERA [dip'te-rah], *n.*(*pl.*) (*entom.*) two-winged order of insects, including the house-fly. [Gk.].

DIPTEROUS [dip'te-rŏŏs], *adj.* (*bot.*) (of seeds) having two wings; (*entom.*) two-winged, belonging to the diptera.

DIPTYCH [dip'tik], *n.* picture on two leaves opening like a screen. [Gk.].

DIPUS [dī'pus], *n.* (*zool.*) genus of rodents, the jerboas; small Australian marsupial. [Gk.].

DIRE [dīer], *adj.* evil, dreadful, horrible. [L.].

DIRECT (1) [di-rekt'], *v.t. and i.* to conduct, control, manage, supervise, be in charge of, govern the actions or movements of; give orders, command; turn, cause to be focused upon; draw to, attract to; address postal matter; address to, aim at; point out the right way to. DIRECT (2), *adj.* straight; without interference; (*fig.*) immediate, without intervening agent; straightforward, plain, frank; (*geneal.*) in uninterrupted succession from father to son; (*astron.*) onward, advancing from west to east; (*mus.*) with both hands moving in the same direction along the keyboard; (*mus.*) not inverted; (*gram.*) in the actual words used by the speaker; **d. action**, strike or

---

The accent ' after a syllable = stress (u-pon'). The mark ‾ over a vowel = length (ā in made; ō in bone).

lock-out action in a labour dispute; **d. current,** (*elect.*) current flowing continuously in one direction only; **d. hit,** impact of a bomb dropped from the air on a building; **d. method,** method of teaching foreign languages by continual conversation and reading in the language, using the native tongue as little as possible; **d. tax,** tax levied upon a person's income or revenue. DIRECT (3), *adv.* in an undeviating line, straight, in a d. manner. [L.].

DIRECTION [di-rek'shn], *n.* act of directing; management, control, leadership, guidance; line or path along which a body moves; point to which, or from which, movement is made, way; group of directors; (often *pl.*) instructions on how to proceed, information as to what to do; order, command; address on a letter; **in the d. of,** towards. [L.].

DIRECTIONAL [di-rek'shn-al], *adj.* pertaining to direction; **d. aerial,** aerial which will transmit or receive radio waves better from one direction than from others.

DIRECTION-FINDER [di-rek'shn-fin-der], *n.* (*radio*) instrument for finding the direction from which radio signals are coming.

DIRECTIVE (1) [di-rek'tiv], *adj.* tending to direct, that directs. DIRECTIVE (2), *n.* an instruction on policy. [Fr.].

DIRECTLY (1) [di-rekt'li], *adv.* in a direct manner; immediately, at once; shortly, presently. DIRECTLY (2), *conj.* as soon as.

DIRECTNESS [di-rekt'nes], *n.* quality of being direct.

DIRECTOIRE [di-rek'twah(r)], *adj.* in the style or fashion of the period of the Directory in France (1795-99). [Fr.].

DIRECTOR [di-rek'ter], *n.* one who directs, instructor, supervisor; person elected to assist in the management of the affairs of a commercial company; instrument that directs the course of anything; one who supervises the making of a film. DIRECTORIAL [di-rek-taw'ri-al], *adj.* relating to directors; containing directions.

DIRECTORATE [di-rek'te-rat], *n.* a board of directors; directorship.

DIRECTORSHIP [di-rek'ter-ship], *n.* the office of director.

DIRECTORY (1) [di-rek'te-ri], *n.* that which directs or instructs; book of directions; book containing classified lists of the inhabitants of a district, of telephone numbers, or of trades and professions; list of the streets in a place; executive council of the French Republic, 1795-99. DIRECTORY (2), *adj.* containing instructions, that directs.

DIRECTRIX [di-rek'triks], *n.* woman director; (*geom.*) fixed line required in drawing a curve, the straight line perpendicular to the axis of a conic section in relation to which its nature may be defined. [MedL.].

DIREFUL [dier'fool], *adj.* dire, horrible, terrible. DIREFULLY, *adv.* in d. fashion. DIREFULNESS, *n.* quality of being d.

DIRENESS [dier'nes], *n.* quality of being dire.

DIRGE [durj], *n.* funeral hymn, song of lament or mourning. [L.].

DIRIGIBLE (1) [di'ri-ji-bl], *adj.* able to be steered. DIRIGIBLE (2), *n.* navigable airship.

DIRK (1) [durk], *n.* short Highland dagger. DIRK (2), *v.t.* to stab with a d. [Uncert.].

DIRT [durt], *n.* unclean matter, filth, mud, dust, soil; refuse or valueless matter; (*fig.*) sordidness, uncleanliness, foulness; thing of no account or value; (*coll.*) earth; **yellow d.,** (*slang*) gold; **d. cheap,** (*coll.*) very cheap. DIRT-TRACK, *n.* track of cinders or other loose material, used for motor-cycle and small-car racing. [OScand.].

DIRTY (1) [dur'ti], *adj.* covered with or containing dirt, not clean, soiled, foul; (of weather) stormy, rainy; (*fig.*) dishonourable, mean, unfair; obscene, indecent; **to do the d. on,** (*coll.*) to treat in a mean fashion. DIRTY (2), *v.t.* to make d., soil. DIRTILY, *adv.* in a d. fashion; meanly, dishonourably. DIRTINESS, *n.* condition of being d.

DIS-, *pref.* indicating or expressing negation; deprivation, removal from; separation, parting from. [L.].

DISABILITY [dis-a-bi'li-ti], *n.* state of being disabled; that which disables.

DISABLE [dis-ā-bl], *v.t.* to render unfit, incapacitate, maim, make unable to perform competently; (*leg.*) render or pronounce legally incapable. DISABLEMENT, *n.* act of disabling, condition of being disabled.

DISABUSE [dis-a-byōōz'], *v.t.* to free from mistaken belief or error, undeceive.

DISACCORD (1) [dis-a-kawd'], *v.i.* to disagree; be

out of accord with. DISACCORD (2), *n.* lack of agreement, variance.

DISADVANTAGE (1) [dis-ad-vahn'tij], *n.* drawback, unfavourable circumstance, position or quality harmful to one's advantage or success; loss, detriment. DISADVANTAGE (2), *v.t.* to act to the prejudice of, affect unfavourably.

DISADVANTAGEOUS [dis-ad-van-tā'jōōs], *adj.* unfavourable to success or prosperity, causing disadvantage, detrimental. DISADVANTAGEOUSLY, *adv.* in a d. fashion. DISADVANTAGEOUSNESS, *n.* quality of being d.

DISAFFECT [dis-a-fekt'], *v.t.* to alienate the affection or loyalty of, discontent, estrange, make dissatisfied. DISAFFECTED, *adj.* disloyal; dissatisfied, unfriendly. DISAFFECTEDLY, *adv.* in a disaffected fashion. DISAFFECTEDNESS, *n.* quality of being disaffected.

DISAFFECTION [dis-a-fek'shn], *n.* state of being disaffected; hostility, dislike; discontent.

DISAFFIRM [dis-a-furm'], *v.t.* to show to be false, deny, contradict; (*leg.*) reverse, annul. DISAFFIRMANCE, *n.* (*leg.*) act of disaffirming.

DISAFFOREST [dis-a-fo'rist], *v.t.* to clear of trees; regard as ordinary land no longer subject to forest laws. DISAFFORESTATION [dis-a-fo-ris-tā'shn], *n.* act of disafforesting; condition of being disafforested.

DISAGREE [dis-a-grē'], *v.i.* to be different; differ in opinion; quarrel; be unsuitable for, upset, make ill.

DISAGREEABLE [dis-a-grē'a-bl], *adj.* bad-tempered, cantankerous; unpleasant, distasteful. DISAGREEABLENESS, *n.* condition of being d. DISAGREEABLY, *adv.* in a d. fashion.

DISAGREEMENT [dis-a-grē'ment], *n.* want of agreement; difference of opinion; dissension, discord; a quarrel.

DISALLOW [dis-a-low'], *v.t.* and *i.* not to permit, refuse to sanction; not to allow or admit as just; not to grant. DISALLOWANCE, *n.* act of disallowing, rejection.

DISAPPEAR [dis-a-pēer'], *v.i.* to vanish from sight, be lost.

DISAPPEARANCE [dis-a-pēer'ans], *n.* state of having disappeared; act of disappearing.

DISAPPOINT [dis-a-point'], *v.t.* to fail to fulfil the expectations of, dash the hopes of; thwart, defeat. DISAPPOINTED, *adj.* with one's hopes or expectations not realized, frustrated in one's wishes. [Fr.].

DISAPPOINTING [dis-a-poin'ting], *adj.* that disappoints, unsatisfactory. DISAPPOINTINGLY, *adv.* in d. fashion.

DISAPPOINTMENT [dis-a-point'ment], *n.* state of being disappointed; that which disappoints; feeling of regret or dejection upon the frustration of one's expectations, intentions or wishes.

DISAPPROBATION [dis-ap-rō-bā'shn], *n.* disapproval; condemnation. DISAPPROBATIVE, DISAPPROBATORY [dis-ap'rō-bā-tiv, dis-ap'rō-bā-te-ri], *adj.* showing disapproval.

DISAPPROVAL [dis-a-prōō'val], *n.* censure, condemnation, adverse opinion.

DISAPPROVE [dis-a-prōōv'], *v.t.* to condemn, have an adverse opinion of, not to approve. DISAPPROVINGLY, *adv.* in disapproving fashion.

DISARM [dis-ahm'], *v.t.* and *i.* to deprive of arms or weapons; (*fig.*) render harmless; deprive of hostile force or intent, allay; reduce armaments. DISARMINGLY, *adv.* in such a way as to d. opposition; frankly; engagingly.

DISARMAMENT [dis-ah'ma-ment], *n.* reduction and limitation of armaments; state of being disarmed.

DISARRANGE [dis-a-rānj'], *v.t.* to cause to be out of place, disturb the order or arrangement of, disorder, upset. DISARRANGEMENT, *n.* confusion, disorder.

DISARRAY [dis-a-rā'], *v.t.* to throw into disorder, confuse, upset; disrobe. DISARRAY (2), *n.* disorder, confusion. [OFr.].

DISASSOCIATE [dis-a-sō'shi-āt], *v.t.* to sever or repudiate connexion or association with.

DISASTER [di-zahs'ter], *n.* calamity, sudden great misfortune, event producing widespread distress, ruin, loss of life etc., severe mishap. [Fr.].

DISASTROUS [di-zahs'trōōs], *adj.* calamitous, causing or resulting in disaster. DISASTROUSLY, *adv.* in d. fashion.

DISAVOW [dis-a-vow'], *v.t.* to disclaim, repudiate, refuse to acknowledge. DISAVOWAL, *n.* act of disavowing; that which disavows; repudiation. [Fr.].

DISBAND [dis-band'], *v.t.* and *i.* to break up or cause to cease as an organized body or band; disperse, cease to exist as an organized band; (of troops) break ranks. DISBANDMENT, *n.* act of disbanding.

ōō is pronounced as in food; ŏŏ as in hood; th as in *think*; ᴛʜ as in *that*; zh as in azure.   ~ = related to

DISBAR (*pres.pt.* **disbarring**, *pret. and p.pt.* **disbarred**) [dis-bah(r)′], *v.t.* (*leg.*) to expel (a barrister) from the Bar, strike off the list of barristers.

DISBELIEF [dis-bi-lēf′], *n.* refusal or disinclination to believe; want of belief.

DISBELIEVE [dis-bi-lēv′], *v.t. and i.* to refuse, or be unable, to believe. **DISBELIEVER**, *n.* one who disbelieves.

DISBENCH [dis-bensh′], *v.t.* (*leg.*) to deprive of membership of an Inn of Court.

DISBURDEN [dis-bur′den], *v.t. and i.* to ease or relieve of a burden, unload, get rid of.

DISBURSE [dis-burs′], *v.t. and i.* to pay out, spend, distribute, contribute sums of money. **DISBURSEMENT**, *n.* act of disbursing money; sum paid out. **DISBURSER**, *n.* one who disburses money. [OFr.].

DISC, see DISK.

DISCAL [dis′kal], *adj.* pertaining to a disk.

DISCARD (1) [dis-kahd′], *v.t. and i.* (*cards*) to throw away a card which is not a trump when unable to follow suit; throw aside as valueless or useless; (of an article of clothing) cease to wear, remove or take off; reject, dismiss, abandon as unworthy or of little account. **DISCARD** (2), *n.* act of discarding, card or cards discarded.

DISCERN [di-surn′], *v.t.* to perceive, distinguish clearly by the sight, see; recognize, perceive. **DISCERNER**, *n.* one who discerns. [L.].

DISCERNIBLE [di-sur′ni-bl], *adj.* capable of being discerned. **DISCERNIBLENESS**, *n.* condition of being d. **DISCERNIBLY**, *adv.* in a d. manner.

DISCERNING (1) [di-sur′ning], *adj.* able to discern. **DISCERNING** (2), *n.* discernment. **DISCERNINGLY**, *adv.* in a d. manner.

DISCERNMENT [di-surn′ment], *n.* act of discerning; ability to discern, insight, penetration.

DISCHARGE (1) [dis-chahj′], *v.t.* to remove or expel the contents of; eject, emit, give off; (of a sore, wound) emit matter; fire (a gun); unload; take away electricity from a charged body; release from service, care or attention; dismiss from employment; acquit, liberate from custody; relieve from legal liability; pay, rid oneself of; perform, carry out (duties etc.). **DISCHARGE** (2), *n.* act of discharging; state or process of being discharged; that which is discharged; testimonial or order certifying freedom from liability; (*med.*) emission of matter from a sore. [OFr.].

DISCHARGING-ROD [dis-chah′jing-rod], *n.* a discharger of electricity.

DISCIPLE [di-sī′pl], *n.* one of the twelve Apostles, an early follower of Jesus; (*fig.*) follower, student, adherent of any particular group holding common principles, or of the leader of such a group; an American sect of Baptists. **DISCIPLESHIP**, *n.* condition of being a d. [L.].

DISCIPLINABLE [di′si-pli-na-bl], *adj.* capable of being disciplined.

DISCIPLINARIAN (1) [di-si-pli-nāer′i-an], *adj.* pertaining to, or involving, discipline. **DISCIPLINARIAN** (2), *n.* one who keeps strict discipline; an expert in the art of discipline.

DISCIPLINARY [di′si-pli-na-ri], *adj.* pertaining to, or involving, discipline.

DISCIPLINE (1) [di′si-plin], *n.* systematic training intended to develop the mind along certain lines, to teach restraint, respect for and willing obedience to recognized authority; result of such training, self-restraint, readiness with which commands etc. are carried out, ability to act in orderly manner in unforeseen or abnormal circumstances; control over the behaviour of a group of persons; corrective punishment, chastisement; (*eccles.*) penance; moral precepts and their enforcement upon members of the Church. **DISCIPLINE** (2), *v.t.* to subject to or enforce d. upon, bring about d. in. [L.].

DISCLAIM [dis-klām′], *v.t. and i.* to renounce or repudiate a claim to, deny connexion with; disown, refuse to admit; repudiate a legal claim. **DISCLAMATION** [dis-kla-mā′shn], *n.* act of disclaiming. [OFr.].

DISCLAIMER [dis-klā′mer], *n.* (*leg.*) refusal to admit; repudiation, renunciation, rejection of a legal claim, right, interest etc.; one who disclaims.

DISCLOSE [dis-klōz′], *v.t.* to reveal, bring to light. **DISCLOSER**, *n.* one who discloses. [OFr.].

DISCLOSURE [dis-klō′zhoor], *n.* act of disclosing; that which is disclosed.

DISCOLORATION, DISCOLOURATION [dis-ku-le-rā′shn], *n.* act of discolouring; state of being discoloured. [OFr.].

DISCOLOUR [dis-ku′ler], *v.t. and i.* to alter or spoil the colour of, stain; become stained or tarnished.

DISCOLOURED, *adj.* stained, tarnished, having its natural colour changed or spoilt. **DISCOLOURMENT**, *n.* alteration in colour. [OFr.].

DISCOLOURATION, see DISCOLORATION.

DISCOMFIT [dis-kum′fit], *v.t.* to defeat, overcome; upset, disconcert. [OFr.].

DISCOMFITURE [dis-kum′fi-tyoor], *n.* act of discomfiting, state of being discomfited, confusion arising from defeat or frustration. [OFr.].

DISCOMFORT (1) [dis-kum′fert], *n.* want of comfort, inconvenience, hardship, unpleasantness. **DISCOMFORT** (2), *v.t.* to cause d. to. **DISCOMFORTABLE**, *adj.* uncomfortable. [OFr.].

DISCOMMEND [dis-ko-mend′], *v.t.* to find fault with, censure, advise against. **DISCOMMENDABLE**, *adj.* censurable; deserving disapproval. **DISCOMMENDATION** [dis-ko-men-dā′shn], *n.* disapproval. [OFr.].

DISCOMMODE [dis-ko-mōd′], *v.t.* to inconvenience annoy. **DISCOMMODITY** [dis-ko-mo′di-ti], *n.* inconvenience.

DISCOMMON [dis-ko′mon], *v.t.* (*leg.*) to appropriate common land by enclosing it; (*fig.*) deprive of a privilege.

DISCOMPOSE [dis-kom-pōz′], *v.t.* to disquiet, disturb, upset the composure of. **DISCOMPOSEDNESS** [dis-kom-pō′zid-nes], *n.* condition of being discomposed. **DISCOMPOSINGLY**, *adv.* in a discomposing fashion.

DISCOMPOSURE [dis-kom-pō′zhoor], *n.* agitation, disturbed state of mind, lack of composure.

DISCONCERT [dis-kon-surt′], *v.t.* to put out of countenance, discompose, abash; upset, frustrate. **DISCONCERTINGLY**, *adv.* in such a way as to d. **DISCONCERTION, DISCONCERTMENT** [dis-kon-sur′shn, dis-kon-surt′ment], *n.* act of disconcerting; state of being disconcerted.

DISCONNECT [dis-ko-nekt′], *v.t.* to separate, disunite, break or remove the connexion between. **DISCONNECTED**, *adj.* separated, disjointed; not connected with, unrelated to; incoherent. **DISCONNECTEDLY**, *adv.* in a disconnected manner. **DISCONNEXION, DISCONNECTION** [dis-ko-nek′shn], *n.* state or quality of being disconnected.

DISCONSOLATE [dis-kon′so-lat], *adj.* unable or unwilling to be consoled, extremely unhappy or dejected, utterly miserable; without comfort or consolation. **DISCONSOLATELY**, *adv.* in d. fashion. [MedL.].

DISCONTENT (1) [dis-kon-tent′], *n.* lack of contentment, dissatisfaction. **DISCONTENT** (2), *v.t.* to dissatisfy, cause to be disquieted in the mind.

DISCONTENTED [dis-kon-ten′tid], *adj.* dissatisfied, not contented. **DISCONTENTEDLY**, *adv.* in d. fashion. **DISCONTENTEDNESS, DISCONTENTMENT**, *n.* condition of being d.

DISCONTINUANCE [dis-kon-ti′nyōō-ans], *n.* act of discontinuing; state of being discontinued; (*leg.*) interruption or dismissal of a suit owing to irregular continuance or breaking off of the proceedings by the plaintiff. **DISCONTINUATION** [dis-kon-ti-nyōō-ā′shn], *n.* d. [AFr.].

DISCONTINUE [dis-kon-ti′nyōō], *v.t. and i.* to interrupt, cease; break off, give up; finish. **DISCONTINUER**, *n.* one who discontinues. [MedL.].

DISCONTINUITY [dis-kon-ti-nyōō′i-ti], *n.* lack of continuity, interrupted sequence.

DISCONTINUOUS [dis-kon-ti′nyōō-ŏŏs], *adj.* not continuous, interrupted, broken off; separated by gaps or intervals. **DISCONTINUOUSLY**, *adv.* in a d. manner.

DISCORD (1) [dis′kawd], *n.* disagreement, variance, dissension, want of harmony; confused, inharmonious jumble of sounds; (*mus.*) dissonant chord, requiring resolution into a concord. **DISCORD** (2) [dis-kawd′], *v.t.* to disagree, differ, be at variance; (*mus.*) be dissonant or inharmonious. [L.].

DISCORDANCE, DISCORDANCY [dis-kaw′dans, dis-kaw′dan-si], *n.* disagreement, lack of harmony, dissonance. [OFr.].

DISCORDANT [dis-kaw′dant], *adj.* not agreeing, at variance, quarrelling; harsh, unmusical, unpleasant to the ear. **DISCORDANTLY**, *adv.* in d. fashion. [OFr.].

DISCOUNT (1) [dis′kownt], *n.* sum of money deducted from the usual price for prompt payment, payment in cash, as a special concession to privileged persons etc.; an allowance off the full amount normally due; charge made by a banker on advancing a sum of money on a bill of exchange or other document not due; **at a d.**, of little account or value. **DISCOUNT** (2) [dis-kownt'], *v.t.* to lend or receive money subject to d. on bills of exchange etc.; diminish in value, depreciate, offset; disregard, refuse to believe or accept. DISCOUNTABLE, *adj.* capable of being discounted. DISCOUNTER, *n.* one who discounts. [OFr.].

DISCOUNT-BROKER [dis'kownt-brō-ker], *n.* one who cashes bills of exchange or advances money on securities at a discount.

DISCOUNT-DAY [dis'kownt-dā], *n.* day on which a bank discounts notes and bills.

DISCOUNTENANCE [dis-kown'ti-nans], *v.t.* to disapprove of, view with disfavour, discourage; disconcert, abash. [OFr.].

DISCOUNTING [dis-kown'ting], *n.* (*comm.*) act or practice of advancing money on discounts.

DISCOURAGE [dis-ku'rij], *v.t.* to dishearten, deter, take away one's enthusiasm, courage or confidence; endeavour to deter from; try to prevent or repress. DISCOURAGEABLE, *adj.* capable of being discouraged. DISCOURAGER, *n.* one who, or that which, discourages. DISCOURAGING, *adj.* tending to d. DISCOURAGINGLY, *adv.* in a d. fashion. [OFr.].

DISCOURAGEMENT [dis-ku'rij-ment], *n.* act of discouraging; that which discourages; state of being discouraged. [OFr.].

DISCOURSE (1) [dis'kaws], *n.* formal speech, address, lecture etc.; written dissertation; conversation, talk. DISCOURSE (2) [dis-kaws'], *v.t. and i.* to converse, talk; speak or write at length in a learned or formal manner; preach, lecture. DISCOURSER, *n.* one who discourses. [L.].

DISCOURTEOUS [dis-kur'ti-ŏŏs], *adj.* rude, illmannered, lacking in courtesy. DISCOURTEOUSLY, *adv.* in a d. fashion. DISCOURTEOUSNESS, *n.* quality of being d.

DISCOURTESY [dis-kur'te-si], *n.* lack of courtesy, discourteous behaviour, incivility; a discourteous act.

DISCOVER [dis-ku'ver], *v.t.* to find out; establish the presence of; (*archaic*) reveal, disclose. DISCOVERER, *n.* one who discovers. [OFr.].

DISCOVERABLE [dis-ku've-ra-bl], *adj.* capable of being discovered. DISCOVERABILITY [dis-ku-ve-ra-bi'li-ti], *n.* quality of being d.

DISCOVERT [dis-ku'vert], *adj.* (*leg.*) of a woman unmarried or widowed. DISCOVERTURE [dis-ku'ver-tyŏŏr], *n.* (*leg.*) condition of being d. [OFr.].

DISCOVERY [dis-ku've-ri], *n.* act of discovering; that which is discovered; (*leg.*) disclosure of evidence or facts affecting the action at issue by one of the parties at the instigation of the other.

DISCREDIT (1) [dis-kre'dit], *v.t.* to bring into ill repute, shake one's confidence in, create an unfavourable opinion about; doubt strongly, refuse to believe. DISCREDIT (2), *n.* loss of credit, ill repute; that which discredits; doubt, disbelief.

DISCREDITABLE [dis-kre'di-ta-bl], *adj.* that discredits; mean, base, unworthy. DISCREDITABLY, *adv.* in a d. fashion.

DISCREET [dis-krēt'], *adj.* circumspect, wary, prudent, endeavouring to avoid ill-advised action or anything likely to produce trouble. DISCREETLY, *adv.* in a d. manner. [LL.].

DISCREPANCE, DISCREPANCY [dis-kre'pans, dis-kre'pan-si], *n.* quality of being discrepant; anything which is discrepant, an inconsistency. [L.].

DISCREPANT [dis-kre'pant, dis'kre-pant], *adj.* inconsistent, disagreeing, contradictory, inconsequent, incompatible. [L.].

DISCRETE [dis-krēt', dis'krēt], *adj.* separate, disconnected; (*path.*) (of spots etc.) scattered singly. [L.].

DISCRETION [dis-kre'shn], *n.* ability to realize and follow the most advantageous line of behaviour; carefulness, avoidance of unnecessary risks; ability or liberty to act or make free decisions as seems best; **to surrender at d.,** to surrender unconditionally; **years of d.,** age at which a person is considered capable of making his own decisions on how to act. DISCRETIONAL, *adj.* discretionary. DISCRETIONALLY, *adv.* discretionarily. [L.].

DISCRETIONARY [dis-kre'shn-a-ri], *adj.* controlled or determined by discretion. DISCRETIONARILY, *adv.* according to discretion.

DISCRIMINATE [dis-kri'mi-nāt], *v.t. and i.* to show, make, or note the difference between, differentiate, distinguish; recognize a difference, see or make a distinction between; deal differently with, show bias and unfair partiality in one's treatment of. DISCRIMINATE (2) [dis-kri'mi-nat], *adj.* exercising, showing or characterized by discrimination. DIS-

CRIMINABLE, *adj.* capable of being discriminated. DISCRIMINATELY, *adv.* in a d. manner. [L.].

DISCRIMINATING [dis-kri'mi-nā-ting], *adj.* able to discriminate, able to distinguish slight differences; (of a duty, tariff) differential; showing discrimination. DISCRIMINATINGLY, *adv.* in a d. manner.

DISCRIMINATION [dis-kri-mi-nā'shn], *n.* act of discriminating; ability to discriminate; acute judgment. [L.].

DISCRIMINATIVE [dis-kri'mi-na-tiv], *adj.* able to discriminate; constituting a mark of difference, that discriminates. DISCRIMINATIVELY, *adv.* with discrimination.

DISCRIMINATOR [dis-kri'mi-nā-ter], *n.* one who discriminates. [L.].

DISCURSIVE [dis-kur'siv], *adj.* rambling, wandering haphazardly from one topic to another, covering a variety of subjects; reasoning. DISCURSIVELY, *adv.* in d. fashion. DISCURSIVENESS, *n.* condition of being d. [L.].

DISCUS [dis'kus], *n.* circular, slightly convex piece of metal, stone or heavy material thrown in athletic contests. [L. from Gk.].

DISCUSS [dis-kus'], *v.t.* to debate, argue about, consider (a topic) in all its aspects and implications, examine the various points of view about a subject upon which diversity of opinion is possible; (*civil leg.*) exhaust the means of, or proceedings against, a principal debtor before taking action against the surety or person secondarily liable. DISCUSSIBLE, *adj.* capable of being discussed. [L.].

DISCUSSION [dis-ku'shn], *n.* act of discussing; state of being discussed; argument, debate, mutual consideration of a problem. [L.].

DISDAIN (1) [dis-dān'], *v.t.* to despise, look down upon, regard or treat with disdain; scorn; consider unworthy of one, refuse to degrade oneself by. DISDAIN (2), *n.* contempt, scorn, haughty disregard of what is considered inferior or derogatory, arrogant indifference. [L.].

DISDAINFUL [dis-dān'fŏŏl], *adj.* haughty, scornful, contemptuous, proudly indifferent or aloof. DISDAINFULLY, *adv.* in a d. fashion.

DISEASE [di-zēz'], *n.* illness, specific form of derangement or disorder of an organ, organism, mind etc., characterized by distinct and recognizable symptoms; abnormal condition of the body, deviation from normal health; disorder of physical, mental, or social structure or function. DISEASED, *adj.* affected by d., not healthy, suffering from d. DISEASEDNESS [di-zēzd'nes], *n.* condition of being diseased. DISEASEFUL, *adj.* bringing on d. [OFr.].

DISEMBARK [dis-em-bahk'], *v.t. and i.* to land, go ashore, put ashore. [Fr.].

DISEMBARKATION [dis-em-bah-kā'shn], *n.* act of disembarking.

DISEMBARRASS [dis-em-ba'ras], *v.t.* to free from embarrassment or trouble; separate. DISEMBARRASSMENT, *n.* act of disembarrassing; state of being disembarrassed.

DISEMBODY [dis-em-bo'di], *v.t.* to free from bodily form; disband, discharge (a military body). DISEMBODIMENT, *n.* act of disembodying; state of being disembodied.

DISEMBOGUE [dis-em-bōg'], *v.t. and i.* (of a river) to discharge or empty its waters at its mouth; (*fig.*) pour or flow forth. DISEMBOGUEMENT, *n.* act of disemboguing; place where a river disembogues. [Span.].

DISEMBOWEL [dis-em-bowl'], *v.t.* to remove the bowels of, eviscerate; wound so as to expose the entrails. DISEMBOWELLED, *adj.* eviscerated; wounded so as to lay open the entrails. DISEMBOWELMENT, *n.* act of disembowelling; state of being disembowelled.

DISENCHANT [dis-en-chahnt'], *v.t.* to disillusion, destroy the power of a charm or spell; remove the enchantment from. DISENCHANTER, *n.* one who disenchants. DISENCHANTMENT, *n.* act of disenchanting; condition of being disenchanted. DISENCHANTRESS, *n.* female disenchanter. [OFr.].

DISENCUMBER [dis-en-kum'ber], *v.t.* to set free o. an encumbrance, relieve of a burden.

DISENDOW [dis-en-dow'], *v.t.* to deprive of endowment. DISENDOWMENT, *n.* act of disendowing; state of being disendowed.

DISENFRANCHISE [dis-en-fran'chiz], *v.t.* to disfranchise.

DISENGAGE [dis-en-gāj'], *v.t.* to set free or unfasten from that which binds or joins, detach, disconnect, release; (*fencing*) transfer one's blade smartly to the

---

ŏŏ is pronounced as in food; ŏŏ as in hood; th as in *think*; TH as in *that*; zh as in azure. ~ = related to.

other side of the opponent's foil. DISENGAGED, *adj.* free, not occupied or engaged at the moment, at liberty. DISENGAGEDNESS, *n.* quality or state of being disengaged. DISENGAGEMENT, *n.* act of disengaging; condition of being disengaged.

DISENTAIL [dis-en-tāl′], *v.t.* to break the entail of.
DISENTANGLE [dis-en-tang′gl], *v.t. and i.* to unravel, untwist, free from entanglement; (*fig.*) straighten out. DISENTANGLEMENT, *n.* act of disentangling; state of being disentangled.
DISENTHRAL (*pres.pt.* disenthralling, *pret. and p.pt.* disenthralled) [dis-en-thrawl′], *v.t.* to release from bondage or oppression. DISENTHRALMENT, *n.* release from bondage.
DISENTOMB [dis-en-tōōm′], *v.t.* to take out of a tomb; (*fig.*) unearth.
DISENTRAIN [dis-en-trān′], *v.t.* (*milit.*) to disembark from a train; detrain.
DISENTWINE [dis-en-twīn′], *v.t.* to untwist, unravel.
DISESTABLISH [dis-es-tab′lish], *v.t.* to remove from an established position or state; sever the connexion between Church and State, remove State control and support from an institution (*esp.* the Church). DISESTABLISHMENT, *n.* act of disestablishing, state of being disestablished.
DISESTEEM (1) [dis-es-tēm′], *v.t.* to hold in slight esteem, think lightly of, disrespect. DISESTEEM (2), *n.* lack of esteem, disrepute.
DISEUSE [dē-zurz′], *n.* actress who entertains by means of spoken monologue. [Fr.].
DISFAVOUR (1) [dis-fā′ver], *n.* dislike, disapproval; lack of favour, discredit. DISFAVOUR (2), *v.t.* to disapprove of, dislike.
DISFIGURE [dis-fi′ger], *v.t.* to spoil or mar the appearance or beauty of, deface; (*fig.*) impair, render ugly, make defective. DISFIGURATION [disfi-ge-rā′shn], *n.* disfigurement. DISFIGURINGLY, *adv.* in such a way as to disfigure. [OFr.].
DISFIGUREMENT [dis-fi′ger-ment], *n.* act of disfiguring; state of being disfigured; that which disfigures, blemish, deformity.
DISFOREST [dis-fo′rist], *v.t.* to disafforest.
DISFRANCHISE [dis-fran′chiz], *v.t.* to deprive of civic rights and privileges, *esp.* of the right to vote, or of representation upon an elected body. DISFRANCHISEMENT, *n.* act of disfranchising; condition of being disfranchised.
DISFROCK [dis-frok′], *v.t.* to unfrock.
DISGORGE [dis-gawj′], *v.t. and i.* to eject from the throat, vomit; discharge violently, pour forth, empty; (*fig.*) give up, hand over. DISGORGEMENT, *n.* act of disgorging. DISGORGER, *n.* instrument for removing a hook from a fish's mouth.
DISGRACE (1) [dis-grās′], *n.* discredit, shame, loss of esteem or honour, ignominy; state of being out of favour; cause of shame, discredit, dishonour or reproach; person who, or thing which, disgraces. DISGRACE (2), *v.t.* to bring d. upon, bring into disrepute; banish from favour or grace. [Fr.].
DISGRACEFUL [dis-grās′fool], *adj.* shameful, discreditable, bringing into disgrace. DISGRACEFULLY, *adv.* in d. fashion.
DISGRUNTLED [dis-grun′tld], *adj.* discontented, dissatisfied, continually grumbling, out of humour. DISGRUNTLEMENT, *n.* state of being d.; ill-humoured dissatisfaction. [DIS and GRUNT].
DISGUISE (1) [dis-gīz′], *v.t.* to alter the normal appearance of, cause to resemble something else for the purposes of deception or concealment; conceal under an assumed outward expression or air, cloak, hide. DISGUISE (2), *n.* act of disguising; state of being disguised; that which disguises. DISGUISEDLY [dis-gī′zid-li], *adv.* in a disguised manner. DISGUISEMENT, *n.* act of disguising; state of being disguised; a d. DISGUISER, *n.* one who, or that which, disguises. DISGUISING, *n.* act of one who disguises. [OFr.].
DISGUST (1) [dis-gust′], *n.* strong feeling of distaste and repugnance, loathing, abhorrence. DISGUST (2), *v.t.* to fill with d., offend the moral feelings, displease profoundly. DISGUSTEDLY, *adv.* in disgusted fashion. DISGUSTFUL, *adj.* offensive to the taste; nauseous; arousing d. DISGUSTFULNESS, *n.* condition of being disgustful. [OFr.].
DISGUSTING [dis-gus′ting], *adj.* arousing disgust, loathsome, revolting, repulsive; (*coll.*) very bad. DISGUSTINGLY, *adv.* in a d. fashion.
DISH (1) [dish], *n.* rimmed shallow vessel with a flat bottom, used for holding food; anything resembling this; the food contained in this; a particular kind of

food. DISH (2), *v.t.* to put in a d., serve in a d.; (*coll.*) spoil upset, defeat; hollow out like a d.; **to d. up,** to present for notice or acceptance; serve (a meal).
DISHABILLE, DESHABILLE [di-sa-bēl′], *n.* undress, state of being partly dressed or undressed (*usu.* **in d.**), loose informal garment. [Fr.].
DISHARMONIOUS [dis-hah-mō′ni-ōōs], *adj.* inharmonious, discordant. DISHARMONIOUSLY, *adv.* in d. fashion.
DISHARMONIZE [dis-hah′mo-nīz], *v.t.* to throw into discord, upset, cause to disagree.
DISHARMONY [dis-hah′mo-ni], *n.* discord, lack of harmony.
DISHCLOTH [dish′kloth], *n.* cloth used for washing dishes.
DISHCOVER [dish′ku-ver], *n.* cover placed over a dish to retain the heat of its contents.
DISHEARTEN [dis-hah′ten], *v.t.* to discourage, dispirit, cause to lack confidence or enthusiasm, depress. DISHEARTENING, *adj.* discouraging, that disheartens.
DISHEVEL (*pres.pt.* dishevelling, *pret. and p.pt.* dishevelled) [di-she′vel], *v.t.* to let the hair hang down loosely and untidily. DISHEVELLED, *adj.* (of hair) loose, disordered; generally untidy in dress and appearance. DISHEVELMENT, *n.* condition of being dishevelled. [OFr.].
DISHFUL [dish′fool], *n.* as much as a dish will contain.
DISHMAT [dish′mat], *n.* a table-mat.
DISHONEST [dis-o′nist], *adj.* not honest, given to cheating or defrauding; unfair, fraudulent, deceitful. DISHONESTLY, *adv.* in a d. fashion. [OFr.].
DISHONESTY [dis-o′nis-ti], *n.* quality of being dishonest; that which is dishonest. [OFr.].
DISHONOUR (1) [dis-o′ner], *v.t.* to bring dishonour or shame upon; treat with indignity, act discreditably towards; violate the chastity of; (*comm.*) decline to pay or accept for payment, refuse to meet (one's debts); go back upon one's promise or word. DISHONOUR (2), *n.* disgrace, ignominy, loss of honour or reputation, shame, disrespect. DISHONOURER, *n.* one who brings d. upon anything. [OFr.].
DISHONOURABLE [dis-o′ne-ra-bl], *adj.* without honour, dishonest, not honourable; discreditable, mean, base. DISHONOURABLENESS, *n.* quality of being d. DISHONOURABLY, *adv.* in a d. fashion.
DISHONOURED [dis-o′nerd], *adj.* disgraced, brought into disrepute; violated; (*comm.*) not accepted for payment; repudiated.
DISHWASHER [dish′wo-sher], *n.* one who washes dishes; the pied wagtail.
DISHWATER [dish′waw-ter], *n.* water in which greasy plates, dishes etc. have been washed.
DISILLUSION (1) [dis-i-lyōō′zhn], *n.* the dispelling of an illusion, state of being disillusioned. DISILLUSION (2), *v.t.* to free from illusion, undeceive, acquaint with the true state of affairs.
DISILLUSIONMENT [dis-i-lyōō′zhn-ment], *n.* act of disillusioning, state of being disillusioned.
DISINCLINATION [dis-in-kli-nā′shn], *n.* want of inclination, unwillingness, reluctance, mild aversion.
DISINCLINE [dis-in-klīn′], *v.t.* to make unwilling or reluctant.
DISINFECT [dis-in-fekt′], *v.t.* to render free from infection. DISINFECTION, *n.* act of disinfecting. DISINFECTOR, *n.* apparatus for spraying disinfectant.
DISINFECTANT (1) [dis-in-fek′tant], *adj.* preventing infection, destroying the germs of infectious disease. DISINFECTANT (2), *n.* a substance used to disinfect. [Fr.].
DISINFLATE [dis-in-flāt′], *v.t.* (*econ.*) to reduce the degree of inflation of (a currency). DISINFLATION [dis-in-flā′shn], *n.* (*econ.*) process of disinflating.
DISINGENUOUS [dis-in-je′nyōō-ōōs], *adj.* insincere, not frank, displaying a crafty meanness. DISINGENUOUSLY, *adv.* in a d. fashion. DISINGENUOUSNESS, *n.* state or quality of being d.
DISINHERIT [dis-in-he′rit], *v.t.* to deprive of inheritance, refuse to allow to inherit. DISINHERITANCE, *n.* act of disinheriting; state of being disinherited.
DISINTEGRATE [dis-in′te-grāt], *v.t. and i.* to separate into constituent parts; break up into fragments or parts, fall to bits. DISINTEGRABLE [dis-in′te-gra-bl], *adj.* able to be disintegrated. DISINTEGRATION [dis-in-te-grā′shn], *n.* process of disintegrating. DISINTEGRATOR, *n.* one who, or that which, disintegrates; machine for grinding to powder.
DISINTER (*pres.pt.* disinterring, *pret. and p.pt.*

disinterred) [dis-in-tur'], *v.t.* to take out of a grave, dig up out of the earth, unearth. DIS-INTERMENT, *n.* act of disinterring.

DISINTERESTED [dis-in'tres-tid], *adj.* unmoved by considerations of personal interest, scrupulously fair and impartial. DISINTERESTEDLY, *adv.* in a d. fashion.

DISJOIN [dis-join'], *v.t.* to part, disunite, separate. [OFr. from L.].

DISJOINT [dis-joint'], *v.t.* to put out of joint, dislocate; sever at the joints, break the natural order or logical arrangement of.

DISJOINTED [dis-join'tid], *adj.* separated at the joints, not connected in compact fashion; out of joint; incoherent, disconnected, not progressing logically or in orderly sequence. DISJOINTEDLY, *adv.* in d. fashion.

DISJUNCTION [dis-jungk'shn], *n.* act of disjoining, state of being disjoined, absence or severance of connexion; (*logic*) proposition offering a choice of alternatives. [L.].

DISJUNCTIVE (1) [dis-jungk'tiv], *adj.* separating, disjoining, severing connexion between; **d. conjunction,** (*gram.*) conjunction linking two or more alternatives, or connecting words, phrases or sentences suggesting opposing ideas (as *either . . . or*); **d. proposition,** (*logic*) proposition offering a choice of alternatives, one of which must be true. DISJUNCTIVE (2), *n.* a d. conjunction or proposition. DISJUNCTIVELY, *adv.* in d. fashion. [L.].

DISK, DISC (1) [disk], *n.* a flat circular surface; thin circular plate; (*coll.*) gramophone record; (*astron.*) the visible face of the sun, moon or a planet; (*bot.*) rounded, flattened part of the flower-head of a radiate composite flower; (*agric.*) disk-plough. DISK (2), *v.t. and i.* to use a disk-plough (upon).

DISK-HARROW [disk'ha-rō], *n.* a disk-plough.

DISK-PLOUGH [disk'plow], *n.* agricultural implement having parallel disks which break up the soil.

DISK-WHEEL [disk-wēl'], *n.* (*motoring*) automobile wheel having circular metal disks in place of spokes.

DISLIKE (1) [dis-līk'], *v.t.* to regard with aversion, not to like. DISLIKE (2), *n.* distaste, aversion, repugnance.

DISLIMN [dis-lim'], *v.t.* to obliterate, efface, make the outlines indistinct.

DISLOCATE [dis'lo-kāt], *v.t.* to displace from its rightful position, put out of joint; (*fig.*) upset the normal course of, disorganize, interrupt the efficient functioning of. [MedL.].

DISLOCATION [dis-lo-kā'shn], *n.* act of dislocating; (*geol.*) displacement of portions of a stratified rock. [MedL.].

DISLODGE [dis-loj'], *v.t.* to remove from its previous established or normal position; drive out from a position after a struggle. DISLODG(E)MENT, *n.* act of dislodging; state of being dislodged.

DISLOYAL [dis-loi'al], *adj.* unfaithful, not loyal, traitorous. DISLOYALLY, *adv.* in d. fashion. DISLOYALTY, *n.* quality or act of being d.

DISMAL [diz'mal], *adj.* depressing, gloomy, dreary, melancholy. DISMALITY [diz-ma'li-ti], *n.* that which is d.; d. condition or quality. DISMALLY, *adv.* in d. fashion; (*coll.*) hopelessly, utterly. DISMALNESS, *n.* condition of being d. [OFr. from L.].

DISMANTLE [dis-man'tl], *v.t.* to strip of furnishings, essential parts, equipment etc.; (*naut.*) remove the sails and rigging of a ship; (*fort.*) pull down defences and fortifications; put out of action by removing the detachable parts, take to pieces. [OFr.].

DISMAST [dis-mahst'], *v.t.* to deprive of masts, carry away the masts of a ship.

DISMAY (1) [dis-mā'], *v.t.* to fill with dismay, alarm and dishearten. DISMAY (2), *n.* surprised alarm and dejection, apprehension and discouragement. DISMAYEDNESS [dis-mād'nes], *n.* condition of being dismayed. [OFr.].

DISMEMBER [dis-mem'ber], *v.t.* to rend limb from limb, tear to pieces, cut off the limbs from; (*fig.*) partition, divide up. DISMEMBERMENT, *n.* act of dismembering; state of being dismembered. [OFr.].

DISMISS [dis-mis'], *v.t.* to send away, allow to depart; (*milit.*) allow to break ranks or organized formation upon the word of command; release from further service or attention; discharge from office or employment; cease to have in one's mind; regard lightly and take no further notice of; (*leg.*) reject, refuse to allow as valid; (*milit.*) **to be dismissed the service,** to be discharged for misconduct or incompetence. DISMISSIBLE, *adj.* liable to be dismissed. DISMISSIVE, *adj.*

relating to dismissal. DISMISSORY, *adj.* dismissive; parting. [L.].

DISMISSAL [dis-mi'sal], *n.* act of dismissing; state of being dismissed.

DISMOUNT [dis-mownt'], *v.t. and i.* to unhorse, get down or cause to get down from a horse, alight; remove or take down from the support on which it is set.

DISOBEDIENCE [dis-ō-bē'di-ens], *n.* quality of being disobedient. [OFr.].

DISOBEDIENT [dis-ō-bē'di-ent], *adj.* refusing to obey what is commanded, defying or wilfully disregarding orders. DISOBEDIENTLY, *adv.* in d. fashion. [OFr.].

DISOBEY [dis-ō-bā'], *v.t. and i.* to refuse to obey, disregard wilfully what is commanded or ordered. [Fr.].

DISOBLIGE [dis-ō-blīj'], *v.t.* to refuse to comply with or meet the wishes of, fail to do that which would help or oblige another, offend, hurt the feelings of. DISOBLIGING, *adj.* not obliging, unwilling or refusing to consult the wishes of others, unaccommodating. DISOBLIGINGLY, *adv.* in d. fashion. [Fr.].

DISORDER (1) [dis-aw'der], *n.* lack of order, untidiness, confusion; political or social disturbance or unrest, breach of the peace, conduct violating law and order; derangement in the bodily health or functions, disease, illness. DISORDER (2), *v.t.* to throw into d.; disturb the normal healthy functioning of mind and body; disarrange. DISORDERED, *adj.* out of order, upset; disarranged; thrown into d. DISORDEREDNESS, *n.* state of d.

DISORDERLY (1) [dis-aw'der-li], *adj. and adv.* confused, untidy, without order; contrary to, or violating, law and order; unruly, creating a public disturbance; **d. house,** brothel. DISORDERLY (2), *adv.* in a d. manner. DISORDERLINESS, *n.* state of being d.

DISORGANIZATION [dis-aw-ga-nī-zā'shn], *n.* act of disorganizing; state of being disorganized.

DISORGANIZE [dis-aw'ga-nīz], *v.t.* to throw into confusion, upset the normal smooth functioning of. DISORGANIZER, *n.* one who, or that which, disorganizes. [Fr.].

DISORIENTATE [dis-aw'ri-en-tāt], *v.t.* to turn away from the east; cause to lose one's sense of direction; (*fig.*) puzzle, perplex.

DISOWN [dis-ōn'], *v.t.* to renounce the ownership of, disclaim, refuse to acknowledge, deny connexion with. DISOWNMENT, *n.* act of disowning.

DISPARAGE [dis-pa'rij], *v.t.* to pour scorn on, depreciate, attempt to discredit. DISPARAGEABLE, *adj.* liable to be disparaged. DISPARAGINGLY, *adv.* in a disparaging manner.

DISPARAGEMENT [dis-pa'rij-ment], *n.* act of disparaging; that which disparages; indignity, loss of credit.

DISPARATE [dis'pa-rāt], *adj.* unequal; dissimilar, totally different, unable to be compared. [L.].

DISPARITY [dis-pa'ri-ti], *n.* inequality, dissimilarity, incongruity. [Fr.].

DISPART (1) [dis-paht'], *n.* (*gunnery*) difference between the thickness of the metal of a gun at its mouth and at its breech; sight placed at the mouth of a gun. [Unkn.].

DISPART (2), *v.t. and i.* to separate, divide, cleave; become separated, part. [L.].

DISPASSIONATE [dis-pa'shn-at], *adj.* calm, not swayed by passion; impartial, uninfluenced by personal feeling, fair and unbiased. DISPASSIONATELY, *adv.* in d. fashion.

DISPATCH (1), **DESPATCH** [dis-pach'], *v.t.* to send off; perform, finish; carry out, transact with alacrity; put to death. DISPATCH (2), DESPATCH, *n.* act of dispatching, state of being dispatched; alacrity, speedy performance; that which is dispatched, official letter, report, document or paper sent by means of a special messenger; **d. box, case,** case for carrying documents; **d. rider,** (*milit.*) special messenger, now on a motor-cycle, entrusted with dispatches. [It.].

DISPEL (*pres.pt.* **dispelling,** *pret. and p.pt.* **dispelled**) [dis-pel'], *v.t.* to drive away, banish, scatter, disperse, cause to depart and vanish. [L.].

DISPENSABLE [dis-pen'sa-bl], *adj.* able to be dispensed with; (*eccles.*) conditional upon dispensation. DISPENSABLENESS, *n.* quality of being d.

DISPENSARY [dis-pen'sa-ri], *n.* place where medicines are dispensed.

DISPENSATION [dis-pen-sā'shn], *n.* act of dispensing; that which is dispensed; (*eccles.*) system of religion, set of divine laws; divine decree, judgment

ōō is pronounced as in food; ŏŏ as in hood; th as in *think*; TH as in *that*; zh as in azure. ∼ = related to.

DSE—G*

or purpose of fate; (*R.C.*) licence from the Pope granting special exemption or privilege; permission granted by a bishop to a clergyman to enjoy certain privileges; (*leg.*) exception or mitigation of a law as a special concession to a particular person. DISPENSATIVE [dis-pen'sa-tiv], *adj.* giving or issuing d. DISPENSATIVELY, *adv.* by d. [L.].

DISPENSATORY (1) [dis-pen'sa-te-ri], *n.* book containing information about the dispensing of medicine. DISPENSATORY (2), *adj.* having power to grant dispensations. [L.].

DISPENSE [dis-pens'], *v.t. and i.* to distribute, deal out; administer; make up medicines from prescriptions; (*R.C.*) issue dispensations; **to d. with**, to do without. DISPENSING, *n.* act of one who dispenses, doing away with. [L.].

DISPENSER [dis-pen'ser], *n.* one who dispenses, one employed in making up medicines from prescriptions. [AFr.].

DISPERSAL [dis-pur'sal], *n.* act of dispersing; state of being dispersed.

DISPERSE [dis-purs'], *v.t. and i.* to scatter, cause to depart or disappear, banish; spread or place with wide gaps between, so as to cover a wide area; (*opt.*) break up (rays of light); depart, disappear in several directions. DISPERSEDLY [dis-pur'sid-li], *adv.* in a dispersed fashion. DISPERSEDNESS, *n.* condition of being dispersed. DISPERSER, *n.* one who, or that which, disperses.

DISPERSION [dis-pur'shn], *n.* act of dispersing; state of being dispersed; diffusion; (*opt.*) the angular separation of light into its different coloured rays; **the D.**, the scattering of the Jewish tribes, *esp.* after the Babylonian Captivity. [L.].

DISPERSIVE [dis-pur'siv], *adj.* tending to disperse or cause dispersion. DISPERSIVELY, *adv.* in a d. fashion.

DISPIRIT [dis-pi'rit], *v.t.* to deject, discourage, depress, dishearten. DISPIRITED, *adj.* dejected, disheartened. DISPIRITEDLY, *adv.* in a dispirited manner or mood. DISPIRITEDNESS, *n.* state of being dispirited. DISPIRITMENT, *n.* that which dispirits.

DISPITEOUS [dis-pi'ti-ŏos], *adj.* without pity, heartless.

DISPLACE [dis-plās'], *v.t.* to put out of the usual or proper place; take the place of; **displaced person,** one exiled from his native land by force of events such as war or political upheaval, *esp.* during the war of 1939–45. DISPLACEABLE, *adj.* able to be displaced.

DISPLACEMENT [dis-plās'ment], *n.* act of displacing; state of being displaced; amount displaced, volume of liquid displaced by anything immersed or floating in it, amount of water a ship displaces.

DISPLAY (1) [dis-plā'], *v.t.* to show, exhibit, spread out prominently to be seen; parade; reveal in a marked manner; (*print.*) arrange and print in a conspicuous way. DISPLAY (2), *n.* a show, exhibition, anything spread out or shown prominently, or to attract attention; art of designing exhibitions; a parade, exaggerated expression of feelings or talents in order to impress; (*print.*) arrangement of a printed page. DISPLAYER, *n.* one who, or that which, displays. [OFr. from L.].

DISPLEASE [dis-plēz'], *v.t.* to offend, make angry, annoy, vex. DISPLEASEDLY [dis-plē'zid-li], *adv.* in a displeased manner. [OFr.].

DISPLEASING [dis-plē'zing], *adj.* disagreeable, unpleasant, arousing anger, annoying. DISPLEASINGNESS, *n.* quality of being d.

DISPLEASURE (1) [dis-ple'zher], *n.* feeling of anger, mild indignation, annoyance, irritation. DISPLEASURE (2), *v.t.* (*archaic*) to displease. [OFr.].

DISPORT (1) [dis-pawt'], *v.i. and reflex.* to play, sport, amuse oneself in pleasurable recreation, frolic. DISPORT (2), *n.* (*archaic*) play, sport, recreation. DISPORTMENT, *n.* sport; diversion; amusement. [OFr.].

DISPOSAL [dis-pō'zal], *n.* act of disposing or disposing of; freedom or power to dispose of as one chooses.

DISPOSE [dis-pōz'], *v.t. and i.* to arrange, set out in order, distribute; bring about, manage, decide; turn, incline, cause to adopt (a line of action, attitude); (*archaic*) prepare, make ready for; **to d. of,** to get rid of, deal effectively with; settle; bestow, give away; sell, part with. DISPOSABLE, *adj.* able to be disposed of, free for one's disposal. DISPOSED, *adj.* arranged; (*fig.*) inclined. DISPOSEDNESS, *n.* disposition; inclination. DISPOSER, *n.* one who, or that which, disposes. DISPOSING, *n.* act of one who disposes. [Fr.].

DISPOSITION [dis-po-zi'shn], *n.* act of disposing,

way in which anything is disposed, arrangement, order, disposal; tendency; temperament, sum of qualities constituting a person's nature; (*psych.*) innate tendency to react in a specific way towards an object. DISPOSITIONAL, *adj.* relating to d. DISPOSITIONED, *adj.* temperamentally inclined. [L.].

DISPOSSESS [dis-po-zes'], *v.t.* to cause to give up, deprive or relieve of the possession of, dislodge from occupation of land etc. DISPOSSESSION, *n.* act of dispossessing; state of being dispossessed. DISPOSSESSOR, *n.* one who dispossesses. [OFr.].

DISPRAISE (1) [dis-prāz'], *v.t.* to disparage, censure, speak ill of, belittle. DISPRAISE (2), *n.* blame, disparagement. DISPRAISINGLY, *adv.* so as to d. [OFr. from L.].

DISPROOF [dis-prŏof'], *n.* act of disproving; state of being disproved; that which disproves.

DISPROPORTION (1) [dis-pro-paw'shn], *n.* ack or absence of proportion, want of symmetry. DISPROPORTION (2), *v.t.* to make or cause to be out of proportion. DISPROPORTIONALLY, *adv.* in a disproportionate manner. DISPROPORTIONED, *adj.* not proportioned; out of proportion.

DISPROPORTIONAL [dis-pro-paw'shn-al], *adj.* disproportionate. DISPROPORTIONALLY, *adv.* in a disproportionate manner.

DISPROPORTIONATE [dis-pro-paw'shn-at], *adj.* not in the proper proportion, incommensurate. DISPROPORTIONATELY, *adv.* in a d. manner; excessively.

DISPROVE [dis-prŏov'], *v.t.* to show to be false or wrong, refute. DISPROVABLE, *adj.* able to be disproved. DISPROVAL, *n.* act of disproving. DISPROVER, *n.* one who disproves. [OFr.].

DISPUTABLE [dis'pyŏo-ta-bl, dis-pyŏo'ta-bl], *adj.* open to question, capable of being argued about, doubtful. DISPUTABLENESS, *n.* condition of being d. DISPUTABLY, *adv.* in a d. fashion. [L.].

DISPUTANT (1) [dis'pyŏo-tant], *adj.* engaged in dispute or argument, disputing. DISPUTANT (2), *n.* one engaged in dispute, debater.

DISPUTATION [dis-pyŏo-tā'shn], *n.* act of disputing, debate, argument, exercise in controversy. [L.].

DISPUTATIOUS [dis-pyŏo-tā'shŏos], *adj.* contentious, fond of disputing, argumentative. DISPUTATIOUSLY, *adv.* in a d. fashion. DISPUTATIOUSNESS, *n.* quality of being d.

DISPUTE (1) [dis-pyŏot'], *v.t. and i.* to debate, discuss; question, contest, oppose, argue about; engage in controversy. DISPUTE (2), *n.* verbal argument, controversy, discussion in which opposing points of view are debated; quarrel, altercation; **in d.,** under discussion. DISPUTED, *adj.* argued about, contested, controversial. DISPUTER, *n.* one who disputes, disputant. [L.].

DISQUALIFICATION [dis-kwo-li-fi-kā'shn], *n.* act of disqualifying, state of being disqualified; that which disqualifies.

DISQUALIFY [dis-kwo'li-fi], *v.t.* to incapacitate, render unfit or ineligible; debar, eliminate on account of failure to comply with rules or conditions.

DISQUIET (1) [dis-kwi'et], *adj.* restless, uneasy, disturbed, unsettled. DISQUIET (2), *v.t.* to make uneasy, disturb, cause to be anxious, trouble, upset. DISQUIET (3), *n.* restlessness, uneasiness, anxiety. DISQUIETER, *n.* one who, or that which, disquiets. DISQUIETNESS, *n.* condition of d.

DISQUIETING [dis-kwi'et-ing], *adj.* such as to cause anxiety, disturbing. DISQUIETINGLY, *adv.* in such a way as to cause disquiet.

DISQUIETUDE [dis-kwi'i-tyŏod], *n.* want of quietude, uneasiness, anxiety, restlessness.

DISQUISITION [dis-kwi-zi'shn], *n.* systematic examination or formal investigation of a subject; learned treatise or account, lengthy discourse. DISQUISITIONAL, DISQUISITIONARY, *adj.* pertaining to, of the nature of, a d. [L.].

DISRANK [dis-rangk'], *v.t.* to reduce in rank.

DISRATE [dis-rāt'], *v.t.* (*nav.*) to reduce in rating or rank.

DISREGARD (1) [dis-ri-gahd'], *v.t.* to take no notice of, refuse to heed, ignore, pay no attention to. DISREGARD (2), *n.* indifference, lack of regard for or attention to; wilful neglect. DISREGARDFUL, *adj.* unmindful of, ignoring, neglectful, heedless. DISREGARDFULLY, *adv.* in disregardful fashion.

DISRELISH (1) [dis-re'lish], *v.t.* to dislike, show distaste for, view with aversion. DISRELISH (2), *n.* dislike, disfavour, distaste.

DISREMEMBER [dis-ri-mem'ber], *v.t.* to forget.

The accent ' after a syllable = stress (u-pon'). The mark ¯ over a vowel = length (ā in made; ō in bone).

DISREPAIR [dis-ri-pāer'], *n.* state of neglect, dilapidation, bad condition caused by lack of proper attention and repair.

DISREPUTABLE [dis-re'pyōō-ta-bl], *adj.* not reputable or respectable, degraded, discreditable. DISREPUTABLY, *adv.* in d. fashion.

DISREPUTE [dis-ri-pyōōt'], *n.* discredit, dishonour, loss of good name, ill repute.

DISRESPECT (1) [dis-ri-spekt'], *v.t.* to fail to respect, treat with d. DISRESPECT (2), *n.* lack of courtesy, impoliteness, absence of due deference or regard.

DISRESPECTABLE [dis-ri-spek'ta-bl], *adj.* not respectable.

DISRESPECTFUL [dis-ri-spekt'fōōl], *adj.* uncivil, rude, impolite, showing want of respect or proper deference. DISRESPECTFULLY, *adv.* in a d. fashion. DISRESPECTFULNESS, *n.* lack of respect.

DISROBE [dis-rōb'], *v.t. and i.* to take off the clothes or robes, undress, strip.

DISRUPT [dis-rupt'], *v.t.* to break asunder, split, shatter, break up. [L.].

DISRUPTION [dis-rup'shn], *n.* act of disrupting; condition of being disrupted.

DISRUPTIVE [dis-rup'tiv], *adj.* tending to disrupt.

DISSATISFACTION [dis-sa-tis-fak'shn], *n.* state of being dissatisfied, discontent; a cause of discontent; feeling of annoyance mingled with disappointment.

DISSATISFACTORY [dis-sa-tis-fak'te-ri], *adj.* unsatisfactory.

DISSATISFIED [dis-sa'tis-fīd], *adj.* discontented; displeased and disappointed with, not satisfied.

DISSATISFY [dis-sa'tis-fī], *v.t.* to fail to please, make discontented, displease by its unsatisfactoriness.

DISSECT [di-sekt'], *v.t.* to cut in pieces, (*anat.*) cut up systematically a dead body, plant etc., in order to examine its structure; (*fig.*) analyse minutely and critically, probe. DISSECTING, *adj.* used in dissection. DISSECTIVE, *adj.* relating to dissection. [L.].

DISSECTION [di-sek'shn], *n.* act of dissecting; that part which is dissected.

DISSECTOR [di-sek'ter], *n.* one who dissects, one employed in making anatomical dissections; a dissecting instrument.

DISSEMBLE [di-sem'bl], *v.t. and i.* to conceal, make anything seem other than it really is, hide under a false exterior; disguise or misrepresent one's real feelings, opinions, motives, plans etc., in order to deceive. DISSEMBLER, *n.* one who dissembles.

DISSEMBLING (1) [di-sem'bling], *n.* dissimulation. DISSEMBLING (2), *adj.* that dissembles, intended to deceive or mislead, hypocritical. DISSEMBLINGLY, *adv.* in a d. manner.

DISSEMINATE [di-se'mi-nāt], *v.t.* to scatter as seed; (*fig.*) spread far and wide. DISSEMINATIVE, *adj.* liable or tending to d., or become disseminated. DISSEMINATOR, *n.* one who disseminates. [L.].

DISSEMINATION [di-se-mi-nā'shn], *n.* act of disseminating. [L.].

DISSENSION [di-sen'shn], *n.* disagreement, quarrel, discord, lack of harmony or unanimity. [L.].

DISSENT (1) [di-sent'], *v.i.* to disagree; (*religion*) observe a form of worship different from that of the Established Church. DISSENT (2), *n.* difference of opinion, disagreement; (*religion*) nonconformity, refusal to accept the form of worship of the Established Church. [L.].

DISSENTER [di-sen'ter], *n.* one who dissents; one who practises a different form of worship from that of the Established Church. DISSENTERISM, *n.* the beliefs of dissenters.

DISSENTIENT (1) [di-sen'shent], *adj.* disagreeing, dissenting. DISSENTIENT (2), *n.* one who holds and expresses a different opinion. [L.].

DISSENTING [di-sen'ting], *adj.* disagreeing, holding a different opinion; nonconformist, practising a different form of worship from that of the Established Church. DISSENTINGLY, *adv.* in d. fashion.

DISSERTATION [di-ser-tā'shn], *n.* written or spoken discourse or systematic treatise upon some particular topic or subject, *esp.* a thesis written for a university degree. DISSERTATIONAL, *adj.* pertaining to a d. DISSERTATOR, *n.* one who writes or delivers a d. [L.].

DISSERVE [di-surv'], *v.t.* to do a disservice to.

DISSERVICE [di-sur'vis], *n.* ill turn; injury, harm. DISSERVICEABLE, *adj.* injurious; hurtful, harmful. DISSERVICEABLENESS, *n.* quality of being disserviceable. DISSERVICEABLY, *adv.* in a disserviceable manner.

DISSEVER [di-se'ver], *v.t.* to separate, divide, part,

cut off. DISSEVERATION, DISSEVERMENT [di-se-ve-rā'shn, di-se'ver-ment], *n.* disseverance. DISSEVERED, *adj.* separated from, cut off, divided.

DISSEVERANCE [di-se've-rans], *n.* act of dissevering; state of being dissevered. [OFr.].

DISSIDENCE [di'si-dens], *n.* disagreement, dissent. [L.].

DISSIDENT (1) [di'si-dent], *adj.* dissenting, disagreeing, differing. DISSIDENT (2), *n.* a dissentient, dissenter. [L.].

DISSIMILAR [di-si'mi-ler], *adj.* unlike, different. DISSIMILARLY, *adv.* in d. fashion.

DISSIMILARITY [di-si-mi-la'ri-ti], *n.* quality of being dissimilar; that which is dissimilar.

DISSIMILATION [di-si-mi-lā'shn], *n.* (*philol.*) the changing of one of two adjacent similar sounds in a word, so as to make them unlike. DISSIMILATE [di-si'mi-lāt], *v.i.* (*philol.*) to undergo d. [L.].

DISSIMILITUDE [di-si-mi'li-tyōōd], *n.* unlikeness; lack of resemblance. [L.].

DISSIMULATE [di-si'myōō-lāt], *v.t. and i.* to conceal or disguise the true nature of anything in order to deceive, dissemble; feign, counterfeit. DISSIMULATOR, *n.* person who dissimulates. [L.].

DISSIMULATION [di-si-myōō-lā'shn], *n.* act of dissimulating. [L.].

DISSIPATE [di'si-pāt], *v.t. and i.* to cause to disappear; squander, waste in wanton gaiety; fritter away one's talents and energies in frivolous pursuits or dissolute pleasures. DISSIPATIVE, *adj.* inclined, tending, to d. DISSIPATOR, *n.* one who dissipates. [L.].

DISSIPATED [di'si-pā-tid], *adj.* scattered; squandered; dissolute, debauched, debilitated by excessive self-indulgence.

DISSIPATION [di-si-pā'shn], *n.* act of dissipating; debauchery, licentiousness, loose and frivolous pursuits. [L.].

DISSOCIAL [dis-sō'shal], *adj.* anti-social, misanthropic. [L.].

DISSOCIATE [dis-sō'shi-āt], *v.t. and reflex.* to separate, disunite; disclaim connexion or association with; (*psych.*) cause to develop additional centres of consciousness; dissociated personality, the simultaneous existence of more than one distinct personality in the same person. DISSOCIATIVE, *adj.* tending to d. [L.].

DISSOCIATION [dis-sō-shi-ā'shn], *n.* act of dissociating, state of being dissociated; (*chem.*) the temporary reduction of a gas into its elements by heating; (*psych.*) the development or existence of a dissociated personality. [L.].

DISSOLUBILITY [di-so-lyōō-bi'li-ti], *n.* quality of being dissoluble.

DISSOLUBLE [di-so'lyōō-bl, di-so'lyōō-bl], *adj.* that may be dissolved. [L.].

DISSOLUTE [di'so-lyōōt], *adj.* loose in thought and behaviour, profligate, given to vice, debauched. DISSOLUTELY, *adv.* in a d. fashion. DISSOLUTENESS, *n.* state or quality of being d. [L.].

DISSOLUTION [di-so-lyōō'shn], *n.* act of dissolving; state of being dissolved; the breaking up of a parliament before an election; (*fig.*) death. [L.].

DISSOLVABLE [di-zol'va-bl], *adj.* capable of being dissolved.

DISSOLVE (1) [di-zolv'], *v.t. and i.* to cause to melt completely, absorb in water or other liquid; terminate, rescind (an arrangement or bond); break up, put an end to; change into a liquid state; (*cinema*) cause one sequence to fade away and another gradually to take its place; (*fig.*) vanish, melt away; disperse, come to an end. DISSOLVE (2), *n.* (*cinema*) method by which one sequence is made to fade into another. DISSOLVER, *n.* that which dissolves, a dissolvent. DISSOLVING, *adj.* melting, disintegrating, fading away. [L.].

DISSOLVENT (1) [di-zol'vent], *adj.* able to dissolve. DISSOLVENT (2), *n.* substance which has the power of dissolving. [L.].

DISSONANCE [di'so-nans], *n.* (*mus.*) a sound which by its introduction changes a concord into a discord; a discord; (*fig.*) disagreement. [L.].

DISSONANT [di'so-nant], *adj.* (*mus.*) inharmonious, harsh-sounding, discordant, unpleasant to the ear; (*fig.*) disagreeing, out of keeping with. DISSONANTLY, *adv.* in d. fashion. [L.].

DISSUADE [di-swād'], *v.t.* to advise against; persuade to refrain, discourage. [L.].

DISSUASION [di-swā'zhn], *n.* act of dissuading; advice against a thing.

DISSUASIVE [di-swā'ziv], *adj.* tending or endeavouring to dissuade. DISSUASIVELY, *adv.* in a d. manner.

ōō is pronounced as in food; ŏŏ as in hood; th as in *th*ink; TH as in *th*at; zh as in azure.   ~ = related to.

DISSYLLABIC, DISYLLABIC [di-si-la'bik], *adj.* containing two syllables.

DISSYLLABLE, DISYLLABLE [di-si'la-bl], *n.* word made up of two syllables.

DISTAFF [dis'tahf], *n.* staff on which the flax, wool or tow was formerly wound in spinning; that part of a spinning-wheel to which the flax or wool was fastened; *(fig.)* the female line; women's occupation; **d. side,** female ancestors or heirs in a pedigree. [OE.].

DISTANCE (1) [dis'tans], *n.* the intervening space between two objects or separate points; amount of such space, *esp.* when considerable; a remote point; remoteness; considerable intervening period of time; difference, degree of remoteness; *(milit.)* space between soldiers in rank, or the space between ranks; *(paint.)* the representation of different relative positions of various objects in a landscape; *(horse-racing)* arbitrary point approximately one furlong from the winning-post; *(archaic)* coldness, reserve, aloofness; **in the d.,** far away; **to keep one's d.,** to keep away from; **to keep at a d.,** to treat with reserve. DISTANCE (2), *v.t.* to separate by some d.; outstrip. [Fr. from L.].

DISTANT [dis'tant], *adj.* far off, separated or removed from by some considerable distance; remote; not closely related; cold, aloof, reserved; **d. signal,** railway signal placed well in advance of a home signal, as an indication of the way in which the latter is set. DISTANTLY, *adv.* remotely, at a distance; coldly.

DISTASTE (1) [dis-tāst'], *n.* dislike, disrelish, feeling of repugnance or disgust. DISTASTE (2), *v.t. (archaic)* to have a d. for; displease, hurt.

DISTASTEFUL [dis-tāst'fōōl], *adj.* unpleasant, offensive, disagreeable. DISTASTEFULLY, *adv.* in d. fashion. DISTASTEFULNESS, *n.* disagreeableness.

DISTEMPER (1) [dis-tem'per], *v.t.* to disorder, indispose; *(archaic)* upset, make bad-tempered. DISTEMPER (2), *n.* catarrhal disease affecting the mucous membrane of dogs; *(fig.)* disturbance, unrest, discontent; *(archaic)* indisposition. [L.].

DISTEMPER (3), *v.t.* to coat or paint with distemper. DISTEMPER (4), *n.* a special preparation of colour mixed with size or a gluey solution, applied to walls and ceilings in interior decoration; method of painting using this. [OFr.].

DISTEMPERED [dis-tem'perd], *adj.* diseased in body or mind; *(fig.)* discontented, disaffected; coated with distemper.

DISTEND [dis-tend'], *v.t. and i.* to cause to swell out, stretch out, inflate, expand in all directions; swell out; be greatly increased in size. [L.].

DISTENSIBLE [dis-ten'si-bl], *adj.* that may be distended. [L.].

DISTENSION, DISTENTION [dis-ten'shn], *n.* act of distending; state of being distended. [L.].

DISTICH [dis'tik], *n. (pros.)* a couplet, pair of lines together forming a unit. [Gk.].

DISTIL *(pres.pt.* **distilling,** *pret. and p.pt.* **distilled)** [dis-til'], *v.t. and i.* to cause to fall in drops; evaporate a liquid and cause it to condense again, extract or refine in this way; manufacture alcoholic spirits etc. by this means; *(fig.)* refine; flow slowly and gently. DISTILLABLE, *adj.* capable of being distilled; fit for distillation. DISTILLATE [dis'ti-lāt], *n.* refined substance extracted by distillation. DISTILLATORY [dis-ti'la-te-ri], *adj.* pertaining to distilling. [L.].

DISTILLATION [dis-ti-lā'shn], *n.* act of distilling; the distillate; *(fig.)* the extracted or refined essence; **fractional d.,** d. of a compound by heating gradually so that all the constituent liquids may be distilled and collected separately; **destructive d.,** d. of substances at high temperature so that the compounds are broken down. [L.].

DISTILLER [dis-ti'ler], *n.* one who distils, *esp.* alcoholic spirits.

DISTILLERY [dis-ti'le-ri], *n.* place where distilling is extensively carried on.

DISTILLING [dis-ti'ling], *n.* act or process of extracting or purifying a fluid by distillation.

DISTINCT [dis-tingkt'], *adj.* separate, individual, distinguishable; clear, plain, well defined; marked, perceptible. [L.].

DISTINCTION [dis-tingk'shn], *n.* act of distinguishing, that which distinguishes, a difference, distinctive traits of pre-eminence or merit; special award or honour as a recognition of superior merit or outstanding conduct; quality of being distinguished by something unusually good. [L.].

DISTINCTIVE [dis-tingk'tiv], *adj.* that distinguishes; peculiar, distinguishable. DISTINCTIVELY, *adv.* in a d. or distinct manner. DISTINCTIVENESS, *n.* state or quality of being d.

DISTINCTLY [dis-tingkt'li], *adv.* in a distinct manner, plainly.

DISTINCTNESS [dis-tingkt'nes], *n.* quality or condition of being distinct.

DISTINGUISH [dis-ting'gwish], *v.t. and i.* to recognize a difference between; separate or make distinct by some characteristic mark or feature; mark out as different, differentiate, perceive; *(reflex.)* become eminent, achieve prominence. [L.].

DISTINGUISHABLE [dis-ting'gwi-sha-bl], *adj.* able to be distinguished. DISTINGUISHABLY, *adv.* in d. manner.

DISTINGUISHED [dis-ting'gwisht], *adj.* marked out by some outstanding trait or feature; celebrated, famous, eminent. DISTINGUISHEDLY, *adv.* in a d. fashion.

DISTINGUISHINGLY [dis-ting'gwi-shing-li], *adv.* with distinction; so as to distinguish.

DISTINGUISHMENT [dis-ting'gwish-ment], *n.* act of distinguishing; state of being distinguished; that which distinguishes.

DISTORT [dis-tawt'], *v.t.* to twist out of the habitual or regular shape or natural position; *(fig.)* cause to seem other than it actually is, misrepresent, warp. DISTORTIVE, *adj.* producing distortion; distorted. [L.].

DISTORTION [dis-taw'shn], *n.* act of distorting; state of being distorted; that which is distorted; degree to which anything is distorted; *(radio)* change of wave form of vibrations during transmission or reception, causing lack of clearness of reception. [L.].

DISTRACT [dis-trakt'], *v.t.* to divert, turn (the attention) away from an object; prevent or hinder from concentrating upon; bewilder or perplex by conflicting alternatives or too many problems and interests; harass the mind to the state of derangement. DISTRACTER, *n.* one who, or that which, distracts. DISTRACTINGLY, *adv.* so as to d. DISTRACTIVE, *adj.* tending to d. [L.].

DISTRACTED [dis-trak'tid], *adj.* perplexed, harassed, extremely worried or disturbed, driven to a state of madness. DISTRACTEDLY, *adv.* in d. fashion. DISTRACTEDNESS, *n.* condition of being d.

DISTRACTION [dis-trak'shn], *n.* act of distracting, state of being distracted; that which distracts; diversion, relaxation from serious affairs; extreme agitation or disturbance of mind; disorder, confusion; **to d.,** to the point of madness. [L.].

DISTRAIN [dis-trān'], *v.i.* to confiscate the goods and possessions of a debtor by way of, or to secure, payment of the debt. DISTRAINABLE, *adj.* liable to be distrained upon. DISTRAINEE [dis-trā-nē'], *n.* person upon whom distraint is levied. DISTRAINER, DISTRAINOR [dis-trā'ner], *n. (leg.)* one who levies distraint. [OFr.].

DISTRAINT [dis-trānt'], *n.* act of distraining a debtor's goods and possessions. [OFr.].

DISTRAIT *(fem.* **distraite)** [dis-trā', *fem.* dis-trāt'], *adj.* absent-minded, thinking of something else. [Fr.].

DISTRAUGHT [dis-trawt'], *adj.* wildly agitated or upset, beside oneself with anxiety, fear or worry; mad. [ME. from L.].

DISTRESS (1) [dis-tres'], *n.* sorrow, grief, extreme unhappiness; state of danger, peril; source of affliction and anxiety; want of necessaries of life, severe poverty and affliction; physical exhaustion; *(leg.)* right of a creditor or landlord to distrain upon a debtor or tenant for non-payment of debt or rent; distraint. DISTRESS (2), *v.t.* to grieve, pain, cause d. to; harass; cause misery and suffering to; *(leg.)* distrain; *(reflex.)* worry. [OFr.].

DISTRESSED [dis-trest'], *adj.* suffering distress; exhausted, harassed; lacking the bare necessaries of life; **d. area,** industrial area in which there is mass unemployment and widespread poverty. DISTRESSEDNESS [dis-tre'sid-nes], *n.* state or condition of being d.

DISTRESSFUL [dis-tres'fōōl], *adj.* causing distress; showing marked signs of distress. DISTRESSFULLY, *adv.* in a d. manner.

DISTRESSING [dis-tre'sing], *adj.* causing distress, that distresses. DISTRESSINGLY, *adv.* in d. fashion.

DISTRIBUTABLE [dis-tri'byōō-ta-bl], *adj.* able to be distributed.

DISTRIBUTARY (1) [dis-tri'byōō-ta-ri], *adj.* that distributes or is distributed. DISTRIBUTARY (2), *n.*

The accent ' after a syllable = stress (u-pon'). The mark ⁻ over a vowel = length (ā in made; ō in bone).

fork of a river which does not rejoin the main stream after leaving it.

DISTRIBUTE [dis-tri'byōot], *v.t.* to divide among a number, share out, apportion; administer, deal out; give out to a number of people etc.; divide into parts or classes; spread out over a large surface; (*typ.*) separate type used for printing, and replace the letters in their proper boxes; (*log.*) employ a term in all the implications of its meaning. [L.].

DISTRIBUTER, see DISTRIBUTOR.

DISTRIBUTION [dis-tri-byōo'shn], *n.* act of distributing; state of being distributed; way in which anything is distributed; (*political economy*) the distributing of commodities among consumers; the sharing-out of profits on products among those concerned in their production. DISTRIBUTIONAL, *adj.* relating to d. [L.].

DISTRIBUTISM [dis-tri'byōo-tizm], *n.* theory that the ownership of land and capital should be vested in the greatest possible number of individuals. DISTRIBUTIST, *n.* supporter of, or believer in, d.

DISTRIBUTIVE (1) [dis-tri'byōo-tiv], *adj.* pertaining to, or engaged in, distribution; (*log., gram.*) pertaining or referring to each separate individual of a class or group. DISTRIBUTIVE (2), *n.* (*gram.*) a pronoun or adjective. DISTRIBUTIVELY, *adv.* in a d. manner, singly, individually. [L.].

DISTRIBUTOR, DISTRIBUTER [dis-tri'byōo-ter], *n.* one who, or that which, distributes; (*motoring*) that part of a magneto which distributes the current to the plugs.

DISTRICT [dis'trikt], *n.* a limited area of land under the management and authority of an official person or administrative body; region, particular part of a country, city etc., locality; **D. Commissioner**, magistrate or government official exercising semi-judicial authority in India or a British Crown Colony; **d. visitor**, church worker helping a clergyman in a particular area in his parish. [MedL.].

DISTRUST (1) [dis-trust'], *v.t.* to be unable to trust, place no reliance or belief in, suspect. DISTRUST (2), *n.* doubt, want of confidence or trust in, suspicion.

DISTRUSTFUL [dis-trust'fool], *adj.* having no trust in, suspicious, doubtful, provoking or feeling distrust for. DISTRUSTFULLY, *adv.* in a d. fashion.

DISTURB [dis-turb'], *v.t.* to stir from a state of rest or tranquillity, ruffle the calmness of; cause to alter its position or condition; trouble, disquiet, make uneasy; interrupt, upset, unsettle. DISTURBANT, DISTURBING, *adj.* that disturbs, unsettling, upsetting. DISTURBER, *n.* one who, or that which, disturbs. [L.].

DISTURBANCE [dis-tur'bans], *n.* act of disturbing; that which disturbs; anything disturbed; row, disorder, uproar; breach of the peace; (*leg.*) the hindering or disquieting of a person in the lawful and peaceable enjoyment of his rights.

DISTURBED [dis-turbd'], *adj.* agitated, upset; moved or altered from its position or normal condition; ruffled; made uneasy, disquieted.

DISULPHATE [di-sul'fāt], *n.* (*chem.*) substance containing two equivalents of sulphuric acid with one of the base.

DISULPHIDE [di-sul'fīd], *n.* (*chem.*) compound in which two atoms of sulphur are combined with another element or radical.

DISUNION [dis-yōo'nyun], *n.* severance, the breaking of a union, rupture; dissension, lack of concord.

DISUNITE [dis-yōo-nīt'], *v.t. and i.* to separate, part; break the union or bond between; become separate.

DISUNITY [dis-yōo'ni-ti], *n.* lack of unity.

DISUSE (1) [dis-yōoz'], *v.t.* to cease to use. DISUSE (2) [dis-yōos'], *n.* state of being no longer in use, discontinuance of a custom or practice, lack of use. DISUSED [dis-yōozd'], *adj.* no longer used, obsolete.

DISYLLABIC, see DISSYLLABIC.

DISYLLABLE, see DISSYLLABLE.

DITAL [di'tal], *n.* thumb-key on stringed plucked instruments such as the guitar. [It.].

DITCH (1) [dich], *n.* long, narrow trench round a fortified place for purposes of defence; long narrow channel dug as a watercourse or an open drain; any natural channel by the side of a road that drains water. DITCH (2), *v.t. and i.* to construct or repair ditches; (*coll.*) drive into a d. DITCHING, *n.* art of digging and repairing ditches. [OE.].

DITCHER [di'cher], *n.* one who constructs or repairs ditches.

DITCH-WATER [dich'waw-ter], *n.* stagnant water; **dull as d.**, (*coll.*) extremely dull and boring.

DITHEISM [di'thē-izm], *n.* belief in the existence of two gods or supreme powers, *esp.* belief in good and evil as the two guiding forces. DITHEIST, *n.* one who believes in d. DITHEISTIC(AL) [di-thē-is'tik(-al)], *adj.* relating to d.

DITHER (1) [di'тнer], *v.i.* (*coll.*) to shiver, shake or quiver continually, tremble violently, quake; hesitate. DITHER (2), *n.* (*coll.*) state of trembling excitement, *esp.* **all of a d.**

DITHYRAMB [di'thi-ram], *n.* hymn in honour of Bacchus, written in an extravagantly rhapsodical style; ode or chant of a similar boisterous character. DITHYRAMBIC [di-thi-ram'bik], *adj.* of the nature of a d.; wild, impetuous, vehement. DITHYRAMBIC-ALLY, *adv.* in the manner of a d., ecstatically. [Gk.].

DITONE [di'tōn], *n.* (*mus.*) a major third, interval consisting of two tones. [Gk.].

DITTANY [di'ta-ni], *n.* (*bot.*) aromatic plant yielding a sweet-scented oil. [OFr. from Gk.].

DITTO [di'tō], *n.* (contracted into *do.*), that which has been said before; the same thing. [It.].

DITTY [di'ti], *n.* short simple song or poem to be sung. [OFr.].

DITTY-BOX [di'ti-boks], *n.* small box in which sailors keep various personal articles. [Unkn.].

DIURESIS [di-yōo-rē'sis], *n.* (*med.*) excessive discharge of urine. [Gk.].

DIURETIC (1) [di-yōo-re'tik], *adj.* stimulating urination or excretion. DIURETIC (2), *n.* a d. medicine. [Gk.].

DIURNAL (1) [di-ur'nal], *adj.* belonging to the daytime; daily, performed in a day, occurring or recurring each day. DIURNAL (2), *n.* (*eccles.*) service-book containing the offices for the day. DIURNALLY, *adv.* daily; every day.

DIVA [dē'va], *n.* prima donna, leading woman singer. [It.].

DIVAGATE [di'va-gāt], *v.i.* to wander about; digress, stray, ramble. DIVAGATION [di-va-gā'shn], *n.* act of divagating. [L.].

DIVALENT [di-vā'lent], *adj.* (*chem.*) combining with two atoms of a radical, bivalent.

DIVAN [di-van'], *n.* long, low backless couch or raised seat fitted with cushions; Oriental council of state (*esp.* Turkish); chamber in which the former Turkish State Council met; smoking-room; cigar shop. [Pers.].

DIVARICATE (1) [di-va'ri-kāt], *v.t. and i.* to fork, split up into branches, branch off at an angle; spread apart, open. DIVARICATE (2), *adj.* (*bot.*) branching off at a wide angle. DIVARICATION [di-va-ri-kā'shn], *n.* act of divaricating; that which divaricates; state of being divaricated; point of forking. [L.].

DIVE (1) [div], *v.i.* to perform a dive or series of dives; sink down under water suddenly when swimming; go under water in a specially constructed watertight suit etc.; swoop down suddenly in the air from a height; hurl oneself at, dart down or into; thrust one's hand rapidly into a receptacle; (*fig.*) study rapidly and intensely; submerge. DIVE (2), *n.* a plunge head first into water; sudden rush; almost vertical descent made by an aircraft; the submerging of a submarine; (*coll.*) underground place of refreshment; basement or cellar in which drinking, singing etc. are carried on. [OE.].

DIVE-BOMBER [div'bo-mer], *n.* aeroplane designed to dive low in order to drop its bombs. DIVE-BOMB, *v.t.* to attack by d.

DIVER [di'ver], *n.* one who dives, *esp.* one who performs under-water tasks in a specially made diving-dress etc.; one of several species of water-birds that dive.

DIVERGE [di-vurj'], *v.i.* to branch off along different courses at a particular point, proceed in different directions; separate; deviate; vary, differ; depart from the stock form. [L.].

DIVERGENCE [di-vur'jens], *n.* act of diverging; amount anything diverges.

DIVERGENCY [di-vur'jen-si], *n.* divergence.

DIVERGENT [di-vur'jent], *adj.* branching off in different directions, deviating, proceeding along different courses, forking in widening branches.

DIVERS [di'verz], *adj.* (*archaic*) different, various, several, sundry. [OFr.].

DIVERSE [di-vurs', di-vurs'], *adj.* different, varied, unlike. DIVERSELY, *adv.* in d. fashion.

DIVERSIFICATION [di-ver-si-fi-kā'shn], *n.* act of diversifying; state of being diversified.

DIVERSIFORM [di-vur'si-fawm], *adj.* of various forms or shapes.

DIVERSIFY [di-vur'si-fi], *v.t.* to make different, give variety to. DIVERSIFIABLE [di-ver-si-fī′a-bl], *adj.* capable of being diversified.

DIVERSION [di-vur′shn], *n.* act of diverting; that which diverts or distracts the attention pleasantly, relaxation, amusement, recreation; (*milit.*) minor attack intended to divert an enemy from the point where the principal attack is to be made. DIVERSIONIST, *n.* one who attempts to create confusion behind the enemy's lines by sabotage etc. when an attack is in progress. [MedL.].

DIVERSITY [di-vur′si-ti], *n.* considerable difference or differences, variety, unlikeness, state of being diverse. [L.].

DIVERT [di-vurt′], *v.t.* to turn away from a fixed course, change the direction of; cause to move, or be employed in a different way; direct the attention away from, distract the thoughts; entertain, engage the mind or attention in pleasurable relaxation or recreation. [L.].

DIVERTIMENTO [di-ver-ti-men′tō], *n.* (*mus.*) short, light composition, vocal or instrumental. [It.].

DIVERTING [di-vur′ting], *adj.* amusing, entertaining. DIVERTINGLY, *adv.* in d. fashion.

DIVERTISSEMENT [di-vāer′tēs-mah(ng)], *n.* short ballet or other entertainment, often introduced between the acts of a longer piece. [Fr.].

DIVEST [di-vest′, di-vest′], *v.t.* to strip, remove, rid of; dispossess, deprive of; (*leg.*) take away; (*reflex.*) shed; give up. DIVESTIBLE, *adj.* able to be divested. DIVESTITURE, DIVESTMENT, DIVESTURE, *n.* act of divesting; state of being divested; (*leg.*) surrender of property. [OFr.].

DIVET, see DIVOT.

DIVI, DIVVY [di′vi], *n.* (*slang*) a dividend paid to shareholders etc. [~DIVIDEND].

DIVIDE (1) [di-vīd′], *v.t.* to split up or mark out into parts; separate into different groups, classify; share out; split up into rival factions, make discordant or at variance; waver between two alternatives; cut off from, cause to be separated from, part; take or ask for a vote on a motion under discussion; (*math.*) find out how many times a number is contained in another; *v.i.* to become split up or separated, part; separate to take a vote on a motion; (*math.*) be contained an exact number of times in another number. DIVIDE (2), *n.* that which divides; watershed, dividing ridge. DIVIDABLE, *adj.* capable of being divided. [L.].

DIVIDED [di-vī′did], *adj.* separated or split up into parts; parted, disunited, at variance; **d. consonant,** (*phon.*) consonant formed by the tongue touching the palate in such a way that the flow of air passes on either side of the tongue. DIVIDEDLY, *adv.* separately.

DIVIDEND [di′vi-dend], *n.* profits of a limited company proportionally divided among, and paid at certain periods to, proprietors and holders of shares; share assigned to creditors out of the estate of a bankrupt; discount on purchases made, paid to members of a co-operative society out of trading profits; (*arith.*) the number to be divided by another. [L.].

DIVIDER [di-vī′der], *n.* one who, or that which, divides; (*pl.*) pair of compasses with steel points for marking or measuring off small spaces.

DIVIDING [di-vī′ding], *adj.* that divides.

DIVIDUAL [di-vi′dyŏō-al], *adj.* separate; shared or divided in common with others, divisible. DIVIDUALLY, *adj.* separately.

DIVINATION [di-vi-nā′shn], *n.* act of divining; prophecy, prediction; inspired guesswork. [L.].

DIVINE (1) [di-vin′], *adj.* belonging to God, or a god; issuing from, or conferred by, God; as befits a god or God; heavenly, godlike; (*coll.*) wonderful, marvellous, superb. DIVINE (2), *n.* theologian, one versed in divinity; (*coll.*) clergyman. DIVINE (3), *v.t. and i.* to conjecture or discover by intuition, guess, foretell; foretell the future or make a revelation or decision by supernatural aid; imagine. DIVINELY, *adv.* in d. fashion. DIVINENESS, *n.* quality of being d. [L.].

DIVINER [di-vī′ner], *n.* one who divines, *esp.* one who reveals the presence of subterranean sources of water, oil etc. by means of a twig or rod held in the hand.

DIVING [di′ving], *n.* act of making a dive or dives; performance of under-water work in special watertight suits or compartments.

DIVING-BELL [di′ving-bel], *n.* hollow vessel in which persons may be lowered into, and remain under, water for some time.

DIVING-BOARD [di′ving-bawd], *n.* a plank, projecting over the water, from which swimmers dive.

DIVING-DRESS [di′ving-dres], *n.* special, waterproof dress worn by divers.

DIVINING-ROD [di-vī′ning-rod], *n.* forked twig held in the hands to detect the presence of underground sources of water, oil etc.

DIVINITY [di-vi′ni-ti], *n.* state or quality of being divine; divine nature, force or power; divine being, god; study of theology; **d. calf,** (*bookbinding*) darkbrown calf leather. [L.].

DIVISIBLE [di-vi′zi-bl], *adj.* capable of division; (*math.*) capable of being divided exactly. DIVISIBILITY, DIVISIBLENESS [di-vi-zi-bi′li-ti, di-vi′zibl-nes], *n.* quality of being d. DIVISIBLY, *adv.* in a d. fashion.

DIVISION [di-vi′zhn], *n.* act of dividing, state of being divided; that which divides, a partition; difference, dissension, discord; (*parl.*) separation of the members of a legislative or deliberative assembly for the purpose of voting, act of taking a vote on a motion; that which is divided, a portion; political, social, administrative etc. unit; class, separate group, special department etc.; (*milit.*) the smallest formation containing all branches of troops capable of independent action, about 10,000 to 15,000 men; (*nav.*) part of a fleet, usually under a commander. DIVISIONAL, *adj.* pertaining to a d., belonging to a d., dividing. [L.].

DIVISIVE [di-vī′siv], *adj.* able to make divisions, distinctions etc.; tending to produce dissension.

DIVISOR [di-vī′zer], *n.* (*arith.*) the number by which another is divided; a factor. [L.].

DIVORCE (1) [di-vaws′], *n.* legal dissolution of marriage; (*fig.*) separation or disunion, breaking of connexion between. DIVORCE (2), *v.t.* to obtain a d. from; (*fig.*) disunite, separate, break the connexion between. DIVORCEABLE, *adj.* capable of being divorced. DIVORCEE [di-vaw-sē′], *n.* divorced person. DIVORCEMENT, *n.* act or process of divorcing, state of being divorced. DIVORCER, *n.* one who divorces. DIVORCIVE, *adj.* tending to, or causing, d. [L.].

DIVOT, DIVET [di′vot], *n.* sod, piece of turf used for thatching or as fuel; (*golf*) piece of turf sometimes dislodged by the head of a golf-club in hitting the ball. [Unkn.].

DIVULGE [di-vulj′], *v.t.* to reveal, tell or make known (a secret etc.); disclose. DIVULGEMENT, DIVULGENCE, *n.* act of divulging. DIVULGER, *n.* one who divulges. [L.].

DIVULSION [di-vul′shn], *n.* act of tearing or pulling apart; state of being torn apart. [L.].

DIVVY, see DIVI.

DIXIE [dik′si], *n.* (*coll.*) camp-kettle or stew-pot. [Hind.].

DIZZY (1) [di′zi], *adj.* giddy, with the head reeling, attacked by vertigo; bewildered, dazed, confused in mind, causing giddiness. DIZZY (2), *v.t.* to make d., confuse. DIZZILY, *adv.* in a d. manner. DIZZINESS, *n.* state of being d. DIZZYING, *adj.* whirling round; making d. [OE.].

DO (1), **DOH** [dō], *n.* (*mus.*) the first note in the scale in the tonic sol-fa method of reading or singing music.

DO (2) (*pret.* **did,** *p.pt.* **done**) [dōō], *v.t.* to perform; be occupied with, engaged upon; carry (an action, task or activity) to completion, perform as work, carry into effect (instructions, mode of conduct etc.); affect (something) in some way, perform the work connected with, work upon, *esp.* cook or prepare food; make use of, employ; offer, bestow; bring to disaster, ruin; deceive, cheat; visit as a tourist, see the sights of; act (a play or rôle); meet the needs or requirements of; travel or traverse (a distance or at a given speed); (*p.pt.*) complete, finish; cause the undoing, defeat or ruin of; (*coll.*) entertain, treat; (*slang*) serve (a sentence); put, bring to pass, have; *v.i.* to act or behave; succeed, prosper; be in a state or condition (of health or prosperity); be suitable, suffice; *also used as an auxiliary verb in negative and interrogative sentences to indicate an urgent request or command, express emphasis, avoid the repetition of a verb, and for inversion;* **well-to-d.,** prosperous, rich; **to d. away with,** to destroy, abolish; **to d. down,** to get the better of, cheat; **to d. for,** (*coll.*) to kill; look after, attend to personally; **to d. in,** (*coll.*) to murder, kill; **to d. in the eye,** (*coll.*) to outwit; **to d. out, to** clean and make tidy; **to d. out of,** to prevent from getting, cheat of; **to d. time,** (*slang*) to be in prison; **to d. up,** to fasten; decorate anew, adorn; **to d. with,** to tolerate, put up with; be in need of, feel ready for; manage with; **to have to d. with,** to have dealings with, be related to or concerned with;

---

to d. without, to forgo; nothing doing, (coll.) certainly not. DO-ALL, person who attends to everything. DO (3), n. (coll.) a social entertainment, esp. on a rather elaborate scale; business, affair, event; (slang) fraud, swindle. [OE.].

DO (4), short form of DITTO.

DOBBIN [do'bin], n. pet name for a horse. [~ROBIN].

DOCILE [dō'sīl], adj. easily managed, tractable, readily submissive to authority; eager to learn. DOCILELY, adv. in a d. manner. [L.].

DOCILITY [dō-sī'li-ti], n. quality of being docile. [L.].

DOCK (1) [dok], n. (bot.) name of several species of coarse plants of the genus Rumex. [OE.].

DOCK (2), n. the short fleshy part of an animal's tail; piece of leather harness over the stump of a horse's tail when cut short. DOCK (3), v.t. to cut off, shorten (esp. a tail); curtail, cut down. [OIcel.].

DOCK (4), n. enclosed place in a criminal court where the prisoner stands for trial; enclosure where ships are loaded, unloaded or repaired; (theatre) storage for scenery at the side of the stage; dry or graving docks, docks from which the water can be pumped, leaving the ship on a row of keel blocks; floating docks, docks with hollow walls which can be raised or sunk, and with pumps to remove the water as in a dry dock. DOCK (5), v.t. and i. to enter or cause to enter a d. DOCKAGE, n. d. accommodation for a ship; dues payable for this. [Uncert.].

DOCKER [do'ker], n. a dock worker.

DOCKET (1) [do'kit], n. (leg.) register or list of legal judgments; summarized account of the contents at the foot of letters patent for the Great Seal; list of court cases and litigants; label tied to goods with directions for delivery or particulars of the contents; memorandum attached to a document, summarizing its contents; ticket or coupon authorizing purchase etc. DOCKET (2), v.t. to make an abstract of for entry in a book, enter on a d., write out a d. or summary of contents and affix it to a letter or parcel. [ME.].

DOCK-MASTER [dok'mahs-ter], n. overseer of a dock.

DOCKSIDE (1) [dok'sīd], n. the side of a dock. DOCKSIDE (2), adj. situated, employed, beside a dock.

DOCKYARD [dok'yahd], n. establishment along a river bank or sea coast, fully equipped for the repairing and building of ships.

DOCTOR (1) [dok'ter], n. (archaic) teacher, instructor, learned man, esp. one of the learned Fathers of the Church, medieval philosopher; holder of the highest degree in any faculty of a university; (pop.) physician or surgeon; mechanical contrivance for adjusting or regulating; fish of the genus Acanthurus; artificial fly used for fishing; (naut.) ship's cook; Doctors' Commons, originally the dining-hall, buildings and college of the Doctors of Civil Law in London and later the seat of a number of law courts. DOCTOR (2), v.t. to treat medically; repair; adulterate, tamper with, esp. by adding a drug; falsify. DOCTORAL, adj. pertaining to a d. [L.].

DOCTORATE [dok'te-rat], n. the degree of a doctor.

DOCTORING [dok'te-ring], n. medical treatment; adulteration of liquids, falsification of facts.

DOCTORSHIP [dok'ter-ship], n. the degree of a doctor, status of a doctor; great learning or scholarship; medical skill or care.

DOCTRINAIRE (1) [dok-tri-nãer'], n. unpractical theorist; (hist.) one of a group of French politicians who in 1816 wished to set up a constitutional government in France. DOCTRINAIRE (2), adj. seeking to apply theories irrespective of their practicability. DOCTRINARIANISM, n. programme of the Doctrinaires; unpractical theorizing. [Fr.].

DOCTRINAL [dok-tri'nal, dok'tri-nal], adj. pertaining to doctrine. DOCTRINALLY, adv. in a d. fashion.

DOCTRINE [dok'trin], n. a thing taught, teaching; a belief, principle taught as true; set of accepted beliefs or principles in religion, politics or science. DOCTRINISM, n. obstinate belief in a particular d. DOCTRINIST, n. one who wholeheartedly maintains a certain d. [L.].

DOCUMENT (1) [do'kyōō-ment], n. any writing or inscription, esp. one which may be used to verify or establish fact. DOCUMENT (2), v.t. to furnish or support with evidence from documents. DOCUMENTAL [do-kyōō-men'tal], adj. relating to documents. [L.].

DOCUMENTARY [do-kyōō-men'ta-ri], adj. pertaining to or supported by documents; d. film, short

film concerned solely with giving a realistic, accurate picture of some aspect of life and work or of a technical process.

DOCUMENTATION [do-kyōō-men-tā'shn], n. act of documenting, state of being documented. [MedL.].

DODDER (1) [do'der], n. (bot.) leafless parasitic plant of the genus Cuscuta. [ME.].

DODDER (2), v.i. to totter, tremble, move in an unsteady fashion like one in a state of extreme mental or physical decay. DODDERER, n. one who dodders, senile semi-invalid. DODDERING, adj. tottering and foolish with extreme age or infirmity. DODDERY, adj. shaky, unsteady with age or infirmity; (fig.) foolish. [Uncert.].

DODDERED [do'derd], adj. (of a tree) having the top lopped off, decayed through age. [ME.].

DODECA-, pref. twelve. [Gk.].

DODECAGON [dō-de'ka-gon], n. polygon with twelve equal sides and angles. [Gk.].

DODECAHEDRON [dō-de-ka-hē'dron], n. a regular solid having twelve equal pentagonal bases. DODECAHEDRAL, adj. having twelve equal sides.

DODECANE [dō'de-kān], n. (chem.) a hydrocarbon of the paraffin group.

DODECASYLLABLE [dō-de-ka-si'la-bl], n. verse or word containing twelve syllables.

DODGE (1) [doj], v.t. and i. to get out of the way of, elude by sudden rapid swerves or twists of the body; shirk or escape by artifices or mean ingenious tricks; twist and turn about to evade something; shuffle, quibble; shirk; (in change-ringing, of a bell) have its normal position in a chime transposed. DODGE (2), n. a sudden evasive movement; (coll.) trick, deception, quibble, plan, tip; (slang) gadget. DODGY, adj. full of dodges, artful, dishonest. [Unkn.].

DODGER [do'jer], n. one who dodges; evasive rogue; (naut.) sheltering screen on the bridge of a ship.

DODO [dō'dō], n. extinct flightless pigeon of Mauritius. [Portug.].

DOE [dō], n. female of the fallow deer, the rabbit and certain other animals. [OE.].

DOER [dōō'er], n. one who does; man of action.

DOES [duz], third person sg. pres. ind. of DO.

DOESKIN [dō'skin], n. the skin of a doe; soft leather made from this; compact twilled woollen cloth.

DOFF [dof], v.t. to take off, raise (the hat), divest oneself of. [DO and OFF].

DOG (1) [dog], n. carnivorous quadruped of the genus Canis, existing in both a domesticated and wild state, often used to denote the male of this species and of certain similar animals; (fig.) worthless rogue; (coll.) fellow, gay young man about town; (astron.) one of the two constellations Canis major or minor; (pl.) pair of andirons used to support logs on a fire; mechanical grappling or clutching contrivance; to go to the dogs, to sink into degeneracy, go to ruin; to put on d., (slang) to affect superior airs; to rain cats and dogs, to rain extremely heavily; to throw to the dogs, to cast off as useless; to lead a d.'s life, to lead a miserable, perpetually harassed existence; to turn d. on, to turn against; d. in the manger, one who does not use a thing himself but prevents others from doing so; hot d., (U.S. slang) sandwich containing hot sausage-meat. DOG (2), v.t. to follow or attend constantly and closely. [OE.].

DOGCART [dog'kaht], n. light, high, two- or four-wheeled vehicle, drawn by one horse, for two persons, originally with a box below for dogs.

DOG-COLLAR [dog'ko-ler], n. collar for a dog; (coll.) high, stiff, white collar fastening at the back, as worn by clerics.

DOG-DAYS [dog'dāz], n. † period of forty days at the time when Sirius, the Dog-star, rises and sets with the sun; this period as comprising the hottest part of the year, during July and August.

DOGE [dōj], n. (hist.) chief magistrate of Venice and Genoa. [It. from L.].

DOG-EARED [dog'ēerd], adj. (of a book etc.) having the corners of the leaves turned down.

DOG FANCIER [dog'fan-si-er], n. connoisseur of dogs, one who breeds and rears dogs for sale.

DOG FIGHT [dog'fit], n. (aeron.) all-in battle between fighter planes.

DOGFISH [dog'fish], n. variety of small shark.

DOG-FOX [dog'foks], n. male fox.

DOGGED [do'gid], adj. determined, resolute, tenacious; (archaic) sullen, surly. DOGGEDLY, adv. in a d. fashion. DOGGEDNESS, n. quality of being d.

DOGGEREL (1) [do'ge-rel], n. fluent but feeble verse,

burlesque. DOGGEREL (2), *adj.* (of verse) trivial, inferior. [Unkn.].

DOGGINESS [do'gi-nes], *n.* quality of resembling a dog or being fond of dogs.

DOGGO [do'gō], *adv.* (*coll.*) in such a manner as to escape attention. [Unkn.].

DOGGONE [dog-gon'], *adj.* (*U.S. slang*) confounded, wretched. [~GOD DAMNED].

DOG-GRASS [dog'grahs], *n.* (*bot.*) couch-grass.

DOGGY [do'gi], *adj.* like a dog, devoted to dogs.

DOG-LATIN [dog'la-tin], *n.* colloquial, non-classical, barbarous Latin.

DOG-LEG [dog'leg], *adj.* having an angle in the middle, like a dog's hind leg; *esp.* of a hole in golf.

DOGMA [dog'mah], *n.* principle or maxim which must not be disputed; that body of doctrine set forth by the Church as unquestionably true; opinions or tenets propounded by a school of thought and accepted by its members. [Gk.].

DOGMATIC(AL) [dog-ma'tik(-al)], *adj.* pertaining to religious dogma; dictatorial, admitting no argument. DOGMATICALLY, *adv.* in a d. manner; arrogantly. DOGMATICALNESS, *n.* quality of being d.; positiveness. [Gk.].

DOGMATICS [dog-ma'tiks], *n.*(*pl.*) study of religious dogma.

DOGMATISM [dog'ma-tizm], *n.* act of dogmatizing; dogmatic state of mind, excessive positiveness of opinion; (*philos.*) system of philosophy based entirely upon pure reason divorced from objective observation.

DOGMATIST [dog'ma-tist], *n.* person who expresses opinions and beliefs in a dogmatic way; philosopher who believes in dogmatism; student or strong supporter of dogma.

DOGMATIZE [dog'ma-tīz], *v.t. and i.* to assert some opinion in an extremely emphatic manner as though admitting no doubt or question, express a belief in an imperious way; advance or formulate as a dogma. DOGMATIZER, *n.* one who dogmatizes.

DOG-ROSE [dog'rōz], *n.* the wild rose.

DOG'S BODY [dogz'bo-di], *n.* (*slang*) inferior underling, stooge.

DOG'S EAR [dogz'ēer], *n.* the turned-down, wrinkled corner of a leaf in a book.

DOGSHORES [dog'shawz], *n.*(*pl.*) pieces of wood used as a brake for a ship ready to be launched from a building slip, and knocked away at the launching.

DOGSKIN [dog'skin], *n.* the skin of a dog, soft leather made from it or sheepskin.

DOG'S NOSE [dogz'nōz], *n.* mixture of beer and gin.

DOG-STAR [dog'stah(r)], *n.* Sirius, the brightest of the stars (in the constellation *Canis major*).

DOG'S-TOOTH VIOLET [dogz-tŏŏth-vī'o-let], *n.* plant of the genus *Erythronium.*

DOG-TIRED [dog-tīerd'], *adj.* tired out.

DOG-TOOTH [dog'tŏŏth], *n.* canine tooth, a sharp-pointed tooth growing between the incisors and premolars; (*arch.*) moulding consisting of four roughly triangular leaves meeting at a raised point in the centre, in the form of a series of raised points, much used in early medieval architecture; **d. spar**, variety of mineral calcium carbonate having pointed, tooth-like crystals.

DOG-VIOLET [dog'vī-o-let], *n.* the wild, scentless violet.

DOG-WATCH [dog'woch], *n.* (*naut.*) either of two watches, from 4 to 6 p.m. and from 6 to 8 p.m.

DOGWOOD [dog'wŏŏd], *n.* tree of the genus *Cornus.*

DOH [dō], *n.* the first note in the tonic sol-fa scale.

DOILY, DOYLEY [doi'li], *n.* small ornamental piece of cloth etc. placed on plates, cruet stands etc. [*Doyley*, inventor].

DOING [dŏŏ'ing], *n.* (*coll.*) a scolding; (*pl.*) activities, things done; (*slang*) objects of any kind.

DOIT [doit], *n.* (*archaic*) small valueless coin. [Du.].

DOITED [doi'tid], *adj.* (*Scots.*) foolish, mentally deranged. [Unkn.].

DOLCE [dol'chi], *adv.* (*mus.*) softly, sweetly and tenderly. [It.].

DOLDRUMS [dol'drumz], *n.* (*naut.*) a tropical zone between the regions of the trade-winds, where calms and variable winds prevail; (*fig.*) depression, the dumps. [Uncert.].

DOLE (1) [dōl], *n.* (*archaic*) sorrow, lamentation. [L.].

DOLE (2), *n.* (*archaic*) portion, share; fate, destiny; something distributed, *esp.* as a charitable gift in scanty portions; weekly payment made for a limited period to certain classes of unemployed from funds contributed by the workman, his employer and the

state; (*coll.*) any system of state-sponsored unemployment assistance; **to be on the d.**, to be out of work and living on unemployment insurance payments. DOLE (3), *v.t.* to deal out in small portions, distribute sparingly. [OE.].

DOLEFUL [dōl'fŏŏl], *adj.* sad, sorrowful, melancholy. DOLEFULLY, *adv.* in a d. fashion. DOLEFULNESS, *n.* state of being d. [DOLE (1) and FULL].

DOLICHOCEPHALIC [do-li-kō-se-fa'lik], *adj.* long-headed, having a skull whose length is at least one-fifth greater than its breadth. [Gk.].

DOLL (1) [dol], *n.* child's toy representing a human or animal figure; (*coll.*) girl or woman possessing an attractive appearance and a vacuous mind. DOLL (2), *v.t. and reflex.* (*slang*) to dress in one's best or smartest clothes (used generally with *up*). [Pet form of *Dorothy*].

DOLLAR [do'ler], *n.* silver or gold coin of the value of 100 cents, which is the monetary unit in U.S.A., Canada etc.; a currency note of this value; silver coins of approximately equal value current in Latin America, China and other countries; (*slang*) five shillings. [Germ.].

DOLLOP [do'lop], *n.* (*coll.*) large quantity or lump, a big, shapeless mass. [Unkn.].

DOLL'S HOUSE [dolz'hows], *n.* toy house suitable for dolls.

DOLLY (1) [do'li], *n.* doll; wooden implement used for beating and stirring clothes in a wash-tub; apparatus for stirring and washing ore; (*eng.*) tapering steel bar having a hollow pointed end shaped to fit the head of a rivet, and held over the rivet while it is fastened; **d. shop**, marine dealer's store, low pawnshop; **d. tub**, wash-tub. DOLLY (2), *v.t.* to stir clothes with a d.

DOLMAN [dol'man], *n.* long, narrow-sleeved robe worn formerly by the Turks; loose jacket with cape-like sleeves formerly worn by ladies; jacket of a hussar's uniform, worn like a cape. [Turk.].

DOLMEN [dol'men], *n.* cromlech, prehistoric stone chamber consisting of a large unhewn stone resting on top of several vertical stones. [Fr. from Corn.].

DOLOROUS [do'le-rŏŏs], *adj.* distressing, sad, mournful. DOLOROUSLY, *adv.* in a d. manner. DOLOROUSNESS, *n.* quality of being d. [OFr.].

DOLOUR [do'ler], *n.* anguish, sorrow. [L.].

DOLPHIN [dol'fin], *n.* cetaceous animal of the genus *Delphinus*; name applied to the fish dorado, noted for its rapid changes of colour just before death; name of a northern constellation; various contrivances similar to a dolphin in shape, as a mooring-post or buoy; **d. striker**, (*naut.*) vertical spar below the bowsprit. DOLPHIN-FLY, louse harmful to beans. [Gk.].

DOLT [dōlt], *n.* blockhead. DOLTISH, *adj.* foolish, dull, stupid. DOLTISHLY, *adv.* in a doltish fashion. DOLTISHNESS, *n.* stupidity. [ME.].

DOM [dom], *n.* title given to certain dignitaries of the Roman Catholic Church, and Benedictine and Carthusian monks. [Portug. from L.].

DOMAIN [dō-mān'], *n.* land under the rule or ownership of some particular person; territory, landed estates; dominions; (*fig.*) sphere of knowledge, work, influence etc. DOMANIAL [dō-mā'ni-al], *adj.* pertaining to domains. [Fr. from L.].

DOME (1) [dōm], *n.* rounded roof in the form of a hemisphere; anything having this shape; (*poet.*) large imposing building. DOME (2), *v.t.* to provide with a d.-shaped roof, form into the shape of a d.; **d. fastener**, a press-stud. DOMELIKE, *adj.* d.-shaped. DOME-SHAPED, *adj.* having the shape of a d.; resembling a d. [L.].

DOMESDAY [dŏŏmz'dā], *n.* doomsday; **D. Book**, survey of the manors of England originally compiled in the reign of William I. [OE.].

DOMESTIC (1) [dō-mes'tik], *adj.* pertaining to the home, family, or household; fond of home; tame; native, not foreign; internal, affecting or pertaining to one's own country. DOMESTIC (2), *n.* servant in a household. [L.].

DOMESTICATE [dō-mes'ti-kāt], *v.t.* to cause to settle down into domestic life, make interested in household life; accustom to life with human beings, tame, bring into the service of man. DOMESTICABLE, *adj.* able to be domesticated. DOMESTICATION [dō-mes-ti-kā'shn], *n.* act of domesticating, condition of being domesticated. [L.].

DOMESTICITY [dō-mes-ti'si-ti, do-mes-ti'si-ti], *n.* home life and the love of it.

DOMICILE (1) [do'mi-sīl], *n.* customary residence, home; (*leg.*) place recognized for official purposes as one's permanent residence; fact of legally residing; (*comm.*) place where a bill of exchange may be paid. DOMICILE (2), *v.t.* to establish in a fixed residence, cause to make a permanent home in a specified locality; (*comm.*) render a bill of exchange payable at a specified place. DOMICILIATE [do-mi-si′li-āt], *v.t.* to d. DOMICILIATED, *adj.* domiciled. [Fr. from L.].

DOMICILIARY [do-mi-si′li-a-ri], *adj.* pertaining to a domicile or residence; **d. visit,** official visit to a private dwelling for the purpose of searching or inspecting it in accordance with the law.

DOMINANCE, DOMINANCY [do′mi-nans, do′mi-nan-si], *n.* state of being dominant; authority, control.

DOMINANT (1) [do′mi-nant], *adj.* ruling, prevailing, having most influence, outstanding in importance; (*mus.*) pertaining to the dominant or fifth above the tonic. DOMINANT (2), *n.* (*mus.*) the fifth note above the tonic; (*biol.*) inheritable characteristic manifesting itself in most of the offspring. [L.].

DOMINATE [do′mi-nāt], *v.t. and i.* to rule over, exercise great influence or authority over, prevail; occupy a position which overlooks or commands. DOMINATOR, *n.* a ruling power. [L.].

DOMINATION [do-mi-nā′shn], *n.* act of dominating; (*pl.*) the fourth order of angels. [L.].

DOMINEER [do-mi-nēer′], *v.i.* to rule, exercise authority in a haughty overbearing manner; act or express oneself in a lordly, imperious style. DOMINEERING, *adj.* overbearing, imperious. [Du.].

DOMINICAL [do-mi′ni-kal], *adj.* relating to the Lord, denoting or pertaining to Sunday; **d. year,** the year as numbered from the birth of Christ; **d. letter,** one of the first seven letters of the alphabet, symbolizing Sunday in an almanac. [LL.].

DOMINICAN (1) [do-mi′ni-kan], *n.* member of the order of preaching friars (and nuns) founded by St. Domingo de Guzman, a Black Friar. DOMINICAN (2), *adj.* belonging to the Dominicans. [MedL.].

DOMINIE [do′mi-ni], *n.* (*Scots*) schoolmaster.

DOMINION [do-mi′ni-on], *n.* supreme power or authority, control, rule, sovereignty; territories under the rule of a king; one of the self-governing territories of the British Commonwealth. [L.].

DOMINO [do′mi-nō], *n.* cape or hood worn by a master, hood worn by a canon in cold weather; loose cloak, with a hood and mask, worn as a disguise at masquerades etc.; person wearing one of these; small, flat, oblong piece of bone, ivory, wood etc., having one side black, the other white or black and divided into halves, either of which may be blank or marked with from one to six spots; (*pl.*) game played with twenty-eight of these. [L.].

DON (1) [don], *n.* Spanish title equivalent to Mr.; (*fig.*) important person; the head, or a fellow or tutor, of a college. [Span. from L.].

DON (2), *v.t.* to put on (articles of clothing). [DO and ON].

DONARY [dō′na-ri], *n.* a gift. [L.].

DONATE [dō-nāt′], *v.t.* to give in charity, present. [L.].

DONATION [dō-nā′shn], *n.* act of giving; that which is given, money for charitable purposes; (*leg.*) contract by which anything is freely transferred to the ownership of another. [L.].

DONATIVE (1) [dō′na-tiv], *n.* gift; (*eccles. leg.*) benefice given and collated to a person by the patron without presentation or institution by the ordinary. DONATIVE (2), *adj.* pertaining to a d. [L.].

DONATOR [dō-nā′ter], *n.* donor. [L.].

DONE [dun], *adj.* finished, performed; completely exhausted, dead beat; cooked sufficiently; agreed, settled; (*slang*) tricked, duped; **not d.,** not in the best of taste; **to be d.,** to be ruined, exhausted; be ready, finished; **d. up,** exhausted; **to have d. with,** to give up, finish. [DO].

DONJON, see DUNGEON.

DONKEY [dong′ki], *n.* the ass; (*coll.*) stupid person; **d. work,** (*coll.*) hard unrewarded work; **d.'s years,** (*coll.*) a long time. [Unkn.].

DONKEY-ENGINE [dong′ki-en-jin], *n.* small steam-engine, as used in a ship for pumping or loading.

DONKEY-PUMP [dong′ki-pump], *n.* pump operated by a donkey-engine.

DONNA [do′nah], *n.* feminine Italian and Portuguese equivalent of DON. [L.].

DONNISH [do′nish], *adj.* characteristic of a university don, pedantic.

DONOR [dō′ner], *n.* one who makes a donation.

DON'T (1) [dōnt], *v.i.* (*coll.*) do not. DON'T (2), *n.* (*coll.*) prohibition; thing not to be done.

DOODAH [dōō′dah], *n.* (*slang*) state of excitement, *esp.* **all of a d.** [Invented].

DOODLE (1) [dōō′dl], *n.* simpleton; aimless scribble. DOODLE (2), *v.i.* to scribble aimlessly and absentmindedly. [LGerm.].

DOODLE-BUG [dōō′dl-bug], *n.* (*slang*) flying bomb; (*U.S.*) tiger-beetle. [Uncert.].

DOOM (1) [dōōm], *n.* (*archaic*) judgment, judicial sentence; judgment day; fate; ruin; **crack of d.,** the end of the world at the Day of Judgment. DOOM (2), *v.t.* to sentence to punishment, condemn. DOOMFUL, *adj.* pregnant with destruction, foreboding d. [OE.].

DOOMSDAY [dōōmz′dā], *n.* the Day of Judgment. [OE.].

DOOR [daw(r)], *n.* sliding or hinged structure closing an entrance; (*fig.*) means of approach to, that which gives access to; **next d.,** in the next house; **next d. to,** nearly, almost; **out of doors,** in the open air; **to lie at the d. of,** to be chargeable or attributable to; **to show a person the d.,** to ask or force a person to depart. DOOR-BELL, bell rung from outside a house to indicate the presence of a person wishing to enter etc. DOOR-KNOCKER, knocker on a d. used by one wishing to enter etc. DOOR-PLATE, plate on the d. of a house bearing the occupant's name. DOOR-POST, one of the uprights of the frame enclosing a d. [OE.].

DOORKEEPER [daw′kē-per], *n.* porter; one who minds the entrance of a building.

DOORMAN [daw′man], *n.* attendant at the door of a building; commissionaire.

DOORMAT [daw′mat], *n.* mat placed inside an outer door, on which those entering may wipe their feet.

DOOR-NAIL [daw′nāl], *n.* large-headed nail with which wooden doors were once studded for additional strength; **dead as a d.,** quite dead.

DOORSTEP [daw′step], *n.* step immediately below the doorway of a house.

DOORWAY [daw′wā], *n.* opening or entrance closed by a door.

DOPE (1) [dōp], *n.* a sluggish oily lubricant; varnish with which the fabric of aeroplanes or the envelope of an airship is coated; (*coll.*) any drug, such as opium, taken as a narcotic, or used to drug horses etc.; (*fig.*) anything intended to deceive or quieten; (*slang*) useful or necessary information; (*slang*) motor spirit; (*U.S. slang*) a fool; **to upset the d.,** to turn out otherwise than was expected. DOPE (2), *v.t. and i.* to treat with d.; (*coll.*) doctor with d., drug; (*fig.*) dupe, deceive, allay or soothe. DOPER, *n.* one who drugs (a racehorse or greyhound). DOP(E)Y, *adj.* (*U.S. slang*) stupid.

DOPPEL-GANGER [do′pel-gang-er], *n.* apparition of a person not yet dead; a double. [Germ.].

DOR, DORR [daw(r)], *n.* the common black-beetle. [OE.].

DORADO [do-rah′dō], *n.* a southern constellation; large fish of the genus *Coryphaena,* often erroneously called the dolphin. [Span. from L.].

DORCAS [daw′kas], *n.* meeting of ladies to make or provide garments for the poor. [*Dorcas,* Acts ix, 36].

DOR-HAWK, DORR-HAWK [daw′hawk], *n.* the nightjar.

DORIAN [daw′ri-an], *n. and adj.* an inhabitant of, pertaining to, Doris in Northern Greece; member of, pertaining to, the race which invaded it from the north about the tenth century B.C. [Gk.].

DORIC (1) [do′rik], *adj.* Dorian; (of dialect) unpolished, rough; **D. order,** (*arch.*) the oldest, strongest and simplest of the three Grecian orders of architecture. DORIC (2), *n.* the D. dialect of Greece; any broad, rough provincial dialect, *esp.* Scots; the D. order of architecture. [Gk.].

DORKING [daw′king], *n.* breed of domestic fowl. [*Dorking,* Surrey].

DORMANT [daw′mant], *adj.* sleeping, in a state of complete inactivity or torpidity; quiescent, at rest, not in use or action; (of a title) not claimed; (*her.*) asleep. DORMANCY [daw′man-si], *n.* state of being d. [OFt.].

DORMER [daw′mer], *n.* (*hist.*) bedroom; **d. window,** vertical window projecting from a sloping roof. [L.].

DORMITIVE [daw′mi-tiv], *n. and adj.* (substance) inducing sleep. [OFr.].

DORMITORY [daw′mi-te-ri], *n.* sleeping apartment for a number of people, one divided into several cubicles or containing many beds. [L.].

DORMOUSE (*pl.* dormice) [daw′mows, daw′mis], *n.*

ōō is pronounced as in f*oo*d; ŏŏ as in h*oo*d; th as in *th*ink; TH as in *th*at; zh as in azure. ~ = related to.

small, hibernating rodent related to the mouse and squirrel. [Uncert.].

DORMY [daw'mi], *adj.* (*golf*) as many holes up on one's opponent as there remain holes to play; **d. house,** sleeping accommodation at a golf club. [Unkn.].

DOROTHY-PERKINS [do-ro-thi-pur'kinz], *n.* a pink rambler rose. [Personal name].

DORR, see DOR.

DORR-HAWK. see DOR-HAWK.

DORSAL [daw'sal], *adj.* pertaining to, near, or on the back. **DORSALLY,** *adv.* at or from the back. [L.].

DORSEL, see DOSSAL.

DORSI-, DORSO-, *pref.* back. [L.].

DORY (1) [daw'ri], *n.* an edible sea fish known as the john dory. [Fr. from L.].

DORY (2), *n.* small flat-bottomed boat used in cod-fishing etc. [Unkn.].

DOSAGE [dō'sij], *n.* act of dosing; quantity of a single dose.

DOSE (1) [dōs], *n.* the quantity of medicine prescribed to be taken at one time; (*fig.*) share or amount, regular definite quantity; (*coll.*) bout (of illness etc.). DOSE (2), *v.t.* to give a d. or series of doses to. [Gk.].

DOSS (1) [dos], *n.* (*slang*) a bed, *esp.* in a registered lodging-house; a sleep. DOSS (2), *v.i.* (*slang*) to sleep; stay the night at a doss-house. DOSSER, *n.* one who sleeps at a doss-house. [Unkn.].

DOSSAL, DORSAL, DOSSEL [do'sal], *n.* (*eccles.*) ornamental cloth hung behind the altar, or at the sides of the chancel. [MedL.].

DOSS-HOUSE [dos'hows], *n.* cheap lodging-house.

DOSSIER [do'si-ā], *n.* a collection of papers or documents on the same subject, *esp.* a personal record. [Fr.].

DOT (1) [dot], *n.* very small, round point or mark made with a pen, pencil etc.; *esp.* one used in punctuation; (*mus.*) a point placed after a rest or note to indicate that its time value is to be increased by one-half; speck, anything like a dot in size; (*coll.*) tiny child; short symbol in signalling, Morse code etc.; **to be off one's d.,** (*slang*) to be crazy. DOT (2) (*pres.pt.* DOTTING, *pret. and p.pt.* DOTTED), *v.t.* to mark with a d. or dots; trace out or draw with dots; place a d. over (i or j) or after (a musical note or rest); scatter about or cover with objects resembling dots from a distance; (*slang*) hit, strike; **to d. one's i's,** to be extremely particular, exact, or scrupulous. [OE.].

DOT (3) [dō], *n.* woman's marriage portion or dowry. [Fr.].

DOTAGE [dō'tij], *n.* senility, feebleness of old age; folly, excessive fondness.

DOTARD [dō'terd], *n.* person feeble in mind and body because of old age. DOTARD, *adj.* like a d., foolish and decrepit. [~DOTE].

DOTE [dōt], *v.i.* to behave or talk foolishly, become weak-minded through old age; adore blindly; **to d. on, upon,** be infatuated with. DOTER, *n.* one who dotes. [MLGerm.].

DOTH [duth], (*archaic*) third person sg. pres. ind. of DO.

DOTING [dō'ting], *adj.* adoring, infatuated; weak-minded, senile. DOTINGLY, *adv.* in a d. fashion.

DOTTED [do'tid], *adj.* marked with a dot or dots; **d. about,** scattered here and there.

DOTTEREL, DOTTREL [do'te-rel], *n.* species of plover. [~DOTE].

DOTTLE [do'tl], *n.* small plug of tobacco ash left in a pipe after a smoke. [DOT (1)].

DOTTREL, see DOTTEREL.

DOTTY [do'ti], *adj.* marked with dots; (*slang*) mad, crazy.

DOUANE [dōō-ahn'], *n.* custom-house, *esp.* on the Continent. [Fr. from Arab.].

DOUBLE (1) [du'bl], *adj.* twice as much, as much again (of quality, strength, amount, size, appearance etc.); for the use of two persons or things; serving two purposes; in pairs, having two similar parts, twofold; having two layers; acting in two ways; having two meanings; (*mus.*) an octave lower in pitch. DOUBLE (2), *adv.* doubly, two at a time, twice over, in pairs. [OFr. from L.].

DOUBLE (3), *n.* twice the quantity or amount; person exactly similar in appearance to another; (*esp. milit.*) an easy running pace, supposed to be twice as fast as a normal "quick" march; (*cards*) an increase, usually twice the amount, in points awarded or stakes decided upon by one of the players; (*tennis*) two faults in succession when serving; (*pl.*) foursome at tennis; actor or singer who takes two parts in the

same piece; act of returning on one's tracks to baffle pursuers; (*racing*) a bet on two horses in different races, the winnings from one race, together with the stake, being carried forward and wagered upon the second race; (*darts*) a throw landing between the two outer circles of a dartboard.

DOUBLE (4), *v.t.* to make double; bend so as to form two layers, fold over; play two parts in one piece; clench (the fists); (*naut.*) sail completely round a point so that the course of the ship is reversed; (*mus.*) play the same melody as another instrument, but an octave higher or lower in pitch; (*milit.*) proceed at double-quick marching time; (*billiards*) pot a ball so that it rebounds from at least one cushion before entering the pocket; (*cards*) increase greatly the points possible to be gained or lost by an opponent; *v.i.* to become twice as much, increase by as much again; run; twist and turn in one's course as one runs; turn back upon one's tracks to elude pursuers; **to d. up,** to cause a person to bend right over in pain etc.; (*fig.*) cause a person to collapse; collapse or crumple up; (*betting*) double the amount staked each time until a win is recorded. [OFr. from L.].

DOUBLE-BANKED [du-bl-bangkt'], *adj.* (*naut.*) having two opposite oars for rowers on the same thwart or two men on the same oar.

DOUBLE-BARRELLED [du-bl-ba'reld], *adj.* (of a gun) furnished with two barrels; (*fig.*) having a twofold effect.

DOUBLE-BASS [du-bl-bās'], *n.* the largest of the stringed instruments of the violin family.

DOUBLE-BREASTED [du-bl-bres'tid], *adj.* (of jackets etc.) cut to have a double thickness in front when buttoned up, and capable of being fastened with either flap outermost.

DOUBLE-CROSS [du-bl-kros'], *v.t.* to act treacherously towards, swindle, betray.

DOUBLE-DEALER [du-bl-dē'ler], *n.* deceitful person who will make contrary professions to fit immediate necessity. DOUBLE-DEALING, *n.* duplicity, treachery.

DOUBLE-DECKER [du-bl-de'ker], *n.* passenger vehicle having two levels of seating accommodation; (*aeron.*) biplane; stand having seating accommodation on two levels or floors.

DOUBLE-DECLUTCH [du-bl-dē-kluch'], *v.i.* (*motoring*) to let out the clutch both before leaving whatever gear the car is already in, and going into neutral, and again before going from neutral into the next gear desired.

DOUBLE-DUTCH [du-bl-duch'], *n.* (*coll.*) unintelligible talk; anything unintelligible.

DOUBLE-DYE [du-bl-dī'], *v.t.* to dye twice. DOUBLE-DYED, *adj.* having been dyed twice; (*fig.*) deeply involved, habitually practising, out-and-out.

DOUBLE-EDGED [du-bl-ejd'], *adj.* having two edges; (*fig.*) having a twofold effect.

DOUBLE-ENTENDRE [dōōb-lah(ng)-tah(ng)dr'], *n.* statement with two meanings, one of which is often improper.

DOUBLE-ENTRY [du-bl-en'tri], *n.* (*comm.*) book-keeping system by which every transaction is entered twice, as a debit to one account, and a credit to another.

DOUBLE-FACED [du-bl-fāst'], *adj.* having or showing two faces; (*fig.*) insincere, hypocritical.

DOUBLE-FIRST [du-bl-furst'], *n.* university degree with first-class honours in two sections of the examination, or in two different subjects.

DOUBLE-LOCK [du-bl-lok'], *v.t.* to lock twice; fasten with double security.

DOUBLENESS [du'bl-nes], *n.* condition or quality of being double.

DOUBLE PLEA [du-bl-plē'], *n.* (*leg.*) defending plea which alleges two different matters in bar of the action.

DOUBLE-QUICK [du-bl-kwik'], *adj. and adv.* very quick(ly), at the speed of the double.

DOUBLE-STOP [du-bl-stop'], *v.i.* (*mus.*) to play chords on a violin on two or more stopped strings.

DOUBLET [dub'let], *n.* (*archaic*) tight garment covering the upper part of the trunk; (*pl.*) throw at dice of the same number on both dice; (*philol.*) one of several words having a common origin, but entering a language at different periods or through different sources, having acquired a different form and often a separate meaning; two birds killed by one discharge from a double-barrelled gun; a combination of two simple lenses; imitation gem consisting of two pieces of crystal with a colour or a small piece of precious stone between them. [Fr.].

DOUBLE-THROW [du-bl-thrō'], *adj.* (of a switch) operating in two ways.

DOUBLETON [du'bl-ton], *n.* (cards) two cards only of a suit.

DOUBLE-TONGUED [du-bl-tungd'], *adj.* treacherous, backbiting.

DOUBLE-TONGUING [du-bl-tung'ing], *n.* (mus.) method of playing rapidly repeated or staccato notes on the cornet or flute.

DOUBLING [dub'ling], *n.* act of one who doubles; a fold; (her.) ornamental lining of a robe etc.

DOUBLOON [dub-loon'], *n.* Spanish and South American gold coin of about the value of a guinea. [Span.].

DOUBLURE [doob'lyoor], *n.* ornamental leather binding inside a book. [Fr.].

DOUBLY [dub'li], *adv.* twice as much, to twice the extent.

DOUBT (1) [dowt], *n.* hesitancy or disinclination to believe, lack of conviction; state of being undecided; misgiving, uncertainty, suspicion; **to give the benefit of the d.**, to take a lenient or charitable view in the absence of proof. DOUBT (2), *v.t.* to be disinclined to believe or recognize as true; suspect, view with distrust; (archaic) fear; *v.i.* to waver in opinion; be undecided about and disinclined to believe the truth of, esp. of religious doctrine; be unconvinced; think something to be unlikely. DOUBTABLE, *adj.* questionable, doubtful. DOUBTER, *n.* person who doubts. [OFr., L.].

DOUBTFUL [dowt'fool], *adj.* not proved or certain, not clear in meaning; undecided, not determined or resolute; disreputable. DOUBTFULLY, *adv.* in a d. way. DOUBTFULNESS, *n.* condition of being d.

DOUBTLESS [dowt'les], *adv.* unquestionably, probably. DOUBTLESSLY, *adv.* unquestionably, indubitably.

DOUCEUR [doo-sur'], *n.* a tip. [Fr.].

DOUCHE (1) [doosh], *n.* shower of water, or stream of vapour, directed on some part of the body; shower-bath; (fig.) unpleasant shock; **to throw a cold d. upon**, (fig.) to discourage. DOUCHE (2), *v.t.* to spray with a d. [Fr.].

DOUGH [dō], *n.* thick mass of flour or meal, kneaded ready for baking; (slang) money. [OE.].

DOUGHBOY [dō'boi], *n.* boiled dumpling; (U.S. slang) American soldier.

DOUGHNUT [dō'nut], *n.* small fried cake.

DOUGHTY [dow'ti], *adj.* (archaic) brave, valiant. DOUGHTILY, *adv.* in a d. manner. DOUGHTINESS, *n.* quality of being d. [OE.].

DOUGHY [dō'i], *adj.* like dough, soft, half-baked.

DOUR [door], *adj.* stern, obstinate. DOURLY, *adv.* in d. fashion. DOURNESS, *n.* quality of being d. [L.].

DOUSE [dows], *v.t.* to plunge into water, drench, squirt water on; (naut.) slacken suddenly (a sail); (coll.) put out (a light). [Unkn.].

DOUT [dowt], *v.t.* to extinguish. [DO and OUT].

DOVE [duv], *n.* a species of pigeon; (fig.) the Holy Spirit; emblem of innocence or peace; term of endearment. DOVE-COLOUR, purplish or pinkish grey. [OE.].

DOVECOT(E) [duv'kot], *n.* wooden hutch on a pole, with roosting boxes for pigeons.

DOVELIKE [duv'lik], *adj.* innocent, meek.

DOVER'S POWDER [dō'verz-pow-der], *n.* compound of ipecacuanha, opium and potassium sulphate, used medicinally as a sedative. [Dr. T. Dover, inventor].

DOVETAIL (1) [duv'tāl], *n.* (carp.) method of fastening pieces of timber together, by pushing a wedge-shaped projection on one piece into a corresponding incision in another piece. DOVETAIL (2), *v.t. and i.* to fasten together by means of d. joints; (fig.) fit neatly and closely together. DOVETAILING, *n.* a d. joint.

DOWAGER [dow'a-jer], *n.* widow with a dower; titled widow. [OFr.].

DOWDY (1) [dow'di], *n.* woman dressed in a slovenly or unfashionable way. DOWDY (2), *adj.* ill-dressed; inelegant. DOWDILY, *adv.* in d. fashion. DOWDINESS, *n.* state or quality of being d. DOWDYISH, *adj.* rather d. [ME.].

DOWEL (1) [dow'el], *n.* pin or peg of metal, stone etc., without a head, used for making joins and fastenings. DOWEL (2), *v.t.* to fasten by dowels. DOWELLING, *n.* method of fastening by dowels. [LGerm.].

DOWER (1) [dow'er], *n.* part of a husband's estate which falls to his widow for life, reverting to his heirs at her death; property which a woman brings to her husband in marriage; gift made by a husband to a wife; endowment; **d. house**, house reserved for the widow. DOWER (2), *v.t.* to provide with a d.; endow. DOWERED, *adj.* having a d. DOWERLESS, *adj.* without a d. [OFr. from MedL.].

DOWLAS [dow'las], *n.* coarse kind of calico. [Daoulas, Brittany].

DOWN (1) [down], *n.* first plumage or soft feathers of birds; any soft substance resembling this, the first hair appearing on a youth's face, hairy covering on certain plants, fruits etc. [OIcel.].

DOWN (2), *n.* tract of open, treeless, high land; **The Downs**, sea between the Goodwin Sands and the east coast of Kent. [OE.].

DOWN (3), *adv.* from a higher to a lower position, from a vertical to a horizontal position; to some place considered as being lower, as from a large city to a smaller place, from the source of a river to the mouth, to a place south of the speaker etc.; in a low position, on the ground; below a level state, below the horizon or surface, denoting loss of money; (sport) indicating defeat or failure (also in an examination); from a higher to a lower social position, from prosperity to misfortune; indicating decrease or weakening; from earlier to later times; from the beginning; (coll.) on the spot, there and then; (universities) not in residence; **to be d. on**, to be strongly opposed to; **d. at heel**, dejected, shabby, poor; **d. in the mouth**, dispirited, miserable; **a d.-and-out**, person with no money or prospects; **to be d. on one's luck**, to be in straitened circumstances; **d. with !** abolish, put an end to; **to be d.**, (sport) to be behind, be in arrears, have lost money; **d. under**, at the Antipodes, esp. in Australia and New Zealand. DOWN (4), *prep.* from a higher to a lower position on, in a descending direction in; away from the speaker or a given point; along; from an earlier to a later time. DOWN (5), *n.* (coll.) a grudge; reversal of fortune. DOWN (6), *adj.* descending; (fig.) dejected; (of a train etc.) travelling away from the chief terminus, esp. London. DOWN (7), *v.t.* (coll.) to bring, put, or knock down, defeat; drink; **to d. tools**, to cease work. [OE.].

DOWNCAST (1) [down'kahst], *n.* shaft for admitting air into a mine; (geol.) downthrow. DOWNCAST (2), *adj.* (of looks) directed downwards; dejected, dispirited.

DOWNFALL [down'fawl], *n.* act of falling; (fig.) ruin, overthrow; heavy fall of rain. DOWNFALLEN, *adj.* ruined, decrepit.

DOWN-GRADE (1) [down'grād], *n.* downward path or trend. DOWN-GRADE (2) [down-grād'], *v.t.* to lower the rank or status of.

DOWNHAUL [down'hawl], *n.* (naut.) rope fastened to the upper corner of a sail to haul it down.

DOWNHEARTED [down-hah'tid], *adj.* dispirited, dejected.

DOWNHILL (1) [down'hil], *n.* declivity, the downward slope of a hill. DOWNHILL (2), *adj.* sloping downwards, descending the slope. DOWNHILL (3) [down-hil'], *adv.* towards the bottom of a hill; (fig.) so as to decline or deteriorate, on the downward path.

DOWN-LINE [down'lin], *n.* railway line along which travel trains outward-bound from the main terminus.

DOWNPOUR [down'paw(r)], *n.* heavy continuous fall of rain, deluge.

DOWN-QUILT [down-kwilt'], *n.* quilt of eiderdown.

DOWNRIGHT (1) [down'rit], *adj.* plain, frank, direct, unceremonious; complete, utter. DOWNRIGHT (2), *adv.* completely, utterly. DOWNRIGHTLY, *adv.* in a d. fashion. DOWNRIGHTNESS, *n.* quality of being d.

DOWNRUSH [down'rush], *n.* a sudden rushing down.

DOWNSTAIRS (1) [down-stäerz'], *adj.* situated on a lower floor. DOWNSTAIRS (2), *adv.* to or on a lower floor.

DOWNSTREAM [down-strēm'], *adv.* in the same direction as the flow of the stream.

DOWNTHROW [down'thrō], *n.* (geol.) sinking of the strata where a fault occurs, amount the strata sinks.

DOWN-TRAIN [down'trān], *n.* train travelling away from the main terminus.

DOWNTRODDEN [down'tro-den], *adj.* trampled or beaten down; (fig.) oppressed.

DOWNWARD (1) [down'weerd], *adj.* descending; (fig.) degenerate, leading to ruin. DOWNWARD (2),

---

ōō is pronounced as in food; ŏŏ as in hood; th as in think; TH as in that; zh as in azure. ~ = related to.

adv. to a lower place, down; towards ruin or depravity.

DOWNWARDS [down'werdz], *adj. and adv.* downward.

DOWNY (1) [dow'ni], *adj.* soft and fluffy like down; made of, or covered with, down; (*slang*) artful, wily, alert. DOWNY (2), *adj.* resembling downland.

DOWRY [dow'ri], *n.* property or portion which a woman brings to her husband as a dower; (*fig.*) natural gift or talent. [OFr.].

DOWSE [dows], *v.i.* to seek for subterranean sources of water or mineral ores with a divining-rod. DOWSER, *n.* one who dowses. DOWSING, *n.* art of discovering water or minerals by the divining-rod. DOWSING-ROD, twig used by diviners. [Unkn.].

DOXOLOGY [dok-so'lo-ji], *n.* hymn of praise to God, *esp.* the short formula used at the end of canticles and psalms. DOXOLOGICAL [dok-sō-lo'ji-kal], *adj.* relating to a d. DOXOLOGIZE [dok-so'lo-jiz], *v.i.* to praise God, utter a d. [Gk.].

DOXY [dok'si], *n.* loose woman, beggar's mistress. [Unkn.].

DOYEN [dwa'ya(ng)], *n.* the senior member of a profession or society, *esp.* of a diplomatic corps. [Fr.].

DOYLEY, see DOILY.

DOZE (1) [dōz], *v.i.* to slumber or sleep lightly for short periods, drowse off into a light sleep. DOZE (2), *n.* a short light sleep. DOZER, *n.* one who dozes. [Dan.].

DOZEN [du'zen], *n.* a group of twelve; (*pl.*) (*coll.*) a considerable number; **baker's d.**, thirteen; **to talk nineteen to the d.**, (*coll.*) to talk incessantly and quickly. [OFr.].

DOZY [dō'zi], *adj.* drowsy, half asleep. DOZINESS, *n.* state of being d., drowsiness.

DRAB (1) [drab], *n.* slovenly woman; prostitute. [Ir.].

DRAB (2), *n.* thick woollen cloth of a dun colour; dull brownish-grey colour. DRAB (3), *adj.* of a dull brown or dun colour; (*fig.*) dingy, dreary, monotonous. DRABLY, *adv.* colourlessly, uninterestingly. [Fr.].

DRABBLE [dra'bl], *v.t. and i.* to make wet or dirty by dragging through mud and water; wade through mud and mire; (*angling*) fish for barbel with a rod and line weighted with a bullet. [LGerm.].

DRACANTH, see TRAGACANTH.

DRACHM [dram], *n.* drachma; eighth of a fluid ounce in apothecaries' weight, sixteenth of an ounce in avoirdupois weight; (*fig.*) minute amount or quantity. [Gk.].

DRACHMA (*pl.* **drachmae, drachmas**) [drak'mah], *n.* chief silver coin of the ancient Greeks; modern Greek standard silver coin; ancient Greek unit of weight. [Gk.].

DRACONIAN [dra-kō'ni-an], *adj.* (*leg.*) harsh, rigorous. [*Drakon*, Athenian Greek who introduced a code of severe laws].

DRACONIC [dra-ko'nik], *adj.* Draconian.

DRAFF [draf], *n.* refuse, dregs, *esp.* of malt after the liquor has been drawn off; hogwash. DRAFFISH, DRAFFY, *adj.* worthless like d. [ME.].

DRAFT (1) [drahft], *n.* act of drawing; that which is drawn; body of men selected for special service; written order authorizing payment by a banker, act of drawing money with this; preliminary outline or plan, rough first copy. DRAFT (2), *v.t.* to select a body of men for special service; make a rough copy of, prepare plans for, draw up subject to later revision (a Parliamentary Bill). [DRAUGHT].

DRAFT-HORSE, see DRAUGHT-HORSE.

DRAFT-OX, see DRAUGHT-OX.

DRAFTSMAN, see DRAUGHTSMAN.

DRAG (1) (*pres.pt.* **dragging**, *pret. and p.pt.* **dragged**) [drag], *v.t. and i.* to haul along with an effort; break up land with a harrow; allow (the feet) to trail along the ground; use dredging or grappling instruments, nets etc. to explore (a stretch of water) in search of some object; trail along the ground, pass slowly, be long drawn out; (*mus.*) fail to keep up to time; **to d. on**, to be tedious or protracted; **to d. in**, to insert unnecessarily; **to d. up**, (*coll.*) to bring up (children) in a careless manner; **to d. anchor**, (*naut.*) to trail the anchor along the bottom when it has failed to hold. DRAG (2), *n.* that which is dragged; low cart or car, heavy sledge, four-wheeled coach; contrivance used for recovering objects under water; heavy harrow; strong-smelling substance dragged along a chosen course for hounds to follow instead of chasing a fox; that which drags, iron shoe of a brake; (*fig.*)

hindrance, burden; (*billiards*) method of striking the cue ball so that it travels at a reduced speed; (*aeron.*) air resistance against an aeroplane when flying, reduction in power due to this. [Swed.].

DRAGEE, dragée [drah'zhā], *n.* a chocolate drop. [Fr. from Gk.].

DRAGGLE [dra'gl], *v.t. and i.* to make wet and dirty by dragging through mud; be drawn along the ground, trailed through mud. DRAGGLE-TAILED, *adj.* sluttish, with muddy, trailing skirts. [Unkn.].

DRAG-HUNT [drag'hunt], *n.* hunt in which the hounds follow a drag.

DRAG-NET [drag'net], *n.* net drawn along the bottom of a stretch of water to catch fish, or along the ground to catch game.

DRAGOMAN (*pl.* **dragomans**) [dra'gō-man], *n.* interpreter, *esp.* in Arabic, Turkish or Persian; guide to foreigners in the East. [Arab.].

DRAGON [dra'gon], *n.* fabulous monster having the form of a serpent, with wings, legs and fiery breath; (*her.*) representation of this monster; (*astron.*) the northern constellation, *Draco*; (*fig.*) fierce, unapproachable woman, *esp.* when the chaperon of a young girl; (*zool.*) one of several species of lizard found in South-east Asia; (*bibl.*) name given to various animals in the Authorized Version; (*milit.*) powerful tractor used in hauling artillery. [Fr. from Gk.].

DRAGONET [dra'go-net], *n.* small sea fish. [Fr.].

DRAGON-FLY [dra'gon-fli], *n.* brilliantly coloured insect of the order *Neuroptera*.

DRAGON'S BLOOD [dra'gonz-blud], *n.* reddish-brown resinous juice obtained from certain tropical plants, used for colouring purposes, and in process engraving.

DRAGOON (1) [dra-gōōn'], *n.* mounted infantryman carrying the kind of carbine known as a dragon; trooper belonging to certain cavalry regiments; fierce person; variety of pigeon. DRAGOON (2), *v.t.* to persecute or subject by armed force; compel to submit to, force into. [DRAGON].

DRAIN (1) [drān], *v.t. and i.* to convey away excess water from land by cutting channels, laying pipes etc.; clear of water by drains; (*surg.*) remove morbid matter from a wound; empty of liquor; (*fig.*) empty, exhaust, deprive of (wealth, resources, strength); furnish or provide with drains; flow away gradually; **to d. to the dregs**, to empty completely; (*fig.*) experience to the full. DRAIN (2), *n.* pipe to carry water; (*pl.*) system of pipes and culverts for removing sewerage and waste water etc.; (*surg.*) tube for drawing off morbid matter from a cavity discharging pus; (*fig.*) persistent source of expenditure, steady demand; (*coll.*) small quantity (of liquor). [OE.].

DRAINAGE [drā'nij], *n.* act, process or system of draining, or of being drained; that which is drained away. DRAINAGE-BASIN, territory drained by a river.

DRAINING-BOARD [drā'ning-bawd], *n.* sloping board beside a sink for draining dishes after washing.

DRAINPIPE [drān'pīp], *n.* pipe for drainage purposes.

DRAIN-TRAP [drān'trap], *n.* device preventing the escape of foul air from a drain.

DRAKE (1) [drāk], *n.* male of the duck. [LGerm.].

DRAKE (2), *n.* species of fly used as a bait in angling. [OE.].

DRAM [dram], *n.* weight equivalent to one-eighth of an ounce (apothecaries' measure) or one-sixteenth of an ounce (avoirdupois); liquid measure equal to one-eighth of a fluid ounce; small amount of liquor, a drop, *esp.* (*Scots*) a glass of whisky. DRAM-DRINKER, habitual drinker of spirits. [DRACHM].

DRAMA [drah'mah], *n.* literary composition for stage performance, depicting the story in action and dialogue; a play; dramatic writing; theatrical art; series of vivid, passionate events. [Gk.].

DRAMATIC(AL) [dra-ma'tik(-al)], *adj.* pertaining to the drama, in the form of a drama; resembling a drama in depicting vivid, passionate events; striking, arresting. DRAMATICALLY, *adv.* in a d. way, in an unnatural manner.

DRAMATIS PERSONAE [dra-ma-tis-per-sō'nē], *n.(pl.)* the characters in a play. [L.].

DRAMATIST [dra'ma-tist], *n.* person who writes stage plays. [Gk.].

DRAMATIZE [dra'ma-tiz], *v.t.* to present in the form of a play. DRAMATIZABLE, *adj.* capable of being dramatized. DRAMATIZATION [dra-ma-tī-zā'shn], *n.* process of dramatizing; that which is dramatized.

DRAMATURGY [dra'ma-ter-ji], *n.* technique of writing and producing plays. DRAMATURGE, DRAMATURGIST, *n.* playwright. [Fr. from Gk.].

The accent ′ after a syllable = stress (u-pon′). The mark ¯ over a vowel = length (ā in made; ō in bone).

DRAMBUIE [dram-byōo'ē], *n.* (*prot.*) a whisky liqueur made in Scotland.

DRANK [drangk], *pret.* of DRINK. [OE.].

DRAPE [drāp], *v.t.* to cover with loose-hanging cloth, clothe with some fabric so that it hangs in folds, arrange artistically the folds of a covering. DRAPED, *adj.* clothed in drapery. [OFr.].

DRAPER [drā'per], *n.* dealer in cloth and fabrics, shopkeeper dealing primarily in such commodities. [ME.].

DRAPERY [drā'pe-ri], *n.* draping fabric, the folds or arrangement of something draped, artistic treatment of drapings; trade or stock of a draper. [OFr.].

DRASTIC [dras'tik], *adj.* vigorous, effective, thorough; severe but efficient and thoroughgoing (applied *esp.* to purges or disciplinary action). DRASTICALLY, *adv.* in d. fashion. [Gk.].

DRAT [drat], *int.* a mild, though low, expletive. [*God rot*].

DRAUGHT [drahft], *n.* act of drawing, thing drawn, the drawing of a liquid from a vessel, the amount of liquid swallowed without taking breath, dose of medicine, liquid purgative; amount of water displaced by a ship, or the depth necessary to take her; air current coming from a small aperture; (*pl.*) game for two, played on a board of sixty-four squares with twelve pieces a side; piece used in this game. DRAUGHT-BOARD, board used in the game of draughts. [OE.].

DRAUGHT-HORSE, DRAFT-HORSE [drahft'-haws], *n.* heavy horse used for pulling loads.

DRAUGHT(S)MAN [drahft(s)'man], *n.* a piece used in draughts.

DRAUGHT-OX, DRAFT-OX [drahft'oks], *n.* ox employed for pulling loads etc.

DRAUGHTSMAN, DRAFTSMAN [drahfts'man], *n.* one who drafts documents, Parliamentary Bills etc.; person who draws designs or plans for buildings, structures etc. DRAUGHTSMANSHIP, *n.* practice and technique of a d.; skill in drawing.

DRAUGHTY [drahf'ti], *adj.* unprotected from, full of, draughts of air.

DRAW (1) (*pret.* **drew**, *p.pt.* **drawn**) [draw], *v.t. and i.* to cause to move towards one, drag in one's direction, pull towards oneself, pull out of something; take (liquor) from a cask; pull back the string of a bow before discharging; take (a sword) from its sheath; attract towards oneself, excite and focus (applause etc.); entice; take money habitually from a source; take in (breaths); (*fig.*) get (ideas, feelings) from a thing, form (a conclusion) from evidence; take a ticket in a lottery, pick something at random from several alternatives; make a design, picture or delineation with a pencil, pen or brush; write out (a cheque); take out the entrails; finish a contest without a definite decision; (*coll.*) attract, be an attraction; approach; **to d. back,** to retreat, hesitate at the last moment; **to d. down,** to incur, incite (anger etc.); **to d. the line,** to show scruple, decline; **to d. the long bow,** to exaggerate, lie; **to d. out,** to encourage talk and confidences; **to d. round,** to gather round; **to d. the teeth of,** to render harmless; **to d. up,** to formulate, set out, make a detailed account of, make out (a legal document or commercial statement); put into military formation; come to a stop. DRAW (2), *n.* process of drawing lots, the lot so drawn; contest in which neither side is victorious; (*coll.*) an attraction, *esp.* a dramatic performance which attracts the public; act of drawing a weapon, *esp.* a pistol. [OE.].

DRAWBACK [draw'bak], *n.* inconvenience or disadvantage in something otherwise desirable; import duty repaid on re-export.

DRAWBRIDGE [draw'brij], *n.* bridge hinged at one end, so that it may be closed by being raised, *esp.* across the moat of a castle.

DRAWEE [draw-ē'], *n.* person by whom a bill of exchange is payable.

DRAWER [draw'er], *n.* one who, or that which, draws; lidless container sliding into a receptacle made for the purpose; (*pl.*) legged undergarment.

DRAWING [draw'ing], *n.* act and technique of making a picture with pencil or brush; picture so made.

DRAWING-BOARD [draw'ing-bawd], *n.* board on which to rest paper during drawing.

DRAWING-PAPER [draw'ing-pā-per], *n.* paper to draw on.

DRAWING-PIN [draw'ing-pin], *n.* flat-headed pin used for attaching paper to a board.

DRAWING-ROOM [draw'ing-rōom], *n.* room for

sociability and hospitality, room for use after dinner; court reception at which women are presented. [Short for WITHDRAWING-ROOM].

DRAWL (1) [drawl], *v.t. and i.* to speak in a slow, lazy, monotonous way; say (something) in this way. DRAWL (2), *n.* drawling manner of speech. [OIcel.].

DRAWLING [draw'ling], *n.* act or sound of speaking in a drawl. DRAWLINGLY, *adv.* in d. fashion.

DRAWN [drawn], *adj. and p.pt.* (of a contest) with victory to neither side; (of a weapon) out of its sheath; disembowelled; (of appearance) worn and tense. [OE.].

DRAWN WORK [drawn'werk], *n.* method of ornamenting linen by drawing out certain threads.

DRAW-STRING [draw'string], *n.* cord passed through a hem or eyelets to close the mouth of a bag.

DRAW-WELL [draw'wel], *n.* deep well into which a bucket on a rope is lowered to fetch water.

DRAY [drā], *n.* low cart for heavy loads. [OE.].

DRAY-HORSE [drā'haws], *n.* cart-horse.

DRAYMAN [drā'man], *n.* man in charge of a dray.

DREAD (1) [dred], *v.t. and i.* to feel terror of, fear horribly, in anticipation; be very apprehensive and afraid. DREAD (2), *n.* fearful apprehension, terror and anticipation, fear of something in the future. DREAD (3), *adj.* dreadful, awe-inspiring. DREADER, *n.* one who dreads. [OE.].

DREADFUL [dred'fōol], *adj.* inspiring dread; **penny d.,** cheap lurid tale of murders and fiendish villainies. DREADFULLY, *adv.* in d. fashion. DREADFULNESS, *n.* quality of being d.

DREADLESS [dred'les], *adj.* fearless.

DREADNOUGHT (1) [dred'nawt], *n.* type of powerful, heavily armoured battleship, first built by Gt. Britain in 1906, and afterwards adopted by other countries as the first warship to combine high speed, effective armour and exceptionally heavy armament. [Named from the first ship of this class].

DREADNOUGHT (2), *n.* thick, long-piled cloth; coat made from this.

DREAM (1) [drēm], *n.* thought-processes of the unconscious while the conscious mind is at rest, those parts of this process which force themselves on the consciousness; an abstraction from realities, fantasy; improbable but preoccupying ambition, something far too pleasing to be real; (*pl.*) sleep in general. DREAM (2) (*pret. and p.pt.* DREAMED, DREAMT), *v.t. and i.* to have dreams about; have dreams in sleep, see visions; have aspirations, wild ambitions; imagine, have baseless fancies. [OE.].

DREAMER [drē'mer], *n.* one who dreams, idealist, wild visionary.

DREAMILY [drē'mi-li], *adv.* in dreamy fashion.

DREAMINESS [drē'mi-nes], *n.* state of being dreamy.

DREAMLAND [drēm'land], *n.* the world of unreality, sleep.

DREAMLESS [drēm'les], *adj.* without dreams; (of sleep) completely undisturbed. DREAMLESSLY, *adv.* in d. fashion.

DREAMLIKE [drēm'līk], *adj.* unreal, like a dream.

DREAMY [drē'mi], *adj.* like a dream, full of hazy content, unreal; given to dreams and fanciful ambitions.

DREAR [drēer], *adj.* melancholy, gloomy, desolate. [*Next*].

DREARY [drēer'ri], *adj.* depressingly gloomy, wearisome, dispiriting. DREARILY, *adv.* in d. fashion. DREARINESS, *n.* state of being d. DREARISOME, *adj.* inducing dreariness, wearisome. [OE.].

DREDGE (1) [drej], *n.* mechanism for clearing or dragging ponds, rivers etc., and fetching up things from the bottom. DREDGE (2), *v.t. and i.* to drag, clear, fetch up with a d.; employ a d. DREDGER (1), *n.* ship used for dredging at sea. [OE.].

DREDGE (3), *v.t.* (*cookery*) to sprinkle with flour, sugar etc. DREDGER (2), *n.* (*cookery*) container with a perforated lid for sprinkling. [ME. from Gk.].

DREE [drē], *v.t.* (*archaic*) to endure. [OE.].

DREGS [dregz], *n.(pl.)* sediment, *esp.* of wine, lees; (*fig.*) refuse, scum; criminals. DREGGISH, DREGGY, *adj.* full of dregs, fouled with dregs. [OIcel.].

DRENCH (1) [drensh], *v.t.* to soak, make thoroughly sodden with liquid; administer a draught to a horse or cow. DRENCH (2), *n.* veterinary draught or purgative. DRENCHER, *n.* funnel for giving a veterinary d. [OE.].

DRESDEN [drez'den], *n.* variety of porcelain. [*Dresden*, Germany].

DRESS (1) [dres], *v.t.* to put clothes on, adorn, decorate, put in order; draw up (troops) in straight lines; prepare and season with condiments; clean, bandage (a wound); *v.i.* to put on clothes, *esp.* put on or wear evening dress; wear, arrange, choose clothes; (*milit.*) get into a straight line; **to d. down,** to rub a horse down; (*fig.*) rebuke severely; **to d. up,** to deck oneself out specially for some occasion, wear fancy dress. DRESS (2), *n.* a garment; one-piece, skirted outer garment worn by women; clothing in general; **full d.,** formal uniform; **evening d.,** special garments worn in the evening on certain social occasions; **morning d.,** garments worn on similar occasions earlier in the day; **d. circle,** lowest tier of a theatre above the stalls; **d. rehearsal,** final rehearsal before a public performance, in which all takes place as if the public were present. [OFr.].

DRESSER (1) [dre'ser], *n.* one who dresses, *esp.* one who dresses an actor or actress; a surgeon's assistant. **DRESSER** (2), *n.* stand fitted with drawers and shelves for holding household utensils. [OFr.].

DRESSING [dre'sing], *n.* process of clothing, adorning; decoration, adornment; sauce or seasoning for food (*esp.* green salads); lint and liniment applied to a wound; manure, fertilizer; starch used for stiffening; the cleaning of metals; (*arch.*) moulding round windows or doors; **a d. down,** a severe scolding.

DRESSING-CASE [dre'sing-kās], *n.* box to hold toilet articles.

DRESSING-GOWN [dre'sing-gown], *n.* gown worn over night attire.

DRESSING-ROOM [dre'sing-rōōm], *n.* small room used for dressing and undressing.

DRESSING-TABLE [dre'sing-tā-bl], *n.* table or stand containing mirrors and toilet utensils.

DRESSMAKER [dres'mā-ker], *n.* one who makes dresses, *esp.* for a living, women's garment maker or tailor.

DRESSY [dre'si], *n.* showy; inclined to overdress.

DREW [drōō], *pret.* of DRAW. [ME.].

DRIBBLE [dri'bl], *v.t. and i.* to spill out in a feeble trickle, *esp.* saliva from the mouth; let fall in drips; run with a football on the field, controlling it by frequent light kicks; trickle out. DRIBBLER, *n.* one who dribbles. DRIBLET, *n.* small amount, *esp.* one of a series. [DRIP].

DRIER [drī'er], *n.* that which makes dry; machine for drying hair etc. by warm air; substance employed to dry oil paints quickly.

DRIFT (1) [drift], *n.* state or act of driving, condition of being driven or moved irrespective of volition; *esp.* a slow current in the sea produced by wind, similar movement of loose sand; (*naut.*) rate at which such a current moves; trend, slowly effective tendency in thought, conversation etc.; thing driven, *esp.* a heap of sand, snow, heaped up by the wind; South African ford. DRIFT (2), *v.t. and i.* to cause to move, float along; pile up into a d.; float with the tide or wind; move along without effort or control; (*fig.*) move to some condition or situation gradually and unconsciously, let oneself be carried along by events. [ME.].

DRIFTAGE [drif'tij], *n.* (*naut.*) amount by which a boat drifts off in bearing up against wind and water.

DRIFTER [drif'ter], *n.* one who, or that which, drifts; fishing-vessel used for fishing with a drift-net.

DRIFTING [drif'ting], *n.* act of drifting; the forming of a drift, the drift itself.

DRIFT-MINE [drift'mīn], *n.* coal-mine in which the coal lies near the surface and is reached by an inclined plane run into the ground.

DRIFT-NET [drift'net], *n.* floating or suspended fishing-net permitted to float with the tide.

DRIFT-WAY [drift'wā], *n.* road across a common for cattle; (*naut.*) course of a ship drifting; (*mining*) a drift.

DRIFTWOOD [drift'wŏŏd], *n.* wood washed ashore.

DRILL (1) [dril], *n.* instrument for piercing tough matter by a rapidly turning point; co-ordinated physical exercises performed by a body of persons; trial military manoeuvres, practice or exercise of any kind. DRILL (2), *v.t. and i.* to bore a hole (in) with a d.; do d. or cause to do d.; instruct or train. DRILL-SERGEANT, sergeant who superintends d. and exercises. [Du.].

DRILL (3), *n.* narrow furrow for planting seed; machine for driving and sowing such furrows. DRILL (4), *v.t.* to sow seed in drills. DRILL-HARROW, small harrow used for pulverizing the earth between the drills, and destroying weeds. [Uncert.].

DRILL (5), *n.* twilled linen stuff. [Germ. from L.].

DRILY [drī'li], *adv.* in a dry manner (of speech).

DRINK (1) [dringk], (*pret.* **drank,** *p.pt.* **drunk**) [dringk], *v.t. and i.* to swallow liquid, absorb, draw in deeply;

(*fig.*) accept credulously; perform the action of consuming liquid; consume alcoholic liquor, *esp.* habitually and to excess. DRINK (2), *n.* liquid for drinking, liquid drunk, alcoholic liquor, *esp.* as a vice. [OE.].

DRINKABLE [dring'ka-bl], *adj.* fit to drink.

DRINKER [dring'ker], *n.* one who drinks; one who habitually drinks alcoholic liquors.

DRINKING (1) [dring'king], *n.* act of one who drinks; consumption of alcoholic liquor. DRINKING (2), *adj.* relating to the consumption of alcoholic liquor.

DRINKING BOUT [dring'king-bowt], *n.* session of hard drinking.

DRINKING-FOUNTAIN [dring'king-foun-ten], *n.* public fountain of drinking-water.

DRINKING-SONG [dring'king-song], *n.* song, generally in praise of alcoholic liquor.

DRINKING-WATER [dring'king-waw-ter], *n.* water fit to drink.

DRIP (1) (*pres.pt.* **dripping,** *pret. and p.pt.* **dripped**) [drip], *v.t. and i.* to cause to fall in drops; fall slowly in drops. DRIP (2), *n.* one of a series of small drops, sound made by the continous falling of drops; dripstone. [OE.].

DRIPPING [dri'ping], *n.* fat obtained from roasting or frying meat.

DRIPSTONE [drip'stōn], *n.* (*arch.*) moulding over the heads of doorways and windows to throw off rain.

DRIVE (1) (*pret.* **drove,** *p.pt.* **driven**) [drīv], *v.t. and i.* to give motion to, force into motion by a violent blow, by orders or threatenings, force on or in by a blow, set a ball in motion by a steady, strong stroke; compel, control the motion of animals or vehicles, cause (a machine) to move, convey in a vehicle; (*fig.*) compel, enforce to; cut through, force a way through (by strong, steady effort); be in control of the motion of an animal or vehicle; **to d. at,** to aim at (in conversation); **to d. home,** to force right in; (*fig.*) bring forcefully and definitely to the hearer. DRIVE (2), *n.* state of being driven in a vehicle, trip made for pleasure in a vehicle; broad road made for driving up to a house, carriage-way through a wood; process of driving game towards the hunters or guns; act of striking a ball with the whole bodily force and swing behind the blow, *esp.* the initial stroke from the tee in golf; vigour and energy of personality; manner in which the power of an engine is employed; intensive campaign of any sort. DRIVABLE, *adj.* capable of being driven. [OE.].

DRIVEL (1) (*pres.pt.* **drivelling,** *pret. and p.pt.* **drivelled**) [dri'vel], *v.i.* to dribble, trickle saliva from the mouth; talk or write in a rambling, feeble-minded fashion. DRIVEL (2), *n.* stupid talk or writing. DRIVELLER, *n.* one who drivels, silly, woolly-minded talker. [OE.].

DRIVELLING (1) [dri've-ling], *n.* silly, rambling speech. DRIVELLING (2), *adj.* that drivels; (*coll.*) nonsensical.

DRIVER [drī'ver], *n.* one who, or that which, drives; one who controls a vehicle or machine; that which imparts motion to something else; wooden golf-club used for driving from the tee; drover.

DRIVING [drī'ving], *n.* the controlling of a vehicle; the striking of a golf-ball from the tee.

DRIZZLE (1) [dri'zl], *v.t. and i.* to let fall in a fine, light spray; rain in this fashion. DRIZZLE (2), *n.* fine, light rain. DRIZZLY, *adj.* drizzling spasmodically. [OE.].

DROGUE [drōg], *n.* sea-anchor; wind-sock; target towed by an aircraft; device attached to a bomb to control the speed and direction of its descent; board on a harpoon line to check the speed of the whale. [DRAG (2).].

DROLL (1) [drōl], *adj.* waggish, comical by virtue of an odd mock-seriousness. DROLL (2), *n.* waggish fellow, clown. DROLLERY, *n.* waggishness. DROLLY, *adv.* in a d. fashion. [Fr.].

DROME [drōm], *n.* (*coll.*) aerodrome.

DROMEDARY [dro'me-däer-i], *n.* Arabian one-humped riding camel. [LL. from Gk.].

DRONE (1) [drōn], *n.* male of the honey-bee, with no function beyond the generative; (*fig.*) idle, useless person; low-pitched humming sound produced by the honey-bee, sound resembling this; one of the tubes of a bagpipe producing a deep, humming note. DRONE (2), *v.t. and i.* to utter a deep, monotonous humming sound; live like a d. DRONING, *n.* a deep rhythmical hum. [OE.].

DROOL [drōōl], *v.t. and i.* to let saliva trickle from the mouth; talk incoherent nonsense. [DRIVEL].

The accent ' after a syllable = stress (u-pon'). The mark ‾ over a vowel = length (ā in made; ō in bone).

DROOP (1) [drōŏp], *v.t. and i.* to hang limply forward and down, sag, let the head or top loll limply forward; *(fig.)* languish, wilt, evince complete loss of spirit; allow to hang limply. DROOP (2), *n.* state of drooping, hanging weakly, wilting. DROOPING, *adj.* languishing, wilting. DROOPINGLY, *adv.* in drooping fashion. [OScand.].

DROP (1) [drop], *n.* small globule of liquid in suspension before falling, measurement for small quantities of liquid, *esp.* medicine; *(fig.)* the smallest possible quantity of liquid, anything resembling in shape a globule of liquid, as certain sweets, ornaments etc.; the vertical distance between two objects regarded as the distance to be fallen from the higher to the lower; a falling from a higher to a lower position; *(fig.)* fall in position or rank, sudden lowering in esteem, spirits; lessening in quantity or degree; that which drops, as a stage curtain, gallows platform; *(football)* a drop-kick. DROP (2) *(pres.pt.* DROPPING, *pret. and p.pt.* DROPPED), *v.t.* to let fall in drops; let fall by releasing hold; *(coll.)* set down someone from a vehicle; cause to fall; *(fig.)* give up, stop doing; let fall; lower the voice; *(of animals)* give birth to; *v.i.* to fall in drops; fall, slip to a lower level; be reduced in quantity, intensity etc.; cease to be thought of or discussed; **to d. a brick,** *(slang)* to commit a tactless blunder; **to d. in,** to call, visit casually; **to d. off,** to decline; fall asleep; **to d. out of,** to cease to participate in; **to d. on,** to blame, take to task; **to let d.,** to utter (a remark) with real or assumed casualness. [OE.].

DROP-KICK (1) [drop′kik], *n.* kick in Rugby football in which the ball is dropped and kicked as soon as it leaves the ground. DROP-KICK (2), *v.i.* to make a d.

DROPLET [drop′let], *n.* small drop, *esp.* from sneezing.

DROPPER [dro′per], *n.* that which drops; instrument for releasing liquid drop by drop.

DROPPING [dro′ping], *n.* act of letting drop; that which drops; *(pl.)* excrement of animals.

DROP-SCENE [drop′sēn], *n.* curtain or scenery lowered to cut off part of the stage when desired.

DROP-SCONE [drop′skon], *n.* flat scone made by dropping batter on a griddle.

DROPSICAL [drop′si-kal], *adj.* relating to, suffering from, resembling, dropsy. DROPSICALLY, *adv.* in d. fashion.

DROPSY [drop′si], *n. (med.)* morbid gathering of watery fluid in the tissues or cavities of the body. DROPSIED, *adj.* swollen with d. [Gk.].

DROSHKY, DROSKY [drosh′ki, dros′ki], *n.* open four-wheeled Russian carriage with a bench for seating passengers. [Russ.].

DROSS [dros], *n.* rubbish, refuse; impurities thrown off by molten metal; *(fig.)* that which has no real worth.

DROUGHT, DROUTH [drowt, drowth, drōŏth], *n.* long period of dry weather, extreme dryness of climate. [OE.].

DROUGHTY, DROUTHY [drow′ti, drōŏ′thi], *adj.* dry, thirsty; in a state of drought. DROUGHTINESS, *n.* state of being d.

DROVE (1) [drōv], *n.* number of cattle or sheep driven along in a body. DROVE (2), *v.t. and i.* to drive cattle or sheep, be a drover. [OE.].

DROVE (3), *pret.* of DRIVE (1). [OE.].

DROVER [drō′ver], *n.* one who takes cattle or sheep to market in a drove.

DROWN [drown], *v.t. and i.* to die or cause to suffocate to death by submersion in liquid; *(fig.)* overwhelm, blot out; extinguish by overwhelming. [ONorw.].

DROWSE (1) [drowz], *v.t. and i.* to doze, be in a sleepy, sluggish state; make drowsy. DROWSE (2), *n.* doze, state of sluggishness. [OE.].

DROWSY [drow′zi], *adj.* sleepy, inclined to doze, torpid; tending to induce sleep. DROWSILY, *adv.* sleepily, sluggishly. DROWSINESS, *n.* condition of being d.

DRUB *(pres.pt.* **drubbing,** *pret. and p.pt.* **drubbed)** [drub], *v.t.* to beat with successive blows, belabour thoroughly, cudgel. DRUBBING, *n.* a cudgelling, good beating. [Swed.].

DRUDGE (1) [druj], *n.* ill-used menial, overworked with heavy, mean labour. DRUDGE (2), *v.i.* to perform heavy menial labour like a d. DRUDGINGLY, *adv.* like a d. [OE.].

DRUDGERY [dru′je-ri], *n.* servile labour of a drudge; distasteful work.

DRUG (1) [drug], *n.* a medicine; substance affecting the organs of the body and producing unnatural excitement or unconsciousness etc.; **d. on the market,** unsaleable article. DRUG (2) *(pres.pt.* DRUGGING, *pret. and p.pt.* DRUGGED), *v.t.* to mingle a d. with; add a narcotic drug to (food); cause to consume a d. in order to cause torpor, unconsciousness, or abnormal activity.

DRUGGET [dru′git], *n.* coarse woollen cloth used as a cheap floor-covering. [OFr.].

DRUGGIST [dru′gist], *n.* apothecary.

DRUID [drōŏ′id], *n.* priest of the ancient pagan Celts; Eisteddfod officer. DRUIDESS, *n.* woman Druid. DRUIDIC(AL) [drōŏ-i′dik(-al)], *adj.* relating to Druids or Druidism. DRUIDISM, *n.* the religious system and ceremonial of Druids.

DRUM (1) [drum], *n. (mus.)* instrument consisting of a skin or parchment stretched tightly across the openings of a hollow (usually cylindrical) framework, played by beating with sticks; resonant sound produced by this; anything resembling this in shape; *(anat.)* membrane between the inner and outer ear. DRUM (2) *(pres.pt.* DRUMMING, *p.pt.* DRUMMED), *v.t.* to beat on a d., beat on something resonant so that a drumming sound is produced; thump rapidly and continuously with the fingers or heels; *(fig.)* impart an idea or fact by frequent repetition; **to d. out,** to expel ceremoniously from the army to the beating of drums. [Uncert.].

DRUMFIRE [drum′fīer], *n.* heavy, continuous fire from a large number of guns directed upon one target.

DRUMHEAD [drum′hed], *n.* the parchment stretched over the head of a drum; **d. court-martial,** emergency court-martial held in the field during active service.

DRUM-MAJOR [drum-mā′jer], *n.* senior band sergeant.

DRUMMER [dru′mer], *n.* one who plays the drum; *(U.S. coll.)* commercial traveller.

DRUMSTICK [drum′stik], *n.* stick used to play the drum; *(coll.)* lower part of a cooked chicken's leg.

DRUNK [drungk], *adj., p.pt. and n.* intoxicated with alcohol, inebriated; *(fig.)* overcome by some strong emotion or idea; intoxicated person, *esp.* one taken up by the police. [OE.].

DRUNKARD [drung′kerd], *n.* person seriously addicted to over-indulgence in alcoholic liquors.

DRUNKEN [drung′ken], *adj.* inebriated; habitually drunk; typical of, produced by, drunkenness; *(fig.)* at a perilous angle, liable to overbalance. DRUNKENLY, *adv.* in d. fashion. DRUNKENNESS, *n.* condition of being d.

DRUPE [drōŏp], *n. (bot.)* soft fleshy fruit containing a nutty kernel. DRUPACEOUS [drōŏ-pā′shōŏs], *adj. (bot.)* relating to drupes. DRUPEL(ET), *n.* small d. [Gk.].

DRY (1) [drī], *adj.* lacking moisture or liquid of any sort; having a low rainfall; *(coll.)* thirsty, wanting a drink; *(of places)* where intoxicants are forbidden; *(of wine)* not sweet; *(fig.)* boring, uninteresting; *(of humour)* undemonstrative but keen-witted; **d. bread,** bread without butter; **d. goods,** non-perishable commodities; **d. work,** work inciting thirst; **d. bob,** one at Eton who plays cricket and football instead of rowing; **d. battery,** electric battery composed of sealed cells containing absorbent matter; **d. wall,** one built without mortar. DRY (2) *(pret. and p.pt.* DRIED), *v.t. and i.* to make d.; become d.; **to d. up,** to cease to provide something; *(coll.)* cease talking; *(of a speaker)* forget what to say. [OE.].

DRYAD [drī′ad], *n.* wood-nymph. [Gk.].

DRYASDUST (1) [drī′as-dust], *n.* pedant. DRYASDUST (2), *adj.* dull, pedantic.

DRY-CLEAN [drī-klēn′], *v.t.* to clean (clothes, etc.) with chemicals without using water. DRY-CLEANER, *n.* one who dry-cleans.

DRYER [drī′er], *n.* a drier.

DRY-EYED [drī-īd′], *adj.* tearless.

DRY-FLY [drī′flī], *n. and adj.* artificial fly dangled above the water in fishing; *(of fishing)* using this.

DRYING [drī′ing], *adj.* intended to free from moisture; freeing, becoming free from moisture.

DRYISH [drī′ish], *adj.* somewhat dry.

DRYLY [drī′li], *adv.* in dry fashion.

DRYNESS [drī′ness], *n.* condition of being dry.

DRY-NURSE (1) [drī-nurs′], *n.* nurse who attends to a child but does not suckle it; *(fig.)* assiduous helper and adviser. DRY-NURSE (2), *v.t. (fig.)* to look after with almost ridiculous solicitude.

DRY-POINT (1) [drī′point], *n.* needle used to make a mark on a copper plate in engraving, where acid is not used; print from such an engraving. DRY-POINT (2), v.i. to engrave with a d.

DRY ROT [drī-rot'], n. decaying of timber through the action of fungi.

DRYSALTER [drī-sawl'ter], n. one who trades in chemical preparations or salted foodstuffs. DRY-SALTERY [drī-sawl'te-ri], n. trade of a d.

DRYSHOD [drī'shod], adj. and adv. without wetting the feet.

DUAL [dyōō'al], adj. relating to the numeral two, double; (gram.) applied to the grammatical number by which certain languages express two of a thing. [L.].

DUALISM [dyōō'a-lizm], n. philosophic and religious doctrine of opposing forces in a twofold universe. DUALIST, n. one who believes in d. DUALISTIC [dyōō-a-lis'tik], adj. pertaining to d.

DUALITY [dyōō-a'li-ti], n. state or quality of being dual. [LL.].

DUALIZE [dyōō'a-līz], v.t. to make dual.

DUB (1) (pres.pt. **dubbing**, pret. and p.pt. **dubbed** [dub], v.t. to make a person knight by laying a sword on the shoulder; name, confer (a title or epithet) upon; (cinema) translate dialogue, sub-titles etc. into another language in such a fashion that the words chosen conform with the movements of the lips etc. of the actors; rub with grease.

DUB (2), v.i. (slang) to subscribe, usually with up.

DUBBIN, DUBBING [du'bin], n. thick grease used for softening or waterproofing leather. [DUB (1)].

DUBIETY [dyōō-bī'e-ti], n. doubt. [L.].

DUBIOUS [dyōō'bi-ŏŏs], adj. doubtful, uncertain; questionable; having several interpretations. DUBI-OUSLY, adv. in d. fashion. [L.].

DUBITABLE [dyōō'bi-ta-bl], adj. dubious, to be doubted. DUBITABLY, adv. in d. fashion.

DUBITATIVE [dyōō'bi-ta-tiv], adj. hesitant, doubt-ful, inclined to doubt.

DUCAL [dyōō'kal], adj. relating to a duke. [L.].

DUCAT [du'kat], n. medieval European gold coin. [LL.].

DUCHESS [du'ches], n. duke's wife, female holder of a duchy. [LL.].

DUCHESSE [dōō-shes', du'ches], n. kind of satin; kind of dressing-table; **d. lace**, a Brussels pillow-lace. [Fr.].

DUCHY [du'chi], n. dominions of a ruling duke. [LL. from L.].

DUCK (1) [duk], n. coarse cotton or linen cloth. [Du.].

DUCK (2), n. broad-beaked water-fowl, esp. the female; flesh of this prepared as food; (coll.) likeable person; (slang) score of nought at cricket; act of ducking; **to play ducks and drakes**, to be absurdly wasteful; **like water off a duck's back**, without making the least impression; **like a d. to water**, naturally and confidently. DUCK (3), v.t. and i. to jerk the head and upper body so as to dodge a blow, get out of sight, or present a smaller target; plunge suddenly under water. [OE.].

DUCK-BILL [duk'bil], n. the platypus, an egg-laying amphibious Australasian mammal.

DUCK-BILLED [duk'bild], adj. having a bill resembling that of a duck.

DUCKBOARD [duk'bawd], n. planking to form a path across muddy ground.

DUCKING [du'king], n. a severe wetting by being plunged into water. DUCKING-STOOL, chair on a long lever, in which nagging women were tied and ducked in water.

DUCKLING [duk'ling], n. young duck.

DUCK'S EGG [duks'eg], n. (cricket) score of nought.

DUCK-SHOT [duk'shot], n. ammunition used in shooting wild duck.

DUCKWEED [duk'wēd], n. a plant covering the surface of still water.

DUCT [dukt], n. tube, covered channel carrying liquid; (anat.) channel carrying glandular secretions in animal bodies; (bot.) channel containing air or water. [L.].

DUCTILE [duk'til], adj. (of metals) able to be drawn out into a fine wire; (fig.) easily influenced. DUC-TILELY, adv. in d. fashion. DUCTILITY [duk-ti'li-ti], n. state of being d. [L.].

DUCTLESS [dukt'les], adj. having no duct; **d. gland**, an endocrine gland.

DUD (1) [dud], n. (coll.) shell or bomb etc. which lands but fails to explode; defective instrument or object; useless person; bad coin or note. DUD (2), adj. useless, defective, no good. [Uncert.].

DUDE [dyōōd], n. (U.S. slang) a dandy, fop. [Unkn.].

DUDGEON [du'jon], n. sullen resentment, annoy-ance, anger. [Uncert.].

DUDS [dudz], n. (slang) clothes; tattered garments, cheap clothing. [OScand.].

DUE (1) [dyōō], adj. (of debt, money) owing, requiring settlement, fitting, required by justice etc.; appointed, promised for a certain time, expected in view of custom or promise; **d. to**, caused by, arising from. DUE (2), adv. (used with points of the compass) exactly, precisely. DUE (3), n. sum to be paid, sum legally payable; anything which should be given in justice or respect. [Fr. from L.].

DUEL (1) [dyōō'el], n. single combat between two per-sons, usually armed with similar weapons and fighting in accordance with prearranged rules, to settle a quarrel; (fig.) battle of wits. DUEL (2) (pres.pt. DUEL-LING, pret. and p.pt. DUELLED), v.i. to fight a d., practise duelling. DUELLER, n. one who fights a d. DUELLING, n. custom of fighting duels. DUELLIST, n. one skilled in duelling. [MedL.].

DUENNA [dyōō-e'nah], n. middle-aged woman who looks after the girls of a Spanish upper-class family; chaperon. [Sp. from L.].

DUET [dyōō-et'], n. (mus.) piece for two performers. [It.].

DUFF (1) [duf], n. suet pudding. [DOUGH].

DUFF (2), v.t. (coll.) to strike (a ball) badly, esp. in golf; muff, bungle. [Back-formation from DUFFER].

DUFFEL, DUFFLE [du'fl], n. wool cloth with a heavy nap. DUFFLE-COAT, short outer coat of thick cloth, worn esp. by seamen. [Duffel, Belgium, where originally made].

DUFFER [du'fer], n. clumsy, slow, heavy-witted person. [Unkn.].

DUG (1) [dug], n. teat of female mammals. [Swed.].

DUG (2), pret. and p.pt. of DIG.

DUGOUT [du'gowt], n. canoe made of a hollowed tree-trunk; cavity dug out of the side of a trench for living quarters and shelter against shell-fire etc.; (slang) a retired officer recalled for service.

DUKE [dyōōk], n. member of the highest rank in the peerage; (slang pl.) fists. [OFr. from L.].

DUKEDOM [dyōōk'dum], n. territory, jurisdiction or rank of a duke.

DUKERY [dyōō'ke-ri], n. duke's residential estate; **the Dukeries**, district in the English Midlands.

DULCAMARA [dul-ka-mah'rah], n. (bot.) the woody nightshade, bittersweet. [L.].

DULCET [dul'sit], adj. melodious, sweet. [OFr.].

DULCIMER [dul'si-mer], n. (mus.) instrument con-sisting of metal wires stretched across a sounding board and played by striking with two hammers.

DULL (1) [dul], adj. slow-witted, obtuse, inept in compre-hension; boring, commonplace; dim, cloudy, tarnished, unpolished; blunt. DULL (2), v.t. and i. to make d., become d. DULLISH, adj. rather d. DULLY, adv. in d. fashion. [OE.].

DULLARD [du'lerd], n. stupid person.

DULSE [duls], n. (bot.) edible red seaweed. [Gael.].

DULY [dyōō'li], adv. fitly, promptly.

DUMA [dōō'mah], n. parliament of Imperial Russia from 1906-17. [Russ.].

DUMB [dum], adj. incapable of articulation; silent, not speaking; (U.S. coll.) stupid, incapable of expressing an idea; **d. show**, mime without words. DUMBLY, adv. silently, as if d. [OE.].

DUMB-BARGE [dum-bahj'], n. barge without sails.

DUMB-BELL [dum'bel], n. bar with a heavy knob at each end, held one in each hand during arm exercises; (slang) a dolt.

DUMBFOUND [dum-fownd'], v.t. to strike dumb with amazement, confound.

DUMB-IRON [dum'īern], n. each of the projecting ends of the side elements of a motor-car chassis to which the forward end of the front spring is shackled.

DUMB-WAITER [dum-wā'ter], n. framework of shelves, used for holding dishes etc., and obviating the need for a servant at meals.

DUMDUM [dum'dum], n. soft-nosed bullet which expands when it hits anything hard. [Dumdum, Indian arsenal].

DUMMY (1) [du'mi], n. bogus object; model of a human being; model, empty carton or the like used to advertise goods; artificial teat for young children to suck; (bridge) partner of the declarer, who when play begins exposes his hand on the table and takes no part in the play; actor without a speaking part; **tailor's d.**, person with a dressy appearance but little real worth; tailor's model. DUMMY (2), adj. sham, bogus. [DUMB].

DUMP (1) [dump], v.t. and i. to unload roughly

and casually by tipping out of a car or basket, deposit (refuse) on a rubbish heap; (*comm.*) throw great quantities of goods on a foreign market at unprofitable prices; descend abruptly with a bump. DUMP (2), *n.* heap of refuse, place where refuse may be left; (*coll.*) dirty, untidy place cluttered up with junk; (*milit.*) deposit of supplies for future use. [Dan.].

DUMPLING [dump'ling], *n.* ball of suet and dough etc., boiled in water. APPLE-DUMPLING, an apple cooked in pastry.

DUMPS [dumps], *n.* (*coll.*) low spirits, sullen depression. [Unkn.].

DUMPTY [dump'ti], *n.* large upholstered cushion used as a stool.

DUMPY (1) [dum'pi], *adj.* short and podgy. DUMPY (2), *n.* high hassock; short-legged variety of hen; short-handled umbrella.

DUN (1) [dun], *adj.* of the colour d., drab. DUN (2), *n.* dull, greyish-brown colour; variety of artificial fly for fishing. [OE.].

DUN (3) (*pres.pt.* **dunning**, *pret. and p.pt.* **dunned**), *v.t.* (of a creditor) to pester insistently for payment. DUN (4), *n.* creditor, one who persistently demands to be paid. [ME.].

DUNCE [duns], *n.* a dullard, who can learn nothing, very stupid pupil. DUNCISH, *adj.* like a d., stupid. [*Duns* Scotus, theologian whose followers were opposed to the study of the classics].

DUNDERHEAD [dun'der-hed], *n.* blockhead. [Unkn.].

DUNDREARY [dun-drēer'ri], *n.* (*usually pl.*) long sidewhiskers worn without a beard. [Lord *Dundreary*, character in a Victorian play].

DUNE [dōon], *n.* low hill of loose sand, close to the shore. [ODu.].

DUNG (1) [dung], *n.* excrement. DUNG (2), *v.t. and i.* to manure with d.; drop excrement. [OE.].

DUNGAREE [dung-ga-rē'], *n.* cotton cloth used for sails and coarse working clothes; (*pl.*) overalls etc. of this material. [Hind.].

DUNGEON (1), **†DONJON** [dun'jun], *n.* (*originally*) the strongest tower of a castle; underground prison-cell in a castle. DUNGEON (2), *v.t.* to confine in a d. [OFr.].

DUNG-FORK [dung'fawk], *n.* fork used for throwing dung and spreading it as manure.

DUNGHILL [dung'hil], *n.* pile of dung; (*fig.*) vile disgusting place.

DUNGY [dung'i], *adj.* smeared, tainted with dung.

DUNIWASSAL [dōō'ni-wo-sal], *n.* (*Scots*) Highland gentleman of secondary rank. [Gael.].

DUNLIN [dun'lin], *n.* (*ornith.*) the reddish sandpiper.

DUNNAGE [du'nij], *n.* brushwood, branches etc., placed under a ship's cargo to prevent damage by water etc. [Unkn.].

DUNNING [du'ning], *n.* act of a creditor who presses to be paid.

DUNNOCK [du'nok], *n.* the hedge-sparrow.

DUNT [dunt], *n.* hard thump; blow sustained by aircraft on running into a vertical air current. [OE.].

DUO- (1) [dyōō'ō], *pref.* two. [L.].

DUO (2), *n.* song in two parts; duet; variety act performed by two persons. [L.].

DUODECENNIAL [dyōō-ō-de-se'ni-al], *adj.* occurring every twelve years. [L.].

DUODECIMAL (1) [dyōō-ō-de'si-mal], *adj.* reckoned in twelves, pertaining to twelve. DUODECIMAL (2), *n.*(*pl.*) numerical system reckoning by twelves. DUODECIMALLY, *adv.* in a d. fashion. [L.].

DUODECIMO [dyōō-ō-de'si-mō], *n.* a book, or the size of a book, in which the sheet is folded into twelve leaves. [L.].

DUODENAL [dyōō-ō-dē'nal], *adj.* of, or relating to, the duodenum.

DUODENARY [dyōō-ō-dē'na-ri], *adj.* in twelves. [L.].

DUODENUM [dyōō-ō-dē'num], *n.* upper end of the small intestine, leading out of the stomach. [MedL.].

DUPE (1) [dyōōp], *n.* one who is easily deceived. DUPE (2), *v.t.* to deceive, trick. DUPABLE, *adj.* easy to d. DUPER, *n.* one who dupes. DUPERY, *n.* act of duping.

DUPLE [dyōō'pl], *adj.* (of ratio) having the first element double the second; (*mus.*) having two beats to the bar. [L.].

DUPLEX [dyōō'pleks], *adj.* twofold, having two parts, *esp.* of machinery and in botany. [L.].

DUPLICATE (1) [dyōō'pli-kat], *adj.* being an identical copy of something; (*arith.*) in the ratio of one

square to another. DUPLICATE (2), *n.* a replica. DUPLICATE (3) [dyōō'pli-kāt], *v.t.* to make a copy identical with (the original), repeat (an action etc.) identically; make copies of on a duplicator. [L.].

DUPLICATION [dyōō-pli-kā'shn], *n.* act of duplicating, condition of being duplicated. [L.].

DUPLICATIVE [dyōō'pli-ka-tiv], *adj.* relating to duplication, tending to duplicate.

DUPLICATOR [dyōō'pli-kā-ter], *n.* machine for rapidly making numerous copies from a stencilled original.

DUPLICITY [dyōō-pli'si-ti], *n.* deceit, trickery, hypocrisy. [L.].

DURABLE [dyōō'ra-bl], *adj.* able to withstand long and hard use or exposure. DURABILITY [dyōō-ra-bi'li-ti], *n.* condition of being d. DURABLY, *adv.* in d. fashion.

DURALUMIN [dyōō-ra'lyōō-min], *n.* (*prot.*) a tough alloy of aluminium.

DURA MATER [dōō-rah-mā'ter], *n.* the tough membrane round the brain and spinal cord. [L.].

DURANCE [dyōō'rans], *n.* imprisonment.

DURATION [dyōō-rā'shn], *n.* period of existence or continuance; **for the d.,** until the end of the war. [L.].

DURATIVE [dyōō'ra-tiv], *adj.* (*gram.*) denoting an action going on, imperfective.

DURBAR [dur'bah(r)], *n.* state levee in India formerly held by the King as Emperor of India or by the Viceroy. [Hind.].

DURESS [dyōō-res'], *n.* confinement, forcible compulsion; (*leg.*) compulsion by threat of bodily hurt. [OFr.].

DURING [dyōō'ring], *prep.* in the course of, through the existence or continuance of.

DURST [durst], *archaic pret.* of DARE. [OE.].

DUSK (1) [dusk], *n.* the twilight at the end of the day. DUSK (2), *adj.* (*poet.*) dim, dusky. [OE., OScand.].

DUSKISH [dus'kish], *adj.* tending to be dusky.

DUSKY [dus'ki], *adj.* shadowy; of dark complexion. DUSKILY, *adv.* in a d. fashion. DUSKINESS, *n.* condition of being d.

DUST (1) [dust], *n.* powdery particles of matter; (*fig.*) a dead and crumbled body; **to bite the d.,** to be flung upon the ground in combat; **to throw d. in the eyes of,** to deceive; **to kick up a d.,** (*slang*) to cause a disturbance, protest. DUST (2), *v.t.* to brush or wipe the d. off; sprinkle with powder. [OE.].

DUSTBIN [dust'bin], *n.* container for household refuse.

DUST-BOWL [dust'bōl], *n.* (*orig. U.S.*) area of land turned to useless dust by prolonged drought and neglect.

DUST-CART [dust'kaht], *n.* cart in which refuse is collected and removed.

DUST-COVER [dust'ku-ver], *n.* paper jacket round a new book.

DUSTER [dus'ter], *n.* cloth for wiping away dust.

DUSTINESS [dus'ti-nes], *n.* condition of being dusty.

DUSTING [dus'ting], *n.* act of removing dust; (*coll.*) a thrashing.

DUSTMAN [dust'man], *n.* labourer who collects household refuse.

DUSTPAN [dust'pan], *n.* flat shovel into which dust may be easily brushed.

DUSTY [dus'ti], *adj.* powdery; covered in dust; **not so d.,** (*slang*) fairly good.

DUTCH (1) [duch], *n.* (*slang*) wife. [DUCHESS].

DUTCH (2), *n.*(*pl.*) the inhabitants of Holland; their language. DUTCH (3), *adj.* relating to Holland and its people; **D. courage,** false courage inspired by drink; **double-D.,** (*coll.*) nonsense; incomprehensible.

DUTCHMAN [duch'man], *n.* inhabitant of Holland.

DUTEOUS [dyōō'ti-ōos], *adj.* respectful, obedient. DUTEOUSLY, *adv.* dutifully. DUTEOUSNESS, *n.* dutifulness.

DUTIABLE [dyōō'ti-a-bl], *adj.* chargeable with customs or other duty.

DUTIFUL [dyōō'ti-fool], *adj.* submissive and respectful to one's superiors, attentive to one's (moral) duties. DUTIFULLY, *adv.* in d. fashion. DUTIFULNESS, *n.* d. quality or conduct.

DUTY [dyōō'ti], *n.* moral or legal obligation to pursue some action; some task or action so performed; task or action obligatory upon some rank or office; a fitting expression of homage or respect; particular task or set of tasks; indirect taxation payable on certain imports, exports, legal transactions etc.; (*mech.*) ratio of work done to fuel consumed; **to be on d.,** to be engaged in carrying out

---

ōō is pronounced as in food; ŏŏ as in hood; th as in *think*; TH as in *that*; zh as in azure. ~ = related to.

instructions; **d. officer,** the officer on d. for a set period. [OFr.].

DUUMVIR [dyŏō'um-ver], *n.* one of two equal and joint officers. [L.].

DUX [duks], *n.* leader; in Scotland, head pupil of a ·class or school; (*mus.*) chief subject in a fugue. [L.].

DWARF (1) [dwawf], *n.* (*myth.*) small goblin living underground and often working metals; undersized man, woman or other creature. DWARF (2), *adj.* abnormally small; **d. tree,** tree whose branches shoot near the root. DWARF (3), *v.t.* to make seem tiny or insignificant by comparison, overshadow; stunt or impede normal development in. [OE.].

DWARFISH [dwaw'fish], *adj.* very small, smaller than is proper or normal, underdeveloped. DWARF-ISHLY, *adv.* in a d. fashion. DWARFISHNESS, *n.* condition of being d.

DWELL (1) (*pret. and p.pt.* dwelt) [dwel], *v.i.* to inhabit, reside or live in; pause; **to d. on,** to pause at, ponder over, discuss at length. DWELL (2), *n.* (*mech.*) regular pause in the motion of a machine. [OE.].

DWELLER [dwe'ler], *n.* one who dwells.

DWELLING [dwe'ling], *n.* place to dwell in, the house in which one lives and sleeps.

DWINDLE [dwin'dl], *v.i.* to grow less by wasting or shrinkage, grow smaller, pass slowly into decay or oblivion. [OE.].

DYAD [dī'ad], *n.* a pair, something consisting of two equal parts; (*chem.*) element with atomic weight equalling two atoms of hydrogen. DYADIC [dī-a'dik], *adj.* relating to a d. [Gk.].

DYAK [dī'ak], *n.* **a member of a people in Borneo.** [Malay].

DYARCHY [dī'ah-ki], *n.* a diarchy. [Gk.].

DYE (1) [dī], *n.* any substance for tinting fabrics etc.; the colour produced by this. DYE (2) (DYES, DYE-ING, DYED), *v.t. and i.* to tint or stain with a d.; undergo change of colour by being dyed. [OE.].

DYEING [dī'ing], *n.* act, trade or occupation of a dyer.

DYER [dī'er], *n.* one whose trade is dyeing; **dyer's weed,** (*bot.*) plant from which is obtained a yellow dye.

DYESTUFFS [dī'stufs], *n.(pl.)* substances employed in dyeing.

DYE-WORKS [dī'werks], *n.* place where dyeing is done.

DYING [dī'ing], *adj.* passing in death, approaching death, an end; fading, losing colour, life, vigour, as at the approach of death. [DIE].

DYKE, see DIKE.

DYNA-, *pref.* power, force. [Gk.].

DYNAMIC [dī-na'mik], *adj.* having power, energy; relating to force in motion; (*fig.*) having energy,

force of personality, vigour; (*met.*) relating to dynamism. [Gk.].

DYNAMICAL [dī-na'mi-kal], *adj.* relating to dynamics. DYNAMICALLY, *adv.* in d. fashion.

DYNAMICS [dī-na'miks], *n.* science dealing with energy and the movement of matter.

DYNAMISM [dī'na-mizm], *n.* philosophy basing the universe on the interplay of natural forces.

DYNAMITE (1) [dī'na-mit], *n.* explosive much used in blasting, consisting of nitro-glycerine stabilized by mixture with a porous substance. DYNAMITE (2), *v.t.* to blow up with d. DYNAMITER, *n.* one who endeavours to create terror and social disruption by acts of violence with d. [Gk.].

DYNAMO [dī'na-mō], *n.* machine for changing mechanical into electrical energy. [Gk.].

DYNAMOMETER [dī-na-mo'mi-ter], *n.* instrument for measuring the force of an engine; instrument for measuring magnifying power of a telescope.

DYNAST [dī'nast, dī'nast], *n.* member of a ruling family, ruler by heredity. [Gk.].

DYNASTIC(AL) [dī-nas'tik(-al), dī-nas'tik(-al)], *adj.* relating to a dynasty, or the rule of dynasties. DYNASTICALLY, *adv.* in d. fashion, from the d. point of view.

DYNASTY [dī'nas-ti], *n.* continuous line of related and hereditary rulers. [Gk.].

DYNE [dīn], *n.* a unit of force; the force which, acting for one second, will give one gramme an acceleration of one centimetre per second. [Fr. from Gk.].

DYS-, *pref.* bad. [Gk.].

DYSENTERY [dī'sen-te-ri], *n.* inflammation of the mucous membrane of the large intestine. DYSEN-TERIC [dī-sen-te'rik], *adj.* relating to, suffering from, d. [Gk.].

DYSGENIC [dis-je'nik], *adj.* having a detrimental biological effect. [DYS and (EU)GENIC].

DYSLOGISTIC [dis-lo-jis'tik], *adj.* implying adverse criticism, DYSLOGISTICALLY, *adv.* in disapproving fashion. [Gk.].

DYSMENORRHOEA [dis-me-no-rē'ah], *n.* abnormal or painful menstruation. [Gk.].

DYSPEPSIA [dis-pep'si-ah], *n.* chronic indigestion, inability to digest foods owing to functional derangement. [Gk.].

DYSPEPTIC (1) [dis-pep'tik], *adj.* suffering from dyspepsia; (*fig.*) gloomy and bad-tempered. DYSPEPTIC (2), *n.* person subject to dyspepsia.

DYSPHAGIA [dis-fā'ji-ah], *n.* difficulty in swallowing. [Gk.].

DYSPNOEA [disp-nē'ah], *n.* difficulty in breathing. DYSPNOIC [disp-nō'ik], *adj.* relating to, suffering from, d.

DYSURIA [dis-yōō'ri-ah], *n.* morbid condition of the urine; difficulty in passing water. DYSURIC, *adj.* suffering from, relating to, d. [Gk.].

E

E (1) [ē], fifth letter of the Latin and English alphabets.

E- (2), *pref.* out of, from, without. [L.].

EACH [ēch], *adj. and pron.* every one of any group or number separately considered. [OE.].

EAGER [ē'ger], *adj.* impatient, anxious to act, excited by ardent desire; filled with a lively and alert spirit; earnest, keen. EAGERLY, *adv.* in an e. fashion. EAGERNESS, *n.* quality of being e. [OFr. from L.].

EAGLE [ē'gl], *n.* large bird of prey, having a strong curved beak and powerful wings and talons; any representation of this bird used as a sign, *esp.* as the standard of the Roman legionaries; American gold coin worth ten dollars; church reading-desk in the form of this bird; (*astron.*) a northern constellation; (*coll.*) golf-hole played in two strokes under bogey. EAGLE-EYED, keen-sighted as an e.; of penetrating discernment. [OFr. from L.].

EAGRE [ē'ger], *n.* sudden and unusually high tide in an estuary or river, a bore as in the Severn etc. [Unkn.].

EAR (1) [ēer], *n.* one of the two organs of hearing, particularly the external portion visible at the side of the head; **to be all ears,** to listen attentively; **to**

set by the ears, to cause to quarrel; **to have an e. for music,** to be appreciative of music. [OE.].

EAR (2), *n.* spike of corn; seed receptacle of a cereal plant. [OE.].

EAR-ACHE [ēer'āk], *n.* pain in the internal part of the ear.

EAR-DRUM [ēer'drum], *n.* (*anat.*) membrane in the ear sensitive to sound vibrations.

EARED [ēerd], *adj.* possessing ears.

EARL [url], *n.* rank or title in the British peerage next below that of marquis; person bearing this rank; **E. Marshal,** head of the College of Arms, hereditary title held by the Dukes of Norfolk, with the duty of directing certain national ceremonies. [OE.].

EARLDOM [url'dum], *n.* title, jurisdiction or dignity of an earl.

EARLY (1) [url'li], *adj.* in advance of the usual, expected or specified time; occurring before the customary date, forward, advanced; near the beginning of any particular period of time; **E. Closing Act,** Shop Act ordering shops to close on one half-day a week. EARLY (2), *adv.* at the beginning of any particular period of time, in good time;

The accent ' after a syllable = stress (u-pon'). The mark ‾ over a vowel = length (ā in made; ō in bone).

with the first in a procession or succession, among the leaders; betimes, premature. [OE.].

EARLY DOOR [er-li-daw(r)′], *n.* theatre door and pay-box admitting the public at an extra charge to the cheaper priced seats some time before the performance commences; also (*pl.*).

EARMARK (1) [ĕer′mahk], *n.* mark or notch for identification purposes on the ear of an animal; (*fig.*) stamp or mark of identification, *esp.* on bullion to denote ownership. EARMARK (2), *v.t.* to mark with an e.; reserve for a special purpose.

EARN [urn], *v.t.* to acquire wages, honour or reward by work or performance; deserve, acquire justly and fittingly. [OE.].

EARNEST (1) [ur′nist], *n.* pledge or token of something more to come; payment of money as first instalment, as an indication of good faith; (*fig.*) foretaste. [ME. from ~Heb.].

EARNEST (2), *adj.* determined, intent, zealous; serious-minded, governed by deep, sincere and consistent moral principles; **in e.**, serious, not joking. EARNESTLY, *adv.* in an e. fashion. EARNESTNESS, *n.* state of being e. [OE.].

EARNINGS [ur′nings], *n.(pl.)* that which is earned by work, wages, reward. [OE.].

EARPHONE [ĕer′fŏn], *n.* apparatus applied to the ears by which radio and telephonic communications may be heard; (*coll.*) coil of plaited hair resembling this.

EAR-PIERCING [ĕer′pĕer-sing], *adj.* horribly penetrating; having a shrill or sharp sound.

EAR-RING [ĕer′ring], *n.* ornament designed to hang from the lobe of the ear.

EARSHOT [ĕer′shot], *n.* distance within which sounds, *esp.* speech sounds, are audible.

EAR-SPLITTING [ĕer′spli-ting], *adj.* extremely loud.

EARTH (1) [urth], *n.* the world inhabited by man considered as a planet in the universe, the globe; the hard surface of the globe as distinct from the sea, air or heavens; dry ground, mould, soil, the substance and materials composing the land; the crust of the globe; lair or den of a fox etc.; (*chem.*) mineral oxides of certain metals; (*elect.*) connexion with the e. completing a circuit; **to come back to e.**, to return to realities from idealism or a state of daydreams; **to move heaven and e.**, to make prodigious efforts; **to run to e.**, (*fig.*) to track down. EARTH (2), *v.t. and i.* to surround or cover with e.; burrow; (*elect.*) complete a circuit by connecting with the e. [OE.].

EARTH-BORN [urth′bawn], *adj.* sprung from the soil; born on the earth, earthly.

EARTH-BOUND [urth′bownd], *adj.* firmly planted in the earth; prosaic.

EARTH-CLOSET [urth′klo-zit], *n.* privy in which earth is used to cover the contents.

EARTHEN [ur′then], *adj.* made of earth or of baked clay.

EARTHENWARE [ur′then-wăer], *n.* domestic vessels made of baked clay, crockery, pottery.

EARTHLY [urth′li], *adj.* relating or belonging to the earth; solid, concrete, material; **not an e.**, (*slang*) no chance in the world. EARTHLINESS, *n.* state of being e.

EARTHLY-MINDED [erth-li-mīn′did], *adj.* having a mind devoted chiefly to material interests.

EARTHQUAKE [urth′kwāk], *n.* a rocking, splitting or bursting of the earth's surface caused by subterranean volcanic activity.

EARTHWARD [urth′werd], *adv.* towards the earth.

EARTH-WIRE [urth′wĭer], *n.* (*elect.*) wire connecting a conductor to the earth.

EARTHWORK [urth′werk], *n.* (*eng.*) a cutting or embankment of earth; a fortification of earth.

EARTHWORM [urth′werm], *n.* long tubular-shaped worm which burrows in soil.

EARTHY [ur′thi], *adj.* consisting of, similar to, or relating to earth; inhabiting the earth; gross, not refined.

EAR-TRUMPET [ĕer′trum-pet], *n.* apparatus attached to the ear to aid the hearing.

EAR-WAX [ĕer′wax], *n.* cerumen.

EARWIG [ĕer′wig], *n.* insect having horny forceps and wings folded under protective cases. [OE.].

EAR-WITNESS [ĕer′wit-nes], *n.* person who is able to give testimony based on what was heard.

EASE (1) [ēz], *n.* undisturbed or unrestricted state, freedom from constraint or exertion; comfort, quietness, pleasant peacefulness, freedom from pain, worry or other difficulties; **to stand at e.**, (*milit.*) to stand with the legs apart and the hands behind the back. EASE (2), *v.t.* to free from constraint or restriction; give more room to, loosen; relieve, assuage, give e. or comfort to; facilitate; slacken; **to e. off**, (*naut.*) to slacken a rope gradually; (*coll.*) relax gradually. EASELESS, *adj.* having no e. [OFr.].

EASEFUL [ēz′fŏŏl], *adj.* giving quiet, peaceful, characterized by rest. EASEFULLY, *adv.* in e. manner.

EASEL [ē′zel], *n.* adjustable upright framework to support an artist's canvas or a blackboard. [Du.].

EASEMENT [ēz′ment], *n.* that which affords ease; (*leg.*) any privilege, right or convenience granted to one landowner in connexion with another's land or property. [OFr.].

EAST (1) [ēst], *n.* one of the four main points of the compass; the point on the horizon where the sun rises at the equinox; the countries situated in the eastern part of the globe, the Orient. EAST (2), *adj.* lying in, coming from, the e. EAST (3), *adv.* towards the e. [OE.].

EASTER [ēs′ter], *n.* spring festival of the Christian Church in commemoration of the Resurrection of Christ; **E. eggs**, gifts of confectionery, formerly of painted eggs, given at E.; **E. offerings**, collection taken for, or the payments made to, the incumbent on E. Day; **E. term**, one of the terms during which the High Courts are in session, school or university term extending from the beginning of the year till E. [OE.].

EASTERLY [ēs′ter-li], *adj.* towards or coming from the east.

EASTERN [ēs′tern], *adj.* relating to the east part of the globe, Oriental, being or dwelling in the East; towards the east. [OE.].

EASTERNMOST [ēs′tern-mōst], *adj.* most easterly.

EASTERTIDE [ēs′ter-tīd], *n.* the week or period following Easter Day.

EASTING [ēs′ting], *n.* (*naut.*) course set or covered in an easterly direction, course east of any meridian.

EASTWARD [ēst′werd], *adj.* towards the east.

EASY (1) [ē′zi], *adj.* free from constraint or restriction, loose-fitting, loosened; comfortable, full of ease; slackened; not difficult; fluent; tolerant, not of strict morals; **shares are e.**, demand falls for specific shares; **honours are e.**, in bridge, an equal number of aces held by both sides during a no-trump hand; **to stand e.**, (*milit.*) to stand informally, free to move the limbs; **e. street**, comfortable circumstances. EASY (2), *v.i.* (*rowing*) to stop rowing. [OFr.].

EASY-CHAIR [ē-zi-chāer′], *n.* soft arm-chair.

EASY-GOING [ē-zi-gō′ing], *adj.* casual, uncritical, tolerant.

EAT (*pret.* **ate**, *p.pt.* **eaten**) [ēt], *v.t.* to take into the mouth, chew and swallow; (*coll.*) consume extravagantly; *v.i.* to take food into the system; **to e. away**, to remove gradually by gnawing, corrosion etc.; **to e. into**, to bite into by slow-acting agents such as acid; waste by extravagance; **to e. one's heart out**, to keep a sorrow to oneself and brood over it; **to e. one's terms**, to qualify for the Bar by eating the traditional number of dinners in an Inn of Court; **to e. one's words**, to be forced to retract a statement. EATING, *adj.* (of fruit) suitable for eating raw, as distinct from cooking. EATING-HOUSE, *n.* cheap restaurant. EATS, *n.(pl.)* (*slang*) food. [OE.].

EATABLE (1) [ē′ta-bl], *adj.* fit to be eaten. EATABLES (2), *n.(pl.)* anything fit for or used as food.

EATER [ē′ter], *n.* person or thing that eats or corrodes; an eating apple.

EAU DE COLOGNE [ō-de-ko-lŏn′], *n.* a perfume, originally made at Cologne. [Fr.].

EAU-DE-NIL [ō-de-nēl′], *n.* dull-green colour like the waters of the Nile. [Fr.].

EAVES [ēvz], *n.(pl.)* the edge of the roof of a building, overhanging the wall. EAVES-BOARD, board along the lower end of the rafters to keep the slates flat. EAVESDRIP, *n.* the dripping of water from the e. [OE.].

EAVESDROP (*pres.pt.* **eavesdropping**, *pret. and p.pt.* **eavesdropped**) [ēvz′drop], *v.i.* to remain hidden while listening to the private conversation of others. EAVESDROPPER, *n.* one who eavesdrops. [Prec.].

EBB (1) [eb], *n.* the return of the tide to the sea; (*fig.*) falling off, decay. EBB-TIDE, the receding tide. EBB (2), *v.i.* to flow back; (*fig.*) decline, decay. [OE.].

E-BOAT [ē′bōt], *n.* kind of fast German torpedo boat. [Germ.].

EBON [e′bon], *adj.* (*poet.*) consisting of or resembling ebony; black. [Gk.].

EBONITE [e′bo-nīt], *n.* vulcanite.

EBONY [e′bo-ni], *n.* the hard, dark-coloured wood

of various trees of the genus *Diospyros*; quality of being black like this. EBONIST, *n.* a worker in e. EBONIZE, *v.t.* to make black like e. [EBON].

EBULLIENCE, EBULLIENCY [ĕ-bu'lyens, ĕ-bu'lyen-si], *n.* a boiling over; spontaneity, enthusiasm.

EBULLIENT [ĕ-bu'lyent], *adj.* boiling over; bubbling with energy; exuberant. [L.].

EBULLITION [e-bŏo-li'shn], *n.* act of boiling or bubbling up; (*fig.*) any sudden outburst. [L.].

EC-, *pref.* out of. [Gk.].

ECARTE, écarté [ā-kah'tā], *n.* a game of cards for two. [Fr.].

ECCE HOMO [ek-si-hō'mō], *n.* a representation of Christ crowned with thorns. [L.].

ECCENTRIC (1) [ek-sen'trik], *adj.* not having the same centre, deviating from the centre; odd, unconventional, slightly queer in the mind, having a peculiar character, abnormal. ECCENTRIC (2), *n.* an e. individual; (*mech.*) wheel in which the axis does not pass through the centre. ECCENTRICALLY, *adv.* in an e. fashion. [Gk.].

ECCENTRICITY [ek-sen-tri'si-ti], *n.* condition or quality of being eccentric. [Gk.].

ECCHYMOSIS [e-ki-mō'sis], *n.* (*med.*) inflamed blotches, bruises or livid spots on the skin, caused by the effusion of extravasated blood. [Gk.].

ECCLESIASTES [e-klĕ-zi-as'tēz], *n.* title of a book of the Old Testament. [Gk.].

ECCLESIASTIC [e-klĕ-zi-as'tik], *n.* clerk in Holy Orders, cleric. [Gk.].

ECCLESIASTICAL [e-klĕ-zi-as'ti-kal], *adj.* relating to the Church. ECCLESIASTICALLY, *adv.* in an e. fashion.

ECCLESIOLOGY [e-klĕ-zi-o'lo-ji], *n.* history of church organization, church building and decoration. ECCLESIOLOGICAL [e-klĕ-zi-o-lo'ji-kal], *adj.* relating to e. ECCLESIOLOGIST [e-klĕ-zi-o'lo-jist], *n.* student of e. [Gk.].

ECCRINOLOGY [ek-ri-no'lo-ji], *n.* (*physiol.*) study of the secretions of the body. [Gk.].

ECHELON [e'she-lon], *n.* (*milit.*) formation of troops in which each unit is placed parallel to, but on a different line from, that next to it, so forming a step-like series; used also of guns, ships etc., *esp.* **in e.**, also, parts of the headquarters organization behind the front. [Fr.].

ECHIDNA [e-kid'nah], *n.* the porcupine ant-eater. [Gk.].

ECHINATE [e'ki-nāt], *adj.* having prickles or bristles. [Gk.].

ECHINODERM [e-ki'nŏ-derm], *n.* (*zool.*) one of a species of marine animals having a skin studded with spines. [Gk.].

ECHINUS (*pl.* echini) [e-ki'nus], *n.* the sea-urchin; (*bot.*) the prickly head of a plant; (*arch.*) oval moulding beneath the capital of a Doric column. [Gk.].

ECHO (1) [e'kō], *n.* repetition of a sound heard when its sound waves are reflected from a solid surface; repetition or imitation of a sound or speech; any imitation; (*bridge*) conventional call indicating strength in a certain suit; (*mus.*) repetition of a phrase in sequence. ECHO (2), *v.t. and i.* to make an e.; copy or imitate. ECHOIC [e-kō'ik], *adj.* (*philol.*) (of a word) onomatopoeic. ECHOISM, *n.* onomatopoeia. ECHOLESS, *adj.* without an e. [Gk.].

ECHOMETER [e-ko'mi-ter], *n.* (*mus.*) apparatus for measuring the duration of sounds together with their intervals and ratios; (*naut.*) apparatus for taking soundings by means of wireless. [ECHO and METER].

ECLAIR, éclair [ā-klāer'], *n.* finger-shaped piece of puff pastry filled with cream and coated with chocolate etc. [Fr.].

ECLAMPSIA [e-klamp'si-ah], *n.* (*path.*) abnormal muscular spasms due to toxaemia during pregnancy; epileptic convulsions. [Gk.].

ECLAT, éclat [ā-klah'], *n.* burst of applause; acclamation, renown; **with é.**, with spectacular success.

ECLECTIC (1) [e-klek'tik], *adj.* accepting the principle or right of selection, choosing; given to selecting and collecting aesthetic and national elements from different sources; incorporating what is considered the best and truest of the established discoveries of others. ECLECTIC (2), *n.* philosopher who forms a system by combining elements considered most true in other systems; believer in eclecticism. ECLECTICALLY, *adv.* in an e. manner. ECLECTICISM, *n.* the practice of an e. [Gk.].

ECLIPSE (1) [i-klips'], *n.* total or partial interception of the light of the sun by the interposition of the moon between the earth and the sun, or of the moon by the shadow cast by the earth; (*fig.*) extinction,

obscurity. ECLIPSE (2), *v.t. and i.* to cut off the light from by an e.; (*fig.*) obscure the fame or merit of, dim or extinguish the brilliance of, surpass. [Gk.].

ECLIPTIC (1) [i-klip'tik], *n.* (*astron.*) the apparent orbit traced by the sun in the heavens on its annual journey from west to east; (*geog.*) great circle or line described on the globe, corresponding to this. ECLIPTIC (2), *adj.* relating to the e. or to an eclipse. [*Prec.*].

ECLOGUE [ek'log], *n.* short rural poem of idyllic character and conventional form. [Gk.].

ECOLOGY, OECOLOGY [ē-ko'lo-ji], *n.* study of organisms in relation to their surroundings. [Gk.].

ECONOMIC [ē-ko-no'mik], *adj.* relating to economics; economical; concerned with or from the viewpoint of social utility and productivity. [Gk.].

ECONOMICAL [ē-ko-no'mi-kal], *adj.* relating to or regulated by economy; frugal, thrifty. ECONOMICALLY, *adv.* in an economic or e. manner; with respect to economics.

ECONOMICS [ē-ko-no'miks], *n.(pl.)* study of the laws of production, distribution and exchange of wealth operating in society. [Gk.].

ECONOMIST [e-ko'no-mist], *n.* economical person; expert in economics.

ECONOMIZE [ē-ko'no-mīz], *v.t. and i.* to expend thriftily; avoid unnecessary expenses, cut down expenditure. ECONOMIZATION [ē-ko-no-mī-zā'shn], *n.* act or result of economizing; saving.

ECONOMY [ē-ko'no-mi], *n.* management of domestic resources or finances; judicious management of finances, the practice of thrift; careful or stringent organization of work and wages; the regular laws operating in natural organisms; the operation of laws of judicious management in relation to the affairs of a nation; (*theol.*) dispensation; the way in which a complex system, machine, or organization works. [Gk.].

ECPHORY [ek'fe-ri], *n.* (*psych.*) the bringing into consciousness of a latent disposition. ECPHORIC [ek-fo'rik], *adj.* (*psych.*) pertaining to e. [Gk.].

ECRU [e-krōo'], *adj.* the colour of unbleached linen, pale yellowish light brown. [Fr.].

ECSTASY [ek'sta-si], *n.* an absorbing state of emotion involving intense feelings of exaltation, wonder, delight, degree of delight strong enough to hold in abeyance the sense of reality; excessive enthusiasm, intense feeling of pleasure. [Gk.].

ECSTATIC [ek-sta'tik], *adj.* characterized by or causing ecstasy, rapturous. ECSTATICALLY, *adv.* in e. fashion. [Gk.].

ECTHYMA [ek-thi'mah], *n.* (*med.*) an eruption of pimples on the skin. [Gk.].

ECTO-, *pref.* outside. [Gk.].

ECTOBLAST [ek'tŏ-blast], *n.* (*physiol.*) outer membranous wall of a cell. [Gk.].

ECTODERM [ek'tŏ-derm], *n.* outer layer of the embryo; outer layer of membrane of a cell. [Gk.].

ECTOGENESIS [ek-tŏ-je'ni-sis], *n.* production of offspring outside the organism. [Gk.].

ECTOPIA [ek-tō'pi-ah], *n.* (*med.*) displacement of an organ or member. [Gk.].

ECTOPLASM [ek'tŏ-plazm], *n.* (*biol.*) the outer layer of protoplasm; (*spiritualism*) substance which is supposed to emerge from a medium and assume tangible forms.

ECTROPION [ek-trō'pi-on], *n.* (*med.*) an everted condition of the eyelid. [Gk.].

ECTYPOGRAPHY [ek-ti-po'gra-fi], *n.* art of etching with the lines in relief. [Gk.].

ECUMENICAL, OECUMENICAL [ē-kyŏō-me'ni-kal], *adj.* general, universal (applied to the councils of the Roman Catholic Church). ECUMENICITY, OECUMENICITY [ē-kyŏō-me-ni'si-ti], *n.* the right of being called e. [Gk.].

ECZEMA [ek'si-mah], *n.* (*med.*) eruption of small vesicles on the skin. ECZEMATOUS [ek-zē'ma-tŏos], *adj.* relating to e. [Gk.].

EDACIOUS [e-dā'shŏos], *adj.* relating to, given to, eating; voracious. EDACIOUSLY, *adv.* in a voracious manner. EDACIOUSNESS, EDACITY [e-dā'shŏos-nes, e-da'si-ti], *n.* greediness. [L.].

EDAM [ē'dam], *n.* kind of cheese made at Edam in Holland.

EDDA [e'dah], *n.* Old Icelandic compilation relating to the materials and conventions of Old Scandinavian poetry; ancient collection of Old Scandinavian heroic and mythological poetry. [OIcel.].

EDDISH [e'dish], *n.* pasturing growth of grass which appears after mowing or reaping. [OE.].

EDDY (1) [e'di], *n.* circling movement of water or air

The accent ′ after a syllable = stress (u-**pon**′). The mark ‾ over a vowel = length (ā in made; ō in bone).

deviating from the direction of the main current; current of air, dust etc. caught up in a spiral movement by the wind. **EDDY** (2), v.i. to move like an e. [~OIcel.].

EDELWEISS [ā'del-vīs], n. (bot.) an Alpine plant. [Germ.].

EDEMA, see OEDEMA.

EDEMATOSE, EDEMATOUS, see OEDEMATOUS.

EDEN [ē'den], n. in the Bible story, the Paradise of Adam and Eve immediately after creation; any delightful region. **EDENIC** [ē-de'nik], adj. relating to or resembling E. [Heb.].

EDENTATE(D) [ē-den'tāt(-id)], adj. (zool.) lacking front teeth.

EDGE (1) [ej], n. the extreme section or portion farthest from the centre, margin; the sharp, sheared-off side of anything, esp. the sharp side of a cutting tool; brink, lip, ledge; **to be on e.**, to be in a highly sensitive state, be irritable; **to set one's teeth on e.**, to irritate acutely. **EDGE-BONE**, the aitch-bone. **EDGE** (2), v.t. and i. to provide with a sharp e. for cutting; line, hem, border; (cricket) mishit the ball with the e. of the bat; **to e. away**, to move sideways carefully, little by little; **to e. into**, to move sideways into, enter unobtrusively. **EDGED**, adj. provided with an e. or border; sharp, keen. [OE.].

EDGE-TOOL [ej-tōōl'], n. any sharp cutting instrument.

EDGEWISE [ej'wīz], adv. with the edge upward or forward, in the direction of the edge.

EDGING [e'jing], n. something forming the edge of a garment for ornament; fringe, hem; garden border; act of trimming.

EDGY [e'ji], adj. having a sharp edge; with too hard an outline; easily provoked, with the nerves in an oversensitive state.

EDIBLE [e'di-bl], adj. suitable for food. **EDIBILITY**, **EDIBLENESS** [e-di-bi'li-ti, e'di-bl-nes], n. quality of being e. [LL.].

EDICT [ē'dikt], n. peremptory and authoritative order or command. **EDICTAL** [ē-dik'tal], adj. pertaining to an e. [L.].

EDIFICATION [e-di-fi-kā'shn], n. act of edifying, condition of being edified; moral teaching. [L.].

EDIFICE [e'di-fis], n. a large building. **EDIFICIAL** [e-di-fi'shal], adj. relating to an e. [L.].

EDIFY [e'di-fi], v.t. to provide with instruction of a moral nature. **EDIFICATORY** [e-di-fi-kā'te-ri], adj. serving to e. **EDIFYING**, adj. providing edification. **EDIFYINGLY**, adv. in an edifying fashion. [L.].

EDIT [e'dit], v.t. to prepare for publication with critical apparatus; censor or select for publication; control the publication of. [L.].

EDITION [i-di'shn], n. the format and issue of a book or newspaper, total number of copies issued at one time; republication of a book under the care of a different editor, or by a different press; prototype, copy, replica; reprint of a text with critical apparatus. [L.].

EDITOR [e'di-ter], n. one who edits; one who directs the publication of a newspaper or periodical; person in charge of some special department of a newspaper or periodical.

EDITORIAL (1) [e-di-taw'ri-al], adj. pertaining to editing or editors. **EDITORIAL** (2), n. article in a newspaper or periodical written by, or under the instructions of, the editor. **EDITORIALLY**, adv. in the manner of an editor.

EDITORSHIP [e'di-ter-ship], n. business and position of an editor.

EDITRESS [e'di-tres], n. woman editor.

EDUCABLE [e'dyōō-ka-bl], adj. able to be educated. **EDUCABILITY** [e-dyōō-ka-bi'li-ti], n. ability to be educated or trained.

EDUCATE [e'dyōō-kāt], v.t. to bring up, train; develop the mind, character and body by planned discipline and instruction; provide the money for a person's education. [L.].

EDUCATION [e-dyōō-kā'shn], n. act of educating; the instruction and discipline employed to educate someone; condition of being educated. [L.].

EDUCATIONAL [e-dyōō-kā'shn-al], adj. relating to education; providing instruction. **EDUCATIONALLY**, adv. from the e. point of view, as regards education.

EDUCATIONALIST [e-dyōō-kā'shn-a-list], n. an expert on education.

EDUCATIONIST [e-dyōō-kā'shn-ist], n. educationalist.

EDUCATOR [e'dyōō-kā-ter], n. person who, or thing which, educates.

EDUCE [i-dyōōs'], v.t. to bring or draw out that which

is inherent or latent; infer, make a deduction. **EDUCIBLE**, adj. able to be educed. **EDUCTION** [i-duk'-shn], n. act of educing. [L.].

EDWARDIAN [ed-waw'di-an], adj. and n. characteristic of the reign of Edward VII; person living at that time.

EEL [ēl], n. one of several varieties of snake-like fresh-and sea-water fishes. **EELBUCK**, basket for catching eels. **EEL-FARE**, young eel; passage of eels travelling upstream. [OE.].

E'EN (1) [ēn], n. (poet.) contraction for EVEN (1).

E'EN (2), adv. (poet.) contraction for EVEN (3).

E'ER [âer], adv. (poet.) contraction for EVER.

EERIE, EERY [ēer'i], adj. weird, uncanny, frightening. [OE.].

EFFACE [i-fās'], v.t. to rub out, obliterate. **EFFACE-ABLE**, adj. capable of being effaced. **EFFACEMENT**, n. act of effacing, condition of being effaced. [Fr.].

EFFECT (1) [i-fekt'], n. any condition considered as a consequence in relation to an action; a consequence, result; show, ostentation; a combination of form and colour making a certain impression; (pl.) goods, possessions, movable property; (stage) offstage or studio representation of sounds necessary to complete the realism of a scene; **to this e.**, in this sense; **in e.**, virtually, practically; **to take e.**, to become operative; **to put into e.**, to make operative. **EFFECT** (2), v.t. to cause to happen. **EFFECTIBLE**, adj practicable; feasible. [L.].

EFFECTIVE (1) [i-fek'tiv], adj. capable of effecting or producing the result that is wanted; efficient, fit for action, competent; producing a strong and definite impression, showy. **EFFECTIVE** (2), n. one who is e.; (milit.) a fighting soldier. **EFFECTIVELY**, adv. in an e. fashion. [L.].

EFFECTUAL [i-fek'tyōō-al], adj. producing a desired effect; potent, valid. **EFFECTUALLY**, adv. in an e. fashion. **EFFECTUALNESS**, n. quality of being e.

EFFECTUATE [i-fek'tyōō-āt], v.t. to effect. **EFFEC-TUATION**, n. action of effecting.

EFFEMINACY [i-fe'mi-na-si], n. quality of being effeminate.

EFFEMINATE (1) [i-fe'mi-nat], adj. having characteristics commonly ascribed to women, unmanly, feeble; voluptuous. **EFFEMINATE** (2), n. an e. person. **EFFEMINATELY**, adv. in an e. fashion. [L.].

EFFENDI [i-fen'di], n. Turkish title of respect to officials and learned men. [Turk.].

EFFERVESCE [e-fer-ves'], v.t. (of a liquid) to let off gas in the form of innumerable bubbles; create bubbles, froth; (fig.) (of a person) be irrepressibly excited. **EFFERVESCIBLE**, adj. able to e. **EFFER-VESCING**, adj. bubbling; **effervescing draughts**, refreshing aerated drinks. [L.].

EFFERVESCENCE, EFFERVESCENCY [e-fer-ve'-sens, e-fer-ve'sen-si], n. action of effervescing, condition of being effervescent.

EFFERVESCENT (1) [e-fer-ve'sent], adj. giving out gas in bubbles, sparkling, gaseous. **EFFERVESCENT** (2), n. that which produces effervescence.

EFFETE [e-fēt'], adj. worn out, exhausted of vigour, barren, sterile. **EFFETENESS**, n. state or quality of being e. [L.].

EFFICACIOUS [e-fi-kā'shōōs], adj. capable of producing an intended effect. **EFFICACIOUSLY**, adv. in an e. fashion. **EFFICACIOUSNESS**, n. state of being e. [~L.].

EFFICACY [e'fi-ka-si], n. the power to produce a certain effect, effectiveness.

EFFICIENCY [i-fi'shen-si], n. condition of being efficient, competency; (mech.) ratio of output to input energy of a machine.

EFFICIENT (1) [i-fi'shent], adj. producing effects, producing an intended result, effective, capable, competent. **EFFICIENT** (2), n. capable person, an effective; (mech.) ratio of effective work to the total energy expended. **EFFICIENTLY**, adv. in an e. fashion. [L.].

EFFIGY [e'fi-ji], n. three-dimensional image or likeness of a person. [L.].

EFFLORESCE [e-flaw-res'], v.t. (bot.) to blossom, flower; (chem.) become covered with whitish crystals due to chemical action. **EFFLORESCENT**, adj. (chem.) efflorescing, or liable to e. [L.].

EFFLORESCENCE [e-flaw-re'sens], n. process of efflorescing, condition of being in blossom; period of blossoming; (med.) a skin rash.

EFFLUENCE [e'flōō-ens], n. process of flowing out; that which flows out.

EFFLUENT (1) [e'flōō-ent], adj. flowing outwards. **EFFLUENT** (2), n. stream which flows out of a lake

---

ōō is pronounced as in food; ŏŏ as in hood; th as in think; TH as in that; zh as in azure. ~ = related to.

etc.; discharge of waste water from a factory, sewage tank etc. [EX and FLUENT].

EFFLUVIAL [e-floo'vi-al], *adj.* relating to, or consisting of, effluvia.

EFFLUVIUM (*pl.* **effluvia**) [e-floo'vi-um], *n.* exhalation; obnoxious odour, *esp.* from putrefying substances. [Ll.].

EFFLUX, EFFLUXION [e'fluks, e-fluk'shn], *n.* act of flowing out, that which flows out; the passing of a period of time. [~L.].

EFFORT [e'fert], *n.* an exertion of strength, strenuous action or testing of power; strain; exertion of strength in relation to a deliberate end in view, endeavour, attempt; (*coll.*) feat, performance. [Fr.].

EFFRANCHISE, see ENFRANCHISE.

EFFRONTERY [e-fron'te-ri], *n.* insolent boldness, impudence, audacity. [~L.].

EFFULGENCE [e-ful'jens], *n.* radiance, stream or flood of light, great lustre or brightness. [L.].

EFFULGENT [e-ful'jent], *adj.* emitting a radiant light, brightly shining; (*fig.*) radiant. EFFULGENTLY, *adv.* in an e. manner. [L.].

EFFUSE [i-fyooz'], *v.t. and i.* to pour out, shed, gush out. [L.].

EFFUSION [i-fyoo'zhn], *n.* act of pouring out; that which is poured out; (*fig.*) fluent and tumultuous outpouring in speech, usually of a superficial character. [L.].

EFFUSIVE [i-fyoo'siv], *adj.* gushing, unrestrainedly lavish, demonstrative. EFFUSIVELY, *adv.* in e. fashion. EFFUSIVENESS, *n.* quality of being e. [L.].

EFT† [eft], *n.* a newt.

EFTSOONS† [eft-soonz'], *adv.* soon afterwards, in a short time. [OE.].

EGAD† [i-gad'], *int.* by God.

EGALITARIAN [i-ga-li-tǽer'i-an], *n. and adj.* one who holds, pertaining to, the belief that all men are equal. EGALITARIANISM, *n.* principles of an e. [Fr.].

EGG (1) [eg], *n.* the female germ-cell; spherical or spheroidal body, covered with a membrane or shell, evolved by female birds, fishes etc., and enclosing the germ from which a new animal may develop, *esp.* that of the domestic fowl, used as food; **bad e.**, person with a bad character. [OScand.].

EGG (2), *v.t.* to incite, urge, provoke. [OScand.].

EGG-CUP [eg'kup], *n.* cup, usually of china, for containing a boiled egg at table.

EGG-FLIP [eg-flip'], *n.* drink consisting of eggs beaten up in milk, beer or spirits, sweetened and spiced.

EGG-NOG [eg-nog'], *n.* egg-flip.

EGG-PLANT [eg'plahnt], *n.* the aubergine, which bears an egg-shaped fruit, East Indian plant used in cookery.

EGG-SHELL [eg'shel], *n.* shell of an egg; thin kind of transparent porcelain.

EGG-WHISK [eg'wisk], *n.* kitchen utensil for beating up eggs.

EGLANTINE [eg'lan-tin], *n.* sweetbriar. [Fr.].

EGO [e'gō], *n.* the self-conscious subject: the self in contrast with another person; consciousness of the self and its development; (*psych.*) the part of the mind concerned with the perception of external reality and with adjusting responses to it. [L.].

EGOCENTRIC [e-gō-sen'trik], *adj.* self-centred, egoistic, attempting to gain stability for the personality by concentrating on the satisfaction of personal desires, with indifference to the effect on others. EGOCENTRICITY [e-gō-sen-tri'si-ti], *n.* state of being e. [EGO and CENTRIC].

EGOISM [e'gō-izm], *n.* state or habit of mind which sets the self in a position of first importance; consistent self-regard; practice of selfishness as a creed. [EGO].

EGOIST [e'gō-ist], *n.* selfish, self-centred person; (*philos.*) adherent of egoism.

EGOISTIC(AL) [e-gō-is'tik(-al)], *adj.* relating to egoism; derived from the ego. EGOISTICALLY, *adv.* in an e. fashion.

EGOMANIA [e-gō-mā'ni-ah], *n.* extravagant egotism. EGOMANIAC, *n. and adj.* (one) given to e. [EGO and MANIA].

EGOTISM [e'gō-tizm], *n.* habit of thinking too much about oneself and of inflicting on others the sense of one's own importance, self-conceit, self-pride. [EGO].

EGOTIST [e'gō-tist], *n.* person whose nature is tainted with egotism.

EGOTISTIC(AL) [e-gō-tis'tik(-al)], *adj.* characterized by egotism, deliberately affecting egotism,

self-conceited, self-important. EGOTISTICALLY, *adv.* in an e. fashion.

EGREGIOUS [i-grē'jŏŏs], *adj.* uncommonly bad. EGREGIOUSLY, *adv.* in an e. fashion. EGREGIOUSNESS, *n.* quality of being e. [L.].

EGRESS (1) [ē'gres], *n.* act of going away from or out of; way out, exit. EGRESS (2) [ē-gres'], *v.i.* to go out, leave, depart. EGRESSION [i-gre'shn], *n.* act of going out from a place. [L.].

EGRET [ē'gret], *n.* the lesser white heron; (*bot.*) feathery tuft of seeds of plants such as the dandelion and thistle. [Fr.].

EGYPTIAN (1) [ē-jip'shn], *adj.* relating to Egypt. EGYPTIAN (2), *n.* a native of Egypt; (*archaic*) gipsy; drawing-paper of a large size. [Gk.].

EGYPTOLOGY [ē-jip-to'lo-ji], *n.* study of Egyptian antiquities. EGYPTOLOGICAL [ē-jip-tō-lo'ji-kal], *adj.* relating to E. EGYPTOLOGIST [ē-jip-to'lo-jist], *n.* an expert in E. [Gk.].

EH [ā], *int.* denoting inquiry or slight surprise.

EIDER [I'der], *n.* sea duck living in the Arctic and sub-Arctic regions and noted for its fine down. [OIcel.].

EIDERDOWN [I'der-down], *n.* fine, soft down of the eider-duck; quilt stuffed with this.

EIDETIC [I-de'tik], *adj.* (*psych.*) having, or referring to, the power of re-experiencing a visual impression with the clarity of an hallucination; pertaining to persistently recurring visual imagery. [Gk.].

EIGHT (1) [āt], *n.* cardinal number immediately following seven and preceding nine; figure representing this number 8; rowing team of e. persons, racing boat holding e. oarsmen; **figure of e.**, movement of a skater on the ice following the lines of the figure 8; **to have had one over the e.**, (*slang*) to be drunk. EIGHT (2), *adj.* one more than seven, one less than nine. [OE.].

EIGHTEEN [ā-tēn'], *n.* ten and eight. [OE.].

EIGHTEENTH (1) [ā-tēnth'], *n.* one of eighteen equal parts. EIGHTEENTH (2), *adj.* the ordinal of eighteen; being one of eighteen equal parts.

EIGHTFOLD [āt'fōld], *adj.* eight times the quantity.

EIGHTH (1) [ātth], *n.* one of eight equal parts; unit following the seventh in a series; (*mus.*) of an octave. EIGHTH (2), *adj.* the ordinal of eight; being one of eight equal parts. EIGHTHLY, *adv.* in the e. place.

EIGHTIETH (1) [ā'ti-eth], *n.* one of eighty equal parts, following seventy-nine of a series. EIGHTIETH (2), *adj.* the ordinal of eighty; being one of eighty equal parts.

EIGHTSOME [āt'sum], *n.* Scottish reel for eight persons.

EIGHTY (1) [ā'ti], *n.* the number equal to eight times ten. EIGHTY (2), *adj.* eight times ten, four-score.

EIKON [I'kon], *n.* variant of ICON.

EISTEDDFOD [ās-teth'vod], *n.* national assembly of Welsh poets, musicians etc. to compete for prizes, a tournament of song and music. [Wel.].

EITHER (1) [I'THer], *pron.* one of two. EITHER (2), *adj.* one of two; *sometimes used incorrectly of more than two.* EITHER (3), *adv.* correlative with OR, *indicating the first of two alternatives, the second being indicated by* OR; *sometimes used loosely of more than two.* [OE.].

EJACULATE [i-jak'yōō-lāt], *v.t. and i.* to exclaim, utter suddenly; (*physiol.*) emit liquid. EJACULATIVE, *adj.* ejaculatory. [L.].

EJACULATION [i-jak-yōō-lā'shn], *n.* that which is ejaculated; act of ejaculating.

EJACULATORY [i-jak'yōō-lā-te-ri], *adj.* of or resembling an ejaculation.

EJECT [i-jekt'], *v.t.* to remove suddenly, expel, discharge, dismiss. EJECTIVE, *adj.* relating to ejection; tending to e. [~L.].

EJECTION [i-jek'shn], *n.* act of ejecting; condition of being ejected.

EJECTMENT [i-jekt'ment], *n.* an ejection, dispossession; (*leg.*) writ or action for the recovery of land from which the owner has been ejected.

EJECTOR [i-jek'ter], *n.* person who ejects or dispossesses another of his land; that which ejects; device on a gun which ejects the cartridge.

EKE† (1) [ēk], *adv.* in addition, moreover. [OE.].

EKE (2), *v.t.* to add to; **to e. out**, to make to last by economy. [OE.].

ELABORATE (1) [i-la'bo-rat], *adj.* worked out with attention to detail, characterized by a complex form or pattern, complicated, loaded with ornamentation. ELABORATE (2) [i-la'bo-rāt], *v.t.* to work out with great pains and attention to detail, make more e. ELABORATELY, *adv.* in an e. way. ELABORATENESS, *n.*

state of being e. ELABORATOR, *n.* one who elaborates. [L.].

ELABORATION [i-la-bo-rā'shn], *n.* act of elaborating.

ELABORATIVE [i-la'bo-ra-tiv], *adj.* tending to elaborate; **e. faculty**, faculty of seeing things in relation to each other.

ELAIN [e-lā'in], *n. variant of* OLEIN.

ELAN, élan [ā-lah(ng)'], *n.* impetuosity, high-spirited vigour. [Fr.].

ELAND [ē'land], *n.* large South African antelope. [Du.].

ELAPSE [i-laps'], *v.i.* to pass away silently. [L.].

ELASTIC (1) [i-las'tik], *adj.* possessing resilience, having the power of returning to its original form after being stretched or extended; able to be stretched or expanded; springy, flexible; (*fig.*) adaptable. ELASTIC (2), *n.* material manufactured in strips, composed of rubber and interwoven strands of silk, cotton etc.; strip of plain rubber, rubber band. ELASTICALLY, *adv.* in an e. fashion. ELASTICITY [ē-las-ti'si-ti], *n.* quality of being e. [Gk.].

ELATE (1) [i-lāt'], *adj.* (*archaic*) exhilarated, exultant, elated. ELATE (2), *v.t.* to make exhilarated, raise the spirits of, stimulate. ELATEDLY, *adv.* in an elated manner. ELATEDNESS, *n.* condition of being elated. ELATOR, *n.* person who or thing which elates. [~L.].

ELATION [i-lā'shn], *n.* state of being elated; pride, elevation of spirits. [L.].

ELBOW (1) [el'bō], *n.* the joint and bone formation between the forearm and the upper arm; anything angular and bent like an elbow; **at the e.**, close by, near at hand; **out at e.**, shabby, reduced in circumstances. ELBOW (2), *v.t. and i.* to use the elbows to push through a crowd, push aside; place inside an angle. [OE.].

ELBOW-GREASE [el'bō-grēs], *n.* hard, continuous rubbing; power to work hard.

ELBOW-ROOM [el'bō-rŏŏm], *n.* room for action.

ELD† [eld], *n.* old age; antiquity. [OE.].

ELDER (1) [el'der], *n.* a tree bearing white flowers having a pungent scent and dark berries. ELDER-WINE, wine made from elderberries. [OE.].

ELDER (2), *adj.* having lived a long time, born earlier, older; senior; **E. Brother,** (*naut.*) one of the senior members of Trinity House who judge navigation cases. ELDER (3), *n.* person who is older, senior in age, rank or experience; person who held office in the early Christian Church; administrative member of the Presbyterian Church; (*pl.*) those granted authority by right of age. [OE.].

ELDERBERRY [el'der-be-ri], *n.* fruit of the elder; **e. wine**, wine made from elderberries.

ELDERLY [el'der-li], *adj.* fairly old; advanced beyond middle age; approaching old age. ELDERLINESS, *n.* condition of being e.

ELDERSHIP [el'der-ship], *n.* office of a Presbyterian elder.

ELDEST [el'dest], *n. and adj.* oldest; first-born or oldest surviving member of a family. [OE.].

ELDORADO [el-dō-rah'dō], *n.* imaginary land where the desires of the poor are satisfied with gold and plenty. [Span.].

ELDRITCH [el'drich], *adj.* uncanny, hideous, ghastly. [Uncert.].

ELECAMPANE [e-lē-kam'pān], *n.* composite plant with yellow flowers; sweetmeat made from the root. [L.].

ELECT (1) [i-lekt'], *adj.* selected, chosen, specially marked as the recipient of some privilege, elected to some office or position of rank but not yet installed; (*theol.*) believed to be chosen by God for salvation. ELECT (2), *n.* persons chosen, selected or set apart; (*theol.*) persons believed to be chosen by God for salvation. ELECT (3), *v.t. and i.* to pick out, choose by vote; decide among various possible courses (to). [~L.].

ELECTION [i-lek'shn], *n.* act of electing, choice, selection, discrimination; (*theol.*) state of being predestined to salvation. BYE-ELECTION, e. in one constituency, the seat of which is vacant. **General E.**, parliamentary e. in every constituency at once. [L.].

ELECTIONEER [i-lek-shn-ēer'], *v.i.* to canvass for votes and do work for a candidate at an election. ELECTIONEERING, *n.* act of one who electioneers.

ELECTIVE [i-lek'tiv], *adj.* effected by choice; pertaining to the right of election; having the power of choice.

ELECTOR [i-lek'ter], *n.* person who elects; person who has the right to vote in an election; (*hist.*) one of

the German princes who elected the Holy Roman Emperor.

ELECTORAL [i-lek'te-ral], *adj.* relating to elections or electors.

ELECTORATE [i-lek'te-rat], *n.* (*hist.*) office, authority or territory of an elector in the German or Holy Roman Empire; body of persons entitled to record votes.

ELECTRESS [i-lek'tres], *n.* wife or widow of a German Elector.

ELECTRIC (1) [i-lek'trik], *adj.* pertaining to, producing or worked by electricity, electrical; **e. blue,** brilliant steel blue; **e. chair,** chair used in U.S.A. for electrocuting a criminal sentenced to death; **e. circuit,** path in which e. energy is transmitted; **e. eel,** South American fish able to communicate an e. shock; **e. field,** area round an electrified body affected by the e. charge; **e. ray,** flat-fish of the genus *Torpedo.* ELECTRIC (2), *n.* a non-conductor; any substance in which electricity can be generated by friction. [Gk.].

ELECTRICAL [i-lek'tri-kal], *adj.* relating to electricity; (*fig.*) having a strong sudden effect on the mind or emotions. ELECTRICALLY, *adv.* by electricity.

ELECTRICIAN [e-lek-tri'shn], *n.* one who is expert in electricity and deals with its practical applications.

ELECTRICITY [e-lek-tri'si-ti], *n.* form of energy transmitted in waves, which produces accredited physical phenomena in heat, light and sound; science investigating and recording the operation of these phenomena.

ELECTRIFY [i-lek'tri-fī], *v.t.* to charge with electricity; adapt to an electric system of power; (*fig.*) startle, surprise, shock into a strong and sudden reaction. ELECTRIFIABLE, *adj.* capable of receiving and conducting electricity. ELECTRIFICATION [i-lek-tri-fi-kā'shn], *n.* act of electrifying, condition of being electrified.

ELECTRO (1) [i-lek'trō], *n.* (*print.*) an electrotype.

ELECTRO- (2), *pref.* pertaining to or produced by electricity.

ELECTROCUTE [i-lek'trō-kyōōt], *v.t.* to kill by electricity, *esp.* as a capital punishment for crime. ELECTROCUTION [i-lek-trō-kyōō'shn], *n.* death by electricity. [ELECTRO and (EXE)CUTE].

ELECTRODE [i-lek'trōd], *n.* one of the points at which an electric current passes from a conducting or producing circuit into another conducting medium. [Gk.].

ELECTRO-DYNAMICS [i-lek-trō-dī-na'miks], *n.*(*pl.*) study of the phenomena of electricity operating in active phases. ELECTRO-DYNAMIC, *adj.* relating to e.

ELECTROLYSIS [i-lek-tro'li-sis], *n.* chemical change produced by electric energy. [Gk.].

ELECTROLYTE [i-lek'trō-līt], *n.* compound which is decomposed by an electric current; a substance producing ions in solution. [Gk.].

ELECTRO-MAGNET [i-lek-trō-mag'net], *n.* magnet energized by a coil of wire carrying an electric current round it.

ELECTRO-MAGNETISM [i-lek-trō-mag'ne-tizm], *n.* science which deals with the properties of electricity in producing and communicating a magnetic force.

ELECTRO-METALLURGY [i-lek-trō-me'ta-ler-ji], *n.* branch of metallurgy which is concerned with the utilization of electricity in the various processes of depositing metals held in solution.

ELECTROMETER [e-lek-tro'mi-ter], *n.* instrument by which electricity is measured.

ELECTROMOTIVE [i-lek-trō-mō'tiv], *adj.* producing motion by means of electricity.

ELECTROMOTOR [i-lek-trō-mō'ter], *n.* prime mover energized by electricity.

ELECTRON [i-lek'tron], *n.* the smallest known component of matter; one of the particles of an atom which are charged with negative electricity; alloy of gold and silver, electrum. ELECTRONIC [e-lek-tro'nik], *adj.* (*phys.*) of, or pertaining to, electrons; operated by the agency of electrons. ELECTRONICS [i-lek-tro'niks], *n.* science which deals with the behaviour of electrons.

ELECTROPLATE (1) [i-lek'trō-plāt], *v.t.* to coat with metal by means of electrolysis. ELECTROPLATE (2), *n.* metal articles coated with another metal by an electrical process, silver-plate.

ELECTROSCOPE [i-lek'trō-skōp], *n.* instrument which tests the presence, nature and intensity of electricity. [Gk.].

ELECTROSTATICS [i-lek-trō-sta'tiks], *n.* branch of physics dealing with static electricity.

ŏŏ is pronounced as in food; ŏŏ as in hood; th as in *th*ink; TH as in *th*at; zh as in azure.   ~ = related to.

ELECTROTECHNICS [i-lek-trŏ-tek'niks], *n.* the technics of electricity.

ELECTROTHERAPEUTICS [i-lek-trŏ-the-ra-pyōō'-tiks], *n.* science of the treatment of disease by electricity.

ELECTROTHERAPY [i-lek-trŏ-the'ra-pi], *n.* cure of disease by electricity.

ELECTRO-THERMIC [i-lek-trŏ-thur'mik], *adj.* relating to the production of heat phenomena by electricity.

ELECTROTYPE (1) [i-lek'trŏ-tīp], *n.* (*print.*) a plate used in printing having the representation protected by a thin coating of copper. ELECTROTYPE (2), *v.t.* to reproduce by the e. process. ELECTROTYPIST, *n.* one expert in making or printing from an e.

ELECTRUM [i-lek'trum], *n.* amber; alloy containing gold and silver. [Gk.].

ELECTUARY [i-lek'tyōō-a-ri], *n.* a sweetened medicine. [Gk.].

ELEEMOSYNARY [e-li-ĕ-mo'si-na-ri], *adj.* relating to charity. [Gk.].

ELEGANCE, ELEGANCY [e'li-gans(-i)], *n.* state of being elegant.

ELEGANT [e'li-gant], *adj.* possessing grace, ease, refinement of speech and taste; having a neat, delicate and proportionate form with the surfaces smooth and the colours blending harmoniously; delicately worked, refined and tasteful. ELEGANTLY, *adv.* in an e. way. [Fr.].

ELEGIAC(AL) (1) [e-li-jī'ak(-al)], *adj.* relating to, having a place in, suitable for, an elegy; expressing sorrow, mournful. ELEGIAC (2), *n.* (usually *pl.*) e. verse. [Gk.].

ELEGY [e'li-ji], *n.* poem or song expressive of sorrow or lamentation, dirge. ELEGIST, *n.* writer of elegies. ELEGIZE, *v.t. and i.* to honour or celebrate with an e.; write an e. [Gk.].

ELEMENT [e'li-ment], *n.* one of the basic constituent parts of a thing; a basic principle; (*chem.*) substance consisting entirely of atoms of the same kind; (*pl.*) earth, air, fire and water, in terms of which the ancients believed the whole world could be explained; (*pl.*) the rudiments, basic principles, of a system of thought, a plan, or an idea; the natural powers of the atmosphere; (*astron.*) the numerical and observational data on which astronomical calculations are based; **the Elements**, the bread and wine at Holy Communion. [L.].

ELEMENTAL [e-li-men'tal], *adj.* relating to elements, arising from first principles; primal, simple. ELEMENTALLY, *adv.* in an e. manner.

ELEMENTARY [e-li-men'ta-ri], *adj.* simple, undeveloped, rudimentary; containing or discussing first principles; dealing with elements; **e. school**, formerly a state school for children. [L.].

ELEMI [e'le-mi], *n.* resinous substance secreted by several trees, used in ointments and for toughening varnish. ELEMIN, *n.* oil distilled from e. [Unkn.].

ELEPHANT [e'li-fant], *n.* huge tusked quadruped, the largest of existing land animals; outsize in drawing paper; **white e.**, albino type of e. considered sacred in Thailand; (*fig.*) unprofitable possession or undertaking. [Gk.].

ELEPHANTIASIS [e-li-fan-tī'a-sis], *n.* (*med.*) disease characterized by thickening and inflammation of limbs or part of the body. ELEPHANTIAC [e-li-fan'ti-ak], *adj.* relating to e. [Gk.].

ELEPHANTINE [e-li-fan'tīn], *adj.* relating to, or resembling, an elephant in bulk or action; huge, clumsy.

ELEUSINIAN [e-lyōō-si'ni-an], *adj.* relating to the rites celebrated in honour of Demeter. [Gk. *Eleusis*, Greek city].

ELEVATE [e'li-vāt], *v.t.* to raise from a lower position or state to a higher; promote in rank; improve morally or mentally; delight, cheer. ELEVATED, *adj.* exalted, dignified; (*coll.*) slightly drunk. [L.].

ELEVATION [e-li-vā'shn], *n.* act of elevating; state of being elevated; emotional state of exaltation; high moral or social status, dignity; (*arch.*) scale drawing of one side of a building; (*astron.*) altitude of a heavenly body above the horizon; (*mus.*) raising of the pitch of a note to a sharper tone. [L.].

ELEVATOR [e'li-vā-ter], *n.* person or object which raises or lifts; a lift; machine for conveying corn, hay etc. from one level to a higher level; grain storehouse; (*anat.*) any muscle with the function of raising; (*aeron.*) a pair of movable horizontal surfaces attached to the tailplane of an aircraft.

ELEVATORY [e'li-vā-te-ri], *adj.* tending to raise.

ELEVEN (1) [i-le'ven], *adj.* one more than ten.

ELEVEN (2), *n.* team composed of eleven players. [OE.].

ELEVENSES [i-le'ven-ziz], *n.*(*pl.*) (*coll.*) light refreshments taken about 11 a.m.

ELEVENTH (1) [i-le'venth], *n.* one of eleven equal parts; (*mus.*) the interval of the octave above the fourth. ELEVENTH (2), *adj.* the ordinal of eleven; being one of eleven equal parts.

ELF (*pl.* **elves**) [elf, elvz], *n.* (*myth.*) small creature of the woods like a human dwarf possessing supernatural or magic power; little or mischievous child. ELF-CHILD, child supposed to have been left by the fairies in place of one stolen by them. [OE.].

ELFIN [el'fin], *adj.* pertaining to elves, fairy-like.

ELFISH [el'fish], *adj.* relating to or resembling elves; as if done by an elf, mischievous; small.

ELF-LOCK [elf'lok], *n.* hair twisted into a curl or lock.

ELICIT [i-li'sit], *v.t.* to draw out, bring to light, cause to become apparent. ELICITATION [i-li-si-tā'shn], *n.* act of eliciting. [L.].

ELIDE [i-līd'], *v.t.* (*gram.*) to omit (a syllable, sound etc.). ELIDABLE, *adj.* able to be elided. [L.].

ELIGIBILITY [e-li-ji-bi'li-ti], *n.* quality of being eligible.

ELIGIBLE [e'li-ji-bl], *adj.* fit to be chosen, desirable; having the necessary qualifications. ELIGIBLENESS, *n.* eligibility. ELIGIBLY, *adv.* in an e. fashion. [L.].

ELIMINANT (1) [i-li'mi-nant], *n.* (*math.*) result of eliminating variables between homogeneous equations. ELIMINANT (2), *n. and adj.* (*med.*) (substance) eliminating harmful matter from the system.

ELIMINATE [i-li'mi-nāt], *v.t.* to remove, exclude, obliterate; throw out, expel. ELIMINABLE, *adj.* able to be eliminated. [L.].

ELIMINATION [i-li-mi-nā'shn], *n.* act of eliminating; condition of being eliminated.

ELIMINATOR [i-li'mi-nā-ter], *n.* that which eliminates; (*radio*) device which eliminates batteries by enabling a set to draw power from the mains.

ELISION [i-li'shn], *n.* (*gram.*) act of eliding, state of being elided.

ELITE, élite [ā-lēt'], *n.* select body; the best of anything; aristocracy, smart set. [Fr.].

ELIXIR [i-lik'ser], *n.* a liquid of many ingredients formerly believed to transmute base metal into gold or to prolong life; refined spirit or liquor; invigorating drink. [Arab.].

ELIZABETHAN (1) [i-li-za-bē'than], *adj.* relating to Queen Elizabeth I or her times. ELIZABETHAN (2), *n.* person who lived in the E. era.

ELK [elk], *n.* (*zool.*) the largest of the deer, the moose. [OE.].

ELK-HOUND [elk'hownd], *n.* shaggy-coated hunting dog of Scandinavian origin.

ELL [el], *n.* a measure varying in different countries, used chiefly for measuring cloth, approximately an inch or two over a yard, an arm's length. [OE.].

ELLIPSE [i-lips'], *n.* a plane curved symmetrical figure longer than it is broad, an oval; (*geom.*) oblique section of a cone. [*Next*].

ELLIPSIS (*pl.* **ellipses**) [i-lip'sis], *n.* omission, defect; (*gram.*) omission of word, phrase or thought having an implied presence and relation to the meaning of the sentence. [Gk.].

ELLIPSOID [i-lip'soid], *n.* (*geom.*) elliptical spheroid. [Gk.].

ELLIPTIC(AL) [i-lip'tik(-al)], *adj.* relating to, having the form of, an ellipse; having a part omitted; (*gram.*) omitting something necessary to complete a construction. ELLIPTICALLY, *adv.* in an e. manner, in the form of an ellipse; having a part omitted. ELLIPTICITY [e-lip-ti'si-ti], *n.* quality of being e.

ELM [elm], *n.* tree of the genus *Ulmus*, having serrated leaves and yielding valuable timber; the wood of the e. ELMY, *adj.* abounding in, covered with, elms.

ELOCUTION [e-lŏ-kyōō'shn], *n.* power of oral expression; manner of speaking or oral delivery; art of speaking with clear delivery. ELOCUTIONARY, *adj.* relating to e. ELOCUTIONIST, *n.* an expert in e. [L.].

ELONGATE (1) [ē'long-gāt], *v.t.* to lengthen, stretch out, extend. ELONGATE (2), *adj.* long, drawn-out; (*bot.*) remarkable for length as contrasted with its breadth. [L.].

ELONGATION [ē-long-gā'shn], *n.* act of elongating; condition of being elongated; (*astron.*) distance of a planet from the sun, measured from the earth.

ELOPE [i-lōp'], *v.i.* to run away with one's lover in order to marry without parental knowledge and consent. ELOPEMENT, *n.* act of eloping. [OFr.].

ELOQUENCE [e'lo-kwens], *n.* the power of fluent

The accent ′ after a syllable = stress (u-pon′).　　The mark ¯ over a vowel = length (ā in made; ō in bone).

speech which by its ease, force and brilliance of expression affects the emotions of those who listen. [L.].

ELOQUENT [e'lo-kwent], *adj.* possessing eloquence, having a brilliant control of words when addressing an audience; expressive in language; (*fig.*) affecting, moving. ELOQUENTLY, *adv.* in an e. fashion.

ELSE [els], *adv.* as well, besides, in addition, as an extra; instead; otherwise, in different circumstances, if not. [OE.].

ELSEWHERE [els-wäer'], *adv.* at, to, in a different place. [OE.].

ELUCIDATE [i-lyōō'si-dāt], *v.t.* to throw light upon the meaning of, explain, illustrate. ELUCIDATIVE, ELUCIDATORY, *adj.* tending to elucidate, making clear, explanatory. ELUCIDATOR, *n.* one who elucidates. [L.].

ELUCIDATION [i-lyōō-si-dā'shn], *n.* act of elucidating, of throwing light on any obscurity.

ELUDE [i-lyōōd'], *v.t.* to evade, escape, avoid capture by guile or dexterity; escape being seen; (*fig.*) evade definition in the mind. ELUDIBLE, *adj.* able to be eluded. [L.].

ELUSION [i-lyōō'zhn], *n.* act of eluding.

ELUSIVE [i-lyōō'siv], *adj.* tending to escape a physical or mental contact; evasive, difficult to grasp; hard to remember. ELUSIVENESS, *n.* quality of being e. [L.].

ELUSORY [i-lyōō'se-ri], *adj.* tending to elude. ELUSORINESS, *n.* quality of being e. [L.].

ELVER [el'ver], *n.* a young eel. [EEL and FARE].

ELVES [elvz], *n.* *pl.* of ELF.

ELVISH [el'vish], *adj.* elfish. ELVISHLY, *adv.* in e. fashion.

ELYSIAN [i-li'zi-an], *adj.* relating to or situated in Elysium; heavenly.

ELYSIUM [i-li'zi-um], *n.* (*myth.*) the country beyond death inhabited by the souls of Greek heroes; (*fig.*) imaginary country or emotional condition of extreme and continual happiness. [Gk.].

EM- (1), *pref.* a form of the prefix *en*, used before certain labial consonants.

EM (2) [em], *n.* (*print.*) unit of measurement of width of type matter, being equal to the depth of the type used. [Letter M, originally as wide as it was deep].

'EM (3), *pron.* (*coll.*) *var.* of THEM.

EMACIATE [i-mā'shi-āt], *v.t.* *and i.* to reduce in weight, cause the flesh to waste away; become very thin. [L.].

EMACIATION [i-ma-si-ā'shn], *n.* act of emaciating; state of being emaciated; unnatural slimness due to undernourishment.

EMANATE [e'ma-nāt], *v.i.* to issue, proceed or spring from, have its source in, start from. EMANATIVE, *adj.* that emanates. [L.].

EMANATION [e-ma-nā'shn], *n.* act of emanating; that which emanates, effluvium, efflux; theory of e., doctrine which regards all existence as derived from and part of the essence of God, and not created by Him from a void. [L.].

EMANCIPATE [i-man'si-pāt], *v.t.* to release from a state of slavery, declare to be free after taking the necessary action; grant legal, moral or political freedom to. EMANCIPATED, *adj.* freed; (*fig.*) unconventional, free from inhibitions. EMANCIPATOR, *n.* one who emancipates. [L.].

EMANCIPATION [i-man-si-pā'shn], *n.* act of emancipating; state of being emancipated. EMANCIPATIONIST, *n.* one who advocates the total abolition of religious, political and economic conditions of oppression.

EMARGINATE (1) [i-mah'ji-nāt], *v.t.* to take away the margin or edge; notch. EMARGINATE (2), *adj.* possessing indented edges, notched. [L.].

EMASCULATE [i-mas'kyōō-lāt], *v.t.* to deprive of virility by castrating; (*fig.*) make effeminate, weaken, tone down. EMASCULATION [i-mas-kyōō-lā'shn], *n.* act of emasculating; state of being emasculated. EMASCULATORY [i-mas'kyōō-lā-te-ri], *adj.* tending to e. [L.].

EMBALM [em-bahm'], *v.t.* to preserve a dead body from decay by removing the internal organs and impregnating it with preservatives; (*fig.*) preserve the memory of; scent, fill with fragrance. EMBALMER, *n.* one who embalms. EMBALMING, *n.* occupation of embalmer. EMBALMMENT, *n.* act of embalming; substance used to e. [Fr.].

EMBANK [em-bangk'], *v.t.* to enclose with a bank; build a bank alongside of.

EMBANKMENT [em-bangk'ment], *n.* act of embanking; state of being embanked; long artificial mound

to form the limits of a river or along which a road or railway is built.

EMBARGO (*pl.* **embargoes**) [em-bah'gō], *n.* a state order to prevent ships from entering or leaving a particular port; prohibition of trade by government order; any imposition of restraint. [Span.].

EMBARK [em-bahk'], *v.t.* *and i.* to put on board a ship; go on board a ship; (*fig.*) start, participate in. [LL.].

EMBARKATION [em-bah-kā'shn], *n.* act of embarking; that which is embarked.

EMBARRASS [em-ba'ras], *v.t.* to make a situation difficult, render complex; disconcert, make nervous, perplex; hinder, obstruct; (*fig.*) place in financial difficulties. EMBARRASSING, *adj.* disconcerting, that embarrasses. EMBARRASSINGLY, *adv.* in an embarrassing manner. [Fr.].

EMBARRASSMENT [em-ba'ras-ment], *n.* act of embarrassing; state of being embarrassed; that which embarrasses; awkwardness, nervousness; financial difficulty.

EMBASSY [em'ba-si], *n.* the official staff of an ambassador; position of an ambassador; building in which an ambassador works and resides; particular mission or business undertaken by a visiting ambassador; any message, mission or transaction undertaken by someone. [~L.].

EMBATTLE (1) [em-ba'tl], *v.t.* to arrange in battle order. EMBATTLED (1), *adj.* in battle order. [OFr.].

EMBATTLE (2), *v.t.* to provide with battlements. EMBATTLED (2), *adj.* (*her.*, *arch.*) indented, like a battlement. [EM (1) and OFr.].

EMBAY [em-bā'], *v.t.* to enclose in a bay; landlock; shut in within a bay; surround. EMBAYMENT, *n.* bay; act of forming into a bay.

EMBED, IMBED (*pres.pt.* **embedding**, *pret.* *and p.pt.* **embedded**) [im-bed'], *v.t.* to set firmly into other material; (*fig.*) instil ineradicably into the mind; lay, as in a bed.

EMBELLISH [em-be'lish], *v.t.* to adorn, decorate; improve the appearance of, beautify; make graceful or elegant; add vivid details to; furnish with illustrations. [~Fr.].

EMBELLISHMENT [em-be'lish-ment], *n.* act of embellishing, state of being embellished; anything which embellishes, adornment.

EMBER [em'ber], *n.* a smouldering cinder, glowing piece of coal etc. in a dying fire. [OE.].

EMBER-DAYS [em'ber-dāz], *n.(pl.)* three days set aside by the Western Church four times a year for prayer and fasting. [OE.].

EMBER-GOOSE [em'ber-gōōs], *n.* (*ornith.*) the great northern diver. [OScand.].

EMBER-WEEK [em'ber-wēk], *n.* a week in which ember-days fall.

EMBEZZLE [em-be'zl], *v.t.* to misappropriate funds, goods etc. placed in one's charge. EMBEZZLER, *n.* person who embezzles. [AFr.].

EMBEZZLEMENT [em-be'zl-ment], *n.* act of embezzling.

EMBITTER [em-bi'ter], *v.t.* to make bitter; arouse harsh feelings in; exasperate.

EMBLAZE [em-blāz'], *v.t.* to adorn with brilliant embellishments; adorn with armorial figures; display heraldic devices.

EMBLAZON [em-blā'zon], *v.t.* to paint with heraldic devices; depict (of armorial bearings etc.); decorate with brilliant colours; celebrate, extol. EMBLAZONER, *n.* one who emblazons. EMBLAZONING, *n.* act of adorning with heraldic devices. [EM (1) and BLAZON (2)].

EMBLAZONMENT [em-blā'zon-ment], *n.* emblazoning; that which is emblazoned.

EMBLAZONRY [em-blā'zon-ri], *n.* blazonry, heraldic devices.

EMBLEM [em'blem], *n.* a concrete symbolization of some abstract thing; sign or device standing as a symbol of something. EMBLEMIZE, *v.t.* to represent by means of an e. [Gk.].

EMBLEMATIC(AL) [em-ble-ma'tik(-al)], *adj.* having the nature of or serving as an emblem, using emblems. EMBLEMATICALLY, *adv.* in an e. manner, by means of emblems.

EMBODIMENT [em-bo'di-ment], *n.* act of embodying; condition of being embodied; that which, or a person in whom, some principle or idea is embodied.

EMBODY [em-bo'di], *v.t.* to collect into a body; invest with a material form, represent in any medium, incorporate, include. EMBODIER, *n.* one who embodies.

EMBOLDEN [em-bōl'den], *v.t.* to make bold.

EMBOLISM [em'bo-lizm], *n.* the regularization of time by the insertion of calculated periods such as days, months or years; (*med.*) clot of blood carried in the bloodstream which, when obstructing the flow of blood, may produce inflammation, paralysis or death. EMBOLISMAL, EMBOLISMIC, *adj.* relating to e.; inserted; clotted. [~Gk.].

EMBOLUS [em'bo-lus], *n.* (*mech.*) something inserted or moving in another, as a wedge or a piston; (*med.*) clot of blood in embolism. [Gk.].

EMBONPOINT [ah(ng)-bo(ng)-pwa(ng)'], *n.* superfluous fat, obesity. [Fr.].

EMBOSOM [em-bŏŏ'zom], *v.t.* to clasp to the bosom, hold in one's arms close to the breast; (*fig.*) shelter, surround with, shut in.

EMBOSS [em-bos'], *v.t.* to cause parts of a surface to rise so as to form designs by hammering or from pressure with a die. EMBOSSER, *n.* craftsman skilled in embossing. EMBOSSING, EMBOSSMENT, *n.* act of raising from a surface ornamental figures in relief; figures thus formed. [EM (1) and BOSS (1)].

EMBOSSED [em-bost'], *adj.* having designs standing out in relief; (*bot.*) projecting from the centre of a surface like the boss of a round shield.

EMBOUCHURE [em-bŏŏ-shŏŏr'], *n.* mouth of a river; mouthpiece of a wood instrument; manner of holding and controlling a mouthpiece with the lips, teeth or tongue. [Fr.].

EMBOWEL (*pres.pt.* **embowelling,** *pret.* and *p.pt.* **embowelled**) [em-bow'el], *v.t.* to enclose within something else; to remove the entrails of. EMBOWELLER, *n.* person who removes the bowels. EMBOWELMENT, *n.* state of being enclosed within something, act of removing the entrails. [OFr.].

EMBOWER [em-bow'er], *v.t.* and *i.* to cover with a bower, shelter with plants.

EMBRACE (1) [em-brās'], *v.t.* to hold and clasp in an e.; take, seize eagerly, willingly, avail oneself of; comprehend, include; encompass. EMBRACE (2), *n.* a holding and clasping of another person in one's arms against the breast, a hug. EMBRACEABLE, *adj.* able to be embraced. EMBRACEMENT, *n.* act of embracing; state of being contained. [OFr.].

EMBRASURE [em-brā'zhŏŏr], *n.* (*arch.*) recessed opening for a door or window in an interior having its sides cut back obliquely; (*fort.*) recessed opening in a rampart in which guns or cannon are mounted. [OFr.].

EMBROCATE [em'bro-kāt], *v.t.* (*med.*) to apply embrocation. [~Gk.].

EMBROCATION [em-bro-kā'shn], *n.* (*med.*) act of embrocating; lotion to be rubbed on a sprain.

EMBROGLIO, see IMBROGLIO.

EMBROIDER [em-broi'der], *v.t.* to decorate with designs picked out in different coloured threads; ornament with needlework; (*fig.*) add imaginative details to. EMBROIDERER, *n.* person who embroiders. [EM (1) and OFr.].

EMBROIDERY [em-broi'de-ri], *n.* art of embroidering; work produced by embroidery; imaginative embellishments, *esp.* to a narrative.

EMBROIL [em-broil'], *v.t.* to involve in trouble, entangle with difficulties. EMBROILMENT, *n.* act of embroiling; state of entanglement, confusion. [Fr.].

EMBRYO (1) [em'bri-ō], *n.* the germ of an organism in the first stages of pre-natal development; early stage of development in anything. EMBRYO (2), *adj.* relating to anything in an undeveloped state, rudimentary, incipient, unborn. EMBRYO- (3), *pref.* relating to an e. [Gk.].

EMBRYOLOGY [em-bri-o'lo-ji], *n.* science concerned with the formation and development of embryos. [Gk.].

EMBRYONIC [em-bri-o'nik], *adj.* relating to or resembling an embryo; undeveloped, incipient.

EMEND [e-mend'], *v.t.* to amend; correct (a mistake) or improve a text. EMENDABLE, *adj.* able to be emended. [L.].

EMENDATION [ē-men-dā'shn], *n.* act of emending; the alteration so made. [L.].

EMENDATOR [ē'men-dā-ter], *n.* corrector of errors or faults in writings; person who corrects or improves.

EMENDATORY [ē-men'da-te-ri], *adj.* contributing to emendation, tending to improve.

EMERALD (1) [e'me-rald], *n.* (*min.*) precious stone of a brilliant green colour; mineral aluminium silicate of beryllium; (*fig.*) the colour of an emerald, a brilliant medium-toned green; (*print.*) size of type between minion and nonpareil. EMERALD (2), *adj.* consisting of, having the colour of, an e. EMERALD-GREEN, vivid light-green pigment, produced from arsenate of copper for use in painting. [OFr. from Gk.].

EMERGE [i-murj'], *v.i.* to rise out of some enveloping medium, come into view; issue from, proceed out of; reappear after passing through a stage of obscurity or concealment. EMERGENCE, *n.* act of emerging. [L.].

EMERGENCY (1) [i-mur'jen-si], *n.* situation arising unexpectedly and involving danger and a need for decisive action; (*sport*) extra player to replace a member of a team in case of accident. EMERGENCY (2), *adj.* used, called upon, required in, designed for an e.

EMERGENT [i-mur'jent], *adj.* issuing, arising from. EMERGENTLY, *adv.* in an e. way.

EMERITUS (*pl.* **emeriti**) [i-me'ri-tus], *n.* person who has been granted a title or pension on retirement from public service, *esp.* a university professor. [L.].

EMERSION [i-mur'shn], *n.* process of emerging; emergence; (*astron.*) reappearance of a heavenly body after an eclipse, or of a star which has been concealed by the sun's light. [~L.].

EMERY [e'me-ri], *n.* granular variety of corundum, used for grinding and polishing. EMERY-CLOTH, -PAPER, cloth, paper, coated with e. powder and used for smoothing and polishing. EMERY-WHEEL, wheel with the rim faced with e. for grinding and polishing. [OFr. from Gk.].

EMETIC (1) [i-me'tik], *adj.* causing vomiting. EMETIC (2), *n.* (*med.*) medicine or other treatment to cause vomiting. [Gk.].

EMETIN [e'me-tin], *n.* bitter white powder obtained from the root of the ipecacuanha. [Gk.].

EMICTION [i-mik'shn], *n.* the discharging of urine; urine when voided. [~L.].

EMIGRANT (1) [e'mi-grant], *n.* one who is emigrating or has emigrated. EMIGRANT (2), *adj.* emigrating or emigrated; used by emigrants. [L.].

EMIGRATE [e'mi-grāt], *v.i.* to leave one's native country to settle in another, take up permanent residence in another country. EMIGRATORY, *adj.* emigrating, accustomed to e., as birds. [L.].

EMIGRATION [e-mi-grā'shn], *n.* act of emigrating; people who have emigrated. EMIGRATIONAL, *adj.* relating to e. EMIGRATIONIST, *n.* promoter of or advocate for e.

ÉMIGRÉ, émigré [ā'mi-grā], *n.* an emigrant; refugee, *esp.* from the French or Russian Revolutions. [Fr.].

EMINENCE, EMINENCY [e'mi-nens(-i)], *n.* that which is high, highest part, part ascending from the common to a higher level of a surface; hill; (*fig.*) superiority of rank; outstanding character or abilities, renown; title of honour accorded to a cardinal. [L.].

EMINENT [e'mi-nent], *adj.* exalted in rank, high in general esteem, famous, renowned, distinguished. EMINENTLY, *adv.* in an e. fashion. [L.].

EMIR [e-mēer'], *n.* independent Mohammedan ruler in Arabia, Asia, Africa; male descendant of Mohammed. [Arab.].

EMISSARY [e'mi-sa-ri], *n.* special representative or messenger. [LL.].

EMISSION [i-mi'shn], *n.* act of emitting; that which is discharged. [L.].

EMISSIVE [i-mi'siv], *adj.* having the power of emitting; relating to emission.

EMISSORY [e'mi-se-ri], *adj.* (*physiol.*) denoting those ducts which convey fluids to certain veins.

EMIT (*pres.pt.* **emitting,** *pret.* and *p.pt.* **emitted**) [i-mit'], *v.t.* to send forth, eject, discharge, cause to come forth; issue, as notes and bills of credit, print and send into circulation, as paper money. [L.].

EMMENAGOGUE [e-me'na-gŏg], *n.* medicine which facilitates the menstrual discharge. [Gk.].

EMMENOLOGY [e-me-no'lo-ji], *n.* treatise on or study of menstruation. [Gk.].

EMMET [e'met], *n.* an ant. [OE.].

EMMETROPIA [e-me-tro'pi-ah], *n.* normal condition of the lenses of the eye when the retina focuses parallel rays of light. [Gk.].

EMOLLIENT (1) [i-mo'li-ent], *adj.* having the power to soothe and make soft. EMOLLIENT (2), *n.* (*med.*) oily substance with soothing and softening properties. [L.].

EMOLUMENT [i-mo'lyŏŏ-ment], *n.* remuneration for services given while in office; fees, salary, profit. [L.].

EMOTION [i-mō'shn], *n.* strong instinctive feeling, involuntary wave of such feeling, stirring of one's inner nature by a mood, circumstance or passion. [L.].

EMOTIONAL [i-mo'shn-al], *adj.* relating to the

emotions; exciting or excited by emotion; possessing strong and deep emotions, being quick in emotional response. EMOTIONALLY, *adv.* with regard to the emotions; with emotion.

EMOTIONALISM [i-mō'shn-a-lizm], *n.* habit of emphasizing the importance of free emotional response; excessive cultivation of, or yielding to, emotion. EMOTIONALIST, *n.* one given to e.

EMOTIVE [i-mō'tiv], *adj.* tending to excite emotion.

EMPALE, see IMPALE.

EMPALEMENT, see IMPALEMENT.

EMPANEL, IMPANEL (*pres.pt.* empanelling, *pret. and p.pt.* empanelled) [im-pa'nel], *v.t.* to form a list of jurors, enrol as jurors. [OFr.].

EMPATHY [em'pa-thi], *n.* (*psych.*) power of subjective identification with an object or with another person during contact, having special reference to experience of a work of art. [Gk.].

EMPEROR [em'pe-rer], *n.* the supreme male sovereign of an empire; largest size of drawing paper; **e. butterfly,** the purple e., *Apatura iris;* **e. moth,** *Saturnia carpini.* [L.].

EMPHASIS [em'fa-sis], *n.* any means, device or method used to stress a part in relation to its context, marking its importance, significance or meaning; accent on a word or syllable in speech; a more powerful or distinct element in the medium of a work of art rendering it more apparent than the rest; impressiveness of expression. [Gk.].

EMPHASIZE [em'fa-sīz], *v.t.* to give emphasis to, lay stress on, accentuate, enhance, underline.

EMPHATIC(AL) [em-fa'tik(-al)], *adj.* expressing emphasis, forcible. EMPHATICALLY, *adv.* in an e. way. [Gk.].

EMPHLYSIS [em-flī'sis], *n.* (*med.*) an eruption of vesicular pimples on the skin. [Gk.].

EMPHYSEMA [em-fi-sē'mah], *n.* (*med.*) distension of a tissue due to air blocked up in the cellular tissues. EMPHYSEMATOUS, *adj.* (*med.*) relating to e., swollen. [Gk.].

EMPIRE [em'pīer], *n.* supreme power, complete sovereignty; dominion, wide territories ruled over by a supreme monarch; group of states under the rule of an emperor, the largest unit of lands and peoples bound by one monarchical allegiance; **E. Day,** 24 May, set aside for the celebration of the greatness of the British E. EMPIRE (2), *adj.* of, or relating to, an e.; style in furniture or dress fashionable during the first French E. [Fr. from L.].

EMPIRIC [em-pi'rik], *n.* person relying on personal experience and observation for principles of practice and action; medical practitioner without scientific training, a quack. [Gk.].

EMPIRIC(AL) [em-pi'rik(-al)], *adj.* based on personal experience, or experiment and observation; known only from experience, without reference to the principles or facts put forward by scientists. EMPIRICISM [em-pi'ri-sizm], *n.* methods and point of view of an empiric. EMPIRICIST, *n.* an empiric.

EMPLACEMENT [em-plās'ment], *n.* position, site, ground; gun platform. EMPLACE, *v.t.* (*milit.*) to set (a gun) in position. [Fr.].

EMPLOY (1) [em-ploi'], *v.t.* to make use of as an instrument, means, agent; engage to do work for one, particularly in a weekly capacity; give work, require workmen; spend, occupy (time etc.). EMPLOY (2), *n.* employment, occupation, service. [Fr. from L.].

EMPLOYABLE [em-ploi'a-bl], *adj.* able to be employed. EMPLOYABILITY [em-ploi-a-bi'li-ti], *n.* quality of being employable.

EMPLOYEE [em-ploi'ē], *n.* a person employed.

EMPLOYER [em-ploi'er], *n.* one who hires the service of others.

EMPLOYMENT [em-ploi'ment], *n.* act of employing, state of being employed; work, occupation, business; **e. exchange,** office for finding work for the unemployed and for paying out the money allotted by the government as unemployment benefit.

EMPORIUM [em-paw'ri-um], *n.* trading centre; large general shop stocking every kind of product. [Gk.].

EMPOWER [em-pow'er], *v.t.* to equip with power or authority, authorize.

EMPRESS [em'pres], *n.* wife of an emperor; woman who rules an empire. [L.].

EMPRESSMENT [em-pres'ment], *n.* display of eagerness, cordiality. [Fr.].

EMPRISE [em-prīz'], *n.* (*archaic*) undertaking, chivalrous adventure. [OFr.].

EMPTY (1) [emp'ti], *adj.* containing nothing, bare;

without what it usually contains or is supposed to contain; (*fig.*) futile, worthless; meaningless; senseless, brainless; unsubstantial, poor. EMPTY (2), *n.* (*coll.*) an e. bottle or receptacle. EMPTY (3), *v.t. and i.* to make e., remove the contents of; become e.; (*reflex.*) discharge into.

EMPTY-HANDED [emp-ti-han'did], *adj.* without gifts, booty or valuables.

EMPTY-HEADED [emp-ti-he'did], *adj.* silly and frivolous.

EMPTY-HEARTED [emp-ti-hah'tid], *adj.* without feeling and attachment.

EMPURPLE [em-pur'pl], *v.t.* to make purple, stain with purple.

EMPYEMA [em-pī-ē'mah], *n.* accumulation of pus around the lungs. [Gk.].

EMPYREAN [em-pī-rē'an], *n.* the highest heaven; domain of fire; dwelling place of God; the pure sky, open heavens. EMPYREAL [em-pī-rē'al], *adj.* formed of the fiery elements; relating to the e.; heavenly. [Gk.].

EMU [ē'myōō], *n.* large flightless Australian bird. [Uncert.].

EMULATE [e'myōō-lāt], *v.t.* to strive to equal or surpass, rival enviously and strive to outdo. EMULATIVE, *adj.* tending to e., that emulates. EMULATIVELY, *adv.* in emulation. EMULATOR, *n.* one who emulates, competitor, rival. [L.].

EMULATION [e-myōō-lā'shn], *n.* act of emulating; ambition to rival or surpass another. [L.].

EMULOUS [e'myōō-lŏŏs], *adj.* eager to emulate, striving to surpass or rival, eager to obtain. EMULOUSLY, *adv.* in e. fashion. EMULOUSNESS, *n.* quality of being e. [L.].

EMULSIFY [i-mul'si-fī], *v.t.* to make into an emulsion. EMULSIFIER, *n.* (*chem.*) substance which emulsifies an oil.

EMULSION [i-mul'shn], *n.* a milky substance, the union of oil and water through the use of an albuminous material, *esp.* a medical preparation of this sort; (*phot.*) mixture of silver salts suspended in collodion, used for coating photographic plates etc. EMULSIVE, *adj.* relating to, resembling e. [L.].

EN- (1), *pref.* in; to make, place into.

EN (2) [en], *n.* (*print.*) unit of width equal to half an em. [Letter N, originally half the width of M].

ENABLE [e-nā'bl], *v.t.* to allow, make able, provide means to do something, give suitable circumstances for something. ENABLEMENT, *n.* act of enabling. ENABLING, *adj.* giving power to do something; *esp.* **enabling act,** measure empowering a person or body to take certain action. [EN (1) and ABLE].

ENACT [e-nakt'], *v.t.* to decree; make into a legal measure; act, perform; do, make to happen. ENACTING, *n.* a decreeing, performing. ENACTIVE, *adj.* having competence to decree, making an enactment. ENACTOR, *n.* one who enacts. [EN (1) and ACT].

ENACTMENT [e-nakt'ment], *n.* act of enacting; that which is enacted.

ENAMEL (1) [i-na'mel], *n.* melted glass-like substance applied to the surface of objects, which forms a hard, glossy, opaque surface; kind of varnish producing an effect similar to this; any smooth, hard glazed covering, *esp.* that covering the crown of a tooth. ENAMEL (2), *adj.* made of, coated with e.; resembling e. ENAMEL (3) (*pres.pt.* ENAMELLING, *pret. and p.pt.* ENAMELLED), *v.t.* to coat with, or as if with, e.; work in enamels; (*fig.*) adorn with varied and bright colouring. ENAMELLER, *n.* worker, designer in enamels. ENAMELLING, *n.* art of laying on e. [OFr.].

ENAMOUR [e-na'mer], *v.t.* (*usually pass.*) to attract deeply, inspire with love. [OFr.].

ENCAENIA [en-sē'ni-ah], *n.*(*pl.*) commemorative celebrations held on anniversaries, *esp.* those of foundations, consecrations etc. [L.].

ENCAGE [en-kāj'], *v.t.* to shut up in a cage, coop up.

ENCAMP [en-kamp'], *v.t. and i.* to pitch camp, take up an encamped position.

ENCAMPMENT [en-kamp'ment], *n.* act of encamping, place where an army or company is encamped; the camp itself.

ENCASE [en-kās'], *v.t.* to put into a case or similar covering; envelop, surround. ENCASEMENT, *n.* act of encasing; state of being encased; thing encasing.

ENCASH [en-kash'], *v.t.* to turn into cash, obtain ready money for (a draft etc.). ENCASHABLE, *adj.* able to be encashed. ENCASHMENT, *n.* act of encashing.

ENCAUSTIC (1) [en-kaws'tik], *adj.* burnt in, pertaining to the art of painting with heated wax, or to the art of burning coloured designs into a tile.

ŏŏ is pronounced as in food; ŏŏ as in hood; th as in *think*; TH as in *that*; zh as in azure.   ~ = related to.

ENCAUSTIC (2), *n.* method or process of e. painting; tile so painted. [Gk.].

ENCEINTE [ah(ng)-sa(ng)t′], *adj.* (of women) pregnant. [Fr.].

ENCEPHAL-, *pref.* brain. [Gk.].

ENCEPHALIC [en-se-fa′lik], *adj.* (med.) relating to the brain. [Gk.].

ENCEPHALITIS [en-se-fa-lī′tis], *n.* (med.) inflammation of the brain; **e. lethargica**, sleeping sickness. [Gk.].

ENCEPHALOCELE [en-se′fa-lō-sēl], *n.* tumour of the brain. [Gk.].

ENCEPHALOID [en-se′fa-loid], *adj.* resembling brain-matter, like the cellular brain-structure of a cancer. [Gk.].

ENCEPHALON [en-se′fa-lon], *n.* (med.) the brain-structure.

ENCEPHALOTOMY [en-se-fa-lo′to-mi], *n.* dissection of the brain, surgical removal of part of the brain. [Gk.].

ENCHAIN [en-chān′], *v.t.* to chain, bind with chains; (fig.) enslave (by fascination), captivate. ENCHAINMENT, *n.* act of enchaining, condition of being enchained. [OFr.].

ENCHANT [en-chahnt′], *v.t.* and *i.* to bewitch, influence, bind with a spell or incantation; (fig.) fascinate, captivate. [OFr. from L.].

ENCHANTER [en-chahn′ter], *n.* one who enchants.

ENCHANTING [en-chahn′ting], *adj.* delightful, charming, captivating. ENCHANTINGLY, *adv.* in e. fashion.

ENCHANTMENT [en-chahnt′ment], *n.* act of enchanting, condition of being enchanted; spell, incantation; (fig.) charm, extraordinary attraction.

ENCHANTRESS [en-chahnt′res], *n.* female enchanter; delightful woman.

ENCHASE [en-chās′], *v.t.* to set in, encase in (usually a jewel in some precious metal); chase, emboss. [Fr.].

ENCIRCLE [en-sur′kl], *v.t.* to stand round or move round in a circle or so as to encompass. ENCIRCLEMENT, *n.* act of encircling, state of being encircled.

EN CLAIR [ah(ng)-klāer′], *adj.* not in cipher. [Fr.].

ENCLAVE [en-klāv′, ah(ng)-klahv′], *n.* territory belonging to one country encircled by that of another. [L.].

ENCLITIC (1) [en-kli′tik], *adj.* (gram.) attached to a word as an unaccented suffix. ENCLITIC (2), *n.* (gram.) an e. particle. ENCLITICALLY, *adv.* in the manner of an e. [Gk.].

ENCLOSE, INCLOSE [en-klōz′], *v.t.* to shut in, off; surround and close in, shut in a receptacle, surround, frame; put in, send along with something else. ENCLOSER, *n.* one who encloses.

ENCLOSURE [en-klō′zhōōr], *n.* act of enclosing, state of being enclosed; the fencing in of common land for private ownership, land so fenced in; open space enclosed by a barrier; something enclosed with a letter or package. [OFr.].

ENCOMIAST [en-kō′mi-ast], *n.* writer or speaker of an encomium. [Gk.].

ENCOMIASTIC(AL) [en-kō-mi-as′tik(-al)], *adj.* relating to an encomium.

ENCOMIUM [pl. encomiums] [en-kō′mi-um], *n.* panegyric, ceremonious eulogy. [Gk.].

ENCOMPASS [en-kum′pas], *v.t.* to surround, go round, encircle, enclose on every side.

ENCORE (1) [on-kaw(r)′], *n.* a call of applause, demand for the repetition of some admired performance, the repetition itself, or an additional item performed in response to applause. ENCORE (2), *v.t.* and *i.* to demand the repetition of a performance; call "encore" in appreciation. ENCORE (3), *int.* again! once more! [Fr.].

ENCOUNTER (1) [en-kown′ter], *v.t.* to meet, esp. by chance or unexpectedly; meet in conflict, battle; come up against, meet as an opponent or source of difficulty. ENCOUNTER (2), *n.* unexpected meeting; hostile meeting, conflict. [OFr. from LL.].

ENCOURAGE [en-ku′rij], *v.t.* to inspire with courage, give confidence to, foster, cause to arise, help to grow and spread. [Fr.].

ENCOURAGEMENT [en-ku′rij-ment], *n.* act of encouraging, that which encourages; stimulus, exhortation to be confident.

ENCOURAGING [en-ku′ri-jing], *adj.* offering encouragement, inspiring confidence. ENCOURAGINGLY, *adv.* in an e. fashion.

ENCRIMSON [en-krim′zun], *v.t.* to colour crimson, stain with crimson, make wholly crimson.

ENCROACH [en-krōch′], *v.i.* (with on or upon) to go beyond one's just rights and invade the territory or privileges of another, invade or go where one has no right, usurp by slow degrees. ENCROACHER, *n.* person or thing that encroaches. ENCROACHINGLY, *adv.* by encroachment. [OFr.].

ENCROACHMENT [en-krōch′ment], *n.* act of encroaching; (leg.) taking more than is one's due. [OFr.].

ENCRUST, INCRUST [in-krust′], *v.t.* to cover with or as with a crust, become like a crust. ENCRUSTMENT, *n.* act of encrusting

ENCUMBER [in-kum′ber], *v.t.* to cumber up, obstruct with unnecessary matter, hamper, burden, impede. [Fr.].

ENCUMBRANCE [in-kum′brans], *n.* that which encumbers; (leg.) a charge, mortgage upon property, dependent person. ENCUMBRANCER, *n.* (leg.) person having a legal claim on an estate. [OFr.].

ENCYCLIC(AL) (1) [en-sik′lik(-al)], *n.* Papal letter issued to the whole Roman Church. ENCYCLIC(AL) (2), *adj.* pertaining to encyclicals. [Gk.].

ENCYCLOPEDIA, ENCYCLOPAEDIA [en-sī-klō-pē′di-ah], *n.* complete classified compendium of all knowledge or of some particular subject. ENCYCLOPEDIACAL, ENCYCLOPAEDIACAL, ENCYCLOPEDIAN, *adj.* encyclopedic. [Gk.].

ENCYCLOPEDIC(AL), ENCYCLOPAEDIC(AL) [en-sī-klō-pē′dik(-al)], *adj.* covering the whole field of knowledge or of a particular subject.

ENCYCLOPEDISM, ENCYCLOPAEDISM [en-sī-klō-pē′dizm], *n.* the movement centred round Diderot and the French *Encyclopédie*, comprehensive knowledge. ENCYCLOPEDIST, ENCYCLOPAEDIST, *n.* compiler of an encyclopedia; (specif.) one of the compilers of the French *Encyclopédie*.

ENCYSTED [en-sis′tid], *adj.* enclosed in a cyst.

END (1) [end], *n.* the conclusion, finish, final point or part of a thing, extreme point, ultimate state, cessation, limit, last remaining part or thing, final part of a period of time; (philos.) final purpose towards which will and action aim; (fig.) death; (slang) buttocks: **bitter e.**, conclusion, however unpleasant; **at a loose e.**, with nothing special to do; **on e.**, continuously; **to make ends meet**, to make do with a bare sufficiency; **to keep one's e. up**, to do one's share fully and successfully; **wrong e. of the stick**, mistake caused by confusing of opposites; **e. play**, technique of play in the last stages of a game of chess or bridge; **no e.**, (coll.) extremely. END (2), *v.t.* and *i.* to finish, bring to an e., complete, discontinue; come to an e., reach a termination, result in, conclude, die. END-ALL, *n.* final aim, object. ENDER, *n.* that which ends. [OE.].

ENDANGER [en-dān′jer], *v.t.* to expose to danger.

ENDEAR [en-dēer′], *v.t.* to make dear, bind by ties of affection. ENDEARING, *adj.* tending to gain affection. ENDEARINGLY, *adv.* in an endearing fashion.

ENDEARMENT [en-dēer′ment], *n.* act of endearing; state of being endeared; a caress.

ENDEAVOUR (1) [en-de′ver], *v.i.* to try, make an attempt, to accomplish something. ENDEAVOUR (2), *n.* an attempt to attain an object. [Fr.].

ENDEMIC (1) [en-de′mik], *adj.* (med.) local, affecting or usually found in one district or class; (zool., bot.) peculiar to, or native to, a certain region. ENDEMIC (2), *n.* an e. disease. ENDEMICAL, *adj.* e. ENDEMICALLY, *adv.* in e. fashion. ENDEMICITY [en-de-mi′si-ti], *n.* quality of being e.

ENDERMIC, ENDERMATIC [en-dur′mik, en-der-ma′tik], *adj.* acting through the skin; applied to the skin after a blister. [Gk.].

ENDING [en′ding], *n.* termination, conclusion; death; (gram.) inflexional suffix.

ENDIRON, see ANDIRON.

ENDIVE [en′div], *n.* a species of chicory. [Fr.].

ENDLESS [end′les], *adj.* without end, everlasting; unlimited, infinite; (coll.) excessively long, interminable; **e. chain**, (mech.) chain in which the ends are joined, and which revolves continuously over pulleys etc. ENDLESSLY, *adv.* so as to be e., unceasingly. ENDLESSNESS, *n.* quality of being e.

ENDLONG [end′long], *adv.* lengthwise, from end to end; on end, vertically. [ME.].

ENDMOST [end′mōst], *adj.* farthest; placed at the end.

ENDO-, *pref.* within. [Gk.].

ENDOCARDITIS [en-dō-kah-dī′tis], *n.* inflammation of the endocardium. [Gk.].

ENDOCARDIUM [en-dō-kah′di-um], *n.* (anat.) membrane which lines the internal surface of the heart. ENDOCARDIAL, *adj.* relating to the e. [Gk.].

ENDOCARP [en'dō-kahp], *n.* (*bot.*) inner layer of the lining of a seed-vessel. [Gk.].

ENDOCRINE (1) [en'dō-krīn], *adj.* (*anat.*) (of certain glands) ductless, secreting internally; (of secretions) secreted internally. ENDOCRINE (2), *n.* an e. gland. [Gk.].

ENDODERM [en'dō-derm], *n.* (*anat., biol.*) inner lining of the alimentary canal, inner germ-layer of an embryo; (*bot.*) innermost layer of the cortex. ENDODERMIC [en-dō-dur'mik], *adj.* relating to the e. [Gk.].

ENDOGAMY [en-do'ga-mi], *n.* restriction of marriage to members of the same tribe. ENDOGAMOUS, *adj.* pertaining to e. [Gk.].

ENDOGASTRITIS [en-dō-gas-trī'tis], *n.* (*med.*) inflammation of the internal membrane of the stomach.

ENDOGEN [en'dō-jen], *n.* (*bot.*) plant, such as a palm, which is supposed to grow from within and in which the stem cannot increase in thickness when the outside becomes hard. [Gk.].

ENDOGENOUS [en-do'je-nŏos], *adj.* relating to endogens; growing from within, arising in the interior.

ENDOPLASM [en'dō-plazm], *n.* the inner layer of protoplasm.

ENDORSE, INDORSE [en-daws'], *v.t.* to write on the back of (a document), *esp.* to sign one's name on the back of a cheque, bill of exchange etc. by way of ratification; (*fig.*) confirm, approve of, sanction; (*U.S.*) praise in an advertisement; write on (a driving licence) so as to show that the owner has been convicted of a motoring offence. ENDORSEE, INDORSEE [en-daw-sē'], *n.* person for whom a document is endorsed. ENDORSER, INDORSER [en-daw'ser], *n.* one who endorses. [MedL.].

ENDORSEMENT, INDORSEMENT [en-daws'ment], *n.* act of endorsing, that which is written on the back of a document; (*fig.*) support, confirmation.

ENDOSCOPE [en'dō-skōp], *n.* optical instrument for examining internal organs. [Gk.].

ENDOSMOSIS [en-dos-mō'sis], *n.* transmission of liquids or gases through a membranous or porous partition from the exterior to the interior. ENDOSMOMETER [en-dos-mo'mi-ter], *n.* instrument for measuring the force of endosmotic action. ENDOSMOTIC [en-dos-mo'tik], *adj.* pertaining to e. [Gk.].

ENDOSPERM [en'dō-sperm], *n.* nutritive tissue surrounding the embryo in many seeds. ENDOSPERMIC [en-dō-spur'mik], *adj.* containing or relating to e. [Gk.].

ENDOTHELIUM [en-dō-thē'li-um], *n.* (*anat.*) the lining of blood-vessels. [Gk.].

ENDOW [en-dow'], *v.t.* to bestow money or property upon, *esp.* so as to provide continued financial support for (an institution, person etc.); provide with (gift, talent, quality etc.). ENDOWER, *n.* one who endows. [EN (1) and Fr.].

ENDOWMENT [en-dow'ment], *n.* act of endowing, state of being endowed; property or money given to endow a person or institution; natural talents or mental quality; **e. policy,** insurance policy by which a fixed sum is payable at a certain date or upon the previous death of the holder.

END-PAPERS [end'pā-perz], *n.*(*pl.*) the blank leaves at the beginning and end of a book.

END-STOPPED [end'stopt], *adj.* (*pros.*) having a pause at the end of each line.

ENDUE [en-dyōo'], *v.t.* to invest or endow with, bestow upon; (*archaic*) put on, clothe. [OFr.].

ENDURABLE [en-dyōo'ra-bl], *adj.* able to be endured. ENDURABLENESS, *n.* quality of being e. ENDURABLY, *adv.* in e. fashion.

ENDURANCE [en-dyōo'rans], *n.* act of enduring, power of enduring, fortitude.

ENDURE [en-dyōor'], *v.t. and i.* to bear with fortitude, support without yielding, sinking or breaking up; tolerate, undergo, suffer; continue, remain; suffer without succumbing, bear up under hardship etc. [L.].

ENDURING [en-dyōo'ring], *adj.* permanent, long-lasting. ENDURINGLY, *adv.* in an e. manner.

ENDWAYS [end'wāz], *adv.* on end, with the end facing front.

ENDWISE [end'wīz], *adv.* endways.

ENEID, see AENEID.

ENEMA [e'ni-mah], *n.* (*med.*) liquid injected into the rectum; apparatus for injecting this. [Gk.].

ENEMY (1) [e'ne-mi], *n.* foe, antagonist, one who hates or endeavours to harm another as much as possible; nation at war with another; the opposing armed forces or a section of them; person strongly opposed to anything, opponent; force or factor harmful to another. ENEMY (2), *adj.* pertaining to an e., hostile. [OFr. from L.].

ENEMY-OCCUPIED [e-ne-mi-o'kyōo-pīd], *adj.* occupied by hostile forces.

ENERGETIC(AL) [e-ner-je'tik(-al)], *adj.* full of energy, exhibiting great vigour, extremely active, forceful. ENERGETICALLY, *adv.* in an e. fashion. [Gk.].

ENERGETICS [e-ner-je'tiks], *n.*(*pl.*) science concerned with the principles and nature of physical energy.

ENERGIZE [e'ner-jīz], *v.t. and i.* to rouse to activity, fill with energy, make vigorous; act with force and effect. ENERGIZER, *n.* person or thing that imparts energy.

ENERGY [e'ner-ji], *n.* power, force which is able to effect change; capacity to cause action or motion, inherent ability or strength; vigour, drive; (*mech.*) capacity to do effective work; **conservation of e.,** (*phys.*) law expressing the theory that the capacity for e. in the material world remains constant regardless of the forms it takes. [Gk.].

ENERVATE [e'ner-vāt], *v.t.* to deprive of strength in any form, sap the vigour of. ENERVATIVE, *adj.* enervating. [L.].

ENERVATION [e-ner-vā'shn], *n.* act of enervating; state of being enervated.

ENFEEBLE [en-fē'bl], *v.t.* to render feeble. ENFEEBLEMENT, *n.* act of enfeebling; state of being enfeebled. [OFr.].

ENFEOFF [en-fef'], *v.t.* to invest with the fee of an estate, give freehold property in fee-simple or tail. ENFEOFFMENT, *n.* act of enfeoffing; deed authorizing the investment with the fee of an estate. [OFr.].

ENFILADE (1) [en-fi-lād'], *n.* (*milit.*) use of fire-power upon the enemy from a flank. ENFILADE (2), *v.t.* (*milit.*) to fire from a flank across the line of the enemy's advance or retreat. ~Fr.].

ENFOLD [en-fōld'], *v.t.* to envelop, embrace, fold round.

ENFORCE [en-faws'], *v.t. and i.* to compel obedience, subdue opposition by force, cause to take effect by forms of authority; attempt by force. ENFORCEDLY [en-faw'sid-li], *adv.* by means of force. [OFr.].

ENFORCEABLE [en-faw'sa-bl], *adj.* capable of being enforced. ENFORCEABILITY [en-faw-sa-bi'li-ti], *n.* quality of being e.

ENFORCEMENT [en-faws'ment], *n.* act of enforcing; condition of being enforced; compulsion.

ENFRANCHISE [en-fran'chīz], *v.t.* to grant the right to vote; release, set free, emancipate; grant the privileges of a free man; convert into a freehold. ENFRANCHISER, *n.* person who enfranchises. [OFr.].

ENFRANCHISEMENT [en-fran'chiz-ment], *n.* act of enfranchising; condition of being enfranchised.

ENGAGE [en-gāj'], *v.t.* to bind by pledge or promise, agree to preliminary conditions in a mutual contract, *esp.* bind (oneself) to marry; hire, reserve for occupation or use; occupy, use, employ; secure, attach; attack, enter into combat with; *v.i.* to commence hostilities, come to grips; pledge oneself; undertake; take part in an enterprise. [Fr.].

ENGAGED [en-gājd'], *adj.* betrothed, promised; employed, reserved, hired, in use; **e. column,** column half sunk in a wall.

ENGAGEMENT [en-gāj'ment], *n.* act of engaging; state of being engaged; that which engages; obligation, mutual arrangement; betrothal; occupation, employment; encounter between armed forces, battle.

ENGAGING [en-gā'jing], *n.* tending to attract the attention or the affections, pleasing. ENGAGINGLY, *adv.* in an e. fashion.

ENGENDER [en-jen'der], *v.t.* to create between the sexes, breed; stir up, rouse; produce. [Fr. from L.].

ENGINE [en'jin], *n.* one of many kinds of apparatus for converting sources of natural power such as heat, gas, steam, into mechanical energy, *esp.* a steam-engine, locomotive; instrument of war, device. ENGINE-DRIVER, person who controls a locomotive on a railway. [L.].

ENGINEER (1) [en-ji-nēer'], *n.* an expert in engineering, person trained in the scientific principles and possessing practical experience of constructing or supervising all kinds of engines and machines; supervisor of the machinery in a ship; member of a military corps which constructs fortifications etc. ENGINEER (2), *v.t. and i.* to direct and superintend the construction of anything as an e.; devise and carry out an intricate scheme or plan of action; be engaged in engineering work. [OFr. from L.].

ENGINEERING [en-ji-nēer'ing], *n.* science concerned with the principles, design, manufacture and control of all types of engines and mechanical appliances; profession of an engineer; **civil e.**, science of designing and constructing bridges, railways, roads etc.; **military e.**, construction of fortifications and the maintenance of lines of communication.

ENGINE-TURNING [en'jin-ter-ning], *n.* mode of metal engraving by machinery.

ENGLISH (1) [ing'glish], *adj.* of or relating to England, its native inhabitants or their language. ENGLISH (2), *n.* the people of England, their language. ENGLISH (3), *v.t.* to translate into the E. language.

ENGLISHRY [ing'glish-ri], *n.* state of being English; people of English descent, particularly those living in Ireland.

ENGLISHISM [ing'gli-shizm], *n.* behaviour characteristic of the English; a form of speech typical of the English spoken in England.

ENGORGE [en-gawj'], *v.t.* to swallow with greediness; fill to excess. ENGORGEMENT, *n.* act of gorging; state of being gorged, *esp.* of an organ of the body.

ENGRAFT [en-grahft'], *v.t.* to insert, as a tree is grafted; (*fig.*) introduce.

ENGRAIN [en-grān'], *v.t.* to dye in the grain, saturate. ENGRAINED, *adj.* thorough, having a permanent tendency, completely impregnated or saturated.

ENGRAM [en'gram], *n.* (*psych.*) permanent change brought about in an organism by a particular stimulus. [Gk.].

ENGRAVE [en-grāv'], *v.t.* to cut lines in stone, metal or wood with a graver; reproduce a pattern or picture by taking impressions from an inked metal plate in which the pattern or picture has been cut or etched in lines. [EN- (1) and GRAVE (4)].

ENGRAVER [en-grā'ver], *n.* person who engraves; cutter of letters, figures or pictures in stone, metal or wood.

ENGRAVING [en-grā'ving], *n.* art of an engraver; art of cutting or etching patterns or pictures in a hard medium and taking impressions from the inked surface; picture so made.

ENGROSS, INGROSS [en-grōs'], *v.t.* to take up exclusively, monopolize (the mind, attention etc.); (*leg.*) copy in clear writing for record purposes; express formally in writing. ENGROSSER, *n.* he who or that which exclusively occupies or monopolizes the whole; (*leg.*) one who engrosses documents. [AFr.].

ENGROSSING (1) [en-grō'sing], *n.* (*leg.*) a copy in legible characters. ENGROSSING (2), *adj.* all-absorbing, exclusively engaging the attention.

ENGROSSMENT [en-grōs'ment], *n.* act of engrossing; (*leg.*) that which has been engrossed; state of being engrossed.

ENGULF [en-gulf'], *v.t.* to swallow up; overwhelm.

ENHANCE [en-hahns'], *v.t.* to raise, advance; increase, heighten, exaggerate. ENHANCEMENT, *n.* act of enhancing; state of being enhanced. ENHANCER, *n.* person who enhances. [OFr.].

ENHARMONIC (1) [en-hah-mo'nik], *adj.* (*mus.*) composed of enharmonic intervals. ENHARMONIC (2), *n.* (*mus.*) interval smaller than a semitone. ENHARMONICALLY, *adv.* in an e. way; by means of e. intonation.

ENHYDROUS [en-hī'drŏŏs], *adj.* (*min.*) containing or enclosing drops of water. [EN- (1) and HYDROUS].

ENIGMA [e-nig'mah], *n.* puzzle, riddle; (*fig.*) puzzling situation or circumstance; one who is difficult to understand. [Gk.].

ENIGMATIC(AL) [e-nig-ma'tik(-al)], *adj.* pertaining to, or containing, an enigma; puzzling, mysterious. ENIGMATICALLY, *adv.* in an e. way.

ENISLE [e-nīl'], *v.t.* to make into or set on an island; (*fig.*) set apart.

ENJAMBEMENT [en-jamb'ment], *n.* (*pros.*) the carrying over of a sentence or clause from one line of verse to the next. [Fr.].

ENJOIN [en-join'], *v.t.* to lay down as a rule to be strictly carried out, give orders or instructions for. ENJOINER, *n.* person who enjoins. ENJOINMENT, *n.* a strict and urgent command. [Fr.].

ENJOY [en-joi'], *v.t.* to use, possess or experience with joy, have as one's lot; have a right to the use of; (*archaic*) have sexual relations with; **to e. oneself**, to find delight in what one is doing or the things or persons about one. [OFr.].

ENJOYABLE [en-joi'a-bl], *adj.* affording enjoyment. ENJOYABLY, *adv.* in an e. way.

ENJOYMENT [en-joi'ment], *n.* delight, pleasure.

ENKINDLE [en-kin'dl], *v.t.* to set alight or on fire; (*fig.*) put vigour or enthusiasm into.

ENLACE [en-lās'], *v.t.* to embrace or enfold. ENLACEMENT, *n.* act of enlacing; condition of being enlaced.

ENLARGE [en-lahj'], *v.t.* and *i.* to make bigger or more capacious, add to; (*phot.*) make a print larger than the negative of; become bigger, more extensive or capacious; **to e. upon**, to discuss very fully. ENLARGER, *n.* one who or that which enlarges, amplifier; (*phot.*) apparatus for enlarging. ENLARGING, *n.* enlargement; amplification.

ENLARGEMENT [en-lahj'ment], *n.* action of making larger, condition of being larger; (*phot.*) a print larger than its negative.

ENLIGHTEN [en-lī'ten], *v.t.* to impart knowledge to; liberate from prejudice or superstition; (*poet.*) illuminate. ENLIGHTENED, *adj.* elevated by, advanced in, knowledge; not barbarous in outlook. ENLIGHTENER, *n.* one who or that which imparts knowledge. ENLIGHTENING, *adj.* that enlightens; illuminating.

ENLIGHTENMENT [en-lī'ten-ment], *n.* act of enlightening; condition of being enlightened.

ENLIST [en-list'], *v.t.* and *i.* to receive as a member of a fighting force; win or engage the active co-operation of; join one of the fighting forces voluntarily; **enlisted men**, (*U.S. milit.*) the rank and file of an army, as distinguished from officers.

ENLISTMENT [en-list'ment], *n.* act of enlisting.

ENLIVEN [en-lī'ven], *v.t.* to put life or vigour into; give gaiety or pleasant diversity to; make cheerful. ENLIVENER, *n.* person or thing that enlivens. ENLIVENING, *adj.* act of making lively. ENLIVENMENT, *n.* act of enlivening; condition of being enlivened.

ENMESH [en-mesh'], *v.t.* to catch in a mesh, entangle, entrap. ENMESHMENT, *n.* action or process of enmeshing; condition of being enmeshed.

ENMITY [en'mi-ti], *n.* antagonistic feelings or actions, ill-will, opposition, hostility. [~OFr. from L.].

ENNEA-, *pref.* nine. [Gk.].

ENNEAGON [e'ni-a-gon], *n.* polygon or plane figure with nine angles. [Gk.].

ENNEAHEDRAL [e-ni-a-hē'dral], *adj.* (*geom.*) with nine sides or faces. [Gk.].

ENNOBLE [en-nō'bl], *v.t.* to elevate to the nobility; impart noble qualities to. ENNOBLEMENT, *n.* act of ennobling; condition of being ennobled.

ENNUI [ahn-wē'], *n.* boredom, feeling of being tired or uninterested in a thing. [Fr.].

ENORMITY [i-naw'mi-ti], *n.* state of being enormous; something which is enormous; an atrocious crime; wicked act or behaviour. [Fr.].

ENORMOUS [i-naw'mŏŏs], *adj.* of huge dimensions, vast, tremendous. ENORMOUSLY, *adv.* to an e. extent; very much. [L.].

ENOUGH (1) [i-nuf'], *adj.* neither too much nor too little, sufficient. ENOUGH (2), *n.* a fit and proper quantity, neither too much nor too little; the exact amount required. ENOUGH (3), *adv.* sufficiently, neither inadequately nor to excess. [OE.].

ENOUNCE [i-nowns'], *v.t.* and *i.* to utter, speak, pronounce. ENOUNCEMENT, *n.* enunciation; utterance. [Fr.].

ENOW†, *adj. and adv.* enough. [OE.].

EN PASSANT [ah(ng)-pa'sah(ng)], *adv. phrase* in passing; (*chess*) used of a particular manner in which one pawn may take another. [Fr.].

EN PRISE [ah(ng)-prēz'], *adv.* (*chess*) liable to be taken. [Fr.].

ENQUIRE, see INQUIRE.

ENQUIRER, see INQUIRER.

ENQUIRY, see INQUIRY.

ENRAGE [en-rāj'], *v.t.* to arouse rage in, make angry. [OFr.].

ENRAPT [en-rapt'], *adj.* enraptured, delighted to ecstasy.

ENRAPTURE [en-rap'tyŏŏr], *v.t.* to make spellbound with delight.

ENREGISTRATION [en-re-jis-trā'shn], *n.* (*psych.*) the registering in the brain of frequent actions, so that they become habitual or automatic.

ENRICH [en-rich'], *v.t.* to make wealthy; improve the quality of; add richness to, make gorgeous or beautiful. ENRICHER, *n.* person who enriches.

ENRICHMENT [en-rich'ment], *n.* act of enriching or of acquiring riches; that which enriches; increase of quality or value.

ENROL [en-rōl'], *v.t.* to enter by name in a list, register etc. ENROLLER, *n.* one who enrols. [OFr.].

The accent ′ after a syllable = stress (u-pon′). The mark ¯ over a vowel = length (ā in made; ō in bone).

ENROLMENT [en-rōl'ment], *n.* act of enrolling; condition of being enrolled; that in which anything is enrolled.

ENSAMPLE [en-sahm'pl], *n.* (*archaic*) an example or pattern. [OFr.].

ENSANGUINE [en-sang'gwin], *v.t.* to stain with blood. ENSANGUINED, *adj.* bloody, blood-stained.

ENSCONCE [en-skons'], *v.t.* to set or stow in a safe place. [EN-(1) and SCONCE].

ENSEMBLE [on-sombl'], *n.* the total effect or general appearance; two or more female garments designed to be worn together; (*mus.*) any part of a musical composition in which all the performers are concerned; the quality of such a performance. [Fr.].

ENSHRINE [en-shrin'], *v.t.* to set in a shrine; preserve with great care and reverence. ENSHRINEMENT, *n.* act of enshrining; condition of being enshrined.

ENSHROUD [en-shrowd'], *v.t.* to veil or shroud.

ENSIGN [en'sin, en'sn], *n.* any crest or symbol indicating the rank or office of the bearer; flag of a regiment or country; (*U.S. navy*) officer holding the lowest commissioned rank; †(*British Army*) former rank equivalent to second lieutenant. ENSIGNCY, *n.* rank of an e. [OFr. from L.].

ENSILAGE (1) [en'si-lij], *n.* way of preserving green fodder in a silo; fodder preserved in this way. ENSILAGE (2), *v.t.* to keep green fodder by e. [~SILO].

ENSILE [en-sil'], *v.t.* to store in a silo. [~ SILO].

ENSLAVE [en-slāv'], *v.t.* to reduce to slavery; obtain the mastery over; subject to one's will. ENSLAVEMENT, *n.* action of enslaving; condition of being enslaved.

ENSNARE [en-snāer'], *v.t.* to trap in a snare; (*fig.*) trick into a false position.

ENSPHERE [en-sfēer'], *v.t.* to put in or surround with a sphere.

ENSUE [en-syōō'], *v.t. and i.* to occur as a consequence, follow as a result; †endeavour to obtain. ENSUING, *adj.* following; resultant.

ENSURE [en-shōōr'], *v.t.* to make secure, insure.

ENTABLATURE [en-tab'la-tyōōr], *n.* (*arch.*) that part of a structure which includes architrave, frieze and cornice.

ENTABLEMENT [en-tā'bl-ment], *n.* slab on top of a pedestal bearing a statue. [Fr.].

ENTAIL (1) [en-tāl'], *v.t.* to bequeath by entail; involve, result inevitably in. ENTAIL (2), *n.* the settlement of the succession of a landed estate so that it cannot be bequeathed at will, but must be passed on in a specified order; estate which is so entailed. ENTAILMENT, *n.* act of entailing; condition of being entailed. [EN-(1) and OFr.].

ENTANGLE [en-tang'gl], *v.t.* to make tangled; cause to be caught in a mesh or net-like obstacle; (*fig.*) obtain a steadily increasing influence over or control of. ENTANGLEMENT, *n.* state of being entangled; perplexity; wire barrier to impede the progress of an enemy. [EN- (1) and TANGLE].

ENTENTE [ah(ng)-tah(ng)t'], *n.* friendly understanding, *esp.* between nations; E. cordiale, unofficial alliance established between Britain and France in the early 20th century. [Fr.].

ENTER [en'ter], *v.t.* to go or come in, pass inside; penetrate, pierce; become a member of; write or record in a book; take down the name of an entrant; enrol as a member or prospective member; break in (a horse); *v.i.* to go in, come in, pass inside, come upon the stage; **to e. for,** to compete for; **to e. into,** to engage in, embark upon; become a party to; sympathize with, understand; take part in; **to e. upon,** to begin to deal with; assume possession of, begin, embark upon. ENTERED, *adj.* recorded; inserted in a list of members etc. ENTERING, *n.* act of coming in or going in. [OFr.].

ENTERIC [en-te'rik], *adj.* relating to the intestines; e. fever, typhoid. [Gk.].

ENTERITIS [en-te-ri'tis], *n.* inflammation of the intestines. [Gk.].

ENTEROLOGY [en-te-ro'lo-ji], *n.* study of the bowels or internal parts of the body. [Gk.].

ENTEROTOMY [en-te-ro'to-mi], *n.* (*anat.*) dissection of the intestines; (*surg.*) incision of the intestines for the removal of strangulation etc. [Gk.].

ENTERPRISE [en'ter-priz], *n.* undertaking, task, adventure, *esp.* one of a bold or difficult nature; courageous and adventurous character; ability to think out and make a start upon new schemes; initiative. ENTERPRISER, *n.* one who undertakes an enterprise, *esp.* a bold or dangerous one. [OFr.].

ENTERPRISING [en'ter-pri-zing], *adj.* bold or venturesome in undertaking; having initiative. ENTERPRISINGLY, *adv.* in an e. way.

ENTERTAIN [en-ter-tān'], *v.t. and i.* to provide hospitality (for); provide light amusement (for) as by conversation, wit etc.; amuse; give mental consideration to, ponder. ENTERTAINER, *n.* person who entertains. [Fr.].

ENTERTAINING [en-ter-tā'ning], *adj.* pleasant, amusing. ENTERTAININGLY, *adv.* in an e. way.

ENTERTAINMENT [en-ter-tān'ment], *n.* act of entertaining; condition of being entertained; amusement, entertaining dramatic performance.

ENTHRAL, ENTHRALL (*pres.pt.* enthralling, *pret. and p.pt.* enthralled) [en-thrawl'], *v.t.* to enslave; enchant; interest intensely. ENTHRALMENT, *n.* act of enthralling; condition of being enthralled.

ENTHRONE [en-thrōn'], *v.t.* to set on a throne; invest with sovereign authority; install as a bishop. ENTHRONEMENT [en-thrōn'ment], *n.* act of enthroning; condition of being enthroned.

ENTHUSE [en-thyōōz'], *v.i.* (*coll.*) to be enthusiastic; gush. [Next].

ENTHUSIASM [en-thyōō'zi-azm], *n.* keen zeal or admiration; religious fervour and exaltation. [Gk.].

ENTHUSIAST [en-thyōō'zi-ast], *n.* enthusiastic person.

ENTHUSIASTIC [en-thyōō-zi-as'tik], *adj.* animated by intense zeal; zealous, eager, hearty. ENTHUSIASTICALLY, *adv.* in an e. fashion.

ENTICE [en-tis'], *v.t.* to tempt, *esp.* to evil, by exciting hopes or desires; allure; lead astray. [OFr.].

ENTICEMENT [en-tis'ment], *n.* act of enticing; condition of being enticed; that which entices.

ENTICING [en-ti'sing], *adj.* having qualities which entice; alluring. ENTICINGLY, *adv.* in an e. way.

ENTIRE (1) [en-tier'], *adj.* complete, having no flaw or imperfection; unbroken; not castrated. ENTIRE (2), *n.* anything which is unmixed; a blend of beer; uncastrated animal. ENTIRELY, *adv.* wholly, fully; utterly. ENTIRENESS, *n.* state of being e. [Fr.].

ENTIRETY [en-tier'ti], *n.* condition of being entire; the whole.

ENTITLE [en-ti'tl], *v.t.* to give a title or name to; style; give a claim or right to. [OFr.].

ENTITY [en'ti-ti], *n.* thing complete in itself, its actual existence as opposed to its qualities and attributes; something with a real existence of its own. [Fr.].

ENTO-, *pref.* within. [Gk.].

ENTOBLAST [en'tō-blahst], *n.* nucleolus or little nucleus of a cell. [Gk.].

ENTOMB [en-tōōm'], *v.t.* to bury in a tomb; shut as in a tomb. ENTOMBMENT, *n.* condition of being entombed; act of laying (something) in a tomb.

ENTOMIC [en-to'mik], *adj.* connected with insects.

ENTOMO-, *pref.* relating to insects. [Gk.].

ENTOMOID [en'to-moid], *adj.* resembling an insect. [Gk.].

ENTOMOLOGY [en-to-mo'lo-ji], *n.* science dealing with insects. ENTOMOLOGICAL, [en-to-mo-lo'ji-kal], *adj.* relating to e. ENTOMOLOGICALLY, *adv.* in an entomological way. ENTOMOLOGIST [en-to-mo'lo-jist], *n.* one expert in e. ENTOMOLOGIZE, *v.i.* to collect insects for scientific observation. [Gk.].

ENTOURAGE [ahn'tōō-rahzh], *n.* persons, circumstances and things which together make up an individual's immediate surroundings; immediate circle of servants and friends. [Fr.].

EN-TOUT-CAS [ah(ng)-tōō-kah'], *n.* contrivance which can be used as either an umbrella or a sunshade; tennis-court for use in all weather. [Fr.].

ENTOZOON (*pl.* entozoa) [en-tō-zō'on], *n.* parasitic animal living inside another animal. ENTOZOAL, ENTOZOIC, *adj.* pertaining to the entozoa. ENTOZOOLOGIST [en-tō-zō-o'lo-jist], *n.* one skilled in entozoology. ENTOZOOLOGY, *n.* scientific study of entozoa. [Gk.].

ENTR'ACTE [on'trakt], *n.* interval between the acts of a play; performance given then. [Fr.].

ENTRAILS [en'trālz], *n.*(*pl.*) the internal parts of animal bodies, the bowels; (*fig.*) internal parts or inside of anything. [OFr.].

ENTRAIN [en-trān'], *v.t. and i.* to dispatch by train; board a train.

ENTRAMMEL [en-tra'mel], *v.t.* to entangle.

ENTRANCE (1) [en'trans], *n.* act of one who enters; right to be admitted; price of admission; action of an actor in coming on the stage; way in, doorway; (*fig.*) commencement or beginning.

ENTRANCE (2) [en-trahns'], *v.t.* to fill with delight

---

or joyous fascination. ENTRANCEMENT, *n.* act of entrancing, condition of one who is entranced; that which entrances. ENTRANCING, *adj.* delightfully fascinating, charming. [EN- (1) and TRANCE].

ENTRANT [en'trant], *n.* one who enters, candidate.

ENTRAP [en-trap'], *v.t.* to snare in a trap; gain an advantage or ascendancy over by trickery.

ENTREAT [en-trēt'], *v.t.* to make an urgent petition to, implore; (*archaic*) use, treat. ENTREATING, *adj.* expressing an urgent appeal. ENTREATINGLY, *adv.* in an entreating way. [OFr.].

ENTREATY [en-trē'ti], *n.* earnest petition; act of one who entreats.

ENTRECOTE, entrecôte [ah(ng)tr'kōt], *n.* (*cookery*) a steak cut off the ribs. [Fr.].

ENTREE, entrée [ah(ng)'trā], *n.* right of access or entry; light dish served between the main courses of a dinner. [Fr.].

ENTREMETS [ah(ng)tr'mā], *n.(pl.)* subsidiary dishes between the main courses of a dinner. [Fr.].

ENTRENCH, INTRENCH [en-trench'], *v.t.* to surround with a trench; make and occupy a trench; (*fig., reflex.*) make a stout resistance. ENTRENCHMENT, *n.* act of entrenching; condition of being entrenched; military trench or system of trenches.

ENTREPOT, entrepôt [ah(ng)tr'pō], *n.* store, warehouse. [Fr.].

ENTREPRENEUR [ah(ng)tr-pre-nur'], *n.* one who undertakes an artistic or commercial venture. [Fr.].

ENTRESOL [ah(ng)tr'sol], *n.* small extra storey between the first and ground floors; small window of such a storey. [Fr.].

ENTROPY [en'tro-pi], *n.* the measure of the thermal energy of a system which cannot be converted into work. [Gk.].

ENTRUST, INTRUST [en-trust'], *v.t.* to commit to a person for safe keeping; commit something to. ENTRUSTMENT, *n.* act of entrusting; that which is entrusted.

ENTRY [en'tri], *n.* action or right of entering; way in, doorway; memorandum or record written down; (*leg.*) the taking possession of property by entering it. [Fr.].

ENTWINE, INTWINE [en-twīn'], *v.t. and i.* to twine or interlace; twine round. ENTWINEMENT, *n.* an interweaving or twisting round.

ENTWIST, INTWIST [en-twist'], *v.t. and i.* to interweave.

ENUCLEATE [i-nyōō'kli-āt], *v.t.* to extricate and make clear, explain; extract. ENUCLEATION [i-nyōō-kli-ā'shn], *n.* act of enucleating.

ENUMERATE [i-nyōō'me-rāt], *v.t.* to reckon, count up or name one by one; tell in detail. ENUMERATIVE, *adj.* connected with enumeration, summing up. ENUMERATOR, *n.* one who enumerates. [L.].

ENUMERATION [i-nyōō-me-rā'shn], *n.* condition of being enumerated; act of enumerating; a reckoning up; detailed list or statement.

ENUNCIATE [i-nun'si-āt], *v.t.* to proclaim, propound; pronounce, articulate. ENUNCIABLE, *adj.* able to be enunciated. ENUNCIATIVE, *adj.* relating to enunciation. ENUNCIATIVELY, *adv.* in an enunciative manner. ENUNCIATOR, *n.* one who enunciates. [L.].

ENUNCIATION [i-nun-si-ā'shn], *n.* act of enunciating; condition of being enunciated; style or manner of enunciating; (*geom.*) formal statement of a proposition.

ENURE, see INURE.

ENURESIS [e-nyōō-rē'sis], *n.* (*med.*) incontinence of urine. [Gk.].

ENVELOP [en-ve'lop], *v.t.* to surround, cover up, hide; (*fig.*) make almost unintelligible. [Fr.].

ENVELOPE [en've-lōp, on've-lōp], *n.* wrapping, outer covering; paper cover for sending a letter in; outer cover of the gas-bag of a balloon or airship; (*bot.*) one of the reproductive organs of a plant, surrounding the stamens and pistils. [Fr.].

ENVELOPMENT [en-ve'lop-ment], *n.* act of enveloping; condition of being enveloped; a wrapping; complete covering.

ENVENOM [en-ve'nom], *v.t.* to poison, impregnate with venom; (*fig.*) embitter; exasperate.

ENVIABLE [en'vi-a-bl], *adj.* liable to excite envy; very desirable. ENVIABLENESS, *n.* state of being e. ENVIABLY, *adv.* in an e. way.

ENVIED [en'vid], *adj.* made the object of envy.

ENVIER [en'vi-er], *n.* one who envies.

ENVIOUS [en'vi-oos], *adj.* feeling envy; animated or motivated by envy. ENVIOUSLY, *adv.* in an e. fashion.

ENVIRON [en-vī'ron], *v.t.* to stand or be placed around, encompass. [Fr.].

ENVIRONMENT [en-vī'ron-ment], *n.* act of environing, condition of being environed; surroundings, conditions in which one grows up or lives and which influence one's development. ENVIRONMENTAL [en-vī-ron-men'tal], *adj.* pertaining to, occasioned by, e. ENVIRONMENTALLY, *adv.* with respect to e.

ENVIRONS [en-vī'ronz], *n.(pl.)* the places and district in the immediate neighbourhood of a particular place; suburbs, outskirts, surroundings.

ENVISAGE [en-vi'zij], *v.t.* to imagine, visualize. ENVISAGEMENT, *n.* act of envisaging. [OFr.].

ENVOY (1) [en'voi], *n.* a diplomatic representative, *esp.* a minister as distinguished from an ambassador; any agent, messenger or representative. ENVOYSHIP, *n.* office of an e. [Fr.].

ENVOY (2), *n.* concluding part, forming a kind of postscript to a poetical composition. [OFr.].

ENVY (1) [en'vi], *n.* feeling of ill-will excited by grudging contemplation of another's good fortune; the object of such feeling. ENVY (2), *v.t.* to feel e. of, cherish envious feelings against. [Fr. from L.].

ENWIND [en-wīnd'], *v.t.* to twine round something else.

ENWRAP, INWRAP (*pres.pt.* enwrapping, *pret. and p.pt.* enwrapped [en-rap'], *v.t.* to envelop, enfold.

ENWREATHE, INWREATHE [en-rērн'], *v.t.* to wreathe, encompass with or as with a wreath or garland.

ENZYME [en'zīm], *n.* (*chem.*) a chemical ferment. ENZYMIC [en-zī'mik], *adj.* characteristic of the action of an e. [Gk.].

EO-, *pref.* in the beginning. [Gk.].

EOCENE [ē'ō-sēn], *n. and adj.* (*geol.*) the earliest division of the Tertiary era or group of strata, pertaining to this. [Gk.].

EOLITH [ē'ō-lith], *n.* flint implement of the earliest age in human history. EOLITHIC, *adj.* relating to the age of eoliths. [Gk.].

EOSIN(E) [ē'ō-sin], *n.* pink dyestuff used for staining objects for microscopic examination. [EO].

EOZOIC [ē-ō-zō'ik], *n. and adj.* (*geol.*) the earliest of the Pre-Cambrian eras or group of rocks, pertaining to this. [Gk.].

EP-, EPI- *pref.* on, upon, at, besides, in addition, on account of. [Gk.].

EPACT [ē'pakt], *n.* amount by which the solar exceeds the lunar year; age of the moon on 1 January. [Gk.].

EPAULETTE, EPAULET [e'paw-let], *n.* piece of ornamentation on the shoulder of a uniform. EPAULETTED, *adj.* provided with epaulettes.

EPEE, épée [e'pā], *n.* sharp-pointed sword for duelling, one with the point blunted for fencing. [Fr.].

EPENTHESIS [e-pen'thi-sis], *n.* (*gram.*) insertion of a letter or syllable in the middle of a word. [Gk.].

EPERGNE [ā-pāern'], *n.* tall branched stand for holding flowers or fruit in the centre of a table. [Fr.].

EPEXEGESIS [e-pek-si-jē'sis], *n.* additional explanation; additional words to make the meaning clearer. [EP and EXEGESIS].

EPHEDRIN(E) [e'fe-drin], *n.* (*med.*) drug extracted originally from the Chinese plant *Ma Huang*, and now also from other plants of the genus *Ephedra*.

EPHEMERA (*pl.* **ephemerae**) [e-fē'me-rah, -rē], *n.* insect which lives only for a day; the order comprising such insects; (*fig.*) anything very shortlived. [Gk.].

EPHEMERAL [e-fē'me-ral], *adj.* lasting only for a day, or a day or two; shortlived, transitory.

EPHEMERON (*pl.* **ephemera**) [e-fē'me-ron], *n.* anything, particularly an insect, which lives only for a day, or has a short, fleeting existence.

EPHESIAN (1) [i-fē'zhn], *adj.* pertaining to Ephesus or its inhabitants. EPHESIAN (2), *n.* inhabitant of Ephesus; (*fig.*) †noisy, riotous fellow.

EPHOD [ē'fod], *n.* garment like an apron, worn by a Jewish priest; vestment worn by any priest. [Heb.].

EPI-, see EP-.

EPIBLAST [e'pi-blahst], *n.* (*physiol.*) the outer wall of a cell, ectoderm. [Gk.].

EPIC (1) [e'pik], *n.* long poem describing the adventures and achievements of a hero or group of heroes; anything resembling this in scale or heroic character. EPIC (2), *adj.* pertaining to, resembling an e.; heroic. EPICAL, *adj.* e. EPICALLY, *adv.* in e. fashion. [Gk.].

EPICENE (1) [e'pi-sēn], *adj.* of the nature of both sexes; of vague and uncertain quality or character; (*gram.*) having a common gender. EPICENE (2),

---

The accent ' after a syllable = stress (u-pon'). The mark ‾ over a vowel = length (ā in made; ō in bone)

n. person having characteristics and attributes of both sexes. [Gk.].

EPICURE [e'pi-kyŏŏr], *n.* one who is fastidious about what he eats and drinks, one who appreciates good food and drink. EPICURISM, *n.* state or quality of being an e.; tastes and habits of an e. [*Epicurus,* Greek philosopher].

EPICUREAN (1) [e-pi-kyŏŏ-rē'an], *adj.* pertaining to Epicurus, his philosophy or followers; relating to an epicure or epicurism; possessing qualities which would delight an epicure. EPICUREAN (2), *n.* follower of Epicurus; epicure. EPICUREANISM, *n.* epicurism.

EPICYCLE [e'pi-si-kl], *n.* small circle with its centre situated and moving on the circumference of a larger circle. [Gk.].

EPICYCLIC [e-pi-si'klik], *adj.* relating to an epicycle; **e. gear,** (*mech.*) change-speed gear consisting of three or more small cogged wheels arranged round and meshing with a larger and central wheel.

EPICYCLOID [e-pi-si'kloid], *n.* the curved path of a point situated on the circumference of an epicycle. [Gk.].

EPIDEMIC (1) [e-pi-de'mik], *adj.* having the nature of an epidemic. EPIDEMIC (2), *n.* occurrence of a disease afflicting many people at once; anything common and temporary (opinion, state of affairs etc.). EPIDEMICALLY, *adv.* as an e. [Gk.].

EPIDEMIOLOGY [e-pi-dē-mi-o'lo-ji], *n.* scientific study of epidemics. [Gk.].

EPIDERMIS [e-pi-dur'mis], *n.* cuticle or outer layer of skin on human beings and animals; (*bot.*) outer covering of leaves and stems of plants. EPIDERMAL, EPIDERMIC, *adj.* connected with the e. EPIDERMOID, *adj.* resembling the e. [Gk.].

EPIDIASCOPE [e-pi-di'a-skōp], *n.* lantern with a system of reflecting mirrors for projecting an image of an opaque body on a screen and for projecting transparent lantern slides. [Gk.].

EPIGASTRIUM [e-pi-gas'tri-um], *n.* that part of the abdomen extending from the sternum towards the navel. EPIGASTRIC, *adj.* pertaining to the upper part of the e. [Gk.].

EPIGLOTTIS [e-pi-glo'tis], *n.* (*anat.*) small cartilage covering the top of the windpipe. EPIGLOTTIC, *adj.* pertaining to the e. [Gk.].

EPIGRAM [e'pi-gram], *n.* short poem or prose passage containing a neatly expressed satirical or witty thought; pointed remark. EPIGRAMMATIST [e-pi-gra'ma-tist], *n.* one who is skilful at making epigrams. EPIGRAMMATIZE [e-pi-gra'ma-tiz], *v.t.* to express epigrammatically; compose an e. on. [Gk.].

EPIGRAMMATIC(AL) [e-pi-gra-ma'tik(-al)], *adj.* relating to, skilful in, epigrams; terse like an epigram. EPIGRAMMATICALLY, *adv.* in an e. way.

EPIGRAPH [e'pi-grahf], *n.* engraved inscription; inscription or quotation at the beginning of a book or section of a book. EPIGRAPHIC [e-pi-gra'fik], *adj.* relating to epigraphs. EPIGRAPHICS, *n.*(*pl.*) epigraphy. EPIGRAPHY [e-pi'gra-fi], *n.* study of ancient inscriptions. EPIGRAPHIST [e-pi'gra-fist], *n.* an expert on epigraphs. [Gk.].

EPILEPSY [e'pi-lep-si], *n.* (*med.*) nervous affliction expressing itself from time to time by foaming at the mouth, convulsions and unconsciousness, the falling sickness. EPILEPTOID [e-pi-lep'toid], *adj.* resembling e. [Gk.].

EPILEPTIC (1) [e-pi-lep'tik], *adj.* relating to, having, epilepsy. EPILEPTIC (2), *n.* one suffering from epilepsy. EPILEPTICAL, *adj.* e.

EPILOGUE [e'pi-log], *n.* short speech by one of the actors at the end of a play; a concluding section in a literary work. EPILOGICAL, EPILOGISTIC [e-pi-lo'ji-kal, e-pi-lo-jis'tik], *adj.* relating to an e. [Gk.].

EPIPHANY [e-pi'fa-ni], *n.* the manifestation of Christ to the Gentiles, represented by three Magi; Christian festival kept on 6 January. [Gk.].

EPIPHYSIS (*pl.* **epiphyses**) [e-pi'fi-sis], *n.* (*anat.*) part of a bone separated by a cartilage which becomes osseous; pineal gland. [Gk.].

EPIPHYTE [e'pi-fīt], *n.* plant growing upon other plants but not parasitic. [Gk.].

EPISCOPACY [e-pis'kŏ-pa-si], *n.* government of a church by bishops; the bishops in a body. [~Gk.].

EPISCOPAL [e-pis'kŏ-pal], *adj.* pertaining to or governed by bishops; member of the Established Church of England. EPISCOPALLY, *adv.* in an e. way.

EPISCOPALIAN (1) [e-pis-ko-pā'li-an], *adj.* relating to, governed by, bishops; relating to the Established Church of England. EPISCOPALIAN (2), *n.* upholder of episcopacy; member of a church governed by bishops; member of the Church of England. EPIS-

COPALIANISM, *n.* system of church government by bishops.

EPISCOPATE [e-pis'ko-pāt], *n.* bishopric; office and rank of a bishop; the bishops as a body. [L.].

EPISODE [e'pi-sōd], *n.* incidental narrative temporarily overshadowing the main story; one of a series of events; any unimportant occurrence; (*Gk. drama*) action of a tragedy between two choric songs. EPISODIAL, *adj.* episodic. [Gk.].

EPISODIC(AL) [e-pi-so'dik(-al)], *adj.* pertaining to, or resembling, an episode; told in a series of short disjointed narratives. EPISODICALLY, *adv.* in an e. fashion.

EPISTLE [i-pi's'l], *n.* letter; apostolic letter forming one of the books of the New Testament; extract from one of these, or some other portion of scripture not in the four gospels, appointed to be read at Holy Communion. EPISTLER, EPISTOLLER, *n.* one who writes or reads out epistles. [Gk.].

EPISTOLARY [i-pis'to-la-ri], *adj.* relating to epistles or letter-writing.

EPISTOLOGRAPHY [i-pis-to-lo'gra-fi], *adj.* art and practice of letter-writing. EPISTOLOGRAPHIC [i-pis-to-lo-gra'fik], *adj.* connected with letter-writing.

EPISTYLE [e'pi-stil], *n.* (*arch.*) architrave. [Gk.].

EPITAPH [e'pi-tahf], *n.* short memorial passage inscribed on a tomb or one suitable for such use. EPITAPHIC, *adj.* pertaining to an e. EPITAPHIST, *n.* one who writes epitaphs. [Gk.].

EPITHALAMIUM (*pl.* **epithalamia**) [e-pi-tha-lā'mi-um], *n.* poem or song celebrating a marriage. EPITHALAMIAL, EPITHALAMIC [e-pi-tha-lā'mi-al, e-pi-tha-la'mik], *adj.* relating to an e. [Gk.].

EPITHELIOMA [e-pi-thē-li-ō'mah], *n.* cancerous condition of the epithelium.

EPITHELIUM [e-pi-thē'li-um], *n.* (*anat.*) thin covering of cells enveloping the mucous membrane; (*bot.*) thin epidermis formed of young cells lining the inner cavities of plants. EPITHELIAL, *adj.* relating to the e. [Gk.].

EPITHET [e'pi-thet], *n.* descriptive phrase or word. EPITHETIC(AL) [e-pi-the'tik(-al)], *adj.* relating to an e. [Gk.].

EPITOME [e-pi'to-mi], *n.* brief recapitulation, abridgement or summary in which nothing essential is omitted; (*fig.*) any similar miniature copy. EPITOMIST, *n.* one who writes epitomes. [Gk.].

EPITOMIZE [e-pi'to-mīz], *v.t.* and *i.* to make an epitome of; précis. EPITOMIZER, *n.* epitomist.

EPOCH [ē'pok], *n.* an era in history; period of time characterized by special events, movements etc.; (*astron.*) heliocentric longitude of a planet at a given date; (*geol.*) one of the minor divisions of time. EPOCH-MAKING, *adj.* marking the commencement of a new era; of outstanding importance and influence. EPOCHAL, *adj.* pertaining to or marking an e.

EPODE [e'pōd], *n.* third or last part of an ode following the strophe and antistrophe. EPODIC [e-pō'dik], *adj.* pertaining to or like an e.

EPONYM [e'po-nim], *n.* historical or fabulous person from whose name the name of a race, family or place is derived. EPONYMIC, EPONYMOUS [e-po-ni'mik, e-po'ni-mŏŏs], *adj.* having a name from which a racial or family name is derived. [Gk.].

EPOS [e'pos], *n.* traditional epic of great antiquity. [Gk.].

EPSOMITE [ep'so-mīt], *n.* hydrated sulphate of magnesium, commonly called Epsom salts. [*Epsom,* where first extracted from local water].

EQUABLE [e'kwa-bl], *adj.* even, steady, uniform; not liable to sudden or excessive changes; not easily disturbed or upset.

EQUAL (1) [ē'kwal], *adj.* the same in number, size, degree etc.; of like amount, quality etc.; uniform; evenly balanced; equable; **to be e. to,** to have necessary strength or ability for. EQUAL (2), *n.* person of e. standing, capabilities, rank, age etc.; person of the same social standing. EQUAL (3), *v.t.* to be e. to in number or quality; come up to, be as good as; be the same in size, number etc. [L.].

EQUALITARIAN [ē-kwo-li-tāer'i-an], *n.* and *adj.* egalitarian. EQUALITARIANISM, *n.* egalitarianism.

EQUALITY [ē-kwo'li-ti], *n.* condition of being equal. [OFr.].

EQUALIZE [ē'kwa-līz], *v.t.* to make even or equal. EQUALIZATION [ē-kwa-lī-zā'shn], *n.* act of equalizing; state of being equalized. EQUALIZER, *n.* one who or that which equalizes.

EQUALLY [ē'kwa-li], *adv.* in equal quantity or degree.

EQUANIMITY [ē-kwa-ni'mi-ti], *n.* steadiness of

ŏŏ is pronounced as in food; ŏŏ as in hood; th as in *think*; TH as in *that*; zh as in azure. ~ = related to.

DSE—H*

disposition, composure of mind, outlook etc.; calm courage. EQUANIMOUS [ē-kwa'ni-mŏŏs], *adj.* possessing the quality of e. [L.].

EQUATE [ē-kwāt'], *v.t.* to look upon or refer to as equal, make no distinction between. [L.].

EQUATION [ē-kwā'zhn], *n.* act of equating, process of being equated; (*alg.*) formal statement of equality. EQUATIONAL, *adj.* relating to an e. EQUATIONALLY, *adv.* in the form of or by means of an e. [~L.].

EQUATOR [i-kwā'ter], *n.* imaginary line encircling the earth so that it is always equidistant from either pole; (*astron.*) corresponding circle in the celestial sphere. [L.].

EQUATORIAL [e-kwa-taw'ri-al], *adj.* close to or relating to the equator.

EQUERRY [e'kwe-ri], *n.* royal household officer in close attendance upon a royal personage; (*archaic*) a master of the royal stables. [Fr.].

EQUESTRIAN (1) [i-kwes'tri-an], *adj.* pertaining to horsemanship; mounted, on horseback; **e. statue,** statue of a person on horseback. EQUESTRIAN (2), *n.* a horseman. EQUESTRIANISM, *n.* riding, horsemanship. [L.].

EQUI-, *pref.* equal. [L.].

EQUIANGULAR [ē-kwi-ang'gyŏŏ-ler], *adj.* (*geom.*) having equal angles.

EQUIDISTANT [ē-kwi-dis'tant], *adj.* equally distant. EQUIDISTANCE, *n.* state of being e., equal distance. EQUIDISTANTLY, *adv.* at an equal distance.

EQUILATERAL [ē-kwi-la'te-ral], *n.* and *adj.* (figure) having all its sides equal.

EQUILIBRATE [ē-kwi-li'brāt], *v.t.* and *i.* to bring into a state of balance; balance. EQUILIBRATION [ē-kwi-li-brā'shn], *n.* act of keeping the balance even; condition of being balanced. EQUILIBRATER [ē-kwi'li-brā-ter], *n.* plane which balances an aeroplane. [~L.].

EQUILIBRIST [ē-kwi'li-brist], *n.* one who performs feats of balancing. [Fr.].

EQUILIBRIUM [ē-kwi-li'bri-um], *n.* state of poise, balance; state of being kept at rest by equal but opposite forces; (*fig.*) balance of power; equanimity. EQUILIBRITY, *n.* condition of being balanced. [L.].

EQUINE [e'kwin], *adj.* relating to horses. [L.].

EQUINOCTIAL (1) [ē-kwi-nok'shal], *adj.* relating to an equinox; **e. line,** circle of the celestial sphere, corresponding to the terrestial equator and having its plane perpendicular to the axis of the earth; **e. points,** the two points of intersection of the equator and the ecliptic. EQUINOCTIAL (2), *n.* e. line. EQUINOCTIALLY, *adv.* towards the equinox. [L.].

EQUINOX [ē'kwi-noks], *n.* the time when the sun passes over the equator, and day and night are of equal length; **spring, vernal, e.,** 20 March; **autumnal e.,** 22 or 23 September. [L.].

EQUIP [i-kwip'], *v.t.* to furnish with what is necessary. [Fr.].

EQUIPAGE [e'kwi-pij], *n.* band of servants and officers attending a great person on a journey; travelling requisites.

EQUIPMENT [i-kwip'ment], *n.* act of equipping; condition of being equipped; that with which one is equipped, outfit, requisites.

EQUIPOISE (1) [ē'kwi-poiz], *n.* perfect balance; that which counterbalances; (*fig.*) equanimity. EQUIPOISE (2), *v.t.* to counterbalance; (*fig.*) keep in suspense.

EQUIPOLLENCE [ē-kwi-po'lens], *n.* equality of force or meaning; that which is equipollent.

EQUIPOLLENT [ē-kwi-po'lent], *adj.* of equal force; equivalent. EQUIPOLLENTLY, *adv.* with equal force.

EQUIPONDERANCE [ē-kwi-pon'de-rans], *n.* state of being equiponderant.

EQUIPONDERANT [ē-kwi-pon'de-rent], *adj.* equal in weight.

EQUIPOTENTIAL [ē-kwi-pō-ten'shal], *adj.* (*phys.*) possessing at every point the same potential force.

EQUITABLE [e'kwi-ta-bl], *adj.* according to justice and equity. EQUITABLENESS, *n.* state of being e. EQUITABLY, *adv.* in an e. fashion. [Fr.].

EQUITATION [e-kwi-tā'shn], *n.* skill in horsemanship. [L.].

EQUITY [e'kwi-ti], *n.* quality or condition of being just and unbiased; principle of fair-mindedness and impartial unprejudiced judgment; (*leg.*) judicial system supplementing and differing from Common Law. [L.].

EQUIVALENCE, EQUIVALENCY [i-kwi'va-lens(-i)], *n.* state of being equivalent.

EQUIVALENT (1) [i-kwi'va-lent], *adj.* equal in value, meaning etc.; tantamount; (*chem.*) equal in

combining value, producing the same result. EQUIVALENT (2), *n.* that which is e. EQUIVALENTLY, *adv.* in an equal way.

EQUIVOCAL [i-kwi'vo-kal], *adj.* liable to be interpreted in more than one way, ambiguous; giving rise to suspicion or doubt. EQUIVOCALLY, *adv.* in an e. fashion. EQUIVOCALNESS, *n.* state of being e. [L.].

EQUIVOCATE [i-kwi'vo-kāt], *v.i.* to use words of doubtful meaning; use ambiguous expressions with a view to mislead; lie; quibble. EQUIVOCATOR, *n.* person who equivocates. EQUIVOCATORY, *adj.* of an equivocating character.

EQUIVOCATION [i-kwi-vo-kā'shn], *n.* act or practice of equivocating.

ERA [ē'rah], *n.* system of dating, starting from some selected event or point of time; epoch, period. [L.].

ERADIATE [i-rā'di-āt], *v.i.* to shoot out like rays of light. ERADIATION [i-rā-di-ā'shn], *n.* sending forth, emission, as of rays.

ERADICATE [i-ra'di-kāt], *v.t.* to tear up by the roots; wipe out, extirpate. ERADICABLE, *adj.* able to be eradicated. ERADICATIVE [i-ra'di-ka-tiv], *adj.* able to e. [L.].

ERADICATION [i-ra-di-kā'shn], *n.* act of eradicating; condition of being eradicated.

ERASE [i-rāz'], *v.t.* to scratch, or otherwise remove, from the surface on which it is written or cut; (*fig.*) remove, wipe out. ERASABLE, *adj.* able to be erased. ERASED, *adj.* effaced; (*her.*) with a jagged edge. ERASER, *n.* person who or thing which erases. ERASION, *n.* act of erasing; place where something has been erased. [~L.].

ERASTIAN (1) [i-ras'ti-an], *adj.* pertaining to Erastus or his teaching. ERASTIAN (2), *n.* one who adheres to the principles of Erastus. ERASTIANISM, *n.* doctrine which advocates the subjection of Church to State. [*Erastus,* sixteenth-century Swiss theologian].

ERASURE [i-rā'zhŏŏr], *n.* act of erasing; place from which something has been erased.

ERE (1) [āer], *adv.* sooner; rather than. ERE (2), *prep.* before. [OE.].

EREBUS [e'ri-bus], *n.* (*myth.*) the cavern between earth and hell; the nether regions. [L.].

ERECT (1) [i-rekt'], *adj.* vertically upright, standing up. ERECT (2), *adv.* in vertical position. ERECT (3), *v.t.* to set up in an e. position; elevate; build. ERECTABLE, *adj.* able to be erected. ERECTED, *adj.* upright. ERECTER, *n.* one who erects, builder. ERECTIVE, *adj.* serving to e. [L.].

ERECTILE [i-rek'til], *adj.* able to be erected; (*anat.*) (of tissue) capable of becoming rigid.

ERECTION [i-rek'shn], *n.* act of erecting; condition of being erected; thing erected, building.

ERECTLY [i-rekt'li], *adv.* in an erect position.

ERECTNESS [i-rekt'nes], *n.* state of being erect.

ERECTOR [i-rek'ter], *n.* engineer who assembles machinery; machine used in building tunnels etc.; (*anat.*) muscle which erects a part or organ; (*phot.*) reversing lens.

ERELONG [āer'long], *adv.* soon.

EREMITE [e'ri-mīt], *n.* hermit. EREMITIC(AL) [e-ri-mi'tik(-al)], *adj.* relating to an e. EREMITISM [e'ri-mi-tizm], *n.* way of life of a hermit.

EREWHILE [āer-wīl'], *adv.* some time before.

ERG [urg], *n.* unit of work equal to the amount performed by one dyne through one centimetre. [Gk.].

ERGO [ur'gō], *adv.* hence, therefore. [L.].

ERGOT [ur'got], *n.* (*bot.*) fungus causing a disease in rye and other cereals; this disease; medicinal drug from this fungus. ERGOTIN, *n.* (*chem.*) medicinal substance with bitter taste found in e. ERGOTISM, *n.* malady caused by e. [Fr.].

ERICA [e'ri-kah], *n.* (*bot.*) genus of plants which includes heather. [Gk.].

ERMINE [ur'min], *n.* the stoat, which in summer has a brown coat, and in winter in cold climates a white one, with a black tip on the tail; winter fur of this animal, used for the robes of judges and peers; (*her.*) white field with black daggers; (*fig.*) office and duties of a judge of the High Court; (*poet.*) symbol of purity and integrity. ERMINED, *adj.* wearing or trimmed with e.; (*her.*) displaying ermine. [OFr.].

ERNE [urn], *n.* eagle, *esp.* the sea-eagle. [OE.].

ERODE [i-rōd'], *v.t.* to gnaw away, fret, wear away slowly and gradually, destroy by attrition, corrode. ERODED, EROSE, *adj.* (*bot.*) having a jagged edge. [L.].

EROSION [i-rō'zhn], *n.* act of eroding; state of being

eroded; destruction of the coastline by the sea. [L.].

EROSIVE [i-rō'siv], *adj.* capable of eroding.

EROTIC [i-ro'tik], *adj.* relating to love and sexual passion; sexually passionate, amorous. EROTICISM, *n.* e. character or cast of mind. EROTOMANIA [i-ro-tō-mā'ni-ah], *n.* madness arising from e. propensities. [Gk.].

ERPETOLOGY, see HERPETOLOGY.

ERR [ur], *v.i.* to make a mistake; sin. [L.].

ERRAND [e'rand], *n.* charge, mission, short journey with a message, usually entrusted to an inferior. ERRAND-BOY, boy employed by a shop or firm to deliver goods, run messages etc.

ERRANT [e'rant], *adj.* travelling on no fixed course or definite mission; *(fig.)* wandering from the business in hand or from upright conduct. KNIGHT-ERRANT, medieval knight travelling in search of adventure, one who performs a chivalrous act. ERRANTRY, *n.* mode of life of a knight-errant.

ERRATIC (1) [i-ra'tik], *adj.* wandering; roving; irregular, not pursuing a steady or settled course. ERRATIC (2), *n.* e. person; *(geol.)* boulder carried by glacier ice from one formation to another. ERRATICALLY, *adv.* in an e. manner. [L.].

ERRATUM (*pl.* **errata**) [i-rā'tum, i-rā'tah], *n.* slip or blunder in printing or writing.

ERRONEOUS [i-rō'ni-ŏŏs], *adj.* incorrect, mistaken. ERRONEOUSLY, *adv.* in an e. fashion. [L.].

ERROR [e'rer], *n.* condition of erring; deviation from the right way; mistake; fault; sin. [L.].

ERSATZ [āer'zats], *adj.* artificial, substituted for a natural product. [Germ.].

ERSE [urs], *n.* Gaelic language spoken in Ireland and sometimes in the Scottish Highlands. [Scots *var.* of IRISH].

ERST [urst], *adv.* (*archaic*) formerly. [OE.].

ERSTWHILE [urst'wil], *adv.* formerly, up till then.

ERUCT [i-rukt'], *v.t. and i.* to belch wind. ERUCTATION, [ē-ruk-tā'shn], *n.* act of belching. [L.].

ERUDITE [e'rŏŏ-dīt], *adj.* learned, scholarly. ERUDITELY, *adv.* in an e. fashion. ERUDITENESS, *n.* state of being e. [L.].

ERUDITION [e-rŏŏ-di'shn], *n.* book learning; scholarly knowledge. [L.].

ERUPT [i-rupt'], *v.i.* to break through, break out, burst forth. [~L.].

ERUPTION [i-rup'shn], *n.* act of erupting; volcanic upheaval; *(med.)* rash or sore. [L.].

ERUPTIVE [i-rup'tiv], *adj.* bursting forth; liable to erupt; *(med.)* accompanied by an eruption on the skin. ERUPTIVELY, *adv.* in an e. way. [Fr.].

ERYSIPELAS [e-ri-si'pe-las], *n.* *(med.)* feverish disease causing irritation and inflammation of the skin. [Gk.].

ERYTHEMA [e-ri-thē'mah], *n.* *(med.)* patchy inflammation of the skin. ERYTHEMATOUS, *adj.* relating to e. [Gk.].

ESCALADE [es-ka-lād'], *n.* act of scaling walls with ladders. [Fr.].

ESCALATOR [es'ka-lā-ter], *n* staircase with an endless belt of steps moved continuously by machinery. [ESCAL(ADE) and (ELEV)ATOR].

ESCALLOP [es-ka'lop], *n.* scallop. [OFr.].

ESCALLOPE [es-ka-lop'], *n.* *(cookery)* slice of lean veal etc., fried with egg and breadcrumbs. [OFr.].

ESCAPADE [es-ka-pād'], *n.* any breaking loose from convention; rash and heedless action. [Fr.].

ESCAPE (1) [es-kāp'], *v.t.* to avoid, evade, get away from; issue unawares from; *v.i.* to get free; get away safely; find a way out. ESCAPE (2), *n.* act of escaping; state or fact of having escaped; leakage; outlet, *esp.* for canal water; garden plant growing wild. ESCAPER, *n.* one who escapes. [OFr.].

ESCAPEMENT [es-kāp'ment], *n.* mechanism by which the action of the mainspring of a watch or the weights of a clock is regulated.

ESCAPIST (1) [es-kā'pist], *adj.* of, or pertaining to, an escapist; *(coll.)* tending, by way of entertainment, to divert the attention from unpleasant realities. ESCAPIST (2), *n.* *(psych.)* one who takes refuge in other activities, *esp.* fantasy, to avoid facing disagreeable facts. ESCAPISM, *n.* *(psych.)* state or quality of being e.

ESCARP (1) [es-kahp'], *n.* steep bank or slope; *(fort.)* side of the ditch in front of and below the rampart. ESCARP (2), *v.t.* to cut into a steep slope or e. [Fr.].

ESCARPMENT [es-kahp'ment], *n.* precipitous side of a hill; steep slope; escarp. [Fr.].

ESCHALOT [es-sha-lot'], *n.* shallot.

ESCHATOLOGY [es-ka-to'lo-ji], *n.* study of the last

things, death, judgment and the after-life. ESCHATOLOGICAL [es-ka-to-lo'ji-kal], *adj.* relating to e. ESCHATOLOGIST [es-ka-to'lo-jist], *n.* student of e. [Gk.].

ESCHEAT (1) [es-chēt'], *n.* *(leg.)* lapsing of property to the Crown or the lord of the manor when there are no heirs; property thus lapsing. ESCHEAT (2), *v.t.* to confiscate; hand over as an e.; *v.i.* to lapse, fall to the Crown or lord of the manor by e. [OFr.].

ESCHEW [es-chōō'], *v.t.* to shun; refrain from. ESCHEWAL, ESCHEWANCE, *n.* act of eschewing or shunning. [OFr.].

ESCHSCHOLTZIA [i-sholt'zi-ah], *n.* Californian poppy, Noah's Nightcap, a plant of the poppy family with deep yellow flowers. [*Eschscholtz*, botanist].

ESCORT (1) [es'kawt], *n.* person or body of persons or war machines accompanying another for protection or from courtesy. ESCORT (2) [es-kawt'], *v.t.* to accompany as an e. [Fr.].

ESCRITOIRE [es-kri-twah(r)'], *n.* kind of writing table, desk. [Fr.].

ESCULAPIAN, see AESCULAPIAN.

ESCULENT (1) [es'kyŏŏ-lent], *adj.* eatable. ESCULENT (2), *n.* something which may be eaten. [L.].

ESCUTCHEON [es-ku'chn], *n.* *(her.)* shield with coat of arms; place on the stern of a ship where the name is written; movable cover of a keyhole; blot on one's e., stain upon one's reputation. [ONFr.].

ESKIMO (1), **ESQUIMAU** (*pl.* **Eskimos**, **Esquimaux**) [es'ki-mō], *n.* member of a people inhabiting the extreme north of America and the Arctic islands; language of this people. ESKIMO (2), ESQUIMAU, *adj.* relating to the Eskimos or their language. [Dan. from AmerInd].

ESO-, *pref.* within. [Gk.].

ESOPHAGEAL, see OESOPHAGEAL.

ESOPHAGUS, see OESOPHAGUS.

ESOTERIC [ē-sō-te'rik], *adj.* for the initiated only; confidential; secret. ESOTERICISM [ē-sō-te'ri-sizm], *n.* practice of having different doctrines for the initiated and the uninitiated. [Gk.].

ESPALIER [es-pa'li-er], *n.* lattice work up which trees and shrubs are grown; tree or shrub trained in this way. [Fr.].

ESPARTO [es-pah'tō], *n.* grass growing in Spain and Algeria and manufactured into paper, ropes etc. [Span.].

ESPECIAL [es-pe'shal], *adj.* particular, special. ESPECIALLY, *adv.* particularly. [OFr.].

ESPERANTO [es-pe-ran'tō], *n.* an artificial language intended as a universal medium of communication. ESPERANTIST, *n.* person who studies and uses E. [*Esperanto*, hoping one, pseudonym of the Polish inventor, Dr. Zamenhof].

ESPIAL [es-pī'al], *n.* act of espying.

ESPIEGLERIE, **espièglerie** [es-pyā'le-rē], *n.* roguishness, playfulness. [Fr.].

ESPIONAGE [es'pi-o-nahzh], *n.* practice of spying, or employment of spies. [Fr.].

ESPLANADE [es-pla-nād'], *n.* level place for walking, public promenade; level space between the citadel of a fortress and the town. [Fr.].

ESPOUSAL [es-pow'zal], *n.* betrothal, marriage; *(fig.)* act of enlisting in support of a cause etc. [OFr.].

ESPOUSE [es-powz'], *v.t.* to marry, wed; give in marriage; *(fig.)* adopt, support. [OFr.].

ESPRESSIVO [es-pre-sē'vŏ], *adv.* *(mus.)* with great expression or passion. [It.].

ESPRIT [es-prē'], *n.* liveliness, spirit; wit; e. de corps, loyalty to the community to which one belongs. [Fr.].

ESPY [es-pī'], *v.t.* to see, catch sight of. [OFr.].

ESQUIMAU, see ESKIMO.

ESQUIRE [es-kwier'], *n.* gentleman, squire; courtesy distinction added after a gentleman's name. [OFr.].

ESS [es], *n.* nineteenth letter of the alphabet, S; anything shaped like this.

ESSAY (1) [e'sā], *n.* an attempt or experiment; short composition, usually in prose. ESSAY (2) [e-sā'], *v.t.* to try, test; attempt. [OFr., Fr.].

ESSAYIST [e'sā-ist], *n.* one who writes essays.

ESSENCE [e'sens], *n.* an entity, being; distinctive qualities or nature of anything; indispensable element; extract obtained by distillation; scent, perfume. [Fr. from L.].

ESSENTIAL (1) [i-sen'shal], *adj.* constituting the essence of; indispensable; characteristic; distinguishing. ESSENTIAL (2), *n.* indispensable quality or element. ESSENTIALITY [i-sen-shi-a'li-ti], *n.* quality of being e. ESSENTIALLY, adv. in an e. fashion. [L.].

ESSONITE [e'so-nīt], n. (min.) cinnamon-stone or yellow garnet. [Gk.].

ESTABLISH [es-tab'lish], v.t. to settle on a fixed basis; settle beyond dispute; prove finally as true or valid; set in a particular position; admit to the permanent staff of a government department. ESTABLISHED, adj. instituted and recognized, esp. by the state; (of civil servants) enrolled on the permanent staff. ESTABLISHER, n. one who establishes. [OFr.].

ESTABLISHMENT [es-tab'lish-ment], n. act of establishing; condition of being established; that which is established; institution, business house; residence or household; total strength of a military unit or civil government department; **the E.**, Church of England.

ESTAMINET [es-ta'mi-nā], n. cheap French restaurant selling drinks. [Fr.].

ESTANCIA [es-tahn'si-ah], n. ranch in South America. [Span.].

ESTATE [es-tāt'], n. order; class; rank; condition; part of the body politic, with a share in the government; landed property; total collective assets and liabilities; **the Three Estates**, Lords Spiritual, Lords Temporal and the Commons; **the third e.**, French bourgeoisie before the Revolution; **the fourth e.**, (coll.) the Press; **real e.**, landed property; **personal e.**, movable property. [OFr.].

ESTEEM (1) [es-tēm], v.t. to have a high opinion of, respect; consider, value. ESTEEM (2), n. high opinion, regard, respect. [Fr.].

ESTIMABLE [es'ti-ma-bl], adj. deserving esteem. ESTIMABLENESS, n. state of being e. ESTIMABLY, adv. in an e. way. [Fr.].

ESTIMATE (1) [es'ti-mat], n. approximate judgment of worth or size; rough calculation; contractor's statement of sum for which he will undertake a job; estimation. ESTIMATE (2) [es'ti-māt], v.t. to form an e. of; calculate roughly. ESTIMATIVE, adj. having the power of comparing and adjusting values. ESTIMATOR, n. one who or that which estimates. [L.].

ESTIMATION [es-ti-mā'shn], n. act of estimating; judgment of value etc.; esteem. [OFr.].

ESTOP [es-top'], v.t. (leg.) to hinder, bar from doing something. [OFr.].

ESTRANGE [es-trānj'], v.t. to alienate, destroy affection between. ESTRANGEDNESS, n. condition of being estranged. [OFr.].

ESTRANGEMENT [es-trānj'ment], n. act of estranging; condition of being estranged.

ESTREAT [es-trēt'], v.t. (leg.) to take out or copy the record of a fine etc., and return to Court of Exchequer for prosecution. [AFr.].

ESTUARY [es'tyōō-a-ri], n. the expanding tidal mouth of a river. ESTUARINE, adj. relating to an e. [L.].

ESURIENT [i-syōō'ri-ent], adj. hungry; necessitous; grasping. [L.].

ETCETERA [et-set'rah], n. and so on; and so forth; and the rest (usually written etc.). ETCETERAS, n. extras, sundries, minor items. [L.].

ETCH [ech], v.t. to produce pictures or designs by engraving a plate of metal with corrosives and then taking prints from the plate; v.i. to practise the art of etching. ETCHED, adj. marked on metal, glass etc., by corrosion of an acid. ETCHER, n. artist who makes etchings. [Du.].

ETCHING [e'ching], n. process of etching; impression taken from an etched plate; **e. ground**, the coating of wax or polish on the e. plate; **e. needle**, pointed steel instrument for tracing outlines on the e. ground.

ETERNAL [i-tur'nal], adj. everlasting; perpetual; timeless; that always has been and always will be; without end; ceaseless, incessant; **the E.**, God; **the E. City**, Rome; **the e. triangle**, (coll.) two men and a woman or two women and a man whose relationships present a problem. ETERN(AL)IZE, v.t. to render e.; give endless duration to. ETERNALLY, adv. without beginning or end; perpetually, for ever; unchangeably. [OFr.].

ETERNITY [i-tur'ni-ti], n. state of being eternal; infinite time; the future life; **the eternities**, the eternal truths. [Fr.].

ETESIAN [i-tē'zhn], adj. occurring regularly and annually; **e. winds**, north-westerly winds prevailing in the Levant for about forty days each summer. [L.].

ETHANE [ē'thān], n. ethyl hydride, a colourless, odourless and insoluble gas. [~ETHER.].

ETHER [ē'ther], n. clear sky; upper regions of air

beyond the clouds; (chem.) colourless, light, volatile and inflammable fluid, the oxide of ethyl, used as an anaesthetic; (phys.) hypothetical subtle material pervading all space, the medium for the transmission of light and radio waves. [Gk.].

ETHEREAL [i-thē'ri-al], adj. airy; heavenly; delicate; spiritual. ETHEREALITY [i-thē-ri-a'li-ti], n. quality of being e. ETHEREALIZE, v.t. to convert into ether; make e. ETHEREALLY, adv. in an e. way. [L. from Gk.].

ETHERIZE [ē'the-rīz], v.t. to make into ether; put under the influence of ether. ETHERIZATION [ē-the-rī-zā'shn], n. act or process of making ether; medical administration of ether.

ETHIC [e'thik], n. a system of morality. [Gk.].

ETHIC(AL) [e'thik(-al)], adj. relating to or treating of ethics; in accordance with a code of morals. ETHICALLY, adv. in accordance with ethics. [Gk.].

ETHICS [e'thiks], n.(pl.) science treating of morals; system of morality. [ETHIC].

ETHIOPIAN (1) [ē-thi-ō'pi-an], n. a native of Ethiopia, Abyssinian; †Negro. ETHIOPIAN (2), adj. pertaining to Ethiopia or the black races generally.

ETHMOID [eth'moid], adj. like a sieve; **e. bone**, (anat.) perforated bone, between the orbits of the eye, which forms the roof of the nose. ETHMOIDAL, adj. e. [Gk.].

ETHNIC(AL) [eth'nik(-al)], adj. pertaining to races or nations; pertaining to pagans, heathen. ETHNIC-ALLY, adv. racially, by race. [Gk.].

ETHNOGRAPHY [eth-no'gra-fi], n. scientific study and description of human races. ETHNOGRAPHER, n. one skilled in e. ETHNOGRAPHIC(AL) [eth-nō-gra'fik(-al)], adj. relating to e. [Gk.].

ETHNOLOGY [eth-no'lo-ji], n. science which deals with the races of mankind. ETHNOLOGICAL [eth-nō-lo'ji-kal], adj. relating to e. ETHNOLOGICALLY, adv. as regards e. ETHNOLOGIST [eth-no'lo-jist], n. one skilled in e. [Gk.].

ETHOS [ē'thos], n. general disposition, characteristic spirit, of a community. [Gk.].

ETHYL [e'thil, ē'thil], n. (chem.) the radical or alkyl of common (ethyl) alcohol. [~ETHER.]

ETHYLENE [e'thi-lēn], n. an unsaturated hydrocarbon gas in which two atoms of carbon are combined with four atoms of hydrogen.

ETIOLATE [ē'ti-ō-lāt], v.t. (bot.) to make pale by exclusion of light; (med.) make pale through sickness or malnutrition. ETIOLATION [ē-ti-ō-lā'shn], n. act or process of becoming etiolated. [Fr.].

ETIOLOGY [ē-ti-o'lo-ji], n. study of the causes of disease. ETIOLOGICAL [ē-ti-ō-lo'ji-kal], adj. relating to e.

ETIQUETTE [e'ti-ket], n. conventional rules of conduct. [Fr.].

ETNA [et'nah], n. small spirit-stove, with a reversed cone for the boiler. [Mount Etna, volcano].

ETRUSCAN [i-trus'kan], n. and adj. native of, pertaining to, the ancient Italian district of Etruria. [L.].

ETUDE, étude [ā-tyōōd'], n. (mus.) piece of music intended as a technical exercise. [Fr.].

ETYMOLOGY [e-ti-mo'lo-ji], n. (study of the) derivation and origin of words. ETYMOLOGICAL [e-ti-mo-lo'ji-kal], adj. relating to e. ETYMOLOGI-CALLY, adv. according to etymological principles. ETYMOLOGIST [e-ti-mo'lo-jist], n. one skilled in e. ETYMOLOGIZE, v.i. to study e.; inquire into the origin of words. [Gk.].

ETYMON [e'ti-mon], n. primary or root-word from which others are derived. [Gk.].

EU-, pref. well. [Gk.].

EUCALYPTUS [yōō-ka-lip'tus], n. (bot.) genus of plants of which one is the Australian gum-tree; oil of eucalyptus; **e. oil, oil of e.**, oil prepared from these trees, useful as a disinfectant for colds etc. EUCA-LYPTOL, n. the essential oil of e. [Gk.].

EUCHARIST [yōō'ka-rist], n. sacrament of the Lord's Supper; the consecrated elements, esp. the bread. EUCHARISTIC [yōō-ka-ris'tik], adj. expressing thanks; pertaining to the E. [Gk.].

EUCHRE [yōō'ker], n. card-game in which all cards below the sevens are left out. [Unkn.].

EUCLIDEAN [yōō-kli'di-an], adj. pertaining to Euclid; geometric; three-dimensional. [Euclid, Alexandrian mathematician].

EUDIOMETER [yōō-di-o'mi-ter], n. instrument for ascertaining the condition of the atmosphere, used in analysing gases. [Gk.].

EUGENIC [yōō-je'nik], adj. concerned with the improvement of the stock or race; tending to promote eugenics. EUGENICALLY, *adv.* with respect to eugenics. [Gk.].

EUGENICS [yōō-je'niks], *n.(pl.)* science which is concerned with the best means of producing a healthy stock. EUGENIST [yōō'je-nist], *n.* person who believes in the value of e. [Gk.].

EULOGISTIC [yōō-lo-jis'tik], *adj.* full of praise, laudatory. EULOGISTICALLY, *adv.* laudatorily; in a e. manner.

EULOGY [yōō'lo-ji], *n.* speech or written testimony greatly praising some person or thing; panegyric; high commendation. EULOGIST, *n.* one who writes or pronounces a e. EULOGIZE, *v.t.* to praise highly, commend, speak well of another. [Gk.].

EUNUCH [yōō'nuk], *n.* castrated man, formerly employed as a domestic officer of state by Eastern rulers. [Gk.].

EUPEPSIA, EUPEPSY [yōō-pep'si(-ah)], *n.* good digestion. EUPEPTIC, *adj.* with a good digestion; *(fig.)* optimistic.

EUPHEMISM [yōō'fe-mizm], *n.* use of a mild, pleasant word to express an unpleasant idea. EUPHEMIZE, *v.t.* to express in a euphemistic manner. [Gk.].

EUPHEMISTIC [yōō-fe-mis'tik], *adj.* characterized by euphemism. EUPHEMISTICALLY, *adv.* in e. fashion.

EUPHONIC(AL) [yōō-fo'nik(-al)], *adj.* euphonious. [Fr.].

EUPHONIOUS [yōō-fō'ni-ŏŏs], *adj.* with euphony; of an agreeable sound. EUPHONIOUSLY, *adv.* in a e. way.

EUPHONIUM [yōō-fō'ni-um], *n.* bass instrument of the saxhorn type.

EUPHONY [yōō'fo-ni], *n.* sweetness of sound; smooth enunciation of sounds. EUPHONISM, *n.* well-sounding combination of sounds. EUPHONIZE, *v.t.* to make euphonious. [Gk.].

EUPHORBIA [yōō-faw'bi-ah], *n.* (*bot.*) genus of plants which includes the spurges. [Gk.].

EUPHRASIA [yōō-frā'zi-ah], *n.* (*bot.*) genus of plants, one species of which is the herb eyebright. [Gk.].

EUPHUISM [yōō'fyōō-izm], *n.* precious, affected style of writing or speech. EUPHUIST, *n.* person who writes or speaks in a euphuistic manner. EUPHUISTIC [yōō-fyōō-is'tik], *adj.* characterized by e.; excessively refined in speech or writing. [Lyly's novel *Euphues*].

EURASIAN [yōō-rā'shn], *n.* one born of a European and an Asiatic parent. [*Europe* and *Asia*].

EUREKA [yōō-rē'kah], *int.* I have found it. [Gk.].

EURHYTHMICS [yōō-rith'miks], *n.(pl.)* art or practice of gracefully moving the body in harmony with music. [Gk.].

EUSTACHIAN [yōōs-tā'shn], *adj.* used of certain parts of the body first described by Eustachius; e. tube, small duct running from a cavity of the ear into the back of the mouth. [*Eustachius*, Italian anatomist].

EUTERPE [yōō-tur'pi], *n.* classical name for the Muse of music; (*bot.*) genus of palms. EUTERPEAN, *adj.* pertaining to E. or to music. [Gk.].

EUTHANASIA [yōō-tha-nā'zi-ah], *n.* practice or method of making death painless; practice, advocated by some, of inducing painless death in incurable invalids. [Gk.].

EVACUANT (1) [i-va'kyōō-ant], *adj.* (*med.*) emptying, promoting evacuation or purgation. EVACUANT (2), *n.* (*med.*) medicine which promotes evacuation; a purgative. [L.].

EVACUATE [i-va'kyōō-āt], *v.* . to empty out, discharge, rid of its contents; (*milit.*) move troops away from; remove from a dangerous area. EVACUATIVE, *adj.* cathartic, purgative. [L.].

EVACUATION [i-va-kyōō-ā'shn], *n.* act or process of evacuating; matter which is evacuated; e. area, area from which persons are to be evacuated. [LL.].

EVACUEE [i-va-kyōō-ē'], *n.* one who has been evacuated.

EVADE [i-vād'], *v.t.* to escape, elude; avoid by dexterity, artifice or trickery. EVADIBLE, *adj.* that may be evaded or eluded. [L.].

EVALUATE [i-va'lyōō-āt], *v.t.* to determine the value of; appraise. [Fr.].

EVALUATION [i-va-lyōō-ā'shn], *n.* act of evaluating; result of such an act. [Fr.].

EVANESCE [ē-va-nes'], *v.i.* to fade or melt away, disappear. [L.].

EVANESCENCE [ē-va-ne'sens], *n.* a fading away, disappearance.

EVANESCENT [ē-va-ne'sent], *adj.* that quickly

---

vanishes; impermanent. EVANESCENTLY, *adv.* in an e. way.

EVANGELIC(AL) (1) [ē-van-je'lik(-al)], *adj.* of, or pertaining to, the gospel, or to the Christian religion; belonging to the Low Church party. EVANGELICAL (2), *n.* a Protestant; member of the E. party in the Church of England. EVANGELICALISM, *n.* system or practice of Evangelicals. EVANGELICALLY, *adv.* in an e. manner.

EVANGELIST [i-van'je-list], *n.* writer of one of the gospels; evangelizing preacher of the gospel; person authorized to preach. EVANGELISM, *n.* the preaching of the gospel. EVANGELISTIC [i-van-je-lis'tik], *adj.* connected with an e. [L.].

EVANGELIZE [i-van'je-līz], *v.t.* to preach the gospel to; convert to Christianity and the gospel. EVANGELIZATION [i-van-je-lī-za'shn], *n.* propagating the Christian gospel. [EcclesL.].

EVANISH [i-va'nish], *v.t.* to vanish away. EVANITION [ē-va-ni'shn], *n.* disappearance. [OFr.].

EVAPORATE [i-va'po-rāt], *v.t.* to change to vapour; *v.i.* turn into vapour; (*fig.*) disappear; dissipate uselessly; evaporated milk, milk from which a large proportion of the water contained in it has been removed by evaporation. EVAPORABLE, capable of evaporation. EVAPORATIVE, *adj.* of, or conducive to, evaporation. EVAPORATOR, *n.* one who, or that which, evaporates; apparatus for evaporating. [L.].

EVAPORATION [i-va-po-rā'shn], *n* act of evaporating; condition of being evaporated; whatever is evaporated. [L.].

EVASION [i-vā'zhn], *n.* escape; act of evading; prevarication. [L.].

EVASIVE [i-vā'siv], *adj.* tending to evade one, difficult to grasp; equivocal. EVASIVELY, *adv.* in an e. way. EVASIVENESS, *n.* quality of being e. [Fr.].

EVE (1) [ēv], *n.* the wife of Adam; personification of womankind. [Heb.].

EVE (2), *n.* latter part or close of the day; evening, or day, before a Saint's day or church festival; time immediately preceding an event. [OE.].

EVEN (1) [ē'ven], *n.* (*poet.*) evening. [OE.].

EVEN (2), *adj.* level, smooth, flat; regular, rhythmical (of sounds); any whole multiple of two; (*fig.*) not easily ruffled or disturbed; monotonous, uneventful; to be e. with, to square accounts with; e. money, (*betting*) return of double the sum risked. EVEN (3), *adv.* evenly; just as; at the same time as; according; expressing a strong assertion and prefixed to words etc. on which the emphatic character of the statement depends, as he e. insulted him; e. though. EVEN (4), *v.t.* to make e., level, make smooth; to e. up, to balance; to e. up on, to requite. EVENER, *n.* one who, or that which, makes e. [OE.].

EVEN-HANDED [ē-ven-han'did], *adj.* impartial, equitable, just. EVEN-HANDEDLY, *adv.* in a just and impartial manner. EVEN-HANDEDNESS, *n.* quality or condition of being e.

EVENING [ēv'ning], *n.* time between sunset and darkness; time from the close of the afternoon until bedtime; e. clothes, dress, suit, conventional clothes for wearing in public in the evening; e. primrose, species of plant in which the flowers open at night; e. star, planet seen in the west soon after sunset. [OE.].

EVENLY [ē'ven-li], *adv.* in an even manner; tranquilly.

EVENNESS [ē'ven-nes], *n.* quality or state of being even.

EVENSONG [ē'ven-song], *n.* (*eccles.*) name of the church office read daily shortly before sunset; in the Church of England, "Evening Prayer."

EVENT [i-vent'], *n.* a happening; result of an action, its outcome; item in a programme; in the e. of, in case of; at all events, in any case. [L.].

EVENTFUL [i-vent'fŏŏl], *adj.* full of incidents; momentous.

EVENTLESS [i-vent'les], *adj.* devoid of incident.

EVEN-TEMPERED [ē-ven-tem'perd], *adj.* having an equable temper.

EVENTIDE [ē'ven-tīd], *n.* (*poet.*) evening.

EVENTRATION [ē-ven-trā'shn], *n.* action of opening the abdomen; intestinal hernia. [Fr.].

EVENTUAL [i-vent'yŏŏ-al], *adj.* happening or likely to happen as a consequence of a series of incidents; contingent; ultimate. EVENTUALLY, *adv.* ultimately. [Fr.].

EVENTUALITY [i-ven-tyŏŏ-a'li-ti], *n.* a possible event, one which may happen as a consequence.

EVENTUATE [i-vent'yŏŏ-āt], *v.i.* to happen; result.

EVER [e'ver], *adv.* always; repeatedly; at any time;

ŏŏ is pronounced as in food; ŏŏ as in hood; th as in *think*; TH as in *that*; zh as in azure. ~ = related to.

in any degree or condition; **e. and anon**, at one time and another; (*coll.*) **e. so, very**, in a great degree; **for e. and e.**, always; **for e. and a day**, eternally. [OE.].

EVERGREEN (1) [e′ver-grēn], *adj.* of a tree or plant which remains green all the year round; (*fig.*) always fresh and vigorous. **EVERGREEN** (2), *n.* plant which has green leaves all the year round.

EVERLASTING [e-ver-lahs′ting], *adj.* lasting for ever, eternal; durable; constantly recurring; repeated until one tires of it. **EVERLASTINGLY**, *adv.* eternally, perpetually, repeatedly. **EVERLASTING-NESS**, *n.* quality or state of being e.

EVERMORE [e-ver-maw(r)′], *adv.* always, for ever.

EVERY [e′ve-ri], *adj.* each one, all, each of a number, singly or one by one; **e. now and then**, at intervals, from time to time; **e. time**, without exception. [ME.].

EVERYBODY [e′ve-ri-bo-di], *n.* every person, all people (with *sg.* verb).

EVERYDAY [e-ve-ri-dā′], *adj.* happening every day, commonplace, usual.

EVERYMAN [e′ve-ri-man], *n.* the ordinary man, "man in the street." [Character in a sixteenth-century morality play].

EVERYONE [e′ve-ri-wun], *n.* everybody.

EVERYTHING [e′ve-ri-thing], *n.* all, each thing omitting nothing; the main thing.

EVERYWAY [e′ve-ri-wā], *adv.* in all ways.

EVERYWHERE [e′ve-ri-wāer], *adv.* in all places.

EVICT [i-vikt′], *v.t.* to dispossess, turn a tenant out of property. **EVICTOR**, *n.* one who evicts. [L.].

EVICTION [i-vik′shn], *n.* act of evicting. [L.].

EVIDENCE [e′vi-dens], *n.* testimony; information or facts which make evident; proof on the authority of sense, reason or the witness of others; a witness; **to hear, call e.**, to listen to, ask for evidence; **circumstantial e.**, indirect evidence which is sufficient only for a judgment of probability; **Queen's e.**, information from a prisoner against his accomplices. [L.].

EVIDENT [e′vi-dent], *adj.* clear, visible, plain; obvious. **EVIDENTLY**, *adv.* plainly, obviously, clearly. [L.].

EVIDENTIAL [e-vi-den′shal], *adj.* of the nature of, affording, evidence. **EVIDENTIALLY**, *adv.* by means of evidence, in an e. manner.

EVIDENTIARY [e-vi-den′sha-ri], *adj.* evidential.

EVIL (1) [ē′vil], *adj.* bad; morally depraved. **EVIL** (2), *n.* the bad; the harmful; moral depravity. **EVILLY**, *adv.* in an e. fashion. **EVILNESS**, *n.* wickedness; viciousness; depravity. [OE.].

EVIL-DOER [ē-vil-dōō′er], *n.* one who does evil; sinner.

EVIL-EYE [ē-vil-I′], *n.* supposed magical power of fascinating, bewitching, or otherwise injuring, by the look.

EVIL-MINDED [ē-vil-mīn′did], *adj.* wicked, malicious.

EVIL-SPEAKING [ē-vil-spē′king], *n.* wicked talk; slander; defamation.

EVINCE [i-vins′], *v.t.* to show, make evident, exhibit; prove beyond doubt. **EVINCIBLE**, *adj.* that may be evinced, demonstrable. **EVINCIBLY**, *adv.* in a manner to compel conviction. **EVINCIVE**, *adj.* giving proof; tending to demonstrate. [L.].

EVISCERATE [i-vi′se-rāt], *v.t.* to disembowel. **EVISCERATION** [i-vi-se-rā′shn], *n.* act of eviscerating; state of being eviscerated. [L.].

EVOCATION [e-vo-kā′shn], *n.* a calling forth, summoning. [L.].

EVOKE [i-vōk′], *v.t.* to call forth, summon; produce (a reply etc.). **EVOCATIVE** [i-vo′ka-tiv], *adj.* tending to e., reminiscent. [L.].

EVOLUTE [e′vo-lyōōt], *n.* (*math.*) a curve which is the locus of the centres of curvature of another curve, its involute.

EVOLUTION [ē-vo-lyōō′shn], *n.* action, condition, or process of evolving, unfolding, developing; series of things unfolded or developed; development of higher forms of life from lower, or conversely; theory that such development is natural and any divine agency is an unnecessary postulate; **emergent e.**, theory that an evolutionary movement can produce something entirely new and not in the initial state; (*biol.*) theory that generation is the separate development of a pre-existent germ; (*geom.*) the unfolding of a curve, and making it describe an evolvent or involute; (*arith.*) extraction of roots; (*milit.*) manoeuvre to change the disposition of troops. **EVOLUTIONAL**, *adj.* connected with e. **EVOLUTIONARY**, *adj.* of or pertaining to e. **EVOLU-**

TIONISM, *n.* belief in evolutionary theories. **EVOLUTIONIST**, *n.* one who advocates evolutionary theories; (*milit.*) one skilled in manoeuvres. [L.].

EVOLVE [i-volv′], *v.t.* to unfold, display, develop step by step; (*fig.*) bring (an idea etc.) to maturity; *v.i.* to unfold; reach a better or more complex state by gradual process from a worse or simpler one. **EVOLVEMENT**, *n.* evolving. **EVOLVENT**, *n.* (*geom.*) the involute. [L.].

EVULSION [i-vul′shn], *n.* action of plucking or tearing out by force. [L.].

EVZONE [ev′zōn], *n.* Greek light infantryman, who wears a skirted uniform. [Gk.].

EWE [yōō], *n.* female of the sheep; (*fig.*) **e. lamb**, specially treasured possession; person very dear to or valued by another. [OE.].

EWER [yōō′er], *n.* jug or pitcher, *esp.* a large one to hold water for washing. [AFr. from OFr. from L.].

EX-, *pref.* from off, drawn from; since, after; from out of, away from, forth from; former. [L.].

EXACERBATE [ek-sa′ser-bāt], *v.t.* to irritate; increase the pain of, aggravate; (*fig.*) exasperate, embitter. **EXACERBATION** [ek-sa-ser-bā′shn], *n.* an exacerbating or a being exacerbated; source of aggravation. [L.].

EXACT (1) [ek-sakt′], *adj.* finished off, complete; correct; accurate; precise; observing strict method, rule or order. **EXACT** (2), *v.t.* to force from; demand or extort by means of authority; demand or require (attention). **EXACTABLE**, *adj.* that can be exacted. **EXACTER, -OR**, *n.* one who exacts payment, often excessively. [L.].

EXACTING [ek-sak′ting], *adj.* making severe or excessive demands; arduous, exhausting.

EXACTION [ek-sak′shn], *n.* act of exacting; tyrannous authoritative demand; extortion; that which is exacted; excessive service or tribute. [L.].

EXACTITUDE [ek-sak′ti-tyōōd], *n.* exactness, correctness, accuracy.

EXACTLY [ek-sakt′li], *adv.* in an exact manner; precisely; accurately; as a conversational interjection, quite so!

EXACTNESS [ek-sakt′nes], *n.* a being exact; accuracy; precision.

EXAGGERATE [eg-za′je-rāt], *v.t.* to represent as greater than the reality; over-emphasize, overstate; increase and render abnormal; *v.i.* to use overstatement. **EXAGGERATEDLY**, *adv.* in an exaggerated fashion. **EXAGGERATIVE**, *adj.* marked by exaggeration. **EXAGGERATOR**, *n.* person who exaggerates. **EXAGGERATORY**, *adj.* containing or tending to exaggeration. [L.].

EXAGGERATION [eg-za-je-rā′shn], *n.* act of exaggerating; exaggerated remark. [L.].

EXALT [eg-zawlt′], *v.t.* to raise up high; heighten in rank, ennoble; praise. **EXALTER**, *n.* one who, or that which, exalts. [L.].

EXALTATION [eg-zawl-tā′shn], *n.* act of exalting; state of being exalted; high spirits, elation; (*astrol.*) influence which a planet is supposed to acquire in certain signs or parts of the Zodiac; **E. of the Cross**, Christian festival observed on 14 September. [L.].

EXALTED [eg-zawl′tid], *adj.* lofty, elevated; of high rank; enraptured; inspired. **EXALTEDLY**, *adv.* in an e. manner. **EXALTEDNESS**, *n.* condition of being e.

EXAM [eg-zam′], *n.* examination. [Shortened.]

EXAMINABLE [eg-za′mi-na-bl], *adj.* capable of being examined; (*leg.*) cognizable.

EXAMINATION [eg-za-mi-nā′shn], *n.* investigation, careful inspection; a test by question and answer. **EXAMINATIONAL**, *adj.* of or pertaining to examinations. **EXAMINATORIAL** [eg-za-mi-na-taw′ri-al], *adj.* pertaining to an examiner or an examination. [L.].

EXAMINE [eg-za′min], *v.t.* to inspect carefully and critically; inquire into by interrogation; test knowledge or capacity by question and answer; put to a test. **EXAMINEE**, *n.* one subject to examination.

EXAMINER [eg-za′mi-ner], *n.* person who examines or inspects; one who marks examination papers; one who interrogates a witness or an offender.

EXAMPLE [eg-zahm′pl], *n.* a particular instance illustrating or dependent on rule or statement; someone or something to be imitated or the reverse; precedent; warning; **for e.**, by way of illustration, often abbreviated to e.g. (L. *exempli gratia*); **to make an e. of**, to punish in order to deter others; **to set an e.**, to conduct oneself so as to be an object of imitation. [L.].

EXANTHEMA (*pl.* **exanthemata**) [eks-an-thē′mah], *n.* (*med.*) febrile disease such as smallpox or measles.

manifesting itself in a distinctive eruption on the skin. EXANTHEMATOUS, *adj.* of, or pertaining to, e. [Gk.].

EXARCH [ek'sahk], *n.* a viceroy of the Byzantine emperors; in the Greek Church, title of certain bishops as primates over others, inspector of the clergy appointed by the Eastern patriarchs; head of certain Orthodox churches. EXARCHATE, *n.* office, dignity or province of an e. [Gk.].

EXASPERATE [eg-zas'pe-rāt], *v.t.* to rouse to anger; provoke and infuriate. EXASPERATER, -OR, *n.* person who exasperates. [L.].

EXASPERATING [eg-zas'pe-rā-ting], *adj.* such as to exasperate. EXASPERATINGLY, *adv.* in an e. manner.

EXASPERATION [eg-zas-pe-rā'shn], *n.* action of exasperating or irritating; state of being exasperated; provocation; rage; exacerbation; extreme irritation. [L.].

EXCAVATE [eks'ka-vāt], *v.t.* to dig a pit; dig out; unearth, *esp.* in archaeological investigations. [L.].

EXCAVATION [eks-ka-vā'shn], *n.* a pit; a digging; a digging out; anything revealed by digging, particularly an archaeological site. [L.].

EXCAVATOR [eks'ka-vā-ter], *n.* person who excavates; machine used for excavating; steam navvy; dredger.

EXCEED [ek-sēd'], *v.t.* to overstep any limit; surpass; *v.i.* to go too far; be guilty of excess; be more or larger than. [L.].

EXCEEDING (1) [ek-sē'ding], *adj.* in surpassing measure, extreme. EXCEEDING (2)†, *adv.* exceedingly. EXCEEDINGLY, *adv.* extremely, surpassingly.

EXCEL (*pres.pt.* excelling, *pret. and p.pt.* excelled) [ek-sel'], *v.t.* to go beyond; exceed; surpass; *v.i.* to have good qualities or to perform good or clever actions to an unusual degree; be surpassingly clever or eminent. [L.].

EXCELLENCE [ek'se-lens], *n.* superiority; notable proficiency; meritorious quality. [L.].

EXCELLENCY [ek'se-len-si], *n.* title of honour given to ambassadors, governors and other eminent persons. [L.].

EXCELLENT [ek'se-lent], *adj.* excelling; fine; surpassingly good of its kind. EXCELLENTLY, *adv.* in an e. manner.

EXCELSIOR [ek-sel'si-aw(r)], *int.* higher! still higher! [L.].

EXCEPT (1) [ek-sept'], *v.t.* to leave out; *v.i.* to object. EXCEPT (2), *prep.* exclusive of, but for, omitting, apart from. EXCEPT (3), *conj.* unless. [L.].

EXCEPTING [ek-sep'ting], *prep.* excluding, except.

EXCEPTION [ek-sep'shn], *n.* action of excluding from a specified number; that which a rule does not include; objection; offence; (*leg.*) denial of what is alleged; **bill of exceptions**, statement of objections to the decision or instructions of a judge. [L.].

EXCEPTIONABLE [ek-sep'shn-a-bl], *adj.* open to objection. EXCEPTIONABLENESS, *n.* quality of being e.

EXCEPTIONAL [ek-sep'shn-al], *adj.* extraordinary, unusual; constituting an exception. EXCEPTIONALLY, *adv.* in an e. way; unusually; extraordinarily.

EXCEPTIVE [ek-sep'tiv], *adj.* forming or including an exception.

EXCERPT (1) [ek-surpt'], *v.t.* to make an extract from, pick out, select. EXCERPT (2) [ek'serpt], *n.* passage selected from a writing or book; reprint of a paper in a technical publication. EXCERPTION [ek-surp'shn], *n.* action of excerpting, selecting one or more extracts. [L.].

EXCESS (1) [ek-ses'], *n.* that which is beyond what is necessary; that which is beyond the common measure or due quantity; superabundance; any transgression of due limits; undue indulgence; intemperance; (*math.*) that by which one number or quantity exceeds another. EXCESS (2), *adj.* excessive, in e. of; **e. profits**, profits made in a stated period in e. of those made over a period laid down as standard. EXCESS (3), *v.t.* to make an additional charge, *esp.* for any luggage over the weight ordinarily allowed. [L.].

EXCESSIVE [ek-se'siv], *adj.* beyond any given, or the ordinary, measure or proportion; beyond the bounds of justice, fitness, propriety or utility; extravagant; unreasonable. EXCESSIVELY, *adv.* in an extreme degree. EXCESSIVENESS, *n.* state or quality of being e. [Fr.].

EXCHANGE (1) [eks-chānj'], *n.* act of exchanging, in which the thing received is claimed to be equivalent to the thing given; act of giving up without contract one thing or state for another; act of giving

and receiving reciprocally; thing given or the thing received in exchange; form of exchanging one debt or credit for another, or settling by order, draft or bill of exchange; foreign currency, or the place where it is bought; place where the merchants, brokers and bankers of a city meet to transact business, sometimes abbreviated *change*; central telephone office of a particular district; **arbitration of e.**, calculation of the profits of exchanges at different places; **bill of e.**, written order directing one party to pay a sum of money to another; **course of e.**, movement of price between two places; **e. control**, limitation by the state of payments abroad in order to conserve currency. EXCHANGE (2), *v.t. and i.* to barter or give one thing in return for another; surrender one thing, state or condition in return for another; interchange; deal in money by changing the currency of one country for the appropriate amount in the currency of another; make an e. EXCHANGER, *n.* person who exchanges or practises e.; money-changer. [LL.].

EXCHANGEABLE [eks-chān'ja-bl], *adj.* that can be exchanged; estimable by what could be got in exchange.

EXCHEQUER [eks-che'ker], *n.* (*hist.*) a court of record, which consisted of two divisions, one with jurisdiction in revenue matters and the other a court of Common Law for the administration of justice; the British Treasury; a treasury; **Chancellor of the E.**, Finance Minister of Great Britain; **E. bill**, bill for money or promissory bills issued by the E. as a floating debt. [OFr. from MedL.].

EXCIPIENT [ek-si'pi-ent], *n.* substance used as a vehicle in administering a medicine. [L.].

EXCISABLE [eks-sī'za-bl], *adj.* liable to excise duty.

EXCISE (1) [ek'sīz], *n.* duty payable to the state on articles manufactured under licence; licence to manufacture; that branch of the Department of Inland Revenue which collects the duty. EXCISE (2), *v.t.* to levy e. duty on. [MDu.].

EXCISE (3) [ek-sīz'], *v.t.* to cut out, cut away or remove. [L.].

EXCISEMAN [ek'sīz-man], *n.* collector of excise duty.

EXCISION [ek-si'zhn], *n.* action of cutting out; what is cut out. [L.].

EXCITABLE [ek-sī'ta-bl], *adj.* easily excited. EXCITABILITY [ek-sī-ta-bi'li-ti], *n.* capacity for being easily excited or stimulated to activity. [L.].

EXCITANT [ek'si-tant, ek-sī'tant], *n.* that which produces or can produce increased action in a living body or organ; a stimulant. [L.].

EXCITE [ek-sīt'], *v.t.* to rouse something into activity; increase in activity; stimulate, provoke. EXCITATION [ek-si-tā'shn], *n.* action of exciting. EXCITATIVE, EXCITATORY [ek-sī'ta-tiv, ek-sī'ta-te-ri], *adj.* such as to e. EXCITER, *n.* agent or cause of excitement. [L.].

EXCITEMENT [ek-sīt'ment], *n.* action of exciting; stimulation; state of being excited; that which excites or produces agitation.

EXCITING [ek-sī'ting], *adj.* producing excitement, thrilling, of absorbing interest. EXCITINGLY, *adv.* in an e. fashion.

EXCLAIM [eks-klām'], *v.t. and i.* to utter a sudden sharp cry of surprise, utter an ejaculation; **to e. against**, to accuse warningly, protest, blame; **to e. at**, to express surprise at. [L.].

EXCLAMATION [eks-kla-mā'shn], *n.* outcry; clamour; vehement or emphatic utterance; note by which emphatic utterance is marked, thus (!); (*gram.*) interjection expressive of some emotion, as wonder. [L.].

EXCLAMATORY [eks-kla'ma-te-ri], *adj.* full of exclamations, tending to exclaim. EXCLAMATORILY, *adv.* in e. fashion.

EXCLUDE [eks-klōōd'], *v.t.* to push or thrust out; hinder from entering; shut out; debar; hinder from participation or enjoyment; except; not to comprehend or include. [L.].

EXCLUSION [eks-klōō'zhn], *n.* act of excluding, thing excluded. EXCLUSIONARY, *adj.* connected with e. EXCLUSIONISM, *n.* exclusivism. EXCLUSIONIST, *n.* one who would exclude someone from a right or privilege. [L.].

EXCLUSIVE [eks-klōō'siv], *adj.* excluding, or tending to exclude, others; maintaining sole privilege; reserved for a few, unapproachable; appearing only in one particular newspaper, film or the like; sold by a particular firm; (*coll.*) *esp.* in *advertising*, out of the common, of superior quality; **e. rights**, rights involving a lack of the same rights by others. EXCLUSIVELY, *adv.* in an e. or superior manner; solely. EXCLUSIVE- NESS, *n.* quality or condition of being e.; snobbish feeling or expression of superiority. EXCLUSIVISM, *n.* adherence to some e. theory or practice. [L.].

EXCOGITATE [eks-ko'ji-tāt], *v.t.* to think out, devise. EXCOGITATION [eks-ko-ji-tā'shn], *n.* the thinking out or devising of anything. [L.].

EXCOMMUNICATE [eks-ko-myōō'ni-kāt], *v.t.* to exclude by authority and rite from Christian privi- leges and sacraments; exclude officially, expel. EXCOMMUNICATORY, *adj.* effecting excommunication. [L.].

EXCOMMUNICATION [eks-ko-myōō-ni-kā'shn], *n.* rite or act of excommunicating ecclesiastically, or expelling generally; **major e.,** complete ecclesiastical e.; **minor e.,** debarring officially from the sacra- ments.

EXCORIATE [eks-kaw'ri-āt], *v.t.* to strip off a skin, rind or bark. EXCORIATION [eks-kaw-ri-ā'shn], *n.* the abrasion of the skin, the stripping off of a skin, rind or bark. [L.].

EXCORTICATE [eks-kaw'ti-kāt], *v.t.* to strip off the bark of. EXCORTICATION [eks-kaw-ti-kā'shn], *n.* process of excorticating. [L.].

EXCREMENT [eks'kre-ment], *n.* waste matter excreted from the body; ordure; dung. EXCRE- MENTAL [eks-kre-men'tal], *adj.* excreted or ejected. EXCREMENTITIOUS [eks-kre-men-ti'shŏŏs], *adj.* per- taining to, consisting of or containing e.; excre- ment. [L.].

EXCRESCENCE [eks-kre'sens], *n.* natural or abnormal protuberance or outgrowth; (*fig.*) an un- necessary, often disagreeable, development. [L.]. **EXCRESCENT** [eks-kre'sent], *adj.* growing out of something else in an abnormal manner. [L.].

EXCRETA [eks-krē'tah], *n.(pl.)* excreted matter or waste.

EXCRETE [eks-krēt'], *v.t.* to separate and expel, usually of waste matter from animal bodies. EXCRE- TIVE, *adj.* capable of excreting or causing excretion. **EXCRETION** [eks-krē'shn], *n.* action of excreting matter from the body; that which is excreted. **EXCRETORY** (1) [eks-krē'te-ri], *adj.* serving to excrete. EXCRETORY (2), *n.* (*anat.*) duct or vessel for the reception and expulsion of waste matter from an animal body.

EXCRUCIATE † [eks-krōō'shi-āt], *v.t.* to torture physically or mentally; (*fig.*) give great pain to. EXCRUCIATION [eks-krōō-shi-ā'shn], *n.* torture, anguish; the giving of such pain. [L.].

EXCRUCIATING [eks-krōō'shi-ā-ting], *adj.* causing intense physical or mental pain; very distressing. EXCRUCIATINGLY, *adv.* in an e. fashion; (*coll.*) very. **EXCULPATE** [eks'kul-pāt], *v.t.* to free from blame or guilt. EXCULPATION [eks-kul-pā'shn], *n.* a clearing from blame or guilt; the grounds for such a clearing. EXCULPATORY [eks-kul'pa-te-ri], *adj.* tending to clear of blame or guilt. [EX- and L.].

EXCURSION [eks-kur'shn], *n.* deviation or wander- ing from a prescribed course; digression; ramble; brief tour; trip for health or pleasure; † (*milit.*) sortie, hence commotion, now only in *phr.* **alarms and excursions; e. train,** train for excursionists at a reduced fare. EXCURSIONIST, *n.* one who is on an e.; a tripper or organizer of trips. [L.].

EXCURSIVE [eks-kur'siv], *adj.* tending to digress. EXCURSIVELY, *adv.* in an e. fashion. EXCURSIVENESS, *n.* tendency to be e.

EXCURSUS [eks-kur'sus], *n.* supplemental treatise or appendix on some important point referred to in the main work. [L.].

EXCUSABLE [eks-kyōō'za-bl], *adj.* deserving excuse; pardonable. EXCUSABLENESS, *n.* state of being able to be excused or forgiven. EXCUSABLY, *adv.* in an e. fashion, so as to allow of forgiveness. [L.].

EXCUSE (1) [eks-kyōōz'], *v.t.* to try to clear someone of blame; overlook a fault, accept an excuse; free from an obligation; ask pardon for a breach of etiquette; **e. me,** polite formula prefixed as an extenuation to a breach of manners or strict etiquette; polite or ironical way of disputing a statement. EXCUSE (2) [eks-kyōōs'], *n.* action of excusing; plea offered in extenuation of a fault or irregularity; pretext. EXCUSATORY [eks-kyōō'za-te-ri], *adj.* tending to e. EXCUSELESS [eks-kyōōs'les], *adj.* without e., inexcus- able. [L.].

EXEAT [ek'si-at], *n.* formal permission given either to an undergraduate to leave his college, or to a priest to leave his diocese. [L.].

EXECRABLE [ek'si-kra-bl], *adj.* worthy to be

excrated; abominable; hateful. EXECRABLENESS, *n.* condition of being e. EXECRABLY, *adv.* in an e. manner.

EXECRATE [ek'si-krāt], *v.t.* to detest or to express detestation; *v.i.* to curse. EXECRATORY, *adj.* of or per- taining to execration; cursing. [L.].

EXECRATION [ek-si-krā'shn], *n.* detestation and its expression in words; object execrated; cursing.

EXECUTANT [eg-ze'kyōō-tant], *n.* agent; one who executes or performs, *esp.* a musician. [Fr.].

EXECUTE [ek'si-kyōōt], *v.t.* to carry out; of an artist or musician, perform; inflict capital punish- ment on; (*leg.*) put into effect any legal provision; fulfil the provisions of a will or instrument conveying property from one person to another. EXECUTABLE [eg-ze'kyōō-ta-bl], *adj.* capable of execution. [L.].

EXECUTION [ek-si-kyōō'shn], *n.* the performance of any act; the putting into practice of a previously calculated policy or line of conduct; performance of a piece of music; exercise of technique in sculpture or painting; a killing after capital sentence; the fulfilling of the provisions of a legal enactment or document. [L.].

EXECUTIONER [ek-si-kyōō'shn-er], *n.* one who executes; man who executes a sentence of capital punishment.

EXECUTIVE (1) [eg-ze'kyōō-tiv], *adj.* concerned with carrying out policies rather than planning them. EXECUTIVE (2), *n.* administrative side of a govern- ment; any administrative body; (*U.S.*) member of a business organization who is allowed to exercise his own initiative. EXECUTIVELY, *adv.* in a fashion concerned with execution; so far as concerns execu- tion.

EXECUTOR [eg-ze'kyōō-ter], *n.* one who carries out a plan or policy; one appointed by a testator to execute his will. EXECUTORIAL [eg-ze-kyōō-taw'ri- al], *adj.* pertaining to an e. EXECUTORSHIP [eg-ze'- kyōō-ter-ship], *n.* office of an e. of a will. EXECU- TORY, *adj.* connected with the carrying out of com- mands, laws etc.; in operation. [L.].

EXECUTRIX [eg-ze'kyōō-triks], *n.* female executor. [MedL.].

EXEGESIS [ek-si-jē'sis], *n.* elucidatory note, *esp.* on the scriptures; elucidation. EXEGETIC(AL) [ek-si- je'tik(-al)], *adj.* explanatory. EXEGETICALLY, *adv.* by way of elucidation. [Gk.].

EXEGETICS [ek-si-je'tiks], *n.(pl.)* art or study of biblical interpretation.

EXEMPLAR [eg-zem'plah(r)], *n.* model to be followed and imitated; specimen. [ME. from OFr.].

EXEMPLARY [eg-zem'pla-ri], *adj.* worthy to be imitated; serving for a warning; commendable. EXEMPLARILY, *adv.* in e. fashion. [LL.].

EXEMPLIFICATION [eg-zem-pli-fi-kā'shn], *n.* act of exemplifying; illustrating by examples. [MedL.].

EXEMPLIFY [eg-zem'pli-fī], *v.t.* to illustrate with examples; take an attested copy of. EXEMPLIFIABLE [eg-zem-pli-fī'a-bl], *adj.* capable of being illustrated by example. [MedL.].

EXEMPT (1) [eg-zempt'], *adj.* exempted, excused from the performance of some duty. EXEMPT (2), *v.t.* to excuse from the performance of some duty. EXEMPTIBLE, *adj.* able to be exempted. EXEMPTIVE, *adj.* tending to e. [Fr. from L.].

EXEMPTION [eg-zemp'shn], *n.* an exempting; being exempt; immunity. [L.].

EXEQUATUR [ek-si-kwä'ter], *n.* document recog- nizing a consul or commercial agent issued by the government to which he comes accredited, and authorizing him to exercise his powers. [L.].

EXEQUIES [ek'si-kwiz], *n.(pl.)* funeral rites. [L.].

EXERCISE (1) [ek'ser-sīz], *n.* a putting in use or practice; exertion of the body for health, strength or dexterity; performance; practice for the acquisition of skill; task appointed one to perform; act of divine worship; lesson for practice; (*mus.*) any composition calculated to improve the voice or fingers. EXER- CISE (2), *v.t.* to use; cause something to move or function, often to keep it in good order or healthy; perplex; discipline; *v.i.* to engage in bodily activity with the purpose of keeping healthy. [L.].

EXERCITATION [ek-ser-si-tā'shn], *n.* exercise, practice. [L.].

EXERT [eg-zurt'], *v.t.* to bring into active operation; **to e. oneself,** to use effort, strive. EXERTIVE, *adj.* rousing into activity. [L.].

EXERTION [eg-zur'shn], *n.* act of exerting or exer- cising something; output of force; great physical activity.

EXES [ek'sez], *n.(pl.)* (*slang*) expenses.

EXEUNT [ek'si-unt], *v.i.* they go, a stage direction. [L.].

EXFOLIATE [eks-fō'li-āt], *v.i.* to split off in scales; peel off. **EXFOLIATION** [eks-fō-li-ā'shn], *n.* a peeling off in scales; act of exfoliating. **EXFOLIATIVE** [eks-fō'li-a-tiv], *adj.* that has the power to cause exfoliation. [L.].

EXHALANT, EXHALENT [eks-hā'lent], *adj.* exhaling. [L.].

EXHALATION [eks-ha-lā'shn], *n.* an exhaling; that which is exhaled; mist, vapour, effluvium. [L.].

EXHALE [eks-hāl'], *v.t.* to give off, emit a vapour; *v.i.* to breathe out. **EXHALABLE**, *adj.* able to be exhaled. [L.].

EXHALENT, see **EXHALANT**.

EXHAUST (1) [eg-zawst'], *v.t.* to draw out or drain off the whole of; empty by drawing off; use or expend the whole of; consume completely; tire out; treat of, as a subject, so completely as to leave nothing unsaid. **EXHAUST** (2). *n.* exhaust-pipe; exhausted gases escaping through it; **e. gas,** gaseous products of combustion in an internal combustion engine. [L.].

EXHAUSTED [eg-zaws'tid], *adj.* empty; used up; finished; that has lost its virtue or strength; tired out; completely dealt with.

EXHAUSTIBLE [eg-zaws'ti-bl], *adj.* that can be exhausted. **EXHAUSTIBILITY** [ig-zaws-ti-bi'li-ti], *n.* capacity of being exhausted.

EXHAUSTING [eg-zaws'ting], *adj.* causing exhaustion; wearying.

EXHAUSTION [eg-zaws'chn], *n.* act of exhausting; condition of being exhausted; (*math.*) method of proving the equality of two magnitudes by a *reductio ad absurdum*; (*log.*) method of proving a point by demonstration of the absurdity of every other possible hypothesis.

EXHAUSTIVE [eg-zaws'tiv], *adj.* that which exhausts; thorough. **EXHAUSTIVELY,** *adv.* in an e. manner, thoroughly. **EXHAUSTIVENESS,** *n.* quality of being e.; thoroughness.

EXHAUSTLESS [eg-zawst'les], *adj.* that cannot be exhausted; boundless; tireless.

EXHAUST-PIPE [eg-zawst'pīp], *n.* pipe from an engine through which the exhausted gases escape.

EXHIBIT (1) [eg-zi'bit], *v.t.* to show, display; display publicly in an exhibition; manifest signs of. **EXHIBIT** (2), *n.* anything displayed; (*leg.*) sworn deed or a material object produced in court as evidence. [L.].

EXHIBITION [ek-si-bi'shn], *n.* act of exhibiting or showing; display; the producing of papers before a tribunal in proof of facts; that which is exhibited; public show, *esp.* of art or manufacture, natural products etc.; bursary to a student in an English university or school. [L.].

EXHIBITIONER [ek-si-bi'shn-er], *n.* one who receives an annual grant for his support in a school or college, as a student.

EXHIBITIONISM [ek-si-bi'shn-izm], *n.* (*psych.*) psychological condition causing the sufferer to exhibit the genital organs; tendency to perform acts which draw attention to one.

EXHIBITIONIST [ek-si-bi'shn-ist], *n.* person who exhibits at an exhibition; one subject to exhibitionism.

EXHIBITOR [eg-zi'bi-ter], *n.* one whose exhibit is included in an exhibition. [L.].

EXHIBITORY [eg-zi'bi-te-ri], *adj.* showing, displaying; pertaining to display. [L.].

EXHILARATE [eg-zi'la-rāt], *v.t.* to make cheerful, enliven, invigorate. **EXHILARATIVE,** *adj.* tending to cause exhilaration. [L.].

EXHILARATING [eg-zi'la-rā-ting], *adj.* enlivening, invigorating. **EXHILARATINGLY,** *adv.* in an e. manner.

EXHILARATION [eg-zi-la-rā'shn], *n.* act of exhilarating; state of being exhilarated; means employed in exhilarating. [LL.].

EXHORT [eg-zawt'], *v.t.* to urge to good conduct; admonish; entreat. **EXHORTATIVE, EXHORTATORY** [eg-zaw'ta-tiv, eg-zaw-tā'te-ri], *adj.* tending to e. **EXHORTATOR** [eg'zaw-tā-ter], *n.* person who exhorts.

EXHORTATION [eg-zaw-tā'shn], *n.* art or practice of exhorting to laudable deeds; form of words intended to incite and encourage; warning, admonition. [L.].

EXHUMATION [eks-hyōō-mā'shn], *n.* process of exhuming.

EXHUME [eks-hyōōm'], *v.t.* to dig up, disinter (*esp.* a body which has been buried). [Fr. from MedL.].

EXIGEANT [eg'zē-zhah(ng)], *adj.* exacting. [Fr.].

EXIGENCE [ek'si-jens], *n.* quality or process of being exigent; urgency.

EXIGENCY [ek'si-jen-si], *n.* exigence; any circumstances demanding immediate attention, a crisis. [L.].

EXIGENT [ek'si-jent], *adj.* urgent, pressing. [L.].

EXIGUOUS [eg-zi'gyōō-ōōs], *adj.* scanty, very small, insufficient. **EXIGUITY, EXIGUOUSNESS** [ek-si-gyōō'i-ti, eg-zi'gyōō-ōōs-nes], *n.* scantiness, paucity, insufficiency. [L.].

EXILE (1) [ek'sīl, eg'zīl], *n.* banishment or absence from one's native land; place to which one then retires. **EXILE** (2), *n.* one banished or absent from his own country. **EXILE** (3), *v.t.* to banish, exclude a person from his own country, or from his customary surroundings. **EXILIAN, EXILIC** [eg-zi'li-an, ek-si'lik], *adj.* of, or pertaining to, e., *esp.* the Jewish e. in Babylon. [L.].

EXIST [eg-zist'], *v.i.* to be; have material being; occur; continue in being; (*coll.*) live poorly. [L.].

EXISTENCE [eg-zis'tens], *n.* state of being; occurrence; life; **mere e.,** continuance of life without pleasure or purpose. [OFr.].

EXISTENT [eg-zis'tent], *adj.* that exists. [L.].

EXISTENTIAL [eg-zis-ten'shal], *adj.* connected with existence; (*log.*) predicating existence. [LL.].

EXISTENTIALISM [eg-zis-ten'sha-lizm], *n.* philosophic doctrine which holds that the perceived fact of human existence is the only valid basis of knowledge, and that "existence is more important than essence." **EXISTENTIALIST,** *n.* one who believes in e.

EXIT (1) [ek'sit], *n.* departure of an actor from the stage; any departure; door or outlet. **EXIT** (2), *v.i.* to make one's departure; (*fig.*) die. [L.].

EX-LIBRIS [eks-li'bris], *n.* motto customary on a bookplate; the bookplate. [L.].

EXO-, *pref.* outside. [Gk.].

EXODUS [ek'so-dus], *n.* title of the second book of the Old Testament which records the departure from Egypt of the Israelites; (*fig.*) any departure. [Gk.].

EX-OFFICIO [eks-o-fi'shi-ō], *adj.* official, in virtue of, or because of, office or authority; **e. member,** one who is a member of a committee in virtue of some other office. [L.].

EXOGAMY [ek-so'ga-mi], *n.* tribal convention which compels all tribesmen to marry wives from other tribes. **EXOGAMOUS,** *adj.* relating to e. [Gk.].

EXOGENOUS [ek-so'je-nōōs], *adj.* growing by additions to the outside; (*bot.*) with the wood augmented by annual external accretions. [Gk.].

EXON [ek'son], *n.* title of the four chief officers of the yeomen of the royal guard. [Fr.].

EXONERATE [eg-zo'ne-rāt], *v.t.* to free from blame or obligation. **EXONERATIVE,** *adj.* tending to e. [L.].

EXONERATION [eg-zo-ne-rā'shn], *n.* an exonerating; the grounds for this. [L.].

EXOPHTHALMIA [ek-sof-thal'mi-ah], *n.* (*med.*) abnormal protrusion of the eyeball, so that the eyelid cannot cover it. **EXOPHTHALMIC,** *adj.* of, pertaining to, or characterized by e. [Gk.].

EXORBITANCE, EXORBITANCY [eg-zaw'bi-tans(-i)], *n.* quality of being exorbitant, excessive, or exceeding due bounds, extravagance; excess.

EXORBITANT [eg-zaw'bi-tant], *adj.* making excessive demands; exceedingly large. **EXORBITANTLY,** *adv.* in an e. fashion, excessively. [L.].

EXORCISM [ek'saw-sizm], *n.* expulsion of an evil spirit by religious rite. [Eccles. Gk.].

EXORCIZE [ek'saw-sīz], *v.t.* to perform an exorcism; (*fig.*) dispel or banish. **EXORCIZER, EXORCIST,** *n.* one who claims to cast out evil spirits. [LL. from Gk.].

EXORDIUM [eg-zaw'di-um], *n.* introductory part of a discourse or a composition; the beginning. **EXORDIAL,** *adj.* having the character of an e. [L.].

EXOSTOSIS [ek-sos-tō'sis], *n.* (*anat.*) unnatural protuberance of a bone; (*bot.*) disease in which knots form in wood. [Gk.].

EXOTERIC(AL) [ek-sō-te'rik(-al)], *adj.* external; of doctrines, rites etc., such as are taught to the uninitiated; (*fig.*) popular. [Gk.].

EXOTIC (1) [eg-zo'tik], *adj.* having foreign characteristics; not yet naturalized; foreign-looking. **EXOTIC** (2), *n.* plant, word etc., of foreign origin. **EXOTICISM** [eg-zo'ti-sizm], *n.* condition of being e.; foreign expression or idiom. [Gk.].

EXPAND [eks-pand'], *v.t. and i.* to spread out; enlarge upon a statement; grow larger, develop; become communicative; **expanded metal,** sheet metal slit and stretched into lattice work sheets and used in making reinforced concrete. [L.].

EXPANSE [eks-pans'], *n.* a wide extent.

EXPANSIBLE [eks-pan'si-bl], *adj.* that may be expanded. EXPANSIBILITY [eks-pan-si-bi'li-ti], *n.* capacity of being expanded. EXPANSIBLY, *adv.* in an e. fashion.

EXPANSILE [eks-pan'sil], *adj.* tending to expansion.

EXPANSION [eks-pan'shn], *n.* process of expanding; state of being expanded; distension, extent; extension of the territory of a state. EXPANSIONISM, *n.* policy of an expansionist. EXPANSIONIST, *n. and adj.* one who advocates or pursues a policy of territorial aggrandizement; of, or tending towards, (territorial) e. [L.].

EXPANSIVE [eks-pan'siv], *adj.* tending to expand, capable of expansion; (*fig.*) genial, unreserved. EXPANSIVELY, *adv.* in an e. fashion. EXPANSIVENESS, *n.* capacity for, or tendency to, expansion; (*fig.*) geniality.

EXPATIATE [eks-pā'shi-āt], *v.i.* to dilate upon, usually in speech or writing. EXPATIATION [eks-pā-shi-ā'shn], *n.* process of expatiating. EXPATIATIVE, *adj.* tending to e. EXPATIATOR, *n.* one who expatiates. EXPATIATORY, *adj.* expatiating. [L.].

EXPECT [eks-pekt'], *v.t.* to wait for; look for as likely to happen; calculate on being done; *v.i.* to wait; suppose. EXPECTINGLY, *adv.* in an expectant fashion. [L.].

EXPECTANCY [eks-pek'tan-si], *n.* a being expectant; that which is expected.

EXPECTANT [eks-pek'tant], *adj.* waiting, looking out; **e. mother,** pregnant woman. EXPECTANTLY, *adv.* with expectation.

EXPECTATION [eks-pek-tā'shn], *n.* act of expecting; state of being expected; that which is expected; an awaiting, looking forward to good to come. [L.].

EXPECTATIVE [eks-pek'ta-tiv], *adj.* anticipatory; expectant. [LL.].

EXPECTORANT (1) [eks-pek'te-rant], *adj.* that promotes expectoration. EXPECTORANT (2), *n.* (*med.*) an e. medicine.

EXPECTORATE [eks-pek'te-rāt], *v.t.* to cough up (phlegm etc.); *v.i.* to eject phlegm; spit. EXPECTORATION [eks-pek-te-rā'shn], *n.* act of expectorating. EXPECTORATIVE [eks-pek'te-rā-tiv], *adj.* pertaining to expectoration. [L.].

EXPEDIENCE, EXPEDIENCY [eks-pē'di-ens(-i)], *n.* fitness for effecting a purpose; propriety under particular circumstances; convenience rather than justice. EXPEDIENTIAL [eks-pē-di-en'shal], *adj.* based on, dictated by, considerations of e. or advantage. [Fr.].

EXPEDIENT (1) [eks-pē'di-ent], *adj.* serviceable for a purpose, useful; proper in the circumstances. EXPEDIENT (2), *n.* a means to an end; means devised in an emergency. EXPEDIENTLY, *adv.* in an e. manner. [L.].

EXPEDITE [eks'pi-dīt], *v.t.* to hasten; facilitate; accelerate. [L.].

EXPEDITION [eks-pi-di'shn], *n.* promptness, dispatch; journey undertaken, *esp.* for warfare or exploration; the collective body on an expedition. EXPEDITIONARY, *adj.* connected with a military e. [L.].

EXPEDITIOUS [eks-pi-di'shŏŏs], *adj.* accomplished, done, with expedition or dispatch. EXPEDITIOUSLY, *adv.* in an e. fashion. EXPEDITIOUSNESS, *n.* celerity.

EXPEL [eks-pel'], *v.t.* to drive out, compel to leave; eject, banish; compel to leave school in disgrace. EXPELLABLE, *adj.* capable of being expelled. [L.].

EXPEND [eks-pend'], *v.t. and i.* to lay out, spend; use; consume, use up; be laid out, used, consumed. [L.].

EXPENDABLE [eks-pen'da-bl], *adj.* that may be expended; (*milit.*) (of personnel or equipment) not sufficiently essential for the future conduct of a war to be rescued from the enemy at all costs.

EXPENDITURE [eks-pen'di-tyŏŏr], *n.* act of spending; anything expended (as money, time, energy etc.).

EXPENSE [eks-pens'], *n.* that which is expended; cost; disbursement; price paid. [LL.].

EXPENSIVE [eks-pen'siv], *adj.* involving expense; costly. EXPENSIVELY, *adv.* in an e. manner. EXPENSIVENESS, *n.* quality of being e.; costliness.

EXPERIENCE (1) [eks-pēer'i-ens], *n.* the ascertained result of a series of trials or experiments; observation of a fact or of the same facts or events happening in like circumstances; what one has felt and learned by enjoying or suffering; being well versed in anything; often, an experiencing, a suffering; (*coll.*) a disastrous or disturbing occasion in life in general, sexual relationship etc.; **e. table,** table of normal expectation of life used by insurance companies in assessing their policies. EXPERIENCE (2), *v.t.* to have e. of; undergo, suffer; meet with. EXPERIENCED, *adj.* versed in, practised; knowing. [L.].

EXPERIENTIALISM [eks-pēer-i-en'sha-lizm], *n.* doctrine which derives all our ideas from experience, or would refer all knowledge to the test of experience. EXPERIENTIALIST, *n.* supporter of e.

EXPERIMENT (1) [eks-pe'ri-ment], *n.* investigation by trial and error, *esp.* scientific investigation. EXPERIMENT (2), *v.t.* to make an e. or experiments. EXPERIMENTATIVE [eks-pe-ri-men'ta-tiv], *adj.* tending to make experiments. EXPERIMENTER, EXPERIMENTIST, *n.* one who experiments. [L.].

EXPERIMENTAL [eks-pe-ri-men'tal], *adj.* connected with experiment; founded on experiment; derived from experience; of scientific institutions, engaged in research by experiment. EXPERIMENTALISM, *n.* empiricism. EXPERIMENTALIST, *n.* one who devotes himself to e. research in science; one who tries new schemes; empiricist. EXPERIMENTALIZE, *v.i.* to perform experiments. EXPERIMENTALLY, *adv.* in an e. fashion.

EXPERIMENTATION [eks-pe-ri-men-tā'shn], *n.* the making of experiments.

EXPERT (1) [eks'pert], *adj.* possessing skill or knowledge in any work or branch of knowledge; skilful, dexterous; **e. work,** work skilfully done. EXPERT (2), *n.* person specially trained and qualified in any department of science or art; one who professes to have such special qualification. EXPERTLY, *adv.* in an e. way. EXPERTNESS, *n.* quality or condition of being e. [L.].

EXPERTISE [eks-per-tēz'], *n.* skill, expertness. [Fr.].

EXPIATE [eks'pi-āt], *v.t.* to atone for; make amends for. EXPIABLE, *adj.* capable of being expiated. EXPIATOR, *n.* one who expiates. EXPIATORY [eks-pi-ā'te-ri], *adj.* tending to e. [L.].

EXPIATION [eks-pi-ā'shn], *n.* act of expiating, or the means employed; atonement. [L.].

EXPIRATION [eks-pi-rā'shn], *n.* the physical movement of breathing out; the last emission of breath, death; (*fig.*) the end. [L.].

EXPIRE [eks-pīer'], *v.t.* to breathe out from the lungs; *v.i.* to die down, die out; emit the last breath; die; come to an end. EXPIRATORY, *adj.* pertaining to the process of expiration. EXPIRING, *adj.* breathing out air; dying; uttered when dying. [L.].

EXPIRY [eks-pīer'i], *n.* expiration; end; death.

EXPLAIN [eks-plān'], *v.t.* to make plain or intelligible; justify by giving reasons; excuse; *v.i.* to give explanations; **to e. away,** to attempt to prove that a statement or situation was misunderstood. EXPLAINABLE, *adj.* capable of explanation. [L.].

EXPLANATION [eks-pla-nā'shn], *n.* action of explaining, or the means employed; an excuse; justification; any reason or cause. [L.].

EXPLANATORY [eks-pla'na-te-ri], *n.* serving to explain. EXPLANATORINESS, *n.* quality of being e.

EXPLETIVE [eks-plē'tiv], *n.* (*gram.*) particle which rounds out the sense of a sentence; exclamation, oath. EXPLETIVELY, *adv.* in an e. fashion. [L.].

EXPLICABLE [eks'pli-ka-bl], *adj.* that can be explained. [L.].

EXPLICATE [eks'pli-kāt], *v.t.* to explain anything complicated; develop an argument. EXPLICATION [eks-pli-kā'shn], *n.* action of explicating or the complicated reasoning involved. EXPLICATIVE, EXPLICATORY [eks'pli-kā-tiv, eks'pli-kā-te-ri], *adj.* serving to explain, explanatory. [L.].

EXPLICIT (1) [eks'pli-sit], *n.* word used to mark the end of a book or section in a manuscript or printed work. [MedL.].

EXPLICIT (2) [eks-pli'sit], *adj.* distinctly stated, not merely implied; express; outspoken. EXPLICITLY, *adv.* in an e. fashion. EXPLICITNESS, *n.* quality of being e.; outspokenness. [L.].

EXPLODE [eks-plōd'], *v.t. and i.* to burst or expand with violence and a loud report; utter a burst of laughter; cause to burst; prove to be fallacious; demonstrate as absurd. EXPLODER, *n.* one who, or that which, causes an explosion; **magneto e.,** portable electrical apparatus used to detonate high-explosive charges. [L.].

EXPLOIT (1) [eks'ploit], *n.* notable heroic or adventurous deed or achievement. EXPLOIT (2) [eks-ploit'], *v.t.* to turn, possibly unfairly, to use and profit; use selfishly; make an unfair use of (another's services). **EXPLOITER**, *n.* one who exploits. [Fr. from L.].

EXPLOITATION [eks-ploi-tā'shn], *n.* act of exploiting; condition of being exploited. [Fr.].

EXPLORATION [eks-plaw-rā'shn], *n.* act of exploring; close and thorough search; travel for purposes of investigation; preliminary theoretic discussion before putting any policy into action. [L.].

EXPLORE [eks-plaw(r)'], *v.t. and i.* to search and examine with care; travel for purposes of investigation; investigate; discuss; (*surg.*) probe (a wound). **EXPLORATORY**, *adj.* pertaining to exploration; preliminary, tentative. **EXPLORING**, *adj.* engaged in, or fond of, exploring. [L.].

EXPLORER [eks-plaw'rer], *n.* one who explores; instrument used to explore a cavity in a tooth; instrument for sounding in mines or water; (*surg.*) instrument for probing a wound; (*elect.*) device to ascertain leakage in a dynamo.

EXPLOSION [eks-plō'zhn], *n.* a bursting with violence and a loud report; the firing of gunpowder, dynamite etc.; any loud burst of sound; a relieving of the feelings in any sudden violent manner. [L.].

EXPLOSIVE (1) [eks-plō'siv], *adj.* tending to explode or burst with noise and violence; irascible; coming in sudden eruptive bursts, as of laughter. **EXPLOSIVE** (2), *n.* substance whose sudden expansion causes an explosion; the motive principle in the firing of shells etc.; **high e.**, e. in which the chemical change is very rapid and violent. **EXPLOSIVELY**, *adv.* in an e. fashion.

EXPONENT [eks-pō'nent], *n.* person who, or that which, expounds or explains; (*alg.*) number placed above a quantity on the right hand, to indicate how often that quantity is to be multiplied by itself. [L.].

EXPONENTIAL [eks-pō-nen'shal], *adj.* relating to, or involving, exponents; **e. curve**, one whose nature is defined by means of an e. equation; **e. equation**, equation which contains an e. quantity; **e. quantity**, quantity whose exponent is variable.

EXPORT (1) [eks'pawt, eks-pawt'], *v.t.* to send out of a country by way of trade. **EXPORT** (2) [eks'pawt], *n.* act of exporting; merchandise conveyed from one country to another; **invisible e.**, e. of services involving no transfer of goods; (*pl.*) yearly value of such exports. **EXPORTABLE**, *adj.* that can be exported. **EXPORTATION** [eks-paw-tā'shn], *n.* act of exporting. [L.].

EXPORTER [eks-paw'ter], *n.* one who exports goods as a business.

EXPOSE [eks-pōz'], *v.t.* to remove the covering or protection from, reveal, make defenceless; lay open (to some danger or influence); (*phot.*) allow light to reach (a sensitized plate, paper etc.); make public, unmask, declare the villainy of. **EXPOSAL**, *n.* exposure; setting forth. [Fr.].

EXPOSE, **exposé** [eks-pō'zā], *n.* explanatory analysis; exposing of something discreditable. [Fr.].

EXPOSED [eks-pōzd'], *adj.* open; open to attack; open to the severity of the weather. **EXPOSEDNESS**, *n.* condition of being e.

EXPOSITION [eks-pō-zi'shn], *n.* act of exposing, laying open or exhibiting; exhibition, explanation, elucidation or interpretation. [L.].

EXPOSITIVE [eks-po'si-tiv], *adj.* expository, explanatory. [L.].

EXPOSITOR [eks-po'zi-ter], *n.* person who, or book which, expounds. [L.].

EXPOSITORY [eks-po'zi-te-ri], *adj.* serving to set forth the meaning.

EXPOSTULATE [eks-pos'tyōō-lāt], *v.i.* to reason seriously (with a person) on some impropriety of conduct or words, remonstrate; protest. **EXPOSTULATOR**, *n.* one who expostulates. **EXPOSTULATORY**, *adj.* characterized by expostulation. [L.].

EXPOSTULATION [eks-pos-tyōō-lā'shn], *n.* act of expostulating; remonstrance; protest. [L.].

EXPOSURE [eks-pō'zhōōr], *n.* act of exposing, or laying open, to the action of the elements or, figuratively, to public knowledge; the being so exposed; (*phot.*) the period of time light is allowed to operate on a sensitive emulsion; act of taking a photograph.

EXPOUND [eks-pownd'], *v.t.* to lay open the meaning of; explain; interpret. [OFr. from L.].

EXPRESS (1) [eks-pres'], *v.t.* to press out; utter or set forth in words or symbols; make manifest; depict; signify; make (one's thoughts or feelings)

manifest; (*reflex.*) explain one's opinions correctly; (*U.S.*) send by e. **EXPRESS** (2), *adj.* clear, definite, precise, explicit; exactly resembling; intended or sent for a particular purpose; travelling unusually fast. **EXPRESS** (3), *adv.* on purpose; by e. messenger, train etc. **EXPRESS** (4), *n.* a specially fast messenger or way of conveyance; fast train which does not stop at intermediate stations. **EXPRESSED**, *adj.* pressed out; uttered, or set forth, in words, symbols, or pictures. **EXPRESSIBLE**, *adj.* capable of being expressed. [OFr. from L.].

EXPRESSAGE [eks-pre'sij], *n.* fee for an article sent by express.

EXPRESSION [eks-pre'shn], *n.* act of expressing; act or method of giving utterance or form; artistic style or method; modulation of the voice, mood or phrasing of a musical performance; turn of phrase, a phrase or idiom; general look of a person's face, *esp.* as expressing his mood or character. **EXPRESSIONAL**, *adj.* pertaining to e. **EXPRESSIONLESS**, *adj.* without e., inexpressive. [L.].

EXPRESSIONISM [eks-pre'shn-izm], *n.* (*art*) that quality of some modern artists whereby they seek to avoid a realistic technique and to express their meaning symbolically, seeking to bring out the meaning by suggestion rather than by naturalistic representation. **EXPRESSIONIST**, *n.* one who practises expressionism. **EXPRESSIONISTIC** [eks-pre-shn-is'tik], *adj.* characterized by e.

EXPRESSIVE [eks-pre'siv], *adj.* serving to express; full of feeling and character (of the face, voice or of a work of art); vivid. **EXPRESSIVELY**, *adv.* in an e. fashion. **EXPRESSIVENESS**, *n.* quality of being e. [Fr.].

EXPRESSLY [eks-pres'li], *adv.* in direct, plain terms; unequivocally; intentionally.

EXPROPRIATE [eks-prō'pri-āt], *v.t.* to take (property) away from. **EXPROPRIATION** [eks-prō-pri-ā'shn], *n.* act of expropriating, depriving of property. [L.].

EXPULSION [eks-pul'shn], *n.* act of expelling; state of being expelled; banishment; dismissal. [L.].

EXPULSIVE [eks-pul'siv], *adj.* tending or serving to expel. [Fr.].

EXPUNCTION [eks-pungk'shn], *n.* act of expunging; condition of being expunged. [L.].

EXPUNGE [eks-punj'], *v.t.* to wipe out, erase. [L.].

EXPURGATE [eks'per-gāt], *v.t.* to purify; remove offensive matter from a book. **EXPURGATION** [eks-per-gā'shn], *n.* action of expurgating. **EXPURGATOR**, *n.* person who expurgates. **EXPURGATORIAL** [eks-per-ga-taw'ri-al], *adj.* concerned with expurgation, pertaining to an expurgator. **EXPURGATORY** [eks-pur'ga-te-ri], *adj.* pertaining to expurgation; tending to e. [L.].

EXQUISITE (1) [eks'kwi-zit], *adj.* choice; refined, delicate; highly finished; excellent; of keen delicacy of discrimination; acutely felt. **EXQUISITE** (2), *n.* a dandy; precious person. **EXQUISITELY**, *adv.* in an e. fashion. [L.].

EXTANT [eks-tant', eks'tant], *adj.* still in existence. [L.].

EXTEMPORANEOUS [eks-tem-pe-rā'ni-ŏŏs], *adj.* without premeditation; extempore. **EXTEMPORANEOUSLY**, *adv.* in an e. manner. [LL.].

EXTEMPORARY [eks-tem'paw-ra-ri], *adj.* unpremeditated, without previous preparation. **EXTEMPORARILY**, *adv.* in an e. manner. **EXTEMPOR(AR)INESS**, *n.* e. condition.

EXTEMPORE [eks-tem'pe-ri], *adv.* without previous study or meditation; without notes; on the spur of the moment. [L.].

EXTEMPORIZE [eks-tem'pe-rīz], *v.i.* to do something without preparation.

EXTEND [eks-tend'], *v.t. and i.* to reach or stretch out; lengthen; make last longer; make larger, cause to have wider influence or to be more inclusive; (*fig.*) offer; be stretched out; be capable of stretching out; last, endure; (*reflex.*) strive hard. **EXTENDEDLY**, *adv.* in an extended fashion. **EXTENDER**, *n.* one who, or something which, extends. **EXTENDIBLE**, *adj.* able to be extended. [L.].

EXTENSIBLE [eks-ten'si-bl], *adj.* capable of being extended or enlarged. **EXTENSIBILITY** [eks-ten-si-bi'li-ti], *n.* quality of being e. [Fr.].

EXTENSILE [eks-ten'sīl], *adj.* able to be extended or stretched out.

EXTENSION [eks-ten'shn], *n.* act of extending; state of being extended; amount extended; branch or addition; continuation in time; widening; enlargement; continuation; (*phys.*) that property of a body by which it occupies a portion of space in each of its three dimensions—length, breadth and thickness; (*comm.*) written engagement on the part of creditors allowing a debtor further time for the payment of his debts; (*surg.*) operation of straightening a limb which has been bent or dislocated; (*log.*) range of the application of a term in contrast to its comprehension; **university e.**, system which provides university teaching to adult students not actually members of a university. EXTENSIONAL, *adj.* having e. [L.].

EXTENSIVE [eks-ten'siv], *adj.* wide in extent, comprehensive. EXTENSIVELY, *adv.* to a wide extent; comprehensively. EXTENSIVENESS, *n.* e. character; comprehensiveness. [L.].

EXTENSOR [eks-ten'ser], *n.* (*anat.*) muscle whose function is to extend or straighten any part of the body. [LL.].

EXTENT [eks-tent'], *n.* space over which, or degree to which, anything is extended; scope; limit; (*leg.*) inventory of lands; writ of execution against the body, lands and goods of a debtor. [AFr.].

EXTENUATE [eks-te'nyōō-āt], *v.t. and i.* to make thin or tenuous, diminish; excuse or minimize a fault. EXTENUATING, *adj.* that extenuates. EXTENUATINGLY, *adv.* in an extenuating way. EXTENUATOR, *n.* one who extenuates. EXTENUATORY, *adj.* having the function of extenuating. [L.].

EXTENUATION [eks-te-nyōō-ā'shn], *n.* act of extenuating; an excuse. [L.].

EXTERIOR (1) [eks-tēer'i-er], *adj.* external; on the outside; extrinsic. EXTERIOR (2), *n.* the outside, *esp.* of a building; picture of the outside of a building. EXTERIORITY [eks-tēer-i-o'ri-ti], *n.* outwardness, superficies. EXTERIORLY, *adv.* outwardly, superficially. [L.].

EXTERMINATE [eks-tur'mi-nāt], *v.t.* to destroy completely; extirpate. EXTERMINATOR, *n.* one who, or that which, exterminates. EXTERMINATORY, *adj.* tending to e. [L.].

EXTERMINATION [eks-ter-mi-nā'shn], *n.* act of exterminating; total destruction. [L.].

EXTERNAL (1) [eks-tur'nal], *adj.* outward; visible; connected with foreign nations; (*fig.*) inessential, incidental; **e. evidence**, evidence obtained from independent sources; **e. nature**, the outward universe as distinct from man. EXTERNAL (2), *n.* some e. person or thing, a non-resident; (*pl.*) outward appearance; (*fig.*) inessential aspects. EXTERNALITY [eks-ter-na'li-ti], *n.* state or quality of being e. EXTERNALLY, *adv.* in an e. manner; from the outside; outwardly. [L.].

EXTERNALIZE [eks-tur'na-līz], *v.t.* to embody in outward form, attribute external existence to. EXTERNALIZATION [eks-ter-na-li-zā'shn], *n.* act or process of embodying in outward form.

EXTERRITORIAL [eks-te-ri-taw'ri-al], *adj.* outside the jurisdiction of the country; extraterritorial.

EXTINCT [eks-tingkt'], *adj.* quenched, extinguished, no longer alive or active; of animal species etc., having died out, no longer existing and propagating. [L.].

EXTINCTION [eks-tingk'shn], *n.* act of extinguishing; state of being extinct. [L.].

EXTINGUISH [eks-ting'gwish], *v.t.* to put out, quench, destroy, suppress; obscure by superior splendour, eclipse; reduce to silence. EXTINGUISHABLE, *adj.* capable of being extinguished. EXTINGUISHMENT †, *n.* extinction. [L.].

EXTINGUISHER [eks-ting'gwi-sher], *n.* that which extinguishes; hollow conical cap with which to put out the light of a candle; apparatus for putting out fires.

EXTIRPATE [eks'ter-pāt], *v.t.* to root out, destroy; (*surg.*) remove completely. EXTIRPABLE [eks-tur'pa-bl], *adj.* capable of being extirpated. EXTIRPATOR, *n.* one who extirpates. [L.].

EXTIRPATION [eks-ter-pā'shn], *n.* act of extirpating, rooting out or completely destroying. [L.].

EXTOL [eks-tōl'], *v.t.* to praise highly, magnify, laud. EXTOLLER, *n.* one who extols. [L.].

EXTORT [eks-tawt'], *v.t.* to force from a person or thing; obtain by undue pressure. [L.].

EXTORTION [eks-taw'shn], *n.* oppressive or illegal exaction; that which is so exacted. EXTORTIONARY, *adj.* pertaining to, or exercising, e. EXTORTIONER, *n.* one who practises e. [L.].

EXTORTIONATE [eks-taw'shn-at], *adj.* characterized by extortion; exorbitant.

EXTRA- (1) [eks'tra], *pref.* outside of, beyond the usual, in excess. [L.].

EXTRA (2), *n. and adj.* in addition; more than;

something added on beyond the agreed upon, or customary, charge; perquisite; supernumerary; (*cricket*) run scored otherwise than by a stroke of the bat; special issue of a newspaper. EXTRA (3), *adj.* in addition; more than normal. EXTRA (4), *adv.* additionally, especially, particularly.

EXTRACT (1) [eks-trakt'], *v.t.* to draw out by force or persuasion; take out or select a part from. EXTRACT (2) [eks'trakt], *n.* something which is extracted; passage taken from a book; (*chem.*) solution containing one or more substances removed from a mixture by means of a solvent. EXTRACTABLE, *adj.* that may be extracted; suitable for quotation or extracting. [L.].

EXTRACTION [eks-trak'shn], *n.* act or process of extracting, *esp.* the pulling of a tooth; an extract; racial or family descent; the eliciting of information. [MedL.].

EXTRACTIVE [eks-trak'tiv], *adj.* capable of being extracted; of the nature of an extract; concerned with obtaining natural productions. [L.].

EXTRACTOR [eks-trak'ter], *n.* person who, or that which, extracts; (*surg.*) forceps, or instrument for extracting.

EXTRADITE [eks'tra-dīt], *v.t.* to surrender someone to a foreign country in conformity with the terms of an extradition treaty. EXTRADITABLE, *adj.* liable to extradition. [Back-formation from *next*].

EXTRADITION [eks-tra-di'shn], *n.* surrender, by one government to another, of fugitives from justice. [Fr.].

EXTRAJUDICIAL [eks-tra-jōō-di'shal], *adj.* (*leg.*) outside the ordinary course of legal procedure. EXTRAJUDICIALLY, *adv.* in an e. manner.

EXTRAMUNDANE [eks-tra-mun'dān], *adj.* beyond the bounds of this world; (*fig.*) remote.

EXTRAMURAL [eks-tra-myōō'ral], *adj.* outside the walls of a city; relating to the external teaching of a university.

EXTRANEOUS [eks-trā'ni-ŏŏs], *adj.* foreign; not connected with, external to; not essential; not germane, unrelated. EXTRANEOUSLY, *adv.* in an e. manner. EXTRANEOUSNESS, *n.* state or quality of being e. [L.].

EXTRA-OFFICIAL [eks-tra-o-fi'shal], *adj.* outside the limits of official duty.

EXTRAORDINARY [eks-tra-aw'di-na-ri], *adj.* out of the ordinary; unusual; outstanding, brilliant; strange; rare; of a person employed on special service, as **ambassador e.** EXTRAORDINARILY, *adv.* in an e. manner. [L.].

EXTRA-PAROCHIAL [eks-tra-pa-rō'ki-al], *adj.* outside the limits of a parish.

EXTRAPHYSICAL [eks-tra-fi'zi-kal], *adj.* outside the province of physics.

EXTRAPOLATION [eks-tra-po-lā'shn], *n.* (*math.*) the calculation, from the known terms in a series, of those which are unknown.

EXTRA-PROFESSIONAL [eks-tra-pro-fe'shn-al], *adj.* foreign to a profession; outside the ordinary limits of professional duty.

EXTRA-PROVINCIAL [eks-tra-pro-vin'shal], *adj.* outside the limits of a province.

EXTRA-SPECIAL [eks-tra-spe'shal], *adj.* (*coll.*) exceptionally good.

EXTRATERRITORIAL [eks-tra-te-ri-taw'ri-al], *adj.* outside a local jurisdiction; **e. waters**, the open sea beyond the territorial limit. EXTRATERRITORIALITY [eks-tra-te-ri-taw-ri-a'li-ti], *n.* state of being outside any local jurisdiction; immunity from a country's laws.

EXTRAVAGANCE, EXTRAVAGANCY [eks-tra'va-gans(-i)], *n.* irregularity; excess; lavish wastefulness of one's money or means; outlandishness in behaviour or opinions. [Fr.].

EXTRAVAGANT [eks-tra'va-gant], *adj.* exceeding due limits; excessive, immoderate; wasteful of one's resources; exaggerated. EXTRAVAGANTLY, *adv.* in an e. manner. [Fr.].

EXTRAVAGANZA [eks-tra-va-gan'zah], *n.* (*mus.*) musical composition distinguished by its absurdity and irregularity; any wild, capricious flight of fancy. [It.].

EXTRAVASATE [eks-tra'va-sāt], *v.t.* (*med.*) to let or force out of the proper vessels. EXTRAVASATION [eks-tra-va-sā'shn], *n.* (*med.*) action of letting out of its proper vessel any fluid of the body, *esp.* the blood, through rupture or injury. [L.].

EXTRAVERT, see EXTROVERT.

EXTREME (1) [eks-trēm'], *adj.* outermost, furthest off, most pressing; worst or best that can exist or be

---

The accent ′ after a syllable = stress (u-pon′). The mark ⁻ over a vowel = length (ā in made; ō in bone).

supposed; very highest; having uncompromising opinions; drastic; **the e. penalty**, capital punishment; **E. Unction**, unction administered to one at the point of death. EXTREME (2), n. the furthest limit, extremity, utmost possible degree; (*math.*) first or last terms of a proportion; (*log.*) first and last terms of a syllogism; **to go to extremes**, to act immoderately. EXTREMELY, adv. in an e. degree; very. EXTREMENESS, n. violent nature. EXTREMISM, n. the holding of e. opinions. [L.].

EXTREMIST [eks-trē'mist], adj. and n. (characteristic of) a supporter of extreme doctrines or action; revolutionist.

EXTREMITY [eks-tre'mi-ti], n. the utmost point or bound; the utmost or highest degree; extreme or utmost distress; the end; (*pl.*) the hands and feet. [Fr.].

EXTRICATE [eks'tri-kāt], v.t. to unravel; disentangle; release; (*chem.*) liberate. EXTRICATION [eks-tri-kā'shn], n. action of extricating, disentangling. [L.].

EXTRINSIC [eks-trin'sik], adj. external, outward, not contained in, or belonging to, a body; foreign; inessential. EXTRINSICALITY [eks-trin-si-ka'li-ti], n. condition of being e. EXTRINSICALLY, adv. in an e. fashion.

EXTROVERSION [eks-tro-vur'shn], n. a turning or being turned outwards; (*path.*) malformation of the bladder; (*psych.*) state of mind not prone to introspection.

EXTROVERT, EXTRAVERT [eks'tro-vert], n. (*psych.*) person mentally unaccustomed to turning the thoughts inwards upon himself, one averse to introspection. [L.].

EXTRUDE [eks-trōōd'], v.t. to thrust, press or force out; expel; shape (metal) by forcing through dies. [L.].

EXTRUSION [eks-trōō'zhn], n. action of extruding. [L.].

EXUBERANCE, EXUBERANCY [eg-zyōō'be-rans(-i)], n. rich, luxuriant growth; overflowing fulness of feeling or expression; superabundance of vitality. [L.].

EXUBERANT [eg-zyōō'be-rant], adj. abundant, over-abundant, overflowing. EXUBERANTLY, adv. in an e. manner. [L.].

EXUDE [eg-zyōōd'], v.t. to discharge slowly; v.i. to ooze out; pass off through the pores as sweat or through corresponding organs or incisions in animals and plants. EXUDATION [eks-yōō-dā'shn], n. action of exuding fluid matter through pores; matter exuded. [L.].

EXULT [eg-zult'], v.i. to rejoice greatly or excessively; triumph. EXULTINGLY, adv. in an exulting fashion. [L.].

EXULTANCE, EXULTANCY [eg-zul'tans(-i)], n. exultant condition; rapture, triumph. [LL.].

EXULTANT [eg-zul'tant], adj. rejoicing triumphantly. EXULTANTLY, adv. in an e. fashion. [L.].

EXULTATION [eg-zul-tā'shn], n. joy at success; intense delight; triumph. [L.].

EXUVIAE [eg-zyōō'vi-ē], n.(*pl.*) the cast-off skins, shells or coverings of animals. EXUVIAL, adj. of the nature of e. [L.].

EXUVIATE [eg-zyōō'vi-āt], v.i. to cast off, slough, shed. EXUVIATION [eg-zyōō-vi-ā'shn], n. act or process of exuviating or sloughing off. [L.].

EYALET [ī'a-let], n. administrative area in the Turkish Republic, presided over by a pasha; vilayet.

EYAS [ī'as], n. young hawk recently taken from the nest. [OFr.].

EYE (1) [ī], n. the organ of sight, the eyeball with its nerves; visible part of the eye; eyesight; power of observation; object thought to resemble an eye in form, as the hole in a needle, small catch on clothes for a hook etc.; **to keep one's e. on**, to watch; **to turn a blind e. to**, to ignore; **to open a person's eyes to something**, to make him aware of it; **to make eyes at**, to ogle; **to have an e. for**, to know how to judge; notice; **to do in the e.**, (*coll.*) to spoil; cheat; **all my e.**, (*coll.*) nonsense; **up to the eyes in it**, extremely busy; **with half an e.**, with slight effort, easily; **sheep's eyes**, amorous glances. EYE (2), v.t. to fix the eyes on; look fixedly at; regard narrowly. [OE.].

EYEBALL [ī'bawl], n. the globular organ of sight.

EYE-BATH [ī'bahth], n. small glass vessel shaped to facilitate douching the eye.

EYE-BOLT [ī'bōlt], n. (*naut.*) bar of iron, having an eye at one end, formed to be screwed into the deck or sides of a ship etc. for fastening ropes.

EYEBRIGHT [ī'brīt], n. (*bot.*) popular name for the wild flower, *Euphrasia officinalis*.

EYEBROW [ī'brow], n. hairy arch which overhangs the eye. EYEBROW-PENCIL, cosmetic pencil for darkening the eyebrows.

EYE-GLASS [ī'glahs], n. lens to assist the sight, the glass next to the eye in an optical instrument; (*pl.*) pair of lenses arranged to clip upon the bridge of the nose.

EYELASH [ī'lash], n. hair fringing the eyelid; single hair of the fringe.

EYELET [ī'let], n. eyelet-hole. [OFr.].

EYELET-HOLE [ī'let-hōl], n. small hole or perforation to receive a lace or small rope or cord; metal ring which lines this hole.

EYELID [ī'lid], n. upper or lower movable cover of skin which serves as a protection to the front of the eyeball.

EYE-OPENER [ī'ō-pe-ner], n. (*coll.*) something calculated to cause extreme surprise; an early drink.

EYEPIECE [ī'pēs], n. in a telescope or microscope, the lens or combination of lenses with which the image is seen and magnified.

EYESHOT [ī'shot], n. range of vision.

EYESIGHT [ī'sīt], n. the sight of the eye; vision; range of vision.

EYESORE [ī'saw(r)], n. anything ugly or offensive to the eye.

EYE-SPLICE [ī'splīs], n. (*naut.*) eye or circle formed by splicing the end of a rope into itself.

EYE-TOOTH [ī'tōōth], n. (*anat.*) one of the upper canine teeth; **to cut one's eye-teeth**, to grow up; **to draw (someone's) eye-teeth**, to take the conceit out of (someone).

EYE-WASH [ī'wosh], n. lotion for bathing the eyes; (*coll.*) humbug, deception, fraudulent pretences.

EYE-WITNESS [ī'wit-nes], n. one who sees a thing happen.

EYOT [ā'ot], n. small island in a river or lake. [OE.].

EYRE [āer], n. (*hist.*) circuit; court of itinerant justices. [OFr.].

EYRIE, see AERIE.

F

F [ef], sixth letter of the Latin, English and other alphabets.

FABIAN (1) [fā'bi-an], adj. wearing out an enemy by a policy of caution and waiting; **F. Society**, society of socialists employing such a policy for the propagation of socialism. FABIAN (2), n. member of the F. Society.

FABLE (1) [fā'bl], n. a story of a supernatural or improbable character, *esp.* a short story in which animals are represented as speaking and acting like human beings in order to convey a moral; myth, legend; idle tale; lie; anything which is merely supposed to exist; plot of a play or epic poem.

FABLE (2), v.i. (*poet.*) to tell fictitious stories. FABLED, adj. celebrated in fables, legendary. [L.].

FABRIC [fab'rik], n. structure, frame; texture, tissue; woven material; edifice, building. [L.].

FABRICATE [fab'ri-kāt], v.t. to construct, manufacture; forge; state falsely, invent (an account or description). FABRICATOR, n. person who fabricates. [L.].

FABRICATION [fab-ri-kā'shn], n. act or process of fabricating; manufacture; forgery; that which is fabricated; a falsehood. [L.].

FABULOUS [fab'yōō-loŏs], adj. fictitious, legendary; unreal, incredible, exaggerated; celebrated in fable.

FABULOUSLY, *adv.* in a f. way. FABULOUSNESS, *n.* quality of being f. [L.].

FACADE, façade [fa-sahd'], *n.* front view of a building, face of a building looking out into the street or any open space. [Fr.].

FACE (1) [fās], *n.* the front of the head; visage; look, expression; front of anything; surface which presents itself to the view; plane surface of a solid; outward aspect; dial of a watch or clock; (*coll.*) coolness, effrontery; **f. to f.**, confronted; **in f. of**, opposite to; in spite of; **to fly in the f. of**, to flout openly; **to show one's f.**, to make an appearance; **to one's f.**, in one's hearing; **to look in the f.**, to confront squarely; **to set one's f. against**, to oppose; **to make, pull, a f.**, to distort the features, grimace; **to wear, pull, a long f.**, to look gloomy or discontented; **to have (the) f. to**, to be pert or shameless enough to; **to lose f.**, to be openly shamed, suffer a loss in prestige; **to save (one's) f.**, to avoid being openly shamed, preserve one's prestige; **on the f. of it**, to judge by outward appearances; **f. value**, surface value, nominal value. FACE (2), *v.t.* to meet, confront firmly or defiantly; oppose; stand with the face or front surface towards; not be dismayed by; cover the outer surface of; attach facings to; dress the surface of; *v.i.* to be turned; **to f. out**, to carry through boldly in the face of difficulty; meet unashamedly, brave unblushingly; **to f. up to**, to realize frankly (disagreeable facts). [Fr. from LL.].

FACE-ACHE [fās'āk], *n.* neuralgia; (*slang*) humorously abusive appellation.

FACE-CLOTH [fās'kloth], *n.* a cloth laid upon the face of a corpse; a cloth used for washing the face; woollen cloth with a smooth surface.

FACE-CREAM [fās'krēm], *n.* a greasy preparation for application to the face, for the purpose of preserving or improving the skin.

FACED [fāst], *adj.* having a face; having the surface treated or covered.

FACE-LIFTING [fās'lif-ting], *n.* operation carried out by beauty specialists to tighten the skin, smooth out wrinkles etc.

FACE-MASSAGE [fās'ma-sahzh], *n.* massage of the face intended to enhance beauty.

FACER [fā'ser], *n.* (*coll.*) a sharp blow in the face; serious difficulty; ticklish problem; a card facing the wrong way in a pack of playing-cards.

FACET [fa'set], *n.* one of the small surfaces of a cut gem; one side of any many-sided object. FACETED, *adj.* with facets. [Fr.].

FACETIOUS [fa-sē'shŏŏs], *adj.* waggish, addicted to pleasantries. FACETIOUSLY, *adv.* in a f. manner. FACETIOUSNESS, *n.* condition of being f. [L.].

FACIA, see FASCIA.

FACIAL (1) [fā'shal], *adj.* pertaining to the face; **f. angle**, (*anthrop.*) the angle formed by a line drawn from the nostril to the forehead. FACIAL (2), *n.* a treatment of face-massage. FACIALLY, *adv.* in a f. way.

FACIES [fā'shi-ēz], *n.* outer appearance; (*anat.*) face; (*geol.*) appearance, general aspect of any period, among rocks and their contents. [L.].

FACILE [fa'sīl, fa'sil], *adj.* easily performed or won; fluent, ready; glib; compliant, yielding. FACILENESS, *n.* quality of being f. [L.].

FACILITATE [fa-si'li-tāt], *v.t.* to make easy, or less difficult; help forward. FACILITATION [fa-si-li-tā'-shn], *n.* process of facilitating. [Fr.].

FACILITY [fa-si'li-ti], *n.* ease, absence of difficulty; readiness, aptitude, fluency, dexterity; opportunity; (*pl.*) means by which anything is made easier; convenient opportunities. [L.].

FACING [fā'sing], *n.* outer layer or covering of a different material; (*pl.*) cuffs and collar of a soldier's uniform, coloured differently from the rest; trimmings of a garment; turning movements in military drill; **to put a soldier through his facings**, to test his smartness in drill.

FACSIMILE (1) [fak-si'mi-li], *n.* a perfectly accurate reproduction, as of handwriting. FACSIMILE (2), *v.t.* to make a f. of. [L.].

FACT [fakt], *n.* something performed, or which has occurred, deed, act, event; something certainly known to be true, to exist or to have occurred; something assumed as a basis for inferences, or brought forward as truth; **a matter of f.**, something pertaining to the sphere of f., not conjecture or inference; **as a matter of f., in f., in point of f.**, in reality, actually; **the f. of the matter**, the truth about the matter. [L.].

FACTION [fak'shn], *n.* a turbulent minority; troublesome clique in a party; partisan strife. FACTIONAL, *adj.* of or pertaining to a f. or factions. FACTIONARY, FACTIONIST, *n.* one belonging to a f. [L.].

FACTIOUS [fak'shŏŏs], *adj.* connected with a faction; tending to promote dissension. FACTIOUSLY, *adv.* in a f. way. FACTIOUSNESS, *n.* quality of being f.; behaviour in the spirit of faction. [L.].

FACTITIOUS [fak-ti'shŏŏs], *adj.* produced by art as distinct from nature; artificial, sham. FACTITIOUSLY, *adv.* artificially, in a f. way. FACTITIOUSNESS, *n.* state of being f. [L.].

FACTITIVE [fak'ti-tiv], *adj.* **f. verb**, (*gram.*) verb which expresses the act of changing the character of, or imparting a specific character to, the object. [L.].

FACTOR [fak'ter], *n.* a proxy or representative; middleman; any circumstance, influence etc. which helps towards a certain result; (*arith.*) one of two numbers which when multiplied together produce a third, the product. FACTORIAL [fak-taw'ri-al], *adj.* (*math.*) pertaining to factors. FACTORSHIP, *n.* business or office of a f. [L.].

FACTORY [fak'te-ri], *n.* building or group of buildings where commodities are manufactured; trading station in a foreign country; **F. Acts**, acts regulating working conditions. [L.].

FACTOTUM [fak-tō'tum], *n.* man of all work; servant discharging all sorts of duties. [L.].

FACTUAL [fak'tyŏŏ-al], *adj.* relating to, concerned with facts; real. FACTUALLY, *adv.* in a f. way.

FACULTY [fa'kul-ti], *n.* special aptitude; proficiency; natural function; one of the main divisions of knowledge comprised in the studies at a university; the body of teachers of one such division; (*leg.*) dispensation, authorization by law; (*eccles.*) dispensation to do something accorded by the chancellor of a diocese; **the f.**, (*coll.*) the medical profession. [L.].

FAD [fad], *n.* a whim; craze; pet notion. FADDIST, *n.* person given to fads. [Unkn.].

FADDISH [fa'dish], *adj.* inclined to be faddy.

FADDY [fa'di], *adj.* given to fads; fussy; overfastidious. FADDINESS, *n.* quality of being f.

FADE [fād], *v.t.* to cause to lose its colour; (*radio*) diminish the volume in transmission, cause one item to disappear against another; **to f. in, out**, (*cinema and television*) cause a picture to become gradually clearer, less clear; (*radio*) increase, decrease, volume gradually; *v.i.* to droop, lose youth, bloom or vigour; wane; become paler or dimmer in colour, or more indistinct; become fainter, die away gradually; become inaudible; (*cinema and television*) of a picture, to become gradually clearer or less distinct; (*radio*) of signals, to vary and lose strength, *esp.* periodically. [OFr.].

FADELESS [fād'les], *adj.* unfading; not liable to fade.

FADING [fā'ding], *n.* withering, drooping; loss of freshness or colour; (*radio*) decrease in volume. FADINGLY, *adv.* in a f. way.

FAECAL, FECAL [fē'kal], *adj.* composed of dregs or sediment; excremental. [L.].

FAECES, FECES [fē'sēz], *n.*(*pl.*) waste matter, excrement; sediment after infusion or distillation. [L.].

FAERIE (1) [fāer'i], *n.* enchantment; fairyland. FAERIE (2), *adj.* of or relating to the fairies or fairyland; fanciful, imaginary. [ME.].

FAG [fag] (*pres.pt.* **fagging**, *pret. and p.pt.* **fagged**) [fag], *v.t. and i.* to labour painfully; fatigue, exhaust; (of a senior boy at a public school) employ a junior as a fag; (of a junior) perform certain tasks for a senior; **to f. out**, (*cricket*) to field. FAG (2), *n.* painful toil; trying, tedious work; fatigue, weariness; junior boy at a public school who performs certain services for a senior; (*slang*) cigarette. FAGGING, *n.* performance of certain duties for a senior by a junior at a public school. [Unkn.].

FAG-END [fag'end], *n.* tedious conclusion; cigarette-end.

FAGGOT (1) [fa'got], *n.* bundle of sticks bound together; bundle of metal rods; savoury rissole of chopped and seasoned liver. FAGGOT (2), *v.t. and i.* to make faggots (of). [Fr.].

FAGGOT-VOTE [fa'got-vōt], *n.* (*hist.*) vote formerly obtained by temporarily transferring sufficient property to a person otherwise not qualified to vote.

FAHRENHEIT (1) [fah'ren-hīt], *n.* thermometer with a freezing point at 32 deg. and boiling point at 212 deg. FAHRENHEIT (2), *adj.* reckoned or calibrated according to the system invented by Fahrenheit. [German inventor].

FAIENCE, FAYENCE [fah-yah(ng)s'], *n.* kind of

glazed porcelain embellished with painted designs. [Fr. form of Faenza, Italian town where first manufactured].

FAIL (1) [fāl], *v.t.* to disappoint, let down; desert; cause to fail in an examination, declare unsuccessful; *v.i.* to be inadequate, run short; grow feeble, lose strength; be wanting, lack, come short; neglect; omit; be unsuccessful, *esp.* in an examination; become insolvent. FAIL (2), *n. (rare)* failure; **without f.,** for certain, quite definitely. [OFr.].

FAILING (1) [fā'ling], *n.* defect, shortcoming, imperfection, weakness. FAILING (2), *prep.* in the lack of. without. FAILINGLY, *adv.* through or by f.

FAILLE [fah'ĕ], *n.* a ribbed Flemish silk. [Fr.].

FAILURE [fā'lyŏŏr], *n.* a failing; deficiency; cessation of supply; omission; non-performance; decay; lack of success; person who fails; insolvency.

FAIN (1)†[fān], *adj.* willing; **f. to,** obliged to, having no alternative but to. FAIN (2) †, *adv.* gladly, willingly. [OE.].

FAIN (3), **FAINS** [fān(z)], *v.i.* school children's formula, claiming exemption from some unwelcome task for those who say it first, as **fains I batting first.** [Unkn.].

FAINT (1) [fānt], *adj.* feeble, nervous, unenterprising; giddy, dizzy, about to swoon; lacking in vividness, dull, insipid; vague, indistinct; **ruled f.,** term applied to paper ruled with f. lines. FAINT (2), *v.i.* to feel sick, giddy or weak; become weak; fall unconscious in a swoon. FAINT (3), *n.* swoon, fainting fit; **in a dead f.,** completely unconscious. [OFr.].

FAINT-HEARTED [fānt-hah'tid], *adj.* fearful, timid; discouraged; easily depressed or yielding to fear. FAINT-HEARTEDLY, *adv.* in a f. way. FAINT-HEARTEDNESS, *n.* quality of being f.

FAINTING [fān'ting], *n.* act of swooning, loss of consciousness.

FAINTISH [fān'tish], *adj.* somewhat faint.

FAINTLY [fānt'li], *adv.* in a faint way; slightly.

FAINTNESS [fānt'nes], *n.* condition of being faint.

FAIR (1) [fāer], *n.* a periodical gathering for sale of articles of various kinds, often accompanied by sideshows and other entertainments; **a day after the f.,** too late for some important occasion. [OFr. from L.].

FAIR (2), *adj.* lovely, beautiful; fresh, clean, clear; fine, dry, sunny; favourable, promising; just, equitable, unprejudiced; moderately good, not bad; light-coloured; having light-coloured hair or complexion; plausible, specious; **f. and square,** above board, without finesse; **a f. copy,** a clean and perfect copy transcribed from a rough one; **the f. sex,** women; **f. game,** a legitimate object of attack; **to be in a f. way to,** to be likely to; **set f.,** of a barometer, indicating a spell of good weather; *(fig.)* propitious. FAIR (3), *n. (poet., archaic)* women; a woman. FAIR (4), *adv.* justly, honestly; courteously; directly; **to bid f. to,** to appear likely to. [OE.].

FAIR-FACED [fāer-fāst'], *adj.* with a fair face; fairspoken with intent to deceive.

FAIRILY [fāer'i-li], *adv.* in a fairy-like fashion.

FAIRING (1) [fāer'ing], *n.* gift bought at a fair. [FAIR (1)].

FAIRING (2), *n.* process of making the surface of a ship or aeroplane smooth or stream-lined; something added to the structure of an aeroplane or motor-car body in order to achieve a stream-lined surface. [FAIR (2)].

FAIRISH [fāer'ish], *adj.* reasonably good; moderately fair.

FAIR ISLE [fāer'īl], *adj.* denoting knitted articles of characteristic pattern made in *Fair Isle* in the Shetlands.

FAIRLY [fāer'li], *adv.* in a fair manner; clearly; nearly, almost; moderately, reasonably.

FAIR-MINDED [fāer-mīn'did], *adj.* unbiased, impartial.

FAIRNESS [fāer'nes], *n.* quality of being fair; justice; impartiality.

FAIR-SPOKEN [fāer-spō'ken], *adj.* using fair words; plausible, specious.

FAIRWAY [fāer'wā], *n.* the navigable channel of a river; smooth stretch of trimmed turf between rough and hazards, from green to green, on a golf course.

FAIRWEATHER [fāer'we-THer], *adj.* only fitted or use for easy circumstances, not to be relied on in trouble or difficulty.

FAIRY (1) [fāer'i], *n.* small supernatural being conceived to have a human form and to exercise magical powers. FAIRY (2), *adj.* pertaining to fairies or fairyland; fairy-like, dainty, delicate, small; **f. cycle,**

small children's bicycle; **f. lights,** see FAIRY-LAMP

FAIRYISM [fāer'i-izm], *n.* belief in fairies.

FAIRY-LAMP [fāer'i-lamp], *n.* small coloured lamp used for illuminations.

FAIRYLAND [fāer'i-land], *n.* domain or abode of the fairies.

FAIRY-LIKE [fāer'i-līk], *adj.* after the manner of fairies; dainty, ethereal, resembling a fairy.

FAIRY-RINGS [fāer'i-ringz], *n.(pl.)* circles of darker green grass caused by fungi, but traditionally supposed to be caused by the dancing of the fairies.

FAIRY TALE [fāer'i-tāl], *n.* tale told about fairies; fib, preposterous story.

FAITH [fāth], *n.* confidence, trust; belief, *esp.* in religious doctrines; a system of religious belief; the accepting of divine truth without actual proof; promise, undertaking; sincerity; loyalty; **Defender of the F.,** title conferred upon Henry VIII by the Pope and borne by sovereigns of England ever since; **in good f.,** sincerely, with honest intent; **bad f.,** deceit; **Punic f.,** treachery. [ME., ~ OFr.].

FAITHFUL [fāth'fool], *adj.* loyal, constant, keeping faith; reliable, accurate; not false or deceitful; **the f.,** true believers, *esp.* of Islam. FAITHFULLY, *adv.* in a f. way. FAITHFULNESS, *n.* condition of being f.

FAITH-HEALING [fāth'hē-ling], *n.* practice of attempting to cure sickness by faith rather than by medical aid.

FAITHLESS [fāth'les], *adj.* lacking faith; disloyal; not true to one's promise or vow; fickle. FAITHLESSLY, *adv.* in a f. way. FAITHLESSNESS, *n.* condition of being f.

FAKE (1) [fāk], *v.t.* to make a sham copy of, touch up so as to raise the apparent value of. FAKE (2), *n.* sham, imitation, piece of faking, cooked report. FAKER, *n.* one who fakes; a cheat. [Uncert.].

FAKIR [fa-kēer'], *n.* Hindu or Mohammedan ascetic beggar, looked upon as a very holy man. [Arab.].

FALANGE [fa-lahn'khe], *n.* the Spanish Fascist party. FALANGIST (1), *n.* member of the F. FALANGIST (2), *adj.* of or pertaining to the F. or the Falangists.

FALCON [fawl'kon], *n.* bird of prey, allied to the hawk, formerly trained and much used for hunting game. [OFr.].

FALCONER [fawl'ko-ner], *n.* one who breeds and trains falcons; one who hunts with falcons.

FALCONET [fawl'ko-net], *n.* a pygmy falcon.

FALCON-GENTLE [fawl-kon-jen'tl], *n.* female of the goshawk.

FALCONRY [fawl'kon-ri], *n.* art of training falcons; sport of hunting with falcons.

FALDSTOOL [fawld'stool], *n.* folding-stool like a camp-stool; armless chair used by a bishop, when not in his own cathedral; kneeling-stool; small desk at which litany is read. [MedL.].

FALL (1) [*pret.* fell, *p.pt.* fallen] [fawl], *v.i.* to drop, descend unhindered from a high to a low level; collapse, come down; lose high office; (of lambs) be born; (of the face) express dismay; sink to a lower level, diminish in value; be killed in battle; sin, yield to temptation, (of women) lose chastity; hang down; abate, grow milder; come by chance, alight upon; pass into a specified condition, become; occur; be uttered; **to f. away,** to withdraw (friendship, support etc.), desert; decay, disappear; **to f. back,** to retreat; **to f. back upon,** to withdraw, have recourse to; **to f. flat,** to fail to produce the desired effect, fail to evoke laughter; **to f. foul of,** *(naut.)* to collide with; quarrel with, get on the wrong side of; **to f. for,** to be captivated, attracted by; fall in love with; be deceived by; **to f. in,** to collapse inwards, give way; come to an end, lapse; *(milit.)* take up correct position in the ranks, get into line; **to f. in with,** to come across by chance; acquiesce in, comply with; **to f. off,** to diminish, grow less in quantity or quality; *(naut.)* of a ship, not to answer to the helm; **to f. on,** to attack; **to f. out,** to happen, turn out; disagree, quarrel; *(milit.)* leave one's position in the ranks; **to f. short,** to be insufficient, run out; **to f. to,** to begin eating; **to f. through,** to come to naught. FALL (2), *n.* act of falling, drop; quantity of rain etc. that falls; surrender; a succumbing to temptation; a lessening in values, drop in prices; waterfall or cataract of water; wrestling match; throw in wrestling; autumn; **the F., the F. of man,** the sin of Adam; **to try a f. with,** *(fig.)* to pit oneself against. [OE.].

FALLACIOUS [fa-lā'shŏŏs], *adj.* founded on a fallacy; deceptive and misleading; producing disappointment; false; compounded of fallacies.

FALLACIOUSLY, *adv.* in a f. way. FALLACIOUSNESS, *n.* condition of being f.

FALLACY [fal'la-si], *n.* deceptive appearance; sophism; misleading argument which sounds plausible. [L.].

FAL-LALS [fal'lalz], *n.(pl.)* showy trifles; gewgaws. [Unkn.].

FALLEN [faw'len], *adj.* abandoned; degraded; *(pl.)* those killed in battle.

FALLIBLE [fa'li-bl], *adj.* inclined, liable to err; liable to deceive, unreliable. FALLIBLY, *adv.* in a f. way. [LL.].

FALLIBILITY [fa-li-bi'li-ti], *n.* quality of being fallible.

FALLOPIAN [fa-lō'pi-an], *adj.* pertaining to, discovered by, Fallopio; **F. tubes,** the oviducts of mammals. [*Fallopio,* Italian anatomist].

FALLOW (1) [fa'lō], *n. and adj.* (land) ploughed and harrowed but left uncropped for a season; *(fig.)* of the mind, uncultivated, untrained; **to lie f.,** to remain uncultivated. FALLOW (2), *v.t.* to plough and harrow land without cropping it. FALLOWNESS, *n.* state of lying untilled or f. [ME.].

FALLOW (3), *adj.* brownish-yellow, dun. [OE.].

FALLOW DEER [fa-lō-dēer'], *n.* species of deer, smaller than the red deer, of a yellowish-brown colour.

FALSE (1) [fawls], *adj.* not true; wrong, incorrect, mistaken; deceitful, lying, treacherous, unfaithful, disloyal, misleading, sham, spurious, artificial; **f. quantity,** an inaccurate vowel-length; **f. position,** an awkward position which may lead to misunderstanding, or necessitate action against one's principles; **f. pretences,** misrepresentations made with intent to deceive. FALSE (2), *adv.* **to play someone f.,** to betray, deceive, let down. [L.].

FALSE-HEARTED [fawls-hah'tid], *adj.* shallow, insincere, perfidious. FALSE-HEARTEDNESS, *n.* insincerity; treachery.

FALSEHOOD [fawls'hŏŏd], *n.* an untruth, lie.

FALSELY [fawls'li], *adv.* in a false way.

FALSENESS [fawls'nes], *n.* quality of being false.

FALSETTO (1) [fawl-se'tō], *n.* high male voice, resembling the female voice in pitch; forced shrill voice above the natural pitch. FALSETTO (2), *adj.* of the quality of f., shrill, forced, squeaky. [It.].

FALSIFICATION [fawl-si-fi-kā'shn], *n.* act or process of falsifying; condition of being falsified.

FALSIFY [fawl'si-fi], *v.t.* to give a false impression of or appearance to, misrepresent, distort; prove to be false; disappoint; alter fraudulently, tamper with. FALSIFIABLE, *adj.* that can be falsified. FALSIFIER, *n.* one who falsifies. [LL.].

FALSITY [fawl'si-ti], *n.* condition of being false; a false assertion.

FALTER [fawl'ter], *v.i.* to be unsteady, stumble, totter, move uncertainly and with hesitation; speak hesitantly, stammer, speak in a broken voice; hesitate, waver, lose confidence. FALTERING, *adj.* hesitating; speaking with an uncertain trembling utterance. FALTERINGLY, *adv.* in a faltering way. [ME.].

FAME [fām], *n.* rumour, report; good repute; reputation; renown. FAMED, *adj.* famous, renowned. [L.].

FAMILIAR (1) [fa-mi'li-ah(r)], *adj.* relating to the family, private, domestic, intimate; well known; common, usual; well versed in, conversant; impudent, presumptuous, over-cordial; **f. spirit,** demon supposed to attend on a witch, magician etc. FAMILIAR (2), *n.* an official in a Pope's or Roman Catholic bishop's household; f. spirit. FAMILIARLY, *adv.* in a f. way. [L.].

FAMILIARITY [fa-mi-li-a'ri-ti], *n.* close acquaintance, intimacy; accurate knowledge; intimate gesture, caress; unceremoniousness, informality; impudence, presumption. [L.].

FAMILIARIZE [fa-mi'li-a-rīz], *v.t.* to make familiar. FAMILIARIZATION [fa-mi-li-a-rī-zā'shn], *n.* act or process of making or becoming familiar.

FAMILY [fa'mi-li], *n.* the members of a household, parents, children, domestics etc.; group of parents and children; set of relations; one's children or other relatives; the descendants of a common ancestor; group of people of the same stock; group of objects having features in common; in botany and zoology, a division of an order; **f. likeness,** a resemblance often observable between relations; **f. man,** man with a family or with domestic proclivities; **f. tree,** a pedigree; *(coll.)* **in the f. way,** pregnant. [L.].

FAMINE [fa'min], *n.* desperate scarcity of food in a district; shortage, dearth of food or water; starvation. [Fr.].

FAMISH [fa'mish], *v.t.* to reduce to extreme hunger; *v.i.* to be reduced to extreme hunger; **to be famished,** *(coll.)* to feel very hungry. FAMISHING, *adj.* starving; perishing by hunger; *(coll.)* very hungry. [~L.].

FAMOUS [fā'mŏŏs], *adj.* renowned, celebrated, usually in a good sense; *(coll.)* excellent, fine. FAMOUSLY, *adv.* in a f. manner; *(coll.)* very well. [L.].

FAN (1) [fan], *n.* machine for winnowing corn; device for cooling the face by winnowing the air; anything spread out like a fan; device which rotates to provide a current of air for the purpose of cooling or ventilation; small sail of a windmill for keeping the main sails across the wind; *(naut.)* propeller, screw. FAN (2) *(pres.pt.* FANNING, *pret. and p.pt.* FANNED), *v.t.* to move (the air) with a f.; winnow, blow the chaff away from; cool (oneself) by means of a f.; kindle a flame by making a current of air as with a f.; blow gently on; spread out in a shape like a f.; *v.i.* to spread out in the shape of a f.; **to f. the flame,** to increase the excitement, feed the anger or indignation etc. [OE. from L.].

FAN (3), *n. (slang)* ardent admirer or devotee; **f. mail,** admiring letters written by fans to a celebrity. [FAN(ATIC)].

FANATIC (1) [fa-na'tik], *adj.* affected with or prompted by excessive and exclusive zeal, *esp.* religious zeal; animated by or proceeding from fanaticism. FANATIC (2), *n.* person filled with extreme ardour for something; person filled with excessive and usually mistaken enthusiasm, *esp.* in religious matters. [L.].

FANATICAL [fa-na'ti-kal], *adj.* fanatic. FANATICALLY, *adv.* in a f. manner. FANATICALNESS, *n.* quality of being f.

FANATICISM [fa-na'ti-sizm], *n.* the violent zeal of a fanatic.

FANCIED [fan'sid], *adj.* imaginary; favoured, preferred.

FANCIER [fan'si-er], *n.* connoisseur, *esp.* of some kind of animal; one who has a fancy for something.

FANCIFUL [fan'si-fŏŏl], *adj.* dictated by fancy; fantastic; whimsical. FANCIFULLY, *adv.* in a f. way. FANCIFULNESS, *n.* quality or condition of being f.

FANCY (1) [fan'si], *n.* baseless belief, delusion; imagination, faculty of calling up mental images; supposition; whim, caprice; inclination, liking; **the f.,** those who have a f. for a certain pastime, *esp.* boxing enthusiasts. FANCY (2), *adj.* not plain or simple, decorative, elaborate; whimsical, extravagant; based on imagination rather than fact; **f. dog, pigeon** etc., dog etc., bred to special points of excellence; **f. dress,** fanciful or picturesque costume, often representing fictitious or historical characters, worn at parties, balls etc.; **f. man,** *(slang)* man who lives on the earnings of a prostitute. FANCY (3), *v.t.* to have a liking, predilection for; picture to oneself, imagine, think of; be inclined to think, suppose; breed, with attention to special points; *(coll.)* have a good opinion of, be conceited about. [Short form of FANTASY].

FANCY-FREE [fan'si-frē], *adj.* not in love, heart-whole.

FANCY-GOODS [fan'si-gŏŏdz], *n.(pl.)* decorative fabrics and oddments of various kinds, as ribbons, silks etc., as distinct from those plain and useful.

FANDANGO [fan-dang'gō], *n.* old Spanish national dance, in which the dancers beat time with castanets. [Span.].

FANE [fān], *n.* a temple. [L.].

FANFARE [fan'fāer], *n.* short flourish of trumpets; lively piece of music performed on hunting-horns. [Fr.].

FANFARONADE [fan-fa-ro-nād'], *n.* ostentation; bragging; vain boasting; bluster. [Fr.].

FANG (1) [fang], *n.* long sharp tooth, *esp.* the canine tooth in dogs and wolves; venom-tooth of a snake; the pronged root of a tooth. FANG (2), *v.t.* to run water into a pump to start it. FANGED, *adj.* having fangs. FANGLESS, *adj.* having no fangs. [OE.].

FANLIGHT [fan'līt], *n.* window shaped like an extended fan, over a door.

FANNER [fa'ner], *n.* winnowing-machine; one who, or that which, fans.

FANON [fa'non], *n.* embroidered scarf worn on the left arm of a Roman Catholic priest at Mass; church banner. [Fr. from L.].

FANTAIL [fan'tāl], *n.* pigeon with a fan-shaped tail; species of Australian bird; gas-burner which emits a fan-like flame. FANTAILED, *adj.* having a fan-shaped tail.

FANTASIA [fan-ta-zē'ah], *n.* free musical composition in which the composer follows his fancy; similarly free literary composition. [It.].

FANTASTIC(AL) [fan-tas'tik(-al)], *adj.* extravagant; whimsical; preposterous. FANTASTICALLY, *adv.* in a f. way. FANTASTICALNESS, *n.* quality of being f. [Gk.].

FANTASY, PHANTASY [fan'ta-zi], *n.* fancy; a dream; hallucination, illusion. [Gk.].

FANTEE [fan'tē], *n.* member of a West African negro tribe; language of this tribe; to go f., to live like a native.

FANTOCCINI [fan-to-chē'ni], *n.(pl.)* puppets, marionettes; a puppet show. [It.].

FAN-TRACERY [fan-trā'se-ri], *n.* (*arch.*) elaborate and delicate carved work on a vaulted roof in the form of a fan.

FAR (1) [fah(r)], *adv.* at a distance, a long way off; by a great interval, by much; to a great distance; f. and away, very much; f. be it from me, I would on no account; I have not the audacity, or inclination to; f. gone, advanced; in an advanced state of drunkenness, disease etc.; to go f., to do much, progress, be successful. FAR (2), *adj.* remote, distant, not close at hand; a f. cry, a long way; few and f. between, rare. [OE.].

FARAD [fa'rad], *n.* (*elect.*) the unit of electrical capacity. FARADAIC, FARADIC [fa-ra-dā'ik, fa-ra'dik], *adj.* susceptible to, or producing, induction; inductive. [*Faraday*, scientist].

FARADIZATION [fa-ra-di-zā'shn], *n.* method of treating disease by the application of electric currents. [*Faraday* who discovered it].

FARAWAY [fah'ra-wā], *adj.* remote; distant; (*fig.*) dreamy.

FARCE [fahs], *n.* a dramatic work, solely intended to promote laughter; a comedy of the more uproarious kind; such plays in general; absurd proceeding; mockery; travesty. [OFr.].

FARCICAL [fah'si-kal], *adj.* pertaining or appropriate to a farce, ridiculous. FARCICALITY [fah-si-ka'li-ti], *n.* state or quality of being f. FARCICALLY, *adv.* in a f. way.

FARDEL [fah'del], *n.* (*archaic*) a bundle. [OFr.].

FARE (1) [fāer], *n.* price of a passenger's conveyance, passage-money; person conveyed for this; food, provisions. FARE (2), *v.i.* to travel, journey; get on; happen, turn out; be entertained, be fed; feed. [OE.].

FAR EAST [fah(r)-ēst'], *n.* the parts of the world in the extreme east, relative to western Europe; *esp.* China and Japan.

FAREWELL (1) [fāer-wel'], *int.* good-bye! adieu! FAREWELL (2), *n.* good wishes on parting, leave-taking. [FARE (2) and WELL (3)].

FAR-FETCHED [fah-fecht'], *adj.* not naturally deduced or introduced; forced; strained, unlikely.

FAR-FLUNG [fah-flung'], *adj.* extending to a great distance.

FARINA [fa-rē'nah], *n.* the pollen of plants; the flour of any kind of corn or starchy root; starch. [L.].

FARINACEOUS [fa-ri-nā'shōos], *adj.* consisting of, or containing, farina or flour; mealy; floury. FARINACEOUSLY, *adv.* in a floury manner. [L.].

FARINOSE [fa'ri-nōs], *adj.* producing farina; covered with farina.

FARM (1) [fahm], *n.* a group of fields and buildings devoted to agriculture and dairy produce. FARM (2), *v.t.* to till, cultivate, grow; care for, for a fixed sum of money; take proceeds of, after paying a fixed sum of money; *v.i.* to be a farmer; to f. out, to let out the labour of, for hire; let out proceeds in return for a fixed sum. FARMABLE, *adj.* that can be farmed. [OFr. from MedL.].

FARMER [fah'mer], *n.* one who earns his living by tilling the soil, breeding stock etc.; one who farms.

FARM-HAND [fahm'hand], *n.* farm-labourer.

FARMHOUSE [fahm'hows], *n.* house belonging to a farm.

FARMING [fah'ming], *n.* the occupation of a farmer.

FARM-LABOURER [fahm-lā'be-rer], *n.* man employed on a farm.

FARMSTEAD [fahm'sted], *n.* the buildings about a farm.

FARMYARD [fahm'yahd], *n.* the yard close to the farm buildings.

FARO [fāer'ō], *n.* old game of hazard played with cards. [The name *Pharaoh*].

FARRAGO [fa-rā'gō], *n.* mixture of various materials;

medley; hodge-podge. FARRAGINOUS [fa-ra'ji-nōōs], *adj.* made of various materials; mixed. [L.].

FAR-REACHING [fah-rē'ching], *adj.* extending far, carrying many consequences.

FARRIER [fa'ri-er], *n.* shoe-smith, one who shoes horses; horse-doctor; non-commissioned officer whose duty it is to look after the horses of a cavalry regiment. FARRIERY, *n.* trade of a f. [L.].

FARROW (1) [fa'rō], *n.* litter of young pigs. FARROW (2), *v.t.* to produce, give birth to (pigs); *v.i.* to give birth to young pigs. [OE.].

FAR-SIGHTED [fah-sī'tid], *adj.* able to see a great distance; foreseeing remote issues. FAR-SIGHTED-NESS, *n.* quality of being f.

FARTHER [fah'THer], *adj. and adv.* more far, more remote. FARTHERMOST, *adj.* most remote, farthest.

FARTHEST [fah'THest], *adj.* most remote, most distant.

FARTHING [fah'THing], *n.* the fourth part of a penny; small bronze coin worth this amount. [OE.].

FARTHINGALE [fah'THing-gāl], *n.* petticoat spread out by hoops formed of whalebone. [~OFr. from Span.].

FASCES [fa'sez], *n.(pl.)* bundle of rods bound together round an axe, in Roman times carried by the lictors before a magistrate; emblem of the Fascists in Italy. [L.].

FASCIA, FACIA [fa'shi-ah], *n.* a band, fillet, stripe; (*arch.*) long flat surface under the eaves of a house or shop, on which the name of the shopkeeper is usually placed. [L.].

FASCICLE, FASCICULE [fa'si-kl, fa'si-kyōol], *n.* (*bot.*) small bundle; close cluster; instalment of a book etc. [L.].

FASCINATE [fa'si-nāt], *v.t.* to exercise a powerful influence over; charm, attract; deprive of will-power, so that the victim is unable to resist, escape etc. FASCINATING, *adj.* entrancing; captivating. FASCINATINGLY, *adv.* in a fascinating fashion. FASCINATOR, *n.* person who fascinates; formerly, a kind of head-covering worn by women. [L.].

FASCINATION [fa-si-nā'shn], *n.* act of fascinating; quality of attracting or enchanting others; charm; attractiveness. [L.].

FASCINE [fa-sēn'], *n.* long faggot bound with withes, used for engineering and military purposes. [L.].

FASCISM [fa'shizm], *n.* political creed of the Fascists.

FASCIST [fa'shist], *n.* member of the former Nationalist anti-Communist movement in Italy, which arose after the First World War under Benito Mussolini; member of an anti-Communist party with similar aims in any other country; in Britain, sympathiser with a similar movement founded by Sir Oswald Mosley. [It.].

FASH [fash], *v.t.* (*Scots and northern dial.*) to vex; annoy; trouble; upset. [OFr.].

FASHION (1) [fa'shn], *n.* form; shape; pattern; style; manner, the prevailing mode of dress; prevailing custom or usage; after a f., somehow, anyhow, not well. FASHION-PLATE, design showing a f. in dress. FASHION (2), *v.t.* to shape, make. FASHIONER, *n.* one who fashions.

FASHIONABLE [fa'shn-a-bl], *adj.* following the prevailing mode or usage; stylish, smart; characteristic of, approved by, people of fashion. FASHION-ABLENESS, *n.* quality of being f. FASHIONABLY, *adv.* in a f. way.

FAST (1) [fahst], *adj.* firm, secure; firmly attached, steady; unfading; fixed; rapid, quick; inducing rapid motion; dissipated. FAST (2), *adv.* firmly, securely, fixedly; tightly; soundly (of sleep); rapidly, quickly. [OE.].

FAST (3), *v.i.* to abstain from eating, *esp.* as a religious observance; go without food. FAST (4), *n.* act of fasting; time appointed for fasting. FAST-DAY, day appointed for a f. [OE.].

FASTEN [fah'sn], *v.t. and i.* to attach, fix, tie, bind, close; become or be capable of becoming fastened or fixed; to f. off, to secure a thread with a knot etc.; to f. on, to seize upon, single out for emphasis (*esp.* in order to pick a quarrel, or criticize). [OE.].

FASTENER [fah'sn-er], *n.* one who, or that which, fastens; device for fastening garments; any contrivance for holding objects together.

FASTENING [fah'sn-ing], *n.* anything which fastens.

FASTIDIOUS [fas-ti'di-ōōs], *adj.* squeamish; particular; hard to please. FASTIDIOUSLY, *adv.* in a f. way. FASTIDIOUSNESS, *n.* quality or state of being f. [L.].

FASTING [fahs'ting]. *n.* act of one who fasts.

FASTNESS [fahst'nes], *n.* stronghold, fortified place; quality of being fast.

FAT (1) [fat], *adj.* corpulent, obese; well fed; plump; thick, substantial, heavy; prosperous, thriving; oily, greasy; fertile, fruitful; (*print.*) easy to set up and well paid; (*fig.*) dull, stupid, slow; **a f. lot,** (*coll.*) a great deal, usually used sarcastically for hardly any; **to cut up f.,** to leave a lot of money. FAT (2), *n.* oily substance which makes up the f. parts of animal bodies; f. part of anything; (*fig.*) the best, choicest part of anything; (*print.*) copy easy and profitable for the compositor; (*theatre*) the part of a role which shows off an actor to best advantage; (*chem.*) a compound of glycerine with an acid; **the f. is in the fire,** there will be trouble soon; **to live on the f. of the land, to** live in comfort and prosperity. FAT (3), *v.t.* to fatten, feed up, make f.; cover, smear with f.; *v.i.* to grow f. [O.E.].

FATAL [fā'tal], *adj.* causing death or ruin, deadly, disastrous; fated, fateful. FATALLY, *adv.* so as to prove f.; so as to cause death. [L.].

FATALISM [fā'ta-lizm], *n.* doctrine or belief that all events are predetermined by the arbitrary decrees of God or fate; submission to all that happens as predetermined. **FATALIST** [fā'ta-list], *n.* one who believes in fatalism. FATALISTIC [fā-ta-lis'tik], *adj.* like a f., involving fatalism. FATALISTICALLY, *adv.* in a fatalistic fashion.

FATALITY [fa-ta'li-ti], *n.* the inevitable course of events; subjection to fate; supremacy of fate; predetermined disaster; calamity; death by accident, war or violence of any kind. [LL.].

FATE (1) [fāt], *n.* the power which orders events beforehand from eternity; destiny, fortune; that which must inevitably happen; that which is predestined; one's ultimate appointed condition; calamity, death, destruction; **the Fates,** (*myth.*) three goddesses supposed by the ancients to preside over the destinies of men. FATE (2), *v.t.* to preordain, predestine. FATED, *adj.* destined, *esp.* to disaster.

FATEFUL [fāt'fōōl], *adj.* having fatal power; producing fatal events; unalterable, irrevocable. FATEFULLY, *adv.* in a f. way. FATEFULNESS, *n.* quality of being f.

FAT-HEAD [fat'hed], *n.* dolt, stupid fellow. FAT-HEADED, *adj.* (*coll.*) having a fat head; crassly stupid.

FATHER (1) [fah'THer], *n.* male parent, begetter; ancestor, progenitor; originator, creator; early leader; one who deserves filial respect and veneration; doyen; mode of addressing a priest or confessor; the F., the First Person of the Trinity; **the Holy F.,** the Pope; **F. of the faithful,** title of a Caliph; **the F. of lies,** the devil, Satan; **Fathers of the Church,** early Christian writers; **the Pilgrim Fathers,** those who sailed in the *Mayflower* to settle in America in 1620; **Conscript Fathers,** members of the Roman Senate. FATHER (2), *v.t. and i.* to beget; be a f. to; behave like a f. to; treat with paternal care, cherish as a f.; **to f. on,** to ascribe paternity to. [O.E.].

FATHERHOOD [fah'THer-hŏŏd], *n.* condition of being a father; character or authority of a father.

FATHER-IN-LAW [fah'THer-in-law], *n.* the father of a person's husband or wife.

FATHERLAND [fah'THer-land], *n.* land of one's fathers; one's native country.

FATHERLESS [fah'THer-les], *adj.* having no father living; without a known author.

FATHERLY [fah'THer-li], *adj.* paternal; like a father; kind, affectionate; protective. FATHERLINESS, *n.* f. kindness; the benevolent feelings appropriate to a father.

FATHOM (1) [fa'THom], *n.* a nautical and mining measure of depth, 6 ft.; measure of quantity of wood 6 ft. square or any length; (*fig.*) depth, profundity; penetration. FATHOM (2), *v.t.* to sound, measure (water); (*fig.*) to get to the bottom of; penetrate; understand. FATHOMABLE, *adj.* able to be fathomed. [O.E.].

FATHOMLESS [fa'THom-les], *adj.* that cannot be fathomed; (*fig.*) incomprehensible.

FATIGUE (1) [fa-tēg'], *n.* exhaustion, weariness after exertion; (of metal) weakness after blows or strain; task or exertion causing weariness; duty carried out by a soldier, in addition to military routine. FATIGUE (2), *v.t.* to make weary; (of metal) weaken by repeated blows or strain. FATIGUING, *adj.* exhausting. [Fr.].

FATLING [fat'ling], *n.* young animal fattened for the table; any fat animal.

FATLY [fat'li], *adv.* coarsely, grossly; greasily.

FATNESS [fat'nes], *n.* condition of being fat; richness; fruitfulness; abundance.

FATTED [fa'tid], *adj.* fattened.

FATTEN [fa'ten], *v.t.* to make fat, *esp.* for slaughtering; make more fertile; *v.i.* to grow fat.

FATTY (1) [fa'ti], *adj.* greasy, like or consisting of fat; having unhealthy deposits of fat. FATTY (2), *n.* familiar and rather contemptuous mode of addressing a corpulent person. FATTINESS, *n.* quality of being f.

FATUITY [fa-tyŏo'i-ti], *n.* weakness of intellect; foolishness. [L.].

FATUOUS [fa'tyŏo-ŏos], *adj.* silly, foolish; weak in mind. FATUOUSLY, *adv.* in a f. way. [L.].

FAUBOURG [fō'bŏŏrg], *n.* outlying district or suburb in French cities. [Fr.].

FAUCES [faw'sēz], *n.(pl.)* upper portion of the throat, passage from the root of the tongue to the gullet. FAUCAL [faw'kal], *adj.* guttural, uttered deep in the throat; pertaining to the f. [L.].

FAUCET [faw'set], *n.* a tap; tube inserted in a cask for extracting the liquid. [Fr.].

FAULT (1) [fawlt], *n.* blemish, imperfection; failing, error; offence, wrongdoing; (*geol.*) displacement of the strata; (*hunting*) loss of the scent; (*tennis*) failure to serve the ball over the net into the proper court; **to find f. with,** to criticize adversely, nag. FAULT (2), *v.t. and i.* (*geol.*) to displace strata; show a displacement of strata; (*tennis*) serve a f.; (*coll.*) impute a f. to. FAULTED, *adj.* having a f., displaced. FAULTFUL, *adj.* full of mistakes; faulty. [OFr.].

FAULT-FINDER [fawlt'fin-der], *n.* one given to finding fault.

FAULTLESS [fawlt'les], *adj.* with no fault or blemish. FAULTLESSLY, *adv.* in a f. way. FAULTLESSNESS, *n.* freedom from faults or blemishes.

FAULTY [fawl'ti], *adj.* having faults; imperfect; defective; wrong; inaccurate. FAULTILY, *adv.* in a f. way. FAULTINESS, *n.* condition or quality of being f.

FAUN [fawn], *n.* in Roman *myth.,* woodland deity having a tail and horns.

FAUNA [faw'nah], *n.* the animal life of any district or geological period. [L.].

FAUTEUIL [fō'til, fō-tu(r)'ē], *n.* arm-chair; seat in the stalls at a theatre. [Fr.].

FAUX PAS [fō-pah'], *n.* a false step; tactless remark or action. [Fr.].

FAVOUR (1) [fā'ver], *n.* goodwill; act of goodwill; undue kindness; preference; partiality; something worn or given as a sign of favour; **to curry f.,** to insinuate oneself into the good graces of someone; **in f. of,** in support of; to the account of; **without fear or f.,** boldly and impartially. FAVOUR (2), *v.t.* to show goodwill towards; prefer; treat with undue kindness; support, help; facilitate, prove advantageous to. FAVOURER, *n.* one who, that which, favours. [L.].

FAVOURABLE [fā've-ra-bl], *adj.* showing favour or goodwill; propitious; conducive; kindly, friendly; advantageous. FAVOURABLENESS, *n.* quality of being f. FAVOURABLY, *adv.* in a f. way.

FAVOURING [fā've-ring], *adj.* wishing well to; promoting; showing partiality to. FAVOURINGLY, *adv.* in a partial way, so as to favour.

FAVOURITE (1) [fā've-rit], *n.* person or thing regarded with especial favour; the competitor generally expected to win. FAVOURITE (2), *adj.* held in particular favour or esteem, most preferred. [OFr.].

FAVOURITISM [fā've-ri-tizm], *n.* habit of having, and discriminating to the advantage of, favourites; bias, partiality.

FAVUS [fā'vus], *n.* a disease of the scalp causing incrustations resembling a honeycomb. [L.].

FAWN (1) [fawn], *n.* young deer, fallow deer of the first year; light yellowish-brown. FAWN (2), *adj.* of the colour of a f., light yellowish-brown. FAWN (3), *v.i.* to bring forth, give birth to, a f. [OFr.].

FAWN (4), *v.i.* (of animals) to show delight or affection by wagging the tail, pawing etc.; cringe, flatter servilely in order to gain favour. FAWNER, *n.* one who fawns. FAWNING, *n.* servile cringing and flattery; gross flattery to obtain favours. FAWNINGLY, *adv.* in a servile manner. [O.E.].

FAY (1) [fā], *n.* a fairy. [OFr.].

FAY (2), *v.t.* to fit two pieces of wood closely together, in shipbuilding; *v.i.* to fit together very closely. [O.E.].

FAYENCE, see FAIENCE.

FEALTY [fē'al-ti], *n.* loyalty of a feudal vassal to his lord. [OFr.].

FEAR (1) [fēer], *n.* mental distress in the presence of real or imagined danger; terror, cowardice; apprehension for the future; worry, anxiety; a grave probability that the unpleasant will occur; profound and submissive respect. FEAR (2), *v.t.* to be afraid of; revere, hold in awe; shrink from; have an uneasy anticipation of ; *v.i.* to be afraid. [OE.].

FEARFUL [fēer'fŏŏl], *adj.* filled with fear, frightened, timid; anxious; terrible, inspiring fear; (*coll.*) annoying, extreme. FEARFULLY, *adv.* in a f. fashion; (*coll.*) very. FEARFULNESS, *n.* condition of being f.

FEARLESS [fēer'les], *adj.* without fear; intrepid. FEARLESSLY, *adv.* in a f. way. FEARLESSNESS, *n.* quality of being f.

FEARSOME [fēer'sŭm], *adj.* inspiring fear and awe, terrible, appalling. FEARSOMELY, *adv.* in a f. manner. FEARSOMENESS, *n.* state or quality of being f.

FEASIBLE [fē'zi-bl], *adj.* that may be done, practicable. FEASIBILITY, FEASIBLENESS [fē-zi-bi'li-ti, fē'zi-bl-nes], *n.* quality of being f. FEASIBLY, *adv.* possibly, practicably. [OFr.].

FEAST (1) [fēst], *n.* a religious festival of rejoicing; a joyful anniversary; banquet, sumptuous meal; (*fig.*) plentiful and enjoyable quantity of anything; something very gratifying to the senses or mind; **movable f.**, religious festival which has no fixed date. FEAST (2), *v.t.* to regale; pass, spend, in feasting; *v.i.* to take part in, partake of, a f.; fare sumptuously, regale oneself. FEASTER, *n.* one who fares sumptuously or entertains magnificently. FEASTING, *n.* eating sumptuously; rejoicing as at a f. [OFr.].

FEAST-DAY [fēst'dā], *n.* a day of feasting; festival; holiday.

FEAT [fēt], *n.* act or deed, *esp.* one demanding extraordinary strength, skill or courage. [OFr. from L.].

FEATHER (1) [fe'THer], *n.* an appendage consisting of a quill, shaft and two sets of barbs, growing with many others on a bird's skin; a plume; plumage; something like, light as, a feather; **birds of a f.**, people of the same kind; **to show the white f.**, to behave like, be, a coward; **a f. in one's cap,** a deed one is proud of and which will raise one's standing with other people. FEATHER (2), *v.t.* to cover, line, adorn, with feathers; (*rowing*) turn (the oar) so that it passes through the air edgeways; (*shooting*) shoot the feathers off (a bird) without killing it; *v.i.* to move like a f.; turn the oar so that it passes through the air edgeways; (*aeron.*) of an airscrew, revolve at such an angle that no pull is exerted; (*hunting*) of a hound, quiver while seeking a scent; **to f. one's nest.** to get rich, enrich oneself. [OE.].

FEATHER-BED [fe'THer-bed'], *n.* mattress stuffed with feathers; **f. bedding,** feathers used for stuffing mattresses.

FEATHER-BRAINED [fe'THer-brānd], *adj.* heedless, irresponsible.

FEATHERED [fe'THerd], *adj.* furnished, covered with, feathers; winged.

FEATHERINESS [fe'THe-ri-nes], *n.* state or quality of being feathery.

FEATHERING (1) [fe'THe-ring], *n.* act of turning the blade of an oar or scull to the horizontal as it leaves the water; (*pl.*) (*arch.*) ornamental cusps formed by the junction of small arcs. FEATHERING (2), *adj.* (*mech.*) acting in the same way as an oar when feathering.

FEATHERLESS [fe'THer-les], *adj.* without feathers; unfledged.

FEATHERSTITCH [fe'THer-stich], *n.* kind of embroidery in which the stitches are made in a series of branching zigzags.

FEATHERWEIGHT [fe'THer-wāt], *n.* anything very light; jockey weighing not more than 4 st. 7 lb.; boxer weighing between 8 st. 6lb. and 9 st.

FEATHERY [fe'THe-ri], *adj.* covered with feathers; looking like feathers.

FEATLY [fēt'li], *adv.* (*archaic*) neatly; skilfully.

FEATNESS [fēt'nes], *n.* (*archaic*) neatness; adroitness.

FEATURE (1) [fē'tyŏŏr], *n.* a part of the face; characteristic; trait; part which arrests attention; something given prominence; a newspaper article, radio programme, cinema film or the like of more than ordinary importance. FEATURE (2), *adj.* specially prepared and given prominence; **f. film,** the main film of a cinema programme. FEATURE (3), *v.t.* to characterize, be the distinctive mark of; show the prominent points of; make into a "feature," give prominence to; exhibit in a conspicuous role in a cinema film or the like, star. FEATURED, *adj.* having a certain cast of f.; shaped; figured prominently in a film. FEATURELESS, *adj.* without distinctive features.

FEBRIFUGE [feb'ri-fyŏŏj], *n.* medicine which cures

fever. FEBRIFUGAL [feb-ri'fyŏŏ-gal], *adj.* possessing the quality of curing fever. [Fr.].

FEBRILE [feb'ril], *adj.* pertaining to, or indicating, fever; feverish. [L.].

FEBRUARY [feb'rŏŏ-a-ri], *n.* second month of the year. [L.].

FECAL, see FAECAL.

FECES, see FAECES.

FECIT [fē'sit], *v.t.* word inscribed on a monument or other work after the name of the man who carried out the work or designed it. [L.].

FECKLESS [fek'les], *adj.* reckless, careless; helpless. FECKLESSNESS, *n.* quality of being f.

FECULENT [fe'kyŏŏ-lent], *adj.* fetid, muddy. FECULENCE, FECULENCY, *n.* state of being f.; f. matter. [L.].

FECUND [fē'kund, fe'kund], *adj.* fruitful; fertile; prolific. [L.].

FECUNDATE [fē'kun-dāt, fe'kun-dāt], *v.t.* to make fruitful or prolific; impregnate; fertilize. FECUNDATION [fē-kun-dā'shn, fe-kun-dā'shn], *n.* act of making fruitful or prolific; impregnation; fertilization. [L.].

FECUNDITY [fē-kun'di-ti, fe-kun'di-ti], *n.* fruitfulness; fertility. [L.].

FED [fed], *pret and p.pt.* of FEED; **f. up,** sated, having had more than enough (of), sick (of). [ME.].

FEDERACY [fe'de-ra-si], *n.* a federation.

FEDERAL (1) [fe'de-ral], *adj.* relating to the political system by which several internally independent states unite under a central government for the management of interests or affairs which concern them all; (*U.S. hist.*) of the Northern party in the Civil War; in favour of central government; (*theol.*) relating to, founded on, the doctrine of Covenants. FEDERAL (2), *n.* supporter of the f. principle in the constitution of the U.S.A.; member of a f. state. [Fr.].

FEDERALIST [fe'de-ra-list], *n.* one who supports the doctrine of federal union, *esp.* of the U.S.A. FEDERALISM, *n.* principles of the federalists; federal union as a political policy or theory. [Fr.].

FEDERALIZE [fe'de-ra-līz], *v.t.* to unite, league (independent states) together under a federal government.

FEDERATE (1) [fe'de-rat], *adj.* joined in confederacy, united under a federal government. FEDERATE (2) [fe'de-rāt], *v.t. and i.* to unite under a federal government. FEDERATIVE, *adj.* relating to federation; federal. [L.].

FEDERATION [fe-de-rā'shn], *n.* act of federating; state of being federated; a group of independent states united under a federal government; league or confederation. [L.].

FEE (1) [fē], *n.* a feudal benefice; inherited estate; sum payable to a public officer, physician, lawyer etc. for his services; entrance-money for a club, society, examination etc.; (*pl.*) amount payable each term to a school or college. FEE (2), *v.t.* to pay a f. to, hire. [ME.].

FEEBLE [fē'bl], *adj.* weak; unstable; infirm; irresolute; dim, indistinct. FEEBLENESS, *n.* condition of being f. FEEBLISH, *adj.* rather f. FEEBLY, *adv.* in a f. way. [OFr. from L.].

FEEBLE-MINDED [fē-bl-mīn'did], *adj.* of weak intellect; deficient in intelligence. FEEBLE-MINDEDNESS, *n.* condition of being f.

FEED (1) [fēd], *v.t.* to supply with food; satisfy, gratify; serve as food for; keep supplied; supply with material; *v.i.* to eat, take food; graze. FEED (2), *n.* act of feeding, of taking or giving food; green crops; a horse's allowance of food; fodder; a meal; the fuelling, feeding, of a machine; the apparatus which does this; the charge of a gun; man who in a comedy act supplies the comedian with cues etc.; **to be off one's f.,** to have no appetite. FEEDING, *adj.* that supplies with food, or material; (*slang*) annoying, tiresome, that makes one fed up. [OE.].

FEEDER [fē'der], *n.* one who or that which feeds; feeding apparatus in a machine; feeding bottle for a child; child's bib; tributary of a larger river; main supplying electricity, gas etc. to branch lines; person who throws the ball to the striker in such games as rounders.

FEED-PIPE [fēd'pīp], *n.* pipe which supplies a machine with material.

FEEL (1) (*pret. and p.pt.* **felt**) [fēl], *v.t.* to perceive, become aware of, by touch; handle, test by touch; experience; be affected, moved by; be conscious of; *v.i.* to produce a sensation of being; have the sense of touch; be physically or emotionally aware; **to f. for**

someone, to have sympathy with someone; **to f. in one's bones,** to have a deep conviction; **to f. one's way,** to grope one's way, go carefully. FEEL (2), *n.* sense of touch; sensation characteristic of something; intuitive understanding. [OE.].

FEELER [fē'ler], *n.* organ of touch found on the heads of certain insects; (*fig.*) remark uttered tentatively in order to sound the opinions of others, a hint.

FEELING [fē'ling], *n.* act of perceiving or exploring by touch; sense of touch; physical sensation; emotion; tenderness; sensibility; sentiment; emotional effect produced by a work of art.

FEELINGLY [fē'ling-li], *adv.* in a feeling manner, sympathetically.

FEE-SIMPLE [fē-sim'pl], *n.* estate held by a person in his own right; freehold, absolute property.

FEET [fēt], *n.(pl.)* of FOOT (1). [OE.].

FEE-TAIL [fē-tāl'], *n.* estate entailed to the possessor's heirs, and thus held with limitation.

FEEZE (1) [fēz], *v.t.* to turn or twist as when driving a screw; screw. FEEZE (2), *n.* (*U.S.*) a rush; (*coll.*) state of perturbation. [OE.].

FEIGN [fān], *v.t.* to invent, fabricate; pretend, sham; *v.i.* to sham, pretend; dissimulate. FEIGNING, *n.* deception; pretence. FEIGNINGLY, *adv.* with false appearance; insincerely. [ME. from OFr. from L.].

FEIGNED [fānd], *adj.* pretended; false; counterfeited. FEIGNEDLY [fā'nid-li], *adv.* in pretence; insincerely. FEIGNEDNESS [fā'nid-nes], *n.* condition of being f.

FEINT (1) [fānt], *n.* a sham attack intended to outwit an opponent; false show; pretence. FEINT (2), *v.i.* to make a sham attack in order to deceive an enemy or opponent. [Fr.].

FELDSPAR, see FELSPAR.

FELICITATE [fe-li'si-tāt], *v.t.* to congratulate. FELICITATOR, *n.* one who felicitates. [L.].

FELICITATION [fe-li-si-tā'shn], *n.* act of felicitating, congratulation.

FELICITOUS [fe-li'si-tŏŏs], *adj.* very happy; fortunate; ingenious; most appropriate. FELICITOUSLY, *adv.* in a f. way.

FELICITY [fe-li'si-ti], *n.* state of being intensely happy; contentment; blissfulness; appropriateness, tact. [L.].

FELINE (1) [fē'līn], *adj.* pertaining to cats or the cat family; cat-like; catty. FELINE (2), *n.* member of the cat family. FELINITY [fē-li'ni-ti], *n.* quality of being f.; cattishness. [L.].

FELL (1) [fel], *n.* the hide of an animal; matted hair. [OE.].

FELL (2), *n.* a mountain side; barren or rocky hill. [~OIcel.].

FELL (3), *adj.* cruel; fierce; ruthless. [OFr.].

FELL (4), *v.t.* to cause to fall; bring down (*esp.* trees) by cutting or striking. FELLABLE, *adj.* suitable for being felled. FELLER (1), *n.* one who fells trees. [OE.].

FELL (5), *v.t.* to sew a hem laid level with the cloth. FELL (6), *n.* act of felling a seam; a felled seam. FELLER (2), *n.* hemming device used in a sewing machine. [Uncert.].

FELL (7), *pret.* of FALL (1). [OE.].

FELLAH (*pl.* **fellahin**) [fe'lah, fe'lah-hēn], *n.* member of the peasant or labouring class in Egypt. [Arab.].

FELLMONGER [fel'mung-ger], *n.* dealer in skins; one who works skins.

FELLOE, FELLY [fe'lō, fe'li], *n.* one of the curved strips joined together to form the rim of a wheel, to which the tyre is fixed; rim of a wheel. [OE.].

FELLOW [fe'lō], *n.* a partner or sharer in anything; person associated with another; comrade; accomplice; equal; uncultured person; man or boy, chap; member of the governing body of some colleges and universities; member of various learned and professional societies; graduate holding certain grants on condition of research. FELLOW-FEELING, feeling in common, sympathy. [OE.].

FELLOWSHIP [fe'lō-ship], *n.* state of being fellows; comradeship; sharing; participation; group of people bound by some common aim or belief; rank of a fellow of a college or university, or learned professional society; (*coll.*) examination which must be passed before one can become a Fellow of the Royal College of Surgeons.

FELLOW-TRAVELLER [fe-lō-trā've-ler], *n.* a travelling companion; (*fig.*) one who, though not a member of the Communist Party, shares and supports its views.

FELO-DE-SE [fe'lō-de-sē'], *n.* suicide by one of sound mind. [LL.].

FELON (1) [fe'lon], *adj.* (*poet.*) criminal; evil;

treacherous; murderous. FELON (2), *n.* a criminal; ruffian; one who has committed felony. FELONRY, *n.* felons in general. [OFr.].

FELON (3), *n.* a whitlow. [Uncert.].

FELONIOUS [fe-lŏ'ni-ŏŏs], *adj.* wicked; worthy of a felon; (*leg.*) done with the deliberate purpose of committing a crime. FELONIOUSLY, *adv.* in a f. way. FELONIOUSNESS, *n.* quality or condition of being f.

FELONY [fe'lo-ni], *n.* (*leg.*) one of the most serious kind of crimes or offences, regarded as more serious than a misdemeanour. [Fr.].

FELSPAR, FELDSPAR [fel'spah(r), feld'spah(r)], *n.* group of minerals consisting of anhydrous aluminium silicates, combined with potassium, calcium, sodium or barium, and forming a constituent part of many igneous and metamorphic rocks. FELSPATHIC, FELSPATHOSE [fel-spa'thik, -'thōs], *adj.* consisting of, containing, f. [Germ.].

FELT (1) [felt], *n.* a compact tough fabric, made by rolling and pressing together wool, size etc., much used for making hats. FELT (2), *v.t.* to cover with f.; mat together; make into f., *v.i.* to become matted, as f. [OE.].

FELT (3), *pret. and p.pt.* of FEEL (1).

FELTING [fel'ting], *n.* act or process of making felt; felt.

FELUCCA [fe-lu'kah], *n.* sailing vessel with oars used in the Mediterranean. [Arab.].

FEMALE (1) [fē'māl], *adj.* of the sex which bears offspring; pertaining to, of, women; (of screws etc.) made so as to receive the corresponding "male" part; (*bot.*) fruit-bearing, having a pistil and ovary but no stamens. FEMALE (2), *n.* a f. person or animal; person or animal of the sex which bears offspring; (*vulg.*) woman. FEMALIZED, *adj.* made f. [L.].

FEMINEITY [fe-mi-nē'i-ti], *n.* quality of being feminine, womanliness.

FEMININE [fe'mi-nin], *adj.* pertaining to the female sex, pertaining to women; characteristic of or befitting a woman; womanly; (*gram.*) of the gender or form proper to females; **f. caesura,** (*pros.*) a caesura which does not immediately follow a stress; **f. ending,** (*pros.*) an ending having the last accent in the line on the penultimate syllable; **f. rhyme,** (*pros.*) rhyme consisting of a stressed syllable followed by an unstressed syllable. FEMININELY, *adv.* in a f. way. FEMININENESS, *n.* condition or quality of being f. FEMININISM, *n.* f. idiom or turn of phrase; tendency towards effeminacy. FEMINIZE, *v.t.* to make f. or effeminate.

FEMININITY [fe-mi-ni'ni-ti], *n.* quality of being feminine.

FEMINIST [fe'mi-nist], *n.* advocate of women's claims to equal privileges with men etc. FEMINISM, *n.* policy of feminists.

FEMORAL [fe'mo-ral], *adj.* relating to the thigh.

FEMUR [fē'mer], *n.* the thigh or thigh bone. [L.].

FEN [fen], *n.* low marshy land; a bog or marsh. FEN-CRICKET, the mole-cricket. FEN-DUCK, the shoveller duck. FEN-GOOSE, the greylag goose. [OE.].

FENCE (1) [fens], *n.* art of swordsmanship; hedge, wall, barrier, enclosing an area, *esp.* one made of wood; guard or guide of some kinds of machine; (*slang*) receiver of stolen goods. FENCE-MONTH, close time for fish or game; **master of f.,** skilful swordsman; (*fig.*) brilliant debater; **to sit on the f.,** not to take sides; **to come down on the right side of the f.,** to join the winning side. FENCE (2), *v.t.* to screen, protect; enclose with a f.; fortify; *v.i.* to fight man against man with swords; repel, keep out; jump fences; (*slang*) receive stolen goods. FENCELESS, *adj.* without a f., unenclosed. [(DE)FENCE].

FENCER [fen'ser], *n.* person who fences or teaches fencing; maker of fences.

FENCING [fen'sing], *n.* art of self-defence with a sword; barrier or railing, *esp.* of wood, fences; material suitable for fences; **f. cully,** (*slang*) one who stores stolen goods; **f. ken,** (*slang*) a store for stolen goods.

FEND [fend], *v.i.* to repel; keep (off); provide (for). [(DE)FEND].

FENDER [fen'der], *n.* protective frame round a hearth; protection from injury by collision etc.

FENESTELLA [fe-nes-te'lah], *n.* (*arch.*) niche like a window in the wall on the south side of an altar. [L.].

FENESTRAL [fe-nes'tral], *adj.* relating to windows. [OFr.].

FENESTRATION [fe-nes-trā'shn], *n.* architectural

The accent ′ after a syllable = stress (u-pon′). The mark ‾ over a vowel = length (ā in made; ō in bone).

arrangement of windows; (*bot.*, *zool.*) condition of being perforated with holes like windows. [L.].

FENIAN [fē′ni-an], *n.* member of a revolutionary organization formed to overthrow English rule and set up a native republic in Ireland. FENIANISM, *n.* political tenets of the Fenians. [OIr.].

FENNEL [fe′nel], *n.* fragrant umbelliferous plant with finely divided leaves. [OE.].

FENUGREEK, FENUGREC [fe′nyōō-grēk], *n.* leguminous plant related to clover. [L.].

FEOD, see FEUD (2).

FEOFF, see FIEF.

FEOFFEE [fĕ-fē′], *n.* one who is enfeoffed. [AFr.].

FEOFFMENT [fĕf′ment], *n.* grant of a fief. [AFr.].

FEOFFOR [fĕ′fer], *n.* person who grants a fief. [AFr.].

FERAL (1) [fē′ral], *adj.* fatal, deadly. [L.].

FERAL (2), *adj.* wild, untamed; uncultivated; escaped from a domesticated condition. [~L.].

FER-DE-LANCE [fāer-de-lahns′], *n.* poisonous pit-viper of South America. [Fr.].

FERIAL [fē′ri-al], *adj.* relating to holidays. [MedL.].

FERINE [fē′rīn], *adj.* untamed; savage. FERINELY, *adv.* after the manner of wild animals. [L.].

FERINGHEE [fe-ring′gē], *n.* Hindu term for Europeans generally used derogatorily. [Pers.].

FERMENT (1) [fur′ment], *n.* that which causes fermentation, leaven; fermentation; (*fig.*) agitation, uproar. FERMENT (2) [fer-ment′], *v.t.* to leaven; (*fig.*) stir up, agitate, excite; *v.i.* to undergo fermentation; effervesce. FERMENTESCIBLE [fer-men-te′si-bl], *adj.* capable of being fermented. [L.].

FERMENTABLE [fer-men′ta-bl], *adj.* capable of being fermented. FERMENTABILITY [fer-men-ta-bi′li-ti], *n.* capacity for being fermented.

FERMENTATION [fer-men-tā′shn], *n.* chemical process in which effervescence takes place, induced by the presence of yeast or enzymes; (*fig.*) agitation, turmoil, tumult. [L.].

FERMENTATIVE [fer-men′ta-tiv], *adj.* inducing, or consisting in, fermentation.

FERN [furn], *n.* flowerless cryptogamous plant with feathery fronds. FERNERY, *n.* place where ferns are grown. FERNY, *adj.* abounding in ferns. [OE.].

FERN-OWL [furn′owl], *n.* the goatsucker or nightjar.

FEROCIOUS [fe-rō′shŏŏs], *adj.* fierce, brutal, savage. FEROCIOUSLY, *adv.* in a f. way. FEROCIOUSNESS, *n.* quality or condition of being f. [L.].

FEROCITY [fe-ro′si-ti], *n.* state or quality of being ferocious. [L.].

FERREOUS [fe′ri-ŏŏs], *adj.* containing, pertaining to or made of iron. [L.].

FERRET (1) [fe′rit], *n.* partially domesticated variety of pole-cat used to chase rabbits and rats from their holes. FERRET (2), *v.i.* to hunt with ferrets; (*fig.*) make a thorough search; **to f. out**, to discover after a persistent search. FERRETER, *n.* one who hunts with ferrets; one who ferrets something out. [OFr.].

FERRET (3), *n.* tape made of woollen thread or sometimes of cotton or silk. [It.].

FERRIAGE [fe′ri-ij], *n.* fare due to be paid at a ferry.

FERRIC [fe′rik], *adj.* relating to, belonging to, iron in its quadrivalent state.

FERRIFEROUS [fe-ri′fe-rŏŏs], *adj.* yielding iron. [L.].

FERRIS-WHEEL [fe′ris-wēl], *n.* giant vertical revolving wheel at a fair, with passenger cars on its periphery. [*Ferris* American engineer].

FERRO-CONCRETE [fe-rō-kon′krēt], *n.* concrete reinforced with iron.

FERROTYPE [fe′rō-tīp], *n.* a positive photograph taken on a sensitized iron plate.

FERROUS [fe′rŏŏs], *adj.* containing, pertaining to, iron in its divalent state.

FERRUGINOUS [fe-rŏŏ′ji-nŏŏs], *adj.* containing iron or iron rust; of the colour of iron rust. [L.].

FERRULE [fe′rŏŏl], *n.* metal cap or tip strengthening the end of a stick, tube or umbrella shaft; metal band strengthening a joint. [ME. from OFr. from MedL.].

FERRY (1) [fe′ri], *v.t. and i.* to cross or carry across water in a boat or ferry; to fly (aircraft) in an operational base. FERRY (2), *n.* boat used as a floating bridge; place of passage where one may be rowed across water; the right of ferrying across; **f. pilot**, one who flies an aircraft to its base of operations. [OE.].

FERRY-BOAT [fe′ri-bōt], *n.* boat for conveying passengers or goods across a ferry.

FERRYMAN [fe′ri-man], *n.* man who keeps or works a ferry.

FERTILE [fur′til], *adj.* productive; rich in resources; inventive; prolific. FERTILELY, *adv.* in a f. way. [L.].

FERTILITY [fer-ti′li-ti], *n.* quality or condition of being fertile. [L.].

FERTILIZATION [fer-ti-lī-zā′shn], *n.* act or process of rendering fertile; impregnation.

FERTILIZE [fur′ti-līz], *v.t.* to render fertile or fruitful; enrich; pollinate.

FERTILIZER [fur′ti-lī-zer], *n.* that which fertilizes; manure.

FERULA [fe′rŏŏ-lah], *n.* a ferule, genus of plants containing the giant fennel. [L.].

FERULE [fe′rŏŏl], *n.* the giant fennel; flat rod (*orig.* made from this) for punishing children. [L.].

FERVENCY [fur′ven-si], *n.* state or quality of being fervent; ardour; zeal.

FERVENT [fur′vent], *adj.* hot, glowing; ardent, zealous, passionate. FERVENTLY, *adv.* in a f. way.

FERVID [fur′vid], *adj.* burning; ardent. FERVIDLY, *adv.* in a f. way. FERVIDNESS, *n.* state of being f. [L.].

FERVOUR [fur′ver], *n.* great heat; ardour, warm devotion; zeal. [L.].

FESCUE [fes′kyŏŏ], *n.* small straw formerly used to point out letters to children when learning to read; **f. grass**, a species of the genus *Festuca*, the stem of which was used as a pointer. [OFr.].

FESSE, FESS [fes], *n.* (*her.*) a broad band crossing the shield horizontally and occupying a third of it. FESSE-POINT, (*her.*) the middle point of an escutcheon. [L.].

FESTAL [fes′tal], *adj.* belonging, suitable, to a feast; joyous. FESTALLY, *adv.* in a festive way. [OFr.].

FESTER (1) [fes′ter], *n.* inflamed tumour or sore containing purulent matter. FESTER (2), *v.i.* to suppurate, grow septic; corrupt; rankle. [OFr. from L.].

FESTIVAL (1) [fes′ti-val], *n.* a feast; festive celebration; day of religious rejoicing; series of elaborately organized musical, dramatic or similar performances, usually recurring at intervals. FESTIVAL (2), *adj.* pertaining or appropriate to a feast; gay, joyous. [MedL.].

FESTIVE [fes′tiv], *adj.* pertaining to or appropriate to a feast; merry. FESTIVELY, *adv.* in a f. way. FESTIVOUS, *adj.* relating to a feast; joyous. [L.].

FESTIVITY [fes-ti′vi-ti], *n.* feasting; joyous celebration as at a feast; a festival. [L.].

FESTOON (1) [fes-tŏŏn′], *n.* garland of flowers etc., suspended so as to hang in a loop and with the ends hanging down; sculptured ornament in imitation of such a garland; curve on the cutting edge of a falcon's beak. FESTOON (2), *v.t.* to form in festoons, adorn with festoons. [OFr.].

FESTUCA [fes-tyŏŏ′ka], *n.* genus of ninety species of grasses; fescue grass. [L.].

FETCH (1) [fech], *v.t.* to go for and bring back a person or thing; cause to come; bring in, realize; (*coll.*) charm, captivate; **to f. and carry**, to run errands, perform the duties of a servant; **to f. a sigh**, to heave a sigh; **to f. someone a blow**, to deal someone a blow; **to f. up**, *v.i.* (*coll.*) to come to a stop. FETCH (2), *n.* a dodge; trick; artifice; **f. of the sea**, distance of a coast from the closest weather shore; **f. of wind**, distance of uninterrupted sea over which the wind blows. FETCHER, *n.* person who fetches. [OE.].

FETCH (3), *n.* a wraith, apparition. FETCH-CANDLE, a light like a moving candle seen at night and supposed to bode death. [Unkn.].

FETCHING [fe′ching], *adj.* alluring, attractive.

FETE, fête [fāt], *n.* a festival or holiday; kind of fair held in a charitable cause. FETED, *adj.* honoured with a f.; made a fuss of. [Fr.].

FETIAL [fē′shal], *adj.* **f. law**, international law concerning the declaration of war or peace. [L.].

FETICH(E), see FETISH.

FETID, see FOETID.

FETISH, FETICH(E) [fe′tish, fē′tish], *n.* an inanimate object believed to be inhabited by spirits, and therefore worshipped by savages; (*fig.*) any object of excessive devotion or veneration. FETICHISM, *n.* the worship of a f.; system of fetishes; juju. FETISHISTIC [fe-ti-shis′tik, fē-ti-shis′tik], *adj.* relating to fetichism. [Fr.].

FETLOCK [fet′lok], *n.* tuft of hair which grows behind the pastern joints of horses; part where it grows. FETLOCKED, *adj.* having a f. [ME.].

FETTER (1) [fe′ter], *n.* a shackle restraining the feet; anything which confines or restrains. FETTER (2), *v.t.* to chain, shackle (*esp.* the feet); confine, put under restraint. FETTERED, *adj.* (*zool.*) applied to the feet of animals, as seals, when they are stretched backwards and appear unsuitable for walking. FETTERLESS, *adj.* without, free from, fetters. [O.E.].

FETTERLOCK [fe'ter-lok], *n.* a shackle or fetter for a horse's feet, sometimes used as a heraldic charge.

FETTLE [fe'tl], *n.* condition; fitness. [ME.].

FETUS, see FOETUS.

FEUD (1) [fyōōd], *n.* a fierce and deadly quarrel between two families, persons or groups of persons. [OFr. from OHGerm.].

FEUD (2), FEOD, *n.* a fief; land held on condition of man-service. [MedL.].

FEUDAL [fyōō'dal], *adj.* relating to feuds or fiefs; consisting of feuds or fiefs; **the f. system,** the social system in medieval Europe by which vassals held their lands from the lord superior on condition of military service when required. FEUDALISM, *n.* the f. system. FEUDALIST, *n.* an authority on feudalism. FEUDALISTIC [fyōō-da-lis'tik], *adj.* pertaining to feudalism. FEUDALLY, *adv.* in the f. way. [MedL.].

FEUDALITY [fyōō-da'li-ti], *n.* condition or quality of being feudal; feudal constitution. [Fr.].

FEUDALIZE [fyōō'da-liz], *v.t.* to make feudal, reduce to a feudal tenure. FEUDALIZATION [fyōō-da-li-zā'shn], *n.* act or process of feudalizing.

FEUDATORY [fyōō'da-te-ri], *n.* vassal who held his lands of a superior on condition that he gave military service when required. [MedL.].

FEUDIST [fyōō'dist], *n.* one versed in feudal law.

FEUILLEMORT(E) [fer-i-mawt'], *n.* the colour of dead leaves; yellowish-brown. [Fr.].

FEUILLETON [fur'i-ton], *n.* space in a French journal devoted to light literature or criticism; in an English journal, a serial story. FEUILLETONIST, *n.* writer on light topics; writer of light criticism or serial stories. [Fr.].

FEVER [fē'ver], *n.* morbid condition of the system characterized by high temperature; one of various diseases characterized by a rise in temperature; state of great nervous excitement; **f. heat,** abnormally high temperature of the body, as in a fever; (*fig.*) high pressure of work, great speed or excitement. [O.E.].

FEVERFEW [fē'ver-fyōō], *n.* the plant *Matricaria Parthenium* and other species of the same genus, formerly used as a febrifuge. [L.].

FEVERISH [fē've-rish], *adj.* slightly fevered; showing, indicating fever; excited, nervous, agitated. FEVERISHLY, *adv.* in a f. way. FEVERISHNESS, *n.* quality of being f.

FEW (1) [fyōō], *adj.* not many; a small number of; **every f. days, hours etc.,** once in every group, or at intervals, of a f. days, hours etc.; **some f.,** quite a good number. FEW (2), *n.* a small number; not many; **the f.,** the minority; **a good f.,** (*coll.*) a good many; quite a number. FEWNESS, *n.* a small quantity; paucity. [O.E.].

FEY [fā], *adj.* doomed to die; epithet applied when a person acts in a remarkably light-hearted, happy way, popularly supposed to be a prelude to death. [O.E.].

FEZ [fez], *n.* a tall brimless red cap. [Turk.].

FIACRE [fē-ahkr'], *n.* French hackney carriage. [Fr.].

FIANCE, fiancé [fē-ahn'sā], *n.* betrothed man, man to whom one is betrothed. [Fr.].

FIANCEE, fiancée [fē-ahn'sā], *n.* betrothed woman, woman to whom one is betrothed. [Fr.].

FIANNA FAIL [fyahn-nah-foil'], *n.* name of the Irish political party led by Eamon de Valera. [Ir.].

FIASCO [fē-as'kō], *n.* any signal failure; an attempt which comes to nothing. [It.].

FIAT [fī'at], *n.* an order to do something; decree; **f. money,** in U.S.A., inconvertible paper money made legal tender by government decree. [L.].

FIB (1) [fib], *n.* a trivial falsehood; harmless inexactitude. FIB (2) (*pres.pt.* **fibbing,** *pret. and p.pt.* **fibbed**), *v.i.* to tell trivial falsehoods. FIBBER, FIBSTER, *n.* one who tells fibs.

FIBRE [fī'ber], *n.* thread-like filament in plants and animals; (*comm.*) the raw material in textile manufacture; **f. needle,** gramophone needle made of bamboo. FIBRED, *adj.* having fibres. FIBRELESS, *adj.* without fibres. [L.].

FIBRIL [fī'bril], *n.* a small fibre; slender thread. FIBRILLAR, *adj.* pertaining to a f. or to fibrils. FIBRILLOSE, *adj.* made up of, or covered with, fibrils.

FIBRILLATION [fī-bri-lā'shn], *n.* (*med.*) quality of being fibrillar; muscular tremor.

FIBRIN [fī'brin], *n.* coagulable lymph found in animals and vegetables; gluten. FIBRINATION [fī-bri-nā'shn], *n.* (*med.*) excessive formation of f. FIBRINOUS, *adj.* containing, of the nature of, f.

FIBROCELLULAR [fī-brō-se'lyōō-ler], *adj.* composed of fibrous and cellular tissues.

FIBROID (1) [fī'broid], *adj.* like fibre. FIBROID (2), *n.* (*path.*) a f. tumour.

FIBROIN [fī'brō-in], *n.* substance which forms the chief constituent of silk, cobwebs etc.

FIBROMA [fī-brō'mah], *n.* (*path.*) a fibrous tumour.

FIBROMUSCULAR [fī-brō-mus'kyōō-ler], *adj.* composed of muscular and connective tissue.

FIBROSE [fī'brōs], *adj.* fibrous.

FIBROSIS [fī-brō'sis], *n.* morbid growth of fibroid matter.

FIBROSITIS [fī-brō-sī'tis], *n.* (*path.*) inflamed condition of muscle fibres.

FIBROUS [fī'brōs], *adj.* consisting of or containing fibres. FIBROUSNESS, *n.* state or quality of being f.

FIBULA [fī'byōō-lah], *n.* (*anat.*) the outer and smaller bone of the leg. FIBULAR [fī'byōō-ler], *adj.* pertaining to the f. [L.].

FICHU [fī'shōō], *n.* piece of silk or lace etc. draped on the shoulders of a dress. [Fr.].

FICKLE [fi'kl], *adj.* changeable, vacillating, inconstant. FICKLENESS, *n.* quality or state of being f. [O.E.].

FICTILE [fik'til], *adj.* moulded or mouldable into form by the potter; of pottery. [L.].

FICTION [fik'shn], *n.* an invented statement or narrative; that type of literature which tells imaginary stories; anything based on imagination; **legal f.,** an accepted falsehood or inaccuracy by which the raising of an awkward or irrelevant issue is avoided. FICTIONAL, *adj.* based on f. FICTIONIST, *n.* writer of f.; novelist. [L.].

FICTITIOUS [fik-ti'shōōs], *adj.* invented; imagined; unreal; not true or genuine; assumed, pretended; occurring in fiction; regarded as, or relating to, a legal fiction. FICTITIOUSLY, *adv.* in a f. way. FICTITIOUSNESS, *n.* quality or state of being f. [L.].

FICTIVE [fik'tiv], *adj.* pertaining to fiction; false, imagined. FICTIVELY, *adv.* in a f. way. [Fr.].

FID [fid], *n.* (*naut.*) conical wooden pin used as a splicing tool; bar of wood or iron put through a hole to hold a spar in place. [Unkn.].

FIDDLE (1) [fi'dl], *n.* familiar or derogatory name for a violin; general term for an instrument of the family which comprises the violin, viola, violoncello and double bass; (*naut.*) wooden device fitted to tables to prevent things from sliding off; (*slang*) an illegal trading operation, a wangle; **as fit as a f.,** in good health; **to play second f.,** to take a subordinate place. FIDDLE (2), *v.i.* to play the f. or violin; make aimless, fidgety movements; waste time; (*slang*) acquire or dispose of goods illegally, wangle. [ME.].

FIDDLE-HEAD [fi'dl-hed], *n.* ornament on a ship's prow, shaped off like the head of a fiddle.

FIDDLER [fid'ler], *n.* one who plays on a fiddle; violinist; small American crab; (*slang*) one who fiddles or wangles. [O.E.].

FIDDLESTICK [fi'dl-stik], *n.* the bow of a fiddle. FIDDLESTICKS! (*int.*) rubbish! nonsense!

FIDDLE-STRING [fi'dl-string], *n.* one of the strings of a fiddle.

FIDDLING [fid'ling], *adj.* trifling in a fussy way; fidgety; petty; trivial.

FIDELITY [fi-de'li-ti], *n.* state or quality of being faithful; strict adherence to fact or truth; accuracy of detail; exact conformity with the original. [L.].

FIDGET (1) [fi'jit], *n.* toying fussiness; mental uneasiness or nervousness; a restless person; **the fidgets,** a fit of restlessness or anxiety. FIDGET (2) (*pres.pt.* FIDGETING, *pret. and p.pt.* FIDGETED), *v.t.* to make restless or nervy; get on the nerves of; disturb, upset; *v.i.* to make restless, spasmodic movements; fuss; be anxious or nervous. [Uncert.].

FIDGETY [fi'ji-ti], *adj.* moving restlessly about; uneasy. FIDGETINESS, *n.* quality of being f.

FIDUCIAL [fi-dyōō'shl], *adj.* confident; undoubting; of the nature of a trust; **f. line, point,** a line etc. assumed, or taken on trust, as a fixed basis of comparison. FIDUCIALLY, *adv.* with confidence; on trust. [L.].

FIDUCIARY (1) [fi-dyōō'sha-ri], *adj.* confident; undoubting; held or given in trust; (of currency) depending for its value on public confidence or securities. FIDUCIARY (2), *n.* one who holds something in trust; trustee. [L.].

FIE [fī], *int.* expression of disapproval or disgust. [Fr.].

FIEF, FEOFF [fēf], *n.* a fee; feud; estate held of a

superior in return for military service. [OFr. from MedL.].

FIELD (1) [fēld], *n.* a tract of land, usually enclosed and used for agricultural purposes; stretch of land rich in some mineral product; ground where a battle is fought; the open country; background of shields, flags, coins etc.; area of observation or operation; scope, range; province, realm, department (of knowledge, study etc.); ground on which games are played; the participants or competitors in outdoor sports, except the favourite; the fielding side in cricket; (*phys.*) volume of space under the influence of a force; **to take the f.,** to commence hostilities; **to hold the f.,** to have an unchallenged position; **in the f.,** on active service, at work at the scene of operations. FIELD (2), *v.t.* (cricket, baseball etc.) to stop a ball and return it to the bowler or pitcher; put (an army, team, side etc.) into the f.; *v.i.* to act as a fielder while the other side is batting. [OE.].

FIELD-ALLOWANCE [fēld'a-low-ans], *n.* special allowance made to officers and warrant officers while on field duty.

FIELD AMBULANCE [fēld-am'byōō-lans], *n.* an Army unit of medical equipment, personnel etc. for emergency treatment of wounded on a battlefield.

FIELD-ARTILLERY [fēld-ah-ti'le-ri], *n.* artillery to co-operate with infantry in the field.

FIELD-BATTERY [fēld'ba-te-ri], *n.* battery composed of field-guns.

FIELD BOOK [fēld'bŏŏk], *n.* book used in surveying, for setting down angles, distances etc.

FIELD-CLUB [fēld'klub], *n.* club devoted to open-air nature study.

FIELD-COLOURS [fēld'ku-lerz], *n.*(*pl.*) small flags, used for marking out the ground for squadrons and battalions.

FIELD-DAY [fēld'dā], *n.* (*milit.*) day when troops are drawn out for review in field exercises and manoeuvres; day when all take the field; (*fig.*) day marked by some celebration or display beyond the ordinary.

FIELDER [fēl'der], *n.* (*cricket*) one who fields.

FIELDFARE [fēld'fāer], *n.* migratory bird of the thrush family.

FIELD-GLASS [fēld'glahs], *n.* the lens of an eyepiece which is nearest the object; (*pl.*) a binocular telescope; large opera-glass.

FIELD-GUN [fēld'gun], *n.* (*milit.*) gun to be used on the battlefield as distinct from a siege-gun.

FIELD-MARSHAL [fēld-mah'shal], *n.* (*milit.*) the highest rank of army officer.

FIELD-MOUSE [fēld'mows], *n.* small rodent of the genus *Microtus.*

FIELD-OFFICER [fēld'o-fi-ser], *n.* (*milit.*) officer of, or senior to, the rank of major but below general rank.

FIELD-PIECE [fēld'pēs], *n.* (*milit.*) a piece of field-artillery, field-gun.

FIELD PREACHER [fēld'prē-cher], *n.* person who preaches in the open air.

FIELDSMAN [fēldz'man], *n.* (*cricket*) a fielder.

FIELD-SPORTS [fēld'spawts], *n.*(*pl.*) open-air sports, as shooting, fishing and hunting.

FIELD-WORKS [fēld'werks], *n.*(*pl.*) (*milit.*) works thrown up in the siege or defence of a place.

FIEND [fēnd], *n.* devil; evil spirit; Satan, Devil; very wicked or cruel person; (*coll.*) devotee, addict. FIENDLIKE, *adj.* like a f. [OE.].

FIENDISH [fēn'dish], *adj.* like a fiend, cruel, devilish, malicious. FIENDISHLY, *adv.* in a f. way.

FIERCE [fēers], *adj.* cruel, savage, ferocious; uncontrolled, violent; strong, intense. FIERCELY, *adv.* in a f. way. FIERCENESS, *n.* quality or condition of being f. [OFr. from L.].

FIERY [fīer'i], *adj.* burning, full of flames, carrying or containing fire; like fire; hot, glowing, red; (*fig.*) impetuous; quick-tempered, vehement; passionate, ardent; (of horses) high-spirited; (*min.*) inflammable. FIERILY, in a f. manner. [FIRE (1)].

FIERY-CROSS [fīer-i-kros'], *n.* a cross charred and dipped in blood, sent round in the Scottish Highlands to summon the clans to war.

FIESTA [fē-es'tah], *n.* a festivity, holiday. [Span.].

FIFE (1) [fīf], *n.* kind of small shrill flute used chiefly in martial music. FIFE (2), *v.i.* to play a f. FIFER, *n.* one who plays a f. [Uncert.].

FIFTEEN (1) [fif-tēn'], *n.* cardinal number next above fourteen; team of Rugby football players; **the F.,** the Jacobite rebellion of 1715. FIFTEEN (2), *adj.* one more than fourteen. [OE.].

FIFTEENTH (1) [fif-tēnth'], *n.* a fifteenth part; (*mus.*) the interval of the double octave. FIFTEENTH (2), *adj.* the ordinal of fifteen; being one of fifteen equal parts.

FIFTH (1) [fifth], *n.* a fifth part; one of five equal parts; (*mus.*) an interval of three tones and a semitone. FIFTH (2), the ordinal of five; being one of five equal parts: **f. wheel,** something superfluous; **F. Monarchy,** the last of the five great empires; **F. Monarchy men,** seventeenth-century fanatics expecting the immediate coming of Christ. [OE.].

FIFTH COLUMN [fifth-ko'lum], *n.* body of traitors within a given area or country. FIFTH COLUMNIST, *n.* member of the f.

FIFTHLY [fifth'li], *adv.* fifth in order, in the fifth place.

FIFTIETH [fif'ti-eth], *adj.* the ordinal of fifty; being one of fifty equal parts.

FIFTY (1) [fif'ti], *n.* cardinal number next above forty-nine; **the fifties,** the sixth decade in a century or a lifetime. FIFTY-FIFTY, (*coll.*) equal sharing; **to go fifty-fifty,** to share equally. FIFTY (2), *adj.* five times ten; one more than forty-nine. [OE.].

FIG [fig], *n.* the fig-tree; soft, pear-shaped many-seeded fruit of the fig-tree; thing of no worth; abbreviation of *figure*; **under one's vine and f.-tree,** safely at home. [OFr. from L.].

FIGHT (1) (*pret. and p.pt.* **fought**) [fīt], *v.t.* to contend against, oppose with violence, physically or figuratively; conduct vigorously (a case, election etc.); manoeuvre in battle (a ship etc.); *v.i.* to engage in a contest, battle or struggle of any kind; **to f. it out,** to settle (a dispute) by fighting; **to f. shy of,** to avoid, keep aloof from. FIGHT (2), *n.* act of fighting; struggle; contest; battle; conflict; ability, inclination to f.; pugnacity; **prize f.,** pugilistic contest; **stand-up f.,** formal, open combat; **free f.,** f. without clearly defined sides; **to put up a good f.,** to f. pluckily; **to show f.,** to show readiness to f. [OE., ME.].

FIGHTER [fī'ter], *n.* person who fights; a combatant; warrior; (*aeron.*) aeroplane designed to attack other aeroplanes; person who does not give in easily.

FIGHTER-BOMBER [fī-ter-bo'mer], *n.* (*aeron.*) aeroplane combining the capabilities of a fighter and a bomber.

FIGHTING [fī'ting], *adj.* trained or designed to fight; engaged in war or combat; **f. chance,** possibility of success if every effort is made. FIGHTING-TOP, circular gun platform fixed to the mast of a battleship.

FIG-LEAF [fig'lēf], *n.* leaf of a fig-tree; device for covering the sexual organs in statuary etc.

FIGMENT [fig'ment], *n.* an invention; fiction; anything feigned or imagined. [L.].

FIGURABLE [fi'gyōō-ra-bl], *adj.* capable of being fashioned into a fixed shape; describable.

FIGURANT [fi'gyōō-rant], *n.* male ballet-dancer, member of a ballet-company. [Fr.].

FIGURANTE (1) [fi'gyōō-rant], *n.* female ballet-dancer, member of a ballet-company. [Fr.].

FIGURANTE (2) (*pl.* **figuranti**) [fi-gyōō-ran'tā], *n.* figurant or figurante (1); ballet-dancer. [It.].

FIGURATE [fi'gyōō-rāt], *adj.* of, or according to, a determinate form. FIGURATED, *adj.* of, possessing, a determinate form. FIGURATELY, *adv.* in a f. way.

FIGURATION [fi-gyōō-rā'shn], *n.* act or process of giving figure or determinate form; determination to a certain form; (*mus.*) mixture of concords and discords or ornamental treatment. [L.].

FIGURATIVE [fi'gyōō-ra-tiv], *adj.* representing something else; representing by resemblance, parable or symbol; not literal or direct; abounding in figures of speech; flowery. FIGURATIVELY, *adv.* metaphorically, not literally. FIGURATIVENESS, *n.* quality of being f. [LL.].

FIGURE (1) [fi'ger], *n.* outer shape or appearance; form; the human form, bodily shape; a representation of the human form; statue; image, likeness; a person as actually seen, or as contemplated mentally; emblem, type; illustration, descriptive diagram or drawing; numerical symbol; a movement or series of movements in skating, set of steps in, division of, a dance; (*geom.*) space enclosed by lines or surfaces; (*log.*) particular form of syllogism; (*gram.*) permissible deviation from the ordinary construction; (*mus.*) short series of notes producing a single impression, phrase; (*rhet.*) recognized mode of expression, in which words are used in some abnormal sense for the sake of emphasis, variety etc.; (*astrol.*) horoscope; **at a low (high) f.,** cheap (dear); **to cut a f.,** to make an impression. FIGURE (2), *v.t.* to represent pictorially or diagrammatically; decorate, embellish with a pattern; be a symbol of; (*U.S.*) reckon, calculate; *v.i.* to appear; be conspicuous; **to f. out,** to work out; give results in figures; **to f. up,** to reckon up, calculate the amount of; **to f. to oneself,** to imagine. FIGURED, *adj.* adorned with figures; having a pattern or design; figurative. [L.].

FIGURE-HEAD [fi'ger-hed], *n.* figure, statue or bust on the projecting part of a ship's prow; person occupying an eminent position but possessing no real authority.

FIGURE-MAKER [fi'ger-mā-ker], *n.* one who makes figures; modeller.

FIGURE-OF-EIGHT [fi-ger-ov-āt'], *n.* knot made in the form of an 8; skating figure in the form of a large 8.

FIGURINE [fi'gyōō-rēn], *n.* a statuette. [Fr.].

FILAGREE, see FILIGREE.

FILAMENT [fi'la-ment], *n.* slender thread or fibre; (*bot.*) long thread-like part which supports the anther; fine wire used in electric light bulbs or radio valves. FILAMENTARY [fi-la-men'ta-ri], *adj.* pertaining to, of the nature of, a f. FILAMENTOUS [fi-la-men'tōōs], *adj.* like a thread. [L.].

FILAR [fi'ler], *adj.* having threads.

FILATURE [fi'la-tyōōr], *n.* process of reeling silk from cocoons; reel so used; place where it is done. [Fr.].

FILBERT [fil'bert], *n.* nut of the cultivated hazel. [Fr.].

FILCH [filch], *v.t.* to steal (*esp.* some petty object). FILCHER, *n.* one who commits a petty theft. [Uncert.].

FILE (1) [fil], *n.* steel instrument with roughened surface for smoothing or reducing hard objects. FILE (2), *v.t.* to reduce, smooth, with a f. [OE.].

FILE (3), *n.* stiff wire on which papers, documents etc. are threaded for keeping; box or folder for a similar purpose; documents, newspapers, periodicals or the like so kept. FILE (4), *v.t.* to put on a f.; keep in a f.; place among public records; send (a message) by cable. [L.].

FILE (5), *n.* row of people or things one behind the other; (*milit.*) row of soldiers ranged one behind the other; (*chess*) line of squares reaching from player to player; **in f.** (*milit.*) drawn up or marching in a line, one behind the other; **Indian, single f.,** a single line of men in f.; **rank and f.,** (*milit.*) soldiers who are not commissioned or warrant officers; (*fig.*) the lower classes; the general body as distinct from the leaders. FILE (6), *v.t.* to command to march in f.; *v.i.* to march in f. [Fr.].

FILER [fi'ler], *n.* one who files.

FILIAL [fi'li-al], *adj.* pertaining to a son or daughter; becoming, proper to, expected from, a son or daughter; (*fig.*) related as a child or offspring. FILIALLY, *adv.* in f. fashion.

FILIATION [fi-li-ā'shn], *n.* state of being a son or daughter, relationship of a child to its parents; fact of being a descendant of; genealogical relationship; development of new branches or subsidiary organizations. [MedL.].

FILIBEG, FILLIBEG, PHILIBEG [fi'li-beg], *n.* a kilt. [Gael.].

FILIBUSTER (1) [fi'li-bus-ter], *n.* pirate, freebooter, buccaneer, military adventurer who unlawfully attacks the possessions of a foreign state; (*U.S.*) political obstructionist; act of obstruction in a legislative assembly. FILIBUSTER (2), *v.i.* to act as, behave like, a f. FILIBUSTERISM, *n.* the practices of the filibusters. [Span. from Du.].

FILICOID [fi'li-koid], *n. and adj.* (plant) resembling a fern. [L. and Gk.].

FILIFORM [fi'li-fawm], *adj.* like a thread. [L.].

FILIGREE, FILAGREE [fi'li-grē], *n.* fine ornamental open-work in gold and silver, so delicate as to resemble lacework; (*fig.*) fine delicate work of any kind. FILIGREED, *adj.* ornamented with f. work. [It.].

FILING [fi'ling], *adj.* designed to store documents or other records; **f. clerk,** one concerned with keeping records.

FILINGS [fi'lingz], *n.(pl.)* minute fragments or particles accumulated by filing.

FILIPINO [fi-li-pē'nō], *n. and adj.* a native of, pertaining to natives of, the Philippine Islands. [Span.].

FILL (1) [fil], *v.t. and i.* to put into a receptacle etc. such a quantity as to leave no space in it unoccupied; stuff, pack, crowd; close with some repairing material (a cavity in a tooth); make full, occupy a space completely; perform the duties of (an office or

position); appoint someone to (a vacant post); (*naut.*) cause to swell out (of sails); provide with abundant supplies of; become full; **to f. in,** to complete by inserting some information required; level out a hollow etc.; **to f. out,** to become distended; (*coll.*) become plump or fatter; **to f. up,** to make completely full; complete by adding necessary information in the appropriate spaces; become full; **to f. the bill,** (*coll.*) to meet the case or requirements satisfactorily. FILL (2), *n.* that which fills; full supply or amount. [OE.].

FILLER [fi'ler], *n.* one who or that which fills; vessel or tube used in filling bottles, casks etc.; (*motoring*) narrow opening by which a petrol or oil tank etc. is filled.

FILLET (1) [fi'lit], *n.* small band of ribbon tied round the hair; portion of fish which has been filleted; thick, fleshy portion of meat; (*pl.*) loins of a horse; (*arch.*) narrow band separating two mouldings, or between the flutes of a column; (*her.*) horizontal band across a chief; (*carp.*) narrow strip of wood or scantling; (*print.*) narrow line made upon the cover of a book. FILLET (2), *v.t.* to bind or adorn with a headband or ribbon; remove the bones from (fish or meat) and slice. [Fr. from L.].

FILLIBEG, see FILIBEG.

FILLING [fi'ling], *n.* that which is used to fill or stop up a cavity, *esp.* in a tooth.

FILLING-STATION [fi'ling-stā-shn], *n.* place where petrol is sold for use in motor vehicles.

FILLIP (1) [fi'lip], *n.* a flick or sharp jerk of the finger when released suddenly from the thumb, which has been pressing upon it; incentive, stimulus, incitement; light blow or tap; trifle, something of small account. FILLIP (2), *v.t. and i.* to strike with a f.; spin (a coin) with a f.; give a f. to. [Imitative].

FILLY [fi'li], *n.* female foal, young mare; (*fig.*) high-spirited young girl. [OIcel.].

FILM (1) [film], *n.* a thin layer, coating or skin; fine, slender, gossamer-like thread; (*phot.*) flexible sheet or ribbon of cellulose or similar substance, sensitized on one surface; reel or spool of this on which a cinematograph picture is photographed; any of the separate screen items composing a cinema entertainment. FILM (2), *v.t. and i.* to cover with a f.; (*phot.*) make a f. of, photograph; become clouded over with a f.; make films. FILMABLE, *adj.* suitable for making into a cinema f. [OE.].

FILM-ACTOR [film'ak-ter], *n.* actor engaged in acting for the screen as opposed to the stage.

FILM-PACK [film'pak], *n.* set of photographic films packed flat instead of rolled, and able to be inserted into, or withdrawn from, a camera in daylight.

FILM-STAR [film'stah(r)], *n.* film-actor or actress who has achieved a pre-eminent position in the profession.

FILM-STUDIO [film'styoo-di-ō], *n.* permanent building in which cinema films are made.

FILM-TEST [film'test], *n.* series of photographs taken to discover whether a person is suitable for acting on the films or in a particular film.

FILMY [fil'mi], *adj.* resembling a film in nature or appearance, clouded over with a film. FILMINESS, *n.* condition of being f.

FILOSELLE [fi'lo-sel], *n.* floss silk. [Fr.].

FILTER (1) [fil'ter], *n.* substance or apparatus used for ridding liquids of impurities or solid matter; apparatus for purifying air; plate of coloured glass, gelatine etc. through which light of only a selected colour, intensity or character may pass; (*radio*) circuit along which a limited number of frequencies only may pass. FILTER (2), *v.t. and i.* to strain or purify by passing through a f. or porous substance; rid of impurities or solid matter; (of light) modify by passing through a f.; trickle as through a f.; (*fig.*) pass or be received slowly and intermittently as through a f. [MedL.].

FILTERABLE [fil'te-ra-bl], *adj.* that may be filtered; **f. virus,** micro-organism able to pass through a fine filter.

FILTER-BED [fil'ter-bed], *n.* reservoir with an artificial lining of some porous substance through which water, sewage etc. may be filtered.

FILTERING [fil'te-ring], *n.* act of straining, purifying or modifying by means of a filter. FILTERING-CUP, *n.* pneumatic apparatus used to demonstrate the pressure of the atmosphere upon water.

FILTER-PAPER [fil'ter-pā-per], *n.* porous paper used for filtering liquids.

FILTH [filth], *n.* foul, unclean matter; anything which defiles; dirt, dust, mud etc.; (*fig.*) obscenity, indecency; (*coll.*) trash, rubbish. [OE.].

FILTHY [fil'thi], *adj.* foul, unclean, dirty, abounding

---

in filth; obscene; indecent; depraved; (*coll.*) vile, very bad; **f. lucre**, money. **FILTHILY**, *adv.* in a f. fashion.

FILTRATE (1) [fĭl'trāt], *v.t.* to filter. **FILTRATE** (2), *n.* liquid which has been run through a filter. **FILTRATION** [fĭl-trā'shn], *n.* act or process of filtering.

FIN [fĭn], *n.* flat ribbed projecting organ of locomotion of a fish or cetacean; similar flat projection attached to the vertical part of the tail of an aeroplane or to an airship for balancing or steering purposes; (*slang*) the hand. [OE.].

FINABLE [fī'na-bl], *adj.* liable to a fine or penalty.

FINAL (1) [fī'nal], *adj.* pertaining to the end, last, concluding, ultimate; conclusive, decisive; **f. clause**, (*gram.*) clause expressing purpose; **f. newspaper**, (*coll.*) the last edition of a newspaper published during the day. **FINAL** (2), *n.* the concluding stage, that which is f., the last heat, round or match in a knockout competition or event; (*pl.*) the f. examination for a university degree, diploma or certificate. **FINALLY**, *adv.* lastly, in conclusion; completely. [L.].

FINALE [fi-nah'li], *n.* (*mus.*) the last movement in a symphony, concerto, sonata etc.; last song or chorus of an act of an opera; that which concludes or finishes, the end, close. [It.].

FINALIST [fī'na-list], *n.* competitor who has reached the final of a competition, tournament etc.

FINALITY [fī-na'li-ti], *n.* quality of being final, conclusiveness; that which is final. [L.].

FINALIZE [fī'na-līz], *v.t.* (*mostly U.S. and Dominions*) to bring to an end, complete (arrangements etc.).

FINANCE (1) [fi-nans', fī-nans'], *n.* science of managing money matters, *esp.* public money or revenue; (*pl.*) funds, wealth, monetary resources. **FINANCE** (2), *v.t.* to find the capital for, furnish with the necessary money or funds. [OFr.].

FINANCIAL [fi-nan'shal, fī-nan'shal], *adj.* pertaining to finance or to money matters. **FINANCIALLY**, *adv.* as regards money matters, from the point of view of f.

FINANCIER [fi-nan'si-er, fī-nan'si-er], *n.* one skilled or versed in finance; person engaged in large-scale monetary dealings. [Fr.].

FINCH [finch], *n.* one of a family of small perching birds. [OE.].

FIND (1) [*pret. and p.pt.* **found**] [fīnd], *v.t. and i.* to discover, perceive that which was hidden or lost; discover by experiment, experience, study; detect; provide, furnish with; (*leg.*) judge, decide and declare; obtain, get hold of; discover game; (*leg.*) give a verdict, decide in favour of, or against; **to f. a true bill**, (*leg.*) to establish grounds of accusation; **to f. oneself**, (of health etc.) be, fare; **to f. a ship's trim**, (*naut.*) discover how a ship sails best; **to f. one's way**, to make one's way. **FIND** (2), *n.* a discovery, *esp.* one of a peculiarly satisfying or important nature; an unexpected and profitable acquisition. **FINDABLE**, *adj.* discoverable, that may be found.

FINDER [fīn'der], *n.* one who, or that which, finds; small lens attached to a camera in which can be seen an image of the object or scene to be photographed; small telescope attached to a larger one for sighting purposes.

FINDING [fīn'ding], *n.* that which is found; (*leg.*) decision reached by a judge, jury etc.; (*pl.*) conclusions arrived at by a commission or tribunal of inquiry.

FINDON, see FINNAN.

FINE (1) [fīn], *n.* a payment of a sum of money imposed by law as punishment for an offence; payment made by a person renewing a lease; **in f.**, finally, in short. **FINE** (2), *v.t.* to impose a f. upon, punish by a f. [OFr.].

FINE (3), *adj.* slender, small, thin; rare; minute; delicately wrought, displaying dexterous workmanship; polished, refined, finished; delicate, not coarse; sharp, keen; elegant, handsome; accomplished, extremely good; superb, splendid, excellent, compelling admiration; well developed, in excellent condition; free from impurities, pure; bright, not raining; subtle, requiring discrimination; acute, keen, discriminating; ostentatious, showy; **one of these f. days**, upon some future unspecified occasion; **f. arts**, arts cultivated for their aesthetic, non-utilitarian, qualities; **f. chemicals**, chemicals made in small quantities and refined to a high degree of purity. **FINE** (4), *adv.* finely, very well; **to cut it f.**, (*coll.*) to allow oneself a bare minimum or hardly enough. **FINE** (5), *v.t. and i.* to become more pure or clear; become finer in texture, quality etc.; purify, refine. **FINELY**, *adv.* in f. fashion. [Fr.].

FINE-DRAW [fīn-draw'], *v.t.* to sew together or mend so that the join or mending is not noticeable;

draw out to a high degree of thinness or fineness. **FINE-DRAWN**, *adj.* having the edge joined or sewn in such a way as to be unnoticeable; drawn out very finely; over-subtle, requiring keen discrimination.

FINERY (1) [fī'ne-ri], *n.* that which is fine; splendour or elaborateness of personal attire; resplendent array.

FINERY (2), *n.* hearth used in the manufacture of steel from pig-iron, or in making cast-iron malleable. [Fr.].

FINE-SPUN [fīn-spun'], *adj.* spun out to a high degree of fineness, delicate; (*fig.*) elaborated with excessive subtlety.

FINESSE (1) [fi-nes'], *n.* subtlety of action, diplomatic management, tact, dexterity; artfulness, cunning; (*cards*) an attempt to take a trick with a low card, while the opponents hold a higher one in that suit, in order to make an extra trick. **FINESSE** (2), *v.t. and i.* to act with f., use f.; (*cards*) make a f.; deal with by f.; (*whist*) play as a f. **FINESSER**, *n.* one who finesses. [Fr.].

FINE-TOOTH [fīn'tōōth], *adj.* (of a comb) having fine, closely-set teeth.

FINGER (1) [fing'ger], *n.* one of the five digits in which the hand terminates, *esp.* any one of these other than the thumb; the breadth of one of these; part of a glove into which a finger fits; anything shaped like a finger; a long thin slice; one of the pointers of a clock or watch; **not to lift a f.**, to make no attempt to help; **to have a f. in the pie**, to have a share in; **to lay a f. on**, to harm, injure; **to have at one's f. ends**, to have certain knowledge ready for immediate use; be thoroughly conversant with. **FINGER** (2), *v.t.* to hold, touch or handle with the fingers; (*mus.*) play an instrument with the fingers, play a passage using a particular fingering; indicate, on the music itself, the fingering to be used; (*coll.*) pilfer, take or accept illegally. [OE.].

FINGER-ALPHABET [fing-ger-al'fa-bet], *n.* various signs or positions of the fingers and hands representing the different letters of the alphabet, and used by deaf and dumb persons in conversing.

FINGERBOARD [fing'ger-bawd], *n.* board at the neck of a violin, guitar or the like, where the fingers are pressed against the strings; a keyboard.

FINGER-BOWL [fing'ger-bōl], *n.* small bowl containing water in which the fingers may be dipped after dessert at the dinner-table.

FINGERBREADTH [fing'ger-bredth], *n.* the sixteenth part of a foot.

FINGERED [fing'gerd], *adj.* having fingers; (*bot.*) digitate; **light-f. gentry**, (*coll.*) pickpockets.

FINGERING (1) [fing'ge-ring], *n.* act or method of playing a musical instrument with the fingers, use of the proper finger in playing each note of a musical composition; written instructions on the music as to the proper fingers to use in playing each note; act of touching or handling with the fingers. **FINGERING** (2), *n.* loose-twisted fine kind of wool. [Fr.].

FINGER-LANGUAGE [fing'ger-lang-gwij], *n.* the deaf and dumb alphabet.

FINGER-MARK [fing'ger-mahk], *n.* mark or impression made by the finger.

FINGERNAIL [fing'ger-nāl], *n.* the thin layer of horny substance at the tip of the finger.

FINGERPLATE [fing'ger-plāt], *n.* plate fixed to a door, near the handle, to protect the paint from finger-marks.

FINGERPOST [fing'ger-pōst], *n.* sign-post at cross-roads etc., *esp.* one whose signs end in the representation of a finger.

FINGERPRINT (1) [fing'ger-print], *n.* impression taken from, or left by, the ball of the finger, used to identify criminals. **FINGERPRINT** (2), *v.t.* to take the fingerprints of.

FINGERSTALL [fing'ger-stawl], *n.* a cover or protection for the finger when hurt.

FINGER-TIP [fing'ger-tip], *n.* the tip of a finger; **to one's finger-tips**, completely, through and through; **f. control**, arrangement of the controls of a machine so that they are easily operated and well within the reach of the hand.

FINIAL [fī'ni-al], *n.* (*arch.*) ornamental projection surmounting a gable, pinnacle etc.

FINICAL [fī'ni-kal], *adj.* extremely fastidious, fussy, too particular about unimportant details; containing a superfluity of highly finished, elaborate detail. **FINICALLY**, *adv.* in a f. fashion. **FINICALNESS**, *n.* quality of being f. [Uncert.].

FINICKING [fī'ni-king], *adj.* finical, affectedly refined, over-precise, *esp.* about trifling details; paltry, mean, insignificant. **FINICKY**, *adj.* f., fussy.

ōō is pronounced as in f*oo*d; ŏŏ as in h*oo*d; th as in *th*ink; TH as in *th*at; zh as in azure.   ~ = related to.

DSE—I

FINING [fī'ning], *n.* process of refining or purifying; solution used for clarifying wines. FINING-POT, receptacle in which metals are refined.

FINIS [fī'nis], *n.* the end, conclusion. [L.].

FINISH (1) [fī'nish], *v.t. and i.* to bring to an end, complete, cease, conclude; come to the end of; make as perfect as possible; kill, destroy; put an end to; come to an end, terminate; (*coll.*) be dispatched; **to f. with,** to cease to have further dealings or relations with. FINISH (2), *n.* the concluding stage, end, close; final attention, care or preparation to **make as perfect as possible;** that which completes or makes perfect; style in which a thing is finished; **to fight to a f.,** to fight until a decisive result is reached. FINISHED, *adj.* complete; perfect, highly wrought, consummate. FINISHER, *n.* one who, or that which, finishes, a workman or machine that performs the final processes in the manufacture of an article. FINISHING, *adj.* completing, giving a f. to, ending. [ME. from OFr. from L.].

FINITE [fī'nīt], *adj.* limited, having a fixed boundary, bounded; (*math.*) that has ends determinable; (*gram.*) (of a part of a verb) limited as regards number and person. FINITELY, *adv.* in a limited degree. [L.].

FINITUDE [fī'ni-tyōōd], *n.* finiteness.

FINLET [fin'let], *n.* a small fin.

FINNAN, FINDON [fi'nan], *n.* a haddock cut open, salted and smoke-dried over a special fire. [*Findhorn,* Scottish river or fishing village on the river].

FINNER [fi'ner], *n.* fin-backed whale, rorqual.

FINNIC [fi'nik], *adj.* pertaining to the Finns, their language, or the group of languages to which it belongs.

FINSEN LIGHT [fin'sen-līt], *n.* special electric light used in ultra-violet ray treatment of disease. [Danish doctor, *Finsen*].

FIORD [fē'awd], *n.* long, narrow, rock-bound inlet in the coast; drowned glacier valley. [Norw.].

FIR [fur], *n.* any of several species of cone-bearing trees of various genera; the wood of these trees. [ME.].

FIRE (1) [fīer], *n.* the visible activity of incandescent combustion, characterized by flame, smoke and heat; a quantity of fuel burning in a hearth or enclosed space to provide heat, or by way of celebration; a conflagration, burning of a building etc.; discharge of fire-arms; state of combustion; (*fig.*) light, lustre; strong feeling, fervour, ardent zeal or passion; spirit, animation; **to set f. to,** to cause to burn; **to play with f.,** to meddle with dangerous things; **to catch f.,** to start to burn; **to set the Thames on f.,** to accomplish some startling exploit; **to go through f. and water,** to endure all manner of dangers or hardships; **out of the frying pan into the f.,** from an unpleasant situation to one still more unenviable; **on f.,** burning, in a state of ignition; wildly excited or eager; **under f.,** exposed to shooting; **to open f.,** to begin shooting; **between two fires,** attacked from two sides. FIRE (2), *v.t. and i.* to set on f., light; supply with fuel; apply heat to; bake (bricks), dry (tea); (*fig.*) direct a continual stream (of questions etc.); rouse, stir violently, inflame; (*slang*) dismiss from a post or from service; become ignited; discharge fire-arms; **to f. away,** (*coll.*) to begin, go ahead; **to f. up,** to burst into sudden violent anger; **to f. off,** to cause to cease burning (a kiln). [OE.].

FIRE-ALARM [fīer'a-lahm], *n.* apparatus for giving the alarm in case of fire.

FIRE-ARM [fīer'ahm], *n.* weapon from which a missile is discharged by the combustion or detonation of an explosive.

FIRE-BALL [fīer'bawl], *n.* large explosive meteor; ball of lightning; (*milit.*) receptacle filled with combustibles and hurled among the enemy.

FIRE-BOMB [fīer'bom], *n.* an incendiary bomb.

FIREBRAND [fīer'brand], *n.* piece of wood kindled or on fire; an incendiary; (*fig.*) one who inflames the minds of others and incites them to revolt; a troublemaker.

FIREBRICK [fīer'brik], *n.* brick which will not disintegrate under the action of intense heat.

FIRE-BRIGADE [fīer'bri-gād], *n.* an organized body of men, properly equipped and trained for dealing with outbreaks of fire.

FIRE-BUCKET [fīer'bu-kit], *n.* bucket in which to carry water for extinguishing fire.

FIRE-BUG [fīer'bug], *n.* a firefly; (*U.S.*) an incendiary.

FIRECLAY [fīer'klā], *n.* clay used in making firebricks.

FIRE-COMPANY [fīer'kum-pa-ni], *n.* fire-brigade; company which issues insurance against fire.

FIRE-CONTROL [fīer'kon-trol], *n.* system by which the guns of a ship can be controlled from one central position.

FIRE-DAMP [fīer'damp], *n.* explosive mixture of gases occurring in coal-mines.

FIREDOG [fīer'dog], *n.* andiron, piece of metal supporting burning fuel on an open hearth.

FIRE-DRILL [fīer'dril], *n.* practice in fire-fighting for the members of a fire-brigade; practice in the routine to be observed in case of fire.

FIRE-EATER [fīer'ē-ter], *n.* performer who claims to eat fire; hot-headed, quick-tempered, contentious person.

FIRE-ENGINE [fīer'en-jin], *n.* vehicle for transporting firemen and equipment to an outbreak of fire, and provided with an engine for pumping water at high pressure to a considerable height.

FIRE-ESCAPE [fīer'es-kāp], *n.* contrivance for enabling persons to escape from the upper part of a building on fire; iron staircase on the outside of a building, to be used in case of fire.

FIRE-EXTINGUISHER [fīer'eks-ting-gwi-sher], *n.* portable metal receptacle containing a chemical liquid for extinguishing an outbreak of fire.

FIREFLY [fīer'flī], *n.* winged insect emitting a phosphorescent light.

FIRE-GUARD (1) [fīer'gahd], *n.* framework placed in front of a fireplace to prevent small children from approaching too near a fire. FIRE-GUARD (2), *n.* a fire-watcher or body of fire-watchers.

FIREHOSE [fīer'hōz], *n.* hose through which water is pumped at high pressure by a fire-engine.

FIRE-INSURANCE [fīer'in-shōō-rans], *n.* indemnity against loss from fire.

FIRE-IRONS [fīer'īernz], *n.(pl.)* metal implements for use in tending a domestic fire.

FIRE-LEAF [fīer'lēf], *n.* incendiary leaf-shaped object dropped from raiding aircraft.

FIRELESS [fīer'les], *adj.* devoid of fire or a fire.

FIRELIGHT [fīer'līt], *n.* the light given off from a fire.

FIRE-LIGHTER [fīer'lī'ter], *n.* combustible substance with which a fire may be kindled.

FIRELOCK [fīer'lok], *n.* old-fashioned musket in which powder was ignited by sparks produced by percussion or friction of a steel and flint.

FIREMAN [fīer'man], *n.* person specially trained for dealing with outbreaks of fire; a stoker.

FIRE-OFFICE [fīer'ō-fis], *n.* office of a fire-insurance company.

FIRE-OPAL [fīer'ō-pal], *n.* variety of opal reflecting a vivid flame-coloured light.

FIREPLACE [fīer'plās], *n.* small recess in the wall at the bottom of a chimney, in which a fire may be lighted, together with the ornamental structure built above and at each side of this.

FIRE-PLUG [fīer'plug], *n.* the valve in a water-main to which the firehose is connected.

FIRE-POLICY [fīer'po-li-si], *n.* insurance policy against loss or damage by fire.

FIREPROOF [fīer'prōōf], *adj.* proof against fire, non-inflammable and heat-resisting; **f. curtain,** safety curtain made of some fire-resisting material, installed in theatres as a protection against fire.

FIRE-RAISING [fīer'rā-zing], *n.* arson, incendiarism.

FIRE-SCREEN [fīer'skrēn], *n.* movable screen placed before a fire as a shield against the heat; a protection against fire.

FIRESHIP [fīer'ship], *n.* ship containing lighted combustibles, sent among enemy ships to ignite them.

FIRESIDE [fīer'sīd], *n.* that part of a room near the fireplace, hearth; (*fig.*) home, home life. FIRESIDE-CHAT, -TALK, informal broadcast address.

FIRE-SPOTTER [fīer'spo-ter], *n.* one detailed to watch for fires caused by raiding aircraft.

FIRE-STONE [fīer'stōn], *n.* a fireproof stone, hearthstone; any of several varieties of sandstone, granite etc.

FIRE-WARDEN [fīer'waw-den], *n.* official responsible for supervising fire-fighting operations.

FIRE-WATCHER [fīer'wo-cher], *n.* one detailed to guard against fires caused by raiding aircraft.

FIREWATER [fīer'waw-ter], *n.* (*coll.*) strong spirits.

FIRE-WEED [fīer'wēd], *n.* plant springing up rapidly where brushwood has been burned.

FIREWOOD [fīer'wŏŏd], *n.* wood for fuel, *esp.* when chopped into small sticks.

FIREWORKS [fīer'werks], *n.(pl.)* preparations of gunpowder and other inflammable materials packed in containers and discharged by the lighting of a small fuse; (*slang*) startling occurrences.

FIRE-WORSHIP [fīer'wer-ship], *n.* the worship of

The accent ' after a syllable = stress (u-pon')   The mark ¯ over a vowel = length (ā in made; ō in bone

fire, *esp.* as embodied in the sun. FIRE-WORSHIPPER, *n.* one who worships fire.

FIRING [fīer'ing], *n.* the discharge of fire-arms; fuel; action of setting on fire, or subjecting to heat in order to bake. FIRING-LINE, line of trenches and soldiers nearest to those of the enemy. FIRING-PARTY, group of soldiers selected to shoot a condemned soldier or spy, or to discharge a salute over the grave of a soldier.

FIRKIN [fur'kin], *n.* small cask or barrel; a measure the fourth part of a barrel, approximately 9 gallons. [ME., Du.].

FIRM (1) [furm], *n.* an association of two or more persons in partnership for conducting the affairs of a business organization; name or title under which a company operates. [It.].

FIRM (2), *adj.* solid, compact, resisting, resolute, steadfast; unflinching; steady, fixed, stable; strong, determined; (*comm.*) not subject to sudden variations, not tending to drop. FIRM (3), *adv.* firmly. FIRM (4), *v.t. and i.* to fix, make f.; become f. FIRMLY, *adv.* in f. fashion. FIRMNESS, *n.* condition of being f. [L.].

FIRMAMENT [fur'ma-ment], *n.* the sky, the heavens. FIRMAMENTAL, *adj.* relating to the f., celestial. [L.].

FIRST (1) [furst], *adj.* beginning a series; taking place, performing something before anything or anyone else; foremost in position, preceding all others in a series; earliest; principal, chief; taking precedence over all others; original; **f. thing,** as early as possible. FIRST (2), *adv.* before anything else in time, place, rank etc.; before something may take place; for the f. time; (*coll.*) rather, preferably. FIRST (3), *n.* the beginning; one who, or that which, is f. in number or quality; f. place or prize in a contest, f. class in an examination; (*mus.*) highest part of a piece of music written for different voices, the instrument playing the highest part of an orchestral work. [OE.].

FIRST AID [ferst-ād'], *n.* immediate simple treatment given to an injured person.

FIRST-BORN (1) [furst'bawn], *adj.* eldest. FIRST-BORN (2), *n.* the eldest child.

FIRST-CLASS (1) [ferst-klahs'], *adj.* of the best quality, of the highest standard; (*coll.*) splendid, excellent. FIRST-CLASS (2), *adv.* excellently, very well; by f. accommodation.

FIRST-FLOOR [ferst-flaw(r)'], *adj.* relating to the floor immediately above the ground floor.

FIRST-FOOT [furst'foot], *n. and v.i.* (*Scots*) the first caller to enter a house on New Year's Day; to perform the action of a f.

FIRST FRUITS [furst'froots], *n.* the first harvest products collected in any season, *esp.* when offered for religious purposes; (*fig.*) first results, effects.

FIRST-HAND [ferst-hand'], *adj.* direct; **at f.,** without the intervention of an intermediary.

FIRSTLING [furst'ling], *n.* the first to be produced, first result, effect etc.; first-born of an animal.

FIRST NIGHT [ferst-nīt'], *n.* the first performance in the run of a play etc. FIRST-NIGHTER, *n.* (*coll.*) person who makes a practice of attending first performances of plays.

FIRST-RATE (1) [ferst-rāt'], *adj.* of the highest degree of excellence, pre-eminent; (*nav.*) belonging to the largest and most powerful class. FIRST-RATE (2), *adv.* excellently, extremely well. FIRST-RATE (3), *n.* ship of war of the largest and most powerful class.

FIRST WATER [ferst-waw'ter], *n.* the finest quality, *esp.* of gems.

FIRTH [furth], *n.* long narrow inlet stretching into the coast. [OIcel.].

FISCAL (1) [fis'kal], *adj.* relating to the public revenue; **Procurator f.,** (*Scots*) the public prosecutor for cases involving the less serious crimes. FISCAL (2), *n.* a public prosecutor; (*Scots*) Procurator fiscal. [L.].

FISH (1) [fish], *n.* cold-blooded finned creature dwelling in water and equipped with gills by which it breathes; any creature living entirely in water; edible flesh of such creatures; (*coll.*) person; torpedo; **f. out of water,** person obviously ill at ease with his surroundings; **to have other f. to fry,** (*coll.*) to have something else to attend to; **a pretty kettle of f.,** (*coll.*) a nice mix-up; **to drink like a f.,** to indulge to excess in alcoholic beverages; **to cry stinking f.,** to indulge in self-depreciation. FISH (2), *v.t. and i.* to catch, or try to catch f.; (*fig.*) angle for, seek to obtain by indirect means, hints etc.; search for various animals living in water; try to catch f. in; seek to catch; **to f. the anchor,** (*naut.*) to secure the anchor to the gunwale after catting; **to f. in**

troubled waters, to endeavour to reap personal gain from unsettled conditions. FISHABLE, *adj.* able to be fished in. [OE.].

FISH (3), *n.* flat piece of wood or iron fastened to another to strengthen it, a fishplate. FISH (4), *v.t.* to strengthen or join by means of a f. or fishplate. [Fr.].

FISH-BALL [fish'bawl], *n.* a fish-cake.

FISH-BASKET [fish'bahs-kit], *n.* a creel.

FISH-CAKE [fish'kāk], *n.* fried dish of shredded fish and potato served in the form of a cake.

FISH-CARVER [fish'kah-ver], *n.* a fish-slice.

FISHERMAN [fi'sher-man], *n.* person who catches fish; skilful angler; fishing boat.

FISHERY [fi'she-ri], *n.* occupation of catching fish, fishing industry; place where fish are caught; (*leg.*) legal authority to fish in certain waters.

FISH-GLUE [fish'gloo], *n.* glue made by boiling the skins and bones of fish.

FISH-HAWK [fish'hawk], *n.* the osprey.

FISH-HOOK [fish'hook], *n.* barbed hook for catching fish.

FISHING [fi'shing], *n.* art or practice of catching fish; legal authority to catch fish in particular waters; stretch of water over which such rights are held.

FISHING BOAT [fi'shing-bōt], *n.* boat used for fishing.

FISHING-LINE [fi'shing-līn], *n.* line to which is attached a fish-hook for catching fish.

FISHING-NET [fi'shing-net], *n.* net used for catching fish.

FISHING-ROD [fi'shing-rod], *n.* pliable rod to which are attached a line and hook for angling.

FISHING-TACKLE [fi'shing-ta-kl], *n.* implements used in fishing.

FISH-KETTLE [fish'ke-tl], *n.* large oval kitchen utensil in which fish may be boiled whole.

FISH-KNIFE [fish'nīf], *n.* blunt knife with a broad flat tapering blade used for eating fish; fish-slice.

FISH-MEAL [fish'mēl], *n.* dried fish ground to a fine powder.

FISHMONGER [fish'mung-ger], *n.* one who sells fish.

FISH-PASTE [fish'pāst], *n.* savoury paste made of fish or shell-fish, eaten on bread and butter.

FISHPLATE [fish'plāt], *n.* steel plate by which the rails are joined end to end on a railway line. [FISH (3)].

FISH-POND [fish'pond], *n.* pond in which fish are reared.

FISH-SAUCE [fish-saws'], *n.* sauce to be eaten with fish; sauce made from fish.

FISH-SKIN [fish'skin], *n.* skin of a fish; **f. disease,** (*med.*) ichthyosis.

FISH-SLICE [fish'slīs], *n.* broad knife for serving fish at a dinner-table; implement for turning fish when cooking.

FISH-TAIL [fish'tāl], *adj.* in the shape of the tail of a fish; **f. burner,** gas-burner producing a flat flame of this shape; **f. wind,** wind continually changing direction.

FISHWIFE [fish'wīf], *n.* woman who hawks fish; (*fig.*) vulgar woman.

FISHY [fi'shi], *adj.* consisting of, or full of, fish; like fish; resembling the smell of a fish; (of eyes) cold, glassy and vacant; (*coll.*) dubious, questionable.

FISSI-, *pref.* divided, cleft. [L.].

FISSILE [fi'sīl], *adj.* capable of being split; dividing readily. FISSILITY [fi-si'li-ti], *n.* quality of being f. [L.].

FISSION (1) [fi'shn], *n.* a cleaving or breaking up into parts; process by which cells and certain simple organisms spontaneously split up into two independent new creatures; (*phys.*) the splitting of atoms. FISSION (2), *v.i.* (*phys.*) to undergo f., split. FISSIONABLE, *adj.* (*phys.*) (of elements) composed in such a way that the component atoms may readily be split. [L.].

FISSIPAROUS [fi-si'pa-roos], *adj.* reproducing by fission. FISSIPARISM, *n.* reproduction by fission. FISSIPAROUSLY, *adv.* in a f. fashion.

FISSIPED (1) [fi'si-ped], *adj.* having the toes separated. FISSIPED (2), *n.* a f. animal. [L.].

FISSURE (1) [fi'shoor], *n.* a cleft, split; (*anat.*) natural deep narrow opening in an organ, narrow depression dividing the anterior and middle lobes of the cerebrum; (*path.*) crack in a bone or other tissue; (*her.*) fourth part of the bend sinister. FISSURE (2), *v.t. and i.* to cleave, split open, form a f. in. [L.].

FIST (1) [fist], *n.* the hand when clenched and with the fingers bent over to touch the palm; (*coll.*)

handwriting, the hand; **to make a good f. at**, to do competently. FIST (2), *v.t.* to strike with the f., grasp, seize. FISTIC, *adj.* pertaining to, involving the use of, the fists, referring to boxing. [OE.].

FISTICUFFS [fis'ti-kufs], *n.(pl.)* blows, a fight with the fists. [FIST and CUFF].

FISTULA [fis'tyŏŏ-lah], *n.* (*path.*) an abnormal channel or opening between two organs, or between an organ and the skin, caused by the discharge of pus from an ulcer; slender winding ulcer; organ resembling a pipe in certain insects; (*eccles.*) tube through which the Pope partakes of the consecrated wine. FISTULAR, *adj.* pertaining to a f.; shaped like a f., pipe-like, tubular. FISTULOSE, FISTULOUS, *adj.* pertaining to a f.; resembling a pipe or reed; containing long, narrow, hollow cylinders. [L.].

FIT (1) [fit], *n.* a sudden and violent derangement of the nerves due to disease and often accompanied by convulsions, nervous spasms and insensibility; seizure, paroxysm; any sudden violent bout; whim, fancy of the moment; any impulsive, intermittent exertion. [ME.].

FIT (2), *n.* (*archaic*) group of verses in a poem, canto. [OE.].

FIT (3), *adj.* appropriate, suitable, worthy; agreeable or adapted to some purpose; seemly, becoming; competent, in a proper state; ready, healthy, in sound mental and physical condition; well-trained. FIT (4) (*pres.pt.* FITTING, *pret. and p.pt.* FITTED), *v.t.* to be of the right proportions or dimensions for; suit, conform to; adjust or fashion to the proper size or dimensions; prepare, make competent to undertake; supply with what is necessary, suitable or desired; try on an incomplete garment for adjustment if necessary; qualify, make to conform with; *v.i.* to suit exactly; conform to the proportions or contours of something else; be proper, becoming or seemly; **to f. out**, to furnish, equip; **to f. up**, to get ready, provide with necessary or suitable furnishings, equipment etc. FIT (5), *n.* the way in which a thing fits; that which fits; adjustment, *esp.* of dress to the body. [ME.].

FITCH (1) [fich], see VETCH.

FITCH (2), *n.* the polecat; brush made of the hair of the fitch; fur or hair of the polecat. [MDu.].

FITCHEW [fi'chŏŏ], *n.* the polecat. [OFr.].

FITFUL [fit'fŏŏl], *adj.* intermittent, spasmodic, impulsive and irregular; changeful. FITFULLY, *adv.* by fits, in a f. manner. FITFULNESS, *n.* quality of being f.

FITLY [fit'li], *adv.* in a fit fashion.

FITMENT [fit'ment], *n.* article of furniture; a fitting.

FITNESS [fit'nes], *n.* state or quality of being fit.

FIT-OUT [fit'owt], *n.* (*coll.*) equipment.

FITTER [fit'er], *n.* one who fits; tailor who fits and tries on clothes; mechanic or engineer who adjusts or assembles the fittings of a machine.

FITTING (1) [fit'ting], *n.* act of one who, or that which, fits; (*pl.*) necessary or suitable fixtures, furniture or equipment; detachable parts of a machine. FITTING (2), *adj.* suitable, proper, appropriate. FITTINGLY, *adv.* in a f. manner.

FITTING-UP [fit-ting-up'], *n.* act of equipping with things suitable or necessary.

FIT-UP [fit'up], *n.* (*slang*) any theatrical accessory which can be adapted to temporary circumstances; f. company, theatrical company which travels with makeshift equipment.

FITZ-, *pref.* the son of; used only in proper names. [AFr. from L.].

FIVE (1) [fīv], *n.* number between four and six; playing card etc. marked with five spots; that which comprises five things. FIVE (2), *adj.* one more than four, one less than six. [OE.].

FIVE-FINGER (1) [fīv-fing'ger], *n.* (*bot.*) the cinquefoil; the oxlip. FIVE-FINGER (2), *adj.* of piano exercises, designed to give practice to all fingers.

FIVEFOLD (1) [fīv'fōld], *adj.* five times repeated; having five component parts. FIVEFOLD (2), *adv.* to a degree five times as great, by five times.

FIVER [fī'ver], *n.* (*coll.*) five-pound note issued by the Bank of England.

FIVES [fīvz], *n.* game played in a walled court by two or four persons, in which a small, hard ball is struck against the walls by the hands ("hand-ball") or a bat. FIVES-BALL, ball used in playing f. FIVES-COURT, walled court in which the game of f. is played. [Unkn.].

FIX (1) [fiks], *v.t.* to fasten, secure in position; set, place; cause to be firmly implanted in; help, concentrate; catch and hold; cause to remain unchanged,

establish in a permanent form; determine, settle; arrange, decide, appoint; attribute, lay to the responsibility of; ascertain; (*coll.*) adjust, put right; attend to; (*chem.*) make solid, non-fluid; (*phot.*) give permanency to, secure against change or fading; preserve; *v.i.* to settle, become firm or set; congeal; **to f. up**, to arrange; decide on; settle, smooth out; (*coll.*) make arrangements for. FIX (2), *n.* (*coll.*) predicament, awkward situation. FIXABLE, *adj.* capable of being fixed. FIXER, *n.* one who, or that which, fixes. FIXING, *n.* act of anyone or anything that fixes. [L.].

FIXATION [fik-sā'shn], *n.* act of fixing, state of being fixed; (*psych.*) affection abnormal in degree or kind. [MedL.].

FIXATIVE (1) [fik'sa-tiv], *adj.* tending to fix. FIXATIVE (2), *n.* anything used for fixing; gummy composition for fixing the hair in the required position.

FIXED [fikst], *adj.* unwavering, steady; determined, settled, definitely decided; made fast, established in permanent form; not subject to fluctuation, stationary; inflexible, rigid, unalterable; (*chem.*) solidified. FIXEDLY [fik'sid-li], *adv.* in a f. manner.

FIXITY [fik'si-ti], *n.* permanence, state of being fixed.

FIXTURE [fiks'tyoor], *n.* that which is permanently attached to something as a necessary part of it; (*pl., leg.*) fittings or accessories attached to a building or land so as to form part of the real property, not removable at will by the occupier; (*coll.*) one who, or that which, seems to have become established as a permanent feature of some place; appointment, event or engagement of a sporting nature for a specified future date; the means of fixing.

FIZZ (1) [fiz], *v.i.* to make a quick bubbly hissing sound; effervesce. FIZZ (2), *n.* spluttering or hissing sound; effervescence; that which fizzes; (*coll.*) champagne; wine or drink which effervesces strongly. [Imitative].

FIZZLE (1) [fiz'l], *v.i.* to fizz feebly; **to f. out**, to extinguish itself by a series of diminishing explosions; (*fig.*) end feebly. FIZZLE (2), *n.* act of fizzling; (*coll.*) failure, fiasco. [Echoic].

FLABBERGAST [fla'ber-gahst], *v.t.* (*coll.*) to confound, astonish completely. [Uncert.].

FLABBY [fla'bi], *adj.* wanting firmness; limp, soft and yielding; hanging loose; (*fig.*) weak. FLABBILY, *adv.* in a f. fashion. FLABBINESS, *n.* condition of being f. [LGerm.].

FLACCID [flak'sid], *adj.* flabby; soft and yielding, loose, limp; (*fig.*) weak, lacking in energy or force. FLACCIDITY, FLACCIDNESS [flak-si'di-ti, flak'sid-nes], *n.* condition of being f. FLACCIDLY, *adv.* in a f. fashion. [L.].

FLAG (1) [flag], *n.* (*bot.*) any of several plants, growing in marshy places, having long, thin, flat leaves; plant of the genus *Iris*; the blade of a plant; kind of rough grass. [ME.].

FLAG (2), *n.* large flat slab of stone used for paving; flag-stone; (*pl.*) pavement of flag-stones. FLAG (3), *v.t.* to pave with flags. [OScand.].

FLAG (4), *n.* piece of bunting or other similar cloth usually containing a distinctive emblem in colours and attached to a pole or halyard; slip of paper marking the position in a file of a document required for reference; attachment to a taximeter indicating whether or not the taxi is engaged; **black f.**, emblem of piracy; former signal of smallpox cases; signal of the execution of a prisoner; **red f.**, danger signal; symbol of defiance or challenge; Communist or Socialist f.; **yellow f.**, signal of quarantine and infectious illness; **white f.**, signal of surrender, parley or truce; **to strike the f.**, (*fig.*) to surrender. FLAG (5), *v.t.* to decorate with flags; signal to with flags; mark (a document) by a f. [Uncert.].

FLAG (6) (*pres.pt.* flagging, *pret. and p.pt.* flagged), *v.t. and i.* to droop, stand limply; grow spiritless or enervated; abate, diminish. [ME.].

FLAG-CAPTAIN [flag'kap-tin], *n.* captain of a flag-ship.

FLAG-DAY [flag'dā], *n.* day on which street-collectors give a small flag or imitation flower in return for contributions towards some charitable organization.

FLAGELLANT [fla'je-lant], *n.* one who scourges himself in religious discipline; (*pl.*) fanatical thirteenth-century sect who believed in flagellation as a punishment for sin. [L.].

FLAGELLATE [fla'je-lāt], *v.t.* to whip, scourge, flog. FLAGELLATION [fla-je-lā'shn], *n.* act of scourging. FLAGELLATOR [fla'je-lā-ter], *n.* one who flagellates. [L.].

FLAGELLUM (*pl.* flagella) [fla-je'lum], *n.* (*biol.*) long flexible appendage of a cell, shaped like a whip-thong; (*bot.*) creeping shoot, whip-like process. [L.].

FLAGEOLET [flă′ji-ō-let], *n.* small wind instrument resembling a pipe and provided with six holes.

FLAGGING [flă′ging], *n.* act of paving with flag-stones; pavement of flag-stones; flag-stones.

FLAGGY (1) [flă′gi], *adj.* relating to flag-stones.

FLAGGY (2), *adj.* (*bot.*) overgrown with flags.

FLAGITIOUS [flă′ji-shŏos], *adj.* deeply criminal, grossly wicked, guilty of atrocious crimes, disgraceful. FLAGITIOUSLY, *adv.* in a f. manner. FLAGITIOUSNESS, *n.* extreme wickedness and cruelty. [L.].

FLAG-LIEUTENANT [flag-lef-te′nant], *n.* adjutant assisting a flag-officer.

FLAGMAN [flag′man], *n.* one who signals with flags.

FLAG-OFFICER [flag′o-fi-ser], *n.* naval officer in command of a squadron; admiral, vice-admiral or rear-admiral; commodore of the squadron of a yacht-club.

FLAGON [flă′gon], *n.* large vessel with a handle, lid and narrow mouth, used for wine, *esp.* at Holy Communion; large bottle. [OFr.].

FLAGRANT [flā′grant], *adj.* glaringly evil, notorious, scandalous, obvious; unqualified. FLAGRANCY, *n.* quality of being f., enormity, glaring, obtrusive nature. FLAGRANTLY, *adv.* in a f. fashion. [L.].

FLAG-SHIP [flag′ship], *n.* ship in which the commander of a squadron sails, and in which his flag is flown.

FLAGSTAFF [flag′stahf], *n.* staff from which a flag is hung.

FLAG-STONE [flag′stŏn], *n.* large flat stone used in paving.

FLAGWAGGING [flag′wa-ging], *n.* (*coll.*) hand signalling with flags; (*fig.*) bellicose, boastful talk.

FLAIL [flāl], *n.* wooden implement for threshing grain by hand; **f. tank**, (*milit.*) tank fitted with steel chains which revolve in front of it like flails and detonate land-mines. [OFr.].

FLAIR [flāer], *n.* intuitive appreciation or discernment, natural aptitude or gift. [Fr.].

FLAK [flak], *n.* anti-aircraft fire; **f. boat,** small German vessel equipped with anti-aircraft guns; **f. tower,** tower equipped with anti-aircraft guns. [Germ.].

FLAKE (1) [flāk], *n.* small light mass of anything which floats about in the air, as snow, wool etc.; thin, light, flat piece of some substance which scales or peels off. FLAKE-WHITE, white pigment obtained from white lead in a flaky or scaly form. FLAKE (2), *v.t. and i.* to form into flakes, separate or peel off into flakes; cover with flakes; fall in flakes. [OIcel.].

FLAKY [flā′ki], *adj.* composed of flakes; breaking off in flakes. FLAKINESS, *n.* condition of being f.

FLAM (1) [flam], *v.t.* to deceive by means of lies, trick, hoax. FLAM (2), *n.* a sham, humbug. [Unkn.].

FLAMBEAU (*pl.* **flambeaux** [flahm′bō], *n.* large ceremonial torch. [Fr.].

FLAMBOYANT [flam-boi′ant], *adj.* (*arch.*) denoting a French Gothic style with flame-like wavings in its tracery; (*fig.*) florid to excess, showy, over-ornate. FLAMBOYANTLY, *adv.* in a flamboyant manner. FLAMBOYANCY, *n.* ornateness, floridness, showy elaborateness. [Fr.].

FLAME (1) [flām], *n.* luminous heat or blaze rising from a burning substance or incandescent gas; anything resembling this in its fierce brightness or glow, anything of a fiery red or yellow colour; (*fig.*) ardour, heat of passion or other strong emotion; vigour and keenness of thought, glow of imagination; (*coll.*) a sweetheart; **f.-coloured,** of the colour of a f., vivid fiery red. FLAME (2), *v.i.* to blaze, give off flames in burning; emit a fiery glow or flame-like luminosity, flare, show or appear as a blaze of colour; blush vividly; break out in violence of passion or excitement. [L.].

FLAMEN [flā′men], *n.* (*Rom. antiq.*) priest devoted to some particular god. [L.].

FLAME-THROWER [flām′thrō-er], *n.* (*milit.*) apparatus for discharging blazing liquid or flame on to the enemy lines.

FLAMING [flā′ming], *adj.* blazing, emitting flames; very bright, lurid, glaring; passionate, ardent; *also used as a substitute for a profane expletive*; **f.-onions,** (*slang*) anti-aircraft projectile comprising a number of balls of fire.

FLAMINGO [fla-ming′gō], *n.* genus of birds with very long necks and legs and, when in full plumage, of a vivid red colour. [Portug.].

FLAMY [flā′mi], *adj.* like a flame in nature or colour.

FLAN [flan], *n.* shallow tart of pastry filled with fruit, treacle etc. [Fr.].

FLANEUR, flâneur [flah-nur′], *n.* lounger, idler. [Fr.].

FLANGE (1) [flanj], *n.* projecting edge, rib or rim on a wheel, girder, pipe etc.; tool employed in making flanges. FLANGE (2), *v.t.* to provide with a f. [OFr.].

FLANK (1) [flangk], *n.* the fleshy part of an animal or human being between the ribs and the hip; side of a mountain, hill, building etc.; (*milit.*) side of an army or body of troops; **to turn the f. of,** (*milit.*) to get round the side of; **f. movement,** (*milit.*) movement made in order to turn the enemy's flank. FLANK (2), *v.t. and i.* to command or be situated at the f. of; attack the f. of; place troops at the f. of; secure, protect on the f.; border, touch, be placed on the side. FLANKERS, *n.(pl.)* skirmishers posted on the flanks of an army on the march. [Fr.].

FLANNEL (1) [fla′nel], *n.* soft plain woollen cloth of loose texture; piece of flannel used for polishing or cleaning; (*pl.*) clothes made of flannel, particularly trousers worn for games or as informal attire. FLANNEL (2), *adj.* made of f. FLANNELLED, *adj.* dressed in flannels. FLANNELLY, *adj.* like f. [OFr.].

FLANNELETTE [fla-ne-let′], *n.* cotton fabric similar in texture to fine flannel.

FLAP (1) [flap], *v.t. and i.* to give a light slap with a broad, flat, flexible object; move (some broad flat object) rapidly up and down, beat (as a bird's wings); cause to flap or flutter; move lightly and loosely up and down or to and fro, often with a sharp light recurring sound; fall or hang down as a flap. FLAP (2), *n.* a slight sharp blow with a broad flat object; noise made by anything flapping; anything broad and flexible, fastened at one end or side, and wrapping over and covering some aperture; thin membranous substance covering the eyes and gills of fishes; soft flexible brim of a hat, or a hanging portion of a garment; (*coll.*) excitement, an access of panic. [Imitative].

FLAPDOODLE [flap-dōō′dl], *n.* (*coll.*) nonsense, rubbish, humbug.

FLAP-EARED [flap′ēerd], *adj.* having broad, loose, pendulous ears.

FLAP-JACK [flap′jak], *n.* a broad pancake; lady's flat powder compact.

FLAPPER [fla′per], *n.* one who, or that which, flaps; fly-whisk, flexible striking part of a flail, broad flat object used for striking, and making a noise to scare away birds; flipper or broad fin of a seal etc.; young wild duck or partridge; (*coll.*) young girl; **f. bracket,** (*coll.*) pillion seat on a motor-cycle.

FLARE (1) [flāer], *v.i.* to blaze up with or emit a flare or flash; (of a candle, lamp etc.) burn up too high; (of a skirt, sides of a ship) spread or swell outwards as a bowl etc.; **to f. up,** to blaze up suddenly; fly suddenly into a passionate display of temper. FLARE (2), *n.* unsteady, fitful glare of light of brief duration and rapidly increasing intensity or size; combustible substance which, when ignited, emits a brief dazzling glare of light, used as a signal or in flashlight photography, or by aircraft to illuminate targets; bright naked flame burning continuously, sometimes used as a guide to traffic in fog; outward curve or bulge; (*fig.*) sudden display of temper. FLARE-PATH, lighted track to enable aircraft to land at night. FLARING, *adj.* emitting a f. or series of flares; swelling or curving outwards; (*fig.*) showy, gaudy. FLARINGLY, *adv.* in a flaring fashion. [Norw.].

FLASH (1) [flash], *v.t. and i.* to emit a flash or series of flashes; burst into, or reflect as, a sudden instantaneous gleam of light; light up, gleam; pass like a flash; (*fig.*) burst forth with sudden brilliance; occur suddenly, pass rapidly through the mind; emit in flashes; direct a light suddenly upon an object; (*fig.*) direct a sudden fleeting glance, smile etc. at; transmit by radio, telephony, signalling apparatus etc.; cause to travel with the speed of a flash; (*coll.*) display in a showy manner. FLASH (2), *n.* sudden instantaneous blaze or gleam of light; an instant, time occupied by a flash; vulgar ostentation; sudden inspiration, brief outburst of brilliance, anger etc.; piece of black velvet worn at the back of the collar by the Royal Welch Fusiliers; distinguishing mark of cloth worn on the uniform of many military and other formations; ornamental tassel hanging from a garter; (*cinema*) short portion of a film; preliminary brief announcement of an item of news; **f. in the pan,** sudden show of brilliance etc., which quickly goes out. FLASH (3), *adj.* showy, ostentatious, smart;

counterfeit; (*slang*) wide awake, cute; pertaining to a class of thieves, rogues, sharpers etc.; **f. steam**, (*eng.*) steam reheated to an extremely high temperature for high-speed engines. [Unkn.].

FLASHBACK [flash'bak], *n.* (*cinema*) sudden switch-over to an earlier part of the story.

FLASHER [fla'sher], *n.* one who, or that which, flashes; mechanism for automatically switching on and off the lamps of electric signs.

FLASHILY [fla'shi-li], *adv.* in a flashy fashion.

FLASHINESS [fla'shi-nes], *n.* condition of being flashy.

FLASHING [fla'shing], *n.* act of that which, or of one who, flashes; pieces of lead or other material lapping over portions of roofs or walls, to prevent rain from entering.

FLASHLIGHT [flash'lit], *n.* an intermittent light; lamp used for signalling by means of flashes; electric torch which can be switched off and on as required; brief dazzling light used in taking photographs of subjects otherwise inadequately lighted.

FLASHPOINT [flash'point], *n.* lowest temperature at which gas or vapour is spontaneously combustible.

FLASHY [fla'shi], *adj.* cheap, showy but worthless, possessing a shallow brilliance, vulgarly ostentatious.

FLASK [flahsk], *n.* small flattened bottle for wine, spirits or other liquid; narrow-necked spherical vessel usually of glass. **Florence f.**, a thin glass f. with a flat bottom. [LL.].

FLAT (1) [flat], *n.* floor or storey in a house; suite of rooms on one floor arranged as a separate, complete dwelling place; an area of flat land. [~OE.].

FLAT (2), *adj.* having an even, level surface, and usually horizontal; only slightly raised from the adjacent surface; prostrate, stretched out on the ground; (*paint.*) without relief, not suggesting distance; uniform; having no prominent contours; dull, dispirited; monotonous; having lost its sparkle or freshness; unqualified, downright, absolute; (*mus.*) out of tune because of a drop in pitch; (*phon.*) pronounced or made with a more or less level tongue; (*golf*) (of a club) having the head jointed to the shaft at a wide angle; **that's f.**, that is final; **a f. spin**, (*fig.*) a state of agitation. FLAT (3), *adv.* prone, so as to be f.; resting against and touching at all points; entirely, directly; without interest; (*coll.*) bluntly, definitely; **to fall f.**, to fail to produce the intended effect; **to go f. out**, (*coll.*) to travel as quickly as possible, strain every nerve in order to achieve something. FLAT (4), *n.* that which is f., the f. side or part of anything, a level surface; shoal or shallow; (*arch.*) horizontal part of a roof; (*paint.*) surface painted without gloss; stage scenery set on a frame, and pushed on the stage into position; (*horse-racing*) level ground without hedges or ditches; (*mus.*) a semitone below a natural; (*coll.*) one who is easily duped. [OScand.].

FLATFISH [flat'fish], *n.* fish with a flat body, which has both eyes on one side, as the flounder, halibut etc.

FLATFOOTED [flat-foo'tid], *adj.* having flat-soled feet with little or no arched instep.

FLAT-IRON [flat'iern], *n.* implement used for ironing clothes.

FLATLET [flat'let], *n.* small self-contained flat.

FLATLY [flat'li], *adv.* in a flat manner; plainly, positively.

FLATNESS [flat'nes], *n.* state or quality of being flat; (*radio*) low degree of selectivity in a radio receiver.

FLAT-RACE [flat'rās], *n.* race run on level ground, without obstacles to be jumped.

FLAT-SPOT [flat'spot], *n.* (*motoring*) temporary lack of response of the carburettor to acceleration.

FLATTEN [fla'ten], *v.t. and i.* to make flat or level and less thick; depress, dispirit; (*mus.*) lower the pitch of; (*fig.*) crush, overwhelm with dismay; (*naut.*) make (a sail) flat; become flat; **f. out**, (*aeron.*) cause an aeroplane to assume a more or less horizontal position after climbing or falling.

FLATTER [fla'ter], *v.t. and i.* to praise insincerely, pay artful compliments to; give too favourable an impression or representation of; (*reflex.*) obtain self-satisfaction from the fact, feel convinced of one's ability to do a certain thing; please, gratify.

FLATTERING [fla'te-ring], *adj.* that flatters, sycophantic; representing too favourably; pleasing to pride or vanity. FLATTERINGLY, *adv.* in a f. fashion.

FLATTERY [fla'te-ri], *n.* false or excessive praise, insincere compliment. [OFr.].

FLATTING [fla'ting], *n.* process of making flat;

mode of painting, in which the paint leaves the work without gloss; method of preserving gilding unburnished; rolling out metals by cylindrical pressure.

FLATULENCE, FLATULENCY [fla'tyoo-lens(-i)], *n.* (*med.*) windiness caused by gases generated in the stomach and intestines; (*fig.*) emptiness, vanity.

FLATULENT [fla'tyoo-lent], *adj.* affected with, or causing, flatulence; (*fig.*) empty, without substance.

FLATUS [fla'tus], *n.* accumulation of wind in the stomach or bowels. [L.].

FLAUNT [flawnt], *v.t. and i.* to make a brave show; wave or move proudly; display showily; flourish or parade offensively; boast of. [Uncert.].

FLAUNTING [flawn'ting], *adj.* making an ostentatious display, waving or moving proudly. FLAUNTINGLY, *adv.* in a f. manner.

FLAUTIST [flaw'tist], *n.* person who plays the flute.

FLAVINE [fla'vēn], *n.* vegetable extract which imparts a yellow colour to cloth; yellow crystalline antiseptic. [L.].

FLAVOUR (1) [fla'ver], *n.* fragrance, taste, savour, that quality of a substance which arouses a distinctive sensation in the organs of taste and smell; (*fig.*) strong suggestion, distinctive atmosphere. FLAVOUR (2), *v.t.* to season, give a f. to; (*fig.*) give a distinctive quality or atmosphere to. FLAVOURED, *adj.* having a distinctive f. [OFr.].

FLAVOURING [fla've-ring], *n.* substance added to give flavour to anything; slight but distinctive flavour.

FLAW (1) [flaw], *n.* defect, blemish, disfigurement; break, crack; fault, error; that which detracts from the excellence or correctness of anything; (*leg.*) fallacy, omission etc., which makes a legal document invalid. FLAW (2), *v.t.* to break, crack, produce a f. in. [ME., OIcel.].

FLAW (3), *n.* sudden gust, squall; (*fig.*) sudden commotion or agitation. [Norw.].

FLAWLESS [flaw'les], *adj.* free from flaws, perfect, unblemished. FLAWLESSLY, *adv.* in a f. manner.

FLAX [flaks], *n.* (*bot.*) annual plant, *Linum usitatissimum*, the stalks of which yield a fibre used for making linen, cambric etc., and from the seeds of which linseed oil is made; fibrous part of the plant; flax-lily. [OE.].

FLAXEN [flak'sen], *adj.* made of or like flax; of the colour of flax; pale yellow. [OE.].

FLAX-LILY [flaks'li-li], *n.* New Zealand flax, a lily-like plant, the fibre of which is used for textile weaving.

FLAX-SEED [flaks'sēd], *n.* the seed of flax, linseed.

FLAY [fla], *v.t.* to strip the skin from; beat severely; (*fig.*) criticize unmercifully. [OE.].

FLEA [flē], *n.* small blood-sucking insect, possessing a troublesome bite; small insect resembling a flea.

FLEA-BAG [flē'bag], *n.* (*slang*) sleeping-bag.

FLEA-BITE [flē'bīt], *n.* the bite of a flea, small red spot on the skin caused by this; (*coll.*) trifle, something of no account.

FLEA-BITTEN [flē'bi-ten], *adj.* bitten by a flea; (of the colour of a horse) light with reddish flecks; (*coll.*) poor, dingy, shabby.

FLECHE, flèche [flāsh], *n.* (*arch.*) tall slender spire of a Gothic church. [Fr.].

FLECK (1) [flek], *n.* a spot, streak, speck, small particle. FLECK (2), *v.t.* to spot, streak or speck, variegate; dapple. FLECKED, *adj.* spotted, marked with flecks. [OIcel.].

FLECTION, see FLEXION.

FLED, *pret. and p.pt.* of FLEE. [ME.].

FLEDGE [flej], *v.t. and i.* (of a bird) to grow feathers; rear until it has grown feathers; **fully fledged**, (*fig.*) properly qualified. [~OE.].

FLEDGELING [flej'ling], *n.* young bird just fledged; (*fig.*) young inexperienced person.

FLEE (*pret. and p.pt.* **fled**) [flē], *v.t. and i.* to run away as quickly as possible, retreat with all speed; (*fig.*) avoid, hasten (from); pass away, depart in haste from, shun. [OE.].

FLEECE (1) [flēs], *n.* woolly coat or covering of a sheep, *esp.* when detached whole by shearing; (*fig.*) any similar soft, downy covering. FLEECE (2), *v.t.* to shear the wool from (a sheep), furnish with a f., spread over as a f.; (*fig.*) strip, rob, plunder by crooked dealing or extortion. [OE.].

FLEECY [flē'si], *adj.* covered with wool or a fleece, woolly, soft.

FLEER [flēer], *v.i.* to mock, grimace derisively, jeer. FLEERING, *adj.* mocking, derisive. [~Norw.].

FLEET (1) [flēt], *n.* a number of vessels sailing or

The accent ' after a syllable = stress (u-pon'). The mark ¯ over a vowel = length (ā in made; ō in bone).

collected together for a common purpose; a wide stretch of shallow water; (*nav.*) large body of warships under one command; unit; navy; (*fig.*) collection of vehicles usually under one ownership and used for a common purpose. [OE.].

FLEET (2), *v.t. and i.* to fly swiftly and lightly, hasten silently, flit; cause to pass swiftly and imperceptibly; (*naut.*) move, *esp.* cables, tackle etc. FLEET (3), *adj.* swift of pace, moving rapidly and lightly. [OE.].

FLEET-FOOTED [flēt-fŏŏ'tid], *adj.* swift of foot, able to run very quickly.

FLEETING [flē'ting], *adj.* passing away quickly and easily, hastening swiftly and imperceptibly. FLEETINGLY, *adv.* in a f. fashion.

FLEETLY [flēt'li], *adv.* swiftly, rapidly.

FLEETNESS [flēt'nes], *n.* quality of being fleet.

FLEMING [fle'ming], *n.* native of Flanders. [MDu.].

FLEMISH [fle'mish], *adj.* pertaining to Flanders, its inhabitants or language. [MDu.].

FLESH (1) [flesh], *n.* the soft tissue covering the bones of an animal body; edible muscular tissue and fat of certain animals; pulpy soft part of fruit or vegetables; the physical human body; the sensual nature, bodily cravings; human nature, mankind; **one's own f. and blood**, one's relatives; **in the f.**, as a living person or thing; **proud f.**, rapidly growing granular tissue forming over a wound. FLESH (2), *v.t.* to whet the appetite of (a hawk or hound) for hunting, by feeding it with the game it has taken; thrust into flesh (a sword); (*fig.*) initiate or harden to bloodshed or fighting. FLESHED, *adj.* fat, fleshy; accustomed to bloodshed or fighting. [OE.].

FLESH-COLOURED [flesh'ku-lerd], *adj.* of the colour of flesh, pale pinkish.

FLESHINESS [fle'shi-nes], *n.* condition of being fleshy.

FLESHING [fle'shing], *n.* act of whetting the appetite (of a hound, hawk etc.) for hunting by a taste of the game killed; (*pl.*) close-fitting flesh-coloured tights.

FLESHLESS [flesh'les], *adj.* lean, bony.

FLESHLINESS [flesh'li-nes], *n.* state of being fleshly; sensuality.

FLESHLY [flesh'li], *adj.* (*archaic*) pertaining to the flesh; pertaining to the physical body and its attributes; carnal, sensual. [OE.].

FLESH-POT [flesh'pot], *n.* vessel in which flesh is cooked; (*fig.*) a luxury greatly desired.

FLESH-WOUND [flesh'wŏŏnd], *n.* superficial wound which injures the flesh only, and does not affect an internal organ or bone.

FLESHY [fle'shi], *adj.* consisting of flesh; like flesh; fat, corpulent; bodily, corporeal; pulpy.

FLEUR-DE-LIS (*pl.* **fleurs-de-lis**) [fler-de-lē'], *n.* (*bot.*) flower of a plant of the genus *Iris*; (*her.*) representation of a lily. [Fr.].

FLEW [flŏŏ], *pret.* of FLY (2). [OE.].

FLEWS [flŏŏz], *n.(pl.)* the large chaps of a deep-mouthed dog. [Unkn.].

FLEX (1) [fleks], *n.* flexible insulated wire to carry electricity. [FLEX(IBLE)].

FLEX (2), *v.t. and i.* to bend (as of joints, limbs); (*geol.*) fold (as of strata). [L.].

FLEXIBILITY [flek-si-bi'li-ti], *n.* pliability, quality of being flexible. [L.].

FLEXIBLE [flek'si-bl], *adj.* pliant, easily bent; expressive, supple (of a voice) modulating easily; able to be influenced by, and readily adapting oneself to, new influences or circumstances; easily persuaded; not fixed. FLEXIBLENESS, *n.* flexibility. FLEXIBLY, *adv.* in a f. fashion. [L.].

FLEXION, FLECTION [flek'shn], *n.* act of bending; state of being bent; that which is bent, a fold; (*anat.*) the bending of a joint or limb by the flexor muscles; (*gram.*) inflexion; (of a voice) modulation or modification of the sound or tone. [L.].

FLEXOR [flek'ser], *n.* (*anat.*) muscle which bends a limb or joint, as opposed to an extensor. [~FLEX (2).]

FLEXUOUS [flek'syŏŏ-ŏŏs], *adj.* bending, curving. [L.].

FLEXURE [flek'sher], *n.* act of bending or curving; a bend, fold; condition of being bent or curved. [L.].

FLIBBERTIGIBBET [fli-ber-ti-ji'bit], *n.* flighty, restless person, unable to settle down to any one thing. [Invented].

FLICK (1) [flik], *n.* smart light jerk or snap, as with a whip, the fingers etc.; quick, jerky turn of the wrist in making certain strokes at cricket, playing one of the backhand shots at table tennis, or delivering a cricket ball. FLICK (2), *v.t.* to strike lightly and smartly with a quick, jerky movement; jerk rapidly and smartly.

FLICK (3), *n.* (*slang*) cinematograph film; (*pl.*) cinematograph performance, the cinema. [~FLICKER (1)].

FLICKER (1) [fli'ker], *v.i.* to burn with a flicker; flutter, quiver, waver. FLICKER (2), *n.* a wavering, fitful gleam of light; unsteady, intermittent light; fluttering, or rapid, agitated movement. [OE.].

FLICKERING [fli'ke-ring], *adj.* that flickers. FLICKERINGLY, *adv.* in a f. fashion.

FLIER, FLYER [flī'er], *n.* one who, or that which, flies or flees.

FLIGHT (1) [flīt], *n.* action of flying, movement through the air by natural or mechanical means; a journey through the air; the manner of flying, path described in moving through the air; migration of birds; distance flown; a number of creatures or things flying together, volley (of missiles); unit or formation of aeroplanes; series of stairs, terraces etc.; (*fig.*) process of passing away or elapsing; contest in long-distance shooting; arrow used in such a contest; (*cricket*) control or variation of the trajectory of the delivery of a cricket ball; **in the first f.**, in the highest class or topmost rank. FLIGHT-FEATHER, quill-feather in the wing of a bird. FLIGHT (2), *v.t.* to shoot (birds) when flying in a f.; feather (an arrow); (*cricket*) deliver (a cricket ball) with particular reference to height and trajectory. [OE.].

FLIGHT (3), *n.* act of fleeing, hasty departure or retreat; **to put to f.**, defeat and cause to flee. [ME.].

FLIGHT-COMMANDER [flīt'ko-mahn-der], *n.* officer of the R.A.F. in charge of a flight.

FLIGHT DECK [flīt'dek], *n.* (*nav.*) flat deck of an aircraft-carrier where aircraft take off and land.

FLIGHTED [flī'tid], *adj.* (of an arrow) furnished with feathers; (*cricket*) cunningly varied in speed and trajectory through the air.

FLIGHTILY [flī'ti-li], *adv.* capriciously, in a flighty fashion.

FLIGHTINESS [flī'ti-nes], *n.* state of being flighty.

FLIGHT-LIEUTENANT [flīt-lef-te'nant], *n.* rank in the R.A.F. corresponding to captain in the army.

FLIGHT-SERGEANT [flīt'sah-jant], *n.* rank next above sergeant in the R.A.F.

FLIGHTY [flī'ti], *adj.* capricious, volatile, fickle, frivolous.

FLIMSY (1) [flim'zi], *adj.* light, fragile, without strength or substance, of loose or unsubstantial texture or nature; weak, trivial, incapable of withstanding close investigation. FLIMSY (2), *n.* (*coll.*) that which is f.; thin sheet of paper, carbon or transfer paper; paper used by newspaper reporters, newspaper copy; (*slang*) banknote; telegram. FLIMSILY, *adv.* in a f. fashion. FLIMSINESS, *n.* state of being f. [Unkn.].

FLINCH [flinsh], *v.i.* to shrink back in fear or pain, wince, fail to stand up (to). [OFr.].

FLING (1) (*pret. and p.pt.* flung) [fling], *v.t.* to cast, throw with an energetic or violent movement; move (a limb, head etc.) in a hasty, impulsive manner; scatter; spread, send forth; (*reflex.*) hurl oneself vigorously into a certain position; (*fig.*) enter into with great enthusiasm and determination; *v.i.* to rush away, hurl oneself in an impetuous manner, kick (of a horse); **to f. in one's teeth**, to reproach or taunt with; **to f. caution to the winds**, to abandon all care and discretion; **to f. out**, (*fig.*) to fly into a sudden outburst of abuse etc. FLING (2), *n.* a throw, sudden violent agitated movement, *esp.* of the limbs; (*fig.*) taunt, gibe; period of gratification of one's desires or impulses, bout of pleasure; **Highland f.**, Scottish dance characterized by rapid energetic movements of the legs and arms in time to music. [ME.].

FLINT (1) [flint], *n.* opaque dark-grey or brown variety of mineral silica; piece of flint used to produce a spark in a tinderbox, musket etc.; small piece of flint; ancient tool or weapon made from flint; anything hard, unyielding or untouched by the gentler feelings or emotions.; **to skin a f.**, to be extremely miserly. FLINT-GLASS, species of lustrous crystalline glass. FLINT (2), *adj.* made of f., resembling f. [OE.].

FLINT-LOCK [flint'lok], *n.* ancient type of musket-lock in which a flint strikes on a steel pan to produce a spark for igniting the powder.

FLINTY [flin'ti], *adj.* consisting of, resembling, flint, abounding in flint; hard, unfeeling. FLINTINESS, *n.* quality of being f. or extremely hard.

FLIP (1) [flip], *v.t. and i.* to flick, jerk, toss with the

ŏŏ is pronounced as in food; ŏŏ as in hood; th as in *think*; TH as in *that*; zh as in azure.   ~ = related to.

thumb or fingernail; move jerkily. FLIP (2), *n.* slight quick stroke; (*gunnery*) recoil of a gun-barrel when fired; (*slang*) short flight in an aeroplane. FLIP (3), *n.* drink consisting of a mixture of milk, egg and spirits or wines. [Uncert.].

FLIPPANT [fli'pant], *adj.* frivolous in mind and speech, wanting in proper seriousness or respect, displaying a too casual light-heartedness. FLIP-PANCY, FLIPPANTNESS, *n.* state or quality of being f. FLIPPANTLY, *adv.* in a f. fashion. [Uncert.].

FLIPPER [fli'per], *n.* limb of a reptile, animal etc., used for swimming, as of a turtle, penguin etc.; (*slang*) the hand.

FLIRT (1) [flurt], *v.t. and i.* to move about with a sudden, jerky motion; endeavour to engage the amorous attentions of the opposite sex without serious intentions, play at courtship; trifle or dally; move with a quick, sharp action; **to f. (a fan)**, to open and close smartly. FLIRT (2), *n.* sudden jerky movement, flick; person who plays at courtship with as many of the opposite sex as will respond, coquette. [Unkn.].

FLIRTATION [fler-tā'shn], *n.* act or practice of flirting, coquetry, pleasant light-hearted love affair.

FLIRTATIOUS [fler-tā'shŏŏs], *adj.* fond of flirting. FLIRTATIOUSLY, *adv.* in a f. fashion.

FLIRTING [flur'ting], *adj.* coquettish, given to f. FLIRTINGLY, *adv.* in a f. fashion.

FLIT (1) (*pres.pt.* **flitting**, *pres. and p.pt.* **flitted**) [flit], *v.i.* to fly quickly from place to place, dart about through the air; move about quickly and quietly; (*fig.*) (of fancies, dreams etc.) pass lightly in rapid succession; remove to another place of residence, often implying a secret change of dwelling to avoid payment of debts. FLIT (2), *n.* change of residence, *esp.* when unexpected and secret. [OScand.].

FLITCH [flich], *n.* the side of a pig, salted and cured. [OE.].

FLITTER [fli'ter], *v.i.* to flutter.

FLITTERMOUSE [fli'ter-mows], *n.* a bat.

FLITTING [fli'ting], *n.* a flying about swiftly and quietly from place to place; removal from one dwelling place to another.

FLIVVER [fli'ver], *n.* (*slang*) cheap or old-fashioned motor-car. [Invented].

FLOAT (1) [flōt], *n.* that which floats, cork or quill of an angling line; raft; flat-bottomed boat; one of the pieces of cork on the edge of a fishing net to prevent it from sinking; air-bladder of a fish; hollow ball indicating or regulating the level of water in a cistern etc.; device to control the quantity of spirit in a carburetter; shallow, low-built cart for conveying milk, livestock and other heavy articles; low platform on wheels on which is grouped a tableau in a procession; trowel for smoothing plaster on walls; (*stage, sg. or pl.*) footlights; (*aviation*) enclosed, hollow watertight compartment enabling a seaplane to float on water. [~OE.].

FLOAT (2), *v.t.* to set afloat (a ship); bear upon the surface, allow to float; cause to float; cover with liquid; (*comm.*) start, put into circulation; *v.i.* to be supported on or near the surface of water or other liquid; glide through or be carried along through the air without making any effort to move; become afloat (of a ship); (*fig.*) hover, move about in an aimless, effortless manner. FLOATABLE, *adj.* able to be floated, that allows a vessel to f. upon it. [OE.].

FLOATAGE [flō'tij], *n.* state of floating; flotsam; right to take anything found floating, ability to float; parts of a ship above the water-line.

FLOATATION, see FLOTATION.

FLOATER [flō'ter], *n.* one who, or that which, floats; (*coll.*) security to be paid to the bearer, stock-certificate, bond etc., recognized and accepted as a security; (*slang*) a blunder.

FLOAT-FISHING [flōt'fi-shing], *n.* angling by means of a float, bottom-fishing.

FLOATING [flō'ting], *adj.* supported on or near the surface of water or other liquid; suspended or gliding through the air; pertaining to sea-cargoes; movable, shifting, fluctuating; (*comm.*) unfunded; **f. bridge**, bridge of logs of timber, having a plank floor, bridge of boats, pontoons etc.; the f. part of a swing bridge; large steam ferry-boat; **f. dock**, dock capable of being submerged to admit a vessel, then raised and converted into a dry dock; **f. harbour**, breakwater formed of large masses of floating timber fastened together; **f. kidney**, kidney liable to displacement; **f. light**, lightship; buoy equipped with a light which serves as a warning of rocks

etc.; **f. policy**, (*comm.*) insurance policy having no specified application at first; **f. rib**, one of the lower, movable ribs, not fastened to the breast-bone.

FLOAT-IRON [flōt'iern], *v.t.* to iron (laundry) by means of a float roll machine.

FLOAT ROLL [flōt'rōl], *n.* resilient roller mounted on springs; **f. machine**, ironing machine fitted with such rollers.

FLOCCULENCE [flo'kyŏŏ-lens], *n.* state of being flocculent.

FLOCCULENT [flo'kyŏŏ-lent], *adj.* woolly, coalescing and adhering in flocks or flakes, fluffy.

FLOCK (1) [flok], *n.* a lock or tuft of wool; (*pl.*) cotton or woollen waste used for stuffing mattresses etc.; (*coll.*) fine particles of wool used in making flock-paper; (*pl.*) flaky, fibrous precipitate forming light, loose masses in solution. FLOCK (2), *v.t.* to stuff or coat with flocks; treat the surface of glass so that it acquires a rough, woolly finish. [L.].

FLOCK (3), *n.* assemblage, collection or company of anything, *esp.* a number of sheep or other domestic animals, pasturing together and under one owner-ship; group under one guardian; the Christian Church considered in relation to Christ; congregation of a church; **flocks and herds**, sheep and cattle. FLOCK (4), *v.i.* to crowd together so as to form a large company or f.; (of birds) assemble together, *esp.* in preparation for a flight. [OE.].

FLOCK-BED [flok-bed'], *n.* bed stuffed with coarse wool or wool refuse.

FLOCK-PAPER [flok'pā-per], *n.* kind of wallpaper made of flock or cloth cut up very finely and dusted on to the paper.

FLOE [flō], *n.* large sheet of floating ice. [Icel.].

FLOG (*pres.pt.* **flogging**, *pret. and p.pt.* **flogged**) [flog], *v.t. and i.* to whip, beat hard, thrash with a stick, whip etc.; urge on by beating; (of a sail) flap in a violent manner; (*army slang*) sell illicitly; **to f. a dead horse**, to seek to revive a well-worn point of controversy, waste energy in unavailing effort; **to f. the water**, to cast a fly continually over a stream in certain kinds of fishing. [~L.].

FLOGGING [flo'ging], *n.* corporal punishment by beating or thrashing with a rod, whip, lash etc.

FLOOD (1) [flud], *n.* large body of water, rising and flowing over land not usually covered with water; the incoming tide; great amount of water or other liquid, quantity of water discharged in torrential fashion; profuse weeping; (*fig.*) great outpouring, profuse stream; **the F.**, the inundation described in Genesis; **at the f.**, (*fig.*) at the highest or most favourable point. FLOOD (2), *v.t.* to cover with a f., inundate, discharge a great amount of water into, cause to be under water; overflow; (*fig.*) fill to excess, overwhelm; *v.i.* to brim over; be at the f.; (*med.*) be afflicted with uterine haemorrhage; **to f. out**, to drive out by water brought or left by floods. [OE.].

FLOOD-GATE [flud'gāt], *n.* sluice or gate which can be opened to allow excess water or floodwater to escape, or shut to prevent water from escaping; lower gates of a lock.

FLOODING [flu'ding], *n.* inundation, overflowing which causes that to be under water which is not normally covered by water; (*med.*) uterine haemorrhage.

FLOOD-LIGHT [flud'lit], *v.t.* to illuminate the exterior of a building by flood-lighting. FLOOD-LIGHTING, *n.* lighting up of the exterior of a building by powerful concealed lights which direct strong beams of light upon the building, giving uniform illumination and absence of shadow.

FLOOD-TIDE [flud'tid], *n.* the tide when coming in.

FLOOK, see FLUKE (1).

FLOOR (1) [flaw(r)], *n.* the flat surface forming the bottom of a building, room or passage, a storey of a building; the base, lowest ground surface of a structure; main area of a hall etc., lowest in position; **to take the f.**, to begin to dance; address a meeting. FLOOR (2), *v.t.* to furnish with a f. or floors; strike to the ground; (*coll.*) confound, defeat or silence; (*slang*) answer successfully. [OE.].

FLOOR-CLOTH [flaw'kloth], *n.* piece of soft woollen fabric used for washing floors.

FLOOR POLISHER [flaw'po-li-sher], *n.* one who, or that which, polishes floors; preliminary dance "to polish the floor" for an ensuing grand ball.

FLOOR-SHOW [flaw'shō], *n.* cabaret entertainment.

FLOOZY, FLOOSIE [flŏŏ'zi], *n.* (*slang, orig. U.S.*) prostitute.

FLOP (1) (*pres.pt.* **flopping**, *pret. and p.pt.* **flopped**)

[flop], v.t. to throw or set down heavily and clumsily; v.i. (coll.) to plump down suddenly, heavily and limply; move heavily and clumsily; flap about; (slang) fail miserably. FLOP (2), n. act of flopping; dull thud made by one who, or that which, flops; (slang) a complete failure. FLOP (3), adv. with a f. [~FLAP].

FLOPPY [flo'pi], adj. inclined to flop, slack, flaccid; careless, limp. FLOPPINESS, n. state of being f.

FLORA [flaw'rah], n. plant life found in a specific region or period; book containing a systematic catalogue or description of such plants; (class. myth.) goddess of flowers. [L.].

FLORAL [flaw'ral], adj. of or pertaining to flora; pertaining to flowers; decorated with representations of flowers. FLORALLY, adv. with flowers, in a f. manner. [L.].

FLORENCE [flo'rens], n. English name for Firenze, in Italy; **f. flask,** spherical glass bottle with a long neck. **FLORENTINE** (1) [flo'ren-tin], adj. pertaining to Florence. FLORENTINE (2), n. native of Florence.

FLORESCENCE [flo-re'sens], n. process of bursting into flower or blossoming; the flowering season. [L.].

FLORET [flaw'ret], n. small flower; (bot.) one of the small separate flowers forming the head of a composite flower. [OFr.].

FLORICULTURE [flaw'ri-kul-tyōōr], n. cultivation of flowering plants. FLORICULTURAL [flaw-ri-kul'-tyōō-ral], adj. relating to f. FLORICULTURIST [flaw-ri-kul'tyōō-rist], n. person who cultivates flowers. [L.].

FLORID [flo'rid], adj. highly embellished, lavishly decorated with ornament; bright in colour, of a lively red; showy, ostentatious. FLORIDITY, FLORID-NESS [flo-ri'di-ti, flo'rid-nes], n. quality of being f. FLORIDLY, adv. in a f. fashion.

FLORIN [flo'rin], n. British silver coin worth two shillings; gold coin of the time of Edward III worth six shillings. [ME. from Ital.].

FLORIST [flo'rist], n. one who cultivates flowers, dealer in flowers, nurseryman.

FLORUIT [flo'rōō-it], n. period when a person lived or flourished. [L.].

FLOSS [flos], n. short rough fibres of silk enveloping the cocoon of a silkworm; silk spun from this; soft fluffy matter resembling this; group of hanging styles in the flower of maize, silky substance in the husks of certain plants. FLOSSY, adj. composed of or like f. [Fr.].

FLOSS SILK [flos-silk'], n. portions of untwisted silk broken off in reeling silk from the cocoons, spun into a soft, fluffy, coarse yarn, and used in embroidery.

FLOTATION, FLOATATION [flō-tā'shn], n. act of floating; study of floating bodies; the launching of a limited company, state of keeping afloat. [Fr.].

FLOTILLA [flō-ti'lah], n. fleet of small vessels; group of destroyers, submarines or other small warships under a single command. [Span.].

FLOTSAM [flot'sam], n. (leg.) goods lost by shipwreck and found floating on the sea. [OFr.].

FLOUNCE (1) [flowns], v.i. to toss oneself about in a jerky, spasmodic manner, fling about the limbs and body. FLOUNCE (2), n. a sudden jerky movement of the body, tossing of the head or a limb. [~MSwed.].

FLOUNCE (3), n. narrow piece of silk, lace etc. sewn by its upper edge round the edge of a skirt or dress as an ornament, and with its lower edge hanging loose. FLOUNCE (4), v.t. to adorn or furnish with a f. or flounces. [Fr.].

FLOUNDER (1) [flown'der], n. small sea flatfish found especially at river-mouths. [~Swed.].

FLOUNDER (2), v.i. to stumble or stagger along with difficulty, as through mud or water; (fig.) blunder or proceed with difficulty in a confused manner. [Unkn.].

FLOUR (1) [flowr], n. the meal of wheat or other grain ground to a fine powder; any soft fine powder resembling this. FLOUR (2), v.t. to reduce to f.; sprinkle or cover with f. [ME.].

FLOURISH (1) [flu'rish], v.t. to decorate with flowery ornament; brandish or wave with an elaborate sweeping gesture; v.i. to prosper, be in a healthy vigorous condition; live, be at the height of one's activity; (mus.) improvise or add passages of elaborate ornament; sound a fanfare. FLOURISH (2), n. brandishing, drawing or waving anything with an elaborate sweeping gesture; piece of showy embellishment in speech or writing, showy parade of rhetoric; bold fanciful curved stroke in handwriting, printing or engraving; (mus.) passage of decorative

notes added for the sake of effect or as a prelude; fanfare of trumpets etc. FLOURISHER, n. person who flourishes. [ME.].

FLOURISHING [flu'ri-shing], adj. thriving, successful, in sound, healthy condition. FLOURISHINGLY, adv. in a f. manner.

FLOURY [flow'ri], adj. covered with flour; like flour; consisting of, relating to, flour.

FLOUT (1) [flowt], v.t. and i. to treat with contempt, mock at, ignore disdainfully; behave in an insulting manner. FLOUT (2), n. a jeer, insult. FLOUTER, n. one who flouts. [~Du.].

FLOW (1) [flō], v.i. to move along with a smooth continuous motion; run freely, gush; (of blood) circulate, run copiously; melt and run as a liquid; move in a steady stream; proceed effortlessly; (of the tide) rise, come in; be poured out in copious amounts; fall in loose masses, hang in loose folds; (fig.) issue, emanate in continual profuseness. FLOW (2), n. that which flows, a stream; act of flowing; quantity or volume which flows; rise of a tide; (fig.) uninterrupted sequence or supply. [OE.].

FLOWER (1) [flow'er], n. the brightly coloured leaves or petals forming the head of a plant; any of certain herbaceous plants producing these; (bot.) reproductive organs of a seed-plant; ornamental representation of a flower; (fig.) adornment, embellishment; the finest part; the prime of life; state or period of blooming; (pl.) (chem.) fine powdery deposits remaining after sublimation; scum or growth formed in fermentation. FLOWER (2), v.t. to cause to produce flowers; v.i. to produce a f., blossom. [L.].

FLOWERBED [flow'er-bed], n. plot in a garden, in which flowers are cultivated.

FLOWERED [flow'erd], adj. formed into flowers; embellished with figures of flowers.

FLOWERET [flow'er-et], n. small flower; floret.

FLOWERING [flow'e-ring], adj. producing flowers; cultivated for the flower.

FLOWERPOT [flow'er-pot], n. earthenware pot in which certain plants are grown.

FLOWER-SHOW [flow'er-shō], n. horticultural display or exhibition.

FLOWERY [flow'e-ri], adj. full of, covered with, flowers, composed of flowers, resembling flowers; florid, full of elaborate ornamentation.

FLOWING [flō'ing], adj. that flows; fluent; waving in loose folds; curving smoothly and naturally; proceeding readily and without effort. FLOWINGLY, adv. in a f. fashion.

FLOWN [flōn], p.pt. of FLY (2). [OE.].

FLUCTUATE [fluk'tyōō-āt], v.t. and i. to rise and fall, or move backwards and forwards, periodically; (fig.) vary, vacillate; cause to vary. FLUCTUATING, adj. unsteady, wavering, variable. [L.].

FLUCTUATION [fluk-tyōō-ā'shn], n. act of fluctuating. [L.].

FLUE (1) [flōō], n. pipe or shaft for conveying hot air, smoke etc.; small chimney or branch of a chimney; tube conveying heat to water in a boiler; (mus.) mouthpiece of an organ pipe. [Uncert.].

FLUE (2), n. loose fluffy mass of particles of some downy substance or dust. [~Flem.].

FLUE (3), n. variety of fishing-net. [~Du.].

FLUENCY [flōō'en-si], n. quality of being fluent. [L.].

FLUENT (1) [flōō'ent], adj. having a ready command and flow of words; spoken easily, readily and without hesitation; flowing smoothly. FLUENT (2), n. (math.) a constantly varying quantity in fluxions. FLUENTLY, adv. in a f. manner. [L.].

FLUFF (1) [fluf], n. a light soft downy substance; soft fur; first growth of hair on the face; woolly mass of dust particles. FLUFF (2), v.t. and i. to spread or shake into a soft fluffy mass; (slang) bungle, perform in an unskilful way; (theatre) bungle a part imperfectly learned; float or settle like f.; become fluffy. [~FLUE (2)].

FLUFFY [flu'fi], adj. consisting of, relating to, or resembling, fluff; covered with fluff or down; (slang) liable to bungle a theatrical part.

FLUID (1) [flōō'id], adj. flowing, liquid or gaseous; (fig.) mobile, yielding readily to forces tending to change it; flowing easily and gracefully. FLUID (2), n. a liquid or gaseous substance, substance which cannot permanently resist forces tending to change its shape. [L.].

FLUIDIFY [flōō-i'di-fi], v.t. to make fluid.

FLUIDITY [flōō-i'di-ti], n. quality or state of being fluid; a fluid substance. [Fr.].

FLUKE (1), **FLOOK** [flōōk], n. triangular tip of the

ōō is pronounced as in food; ŏŏ as in hood; th as in think; TH as in that; zh as in azure.   ~ = related to.

DSE—I*

shank of an anchor; barbed head of a harpoon, lance etc.; lobe of the tail of a whale.

FLUKE (2), *n.* a flatfish, *esp.* the flounder; parasitic worm causing liver-rot in sheep; kind of kidney potato. [OE.].

FLUKE (3), *n.* (*coll.*) lucky unintentional scoring shot at billiards or other games; (*fig.*) piece of luck, chance successful stroke. FLUKE (4), *v.t. and i.* (*coll.*) to make a f. or series of flukes; score by means of a f.; gain by a f. [Unkn.].

FLUKY (1) [floo'ki], *adj.* (*coll.*) lucky, accidentally successful, of the nature of a fluke. FLUKILY, *adv.* luckily, by a lucky chance. FLUKINESS, *n.* quality of being f.

FLUKY (2), *adj.* attacked by flukes.

FLUME [floom], *n.* the passage for the water which drives a mill-wheel; artificial channel down which water may be directed for industrial purposes; deep ravine through which a stream flows. [ME. from OFr.].

FLUMMERY [flu'me-ri], *n.* kind of blancmange; (*fig.*) nonsense, idle talk; empty flattery. [Unkn.].

FLUNG [flung], *pret. and p.pt.* of FLING (1). [OE.].

FLUNK [flungk], *v.t. and i.* (*U.S. coll.*) to shirk; fail (an examination); cause to fail, plough. [Unkn.].

FLUNKEY [flung'ki], *n.* man-servant in livery, footman; (*fig.*) toady. FLUNKEYDOM, *n.* state of being a f. FLUNKEYISM, *n.* character of a f.

FLUOR [floo'er], *n.* any variety of mineral containing calcium fluoride. [L.].

FLUORENE [floo'e-rēn], *n.* a coal-tar product.

FLUORESCENCE [floo-e-re'sens], *n.* property of certain substances of emitting light of longer wavelength than the light directed upon them, giving the effect of a coloured luminosity. [Fr.].

FLUORESCENT [floo-e-re'sent], *adj.* possessing or exhibiting fluorescence.

FLUORINE [floo'e-rēn], *n.* an elementary greenishyellow gas of great chemical activity, one of the halogens.

FLUOROSCOPE [floo'e-rō-skōp], *n.* apparatus used to observe the effect of X-rays by means of a fluorescent screen. FLUOROSCOPY [floo-e-ro'skō-pi], *n.* examination of a substance by means of a f.

FLURRY (1) [flu'ri], *n.* sudden gust of wind; sudden commotion or bustle, restless hurry and confusion; convulsive movements of a dying whale. FLURRY (2), *v.t.* to bewilder, fluster by restless unceasing bustle. [Echoic].

FLUSH (1) [flush], *v.t.* to cleanse by a sudden rush of water or other liquid; suffuse with a ruddy glow; (*pass.*) be wildly elated at or with; *v.i.* to fly up suddenly in startled fashion; flow suddenly, quickly and in a large volume; (of blood) rush to the skin; blush; send forth sprouts or shoots; (*fig.*) glow. FLUSH (2), *n.* flock of birds suddenly started in flight; sudden rush of water or other liquid; sudden flow of blood to the face; ruddy glow of colour; sudden blooming or sprouting; impulsive feeling of elation; height of vigour or freshness; abundance. [ME.].

FLUSH (3), *adj.* brimming, full; level, forming one even surface on the same plane; (*coll.*) well supplied with money; plentiful; lavish. FLUSH (4), *adv.* in a f. manner, so as to form one even surface on the same plane. FLUSH (5), *v.t.* to make f. or level. [Uncert.].

FLUSH (6), *n.* (*cards*) a hand containing only cards of the same suit; run of cards of the same suit. FLUSH (7), *adj.* made up of cards of the same suit.

FLUSHING [flu'shing], *n.* blushing.

FLUSTER (1) [flus'ter], *v.t. and i.* to agitate and confuse, make hot and bothered; be confused and agitated; be muddled with drink. FLUSTER (2), *n.* state of being flustered, agitation, confusion. [~Icel.].

FLUTE (1) [floot], *n.* musical wind-instrument consisting of a wooden pipe containing holes to be covered by the fingers or keys, and played by blowing across a hole in the side of the instrument; organ stop producing a sound similar to that of a flute; flautist in an orchestra; narrow vertical groove along the shaft of a column. FLUTE (2), *v.t. and i.* to play the f., sing in f.-like tones; play (an air) on a f.; sound as a f.; form flutes in. FLUTED, *adj.* grooved, decorated with flutes; f.-like. [Fr.].

FLUTING [floo'ting], *n.* (*arch.*) fluted work; shallow groove in a column or in a ruffle; (*mus.*) action of playing the flute.

FLUTIST [floo'tist], *n.* a flautist.

FLUTTER (1) [flu'ter], *v.t.* to throw into a state of

agitation, disturb, perturb; *v.i.* to move the wings quickly and nervously; make short flights flapping the wings in this way; vibrate with a rapid irregular motion, flap rapidly; throb faintly, quickly and unevenly; be in a state of nervous bustle and excitement. FLUTTER (2), *n.* act of fluttering; condition of being nervously agitated; (*coll.*) a small gamble. FLUTTERER, *n.* one who flutters; one who acts in a nervously excited way. [OE.].

FLUTY [floo'ti], *adj.* having the sound or timbre of a flute.

FLUVIAL [floo'vi-al], *adj.* belonging to rivers; living in a river. [L.].

FLUX (1) [fluks], *n.* act or state of flowing, fluidity; excessive discharge of morbid matter, blood etc.; flowing in of a tide; (*phys.*) amount flowing over a certain area in a specified time; (*math.*) continual motion (of a point); (*metal.*) any substance mixed with a metal or mineral to promote fusion. FLUX (2), *v.t. and i.* to flow; fuse, melt; melt by using a f. [L.].

FLUXION [fluk'shn], *n.* flux; (*math.*) rate of increase in magnitude of a variable quantity; (*pl.*) Newtonian calculus. FLUXIONAL, *adj.* relating to fluxions. FLUXIONARY, *adj.* variable. [L.].

FLY (1) [fli], *n.* two-winged flying insect; imitation of such an insect, fastened to a fish-hook to attract fish; plant-disease caused by insects; (*print.*) person or device that removes the printed sheets from a press; **f. in the ointment,** a drawback. [OE.].

FLY (2) (*pret.* flew, *p.pt.* flown), *v.t.* to cause to fly; navigate or control during flight; traverse by aircraft; transport by aircraft; hang up (a flag) from a mast or staff; flee from; *v.i.* to move through the air by wings or mechanical means; float in the air; move rapidly through the air; flutter in the wind; hasten, travel at an extremely quick rate; flee; move with a violent motion; **to f. at,** (*fig.*) to attack fiercely, abuse; **to f. into,** to develop (a rage) quickly and violently; **to f. out at,** to burst into a storm of abuse against; **to let f.,** to shoot, hurl; **as the crow flies,** in a direct line; **to f. in the face of,** to flout; **to f. high,** to be ambitious. [OE.].

FLY (3), *n.* act of flying; flight through the air; hackney carriage drawn by one horse; strip of cloth covering a row of buttons on a garment; canvas sheet slung above a tent as an extra roof; canvas flap covering the entrance to a tent; edge of a flag etc. farthest away from the staff; width of a flag etc., from the staff to the further edge; (*pl.*) place above the stage of a theatre from which scenery is moved; (*baseball*) flight of a ball before touching the ground. [*Prec.*].

FLYAWAY [fli'a-wā], *adj.* flighty, capricious; (of garments etc.) streaming loosely.

FLY-BLOW (1) [fli'blō], *n.* egg or larva of a fly laid in flesh. FLY-BLOW (2), *v.t.* to taint or corrupt by depositing eggs in.

FLY-BLOWN [fli'blōn], *adj.* corrupted or tainted with fly-blow; (*fig.*) discredited, sullied.

FLY-BOOK [fli'book], *n.* container in which artificial flies for angling are kept.

FLY-BUTTON [fli'bu-ton], *n.* one of the buttons covered by the fly of a pair of trousers.

FLY-CATCHER [fli'ka-cher], *n.* any of various birds which feed on flies; plant which traps and eats flies; a cage of wire gauze for trapping flies.

FLYER, see FLIER.

FLY-FISHING [fli'fi-shing], *n.* art or practice of catching fish by means of artificial flies fastened to the fish-hook.

FLY-HALF [fli-hahf'], *n.* (*Rugby football*) half-back who stands at some distance from the scrum-half.

FLYING (1) [fli'ing], *n.* act or practice of one who, or that which, flies, aviation. FLYING (2), *adj.* that flies; hasty, of short duration; streaming out into the air; resembling anything which flies; very fast; **with f. colours,** with distinction; **f. squad,** branch of the police equipped with high-powered motor vehicles for the pursuit of criminals; **f. start,** start to a race in which the competitors approach the starting line on the move; (*fig.*) auspicious beginning resulting in an early advantage or rapid progress.

FLYING-BOAT [fli-ing-bōt'], *n.* (*aeron.*) aeroplane so constructed that the fuselage can rest directly on the water.

FLYING-BOMB [fli-ing-bom'], *n.* weapon consisting of a winged body containing explosive and a motor to carry it to its objective.

FLYING-BRIDGE [fli-ing-brij'], *n.* bridge of pontoons.

FLYING-BUTTRESS [fli-ing-but'res], *n.* (*arch.*) a

The accent ´ after a syllable = stress (u-pon´). The mark ‾ over a vowel = length (ā in made; ō in bone).

buttress, the base of which stands away from the wall it is supporting.

FLYING-COLUMN [flī-ing-ko'lum], *n.* body of troops kept moving from one place to another, and practically independent of the main base.

FLYING-FISH [flī-ing-fish'], *n.* fish which is able to sustain itself in the air for a time by means of its long pectoral fins.

FLYING-FOX [flī-ing-foks'], *n.* kind of fruit-eating bat.

FLYING-OFFICER [flī'ing-o-fi-ser], *n.* rank in the R.A.F. immediately below that of flight-lieutenant.

FLY-LEAF [flī'lēf], *n.* leaf of blank paper at the beginning and end of a book; printed circular contained on a single sheet.

FLY-OVER [flī'ō-ver], *n.* method of avoiding crossroads etc., whereby one road or set of rails crosses over another by means of a shallow bridge.

FLYPAPER [flī'pā-per], *n.* paper coated with a sticky or poisonous substance, hung up to catch flies.

FLY-PAST [flī'pahst], *n.* ceremonial flight of aircraft past a given point, corresponding to a march-past of troops.

FLY-SWAT [flī'swot], *n.* instrument for killing flies.

FLY-TRAP [flī'trap], *n.* plant which traps and eats small insects and flies.

FLY-WHEEL [flī'wēl], *n.* heavy-rimmed revolving wheel used to regulate the speed of a machine.

FOAL (1) [fōl], *n.* the young of a horse, ass or other related animal. FOAL (2), *v.t. and i.* to give birth to a f. FOALING, *n.* act of bringing forth a f.

FOAM (1) [fōm], *n.* white frothy collection of small bubbles forming on the surface of liquids in a state of fermentation, effervescence or agitation; anything resembling this; (*poet.*) the sea. FOAM-BATH, bath of f. taken for medicinal purposes. FOAM (2), *v.i.* to form or produce f.; emit thick saliva or profuse perspiration resembling f.; run in the form of f. (of liquids); **to f. at the mouth**, (*fig.*) to be in a furious rage. [OE.].

FOAMY [fō'mi], *adj.* covered with, or like, foam.

FOB (1) [fob], *n.* small pocket in the waistband of breeches or trousers. [~LGerm.].

FOB (2) [*pres.pt.* fobbing, *pret. and p.pt.* fobbed], *v.t.* (*archaic*) to cheat; **to f. off**, to put off by an excuse, pretence or trick. [~ME.].

FOCAL [fō'kal], *adj.* relating to a focus; **f. length**, (*opt.*) distance between the centre of a lens and the point where the rays meet.

FOCALIZE [fō'ka-liz], *v.t.* to focus.

FO'C'SLE [fōk'sl], *n.* the forecastle of a ship.

FOCUS (1) (*pl.* foci) [fō'kus, fō'sī], *n.* (*phys.*) a point in which rays of light, heat, sound etc., meet after being reflected or refracted; adjustment or position required to produce a sharply defined image; focal length or distance; (*math.*) a point from which distances to all points on a given curve are linearly related; (*fig.*) the point where anything is gathered to a head, area of greatest activity; **in f.**, (*phot.*) correctly adjusted so that the image is sharply defined; (*fig.*) undistorted. FOCUS (2) (*pres.pt.* FOCUSING, *pret. and p.pt.* FOCUSED), *v.t. and i.* to bring to a f.; bring into f.; (*fig.*) concentrate; converge. [L.].

FODDER (1) [fo'der], *n.* food for horses, cattle or sheep, *esp.* dried food such as hay, straw etc. FODDER (2), *v.t.* to feed or supply with f. [OE.].

FOE [fō], *n.* enemy, adversary. [OE.].

FOEHN [furn], *n.* dry, hot wind of the Northern Alps. [Germ.].

FOETAL [fē'tal], *adj.* relating to the foetus.

FOETICIDE [fē'ti-sīd], *n.* criminal abortion.

FOETID, FETID [fē'tid], *adj.* having an offensive smell. [L.].

FOETUS, FETUS [fē'tus], *n.* the young of viviparous animals before birth, and of oviparous ones in the shell, after the embryo has developed. [L.].

FOG (1) [fog], *n.* dense mass of low-lying watery vapour, smoky particles etc., reducing or obliterating visibility; (*phot.*) blurred condition of a photographic negative; (*fig.*) state of perplexity and bewilderment. FOG (2) (*pres.pt.* FOGGING, *pret. and p.pt.* FOGGED), *v.t.* to surround or envelop with f.; (*phot.*) make blurred; (*fig.*) perplex, baffle; *v.i.* to become foggy; (*phot.*) cloud over. [Uncert.].

FOG (3), *n.* long grass unpastured and left untouched during winter. [ME.].

FOG-BANK [fog'bangk], *n.* dense mass of fog at sea, resembling land at a distance.

FOGEY, FOGY [fō'gi], *n.* elderly, fussy, old-fashioned person. [Unkn.].

FOGGY [fo'gi], *adj.* pertaining to, clouded with, or

resembling fog; (*phot.*) blurred; (*fig.*) obscure, baffling; confused; vague. FOGGILY, *adv.* in a f manner. FOGGINESS, *n.* state of being f.

FOGHORN [fog'hawn], *n.* powerful siren on a ship, lighthouse etc., used as a warning signal in fog.

FOG-LAMP [fog'lamp], *n.* lamp fitted to the front of a motor vehicle, emitting a ray which penetrates fog.

FOG-SIGNAL [fog'sig-nal], *n.* any audible warning signal used in the event of fog.

FOGY, see FOGEY.

FOIBLE [foi'bl], *n.* an unworthy feature in one's character, small failing; idiosyncrasy; (*fencing*) part of a sword-blade, from middle to tip. [OFr.].

FOIL (1) [foil], *n.* (*arch.*) leaf-like space between the cusps in window tracery; plate of metal beaten out into a thin sheet; thin leaf of metal placed under precious stones to heighten their brilliancy; thin coating of tin and quicksilver laid on the back of a sheet of glass to make a mirror; (*fig.*) anything which serves to set off another thing to advantage by contrast. FOIL (2), *v.t.* to decorate or provide with a f.; back or cover with f.; (*fig.*) set off by contrast. [OFr. from L.].

FOIL (3), *n.* light rapier or tapering sword used as a weapon in fencing, and tipped with a leather-covered button. [Uncert.].

FOIL (4), *v.t. and i.* to frustrate, defeat; repulse; (*hunting*) cross and recross so as to obliterate or confuse the scent. FOIL (5), *n.* track or trail of game when pursued; (*fig.*) defeat, check. [~OFr.].

FOIST [foist], *v.t.* to insert secretly or wrongfully, palm off (something bad) in an underhand way. [Du.].

FOLD (1) [fōld], *n.* pen or enclosure for sheep; flock of sheep in such an enclosure; (*fig.*) the Church, flock of believers. FOLD (2), *v.t.* to pen, enclose in a f.; manure land by enclosing sheep in folds upon it. [OE.].

FOLD (3), *v.t. and i.* to lay or bend one part of (something flexible) over another, double over or up; wrap round, coil; envelop; embrace; close or bend back over another part, be capable of being folded; **to f. one's arms**, to cross one's arms over the breast with the elbows bent. FOLD (4), *n.* a bend or part of some flexible material which is doubled over; crease or mark made by such folding; layer; (*geol.*) curvature or warping of strata. [OE.].

FOLDER [fōl'der], *n.* instrument used in folding paper; container for papers; advertisement or other document which folds up.

FOLDING (1) [fōl'ding], *n.* act of doubling one part of a substance over another; penning of sheep or cattle. FOLDING (2), *adj.* that folds or can be folded.

FOLDING DOOR [fōl-ding-daw(r)'], *n.* door hinged down the centre to form two leaves which can be folded flat against one wall.

FOLIACEOUS [fō-li-ā'shôos], *adj.* relating to, or like, foliage. [L.].

FOLIAGE [fō'li-ij], *n.* the leaves of a plant, leaves collectively; ornamentation in the form of leaves; **f. leaf**, leaf itself as distinct from petal, sepal etc. [OFr.].

FOLIATE (1) [fō'li-āt], *adj.* resembling a leaf; provided with leafage. FOLIATE (2), *v.t.* to beat into a leaf or thin plate; spread (a mirror) over with a coat of tin and quicksilver; decorate with foils or foliage; number the leaves or folios of a book; *v.i.* to split into leaves. [L.].

FOLIATED [fō'li-ā-tid], *adj.* spread or covered with a thin plate or foil; (*min.*) consisting of plates or thin layers; (*arch.*) adorned with foils; (*zool.*) shaped like a leaf; (*her.*) consisting of leaves; (*mus.*) decorated with slurred notes.

FOLIATION [fō-li-ā'shn], *n.* act of springing into leaf, state of being in leaf; process of beating into foil; (*geol.*) quality of splitting into thin layers; decoration in the form of foils; numbering of the folios of a book.

FOLIO (1) [fō'li-ō], *n.* sheet of paper folded once; book of the largest size; (*print.*) leaf of a printed book; page number of a book; (*comm.*) right- and left-hand pages of an account book, used for both sides of an account; (*leg.*) seventy-two or ninety words of manuscript. FOLIO (2), *adj.* having the sheets of paper folded once only. [L.].

FOLK [fōk], *n.* people in general; nation, race; class or division of people; (*pl., coll.*) relatives, relations.

FOLK-DANCE [fōk'dahns], *n.* traditional popular dance. FOLK-DANCING, *n.* performance of folk-dances.

FOLKLORE [fōk'law(r)], *n.* legendary traditions,

ōō is pronounced as in food; ŏŏ as in hood; th as in *think*; TH as in *that*; zh as in azure. ~ ═ related to.

popular beliefs, sayings and customs prevailing among a people; study of these.

FOLKSONG [fōk'song], *n.* popular traditional song and air.

FOLKTALE [fōk'tāl], *n.* popular traditional tale.

FOLKWEAVE [fōk'wēv], *n.* loosely-woven fabric supposed to resemble hand-woven cloth.

FOLLICLE [fo'li-kl], *n.* (*bot.*) pod opening on the ventral side; vessel distended with air; little bag or secreting recess in animal bodies; (*entom.*) cocoon. FOLLICULATE(D) [fo-li'kyōō-lāt, -lā-tid], *adj.* (*bot.*) having a f.; (*entom.*) contained in a cocoon. FOLLICULOUS [fo-li'kyōō-lōōs], *adj.* containing or consisting of follicles; resembling a f. [L.].

FOLLICULAR [fo-li'kyōō-ler], *adj.* in the form of a follicle, pertaining to a follicle, consisting of, containing, follicles.

FOLLOW (1) [fo'lō], *v.t.* to go or come after; pursue; be next in order; be engaged in (a particular profession or career); pursue with the eye, watch; imitate, be an adherent of; (*fig.*) obey; keep in touch with, make a study of; understand clearly, grasp the stages of (an argument etc.); *v.i.* to come after; happen later; result; **to f. suit,** (*cards*) to play a card of the same suit as the one led; (*fig.*) do likewise; **to f. on,** (*coll.*) to come at some later time; (*cricket*) take the second innings immediately after the first (of a side which does not bat first); **to f. through,** (*billiards*) play a stroke so that the cue-ball continues in the same straight line or the same general direction after striking another ball; (*sport*) continue and complete the motion of a stroke after the ball has been hit; **to f. up,** to pursue steadily and persistently; carry out to a conclusion, investigate thoroughly; (*football*) keep near the player with the ball so as to render help. FOLLOW (2), *n.* act of following. FOLLOW-ON, (*cricket*) second innings taken immediately after the first. FOLLOW-THROUGH, (*billiards*) stroke in which the ball continues in the same direction after striking a ball; (*sport*) continuation and completion of the swing of a stroke after impact. FOLLOW-UP, action of following up; continuation of something begun. [OE.].

FOLLOWER [fo'lō-er], *n.* one who follows, disciple; retainer, supporter; (*coll.*) lover.

FOLLOWING (1) [fo'lō-ing], *n.* act of one who follows; body of followers, crowd of supporters. FOLLOWING (2), *adj.* that follows next after, succeeding; (of wind) moving in the same direction as the course of a ship, runner in a race etc.; mentioned next.

FOLLY [fo'li], *n.* foolish act, utterance, or piece of behaviour; want of sense, foolishness or weakness of mind; costly, impractical structure. [OFr.].

FOMENT [fō-ment'], *v.t.* to apply warm lotions or poultices (to); (*fig.*) excite, stir up, encourage. FOMENTER, *n.* one who foments. [LL.].

FOMENTATION [fō-men-tā'shn], *n.* act of fomenting; lotion etc. applied; (*fig.*) incitement. [L.].

FOND [fond], *adj.* vain, credulous, misguided; foolishly tender, doting; loving, affectionate; **to be f. of,** to like, derive pleasure from; regard with great affection. FONDLY, *adv.* in a f. manner, misguidedly; lovingly. FONDNESS, *n.* condition of being f. [ME.].

FONDANT [fon'dant], *n.* kind of sweetmeat. [Fr.].

FONDLE [fon'dl], *v.t. and i.* to caress, stroke or play with lovingly. FONDLER, *n.* one who fondles. [FOND].

FONT (1) [font], *n.* receptacle for containing the holy water used in baptism; reservoir of an oil-lamp; (*poet.*) fountain, spring. [OE. from L.].

FONT (2), see FOUNT (2).

FONTAL [fon'tal], *adj.* relating to a fount or source, baptismal.

FOOD [fōōd], *n.* that which can be eaten or absorbed by an animal or plant as nutriment; solid edible matter; a particular kind of nourishment; (*fig.*) matter to be reflected upon or assimilated mentally.

FOODSTUFF [fōōd'stuf], *n.* an article commonly regarded as food.

FOOL (1) [fōōl], *n.* an imbecile, idiot; stupid, silly person; dupe, butt; clown or jester formerly kept in a noble household to provide amusement; (*coll.*) light-hearted, mischievous person who makes people laugh; **fool's paradise,** (*fig.*) state of happiness founded on illusion and vain hopes; **All Fools' Day,** 1 April; **April f.,** person hoaxed on 1 April. FOOL (2), *v.t. and i.* to dupe, make a f. of; act like a f. [OFr. from L.].

FOOL (3), *n.* dish of fruit stewed, pounded to a pulp and mixed with cream, custard etc. [Uncert.].

FOOLERY [fōō'le-ri], *n.* foolish behaviour, habitual folly; act of folly, foolish idea etc.

FOOLHARDY [fōōl'hah-di], *adj.* taking or involving unnecessary, foolish risks. FOOLHARDILY, *adv.* in a f. way. FOOLHARDINESS, *n.* courage without sense or judgment; rashness. [OFr.].

FOOLISH [fōō'lish], *adj.* weak in intellect; silly, stupid; exhibiting little intelligence, forethought or judgment; rash, ill-advised; (*Bible*) impious. FOOLISHLY, *adv.* in a f. fashion.

FOOL-PROOF [fōōl'prōōf], *adj.* (*coll.*) so simple as to be manageable even by the most incompetent.

FOOLSCAP [fōōlz'kap, fōōls'kap], *n.* cap furnished with bells, formerly worn by a professional fool; dunce's cap; size of paper, about 17 x 14 in.

FOOL'S PARSLEY [fōōlz-pahs'li], *n.* (*bot.*) an umbelliferous plant.

FOOT (1) (*pl.* **feet**) [fōōt], *n.* that end of the leg on which an animal stands and walks; anything like this in shape or function; part of a stocking or sock which receives this; the lower part, base; infantry soldiers; lineal measure of 12 in.; shortest unit of the metre of a verse; **cubic f.,** cube with a side of 1 sq. ft.; **square f.,** square whose side measures 1 ft.; **on f.,** walking; **at one's feet,** captive or captivated; **to fall on one's feet,** to have good luck; **to find one's feet,** to gain experience; **to set on f.,** to originate; **to put one's f. down.,** (*coll.*) to forbid, threaten to take preventive measures; **to put one's f. in it,** to act tactlessly; **to put one's best f. foremost,** (*coll.*) to do one's utmost. FOOT (2), *v.t.* to walk; supply a new foot to (stockings); **to f. the bill,** to pay; **to f. a measure,** to dance. [OE.].

FOOTAGE [fōō'tij], *n.* (*mining*) method of payment of miners according to the length of seam cut; quantity mined; (*cinema*) length of film used in photographing a scene, play etc.

FOOTBALL [fōōt'bawl], *n.* inflated round or egg-shaped ball of thin rubber, cased in leather and kicked by the feet; team games played with it.

FOOTBALLER [fōōt'baw-ler], *n.* one who plays football.

FOOT-BATH [fōōt'bahth], *n.* small bath in which to wash the feet.

FOOTBOARD [fōōt'bawd], *n.* sloping board on which a coachman or motorist supports his feet when driving; step running alongside a railway-coach; board at the foot of a bed.

FOOT-BRAKE [fōōt'brāk], *n.* brake, *esp.* on a motor-car, operated by the foot.

FOOT-BRIDGE [fōōt'brij], *n.* bridge for foot-passengers.

FOOTED [fōō'tid], *adj.* having feet or a foot.

FOOTER [fōō'ter], *n.* (*slang*) football.

FOOTFALL [fōōt'fawl], *n.* the sound of a footstep.

FOOT-FAULT (1) [fōōt'fawlt], *n.* (*tennis*) a service illegal on account of the position of the server's feet when striking the ball. FOOT-FAULT (2), *v.t.* to penalize for committing a f.; *v.i.* to commit a f.

FOOT-GUARDS [fōōt'gahdz], *n.(pl.)* (*milit.*) five infantry regiments which form part of the household troops.

FOOTHILL [fōōt'hil], *n.* hill at the base of a mountain or range of mountains.

FOOTHOLD [fōōt'hōld], *n.* that which offers a secure position for the feet; (*fig.*) support, stable position.

FOOTING [fōō'ting], *n.* act of setting down the feet; foothold; firm foundation; basis, status or condition; **to pay one's f.,** to discharge a fee or obligation on gaining admission to a club, society, trade etc.

FOOTLE (1) [fōō'tl], *v.i.* (*coll.*) to talk or act foolishly. FOOTLE (2), *n.* nonsense, twaddle. [Unkn.].

FOOTLIGHTS [fōōt'līts], *n.(pl.)* row of lights across the front of a stage; (*fig.*) actor's profession.

FOOTLING [fōōt'ling], *adj.* trifling, foolish.

FOOTMAN [fōōt'man], *n.* liveried manservant.

FOOTMARK [fōōt'mahk], *n.* footprint.

FOOTMUFF [fōōt'muf], *n.* bag lined with fur, for keeping the feet warm in winter.

FOOTNOTE [fōōt'nōt], *n.* note or comment at the foot of a page.

FOOTPACE [fōōt'pās], *n.* walking pace; raised portion of a floor; top step in the sanctuary of a church, on which the altar stands.

FOOTPAD [fōōt'pad], *n.* highway robber who goes on foot.

FOOTPATH [fōōt'pahth], *n.* path for pedestrians only.

FOOTPLATE [fōōt'plāt], *n.* platform on a loco-motive on which the driver and fireman stand.

FOOT-POUND [fŏŏt-pownd'], *n.* unit of work, work required to raise 1 lb. through 1 ft.

FOOTPRINT [fŏŏt'print], *n.* print or mark of a foot.

FOOT-ROT [fŏŏt'rot], *n.* a disease of the feet of sheep and cattle.

FOOTRULE [fŏŏt-rōŏl'], *n.* ruler 12 in. long.

FOOT-SLOG [fŏŏt'slog], *v.i.* (*slang*) to tramp, march laboriously. **FOOT-SLOGGER**, *n.* (*slang*) infantryman.

FOOT-SOLDIER [fŏŏt'sōl-jer], *n.* infantryman.

FOOTSORE [fŏŏt'saw(r)], *adj.* having sore feet, tired with walking.

FOOTSTEP [fŏŏt'step], *n.* a step of the foot; footfall; footmark; **to follow in a person's footsteps**, to follow an example or precedent.

FOOTSTOOL [fŏŏt'stŏŏl], *n.* stool on which to rest the feet when sitting.

FOOTWARMER [fŏŏt'wah-mer], *n.* any appliance for warming the feet.

FOOTWAY [fŏŏt'wā], *n.* footpath.

FOOTWEAR [fŏŏt'wāer], *n.* boots, shoes etc.

FOOTWORK [fŏŏt'werk], *n.* skilful use of the feet in sport.

FOOZLE (1) [fŏŏ'zl], *v.t.* to bungle; (*golf*) spoil a stroke. **FOOZLE** (2), *n.* a bungling stroke. [Unkn.].

FOP [fop], *n.* dandy, coxcomb. [ME.].

FOPPERY [fo'pe-ri], *n.* affectation.

FOPPISH [fo'pish], *adj.* affected, like a fop. **FOPPISHLY**, *adv.* in f. fashion. **FOPPISHNESS**, *n.* quality of being f.

FOR (1) [faw(r)], *prep.* instead of; as being; towards; for the sake of; on account of; in favour of; towards the obtaining of; by reason of; through a certain space or time; in order to obtain; notwithstanding; **to be f. it**, (*coll.*) to be due for punishment, about to get into trouble. **FOR** (2), *conj.* because, since; on this account that.

FOR- (3), *pref.* forward, through; out beyond; thoroughly, to excess; to a wrong end. [OE.].

FORAGE (1) [fo'rij], *n.* food for horses and cattle; search by soldiers for provisions. **FORAGE** (2), *v.t.* to provide f. for; plunder for f.; *v.i.* to search for f.; (*fig.*) rummage. **FORAGER**, *n.* one who forages. **FORAGING**, *n.* act of searching for f. [OFr.].

FORAGE-CAP [fo'rij-kap], *n.* (*milit.*) peaked undress infantry cap.

FORAMEN (*pl.* **foramina**) [faw-rā'men], *n.* a small hole; (*anat.*) opening in a bone for a vessel to pass through; (*bot.*) orifice of an ovule. **FORAMINATED** [faw-ra'mi-nā-tid], *adj.* having a f.; perforated. [L.].

FORASMUCH [faw-raz-much'], *conj.* considering that.

FORAY (1) [fo'rā], *n.* a raid, plundering expedition. **FORAY** (2), *v.t. and i.* to make a f. upon. [ME.].

FORBAD(E) [faw-bad'], *pret.* of FORBID. [~OE.].

FORBEAR (1), see FORBEAR.

FORBEAR (2) (*pret.* **forbore**, *p.pt.* **forborne**) [faw-bāer'], *v.t.* to abstain from; treat leniently; *v.i.* to hold oneself in check; refrain; be patient. **FORBEARINGLY**, *adv.* in a forebearing fashion. [OE.].

FORBEARANCE [faw-bāer'ans], *n.* act of forbearing; patience and understanding, leniency, self-control.

FORBID (*pres.pt.* **forbidding**, *pret.* **forbade**, *p.pt.* **forbidden**) [faw-bid'], *v.t.* to order not to do; refuse entry; prevent; prohibit; *v.i.* to utter a prohibition. [OE.].

FORBIDDEN [faw-bi'den], *adj.* not allowed, prohibited.

FORBIDDING [faw-bi'ding], *adj.* awesome; repulsive. **FORBIDDINGLY**, *adv.* in f. fashion. **FORBIDDINGNESS**, *n.* quality of being f.

FOR-BY [faw-bi'], *prep.* (*Scots*) near to, adjacent. [ME.].

FORCE (1) [faws], *n.* a waterfall. [OIcel.].

FORCE (2), *n.* power or energy exerted so as to issue in change or movement; physical or moral pressure or constraint; compulsory power; moral power to convince the mind; validity; body of troops; one of the fighting services; body organized for action; (*leg.*) unlawful violence to person or property; **mechanical f.**, any cause which tends to alter a body's state of rest or of uniform motion in a straight line; **brutef.**, physical violence; **the F.**, the police f. [OE.]. **FORCE** (3), *v.t.* to constrain by the exertion of f.; overpower by strength; draw, push or open by f.; compel; take by f.; violate; overstrain; distort; cause to ripen prematurely; *v.i.* to use violence; lay stress on; strive; **to f. from**, to wrest from; **to f. a smile**, to compel the features to assume a smile unwillingly. [Fr. from L.].

FORCED [fawst], *adj.* performed by means of external force; not spontaneous, unnatural, compulsory. **FORCEDLY** [faw'sid-li], *adv.* in a f. fashion. **FORCEDNESS**, *n.* condition of being f.

FORCEFUL [faws'fŏŏl], *adj.* full of force; forcible, effective; of a strong personality. **FORCEFULLY**, *adv.* in a f. manner. **FORCEFULNESS**, *n.* state or quality of being f.

FORCE MAJEURE [faws-mah-zhur'], *n.* power exerted by a strong state over a weaker one; coercion. [Fr.].

FORCEMEAT [faws'mēt], *n.* meat chopped finely and highly seasoned, as a stuffing.

FORCEPS [faw'seps], *n.* pair of pincers or small tongs, *esp.* as used in surgery, dentistry etc.; (*zool.*) organ resembling these in shape or function. [L.].

FORCE-PUMP [faws'pump], *n.* pump from which water is forced out under pressure of a plunger.

FORCIBLE [faw'si-ble], *adj.* effected by force or compulsion; powerful; convincing. **FORCIBLENESS**, *n.* quality of being f. **FORCIBLY**, *adv.* in a f. fashion.

FORCING [faw'sing], *n.* action of a person or thing that forces; (*hort.*) art of raising plants etc. by the use of artificial heat; (*fig.*) any hastening of development. **FORCING-HOUSE**, (*hort.*) hot-house. **FORCING-PIT**, (*hort.*) pit for holding the fermenting materials used to produce bottom heat for forcing plants.

FORD (1) [fawd], *n.* shallow place where a river or other water may be crossed by wading. **FORD** (2), *v.t.* to cross by a f. **FORDABLE**, *adj.* that can be forded. [OE.].

FORDONE [faw-dun'], *adj.* (*archaic*) wearied, exhausted. [OE.].

FORE (1) [faw(r)], *adj.* situated in front of. **FORE** (2), *n.* the front; **to the f.**, into prominence. **FORE** (3), *adv.* before, in front; **f. and aft**, (*naut.*) from one end to the other of a ship. [OE.].

FORE- (4), *pref.* before, in front of; at the front part of; before in time; prior.

FORE (5), *int.* warning cry to move out of the way, at golf.

FOREARM (1) [faw(r)'ahm], *n.* (*anat.*) the arm between elbow and wrist. **FOREARM** (2) [faw(r)-ahm'], *v.t.* to arm beforehand; prepare in advance for.

FOREBEAR, **FORBEAR** [faw'bāer], *n.* ancestor, forefather. [FORE (3) and BE, with -ER ending].

FOREBODE [faw-bōd'], *v.t.* to foretell or prognosticate; feel a strong inward sense of something future. **FOREBODER**, *n.* person who forbodes. [OE.].

FOREBODING [faw-bō'ding], *n.* prediction, presage; presentiment, *esp.* of ill; dread. **FOREBODINGLY**, *adv.* in a f. manner.

FORECAST (1) (*pret. and p.pt.* **forecast**) [faw-kahst'], *v.t.* to estimate beforehand; foresee; foretell. **FORECAST** (2) [faw'kahst], *n.* a prediction of future events; weather prediction; estimate.

FORECASTLE [fōk'sl], *n.* (*naut.*) that part of the upper deck of a ship forward of the foremast; forward part of a merchant vessel under the deck, where the seamen eat and sleep.

FORECLOSE [faw-klōz'], *v.t.* (*leg.*) to preclude; cut off a mortgager from the power of redeeming mortgaged goods; close prematurely. **FORECLOSURE** [faw-klō'zher], *n.* action of foreclosing. [ME. from OFr.].

FORECOURT [faw'kawt], *n.* a court in front of, or near, the entrance to a building.

FOREDOOM [faw-dōŏm'], *v.t.* to condemn in advance.

FOREFATHER [faw'fah-THer], *n.* ancestor, progenitor.

FOREFINGER [faw'fing-ger], *n.* finger next the thumb.

FOREFOOT [faw'fŏŏt], *n.* one of the front feet of a quadruped.

FOREFRONT [faw'frunt], *n.* the principal or foremost part of anything, prominence.

FOREGATHER, see FORGATHER.

FOREGO (*pret.* **forewent**, *p.pt.* **foregone**) [faw-gō'], *v.t.* to go before; precede. **FOREGONE** [faw'gon], *adj.* past; determined beforehand; certain, settled. [OE.].

FOREGROUND [faw'grownd], *n.* that part of anything nearest the spectator; the part of a picture representing this; (*fig.*) a conspicuous position.

FOREHAND (1) [faw'hand], *n.* the part of a horse in front of the rider; (*tennis*) the right-hand side of a right-handed player, and vice versa; the range of a player's strokes played on that side. **FOREHAND** (2), *adj.* done beforehand, forward; (*tennis*) executed with the palm of the hand facing the front, the ball being taken on the right-hand side of a right-handed player. FOREHANDED, *adj.* with a f. stroke (also *adv.*). FOREHANDER, *n.* a f. stroke.

FOREHEAD [fo'rid, faw'hed], *n.* the front part of the face above the eyes. [OE.].

FOREIGN [fo'rin], *adj.* not belonging to; of another nation; alien; not to the purpose; strange. [OFr.].

FOREIGNER [fo'ri-ner], *n.* person belonging to a foreign country; an alien; stranger.

FOREJUDGE [faw-juj'], *v.t.* to prejudge, give judgment before hearing the facts and proof. FOREJUDGMENT, *n.* judgment determined beforehand.

FOREKNOW (*pret.* **foreknew**, *p.pt.* **foreknown**) [faw-nō'], *v.t.* to know beforehand.

FOREKNOWLEDGE [faw'no-lij], *n.* knowledge of an event before it happens; prescience.

FORELAND [faw'land], *n.* a cape, headland.

FORELEG [faw'leg], *n.* one of the front legs of a quadruped.

FORELOCK [faw'lok], *n.* the lock of hair which grows from the fore part of the head; **to take time by the f.**, to seize an opportunity.

FOREMAN [faw'man], *n.* the chief man; principal juror and spokesman of a jury; supervisor, overseer.

FOREMAST [faw'mahst], *n.* the mast nearest the bow. FOREMASTMAN, *n.* (*naut.*) an able seaman.

FOREMENTIONED [faw-men'shnd], *adj.* previously referred to.

FOREMOST [faw'mōst], *adj.* first in place; first in dignity or importance; chief. [OE.].

FORENOON [faw'nōon], *n.* the earlier part of the day from sunrise to noon; morning.

FORENSIC [fo-ren'sik], *adj.* of the law court; **f. medicine**, medical jurisprudence. [L.].

FORE-ORDAIN [faw(r)-aw-dān'], *v.t.* to ordain beforehand; predestinate.

FORE-ORDINATION [faw(r)-aw-di-nā'shn], *n.* act of fore-ordaining; state of being fore-ordained.

FORE-QUARTER [faw'kwaw-ter], *n.* one of the two front sections of the carcase of an animal, including a foreleg.

FORERUNNER [faw'ru-ner], *n.* messenger sent on ahead; harbinger, predecessor.

FORESAIL [faw'sl], *n.* (*naut.*) the principal sail set on the foremast.

FORESEE (*pret.* **foresaw**, *p.pt.* **foreseen**) [faw-sē'], *v.t. and i.* to see beforehand, have foreknowledge of; anticipate. [OE.].

FORESHADOW [faw-sha'dō], *v.t.* to typify beforehand, prefigure.

FORESHORE [faw'shaw(r)], *n.* the part of the seashore between the high- and low-water marks.

FORESHORTEN [faw-shaw'ten], *v.t.* (*art*) to represent objects as they appear in perspective. FORESHORTENING, *n.* effect of perspective upon lines or planes receding from the observer.

FORESHOW (*pret.* **foreshowed**, *p.pt.* **foreshown**) [faw-shō'], *v.t.* to show beforehand, foreshadow. [OE.].

FORESIGHT (1) [faw'sīt], *n.* action of foreseeing what will happen; provident care, prudence, intelligent anticipation. FORESIGHT (2), *n.* the foremost of the two sights of a gun. FORESIGHTED, *adj.* manifesting f.

FORESKIN [faw'skin], *n.* (*anat.*) the skin covering the glans of the penis.

FOREST (1) [fo'rist], *n.* an extensive wood, large stretch of land covered with trees; uncultivated tract of woodland and heath; (*hist.*) unenclosed royal hunting-ground; (*fig.*) large number of tree-like objects, closely clustered. FOREST (2), *adj.* belonging to a f.; sylvan. FOREST (3), *v.t.* to plant with trees.

FORESTALL [faw-stawl'], *v.t.* to act before another and thus frustrate his intention; anticipate. [ME.].

FORESTAY [faw'stā], *n.* (*naut.*) stout rope reaching from the foremast head of a ship towards the bow to support the mast.

FORESTER [fo'ris-ter], *n.* officer in charge of a forest; inhabitant of a forest; one skilled in forestry; member of the Ancient Order of Foresters. [OFr.].

FORESTRY [fo'ris-tri], *n.* art of cultivating forests; forests collectively.

FORETASTE (1) [faw'tāst], *n.* a taste beforehand; anticipation; enjoyment in advance. FORETASTE (2) [faw-tāst'], *v.t.* to taste beforehand; anticipate.

FORETELL (*pret. and p.pt.* **foretold**) [faw-tel'], *v.t.* to tell beforehand; predict, prophesy.

FORETHOUGHT [faw'thawt], *n.* a thinking out beforehand; prudence, wise anticipation. FORETHOUGHTFUL [faw-thawt'fool], *adj.* full of f.; provident.

FORETOKEN (1) [faw'tō-ken], *n.* a warning token.

FORETOKEN (2) [faw-tō'ken], *v.t.* to foreshadow, indicate in advance.

FORETOP [faw'top], *n.* (*naut.*) platform at the head of the foremast. FORETOPMAN, *n.* (*naut.*) sailor stationed in the f.

FORETOPGALLANT [faw-top-ga'lant], *n.* (*naut.*) the mast above the foretopmast.

FORETOPMAST [faw-top'mahst], *n.* (*naut.*) the mast which rises from the head of the foremast, and is surmounted by the foretopgallant mast.

FORETOPSAIL [faw-top'sl], *n.* the sail above the topsail.

FOREVER [fo-re'ver], *adv.* for ever.

FOREWARN [faw-wawn'], *v.t.* to warn beforehand.

FOREWOMAN [faw'wŏo-man], *n.* female supervisor or overseer.

FOREWORD [faw'werd], *n.* a preface; note or preface before the introduction.

FORFEIT (1) [faw'fit], *n.* something risked, and liable to be lost if one fails; anything so lost, a small penalty; (*pl.*) parlour game, whose interest lies in the exaction of mock penalties. FORFEIT (2), *v.t.* to be deprived of through breach of conditions; lose in consequence of any act; surrender, often voluntarily. FORFEITABLE, *adj.* subject to forfeiture. FORFEITER, *n.* person who forfeits. [OFr.].

FORFEITURE [faw'fi-tyŏor], *n.* act of forfeiting; thing which is forfeited. [OFr.].

FORFEND [faw-fend'], *v.t.* to avert, prevent. [ME.].

FORGATHER, FOREGATHER [faw-ga'ther], *v.i.* to assemble; meet and talk together.

FORGE (1) [fawj], *n.* furnace or workshop in which iron or other metal is heated in order to be hammered into form; smithy; blacksmith's furnace. FORGE (2), *v.t.* to soften and work metal; produce by such a process; (*fig.*) mould and form with effort; counterfeit, fabricate; **to f. ahead**, to move forward in spite of opposition, make notable progress. [OFr.].

FORGER [faw'jer], *n.* person who forges; one guilty of forging signatures, paper money etc.

FORGERY [faw'je-ri], *n.* act of forging; that which is forged.

FORGET (*pres.pt.* **forgetting**, *pret.* **forgot**, *p.pt.* **forgotten**) [faw-get'], *v.t.* to lose the remembrance of something, fail to recall to mind; neglect; leave behind inadvertently; leave unnoticed by accident; *v.i.* to fail to remember; **to f. oneself**, to omit to behave with due self-respect.

FORGETFUL [faw-get'fool], *adj.* liable to forget, neglectful, inattentive. FORGETFULLY, *adv.* in f. fashion.

FORGET-ME-NOT [faw-get'mi-not], *n.* small blue flower of the genus *Myosotis*. [Transl. of OFr.].

FORGIVABLE [faw-gi'va-bl], *adj.* pardonable.

FORGIVE [faw-giv'], *v.t.* to pardon; remit, *esp.* of a debt, overlook a fault; *v.i.* to disregard injuries, slights etc. [OE.].

FORGIVENESS [faw-giv'nes], *n.* action of forgiving; character of being habitually forgiving.

FORGIVING [faw-gi'ving], *adj.* merciful, willing to forgive. FORGIVINGNESS, *n.* quality of being f.

FORGO (*pret.* **forwent**, *p.pt.* **forgone**) [faw-gō'], *v.t.* to refrain from, go without; abstain from something pleasurable or profitable. [OE.].

FORK (1) [fawk], *n.* implement with a handle and two or more prongs; any object of similar shape; the branch caused by the meeting of two roads or rivers; junction of a branch with the trunk of a tree; junction of the legs with the human trunk; part of a bicycle frame in which each wheel is set. FORK (2), *v.t.* to use a f. for or upon; make to bifurcate; loosen with a f.; *v.i.* to divide into two branches; **to f. in**, to dig in; **to f. out**, (*slang*) to pay out money. [OE.].

FORKFUL [fawk'fool], *n.* as much as a fork will hold.

FORLORN [faw-lawn'], *adj.* forsaken, bereft, wretched; desolate, neglected; **a f. hope**, a very faint hope; a desperate enterprise undertaken as a last hope. FORLORNLY, *adv.* in a f. fashion. [OE.].

FORM (1) [fawm], *n.* shape, external appearance; the human body; state in which one displays one's abilities to the full; essential structure or plan of anything; kind, type, in which anything is manifested; grouping or arrangement of particular things in a pattern or to serve a purpose; mould; formula; artistic expression, style; established conventional practice, etiquette; official document prescribing the plan of an answer to a request for information; a long bench; class in school; lair of a hare; (*racing etc.*) estimate of the current potentialities of race-horses, sports teams etc. FORM (2), *v.t.* to make, give shape to, mould; educate; plan, arrange; contrive;

make up; frame; combine; establish; compile; constitute; (*gram.*) build up; *v.t.* to take a f. [L.].

FORMAL [faw'mal], *adj.* in accordance with form or established mode; methodical; strictly ceremonious; done in due form; having the form without the substance; depending on customary forms; corresponding strictly to some pattern. [L.].

FORMALDEHYDE [faw-mal'di-hid], *n.* (*chem.*) a compound produced by the oxidation of methyl alcohol. [FORM(IC) and ALDEHYDE].

FORMALIN [faw'ma-lin], *n.* a solution of formaldehyde in spirit and water.

FORMALISM [faw'ma-lizm], *n.* habitual observance of external forms, tending to the neglect of spiritual realities.

FORMALIST [faw'ma-list], *n.* person who insists excessively on forms in art or religion.

FORMALITY [faw-ma'li-ti], *n.* rigid observance of forms; precise conformity to customary modes; conventionality; an official regulation, or the compliance with it; a matter of form, of little real significance.

FORMALIZE [faw'ma-liz], *v.t.* to form, make formal; *v.i.* to behave formally. FORMALIZATION [faw-ma-li-zi'shn], *n.* action of formalizing.

FORMALLY [faw'ma-li], *adv.* in a formal fashion, officially.

FORMAT [faw'mat], *n.* the shape and size in which a book is produced. [Fr.].

FORMATION [faw-mā'shn], *n.* action of forming; manner in which a thing is formed, arrangement; something formed, an organization; group of aeroplanes flying in a fixed order; (*geol.*) group of strata united by community of age, origin or composition. [L.].

FORMATIVE (1) [faw'ma-tiv], *adj.* having the power of forming and of regulating development; serving to form. FORMATIVE (2), *n.* (*gram.*) element helping to form a word.

FORM(E) [fawm], *n.* (*print.*) a body of type set up, locked in a chase and ready to be printed. [FORM (1)].

FORMED [fawmd], *adj.* arranged; matured; definite, decided.

FORMER (1) [faw'mer], *n.* person who, or thing which, forms; anything which determines the shape of a product; support on which electrical coils are wound.

FORMER (2), *adj.* preceding in time, earlier; the first mentioned; in days gone by, one-time. FORMERLY, *adv.* in times past, of old. [ME.].

FORMIC [faw'mik], *adj.* of, or pertaining to, ants; **f. acid**, acid obtained originally from red ants. [L.].

FORMIDABLE [faw'mi-da-bl], *adj.* inspiring, or such as to inspire, fear; difficult; awe-inspiring. FORMIDABILITY, FORMIDABLENESS [faw-mi-da-bi'li-ti, faw'-mi-da-bl-nes], *n.* quality of being f. FORMIDABLY, *adv.* in a f. manner. [L.].

FORMLESS [fawm'les], *adj.* without determinate form. FORMLESSLY, *adv.* in f. fashion.

FORMULA (*pl.* **formulae, formulas**) [faw'myōō-lah, -lē], *n.* a precise form of words; a prescribed form; rule of thumb, enabling one to act without reasoning; oft-repeated phrase; (*math.*) a general expression for solving certain cases or problems; (*chem.*) set of symbols representing the constituents of a compound body. [L.].

FORMULARY (1) [faw'myōō-la-ri], *n.* book made up of stated and prescribed forms; a prescribed form. FORMULARY (2), *adj.* prescribed, according to formula. [L.].

FORMULATE [faw'myōō-lāt], *v.t.* to express in a formula; express in clear definite terms.

FORMULISM [faw'myōō-lizm], *n.* study of formulae; action governed purely by formulae.

FORNICATE [faw'ni-kāt], *v.i.* to commit fornication. [EcclesL.].

FORNICATION [faw-ni-kā'shn], *n.* sexual intercourse between unmarried persons. [EcclesL.].

FORNICATOR [faw'ni-kā-ter], *n.* person guilty of fornication. [EcclesL.].

FORRADER [fo'ra-der], *adv.* (*slang*) more advanced, more forward. [FORWARD].

FORSAKE (*pret.* **forsook**, *p.pt.* **forsaken**) [faw-sāk'], *v.t.* to abandon, desert; withdraw from. [OE.].

FORSAKEN [faw-sā'ken], *adj.* deserted, abandoned, left desolate.

FORSOOK [faw-sōōk'], *pret. of* FORSAKE. [OE.].

FORSOOTH [faw-sōōth'], *adv.* in truth, no doubt. [ME.].

FORSWEAR (*pret.* **forswore**, *p.pt.* **forsworn**) [faw-swāer'], *v.t.* to renounce or disown upon oath; *v.i.* to swear falsely; (*reflex.*) perjure oneself.

FORSYTHIA [faw-si'thi-ah], *n.* (*bot.*) spring-flowering shrub bearing bright yellow sprays of blossom. [W. *Forsyth*, English botanist].

FORT [fawt], *n.* fortified building or position from which to resist an enemy. [Fr.].

FORTE (1) [fawt], *n.* quality in which one excels; one's strong point; (*fencing*) the part of a sword blade between hilt and middle. [Fr.].

FORTE (2) [faw'tā], *adv.* (*mus.*) loudly. [It.].

FORTH [fawth], *adv.* forwards, onwards in time, place or order; away; out into view; **so far f.**, to that degree or extent. [OE.].

FORTHCOMING [fawth-ku'ming], *adj.* about to appear; available; (*fig.*) communicative; generous.

FORTHRIGHT (1) [fawth'rit], *adj.* direct, straightforward, downright. FORTHRIGHT (2), *adv.* at once, straightway. [ME.].

FORTHWITH [fawth-wITH'], *adv.* without delay.

FORTIETH (1) [faw'ti-eth], *n.* one of forty equal parts. FORTIETH (2), *adj.* the ordinal of forty; being one of forty equal parts. [OE.].

FORTIFIABLE [faw'ti-fi-a-bl], *adj.* capable of being fortified.

FORTIFICATION [faw-ti-fi-kā'shn], *n.* act of fortifying; (*pl.*) works erected to fortify a place; a place fortified. [L.].

FORTIFY [faw'ti-fi], *v.t.* to make stronger; (*milit.*) strengthen and secure against enemy attack; strengthen liquor with alcohol; confirm, corroborate; *v.i.* to raise defence works. FORTIFIER, *n.* one who, or that which, fortifies. [L.].

FORTISSIMO [faw-ti'si-mō], *adv.* (*mus.*) with the greatest strength or loudness. [It.].

FORTITUDE [faw'ti-tyōōd], *n.* patience combined with strength of mind and courage to face or suffer adversity. [L.].

FORTNIGHT [fawt'nit], *n.* period of two weeks. FORTNIGHTLY, *adv. and adj.* (appearing or occurring) every f. [OE.].

FORTRESS [faw'tres], *n.* fortified town or place; fort; any place of defence or security. [OFr.].

FORTUITOUS [faw-tyōō'i-tōōs], *adj.* that happens by chance, accidental. FORTUITOUSLY, *adv.* in f. fashion. FORTUITOUSLY, *n.* quality of being f. [L.].

FORTUNATE [faw'tyōō-nat], *adj.* lucky; bringing or boding good luck or success, auspicious. FORTUNATELY, *adv.* successfully; by good fortune, luckily. [L.].

FORTUNE (1) [faw'tyōōn], *n.* chance, luck; the good or ill that befalls one, one's lot; good luck, success; considerable private means; great wealth. FORTUNE (2), *v.i.* (*archaic*) to chance, happen. [L.].

FORTUNE-HUNTER [faw'tyōōn-hun-ter], *n.* person who seeks a fortune, *esp.* by a suitable marriage.

FORTUNE-TELLER [faw'tyōōn-te-ler], *n.* person who professes to tell one's future.

FORTY (1) [faw'ti], *n.* the number equal to four times ten; **the Roaring Forties**, stormy region of the Atlantic Ocean between 40 deg. and 50 deg. north latitude; **the Forty-five**, the Jacobite rising of 1745. FORTY (2), *adj.* four times ten; **f. winks**, a short nap in the daytime. [OE.].

FORUM [faw'rum], *n.* market-place in Roman cities; place of common judgment or justice; (*fig.*) place or occasion of open discussion. [L.].

FORWARD (1) [faw'werd], *adj.* onward; in the front part of; in advance of something else; progressive, active, energetic; early, unusually advanced in development; quick to mature; too ready, presumptuous. FORWARD (2), *adv.* towards what is in front, onward; (*fig.*) progressively; into notice; (*naut.*) [fo'rud], in the fore part of a ship; **carriage f.**, payment for carriage on delivery. FORWARD (3), *n.* one who plays in the front line in football, polo or hockey. FORWARD (4), *v.t.* to advance, help onward; send on, transmit; re-direct a letter etc. [OE.].

FORWARDLY [faw'werd-li], *adv.* in a forward fashion.

FORWARDNESS [faw'werd-nes], *n.* quality of being forward.

FORWARDS [faw'werdz], *adv.* forward.

FORWENT [faw-went'], *pret. of* FORGO.

FOSSE [fos], *n.* ditch; (*anat.*) depression in a bone. [L.].

FOSSICK [fo'sik], *v.i.* (*coll.*) to rummage, hunt about for odds and ends; (*Australian*) seek gold in old diggings, crevices etc. FOSSICKER, *n.* one who fossicks for gold. [E.dial.].

FOSSIL (1) [fo'sil], *n.* (*geol.*) the form of the body of a plant or animal petrified and preserved in the strata of the earth's surface; an impression or cast of this;

ōō is pronounced as in food; ŏŏ as in hood; th as in *think*; TH as in *that*; zh as in azure. ～ = related to.

(fig.) person or thing out of harmony with the present. FOSSIL (2), *adj.* having the character of a f.

FOSSILIZE [fo'si-līz], *v.t.* to reduce to a fossil or fixed state; *v.i.* to be converted into a fossil or fixed state. FOSSILIZATION [fo-si-lī-zā'shn], *n.* act of fossilizing.

FOSTER (1) [fos'ter], *v.t.* to nourish, nurse, rear; *(fig.)* encourage, cherish. FOSTER (2), *adj.* connected through nursing or rearing. FOSTERAGE, *n.* the rearing of the child of another. FOSTERER, *n.* person who fosters; one who takes the place of a parent. [O.E.].

FOSTER-BROTHER [fos'ter-bru-THer], *n.* brother by nursing though not by birth.

FOSTER-CHILD [fos'ter-chīld], *n.* child nursed and reared by one who is not its parent.

FOSTER-DAUGHTER [fos'ter-daw-ter], *n.* girl nursed and brought up as a daughter by foster-parents.

FOSTER-FATHER [fos'ter-fah-THer], *n.* man who takes the place of a father in bringing up a child.

FOSTERLING [fos'ter-ling], *n.* foster-child.

FOSTER-MOTHER [fos'ter-mu-THer], *n.* woman who acts as mother to another's child.

FOSTER-PARENT [fos'ter-pāer-ent], *n.* foster-father or foster-mother.

FOSTER-SISTER [fos'ter-sis-ter], *n.* sister by nursing though not by birth.

FOSTER-SON [fos'ter-sun], *n.* boy nursed and brought up as a son by foster-parents.

FOUGHT [fawt], *pret. and p.pt.* of FIGHT. [O.E.].

FOUL (1) [fowl], *adj.* dirty, muddy; offensive; abominable; obscene; *(naut.)* (of a ship's bottom) covered with weeds and barnacles; (of ropes and cordage) entangled; (of weather) squally; *(sport)* against the rules; *(slang)* disagreeable; unsatisfactory; **f. play**, violence; **by fair means or f.**, without scruple. FOUL (2), *n. (naut.)* slight collision; *(sport)* breach of the rules of a game, unlawful blow, tackle, stroke or action. FOUL (3), *v.t.* to make f.; collide with; *(sport)* commit a f. upon; *v.i.* to become f.; become entangled, collide; *(sport)* commit a f. [O.E.].

FOULARD [foo'lahd], *n.* light dress material of silk or silk and cotton. [Fr.].

FOULLY [fowl'li], *adv.* in a foul fashion.

FOUL-MOUTHED [fowl-mowTHd'], *adj.* habitually indulging in bad language.

FOULNESS [fowl'nes], *n.* quality of being foul.

FOUMART [foo'maht], *n.* the polecat. [M.E.].

FOUND (1) [fownd], *v.t.* to lay the basis of; begin the building and construction of; establish; endow; originate. [L.].

FOUND (2), *v.t.* to cast; form by melting a metal and pouring it into a mould. [Fr.].

FOUND (3), *pret. and p.pt.* of FIND. [O.E.].

FOUNDATION [fown-dā'shn], *n.* act of founding; that part of a structure which rests on or below the ground; base or substructure on which anything rests; basis; origin; endowment appropriated to support an institution; an endowed institution; **f. stone**, stone laid with ceremony to celebrate the founding of a building. [L.].

FOUNDATIONER [fown-dā'shn-er], *n.* student who is supported from the funds of an endowed school or college.

FOUNDER (1) [fown'der], *n.* person who founds anything; endower of an institution. [O.Fr.].

FOUNDER (2), *n.* man who founds metal. [FOUND (2)].

FOUNDER (3), *v.i.* to fill with water and sink, as a ship; *(fig.)* fail, miscarry; trip up; fall through soreness in the feet; give way, collapse. [O.Fr.].

FOUNDLING [fownd'ling], *n.* a deserted child of unknown parents. [M.E.].

FOUNDRESS [fown'dres], *n.* woman who is a founder.

FOUNDRY [fown'dri], *n.* process of casting metals; place where metals are cast [A.Fr.].

FOUNT (1) [fownt], *n.* a spring, source, fountain. [A.Fr.].

FOUNT, FONT (2), *n. (typ.)* set of type of a uniform size and design.

FOUNTAIN [fown'tin], *n.* a spring or source; spout of water issuing from a pipe, series of these contrived as an ornament; jet of drinking-water; reservoir for holding ink, oil etc.; *(fig.)* source or inspiration; **soda f.**, apparatus or bar for supplying soft drinks. [A.Fr.].

FOUNTAIN-HEAD [fown'tin-hed], *n.* source; *(fig.)* ultimate origin.

FOUNTAIN-PEN [fown-tin-pen'], *n.* pen with a reservoir which can be filled with ink which flows to the nib as the pen is used.

FOUR (1) [faw(r)], *n.* cardinal number next after three; four-oared boat; *(pl.)* races rowed in such boats; *(pl.) (milit.)* formation for marching four deep; **on all fours**, on hands and knees; *(fig.)* equivalent, parallel. FOUR (2), *adj.* of the cardinal number next after three; **to the f. winds**, in all directions. [O.E.].

FOUR-ALE [faw-rāl'], *n.* ale formerly sold at four-pence a quart; **f. bar**, the public bar.

FOUR-FLUSHER [faw-flu'sher], *n. (U.S. slang)* deceiver, humbug.

FOURFOLD [faw'fōld], *adj.* quadruple, made up of four parts.

FOUR-FOOTED [faw-foo'tid], *adj.* quadruped.

FOUR-HANDED [faw-han'did], *adj.* having four hands, designed for four persons; played by four persons.

FOUR-IN-HAND [faw(r)'in-hand], *n.* vehicle with four horses driven by one man; kind of necktie, worn knotted loosely with hanging ends.

FOUR-LEGGED [faw-le'gid], *adj.* with four legs.

FOUR-POSTER [faw-pōs'ter], *n.* bedstead with upright pillars at each corner, and often a canopy.

FOUR-POUNDER [faw-pown'der], *n.* gun throwing shot of 4 lb. weight.

FOURSCORE [faw-skaw(r)'], *adj.* four times twenty, eighty.

FOURSOME [faw'sum], *n.* game or dance in which four persons take part in two opposing pairs; *(golf)* game in which there are two players on each side who play the ball alternately; **mixed f.**, one with a man and a woman on each side.

FOUR-SQUARE [faw-skwāer'], *adj.* with sides and four angles equal; square.

FOUR-STROKE [faw'strōk], *adj. (mech.)* having a cycle of four strokes (of an internal combustion engine).

FOURTEEN (1) [faw-tēn'], *n.* the sum of four and ten; the symbol for this sum. FOURTEEN (2), *adj.* of f.

FOURTEENTH (1) [faw-tēnth'], *n.* one of fourteen equal parts; *(mus.)* interval extending to the octave of the seventh. FOURTEENTH (2), *adj.* the ordinal of fourteen; being one of fourteen equal parts.

FOURTH (1) [fawth], *n.* a quarter; one who makes up a party to four; *(mus.)* interval composed of two tones and a semitone. FOURTH (2), *adj.* the ordinal of four; being one of four equal parts; **the F.,** *(U.S.)* 4 July, anniversary of the Declaration of Independence. [O.E.].

FOURTH DIMENSION [fawth-di-men'shn], *n.* a supposed dimension in addition to length, breadth and thickness, often associated with time. FOURTH-DIMENSIONAL, *adj.* pertaining to the supposed f.; superhuman; mysterious, unintelligible.

FOURTHLY [fawth'li], *adv.* in the fourth place.

FOUR-WHEELED [faw-wēld'], *adj.* having or running on four wheels. FOUR-WHEELER, *n.* a f. vehicle.

FOWL (1) [fowl], *n.* a bird, *esp.* an edible bird, poultry; a cock or hen; the flesh of such birds. FOWL (2), *v.i.* to shoot or snare wildfowl.

FOWLER [fow'ler], *n.* sportsman who snares or shoots wildfowl.

FOWLING [fow'ling], *n.* art or practice of snaring or shooting wildfowl. FOWLING-PIECE, light shot-gun for shooting wildfowl.

FOX (1) [foks], *n.* small reddish-brown animal hunted for sport etc.; fur of this animal; *(fig.)* sly cunning fellow. FOX (2), *v.t.* to deceive, hoax; discolour (paper); *v.i.* to pretend, simulate. [O.E.].

FOX-BRUSH [foks'brush], *n.* the bushy tail of the fox.

FOX-EARTH [foks'erth], *n.* the burrow of the fox.

FOXGLOVE [foks'gluv], *n.* a medicinal plant, *Digitalis purpurea.* [O.E.].

FOXHOUND [foks'hownd], *n.* a type of hound used in foxhunting.

FOXHUNT [foks'hunt], *n.* the hunting of a fox with hounds. FOXHUNTER, *n.* one who hunts the fox.

FOXHUNTING (1) [foks'hun-ting], *n.* the sport of hunting the fox with hounds. FOXHUNTING (2), *adj.* of, or pertaining to, f.

FOXINESS [fok'si-nes], *n.* quality of being foxy.

FOX-TERRIER [foks-te'ri-er], *n.* terrier originally used to drive the fox into the open.

FOX-TROT [foks'trot], *n.* a ballroom dance; music suitable for this.

FOXY [fok'si], *adj.* of, or pertaining to, foxes; wily;

The accent ' after a syllable = stress (u-pon'). The mark ‾ over a vowel = length (ā in made; ō in bone).

having a dun, fox-like colour; sour; marked with brown stains.

FOYER [fwa'yā], *n.* lobby or anteroom in a theatre; any anteroom used for waiting. [Fr.].

FRABJOUS [frab'jŏŏs], *adj.* egregious. [Nonsense word invented by Lewis Carroll].

FRACAS [fra'kah], *n.* an uproar; noisy quarrel, brawl. [Fr.].

FRACTION [frak'shn], *n.* act of breaking; state of being broken; fragment; very small quantity, degree etc.; (*math.*) one or more of aliquot parts into which a whole number is divided; **decimal f.**, a f. in which the unit is divided by 10 or a power of 10 and in which the denominator is a power of 10 and is not stated; **vulgar f.**, a f. in which the unit is divided by any number; **compound f.**, a f. of a f. [L.].

FRACTIONAL [frak'shn-al], *adj.* belonging to or containing a fraction or fractions; (*chem.*) denoting the separation, by heating etc., of various substances which have different boiling points etc.

FRACTIONARY [frak'shn-a-ri], *adj.* fractional.

FRACTIOUS [frak'shŏŏs], *adj.* unruly; cross; fretful, peevish. FRACTIOUSLY, *adv.* in a f. fashion. FRACTIOUSNESS, *n.* condition of being f. [FRACTION].

FRACTURE (1) [frak'tyŏŏr], *n.* a breaking, *esp.* one caused by violence; a crack; (*surg.*) the breaking of a bone; **simple f.**, a f. in which the bone is merely divided; **compound f.**, a f. in which the bone is broken and the skin is lacerated. FRACTURE (2), *v.t.* to break; *v.i.* to break or to be liable to break. [L.].

FRAGILE [fra'jīl], *adj.* easily broken, delicate, brittle. FRAGILELY, *adv.* in a f. fashion. [L.].

FRAGILITY [fra-ji'li-ti], *n.* the condition of being fragile; frailty.

FRAGMENT [frag'ment], *n.* a part broken off; small detached portion; unfinished work of art. FRAGMENTAL [frag-men'tal], *adj.* fragmentary. FRAGMENTED [frag-men'tid], *adj.* broken into fragments. [L.].

FRAGMENTARY [frag'men-ta-ri], *adj.* consisting of fragments; **f. rocks,** (*geol.*) rocks formed of the fragments of other rocks.

FRAGRANCE [frā'grans], *n.* quality of being fragrant.

FRAGRANT [frā'grant], *adj.* diffusing an agreeable odour; sweet smelling; (*fig.*) fresh and sweet. FRAGRANTLY, *adv.* in a f. manner. [L.].

FRAIL (1) [frāl], *n.* rush basket in which figs, raisins etc. are packed. FRAIL (2), *adj.* delicate, fragile; weak; weak of will; (formerly) not chaste. FRAILLY, *adv.* in a f. fashion. FRAILNESS, *n.* state of being f. [OFr.].

FRAILTY [frāl'ti], *n.* weakness in resisting temptation; infirmity; a foible.

FRAME (1) [frām], *v.t.* to fit together, construct; shape; devise (a policy); compose (a sentence, law); adapt; surround and support with a frame; serve as a frame or background to; (*slang*) contrive someone's defeat by a trick, compromise falsely; *v.i.* to contrive, progress. FRAME (2), *n.* fabric or structure designed to surround and support; skeleton structure round which a thing is built; form, system, shape; bony structure of a human or animal body; background; temper or disposition of mind; forcing-box for plants; (*cinema*) one of the small pictures comprising a film; **f. aerial,** aerial wound on a flat f. and adapted for directional reception. [OE.].

FRAME-HOUSE [frām'hows], *n.* framework of timber covered with boards; half-timbered house.

FRAMER [frā'mer], *n.* person who frames.

FRAME-SAW [frām'saw], *n.* saw stretched and kept rigid in a hand-frame.

FRAME-UP [frām'up], *n.* (*slang, orig. U.S.*) underhand arrangement; false charge.

FRAMEWORK [frām'werk], *n.* frame which supports or encloses a thing; skeleton; understructure; (*fig.*) organization, scope.

FRANC [frangk], *n.* French coin, the monetary unit of France, worth 100 centimes; corresponding coin of Belgium and Switzerland. [Fr.].

FRANCHISE, EFFRANCHISE [fran'chīz], *n.* a privilege, immunity or right granted to an individual or to a number of persons; citizenship; right to vote in a public election, *esp.* in a parliamentary election; (*insurance*) percentage of loss below which the underwriter does not pay. [Fr.].

FRANCISCAN (1) [fran-sis'kan], *adj.* of, or pertaining to, St. Francis of Assisi or to the Franciscans. FRANCISCAN (2), *n.* friar of the order of St. Francis of Assisi. [St. *Francis*, founder of the order].

FRANCO-, *pref.* French; Frankish. [LL.].

FRANCOLIN [frang'ko-lin], *n.* bird somewhat like a partridge. [It.].

FRANCOPHIL(E) [frang'kŏ-fīl], *n.* lover of France and all things French. [FRANCO and Gk.].

FRANCOPHOBE [frang'kŏ-fōb], *n.* one who dreads French influences; one who hates the French or what is French. [FRANCO and Gk.].

FRANC-TIREUR [frah(ng)-tē-rur'], *n.* combatant who lacks military status; guerrilla fighter. [Fr.].

FRANGIBLE [fran'ji-bl], *adj.* easily broken. [L.].

FRANGIPANI, FRANGIPANE [fran-ji-pah'ni], *n.* kind of rich pastry; perfume prepared from the red jasmine. [Fr.].

FRANK (1) [frangk], *n.* Eastern term for a West-European; member of a Germanic people who overran, and gave their name to, France. [OE.].

FRANK (2), *adj.* free and open in manner and speech; sincere; candid. FRANK (3), *v.t.* to render free; be responsible for a person's expenses; exempt a letter from postage by means of a signature or official stamp. FRANK (4), *n.* signature exempting from postage; letter or parcel so exempted. [Fr.].

FRANKENSTEIN [frang'ken-stīn], *n.* one who creates a thing or situation he is afterwards unable to control, thing so created. [Count *Frankenstein* in a novel by Mary Shelley].

FRANKFURTER [frangk'fer-ter], *n.* small smoked German sausage. [*Frankfurt,* Germany].

FRANKINCENSE [frang'kin-sens], *n.* resinous substance which gives off a fragrant smell when burning. [OFr.].

FRANKLIN [frangk'lin], *n.* old English freeholder; yeoman. [AFr.].

FRANKLY [frangk'li], *adv.* in a frank fashion, candidly.

FRANKNESS [frangk'nes], *n.* quality of being frank.

FRANTIC [fran'tik], *adj.* violently excited, disordered wild; distraught; (*coll.*) in a hurry; awful, terrible. FRANTICALLY, *adv.* in a f. fashion. FRANTICNESS, *n.* condition of being f. [OFr.].

FRAPPE, frappé [fra'pā], *adj.* iced, cooled. [Fr.].

FRATERNAL [fra-tur'nal], *adj.* brotherly; pertaining to brothers; very friendly. FRATERNALLY, *adv.* in f. fashion. [L.].

FRATERNITY [fra-tur'ni-ti], *n.* state of being brothers; brotherhood; company of men associated for a common interest; men of the same class or profession; (*U.S.*) a student association. [Fr.].

FRATERNIZATION [fra-ter-ni-zā'shn], *n.* action of fraternizing.

FRATERNIZE [fra'ter-nīz], *v.i.* to associate together as brothers or in friendly intimacy. [MedL.].

FRATRICIDE [frat'ri-sīd], *n.* one who wilfully kills his brother; the murder thus committed. FRATRICIDAL, *adj.* of, or pertaining to, f. [L.].

FRAU [frow], *n.* German title for a married woman. [Germ.].

FRAUD [frawd], *n.* trick or subterfuge by which the right or interest of another is injured; stratagem intended to obtain some undue advantage; cheat, impostor; cheating, deceit. [Fr.].

FRAUDULENCE, FRAUDULENCY [fraw'dyŏŏlens-(i)], *n.* quality of being fraudulent.

FRAUDULENT [fraw'dyŏŏ-lent], *adj.* committing fraud; addicted to fraud; obtained by fraud; dishonest. FRAUDULENTLY, *adv.* in a f. fashion. [L.].

FRAUGHT [frawt], *adj.* freighted, laden; (*fig.*) stored; full of. [ME.].

FRAULEIN, fraülein [froi'līn], *n.* in Germany, an unmarried woman. [Germ.].

FRAY (1) [frā], *n.* brawl; the thick of a fight; (*fig.*) any struggle. [ME.].

FRAY (2), *v.t.* to wear into loose ends by rubbing, ravel; (*fig.*) try the temper; *v.i.* to become ravelled. [Fr.].

FRAZZLE (1) [fra'zl], *n.* a shred, tatter; **to reduce to a f.,** to make thoroughly weary; **to beat to a f.,** to beat thoroughly. FRAZZLE (2), *v.t.* to fray, reduce to tatters; *v.i.* to become frayed; (*slang*) be worn out. [Unkn.].

FREAK (1) [frēk], *n.* sudden, non-rational change of mind; capricious humour; an abnormality, monstrosity; (*slang*) eccentric or curiously ugly person. FREAK (2), *adj.* unusual, abnormal. [Uncert.].

FREAKISH [frē'kish], *adj.* full of freaks; capricious; unusual. FREAKISHLY, *adv.* in a f. manner. FREAKISHNESS, *n.* quality of being f.

FRECKLE (1) [fre'kl], *n.* brown spot on the skin caused by the action of the sun's rays; any small spot or discoloration. FRECKLE (2), *v.t.* to cover with freckles; *v.i.* to become freckled; be liable to freckles. FRECKLED, FRECKLY, *adj.* marked with freckles. [~ME.].

FREE (1) [frē], *adj.* able to move; enjoying liberty; not enslaved, not imprisoned; self-determining; released from obligations, exempt; unrestricted; uncontrolled by rule or convention; unattached; unreserved; liberal, lavish; outspoken; abundant; with no price to be paid; not engaged, unoccupied; (*chem.*) uncombined; **f. fight,** haphazard general fight or struggle; **f. hand,** liberty of action; **a f. place,** f. education at a secondary school; **f. port,** port serving international trade at which no duties are levied on goods; **f. verse,** verse not conforming to a recognized pattern; **f. wheel,** wheel driven by a gear in which the driven member may freely outrun the driving member; **F. Church,** a dissenting Scottish body; (*pl.*) the Nonconformist churches. FREE (2), *adv.* freely. FREE (3), *v.t.* to rid, liberate. [O.E.].

FREE AGENT [frē-ā'jent], *n.* person acting freely in any matter.

FREEBOARD [frē'bawd], *n.* (*naut.*) the part of a vessel's hull which rises from the waterline.

FREEBOOTER [frē'bōō-ter], *n.* pirate; person or ship out for plunder. [Du.].

FREEBORN [frē'bawn], *adj.* born free.

FREEDOM [frē'dum], *n.* state of being free; liberty; exemption from slavery, servitude or confinement; franchise; immunity; ease or facility of doing anything; frankness; licence; improper familiarity; **f. of a city,** admission to citizenship with participation in its privileges. [O.E.].

FREE-HAND [frē'hand], *adj.* (*art*) drawn without the use of instruments.

FREE-HANDED [frē-han'did], *adj.* generous, liberal.

FREE-HEARTED [frē-hah'tid], *adj.* open-hearted, generous.

FREEHOLD [frē'hōld], *n.* land or tenement which is held in fee-simple, fee-tail or for term of life; estate or appointment thus held. FREEHOLDER, *n.* one who possesses a f.

FREE HOUSE [frē'hows], *n.* independent public house not "tied" to a particular brewery.

FREELANCE (1) [frē'lahns], *n.* journalist, politician etc., not attached to a particular paper, party or organization. FREELANCE (2), *v.i.* to work as a f.

FREE LIVER [frē-li'ver], *n.* person who indulges his appetites freely.

FREE LOVE [frē-luv'], *n.* doctrine that sexual relations should not be limited by marriage; practice of that doctrine.

FREELY [frē'li], *adv.* in a free manner.

FREEMAN [frē'man], *n.* one who is personally free; full member of a state; one on whom the freedom of a city, town etc. has been conferred. [O.E.].

FREEMASON [frē-mā'sun], *n.* member of an ancient and secret fraternity, originally an association of masons or builders in stone, now a mutual assistance society.

FREEMASONRY [frē-mā'sun-ri], *n.* the spirit and institutions of freemasons; (*fig.*) a natural understanding and comradeship.

FREER [frē'er], *n.* liberator.

FREESIA [frē'si-ah], *n.* (*bot.*) South African bulbous plant of the iris family. [MdL.].

FREE-SPOKEN [frē-spō'ken], *adj.* speaking without seemly reserve, embarrassingly frank.

FREESTONE [frē'stōn], *n.* a building stone which can be cut with equal ease in any direction; oolitic limestone.

FREETHINKER [frē-thing'ker], *n.* one who rejects the teachings of the churches in religious matters; a deist or rationalist. FREETHINKING, *n.* rationalism; deism; irreligion.

FREE TRADE [frē-trād'], *n.* (*econ.*) trade or commerce exempt from Government control, *esp.* international trade unrestricted by customs duties, quotas etc. FREE-TRADER, *n.* an advocate of f.; (*slang*) a smuggler.

FREE-WHEEL [frē-wēl'], *v.i.* to ride a bicycle fitted with a free wheel without moving the pedals; allow a car with a similar device to run downhill with engine unconnected to wheels.

FREE-WILL (1) [frē-wil'], *n.* the philosophic belief that one's will is entirely self-determined. FREE-WILL (2), *adj.* spontaneous, voluntary; appertaining to the doctrine of f.

FREEZE (*pret.* **froze,** *p.pt.* **frozen**) [frēz], *v.t.* to congeal (a liquid) into a solid state; kill by cold; chill; (*fig.*) quench the vigour of; forbid or prevent the free circulation of (currency, credits etc.); **to f. on to,**

to seize and hold firmly; **to f. off, out,** to snub, get rid of; *v.i.* (*impers.*) to be cold enough to turn water into ice; be congealed by cold; be chilled; (*coll.*) feel the cold; (*fig.*) become rigid; **to f. up,** to become congealed or immobile through cold. [O.E.].

FREEZER [frē'zer], *n.* freezing apparatus, refrigerator.

FREEZE-UP [frēz'up], *n.* (*coll.*) an extended period of hard frost; immobility caused by frost.

FREEZING-MIXTURE [frē'zing-miks-tyōōr], *n.* a mixture of two or more substances which, in combining, absorb heat from contiguous bodies and thus produce intense cold.

FREEZING-POINT [frē'zing-point], *n.* the temperature at which a fluid, *esp.* water, freezes.

FREIGHT (1) [frāt], *n.* load, goods loaded for transport; monetary recompense for carrying goods; transport of goods; (*fig.*) load, burden; **f. train,** (*U.S.*) goods train. FREIGHT (2), *v.t.* to load with goods for transport; hire for this purpose. [ME.].

FREIGHTAGE [frā'tij], *n.* freight, charge for freight.

FREIGHTER [frā'ter], *n.* man who freights a ship; one who transports goods by rail; ship or aircraft which does not primarily carry passengers.

FRENCH (1) [frensh], *adj.* of, or pertaining to, France or her inhabitants. FRENCH (2), *n.* the F. language; **the F.,** (*pl.*) the F. people. [O.E.].

FRENCH BEAN [frensh-bēn'], *n.* the common kidney bean.

FRENCH CHALK [frensh-chawk'], *n.* a hardened talc used for drawing lines on cloth, and for various dusting purposes when powdered.

FRENCH GREY [frensh-grā'], *n.* a blue-grey colour.

FRENCH HORN [frensh-hawn'], *n.* musical wind-instrument of brass or silver.

FRENCHIFY [fren'shi-fī], *v.t.* to make to appear French.

FRENCH LEAVE [frensh-lēv'], *n.* departure, holiday, taken without permission.

FRENCH-POLISH (1) [frensh-po'lish], *n.* spirit polish for wood. FRENCH-POLISH (2), *v.t.* to give a high finish to wood with f. FRENCH-POLISHER, *n.* one who french-polishes for a living.

FRENCH WINDOW [frensh-win'dō], *n.* glass door opening on to a garden or balcony.

FRENZIED [fren'zid], *adj.* affected with frenzy, distraught; wildly excited.

FRENZY (1) [fren'zi], *n.* mental disturbance, uncontrollable rage or mania; any great excitement, delirious fury. FRENZY (2), *v.t.* to fill with f. [OFr.].

FREQUENCY [frē'kwen-si], *n.* regular or repeated occurrence; (*phys.*) rate of such occurrence, *esp.* the number of cycles per second of an alternating electric current. [L.].

FREQUENT (1) [frē'kwent], *adj.* oft repeated; regularly repeated; plentiful. [L.].

FREQUENT (2) [frē-kwent'], *v.t.* to resort to often, be often in the society of. [L.].

FREQUENTATIVE [frē-kwen'ta-tiv], *adj.* (*gram.*) (of verbs) signifying the frequent repetition of an action. [L.].

FREQUENTER [frē-kwen'ter], *n.* one who frequents.

FREQUENTLY [frē'kwent-li], *adv.* often.

FRESCO [fres'kō], *n.* method of painting on fresh plaster; picture so painted; **al f.,** in the open air. [It.].

FRESH [fresh], *adj.* not used, not worn out; blooming; recently made or grown; (of horses) lively; not faded; in a good state; not forgotten or obliterated; not salt; (of wind) brisk and cool; having new vigour, invigorating; healthy; (*coll.*) slightly intoxicated; (*slang*) cheeky; **f. way,** (*naut.*) increased velocity of a vessel. FRESHLY, *adv.* in a f. manner; newly, recently. FRESHNESS, *n.* quality of being f. [O.E.].

FRESHEN [fresh'en], *v.t. and i.* to make fresh; refresh; grow fresh. FRESHENER, *n.* that which refreshes; refreshing drink; (*journ.*) fresh handling of a story.

FRESHER [fresh'er], *n.* (*slang*) freshman.

FRESHES [fresh'iz], *n.* (pl.) the intermingling of fresh water with salt water in rivers or bays; a flood; freshet. [OFr.].

FRESHET [fresh'et], *n.* a clear brook; flooding of a river by heavy rains or melted snow. [OFr.].

FRESHMAN [fresh'man], *n.* newcomer; student in his first year at a university.

FRESHWATER [fresh'waw-ter], *adj.* formed or living in fresh water; accustomed to sail on fresh water only; **f. sailor,** a poor, fair-weather sailor.

FRET (1) [fret], *n.* criss-cross pattern of ornament; piece of wood cut to a fine ornamental pattern by

---

The accent ' after a syllable = stress (u-pon'). The mark ¯ over a vowel = length (ā in made; ō in bone).

sawing out the interstices; the cut made by a fine saw or any similar action; (*mus.*) raised pattern which assists fingering on the guitar; (*her.*) series of interlacing narrow bands. FRET (2) (*pres.pt.* FRETTING, *pret.* and *p.pt.* FRETTED), *v.t.* to pattern with a f.; (*arch.*) decorate a vault etc. in relief. [ME. from OFr.].

FRET (3) (*pres.pt.* fretting, *pret.* and *p.pt.* fretted), *v.t.* and *i.* to eat away; wear away a passage by erosion; stir up; cause agitation to, irritate; be uneasy and agitated, grieve, repine. FRET (4), *n.* a frayed state of nerves; irritation; uneasiness. [O.E.].

FRETFUL [fret'fŏŏl], *adj.* inclined to fret, restlessly irritable, peevish. FRETFULLY, *adv.* in a f. manner. FRETFULNESS, *n.* condition of being f.

FRET-SAW [fret'saw], *n.* light saw used for fret cutting and fretwork.

FRETTED [fre'tid], *adj.* decorated with fretwork; (*her.*) interlaced with narrow bands.

FRETWORK [fret'werk], *n.* interlaced ornament; ornamental woodwork in which the pattern has been cut out by a fine saw; work decorated with frets.

FRIABLE [frī'a-bl], *adj.* crumbling easily; pulverizable. FRIABILITY, FRIABLENESS [frī-a-bi'li-ti, frī'a-bl-nes], *n.* condition of being f. [L.].

FRIAR [frī'er], *n.* member of a religious mendicant order. [OFr.].

FRIAR'S BALSAM [frī-erz-bawl'sam], *n.* compound tincture of benzoin.

FRIARY [frī'a-ri], *n.* a convent of friars.

FRIBBLE [fri-bl], *v.i.* to spend one's time in foolish frivolity. [Imitative].

FRICASSEE [fri'ka-sē], *n.* dish of meat and vegetables cut small and stewed in a thick gravy. [Fr.].

FRICATIVE (1) [fri'ka-tiv], *adj.* (*phon.*) (of a consonant sound) produced by the friction of the breath passing through a narrow passage in the mouth, as in f. FRICATIVE (2), *n.* (*phon.*) a f. consonant. [L.].

FRICTION [frik'shn], *n.* act of rubbing the surface of one body against that of another; attrition; (*fig.*) clash of two personalities; (*mech.*) resistance offered to a moving body by the surface on which it moves; (*med.*) act of rubbing any part of the surface of the body to promote circulation. FRICTION-CLUTCH, (*eng.*) clutch in which one member is driven by f. FRICTION-CONES, (*eng.*) conical-shaped members of a f.-clutch. FRICTION-WHEEL, (*eng.*) wheel moved by frictional contact. FRICTIONAL, *adj.* connected with, caused by, f. [L.].

FRIDAY [frī'dā], *n.* the sixth day of the week; Good F., the last F. before Easter, commemorating the death of Christ. [O.E.].

FRIEND [frend], *n.* one who is attached to another by ties of affection, an intimate companion; one who assists another; an acquaintance; member of the Society of Friends (Quakers); colleague. [O.E.].

FRIENDLESS [frend'les], *adj.* without friends.

FRIENDLY [frend'li], *adj.* having the disposition of a friend; courteous, kind; disposed to peace; favourable; propitious; F. Society, mutual-aid society, whose contributions provide sickness and other benefits for its members. FRIENDLILY, *adv.* in a f. manner. FRIENDLINESS, *n.* quality of being f.

FRIENDSHIP [frend'ship], *n.* the relationship of friends; friendly affection. [O.E.].

FRIESIAN [frē'zhn], *adj.* (of cattle) of the Friesland breed.

FRIEZE (1) [frēz, friz], *n.* kind of coarse woollen material with a nap. [~Fr.].

FRIEZE (2) [frēz], *n.* (*arch.*) that part of the entablature of a column which is between the architrave and cornice; decorative band placed immediately below the ceiling or cornice. [Fr.].

FRIGATE [fri'gat], *n.* (*naut.*) naval vessel smaller than a destroyer and similar to a sloop; formerly a ship of war rating next below a ship of the line. [It.].

FRIGATE-BIRD [fri'gat-berd], *n.* large and rapacious tropical sea-bird.

FRIGHT (1) [frīt], *n.* sudden fear, violent terror; (*coll.*) any person or thing of a shocking or curious appearance. FRIGHT (2), *v.t.* (*poet.*) to frighten. [O.E.].

FRIGHTEN [frī'ten], *v.t.* to fill with fear, terrify.

FRIGHTFUL [frīt'fŏŏl], *adj.* fearful, dreadful, shocking; (*coll.*) appalling. FRIGHTFULLY, *adv.* in a f. manner; (*coll.*) very.

FRIGHTFULNESS [frīt'fŏŏl-nes], *n.* quality or act of being frightful; *esp.* the policy of terror used by invaders in occupied countries.

FRIGID [fri'jid], *adj.* so cold as to be almost frozen; wanting warmth of affection; wanting animation or

life; stiff, formal; aloof; wanting feeling; sexually impotent; f. zone, the parts of the earth between the polar circles and the poles. FRIGIDLY, *adv.* in a f. fashion. FRIGIDNESS, *n.* frigidity. [L.].

FRIGIDITY [fri-ji'di-ti], *n.* state of being frigid.

FRILL (1) [fril], *n.* a loose, protruding edging on a garment; a ruffle; anything resembling this, *esp.* when used as an ornament; (*pl.*) (*fig.*) affected airs, mannerisms; ornament; elaboration. FRILL (2), *v.t.* to decorate with a f.; *v.i.* to form into a f.; ruffle. FRILLING, *n.* frilled edges; act of putting frills on to anything. FRILLY, *adj.* adorned with frills. [Unkn.].

FRINGE (1) [frinj], *n.* ornamental bordering of hanging threads or tassels; anything resembling this; border, outer edge; border of hair worn over the forehead; (*fig.*) the initial stages of anything. FRINGE (2), *v.t.* to decorate with a f.; form a f. to. [OFr.].

FRIPPERY [fri'pe-ri], *n.* tawdry finery; showy trifles; (*fig.*) empty rhetoric. [Fr.].

FRISK (1) [frisk], *v.t.* and *i.* to caper, gambol; (*slang*) search (someone). FRISK (2), *n.* a caper; lively frolic; fit of boisterous gaiety. [OFr.].

FRISKY [fris'ki], *adj.* given to frisking; frolicsome; lively. FRISKILY, *adv.* in a f. fashion. FRISKINESS, *n.* state of being f.

FRITH [frith], *n.* firth. [OIcel.].

FRITILLARY [fri-ti'la-ri], *n.* genus of liliaceous plants, including the crown-imperial; any of several species of British butterflies. [MedL.].

FRITTER (1) [fri'ter], *n.* pancake of batter, often containing a slice of fruit or meat. [Fr.].

FRITTER (2), *v.t.* and *i.* to cut into small pieces; to f. away, (*fig.*) to waste, squander aimlessly and futilely. [Uncert.].

FRIVOL (*pres.pt.* frivolling, *pret.* and *p.pt.* frivolled) [fri'vol], *v.i.* to act frivolously, trifle. [FRIVOLOUS].

FRIVOLITY [fri-vo'li-ti], *n.* frivolousness, idle trifling.

FRIVOLOUS [fri'vo-lŏŏs], *adj.* of little worth or consequence; trifling, silly; superficial, without depth of character. FRIVOLOUSLY, *adv.* in a f. fashion. FRIVOLOUSNESS, *n.* state of being f. [L.].

FRIZZ (1) [friz], *v.t.* to curl or crisp (the hair). FRIZZ (2), *n.* a crisped lock of hair; fuzzy curls. [Fr.].

FRIZZLE (1) [fri'zl], *v.t.* and *i.* to curl the hair into frizzes; (of hair) to curl into a frizz. [Fr.].

FRIZZLE (2), *v.t.* and *i.* to sputter; fry, toast or grill with a sputtering sound; (*fig.*) to be baked by the sun. [Echoic.].

FRIZZY [fri'zi], *adj.* frizzed; consisting of or resembling frizzes.

FRO [frō], *adv.* from, away, backwards; to and f., alternately forwards and backwards. [OIcel.].

FROCK (1) [frok], *n.* long outer garment; woman's or child's dress; garment indicative of their order, worn by monks and priests. FROCK (2), *v.t.* to clothe in a f.; make a priest or monk of. [Fr.].

FROCK-COAT [frok-kōt'], *n.* half-length skirted coat for men.

FROEBELISM [frur'be-lizm], *n.* a system of education for young children; kindergarten education. [*Froebel*, German educationalist].

FROG (1) [frog], *n.* a tailless amphibian; tender horn growing in the middle of the sole of a horse's foot; grooved iron plate replacing railway lines at points where they cross; (*coll.*) Frenchman. FROG-MARCH, punishment of being carried face downwards by four men each holding an arm or leg. [O.E.].

FROG (2), *n.* attachment to the belt by which the sword is held; braided coat fastening on uniforms; small barrel-shaped silk ornament with tassels, used in the decoration of clothes. FROGGED, *adj.* adorned with frogs. [Uncert.].

FROGGY (1) [fro'gi], *n.* (*coll.*) Frenchman. [FROG (1)].

FROGGY (2), *adj.* resembling or containing frogs.

FROG-SPAWN [frog'spawn], *n.* the ova or spawn of frogs.

FROLIC (1) [fro'lik], *adj.* gay, merry, light-hearted. FROLIC (2), *v.i.* to indulge in merry, light-hearted play. FROLIC (3), *n.* joyful, light-hearted game; merry-making; party, light entertainment. [Du.].

FROLICSOME [fro'lik-sum], *adj.* full of frolics; sportive; full of fun and high spirits.

FROM [from], *prep.* expressing motion away; subtraction; exclusion; difference; continued action; point of origin; out of; starting at; leaving behind; by reason of; since; f. time to time, occasionally. [O.E.].

FROND [frond], *n.* (*bot.*) leaf-like organ of a fern or

similar plant, which bears the reproductive cells; any leaf, or leaf-like object. [L.].

FRONDESCENCE [fron-de'sens], *n.* (*bot.*) time of the year when each plant unfolds its leaves; act of putting forth leaves.

FRONT (1) [frunt], *n.* (*poet.*) forehead; the forepart of anything; the foremost rank, van; area of military operations; position directly before the face of a person; false hair or curls worn on the forepart of the head; dickey or separate shirtfront; face of a building; promenade along the sea, above the shore; **to come to the f.,** to achieve eminence. FRONT (2), *adj.* first; advanced, prominent, eminent; (of sounds) palatal; **f.-page news,** important or sensational news. FRONT (3), *v.t.* to oppose face to face; stand in front of or against; face; supply with a f.; (*phon.*) pronounce further forward in the mouth; *v.i.* to have the face in a certain direction. [L.].

FRONTAGE [frun'tij], *n.* the front part of a building; the side of a piece of land which abuts on a road or river; building line.

FRONTAL (1) [frun'tal], *adj.* in front; (*anat.*) connected with the forehead or brow; (*milit.*) (of an attack) from the front. FRONTAL (2), *n.* (*eccles.*) hanging ornamental panel in the front of an altar.

FRONT BENCH [frunt-bensh'], *n.* either of the foremost benches in the House of Commons, occupied respectively by ministers and leading members of the Opposition.

FRONTIER (1) [frun'ti-er], *n.* that part of a country bordering on another country; (*pl.*) (*fig.*) the extreme limits. FRONTIER (2), *adj.* lying on the border; (*Canadian*) connected with pioneer days. [Fr.].

FRONTISPIECE [frun'tis-pēs], *n.* (*arch.*) main façade of a building; (*print.*) illustration or ornamental design facing the title-page of a book. [Fr.].

FRONTLET [frunt'let], *n.* band worn on the forehead; (*ornith.*) margin of the head behind the bill of birds; strip of cloth etc., completing the frontal of an altar.

FRONTWARD(S) [frunt'werd(z)], *adv.* towards the front.

FROST (1) [frost], *n.* temperature of the air, at or below 32 deg. Fahrenheit, which causes freezing of water; frozen dew or moisture; (*fig.*) frigidity; (*coll.*) complete failure. FROST (2), *v.t.* to nip with f.; give the appearance of being covered with hoar f.; roughen the surface of metal or glass; (*fig.*) chill. [OE.].

FROST-BITE (1) [frost'bīt], *n.* gangrenous condition of flesh set up by continued exposure to extreme cold; damage done to plants by frost. FROST-BITE (2), *v.t.* to nip with frost; produce f. in. FROST-BITTEN, *adj.* nipped by the frost; suffering from f.

FROSTED [frost'id], *adj.* having been subjected to frost; covered with hoar frost; (of glass or metal) roughened.

FROSTING [fros'ting], *n.* a preparation of sugar for covering a cake; light covering of white paint or alum solution dabbed on glass, to render it opaque.

FROSTY [fros'ti], *adj.* freezing, or containing frost; ice-cold; resembling hoar frost; (of the hair) hoary; (*fig.*) chill, frigid. FROSTILY, *adv.* in a f. manner. FROSTINESS, *n.* condition of being f.

FROTH (1) [froth], *n.* foam; bubbles on liquids caused by fermentation or agitation, similar bubbles forming in saliva; (*fig.*) empty show of wit or eloquence; light, unsubstantial matter. FROTH (2), *v.t.* to form f. on; beat to a f.; (*fig.*) talk superficially; *v.i.* to form a f., foam. [OIcel.].

FROTHY [fro'thi], *adj.* full of, or covered with, froth; (*fig.*) unsubstantial, empty. FROTHILY, *adv.* in a f. manner. FROTHINESS, *n.* condition of being f.

FROU-FROU [froo'froo], *n.* rustling of silk. [Fr.].

FROWARD [frō'ahd], *adj.* perverse, wayward. FROWARDLY, *adv.* in a f. way. FROWARDNESS, *n.* quality of being f. [FRO and WARD].

FROWN (1) [frown], *v.i.* to contract the brows in displeasure or concentration; look gloomy; **to f. on,** to regard with displeasure, be opposed to. FROWN (2), *n.* a knitting of the brows; look denoting displeasure or censure. [ME. from OFr.].

FROWNING [frow'ning], *adj.* exhibiting or wearing a frown; gloomy and forbidding. FROWNINGLY, *adv.* in a f. manner.

FROWST (1) [frowst], *n.* close stuffy atmosphere in a room, fog. FROWST (2), *v.i.* to lounge in an over-heated room. [Unkn.].

FROWSY, FROWZY [frow'zi], *adj.* fusty, ill-smelling; bedraggled, slatternly. [Unkn.].

FROZE [frōz], *pret. of* FREEZE. [ME.].

FROZEN [frō'zen], *adj.* congealed by cold; extremely

cold, icy; frigid; (of credits etc.) temporarily unrealizable. FROZENNESS, *n.* condition of-being f. [ME., *p.pt.* of FREEZE].

FRUCTIFICATION [fruk-ti-fi-kā'shn], *n.* (*bot.*) act or process of fructifying; group of organs employed in the reproduction of a plant.

FRUCTIFY [fruk'ti-fī], *v.t.* to make fruitful, fertilize; *v.i.* to bear fruit, become fruitful. [Fr.].

FRUCTOSE [fruk'tōs], *n.* sugar present in ripe fruit and honey; fruit sugar. [~L.].

FRUGAL [froo'gal], *adj.* careful in the use of means, goods or food; thrifty; meagre; living poorly. FRUGALLY, *adv.* in a f. manner. [L.].

FRUGALITY [froo-ga'li-ti], *n.* quality of being frugal.

FRUIT (1) [froot], *n.* produce of a tree or other plant; seed of plants, part which contains the seed; that which is produced, offspring; (*fig.*) effect, consequence; reward. FRUIT (2), *v.i.* to produce f. [OFr.].

FRUITAGE [froo'tij], *n.* fruit collectively; product. [OFr.].

FRUITARIAN [froo-tāer'i-an], *n.* one who eats mainly fruit.

FRUIT-CAKE [froot'kāk], *n.* cake containing several kinds of dried fruits.

FRUITERER [froo'te-rer], *n.* person who deals in fruit.

FRUITFUL [froot'fool], *adj.* productive of fruit, offspring or profit; useful; effective, successful. FRUITFULLY, *adv.* in a f. fashion.

FRUITION [froo-i'shn], *n.* pleasurable realization, enjoyment; pleasure derived from use or possession or the maturing of an idea or scheme. [L.].

FRUITLESS [froot'les], *adj.* not bearing fruit; unprofitable; barren, useless; unproductive; unsuccessful; abortive. FRUITLESSLY, *adv.* in a f. fashion.

FRUIT SALAD [froot-sa'lad], *n.* compote of mixed fruit.

FRUIT-TREE [froot'trē], *n.* tree which bears edible fruit.

FRUITY [froo'ti], *adj.* like fruit; having the flavour of fruit; ripe; luscious; (*slang*) suggestive, salacious; (*slang*) (of a voice) over-rich in quality.

FRUMENTY [froo'men-ti], *n.* dish of wheat boiled in milk. [OFr.].

FRUMP [frump], *n.* plain and dowdy woman. FRUMPISH, FRUMPY, *adj.* old-fashioned; like a f. [Unkn.].

FRUSTRATE [frus-trāt'], *v.t.* to hinder; render of no avail; baffle, foil, baulk. [L.].

FRUSTRATION [frus-trā'shn], *n.* act of frustrating; state of being frustrated.

FRUSTUM (*pl.* **frusta**) [frus'tum], *n.* (*geom.*) that part of a solid next the base, formed by cutting off the top parallel to the base; the part of any solid between two planes. [L.].

FRUTICOSE, FRUTICOUS [froo'ti-kōs, -kōos], *adj.* branching in the manner of a shrub; pertaining to shrubs; shrubby. [L.].

FRY (1) [frī], *n.* the small young, *esp.* of fish; **small f.,** insignificant persons; children. [OIcel.].

FRY (2), *v.t.* to cook with fat in a pan over a fire; *v.i.* to cook in a frying-pan in fat; (*fig.*) seethe with passion; scorch. FRY (3), *n.* fried food; edible inwards of a pig or lamb. FRYER, *n.* person who fries; frying-pan. [Fr.].

FRYING-PAN [frī'ing-pan], *n.* shallow pan for frying food.

FUCHSIA [fyoo'shah], *n.* (*bot.*) ornamental shrub with pendulous flowers. [L. *Fuchs*, German botanist].

FUCUS (*pl.* **fuci**) [fyoo'kus], *n.* kind of seaweed. [L.].

FUDDLE [fu'dl], *v.t.* to confuse by means of drink; (*fig.*) confuse the thoughts of; *v.i.* to get drunk. [Unkn.].

FUDGE (1) [fuj], *v.t.* to fake, fabricate. FUDGE (2), *n.* made-up story; soft, crumbly sweetmeat; (*coll.*) stop-press news. FUDGE (3), *int.* stuff and nonsense! [Uncert.].

FUEL (1) [fyoo'el], *n.* any combustible material which feeds a fire or internal combustion engine; firing; (*fig.*) anything which inflames the mind; **to add f. to the flames,** to aggravate, keep a passion raging. FUEL (2) [*pres.pt.* FUELLING, *pret. and p.pt.* FUELLED], *v.t.* to supply with f.; *v.i.* to get provision of fuel. FUELLING, *n.* act of providing with f.; material used for f. [OFr.].

FUEL-OIL [fyoo'el-oil], *n.* oil used as fuel.

FUG [fug], *n.* (*coll.*) hot dense atmosphere; stuffy

The accent ' after a syllable = stress (u-pon'). The mark ‾ over a vowel = length (ā in made; ō in bone).

heat. **FUGGY**, *adj.* stuffy, badly ventilated. [Unkn.].

FUGAL [fyoo'gal], *adj.* of or pertaining to fugues.

FUGITIVE (1) [fyoo'ji-tiv], *adj.* fleeing; fleeting; swiftly passing, evanescent; escaping from justice; connected with fugitives. **FUGITIVE** (2), *n.* one who flees from danger, captivity or justice. **FUGITIVELY**, *adv.* in a f. manner. [L.].

FUGUE [fyoog], *n.* (*mus.*) composition in contrapuntal form developing a first theme, an answering theme and counter subjects according to the acknowledged devices of counterpoint. **FUGUIST**, *n.* one who composes fugues. [L.].

FUHRER, führer [fyoo'rer], *n.* leader, *esp.* applied to Adolf Hitler, former Chancellor and Leader of Nazi Germany. [Germ.].

FULCRUM (*pl.* **fulcra, fulcrums**) [ful'krum], *n.* (*bot.*) the part of a plant which serves to defend or support it; (*mech.*) support on which a lever rests; (*fig.*) any means to an end. [L.].

FULFIL (*pres.pt.* **fulfilling**, *pret. and p.pt.* **fulfilled**) [fool-fil'], *v.t.* to accomplish; carry out, complete; perform what is required, discharge (a duty); (*reflex.*) develop one's inherent capacity completely. **FULFILLER**, *n.* person who fulfils. **FULFILLING**, *n.* fulfilment. [OE.].

FULFILMENT [fool-fil'ment], *n.* accomplishment; satisfaction, realization in experience of spiritual or psychological potentialities.

FULGENT [ful'jent], *adj.* radiant, dazzling, bright with light. **FULGENTLY**, *adv.* in a f. way.

FULL (1) [fool], *adj.* having no space empty, containing as much as capacity permits; crowded; sated; well-provided, abounding in; occupied with; overwhelmed by emotion; having reached the highest degree or state of some quality, process or characteristic; resonant; plump; roomy; extended; **in f. cry**, hard on the scent of the hunted; **f. dress**, elaborate ceremonial uniform; **f. up**, completely filled. **FULL** (2), *n.* the highest or utmost degree or state of any quality, attribute or characteristic; **in f.**, fully, completely; **to the f.**, completely. **FULL** (3), *adv.* completely. [OE.].

FULL (4), *v.t.* to cleanse and thicken cloth after weaving. [OE.].

FULL-BLOODED [fool-blu'did], *adj.* of unmixed descent; vigorous, virile, robust.

FULL-BLOWN [fool-blon'], *adj.* fully expanded; (*fig.*) past maturity.

FULL-BOTTOMED [fool-bo'tomd], *adj.* having a large bottom, as a wig worn by a Q.C.

FULLER [foo'ler], *n.* person whose business consists in fulling cloth. [OE.].

FULLER'S EARTH [foo-lerz-urth'], *n.* kind of soft clay which absorbs grease, used in fulling cloth and as a dusting powder.

FULL FACE [fool-fas'], *adj. and adv.* (of a portrait) with the sitter directly facing the camera or artist. **FULL-FACED** [fool-fast'], *adj.* with a broad-boned or plump face.

FULL-GROWN [fool-gron'], *adj.* mature in development, grown to full size.

FULL-LENGTH [fool-length'], *adj.* extending the whole length, stretched out to the full.

FULLNESS, see **FULNESS**.

FULL-PITCHER [fool-pi'cher], *n.* (*cricket*) ball which pitches inside the batting crease, or which hits the stumps without previously touching the ground.

FULL-RIGGED [fool-rigd'], *adj.* set with square rig on all three masts.

FULL STOP [fool-stop'], *n.* the period (.) used in punctuation, *esp.* to denote the end of a sentence.

FULL-SWING (1) [fool-swing'], *n.* the highest activity and efficiency. **FULL-SWING** (2), *adv.* at the highest pitch of organized movement.

FULL-TIME [fool-tim'], *adj. and adv.* occupying or employed during all normal working hours.

FULLY [foo'li], *adv.* to the full, in full manner; entirely.

FULLY-FASHIONED [foo-li-fa'shnd], *adj.* shaped to conform to the curves of the body (*esp.* of women's stockings).

FULMAR [fool'mah(r)], *n.* sea-bird resembling the gull, a kind of petrel. [OIcel.].

FULMINANT [ful'mi-nant], *adj.* thundering; (*med.*) developing extremely quickly. [L.].

FULMINATE [ful'mi-nat], *v.t.* to cause to explode, detonate; *v.i.* to explode loudly, detonate; flash; utter vehement denunciations. [L.].

FULMINATION [ful-mi-na'shn], *n.* act of fulmina-ting; a chemical explosion; violent threats or censure. [L.].

FULMINATORY [ful'mi-na-te-ri], *adj.* characterized by, or given to, fulmination.

FULNESS, **FULLNESS** [fool'nes], *n.* condition of being full; abundance; completion, fulfilment.

FULSOME [fool'sum], *adj.* gushing; (of flattery) excessive. **FULSOMELY**, *adv.* in a f. way. **FULSOMENESS**, *n.* condition of being f.

FULVOUS [ful'voos], *adj.* tawny. [L.].

FUMBLE [fum'bl], *v.t. and i.* to manage awkwardly, bungle; fail to pick up something cleanly, make awkward clumsy movements. **FUMBLER**, *n.* person who fumbles. [Unkn.].

FUMBLING [fum'bling], *adj.* groping, controlling the hands awkwardly. **FUMBLINGLY**, *adv.* in a f. way.

FUME (1) [fyoom], *n.* pungent smoke, strong bitter smell, acidulous vapour, exhalation; outbreak of rage, turmoil of emotion. **FUME** (2), *v.t.* to dry in smoke; give a smoky finish or colour to a wood surface; fumigate; *v.i.* to give off fumes, smoke, pass off in the form of vapour; be in a rage, be in a turmoil of emotion, fret, chafe. [L.].

FUMIGATE [fyoo'mi-gat], *v.t.* to disinfect by smoke or vapour.

FUMIGATION [fyoo-mi-ga'shn], *n.* act of fumigating. [L.].

FUMIGATORY [fyoo'mi-ga-te-ri], *adj.* having the power of fumigating.

FUMITORY [fyoo'mi-te-ri], *n.* a herb plant. [OFr. from MedL.].

FUMY [fyoo'mi], *adj.* full of fumes.

FUN [fun], *n.* matter for laughter, sport, cause or source of merriment; amusement, spontaneous entertainment, jollity. [~ME.].

FUNAMBULIST [fyoo-nam'byoo-list], *n.* performer on a tight-rope.

FUNCTION (1) [fungk'shn], *n.* the activity, or line of progress, pertaining to a person or object which is peculiarly vital to its nature; action or vitality natural to a physiological or biological organ; specially designed activity; series of duties attached to a particular office; something carried out or performed; a gathering of people under official control; a ceremony; large social gathering; (*math.*) a quantity related to another having corresponding values. **FUNCTION** (2), *v.i.* to act, fulfil in action characteristic powers of work or vitality; operate, work. [L.].

FUNCTIONAL [fungk'shn-al], *adj.* relating to, or affecting, functions but not structure; having a practical purpose in action; designed with regard to utility only, without irrelevant ornament. **FUNCTIONALLY**, *adv.* by means of the functions, in relation to the functions. **FUNCTIONALISM**, *n.* theory of design which makes practical utility determine form.

FUNCTIONARY [fungk'shn-a-ri], *n.* public official; anyone entrusted to perform a duty.

FUND (1) [fund], *n.* a stock, store, *esp.* a sum of money; money loaned to the government and constituting a national debt; (*pl.*) capital, cash resources; government securities. **FUND** (2), *v.t.* to provide a f. for paying interest; add to a f. **FUNDABLE**, *adj.* able to be funded. [L.].

FUNDAMENT [fun'da-ment], *n.* the buttocks, the anus. [L.].

FUNDAMENTAL (1) [fun-da-men'tal], *adj.* relating to, or connected with, the basic principles or foundations of anything, primary, essential; **f. bass**, (*mus.*) the lowest note sustaining a chord. **FUNDAMENTAL** (2), *n.* basic principle, radical element, an essential.

FUNDAMENTALISM [fun-da-men'ta-lizm], *n.* firm belief in the necessity to resort to considered fundamental principles as a guidance to thought and action; *esp.* entire acceptance of the truth of the story of the Creation in the Old Testament. **FUNDAMENTALIST**, *n.* person whose attitude is based on f.

FUNDAMENTALITY [fun-da-men-ta'li-ti], *n.* that which is fundamental.

FUNDAMENTALLY [fun-da-men'ta-li], *adv.* in a fundamental way, basically.

FUNDED [fun'did], *adj.* invested in state securities; deposited in a fund from which payments or interest are drawn; **f. debt**, public debt in the form of securities issued for a term of years.

FUNERAL (1) [fyoo'ne-ral], *n.* burial of the dead with ceremonial rites; procession attending the corpse on the way to the cemetery. **FUNERAL** (2), *adj.* relating to a f. [L.].

FUNEREAL [fyoo-ne'ri-al], *adj.* suitable for, or

---

oo**i**s pronounced as in food; oo as in hood; th as in *think*; TH as in *that*; zh as in azure. ~ = related to.

relating to, a funeral; mournful. FUNEREALLY, *adv.* in a f. way. [L.].

FUNGI [fun'jī], *n. pl. of* FUNGUS.

FUNGICIDE [fun'ji-sīd], *n.* a preparation for killing fungi.

FUNGOID [fung'goid], *adj.* having the characteristics of a mushroom. [L. and Gk.].

FUNGOLOGY [fung-go'lo-ji], *n.* study of fungi. [L. and Gk.].

FUNGOUS [fung'gŏŏs], *adj.* having the characteristics of a fungus, of mushroom growth and structure. [L.].

FUNGUS (*pl.* **fungi, funguses**) [fung'gus, fun'jī, fung'gu-siz], *n.* one of a class of flowerless plants comprising the mushrooms, toadstools and those cellular plants formed as mould, mildew etc.; (*med.*) spongy growth on a wound. [L.].

FUNICULAR [fyŏŏ-ni'kyŏŏ-ler], *adj.* joined by, worked by, a rope; pertaining to cords or fibres; **f. railway,** railway consisting of two carriages connected by a system of metal cables running over pulley wheels, so weighted that the carriage descending causes the other to ascend. [L.].

FUNK (1) [fungk], *n.* (*slang*) fear, timidity, a coward; **blue f.,** state of utter terror. FUNK (2), *v.t. and i* (*slang*) to fear, be afraid of, be frightened by; act as a coward, feel fear. FUNKY, *adj.* frightened, timid. [Unkn.].

FUNNEL [fu'nel], *n.* metal chimney or smoke stack; conical metal bowl tapering down to a tube and used for transferring liquid into a container with a narrow neck. FUNNELLED, *adj.* provided with, or like, a f. [ME. from L.].

FUNNILY [fu'ni-li], *adv.* in a funny way; **f. enough,** peculiar as it may seem.

FUNNINESS [fu'ni-nes], *n.* quality of being funny.

FUNNY [fu'ni], *adj.* laughable, full of fun; queer; peculiar; having the appearance of dishonesty; **f. business,** actions of a comedian meant to be f.; (*coll.*) nonsense, foolery; crooked dealing.

FUNNYBONE [fu'ni-bōn], *n.* part of the elbow over which the ulnar nerve passes, and which is markedly sensitive to knocks.

FUR (1) [fur], *n.* short, closely set hair growing on the skin and forming the protective coat of certain animals; animals growing this; such animal skin prepared for use as a coat, or for lining or ornamenting garments; coating or deposit of morbid matter collecting on the tongue; chalky deposit left when undistilled water is boiled; **to make the f. fly,** to provoke enmity or actual hostilities. FUR (2) (*pres.pt.* FURRING, *pret. and p.pt.* FURRED), *v.t. and i.* to line, trim, cover with f.; cover, coat with a morbid deposit; level a surface by covering with thin strips of wood or casing to take plaster; form a coating, become covered with a deposit, as a kettle or pipe. [OFr.].

FURBELOW [fur'be-lō], *n.* pleated flounce attached to a gown or petticoat. [~Fr.].

FURBISH [fur'bish], *v.t.* to rub or scour to brightness, polish; **to f. up,** to clean up, smarten up. [ME. from OFr.].

FURCATE(D) [fur'kāt(-id)], *adj.* forked; dividing like the prongs of a fork.

FURCATION [fer-kā'shn], *n.* process of furcating; a branching like a fork.

FURIOSO [fyŏŏ-ri-ō'zo], *adv.* (*mus.*) with great energy. [It.].

FURIOUS [fyŏŏ'ri-ös], *adj.* raging; rushing with impetuosity; transported with passion; mad with rage, savagely angry. FURIOUSLY, *adv.* in a f. fashion. FURIOUSNESS, *n.* state of being f. [L.].

FURL [furl], *v.t.* to fold, roll up, as a sail; roll up closely, fold up compactly. [Uncert.].

FURLONG [fur'long], *n.* a measure of distance, eighth of a mile, 220 yd. [OE.].

FURLOUGH [fur'lō], *n.* leave of absence granted to members of the armed forces or officials. [~Du.].

FURMETY [fur'mi-ti], *n.* frumenty.

FURNACE [fur'nis], *n.* enclosed fireplace for concentrating combustible matter to generate heat at high temperatures. [OFr.].

FURNISH [fur'nish], *v.t.* to supply with anything necessary, equip, stock, supply, *esp.* fill (a house) with furniture and fittings. FURNISHER, *n.* person who furnishes; dealer in furniture. [OFr.].

FURNISHING [fur'ni-shing], *n.* act of equipping a house with furniture; (*pl.*) articles of furniture and fittings.

FURNITURE [fur'ni-tyŏŏr], *n.* articles of equipment, movable articles of domestic utility and convenience

having a place in the rooms of a house; articles with a functional value constituting the equipment of a ship; (*archaic*) armour and equipment for horse and man. [Fr.].

FURORE [fyŏŏ-raw'ri], *n.* outburst of enthusiasm; excited disturbance; a sensation. [It.].

FURRIER [fu'ri-er], *n.* dealer in, or dresser of, furs.

FURROW (1) [fu'rō], *n.* the trench or channel in the ground made by a plough; rut, long groove, cart-rut; wrinkle on the face. FURROW (2), *v.t.* to make furrows in, make grooves in, plough; cause deep wrinkles. FURROWY, *adj.* full of furrows, with furrows. [OE.].

FURRY [fur'i], *adj.* covered with fur; dressed in fur; consisting of or resembling fur.

FURTHER (1) [fur'THer], *adj.* farther, more distant, more remote; additional, more. FURTHER (2), *adv.* to a greater distance or degree; besides, also, moreover. FURTHER (3), *v.t.* to bring to a higher, more forward, stage of development, progress or maturity; promote, help forward. [OE.].

FURTHERANCE [fur'THe-rans], *n.* act of advancing; distance advanced.

FURTHERER [fur'THe-rer], *n.* person who furthers.

FURTHERMORE [fur'THer-maw(r)], *adv.* moreover, besides, in addition.

FURTHERMOST [fur'THer-mōst], *adj.* remotest, furthest.

FURTHEST (1) [fur'THest], *adj.* most remote, most distant either in time or in place. FURTHEST (2), *adv.* at, or to, the greatest distance.

FURTIVE [fur'tiv], *adj.* covert, stealthy; secret, surreptitious. FURTIVELY, *adv.* in a f. way. FURTIVENESS, *n.* quality of being f. [L.].

FURUNCULOSIS [fur-rung-kyŏŏ-lō'sis], *n.* (*med.*) disease characterized by extensive boils. [L. and Gk.].

FURY [fyŏŏ'ri], *n.* violent emotional agitation, rage, frenzy; violent person; (*myth.*) goddess of vengeance. [L.].

FURZE [furz], *n.* thorny, matted, branched evergreen shrub, having yellow flowers, and spines instead of leaves; gorse, whin. FURZY, *adj.* covered, overgrown, with, f. [OE.].

FUSCOUS [fus'kŏŏs], *adj.* dark in colour, brownish-black. [L.].

FUSE (1), **FUZE** [fyŏŏz], *n.* tube filled with explosive or ignitable matter used to start the explosion of dynamite etc.; device to explode a shell; (*elect.*) safety device, consisting of fusible metal, inserted into an electric circuit, which melts when the current exceeds a specific power. [L.].

FUSE (2), *v.t. and i.* to melt, liquefy by heat; cause to mingle together, unite as by melting together; be melted; be liquefied, become blended; (of electric light or other apparatus) fail owing to the blowing of a fuse. [L.].

FUSEE [fyŏŏ-zē'], *n.* grooved conical wheel of a watch or clock, round which the chain is wound; match with a head which glows for a long time. [Fr. from ~L.].

FUSELAGE [fyŏŏ'zi-lahzh], *n.* the body part of an aeroplane. [Fr.].

FUSEL-OIL [fyŏŏ'zel-oil], *n.* crude form of mixed alcohols obtained in distilling spirits. [Germ.].

FUSIBILITY [fyŏŏ-zi-bi'li-ti], *n.* quality of being fusible; degree of fusible capacity. [Fr.].

FUSIBLE [fyŏŏ'zi-bl], *adj.* able to be fused.

FUSIL [fyŏŏ'zil], *n.* a light, flint-lock musket.

FUSILIER [fyŏŏ-zi-lēer'], *n.* in olden days, a soldier belonging to a regiment armed with fusils; now sometimes applied to riflemen.

FUSILLADE (1) [fyŏŏ-zi-lād'], *n.* a sustained discharge of fire-arms. FUSILLADE (2), *v.t.* to attack by a f.

FUSION [fyŏŏ'zhn], *n.* process of melting by heat; condition of being melted; act of blending; coalition. [L.].

FUSS (1) [fus], *n.* an excited, nervous and anxious state of mind, commotion, bustle; unnecessary ado about trifles, angry complaint. FUSS (2), *v.i.* to make a fuss, become nervously excited; make much of trivialities. [Unkn.].

FUSSY [fu'si], *adj.* making a fuss, finicky over detail; fidgety. FUSSILY, *adv.* in a f. way. FUSSINESS, *n.* condition of being f.

FUSTIAN (1) [fus'ti-an], *n.* kind of twilled cloth, corduroy; (*fig.*) bombastic style of writing. FUSTIAN (2), *adj.* made of f.; (*fig.*) bombastic in style. [OFr.].

FUSTIC [fus'tik], *n.* wood of a tropical American tree which yields a yellow dye. [Pers.].

The accent ' after a syllable = stress (u-pon'). The mark ‾ over a vowel = length (ă in made; ō in bone).

FUSTY [fus'ti], *adj.* smelling stale, mouldy; (*fig.*) old-fashioned, pedantic. FUSTINESS, *n.* state or quality of being f. [OFr.].

FUTILE [fyōō'til], *adj.* ineffectual, fruitless; superficial, inept. FUTILELY, *adv.* in a f. fashion. [L.].

FUTILITY [fyōō-ti'li-ti], *n.* quality of being futile; a futile act. [L.].

FUTURE (1) [fyōō'tyŏŏr], *adj.* occurring after the present, having an existence in time later than the present; pertaining to life after death; **f. perfect,** (*gram.*) expressing the past in relation to an assumed future; **f. tense,** a modification of the verb expressing time to come. FUTURE (2), *n.* the time which lies ahead; events which will occur; (*pl.*) (*comm.*) goods paid for at their price when the deal was made and not at their price at the time of delivery. [L.].

FUTURELESS [fyōō'tyŏŏr-les], *adj.* having a grim, comfortless future, without hope.

FUTURISM [fyōō'tyŏŏ-rizm], *n.* faith in the fulfilment of the prophecies made in the Bible; a movement in art rejecting convention and based on the free exploitation of line and colour according to non-realist vision.

FUTURIST(IC) (1) [fyōō'tyŏŏ-rist, fyōō-tyŏŏ-ris'tik], *adj.* pertaining to, characteristic of, the futurists, *esp.* in art. FUTURIST (2), *n.* an advocate of futurism.

FUTURITY [fyōō-tyŏŏ'ri-ti], *n.* future time, time to come; state of being yet to come.

FUZE, see FUSE (1).

FUZZ [fuz], *n.* mass of fluff, small tangle of fibre, hairs, threads. FUZZ-BALL, puff-ball.

FUZZY [fu'zi], *adj.* fluffy; frizzy; blurred.

FUZZY-WUZZY [fu'zi-wu-zi], *n.* slang name for a member of one of the savage tribes of the Sudan.

FYLFOT [fil'fot], *n.* symbol used as decoration in the Middle Ages, the swastika. [Uncert.].

G

G [jē], seventh letter and fifth consonant of the English alphabet; (*mus.*) sign of the treble clef. G.-MAN, (*U.S.*) Federal Government police-agent.

GAB (1) [gab], *n.* (*coll.*) idle chatter, talkativeness; **the gift of the g.,** ability to speak fluently and at great length. GAB (2) (*pres.pt.* GABBING, *pret. and p.pt.* GABBED), *v.i.* to chatter, prattle, talk volubly and pointlessly. [~Du.].

GABARDINE, see GABERDINE.

GABBLE (1) [ga'bl], *v.t. and i.* to chatter, jabber; talk rapidly and in confused manner; utter rapidly, indistinctly and incoherently. GABBLE (2), *n.* loud, rapid incoherent talk; inarticulate sounds rapidly uttered. GABBLER, *n.* one who gabbles. [Echoic].

GABERDINE [ga'ber-dēn], *n.* long coarse coat, *esp.* as traditionally worn by Jews; thin woollen material with a fine parallel rib. [OFr., ~MHGerm.].

GABLE [gā'bl], *n.* triangular top part of the end wall of a building; end wall of a building having a top of this shape; piece of architecture in this form. GABLED, *adj.* having gables. [OFr. from OIcel.].

GABY [gā'bi], *n.* simpleton. [Unkn.].

GAD (1) [gad], *pres.pt.* **gadding,** *pret. and p.pt.* **gadded**) [gad], *v.i.* to wander about aimlessly in pursuit of pleasure or diversion. GADDER, *n.* gadabout. [~OE.].

GAD (2), *int.* (*old-fashioned slang*) God.

GADABOUT [ga'da-bowt], *n.* person fond of gadding.

GADFLY [gad'fli], *n.* horsefly, the bite of which is often maddening to animals; (*fig.*) person who annoys or torments. [ON.].

GADGET [ga'jet], *n.* (*coll.*) ingenious contrivance or appliance, cunning mechanical device. [Unkn.].

GADOID [ga'doid], *adj. and n.* pertaining to, a member of, the cod-fish family. [Gk.].

GAEKWAR, GAIKWAR [gi'kwah(r)], *n.* title of the ruler of Baroda. [Marathi].

GAEL [gāl], *n.* a Scottish or Irish Celt. [Scots Gael.].

GAELIC (1) [gā'lik, ga'lik], *adj.* pertaining to the Gaels or to their language; *esp.* pertaining to the Scottish Gaels. GAELIC (2), *n.* Celtic language spoken by the Gaels of Scotland, Ireland and the Isle of Man.

GAFF (1) [gaf], *n.* light barbed fishing spear; stick fitted with an iron hook for landing salmon etc.; (*naut.*) boom or yard used to extend the top portion of certain fore-and-aft sails. GAFF (2), *v.t.* to land (a fish) with a g. [Fr.].

GAFF (3), *n.* (*slang*) inferior type of theatre or place of entertainment.

GAFF (4), *n.* (*slang*) nonsense, foolish talk; **to blow the g.,** (*slang*) to reveal a secret. [Uncert.].

GAFFE [gaf], *n.* blunder, indiscretion, embarrassing mistake. [Fr.].

GAFFER [ga'fer], *n.* old rustic; elderly fellow; foreman. [Contraction of GODFATHER or GRANDFATHER].

GAG (1) [gag], *n.* something thrust into, or placed over, a person's mouth to prevent him from speaking or crying out; (*surg.*) device for keeping the mouth wide open during an operation; (*parl.*) closure of a debate; (*theatre*) impromptu remark by an actor, not included in the script; (*slang*) joke, funny story; wheeze, excuse; hoax, lie. GAG (2) (*pres.pt.* GAGGING, *pret. and p.pt.* GAGGED), *v.t.* to silence by means of a g.; (*fig.*) deny freedom of speech or expression to; (*slang*) deceive, hoax; *v.i.* to add or substitute one's own remarks in acting. [ME.].

GAGA [gah'gah], *adj.* (*slang*) gibbering incoherently; crazy, deranged, senile. [Imitative].

GAGE (1) [gāj], *n.* a pledge, something given as a security; something thrown down as a challenge; a challenge. GAGE (2), *v.t.* to pledge, offer as security. [Fr.].

GAGE (3), see GAUGE.

GAGGLE [ga'gl], *n.* flock (of geese). [~OIcel.].

GAIETY [gā'e-ti], *n.* state or quality of being gay, merriment, cheerfulness; (*pl.*) that which is gay, festivities. [Fr.].

GAIKWAR, see GAEKWAR.

GAILY [gā'li], *adv.* in a gay manner.

GAIN (1) [gān], *v.t.* to obtain, acquire (something advantageous); obtain by industry, earn; acquire as an addition, increase, profit or reward; obtain by merit, superiority; win; reach, attain; (of a watch etc.) increase in rate by; save (time); *v.i.* to derive advantage from; improve; increase; (of a clockwork mechanism) work at a faster rate than is accurate; **to g. on, upon,** to overtake; outdistance; encroach upon; **to g. ground,** to move faster than; (*fig.*) make progress; **to g. time,** to secure the delay or putting-off of something; **to g. the wind,** (*naut.*) to reach the windward side of another ship. GAIN (2), *n.* act or process of gaining; that which is gained, profit, earnings, rewards. [OFr.].

GAIN-CONTROL [gān'kon-trōl], *n.* (*radio*) volume-control on a radio receiver.

GAINFUL [gān'fŏŏl], *adj.* profitable, advantageous. GAINFULLY, *adv.* profitably, for gain.

GAININGS [gā'ningz], *n.*(*pl.*) that which is gained, earnings, profits, winnings.

GAINSAY [gān-sā'], *v.t.* to contradict, deny what another says, dispute. [ME.].

GAIT [gāt], *n.* manner of walking or moving. [GATE (3).].

GAITER (1) [gā'ter], *n.* a covering of leather or cloth fitting over the ankle and the leg below the knee. GAITER (2), *v.t.* to dress or furnish with gaiters. [Fr.].

GALA [gah'lah, gā'lah], *n.* an occasion for merry-making, feasting and entertainment, festival. [It.].

GALACTIC [ga-lak'tik], *adj.* lactic; pertaining to the Milky Way. [Gk.].

GALACTIN [ga-lak'tin], *n.* vegetable substance extracted from the sap of the cow-tree of tropical America; the element in milk causing coagulation. [Gk.].

GALACTO-, *pref.* milk. [Gk.].

GALANTHUS [ga-lan'thus], *n.* the snowdrop genus of plants. [Gk.].

GALANTINE [ga-lan-tēn'], *n.* dish of veal, chicken etc. boned, minced, boiled and served cold. [Fr.].

ōō is pronounced as in food; ŏŏ as in hood; th as in *th*ink; TH as in *th*at; zh as in azure.   ~ = related to.

GALAXY [ga′lak-si], *n.* the Milky Way; (*fig.*) assemblage of outstanding persons or things; spectacular array. [Gk.].

GALBANUM [gal′ba-num], *n.* a resinous juice or gum, used medicinally. [~Gk.].

GALE (1) [gāl], *n.* violent blustery wind; (*poet.*) gentle breeze. [Uncert.].

GALE (2), *n.* the bog-myrtle. [~GAVEL].

GALEENY [ga-lē′ni], *n.* guinea-fowl. [Span.].

GALENA [ga-lē′nah], *n.* mineral sulphide of lead.

GALENIC [ga-lē′nik], *adj.* pertaining to *Galen*, Greek physician, or to his methods.

GALILEAN [ga-li-lē′an], *adj.* pertaining to *Galileo*, Italian mathematician and physicist.

GALILEE [ga′li-lē], *n.* (*eccles. antiq.*) porch or chapel, usually at the west end of a church. [*Galilee*, Israel].

GALINGALE [ga′ling-gāl], *n.* a sedge, the sweet cyperus; aromatic roots of an Asiatic plant. [~Arab.].

GALIPOT [ga′li-pot], *n.* white viscid resin issuing from, and hardening upon, fir-trees. [Fr.].

GALL (1) [gawl], *n.* the bile, a liquid secreted in the glandular substance of the liver; gall-bladder; (*fig.*) bitterness of mind, rancour, malignity. [~OE., ~OIcel.].

GALL (2), *n.* painful swelling or blister, *esp.* on a horse; sore or wound on the skin caused by rubbing; (*fig.*) something maddeningly irritating. GALL (3), *v.t.* to chafe or break ᵗʰe skin by rubbing; (*fig.*) chagrin, exasperate; ha̱ss; *v.i.* to become sore or chafed; rankle. [~OE.].

GALL (4), *n.* hard round growth on trees, *esp.* oaks, caused by insects. OAK-GALL, a g. used in making ink, dyeing etc. [L.].

GALLANT (1) [ga′lant], *adj.* brave, high-spirited, noble; chivalrous; having a fine appearance; (*parl.*) applied to a Member of Parliament who is also an officer in the forces; (*also* ga-lant′) courtly, attentive and courteous to ladies; relating to love, amorous. GALLANT (2) [ga-lant′], *n.* smart, dashing young man, fine gentleman; lady's man; suitor, lover. GALLANT (3) [ga-lant′, ga′lant], *v.t. and i.* to escort; pay excessive attention to; flirt with; play the g. GALLANTLY, *adv.* in a g. manner. [Fr.].

GALLANTRY [ga′lan-tri], *n.* bravery, daring; courageous bearing; courtliness of behaviour; courteous act or speech, compliment; love affairs. [Fr.].

GALL-BLADDER [gawl′bla-der], *n.* small, pear-shaped membranous sac on the underside of the liver, to receive the bile.

GALLEON [ga′li-on], *n.* large sailing ship with three or four decks, formerly used by the Spaniards and others. [Span.].

GALLERY [ga′le-ri], *n.* narrow balcony, partly open in front, on the outside of a building; long narrow passage built into, or projecting from, the walls of a room, at some height from the ground, and partly open on the side which faces inwards; long, narrow semi-covered court or cloister; long narrow passage or corridor; raised structure projecting from the back and side walls above the floor of a hall etc., forming a kind of second storey; uppermost and cheapest seats in a theatre; (*fig.*) the part of the audience occupying these seats; spectators at a golf match etc.; building or room which contains a collection or display of works of art; **to play to the g.**, to make a display for the purpose of pleasing popular taste. [Fr.].

GALLEY [ga′li], *n.* ancient war vessel propelled by oars; low, flat-built vessel with one deck, driven by oars and sails; large rowing boat; kitchen of a ship; (*print.*) oblong tray in which lines of type are placed, a galley-proof. [ME. from MedL.].

GALLEY-PROOF [ga′li-proof], *n.* (*print.*) proof taken straight from the galley, before the printed matter is made up into pages or columns.

GALLEY-SLAVE [ga′li-slāv], *n.* slave condemned to work at the oar on board a galley.

GALLIC (1) [ga′lik], *adj.* pertaining to Gaul or the Gauls; pertaining to France or the French. [L.].

GALLIC (2) [gaw′lik], *adj.* pertaining to galls or oak-apples; derived from galls. [GALL (4)].

GALLICAN (1) [ga′li-kan], *adj.* pertaining to Gaul or France; (*eccles.*) pertaining to the national Roman Catholic Church of France; pertaining to the Gallicans. GALLICAN (2), *n.* member of the French Roman Catholic party resisting complete Papal control. [L.].

GALLINACEOUS [ga-li-nā′shoos], *adj.* pertaining

to the family of birds including the domestic fowl, pheasant, grouse etc. [L.].

GALLING [gaw′ling], *adj.* vexing, irritating, rankling.

GALLIPOT [ga′li-pot], *n.* glazed earthenware pot.

GALLIVANT [ga′li-vant], *v.i.* to gad about; flirt or idle with members of the opposite sex. [GALLANT].

GALLON [ga′lun], *n.* measure of capacity equivalent to four quarts. [AFr.].

GALLOON [ga-loon′], *n.* narrow close braid for trimming garments. [Fr.].

GALLOP (1) [ga′lop], *n.* the fastest moving pace of a horse etc., in which both forelegs or hind legs touch the ground together, and all four legs are in the air at some period of the stride; a quick ride at this pace. GALLOP (2), *v.t. and i.* to move, ride or run at a g.; progress at a rapid pace; hurry; cause to g. GALLOPER, *n.* one who, or that which, gallops; aide-de-camp, orderly officer. [OFr.].

GALLOWAY [ga′lō-wā], *n.* species of small horse originally bred in Galloway, Scotland; one of a breed of cattle native to Galloway.

GALLOWS [ga′lōz], *n.* structure provided with a crossbeam from which criminals are hanged; any object or structure resembling this. GALLOWS-BIRD, one who deserves, or is destined for, the g. GALLOWS-TREE, a g. [OE.].

GALL-STONE [gawl′stōn], *n.* a concretion formed in the gall-bladder or duct.

GALOP (1) [ga′lop], *n.* quick lively dance in two-four time; music suitable for this. GALOP (2), *v.i.* to dance a g. [Fr.].

GALORE [ga-law(r)′], *adv.* in abundance, in great quantities. [Ir.].

GALOSH [ga-losh′], *n.* *see* GOLOSH.

GALUMPH [ga-lumf′], *v.i.* to dance about heavily with joy and triumph. [Invented by Lewis Carroll, from GALLOP and TRIUMPH].

GALVANIC [gal-va′nik], *adj.* (*elect.*) pertaining to, produced by, galvanism; producing electricity by galvanism; (*fig.*) convulsive, produced by a sudden burst of energy or effort.

GALVANISM [gal′va-nizm], *n.* electricity produced by chemical action; that aspect of the science of electricity dealing with this; remedial treatment by this kind of electricity. GALVANIST, *n.* student of g. [*Galvani*, its discoverer].

GALVANIZE [gal′va-nīz], *v.t.* to treat by means of galvanism; coat with a covering of metal, especially by galvanic action; (*fig.*) startle, shock into energetic action. GALVANIZED, *adj.* electrified by galvanism; coated with metal; **galvanized iron**, iron plates coated with zinc to prevent rusting.

GALVANO-, *pref.* galvanism, galvanic.

GALVANOMETER [gal-va-no′mi-ter], *n.* instrument for measuring the strength of a galvanic current of electricity. [GALVANO and METER].

GAMBA [gam′bah], *n.* viola-da-gamba. [LL.].

GAMBIT [gam′bit], *n.* an opening move in the game of chess in which a pawn or minor piece is sacrificed for a possible subsequent advantage; (*fig.*) opening move in a piece of strategy, transaction etc. [It.].

GAMBLE (1) [gam′bl], *v.i.* to play games of chance for money, *esp.* for high stakes; risk money in financial speculation; (*fig.*) base action upon some fortuitous uncertain event. GAMBLE (2), *n.* act of gambling; something dependent upon chance, a risk.

GAMBLER [gam′bler], *n.* one who gambles habitually.

GAMBLING [gam′bling], *n.* the playing of games of chance for money. G-HOUSE, place used for g.

GAMBOGE [gam-bōzh′], *n.* a gum-resin used as a yellow pigment. [MdL.].

GAMBOL (1) [gam′bol], *n.* a skipping or leaping about in frolic, rhythmical bodily expression of high spirits. GAMBOL (2) (*pres.pt.* GAMBOLLING, *pret. and p.pt.* GAMBOLLED), *v.i.* to frisk, caper, dance and skip about. [It.].

GAME (1) [gām], *n.* amusement, sport, pastime; sporting contest played according to certain rules; a single round, part or match of such a contest; the scoring of a definite number of points constituting this; the state of a game; (*pl.*) organized athletic sports; (*pl.*) (*antiq.*) public athletic, musical or dramatic contests as a recreation, spectacle or celebration; joke, prank; intention, aim; trick, artful scheme; business, undertaking; wild animals or birds which are hunted in the chase or sports of the field; edible flesh of such animals or birds; (*fig.*) object of pursuit, quarry; **the g. is not worth the candle**, the reward does not justify the effort spent or risks incurred; **to play the g.**, to behave in an honest, decent manner; **to have a g. with**, to fool; **to be on**

(off) one's g., to play well (badly); **to make g. of,** to mock, laugh at. GAME (2), *adj.* plucky, courageous; eager, willing. GAME (3), *v.i.* to gamble; (*archaic*) play, sport. [OE.].

GAME (4), *adj.* crippled, lame, disabled. [Uncert.].

GAMEBAG [gām'bag], *n.* receptacle for carrying game when killed.

GAMECOCK [gām'kok], *n.* a fighting-cock.

GAMEKEEPER [gām'kē-per], *n.* person employed to look after game.

GAME-LAWS [gām'lawz], *n.(pl.)* laws for the protection or preservation of game.

GAMELY [gām'li], *adv.* in a game manner, pluckily.

GAMENESS [gām'nes], *n.* quality of being game, pluck.

GAME-PRESERVE [gām'pri-zerv], *n.* tract of land used as a breeding, rearing or dwelling place for game.

GAMESOME [gām'sum], *adj.* gay, sportive, playful. GAMESOMELY, *adv.* in a g. fashion. GAMESOMENESS, *n.* quality of being g.

GAMESTER [gām'ster], *n.* person addicted to gaming, gambler; (*pl.*) (*billiards*) two opponents who have scored the same number of points at some stage of the game.

GAMETE [ga-mēt'], *n.* (*biol.*) a sexual reproductive cell uniting with another to produce a zygote. [Gk.].

GAMETOGENESIS [ga-me-tō-je'ni-sis], *n.* reproduction through gametes. [GAMETE and GENESIS].

GAMIC [ga'mik], *adj.* (*biol.*) sexual. [Gk.].

GAMIN (*fem.* **gamine**) [ga'ma(ng), ga-mēn'], *n.* mischievous urchin of the streets. [Fr.].

GAMING [gā'ming], *n.* gambling. GAMING-HOUSE, house where g. is carried on. GAMING-TABLE, table used for various gambling games.

GAMMA [ga'mah], *n.* third letter of the Greek alphabet γ; a common European moth; **g. rays,** penetrating rays emitted by radium and other radioactive substances.

GAMMER [ga'mer], *n.* old woman. [GRANDMOTHER].

GAMMON (1) [ga'mun], *n.* the lower part of a flitch of bacon, containing the hind leg; a cured ham. GAMMON (2), *v.t.* to cure bacon. [ONFr.].

GAMMON (3), *n.* victory at backgammon by which all one's men are withdrawn from the board before one's opponent has withdrawn any. GAMMON (4), *v.t.* to defeat at backgammon by making a g. [ME.].

GAMMON (5), *n.* a hoax, deception. GAMMON (6), *v.t.* and *i.* to hoax, deceive, dupe; pretend, dissemble. [GAMMON (3)].

GAMMON (7), *int.* nonsense, humbug. [GAME (4)].

GAMMY [ga'mi], *adj.* (*coll.*) crippled, lamed, injured.

GAMOGENESIS [ga-mō-je'ni-sis], *n.* sexual reproduction. [Gk.].

GAMP [gamp], *n.* large, badly rolled umbrella; (*coll.*) any umbrella. [Mrs. Gamp, in *Martin Chuzzlewit*].

GAMUT [ga'mut], *n.* the range of a voice or instrument; (*fig.*) scope, compass, range; (*mus.*) any scale used at some particular period in history; (*fig.*) **to run the g.,** to cover the whole field. [MedL.].

GAMY [gā'mi], *adj.* having the taste of game, high.

GANDER [gan'der], *n.* male of the goose; (*fig.*) fool. [OE.].

GANG (1) [gang], *n.* a band, group of persons associated together for some common purpose; set, clique; complete set of tools for some particular process; the cutting blade of a mechanical mower. GANG (2), *v.i.* (*U.S. coll.*) to form an association (with); **to g. up,** (*coll.*) to join together in a clique (against). [OE.].

GANGER [gang'er], *n.* foreman of a gang of labourers or platelayers.

GANGLION (*pl.* **ganglia**) [gang'gli-on], *n.* (*anat.*) a nucleus of nerve-cells, centre from which nerve-cells radiate; (*med.*) encysted tumour or sac, usually on a tendon or sinew; (*fig.*) meeting point of several converging forces or branches of activity. GANGLION-CELL, a single cell of a mass of nerve-cells. [Gk.].

GANGLIONIC [gang-gli-o'nik], *adj.* pertaining to, composed of, ganglia.

GANG-PLANK [gang'plangk], *n.* board or plank used as a ship's gangway.

GANGRENE (1) [gang'grēn], *n.* mortification affecting a considerable area of animal tissue; (*fig.*) a decaying force. GANGRENE (2), *v.t.* and *i.* to cause g. in; become mortified. [Gk.].

GANGRENOUS [gang'gri-nŏŏs], *adj.* of the nature of, affected by, gangrene.

GANGSTER [gang'ster], *n.* armed member of a criminal gang, unhesitatingly resorting to violence to perpetrate some crime or avoid capture.

GANGUE [gang], *n.* (*mining*) the substance which contains the ore of metals. [Germ.].

GANGWAY [gang'wā], *n.* board or movable bridge placed between a ship and the landing-stage; opening of the bulwarks of a ship into which this fits; passage, way of approach; passage separating blocks of seats in a hall, theatre etc.; (*parl.*) passage across the House of Commons separating the front benches from the back benches.

GANNET [ga'net], *n.* large sea-bird, the solan-goose. [OE.].

GANOID (1) [ga'noid], *adj.* (of a scale) smooth, shining and enamel-like; (of fishes) having hard, enamel-like scales of bone. GANOID (2), *n.* a g. fish. [Gk.].

GANTRY, GAUNTRY [gan'tri], *n.* framework of two upright members some distance apart, spanned by a horizontal piece, *esp.* one crossing several sets of railway lines and bearing signals, or carrying a travelling crane; stand used for supporting barrels. [OFr.].

GAOL (1), **JAIL** [jāl], *n.* prison; confinement in prison. GAOL (2), JAIL, *v.t.* to put into g. GAOL-BIRD, hardened criminal. GAOL-FEVER, typhus fever formerly widespread among prisoners. [OFr.].

GAOLER, JAILER [jā'ler], *n.* the head of a gaol; prison warder.

GAP [gap], *n.* hole, breach, opening in anything; opening in a range of mountains or hills; interval, vacant place, blank space, deficiency caused by a break in a sequence. GAP-TOOTHED, having the teeth irregularly set, with intervening gaps. [OIcel.].

GAPE (1) [gāp], *v.i.* to stare in open-mouthed astonishment or stupidity; (of a bird) open the mouth wide for food; yawn; (of the earth) open in a fissure; **to g. at,** to gaze in amazement at. GAPE (2), *n.* act of gaping, a vacant stare accompanied by an opening of the mouth; yawn; (*pl.*) a poultry disease; (*coll.*) yawning fit; (*fig.*) an opening. [OIcel.].

GAPER [gā'per], *n.* one who gapes; a bivalve mollusc; a sea-fish, the comber.

GARAGE (1) [ga'rahj, ga'rij], *n.* building in which motor vehicles are kept when not in use; establishment where motor vehicles may be housed, repaired etc., and at which petrol and motor accessories may be purchased. GARAGE (2), *v.t.* to put away in a g. [Fr.].

GARB (1) [gahb], *n.* mode or style of dress, attire, *esp.* distinctive type of dress of a class, occupation etc. GARB (2), *v.t.* and *reflex.* to dress, clothe. [It.].

GARBAGE [gah'bij], *n.* refuse, offal; (*fig.*) sordid rubbish. [Uncert.].

GARBLE [gah'bl], *v.t.* to present (facts etc.) tendentiously; mutilate, distort, misrepresent. GARBLER, *n.* person who garbles. [Arab.].

GARDEN (1) [gah'den], *n.* plot of land devoted to the cultivation of flowers, fruits and plants; (*pl.*) public enclosure for the cultivation of flowers, trees etc., serving as a place of recreation or rest; (*fig.*) richly fertile and well-cultivated region; **market g.,** large g. in which fruit, flowers or vegetables are grown for sale; **to lead up the g.,** (*slang*) to befool, deceive. GARDEN (2), *adj.* pertaining to a g., cultivated in a g. GARDEN (3), *v.i.* to cultivate, work in, a g. [AFr.].

GARDEN-CITY, -SUBURB [gah-den-si'ti,-su'berb], *n.* town, suburb, built in a harmonious style of architecture, having ample provision for gardens for the houses.

GARDENER [gah'de-ner], *n.* one whose occupation is to cultivate a garden; person interested in gardening.

GARDENIA [gah-dē'ni-ah], *n.* tropical and subtropical shrub with yellow and white fragrant flowers. [A. *Garden,* American botanist].

GARDENING [gah'de-ning], *n.* art of cultivating a garden.

GARDEN-PARTY [gah'den-pah-ti], *n.* social gathering held in the open, on the lawn of a garden or park.

GARFISH [gah'fish], *n.* a slender sea-fish with long, beak-like jaws. [ME. from OE.].

GARGANTUAN [gah-gan'tyŏŏ-an], *adj.* prodigious, of extremely large proportions. [*Gargantua,* giant in *Gargantua and Pantagruel* by Rabelais].

GARGLE (1) [gah'gl], *v.t.* and *i.* to cleanse the mouth and throat with a liquid preparation, while breathing out steadily and forcefully, so that the liquid is constantly agitated and not swallowed. GARGLE

(2), *n.* act of gargling; any antiseptic liquid preparation used for washing the mouth and throat. [Fr.].

GARGOYLE [gah'goil], *n.* a projecting rain-spout of the gutter of a building, *esp.* one carved in the form of a grotesque figure. [OFr.].

GARIBALDI [gah-ri-bahl'di], *n.* loose blouse of vivid cerise material; **g. biscuit**, biscuit containing a layer of currants. [*Garibaldi*, Italian patriot].

GARISH [gãer'ish], *adj.* gaudy, showy, glaringly bright. GARISHLY, *adv.* in a g. fashion. GARISHNESS, *n.* quality of being g. [~ME.].

GARLAND (1) [gah'land], *n.* wreath or chaplet of flowers, leaves etc., worn round the head or neck, or hung around any object; anything resembling or representing this; band or wreath worn as a mark of success or merit; (*fig.*) sign of victory or success. GARLAND (2), *v.t.* to adorn or wreathe with a g. [OFr.].

GARLIC [gah'lik], *n.* bulbous culinary plant, possessing a strong taste and smell. GARLICKY, *adj.* like or containing g. [OE.].

GARMENT [gah'ment], *n.* article of clothing; (*pl.*) dress, attire. [OFr.].

GARNER (1) [gah'ner], *n.* storehouse, *esp.* for grain. GARNER (2), *v.t.* to store up as in a g. [L.].

GARNET [gah'nit], *n.* a siliceous stone, crystallizing in the cubical system; deep-red variety of this, cut as a gem. [ME. from MedL.].

GARNISH (1) [gah'nish], *v.t.* to decorate, adorn, embellish; make a dish of food more attractive by serving a sauce, relish etc. with it. GARNISH (2), *n.* ornament, decoration; articles served with food to g. it; literary adornment. GARNISHING, *n.* anything which garnishes. [Fr.].

GARNITURE [gah'ni-tyoōr], *n.* ornamental appendages, decoration, dress.

GARRET [ga'rit], *n.* attic, small room at the top of a house. [OFr.].

GARRISON (1) [ga'ri-sun], *n.* body of troops quartered in a fortress or fortified town for its defence; fortress or fortified town defended in this way. GARRISON (2), *v.t.* to provide with a g.; occupy as a g.; send (troops) as a g. [OFr.].

GARRISON-ARTILLERY [ga-ri-sun-ah-ti'le-ri], *n.* heavy artillery firing large-calibre shells.

GARROTTE (1), **GAROTTE** [ga-rot'], *n.* means of execution in Spain and Portugal by strangulation; strangulation by means of a cord wound tightly round the victim's neck. GARROTTE (2), *v.t.* to strangle with a g., *esp.* preparatory to robbing. GARROTTER, *n.* robber who strangles his victims by means of a g. GARROTTING, *n.* punishment by strangulation; throttling by means of a g. [Span.].

GARRULITY [ga-roō'li-ti], *n.* quality of being garrulous.

GARRULOUS [ga'ryoō-loōs], *adj.* talkative, inclined to discourse at great length upon topics of slight interest or importance. GARRULOUSLY, *adv.* in a talkative fashion. GARRULOUSNESS, *n.* quality of being g. [L.].

GARTER [gah'ter], *n.* elastic band worn round the leg to keep the stocking in position; highest order of knighthood in Great Britain; badge of the order; membership of this order; **G. King of Arms**, principal herald of the College of Arms of England. [OFr.].

GARTH [gahth], *n.* yard, court, enclosed lawn. [OIcel.].

GAS (1) [gas], *n.* one of various elastic air-like substances, *esp.* that obtained from coal and used for heating and illumination; nitrous oxide gas when used as an anaesthetic in dentistry; any poisonous chemical vapour used in modern warfare; (*min.*) fire-damp mixed with air and forming an explosive mixture; (*U.S.*) gasoline; (*coll.*) idle talk; **to step on the g.**, (*slang*) to accelerate; **g. proof**, impervious to poison gas. GAS (2) (*pres.pt.* GASSING, *pret.* and *p.pt.* GASSED), *v.t.* to poison or kill by the fumes of g.; *v.i.* (*coll.*) to gossip. [Invented by Van Helmont, Belgian chemist, based on Gk. (CHAOS).]

GAS-ATTACK [gas'a-tak], *n.* an attack with poison gas.

GAS-BAG [gas'bag], *n.* bag for holding gas; (*slang*) talkative person, gossip.

GAS-BRACKET [gas'bra-kit], *n.* fixed or jointed gas pipe with a burner, attached to a wall etc.

GAS-BURNER [gas'ber-ner], *n.* jet fitted at the end of a gas pipe, from which the flame appears.

GASCON [gas'kon], *n.* a native of Gascony in France; boaster. [Fr.].

GASCONADE (1) [gas-ko-nãd'], *n.* boastful,

bragging talk. GASCONADE (2), *v.i.* to boast, brag. [Fr.].

GAS-CHAMBER [gas'chãm-ber], *n.* a gas-tight chamber used for the asphyxiation of animals or human beings by poison gas.

GAS-COOKER [gas'koō-ker], *n.* stove in which the heat for cooking is supplied by gas.

GASEITY [ga-sē'i-ti], *n.* gaseousness.

GAS-ENGINE [gas'en-jin], *n.* internal combustion engine driven by gas.

GASEOUS [gã'si-oōs], *adj.* in the form of gas, like gas. GASEOUSNESS, *n.* condition of being g.

GAS-FIRE [gas'fier], *n.* a fire burning gas as fuel.

GAS-FITTER [gas'fi-ter], *n.* workman who installs gas-fittings.

GAS-FITTINGS [gas'fi-tingz], *n.(pl.)* pipes, brackets, jets etc. necessary for the use of gas for heating and lighting purposes.

GASH (1) [gash], *n.* a narrow, deep and long cut; cleft. GASH (2), *v.t.* to make a g. in. [OFr.].

GASIFY [ga'si-fi], *v.t.* and *i.* to turn into gas; manufacture gas from. GASIFICATION [ga-si-fi-kã'shn], *n.* act of gasifying.

GAS-JET [gas'jet], *n.* a gas-burner.

GASKET [gas'ket], *n.* piece of plaited hemp etc., used for packing the piston of a steam engine or stopping up a joint; a copper-asbestos joint; (*naut.*) cord or canvas strip with which a furled sail is tied to a yard. [It.].

GAS-LAMP [gas'lamp], *n.* lamp which burns gas.

GAS-LIGHT [gas'lit], *n.* light produced by burning coal-gas; lamp burning gas; **g. paper**, (*phot.*) sensitized printing paper which can be manipulated in subdued artificial light, or on which prints are made by exposure to artificial light.

GAS-MAINS [gas'mãnz], *n.(pl.)* the principal pipes which carry the gas from the gas-works.

GAS-MANTLE [gas'man-tl], *n.* small gauze-like net of cotton fabric fitted to a gas-burner, and becoming incandescent when heated by the flame.

GAS-MASK [gas'mahsk], *n.* respirating apparatus worn over the face and head as a protection against the inhaling of poisonous gas.

GAS-METER [gas'mē-ter], *n.* mechanical contrivance for measuring and recording the quantity of gas consumed.

GASOLINE [ga'sō-lēn], *n.* inflammable product obtained from the refining of crude petroleum and used for heating and lighting; (*U.S.*) petrol.

GASOMETER [ga-so'mi-ter], *n.* (*coll.*) reservoir or storage tank for gas; (*chem.*) apparatus for holding or measuring a quantity of gas. [GAS and METER].

GASP (1) [gahsp], *v.t.* and *i.* to breathe by a series of gasps, fight for breath, catch the breath in fear or amazement; utter in a gasp. GASP (2), *n.* sudden convulsive effort to catch one's breath; **at the last g.**, at the limit of one's powers or strength. [ME. from OIcel.].

GASPER [gahs'per], *n.* (*slang*) cigarette, *esp.* of inferior quality.

GASPING [gahs'ping], *adj.* that gasps, convulsive, laborious and spasmodic.

GAS PIPE [gas'pip], *n.* pipe along which gas is conveyed.

GAS-RING [gas'ring], *n.* metal ring pierced with holes through which gas is burnt for cooking purposes.

GAS-SHELL [gas'shel], *n.* explosive shell containing poison gas or chemicals emitting deadly fumes.

GAS-STOVE [gas'stōv], *n.* cooking-stove heated by burning gas.

GASSY [gas'i], *adj.* gaseous; full of gas; (*coll.*) talkative.

GASTEROPOD, GASTROPOD [gas'te-ro-pod], *n.* member of the class of gasteropoda.

GASTEROPODA, GASTROPODA [gas-te-ro'po-dah], *n.(pl.)* class of univalve molluscs, including snails, slugs, limpets etc. GASTEROPODOUS, GASTROPODOUS, *adj.* pertaining to the g. [Gk.].

GASTRIC [gas'trik], *adj.* belonging to the stomach; **g. juice**, acid secretion from glands in the stomach, which aids digestion; **g. fever**, former name for typhoid fever.

GASTRITIS [gas-tri'tis], *n.* (*med.*) inflammation of the stomach. [Gk.].

GASTRO(O)-, *pref.* stomach, belly. [Gk.].

GASTRO-ENTERITIS [gas-trō-en-te-ri'tis], *n.* (*med.*) inflammation of the stomach and intestines.

GASTRONOME, GASTRONOMER, GASTRONOMIST [gas'trō-nōm, gas-tro'no-mer, gas-tro'no-mist], *n.* epicure, one who enjoys and appreciates good food and cookery. [Fr.].

The accent ' after a syllable = stress (u-pon'). The mark ¯ over a vowel = length (ã in made; ō in bone).

GASTRONOMIC(AL) [gas-trŏ-no′mik(-al)], *adj.* relating to gastronomy.

GASTRONOMY [gas-tro′no-mi], *n.* art of gratifying the palate by good food and cooking.

GASTROPOD, GASTROPODA, GASTROPODOUS, see GASTEROPOD, GASTEROPODA, GASTEROPODOUS.

GASTROSCOPY [gas-tro′sko-pi], *n.* (*med.*) inspection of the interior of the stomach. [Gk.].

GASTROSTOMY [gas-tro′sto-mi], *n.* (*surg.*) operation of making an opening in the stomach by which food may be introduced. [Gk.].

GASTROTOMY [gas-tro′to-mi], *n.* (*surg.*) operation of cutting into or opening the abdomen. [Gk.].

GAS-WORKS [gas′werks], *n.(pl.)* works where coal-gas is manufactured for heating and lighting.

GAT (1) [gat], *n.* channel between sandbanks. [OIcel.].

GAT (2), *n.* (*U.S.*) a Gatling gun; (*coll.*) a gun.

GATE (1) [gāt], *n.* a framework swinging on hinges and used to open or close the entrance to an enclosure, drive etc., or to bar progress along a path; gateway; structure to regulate or stop the flow of water through a lock, dock etc.; the number of persons assembled to watch a sporting contest; the total amount of money paid by such spectators; (*motoring*) metal plate controlling the rectangular series of movements made by a gear lever in changing gear. GATE (2), *v.t.* to prohibit students or schoolboys from leaving their colleges, schools or grounds after a certain hour. GATED, *adj.* provided with gates; confined to college or school. [OE.].

GATE (3), *n.* road, way. [OIcel.].

GATEAU [ga′tō], *n.* a fancy cake. [Fr.].

GATE-BILL [gāt′bil], *n.* a record of the times at which an Oxford or Cambridge undergraduate returns to college after hours, or of fines imposed for this.

GATE-CRASH [gāt′krash], *v.t. and i.* to gain admittance to a social gathering without invitation or ticket of admission. GATE-CRASHER, *n.* one who gate-crashes.

GATEHOUSE [gāt′hows], *n.* house built adjacent to, or over, a gate giving entrance to an enclosure, city etc.

GATEKEEPER [gāt′kē-per], *n.* person in charge of a gate.

GATE-LEGGED TABLE [gāt-legd-tā′bl], *n.* table having legs which fold inwards, and a top whose end leaves fold downwards, when not in use.

GATEMAN [gāt′man], *n.* gatekeeper; person collecting gate-money or the levy at a toll-gate.

GATE-MONEY [gāt′mu-ni], *n.* money taken as charge for admission to a sporting contest etc.

GATE-POST [gāt′pōst], *n.* one of the two posts on either side of an opening closed by a gate.

GATEWAY [gāt′wā], *n.* opening in a wall, hedge etc., closed by a gate; (*fig.*) means of access.

GATHER (1) [gaTHer], *v.t.* to bring together, collect; pick; acquire, accumulate; muster, summon up; infer, conclude; draw together in small folds by means of a thread; contract, pucker; (*v.i.*) to assemble; increase; come to a head; generate pus or morbid matter; **to g. way,** (*naut.*) to start moving. GATHER (2), *n.* small pleat or fold in cloth etc., made by drawing a thread through the material. GATHERER, *n.* one who, or that which, gathers. [OE.].

GATHERING [gaTHe-ring], *n.* act of one who gathers; assembly; congregation; swelling generating pus.

GATLING [gat′ling], *n.* rapid-firing American machine gun. [Dr. R. J. *Gatling*, its inventor].

GAUCHE [gōsh], *adj.* awkward, lacking in tact. [Fr.].

GAUCHERIE [gō′she-rē], *n.* awkwardness, clumsiness, want of tact. [Fr.].

GAUCHO [gow′chō], *n.* a native of the South American pampas, of mixed Spanish and Indian descent. [Span.].

GAUD [gawd], *n.* trinket, showy knick-knack; (*pl.*) gaieties. [L.].

GAUDY (1) [gaw′di], *n.* feast, *esp.* an annual commemorative dinner or reunion at a college. GAUDY (2), *adj.* showy, gay, unpleasantly brilliant, too highly coloured. GAUDILY, *adv.* in a g. fashion. GAUDINESS, *n.* state of being g. [L.].

GAUFFER, GAUFFERING, GAUFFRE, see GOFFER (1), GOFFERING, GOFFER (1).

GAUGE, GAGE (3) [gāj], *n.* a standard measure, *esp.* the distance between the rails of a railway, the diameter of wire, tubing, bullets etc.; (*naut.*) position of one vessel with respect to another and to the wind; depth to which a ship sinks in the water; instrument for measuring the force, quantity etc. of such constantly varying things as wind, rain, steam-pressure etc.; instrument for testing the size of tools, instruments etc.; (*fig.*) means of estimating, criterion; **to have the weather g. of.** (*naut.*) to lie to windward of; (*fig.*) have the advantage over. GAUGE (2), GAGE, *v.t.* to measure the force, volume etc. by means of a g.; measure exactly anything made to standard requirements; cause to conform to standard dimensions; (*fig.*) estimate, judge. [AFr.].

GAUGER [gā′jer], *n.* one who gauges; excise officer who gauges casks of liquor.

GAUGING [gā′jing], *n.* act of one who gauges; **g. rod, rule,** instrument used to determine the capacity of a cask of liquor.

GAULEITER [gow′lī-ter], *n.* governor of a district in Nazi Germany or German-occupied territory. [Germ.].

GAUNT [gawnt], *adj.* lean, thin; grim, austere. [~Norw.].

GAUNTLET (1) [gawnt′let], *n.* (*hist.*) leather glove covered with small steel plates; strong glove with a wide sheath to protect the wrist; **to fling down the g.,** to issue a challenge. [Fr.].

GAUNTLET (2), *n.* former naval or military punishment, in which the offender was compelled to run between two lines of men armed with rods, who struck him as he passed; **to run the g.,** to undergo this punishment; (*fig.*) be liable to hostile attacks or criticism. [Earlier *gantelope* from Swed., influenced by GAUNTLET (1)].

GAUNTRY, see GANTRY.

GAUSS [gows], *n.* (*magn.*) unit of strength of a magnetic field. [K. *Gauss*, German physicist].

GAUZE [gawz], *n.* very thin, transparent stuff, of silk, cotton, wire etc. [Fr.].

GAVE [gāv], *pret.* of GIVE.

GAVEL [ga′vel], *n.* small mallet used by a chairman at a meeting; auctioneer's hammer. [Uncert.].

GAVOTTE [ga-vot′], *n.* a stately dance danced to music written in common time; music suitable for this dance. [Provenc.].

GAWK [gawk], *n.* awkward, clumsy person [Uncert.].

GAWKY [gaw′ki], *adj.* clumsy, ungainly.

GAY [gā], *adj.* lively, cheerful, vivacious, light-hearted; fond of pleasure; showy; brilliant. [Fr.].

GAZE (1) [gāz], *v.i.* to look steadily, thoughtfully and continually. GAZE (2), *n.* a steady, thoughtful look; **at g.,** gazing, in a wondering attitude; (*her.*) full-faced. GAZER, *n.* one who gazes. [ME. ~Swed.].

GAZEBO [ga-zē′bō], *n.* balcony, turret or window with a wide outlook; summer-house. [Unkn.].

GAZELLE [ga-zel′], *n.* genus of small, swift antelopes with large, gentle eyes. [Arab.].

GAZETTE (1) [ga-zet′], *n.* (*hist.*) news-sheet; official publication in which public appointments, promotions and other public notices are recorded; similar official publication of a university etc. GAZETTE (2), *v.t.* to publish in the *Gazette*. [It.].

GAZETTEER [ga-ze-tēer′], *n.* official journalist who writes for the *Gazette*; geographical dictionary. [It.].

GAZOGENE, GASOGENE [ga′zo-jēn, ga′so-jēn], *n.* apparatus for making aerated water. [Fr.].

GEAR (1) [gēer], *n.* harness, trappings; tools, apparatus; (*archaic*) equipment, clothes; (*naut.*) rigging; (*machinery*) piece of machinery consisting of a combination of toothed wheels for transmitting or regulating motion; **high (low) g.,** mechanical contrivance whereby the driving part of machinery moves relatively slowly (quickly) compared with the driven part; **out of g.,** disconnected from the gear; (*fig.*) not proceeding smoothly and easily. GEAR (2), *v.t.* to harness, equip; put into g.; *v.i.* to be connected in the gearing system (with). [ME. from OIcel.].

GEAR-BOX [gēer′boks], *n.* the case in which the gearing mechanism is encased.

GEAR-CASE [gēer′kās], *n.* the chain guard of a bicycle.

GEAR-CHANGE [gēer′chānj], *n.* (*mech.*) act of changing gear; means or system of changing gear.

GEARING [gēer′ing], *n.* act of fitting a machine with gears; manner in which the gears work; arrangement of gears in a piece of machinery.

GEAR-WHEEL [gēer′wēl], *n.* wheel with cogs, forming part of a gearing system.

GEE (1) [jē], *int.* word of encouragement or command to a horse; also GEE-UP.

GEE (2), *int.* (*U.S.*) exclamation of astonishment.

appreciation etc. [Short for *gee whiz*, possibly from Germ. *gewisz* !].

GEE-GEE [jē'jē], *n.* childish word for a horse.

GEESE [gēs], *n. pl. of* GOOSE.

GEEZER [gē'zer], *n.* (*coll.*) old man or woman. [GUISER].

GEHENNA [ge-he'nah], *n.* hell; place of torture or torment. [Eccles L. from Heb.].

GEISHA [gā'shah], *n.* Japanese dancing girl. [Jap.].

GEL [jel], *n.* (*chem.*) a colloid which has hardened and set as a jelly.

GELATINATE [je-la'ti-nāt], *v.t.* to convert into gelatine; *v.i.* to be transformed into gelatine. GELATINATION [je-la-ti-nā'shn], *n.* act of gelatinating; state of being gelatinated.

GELATIN(E) [je'la-tin, -tēn], *n.* brittle, translucent substance which can be melted, obtained by boiling certain animal tissues in hot water; **vegetable g.**, substance found in gluten; **blasting g.**, explosive compound containing nitro-glycerine. [It.].

GELATINIZE [je-la'ti-niz], *v.t.* to cause to set into a jelly. GELATINIZATION, the process of setting or causing to set into a jelly.

GELATINOUS [je-la'ti-noŏs], *adj.* relating to, consisting of, gelatine; of the nature of jelly.

GELD [geld], *v.t.* to castrate, emasculate. [OIcel.].

GELDER-ROSE. see GUELDER-ROSE.

GELDING [gel'ding], *n.* act of castrating; castrated animal, *esp.* a horse. [OIcel.].

GELID [je'lid], *adj.* icy cold; (*fig.*) frigidly aloof. GELIDLY, *adv.* in a g. manner. GELIDNESS, *n.* quality of being g.

GELIGNITE [je-lig'nīt], *n.* gelatine dynamite, highly explosive substance used for blasting.

GEM (1) [jem], *n.* precious stone, *esp.* when cut and polished; precious or semi-precious stone on which is engraved a design; anything of outstanding quality, worth or beauty; (*fig.*) the best, choicest. GEM (2) (*pres.pt.* GEMMING, *pret. and p.pt.* GEMMED), *v.t.* to adorn with gems. [Fr. from L.].

GEMINATE (1) [je'mi-nāt], *adj.* (*bot.*) (of leaves) issuing in pairs from the same point; twin. GEMINATE (2), *v.t.* to double, pair. GEMINATION [je-mi-nā'shn], *n.* (*gram.*) the doubling of a letter or consonant sound. [L.].

GEMINI [je'mi-ni], *n.* (*astrol.*) the constellation Castor and Pollux; third sign of the Zodiac. [L.].

GEMMA (*pl.* **gemmae**) [je'mah], *n.* (*bot.*) a leaf-bud; (in mosses etc.) small cellular nodule; (*zool.*) bud-like development which separates and becomes a new organism. [L.].

GEMMATE (1) [je'māt], *adj.* (*bot.*) reproducing by buds. GEMMATE (2), *v.i.* (*bot.*) to reproduce itself by buds. [L.].

GEMMATION [je-mā'shn], *n.* (*bot.*) process of reproduction by gemmae; budding-time; arrangement of leaves in the bud and of buds on the stalk; (*zool.*) reproduction by budding off.

GEMMIPAROUS [je-mi'pa-roŏs], *adj.* reproducing by budding; pertaining to the process of budding. [L.].

GEMMY [je'mi], *adj.* full of gems; set with gems; glittering.

GEN [jen], *n.* (*R.A.F. slang*) (reliable) information. [GENERAL INFORMATION].

GENDARME [zhahn-dahm'], *n.* member of a body of soldiers in France who perform police duties. GENDARMERIE [zhahn-dah'me-rē], *n.* the collective body of gendarmes. [Fr.].

GENDER [jen'der], *n.* a grammatical classification of nouns and pronouns sometimes corresponding to that of sex. [ME. from OFr.].

GENE [jēn], *n.* (*biol.*) factor determining hereditary characteristics. [Gk.].

GENEALOGICAL [jē-ni-a-lo'ji-kal], *adj.* pertaining to genealogy, showing genealogy; **g. tree**, diagram representing the origin and descent of a family by means of a tree with branches. GENEALOGICALLY, *adv.* in a g. fashion.

GENEALOGIST [jē-ni-a'lo-jist], *n.* one who studies genealogy.

GENEALOGY [jē-ni-a'lo-ji], *n.* history of the descent of a person or family from the earliest known ancestor, pedigree; account or diagrammatic representation of this; way in which animals, plants etc. have evolved from primitive types; the making of pedigrees, study of the descent of persons or families. [Gk.].

GENERA [je'ne-rah], *n. pl. of* GENUS.

GENERAL (1) [je'ne-ral], *adj.* not confined to any particular section, aspect or part; relating to a whole

class, involving all or many parts of a whole; referring to, affecting or applicable to, a large number of instances; summarizing all aspects; widespread, prevalent, common; usual; miscellaneous, vague; considered as a whole; (*milit.*) above the rank of colonel (of an officer or rank); (*coll.*) complete, utter; **g. meeting**, meeting all members are invited to attend; **G. Election**, election held at the same time in every constituency throughout the country; **g. strike**, concerted strike of the workers employed in all major trades and industries; **G. Council**, council summoned by the Pope, at which all Catholic bishops are requested to be present; **as a g. rule**, usually; in **g.**, on the whole; **G. Headquarters**, headquarters of the Commander-in-Chief; **G. Hospital**, military hospital receiving casualties from field hospitals; (in certain cities) hospital which does not specialize in any particular type of malady. GENERAL (2), *n.* a class or group considered collectively; *orig.*, the commander of an army, now an officer next in rank below a field-marshal, and also (*pop.*) lieutenant-g. and major-g.; the head of certain religious organizations, as the Salvation Army, Jesuits etc.; one skilful in manoeuvring and marshalling his resources; a general maid. [L.].

GENERALISSIMO [je-ne-ra-li'si-mō], *n.* the chief commander of a large army, *esp.* of the combined forces of allies. [It.].

GENERALITY [je-ne-ra'li-ti], *n.* quality of being general; that which is general; a general statement; the greater part. [L.].

GENERALIZATION [je-ne-ra-lī-zā'shn], *n.* act of generalizing; inference or deduction of general applicability; statement which seeks to summarize all aspects; process of becoming widespread.

GENERALIZE [je'ne-ra-liz], *v.t.* to infer or express in general terms; depict the general aspect of; cause to be widespread; *v.i.* to make general inferences from specific examples; extend from the particular to the general.

GENERALLY [je'ne-ra-li], *adv.* in a general fashion; usually, as a rule; without being specific; widely, commonly.

GENERALSHIP [je'ne-ral-ship], *n.* rank or dignity of a general; skill in military tactics, strategy and leadership; ability to manage or direct.

GENERANT [je'ne-rant], *n.* that which generates; (*math.*) point, line or surface which, as it moves, forms a line, surface or solid. [L.].

GENERATE [je'ne-rāt], *v.t.* to produce, cause the existence of; (*fig.*) bring about; (*math.*) produce or form (a line, surface or solid) as it moves. GENERATING, *adj.* producing; **generating station**, electric power-house.

GENERATION [je-ne-rā'shn], *n.* act of generating; single distinct step in the line of descent; all the persons who form such a stage; period of time, about thirty years, which, as a general rule, marks off each stage in the line of descent; people considered as belonging to such a period; **the rising g.**, the younger members of a period or age. [L.].

GENERATIVE [je'ne-ra-tiv], *adj.* having the power of generating, pertaining to generation.

GENERATOR [je'ne-rā-ter], *n.* one who, or that which, generates; apparatus for generating gas, electricity, steam etc. [L.].

GENERIC(AL) [je-ne'rik(-al)], *adj.* pertaining to, or comprising, a genus or class; common to all members of a genus.

GENEROSITY [je-ne-ro'si-ti], *n.* quality of being generous; liberality, magnanimity. [L.].

GENEROUS [je'ne-roŏs], *adj.* liberal, munificent; of noble nature, magnanimous; freely given, abundant; large; (of wine) strong, invigorating. GENEROUSLY, *adv.* in g. fashion. [L.].

GENESIS [je'ne-sis], *n.* origin, birth, beginning; first book of the Old Testament, which tells of the creation of the world. [Gk.].

GENET [je'net], *n.* variety of civet-cat; fur from this animal; cat-skin made to resemble this fur. [Arab.].

GENETIC(AL) [je-ne'tik(-al)], *adj.* arising from, caused by, or relating to, the genesis of a thing. GENETICALLY, *adv.* in a g. manner, according to genetics.

GENETICS [je-ne'tiks], *n.(pl.)* study of heredity.

GENEVA [je-nē'vah], *n.* spirit distilled from grain, flavoured with juniper berries; gin, hollands. [Du. from L.].

GENEVA BANDS [je-nē'va-bandz], *n.* a pair of white linen tabs worn at the neck as a mark of authority, *esp.* by Presbyterian ministers.

The accent ' after a syllable = stress (u-pon'). The mark ‾ over a vowel = length (ā in made; ō in bone).

GENIAL [jē'ni-al], *adj.* cheerful, kindly, affably good-natured; (of climate) pleasant, mild. GENIALLY, *adv.* in a g. fashion. [L.].

GENIALITY [jē-ni-a'li-ti], *n.* state or quality of being genial. [L.].

GENIE (*pl.* **genii**) [jē'ni], *n.* Arabian sprite or goblin.

GENISTA [je-nis'tah], *n.* genus of leguminous shrubs with yellow flowers. [L.].

GENITAL [je'ni-tal], *adj.* relating to, connected with, generation. GENITALS, *n.*(*pl.*) external organs of procreation.

GENITIVAL [je-ni-tī'val], *adj.* pertaining to, having the form of or derived from, the genitive.

GENITIVE [je'ni-tiv], *adj.* (*gram.*) **g. case**, a grammatical form of nouns, pronouns or adjectives indicating origin, source, ownership, possession etc. [L.].

GENIUS (*pl.* **geniuses**) [jē'ni-us], *n.* spiritual atmosphere, traditional associations or feeling conjured up by the essential nature of anything; natural aptitude for a particular thing; natural ability of the highest order, unsurpassed intellectual, creative or expressive power; person displaying such power; (*myth.*) spirit presiding over a place or person; (*fig.*) person wielding a powerful influence over the life of another; **g. loci**, atmosphere or group of associations native to a place; presiding spirit of a place. [L.].

GENOCIDE [je'nō-sīd], *n.* the crime, in international law, of committing acts intended to destroy, in whole or in part, national, ethnical, racial or religious groups. [Gk. and L.].

GENRE [zhah(ng)r], *n.* type, species, style; style of painting or writing depicting scenes or subjects in everyday life. [Fr.].

GENT [jent], *n.* (*vulg.*) gentleman.

GENTEEL [jen-tēl'], *adj.* mincing, affecting a mode of life or deportment considered suitable for, or typical of, the upper classes; (*formerly*) stylish, elegant; having the bearing and behaviour of a well-bred person. GENTEELLY, *adv.* in a g. fashion. GENTEELNESS, *n.* quality of being g. [Fr.].

GENTIAN [jen'shan], *n.* species of plants of the genus *Gentiana* possessing bitter roots and bright, usually blue, flowers. GENTIAN-BITTER, medicinal tonic obtained from the roots of the g. [L.].

GENTILE (1) [jen'tīl], *adj.* not a member of the Jewish race. GENTILE (2), *n.* a non-Jew; (*archaic*) a heathen. [L.].

GENTILITY [jen-ti'li-ti], *n.* (*archaic*) gentle birth; the manners, behaviour and mode of life of well-bred persons. [L.].

GENTLE [jen'tl], *adj.* well-bred; mild, kindly, tender; peace-loving, placid; moderate, slight; soft, soothing; not excessive; not rough or rapid; gradual; docile, quiet; (*her.*) having the right to bear arms. [L.].

GENTLEFOLK [jen'tl-fōk], *n.*(*pl.*) persons of good or noble breeding and family.

GENTLEMAN [jen'tl-man], *n.* chivalrous, well-mannered man; well-born man belonging to the upper classes of society; man of means and leisure; (*hist.*) man who has the right to bear arms, although not a nobleman; (*hist.*) man of high birth and breeding attached to the court, or to the household of a person of high rank; (*leg.*) man of independent means; (*pl.*) courteous form of address; **gentlemen's agreement**, an agreement not legally enforceable, but binding on the honour of the parties. [ME.].

GENTLEMAN-AT-ARMS [jen-tl-man-at-ahmz'], *n.* member of the sovereign's bodyguard on state occasions.

GENTLEMAN-COMMONER [jen-tl-man-ko'mo-ner], *n.* one of a privileged class of undergraduates formerly recognized at Oxford University.

GENTLEMAN-FARMER [jen-tl-man-fah'mer], *n.* in England, gentleman farming his own or leased land; (*U.S.*) man of independent means who farms for pleasure or diversion.

GENTLEMANLIKE [jen'tl-man-līk], *adj.* gentlemanly.

GENTLEMANLY [jen'tl-man-li], *adj.* characteristic or worthy of a gentleman. GENTLEMANLINESS [jen'tl-man-li-nes], *n.* quality of being g.

GENTLEMAN-USHER [jen-tl-man-u'sher], *n.* one who is usher to a person of high rank.

GENTLENESS [jen'tl-nes], *n.* quality of being gentle.

GENTLEWOMAN [jen'tl-woo-man], *n.* lady, woman of good family or breeding; woman who waits upon one of high rank.

GENTLY [jent'li], *adv.* in a gentle manner.

GENTRY [jen'tri], *n.* untitled people of good birth

and high social position; type of people, class of folk. [OFr.].

GENUFLECT [je-nyōō-flekt'], *v.i.* to bend the knee in worship. GENUFLEXION, GENUFLECTION, *n.* the bending of the knee in reverence. [MedL.].

GENUINE [je'nyōō-in], *adj.* real, valid, authentic; honest, not assumed or counterfeit; belonging to the original stock, pure-bred. GENUINELY, *adv.* in a g. fashion. GENUINENESS, *n.* quality of being g. [L.].

GENUS (*pl.* **genera**) [jē'nus, je'ne-rah], *n.* (*bot.*, *zool.*) group of species possessing certain distinctive structural characters in common; (*logic*) class made up of several species, each distinguished slightly from the others; kind, sort, class. [L.].

GEO-, *pref.* the earth. [Gk.].

GEOCENTRIC(AL) [jē-ō-sen'trik(-al)], *adj.* regarded as seen or reckoned from the centre of the earth; having the earth for centre.

GEODESY [jē-o'de-si], *n.* science of measuring the earth, or surveying any large portion of it. GEODESIC(AL), GEODETIC(AL) [jē-ō-de'sik(-al), jē-ō-de'tik(-al)], *adj.* pertaining to, produced by, g. [Gk.].

GEOGNOSY [jē-og'no-si], *n.* science of the constitution and structure of the earth, and of the arrangement and distribution of its strata; geology of a particular locality. GEOGNOSTIC(AL) [jē-og-nos'tik(-al)], *adj.* relating to g.; geological. [Gk.].

GEOGRAPHER [jē-o'gra-fer], *n.* one who studies or writes about geography.

GEOGRAPHIC(AL) [jē-ō-gra'fik(-al)], *adj.* pertaining to geography; **g. mile**, one sixtieth of a degree of latitude, which varies according to the latitude but may be taken as approximately equal to 6,080 ft. GEOGRAPHICALLY, *adv.* in a g. manner, from the point of view of geography.

GEOGRAPHY [jē-o'gra-fi], *n.* science which deals with the description of the earth's surface, its physical features, people, products, climate etc.; arrangement and relative position of the different parts of a place, building etc.; book about geography. [Gk.].

GEOLOGICAL [jē-ō-lo'ji-kal], *adj.* relating to geology.

GEOLOGIST [jē-o'lo-jist], *n.* student of geology.

GEOLOGIZE [jē-o'lo-jīz], *v.t. and i.* to study geology; make geological investigations; study the geology of.

GEOLOGY [jē-o'lo-ji], *n.* science which deals with the structure of the earth's crust, with its rocks and their contents and the successive changes which have undergone; geological features of a district; book about geology. [Gk.].

GEOMETER [jē-o'mi-ter], *n.* one skilled in geometry; (*entom.*) any one of the looper moths. [Gk.].

GEOMETRIC(AL) [jē-ō-me'trik(-al)], *adj.* pertaining to, according to, the principles of geometry; regular, symmetrical, made up of figures and shapes used in geometry; **g. progression**, progression in which the quantities increase by a common multiplier or decrease by a common division. GEOMETRICALLY, *adv.* in accordance with geometry.

GEOMETRICIAN [jē-ō-me-tri'shn], *n.* one learned in geometry.

GEOMETRY [jē-o'me-tri], *n.* that part of mathematics which deals with points, lines, surfaces and solids; book about geometry. [Gk.].

GEOPHYSICS [jē-ō-fi'ziks], *n.* science dealing with the physical principles, causes or forces involved in, or affecting, the structure of the earth. GEOPHYSICAL, *adj.* pertaining to g. [GEO and PHYSICS].

GEOPOLITICS [jē-ō-po'li-tiks], *n.*(*pl.*) study of the effect of geographic conditions upon world politics. GEOPOLITICAL [jē-ō-po-li'ti-kal], *adj.* pertaining to g. [GEO and POLITICS].

GEORGE [jawj], *n.* jewelled figure of St. George worn by Knights of the Garter; **St. George's cross**, vertical and horizontal bars of red, intersecting in their centres. [St. *George*, Cappadocian martyr].

GEORGETTE [jaw-jet'], *n.* thin, light, partially transparent silk and cotton fabric. [Mme. *Georgette*, French dressmaker].

GEORGIAN (1) [jaw'ji-an], *adj.* pertaining to Georgia in the Caucasus or to Georgia, U.S.A. GEORGIAN (2), *n.*, a native or the language of Georgia in the Caucasus, or Georgia, U.S.A.

GEORGIAN (3), *adj.* belonging to the reigns of the Georges, Kings of England.

GEORGIC [jaw'jik], *n.* poetical composition on rural husbandry, one of the books of Virgil's poem upon husbandry. [Gk.].

GERANIUM [je-rā'ni-um], *n.* one of a large genus of plants having lobed leaves and red, pink or white flowers; plant of the genus *Pelargonium*. [Gk.].

GERFALCON [jur'fawl-kon], n. large falcon found in the northern regions.

GERM (1) [jarm], n. origin of an embryo, rudimentary form of an organism from which a new similar individual being can develop; microbe, esp. one which helps to cause disease; (fig.) the primitive, undeveloped form from which anything springs or grows. GERM (2), v.i. (fig.) to bud, sprout; form. [L.].

GERMAN (1) [jur'man], adj. pertaining to Germany, the German people or language; made in, characteristic of, Germany; **G. text**, black letter; **G. measles**, mild infectious disease resembling measles; **High G.**, standard literary language in Germany; **Low G.**, G. dialects other than High G. [L.].

GERMAN (2), adj. having the same grandparents; born of the same parents. [L.].

GERMANDER [jer-man'der], n. one of the labiate, aromatic plants of the genus Teucrium. [MedL.].

GERMANE [jer-mān'], adj. related, appropriate, pertinent. [GERMAN (2)].

GERMANIC (1) [jer-ma'nik], adj. pertaining to Germany or to the Germans; relating to the Teutonic peoples. GERMANIC (2), n. the language of the Teutonic peoples, esp. in its earliest stage. [L.].

GERMANISM [jur'ma-nizm], n. a German idiom; German quality or characteristic; love of Germany and that which is German.

GERMANIZE [jur'ma-nīz], v.t. and i. to make German.

GERMANOPHIL(E) [jer-ma'nō-fil], n. and adj. (person) fervently admiring the Germans or that which is German. [GERMAN and Gk.].

GERMANOPHOBE [jer-ma'nō-fōb], n. and adj. (person) hating Germans and things German. [GERMAN and Gk.].

GERMAN-SILVER [jer-man-sil'ver], n. alloy containing copper, zinc and nickel.

GERM-CELL [jurm'sel], n. a reproductive cell.

GERMICIDAL [jer-mi-sī'dal], adj. able to, or tending to, destroy germs.

GERMICIDE [jur'mi-sīd], n. and adj. (substance) destroying germs, esp. disease germs. [L.].

GERMINAL [jur'mi-nal], adj. pertaining to, of the nature of, a germ; (fig.) in an undeveloped, rudimentary stage. [MdL.].

GERMINATE [jur'mi-nāt], v.t. and i. to sprout, bud, begin to develop; cause to do this. GERMINATIVE [jur'mi-na-tiv], adj. pertaining to germination, able to germinate, causing germination. [L.].

GERMINATION [jer-mi-nā'shn], n. process of germinating; state or period of germinating. [L.].

GERM-PLASM [jurm'plazm], n. (biol.) that part of the nucleus of a germ-cell transmitted unchanged from generation to generation.

GERRY, see JERRY.

GERRYMANDER (1) [ge-ri-man'der], n. unfair manipulation, wangling, esp. of electoral districts in politics. GERRYMANDER (2), v.t. to manipulate unfairly, wangle. [E. Gerry, Governor of Massachusetts, who unfairly divided a county into electoral divisions].

GERUND [je'rund], n. the verbal noun in Latin, having the nature of a noun but expressing the action of a verb; the English verbal noun ending in -ing. GERUNDIAL [je-run'di-al], adj. pertaining to, or resembling, a gerund. [L.].

GERUNDIVE (1) [je-run'div], adj. pertaining to a gerund. GERUNDIVE (2), n. the verbal adjective formed from the gerund, used to indicate necessity etc. [LL.].

GESSO [je'sō], n. gypsum or plaster-of-Paris, prepared for use in sculpture and painting; a surface of this. [It. from L.].

GESTAPO [ges-tah'pō], n. Nazi secret police; any organization resembling this. [Germ.].

GESTATION [jes-tā'shn], n. act of carrying or the state of being carried in the womb; period of pregnancy. [L.].

GESTICULATE [jes-ti'kyōō-lāt], v.t. and i. to make rapid brisk movements of the arms or body as a means of emphasis or vivid expression when speaking, or as a means of communication in place of speech; express by gesture. GESTICULATOR, n. person who gesticulates. GESTICULATORY, adj. pertaining to gesticulation, representing by gesture. [L.].

GESTICULATION [jes-ti-kyōō-lā'shn], n. act of gesticulating, forceful gesture. [L.].

GESTURE (1) [jes'tyoor], n. a movement of the limbs or body, expressing an idea, feeling etc., or to emphasize what is being said, facial movement used in such a way; action performed to convey an impression or to suggest a particular attitude. GESTURE (2), v.t. and i. to make gestures; express by means of g. [MedL.].

GET (pres.pt. **getting**, pret. and p.pt. **got**) [get], v.t. to acquire possession of, procure, obtain; succeed in doing something; score; beget; put in a certain condition; persuade to do; be put into communication with; (coll.) understand; v.i. to become, grow; arrive at any place; accomplish something; undergo an experience; earn, make money; **to have got**, to own, possess; **to have got to**, (coll.) to be obliged to; **to g. about**, to resume normal activity; visit many places; **to g. along**, to depart; prosper, manage; **to g. at**, to obtain access to; reach; grasp, understand; attack; find out; suborn, influence surreptitiously; **to g. away**, to leave; escape; **to g. away with**, to succeed in making off with; pass off successfully; escape discovery in connexion with; **to g. down**, to depress; **to g. down to**, to concentrate upon; **to g. home**, to find its mark; **to g. in**, to enter; be elected; succeed in gaining admission to; **to g. in with**, to associate with; **to g. into**, to enter; put on; involve oneself in; **to g. off**, to dismount; succeed in avoiding punishment for a person; escape; **to g. off with**, to be punished leniently; (slang) flirt with, have an affair with; **to g. on**, to make progress; depart; establish friendly relations with; be successful; **to be getting on**, to fare; become old; (of the hour) be late; **to be getting on for**, (coll.) to approach; **to g. on to**, (coll.) to approach (someone) about, speak to (someone) by telephone; **to g. on with**, to be on friendly terms with; start and make progress with; **to g. over**, to surmount; recover from (a shock, illness etc.); **to g. out**, to extract; (coll.) draw up, work out; produce; (cricket) be dismissed; dismount; **to g. out of**, to escape, avoid; alight from; **to g. round**, to cajole, win the good favour of; overcome; **to g. together**, to collect; assemble; **to g. up**, to arise from bed; stand up; study, cram; develop; adorn oneself; decorate, ornament; organize; launder; **to g. up to**, to involve oneself in (mischief etc.); scheme; **to g. through**, to penetrate; succeed in an examination or test; finish; **to g. hold of**, to grasp; find; **to g. away from**, to avoid, leave behind; **to g. back**, to return, retreat; **to g. back to**, to resume; **to g. across**, (coll.) to fall into disfavour; **to g. there**, to succeed; **to tell someone where he gets off**, (coll.) to give a person a piece of one's mind, put him in his proper place. [OIcel.].

GET-AT-ABLE [get-at'a-bl], adj. accessible, that can be approached or reached.

GETAWAY [ge'ta-wā], n. (slang) escape; departure.

GETTERING [ge'te-ring], n. (radio) process of absorbing any gases remaining in a thermionic valve after exhaustion by igniting a small piece of magnesium inside the valve envelope. [Unkn.].

GET-UP [get'up], n. way in which a person is dressed, clothes; general appearance.

GEUM [jē'um], n. hardy genus of plants related to the rose. [L.].

GEW-GAW [gyōō'gaw], n. showy, worthless trifle, bauble, knick-knack. [ME.].

GEYSER [gē'zer, gā'zer, gī'zer (first sense)], n. natural jet of hot water and steam rising from a hot spring; metal cylinder in which water is heated quickly by means of lighted gas etc. [Icel.].

GHASTLY [gahst'li], adj. horrible, terrifying, death-like, pale; (coll.) dreadful, shocking; frightful. GHASTLINESS, n. condition of being g. [OE.].

GHAZI [gah'zē], n. Mohammedan fanatic; title of honour in Turkey. [Arab.].

GHEE [gē], n. in the East Indies, clarified butter made from the milk of buffaloes. [Hind.].

GHERKIN [gur'kin], n. small cucumber commonly used for pickling. [~Du.].

GHETTO [ge'tō], n. Jewish quarter in a city; (coll.) place frequented by large numbers of Jews. [It.].

GHOST (1) [gōst], n. the soul, spiritual essence of life; spirit of a dead person appearing before the living in visible form, spectre; shadow, pale, emaciated image of a person's former self; unknown person who does literary or artistic work for another who takes the credit for it; (fig.) shadowy recollections of times past; spirit of man or God; **to give up the g.**, to die; **the g. walks**, (theatrical slang) salaries are paid. GHOST (2), v.i. (coll.) to do literary or artistic work for another and under his name. [OE.].

GHOSTLY [gōst'li], adj. spiritual, relating to the soul;

The accent ′ after a syllable = stress (u-pon′). The mark ‾ over a vowel = length (ā in made; ō in bone).

holy; pertaining to, like, a ghost; shadowy, unsubstantial; suggesting the presence of ghosts. GHOSTLINESS, *n.* quality of being g. [OE.].

GHOUL [gōōl], *n.* demon in Eastern countries supposed to frequent burial places and devour corpses; *(fig.)* fiendish monster. GHOULISH, *adj.* like a g.; fiendish, cruelly horrible, gloating over misfortune to others. [Arab.].

GHYLL [gil], *n.* ravine, gully. [GILL (3)].

GIANT (1) [ji'ant], *n.* fabulous being in human form possessing extraordinary bulk, stature and strength; person of exceptional height and size; peculiarly large plant or animal; person outstanding in merit or genius. GIANT (2), *adj.* of extraordinary dimensions or proportions, enormous. [OFr.].

GIANTESS [ji'an-tes], *n.* female giant

GIANTISM [ji'an-tizm], *n.* excessive and usually misproportioned growth in man and animals, due to abnormal secretion of the pituitary gland.

GIAOUR [jow(r)], *n.* Turkish name for an unbeliever, *esp.* for a Christian. [Pers.].

GIBBER [ji'ber], *v.i.* to chatter in a rapid incoherent manner; jabber. [Imitative].

GIBBERISH [ji'be-rish], *n.* rapid, incoherent, inarticulate talk; a language unintelligible to the hearer or reader.

GIBBET (1) [ji'bet], *n.* gallows, post with an arm at the top from which the body of an executed person was hung. GIBBET (2), *v.t.* to hang on a g.; *(fig.)* exhibit to public contempt. [OFr.].

GIBBON [gi'bon], *n.* long-armed, tailless, small ape. [Fr.].

GIBBOSITY [gi-bo'si-ti], *n.* quality of being gibbous; protuberance.

GIBBOUS [gi'bŏŏs], *adj.* protuberant, convex; hump-backed; (of the moon, planets) greater than half but less than full. [L.].

GIBE (1) [jib], *v.i.* to sneer, scoff, utter a taunt; **to g. at,** to deride; gybe. GIBE (2), *n.* taunt, sneer; gybe. GIBINGLY, *adv.* in gibing fashion. [Unkn.].

GIBLETS [jib'lits], *n.(pl.)* edible, but not relished, parts of poultry, as the gizzard, liver etc. [OFr.].

GIBUS [ji'bus], *n.* collapsible opera-hat. [*Gibus,* inventor].

GIDDILY [gi'di-li], *adv.* in a giddy fashion.

GIDDINESS [gi'di-nes], *n.* quality of being giddy; vertigo.

GIDDY [gi'di], *adj.* dizzy, having the impression that stationary objects are reeling about; tending to cause vertigo; thoughtless, irresponsible, light-headed, flighty; frivolous. [OE.].

GIFT (1) [gift], *n.* that which is given, a present; natural endowment or talent, inherent aptitude; act of giving; right of giving; *(leg.)* voluntary transference to the possession of others without reasonable return; *(slang)* an easy thing, cinch. GIFT (2), *v.t.* to endow with a particular talent or aptitude. GIFTED, *adj.* having a specified g., talented. [OIcel.].

GIFT-HORSE [gift'haws], *n.* horse given as a gift; *(fig.)* favourable opportunity or chance; **look a g. in the mouth,** criticize the quality of a gift.

GIG [gig], *n.* light, two-wheeled carriage; light, speedy ship's boat; racing boat of similar design. [Uncert.].

GIGANTIC [ji-gan'tik], *adj.* like a giant, enormous, colossal. GIGANTICALLY, *adv.* in a g. fashion. [Gk.].

GIGGLE (1) [gi'gl], *v.i.* to utter nervous, partly repressed, ill-controlled bursts of laughter. GIGGLE (2), *n.* a giggling laugh. GIGGLER, *n.* one who giggles. [Imitative].

GIGOLO [ji'go-lō], *n.* hired male dancing partner, lounge lizard. [Fr.].

GIGUE [zhēg], *n.* a brisk old-fashioned dance; lively tune to which this was performed. [OFr.].

GILBERTIAN [gil-bur'ti-an], *adj.* resembling the absurd situations characteristic of the comic operas written by W. S. Gilbert.

GILD (1), see GUILD.

GILD (2) *(pret. and p.pt.* **gilded, gilt),** *v.i.* to cover with a veneer of gold leaf; colour with gold paint or any similar substance; brighten and give lustre to; adorn, add beauty to; **to g. the pill,** to make an unpleasant thing more palatable. [OE.].

GILDED [gil'did], *adj.* covered or adorned with gilt, having a golden colour; **G. Chamber,** House of Lords; **g. youth,** smart rich young men of social standing.

GILDING [gil'ding], *n.* act or process of one who gilds; gold, gold leaf, gold paint or dust laid on a substance to gild it; gilt appearance; adornment.

GILL (1) [gil], *n.* organ of respiration in fishes and water animals; flesh under the chin; plates on the underside of the head of fungus. [ME. ~ODan. ~OSwed.].

GILL (2) [jil], *n.* measure equivalent to a quarter pint liquid measure; vessel holding this amount. [ML.].

GILL (3) [gil], *n.* ravine, gully; narrow stream. [OIcel.].

GILLIE [gi'li], *n.* sportsman's outdoor attendant or servant in the Highlands. [Gael.].

GILLYFLOWER [ji'li-flow-er], *n.* one of several British flowers whose scent is similar to that of a clove; clove-pink; white stock; wallflower. [~ME. from OFr.].

GILT (1) [gilt], *n.* gold leaf, paint, dust or plate used for gilding; *(fig.)* lustre, surface beauty. [GILD].

GILT (2), *adj.* gilded.

GILT-EDGED [gilt-ejd'], *adj.* having the edges gilded; *(fig.)* extremely favourable or valuable; *(comm.)* sound, safe, reliable; **g. security,** originally Government stock, now any stock resembling this in its soundness.

GIMBALS [gim'balz], *n.(pl.)* two brass rings moving within each other, used in suspending a mariner's compass, barometer etc. in a horizontal position. [Fr. from L.].

GIMCRACK (1) [jim'krak], *n.* superficially attractive, worthless object; trifling, showy toy. GIMCRACK (2), *adj.* showy, cheap, trifling. [ME.].

GIMLET [gim'lit], *n.* boring tool consisting of a slender piece of steel terminating in a pointed spiral, and provided with a cross-handle set at right angles; **g.-eyed,** having a sharp, penetrating gaze. [ME. from OFr.].

GIMP [gimp], *n.* trimming of twisted cord, silk etc., stiffened by wire; fishing line bound with wire. [Du.].

GIN (1) [jin], *n.* spirituous liquor distilled from grain or malt and flavoured with juniper berries. GIN-FIZZ, drink consisting of g., soda-water and lemon. GIN-SLING, iced drink of g. and sweetened water, flavoured in various ways. [Fr. from L.].

GIN (2), *n.* mechanical contrivance of various kinds; snare, trap for catching game; kind of crane; machine used to remove cotton from the seeds. [ENGINE].

GINGER (1) [jin'jer], *n.* tropical aromatic plant; hot spicy root of this; *(coll.)* energy, spirit. GINGER (2), *adj. (coll.)* (of hair) bright red. GINGER (3), *v.t.* to flavour with g.; dose (a horse) with g.; *(coll.)* liven up, stir to increased activity. [OE.].

GINGER-ALE [jin-jer-āl'], *n.* sparkling aerated beverage flavoured with ginger.

GINGER-BEER [jin-jer-bēer'], *n.* aerated drink made from ginger, cream of tartar, sugar and yeast.

GINGERBREAD [jin'jer-bred], *n.* kind of cake, containing treacle and flavoured with ginger, formerly often gilded; **to take the gilt off the g.,** to disillusion. [ME. from OFr.].

GINGERLY (1) [jin'jer-li], *adj.* careful, cautious, delicate. GINGERLY (2), *adv.* in a cautious, g. way. [OFr.].

GINGER-POP [jin-jer-pop'], *n.* ginger beer.

GINGER-WINE [jin-jer-win'], *n.* brown fermented drink containing ginger.

GINGERY [jin'je-ri], *adj.* resembling ginger; spicy, pungent; of a light reddish-brown colour; *(fig.)* irascible.

GINGHAM [ging'am], *n.* cotton or linen cloth made from dyed yarn, often striped or chequered. [Malay].

GINGIVITIS [jin-ji-vī'tis], *n. (med.)* inflammation of the gums. [L. and Gk.].

GINGKO [ging'kō], *n.* Japanese tree producing fan-shaped leaves and a yellow fruit. [Jap.].

GINNING [ji'ning], *n.* process by which cotton is separated from its seeds.

GIPSY (1), **GYPSY** [jip'si], *n.* member of a wandering race of people of Indian origin; the gipsy language, Romany; *(fig.)* dark-complexioned person; untrustworthy person of erratic habits. GIPSY (2), *adj.* relating to, or resembling, the gipsies. [ME. from LL.].

GIPSY-MOTH [jip'si-moth], *n.* large species of European moth.

GIRAFFE [ji-rahf'], *n.* long-necked, four-legged animal with a spotted skin and small, narrow head. [Arab.].

GIRANDOLE [ji'ran-dōl], *n.* any of various circular objects; branched candlestick or chandelier; series of fireworks arranged to form a wheel; revolving water-jet; pendant in the form of a large central stone set round with smaller ones. [Fr.].

GIRASOL(E) [ji'ra-sol], *n.* the fire-opal. [It.].

GIRD (1) (*pret. and p.pt.* **girded, girt**) [gurd], *v.t.* to bind round with a flexible substance such as a belt etc., *esp.* at the waist; fasten by a girdle; surround, encircle; invest, endue; (*fig.*) (*reflex.*) prepare; **to g. up one's loins,** to prepare oneself for vigorous action. [OE.].

GIRD (2), *v.i.* **to g. at,** to reproach, deride, sneer at. [ME.].

GIRDER [gur'der], *n.* strong beam of wood or steel, used in building and engineering as a main support.

GIRDLE (1) [gur'dl], *n.* belt, cord or band used to encircle the waist and confine the clothing; kind of corset; (*fig.*) that which surrounds or encompasses; (*bot.*) ring round the trunk of a tree made by removing bark. GIRDLE (2), *v.t.* to bind with a g.; make a ring round a tree by removing bark; (*fig.*) surround, encompass. [OE.].

GIRDLE (3), *n.* round metal plate on which cakes may be baked over a fire. [GRIDDLE].

GIRDLING [gurd'ling], *n.* method of killing trees by removing rings of bark.

GIRL [gurl], *n.* female child; young or unmarried female; maidservant; female member of a business staff, company etc.; (*coll.*) sweetheart. [ME.].

GIRLHOOD [gurl'hŏŏd], *n.* period of being a girl.

GIRLIE [gur'li], *n.* (*coll.*) term of affection for a girl.

GIRLISH [gur'lish], *adj.* of or like a girl. GIRLISHLY, *adv.* in a g. fashion. GIRLISHNESS, *n.* quality of being g.

GIRONDIST, GIRONDIN [zhi-ron'dist, zhi-ron'dan(g)], *n.* one of the moderate Republican party in the French Revolution, called the Gironde. [Fr.].

GIRT, *pret. and p.pt. of* GIRD.

GIRTH (1) [gurth], *n.* band or strap passing under the belly of a horse or other beast of burden, by which a saddle, load etc. is made fast; measurement round that which is more or less circular or spherical, circumference, distance round the middle; (*fig.*) that which encircles. GIRTH (2), *v.t.* to put on girths, fasten by means of a g.; **to g. up,** to tighten the girths. [ME. ~OIcel.].

GIST [jist], *n.* the main point of a question or argument; essence; (*leg.*) foundation or essential point of an action. [OFr.].

GIVE (1) (*pret.* **gave,** *p.pt.* **given**) [giv], *v.t.* to convey to the possession of another without requiring a recompense, provide with; award as a punishment, pronounce a verdict; deliver into the temporary possession of; dedicate, sacrifice; impart; deliver over something in return or exchange for something else; pay; recite, sing; assign, allot; arrange, provide; portray; produce; concede, allow; announce; offer; show; attribute; *v.i.* to make donations; break down under pressure; yield slightly to pressure; **to g. away,** to transfer unconditionally; sacrifice; disclose; **to g. back,** to restore; repay; **to g. forth,** to proclaim; **to g. in,** to hand in; acknowledge oneself beaten; **to g. best to,** to acknowledge the superiority of; **to g. out,** to distribute; announce; come to an end; **to g. over,** to deliver up; refrain completely from; **to g. up,** to abandon; relinquish; regard as beyond hope of recovery etc.; confess oneself beaten; **to g. oneself up to,** to devote oneself to; **to g. one's word,** to promise faithfully; **to g. it to,** to punish severely; **to g. a horse, man, his head,** to allow to proceed without restraint; **to g. a piece of one's mind,** to say just what one thinks about a certain thing; **to g. way,** to yield; **to g. way to,** to abandon oneself to; **to g. ground,** to retreat; **to g. tongue,** to bay as a hound; **to g. rise to,** to cause, start; **to g. place to,** to be succeeded by. GIVE (2), *n.* resilience, elasticity. [OE. ~OIcel.].

GIVE AND TAKE [giv-and-tāk'], *n.* the mutual making and receiving of concessions; compromise.

GIVE-AWAY, [giv'a-wā], *n.* (*coll.*) exposure, revelation, *esp.* accidental.

GIVEN [gi'ven], *adj.* specified, stated; taken for granted; **g. to,** addicted to; **g. name,** (*Scots and U.S.*) Christian name.

GIVER [gi'ver], *n.* one who gives.

GIZZARD [gi'zerd], *n.* second stomach of a bird in which the food is ground; (*coll.*) throat; **to stick in one's g.,** to be unpalatable. [OFr.].

GLACE, glacé [gla'si], *adj* having a shiny, highly polished surface; covered with sugar, iced. [Fr.].

GLACIAL [glā'shi-al], *adj.* pertaining to, like, ice; due to ice, consisting of ice; pertaining to glaciers; geological epoch when the northern hemisphere was largely under ice. [L.].

GLACIER [gla'si-er], *n.* mass of frozen snow formed on mountains and slowly moving down along a

---

definite track, until it reaches a point at which it gradually melts. [Fr.].

GLAD (1) [glad], *adj.* pleased, relieved; happy, willing; joyful; **g. rags,** (*slang*) one's best attire; evening dress; **to give the g. eye to,** (*coll.*) to cast inviting glances at. GLAD (2), *v.t.* (*archaic*) to make g. [OE.].

GLADDEN [gla'den], *v.t. and i.* to make glad; become glad.

GLADE [glād], *n.* open space in a forest. [Uncert.].

GLADIATOR [gla'di-ā-ter], *n.* (*Rom. antiq.*) one who fought in an arena to provide entertainment; (*fig.*) warrior, contentious debater. GLADIATORIAL [gla-di-a-taw'ri-al], *adj.* relating to gladiators. [L.].

GLADIOLUS [gla-di-ō'lus], *n.* genus of sword-lilies or corn-flags. [L.].

GLADLY [glad'li], *adv.* willingly, with gladness.

GLADSOME [glad'sum], *adj.* radiating gladness, inspiring with gladness. [ME.].

GLADSTONE [glad'stun], *n.* **g. bag,** leather bag opening along the middle and secured with clasps. [W. E. *Gladstone*].

GLAIR (1) [glâer], *n.* white of egg used as a varnish; any substance resembling white of egg in character or appearance. GLAIR (2), *v.t.* to paint with g. GLAIRY, *adj.* like, painted with, g. [Fr.].

GLAMOROUS [gla'me-rŏŏs], *adj.* possessing glamour, attracting by glamour.

GLAMOUR [gla'mer], *n.* allure, charm, deceptive and fascinating quality, seductive fascination. [Scots, corruption of GRAMMAR].

GLANCE (1) [glahns], *v.t.* (*coll.*) to glimpse; (*cricket*) deflect a ball on the leg side; *v.i.* to cast a glance; strike obliquely so as to be deflected; flicker briefly; reflect bright light. GLANCE (2), *n.* brief look, hasty or furtive look; oblique impact deflecting the course of the object; swift flash of brightness; (*cricket*) stroke on the leg side by which the course of the ball is slightly diverted. GLANCINGLY, *adv.* in a glancing way. [Uncert.].

GLAND [gland], *n.* one of many animal organs attracting substances from the blood and turning them into vital chemical fluids; (*bot.*) secretory organ in plants. [Fr.].

GLANDERS [glan'derz], *n.* (*med.*) contagious and malignant disease affecting the mucous membrane in horses and communicable to man. GLANDERED, GLANDEROUS, *adj.* suffering from g. [OFr.].

GLANDULAR [glan'dyŏŏ-ler], *adj.* relating to the glands. GLANDULARLY, *adv.* from the g. aspect.

GLARE (1) [glâer], *v.i.* to give out a blinding, harsh light; blaze with vulgar brightness; stare fiercely and angrily. GLARE (2), *n.* brightness which blinds and strains the eyes; (*fig.*) annoying publicity; fierce stare. GLARY, *adj.* glaring. [ME.].

GLARING [glâer'ing], *adj.* blazing brightly, blinding; vulgar, garish; obvious, patent. GLARINGLY, *adv.* in g. fashion; (*fig.*) obviously.

GLASS (1) [glahs], *n.* brittle translucent substance made by the fusions of silicates with alkalis; object, *esp.* a drinking-vessel, made of this; such objects collectively; capacity or contents of such a vessel; mirror; magnifying lens, telescope, optical instrument; barometer; sand clock; (*pl.*) spectacles, binoculars; **ground g.,** glass so roughened as to lose its transparency. GLASS (2), *adj.* made of g.; brittle, transparent. GLASS (3), *v.t.* to cover with g. [OE.].

GLASSBLOWER [glahs'blō-er], *n.* one who shapes and moulds glass by blowing.

GLASSCLOTH [glahs'kloth], *n.* soft cloth for polishing glass.

GLASSCUTTER [glahs'ku-ter], *n.* workman employed in cutting glass into patterns or sizes; tool used for cutting glass.

GLASSFUL [glahs'fŏŏl], *n.* the quantity of liquid which fills a glass.

GLASSHOUSE [glahs'hows], *n.* hothouse; conservatory; factory where glass is made; (*fig.*) state of insecure self-satisfaction; (*slang*) military prison.

GLASSILY [glahs'si-li], *adv.* in glassy fashion.

GLASS-PAPER [glahs'pā-per], *n.* paper on which glass dust has been gummed to render it abrasive.

GLASSWARE [glahs'wâer], *n.* vessels and ornaments made from glass.

GLASSY [glahs'si], *adj.* smooth, cold and expressionless as glass; resembling glass; still and without feeling.

GLASWEGIAN [glas-wē'jan], *n. and adj.* a native of, pertaining to, Glasgow. [Uncert.].

GLAUBER'S SALT [glaw-ber-sawlt'], *n.* sulphate of sodium, an aperient. [J. *Glauber*, German chemist].

GLAUCOMA [glaw-kŏ′mah], *n.* a disease of the eyeball. GLAUCOMATOUS [glaw-kŏ′ma-tŏŏs], *adj.* relating to g. [Gk.].

GLAUCOUS [glaw′kŏŏs], *adj.* greenish-blue; (*bot.*) with a bluish bloom. [Gk.].

GLAZE (1) [glāz], *v.t. and i.* to cover with glass, fit glass to; coat or cover with a glassy surface; become glassy and expressionless. GLAZE (2), *n.* glassy surface imparted to earthenware, paper etc.; thin wash of varnish over paint; glossy surface applied to anything; shiny film; coating of jelly over cold meat. GLAZED, *adj.* coated with jelly; having a shiny surface; provided with glass windows. [ME.].

GLAZER [glā′zer], *n.* one whose trade is to glaze pottery; glazing tool.

GLAZIER [glā′zi-er], *n.* one who cuts, fits and trades in window- or picture-glass.

GLAZING [glā′zing], *n.* act of applying a glaze or fitting window-glass; substance used to glaze pottery; thin coat of varnish applied over paint.

GLAZY [glā′zi], *adj.* showing a glaze.

GLEAM (1) [glēm], *n.* transitory glint or beam of light; reflection from polished metal or glass; (*fig.*) sudden slight showing of understanding or emotion. GLEAM (2), *v.i.* to emit or reflect light; glow brightly, flash; (*fig.*) (of a quality) show itself. [ME.].

GLEAMING [glē′ming], *adj.* shining brightly.

GLEAN [glēn], *v.t. and i.* to gather up scattered ears of corn left by the reapers; gather up unconsidered leavings; (*fig.*) obtain, discover, by diligent search. GLEANING, *n.* act of one who gleans; trifle so gathered. [ME.].

GLEANER [glē′ner], *n.* one who gleans.

GLEBE [glēb], *n.* (*eccles.*) land attached to a living and held by the incumbent. [L.].

GLEE [glē], *n.* mirthful jollity, gaiety; (*mus.*) part-song for three or more voices, usually unaccompanied. [OE.].

GLEEFUL [glē′fŏŏl], *adj.* full of glee, displaying pleasure; inspiring glee. GLEEFULLY, *adv.* in g. fashion.

GLEET [glēt], *n.* morbid discharge from the urethra. [OFr.].

GLEN [glen], *n.* narrow valley in the hills. [OIr.].

GLENGARRY [glen-ga′ri], *n.* boat-shaped Highland cap. [*Glengarry*, Scotland].

GLIB [glib], *adj.* over-facile of speech, fluent, plausible. GLIBLY, *adv.* in g. fashion. GLIBNESS, *n.* quality of being g.

GLIDE (1) [glīd], *v.i.* to slide smoothly down an incline, progress easily and noiselessly; (of persons) move smoothly and silently; float easily over water; (*aeron.*) plane down or along without using the engine, or in a glider. GLIDE (2), *n.* a gliding movement, progression by gliding; easy descent; (*cricket*) glancing stroke to leg. GLIDINGLY, *adv.* by, as if by, gliding. [OE.].

GLIDER [glī′der], *n.* engineless heavier-than-air craft.

GLIM [glim], *n.* (*dial.*) light, lamp. [GLEAM].

GLIMMER (1) [gli′mer], *v.i.* to shine feebly and fitfully, flicker. GLIMMER (2), *n.* very faint gleam, fitful flicker of light; (*fig.*) faint and infrequent flicker of intelligence etc. [ME.].

GLIMMERING [gli′me-ring], *n.* glimmer; (*fig.*) faint comprehension.

GLIMPSE (1) [glimps], *v.t.* to catch sight of briefly and incompletely, perceive in a glimpse or glimpses. GLIMPSE (2), *n.* brief sight, fleeting vision; fugitive visual impression of something. [ME.].

GLINT (1) [glint], *v.i.* to flash briefly, flicker brightly and intermittently. GLINT (2), *n.* brief and intermittent flash; gleam of suppressed anger or amusement in the eye. [ME.].

GLISSADE (1) [gli-sahd′, -sād′], *n.* a downhill upright glide over snow or ice on skis; sidelong glide in dancing. GLISSADE (2), *v.i.* to execute a g. [Fr.].

GLISSANDO [gli-sahn′dŏ], *n.*, *adj. and adv.* (*mus.*) (*with*) a rapid slur or quick succession of notes. [It. from Fr.].

GLISTEN [gli′sen], *v.i.* to glitter, sparkle with reflected light. GLISTENINGLY, *adv.* in glistening fashion.

GLISTER (1) [glis′ter], *v.i.* to gleam, sparkle. GLISTER (2), *n.* a sparkle. GLISTERINGLY, *adv.* in glistering fashion. [ME.].

GLITTER (1) [gli′ter], *v.i.* to shine brightly, sparkle with light; (*fig.*) blaze with splendour, make a dazzling show. GLITTER (2), *n.* sparkle, brightness; (*fig.*) blazing splendour. [ME.].

GLITTERING [gli′te-ring], *adj.* sparkling, gleaming; falsely brilliant. GLITTERINGLY, *adv.* in g. fashion.

GLOAMING [glō′ming], *n.* (*poet.*) twilight, dusk. [Scots.].

GLOAT (1) [glōt], *v.i.* to feel or display unpleasant exultation in or over something; take pleasure in another's misfortune. GLOAT (2), *n.* act of gloating. GLOATINGLY, *adv.* in gloating fashion.

GLOBAL [glō′bal], *adj.* total, comprehensive, embracing all parts; world-wide.

GLOBE [glōb], *n.* a sphere, ball; the earth; spherical model of the earth; anything shaped like a ball; orb; spherical glass vessel. [L.].

GLOBE-TROTTER [glŏb′tro-ter], *n.* inveterate world traveller, continual sightseer.

GLOBULAR [glo′byŏŏ-ler], *adj.* having the shape of a globe, spherical. [L.].

GLOBULE [glo′byŏŏl], *n.* minute spherical particle of liquid, a drop; blood corpuscle. [L.].

GLOBULIN [glo′byŏŏ-lin], *n.* the protein constituent of haemoglobin.

GLOCKENSPIEL [glo′ken-shpēl], *n.* musical instrument played by striking a series of hanging metal bars with a hammer. [Germ.].

GLOMERATE [glo′me-rat], *adj.* accumulated, rolled together; **g. gland,** gland secreting immediately into a duct. [L.].

GLOOM (1) [glŏŏm], *n.* darkness, absence of light; despondency; conditions conducive to melancholy and depression. GLOOM (2), *v.i.* to become or to look gloomy. [ME.].

GLOOMY [glŏŏ′mi], *adj.* dark, obscure, shadowed; despondent, pessimistic; dismal. GLOOMILY, *adv.* in g. fashion. GLOOMINESS, *n.* state of being g.; conditions inducing gloom.

GLORIA [glaw′ri-ah], *n.* (*eccles.*) doxology commencing with the word *gloria*. [L.].

GLORIFICATION [glaw-ri-fi-kā′shn], *n.* act of glorifying; condition of being glorified. [L.].

GLORIFY [glaw′ri-fi], *v.t.* to magnify and worship, give praise and glory (*esp.* to God); exalt beyond reason; praise some rather sorry act or person; make more glorious, enhance. [ME. from L.].

GLORIOLE [glaw′ri-ōl], *n.* nimbus, halo. [L.].

GLORIOUS [glaw′ri-ŏŏs], *adj.* splendid, full of glory; overwhelmingly beautiful, illustrious; (*coll.*) completely satisfactory. GLORIOUSLY, *adv.* in g. fashion. GLORIOUSNESS, *n.* quality of being g. [L.].

GLORY (1) [glaw′ri], *n.* radiant, heavenly splendour; magnificent majesty; triumph; illustrious renown; brilliant beauty; nimbus. GLORY (2), *v.i.* to exult, rejoice in; boast. GLORYINGLY, *adv.* in glorying fashion. [L.].

GLORY-HOLE [glaw′ri-hōl], *n.* (*coll.*) cupboard where everything is allowed to be in disorder; cramped quarters. [Unkn.].

GLOSS (1) [glos], *n.* a comment on, explanation of, some difficulty in a text; translation of a word or short phrase; (*fig.*) excuse, explanation of bad conduct. GLOSS (2), *v.t.* to make a g. on; put as a g. for; extenuate, explain (bad conduct). [L.].

GLOSS (3), *n.* smooth sheen, bright, reflecting surface; (*fig.*) false surface lustre. GLOSS (4), *v.t.* to impart a g. to, make shiny; **to g. over,** to give a superficially fair appearance to (faults etc.). [OIcel.].

GLOSSARIAL [glo-sāer′i-al], *adj.* relating to a glossary.

GLOSSARY [glo′sa-ri], *n.* vocabulary of foreign or difficult words occurring in a text. [L.].

GLOSSILY [glo′si-li], *adv.* in glossy fashion.

GLOSSINESS [glo′si-nes], *n.* state of being glossy; gloss on a surface.

GLOSSY [glo′si], *adj.* having a smooth, highly polished surface.

GLOTTAL [glo′tal], *adj.* relating to the glottis; **g. stop,** clicking sound made by the sudden opening or closing of the glottis.

GLOTTIS [glo′tis], *n.* the opening between the vocal cords in the larynx. [Gk.].

GLOVE (1) [gluv], *n.* a covering for the hand, *esp.* one with separate compartments for the fingers; **with the gloves off,** in deadly earnest, belligerently; **to throw down the g.,** to challenge to a duel. GLOVE (2), *v.t.* to cover with a g. GLOVER, *n.* merchant or maker of gloves. [OE.].

GLOW (1) [glō], *v.i.* to give off, emit, a heat with neither flames nor smoke; feel a bodily glow; feel mental vigour, enthusiasm or pride; blaze with colour; (of the cheeks) redden. GLOW (2), *n.* red heat, combustion at great heat without flames or smoke; steady luminosity; (*fig.*) bodily feeling of warmth and satisfaction; ardent enthusiasm, fervour; intensity of colour; a blush. [OE.].

ŏŏ is pronounced as in f*oo*d; ŏŏ as in h*oo*d; th as in *th*ink; TH as in *th*at; zh as in azure. ~ = related to.

GLOWER [glow'er], *v.i.* to scowl, gaze sullenly and ominously. GLOWERINGLY [glow'er-ing-li], *adv.* in the manner of one who glowers. [ME.].

GLOWING [glō'ing], *adj.* shining with heat, in a glow; *(fig.)* ardent, enthusiastic; vivid, vehement. GLOWINGLY, *adv.* in g. fashion.

GLOW-LAMP [glō'lamp], *n.* incandescent lamp.

GLOW-WORM [glō'werm], *n.* female of a kind of beetle which emits a glow in the dark.

GLOXINIA [glok-si'ni-ah], *n.* tropical American plant. [B. *Gloxin*, German botanist].

GLOZE [glōz], *v.i.* **to g. over**, to explain away, palliate, interpret favourably. GLOZING, *n.* specious palliation, deceitful and facile explanation. [Fr.].

GLUCOSE [glōō'kōs], *n.* form of sugar made by acting upon starch with dilute sulphuric acid; diabetic sugar. [Gk.].

GLUCOSID(E) [glōō'kō-sīd], *n.* compound producing glucose by fermentation.

GLUE (1) [glōō], *n.* sticky, viscous gelatine made by boiling hides, bones etc.; any strong adhesive. GLUE (2), *v.t.* to fasten together with g., cause to adhere to; *(fig.)* have the attention fixed firmly upon; *(pass.)* be constantly associated with

GLUEY [glōō'i], *adj.* sticky, adhesive, like glue. GLUEYNESS, *n.* property of being g.

GLUM [glum], *adj.* dully sullen, silently bad-tempered or depressed, morose. GLUMLY, *adv.* in g. fashion. GLUMNESS, *n.* condition or quality of being g. [L.].

GLUT (1) [*pres.pt.* glutting, *pret. and p.pt.* glutted) [glut], *v.t.* to stuff down food; surfeit; flood the market with a superabundance of a commodity. GLUT (2), *n.* a superabundance of anything; quantity too great for consumption. [L.].

GLUTEN [glōō'ten], *n.* a viscid, albuminous substance, the protein in wheat. [L.].

GLUTINOUS [glōō'ti-nōōs], *adj.* sticky, viscous, resembling glue. GLUTINOSITY, GLUTINOUSNESS [glōō-ti-no'si-ti, glōō'ti-nōōs-nes], *n.* condition of being g.

GLUTTON [glu'ton], *n.* one who overeats grossly; *(fig.)* one who indulges excessively in anything without being sated; *(zool.)* wolverine. [L.].

GLUTTONOUS [glu'to-nōōs], *adj.* grossly greedy, given to gluttony. GLUTTONOUSLY, *adv.* in g. fashion.

GLUTTONY [glu'to-ni], *n.* gross appetite of a glutton.

GLYCERIN(E) [gli'se-rēn], *n.* sweet viscous liquid extracted from fats, used in medicine and the manufacture of explosives etc. [Gk.].

GLYCOGEN [gli'kō-jen], *n.* *(chem.)* a carbohydrate present in animal tissues.

GLYCOL [gli'kol], *n.* group of viscous, sweet-tasting alcohols, *esp.* ethylene glycol.

GLYCOSURIA [gli-kō-syōō'ri-ah], *n.* *(med.)* presence of sugar in wine. [Gk.].

GLYPHOGRAPHY [gli-fo'gra-fi], *n.* process for transforming etching into relief for printing, by means of electrotyping. [Gk.].

GLYPTIC [glip'tik], *adj.* relating to carving, *esp.* to engravings on ivory or precious stones.

GLYPTOGRAPHY [glip-to'gra-fi], *n.* study or practice of engraving upon gems. [Gk.].

GNARL [nahl], *n.* knot in wood, *esp.* on the trunk of a tree. [~OIcel.].

GNARLED [nahld], *adj.* knotted, covered with gnarls; *(fig.)* rugged, weatherbeaten of appearance and complexion.

GNASH [nash], *v.t.* to grind the teeth together with rage or emotion. [Echoic].

GNAT [nat], *n.* any of the small two-winged insects of the family *Culex*. [OE.].

GNATHIC [na'thik], *adj.* relating to the jaw. [Gk.].

GNAW [naw], *v.t. and i.* to wear away by scratching with the teeth or by biting; bite up (food) like an animal; *(fig.)* wear away; torment continually. GNAWER, *n.* one who, or that which, gnaws; a rodent. GNAWINGLY, *adv.* by gnawing. [OE.].

GNEISS [nīs], *n.* *(min.)* a metamorphic rock similar in composition to granite but with foliated structure. [Germ.].

GNOME (1) [nōm], *n.* mythical subterranean supernatural dwarf; dwarfish person resembling such a being. [Fr.].

GNOME (2), *n.* a moral aphorism. [Gk.].

GNOMIC(AL) [nō'mik(-al)], *adj.* aphoristic, didactic. [Gk.].

GNOMON [nō'mon], *n.* the rod of a sundial by whose shadow the time is shown; interpreter; *(geom.)* the

part of a parallelogram left when one quarter of it has been removed from one corner. [Gk.].

GNOSIS [nō'sis], *n.* mystical knowledge obtained by direct spiritual ecstasy and experience. [Gk.].

GNOSTIC (1) [nos'tik], *adj.* relating to gnosis and to gnosticism. GNOSTIC (2), *n.* believer in gnosticism, *esp.* a believer in the second-century gnostic heresy. [Gk.].

GNOSTICISM [nos'ti-sizm], *n.* belief in gnosis and its implications, *esp.* the philosophy built up from the combination of Christian mysticism and Platonic speculation.

GNU [nyōō], *n.* kind of antelope, the wildebeest. [Hottentot].

GO (1) (*pret.* went, *p.pt.* gone) [gō], *v.i.* to move, walk; proceed away from the speaker, depart; be educated in a place; (of machinery) work, function; break down; disappear; die; carry on, take place; become, change to; behave in a particular manner; be available for; lead to; (of wagers etc.) contract to achieve something; be sold; be put; **going to,** about to (used to express action in the near future); **to g. about,** *(naut.)* to tack; begin work upon; be current; **to g. at,** to undertake furiously; **to g. back on,** to withdraw, back down; **to g. down,** to sink; leave a university; **to g. for,** to be considered as; attack; **to g. in for,** to devote oneself to; **to g. into,** to investigate, undertake; **to g. off,** to explode; decline, decay; take place; **to g. on,** to continue; **going on for,** approaching; **to g. out,** to become extinguished; endeavour eagerly; become unfashionable; **to g. over,** to study; correct, criticize; make a (good or bad) impression; **to g. through with,** to persist to the end in; **to g. under,** to succumb; **to g. with,** to harmonize; **to g. without,** to endure the lack of. GO (2), *n.* movement, performance; undertaking, occurrence; endeavour, action; spirit, energy; bargain; **no g.,** impossible. [OE.].

GOAD (1) [gōd], *n.* sharp instrument for driving animals; *(fig.)* pressing incentive. GOAD (2), *v.t.* to drive with a g.; *(fig.)* prick on; incite, provoke. [OE.].

GO-AHEAD [gō-a-hed'], *adj.* active, pushing, ambitious.

GOAL (1) [gōl], *n.* aim, final purpose, ambition; two posts between which the ball has to be driven in various team games, score obtained by so driving the ball; mark set up at the end of a race track; winning-post. [ME.].

GOALIE [gō'li], *n.* *(coll.)* goalkeeper.

GOALKEEPER [gōl'kē-per], *n.* player guarding the goal in football and hockey.

GOAL-LINE [gōl'līn], *n.* line between the goal-posts, which is extended in either direction to mark the terminal boundary of the playing-field.

GOAL-POST [gōl'pōst], *n.* one of the two posts between which the ball must be driven in order to score.

GOAT [gōt], *n.* hollow-horned, bearded ruminant quadruped; one of the signs of the Zodiac; *(fig.)* lecher; **to get one's g.,** to make one angry; **to act the g.,** to act in a foolish, excited fashion. [OE.].

GOATEE [gō-tē'], *n.* short, straggling, goat-like beard.

GOATHERD [gōt'herd], *n.* one in charge of a herd of goats.

GOATISH [gō'tish], *adj.* like a goat, lecherous. GOATISHLY, *adv.* in g. fashion. GOATISHNESS, *n.* state of being g.

GOATSUCKER [gōt'su-ker], *n.* the nightjar.

GOB [gob], *n.* *(prov.)* large bite of food; *(slang)* mouth; *(vulg.)* globule of saliva; *(U.S.)* sailor. [OFr.].

GOBANG [gō-bang'], *n.* Japanese game played on a board. [Chin.].

GOBBET [go'bet], *n.* lump of food or spittle; small portion of something, *esp.* passage set for translation or comment in an examination. [ME.].

GOBBLE (1) [go'bl], *v.t. and i.* to bolt down food; eat rapidly and noisily. GOBBLER (1), *n.* one who gobbles. [Fr.].

GOBBLE (2), *v.i.* to utter a noise as a turkey. GOBBLE (3), *n.* gobbling sound or action. GOBBLER (2), *n.* turkey-cock. [GABBLE (1)].

GOBELIN (1) [go'be-la(ng)], *n.* fine tapestry originally made by the brothers Gobelin in 15th-century Paris. GOBELIN (2), *adj.* made by, or similar to, the work of the brothers Gobelin.

GO-BETWEEN [gō'be-twēn], *n.* an intermediary, a pander.

GOBLET [gob'lit], *n.* drinking vessel, *esp.* one without handles and with a pedestal base. [Fr.].

GOBLIN [gob'lin], *n.* ugly malicious sprite. [OFr.].

The accent ′ after a syllable = stress (u-pon′). The mark ¯ over a vowel = length (ā in made; ō in bone).

GO-CART [gō'kaht], *n.* wheeled framework in which children learn to walk; perambulator.

GOD [god], *n.* powerful supernatural being controlling an aspect of the universe, male deity; creator of the universe; (*fig.*) one of superhuman qualities or stature; idolized ideal, object of worship; **God's acre**, churchyard. [OE.].

GODCHILD [god'child], *n.* child sponsored at baptism. [ME.].

GODDAUGHTER [god'daw-ter], *n.* female godchild. [OE.].

GODDESS [go'des], *n.* female divinity; idolized woman.

GODETIA [gō-dē'shi-ah], *n.* showy annual garden flower. [*Godet*, Swiss botanist].

GODFATHER [god'fah-THer], *n.* male sponsor at baptism.

GODFEARING [god'fēer-ing], *adj.* pious.

GODFORSAKEN [god'faw-sā-ken], *adj.* abandoned, desolate.

GODHEAD [god'hed], *n.* divinity of a god or of God.

GODLESS [god'les], *adj.* impious, irreligious, atheistical. GODLESSLY, *adv.* in g. fashion.

GODLY [god'li], *adj.* pious, religious.

GODMOTHER [god'mu-THer], *n.* female sponsor at baptism.

GODPARENT [god'pāer-ent], *n.* sponsor at baptism.

GODSEND [god'send], *n.* sudden, unexpected and extremely welcome piece of good fortune.

GODSON [god'sun], *n.* male godchild.

GOD-SPEED [god-spēd'], *n.* parting wish for success.

GODWARD [god'werd], *adv.* towards God.

GODWIT [god'wit], *n.* a coastal snipe. [Uncert.].

GOER [gō'er], *n.* one who goes; fast horse; (*slang*) active, ambitious person.

GOFFER, GAUFFRE, GAUFFRE [gō'fer], *v.t.* to gather cloth in pleats. GOFFER (2), *n.* an edging of frills or pleats. GOFFERING, GAUFFERING, *n.* g. work; act of gathering in pleats. [Fr.].

GO-GETTER [gō'ge-ter], *n.* (*U S.*) person of energy and successful determination. [GO and GET].

GOGGLE [go'gl], *v.i.* to roll the eyes in amazement or terror, stare with stupid, popping eyes. GOGGLED, *adj.* staring, goggle-eyed; wearing goggles. [~Ir.].

GOGGLE-EYED [go-gl-īd'], *adj.* having staring, popping eyes.

GOGGLES [go'glz], *n.(pl.)* spectacles with guards to protect the eyes against dust and glare, worn in motor-racing etc.; (*coll.*) ordinary spectacles.

GOING (1) [gō'ing], *n.* act of progressing; departure; condition of the ground for walking, riding etc. GOING (2), *adj.* in working order; prospering.

GOITRE [goi'ter], *n.* bronchocele of the thyroid, a pathological condition accompanied by swelling in the forepart of the neck. GOITROUS, *adj.* relating to, suffering from, g. [Fr.].

GOLCONDA [gol-kron'dah], *n.* fabulous repository of enormous treasure. [*Golconda*, treasure house of the Nizam of Hyderabad].

GOLD (1) [gold], *n.* soft, heavy, yellow precious metal, chemical element Au; coins made of this; colour resembling that of the metal; (*fig.*) wealth, riches; purchasing power, prosperity; worth, virtues; (*archery*) gilt bull's-eye of the target; **g. rush**, rush to stake out claims on a newly discovered goldfield; **g. standard**, the legal fixing of a currency at an equivalent in g. GOLD (2), *adj.* made of, resembling g.; golden. [OE.].

GOLDBEATER [gold'bē-ter], *n.* craftsman who hammers gold into leaf.

GOLDCREST [gold'krest], *n.* golden-crested wren.

GOLD-DIGGER [gold'di-ger], *n.* a gold prospector; (*slang*) adventuress who wheedles money out of rich men.

GOLD-DUST [gold'dust], *n.* particles of gold sifted from the ore.

GOLDEN [gol'den], *adj.* made of gold, resembling gold in colour; (*fig.*) valuable, promising; virtuous, happy; **g. calf**, false material idol; **g. age**, period of perfection; **g. number**, number of a year as used in reckoning Easter; **g. opportunity**, best possible chance for something; **g. syrup**, refined treacle; **g. wedding**, 50th anniversary of one's wedding.

GOLDEN-ROD [gol-den-rod'], *n.* perennial yellow-flowered plant.

GOLDFIELD [gold'fēld], *n.* tract of land rich in gold-bearing ore.

GOLDFINCH [gold'finch], *n.* a gold-winged songbird.

GOLDFISH [gold'fish], *n.* small Far-eastern fish of the carp family with golden scales.

GOLD-FOIL [gold'foil], *n.* gold beaten into thin sheets, somewhat thicker than gold leaf.

GOLDILOCKS [gol'di-loks], *n.* child with golden hair; the woodland buttercup.

GOLD LEAF [gold'lēf], *n.* gold beaten into very thin sheets.

GOLD-MINE [gold'min], *n.* workings from which gold is dug; (*fig.*) very profitable enterprise.

GOLD PLATE [gold-plāt'], *n.* coating of gold plated on another metal; articles so plated; silver gilt.

GOLDSMITH [gold'smith], *n.* worker in gold, trader in gold work.

GOLDY [gol'di], *adj.* like gold, of golden colour.

GOLF (1) [golf], *n.* game in which a ball has to be struck successively into 9 or 18 holes along a specially laid-out course, by means of long clubs. GOLF (2), *v.i.* to play g. [Uncert.].

GOLF-CLUB [golf'klub], *n.* club used in striking the ball in golf; association for the purpose of playing golf; links and buildings held by such an association.

GOLFER [gol'fer], *n.* one who plays golf.

GOLF-LINKS [golf'lingks], *n.(pl.)* land laid out for golf.

GOLLIWOG [go'li-wog], *n.* grotesque black, pop-eyed doll; (*coll.*) fuzzy-haired person. [Invented].

GOLLOP [go'lop], *v.t.* (*coll.*) to swallow greedily. [Imitative].

GOLLY [go'li], *int.* (*coll.*) good God! [Amer.Negro].

GOLOSH, GALOSH [go-losh'], *n.* rubber overshoe for keeping out damp. [Fr.].

GONAD [go'nad], *n.* a reproductive gland. [Gk.].

GONDOLA [gon'do-lah], *n.* long, narrow flat-bottomed Venetian boat with a high curving prow and stern; car of an airship. [Uncert.].

GONDOLIER [gon-do-lēer'], *n.* one who propels a gondola.

GONE [gon], *p.pt.* of GO. [OE.].

GONER [go'ner], *n.* (*slang*) one inevitably doomed or ruined; one on the point of destruction or defeat.

GONFALON [gon'fa-lon], *n.* banner with several streamers, hanging from a crosspiece. [Fr. from It.].

GONG (1) [gong], *n.* metal disk with raised rim, giving out a sonorous sound when struck; (*slang*) medal. GONG (2), *v.t.* (*coll.*) to strike on a g.; (*coll.*) of police, sound a g. as a summons (to a car) to stop. [Malay].

GONIOMETER [go-ni-o'mi-ter], *n.* instrument for measuring angles, *esp.* of crystals. [Gk.].

GONOCOCCUS [go-no-ko'kus], *n.* (*path.*) the micrococcus which causes gonorrhoea. [Gk.].

GONORRHOEA [go-ne-rē'ah], *n.* contagious venereal disease symptomized by inflammation of the urethra and a morbid discharge. GONORRHOEAL, *adj.* pertaining to g. [Gk.].

GOOD (1) [good], *adj.* having worth; possessing merit or desirability; suitable for its purpose; tending to promote health, comfort etc.; virtuous, having high moral standards; well-behaved; competent, skilled; in sound condition; valid; capable of supplying, maintaining, undertaking; thorough, satisfactory; considerable; **a g. deal**, a considerable amount; **a g. many**, a considerable number; **g. for**, beneficial to; worth, able to pay; **in g. time**, punctually; **all in g. time**, in due course; **to make g.**, to compensate for (loss of), succeed in life; **to be as g. as one's word**, to keep one's promise. GOOD (2), *n.* a merit, virtue; advantage, benefit; (*pl.*) material possessions; articles of use or commerce, *esp.* other than livestock; **for g. (and all)**, finally, for ever; **the goods**, (*slang*) the real thing; **to deliver the goods**, to carry out one's promise. [OE.].

GOOD-BYE [good-bi'], *int.* farewell! as a greeting given on parting. GOOD-BYE (2), *n.* a farewell. [*Good* (*day* etc.) and (*God*) *be with you* (or *ye*)].

GOOD FELLOWSHIP [good-fe'lō-ship], *n.* conviviality, sentimentally hearty companionship.

GOOD-FOR-NOTHING [good-faw-nu'thing], *n.* and *adj.* (one who is) worthless.

GOOD-HUMOURED [good-hyōō'merd], *adj.* cheerful, good-tempered. GOOD-HUMOUREDLY, *adv* in a g. way.

GOODISH [good'ish], *adj.* (*coll.*) considerable, fair.

GOODLY [good'li], *adj.* pleasing agreeable; moderately large.

GOODMAN [good'man'], (*archaic Scots*) householder, husband, master of a house.

GOOD-NATURED [good-nā'yerd], *adj.* agreeable, naturally kindly of temper. GOOD-NATUREDLY, *adv.* in a g. way. GOOD-NATUREDNESS, *n.* state of being g.

GOODNESS [good'nes], *n.* quality of being good; holiness, moral worth; excellence of quality; that which does good, *esp.* nourishment; **for g. sake,** (*slang*) at all costs; **g** ! (*int.*) exclamation of surprise: **g. gracious** ! (*int.*) exclamation of surprise or disgust.

GOODS TRAIN [gŏŏdz′trān], *n.* train carrying only merchandise.

GOOD-TEMPERED [gŏŏd-tem′perd], *adj.* of level temper, not easily angered.

GOODWIFE [gŏŏd-wīf′], *n.* (*archaic, Scots*) mistress of a household.

GOODWILL [gŏŏd-wil′], *n.* benevolence, kindly approval; (*leg.*) that value of a business lying in its name, reputation and trade.

GOODY [gŏŏ′di], *n.* sweetmeat; person who is prim and narrow-minded; †old woman.

GOODY-GOODY [gŏŏ′di-gŏŏ-di], *n. and adj.* (one who is) primly pious, smugly narrow-minded; namby-pamby.

GOOGLY [gŏŏ′gli], *n.* (*cricket*) an off-break bowled with a leg-break action, or the reverse. [Unkn.].

GOOSE (*pl.* **geese**) [gŏŏs, gēs], *n.* web-footed bird of the genus *Anser, esp.* the domestic variety; (*coll.*) silly person; tailor's iron (*pl.* **gooses**); **to cook someone's g.,** to frustrate or deal with someone. [OE.].

GOOSEBERRY [gŏŏz′be-ri], *n.* edible berry of a thorny shrub; the shrub itself; **to play g.,** (*coll.*) to hamper a flirtation by unwelcome intrusion, to chaperon lovers; **g. fool,** dish of pulped gooseberries and cream. [GOOSE and BERRY].

GOOSE-FLESH [gŏŏs′flesh], *n.* prickly roughening of the skin in cold or fear.

GOOSEGOG [gŏŏz′gog], *n.* (*dial. and coll.*) gooseberry. [Unkn.].

GOOSE-GRASS [gŏŏs′grahs], *n.* a trailing burr-bearing weed; cleavers.

GOOSE-STEP [gŏŏs′step], *n.* German military marching step in which the legs are raised parallel to the ground at each step, without bending the knees.

GOPHER [gō′fer], *n.* small burrowing American rodent. [Fr.].

GORDIAN [gaw′di-an], *adj.* **to cut the G. knot,** to get out of a difficulty by drastic and direct means. [*Gordius,* who tied an intricate knot which no one could untie and which Alexander the Great cut with his sword].

GORE (1) [gaw(r)], *n.* human blood, *esp.* from a wound; clotted blood. [OE.].

GORE (2), *n.* wedge-shaped piece of material let into a garment to make it wider. GORE (3), *v.t.* to let a g. into a garment. [OE.].

GORE (4), *v.t.* to pierce with the horns or tusks. [OE.].

GORGE (1) [gawj], *n.* throat, food-passage; narrow, deep valley between rocks. GORGE (2), *v.t. and i.* to eat heavily and greedily, cram to repletion. GORGED, *adj.* stuffed, crammed; (*her.*) (of animals) having a collar. [Fr.].

GORGEOUS [gaw′ji-ŏŏs], *adj.* richly splendid, magnificent; (*coll.*) marvellous. GORGEOUSLY, *adv.* in g. fashion. GORGEOUSNESS, *n.* quality of being g. [OFr.].

GORGET [gaw′jet], *n.* throat armour; ornamental neck-plate; kind of ruff; coloured patch on the throat of a bird. [OFr.].

GORGON [gaw′gon], *n.* (*class. myth.*) one of three hideous woman-like creatures whose hair consisted of snakes, and whose eyes petrified all who saw them; (*fig.*) alarmingly fierce elderly woman. GORGONIZE, *v.t.* to petrify. [Gk.]

GORGONZOLA [gaw-gon-zō′lah], *n.* a highly flavoured cheese. [*Gorgonzola,* near Milan].

GORILLA [go-ri′lah], *n.* great anthropoid ape found in the Congo. [Native].

GORMAND, see GOURMAND

GORMANDIZE [gaw′man-dīz], *v.i.* to take pleasure in food; eat gluttonously. GORMANDIZER, *n.* gourmand. [Fr.].

GORSE [gaws], *n.* spiny, yellow-flowered shrub, furze; cluster of such plants. GORSY, *adj.* thick with g. [OE.].

GORY [gaw′ri], *adj.* covered with gore, bloody; (*fig.*) murderous.

GOSHAWK [gos′hawk], *n.* powerful, short-winged bird formerly used in hawking. [OE.].

GOSLING [goz′ling], *n.* young goose. [OE.].

GO-SLOW [gō-slō′], *n. and adj.* (characteristic of) a policy among workers of deliberately limiting output.

GOSPEL (1) [gos′pel], *n.* any of the first four books of the New Testament, giving the life and teachings of Christ; the portion of these read at the Communion Service each day; the teachings of Christ; statement of some absolute and holy truth. GOSPEL (2), *adj.* sacred and inviolable. [OE.].

GOSPELLER [gos′pe-ler], *n.* evangelist; priest or deacon reading the gospel for the day.

GOSSAMER [go′sa-mer], *n.* light substance formed of filmy strands of cobweb found floating or caught in bushes; anything very light, filmy and insubstantial. GOSSAMERY, *adj.* flimsy, like g. [ME.].

GOSSIP (1) [go′sip], *n.* one who gossips, busybody; unfounded rumours about others bandied about in conversation, *esp.* ill-natured tittle-tattle. GOSSIP (2), *v.i.* to chat casually and intimately; spread rumours, *esp.* ill-natured, about the private concerns of others. GOSSIPY, *adj.* of the nature of g.; fond of gossiping. [OE.].

GOT [got], *pret. and p.pt.* of GET. [ME.].

GOTH [goth], *n.* member of a Germanic people who overran much of the Roman Empire; (*fig.*) barbarous person. [Gk.].

GOTHIC (1) [go′thik], *adj.* relating to, derived from, the Goths; (*arch.*) in the late medieval style of pointed arches; (*typog.*) having heavy, complex characters as in modern German; (*fig.*) barbarous. GOTHIC (2), *n.* G. architecture; language of the Goths. GOTHICALLY, *adv.* in the G. manner. GOTHICISM [go′thi-sizm], *n.* affectation of the G. GOTHICIZE [go′thi-sīz], *v.t. and i.* to make G.; affect the G. style.

GOTTEN [go′ten], *archaic and U.S. p.pt.* of GET. [ME.].

GOUGE (1) [gowj], *n.* concave-bladed chisel used for cutting grooves. GOUGE (2), *v.t. and i.* to make grooves with a g.; prise out as if with a g.; force out the eye with the thumb. [Fr.].

GOULASH [gŏŏ′lash], *n.* rich spiced stew of meat and vegetables; (*bridge*) redeal in which the hands are not shuffled, but left arranged in order of suits. [Hung.].

GOURD [gŏŏrd], *n.* any of several plants of the order *Cucurbitaceae*; rounded fruit of such plants; drinking vessel made from the dried hollowed husk of this. [Fr.].

GOURMAND, GORMAND [gŏŏr′mahn(g)], *n.* glutton; lover of good fare. GOURMANDISM, *n.* delight in good food. [Fr.].

GOURMET [gŏŏr′mā], *n.* one with a delicate and fastidious delight in food. [Fr.].

GOUT [gowt], *n.* painful inflammation of the joints produced by an excess of uric acid. [Fr.].

GOUTY [gow′ti], *adj.* suffering from, arising from gout. GOUTILY, *adv.* in g. fashion. GOUTINESS, *n.* state of being g.; g. diseases.

GOVERN [gu′vern], *v.t. and i.* to rule, direct, control, have authority over; determine; check, restrain; (*gram.*) cause a subordinate word to adopt a certain case etc.; modify the sense or force of a statement. GOVERNABLE, *adj.* amenable to government. [Fr.].

GOVERNANCE [gu′ver-nans], *n.* (*archaic*) control, authority.

GOVERNESS [gu′ver-nes], *n.* private instructress of young children.

GOVERNING [gu′ver-ning], *adj.* controlling, ruling; exercising government.

GOVERNMENT [gu′vern-ment], *n.* act or power of governing; power, rule; governing machinery or body of a state; the state itself. GOVERNMENTAL [gu-vern-men′tal], *adj.* relating to g. or to the G. [Fr.].

GOVERNOR [gu′ver-ner], *n.* one who governs; one who exercises the supreme authority of a state in part of its territory; member of the governing body of an institution; (*mech.*) device for regulating the speed or motion of a machine; (*slang*) father, chief, sir. [OFr.].

GOVERNOR-GENERAL [gu-ver-ner-ge′ne-ral], *n.* principal governor of a subject territory; viceroy; Sovereign's representative in a British dominion.

GOVERNORSHIP [gu′ver-ner-ship], *n.* office of a governor.

GOWAN [gow′an], *n.* (*Scots*) daisy; **luckan g.,** marsh marigold. [Uncert.].

GOWK [gowk], *n.* (*Scots and northern dial.*) cuckoo; (*coll.*) clumsy, gaping adolescent. [~Olcel.].

GOWN (1) [gown], *n.* loose, body-length garment; woman's one-piece dress; academic robe; official robe of an alderman, barrister etc. GOWN (2), *v.t.* to clothe in a g. [OFr.].

GOWNSMAN [gownz′man], *n.* one in residence at a university.

GRAB (1) (*pres.pt.* **grabbing**, *pret. and p.pt.* **grabbed**

The accent ′ after a syllable = stress (u-pon′). The mark ̄ over a vowel = length (ā in made; ō in bone).

[grab], *v.t.* to snatch, seize hold of hastily and force-fully. **GRAB** (2), *n.* sudden, clutching snatch; mechanical device for clutching up rubble etc.; children's card-game which depends on speed in seizing like cards. **GRABBER**, *n.* one who, or that which, grabs. [~Swed.].

GRABBLE [gra'bl], *v.t.* to scrabble.

GRACE (1) [grās], *n.* pleasing symmetry, poise; polished elegance, felicity; clemency; respite, allowance of extra time for the fulfilment of an obligation; God's mercy; state of enjoying Divine favour; declaration of thanksgiving made at meal-times; decree granting a privilege; (*mus.*) ornamental flourish; (*myth.*) one of the goddesses of the arts; **g. note**, (*mus.*) an embellishing note. **GRACE** (2), *v.t.* to give g., charm or attractiveness to. [OFr.].

GRACEFUL [grās'fŏŏl], *adj.* displaying grace, elegant of movement, easy and pleasing in motion. **GRACE-FULLY**, *adv.* in g. fashion.

GRACELESS [grās'les], *adj.* lacking grace; beyond grace. **GRACELESSLY**, *adv.* in g. fashion. **GRACE-LESSNESS**, *n.* state of being g.

GRACIOUS [grā'shŏŏs], *adj.* exhibiting grace; dispensing grace; kindly condescending, nobly forgiving. **GRACIOUSLY**, *adv.* in g. fashion. **GRA-CIOUSNESS**, *n.* quality of being g. [OFr.].

GRADATE [gra-dāt'], *v.t.* to arrange in grades; arrange colours so that one gradually merges into another; *v.i.* to merge in gradation.

GRADATION [gra-dā'shn], *n.* series of stages of advance, gradual progression or changing by imper-ceptible degrees; regular grading in order; (*philol.*) change of vowel caused by difference of accent or tone; (*mus.*) diatonic progression of chords. **GRADA-TIONAL**, *adj.* pertaining to g. [L.].

GRADE (1) [grād], *n.* a stage in a classification; degree of rank, quality, educational proficiency etc.; (*biol.*) variation effected by crossbreeding; gradient; (*philol.*) one of the possible ways in which the vowel of a base may vary. **GRADE** (2), *v.t. and i.* to put into grades, classify; crossbreed; **make the g.** to reach a standard of success. [L.].

GRADELY (1) [grād'li], *adj.* (*dial.*) attractive, pleasant. **GRADELY** (2), *adv.* (*dial.*) decently, in handsome fashion. [ME.].

GRADIENT [grā'di-ent], *n.* slope or incline; the measurement or inclination of this.

GRADUAL (1) [gra'dyŏŏ-al], *adj.* proceeding step by step, happening slowly and by degrees; sloping gently. **GRADUAL** (2), *n.* antiphon formerly sung on the steps of the altar; book containing musical settings of parts of the Mass. **GRADUALLY**, *adv.* slowly, by degrees. [L.].

GRADUATE (1) [gra'dyŏŏ-āt], *v.t. and i.* to arrange in grades; take a degree at a university, *esp.* the Bachelor's degree; mark with gradations. **GRADUATE** (2) [gra'dyŏŏ-at], *n.* one who has graduated at a university. **GRADUATED**, *adj.* marked with gradua-tions. [MedL.].

GRADUATION [gra-dyŏŏ-ā'shn], *n.* act of graduat-ing; classification; regular progression in degree; mark indicating measure, *esp.* on a medicine bottle; state of being so marked. [L.].

GRADUATOR [gra'dyŏŏ-ā-ter], *n.* instrument for dividing lines into regular sections. [LL.].

GRADUS [grā'dus], *n.* list of Latin synonyms with quantities marked, used in writing Latin verse. [L.].

GR(A)ECISM [grē'sizm], *n.* affectation of Greek style or idiom; a Greek turn of phrase.

GR(A)ECIZE [grē'sīz], *v.t. and i.* to make Greek; put into Greek style or idiom; affect the classical.

GRAFFITO (*pl.* **graffiti**) [gra-fē'tō], *n.* a scribbling on a wall, *esp.* when ancient. [It.].

GRAFT (1) [grahft], *n.* a shoot from a plant trans-planted into another, to form a new growth; piece of living tissue used to replace injured or defective tissue; (*coll.*) payments made as a bribe; unfair influence or manipulation, political jobbery; (*Austra-lian*) hard work. **GRAFT** (2), *v.t.* to transfer as a horticultural or surgical g.; join one thing to another so that they merge; *v.i.* (*coll.*) practise g.; (*Australian*) work hard. [~OFr.].

GRAFTER [grahf'ter], *n.* one who grafts; tool used in grafting.

GRAFTING [grahf'ting], *n.* act of making a horticul-tural or surgical graft; the part so grafted.

GRAIL (1) [grāl], *n.* vessel in which Joseph of Arima-thea collected Christ's blood; a priceless object of vain quest. [OFr.].

GRAIL (2), *n.* (*eccles.*) a gradual. [OFr.].

GRAIN (1) [grān], *n.* plant-seed, cereal produce;

small round body; smallest possible quantity of anything; smallest unit of troy and apothecaries' measure; fibres of wood; direction in which the fibres run; **against the g.**, repugnant to nature. **GRAIN** (2), *v.t.* to rub down to small particles; impart a granular surface to; paint so as to represent the grain of wood. [L.].

GRAINING [grā'ning], *n.* process of surfacing in tanning; arrangement of the grain in wood; artificial reproduction of this.

GRAINY [grā'ni], *adj.* having a grain; full of grains.

GRAM (1) [gram], *n.* any pulse used as fodder for horses. [~Portug.].

GRAM (2), see GRAMME.

GRAMERCY† [gra-mur'si], *int.* many thanks. [Fr.].

GRAMINACEOUS [gra-mi-nā'shŏŏs], *adj.* relating to grasses. [L.].

GRAMINIVOROUS [gra-mi-ni've-rŏŏs], *adj.* feed-ing wholly on plants. [L.].

GRAMMALOGUE [gra'ma-log], *n.* word symbolized by a logogram. [Gk.].

GRAMMAR [gra'mer], *n.* study and history of the forms of a language; rules governing the forms of words in their relations to each other, and their arrangement as members of a sentence; treatise on this subject; (*fig.*) rudiments of a subject; **g. school**, endowed secondary day school, founded originally to instruct boys in classical g. [OFr.].

GRAMMARIAN [gra-māer'i-an], *n.* one versed in the study of grammar.

GRAMMATIC(AL) [gra-ma'tik(-al)], *adj.* conforming to the rules of grammar; relating to grammar. **GRAMMATICALLY**, *adv.* in g. fashion, according to grammar.

GRAMME, GRAM [gram], *n.* metric unit of weight, equal to the weight of one cubic centimetre of water, or 15·432 grains. [Gk.].

GRAMOPHONE [gra'ma-fōn], *n.* machine for reproducing sounds by means of a needle connected to a vibrating plate and moving across a revolving grooved disk. [Gk.].

GRAMOPHONIC [gra-ma-fo'nik], *adj.* pertaining to, resembling, a gramophone. **GRAMOPHONICALLY**, *adv.* in the manner of a gramophone.

GRAMPUS [gram'pus], *n.* the spouting whale. [~OFr. from L.].

GRANADILLA [gra-na-di'lah], *n.* fruit of the passion-flower. [Span.].

GRANARY [gra'na-ri], *n.* storehouse for grain, barn; (*fig.*) place rich in grain. [L.].

GRAND (1) [grand], *adj.* great; splendid, magnificent; important, haughty; lofty, majestic; (*slang*) ex-tremely good. **GRAND** (2), *n.* a g. piano; (*U.S. slang*) thousand dollars. [ME. from L.].

GRANDAM [gran'dam], *n.* grandmother. [AFr.].

GRAND-AUNT [grand'ahnt], *n.* sister of a grand-parent.

GRANDCHILD [grand'chīld], *n.* son's or daughter's child.

GRANDDAUGHTER [grand'daw-ter], *n.* son's or daughter's daughter.

GRAND DUCHESS [grand-du'ches], *n.* female holder of a Grand Duchy; wife of a Grand Duke.

GRAND DUCHY [grand-du'chi], *n.* Continental exalted rank of duke; honour or possessions attached to this.

GRAND DUKE [grand-dyŏŏk'], *n.* holder of a Grand Duchy.

GRANDEE [gran-dē'], *n.* Spanish noble; great and illustrious noble. [Span.].

GRANDEUR [gran'dyer], *n.* splendour, glory, magnificence; noble elevation; breadth of conception. [Fr.].

GRANDFATHER [grand'fah-THer], *n.* parent's father; **g. clock**, tall pendulum clock standing on the floor.

GRANDILOQUENCE [gran-di'lō-kwens], *n.* pom-posity of speech, bombast. [L.].

GRANDILOQUENT [gran-di'lō-kwent], *adj.* pom-pous of speech, having a lofty and exaggerated style. [L.].

GRANDIOSE [gran'di-ōs], *adj.* pretentiously im-posing, bombastic. **GRANDIOSITY** [gran-di-o'si-ti], *n.* state of being g. [Fr.].

GRANDLY [grand'li], *adv.* in grand style.

GRANDMOTHER [grand'mu-THer], *n.* mother of a parent.

GRANDNEPHEW [grand-ne'vyŏŏ], *n.* grandson of a brother or sister.

GRANDNESS [grand'nes], *n.* quality of being grand.

ŏŏ is pronounced as in food; ŏŏ as in hood; th as in *think*; TH as in *that*; zh as in azure.   ~ = related to.

GRANDNIECE [grand-nēs'], *n.* granddaughter of a brother or sister.

GRANDPARENT [grand'pãer-ent], *n.* parent's parent.

GRANDSIRE [grand'sīer], *n.* grandfather.

GRANDSON [grand'sun], *n.* son's or daughter's son.

GRANDSTAND [grand'stand], *n.* principal accommodation for spectators on a racecourse or similar arena, provided with seats in rising tiers.

GRAND-UNCLE [grand'ung-kl], *n.* grandparent's brother.

GRANGE [grānj], *n.* country house joined to farm buildings. [AFr.].

GRANGERIZE [grān'je-rīz], *v.t.* to illustrate a book by inserting pictures, cuttings etc. after publication. GRANGERISM, *n* practice of grangerizing. [James *Granger*].

GRANITE (1) [gra'nit], *n.* hard igneous rock, of granular texture. GRANITE (2), *adj.* made of g.; *(fig.)* inflexible. GRANITIC(AL) [gra-ni'tik(-al)], *adj.* relating to g. [It.].

GRANNY [gra'ni], *n.* childish abbreviation of grandmother.

GRANOLITHIC [gra-nō-li'thik], *adj. and n.* (of) concrete composed of cement and granite.

GRANT (1) [grahnt], *v.t.* to permit, concede a favour or request; confer on, award; concede a point; assume for argument's sake; *(leg.)* make a legal assignment. GRANT (2), *n.* something granted; sum of money granted to enable the pursuit of some specified object or study; *(leg.)* assignment by deed. [OFr.].

GRANTEE [grahn-tē'], *n.* *(leg.)* person to whom a grant is made.

GRANTOR [grahn-taw(r)'], *n.* *(leg.)* one who assigns.

GRANULAR [gra'nyōō-ler], *adj.* consisting of grains; grained, of rough texture. GRANULARLY, *adv.* in g. style.

GRANULARITY [gra-nyōō-la'ri-ti], *n.* state or quality of being granular.

GRANULATE [gra'nyōō-lāt], *v.t. and i.* to rub to grains; roughen; become grained, rough of surface. GRANULATED, *adj.* consisting of grains; granular.

GRANULATION [gra-nyōō-lā'shn], *n.* act of granulating; *(med.)* granular formation on the surface of a wound.

GRANULE [gra'nyōōl], *n.* tiny granular particle. [LL.].

GRAPE [grāp], *n.* fruit of the vine; the vine itself; *(coll.)* wine; grapeshot; *(pl.)* *(med.)* morbid growths on the leg of a horse.

GRAPEFRUIT [grāp'frōōt], *n.* a citrus fruit.

GRAPE-HYACINTH [grāp-hī'a-sinth], *n.* dark blue hyacinth, *Muscari.*

GRAPESHOT [grāp'shot], *n.* round of small shot in a bag fired simultaneously from a cannon.

GRAPE-VINE [grāp'vīn], *n.* vine on which grapes grow.

GRAPH [graf], *n.* linear diagram to express mathematical relationships, and based on two graduated scales. [Gk.].

GRAPHIC(AL) [gra'fik(-al)], *adj.* relating to, expressed in, writing, drawing or by visual means; *(fig.)* very vivid, realistic; *(science)* diagrammatic. GRAPHICALLY, *adv.* in g. fashion. [Gk.].

GRAPHICS [gra'fiks], *n.* art of drawing; art of calculating stresses etc., by means of graphs and geometrical plans.

GRAPHITE [gra'fīt], *n.* a form of carbon, used as pencil lead and as a lubricant.

GRAPHO-, *pref.* writing, drawing. [Gk.].

GRAPHOLOGY [gra-fo'lo-ji], *n.* art of deducing character from handwriting; art of calculating by graphs. [Gk.].

GRAPNEL [grap'nel], *n.* anchor with radiating flukes, used for grappling an enemy, or in emergency mooring. [ME. from OFr.].

GRAPPLE (1) [gra'pl], *n.* grapnel; seizure with a grapple; firm grip; fight at close quarters, wrestle. GRAPPLE (2), *v.t. and i.* to seize with a grapnel; seize in a strong, clutching hold; *(naut.)* come close to for boarding; wrestle, engage hand-to-hand; *(fig.)* get to grips (with). [OFr.].

GRAPPLING-IRON [grap'ling-īern], *n.* grapnel.

GRASP (1) [grahsp], *v.t. and i.* to seize in one's grasp, clasp firmly, clutch; comprehend, understand. GRASP (2), *n.* firm grip, clasp; firm handshake; control, power; comprehension, intellectual understanding; ability of getting. GRASPER, *n.* grasping person. [ME.].

GRASPING [grahs'ping], *adj.* meanly avaricious,

eager for gain. GRASPINGLY, *adv.* in g. fashion.

GRASS (1) [grahs], *n.* low-growing, green herbage covering the ground; *(bot.)* any plant of the monocotyledonous group of the *Gramineae*; ground covered with such herbage. GRASS (2), *v.t.* to sow with g.; shoot down an animal; land a fish. [OE.].

GRASSCUTTER [grahs'ku-ter], *n.* lawn-mower.

GRASSHOPPER [grahs'ho-per], *n.* leaping insect related to the locust. [ME.].

GRASS-SNAKE [grahs'snāk], *n.* a harmless British snake.

GRASS-WIDOW [grahs-wi'dō], *n.* wife whose husband is absent from her.

GRASS-WIDOWER [grahs-wi'dō-er], *n.* husband whose wife is absent from him.

GRASSY [grah'si], *adj.* covered with, abounding in, grass; relating to grass.

GRATE (1) [grāt], *n.* metal frame used for holding fuel in the fireplace; the fireplace itself. [ME. from LL.].

GRATE (2), *v.t. and i.* to scrape on or with a rough surface; scrape and rub into small fragments; produce a harsh noise by the friction of rough objects; produce irritation or pain by harsh sound; *(fig.)* produce an unpleasant impression (upon). [OFr.].

GRATEFUL [grāt'fōōl], *adj.* feeling or expressing gratitude; gratifying, pleasing. GRATEFULLY, *adv.* in g. fashion. GRATEFULNESS, *n.* quality of being g.

GRATER [grā'ter], *n.* rough-surfaced instrument for grating substances.

GRATIFICATION [gra-ti-fi-kā'shn], *n.* feeling of pleasurable satisfaction; act of gratifying; that which gratifies; state of being gratified. [L.].

GRATIFY [gra'ti-fī], *v.t.* to please, satisfy, make content; indulge (some desire). GRATIFIER, *n.* one who, or that which, gratifies. GRATIFYINGLY, *adv.* in gratifying fashion. [L.].

GRATIN [gra'ta(ng)], *n.* grated surface of breadcrumbs, cheese etc. topping certain dishes. [Fr.].

GRATING (1) [grā'ting], *n.* frame of parallel or intersecting bars used as the covering of a window etc.; *(opt.)* a piece of glass on which fine parallel lines have been ruled. [GRATE (1)].

GRATING (2), *adj.* producing a harsh, unpleasant sound, irritating, jarring. GRATINGLY, *adv.* in g. fashion. [GRATE (2)].

GRATIS [grā'tis], *adv.* free of charge. [L.].

GRATITUDE [gra'ti-tyōōd], *n.* thankfulness for benefits received, appreciation of the kindness of a benefactor. [LL.].

GRATUITOUS [gra-tyōō'i-tŏŏs], *adj.* free, obtained or given without payment; uncalled for, unnecessary. GRATUITOUSLY, *adv.* in g. fashion. [L.].

GRATUITY [gra-tyōō'i-ti], *n.* something given without obligation, a tip; gift made to members of the armed forces at the end of their services. [LL.].

GRATULATORY [gra'tyōō-la-te-ri], *adj.* congratulatory.

GRAVAMEN [gra-vā'men], *n.* the fundamental, substantial part (of a charge, accusation, problem); *(eccles.)* grievance laid before the Upper House of Convocation by the Lower. [LL.].

GRAVE (1) [grāv], *n.* hole dug in the ground for the burial of a corpse; mound etc. marking this; tomb, monumental place of sepulture; the g., *(fig.)* death, mortality. GRAVE-CLOTHES, winding sheets. [OE.].

GRAVE (2), *adj.* momentous, of weighty importance, ominous; serious; solemn; austere; *(mus.)* low-pitched. [L.].

GRAVE (3) [grahv], *adj.* *(gram.)* low-pitched, pronounced with a falling tone; of, or pertaining to, the symbol (`) used to denote this. [Fr.].

GRAVE (4) [grāv], *v.t. and i.* to engrave, carve; *(fig.)* impress deeply on. [OE.].

GRAVE (5), *v.t.* to clean a ship's hull and apply fresh pitch and tar to it. [OFr.].

GRAVEL (1) [gra'vel], *n.* mixture of sand and small stones used to make paths etc.; *(med.)* collection of small concretions in the bladder. GRAVEL (2) *(pres.pt.* GRAVELLING, *pret. and p.pt.* GRAVELLED), *v.t.* to cover a road with g.; *(fig.)* disconcert, nonplus. GRAVELLY, *adj.* abounding in g.

GRAVELY [grā'vli], *adv.* in grave fashion.

GRAVEN † [grā'ven], *adj.* carved, sculptured. [Old *p.pt. of* GRAVE (4)].

GRAVES (1) [grahv], *n.* a white Bordeaux wine. [*Graves*, district where grown].

GRAVES (2), see GREAVES (2).

GRAVESTONE [grāv'stōn], *n.* tombstone.

GRAVEYARD [grāv'yahd], *n.* burial ground.

GRAVING [grā'ving], *n.* act of cleaning a ship's hull

in dry dock. GRAVING-DOCK, dock into which ships are floated to be graved. [GRAVE (5).].

GRAVITATE [gra'vi-tāt], *v.t.* (*phys.*) to move according to gravity; sink, fall; (*fig.*) move naturally in a certain direction. [MdL.].

GRAVITATION [gra-vi-tā'shn], *n.* force exercised by gravity; movement impelled by gravity; act of gravitating. GRAVITATIONAL, *adj.* of, or pertaining to, gravity.

GRAVITY [gra'vi-ti], *n.* seriousness; solemnity of mien; seriousness of mind and character; (*phys.*) natural attraction of bodies by virtue of their mass, *esp.* the force by which bodies tend to move towards the centre of the earth; **specific g.**, the gravimetric proportion of substances to an equal volume of water. [L.].

GRAVY [grā'vi], *n.* juice from roasting meat; sauce consisting largely of such juice. [ME.].

GRAY, see GREY.

GRAYLING [grā'ling], *n.* freshwater fish of the trout family; a British butterfly. [GREY].

GRAZE (1) [grāz], *v.t. and i.* to feed on growing herbage; put out to grass; allot land for use as pasture. [OE.].

GRAZE (2), *v.t.* to touch lightly during passage. scrape lightly across; cause a graze in. GRAZE (3), *n.* slight scratch or contusion; very slight contact in passing. [Uncert.].

GRAZIER [grā'zi-er], *n.* one who grazes cattle or sheep.

GRAZING [grā'zing], *n.* pasturage.

GREASE (1) [grēs], *n.* animal fat obtained by melting; fat produced by cooking meat; oily matter used in the lubrication of machines; wool which has not been washed; (*med.*) inflammation of a horse's fetlock. GREASE (2), *v.t.* to coat, lubricate, with g.; put g. on.; (*slang*) bribe. [OFr.].

GREASE-GUN [grēs'gun], *n.* pump used to force lubricating grease into machinery.

GREASE-PAINT [grēs'pānt], *n.* greasy make-up used by actors.

GREASE-PROOF [grēs'prōōf], *adj.* impervious to grease.

GREASER [grē'zer], *n.* one who lubricates machinery.

GREASY [grē'zi, grē'si], *adj.* containing grease, smeared with grease; slimy, slippery; (*coll.*) unctuous, obsequious; (*naut.*) (of weather) dirty. GREASILY, *adv.* in g. fashion. GREASINESS, *n.* condition of being g.

GREAT [grāt], *adj.* large in amount, size, extent, number; of excelling qualities, exceedingly distinguished; (of nations) powerful; of high social rank; sublime; (*slang*) fine, splendid. GREAT-HEARTED, noble, magnanimous.

GREATCOAT [grāt'kōt], *n.* heavy overcoat.

GREAT-GRANDDAUGHTER [grāt-grand'daw-ter], *n.* daughter of one's grandson or granddaughter.

GREAT-GRANDFATHER [grāt-grand'fah-тнer], *n.* father of one's grandfather or grandmother.

GREAT-GRANDMOTHER [grāt-grand'mu-тнer], *n.* mother of one's grandfather or grandmother.

GREAT-GRANDSON [grāt-grand'sun], *n.* son of one's grandson or granddaughter.

GREATLY [grāt'li], *adv.* to a great extent, in great degree, style.

GREATNESS [grāt'nes], *n.* quality of being great.

GREATS [grāts], *n.* (*coll.*) School of Philosophy and Ancient History at Oxford; **Modern G.,** School of Modern Philosophy, Politics and Economics.

GREAVES (1) [grēvz], *n.(pl.)* metal armour for the leg between knee and ankle.

GREAVES (2) **GRAVES** (2) [grēvz, grāvz], *n.(pl.)* sediment of tallow used as fish bait. [LGerm.].

GREBE [grēb], *n.* a tailless diving bird. [Fr.].

GRECIAN (1) [grē'shan], *adj.* Hellenic, relating to ancient Greece. GRECIAN (2), *n.* † a Greek; scholar of ancient Greek; member of the highest form at Christ's Hospital. [OE. from Gk.].

GRECISM, see GRAECISM.

GRECIZE, see GRAECIZE.

GREED [grēd], *n.* covetousness, excessive desire to obtain; gluttony. [GREEDY].

GREEDY [grē'di], *adj.* over-eager to obtain and possess, avaricious; inclined to gluttony. GREEDY-GUTS, (*slang*) glutton. GREEDILY, *adv.* with greed. GREEDINESS, *n.* state of being g. [OE.].

GREEK (1) [grēk], *n.* a native of Greece; the language of Greece. GREEK (2), *adj.* relating to Greece, its inhabitants, culture etc.; relating to the Orthodox Church. [OE. from Gk.].

GREEN (1) [grēn], *adj.* of a colour between yellow and

blue; made up of fresh vegetables; (of a salad) consisting of leaf vegetables; of a sickly complexion; unripened, unseasoned; (*fig.*) callow, inexperienced; verdant; **g. belt,** land around a town on which building is forbidden by the local authority. GREEN (2), *n.* colour of grass and foliage; (*pl.*) vegetable leaves cooked for food; common plot of grassy ground in the middle of a village; plot of smooth grass in certain sports; smooth turf round the hole in golf; green badge of Irish Republicanism. GREEN (3), *v.t. and i.* to make or become g. [OE.].

GREENBACK [grēn'bak], *n.* (*coll.*) American banknote.

GREENERY [grē'ne-ri], *n.* mass of leafy plants.

GREENFINCH [grēn'finch], *n.* green-plumed finch. green linnet.

GREENFLY [grēn'flī], *n.* the green aphis.

GREENGAGE [grēn'gāj], *n.* sweet green plum. [Sir W. *Gage,* who introduced it into England].

GREENGROCER [grēn'grō-ser], *n.* one who trades in vegetables and fruit.

GREENHORN [grēn'hawn], *n.* (*coll.*) raw novice.

GREENHOUSE [grēn'hows], *n.* glass building used to rear delicate plants or produce fruit out of season.

GREENISH [grē'nish], *adj.* tending to greenness.

GREENROOM [grēn'rōōm], *n.* room behind the stage of a theatre for the use of the players.

GREENSTICK [grēn'stik], *n.* (*med.*) fracture occurring in young children in which part of the bone bends without breaking.

GREENSTUFF [grēn'stuf], *n.* green vegetables or grass used for food or fodder.

GREENSWARD [grēn'swawd], *n.* turf, lawn.

GREENWOOD [grēn'wōōd], *n.* leafy woodland.

GREET (1) [grēt], *v.i.* (*Scots and northern dial.*) to weep, wail, mourn. [OE.].

GREET (2), *v.t.* to address when meeting; welcome; express or feel an emotion at. [OE.].

GREETING [grē'ting], *n.* salutation on meeting. welcome.

GREGARIOUS [gre-gāer'i-ōōs], *adj.* relating to a flock; living in herds or communities; (*fig.*) fond of company, sociable. GREGARIOUSLY, *adv.* in a flock. GREGARIOUSNESS, *n.* quality of being g.

GREGORIAN [gri-gaw'ri-an], *adj.* (of a chant, tones etc.) relating to, introduced by, Pope Gregory I; (of a calendar or epoch) introduced by Pope Gregory XIII.

GREGORY-POWDER [gre'ge-ri-pow-der], *n.* aperient compounded of rhubarb and magnesia. [Dr. J. *Gregory,* its inventor].

GREMLIN [grem'lin], *n.* (*R.A.F. slang*) imp or goblin alleged to be responsible for mysterious faults in an aeroplane. [Uncert.].

GRENADE [gre-nād'], *n.* hand bomb thrown at short range; small spherical fire-extinguisher. [Span.].

GRENADIER [gre-na-dēer'], *n.* soldier throwing grenades; (*hist.*) member of the right flank company of a battalion; member of the Grenadier Guards. [Fr.].

GRENADINE (1) [gre'na-dēn], *n.* larded and glazed fricassee of veal; a scented carnation. [Fr.].

GRENADINE (2), *n.* syrup made from pomegranates; light dress material. [Fr.].

GREW [grōō], *pret. of* GROW. [OE.].

GREY (1), **GRAY** [grā], *adj.* of a colour between black and white, ashy; cloudy, sunless; (*fig.*) gloomy; dreary; hopeless; dull, lustreless; **g. matter,** (*slang*) brains. GREY (2), GRAY, *n.* colour of ashes; a g. horse; **The Greys,** 2nd Dragoons. GREY (3), GRAY, *v.t. and i.* to make or become g. [OE.].

GREYBEARD [grā'bēerd], *n.* old man; earthenware liquor jug; a straggling lichen.

GREYFRIAR [grā'frī-er], *n.* member of the Order of Franciscans; **Greyfriars,** convent of this order.

GREY-GOOSE [grā'gōōs], *n.* the greylag goose.

GREYHEN [grā'hen], *n.* female black-grouse.

GREYHOUND [grā'hownd], *n.* slender, very swift breed of dog, now bred and specialized for racing; **ocean g.,** (*fig.*) speedy liner. [OE.].

GREYISH [grā'ish], *adj.* somewhat grey.

GREYLAG [grā'lag], *n.* a migrating goose.

GRID [grid], *n.* grating; gridiron; network of wires between filament and plate of a radio valve; network of cables to distribute electricity over a wide area; network of lines to facilitate reference to a map; framework to hold luggage on a motor-car. [GRID-(IRON)].

GRIDDLE [gri'dl], *n.* iron baking-plate; mining-sieve. GRIDDLE-CAKE, oatmeal cake cooked on a g. [AFr.].

GRIDIRON [gri'diern], *n.* iron frame for grilling over

ōō is pronounced as in f*oo*d; ŏŏ as in h*oo*d; th as in *th*ink; тн as in *th*at; zh as in a*z*ure. ~ = related to

a fire; *(railways)* set of parallel rails for shunting; *(elect.)* network of power cables; framework over a stage from which are worked drop-scenes etc. [ME.].

GRID-LEAK [grid′lēk], *n.* *(elect.)* high resistance joined from grid to filament to allow the escape of electrons.

GRIEF [grēf], *n.* misfortune; sorrow; a cause of sorrow; mental distress; **to come to g.**, to fail. [OFr.].

GRIEVANCE [grē′vans], *n.* ground of complaint; injury giving ground for complaint. [OFr.].

GRIEVE [grēv], *v.t. and i.* to distress with grief, feel sorrow, lament. [OFr.].

GRIEVOUS [grē′vŏŏs], *adj.* woeful, causing grief or great distress, lamentable. GRIEVOUSLY, *adv.* in g. fashion. GRIEVOUSNESS, *n.* quality of being g. [OFr.].

GRIFFIN [gri′fin], *n.* heraldic monster, a composite of lion and eagle. [OFr.].

GRIFFON [gri′fon], *n.* small, rough-haired hunting dog. [GRIFFIN].

GRIG [grig], *n.* sand-eel; grasshopper. [Uncert.].

GRILL (1) [gril], *n.* gridiron; grill-room. GRILL (2), *v.t. and i.* to cook or be cooked on a g.; subject or be subjected to extreme heat; *(U.S.)* put through a thorough and violent cross-examination. GRILL-ROOM, room in a restaurant where food is publicly cooked on a g.; room where meals are served à la carte. [OFr.].

GRILLE [gril], *n.* crosswork of bars over an aperture, a grating. [Fr.].

GRILSE [grils], *n.* salmon in its second year. [AFr.].

GRIM [grim], *adj.* sternly fierce, ominous; horrifying, terrible; *(slang)* very unpleasant. [OE.].

GRIMACE (1) [gri-mās′], *n.* horrifying or humorous facial contortion. GRIMACE (2), *v.i.* to make a g. [Fr.].

GRIME (1) [grīm], *n.* thick, coated, ingrained dirt or soot; general filth. GRIME (2), *v.t.* to cover or coat with g. [ME.].

GRIMY [grī′mi], *adj.* covered with grime, filthy.

GRIN (1) *(pres.pt.* **grinning,** *pret. and p.pt.* **grinned)** [grin], *v.i.* to smile showing the teeth, smile crudely or with cruel delight. GRIN (2), *n.* a distorted smile; broad smile showing the teeth. [OE.].

GRIND (1) *(pret. and p.pt.* **ground)** [grīnd], *v.t. and i.* to reduce to powder or fragments by friction and pressure; shape, sharpen, roughen or make smooth by friction; grit the teeth together; *(fig.)* oppress; *(coll.)* turn the handle of a barrel-organ; toil tediously at a task. GRIND (2), *n.* act of grinding; tedious work, difficult study; gruelling race; *(slang)* steeplechase. GRINDER, *n.* one who, that which, grinds; a molar. [OE.].

GRINDSTONE [grīnd′stōn], *n.* revolving disk of hard sandstone used for grinding; *(fig.)* tedious and laborious work.

GRIP (1) [grip], *n.* a clutch, grasp, *esp.* a wrestling hold; thing meant to be gripped, handle; handbag; *(fig.)* grasp, intellectual mastery; psychological control of oneself and others; **to get to grips with**, to tackle. GRIP (2) *(pres.pt.* **GRIPPING,** *pret. and p.pt.* **GRIPPED),** *v.t. and i.* to clutch firmly, hold tightly; *(fig.)* hold the attention and interest; seize; grasp. [OE.].

GRIPE (1) [grīp], *v.t.* to distress with colic pains in the bowels; †clutch. GRIPE (2), *n.* act of griping or clutching; *(chiefly pl.)* colic; *(mech.)* brake on a wheel. [~GRIP].

GRISETTE [gri-zet′], *n.* French working-girl. [Fr.].

GRISKIN [gris′kin], *n.* loin of pork. [~OIcel.].

GRISLY [griz′li], *adj.* fear-inspiring, horrifying. GRISLINESS, *n.* quality of being g. [OE.].

GRIST [grist], *n.* ground corn; corn about to be ground. [OE.].

GRISTLE [gri′sl], *n.* animal cartilage, *esp* in food. GRISTLY, *adj.* containing g. [OE.].

GRIT (1), *n.* stone-dust, small fragments of stone; *(geol.)* hard sandstone; *(fig.)* something small which impedes action; *(coll.)* pluck, courageous endurance. GRIT (2) *(pres.pt.* GRITTING, *pret. and p.pt.* GRITTED), *v.t. and i.* to grind together, *esp.* the teeth; produce a grating noise by friction. [OE.].

GRITTY [gri′ti], *adj.* containing, full of, grit.

GRIZZLE (1) [gri′zl], *n.* grey horse. GRIZZLED, *adj.* grey; marked with grey. [OFr.].

GRIZZLE (2), *v.i.* to cry, whimper in a sullen, fretting way; grumble. [Unkn.].

GRIZZLY [griz′li], *n.* large and ferocious North American bear.

GROAN (1) [grōn], *v.i.* to utter a deep, moaning sound of sorrow, pain or distress; (of timber) creak;

(fig.) suffer and complain under oppression. GROAN (2), *n.* deep, moaning sound of pain or distress; the creaking of timber under stress; *(fig.)* loud complaint. [OE.].

GROAT [grōt], *n.* former fourpenny piece; small medieval coin of the Netherlands etc. [MDu.].

GROATS [grōts], *n.(pl.)* hulled grain. [OE.].

GROCER [grō′ser], *n.* dealer in dry stores and household necessities. [ME. from OFr.].

GROCERY [grō′se-ri], *n.* business of a grocer; *(pl.)* the goods he sells. [OFr.].

GROG [grog], *n.* rum diluted with water. [*Grogram*, nickname of Admiral Vernon].

GROGGY [gro′gi], *adj.* unsteady on the feet, shaky; not firm or well made. [GROG].

GROGRAM [grog′ram], *n* coarse material made of silk and mohair. [Fr].

GROIN [groin], *n.* that part of the body where the thighs join the abdomen; *(arch.)* intersection of two arches. GROINED, *adj.* *(arch.)* with an angular curve formed by the intersection of two arches. [ME.].

GROOM (1) [grŏŏm], *n.* man-servant in charge of horses; bridegroom; one of several officials in the Royal Household. GROOM (2), *v.t.* to rub down, brush and comb a horse; keep one's clothes and person neat and tidy; prepare (a person) for an office or employment. [ME.].

GROOMSMAN [grŏŏmz′man], *n.* person who attends the bridegroom, best man or an assistant.

GROOVE (1) [grŏŏv], *n.* furrow or elongated hollow cut by a tool; narrow channel running spirally round the bore of a gun; **to get into a g.**, to become set in habits. GROOVE (2), *v.t.* to cut a g. in. [Du.].

GROPE [grōp], *v.t. and i.* to search for one's way by touch, as though blind; *(fig.)* work cautiously towards a settlement of doubts or difficulties; fumble. GROPINGLY, *adv.* in a groping fashion. [OE.].

GROSBEAK [grōs′bēk], *n.* bird with a large, broad beak, related to the bullfinch. [Fr.].

GROSCHEN [grō′shen], *n.* former German coin. [Germ.].

GROSGRAIN [gros′grān, grō′gra(ng)], *n.* kind of corded cloth. [Fr.].

GROSS (1) [grōs], *adj.* thick, bulky, stout; coarse; vulgar, disgusting; clumsy; total, including everything; *(leg.)* inexcusable; patently obvious. GROSS (2), *n.* twelve dozen. GROSSLY, *adv.* in g. fashion. GROSSNESS, *n.* quality of being g. [Fr.].

GROT [grot], *n.* *(poet.)* grotto, cave. [It.].

GROTESQUE (1) [grō-tesk′], *n.* style of creative expression concentrating on the quaint and incongruous; work containing such elements; grotesque person. GROTESQUE (2), *adj.* (of art, ornamentation etc.) characterized by combinations of incongruities, fantastic images and bizarre extravagances; ludicrous, fantastic. GROTESQUELY, *adv.* in a g. way. GROTESQUENESS, *n.* quality of being g. [It.].

GROTTO *(pl.* **grottoes, grotts)** [gro′tō], *n.* cavern in the earth, cave with a decorative interior; miniature shrine built of shells. [It.].

GROUCH (1) [growch], *n.* grumble; *(U.S. slang)* person perpetually grumbling. GROUCH (2), *v.i.* to grumble. [GRUDGE].

GROUND (1) [grownd], *n.* the earth, land; surface of the earth; piece of land, *esp.* a field for sports; surface used as a background in painting; dominant colour in a colour scheme; foundation; intellectual basis for an argument, reason etc.; *(pl.)* estate surrounding a house; *(pl.)* undissolved particles at the bottom of a vessel containing liquid, dregs; *(pl.)* reason(s), cause, pretext; **g. frost**, frost on the surface of the ground but not in the air; **g. staff**, mechanics etc. responsible on the ground for the maintenance of aircraft; **to break g.**, to initiate a movement; **to gain, lose g.**, to advance or retreat from a point of advantage; **down to the g.**, *(coll.)* entirely, absolutely. GROUND (2), *v.t.* to place on the g.; base; educate in basic principles; *(elect.)* earth; *(naut.)* cause to run aground; *(aeron.)* prevent or prohibit from flying; *v.i.* *(naut.)* run aground. [OE.].

GROUND (3), *adj.* reduced to powder by grinding; having the surface prepared, smoothed or roughened by grinding. [GRIND].

GROUND (4), *pret. and p.pt. of* GRIND. [OE.].

GROUNDBAIT [grownd′bāt], *n.* bait dropped to the bottom of the water to attract the fish.

GROUND-BASS [grownd′bās], *n.* *(mus.)* bass of a few bars recurring as a pattern for accompaniment.

GROUND FLOOR [grownd′flaw(r)], *n.* the floor of a building level with the ground.

GROUNDING [grown′ding], *n.* act of placing on, or

The accent ′ after a syllable = stress (u-pon′).   The mark ‾ over a vowel = length (ā in made; ō in bone).

coming down to, the ground; act of preparing a surface as a ground; the prepared surface; thorough instruction in the first principles of a subject; (elect.) act of making an earth-connexion; (golf) act of touching the ground just behind the ball with one's club.

GROUNDLESS [grownd'les], adj. without reason, unfounded. GROUNDLESSLY, adv. without ground or reason. GROUNDLESSNESS, n. quality of being g.

GROUNDLING [grownd'ling], n. member of the audience who stood in the pit of an Elizabethan theatre; (fig.) person of little taste; one of several fishes which keep close to the ground.

GROUNDNUT [grownd'nut], n. South American earthnut; peanut.

GROUND PLAN [grownd'plan], n. (arch.) horizontal plan of the ground storey of a building.

GROUND-RENT [grownd'rent], n. rent paid to the owner of land for the privilege of building on it.

GROUNDSEL [grownd'sel], n. the composite plant, Senecio vulgaris. [OE.].

GROUNDSHEET [grownd'shēt], n. sheet of waterproof material for laying on the ground to protect bedding etc. from damp.

GROUNDSMAN [growndz'man], n. man responsible for looking after a sports ground.

GROUND SPEED [grownd'spēd], n. (aviation) speed of aircraft measured in terms of its position relative to the ground

GROUND-SWELL [grownd'swel], n. heavy swell of the sea continuing after the wind has fallen.

GROUNDWORK [grownd'werk], n. work which forms the foundation of anything, basis.

GROUP (1) [grōōp], n. collection or assemblage of components, cluster; number of persons having the same view or objects; aggregation of objects or organisms related to, or resembling, each other; (paint., sculp.) collection of figures or images related to one another to form an artistic whole; (geol.) the strata laid down in an era. GROUP (2), v.t. and i. to form a g.; cluster, cause to come together; classify, arrange in groups. [It.].

GROUP CAPTAIN [grōōp'kap-tin], n. commissioned rank in the R.A.F. of the same status as captain in the Navy and colonel in the Army.

GROUSE (1) [grows], n. one of several varieties of wildfowl shot as game, including the ptarmigan and the red grouse. GROUSE-SHOOTING, the shooting of driven red g. during a season beginning on 12 August. [Unkn.].

GROUSE (2), v.t. (slang) to grumble. GROUSER, n. (slang) person who grouses. [Unkn.].

GROUT (1) [growt], n. coarse liquid mortar. GROUT (2), v.t. to fill in with g. [Unkn.].

GROVE [grōv], n. small shady wood. [OE.].

GROVEL (pres.pt. grovelling, pret. and p.pt. grovelled) [gro'vel], v.i. to fawn (on someone) for favours or from fear, crawl on the earth;(fig.) abase oneself. GROVELLER, n. one who grovels. GROVELLING, adj. servile, abject. [ME.].

GROW (pret. grew, p.pt. grown) [grō], v.t. to cultivate, raise; v.i. to increase in size; flourish; be changed in condition, features etc.; increase in quantity or quality; to g. on, to gain influence over; to g. out of, to pass beyond, become too old for; to g. up, to develop to a mature stage. GROWER, n. person whose business is the cultivation of plants and produce; that which grows. [OE.].

GROWL (1) [growl], v.t. to utter a low roar of anger, fear or hostility; grumble; snarl. GROWL (2), n. low roar; angry murmur, snarl; menacing rumble. [AFr.].

GROWLER [grow'ler], n. one who growls; (slang) old-fashioned horse-drawn cab with four wheels.

GROWTH [grōth], n. act of growing; stage of development attained by an organism; increase, development; anything produced by growing; increase in size or numbers; (new) g., (path.) core of morbid tissue, cancer. [OIcel.].

GROYNE [groin], n. a barrier erected down a beach to prevent the removal of the beach by longshore drifting. [Perhaps GROIN].

GRUB (1) [grub], n. larva of an insect; (coll.) dirty small child; (cricket) ball which fails to rise after pitching when bowled; (coll.) food, tuck. [ME.].

GRUB (2) (pres.pt grubbing, pret. and p.pi. grubbed), v.i. to dig up; grope in dust or dirt; work at tedious jobs; to g. up, to dig up by the roots. GRUBBER, n. person who grubs; implement to stir up soil. [ME.].

GRUBBY [gru'bi], adj. dirty, slovenly, full of grubs. GRUBBINESS, n. condition of being g.

GRUB STREET [grub'strēt], n. street frequented in the seventeenth century by jobbing literary men; authors living by hack work. [Grub Street, now Milton Street, London].

GRUDGE (1) [gruj], v.t. to show envy and resentment at; envy a person some advantage. GRUDGE (2), n. feeling of envy, resentment, secret hostility to another person; reason or pretext for bearing ill-will. [ME.].

GRUDGING [gru'jing], adj. ungenerous, mean; ungracious, reluctant. GRUDGINGLY, adv. in a g. fashion. [ME.].

GRUEL (1) [grōō'el], n. thin porridge of meal boiled in water; to get one's g., to be severely punished, or killed. GRUEL (2) (pres.pt. GRUELLING, pret. and p.pt. GRUELLED), v.t. (slang) to treat harshly, make undergo a severe experience. [OFr.].

GRUELLING (1) [grōō'el-ing], n. (slang) exhausting punishment or defeat; harsh handling. GRUELLING (2), adj. harsh, exhausting.

GRUESOME [grōō'sum], adj. evoking horror, horrible. GRUESOMELY, adv. in a g. fashion. GRUESOMENESS, n. condition or quality of being g. [ME.].

GRUFF [gruf], adj. of a rough, surly manner; ungracious; hoarse, deep in tone. GRUFFLY, adv. in a g. fashion. GRUFFNESS n. quality of being g. [Scots].

GRUMBLE [grum'bl], v.i. to mutter complaints, murmur with discontent; rumble. GRUMBLER, n. person who grumbles. [Fr.].

GRUMPY [grum'pi], adj. surly, bad-tempered. GRUMPILY, adv. in a g. fashion. GRUMPINESS, n. state of being g. [Echoic].

GRUNDYISM [grun'di-izm], n. excessive emphasis on respectable conventions, prudery. [Mrs. Grundy, character in a play].

GRUNT (1) [grunt], v.t. and i. to make a deep guttural sound, as a hog. GRUNT (2), n. forced, throaty ejaculation; guttural sound. GRUNTER, n. person or animal that grunts. [OE.].

GRUYERE, Gruyère [grōō'yaér], n. kind of cheese with many holes. [Gruyère, district in Switzerland].

GUAIACOL [gwi'a-kol], n. liquid distilled from guaiacum and creosote, used in treating phthisis.

GUAIACUM [gwi'a-kum], n. genus of tropical American trees, the wood of one species being lignum vitae; resin of this tree used medicinally. [Span.].

GUANO [gwah'nō], n. rich manure, composed of the dung of sea-birds. [Peruvian].

GUARANTEE (1) [ga-ran-tē'], n. agreement to conclude or observe strictly some arrangement or contract; pledge or security handed over in support of this; person accepting a surety; person offering the surety; undertaking by a manufacturer to make good defects in his products. GUARANTEE (2),v.t. to take on the office of a guarantor for, give security for; protect against losses, indemnify; promise, undertake. GUARANTEED, adj. warranted; covered by g. [GUARANTY].

GUARANTOR [ga'ran-taw(r)], n. person who gives a guarantee.

GUARANTY [ga'ran-ti], n. undertaking in writing to be responsible for the liabilities of another person; promise to observe a right or agreement; pledge. [AFr.].

GUARD (1) [gahd], n. means of defence; state of watchful precaution; posture of defence; body of men keeping watch against attack or danger; sentry; armed escort in charge of prisoners etc.; official in charge of a railway train; wire frame shielding a fireplace; (pl.) regiments of household troops whose duty it was to protect the royal person; off one's g., unprepared, defenceless. GUARD (2), v.t. and i. to protect, act as g. for; restrain by watching; be on the defensive; (fencing) take up a posture of defence; to g. against, to prevent by taking precautions. [OFr.].

GUARDED [gah'did], adj. defended; discreet, circumspect. GUARDEDLY, adv. in a g. way. GUARDEDNESS, n. quality of being g.

GUARD-HOUSE [gahd'hows], n. building inhabited by the guard, or in which military prisoners are detained.

GUARDIAN (1) [gah'di-an], n. person who guards, defender; (leg.) person appointed to the legal custody of the estate, welfare and upbringing of a minor or person legally incapable of managing his affairs. GUARDIAN (2), adj. protecting, acting as a g. GUARDIANSHIP, n. office of a g.; protection.

GUARD-ROOM [gahd'rōōm], n. guard-house.

ōō is pronounced as in food; ŏŏ as in hood; th as in think; TH as in that; zh as in azure.   ~ = related to.

GUARDSMAN [gahdz'man], *n.* soldier or officer of the household troops.

GUAVA [gwah'vah], *n.* tree of the myrtle family, with a small pear-shaped fruit. [Span.].

GUBERNATORIAL [gyōō-ber-na-taw'ri-al], *adj.* belonging to government, or to a governor. [L.].

GUDGEON (1) [gu'jon], *n.* small freshwater fish allied to the carp. [Fr.].

GUDGEON (2), *n.* pivot or collar at the end of an axle; pin fixing the piston rod to the connecting rod; socket in which the rudder turns. [OFr.].

GUELDER ROSE [gel'der-rōz], *n.* the snowball tree. [Fr.].

GUELF, GUELPH [gwelf], *n.* member of a militant political party in Italy during the Middle Ages. [From Germ. *Welf*, ancestor of the family from which the Hanoverian dynasty in Britain is descended].

GUERDON [gur'don], *n.* a reward. [OFr.].

GUERILLA, see GUERRILLA.

GUERNSEY [gurn'zi], *n.* thick jersey; breed of dairy cattle. [*Guernsey*, one of the Channel Islands].

GUERRILLA, GUERILLA [ge-ri'lah], *n.* form of warfare carried on by armed bands, usually of irregulars, volunteers or insurgents, making sporadic attacks and raids; member of such a band. [Span.].

GUESS (1) [ges], *v.t. and i.* to make a judgment without real evidence; surmise, consider likely. GUESS (2), *n.* act of guessing; a conjecture. [ME.].

GUESSWORK [ges'werk], *n.* conjecture or opinion arrived at by guessing; work dependent on, or done by, guesses.

GUEST [gest], *n.* person entertained in the house or invited to a meal by another; lodger paying for accommodation at an hotel; **g. night**, night on which guests are received at a club, college etc. GUEST-HOUSE, house providing accommodation for paying guests. [OE.].

GUFFAW (1) [gu-faw'], *n.* loud vulgar laugh. GUFFAW (2), *v.i.* to utter a g. [Echoic].

GUGGLE (1) [gu'gl], *v.t.* to gurgle. GUGGLE (2), *n.* a gurgle. [Echoic].

GUIDANCE [gi'dans], *n.* act of guiding, instruction.

GUIDE (1) [gid], *n.* person who helps another by showing him the way; person who conducts visitors or sightseers; person accepted as a moral preceptor; that which directs; book containing directions; guide-book; member of the Girl Guides. GUIDE (2), *v.t.* to direct, conduct another on the way; give physical support or moral example to; control the activity of a person or country; superintend. GUIDE-BOOK, book describing places and routes. [OFr.].

GUIDON [gi'don], *n.* (*milit.*) pennant or cavalry flag with an indented fly. [Fr.].

GUILD, GILD [gild], *n.* (*hist.*) association of craftsmen following the same craft; incorporated society; **g. socialism**, form of socialism based on guilds. [ME.].

GUILDER [gil'der], *n.* Dutch silver coin. [Du.].

GUILDHALL [gild'hawl], *n.* hall in which the meetings of a guild were held; town hall; great assembly-hall of the Corporation of London.

GUILE [gil], *n.* wiliness, craft, duplicity. [OFr.].

GUILEFUL [gil'fōōl], *adj.* wily, crafty, treacherous. GUILEFULLY, *adv.* in a g. way.

GUILELESS [gil'les], *adj.* without guile, innocent.

GUILLEMOT [gi'li-mot], *n.* web-footed sea bird of the auk family. [Fr.].

GUILLOTINE (1) [gi-lo-tēn'], *n.* instrument for decapitating persons, consisting of a knife-blade running down two grooved posts towards the head-rest; machine for cutting sheets of paper evenly; surgical cutting instrument; (*Parl., coll.*) resolution to conclude a debate and take a vote at a fixed time. GUILLOTINE (2), *v.t.* to behead by means of the g.; cut with a g.; (*Parl., coll.*) to cut short (a debate) at a fixed time. [Dr. *Guillotin*, who urged its use during the French Revolution].

GUILT [gilt], *n.* fact or consciousness of having committed a crime or offence, culpability; (*leg.*) violation of criminal law; (*theol.*) sin. [OE.].

GUILTLESS [gilt'les], *adj.* free from guilt, blameless. GUILTLESSLY, *adv.* in a g. way. GUILTLESSNESS, *n.* quality of being g.

GUILTY [gil'ti], *adj.* pertaining to guilt, arising from, expressing, guilt, blameworthy; having committed a crime. [OE.].

GUINEA [gi'ni], *n.* gold coin, formerly current in Great Britain, worth 21s.; a nominal value of 21s. [Portug.].

GUINEA-FOWL [gi'ni-fowl], *n.* an African fowl of the pheasant family.

GUINEA-PIG [gi'ni-pig], *n.* small domesticated variety of rodent mammal of the genus *Cavia*; the cavy; (*slang*) one who receives a guinea as a fee for his services; one on whom experiments are performed; **g. director**, one paid for the use of his name on a board of directors.

GUINEA-WORM [gi'ni-werm], *n.* parasitic worm afflicting man and cattle.

GUIPURE [gē-pyōōr'], *n.* kind of large patterned lace; gimp. [Fr.].

GUISE [gīz], *n.* a masking of external appearance; style of dress and manner, disguise, pretence. GUISER, *n.* mummer. [OFr. from OHGerm.].

GUITAR [gi-tah(r)'], *n.* musical instrument with a flat back and six strings, played with the fingers stopping the strings against a fretted fingerboard. GUITARIST, *n.* player on a g. [Span.].

GULCH [gulch], *n.* ravine; deep bed filled by a torrent. [ME.].

GULDEN [gōōl'den], *n.* florin formerly current in Austria-Hungary; Dutch guilder. [MHGerm.].

GULES [gyōōlz], *n.* (*her.*) the colour red. [OFr.].

GULF [gulf], *n.* large deep bay; deep place in the earth, abyss; impassable barrier; whirlpool; **G. stream**, warm current crossing the Atlantic Ocean from the G. of Mexico. [OFr.].

GULL (1) [gul], *n.* any of several species of sea-bird with long wings and webbed feet. [Cornish].

GULL (2), *n.* person easily cheated, dupe. GULL (3), *v.t.* to dupe, deceive. [Uncert.].

GULLET [gu'let], *n.* passage by which food enters the stomach. [OFr.].

GULLIBLE [gu'li-bl], *adj.* able to be deceived easily, credulous. GULLIBILITY [gu-li-bi'li-ti], *n.* quality of being g. [GULL (3)].

GULLY [gu'li], *n.* small ravine or hollow worn by water; gutter; (*cricket*) a fielding position.

GULP (1) [gulp], *v.t. and i.* to swallow noisily and quickly, or convulsively and greedily; check as if by swallowing back. GULP (2), *n.* action of gulping, a swallow; noise made at the back of the throat when swallowing; large mouthful. [ME.].

GUM (1) [gum], *n.* firm flesh round each of the jaws in which the teeth are imbedded. [OE.].

GUM (2), *n.* one of the various sticky, soluble resins exuded from trees; any sticky substance for use as an adhesive; sweetmeat made of coloured gelatine; **chewing g.**, sweet with a rubbery texture made of chicle coated with sugar and flavoured; **g. arabic**, a g. extracted from kinds of acacia. GUM (3) (*pres.pt.* GUMMING, *pret. and p.pt.* GUMMED), *v.t. and i.* to smear with g ; stick, fasten, stiffen with g.; exude g. [L.].

GUMBO [gum'bō], *n.* preparation made from the young capsules of okra, stewed and served with melted butter; soup thickened with these capsules. [Native].

GUM-BOIL [gum'boil], *n.* a boil on the gum.

GUMBOOTS [gum'bōōts], *n.(pl.)* rubber boots with high leggings; waders.

GUM-DRAGON [gum'dra-gon], *n.* tragacanth.

GUM-ELASTIC [gum-i-las'tik], *n.* rubber. [MdL.].

GUMMA (*pl.* **gummata**) [gu'mah, gu'mah-tah], *n.* (*path.*) a syphilitic tumour. [L.].

GUMMY [gu'mi], *adj.* relating to, consisting of, gum; covered with gum. GUMMINESS, *n.* quality of being g.

GUMPTION [gump'shn], *n.* shrewd sense, resourceful common sense. [Scots].

GUM-RESIN [gum-re'zin], *n.* mixture of gum and resin partially soluble in water or alcohol.

GUM-TREE [gum'trē], *n.* any species of *Eucalyptus*; **to be up a g.**, (*coll.*) to be in a desperate quandary.

GUN (1) [gun], *n.* mounted tube of metal from which explosives are fired; cannon; (*coll.*) any fire-arm, including a pistol; sporting fire-arm without rifling; similar weapon fired without explosives; member of a shooting party; tool expelling some fluid or viscous substance, as paint-spray or lubricating grease; a **big g.**, (*slang*) important person; **to blow great guns**, (*naut.*) to blow a gale; **to stick to one's guns**, to hold to one's opinions in a vigorous argument. GUN (2), *v.i.* to shoot; (*fig.*) **to g. for**, (*slang*) to seek with hostile intent. [ME.].

GUNBOAT [gun'bōt], *n.* small armed vessel of light draught.

GUN-CARRIAGE [gun'ka-rij], *n.* wheel-carriage for carrying and transporting cannon.

GUN-COTTON [gun'ko-ton], *n.* high explosive obtained by saturating cotton, cellulose or any other vegetable fibre with nitro-glycerine.

The accent ' after a syllable = stress (u-pon'). The mark ¯ over a vowel = length (ă in made; ō in bone)

GUN-FIRE [gun'fier], n. the discharge of guns; (milit., naut.) the firing of guns to announce the time.
GUN-LAYER [gun'lā-er], n. one who aims a gun.
GUNMAN [gun'man], n. an armed bandit.
GUN-METAL [gun'me-tal], n. an alloy of copper and tin; metal used in cheap manufacture resembling this.
GUNNAGE [gu'nij], n. the number of guns on one ship.
GUNNEL [gu'nel], n. the butter-fish, *Centronotus gunnellus*, a kind of blenny found in the Atlantic. [Unkn.].
GUNNER [gu'ner], n. person who operates a gun; artilleryman; (naut.) warrant officer in charge of the ship's ordnance.
GUNNERY [gu'ne-ri], n. science of artillery, ballistics; the firing of guns.
GUNPOWDER [gun'pow-der], n. explosive mixture of granulated nitre, sulphur and charcoal.
GUN-ROOM [gun'rōōm], n. room in which fire-arms are stored; (nav.) junior officers' messroom.
GUN-RUNNER [gun'ru-ner], n. one who smuggles fire-arms.
GUNSHOT [gun'shot], n. the range of a gun.
GUN-SHY [gun'shī], adj. liable to take fright at the noise of shooting.
GUNSMITH [gun'smith], n. maker and repairer of small fire-arms.
GUNTER [gun'ter], n. (naut.) movable topmast; sail carried by this; **Gunter's chain**, chain 66 ft. long used for land measurement; **Gunter's line**, calculating instrument for multiplying and dividing; **Gunter's scale**, two-foot rule used in surveying and navigation. [E. *Gunter*, inventor].
GUN-TURRET [gun'tu-rit], n. armed rotating gun-emplacement in a warship, tank or aircraft.
GUNWALE, GUNNEL [gu'nl], n. (naut.) upper edge of timber running round an open boat's side; the strake immediately below the bulwarks.
GUP [gup], n. (slang) rubbish, nonsense. [Hind.].
GURGITATION [ger-ji-tā'shn], n. violent surging or boiling up of a liquid. [L.].
GURGLE (1) [gur'gl], v.i. to flow in a broken current making bubbling sounds; make a throaty gurgle or series of gurgles. **GURGLE** (2), n. bubbling sound as of rippling liquid. [OFr.].
GURKHA [gōōr'kah], n. member of a native Indian regiment from Nepal.
GURNARD [gur'nerd], n. a gurnet. [OFr.].
GURNET [gur'net], n. small sea-fish, having a large head and six feelers growing from the breast. [OFr.].
GURU [gōō'rōō], n. Indian religious teacher. [Skr.].
GUSH (1) [gush], v.i. to flood suddenly, stream out; flow in an unrestrained and copious stream; talk effusively; be extravagantly emotional, enthusiastic or sentimental. **GUSH** (2), n. sudden flood of fluid from an enclosed space; (fig.) spate of effusive phrases; outburst of insincere emotion or sentimentality. [ME.].
GUSHER [gu'sher], n. one who, or that which, gushes, esp. an oil-well which flows abundantly when first tapped.
GUSHING [gu'shing], adj. that gushes, flowing copiously; effusive, overpoweringly demonstrative. GUSHINGLY, adv. in a g. way.
GUSSET [gu'set], n. triangular piece of cloth or material let into a garment to enlarge it; iron brace for supporting corners. [OFr.].
GUST [gust], n. sudden squall, violent and sudden blast of wind; (fig.) violent outburst of passion. [OIcel.].
GUSTO [gus'tō], n. relish, enjoyment, zest. [It.].
GUSTY [gus'ti], adj. subject to gusts of wind, squally; (fig.) passionate. GUSTILY, adv. in g. fashion. GUSTINESS, n. quality of being g.
GUT (1) [gut], n. (anat.) that part of the alimentary canal extending from the pylorus to the anus; (pl.) bowels, intestines; narrow channel in a river or passage in a street; thin cord prepared from a sheep's intestines and used as a string for musical instruments etc., catgut; intestine of a silkworm used for making fishing casts; (pl.) (fig.) stamina, will-power; courage and determination; body, substance. GUT (2) (pres. pt. GUTTING, pret. and p.pt. GUTTED), v.t. to remove the guts from; (fig.) remove everything inside, esp. of a building by fire; get the essence of a book. [OE.].
GUTLESS [gut'les], adj. (coll., fig.) lacking stamina or courage.
GUTTA-PERCHA [gu-tah-pur'chah], n. hardened elastic milky juice of several Malayan trees. [Malay].
GUTTER (1) [gu'ter], n. open channel for carrying

away water, esp. a metal trough at the edge of a roof for drainage; channel in the roadway next to the pavement, down which rainwater runs; (print.) the groove between the inner margins of the open pages of a book; (fig.) the most degraded stage in the social scale; **g. press**, cheap scurrilous newspapers. GUTTER (2), v.t. and i. to provide with a g.; form into a series of small channels; (of a candle) run down one side with melted wax. [ME. from OFr.].
GUTTERING [gu'te-ring], n. action of making gutters; a system of gutters.
GUTTER-SNIPE [gu'ter-snīp], n. slum child, street arab.
GUTTURAL (1) [gu'te-ral], adj. relating to the throat; (phon.) formed in, or at the back of, the throat; (of speech) harsh, rasping. GUTTURAL (2), n. (phon.) a g. consonant or vowel. GUTTURALLY, adv. in a g. way. [L.].
GUY (1) [gī], n. rope attached to anything to guide or steady it. GUY (2), v.t. to steady by means of a rope. [OFr.].
GUY (3), n. effigy of Guy Fawkes; any absurd effigy; badly dressed person; person who is ridiculed; (U.S. slang) fellow. GUY (4), v.t. to ridicule by representing in grotesque effigy; (fig.) mock. [Guy Fawkes, who attempted to blow up the Houses of Parliament].
GUZZLE [gu'zl], v.t. and i. to swallow liquor greedily; eat or drink in noisy, gluttonous fashion. GUZZLER, n. person who guzzles. [~OFr.].
GYBE, GIBE [jīb], v.t. and i. (naut.) (of a boom or sail) to swing from one side to another when running before the wind; cause to gybe. GYBE (2), n. act or process of gybing. [JIB.].
GYM [jim], n. (coll.) a gymnasium; gymnastics.
GYMKHANA [jim-kah'nah], n. a meeting for an athletic display, esp. for races. [Hind.].
GYMNASIUM (pl. gymnasiums, gymnasia) [jim-nā'zi-um], n. hall or building specially equipped for the performance of physical exercises; (in Germany and other Continental countries) school for the higher branches of literature and science. [L.].
GYMNAST [jim'nast], n. person expert in gymnastic exercises. [Gk.].
GYMNASTIC(AL) [jim-nas'tik(-al)], adj. relating to physical exercises; (fig.) agile, quick-thinking. GYMNASTICALLY, adv. in a g. way.
GYMNASTICS [jim-nas'tiks], n.(pl.) art of teaching exercises designed to promote a perfectly developed body; gymnastic feats; feats of agility.
GYMNO- [jim'nō], pref. naked, uncovered. [Gk.].
GYNANDRIA [ji-nan'dri-ah], n.(pl.) (bot.) plants with stamens and pistils united. GYNANDROUS, adj. having stamens united with the carpels in the pistils. [Gk.].
GYNARCHY [ji'nah-ki], n. government by women. [Gk.].
GYNECOLOGICAL [gī-ni-ko-lo'ji-kal], adj. pertaining to gynecology.
GYNECOLOGIST [gī-ni-ko'lo-jist], n. specialist in gynecology.
GYNECOLOGY [gī-ni-ko'lo-ji], n. (med.) study of the diseases of women. [Gk.].
GYNO- [jī'nō], pref. woman, female. [Gk.].
GYP (1) [jip], n. (coll.) college servant at Cambridge or Durham Universities. [Uncert.].
GYP (2), n. (dial. and slang) **to give (someone) g.**, to punish or hurt someone. [~GEE-UP].
GYPSOPHILA [jip-so'fi-lah], n. genus of garden flowers having sprays of white or pink blooms. [Gk.].
GYPSUM [jip'sum], n. sulphate of lime, which when burnt yields plaster-of-Paris. [L.].
GYPSY, see GIPSY (1).
GYRATE [jī-rāt'], v.i. to revolve round a central point, whirl round. GYRATORY [ji-rā'te-ri], adj. revolving, moving in a circle. [L.].
GYRATION [ji-rā'shn], n. act or process of gyrating; (zool.) whorl of a spiral shell.
GYRO-, pref. relating to gyration. [Gk.].
GYRO-COMPASS [jī-rō-kum'pus], n. a compass controlled by one or more gyroscopes.
GYROPTER† [jī-rop'ter], n. flying machine with revolving planes; a helicopter. [Gk.].
GYROSCOPE [jī'rō-skōp], n. heavy stabilizing fly-wheel which tends to remain stationary when revolving; an adaptation of this used to stabilize ships, aircraft etc. or to keep automatic machines on a straight course. [Gk.].
GYROSTAT [jī'rō-stat], n. form of gyroscope with the fly-wheel fixed in a rigid case. [Gk.].
GYVE (1) **GIVE** [jīv], n. fetter, shackle or handcuff. GYVE (2), v.t. to shackle or bind with gyves. [AFr.].

H

H [āch], eighth letter of the English alphabet.
HA [hah], *int.* exclamation of surprise, joy, scorn, grief or laughter.
HABERDASHER [ha'ber-da-sher], *n.* dealer in drapery and small articles connected with dress-wear. [ME.].
HABERDASHERY [ha'ber-da-she-ri], *n.* goods sold by a haberdasher; business of a haberdasher.
HABERGEON [ha'ber-jon], *n.* short coat of chain mail without sleeves. [OFr.].
HABILIMENT [ha-bi'li-ment], *n.* garment, clothing. [Fr.].
HABILITATE [ha-bi'li-tāt], *v.t.* to qualify, make capable. [L.].
HABIT [ha'bit], *n.* ordinary condition or disposition of mind or body; normal behaviour; action or tendency which has become instinctive through frequent repetition; practice, custom; garment, *esp.* as distinctive of a class; wide skirt for women who ride on horseback. [L.].
HABITABLE [ha'bi-ta-bl], *adj.* capable of being dwelt in. HABITABILITY, HABITABLENESS [ha-bi-ta-bi'li-ti, ha'bi-ta-bl-nes], *n.* quality of being h. HABITABLY, *adv.* in a h. fashion. [L.].
HABITANT [ha'bi-tant], *n.* inhabitant, *esp.* [a-bi-tah(ng)'] a French Canadian. [Fr.].
HABITAT [ha'bi-tat], *n.* natural environment of an animal or plant. [L.].
HABITATION [ha-bi-tā'shn], *n.* act of inhabiting; place of abode; natural locality or environment. [L.].
HABITUAL [ha-bi'tyōō-al], *adj.* formed or acquired by habit, usual, customary; having a special tendency which recurs. HABITUALLY, *adv.* in an h. manner. HABITUALNESS, *n.* condition of being h. [L.].
HABITUATE [ha-bi'tyōō-āt], *v.t.* to accustom, make used to. HABITUATION [ha-bi-tyōō-ā'shn], *n.* state of being habituated; act of habituating. [L.].
HABITUDE [ha'bi-tyōōd], *n.* customary manner or mode; habit. [L.].
HABITUE, habitué [ha-bi'tyōō-ā], *n.* person who frequents a place, regular attender. [Fr.].
HACHURES [ha'shōōrz], *n.(pl.)* small, close-set lines of variable thickness used to indicate graphically the relief of the land on a map.
HACIENDA [(h)a-si-en'dah], *n.* (in Spain or Spanish America) stock-raising farm; estate in the country. [Span.].
HACK (1) [hak], *n.* action of hacking; cut, gash or notch, crudely made; kick on the shin. HACK (2), *v.t.* to chop with an axe; gash, notch or cut clumsily; kick the shins; break up clods of earth; rack the chest by coughing. [OE.].
HACK (3), *n.* horse kept for hire, *esp.* as a mount; horse put to all kinds of work; decrepit horse; (*fig.*) writer employed in work of poor quality or of no creative intention. HACK (4), *adj.* fit for a h.; hired out; over-worked. HACK (5), *v.t. and i.* to let out on hire; engage to do h. work; ride a h., work as a literary h. [Span.].
HACK (6), *n.* mining tool, mattock. [Germ.].
HACKING [ha'king], *adj.* harsh and dry, as a cough, racking.
HACKLE [ha'kl], *n.* long feathers on the neck of certain birds, as a cock or peacock; artificial fly made of these; comb used for treating flax. [ME.].
HACKLY [hak'li], *adj.* rough, broken crudely, jagged.
HACKNEY (1) [hak'ni], *n.* horse of medium size and quality; horse hired out as a hack; hackney-coach. HACKNEY (2), *adj.* let out on hire. [ME. from OFr.].
HACKNEY-CARRIAGE [hak'ni-ka-rij], *n.* vehicle, including a motor-car, plying for hire.
HACKNEY-COACH [hak'ni-kōch], *n.* four-wheeled horse-drawn carriage for hire.
HACKNEYED [hak'nid], *adj.* commonplace, much used, trite.
HAD [had], *pret. and p.pt.* of HAVE. [OE.].
HADDOCK [ha'dok], *n.* a sea-fish much used for food. [Unkn.].
HADES [hā'dēz], *n.* region believed to be inhabited by the dead, the underworld, hell. [Gk.].
HADJI [ha'jē], *n.* Moslem who has made a pilgrimage

to Mecca; Eastern Orthodox Christian who has made a pilgrimage to Jerusalem. [Arab.].
HAEMA-, *pref.* blood. [Gk.].
HAEMAL [hē'mal], *adj.* pertaining to the blood.
HAEMATEMESIS [hē-ma-te'mi-sis], *n.* (*med.*) vomiting of blood. [Gk.].
HAEMATIC [hē-ma'tik], *adj.* (*med.*) relating to, assembling, acting on, the blood. [Gk.].
HAEMATIN, HEMATIN [hē'ma-tin], *n.* (*chem.*) the colouring principle in blood.
HAEMATITE, HEMATITE [hē'ma-tīt], *n.* an iron ore, red or brown ferric oxide, red ochre. [Gk.].
HAEMATO-, *pref.* relating to or consisting of blood. [Gk.].
HAEMIC [hē'mik], *adj.* relating to the blood.
HAEMO-, *pref.* short form of HAEMATO-.
HAEMOGLOBIN [hē-mō-glō'bin], *n.* (*physiol.*) red substance in the red corpuscles of the blood, which takes in and distributes the oxygen. [HAEMO and GLOBE].
HAEMOPHILIA [hē-mō-fi'li-ah], *n.* (*med.*) hereditary disease marked by a tendency to excessive haemorrhage. [Gk.].
HAEMOPTYSIS [hē-mop'ti-sis], *n.* (*med.*) a coughing up of blood from the lungs. [Gk.].
HAEMORRHAGE, HEMORRHAGE [he'me-rij], *n.* (*med.*) discharge of blood from a blood-vessel, *esp.* when violent. HAEMORRHAGIC [he-me-ra'jik], *adj.* relating to h. [Gk.].
HAEMORRHOIDS, HEMORRHOIDS [he'me-roidz], *n.(pl.)* piles. HAEMORRHOIDAL [he-me-roi'dal], *adj.* relating to h. [L.].
HAFT [hahft], *n.* handle or shaft of a tool. [OE.].
HAG [hag], *n.* ugly, dirty, vindictive old woman; witch. [ME.].
HAGGARD [ha'gerd], *adj.* hollow-eyed and tired-looking, worn out, drawn, gaunt; (*falconry*) wild. HAGGARD (2), *n.* untrained hawk. [Fr.].
HAGGIS [ha'gis], *n.* Scottish dish of certain internal organs of a sheep, chopped up with oatmeal, highly seasoned and boiled in a sheep's stomach-bag. [ME.].
HAGGISH [ha'gish], *adj.* like a hag; ugly, vindictive.
HAGGLE [ha'gl], *v.i.* to argue, wrangle, bargain, *esp.* over a money payment. HAGGLER, *n.* person who haggles. [Uncert.].
HAGIARCHY [ha'gi-ah-ki], *n.* government by saints; the order of saints. [Gk.].
HAGIO-, *pref.* holy, sacred. [Gk.].
HAGIOGRAPHA [ha-gi-o'gra-fah], *n.* (*bibl.*) those Old Testament books not grouped under the Law and the Prophets. [Gk.].
HAGIOLOGY [ha-gi-o'lo-ji], *n.* study of the lives of saints; collection of writings recording the lives and traditional legends of the saints. [Gk.].
HAG-RIDDEN [hag'ri-den], *adj.* afflicted with nightmare.
HAH [hah], *int.* exclamation of surprise, triumph or effort.
HA-HA (1) [hah-hah'], *n.* a laugh. [Echoic].
HAHA (2) [hah'hah, hav'haw], *n.* low boundary fence or wall sunk between ditches. [Fr.].
HAIL (1) [hāl], *n.* round nodules of ice falling in showers from the sky, a shower of this; anything which strikes sharply in rapid succession. HAIL (2), *v.t. and i.* to hurl a rapid succession of; shower down h. [OE.].
HAIL (3), *int.* cry of greeting and salutation. HAIL (4), *v.t.* to shout or say "hail" as a greeting, salute, welcome; attract the attention of by shouting or waving; signal; *v.i.* **to h. from, to come from.** HAIL (5), *n.* action of greeting; salutation, call; range of hearing of a shout. [OIcel.].
HAIL-FELLOW [hāl'fe-lō], *n. and adj.* (befitting) an intimate companion; **h. well met,** on familiar terms.
HAILSTONE [hāl'stōn], *n.* a nodule of hail.
HAILSTORM [hāl'stawm], *n.* a storm of hail.
HAIR [hāer], *n.* one of the many fine, threadlike filaments which grow from the skin of an animal or human being; the whole growth of such filaments covering the scalp of a human being; fine fibre growing from the surface of a stem, stalk or leaf; **to keep one's h. on,** (*slang*) to remain calm; **to make one's**

The accent ' after a syllable = stress (u-pon'). The mark ‾ over a vowel = length (ā in made; ō in bone).

h. stand on end, to horrify; **not to turn a h.**, to remain composed, show no sign of fear; **to split hairs**, to argue over trivial details or over-subtle distinctions. [OE.].

HAIRBELL, see HAREBELL.

HAIRBREADTH [häer′bredth], *adj.* very narrow.

HAIRBRUSH [häer′brush], *n.* brush used for the hair.

HAIR-CLOTH [häer′kloth], *n.* textile woven chiefly of horsehair.

HAIR-CUT [häer′kut], *n.* process of having the hair cut by a hairdresser.

HAIR-DO [häer′dōō], *n.* (*coll.*) woman's style of hairdressing.

HAIRDRESSER [häer′dre-ser], *n.* barber.

HAIRINESS [häer′i-nes], *n.* condition of being hairy.

HAIRLESS [häer′les], *adj.* without hair; bald.

HAIRLINE [häer′lin], *n.* rope or line made of hair; hairstroke, very thin line.

HAIR-NET [häer′net], *n.* fine net for keeping a woman's hair in place.

HAIR-OIL [häer′oil], *n.* perfumed oil for dressing and setting the hair.

HAIR-PENCIL [häer′pen-sil], *n.* brush made of very fine hair used in water-colour painting.

HAIRPIN [häer′pin], *n.* two-pronged pin used for keeping the hair in place; **h. bend**, sharp bend in a road which almost doubles back on itself.

HAIR-RAISING [häer′rā-zing], *adj.* capable of making the hair stand on end; thrilling; frightening.

HAIRSBREADTH [häerz′bredth], *n.* the breadth of a hair; a minute distance.

HAIR-SLIDE [häer′slid], *n.* clip made of metal, tortoiseshell etc. used to keep a woman's hair in place.

HAIR-SPLITTING (1) [häer′spli-ting], *n.* the making of over-subtle distinctions in argument, quibbling. HAIR-SPLITTING (2), *adj.* characterized by quibbling.

HAIRSPRING [häer′spring], *n.* very fine spring controlling the balance-wheel of a watch.

HAIRSTROKE [häer′strōk], *n.* thin upward stroke of the pen in copy-book handwriting.

HAIR-TRIGGER [häer′tri′ger], *n.* trigger actuated by very slight pressure.

HAIRY [häer′i], *adj.* covered with, relating to or resembling, hair.

HAKE [hāk], *n.* a sea-fish allied to the cod. [ME., ~OE.].

HALATION [ha-lā′shn], *n.* (*phot.*) blurring caused by strong light reflected from the back of a negative. [HALO and -ATION.]

HALBERD [hal′berd], *n.* obsolete military weapon combining the blade of a battle-axe with a spearhead mounted on a long handle. HALBERDIER [hal-ber-dēer′], *n.* soldier armed with a h. [Uncert.].

HALCYON (1) [hal′si-on], *n.* kingfisher. HALCYON (2), *adj.* relating to the kingfisher; calm, peaceful, happy; **h. days**, 14 days divided by the winter solstice, believed in folklore always to be accompanied by fine weather, to enable the kingfisher to breed peacefully; (*fig.*) time of exceeding happiness and peace. [Gk.].

HALE (1) [hāl], *adj.* sound in body, healthy, robust, vigorous; **h. and hearty**, healthy, fit. [OE.].

HALE (2)†, *v.t.* to haul, drag along. [Fr.].

HALF (1) (*pl.* halves) [hahf, hahvz], *n.* one of two equal parts into which a thing may be divided; one of two complementary portions, weights, values, *esp.* when of the same size; (*sport*) half-back; **better h.**, (*coll.*) wife; **by halves**, not thoroughly; **to go halves**, to share equally. HALF (2), *adj.* consisting of, equal to, a h.; incomplete, imperfect. HALF (3), *adv.* in part, to the extent of a h.; imperfectly; **not h.**, (*coll.*) rather, indeed, very much. [OE.].

HALF-AND-HALF [hahf-and-hahf′], *n.* mixture of two components in equal quantities, *esp.* of stout and ale; a compromiser.

HALF-BACK [hahf′bak], *n.* player who takes up a position immediately behind the forwards at football or hockey.

HALF-BLOOD [hahf′blud], *n.* blood relationship through one parent only; person related in this way; half-breed. HALF-BLOODED, *adj.* having parents of different breeds.

HALF-BLUE [hahf-blōō′], *n.* colour awarded at Oxford or Cambridge for minor sports; representative who has won this.

HALF-BOUND [hahf-bownd′], *adj.* (*bookbinding*) bound with leather only on the back and corners.

HALF-BRED [hahf′bred], *adj.* of mixed breeding; imperfectly bred.

HALF-BREED [hahf′brēd], *n.* and *adj.* (person) whose parents are of mixed races, *esp.* of white and black races.

HALF-BROTHER [hahf′bru-THer], *n.* brother by one parent only.

HALF-CASTE [hahf′kahst], *n.* and *adj.* (person) born of a white parent and a coloured parent.

HALF-COCK [hahf′kok], *n.* position of the trigger of a gun when retained by the first notch; **to go off at h.**, (*coll.*) to act, or to be done, prematurely and so unsuccessfully.

HALF-CROWN [hahf-krown′], *n.* silver coin worth 2s. 6d.; sum of money having this value.

HALF-DOLLAR [hahf-do′ler], *n.* American coin worth 50 cents; (*coll.*) half-crown.

HALF-HEARTED [hahf-hah′tid], *adj.* unenthusiastic, not resolute, having mixed sympathies. HALF-HEARTEDLY, *adv.* in a h. manner. HALF-HEARTED-NESS, *n.* quality of being h.

HALF-HITCH [hahf′hich], *n.* kind of hitch formed by looping the rope, string etc. and drawing the end through the loop.

HALF-HOLIDAY [hahf-ho′li-dā], *n.* holiday from work or school, beginning at noon or one o'clock.

HALF-HOSE [hahf′hōz], *n.* men's socks reaching to the calf.

HALF-LENGTH [hahf′length], *n.* and *adj.* (portrait) taking in only the top half of the body.

HALF-MAST [hahf-mahst′], *adv.* (of a flag) lower than the masthead, in sign of mourning.

HALF-MOON [hahf-mōōn′], *n.* moon when only half of its face can be seen; anything in the shape of this.

HALF-MOURNING [hahf-maw′ning], *n.* mode of dress, of black relieved by white, grey or purple, worn for a period after full mourning.

HALF-NELSON [hahf-nel′sun], *n.* hold in wrestling with one arm held under the opponent's armpit while facing his rear, and the hands pressing on the nape of his neck. [NELSON.]

HALF-PAY (1) [hahf-pā′], *n.* reduced pay given to a retired officer. HALF-PAY (2), *adj.* retired on h.

HALFPENNY (1) (*pl.* halfpence, halfpennies) [hāp′ni, hā′pens], *n.* British copper coin worth half a penny. HALFPENNY (2), *adj.* of the value of half a penny; cheap, trivial, worthless.

HALF-SEAS [hahf-sēz′], *adj.* (*naut.*) halfway across the sea. HALF-SEAS-OVER, (*slang*) almost drunk.

HALF-SISTER [hahf′sister], *n.* sister by one parent only.

HALF-SOVEREIGN [hahf-sov′rin], *n.* (gold coin worth) ten shillings.

HALF-TIMBERED [hahf-tim′berd], *adj.* (*arch.*) having the main supports of a wall in timber, and the remaining parts filled in with brick, stone or plaster.

HALF-TIME [hahf-tim′], *n.* half the usual working time; interval between the two halves of a game of football etc.

HALF-TONE [hahf′tōn], *n.* process block obtained by photographing the drawing or other object through a glass screen covered with a network of fine lines.

HALF-TRACK [hahf′trak], *n.* (*orig. U.S.*) motor truck having a short caterpillar track instead of back wheels.

HALF-VOLLEY [hahf-vo′li], *n.* (*sport*) stroke made, kick taken, when the ball has just left the ground.

HALFWAY [hahf-wā′], *adj.* and *adv.* equally distant from the extremes, in the middle.

HALF-WIT [hahf′wit], *n.* an imbecile, fool. HALF-WITTED, *adj.* mentally deficient, foolish.

HALF-YEARLY [hahf-yēer′li], *adj.* and *adv.* (occurring) every half-year.

HALIBUT [ha′li-but], *n.* an edible fish, the largest of the flatfish. [ME.].

HALIDOM† [ha′li-dum], *n.* holy relic; anything sacred. [OE.].

HALITOSIS [ha-li-tō′sis], *n.* (*med.*) bad breath. [L.].

HALL [hawl], *n.* formerly, large chamber used as a living-room in a castle etc.; spacious dining-room in a palace or castle; apartment, corridor or passage into which the entrance opens; mansion, large residence; public building used for municipal administrative purposes, assemblies etc.; college.

HALLELUJAH, HALLELUIAH [ha-li-lōō′yah], *int.* word of praise used in religious worship as a shout, peal or refrain. [Heb.].

HALLIARD, see HALYARD.

HALL-MARK (1) [hawl′mahk], *n.* small embossed mark stamped on gold, silver or plate, *esp.* at Goldsmiths' Hall, as an official guarantee of quality; (*fig.*) any sign of distinction or characteristic of quality.

ōō is pronounced as in food; ŏŏ as in hood; th as in think; TH as in that; zh as in azure.   ~ = related to.

HALL-MARK (2), *v.t.* to stamp gold, silver or plate with the official h.; (*fig.*) provide with a guarantee of high quality.

HALLO [ha-lō', hu-lō'], *int.* an introductory remark when meeting someone; call for attention. [Echoic].

HALLOO (1) [ha-lōō'], *n.* cry to attract the attention of someone in the distance; call to hounds at a hunt. HALLOO (2), *v.t. and i.* to stimulate a pack of hounds to the chase; shout halloos; shout. [ME.].

HALLOW [ha'lō], *v.t.* to set apart for sacred use; consecrate; regard as sacred; render holy. [OE.].

HALLOWEEN [ha-lō-ēn'], *n.* eve of All Saints' Day, falling on 31 October. [HALLOW and E(V)EN].

HALLUCINATION [ha-lyōō-si-nā'shn], *n.* effect of a deranged mind by which the senses create and present to themselves an object which in reality does not exist; object of such a subjective perception. HALLUCINATORY [ha-lyōō'si-nā-te-ri], *adj.* resembling, or pertaining to, an h. [L.].

HALM, see HAULM.

HALMA [hal'mah], *n.* game for 2 or 4 players on a board of 256 squares. [Gk.].

HALO [hā'lō], *n.* luminous circle surrounding the sun or moon; ring of light or a white, gold or silver disk encircling the head of Christ, a saint etc., in paintings; (*fig.*) glory or attractiveness associated with a romantic ideal, act etc. [Gk.].

HALT (1) [hawlt], *n.* temporary stoppage of any act of work or movement; pause; place to stop at, stage on a route where buses etc. stop to pick up passengers; small wayside railway station. HALT (2), *v.t. and i.* (*milit.*) to bring a body of troops to a h. by a command; cease marching, moving or any activity for the time being. [Fr.].

HALT (3), [*adj.* lame, crippled. HALT (4) *v.i.* to be lame, walk with a limp; (*fig.*) hesitate; speak falteringly; be faulty in metre. [OE.].

HALTER (1) [hawl'ter], *n.* short rope for leading a horse; rope ending in a slip noose for hanging condemned persons. HALTER (2), *v.t.* to put a h. on; bind with a h. [OE.].

HALTING [hawl'ting], *adj.* stumbling, faltering, hesitating. HALTINGLY, *adv.* in h. fashion.

HALVE [hahv], *v.t.* to divide into two equal parts; lessen to a half; offer or take an equal share; to h. a hole or match, (*golf*) to complete the hole or match in an equal number of strokes or holes. [ME.].

HALYARD, HALLIARD [hal'yahd], *n.* (*naut.*) rope for hoisting flags or sails up the mast. [ME.].

HAM [ham], *n.* inner or hind part of the thigh; thigh of an animal, *esp.* of a pig, salted and dried in smoke; portion or dish of slices of this meat; h. actor, (*slang*) actor so bad as to be absurd. [OE.].

HAMADRYAD [ha-ma-drī'ad], *n.* (*myth.*) woodnymph believed to live in a tree and die with it; (*zool.*) Indian king cobra; Arabian baboon. [Gk.].

HAMBURGER [ham'ber-ger], *n.* steak of minced beef usually cooked or eaten with onions; kind of breakfast sausage. [*Hamburg*, Germany].

HAMITE [ha'mīt], *n.* member of a race supposed to be descended from Noah's son, Ham, including Egyptians and Somalis. HAMITIC [ha-mi'tik], *adj.* relating to the Hamites or their languages.

HAMLET [ham'lit], *n.* small village; group of cottages in the country. [AFr.].

HAMMER (1) [ha'mer], *n.* tool for striking, beating, or driving in by blows; anything which resembles this in function; one of the mechanical felted heads of a piano action; striking device of a bell; auctioneer's mallet; heavy piece of machinery for crushing, beating etc.; percussion head of a gun-lock released by the trigger; to come under the h., to be sold by auction; to go at it h. and tongs, to set about anything with great energy. HAMMER (2), *v.t.* to beat, strike, drive with a h.; strike repeatedly; (*coll.*) defeat crushingly; declare (a Stock Exchange member) a defaulter; *v.i.* to wield a h.; to h. into, (*fig.*) to fix in the mind by forceful repetition; to h. out, (*fig.*) to force a solution to a problem by assiduous application. [OE.].

HAMMERCLOTH [ha'mer-kloth], *n.* cloth covering the box containing the repair outfit of a coach or carriage.

HAMMERHEAD [ha'mer-hed], *n.* head of a hammer; species of shark; a shell-fish; an African bird.

HAMMER-LOCK [ha'mer-lok], *n.* hold in wrestling in which the opponent's arm is bent and held behind his back.

HAMMER-TOE [ha-mer-tō'], *n.* (*med.*) deformed toe with the joint abnormally bent.

HAMMOCK [ha'mok], *n.* hanging bed, usually of

canvas or network, suspended by cords from hooks; h. chair, folding chair with a canvas seat and back. [Span.].

HAMPER (1) [ham'per], *n.* large basket with a lid. [~OFr.].

HAMPER (2), *v.t.* to impede, hinder, cramp. HAMPER (3), *n.* (*naut.*) obstructive but necessary objects. [ME.].

HAMSHACKLE [ham'sha-kl], *v.t.* to fasten the head of an animal to one of its forelegs with a rope.

HAMSTER [ham'ster], *n.* large rat with cheekpouches for holding grain. [OHGerm.].

HAMSTRING (1) [ham'string], *n.* one of the tendons behind the knee; large tendon behind the hock of a horse. HAMSTRING (2), *v.t.* to lame by severing a h.; (*fig.*) put out of action.

HAND (1) [hand], *n.* end portion of the arm below the wrist; approximate unit of measurement being the width of this; agency; skill, artistry; workman; style of work, artistic touch; position at the side to right or left; handwriting; indicator on a clock or watch; number of cards dealt to a player; (*fig.*) custody, jurisdiction; at h., nearby, handy; old h., experienced person; at first h., with the authority of an original; from h. to mouth, with no margin of safety; h. in glove, intimate; to wait on h. and foot, to attend assiduously; in h., in the process of completion; under control; upper h., advantage; to feed out of one's h., (*fig.*) to be subservient to one; to get out of h., to get out of control; to have in h., to have in reserve; off h., on the spur of the moment; indifferent; out of h., without hesitation; to give, lend, a h., to help; to play into another's hands, to surrender an advantage; to take a h., to join in; to win hands down, to win easily. HAND (2), *v.t.* to give, pass, offer with the h.; transmit, transfer; to h. down, to transmit as an inheritance; to h. in, to deliver; to h. on, to pass on its way; to h. out, to distribute; to h. over, to give up to another; to h. it to (someone), (*slang*) to give due credit to. [OE.].

HANDBAG [hand'bag], *n.* small light bag for carrying on the wrist or in the hand.

HANDBELL [hand'bel], *n.* small bell rung by the hand.

HANDBILL [hand'bil], *n.* loose sheet containing some announcement and given out by hand.

HANDBOOK [hand'book], *n.* book serving as a guide to a particular subject, a manual.

HANDBRACE [hand'brās], *n.* boring tool into which a bit is fitted for drilling.

HAND-BRAKE [hand'brāk], *n.* brake on a vehicle, worked by a hand-lever.

HANDCART [hand'kaht], *n.* small cart pushed or drawn by hand.

HANDCUFF (1) [hand'kuf], *n.* (*usu.pl.*) iron manacle for the wrist consisting of a ring connected by a bar which fits into a lock. HANDCUFF (2), *v.t.* to put handcuffs on.

HANDED [han'did], *adj.* having hands; having a specified number of players. HEAVY-HANDED, clumsily forceful.

HANDFUL [hand'fool], *n.* as much as the hand will grasp; small quantity or number; (*coll.*) child or horse difficult to control.

HAND-GALLOP [hand'ga-lop], *n.* slow and easy gallop.

HAND-GLASS [hand'glahs], *n.* frame of glass for protecting plants; small portable mirror.

HAND-GRENADE [hand'gre-nād], *n.* (*milit.*) small bomb thrown by hand.

HANDICAP (1) [han'di-kap], *n.* penalty or drawback imposed on a competitor in a sporting contest etc. to place him on an equal footing with the rest of the competitors; race or contest under these conditions; (*fig.*) any disability or disadvantage. HANDICAP (2) (*pres.pt.* HANDICAPPING, *pret. and p.pt.* HANDICAPPED), *v.t.* to allot a h. to; be a disadvantage to. HANDICAPPER, *n.* person who allots handicaps to competitors. [Uncert.].

HANDICRAFT [han'di-krahft], *n.* skilled and artistic hand work; manual occupation. HANDICRAFTSMAN, *n.* man occupied or skilled in handicrafts. [OE.].

HANDIWORK [han'di-werk], *n.* work, *esp.* skilled artistic work done by hand; something due to work specified agency.

HANDKERCHIEF [hang'ker-chif], *n.* square of cotton, linen, silk etc. for wiping the nose.

HANDLE (1) [han'dl], *n.* that part of a tool, utensil etc. gripped by the hand; (*slang*) name; to give a h. to, to provide with an excuse to attack or put at a disadvantage. HANDLE (2), *v.t.* to touch, feel, move with the hands; manage, work on with the hands; cope with, control, direct the movements of; treat, behave towards; deal in. [OE.].

HANDLE-BAR [han'dl-bah(r)], *n.* control part of the steering apparatus of a bicycle.

HANDLING [hand'ling], *n.* way in which anything is handled, treatment, management.

HANDMAID(EN) [hand'mād(-en)], *n.* (*archaic*) female servant; (*fig.*) anything subordinate to and helping something else.

HAND-MICROPHONE [hand-mi'kro-fōn], *n.* portable microphone, *esp.* as used by speakers; telephone mouthpiece and receiver which can be held with one hand.

HANDOUT [han'dowt], *n.* (*coll.*) prepared statement issued to the Press, *esp.* by a government department; (*U.S.*) gift to a beggar.

HAND-PICKED [hand-pikt'], *adj.* carefully selected.

HANDRAIL [hand'rāl], *n.* rail which may be gripped for support, *esp.* on a staircase.

HANDSAW [hand'saw], *n.* saw worked with one hand.

HANDSEL (1) [hand'sel], *n.* New Year's gift, gift for luck; (*archaic*) first sale; first payment. HANDSEL (2) (*pres.pt.* HANDSELLING, *pret.* and *p.pt.* HANDSELLED), *v.t.* to offer a h. to; inaugurate. [OIcel.].

HANDSET [hand'set], *n.* and *adj.* (telephone instrument) designed to rest on a table and fitted with a hand-microphone; (of a saw etc), with the teeth, blade etc. set by hand.

HANDSHAKE [hand'shāk], *n.* the grasping of another's hand in greeting.

HANDSOME [hand'sum], *adj.* good-looking; generous, ample. HANDSOMELY, *adv.* in a h. fashion. HANDSOMENESS, *n.* quality of being h. [ME.].

HAND-TO-HAND [hand-too-hand'], *adj.* and *adv.* (fought) at close quarters.

HANDWRITING [hand'rī-ting], *n.* that which is written by the hand; penmanship.

HANDY (1) [han'di], *adj.* dexterous, expert with the hands; near, close at hand; convenient, useful. HANDY (2), *adv.* nearby, close at hand.

HANDYMAN [han'di-man], *n.* man with a knowledge of practical things; jack of all trades.

HANG (1) (*pret.* and *p.pt., usu.* hung, but hanged in sense *executed*) [hang], *v.t.* to fasten something to a high point of support, suspend by a cord etc., suspend game or meat till fit to eat; put to death by hanging; support on hinges; paste (wallpaper) to the wall; *v.i.* to be suspended, dangle; fall into a form, as clothes round the body; be deprived of life by hanging; **to h. about, around,** to frequent; keep close to; loiter; **to h. back,** to hesitate to act; remain behind; **to h. fire,** to delay, be slow in maturing; **to h. out,** (*slang*) to live; **to h. together,** to be closely associated; have all the parts in working order; **to h. up,** to delay, retard progress; conclude a telephone conversation; **to h. upon someone's words,** to be attentive in the extreme; **to h. the head,** to incline the head forward in shame; **to let go h.,** to be indifferent to. HANG (2), *n.* way a thing hangs; way the component parts of anything are interdependent; knack; way a mechanism works; meaning, significance; **to get the h. of,** to understand, grasp. [OE.].

HANGAR [hang'er], *n.* shed for housing aircraft. [Fr.].

HANGDOG [hang'dog], *adj.* sullen, dejected.

HANGER [hang'er], *n.* support from which a thing is hung; that which hangs; a small compact wood on the slope of a hill; short curved broadsword; one who hangs. HANGER-ON, person who persists in associating with another in expectation of favours.

HANGING (1) [hang'ing], *n.* action of that which hangs; state or event of being hanged or hung; object which is hung; (*pl.*) curtains used in interior decoration. HANGING (2), *adj.* being in a state of suspension; **h. gardens,** gardens laid out in terraces.

HANGMAN [hang'man], *n.* public executioner.

HANGNAIL [hang'nāl], *n.* loose piece of skin hanging from the cuticle covering a finger-nail.

HANG-OVER [hang'ō-ver], *n.* (*slang*) uncomfortable after-effects of intoxication.

HANK [hangk], *n.* coil or loop; skein of yarn, string etc. of a particular length; (*naut.*) ring attached to a stay to secure the luff of the fore-and-aft sails. [OIcel.].

HANKER [hang'ker], *v.i.* to yearn for, crave for. [Unkn.].

HANKERING [hang'ke-ring], *n.* yearning, craving.

HANKY-PANKY [hang'ki-pang-ki], *n.* trickery.

HANSE [han'se], *n.* league of merchants in medieval Europe; **H. towns,** certain cities of Germany, associated in the Middle Ages for the protection of their commercial interests. HANSEATIC [han-si-a'-tik], *adj.* relating to the H. towns. [OHGerm.].

HANSOM [han'som], *n.* light two-wheeled cab for two passengers, with the driver mounted on a raised seat behind. [J. A. *Hansom,* its inventor].

HAP (1) [hap], *n.* (*archaic*) that which happens by chance, luck. HAP † (2) (*pres.pt.* HAPPING, *pret.* and *p.pt.* HAPPED), *v.i.* to happen. [OIcel.].

HAPHAZARD (1) [hap'ha-zerd], *adj.* accidental, random, unmethodical. HAPHAZARD (2), *n.* chance, accident. HAPHAZARD (3), *adv.* casually.

HAPLESS [hap'les], *adj.* unfortunate, unlucky.

HA'P'ORTH [hā'puth], *n.* (*slang*) a halfpenny-worth.

HAPPEN [ha'pen], *v.t.* to come to pass, take place; do anything by chance; **to h. on,** to find by chance; **to h. to,** to occur to. [ME.].

HAPPENING [ha'pe-ning], *n.* event, occurrence.

HAPPILY [ha'pi-li], *adv.* in a happy manner; luckily.

HAPPINESS [ha'pi-nes], *n.* state of being happy, good fortune; joy.

HAPPY [ha'pi], *adj.* joyful, contented, cheerful; pleased with success or good fortune; well adapted to a purpose, apt; bringing about or indicating joy and delight. [ME.].

HAPPY-GO-LUCKY [ha-pi-gō-lu'ki], *adj.* carefree, thoughtless and light-hearted; haphazard.

HARA-KIRI [hah-rah-kē'ri], *n.* Japanese way of committing suicide by slitting the abdomen. [Jap.].

HARANGUE (1) [ha-rang'], *n.* speech made to a crowd; public speech, *esp.* one with popular and emotional appeal, tirade. HARANGUE (2), *v.t.* and *i.* to address by means of an h.; pronounce an h. [Fr.].

HARASS [ha'ras], *v.t.* to weary, annoy or exhaust by repetitions or persistence; worry, distract. HARASSMENT, *n.* act of harassing; state of being harassed. [OFr.].

HARBINGER (1) [hah'bin-jer], *n.* precursor, forerunner. HARBINGER (2), *v.t* to herald, be the h. of. [~OFr.].

HARBOUR (1) [hah'ber], *n.* natural or artificial inlet, bay or stretch of water on the coastline, giving shelter and smooth anchorage to ships; sheltered place, haven. HARBOUR (2), *v.t.* to shelter; provide a refuge for, conceal; keep in the mind; *v.i.* to lodge, take cover; come to rest in a h. HARBOUR-DUES, *n.*(*pl.*) fees charged for anchorage in a h. HARBOUR-MASTER, *n.* officer who superintends the mooring of ships etc. at a port. [OIcel.].

HARBOURAGE [hah'be-rij], *n.* place of shelter.

HARBOURER [hah'be-rer], *n.* person who harbours.

HARD (1) [hahd], *adj.* firm, not easily penetrated or pressed, unyielding; harsh, unfeeling, exacting; painful, distressing, difficult; involving intense mental effort, complex; full of force, vigorous; severe; lacking resonance; strenuous; bitter, angry; **h. and fast,** rigid, inflexible; **h. cash,** ready money; **h. currency,** currency of a country whose products are in great demand, which it is h. to obtain owing to the difficulty of selling enough goods to that country; **h. food,** corn fodder; **h. luck,** bad fortune; **h. of hearing,** deaf; **h. water,** water containing a good deal of lime or chalk; **h. up,** having little or no money. HARD (2), *adv.* close, near; to the point of hardness; strenuously; severely, sorely; painfully, with difficulty; excessively; **it will go h.,** it will be serious. [OE.].

HARDBAKE [hahd'bāk], *n.* almond toffee.

HARDBITTEN [hahd-bi'ten], *adj.* stubborn, tough; of a coarse but capable character.

HARD-BOILED [hahd-boild'], *adj.* (of an egg) boiled until the yolk and white are solid; (*slang*) callous, brutally efficient.

HARD COURT [hahd'kawt], *n.* tennis-court with a hard playing surface instead of grass.

HARD-EARNED [hahd-urnd'], *adj.* earned with much labour, *esp.* for a low rate of pay.

HARDEN [hah'den], *v.t.* to make hard or harder, solidify; make hardy; make insensitive, callous, obstinate; *v.i.* to become hard or harder, grow solid; become callous; (*comm.*) (of prices) to remain stable at a high level; **to h. off,** to expose seedlings gradually to the cold. HARDENED, *adj.* confirmed. HARDENER, *n.* one who, or that which, hardens. HARDENING, *n.* act of making hard or hardy; that which hardens. [OIcel.].

HARD-FACED, -FAVOURED, -FEATURED

ōō is pronounced as in *food*; ŏŏ as in *hood*; th as in *think*; TH as in *that*; zh as in *azure*   ~ = related to [hahd-fãst′, -fã′verd, -fẽ′tyōõrd]. *adj.* having a harsh and stern expression.

HARD-HEADED [hahd-he′did]. *adj.* unsentimental, practical; realistic.

HARD-HEARTED [hahd-hah′tid], *adj.* merciless, cruel; unfeeling. HARD-HEARTEDLY, *adv.* in a h. fashion. HARD-HEARTEDNESS, *n.* quality of being h.

HARDIHOOD [hah′di-hōōd], *n.* boldness, daring, effrontery; hardiness.

HARDILY [hah′di-li], *adv.* in hardy fashion.

HARDINESS [hah′di-nes], *n.* quality of being hardy.

HARD LABOUR [hahd-lã′ber], *n.* formerly the most rigorous form of ordinary imprisonment.

HARDLY [hahd′li], *adv.* with difficulty, only just; barely; harshly.

HARDMOUTHED [hahd-mowтнd′], *adj.* (of a horse) insensible to the bit; (of a dog, *esp.* a retriever) unable to carry game in the mouth without biting it; *(fig.)* obstinate.

HARD-PRESSED [hahd-prest′], *adj.* in severe difficulties; almost overwhelmed by the enemy; short of time.

HARDSHIP [hahd′ship], *n.* arduous conditions of living, privation, discomfort; unfair treatment or deprivation; a particular example of this.

HARD TACK [hahd′tak], *n.* ship's biscuit.

HARDWARE [hahd′wãer], *n.* ironmongery.

HARDY [hah′di], *adj.* able to endure hardship, tough, robust, audacious; (of plants) resisting frost and bad weather. [Fr.].

HARE (1) [hãer], *n.* long-eared rodent with a divided upper lip. HARE-AND-HOUNDS, paper-chase. HARE (2), *v.i.* (*slang*) to run very fast.

HAREBELL, HAIRBELL [hãer′bel], *n.* the plant *Campanula rotundifolia*, bearing blue, bell-shaped flowers; the bluebell of Scotland.

HAREBRAINED [hãer′brãnd]. *adj.* empty-headed, careless.

HARE-LIP [hãer′lip], *n.* (*med.*) deformity of the lip, in which the upper lip is cleft.

HAREM [hah-rẽm′, hã′rem], *n.* part of a Moslem house in which wives and concubines are secluded; wives and concubines of a potentate. [Arab.].

HARICOT [ha′ri-kō], *n.* a small kidney-bean; savoury hash containing kidney-beans. [Fr.].

HARK [hahk], *v.t. and i.* to listen, hear; **to h. back,** to return to the point at which one started; refer repeatedly to what is past. [ME.].

HARLEQUIN [hah′li-kwin], *n.* fantastic masked character in Italian comedy and pantomime. [OFr.].

HARLEQUINADE [hah-li-kwi-nãd′], *n.* scene in which Harlequin appears; frolics and buffoonery.

HARLOT [hah′lot], *n.* prostitute. HARLOTRY, *n.* trade and manners of a h. [ME.].

HARM (1) [hahm], *n.* injury, ill, damage. HARM (2), *v.t.* to do h. to. [OE.].

HARMFUL [hahm′fōōl], *adj.* hurtful, causing harm. HARMFULLY, *adv.* in h. fashion. HARMFULNESS, *n.* quality of being h.

HARMLESS [hahm′les], *adj.* doing no harm, unable or unwilling to hurt; inoffensive. HARMLESSLY, *adv.* in h. fashion. HARMLESSNESS, *n.* quality of being h.

HARMONIC (1) [hah-mo′nik], *adj.* relating to harmony; harmonious; (*arith.*) with reciprocals in arithmetical progression. HARMONIC (2), *n.* (*mus.*) one of a series of additional and superimposed frequencies set up when a note is played, overtone; (*pl.*) (*radio*) secondary frequencies of an oscillating circuit. HARMONICALLY, *adv.* in h. fashion. [Gk.].

HARMONICA [hah-mo′ni-kah], *n.* musical instrument consisting of a series of hemispherical glasses rubbed with a wet finger, or of glass or steel plates struck with hammers; kind of mouth-organ. [L.].

HARMONICS [hah-mo′niks], *n.*(*pl.*) (*mus.*) science of harmony.

HARMONIOUS [hah-mō′ni-ŏŏs], *adj.* in harmony, melodious; (*fig.*) justly proportioned and agreeably combined, suitable, well adapted to each other. HARMONIOUSLY, *adv.* in h. fashion. HARMONIOUSNESS, *n.* condition of being h.

HARMONIST [hah′mo-nist], *n.* (*mus.*) one skilled in harmonics or in the writing of harmony; one who reconciles apparent literary and religious inconsistencies. HARMONISTIC [hah-mo-nis′tik], *adj.* relating to a h. and his work.

HARMONIUM [hah-mō′ni-um], *n.* small organ with a keyboard and free metal reeds, pumped by means of pedals. [L.].

HARMONIZE [hah′mo-nīz], *v.t. and i.* to bring into harmony; be harmonious; get on well together.

HARMONY [hah′mo-ni], *n.* just proportion of the parts or qualities of a thing so as to produce an aesthetic whole; (*mus.*) combination of different notes into a chord; music characterized by combinations and progressions of chords; art of composing such music and rules governing its composition; music in general; concord; a combining of several narratives to produce a complete account. [Gk.].

HARNESS (1) [hah′nes], *n.* trappings of a horse, by which it is driven and by which it draws; †armour; **to die in h.,** to die still working. HARNESS (2), *v.t.* to put into harness; tie to some work; bring under control for practical use. [OFr.].

HARP (1) [hahp], *n.* (*mus.*) instrument consisting of strings stretched over a triangular frame and played by plucking with the fingers. HARP (2), *v.i.* to play upon the h.; **to h. on**, (*coll.*) to reiterate tediously and persistently. HARPER, HARPIST, *n.* one who plays the h. [OE.].

HARPOON (1) [hah-pōōn′], *n.* fish-spear, barbed throwing-spear used in whale-hunting. HARPOON (2), *v.t.* to spear with a h. [OFr.].

HARPSICHORD [hahp′si-kawd], *n.* (*mus.*) old-fashioned keyboard instrument in which the strings are plucked by quills. [Fr.].

HARPY [hah′pi], *n.* (*Gk. myth.*) filthy creature with the head and breasts of a woman and the wings and claws of a bird; (*fig.*) cruel woman. [Fr.].

HARQUEBUS, see ARQUEBUS.

HARRIDAN [ha′ri-dan], *n.* fierce and filthy old woman, old prostitute, hag. [Unkn.].

HARRIER (1) [ha′ri-er], *n.* dog used for hunting hares; cross-country runner. [HARE].

HARRIER (2), *n.* a small fierce hawk. [HARRY].

HARRIS TWEED [ha-ris-twēd′], *n.* hand-woven tweed made in Harris, Lewis and other islands of the Outer Hebrides.

HARROVIAN (1) [ha-rō′vi-an], *adj.* of, or pertaining to, Harrow School. HARROVIAN (2), *n.* pupil of Harrow. [MdL.].

HARROW (1) [ha′rō], *n.* agricultural instrument with tines or disks for levelling ploughed land and breaking soil. HARROW (2), *v.t.* to smooth, break up ground with a h.; (*fig.*) torment the feelings; move to horror and distress.

HARROWING (1) [ha′rō-ing], *n.* a ravaging and distressing. HARROWING (2), *adj.* causing horror and distress, moving to mental anguish.

HARRY [ha′ri], *v.t.* to ravage, despoil; (*fig.*) worry and disturb, pester.

HARSH [hahsh], *adj.* rough, coarse of texture; discordant of sound; inharmonious, crude; unfeeling, severe; rigorous, savagely stern; angry and bitter. HARSHLY, *adv.* in h. fashion. HARSHNESS, *n.* quality of being h. [ME.].

HART [haht], *n.* a stag from its sixth year. [OE.].

HARTEBEEST [hah′ti-bēst], *n.* large reddish South African antelope. [Afrik.].

HARTSHORN [hahts′hawn], *n.* ammonium carbonate prepared from the horns of stags.

HART'S-TONGUE [hahts′tung], *n.* a narrow-leaved fern.

HARUM-SCARUM [hãer-um-skãer′um], *adj.* flighty, irresponsible, madcap. [Scots].

HARVEST (1) [hah′vest], *n.* the gathering in of crops; season when crops are gathered; crops so gathered in; (*fig.*) fruits of labour or action. HARVEST (2), *v.t.* to gather in crops, garner; store up what has been gathered. [OE.].

HARVESTER [hah′ves-ter], *n.* one who gathers a harvest; reaping machine; harvest-mite.

HARVEST FESTIVAL [hah-vest-fes′ti-val], *n.* service at which flowers and fruit are brought to church as a thankoffering for the harvest.

HARVEST HOME [hah-vest-hōm′], *n.* festivities at the completion of harvest; religious thanksgiving service at the time of harvest.

HARVEST-MITE [hah′vest-mīt], *n.* small tick, found in grass stalks, which burrows under the skin.

HARVEST-MOON [hah′vest-mōōn], *n.* moon near the autumnal equinox.

HARVEST-MOUSE [hah′vest-mows], *n.* small field-mouse nesting among corn stalks.

HAS [haz], *3rd person pres. ind. sg.* of HAVE.

HAS-BEEN [haz′bēn], *n.* (*coll.*) person who has passed his heyday.

HASH (1) [hash], *v.t.* to cut up (meat), make into a h.; (*fig.*) make an utter mess of. HASH (2), *n.* stew of vegetables and reheated meat; (*fig.*) mess, muddle, mismanagement of something. [Fr.].

HASHISH [ha′shĕsh], *n.* preparation of Indian hemp used as a stimulating and narcotic drug. [Arab.].

The accent ′ after a syllable = stress (u-pon′). The mark ¯ over a vowel = length (ã in made; ō in bone)

HASLETS [haz'litz]. *n.(pl.)* edible entrails of an animal, *esp.* of a pig. [OFr.].

HASP (1) [hahsp]. *n.* clasp, catch for closing a door, book etc.; metal flag for hanging over a staple; spindle for thread; hank of yarn etc. HASP (2), *v.t.* to close, hold with a h. [OE.].

HASSOCK [ha'sok]. *n.* tussock of grass; stuffed, solid cushion for kneeling. [OE.].

HASTE (1) [hāst]. *n.* speed, quickness of motion; an endeavouring to accomplish something in the shortest possible time; precipitancy. HASTE (2), *v.t. and i.* to hasten. [OFr.].

HASTEN [hā'sen], *v.t. and i.* to make to haste, speed up, cause to happen at the earliest possible time; be in haste, hurry. [*Prec.*].

HASTY [hās'ti]. *adj.* exhibiting haste, in too great haste; rash; quick-tempered. HASTILY, *adv.* in h. fashion. HASTINESS, *n.* quality of being h. [OFr.].

HASTY-PUDDING [hās-ti-poo'ding]. *n.* thin batter made of flour and water or milk.

HAT [hat]. *n.* covering for the head; **to talk through one's h.**, (*coll.*) to talk complete nonsense. HAT-BAND, band round the crown of a h. HAT-PIN, pin to attach a h. to the hair. HAT-TRICK, (*cricket*) the taking of three wickets in successive balls; (*coll.*) a triple success. [OE.].

HATCH (1) [hach]. *n.* movable covering above a hole, *esp.* (*naut.*) in the deck of a ship; (*naut.*) hatchway; door with an open space above or below a wicket. [OE.].

HATCH (2), *v.t. and i.* to produce young from eggs by incubation; (*fig.*) plan secretly; be in process of incubation. HATCH (3), *n.* process of hatching eggs; brood hatched at one time. [ME.].

HATCH (4), *v.t.* to mark, shade or decorate with very fine lines. CROSS-HATCH, to h. with lines crossing each other. [Fr.].

HATCHET [ha'chet]. *n.* light chopping axe held in one hand; tomahawk; **to bury the h.**, to make peace. HATCHET-FACED, *adj.* having a thin, narrow face with prominent features. [Fr.].

HATCHING [ha'ching]. *n.* process of shading by fine crossed lines; decoration so produced. [HATCH (4)].

HATCHMENT [hach'ment]. *n.* (*her.*) escutcheon of a deceased person, painted on wood and hung in front of his house, later in church. [ME.].

HATCHWAY [hach'wā]. *n.* (*naut.*) opening from the deck to the interior of a vessel.

HATE (1) [hāt]. *n.* extreme ill-feeling, violent hostility, loathing. HATE (2), *v.t. and i.* to loathe, abominate. HATER, *n.* one who hates. [OE.].

HATEFUL [hāt'fool]. *adj.* arousing hatred, detestable. HATEFULLY, *adv.* in h. fashion. HATEFULNESS, *n.* quality of being h.

HATRED [hā'trid]. *n.* hate, strong and enduring ill-will. [ME.].

HATTER [ha'ter]. *n.* maker of, or dealer in, hats.

HAUBERK [haw'berk]. *n.* coat of mail. [OFr. from OHGerm.].

HAUGHTY [haw'ti]. *adj.* proud, arrogant, supercilious. HAUGHTILY, *adv.* in h. fashion. HAUGHTINESS, *n.* quality of being h. [OFr.].

HAUL (1) [hawl], *v.t. and i.* to pull, heave, drag along or up with effort; (*naut.*) bring a vessel close to the wind; (*naut.*) alter the course of a ship; **to h. over the coals,** to reprimand severely. HAUL (2), *n.* act of hauling; catch of fish; booty, profits. [Fr.].

HAULAGE [haw'lij]. *n.* act of hauling; force employed in hauling; cost of hauling.

HAULIER, HAULER [haw'l(i)er]. *n.* one employed in hauling; carter.

HAU(L)M, HALM [hawm]. *n.* stubble of grain; straw; plant stalk. [OE.].

HAUNCH [hawnsh]. *n.* that part of the body including the upper thigh, hip and buttock. [OFr.].

HAUNT (1) [hawnt]. *v.t.* to visit frequently, *esp.* as a ghost; pester by continual visits, follow; trouble the mind continually. HAUNT (2), *n.* a resort, place frequented by a person or animal. HAUNTED, *adj.* subject to supernatural manifestations. HAUNTER, *n.* one who haunts. [Fr.].

HAUTBOY [ō'boi], *n.* wood-wind musical instrument with a double reed, the oboe. [Fr.].

HAUTEUR [ō-tur']. *adj.* haughtiness. [Fr.].

HAVANA [ha-vah'nah], *n.* name of the capital of Cuba, used to designate cigars etc. produced there.

HAVE (*3rd person sg. pres.* **has,** *pret. and p.pt.* **had**) [hav], *v.t.* to possess, own; possess as a function or characteristic; experience; encounter; assert; allow; cause (to be done); take; consume; dupe; outwit; be compelled; **to h. at,** to attack; **to h. to do with,** to

concern, be related to; associate with; **to h. up,** to charge before a court; **to h. it out,** to discuss and settle a dispute; *used also as an auxil. verb with past participles to form perfect and pluperfect tenses.* [~OE.].

HAVEN [hā'ven], *n.* harbour; (*fig.*) refuge. [OE.].

HAVER [hā'ver], *v.i.* (*Scots and northern dial.*) to talk nonsense.

HAVERSACK [ha'ver-sak], *n.* canvas bag for provisions etc. during marching or travelling, carried slung on the back or by the side. [Germ.].

HAVOC [ha'vok], *n.* devastation, extensive, indiscriminate damage. [AFr. from OFr.].

HAW (1) [haw], *n.* a hawthorn berry. [OFr.].

HAW (2), *n.* an inarticulate noise of embarrassment or nervousness. HAW (3), *v.i.* to utter a h. or series of haws in speaking. [Echoic].

HAWFINCH [haw'finch], *n.* the large-beaked British finch.

HAW-HAW (1) [haw'haw], *n.* stupid guffaw. [Echoic].

HAWHAW (2), see HAHA (2).

HAWK (1) [hawk], *n.* any of the smaller members of the falcon family, *esp.* the short-winged hunting falcon; (*fig.*) a sharper. HAWK (2), *v.i.* to hunt with the h., practise falconry; swoop down on its prey in flight. [OE.].

HAWK (3), *v.t. and i.* to cough up phlegm; clear the throat thickly. HAWK (4), *n.* noise made in clearing the throat. [Echoic].

HAWK (5), *v.t. and i.* to offer for sale from door to door, cry for sale in the streets; (*fig.*) circulate, spread. [*Next*].

HAWKER [haw'ker], *n.* pedlar who hawks his wares, *esp.* in a cart or barrow. [ME.].

HAWK-EYED [hawk-īd'], *adj.* keen-eyed and vigilant.

HAWKMOTH [hawk'moth], *n.* a large quick-darting, hovering moth.

HAWK-OWL [hawk'owl], *n.* owl which hunts by daylight.

HAWSE [hawz], *n.* (*naut.*) hawseholes of a ship; part of the bows where the hawseholes are situated. [~OIcel.].

HAWSEHOLE [hawz'hōl], *n.* (*naut.*) hole in a ship's bows through which the anchor cables run.

HAWSER [haw'zer], *n.* (*naut.*) mooring rope or steel cable with a right-handed twist. [~OFr.].

HAWTHORN [haw'thawn], *n.* spiny tree related to the rose, the may-tree, whitethorn.

HAY (1) [hā], *n.* cut grass dried for fodder; grass grown for this purpose; **to make h. of,** to make a mess of. [OE.].

HAY (2), *n.* figure in many country-dances; kind of country-dance. [OFr.].

HAYBOX [hā'boks], *n.* box packed with hay, in which food may be maintained at cooking heat.

HAYCOCK [hā'kok], *n.* pile of hay ready for carting.

HAY-FEVER [hā-fē'ver], *n.* irritating persistent catarrh caused by the inhalation of pollen and dust.

HAYMAKER [hā'mā-ker], *n.* man or machine that makes hay; (*slang*) vigorous unscientific blow.

HAYMAKING [hā'mā-king], *n.* act of tending cut grass to convert it into hay.

HAYRICK [hā'rik], *n.* haystack.

HAY-SEED [hā'sēd], *n.* grass seed; (*slang*) simple rustic.

HAYSTACK [hā'stak], *n.* stacked mass of hay.

HAYTEDDER [hā'te-der], *n.* machine which scatters hay for drying. [TED.].

HAYWIRE [hā'wier], *adj.* (*U.S. slang*) **to go h.,** to run riot, behave in a wild and unmanageable fashion.

HAZARD (1) [ha'zerd], *n.* a risk, chance, gamble; a danger; gambling game played with dice; shot in billiards in which one of the balls is played into a pocket; (*tennis*) a winning opening; **losing h.,** (*billiards*) in-off shot; **winning h.,** (*billiards*) pot. HAZARD (2), *v.t.* to expose to risks; venture. [OFr.].

HAZARDOUS [ha'zer-doos], *adj.* dangerous, risky; highly speculative. HAZARDOUSLY, *adv.* in h. fashion. HAZARDOUSNESS, *n.* quality or state of being h.

HAZE (1) [hāz], *n.* faint obscurity of the atmosphere, light mist; (*fig.*) state of mental cloudiness. HAZE (2), *v.t. and i.* to make hazy; be or become misty. [Unkn.].

HAZE (3), *v.t.* to make unpleasant sport of. [OFr.].

HAZEL (1) [hā'zel], *n.* tree with edible nuts; colour of these nuts, light brown. HAZEL (2), *adj.* made of h. wood; light brown. [OE.].

HAZY [hā'zi], *adj.* obscured by haze, misty; (*fig.*)

confused, dim, vague. HAZILY, *adv.* in h. fashion. HAZINESS, *n.* mistiness; (*fig.*) state of mental confusion.

H-BOMB [āch'bom], *n.* hydrogen-bomb.

HE [hē], *pron. 3rd person sg. masc. nom. case.* [OE.].

HEAD (1) [hed], *n.* part of the body containing the brain, mouth, nose, ears and eyes; the topmost or foremost part of a thing; side of a coin bearing the ruler's portrait or emblem and the superscription, the obverse; source, fount of a thing; froth on the top of a liquid; pustulent top of a pimple or boil; individual person or animal; the foremost person, the senior, of a group; principal master of a school; position of seniority, rank of leadership; division of a thesis or statement; aptitude, intelligence; **to bring to a h.,** to bring to its climax; **off one's h.,** mad; **to give someone his h.,** to release from restraint. HEAD (2), *adj.* chief, principal, senior. HEAD (3), *v.t. and i.* to lead, be at the h. of; provide with a h.; (*football*) propel the ball with the h.; **to h. off,** to divert; **to h. for,** to go towards, be about to meet with.

HEADACHE [he'dāk], *n.* dull pain in the head; (*fig.*) a difficulty or problem.

HEAD-BAND [hed'band], *n.* band at each end of the spine of a book; band worn round the head.

HEAD-DRESS [hed'dres], *n.* elaborate covering or decoration worn on the head.

HEADER [he'der], *n.* a dive head-foremost; brick laid at right angles to the face of a wall; a striking of a football with the head.

HEADGEAR [hed'gēer], *n.* a hat, hats; any covering for the head.

HEAD-HUNTER [hed'hun-ter], *n.* savage belonging to a tribe which practises decapitating enemies and preserving their heads.

HEADILY [he'di-li], *adv.* in heady fashion.

HEADINESS [he'di-nes], *n.* quality of being heady.

HEADING [he'ding], *n.* act of one who heads; title, headwords, at the top of a page of writing.

HEADLAMP [hed'lamp], *n.* a powerful driving lamp on the front of a car.

HEADLAND [hed'land], *n.* steep promontory.

HEADLESS [hed'les], *adj.* without a head.

HEADLIGHT [hed'līt], *n.* directing light fixed to the front of a vehicle or ship.

HEADLINE [hed'līn], *n.* bold heading across the top of a newspaper report, or at the beginning of a new subject; (*naut.*) rope used to fasten a sail to the yard.

HEADLONG (1) [hed'long], *adv.* head-foremost, precipitously, impetuously. HEADLONG (2), *adj.* head-first, impetuous. [ME.].

HEADMASTER [hed-mahs'ter], *n.* chief master of a school.

HEADMISTRESS [hed-mis'tres], *n.* chief mistress of a school.

HEAD-ON (1) [hed-on'], *adv.* from opposite directions. HEAD-ON (2), *adj.* coming from opposite directions.

HEADPHONE [hed'fōn], *n.* (*usu. pl.*) earphone.

HEADPIECE [hed'pēs], *n.* helmet; decoration at the head of a page; (*slang*) intelligence.

HEADQUARTERS [hed-kwaw'terz], *n.(pl.)* residence or station of the commander-in-chief of an army; central office of any organization.

HEADROOM [hed'rōōm], *n.* space above the head.

HEADSHIP [hed'ship], *n.* position or office of head.

HEADSMAN [hedz'man], *n.* executioner who decapitates.

HEADSTONE [hed'stōn], *n.* keystone of an arch; stone at the head of a grave.

HEADSTRONG [hed'strong], *adj.* stubbornly self-willed; impetuously obstinate.

HEADWAY [hed'wā], *n.* progress in a forward direction, *esp.* against opposition; forward motion of a ship.

HEAD-WIND [hed'wind], *n.* wind blowing against one's course.

HEADWORD [hed'werd], *n.* word in bold type forming a heading.

HEADWORK [hed'werk], *n.* mental work; use of the head at association football.

HEADY [he'di], *adj.* intoxicating; inflaming, rashly headstrong.

HEAL [hēl], *v.t. and i.* to restore to health, cure injury or sickness; become healthy; (of wounds) grow a new skin. HEALING, *adj.* that heals. HEALINGLY, *adv.* in healing fashion. [OE.].

HEALER [hē'ler], *n.* one who heals, *esp.* by non-medical means.

HEALTH [helth], *n.* state of being free from disease

or injury; bodily condition; toast drunk to someone's prosperity and well-being. [OE.].

HEALTHFUL [helth'fōōl], *adj.* conducive to good health; healthy. HEALTHFULLY, *adv.* in h. fashion. HEALTHFULNESS, *n.* condition of being h.

HEALTHY [hel'thi], *adj.* enjoying good health; conducive to good health; displaying good health; (*fig.*) wholesome. HEALTHILY, *adv.* in h. fashion. HEALTHINESS, *n.* condition of being h.

HEAP (1) [hēp], *n.* pile or mound of things; (*slang*) (*pl.*) large quantity or number. HEAP (2), *v.t. and i.* to pile up into a h.; accumulate in great quantities; fill with a h. or heaps. [OE.].

HEAR [hēer], *v.t. and i.* to perceive sounds with the ear; listen to; grant (a request); (*leg.*) judge; **to h. from,** to receive a communication from; **to h. of,** to get news of; (**someone**) **will not h. of it,** will not consider allowing it. HEARER, *n.* one who hears. [OE.].

HEARING [hēer'ing], *n.* faculty of perceiving sound; attention, chance of speaking; earshot; (*leg.*) judgment of a case.

HEARKEN, HARKEN [hah'ken], *v.i.* to listen; attend to. [OE.].

HEARSAY [hēer'sā], *n.* report, rumour; **h. evidence,** (*leg.*) statement of what a witness has heard said, without himself seeing the event.

HEARSE [hurs], *n.* vehicle carrying a corpse to the grave; framework bearing the pall. [OFr.].

HEART (1) [haht], *n.* organ of the body which maintains the blood circulation by its pulsations; (*fig.*) seat of the emotions and affections; courage, enthusiasm; core of anything; vital part of a thing; anything resembling the heart in shape; (*pl.*) firm centre of a vegetable, as lettuce; (*cards*) suit marked by red heart-shaped figures; **by h.,** by rote, by memory; **to take to h.,** to take very seriously; **to eat one's h. out,** to pine away in secret; **h. to h.,** intimate; **to take h.,** to cheer up. HEART (2), *v.i.* **to h. up,** of vegetables, to develop a firm centre. [OE.].

HEARTACHE [haht'tāk], *n.* sorrow, grief.

HEARTBROKEN [haht'brō-ken], *adj.* overwhelmed by sorrow or disappointment.

HEARTBURN [haht'bern], *n.* acidity of the stomach producing a burning sensation in the throat.

HEARTBURNING [haht'ber-ning], *n.* secret discontent and envy.

HEARTEN [hah'ten], *v.t. and i.* to encourage, cheer up.

HEARTFELT [haht'felt], *adj.* felt deeply.

HEARTH [hahth], *n.* stone or bricks on which household fires are made; (*fig.*) the home, domestic life and comfort. [OE.].

HEARTHRUG [hahth'rug], *n.* rug laid in front of the hearth.

HEARTHSTONE [hahth'stōn], *n.* stone forming the hearth; soft stone or pumice used to clean the hearth and other stone surfaces.

HEARTILY [hah'ti-li], *adv.* in hearty fashion.

HEARTINESS [hah'ti-nes], *n.* quality of being hearty.

HEARTLESS [haht'les], *adj.* pitiless, unfeeling. HEARTLESSLY, *adv.* in h. fashion.

HEARTRENDING [haht'ren-ding], *adj.* moving to the deepest grief and pity.

HEART'S BLOOD [hahts'blud], *n.* life-blood; life itself.

HEARTSEASE [haht'sēz], *n.* the wild pansy.

HEART-SICK [haht'sik], *adj.* distressed, grieved.

HEARTSTRINGS [haht'stringz], *n.* the profoundest feelings.

HEART-WHOLE [haht'hōl], *adj.* not in love.

HEARTY (1) [hah'ti], *adj.* in fine physical condition, vigorous, strong; proceeding from good condition; sincere; philistine. HEARTY (2), *n.* (*coll.*) brave, vigorous fellow, *esp.* **my hearties!** (*slang*) one who prefers sport and social life to intellectual pursuits.

HEAT (1) [hēt], *n.* form of energy connected with molecular activity; condition of matter characterized by high temperature, warmth; state of being hot; sensation produced by contact with, or exposure to, high temperature; passion, wrath; (*athletics*) preliminary eliminating contest. HEAT-SPOT, pimple supposed to be produced by h. HEAT-WAVE, spell of excessive h. HEAT (2), *v.t. and i.* to impart h. to; rouse, stir; become hot. HEATED, *adj.* that has been made warm or hot; (*fig.*) passionate, with warmth. HEATEDLY, *adv.* with acrimony. [OE.].

HEATER [hē'ter], *n.* machine or apparatus for heating something.

HEATH [hēth], *n.* stretch of open, uncultivated land,

---

esp. if covered with heather; pinkish-flowered shrub of the genus *Erica*. HEATH-COCK, male of the black-grouse. HEATHY, *adj.* covered with h. [OE.].

HEATHEN (1) [hē'THen], *adj.* pertaining to, or characteristic of, a heathen; impious; (*coll.*) uncultured and unenlightened. HEATHEN (2), *n.* (*sg. and collect.*) (*O.T.*) anyone not observing the Jewish religion; any non-Christian; anyone not observing one of the major religions; a savage; (*fig.*) barbarous person. [OE.].

HEATHENDOM [hē'THen-dum], *n.* heathen parts of the world; heathenism. [OE.].

HEATHENISH [hē'THe-nish], *adj.* idolatrous, barbarous. HEATHENISHLY, *adv.* in h. fashion. HEATHENISHNESS, *n.* condition of being h. [OE.].

HEATHENISM [hē'THe-nizm], *n.* state of being heathen.

HEATHER [he'THer], *n.* ling; plant related to the heath; stretch of land covered with this. HEATHERY, *adj.* prolific in h.

HEATING (1) [hē'ting], *n.* apparatus for keeping warm a building; means for raising the temperature of anything. HEATING (2), *adj.* that heats.

HEAVE (1) [pret. and p.pt. (naut.) hove) [hēv], *v.t.* to raise, swing up with effort; move, drag laboriously; throw; (*naut.*) haul; (*naut.*) move (a ship); *v.i.* to rise in long, high waves; rise and fall deeply and regularly; retch; (*naut.*) haul a rope; (of a ship) move; **to h. to**, to stop a ship's progress. HEAVE (2), *n.* act of heaving; swelling, upward movement; retching; (*geol.*) displacement caused by a fault in the stratum. [∼OE.].

HEAVEN [he'ven], *n.* abode of God or of the gods, place to which the blessed soul goes after death; the sky; (*pl.*) the universe; (*fig.*) place or state of extreme joy and blessedness. HEAVEN-BORN, *adj.* divine. [OE.].

HEAVENLY [he'ven-li], *adj.* relating to heaven; having the joys of heaven; delightful, adorable. HEAVENLINESS, *n.* quality of being h.

HEAVENWARD [he'ven-werd], *adv.* towards heaven.

HEAVER [hē'ver], *n.* one who shifts heavy objects; (*naut.*) lever for heaving rope.

HEAVILY [he'vi-li], *adv.* in heavy fashion.

HEAVINESS [he'vi-nes], *n.* quality of being heavy

HEAVY [he'vi], *adj.* having weight, ponderous; crushing, burdensome; excessive, considerable, powerful, of the largest class; forceful, violent; overcast; depressing; depressed; solid, indigestible; (of troops) elaborately armed and equipped; thick, muddy; over-serious, dull; produced with effort; clumsy; lifeless, torpid; pregnant; pompous. HEAVY-HANDED, oppressive; clumsy. HEAVY-LADEN, heavily burdened. [OE.].

HEAVY WATER [he-vi-waw'ter], *n.* deuterium oxide; water having a density ten per cent greater than the normal.

HEAVYWEIGHT [he'vi-wāt], *n.* boxer weighing more than 12 stone 7 lb.; person or animal of the largest class.

HEBDOMADAL [heb-do'ma-dal], *adj.* weekly. [Gk.].

HEBE [hē'bi], *n.* (*coll.*) barmaid. [Gk. *Hebe*, Goddess of Youth, cupbearer of the gods].

HEBRAIC [hē-brā'ik], *adj.* relating to the Hebrews. HEBRAICALLY, *adv.* in Hebrew fashion.

HEBRAISM [hē'brā-izm], *n.* Judaism; Hebrew ideology; Hebrew word or turn of phrase. HEBRAIST, *n.* student of the Hebrew language, religion and culture; follower of H. HEBRAISTIC [hē-brā-is'tik], *adj.* relating to H.

HEBREW (1) [hē'brōō], *n.* Israelite; Jew; language of the Israelites. HEBREW (2), *adj.* relating to the Hebrews. [ME. from Aramaic].

HECKLE [he'kl], *v.t.* to dress flax; harass a speaker with taunts, interjections and difficult questions. HECKLER, *n.* one who heckles. [ME.].

HECTIC [hek'tik], *adj.* consumptive, feverish; agitated, excited; wildly exciting. HECTICALLY, *adv.* in h. fashion. [Gk.].

HECTO-, *pref.* hundred. [Gk.].

HECTOGRAM, HECTOGRAMME [hek'tō-gram], *n.* a hundred grammes.

HECTOLITRE [hek'tō-lē-ter], *n.* a hundred litres.

HECTOMETRE [hek'tō-mē-ter], *n.* a hundred metres.

HECTOR [hek'ter], *v.t. and i.* to bully, browbeat; bluster. [*Hector*, Trojan warrior].

HEDGE (1) [hej], *n.* barrier or boundary of closely planted shrubs or bushes set in line; thickest row of

anything; (*fig.*) that which restricts or shuts off. HEDGE-HOP, (*coll.*) to fly low in an aircraft. HEDGE-SPARROW, grey and brown passerine bird. HEDGE (2), *v.t. and i.* to surround with a h.; shut in, restrict; avoid committing oneself; (*betting*) place secondary stakes in order to cover one's losses if the main gamble fails. HEDGER, *n.* maker or trimmer of hedges. [OE.].

HEDGEHOG [hej'hog], *n.* insectivorous mammal, notable for its covering of quills.

HEDGEROW [hej'rō], *n.* hedge; row of small trees set in a hedge.

HEDONIC [hē-do'nik], *adj.* hedonistic. [Gk.].

HEDONISM [hē'do-nizm], *n.* (*eth.*) theory that pleasure is the chief good and final cause; devotion to cultivated pleasure. HEDONIST, *n.* adherent of h.; one constantly engaged in the pursuit of pleasure. HEDONISTIC [hē-do-nis'tik], *adj.* relating to, following, h. [Gk.].

HEED (1) [hēd], *v.t. and i.* to pay attention to, observe, have care. HEED (2), *n.* watchful care, attention, obedience. [OE.].

HEEDFUL [hēd'fool], *adj.* taking heed, watchful, obedient. HEEDFULLY, *adv.* in h. fashion. HEEDFULNESS, *n.* quality of being h.

HEEDLESS [hēd'les], *adj.* careless, disregardful, inattentive. HEEDLESSLY, *adv.* in h. fashion. HEEDLESSNESS, *n.* quality of being h.

HEE-HAW (1) [hē'haw], *n.* bray of a donkey HEE-HAW (2), *v.i.* to utter hee-haws.

HEEL (1) [hēl], *n.* back part of the foot behind and below the ankle; raised piece supporting this in a shoe; the part of any footgear covering this; hock or hoof of an animal; tail end of a thing; **head over heels**, completely over; **down at h.**, shabby; **to take to one's heels**, to run away; **to come to h.**, to submit to discipline; **to lay by the heels**, to capture; **to cool, kick, one's heels**, to be kept waiting. HEEL (2), *v.t.* to provide with a h.; (*football*) kick with the h. [OE.].

HEEL (3), *v.t. and i.* to tilt over to the side, list, reel over; cause to do this. HEEL (4), *n.* heeling, list of a ship. [OE.].

HEEL-TAP [hēl'tap], *n.* last drops of liquid left in a glass after drinking; layer of leather on the heel of a boot.

HEFTY [hef'ti], *adj.* (*coll.*) strong, big and of powerful physique. HEFTILY, *adv.* in h. fashion. HEFTINESS, *n.* quality of being h. [HEAVE].

HEGEMONY [hē'ge-mo-ni], *n.* political supremacy of one state in a group or confederacy. HEGEMONIC(AL), *adj.* relating to a h.; exercising a h. [Gk.].

HEIFER [he'fer], *n.* cow which has not yet calved. [OE.].

HEIGH [hā], *int.* exclamation of exhortation or to attract attention. HEIGH-HO [hā-hō'], expression of surprise or weariness.

HEIGHT [hīt], *n.* condition of being high; altitude, vertical extent; (*fig.*) peak, highest degree of a thing; mountain, high hill. [OE.].

HEIGHTEN [hī'ten], *v.t. and i.* to make higher, augment; (*fig.*) intensify, enhance; become higher.

HEINOUS [hā'nŏŏs], *adj.* wicked, hateful, detestable. HEINOUSLY, *adv.* in h. fashion. HEINOUSNESS, *n.* quality of being h. [OFr.].

HEIR [āer], *n.* one who succeeds to the property of another; one entitled or appointed by will to succeed to property on the death of the holder; successor to anything. HEIR-APPARENT, one who, failing his own death, is bound to succeed. HEIR-AT-LAW, natural h. of another. HEIR-PRESUMPTIVE, one who is h. failing a birth into a more direct line of succession. HEIRDOM, *n.* state of being an h.; succession by right or by will. HEIRSHIP, *n.* status or rights of an h. [OFr.].

HEIRESS [āer'es], *n.* female heir.

HEIRLOOM [āer'lŏōm], *n.* something inherited, *esp.* inherited chattel which cannot be alienated.

HELD [held], *pret. and p.pt.* of HOLD. [OE.].

HELICAL [he'li-kal], *adj.* spiral; **h. gear**, gearing with the teeth so cut that if extended they would form a series of spirals or helices about the axis of the wheel. [L.].

HELICOPTER [he'li-kop-ter], *n.* flying machine with horizontal rotors, by means of which it can ascend and descend vertically. [Gk.].

HELIO-, *pref.* relating to the sun.

HELIOGRAPH [hē'li-ō-grahf], *n.* device for transmitting messages by flashing a mirror or polished surface; method of engraving by exposing a chemically treated plate to sunlight. HELIOGRAPHIC [hē-li-ō-gra'fik], adj. relating to a h. HELIOGRAPHIC-ALLY, adv. by means of the h.

HELIO-THERAPY [hē-li-ō-the'ra-pi], n. sunshine treatment.

HELIOTROPE (1) [hē'li-ō-trōp], n. plant with pale purple flowers which turn towards the sun; scent of this flower; the bloodstone; light purple colour. HELIOTROPE (2), adj. having the colour or scent of the h. [Gk.].

HELIOTROPIC [hē-li-ō-tro'pik], adj. turning towards the light. [Gk.].

HELIOTROPISM [hē-li-o'tro-pizm], n. tendency of plants to turn towards the sun. [Gk.].

HELIUM [hē'li-um], n. a non-inflammable gas, the element He, the second-lightest known substance. [Gk.].

HELIX (pl. **helices**) [hē'liks, hē'li-sēz], n. spiral line, coil, convolution; rim of the external ear; genus of snails. [Gk.].

HELL [hel], n. eternal abode of the damned, according to the Christian religion; (fig.) extreme pain and distress; haunt of vice; **a h. of a**, very large, bad etc.; **what the h.**, used to express surprise or indignation; **like h.**, very much; **to give h. to**, to treat roughly; **h. for leather**, at top speed. HELL-CAT, violent and evil-tempered woman. [OE.].

HELLEBORE [he'li-baw(r)], n. the Christmas rose; medicinal drug extracted from this; poisonous plant of the same genus. [Gk.].

HELLENE [he'lēn], n. a Greek. HELLENIAN [he-lē'ni-an], adj. Hellenic. [Gk.].

HELLENIC [he-lē'nik], adj. relating to Greece, its people and language. [Gk.].

HELLENISM [he'le-nizm], n. Greek culture; a Greek turn of phrase; Greek nationality. [Gk.].

HELLENIST [he'le-nist], n. devotee of Hellenism; Greek Jew. HELLENISTIC [he-le-nis'tik], adj. relating to the kingdom and culture of the Asiatic Greeks, esp. to the successors of Alexander in Egypt and Asia Minor; **H. Greek**, language of Greek-speaking Jews, as of the N.T. HELLENISTICALLY, adv. in H. fashion.

HELLHOUND [hel'hownd], n. horrible and wicked person; demoniacal dog.

HELLISH [he'lish], adj. relating to, resembling, hell; (coll.) extremely unpleasant. HELLISHLY, adv. in h. fashion. HELLISHNESS, n. quality of being h.

HELLO [he-lō'], int. exclamation expressing greeting or surprise.

HELM (1) [helm], n. helmet. HELMED, adj. helmeted. [OE.].

HELM (2), n. tiller, steering wheel or steering mechanism of a vessel; control, leadership of anything. [OE.].

HELMET [hel'mit], n. metal head armour; protective headgear worn by police, firemen, people in hot climates etc.; top of a retort. HELMETED, adj. having a h. on. [OFr.].

HELMINTH [hel'minth], n. intestinal worm. [Gk.].

HELMSMAN [helmz'man], n. one who controls the helm.

HELOT [he'lot], n. (Gk. antiq.) member of a subject and oppressed race in Sparta; (fig.) slave-like subject. [Gk.].

HELP (1) [help], v.t. and i. to aid, assist; co-operate with in achieving some end; serve food to; (following **can't** or **can**) avoid, prevent; **I can't h. it**, it is not my fault; **not more than one can h.**, not more than is inevitable; **to h. oneself to**, to take. HELP (2), n. aid, assistance; act of helping; one who, or that which, helps; domestic servant. HELPER, n. one who helps. [OE.].

HELPFUL [help'fool], adj. helping, obliging. HELP-FULLY, adv. in a h. manner. HELPFULNESS, n. quality of being h.

HELPING [hel'ping], n. portion of food served to one person.

HELPLESS [help'les], adj. unable to help oneself. HELPLESSLY, adv. in a h. manner.

HELPMATE [help'māt], n. helpmeet.

HELPMEET [help'mēt], n. helper; wife. [Wrongly formed from Gen. ii. 18, an help meet for him, where meet means "fitting"].

HELTER-SKELTER (1) [hel'ter-skel-ter], adv. in confused, noisy haste. HELTER-SKELTER (2), n. circular tower fitted with an external spiral slide, common at fairs etc. [Echoic].

HELVE [helv], n. handle, haft. [OE.].

HELVETIAN [hel-vē'shn], adj. Swiss. [L.].

HEM (1) [hem], n. edge of cloth folded over and sewn down; border of a garment. HEM (2) (pres.pt.

HEMMING, pret. and p.pt. HEMMED), v.t. to make a h. round; **to h. in**, to surround closely on all sides. [OE.].

HEM (3), int. sound expressing hesitation, nervousness. [OE.].

HEMATIN, see HAEMATIN.

HEMATITE, see HAEMATITE.

HEMI-, pref. half. [Gk.].

HEMIPLEGIA [he-mi-plē'ji-ah], n. (med.) paralysis affecting one side of the body. [Gk.].

HEMISPHERE [he'mi-sfēer], n. half-sphere; half of the earth's surface. HEMISPHERIC(AL) [he-mi-sfe'rik(-l)], adj. having the form of a h. [Gk.].

HEMLOCK [hem'lok], n. a poisonous herb; poison made from this herb. HEMLOCK-SPRUCE, a coniferous tree. [OE.].

HEMORRHAGE, see HAEMORRHAGE.

HEMORRHOIDS, see HAEMORRHOIDS.

HEMP [hemp], n. a herbaceous plant; narcotic drug obtained from this; coarse cloth and rope woven from the fibres of this and similar plants. HEMPEN, adj. made of h.

HEMSTITCH [hem'stich], v.t. to decorate the border of a woven material with a particular kind of ornamental stitch. [HEM and STITCH].

HEN [hen], n. female of any bird, female of the domestic fowl; (coll.) fussy elderly person of either sex. HEN-COOP, coop for fowls. HEN-HOUSE, shed or hut for fowls. HEN-ROOST, place in which poultry roost. [OE.].

HENBANE [hen'bān], n. a poisonous herb. [HEN and BANE].

HENCE [hens], adv. away from this place; from this time; from this; for this reason. [ME.].

HENCEFORTH [hens-fawth'], adv. from this time onward. [~OE.].

HENCEFORWARD [hens-faw'werd], adv. hence-forth.

HENCHMAN [hench'man], n. close and trusted follower or retainer. [ME.].

HENDECAGON [hen-de'ka-gon], n. (geom.) plane figure having eleven sides. [Gk.].

HENDECASYLLABLE [hen-de-ka-si'la-bl], n. (pros.) metrical form employing a line of eleven syllables. [Gk.].

HENNA [he'nah], n. white-flowered Asiatic shrub; reddish nail-tint and hair shampoo made from this.

HEN-PARTY [hen'pah-ti], n. (coll.) party for women only.

HENPECKED [hen'pekt], adj. nagged by one's wife.

HENRY [hen'ri], n. (elect.) international unit of inductance. [Joseph Henry, American physicist].

HEPAT-, HEPATO-, pref. relating to the liver. [~Gk.].

HEPATIC [hi-pa'tik], adj. relating to the liver; liver-coloured. [Gk.].

HEPATICA [hi-pa'ti-kah], n. European anemone. [L.].

HEPATO-, see HEPAT-.

HEPPLEWHITE [he'pl-wīt], adj. of furniture, in the style of the eighteenth-century designer George Hepplewhite.

HEPTA-, pref. seven. [Gk.].

HEPTACHORD [hep'ta-kawd], n. (mus.) a major seventh; series of seven consecutive notes; instrument having seven strings. [Gk.].

HEPTAD(E) [hep'tad, -tād], n. group of seven. [Gk.].

HEPTAGON [hep'ta-gon], n. (geom.) plane figure of seven sides. HEPTAGONAL [hep-ta'go-nal], adj. in the form of a h. [Gk.].

HEPTAHEDRON [hep-ta-hē'dron], n. a seven-faced solid. [Gk.].

HEPTARCHY [hep'tah-ki], n. government by seven rulers; period in Anglo-Saxon history when England was divided into seven kingdoms. [Gk.].

HEPTASYLLABIC [hep-ta-si-la'bik], adj. of seven syllables. [Gk.].

HEPTATEUCH [hep'ta-tyōōk], n. first seven books of the Bible. [Gk.].

HER (1) [hur], possessive adj. belonging to, relating to her. HER (2), pron. objective case of SHE. [OE.].

HERALD (1) [he'rald], n. one who makes public announcements on behalf of a potentate; officer entrusted with the granting or withdrawing of armorial bearings; anyone announcing anything, esp. for the first time; forerunner; anticipation. HERALD (2), v.t. to proclaim as a h., announce. [OFr.].

HERALDIC [he-ral'dik], adj. relating to heraldry. HERALDICALLY, adv. according to heraldry.

HERALDRY [he'ral-dri], n. art and study of armorial

bearings; heraldic devices; position of a herald. [OFr.].

HERB [hurb], *n.* low-growing seasonal plant; plant possessing aromatic or medical qualities; (*poet.*) grass. [L.].

HERBACEOUS [her-bā′shŏŏs], *adj.* relating to herbs; dying in winter like a h.; covered with, composed of or resembling herbs; not woody. [L.].

HERBAGE [hur′bij], *n.* herbs, pasturage, plants growing in fields; juicy tops of herbs; (*leg.*) right of grazing. [Fr.].

HERBAL (1) [hur′bal], *n.* book on medicinal herbs. HERBAL (2), *adj.* relating to herbs. [L.].

HERBALIST [hur′ba-list], *n.* one skilled in the use of herbs; dealer in herbs.

HERBARIUM [her-bāer′i-um], *n.* collection of dried plants; room or building in which this is housed. [L.].

HERBIVOROUS [her-bi′ve-rŏŏs], *adj.* feeding on herbage.

HERCULEAN [her-kyŏŏ-lē′an, her-kyŏŏ′li-an], *adj.* relating to Hercules, resembling him in size and strength; tremendously laborious, requiring a Hercules. [L.].

HERCULES [hur′kyŏŏ-lēz], *n.* (*class. myth.*) hero notable for his strength; man of immense physical strength and size.

HERD (1) [hurd], *n.* large group of gregarious animals living and moving together; group of domestic animals of one breed, usually under one ownership; (*fig.*) crowd of sheep-like human beings. HERD-BOOK, *n.* book of the pedigrees of stud cattle. HERD (2), *n.* herdsman. HERD (3), *v.t. and i.* to gather, drive together in one h.; come together in a h.; huddle together in a close mass. [OE.].

HERD INSTINCT [hurd′in-stingkt], *n.* tendency to crowd together, act, feel and think as a herd.

HERDSMAN [hurdz′man], *n.* one who looks after a domestic herd.

HERE [hēer], *adv.* at this place; towards this place; **h. and there,** thinly scattered. [OE.].

HEREABOUT, HEREABOUTS [hēer′a-bowt(z)], *adv.* somewhere near this place.

HEREAFTER (1) [hēer-ahf′ter], *adv.* after the present, later on; after death, in the next world. HEREAFTER, *n.* the next life. [OE.].

HEREAT [hēer-at′], *adv.* at this, when this occurred.

HEREBY [hēer-bī′], *adv.* near this, near here; as a result of this, by (means of) this.

HEREDITABLE [hi-re′di-ta-bl], *adj.* heritable. [L.].

HEREDITAMENT [hi-re-di′ta-ment], *n.* (*leg.*) hereditable property.

HEREDITARY [hi-re′di-ta-ri], *adj.* descending by inheritance; inherited; derived from one's ancestors. HEREDITARILY, *adv.* by inheritance. [L.].

HEREDITY [hi-re′di-ti], *n.* ability of organisms to transmit characteristics to their offspring; process by which this transmission takes place. [L.].

HEREFORD [he′ri-ferd], *n.* name of a breed of red-and-white cattle. [*Hereford*, English county].

HEREIN [hēer′in, hēer-in′], *adv.* in this. [OE.].

HEREINAFTER [hēer-in-ahf′ter], *adv.* afterwards, after this, henceforward, in this document.

HEREOF [hēer-ov′], *adv.* of this.

HERESY [he′re-si], *n.* doctrine or religious belief contrary to the teachings of the Church, *esp.* of the Christian Church; theory contrary to that officially approved. [L.].

HERETIC [he′re-tik], *n.* believer in a heresy, one who will not subscribe to official doctrine. HERETICAL [hi-re′ti-kal], *adj.* relating to, believing in, heresy; contrary to official doctrine. HERETICALLY, *adv.* in heretical fashion. [L.].

HERETO [hēer-tŏŏ′], *adv.* hereunto, to this.

HERETOFORE [hēer-tŏŏ-faw(r)′], *adv.* hitherto; before this.

HEREUNTO [hēer′un-tŏŏ], *adv.* to this.

HEREUPON [hēer′u-pon], *adv.* upon this, at this.

HEREWITH [hēer-wiTH′], *adv.* with this, at this time, now.

HERITABLE [he′ri-ta-bl], *adj.* possible to be inherited. [Fr.].

HERITAGE [he′ri-tij], *n.* that which is inherited. [OFr.].

HERITOR [he′ri-ter], *n.* one who inherits. [Fr.].

HERMAPHRODISM, HERMAPHRODITISM [her-ma′frŏ-dizm, her-ma′frŏ-di-tizm], *n.* state of being a hermaphrodite.

HERMAPHRODITE [her-ma′frŏ-dīt], *n.* (*biol.*) organism containing both fertilizing and generative organs; person or animal with indeterminate sexual organs, or with those of both sexes. HERMAPHRODITIC(AL) [her-ma-frŏ-di′tik(-al)], *adj.* having the organs of both sexes; relating to a h. [Gk.].

HERMES [hur′mēz], *n.* (*myth.*) messenger of the gods; (*fig.*) swift, fluent person. [Gk.].

HERMETIC [her-me′tik], *adj.* airtight, sealed so securely as to forbid the passage of air. HERMETICALLY, *adv.* so as to be airtight. [LL.].

HERMIT [hur′mit], *n.* one living alone in seclusion in order to pursue his religious life undisturbed; (*fig.*) one who shuns human society. HERMIT-CRAB, soft-bodied crab inhabiting a discarded mollusc shell. [ME.].

HERNIA [hur′ni-ah], *n.* (*med.*) protrusion of an internal organ through the side of its protective wall. HERNIAL, *adj.* relating to h. [L.].

HERO [hēer′o], *n.* one outstandingly brave and victorious in war; one idolized as a model of prowess and virtue; leading male character in a story or drama. HERO-WORSHIP, worship of a h.; excessive idolization of someone. [Gk.].

HEROIC [hi-rō′ik], *adj.* possessing, displaying, the qualities of a hero; (of actions) daring and brave; on a great scale; (of representations in art) larger than life; relating to epic poetry; **h. couplets,** (*pros.*) rhymed couplets of ten syllables and five regular stresses. HEROICALLY, *adv.* in h. fashion.

HEROIN [he′rō-in], *n.* a narcotic derivative of morphine. [HERO].

HEROINE [he′rō-in], *n.* female hero; principal young female character of a story or drama. [Gk.].

HEROISM [he′rō-izm], *n.* qualities displayed by. a hero, extreme bravery. [Fr.].

HERON [he′ron], *n.* large wading bird distinguished by its long legs, neck and beak. HERONRY, *n.* colony of herons. [OFr.].

HERPES [hur′pēz], *n.* (*path.*) sk'n disease marked by clusters of vesicles. [Gk.].

HERPETOLOGY [her-pi-to′lo-ji], *n.* scientific study of reptiles. [Gk.].

HERR [hāer], *n.* German title for a man, Mr. [Germ.].

HERRING [he′ring], *n.* an edible marine shoal-fish; any of several fish resembling this; **red h.,** (*fig.*) irrelevant fact or suggestion introduced to divert attention from the point at issue. HERRING-POND, (*coll.*) North Atlantic Ocean. [OE.].

HERRING-BONE [he′ring-bōn], *n.* herring's spine; pattern resembling this; (*arch.*) method of bricklaying in which courses are laid in alternate diagonals; a cross-stitch; method of climbing on skis which leaves this pattern.

HERS [hurz], *possessive pron.* belonging to her. [ME.].

HERSELF [her-self′], *pron. emphatic and reflexive form of* HER. [OE.].

HERTZIAN [hurt′zi-an], *adj.* relating to the etheric wave movements investigated by H. *Hertz,* German physicist.

HESITANCY [he′zi-tan-si], *n.* hesitation. [L.].

HESITANT [he′zi-tant], *adj.* hesitating, doubtful. HESITANTLY, *adv.* in h. fashion. [L.].

HESITATE [he′zi-tāt], *v.i.* to pause doubtfully; falter; be unwilling. HESITATING, *adj.* doubtful, undecided. HESITATINGLY, *adv.* in hesitating fashion. HESITATIVE, *adj.* tending to h. [L.].

HESITATION [he-zi-tā′shn], *n.* act or state of hesitating; indecision, unwillingness; a speech defect. [L.].

HESPER [hes′per], *n.* the planet Venus. [Gk.].

HESPERIAN [hes-pēer′i-an], *adj.* western, pertaining to the west. [*Prec.*].

HESSIAN [he′shn], *n.* coarse cloth made from jute or hemp; high boot. [*Hesse*, Germany].

HEST [hest], *n.* (*archaic*) a command. [OE.].

HETER(O)-, *pref.* irregular, of another kind. [Gk.].

HETERODOX [he′te-rō-doks], *adj.* unorthodox, heretical. HETERODOXY [he′te-rō-dok-si], *n.* h. opinions; the holding of such opinions. [Gk.].

HETERODYNE [he′te-rō-dīn], *n.* (*radio*) a beat note due to differences in frequency between the transmitted waves and those created in the receiver, with which they are combined. [HETERO and DYNE].

HETEROGENEITY [he-te-rō-je-nē′i-ti], *n.* condition of being heterogeneous.

HETEROGENEOUS [he-te-rō-jē′ni-ŏŏs], *adj.* of dissimilar kind; consisting of unrelated parts; unable to be compared; (*math.*) having no common measure. HETEROGENEOUSLY, *adv.* in h. fashion. [Gk.].

HETEROGENESIS [he-te-rō-je′ni-sis], *n.* (*biol.*) production of an organism from a dissimilar parent. [HETERO and GENESIS].

HETEROSEXUAL [he-te-rō-sek′shŏŏ-al], *adj.*

ŏŏ is pronounced as in food; ŏŏ as in hood; th as in *think*; TH as in *that*; zh as in azure.   ~ = related to.

normally sexual, sexually attracted by the opposite sex. [HETERO and SEXUAL].

HETMAN [het'man], *n.* Cossack leader; Polish commander. [Polish].

HEW (*pret.* **hewed**, *p.pt.* **hewn, hewed**) [hyōō], *v.t. and i.* to chop, cut with heavy strokes; carve or shape in this way. HEWER, *n.* one who hews. [OE.].

HEWN [hyōōn], *p.pt.* of HEW.

HEX-, HEXA-, *pref.* six, relating to six. [Gk.].

HEXACHORD [hek'za-kawd], *n.* (*mus.*) diatonic scale of six notes; a major sixth. [Gk.].

HEXAD [hek'zad], *n.* series containing six numbers. [Gk.].

HEXAGON [hek'za-gon], *n.* plane figure having six sides. HEXAGONAL [hek-za'go-nal], *adj.* like a h., six-sided. [Gk.].

HEXAHEDRON [hek-za-hē'dron], *n.* (*geom.*) a six-sided solid, *esp.* a cube. [Gk.].

HEXAMETER [hek-za'mi-ter], *n.* (*pros.*) classical heroic metre of six feet; any metrical line of six feet. HEXAMETRIC(AL) [hek-za-met'rik(-al)], *adj.* written in hexameters. [Gk.].

HEXASYLLABLE [hek'za-si-la-bl], *n.* word containing six syllables. [Gk.].

HEXATEUCH [hek'za-tyōōk], *n.* first six books of the Bible. [Gk.].

HEYDAY [hā'dā], *n.* acme, height, period of greatest prosperity or activity. [HIGH DAY].

HI [hī], *int.* a call to attract attention.

HIATUS [hī-ā'tus], *n.* gap, space; (*gram.*) unelided pronunciation of two adjacent vowels. [L.].

HIBERNATE [hī'ber-nāt], *v.i.* to pass the winter in sleep; retire into warm inactivity during the winter. HIBERNATION, [hī-ber-nā'shn], *n.* practice or condition of hibernating. [L.].

HIBERNIAN (1) [hī-bur'ni-an], *adj.* Irish. HIBERNIAN (2), *n.* member of the Irish people. HIBERNIANISM, HIBERNICISM [hī-bur'ni-a-nizm, hī-bur'ni-sizm], *n.* an Irishism. [L.].

HIBISCUS [hi-bis'kus], *n.* cultivated mallow. [Gk.].

HICCOUGH, HICCUP (1) [hi'kup], *n.* sudden involuntary drawing together of the diaphragm, resulting in a coughing sound; sound so produced. HICCOUGH, HICCUP (2), *v.t. and i.* to utter a h. or series of hiccoughs; speak with a h. [ME.].

HICKORY [hi'ke-ri], *n.* American hardwood tree; wood from this tree. [Native].

HID [hid], *pret. and archaic p.pt.* of HIDE (3). [OE.].

HIDALGO [hi-dal'gō], *n.* Spanish gentleman of noble descent. [Span.].

HIDDEN (1) [hi'den], *p.pt.* of HIDE (3). HIDDEN (2), *adj.* secret, mysterious, not plain or obvious. [ME.].

HIDE (1) [hīd], *n.* skin of a beast, *esp.* when flayed off; (*fig.*) human skin; (*coll.*) thickness of skin, insolence. HIDE (2), *v.t.* to flay; (*coll.*) thrash. [OE.].

HIDE (3) (*pret.* **hid**, *p.pt.* **hidden**), *v.t. and i.* to conceal; keep out of view; keep from being known or understood; withhold; go into concealment. HIDE-AND-SEEK, children's game in which some h. and others try to find them. HIDE (4), *n.* place of concealment, *esp.* one from which to observe wild life. HIDER, *n.* one who hides. [OE.].

HIDEBOUND [hīd'bownd], *adj.* rigidly conservative, obstinately conventional; (of an animal) having too close a hide.

HIDEOSITY [hi-di-o'si-ti], *n.* hideousness.

HIDEOUS [hi'di-ōōs], *adj.* very ugly; revolting. HIDEOUSLY, *adv.* in h. fashion. HIDEOUSNESS, *n.* quality of being h. [OFr.].

HIDEOUT [hī'dowt], *n.* (*coll.*) safe retreat or hiding place.

HIDING (1) [hī'ding], *n.* concealment. [HIDE (3)].

HIDING (2), *n.* a flogging, beating. [HIDE (2)].

HIE [hī], *v.i.* (*archaic*) to go in haste. [OE.].

HIER-, HIERO-, *pref.* sacred; relating to priesthood. [Gk.].

HIERARCH [hīer'ahk], *n.* chief priest. HIERARCHAL, HIERARCHIC(AL), *adj.* relating to a h. or a hierarchy. [Gk.].

HIERARCHY [hīer'ah-ki], *n.* an order of angels or other sacred persons; order of priests; organization of such an order; government by a body of persons graded so that each rank controls that immediately inferior to it; graded system of organization, *esp.* ecclesiastical. [Gk.].

HIERO-, see HIER-.

HIEROGLYPH [hīer'ō-glif], *n.* a character in the picture writing of the ancient Egyptians; character in any picture script; (*fig.*) incomprehensible symbol.

HIEROGLYPHIC(AL) (1) [hīer-ō-gli'fik(-al)], *adj.*

written in hieroglyphs. HIEROGLYPHIC (2), *n.* a hieroglyph; (*pl.*) writing in h. characters. HIEROGLYPHICALLY, *adv.* in hieroglyphics. [Gk.].

HIEROPHANT [hīer'ō-fant], *n.* one who initiates into mysteries. HIEROPHANTIC [hier-ō-fan'tik], *adj.* relating to the office of h. [Gk.].

HIGGLE [hi'gl], *v.i.* to haggle over small transactions, drive a mean bargain. [HAGGLE].

HIGGLEDY-PIGGLEDY [hi-gl-di-pi'gl-di], *adv.* in complete disorder, jumbled haphazardly. [Symbolic].

HIGH (1) [hī], *adj.* lofty, extending a good distance upwards; of a certain altitude; at a specified distance above the ground; of important status or position; chief, principal; very good; sublime; advanced, developed; extreme in opinion; intense; exaggerated in colour or sound, shrill, sharp; (of food) beginning to decay; (of explosives) rapid in action; **h. and dry**, stranded (also *fig.*); **to ride the h. horse**, to behave arrogantly; **h. living**, luxury; **h. noon**, full noon; **h. sea**, the sea outside territorial waters; **h. speed**, great speed; **h. table**, table on a dais where senior members of a college etc. dine in hall; **h. tea**, late tea with meat, fish etc.; **h. time**, time when action should no longer be delayed; **h. old time**, uproarious entertainment; **h. words**, a quarrel; **ace h.**, (*cards*) with an ace as highest card; (*U.S. slang*) h. level, record. HIGH (2), *adv.* highly, to a h. extent, level or degree. [OE.].

HIGHBALL [hī'bawl], *n.* (*U.S. slang*) whisky and soda.

HIGHBORN [hī-bawn'], *adj.* of noble birth.

HIGHBROW (1) [hī'brow], *n.* one having rather exalted intellectual interests. HIGHBROW (2), *adj.* relating to a h., his interests and tastes.

HIGH-CHURCH [hī-church'], *adj.* ritualistically Anglican. HIGH-CHURCHMAN, *n.* one believing in or practising elaborate ritual in the Anglican Church.

HIGHDAY [hī'dā], *n.* holiday, festival.

HIGHFALUTIN(G) [hī-fa-lōō'tin(g)], *adj.* pretentious, bombastic, high-sounding. [Uncert.].

HIGH-FLIER [hī'flī-er], *n.* ambitious person; one tending to go to extremes; purple emperor butterfly.

HIGHFLOWN [hī-flōn'], *adj.* (of language) extravagant; bombastic.

HIGH-GRADE [hī'grād], *adj.* of high quality.

HIGH-HANDED [hī-han'did], *adj.* overbearing, arbitrary.

HIGH-HEARTED [hī-hah'tid], *adj.* full of courage.

HIGH-JUMP [hī'jump], *n.* athletic contest in jumping high; **for the h.**, (*slang*) up for trial, in serious trouble.

HIGHLAND [hī'land], *n.* hilly or mountainous district. HIGHLANDS, *n.* elevated region of the north and north-west of Scotland. HIGHLAND (2), *adj.* relating to the Highlands.

HIGHLANDER [hī'lan-der], *n.* a native of the Scottish Highlands; soldier of a Highland regiment.

HIGH-LIFE [hī'līf], *n.* life of the rich and aristocratic.

HIGHLIGHT [hī'līt], *n.* brightest part of a painting etc.; best or outstanding part of a performance.

HIGHLY [hī'li], *adv.* to or at a height; extreme; with esteem; very favourably; well. [OE.].

HIGH-METTLED [hī-me'tld] *adj.* high-spirited; high-hearted.

HIGH-MINDED [hī-mīn'did], *adj.* nobly minded; (*archaic*) haughty.

HIGHNESS [hī'nes], *n.* height, state or extent of being high; title of respect given to princes and princesses. [OE.].

HIGH-PRESSURE [hī-pre'shyōōr], *adj.* driven by high pressure of steam etc.; designed for use under h. conditions; (*fig.*) done with great speed and energy.

HIGH PRIEST [hī-prēst'], *n.* chief priest.

HIGH-PRINCIPLED [hī-prin'si-pld], *adj.* high-minded, honourable.

HIGHROAD [hī'rōd], *n.* main road; (*fig.*) quickest and most direct way.

HIGH-SOUNDING [hī-sown'ding], *adj.* high-falutin; lofty in word.

HIGH-SPEED [hī-spēd'], *adj.* working or travelling fast.

HIGH-SPIRITED [hī-spi'ri-tid], *adj.* vivacious, daring, ardent; full of vigour.

HIGH-STEPPER [hī-ste'per], *n.* a high-stepping horse; (*slang*) attractive and socially brilliant woman.

HIGH(LY)-STRUNG [hī-(li)-strung'], *adj.* nervous, excitable.

HIGHT [hīt], *adj.* (*archaic*) named. [ME.].

HIGH-TIDE [hī-tīd'], *n.* highest level to which a tide

rises; time of this maximum rising; state of tidal water at this time; (*fig.*) fullest extent of anything.
HIGH-TONED [hī-tōnd'], *adj.* full of high moral feeling; elevated, honourable.
HIGH-UP [hī-up'], *n. and adj.* (*coll.*) (person) of high rank.
HIGH-WATER [hī-waw'ter], *n.* high-tide; **h. mark**, mark showing the highest limit reached by a tide; (*fig.*) highest point of development, acme.
HIGHWAY [hī'wā], *n.* public road; (*fig.*) best and quickest way to something.
HIGHWAYMAN [hī'wā-man], *n.* (often mounted) bandit who held up and robbed travellers.
HIJACKER [hī'ja-ker], *n.* (*U.S. slang*) parasitical criminal robbing bootleggers of their liquor etc.
HIKE (1) [hīk], *n.* long country walk, taken for pleasure. HIKE (2), *v.i.* to go on a h.; tramp. [Dial.].
HIKER [hī'ker], *n.* devotee of hiking; a tramp.
HILARIOUS [hi-lāer'i-ōos], *adj.* very merry, boisterously gay; exciting great merriment. HILARIOUSLY, *adv.* in h. fashion. [Gk.].
HILARITY [hi-la'ri-ti], *n.* state of being hilarious. [L.].
HILARY [hi'la-ri], *n.* the January legal term; university term from Christmas to Easter. [St. *Hilarius*, whose festival is on 13 January].
HILL [hil], *n.* smallish natural elevation on the surface of the earth; artificial hillock or mound. HILL-CLIMB, act of climbing a h.; *esp.* as a test for motor vehicles. [OE.].
HILL-BILLY [hil'bi-li], *n. and adj.* (*U.S. coll.*) (pertaining to) a mountain farmer or cowboy; type of popular song characteristic of the American ranching country.
HILLO [hi-lō'], *int.* a cry to attract attention
HILLOCK [hi'lok], *n.* small hill, mound.
HILT [hilt], *n.* handle of a sword, dagger etc.; **up to the h.**, utterly, completely. [OE.].
HIM [him], *pron. objective case of* HE. [OE.].
HIMSELF [him-self'], *pron. 3rd person sg. masc. used reflexively or emphatically;* **by h.**, alone; **he is h. again**, he has recovered. [OE.].
HIND (1) [hīnd], *n.* female red deer. [OE.].
HIND (2), *n.* farm servant; a rustic. [OE.].
HIND (3), *adj.* posterior; situated behind. [ME.].
HINDER (1) [hīn'der], *adj.* that is at the rear or at the back, posterior. [OE.].
HINDER (2) [hin'der], *v.t.* to prevent; delay, thwart. [OE.].
HINDERMOST, HINDMOST [hīnd'(er-)mōst], *adj.* farthest behind.
HINDI (1) [hin'di], *adj.* pertaining to northern India, or to the vernacular language spoken there. HINDI (2), *n.* Aryan vernacular language spoken in northern India. [Hind.].
HIND-QUARTERS [hīnd'kwaw-terz], *n.(pl.)* hind part of an animal, including the hind legs.
HINDRANCE [hin'drans], *n.* act of hindering; one who, or that which, hinders; obstacle.
HINDU (1) [hin-dōo'], *n.* non-Moslem Aryan inhabitant of northern India; believer in Hinduism; native of Hindustan. HINDU (2), *adj.* of, or pertaining to, the Hindus or Hinduism. [Pers.].
HINDUISM [hin'dōo-izm], *n.* religion of the Hindus.
HINDUSTANI [hin-dōo-stah'ni], *n. and adj.* native inhabitant of, pertaining to, Hindustan; most widespread language of India, Urdu, being a variety of Hindi mixed with Persian etc. [HINDU and Pers.].
HINGE (1) [hinj], *n.* joining device by which one or both of two objects so connected may move in relation to the other; (*fig.*) pivot. HINGE (2), *v.t. and i.* to fasten or connect with a h.; (*fig.*) turn or depend on. [ME.].
HINNY (1) [hi'ni], *n.* offspring of a she-ass and a stallion. [L.].
HINNY (2), *v.i.* to neigh. [Fr.].
HINT (1) [hint], *n.* suggestion or allusion; faint intimation; short useful item of advice. HINT (2), *v.t. and i.* to intimate, suggest. [~OE.].
HINTERLAND [hin'ter-land], *n.* land behind a stretch of coast or river-bank; region served by a port. [Germ.].
HIP (1) [hip], *n.* projection made by the side of the pelvis and the top end of the thigh-bone; the sloping timber forming the corner of a roof; **on the h.**, at a disadvantage; **h. and thigh**, utterly, remorselessly. HIP-BATH, bath to be sat in. HIP-BONE, haunch-bone. [OE.].
HIP (2), *n.* fruit of the dog-rose. [OE.].
HIP (3), *n.* (*coll.*) melancholy. HIP (4) (*pres.pt.* HIPPING,

pret. and p.pt. HIPPED), *v.t.* to depress in spirits. HIPPED, *adj.* depressed. [HYP(OCHONDRIA)].
HIP (5), *int.* exclamation twice given as a signal for a general cheer.
HIPPO (1) [hi'pō], *n.* (*coll.*) hippopotamus.
HIPPO- (2), *pref.* horse. [Gk.].
HIPPOCAMPUS (*pl.* hippocampi) [hi-pō-kam'pus], *n.* sea-horse, small fish with a head like that of a horse. [Gk.].
HIPPOCRAS [hi'po-kras], *n.* spiced wine. [Fr. from *Hippocrates*, ancient Greek physician].
HIPPOCRATIC [hi-po-kra'tik], *adj.* pertaining to Hippocrates; relating to the pinched and livid appearance of the human face shortly before death; **H. oath**, the medical oath. [*Hippocrates*, Greek physician].
HIPPODROME [hi'pō-drōm], *n.* circus or arena for horseshows, riding displays etc.; (*hist.*) course for chariot races in ancient Greece and Rome. [Gk.].
HIPPOGRIFF, HIPPOGRYPH [hi'pō-grif], *n.* fabulous monster, mixture of horse and griffin. [Fr.].
HIPPOPOTAMUS [hi-pō-po'ta-mus], *n.* large African river-animal related to the pig. [Gk.].
HIRE (1) [hīer], *n.* act of hiring; payment made to hire something; rights or benefits acquired by hiring something. HIRE (2), *v.t.* to obtain services or temporary possession and use of something in exchange for payment; lend out in exchange for payment; engage under promise of monetary payment. [OE.].
HIRELING [hīer'ling], *n.* paid supporter or follower; one who, or that which, is hired. [OE.].
HIRE-PURCHASE [hīer-pur'chas], *n.* purchase by instalments, use of the object being given on the first payment.
HIRSUTE [hur'syōot], *adj.* hairy. [L.].
HIS [hiz], *possessive pron. and adj.* belonging or pertaining to him. [OE.].
HISS (1) [his], *v.t. and i.* to emit a prolonged sibilant sound; show disapproval by such a sound. HISS (2), *n.* sibilant sound, sometimes indicating annoyance, disapproval etc.; any similar sound produced mechanically; noise made by a snake or cat when alarmed. [ME.].
HISSING [hi'sing], *n.* act of one who, or that which, hisses; sound thus produced, *esp.* when indicating disapproval. HISSINGLY, *adv.* with a h. noise.
HIST [hist], *int.* hush, be quiet. [Echoic].
HISTO- *pref.* tissue. [Gk.].
HISTOLOGY [his-to'lo-ji], *n.* scientific study of organic tissue. HISTOLOGIST, *n.* one versed in h. HISTOLOGICAL [his-to-lo'ji-kal], *adj.* relating to h. [Gk.].
HISTORIAN [his-taw'ri-an], *n.* one versed in history.
HISTORIC [his-to'rik], *adj.* pertaining to, recorded in, history; momentous, memorable, famous. [L.].
HISTORICAL [his-to'ri-kal], *adj.* true to history; historic; according to history; displaying the whole development of something step by step.
HISTORY [his'te-ri], *n.* narrative of events recorded chronologically; study of human activities and events arising from them, from the earliest times, *esp.* the study of past times and events; whole course of development of anything, an account of this. [L.].
HISTRIONIC(AL) [his-tri-o'nik(-al)], *adj.* pertaining to actors or acting; dramatic; theatrical. [L.].
HIT (1) (*pres.pt.* hitting, *pret. and p.pt.* **hit**) [hit], *v.t.* to strike, knock, come in sharp contact with; **to h. on**, to find, *esp.* unexpectedly; **to h. off**, to imitate exactly; **to h. it**, (*slang*) to depart; guess right; **to h. it off with**. (*coll.*) to get on well with. HIT (2), *n.* a blow, stroke etc. which hits its mark; stroke of success, *esp.* if unexpected; happy or witty remark, *esp.* in sarcasm, taunt; (*coll.*) popular success; **to make a h. with**, to impress favourably. [OE.].
HITCH (1) [hich], *v.t.* to move with a jerk or jerks; fasten by something which catches on; **to h. up**, to pull up sharply. HITCH (2), *n.* a jerky motion; a limp; temporary dislocation of arrangements; class of knot used by sailors. [ME.].
HITCH-HIKE [hich'hīk], *v.i.* (*coll.*) to travel by road obtaining lifts where possible.
HITHER (1) [hi'THer], *adv.* to this place, in this direction; **h. and thither**, on an uncertain, varying course. HITHER (2), *adj.* lying on this side, nearer. [OE.].
HITHERMOST [hi'THer-mōst], *adj.* nearest in this direction.
HITHERTO [hi-THer-tōo'], *adv.* up to this time; up till now.
HIT-OR-MISS [hit-aw-mis'], *adj.* careless, haphazard.

HITTER [hi'ter], *n.* one who hits, *esp.* one who hits hard.

HIVE (1) [hiv], *n.* receptacle in which live bees are kept; (*fig.*) place swarming with busy people. HIVE (2), *v.t. and i.* to collect (bees) into a h.; store up (honey) in a h.; enter, live in, a h. [OE.].

HIVES [hivz], *n.(pl.)* a rash on the skin. [Unkn.].

HO [hō], *int.* a cry to attract attention; an expression of astonishment.

HOAR (1) [haw(r)], *adj.* greyish-white; white-haired; (*fig.*) venerable and ancient. HOAR (2), *n.* white, powdery coating of frost, rime. [OE.].

HOARD (1) [hawd], *n.* store of treasure; accumulation, secret collection; store, fund. HOARD (2), *v.t. and i.* to gather together, store away. HOARDER, *n.* one who hoards. [OE.].

HOARDING (1) [haw'ding], *n.* act of making a hoard. [HOARD (2).].

HOARDING (2), *n.* high wooden fence; such a fence used for exhibiting posters. [Uncert.].

HOAR FROST [haw'frost], *n.* white frost.

HOARHOUND, see HOREHOUND.

HOARINESS [haw'ri-nes], *n.* quality of being hoary

HOARSE [haws], *adj.* husky in speech; harsh-sounding. HOARSELY, *adv.* in a h. voice. HOARSE-NESS, *n.* condition of being h. [OE.].

HOARY [haw'ri], *adj.* greyish-white in colour; white-haired; (*fig.*) venerable, ancient, of long standing. [ME.].

HOAX (1) [hōks], *v.t.* to deceive or trick; play a practical joke upon. HOAX (2), *n.* deceiving trick or statement; practical joke. HOAXER, *n.* person who hoaxes. [HOCUS].

HOB (1) [hob], *n.* hub, nave of a wheel; flat part of a grate, at the side. [Uncert.].

HOB (2)†, *n.* imp; fairy. [~ROB from ROBIN].

HOBBLE (1) [ho'bl], *v.t. and i.* to check a horse etc. by tying two of its legs together; limp or stumble along laboriously and painfully. HOBBLE (2), *n.* a lame, stumbling walk; shackle used for hobbling. HOBBLINGLY, *adv.* with a hobbling gait. [ME.].

HOBBLEDEHOY [ho'bl-di-hoi], *n.* clumsy, awkward youth. [Uncert.].

HOBBY [ho'bi], *n.* hobby-horse; an occupation for one's leisure; fad. [ME.].

HOBBY-HORSE [ho'bi-haws], *n.* children's toy consisting of a stick with the head of a horse at one end; early kind of bicycle; rocking-horse; morris-dancer wearing the head of a horse; hobby; pet theme. [*Prec.*].

HOBGOBLIN [hob'gob-lin], *n.* imp; alarming apparition; bogey. [HOB (2) and GOBLIN].

HOBNAIL [hob'nāl], *n.* nail with a thick head, used for the soles of boots. HOBNAILED, *adj.* having hobnails; **hobnailed liver**, liver covered with small projections, due to cirrhosis. [HOB (1)].

HOBNOB (1) (*pres.pt.* **hobnobbing**, *pret. and p.pt.* **hobnobbed**) [hob'nob], *v.i.* to be very friendly; converse amicably. HOBNOB (2), *n.* (*slang*) friendly chat. [ME.].

HOBO [hō'bō], *n.* (*U.S.*) tramp; professional vagabond. [Unkn.].

HOCK (1) **HOUGH** [hok], *n.* joint between the true knee and the fetlock in the hind leg of a horse; in man, the back of the knee; the ham. HOCK (2), *v.t.* to hamstring. [HOUGH].

HOCK (3), *n.* a German white wine. [Germ., wine of Hochheim].

HOCK (4), *n.* **in h.**, (*slang*) in pawn, in prison or in debt. HOCK (5), *v.t.* (*U.S. slang*) to pawn; pledge as a security. [Du.].

HOCKEY (1) [ho'ki], *n.* game played between two teams of eleven, with a small hard ball driven by curved sticks. HOCKEY (2), *adj.* belonging to the game of h. [Uncert.].

HOCUS-POCUS [hō'kus-pō-kus], *n.* meaningless jargon used by a conjurer while performing a trick; silly mystification; nonsense; swindling, underhand work. [Uncert.].

HOD [hod], *n.* wooden trough on a long handle for carrying mortar and bricks over the shoulder. [ME. ~MDu.].

HODDEN [ho'den], *n.* (*Scots*) coarse undyed woollen material; **h. grey**, mixed black and white woollen cloth used for the kilts of the London Scottish. [Unkn.].

HODGE [hoj], *n.* (*coll.*) agricultural labourer. [*Hodge*, character in a play].

HODGE-PODGE, HOTCH-POTCH [hoj'poj, hoch'poch], *n.* mixture, medley, miscellany. [Fr.].

HOE (1) [hō], *n.* garden tool for weeding and loosening the earth. HOE (2), *v.t. and i.* to use a h. for weeding or turning the surface of the soil. [Fr.].

HOG (1) [hog], *n.* castrated boar; pig; (*Scots and dial.*) hogget; (*fig.*) coarse, self-indulgent or filthy person; (*curling*) stone which fails to pass the hog-score; **to go the whole h.**, to do something very thoroughly; **road h.**, motorist inconsiderate of other road users. HOG (2) (*pres.pt.* HOGGING, *pret. and p.pt.* HOGGED), *v.t. and i.* to arch like the back of a h.; act or eat like a h., seize greedily. [OE.].

HOG(S)BACK [hog(z)-bak'], *n.* level ridge (of land or rock) with steep sides.

HOGGET [ho'get], *n.* yearling sheep before its first shearing; colt of a year old; young boar of the second year.

HOGGISH [ho'gish], *adj.* like a hog; greedy, filthy. HOGGISHLY, *adv.* in a h. way. HOGGISHNESS, *n.* quality of being h.

HOGMANAY [hog'ma-nā], *n.* (*Scots*) New Year's Eve; festivities then held. [OFr.].

HOGSHEAD [hogz'hed], *n.* large cask; liquid measure equal to 52½ imperial gallons, or 54 gallons of beer or cider.

HOGSKIN [hog'skin], *n.* leather made from the skins of swine.

HOGWASH [hog'wosh], *n.* kitchen refuse made into swill for swine; (*fig.*) silly talk.

HOICK [hoik], *v.t.* (*coll.*) to lift or hoist with a jerk. [Uncert.].

HOIST (1) [hoist], *v.t.* to raise, heave up, *esp.* by means of tackle. HOIST (2), *n.* act of hoisting; lift, apparatus for hoisting. [ME. ~MDu.].

HOITY-TOITY [hoi-ti-toi'ti], *int. and adj.* cry of protest, *esp.* at arrogance; touchy, arrogant.

HOKEY-POKEY [hō-ki-pō'ki], *n.* kind of ice-cream. [HOCUS-POCUS].

HOLD (1) [hōld], *n.* space below deck in a ship, for storing cargo. [Du.].

HOLD (2) (*pret. and p.pt.* held), *v.t.* to seize with and retain by the hand; grasp; catch; retain; possess; occupy; be in charge of; defend, *esp.* successfully; keep inviolate, abide by; contain; retain pending use; restrain, keep from escaping; dominate; be a match for; attract and retain the attention of; retain in the mind; believe; decide; organize, institute; *v.i.* to withstand strain; be valid, last; continue to do or to be; **to h. forth**, to talk at length; **to h. on**, to persevere; (*teleph.*) maintain a connexion; **to h. one's own**, to be the equal of one's opponents; **to h. out**, to proffer; present; defend amid difficulties; **to h. over**, to threaten with; postpone; **to h. to**, to abide by; compel to abide by; **to h. up**, to stop a vehicle on a road or railway for any nefarious purpose, but *esp.* for robbery; delay; **to h. water**, (*fig.*) (of an idea, statement etc.) to be sound and valid; (*naut.*) stop a rowing boat by holding the oars vertical in the water; **to h. with**, to approve of. HOLD (3), *n.* action of holding; manner or power of holding; that by which one may h. on; socket; (*fig.*) control; mental grip; influence; **to get h. of**, to obtain; (*slang*) obtain an interview with. [OE.].

HOLDALL [hōl'dawl], *n.* large bag for conveniently carrying all manner of things.

HOLDER [hōl'der], *n.* one who, or that which, holds; tenant; receptacle.

HOLDFAST [hōld'fahst], *n.* something to which one may hold on; that which holds fast, clamp etc.

HOLDING [hōl'ding], *n.* action of one who holds; land or property owned.

HOLD-UP [hōld'up], *n.* stoppage or delay, *esp.* in traffic; armed robbery.

HOLE (1) [hōl], *n.* cavity, depression in a solid surface; empty space; receptacle; excavation; lair, den or burrow of an animal; small mean dwelling, unpleasant place; break, gap or rent; opening, orifice; (*fig.*) flaw, inaccuracy; (*golf*) cup cut in the green into which the players try to hit the ball; point scored in a holing game; (*slang*) difficult situation; **to make a h. in**, to reduce, consume a considerable part of; **to pick holes in**, to make adverse criticism of. HOLE (2), *v.t. and i.* to make a h. in, hollow out; make a tunnel through; drive into a h. [OE.].

HOLE-AND-CORNER [hōl-and-kaw'ner], *adj.* (*coll.*) underhand, secret.

HOLEY [hō'li], *adj.* having holes; full of holes.

HOLIDAY (1) [ho'li-dā], *n.* religious festival; day of festivity, rest or recreation when work temporarily ceases; period of rest from work and duty; **Bank H.**, general national h. in England appointed by Act of Parliament. HOLIDAY-MAKER, someone on h., tripper. HOLIDAY (2), adj. belonging to, or befitting, a h. HOLIDAY (3), v.i. to take a h. [OE.].

HOLILY [hō'li-li], adv. in a holy manner.

HOLINESS [hō'li-nes], n. quality of being holy; **His H.**, the Pope's title.

HOLLA [ho'lah], int. a call of greeting or to attract attention. [Fr.].

HOLLAND [ho'land], n. kind of coarse unbleached linen. [Holland, where first made].

HOLLANDS [ho'landz], n. gin made in Holland. [Du.].

HOLLER [ho'ler], n. and v.i. (dial. and U.S.) a holla; to hollo.

HOLLO(W) [ho-lō'], v.t. and i. (coll.) to shout loudly.

HOLLOW (1) [ho'lō], n. a depression, wide groove, shallow cavity; little valley. HOLLOW (2), adj. having a cavity or depression in the surface; (of eyes) deep-set; (of the face) lean; not solid; having an outer bulk or husk but nothing inside; empty; re-echoing, resonant; (fig.) insubstantial, false; (of laughter) mirthless, unreal. HOLLOW-EYED, having sunken eyes. HOLLOW (3), v.t. to render h.; make a h. in. HOLLOWLY, adv. in a h. way. HOLLOWNESS, n. quality of being h. [OE.].

HOLLY [ho'li], n. evergreen tree with dark-green prickly leaves and scarlet berries. [OE.].

HOLLYHOCK [ho'li-hok], n. tall plant related to the mallow. [ME.].

HOLM [hōm], n. low, flat river bank; small island, esp. in an estuary or river. [OE.].

HOLM-OAK [hōm'ōk], n. the evergreen oak.

HOLO-, pref. entire, whole; (geol.) relating to the most recent strata. [Gk.].

HOLOCAUST [ho'lō-kawst], n. sacrifice by fire; massacre, mass destruction. [Fr.].

HOLOGRAPH [ho'lō-grahf], n. document entirely in the handwriting of the signatory. HOLOGRAPHIC [ho-lō-gra'fik], adj. pertaining to a h.; written throughout by the author. [Gk.].

HOLPEN† [hōl'pen], p.pt. of HELP (1).

HOLSTER [hōl'ster], n. leather pistol case, hung from the belt or saddle-bow. [Swed.].

HOLT [hōlt], n. grove, small wood or thicket. [OE.].

HOLY (1) [hō'li], adj. sacred; spiritually noble and pure; blessed by the Church; connected with religion; pious. HOLY (2), n. a h. place; **H. of Holies**, inmost sanctuary of the Jewish temple or tabernacle; any h. place; (slang) inaccessible sanctum. [OE.].

HOLY-DAY [hō'li-dā], n. religious feast or fast; day in the Church's calendar.

HOLY GHOST [hō-li-gōst'], n. third person of the Trinity, the comforter bequeathed by Christ after His resurrection.

HOLYSTONE (1) [hō'li-stōn], n. (naut.) soft stone used to scour the decks of ships. HOLYSTONE (2), v.t. to scour with h.

HOMAGE [ho'mij], n. ritual act by which one declares oneself the vassal of another; (fig.) deference, respect; an expression of these. [OFr.].

HOMBURG [hom'berg], n. soft, felt, brimmed hat for men. [Homburg, Germany].

HOME (1) [hōm], n. house of one's birth and nurture, or that belonging to one's parents; house or apartment where one lives; house where one is welcomed as a member of the family; one's habitual haunt; household, family circle; contents, esp. furniture, of a house; mother-country, in British overseas countries, the British Isles; town etc. where one was born; place or state in which one finds happiness and satisfaction; asylum or institute where the sick and poor are cared for; small private hospital; place where anything is found or fostered; goal or base in a game; **at h.**, receiving visitors; **at h. with**, at one's ease with; **nothing to write h. about**, not exciting or unusual. HOME (2), adj. pertaining to one's h. or to one's native country; internal; appropriate; **H. Counties**, counties round London. HOME (3), v.i. to go h. (esp. of pigeons); (poet.) dwell; v.t. to establish in a h. HOME (4), adv. towards h.; accurately, right on the mark; movingly; **to bring h. to**, to impress with rational force, to convince. [OE.].

HOME-BIRD [hōm'berd], n. (coll.) person who loves to be at home.

HOME-BREWED [hōm-brōōd'], n. and adj. (ale) brewed at home.

HOMECOMING [hōm'ku-ming], n. return to or arrival at home, or one's native land.

HOME-FARM [hōm-fahm'], n. farm attached to the dwelling-house of the occupier of an estate.

HOME GUARD [hōm-gahd'], n. body of part-time soldiers enrolled for defence against invasion esp. in the U.K. in 1940; member of this body.

HOMELAND [hōm'land], n. native land; mother-country.

HOMELESS [hōm'les], adj. having no home.

HOMELIKE [hōm'līk], adj. like home; homely; informal.

HOMELY [hōm'li], adj. like home; informal, friendly; lacking polish; familiar, everyday; (U.S.) plain-looking. HOMELINESS, n. quality of being h.

HOMEMADE [hōm-mād'], adj. (as if) made at home.

HOMER [hō'mer], n. homing pigeon.

HOMERIC [hō-me'rik], adj. pertaining to the Greek poet Homer or his poetry; resembling his poetry; epic. [Gk.].

HOME RULE [hōm-rōōl'], n. autonomy, independent and local government without outside control.

HOMESICK [hōm'sik], adj. miserable with the longing to be at home. HOMESICKNESS, n. state of being h., nostalgia.

HOMESPUN (1) [hōm'spun], adj. woven by hand in the home; (fig.) simple, honest. HOMESPUN (2), n. cloth of handwoven yarn.

HOMESTEAD [hōm'sted], n. dwelling-house, esp. farmhouse, with outbuildings and surrounding land.

HOMEWARD [hōm'werd], adj. and adv. in the direction of home. [OE.].

HOMICIDAL [ho-mi-sī'dal], adj. pertaining to homicide; like homicide; murderous.

HOMICIDE [ho'mi-sīd], n. the killing of one man by another; person who kills another. [L.].

HOMILETICS [ho-mi-le'tiks], n.(pl.) art of preaching; religious oratory. HOMILETIC(AL), adj. pertaining to sermons or preaching. [Gk.].

HOMILY [ho'mi-li], n. sermon, moral discourse, instructive lecture. [Gk.].

HOMING [hō'ming], adj. going home, esp. (of pigeons) trained to fly home from great distances.

HOMINY [ho'mi-ni], n. meal prepared from Indian corn, boiled maize. [Native].

HOMO-, pref. the same, of the same sort. [Gk.].

HOMOEO-, pref. the same, like. [Gk.].

HOMOEOPATHIC hō-mi-ō-pa'thik], adj. relating to homoeopathy. HOMOEOPATHICALLY, adv. according to the methods of homoeopathy.

HOMOEOPATHIST [hō-mi-o'pa-thist], n. one who practises or believes in homoeopathy.

HOMOEOPATHY [hō-mi-o'pa-thi], n. treatment of disease by frequent very small doses of some drug producing symptoms similar to those of the illness treated. [Gk.].

HOMOGENEITY [ho-mō-je-nē'i-ti], n. state of being homogeneous.

HOMOGENEOUS [ho-mō-jē'ni-ōōs], adj. alike, similar; uniform; of the same kind, of like parts throughout; (math.) commensurable. HOMOGENE-OUSLY, adv. in a h. way. [MedL.].

HOMOLOGOUS [ho-mo'lo-gōōs], adj. corresponding in character, position, proportion, value, structure etc. HOMOLOGY [ho-mo'lo-ji], n. quality of being h.; (biol.) affinity of structure, though not of form and function. [Gk.].

HOMONYM [ho'mō-nim], n. one of a pair or series of words identical in sound but different in meaning. HOMONYMIC, HOMONYMOUS [ho-mō-ni'mik, ho-mo'ni-mōōs], adj. possessing the same name; like, or that are, homonyms. [Gk.].

HOMOPHONE [ho'mō-fōn], n. letter or symbol representing the same sound as another; homonym. HOMOPHONIC, HOMOPHONOUS [ho-mō-fo'nik, ho-mo'fo-nōōs], adj. having the same sound; (mus.) monodic; unisonant. [Gk.].

HOMOSEXUAL [ho-mō-sek'shōō-al], n. and adj. (one) possessing a sexual propensity for persons of one's own sex. HOMOSEXUALITY [ho-mō-sek-shōō-a'li-ti], n. state of being h. [HOMO and SEXUAL].

HOMUNCULUS [ho-mung'kyōō-lus], n. dwarf or mannikin. [L.].

HONE (1) [hōn], n. whetstone; stone of fine grain used for sharpening blades. HONE (2), v.t. to sharpen by means of a h. [OE.].

HONEST [o'nest], adj. to be trusted, not given to immoral or illegal actions; fair-minded; sincere; not given to lying; legally or conscientiously earned or done; virtuous, decent. HONEST-TO-GOODNESS, (coll.) genuine. HONESTLY, adv. in an h. fashion. [OFr.].

HONESTY [o'nes-ti], n. quality of being honest; garden plant with silvery pods. [OFr.].

HONEY (1) [hu'ni], n. sweet, yellow, glutinous substance which bees make from the nectar of flowers;

(*fig.*) anything very sweet or delightful; (*coll.*) darling. HONEY-BAG, sac or receptacle for h. in a h-bee. HONEY (2), *adj.* pertaining to, productive of, h. [OE.].
HONEY-BEE [hu'ni-bē], *n.* bee kept for its honey.
HONEY-BUZZARD [hu'ni-bu-zerd], *n.* hawk which feeds on the grubs of bees and other insects.
HONEYCOMB (1) [hu'ni-kōm], *n.* structure of hexagonal wax cells made by bees to contain honey or larvae; any perforated object resembling this in its pattern. HONEYCOMB (2), *v.t.* to perforate excessively; riddle with holes or passages. [OE.].
HONEYDEW [hu'ni-dyōō], *n.* sweet substance secreted mainly by aphides on leaves of plants; sweetish tobacco; ambrosia.
HONEYED [hu'nid], *adj.* covered with honey; (*fig.*) sweet; ingratiating, flattering.
HONEYMOON (1) [hu'ni-mōōn], *n.* holiday spent by a bridal pair immediately after marriage. HONEYMOON (2), *v.i.* to spend a h.
HONEYSUCKLE [hu'ni-su-kl], *n.* climbing plant with fragrant yellowish flowers. [ME.].
HONEY-TONGUED [hu-ni-tungd'], *adj.* softspoken.
HONITON [hu'ni-ton], *n.* hand-made lace from *Honiton*, in Devonshire.
HONK (1) [hongk], *n.* cry of a wild goose; harsh sound of a motor-horn. HONK (2), *v.i.* to utter a h.; blow on a motor-horn. [Echoic].
HONORARIUM [o-ne-räer'i-um], *n.* voluntary payment for services rendered; gratuity. [L.].
HONORARY [o'ne-ra-ri], *adj.* pertaining to, or denoting, honour; conferred as an honour, but not producing profit; holding a post of this kind. [L.].
HONORIFIC [o-ne-ri'fik], *adj.* conferring honour; expressing honour. [L.].
HONOUR (1) [o'ner], *n.* complex virtue or idea compounded of truth, purity, courage and generosity of spirit; elevation of character; deference or veneration; reverence and esteem; glory, renown; that which does credit to or confers respect; special distinction gained; token symbolizing this; high rank, exalted position; courtesy rendered; (*pl.*) acts expressing reverence or admiration; acts of hospitality; specialized university degree; (*golf*) right of making the first stroke off the tee; (*bridge*) playing-cards above the nine; (of a woman) good reputation; (of a man) sensitiveness to disgrace or affront; **debt of h.,** debt which is morally but not legally due to be paid; **h. bright,** indeed, truly; **to do the honours,** to act as host or hostess; **to have the h.,** to be allowed. HONOUR (2), *v.t.* to bestow h. upon; esteem, respect; (of a debt) pay according to agreement; (of a cheque etc.) recognize as valid, accept and pay; (of a promise) keep. [AFr.].
HONOURABLE [o'ne-ra-bl], *adj.* worthy to be honoured; having principles of honour, high-minded; based upon principles of honour; courtesy title given to the children of barons, younger sons or eldest daughter of a viscount, younger sons of earls or to the wife of such a person; epithet of courtesy used when one member of the House of Commons or similar governing body refers to another; used in addressing a High Court Judge, Judge of the High Court of Scotland or a Royal Maid of Honour; **Right H.,** phrase used in the title of earls, viscounts and barons, Privy Councillors, Lords Justices of Appeal, Lords Mayor of London, York and Belfast, Lords Provost of Edinburgh and Glasgow and Chairman of the London County Council; **Most H.,** style of a marquis or member of the Order of the Bath. HONOURABLE-NESS, *n.* condition of being h. HONOURABLY, *adv.* in an h. way. [OFr.].
HOOCH [hōōch], *n.* (*U.S. slang*) alcoholic liquor, *esp.* when synthetic. [Alaskan Indian].
HOOD (1) [hōōd], *n.* soft brimless covering for the head and neck, often attached to a cloak; academic cowl worn hanging at the back from the neck, denoting the degree and university of the wearer; anything resembling a h. in shape; collapsible cover on a motor-car etc. HOOD (2), *v.t.* to cover as with a h.; supply with a h. HOODED, *adj.* covered with, wearing, a h.; (*bot.*) h.-shaped; (*zool.*) having a crest or markings like a h. [OE.].
HOODLUM [hōōd'lum], *n.* (*U.S. slang*) rowdy youth; hooligan. [Unkn.].
HOODOO (1) [hōō'dōō], *n.* (*orig. U.S.*) hidden malevolent influence. HOODOO (2), *adj.* mysteriously unlucky. [VOODOO].
HOODWINK [hōōd'wingk], *v.t.* to bind or partly cover the eyes of a horse; deceive, mislead, trick.
HOOEY [hōō'i], *n.* (*U.S. slang*) nonsense.

HOOF (1) (*pl.* **hoofs, hooves**) [hōōf(s), hōōvz], *n.* horny protection to the extremity of the feet of horses, swine, or other animals; (*slang*) human foot. HOOF (2), *v.t.* (*slang*) to h. it, to walk; dance; **to h. out,** to eject violently; dismiss from employment. HOOFED, HOOVED, *adj.* having hoofs. [OE.].
HOOK (1) [hōōk], *n.* piece of metal bent in the shape of the letter J, used for catching, hanging, fastening etc.; (*writing*) a curved line resembling this; bent metal contrivance fitting into a metal loop to fasten a garment; chopping tool with a curved blade; stroke in golf or cricket in which the ball is hit sharply to the left (of a right-handed player); blow in boxing with the arm bent; **h. up,** (*radio*) temporary connexion enabling radio programmes to be transmitted simultaneously from several stations; **by h. or by crook,** somehow or other; **to sling one's h.,** (*slang*) to depart. HOOK (2), *v.t. and i.* to shape or be shaped like a h., catch or fasten with a h.; be attached by a h. or hooks; make a h. stroke at golf, cricket or boxing; (*Rugby football*) take up the position of hooker; (*fig.*) beguile; (*slang*) steal; **to h. it,** (*slang*) to make off. HOOKED, *adj.* bent or curved like a h.; having hooks. [OE.].
HOOKAH [hōō'kah], *n.* long Oriental tobacco pipe, consisting of a tobacco receptacle, bowl and flexible tube, in which the smoke is made to pass through water.
HOOKER (1) [hōō-ker], *n.* Dutch two-masted fishing boat; Irish fishing smack. [Du.].
HOOKER (2), *n.* one who hooks; one of the players in Rugby football whose duty it is to try to win possession of the ball with their feet, when it is put into the scrummage.
HOOKWORM [hōōk'werm], *n.* parasitic worm infesting the intestines in hot climates.
HOOLIGAN [hōō'li-gan], *n.* rough boy; rowdy vandal. [*Houlihan,* name of a noisy family in an Irish music-hall song].
HOOP (1) [hōōp], *n.* ring of wood, metal etc.; one of the circular horizontal pieces binding a cask; whalebone or wooden ring at one time worn under petticoats to extend them; large wooden or metal ring trundled along the ground by children; rounded metal arch through which a croquet ball is struck. HOOP (2), *v.t.* to encircle with a h. [OE.].
HOOP (3), *v.i.* to utter a wheezy cry as when suffering from whooping-cough; shout. HOOP (4), *n.* a shout. [OFr.].
HOOPING-COUGH, see WHOOPING-COUGH
HOOP-LA [hōōp'lah], *n.* game at fairs in which wooden rings are tossed at an array of various objects to encircle and so win them.
HOOPOE [hōō'pōō], *n.* a crested bird. [Echoic].
HOOT (1) [hōōt], *v.t. and i.* to utter a shout of contempt or derision; (of an owl) cry; (of a hooter) sound. HOOT (2), *n.* shout of dislike or derision; cry of an owl; note of a hooter. [ME. ~MSwed.].
HOOTER [hōō'ter], *n.* one who, or that which, hoots; steam whistle; horn sounded as a signal; siren.
HOP (1) [hop], *n.* plant of which the female plant bears green cones, which when ripened are used in brewing to give a bitter flavour; one of these cones. HOP-BINE, twining stem of the h. plant. HOP-GARDEN, field planted with hops. HOP-KILN, kiln for drying hops. HOP-POLE, pole up which hops are trained. HOP (2), (*pres.pt.* HOPPING, *pret. and p.pt.* HOPPED), *v.t.* to impregnate with hops; *v.i.* to gather hops. [MDu.].
HOP (3), (*pres.pt.* **hopping,** *pret. and p.pt.* **hopped**), *v.i.* to jump on one leg; dance about; progress by a series of short leaps, skip; **to h. it,** (*slang*) to depart quickly. HOP (4), *n.* jump achieved on one leg; small jump; (*slang*) dance; (*aeron.*) stage in a long-distance flight. [OE.].
HOPE (1) [hōp], *n.* confident expectation that something longed for will come; state of mind entertaining such expectation; someone or something that inspires such expectation or upon which success depends; likelihood. HOPE (2), *v.i.* to desire and expect that something will come to pass; be hopeful, trust, desire. [OE.].
HOPEFUL [hōp'fŏŏl], *adj.* full of hope; hoping; promising; **young h.,** promising young person. HOPEFULLY, *adv.* in a h. manner. HOPEFULNESS, *n.* condition of being h.
HOPELESS [hōp'les], *adj.* without hope; desponding; desperate; incurable. HOPELESSLY, *adv.* in a h. way. HOPELESSNESS, *n.* quality of being h.
HOPPER [ho'per], *n.* one who hops; insect which hops; funnel by which grain passes into a mill; barge

which empties its contents through its bottom; picker of hops.

HOP-PICKER [hop'pi-ker], *n.* person who picks hops; machine for picking hops.

HOPPLE [ho'pl], *v.t.* to hobble (an animal). [~MDu.].

HOP-POCKET [hop'po-kit], *n.* sack holding from 1½ cwt. to 2 cwt. of hops.

HOP-SCOTCH [hop'skoch], *n.* children's game in which one hops along on one leg, pushing forward a small slab of stone etc. into numbered squares. [HOP (4) and SCOTCH (3)].

HORDE (1) [hawd], *n.* nomadic warlike tribe; barbarian host; large mob; vast herd or collection of animals; (*pl.*) (*coll.*) crowds, swarms. HORDE (2), *v.i.* gather as in a h. [Turk.].

HOREHOUND, HOARHOUND [haw'hownd], *n.* a labiate plant, the bitter juice of which is used as a remedy for coughs. [OE.].

HORIZON [ho-rī'zon], *n.* line at which earth and sky seem to meet and beyond which it is not possible to see; (*geol.*) any level in a rock formation parallel with the bedding; (*fig.*) limit of one's intellectual perception or experience. [Gk.].

HORIZONTAL (1) [ho-ri-zon'tal], *adj.* at right angles with the vertical; parallel with the horizon; flat, level; **h. bars,** bars used in gymnastic exercises. HORIZONTAL (2), *n.* something h. HORIZONTALLY, *adv.* in a h. direction or position. [Fr.].

HORMONE [haw'mōn], *n.* (*physiol.*) one of various endocrine secretions which stimulate organs of the body. [Gk.].

HORN (1) [hawn], *n.* one of the projections on the heads of cattle and other animals; tusk or bony snout; the hard substance composing this; object made of or resembling this; projection, cusp; end of a crescent, *esp.* of the new moon; a musical wind-instrument; any instrument used to utter a note of warning resembling that of a trumpet, hooter, siren; **h. of plenty,** cornucopia, any source of wealth and well-being; **French h.,** musical instrument of the trumpet type; **English h.,** tenor oboe; **to take the bull by the horns,** to face a problem boldly. HUNTING-HORN, shrill-toned instrument blown during a hunt. HORN (2), *adj.* of h., made of h. HORN (3), *v.t.* to provide with horns; strike or gore with the horns. HORNED, *adj.* furnished with antlers or horns; having horny or h.-like projections; crescent-shaped. [OE.].

HORNBEAM [hawn'bēm], *n.* deciduous tree with a wood of horny toughness. [HORN (1) and OE.].

HORNBILL [hawn'bil], *n.* tropical bird with a horny growth on head and bill.

HORNBLENDE [hawn'blend], *n.* a mineral found in igneous rocks. [Germ.].

HORNBOOK [hawn'bŏŏk], *n.* sheet of paper inscribed with the alphabet etc. backed with wood and covered with a thin sheet of transparent horn, used formerly to give a child its first lessons.

HORNET [haw'net], *n.* large species of wasp; (*fig.*) irritating or oppressive person. [~OE.].

HORN-OWL [hawn'owl], *n.* owl with tufted feathers like horns on its head.

HORNPIPE [hawn'pīp], *n.* former reed instrument; energetic dance originally performed to an accompaniment on this, *esp.* by sailors; music to accompany such a dance.

HOROSCOPE [ho'rō-skōp], *n.* observation of the position of the stars and planets at some particular moment, *esp.* at a child's birth, in order to foretell its future; diagram showing this. [Gk.].

HORRIBLE [ho'ri-bl], *adj.* causing, or liable to cause, horror; dreadful; shocking; (*coll.*) not at all pleasant. HORRIBLY, *adv.* in a h. fashion; (*coll.*) very. [L.].

HORRID [ho'rid], *adj.* liable to excite horror; frightful; offensive or disgusting; (*coll.*) annoying, disagreeable. HORRIDLY, *adv.* in a h. fashion. HORRIDNESS, *n.* quality of being h. [L.].

HORRIFIC [ho-ri'fik], *adj.* horrible, frightening. [L.].

HORRIFY [ho'ri-fī], *v.t.* to fill with horror; (*coll.*) shock. [L.].

HORROR [ho'rer], *n.* powerful feeling of fear or loathing; that which excites this feeling; (*coll.*) unpleasant sight; disagreeable person; (*pl.*) extreme terror, *esp.* in delirium tremens; **h. film,** (*cinema*) film dealing with terrifying subjects and licensed for showing to adults only. HORROR-STRICKEN, smitten with terror, horrified. [OFr.].

HORS [aw(r)], *prep.* out of; **h. de combat** [aw(r)-de-kom'bah], disabled; **h. d'oeuvre** [aw(r)-durvr'],

small dishes served as relish usually at the beginning of a meal, and normally served cold. [Fr.].

HORSE (1) [haws], *n.* large hoofed quadruped, commonly domesticated and used for pulling, carrying and riding upon; adult male of the species stallion; (*zool.*) any member of the family *Equidae*; cavalry; something resembling a horse; **clothes h.,** frame on which clothes are hung for drying and airing; **vaulting h.,** gymnastic apparatus used for jumping exercises; **dark h.,** person whose qualities are unknown. HORSE (2), *adj.* pertaining to a h. strong and large as a h. HORSE (3), *v.t.* to furnish with a h. or horses. [OE.].

HORSE-BLOCK [haws'blok], *n.* step to assist persons in mounting and dismounting from a horse.

HORSEBOX [haws'boks], *n.* railway or road van constructed to carry horses.

HORSE-CHESTNUT [haws-ches'nut], *n.* deciduous tree bearing cone-shaped clusters of white or pink flowers; fruit or nut of this tree.

HORSECLOTH [haws'kloth], *n.* blanket to cover a horse's back; saddle-cloth.

HORSECOPER [haws'kō-per], *n.* dealer in horses *esp.* a dishonest one.

HORSEFLESH [haws'flesh], *n.* edible flesh of a horse; horses collectively.

HORSEFLY [haws'flī], *n.* fly which stings horses; gadfly.

HORSE GUARDS [haws'gahdz], *n* (*pl.*) household cavalry, *esp.* the cavalry brigade of the British Guards; their headquarters in Whitehall.

HORSE LATITUDES [haws'la-ti-tyŏŏdz], *n.(pl.)* belt of calms at about 30 degrees N. and S. of the equator, *esp.* in the N. Atlantic. [Unkn.].

HORSE-LAUGH [haws'lahf], *n.* loud boisterous laugh; guffaw.

HORSEMANSHIP [haws'man-ship], *n.* art of riding a horse, or of training and managing horses.

HORSE MARINE [haws'ma-rēn], *n.* fictitious rating, mentioned jocularly to hint at disbelief on the part of the speaker.

HORSEPLAY [haws'plā] *n.* rough boisterous play.

HORSE-POWER [haws'pow-er], *n.* unit for measuring power standardized as the power needed to lift 550 lb. one foot per second.

HORSE-RADISH [haws'ra-dish], *n.* cruciferous plant with a hot, pungent root.

HORSE-SENSE [haws'sens], *n.* practical common sense.

HORSESHOE (1) [haws'shŏŏ], *n.* iron shoe for horses; anything of the same shape. HORSESHOE (2), *adj.* shaped like a h.

HORSE-TAIL [haws'tāl], *n.* tail of a horse, used as a Turkish standard. or badge of rank; (*bot.*) genus of flowerless plants.

HORSEWHIP (1) [haws'wip], *n.* long whip used in driving a team of horses. HORSEWHIP (2) (*pres.pt.* HORSEWHIPPING, *pret. and p.pt.* HORSEWHIPPED), *v.t.* to flog severely, *esp.* with a h.

HORST [hawst], *n.* a block-mountain; a mountain surrounded by precipices. [Germ.].

HORSY [haw'si], *adj.* interested in, accustomed to, horses; having the appearance of a person with such interests and habits.

HORTATIVE [haw'ta-tiv], *adj.* exhorting, admonishing, encouraging. [L.].

HORTATORY [haw'ta-te-ri], *adj.* hortative. [L.].

HORTICULTURAL [haw-ti-kul'tyŏŏ-ral] *adj.* of, or relating to, horticulture.

HORTICULTURE [haw'ti-kul-tyŏŏr], *n.* art of growing flowers and fruits; craft of making and keeping a garden. HORTICULTURIST [haw-ti-kul'tyŏŏ-rist], *n.* one skilled in h. [L.].

HOSANNA [hō-za'nah], *int.* a cry of adoration. [Heb.].

HOSE (1) [hōz], *n.(pl.)* socks and stockings; † divided garment for the legs. [OE.].

HOSE (2), *n.* long flexible tube for conveying water. HOSE (3), *v.t.* to water with a h. [Du.].

HOSEPIPE [hōz'pīp], *n.* a hose.

HOSIER [hō'zi-er], *n.* dealer in hosiery.

HOSIERY [hō'zhe-ri], *n.* lighter articles of men's clothing, as socks, collars, underwear; the trade dealing in these articles. [HOSE (1)].

HOSPICE [hos'pis], *n.* travellers' house of rest kept by monks; home for the sick and poor. [Fr.].

HOSPITABLE [hos'pi-ta-bl], *adj.* liberal in entertaining guests; affording shelter and hospitality.

HOSPITAL [hos'pi-tal], *n.* institution where sick and injured persons are received and attended to; charitable institution for sick, poor, or aged. [L.].

HOSPITALITY [hos-pi-ta'li-ti], *n.* generous entertainment of guests; entertainment provided for guests on either a friendly or a commercial basis; cheerful willingness to receive guests. [Fr.].

HOSPITALLER [hos'pi-ta-ler], *n.* member of a charitable order; member of the order of St. John of Jerusalem.

HOST (1) [hōst], *n* (*archaic*) army; (*fig.*) great number. [L.].

HOST (2), *n.* one who receives guests; innkeeper; (*biol.*) plant or animal on which a parasite lives. [OFr.].

HOST (3), *n.* (*eccles.*) the consecrated wafer of the Eucharist. [L.].

HOSTAGE [hos'tij], *n.* member of one of two warring states, armies etc. handed over to, or seized by, the other as a pledge of good faith; (*fig.*) a security. [OFr.].

HOSTEL [hos'tel], *n.* hall of residence or temporary accommodation for members of a particular society, group or institution. [OFr.].

HOSTELRY [hos'tel-ri], *n.* hotel, inn. [ME.].

HOSTESS [hōs'tes], *n.* female host; host's wife; female innkeeper.

HOSTILE [hos'tīl], *adj.* of, or pertaining to, an enemy; inimical; showing unfriendliness and dislike, opposed to. HOSTILELY, *adv.* in a h. way.

HOSTILITY [hos-ti'li-ti], *n.* animosity, hatred, enmity; the feeling or expression of these; (*pl.*) acts of war. [Fr.].

HOSTLER, see OSTLER.

HOT (1) [hot], *adj.* having heat to such an extent as may be felt; giving a sense of burning in the mouth; (of food) newly cooked; (*fig.*) eager and impetuous; (*slang*) extremely clever, expert; (of music) elaborately syncopated; (*slang*) hectic, dangerous; sexually aroused; (*coll.*) pornographic, indecent; (of scent) strong and well marked; **to be h. on the track,** to be on the heels of the quarry; **to be h. on,** (*coll.*) to be addicted to; **to get h.,** to be very near the place where something is hidden, very near guessing the right answer; **h. air,** pointless talk; **h. dog,** (*U.S.*) hot sausage sandwich; **h. water,** (*coll.*) trouble, difficulties; **h. news,** report of a very recent event; **h. stuff,** (*slang*) person or thing of exceptional quality; **not so h.,** (*slang*) not very good. HOT (2), *adv.* in a h. manner; so as to render h.; hotly, severely; **to blow h. and cold,** to hesitate, waver. HOT (3), *v.t. and i.* (*slang*) **to h. up,** to become more exciting; increase the power of; heat up. [OE.].

HOTBED [hot'bed], *n.* (*hort.*) layer of fermenting manure covered with earth, used to encourage the growth of seeds and plants; (*fig.*) place where something evil is fostered and unusually rife.

HOT-BLOODED [hot-blu'did], *adj.* passionate.

HOT-BULB [hot-bulb'], *n.* a hot-spot.

HOTCH-POTCH, see HODGE-PODGE.

HOTEL [hō-tel'], *n.* large inn of a superior kind.

HOTELIER [ō-te'lyā], *n.* hotel-keeper. [Fr.].

HOT-FOOT [hot-fŏŏt'], *adv.* in great haste.

HOT-HEADED [hot-he'did], *adj.* excitable, impetuous, stupidly rash.

HOTHOUSE [hot'hows], *n.* artificially heated glasshouse in which tender or exotic plants are reared.

HOTPOT [hot'pot], *n.* stew of various meats and vegetables baked in a casserole.

HOT-PRESS (1) [hot'pres], *n.* machine for giving a gloss to linen or paper by pressing it between hot metal plates. HOT-PRESS (2), *v.t.* to put through a h.

HOT-SPOT [hot'spot], *n.* (in an oil fuel engine) heated point or chamber where the oil is vaporized.

HOUDAH, HOWDAH [how'dah], *n.* seat carried on an elephant's back. [Pers.].

HOUGH, see HOCK (1) and (2).

HOUND (1) [hownd], *n.* a dog, *esp.* a large or a hunting dog; one of the pursuers in a paper-chase; (*pl.*) a hunt; (*coll.*) blackguard. HOUND (2), *v.t.* to pursue unremittingly; incite. [OE.].

HOUR [owr], *n.* twenty-fourth part of a day and a night, 60 minutes; an occasion; an opportunity; a limited space of time; the time; present moment; distance which can be travelled in one hour; (*astron.*) 15 deg. of longitude; (*pl.*) (*eccles.*) prayers said at the canonical hours; (*pl.*) period fixed for the transaction of business; **canonical hours,** (*eccles.*) seven periods of the day appointed for prayer; **the eleventh h.,** the last moment; **his h. has come,** his death is imminent; he has now his greatest chance. HOUR-CIRCLE, a meridian. HOUR-HAND, hand of a watch or clock which shows the h. [L.].

HOUR-GLASS [owr'glahs], *n.* device for measuring intervals of time by running sand between two glass bulbs.

HOURI [hŏŏ'ri], *n.* female inhabitant of the Mohammedan paradise; (*fig.*) voluptuous, fascinating woman. [Pers.].

HOURLY (1) [owr'li], *adj.* occurring or done every hour; lasting an hour; continual. HOURLY (2), *adv.* every hour; continually; frequently.

HOUSE (1) [hows], *n.* building designed for human habitation; dwelling place; hotel, inn or boarding-house; boarding-house attached to a public school, or its inmates; one of several divisions in which the pupils are grouped in a day school; hall or college attached to a university, or its members; educational institution providing residence for its members; household, domestic circle; lineage, *esp.* an ancient or noble family; lair, nest, shell of an animal, bird, insect etc.; commercial firm; theatre or its audience; religious establishment for nuns, monks etc., or its inmates; building for the meeting of a deliberative or legislative body; the members of such a body; **h. of ill fame,** brothel; **the H.,** House of Commons, Parliament; House of Lords; Stock Exchange; Christ Church, Oxford; Peterhouse, Cambridge; workhouse; **like a h. on fire,** with extreme rapidity; **as safe as houses,** very safe indeed; **to make a h.** (of a legislative assembly etc.) to have sufficient members present for a quorum; arrange for this to happen; **to bring the h. down,** to provoke storms of applause from the audience; **on the h.,** (*coll.*) at the expense of the inn etc.; **h. charge,** basic charge made to diners in a restaurant in addition to the bill for food consumed. HOUSE (2) [howz], *v.t. and i.* to provide with a h. or houses; give food and lodging to; offer or find room for; store. [OE.].

HOUSE-AGENT [hows'ā-jent], *n.* one employed to let or sell property.

HOUSEBOAT [hows'bōt], *n.* covered boat for living in; barge with a wooden house built on it.

HOUSEBREAKER [hows'brā-ker], *n.* one who breaks into a house before sunset with intent to steal; one who pulls down buildings. HOUSEBREAKING, *n.* burglary by day; act of pulling down a building.

HOUSE-DOG [hows'dog], *n.* dog trained to guard a house.

HOUSE-FLAG [hows'flag], *n.* ship's flag indicating to which commercial house it belongs.

HOUSE-FLY [hows'flī], *n.* common dipterous insect, *Musca domestica.*

HOUSEHOLD (1) [hows'hōld], *n.* the members of one family, together with servants etc., living under one roof; home. HOUSEHOLD (2), *adj.* of, or pertaining to, a h., *esp.* to the Royal H.; **h. word,** word of everyday usage; **H. troops,** the regiments of the Brigade of Guards whose duty it is to guard the Sovereign. [ME.].

HOUSEHOLDER [hows'hōl-der], *n.* one who occupies a house; head of a household.

HOUSEKEEPER [hows'kē-per], *n.* mistress of a household; hired servant who manages a household.

HOUSEKEEPING [hows'kē-ping], *n.* science or act of keeping house.

HOUSELEEK [hows'lēk], *n.* plant with pink flowers, growing on walls and roofs.

HOUSEMAID [hows'mād], *n.* female domestic servant whose main duty is the cleaning of rooms; **h. 's knee,** affection of the knee produced by much kneeling.

HOUSE-PARTY [hows'pah-ti], *n.* a number of guests entertained for several days, usually at a country residence; entertainment of such guests.

HOUSE-PHYSICIAN [hows'fi-zi-shn], *n.* junior physician residing in a hospital.

HOUSEPROUD [hows'prowd], *adj.* taking a great interest in the clean and orderly appearance of one's house and furniture.

HOUSEROOM [hows'rŏŏm], *n.* accommodation in the house.

HOUSE-SURGEON [hows'ser-jn], *n.* junior surgeon residing in a hospital.

HOUSE-WARMING [hows'waw-ming], *n.* party given by occupants of a new house to celebrate their arrival.

HOUSEWIFE, HUSSIF [hows'wif, hu'zif], *n.* mistress of a household; female domestic manager; case for holding needles, thread etc. [ME.].

HOUSEWIFERY [hows'wi-fe-ri, hu'zi-fe-ri], *n.* the occupation of a housewife; domestic economy.

HOUSING [how'zing], *n.* act of providing a house or houses; accommodation.

HOVE [hōv], (*naut.*) *pret. and p.pt.* of HEAVE. [ME.].

The accent ′ after a syllable = stress (u-pon′). The mark ‾ over a vowel = length (ā in made; ō in bone).

HOVEL [ho'vel], *n.* hut, mean and squalid dwelling. [ME.].

HOVER [ho'ver], *v.i.* (of a bird etc.) to hang poised in the air without forward motion; **to h. about,** (of persons) to loiter; (*fig.*) show irresolution. HOVER-INGLY, *adv.* in a hovering way. [ME.].

HOW (1) [how], *n.* hillock; mound, barrow. [~OScand.].

HOW (2), *adv., interrogative,* in what manner? by what method or means? to what extent? **and h.,** (*U.S.*) *meaningless phrase expressing emphasis; relative,* in what manner, by what method or means; to what extent; that; **for all you know h.,** with your utmost endeavour; *of degree, introducing exclamatory phrases,* to what degree. HOW (3), *n.* the means, method. [OE.].

HOWBEIT [how-bē'it], *adv.* (*archaic*) nevertheless. [HOW, BE and IT].

HOWDAH, see HOUDAH.

HOWEVER (1) [how-e'ver], *adv.* by whatever means or method, in whatever manner, to whatever degree. HOWEVER (2), *conj.* nevertheless.

HOWITZER [how'it-ser], *n.* short gun of high trajectory and low muzzle velocity. [Germ.].

HOWL (1) [howl], *v.i.* to utter a loud long wailing cry or series of such cries; yell, wail; (*coll.*) laugh heartily. HOWL (2), *n.* long wailing cry, yell, wail; loud outburst of laughter or tears. [ME. ~Du.].

HOWLER [how'ler], *n.* a South American monkey; one who howls; (*slang*) glaring blunder.

HOWLING (1) [how'ling], *n.* act of uttering howls. HOWLING (2), *adj.* uttering howls; (*slang*) excessive, glaring; **h. wilderness,** wild and dangerous wilderness.

HOWSOEVER [how-sō-e'ver], *adv.* in what way or manner so ever.

HOY (1) [hoi], *n.* small coasting vessel. [MDu.].

HOY (2), *int.* a cry uttered to attract attention; (*naut.*) cry used to call aloft. [Echoic].

HOYDEN [hoi'den], *n.* lively, boisterous girl. [Unkn.].

HUB [hub], *n.* boss at the centre of a wheel; (*fig.*) centre of activity. [Uncert.].

HUBBUB [hu'bub], *n.* confused noise; uproar. [Echoic].

HUBBY [hu'bi], *n.* affectionate *dim.* of HUSBAND.

HUCKABACK [hu'ka-bak], *n.* coarse kind of linen with raised figures on it, used for towels. [Unkn.].

HUCKSTER (1) [huk'ster], *n.* vendor of small goods; hawker. HUCKSTER (2), *v.i.* to trade as a h.; haggle. [MDu.].

HUDDLE (1) [hu'dl], *v.t. and i.* to push, drive into a promiscuous heap or crowd; **to h. on,** (of clothes) to put on in a hurried and untidy fashion; **to h. together,** to gather close together in an unceremonious fashion. HUDDLE (2), *n.* group of people or objects crowded together without plan or order; **to go into a h.,** (*slang*) to consult together in private. [Uncert.].

HUE (1) [hyōō], *n.* tint or colour; shade. [OE.].

HUE (2), *n.* **h. and cry,** outcry of pursuit; widely expressed and noisy disapproval. [OFr.].

HUFF (1) [huf], *v.t. and i.* to behave in a bullying, insolent fashion; cause to sulk by rude behaviour; (*draughts*) take one of an opponent's pieces from the board if he fails to take one of one's own when the chance occurs. HUFF (2), *n.* sulky mood, sulkiness; (*draughts*) act of huffing. [ME.].

HUFFY [hu'fi], *adj.* petulant; inclined to take offence. HUFFILY, *adv.* in a h. manner.

HUG (1) [*pres.pt.* **hugging,** *pret. and p.pt.* **hugged**) [hug], *v.t.* to embrace warmly and closely; move in a direction closely parallel to; (*fig.*) cherish, refuse to be parted from. HUG (2), *n.* close or loving embrace; a grip in wrestling. [Uncert.].

HUGE [hyōōj], *adj.* enormous; very big. HUGELY, *adv.* to a h. degree. [OFr.].

HUGGER-MUGGER (1) [hu'ger-mu-ger], *n.* secrecy; confusion. HUGGER-MUGGER (2), *adj. and adv.* secret; confused; in a muddled way. [Unkn.].

HUGUENOT [hyōō'ge-nō], *n.* sixteenth-century French Protestant. [Fr.].

HULA [hōō'lah], *n.* native dance by women of Hawaii. [Native].

HULK [hulk], *n.* body of an old, dismantled ship; (*pl.*) such ships formerly used as prisons; unwieldy ship; (*fig.*) large ungainly person. [OE.].

HULKING [hul'king], *adj.* large; clumsy, unwieldy.

HULL (1) [hul], *n.* seed-pod, shell of a fruit, vegetable etc.; outer part of a matchbox. HULL (2), *v.t.* to remove (seeds) from their pod. [OE.].

HULL (3), *n.* body of a ship or boat; space below deck. HULL (4), *v.t.* to strike the h. of a ship. [Uncert.].

HULLABALOO [hu'la-ba-lōō], *n.* outcry, clamour, uproar. [Echoic].

HULLO [hu-lō'], *int.* word of greeting, cry of surprise.

HUM (1) (*pres.pt.* **humming,** *pret. and p.pt.* **hummed**) [hum], *v.t.* to make a prolonged musical sound of nasal quality; sing with the lips closed; make a steady buzzing sound; (*slang*) to stink; **to make things h.,** to excite lively activity; **to h. along,** (*esp.* of motor vehicles) to proceed at a rapid, even pace; **to h. and haw,** to utter short ejaculations expressive of doubt, hesitation or embarrassment. HUM (2), *n.* act of humming; buzzing sound; continuous, steady but indistinct noise; (*coll.*) unpleasant odour. [ME.].

HUMAN (1) [hyōō'man], *adj.* of, or pertaining to, mankind; resembling, consisting of, men, women or children; sympathetic and understanding; pathetic, touching. HUMAN (2), *n.* a h. being. [L.].

HUMANE [hyōō-mān'], *adj.* tender and sympathetic; merciful; pertaining to humanism; cultured, civilized; **h. killer,** device for the painless slaughtering of cattle. HUMANELY, *adv.* in a h. way. [HUMAN].

HUMANISM [hyōō'ma-nizm], *n.* learning concerned with such studies as are connected with human culture, *esp.* classical culture; view of knowledge which ranks the study of man as of first consideration.

HUMANIST [hyōō'ma-nist], *n.* one who adopts the outlook, ethics and ideals of humanism, *esp.* a Renaissance scholar having such an outlook. HUMANISTIC [hyōō-ma-nis'tik], *adj.* relating to humanists or humanism.

HUMANITARIAN (1) [hyōō-ma-ni-tāer'i-an], *n.* one who professes or practises humanitarian principles; one who doubts or rejects the Divine Nature of Christ. HUMANITARIAN (2), *adj.* merciful, striving to mitigate or eliminate pain and suffering in human beings or animals; doubting the Divine Nature of Christ. HUMANITARIANISM, *n.* devotion to the good of humanity; religious doctrine of the humanitarians.

HUMANITY [hyōō-ma'ni-ti], *n.* the human race; quality of being human; quality of being humane; a humane act; human nature; (in Scots universities) study of Latin; (*pl.*) study of literature *esp.* classical literature. [L.].

HUMANIZE [hyōō'ma-nīz], *v.t. and i.* to make humane; make human; become humane; **humanized milk,** cow's milk treated so as to resemble human milk. HUMANIZATION [hyōō-ma-nī-za'shn], *n.* act or process of humanizing.

HUMBLE (1) [hum-bl], *adj.* meek and unassuming; modest; obsequious; of lowly origin; poor, unpretentious; unimportant. HUMBLE (2), *v.t.* to abase, humiliate. [OFr.].

HUMBLE-BEE [hum'bl-bē], *n.* bumble-bee.

HUMBLE-PIE, UMBLE-PIE [(h)um-bl-pī'], *n.* †pie made of the entrails of deer; **to eat h.,** to suffer humiliation; offer a humiliating apology. [UMBLES and HUMBLE].

HUMBUG (1) [hum'bug], *n.* hoax, sham; empty, insincere talk; deliberate mis-statement; pretentious, hypocritical person; specious rogue; peppermint sweetmeat. HUMBUG (2) (*pres.pt.* HUMBUGGING, *pret. and p.pt.* HUMBUGGED), *v.t.* to dupe, delude. [Uncert.].

HUMDRUM [hum'drum], *adj.* tedious and dull; uneventful.

HUMERAL [hyōō'me-ral], *adj.* (*anat.*) of, or pertaining to, the shoulder. [LL.].

HUMERUS [hyōō'me-rus], *n.* (*anat.*) bone of the arm from shoulder to forearm. [L.].

HUMID [hyōō'mid], *adj.* damp, moist. [L.].

HUMIDITY [hyōō-mi'di-ti], *n.* quality of being humid.

HUMILIATE [hyōō-mi'li-āt], *v.t.* to lower the pride of, humble; hurt the feelings of; disgrace. HUMILIAT-ING, *adj.* causing humiliation.

HUMILIATION [hyōō-mi-li-ā'shn], *n.* act of humiliating; condition of having been humiliated; feeling of defeat or mortification. [L.].

HUMILITY [hyōō-mi'li-ti], *n.* quality of being humble. [L.].

HUMMING (1) [hu'ming], *n.* sound of anything which hums. HUMMING (2), *adj.* that hums. HUM-MING-BIRD, *n.* American bird which produces a h noise with its rapidly vibrating wings. HUMMING-TOP, *n.* hollow top with a hole at the side which makes it hum when spinning.

HUMMOCK [hu'mok], *n.* hillock. [Uncert.].

HUMORIST, HUMOURIST [hyōō'me-rist], *n.*

person given to making jokes, one who always sees the funny side of things; professional purveyor of humour. [MedL.].

HUMORLESS, see HUMOURLESS.

HUMOROUS [hyōō'me-rŏŏs], adj. funny, amusing; having a sense of humour. HUMOROUSLY, adv. in a h. way. HUMOROUSNESS, n. quality of being h.

HUMORSOME, see HUMOURSOME.

HUMOUR (1) [hyōō'mer], n. fun, jesting, comical absurdity; ability to enjoy the ludicrous; temperament, whim; liquids of the eye; one of the four liquids formerly supposed to be in the human body and to determine a person's temperament and character; lymph exuding from a wound or festering sore; **out of h.,** depressed, annoyed. HUMOUR (2), v.t. to indulge the whims of; manipulate to one's own ends by tact and diplomacy.

HUMOURIST, see HUMORIST.

HUMOURLESS, HUMORLESS [hyōō'mer-les] adj. lacking humour.

HUMOURSOME, HUMORSOME [hyōō'mer-sum], adj. capricious.

HUMOUS [hyōō'mŏŏs], adj. found in, or derived from, vegetable mould.

HUMP (1) [hump], n. lump or protuberance; lump on the backs of certain animals; lump on a person's back due to deformity of the spine; knoll; (slang) fit of melancholy. HUMP (2), v.t. to stoop so as to arch the back into a h.; (Australian) carry on one's back, esp. **to h. one's swag,** to be a tramp. [~Du.].

HUMPBACK [hump'bak], n. a back with a hump; person having such a back. HUMP-BACKED, adj. having a back with a hump.

HUMPTY [hump'ti], n. large padded cushion used as a seat.

HUMUS [hyōō'mus], n. vegetable mould forming soil. [L.].

HUN [hun], n. one of the Asiatic invaders of Europe in the fourth century.

HUNCH (1) [hunch], n. hump on the back; hunk; (U.S. slang) suspicion, notion. HUNCH (2), v.t. to stoop and arch the back; **to h. up,** (the shoulders) to draw them together so as to make a hump on the back.

HUNCHBACK [hunch'bak], n. a back which is hunched up or humped, as in a person suffering from spinal curvature; person so afflicted. HUNCH-BACKED, adj. humpbacked.

HUNDRED (1) [hun'dred], n. ten times ten; a great many; former subdivision of an English county; **long h.,** 120, six score. HUNDRED (2), adj. ten times ten; (pl.) very many; **a h. and one,** very many. [OE.].

HUNDREDTH (1) [hun'dredth], adj. the ordinal of a hundred; being one of a hundred equal parts. HUNDREDTH (2), n. one of a hundred equal parts, a hundredth part; the hundredth member of a series; **Old H.,** metrical paraphrase of the H. Psalm; the tune to which this was sung.

HUNDREDWEIGHT [hun'dred-wāt], n. eight stone, or 112 lb. avoirdupois; (U.S.) 100 lb.

HUNG [hung], pret. and p.pt. of HANG. [Analogical].

HUNGER (1) [hung'ger], n. lack of food; physical pain and weakness due to lack of food; famine; craving for food; (fig.) great craving or desire. HUNGER (2), v.i. to lack food and nourishment; **to h. for, h. after,** to crave violently for. [OE.].

HUNGER-STRIKE [hung'ger-strik], n. refusal to eat, esp. by a prisoner.

HUNGRY [hung'gri], adj. lacking food; ready and eager to eat; (fig.) keenly desiring, craving for; (of a look) avid. HUNGRILY, adv. in a h. way. [OE.].

HUNK [hungk], n. large slice or chunk. [~Flem.].

HUNT (1) [hunt], v.t. and i. to chase wild animals and kill them, esp. to chase foxes, hares, stags etc. with hounds and horses; follow the chase; act as master of the hounds; drive away, pursue; search intensely for; (of machinery) oscillate abnormally. HUNT (2), n. act of hunting; association of persons who h.; area over which they h.; body of persons, hounds and horses engaged in hunting; (fig.) a vigorous search. [OE.].

HUNTER [hun'ter], n. one who hunts, horse ridden for fox-hunting; a watch in a hinged case protecting the glass.

HUNTING [hun'ting], n. act of one who hunts; the chase. HUNTING-BOX, small house lived in during the h. season. HUNTING-CROP, whipstock with a loop at one end and a handle at the other. HUNTING-HORN, horn used by huntsmen.

HUNTRESS [hunt'res], n. woman who hunts.

HUNTSMAN [hunts'man], n. hunter; man in charge of a pack of hounds.

HURDLE (1) [hur'dl], n. light oblong framework, used to make a temporary barrier, or for jumping over in a race; (pl.) hurdle race, hurdle racing; **h. race,** race in which the competitors must jump a number of hurdles. HURDLE (2), v.t. and i. to make hurdles; enclose with hurdles; jump over hurdles in a h. race. HURDLER, n. maker of hurdles; one who runs in h. races. [OE.].

HURDY-GURDY [hur'di-ger-di], n. barrel-organ.

HURL (1) [hurl], v.t. to throw with great force. HURL (2), n. action of hurling. [ME.].

HURLY-BURLY [hur'li-ber-li], n. tumult; bustle; commotion. [Imitative].

HURRICANE [hu'ri-kan], n. cyclonic storm common in the W. Indies; very violent wind; (meteor.) wind blowing at 75 or more miles per hour. HURRICANE-LAMP, oil lamp having its flame well shielded from wind. [Span.].

HURRIED [hu'rid], adj. moving with haste; done in a hurry. HURRIEDLY, adv. in a h. way.

HURRY (1) [hu'ri], n. act of hurrying; bustling speed; **in a h.,** eager and impatient. HURRY (2), v.t. and i. to do or go quickly; hasten; cause to hasten; do, or cause to be done, with increased speed; bustle; **to h. up,** to accelerate. HURRYINGLY, adv. in a hurrying way.

HURST [hurst], n. thicket; wood on a hill. [OE.].

HURT (1) [hurt], v.t. and i. to cause pain to; damage, injure; (fig.) wound the feelings of; come to harm; **it won't h.,** (coll.) it does not matter. HURT (2), n. pain, injury, damage. [OFr.].

HURTFUL [hurt'fŏŏl], adj. causing hurt, harmful, injurious. HURTFULLY, adv. in a h. way.

HURTLE [hur'tl], v.i. to fly, rush or be projected through the air with great violence. [ME.].

HURTLEBERRY, see WHORTLEBERRY.

HUSBAND (1) [huz'band], n. man joined to a woman by marriage. HUSBAND (2), v.t. to manage with skill and economy. [OE.].

HUSBANDMAN [huz'band-man], n. farmer.

HUSBANDRY [huz'ban-dri], n. farming, agriculture; thrift, good management.

HUSH (1) [hush], v.t. to make or become calm and silent; soothe; **to h. up,** to keep from public knowledge or discussion. HUSH (2), n. a silence. HUSH-HUSH, adj. (coll.) very secret.

HUSHMONEY [hush'mu-ni], n. money paid to secure silence.

HUSK (1) [husk], n. dry outer covering of some seeds and fruits; (fig.) dull framework of some subject. HUSK (2), v.t. to strip the h. from. HUSKED, adj. having husks; stripped of husks. [ME.].

HUSKY (1) [hus'ki], n. an Eskimo; his language; Eskimo dog. [ESKIMO].

HUSKY (2), adj. having a hoarse dry rasping quality in the speech. [Dial E.].

HUSKY (3), adj. covered with, like a husk; (coll.) strong, vigorous.

HUSSAR [hu-zah(r)'], n. member of certain regiments of light cavalry. [Hungarian].

HUSSIF, see HOUSEWIFE.

HUSSY [hu'zi], n. roguish, pert girl; woman of dubious reputation. [HUSSIF].

HUSTINGS [hus'tingz], n.(pl.) platform on which parliamentary candidates were nominated and from which they addressed meetings; election proceedings. [OE.].

HUSTLE (1) [hu'sl], v.t. and i. to jostle, push quickly and unceremoniously; hurry, bustle; push, push oneself forward; get things done quickly. HUSTLE (2), n. rapid, vigorous action; restless activity. HUSTLER, n. man of energy who gets things done quickly. [Uncert.].

HUT (1) [hut], n. small wooden building; cabin. HUT (2) (pres.pt. HUTTING, pret. and p.pt. HUTTED), v.t. and i. to inhabit a h.; provide with a h. or huts. [Fr.].

HUTCH [huch], n. bin for flour or grain; trough for kneading dough; truck for hewn coal; wooden cage or box for tame animals; (coll.) cottage.

HUTMENT [hut'ment], n. group of huts; camp or settlement.

HYACINTH [hi'a-sinth], n. one of a group of bulbous plants which flower with numerous bell-shaped blossoms set in a conical spike. [Gk.].

HYACINTHINE [hi-a-sin'thin], adj. like a hyacinth; of the colour of hyacinths.

HYAENA, see HYENA.

HYALO-, pref. glass. [Gk.].

HYALOID [hi'a-loid], adj. like glass, glassy. [Gk.].

HYBRID (1) [hī'brĭd], *n.* plant or animal which is a crossbreed from different species; anything of mixed origin. **HYBRID** (2), *adj.* possessing the nature of a h.; of mixed parentage; of mixed elements. [L.].

HYBRIDIZE [hī'brĭ-dīz], *v.t. and i.* to produce hybrids, interbreed.

HYDATID [hī'da-tĭd], *n. (path.)* cyst containing watery fluid; bladder-worm stage of certain tapeworms. [Gk.].

HYDRA [hī'drah], *n. (Gk. myth)* many-headed serpent slain by Hercules; *(zool.)* a freshwater polyp; *(fig.)* an evil which always reappears despite every effort to exterminate it. [Gk.].

HYDRANGEA [hī-drān'jĭ-ah], *n.* a kind of shrub, whose flowers, white, pink and blue, blossom in large clusters. [MdL.].

HYDRANT [hī'drănt], *n.* pipe to which a hose may be attached, to draw water from a main. [HYDRO].

HYDRARGYRUM [hī-drah'jĭ-rum], *n.* mercury or quicksilver, the chemical element Hg. [Gk.].

HYDRATE (1) [hī'drāt], *n. (chem.)* compound of which the OH radical is a constituent. **HYDRATE** (2), *v.t. (chem.)* to make a h. of; combine with water. **HYDRATED** [hī-drā'tĭd], *adj. (chem.)* combined with water. **HYDRATION** [hī-drā'shn], *n. (chem.)* process of forming a h.

HYDRAULIC [hī-draw'lĭk], *adj.* of, or pertaining to, the properties of water or other liquids when conveyed through a pipe; operating by the passage of water through a pipe; connected with, worked by, or containing, water; (of cement) tending to harden or solidify in water. **HYDRAULICALLY**, *adv.* by means of water-power or hydraulics. [Gk.].

HYDRAULICS [hī-draw'lĭks], *n.* science of the motive power of liquids.

HYDRIC [hī'drĭk], *adj. (chem.)* pertaining to hydrogen. [HYDROGEN].

HYDRO (1) [hī'drō], *n.* a hydropathic.

HYDRO- (2), *pref.* water. [Gk.].

HYDROCARBON [hī-drō-kah'bon], *n.* compounds of hydrogen and carbon only.

HYDROCEPHALUS [hī-drō-sĕf'a-lus], *n. (med.)* water on the brain. **HYDROCEPHALIC** [hī-drō-sĕ-fa'lĭk], *adj.* relating to, affected with, h. [Gk.].

HYDROCHLORIC [hī-drō-klo'rĭk], *adj. (chem.)* consisting of chlorine and hydrogen.

HYDROCYANIC [hī-drō-sī-a'nĭk], *adj.* consisting of hydrogen and cyanogen.

HYDRODYNAMICS [hī-drō-dī-na'mĭks], *n.* the dynamics of liquids. **HYDRODYNAMIC**, *adj.* relating to the dynamics of fluids. [MdL.].

HYDRO-ELECTRICITY [hī-drō-e-lek-trĭ'sĭ-tĭ], *n.* electricity generated by water-power. **HYDRO-ELECTRIC** [hī-drō-ĭ-lek'trĭk], *adj.* pertaining to h.

HYDROGEN [hī'dro-jen], *n. (chem.)* a highly inflammable gas, the lightest known substance, the chemical element H. **HYDROGEN-BOMB**, bomb deriving its immense explosive power from the fusion of hydrogen atoms. **HYDROGENIZE** [hī-dro'je-nīz, hī-drō-je-nīz], *v.t. (chem.)* to combine with h. **HYDROGENOUS** [hī-dro'je-nŏŏs], *adj. (chem.)* relating to, containing, h. [Fr.].

HYDROGRAPHER [hī-dro'gra-fer], *n.* one who draws maps of the sea, lakes or other waters; chartmaker. [Gk.].

HYDROGRAPHY [hī-dro'gra-fĭ], *n.* science which treats of the waters of the earth; technique of measuring and making maps of these. [Gk.].

HYDROLOGY [hī-dro'lĭ-jĭ], *n.* scientific study of water. [Gk.].

HYDROLYSIS [hī-dro'lĭ-sĭs], *n.* decomposition by water. [Gk.].

HYDROMETER [hī-dro'mĭ-ter], *n.* instrument for measuring the specific gravity of liquids, or the velocity of water.

HYDROPATHIC (1) [hī-drō-pa'thĭk], *adj.* relating to hydropathy. **HYDROPATHIC** (2), *n.* hotel with special facilities for those taking a water-cure.

HYDROPATHY [hī-dro'pa-thĭ], *n. (med.)* a medical cure by the external and internal application of water; the water-cure. [Germ.].

HYDROPHOBIA [hī-drō-fō'bĭ-ah], *n. (path.)* difficulty in swallowing water and intense dread of it, *esp.* as a symptom of rabies; rabies, form of madness attacking dogs etc. or caused by a bite from a rabid animal. **HYDROPHOBIC**, *adj.* relating to h. [Gk.].

HYDROPHONE [hī'drō-fōn], *n.* instrument for detecting by sounds through water, *esp.* those made by the engines of a submarine. [Gk.].

HYDROPHYTE [hī'drō-fīt], *n.* water-plant. [Gk.].

HYDROPLANE [hī'drō-plān], *n.* rudder controlling the vertical movement of a submarine; plane or board fixed to a motor-boat by which it can skim over the surface of the water; motor-boat with this attachment; seaplane.

HYDROSTATIC [hī-drō-sta'tĭk], *adj.* concerning the equilibrium of liquids; employing the pressure of water as a driving force. **HYDROSTATICALLY**, *adv.* according to the principles of hydrostatics.

HYDROSTATICS [hī-drō-sta'tĭks], *n.(pl.)* science treating of the equilibrium of fluids.

HYDROUS [hī'drŏŏs], *adj. (chem.)* containing or compounded of water. [Gk.].

HYENA, HYAENA [hī-ē'nah], *n.* flesh-eating quadruped allied to the dog tribe; *(fig.)* cruel or repulsive person. [L.].

HYGIENE [hī'jēn], *n.* theory and practice of the maintenance of public and private health. [Gk.].

HYGIENIC [hī-jē'nĭk], *adj.* pertaining to hygiene; in accordance with good hygiene; sanitary, wholesome. **HYGIENICALLY**, *adv.* in a h. fashion.

HYGRO-, *pref.* damp, moist. [Gk.].

HYGROMETER [hī-gro'mĭ-ter], *n.* device for measuring the moisture of the atmosphere.

HYGROSCOPE [hī'grō-skōp], *n.* instrument to show the variation in the quantity of moisture in the air. [Gk.].

HYMEN [hī'men], *n. (anat.)* virginal membrane at the external orifice of the vagina, the maidenhead; *(myth.)* god of marriage. **HYMENEAL** [hī-me-nē'al], *adj.* relating to marriage or to the h. [Gk.].

HYMENOPTERA [hī-me-nop'te-rah], *n.(pl.) (entom.)* the highest order of insects, those with four membranous wings. [Gk.].

HYMN (1) [hĭm], *n.* song of praise, usually in a religious service. **HYMN-BOOK**, a hymnal. **HYMN** (2), *v.t. and i.* to give praise, celebrate in hymns; sing a h. [L.].

HYMNAL (1) [hĭm'nal], *adj.* relating to hymns. **HYMNAL** (2), *n.* a collection of hymns for worship, hymn-book.

HYMNODY [hĭm'no-dĭ], *n.* hymnology; singing of hymns. [Gk.].

HYMNOGRAPHER [hĭm-no'gra-fer], *n.* writer about hymns; composer of hymns. [Gk.].

HYMNOLOGY [hĭm-no'lo-jĭ], *n.* study of hymns; a collection of hymns. **HYMNOLOGIST**, *n.* student of hymns; composer of hymns. [Gk.].

HYOSCINE [hī'o-sēn], *n. (med.)* a poisonous alkaloid of henbane used as a local anaesthetic. [Gk.].

HYOSCYAMINE [hī-o-sī'a-min], *n.* an alkaloid extracted from henbane.

HYOSCYAMUS [hī-o-sī'a-mus], *n.* henbane. [Gk.].

HYPER-, *pref.* in excess of; going beyond; above. [Gk.].

HYPERBOLA [hī-pur'bo-lah], *n. (geom.)* curve formed by the section of a cone so that the plane is at a greater angle to the base than that made by the side of the cone. [Gk.].

HYPERBOLE [hī-pur'bo-lĭ], *n. (gram.)* figure of speech which expresses more or less than the truth by overstatement or understatement; exaggerated statement. [Gk.].

HYPERBOLIC(AL) [hī-per-bo'lĭk(-al)], *adj.* relating to, of the nature of, hyperbole; *(geom.)* relating to a hyperbola. **HYPERBOLICALLY**, *adv.* in a h. way.

HYPERBOREAN (1) [hī-per-baw'rĭ-an], *adj.* northern; bitterly cold. **HYPERBOREAN** (2), *n.* inhabitant of the northern regions; *(Gk. myth.)* member of a happy people believed to live on the edge of the world. [Gk.].

HYPERCRITICAL [hī-per-krĭ'tĭ-kal], *adj.* over-critical, excessively severe in judgment.

HYPERICUM [hī-pe'rĭ-kum], *n.* genus of plants including the St. John's wort. [Gk.].

HYPERMETROPIA [hī-per-me-trō'pĭ-ah], *n. (opt.)* long sight. [Gk.].

HYPERPHYSICAL [hī-per-fĭ'zĭ-kal], *adj.* beyond material limits, supernatural.

HYPERTHYROIDISM [hī-per-thī'roi-dizm], *n. (path.)* condition caused by overactivity of the thyroid gland, Graves' disease. **HYPERTHYROID**, *adj. (psych.)* relating to, derived from, h.

HYPERTROPHY [hī-pur'tro-fĭ], *n. (path.)* morbid enlargement of an organ or part of an organism. **HYPERTROPHIED**, *adj.* morbidly enlarged; *(fig.)* over-developed. [Gk.].

HYPHEN (1) [hī'fen], *n.* short, horizontal dash connecting words or syllables. **HYPHEN** (2), *v.t.* to hyphenate. **HYPHENATE**, *v.t.* to connect by a h. [Gk.].

HYPNOSIS [hĭp-nō'sĭs], *n.* deep sleep artificially

induced, in which the sleeper is sensitive to external suggestions. [Gk.].

HYPNOTIC (1) [hip-no′tik], *adj.* inducing sleep, narcotic; relating to hypnosis or to hypnotism. HYPNOTIC (2), *n.* medicine or drug which induces sleep, soporific; person who is easily hypnotized. [Gk.].

HYPNOTISM [hip′no-tizm], *n.* artificially induced state of sleep; theory and practice of inducing hypnosis; (*fig.*) power to render a person fascinated or open to suggestion. HYPNOTIST, *n.* one skilled in inducing hypnosis in others.

HYPNOTIZE [hip′no-tiz], *v.t.* to put into a state of hypnosis; (*fig.*) dominate the will of, reduce to unquestioning obedience.

HYPO (1) [hi′pō], *n.* sodium thiosulphate, formerly called hyposulphite of soda, used for fixing photographic prints and negatives. [HYPO (SULPHITE)].

HYPO- (2), *pref.* beneath. [Gk.].

HYPOCHONDRIA [hī-pō-kon′dri-ah], *n.* chronic nervous and mental disorder characterized by depression and excessive concern for health. [Gk.].

HYPOCHONDRIAC (1) [hī-pō-kon′dri-ak], *adj.* relating to hypochondria. HYPOCHONDRIAC (2), *n.* person who suffers from hypochondria.

HYPOCHONDRIACAL [hī-pō-kon-drī′a-kal], *adj.* hypochondriac. HYPOCHONDRIACALLY, *adv.* in a h. fashion.

HYPOCHONDRIASIS [hī-pō-kon-drī′a-sis], *n.* (*med.*) hypochondria.

HYPOCRISY [hi-pok′ri-si], *n.* practice of disguising one action or emotion by simulating another, dissimulation; insincere profession of goodness, piety etc. [ME. from Gk.].

HYPOCRITE [hi′pō-krit], *n.* person who uses hypocrisy. [ME. from Gk.].

HYPOCRITICAL [hi-pō-kri′ti-kal], *adj.* relating to

hypocrisy; practising hypocrisy. HYPOCRITICALLY, *adv.* in a h. fashion. [Gk.].

HYPODERMIC (1) [hī-pō-dur′mik], *adj.* beneath the skin; **h. syringe**, syringe to inject drugs etc. beneath the skin. HYPODERMIC (2), *n.* drug injected under the skin; injection of such a drug. [HYPO and DERM.].

HYPOGASTRIUM [hī-pō-gas′tri-um], *n.* (*anat.*) middle part of the abdomen HYPOGASTRIC *adj.* pertaining to the h. [Gk.].

HYPOSTASIS [hi-pos′ta-sis], *n.* (*philos.*) the reality or basis behind all being; (*theol.*) any of the persons of the Trinity; (*med.*) excess of blood. [Gk.].

HYPOTENUSE [hi-po′te-nyōōz], *n.* (*geom.*) that side of a right-angled triangle which faces and closes the right angle. [Gk.].

HYPOTHECATE [hi-po′thi-kāt], *v.t.* (*leg.*) to pledge as security for a debt. [LL.].

HYPOTHESIS (*pl.* **hypotheses**) [hī-po′thi-sis, -sēz], *n.* assumption adopted as a basis for argument and which, though admitted, is not backed by a proof of its correctness. [Gk.].

HYPOTHETIC(AL) [hī-po-the′tik(-al)], *adj.* assumed for the sake of argument. [Gk.].

HYPOTHYROIDISM [hī-pō-thī′roi-dizm], *n.* (*med.*) condition of morbid underactivity of the thyroid gland.

HYSSOP [hi′sop], *n.* a kind of mint; popular name of various aromatic herbs. [Gk.].

HYSTERECTOMY [his-te-rek′to-mi], *n.* excision of the womb. [Gk.].

HYSTERIA [his-tēer′i-ah], *n.* nervous disorder characterized by excessive emotional excitement; (*fig.*) wild excitement.

HYSTERIC(AL) [his-te′rik(-al)], *adj.* pertaining to, affected by, hysteria; (*fig.*) excessively emotional. HYSTERICALLY, *adv.* in an h. fashion. [Gk.].

HYSTERICS [his-te′riks], *n.* a fit of hysteria.

I (1) [I], ninth letter and third vowel of the English and related alphabets.

I (2), *pron.*, *1st person sg. nom.* [OE.].

IAMB [I-amb′], *n.* iambus.

IAMBIC (1) [i-am′bik], *adj.* consisting of iambuses; composed in iambuses. IAMBIC (2), *n.* an i. foot or verse; (*pl.*) verses containing, or composed of, i. feet. IAMBICALLY, *adv.* in the fashion of iambics. [Gk.].

IAMBUS [I-am′bus], *n.* (*pros.*) metrical foot consisting of a short syllable followed by a long or an unaccented syllable followed by an accented. [Gk.].

IBERIAN (1) [I-bēer′i-an], *adj.* pertaining to Iberia or the Iberians. IBERIAN (2), *n.* inhabitant of Iberia, i.e. Spain, Portugal and the Pyrenees; language of Iberia; (*anthrop.*) member of the prehistoric neolithic race of Western Europe, North Africa and Britain. [L.].

IBEX [I′beks], *n.* a species of mountain goat. [L.].

IBID [i′bid], *adv.* abbreviation of IBIDEM.

IBIDEM [i-bi′dem], *adv.* in the same place, on the same page etc.; from the same author, work etc. [L.].

IBIS [I′bis], *n.* genus of wading birds related to the storks. [Gk.].

ICE (1) [Is], *n.* frozen water; an ice-cream; **to cut no i.**, to fail to impress; **to break the i.**, to overcome natural reserve or formal politeness; make a beginning; **on thin i.**, on delicate ground. ICE (2), *v.t. and i.* to freeze; chill with i.; cover with i. or icing; (*aeron.*) become covered with i. [OE.].

ICE AGE [is′āj], *n.* (*geol.*) any of the epochs in which ice-fields and glaciers covered much of the surface of the earth.

ICEBERG [Is′berg], *n.* huge mass of floating ice. [~Dan., Du.].

ICEBLINK [Is′blingk], *n.* shining whiteness on the horizon caused by the reflection of light from ice.

ICE-BOAT [Is′bōt], *n.* ice-breaker; light boat equipped with runners for sailing over ice.

ICEBOUND [Is′bownd], *adj.* hemmed in and brought to a standstill by ice.

ICE-BREAKER [Is′brā-ker], *n.* ship strongly built for the purpose of forcing a way through floating ice.

ICE-CAP [Is′kap], *n.* permanent sheet of ice covering the top of a mountain; the ice-sheets covering the North and South Poles.

ICE-CREAM [Is-krēm′], *n.* flavoured and sweetened mixture of frozen cream, custard or similar foodstuff.

ICE-FIELD [Is′fēld], *n.* wide region of ice.

ICE-FLOE [Is′flō], *n.* large mass of floating ice.

ICE-HOCKEY [Is-ho′ki], *n.* game like hockey played by skaters on ice.

ICELAND MOSS [Is-land-mos′], *n.* a North European lichen, used medicinally and as food.

ICELAND-SPAR [Is-land-spah(r)′], *n.* one of the transparent varieties of calcite.

ICE-PACK [Is′pak], *n.* large, solid body formed by masses of broken floating ice packed tightly together.

ICE-RINK [Is′ringk], *n.* indoor skating floor of artificial ice.

ICHABOD [i′ka-bod], *int.* exclamation of regret. [I Samuel iv, 21].

ICHNEUMON [ik-nyōō′mon], *n.* small Eastern carnivore which feeds on the eggs of crocodiles; **i. fly**, parasite insect laying its eggs on the larvae of other insects. [Gk.].

ICHOR [I′kaw(r)], *n.* (*Gk. myth.*) ethereal fluid in the veins of the gods; (*path.*) watery discharge from a wound or sore. [Gk.].

ICHTHY(O)-, *pref.* pertaining to a fish. [Gk.].

ICHTHYOGRAPHY [ik-thi-o′gra-fi], *n.* a dissertation on fishes. [Gk.].

ICHTHYOLOGY [ik-thi-o′lo-ji], *n.* scientific study of fishes. [Gk.].

ICHTHYOSAURUS [ik-thi-ō-saw′rus], *n.* extinct marine animal with an immense head and four paddle-like limbs. [Gk.].

ICHTHYOSIS [ik-thi-ō′sis], *n.* (*path.*) skin disease in which the part affected becomes hard, dry and scaly. [Gk.].

ICICLE [I′si-kl], *n.* slender, tapering pendant of ice formed by the freezing of dripping or slowly running water. [OE.].

ICING [I′sing], *n.* powdered sugar mixed with white of egg etc., used as a covering for cakes.

The accent ′ after a syllable = stress (u-pon′). The mark ˉ over a vowel = length (ā in made; ō in bone).

ICON, IKON [ī'kon], *n.* representation of some holy person in painting or low relief, honoured as a sacred object, *esp.* in the Eastern Orthodox Church. [Gk.].

ICONO-, *pref.* relating to an image. [Gk.].

ICONOCLASM [ī-ko'nō-klazm], *n.* the breaking of images or sacred objects; (*fig.*) destruction of popular beliefs, customs etc. [Gk.].

ICONOCLAST [ī-ko'nō-klast], *n.* breaker of images or idols; one who wished to abolish images in the Eastern Christian churches in the eighth and ninth centuries; (*fig.*) destroyer of beliefs, institutions etc. generally considered sacrosanct. [Gk.].

ICONOGRAPHY [ī-ko-no'gra-fi], *n.* representation of objects or persons by portraits, images etc.; art of illustration; study of the portraits, statues etc. of a particular person. [Gk.].

ICONOMETER [ī-ko-no'mi-ter], *n.* (*phot.*) view-finder through which the object is seen directly and not as a reflected image; (*surveying*) instrument used in finding the size and distance of an object.

ICONOSCOPE [ī-ko'nō-skōp], *n.* television camera. [Gk.].

ICTUS [ik'tus], *n.* (*pros.*) rhythmical stress. [L.].

ICY [ī'si], *adj.* covered with, consisting of, resembling, ice; extremely cold.

ID [id], *n.* (*psychol.*) the total of instinctive impulses in the individual. [L.].

IDEA [ī-dē'ah], *n.* that which exists in the mind as a result of mental activity, a mental conception; notion; vague impression, fancy; opinion; plan, intention; principle behind anything; (*Gk. philos.*) universal, eternal, immaterial pattern of which a material thing is but an imperfect copy; (*modern philos.*) immediate object of thought, understanding or perception; absolute truth which lies behind the existence of a phenomenon. [Gk.].

IDEAL (1) [ī-dē'al], *adj.* existing only as an idea; realized only in the imagination; typifying or realizing one's notion of supreme excellence, perfect; representing an idea. IDEAL (2), *n.* a conception of supreme excellence, *esp.* when set up in the mind as a standard to be aspired to; anything or anyone who exemplifies such a conception; something which exists only in the mind. [LL.].

IDEALISM [ī-dē'a-lizm], *n.* (*philos.*) theory which resolves the universe into ideas as the only existences or objects of perception; tendency to form ideals or to idealize; ideal treatment in art or literature.

IDEALIST [ī-dē'a-list], *n.* one who bases his conduct and mode of thought upon ideals, a visionary; artist or writer treating his subjects from an ideal point of view; (*philos.*) upholder of idealism.

IDEALIZE [ī-dē'a-līz], *v.t. and i.* to make ideal, treat from an ideal point of view; form ideals. IDEALIZATION [ī-dē-a-lī-zā'shn], *n.* act of idealizing, state of being idealized; idealized representation or treatment of anything.

IDEALLY [ī-dē'a-li], *adv.* in an ideal fashion; in accordance with the ideal.

IDEE FIXE, idée fixe [ē-dā-fēks'], *n.* obsession. [Fr.].

IDEM [ī'dem], *n.* the same book, author, reference etc. [L.].

IDENTICAL [ī-den'ti-kal], *adj.* the very same; exactly alike. IDENTICALLY, *adv.* in an i. fashion. [MedL.].

IDENTIFICATION [ī-den-ti-fi-kā'shn], *n.* act of identifying; state of being identified.

IDENTIFY [ī-den'ti-fī], *v.t.* to establish the identity of, prove to be a particular thing or person; (*reflex.*) associate oneself closely (with). IDENTIFIABLE, *adj.* able to be identified. [LL.].

IDENTITY [ī-den'ti-ti], *n.* fact or state of being a given person or thing; quality of being identical; **i. card, disk etc.**, card, disk etc. to prove one's i. [LL.].

IDEO-, *pref.* kind, idea. [Gk.].

IDEOGRAPH [i'di-ō-grahf], *n.* character used in writing, in certain languages as Chinese, which symbolizes the idea of an object or the object itself, and is not merely an orthographical representation of a speech sound. IDEOGRAPHIC [i-di-ō-gra'fik], *adj.* representing or expressing ideas or things directly by ideographs. [Gk.].

IDEOLOGY [i-di-o'lo-ji], *n.* science of ideas; theory deriving all ideas from sensations; impractical speculation; (*pol.*) set of ideas or theories governing a political, religious or economic system. IDEOLOGIST, *n.* one who studies or is guided by i. [Gk.].

IDES [idz], *n.(pl.)* (*Rom. hist.*) 15 March, May, July and October, and 13th of other months, being one of the three days in each month of the Roman calendar used in reckoning dates. [L.].

IDIO-, *pref.* one's own, distinct, individual. [Gk.].

IDIOCY [i'di-o-si], *n.* state of being an idiot, extreme mental defectiveness; extremely stupid behaviour. [Gk.].

IDIOM [i'di-om], *n.* special turn of phrase, expression etc. characteristic of a particular language; language of a particular people; dialect; essential spirit or nature of a language. [Gk.].

IDIOMATIC [i-di-ō-ma'tik], *adj.* peculiar to a language; exhibiting the idioms of a language; characterized by idioms; of the nature of an idiom. IDIOMATICALLY, *adv.* in an i. fashion. [Gk.].

IDIOPLASM [i'di-ō-plazm], *n.* that section of protoplasm held to determine the nature of the organism which will result from a cell.

IDIOSYNCRASY [i-di-ō-sing'kra-si], *n.* a peculiarity of mental constitution, temperament or character; characteristic and individualistic mannerism or mode of expression; (*med.*) physical constitution of a particular individual. IDIOSYNCRATIC [i-di-ō-sing-kra'tik], *adj.* peculiar to a particular individual or thing. [Gk.].

IDIOT [i'di-ot], *n.* imbecile, extremely mentally defective person; (*coll.*) utter fool. [Gk.].

IDIOTIC [i-di-o'tik], *adj.* like, characteristic of, relating to, an idiot; extremely stupid. [Gk.].

IDLE (1) [ī'dl], *adj.* unoccupied, doing nothing; inactive; lazy; unprofitable; frivolous; unfounded. IDLE (2), *v.i.* to remain i., waste time. [OE.].

IDLER [īd'ler], *n.* one who wastes his time in idleness.

IDO [ē'dō], *n.* artificial language after the manner of Esperanto. [Invented].

IDOL [ī'dol], *n.* image, statue etc. of an unseen deity or object of worship; false god; person or object devoutly admired. [Gk.].

IDOLATER [ī-do'la-ter], *n.* worshipper of idols; devout admirer.

IDOLATRESS [ī-do'la-tres], *n.* female idolater.

IDOLATROUS [ī-do'la-troŏs], *adj.* of the nature of, practising, idolatry.

IDOLATRY [ī-do'la-tri], *n.* worship of idols, images or false gods; (*fig.*) extravagant admiration. [Gk.].

IDOLIZE [ī'do-līz], *v.t.* to make an idol of; worship blindly. IDOLIZATION [ī-do-lī-zā'shn], *n.* act of idolizing. IDOLIZER, *n.* person who idolizes.

IDYLL, IDYL [ī'dil, i'dil], *n.* short simple poem, *esp.* one describing everyday life amid natural or pastoral surroundings; incident or scene providing an admirable subject for such a poem. [Gk.].

IDYLLIC [i-di'lik, i-di'lik], *adj.* of the nature of an idyll; suitable for an idyll; charmingly picturesque, peaceful and rural.

IF [if], *conj.* supposing that; provided that; even though, although; whether. [OE.].

IGLOO [ig'loō], *n.* dome-shaped dwelling of an Eskimo, built of snow. [Eskimo].

IGNEOUS [ig'ni-ōos], *adj.* pertaining to, consisting of, like, fire; (*geol.*) produced by the action of fire, primeval heat or volcanic activity. [L.].

IGNIS FATUUS [ig-nis-fa'tyōō-us], *n.* phosphorescence appearing at night over marshy places, will-o'-the-wisp; object of aspiration never attained, but misleading pursuers. [L.].

IGNITE [ig-nīt'], *v.t. and i.* to kindle, set on fire; (*chem.*) heat until combustion takes place; take fire. IGNITABLE, IGNITIBLE, *adj.* able to be ignited. [L.].

IGNITION [ig-ni'shn], *n.* act of igniting; state of being ignited; means of firing the explosive mixture in the cylinder of an internal combustion engine. [MedL.].

IGNOBLE [ig-nō'bl], *adj.* of mean character, dishonourable, despicable; (*archaic*) of low birth. [L.].

IGNOMINIOUS [ig-no-mi'ni-ōos], *adj.* contemptible, base, disgraceful, inglorious. [L.].

IGNOMINY [ig'no-mi-ni], *n.* public disgrace, degradation; base conduct. [L.].

IGNORAMUS [ig-ne-rā'mus], *n.* ignorant person. [L.].

IGNORANCE [ig'ne-rans], *n.* lack of general knowledge or experience; lack of particular knowledge of some specific thing. [L.].

IGNORANT [ig'ne-rant], *adj.* uneducated, lacking general knowledge; proceeding from ignorance; unaware of some particular thing. [L.].

IGNORE [ig-naw(r)'], *v.t.* to take no notice of, disregard deliberately; refuse to recognize or consider. [L.].

IGUANA [i-gwah'nah], *n.* any of a large family of American lizards. [Span.].

ōō is pronounced as in food; ŏŏ as in hood; th as in *think*, TH as in *that*; zh as in azure. ~ = related to.

IL-, *pref.* form of negative prefix IN-, used before *l*. [L.].

ILEUM [I'li-um], *n.* (*anat.*) lower portion of the small intestine. [ILIUM].

ILEUS [I'li-us], *n.* colic caused by a stoppage in the intestines. [Gk.].

ILEX [I'leks], *n.* the evergreen or holm-oak. [L.].

ILIAC [I'li-ak], *adj.* pertaining to the ileum; pertaining to the ilium; **i. process,** the hip-bone; **i. region,** region of the abdomen between the ribs and the hips. [L.].

ILIAD [i'li-ad], *n.* epic poem, attributed to Homer, describing the events of the siege of Troy. [L.].

ILIUM (*pl.* **ilia**) [I'li-um], *n.* (*anat.*) the upper partly-flattened portion of the hip-bone. [L.].

ILK [ilk], *adj.* same; **of that i.,** (*Scots*) denotes that a person's surname is the same as that of his estate or of the clan of which he is the head; *erroneously used for* of that class, sort. [OE.].

ILL (1) [il], *adj.* sick, suffering from a disease; evil, wicked; producing evil, harmful; unfavourable; bad; poor; troublesome. ILL (2), *n.* wickedness, misfortune, ailment; unpleasant happening. ILL (3), *adv.* not well, badly; faultily; unfavourably; inadequately; with difficulty; **i. at ease,** uncomfortable. [OIcel.].

ILL-ADVISED [il-ad-vīzd'], *adj.* injudicious, rash.

ILL-BRED [il-bred'], *adj.* badly brought up, discourteous, displaying a lack of good manners.

ILL-CONDITIONED [il-kon-di'shnd], *adj.* having a nasty or wicked disposition.

ILLEGAL [i-lē'gal], *adj.* unlawful.

ILLEGALITY [i-lē-ga'li-ti], *n.* unlawfulness.

ILLEGIBILITY [i-le-ji-bi'li-ti], *n.* quality of being illegible.

ILLEGIBLE [i-le'ji-bl], *adj.* unable to be read. ILLEGIBLY, *adv.* in an i. fashion. [IL and LEGIBLE].

ILLEGITIMACY [i-li-ji'ti-ma-si], *n.* condition of being illegitimate.

ILLEGITIMATE (1) [i-li-ji'ti-mat], *adj.* unlawful, irregular; born out of wedlock; illogical. ILLEGITIMATE (2), *n.* an i. child. ILLEGITIMATE (3), *v.t.* to render or declare i.

ILL FAME [il-fām'], *n.* bad repute; **house of i.,** brothel.

ILL-FATED [il-fā'tid], *adj* doomed to misfortune; resulting in misfortune.

ILL-FAVOURED [il-fā'verd], *adj.* ugly.

ILL-GOTTEN [il-go'ten], *adj.* obtained by wrongdoing.

ILL-HUMOUR [il-hyōō'mer], *n.* irritability, anger, moroseness. ILL-HUMOURED, *adj.* irritable, bad-tempered.

ILLIBERAL [i-li'be-ral], *adj.* not generous; narrow-minded, intolerant; not enlightened.

ILLIBERALITY [i-li-be-ra'li-ti], *n.* quality of being illiberal.

ILLICIT [i-li'sit], *adj.* prohibited, illegal. [L.].

ILLIMITABLE [i-li'mi-ta-bl], *adj.* that cannot be limited, boundless, unrestricted. ILLIMITABLY, *adv.* in an i. fashion. [IL and LIMITABLE].

ILLITERACY [i-li'te-ra-si], *n.* state of being illiterate.

ILLITERATE (1) [i-li'te-rat], *adj.* unlearned, uneducated; unable to read or write. ILLITERATE (2), *n.* an i. person, *esp.* one unable to read or write. [L.].

ILL-MANNERED [il-ma'nerd], *adj.* badly behaved, rude.

ILL-NATURE [il-nā'tyōōr], *n.* maliciousness, bad temper. ILL-NATURED, *adj.* spiteful, morose.

ILLNESS [il'nes], *n.* state of being ill; a particular kind of disease or sickness.

ILLOGICAL [i-lo'ji-kal], *adj.* irrational, not reasonable.

ILL-OMENED [il-ō'mend], *adj.* attended with misfortune, inauspicious.

ILL-STARRED [il-stahd'], *adj.* unfortunate, ill-omened.

ILL-TEMPERED [il-tem'perd], *adj.* cross, morose.

ILL-TIMED [il-tīmd'], *adj.* coming at the wrong time, tactless.

ILL-TREAT [il-trēt'], *v.t.* to treat in a cruel, brutal fashion. ILL-TREATMENT, *n.* cruelty.

ILLUMINANT (1) [i-lyōō'mi-nant], *adj.* giving light, illuminating. ILLUMINANT (2), *n.* anything which illuminates.

ILLUMINATE [i-lyōō'mi-nāt], *v.t.* to light up, make light; adorn with bright lights and coloured lamps; decorate (a manuscript) with ornamental initial letters and miniature illustrations in gold, silver and colours; (*fig.*) enlighten, make clear. [L.].

ILLUMINATI [i-lōō-mi-nā'ti, -nah'tē], *n.(pl.)* persons claiming to be specially enlightened, *esp.* any of several religious societies, priding themselves on their supposed enlightenment as to certain beliefs. [L.].

ILLUMINATION [i-lyōō-mi-nā'shn], *n.* act of illuminating; state of being illuminated; (*pl.*) display of bright lights and coloured lamps; (*fig.*) divine inspiration; intellectual enlightenment; decorated initial letter in a manuscript or book. [L.].

ILLUMINATIVE [i-lyōō'mi-na-tiv], *adj.* that illuminates.

ILLUMINATOR [i-lyōō'mi-nā-ter], *n.* person who or thing which illuminates; one who illuminates manuscripts. [L.].

ILLUMINE [i-lyōō'min], *v.t.* to light up; throw light upon; make a meaning clear. [L.].

ILLUSION [i-lōō'shn], *n.* that which appears to the eye other than it actually is; anything which conveys a deceptive impression to the senses; delusion, mistaken belief. ILLUSIONIST, *n.* one who believes that the external world consists entirely of illusions; a conjurer. [L.].

ILLUSIVE [i-lōō'siv], *adj.* deceptive.

ILLUSORY [i-lōō'ze-ri], *adj.* deceptive; produced by, or consisting of, an illusion, not real. [LL.].

ILLUSTRATE [i'lus-trāt], *v.t.* to make more clear by giving examples; bring out the truth of by performing some action, or producing supporting evidence; provide with pictures or drawings. ILLUSTRATED, *adj.* containing pictures or drawings. [L.].

ILLUSTRATION [i-lus-trā'shn], *n.* example which illustrates something; drawing or picture in a book etc; act of illustrating. [L.].

ILLUSTRATIVE [i'lus-trā-tiv, i-lus'tra-tiv], *adj.* that illustrates. ILLUSTRATIVELY, *adv.* in an i. way.

ILLUSTRATOR [i'lus-trā-ter], *n.* one who illustrates, *esp.* one who draws illustrations. [LL.].

ILLUSTRIOUS [i-lus'tri-ōōs], *adj.* renowned, celebrated, noble. ILLUSTRIOUSLY, *adv.* in i. fashion. ILLUSTRIOUSNESS, *n.* quality of being i. [L.].

ILL-WILL [il-wil'], *n.* enmity, malice, spite.

IM-, *pref.* form of the Latin prefix IN- used before *b, m* and *p.* [L.].

IMAGE (1) [i'mij], *n.* material representation of a person or other object, in the form of a statue, carved figure etc.; idol; person who is extraordinarily like someone else; figure of speech; likeness; embodiment; mental picture, idea; (*optics*) reflection of an object in a mirror; the visible form of an object projected in the focal plane of a mirror or lens, *esp.* if manifest on a screen. IMAGE (2), *v.t.* to make or form an i. of; mirror in the mind; imagine; reflect. [L.].

IMAGERY [i'mij-ri, i'mi-je-ri], *n.* images, statues, effigies etc.; (*rhet.*) figures of speech and their use, figurative description. [Fr.].

IMAGINABLE [i-ma'ji-na-bl], *adj.* that may be imagined, conceivable. IMAGINABLY, *adv.* in an i. fashion.

IMAGINARY [i-ma'ji-na-ri], *adj.* existing only in imagination, not real. [L.].

IMAGINATION [i-ma-ji-nā'shn], *n.* ability of the mind to call up images which vividly recreate some past experience, or to form mental pictures of some object not present; power of the mind to create images or form concepts of things which have not been or cannot be experienced; mental image; fanciful notion. [L.].

IMAGINATIVE [i-ma'ji-na-tiv], *adj.* displaying, proceeding from, imagination; possessing a powerful imagination. IMAGINATIVENESS, *n.* quality of being i. [LL.].

IMAGINE [i-ma'jin], *v.t.* to form a mental image of; fancy, conjecture, suppose. [L.].

IMAGO (*pl.* **imagines, imagos**) [i-mā'gō, *pl* i-mā'ji-nēz, i-mā'gōz], *n.* (*entom.*) adult or completely developed state of an insect. [L.].

IMAM, IMAUM [i-mahm'], *n.* officer in charge of a Mohammedan mosque; Mohammedan prince, chief or religious leader. [Arab.].

IMBECILE (1) [im'bi-sēl], *adj.* feeble-minded, mentally deficient; (*coll.*) foolish, silly. IMBECILE (2), *n.* mentally deficient person; (*coll.*) fool, idiot. [Fr.].

IMBECILITY [im-bi-si'li-ti], *n.* state of being imbecile; imbecile act. [L.].

IMBED, see EMBED.

IMBIBE [im-bīb'], *v.t.* to drink in, absorb into the system (liquid nourishment); take in (moisture); (*fig.*) assimilate mentally; (*coll.*) indulge in alcoholic beverages. [L.].

IMBOSOM, see EMBOSOM.

IMBRICATE (1) [im'bri-kāt], *adj.* (*nat. hist.*) composed of overlapping scales. IMBRICATE (2), *v.t. and i.* to overlap like tiles; arrange so as to overlap. IMBRICATED, *adj.* composed of parts overlapping like tiles; arranged so as to overlap. [L.].

IMBROGLIO, EMBROGLIO [im-brō'li-ō], *n.* confused, complicated state of affairs; perplexing muddle. [It.].

IMBRUE [im-brōō'], *v.t.* to stain, drench, soil (in blood etc.). [OFr.].

IMBUE [im-byōō'], *v.t.* to soak, saturate; dye, stain; (*fig.*) fill, inspire with. [L.].

IMITATE [i'mi-tāt], *v.t.* to copy exactly, follow in manner of conduct or behaviour; reproduce closely; mimic; counterfeit. [L.].

IMITATION [i-mi-tā'shn], *n.* act of imitating; that which imitates; counterfeit, copy intended to be taken for the real thing; likeness. [L.].

IMITATIVE [i'mi-ta-tiv], *adj.* formed after a model; reproducing, copying; tending to imitate something or someone else. [LL.].

IMITATOR [i'mi-tā-ter], *n.* one who imitates. [L.].

IMMACULATE [i-ma'kyōō-lat], *adj.* spotless; extremely neat, faultless; pure, undefiled by sin; (*zool.*) without markings; (of the conception of the Virgin Mary) devoid of original sin. [L.].

IMMANENCE, IMMANENCY [i'ma-nens(-i)], *n.* condition of being immanent, inherence.

IMMANENT [i'ma-nent], *adj.* inherent; (*theol.*) (of God) present throughout the whole universe. [L.].

IMMATERIAL [i-ma-tēer'i-al], *adj.* not consisting of matter, spiritual; unimportant. [MedL.].

IMMATURE [i-ma-tyōōr'], *adj.* not ripe, not fully formed. [L.].

IMMATURITY [i-ma-tyōō'ri-ti], *n.* condition of being immature.

IMMEASURABLE [i-me'zhe-ra-bl], *adj.* unable to be measured, enormous.

IMMEDIACY [i-mē'di-a-si], *n.* state or quality of being immediate; directness.

IMMEDIATE [i-mē'di-at], *adj.* with nothing intervening; instant, without delay; present at this or that particular moment; very near; nearest; adjacent; direct, next in succession. IMMEDIATELY, *adv.* at once, without delay; directly; without anything intervening. [L.].

IMMEMORIAL [i-me-maw'ri-al], *adj.* extremely ancient, beyond memory or record. [MedL.].

IMMENSE [i-mens'], *adj.* vast, huge; (*coll.*) splendid. IMMENSELY, *adv.* to an i. degree; (*coll.*) exceedingly. [L.].

IMMENSITY [i-men'si-ti], *n.* quality of being immense; infinity, the infinite universe. [L.].

IMMENSURABLE [i-men'she-ra-bl], *adj.* incapable of being measured. IMMENSURABILITY [i-men-she-ra-bi'li-ti], *n.* quality of being i. [LL.].

IMMERSE [i-murs'], *v.t.* to plunge or dip deep into liquid; **to be immersed in,** to have one's whole attention absorbed by. [L.].

IMMERSION [i-mur'shn], *n.* act of immersing; condition of being immersed; baptism by covering the whole body with water; (*astron.*) disappearance of a celestial body behind, or in the shadow of, another.

IMMIGRANT (1) [i'mi-grant], *adj.* coming to live in a foreign country. IMMIGRANT (2), *n.* one who immigrates. [L.].

IMMIGRATE [i'mi-grāt], *v.t. and i.* to come to live in a foreign country permanently; bring as a settler into a foreign country. [L.].

IMMIGRATION [i-mi-grā'shn], *n.* act of immigrating; entrance into a country of bodies of immigrants.

IMMINENCE [i'mi-nens], *n.* quality of being imminent. [LL.].

IMMINENT [i'mi-nent], *adj.* impending, close at hand, about to take place. [L.].

IMMITIGABLE [i-mi'ti-ga-bl], *adj.* impossible to mitigate. IMMITIGABLY, *adv.* in an i. way. [L.].

IMMOBILE [i-mō'bil], *adj.* unable to move or be moved, fixed; stationary, motionless.

IMMOBILITY [i-mō-bi'li-ti], *n.* condition or quality of being immobile. [L.].

IMMOBILIZE [i-mō'bi-līz], *v.t.* to make immobile; make (a body of troops) incapable of being mobilized; keep stationary; withdraw from circulation. [Fr.].

IMMODERATE [i-mo'de-rat], *adj.* excessive, extravagant, extreme. [L.].

IMMODEST [i-mo'dest], *adj.* improper, lewd; lacking modesty; impudent, forward.

IMMODESTY [i-mo'des-ti], *n.* quality of being immodest. [L.].

IMMOLATE [i'mō-lāt], *v.t.* to kill as a sacrifice;

(*fig.*) sacrifice. IMMOLATOR, *n.* one who immolates. [L.].

IMMOLATION [i-mō-lā'shn], *n.* act of sacrificing; state of being sacrificed; a sacrifice. [L.].

IMMORAL [i-mo'ral], *adj.* not moral; having no moral principles; licentious, vicious; obscene.

IMMORALITY [i-mo-ra'li-ti], *n.* quality of being immoral; licentiousness; an immoral action.

IMMORTAL (1) [i-maw'tal], *adj.* living for ever, not subject to death; imperishable, eternal; renowned for ever. IMMORTAL (2), *n.* person who is i.; one whose fame is everlasting. [L.].

IMMORTALITY [i-maw-ta'li-ti], *n.* quality of being immortal. [L.].

IMMORTALIZE [i-maw'ta-līz], *v.t.* to make immortal, cause to be renowned for ever.

IMMORTELLE [i-maw-tel'], *n.* any of several genera of flowers whose petals retain their colour and shape when dried. [Fr.].

IMMOVABLE [i-mōō'va-bl], *adj.* not able to be moved; unalterable, unshakable; motionless; (*leg.*) that cannot be removed.

IMMUNE [i-myōōn'], *adj.* safe, not likely to be harmed; **i. serum,** serum containing an antibody. [L.].

IMMUNITY [i-myōō'ni-ti], *n.* quality of being immune; (*leg.*) exemption from liability, tax etc. [L.].

IMMUNIZE [i'myōō-nīz], *v.t.* to make immune. [L.].

IMMURE [i-myōōr'], *v.t.* to shut up, imprison; (*reflex.*) shut oneself up, remain in seclusion. [MedL.].

IMMUTABLE [i-myōō'ta-bl], *adj.* steadfastly the same, not alterable, fixed. IMMUTABILITY [i-myōō-ta-bi'li-ti], *n.* quality of being i. IMMUTABLY, *adv.* unchangeably. [L.].

IMP (1) [imp], *n.* little demon, mischievous sprite; (*coll.*) mischievous child. [OE.].

IMP (2), *v.t.* to introduce feathers into a bird's wing to repair or strengthen it; repair; enlarge. [OE.].

IMPACT (1) [im'pakt], *n.* collision, violent contact. IMPACT (2) [im-pakt'], *v.t.* to pack closely together, drive firmly in. IMPACTION, *n.* condition of being impacted. [L.].

IMPAIR [im-pāer'], *v.t.* to weaken, sap, make worse. [OFr.].

IMPALE, EMPALE [im-pāl'], *v.t.* to put to death by fixing on an upright sharp stake, transfix; (*her.*) place side by side on one shield, divided by a vertical line down the centre. IMPALEMENT, EMPALEMENT, *n.* act of impaling; state of being impaled; (*her.*) representation of two coats of arms on one shield, divided by a vertical line. [MedL.].

IMPALPABLE [im-pal'pa-bl], *adj.* not able to be felt or experienced by touch; (*fig.*) not easily grasped by the mind. [MedL.].

IMPANEL, see EMPANEL.

IMPART [im-paht'], *v.t.* to bestow; make known, tell. [L.].

IMPARTIAL [im-pah'shal], *adj.* not prejudiced, fair, disinterested.

IMPARTIALITY [im-pah-shi-a'li-ti], *n.* quality of being impartial.

IMPASSABLE [im-pah'sa-bl], *adj.* that cannot be passed over or crossed.

IMPASSE [im-pahs', am-pas'], *n.* deadlock, stalemate; blind alley. [Fr.].

IMPASSIBLE [im-pa'si-bl], *adj.* incapable of suffering, insensitive to pain; that cannot be injured; incapable of feeling or passion. [L.].

IMPASSION [im-pa'shn], *v.t.* to stir to strong feeling or passion. IMPASSIONED, *adj.* displaying passion, animated, fiery. [It.].

IMPASSIVE [im-pa'siv], *adj.* unemotional, unmoved by feeling; calm and unruffled.

IMPASTE [im-pāst'], *v.t.* to lay colours on thickly and boldly in painting. [It.].

IMPATIENCE [im-pā'shns], *n.* lack of ability to endure delay, opposition, restraint etc., irritability; restless desire to engage in activity. [L.].

IMPATIENT [im-pā'shnt], *adj.* displaying or indicating impatience, restive. [L.].

IMPEACH [im-pēch'], *v.t.* to charge or accuse, *esp.* of high treason or similar crime; call into question, discredit; inform against. [OFr.].

IMPEACHMENT [im-pēch'ment], *n.* act of impeaching; condition of being impeached; censure, disparagement. [OFr.].

IMPECCABLE [im-pe'ka-bl], *adj.* sinless, not liable to do wrong; irreproachable. [MedL.].

IMPECUNIOUS [im-pi-kyōō'ni-ōōs], *adj.* penniless;

poverty-stricken. IMPECUNIOSITY [im-pi-kyōō-ni-o'si-ti], *n.* condition of being i. [L.].

IMPEDANCE [im-pē'dans], *n.* (*elect.*) resistance arising from self-induction, offered by a coil of wire to an alternating current of electricity passing through it.

IMPEDE [im-pēd'], *v.t.* to hinder, hamper, obstruct. [L.].

IMPEDIMENT [im-pe'di-ment], *n.* obstacle, hindrance; the cause of a defective or indistinct articulation. IMPEDIMENTAL [im-pe-di-men'tal], *adj.* obstructing. [L.].

IMPEDIMENTA [im-pe-di-men'tah], *n.* baggage. [L.].

IMPEL (*pres.pt.* **impelling**, *pret. and p.pt.* **impelled**) [im-pel'], *v.t.* to drive or urge forward; constrain, stir to action. [L.].

IMPEND [im-pend'], *v.i.* to hang over, threaten, be about to take place. IMPENDENT, IMPENDING, *adj.* threatening, approaching. [L.].

IMPENETRABILITY [im-pe-ni-tra-bi'li-ti], *n.* quality of being impenetrable.

IMPENETRABLE [im-pe'ni-tra-bl], *adj.* unable to be penetrated or pierced; unable to be understood, inscrutable; insensible to ideas, feelings etc.; unable to be passed through; (*philos.*) not admitting the presence of two substances in the same place at the same time. [L.].

IMPENITENCE, IMPENITENCY [im-pe'ni-tens (-i)], *n.* absence of repentance, refusal to be penitent. [LL.].

IMPENITENT (1) [im-pe'ni-tent], *adj.* unrepentant. IMPENITENT (2), *n.* unrepentant person.

IMPERATIVE (1) [im-pe'ra-tiv], *adj.* authoritative, commanding; necessary, vital; (*gram.*) expressing a command. IMPERATIVE (2), *n.* (*gram.*) the i. mood, that form of the verb used to indicate a command; word, sentence etc. expressing a command. [LL.].

IMPERCEPTIBLE [im-per-sep'ti-bl], *adj* unable to be perceived or discerned; very small or gradual, unnoticeable. [L.].

IMPERFECT [im-pur'fekt], *adj.* not perfect, faulty; incomplete; (*leg.*) not legally binding; **i. tense,** (*gram.*) tense used to express action continuing and not complete; **i. cadence,** (*mus.*) cadence not ending on the chord of the tonic. [L.].

IMPERFECTION [im-per-fek'shn], *n.* state of being imperfect; defect, shortcoming. [L.].

IMPERFORATE(D) [im-pur'fe-rāt(-id)], *adj.* having no perforation; (*anat.*) having no opening, with the normal openings closed; (of postage stamps) not having a perforated edge.

IMPERIAL (1) [im-pēer'i-al], *adj.* pertaining to an empire or to an emperor; pertaining to Great Britain or to the British Empire; standardized throughout Great Britain; like or befitting an emperor, majestic. IMPERIAL (2), *n.* tuft of beard cultivated beneath the lower lip, after the fashion of Napoleon III; a size of paper or of roofing slate. IMPERIALLY, *adv.* in an i. way; from the point of view of imperialism. [L.].

IMPERIALISM [im-pēer'i-a-lizm], *n.* doctrine which seeks to weld the different portions of an empire into a closely bound whole; the increasing of the power and extent of an empire; rule by an emperor.

IMPERIALIST [im-pēer'i-a-list], *n.* supporter of an emperor or imperial government; advocate of imperialism.

IMPERIL (*pres.pt.* **imperilling**, *pret. and p.pt.* **imperilled**) [im-pe'ril], *v.t.* to endanger, place in peril.

IMPERIOUS [im-pēer'i-ōōs], *adj.* domineering, dictatorial; urgent; irresistible. [L.].

IMPERISHABLE [im-pe'ri-sha-bl], *adj.* not subject to decay; eternal.

IMPERMANENT [im-pur'ma-nent], *adj.* not permanent, transitory. IMPERMANENCE, *n.* transitoriness.

IMPERMEABLE [im-pur'mi-a-bl], *adj.* not porous. [L.].

IMPERSONAL [im-pur'so-nal], *adj.* having no personality or individuality; having no personal significance; (*gram.*) (of verbs) used only in the third person singular without a subject. IMPERSONALITY [im-per-so-na'li-ti], *n.* quality of being i. IMPERSONALLY, *adv.* in an i. way. [LL.].

IMPERSONATE [im-pur'so-nāt], *v.t.* to embody, represent in one's person; pretend to be someone else. IMPERSONATOR, *n.* one who impersonates. [L.].

IMPERSONATION [im-per-so-nā'shn], *n.* act of impersonating; manner of acting the part of a character in a play; imitation of another person.

IMPERTINENCE [im-pur'ti-nens], *n.* quality of being impertinent, presumptuousness; an impertinent act or speech; irrelevancy.

IMPERTINENT [im-pur'ti-nent], *adj.* rude, disrespectful; irrelevant; inappropriate. [L.].

IMPERTURBABLE [im-per-tur'ba-bl], *adj.* not liable to be ruffled or excited; cool, collected. [LL.].

IMPERVIOUS [im-pur'vi-ōōs], *adj.* not to be passed through, (of rocks) not porous, proof against; (*fig.*) heedless of, not open to influence by. [L.].

IMPETIGO [im-pi-ti'gō], *n.* skin disease characterized by an eruption of yellow-scaled pustules. IMPETIGINOUS [im-pe-ti'ji-nōōs], *adj.* resembling i. [L.].

IMPETUOSITY [im-pe-tyōō-o'si-ti], *n.* quality of being impetuous; impetuous act or speech.

IMPETUOUS [im-pe'tyōō-ōōs], *adj.* rushing violently; rash, hasty; vehement, dashing; inclined to act on sudden impulse. [L.].

IMPETUS [im'pe-tus], *n.* force with which a body moves, momentum; driving force, spur. [L.].

IMPI [im'pi], *n.* large organized body of Zulu warriors. [Zulu].

IMPIETY [im-pī'e-ti], *n.* condition or quality of being impious; impious act or speech. [L.].

IMPINGE [im-pinj'], *v.i.* to fall, dash or strike (upon, against); encroach (upon), come into contact. IMPINGEMENT, *n.* act of impinging. [L.].

IMPIOUS [im'pi-ōōs], *adj.* irreverent, profane, ungodly. IMPIOUSLY, *adv.* in an i. way. [L.].

IMPISH [im'pish], *adj.* like an imp, mischievous.

IMPLACABILITY [im-pla-ka-bi'li-ti], *n.* quality of being implacable.

IMPLACABLE [im-pla'ka-bl], *adj.* not to be appeased, relentless, inexorable. [L.].

IMPLANT [im-plahnt'], *v.t.* to set or plant deeply, insert; (*fig.*) instil, inculcate. IMPLANTATION [im-plahn-tā'shn], *n.* act of implanting; that which is implanted. [Fr.].

IMPLAUSIBLE [im-plaw'zi-bl], *adj.* not plausible, unlikely. IMPLAUSIBLY, *adv.* in an i. way.

IMPLEMENT (1) [im'pli-ment], *n.* tool, instrument etc. for carrying out some task. IMPLEMENT (2), *v.t.* to accomplish, complete; (*Scots leg.*) fulfil. [L.].

IMPLICATE [im'pli-kāt], *v.t.* to entangle; involve; show to be connected with. [L.].

IMPLICATION [im-pli-kā'shn], *n.* act of implicating; state of being implicated; something implied; act of implying. [L.].

IMPLICIT [im-pli'sit], *adj.* implied though not definitely stated; absolute, unquestioning. [L.].

IMPLIED [im-plīd'], *adj.* understood, intended to be inferred. IMPLIEDLY [im-plī'ed-li], *adv.* by implication. [IMPLY].

IMPLORE [im-plaw(r)'], *v.t.* to beg earnestly; entreat, beseech. IMPLORING, *adj.* beseeching. [L.].

IMPLY [im-plī'], *v.t.* to suggest, have a certain intended meaning not directly expressed; hint; necessitate as a logical conclusion. [OFr.].

IMPOLITE [im-po-līt'], *adj.* not polite; uncivil. IMPOLITELY, *adv.* in an i. way. [L.].

IMPOLITIC [im-po'li-tik], *adj.* not wise, inexpedient, imprudent.

IMPONDERABLE (1) [im-pon'de-ra-bl], *adj.* unable to be weighed; extremely light; (*fig.*) incalculable; incapable of material assessment. IMPONDERABLE (2), *n.* an i. body or thing.

IMPORT (1) [im-pawt'], *v.t.* to bring in, *esp.* to bring into a country in the course of international trade; introduce from an external or foreign source; mean, imply. IMPORT (2) [im'pawt], *n.* that which is imported; (*pl.*) goods brought into a country; meaning, implication; importance, consequence. IMPORTABLE, *adj.* able to be imported. [L.].

IMPORTANCE [im-paw'tans], *n.* quality or state of being important; reason why a particular thing is important. [MedL.].

IMPORTANT [im-paw'tant], *adj.* eminent, notable; of great consequence or significance; momentous; essential; pompous. [MedL.].

IMPORTATION [im-paw-tā'shn], *n.* act or practice of importing; that which is imported.

IMPORTUNATE [im-paw'tyōō-nat], *adj.* persistently entreating, demanding with pertinacity; insistent. [L.].

IMPORTUNE [im-paw-tyōōn', im-paw'tyōōn], *v.t.* to weary with persistent begging or demands. [MedL.].

IMPORTUNITY [im-paw-tyōō'ni-ti], *n.* quality of being importunate.

IMPOSE [im-pōz'], *v.t.* to force to accept; inflict;

levy, exact; (*print.*) arrange (pages) for printing and prepare the forme for press; *v.i.* to impress; **to i. on, upon,** to dupe, take a mean advantage of. [Fr.].

IMPOSING [im-pō′zing], *adj.* striking, compelling attention.

IMPOSITION [im-po-zi′shn], *n.* act of imposing; tax, duty; task set as a punishment for misbehaviour in school; disagreeable request or instruction; deception; (*eccles.*) the laying on of hands by a bishop etc. in ordination or confirmation. [L.].

IMPOSSIBILITY [im-po-si-bi′li-ti], *n.* state of being impossible; anything which is impossible. [L.].

IMPOSSIBLE [im-po′si-bl], *adj.* not possible; (*coll.*) insufferable, outrageous. **IMPOSSIBLY,** *adv.* not possibly; (*coll.*) in an apparently i. manner.

IMPOST (1) [im′pōst], *n.* tax, duty; (*racing*) weight carried by a horse as a handicap in a race. **IMPOST** (2), *n.* (*arch.*) moulding on the top of a pillar or pier from which an arch springs. [AFr.].

IMPOSTOR [im-pos′ter], *n.* one who attempts to trick people into believing that he is some other person, cheat, fraud. [LL.].

IMPOSTURE [im-pos′tyŏor], *n.* swindle, hoax, deception. [LL.].

IMPOTENCE [im′po-tens], *n.* condition of being impotent. [L.].

IMPOTENT [im′po-tent], *adj.* weak, feeble, lacking physical strength; (of males) unable to perform the sexual act; helpless. [L.].

IMPOUND [im-pownd′], *v.t.* to shut up (cattle) in a pound; hold in security; seize by legal authority.

IMPOVERISH [im-po′ve-rish], *v.t.* to make poor; exhaust the resources of; weaken. **IMPOVERISHMENT,** *n.* act of impoverishing; condition of being impoverished. [OFr.].

IMPRACTICABLE [im-prak′ti-ka-bl], *adj.* that cannot be done, unworkable; (of persons) intractable; (of roads) impassable.

IMPRECATE [im′pri-kāt], *v.t.* to invoke (an evil), pray that a misfortune fall on. [L.].

IMPRECATION [im-pri-kā′shn], *n.* act of imprecating; a curse, misfortune imprecated. [L.].

IMPREGNABLE [im-preg′na-bl], *adj.* able to withstand any attack; (*fig.*) proof against pressure or temptation. [~Fr.].

IMPREGNATE [im′preg-nāt], *v.t.* to make pregnant, fertilize; imbue, instil; saturate. [L.].

IMPREGNATION [im-preg-nā′shn], *n.* act of impregnating; state of being impregnated; that which impregnates.

IMPRESARIO [im-pre-sah′ri-ō], *n.* manager, organizer and producer of concerts and dramatic and operatic performances etc. [It.].

IMPRESCRIPTIBLE [im-pri-skrip′ti-bl], *adj.* that cannot be lost; unchallengeable, inviolable.

IMPRESS (1) [im-pres′], *v.t. and i.* to mark by applying pressure, imprint; fix deeply in a person's mind; strike the mind forcibly; evoke a strong feeling of approval. **IMPRESS** (2) [im′pres], *n.* act of impressing; mark or impression; seal, imprint; result of some powerful influence or force. [L.].

IMPRESS (3) [im-pres′], *v.t.* to force into public service, *esp.* compel to serve in the army or navy; seize for public service; (*fig.*) enforce the assistance of. [IM and PRESS (3)].

IMPRESSIBLE [im-pre′si-bl], *adj.* that may be impressed, susceptible to impression. **IMPRESSIBILITY** [im-pre-si-bi′li-ti], *n.* quality of being i.

IMPRESSION [im-pre′shn], *n.* act of impressing; state of being impressed; mark or stamp made by pressure; effect upon anything produced by some external influence; notion, vague feeling; printed copy; (*print.*) number of copies of a book etc. printed for a single issue; reprint of a book without additions or alterations; **to be under an i.,** to think, believe. [L.].

IMPRESSIONABLE [im-pre′shn-a-bl], *adj.* readily sensitive to impressions. [Fr.].

IMPRESSIONISM [im-pre′shn-izm], *n.* artistic doctrine which maintains that a painter should attempt to convey the general impression immediately produced on the mind by an object, rather than reproduce a detailed objective representation of it; application of this theory in art and literature.

IMPRESSIONIST (1) [im-pre′shn-ist], *n.* painter or writer who carries into practice the doctrine of impressionism. **IMPRESSIONIST** (2), *adj.* of, or pertaining to, impressionism and its exponents.

IMPRESSIVE [im-pre′siv], *adj.* creating a deep impression, striking, stirring.

IMPREST [im′prest], *n.* sum of money advanced to a

person to enable him to perform some State business or duties. [OFr.].

IMPRIMATUR [im-pri-mā′ter], *n.* licence to print a book, *esp.* one granted by the Roman Catholic Church; (*fig.*) sanction. [L.].

IMPRIMIS [im-pri′mis], *adv.* first of all. [L.].

IMPRINT (1) [im-print′], *v.t.* to stamp, make or mark by pressure; press, print; (*fig.*) fix clearly in the mind. **IMPRINT** (2) [im′print], *n.* that which is imprinted, impression; name of the printer or publisher of a book, usually with the date of printing or publication, printed at the front or the end of the book; (*fig.*) feature impressed upon something. [OFr.].

IMPRISON [im-pri′zon], *v.t.* to confine in a prison, shut up.

IMPRISONMENT [im-pri′zon-ment], *n.* act of imprisoning; state of being imprisoned; period of detention. [OFr.].

IMPROBABLE [im-pro′ba-bl], *adj.* not likely to be true.

IMPROMPTU (1) [im-promp′tyŏo], *adv.* without previous preparation. **IMPROMPTU** (2), *n.* anything done or made i. **IMPROMPTU** (3), *adj.* performed on the spur of the moment, improvised. [Fr.].

IMPROPER [im-pro′per], *adj.* not proper, unsuitable; incorrect; indecent.

IMPROPRIATE [im-prō′pri-āt], *v.t.* to transfer or annex an ecclesiastical benefice for private use; place ecclesiastical property in the hands of a layman. [MedL.].

IMPROPRIETY [im-prō-pri′i-ti], *n.* quality or condition of being improper; an improper act, speech etc. [L.].

IMPROVE [im-prŏov′], *v.t.* to make more valuable or better; use to advantage; *v.i.* to become better. **IMPROVER,** *n.* one who or that which improves, an apprentice. [AFr.].

IMPROVEMENT [im-prŏov′ment], *n.* act of improving; state of being improved; that which constitutes an increase in value or good qualities. [AFr.].

IMPROVIDENCE [im-pro′vi-dens], *n.* quality of being improvident. [L.].

IMPROVIDENT [im-pro′vi-dent], *adj.* thriftless, wanting in foresight.

IMPROVISATION [im-prō-vi-zā′shn], *n.* act of improvising; whatever is improvised.

IMPROVISE [im′prō-vīz], *v.t. and i.* to compose and perform on the spur of the moment; rig up in a makeshift way. [It.].

IMPRUDENCE [im-prŏo′dens], *n.* quality of being imprudent; that which is imprudent. [L.].

IMPRUDENT [im-prŏo′dent], *adj.* rash, indiscreet.

IMPUDENCE [im′pyŏo-dens], *n.* quality of being impudent. [L.].

IMPUDENT [im′pyŏo-dent], *adj.* wanting modesty, shameless, cheeky.

IMPUGN [im-pyŏon′], *v.t.* to attack in argument; call in question. [L.].

IMPULSE [im′puls], *n.* act of impelling, thrust, push; sudden emotional urge to action; large force applied for a very short time. [L.].

IMPULSIVE [im-pul′siv], *adj.* able or tending to impel; liable to act on impulse without considering the possible consequences; based on an impulse. [MedL.].

IMPUNITY [im-pyŏo′ni-ti], *n.* exemption or freedom from penalty, punishment, injury or loss; **with i.,** without fear of the consequences. [L.].

IMPURE [im-pyŏor′], *adj.* not pure; dirty; unhallowed; unchaste; mixed with some foreign matter; adulterated.

IMPURITY [im-pyŏo′ri-ti], *n.* quality or state of being impure; that which is impure, foreign element which adulterates. [L.].

IMPUTABLE [im-pyŏo′ta-bl], *adj.* able to be imputed, charged, or attributed.

IMPUTATION [im-pyŏo-tā′shn], *n.* act of imputing, attribution, *esp.* of something bad, to a person; accusation made against a person. [LL.].

IMPUTE [im-pyŏot′], *v.t.* to attribute, ascribe to (*esp.* something bad); lay to the blame of. [L.].

IN (1) [in], *prep.* inside of, within; enclosed by; during; at the end of; by means of; because of; by way of; having regard to; *also used to express state, condition, place, time, manner, action, limitation, method of arrangement.* **IN** (2), *adv.* within, inside, into; along, close to; into the bargain; (of a fire) alight; (*pol.*) holding office; (*cricket*) batting; arrived at a place; **i. for,** committed to; about to receive; entered or applied for; (*coll.*) due for; **i. with,** on

friendly terms with. IN (3), *adj.* interior, internal.
IN (4), *n.* **the ins and outs,** the full details, complexities etc. [OE.].
IN- (5), *pref.* not. [L.].
IN- (6), *pref.* in, upon; into, against, towards. [L.].
INABILITY [in-a-bi′li-ti], *n.* incapacity, lack of ability.
INACCESSIBILITY [in-ak-se-si-bi′li-ti], *n.* quality of being inaccessible.
INACCESSIBLE [in-ak-se′si-bl], *adj.* out-of-the-way, remote, difficult to get at; unattainable; reserved, aloof. INACCESSIBLY, *adv.* in an i. way. [LL.].
INACCURACY [in-a′kyōō-ra-si], *n.* quality of being inaccurate; a mistake.
INACCURATE [in-a′kyōō-rat], *adj.* not accurate, incorrect.
INACTION [in-ak′shn], *n.* want of action; inertness; state of doing nothing.
INACTIVE [in-ak′tiv], *adj.* not active, indisposed to exertion or effort; quiescent, dormant; indolent; unemployed; not operating.
INACTIVITY [in-ak-ti′vi-ti], *n.* state or period of being inactive.
INADEQUACY [in-a′di-kwa-si], *n.* quality of being inadequate.
INADEQUATE [in-a′di-kwat], *adj.* not adequate, not equal to the purpose; not competent.
INADMISSIBLE [in-ad-mi′si-bl], *adj.* that cannot be admitted.
INADVERTENCE, INADVERTENCY [in-ad-vur′tens(-i)], *n.* quality of being inadvertent; anything done inadvertently, an oversight.
INADVERTENT [in-ad-vur′tent], *adj.* heedless, not paying attention; unintentional, due to an accidental error or miscalculation.
INALIENABLE [in-ā′li-e-na-bl], *adj.* that may not be alienated.
INAMORATO, INAMORATA [in-a-maw-rah′tō, ′tah], *n.* lover, beloved man (woman). [It.].
INANE (1) [in-ān′], *adj.* vacant, silly, brainless. INANE (2), *n.* the limitless void. [L.].
INANIMATE [in-a′ni-mat], *adj.* without life or animation; (*fig.*) inactive. [LL.].
INANITION [in-a-ni′shn], *n.* exhaustion from lack of nourishment. [L.].
INANITY [in-a′ni-ti], *n.* quality of being inane; inane remark or act. [L.].
INAPPLICABLE [in-ap′li-ka-bl], *adj.* not applicable, unsuitable.
INAPPOSITE [in-a′pō-zit], *adj.* not apposite, irrelevant.
INAPPRECIABLE [in-a-prē′sha-bl], *adj.* imperceptible, negligible.
INAPPROPRIATE [in-a-prō′pri-at], *adj.* not appropriate, unsuitable.
INAPT [in-apt′], *adj.* unskilful, clumsy; incongruous. INAPTLY, *adv.* in an i. fashion.
INAPTITUDE [in-ap′ti-tyōōd], *n.* quality of being inapt.
INARTICULATE [in-ah-ti′kyōō-lat], *adj.* (*anat.*) not jointed or articulated; (of speech) not clear or distinct; unable to speak or express oneself clearly and fluently.
INARTISTIC [in-ah-tis′tik], *adj.* lacking in artistry; lacking a taste for or appreciation of the arts.
INASMUCH [in-az-much′], *adv.* **i. as,** seeing that, because, since; in so far as.
INATTENTION [in-a-ten′shn], *n.* want of attention; failure to concentrate; lack of courtesy or consideration.
INATTENTIVE [in-a-ten′tiv], *adj.* not paying attention; heedless; negligent.
INAUDIBILITY [in-aw-di-bi′li-ti], *n.* condition of being inaudible.
INAUDIBLE [in-aw′di-bl], *adj.* unable to be heard. [L.].
INAUGURAL [in-aw′gyōō-ral], *adj.* pertaining to inauguration, given on entering into office or at an opening ceremony. [Fr.].
INAUGURATE [in-aw′gyōō-rāt], *v.t.* to install or induct into office with suitable ceremonies; introduce or commence formally; open to the public by a special ceremony. INAUGURATOR, *n.* one who inaugurates. [L.].
INAUGURATION [in-aw-gyōō-rā′shn], *n.* act of inaugurating; condition of being inaugurated.
INAUSPICIOUS [in-aw-spi′shŏŏs], *adj.* ill-omened, unfortunate.
INBOARD [in′bawd], *adj.* (*naut.*) within the ship, towards the centre line of the ship.
INBORN [in′bawn], *adj.* innate, inherent, instinctive.

INBRED [in′bred], *adj.* innate, inherent, natural; bred from the mating of individuals sprung from common ancestors.
INBREED [in-brēd′], *v.t.* to breed from the same stock; engender within.
INCA [ing′kah], *n.* member of a highly civilized people who occupied Peru before it was conquered by the Spaniards; the ruler of this people. [Peruvian].
INCALCULABLE [in-kal′kyōō-la-bl], *adj.* unable to be calculated, untold, unable to be forecast; volatile, fickle. INCALCULABLY, *adv.* in an i. way.
INCANDESCE [in-kan-des′], *v.t.* to cause to glow; *v.i.* to become incandescent, emit light when strongly heated.
INCANDESCENT [in-kan-de′sent], *adj.* glowing with a white heat, emitting light because of its high temperature; luminous, shining; (*fig.*) ardent. [L.].
INCANTATION [in-kan-tā′shn], *n.* magical formula chanted or recited, a spell. [L.].
INCAPABLE [in-kā′pa-bl], *adj.* not capable, unable; helpless; incompetent; (*leg.*) disqualified or barred from.
INCAPACITATE [in-ka-pa′si-tāt], *v.t.* to render unfit for or incapable of, disable; (*fig.*) disqualify.
INCAPACITY [in-ka-pa′si-ti], *n.* want of capacity, inability, incompetence; (*leg.*) disqualification.
INCARCERATE [in-kah′se-rāt], *v.t.* to shut up in a prison. INCARCERATION [in-kah-se-rā′shn], *n.* act of incarcerating; state or period of being incarcerated. [L.].
INCARNATE (1) [in-kah′nat], *adj.* invested with or embodied in flesh, in bodily form; personified. INCARNATE (2) [in-kah′nāt], *v.t.* to embody in flesh, take on bodily form; express in concrete form. [L.].
INCARNATION [in-kah-nā′shn], *n.* act of incarnating; assumption of a human body and personality; personification of an abstract quality. [LL.].
INCAUTIOUS [in-kaw′shŏŏs], *adj.* not cautious, indiscreet, rash.
INCENDIARISM [in-sen′di-e-rizm], *n.* arson, act of wilfully setting fire to property; (*fig.*) an inflaming of passions.
INCENDIARY (1) [in-sen′di-e-ri], *adj.* pertaining to, given to, the malicious burning of property; capable of causing a fire; (*fig.*) inflammatory. INCENDIARY (2), *n.* one who indulges in incendiarism; incendiary bomb. [L.].
INCENSE (1) [in′sens], *n.* fragrant odours or smoke arising from aromatic herbs, spices etc., burned in religious rites; materials thus burned; any fragrant odour; (*fig.*) flattery, homage. INCENSE (2) [in-sens′], *v.t.* to perfume, fumigate with i.; burn or offer i. to; enrage, make furious. [OFr. from L.].
INCENTIVE (1) [in-sen′tiv], *adj.* tending to stimulate or stir up. INCENTIVE (2), *n.* stimulus, spur, incitement. [L.].
INCEPTION [in-sep′shn], *n.* beginning. [L.].
INCEPTIVE [in-sep′tiv], *adj.* beginning, initial; (*gram.*) expressing the beginning of an action. [L.].
INCERTITUDE [in-sur′ti-tyōōd], *n.* uncertainty; insecurity. [Fr.].
INCESSANT [in-se′sant], *adj.* unceasing, continual. [LL.].
INCEST [in′sest], *n.* sexual intercourse within the prohibited degrees of relationship. [L.].
INCESTUOUS [in-ses′tyŏŏ-ŏŏs], *adj.* guilty of incest, of the nature of incest. [L.].
INCH (1) [inch], *n.* a twelfth of a foot; (of rain) quantity sufficient to cover a surface to the depth of an inch; small amount, distance etc.; (*pl.*) height, stature; **by inches, i. by i.,** gradually; **every i.,** completely, entirely. INCH (2), *v.t.* measure the number of inches in; drive by small degrees; *v.i.* to move by inches. [OE. from L.].
INCHOATE (1) [in′kō-āt, in-kō′āt], *adj.* just begun, in an early stage; unfinished. INCHOATE (2), *v.t. and i.* to begin, initiate. INCHOATELY, *adv.* in an i. manner. INCHOATION [in-kō-ā′shn], *n.* beginning. INCHOATIVE [in-kō′a-tiv], *adj.* (*gram.*) expressing the beginning of an action; initial, rudimentary. [L.].
INCIDENCE [in′si-dens], *n.* fact of falling upon; manner of falling upon; extent to which a thing affects anything; direction in which a line or moving body falls upon another; **angle of i.,** angle which a ray of light, line etc., falling on a surface, makes with a perpendicular to that surface. [Fr.].
INCIDENT (1) [in′si-dent], *adj.* liable to happen to, naturally belonging to; (*phys.*) striking or falling on; (*leg.*) attached to. INCIDENT (2), *n.* event; occurrence considered as a separate circumstance; subordinate episode in a literary composition; (*leg.*) privilege,

---

The accent ′ after a syllable = stress (u-pon′). The mark ⁻ over a vowel = length (ā in made; ō in bone).

right etc. attaching to an office or estate; **i. officer,** person deputed to take charge of an individual i. caused by the dropping of a bomb. [L.].

INCIDENTAL (1) [in-si-den'tal], *adj.* attendant on, liable to happen in; (of expenses) incurred in addition to the main expense; occasional, subordinate; (of music) accompanying a spoken play. INCIDENTAL (2), *n.* that which is i.

INCINERATE [in-si'ne-rāt], *v.t.* to burn to ashes. INCINERATION [in-si-ne-rā'shn], *n.* a burning to ashes. [MedL.].

INCINERATOR [in-si'ne-rā-ter], *n.* furnace for burning refuse; cremation furnace.

INCIPIENT [in-si'pi-ent], *adj.* beginning, in the earliest stages.

INCISE [in-sīz'], *v.t.* to make a cut in; carve, engrave. INCISED, *adj.* cut, gashed; (*bot., zool.*) indented along the margin. [L.].

INCISION [in-si'zhn], *n.* act of incising; a cut, *esp.* one made for surgical purposes; (*bot., zool.*) deep marginal indentation. [L.].

INCISIVE [in-sī'siv], *adj.* cutting sharply into; (*fig.*) keen, vigorous; sharp, trenchant. [MedL.].

INCISOR [in-sī'zer], *n.* any of those front teeth occurring between the canine teeth, in the upper or lower jaws of mammals. INCISORY, *adj.* sharp, able to cut. [MedL.].

INCITE [in-sīt'], *v.t.* to stir up, stimulate. [L.].

INCITEMENT [in-sīt'ment], *n.* act of inciting; condition of being incited; that which incites, a stimulus.

INCIVILITY [in-si-vi'li-ti], *n.* want of courtesy; an act of rudeness. [LL.].

INCLEMENCY [in-kle'men-si], *n.* lack of clemency; harshness; severity of weather. [L.].

INCLEMENT [in-kle'ment], *adj.* (of weather) severe, cold, stormy. INCLEMENTLY, *adv.* in an i. way. [L.].

INCLINATION [in-kli-nā'shn], *n.* act of inclining, a sloping; state of being inclined, slanting position; amount of deviation from the horizontal; favourable disposition towards; fondness, partiality; dip of the magnetic needle; (*geom.*) angle made by two lines or planes which meet, or which would meet if produced. [L.].

INCLINE (1) [in-klīn'], *v.t.* to cause to slant or deviate from a horizontal position, tilt; bow, bend downwards; *v.i.* to lean, slope or slant; tend, be disposed, prone or liable; **to be or feel inclined to,** to feel as if one ought or one would like to. INCLINE (2) [in'klīn], *n.* slope, gradient. INCLINED, *adj.* slanting, deviating from the horizontal; tending to; favourable towards. [L.].

INCLUDE [in-klood'], *v.t.* to comprise, comprehend; consider as a constituent part of. INCLUDING, *adj. and prep.* that includes; counting, reckoning in, together with. [L.].

INCLUSION [in-kloo'zhn], *n.* act of including; state of being included. [L.].

INCLUSIVE [in-kloo'siv], *adj.* including, together with; including both extremes mentioned; reckoning in everything. [L.].

INCOGNITO (1) [in-kog'ni-tō], *adj.* adopting or travelling under an assumed name. INCOGNITO (2), *adv.* under an assumed name. INCOGNITO (3), *n.* person who endeavours to keep secret his identity; assumed name adopted to conceal identity. [It.].

INCOHERENCE [in-kō-hēer'ens], *n.* state or quality of being incoherent; incoherent statement, idea etc.

INCOHERENT [in-kō-hēer'ent], *adj.* disconnected, not proceeding by a logical progression, inconsistent.

INCOMBUSTIBLE [in-kom-bus'ti-bl], *adj.* unable to be burnt. INCOMBUSTIBILITY [in-kom-bus-ti-bi'li-ti], *n.* quality of being i. [MedL.].

INCOME [in'kum], *n.* the total amount of money periodically accruing to a person or body in the form of wages, interest, profit, rent etc.; **i. tax,** tax levied on annual i., earned or unearned.

INCOMING (1) [in'ku-ming], *n.* arrival; (*pl.*) income. INCOMING (2) [in-ku'ming], *adj.* coming in; succeeding; (of profit, payment) falling due, resulting; settling in from abroad; (of a period of time) about to start.

INCOMMENSURABLE [in-ko-men'shyoo-ra-bl], *adj.* having no common standard for comparative measurement; unworthy to be compared with; (*math.*) (of two quantities) having no common measure.

INCOMMENSURATE [in-ko-men'shyoo-rat], *adj.* incommensurable; disproportionate, unequal.

INCOMMODE [in-ko-mōd'], *v.t.* to inconvenience, cause discomfort or trouble to, annoy. [L.].

INCOMMODIOUS [in-ko-mō'di-oos], *adj.* inconvenient, troublesome; uncomfortably small.

INCOMMUNICABLE [in-ko-myoo'ni-ka-bl], *adj.* unable to be communicated or imparted to others.

INCOMMUNICATIVE [in-ko-myoo'ni-ka-tiv], *adj.* not communicative, disinclined to impart information; not disposed to converse freely.

INCOMPARABLE [in-kom'pa-ra-bl], *adj.* not able to be compared (with); matchless, unrivalled.

INCOMPATIBILITY [in-kom-pa-ti-bi'li-ti], *n.* quality or condition of being incompatible.

INCOMPATIBLE [in-kom-pa'ti-bl], *adj.* not compatible, mutually opposed, inconsistent.

INCOMPETENCE [in-kom'pi-tens], *n.* state or quality of being incompetent.

INCOMPETENT [in-kom'pi-tent], *adj.* lacking the necessary qualifications or ability; unsatisfactory, totally inefficient; (*leg.*) incapable. [LL.].

INCOMPLETE [in-kom-plēt'], *adj.* not complete, unfinished; having some part missing.

INCOMPREHENSIBLE [in-kom-pri-hen'si-bl], *adj.* that cannot be understood, unintelligible; boundless, infinite. [L.].

INCOMPRESSIBLE [in-kom-pre'si-bl], *adj.* unable to be compressed.

INCONCEIVABLE [in-con-sē'va-bl], *adj.* unimaginable, that cannot be conceived; (*coll.*) extremely unlikely.

INCONCLUSIVE [in-kon-kloo'siv], *adj.* not conclusive; indecisive.

INCONDENSABLE [in-kon-den'sa-bl], *adj.* that cannot be condensed.

INCONGRUITY [in-kong-groo'i-ti], *n.* want of congruity, inappropriateness, inconsistency; that which is incongruous.

INCONGRUOUS [in-kong'groo-oos], *adj.* unsuitable; inappropriate; inconsistent. [L.].

INCONSEQUENCE [in-kon'si-kwens], *n.* quality of being inconsequent; that which is inconsequent.

INCONSEQUENT [in-kon'si-kwent], *adj.* not consequent, disconnected, irrelevant, illogical. [L.].

INCONSEQUENTIAL [in-kon-si-kwen'shal], *adj.* inconsequent; of no importance.

INCONSIDERABLE [in-kon-si'de-ra-bl], *adj.* not worthy of consideration, unimportant, trifling; small.

INCONSIDERATE [in-kon-si'de-rat], *adj.* rash, indiscreet; indifferent to the feelings or wishes of others, thoughtless.

INCONSISTENCY [in-kon-sis'ten-si], *n.* state of being inconsistent; that which is inconsistent, discrepancy.

INCONSISTENT [in-kon-sis'tent], *adj.* not concic nsistent, incompatible; irreconcilable, logically opposed; illogically or haphazardly variable or changeable.

INCONSOLABLE [in-kon-sō'la-bl], *adj.* not to be consoled or comforted.

INCONSPICUOUS [in-kon-spi'kyoo-oos], *adj.* not conspicuous, not strikingly noticeable. [L.].

INCONSTANCY [in-kon'stan-si], *n.* quality of being inconstant.

INCONSTANT [in-kon'stant], *adj.* fickle, unfaithful; prone to change; variable; irregular.

INCONTESTABLE [in-kon-tes'ta-bl], *adj.* undeniable, undisputed, unquestionable. [Fr.].

INCONTINENCE [in-kon'ti-nens], *n.* state or quality of being incontinent. [L.].

INCONTINENT (1) [in-kon'ti-nent], *adj.* lacking self-control or restraint; given to unrestrained sexual indulgence; unable to restrain the natural discharges. [L.].

INCONTINENT (2), *adv.* (*archaic*) straightway, instantly. [LL.].

INCONTROVERTIBLE [in-kon-trō-vur'ti-bl], *adj.* indisputable, that cannot be argued about.

INCONVENIENCE (1) [in-kon-vē'ni-ens], *n.* state or quality of being inconvenient; that which is inconvenient; discomfort, awkwardness. INCONVENIENCE (2), *v.t.* to put to i., trouble. [LL.].

INCONVENIENT [in-kon-vē'ni-ent], *adj.* not convenient, troublesome, causing discomfort or embarrassment, awkward. [L.].

INCONVERTIBLE [in-kon-vur'ti-bl], *adj.* not convertible, unable to be changed into, or exchanged for, something else; (*esp.* of paper money) unable to be converted into coin. [LL.].

INCORPORATE (1) [in-kaw'pe-rāt], *v.t.* to embody;

adopt into, include and make a homogeneous part of; blend into a uniform mass; make a member of a corporation or society; form into a legal corporation; *v.i.* to unite, mix or blend so as to form one substance. INCORPORATE (2) [in-kaw'pe-rat], *adj.* united in a body or corporation; formally established as a corporation. [LL.].

INCORPORATION [in-kaw-pe-rā'shn], *n.* act of incorporating; condition of being incorporated; association in a corporate body. [L.].

INCORPOREAL [in-kaw-paw'ri-al], *adj.* not in bodily form, spiritual; pertaining to immaterial beings; (*leg.*) having no tangible existence itself, but inseparably connected with some actual thing. [L.].

INCORRECT [in-ko-rekt'], *adj.* not correct; not conforming to a recognized standard or custom; inaccurate; untrue. [L.].

INCORRIGIBLE [in-ko'ri-ji-bl], *adj.* unable to be corrected, reformed or improved.

INCORRUPTIBLE [in-ko-rup'ti-bl], *adj.* everlasting, not subject to decay; unable to be bribed. [L.].

INCORRUPTION [in-ko-rup'shn], *n.* immunity from decay.

INCREASE (1) [in-krēs'], *v.t.* to make greater or more numerous, extend, enlarge, multiply; intensify, aggravate; *v.i.* to become larger or more numerous, multiply; grow, advance in. INCREASE (2) [in'krēs], *n.* growth, augmentation; fact of becoming larger, more numerous or extensive; amount by which anything is increased; (*archaic*) crops. INCREASINGLY, *adv.* to an increasing extent. [OFr.].

INCREDIBLE [in-kre'di-bl], *adj.* not credible, unbelievable; (*coll.*) tremendous; extraordinary. INCREDIBILITY [in-kre-di-bi'li-ti], *n.* quality of being i. INCREDIBLY, *adv.* in an i. manner, to an i. extent; (*coll.*) extraordinarily. [L.].

INCREDULITY [in-kre-dyōō'li-ti], *n.* quality of being incredulous. [LL.].

INCREDULOUS [in-kre'dyōō-loŏs], *adj.* sceptical, unwilling to believe; indicating lack of belief. INCREDULOUSLY, *adv.* in an i. fashion. [LL.].

INCREMENT [in'kre-ment], *n.* act of increasing; increase; addition; amount by which a thing is increased; (*math.*) the regular increase of a variable quantity. [L.].

INCRIMINATE [in-kri'mi-nāt], *v.t.* to charge with a crime; render a person liable to be accused of a crime, implicate in a charge of crime or guilt. INCRIMINATORY, *adj.* tending to i., that incriminates. [MedL.].

INCRUST, see ENCRUST.

INCRUSTATION [in-krus-tā'shn], *n.* act of incrusting; state of being incrusted; crust or coating; mosaic or inlaid covering. [LL.].

INCUBATE [in'kyōō-bāt], *v.t. and i.* to sit upon eggs in order to hatch them out, hatch artificially; (*fig.*) ponder over; (*med.*) (of a disease) undergo the stage of incubation. [L.].

INCUBATION [in-kyōō-bā'shn], *n.* act or process of incubating; (*path.*) stage or period of an infectious disease occurring between the time of infection and the first appearance of symptoms. [L.].

INCUBATOR [in'kyōō-bā-ter], *n.* heated apparatus for hatching eggs artificially; apparatus for cultivating bacteria; apparatus for rearing children prematurely born. [L.].

INCUBUS (*pl.* incubi) [in'kyōō-bus], *n.* nightmare; demon believed to haunt women when asleep; troublesome obsession or encumbrance. [LL.].

INCULCATE [in'kul-kāt], *v.t.* to impress forcibly upon the mind of someone else. INCULCATION [in-kul-kā'shn], *n.* process of inculcating. [L.].

INCULPATE [in'kul-pāt], *v.t.* to censure, lay a charge against; implicate in an accusation. INCULPATION [in-kul-pā'shn], *n.* censure, act of inculpating. INCULPATORY [in-kul'pa-te-ri], *adj.* tending to i. [MedL.].

INCUMBENCY [in-kum'ben-si], *n.* the holding of an ecclesiastical office, *esp.* a benefice; period during which it is held; an ecclesiastical office.

INCUMBENT (1) [in-kum'bent], *adj.* lying or resting upon; obligatory, as a duty; **i. upon,** required of as a duty, morally compulsory for. INCUMBENT (2), *n.* (*eccles.*) person who holds a benefice. [L.].

INCUNABULA [in-kyōō-na'byōō-lah], *n.*(*pl.*) the first stages of anything; books printed in the earliest stages of printing, *i.e.* before 1500. [L.].

INCUR (*pres.pt.* incurring, *pret. and p.pt.* incurred) [in-kur'], *v.t.* to become liable to, bring upon oneself. [L.].

INCURABLE (1) [in-kyōō'ra-bl], *adj.* that cannot

be cured. INCURABLE (2), *n.* person afflicted with an i. disease.

INCURIOUS [in-kyōō'ri-oŏs], *adj.* not inquisitive; not interested. [L.].

INCURSION [in-kur'shn], *n.* attack, raid, sudden invasion. [L.].

INDEBTED [in-de'tid], *adj.* owing money; under an obligation, extremely grateful. [OFr.].

INDECENCY [in-dē'sen-si], *n.* quality of being indecent; an indecent action or expression.

INDECENT [in-dē'sent], *adj.* not decent, unbecoming; obscene, lewd.

INDECIPHERABLE [in-di-sī'fe-ra-bl], *adj.* unable to be deciphered; illegible.

INDECISION [in-di-si'zhn], *n.* want of decision, hesitation.

INDECISIVE [in-di-sī'siv], *adj.* inconclusive, not deciding one way or another; irresolute. INDECISIVELY, *adv.* in an i. fashion.

INDECLINABLE [in-di-klī'na-bl], *adj.* (*gram.*) that cannot be declined, uninflected. [L.].

INDECOROUS [in-di-kaw'roŏs, in-de'ke-roŏs], *adj.* not in good taste, unseemly. [L.].

INDECORUM [in-di-kaw'rum], *n.* quality of being indecorous, impropriety; indecorous act or speech.

INDEED (1) [in-dēd'], *adv.* in reality; as a matter of fact; certainly, in truth; *used also for emphasis.* INDEED (2), *int. expressing surprise, indignation etc.*

INDEFATIGABLE [in-di-fa'ti-ga-bl], *adj.* unable to be wearied; tireless. [L.].

INDEFEASIBLE [in-di-fē'zi-bl], *adj.* that cannot be set aside, forfeited or declared void.

INDEFENSIBLE [in-di-fen'si-bl], *adj.* that cannot be defended; unjustifiable, inexcusable.

INDEFINABLE [in-di-fī'na-bl], *adj.* that cannot be defined, indescribable.

INDEFINITE [in-de'fi-nit], *adj.* not clearly defined, vague; not expressly stated or specified; (*gram.*) (of *adj., pron.*) not indicating precisely the number, place, person etc. to which they refer; (of *v.*) not stating whether an action is complete or continuous.

INDELIBLE [in-de'li-bl], *adj.* that cannot be effaced or rubbed out; producing an inerasable mark; that cannot be wiped out or lived down. [L.].

INDELICACY [in-de'li-ka-si], *n.* quality of being indelicate; an indelicate act or speech.

INDELICATE [in-de'li-kat], *adj.* not delicate, offensive to decency, coarse.

INDEMNIFICATION [in-dem-ni-fi-kā'shn], *n.* act of indemnifying; that which indemnifies; state of being indemnified.

INDEMNIFY [in-dem'ni-fī], *v.t.* to safeguard against, render immune from (loss, damage etc.); free from (liability or responsibility); compensate for. [L.].

INDEMNITY [in-dem'ni-ti], *n.* security or compensation against loss or damage; amount paid or demanded as compensation; exemption or immunity from liability or responsibility. [LL.].

INDENT (1) [in-dent'], *v.t.* to cut the edge of into a series of tooth-like points; make sharp recesses in; separate (a document drawn up in duplicate) into corresponding halves by means of a jagged or zigzag line; write out in duplicate; (*print.*) begin farther in from the margin than the remainder of the section; *v.i.* to draw upon (stores etc.) by making out an official order (together with a duplicate copy). INDENT (2) [in-dent', in'dent], *n.* a notch or cut in the margin of anything; indenture; official application for goods; (*comm.*) order for goods. [Fr.].

INDENT (3) [in-dent'], *v.t.* to make a dent in; imprint. INDENT (4) [in'dent], *n.* depression, dent. [IN and DENT].

INDENTATION [in-den-tā'shn], *n.* act of indenting, condition of being indented; tooth-shaped cut in the edge of anything; narrow opening in a coastline etc.

INDENTURE (1) [in-den'tyōōr], *n.* indentation, notch, document drawn up in duplicate and cut by means of a jagged line into corresponding halves; deed, contract etc. between two or more parties, *esp.* one which binds an apprentice to his employer; official deed, certificate etc. INDENTURE (2), *v.t.* to bind by an i., draw up a formal contract with. [OFr.].

INDEPENDENCE [in-di-pen'dens], *n.* condition or quality of being independent.

INDEPENDENT (1) [in-di-pen'dent], *adj.* not dependent on or subject to the authority of others; not conditional upon something; not influenced by others; (of an income) such that the possessor has no need to earn his living; (of a person) possessing such an income; self-supporting; unwilling to accept help or advice; irrespective (of). INDEPENDENT (2), *n.* person who supports no particular political party etc.; Congregationalist.

INDESCRIBABLE [in-di-skrī'ba-bl], *adj.* that cannot be described.

INDESTRUCTIBLE [in-di-struk'ti-bl], *adj.* that cannot be destroyed.

INDETERMINABLE [in-di-tur'mi-na-bl], *adj.* that cannot be determined or fixed.

INDETERMINATE [in-di-tur'mi-nat], *adj.* not fixed, uncertain; indefinite, vague; (*math.*) possessing no fixed value; (*math.*) capable of an indefinite number of solutions.

INDETERMINATION [in-di-ter-mi-nā'shn], *n.* lack of determination, vacillation, irresoluteness.

INDEX (1) (*pl.* (*math.*) **indices**, (*of books*) **indexes**) [in'deks, (*pl.*) in'di-sēz], *n.* that which indicates anything, *esp.* a pointer on a dial or graduated scale; alphabetical list of topics, persons mentioned etc. in a book, with references; (*fig.*) indication, guide; (*anat.*) forefinger; (*math.*) number placed above and to the right of another number or letter to indicate the power to which it is raised or before a root sign to denote a root; number or formula expressing some ratio; **the I.**, list of books which may not be read by Roman Catholics without special permission. INDEX (2), *v.t.* to provide with an i.; enter in an i. INDEXER, *n.* person who compiles an i. [L.].

INDIAMAN [in'di-a-man], *n.* large ship engaged in trade with the East or West Indies.

INDIAN (1) [in'di-an], *adj.* pertaining to India or the East Indies; pertaining to an Indian; made in India; **I. club**, bottle-shaped club swung in the hands in certain gymnastic exercises; **I. corn**, maize; **I. file**, single file; **I. ink**, ink made of lampblack and animal glue; **I. summer**, spell of fine, warm weather occurring towards the end of autumn; (*fig.*) revival of youthful vigour and feeling in old age. INDIAN (2), *n.* a native of India or the East Indies; aboriginal of North or South America, or of the West Indies; language of the aboriginal inhabitants of America; **Red I.**, North American aboriginal.

INDIA PAPER [in-di-a-pā'per], *n.* soft, fine, pale yellow paper, used for impressions of engravings; very thin opaque paper used for printing books.

INDIARUBBER [in-di-a-ru'ber], *n.* substance obtained from the juice of certain tropical plants; small piece of this used for erasing pencil marks.

INDICATE [in'di-kāt], *v.t.* to point out, show; make known, express; imply; reveal; **to be indicated**, (*esp. med.*) to be shown by circumstances to be desirable. [L.].

INDICATION [in-di-kā'shn], *n.* act of indicating, condition of being indicated; sign, token.

INDICATIVE (1) [in-di'ka-tiv], *adj.* that indicates; **i. mood**, (*gram.*) that mood of a verb used to express a statement of fact, or to ask a question implying a fact. INDICATIVE (2), *n.* (*gram.*) the i. mood.

INDICATOR [in'di-kā-ter], *n.* that which, or one who, indicates, *esp.* a needle or finger on a dial, registering some specific information; (*chem.*) a chemical reagent. INDICATORY [in'di-kā-te-ri, in-di'ka-te-ri], *adj.* serving to indicate.

INDICT [in-dīt'], *v.t.* to charge with a crime, accuse formally. INDICTABLE [in-dī'ta-bl], *adj.* that may be indicted; exposed to indictment. [OFr.].

INDICTMENT [in-dīt'ment], *n.* act of indicting; formal written charge or accusation; document containing this.

INDIFFERENCE [in-di'fe-rens], *n.* state of being indifferent, unconcern; apathy; unimportance.

INDIFFERENT [in-di'fe-rent], *adj.* displaying no active feeling towards; not interested in; apathetic; unmoved by; unimportant; commonplace, mediocre; (*elect.*) neutral; (*archaic*) impartial. [L.].

INDIGENCE [in'di-jens], *n.* state of being indigent, extreme want. [L.].

INDIGENOUS [in-di'je-nŏŏs], *adj.* native, belonging naturally to. [LL.].

INDIGENT [in'di-jent], *adj.* lacking means of subsistance, extremely poor. [L.].

INDIGESTED [in-di-jes'tid], *adj.* not digested, not properly sorted out or assimilated mentally.

INDIGESTIBLE [in-di-jes'ti-bl], *adj.* that may not be easily digested.

INDIGESTION [in-di-jes'chn], *n.* improper digestion of food, dyspepsia; state of being undigested. [LL.].

INDIGNANT [in-dig'nant], *adj.* inflamed with anger at some real or imaginary injustice or insult.

INDIGNATION [in-dig-nā'shn], *n.* strong feeling of resentful anger, tinged with disgust. [L.].

INDIGNITY [in-dig'ni-ti], *n.* insult, affront or uncivil action intended to humiliate or discredit. [L.].

INDIGO (1) [in'di-gō], *n.* deep blue dye, primarily obtained from the indigo plant; the indigo plant. INDIGO (2), *adj.* deep blue. [Gk.].

INDIRECT [in-di-rekt'], *adj.* not direct; devious; implied rather than stated; not first-hand; **i. tax**, tax levied on commercial goods etc., in which the consumer pays for both the article and the tax; **i. speech**, (*gram.*) reported speech; **i. object**, (*gram.*) object affected in turn by an action which primarily affects a direct object.

INDISCERNIBLE [in-di-sur'ni-bl], *adj.* that may not be discerned, imperceptible.

INDISCIPLINE [in-di'si-plin], *n.* lack of discipline.

INDISCREET [in-dis-krēt'], *adj.* not discreet, imprudent, ill-advised.

INDISCRETION [in-dis-kre'shn], *n.* want of discretion; an indiscreet act. [LL.].

INDISCRIMINATE [in-dis-kri'mi-nat], *adj.* not displaying discrimination, promiscuous.

INDISPENSABLE [in-dis-pen'sa-bl], *adj.* that may not be done without, absolutely necessary; not able to be annulled or disregarded.

INDISPOSE [in-dis-pōz'], *v.t.* to disincline, make unwilling; render unfit for; make unwell. INDISPOSED, *adj.* disinclined; unwell.

INDISPOSITION [in-dis-po-zi'shn], *n.* slight illness, ill health; aversion, unwillingness.

INDISPUTABLE [in-dis'pyŏŏ-ta-bl, in-dis-pyŏŏ'-ta-bl], *adj.* undoubted, not admitting of dispute.

INDISSOLUBLE [in-di-so'lyŏŏ-bl, in-di'so-lyŏŏ-bl], *adj.* that may not be dissolved; indestructible; permanent. INDISSOLUBLY, *adv.* in an i. way. [L.].

INDISTINCT [in-dis-tingkt'], *adj.* not distinct or clear, dim, confused.

INDISTINGUISHABLE [in-dis-ting'gwi-sha-bl], *adj.* that may not be distinguished.

INDITE [in-dīt'], *v.t.* to put into words, write. [OFr.].

INDIVIDUAL (1) [in-di-vi'dyŏŏ-al], *adj.* single, separate; distinctive, peculiar; relating to, or characteristic of, one person, animal or thing. INDIVIDUAL (2), *n.* a single person, animal, thing etc.; a single member of a class; (*coll.*) a person. [MedL.].

INDIVIDUALISM [in-di-vi'dyŏŏ-a-lizm], *n.* egoism; social doctrine advocating the limitation of state control or organization of society in favour of individual freedom of action; (*philos.*) theory that only individuals have an independent existence.

INDIVIDUALIST [in-di-vi'dyŏŏ-a-list], *n.* supporter of individualism; person who displays marked individual traits; one who prefers to work on his own rather than under instructions.

INDIVIDUALITY [in-di-vi-dyŏŏ-a'li-ti], *n.* the sum of those distinctive personal qualities which render an individual different from others; fact of having a separate existence as an individual.

INDIVIDUALIZE [in-di-vi'dyŏŏ-a-līz], *v.t.* to make individual, characterize; consider individually.

INDIVIDUALLY [in-di-vi'dyŏŏ-a-li], *adv.* one by one, singly; as a separate, distinct individual.

INDIVISIBLE (1) [in-di-vi'zi-bl], *adj.* that may not be divided, infinitely small. INDIVISIBLE (2), *n.* an i. quantity or thing.

INDO- [in'dō], *pref.* Indian. [Gk.].

INDOCTRINATE [in-dok'tri-nāt], *v.t.* to fill the mind with a particular doctrine or set of principles; teach. INDOCTRINATION [in-dok-tri-nā'shn], *n.* act of indoctrinating.

INDO-EUROPEAN (1) [in-dō-yŏŏ-rō-pē'an], *n.* group of related languages including most of those spoken in Europe and part of Asia; the original language from which these have evolved; member of a race speaking one of these languages. INDO-EUROPEAN (2), *adj.* pertaining to I.

INDOLENCE [in'dō-lens], *n.* quality of being indolent.

INDOLENT [in'dō-lent], *adj.* idle, slothful.

INDOMITABLE [in-do'mi-ta-bl], *adj.* that cannot be subdued, untamable, unyielding. [LL.].

INDONESIAN [in-dō-nē'shan], *n. and adj.* (a native) of the East Indian islands. [Gk.].

INDOOR [in'daw(r)], *adj.* within the house, situated, performed, suitable for, inside a house.

INDORSABLE, INDORSE, INDORSEE, INDORSEMENT, INDORSER, see ENDORSABLE, ENDORSE, ENDORSEE, ENDORSEMENT, ENDORSER.

INDUBITABLE [in-dyōō′bi-ta-bl], *adj.* undoubted, absolutely certain. **INDUBITABLY**, *adv.* undoubtedly. [L.].

INDUCE [in-dyōōs′], *v.t.* to persuade, prevail upon; bring on, occasion; infer by reasoning from particular instances to general principles; (*elect.*) bring about by induction. [L.].

INDUCEMENT [in-dyōōs′ment], *n.* that which induces, means of persuasion, incentive.

INDUCT [in-dukt′], *v.t.* to install formally into office, *esp.* into an ecclesiastical office; place in, conduct to a position or seat. [L.].

INDUCTANCE [in-duk′tans], *n.* (*elect.*) the setting up of a magnetic field or flux by induction when an electric current is passed continuously through a conductor or circuit, the coefficient of self-induction.

INDUCTION [in-duk′shn], *n.* act of inducting into office; method of reasoning from particular instances to general principles; an example of this; statement, fact etc. brought forward to bear out a general statement; (*elect.*) production of an electrical or magnetic force in a circuit or conductor without direct contact; **i. coil,** apparatus for producing a flow of electricity by induction, or for transforming intermittent currents of one voltage into currents of another voltage; **i. pipe,** pipe through which gas or steam is admitted to the cylinder; **i. stroke,** (*mech.*) that stroke of the piston in an internal combustion engine which draws gas from the carburettor. [L.].

INDUCTIVE [in-duk′tiv], *adj.* pertaining to, using, induction; inducing; (*elect.*) produced by, producing electricity by, induction.

INDUCTOR [in-duk′ter], *n.* one who inducts a person into office; that part of an electrical apparatus which sets up induction. [L.].

INDULGE [in-dulj′], *v.t.* to satisfy wholeheartedly one's longing for; pamper, yield to every wish of; (*eccles.*) grant an indulgence to; *v.i.* (*coll.*) to drink heavily; **to i. in,** to allow oneself the pleasure of having. [L.].

INDULGENCE [in-dul′jens], *n.* act of indulging one's desires; forbearance, kindliness; a favour; (*R.C. Church*) remission of temporal punishment granted through the Church to a penitent. [L.].

INDULGENT [in-dul′jent], *adj.* showing indulgence; that indulges; inclined to overlook faults etc. too easily. **INDULGENTLY**, *adv.* in an i. way.

INDURATE [in′dyōō-rāt], *v.t. and i.* to harden; (*fig.*) make or become callous. [MedL.].

INDUSTRIAL [in-dus′tri-al], *adj.* pertaining to, characterized by, engaged in, industry; prepared specially for use in industry; **i. school,** school to which neglected or delinquent children are sent to learn a trade. **INDUSTRIALS**, *n.*(*pl.*) i. shares.

INDUSTRIALISM [in-dus′tri-a-lizm], *n.* employment in industrial pursuits; social system characterized by this.

INDUSTRIALIST [in-dus′tri-a-list], *n.* one engaged in industry; industrial worker or magnate.

INDUSTRIALIZE [in-dus′tri-a-liz], *v.t.* to make industrial.

INDUSTRIALLY [in-dus′tri-a-li], *adv.* from the point of view of industry.

INDUSTRIOUS [in-dus′tri-ōōs], *adj.* hard-working, assiduous, showing zealous application to one's work.

INDUSTRY [in′dus-tri], *n.* quality of being industrious; work devoted to the production of resources or wealth; a particular branch of trade or manufacture. [L.].

INDWELLING [in-dwe′ling], *n.* act of dwelling within, *esp.* the dwelling of the Holy Spirit within the soul.

INEBRIATE (1) [in-ē′bri-āt], *v.t.* to intoxicate, make drunk; (*fig.*) excite the mind. **INEBRIATE** (2) [in-ē′bri-at], *adj.* drunken, intoxicated. **INEBRIATE** (3), *n.* habitual drunkard. [L.].

INEBRIETY [in-ē-bri′i-ti], *n.* habitual drunkenness; intoxication.

INEDIBLE [in-e′di-bl], *adj.* not fit for eating.

INEDUCABLE [in-e′dyōō-ka-bl], *adj.* incapable of being educated.

INEFFABLE [in-e′fa-bl], *adj.* unspeakable, indescribable. **INEFFABILITY** [in-e-fa-bi′li-ti], *n.* quality of being i.

INEFFECTIVE [in-i-fek′tiv], *adj.* useless, having no effect, not producing the right effect; incompetent.

INEFFECTUAL [in-i-fek′tyōō-al], *adj.* ineffective, unsuccessful, unavailing.

INEFFICIENCY [in-i-fi′shn-si], *n.* quality of being inefficient.

INEFFICIENT [in-i-fi′shnt], *adj.* not efficient, unable

to perform something satisfactorily; not in sound working order.

INELASTIC [in-i-las′tik], *adj.* not elastic; (*fig.*) unyielding, unadaptable. **INELASTICITY** [in-i-las-ti′si-ti], *n.* quality of being i.

INELEGANCE [in-e′li-gans], *n.* want of elegance, clumsiness.

INELEGANT [in-e′li-gant], *adj.* wanting in elegance; uncouth, awkward.

INELIGIBLE [in-e′li-gi-bl], *adj.* not eligible; unworthy.

INELUCTABLE [in-i-luk′ta-bl], *adj.* from which one may not escape by struggling, unavoidable. [L.].

INEPT [in-ept′], *adj.* stupid, fatuous; not apt. [L.].

INEPTITUDE [in-ep′ti-tyōōd], *n.* condition of being inept; inept act or speech. [L.].

INEQUALITY [in-ē-kwo′li-ti], *adj.* lack of equality, disparity; unevenness; tendency to vary; lack of uniformity.

INEQUITABLE [in-e′kwi-ta-bl], *adj.* not equitable, unfair.

INEQUITY [in-e′kwi-ti], *n.* unfairness.

INERADICABLE [in-i-ra′di-ka-bl], *adj.* that may not be eradicated.

INERT [in-urt′], *adj.* unable to move itself or resist motion; sluggish, lifeless; (*sci.*) displaying no activity. **INERTLY**, *adv.* in an i. way. [L.].

INERTIA [in-ur′shah], *n.* (*phys.*) that property of matter by which it tends to remain at rest or to continue in uniform motion in a straight line; sluggishness, inactivity. [L.].

INESCAPABLE [in-es-kā′pa-bl], *adj.* from which one may not escape.

INESSENTIAL (1) [in-i-sen′shal], *adj.* not essential. **INESSENTIAL** (2), *n.* that which is i.

INESTIMABLE [in-es′ti-ma-bl], *adj.* that may not be estimated; invaluable. **INESTIMABLY**, *adv.* in an i. way.

INEVITABLE [in-e′vi-ta-bl], *adj.* unavoidable, bound to come or follow. [L.].

INEXACT [in-ig-zakt′], *adj.* not exact or precise.

INEXACTITUDE [in-ig-zak′ti-tyōōd], *n.* quality of being inexact; something which is inexact.

INEXCUSABLE [in-eks-kyōō′za-bl], *adj.* not to be excused, unpardonable.

INEXHAUSTIBLE [in-ig-zaws′ti-bl], *adj.* that cannot be exhausted.

INEXORABLE [in-ek′se-ra-bl], *adj.* relentless, not to be shaken from one's purpose, or its course; unmoved by entreaty. [L.].

INEXPEDIENCY [in-eks-pē′di-en-si], *n.* state of being inexpedient.

INEXPEDIENT [in-eks-pē′di-ent], *adj.* not expedient, impolitic.

INEXPENSIVE [in-eks-pen′siv], *adj.* not expensive; not extravagant.

INEXPERIENCE [in-eks-pēer′i-ens], *n.* lack of experience, or of knowledge by experience.

INEXPERT [in-eks′pert], *adj.* not expert, unskilled.

INEXPIABLE [in-eks′pi-a-bl], *adj.* that may not be expiated or atoned for; implacable.

INEXPLICABLE [in-eks′pli-ka-bl], *adj.* that cannot be explained, unaccountable. [L.].

INEXPRESSIBLE [in-eks-pre′si-bl], *adj.* that may not be expressed, indescribable.

INEXPRESSIVE [in-eks-pre′siv], *adj.* not expressing anything.

INEXTINGUISHABLE [in-eks-ting′gwi-sha-bl], *adj.* that cannot be extinguished.

INEXTRICABLE [in-eks′tri-ka-bl], *adj.* from which one may not be extricated; unable to be disentangled or straightened out.

INFALLIBILITY [in-fa-li-bi′li-ti], *n.* quality of being infallible, *esp.* in regard to faith and morals, as claimed by Roman Catholics for their Church as a whole, and for the Pope when speaking officially upon matters of doctrine.

INFALLIBLE [in-fa′li-bl], *adj.* incapable of error, always right; that cannot go wrong, unfailing. [L.].

INFAMOUS [in′fa-mōōs], *adj.* notoriously wicked, having a very bad reputation; shameful, vile. [MedL.].

INFAMY [in′fa-mi], *n.* quality of being infamous; public disgrace; infamous behaviour. [L.].

INFANCY [in′fan-si], *n.* state or period of being an infant; legal minority; the rudimentary stages of anything. [L.].

INFANT (1) [in′fant], *n.* young child; (*leg.*) minor, person under the age of 21 years. **INFANT** (2), *adj.* pertaining to infancy or to infants. [L.].

INFANTA, INFANTE [in-fahn′tah, ′tā], *n.*

(formerly in Spain and Portugal) daughter, son, of the king and queen, other than the heir to the throne. [Span.].

INFANTICIDE [in-fan'ti-sīd], *n.* murder of an infant, *esp.* of a newly-born child; murderer of an infant. [Ll.].

INFANTILE [in'fan-tīl], *adj.* belonging to, affecting, infants; rudimentary; childish; **i. paralysis,** an infectious disease, poliomyelitis, which often causes paralysis.

INFANTRY [in'fan-tri], *n.* foot soldiers. [It.].

INFATUATE [in-fa'tyōo-āt], *v.t.* to deprive of sound judgment; cause to fall madly in love with.

INFATUATION [in-fa-tyōo-ā'shn], *n.* act of infatuating; state of being infatuated; fierce unreasoning passion.

INFECT [in-fekt'], *v.t.* to taint or pollute with disease germs; communicate a disease to; *(fig.)* imbue with, by example. [L.].

INFECTION [in-fek'shn], *n.* act of infecting; state or process of being infected with disease; that which infects; *(fig.)* mental or moral influence readily communicated; contamination. [L.].

INFECTIOUS [in-fek'shōos], *adj.* that infects; readily transmitted through the air etc. without actual contact; caught by proximity to a source of infection; *(fig.)* catching, easily communicated. [L.].

INFECTIVE [in-fek'tiv], *adj.* infectious.

INFELICITOUS [in-fe-li'si-tōos], *adj.* unhappy; inappropriate, unfortunate.

INFELICITY [in-fe-li'si-ti], *n.* quality of being infelicitous; an infelicitous act or remark. [L.].

INFER (*pres.pt.* **inferring,** *pret. and p.pt.* **inferred**) [in-fur'], *v.t.* to deduce, conclude; imply. [L.].

INFERENCE [in'fe-rens], *n.* act of inferring; that which is inferred; implication. [MedL.].

INFERENTIAL [in-fe-ren'shal], *adj.* ascertained by inference.

INFERIOR (1) [in-fēer'i-er], *adj.* lower in position, place or quality; below something else; poor, mediocre; low in rank, status or value, subordinate. INFERIOR (2), *n.* person who is i. [L.].

INFERIORITY [in-fēer-i-o'ri-ti], *n.* state of being inferior; **i. complex,** *(psych.)* morbid mental condition characterized by feeling of i. and a lack of self-confidence; *(pop.)* sense of i.

INFERNAL [in-fur'nal], *adj.* pertaining to hell or the lower regions; fiendish, diabolical; *(coll.)* confounded, deuced; **i. machine,** explosive bomb or machine. INFERNALLY, *adv. (coll.)* in an i. manner, to an i. degree.

INFERNO [in-fur'nō], *n.* hell; *(fig.)* anything resembling hell. [It.].

INFERTILE [in-fur'tīl], *adj.* not fertile, arid.

INFEST [in-fest'], *v.t.* to trouble greatly, overrun, swarm on in troublesome manner. [L.].

INFESTATION [in-fes-tā'shn], *n.* act of infesting; state of being infested. [Ll.].

INFIDEL (1) [in'fi-del], *n.* one who does not believe in religion, heathen; *(hist.)* one who does not believe in Christianity; (among Moslems or Jews) one who believes in some other religion; unbeliever. INFIDEL (2), *adj.* unbelieving, heathen; practising a false religion.

INFIDELITY [in-fi-de'li-ti], *n.* want of faith or belief, *esp.* in Christianity; unfaithfulness, *esp.* of a husband or wife. [L.].

INFIELD [in'fēld], *n.* farm land immediately surrounding the farm buildings; land kept in crop; *(cricket)* that part of the field near the wicket; one who fields near the wicket; *(baseball)* space enclosed by the base-lines.

INFILTRATE [in'fil-trāt], *v.t. and i.* to cause to filter through; filter through, permeate; *(milit.)* penetrate hostile positions gradually by stealth; *(pol.)* introduce one's supporters secretly into a rival party for disruptive ends.

INFILTRATION [in-fil-trā'shn], *n.* act of infiltrating; state of being infiltrated; an infiltrated substance; gradual penetration.

INFINITE (1) [in'fi-nit], *adj.* boundless, unlimited; immeasurable; innumerable; *(gram.)* not limited by number and person; *(math.)* having no limit. INFINITE (2), *n.* that which is i.; the supreme deity; *(math.)* an i. quantity. INFINITELY, *adv.* to an i. extent. [L.].

INFINITESIMAL [in-fi-ni-te'si-mal], *adj.* too small to be measured or calculated; infinitely small.

INFINITIVE (1) [in-fi'ni-tiv], *adj. (gram.)* pertaining to that form of the verb expressing its mere action without limitation of person, number, tense or voice.

INFINITIVE (2), *n. (gram.)* the i. form of the verb. [L.].

INFINITUDE [in-fi'ni-tyōod], *n.* quality of being infinite; infinite number, quantity or size.

INFINITY [in-fi'ni-ti], *n.* quality of being infinite; that which is infinite; *(math.)* an infinite quantity; infinite space, time or distance. [L.].

INFIRM [in-furm'], *adj.* not strong physically, weak, decrepit, *esp.* through age; irresolute. [L.].

INFIRMARY [in-fur'ma-ri], *n.* hospital; sick room of a public institution, school etc. [MedL.].

INFIRMITY [in-fur'mi-ti], *n.* state of being infirm; a particular form of weakness; moral defect. [L.].

INFLAME [in-flām'], *v.t. and i.* to suffuse with a fiery glow; make or become hot, red, swollen and tender; *(fig.)* excite to strong anger, passion or indignation. [L.].

INFLAMMABLE [in-fla'ma-bl], *adj.* readily catching fire, easily combustible; *(fig.)* highly excitable, easily roused. [Fr.].

INFLAMMATION [in-fla-mā'shn], *n.* act of inflaming; state of being inflamed; *(path.)* redness and swelling, with pain and an increase of heat in the affected part. [L.].

INFLAMMATORY [in-fla'ma-te-ri], *adj.* tending to inflame or cause inflammation; accompanied by inflammation.

INFLATE [in-flāt'], *v.t.* to cause to swell, distend with air or gas; *(fig.)* make haughty; *(comm.)* raise artificially beyond the normal or natural level; increase the amount of money, *esp.* paper money, in circulation. INFLATED, *adj.* distended with air or gas; *(fig.)* turgid, bombastic; swollen with pride; *(comm.)* increased beyond the natural limits. [L.].

INFLATION [in-flā'shn], *n.* act of inflating; state of being inflated. INFLATIONARY, *adj. (econ.)* tending towards, pertaining to, i. INFLATIONISM, *n. (econ.)* policy of inflating currency. [L.].

INFLECT [in-flekt'], *v.t.* to bend inwards, curve; *(gram.)* vary the endings of a word in order to express differences of number, case, tense etc.; *(mus.)* modulate (the voice). INFLECTED, *adj.* bent inwards; *(gram.)* exhibiting inflexion.

INFLECTION, INFLECTIONAL, see INFLEXION, INFLEXIONAL.

INFLECTIVE [in-flek'tiv], *adj.* that inflects; *(gram.)* modified by inflection.

INFLEXIBILITY [in-flek-si-bi'li-ti], *n.* quality of being inflexible.

INFLEXIBLE [in-flek'si-bl], *adj.* that may not be bent, rigid; *(fig.)* not to be turned aside, relentless, unyielding; immovably fixed. INFLEXIBLY, *adv.* in an i. way. [L.].

INFLEXION, INFLECTION [in-flek'shn], *n.* act of inflecting; state of being inflected; *(gram.)* variation in the endings of words which inflect; an inflected form; termination used to inflect; modulation. INFLEXIONAL, INFLECTIONAL, *adj.* pertaining to i. [L.].

INFLICT [in-flikt'], *v.t.* to deal, cause to suffer (a blow, wound etc.); impose (something unpleasant). [L.].

INFLICTION [in-flik'shn], *n.* act of inflicting; that which is inflicted. [Ll.].

INFLORESCENCE [in-flaw-re'sens], *n. (bot.)* the method of flowering of a plant; arrangement of the flowers on the stalks; the whole mass of flowers blossoming on a plant; process of blossoming. [MdL.].

INFLUENCE (1) [in'flōo-ens], *n.* any power, force or agency producing an effect in such a way that its action is not apparent; effect so produced; control or authority indirectly manifested; power of affecting action, thought etc.; thing or person exercising such power; *(astrol.)* effect of the stars upon human destiny. INFLUENCE (2), *v.t.* to exert i. upon, affect, or persuade by one's i. [Fr.].

INFLUENTIAL [in-flōo-en'shal], *adj.* that influences; possessing and able to exert strong influence, powerful. INFLUENTIALLY, *adv.* in an i. way.

INFLUENZA [in-flōo-en'zah], *n.* infectious and contagious epidemic disease, characterized by catarrh accompanied by fever and exhaustion. [It.].

INFLUX [in'fluks], *n.* act of flowing in, *esp.* of a tributary or stream into a river; place where this occurs; constant flow of anything, *esp.* in large quantities, into a place. [Ll.].

INFORM [in-fawm'], *v.t.* to inspire; pervade; communicate some knowledge or fact to, acquaint with; **to i. against,** to bring a charge against, communicate facts resulting in a charge being made against. [L.].

INFORMAL [in-faw'mal], *adj.* not in the usual,

customary or recognized form; without formality; familiar.

INFORMALITY [in-faw-ma′li-ti], *n.* quality of being informal; that which is informal.

INFORMANT [in-faw′mant], *n.* one who gives information. [L.].

INFORMATION [in-faw-mā′shn], *n.* act of informing; something told, knowledge of a fact or facts communicated or learnt; news; knowledge; (*leg.*) charge or accusation made to a magistrate or a court instead of a formal indictment. [L.].

INFORMATIVE [in-faw′ma-tiv], *adj.* that informs, instructive; (*leg.*) pertaining to, of the nature of, an information. INFORMATIVELY, *adv.* so as to provide information; for information and not for publication.

INFORMATORY [in-faw′ma-te-ri], *adj.* containing information.

INFORMED [in-fawmd′], *adj.* possessing information; enlightened; educated.

INFRA (1) [in′frah], *adj.* below; further down or on; **i. dig.,** beneath one's dignity. [L.].

INFRA- (2), below. [L.].

INFRACTION [in-frak′shn], *n.* violation, infringement; breach. [L.].

INFRA-RED [in-frah-red′], *adj.* (*phys.*) relating to the invisible rays beyond the red rays of the spectrum; **i. photography,** photography by the use of i. rays.

INFREQUENCY [in-frē′kwen-si], *n.* state of being infrequent, rarity. [L.].

INFREQUENT [in-frē′kwent], *adj.* not frequent, rare, sparse. INFREQUENTLY, *adv.* rarely.

INFRINGE [in-frinj′], *v.t.* to break, violate, transgress. [L.].

INFURIATE [in-fyōō′ri-āt], *v.t.* to make furious, enrage, madden. [MedL.].

INFUSE [in-fyōōz′], *v.t.* to pour into; steep or soak in liquid to extract its properties; (*fig.*) cause to enter, inspire with. [L.].

INFUSION [in-fyōō′zhn], *n.* act of infusing; that which is infused; liquid in which vegetable substances have been infused; blend. [L.].

INFUSORIA [in-fyōō-zaw′ri-ah], *n.* (*pl.*) class of microscopic motile protozoa present in infusions of animal or vegetable matter. [MdL.].

INGENIOUS [in-jē′ni-ŏŏs], *adj.* clever, artful; good at inventing or contriving things; artfully contrived. [L.].

INGÉNUE, ingénue [a(ng)-zhā-nyōō′], *n.* simple, unsophisticated girl; actress playing such a part. [Fr.].

INGENUITY [in-ji-nyōō′i-ti], *n.* quality of being ingenious. [L.].

INGENUOUS [in-je′nyōō-ŏŏs], *n.* frank, candid; simple, innocent, guileless. [L.].

INGLE [ing′gl], *n.* fire burning on a hearth; fireplace. INGLE-NOOK, chimney corner. [Gael.].

INGLORIOUS [in-glaw′ri-ŏŏs], *adj.* not bringing honour, shameful, ignominious; not renowned. [L.].

INGOT [in′got], *n.* block of gold, silver or other metal, cast in a mould. [IN (6) and OE.].

INGRAIN [in-grān′], *adj.* dyed in the grain; dyed in the yarn with fast colours before manufacture; (*fig.*) innate, inborn. INGRAINED, *adj.* firmly fixed in, impregnating every part; deeply rooted, inveterate.

INGRATE (1) [in′grāt], *adj.* (*archaic*) ungrateful. INGRATE (2), *n.* ungrateful person. [L.].

INGRATIATE [in-grā′shi-āt], *v.reflex.* to get into the good graces of another person. INGRATIATING, *adj.* seeking to curry favour, winning. [It.].

INGRATITUDE [in-gra′ti-tyōōd], *n.* want of gratitude.

INGREDIENT [in-grē′di-ent], *n.* that which goes to make up a compound, component part. [L.].

INGRESS [in′gres], *n.* act of going in; means of entrance; (*leg.*) power or right of entrance. [L.].

INGUINAL [in′gwi-nal], *adj.* relating to the groin. [L.].

INGURGITATE [in-gur′ji-tāt], *v.t. and i.* to swallow up greedily; (*fig.*) engulf; gorge. [L.].

INHABIT [in-ha′bit], *v.t.* to live or dwell in, occupy as a residence; (*fig.*) be present in. [L.].

INHABITANT [in-ha′bi-tant], *n.* one who lives in a certain place etc., a resident. [L.].

INHALANT (1) [in-hā′lant], *adj.* inhaling, breathing in. INHALANT (2), *n.* medicine to be taken by inhalation. [L.].

INHALATION [in-ha-lā′shn], *n.* act of inhaling; that which is inhaled.

INHALE [in-hāl′], *v.t. and i.* to breathe in, draw into

the lungs; do this habitually with tobacco smoke. [L.].

INHERE [in-hēer′], *v.i.* to exist in as a natural and permanent feature, form an intrinsic part of; be vested in; be naturally implied in. [L.].

INHERENCE [in-hēer′ens], *n.* state of being inherent.

INHERENT [in-hēer′ent], *adj.* natural to, existing in as an essential, inseparable element; vested in.

INHERIT [in-he′rit], *v.t.* to receive from an ancestor or former possessor, as an heir; acquire from a predecessor as a gift; possess as an hereditary characteristic; obtain; *v.i.* to become an heir, take possession as an heir. [OFr.].

INHERITABLE [in-he′ri-ta-bl], *adj.* that may be inherited; able or entitled to inherit. [OFr.].

INHERITANCE [in-he′ri-tans], *n.* act of inheriting; that which is inherited or possessed as a birthright; (*biol.*) transmission of hereditary characteristics. [OFr.].

INHERITOR [in-he′ri-ter], *n.* one who inherits as an heir.

INHIBIT [in-hi′bit], *v.t.* to prohibit, prevent, *esp.* (*eccles. leg.*) forbid a priest to carry out ecclesiastical duties; hinder, delay; (*psych.*) keep in check by inhibition. [L.].

INHIBITION [in-hi-bi′shn], *n.* act of inhibiting, formal prohibition; (*psych.*) unconscious force forbidding what would otherwise be an impulse or urge; (*eccles. leg.*) court order forbidding further proceedings in an inferior court; official order inhibiting a clergyman; (*physiol.*) deliberate or involuntary temporary restraining of the functions of a structure or organism. [OFr.].

INHOSPITABLE [in-hos′pi-ta-bl], *adj.* affording no hospitality; bleak, cheerless. [MedL.].

INHUMAN [in-hyōō′man], *adj.* void of human or humane feelings or qualities, brutal, savage; pertaining to that which is not human. [L.].

INHUMANITY [in-hyōō-ma′ni-ti], *n.* quality of being inhuman; an inhuman act. [L.].

INHUMATION [in-hyōō-mā′shn], *n.* burial in the ground, interment.

INHUME [in-hyōōm′], *v.t.* to bury, inter. [L.].

INIMICAL [i-ni′mi-kal], *adj.* hostile; unfavourable, injurious. [LL.].

INIMITABLE [i-ni′mi-ta-bl], *adj.* that cannot be imitated, unique, without rival. [L.].

INIQUITOUS [i-ni′kwi-tŏŏs], *adv.* wicked, unjust.

INIQUITY [i-ni′kwi-ti], *n.* quality of being iniquitous, injustice, sin; iniquitous conduct. [L.].

INITIAL (1) [i-ni′shal], *adj.* pertaining to, constituting, or occurring at, the beginning; first, earliest. INITIAL (2), an an i. letter; (*pl.*) the first letter of the Christian name(s) and surname of a person; (*mus.*) any of the notes on which the melody of a plainsong may begin. INITIAL (3) (*pres.pt.* INITIALLING, *pret. and p.pt.* INITIALLED), *v.t.* to write one's initials on. INITIALLY, *adv.* at the beginning, in the first place.

INITIATE (1) [i-ni′shi-āt], *v.t.* to originate, set on foot; admit into some society etc., *esp.* with appropriate rites and ceremonies; instruct in the first principles of anything. INITIATE (2) [i-ni′shi-at], *adj.* having been initiated. INITIATE (3) [i-ni′shi-at], *n.* one who has been initiated.

INITIATION [i-ni-shi-ā′shn], *n.* act or ceremony of initiating; state of being initiated. [L.].

INITIATIVE (1) [i-ni′shi-a-tiv], *n.* initial move, first step; right of making the first move; the lead; ability to transcend routine and initiate things; enterprise. INITIATIVE (2), *adj.* serving to initiate.

INITIATORY [i-ni′shi-a-te-ri], *adj.* that initiates, introductory.

INJECT [in-jekt′], *v.t.* to cause to enter by pressure, force in (fluid) as by a syringe etc.; fill (a bodily cavity or tissue) by this means. [L.].

INJECTION [in-jek′shn], *n.* act of injecting, *esp.* a liquid by means of a syringe etc.; a medicinal preparation to be injected. [L.].

INJECTOR [in-jek′ter], *n.* apparatus for injecting; device for forcing water into the boiler of a steam-engine.

INJUDICIOUS [in-jŏŏ-di′shŏŏs], *adj.* unwise, not displaying judgment, ill-advised.

INJUNCTION [in-jungk′shn], *n.* act of enjoining; that which is enjoined; order, instruction; (*leg.*) writ restraining a person from committing a wrong against, or infringing the rights of, another person. [LL.].

INJURE [in′jyŏŏr], *v.t.* to do harm to, wrong; hurt, do physical injury to. INJURED, *adj.* wronged.

offended; expressing a sense of injustice or hurt; damaged. [INJURY].

INJURIOUS [in-jŏō'ri-ŏŏs], *adj.* unjust, causing injury; tending or intended to injure; (of language) slanderous; detrimental. [L.].

INJURY [in'jўŏō-ri], *n.* wrong done to a man's person, rights, reputation or goods; physical hurt or damage; moral or mental hurt. [L.].

INJUSTICE [in-jus'tis], *n.* a wrong, an unjust act; unfairness. [L.].

INK (1) [ingk], *n.* coloured fluid used in writing; black or coloured paste used for printing; black liquid emitted by a squid and other related fishes when attacked. INK (2), *v.t.* to mark or trace over with i.; cover (types etc.) with i. [Gk.].

INKLING [ingk'ling], *n.* hint, intimation, vague notion or suspicion. [Uncert.].

INLAID [in-lād'], *adj.* laid into the surface of a thing, *esp.* so as to form a decorative pattern.

INLAND (1) [in'land], *n.* the interior part of a country. INLAND (2), *adj.* remote from the sea; situated in the interior of a country; carried on within a country; **i. revenue,** revenue derived from taxes and duties imposed inside the country. IN-LAND (3), *adv.* in or towards the interior of a country.

INLAY (1) [*pret. and p.pt.* **inlaid**] [in-lā'], *v.t.* to insert pieces of hard material into differently coloured, or different kinds of, material so as to form an ornamental pattern; lay or embed into the surface of something else so as to form one continuous level upper surface. INLAY (2) [in'lā], *n.* inlaid work.

INLET [in'let], *n.* small opening in the coastline or in the bank of a river or lake; means of entrance, opening allowing passage inwards; anything inserted or let in.

INLY [in'li], *adv.* deeply, inwardly, sincerely. [OE.].

INMATE [in'māt], *n.* occupant of a house, asylum or institution.

INMOST [in'mōst], *adj.* deepest or farthest within; most private or secret.

INN [in], *n.* house providing bedroom accommodation and catering for travellers, hotel; **Inns of Court,** four incorporated legal societies in London, to join which provides the exclusive means of qualifying for the Bar; the buildings belonging to these societies. [OE.].

INNATE [i-nāt'], *adj.* inborn, instinctive. [L.].

INNER (1) [i'ner], *adj.* farther in, inside, interior; nearer the centre. INNER (2), *n.* the ring, on a target, immediately surrounding the bull's-eye; shot striking this area. [OE.].

INNINGS [i'ningz], *n.* the turn of a particular side to bat in cricket; turn of one player to bat.

INNOCENCE [i'nō-sens], *n.* quality of being innocent. [L.].

INNOCENT (1) [i'nō-sent], *adj.* innocuous, harmless, free from guilt or sin; lawful; guileless; simple and inexperienced. INNOCENT (2), *n.* ingenuous person; idiot. [L.].

INNOCUOUS [i-no'kyŏō-ŏŏs], *adj.* harmless in effect; inoffensive. [L.].

INNOVATE [i'nō-vāt], *v.i.* to introduce new things or methods into established practice. INNOVATOR, *n.* introducer of changes. [L.].

INNOVATION [i-nō-vā'shn], *n.* act or process of innovating; that which is newly introduced, a novelty. [L.].

INNUENDO [i-nyŏō-en'dō], *n.* suggestive allusion; indirect reference of a malicious character; insinuation. [L.].

INNUMERABLE [i-nyŏō'me-ra-bl], *adj.* not able to be counted, countless.

INOCULATE [i-no'kyŏō-lāt], *v.t.* (*med.*) to introduce the weakened germ or virus of a specific disease into a person's system so as to generate its antitoxins or antibodies. INOCULATOR, *n.* person who inoculates. [L.].

INOCULATION [i-no-kyŏō-lā'shn], *n.* act of inoculating.

INOFFENSIVE [in-o-fen'siv], *adj.* giving no offence, harmless, innocent; having no positive characteristics.

INOPERABLE [in-o'pe-ra-bl], *adj.* (*med.*) not able to be operated upon; that does not operate. [IN (5) and Fr.].

INOPERATIVE [in-o'pe-ra-tiv], *adj.* having no force or effect.

INOPPORTUNE [in-o'per-tyŏōn], *adj.* not opportune, untimely.

INORDINATE [in-aw'di-nat], *adj.* excessive, extravagant. INORDINATELY, *adv.* in an i. way.

INORGANIC [in-aw-ga'nik], *adj.* not organic, not possessing parts in a functioning or developing relationship; (*chem.*) consisting of inanimate matter; dealing with all substances other than the carbon compounds.

INOSCULATE [in-os'kyŏō-lāt], *v.t.* to join; *v.i.* to unite parts of a body or organism by their ends; intertwine, amalgamate. INOSCULATION, *n.* state of being inosculated. [IN (6) and L.].

IN-PATIENT [in'pā-shent], *n.* patient living in hospital during treatment.

INPUT [in'pŏŏt], *n.* (*elect.*) current taken in by or put into an electrical apparatus.

INQUEST [in'kwest], *n.* judicial inquiry held with a jury present for the purpose of establishing facts; **coroner's i.,** such an inquiry into the circumstances of a death, of a fire in the City of London, or to find the owner of treasure trove. [MedL.].

INQUIETUDE [in-kwī'i-tyŏōd], *n.* disturbed state of body or mind, restlessness, uneasiness. [L.].

INQUIRE, ENQUIRE [in-kwier'], *v.t. and i.* to ask; ask questions about; **to i. after,** to ask about the state of someone's health; **to i. into,** to investigate. [L.].

INQUIRING [in-kwier'ing], *adj.* given to inquiry, curious.

INQUIRY, ENQUIRY [in-kwier'i], *n.* act of inquiring; a single question; official investigation of facts.

INQUISITION [in-kwi-zi'shn], *n.* official inquiry, investigation; (*R.C.*) medieval ecclesiastical tribunal established to discover and punish heretics; any aggressive or rigorous examination. INQUISITIONAL, *adj.* relating to an examination; pertaining to or resembling the I. [L.].

INQUISITIVE [in-kwi'zi-tiv], *adj.* having a desire to increase one's knowledge, curious to know; curious about other people's business, prying. [LL.].

INQUISITOR [in-kwi'zi-ter], *n.* person who inquires, *esp.* officially; member of the Inquisition. [L.].

INQUISITORIAL [in-kwi-zi-taw'ri-al], *adj.* relating to inquiry, or to the Inquisition; searching; prying.

INRIGGED [in'rigd], *adj.* (*naut.*) having rowlocks on the gunwale.

INROAD [in'rōd], *n.* sudden, aggressive advance into an enemy's country; invasion; encroachment.

INSALIVATE [in-sa'li-vāt], *v.t.* to mingle food with saliva in mastication.

INSALUBRIOUS [in-sa-lŏō'bri-ŏŏs], *adj.* unhealthy, unwholesome.

INSANE [in-sān'], *adj.* mad, not of a sound mind. INSANELY, *adv.* in an i. way. [L.].

INSANITARY [in-sa'ni-ta-ri], *adj.* not sanitary, unhealthy, likely to carry infection.

INSANITY [in-sa'ni-ti], *n.* condition of being insane.

INSATIABLE [in-sā'sha-bl], *adj.* impossible to be satisfied or appeased. [L.].

INSATIATE [in-sā'shi-at], *adj.* never satisfied, insatiable. [L.].

INSCRIBE [in-skrīb'], *v.t.* to write on, engrave letters, symbols or figures upon; record in a register; (*geom.*) draw a figure within another. [L.].

INSCRIPTION [in-skrip'shn], *n.* act of inscribing; that which is inscribed; lettering on a coin, scroll etc.; dedication in the front of a book. [L.].

INSCRUTABLE [in-skrŏō'ta-bl], *adj.* impossible to understand or unravel; enigmatic; impenetrable.

INSECT [in'sekt], *n.* (*entom.*) one of the small arthropod animals, often winged, having a body in three sections, set on six legs arranged in three pairs. [L.].

INSECTICIDE [in-sek'ti-sīd], *n.* a preparation for killing insects. [L.].

INSECTIVOROUS [in-sek-ti've-rŏŏs], *adj.* feeding on insects. [L.].

INSECTOLOGY [in-sek-to'lo-ji], *n.* study of insects and their habits. [INSECT and Gk.].

INSECURE [in-si-kyŏŏr'], *adj.* open to peril; unsafe; not effectively protected; having inadequate support; unreliable. INSECURELY, *adv.* in an i. way.

INSECURITY [in-si-kyŏŏ'ri-ti], *n.* condition of being insecure.

INSEMINATE [in-se'mi-nāt], *v.t.* to sow, plant, impregnate. [L.].

INSENSATE [in-sen'sāt], *adj.* wanting sensibility; stupid, irrational, senseless. [LL.].

INSENSIBLE [in-sen'si-bl], *adj.* unable to partake of sensory experience; unconscious; devoid of sympathetic feeling; imperceptible. INSENSIBLY, *adv.* imperceptibly; gradually.

INSENSITIVE [in-sen'si-tiv], *adj.* not sensitive,

incapable of experiencing particular sensations or emotions.

INSENTIENT [in-sen'shi-ent], *adj.* not having perception, inanimate.

INSEPARABLE [in-se'pa-ra-bl], *adj.* not capable of being separated, joined firmly together; always accompanying one another; (*gram.*) not existing as an independent word. [LL.].

INSERT (1) [in-surt'], *v.t.* to set or place in or among, introduce into something else. INSERT (2) [in'sert], *n.* something inserted. [L.].

INSERTION [in-sur'shn], *n.* act of inserting; state of being inserted; something, *esp.* a word or printed matter, inserted; piece of lace etc. inserted in some other material. [L.].

INSET [in'set], *n.* an insertion; something set in, *esp.* a leaf or batch of leaves inserted in a book; small picture, map etc. set within a larger.

INSHORE (1) [in'shaw(r)], *adv.* near the shore. INSHORE (2), *adj.* situated near the shore.

INSIDE (1) [in-sid'], *n.* inner part, edge etc., interior; (*slang*) stomach. INSIDE (2), *adj.* placed on the inner side, within, having a position on the inside; secret, privileged. INSIDE (3), *prep.* on the inner side, within.

INSIDER [in-si'der], *n.* person having inside knowledge, or having access to a particular class or group.

INSIDIOUS [in-si'di-oos], *adj.* working or progressing imperceptibly; deceitful, treacherous. [L.].

INSIGHT [in'sit], *n.* mental faculty of sharp discernment, clear perception; intuitive grasp of a situation.

INSIGNIA [in-sig'ni-ah], *n.(pl.)* symbols, tokens, badges of office or honour; distinguishing marks. [L.].

INSIGNIFICANCE [in-sig-ni'fi-kans], *n.* quality of being insignificant.

INSIGNIFICANT [in-sig-ni'fi-kant], *adj.* having no sense or meaning; unimpressive; unimportant, trivial, contemptible. INSIGNIFICANTLY, *adv.* in an i. way.

INSINCERE [in-sin-seer'], *adj.* not expressing real feeling or thought, not sincere, hypocritical.

INSINCERITY [in-sin-se'ri-ti], *n.* quality of being insincere.

INSINUATE [in-si'nyoo-āt], *v.t. and i.* to penetrate, worm oneself in (to favour etc.) gradually and imperceptibly; suggest by allusion or indirect reference, hint. INSINUATING, *adj.* that insinuates, characterized by insinuation. [L.].

INSINUATION [in-si-nyoo-ā'shn], *n.* act of insinuating; suggestion, hint. [L.].

INSIPID [in-si'pid], *adj.* without a well-defined flavour, tasteless; (*fig.*) dull, spiritless. INSIPIDLY, *adv.* in an i. way. [LL.].

INSIPIDITY [in-si-pi'di-ti], *n.* quality of being insipid.

INSIST [in-sist'], *v.t. and i.* to persist in; urge as a command, demand with urgency; emphasize in argument; assert. [L.].

INSISTENCE [in-sis'tens], *n.* act of insisting; quality of being insistent.

INSISTENT [in-sis'tent], *adj.* emphatic, imperative; commanding. INSISTENTLY, *adv.* in an i. way.

INSOBRIETY [in-sō-bri'i-ti], *n.* lack of sobriety.

INSOLENCE [in'so-lens], *n.* quality of being insolent; insulting behaviour, impertinence. [L.].

INSOLENT [in'so-lent], *adj.* offensively contemptuous, insulting, arrogantly rude.

INSOLUBLE [in-so'lyoo-bl], *adj.* not able to be dissolved; that cannot be solved. INSOLUBILITY [in-so-lyoo-bi'li-ti], *n.* condition of being i. INSOLUBLY, *adv.* in an i. way. [L.].

INSOLVENCY [in-sol'ven-si], *n.* state of being insolvent, bankruptcy.

INSOLVENT (1) [in-sol'vent], *adj.* not able to pay debts, bankrupt; relating to bankruptcy. INSOLVENT (2), *n.* person who is i.

INSOMNIA [in-som'ni-ah], *n.* sleeplessness.

INSOMUCH [in-sō-much'], *adv.* in as far as, to such a degree.

INSOUCIANCE [in-soo'si-ans], *n.* indifference expressed freely and easily, unconcern. [Fr.].

INSOUCIANT [in-soo'si-ant], *adj.* careless, unconcerned. [Fr.].

INSPAN (*pres.pt.* **inspanning**, *pret. and p.pt.* **inspanned**) [in-span'], *v.t.* to yoke (oxen etc.). [Du.].

INSPECT [in-spekt'], *v.t.* to look into; examine carefully, *esp.* as an official; superintend. [L.].

INSPECTION [in-spek'shn], *n.* act of inspecting; scrutiny, official examination. [L.].

INSPECTOR [in-spek'ter], *n.* one who inspects, *esp.*

an official whose duty it is to inspect and send in reports; police officer ranking immediately above a sergeant.

INSPECTORATE [in-spek'te-rat], *n.* body of official inspectors; inspectorship.

INSPECTORIAL [in-spek-taw'ri-al], *adj.* relating to an inspector.

INSPECTORSHIP [in-spek'ter-ship], *n.* office of inspector; period of office of an inspector.

INSPIRATION [in-spi-rā'shn], *n.* act of breathing in; act of inspiring; state of being inspired; the fusion of intellectual and emotional activity which controls one's creative, visionary power; that which, or one who, inspires; intuitional impulse, original idea; divine guidance. INSPIRATIONAL, *adj.* having the power to inspire; relating to i. [L.].

INSPIRATORY [in-spier'a-te-ri], *adj.* relating to the inhaling of air into the lungs.

INSPIRE [in-spier'], *v.t.* to draw air into the lungs, breathe in; influence a person to attain a state of controlled excitement; instil into the mind; fill with creative power; communicate divine power. INSPIRED, *adj.* moved by inspiration. INSPIRING, *adj.* that inspires, animating. [L.].

INSPIRIT [in-spi'rit], *v.t.* to infuse spirit into, give new life to, animate, stimulate.

INSPISSATE [in-spi-sāt], *v.t.* to thicken, *esp.* a fluid, by boiling, evaporation etc. INSPISSATION [in-spi-sā'shn], *n.* process of inspissating.

INSTABILITY [in-sta-bi'li-ti], *n.* lack of stability; shakiness; inconstancy; irresolution. [L.].

INSTALL [in-stawl'], *v.t.* to place in office, invest with a rank, with formal ceremony; establish in a place or seat; place in position ready for use. [MedL.].

INSTALLATION [in-sta-lā'shn], *n.* act of installing; apparatus fitted in position. [MedL.].

INSTALMENT [in-stawl'ment], *n.* part payment of a debt made regularly until the whole is paid off; part of a whole, appearing serially or supplied periodically until complete.

INSTANCE (1) [in'stans], *n.* a particular example, occurrence, illustrative fact; suggestion, request; for i., as an example. INSTANCE (2), *v.t.* to mention as an example or illustration. [L.].

INSTANCY [in'stan-si], *n.* insistence, urgency.

INSTANT (1) [in'stant], *adj.* pressing, urgent; immediate; present; current; of the current month. INSTANT (2), *n.* a point of time, exact moment, particular second; extremely brief period of time. [L.].

INSTANTANEOUS [in-stan-tā'ni-oos], *adj.* occurring or done in an instant, immediate; at some particular instant. INSTANTANEOUSLY, *adv.* in an instant; without a second wasted.

INSTANTER [in-stan'ter], *adv.* immediately. [L.].

INSTANTLY [in'stant-li], *adv.* at once, immediately.

INSTEAD [in-sted'], *adv.* in place of, substitute for.

INSTEP [in'step], *n.* top curved side of the human foot at the base of the shinbone; that which covers this part in a stocking, boot or shoe. [Uncert.].

INSTIGATE [in'sti-gāt], *v.t.* to incite, urge on; stir up, foment. INSTIGATOR, *n.* person who instigates.

INSTIGATION [in-sti-gā'shn], *n.* act of instigating; incitement; provocation. [L.].

INSTIL(L) (*pres.pt.* **instilling**, *pret. and p.pt.* **instilled**) [in-stil'], *v.t.* to pour in by drops; infuse slowly but firmly into the mind. INSTILLATION [in-sti-lā'shn], *n.* act of instilling; that which is instilled.

INSTINCT (1) [in'stingkt], *n.* intuition, natural inclination; (*psych.*) natural urge compelling a more or less definite mode of behaviour, congenital impulse towards specific immediate ends, pattern of conduct derived from a congenital organization of energy. INSTINCT (2) [in-stingkt'], *adj.* filled with; possessing by nature; animated by. [L.].

INSTINCTIVE [in-stingk'tiv], *adj.* prompted by, arising from, instinct; intuitional. INSTINCTIVELY, *adv.* in an i. manner.

INSTITUTE (1) [in'sti-tyoot], *v.t.* to set up, establish, found; begin proceedings; install, appoint, invest. INSTITUTE (2), *n.* society with some scientific, educational or recreational purpose; organization giving a social service; building housing such an organization; settled or established principle, law or order; (*pl.*) book of fundamental principles of law or medicine. [L.].

INSTITUTION [in-sti-tyoo'shn], *n.* act of instituting; state of being instituted; something which has been instituted; custom or established order; scientific, educational etc. organization or society set up to provide a public service; building which is the headquarters for such work; (*coll.*) something or someone [L.].

regarded as a noteworthy, accepted public feature. INSTITUTIONAL, *adj.* relating to an i.; instituted by authority. [L.].

INSTITUTIONALISM [in-sti-tyōō'shn-a-lizm], *n.* the principles of organized religion; characteristics of life in a charitable institution.

INSTITUTOR [in'sti-tyōō-ter], *n.* person who institutes; founder. [L.].

INSTRUCT [in-strukt'], *v.t.* to impart knowledge or information to, teach; give orders to, command; (*leg.*) direct and authorize. [L.].

INSTRUCTION [in-struk'shn], *n.* act of instructing; teaching; direction, command. INSTRUCTIONAL, *adj.* containing i. [L.].

INSTRUCTIVE [in-struk'tiv], *adj.* serving to instruct, containing information.

INSTRUCTOR [in-struk'ter], *n.* teacher, one appointed to instruct others.

INSTRUCTRESS [in-struk'tres], *n.* female instructor.

INSTRUMENT [in'strōō-ment], *n.* something used as a mechanical aid; tool, implement; measuring, detecting or recording apparatus; (*mus.*) contrivance designed to produce musical sounds when played; (*leg.*) formal document or deed; (*fig.*) person acting as an agent or tool of another. [L.].

INSTRUMENTAL [in-strōō-men'tal], *adj.* acting as a means to an end, effective (in); produced by or for a musical instrument or instruments; due to, made by, an instrument. INSTRUMENTALIST, *n.* person who plays a musical instrument. INSTRUMENTALLY, *adv.* by means of an instrument; with musical instruments.

INSTRUMENTALITY [in-strōō-men-ta'li-ti], *n.* means, agency, by which something is accomplished.

INSTRUMENTATION [in-strōō-men-tā'shn], *n.* (*mus.*) arrangement of a composition for musical instruments, orchestration; use of instruments in surgery etc.

INSUBORDINATE [in-su-baw'di-nat], *adj.* defying discipline or authority, disobedient, rebellious.

INSUBORDINATION [in-su-baw-di-nā'shn], *n.* state of being insubordinate, disobedience.

INSUBSTANTIAL [in-sub-stan'shal], *adj.* having no substance, not real.

INSUFFERABLE [in-su'fe-ra-bl], *adj.* not to be suffered or endured, intolerable.

INSUFFICIENCY [in-su-fi'shen-si], *n.* quality of being insufficient; insufficient amount, lack.

INSUFFICIENT [in-su-fi'shent], *adj.* not sufficient, inadequate.

INSUFFLATE [in'su-flāt], *v.t.* to blow air into the body, *esp.* into the lungs; fill with air. INSUFFLATION [in-su-flā'shn], *n.* act of insufflating. [L.].

INSULAR [in'syōō-lah(r)], *adj.* belonging to, of the nature of, an island; (*fig.*) self-contained, narrow-minded. [L.].

INSULARITY [in-syōō-la'ri-ti], *n.* quality of being insular.

INSULATE [in'syōō-lāt], *v.t.* to make into an island; place in an isolated position; (*elect.*) isolate by means of a non-conducting substance. [L.].

INSULATION [in-syōō-lā'shn], *n.* act of insulating; state of being insulated, *esp.* by a non-conductor; that which insulates.

INSULATOR [in'syōō-lā-ter], *n.* non-conductor; device consisting of some substance which does not readily conduct electricity; such a substance.

INSULIN [in'syōō-lin], *n.* (*med.*) preparation from the pancreas of sheep etc., used in the treatment of diabetes. [L.].

INSULT (1) [in'sult], *n.* word, act or gesture which offends the feelings, dignity or sense of honour; abuse, affront. INSULT (2) [in-sult'], *v.t.* to offer an i. or insults to, affront. [L.].

INSULTING [in-sul'ting], *adj.* that conveys or expresses an insult, insolent.

INSUPERABLE [in-syōō'pe-ra-bl], *adj.* unable to be overcome or surmounted. [L.].

INSUPPORTABLE [in-su-paw'ta-bl], *adj.* intolerable.

INSURABLE [in-shyōōr'a-bl], *adj.* capable of being insured against loss or damage.

INSURANCE [in-shōōr'ans], *n.* state of being insured; act of insuring; contract to make good a specified loss on certain conditions in return for a stipulated premium; the premium itself.

INSURE [in-shōōr'], *v.t.* to contract to pay or receive under specified conditions in return for a stated premium a sum of money at a prescribed date, or indemnification against stipulated liabilities, or compensation for injury to or loss (of life, health,

goods etc.). INSURANT, *n.* holder of an insurance policy. INSURER, *n.* person who insures. [ENSURE].

INSURGENCY [in-sur'jen-si], *n.* state of being insurgent, insurrection.

INSURGENT (1) [in-sur'jent], *adj.* rising against established authority in an endeavour to usurp it, participating in rebellion; surging. INSURGENT (2), *n.* person who is in revolt, rebel. [L.].

INSURMOUNTABLE [in-ser-mown'ta-bl], *adj.* not to be surmounted or overcome.

INSURRECTION [in-se-rek'shn], *n.* act of rising up against authority; rebellion. INSURRECTIONAL, INSURRECTIONARY, *adj.* relating to, or participating in, i. [L.].

INTACT [in-takt'], *adj.* uninjured, untouched; entire, unimpaired. [L.].

INTAGLIO [in-ta'li-ō], *n.* design or figure which has been cut or engraved into a hard surface; jewel with an incised design. [It.].

INTAKE [in'tāk], *n.* act of taking in; anything taken in; inlet of a pipe or channel; valve through which the explosive mixture enters the cylinder of an internal-combustion engine; ventilation shaft of a mine; point at which a tube narrows.

INTANGIBLE [in-tan'ji-bl], *adj.* not able to be sensed by the touch, not tangible; (*fig.*) indefinite, vague.

INTEGER [in'ti-jer], *n.* a complete, undivided whole; (*math.*) whole number. [L.].

INTEGRAL [in'ti-gral], *adj.* having all the component parts, entire, whole; indispensable in order to be complete; (*math.*) relating to, consisting of, integers. INTEGRALITY [in-ti-gra'li-ti], *n.* state of being i.; wholeness, entirely. [LL.].

INTEGRATE [in'ti-grāt], *v.t.* to form parts into a whole, complete; give the total. [L.].

INTEGRITY [in-teg'ri-ti], *n.* state of being complete or unimpaired, wholeness, entireness; (*fig.*) moral soundness, uprightness; honesty. [L.].

INTEGUMENT [in-teg'yōō-ment], *n.* that which naturally covers anything, *esp.* the outer shell, skin, rind. INTEGUMENTARY [in-teg-yōō-men'ta-ri], *adj.* relating to, composed of, integuments. [L.].

INTELLECT [in'te-lekt], *n.* faculty of thinking, ability to reason; power of perceiving or knowing through the mind; an intellectual person. [L.].

INTELLECTUAL (1) [in-te-lek'tyōō-al], *adj.* relating to, appreciated by, exercised by, the intellect; able to follow or create a difficult line of reasoning; tending to devote oneself to mental activity. INTELLECTUAL (2), *n.* an i. person. [L.].

INTELLECTUALISM [in-te-lek'tyōō-a-lizm], *n.* theory that knowledge can lead to truth only when the intellect is free of emotional interference; belief in the primary importance of the intellect.

INTELLIGENCE [in-te'li-jens], *n.* faculty of understanding, quickness of mental apprehension, common sense with a good basis of intellectual control, sagacity; information, *esp.* of military value; news; an intelligent person.

INTELLIGENT [in-te'li-jent], *adj.* possessing intelligence; able to reason and understand; having a quick or acute intellect. INTELLIGENTIAL, *adj.* of, or relating to, the intellect. [L.].

INTELLIGENTSIA [in-te-li-jent'si-ah], *n.(pl.)* the educated and intellectual classes. [Russ.].

INTELLIGIBLE [in-te'li-ji-bl], *adj.* able to be understood; (*philos.*) clear to the mental understanding only. [L.].

INTEMPERANCE [in-tem'pe-rans], *n.* lack of control or moderation; excess; over-indulgence, *esp.* in drinking, habitual drunkenness. [L.].

INTEMPERATE [in-tem'pe-rat], *adj.* immoderate, extravagant; over-indulgent, *esp.* in intoxicating drink. [L.].

INTEND [in-tend'], *v.t.* to hold in the mind a thought which has a practical end in view, mean, purpose. [L.].

INTENDED [in-ten'did], *n.* (*coll.*) affianced lover.

INTENSE [in-tens'], *adj.* having a specific quality to an extreme degree; keen, deep, violent, excessive; deeply emotional; (of feeling) wrought to a high pitch. INTENSELY, *adv.* in an i. manner, to an i. degree. [L.].

INTENSIFICATION [in-ten-si-fi-kā'shn], *n.* act of making intense or more intense.

INTENSIFY [in-ten'si-fi], *v.t.* to make more intense; (*phot.*) increase the contrast in a negative by chemical means.

INTENSITY [in-ten'si-ti], *n.* quality of being intense; degree to which anything is intense.

INTENSIVE [in-ten'siv], *adj.* concentrated, intense; relating to, characterized by, intensity; admitting of intensification; relating to concentrated work; (*gram.*) giving emphasis; (*med.*) progressively increasing in force. INTENSIVELY, *adv.* in an i. fashion.

INTENT (1) [in-tent'], *n.* purpose, intention. INTENT (2), *adj.* having the mind concentrated on some object or action; having concentrated the attention on; fixed, earnest. [L.].

INTENTION [in-ten'shn], *n.* that which is intended, design, purpose; (*eccles.*) fixedness of attention to accomplish something; (*philos.*) idea, concept; (*surg.*) a process of healing. [L.].

INTENTIONAL [in-ten'shn-al], *adj.* intended, done designedly.

INTER (1) (*pres.pt.* interring, *pret. and p.pt.* interred) [in-tur'], *v.t.* to bury. [LL.].

INTER- (2), *pref.* among, between; *expressing a mutual relationship.* [L.].

INTERACT [in-te-rakt'], *v.i.* to act and react upon each other. INTERACTIVE, *adj.* interacting.

INTERACTION [in-te-rak'shn], *n.* process of interacting, reciprocal action.

INTERBREED [in-ter-brēd'], *v.t. and i.* to crossbreed.

INTERCEDE [in-ter-sēd'], *v.i.* to plead for someone else, mediate. [L.].

INTERCEPT [in-ter-sept'], *v.t.* to seize, halt a person or object on its journey from one point to another; hinder, obstruct; interrupt a communication with; (*math.*) mark off between two points or lines. [L.].

INTERCEPTION [in-ter-sep'shn], *n.* act of intercepting; obstruction, hindrance.

INTERCEPTOR [in-ter-sep'ter], *n.* one who intercepts; **i. plane**, aeroplane designed to intercept enemy planes, fighter plane.

INTERCESSION [in-ter-se'shn], *n.* act of interceding, reconciliatory mediation, entreaty on behalf of another; prayer offering this. INTERCESSIONAL, *adj.* relating to, containing, i. INTERCESSORIAL [in-ter-se-saw'ri-al], *adj.* relating to an intercessor, or to i. [L.].

INTERCESSOR [in-ter-se'ser], *n.* one who intercedes. INTERCESSORY, *adj.* that intercedes. [L.].

INTERCHANGE (1) [in-ter-chānj'], *v.t. and i.* to give and take mutually, exchange with each other; put one in place of the other; cause to take each other's place alternately; follow alternately. INTERCHANGE (2) [in'ter-chānj], *n.* mutual exchange; alternate succession. [OFr.].

INTERCHANGEABLE [in-ter-chān'ja-bl], *adj.* able to be interchanged.

INTERCOM [in-ter-kom'], *n.* (*coll.*) system of telephonic communication among the members of the crew of an aircraft. [INTERCOM(MUNICATION)].

INTERCOMMUNICATE [in-ter-ko-myōō'ni-kāt], *v.i.* to hold intercourse together; (of rooms) lead into one another.

INTERCOMMUNICATION [in-ter-ko-myōō-ni-kā'shn], *n.* reciprocal communication.

INTERCOMMUNION [in-ter-ko-myōō'ni-on], *n.* mutual communion.

INTERCONNECT [in-ter-ko-nekt'], *v.t. and i.* to join together; be linked together.

INTERCOSTAL [in-ter-kos'tal], *adj.* (*anat.*) lying between the ribs; (*bot.*) occurring between the veins.

INTERCOURSE [in'ter-kaws], *n.* social relationship of reciprocal dealings; communion; fellowship; sexual connexion. [OFr.].

INTERDEPENDENT [in-ter-di-pen'dent], *adj.* depending upon each other, mutually dependent.

INTERDICT (1) [in'ter-dikt], *v.t.* to forbid or prohibit by authority; place under an interdict; prevent. INTERDICT (2), *n.* official decree prohibiting something, *esp.* one forbidding participation in the Church ceremonies. INTERDICTORY, *adj.* that interdicts; relating to, of the nature of, an i. [L.].

INTERDICTION [in-ter-dik'shn], *n.* act of interdicting; prohibition. [L.].

INTEREST (1) [in'te-rest], *n.* state of mind or emotion strong enough to control and focus the attention; preoccupation; thing which engages the attention; advantage, benefit; consequence, importance; group of people sharing the same business or political aims; premium paid for the use of money; share, legal or financial claim; something added. INTEREST (2), *v.t.* to awaken i. in, engage the attention; induce to take part in. [L.].

INTERESTED [in'te-res-tid], *adj.* having or taking an interest in something; exhibiting interest; personally concerned in and thus liable to be biased.

INTERESTING [in'te-res-ting], *adj.* arousing interest, engaging the attention.

INTERFERE [in-ter-fēer'], *v.i.* to interpose; intervene in another's business, meddle; come into collision; (*phys.*) modify each other, interact; **to i. with,** to hinder; molest; prevent. [L.].

INTERFERENCE [in-ter-fēer'ens], *n.* act of interfering; meddling, unwarranted intervention; hindrance; (*phys.*) cancellation of effect when two waves overlap out of phase; (*radio*) distortion or obliteration of reception by electric disturbances from apparatus or signals from other transmitters.

INTERFERING [in-ter-fēer'ing], *adj.* that interferes, meddlesome.

INTERFUSE [in-ter-fyōōz'], *v.t. and i.* to blend, intermix, mix together. [L.].

INTERIM (1) [in'te-rim], *n.* intermediate period, time intervening. INTERIM (2), *adj.* relating to, occurring in an i.; temporary, in the meantime. [L.].

INTERIOR (1) [in-tēer'i-er], *adj.* placed, lying, in the inside of anything, internal, inner; relating to the inside of a house; remote from boundaries or coasts. INTERIOR (2), *n.* the inside of anything, *esp.* of a room or body; inland part of a country; state department dealing with home affairs; picture of part of the inside of a building. INTERIORLY, *adv.* internally. [L.].

INTERJECT [in-ter-jekt'], *v.t.* to throw between; insert; interrupt a conversation with. [L.].

INTERJECTION [in-ter-jek'shn], *n.* act of interjecting; word expressing some sudden emotion; exclamation. INTERJECTIONAL, INTERJECTORY, *adj.* relating to, of the nature of, an i. [L.].

INTERLACE [in-ter-lās'], *v.t. and i.* to twist together, interweave; be interwoven. [Fr.].

INTERLARD [in-ter-lahd'], *v.t.* to mix with alternate layers of fat; interpose; intersperse.

INTERLEAVE [in-ter-lēv'], *v.t.* to insert a blank leaf or leaves in a book and bind them up with the other leaves.

INTERLINE [in-ter-līn'], *v.t.* to print in alternate lines; insert between the printed lines. INTERLINEAR [in-ter-li'ni-er], *adj.* written, inserted or printed between lines. [MedL.].

INTERLOCK [in-ter-lok'], *v.t. and i.* to lock, clasp, join together by means of alternate projections.

INTERLOCUTION [in-ter-lo-kyōō'shn], *n.* conference; conversation, dialogue. [L.].

INTERLOCUTOR [in-ter-lo'kyōō-ter], *n.* person who speaks in dialogue. INTERLOCUTORY, *adj.* relating to, consisting of, dialogue; (*leg.*) intermediate, limited to the earliest stages.

INTERLOPER [in'ter-lō-per], *n.* person who interferes in another's business, intruder.

INTERLUDE [in'ter-lyōōd], *n.* short performance between the acts of a play; interval between two acts; intervening period; (*mus.*) passage played by instruments, to link up two stanzas. [MedL.].

INTERMARRY [in-ter-ma'ri], *v.i.* to marry, *esp.* of persons of different races, tribes, castes etc.

INTERMEDDLE [in-ter-me'dl], *v.i.* to meddle in the affairs of others, interfere.

INTERMEDIARY (1) [in-ter-mē'di-a-ri], *adj.* intermediate, lying between; acting as agent or go-between. INTERMEDIARY (2), *n.* an i. object or person. [L.].

INTERMEDIATE (1) [in-ter-mē'di-āt], *adj.* situated in the middle between extremes; situated or occurring between two things or points of time; interposed. INTERMEDIATE (2), *n.* examination to be taken between matriculation and a final degree; an i. object. INTERMEDIATE (3) [in-ter-mē'di-āt], *v.i.* to intervene, be an intermediary. INTERMEDIATELY, *adv.* in an i. position. [L.].

INTERMEDIATION [in-ter-mē-di-ā'shn], *n.* act of intermediating, intervention.

INTERMEDIATOR [in-ter-mē'di-ā-ter], *n.* person who intermediates.

INTERMENT [in-tur'ment], *n.* burial.

INTERMEZZO [in-ter-met'zō], *n.* interlude; (*mus.*) short piece played between acts, or linking the movements of a symphony etc. [It.].

INTERMINABLE [in-tur'mi-na-bl], *adj.* endless, without limit; tediously prolonged, boring.

INTERMINGLE [in-ter-ming'gl], *v.t.* to blend, mingle together; *v.i.* to be mixed or blended.

INTERMISSION [in-ter-mi'shn], *n.* cessation for a time, respite, interval, pause. [L.].

INTERMIT (*pres.pt.* intermitting, *pret. and p.pt.* intermitted) [in-ter-mit'], *v.t.* to cause to cease for a time; *v.i.* to cease for a time, pause. [L.].

INTERMITTENT [in-ter-mi'tent], *adj.* ceasing at intervals; alternately weak or strong, active or quiescent.

INTERMIX [in-ter-miks'], *v.t. and i.* to intermingle. **INTERMIXTURE** [in-ter-miks'tyŏŏr], *n.* mass formed by mixture, compound, blend.

INTERN (1) [in-turn'], *n.* (*U.S.*) house surgeon or house physician in a hospital. [Fr.].

INTERN (2), *v.t.* to imprison, confine in custody, *esp.* aliens in time of war, prisoners of war etc. [Fr.].

INTERNAL [in-tur'nal], *adj.* pertaining to, present in, the inside of anything; inner, inward; relating to, derived from, the nature of anything, intrinsic; relating to, concerned with, the home affairs of a country; **i.-combustion engine,** engine driven by the recurrent explosions of gas in air chambers. **INTERNALLY,** *adv.* in the inside, inwardly. [L.].

INTERNATIONAL (1) [in-ter-na'shn-al], *adj.* relating to, affecting, common to, carried on between, administered by, different nations. **INTERNATIONAL** (2), *n.* player representing his country in any sport; **i.** body for the propagation of socialism.

INTERNATIONALE [in-ter-na-shn-ahl'], *n.* song adopted as the anthem of the international socialist movement and the national anthem of the U.S.S.R. [Fr.].

INTERNATIONALISM [in-ter-na'shn-a-lizm], *n.* political doctrine and aims of the socialist Internationals; belief in the benefits of co-operation among nations. **INTERNATIONALIST,** *n.* believer in the power and validity of i.; one expert in international law.

INTERNECINE [in-ter-nē'sin], *adj.* mutually destructive, deadly. [L.].

INTERNEE [in-ter-nē'], *n.* one who is or has been interned.

INTERNMENT [in-turn'ment], *n.* act of interning; state of being interned; **i. camp,** camp in which aliens, political prisoners or prisoners of war are interned.

INTERPENETRATE [in-ter-pe'ni-trāt], *v.t.* to penetrate mutually, pervade each other.

INTERPLAY [in'ter-plā], *n.* action and reaction of two sides, elements, factors etc. upon one another.

INTERPOLAR [in-ter-pō'ler], *adj.* placed or occurring between the poles, *esp.* of an electric cell or battery.

INTERPOLATE [in-tur'po-lāt], *v.t.* to insert (words or passages) in a book or manuscript, corrupt (a text); (*math.*) insert intermediate terms in a series. **INTERPOLATOR,** *n.* person who interpolates. [L.].

INTERPOLATION [in-ter-po-lā'shn], *n.* act of interpolating; state of being interpolated; that which is interpolated. [L.].

INTERPOSE [in-ter-pōz'], *v.t. and i.* to place, put between, insert; put forward suddenly an offer, objection etc.; butt in with a remark, interruption etc.; intervene; interrupt.

INTERPOSITION [in-ter-po-zi'shn], *n.* act of interposing; intervention; anything interposed. [L.].

INTERPRET [in-tur'prit], *v.t. and i.* to explain the significance of, elucidate; represent in practical fashion by artistic means; translate; take to mean, regard; act as an interpreter. **INTERPRETABLE,** *adj.* able to be interpreted. [L.].

INTERPRETATION [in-ter-pri-tā'shn], *n.* act or power of interpreting; way in which anything is interpreted; significance, meaning. [L.].

INTERPRETATIVE [in-tur'pri-ta-tiv], *adj.* that interprets, explanatory, pertaining to interpretation.

INTERPRETER [in-tur'pri-ter], *n.* one who interprets; one employed in translating foreign languages orally and instantaneously.

INTERRACIAL [in-ter-rā'shal], *adj.* taking place between races.

INTERREGNUM [in-ter-reg'num], *n.* time between two reigns, governments or ministries; interval, break. [L.].

INTERRELATION [in-ter-ri-lā'shn], *n.* mutual relation.

INTERROGATE [in-te'ro-gāt], *v.t. and i.* to question, cross-examine. [L.].

INTERROGATION [in-te-ro-gā'shn], *n.* act of interrogating; question; **note of i.,** punctuation mark (?) denoting a question. [L.].

INTERROGATIVE (1) [in-te-ro'ga-tiv], *adj.* relating to, denoting, a question; expressed in the form of a question, inquiring. **INTERROGATIVE** (2), *n.* an i. pronoun or word.

INTERROGATOR [in-te'ro-gā-ter], *n.* questioner.

INTERROGATORY (1) [in-te-ro'ga-te-ri], *adj.* relating to, containing, expressing, a question.

INTERROGATORY (2), *n.* question or inquiry; formal series of questions to be answered on oath as part of the preliminaries before a trial. [L.].

INTERRUPT [in-te-rupt'], *v.t.* to cause to stop by breaking in upon, hinder by intervention; obstruct; break the continuity of, cut off. [L.].

INTERRUPTED [in-te-rup'tid], *adj.* not continuous; broken; intermitted. **INTERRUPTEDLY,** *adv.* in an i. way.

INTERRUPTION [in-te-rup'shn], *n.* act of interrupting; state of being interrupted; that which interrupts. [L.].

INTERSECT [in-ter-sekt'], *v.t. and i.* to divide by cutting or passing across; cut, cross; cross each other. [L.].

INTERSECTION [in-ter-sek'shn], *n.* act of intersecting; point or line in which two lines or planes intersect; cross-road. **INTERSECTIONAL,** *adj.* of or relating to i.

INTERSEXUAL [in-ter-sek'shŏŏ-al], *adj.* existing between the sexes; of intermediate sex.

INTERSPACE (1) [in'ter-spās], *n.* space situated between. **INTERSPACE** (2) [in-ter-spās'], *v.t.* to put space between.

INTERSPERSE [in-ter-spurs'], *v.t.* to scatter or set here and there; diversify. **INTERSPERSION,** *n.* act of interspersing, condition of being interspersed. [L.].

INTERSTELLAR [in-ter-ste'ler], *adj.* passing between, situated among, the stars.

INTERSTICE [in-tur'stis], *n.* small space between things closely set, intervening space; chink, narrow gap. [L.].

INTERSTITIAL [in-ter-sti'shal], *adj.* relating to or containing interstices.

INTERTWINE [in-ter-twīn'], *v.t. and i.* to twine together.

INTERVAL [in'ter-val], *n.* a space between; the extent of separation or difference; intervening amount of time, period between two fixed periods; pause between two acts of a play; intermission; (*mus.*) difference of pitch between two notes. [L.].

INTERVENE [in-ter-vēn'], *v.i.* to take place, occur, come between; be interposed; interfere; (*leg.*) become a party to an action. [L.].

INTERVENTION [in-ter-ven'shn], *n.* act of intervening; interposition; mediation; the taking of sides in a foreign dispute or war. **INTERVENTIONIST,** *adj. and n.* (characteristic of) one who favours i. (in foreign affairs). [L.].

INTERVIEW (1) [in'ter-vyŏŏ], *n.* meeting between persons or groups to discuss a specified question; *esp.* meeting between a reporter and a person who is to be the subject of an article; meeting between a prospective employer and a candidate for employment to test the applicant's qualities. **INTERVIEW** (2), *v.t.* to have an i. with. [~Fr.].

INTERVIEWER [in'ter-vyŏŏ-er], *n.* person who interviews, newspaper reporter who specializes in interviewing.

INTERWEAVE (*pret.* **interwove,** *p.pt.* **interwoven**) [in-ter-wēv'], *v.t.* to twine or weave together, intermingle.

INTESTACY [in-tes'ta-si], *n.* condition of dying intestate.

INTESTATE (1) [in-tes'tāt], *adj.* leaving no will; not disposed of by will. **INTESTATE** (2), *n.* person who dies i. [L.].

INTESTINAL [in-tes'ti-nal, in-tes-tī'nal], *adj.* relating to the intestines.

INTESTINE (1) [in-tes'tin], *adj.* internal, *esp.* inside a country, domestic. **INTESTINE** (2), *n.* the part of the alimentary canal situated beneath the stomach, bowel, gut. [L.].

INTIMACY [in'ti-ma-si], *n.* condition of being intimate; close familiarity; sexual intercourse.

INTIMATE (1) [in'ti-mat], *adj.* relating to the private and deepest recesses of mind and feelings; having a close emotional relationship as friends; private, personal; joined in sexual intercourse. **INTIMATE** (2), *n.* close friend. [L.].

INTIMATE (3) [in'ti-māt], *v.t.* to announce, make known, declare; hint, suggest, imply. [LL.].

INTIMATION [in-ti-mā'shn], *n.* act of intimating; announcement. [LL.].

INTIMIDATE [in-ti'mi-dāt], *v.t.* to make afraid, terrorize, coerce. **INTIMIDATORY,** *adj.* that intimidates. [MedL.].

INTIMIDATION [in-ti-mi-dā'shn], *n.* act of intimidating; condition of being intimidated.

INTO [in'tŏŏ], *prep. expressing movement towards an*

ŏŏ is pronounced as in *food*; ŏŏ as in *hood*; th as in *think*; TH as in *that*; zh as in azure.   ~ = related to.

inner point, denoting passage from outside to inside, or from one state to another.

INTOLERABLE [in-to′le-ra-bl], *adj.* that cannot be tolerated or endured. [L.].

INTOLERANCE [in-to′le-rans], *n.* quality of being intolerant. [L.].

INTOLERANT [in-to′le-rant], *adj.* not able or refusing to endure; not able to tolerate difference of opinion, impatient of opposing beliefs.

INTONATION [in-tō-nā′shn], *n.* act of intoning; modulation of the voice; fluctuation of the pitch of the voice; (*mus.*) production of musical tones; introductory phrase in plainsong.

INTONE [in-tōn′], *v.t. and i.* to utter in a singing tone with fluctuating pitch of the voice, recite in a singsong manner, chant. [L.].

INTOXICANT (1) [in-tok′si-kant], *adj.* that intoxicates. INTOXICANT (2), *n.* anything intoxicating, *esp.* an intoxicating liquor. [L.].

INTOXICATE [in-tok′si-kāt], *v.t.* to make drunk; (*fig.*) excite the senses to an abnormal emotional pitch. [MedL.].

INTOXICATION [in-tok-si-kā′shn], *n.* condition of being intoxicated; act of intoxicating.

INTRA-, *pref.* within. [L.].

INTRACTABLE [in-trak′ta-bl], *adj.* ungovernable, stubborn; awkward, difficult. [L.].

INTRAMURAL [in-tra-myōō′ral], *adj.* within the walls, as of a city.

INTRANSIGENT (1) [in-tran′si-jent], *adj.* refusing to be reconciled, uncompromising in hostility. INTRANSIGENT (2), *n.* an i. person. [Span.].

INTRANSITIVE (1) [in-tran′si-tiv], *adj.* (*gram.*) not governing a direct object, expressing an action limited to the agent. INTRANSITIVE (2), *n.* an i. verb. INTRANSITIVELY, *adv.* in an i. way.

INTRENCH, see ENTRENCH.

INTREPID [in-tre′pid], *adj.* not to be frightened, without fear, undaunted. [L.].

INTREPIDITY [in-tre-pi′di-ti], *n.* quality of being intrepid.

INTRICACY [in′tri-ka-si], *n.* quality of being intricate.

INTRICATE [in′tri-kat], *adj.* difficult to disentangle, involved, complicated. [L.].

INTRIGUE (1) [in-trēg′], *n.* secret plot; secret love affair. INTRIGUE (2), *v.t.* to puzzle, mystify; fascinate by its unusualness or complexity; *v.i.* to participate in, or originate, an i. [Fr.].

INTRINSIC [in-trin′sik], *adj.* relating to the essential nature, inherent; real. [L.].

INTRO-, *pref.* within. [L.].

INTRODUCE [in-trō-dyōōs′], *v.t.* to lead, bring in; present, cause to make the acquaintance of; present formally for debate; bring up in conversation; place or put in, inaugurate. [L.].

INTRODUCTION [in-trō-duk′shn], *n.* act of introducing; state of being introduced; preliminary statement, preface; elementary text book. [L.].

INTRODUCTORY [in-trō-duk′te-ri], *adj.* serving to introduce something, opening.

INTROIT [in-trō′it], *n.* (*R.C. Church*) verses of Scripture sung as the priest enters within the altar-rails to celebrate Mass. [L.].

INTROSPECTION [in-trō-spek′shn], *n.* act of observing one's own thoughts and feelings; self-analysis. [L.].

INTROSPECTIVE [in-trō-spek′tiv], *adj.* relating to, based on, given to, introspection.

INTROVERSION [in-trō-vur′shn], *n.* act of introverting; condition of being introverted.

INTROVERT (1) [in-trō-vurt′], *v.t.* to turn inwards. INTROVERT (2) [in′trō-vert], *n.* (*psych.*) introspective person who tends to alter external reality in his imagination to make it correspond more closely with his own ideas and desires. [L.].

INTRUDE [in-trōōd′], *v.t. and i.* to thrust in; enter without permission; encroach, trespass. [L.].

INTRUDER [in-trōō′der], *n.* person who intrudes; single raiding aircraft.

INTRUSION [in-trōō′zhn], *n.* act of intruding; an instance of this; state of being intruded. [MedL.].

INTRUSIVE [in-trōō′siv], *adj.* tending to intrude; that intrudes.

INTRUST, see ENTRUST.

INTUITION [in-tyōō-i′shn], *n.* faculty of consciousness directed by unreasoning feeling or instinct, characterized by immediate perception; that which is so apprehended. [MedL.].

INTUITIVE [in-tyōō′i-tiv], *adj.* perceived or perceiving by intuition. INTUITIVELY, *adv.* in an i. way.

INTUMESCENCE [in-tyōō-me′sens], *n.* process of swelling; a swelling; state of being swollen. [L.].

INTUMESCENT [in-tyōō-me′sent], *adj.* swelling up. [L.].

INTUSSUSCEPTION [in-tus-su-sep′shn], *n.* (*path., biol.*) the taking in of one part of the intestine by an adjacent part; conversion of foreign matter into tissue by an organism. [L.].

INTWINE, see ENTWINE.

INTWIST, see ENTWIST.

INUNDATE [in′un-dāt], *v.t.* to flood; overflow; (*fig.*) overwhelm. [L.].

INUNDATION [in-un-dā′shn], *n.* act of inundating; flood, deluge. [L.].

INURBANITY [in-er-ba′ni-ti], *n.* incivility.

INURE, ENURE [in-yōōr′], *v.t. and i.* to expose to the discipline of use and practice, harden, accustom; (*leg.*) become operative. [IN (6) and Fr.].

INVADE [in-vād′], *v.t.* to enter a country with hostile intentions; attack; (*fig.*) encroach upon; swarm into. [L.].

INVALID (1) [in′va-lid], *adj.* suffering from bad health, ill, weak; used by, suitable for, an ailing person. INVALID (2), *n.* person who is sick or in poor health. INVALID (3) [in′va-lid, in-va-lid′], *v.t.* to make an i., *esp.* to draft out of active service for reasons of ill-health or wounds. [L.].

INVALID (4) [in-va′lid], *adj.* not valid; null, having no legal cogency. [L.].

INVALIDATE [in-va′li-dāt], *v.t.* to destroy the validity of, deprive of legal force.

INVALIDATION [in-va-li-dā′shn], *n.* act of invalidating; condition of being invalidated.

INVALIDISM [in′va-li-dizm], *n.* state of being an invalid, time during which one is an invalid.

INVALIDITY [in-va-li′di-ti], *n.* state of being not valid.

INVALUABLE [in-va′lyōō-a-bl], *adj.* that cannot be valued, very precious, priceless.

INVARIABLE [in-vāer′i-a-bl], *adj.* not variable; constant, unalterable; (*math.*) fixed. INVARIABLY, *adv.* in i. fashion, regularly, unchangingly.

INVASION [in-vā′zhn], *n.* act of invading; state of being invaded; aggressive intrusion. [LL.].

INVECTIVE [in-vek′tiv], *n.* vehement and reviling language, abuse. [MedL.].

INVEIGH [in-vā′], *v.i.* to attack with invective, rail against with bitterness. [L.].

INVEIGLE [in-vē′gl], *v.t.* to persuade or coax by means of artful cajolery, wheedle, lure. [OFr.].

INVENT [in-vent′], *v.t.* to devise something original; fabricate; make up. [L.].

INVENTION [in-ven′shn], *n.* act of inventing; state of being invented; that which is invented, original contrivance; fiction, lie; ability to invent things. [L.].

INVENTIVE [in-ven′tiv], *adj.* able to invent; quick at contriving new things.

INVENTOR [in-ven′ter], *n.* person who invents; discoverer of new principles or applications, constructor of original mechanical devices. [L.].

INVENTORY [in′ven-te-ri], *n.* list, catalogue, *esp.* of goods or chattels; things named in such a list. [MedL.].

INVERSE (1) [in-vurs′], *adj.* contrary, reversed, inverted; **i. proportion**, (*math.*) increase in one quantity to the extent another decreases; **i. ratio**, (*math.*) ratio of the reciprocals of two quantities. INVERSE (2), *n.* condition of being inverted; that which is the exact opposite of something else. INVERSELY, *adv.* in an i. way. [L.].

INVERSION [in-vur′shn], *n.* act of inverting; state of being inverted; something inverted; change of order or position into its opposite. [L.].

INVERT (1) [in-vurt′], *v.t.* to turn upside down; reverse, transpose; (*gram.*) reverse the normal order of words; (*math.*) transpose the antecedent and consequent terms of a proposition; (*mus.*) raise the lower note of an interval an octave in pitch; (*psych.*) reverse the sex instincts of. INVERT (2) [in′vert], *n.* (*arch.*) inverted arch; one whose sex instincts are inverted; **i. sugar**, compound of laevulose and dextrose. [L.].

INVERTEBRATE (1) [in-vur′ti-brat], *adj.* (*zool.*) lacking a spinal column or backbone. INVERTEBRATE (2) [in-vur′ti-brāt], *n.* an i. animal. [IN (5) and L.].

INVEST [in-vest′], *v.t.* to array, clothe, *esp.* decorate with the dress or symbols of rank or office; surround; lay siege to; lay out a sum of money with a view to obtaining a subsequent profit on it. [L.].

The accent ′ after a syllable = stress (u-pon′). The mɐrk ‾ over a vowel = length (ā in made; ō in bone).

INVESTIGATE [in-ves'ti-gāt], *v.t.* to examine into with care; make a systematic inquiry into. [L.].

INVESTIGATION [in-ves-ti-gā'shn], *n.* act of investigating; research, inquiry. [L.].

INVESTIGATOR [in-ves'ti-gā-ter], *n.* person who investigates. [L.].

INVESTITURE [in-ves'ti-tyoor], *n.* act or right of investing with a rank etc.; formal occasion when a person is so invested; state of being invested with. [MedL.].

INVESTMENT [in-vest'ment], *n.* act of nvesting money, money so invested; something in which one may invest money; act of laying siege to; investiture.

INVESTOR [in-ves'ter], *n.* one who invests money.

INVETERATE [in-ve'te-rat], *adj.* firmly established by long custom, confirmed; obstinate; of long standing. [L.].

INVIDIOUS [in-vi-di-oos], *adj.* likely to arouse ill-will, provoke envy or give offence. INVIDIOUSLY, *adv.* in an i. way. [L.].

INVIGILATE [in-vi'ji-lāt], *v.i.* to supervise candidates taking an examination. INVIGILATION [in-vi-ji-lā'shn], *n.* act of invigilating. INVIGILATOR, *n.* person who invigilates. [L.].

INVIGORATE [in-vi'ge-rāt], *v.t.* to impart vigour to, refresh, stimulate. INVIGORATION [in-vi-ge-rā'shn], *n.* act of invigorating; condition of being invigorated. [L.].

INVINCIBILITY [in-vin-si-bi'li-ti], *n.* condition of being invincible.

INVINCIBLE [in-vin'si-bl], *adj.* not able to be conquered or subdued. INVINCIBLY, *adv.* in an i. way. [L.].

INVIOLABILITY [in-vī-ō-la-bi'li-ti], *n.* state of being inviolable.

INVIOLABLE [in-vī'ō-la-bl], *adj.* not to be violated or damaged. [L.].

INVIOLATE [in-vī'ō-lat], *adj.* not violated, unprofaned, unharmed, unimpaired. [L.].

INVISIBILITY [in-vi-zi-bi'li-ti], *n.* condition of being invisible.

INVISIBLE [in-vi'zi-bl], *adj.* not able to be seen; imperceptible; **i. exports,** overseas investments, shipping and other services performed for foreigners. INVISIBLY, *adv.* in an i. way. [L.].

INVITATION [in-vi-tā'shn], *n.* act of inviting; request for a visit etc.; proposal which invites. [L.].

INVITE [in-vīt'], *v.t.* to request the company of, ask (a person) to come to a social gathering; request; encourage; solicit; provoke. [L.].

INVITING [in-vī'ting], *adj.* alluring, tempting. INVITINGLY, *adv.* in an i. way.

INVOCATION [in-vō-kā'shn], *n.* act of invoking, *esp.* God or some supernatural being; prayer or words expressing this. [L.].

INVOCATORY [in-vo'ka-te-ri], *adj.* that invokes; relating to invocation.

INVOICE (1) [in'vois], *n.* detailed list of goods delivered, together with their prices, sent to their purchaser. INVOICE (2), *v.t.* to make an i. of, enter in an i. [OFr.].

INVOKE [in-vōk'], *v.t.* to address in prayer, summon aid from; call upon; implore; conjure up. [L.].

INVOLUCRE [in'vo-lyoo-ker], *n.* (*anat.*) covering of membrane; (*bot.*) group of bracts enclosing buds or the leaves at the base of the flowers. [L.].

INVOLUNTARY [in-vo'lun-ta-ri], *adj.* not arising from the functioning of the will power, instinctive; unwilling, without intention. INVOLUNTARILY, *adv.* in an i. way. [L.].

INVOLUTE [in'vo-loot], *adj.* involved; (*bot.*) possessing edges curved inwards or rolled under; (*zool.*) curving spirally. [L.].

INVOLUTION [in-vo-loo'shn], *n.* act of involving; condition of being involved; that which is involved or involute; (*gram.*) the addition of clauses complicating the construction of a sentence; (*math.*) the raising of a quantity to any given power; (*biol.*) degeneration, atrophy. [L.].

INVOLVE [in-volv'], *v.t.* to entangle; overwhelm with intricate details; be placed inextricably in a position; cause to happen as a necessity, entail. INVOLVED, *adj.* complicated, complex to the point of being obscure; difficult to sort out. [L.].

INVULNERABLE [in-vul'ne-ra-bl], *adj.* that cannot be wounded, damaged or assailed; (*bridge*) of the state of a team before it has won a game. INVULNERABILITY [in-vul-ne-ra-bi'li-ti], *n.* quality of being i. INVULNERABLY, *adv.* in an i. way. [L.].

INWARD (1) [in'werd], *adj.* placed or existing on the inside, inner, internal; progressing towards the interior; spiritual, subjective. INWARD(S) (2), *adv.* towards the inside; in the imagination or the mind. [OE.].

INWARDLY [in'werd-li], *adv.* in the inner parts; privately, intimately; in the inner self.

INWARDNESS [in'werd-nes], *n.* condition of being inward; inner significance or nature.

INWARDS [i'nerdz], *n.*(*pl.*) (*coll.*) inner parts of an animal, viscera, entrails.

INWRAP, see ENWRAP.

INWREATHE, see ENWREATHE.

IODINE [ī'ō-dēn, ī'ō-dīn], *n.* non-metallic element with important medical and chemical uses. [Gk.].

IODIZE [ī'ō-dīz], *v.t.* to permeate with iodine.

IODOFORM [ī-ō'dō-fawm], *n.* antiseptic containing iodine.

ION [ī'on], *n.* (*phys.*) an electrically charged atom or group of atoms. [Gk.].

IONIC (1) [i-o'nik], *adj.* Ionian; **I. order,** (*arch.*) style characterized by flutings and scrolled capitals. [Gk.].

IONIC (2), *adj.* of, pertaining or relating to an ion or ions. [ION].

IONIUM [ī-ō'ni-um], *n.* (*chem.*) radio-active element obtained from uranium. [ION].

IONIZE [ī'o-nīz], *v.t. and i.* to charge a liquid or gas with ions; split into ions.

IOTA [ī-ō'tah], *n.* the Greek letter i; (*fig.*) very small quantity, jot. [Gk.].

I O U [ī-ō-yoo'], *n.* writing acknowledging a debt or loan. [*I owe you*].

IPECACUANHA [i-pi-ka-kyoo-a'nah], *n.* South American plant, an extract of whose root is used as an emetic etc. [Native].

IRANIAN [i-rā'ni-an], *n. and adj.* (a) Persian; (*philol.*) (pertaining to) that division of Indo-European including Zend and Old Persian. [Pers.].

IRASCIBLE [i-ra'si-bl], *adj.* irritable, quickly angered. IRASCIBLY, *adv.* in i. fashion. [L.].

IRATE [ī-rāt'], *adj.* angered, enraged. [L.].

IRE [īer], *n.* rage, angry resentment. [L.].

IREFUL [īer'fool], *adj.* full of anger.

IRIDACEOUS [i-ri-dā'shoos], *adj.* (*bot.*) belonging to the order *Iridaceae*; related to plants of the genus *Iris.*

IRIDESCENCE [i-ri-de'sens], *n.* state of being iridescent.

IRIDESCENT [i-ri-de'sent], *adj.* shining with the colours of the rainbow; reflecting light in differing colours and intensities. [Gk.].

IRIS (*pl.* irises, (*of eyes*) irides) [ī'ris], *n.* coloured area surrounding the pupil of the eye; (*bot.*) genus of plants with blade-shaped leaves and brightly coloured flowers; iridescent colouring; rainbow; diaphragm of a camera. [Gk.].

IRISH [īer'ish], *adj.* relating to Ireland, its people, language, customs and characteristics; **I. stew,** boiled hash of mutton, potatoes and onions. [~OE.].

IRITIS [ī-rī'tis], *n.* (*med.*) morbid inflammation of the iris. [Gk.].

IRK [urk], *v.t.* (*archaic*) to worry, tire; irritate, fret. [ME.].

IRKSOME [urk'sum], *adj.* that irks, wearisome, vexatious.

IRON (1) [īern], *n.* the element Fe, a malleable, hard, tough metal; tool made of this, *esp.* one with a flat surface, heated and used to smooth cloth; stirrup; iron-headed golf-club; medicinal preparation containing an i. compound as a tonic; (*fig.*) something very hard, ruthless and unyielding; (*pl.*) chains, fetters; supports for crippled legs; **to strike while the i. is hot,** to act promptly and at the right moment. IRON (2), *adj.* made of i., resembling i.; (*fig.*) very hard, ruthless; **i. rations,** rations to be retained for use in an emergency. IRON (3), *v.t.* to smooth (cloth) with an i.; furnish with i. parts; fit i. on the heel of a shoe; put into fetters; **to i. out,** (*fig.*) to smooth away, remove (differences, difficulties etc.). [OE.].

IRON-BOUND [īern'bownd], *adj.* bound, belted, with iron; (*fig.*) ruthless, unyielding; savagely rocky.

IRON-CURTAIN [īern-kur'tan], *n.* (*coll.*) the political frontier between Russia and her satellites on the one hand, and the Western European states on the other.

IRONFOUNDRY [īern'fownd-ri], *n.* place where iron is melted and cast.

IRON-GREY [īern-grā'], *adj.* of the hard grey colour of newly broken iron.

IRONIC(AL) [ī-ro'nik(-al)], *adj.* relating to irony,

said in irony. IRONICALLY, adv. in i. fashion. [Gk.].

IRONING [iern'ing], n. process of smoothing cloth with a heated iron; clothes etc. to be ironed.

IRONIST [ier'o-nist], n. one fond of or using irony.

IRON LUNG [iern-lung'], n. (med.) device for inducing breathing artificially, consisting of an iron casing in which the pressure can be regulated and into which the patient's body is put.

IRONMASTER [iern'mah-ster], n. owner of an ironfoundry.

IRONMONGER [iern'mung-ger], n. dealer in metal goods.

IRONMONGERY [iern'mung-ge-ri], n. metal goods; trade of an ironmonger.

IRONMOULD [iern'mōld], n. stain made by iron rust.

IRONSIDE [iern'sīd], n. member of Cromwell's cavalry; fierce, humourless person.

IRONSTONE [iern'stōn], n. impure iron ore.

IRONWARE [iern'wāer], n. ironmongery.

IRONWORK [iern'werk], n. iron structure; objects made of iron; (pl.) place where iron is smelted.

IRONY [ier'o-ni], n. satiric mode of speaking in which words are used with an intention exactly opposite to their normal meaning; (fig.) result precisely opposite in effect from what might have been expected from its cause; dramatic i., the placing in characters' mouths of speeches which the audience know to have a special significance for the outcome of the plot of which the speaker is deemed to be ignorant; Socratic i., pretence of ignorance as a technique for confuting an opponent in argument. [Gk.].

IRRADIANCE, IRRADIANCY [i-rā'di-ans(-i)], n. condition of being irradiant.

IRRADIANT [i-rā'di-ant], adj. radiating light, brightly gleaming. [L.].

IRRADIATE [i-rā'di-āt], v.t. to shine upon, illumine with beams of light; light up; give out, pour forth; (phys.) subject to radiation; (med.) treat with therapeutic rays; (fig.) explain, illuminate. [L.].

IRRADIATION [i-rā-di-ā'shn], n. process of irradiating; condition of being irradiated; beam of light; (opt.) apparent magnification of a bright body against darkness.

IRRATIONAL (1) [i-ra'shn-al], adj. unreasoning; not rational or logical, contrary to sense; (math.) incapable of expression by integer or vulgar fraction. IRRATIONAL (2), n. (math.) an i. number or quantity. IRRATIONALLY, adv. in an i. fashion. [L.].

IRRECLAIMABLE [i-ri-klā'ma-bl], adj. impossible to be reclaimed.

IRRECONCILABLE [i-re-kon-sī'la-bl], adj. not able to be reconciled; hopelessly incompatible.

IRRECOVERABLE [i-ri-ku've-ra-bl], adj. impossible to recover or be recovered, beyond recovery.

IRREDEEMABLE [i-ri-dē'ma-bl], adj. not to be redeemed; not to be converted into cash.

IRREDENTISM [i-ri-den'tizm], n. political belief which demands the inclusion in the state of all fellow-countrymen subject to foreign control.

IRREDENTIST (1) [i-ri-den'tist], n. believer in irredentism. IRREDENTIST (2), adj. of, or pertaining to, irredentism or irredentists. [It.].

IRREDUCIBLE [i-ri-dyōō'si-bl], adj. not to be reduced, already brought to the lowest possible level, form or degree.

IRREFRAGABLE [i-ri-fra'ga-bl], adj. beyond dispute, unanswerable, irrefutable. [L.].

IRREFRANGIBLE [i-ri-fran'ji-bl], adj. inviolable, unbreakable.

IRREFUTABLE [i-re'fyōō-ta-bl, i-ri-fyōō'ta-bl], adj. impossible to refute. IRREFUTABLY, adv. beyond refutation.

IRREGULAR (1) [i-re'gyōō-ler], adj. not regular; unsymmetrical, not evenly ordered; out of form and order; not conforming to rule or general type; contrary to normal practice or standards; unlawful. IRREGULAR (2), n. member of a loosely organized, casually disciplined body of troops outside the regular army. IRREGULARLY, adv. in i. fashion. [MedL.].

IRREGULARITY [i-re-gyōō-la'ri-ti], n. state of being irregular; that which is irregular. [MedL.].

IRRELEVANCE, IRRELEVANCY [i-re'li-vans(-i)], n. state of being irrelevant; that which is irrelevant.

IRRELEVANT [i-re'li-vant], adj. not relevant, inapplicable, beside the point. IRRELEVANTLY, adv. in i. fashion.

IRRELIGION [i-ri-li'jn], n. contempt of religion, want of reverence.

IRRELIGIOUS [i-ri-li'jŏŏs], adj. without or despising religion; impious. IRRELIGIOUSLY, adv. in i. fashion. [L.].

IRREMEDIABLE [i-ri-mē'di-a-bl], adj. impossible to be remedied or repaired. [L.].

IRREMOVABLE [i-ri-mōō'va-bl], adj. impossible to be removed.

IRREPARABLE [i-re'pa-ra-bl], adj. impossible to be rectified or repaired. IRREPARABLY, adv. in i. fashion. [L.].

IRREPLACEABLE [i-ri-plā'sa-bl], adj. impossible to replace.

IRREPRESSIBLE [i-ri-pre'si-bl], adj. impossible to repress, beyond control. IRREPRESSIBLY, adv. in i. fashion.

IRREPROACHABLE [i-ri-prō'cha-bl], adj. blameless, beyond reproach. IRREPROACHABLY, adv. in i. fashion.

IRRESISTIBLE [i-ri-zis'ti-bl], adj. impossible to be resisted, overpowering; irrefutable. IRRESISTIBLY, adv. in i fashion.

IRRESOLUTE [i-re'zŏ-lyŏŏt], adj. lacking resolution, hesitant, vacillating. IRRESOLUTELY, adv. in i. fashion.

IRRESOLUTION [i-re-zŏ-lyŏŏ'shn], n. irresoluteness; irresolute state of mind.

IRRESPECTIVE (1) [i-ri-spek'tiv], adj. without reference to, without taking account of, independent of. IRRESPECTIVE (2), adv. irrespectively. IRRESPECTIVELY, adv. without regard to, without account of.

IRRESPONSIBLE [i-ri-spon'si-bl], adj. not responsible; having no sense of responsibility or no capacity for bearing responsibility, unreliable. IRRESPONSIBLY, adv. in i. fashion.

IRRESPONSIVE [i-ri-spon'siv], adj. not responsive; not responding.

IRRETRIEVABLE [i-ri-trē'va-bl], adj. impossible to retrieve, beyond recovery; irremediable. IRRETRIEVABLY, adv. in i. fashion.

IRREVERENCE [i-re've-rens], n. state of being irreverent; irreverent behaviour or speech. [L.].

IRREVERENT [i-re've-rent], adj. impious, unreligious, without reverence, disrespectful. IRREVERENTLY, adv. in i. fashion.

IRREVOCABLE [i-re'vo-ka-bl], adj. beyond recall, unalterable. IRREVOCABLY, adv. in i. fashion. [L.].

IRRIGATE [i'ri-gāt], v.t. to provide (land) with water, esp. by a system of artificial canals etc.; (med.) keep a wound moist by a constant spray of water; inject liquid into an orifice of the body. IRRIGATOR, n. one who, or that which, irrigates. [L.].

IRRIGATION [i-ri-gā'shn], n. act of irrigating; condition of being irrigated. [L.].

IRRITABILITY [i-ri-ta-bi'li-ti], n. state of being irritable.

IRRITABLE [i'ri-ta-bl], adj. easily irritated, nervously petulant; inflamed, excited. IRRITABLY, adv. in i. fashion. [L.].

IRRITANT (1) [i'ri-tant], adj. producing irritation. IRRITANT (2), n. an i. substance, action or circumstance. [L.].

IRRITATE [i'ri-tāt], v.t. to anger, provoke; exasperate by small annoyances; cause morbid itching or excitement in a part of the body; (physiol.) stimulate to activity. IRRITATIVE, adj. producing, marked by, irritation. [L.].

IRRITATING [i'ri-tā-ting], adj. that irritates; annoying. IRRITATINGLY, adv. in i. fashion.

IRRITATION [i-ri-tā'shn], n. act of irritating; state of being irritated; an itching; (fig.) state of mind in which small things excite and infuriate; that which irritates. [L.].

IRRUPTION [i-rup'shn], n. a violent bursting in, overwhelming invasion. [L.].

IRRUPTIVE [i-rup'tiv], adj. rushing in, bursting upon.

IS [iz], 3rd person sg. pres. ind. of BE.

ISHMAELITE [ish'māl-īt], n. social outcast, hater of humanity. [Ishmael, Gen. XVI, 11].

ISINGLASS [ī'sing-glahs], n. gelatinous substance prepared from the bladders and viscera of certain fishes, and used in the manufacture of glues and jellies. [ODu.].

ISLAM [iz'lahm], n. the religion of Mohammed; the countries under Mohammedan rule or religion. ISLAMIC, ISLAMITIC [iz-lah'mik, iz-lah-mi'tik], adj. relating to I. or Islamism. [Arab.].

ISLAND (1) [ī'land], n. piece of land completely surrounded by water; anything, esp. cellular tissue, completely isolated; refuge for pedestrians in the middle of a roadway. ISLAND (2), pertaining

The accent ' after a syllable = stress (u-pon'). The mark ¯ over a vowel = length (ā in made; ō in bone).

to islands, found on, living on, an i.   ISLAND (3), *v.t.* to make into an i., isolate; set with islands.   [OE.].

ISLANDER [I'lan-der], *n.* one who inhabits an island.

ISLE [Il], *n.* (*poet.*) island.

ISLET [I'let], *n.* little island.

ISM [izm], *n.* theory, science, *esp.* one supposed to be difficult, impractical or eccentric.   [Gk.].

ISO-, *pref.* equal.   [Gk.].

ISOBAR [I'sō-bah(r)], *n.* line on a map joining places of similar barometric pressure.   ISOBARIC [I-sō-ba'-rik], *adj.* containing, relating to, isobars.   [Gk.].

ISOCLINAL [I-sō-klī'nal], *adj.* pertaining to places where the magnetic needle has similar inclination.   [Gk.].

ISOLATE [I'sō-lāt], *v.t.* to set apart, make separate; (*chem.*) separate an element from a compound; (*med.*) put into quarantine, remove (an infectious case) from contact with others; (*elect.*) insulate.   [It.].

ISOLATION [I-sō-lā'shn], *n.* state of being isolated; act of isolating.

ISOLATIONISM [I-sō-lā'shn-izm], *n.* policy of avoiding political commitments to foreign countries.

ISOLATIONIST [I-sō-lā'shn-ist], *n. and adj.* (characteristic of) one who believes in isolationism.

ISOMERIC [I-sō-me'rik], *adj.* (*chem.*) (of compounds) having similar elements in similar proportion but possessing different properties.   [Gk.].

ISOSCELES [I-so'si-lēz], *adj.* (*geom.*) (of a triangle) having two equal sides.   [Gk.].

ISOTHERM [I'sō-therm], *n.* line on a map joining places of the same thermometer readings.   ISOTHERMAL [I-sō-thur'mal], *adj.* of equal heat.   [Gk.].

ISOTOPE [I'sō-tōp], *n.* (*chem.*) one of two or more states of an element, chemically identical, but differing in their atomic weight.   [Gk.].

ISRAELITE [iz'rāl-īt], *n.* inhabitant of Biblical Israel; Jew, *esp.* an orthodox Jew.   [Heb.].

ISSUE (1) [i'syōō], *n.* act of issuing; that which is issued or which issues; flow, bursting out; place or time of flowing; publications sent out at one particular time; children; point arising from a situation, depending upon certain events; main point of an argument; question, problem; result, outcome; **at i.**, in dispute; **to join i. with**, to express disagreement with.   ISSUE (2), *v.t. and i.* to give or send out, publish, circulate, distribute; flow from, emerge; be derived or descended from; result in; (*coll.*) supply with.   [OFr.].

ISSUELESS [i'syōō-les], *adj.* without children.

-IST, *suff.* implying adherence to a particular doctrine or the practice of a particular habit.

ISTHMIAN [is(th)'mi-an], *adj.* relating to an isthmus.

ISTHMUS [is(th)'mus], *n.* strip of land linking two

continental masses or a peninsula with the mainland; narrow strip joining two larger parts.   [Gk.].

IT (1) [it], *pron.* 3rd person *sg.* neut., *used to signify* anything impersonal or non-human.   IT (2), *n.* the ideal, acme of perfection; (*U.S.*) (*slang*) personal charm.   [OE.].

IT (3), *n.* (*coll.*) Italian vermouth.   [IT(ALIAN)].

ITALIANATE [i-ta'lya-nāt], *adj.* affecting the manners and culture of Italy.

ITALIC [i-ta'lik], *adj.* relating to ancient Italy; **i. type**, sloping type first used in Venice.   [L.].

ITALICIZE [i-ta'li-sīz], *v.t.* to emphasize by putting into italic type.

ITALICS [i-ta'liks], *n.*(*pl.*) italic type or characters.

ITALO-, *pref.* Italian.   [L.].

ITCH (1) [ich], *n.* irritation of the skin, tickling; (*fig.*) irrepressible urge to do something; (*med.*) contagious skin disease accompanied by violent irritation.   ITCH (2), *v.i.* to feel a violent skin irritation; (*fig.*) experience an i.; (*med.*) have the i.   ITCHY, *adj.* itching, feeling irritation.   [OE.].

ITEM (1) [I'tem], *n.* a particular article or detail of a list; a particular selected from many; a part of a programme, agenda etc.   ITEM (2), *adv.* also, likewise.   [L.].

ITEMIZE [I'te-mīz], *v.t.* to set out in items; instance item by item.

ITERATE [i'te-rāt], *v.t.* to repeat, say again.   [L.].

ITERATION [i-te-rā'shn], *n.* repetition; act of repeating; something repeated.   [L.].

ITERATIVE [i'te-ra-tiv], *adj.* repetitive; (*gram.*) indicating repetition of an action.

ITINERA(N)CY [i-ti'ne-ra(n)-si], *n.* state of being itinerant.

ITINERANT (1) [i-ti'ne-rant], *adj.* moving from place to place; wandering without fixed headquarters.   ITINERANT (2), *n.* one who wanders from place to place, a tramp.   [L.].

ITINERARY (1) [i-ti'ne-ra-ri], *n.* route, way of going from place to place; an account of this, guide book.   ITINERARY (2), *adj.* relating to a journey.   [L.].

ITINERATE [i-ti'ne-rāt], *v.i.* to wander from place to place without fixed abode.   [L.].

ITS [its], *pron. possessive of* IT (1).

ITSELF [it-self'], *pron. emphatic and reflexive form of* IT (1).

IVIED [I'vid], *adj.* covered with ivy.

IVORY (1) [I've-ri], *n.* hard, white, bony substance composing the tusks of the elephant, walrus and narwhal; whitish colour; (*pl.*) (*slang*) teeth; pianokeys.   IVORY (2), *adj.* made of i.; of an i. colour.   [OFr.].

IVY [I'vi], *n.* a dark green glossy-leaved, climbing, evergreen plant, *Hedera Helix*.   [OE.].

J

J [jā], tenth letter in the English alphabet.

JAB (1) [jab], *v.t.* to poke roughly, stab.   JAB (2), *n.* a poke, sharp thrust, stab.   [Unkn.].

JABBER (1) [ja'ber], *v.t. and i.* to utter rapidly or indistinctly; talk rapidly, chatter.   JABBER (2), *n.* a stream of rapid, semi-intelligible talk, voluble chatter.   [Imitative].

JABOT [zha'bō], *n.* frill on the front of a bodice or shirt.   [Fr.].

JACARANDA [ja-ka-ran'dah], *n.* genus of South American hardwood trees with scented wood.   [Braz.].

JACINTH [ja'sinth, jā'sinth], *n.* transparent reddish-orange silicate of zirconium used as a semi-precious stone.   [OFr. from Gk.].

JACK (1) [jak], *n.* rank and file sailor, jack tar; man of the common people; knave in a suit of cards; contrivance for turning a spit; apparatus for lifting heavy weights, *esp.* for raising the wheel of a motor-car off the ground; small white ball used in the game of bowls; (*naut.*) flagstaff in the bows of a ship; flag flown from this staff; **before you can say J. Robinson**, in the fraction of a second; **cheap-j.**, hawker, pedlar; **every man j.**, the whole company; **j.-o'-lantern**, will-o'-the-wisp; **j. of all trades**, person

who can cope with any kind of practical job; **j.-in-the-box**, child's toy consisting of a doll on a spring which jumps out of a box when the lid is raised; **J. Frost**, personification of frost; **Union J.**, national flag of the United Kingdom of Great Britain and Northern Ireland.   JACK (2), *v.t.* to lift with a j.   [ME., *dim. of* JOHN].

JACKAL [ja'kawl], *n.* animal resembling a dog, with the colour and bushy tail of a fox; (*fig.*) a drudge who prepares for the tasks of other menials.   [Pers.].

JACKANAPES [ja'ka-nāps], *n.* monkey; mischievous boy; conceited fop.   [Unkn.].

JACKAROO [ja'ka-rōō], *n.* (*slang*) in the Australian bush, a novice or new hand.   [JACK (1) and (KANG)AROO].

JACKASS [ja'kas], *n.* male ass or donkey; blockhead, dolt; **laughing j.**, laughing kingfisher found in Australia.   [JACK (1) and ASS].

JACK-BOOT [jak'bōōt], *n.* large boot which extends above the knees.

JACKDAW [jak'daw], *n.* a British bird, the daw.   [JACK (1) and DAW].

JACKET (1) [ja'kit], *n.* short coat; outer covering, with sleeves, to protect the torso; outer covering round a pipe, boiler etc.; coat of an animal; skin of a potato; loose paper wrapper to protect a book from dust; any similar covering. JACKET (2), *v.t.* to cover with a j. [OFr.].

JACK-IN-OFFICE [jak-in-o'fis], *n.* overbearing minor official.

JACK-KNIFE [jak'nif], *n.* large clasp-knife for the pocket.

JACKPOT [jak'pot], *n.* pool at the card game of poker.

JACK-SCREW [jak'skrōō], *n.* lifting jack operated by a screw. [JACK (1) and SCREW].

JACK TAR [jak-tah(r)'], *n.* (*coll.*) sailor of the Royal Navy.

JACOBEAN [ja-kō-bē'an], *adj.* belonging or relating to the reign of James I. [L.].

JACOBIN [ja'kō-bin], *n.* monk of the order of St. Dominic; member of a revolutionary party in the French Revolution which met in a Jacobin convent. JACOBINISM, *n.* J. principles based on belief in the necessity of overthrowing the established government by force. [MedL.].

JACOBITE [ja'kō-bit], *n.* follower of James II after his dethronement; adherent of the party believing in the rightness of the cause of his descendants in claiming the throne of England. JACOBITICAL [ja-kō-bi'ti-kal], *adj.* pertaining to the Jacobites or their principles. JACOBITISM [ja'kō-bit-izm], *n.* political principles of the Jacobites. [L.].

JACOB'S LADDER [jā-kobz-la'der], *n.* plant having blue flowers; (*naut.*) rope ladder with wooden steps for climbing rigging.

JACONET [ja'ko-net], *n.* light, soft, open-textured muslin. [Hind.].

JADE (1) [jād], *n.* badly bred, aged or worn-out horse; unkempt woman, old before her time; (*playfully*) hussy, wench. JADE (2), *v.t. and i.* to make exhausted by overwork; become tired and weary. [Unkn.].

JADE (3), *n.* nephrite, the green mineral silicate of calcium and magnesium, containing a trace of iron and used for carving ornaments. [Span.].

JAFFA [ja'fah], *adj.* relating to, grown in, Jaffa, *esp.* of a sweet, large variety of orange. [*Jaffa*, Israel].

JAG (1) [jag], *n.* projection with a sharp, ragged edge; notch, tooth; slit or tear in material; (*slang*) binge. JAG (2) (*pres.pt.* **JAGGING**, *pret. and p.pt.* **JAGGED**), *v.t.* to cut, tear or slit so that a ragged edge is left. [Unkn.].

JAGGED [ja'gid], *adj.* having an uneven edge, notched.

JAGUAR [ja'gyōō-ah(r)], *n.* largest of the American carnivores, belonging to the cat family. [Braz.].

JAH [jah, yah], *n.* Jehovah. [Heb.].

JAIL, GAOL [jāl], *n.* building for the detention and confinement of people convicted of crime, prison; **j. fever**, typhus fever. [OFr.].

JAILBIRD [jāl'berd], *n.* prisoner; person who has been in prison, *esp.* more than once. [JAIL and BIRD].

JAILER, see GAOLER.

JAIN [jān, jīn], *n.* believer in Jainism.

JAINISM [jā'nizm, jī'nizm], *n.* Indian religion based on the belief that all matter is animated by soul. [Skr.].

JALAP [ja'lap], *n.* root of a Mexican plant used as a cathartic. [*Xalapa*, Mexico].

JALOUSIE [zha'lōō-zē], *n.* blind of sloping wooden slats; Venetian blind. [Fr.].

JAM (1) [jam], *n.* conserve of fruits boiled with sugar and left to stand in jars till firm and cold. [Uncert.].

JAM (2), *v.t. and i.* to press, crowd, squeeze tight into a small space; form or force into a compact mass or body; block movement; become wedged; (*radio*) make a transmission unintelligible by transmitting on the same wavelength. JAM (3), *n.* state of being squeezed together; that which is squeezed together, forcibly compact mass or body; crush; (*slang*) difficult position. [~CHAMP].

JAMB [jam], *n.* sidepiece or post of a door or fireplace. [Fr.].

JAMBOK [sham'bok], *n.* strip of hide used as a whip in South Africa. [Du.].

JAMBOREE [jam-be-rē'], *n.* jolly gathering, spree, great concourse of boy scouts. [Uncert.].

JAMMING [ja'ming], *n.* (*radio*) interference with reception by outside signals on the same wavelength.

JAMMY [ja'mi], *adj.* covered with jam, sticky like jam. [JAM (1)].

JANGLE (1) [jang'gl], *v.t. and i.* to make a noise with the different sounds out of tune, particularly of bells ringing; make a harsh noise; talk all at once noisily. JANGLE (2), *n.* noise made by discordant sounds, clash of noises. JANGLING, *n.* noisy dispute; wrangling. [OFr.].

JANISSARY, JANIZARY [ja'ni-sāer-i], *n.* soldier of

the Turkish infantry formerly a bodyguard of the Sultan. [Turk.].

JANITOR [ja'ni-ter], *n.* doorkeeper, porter. [L.].

JANSENISM [jan'se-nizm], *n.* doctrine of the perverseness of man's natural will in opposition to the R.C. authorities. JANSENIST, *n.* supporter of J. [*Jansen*, Bishop of Ypres].

JANUARY [ja'nyōō-a-ri], *n.* first month of the year according to the present computation. [L.].

JANUS [jā'nus], *n.* ancient Roman god credited with the faculty of looking both ways, into the future and the past, and represented as having two faces. [L.].

JAPAN (1) [ja-pan'], *n.* hard varnish or lacquer used to cover and decorate woodwork by the Japanese; work in this varnish. JAPAN (2), *adj.* relating to J. JAPAN (3) (*pres.pt.* **JAPANNING**, *pret. and p.pt.* **JAPANNED**), *v.t.* to cover with a hard coat of black varnish, lacquer. [Chin.].

JAPE (1) [jāp], *v.i.* to joke, jest. JAPE (2), *n.* comic trick; joke, jest. [OFr.].

JAPONICA [ja-po'ni-kah], *n.* Japanese quince. [MdL.].

JAR (1) [jah(r)], *n.* glass or earthenware pot without a spout, generally cylindrical and upright. [Arab.].

JAR (2) (*pres.pt.* **jarring**, *pret. and p.pt.* **jarred**), *v.i. and i.* to shake, cause to tremble by sharp impact, upset the functional equilibrium of a person, body or mechanism; cause mental disturbance; give out a discordant sound; be a cause of contention; work as an irritant on a person's nerves. JAR (3), *n.* harsh, discordant sound, discord of rattling sounds; sudden shock and its after effects on the nerves caused by collision of two bodies; physical impact causing shock; unexpected obstruction to accepted ideas; (*fig.*) contention. [Uncert.].

JARDINIERE, jardinière [zhah-di-nyāer'], *n.* ornamental flower stand. [Fr.]

JARGON [jah'gon], *n.* technical terminology unintelligible to the inexpert reader or listener; muddled incantatory speech, gibberish; wordy and ill-constructed language heavily laden with clichés. [OFr.].

JARGONELLE [jah-go-nel'], *n.* an early-ripening variety of pear. [Fr.].

JARRING [jah'ring], *adj.* harshly discordant; disturbing to the nerves.

JASMINE, JESSAMINE [jaz'min], *n.* (*bot.*) climbing shrub with delicate and fragrant white or yellow flowers. [Pers.].

JASPER [jas'per], *n.* opaque variety of quartz found in different colours. [Gk.].

JAUNDICE [jawn'dis], *n.* disease due to obstruction of bile and a disordered liver characterized by yellow pigment forming in the whites of the eyes and under the skin; (*fig.*) jealousy. JAUNDICE (2), *v.t.* to cause to become jealous, distort the power of judgment of, owing to ill-temper, envy etc. [OFr from L.].

JAUNT (1) [jawnt], *n.* trip taken for pleasure, short journey or excursion. JAUNT (2), *v.i.* to take a j., go for a day's outing. [Uncert.].

JAUNTING-CAR [jawn'ting-kah(r)], *n.* low light car with seats back to back at right angles to the axle, used in Ireland.

JAUNTY [jawn'ti], *adj.* expressing or feeling free and easy confidence, sprightly in bearing. JAUNTILY, *adv.* in a j. manner. [Fr.].

JAVANESE [jah-vah-nēz'], *adj.* relating to Java. JAVANESE (2), *n.* a native of Java, or the language.

JAVELIN [ja've-lin], *n.* short light spear with a barbed head, dart. [Fr.].

JAW (1) [jaw], *n.* the bones in which the teeth are fixed; mouth; anything like the jaw, such as a crushing or gripping device in machinery; (*pl.*) the sides of a narrow valley, pass etc.; (*slang*) talk, continuous talking; (*slang*) formal and tedious reproof. JAW (2), *v.t. and i.* (*slang*) to reprove, lecture; talk rapidly, be garrulous. [Uncert.].

JAWBONE [jaw'bōn], *n.* one of the bones of the jaw forming the framework of the mouth.

JAY [jā], *n.* chattering bird of the crow family. [OFr. from MedL.].

JAY-WALKER [jā'waw-ker], *n.* (*coll., orig. U.S.*) pedestrian who steps carelessly into the way of traffic.

JAZZ (1) [jaz], *n.* syncopated ragtime music derived from negro spirituals and developed in a popular form as an accompaniment for dancing during the war of 1914-18. JAZZ (2), *adj.* relating to, consisting of, j; (of a pattern) jumbled and brightly coloured in contrasting hues. JAZZ (3), *v.t.* to dance to j. music; transcribe into a syncopated form. JAZZY,

---

The accent ' after a syllable = stress (u-pon'). The mark ⁻ over a vowel = length (ā in made; ō in bone).

adj. j.; resembling, having the characteristics of, j. [U.S., origin doubtful].

JEALOUS [je'lŏŏs], *adj.* experiencing feelings of envy and enmity towards another person who is believed to be better off in some way; afraid of or hostile to a rival in love or friendship; envious; eagerly vigilant, solicitous. JEALOUSLY, *adv.* in a j. manner, with jealousy. [OFr. from LL.].

JEALOUSY [je'lŏŏ-si], *n.* emotional condition aroused by the envious and hostile recognition of another's success in matters in which personal success is desired; eager vigilance. [OFr.].

JEAN [jēn], *n.* twilled cotton cloth; (*pl.*) overalls, a kind of slacks. [ME.].

JEEP [jēp], *n.* small high-powered open military car. [G.P. initials of *general purpose* car].

JEER (1) [jēr], *v.t. and i.* to make rude and contemptuous remarks, sneer at someone, mock derisively. JEER (2), *n.* sneering remark; derision, mockery. [Unkn.].

JEHAD, JIHAD [ji-hahd'], *n.* holy war waged by Mohammedans against unbelievers; (*fig.*) crusade for or against a doctrine. [Arab.].

JEHOVAH [ji-hō'vah], *n.* the God of Israel, Yahweh. [Heb.].

JEHU [jē'hyŏŏ], *n.* skilful or reckless driver. [2 Kings ix. 20].

JEJUNE [ji-jyŏŏn'], *adj.* empty, void of interest; meagre, barren. [L.].

JEJUNUM [ji-jŏŏ'num], *n.* (*anat.*) small intestine between the duodenum and the ileum. [*Prec.*].

JELL [jel], *v.i.* (of jelly) to set.

JELLIED [je'lid], *adj.* brought to the consistency of jelly; thickened with jelly; prepared in or with jelly.

JELLY [je'li], *n.* any substance, but *esp.* foodstuff, in a semi-liquid elastic state, due to the separation from solution of non-crystalline substances such as gelatine and starch. [~L.].

JELLYFISH [je'li-fish], *n.* free-swimming polyp, medusa or similar animal, resembling a jelly in consistency and transparency.

JEMMY, JIMMY [je'mi], *n.* small crowbar used by burglars. [*Var. of James*].

JENNET, GENET, GENNET [je'nit], *n.* small Spanish horse. [OFr.].

JENNY [je'ni], *n.* machine for spinning which takes a number of threads simultaneously. [*Jenny*, woman's name].

JEOPARDIZE [je'per-diz], *v.t.* to expose to jeopardy.

JEOPARDY [je'per-di], *n.* exposure to loss or injury, peril, danger. [OFr.].

JERBOA [jer-bō'ah], *n.* small African rodent having long hind legs. [Arab.].

JEREMIAD [je-ri-mi'ad], *n.* lamentation or complaining tirade. [*Jeremiah*, Hebrew prophet].

JERFALCON, see GERFALCON.

JERK (1) [jurk], *n.* sharp quick pull or tug, sudden brief movement; brief sharp contraction of a muscle, nervous twitch; physical jerks, (*slang*) gymnastics, physical training. JERK (2), *v.t. and i.* to perform any action with a j., give a sudden sharp pull, twitch or jolt to; progress in jolts and jerks. [Unkn.].

JERKIN [jur'kin], *n.* man's leather jacket; short waistcoat cut close to the body. [Uncert.].

JERKY [jur'ki], *adj.* characterized by jerks.

JEROBOAM [je-ro-bō'am], *n.* large bottle for holding wine; large bottle of champagne. [Heb. I Kings xi. 28, xiv. 16].

JERRY-BUILDER [je'ri-bil-der], *n.* builder of cheap, insubstantial houses with poor material.

JERSEY [jur'zi], *n.* close-fitting, knitted jumper; Jersey cow. [Isle of *Jersey*].

JERUSALEM ARTICHOKE [je-rŏŏ-sa-lem-ah'ti-chōk], *n.* a sunflower or its edible root. [It.].

JESS [jes], *n.* short strap round the legs of a hawk, whereby it is held and let fly. [OFr.].

JESSAMINE, see JASMINE.

JEST (1) [jest], *n.* a joke; banter; act intended to excite laughter; in j., not in earnest. JEST (2), *v.i.* to make jokes; not to be in earnest. JESTINGLY, *adv.* in jest.

JESTER [jes'ter], *n.* person who jests; attendant in absurd livery kept for making jests.

JESUIT [je'zyŏŏ-it], *n.* member of the Society of Jesus, founded by Ignatius Loyola in 1534; (*coll.*) crafty person, casuist; J's bark, cinchona. [Fr.].

JESUITIC(AL) [je-zyŏŏ-i'tik(-al)], *adj.* of or pertaining to the Jesuits; (*coll.*) casuistic, crafty.

JET (1) [jet], *n.* hard, black, velvety form of lignite; set of beads or ornaments of it; deep glossy black. JET (2), *adj.* of j., of a j.-black colour. [OFr.].

JET (3), *v.t. and i.* to emit in a single stream; spurt. JET (4), *n.* single column of liquid or gas forced from a narrow opening; any narrow passage through which liquid or gas is forced. [Fr.].

JET-BLACK [jet-blak'], *adj.* of the colour of jet, the deepest, purest black.

JET ENGINE [jet'en-jin], *n.* engine, used *esp.* in aircraft, which exerts power by the expulsion of jets of gas.

JET-PROPELLED [jet-prō-peld'], *adj.* driven by a jet engine.

JET PROPULSION [jet-prō-pul'shn], *n.* propulsion by jet engines.

JETSAM [jet'sam], *n.* goods thrown overboard to lighten a vessel in distress; such goods washed up; flotsam and j., (*fig.*) the waifs and strays of society. [~JETTISON].

JETTISON [je'ti-son], *v.t.* to throw goods overboard so as to lighten a ship; (*fig.*) forgo, abandon. [~AFr.].

JETTY (1) [je'ti], *n.* small pier; projection. [OFr.].

JETTY (2), *adj.* made of jet; jet-black.

JEW (1) [jŏŏ], *n.* member of the Hebrew branch of the Semitic race; Israelite; believer in the Hebrew religion;

JEWEL (1) [jŏŏ'el], *n.* ornament of dress, usually containing a precious stone; precious stone; anything highly valued or dear to one; j. box, case, casket or safe for holding jewels. JEWEL (2), *v.t.* to adorn or set with jewels; (*fig.*) decorate brightly. [AFr.].

JEWELLER [jŏŏ'el-er], *n.* one who deals in or sets jewels.

JEWELLERY, JEWELRY [jŏŏ'el-(e-)ri], *n.* jewels in general; the jewel trade.

JEWRY [jŏŏ'ri], *n.* land of the Jews; district inhabited by Jews in a town, ghetto; Jews collectively; the Jewish religion. [AFr.].

JEW'S HARP [jŏŏz'hahp], *n.* small harp-shaped musical instrument, with a spring or metal tongue, which, if placed between the teeth and struck by the fingers, gives modulated sounds.

JEZEBEL [je'ze-bel], *n.* name of the infamous queen of Ahab, king of Israel; vicious temptress; painted j., vicious woman who is artificially beautiful.

JIB (1) [jib], *n.* (*naut.*) foremost sail of a ship, extending from the outer end of the jib-boom; extended arm of a crane; flying j., sail sometimes set upon a boom rigged out beyond the jib-boom; cut of one's j., one's character and personal appearance, physique. JIB (2), *v.t. and i.* (of a j.) to swing over, pull round in tacking. JIB (3), *v.i.* to stop, (of a horse) shy; move restively back and forth; (*fig.*) to j. at, to hesitate at, raise objections to. [Uncert.].

JIB-BOOM [jib'bŏŏm], *n.* (*naut.*) the continuation of the bowsprit; flying j., boom extended beyond the j. by means of two boom irons.

JIBE [jib], *v.t. and i.* to taunt, sneer; (of sailing) to come to a standstill by turning into the wind, to luff. [~GIBE].

JIFFY [ji'fi], *n.* (*coll.*) a very short space of time. [Unkn.].

JIG (1) [jig], *n.* brisk dance or tune, usually in 6-8 time. JIG (2) (*pres.pt.* JIGGING, *pret. and p.pt.* JIGGED), *v.t.* to jerk; clean (ore) by shaking under water in a sieve; *v.i.* to dance a j., move jerkily. [Fr.].

JIG (3), *n.* one of a considerable variety of mechanical devices; guide for a machine or other tool in repetitive work. [Unkn.].

JIGGER (1) [ji'ger], *n.* one who dances jigs; potter's wheel; miner who cleans ore in a sieve; sieve for cleaning ore; machine for holding the cable when it is hauled into the ship by the windlass; small lug-sail on the mizzen-mast of a yawl etc.; (*slang*) rest for a billiard-cue; measure for liquor; (*coll.*) any small mechanical device; (*golf*) iron-headed club.

JIGGER (2), *n.* the sand-flea, minute insect which lays its eggs underneath the skin of men and animals. [~CHIGOE].

JIGGERED [ji'gerd], *adj.* suffering from the burrowing of the jigger; (*coll.*) dumbfounded; jumbled, spoilt.

JIGGERY-POKERY [ji-ge-ri-pō'ke-ri], *n.* (*coll.*) humbug, underhand scheming, wire-pulling. [Unkn.].

JIGGING [ji'ging], *n.* the dancing of jigs; (*mining*) process of sorting ore by passing it through a wire-bottomed sieve.

JIG-SAW [jig'saw], *n.* saw for cutting fretwork; j. puzzle, picture pasted on thin board and cut into interlocking pieces to be fitted into one another.

JIHAD, see JEHAD.

JILT (1) [jilt], *v.t.* to discard a lover. JILT (2), *n.*

ōō is pronounced as in food; ŏŏ as in hood; th as in think; ᴛʜ as in that; zh as in azure. ~ = related to.

young woman who dismisses her lover; coquette. [~*Jill*, girl's name].

JIM CROW [jim-krō'], *n. (U.S. coll.)* negro; tool for binding iron rails etc.; look-out appointed to watch for the approach of hostile aircraft. [*Jim, dim. of James*].

JIMMY, see JEMMY.

JINGLE (1) [jing-gl], *n.* a clinking sound, as of little bells or pieces of metal knocking together; that which jingles; little bell or rattle; correspondence of sound in rhymes. JINGLE (2), *v.t.* to cause to j.; *v.i.* to sound like a j. [Echoic].

JINGO [jing'gō], *n.* exclamation of surprise; anyone who advocates a warlike policy or brags of his country's readiness to fight. [Uncert.].

JINGOISM [jing'gō-izm], *n.* militaristic spirit. JINGOISTIC [jing-gō-is'tik], *adj.* expressing or resembling j.

JINK [jink], *n.* act of turning quickly; **high jinks,** merrymaking. [Symbolic].

JINN [jin], *n.* demon; sprite of Mohammedan demonology. [Arab.].

JITTERBUG (1) [ji'ter-bug], *n. (coll.)* one who dances to jazz music with spasmodic energy; *(coll.)* an alarmist. JITTERBUG (2), *v.i. (slang)* to dance wildly.

JITTERS [ji'terz], *n.(pl.) (U.S.)* shudderings; feeling of nervous alarm.

JITTERY [ji'te-ri], *adj.* panicky; shaking.

JIU-JITSU, see JU-JITSU.

JOB (1) [job], *n.* piece of work; anything to be done; undertaking professedly for the public good but really for one's own; occupation, profession, employment, post; **to make a good j. of it,** to do a thing well; **j. lots,** odd lots; odd j., isolated piece of work; **a good j.,** fortunate; **to be on the j.,** *(coll.)* to be doing one's best, be very busy. JOB (2), *v.t. (pres.pt.* JOBBING, *pret. and p.pt.* JOBBED), to use personal influence in public appointments; hire out; act as broker in; *v.i.* to undertake small pieces of work, work casually; act as a small broker; let or hire. [Unkn.].

JOBBER [jo'ber], *n.* one who does odd jobs; dealer in stock-exchange securities; one who uses a public office for private gain. JOBBERY, *n.* intriguing for private profit, *esp.* in public transactions.

JOBMASTER [job'mah-ster], *n.* person who lets out horses and carriages; livery-stable keeper.

JOB'S COMFORTER [jōbz-kum'fer-ter], *n.* friend whose commiserations serve only to augment one's grief. [Job xvi. 2].

JOCKEY (1) [jo'ki], *n.* the rider of a racehorse; man trained for that purpose; **J. Club,** club of owners which controls horseracing. JOCKEY (2), *v.t. and i.* to use unfair means, outwit; jostle by riding against one; **to j. (a person) into doing something,** to persuade him into it by manoeuvres; **to j. for position,** to try to obtain an advantage by preliminary manoeuvring. [*Jock,* Scots name].

JOCOSE [jo-kōs'], *adj.* given to joking; facetious. [L.].

JOCULAR [jo'kyoo-ler], *adj.* given to joking; waggish; merry; bantering. JOCULARITY [jo-kyoo-la'ri-ti], *n.* merriment, fun, waggishness. JOCULARLY, *adv.* in a j. fashion. [L.].

JOCUND [jo'kund], *adj.* gay, sportive, light-hearted, sprightly. JOCUNDITY [jo-kun'di-ti], *n.* condition of being j. JOCUNDLY, *adv.* in a j. fashion. [LL.].

JODHPURS [jod'perz], *n.(pl.)* tight-legged riding breeches which reach to the ankles [*Jodhpur,* state in India].

JOG (1) *(pres.pt.* jogging, *pret. and p.pt.* jogged) [jog], *v.t.* to give a slight push to, nudge; *(fig.)* arouse the attention, remind; *v.i.* to ride or move at a slow trot; proceed slowly; **to j. along,** *(fig.)* to continue steadily with one's way of life or occupation. JOG (2), *n.* slight, sudden push; nudge. [Symbolic].

JOGGLE (1) [jo'gl], *v.t.* to jolt, jar, shake; give a sudden slight push to; *v.i.* to shake, move in jolts. JOGGLE (2), *n.* a jolt. [~JOG].

JOGGLE (3), *n. (building, carp.)* notch in a joint; *(eng.)* kink or set in sheet metal. JOGGLE (4), *v.t.* to join by the use of a j. [Uncert.].

JOG-TROT (1) [jog'trot], *n.* a slow regular pace; *(fig.)* slow, monotonous but steady progress. JOG-TROT (2), *adj.* at a j. pace; *(fig.)* monotonously regular; humdrum.

JOHANNINE [jō-ha'nīn], *adj.* pertaining to St. John.

JOHANNISBERGER [jō-ha'nis-ber-ger], *n.* hock from Johannisberg on the Rhine.

JOHN [jon], *n.* man's name; **J. Barleycorn,** malt liquor; **J. Bull,** the typical Englishman; **J. Doe,** fictitious character in legal parlance; **J. dory,** the dory; **J. Collins,** drink of gin, lemon and soda. [OFr., L., Heb.].

JOIE DE VIVRE [zhwa-de-vēvr'], *n.* gusto; zest. [Fr.].

JOIN (1) [join], *v.t.* to fasten together; connect along a whole line of juxtaposition; unite; adjoin; *(fig.)* combine; unite oneself with; *v.i.* to be in contact, combine; **to j. battle,** to begin fighting, fight; **to j. forces with,** to unite with; **to j. up,** to enlist JOIN (2), *n.* act of joining; junction, joint, seam. [Fr. from L.].

JOINER (1) [joi'ner], *n.* one who, that which, joins; craftsman doing woodwork of a lighter and more decorative kind than that of a carpenter. JOINER (2), *v.i.* to practise joinery.

JOINERY [joi'ne-ri], *n.* craft or product of a joiner; fine woodwork.

JOINT (1) [joint], *n.* place where two or more things join; any constituent part of a jointed whole; juncture which admits of motion of the parts as in a body or in a machine; hinge; one of the parts into which a butcher divides a carcase for cooking purposes; *(U.S. slang)* low drinking house; any building; **out of j.,** (of a bone) dislocated; (of the times) unhappy, disorderly; **to put one's nose out of j.,** to supplant one in favour of another, outshine one. JOINT (2), *adj.* shared by two or more. JOINT (3), *v.t.* to provide with joints; unite by joints; divide a carcase into joints; form the edges of boards so that they may fit closely together; fit closely. [OFr.].

JOINTED [join'tid], *adj.* with joints, not in a continuous, unbroken line. JOINTEDLY, *adv.* connectedly.

JOINTER [join'ter], *n.* plane used by carpenters in making joints; metal bar for joining stones; mason's tool used in jointing.

JOINTLY [joint'li], *adv.* together; unitedly; in concert; in conjunction.

JOINTRESS [joint'res], *n.* woman who holds a jointure.

JOINT-STOCK [joint-stok'], *n. (comm.)* stock contributed by a number of people in company; **j. company, j. bank,** company or bank where the stock is divided into shares which are transferable by each owner without the consent of the other holders.

JOINTURE [join'tyoor], *n. (leg.)* estate settled on a married woman for her lifetime. [Fr.].

JOIST [joist], *n.* one of the parallel timbers to which the boards of a floor or the laths of a ceiling are fastened. [OFr.].

JOKE (1) [jōk], *n.* funny, humorous or witty phrase, anecdote or trick; jest; something not serious or in earnest; any thing or person meriting laughter; **no j.,** a serious matter; **practical j.,** trick played on a person so as to raise a laugh or to tease; **to crack a j.,** to make a joke. JOKE (2), *v.i.* to make jokes; jest, make fun. JOKINGLY, *adv.* in a joking manner. [L.].

JOKER [jō'ker], *n.* one who jokes; fifty-third card in a pack used in some games.

JOLLITY [jo'li-ti], *n.* condition of being jolly; merriment; joviality; revelry. [OFr.].

JOLLY (1) [jo'li], *adj.* cheerful, gay; full of life and mirth; expressing or inspiring mirth; plump and cheerful in appearance; fond of jollity; *(coll.)* slightly drunk; enjoyable, agreeable. JOLLY (2), *adv.* in a j. fashion, merrily; *(coll.)* extremely, very. [OFr.].

JOLLY-BOAT [jo'li-bōt], *n. (naut.)* small ship's boat. [Uncert.].

JOLT (1) [jōlt], *v.t.* to shake with sudden jerks, jar, jog; *v.i.* to move along bumping. JOLT (2), *n.* sudden jerk or jar; *(fig.)* shock, jerk to the mind. [Unkn.].

JONAH [jō'nah], *n.* an unlucky person; one who brings bad luck. [The prophet *Jonah*].

JONQUIL [jon'kwil], *n.* variety of narcissus. [Fr. ~L.].

JORAM, see JORUM.

JORDAN ALMOND [jaw-dan-ah'mond], *n.* fine variety of cultivated almond. [Fr. *jardin* garden and ALMOND].

JORUM, JORAM [jaw'rum], *n.* large drinking vessel; bowl of drink; large quantity; dose. [King *Joram,* 2 Kings viii. 16].

JOSS [jos], *n.* Chinese idol. JOSS-HOUSE, Chinese temple. JOSS-STICK, odoriferous stick which the Chinese burn before their idols. [Portug., L.].

JOSTLE (1) [jo'sl], *v.t. and i.* to push against, elbow, hustle. JOSTLE (2), n. a rough push, such as one gets in a crowd; jog. [~JOUST].

JOT (1) [jot], n. an iota, negligible quantity. JOT (2), v.t. to make a written note of. JOTTING, n. brief note. [FOTA].

JOURNAL [jur'nal], n. daily record of events; diary, day-book; book in which this record is kept; (book-keeping) book in which each transaction is referred to the relevant accounts before posting to the ledger; daily newspaper; periodical or magazine; (mech.) neck of the bearing portion of the shaft in machinery; passage in the interior of a piece of machinery. [OFr. from L.].

JOURNALESE [jer-na-lēz'], n. style of writing such as occurs in inferior newspapers, highly coloured, loose and full of stock phrases. [Prec.].

JOURNALISM [jur'na-lizm], n. profession of a journalist; writing for newspapers or periodicals.

JOURNALIST [jur'na-list], n. one who writes for or edits a newspaper or periodical. JOURNALISTIC [jer-na-lis'tik], adj. pertaining to, or resembling, journals or journalism.

JOURNEY (1) [jur'ni], n. route or the traversing of a route from one place to another; excursion or expedition of some distance. JOURNEY (2), v.i. to travel, usually for some considerable distance. [OFr.].

JOURNEYMAN [jur'ni-man], n. artisan who has learnt his craft; (fig.) indifferent performer.

JOUST (1) [jowst], n. an encounter, properly a tournament. JOUST (2), v.i. to engage in a j., tilt. [OFr. from L.].

JOVE [jōv], n. name of Jupiter, supreme deity of the Romans; (coll.) by J.! (to register surprise, strong assertion etc.) good gracious! [L.].

JOVIAL [jō'vi-al], adj. cheerful, merry. JOVIALLY, adv. in a j. fashion. [Prec.].

JOVIALITY [jō-vi-a'li-ti], n. quality of being jovial; conviviality.

JOVIAN [jō'vi-an], adj. pertaining to Jove or to the planet Jupiter; godlike, majestic. [~JOVE].

JOWL [jowl], n. the cheek; jaw; heavy and pendulous chin; cheek by j., close together, head to head. [OE.].

JOY (1) [joi], n. feeling of quiet continuous exaltation, inward happiness; gladness, delight; object promoting such a feeling. JOY (2), v.t. to give happiness to, gladden; v.i. to rejoice, exult. [OFr. from L.].

JOYFUL [joi'fool], adj. full of joy, happy, glad; bringing joy. JOYFULLY, adv. in a j. fashion.

JOYLESS [joi'les], adj. miserable; causing misery.

JOYOUS [joi'ōos], adj. joyful, giving joy, gay. JOYOUSLY, adv. in a j. fashion.

JOY-RIDE (1) [joi'rīd], n. ride for pleasure, esp. in a motor vehicle appropriated without the owner's leave. JOY-RIDE (2), v.i. to go for a j.

JOYSTICK [joi'stik], n. control lever of an aircraft.

JUBATE [jōo'bāt], adj. (zool.) having a mane or fringe of hair. [L.].

JUBILANT [jōo'bi-lant], adj. rejoicing, uttering sounds of triumph, exultant. [~L.].

JUBILATION [jōo-bi-lā'shn], n. triumphant rejoicing; exultation. [L.].

JUBILEE [jōo'bi-lē], n. festival of emancipation among the Jews held every fifty years; (R.C.) year of plenary indulgence; fiftieth anniversary of a notable event; silver j., twenty-fifth anniversary; diamond j., sixtieth anniversary, esp. of Queen Victoria's commemoration in 1897. [L. ~Heb.].

JUDAEO-, pref. Jewish. [L.].

JUDAIC(AL) [jōo-dā'ik(-al)], adj. pertaining to the Jews, Jewish. [Gk.].

JUDAISM [jōo'dā-izm], n. Jewish religion and its practices. [Gk.].

JUDAS [jōo'das], n. an abominable traitor. JUDAS-TREE, a leguminous tree, traditionally the tree on which J. hanged himself. [Judas, disciple who betrayed Christ].

JUDGE (1) [juj], n. officer of the crown appointed to preside over a court of justice and to hear and decide causes; arbiter, person chosen to settle a dispute; one competent to appreciate and to decide merit in any given direction; person appointed to estimate success in a competition or contest. JUDGE (2), v.t. to hear and determine a case in a law court; examine and pass sentence on; try; reckon; consider; v.i. to act the j.; pass sentence; consider. [Fr. from L.].

JUDGE ADVOCATE [juj-ad'vō-kat], n. (leg.) legal official acting at a court-martial.

JUDGEMENT, see JUDGMENT.

JUDGMENT, JUDGEMENT [juj'ment], n. a

judging; legal sentence of a judge; divinely inflicted penalty; any authoritative decision; criticism, censure; capacity for sound discrimination; discernment, appreciation; the (Last) J., ultimate trial of the human race by God. [OFr.].

JUDGMENT DAY [juj'ment-dā], n. the last day, doomsday.

JUDGMENT DEBT [juj'ment-det], n. security debt, legalized by the c'der of a judge, under which execution can be issued at any time.

JUDGMENT-SEAT [juj'ment-sēt], n. seat of a judge; judgeship; tribunal.

JUDICATORY [jōo'di-ka-te-ri], n. a court; body of judges; judicial system. [LL.].

JUDICATURE [jōo'di-ka-tyōor], n. power of jurisdiction; body of judges or the judicial system of a country. [MedL.].

JUDICIAL [jōo-di'shal], adj. pertaining to judgment, or to courts of justice; judge-like. JUDICIALLY, adv. in a j. manner. [L.].

JUDICIARY [jōo-di'sha-ri], n. judges collectively; department of government which is concerned in the trial and determination of causes. [L.].

JUDICIOUS [jōo-di'shōos], adj. having or exercising sound judgment, wise, discerning; well-timed. JUDICIOUSLY, adv. in a j. fashion. [Fr.].

JUDO [jōo'dō], n. a modified form of ju-jitsu. [Jap.].

JUG (1) [jug], n. any deep pouring vessel; (slang) stone j., prison; in j., in gaol. JUG (2), v.t. to stew in a covered jar, esp. a hare; (slang) put into gaol. [Unkn.].

JUGGERNAUT [ju'ger-nawt], n. a title of the Hindu god, Vishnu; image of this god which, mounted on its chariot at certain seasons, is taken in procession, on which occasion many devotees are said to have formerly thrown themselves under its wheels; relentless inhuman force which destroys blindly anything that comes in its way. [Hind.].

JUGGLE (1) [ju'gl], v.i. to perform tricks of manual dexterity; to j. with, to manipulate, perform tricks with; (fig.) distort. JUGGLE (2), n. a piece of juggling; imposture. JUGGLING, n. sleight of hand; juggler's trade; trickery. [OFr. from L.].

JUGGLER [jug'ler], n. one who gives exhibitions of jugglery; (fig.) deceiver, trickster.

JUGGLERY [jug'le-ri], n. manual dexterity; trickery. [OFr.].

JUGULAR (1) [jug'yōo-ler], adj. pertaining to the neck or throat; j. veins, large veins in the throat. JUGULAR (2), n. the j. vein. [MedL.].

JUICE [jōos], n. sap, liquid part of vegetable matter, moisture in cooked meat; (fig.) essential part of anything; (slang) any motive power, electricity, petrol etc. [L.].

JUICY [jōo'si], adj. full of juice, succulent; (slang) full of interest, racy, suggestive.

JU-JITSU, JIU-JITSU, JU-JUTSU [jōo-jit'sōo], n. Japanese system of wrestling. [Jap.].

JUJU [jōo'jōo], n. African magic; charm or taboo connected with this; animism. [Uncert.].

JUJUBE [jōo'jōob], n. (bot.) shrub of the genus Zizyphus, or its fruit; lozenge of gum arabic and sugar. [MedL.].

JULEP [jōo'lep], n. sweet liquid forming a foundation for medicines; drink of spirituous liquor, water and sugar with a seasoning of mint. [Pers.].

JULIAN [jōo'li-an], adj. pertaining to Julius Caesar, usually of his calendar. [L.].

JULIENNE [zhōo-li-en'], n. a clear meat soup with finely shredded vegetables. [Fr.].

JULY [jōo-lī'], n. seventh month of the year, named after Julius Caesar. [OFr. from L.].

JUMBLE (1) [jum'bl], n. a thin, hollow, cylindrical, crisp sweet cake. [Uncert.].

JUMBLE (2), v.t. to mix, confuse; v.i. to act or think confusedly. JUMBLE (3), n. a confused collection of heterogeneous objects; j. sale, sale of cast-off goods for charity. [Echoic].

JUMP (1) [jump], v.i. to make or take a jump, leap, spring; to miss one or more of a sequence; to start as a result of shock; (of a nerve) to throb, give spasmodic pain; to j. at, to seize eagerly; to j. into, to rush into; to j. on, to blame instantly; to j. with, (fig.) to agree with, correspond to; to j. to it, (coll.) to hurry; v.t. to jump over; make to jump; to j. a claim, to seize summarily without the normal formalities. JUMP (2), n. sudden motion upwards, a leap, spring, bound; a nervous start; sudden acceleration or change of direction in any ordered progress or motion; (geol.) fault. [Echoic].

JUMPER (1) [jum'per], n. one who, or that which,

jumps; member of religious sects who jump as part of worship; (coll.) ticket-inspector on a public conveyance; **counter j.,** (coll.) shop-assistant.
JUMPER (2), n. sailor's loose tunic; blouse, usu. of knitted material, reaching over the top of the skirt; similar loose garment worn by men. [Fr.].
JUMPY [jum'pi], adj. nervous; erratic.
JUNCTION [jungk'shn], n. act of joining; state of being joined, union, meeting; place or point of union; meeting point of two or more sets of railway lines. [L.].
JUNCTURE [jungk'tyŏor], n. a joining; union; line or point at which two bodies are joined; point of time, critical moment, position of affairs. [L.].
JUNE [jŏon], n. sixth month of the year. [OFr. from L.].
JUNGLE [jung'gl], n. wild, heavily overgrown, trackless ground in tropical countries; (fig.) anything through which it is hard to find one's way. JUNGLE-FEVER, tropical fever; malaria. JUNGLE-FOWL, game-bird of the j. JUNGLY, adj. covered with j. [Hind.].
JUNIOR (1) [jŏo'ni-er], adj. younger in years or practice; of the younger of two brothers, or son with the same name as his father; subordinate; of less standing. JUNIOR (2), n. person who is younger in years or practice, subordinate. [L.].
JUNIPER [jŏo'ni-per], n. (bot.) evergreen tree bearing dark, purple berries, the oil of which is used in medicines and in flavouring gin. [L.].
JUNK (1) [jungk], n. piece of old cable or cordage put to secondary uses; hard, salt beef; source of spermacetti in the sperm-whale; (slang) cast-off, broken things; **j. shop,** shop dealing in second-hand goods, usually of little value. [Unkn.].
JUNK (2), n. large flat-bottomed vessel with flat matting sails used in China Seas. [Malay].
JUNKER [yŏong'ker], n. former Prussian or North-German landed aristocrat. [Germ.].
JUNKET (1) [jung'kit], n. soft curds made by treating milk with rennet; feast, entertainment. JUNKET (2), v.i. to attend a junketing. JUNKETING, n. a merry entertainment. [AFr.].
JUNO [jŏo'nō], n. (Roman myth.) wife of Jupiter and Queen of Heaven; queenly and statuesque woman; (astron.) one of the minor planets. [L.].
JUNTA, JUNTO [jun'tah('to)], n. the former Spanish Grand Council; secret political convention; a cabal. [Span.].
JUPITER [jŏo'pi-ter], n. (Roman myth.) the supreme deity, Jove; (astron.) the largest of the planets. [L.].
JURIDICAL [jŏo-ri'di-kal], adj. of, or pertaining to, a judge or justice. [~L.].
JURISCONSULT [jŏo-ris-kon-sult'], n. an authority on law, esp. civil or international; jurist. [L.].
JURISDICTION [jŏo-ris-dik'shn], n. authority or power to try causes; district or sphere where such a right runs; the trying of causes; (more generally) administration, realm, province. [L.].
JURISPRUDENCE [jŏo-ris-prŏo'dens], n. knowledge of the practice and history of laws, rights, usages and so forth; study in this. JURISPRUDENT, adj. versed in the science of law. [L.].
JURIST [jŏo'rist], n. one versed in law; student of,

writer on, law, esp. civil or international law. [MedL.].
JUROR [jŏo'rer], n. juryman, or anyone with similar functions; one who swears an oath. [AFr.].
JURY [jŏo'ri], n. a sworn body of men and women who must pronounce a verdict on the facts of a cause from the evidence adduced in court after direction by a judge; any body of judges, umpires etc. JURY-BOX, jury's enclosed seats. [OFr.].
JURYMAN [jŏo'ri-man], n. member of a jury.
JURYMAST [jŏo'ri-mahst], n. (naut.) a temporary mast. [Uncert.].
JUSSIVE [ju'siv], adj. (gram.) conveying a command. [L.].
JUST (1) [just], adj. righteous; in conformity with abstract right, one's rights as a man or citizen, or to the rules, principles and practice of a juridical system; equitable, due, impartial; in conformity with what is good or fitting; honest, fair, sporting; of a correct, equivalent or equal size, amount or extent. JUST (2), adv. exactly; nearly, barely; almost. [Fr. from L.].
JUSTICE [jus'tis], n. the ideal principle determining what is fitting and right; quality of being just; rectitude in the dealings of men one with another; accordance with truth and fact; just desert; (leg.) the administration of law; jurisdiction, due punishment; person commissioned to hold courts, or to try and decide controversies and administer justice; judge; **J. of the Peace,** unpaid local magistrate.
JUSTICIARY [jus-ti'sha-ri], n. the High Court in Scotland, of supreme jurisdiction in all criminal cases.
JUSTIFIABLE [jus'ti-fi-a-bl], adj. that can be justified; defensible, excusable. JUSTIFIABLY, adv. so as to be j.; in a j. manner; rightly. [Fr.].
JUSTIFICATION [jus-ti-fi-kā'shn], n. act of justifying; vindication, defence; (theol.) acceptance of a sinner as righteous through the merits of Christ. [LL.].
JUSTIFY [jus'ti-fi], v.t. to prove; show to be just, right, allowable, excusable, reasonable; exculpate, exonerate; (print.) space out type. [Fr. from L.].
JUT (1) [jut], v.i. to project sharply. JUT (2), n. sharp, well-defined projection. [~JET (3)].
JUTE (1) [jŏot], n. vegetable fibre serving as coarse hemp for canvas, ropes etc.; Bengal trees from which it is derived. [Bengali].
JUTE (2), n. member of one of the Low German invading tribes which settled in Britain. [L.].
JUVENESCENT [jŏo-ve-ne'sent], adj. immature, becoming young. JUVENESCENCE [jŏo-ve-ne'sens], n. process of becoming young. [L.].
JUVENILE (1) [jŏo've-nil], adj. young, youthful, pertaining to or suited to youth; adolescent; **j. offender,** guilty person, not yet of age, tried in a special court and liable to special penalties. JUVENILE (2), n. official term for a youth; j. offender; book for children. [L.].
JUVENILIA [jŏo-ve-ni'li-ah], n.(pl.) books written, or works of art executed, in youth. [L.].
JUVENILITY [jŏo-ve-nil'li-ti], n. juvenile condition; youthfulness. [L.].
JUXTAPOSITION [juks-ta-pō-zi'shn], n. state of being placed side by side. [Fr.].

K

K [kā], eleventh letter of the English alphabet.
KAAMA [kah'mah], n. a South African antelope, Bubalis caama. [Bechuana].
KABBALA, see CABALA.
KAFFIR, KAFIR, CAFFRE [ka'fer], n. member of the chief native race in South-East Africa, a branch of the Bantus, esp. one living between Natal and Cape Province; their language; a native of Kafristan in Afghanistan; (pl.) South African mining shares. [Arab.].
KAFTAN, see CAFTAN.
KAIL, see KALE.
KAINOZOIC, see CAINOZOIC.
KAISER [kī'zer], n. title taken by the sovereigns of

the Holy Roman Empire, and in 1871 adopted by the first Emperor of the new German Empire. [Germ. form of CAESAR].
KAKA [kah'kah], n. the parrot, Nestor meridionalis, of New Zealand. [Maori].
KAKODYL, see CACODYL.
KALE, KAIL [kāl], n. a curly-leafed cabbage, cole. [Scots form of COLE].
KALEIDOSCOPE [ka-lī'dō-skōp], n. optical instrument in the form of a tube containing reflecting surfaces, having an eye-hole at one end and, at the other, pieces of coloured glass, forming constantly changing symmetrical figures as the tube is turned or shaken; (fig.) constantly changing scene of colour.

The accent ' after a syllable = stress (u-pon'). The mark ‾ over a vowel = length (ā in made; ō in bone).

KALEIDOSCOPIC [ka-lī-dō-sko′pik], *adj.* of, pertaining to, or resembling, a k., rapidly changing in colour or appearance. [Gk.].

KALENDS, see CALENDS.

KALEYARD [kāl′yahd], *n.* Scottish kitchen garden; **k. school**, group of authors writing, with much use of dialect, about humble Scottish domestic life.

KALIF, see CALIPH.

KALSOMINE, see CALCIMINE.

KAM, see CAM (2).

KAMARBAND, see CUMMERBUND.

KANAKA [ka-na′kah, ka′na-kah], *n.* a native of the South Sea Islands, *esp.* one brought under contract to Australia as a labourer on the sugar plantations. [Hawaiian].

KANGAROO [kang-ga-rōō′], *n.* herbivorous marsupial mammal, native to Australia, having short forelegs and powerful hind legs, by which it travels in a series of leaps; (*pl.*) West Australian mining shares; method of procedure in the House of Commons by which the Chairman of a committee can choose the amendments to be discussed. KAN-GAROO-RAT, species of small marsupial animals; North American rodent. [Native].

KANTIAN (1) [kan′ti-an], *adj.* relating to the philosophical system of Kant. KANTIAN (2), *n.* follower of Kant. [~*Kant*, German philosopher].

KANTISM [kan′tizm], *n.* Kantian doctrine or theory; Kantian criticism.

KAOLIN [kā′o-lin], *n.* fine white clay used medicinally and in the manufacture of porcelain, china-clay. [Chin.].

KAPOK [kā′pok], *n.* soft, light, downy, oily fibre obtained from the silk-cotton tree. [Malay].

KAROO [ka-rōō′], *n.* South African barren tableland or dry plateau. [Hottentot].

KAROSS, CAROSS [ka-ros′], *n.* South African native cloak or rug of animal skin with the hair or fur left on. [S. African].

KATABATIC [ka-ta-ba′tik], *adj.* (*meteor.*) due to the downward flow of air. [Gk.].

KATABOLISM [ka-ta′bo-lizm], *n.* process by which complex organic compounds of living bodies are broken up into simpler ones. [Gk.].

KATYDID [kā′ti-did], *n.* North American tree-grass-hopper, so called from the peculiar sound made by its wing covers. [Echoic].

KAYAK [kī′ak], *n.* covered Eskimo canoe. [Eskimo].

KEDGE (1) [kej], *v.i.* to move a ship by winding in a hawser which is fastened to a small anchor. KEDGE (2), *n.* small anchor for mooring or warping a ship. [Uncert.].

KEDGEREE [ke-je-rē′], *n.* spiced dish of stewed fish, rice and eggs. [Hind.].

KEEL (1) [kēl], *n.* the lowest set of plates or timbers in a ship's structure, extending from stem to stern, upon which the framework of the ship ship is built; **false k.**, second k. bolted under the main k.; **sliding k.**, centreboard working in a trunk along the line of the keel so as to deepen it when necessary. KEEL (2), *v.t.* to turn up the k. of so as to show the bottom of; **to k. over**, to capsize. [OIcel.].

KEEL (3), *n.* flat-bottomed coal barge, as used on the Tyne; quantity of coal carried in one of these. [MDu.].

KEEL-HAUL [kēl-hawl′], *v.t.* to hang to the yard-arm, drop over the side of the ship, and haul under the keel to the other side as a punishment. [Du.].

KEELSON, KELSON [kel′son], *n.* set of timbers or plates placed above and parallel to the keel, and by which the keel is bolted to the floor-timbers.

KEEN (1) [kēn], *adj.* sharp, having a fine cutting edge; sensitive, highly developed; poignant, intense; biting, severe; incisive, acute; piercing; eager, zealous, enthusiastic; shrewd, searching; desirous of; hard and closely contested; strong, well-marked; **to be k. on**, to be anxious to, desire eagerly; have a strong affection for. KEENLY, *adv.* in a k. fashion. [OE.].

KEEN (2), *v.i.* to lament loudly and bitterly for the dead. KEEN (3), *n.* lamentation and wailing set up by the Irish upon the death of some person or over a corpse. [Ir.].

KEEP (1) (*pret. and p.pt.* kept) [kēp], *v.t.* to retain in one's possession, hold; continue to hold; cause to remain, deposit in a particular place; fulfil, abide by; celebrate; maintain, provide means of sustenance and residence for, *esp.* maintain for personal use or enjoyment; manage, be in charge of; maintain in proper order, preserve a record of; defend from attack; detain; preserve; continue to (*with another*

v.); have in stock for sale; *v.i.* to remain in a certain (*esp.* good) condition; stay in a certain place; continue; remain; **to k. at**, to continue to, stick to; compel to remain at; **to k. from**, to withhold, conceal from; prevent access to, prevent doing; **to k. away from**, not to go near; **to k. to**, to stick to; **to k. away**, to prevent from approaching close to; **to k. back**, to restrain, repress; conceal, withhold; **to k. in**, to detain (*esp.* after normal hours at school), compel to stay; restrain; **to k. off**, to abstain from; ward off; **to k. on**, to continue to; retain in employment; not to take off; **to k. out**, to prevent, refrain, from entering; take no part in, avoid; **to k. up**, not to let slide or lapse; maintain; continue, preserve; remain unsubdued; prevent from falling (*esp.* of courage or spirits); **to k. up with**, to progress at the same rate as; **to k. down**, to suppress; **to k. an eye on**, (*coll.*) to look after; **to k. one's eyes open**, (*coll.*) to be on the alert for, observe carefully. KEEP (2), *n.* act of keeping; fact or condition of being kept; maintenance, sustenance, attention and lodging necessary to k. anyone or anything, money etc. required in return for this; the innermost and most strongly fortified tower of a castle, donjon; **for keeps**, (*coll.*) for ever. [OE.].

KEEPER [kē′per], *n.* one who keeps or guards, custodian, protector; attendant in charge of a lunatic; employee responsible for the care and upkeep of a park or other enclosure; one who is in charge; ring worn above another to keep it from slipping off the finger; clasp; loop to hold a belt in place.

KEEPING [kē′ping], *n.* act of holding or retaining; protection, guardianship; observance; preservation; completing and maintaining in proper condition; just proportion; **in k.**, fitting, suitable, consistent.

KEEPSAKE [kēp′sāk], *n.* token of remembrance, memento.

KEG [keg], *n.* small barrel. [~Icel.].

KELP [kelp], *n.* ashes of seaweed used in the manufacture of iodine; seaweed, *esp.* the large seaweeds burned because of their valuable ashes. [ME.].

KELPIE [kel′pi], *n.* (*Scots*) imaginary sprite or demon haunting lakes or rivers. [Uncert.].

KELSON, see KEELSON.

KELT, see CELT (1).

KEN (1) (*pres.pt.* kenning, *pret. and p.pt.* kenned) [ken], *v.t.* (*Scots*) to know; recognize. KEN (2), *n.* range of vision; range of knowledge or experience. [OE.].

KENNEL (1) [ke′nel], *n.* hut for a dog; dwelling-hole of other animals; pack of hounds; band of animals; mean dwelling. KENNEL (2) (*pres.pt.* KENNELLING, *pret. and p.pt.* KENNELLED), *v.t.* to confine or put into a k. or kennels; *v.i.* to live in a k. [NFr.].

KENNEL (3), *n.* gutter, open drain or watercourse of a street. [~CANAL].

KENTISH [ken′tish], *adj.* belonging to Kent; **K. man**, person born West of the Medway, as opposed to **man of Kent**: **K. rag**, limestone of the lower greensand found in Kent. [*Kent*, English county].

KERAMIC, see CERAMIC.

KERARGYRITE, see CERARGYRITE.

KERATIN [ke′ra-tin], *n.* the principal constituent of hair and horn. [Gk.].

KERATITIS [ke-ra-tī′tis], *n.* (*path.*) chronic inflammation of the cornea. [Gk.].

KERB [kurb], *n.* the edge of the pavement of a street, raised path etc.; **on the k.**, Stock Exchange business transacted in the street, *esp.* after the exchange has closed. [~CURB (1)].

KERBSTONE [kurb′stōn], *n.* one of the stones forming the kerb; **k. broker**, broker who is not a member of the Stock Exchange.

KERCHIEF [kur′chēf], *n.* cloth worn by women to cover the head; scarf. [OFr.].

KERF [kurf], *n.* slit or notch made by a saw, axe etc.; place at which a tree or branch has been cut; a cutting. [OE.].

KERMES [kur′mēz], *n.* female of the insect *Coccus ilicis*, the dried bodies of which are used in making a crimson dye; dye obtained from these. [Arab.].

KERNEL [kur′nel], *n.* the seed of a fruit, *esp.* when enclosed within a hard husk or shell; grain of wheat or other grassy plant; (*fig.*) the essential point, central part of anything. [OE.].

KEROSENE [ke′rō-sēn], *n.* oil for illumination obtained from petroleum. [Gk.].

KERRY [ke′ri], *n.* name of an Irish county used to denote a breed of terrier or of dairy cattle.

KERSEY [kur′zi], *n.* coarse, closely woven, ribbed variety of woollen cloth. [*Kersey*, Suffolk].

ŏŏ is pronounced as in *food*; ŏŏ as in *hood*; th as in *think*; TH as in *that*; zh as in azure.   ~ = related to.

KINDLE [kin'dl], *v.t.* to set fire to, light; (*fig.*) illuminate; provoke, incite; *v.i.* to take fire; (*fig.*) glow, shine; become excited, flare up. KINDLER, *n.* one who, or that which, kindles. [~OIcel.].

KINDLING [kind'ling], *n.* act of setting fire to or of becoming inflamed; fuel for lighting a fire.

KINDLY (1) [kind'li], *adj.* benevolent and sympathetic; expressing or displaying kindness of heart. KINDLY (2), *adv.* in a kind manner. [OE.].

KINDRED (1) [kin'dred], *n.* relationship by blood or birth, now loosely including relationship by marriage; group of persons related by blood; kinsfolk. KINDRED (2), *adj.* belonging to the same family, related by blood or birth; congenial, having similar qualities or properties; related, allied. [OE.].

KINE [kin], *n.*(*pl.*) (*poet.*) cows, cattle. [ME. from OE.].

KINEMA, see CINEMA.

KINEMATIC(AL) [ki-ni-ma'tik(-al)], *adj.* pertaining to kinematics. [Gk.].

KINEMATICS [ki-ni-ma'tiks], *n.*(*pl.*) (*phys.*) science dealing with pure motion, irrespective of the force producing it or the mass moved.

KINEMATOGRAPH, KINEMATOGRAPHY, see CINEMATOGRAPH, CINEMATOGRAPHY.

KINETIC [ki-ne'tik], *adj.* (*phys.*) pertaining to or due to motion. [Gk.].

KINETICS [ki-ne'tiks], *n.*(*pl.*) (*phys.*) that branch of dynamics which deals with the motions of bodies considered in relation to the forces acting upon them.

KING (1) [king], *n.* male sovereign of a nation, monarch, usually succeeding by hereditary right; one who holds a position of influence in a certain sphere; (*fig.*) the chief, supreme example; (*cards*) card bearing the picture of a king and generally ranking in value above a queen; the principal piece in chess; (*draughts*) piece which has been crowned by having a similar piece placed on it; **k. of beasts,** the lion; **k. of birds,** the eagle; **K. of Kings,** God; **K. of Arms,** one of the three chief officers of the College of Arms, being Garter, Norroy and Clarenceux; also Lyon for Scotland and Ulster for Ireland; **king's evil,** scrofula, formerly thought to be cured by the touch of a k.; **K. Charles's head,** a fixed idea, obsession. KING (2), *v.t. and i.* to make a k.; occupy a position comparable with that of a k. [OE.].

KINGCRAFT [king'krahft], *n.* art of ruling as a king.

KINGCUP [king'kup], *n.* the marsh marigold.

KINGDOM [king'dom], *n.* territory ruled over by a king, the realm; rule of God in heaven or on earth; (*nat. hist.*) one of the three main divisions of nature; **k. come,** heaven, the life hereafter.

KINGFISH [king'fish], *n.* name given to various fishes distinguished by their size, appearance etc.

KINGFISHER [king'fi-sher], *n.* bird distinguished by its long beak and brightly coloured plumage, dwelling near streams and rivers and feeding on fish.

KINGLY (1) [king'li], *adj.* pertaining to a king; becoming a king; regal, majestic, noble; worthy of a king. KINGLY (2), † *adv.* in the manner of a king.

KING-PIN [king'pin], *n.* the main bolt in a machine or structure; (*fig.*) a leading figure.

KINGPOST [king'post], *n.* (*carp.*) the main perpendicular beam supporting the ridge of a roof; (*aeron.*) strut to which the bracing wires are secured.

KING'S BENCH, KING'S COUNSEL, KING'S EVIDENCE, see QUEEN'S BENCH, QUEEN'S COUNSEL, QUEEN'S EVIDENCE.

KINK (1) [kingk], *n.* short twist, bend or curl in a rope, hair, wire etc., at which it is doubled upon itself; (*fig.*) mental or moral twist, oddity or irregularity. KINK (2), *v.t. and i.* to twist or curl so as to form a k. in. [~Du.].

KINSFOLK [kinz'fōk], *n.*(*pl.*) persons of the same family, relatives.

KINSHIP [kin'ship], *n.* blood relationship; (*fig.*) affinity, close connexion or similarity.

KINSMAN [kinz'man], *n.* male relation, *esp.* one related by blood or birth.

KINSWOMAN [kinz'woo-man], *n.* female relation, *esp.* one related by blood or birth.

KIOSK [kē-osk'], *n.* Turkish or Persian open summerhouse; light, open building resembling this, used as a bandstand, refreshment place or newspaper stall. [Turk.].

KIP (1) [kip], *n.* (*slang*) bed; sleep. KIP (2) (*pres.pt.* KIPPING, *pret. and p.pt.* KIPPED), *v.i.* (*slang*) to sleep, go to bed. [~Du.].

KIPPER (1) [ki'per], *n.* herring or mackerel cleaned, dried, smoked and salted. KIPPER (2), *v.t.* to cure

(fish) by cleaning, drying, smoking and salting. [~OE.].

KIRK [kurk], *n.* (*Scots and northern dial.*) church. [OScand.].

KIRSH(WASSER) [kēersh'(va-ser)], *n.* intoxicating spirit made in Germany from the fermented juice and crushed stones of cherries. [Germ.].

KIRTLE [kur'tl], *n.* (*hist.*) woman's gown, skirt or petticoat; man's tunic. [OE.].

KISMET [kiz'met], *n.* fate or destiny. [Arab.].

KISS (1) [kis], *n.* salute given with the lips as a sign of reverence or homage, or as a caress of love and affection; (*fig.*) gentle touch or pressure; (*billiards*) stroke in which the ball struck hits the object ball a second time, contact between moving balls at billiards or bowls. KISS (2), *v.t.* to give a k. to, salute or caress with the lips; (*fig.*) touch lightly, caress gently; (*billiards*) strike a second time; *v. reflex,* to k. each other; **to k. the dust, ground,** to be overthrown; **to k. the rod,** to bow to discipline and punishment. KISS-CURL, small curl on the temple or forehead. [OE.].

KIT (1) [kit], *n.* small round wooden tub; receptacle in which a sailor, soldier or airman carries his outfit and personal belongings; box or bag in which a workman's tools are carried; outfit or personal equipment of a sailor, soldier or airman; set of tools required in some particular occupation; special attire, equipment or outfit for sport, travelling etc. KIT (2), *v.t.* to provide (a sailor, soldier or airman) with k. [MDu.].

KITCHEN (1) [ki'chen], *n.* room or part of a building in which the cookery is done; (*Scots*) cooked dish to accompany high tea. KITCHEN (2), *adj.* pertaining to a k.; **k. garden,** plot of ground in which vegetables are raised for the table. [OE. from L.].

KITCHENER [ki'che-ner], *n.* cooking range.

KITCHENETTE [ki-che-net'], *n.* small combined kitchen and pantry.

KITCHENMAID [ki'chen-mād], *n.* female servant who does the rougher work of a kitchen.

KITE [kit], *n.* bird of prey of the hawk family; (*fig.*) rapacious person; flying toy or contrivance consisting of a light wooden framework covered with paper or cloth, having a long length of string by which the flier retains control over it when it is carried aloft by the wind; (*comm.*) accommodation bill or bill of exchange; (*slang*) an aircraft; **to fly the k.,** to throw out a feeler to test public opinion upon some matter. KITE-BALLOON, captive observation balloon used for obtaining recordings of scientific information. KITE-FLYING, (*comm.*) act or practice of dealing in accommodation paper for the purpose of raising money; (*coll.*) the testing of public opinion by announcing professed plans and awaiting comment. [OE.].

KITH [kith], *n.* (*archaic*) friends, acquaintances; **k. and kin,** close friends and relations, often implying only relatives or family. [OE.].

KITTEN (1) [ki'ten], *n.* young cat. KITTEN (2), *v.i.* to give birth to kittens. [~OFr.].

KITTENISH [ki'te-nish], *adj.* playful, like a kitten, frisky, lively.

KITTIWAKE [ki'ti-wāk], *n.* three-toed variety of seagull, so called from its cry. [Echoic].

KITTY [ki'ti], *n.* pet name for a kitten; pool of stakes to which the players of certain card-games contribute in turn; common fund out of which certain communal expenses of a party are paid; (*bowls*) the jack.

KIWI [kē'wē], *n.* New Zealand flightless bird with a long curved beak and no tail; (*slang*) New Zealander, *esp.* a member of the armed forces abroad; (*aeron. slang*) member of the R.A.F. not actually engaged in flying. [Maori].

KLAXON [klak'sun], *n.* electrically-operated motor horn. [Name of makers].

KLEPTOMANIA [klep-tō-mā'ni-ah], *n.* form of mental disorder expressing itself in an irresistible urge to steal. KLEPTOMANIAC, *n.* one suffering from k. [Gk.].

KLOOF [kloof], *n.* in South Africa, a ravine. [Du.].

KNACK [nak], *n.* trick, dodge; special dexterity or manipulative skill, trick of knowing how to do something and being able to do it well; gift, talent. [Uncert.].

KNACKER [na'ker], *n.* one who buys worn out horses for slaughter and cuts the carcasses up for dogs' meat; one who buys old houses or ships to be broken up for scrap. [Uncert.].

KNAG [nag], *n.* knob or stump projecting from the trunk of a tree, peg, hook; knot in wood. [ME.].

KNAPSACK [nap'sak], *n.* bag or wallet of canvas or leather, strapped to the back and used for carrying food and personal belongings. [LGerm.].

KNAPWEED [nap'wēd], *n.* hardy weed having a purple flower.

KNAVE [nāv], *n.* dishonest person, rogue, rascal; (*cards*) the lowest court-card, the jack, ranking between the queen and ten and bearing a picture of a page. [OE.].

KNAVERY [nā've-ri], *n.* dishonesty, petty villainy, sharp tricks or practices.

KNAVISH [nā'vish], *adj.* worthy of a knave, dishonest, rascally. KNAVISHLY, *adv.* in a k. fashion.

KNEAD [nēd], *v.t.* to work into a soft yielding mass by pressing out and squeezing together with the hands; make soft or supple by similar movements with the hands; (*fig.*) mould, fashion. [OE.].

KNEE (1) [nē], *n.* the joint, together with the part surrounding it, of the thigh and the lower leg bones of a human being; joint corresponding to this, as that in the foreleg of a horse; bent or angular piece of timber or metal, *esp.* one used for connecting the beams of a ship; **to bow the k.,** to submit, yield; **to bend the k. to,** to pray to. KNEE (2), *v.t.* to strike with the k.; stretch out of shape, lose the crease, at the k. [OE.].

KNEE-BREECHES [nē'bri-chez], *n.(pl.)* breeches fastening just below the knee.

KNEECAP [nē'kap], *n.* small, flat, heart-shaped bone, the patella, situated at the forepart of the kneejoint; cover or protection for the knee.

KNEEHOLE [nē'hōl], *adj.* (of a desk, table etc.) with an opening in the front to admit the knees and legs.

KNEEJOINT [nē'joint], *n.* joint of the knee, hinged joint resembling that of the knee.

KNEEL (*pret. and p.pt.* **knelt**) [nēl], *v.i.* to go down on one's bended knees. [OE.].

KNEE-LENGTH [nē'length], *adj.* (of garments) reaching down to the knees.

KNEEPAN [nē'pan], *n.* the kneecap.

KNELL (1) [nel], *n.* sound of a church bell tolling, *esp.* of one rung at a funeral or to announce a death or disaster; (*fig.*) omen of death or ending; **to sound the k. of,** to indicate the end of. KNELL (2), *v.t.* to summon by a k.; *v.i.* to toll as at a death or funeral, sound mournfully. [OE.].

KNEW [nyōō], *pret. of* KNOW.

KNICKERBOCKERS [ni'ker-bo-kerz], *n.(pl.)* loose breeches gathered in under the knee. [*Knickerbocker,* imaginary author of Washington Irving's *History of New York*].

KNICKERS [ni'kerz], *n.(pl.)* knickerbockers; short loose-fitting trousers ending at the knee; woman's undergarment covering the upper part of the legs. [~*Prec.*].

KNICK-KNACK [nik'nak], *n.* trifle, small, dainty, attractive ornamental object.

KNIFE (1) (*pl.* **knives**) [nīf, nīvz], *n.* instrument for cutting, usually consisting of a short handle to which is fastened a blade with a sharp cutting edge; cutting blade of a machine; **war to the k.,** relentless, merciless fighting or hostility; **to have one's k. in a person,** to owe him a perpetual grudge, adopt a hostile attitude towards. KNIFE (2), *v.t.* to stab or cut with a k. so as to wound or kill. [OE.].

KNIFEBOARD [nīf'bawd], *n.* piece of wood for cleaning knives on; two benches placed together lengthwise on the top of an early form of omnibus.

KNIFE-EDGE [nīf'ej], *n.* sharp edge of steel serving as the axis of a balance; edge of a knife; (*fig.*) sharp ridge of rock; anything very sharp, excepting a needle or pin.

KNIGHT (1) [nīt], *n.* non-hereditary title of honour conferred by the sovereign, which entitles the possessor to use the title *Sir* before his name; (*hist.*) one, usually of noble birth, admitted to a certain military rank; rank conferred upon certain of their distinguished members by several organizations; (*fig.*) brave, chivalrous person, *esp.* a lady's champion; (*chess*) piece bearing a horse's head; **K. Bachelor,** lowest class of knights consisting of those who are not members of any order of knighthood; **K. of the Shire,** (*hist.*) representative of a shire or county in Parliament; **k. of the road,** highwayman. KNIGHT-ERRANT, one who travelled in search of adventures to show his military prowess and chivalry; (*fig.*) valorous champion of causes etc. KNIGHT (2), *v.t.* to create a k. [OE.].

KNIGHTAGE [nī'tij], *n.* the body of knights; book containing an account of those who are knights.

KNIGHT-ERRANTRY [nīt'e-ran-tri], *n.* practice or conduct of a knight-errant; act worthy of a knight-errant.

KNIGHTHOOD [nīt'hŏŏd], *n.* rank, dignity and character of a knight; the body of knights.

KNIGHTLY [nīt'li], *adj.* pertaining to a knight; worthy of a knight, chivalrous, brave, courteous.

KNIT (*pres.pt.* **knitting,** *pret. and p.pt.* **knitted, knit**) [nit], *v.t.* to weave or connect (yarn, wool etc.) by a series of interlocking loops and knots made with long eyeless needles; make (a fabric) in this way; cause to grow together, fasten closely together; draw together, contract; unite or link closely; make compact; *v.i.* to practise knitting; unite, become welded together into a whole; **to k. up,** to fasten up dropped stitches in knitting; become closely bound with. [OE.].

KNOB [nob], *n.* small hard rounded protuberance on a stick, branch etc.; hard rounded boss or stud used as a handle etc.; small lump of coal, sugar. [ME.].

KNOBBLE [no'bl], *n.* small knob.

KNOBKERRIE [nob-ke'ri], *n.* round-topped stick used as a weapon by African natives. [Afrik.].

KNOBSTICK [nob'stik], *n.* stick with a knobbed head; (*slang*) blackleg.

KNOCK (1) [nok], *v.t.* to strike, rap, beat; drive against; (*fig.*) startle, flabbergast; (*U.S. coll.*) find fault with; *v.i.* to strike a blow with something hard or heavy, *esp.* to rap on a door with the knocker or the knuckle in order to indicate one's presence; bump or rattle because of some mechanical defect; **to k. about,** to batter; (*coll.*) travel about haphazardly, lead an unsettled life; **to k. down,** to fell; sell at a reduced price; (*of auctioneers*) assign to a bidder by a k. with the hammer; **to k. on,** (*Rugby football*) to strike the ball forward with the hand or arm; **to k. off,** to force off or away by striking; (*coll.*) cease work; complete hurriedly; **to k. out,** to remove by striking; eliminate from a competition; render temporarily unconscious; **to k. together,** to construct in a rough and ready fashion; **to k. up,** to hit in an upward direction; (*tennis*) practise tennis shots; construct roughly and hastily; arouse by knocking; exhaust, wear out by excessive toil or exertion; **to k. on the head,** to put an end to, thwart; **to k. the bottom out of,** to demolish, prove (an argument) false. KNOCK (2), *n.* act of knocking; blow, rap, *esp.* announcing one's presence at a door; shock, disagreeable surprise; (*cricket*) innings; bumping sound made by an engine in imperfect order; **k. for k.,** (of motor insurance) of an agreement between insurance companies to pay for the damage to the vehicles of their respective clients without regard to responsibility. [OE.].

KNOCKABOUT (1) [no'ka-bowt], *adj.* rough, slapstick, boisterous; (of clothes) suitable for hard wear and rough travelling. KNOCKABOUT (2), *n.* rough, slapstick, noisy farce; actor in this.

KNOCK-DOWN [nok'down], *adj.* (of a blow) that strikes to the ground; so constructed as to be easily taken to pieces again; (*fig.*) overwhelming; **k. price,** lowest price that will be accepted by the seller.

KNOCKER [no'ker], *n.* one who, or that which, knocks; metal striker hinged to a door, and struck against a metal plate to attract attention; (*U.S. coll.*) persistent fault-finder.

KNOCK-KNEE [nok-nē'], *n.* deformity in which the legs bend inwards, and the knees touch each other in walking. KNOCK-KNEED, *adj.* with knees which touch each other in walking; weak, feeble.

KNOCK-ON [nok-on'], *n.* (*Rugby football*) infringement of the rules caused by propelling the ball forward with the hand or fist.

KNOCK-OUT (1) [nok'owt], *n.* auction sale in which the bids are arranged beforehand by the dealers present; (*boxing*) blow delivered with such force as to prevent one's opponent from continuing the fight until the timekeeper has counted ten; a k. competition; (*fig.*) striking success, conquest. KNOCK-OUT (2), *adj.* felling, stunning, bringing about a k.; pertaining to, of the nature of, a k. auction sale; of an eliminating tournament or competition in which a single defeat means retirement from the competition.

KNOCK-UP [nok'up], *n.* (*tennis*) preliminary practice shots before the start of a match or game; bout of practice as opposed to a game; *v.t.* to construct roughly of readily-available materials.

KNOLL [nōl], *n.* rounded hillock or mound. [OE.].

KNOT (1) [not], *n.* the tying, intertwining or entangling of one or more threads, cords etc. tightly for the

---

purpose of fastening etc.; bow or tie worn as an ornament; (*fig.*) difficulty, intricate problem, awkward complication; meeting point of a number of converging lines etc.; tie, link, that which unites; hard excrescence or protuberance, nodule; hard mass in a tree trunk where a branch joins it, hard rounded cross-grained mass in a sawn piece of wood; knob, boss, stud; small group of people gathered closely together; (*naut.*) a division of the log-line, marked by a knotted string fastened to it, serving to measure the rate of a vessel's motion. KNOT (2) (*pres.pt.* KNOTTING, *pret. and p.pt.* KNOTTED), *v.t.* to tie a k. or a series of knots in; entangle; unite closely; *v.i.* to tie knots; knit thread etc. into a kind of fringe; become knotty. [OE.].

KNOTGRASS [not'grahs], *n.* a common British weed, so called from the joints on its stems.

KNOTTING [no'ting], *n.* act of tying or forming into a knot or knots; the knitting of thread etc. into a kind of fringe-work formed by a series of knots; act of painting over the knots in wood with a preparation of red lead; the preparation used for this.

KNOTTY [no'ti], *adj.* full of knots; (*fig.*) perplexing, difficult; hard, rugged.

KNOUT (1) [nowt], *n.* Russian whip or scourge. KNOUT (2), *v.t.* to flog with the k. [Russ.].

KNOW (*pret.* **knew**, *p.pt.* **known**) [nō], *v.t.* to be aware of or familiar with, possess knowledge as to; have experience of, be conversant with; understand, apprehend; have learnt; be acquainted with; recognize by remembrance, perception or description as being someone or something; be able to distinguish between; † have sexual relations with; *v.i.* to be certain, be informed; **to k. of,** to have heard about; possess information about; **to k. what's what,** k. a **thing or two** etc., to have a certain degree of common sense or worldly wisdom. [OE.].

KNOWING [nō'ing], *adj.* astute, cunning, wily, well-informed. KNOWINGLY, *adv.* with knowledge, deliberately, consciously; in a k. manner.

KNOWLEDGE [no'lij], *n.* clear and certain mental perception, understanding, fact of being aware of something; experience of, familiarity with, information of; learning, erudition; facts learned by study of; (*leg.*) cognizance, recognition; **carnal k.,** sexual intercourse. [ME.].

KNOWLEDGEABLE [no'li-ja-bl], *adj.* well-informed, clever, learned; intelligent, skilful.

KNUCKLE (1) [nu'kl], *n.* the joint of a finger, protruding at the back of the hand when clenched; corresponding joint in the leg of a quadruped together with the surrounding muscular parts, *esp.* considered as a joint of meat; **near the k.,** (*coll.*) verging on indecency. KNUCKLE (2), *v.t. and i.* to strike or rub with the knuckles; **to k. down to,** to settle down to steady work at; **to k. under,** to yield, submit. [~MDu.].

KNUCKLE-BONE [nu'kl-bōn], *n.* a bone of the knuckles, the protruding end of a joint of a bone in the fingers; joint of meat consisting of a leg bone with the knuckle; small bone from the limb of a sheep etc.; (*pl.*) game played with these bones.

KNUCKLEDUSTER [nu'kl-dus-ter], *n.* metal protection worn over the knuckles by certain roughs in fighting, and often studded with projecting knobs or points.

KNUR(R) [nur], *n.* hard, round protuberance on the trunk of a tree; wooden ball used in certain games. [~MDu.].

KOALA, KOOLAH [kō-ah'lah, kōō'lah], *n.* a bear-like Australian marsupial rodent. [Native].

KOHL [kōl], *n.* powdered antimony sulphide, a black pigment used in the East as a cosmetic. [Arab.].

KOHL-RABI [kōl-rah'bi], *n.* a cabbage having a globular, turnip-shaped stem. [Germ. from It.].

KOLA [kō'lah], *n.* West African tree which bears a fruit whose seeds contain caffeine; drink prepared from the seeds of this fruit.

KOODOO, see KUDU.

KOPECK, see COPECK.

KOPJE [ko'pi], *n.* (*S. Afr.*) hillock, small round-topped hill. [Du.].

KORAN [ko-rahn', kaw'ran], *n.* the sacred book of the Mohammedan religion. [Arab.].

KOSHER [kō'sher], *adj.* pure, clean, fulfilling the requirements of the Jewish sacred law. [Heb.].

KOW-TOW (1) [kow-tow'], *n.* Chinese custom of touching the ground with the forehead as a mark of reverence or deep respect. KOW-TOW (2), *v.i.* to perform the k.; (*fig.*) **to k. to,** to fawn on, treat with servile deference. [Chin.].

KRAAL (1) [krahl], *n.* native village in South Africa consisting of a collection of huts surrounded by a fence or mud walls, and containing a cattle enclosure in the centre of it. KRAAL (2), *v.t.* to enclose in a k. [Du.].

KRIEGSPIEL [krēg'shpēl], *n.* game played by military general staffs, in which pieces representing army units are manoeuvred on a map as a method of instruction in tactics; variety of chess in which neither player sees the other's pieces. [Germ.].

KRIS [kris], *n.* Malay dagger with a wavy blade. [Malay.].

KRISHNAISM [krish'na-izm], *n.* worship of Krishna, a Hindu male deity, one of the incarnations of Vishnu.

KRONE [krō'ner], *n.* Scandinavian silver coin; former German 10-mark gold piece; former Austrian silver coin. [Germ., Dan., Swed.].

KUDOS [kyoo'dos], *n.* (*coll.*) fame, credit, glory. [Gk.].

KUDU, KOODOO [kōō'dōō], *n.* large African antelope with corkscrew horns. [Hottentot].

KUKRI [kōō'kri], *n.* Gurkha knife with a curved blade. [Hind.].

KUMMEL [kü'mel], *n.* German liqueur made from caraway seeds and cumin. [Germ.].

KUMQUAT, see CUMQUAT.

KUOMINTANG [kwō-min-tahng'], *n.* nationalist radical party in China. [Chin.].

KURD [kōord], *n.* a native of Kurdistan, on the borders of Turkey, Iraq and Iran.

KURDISH [kōor'dish], *adj. and n.* of, or pertaining to, the Kurds; their language.

KURSAAL [kōor'sahl], *n.* large building at a watering place, used for public recreation and entertainment. [Germ.].

KYLE [kīl], *n.* (*Scots*) narrow channel separating two islands or an island from the mainland. [ONorw.].

KYRIE(ELEISON) [kē'ri-ā-(e-lā'i-son)], *n.* Greek religious petition, "Lord have mercy," used *esp.* at the beginning of the Mass and as a response; musical setting of this, *esp.* when forming the opening movement of a Mass. [Gk.].

L

L [el], twelfth letter of the English alphabet.

LA [lah], *n.* (*mus.*) sixth note in the tonic sol-fa scale.

LAAGER (1) [lah'ger], *n.* defensive camp formed by a ring of wagons. LAAGER (2), *v.i.* to make a l. [Afrik.].

LABEL (1) [lā'bel], *n.* strip of paper or cardboard attached to anything as an identification tab, *esp.* for parcels, luggage, exhibits; (*fig.*) term or phrase describing and summarizing. LABEL (2) (*pres.pt.* LABELLING, *pret. and p.pt.* LABELLED), *v.t.* to fasten a l. to; apply a descriptive tag to. [OFr.].

LABIAL (1) [lā'bi-al], *adj.* relating to the lips; (*phon.*) articulated by the lips. LABIAL (2), *n.* (*phon.*) a l. consonant or vowel. LABIALLY, *adv.* by means of the lips. [L.].

LABORATORY [la-bo'ra-te-ri], *n.* room or building equipped with apparatus and set apart for experimental work in the sciences. [MedL.].

LABORIOUS [la-baw'ri-ōos], *adj.* taking great pains, caring for detail and accuracy; slow and somewhat clumsy in practical matters; attained by or requiring much labour. [L.].

LABOUR (1) [lā'ber], *n.* work, *esp.* done to earn a living; manual work; prolonged and severe exertion;

ōō is pronounced as in food; ŏŏ as in hood; th as in *think*; TH as in *that*; zh as in azure. ~ = related to.

class of men and women who earn their living by being employed by others, the working class, *esp.* manual workers; section of this class organized into trade unions; the Labour Party; the pangs of childbirth; **hard l.,** former punishment for convicted criminals. LABOUR (2), *v.t.* to repeat with pointless detail and emphasis; *v.i.* to engage in l., work very hard; toil, strive, *esp.* to accomplish something; progress with difficulty; experience the pains of childbirth. LABOURED, *adj.* characterized by extreme effort in the execution; clumsy, not spontaneous in style. [L.].

LABOURER [lā′be-rer], *n.* person who labours, *esp.* a manual worker or farm-hand.

LABOUR-EXCHANGE [lā′ber-eks-chānj], *n.* a branch office of the Ministry of Labour and National Service.

LABOUR-SAVING [lā′ber-sā-ving], *adj.* designed or adapted to save work and conserve energy.

LABRADOR [lab′ra-daw(r)], *n.* name of a peninsula in British North America, used to denote various products of this region, as dog, duck etc.

LABURNUM [la-bur′num], *n.* small tree having large hanging racemes of yellow flowers. [L.].

LABYRINTH [la′bi-rinth], *n.* a complicated arrangement of passages and paths, with one exit extremely difficult to find, a maze; *(fig.)* anything resembling this in its intricacy. LABYRINTHINE [la-bi-rin′thin], *adj.* resembling a l., winding, intricate. [Gk.].

LAC (1) [lak], *n.* resinous substance which yields a fine red dye. [Hind.].

LAC (2) **LAKH,** *n.* in India, 100,000 (rupees). [Hind.].

LACE (1) [lās], *n.* decorative fabric of delicate mesh or network with the threads plaited, knotted and turned to make patterns; string or leather thong used for fastening, *esp.* shoes etc.; dash of spirits in coffee etc.; **point l.,** l. made with a single thread. LACE (2), *v.t. and i.* to fasten by means of a l.; decorate with l.; fortify (coffee etc.) with a dash of spirits. [OFr.].

LACERATE [la′se-rāt], *v.t.* to tear, rend; *(fig.)* affect the feelings painfully. LACERATED, *adj.* torn, rent; *(fig.)* deeply grieved or wounded. [L.].

LACERATION [la-se-rā′shn], *n.* act of lacerating; condition of being lacerated; that which is lacerated. [L.].

LACHES [la′shez], *n. (leg.)* negligence; inexcusable delay in making a claim. [OFr.].

LACHRYMA CHRISTI [lak-ri-mah-kris′ti], *n.* a sweet, rich wine from southern Italy. [L.].

LACHRYMAL [lak′ri-mal], *adj.* relating to tears; secreting tears; tending to stimulate tears. [MedL.].

LACHRYMATORY [lak′ri-ma-te-ri], *adj.* relating to, stimulating, tears.

LACHRYMOSE [lak′ri-mōs], *adj.* given to weeping; tearful.

LACING [lā′sing], *n.* method of fastening with a lace drawn through eyelet holes; cord used in this.

LACK (1) [lak], *n.* deficiency, shortage; absence; need, poverty. LACK (2), *v.t. and i.* to be short of, be without, want; be needy. [~LGerm.].

LACKADAISICAL [la-ka-dā′zi-kal], *adj.* affectedly indifferent or listless, dreamily absent-minded. LACKADAISICALLY, *adv.* in a l. manner. [*Next*].

LACK-A-DAY [lak′a-dā], *int. expressing sorrow, melancholy etc.*

LACKEY (1) [la′ki], *n.* man-servant who wears livery or uniform; footman; *(fig.)* servile follower. LACKEY (2), *v.t.* to perform the duties of a l. for; *(fig.)* fawn round.

LACK-LUSTRE [lak′lus-ter], *adj.* deficient in lustre or brightness, dull, dim.

LACONIC(AL) [la-ko′nik(-al)], *adj.* expressing much in few words, concise, pithy. LACONICALLY, *adv.* in a l. way. [Gk.].

LACQUER (1) [la′ker], *n.* a varnish made of shellac which dries with a hard, bright, polished surface; thickened sap of the lac tree, used in the Far East to coat ornamental articles of wood etc.; articles decorated with this. LACQUER (2), *v.t.* to cover or coat with l. [Fr.].

LACROSSE [lah-kros′], *n.* game played with a rubber ball which is caught in a net-like racket, and thrown through a goal. [Fr.].

LACTATION [lak-tā′shn], *n.* act of giving suck; time of suckling; secretion of milk.

LACTEAL (1) [lak′ti-al], *adj.* resembling, relating to milk; conveying chyle. LACTEAL (2), *n. (anat.)* one of the lymphatic vessels conveying chyle. [L.].

LACTESCENT [lak-te′sent], *adj.* turning to milk; secreting milk or a milky juice. [L.].

LACTIC [lak′tik], *adj.* relating to, derived from, milk; *(chem.)* formed from sour milk, as lactic acid.

LACTIFEROUS [lak-ti′fe-rŏŏs], *adj.* secreting milk or white juice. [L.].

LACTOSE [lak′tōs], *n. (chem.)* sugar of milk.

LACUNA (*pl.* **lacunae**) [la-kyŏŏ′nah], *n.* gap, vacant space. LACUNAL, *adj.* relating to or having lacunae. [L.].

LACUSTRINE [la-kus′trin], *adj.* relating to lakes. [L.].

LAD [lad], *n.* boy, youth; *(coll.)* person of rather dashing and irresponsible habits. [ME.].

LADDER (1) [la′der], *n.* device for climbing, often portable, consisting of two parallel side pieces connected by a series of rungs; a break in the mesh of stockings etc. which resembles this; *(fig.)* means of ascending in the world; **accommodation l.,** light railed staircase for the use of senior naval officers. LADDER (2), *v.t. and i.* to cause a l. to appear in stockings. [OE.].

LADE (*pret.* **laded,** *p.pt.* **laden, laded**) [lād], *v.t.* to store freight in a vehicle or vessel; load. [OE.].

LADEN [lā′den], *adj.* loaded to capacity; *(fig.)* burdened, oppressed. [OE.].

LADING [lā′ding], *n.* cargo, freight.

LADLE (1) [lā′dl], *n.* deep spoon with a long handle for scooping out or serving liquids. LADLE (2), *v.t.* to scoop out or serve with a l.; **to l. out,** *(fig.)* hand round freely. [OE.].

LADY [lā′di], *n.* woman of refined manners, good taste and sympathetic understanding, gentlewoman; woman of aristocratic breeding or title; any woman; mistress of a house; title accorded to a woman whose husband is a titled person ranking below a duke, or whose father holds a rank higher than viscount; **lady's smock,** the cuckoo-flower; **lady's maid,** woman employed as a lady's personal servant; **lady's man,** man who seeks the society of women to pay them attention. LADY-KILLER, man who fancies he has an irresistible way with women. LADY-LOVE, sweetheart. [OE.].

LADYBIRD [lā′di-berd], *n. (entom.)* small flying beetle, generally of a brilliant red or yellow colour and black-spotted.

LADY-CHAPEL [lā′di-cha-pel], *n.* chapel dedicated to the Virgin Mary.

LADY-DAY [lā′di-dā], *n.* day of the Annunciation of the Virgin Mary, 25 March, a quarter day.

LADY-IN-WAITING [lā-di-in-wā′ting], *n.* lady of the court whose duty it is to attend on the queen or princesses.

LADYLIKE [lā′di-līk], *adj.* like a lady in manners; well-bred; soft, delicate, effeminate.

LADYSHIP [lā′di-ship], *n.* rank or title of a lady.

LAEVULOSE [lē′vyŏŏ-lōs], *n. (chem.)* a fruit-sugar the crystals of which rotate polarized light to the left. [~L.].

LAG (1) (*pres.pt.* **lagging,** *pret. and p.pt.* **lagged**) [lag], *v.i.* to fall behind, linger, loiter. LAG (2), *n.* retardation, lapse in time, *esp.* when the effect of a force makes itself felt after its initial action. [Uncert.].

LAG (3) (*pres.pt.* **lagging,** *pret. and p.pt.* **lagged**) *v.t.* to catch, send to prison. LAG (4), *n. (slang)* a convict, *esp.* one who has been in prison more than once. [Uncert.].

LAGER [lah′ger], *n.* light German beer stored some months before being drunk. [Germ.].

LAGGARD [la′gerd], *n.* person who falls behind; loiterer, idler. [LAG (1)].

LAGOON [la-gŏŏn′], *n.* shallow stretch of water near the sea or a river; expanse of sea water enclosed in an atoll. [It.].

LAIC(AL) [lā′ik(-al)], *adj.* relating to the laity. [Gk.].

LAID [lād], *adj.* (of paper) having a ribbed watermark.

LAIN [lān], *p.pt. of* LIE. [OE.].

LAIR [lāer], *n.* place to rest in; bed of a wild beast; den. [OE.].

LAIRD [lāerd], *n.* Scottish landowner. [Scots].

LAISSEZ-FAIRE [lā-sā-fāer′], *n.* policy of non-interference in industry and commerce by the state. [Fr.].

LAITY [lā′i-ti], *n.* the people other than the clergy.

LAKE (1) [lāk], *n.* stretch of water enclosed by land; **l. dwellings,** prehistoric houses built on piles in a lake. [L.].

LAKE (2), *n.* a deep red pigment. [Fr.].

LAKH, see LAC (2).

LAM (*pres.pt.* **lamming.** *pret. and p.pt.* **lammed**), *v.t. (slang)* to beat, thrash. [OIcel.].

LAMA [lah′mah], *n.* Tibetan Buddhist priest. [Tibetan].

LAMASERY [lah-mah′se-ri], *n.* Tibetan monastery where lamas live. [Fr.].

LAMB (1) [lam], *n.* young sheep; edible cooked flesh of this; child. LAMB (2), *v.i.* to bring forth a l. or lambs. [OE.].

LAMBENCY [lam′ben-si], *n.* condition of being lambent.

LAMBENT [lam′bent], *adj.* moving lightly, playing on the surface, touching lightly, flickering. [L.].

LAMBING [la′ming], *n.* the birth of lambs; care given to ewes at this season.

LAMBSKIN [lam′skin], *n.* prepared skin and fleece of the lamb.

LAMB'S-WOOL [lamz′wool], *n.* wool from lambs; hot ale, mixed with sugar and the pulp of roasted apples, and spiced with nutmeg.

LAME (1) [lām], *adj.* disabled in a limb, *esp.* in the legs or feet; not smooth in movement; poor, not convincing. LAME (2), *v.t.* to make l. [OE.].

LAMENT (1) [la-ment′], *n.* the expressing aloud of a deeply felt sorrow; elegy. LAMENT (2), *v.t. and i.* to express deep sorrow at or for, grieve for; deplore; utter a l., mourn. [L.].

LAMENTABLE [la′men-ta-bl], *adj.* to be lamented, grievous; mournful, pitiful; of extremely poor quality.

LAMENTATION [la-men-tā′shn], *n.* act of lamenting; expression of sorrow; (*pl.*) (*O.T.*) book of Scripture, the Lamentations of Jeremiah. [L.].

LAMENTING [la-men′ting], *n.* lamentation.

LAMINA (*pl.* laminae) [la′mi-nah], *n.* thin plate, layer or scale. [L.].

LAMINATE (1) [la′mi-nāt], *v.t. and i.* to form into, cover with, laminae. LAMINATE(D), *adj.* consisting of, arranged in, laminae.

LAMINATION [la-mi-nā′shn], *n.* condition of being laminated; process of laminating; (*elect.*) thin plate of soft iron used in an armature.

LAMMAS [la′mas], *n.* 1 August, as the day of first fruits; the feast celebrated on this day. [OE.].

LAMP [lamp], *n.* contrivance for giving light by burning oil or gas or consuming electricity; (*fig.*) means of enlightenment. [Gk.].

LAMPBLACK [lamp′blak], *n.* fine soot from the condensation of the smoke of burning oil, pitch etc.; jet black pigment from this.

LAMPLIGHTER [lamp′lī-ter], *n.* person employed to light street lamps.

LAMPOON (1) [lam-poon′], *n.* literary composition of a crude, personal, satirical nature. LAMPOON (2), *v.t.* to attack, satirize publicly in a l. [Fr.].

LAMPREY [lam′pri], *n.* eel-like, vertebrate fish having a round mouth by which it fastens itself to rocks etc. [Fr.].

LAMPSHADE [lamp′shād], *n.* covering fitted to a lamp in order to concentrate or diffuse the light.

LANCE (1) [lahns], *n.* weapon consisting of a long shaft with a sharp metal head. LANCE (2), *v.t.* to impale with a l.; (*surg.*) make an incision with a lancet. [L.].

LANCE-CORPORAL [lahns-kaw′pe-ral], *n.* (*milit.*) non-commissioned officer of the lowest grade in the British Army.

LANCEOLATE(D) [lahn′si-ō-lāt(-id)], *adj.* (*bot.*) tapering towards the outer extremity.

LANCER [lahn′ser], *n.* cavalry soldier armed with a lance; (*pl.*) kind of dance with set figures; music for this. [OFr.].

LANCE-SERGEANT [lahns-sah′jent], *n.* corporal acting as sergeant.

LANCET [lahn′set], *n.* thin, sharp surgical instrument for making incisions in flesh; (*arch.*) narrow window or arch with a pointed top. [Fr.].

LAND (1) [land], *n.* the solid dry surface of the earth; a portion of this; a recognized region or specific area of the earth, a country etc.; soil, ground, earth, *esp.* arable soil; specific area of land owned as an estate; **to see how the l. lies,** to sound a person; explore the state or facts of a situation. LAND (2), *v.t.* to set, place on shore or land; bring (an aircraft) to earth; take from a transport vehicle and set down; bring (a fish) to the bank; (*coll.*) strike (a blow); (*fig.*) establish a desired relationship with; place, set; win; *v.i.* to come to rest on or by the land, disembark; arrive at a place. [OE.].

LAND-AGENT [land′ā-jent], *n.* person who manages land for the owner; one who deals in landed property.

LAND ARMY [land′ah-mi], *n.* formerly body of

women formed under Government supervision to work on the land, in full *Women's Land Army.*

LANDAU [lan′daw], *n.* four-wheeled horse-drawn carriage with a roof which folds back in two sections. [*Landau*, Bavaria, where first made].

LANDAULET [lan-daw-let′], *n.* type of motor-car with a landau body.

LAND BREEZE [land′brēz], *n.* current of air blowing from the land towards the sea.

LAND-CRAB [land′krab], *n.* crab mainly frequenting the land, *esp.* one of the genus *Gecarcinus.*

LANDED [lan′did], *adj.* possessing an estate in land; composed of real estate or land; disembarked; (*slang*) in a difficult situation.

LANDFALL [land′fawl], *n.* (*naut.*) first land sighted after a voyage.

LAND-GIRL [land′gerl], *n.* woman employed, *esp.* as a member of the former Women's Land Army, to cultivate the land.

LANDGRAVE [land′grāv], *n.* (*hist.*) count in Germany holding special territorial judicial powers. [MH-Germ.].

LANDHOLDER [land′hōl-der], *n.* freeholder; land-owner; tenant holding land.

LANDING [lan′ding], *n.* act of one who lands; act of going ashore; forcible descent on a coast; the alighting of an aircraft on the ground; place for setting on shore or for stepping on to; intermediate stage between two flights of stairs; passage at the top of a flight of stairs from which rooms are reached. LANDING-CRAFT, (*milit.*) vessel specially built to facilitate the landing of troops and equipment on a hostile coast. LANDING-NET, net fastened to the end of a long handle and used by fishermen for landing heavy fish caught by rod and line. LANDING-STAGE, pier to which passenger boats are secured, jetty; platform built over the water on to which passengers step from a boat.

LANDLADY [land′lā-di], *n.* female landlord; wife of a landlord; woman who owns or manages a boarding house or inn.

LAND-LINE [land′līn], *n.* telephone cable running overland.

LANDLOCKED [land′lokd], *adj.* enclosed by land.

LANDLORD [land′lawd], *n.* owner of land or houses; master or manager of an inn; proprietor of a lodging-house.

LANDLUBBER [land′lu-ber], *n.* (*naut.*) landsman, person with no knowledge of or skill in nautical matters.

LANDMARK [land′mahk], *n.* salient characteristic or mark serving to indicate the boundary of land; object which serves as a guide to a locality; (*fig.*) notable stage or episode; boundary mark.

LAND-MINE [land′mīn], *n.* (*milit.*) mine capable of employment against troops etc.

LANDRAIL [land′rāl], *n.* the corn-crake.

LANDSCAPE [land′skāp], *n.* region of countryside as seen by an observer, a prospect; representation of this in a pictorial art medium, picture of scenery; branch of painting and drawing specializing in this. [Du.].

LANDSCAPE-GARDENER [land-skāp-gah′de-ner], *n.* one who lays out grounds, parks and gardens, so as to produce a natural effect.

LANDSLIDE [land′slīd], *n.* fall of a mass of land due to undermining or erosion, landslip; (*fig.*) serious electoral defeat of a political party.

LANDSLIP [land′slip], *n.* small landslide.

LANDSMAN [landz′man], *n.* one who lives and works on land; (*naut.*) novice on board ship.

LAND-SURVEYING [land′ser-vā-ing], *n.* art of measuring and mapping land, *esp.* landed estates. LAND-SURVEYOR, *n.* person trained to measure and draw plans of landed estates etc.

LAND-TAX [land′taks], *n.* tax assessed on land and buildings.

LAND-VALUE [land′va-lyoo], *n.* (*econ.*) value of land, *esp.* as a basis for taxation or rating.

LAND WIND [land′wind], *n.* wind blowing from the land towards the sea.

LANE [lān], *n.* narrow way, *esp.* in the country; country by-road; narrow street; passage between lines of people; recognized course for shipping. [OE.].

LANG SYNE [lang-sīn′], *n.* (Scots) long ago. [Scots].

LANGUAGE [lang′gwij], *n.* the complete set of articulate sounds and sound combinations used as a means of verbal communication, *esp.* by a particular nation, people or race; the graphical representation of this; any mode of expression, style; the characteristic terminology of a science etc.; any method of

oo is pronounced as in food; oo as in hood; th as in *th*ink; TH as in *th*at; zh as in azure. ~ = related to.

DSE—M

expressing thoughts and feelings; **bad l.**, profanity, swearing. [OFr.].

LANGUID [lang'gwid], *adj.* listless, indisposed to exertion; slow, lifeless, half-hearted. [L.].

LANGUISH [lang'gwish], *v.i.* to become languid, lose health and vigour; grow weak, wane; experience an enervating attack of melancholy. **LANGUISHING**, *adj.* that languishes, fading; wistful and tender. [Fr.].

LANGUOR [lang'ger], *n.* condition of being languid; lassitude, listlessness; state of dreamy inaction. [L.].

LANGUOROUS [lang'ge-rōōs], *adj.* displaying or inducing languor.

LANIARD, see LANYARD.

LANK [langk], *adj.* lean, thin and long; loose and drooping; (of hair) straight and limp. [OE.].

LANKY [lang'ki], *adj.* having a lean figure, tall and thin.

LANOLIN [la'nō-lin], *n.* a grease obtained from wool; ointment made from this. [L.].

LANTERN, LANTHORN† [lan'tern], *n.* portable lamp usually consisting of a case with one or more windows of horn or glass, and enclosing a flame fed by grease or oil; chamber at the top of a lighthouse, housing the lights; (*arch.*) open-sided or glazed structure at the top of a church, dome etc., to provide light or ventilation. LANTERN-JAWED, *adj.* having a square-formed jaw framing a lean, hollow-cheeked face. [L.].

LANYARD, LANIARD [lan'yahd], *n.* (*naut.*) short piece of rope made fast to anything to secure it; length of cord looped round the shoulder in artillery and some other uniforms. [~Fr.].

LAODICEAN [lā-ō-di-sē'an], *adj.* like the Christians of Laodicea, lukewarm in religion or other matters. [Rev. iii, 14-16]

LAP (1) [lap], *n.* overhanging piece of material or garment; space between the knees and the waist available as a seat or support when one is seated; one circuit of a racing track; a definite stage in a line of progress. LAP (2) (*pres.pt.* LAPPING, *pret. and p.pt.* LAPPED), *v.t. and i.* to fold over, wrap; surround; place something so that it partially covers another; fold or turn back; overlap; cover a l.; be a l. ahead of. [OE.].

LAP (3) (*pres.pt.* **lapping**, *pret. and p.pt.* **lapped**), *v.t. and i.* to lick up with the tongue; make a noise like this; **to l. up**, to swallow or assimilate eagerly and readily. LAP (4), *n.* a licking up of liquid with the tongue; the sound thus made. [OE.].

LAPDOG [lap'dog], *n.* small pet dog. [LAP (1)].

LAPEL [la-pel'], *n.* continuation of a coat collar turned back in the form of a flap. [LAP (1)].

LAPIDARY (1) [la'pi-da-ri], *n.* one engaged in the polishing and cutting of stones; connoisseur of precious stones. LAPIDARY (2), *adj.* relating to stones; relating to the art of cutting and polishing precious stones; apt for engraving on stone as an inscription; **l. wheel**, lathe for cutting and polishing precious stones. [L.].

LAPIS LAZULI [la-pis-la'zyōō-li], *n.* light-blue semi-precious stone. [L. and MedL.].

LAPPET [la'pet], *n.* loose flap or fold, *esp.* on a woman's cap or head-dress. [LAP (1)].

LAPSE (1) [laps], *n.* a sliding or imperceptible passing; that which has thus passed by, a period of time; slip, mistake; omission; deviation from strict principles of conduct, morality or truth. LAPSE (2), *v.i.* to pass by degrees, glide, slip; fail to maintain a certain standard of morality, err; (*leg.*) cease to be valid; pass to another. LAPSED, *adj.* fallen; passed to another; (*leg.*) (of a legacy etc.) inoperative because the right or claim to it has passed to another. [L.].

LAPWING [lap'wing], *n.* the crested peewit or green plover. [OE.].

LAR (*pl.* **lares**) [lah(r), lāer'ēz], *n.* (*Rom. antiq.*) household god. [L.].

LARBOARD† (1) [lah'bawd], *n.* (*naut.*) left side of a ship when looking from the stern towards the bows; port. LARBOARD† (2), *adj.* relating to, placed on, the l.; port. [~ME.].

LARCENOUS [lah'se-nŏŏs], *adj.* having the features of theft; thieving. [*Next*].

LARCENY [lah'se-ni], *n.* theft, stealing, *esp.* on a minor scale. [~OFr.].

LARCH [lahch], *n.* coniferous tree of the genus *Larix*. [Germ.].

LARD (1) [lahd], *n.* pig fat, refined and used in cooking. LARD (2), *v.t.* to smear or cover with l.;

cover with pieces of bacon fat before cooking; (*fig.*) enrich, embellish; overdecorate. [OFr.].

LARDER [lah'der], *n.* place where provisions etc. are kept; pantry. [OFr.].

LARGE (1) [lahj], *adj.* big, great in size, bulk, quantity; spacious; numerous, copious; ample, broad; liberal; generous; comprehensive. LARGE (2), *adv.* in a l. manner. LARGE (3), *n. only in phr.* **at l.**, free; unrestricted, not attached to any specific part; discursively. LARGELY, *adv.* to a l. degree or extent. [OFr.].

LARGE-HEARTED [lahj-hah'tid], *adj.* liberal, generous, magnanimous; tolerant; charitable.

LARGESSE [lah-jes'], *n.* present, gift; alms thrown to a crowd. [OFr.].

LARGHETTO [lah-ge'tō], *adv.* (*mus.*) rather slowly. [It.].

LARGO (1) [lah'gō], *adv. and adj.* (*mus.*) in broad, slow and measured time. LARGO (2), *n.* (*mus.*) movement or piece in l. time. [It.].

LARIAT [la'ri-at], *n.* long rope with a slip-noose for picketing horses, or for use as a lasso. [Span.].

LARK (1) [lahk], *n.* genus of small birds including the skylark. [OE.].

LARK (2), *n.* practical joke, bit of fun, frolic. LARK (3), *v.i.* to participate in a l.; indulge in tricks; frolic. [Uncert.].

LARKSPUR [lahk'sper], *n.* (*bot.*) plant of the genus *Delphinium*, with a spur-shaped calyx.

LARRIKIN [la'ri-kin], *n.* (*Australian coll.*) a rough, tough, hooligan, rowdy. [Uncert.].

LARVA (*pl.* **larvae**) [lah'va, 'vē], *n.* (*entom.*) fly, moth, butterfly etc. in its caterpillar, grub or maggot stage; fish, frog etc. in the corresponding stage. LARVAL, *adj.* relating to the l. stage. [L.].

LARYNGEAL [la-rin'ji-al], *adj.* relating to the larynx.

LARYNGITIS [la-rin-ji'tis], *n.* inflammation of the larynx. [Gk.].

LARYNGOSCOPE [la-ring'gō-skōp], *n.* (*med.*) instrument fitted with reflecting mirrors for examining the larynx and throat. LARYNGOSCOPY [la-ring-go'sko-pi], *n.* technique of using the l.; employment of this. [Gk.].

LARYNGOTOMY [la-ring-go'to-mi], *n.* (*surg.*) operation of cutting into the larynx.

LARYNX [la'ringks], *n.* (*anat.*) cartilaginous cavity of the upper part of the windpipe at the back of the throat, containing the vocal cords. [Gk.].

LASCAR [las'kah(r)], *n.* native East Indian employed as a sailor. [Pers.].

LASCIVIOUS [la-si'vi-ŏŏs], *adj.* lustful; wanton; exciting lust. [LL.].

LASH (1) [lash], *v.t.* to strike with a whip, flog; cause to move rapidly in the manner of a wielded whip; fasten tightly with the coils of a rope; (*fig.*) scourge with censure, satirize vehemently; (*fig.*) excite to violence; dash violently against; *v.i.* to lunge out violently with legs or arms; attack violently; (of rain) beat down heavily. LASH (2), *n.* thong, *esp.* one forming part of a whip; stroke given with a whip or anything flexible; (*fig.*) severe satire, cutting retort; a single eyelash. [ME.].

LASHER [la'sher], *n.* one who lashes; vent in a weir.

LASHING [la'shing], *n.* piece of rope for making fast one thing to another; beating, chastisement; (*pl.*) (*slang*) a great deal of anything.

LASS [las], *n.* female child; young woman, girl; sweetheart. [ME.].

LASSIE [la'si], *n.* (*Scots*) young lass; small girl.

LASSITUDE [la'si-tyōōd], *n.* faintness, weariness in body or mind. [L.].

LASSO (1) [la-sōō', la'sō], *n.* long strip of leather or length of rope with a running noose at one end, used by cowboys to catch cattle. LASSO (2), *v.t.* to catch by means of a l. [Span.].

LAST (1) [lahst], *n.* model of the human foot, on which shoes are made or repaired. [OE.].

LAST (2), *n.* load, cargo; a specific weight or measure. [OE.].

LAST (3), *adj.* occurring at the end of a series, coming after all the others, hindmost; latest; final; immediately prior to the present event, or to any specified fact etc.; the least likely or desirable. LAST (4), *adv.* on the l. occasion; in the end, finally. LAST (5), *n.* that which is l., the end. [OE.].

LAST (6), *v.i.* to continue in time, endure, continue unimpaired; **to l. out**, to maintain strength; hold out. [OE.].

LASTING [lah'sting], *adj.* permanent, continuing, durable. LASTINGLY, *adv.* to a l. degree.

The accent ′ after a syllable = stress (u-pon′). The mark ‾ over a vowel = length (ā in made; ō in bone).

LASTLY [lahst'li], *adv.* in the last place, finally.

LATAKIA [la-ta-kē'ah], *n.* a fine Syrian tobacco. [*Latakia*, Syrian port].

LATCH (1) [lach], *n.* movable catch for a door or gate; small lock supplementing the main lock on an outside door. LATCH (2), *v.t.* to fasten with a l. [Uncert.].

LATCHET† [la'chit], *n.* leather shoelace. [OFr.].

LATCH-KEY [lach'kē], *n.* key opening the main door of a house.

LATE (1) [lāt], *adj.* arriving after the expected or settled time, tardy; appearing after the normal season, backward; taking place near the end of a period; existing not long ago; having just previously come to an end; former; deceased; recent. LATE (2), *adv.* after the expected or designated time; towards the end of a particular period or season; at or to a l. hour of the night. [OE.].

LATEEN [la-tēn'], *n.* (*naut.*) triangular sail, extended by a long yard, used on small boats; boat bearing such a sail. [Fr.].

LATELY [lāt'li], *adv.* not long ago, recently, of late.

LATENCY [lā'ten-si], *n.* quality of being latent.

LATENT [lā'tent], *adj.* concealed, lying dormant, present but not visible; l. heat, heat given off or absorbed by a body in changing its state. [L.].

LATERAL [la'te-ral], *adj.* pertaining to, situated at, or proceeding from the side.

LATEST [lā'test], *adj.* most recent. [OE.].

LATEX [lā'teks], *n.* (*bot.*) milky juice of certain plants, *esp.* of the rubber-tree; vegetable milk. [L.].

LATH [lahth], *n.* thin strip of wood, *esp.* one used to form a support for tiles or plaster; strip of wood used for trellis-work or venetian blinds. LATHY, *adj.* thin; long and slender. [Uncert.].

LATHE [lāth], *n.* turner's machine tool which rotates the material to be cut. [Uncert.].

LATHER (1) [lah'THer], *n.* froth made by rubbing soap in water; foam of sweat exuded by a horse. LATHER (2), *v.t. and i.* to cover with l.; form l. [OE.].

LATI-, *pref.* broad. [L.].

LATIN (1) [la'tin], *adj.* relating to Latium, or to the Latins; relating to, written in, Latin; L. Church, the Roman Catholic Church as distinct from the Eastern Orthodox; L. race, race whose members speak a language derived from L.; Ecclesiastical L., L. as used by the R. C. Church; Late L., L. as used from the end of the classical period to about the sixth century; Low L., medieval L.; L. America, the countries of the American continent where Spanish or Portuguese is the principal language. LATIN (2), *n.* language of the ancient Romans; member of one of the L. races. [L.].

LATINISM [la'ti-nizm], *n.* a Latin idiom.

LATINIST [la'ti-nist], *n.* one versed in Latin.

LATINIZE [la'ti-nīz], *v.t. and i.* to give Latin form or terminations to; use words or phrases borrowed from the Latin; make Latin in character.

LATITUDE [la'ti-tyōōd], *n.* the angular distance of a place, or its meridian, from the equator; (*pl.*) regions, climes; scope, extent; freedom from restrictions, *esp.* on thought; (*astron.*) the angular distance of a heavenly body from the ecliptic. LATITUDINAL [la-ti-tyōō'di-nal], *adj.* relating to l.; in the direction of l. [L.].

LATITUDINARIAN (1) [la-ti-tyōō-di-nāer'i-an], *adj.* not restricted, liberal, broad-minded in views and principles; (*theol.*) refusing to restrict oneself to a literal interpretation of religious dogma, tending towards unorthodoxy or laxity of belief. LATITUDINARIAN (2), *n.* person of l. outlook.

LATRINE [lat-rēn'], *n.* camp lavatory. [L.].

LATTER [la'ter], *adj.* later, hinder; happening after something else; last mentioned of two. LATTERLY, *adv.* lately, of late, in time not long past; towards the end of a specified time. [OE.].

LATTICE [la'tis], *n.* network of thin strips of wood or laths set obliquely; window with diamond-shaped panes held secure by lead strips crossing diagonally. LATTICED, *adj.* in the form of a l.; furnished with a l. [OFr.].

LAUD (1) [lawd], *n.* praise, eulogy; (*pl.*) prayer of praise in divine worship, usually recited at dawn; song of praise. LAUD (2), *v.t.* to praise; celebrate. [L.].

LAUDABLE [law'da-bl], *adj.* worthy of praise. [L.].

LAUDANUM [lod'num], *n.* crude opium prepared in spirits, tincture of opium. [MdL.].

LAUDATION [law-dā'shn], *n.* act of praising; state of being praised; eulogy, praise. [L.].

LAUDATORY [law'da-te-ri], *adj.* containing praise; tending to praise; eulogistic. [LL.].

LAUGH (1) [lahf], *v.i.* to utter a sound or sounds expressive of a nervous or reflexive response attendant upon a feeling of happiness, amusement etc., and accompanied by a grin and shaking of the body; be pleased; give expression to good humour; to l. at, to ridicule; take no heed of; to l. in someone's face, to defy someone openly; *v.t.* to produce a certain effect on (a person or thing) by laughing; to l. out of court, to discomfit (an accuser) by ridicule; to l. off, to turn away in pleasantry a remark threatening to be embarrassing. LAUGH (2), *n.* act of laughing; sound thus uttered. [OE.].

LAUGHABLE [lahf'a-bl], *adj.* causing laughter; ludicrous, ridiculous.

LAUGHING-GAS [lah'fing-gas], *n.* nitrous oxide, used as an anaesthetic in dentistry.

LAUGHING HYENA [lah-fing-hī-ē'nah], *n.* the spotted hyena.

LAUGHING JACKASS [lah-fing-ja'kas], *n.* an Australian bird allied to the kingfisher, with a harsh guffawing cry.

LAUGHING-STOCK [lah'fing-stok], *n.* an object of derision.

LAUGHTER [lahf'ter], *n.* the sound of laughing; convulsive merriment. [OE.].

LAUNCH (1) [lawnch, lahnch], *v.t.* to throw, hurl through the air; cause to move; initiate, start; cause to glide into the water, *esp.* a new ship for the first time; *v.i.* to glide into the water; to l. out, (*fig.*) to begin a new set of operations on a large scale. LAUNCH (2), *n.* act of launching a boat; movement of a boat as it is launched. [ME. from OFr.].

LAUNCH (3), *n.* a boat, usually driven by motor, used for pleasure or patrolling purposes; largest boat carried by a warship. [Span.].

LAUNDER [lawn'der], *v.t.* to wash, dry and iron dirty clothes or linen; *v.i.* (of fabrics) to endure washing etc. (well, badly etc.). [OFr.].

LAUNDRESS [lawn'dres], *n.* woman who launders clothes for a living.

LAUNDRY [lawn'dri], *n.* establishment or place where clothes are washed; clothes and other articles to be washed. [OFr.].

LAUREATE (1) [law'ri-at, lo'ri-at], *adj.* crowned with laurel; Poet L., poet appointed for life to an official position in the Royal Household and expected to write suitable poetry on state occasions. LAUREATE (2), *n.* person crowned with laurel; Poet L. [L.].

LAUREL [lo'rel], *n.* a bay-tree, one of several species of evergreen shrubs, the leaves of which were used in ancient Greece to make wreaths of honour and success; (*pl.*) (*fig.*) reward of success, honours. LAURELLED, *adj.* crowned with l., honoured. [L.].

LAURUSTINUS, LAURESTINUS [law-rus-tī'nus], *n.* an ornamental evergreen shrub. [L.].

LAVA [lah'vah], *n.* mineral matter which issues molten from a volcano; (*geol.*) glassy or finely crystalline rocks of eruptive origin. [It.].

LAVAGE [lā'vij, la-vahzh'], *n.* (*med.*) internal washing, *esp.* of a therapeutic nature. [Fr.].

LAVATORY [la'va-te-ri], *n.* place for washing; room fitted with wash-basins and conveniences; privy. [L.].

LAVE [lāv], *v.t. and i.* to wash, bath, bathe. [OE.].

LAVENDER (1) [la'ven-der], *n.* (*bot.*) a fragrant, pale purple-flowered plant; the perfume characteristic of this; light purple colour; l. water, perfume made from l. LAVENDER (2), *adj.* relating to the l. plant, its scent or colour. [OFr.].

LAVISH (1) [la'vish], *adj.* extremely liberal, very generous; extravagant, wasteful; ample, abundant. LAVISH (2), *v.t.* to give with excessive generosity; spend extravagantly, squander. [OFr.].

LAW [law], *n.* the body of rules governing the conduct, affairs and relationships of the members of a nation or community, as established and administered by authority; any one of these rules; system of legal operation, jurisprudence; study of this; body of rules and customs relating to social tradition; an abstract statement formulating the general relationship of a fact to its context; a definition expressing the specific sequence of events peculiar to a given activity under certain conditions. [OE.].

LAW-ABIDING [law'a-bī-ding], *adj.* having a conscientious regard for the law.

LAW COURT [law'kawt], *n.* court where the law is administered; (*pl.*) public buildings (in London) used for this purpose.

LAWFUL [law'fool], *adj.* allowed by, in accordance

ōō is pronounced as in food; ŏŏ as in hood; th as in *th*ink; TH as in *th*at; zh as in azure.   ~ = related to.

with, the law; legitimate, acknowledged or constituted by law; rightful.

LAWGIVER [law'gi-ver], *n.* one who prescribes laws.

LAWLESS [law'les], *adj.* not subject to or governed by law; contrary to law; unruly.

LAWN (1) [lawn], *n.* stretch of more or less flat ground, covered with grass and kept closely mown. [OFr.].

LAWN (2), *n.* fine linen or cambric, *esp.* used for bishops' sleeves. [*Laon*, French town].

LAWN-MOWER [lawn'mō-er], *n.* machine for cutting the grass on a lawn.

LAWN TENNIS [law'n-te'nis], *n.* game played on a specially marked-out lawn or court, in which a small felt-covered rubber ball is hit to and fro over a net by opposing players by means of rackets.

LAWSUIT [law'syōōt], *n.* an action at law.

LAWYER [law'yer], *n.* one expert in legal knowledge and procedure who practises law; legal adviser, *esp.* a solicitor.

LAX [laks], *adj.* loose, slack; not strict, free, *esp.* in morals; careless; loose in the bowels. [L.].

LAXATIVE (1) [lak'sa-tiv], *adj.* loosening the bowels, purging. LAXATIVE (2), *n.* a l. medicine. [L.].

LAXITY [lak'si-ti], *n.* looseness; inexactness; absence of moral correctitude. [L.].

LAY (1) [lā], *n.* short narrative poem; **lyrical** poem; song or ballad. [OFr.].

LAY (2), *adj.* relating to the laity, non-ecclesiastical; non-specialist, non-professional. LAY-BROTHER, *n.* person received into a convent of monks without taking holy orders. LAY-CLERK, *n.* layman who reads the responses in a church service. [Gk.].

LAY (3) (*pret. and p.pt.* **laid**), *v.t.* to put down, set, cause to lie in a particular place or be in a particular condition; place in order, *esp.* eating utensils; prepare (a table); cause to settle; make subside or disappear; strike down; produce (eggs); propose odds for a wager; impose as a tax etc.; charge with; present; assert, as a claim; (*naut.*) place in dock; *v.i.* to produce eggs; make a bet; **to l. about one,** to fight with wild and reckless vigour; **to l. aside,** to discontinue; **to l. by the heels,** to place in custody; **to l. down,** to relinquish; **to l. down the law,** to be dogmatic; **to l. off,** (*slang*) to cease; (*naut.*) cause a ship to move farther away; suspend temporarily from work; **to l. on,** to inflict (blows); strike vigorously; supply (water, power etc.) to houses by means of pipes, wires etc.; (*slang*) arrange; **to l. out,** to plan; expend; render insensible by a blow; prepare (a body) for the grave; **to l. to,** (*naut.*) to bring a ship into a stationary position; **to l. up,** to store; (*pass.*) be confined to bed. LAY (4), *n.* that which is laid; position in which a person or object is found; (*naut.*) direction in which the strands of a rope are twisted; share of profit. [OE.].

LAY-BY [lā'bī], *n.* railway siding; cleared space beside a road in which vehicles may stop without impeding traffic.

LAYER (1) [lā'er], *n.* person who lays, *esp.* odds; bird which lays eggs; section of a substance, placed upon another, a stratum; (*hort.*) undetached shoot laid underground to enable it to take root. LAYER (2), *v.t.* (*hort.*) to bend a branch or stem of a plant so that it is covered by earth and able to take root.

LAYETTE [lā-et'], *n.* new-born baby's outfit. [Fr.].

LAY-FIGURE [lā'fi-ger], *n.* artist's model made of wood etc., in imitation of the human body; (*fig.*) puppet, nonentity. [~Du.].

LAYMAN [lā'man], *n.* one who is not a clergyman; man with no professional skill or status.

LAY-OFF [lā-of'], *n.* temporary period of unemployment for a worker during a slack season.

LAY-OUT [lā'owt], *n.* plan of buildings etc.; ground plan; design or make-up of a publication; rough draft of an advertisement design.

LAZARETTO [la-zah-re'tō], *n.* hospital for diseased beggars or lepers; place of quarantine. [It.].

LAZAR-HOUSE [la'zah-hows], *n.* lazaretto.

LAZE [lāz], *v.t. and i.* to waste time in idleness; indulge in the minimum of exertion. [*Next*].

LAZY [lā'zi], *adj.* unwilling to work, not disposed to exert oneself; **l. tongs,** series of collapsible scissor-like bars opening out in a criss-cross pattern to grasp an object. LAZY-BONES, *n.* l. person. [Uncert.].

LEA [lē], *n.* meadow or pasture. [OE.].

LEAD (1) [led], *n.* the heavy metallic element Pb, a lump of this used for taking soundings at sea; small stick of plumbago used in pencils; (*print.*) thin strip

of metal used to separate lines of type; (*pl.*) sheets of l. for covering roofs; roofs so covered; **red l.,** oxide of l.; **white l.,** carbonate of l.; **to swing the l.,** to sham, malinger. LEAD (2), *adj.* made of l.   LEAD (3), *v.t.* to cover with l.; (*print.*) insert thin metal strips between lines of type. LEADED, *adj.* (*print.*) (of type) fitted with or set in l.; separated by leads. [OE.].

LEAD (4) (*pret. and p.pt.* **led**) [lēd], *v.t.* to conduct, guide, *esp.* by the hand; act as head, controller or principal agent in; bring; persuade to act in a certain way; cause; spend, pass; cause to spend; be at the head of; (*milit.*) command; (*cards*) play as the first card; *v.i.* to proceed in front and show the way; act as chief or principal; be ahead of all other competitors; go; **to l. off,** to make the first move in a game; **to l. out of,** to give on to; **to l. to,** to result in; **to l. up to,** to approach indirectly; provide opportunity for.   LEAD (5), *n.* action of leading; position or right of leading, command; direction, guide; strap, chain or cord for leading a dog etc.; privilege of leading off in a game; card played first; principal rôle in a play or film; actor or actress who plays this; the distance a competitor in a race is in front of his nearest rival; (*elect.*) length of wire acting as a conductor of current. [OE.].

LEADEN [le'den], *adj.* made of lead; (*fig.*) heavy, dull; inert.

LEADER [lē'der], *n.* one who or that which leads; horse at the head of a team; principal player in each section of an orchestra, *esp.* the principal of the first violins; principal article in a newspaper, editorial; (*leg.*) senior counsel; (*pl.*) (*print.*) line of dots.

LEADERETTE [lē-de-ret'], *n.* short leading article or paragraph written by an editor.

LEADERSHIP [lē'der-ship], *n.* office of a leader; qualities of character needed in a leader.

LEAD-IN [lēd-in'], *n.* (*radio*) conductor connecting an aerial to a receiving set.

LEADING (1) [le'ding], *n.* strips of lead used for building purposes, *esp.* in casement windows.

LEADING (2) [lē'ding], *n.* guidance, direction. LEADING (3), *adj.* that leads; chief, principal; front.

LEADING ARTICLE [lē-ding-ah'ti-kl], *n.* any one of a regular series of articles in a newspaper, devoted primarily to expressing editorial opinion.

LEADING QUESTION [lē-ding-kwes'chn], *n.* (*leg.*) question which suggests the answer required.

LEADING-REIN [lē'ding-rān], *n.* control rein held by a riding instructor and connected to the bit of the pupil's horse.

LEADING-STRINGS [lē'ding-stringz], *n.*(*pl.*) strings by which children are supported when beginning to walk; **in l.,** unable to act for oneself.

LEAD PENCIL [led-pen'sil], *n.* slender stick of black-lead encased in a covering and used for drawing or writing.

LEADSMAN [ledz'man], *n.* (*naut.*) sailor appointed to take soundings.

LEAF (1) (*pl.* **leaves**) [lēf, lēvz], *n.* (*bot.*) one of the thin, flat growths from the stem of a plant; anything resembling this in shape or thinness; sheet of a book etc. comprising two pages; insertable or folding flap of a table top; thin sheet of pressed or hammered metal; **to turn over a new l.,** to mend one's ways. LEAF (2), *v.i.* to produce leaves; *v.t.* **to l. through,** to glance through (a book) quickly. [OE.].

LEAFAGE [lē'fij], *n.* leaves collectively, foliage.

LEAFLET [lē'flet], *n.* small pamphlet, handbill of unstitched pages; (*bot.*) little leaf.

LEAF-MOULD [lēf'mōld], *n.* humus formed by decayed leaves.

LEAGUE (1) [lēg], *n.* measure of length equal in England to three miles. [LL.].

LEAGUE (2), *n.* organized alliance of individuals, states etc., for the protection or furtherance of common interests; collective body of such persons, states etc., *esp.* a group of sports clubs in competition for championships. LEAGUE (3), *v.t. and i.* to form into a l.; unite together in a l. LEAGUER, *n.* person who belongs to a l. [Fr.].

LEAK (1) [lēk], *n.* crack or hole in a container or vessel which allows liquid, gas etc. to escape or enter improperly; the water, gas etc. which is thus let in or out; (*elect.*) escape of electricity owing to imperfect insulation; (*coll.*) an unauthorized disclosure of information. LEAK (2), *v.i.* (of water, gas etc.) to enter or escape through a l.; **to l. out,** (*fig.*) to become known gradually, unintentionally or irregularly. [OIcel.].

LEAKAGE [lē'kij], *n.* process of leaking; quantity

lost or entering through a leak; (*fig.*) improper disclosure of information; (*comm.*) loss not accounted for.

LEAL [lēl], *adj.* (*Scots and northern dial.*) loyal, faithful, true; **land of the l.**, heaven. [OFr.].

LEAN (1) [lēn], *adj.* having or consisting of little fat; having relatively little flesh on the body, thin; (*fig.*) poor, unproductive. LEAN (2), *n.* that part of meat or flesh which is free from fat. LEANLY, *adv.* poorly. [OE.].

LEAN (3) (*pret. and p.pt.* **leaned** [lēnd] or **leant** [lent]), *v.t. and i.* to deviate from the perpendicular, incline; incline (towards); rest (against), support oneself (on); be partial (to), disposed (to); (*fig.*) rely (upon). LEAN (4), *n.* slope, inclination. [OE.].

LEANING [lē'ning], *n.* act or state of one who leans, inclination, predisposition.

LEAN-TO [lēn'tōō], *n.* shed with a roof sloping down from a wall.

LEAP (1) (*pret. and p.pt.* **leaped, leapt** [lēp, lēpt, lept], *v.t. and i.* to make a leap or leaps, jump, spring in the air; spring over by a leap; cause to jump; **to l. at,** to accept eagerly. LEAP (2), *n.* a jump, bound, spring into the air; the height or length of this; (*fig.*) sudden upward trend. [OE.].

LEAP-FROG [lēp'frog], *n.* game in which each of the players leaps over the stooping backs of the others in turn.

LEAP YEAR [lēp'yēer], *n.* a year of 366 days formed by adding an extra day to February.

LEARN (*pret. and p.pt.* **learned, learnt** [lurn], *v.t. and i.* to acquire knowledge of; commit to memory; develop skill or technique by practice; gain knowledge, receive information; understand, experience; endeavour by practice to become. [OE.].

LEARNED [lur'nid], *adj.* possessing learning acquired by study; erudite; containing and showing learning; relating to learning and study.

LEARNER [lur'ner], *n.* person who is learning, novice.

LEARNING [lur'ning], *n.* act of studiously acquiring knowledge; knowledge, scholarship, the whole body of knowledge possessed by a scholar. [OE.].

LEASE (1) [lēs], *n.* a letting of land or tenements for a term of years; the contract for such letting; any tenure, term, period or time. LEASE (2), *v t.* to let or hold on l. LEASABLE, *adj.* able to be leased.

LEASEHOLD (1) [lēs'hōld], *n.* tenure held by lease. LEASEHOLD (2), *adj.* held on a lease.

LEASE-LEND, LEND-LEASE [lēs-lend', lend-lēs'], *adj.* used to denote a policy or goods originating from the provisions of the American Lease and Lend Act, 1941-45.

LEASH (1) [lēsh], *n.* thong, strap etc. by which a dog or hawk is held close; set of three hounds, whippets, hares etc.; a brace and a half. LEASH (2), *v.t.* to hold fast by means of a l. [OFr.].

LEAST (1) [lēst], *adj.* smallest. LEAST (2), *n.* the l. amount, the smallest in measurement or estimation; **not in the l.,** not a bit; **at l.,** nevertheless, not less than. LEAST (3), *adv.* in the smallest or lowest degree or extent, below all others. [OE.].

LEASTWISE [lēst'wīz], *adv.* anyhow, at least.

LEATHER (1) [le'THer], *n.* the skin of animals prepared for use by tanning; a football. LEATHER (2), *adj.* consisting of l. LEATHER (3), *v.t.* to beat, thrash, *esp.* with a l. belt. [OE.].

LEATHERETTE [le-THe-ret'], *n.* imitation leather.

LEATHERN [le'THern], *adj.* made of leather; like leather.

LEATHERY [le'THe-ri], *adj.* like leather, tough.

LEAVE (1) [lēv], *n.* permission, temporary freedom granted by permission, *esp.* holiday from work or duty for a member of the armed forces; departure, farewell; (*billiards*) position in which the balls are left after a stroke or break; **French l.,** absence from duty without permission. [OE.].

LEAVE (2) (*pret. and p.pt.* **left**), *v.t.* to depart from; terminate residence in or association with; abandon, desert; let lie or stay; forget to pick up or carry away; possess at one's death; bequeath; entrust; deposit; render, cause to become; forbear; refer; (*arith.*) cause to remain over; *v.i.* to desist; depart; **to l. off,** to cease to wear; cease; **to l. out,** to omit. [OE.].

LEAVEN (1) [le'ven], *n.* substance which makes dough rise, yeast, barm; (*fig.*) anything which effects fresh activity through modification. LEAVEN (2), *v.t.* to mix up or raise with l.; (*fig.*) imbue; modify, lighten.

LEAVES [lēvz], *n. pl. of* LEAF.

LEAVE-TAKING [lēv'tā-king], *n.* formal termination of a meeting, parting compliments.

LEAVINGS [lē'vingz], *n.*(*pl.*) things left or cast away; relics; refuse.

LEBENSRAUM [lā'benz-rowm], *n.* territory viewed by a power as belonging to its indispensable economic domain. [Germ.].

LECHER [le'cher], *n.* one habitually indulging in lewdness. [OFr.].

LECHEROUS [le'che-rŏŏs], *adj.* immoderately given to sexual indulgence, lustful; provoking lust.

LECHERY [le'che-ri], *n.* lecherous behaviour, lewdness.

LECITHIN [le'si-thin], *n.* (*physiol.*) a waxy constituent of nerve tissue and yolk of egg, possessing therapeutic properties. [Gk.].

LECTERN [lek'tern], *n.* reading desk for supporting heavy books, *esp.* one used in church. [LL.].

LECTURE (1) [lek'tyŏŏr], *n.* informative discourse on a particular subject delivered before an audience; formal reproof, reprimand. LECTURE (2), *v.t. and i.* to instruct by means of lectures; reprove; deliver a l. [Fr.].

LECTURER [lek'tyŏŏr-er], *n.* one who lectures, *esp.* a university or college teacher.

LED [led], *pret. and p.pt. of* LEAD.

LEDGE [lej], *n.* narrow shelf; narrow extended projection from any surface, *esp.* from a cliff, rock etc.; (*arch.*) small moulding. [ME.].

LEDGER [le'jer], *n.* (*book-keeping*) book in which the main debit and credit items are entered in summary form; (*arch.*) horizontal, supporting piece of timber used in scaffolding; horizontal slab of stone. LEDGER-LINE, fishing-line with a sinker near the hook; (*mus.*) line added above or below the staff to accommodate notes falling outside the range. [~OE.].

LEE (1) [lē], *n.* (*naut.*) the protected side of the quarter towards which the wind blows; shelter. LEE (2), *adj.* (*naut.*) situated on the side farthest from the wind; **l. anchor,** the anchor to leeward of a ship; **l. shore,** shore to leeward of a ship. [OE.].

LEECH (1) [lēch], *n.* species of blood-sucking worm, used for blood-letting; (*archaic*) a doctor. LEECH (2), *v.t.* to apply a l. to, for the purpose of bloodletting. [OE.].

LEECH (3), *n.* (*naut.*) flying edge of a sail. [Du.].

LEEK [lēk], *n.* vegetable allied to the onion, the national emblem of Wales. [OE.].

LEER (1) [lēer], *v.i.* to look with a furtive, sidelong grin. LEER (2), *n.* sidelong grin. LEERINGLY, *adv.* in leering fashion. LEERY, *adj.* (*slang*) sly, knowing. [OE.].

LEEWARD (1) [lyŏŏ'erd, lē'wawd], *adj.* relating to, placed on, the lee side. LEEWARD (2), *n.* (*naut.*) the lee side.

LEEWAY [lē'wā], *n.* lateral movement of a ship drifting to leeward; (*fig.*) loss of progress or time, arrears of work.

LEFT (1) [left], *adj.* relating to, connected with, that side of the body in which the heart is normally situated, indicating a position or direction corresponding with this side; (*pol.*) radical, socialistic. LEFT (2), *adv.* towards the l. side. LEFT (3), *n.* the l. side, position, or direction; (*pol.*) party or group of parties characterized by advanced radical or socialistic principles. [OE.].

LEFT-HAND (1) [left'hand], *adj.* situated on the left side; performed with the left hand. LEFT-HAND (2), *n.* the left side.

LEFT-HANDED [left-han'did], *adj. and adv.* using the left hand more naturally than the right; (of a marriage) morganatic; awkward, clumsy; with the left hand; **l. compliment,** compliment which has an ambiguous derogatory meaning.

LEFT-HANDER [left-han'der], *n.* left-handed person, *esp.* a cricketer who adopts a left-handed stance; a blow with the left hand.

LEFTIST [lef'tist], *adj. and n.* (*pol.*) pertaining to, a supporter of, the left.

LEFT WING [left-wing'], *adj. and n.* (*pol.*) (pertaining to) that element in a state or a political party which tends more to the left than do the rest; (*sport*) the forward members of a team stationed on the left side of the centre-forward; **left-winger,** *n.* (*pol.*) member of the l.

LEG (1) [leg], *n.* one of the limbs, consisting of the parts between hip and ankle, by means of which an animal supports itself; clothing which covers this; that part of anything which acts as a support; thigh part of a leg of a beast or fowl, prepared as food; (*naut.*) a tack to windward; (*cricket*) area of the field remote from the off-side; **short l., long l.** (position of) the fieldsman at an angle of some 45 deg. to the wicket on the l. side, at a short or long distance

---

ōō is pronounced as in food; ŏŏ as in hood; th as in *think*; TH as in *that*; zh as in azure. ~ = related to.

respectively; **fine l.**, fielding position on the l. side at a more acute angle than these; **square l.**, position on the l. side almost opposite the wicket; **one's last legs**, about to die or come to an end; **to pull someone's l.**, to impose on a person for a joke. LEG (2) (*pres.pt.* LEGGING, *pret.* and *p.pt.* LEGGED), *v.i.* (*slang*) to use one's legs, *esp.* to run away or hurry. [OIcel.].

LEGACY [le'ga-si], *n.* bequest left by will; (*fig.*) that which has been bequeathed; a consequence. [OFr.].

LEGAL [le'gal], *adj.* connected with, relating to, or according to law, lawful; created by law; required by law; **l. offence**, an act defined by statute as unlawful and punishable. LEGALLY, *adv.* according to law. [L.].

LEGALISM [le'ga-lizm], *n.* respect for, or adherence to, the law; excessive respect for legal forms and procedure.

LEGALIST [le'ga-list], *n.* one who relies strictly on the law; one who delights in legalism.

LEGALITY [li-ga'li-ti], *n.* quality of being legal, lawfulness.

LEGALIZE [le'ga-liz], *v.t.* to make lawful.

LEGATE [le'gat], *n.* the Pope's ambassador to a foreign prince or state.

LEGATEE [le-ga-te'], *n.* person to whom a legacy is bequeathed.

LEGATION [le-ga'shn], *n.* a diplomatic mission, lower in rank than an embassy, regularly representing a state at a foreign capital and headed by a minister; the offices of the mission; the minister's official residence. [L.].

LEGATO [le-gah'tō], *adv.* (*mus.*) smoothly and evenly. [It.].

LEG-BAIL [leg'bāl], *n.* escape from custody; (*cricket*) bail on the leg side.

LEG BYE [leg'bī], *n.* (*cricket*) run scored off the batsman's leg or body.

LEGEND [le'jend], *n.* traditional story, usually of oral origin; story based more on fancy than on fact; inscription on a shield, medal or coin. [L.].

LEGENDARY [le'jen-da-ri], *adj.* having the nature of legend; romantic, fabulous. [MedL.].

LEGERDEMAIN [le'jer-de-mān], *n.* sleight of hand; conjuring trick which depends on clever manipulation. [Fr.].

LEGGING [le'ging], *n.* leather cover for the leg fastened by buttons, straps etc.; long supple gaiter.

LEGGY [le'gi], *adj.* having long legs; weedy.

LEGHORN [le-gawn'], *n.* plait of smooth straw, of a kind made in Tuscany, for making hats; hat made of this; breed of poultry. [*Leghorn*, Italy].

LEGIBILITY [le-ji-bi'li-ti], *n.* condition of being legible.

LEGIBLE [le'ji-bl], *adj.* capable of being read; clear and distinct; easily decipherable. LEGIBLY, *adv.* in a l. style. [LL.].

LEGION [le'jn], *n.* a major Roman military unit; any large body of troops; a great number of people, *esp.* in organized order; **British L.**, an association for the protection of the interests of ex-service men who served in the World Wars; **Foreign L.**, corps of volunteers recruited by the French army from foreigners for service abroad; **L. of Honour**, French order awarded for meritorious military or civil activities. [L.].

LEGIONARY [le'jn-e-ri], *n.* and *adj.* member of, relating to, consisting of, a legion or legions. [L.].

LEGIONNAIRE [le-jn-āer'], *n.* member of a legion, *esp.* the Foreign Legion. [Fr.].

LEGISLATE [le'jis-lāt], *v.i.* to make or enact a law or laws.

LEGISLATION [le-jis-lā'shn], *n.* the procedure of legislating. [LL.].

LEGISLATIVE [le'jis-la-tiv], *adj.* appointed to legislate; relating to legislation; done by legislation. LEGISLATIVELY, *adv.* in a l. form.

LEGISLATOR [le'jis-lā-ter], *n.* person who makes laws; member of a legislature. [L.].

LEGISLATURE [le'jis-la-tyŏor], *n.* assembly in a state invested with power to make, amend or repeal laws.

LEGITIMACY [li-ji'ti-ma-si], *n.* quality or fact of being legitimate.

LEGITIMATE (1) [li-ji'ti-mat], *adj.* born in lawful wedlock; lawful, rightful; reasonable, just; having the status and rights of a lawful heir to the throne; **l. theatre**, **drama**, **stage**, that concerned with serious plays of some literary quality, as distinct from variety, farce etc. LEGITIMATE (2) [li-ji'ti-māt], *v.t.* to make l.; declare to be l. [L.].

LEGITIMATION [li-ji-ti-mā'shn], *n.* act of rendering legitimate.

LEGITIM(AT)IZE [li-ji'ti-m(at-)īz], *v.t.* to make legitimate.

LEG-PULL [leg'pŏol], *n.* deception of a person for the sake of a joke.

LEGUME [le'gyŏom], *n.* (*bot.*) fruit which splits into two halves and has the seeds attached to the ventral suture, as the bean, pea etc.; pod of such plants. LEGUMINOUS [le-gyŏo'mi-nŏos], *adj.* pertaining to, of the nature of, a l. [L.].

LEISURE [le'zher], *n.* freedom from occupation; time free from employment. LEISURED, *adj.* of, possessing or displaying, l. [OFr.].

LEISURELY (1) [le'zher-li], *adj.* performed at leisure or at one's ease; slow and deliberate. LEISURELY (2), *adv.* in l. fashion.

LEIT-MOTIV [līt'mō-tēf], *n.* (*mus.*) a recurring theme always associated with a specific person, situation or mood. [MdGerm.].

LEMON (1) [le'mun], *n.* yellow-skinned acidulous fruit; tree which bears this; (*U.S. slang*) unattractive girl; swindle; **salt(s) of l.**, potash combined with oxalic acid. LEMON (2), *adj.* having the colour or characteristics of a l.; made with l. [Arab.].

LEMONADE [le-mu-nād'], *n.* drink consisting of lemon juice mixed with water and sweetened; bottled drink made of a flavoured soda-water. [Fr.].

LEMON SOLE [le-mun-sōl'], *n.* trade name for certain edible fish, a kind of plaice. [Fr.].

LEMON SQUASH [le-mun-skwosh'], *n.* drink made of lemon juice and water or soda-water, sweetened.

LEMUR [le'mer], *n.* nocturnal mammal allied to the monkeys. [L.].

LEND (*pret.* and *p.pt.* **lent**) [lend], *v.t.* to transfer to a person for use over a limited period; contribute; loan money out at interest; (*reflex.*) be adaptable for use as. LENDER, *n.* one who lends; one engaged in lending money. LENDING, *n.* act of making a loan; that which is lent. [OE.].

LEND-LEASE, see LEASE-LEND.

LENGTH [length], *n.* measurement from end to end or from one point to another; duration, total measurement of time taken by an action or activity; extent, size, range; **at l.**, after a time; for a long time; in detail, fully. [OE.].

LENGTHEN [leng'then], *v.t.* and *i.* to make or become longer.

LENGTHWISE [length'wīz], *adv.* in the direction of the length.

LENGTHY [leng'thi], *adj.* long; full and detailed, diffuse. LENGTHILY, *adv.* in a l. manner, at great length.

LENIENCY [lē'ni-en-si], *n.* quality of being lenient.

LENIENT [lē'ni-ent], *adj.* not severe, mild, merciful, tolerant. LENIENTLY, *adv.* in l. fashion. [L.].

LENITIVE (1) [le'ni-tiv], *adj.* having the power to mitigate, soften, assuage; emollient. LENITIVE (2), *n.* (*med.*) medicine alleviating pain and soothing excitement or irritation. [MedL.].

LENITY [le'ni-ti], *n.* quality of being lenient.

LENS [lenz], *n.* piece of glass specially ground so as to modify, in some particular way, the course of rays of light passing through it; (*anat.*) that part of the eye having a similar function. [L.].

LENT (1) [lent], *n.* the 40 weekdays from Ash Wednesday to Easter Day observed by Christians as a time of fasting and abstinence. LENT-LILY, daffodil. [OE.].

LENT (2), *pret.* and *p.pt.* of LEND.

LENTAMENTE [len-tah-men'tā'], *adv.* (*mus.*) slowly. [It.].

LENTEN [len'ten], *adj.* belonging to, or used in, Lent; (*fig.*) sparing, meagre. [OE.].

LENTICULAR [len-ti'kyŏo-ler], *adj.* resembling a lentil; having the form of a double-convex lens; in or of the lens of the eye. [LL.].

LENTIL [len'til], *n.* a leguminous plant, and its seed. [Fr.].

LENTO [len'tō], *adv.* and *adj.* (*mus.*) (played) slowly. [It.].

LEO [le'ō], *n.* the Lion, fifth sign of the Zodiac. [L.].

LEONINE (1) [le'ō-nīn], *adj.* relating to (Pope) Leo; **l. verse**, elegiac verse characterized by internal rhyme.

LEONINE (2), *adj.* pertaining to, resembling, a lion. [L.].

LEOPARD [le'perd], *n.* spotted carnivore of the cat group; **American l.**, the jaguar; **snow l.**, the ounce; **l. moth**, large white moth with black spots. LEOPARD-CAT, small wild cat. [L.].

LEOPARDESS [le'per-des], *n.* female leopard.

LEPER [le'per], *n.* person affected with leprosy; (*fig.*) an outcast. [OFr. from Gk.].

LEPIDO-, *pref.* scaly. [Gk.].

LEPIDOPTERA [le-pi-dop'te-rah], *n.(pl.)* (*entom.*) order of insects, comprising the moths and butterflies, and having four wings covered with scales. LEPIDOPTERAL, LEPIDOPTEROUS, *adj.* belonging to the l. [Gk.].

LEPORINE [le'pe-rīn], *adj.* relating to, or resembling, the hare. [L.].

LEPRECHAUN [le'pre-kawn], *n.* in Ireland, a benevolent brownie in the shape of an old man. [It.].

LEPROSY [le'pro-si], *n.* infectious disease attacking the skin. [*Next*].

LEPROUS [le'prŏŏs], *adj.* infected with leprosy. [LL.].

LESBIAN (1) [lez'bi-an], *adj.* pertaining to female sexual inversion. LESBIAN (2), *n.* female sexual invert. [Sappho of *Lesbos*].

LESE-MAJESTY, **lèse-majesté** [lēz-ma'jes-ti, lāz-mȧ'zhes-tā], *n.* treason. [Fr.].

LESION [lē'zhn], *n.* damage, injury; (*med.*) pathological change in tissue. [L.].

LESS (1) [les], *adj.* smaller in size or amount, not so much; fewer; not so long; not so important; **no l.** a **person than**, no other person than. LESS (2), *n.* the smaller portion or amount; the inferior or younger. LESS (3), *adv.* in a lower degree, to a smaller extent. LESS (4), *prep.* deducting.

LESSEE [le-sē'], *n.* person who holds a lease.

LESSEN [le'sen], *v.t. and i.* to make or become less.

LESSER [le'ser], *adj.* less, smaller.

LESSON [le'son], *n.* set piece of instruction in a subject given by a teacher during a single period; period so allotted; instructions, facts etc. to be learnt for such a period; anything learned, *esp.* through bitter experience; example, warning; portion of Scripture read in divine service; (*pl.*) instruction necessary for one's education. [OFr.].

LESSOR [le-saw(r)'], *n.* one who grants a lease.

LEST [lest], *conj.* for fear that; in case, that . . . not. [OE.].

LET (1) [let], (*pres.pt.* **letting**, *pret. and p.pt.* **let, letted**), [let], *v.i.* to hinder, prevent. LET (2), *n.* a retarding, hindrance; (*lawn tennis, rackets etc.*) accidental obstruction of the game. [OE.].

LET (3) [let], (*pres.pt.* **letting**, *pret. and p.pt.* **let**), *v.t.* to leave; not to disturb or interfere with; grant temporary possession and use of in return for rent; allow to escape (blood); allow, permit; (*imper.*) *expressing command or wish in first or third person;* **to l. alone**, to say nothing of; **to l. down**, to break a promise or fail to fulfil an obligation; **to l. in**, to introduce into a piece of material to lengthen or widen it; **to l. off**, to discharge (firearms); excuse from punishment; **to l. on**, (*coll.*) to reveal a secret; (*dial.*) pretend; **to l. out**, to make bigger by untacking a hem or tuck; disclose; **to l. up**, (*slang*) to pause, relax. [OE.].

LETHAL [lē'thal], *adj.* deadly, mortal, fatal. [L.].

LETHARGIC(AL) [li-thahr'jik(-al)], *adj.* inclined to, affected with, lethargy; dull, apathetic. [Gk.].

LETHARGY [le'thah-ji], *n.* heavy, unnatural state of mental or physical drowsiness; dulness, inaction; torpidity. [Gk.].

LETHE [lē'thē], *n.* oblivion, forgetfulness. [Gk.].

LET-OFF [let'of], *n.* act of excusing; unexpected escape from punishment or retribution.

LETT [let], *n.* a native of Latvia. [Germ.].

LETTER (1) [le'ter], *n.* written, printed or carved symbol representing a speech sound or sounds; a printed type; written communication sent to a person, epistle; (*pl.*) literature, literary learning; any of various legal documents or official certificates; **the l. of the law**, the literal meaning of the law; **letters patent**, official document granting some legal right or privilege. LETTER (2), *v.t.* to draw, mark or form letters. [L.].

LETTER-BOX [le'ter-boks], *n.* receptacle in which letters are posted or delivered.

LETTER-CARD [le'ter-kahd], *n.* postcard which can be folded and sealed.

LETTERED [le'terd], *adj.* engraved, marked with letters; educated, cultured; belonging to learning.

LETTERING [le'te-ring], *n.* act of drawing or painting letters; the letters printed, painted or drawn; style in which they are executed.

LETTER-PERFECT [le'ter-per-fekt], *adj.* reproducing words with absolute accuracy.

LETTERPRESS [le'ter-pres], *n.* (*typ.*) printed words or letters, *esp.* as distinct from illustrations.

LETTER-WEIGHT [le'ter-wāt], *n.* heavy object for holding down letters.

LETTER-WRITER [le'ter-rī-ter], *n.* person who writes letters; instrument for copying letters.

LETTUCE [le'tis], *n.* vegetable plant whose leaves are used as a salad. [Fr.].

LEUCAEMIA [lyŏŏ-kē'mi-ah], *n.* (*path.*) disease characterized by excessive increase of white corpuscles in the blood stream, and producing a general anaemic condition. [Gk.].

LEUCO-, *pref.* white. [Gk.].

LEUCOCYTE [lyŏŏ'kō-sīt], *n.* white corpuscle in the blood stream. [Gk.].

LEUCORRHOEA [lyŏŏ-kō-rē'ah], *n.* (*path.*) disease characterized by a white mucous discharge from the lining of the uterus or of the vaginal canal. [Gk.].

LEVANT (1) [li-vant'], *n.* **the L.**, the eastern coasts of the Mediterranean Sea. LEVANT (2), *v.i.* to disappear without paying one's debts. [Fr.].

LEVANTER (1) [li-van'ter], *n.* strong easterly wind on the North African coast. LEVANTER (2), *n.* (*coll.*) a welsher. [*Prec.*].

LEVANTINE (1) [le'van-tīn, li-van'tīn], *adj.* coming from, pertaining to, the Levant. LEVANTINE (2), *n.* a native of the Levant.

LEVEE [le'vā, le-vē'], *n.* reception by a prince or ruler held in the morning; royal reception at which only men are presented; raised river-bank. [Fr.].

LEVEL (1) [le'vel], *n.* horizontal even surface or plane; flat section of ground; a height identical with something specified; the normal height; similar state of morals, intellect etc.; a standard; (*econ.*) temporarily established state (of prices etc.); (*mech.*) instrument capable of indicating an exact horizontal line, used for testing whether a surface is level; **on the l.**, (*slang*) honest, genuine. LEVEL (2), *adj.* even, of equal height, having a flat horizontal surface; constant in power; equal in quality, rank or degree; well-balanced; (of a note, stress etc.) having a constant pitch or force; **one's l. best**, one's utmost. LEVEL (3) (*pres.pt.* LEVELLING, *pret. and p.pt.* LEVELLED), *v.t.* to make l.; form a straight line between the sight and a target, aim; raze to the ground; (*fig.*) make equal; (*philol.*) combine in a single sound. [OFr.].

LEVEL-HEADED [le-vel-he'did], *adj.* possessing common sense; judicious, controlled in a crisis.

LEVELLER [le've-ler], *n.* person who levels; believer in equal rights and status for all, *esp.* a member of the radical party in the Parliamentary army of the English Civil War which advocated an equalitarian programme.

LEVELLING [le've-ling], *n.* act of making level; art of measuring elevations of objects.

LEVER [lē'ver], *n.* rigid bar working on a fulcrum or pivot to raise or dislodge a weight by pressure on the free end; any device or contrivance functioning similarly; (*fig.*) means of bringing pressure to bear. LEVER (2), *v.t. and i.* to dislodge or lift by using a l.

LEVERAGE [lē've-rij], *n.* an arrangement of levers; principle of a lever; mechanical advantage gained by its use; (*fig.*) means of effecting.

LEVERET [le've-ret], *n.* hare in its first year. [OFr.].

LEVIATHAN [li-vī'a-than], *n.* sea monster; (*fig.*) anything huge or monstrous. [Heb.].

LEVIGATE [le'vi-gāt], *v.t.* to grind, reduce to a fine powder. [L.].

LEVITATE [le'vi-tāt], *v.t. and i.* (to cause) to float or rise in the air; become buoyant. [L.].

LEVITATION [le-vi-tā'shn], *n.* act of levitating or state of being levitated, *esp.* by supernatural means.

LEVITE [lē'vīt], *n.* member of the tribe or family of Levi; assistant to the Jewish priests; priest; (*coll.*) Jew. [Heb.].

LEVITICAL [li-vi'ti-kal], *adj.* connected with, belonging to, the Levites; priestly; **L. degrees**, degrees of affinity within which marriage was forbidden in the book of Leviticus.

LEVITY [le'vi-ti], *n.* lightness of weight, tendency to be buoyant; (*fig.*) lightness of temper or conduct, inconstancy; want of proper seriousness, irresponsibility, frivolity. [L.].

LEVY (1) [le'vi], *n.* imposition of a tax by decree; tax so imposed; conscription for military service; troops thus raised. LEVY (2), *v.t. and i.* to impose a tax, toll, tribute etc.; raise troops by conscription; raise money by a l.; **to l. war**, to declare and commence war; **to l. a fine**, (*leg. hist.*) to institute proceedings to convey lands where the usual procedure was inapplicable. [Fr.].

LEWD [lyŏŏd], *adj.* obscene, licentious, indecent; ignorant. LEWDLY, *adv.* in a l. way. [OE.].

ŏŏ is pronounced as in food; ŏŏ as in hood; th as in *think*; ᴛʜ as in *that*; zh as in azure. ~ = related to.

LEWIS GUN [lōō'is-gun], *n.* type of light automatic machine-gun. [Col. *Lewis*, inventor].

LEWISITE [lōō'i-sīt], *n.* liquid, vesicant poison gas containing arsenic. [Prof. *Lewis*, inventor].

LEXICAL [lek'si-kal], *adj.* relating to a lexicon or lexicography.

LEXICOGRAPHER [lek-si-ko'gra-fer], *n.* one who makes a dictionary. [Gk.].

LEXICOGRAPHY [lek-si-ko'gra-fi], *n.* art or practice of compiling dictionaries. [Gk.].

LEXICON [lek'si-kon], *n.* dictionary, *esp.* a Greek or Semitic dictionary. [Gk.].

LEY, see LYE.

LEYDEN JAR [lā-den-jah(r)'], *n.* glass jar coated inside and out with tinfoil and fitted with a vertical brass rod passing through its lid, used to accumulate static electricity. [*Leyden*, Holland].

LEY FARMING [lā'fah-ming], *n.* (*agric.*) pastoral farming on land previously cropped. [Uncert.].

LIABILITY [lī-a-bi'li-ti], *n.* quality or fact of being liable; that, *esp.* a sum of money, for which one is liable; a charge; disadvantage.

LIABLE [lī'a-bl], *adj.* responsible for, bound, obliged in law and equity; apt, inclined. [~Fr.].

LIAISON [li-ā'zon], *n.* working relationship between two parties, usually of a semi-official nature; bond of union, association; state of intimacy, *esp.* of an illicit sexual nature; co-ordination between allies or military units. [Fr.].

LIANA [li-ah'nah], *n.* (*bot.*) any tropical climbing plant. [Fr.].

LIAR [lī'er], *n.* person who tells lies. [ME.].

LIAS [lī'as], *n.* (*geol.*) a blue-black clay; the lowest division of the Jurassic. [Fr.].

LIBATION [li-bā'shn], *n.* liquid sacrifice to the gods; wine so sacrificed; (*coll.*) a drink. [L.].

LIBEL (1) [lī'bel], *n.* statement in writing judged to harm the reputation of a person; misrepresentation of a person's merits; (*leg.*) any book, writing or representation which, being published, unjustifiably exposes a person to defamation. LIBEL (2) (*pres.pt.* LIBELLING, *pret.* and *p.pt.* LIBELLED), *v.t.* to defame by means of a l.; (*pop.*) misrepresent a person's merits or nature; (*leg.*) bring a l. against. [L.].

LIBELLOUS [lī'be-lōōs], *adj.* constituting a libel, defamatory; habitually publishing libels.

LIBERAL (1) [lī'be-ral], *adj.* giving freely, generous; abundant, plentiful; having broad interests and sympathies, tolerant; enlightened, advanced; (*pol.*) connected with the Liberal Party. LIBERAL (2), *n.* person of tolerant and enlightened views; adherent of the political party so called. [L.].

LIBERALISM [lī'be-ra-lizm], *n.* (*pol.*) theory and practice of the Liberal party.

LIBERALITY [lī-be-ra'li-ti], *n.* quality of being liberal; munificence. [L.].

LIBERALIZE [lī'be-ra-līz], *v.t.* to render liberal or catholic in outlook.

LIBERATE [lī'be-rāt], *v.t.* to set free, release; set in motion; (*chem.*) allow to escape. [L.].

LIBERATION [li-be-rā'shn], *n.* act of liberating; release. [L.].

LIBERATOR [lī'be-rā-ter], *n.* person who liberates, *esp.* a leader who sets his people free from foreign domination. [L.].

LIBERTINE (1) [lī'ber-tēn], *n.* person who spends his life in habitual licentiousness and debauchery. LIBERTINE (2), *adj.* devoid of moral restraint; licentious, dissolute. [L.].

LIBERTY [lī'ber-ti], *n.* freedom; state of being free in one's personal life; absence of undesired restrictive forces governing the life of the community; permission, privilege; instance of bad manners, offensive behaviour; civil l., participation by the civilian members of a nation in communal life at its best; (*pol.*) fruitful interaction of state and social and personal functions on a plane of economic equality; at l., free, not in use; unoccupied; free from captivity. [L.].

LIBIDINAL [li-bi'di-nal], *adj.* connected with, characterized by, libido.

LIBIDINOUS [li-bi'di-nōōs], *adj.* having or implying an immoderate desire for indulgence in lust, sensual; exciting lust. [L.].

LIBIDO [li-bī'dō], *n.* (*psych.*) the basic emotional power in a human being. [L.].

LIBRA [lī'brah], *n.* seventh sign in the Zodiac, the Scales. [L.].

LIBRARIAN [lī-brāer'i-an], *n.* person employed to look after a library. [L.].

LIBRARY [lī'bra-ri], *n.* a collection of books; a collection of books for public use or loan; building or room in which such a collection is housed; series of books forming a homogeneous category. [L.].

LIBRETTIST [li-bret'tist], *n.* writer of a libretto.

LIBRETTO (*pl.* libretti) [li-bret'tō, 'ti], *n.* words of a musical play or opera; book containing them. [It.].

LICENCE [lī'sens], *n.* leave, permission from an authority; certificate giving such permission; irregular behaviour, unrestrained conduct; justifiable deviation from accepted rules. [L.].

LICENSE [lī'sens], *v.t.* to authorize, grant a l. for something.

LICENSED [lī'senst], *adj.* authorized by licence; l. victualler, publican licensed to sell food and drinks.

LICENSEE [lī-sen-sē'], *n.* holder of a licence, *esp.* for the sale of alcoholic drinks.

LICENTIATE [li-sen'shi-at], *n.* person holding a licence, *esp.* a recognized professional practitioner; Presbyterian qualified to preach. [L.].

LICENTIOUS [li-sen'shōōs], *adj.* indulging in unrestrained gratification of sensual appetites, *esp.* of lust; immoral, dissolute. [L.].

LICHEN [lī'ken], *n.* (*bot.*) one of a class of cryptogamic thallophytes in which the individual plant consists of a fungus and an alga living symbiotically; (*med.*) a skin disease. [Gk.].

LICHGATE, LYCHGATE [lich'gāt], *n.* porch or covered gateway at the entrance of a churchyard. [OE.].

LICK (1) [lik], *v.t.* to draw the tongue over; moisten with the tongue; (*fig.*) (of flames etc.) touch lightly and quickly; (*coll.*) flog; defeat; run; to l. the dust, to be slain or triumphed over; to l. someone's boots, to play the toady to someone; to l. into shape, to improve, educate. LICK (2), *n.* act of licking; (*coll.*) an inadequate wash; taste, morsel; daub; (*coll.*) a swift speed. [OE.].

LICKERISH, LIQUORISH [li'ker-ish], *adj.* greedy; nice about food; lecherous. [OFr.].

LICKSPITTLE [lik'spi-tl], *n.* a toady.

LICORICE, see LIQUORICE.

LID [lid], *n.* movable cover to close a vessel or receptacle; eyelid; to put the l. on, (*coll.*) to finish. LIDDED, *adj.* having a l. [OE.].

LIDO [lē'dō, lī'dō], *n.* outdoor bathing pool with a terrace for sunbathing; place of entertainment. [*Lido*, bathing beach near Venice].

LIE (1) [lī], *n.* intentional falsehood, violation of truth; false appearance; white l., justifiable untruth. LIE (2),*v.i.* to utter a l. or lies; present a false appearance. [OE.].

LIE (3) (*pret.* lay, *p.pt.* lain),*v.i.* to assume a recumbent position, recline; lean or press on; be situate; remain, be; be spread out motionless, *esp.* in death; (*leg.*) be sustainable; to l. low, to remain in hiding; to l. at one's door, to appertain to; to l. in, to be in childbed; stay in bed late; to l. up, to be ill in bed; to l. with, to have sexual intercourse with; to l. off, (*naut.*) to ride at anchor off; to l. to, (*naut.*) to come almost to a stop, with head near wind. LIE (4), *n.* the way anything lies; l. of the land, state of affairs. [OE.].

LIEF [lēf], *adv.* gladly, willingly. [OE.].

LIEGE (1) [lēj], *adj.* connected by feudal rights and duties; relating to homage. LIEGE (2), *n.* feudal lord with vassals; vassal bound to perform certain services to his lord. LIEGEMAN, *n.* vassal. [OFr.].

LIEN [lē'en, lēn], *n.* (*leg.*) right to hold the property of another until the satisfaction of a claim. [Fr.].

LIEU [lyōō], *n.* place; in l., instead. [Fr.].

LIEUTENANCY [lef-te'nan-si, *nav.* and *U.S.* lōō-te'nan-si], *n.* rank of lieutenant; possession of this rank; the holders of this rank, as a body.

LIEUTENANT [lef-te'nant, *nav.* and *U.S.* lōō-te'nant], *n.* deputy, substitute; principal assistant; officer acting for another; (*milit.*) junior officer or rank next below a captain; (*nav.*) officer or rank next below a lieutenant-commander. [LIEU and TENANT].

LIEUTENANT-COLONEL [lef-te-nant-kur'nel], *n.* (*milit.*) officer of the rank next below colonel.

LIEUTENANT-COMMANDER [lōō-, lef-te-nant-ko-mahn'der], *n.* (*nav.*) officer of the rank next below commander.

LIEUTENANT-GENERAL [lef-te-nant-ge'ne-ral], *n.* (*milit.*) officer of the rank next below general.

LIEUTENANT-GOVERNOR [lef-te-nant-gu'ver-ner], *n.* subsidiary or assistant governor.

LIEUTENANTSHIP [lef-te'nant-ship], *n.* position of lieutenant.

LIFE (*pl.* lives) [līf], *n.* that condition of an animal or

---

The accent ' after a syllable = stress (u-pon'). The mark ⁻ over a vowel = length (ā in made; ō in bone).

plant organism in which it is capable of performing its natural functions; the source from, or principle by, which it achieves this condition; present state or manner of existence; time from birth to death; period of existence; human affairs and experience; the general state of a man, *esp.* with reference to his social relations; spirit, animation; vitality, energy; joyous living, felicity; inspiration, moving spirit; a biography; subject of an insurance policy; **l. assurance, insurance,** contract for the payment of a specific sum upon a person's death or upon his reaching a certain age; **to see l.,** to enjoy at first-hand the world and its excitements; **for dear l.,** with all one's might; **as large as l.,** unmistakable; **for l.,** until one is dead; (of a legal sentence) indefinitely. [OE.].

LIFE-AND-DEATH [lïf-and-deth'], *adj.* determining life or death; critically important.

LIFEBELT [lïf'belt], *n.* buoyant belt to support the body in water.

LIFE-BLOOD [lïf'blud], *n.* the blood necessary for life; (*fig.*) that which constitutes or provides strength and energy.

LIFEBOAT [lïf'bōt], *n.* a strongly-built, unsinkable, self-righting boat for saving persons from shipwreck; small boat on a ship, for use in case of emergency.

LIFEBUOY [lïf'boi], *n.* circular lifebelt.

LIFE-ESTATE [lïf'es-tāt], *n.* estate which is held by an owner during his life, but which he cannot bequeath.

LIFE-GIVING [lïf'gi-ving], *adj.* giving life or animation; invigorating.

LIFEGUARD [lïf'gahd], *n.* safety device attached to machinery, vehicles etc. to prevent serious accidents; bodyguard of soldiers; (*pl.*) those regiments forming part of the Sovereign's bodyguard in England; member of one of these; strong swimmer trained to save the lives of bathers.

LIFE INTEREST [lïf'in-te-rest], *n.* (*leg.*) interest or claim valid only during one's lifetime.

LIFE-JACKET [lïf'ja-kit], *n.* jacket of buoyant material for support in the water.

LIFELIKE [lïf'lïk], *adj.* resembling life or reality; resembling closely its living original.

LIFELINE [lïf'lïn], *n.* rope for rescue work, *esp.* at sea; one of the lines on the palm of the hand.

LIFELONG [lïf'long], *adj.* throughout life.

LIFE-PRESERVER [lïf'pri-zer-ver], *n.* apparatus for saving lives in cases of shipwreck or fire; stick weighted at one end; a bludgeon.

LIFER [lï'fer], *n.* (*slang*) prisoner undergoing penal servitude for life; a life sentence.

LIFE-SAVING [lïf'sā-ving], *adj. and n.* (applicable or pertaining to) the saving of life, *esp.* from immediate hazards.

LIFETIME [lïf'tïm], *n.* duration of the life of an individual; the time anything lasts.

LIFT (1) [lift], *v.t.* to raise, elevate, hoist; (*sport*) direct upwards; (*fig.*) raise in dignity, rank etc.; dig up; (*slang*) steal; *v.i.* (of mist etc.) to rise, disperse. LIFT (2), *n.* act of lifting, a heave; result of lifting, a rise; an upward spring; rise in status or salary; act of assistance; hoist for carrying persons or goods from floor to floor; free transport in a private vehicle. LIFTER, *n.* person who or thing which lifts; (*slang*) thief. [OIcel.].

LIGAMENT [li'ga-ment], *n.* tie, band; (*anat.*) strong fibrous connecting band in the body. LIGAMENTAL, LIGAMENTOUS [li-ga-men'tal, 'tŏŏs], *adj.* resembling, pertaining to, a l. [L.].

LIGATURE [li'ga-tyŏŏr], *n.* anything which ties; act of tying; (*surg.*) thread used to tie up a blood-vessel etc. to prevent excessive bleeding; (*mus.*) line connecting several notes; character made up of two or more letters joined together. [L.].

LIGHT (1) [lït], *n.* the cause of visibility; the brightness emanating from the sun; a source of this; lamp, window or aperture; degree or strength of the light; day, dawn; (*fig.*) moral, spiritual or intellectual illumination, knowledge, revelation; a point of view; manner in which a situation strikes one; (*phys.*) that form of radiation which produces the sensation of sight, but which manifests itself also in phenomena imperceptible to the naked eye but measurable by a spectroscope; (*paint.*) the representation of the illumination of a subject; **ancient lights,** right to prevent obstruction of light; **l. year,** distance travelled by light in one year; **to stand in one's l.,** to obstruct one's interests; **to come to l.,** to be revealed, transpire; **to throw l. upon,** to make clear, explain. LIGHT (2), *adj.* not dark or shadowed,

bright; pale. LIGHT (3) (*pret. and p.pt.* LIGHTED, LIT), *v.t.* to cause to emit l.; set fire to; supply l. to, upon or for; *v.i.* to begin to emit l.; to be capable of emitting l.; (*fig.*) show signs of animation; **to l. up,** to brighten. [OE.].

LIGHT (4), *adj.* not heavy; below the just or legal weight; not heavily armed; carrying only what is light; nimble, active, dainty; slight, without force; superficial; (of soil) loose, sandy; (of food) easy to digest; (*fig.*) easy to bear or to perform; graceful and elegant; gay; frivolous; unchaste; of little importance or value, trivial; **to make l. of,** to minimize the importance or the difficulty of. LIGHT (5), *adv.* in l. fashion. [OE.].

LIGHT (6), *v.i.* to alight, land; **to l. on,** to find by chance. [OE.].

LIGHTEN (1) [lï'ten], *v.t.* to afford light to, illuminate; *v.i.* (of lightning) flash; increase in luminosity. [LIGHT (1)].

LIGHTEN (2), *v.t.* to make lighter; relieve, cheer. [LIGHT (4)].

LIGHTER (1) [lï'ter], *n.* one who makes a light; device for producing a flame. [LIGHT (1)].

LIGHTER (2), *n.* large, open flat-bottomed boat used in loading and unloading ships. LIGHTERAGE, *n.* act of unloading, or the price for unloading, ships into lighters. [Du.].

LIGHTERMAN [lï'ter-man], *n.* boatman of a lighter.

LIGHT-FINGERED [lït-fing'gerd], *adj.* deft; thievish.

LIGHT-FOOTED [lït-fŏŏ'tid], *adj.* nimble, active.

LIGHT-HANDED [lït-han'did], *adj.* deft; not harsh or emphatic; not carrying anything heavy; (*naut.*) without a full complement of crew.

LIGHT-HEADED [lït-he'did], *adj.* thoughtless, heedless; delirious.

LIGHT-HEARTED [lït-hah'tid], *adj.* free of grief and anxiety; cheerful, gay.

LIGHTHOUSE [lït'hows], *n.* tower or building emitting a powerful light to direct navigation or aviation at night; beacon; **l. keeper,** one in charge of a l.

LIGHTING [lï'ting], *n.* illumination; system of appurtenances for the illumination of a building, stage etc.

LIGHT-MINDED [lït-mïn'did], *adj.* frivolous.

LIGHTNING [lït'ning], *n.* flash, or succession of flashes, of light due to the discharge of atmospheric electricity; **like l.,** very quickly; **l. glance,** quick glance. LIGHTNING-CONDUCTOR, *n.* metal conductor so placed on a building as to attract atmospheric electricity and conduct it harmlessly to earth. [LIGHTEN (1)].

LIGHT-O'-LOVE [lït-o-luv'], *n.* light woman; prostitute.

LIGHTS [lïts], *n.(pl.)* lungs of cattle and pigs, *esp.* when used as food. [LIGHT (4)].

LIGHTSHIP [lït'ship], *n.* vessel anchored near a shoal or dangerous rocks, bearing lights as a warning.

LIGHTSOME [lït'sum], *adj.* gay; nimble; dainty.

LIGHTWEIGHT [lït'wāt], *adj.* of small weight; (of a boxer) between 9 st. and 9 st. 9 lb. in weight; slight, trifling.

LIGNEOUS [lig'ni-ŏŏs], *adj.* made of wood; resembling wood. [L.].

LIGNI-, *pref.* wood, of wood. [L.].

LIGNITE [lig'nït], *n.* brown coal retaining the texture of the wood from which it originated. [L.].

LIGNUM-VITAE [lig-num-vï'tē], *n.* extremely hard, close-grained wood of a tropical American tree. [L.].

LIKE (1) [lïk], *adj.* equal in quality, quantity or degree; resembling, similar, of corresponding kind or nature; in keeping with. LIKE (2), *adv.* in the same manner; likely; (*dial.*) **l. enough,** probably. LIKE (3), *n.* that which resembles something else; copy; (*coll.*) **the likes of,** people l. [OE.].

LIKE (4), *v.t.* to be pleased with, attracted to, fond of; enjoy; approve; want, wish. LIKE (5), *n.* that which one likes, preference.

LIKEABLE [lï'ka-bl], *adj.* that one can like, amiable.

LIKELIHOOD [lïk'li-hŏŏd], *n.* probability.

LIKELY (1) [lïk'li], *adj.* resembling reality; such as may reasonably be expected; probable; suitable; pleasing. LIKELY (2), *adv.* probably.

LIKE-MINDED [lïk-mïn'did], *adj.* of similar views or temperament, in agreement.

LIKEN [lï'ken], *v.t.* to represent as like; make like; compare.

LIKENESS [lïk'nes], *n.* quality of being like, resemblance; portrait, photograph, *esp.* a successful one.

LIKEWISE [lïk'wïz], *adv.* similarly, also, moreover.

ōō is pronounced as in foot; ŏŏ as in hood; th as in think; TH as in that; zh as in azure. ~ = related to.

LIKING [li'king], *n.* feeling of being attracted by; inclination, taste.

LILAC [li'lak], *n.* a sweet-smelling flowering shrub. [Pers.].

LILIACEOUS [li-li-ā-shōōs], *adj.* pertaining to the lily family.

LILIED [li'lid], *adj.* decorated with, having, lilies; white, pale.

LILLIPUTIAN (1) [li-li-pyōō'shan], *n.* inhabitant of Lilliput, where everything was diminutive. LILLIPUTIAN (2), *adj.* of Lilliput; diminutive. [*Lilliput*, fabulous country in Swift's *Gulliver's Travels*].

LILO [li'lō], *n.* (*prot.*) inflatable rubberized mattress.

LILT (1) [lilt], *v.i.* to sing or say with a lilt. LILT (2), *n.* smooth, rhythmic, melodious quality in a song or in a speaking voice; song exhibiting this. [ME.].

LILY [li'li], *n.* a bulbous flowering plant; (*fig.*) pallor; chastity; **l. of the valley**, the plant *Convallaria majalis.* LILY-HANDED, *adj.* with delicate white hands. LILY-LIVERED, *adj.* cowardly. LILY-WHITE, *adj.* white as a l. [OE.].

LIMB (1) [lim], *n.* any corporeal member, as the arm, leg, wing etc.; branch of a tree; (*fig.*) member or section of any organization; (*coll.*) mischievous child; **life and l.**, the whole being. [OE.].

LIMB (2), *n.* edge or border of a surface; (*astron.*) edge of the disk of the sun and moon. [L.].

LIMBER (1) [lim'ber], *n.* (*milit.*) detachable front part of a gun-carriage. LIMBER (2), *v.t.* to attach the l. to (a gun); prepare to move a gun. [Unkn.].

LIMBER (3), *adj.* flexible, pliant; lithe. LIMBER (4), *v.t.* to loosen up the limbs. [Unkn.].

LIMBO [lim'bō], *n.* region intermediate between heaven and hell; any intermediate, ambiguous position; neglect, oblivion. [L.].

LIME (1) [lim], *n.* (*chem.*) quicklime, oxide of calcium obtained by burning limestone; slaked lime; limestone; birdlime. LIME (2), *v.t.* to smear birdlime on; snare; dress (land) with l. [OE.].

LIME (3), *n.* the linden-tree. [OE.].

LIME (4), *n.* the tree, *Citrus medica*; its lemon-like fruit; lime-juice. [Arab.].

LIME-JUICE [lim'jōōs], *n.* antiscorbutic drink made from the fruit of the lime. [LIME (4)].

LIMEKILN [lim'kiln], *n.* kiln in which limestone is burnt and reduced to lime.

LIMELIGHT [lim'līt], *n.* light given off by a cylinder of lime heated to incandescence, formerly used in theatres to pick out leading actors; **in the l.**, (*fig.*) in the public eye.

LIMEN [li'men], *n.* (*psych.*) the dividing line between the conscious and the subconscious. [L.].

LIMERICK [li'me-rik], *n.* verse of five lines, invented by Edward Lear and usually employed for humorous compositions; the first and second lines rhyme with the fifth, and the shorter third and fourth rhyme together.

LIMESTONE [lim'stōn], *n.* (*geol.*) rock whose chief constituent is carbonate of lime.

LIME-TREE (1) [lim'trē], *n.* tree of the genus *Tilia* with fragrant hanging blossoms. [LIME (3)].

LIME-TREE (2), *n.* the tree, *Citrus medica*, prized for its green lemon-like fruit. [LIME (4)].

LIME-WATER [lim'waw-ter], *n.* solution of calcium hydroxide used medicinally.

LIMIT (1) [li'mit], *n.* boundary, edge, terminus; restriction; the utmost extent; the utmost possible; (*coll.*) something or someone utterly intolerable. LIMIT (2), *v.t.* to set a boundary to; restrain, restrict. [L.].

LIMITARY [li'mi-ta-ri], *adj.* placed at the limit; restrained within limits; confining. [L.].

LIMITATION [li-mi-tā'shn], *n.* act of limiting; state of being limited; that which limits, depreciates or qualifies; (*leg.*) period limited by statute within which an action may be brought. [L.].

LIMITED [li'mi-tid], *adj.* narrow, circumscribed, restricted; **l. liability**, in a joint-stock company, liability of the shareholders to the nominal value of their shares; **l. monarchy**, kingdom in which the sovereign must keep within the bounds of the constitution.

LIMITLESS [lim'it-les], *adj.* without limit, immense.

LIMN [lim], *v.t.* to illuminate (letters or manuscripts); draw, paint, describe in glowing colours. LIMNER [lim'ner], *n.* one who limns, a painter. [ME. from Fr.].

LIMOUSINE [li-mōō-zēn'], *n.* covered motor-car in which the driver's seat is divided from the back seats by a glass partition. [Fr.].

LIMP (1) [limp], *adj.* wanting firmness and stiffness,

flaccid; (of fabric) unstiffened; (*fig.*) characterless, without energy; **l. binding**, binding in which no millboard is used. [~OIcel.].

LIMP (2), *v.i.* to walk lamely and unevenly; (of verse) have a faulty rhythm. LIMP (3), *n.* a lameness; act of limping. [~MHighGerm.].

LIMPET [lim'pet], *n.* (*zool.*) univalve mollusc, sticking to rocks; kind of adhesive bomb; (*fig., coll.*) one who clings to a post even when superfluous. [OE.].

LIMPID [lim'pid], *adj.* crystal clear, pellucid; (*fig.*) lucid, easy. [Fr.].

LIMPING [lim'ping], *adj.* halting, lame.

LIMY [li'mi], *adj.* viscous; like lime; containing lime.

LINAGE, LINEAGE (2) [li'nij], *n.* the number of lines on a page, or in a newspaper article; payment for writing according to number of lines; contributions so paid for. [LINE].

LINCHPIN [linch'pin], *n.* pin or peg to keep a wheel in its place on the axle. [~OE.].

LINCRUSTA [lin-krus'tah], *n.* (*prot.*) compound of cellulose paper and pulverized cork soaked with oil and resin, used for floor-cloth and for covering walls, etc. [L.].

LINCTUS [lingk'tus], *n.* thick soothing throat medicine. [L.].

LINDEN [lin'den], *n.* lime-tree, of the genus *Tilia*. [OE.].

LINE (1) [lin], *n.* a slender string or cord; thread-like stroke or trace; such a mark used to trace out a limit or point of division; narrow furrow in the brow, palm etc.; row, series in regular succession, *esp.* of written words, persons etc.; fleet of merchant ships; railroad; railway company; (*pl.*) verses; lineage; outline, lineament; trench or rampart; series of adjoining fortified defensive positions; method; course; direction; occupation; (*coll.*) series of specified goods; (*coll.*) short letter; telephone wire; (*math.*) that which has length without breadth or thickness; (*geog.*) the equator; **l. of battle**, disposition of an army or fleet in face of the enemy; **ship of the l.**, capital ship; **to draw the l. at**, to refuse to contemplate, object to; **to toe the l.**, to obey; **to get a l. on**, (*slang*) to acquire information about. LINE (2), *v.t.* to mark with lines; form into lines; form a line along. [L.].

LINE (3), *v.t.* to cover on the inside with another layer of material; provide a lining for. [OE.].

LINEAGE (1) [li'ni-ij], *n.* a course of descent, ancestry, pedigree; descendants; family, *esp.* with implication of distinction.

LINEAGE (2), see LINAGE.

LINEAL [li'ni-al], *adj.* linear; in a direct line from an ancestor. LINEALLY, *adv.* by direct descent. [L.].

LINEAMENT [li'ni-a-ment], *n.* distinguishing outline of a body or figure, *esp.* of the face; (*pl.*) features; (*fig.*) distinguishing features of the character. [L.].

LINEAR [li'ni-er], *adj.* pertaining to a line; consisting of lines, *esp.* straight lines; in a straight direction; like a line; (*bot.*) narrow and long; **l. perspective**, that which regards only the positions, magnitudes and forms of objects. LINEARLY, *adv.* in a l. manner. [L.].

LINEATION [li-ni-ā'shn], *n.* a dividing with linear marks; manner of doing this; arrangement (of verse) in lines. [L.].

LINED [lind], *adj.* marked with lines or wrinkles; having a lining.

LINE ENGRAVING [lin'en-grā-ving], *n.* engraving by means of fine lines on a surface of metal etc.

LINEN (1) [li'nen], *n.* cloth woven from flax; articles made of this; underclothing; tablecloths; bedclothes. LINEN (2), *adj.* made of l. [OE.].

LINEN DRAPER [li'nen-drā-per], *n.* tradesman who deals in linens, calicos etc., and articles made of these.

LINE-OUT [lin'owt], *n.* (*Rugby football*) formation of the opposing forwards in two parallel lines when the ball is to be thrown in from touch.

LINER [li'ner], *n.* large vessel belonging to a regular line of ships; large passenger aircraft on a regular route.

LINESMAN [linz'man], *n.* man employed in attending to railway, telegraph or telephone lines; judge who watches the boundary lines at tennis or football; soldier of the line.

LINE-UP [lin'up], *n.* formation in line; deploying of opposing forces as a preliminary to battle.

LING (1) [ling], *n.* sea-fish related to the cod. [ME.].

LING (2), *n.* the common heath. [OIcel.].

LINGER [ling'ger], *v.t.* to protract; *v.i.* to delay, remain long; loiter. [~OE.].

The accent ' after a syllable = stress (u-pon'). The mark ¯ over a vowel = length (ā in made; ō in bone).

LINGERIE [la(ng)'zhe-rē], *n.* women's fine under-clothes. [Fr.].

LINGERING [ling'ge-ring], *adj.* that lingers; protracted.

LINGO [ling'gō], *n.* language, jargon; (in contempt) foreign language. [Provenc.].

LINGUA-, LINGUO-, *pref.* relating to the tongue. [L.].

LINGUA FRANCA [ling-gwah-frang'kah], *n.* the international language of the Levant, a mixture of Italian, Arabic, Greek etc.; any language of similar usage or usefulness. [It.].

LINGUAL (1) [ling'gwal], *adj.* of, or pertaining to, the tongue; (*phon.*) formed by the tongue. LINGUAL (2), *n.* a l. sound as *l, d* etc.

LINGUIST [ling'gwist], *n.* person skilled in foreign languages.

LINGUISTIC [ling-gwis'tik], *adj.* pertaining to languages. LINGUISTICS, *n.(pl.)* scientific study of language, its nature and development.

LINGUO-, see LINGUA-.

LINIMENT [li'ni-ment], *n.* medicated liquid for rubbing into the skin to relieve pain or strain; embrocation. [L.].

LINING [lī'ning], *n.* the covering of the inner surface of anything.

LINK (1) [lingk], *n.* ring or loop forming part of a chain; anything doubled or closed like this; device for fastening shirt-cuffs, cuff-link; (*fig.*) person who or thing which bridges a gap; connexion; (*mech.*) short connecting-rod; measure of 7.92 in. LINK (2), *v.t.* to unite or connect as with a l.; *v.i.* to be coupled, go arm in arm; **to l. arms,** to put one's arm in another's. [OE.].

LINK (3), *n.* torch of tow and pitch. [Unkn.].

LINK (4), *n.* (*usually pl.*) grassy undulating ground near the sea; golf course. [OE.].

LINNAEAN [li-nē'an], *adj.* (*nat. hist.*) pertaining to the classification of Linné, Swedish naturalist. [*Linnaeus*, latinized form of *Linné*].

LINNET [li'nit], *n.* a small song-bird. [OFr.].

LINOCUT [lī'nō-kut], *n.* a drawing cut in relief on a linoleum block; print taken from this. [LINO-(LEUM) and CUT (1)].

LINOLEUM [li-nō'li-um], *n.* a covering for floors, of compacted linseed oil on a canvas base. [L.].

LINOTYPE [lī'nō-tīp], *n.* (*prot.*) (*print.*) type-setting machine in which the matter is cast in lines as it is set. [LINE OF TYPE].

LINSEED [lin'sēd], *n.* seed of the flax plant; **l. cake,** hard mass left after the oil has been pressed out of flax-seed; **l. meal,** ground l.; **l. oil,** oil pressed from flax-seed. [OE.].

LINSEY-WOOLSEY [lin-zi-wōōl'zi], *n.* coarse fabric of wool and cotton or linen; garment of this; (*fig.*) incongruous mixture; jargon. [OE.].

LINT [lint], *n.* (*surg.*) linen specially prepared for dressing wounds. [ME.].

LINTEL [lin'tel], *n.* horizontal timber or stone piece over a door or casement. [OFr.].

LION [lī'on], *n.* large, carnivorous, tawny-coloured wild cat; (*fig.*) strong or powerful person; celebrity; (*astron.*) the constellation Leo; (*pl.*) (*coll.*) sights of special interest; **l.'s share,** largest share. [OFr.].

LIONESS [lī'ō-nes], *n.* female lion.

LION-HEARTED [lī-on-hah'tid], *adj.* having great courage.

LION-HUNTER [lī'on-hun-ter], *n.* one who hunts lions; one who seeks the company of celebrities.

LIONIZE [lī'ō-nīz], *v.t.* to treat as a celebrity.

LIP (1) [lip], *n.* either of the red fleshy edges of the mouth; any edge or rim; (*coll.*) impudence; **to hang on someone's lips,** to listen intently to someone. LIP (2) (*pres.pt.* LIPPING, *pret. and p.pt.* LIPPED), *v.t.* to kiss; utter. [OE.].

LIPOMA [li-pō'mah], *n.* (*path.*) fatty tumour. [Gk.].

LIP-READING [lip'rē-ding], *n.* art or practice of following what is said by observing the movements of the speaker's lips.

LIP-SERVICE [lip'ser-vis], *n.* promises, or expressions of admiration, devotion etc., spoken but not sincerely meant.

LIPSTICK [lip'stik], *n.* cosmetic in the shape of a stick for colouring the lips.

LIQUEFACTION [li-kwi-fak'shn], *n.* act, process, of liquefying; state of being liquefied. LIQUEFACTIVE, *adj.* able to be liquefied, to cause liquefaction. [L.].

LIQUEFY [li'kwi-fī], *v.t.* and *i.* to make or become liquid. [L.].

LIQUESCENT [li-kwe'sent], *adj.* in process of melting, becoming fluid. [L.].

LIQUEUR [li-kyōōr', li-kur'], *n.* strong, distilled, aromatic spirit; **l. brandy,** fine brandy. [Fr.].

LIQUID (1) [li'kwid], *adj.* flowing, fluid; in a state intermediate between the solid and the gaseous; (of a fluid) that runs freely; bright, gleaming, clear; (of assets etc.) easily changed into money. LIQUID (2), *n.* any l. substance, watery material; (*phon.*) sonant or consonant such as *l* or *r*. [L.].

LIQUIDATE [li'kwi-dāt], *v.t. and i.* to settle, pay, as a debt; (*comm.*) wind up, as a bankrupt estate, determine the debts and assets of; go into bankruptcy; destroy or stop payment. LIQUIDATOR, *n.* one legally appointed to carry out a liquidation. [L.].

LIQUIDATION [li-kwi-dā'shn], *n.* act of liquidating; state of being liquidated; **to go into l.,** to become bankrupt.

LIQUOR [li'ker], *n.* a fluid; liquid for drinking, *esp.* when alcoholic; the liquid product of any operation; **in l.,** intoxicated. [OFr.].

LIQUORICE, LICORICE [li'ke-ris], *n.* a plant, the dried juice of which is used medicinally and as a sweetmeat. [AFr. from Gk.].

LIQUORISH, see LICKERISH.

LIRA (*pl.* **lire**) [lē'rah], *n.* Italian and Turkish coin and monetary unit. [It.].

LISLE [līl], *n.* cotton thread or fabric used for hose etc. [*Lille*].

LISP (1) [lisp], to speak with a lisp; speak imperfectly, as a child; *v.t.* to utter with a lisp. LISP (2), *n.* speech impediment resulting in the mispronunciation of *s* or *z* as *th*. LISPER, *n.* person who lisps. [OE.].

LISSOM(E) [li'sum], *adj.* lithe, agile. [LITHE].

LIST (1) [list], *n.* an edging; selvedge of cloth; cheap material; (*arch.*) small moulding; (*hist.*) (*pl.*) palisades or barriers surrounding a piece of ground set aside for tilting; the tournament ground itself; **to enter the lists,** to defend a cause or enter a quarrel. [OFr.].

LIST (2), *n.* a roll or catalogue of entries, inventory. [OFr.].

LIST (3), *v.t.* to make a list of; *v.t.* (*coll.*) enlist. [OE.].

LIST (4), *v.i.* (*archaic*) to desire, choose; please.

LIST (5), *n.* a leaning or sloping to one side, *esp.* of a ship. LIST (6), *v.i.* to incline to one side. [OE.].

LIST (7), *v.t. and i.* (*poet.*) to listen, listen to. [OE.].

LISTEN [li'sen], *v.i.* to pay aural attention, direct the hearing towards something; pay heed to; **to l. in,** (*radio*) to radio broadcasts; intercept messages transmitted by radio or telephone. [OE.].

LISTLESS [list'les], *adj.* indifferent, apathetic; languid; spiritless. LISTLESSLY, *adv.* in l. fashion. [ME.].

LIT [lit], *pret. and p.pt.* of LIGHT; **l. up,** (*coll.*) drunk.

LITANY [li'ta-ni], *n.* set form of supplication, being a collection of short prayers recited by clergy with responses from the congregation. [Gk.].

LITERACY [li'te-ra-si], *n.* condition or state of being literate.

LITERAL [li'te-ral], *adj.* in accordance with the letter; accurate, exact; real; strictly following the exact words; relating to an alphabetical letter; (*math.*) expressed in letters. LITERALLY, *adv.* word for word; according to strict grammatical interpretation; (*coll.*) simply, completely. [L.].

LITERALISM [li'te-ra-lizm], *n.* slavish adherence to the letter; addiction to rigid interpretation of formularies, instructions etc. LITERALIST, *n.* one who adheres to l.

LITERARY [li'te-ra-ri], *adj.* relating to letters or literature; devoted to or practising literature; of the written rather than the spoken idiom; **l. property,** rights and profits belonging to l. work. [L.].

LITERATE (1) [li'te-rat], *adj.* acquainted with letters or learning; having learnt to read or write. LITERATE (2), *n.* educated man, able to read and write. [L.].

LITERATI [li-te-rah'ti, li-te-rā'tī], *n.(pl.)* men of letters. [L. from L.].

LITERATIM [li-te-rā'tim], *adv.* letter for letter, literally. [L.].

LITERATURE [li'te-ra-tyōōr], *n.* written works in general, *esp.* non-technical or non-scientific works; such products of a nation, people, age or culture; books or treatises dealing with a particular subject; books of artistic merit written in memorable prose or verse, fine writing, the craft of letters. [L.].

LITHE [līTH], *adj.* easily bent, nimble, supple. [OE.].

LITHIUM [li'thi-um], *n.* (*chem.*) the metallic element, Li, the lightest of metals.

LITHO-, *pref.* stone. [Gk.].

LITHOGRAPH [li'thō-grahf], *n.* a print from a drawing made on specially prepared stone or metal

---

ōō is pronounced as in *food*; ŏŏ as in *hood*; th as in *think*; TH as in *that*; zh as in *azure*. ~ = related to.

plate. LITHOGRAPH (2), v.t. to draw on stone and transfer to paper; make a lithographic print. [Gk.].

LITHOGRAPHER [li-tho′gra-fer], n. one who practises lithography.

LITHOGRAPHIC(AL) [li-thō-gra′fĭk(-al)], adj. pertaining to lithography.

LITHOGRAPHY [li-tho′gra-fi], n. art or process of making lithographs. [Gk.].

LITHOTOMY [li-tho′to-mi], n. (surg.) operation of cutting for stone in the bladder. [Gk.].

LITIGANT (1) [li′ti-gant], adj. engaged in a lawsuit. LITIGANT (2), n. (leg.) party in a lawsuit. [L.].

LITIGATE [li′ti-gāt], v.t. to contest at law; v.i. to carry on a lawsuit. [L.].

LITIGATION [li-ti-gā′shn], n. act of litigating; legal business in general. [L.].

LITIGIOUS [li-ti′jŏŏs], adj. inclined to engage in lawsuits; fond of disputes, contentious. [Fr.].

LITMUS [lit′mus], n. colouring matter extracted from certain lichens; **l. paper**, unsized paper stained with l., used to test acidity or alkalinity by its change of colour. [AF., —ODu.].

LITOTES [lī′to-tēz], n. (rhet.) understatement, figure of speech which consists of the toning down of a statement, esp. when an affirmative is implied by using the negative of the contrary. [Gk.].

LITRE [lē′ter], n. unit of capacity in the metric system, equivalent to rather more than 1¾ pints. [Fr.].

LITTER (1) [li′ter], n. wheel-less vehicle in which a person may be carried; stretcher; straw, hay etc., used as a bed for animals; waste matter, rubbish etc., scattered about untidily; the whole number of the young of certain animals, brought forth at one birth. LITTER (2), v.t. to provide with l.; pile up with l.; v.i. to give birth to a l. [Fr.].

LITTERATEUR [li-te-rah-tur′], n. man of letters. [Fr.].

LITTLE (1) [li′tl], adj. small in height, size, quantity, extent; brief; young; of small power and importance; petty, mean. LITTLE (2), n. a small quantity or amount; short time. LITTLE (3), adv. in a small quantity or degree; not much, slightly. [OE.].

LITTLE-GO [li′tl-gō], n. (coll.) preliminary examination at Cambridge University.

LITTORAL (1) [li′te-ral], adj. pertaining to the seashore. LITTORAL (2), n. seashore; any coastal strip of country. [L.].

LITURGIC(AL) [li-tur′jik(-al)], adj. connected with a liturgy; in accordance with a religious formulary, calendar etc. LITURGICALLY, adv. according to the liturgy.

LITURGY [li′ter-ji], n. body of ritual or established formularies for public worship; the Office for the celebration of the Holy Communion. LITURGIST, n. one who advocates the use of liturgies; an authority on l. [Gk.].

LIVE (1) [liv], adj. having life, living; on fire; loaded; covered with animalculae or filth; (fig.) lively, spirited; **l. broadcast**, transmission made directly from an original performance, not a recording; **l. cartridge**, cartridge containing a bullet; **l. rail**, electrified rail; **l. wire**, electrified wire; (fig.) lively, energetic person. [ALIVE].

LIVE (2) [liv], v.i. to be alive; spend one's life; remain alive; dwell; feed, subsist; gain a livelihood; lead a vivid life; (fig.) be remembered; spend, pass; conform to; **to l. down**, to cause to be forgotten; **to l. up to**, to fulfil expectations; **to l. and let l.**, to be tolerant. [OE.].

LIVELIHOOD [liv′li-hŏŏd], n. means of subsistence. [OE.].

LIVELONG [liv′long], adj. lasting, enduring; all through. [LIVE (2) and LONG (1)].

LIVELY [liv′li], adj. brisk, vigorous, full of vitality; gay, sprightly; fresh; keen; vivid; moving quickly.

LIVEN [li′ven], v.t. to enliven, cheer up, relieve.

LIVER (1) [li′ver], n. one who lives.

LIVER (2), n. organ which secretes the bile; this organ in animals, cooked as food; (coll.) attack of sluggishness of the liver. LIVER (3), adj. dark reddish-brown in colour. [OE.].

LIVER-FLUKE [li′ver-flŏŏk], n. trematoid worm infesting the liver of sheep etc.

LIVERIED [li′ve-rid], adj. wearing livery.

LIVERISH [li′ve-rish], adj. suffering from a disordered liver; irritable, testy.

LIVERPUDLIAN [li-ver-pud′li-an], n. and adj. (coll.) a native of, pertaining to, Liverpool.

LIVERWORT [li′ver-wert], n. member of the Hepaticae, cryptogamic plants related to the mosses.

LIVERY [li′ve-ri], n. uniform worn by servants and retainers; any uniform proper to particular persons on particular occasions; (fig.) garb, dress; (leg.) delivery of property; writ of such delivery; **at l.**, (of a horse) kept for the owner at a fixed charge; **l. company**, company of the City of London whose members were formerly entitled to wear a distinctive l. LIVERY-MAN, member of a l. company and a freeman of the City of London. LIVERY-STABLE, jobmaster's stable in which horses are kept at l. or for hire. [OFr.].

LIVESTOCK [liv′stok], n. cattle, sheep etc.; (coll.) vermin on the person. [LIVE (1) and STOCK (1)].

LIVID [li′vid], adj. bluish; of a leaden colour; discoloured; very pale; (slang) very angry. [L.].

LIVING (1) [li′ving], n. wages, salary or income; livelihood; manner and standard of life; trade, craft or profession; benefice of a parish priest. LIVING (2), adj. alive, existing; (of water) flowing; full of vitality; lifelike; **l. rock**, rock in its natural state.

LIZARD [li′zerd], n. a small reptile. LIZARD-STONE, serpentine marble stone found in Cornwall near L. Point. [OFr.].

LLAMA [lah′mah], n. South American beast of burden, related to the camel. [Span. from Peruvian].

LLOYD'S [loidz], n. headquarters of the London underwriters and insurance brokers. [Lloyd's coffee-house, their original meeting place].

LO [lō], int. see, look, behold. [OE.].

LOACH [lōch], n. a small freshwater fish. [Fr.].

LOAD (1) [lōd], n. that which is laid on or put in anything for conveyance, burden, weight; as much as can be, or is, carted at once, esp. as a unit of measure; (fig.) anything oppressive or depressing; charge of a gun; (elect.) amount of electricity supplied by a generating station or dynamo at any one time; work imposed on an engine. LOAD (2), v.t. to lay a burden on; place a l. on or in; overburden, encumber; oppress; weight at one end or side; charge a gun; adulterate drink. LOADER, n. person employed in loading; attendant who loads guns; machine for loading. LOADING, n. act of one who loads; a load. [OE.].

LOADLINE [lōd′lin], n. (naut.) line on the side of a ship to indicate the limit to which it may be legally loaded.

LOADSTAR, see LODESTAR.

LOADSTONE, LODESTONE [lōd′stōn], n. iron ore which has the power of attracting iron; magnet. [OE.].

LOAF (1) (pl. **loaves**) [lōf, lōvz], n. a certain quantity of bread baked in one mass; cubical mould of sugar; lump of anything. LOAF-SUGAR, sugar refined and formed into small cubical lumps. [OE.].

LOAF (2), v.t. and i. to idle away or about. LOAFER, n. one who spends his time in idleness. [Unkn.].

LOAM (1) [lōm], n. a rich soil, mainly clay with an admixture of sandy soil; paste of clay, sand, water etc., used in making bricks. LOAM (2), v.t. to cover with l. [OE.].

LOAN (1) [lōn], n. the lending of anything; thing lent; money lent at interest; an issue of stock by a government. LOAN (2), v.t. (U.S.) to lend. [OIcel.].

LOATH, LOTH [lōth], adj. unwilling, reluctant; **nothing l.**, not at all unwilling. [OE.].

LOATHE [lōTH], v.t. to hate, detest; feel disgust at. [OE.].

LOATHING [lō′THing], n. extreme dislike or disgust; hatred of.

LOATHLY (1) [lōTH′li], adj. arousing loathing. LOATHLY (2), adv. in a manner to arouse loathing.

LOATHSOME [lōTH′sum], adj. exciting loathing; (coll.) objectionable.

LOB (1) (pres.pt. **lobbing**, pret. and p.pt. **lobbed**) [lob], v.t. to toss as a lob at cricket or tennis. LOB (2), n. slow high-pitched ball bowled underhand at cricket; high-pitched ball at tennis. [Uncert.].

LOBAR [lō′ber], adj. pertaining to a lobe.

LOBBY (1) [lo′bi], n. hall; passage communicating with rooms; anteroom; (parl.) large room in the House of Commons for public interviews with Members of Parliament; corridor for recording votes on a division. LOBBY (2), v.t. and i. (parl.) to interview members of a legislative assembly in the l. in order to obtain their support for some object; canvass. [LL.].

LOBE [lōb], n. lower, soft pendulous part of the ear; any rounded, projecting part, esp. of an organ of the body; a division of a leaf; cotyledon of a plant. [Gk.].

LOBELIA [lō-bē′li-ah], n. (bot.) genus of brightly flowered plants; plant of this genus. [M. de Lobel, botanist].

LOBSTER [lob′ster], n. an edible crustacean, bluish

The accent ′ after a syllable = stress, upon′); ‖The mark ‾ over a vowel = length (ā in made; ō in bone).

black when alive, red when it has been boiled; **l. pot**, trap for lobsters. [OE.].

LOBWORM [lob′werm], *n.* a worm used for bait by anglers.

LOCAL (1) [lō′kal], *adj.* pertaining to place or space; connected with some particular place, area, or district; **l. colour**, background detail and atmosphere in any work of art; **l. option**, regulation of the sale of intoxicants by a l. plebiscite. LOCAL (2), *n.* inhabitant of a particular locality; train or vehicle serving a certain small area; (*pl.*) l. examinations, held by universities at various different centres; (*coll.*) public house. LOCALLY, *adv.* in certain localities; in the surrounding district, near at hand. [L.].

LOCALE [lō-kahl′], *n.* location, *esp.* of a story, film or drama. [Fr.].

LOCALISM [lō′ka-lizm], *n.* attachment to a locality; restricted mental outlook; local peculiarity of idiom or behaviour.

LOCALITY [lō-ka′li-ti], *n.* a particular district; situation, environment.

LOCALIZE [lō′ka-līz], *v.t.* to make local; restrict to a particular region; identify with a particular locality.

LOCATE [lō-kāt′], *v.t.* to set, establish in a particular spot or position; determine, find where a particular thing is. [L.].

LOCATION [lō-kā′shn], *n.* act of locating; act of placing; relative situation; that which is located. [L.].

LOCATIVE (1) [lo′ka-tiv], *adj.* (*gram.*) of, or denoting, position. LOCATIVE (2), *n.* (*gram.*) the l. case. [L.].

LOCH [lokh], *n.* lake or arm of the sea, *esp.* in Scotland. [Gael.].

LOCK (1) [lok], *n.* tress of hair; (*pl.*) hair. [OE.].

LOCK (2), *n.* mechanism for shooting a bar or bolt into a socket so as to hold closed a door, box etc.; part of a firearm by which it is discharged; a grapple in wrestling; enclosure on a river or canal between movable watertight gates through which ships can be moved from one level to another; (*mech.*) any tight coupling; stoppage of any moving part in a machine; limits of the turning-circle of a motor-car's steering wheel. LOCK (3), *v.t.* to fasten with a l.; embrace closely; interlace; set rigidly; cause a stoppage of motion in; (*fig.*) keep fast; *v.i.* to be fastened or be capable of being fastened with a l.; cease to move or revolve; **to l. out**, to prevent from entering a factory to work; **to l. up**, to imprison. [OE.].

LOCKER [lo′ker], *n.* person who locks; cupboard, receptacle etc. which may be closed with a lock; **in Davy Jones's l.**, at the bottom of the sea.

LOCKET [lo′kit], *n.* little case usually of gold or silver containing a miniature etc. and worn as an ornament. [OFr.].

LOCK-GATE [lok′gāt], *n.* one of the gates enclosing the basin of a river or canal lock.

LOCK-HOSPITAL [lok′hos-pi-tal], *n.* hospital for venereal diseases.

LOCKJAW [lok′jaw], *n.* (*path.*) a form of tetanus.

LOCK-KEEPER [lok′kē-per], *n.* man who attends to the lock of a river or canal.

LOCK-KNIT [lok′nit], *n.* material woven so as to resemble knitting and having locked stitches.

LOCK-OUT [lok′owt], *n.* refusal of an employer to allow workmen to resume work until they accept his terms.

LOCKSMITH [lok′smith], *n.* one whose craft is the making and repairing of locks and keys.

LOCK-STITCH [lok′stich], *n.* an interlocking stitch which will not slip.

LOCK-UP (1) [lok′up], *n.* prison, quarters for the detention of arrested persons. LOCK-UP (2), *adj.* able to be locked; **l. shop**, shop without living quarters.

LOCO (1) [lō′kō], *adj.* (*slang*) mad. [Span.].

LOCO- (2), *pref.* by, with or from a place. [L.].

LOCOMOTION [lō-kō-mō′shn], *n.* act or power of moving from place to place. [LOCO (2)].

LOCOMOTIVE (1) [lō-kō-mō′tiv], *adj.* moving by its own power from place to place. LOCOMOTIVE (2), *n.* engine on wheels moving along by its own power, *esp.* a steam railway engine. [LOCO (2)].

LOCOMOTOR [lō′kō-mō-ter], *adj.* pertaining to locomotion.

LOCUM TENENS [lō-kum-te′nenz], *n.* a deputy, *esp.* a doctor or clergyman. [L.].

LOCUS (*pl.* loci) [lō′kus, lō′sī], *n.* seat, place in which something is situated; (*math.*) the line generated by a point, or surface generated by a line, moving according to a fixed law; **l. classicus**, the standard authoritative passage or instance; (*nat. hist.*)

original locality; **l. standi**, official position; (*leg.*) right to intervene in a lawsuit. [L.].

LOCUST [lō′kust], *n.* orthopterous insect allied to the grasshopper; a thorny flowering U.S. tree, carob-tree; **l. bean**, fruit of the carob-tree.

LOCUTION [lo-kyōō′shn], *n.* speech; mode of expression; phrase, idiom. [L.].

LODE [lōd], *n.* a mineral vein. [OE.].

LODESTAR, LOADSTAR [lōd′stah(r)], *n.* star which shows the way; the pole-star; (*fig.*) guiding influence or ideal [*Prec.*].

LODESTONE, see LOADSTONE.

LODGE (1) [loj], *n.* dwelling, *esp.* a temporary habitation; small house for the use of sportsmen when shooting etc.; gatekeeper's cottage; local association, *esp.* of Freemasons and similar societies; place where they meet; meeting held by them. LODGE (2), *v.t.* to deposit, *esp.* in the official custody of; harbour; place, implant; lay a formal statement before the authorities; *v.i.* reside for a time; occupy lodgings; come to rest securely fixed (in). [Fr.].

LODGEMENT, see LODGMENT.

LODGER [lo′jer], *n.* one who lodges, paying guest.

LODGING [lo′jing], *n.* habitation, *esp.* when temporary; (*pl.*) hired apartments in a house; **l. house**, house in which apartments are let out to lodgers.

LODGMENT, LODGEMENT [loj′ment], *n.* act of lodging; state of being lodged; accumulation of something deposited.

LOFT (1) [loft], *n.* room immediately under the roof, *esp.* in a stable; gallery in a church; pigeon-house; flock of pigeons; (*golf*) the inclination of the head of a club; a stroke which lofts. LOFT (2), *v.t.* to place in a l.; (*golf*) hit (a ball) high; (of the face of a club) cause to slope. LOFTER, *n.* (*golf*) iron-headed club for lofting the ball. [ON.].

LOFTY [lof′ti], *adj.* extending to a great height, tall; (*fig.*) elevated, dignified; haughty, frigid.

LOG (1) [log], *n.* large piece of undressed timber; apparatus for measuring speed at sea; daily record of a voyage or flight; book in which the record is kept. LOG (2) (*pres.pt.* LOGGING, *pret.* and *p.pt.* LOGGED), *v.t.* to fell and cut into logs; insert as an entry in a logbook; cruise at (a given speed); cover (a distance) in a day's run; record in official or semi-official manner; *v.i.* to fell and collect timber from a forest; work as a lumberman. [ME.].

LOG (3), *n.* a logarithm.

LOGANBERRY [lō′gan-be-ri], *n.* a cultivated fruit, a cross between a blackberry and raspberry and resembling the latter in appearance; bush on which this grows. [Judge *Logan*, American who introduced it].

LOGANSTONE [lō′gan-stōn], *n.* large stone so balanced on another that it will rock when touched. [DialE.].

LOGARITHM [lo′ga-riᴛʜm], *n.* (of a number) the power to which a base must be raised to give that number. LOGARITHMIC(AL) [lo-ga-riᴛʜ′mik(-al)], *adj.* pertaining to, consisting of, logarithms. [Gk.].

LOGBOOK [log′bŏŏk], *n.* official record of the daily events of a voyage or flight.

LOGGERHEAD [lo′ger-hed], *n.* long handle with a ball at the head, heated and plunged into tar etc. to melt it; **at loggerheads**, at variance. [LOG (1)].

LOGGIA [lo′ji-ah], *n.* gallery, arcade or roofed terrace in front of a building. [It.].

LOGIC [lo′jik], *n.* the formal aspect of cogent reasoning; department of philosophy which determines and evaluates its forms; reasoning; subtlety in thought; (*coll.*) common sense, cogency; rational nature. [Gk.].

LOGICAL [lo′ji-kal], *adj.* belonging to logic; according to logic; skilled in logic; discriminating; consistent. LOGICALLY, *adv.* in l. fashion.

LOGISTICS (1) [lo-jis′tiks], *n.* (*pl.*) subtle argumentation; arithmetical computation; arithmetic of sexagesimal fractions. [Gk.].

LOGISTICS (2), *n.* (*pl.*) (*milit.*) science and technique of moving and quartering troops. [Fr.].

LOGO-, *pref.* words, speech, reason. [Gk.].

LOGOGRAM [lo′gō-gram], *n.* a sign which stands for a whole word. [Gk.].

LOGOS [lo′gos], *n.* (*theol.*) the Divine Word incarnate; the active principle of the universe. [Gk.].

LOG-ROLLING [log′rōl-ing], *n.* (*fig.*) mutual admiration; practice whereby writers etc. praise each other's work reciprocally. LOG-ROLLER, *n.* one who practises l.; lumberman.

LOGWOOD [log′wŏŏd], *n.* an American tree; shavings of this used to make a rich red dye.

ŏŏ is pronounced as in *food*; ŏŏ as in *hood*; th as in *think*; ᴛʜ as in *that*; zh as in azure.   ~ = related to.

LOIN [loin], *n.(pl.)* the fleshy part of an animal or human being surrounding the fork, and connecting the abdomen with the legs or hind legs; meat from this part eaten as food; *(fig.)* male parentage or ancestry; **to gird up one's loins**, to prepare for strenuous effort. LOIN-CLOTH, cloth worn round the loins. [Fr.].

LOITER [loi'ter], *v.i.* to be slow in moving, linger or delay in a suspicious manner. LOITERER, *n.* one who loiters. [Du.].

LOLL [lol], *v.t.* to allow to hang out or down; *v.i.* to lounge, sit or stand lazily about; (of the tongue) hang out. [Symbolic].

LOLLARD [lo'lerd], *n.* medieval follower of John Wyclif. [Du.].

LOLLIPOP [lo'li-pop], *n. (coll.)* hard-boiled sweet. [Uncert.].

LOLLOP [lo'lop], *v.i.* to move with an ungainly loping gait. [LOLL].

LONDON PRIDE [lun-dn-prid'], *n. (bot.)* a garden saxifrage. [(A)LONE].

LONE [lōn], *adj.* lonely; solitary; unfrequented. [(A)LONE].

LONELY [lōn'li], *adj.* solitary, single; standing by itself; unfrequented, remote; sad in solitude, lacking companionship.

LONESOME [lōn'sum], *adj.* desolate; lonely; lone.

LONG (1) [long], *adj.* of notable extension in length or time; tall; lengthy, protracted; lingering, tedious; **l. face**, a dismal face; **l. firm fraud**, fraud in which goods are ordered for remote or non-existent firms, and then appropriated; **l. wave**, *(radio)* band of longest wavelengths used for broadcasting; transmission so broadcast; **in the l. run**, ultimately; **one's l. suit**, *(fig.,* from cards) one's strong point. LONG (2), *adv.* to a great extent in space or time; at a point of time far distant before or after. LONG (3), *v.i.* to be filled with longing or desire; crave (for). [OE.].

LONG-AGO [long-a-gō'], *n.* the distant past.

LONGBOAT [long'bōt], *n.* largest boat carried on a sailing ship.

LONGBOW [long'bō], *n.* powerful bow formerly used by English archers; **to draw the l.,** to exaggerate.

LONGCLOTH [long'kloth], *n.* a tough cotton stuff.

LONGERON [lon'je-ron], *n. (aeron.)* any main girder running lengthwise in a fuselage. [Fr.].

LONGEVITY [lon-je'vi-ti], *n.* long life. [L.].

LONGHAND [long'hand], *n.* ordinary handwriting as distinguished from shorthand.

LONG-HEADED [long-he'did], *adj.* dolichocephalic; *(fig.)* of great discernment.

LONG-HOP [long'hop], *n. (cricket)* short-pitched ball which makes a long bounce.

LONGI-, *pref.* long. [L.].

LONGING (1) [long'ing], *n.* eager desire, yearning. LONGING (2), *adj.* desiring earnestly, yearning.

LONGITUDE [long'gi-tyōod], *n. (geog.)* distance of a place east or west of a given meridian, usually that of Greenwich, expressed in degrees; *(astron.)* distance from the vernal equinox reckoned eastward on the ecliptic. [L.].

LONGITUDINAL [long-gi-tyōo'di-nal], *adj.* lengthwise. LONGITUDINALLY, *adv.* in a l. direction; lengthwise.

LONG-LIVED [long-livd'], *adj.* living long; lasting.

LONG MEASURE [long'me-zher], *n.* lineal measure.

LONGSHOREMAN [long'shaw-man], *n.* man who earns his living in or about boats along the shore.

LONG-SIGHTED [long-si'tid], *adj.* able to see at a great distance; *(fig.)* provident, sagacious; *(med.)* seeing only distant objects distinctly.

LONG-SUFFERING (1) [long-su'fe-ring], *n.* patience in adversity, kindly tolerance. LONG-SUFFERING (2), *adj.* patient in adversity, kind.

LONG-TERM [long'term], *adj.* having in view a considerable time in the future.

LONGWAYS [long'wāz], *adv.* lengthwise.

LONG-WINDED [long-win'did], *adj.* long-breathed; tediously eloquent.

LOO (1) [lōō], *n.* round card-game involving forfeits, the forfeit paid in it. LOO (2), *v.t.* to subject to a forfeit at the game of l. [~Fr.].

LOOFAH [lōō'fah], *n.* fibrous part of the fruit of the towel-gourd, used as a washing-sponge. [Arab.].

LOOK (1) [lōōk], *v.t. and i.* to direct the eyes at an object; direct the mind or attention to; convey an impression; appear, seem; take care; search; expect, hope; **to l. after,** to care for; **to l. down on,** to despise; **to l. at,** to consider; examine; **to l. for,** to seek; expect; **to l. on,** to regard; be a

spectator; remain inactive; **to l. out,** to take care; **to l. up,** *(coll.)* to visit; improve; consult in a book or books; **to l. up to,** to respect. LOOK (2), *n.* act of looking; a consciously directed glance of the eyes; brief inspection; appearance; mien; expression. [OE.].

LOOKER [lōōk'er], *n.* person who looks; **a good l.,** *(slang)* handsome person. LOOKER-ON, spectator.

LOOK-IN [lōōk'in], *n. (coll.)* a chance of success.

LOOKING [lōōk'ing], *adj.* having a specified appearance.

LOOKING-GLASS [lōōk'ing-glahs], *n.* mirror.

LOOK OUT [lōōk'owt, lōōk-owt'], *n.* a careful watching for someone or something; person keeping such a watch; place to look out from; prospect.

LOOK-SEE [lōōk'sē], *n. (slang)* a glance, survey.

LOOM (1) [lōōm], *n.* weaving machine. [ME.].

LOOM (2), *v.i.* to appear above the horizon; appear suddenly, and as though magnified, before the gaze; appear dimly in the distance. LOOMING, *adj.* that looms up suddenly; menacing. [Unkn.].

LOON (1) [lōōn], *n. (Scots and northern dial.)* worthless fellow; boor; *(slang)* foolish person. [Scots].

LOON (2), *n. (ornith.)* the great northern diver; any species of *Colymbus.* [OIcel.].

LOONY [lōō'ni], *adj. (slang)* mad, crazy; **l. bin,** *(slang)* lunatic asylum. [LUNATIC].

LOOP (1) [lōōp], *n.* the doubled part of a string, chain etc.; noose through which a cord may be run for fastening; bend; bight; *(railway)* loop-line. LOOP (2), *v.t.* to form into a l., fasten with a l.; *v.i.* to form a l. or loops; **to l. the l.,** to describe a vertical circle in the air in an aeroplane. LOOPED, *adj.* coiled in a l. or loops; furnished with a l. or loops; having loopholes. LOOPER, *n.* hook which loops; caterpillar of the geometer moth which, in moving along, forms its body into loops.

LOOPHOLE [lōōp'hōl], *n.* hole in a wall, through which small arms may be discharged; *(fig.)* way or means of escape. [~MDu.].

LOOP-LINE [lōōp'lin], *n.* railway line which branches from the main line and then rejoins it at another point.

LOOSE (1) [lōōs], *adj.* unbound, not under restraint; not compact; not close or tight, having play; not stretched tight, slack; unpacked; inaccurate; (of speech) licentious or merely approximate; (of conduct) lax; not strict; not securely fixed in place; not firm; *(med.)* subject to a flux from the bowels; **at a l. end,** unoccupied, idle. LOOSE (2), *adv.* loosely; **fast and l.,** rashly. LOOSE (3), *v.t.* to unfasten; free from fastenings, restraint or obligation; liberate; discharge; fire a weapon. [OScand.].

LOOSE-BOX [lōōs'boks], *n.* stable in which a horse may remain loose.

LOOSE-LEAF [lōōs'lēf], *adj.* (of a ledger, notebook) with each leaf separate and detachable.

LOOSEN [lōō'sen], *v.t. and i.* to make or become loose or looser; **to l. up,** *(fig., coll.)* to become more expansive in conversation.

LOOSESTRIFE [lōōs'strif], *n. (bot.)* plant of the genus *Lysimachia,* or *Lythrum salicaria.*

LOOT (1) [lōōt], *n.* plunder, booty; proceeds of war; *(coll.)* any financial return. LOOT (2), *v.t. and i.* to plunder; take as l. LOOTER, *n.* one who loots. LOOTING, *n.* plundering. [Hind.].

LOP (1) *(pres.pt.* lopping, *pret. and p.pt.* lopped) [lop], *v.t.* to chop; shorten by cutting off a part, *esp.* of trees. LOP (2), *n.* that which is cut from a tree. [Unkn.].

LOP (3) *(pres.pt.* lopping, *pret. and p.pt.* lopped), *v.t.* to let fall; *v.i.* to hang down, droop; move along jerkily. LOP-EARED, *adj.* having pendulous ears. [Echoic].

LOPE [lōp], *v.i.* to run with long, leisurely, effortless stride. [OScand.].

LOPSIDED [lop-si'did], *adj.* asymmetrical, heavier or larger on one side than the other. LOPSIDEDLY, *adv.* so as to appear l., in l. fashion. [LOP (3) and SIDE].

LOQUACIOUS [lō-kwā'shŏos], *adj.* talkative; eloquent. [L.].

LOQUACITY [lō-kwa'si-ti], *n.* quality of being loquacious.

LORD (1) [lawd], *n.* one who controls inferiors and is venerated by them; a feudal superior; a peer; title of address of certain ranks of the aristocracy and hierarchy, and of certain high officials, as judges etc.; **the L., the L. of hosts,** God; **Our L.,** second person of the Trinity; **the Lords,** upper chamber of the British Parliament; **L. Chancellor,** chief judge of England; **L. Mayor,** mayor of certain important cities in the British Commonwealth; **L. Rector,** elected head of certain Scottish universities; **L. of the Bedchamber,** official attending on the Sovereign's person; **my L.,** form of address to bishops and peers below a duke; **good L.,** common exclamation of surprise. LORD (2), *v.i.* to domineer; **to l. it over,** to behave arrogantly to. [OE.].

LORDLING [lawd'ling], *n.* young or unimportant lord.

LORDLY [lawd'li], *adj.* becoming or befitting a lord; haughty, imperious; lavish, sumptuous.

LORDOSIS [law-dō'sis], *n.* (*anat.*) curvature of the bones, *esp.* forward curvature of the spine. [Gk.].

LORDS-AND-LADIES [lawdz-and-lā'diz], *n.* the wild arum lily.

LORDSHIP [lawd'ship], *n.* domain, rule, power of a lord; form used in speaking of a nobleman.

LORE [law(r)], *n.* knowledge gained from reading or tradition; abstruse or specialized knowledge. [OE.].

LORGNETTE [law-nyet'], *n.* pair of eyeglasses on a long handle. [Fr.].

LORN [lawn], *adj.* forlorn, lost; forsaken. [ME.].

LORRY [lo'ri], *n.* large strongly built motor- or steam-wagon for haulage work. [Unkn.].

LOSE (*pret. and p.pt.* **lost**) [looz], *v.t.* to cease to have, be deprived of possession of; to be bereaved of; fail to obtain or win; waste, squander; cause to perish; miss; bewilder; fail to see or find; *v.i.* to be beaten in a contest; **to l. oneself,** to be bewildered, be deeply absorbed in. LOSER, *n.* one who loses; (*billiards*) losing hazard. [OE.].

LOSING [loo'zing], *adj.* bringing or causing loss; **l. hazard,** (*billiards*) stroke in which the cue ball strikes another, and then falls into a pocket. LOSINGLY, *adv.* in a l. fashion.

LOSS [los], *n.* failure to keep or win; act or result of losing; bereavement; damage, waste; that which is lost, or its monetary equivalent; (*milit.*) amount destroyed or number killed. [OE.].

LOST [lost], *adj.* that cannot be found or seen, missing; forfeited, wasted; confused, bewildered; ruined; wrecked or drowned; morally abandoned. [LOSE.].

LOT [lot], *n.* chance; destiny, fate; that which falls to one by fortune; distinct portion or parcel, *esp.* at an auction; a group considered collectively; (*coll.*) a great deal, many; (*coll.*) person or persons; **to cast or draw lots,** to decide by throwing dice or drawing one from a number of objects. [OE.].

LOTH, see LOATH.

LOTION [lō'shn], *n.* (*med.*) a fluid medicinal preparation for outward application. [L.].

LOTOS, see LOTUS.

LOTTERY [lo'te-ri], *n.* scheme for the distribution of prizes by lot; outcome which depends largely on chance. [It.].

LOTTO [lo'tō], *n.* a table game of chance. [It.].

LOTUS, LOTOS [lō'tus], *n.* large genus of leguminous plants; sacred Egyptian water-lily; tree or plant, of unspecified identity, frequently referred to by the ancient writers. LOTUS-EATER, *n.* (*Gk. antiq.*) member of a fabulous race of people who lived a life of dreamy enjoyment; (*fig.*) one who lives in a dreamy, blissful state. [Gk.].

LOUD (1) [lowd], *adj.* characterized by perceptible or considerable noise; heard and pronounced in sound; noisy; (*fig.*) in bad taste, vulgarly gaudy. LOUD (2), *adv.* in a l. manner; aloud. [OE.].

LOUD-SPEAKER [lowd-spē'ker], *n.* vibrant instrument for converting electrical impulses into sound vibrations loud enough to be heard some distance away; amplifier.

LOUGH [lokh], *n.* lake, long arm of the sea. [Ir.].

LOUNGE (1) [lownj], *v.i.* to recline in a lazy manner; loll comfortably; walk in a slovenly, lazy manner. LOUNGE (2), *n.* act of lounging; comfortable but informally furnished sitting-room, *esp.* in a club or hotel; couch or sofa; **l. lizard,** useless, effeminate man; **l. suit,** suit for informal morning wear. LOUNGER, *n.* one who lounges; idler. [Uncert.].

LOUR, LOWER (3) [lowr], *v.i.* to look threatening, frown; (of the sky) threaten, be overcast. [ME.].

LOUSE (*pl.* **lice**) [lows], *n.* small insect, *esp.* of the genus *Pediculus,* parasitic on man etc.

LOUSY [low'zi], *adj.* infested with lice; (*coll.*) extremely poor or bad; highly unpleasant.

LOUT [lowt], *n.* mean, awkward fellow; clumsy bumpkin. [~OE.].

LOUTISH [low'tish], *adj.* like a lout; clumsy, boorish, awkward.

LOUVER, LOUVRE [loo'ver], *n.* opening in a turret or lantern for the escape of smoke, now often

glazed; **l. window,** opening, usually in belfries, crossed by sloping bars of wood. [OFr.].

LOVABLE [lu'va-bl], *adj.* worthy of love; amiable; endearing; attractive.

LOVE (1) [luv], *n.* intense spiritual attraction towards an object, affection; benevolence, goodwill; self-sacrifice; the object beloved; word of endearment; (*tennis etc.*) no score, nothing; **to make l.,** to express feelings of l.; **to give (one's) l. to,** to send affectionate greetings to. LOVE (2), *v.t.* to experience l. for; like very much; regard with affection; *v.i.* to have the feeling of l. [OE.].

LOVEBIRD [luv'berd], *n.* a small parakeet, the budgerigar; (*slang*) lover.

LOVE-CHILD [luv'child], *n.* illegitimate child.

LOVE-IN-A-MIST [luv-in-a-mist'], *n.* the fennel flower, a species of *Nigella.*

LOVE-IN-IDLENESS [luv-in-I'dl-nes], *n.* heartsease, *Viola tricolor.*

LOVE-KNOT [luv'not], *n.* double knot made up of interlacing bows.

LOVELESS [luv'les], *adj.* loving or loved by no one; without love.

LOVE-LETTER [luv'le-ter], *n.* tender letter between lovers.

LOVE-LIES-BLEEDING [luv-liz-blē'ding], *n.* the cultivated plant, *Amaranthus caudatus.*

LOVELOCK [luv'lok], *n.* curl worn by men of fashion in the reign of Elizabeth and James I; any curl trained to lie on the forehead.

LOVE-LORN [luv'lawn], *adj.* forsaken by one's lover; jilted; forlorn.

LOVELY [luv'li], *adj.* such as to excite love or admiration, beautiful, charming; (*coll.*) delightful, splendid.

LOVER [lu'ver], *n.* one who loves; person carrying on an illicit love-affair.

LOVESICK [luv'sik], *adj.* languishing for love.

LOVING [lu'ving], *adj.* animated by love, expressing love for; dutiful, affectionate.

LOVING-CUP [lu'ving-kup], *n.* large two-handled drinking vessel passed round a company.

LOVING-KINDNESS [lu-ving-kind'nes], *n.* deep and tender regard; mercy.

LOW (1) [lō], *adj.* not high, not extending far above any surface; below the usual height; (of a sound) soft and deep; in poor health; dejected; poverty-stricken, mean; humble, poor; vulgar, base; indecent; submissive; weak, feeble; unfavourable; (*biol.*) primitive; (*eccles.*) belonging to the Low Church party; **L. Church,** Evangelical party in the Church of England; **l. water,** the ebb; (*coll.*) financial straits. LOW (2), *adv.* not in a high position, near the ground; in a l. voice or pitch; in a state of poverty, subjection, or disgrace; **to lie l.,** to keep quietly hidden or inconspicuous. [OIcel.].

LOW (3), *v.i.* to utter the characteristic sound of an ox or cow. LOW (4), *n.* cry of the ox or cow. [OE.].

LOW-BORN [lō'bawn], *adj.* of humble birth.

LOWBROW (1) [lō'brow], *n.* non-intellectual person. LOWBROW (2), *adj.* relating to a l., his interests and tastes. [LOW (1) and BROW].

LOW-DOWN (1) [lō'down], *adj.* (*coll.*) mean, dishonourable. LOW-DOWN (2), *n.* (*slang*) inside information; full details.

LOWER (1) [lō'er], *adj.* more low; **l. animals,** all mammals except man; **l. case,** (*print.*) case which contains the small letters; the small letters; **L. Chamber, L. House,** House of Commons; **l. classes,** the poor, working people; **l. deck,** (*nav.*) petty officers and men; **l. regions,** hell; (*coll.*) the basement. LOWER (2), *v.t. and i.* to let down; bring down; reduce; diminish in pitch, price etc.; (*fig.*) humble.

LOWER (3), see LOUR.

LOWERING [lowr'ing], *adj.* cloudy, heavy and threatening. LOWERINGLY, *adv.* in a l. manner.

LOWING (1) [lō'ing], *n.* sound made by an ox or cow. LOWING (2), *adj.* mooing as a cow, or bellowing as an ox.

LOWLAND (1) [lō'land], *n.* flat, low-lying country; **the Lowlands,** the southern counties of Scotland. LOWLAND (2), *adj.* pertaining to low-lying country; pertaining to the Lowlands of Scotland.

LOWLANDER [lō'lan-der], *n.* inhabitant of the lowlands; a native of the Lowlands of Scotland.

LOWLY [lō'li], *adj.* of humble birth; (*fig.*) meek, humble, modest. [ME.].

LOW MASS [lō-mas'], *n.* (*eccles.*) Mass celebrated without music and with the minimum of ceremonial.

LOW-NECKED [lō-nekt'], *adj.* (of a garment) cut so

ōo is pronounced as in food; ŏŏ as in hood; th as in *think*; TH as in *that*; zh as in azure. ~ = related to.

as to lay bare the neck, shoulders and part of the chest.

LOW-PRESSURE [lō-pre′sher], *adj.* (*eng.*) (of steam) exerting a pressure on the piston of less than 50 lb. to the sq. in.; (of a steam engine) employing such a pressure.

LOW-SPIRITED [lō-spi′ri-tid], *adj.* depressed in spirits; dejected.

LOYAL [loi′al], *adj.* faithful in allegiance or in any duty or affection, *esp.* as a subject or soldier of the crown. LOYALLY, *adv.* in a l. manner. [OFr.].

LOYALIST [loi′a-list], *n.* one who is loyal to the Government in a rebellion.

LOYALTY [loi′al-ti], *n.* quality of being loyal. [OFr.].

LOZENGE [lo′zenj], *n.* figure with four equal sides and two acute and two obtuse angles, a rhomb; anything similarly shaped; flat, small, thin pastille which can be dissolved by sucking; (*her.*) square figure set diagonally. [Fr.].

LUBBER [lu′ber], *n.* awkward, clumsy fellow; (*naut.*) clumsy seaman. LUBBERLY, *adj.* and *adv.* like a l., clumsy, ungainly; unseamanlike; in the manner of a l. [~OFr.].

LUBRICANT (1) [loo′bri-kant], *adj.* lubricating. LUBRICANT (2), *n.* oil or grease used for lubricating purposes. [L.].

LUBRICATE [loo′bri-kāt], *v.t.* and *i.* to make slippery or smooth; treat with grease or oil so as to lessen friction; (*slang*) bribe; cause to unbend by filling with drink. [L.].

LUBRICATION [loo-bri-kā′shn], *n.* action of lubricating; lubricating system.

LUBRICATOR [loo′bri-kā-ter], *n.* person who lubricates; a lubricant; instrument for oiling machinery.

LUBRICITY [loo-bri′si-ti], *n.* smoothness, slipperiness, instability; salaciousness. [L.].

LUCCA OIL [look′kah-oil], *n.* a fine olive oil. [*Lucca*, Italy, where produced].

LUCE [lyoos], *n.* a full-grown pike. [LL.].

LUCENT [lyoo′sent], *adj.* bright, shining; clear, transparent. [L.].

LUCERNE [loo-surn′], *n.* clover-like plant cultivated for fodder. [Provenc.].

LUCID [lyoo′sid], *adj.* shining, bright; clear, transparent; easily understood; sane, reasonable; clear-thinking. LUCIDLY, *adv.* in a l. manner. [L.].

LUCIDITY [lyoo-si′di-ti], *n.* quality of being lucid.

LUCIFER [loo′si-fer], *n.* the planet Venus, as morning star; Satan, before his fall; (*obs.*) match tipped with some inflammable substance, and ignited by friction. [L.].

LUCK [luk], *n.* mere chance, unexpected and undeserved fortune; good fortune. [Du.].

LUCKLESS [luk′les], *n.* having no luck, unfortunate.

LUCKY [lu′ki], *adj.* having good luck, fortunate; productive of good luck, auspicious.

LUCRATIVE [loo′kra-tiv], *adj.* bringing gain, profitable. LUCRATIVELY, *adv.* in l. fashion. [L.].

LUCRE [loo′ker], *n.* money, gain, *esp.* base gain; filthy l., ill-gotten money; mere money. [L.].

LUCUBRATE [loo′kyoo-brāt], *v.i.* to do learned work by artificial light; discourse learnedly. LUCUBRATION [loo-kyoo-brā′shn], *n.* work produced as the results of laborious study. [L.].

LUDICROUS [loo′di-kroos], *adj.* suited to raise laughter; funny, laughable, ridiculous. [L.].

LUDO [loo′dō], *n.* game played with counters on a marked board. [L.].

LUFF [luf], *v.i.* to sail near the wind. [Du.].

LUFTWAFFE [looft′vah-fe], *n.* the German Air Force. [Germ.].

LUG (1) (*pres.pt.* **lugging**, *pret.* and *p.pt.* **lugged**) [lug], *v.t.* and *i.* to draw, pull with difficulty; **to l. in**, (*fig.*) to introduce irrelevantly. LUG (2), *n.* act of lugging; any projection resembling an ear, *esp.* on castings etc. in machinery, for holding bolts; (*Scots and northern dial.*) ear. [~Swed.].

LUGE [loozh], *n.* sledge of the simplest type. [Fr.].

LUGGAGE [lu′gij], *n.* baggage of a traveller.

LUGGER [lu′ger], *n.* small vessel carrying two or three masts and having a running bowsprit and lugsails. [Uncert.].

LUGSAIL [lug′sl], *n.* (*naut.*) sail, set fore and aft, bent upon a yard which hangs obliquely to the mast.

LUGUBRIOUS [loo-goo′bri-oos], *adj.* mournful, depressed and depressing, dismal. LUGUBRIOUSLY, *adv.* in l. fashion. [L.].

LUKEWARM [look′wawm], *adj.* moderately warm, tepid; (*fig.*) half-hearted. [ME.].

LULL (1) [lul], *v.t.* to quiet, compose; soothe, allay; *v.i.* to subside, abate. LULL (2), *n.* period of relative calm or quiet in the midst of a storm or busy activity. [Swed.].

LULLABY [lu′la-bī], *n.* cradle song; (*fig.*) soothing sound. [Echoic].

LUMBAGO [lum-bā′gō], *n.* (*med.*) rheumatic affection of the loins. [L.].

LUMBAR [lum′ber], *adj.* pertaining to, or situated near, the loins; **l. region**, the hinder part of the body, from the false ribs to the haunch-bone. [L.].

LUMBER (1) [lum′ber], *n.* timber sawn or split for use; anything valueless and cumbersome. LUMBER (2), *v.t.* to heap together; fill with l.; cut timber for sale; *v.i.* to overcrowd. [*Lombard*, pawnbroker's shop].

LUMBER (3), *v.i.* to move heavily; make a rumbling noise in moving along. LUMBERING, *adj.* clumsy and heavy of movement. [~Swed.].

LUMBERER [lum′be-rer], *n.* lumberman.

LUMBER-JACK [lum′ber-jak], *n.* lumberman.

LUMBERMAN [lum′ber-man], *n.* one who cuts down trees and dresses them for the market.

LUMINARY [loo′mi-na-ri], *n.* body which gives off light, *esp.* a heavenly body; (*fig.*) distinguished person, leading light. [MedL.].

LUMINOSITY [loo-mi-no′si-ti], *n.* quality of being luminous.

LUMINOUS [loo′mi-noos], *adj.* emitting or diffusing light, bright, glowing; (*fig.*) glowing. [L.].

LUMP (1) [lump], *n.* a shapeless mass of matter; a swelling on a surface, *esp.* of the skin; large piece; (*coll.*) boorish lout; **l. sum**, considerable sum of money paid in settlement on the spot. LUMP-SUGAR, loaf sugar formed into small cubes. LUMP (2), *v.t.* to put or throw together unsystematically into one mass; (*coll.*) put up with. LUMPING, *adj* (*coll.*) large, heavy. [ME.].

LUMPFISH [lump′fish], *n.* a clumsily shaped sea-fish.

LUMPISH [lum′pish], *adj.* like a lump; heavy, bulky, clumsy, stupid.

LUMPY [lum′pi], *adj.* full of lumps, heavy, clumsy, shapeless.

LUNACY [loo′na-si], *n.* madness, insanity; extreme foolishness. [LUNATIC].

LUNAR [loo′ner], *adj.* pertaining to the moon; measured by the revolutions of the moon; resembling the moon; influenced by the moon; **l. cycle**, period of time after which the new moons return on the same days of the year; **l. month**, time from new moon to new moon; **l. observation**, observation of the moon's distance from a star to find the longitude of the observer; **l. rainbow**, rainbow caused by the refraction of the light of the moon; **l. year**, period of twelve synodic lunar months, 354½ days. LUNARY, *adj.* lunar; monthly. [L.].

LUNATIC (1) [loo′na-tik], *adj.* suffering from lunacy; devoted to the care and treatment of lunatics. LUNATIC (2), *n.* person suffering from lunacy; (*coll.*) irresponsible fool. [LL.].

LUNATION [loo-nā′shn], *n.* period of time from one new moon to the next. [MedL.].

LUNCH (1) [lunch], *n.* luncheon. LUNCH (2), *v.t.* to give luncheon to; *v.i.* to have luncheon. [Early E.].

LUNCHEON [lun′chun], *n.* meal taken at or about mid-day, originally a snack eaten between breakfast and mid-day dinner; **l. set**, set of table doilies. [Prec.].

LUNETTE [loo-net′], *n.* (*arch.*) opening for the admission of light into a concave ceiling. [Fr.].

LUNG [lung], *n.* one of the two respiratory organs in an air-breathing mammal; (*fig.*) large open space in a city. [OE.].

LUNGE (1) [lunj], *n.* sudden thrust with a weapon, combined with a forward movement of the foot and body; movement resembling this. LUNGE (2), *v.i.* to make a l. [Fr.].

LUNGE (3), *n.* long rope or rein used in training a horse. LUNGE (4), *v.t.* to exercise a horse at the end of a l. [Fr.].

LUNGWORT [lung′wert], *n.* (*bot.*) plant with spotted leaves; species of lichen. [OE.].

LUPIN(E) [loo′pin], *n.* (*bot.*) genus of plants of the order *Leguminosae*. [L.].

LUPINE [lyoo′pīn], *adj.* like a wolf. [L.].

LUPUS [loo′pus], *n.* a tuberculous skin disease. [L.].

LURCH (1) [lurch], *n.* losing position in a game; **in the l.**, in difficulties. [Fr.].

LURCH (2), *n.* a sudden, unsteady, sideways stagger. LURCH (3), *v.i.* to stagger sideways with a l. [Uncert.].

The accent ′ after a syllable = stress (u-pon′). The mark ‾ over a vowel = length (ā in made; ō in bone).

LURCHER [lur'cher], n. breed of dog, a cross between a collie and a greyhound. [LURK].

LURE (1) [lyōor], n. bait used for recalling hawks from hunting; decoy for catching animals or fish; (fig.) enticement. LURE (2), v.t. to recall by means of a l.; attract, entice. [OFr.].

LURID [lyōo'rid], adj. pale, dismal, wan; gleaming unnaturally; (fig.) sensational, highly coloured. LURIDLY, adv. in l. fashion. LURIDNESS, n. quality of being l. [L.].

LURK [lurk], v.i. to lie furtively in wait; lie in such a position as to escape observation; (fig.) be implicit or latent. [Uncert.].

LUSCIOUS [lu'shoos], adj. ripe almost to over-ripeness, rich in taste and soft in touch; delicious, full-flavoured; (fig.) highly sensuous.

LUSH [lush], adj. luxuriant, rich in growth, succulent. [Uncert.].

LUST (1) [lust], n. intense desire, usually physical; sinful appetite or the resultant sin; (fig.) overwhelming passion. LUST (2), v.i. to desire strongly, have carnal desire. LUSTER, n. one inflamed with l. [OE.].

LUSTFUL [lust'fool], adj. full of carnal desire. LUSTFULLY, adv. in l. fashion.

LUSTRATION [lus-trā'shn], n. rites of purification from sin or guilt; ritual cleansing. [L.].

LUSTRE (1) [lus'ter], n. smooth sheen, brightness, esp. of reflected light; chandelier made of crystal pendants; (fig.) distinction, renown. LUSTRE-WARE, pottery to which this has been imparted a metallic sheen. LUSTRELESS, adj. lacking l. [Fr.].

LUSTRE (2), n. lustrum.

LUSTRING, LUTESTRING [lus'tring], n. a glossy silk fabric. [Fr.].

LUSTROUS [lus'trōos], adj. shining, luminous.

LUSTRUM [lus'trum], n. a period of five years. [L.].

LUSTY [lus'ti], adj. full of youthful vigour and animal health; produced by such vigour; spirited; large and strong.

LUSUS NATURAE [lyōo-sus-na-tyōo'rē], n. freak of nature, sport.

LUTANIST [lyōo'ta-nist], n. lute player; composer for the lute. [LL.].

LUTE (1) [lyōot], n. stringed musical instrument resembling a guitar, plucked by the fingers. [OFr.].

LUTE (2), n. composition of cement, clay etc. used for sealing, making airtight or fire-proofing. LUTE (3), v.t. to seal or coat with l. [L.].

LUTESTRING, see LUSTRING.

LUTETIAN [loo-tē'shan], adj. and n. pertaining to Paris; (geol.) a stage in the Eocene, comprising the Lower Bracklesham beds and Boscombe Sands. [L.].

LUXURIANCE [luk-zyōo'ri-ans], n. quality of being luxuriant; the degree of this.

LUXURIANT [luk-zyōo'ri-ant], adj. profuse, abundant; fertile and rich; (fig.) florid; extravagant. LUXURIANTLY, adv. in l. fashion. [L.].

LUXURIATE [luk-zyōo'ri-āt], v.i. to grow profusely; (fig.) revel in; live luxuriously. [L.].

LUXURIOUS [luk-zyōo'ri-oos], adj. indulging freely in, characterized by, luxury; furnished with luxuries. LUXURIOUSLY, adv. in l. fashion. [L.].

LUXURY [luk'zyōo-ri], n. costly ease and comfort; profusion of material aids to pleasure; anything acquired for pleasure at noticeable cost; anything agreeable which is not a basic necessity of life. [L.].

LYCANTHROPY [li-kan'thro-pi], n. form of insanity in which the patient imagines himself to be a wolf, and acts like one; transformation of a man into a wolf by means of magic. [Gk.].

LYCEE lycée [lē'sā], n. state-maintained secondary school in French-speaking countries. [Fr. from Gk.].

LYCEUM [lī-sē'um], n. place devoted to study and instruction, esp. a literary society and its building. [Gk.].

LYCHGATE, see LICHGATE.

LYDDITE [li'dit], n. powerful explosive used in shells. [Lydd, Kent, where first made].

LYDIAN (1) [li'di-an], adj. pertaining to Lydia or Lydians; soft, effeminate, esp. of the Lydian musical mode. LYDIAN (2), n. inhabitant of Lydia; language of Lydia; one of the ancient Greek musical modes. [Lydia, ancient country in Asia Minor].

LYE, LEY [lī], n. strongly alkaline solution, used esp. in the manufacture of soap etc. [OE.].

LYING (1) [lī'ing], adj. reclining, prostrate. [LIE (3)].

LYING (2), adj. false, untrue; telling or given to telling lies. LYINGLY, adv. falsely, without truth. [LIE (2)].

LYING-IN [lī-ing-in'], n. confinement, childbirth.

LYMPH [limf], n. (poet.) water; (physiol.) one of the fluid principles of an animal body, watery in colour; (med.) matter exuded from a sore and used as a vaccine. [L.].

LYMPHATIC (1) [lim-fa'tik], adj. pertaining to, producing, conveying, lymph; sluggish. LYMPHATIC (2), n. (usually pl.) small vessel in animal bodies, which contains or conveys lymph. [L.].

LYNCH [linch], v.t. to put to death by mob action, without legal sentence; l. law, summary punishment by a mob. LYNCHING, n. summary execution by a mob, without legal sentence; instance of this. [Charles Lynch, Virginian who started this practice].

LYNX [lingks], n. any of several species of feline carnivora, proverbial for their keen-sightedness. LYNX-EYED, adj. sharp-sighted. [Gk.].

LYON [lī'on], n. title of the chief Scottish herald, from the royal lion on the shield.

LYRE [līer], n. early form of harp, used by the ancients as an accompaniment to the voice; l. bird, Australian bird with a l.-shaped tail. [Gk.].

LYRIC (1) [li'rik], adj. apt to sing; pertaining to the lyre as the symbol of song; suitable for singing; (of poetry) having the character of a lyric. LYRIC (2), n. poem in manner or matter resembling a song, and written in a metre originally intended to be sung; the words of a song. [Gk.].

LYRICAL [li'ri-kal], adj. lyric; (coll.) eloquent; exuberantly laudatory.

LYRICISM [li'ri-sizm], n. quality of being lyrical, lyrical expression; cult or art of lyric poetry.

LYRIST [li'rist], n. composer of lyrics; [lier'ist] musician who plays on the lyre.

LYSIS [lī'sis], n. (med.) the gradual lessening in severity of an acute disease; (biochem.) the dissolving of a cell by a poisonous substance. [Gk.].

LYSOL [lī'sol], n. (prot.) (med.) liquid mixture used as an antiseptic and disinfectant.

M

M [em], thirteenth letter of the English alphabet.

MA [mah], n. (pop.) mother. [MAMMA].

MA'AM [mam], n. contracted form of MADAM.

MAC [mak], n. (coll.) contracted form of MACKINTOSH.

MACABRE [ma-kah'ber], adj. gruesome. [Fr.].

MACADAM [ma-ka'dam], n. road-surfacing material made from broken stones. MACADAMIZE, v.t. to surface with m. [J. McAdam, inventor].

MACARONI [ma-ka-rō'ni], n. Italian dish of wheat-paste dried into long tubes; (hist.) Italianate dandy. [It.].

MACARONIC (1) [ma-ka-ro'nik], adj. (of verse) composed in a burlesque mixed language using words taken or combined from two languages, esp. English words with Latin endings. MACARONIC (2), n. (usu. in pl.) m. verse. [MdL.].

MACAROON [ma-ka-rōon'], n. sweet cake made from almonds. [Fr.].

MACASSAR [ma-ka'ser], n. vegetable oil originally imported from Mangkasara in Celebes, formerly used as hair-oil.

MACAW [ma-kaw'], n. large tropical parrot. [Portug.].

MACE (1) [mās], n. (hist.) heavy spiked club; symbol of office resembling this. [OFr.].

MACE (2), n. a spice obtained from nutmeg. [OFr.].

---

oo is pronounced as in food; oo as in hood; th as in think; TH as in that; zh as in azure. ~ = related to.

MACEBEARER [mās′bāer-er], *n.* official who carries the mace in a procession.

MACEDOINE [ma-si-dwahn′], *n.* mixture, sometimes in jelly, of various kinds of diced fruit or vegetables. [Fr.].

MACERATE [ma′se-rāt], *v.t.* to soften by soaking; weaken. MACERATION [ma-se-rā′shn], *n.* act of macerating, state of being macerated. [L.].

MACHETE [ma-chā′ti], *n.* heavy chopping knife used in South America. [Span.].

MACHIAVELLIAN [ma-ki-a-ve′li-an], *adj.* following the principles and policy of Machiavelli, subtle, unscrupulous. [N. *Machiavelli*, Italian statesman].

MACHICOLATION [ma-chi-kō-lā′shn], *n.* opening between the corbels of overhanging battlements. MACHICOLATED [ma-chi′kō-lā-tid], *adj.* provided with machicolations. [MedL.].

MACHINATION [ma-ki-nā′shn], *n.* plotting, intrigue. [L.].

MACHINE (1) [ma-shēn′], *n.* apparatus consisting of several interconnecting parts which, by their motion, transform or transmit power into work; mechanically-propelled vehicle, *esp.* a bicycle or aircraft; organization for performing a specified function; **m. tool**, mechanical tool designed for the manufacture of machinery. MACHINE (2), *v.t.* to make, treat, or finish by machinery. MACHINER, *n.* worker operating a m. performing certain mechanical processes. [L.].

MACHINE-GUN (1) [ma-shēn′gun], *n.* relatively small, quick-firing, mechanically-operated gun. MACHINE-GUN (2), *v.t.* to attack with a m.

MACHINERY [ma-shē′ne-ri], *n.* machines; the parts of a machine; means by which some process is carried out.

MACHINIST [ma-shē′nist], *n.* one who operates a machine.

MACKEREL [ma′ke-rel], *n.* an edible sea-fish; **m. (back) sky**, cloud formation resembling the markings on a m. [OFr.].

MACKINTOSH [ma′kin-tosh], *n.* waterproof fabric lined or coated with rubber; raincoat of this material. [C. *Mackintosh*, its inventor].

MACON [mah-kaw(ng)′], *n.* heavy red wine. [*Macon*, France, where made].

MACRAME, macramé [ma-krah′mā], *n.* fringe of twisted thread; twine made in this way. [Turk.].

MACRO-, *pref.* long, large. [Gk.].

MACROCEPHALIC [ma-krō-si-fa′lik], *adj.* long-headed. MACROCEPHALOUS [ma-krō-se′fa-lōos], *adj.* macrocephalic. MACROCEPHALY [ma-krō-se′fa-li], *n.* long-headedness. [Gk.].

MACROCOSM [ma′krō-kozm], *n.* the universe. [Gk.].

MACRON [ma′kron], *n.* long mark (⁻) over a vowel. [Gk.].

MACROSCOPIC [ma-krō-sko′pik], *adj.* visible to the naked eye. [Gk.].

MACULA [ma′kyōō-lah], *n.* a mark or dark stain; sun-spot; flaw in a jewel or mineral; spot on the skin. [L.].

MACULATE [ma′kyōō-lāt], *v.t.* to stain, spot. MACULATION [ma-kyōō-lā′shn], *n.* act of maculating; state of being maculated; spot, blemish. [L.].

MAD [mad], *adj.* insane, out of one's mind; overwrought with passion or emotion; reckless; (*U.S. coll.*) angry. MADLY, *adv.* in m. fashion; intensely. [OE.].

MADAM (*pl.* **mesdames**) [ma′dam, *pl.* mā′dahm], *n.* formal mode of address to ladies, *esp.* to married women. [Fr.].

MADCAP [mad′kap], *n.* impulsive, carefree girl.

MADDEN [ma′den], *v.t.* to drive mad, infuriate.

MADDER [ma′der], *n.* yellow-flowered plant; root of this used in dyeing. [OE.].

MADDING [ma′ding], *adj.* mad; that maddens.

MADE [mād], *pret. and p.pt.* of MAKE; (of the body) built, formed; successful. [OE.].

MADEIRA [ma-dēer′ah], *n.* a heavy, sweet wine. [*Madeira*, island off the west coast of Africa].

MADEMOISELLE [ma-de-mwa-zel′], *n.* French form of address to an unmarried woman; (*coll.*) French governess.

MADHOUSE [mad′hows], *n.* lunatic asylum; (*coll.*) noisy assembly resembling this.

MADONNA [ma-do′nah], *n.* the Virgin Mary; statue or icon of the Virgin; **M. lily**, the white lily. [It.].

MADREPORE [mad′ri-paw(r)], *n.* coral; the coral polyp. [It.].

MADRIGAL [mad′ri-gal], *n.* lyric sung unaccompanied as a part-song; love lyric. [It.].

MAECENAS [mē-sē′nas], *n.* patron of the arts. [*Maecenas*, patron of Horace].

MAELSTROM [māl′strom], *n.* whirlpool; (*fig.*) tumult of passions or events. [*Maelström*, famous Norwegian whirlpool].

MAENAD [mē′nad], *n.* a Bacchante. [Gk.].

MAESTOSO [mah-e-stō′zō], *adv.* (*mus.*) grandly. [It.].

MAESTRO [mah-ē′strō], *n.* master in an art, *esp.* in music. [It.].

MAE WEST [mā-west′], *n.* inflatable live-saving jacket worn by airmen. [*Mae West*, U.S. film star].

MAFFICK [ma′fik], *v.i.* to celebrate riotously. [*Mafeking*, South Africa, the relief of which in 1900 was celebrated thus in London].

MAGAZINE [ma-ga-zēn′], *n.* store for weapons, ammunition etc., *esp.* for explosives; chamber in a repeating rifle holding the cartridges ready for propulsion into the breech; periodical publication containing several unconnected compositions. [Arab.].

MAGENTA [ma-jen′tah], *n.* purplish aniline dye; the colour of this. [*Magenta*, Italy].

MAGGOT [ma′got], *n.* larva of a fly; small larva of certain beetles and moths which attack food-stuffs and fabrics; cheese-mite. [ME.].

MAGI [mā′jī], *n.*(*pl.*) the wise men of the Nativity. MAGIAN (1), *n.* one of the M.; magician. MAGIAN (2) *adj.* relating to the M.; wise in magic. [L.].

MAGIC (1) [ma′jik], *n.* power of supernaturally influencing things and events; witchcraft, sorcery; mystifying conjuring. MAGIC(AL) (2), *adj.* relating to, caused by, employed in, m.; inexplicable, fascinating. MAGICALLY, *adv.* in m. fashion. [Gk.].

MAGICIAN [ma-ji′shan], *n.* one exercising magic power, a wizard. [Fr.].

MAGIC LANTERN [ma-jik-lan′tern], *n.* device for throwing magnified images on to a screen, by shining a powerful light through a transparent picture.

MAGISTERIAL [ma-jis-tēer′i-al], *adj.* relating to a master or to a magistrate; authoritative. MAGISTERIALLY, *adv.* in m. fashion.

MAGISTRACY [ma′jis-tra-si], *n.* the magistrates of a state; office or status of a magistrate.

MAGISTRAL [ma′jis-tral], *adj.* relating to a master. [L.].

MAGISTRATE [ma′jis-trāt], *n.* civil official with judicial and administrative functions, *esp.* a judicial officer dealing summarily with minor cases, Justice of the Peace. [L.].

MAGISTRATURE [ma′jis-tra-tyōōr], *n.* the magistracy; tenure of a magistrate's office.

MAGNA CARTA, MAGNA CHARTA [mag-nah-kah′tah], *n.* charter of privileges extracted by the feudal lords from King John; (*fig.*) a guarantee of rights and liberties. [L.].

MAGNANIMITY [mag-na-ni′mi-ti], *n.* quality of being magnanimous. [L.].

MAGNANIMOUS [mag-na′ni-mōōs], *adj.* noble-spirited, high-minded, generous. [L.].

MAGNATE [mag′nāt], *n.* potentate, *esp.* a man of great position and power in industry, finance etc. [LL.].

MAGNESIA [mag-nē′shah], *n.* oxide of magnesium; powder of magnesium carbonate used as a medical antacid. MAGNESIAN, *adj.* containing m. [Gk.].

MAGNESIUM [mag-nē′si-um], *n.* (*chem.*) the white, metallic element Mg. [Gk.].

MAGNET [mag′nit], *n.* piece of iron, steel or nickel with the property of exercising attraction on these metals; (*fig.*) something exercising strong attraction. [L.].

MAGNETIC [mag-ne′tik], *adj.* having the properties of a magnet; (*fig.*) attracting strongly; **m. mine**, mine exploded by m. action; **m. pole**, location to which the compass needle points.

MAGNETISM [mag′ne-tizm], *n.* magnetic properties and phenomena; scientific study of these; (*fig.*) strong personal attraction.

MAGNETITE [mag′ne-tīt], *n.* magnetic iron oxide.

MAGNETIZE [mag′ne-tiz], *v.t.* to make magnetic by contact with a magnet or by passing electric current through; (*fig.*) attract intensely. MAGNETIZATION [mag-ne-tī-zā′shn], *n.* act of magnetizing; condition of being magnetized.

MAGNETO-, *pref.* magnetic or utilizing magnetism. [MAGNET].

MAGNETO [mag-nē′tō], *n.* contrivance generating the ignition spark in an internal combustion engine. [Gk.].

MAGNETOPHONE [mag-nē′tō-fōn], *n.* microphone

The accent ′ after a syllable = stress (u-pon′). The mark ⁻ over a vowel = length (ā in made; ō in bone).

in which the sound waves strike a flat coil of wire supported in a magnetic field.

MAGNIFICAT [mag-ni'fi-kat], *n.* the song of the Virgin Mary, Luke i. 46-55. [L.].

MAGNIFICATION [mag-ni-fi-kā'shn], *n.* act of magnifying; extent of being magnified. [L.].

MAGNIFICENCE [mag-ni'fi-sens], *n.* splendour, elaborate grandeur. [L.].

MAGNIFICENT [mag-ni'fi-sent], *adj.* splendid, glorious; of outstanding richness, quality, extent etc.; (*coll.*) excellent. [OFr.].

MAGNIFICO [mag-ni'fi-kō], *n.* a Venetian grandee; a magnificent magnate. [It.].

MAGNIFY [mag'ni-fi], *v.t.* (*archaic*) to extol; make great, enlarge; increase the apparent size of, *esp.* by means of a lens; (*fig.*) exaggerate. MAGNIFIER, *n.* that which, one who, magnifies. [OFr.].

MAGNILOQUENCE [mag-ni'lō-kwens], *n.* quality of being magniloquent, *esp.* of speech.

MAGNILOQUENT [mag-ni'lō-kwent], *adj.* bombastic, grandiose in expression. [~L.].

MAGNITUDE [mag'ni-tyōōd], *n.* greatness of size or extent; size; (*astron.*) degree of brilliance of a fixed star. [L.].

MAGNOLIA [mag-nō'li-ah], *n.* genus of flowering trees. [P. *Magnol*, botanist].

MAGNUM [mag'num], *n.* wine bottle holding two quarts. [L.].

MAGPIE [mag'pī], *n.* black and white bird, related to the crow; (*coll.*) chattering or harmlessly predatory person; shot hitting the target between the inner and outer positions. [MAG, *Margaret*, and PIE (2).].

MAGYAR [mag'yah(r)], *n. and adj.* member of, pertaining to, the predominant race in Hungary; Hungarian; language of these people; **m. sleeves**, sleeves of a blouse etc. cut in one piece with the body. [Hungarian].

MAHARAJA(H) [mah-hah-rah'jah], *n.* major Indian ruling prince. [Hind.].

MAHARANEE [mah-hah-rah'nē], *n.* wife of a maharaja, Indian female sovereign. [Hind.].

MAH-JONG(G) [mah-jong'], *n.* Chinese game played with 144 painted blocks. [Chin.].

MAHLSTICK, SEE MAULSTICK.

MAHOGANY [ma-ho'ga-ni], *n.* tropical American tree, producing a fine wood; the wood itself; its reddish-brown colour. [Haiti].

MAHOMETAN, SEE MOHAMMEDAN.

MAHOUT [ma-howt'], *n.* elephant-driver. [Hind.].

MAID [mād], *n.* maiden, virgin; unmarried woman; female servant; **M. of Honour**, unmarried lady attendant upon a queen or princess; almond cheesecake in a pastry shell. [*Next*].

MAIDEN (1) [mā'den], *n.* girl; virgin, young unmarried woman; female attendant; (*cricket*) maiden over. MAIDEN (2), *adj.* relating to a m.; unmarried; (*fig.*) unblemished; experienced or done for the first time; **m. over**, (*cricket*) over in which no runs are scored; **m. name**, woman's surname before marriage; **m. speech**, first speech in Parliament of a new member. [OE.].

MAIDENHAIR [mā'den-hāer], *n.* a species of fern.

MAIDENHEAD [mā'den-hed], *n.* the hymen; virginity. [*Next*].

MAIDENHOOD [mā'den-hōōd], *n.* virginity. [OE.].

MAIDENLY [mā'den-li], *adj.* befitting a maiden, modest.

MAIDSERVANT [mād'ser-vant], *n.* female servant.

MAIL (1) [māl], *n.* armour composed of interlocking rings or links; armour in general. MAILED, *adj.* protected with m.; **the mailed fist**, violence or the threat of it. [Fr.].

MAIL (2), *n.* bag, sack for carrying letters etc. by post; letters etc. so conveyed; postal collection or delivery; postal system for collection and delivery of letters etc.; **m. train**, train carrying mails. MAIL-BOAT, ship carrying mails. MAIL (3), *v.t.* (*U.S.*) to dispatch by post. [OFr.].

MAIL-CART [māl'kaht], *n.* cart for transporting mails; light push-cart for young children.

MAIL-ORDER [māl'aw-der], *adj.* pertaining to the system of buying goods through the post.

MAIM [mām], *v.t.* to mutilate, deprive of a bodily member. [ME. from OFr.].

MAIN (1) [mān], *n.* the most part; principal pipe or cable of gas, water etc. system; (*poet.*) the high seas; strength or force, in phr. **might and m.** [OE.].

MAIN (2), *adj.* chief, most important; † strong; **by m. force**, by simple physical strength; **the m. chance**, one's own interests. MAIN-BOOM, large boom at the

foot of a fore-and-aft mainsail. MAIN-DECK, principal deck. MAIN-TOP, platform at top of the mainmast. MAIN-YARD, mainsail yard. [OIcel.].

MAIN (3), *n.* a cock-fight. [Uncert.].

MAIN-BRACE [mān'brās], *n.* the main-yard brace; **to splice the m.**, to serve out a double ration of rum.

MAINLAND [mān'land], *n.* the continent, major land-mass, as opposed to an island.

MAINLY [mān'li], *adv.* in the main; mostly, chiefly.

MAINMAST [mān'mahst], *n.* the principal mast of a ship.

MAINSAIL [mān-sl], *n.* the principal sail in a ship.

MAINSHEET [mān'shēt], *n.* (*naut.*) rope which extends the mainsail; rope working the main boom.

MAINSPRING [mān'spring], *n.* principal spring of a watch etc.; (*fig.*) main impulse of an event or activity.

MAINSTAY [mān'stā], *n.* the main-top stay; (*fig.*) chief support or prop.

MAINTAIN [mān-tān'], *v.t.* to support, sustain; uphold; preserve; defend; affirm. [OFr.].

MAINTENANCE [mān'te-nans], *n.* process of maintaining; state of being maintained; means of maintaining; livelihood, funds provided for a person's living expenses; (*leg.*) interference in a suit in which one has no interest; **cap of m.**, royal cap of dignity. [OFr.].

MAISON(N)ETTE [mā-zo-net'], *n.* dwelling consisting of two or three floors only of a building. [Fr.].

MAIZE [māz], *n.* edible grain of the plant *Zea Mays*; the plant itself. [Span.].

MAJESTIC(AL) [ma-jes'tik(-al)], *adj.* displaying, possessing, majesty.

MAJESTY [ma'jes-ti], *n.* impressive and magnificent dignity, grandeur; royal power; title of a sovereign. [L.].

MAJOLICA [ma-jo'li-kah], *n.* kind of Italian enamelled pottery. [It.].

MAJOR (1) [mā'jer], *adj.* the more important of two things, groups, issues; elder; (*mus.*) denoting a specific arrangement of semitones in a scale, and a specific number of semitones in an interval; (*log.*) containing the general rule, or the predicate of the conclusion of a syllogism. MAJOR (2), *n.* lowest-ranked field-officer in the British Army, second-in-command of a battalion; person legally of age; (*log.*) the m. premise in a syllogism. [L.].

MAJOR-DOMO [mā-jer-dō'mō], *n.* steward of a great household. [It. from MedL.].

MAJOR-GENERAL [mā-jer-je'ne-ral], *n.* (*milit.*) officer holding military rank next above that of a brigadier.

MAJORITY [ma-jo'ri-ti], *n.* the most part, greater number; in a debate, election etc., the number by which votes cast on one side exceed those cast on the other; rank of a major; age of full legal responsibility. [MedL.].

MAKE (1) (*pret. and p.pt.* **made**) [māk], *v.t.* to construct, put together; cause to appear, happen or become; perform, carry out; prepare; achieve; result in, act as; add up to; reckon to be; compel; create; appoint; reach; (*coll.*) do, manage, succeed in obtaining; *v.i.* to prepare; rise; move; **to m. at**, to move to attack; **to m. away with**, to dispose of, kill; **to m. for**, to go towards; **to m. off**, to go away, escape; **to m. out**, to understand; prove; pretend; **to m. up**, to apply paint and cosmetics; compose a quarrel; indemnify; ingratiate oneself; invent; (*print.*) to set up for the press; **to m. up one's mind**, to decide; **to m. good**, to succeed; replace or provide compensation for; **to m. do (with)**, to content oneself with something not as good as one wants. MAKE (2), *n.* process of making; things made in a certain way; method of making; **on the m.**, (*coll.*) in pursuit of personal profit. [OE.].

MAKE-AND-BREAK [māk-and-brāk'], *adj. and n.* (of) an automatic device for regularly making and breaking an electric contact.

MAKE-BELIEVE [māk'bi-lēv], *n.* act of pretending something not true; that which is pretended; belief in something one knows to be untrue.

MAKER [mā'ker], *n.* one who makes; the Creator.

MAKESHIFT (1) [māk'shift], *n.* a temporary and approximate substitute. MAKESHIFT (2), *adj.* employed as a m.

MAKE-UP [māk'up], *n.* arrangement of a printed page or poster; facial painting, *esp.* for the stage; materials for this; a person's nature.

MAKEWEIGHT [māk'wāt], *n.* something added to bring weights to a specified level.

MAKING [mā′king], *n.* act of one who makes; (*pl.*) elements promising future realization; profits.

MAL-, *pref.* bad, wrong. [L.].

MALACCA [ma-la′kah], *n.* cane made from Malaccan palm; **M. cane**, walking-stick of this. [*Malacca*, Malaya].

MALACHITE [ma′la-kīt], *n.* green carbonate of copper, polished and used for ornaments. [Gk.].

MALADJUSTMENT [ma-la-just′ment], *n.* wrong adjustment; (*psych.*) inability to cope with one's environment.

MALADROIT [ma-la-droit′], *adj.* tactless, clumsy. [Fr.].

MALADY [ma′la-di], *n.* sickness, ailment. [Fr.].

MALAGA [mah′lah-gah], *n.* a sweet Spanish wine. [*Malaga*, Spain].

MALAGASY [ma-la-ga′si], *n. and adj.* a native of, pertaining to, Madagascar; its language. [Uncert.].

MALAISE [ma-lāz′], *n.* slight ailment or physical uneasiness. [Fr.].

MALAPERT [ma′la-pert], *adj.* (*archaic*) saucy, impudent. [OFr.].

MALAPROPISM [ma′la-pro-pizm], *n.* misuse of words through sound-association. [Mrs. *Malaprop*, in Sheridan's "The Rivals."].

MALAPROPOS [ma-la-pro-pō′], *adj. and adv.* ill-timed, out of place. [Fr.].

MALARIA [ma-lāer′i-ah], *n.* a fever transmitted by mosquito-bite. MALARIAL, *adj.* producing, pertaining to, m.; marshy and noxious. [It.].

MALCONTENT (1) [mal′kon-tent], *adj.* discontented. MALCONTENT (2), *n.* discontented person, *esp.* one dissatisfied with the form or administration of government. [OFr.].

MALE (1) [māl], *adj.* having the sexual capability of impregnating the female ovum; virile; composed of men; (*mech.*) screwing into a threaded hollow counterpart made to receive it. MALE (2), *n.* animal or plant of m. sex, man. [OFr.].

MALEDICTION [ma-li-dik′shn], *n.* a curse, imprecation. [L.].

MALEFACTOR [ma′li-fak-ter], *n.* evil-doer. [L.].

MALEVOLENCE [ma-le′vo-lens], *n.* ill-will, malice. [L.].

MALEVOLENT [ma-le′vo-lent], *adj.* wishing evil, malicious. [L.].

MALFEASANCE [mal-fē′zans], *n.* (*leg.*) wrongdoing in connexion with a legal office. [OFr.].

MALFORMATION [mal-faw-mā′shn], *n.* imperfect formation.

MALICE [ma′lis], *n.* spite, desire to injure; (*leg.*) evil or illegal intention. [Fr.].

MALICIOUS [ma-li′shôos], *adj.* feeling or displaying malice, spiteful. [OFr.].

MALIGN (1) [ma-līn′], *adj.* malevolent, of evil influence. MALIGN (2), *v.t.* to defame, slander; disparage. [L.].

MALIGNANCY [ma-lig′nan-si], *n.* state of being malignant.

MALIGNANT [ma-lig′nant], *adj.* evilly disposed, malicious; (*med.*) virulent; threatening life. [L.].

MALIGNITY [ma-lig′ni-ti], *n.* quality of being malignant. [L.].

MALINGER [ma-ling′ger], *v.i.* to pretend illness or incapacity in order to escape a task. [Fr.].

MALL [mawl], *n.* (*hist.*) game of pall-mall; mallet used in this; broad shady walk in a city, originally an alley in London where the game was played. [MAUL (1)].

MALLARD [ma′lahd], *n.* the common wild duck. [OFr.].

MALLEABLE [ma′li-a-bl], *adj.* soft enough to be hammered into shape; (*fig.*) pliable, adaptable. MALLEABILITY [ma-li-a-bi′li-ti], *n.* state of being m. [OFr.].

MALLEOLUS [ma-lē′ō-lus], *n.* (*anat.*) one of the projecting knobs of bone on either side of the ankle. MALLEOLAR, *adj.* (*anat.*) belonging to the ankle. [L.].

MALLET [ma′let], *n.* hammer with a large wooden head; long-handled, wooden-headed striker used in croquet, polo etc. [Fr.].

MALLEUS [ma′lē-us], *n.* (*anat.*) a bone of the middle ear. [L.].

MALLOW [ma′lō], *n.* pink-flowered plant of the genus *Malva*. [OE.].

MALMAISON [mal-mā′zn], *n.* a kind of carnation. [*Malmaison*, residence of the Empress Josephine].

MALMSEY [mahm′zi], *n.* a heavy, sweet wine. [MedL.].

MALNUTRITION [mal-nyōo-tri′shn], *n.* inadequate nutrition; slow starvation.

MALPRACTICE [mal-prak′tis], *n.* evil practice, *esp.* irregular or criminal acts in an official position; (*leg.*) negligent medical treatment of a patient.

MALT (1) [mawlt], *n.* barley soaked in water, allowed to bud, and dried for use in brewing. MALT (2), *v.t.* to make into m.; flavour with m. [OE.].

MALTESE [mawl-tēz′], *n. and adj.* a native of, pertaining to, Malta; its language; **M. cross**, cross with four equal arms broadening and forking at the extremities.

MALT-HOUSE [mawlt′hows], *n.* building in which malt is made.

MALTOSE [mawl′tōs], *n.* sugar obtained from starch by the action of malt ferments.

MALTSTER [mawlt′ster], *n.* one who makes malt.

MALVACEOUS [mal-vā′shôos], *adj.* relating to the group of plants which includes the mallows.

MALVERSATION [mal-ver-sā′shn], *n.* corrupt diversion of public funds to private profit. [Fr.].

MAMBA [mam′bah], *n.* either of two varieties of African tree-snake. [Kaffir].

MAMELUKE [ma′me-lyōōk], *n.* one of the bodyguard, later masters, of the sultans of Egypt, originally Caucasian slaves. [Arab.].

MAMILLA (*pl.* mamillae) [ma-mi′lah, ′lē], *n.* teat or nipple. [L.].

MAMMA (1) [ma-mah′, ma′mah], *n.* childish word for mother. [~L.].

MAMMA (2) (*pl.* mammae) [ma′mah, ′mē], *n.* the milk-secreting gland in female mammals; rudimentary development of this in males. [L.].

MAMMAL [ma′mal], *n.* one of the mammalia.

MAMMALIA [ma-mā′li-ah], *n.*(*pl.*) class of warm-blooded vertebrates which suckle their young. MAMMALIAN (1), *adj.* relating to the m. MAMMALIAN (2), *n.* a mammal. [L.].

MAMMARY [ma′ma-ri], *adj.* relating to the breasts.

MAMMIFEROUS [ma-mi′fe-rôos], *adj.* having mammae.

MAMMON [ma′mon], *n.* god of riches; (*fig.*) wealth, lust after material things. MAMMONISM, *n.* worship of m. MAMMONIST, MAMMONITE, *n.* worshipper of m. [Aram.].

MAMMOTH (1) [ma′moth], *n.* extinct elephant of great size. MAMMOTH (2), *adj.* (*coll.*) enormous. [Russ.].

MAMMY [ma′mi], *n.* mother; (*U.S.*) American negro nurse or mother. [Childish, apparently *orig.* instinctive].

MAN (1) (*pl.* **men**) [man], *n.* adult male of the human species; mankind; individual, person; person with manly qualities; male employee; faithful supporter; husband; male lover; counter used in playing chess, draughts etc.; member of a team; (*pl.*) private soldiers; **best m.**, groomsman at wedding. MAN-AT-ARMS, medieval armed retainer. MAN-IN-THE-STREET, the average person. MAN-OF-WAR, warship. MAN (2) (*pres.pt.* MANNING, *pret. and p.pt.* MANNED), *v.t.* to furnish with men; **to m. up**, to provide (an industry) with the full number of workers required. [OE.].

MANACLE (1) [ma′na-kl], *n.* a fetter for the wrist. MANACLE (2), *v.t.* to bind with a m. [L.].

MANAGE [ma′nij], *v.t. and i.* to control; handle; deal with; direct (an enterprise, business etc.); see to; succeed, accomplish. [It.].

MANAGEABLE [ma′ni-ja-bl], *adj.* that may be managed. MANAGEABILITY [ma-ni-ja-bi′li-ti], *n.* quality of being m.

MANAGEMENT [ma′nij-ment], *n.* act or technique of managing; state of being managed; group of persons managing a business; skilful methods of handling something or someone.

MANAGER [ma′ni-jer], *n.* one who manages, *esp.* a business or other undertaking. MANAGERIAL [ma-ni-jēer′i-al], *adj.* relating to the office of m.

MANAGING DIRECTOR [ma-ni-jing-dī-rek′ter], *n.* director of a company employed to administer its operations.

MANATEE [ma-na-tē′], *n.* the Atlantic sea-cow. [Caribbean].

MANCHU [man-chōo′], *n. and adj.* member of, pertaining to, a race inhabiting Manchuria; their language. [Chin.].

MANCIPLE [man′si-pl], *n.* steward of a household, college etc. [OFr.].

MANCUNIAN [man-kyōo′ni-an], *n. and adj.* a native of, pertaining to, Manchester. [L.].

MANDAMUS [man-dā′mus], *n.* (*leg.*) writ from a high to an inferior court. [L.].

MANDARIN [man′da-rin], *n.* officer of the Imperial

The accent ′ after a syllable = stress (u-pon′).   The mark ‾ over a vowel = length (ā in made; ō in bone).

Chinese civil service; (*fig.*) officious and absolute bureaucrat; small, originally Chinese, orange; orange coal-tar dye; **m. duck**, handsome Chinese duck. [Portug.].

MANDATARY, MANDATORY [man'da-ta-ri, -te-ri], *n.* person or power to whom a mandate is entrusted. [L.].

MANDATE (1) [man'dāt], *n.* command, injunction; commission to exercise power on behalf of another; formerly, the delegation of government by the League of Nations to one of its members, of part of the empire of a defeated enemy state or of a backward people; (*R.C.*) a rescript of the Pope; instruction to adopt a certain policy, supposed to be received by a parliament from the electorate. MANDATE (2) [man-dāt'], *v.t.* to delegate to a mandatory. [L.].

MANDATORY (1) [man'da-te-ri], *adj.* commanding, instructing; entrusted with a mandate. MANDATORY (2), *n.* see MANDATARY. [LL.].

MANDIBLE [man'di-bl], *n.* a jaw, *esp.* the lower jaw; either of the halves of a beak or pair of jaws. MANDIBULAR [man-di'byoō-ler], *adj.* relating to the jaw. MANDIBULATE(D) [man-di'byoō-lāt(-id)], *adj.* having mandibles. [LL.].

MANDOLIN(E) [man'dō-lin], *n.* pear-shaped, metal-stringed instrument, related to the guitar. [It.].

MANDRAKE [man'drāk], *n.* narcotic and emetic herb, used in magic and said to shriek when torn from the ground. [ME.].

MANDREL [man'drel], *n.* the shank of a lathe on which the object to be turned is fixed. [Uncert.].

MANDRILL [man'dril], *n.* West African baboon having red-and-blue pigmentation on its face and buttocks. [MAN (1) and DRILL (5)].

MANDUCATE [man'dyoō-kāt], *v.t.* to chew. MANDUCATION [man-dyoō-kā'shn], *n.* act of chewing. MANDUCATORY [man'dyoō-ka-te-ri], *adj.* relating to chewing. [L.].

MANE [mān], *n.* long, thick hair on the neck of an animal MANED, *adj.* having a m. [OE.].

MANEGE, manège [ma-nāzh'], *n.* horsemanship or the training of horses; school for teaching this. [Fr.].

MANFUL [man'fŏŏl], *adj.* bold, vigorous, manly. MANFULLY, *adv.* in m. fashion.

MANGANESE [mang'ga-nēz], *n.* (*chem.*) soft, grey metallic element, Mn; black oxide of this. MANGANIC [mang-ga'nik], *adj.* pertaining to, containing, m. in its highest valency. [Fr.].

MANGE [mānj], *n.* skin disease in hairy-coated animals, caused by a parasite. [OFr.].

MANGEL-WURZEL, MANGOLD-WURZEL [man'gl-wer-zel], *n.* large coarse beet used as food for cattle. [Germ.].

MANGER [mān'jer], *n.* eating-trough for cattle. [Fr.].

MANGLE (1) [mang'gl], *n.* device of wooden rollers used for pressing linen, cotton etc. after washing and drying. MANGLE (2), *v.t.* to press with a m. [Du.].

MANGLE (3), *v.t.* to cut up, lacerate; (*fig.*) spoil by incompetent rendering. [AFr.].

MANGO [mang'gō], *n.* tropical Asiatic tree; the fruit of this. [Tamil].

MANGOLD-WURZEL, see MANGEL-WURZEL.

MANGOSTEEN [mang'gō-stēn], *n.* an East Indian tree; the fruit of this. [Malay].

MANGROVE [mang'grōv], *n.* genus of tropical swamp-trees. [~Malay].

MANGY [mān'ji], *adj.* afflicted with mange; moth-eaten, squalidly shabby.

MAN-HANDLE [man'han-dl], *v.t.* to ill-treat physically, handle roughly; move by manpower alone.

MANHATTAN [man-ha'tan], *n.* cocktail of whisky, vermouth and bitters. [*Manhattan* Island, New York].

MANHOLE [man'hōl], *n.* covered hole, of sufficient size to admit a man, giving access to sewers etc.

MANHOOD [man'hŏŏd], *n.* state, age or status of being a man; men in general; manliness.

MAN-HOUR [man-owr'], *n.* an hour's work done by one man, as a unit in calculating total working time.

MANIA [mā'ni-ah], *n.* a neurotic state of mental disturbance characterized by fixation, delusion and hallucination; (*fig.*) irrational enthusiasm for one subject, obsession. [Gk.].

MANIAC (1) [mā'ni-ak], *adj.* afflicted with, arising from, characteristic of, mania. MANIAC (2), *n.* violent madman. [L.].

MANIACAL [ma-ni'a-kal], *adj.* maniac.

MANIC [mā'nik], *adj.* pertaining to mania.

MANICHEE [ma-ni-kē'], *n.* adherent of a religious system based on the eternal and universal dualism of good and evil. [Gk., from Mani, third-century Persian founder].

MANICURE (1) [ma'ni-kyoŏr], *n.* act of manicuring; state of being manicured. MANICURE (2), *v.t.* to treat the hands and fingernails, *esp.* to file, polish and trim the fingernails. MANICURIST, *n.* one whose profession is manicuring. [L.].

MANIFEST (1) [ma'ni-fest], *adj.* clearly evident, obvious. MANIFEST (2), *v.t. and i.* to show clearly, express, display; make evident; (*spiritualism*) become visible to the senses; (*naut.*) put down in a m. MANIFEST (3), *n.* inventory of a ship's cargo declared to the customs. [L.].

MANIFESTATION [ma-ni-fes-tā'shn], *n.* act of manifesting; thing manifested; state of being manifested. [L.].

MANIFESTO (*pl.* **manifestos**) [ma-ni-fes'tō], *n.* public declaration of policy and belief issued by a person or body, *esp.* by a political party. [It.].

MANIFOLD (1) [ma'ni-fōld], *adj.* multifarious, many-sided. MANIFOLD (2), *v.t.* to make several copies of a document by carbons etc. [OE.].

MANIKIN, MANNIKIN [ma'ni-kin], *n.* anatomical model of the human body; dwarf; tailor's dummy. [Du.].

MANILLA (1) [ma-ni'lah], *adj.* relating to Manila; **M. hemp**, strong fibre from the plantain, used for making ropes and cables; **M. paper**, strong paper made from M. hemp. MANILLA (2), *n.* cigar made in the Philippines. [*Manila*, capital of the Philippines].

MANIPLE [ma'ni-pl], *n.* Roman military unit of 200 men; embroidered vestment worn on the left wrist at the Eucharist by the celebrant and his assistants. [L.].

MANIPULATE [ma-ni'pyoō-lāt], *v.t.* to work, control or fashion with the hands; handle skilfully; manage or arrange dishonestly. MANIPULATIVE, MANIPULATORY, *adj.* done by, relating to, manipulation. MANIPULATOR, *n.* one who manipulates. [*Next*].

MANIPULATION [ma-ni-pyoō-lā'shn], *n.* act of manipulating; state of being manipulated. [Fr.].

MANKIND [man-kīnd'], *n.* the human race. [OE.].

MANLY [man'li], *adj.* befitting a man, brave, virile; like a man.

MANNA [ma'nah], *n.* the food dropped from heaven to feed Israel in the wilderness; sweet juice from two varities of ash; (*fig.*) providential relief in extremity or want. [Heb.].

MANNEQUIN [ma'ni-kin], *n.* person, usually a woman, trained and employed in wearing new clothes in order to display them for sale. [Fr.].

MANNER [ma'ner], *n.* method, style or mode of performing an action; bearing, behaviour; characteristic style or mode; (*pl.*) observance of the customary social courtesies and conventions; habits and way of life; (*archaic*) sort; **all m. of**, all sorts of. MANNERED, *adj.* having manners; displaying mannerisms, affected. MANNERLESS, *adj.* ill-mannered. [OFr.].

MANNERISM [ma'ne-rizm], *n.* a peculiarity of manner, small distinguishing personal idiosyncrasy; an affectation of manners.

MANNERLY [ma'ner-li], *adj.* displaying good manners, well-bred, polite.

MANNIKIN, see MANIKIN.

MANNISH [ma'nish], *adj.* (of a woman) like a man in manner and appearance.

MANOEUVRABLE [ma-noō'vra-bl], *adj.* (*esp.* of aircraft) capable of being readily and effectively manoeuvred.

MANOEUVRE (1) [ma-noō'ver], *n.* an adroit move to gain advantage; subtle management; (*pl.*) mock warfare carried out by an army or navy as training in strategy and tactics. MANOEUVRE (2), *v.t. and i.* to intrigue and skilfully manipulate oneself or another into or out of some position; carry out subtly a tactical scheme for one's own advantage; move or dispose (troops etc.) according to stratagem; carry out manoeuvres. [Fr.].

MANOMETER [ma-no'mi-ter], *n.* pressure-gauge measuring the density of gases. MANOMETRIC [ma-no-me'trik], *adj.* of, or pertaining to, a m. [Gk.].

MANOR [ma'ner], *n.* feudal landholding unit consisting of a manor-house and a quantity of land over which the seigneur had rights of service, taxation and jurisdiction; large country house surrounded by lands over which its owner has certain rights. MANOR-HOUSE, dwelling of the lord of the m. MANORIAL [ma-naw'ri-al], *adj.* belonging to a m.; based on manors. [OFr.].

MANPOWER [man'power], *n.* the force exerted by a man at work; work done by men without the help of machines; (number of) people available for a particular industrial or military purpose.

MANSARD [man'sahd], *n.* a form of roof built in two steps. [F. *Mansard*, French architect].

MANSE [mans], *n.* house of a Scots Presbyterian or Methodist minister. [MedL.].

MANSION [man'shn], *n.* a great residence; (*pl.*) block of flats. [L.].

MANSLAUGHTER [man'slaw-ter], *n.* (*leg.*) unlawful homicide without malice aforethought.

MANTEL [man'tel], *n.* shelf projecting from, and lying across, the top of a fireplace. [MANTLE (1)].

MANTELPIECE [man'tel-pēs], *n.* mantel.

MANTELSHELF [man'tel-shelf], *n.* mantel.

MANTILLA [man-ti'lah], *n.* Spanish shawl worn round the head and shoulders. [Span.].

MANTIS [man'tis], *n.* genus of orthopterous insects. [Gk.].

MANTISSA [man-ti'sah], *n.* the decimal part of a logarithm. [L.].

MANTLE (1) [man'tl], *n.* loose outer garment, cloak; asbestos mesh cover placed over a gas flame to increase the light by becoming incandescent; (*her.*) cloak behind the escutcheon; (*fig.*) anything covering or hiding. MANTLE (2), *v.t.* and *i.* to cover with a m.; form a coating, cover a surface; suffuse; (of hawks) hide the legs with the wings. [L.].

MAN-TRAP [man'trap], *n.* iron spring trap for catching trespassers by the feet.

MANUAL (1) [ma'nyōō-al], *adj.* performed by hand, relating to the hand. MANUAL (2), *n.* handbook, text book; keyboard of an organ; Roman Catholic service book. MANUALLY, *adv.* with the hand. [L.].

MANUFACTURE (1) [ma-nyōō-fak'tyōōr], *n.* act of manufacturing; thing manufactured; way or style in which a thing is manufactured. MANUFACTURE (2), *v.t.* to make finished goods out of raw materials by means of an organized system of labour under single control, *esp.* with the aid of machinery; (*fig.*) falsify, invent what is untrue. MANUFACTURING, *adj.* pertaining to, employed in, m. MANUFACTORY, *n.* factory. [L.].

MANUFACTURER [ma-nyōō-fak'tyōōr-er], *n.* one who manufactures; the owner of a factory.

MANUMISSION [ma-nyōō-mi'shn], *n.* act of manumitting; state of being manumitted; the deed embodying this. [L.].

MANUMIT (*pres.pt.* **manumitting**, *pret.* and *p.pt.* **manumitted**) [ma-nyōō-mit'], *v.t.* to release from slavery. [L.].

MANURE (1) [ma-nyōōer'], *n.* fertilizer, *esp.* animal excrements, spread on the ground. MANURE (2), *v.t.* to apply m. to. [AFr.].

MANUSCRIPT (1) [ma'nyōō-skript], *adj.* written by hand. MANUSCRIPT (2), *n.* document, book, written by hand; original draft of a work as prepared by the author for printing. [L.].

MANX (1) [mangks], *adj.* relating to the Isle of Man and its inhabitants; **M. cat**, a tailless species of cat. MANX (2), *n.* language of the Isle of Man. [OIcel.].

MANY [me'ni], *adj.* numerous, in considerable number. MANY-SIDED, having m. sides; versatile. [OE.].

MANZANILLA [man-za-nē'lya], *n.* a kind of dry sherry. [Span.].

MAORI (*pl.* **Maoris**) [mow'ri], *n.* and *adj.* member of, pertaining to, the Polynesian race inhabiting New Zealand since some centuries before the arrival of Europeans; their language. [Native].

MAP (1) [map], *n.* plan representing the positions and relations of objects, *esp.* a representation on a plane surface of the earth's surface or the heavens; **on the m.**, important; **off the m.**, out of the way. MAP (2) (*pres.pt.* MAPPING, *pret.* and *p.pt.* MAPPED), *v.t.* to draw a m. of; **to m. out**, to draw up (a scheme, plan etc.). [MedL.].

MAPLE [mā'pl], *n.* tree of the genus *Acer*; the wood of this tree; **m. sugar**, sugar obtained by evaporation from the juice of *Acer saccharinum*. [OE.].

MAQUIS [mah-kē'], *n.* scrubby undergrowth typical of Corsica; a resistance organization in France during the German occupation from 1940-44. [Fr. dial.].

MAR (*pres.pt.* **marring**, *pret.* and *p.pt.* **marred**) [mah(r)], *v.t.* to spoil, damage; stain, disfigure. [OE.].

MARABOU [ma'ra-bōō], *n.* an adjutant stork; soft feathers from this. [Arab.].

MARABOUT [ma'ra-bōōt], *n.* Moslem ascetic or hermit. [Arab.].

MARASCHINO [mah-rah-skē'nō], *n.* sweet liqueur made from black cherries. [It.].

MARASMUS [ma-raz'mus], *n.* bodily atrophy. [Gk.].

MARATHI [mah-rah'ti], *n.* language of the Mahrattas. [Native].

MARATHON [ma'ra-thon], *n.* foot-race of 26 miles 385 yd. by road, named after the famous run from Marathon to Athens to bring news of the defeat of the Persians in 490 B.C.; prolonged, gruelling, sporting contest.

MARAUD [ma-rawd'], *v.i.* to wander in quest of plunder and pillage; go on a looting raid. [OFr.].

MARBLE (1) [mah'bl], *n.* a compact crystalline limestone capable of taking a high polish; imposing sculpture made of this; small glass or stone ball used in children's games. MARBLE (2), *adj.* made of, resembling, m.; (*fig.*) callous; deathly pale. MARBLED, *adj.* veined to resemble m., *esp.* of book boards so treated. MARBLING, *n.* art or practice of veining like m.; variegation like that of m. [Fr.].

MARCASITE [mah'ka-sīt], *n.* a mineral sulphide of iron. [MedL.].

MARCH (1) [mahch], *n.* the third month of the year. [OFr. from L.].

MARCH (2), *n.* the border of a country, *esp.* land of disputed ownership along the frontiers. MARCH (3), *v.i.* to border (on), run contiguous (with). MARCH (4), *v.t.* and *i.* to walk in regular, measured steps, as soldiers in formation; walk strongly and purposefully; order troops to march; make someone walk swiftly and unhesitatingly; go to war. MARCH (5), *n.* act of marching; distance marched; route marched over; a long, steady advance; regular measured step of soldiers marching; musical composition in march time; **m. past**, ceremonial m. past a point at which some distinguished personage takes the salute. [Fr.].

MARCHIONESS [mah'sho-nes], *n.* wife of a marquess. [MedL.].

MARDI-GRAS [mah-di-grah'], *n.* Shrove Tuesday; carnival held on that day. [Fr.].

MARE [māer], *n.* female of the horse; **m.'s nest**, discovery which amounts to nothing. [OE.].

MARGARIC [mah-ga'rik], *adj.* pearly; **m. acid**, a fatty acid of a pearly aspect. [Gk.].

MARGARINE [mah'ja-rēn, mah'ga-rēn], *n.* butter substitute containing animal and vegetable oils. [Fr.].

MARGIN [mah'jin], *n.* edge, border, limit; space round a page of written or printed matter; the additional amount of anything, *esp.* for safety, beyond what is exactly needed; (*comm.*) the difference between the selling and buying price of shares; cover deposited for speculation or market fluctuations. MARGINATE(D), *adj.* having a m. [L.].

MARGINAL [mah'ji-nal], *adj.* set in the margin; pertaining to a margin; concerning the fringe of a subject rather than the core; near a limit dividing one category from another, border line.

MARGINALIA [mah-ji-nā'li-ah], *n.*(*pl.*) marginal notes. [L.].

MARGRAVE [mah'grāv], *n.* title of certain Princes of the Holy Roman Empire. MARGRAVATE, *n.* territory of a m. [Germ.].

MARGUERITE [mah-ge-rēt'], *n.* the ox-eye daisy. [Gk.].

MARIAN (1) [māer'i-an], *adj.* connected with the Virgin Mary; connected with Queen Mary I, or with Mary, Queen of Scots. MARIAN (2), *n.* supporter of Mary, Queen of Scots. [L.].

MARIGOLD [ma'ri-gōld], *n.* a bright yellow composite flower. [*Mary* and GOLD].

MARINADE (1) [ma-ri-nād', ma-ri-nahd'], *n.* fish or meat pickled in vinegar, wine and spice; the pickle itself. MARINADE (2), *v.t.* to marinate. [Span.].

MARINATE [ma'ri-nāt], *v.t.* to pickle as in a marinade.

MARINE (1) [ma-rēn'], *adj.* relating to, found in, the sea; relating to shipping; **m. store**, second-hand junk shop. MARINE (2), *n.* the ships of a state, considered as a whole; soldier serving in the navy. [L.].

MARINER [ma'ri-ner], *n.* sailor, *esp.* one in the merchant service. [MedL.].

MARIOLATRY [māer-i-o'la-tri], *n.* worship of the Virgin Mary. [Gk.].

MARIONETTE [ma-ri-o-net'], *n.* puppet dangled on strings and so made to dance and act. [Fr.].

The accent ' after a syllable = stress (u-pon'). The mark ¯ over a vowel = length (ā in made; ō in bone).

MARITAL [ma'ri-tal], *adj.* relating to marriage or to a husband. **MARITALLY**, *adv.* in m. fashion. [L.].

MARITIME [ma'ri-tim], *adj.* bordering on the sea; relating to, connected with, the sea, relating to ships and ocean trade. [L.].

MARJORAM [mah'je-ram], *n.* an aromatic plant used in seasoning. [MedL.].

MARK (1) [mahk], *n.* a medieval unit of weight for precious metals; a medieval coin; the modern unit of German currency. [Late OE.].

MARK (2), *n.* impression, distinguishing sign, spot etc.; stain, blemish; symbol or sign of ownership or identity; thing aimed at, vital point; standard, level; symbol or score denoting comparative merit of someone or something, *esp.* in an examination, test or competition; starting-point of a race; (*Rugby football*) impression in the ground made with the heel by a player making a fair catch and claiming a free kick. **MARK** (3), *v.t.* to make a m. on, as a distinguishing sign; stain, blemish; award marks of merit to; keep the score in certain games; pay attention to; follow closely an opponent in football; **to m. time,** to move the feet up and down in march rhythm while remaining in the same place; (*fig.*) cease to progress while remaining potentially active; **to m. out,** to trace the boundaries etc. of; destine; **to m. off,** to measure off. **MARKER**, *n.* one marking the score in a game; device for this; bookmark. [OE.].

MARKED [mahkt], *adj.* distinguished with a mark; displaying obvious signs of injury; noticeable. **MARKEDLY** [mah'ked-li], *adv.* in m. manner, noticeably, conspicuously.

MARKET (1) [mah'ket], *n.* meeting-place or meeting for the sale, purchase and exchange of goods; demand for a commodity; actual or potential trade in a saleable product; **m. price,** price at which goods are offered in open m. **MARKET-DAY,** day on which a public m. is held. **MARKET-PLACE,** open space in a town where a m. is held. **MARKET** (2), *v.t.* and *i.* to bring goods to m. for sale; offer for sale; deal at a m. **MARKETING,** *n.* act of bringing goods to m. or of offering goods for sale; the buying of goods in a m. [ONFr.].

MARKET-GARDEN [mah-ket-gah'den], *n.* garden where fruits and vegetables are grown for market. **MARKET-GARDENER,** *n.* one who grows **fruits** and vegetables for sale.

MARKING [mah'king], *n.* a distinctive mark on a surface, *esp.* a natural pattern on the coat of an animal or bird; **m. ink,** indelible ink used to make identifying marks on linen.

MARKSMAN [mahks'man], *n.* one skilled in shooting.

MARL (1) [mahl], *n.* rich soil of clay and lime, used for fertilizing. **MARL-PIT,** pit where m. is dug. **MARL** (2), *v.t.* to treat with m. **MARLACEOUS, MARLY** [mah-lā'shoŏs, mah'li], *adj.* containing, consisting of, resembling, m. [OFr.].

MARL (3), *adj.* (of yarn and cloth) variegated, mottled, owing to the combination of different-coloured strands. **MARLED,** *adj.* mottled, variegated, marbled. [OFr.].

MARLINE (1) [mah'lin], *n.* thin, two-stranded cord used for binding ropes to prevent galling. **MARLINE** (2), *v.t.* to bind round with m. [Du.].

MARLINE-SPIKE, MARLINSPIKE [mah'lin-spīk], *n.* (*naut.*) iron spike used to open the strands of rope in splicing.

MARMALADE [mah'ma-lād], *n.* jam made from citrus fruits. [Fr. from Portug.].

MARMORATUM [mah-me-rā'tum], *n.* cement containing powdered marble; amalgam used in stopping teeth. [L.].

MARMOREAL [mah-maw'ri-al], *adj.* made of, resembling, marble. [L.].

MARMOSET [mah-mō-zet'], *n.* small tropical American monkey. [Fr.].

MARMOT [mah'mot], *n.* rodent related to the squirrel. [Fr.].

MAROCAIN [ma'rō-kān], *n.* heavy dress material with a grained surface. [Fr.].

MAROON (1) [ma-roōn'], *n.* deep brownish crimson; firework exploding with a loud detonation. [Fr.].

MAROON (2), *n.* negro, *esp.* a runaway slave in the West Indies; one who is marooned. **MAROON** (3), *v.t.* to isolate, abandon in a desert island or desolate region. [Fr.].

MARQUEE [mah-kē'], *n.* large tent, *esp.* one erected for refreshment or entertainment purposes. [MARQUISE.].

MARQUESS, MARQUIS [mah'kwis], *n.* title of a peer ranking between earl and duke; courtesy title of the eldest son of a duke; title of nobility in certain European countries. **MARQUISATE,** *n.* rank or dignity of a m. [OFr.].

MARQUETRY, MARQUETERIE [mah'ke-tri], *n.* wood mosaic; design produced by inlaying one wood with others of different texture and colour. [Fr.].

MARQUIS, see **MARQUESS.**

MARQUISE [mah-kēz'], *n.* in foreign countries, the wife of a marquis; finger-ring with an oval cluster of stones. [Fr.].

MARRAM [ma'ram], *n.* coarse grass growing in sand-dunes; also **m. grass.** [OIcel.].

MARRIAGE [ma'rij], *n.* legal or religious ceremony and bond sanctioning and involving cohabitation of, and sexual intercourse between, two persons of opposite sex, the union of husband and wife; (*fig.*) indissoluble union. **MARRIAGEABLE,** *adj.* suitable for m. **MARRIED,** *adj.* united in m.; intimately associated. [Fr.].

MARROW (1) [ma'rō], *n.* soft fatty tissue in the hollow of bones; (*fig.*) the very core, substantial essence; **m. bone,** bone containing a generous proportion of m., used in cookery; (*pl.*) the knees. **MARROW** (2), *n.* an edible gourd. **MARROW** (3), *adj.* containing m. [OE.].

MARROWFAT [ma'rō-fat], *n.* kind of rich pea.

MARRY (1) [ma'ri], *v.t.* and *i.* to take a person of the opposite sex in marriage; unite a couple in marriage; (*fig.*) unite intimately; (*naut.*) splice rope-ends together. [Fr.].

MARRY† (2), *int.* exclamation of surprise or emphasis. [The Virgin *Mary*].

MARS [mahz], *n.* the Roman god of war; fourth planet from the sun; (*fig.*) war. [L.].

MARSALA [mah-sah'lah], *n.* a light Sicilian wine. [*Marsala,* Sicily].

MARSEILLAISE [mah-se-lāz', mah-sā'yāz], *n.* the French national anthem. [Fr.].

MARSH [mahsh], *n.* tract of soft, very damp land, usually low-lying, a swamp. **MARSH-HARRIER,** the moor buzzard. **MARSH-HEN,** the moorhen. **MARSH-TIT,** the small blackheaded tomtit. [OE.].

MARSHAL (1) [mah'shal], *n.* high official in a princely household; (*milit.*) general officer of the highest rank in certain countries. **MARSHAL** (2) (*pres.pt.* **MARSHALLING,** *pret.* and *p.pt.* **MARSHALLED**), *v.t.* to arrange in suitable or systematic order; (*leg.*) arrange so as to settle claims in order of precedence. [OHGerm.].

MARSH-GAS [mahsh'gas], *n.* methane, an inflammable gas given off from decayed vegetation.

MARSH-MALLOW [mahsh-ma'lō], *n.* the pink-flowered mallow; a sweet made from its root.

MARSH-MARIGOLD [mahsh-ma'ri-gōld], *n.* a plant with yellow flowers.

MARSHY [mah'shi], *adj.* waterlogged, like a marsh, full of marshes.

MARSUPIAL (1) [mah-syoō'pi-al], *adj.* relating to mammals who carry their young in an external pouch. **MARSUPIAL** (2), *n.* a m. animal, as the kangaroo. [L.].

MART [maht], *n.* market-place, sale-room. [Du.].

MARTELLO TOWER [mah-te-lō-tower'], *n.* a circular, low, stone tower, *esp.* one built along a coast. [*Mortella,* Corsica].

MARTEN [mah'ten], *n.* a fur-bearing mammal, similar to the weasel. [OFr.].

MARTIAL [mah'shal], *adj.* warlike; military, fitted for war. **MARTIALLY,** *adv.* in m. fashion. [L.].

MARTIN [mah'tin], *n.* a species of swallow. [*Martin,* the personal name].

MARTINET [mah-ti-net'], *n.* a strict and rigid disciplinarian. [*Martinet,* general of Louis XIV.].

MARTINGALE [mah'tin-gāl], *n.* a strap from a horse's girth to hold its head down and prevent rearing; (*naut.*) the jib-boom stay; (*gambling*) practice of doubling up on losses. [Fr.].

MARTINI (1) [mah-tē'ni], *n.* an early breech-loading rifle. [*Martini* and Henry, inventors].

MARTINI (2), *n.* cocktail made of gin, vermouth and bitters. [*Martini,* brand of vermouth].

MARTINMAS [mah'tin-mas], *n.* feast of St. Martin, 11 November.

MARTLET [maht'let], *n.* the swift; the house-martin; (*her.*) imaginary bird without feet. [Fr.].

MARTYR (1) [mah'ter], *n.* one who undergoes death or severe penalty for refusing to abandon principles or beliefs, *esp.* religious beliefs; (*fig.*) severe sufferer. **MARTYR** (2), *v.t.* to put to death for refusal to abandon principles. [OE.].

MARTYRDOM [mah'ter-dom], *n.* state of being a

ōō is pronounced as in food; ŏŏ as in hood; th as in *think*; ᴛʜ as in *that*; zh as in azure. ~ = related to.

martyr; torture or death of a martyr; severe pain. [OE. from Gk.].

MARTYROLOGY [mah-te-ro'lo-ji], *n.* the history, study of martyrs; list of the feasts of martyrs. [Gk.].

MARVEL (1) [mah'vel], *n.* a wonder, thing to cause amazement; (*coll.*) astonishingly able person. **MARVEL** (2) (*pres.pt.* MARVELLING, *pret. and p.pt.* MARVELLED), *v.i.* to wonder, be amazed. [OFr.].

MARVELLOUS [mah've-lŏŏs], *adj.* arousing wonder, causing to marvel, amazing; (*coll.*) extremely good, remarkable. [OFr.].

MARXISM [mahk'sizm], *n.* the doctrine of Karl Marx, that human and political motives are fundamentally economic, and that history is the record of continuous class struggle. MARXIST, *n. and adj.* believer in, pertaining to, M.

MARZIPAN [mah'zi-pan], *n.* sweetmeat made from crushed almonds and sugar. [~Germ.].

MASCOT [mas'kot], *n.* talisman, any thing or person taken with one to bring good luck. [Fr.].

MASCULINE [mas'kyŏŏ-lin], *adj.* male in sex; showing male characteristics, virile; mannish; (*gram.*) belonging to the male gender; **m. rhyme,** rhyming of the final stressed syllables of a line. MASCULINITY [mas-kyŏŏ-li'ni-ti], *n.* quality of being m. [L.].

MASH (1) [mash], *n.* mixture of bran, grain or malt and hot water; any pulped-up substance. MASH (2), *v.t.* to crush or pound into a pulpy mass, *esp.* to prepare potatoes in this way; mix malt and hot water in brewing. [OE.].

MASHER [ma'sher], *n.* one who flirts with a girl; dandy. [Uncert.].

MASHIE [ma'shi], *n.* golf-club with a lofted face. MASHIE-NIBLICK, exceptionally lofted m. [Fr.].

MASK (1) [mahsk], *n.* covering or protection for the face; strip of cloth with eye-holes, worn over the face; elaborate religious head and face covering; wire facial protection in fencing; representation in clay etc. of the human face; head and face of a fox displayed as a hunting trophy; a masker; (*fig.*) a deception, open activity to conceal some secret design. GAS-MASK, apparatus to prevent the breathing of poisonous gases. MASK (2), *v.t. and i.* to conceal with a m.; disguise; (*milit.*) conceal and protect from fire; put on a mask. [Span.].

MASKED [mahskd], *adj.* wearing a mask; disguised; concealed; **m. ball,** ball at which the guests wear masks.

MASKER [mahs'ker], *n.* one who wears a mask; one taking part in a masque or masquerade.

MASOCHISM [ma'sŏ-kizm], *n.* psycho-pathological state in which the suffering of pain, bullying and humiliation is essential for sexual satisfaction. MASOCHIST, *n.* one suffering from m. MASOCHISTIC [ma-sŏ-kis'tik], *adj.* displaying, tending towards, m. [Sacher-*Masoch*, Austrian novelist who described it].

MASON [mā'son], *n.* worker in stone; Freemason. [OFr.].

MASONIC [ma-so'nik], *adj.* pertaining to Freemasonry.

MASONRY [mā'son-ri], *n.* craft or work of a mason; stonework of a building; Freemasonry.

MASQUE [mahsk], *n.* a dramatic performance, originally a combination of ballet and tableau, later containing songs and verse-dialogue; composition written for performance in this way. [Fr.].

MASQUERADE (1) [mahs-ke-rād'], *n.* a dance, party, light-hearted dramatic performance in which the participants are disguised. MASQUERADE (2), *v.i.* to take part in a m.; disguise oneself (as). MASQUERADER, *n.* one who masquerades. [Span.].

MASS (1) [mas], *n.* celebration of the Eucharist, *esp.* by Roman Catholics; **High M.,** this ceremony with music and attendant rites; **Low M.,** simpler ceremony without music. [OE. from L.].

MASS (2), *n.* a coherent, formless collection of matter; large quantity or number of objects or persons, *esp.* close together; the majority; (*pl.*) the proletariat; (*phys.*) the quantity of matter present in a substance. MASS (3), *adj.* pertaining to, involving, characteristic of, a m. of people or things; **m. meeting** large public meeting to hear speeches of popular appeal. MASS (4), *v.t. and i.* to gather together in a m., *esp.* to concentrate troops. [L.].

MASSACRE (1) [ma'sa-ker], *n.* wholesale slaughter, *esp.* of defenceless persons. MASSACRE (2), *v.t.* to slaughter indiscriminately in wholesale fashion. [Fr.].

MASSAGE (1) [ma'sahzh], *n.* medical treatment by

manipulating, rubbing and kneading parts of the body. MASSAGE (2), *v.t.* to apply m. to. [Fr.].

MASSE, massé [ma'sā], *n.* (*billiards*) stroke made with the cue held vertically. [Fr.].

MASSEUR [ma-sur'], *n.* one skilled in massage. [Fr.].

MASSEUSE [ma-surz'], *n.* female masseur. [Fr.].

MASSIF [ma'sēf], *n.* a distinct group of mountains; mountainous mass splitting into peaks towards the summit. [Fr.].

MASSIVE [ma'siv], *adj.* heavy, of great mass and size; ponderous; solid; powerful. MASSIVELY, *adv.* in m. fashion. [MASS (2)].

MASS-PRODUCE [mas-pro-dyŏŏs'], *v.t.* to produce systematically in large quantities, *esp.* mechanically. MASS-PRODUCTION [mas-pro-duk'shn], *n.* production of standardized commodities in large quantities, *esp.* mechanically.

MASSY [ma'si], *adj.* of great mass.

MAST (1) [mahst], *n.* a long upright shaft supporting the sails and yards of a ship; flag-staff; upright pole supporting a radio aerial. [OE.].

MAST (2), *n.* the fruit of various forest trees used as food for animals. [OE.].

MASTER (1) [mahs'ter], *n.* one exercising control and authority over others; captain of a merchant ship; male teacher at a school; teacher or prophet of a religion or philosophy; head of certain secular and religious orders, and of certain Oxford and Cambridge colleges; person holding the second degree in various universities; person pre-eminent in a craft, art or technique; male ruler of a household; any of the various official personages in charge of some specified thing; courtesy title given to the heirs of certain Scottish baronies; form of address given to young boys; **old m.,** (painting by) one of the leading artists of the thirteenth to eighteenth centuries; **m. hand,** skill of an expert; **m. key,** key which opens many different locks; **m. switch,** (*elect.*) switch controlling an entire installation. MASTERMIND, controlling intelligence of an organization etc. MASTER-SPRING, central, controlling spring of a mechanism; vital centre of an enterprise. MASTER-STROKE, critical and brilliant action in an enterprise. MASTER-TOUCH, touch or stroke showing in its brilliance the hand of a m. MASTER (2), *v.t.* to make oneself m. of, subdue; become proficient at. [OFr. and OE.].

MASTER-AT-ARMS [mahs-ter-at-ahmz'], *n.* the police-officer of a warship.

MASTER-BUILDER [mahs-ter-bil'der], *n.* the chief builder; employer of workmen engaged in the building trade.

MASTERFUL [mahs'ter-fŏŏl], *adj.* imposing one's will, overbearing; able to be a master.

MASTERLY [mahs'ter-li], *adj.* showing the skill, talent, and assured touch of a master. MASTERLINESS, *n.* quality of being m.

MASTERPIECE [mahs'ter-pēs], *n.* work of art or craft of the highest excellence and genius; the best work of an artist or craftsman.

MASTERY [mahs'te-ri], *n.* authority, dominance; victory, ascendancy; extreme skill, dexterity or knowledge in a thing. [OFr.].

MASTHEAD [mahst'hed], *n.* the highest part of a mast; the topmast.

MASTIC [mas'tik], *n.* a resin exuding from trees, *esp. Pistacia Lentiscus,* used in varnish; colour of this; tree from which it is obtained. [Gk.].

MASTICATE [mas'ti-kāt], *v.t. and i.* to chew with the teeth. MASTICATOR, *n.* one who, that which, masticates. [L.].

MASTICATION [mas-ti-kā'shn], *n.* act of masticating. [LL.].

MASTICATORY [mas'ti-kā-te-ri], *adj.* relating to, apt for, mastication.

MASTIFF [mas'tif], *n.* large, powerful British dog with slavering lips and heavy muzzle. [OFr.].

MASTITIS [mas-ti'tis], *n.* inflammation of the breasts. [Gk.].

MASTO-, *pref.* breast. [Gk.].

MASTODON [mas'tŏ-don], *n.* gigantic extinct mammal related to the elephant. [Gk.].

MASTOID [mas'toid], *adj.* breast-like; relating to, affecting, the mastoid process; **m. process,** breast-shaped process of the bone behind the ear. [Gk.].

MASTURBATE [mas'ter-bāt], *v.i.* to excite one's own genital organs, *esp.* with the hand. MASTURBATION [mas-ter-bā'shn], *n.* act or practice of masturbating. [L.].

MAT (1) [mat], *n.* coarse fibrous material made from

The accent ' after a syllable = stress (u-pon'). The mark ¯ over a vowel = length (ā in made; ō in bone).

straw, rushes etc.; piece of this used for covering part of a floor, or for wiping the feet on; bolster of this used to dull an impact; small cover on which dishes etc. may be stood; **on the m.**, (slang) in trouble; summoned for reprimand. MAT (2) (pres.pt. MATTING, pret. and p.pt. MATTED), v.t. and i. to tangle together; become tangled like fibre; cover with mats. [OE. from LL.].

MAT (3), **MATT**, adj. dull, lustreless. [Fr.].

MATADOR [ma'ta-daw(r)], n. the performer in a bull-fight who gives the coup de grâce; kind of dominoes in which seven must be made at each play. [Span.].

MATCH (1) [mach], n. object corresponding exactly to another, someone equal in prowess to a rival; someone superior in contest to another; sporting contest; marriage; person suitable for marriage with another; **m. point, ball etc.,** (esp. lawn tennis) the point or ball which may decide the result of a m. MATCH (2), v.t. and i. to bring into contest with another; find a colour or material similar to; correspond with, suit; marry; equal in contest; correspond in form, colour etc. [OE.].

MATCH (3), n. slender piece of wood or wax taper tipped with inflammable material, ignited by friction to give a flame. SLOW-MATCH, touch-paper; lighted rope for firing artillery, mines etc. [OFr.].

MATCH-BOARDING [mach'baw-ding], n. a series of boards fitting into one another by means of a tongue on one edge and a groove on the other.

MATCHET [ma'chet], n. a machete. [Span.].

MATCHLESS [mach'les], adj. unequalled, that cannot be matched. MATCHLESSLY, adv. in m. fashion.

MATCHLOCK [mach'lok], n. gun with a lock holding a match for firing it; lock of such a gun.

MATCHMAKER [mach'mā-ker], n. one intriguing to bring about marriages; one who makes matches.

MATCHWOOD [mach'wood], n. wood from which matches are made; thin or splintered wood.

MATE (1) [māt], n. companion, work-fellow; friend; sexual partner in man or animals; second in command of anything, esp. of a merchant ship. MATE (2), v.t. and i. to take a sexual partner, marry. [OLGerm.].

MATE (3), v.t. and n. (to) checkmate. [CHECKMATE].

MATE (4), **maté** [mah'tā], n. South American plant from the powdered dried leaves of which is made a kind of tea; infusion of this. [Span.].

MATER [mā'ter], n. (anat.) either of two of the membranes enclosing the brain and spinal cord; (slang) mother. [L.].

MATERFAMILIAS [mā-ter-fa-mi'li-as], n. the mother of the household.

MATERIA [ma-tēer'i-ah], n. substances, matter; **m. medica,** substances used in medicine; the study of these. [L.].

MATERIAL (1) [ma-tēer'i-al], adj. made of substance, concrete; relating to tangible reality, corporeal; (of persons) not spiritually inclined; relevant to an issue, important; (leg.) affecting judgment. MATERIAL (2), n. substance of which a thing is made, esp. cloth, fabric of any kind; knowledge necessary for literary work, teaching etc.; human beings regarded as stuff for a purpose. MATERIALLY, adv. in m. fashion, from the m. aspect. [L.].

MATERIALISM [ma-tēer'i-a-lizm], n. belief accepting only the material as valid, and dismissing the spiritual and supernatural as imaginary, or of material origin. MATERIALIST, n. one who professes and practises m. MATERIALISTIC [ma-tēer-i-a-lis'tik], adj. relating to, imbued with, m.

MATERIALITY [ma-tēer-i-a'li-ti], n. quality of being material.

MATERIALIZATION [ma-tēer-i-a-li-zā'shn], n. act of materializing; state of being materialized; a materialized ghost.

MATERIALIZE [ma-tēer'i-a-liz], v.t. and i. to bring into material form; (of a spirit) cause to assume bodily shape; imbue with materialism; assume practical form, be realized.

MATERIEL, matériel [ma-tā-ri-el'], n. the implements or equipment required for some task or operation, esp. the equipment of an army. [Fr.].

MATERNAL [ma-tur'nal], adj. relating to a mother; on the mother's side; characteristic of a mother. MATERNALLY, adv. in m. fashion.

MATERNITY [ma-tur'ni-ti], n. motherhood; condition of being a mother; **m. hospital,** hospital for women during confinement. [L.].

MATEY [mā'ti], adj. (coll.) sociable. [MATE (1)].

MATHEMATICAL [ma-thi-ma'ti-kal], adj. according to, dealing with, relating to, mathematics; (fig.) as exact as if according to mathematics.

MATHEMATICIAN [ma-thi-ma-ti'shan], n. one skilled in mathematics.

MATHEMATICS [ma-thi-ma'tiks], n.(pl.) science of numerical or quantitative properties and relations. [Gk.].

MATINEE, matinée [ma'ti-nā], n. dramatic, cinema etc. performance held in the afternoon; **m. coat,** woollen jacket for infants. [Fr.].

MATINS [ma'tinz], n.(pl.) morning public worship in the Church of England; (R.C.) one of the canonical hours. [Fr.].

MATRIARCH [mā'tri-ahk], n. female head of a family; woman ruling a tribal group. MATRIARCHAL [mā-tri-ah'kal], adj. relating to a m. or to matriarchy. [L., ~PATRIARCH].

MATRIARCHY [mā'tri-ah-ki], n. social system in which inheritance and kinship are through the female line, and the mother is head of the family and tribe.

MATRICES [ma'tri-sēz, mā'tri-sēz], n. pl. of MATRIX.

MATRICIDE [mā'tri-sīd], n. the killing of one's own mother; one who commits this crime. MATRICIDAL [mā-tri-sī'dal], adj. pertaining to m. [L.].

MATRICULATE [ma-tri'kyōo-lāt], v.t. and i. to admit to a university; obtain admittance to a university; pass the examination formerly qualifying for admittance. [L.].

MATRICULATION [ma-tri-kyōo-lā'shn], n. act of matriculating; examination necessary for this. MATRICULAR, adj. relating to m.

MATRIMONIAL [ma-tri-mō'ni-al], adj. relating to marriage. [LL.].

MATRIMONY [ma'tri-mu-ni], n. marriage, state of being married. [L.].

MATRIX (pl. **matrices**) [mā'triks, ma'triks], n. the womb; place where a thing is formed; substance in which objects are embedded, esp. mineral crystals; mould for casting type. [L.].

MATRON [mā'tron], n. married woman, esp. if elderly and a mother; woman in charge of nursing at a hospital etc., or of domestic matters at a boarding school etc. MATRONLY, adj. like or relating to a m.; elderly and motherly; rather fat. [L.].

MATRONYMIC [mā-trō-ni'mik], n. a metronymic. [L. and Gk.].

MATT, see MAT (3).

MATTED [ma'tid], adj. tangled, coarsely twisted together. [MAT (2)].

MATTER (1) [ma'ter], n. substance, material, stuff of which physical objects are made; the subjects, facts of a book, statement etc.; affair, business, concern; amount, distance; pus. MATTER (2), v.i. to be of importance; discharge matter. MATTERY, adj. purulent. [L.].

MATTER-OF-FACT [ma-ter-ov-fakt'], adj. concerned only with facts, unimaginative, casual.

MATTING [ma'ting], n. coarse woven material; sacking woven from hemp etc. [MAT (1)].

MATTOCK [ma'tok], n. kind of pickaxe with a broad edge to one blade and a point to the other. [OE.].

MATTRESS [ma'tres], n. container filled with stuffing and used to lie on; stuffed or sprung contrivance used as a bed or as a support for a bed. [OFr.].

MATURE (1) [ma-tyōor'], adj. ripe; fully developed; wise, carefully considered; due, payable. MATURE (2), v.t. and i. to ripen, make m.; make ready for putting into effect; become m.; become payable. [L.].

MATURITY [ma-tyōor'i-ti], n. state of being mature.

MATUTINAL [ma-tyōo-tī'nal], adj. relating to, occurring in, the morning. [L.].

MAUD [mawd], n. Scots shepherd's plaid. [Unkn.].

MAUDLIN [mawd'lin], adj. tipsily tearful; displaying embarrassing emotionalism or self-pity. [OFr.].

MAUL (1) [mawl], n. heavy wooden mallet. MAUL (2), v.t. and i. to tear savagely, injure brutally. [OFr.].

MAULSTICK, MAHLSTICK [mawl'stik], n. rod used by painters to steady the wrist. [Du.].

MAUNDER [mawn'der], v.i. to mutter vaguely, ramble in speech. [Unkn.].

MAUNDY [mawn'di], n. royal bounty distributed on the Thursday before Easter; silver pence struck for this; former ceremony of washing the feet of the poor by the king. [OFr.].

MAUSOLEUM [maw-sō-lē'um], n. large monumental sepulchre. MAUSOLEAN, adj. relating to, like,

---

ōō is pronounced as in food; ŏŏ as in hood; th as in think; TH as in that; zh as in azure.   ~ = related to.

a m. [L. from *Mausolos*, King of Caria, buried in one].

MAUVE (1) [mōv], *n.* light purple colour. MAUVE (2), *adj.* of this colour. [Fr.].

MAVERICK [ma've-rik], *n.* (*U.S.*) unbranded calf or yearling; masterless man. [*Maverick*, a Texan].

MAVIS [mā'vis], *n.* the song-thrush. [OFr.].

MAVOURNEEN [ma-vōōr'nēn], *n.* Irish term of endearment. [Ir.].

MAW [maw], *n.* stomach of an animal; crop of a bird; (*fig.*) gaping chasm. [OE.].

MAWKISH [maw'kish], *adj.* sickly, insipid; feebly sentimental, emotionally unreal. [ME.].

MAXILLA (*pl.* **maxillae**) [mak-si'lah], *n.* the jaw-bone. [L.].

MAXILLARY [mak-si'la-ri], *adj.* relating to the jaw or to the jawbone. [L.].

MAXIM (1) [mak'sim], *n.* saying giving generalized advice on action and conduct. [L.].

MAXIM (2), *n.* type of machine-gun. [Sir H. *Maxim*, its inventor].

MAXIMUM (1) (*pl.* **maxima**) [mak'si-mum], *n.* the greatest extent, quantity etc.; the greatest possible. MAXIMUM (2), *adj.* greatest possible. [L.].

MAY (1) [mā], *n.* fifth month of the year; hawthorn blossom, the hawthorn. [L.].

MAY (2) (*pret.* **might**), *v. auxil. expressing possibility, permissibility and uncertainty, and also wish, hope or will.* [OE.].

MAYBE [mā'bē], *adv.* possibly, perhaps.

MAY-BUG [mā'bug], *n.* the cockchafer.

MAY-DAY [mā'dā], *n.* first of May.

MAYFLOWER [mā'flower], *n.* the cuckoo-flower.

MAYFLY [mā'flī], *n.* a species of *Ephemera*; synthetic imitation of this insect used in fly-fishing.

MAYHAP † [mā'hap], *adv.* perchance.

MAYHEM [mā'hem], *n.* (*leg.*) injury to any important part of the body, *esp.* as ground for legal action. [AFr.].

MAYING [mā'ing], *n.* celebration of May festivities.

MAYONNAISE [mā-o-nāz'], *n.* dressing made from yolk of eggs, oil, vinegar etc.; cold dish served with this dressing. [Fr.].

MAYOR [māer], *n.* chief officer of a municipal corporation. MAYORALTY [māer'al-ti], *n.* office, status or period of office of a m. [Fr.].

MAYORESS [māer'es], *n.* wife of a mayor; woman chosen to perform the public functions of a mayor's wife if the mayor is unmarried.

MAYPOLE [mā'pōl], *n.* decorated pole, danced round on May-day.

MAY-QUEEN [mā-kwēn'], *n.* girl chosen to preside at May-day festivities.

MAYWEED [mā'wēd], *n.* foetid camomile. [OE.].

MAZARIN (1) [ma'za-rin], *n.* deep blue colour. MAZARIN (2), *adj.* of a deep blue. [Cardinal *Mazarin*].

MAZE (1) [māz], *v.t.* to puzzle, bewilder, perplex. MAZE (2), *n.* complex network of high-hedged, winding paths, designed to puzzle those attempting to reach the centre or make their way out; (*fig.*) tangle of puzzling detail. [ME.].

MAZER [mā'zer], *n.* shallow drinking-bowl. [ME.].

MAZURKA [mah-zoōr'kah], *n.* Polish dance in triple time; music for this. [Polish].

MAZUT [ma-zoōt'], *n.* petroleum residue used as fuel. [Russ.].

MAZY [mā'zi], *adj.* labyrinthine; bewildered.

ME [mē], *pron. acc. and dat. of* I. [OE.].

MEAD (1) [mēd], *n.* drink made from fermented honey. [OE.].

MEAD (2), *n.* (*poet.*) meadow. [OE.].

MEADOW [me'dō], *n.* hayfield, field of grass. MEADOW-GRASS, grass of the genus *Poa*. MEADOW-LARK, titlark. MEADOW-PINK, ragged robin. MEADOW-SAFFRON, *Colchicum autumnale.* MEADOWY, *adj.* resembling, abounding in, meadows. [OE.].

MEADOWSWEET [me'dō-swēt], *n.* a white-flowered plant.

MEAGRE [mē'ger], *adj.* lean, emaciated; poor, barely sufficient; barren, limited. [OFr.].

MEAL (1) [mēl], *n.* repast, taking of food, *esp.* at a customary time; amount of food consumed at this. [OE.].

MEAL (2), *n.* the edible part of grain or pulse, other than wheat, ground to a powder. [OE.].

MEALIE [mē'li], *n.* ear of maize; (*pl.*) a quantity of maize. [Afrik.].

MEALY [mē'li], *adj.* pertaining to, like, meal; covered with meal; (of horses) full of small spots; dullish white, pale; **m. bug,** insect of m. appearance, infesting plants. MEALINESS, *n.* quality of being m.

MEALY-MOUTHED [mē-li-mowтнd'], *adj.* afraid to use blunt or frank expressions.

MEAN (1) [mēn], *adj.* middle; average; intervening; (*math.*) halfway between the extremes of a series: **m. proportional,** the middle of three quantities, standing in the same proportion to the first as does the third to it. MEAN (2), *n.* medium, the middle point, course etc. between extremes or opposites; (*math.*) m. term or quantity; (*pl.*) method by which something is done; resources, income; wealth; **by all means,** certainly. [OFr.].

MEAN (3), *adj.* low in rank or birth; inferior, humble; shabby, dingy; contemptible; miserly. [OE.].

MEAN (4) (*pret. and p.pt.* **meant**), *v.t.* to intend, purpose; design; intend to refer to or indicate; imply; convey, signify; *v.i.* to intend; **to m. business,** (*coll.*) to be in earnest. [OE.].

MEANDER (1) [mē-an'der], *n.* winding course; haphazard leisurely progression; (*pl.*) twists and bends. MEANDER (2), *v.i.* to flow in a winding course; (*fig.*) wander haphazardly. [Gk., river *Maiandros*].

MEANING (1) [mē'ning], *n.* that which is meant, sense; significance; implication. MEANING (2), *adj.* significant, full of m. MEANINGLY, *adv.* significantly, expressively.

MEANINGFUL [mē'ning-fōōl], *adj.* full of meaning, significant. MEANINGFULLY, *adv.* significantly.

MEANINGLESS [mē'ning-les], *adj.* having no meaning, expressing nothing.

MEANS-TEST [mēnz'test], *n.* official inquiry into the means of subsistence of a person seeking a State grant.

MEANT [ment], *pret. and p.pt. of* MEAN (4). [ME.].

MEANTIME (1) [mēn'tīm], *n.* the intervening time. MEANTIME (2), *adv.* in the intervening time.

MEANWHILE (1) [mēn'whīl], *n.* the intervening period of time. MEANWHILE (2), *adv.* during the intervening time. [MEAN (1) and OE.].

MEASLES [mē'zlz], *n.* acute infectious disease with a crimson rash; the rash itself; a disease of swine. MEASLED [mē'zld], *adj.* infected with or marked by m. [ME. —OHigh Germ.].

MEASLY [mēz'li], *adj.* pertaining to, of the nature of, measles; having measles; (*fig.*) paltry, meagre.

MEASURABLE [me'zhe-ra-bl], *adj.* able to be measured; moderate.

MEASURE (1) [me'zher], *n.* size, dimensions, quantity; standard or unit used in determining these; graduated rod, standard-sized vessel, for measuring something; unit of capacity; limit, fixed extent; Parliamentary Bill; (*fig.*) criterion, standard; metre; (*mus.*) group of notes and/or rests comprised within two consecutive bar lines; the time in which a musical composition is written; rhythm; (*archaic*) a dance; (*pl.*) proceedings, means to an end; (*arith.*) a number dividing exactly into another; **to have the m. of,** to have summed up; **made to m.,** made to fit by previous measurement; **greatest common m.,** (*arith.*) the greatest quantity dividing exactly into all of a number of given quantities. MEASURE (2), *v.t.* to find the dimensions, capacity etc. of; mark off, deal out (a specific quantity); test by competition with another; judge by some criterion; *v.i.* to be of certain dimensions; **to m. swords with,** to fight; **to m. one's length,** to fall full length on the ground; **to m. up to,** to conform to. [Fr.].

MEASURED [me'zherd], *adj.* carefully considered, well chosen; steady, deliberate.

MEASURELESS [me'zher-les], *adj.* without measure, boundless.

MEASUREMENT [me'zher-ment], *n.* act of measuring, state of being measured; size, amount etc. which anything measures.

MEAT [mēt], *n.* edible flesh of animals; (*archaic*) food; a meal; (*fig.*) food for thought. MEAT-OFFERING, Jewish offering of flour, oil and frankincense. MEAT-SAFE, cupboard in which m. may be kept. [OE.].

MEATLESS [mēt'les], *adj.* containing no meat; **m. day,** day on which either the sale or the consumption of meat may not or does not take place.

MEATUS [mē-ā'tus], *n.* (*anat.*) passage or duct in the body. [L.].

MEATY [mē'ti], *adj.* full of meat, fleshy but not fat; of meat, like meat; (*fig.*) providing mental nourishment. MEATINESS, *n.* quality of being m.

MECCA [me'kah], *n.* principal city of pilgrimage for Moslems; (*fig.*) place a devotee desires to visit.

MECHANIC [me-ka'nik], *n.* artisan, skilled operative, *esp.* one trained in the use or construction of machinery; (pl.) that branch of applied mathematics dealing with motion, force and matter; the science of machinery. [Gk.].

MECHANICAL [me-ka'ni-kal], adj. of or by machines; acting by physical power, esp. according to the principles of mechanics; non-creative, performed without thought, according to routine; **m. drawing**, drawing done with instruments.

MECHANICIAN [me-ka-ni'shan], n. one skilled in the construction and working of machines.

MECHANISM [me'ka-nizm], n. machinery, the collective parts which by their combined motion operate a piece of machinery; the means by which something functions; (art) technique; (philos.) doctrine that everything is produced by mechanical action.

MECHANIZE [me'ka-niz], v.t. to make mechanical; cause to function by machinery, or like a machine; (milit.) to equip with mechanical weapons and armoured fighting vehicles. MECHANIZATION [me-ka-ni-zā'shn], n. act or process of mechanizing, esp. an army.

MECONIC [mi-ko'nik], adj. obtained from the poppy; **m. acid**, a crystalline acid obtained from opium. [Gk.].

MEDAL [me'dal], n. small metal disk containing a device, inscription etc., issued to commemorate some event, or as a reward or distinction. MEDALLIC [me-da'lik], adj. pertaining to, like, occurring on, a m. [Fr.].

MEDALLION [me-da'lyon], n. large medal; circular bas-relief. [It.].

MEDALLIST [me'da-list], n. one skilled in medals; maker of medals; one who has gained a prize-medal.

MEDDLE [me'dl], v.i. to interfere unnecessarily and objectionably in other people's affairs; busy oneself with something one does not understand. [OFr.].

MEDDLESOME [med'dl-sum], adj. given to meddling, interfering.

MEDIA [mē'di-ah], n. pl. of MEDIUM.

MEDIAEVAL, see MEDIAEVAL.

MEDIAL [mē'di-al], adj. middle; pertaining to a mean; average. MEDIALLY, adv. in a m. position. [LL.].

MEDIAN (1) [mē'di-an], adj. situated in, traversing, the middle of something. MEDIAN (2), n. (anat.) the m. vein; (math.) a line joining any vertex of a triangle to the mid-point of the opposite side. [LL.].

MEDIATE (1) [mē'di-āt], adj. acting through, involving, an intermediary. MEDIATE (2), v.t. to effect by intervention; v.i. to intervene in order to reconcile disputants. [L.].

MEDIATION [mē-di-ā'shn], n. act of mediating; state of being an intermediary. [LL.].

MEDIATIZE [mē'di-a-tiz], v.t. to annex a small state to a larger one, while permitting its ruler to retain his rights and title. MEDIATIZATION [mē-di-a-ti-zā'shn], n. act of mediatizing; state of being mediatized. [Fr.].

MEDIATOR [mē'di-ā-ter], n. one who mediates, a peacemaker. MEDIATORIAL, MEDIATORY [mē-di-a-taw'ri-al, mē'di-ā-te-ri], adj. belonging to a m. or to mediation. [LL.].

MEDICABLE [me'di-ka-bl], adj. that may be cured by medical treatment. [L.].

MEDICAL (1) [me'di-kal], adj. pertaining to the healing of disease; relating to medicine and to treatment of disease by medicine; **m. practitioner**, qualified doctor; **m. school**, institution for training doctors. MEDICAL (2), n. (coll.) a m. student. MEDICALLY, adv. according to, by means of, medicine. [L.].

MEDICAMENT [me-di'ka-ment, med'i-ka-ment], n. a medical remedy. MEDICAMENTAL [me-di-ka-men'tal], adj. healing, of the nature of a m. [L.].

MEDICATE [me'di-kāt], v.t. to tincture with a medicinal substance; treat with medicine. MEDICATION [me-di-kā'shn], n. act of medicating; state of being medicated. MEDICATIVE [me'di-ka-tiv], adj. curative. [L.].

MEDICINAL [me-di'si-nal], adj. relating to medicine; curative, healing.

MEDICINE [med'sn, me'di-sin], n. art of preventing, curing or alleviating disease, esp. by healing compounds, drugs etc. taken internally; any curative preparation taken internally in the treatment of disease, esp. one in liquid form. MEDICINE-BALL, large stuffed leather ball thrown and caught for exercise. MEDICINE-MAN, among savages, a witch-doctor professing supernatural powers and practising magic. [L.].

MEDICO [me'di-kō], n. (slang) medical student; doctor.

MEDICO-LEGAL [me-di-kō-lē'gal], adj. relating to law as concerned with medicine.

MEDIEVAL, **MEDIAEVAL** [me-di-ē'val], adj. belonging to, characteristic of, the Middle Ages. [L.].

MEDIEVALISM [me-di-ē'va-lizm], n. medieval spirit or quality; something surviving from the Middle Ages; affection for, cult of, that which is medieval. MEDIEVALIST, n. student, historian or admirer of the Middle Ages.

MEDIOCRE [mē'di-ō-ker], adj. of moderate quality, neither good nor bad. [L.].

MEDIOCRITY [mē-di-ok'ri-ti], n. quality of being mediocre; mediocre person. [L.].

MEDITATE [me'di-tāt], v.t. to plan, contrive; v.i. to be engrossed in deep thought or serious contemplation. [L.].

MEDITATION [me-di-tā'shn], n. act of meditating; (pl.) work containing one's thoughts or reflections. [L.].

MEDITATIVE [me'di-ta-tiv], adj. thoughtful, contemplative. MEDITATIVELY, adv. in m. fashion.

MEDITERRANEAN [me-di-te-rā'ni-an], adj. (of land) far from the sea; inland, (of a sea) land-locked; pertaining to, situated on, the Mediterranean Sea. [L.].

MEDIUM (1) (pl. **media, mediums**) [mē'di-um], n. that which is medium in quality, size etc.; means, agency; intervening substance through which something may be transmitted; material in which an artist etc. works; substance in which pigments are mixed before painting; (spiritualism) intermediary serving as means of communication between the dead and the living. MEDIUM (2), adj. middling, average, moderate, intermediate; **m. wave**, (radio) (of wavelengths) more than 99 or less than 801 metres. [L.].

MEDIUMISTIC [mē-di-u-mis'tik], adj. relating to spiritualistic mediums, their work and powers.

MEDLAR [med'lar], n. a tree, the fruit of which is eaten when half-rotten; the fruit of this. [OFr.].

MEDLEY [med'li], n. confused mass of dissimilar things; mixed crowd of people; musical composition made up of short extracts from other works. [OFr.].

MEDOC, médoc [me-dok'], n. a kind of claret. [Médoc, France].

MEDULLA [mi-du'lah], n. the marrow of bones; the spinal cord, marrow of this; pith of the hair of mammals; (bot.) pith of plants; (anat.) internal part of certain organs; **m. oblongata**, upper continuation of the spinal cord to form the back section of the brain. [L.].

MEDULLARY [mi-du'la-ri], adj. pertaining to, consisting of, like, marrow; (bot.) filled with pith; **m. rays**, (bot.) plates of tissue causing the grain in oak etc.

MEDUSA [me-dyōō'sah], n. (Gk. myth.) Gorgon whose head was cut off by Perseus; (zool.) a jellyfish. [Gk.].

MEED [mēd], n. (poet.) reward; just portion. [OE.].

MEEK [mēk], adj. mild, gentle, submissive. [~OIcel.].

MEERSCHAUM [mäer'showm], n. fine white clay used in making bowls of tobacco pipes; pipe made of it. [Germ.].

MEET (1) [mēt], adj. (archaic) fitting, suitable. [OE.].

MEET (2) (pret. and p.pt. **met**), v.t. to come face to face with; encounter when approaching from different directions; await the arrival of; come into contact with; come into or join the company of; be formally introduced to; be in opposition against; come together in negotiation; satisfy; pay (debts etc.); v.i. to come together; come into contact; assemble; become formally acquainted; **to m. with**, to experience; find. MEET (3), n. a meeting of hounds and huntsmen to take part in a hunt. [OE.].

MEETING [mē'ting], n. an encounter; public gathering of people for a specific purpose. MEETING-HOUSE, Quaker or other dissenting chapel.

MEGA-, pref. large, great. [Gk.].

MEGACYCLE [me'ga-sī-kl], n. (elect.) a million cycles, a measure of frequency of alternating current or oscillation.

MEGA-ERG [me'ga-erg], n. (elect.) a million ergs.

MEGAFARAD [me-ga-fa'rad], n. (elect.) a million farads.

MEGALITH [me'ga-lith], n. large prehistoric stone monument. MEGALITHIC [me-ga-li'thik], adj. composed of large stones; characterized by the building of megaliths. [Gk.].

MEGALOMANIA [me-ga-lō-mā'ni-ah], n. form of

insanity in which a person thinks he is a great personage. MEGALOMANIAC, *n.* person suffering from m. [Gk.].

MEGAPHONE [me'ga-fōn], *n.* cone-shaped speaking-trumpet used to amplify the sound of the voice. [Gk.].

MEGATHERIUM [me-ga-thēer'i-um], *n.* extinct gigantic edentate resembling a sloth. [Gk.].

MEGOHM [me'gōm], *n.* a million ohms.

MEGRIM [mē'grim], *n.* migraine; whim, fad; (*pl.*) depression, melancholy; a nervous disease in cattle and horses. [MIGRAINE].

MEIOSIS [mī-ō'sis], *n.* figure of speech by which the statement is in milder terms than the meaning intended; (*biol.*) reduction of the number of chromosomes in a reproductive cell. MEIOTIC [mī-o'tik], *adj.* pertaining to, characterized by, m. [Gk.].

MELAN(O)-, *pref.* black. [Gk.].

MELANCHOLIA [me-lan-kō'li-ah], *n.* form of insanity marked by fits of profound depression. [LL.].

MELANCHOLIC [me-lan-ko'lik], *adj.* affected with, resulting from, melancholy, depressed; gloomy, sad. [Gk.].

MELANCHOLY (1) [me'lan-ko-li], *n.* a habitually gloomy state of mind, extremely low spirits. MELANCHOLY (2), *adj.* gloomy, low-spirited; depressing, dismal. [Gk.].

MELANGE, mélange [me-lah(ng)zh'], *n.* confused mixture, medley. [Fr.].

MELANIN [me'la-nin], *n.* black colouring matter in certain tissues, as the negro's skin; black pigment of the skin caused by certain diseases. [Gk.].

MELANISM [me'la-nizm], *n.* excess of dark colouring matter in the skin, hair etc. [Gk.].

MELANOSIS [me-la-nō'sis], *n.* (*path.*) morbid deposit of black pigment in certain bodily tissues. MELANOTIC [me-la-no'tik], *adj.* pertaining to, suffering from, m. [Gk.].

MELEE, melée [me'lā], *n.* confused fight or scuffle, skirmish. [Fr.].

MELINITE [me'li-nīt], *n.* a high explosive. [Fr.].

MELLIFLUENT [me-li'flōō-ent], *adj.* mellifluous. MELLIFLUENCE, *n.* quality of being m. [LL.].

MELLIFLUOUS [me-li'flōō-ōōs], *adj.* (of the voice etc.) sweetly sounding and smoothly flowing. [L.].

MELLOW (1) [me'lō], *adj.* (of fruit) sweet, ripe and juicy; (of earth) soft, loamy; (of wine) fully mature and satisfying to the palate; (of sounds, colour etc.) softened and smooth, yet rich and full; (*fig.*) softened and sweetened in character by maturity; (*slang*) affably drunk. MELLOW (2), *v.t.* to make m.; *v.i.* to become m. MELLOW, *adv.* in m. fashion. [ME.].

MELODEON [me-lō'di-on], *n.* musical wind-instrument similar to a harmonium; kind of accordion. [MELODY].

MELODIC [me-lo'dik], *adj.* relating to or containing melody, tuneful. [Gk.].

MELODIOUS [me-lō'di-ōōs], *adj.* full of melody, tuneful; producing melody. MELODIOUSLY, *adv.* in m. fashion. [Gk.].

MELODIST [me'lo-dist], *n.* composer or singer of melodies.

MELODRAMA [me'lō-drah-mah], *n.* type of play thrilling in incident, and crude and overdrawn in sentiment and emotional appeal; incident or series of happenings resembling this. [Gk.].

MELODRAMATIC [me-lō-dra-ma'tik], *adj.* of the nature of a melodrama, sensational and touching. MELODRAMATICALLY, *adv.* in a m. way.

MELODY [me'lo-di], *n.* a succession of pleasing musical sounds, *esp.* when rhythmically arranged as a tune; the air of a musical composition; art of writing this. [Gk.].

MELON [me'lon], *n.* any of several edible varieties of gourd. [LL.].

MELT (1) [melt], *v.t. and i.* to become or make liquid under heat; dissolve; (*fig.*) fill with pity or compassion; blend, merge; disperse, disappear; (*coll.*) be extremely hot and perspiring. MELT (2), *n.* molten metal; the quantity of metal melted at a time. [OE.].

MELTING (1) [mel'ting], *n.* act of one who, or that which, melts. MELTING (2), *adj.* that melts, full of compassion; deeply affecting; tender; (of sounds) soothing and liquid.

MELTON [mel'ton], *n.* stout woollen cloth for coating; overcoat of this. [*Melton* Mowbray, Leicestershire].

MEMBER [mem'ber], *n.* part, limb or organ of the body; a single component part of a complex whole;

individual belonging to a specific group, organization etc.; (*math.*) series of figures or symbols forming part of an expression or formula; (*gram.*) clause of a sentence; **M. of Parliament**, the elected representative of a constituency in the House of Commons. [L.].

MEMBERSHIP [mem'ber-ship], *n.* state of being a member of a specific group or organization; the total number of such members.

MEMBRANE [mem'brān], *n.* (*anat.*) thin laminar tissue which covers organs, lines cavities, and connects various bodily structures; (*bot.*) thin white tissue performing similar functions in vegetable bodies. MEMBRANOUS, MEMBRANEOUS [mem'bra-nōōs, mem-brā'ni-ōōs], *adj.* belonging to, consisting of, or resembling m. [L.].

MEMENTO (*pl.* **mementos**) [mi-men'tō], *n.* something kept to remind one of something or someone, keepsake; reminder. [L.].

MEMO [me'mō], *n.* (*coll.*) memorandum.

MEMOIR [mem'wahr], *n.* biography of a person by another; essay embodying research on a learned subject; (*pl.*) written account of one's reminiscences; account of the transactions of a learned society. MEMOIRIST, *n.* writer of memoirs. [Fr.].

MEMORABILIA [me-maw-ra-bi'li-ah], *n.*(*pl.*) things worthy of remembrance or record. [L.].

MEMORABLE [me'me-ra-bl], *adj.* worth remembering, never to be forgotten. MEMORABLY, *adv.* in a m. manner. [L.].

MEMORANDUM (*pl.* **memoranda, memorandums**) [me-me-ran'dum], *n.* a note of certain particulars jotted down for future reference; brief business note sent to another; (*leg.*) document stating the terms of a contract etc.; **m. of association**, legal articles of registration of a joint-stock company. [L.].

MEMORIAL (1) [mi-maw'ri-al], *adj.* pertaining to memory; preserving the memory of, commemorating. MEMORIAL (2), *n.* an object, *esp.* a monument or custom, which preserves the memory of something; (*pl.*) chronicle of historical events; (*leg.*) written statement of the terms of a petition; informal state papers embodying the attitude or suggestions of a State, or containing instructions to an ambassador, in international negotiation. [L.].

MEMORIALIST [mi-maw'ri-a-list], *n.* one who writes a memorial; one who presents a legal memorial.

MEMORIALIZE [mi-maw'ri-a-liz], *v.t.* to preserve the memory of; send up a memorial or petition to.

MEMORIA TECHNICA [mi-maw-ri-ah-tek'ni-kah], *n.* an artificial aid to memory. [L.].

MEMORIZE [me'me-riz], *v.t.* to commit to memory.

MEMORY [me'me-ri], *n.* that aspect of intelligence by which past experience is retained and recollected by the mind; that which is remembered, a recollection; remembrance; fame; time during which one may remember. [L.].

MEMSAHIB [mem'sah-ib], *n.* Hindu address of respect to a white woman. [MA'AM and SAHIB].

MEN [men], *n. pl. of* MAN. [OE.].

MENACE (1) [me'nas], *n.* a threat. MENACE (2), *v.t.* to threaten. [OFr.].

MENACING [me'na-sing], *adj.* threatening. MENACINGLY, *adv.* in threatening fashion.

MENAGE, ménage [me-nahzh'], *n.* housekeeping, a household. [Fr.].

MENAGERIE [me-na'je-ri], *n.* a collection of wild animals kept in cages or special enclosures for public exhibition; place in which they are housed. [Fr.].

MEND (1) [mend], *v.t.* to repair, put right; correct, remedy; improve; reform; *v.i.* to recover from illness; become better; be capable of repair. MEND (2), *n.* a darn or patch in a fabric; **on the m.**, improving. [AMEND].

MENDACIOUS [men-dā'shŏŏs], *adj.* lying, false. [L.].

MENDACITY [men-da'si-ti], *n.* lying, untruthfulness; a falsehood. [L.].

MENDELISM [men'de-lizm], *n.* theory of heredity propounded by Mendel.

MENDICANCY [men'di-kan-si], *n.* state of being a mendicant.

MENDICANT (1) [men'di-kant], *adj.* begging; (of certain religious orders) living solely on alms. MENDICANT (2), *n.* beggar; member of a m. order. [L.].

MENDICITY [men-di'si-ti], *n.* life or condition of a beggar; begging. [L.].

MENHIR [men'hēer], *n.* single, upright, unhewn stone serving as a prehistoric monument. [Breton].

The accent ' after a syllable = stress (u-pon'). The mark ⁻ over a vowel = length (ā in made; ō in bone).

MENIAL (1) [mē'ni-al], *adj.* (of work) base, servile; (of servants) domestic. **MENIAL** (2), *n.* domestic servant; drudge; inferior subordinate. [AFr.].

MENINGEAL [me-nin'ji-al], *adj.* relating to the meninges. [MdL.].

MENINGES [me-nin'jēz], *n.(pl.)* the three membranes which envelop the brain and spinal cord. [L.].

MENINGITIS [me-nin-jī'tis], *n.* inflammation of the membranes of the brain. [MdL.].

MENISCUS (*pl.* **meniscuses**) [me-nis'kus], *n.* a lens, convex on one side and concave on the other; rounded top of liquid in a tube; (*math.*) figure shaped like a crescent. [Gk.].

MENOPAUSE [me'nō-pawz], *n.* the change of life in women when the menses cease. [Gk.].

MENORRHAGIA [me-ne-rā'ji-ah], *n.* (*med.*) excessive menstrual discharge. [Gk.].

MENSES [men'sēz], *n.(pl.)* monthly discharge from the womb. [L.].

MENSHEVIK [men'she-vik], *n.* Russian socialist of the minority party defeated by the Bolsheviks. [Russ.].

MENSTRUAL [men'strōō-al], *adj.* (*astron.*) monthly; pertaining to the menses.

MENSTRUATE [men'strōō-āt], *v.i.* to discharge the menses. **MENSTRUATION** [men-strōō-ā'shn], *n.* act of menstruating. [L.].

MENSTRUOUS [men'strōō-ōōs], *adj.* having or relating to the menses. [OFr.].

MENSTRUUM (*pl.* **menstrua, menstruums**) [men'strōō-um], *n.* a solvent. [L.].

MENSURABLE [men'shōō-re-bl], *adj.* that may be measured; (*mus.*) written in a set rhythm. [L.].

MENSURATION [men-shōō-rā'shn], *n.* act or art of measuring; (*math.*) branch of mathematics concerned with the determination of lengths, areas and volumes. [L.].

MENTAL [men'tal], *adj.* pertaining to the mind; performed in the mind; affected with, specializing in, diseases of the mind; (*coll.*) mentally defective; **m. arithmetic**, sums worked in the mind and not on paper. **MENTALLY**, *adv.* in the mind; as regards the mind. [L.].

MENTALITY [men-ta'li-ti], *n.* intelligence, mental capacity; type of mind, mental outlook.

MENTHOL [men'thol], *n.* mint camphor, crystalline substance, obtained by cooling oil of peppermint. [Germ.].

MENTION (1) [men'shn], *n.* a direct reference to; brief notice of or remarking upon; **honourable m.**, distinction awarded for specially meritorious work which has failed to secure a prize. **MENTION** (2), *v.t.* to speak of, refer to, name. [L.].

MENTOR [men'taw(r)], *n.* a wise and faithful guide and adviser. [*Mentor*, in the *Odyssey*].

MENU [me'nyōō], *n.* bill of fare, list of dishes; the actual meal. [Fr.].

MEPHISTOPHELIAN [me-fis-tō-fē'li-an], *adj.* resembling Mephistopheles, sinister. [*Mephistopheles*, devil to whom Faust sold his soul].

MEPHITIC [mi-fi'tik], *adj.* offensive to the smell, foul. [L.].

MEPHITIS [mi-fi'tis], *n.* noxious exhalation from decomposing substances; foul smell.

MERCANTILE [mur'kan-til], *adj.* commercial, pertaining to, employed in, trade or commerce; **m. marine**, merchant shipping collectively; **m. system**, economic doctrine based on the supposition that money alone is wealth. **MERCANTILISM**, *n.* trade and commerce; (*econ.*) the m. system. [It.].

MERCENARY (1) [mur'se-na-ri], *adj.* hired or procured with money; actuated or moved by love of money; greedy of gain. **MERCENARY** (2), *n.* professional soldier hired by a foreign state. [L.].

MERCER [mur'ser], *n.* dealer in silks, cottons, linens and woollen cloths. [Fr.].

MERCERIZE [mur'se-rīz], *v.t.* to treat (cotton fabrics) with caustic alkali in order to give them a silky finish. [J. *Mercer*, inventor of this process].

MERCHANDISE [mur'chan-dīz], *n.* wares, goods or commodities bought or sold. [OFr.].

MERCHANT (1) [mur'chant], *n.* one who carries on trade, *esp.* with foreign countries and on a large scale. **MERCHANT** (2), *adj.* pertaining to trade or commerce; **m. prince**, powerful, wealthy trader. **MERCHANTABLE**, *adj.* fit for market, that may be sold. [OFr.].

MERCHANTMAN [mur'chant-man], *n.* ship in the merchant service.

MERCHANT SERVICE [mur'chant-ser-vis], *n.* the mercantile marine, consisting of ships engaged solely in commerce or trade.

MERCIFUL [mur'si-fōōl], *adj.* exhibiting mercy, compassionate; lenient; providential. **MERCIFULLY**, *adv.* in a m. manner.

MERCILESS [mur'si-les], *adj.* without mercy, pitiless. **MERCILESSLY**, *adv.* in m. fashion.

MERCURIAL [mer-kyōōr'i-al], *adj.* pertaining to, consisting of, containing, like, due to, mercury; (*fig.*) nimble, alert; unstable.

MERCURIC [mer-kyōōr'ik], *adj.* of, or containing, mercury; (*chem.*) containing mercury in its higher valency state.

MERCUROUS [mer-kyōōr'ōōs], *adj.* mercuric; (*chem.*) containing mercury in its lower valency state.

MERCURY [mur'kyōō-ri], *n.* heavy silvery fluid metallic element, Hg; a medical preparation of this; (*myth.*) the messenger of the gods; (*astron.*) planet nearest the sun; (*coll.*) messenger. [L.].

MERCY [mur'si], *n.* compassion, forbearance, leniency; a blessing, stroke of providence; act of kindness to someone in one's power; **at the m. of**, helpless in the power of. [OFr.].

MERE (1) [mēer], *n.* pool, lake or pond. [OE.].

MERE (2), *adj.* simple, pure, nothing more than **MERELY**, *adv.* only, simply, purely. [L.].

MERETRICIOUS [me-ri-tri'shōōs], *adj.* gaudy, vulgarly ostentatious; deceitfully alluring; (*archaic*) pertaining to, worthy of, a prostitute. **MERETRICIOUSLY**, *adv.* in m. fashion. [L.].

MERGANSER [mer-gan'ser], *n.* (*zool.*) a diving aquatic bird, allied to the duck. [L.].

MERGE [murj], *v.t. and i.* to cause to be, or to become completely absorbed by another; fade or dissolve imperceptibly into; (*leg.*) absorb into a greater. **MERGENCE**, *n.* act of merging; state of being merged. [L.].

MERGER [mur'jer], *n.* (*leg.*) the complete absorption of a smaller property, estate etc. into a greater; commercial combine of several business companies under one head. [OFr.].

MERIDIAN (1) [me-ri'di-an], *n.* (*astron., geog.*) great circle supposed to be drawn so as to pass through the poles of the earth, and the zenith of any place on the surface of the earth, and to intersect the equator at right angles; highest point reached by the sun or a star; (*fig.*) the height of development, peak of perfection; noon; **magnetic m.**, a great circle, parallel with the direction of the magnetic needle, and passing through the magnetic poles. **MERIDIAN** (2), *adj.* pertaining to the sun at its m.; pertaining to a m.; (*fig.*) relating to the peak or zenith; pertaining to noon. [L.].

MERIDIONAL [me-ri'di-o-nal], *adj.* pertaining to the south or to dwellers in the south (of Europe), southerly; pertaining to a meridian. **MERIDIONALLY**, *adv.* towards the meridian.

MERINGUE [me-rang'], *n.* white of egg mixed with powdered sugar; light cake of this. [Fr.].

MERINO (1) [me-rē'nō], *n.* variety of fine-woolled sheep; fine wavy wool from these sheep; mixture of fine wool and cotton; fine woollen fabric used in making stockings. **MERINO** (2), *adj.* made of m.; relating to the m. sheep or to their wool. [Span.].

MERIT (1) [me'rit], *n.* good quality or excellence entitling to commendation or reward; proved ability or worth; (*pl.*) deserts; (*leg.*) rights and wrongs of a question at issue; **Order of M.**, British military and civil order awarded for outstanding eminence. **MERIT** (2), *v.t.* to deserve, earn, be entitled to. **MERITED**, *adj.* earned, deserved. [L.].

MERITORIOUS [me-ri-taw'ri-ōōs], *adj.* deserving reward or commendation; praiseworthy. **MERITORIOUSLY**, *adv.* in a m. manner. [L.].

MERLE [murl], *n.* the blackbird. [OFr.].

MERLIN [mur'lin], *n.* smallest British falcon. [AFr.].

MERMAID [mur'mād], *n.* imaginary marine creature having the head and body of a woman and the tail of a fish. [ME.].

MERMAN [mur'man], *n.* male equivalent of a mermaid.

MEROVINGIAN [me-rō-vin'ji-an], *adj.* relating to the Merovingians, the earliest Frankish dynasty ruling in Gaul. [LL.].

MERRIMENT [me'ri-ment], *n.* mirth, hilarious gaiety.

MERRY [me'ri], *adj.* gay, cheerful, jolly; fond of fun and laughter; (*slang*) slightly intoxicated. **MERRILY**, *adv.* in a m. manner. [OE., ME.].

MERRY-ANDREW [me-ri-an'drōō], *n.* jester, buffoon or clown; mountebank's assistant.

MERRY-GO-ROUND [me'ri-gō-rownd], *n.* circular

ōō is pronounced as in food; ŏŏ as in hood; th as in *think*; TH as in *that*; zh as in azure. ~ = related to.

rotating structure, mounted with imitation vehicles, horses etc. and mechanically propelled, used for entertainment at fairs etc.

MERRYMAKING [me'ri-mā-king], *n.* festival, jovial entertainment.

MERRYTHOUGHT [me'ri-thawt], *n.* the forked upper bone of the breast of a bird, wishbone.

MESALLIANCE, mésalliance [mā-za'li-ah(ng)s], *n.* marriage in which one of the parties is of inferior social status to the other. [Fr.].

MESDAMES [mā-dahm', mā'dahm], used as *pl.* of MADAM and MRS. (*abbr.* of MISSIS). [Fr. *pl.* of *madame*].

MESEEMS [mi-sēmz'], *v. impers.* (*archaic*) it seems to me.

MESENTERY [me-sen'te-ri], *n.* (*anat.*) the part of the peritoneum fastening the intestines to the back wall of the abdomen. MESENTERIC [me-sen-te'rik], relating to the m. [Gk.].

MESH (1) [mesh], *n.* one of the small holes enclosed by the threads of a net, similar hole in a sieve etc.; network, arrangement of threads to form a net; (*fig.*) snare, entanglement. MESH (2), *v.t.* to catch in a net; ensnare; *v.i.* (of gears etc.) to engage with corresponding parts of machinery. [~OE., MDu.].

MESMERISM [mez'me-rizm], *n.* hypnotism, presumed magnetic influence exerted by one person upon another, controlling his thoughts and actions; hypnotic state so induced. MESMERIC [mez-me'rik], *adj.* pertaining to, resembling, resulting from, m. MESMERIST [mez'me-rist], *n.* one who practises m. [*Mesmer*, Austrian physician].

MESMERIZE [mez'me-rīz], *v.t.* to hypnotize. MESMERIZATION, *n.* act of mesmerizing; state of being mesmerized.

MESNE [mēn], *adj.* intermediate; **m. process,** process intervening between the beginning and end of a lawsuit; **m. profits,** intermediate profits of land received by one who is wrongfully in possession. [OFr.].

MESO-, *pref.* middle. [Gk.].

MESOZOIC [me-sō-zō'ik], *adj.* (*geol.*) pertaining to the period between the Palaeozoic and Cainozoic eras. [Gk.].

MESS (1) [mes], *n.* soft, pulpy food for animals; hodge-podge, medley; state of dirty untidiness or disorder; muddle, awkward situation; (*coll.*) a nuisance; group of persons, *esp.* in the fighting forces, who regularly dine together; messroom. MESS (2), *v.t.* to soil, spoil, dirty; muddle, bungle; put into a m.; *v.i.* to take one's meals, *esp.* habitually with the same group of persons; **to m. about,** to waste time doing nothing. [OFr.].

MESSAGE [me'sij], *n.* communication sent by one person to another by means of an intermediary; divine revelation. [Fr.].

MESSENGER [me'sen-jer], *n.* one who bears a message, *esp.* one employed in delivering dispatches or business communications; **Queen's m.,** one carrying British diplomatic mails. [OFr.].

MESSIAH [mi-sī'ah], *n.* the promised redeemer of the Jews; Jesus Christ as this; deliverer of a downtrodden people. MESSIANIC [me-si-a'nik], *adj.* pertaining to a m. [Heb.].

MESSIEURS [mes-yur'], *n. pl. of* MONSIEUR. [Fr.].

MESSMATE [mes'māt], *n.* companion at meals in a mess; (*coll.*) friend, colleague, shipmate.

MESSROOM [mes'rōōm], *n.* room in which a mess assembles.

MESSRS. [me'serz], *n.(pl.)* title placed before the name of a firm, or at the head of a list of men's names. [MESSIEURS].

MESSUAGE [me'swij], *n.* (*leg.*) dwelling-house together with the outbuildings and land attached thereto. [OFr.].

MESSY [me'si], *adj.* (*coll.*) in a mess, dirty, untidy, confused.

MESTIZO [mes-tē'zō], *n.* child of a Spaniard, Portuguese or Creole, and an American Indian. [Span.].

META-, *pref.* beyond; after; with; between; among; frequently expressing change. [Gk.].

METABOLISM [me-ta'bo-lizm], *n.* (*biol.*) continual chemical change in living organisms, by which living matter is gradually built up, and complex substances broken down. METABOLIC [me-ta-bo'lik], *adj.* pertaining to, resulting from, m. METABOLIZE [me-ta'bo-līz], *v.t.* to change by m. [Gk.].

METACARPAL [me-ta-kah'pal], *adj.* pertaining to the metacarpus; **m. bones,** bones between the wrist and the fingers.

METACARPUS [me-ta-kah'pus], *n.* (*anat.*) the part

of the hand lying between the wrist and the fingers. [Gk.].

METAL (1) [me'tal], *n.* a malleable, ductile electropositive element, fusible by heat, a good conductor of heat and electricity, usually lustrous, and usually solid at ordinary temperatures; glass in a state of fusion; stones broken small for road-making; (*pl.*) rails. METAL (2), *adj.* made of m. METAL (3) (*pres.pt.* METALLING, *pret.* and *p.pt.* METALLED), *v.t.* to cover with m.; repair or make roads with stones broken small. [Gk.].

METALLIC [me-ta'lik], *adj.* pertaining to, like, containing, consisting of, metal; having a sound like that produced when metal is struck; **m. currency,** currency in which metal coins are used. [Gk.].

METALLIFEROUS [me-ta-li'fe-rŏŏs], *adj.* producing metal. [L.].

METALLINE [me'ta-līn], *adj.* pertaining to, consisting of, containing, metal, resembling metal.

METALLING [me'ta-ling], *n.* broken stone used in road construction or repair; process of repairing or making roads with this.

METALLIZE [me'ta-līz], *v.t.* to form into metal; give metallic qualities to. METALLIZATION [me-ta-li-zā'shn], *n.* act of metallizing; state of being metallized.

METALLURGY [me-ta'ler-ji], *n.* science of extracting, smelting, refining and generally preparing metals. METALLURGIC [me-ta-lur'jik], *adj.* relating to m. METALLURGIST [me'ta-ler-jist], *n.* worker in metals; one skilled in m. [Gk.].

METAMORPHIC [me-ta-maw'fik], *adj.* displaying change of form; (*geol.*) changed in structure or form under external influence. METAMORPHISM, *n.* state of being m., *esp.* of rocks. [Gk.].

METAMORPHOSIS (*pl.* metamorphoses) [me-ta-maw'fō-sis, -sēs], *n.* change of appearance, character, structure etc., transformation. METAMORPHOSE, *v.t.* to change into a different form, transform. [Gk.].

METAPHOR [me'ta-faw(r)], *n.* figure of speech in which a word or phrase is used to describe or qualify another with which it is not normally associated, so as to imply a comparison. [Gk.].

METAPHORIC(AL) [me-ta-fo'rik(-al)], *adj.* pertaining to, of the nature of, a metaphor; containing metaphors, figurative.

METAPHYSICAL [me-ta-fi'zi-kal], *adj.* relating to, connected with, metaphysics; based on pure reasoning; insubstantial, supernatural; too subtle or nice in making distinctions.

METAPHYSICIAN [me-ta-fi-zi'shan], *n.* one skilled in metaphysics.

METAPHYSICS [me-ta-fi'ziks], *n.(pl.)* study of the ultimate problems and principles behind all being and knowledge. [Gk.].

METAPSYCHIC(AL) [me-ta-sī'kik(-al)], *adj.* pertaining to mental phenomena beyond the range of normal psychology. METAPSYCHICS, *n.(pl.)* study of m. phenomena. [META and PSYCHICS].

METAPSYCHOLOGY [me-ta-sī-ko'lo-ji], *n.* theoretical study of the workings of the mind which are not susceptible of investigation by experiment.

METASTASIS (*pl.* metastases) [me-tas'ta-sis, -sēz], *n.* removal of a bodily function or of the seat of a disease into another part of the body; (*biol.*) metabolism; (*fig.*) change, transformation. [Gk.].

METATARSAL [me-ta-tah'sal], *adj.* pertaining to, involving, the metatarsus.

METATARSUS [me-ta-tah'sus], *n.* the group of five bones between the ankle and toes. [Gk.].

METATHESIS [me-ta'thi-sis], *n.* (*phon.*) transposition of sounds or letters in a word. [Gk.].

METE [mēt], *v.t.* (*poet., archaic*) to measure; deal out, distribute. [OE.].

METEMPSYCHOSIS [me-tem-sī-kō'sis], *n.* the passing over of the soul after death from one body to another.

METEOR [mē'ti-er], *n.* transitory luminous body, heated by friction as it shoots through the atmosphere; (*fig.*) anything which dazzles and does not last. [Gk.].

METEORIC [mē-ti-o'rik], *adj.* pertaining to the atmosphere; pertaining to, resulting from, meteors; (*fig.*) sudden, swift and dazzling. METEORICALLY, *adv.* with m. speed.

METEORITE [mē'ti-o-rīt], *n.* meteor, or part of one, which has fallen upon the earth.

METEOROLOGY [mē-ti-o-ro'lo-ji], *n.* scientific study of the atmosphere and its phenomena, *esp.* with regard to its effect upon the weather; atmospheric conditions of a particular region. METEOROLOGICAL

The accent ' after a syllable = stress (u-pon'). The mark ‾ over a vowel = length (ā in made; ō in bone).

[mē-ti-o-ro-lo′ji-kal], *adj.* relating to m. METEORO-
LOGIST [mē-ti-o-ro′lo-jist], *n.* one versed in m.
[Gk.].
METER (1) [mē′ter], *n.* machine for regulating the
quantity or amount of anything, *esp.* the consumption of gas, water etc. METER (2), *v.t.* to measure
with a m. [Gk.].
METHANE [mē′thān], *n.* an inflammable gas.
[METHYL].
METHINKS [mi-thingks′], *v. impers.* (*archaic*) it
seems to me. [O.E.].
METHOD [me′thod], *n.* manner or way in which
anything is done; systematic arrangement or form of
procedure, *esp.* in scientific inquiry or exposition,
logical orderliness; (*bot., zool.*) classification. [Gk.].
METHODICAL [me-tho′di-kal], *adj.* displaying
method, orderly, systematic. METHODICALLY, *adv.*
in m. fashion.
METHODISM [me′tho-dizm], *n.* the principles,
doctrines and practices of the Methodists.
METHODIST [me′tho-dist], *n.* member of a nonconformist branch of the Christian Church resulting from
the movement of John and Charles Wesley and
George Whitefield. METHODISTICAL [me-tho-dis′ti-
kal], *adj.* resembling the Methodists; strictly and
rather narrowly religious.
METHODIZE [me′tho-dīz], *v.t.* to systematize.
METHOUGHT [mi-thawt′], *pret. of* METHINKS.
[O.E.].
METHYL [mē′thil], *n.* the organic radical CH₃;
m. alcohol, pyroxylic spirit, wood alcohol. [Fr.
from Gk.].
METHYLATE [me′thi-lāt], *v.t.* to mix with methyl,
esp. in order to make unfit for drinking; **methylated
spirit**, rectified spirit of wine denatured by mixing
with wood naphtha or methyl alcohol.
METICULOUS [me-ti′kyōo-lŏos], *adj.* scrupulously
exact; over-punctilious. [L.].
METIER, métier [me′tyā], *n.* profession, trade,
calling; that for which one has a special aptitude.
[Fr.].
METONYMY [me-to′ni-mi], *n.* figure of speech in
which one word is put for another it suggests. [Gk.].
METRE (1) [mē′ter], *n.* poetical rhythm; rhythmic
arrangement of syllables in verse according to some
fixed scheme. [OFr. from Gk.].
METRE (2), *n.* unit of length in the metric system,
corresponding to 39.37 in. [Fr. from Gk.].
METRIC [met′rik], *adj.* pertaining to the decimal
system of measurement based on the metre.
METRICAL [met′ri-kal], *adj.* pertaining to, using
measurement; pertaining to, written in metre.
METRICS [met′riks], *n.* theory and art of verse composition and metre.
METROLOGY [me-tro′lo-ji], *n.* science of weights
and measures. METROLOGICAL [met-ro-lo′ji-kal],
adj. pertaining to m. METROLOGIST [me-tro′lo-jist],
n. one learned in m. [Gk.].
METRONOME [met′rŏ-nōm], *n.* (*mus.*) instrument
consisting of a weighted pendulum worked by clockwork, which can be adjusted to beat time at various
given rates. [Gk.].
METRONYMIC [met-rŏ-ni′mik], *n.* name taken
from the mother's family or from a maternal
ancestor. [Gk.].
METROPOLIS [mi-tro′po-lis], *n.* the capital, chief
city of a country; see of a metropolitan bishop.
[Gk.].
METROPOLITAN (1) [met-rŏ-po′li-tan], *adj.*
belonging to a metropolis; pertaining to a metropolitan or his see; **m. France**, France as distinct from
the French Empire. METROPOLITAN (2), *n.* bishop
who presides over the other bishops of a province;
dweller in a metropolis. [Gk.].
METTLE [me′tl], *n.* disposition, character; spirit,
courage. METTLED, *adj.* mettlesome. [METAL].
METTLESOME [me′tl-sum], *adj.* high-spirited, full
of fire.
MEW (1) [myōo], *n.* a seagull. [O.E.].
MEW (2), *v.t. and i.* to moult. MEW (3), *v.t.* to confine
in a cage during moulting time; imprison. MEW (4),
n. a cage for hawks, *esp.* during moulting time; (*pl.*)
(*hist.*) royal stables in London, built upon the site
where the king's hawks were mewed; (*pl. treated
grammatically as sg.*) series of stables built round an
open yard. [Fr.].
MEW (5), *n.* the cry of a cat. MEW (6), *v.i.* to cry as a
cat. [Echoic.].
MEWL [myōol], *v.i.* to cry as an infant, whimper;
mew like a cat. [Echoic.].
MEZZANINE [me′za-nēn], *n.* storey of small height

between two higher ones; (*arch.*) window in this;
floor below the stage of a theatre used in working
traps etc. [It.].
MEZZO [med′zō], *adj.* middle, mean; (*mus.*)
moderately; **m. rilievo**, carving in half relief. [It.].
MEZZO-SOPRANO [med-zō-sō-prah′nō], *n.* voice
between a soprano and a contralto; singer with such
a voice; part suitable in range for such a singer.
MEZZOTINT (1) [med′zō-tint], *n.* mode of engraving
on steel or copper, in which the surface of the plate
is first roughened completely, the intended lighter
parts being then scraped away; engraving so produced. MEZZOTINT (2), *v.t. and i.* to engrave in m.
[It.].
MHO [mō], *n.* the unit of electrical conductance, the
reciprocal of the ohm. [Reversed spelling of OHM].
MI [mē], *n.* (*mus.*) third note in the tonic sol-fa scale.
[L.].
MIAOW (1) [mi-ow′], *n.* the cry of a cat. MIAOW (2),
v.i. to cry as a cat. [Echoic].
MIASMA (*pl.* **miasmas, miasmata**) [mi-az′mah(z),
mi-az′ma-tah], *n.* infectious matter or pestilential
vapours floating in the air. MIASMAL, *adj.* containing m. MIASMATIC [mē-az-ma′tik], *adj.* pertaining
to, containing, caused by, m. [Gk.].
MIAUL [mi-awl′], *v.i.* to cry as a cat. [Fr.].
MICA [mī′kah], *n.* group of mineral silicates, crystal-
lizing in hexagonal transparent plates. [L.].
MICE [mīs], *n. pl. of* MOUSE. [O.E.].
MICHAELMAS [mi′kl-mas], *n.* feast of St. Michael,
29 September; **M. daisy**, composite plant bearing
pinkish-blue flowers; **M. term**, first university term
of the academic year. [The archangel *Michael*].
MICKLE, MUCKLE [mi′kl, mu′kl], *n., adj. and adv.*
(*Scots*) great; much. [OIcel.].
MICRO-, *pref.* small, minute; (*elect.*) millionth of.
[Gk.].
MICROBE [mī′krōb], *n.* a micro-organism, *esp.*
disease-producing bacteria. MICROBIAL [mī-krō′bi-
al], *adj.* pertaining to or like microbes. [Gk.].
MICRO-BIOLOGY [mī-krō-bī-o′lo-ji], *n.* study of
bacteria, schizomycetes and other micro-organisms
visible under the microscope.
MICROCEPHALIC [mī-krō-si-fa′lik], *adj.* having
an unusually small skull. [Gk.].
MICROCEPHALOUS [mī-krō-se′fa-lŏos], *adj.*
microcephalic.
MICROCOSM [mī′krō-kozm], *n.* man considered as
an epitome of the world; any community etc. regarded as constituting in itself a world on a small scale.
MICROCOSMIC(AL) [mī-krō-koz′mik(-al)], *adj.* pertaining to or constituting a m. [Gk.].
MICROFARAD [mī-krō-fa′rad], *n.* (*elect.*) the
millionth part of a farad, the practical unit of electrical capacity.
MICROHM [mī′krōm], *n.* the millionth part of an
ohm.
MICROMETER [mī-kro′mi-ter], *n.* instrument for
measuring extremely small objects or for taking
extremely fine measurements. [MICRO and METER].
MICRON [mī′kron], *n.* the millionth part of a metre.
[Gk.].
MICRO-ORGANISM [mī-krō-aw′ga-nizm], *n.* organism visible (if at all) only under the microscope.
MICROPHONE [mī′krō-fōn], *n.* instrument by
which sound is transmitted, the sound waves being
converted into electrical energy. [Gk.].
MICROPHOTOGRAPH [mī-krō-fō′to-grahf], *n.*
photograph taken on a small negative and intended
to be enlarged; a photograph taken through a
microscope. MICROPHOTOGRAPHY [mī-krō-fō-to′gra-
fi], *n.* the making of microphotographs. [MICRO and
PHOTOGRAPH].
MICRO-RAYS [mī′krō-rāz], *n.*(*pl.*) (*radio*) micro-
waves.
MICROSCOPE [mī′krō-skōp], *n.* optical or electronic
instrument for magnifying, and rendering visible,
minute objects invisible to the naked eye. MICRO-
SCOPY [mī-kro′sko-pi], *n.* use of the m.; investigation
by means of the m. [Gk.].
MICROSCOPIC(AL) [mī-krō-sko′pik(-al)], *adj.* magnifying as a microscope; visible only under the
microscope; extremely small. MICROSCOPICALLY,
adv. by or as by the microscope, extremely minutely.
MICROVOLT [mī′krō-vōlt], *n.* (*elect.*) the millionth
part of a volt.
MICRO-WAVES [mī′krō-wāvz], *n.*(*pl.*) (*radio*) ultra-
short waves, *esp.* those having a wavelength of less
than one metre.
MICTURITION [mik-tyŏor-i′shn], *n.* morbid desire
to pass water; act of urinating. [L.].

ŏō is pronounced as in *food*; ŏō as in *hood*; th as in *think*; TH as in *that*; zh as in azure. ～ = related to.

MID (1) [mid], *adj.* middle, at equal distance from extremes. [OE.].

MID (2), *prep. (poet.)* amidst. [AMIDST].

MID-DAY [mid-dā'], *n. and adj.* noon. [OE.].

MIDDEN [mi'den], *n.* pile of kitchen refuse; dunghill. [ME. ~Dan.].

MIDDLE (1) [mi'dl], *adj.* equally distant from the extremes, halfway between the beginning and the end, or between two points, intermediate; *(philol.)* (of a period in the development of a language) between the earliest stage and the modern; **m. distance**, *(paint.)* the part of a picture between foreground and background; **m. ear**, the tympanum; **m. term**, *(log.)* term common to both premises in a syllogism, with which those of the conclusion are successively compared; **m. watch**, *(naut.)* watch between midnight and 4 a.m.; **m. weight**, *(boxing)* boxer weighing more than 10 stone 7 lb. and less than 11 stone 6 lb. MIDDLE (2), *n.* the m. part or point, centre; the waist; *(log.)* a m. term; *(cricket)* guard in which the bat covers the m. stump. MIDDLE (3), *v.t.* to place in the m.; *(cricket)* hit (the ball) with the full face of the bat; *(football)* kick (the ball) into the centre of the field from the wings. [OE.].

MIDDLE AGE [mi-dl-āj'], *n.* period of life between youth and old age. MIDDLE-AGED, *adj.* having arrived at this period.

MIDDLE AGES [mi-dl-ā'jiz], *n.(pl.)* period of history between the fall of the Western Roman Empire and the Renaissance.

MIDDLEMAN [mi'dl-man], *n.* intermediate dealer, *esp.* one who buys from the producer to sell to the retailer.

MIDDLING [mid'ling], *adj.* of middle size or quality; fair, moderate; rather mediocre.

MIDDLINGS [mid'lingz], *n.(pl.)* second-class goods.

MIDDY [mi'di], *n. (coll.)* midshipman.

MIDGE [mij], *n.* fly of the family *Chironomidae*; small singing gnat. [OE.].

MIDGET (1) [mi'jet], *n.* very small person, dwarf. MIDGET (2), *adj.* tiny, miniature. [*Prec.*].

MID-IRON [mid'īern], *n. (golf)* metal-headed club of medium weight, with the head inclined so as to direct the golf-ball with a moderately low flight.

MIDLAND [mid'land], *adj.* in the interior of a country; pertaining to the Midlands; surrounded by land.

MIDLANDS [mid'landz], *n.(pl.)* the middle counties of England.

MIDNIGHT (1) [mid'nīt], *n.* the middle of the night; twelve o'clock at night; complete darkness. MIDNIGHT (2), *adj.* in the middle of the night, at m.; intensely dark; **to burn the m. oil**, to sit up late working.

MID-OFF [mid-of'], *n. (cricket)* (position of) fieldsman stationed on the off-side of the pitch, near to the bowler.

MID-ON [mid-on'], *n. (cricket)* (position of) the fieldsman stationed on the on-side of the pitch, near to the bowler.

MIDRIFF [mid'rif], *n. (anat.)* the diaphragm. [OE.].

MIDSHIP [mid'ship], *adj.* situated in, pertaining to, the middle part of a ship.

MIDSHIPMAN [mid'ship-man], *n.* naval officer ranking below a sub-lieutenant and above a cadet.

MIDSHIPS [mid'ships], *adj. and adv. (naut.)* in the middle of a ship.

MIDST (1) [midst], *n.* the middle; **in the m.**, among; completely involved or occupied in. [ME.].

MIDST (2), *prep. (poet.)* amidst.

MIDSUMMER [mid'su-mer], *n.* the summer solstice, occurring about 21 June; **M. Day**, feast of the nativity of St. John the Baptist, 24 June; **m. madness**, utter folly and recklessness.

MIDWAY [mid'wā], *adj. and adv.* (situated) halfway.

MIDWEEK [mid-wēk'], *adj.* taking place in the middle of the week.

MID-WICKET [mid-wi'kit], *n. (cricket)* (position of) the fieldsman about halfway down the wicket on the on side.

MIDWIFE (1) [mid'wīf], *n.* woman specially trained to assist women in childbirth. MIDWIFE (2), *v.t. and i.* to act as m. (to).

MIDWIFERY [mid'wi-fe-ri], *n.* art or practice of attending women in childbirth; obstetrics.

MIDWINTER [mid-win'ter], *n.* the winter solstice, falling about 21 December.

MIEN [mēn], *n.* external appearance, demeanour, bearing. [Uncert.].

MIGHT (1) [mīt], *n.* power, strength, force. [OE.].

MIGHT (2), *pret. of* MAY. [OE.].

MIGHTY (1) [mī'ti], *adj.* strong, powerful, having great authority; *(coll.)* great. MIGHTY (2), *adv. (coll.)* very, greatly. MIGHTILY, *adv.* in m. fashion; *(coll.)* greatly. [OE.].

MIGNON (*fem.* **mignonne**) [mē-nyaw(ng)', mē-nyon'], *adj.* delicate and pretty, dainty. [Fr.].

MIGNONETTE [mi-nyo-net'], *n.* a fragrant plant. [Fr.].

MIGRAINE [mi'grān, mi-grān'], *n. (med.)* sick headache, hemicrania. [Fr.].

MIGRANT (1) [mi'grant], *adj.* migratory. MIGRANT (2), *n.* creature which migrates. [L.].

MIGRATE [mi-grāt'], *v.i. (zool.)* to make an annual passage from one climate to another; move to a fresh country or district. [L.].

MIGRATION [mi-grā'shn], *n.* act of migrating; group of persons or birds who or which migrate. [L.].

MIGRATORY [mī'gra-te-ri], *adj.* that migrates.

MIKADO [mi-kah'dō], *n.* Emperor of Japan. [Jap.].

MIKE (1) [mīk], *n. (slang)* microphone.

MIKE (2), *v.i. (slang)* to idle. MIKE (3), *n. (slang)* **to be on the m.**, to have a m., to idle. [Unkn.].

MILANESE [mi-la-nēz'], *n. and adj.* inhabitant of, pertaining to, Milan; a silk or artificial silk fabric.

MILCH [milch], *adj.* yielding milk. [ME.].

MILD [mīld], *adj.* moderate, not extreme, harsh or bitter; gentle; even-tempered, not aggressive; temperate, warm. [OE.].

MILDEW (1) [mil'dyōō], *n.* whitish, small fungus appearing on plants, food etc. exposed to damp. MILDEW (2), *v.t. and i.* to affect with m.; go mildewy. [OE.].

MILE [mīl], *n.* unit of linear measurement, 1760 yards; **geographical, nautical m.**, distance of 6080 feet. [OE. from L.].

MILEAGE [mī'lij], *n.* distance travelled, measured in miles; rate of travelling, measured in miles.

MILESIAN [mi-lē'zi-an], *adj. and n.* Irish; Irishman. [*Milesius*, legendary king, supposed to have conquered Ireland].

MILESTONE [mīl'stōn], *n.* stone by the roadside to mark the end of a mile, and giving the distance to the place or places mentioned on it; *(fig.)* important event in someone's life.

MILFOIL [mil'foil], *n. (bot.)* the yarrow plant. [L.].

MILIARY [mi'li-a-ri], *adj. (path.)* resembling millet seeds; characterized by an eruption of spots like millet seeds. [L.].

MILIEU [mē'lyer], *n.* surroundings, environment. [Fr.].

MILITANCY [mi'li-tan-si], *n.* quality of being militant.

MILITANT [mi'li-tant], *adj.* pugnacious, combative; fighting, at war. MILITANTLY, *adv.* in m. fashion.

MILITARISM [mi'li-ta-rizm], *n.* spirit or opinions of a soldier or warlike person; point of view which regards military matters as of first importance; aggressive patriotism. [Fr.].

MILITARIST [mi'li-ta-rist], *n.* one versed in or concerned in military matters; advocate of militarism. MILITARISTIC [mi-li-ta-ris'tik], *adj.* pertaining to military matters; combative, pugnacious.

MILITARIZE [mi'li-ta-rīz], *v.t.* to organize on a military basis; fill with a spirit of militarism.

MILITARY (1) [mi'li-ta-ri], *adj.* pertaining to warfare and soldiering; connected with the army, warlike; **M. Cross**, army decoration awarded to officers for conspicuous courage under fire; **M. Medal**, similar army decoration for other ranks. MILITARY (2), *n.* soldiers. [L.].

MILITATE [mi'li-tāt], *v.i.* to take warlike action; **to m. against**, to oppose, be unfavourable to. [L.].

MILITIA [mi-li'shah], *n.* army recruited from the civilian population, *esp.* a civilian auxiliary force consisting of contingents from each county, available in an emergency. MILITIAMAN, *n.* member of the m. [L.].

MILK (1) [milk], *n.* white fluid secreted by the mammary glands of female mammals to nourish their young, *esp.* that secreted by cows; medical preparation resembling this; white juice of certain plants. MILK (2), *v.t.* to draw m. from the teats of; *(fig.)* extort all possible money or benefit from; *v.i.* to supply with m. MILKER, *n.* one who, or that which, milks; cow which yields m. MILKING, *n.* act of extracting m. from a m. gland; quantity of m. drawn.

MILK-BAR [milk'bah(r)'], *n.* establishment where attractively flavoured milk drinks may be bought.

The accent ' after a syllable = stress (u-pon'). The mark ‾ over a vowel = length (ā in made; ō in bone).

MILK-FLOAT [milk'flōt], *n.* small flat dray in which milk is carried round to customers.

MILKMAID [milk'mād], *n.* woman employed in milking cows and in dairy work.

MILKMAN [milk'man], *n.* man who sells milk.

MILK-PUNCH [milk-punch'], *n.* milk and spirits sweetened and mixed.

MILKSOP [milk'sop], *n.* cowardly effeminate boy.

MILK SUGAR [milk-shoo'ger], *n.* a sugar present in milk, lactose.

MILK-TEETH [milk'tēth], *n.(pl.)* first and temporary set of teeth in mammals.

MILKY [mil'ki], *adj.* resembling milk; white and opaque; full of, yielding, milk; (*fig.*) timorous, lacking spirit; **M. Way**, broad, luminous path in the heavens formed by millions of stars clustered together.

MILL (1) [mil], *n.* machine for grinding corn to flour, building in which this is done; factory; machine for grinding solid material to fine particles; corn-stamping machine; (*slang*) a fight with the fists; **to go through the m.**, to experience hardship and suffering. MILL (2), *v.t.* to grind in a m.; subject to some manufacturing process; full (cloth); roll out (metal); cut (steel) into shapes; make a raised and serrated rim round the edge of (a coin); stamp (a coin); (*slang*) beat severely with the fists; *v.i.* (of cattle) to go round in circles; (*slang*) fight with the fists. [O.E.].

MILLBOARD [mil'bawd], *n.* strong pasteboard.

MILLENARIAN [mi-le-nāer'i-an], *adj. and n.* pertaining to, one who believes in, the millennium.

MILLENARY (1) [mi-le'na-ri], *adj.* consisting of a thousand, *esp.* years; pertaining to the millennium. MILLENARY (2), *n.* a thousand years; a millenarian; thousandth anniversary. [L.].

MILLENNIUM [mi-le'ni-um], *n.* period of a thousand years, *esp.* that period of a thousand years during which, according to Rev. xx, Christ is to reign in person on earth; golden era of happiness and prosperity. MILLENNIAL, *adj.* relating to the m. [L.].

MILLEPEDE, see MILLIPEDE.

MILLER [mi'ler], *n.* owner or manager of a flour mill; moth with white powdered wings; **m.'s thumb**, small freshwater fish.

MILLESIMAL [mi-le'si-mal], *adj.* thousandth; consisting of, reckoned in, thousandths. [L.].

MILLET [mi'lit], *n.* any of several cereals producing small seeds, *esp. Panicum miliaceum*, an East Indian plant. [Fr.].

MILL-HAND [mil'hand], *n.* subordinate worker in a factory.

MILLIARD [mil'yahd], *n.* a thousand millions. [Fr.].

MILLIGRAMME [mi'li-gram], *n.* thousandth part of a gramme, ·0154 of a grain. [Fr.].

MILLILITRE [mi'li-lē-ter], *n.* thousandth part of a litre, ·06103 cubic in. [Fr.].

MILLIMETRE [mi'li-mē-ter], *n.* thousandth part of a metre, ·03937 in. [Fr.].

MILLINER [mi'li-ner], *n.* one who makes or sells hats and other apparel, such as lace and ribbons, for women. [*Milaner*, dealer in Milan goods].

MILLINERY [mi'li-ne-ri], *n.* articles sold by milliners; business or shop of a milliner.

MILLING [mi'ling], *n.* act of one who mills; serrated rim of a coin.

MILLION [mil'yun], *n.* a thousand thousands; (*fig.*) very great number; **the m.**, the general public. [Fr.].

MILLIONAIRE [mil-yu-nāer'], *n.* man worth a million francs, dollars or pounds; (*pop.*) very rich man. [Fr.].

MILLIONTH (1) [mil'yunth], *adj.* the ordinal of a million; being one of a million equal parts. MILLIONTH (2), *n.* one of a million equal parts.

MILLIPEDE, MILLEPEDE [mi'li-pēd], *n.* species of myriapod with a large number of legs. [L.].

MILLPOND [mil'pond], *n.* reservoir used in working a water-mill.

MILLRACE [mil'rās], *n.* current of water which works a mill-wheel.

MILLS BOMB [milz-bom'], *n.* oval-shaped hand-grenade. [*Mills*, inventor].

MILLSTONE [mil'stōn], *n.* one of a pair of heavy circular flat stones between which corn is milled; (*fig.*) heavy drag or encumbrance.

MILL-STREAM [mil'strēm], *n.* stream used to drive a water-mill.

MILL-WHEEL [mil'wēl], *n.* water-driven wheel which works the machinery of a mill.

MILREIS [mil'rās], *n.* a Portuguese coin; a Brazilian coin. [Portug.].

MILT (1) [milt], *n.* spawn or roe of the male fish. MILT (2), *v.t.* to discharge m. [O.E.].

MIME (1) [mīm], *n.* (*Gk., Rom. antiq.*) kind of farce full of mimicry and burlesque; actor in this; dumb show; buffoon, mimic. MIME (2), *v.i.* to play in a m.; act with expressive gestures; *v.t.* to mimic, *esp.* in dumb show. [Gk.].

MIMEOGRAPH (1) [mi'mi-o-grahf], *n.* apparatus for making a stencil copy to be used in a duplicating machine. MIMEOGRAPH (2), *v.t.* to copy by means of a m. [MIME and GRAPH].

MIMETIC [mi-me'tik], *adj.* imitative; skilful in mimicking; (*bot., zool.*) exhibiting mimicry. [Gk.].

MIMIC (1) [mi'mik], *adj.* imitative; that mimics; counterfeit; mock, copied on a small scale. MIMIC (2), *n.* one who mimics. MIMIC (3), *v.t.* to imitate in exaggerated manner, burlesque, *esp.* in order to ridicule; take on the appearance of, resemble; (*bot., zool.*) resemble its natural surroundings or another animal or plant, *esp.* for protection. [L.].

MIMICRY [mi'mi-kri], *n.* act of, skill in, mimicking; imitation, copy; (*bot., zool.*) characteristic by which an animal or plant mimics another or its surroundings.

MIMOSA [mi-mō'zah], *n.* large genus of leguminous plants, including the sensitive plant. [L.].

MINARET [mi-ne-ret'], *n.* tall turret, attached to a mosque and containing balconies from which the muezzin summons the people to prayer. [Arab.].

MINATORY [mi'na-te-ri], *adj.* threatening. [LL.].

MINCE (1) [mins], *v.t. and i.* to chop into very small pieces; express in mild, watered-down terms; speak, pronounce or walk in an affectedly genteel manner; **not to m. matters**, to speak plainly and directly. MINCE (2), *n.* meat chopped up into very small pieces, served as a dish when cooked. [O.Fr.].

MINCEMEAT [mins'mēt], *n.* mixture of raisins and currants with chopped candied peel, suet, apples etc.; **to make m. of**, to destroy, break up etc.

MINCEPIE [mins-pī'], *n.* pie made with mincemeat.

MINCER [min'ser], *n.* one who minces; mincing-machine.

MINCING [min'sing], *adj.* walking or speaking in an affected dainty manner.

MINCING-MACHINE [min'sing-ma-shēn], *n.* machine for mincing meat etc.

MIND (1) [mīnd], *n.* memory, remembrance; intellect, reason, intelligence; man, as possessing this; will-power; moral, ethical or intellectual outlook; cognitive, emotional and volitional capacities in man; cognitive power alone; opinions, thoughts; intention, desire; (*philos.*) that aspect of reality other than matter; **to have something on one's m.**, to be worried; **to be in two minds**, to hesitate; **to have a good m. to**, to feel strongly inclined to; **presence of m.**, ability to adapt oneself rapidly to unforeseen situations. MIND (2), *v.t.* to pay attention to; care about, object to; be on one's guard against; take care of, look after; (*archaic and dial.*) remember; feel strongly about; *v.i.* to take heed, be careful; object. MINDED, *adj.* having a particular kind of m.; disposed, inclined. [O.E.].

MINDFUL [mīnd'fool], *adj.* attentive, heedful.

MINDLESS [mīnd'les], *adj.* without a mind, unreasoning; heedless.

MINE (1) [mīn], *n.* a deep excavation in the earth from which minerals are dug; this together with its attendant machinery and buildings; a charge of explosive used for blowing up fortifications etc.; container filled with explosives, fitted with a detonator and used for destructive purposes; (*fig.*) abundant store of. MINE (2), *v.t. and i.* to dig a m. in (the earth); dig (minerals) from the earth in a m.; blow up with a m.; lay a m. or mines in or under; (*fig.*) undermine. [Fr.].

MINE (3), *pron. possessive 1st person sg.* belonging or pertaining to me. [O.E.].

MINEFIELD [mīn'fēld], *n.* (*milit., naut.*) area on land or sea which has been mined.

MINELAYER [mīn'lā-er], *n.* vessel for laying mines at sea; member of the crew of this.

MINER [mī'ner], *n.* one who digs in the earth for minerals; (*milit.*) soldier trained in the use of mines. [O.Fr.].

MINERAL (1) [mi'ne-ral], *adj.* pertaining to, consisting of, of the nature of, a mineral; (*chem.*) inorganic; **m. jelly**, petroleum jelly; **m. kingdom**, third great division of natural objects comprising substances other than animal or vegetable; **m. waters**, waters

---

ōō is pronounced as in *food*; ŏŏ as in *hood*; th as in *think*, TH as in *that*; zh as in *azure*. ~ = related to.

DSE—N

impregnated with m. matter; (coll.) aerated drinks. MINERAL (2), n. any substance dug from the earth by mining; (chem.) natural inorganic substance with a definite chemical composition; (coll. pl.) aerated drinks. [MedL.].

MINERALIZE [mi'ne-ra-līz], v.t. to convert into a mineral; impregnate with mineral matter; combine with a metal to form an ore; v.i. to go out collecting minerals.

MINERALOGICAL [mi-ne-ra-lo'ji-kal], adj. relating to mineralogy. MINERALOGICALLY, adv. according to mineralogy.

MINERALOGY [mi-ne-ra'lo-ji], n. scientific study of minerals. MINERALOGIST, n. one learned in m. [MINERAL and Gk.].

MINESWEEPER [mīn'swē-per], n. vessel specially fitted with nets for clearing a minefield; member of the crew of this.

MINE-THROWER [mīn'thrō-er], n. trench mortar firing a high-explosive shell. [Transl. of Germ.].

MINGLE [ming'gl], v.t. and i. to mix, unite, blend; become an indistinguishable part. [ME. from OE.].

MINIATURE (1) [mi'na-tyoor], n. illumination in a manuscript; small-scale portrait in oil or water-colours on vellum or ivory; reproduction on a small scale; in m., on a small scale. MINIATURE (2), adj. in the form of a m.; on a small scale. MINIATURIST, n. painter of miniatures; one who uses m. cameras. [It.].

MINIKIN [mi'ni-kin], n. tiny object; dwarfish person. [Du.].

MINIM [mi'nim], n. (mus.) note equal in time value to half a semibreve; smallest liquid measure, one-sixtieth of a fluid drachm, a single drop; single down stroke in writing. [L.].

MINIMALIST [mi'ni-ma-list], n. a Menshevik; one who is ready to accept temporarily his minimum political demands.

MINIMIZE [mi'ni-mīz], v.t. to reduce as far as possible; under-emphasize, underestimate.

MINIMUM (1) (pl. minima) [mi'ni-mum], n. the least possible quantity or amount. MINIMUM (2), adj. least or smallest possible required or recorded. [L.].

MINIMUS (1) [mi'ni-mus], n. person or thing of the smallest size. MINIMUS (2), adj. (school coll.) denoting the youngest of three or more boys of the same name. [L.].

MINING [mī'ning], n. act of working a mine or laying mines.

MINION [min'yon], n. favourite, darling; servile hireling, toady; small printing-type. [Fr.].

MINISTER (1) [mi'nis-ter], n. agent; person appointed to direct a particular branch of government or state administration; representative of a government at a foreign court, of lower rank than an ambassador; (eccles.) one who conducts the service at public worship, esp. a nonconformist clergyman. MINISTER (2), v.i. to attend to the wants of another; tend to promote; act as a m. of religion. [L.].

MINISTERIAL [mi-nis-tēer'i-al], adj. belonging to a minister or to a ministry; supporting the government ministers; acting or performed at the bidding of a superior. MINISTERIALIST, n. supporter of the ministry in power. MINISTERIALLY, adv. in a m. manner or capacity. [L.].

MINISTRANT (1) [mi'nis-trant], adj. that ministers, helping. MINISTRANT (2), n. person who ministers. [L.].

MINISTRATION [mi-nis-trā'shn], n. act of ministering to or performing services for, esp. as a minister of religion. [L.].

MINISTRY [mi'nis-tri], n. act of ministering; office or duties of a minister; body of ministers; vocation of a minister of religion; (pol.) the Cabinet; a state department; term of office as a minister. [L.].

MINIUM [mi'ni-um], n. red lead.

MINIVER [mi'ni-ver], n. kind of white fur with occasional black markings, used for ceremonial robes. [OFr.].

MINK [mingk], n. carnivore of the weasel family greatly prized for its fur; fur of this animal. [~Swed.].

MINNESINGERS [mi'ni-sing-erz], n.(pl.) a body of lyric poets or singers in medieval Germany. [Germ.].

MINNOW [mi'nō], n. a small freshwater fish; artificial fish resembling this, used as a bait. [Fr.].

MINOAN [mi-nō'an], adj. and n. relating to, a native of, the prehistoric civilization of Crete. [Minos, fabled king of Crete].

MINOR (1) [mī'ner], adj. less, inferior; slight, unimportant; (surg.) (of operations) with no expected danger to life; (mus.) less by a semitone than a major interval; m. canon, clergyman who officiates in the services of a cathedral but is not a member of the chapter; m. orders, (R.C.) lesser orders below that of subdeacon; m. key, key in which the semitones occur between the second and third, and the fifth and sixth notes of the scale; m. term, (log.) subject of the conclusion of a syllogism; m. premise, (log.) premise containing the m. term; m. suit, (bridge) diamonds or clubs. MINOR (2), n. person who has not yet come of age; (mus.) m. key or mode; (log.) m. term or m. premise; (eccles.) Franciscan friar. [L.].

MINORCA [mi-naw'kah], n. one of a breed of domestic fowl originating in Minorca in the Balearic Islands.

MINORITE [mī'ne-rīt], n. Franciscan friar. [L.].

MINORITY [mi-no'ri-ti], n. state of being under legal age; period of life embraced by this state; the smaller number. [MedL.].

MINSTER [min'ster], n. the church of a monastery; cathedral church. [OE.].

MINSTREL [min'strel], n. (hist.) one who earned his living as an itinerant entertainer, esp. one who recited or sang poetry; poet, musician or singer; nigger m., one of a band of singers, banjoists and entertainers with blackened faces. [LL.].

MINSTRELSY [min'strel-si], n. art or occupation of minstrels; group of minstrels; songs or poetry of minstrels. [OFr.].

MINT (1) [mint], n. aromatic plant, producing a pungent essential oil, and used for flavouring. MINT-JULEP, drink of whisky or brandy, sugar and pounded ice, flavoured with m. MINT-SAUCE, sauce made of chopped mint, vinegar and sugar. [OE. from L.].

MINT (2), n. place where money is officially coined and issued; origin, source; (fig.) abundant supply. MINT (3), adj. (of a stamp, coin, book etc.) in its unused state. MINT (4), v.t. to coin and stamp; (fig.) invent. MINTER, n. coiner; (fig.) inventor. [OE. from L.].

MINTAGE [min'tij], n. process of minting money; that which is minted, esp. at a particular mint at a specific time; duty paid for minting.

MINUET [mi-nyoo-et'], n. slow graceful dance in triple time; music for this. [Fr.].

MINUS (1) [mī'nus], prep. with the deduction of; m. quantity, (math.) quantity preceded by a m. sign; m. charge, (elect.) negative charge. MINUS (2), n. sign denoting subtraction. [L.].

MINUSCULE [mi-nus'kyool], n. small letter; small cursive script which arose about the seventh century; (print.) lower-case letter. [L.].

MINUTE (1) [mi'nit], n. sixtieth part of an hour or a degree; moment; brief note or memorandum, esp. a comment on a document in official files; (pl.) summarized record of the business at a formal meeting. MINUTE-BOOK, book in which minutes are recorded. MINUTE-GUN, gun fired every m., as a signal of distress or mourning. MINUTE-HAND, hand which registers the minutes on the dial of a clock or watch. MINUTE (2), v.t. to time exactly; record in a m. or minutes; v.i. to write a m. [L.].

MINUTE (3) [mi-nyoot'], adj. very small; trifling; precise, exact, detailed. MINUTELY, adv. in m. fashion, punctiliously. [L.].

MINUTIAE [mi-nyoo'shi-ē], n.(pl.) particulars or details of lesser importance. [L.].

MINX [mingks], n. pert girl, hussy. [Uncert.].

MIOCENE [mī'ō-sēn], adj. (geol.) of the middle division of the Tertiary era or group of rocks. [Gk.].

MIRACLE [mi'ra-kl], n. event which seems contrary to, or inexplicable by, the laws of nature, and which is thus regarded as the work of a Divine Power; extremely remarkable happening; extraordinary example; m. play, form of drama, popular in the Middle Ages, depicting the fall and redemption of man. [L.].

MIRACULOUS [mi-ra'kyoo-loŏs], adj. of the nature of or approaching a miracle, wonderful, extraordinary. [Fr.].

MIRAGE [mi'rahzh], n. optical illusion, due to certain atmospheric conditions, by which objects appear out of their true position; (fig.) deceptive hope. [Fr.].

MIRE (1) [mīer], n. thick mud, boggy ground; (fig.) defilement, dirt. MIRE (2), v.t. to immerse in m.; daub with mud; defile; v.i. to sink in thick mud. [OIcel.].

MIRK, see MURK.

MIRROR (1) [mi'rer], n. piece of glass backed with metal, or a highly polished surface, which reflects an image; (fig.) pattern, model; reflection, representation. MIRROR (2), v.t. to reflect as in a m. [OFr.].

MIRTH [murth], *n.* merriment, gaiety, laughter. [OE.].
MIRTHFUL [murth'fŏŏl], *adj.* merry, jovial.
MIRTHLESS [murth'les], *adj.* sad, joyless; sardonic.
MIRY [mier'i], *adj.* abounding in mire; muddy.
MIS-, *pref.* wrong, ill, badly, unfavourable. [OE., OFr.].
MISADVENTURE [mi-sad-ven'tyŏŏr], *n.* mishap, ill-luck, accident; **by m.**, accidentally.
MISALLIANCE [mi-sa-li'ans], *n.* improper alliance; unsuitable marriage.
MISANTHROPE [mi'san-thrŏp], *n.* one who hates and shuns mankind. MISANTHROPIC [mi-san-thro'-pik], *adj.* hating mankind. [Gk.].
MISANTHROPY [mi-san'thro-pi], *n.* hatred of mankind. MISANTHROPIST, *n.* misanthrope.
MISAPPLY [mi-sa-pli'], *v.t.* to apply or use wrongly.
MISAPPREHEND [mi-sa-pri-hend'], *v.t.* to misunderstand. MISAPPREHENSION [mi-sa-pri-hen'shn], *n.* a misunderstanding, mistaken idea or belief.
MISAPPROPRIATE [mi-sa-prŏ'pri-āt], *v.t.* to apply to a wrong purpose; (*leg.*) convert wrongfully to one's own use (money etc. entrusted). MISAPPROPRIATION [mi-sa-prŏ-pri-ā'shn], *n.* act of misappropriating.
MISBECOME [mis-bi-kum'], *v.t.* to suit ill.
MISBEGOTTEN [mis-bi-go'ten], *adj.* unlawfully or irregularly begotten, bastard.
MISBEHAVE [mis-bi-hāv'], *v.i.* to behave badly.
MISCALCULATE [mis-kal'kyŏŏ-lāt], *v.t.* and *i.* to calculate wrongly, misjudge.
MISCALL [mis-kawl'], *v.t.* to call by a wrong name; (*dial.*) abuse; (*cards etc.*) call incorrectly.
MISCARRIAGE [mis-ka'rij], *n.* act of miscarrying; instance of this, *esp.* a premature birth.
MISCARRY [mis-ka'ri], *v.i.* to go wrong or astray; fail to be carried out, executed or administered properly; give birth prematurely.
MISCEGENATION [mi-si-je-nā'shn], *n.* interbreeding and mingling of races, *esp.* between whites and blacks. [L.].
MISCELLANEA [mi-se-lā'ni-ah], *n.(pl.)* miscellany; miscellaneous articles. [L.].
MISCELLANEOUS [mi-se-lā'ni-ŏŏs], *adj.* mixed, consisting of various kinds. [L.].
MISCELLANY [mi'se-la-ni, mi-se'la-ni], *n.* a mixture of various kinds; *esp.* a collection of writings or compositions of various kinds, or by various writers. [L.].
MISCHANCE [mis-chahns'], *n.* misfortune, accident, bad luck. [OFr.].
MISCHIEF [mis'chif], *n.* harm, injury, damage; wilful wrongdoing; disorder, unrest; trouble, vexatious action or conduct; roguishness; troublesome child; **to make m.**, to cause ill-feeling. [OFr.].
MISCHIEVOUS [mis'chi-vŏŏs], *adj.* making mischief; naughty, continually getting into mischief; harmful; annoying; arch, roguish. [AFr.].
MISCONCEIVE [mis-kon-sēv'], *v.t.* and *i.* to entertain a false notion, misapprehend.
MISCONCEPTION [mis-kon-sep'shn], *n.* false conception, wrong idea.
MISCONDUCT (1) [mis-kon'dukt], *n.* improper conduct, misbehaviour, adultery. MISCONDUCT [mis-kon-dukt'], *v.t.* to manage badly; (*reflex.*) behave improperly.
MISCONSTRUCTION [mis-kon-struk'shn], *n.* false interpretation of words or actions.
MISCONSTRUE [mis-kon-strŏŏ'], *v.t.* to interpret or translate inaccurately, misunderstand.
MISCREANT (1) [mis'kri-ant], *adj.* scoundrelly, vile. MISCREANT (2), *n.* scoundrel, base fellow, villain. [OFr.].
MISCUE (1) [mis-kyŏŏ'], *n.* (*billiards*) faulty stroke in which the cue-ball is not struck truly. MISCUE (2) (*pres. pt.* MISCUEING), *v.i.* (*billiards*) to make a m.
MISDEED [mis-dēd'], *n.* a wicked deed.
MISDEMEAN [mis-di-mēn'], *v. reflex.* to misbehave oneself. MISDEMEANANT, *n.* one guilty of a misdemeanour.
MISDEMEANOUR [mis-di-mē'ner], *n.* (*leg.*) indictable offence less serious than felony; petty offence.
MISE-EN-SCENE, mise-en-scène [mēz-ah(ng)-sān'], *n.* the setting of a play; external environment. [Fr.].
MISER [mi'zer], *n.* a stingy hoarder of wealth, avaricious person. [L.].
MISERABLE [mi'ze-ra-bl], *adj.* unhappy, sad; in discomfort; depressing; poor; scanty, meagre; squalid, uncomfortable; wretched. MISERABLY, *adv.* in a m. way. [L.].
MISERE, misère [mi-zāer'], *n.* a call in solo whist in

which the caller undertakes to lose every trick. [Fr.].
MISERERE [mi-ze-rēer'i], *n.* the fifty-first Psalm; a musical setting for this; cry for mercy; misericord seat. [L.].
MISERICORD [mi-se'ri-kawd], *n.* projection on the under side of a hinged seat of a church choir stall, made to support a person standing. [L.].
MISERLY [mi'zer-li], *adj.* avaricious; covetous; niggardly, like a miser.
MISERY [mi'ze-ri], *n.* wretchedness; distress, unrelieved unhappiness; extreme pain or anguish. [L.].
MISFEASANCE [mis-fē'zans], *n.* a trespass, wrongful act; (*leg.*) the doing in a wrongful way of a perfectly legal act. [OFr.].
MISFIRE (1) [mis-fier'], *v.i.* to fail to go off; (of an engine) fail to explode the mixture in one or more cylinders, or explode it out of turn; (*fig.*) fail to produce the desired effect. MISFIRE (2), *n.* failure of a firearm to go off; imperfect ignition in one or more of the cylinders of an internal combustion engine; (*fig.*) something which misfires badly.
MISFIT [mis'fit], *n.* a bad fit; anyone or anything not suited to his or its environment or occupation.
MISFORTUNE [mis-faw'tyŏŏn], *n.* bad luck; mishap, disaster.
MISGIVE (*pret.* **misgave**, *p.pt.* **misgiven**) [mis-giv'], *v.t.* to cause fear, suspicion, doubt.
MISGIVING [mis-gi'ving], *n.* a losing of confidence or trust; doubt, scruple.
MISGUIDE [mis-gid'], *v.t.* to mislead, mismanage.
MISGUIDED [mis-gi'did], *adj.* and *p.pt.* led astray, ill-advised, mistaken. MISGUIDEDLY, *adv.* in a m. manner.
MISHANDLE [mis-han'dl], *v.t.* to mismanage; handle wrongly; ill-treat.
MISHAP [mis-hap'], *n.* an accident. [MIS and HAP].
MISINTERPRET [mis-in-tur'prit], *v.t.* and *i.* to interpret incorrectly.
MISJUDGE [mis-juj'], *v.t.* to judge wrongly; fail to appreciate or estimate correctly. MISJUDG(E)-MENT, *n.* act of misjudging; a wrong judgment.
MISLAY (*pret.* and *p.pt.* **mislaid**) [mis-lā'], *v.t.* to forget where one has put something, lose for a time.
MISLEAD (*pret.* and *p.pt.* **misled**) [mis-lēd', -led'], *v.t.* to lead astray, deceive.
MISNOMER [mis-nō'mer], *n.* a wrong or unsuitable name. [OFr.].
MISO-, *pref.* hatred. [Gk.].
MISOGAMIST [mī-so'ga-mist, mi-so'ga-mist], *n.* one who hates marriage.
MISOGAMY [mī-so'ga-mi, mi-so'ga-mi], *n.* hatred of marriage. [Gk.].
MISOGYNIST [mī-so'ji-nist, mi-so'ji-nist], *n.* one who hates women.
MISOGYNY [mī-so'ji-ni, mi-so'ji-ni], *n.* hatred of women. [Gk.].
MISPLACE [mis-plās'], *v.t.* to lay in a wrong place; mislay; misdirect.
MISPRINT (1) [mis-print'], *v.t.* and *i.* to print incorrectly. MISPRINT (2) [mis'print], *n.* mistake in printing, printer's error.
MISPRISION [mis-pri'zhn], *n.* a mistake; (*leg.*) failure of duty, misdemeanour, by a public official; **m. of felony, treason,** concealment of a felony or treason. [OFr.].
MISPROPORTIONED [mis-prŏ-paw'shnd], *adj.*, badly proportioned.
MISQUOTE [mis-kwŏt'], *v.t.* to quote inaccurately.
MISREPRESENT [mis-re-pri-zent'], *v.t.* to represent or describe incorrectly, give a false impression or account of.
MISREPRESENTATION [mis-re-pri-zen-tā'shn], *n.* an (intentionally) inaccurate representation.
MISRULE (1) [mis-rŏŏl'], *n.* bad government; unruliness, insubordination; **Lord of M.,** leader of the Christmas revels in former times. MISRULE (2), *v.t.* to rule badly.
MISS (1) (*pl.* **misses**) [mis], *n.* form of address to an unmarried woman if she does not own any other title; unmarried woman; lively young girl. [MISTRESS]
MISS (2), *v.t.* and *i.* to fail to hit, meet or find, pass without touching; fail to hold, take or catch; fail to achieve or attain; fail to understand, see or hear; omit, overlook; be or do without; discover or regret the loss of; be distressed by the absence of; avoid, escape; misfire; **to m. out,** to omit; **to m. stays,** (*naut.*) to fail to go about from one tack to another. MISS (3), *n.* failure to hit, attain or get; escape;

ŏŏ is pronounced as in food; ŏŏ as in hood; th as in think; TH as in that; zh as in azure. ~ = related to.

(*billiards*) failure to hit a ball with the cue-ball; **to give a m.**, to stay away from, neglect; **near m.**, shot etc. which misses its objective by very little. [O.E.].

MISSAL [mi'sal], *n.* Roman Catholic mass-book; book of prayers or devotions, *esp.* if illuminated. [EcclesL.].

MISSEL-THRUSH [mi'sl-thrush], *n.* largest European thrush, feeding upon mistletoe. [~MISTLETOE].

MISSHAPE [mis-shāp'], *v.t.* to shape badly, deform.
MISSHAPEN [mis-shā'pen], *adj.* badly shaped, deformed.

MISSILE [mi'sīl], *n.* anything thrown or throwable, projectile.

MISSING [mi'sing], *adj.* lost; unaccounted for.

MISSION [mi'shn], *n.* a sending; what one is sent to do; those sent, delegation sent to a foreign country for a specific purpose; body of missionaries sent abroad; their outpost, their field of work; a special effort to quicken religious activity in a particular locality; centre for religious or social work among the poor. [L.].

MISSIONARY (1) [mi'shn-a-ri], *adj.* of, or concerning, missions or missionaries. MISSIONARY (2), *n.* one sent to propagate a religion, *esp.* in a heathen country; police court official whose duty is to assist defendants and those seeking the magistrate's aid.

MISSIONER [mi'shn-er], *n.* a missionary; person belonging to or directing a mission.

MISSIS, MISSUS [mi'siz], *n.* oral form of address prefixed to the name of a married woman with no other title; form of address written MRS.; (*coll.*) wife; mistress. [MISTRESS].

MISSIVE [mi'siv], *n.* a letter, *esp.* of an official character. [L.].

MIS-STATE [mis-stāt'], *v.t. and i.* to describe badly or wrongly, misrepresent.

MISSUS, see MISSIS.

MIST (1) [mist], *n.* cloud of minute particles of water formed near the surface of the earth; a blurring of the vision; (*fig.*) state of doubt; that which 'causes this. MIST (2), *v.t. and i.* to obscure, blur; form a m. [O.E.].

MISTAKABLE [mis-tā'ka-bl], *adj.* that may be mistaken or misunderstood.

MISTAKE (1) (*pret.* mistook, *p.pt.* mistaken) [mis-tāk'], *v.t. and i.* to misunderstand, make a false judgment of; identify inaccurately. MISTAKE (2), *n.* error, blunder; misunderstanding, misconception. [OIcel.].

MISTAKEN [mis-tā'ken], *adj.* wrong, erroneous; misdirected. MISTAKENLY, *adv.* by mistake.

MISTER [mis'ter], *n.* oral form of address prefixed to the name of any man not possessing any other title; form of address written MR.; also prefixed to certain titles held by virtue of office. [MASTER (1)].

MISTLETOE [mi'sl-tō], *n.* parasitic plant with white berries, growing on various trees, *esp.* on the apple and the elm. [O.E.].

MISTRAL [mē-strahl'], *n.* cold north-west wind in the south of France. [Provenc.].

MISTRESS [mis'tres], *n.* woman who rules and supervises; female head of a household or family, *esp.* one employing servants; woman teacher; concubine; woman who has mastered some specific accomplishment; (*fig.*) that which occupies a dominant position; (*archaic*) polite mode of address to a woman; (*archaic*) sweetheart. [OFr.].

MISTRUST (1) [mis-trust'], *v.t.* to suspect, doubt, have fears about. MISTRUST (2), *n.* lack of confidence, suspicion. MISTRUSTINGLY, *adv.* with m.

MISTRUSTFUL [mis-trust'fool], *adj.* suspicious.

MISTY [mis'ti], *adj.* covered with mist; obscure, blurred. [O.E.].

MISUNDERSTAND (*pret. and p.pt.* misunderstood) [mi-sun-der-stand'], *v.t.* to take in a wrong sense.

MISUNDERSTANDING [mi-sun-der-stan'ding], *n.* slight dispute, disagreement, misconception, error.

MISUSE (1) [mis-yōōz'], *v.t.* to use wrongly; maltreat. MISUSE (2) [mis-yōōs'], *n.* ill-treatment, wrong use.

MITE (1) [mīt], *n.* small parasitic arachnid sometimes found in food. [O.E.].

MITE (2), *n.* anything very small, *esp.* a small child or a small portion; (*bibl.*) small copper coin worth about half a farthing. [MDu.].

MITHRAISM [mith'rā-izm], *n.* cult of Mithras, the Persian God of Light.

MITIGABLE [mi'ti-ga-bl], *adj.* able to be mitigated.

MITIGATE [mi'ti-gāt], *v.t.* to soften, moderate or alleviate. MITIGATIVE, MITIGATORY, *adj.* having the

quality of alleviating. MITIGATOR, *n.* someone who or something which mitigates. [L.].

MITIGATION [mi-ti-gā'shn], *n.* act of mitigating; state of being mitigated; abatement.

MITRAL [mī'tral], *adj.* of, or resembling, a mitre; **m. valve**, (*anat.*) left valve of the heart.

MITRE (1) [mī'ter], *n.* (*eccles.*) head-dress of a bishop or archbishop and of certain abbots; (*fig.*) episcopal dignity. MITRE (2), *v.t.* to bestow a m. upon. [Gk.].

MITRE (3), *n.* (*carp.*) the joining of two pieces of wood at an angle, usually of 90 deg., by bevelling the adjacent edges at complementary angles. MITRE (4), *v.t.* (*carp.*) to join with a m. joint. [Uncert.].

MITRED [mī'terd], *adj.* wearing a mitre; (*carp.*) joined with a mitre joint.

MITT [mit], *n.* mitten; (*slang*) hand; (*pl.*) (*slang*) boxing-gloves. [MITTEN].

MITTEN [mi'ten], *n.* fingerless, open glove; glove with a place for the thumb, and one large compartment for the fingers. [OFr.].

MITTIMUS [mi'ti-mus], *n.* (*leg.*) warrant for committal to prison. [L.].

MIX [miks], *v.t.* to blend, mingle together; unite into a compound; prepare by combining ingredients; confuse, muddle; *v.i.* to mingle; (of persons) enjoy each other's society easily; **to m. up**, to muddle, confuse. MIX-UP, (*coll.*) a muddle.

MIXER [mik'ser], *n.* someone who or something which mixes; apparatus for blending sounds in broadcasting and talking-films; **a good m.**, person who easily gets acquainted with others.

MIXTURE [miks'tyoor], *n.* act of mixing; state of being mixed; something mixed, combination; (*chem.*) combination in which each ingredient retains its own properties; (*motoring*) vaporized oil-fuel mixed with air. [L.].

MIZEN, MIZZEN [mi'zen], *n.* (*naut.*) the aftermost sail of a ship. MIZEN-MAST, aftermost mast of a three-or-more masted ship. [Fr.].

MNEMONIC (1) [ni-mo'nik], *adj.* aiding the memory. MNEMONIC (2), *n.* device, formula etc. to aid the memory. [Gk.].

MNEMONICS [ni-mo'niks], *n.(pl.)* science of improving the memory; use of formulae and other devices to assist the memory. [Gk.].

MOAN (1) [mōn], *n.* low continued cry of pain or anguish; lamentation. MOAN (2), *v.i.* to utter a m.; (*slang*) complain; *v.t.* (*poet.*) to lament. [ME.].

MOAT [mōt], *n.* water-filled ditch around the outer wall of a fortress, castle etc. [OFr.].

MOB (1) [mob], *n.* tumultuous crowd bent on disorder; crowd, *esp.* of all types of people; rabble; (*Australian and N.Z.*) flock or herd of animals; **m. law**, rule imposed by a m. MOB (2) (*pres.pt.* MOBBING, *pret. and p.pt.* MOBBED), *v.t.* to crowd round and maltreat in enthusiastic affection or dislike. [L.].

MOB-CAP [mob'kap], *n.* frilled cap covering all the hair, formerly worn indoors by women. [~Du.].

MOBILE [mō'bīl], *adj.* easily movable, moving readily; changeable and adaptable; **m. police**, section of the police force, equipped with cars, whose special duty is to see that traffic regulations are carried out. [L.].

MOBILITY [mō-bi'li-ti], *n.* quality of being mobile.

MOBILIZATION [mō-bi-lī-zā'shn], *n.* action of mobilizing.

MOBILIZE [mō'bi-līz], *v.t. and i.* to put armed forces on a war footing; assemble; make available for use. [Fr.].

MOCCASIN [mo'ka-sin], *n.* footwear made of soft leather and worn by North American Indians; soft-soled house-slipper resembling this. [Amer-Ind.].

MOCHA [mō'kah], *n.* a fine-quality coffee; (*pop.*) coffee. [*Mocha*, Arabia, where grown].

MOCK (1) [mok], *v.t.* to ridicule, scorn, deride; burlesque; render ineffective; befool. MOCK (2), *n.* object of contempt or ridicule. MOCK (3), *adj.* imitation. [OFr.].

MOCKERY [mo'ke-ri], *n.* act of mocking; derision, ridicule; an object of this; travesty, false show.

MOCK-HEROIC [mok-hi-rō'ik], *adj.* burlesquing or mocking the heroic.

MOCKING (1) [mo'king], *n.* ridicule. MOCKING (2), *adj.* derisive, scornful. MOCKINGLY, *adv.* in a m. manner.

MOCKING-BIRD [mo'king-berd], *n.* American bird of the thrush family.

MOCK-TURTLE [mok-tur'tl], *n.* a soup, imitating turtle soup.

MODAL [mō'dal], *adj.* pertaining to a mode; (*leg.*)

(of a contract, legacy etc.) containing clauses defining the manner of its effectiveness; (*gram.*) pertaining to, indicating mood; **m. proposition,** (*log.*) one involving a statement of limitation. [MedL.].

MODE [mōd], *n.* method of procedure, manner of doing; style, custom, convention; the accepted way, current fashion; (*mus.*) system of sounds, scale in ancient Greek or medieval church music; arrangement of tones and semitones in a scale; (*log.*) manner in which a proposition is qualified or limited. [L.].

MODEL (1) [mo'del], *n.* a copy, exact resemblance, *esp.* a miniature reproduction; standard, example, to be copied; three-dimensional plan; someone who poses as a pattern for an artist; mannequin; gown, hat etc. claimed to be of distinctive design; type of construction or design, *esp.* of things which are commonly subject to frequent revision in detail, such as motor-cars. MODEL (2), *adj.* imitating or reproducing identically or to scale; set up as a m. to be imitated. MODEL (3) (*pres.pt.* MODELLING, *pret. and p.pt.* MODELLED), *v.t. and i.* to shape, fashion, mould, *esp.* as, or into, a m. of something; display as a mannequin; **to m. on,** to imitate. [OFr.].

MODELLING [mo'de-ling], *n.* the making of a model; art of working in plastic substances; way in which anything is modelled.

MODERATE (1) [mo'de-rat], *adj.* temperate, not excessive or extreme; reasonable, not rash or rigorous; medium, rather small; mediocre, limited. MODERATE (2), *n.* one who holds m. views. MODERATE [mo'de-rāt], *v.t. and i.* to keep within bounds; make less violent; become less violent; preside over as moderator. [L.].

MODERATION [mo-de-rā'shn], *n.* state of being moderate; act of moderating; abatement or avoidance of excess or extremes; (*Scots*) meeting of a congregation under a moderator to choose a new minister; (*pl.*) first public examination in the University of Oxford.

MODERATO [mo-de-rah'tō], *adv.* (*mus.*) at a moderate pace. [It.].

MODERATOR [mo'de-rā-ter], *n.* someone who or something which moderates; one who arbitrates; one who presides over an assembly; Presbyterian minister chosen to preside over a church assembly; examiner or presiding official in certain degree examinations at Oxford or Cambridge; **m. lamp,** lamp in which the flow of oil to the wick may be regulated. [L.].

MODERN (1) [mo'dern], *adj.* pertaining to, or characteristic of, the present; recent; occurring later than the 15th century; up to date, fashionable; **m. side,** the division in a school which specializes in science and modern languages. MODERN (2), *n.* modernist; one living in m. times. [L.].

MODERNISM [mo'der-nizm], *n.* present-day usage and thought; methods and principles of theologians who interpret the Bible in the light of recent ideas and research.

MODERNIST [mo'der-nist], *n.* admirer of things modern; supporter of Modernism in religion.

MODERNISTIC [mo-der-nis'tik], *adj.* characteristic of modern style or taste; consciously advanced; pertaining to Modernism.

MODERNITY [mo-dur'ni-ti], *n.* quality or condition of being modern.

MODERNIZE [mo'der-nīz], *v.t.* to make modern or adapt to modern taste. MODERNIZATION [mo-der-nī-zā'shn], *n.* act of modernizing, state or result of being modernized.

MODEST [mo'dest], *adj.* having a humble estimate of one's capabilities and merits; unassuming; bashful; chaste, exhibiting a sense of propriety and delicacy; not excessive, moderate. [L.].

MODESTY [mo'des-ti], *n.* quality of being modest; chastity; sense of delicacy and propriety. [L.].

MODICUM [mo'di-kum], *n.* small quantity. [L.].

MODIFICATION [mo-di-fi-kā'shn], *n.* act of modifying; state or result of being modified; a minor change.

MODIFICATORY [mo'di-fi-kā-te-ri], *adj.* that modifies.

MODIFY [mo'di-fī], *v.t.* to moderate, lessen, qualify; alter; (*philol.*) change one vowel by the influence of another which follows. [Fr.].

MODISH [mō'dish], *adj.* stylish; fashionable.

MODISTE [mō-dēst'], *n.* milliner, dressmaker. [Fr.].

MODULATE [mo'dyoo-lāt], *v.t. and i.* to adjust, temper, soften; inflect; vary in pitch, tone etc.; (*mus.*) pass from one key to another. [L.].

MODULATION [mo-dyoo-lā'shn], *n.* act of modulating the voice, pitch, key etc.; example of this; (*elect.*) variation in the amplitude of continuous waves of frequencies below 14,000 cycles per second. [L.].

MODULATOR [mo'dyoo-lā-ter], *n.* someone who or something which modulates; chart to show the relationship of scales and tones in the tonic sol-fa system. [L.].

MODUS [mō'dus], *n.* method or manner; **m. agendi,** way of acting; **m. operandi,** way of operating, manner of procedure; **m. vivendi,** way of living; a working agreement pending settlement. [L.].

MOGUL (1) [mō'gool], *n.* Mongolian follower of Baber or Genghiz Khan in their invasions of India; **the Great M.,** one of the former Emperors of Delhi. MOGUL (2), *adj.* pertaining to the Mongolian Empire in India. [MONGOL].

MOHAIR [mō'hāer], *n.* hair of the Angora goat; fine silky cloth made from this; an imitation of such cloth. [Arab.].

MOHAMMEDAN (1), **MAHOMETAN** [mō-ha'mi-dan], *adj.* pertaining to Mohammedanism. MOHAMMEDAN (2), MAHOMETAN, *n.* follower of Mohammed, a Moslem. [Arab.].

MOHAMMEDANISM [mō-ha'mi-da-nizm], *n.* the religion founded by Mohammed.

MOHAWK [mō'hawk], *n. and adj.* member of, pertaining to, the tribe of Mohawk Red Indians; their language; a figure in skating. [Native].

MOHICAN [mō'i-kan, mō-hē'kan], *n. and adj.* member of, pertaining to, the Mohicans, a tribe of North American Indians now extinct; their language.

MOHOCK [mō'hok], *n.* fashionable ruffian, belonging to a gang which prowled round London streets in the 18th century. [MOHAWK].

MOIDORE [moi'daw(r)], *n.* former Portuguese gold coin, worth about 27s. [Portug.].

MOIETY [moi'i-ti], *n.* a half; one of two more or less equal parts, a part; (*leg.*) exact half-share. [OFr.].

MOIL [moil], *v.t. and i.* to drudge and toil. [OFr.].

MOIRÉ (1), **moiré** [mwah'rā], *n.* a watered silk; any material with a similar appearance. MOIRE (2), *adj.* possessing a watered or clouded appearance, *esp.* of silks. [Fr.].

MOIST [moist], *adj.* somewhat wet, damp, humid.

MOISTEN [moi's(t)n], *v.t.* to make moist, damp.

MOISTURE [moi'styoor], *n.* moistness; condensed water vapour. [OFr.].

MOKE [mōk], *n.* (*slang*) a donkey. [Unkn.].

MOLAR (1) [mō'ler], *adj.* capable of grinding. MOLAR (2), *n.* large grinding tooth. [L.].

MOLAR (3), *adj.* (*mech.*) pertaining to mass. [L.].

MOLASSES [mō-la'siz], *n.* thick syrup extracted during the manufacture of sugar; thickish treacle. [Portug.].

MOLE (1) [mōl], *n.* small dark-brown spot on the human body. [OE.].

MOLE (2), *n.* stone jetty or breakwater. [L.].

MOLE (3), *n.* small burrowing mammal with a thick, blackish-brown velvety fur. [~MDu.].

MOLECAST [mōl'kahst], *n.* molehill.

MOLECULAR [mō-le'kyōo-ler], *adj.* pertaining to, or consisting of, molecules.

MOLECULE [mo'li-kyōol], *n.* (*chem., phys.*) the smallest particle of a substance capable of retaining its distinctive properties; small particle. [Fr.].

MOLEHILL [mōl'hil], *n.* little hillock of earth thrown up by a mole as it burrows.

MOLESKIN (1) [mōl'skin], *n.* skin of the mole prepared for use as a fur; strong cotton fustian the pile of which is shaved; (*pl.*) trousers of this. MOLESKIN (2), *adj.* made of m.

MOLEST [mo-lest'], *v.t.* to interfere with, pester, annoy by accosting illegally. [L.].

MOLESTATION [mō-les-tā'shn], *n.* act of molesting; state of being molested.

MOLLIFY [mo'li-fī], *v.t.* to soften, pacify, soothe.

MOLLUSC [mo'lusk], *n.* anima o the groups *Mollusca.*

MOLLUSCA [mo-lus'kah], *n.(pl.)* (*biol.*) invertebrates with soft unsegmented bodies, often enclosed in a hard shell; shell-fish. MOLLUSCAN, MOLLUSCOUS, *adj.* pertaining to m. MOLLUSCOID, *adj.* like a mollusc.

MOLLY-CODDLE (1) [mo'li-ko-dl], *n.* pampered, effeminate person. MOLLY-CODDLE (2), *v.t.* to fuss over, pamper. [MOLLY, pet-name for MARY, and CODDLE (1)].

MOLOCH [mō'lok], *n.* god of the Ammonites to

whom living human sacrifices were made; (*fig.*) anything demanding unnatural sacrifice. [Heb.].

MOLTEN [mōl'ten], *adj.* made liquid by heat, melted. [OE.].

MOLTO [mōl'tō], *adv.* (*mus.*) very. [It.].

MOLYBDENUM [mo-lib'de-num], *n.* (*chem.*) a metallic element, Mo, used as an alloy in steel manufacture. [Gk.].

MOMENT [mō'ment], *n.* brief space of time; instant; importance; (*mech.*) the measure of the power of a force in causing rotation. [L.].

MOMENTARY [mō'men-ta-ri], *adj.* instantaneous; lasting a very short time; short and quick.

MOMENTLY [mō'ment-li], *adv.* momentarily, every moment. ˉ

MOMENTOUS [mō-men'tŏŏs], *adj.* important, weighty, of moment.

MOMENTUM [mō-men'tum], *n.* the force given to a moving body by its motion; (*dynamics*) the product of mass and velocity; (*fig.*) progressive increase in effect. [L.].

MON-, see MONO-.

MONACHAL [mo'na-kal], *adj.* relating to monks; monastic.

MONACHISM [mo'na-kizm], *n.* monasticism.

MONAD [mo'nad], *n.* an organic unit; (*zool.*) hypothetical, elementary organism; (*chem.*) element having the combining power of one atom of hydrogen; (*philos.*) one of the simple individual entities of which the universe is made up in the philosophy of Leibnitz. MONADIC [mo-na'dik], *adj.* having the nature of a m. [L.].

MONARCH [mo'nahk], *n.* supreme hereditary ruler or head of a state; king, emperor; someone who or something which dominates all others. [L.].

MONARCHIC(AL) [mo-nah'kik(-al)], *adj.* pertaining to monarchy or a monarch; royal.

MONARCHISM [mo'nah-kizm], *n.* principles of monarchy.

MONARCHY [mo'nah-ki], *n.* state ruled by a single person, *esp.* a king; rule of a monarch; the idea of princely rule; **constitutional m.,** system of government in which the powers of the monarch are limited by a constitution. [Gk.].

MONASTERY [mo'nas-te-ri], *n.* abode of a community of monks. MONASTERIAL [mo-nas-tēer'i-al], *adj.* relating to a m. [EcclesL.].

MONASTIC(AL) [mo-nas'tik(-al)], *adj.* pertaining to a monastery or to monks and their way of living.

MONASTICISM [mo-nas'ti-sizm], *n.* monastic life.

MONDAY [mun'dā], *n.* second day of the week. MONDAYISH, *adj.* disinclined for work after the weekend. [OE.].

MONETARY [mu'ni-ta-ri], *adj.* of, or pertaining to, money or currency.

MONETIZE [mu'ni-tīz], *v.t.* to give a basic value to a currency; coin into money, authorize as money.

MONEY [mu'ni], *n.* piece of metal authoritatively stamped for use as a medium of exchange; any material, *esp.* engraved and watermarked paper notes, authorized for a similar use; wealth, riches; **to make m.,** to become rich. MONEY-BAGS, (*slang*) wealthy (*esp.* miserly) person. MONEY-BOX, receptacle for keeping m. or for storing savings. MONEY-BROKER, changer of m. MONEY-GRUBBER, avaricious hoarder of wealth. MONEY-MARKET, sphere of commercial and monetary transactions. MONEY-SPIDER, -SPINNER, small spider considered to bring luck. MONEY'S-WORTH, full value. [OFr.].

MONEY-CHANGER [mu'ni-chān-jer], *n.* one who deals in money, *esp.* one who changes the currency of one country for that of another.

MONEYED [mu'nid], *adj.* well-to-do.

MONEY ORDER [mu'ni-aw-der], *n.* Post Office cash token authorizing the payment of money to the recipient at a particular Post Office.

MONGER [mung'ger], *n.* dealer, trafficker. [OE.].

MONGOOSE, MUNGOOSE (*pl.* **mongooses**) [mong'gŏŏs, mung'gŏŏs], *n.* (*zool.*) the ichneumon, a small ferret-like Indian animal. [Tamil].

MONGREL (1) [mung'grel], *n.* the result of the crossing of several breeds or kinds of animals or plants, *esp.* a dog of very mixed breed. MONGREL (2), *adj.* of undefined breed. [Uncert.].

MONISM [mo'nizm], *n.* (*philos.*) belief which regards all phenomena as developed from a single principle. MONISTIC [mo-nis'tik], *adj.* relating to m. [Gk.].

MONITION [mo-ni'shn], *n.* admonition or warning, *esp.* from an ecclesiastical authority to refrain from some specific conduct.

MONITOR (1) [mo'ni-ter], *n.* one who admonishes or

advises; senior pupil chosen to perform special duties in school; warship of very shallow draught with large guns mounted in turrets; one employed to listen to foreign radio broadcasts. MONITOR (2), *v.t.* to listen to (radio broadcasts) in order to check any deviation from the allotted wavelength; listen to (foreign broadcasts) for the purpose of using or recording the matter broadcast. [L.].

MONITORIAL [mo-ni-taw'ri-al], *adj.* pertaining to monitors; warning, admonishing.

MONITORY [mo'ni-te-ri], *adj.* giving advice or warning.

MONITRESS [mo'ni-tres], *n.* female monitor.

MONK [mungk], *n.* member of a religious order of men vowed to poverty, chastity etc., and living a life of contemplation and good works in a community apart from the world. MONKERY, *n.* (*derogatory*) monasticism; monks in general; monastic practices. [L.].

MONKEY (1) [mung'ki], *n.* mammal of the order *Primates*, other than man and the lemurs, *esp.* a tailed member of this order; (*fig.*) mischievous child; striker of a pile-driver; (*slang*) £500 or $5.0; **to get (someone's) m. up,** to anger. MONKEY (2), *v.t. and i.* to mimic; play about with in a mischievous or destructive way. MONKEYISH, *adj.* mischievous and impudently playful. [Uncert.].

MONKEY-JACKET [mung'ki-ja-kit], *n.* small, close-fitting jacket worn by seamen.

MONKEY-NUT [mung'ki-nut], *n.* peanut.

MONKEY-PUZZLE [mung'ki-pu-zl], *n.* the Chilean pine, so covered with prickles that no monkey can climb it.

MONKEY-WRENCH [mung'ki-rensh], *n.* spanner having adjustable jaws.

MONKHOOD [mungk'hŏŏd], *n.* state, status or character of a monk; monks collectively.

MONKISH [mung'kish], *adj.* pertaining to, like, a monk or his way of life.

MONKSHOOD [mungks'hŏŏd], *n.* the plant *Aconitum Napellus.*

MONO-, MON-, *pref.* single, alone. [Gk.].

MONOCARP [mo'nō-kahp], *n.* (*bot.*) an annual plant. [Gk.].

MONOCHORD [mo'nō-kawd], *n.* instrument with a single string, used for the scientific measurement of musical intervals. [Gk.].

MONOCHROME [mo'nō-krōm], *n.* a painting in a single colour; manner of making or reproducing pictures in which a single colour is used. MONOCHROMATIC [mo-nō-krō-ma'tik], *adj.* in one colour. [MedL.].

MONOCLE [mo'no-kl], *n.* eye-glass for one eye. [Fr.].

MONOCOTYLEDON [mo-nō-ko-ti-lē'don], *n.* (*bot.*) plant with one seed-leaf in the embryo. MONOCOTYLEDONOUS, *adj.* with one cotyledon.

MONOCULAR [mo-no'kyŏŏ-ler], *adj.* with, or for, one eye only.

MONODIC [mo-no'dik], *adj.* relating to, of the nature of, a monody; (*mus.*) for a single voice. [Gk.].

MONODY [mo'nō-di], *n.* ode sung by one actor in a Greek tragedy; poem of lament, usually for a death; (*mus.*) composition for a single voice. [Gk.].

MONOGAMIST [mo-no'ga-mist], *n.* believer in or practicer of monogamy.

MONOGAMY [mo-no'ga-mi], *n.* practice of marriage to only one wife or one husband at one time. MONOGAMOUS, *adj.* having a single living husband or wife; believing in m. [Gk.].

MONOGRAM [mo'nō-gram], *n.* device or cipher composed of two or more letters interwoven. [Gk.].

MONOGRAPH [mo'nō-grahf], *n.* piece of writing confined to one subject or to one aspect of a subject. MONOGRAPHIC [mo-nō-gra'fik], *adj.* relating to a m. [Gk.].

MONOLITH [mo'nō-lith], *n.* monument consisting of a single stone. MONOLITHIC [mo-nō-li'thik], *adj.* of a single stone. [Gk.].

MONOLOGUE [mo'nō-log], *n.* dramatic composition or recitation for one performer; long speech by one person, *esp.* in a play or in social conversation. [Gk.].

MONOMANIA [mo-nō-mā'ni-ah], *n.* mental derangement with regard to one particular subject. MONOMANIAC, *n.* person suffering from m. [Gk.].

MONOMETALLIC [mo-nō-me-ta'lik], *adj.* (of a currency) standardized or based upon one metal. MONOMETALLISM [mo-nō-me'ta-lizm], *n.* use of a m. currency system. MONOMETALLIST [mo-nō-me'ta-list], *n.* one who advocates monometallism.

MONOMIAL [mo-nō′mi-al], *adj.* (*alg.*) of one term only. [MONO and (BINO)MIAL].

MONOPLANE [mo′nō-plān], *n.* an aircraft with one plane.

MONOPOLIST [mo-no′po-list], *n.* one who has a monopoly, or who believes in the system of monopoly.

MONOPOLIZE [mo-no′po-līz], *v.t.* to dominate, gain exclusive possession or control of.

MONOPOLY [mo-no′po-li], *n.* exclusive possession, enjoyment or control; exclusive rights of trade in an article or in certain goods, granted by authority; licence authorizing this; the goods in question. [Gk.].

MONOSYLLABLE [mo′nō-si-la-bl], *n.* word consisting of one syllable only. MONOSYLLABIC [mo-nō-si-la′bik], *adj.* of one syllable; consisting of monosyllables.

MONOTHEISM [mo′nō-thē-izm], *n.* doctrine that there is only one God. MONOTHEIST, *n.* one who believes in m. MONOTHEISTIC [mo-nō-thē-is′tik], *adj.* relating to m.

MONOTINT [mo′nō-tint], *n.* a monochrome.

MONOTONE (1) [mo′nō-tōn], *n.* one pitch or tone; a singing or speaking without variation of pitch; (*fig.*) sameness of manner; steady repetition. MONOTONE (2), *v.t. and i.* to sing or speak without variation of pitch or tone. MONOTONIC [mo-nō-to′nik], *adj.* at one pitch.

MONOTONOUS [mo-no′to-nŏos], *adj.* persisting on the same unvaried note; (*fig.*) dully repetitive, boring in its lack of variety. [Gk.].

MONOTONY [mo-no′to-ni], *n.* absence of variety of pitch or tone; (*fig.*) irksome sameness, dull uniformity. [Gk.].

MONOTYPE [mo′nō-tīp], *n.* (*biol.*) the only type or representative; (*print.*) (*prot.*) type-setting machine in which each letter is cast and set separately as required.

MONOXIDE [mo-nok′sīd], *n.* oxide with only one atom of oxygen.

MONROEISM [mun-rō′izm], *n.* principle enunciated by James Munroe that the U.S.A. should not tolerate any further interference on the American mainland by European Powers. [*J. Munroe*, President of the U.S.A. 1817-25].

MONSEIGNEUR (*pl.* **messeigneurs**) [mo(ng)-sā′nyer, *pl.* me-sā′nyer], *n.* French title of address to princes, cardinals and certain other high ecclesiastical dignitaries. [Fr.].

MONSIGNOR [mon-sē′nyaw:r], *n.* courtesy title granted by the Pope, *esp.* to officers of the Papal household. [It.].

MONSOON [mon-sŏon′], *n.* wind blowing over Southern Asia and the Indian Ocean from October to April from the north-east and from April to October from the south-west; a similar type of seasonal wind; the rainy season. [MdDu.].

MONSTER (1) [mon′ster], *n.* monstrosity, congenitally malformed creature or plant; legendary beast, either part human and part brute, or part one beast and part another; strange, huge animal; anything unusually big; person displaying brutish malice or cruelty. MONSTER (2), *adj.* huge, abnormally big. [OFr.].

MONSTRANCE [mon′strans], *n.* transparent receptacle in which the Host is shown, or in which relics are exhibited. [OFr.].

MONSTROSITY [mon-stro′si-ti], *n.* an abnormal growth or product, freak of nature; condition or quality of being monstrous; atrocious object; outrageous conduct. [LL.].

MONSTROUS [mon′strŏos], *adj.* enormous; horrible; malformed; unnatural; outrageous. [LL.].

MONTAGE [mon′tahzh], *n.* the final choice and arrangement of shots to form a cinematograph film; art of film cutting; art or act of combining photographs into one picture. [Fr.].

MONTESSORIAN [mon-ti-saw′ri-an], *adj.* pertaining to the Montessori system of infant education.

MONTH [munth], *n.* one of the twelve sections which together make up a year; period of time corresponding to any one of these; **lunar m.**, time taken to complete one revolution of the moon; period of four weeks. [OE.].

MONTHLY (1) [munth′li], *adj.* occurring, repeated month by month; **m. nurse**, female attendant on women during, and for a month after, childbirth. MONTHLY (2), *n.* publication appearing once a month. MONTHLY (3), *adv.* every month, once a month, month by month.

MONUMENT [mo′nyŏo-ment], *n.* a memorial, erection to commemorate some event or person; building or other relic of enduring historic interest; great achievement felt to be of permanent value. [L.].

MONUMENTAL [mo-nyŏo-men′tal], *adj.* relating to, serving as, a monument; of the nature of a monument; vast, impressive; **m. mason**, maker and engraver of tombstones and monuments.

MOO (1) [mŏo], *v.i.* to low or call like a cow. MOO (2), *n.* the low of a cow. [Echoic].

MOOCH, MOUCH [mŏoch], *v.i.* (*coll.*) to loiter, idle about; **to m. along**, to saunter leisurely. MOOCHER, MOUCHER, *n.* skulker, loiterer. [OFr.].

MOOD (1) [mŏod], *n.* temporary frame of mind or emotional disposition; **to be in the m. for**, to feel like. [OE.].

MOOD (2), *n.* (*gram.*) a variation in the form of a verb to express the aspect in which the act or fact denoted by the verb is regarded; (*log.*) nature or form of a syllogism; (*mus.*) mode. [MODE].

MOODY [mŏo′di], *adj.* subject to varying moods, temperamental; disgruntled, sullen. [OE.].

MOON (1) [mŏon], *n.* the satellite of the earth which revolves about it; the satellite of another planet; lunar month, four weeks; (*fig.*) object or ideal impossible to attain; **the man in the m.**, the markings visible on the surface of the full moon; **once in a blue m.**, very rarely. MOON (2), *v.i.* to loiter dreamily; **to m. about**, to wander about in an absorbed, aimless or unhappy manner. [OE.].

MOONBEAM [mŏon′bēm], *n.* ray of light reflected from the moon.

MOONCALF [mŏon′kahf], *n.* misshapen creature or abortion; dolt.

MOON-DAISY [mŏon′dā-zi], *n.* the ox-eye daisy.

MOONFACE [mŏon′fās], *n.* a round, full, moon-like face.

MOONLESS [mŏon′les], *adj.* without moonlight or moon.

MOONLIGHT (1) [mŏon′lit], *n.* the light of the moon. MOONLIGHT (2), *adj.* lit by the moon; carried out at night.

MOONLIGHTER [mŏon′li-ter], *n.* member of the Irish Land League which organized nocturnal outrages against property. MOONLIGHTING, *n.* the activities of moonlighters.

MOONLIT [mŏon′lit], *adj.* lighted by the moon.

MOONRAKER [mŏon′rā-ker], *n.* (*naut.*) sail over a skysail; (*coll.*) native of Wiltshire.

MOONSHINE [mŏon′shin], *n.* moonlight; (*coll.*) piece of airy nonsense; (*slang*) smuggled whisky. MOONSHINER, *n.* (*slang*) rum-runner; one who smuggles or distils illicitly whisky or other spirits.

MOONSTONE [mŏon′stōn], *n.* opalescent variety of potash feldspar.

MOONSTRUCK [mŏon′struk], *adj.* supposed to be affected by the moon's influence, dazed and disordered in the mind.

MOONY [mŏo′ni], *adj.* dreamy; mentally unbalanced.

MOOR (1) [mŏor], *n.* wild, open stretch of waste ground overgrown with heather, usually hilly. [OE.].

MOOR (2), *n.* a native of Morocco in North Africa. [L.].

MOOR (3), *v.t. and i.* to fasten a boat to the shore by a cable; fasten an airship to the mast at an airport. MOORAGE, *n.* place for mooring vessels. [Uncert.].

MOORCOCK [mŏor′kok], *n.* the male red grouse.

MOORHEN [mŏor′hen], *n.* the water hen.

MOORING [mŏor′ing], *n.* moorage; (*pl.*) tackle used to moor a vessel; **m. mast**, mast to which an airship may be moored.

MOORLAND [mŏor′land], *n.* moor or heath, country similar to a moor.

MOOSE [mŏos], *n.* the North American elk. [Native].

MOOT (1), **MOTE** [mŏot], *n.* (*hist.*) assembly of freemen to discuss matters affecting the community; (*leg.*) moot-court. MOOT-COURT, meeting of lawyers and law-students for legal debate on points of law. MOOT (2), *adj.* debatable, open to argument. MOOT (3), *v.t.* to propose or raise for discussion or debate. [OE.].

MOP (1) [mop], *n.* bundle of rags etc. on the end of a handle for cleaning floors etc.; (*coll.*) thick and untidy head of hair. MOP (2) (*pres.pt.* MOPPING, *pret. and p.pt.* MOPPED), *v.t.* to swill or clean with a m.; wipe; **to m. up**, (*coll.*) to get through quickly; defeat decisively; round up the remnants of a defeated force. [Uncert.].

MOP (3) (*pres.pt.* **mopping**, *pret. and p.pt.* **mopped**), *v.i.* to grimace like a monkey. MOP (4), *n.* grin or grimace as made by a monkey. [~Du.].

MOPE (1) [mōp], *v.i.* to sulk or mooch in a lifeless, low-spirited manner. MOPE (2), *n.* sulky, low-spirited person. [Uncert.].

MOPPING-UP [mo-ping-up'], *adj. and n. (milit.)* (pertaining to) the operation of rounding up enemy remnants in newly-won territory. [MOP (2)].

MOQUETTE [mo-ket'], *n.* a material used for carpeting and upholstery. [Fr.].

MORAINE [mo-rān'], *n.* accumulated debris deposited by a glacier. [Fr.].

MORAL (1) [mo'ral], *adj.* concerning conduct or habits considered as right or wrong; observing or teaching a high tone of conduct, virtuous; appealing to or accepting the obligations of what is just and right; spiritual; chaste; virtual; **m. victory,** defeat or inconclusive result which can be regarded as a victory. MORAL (2), *n.* the implied meaning, practical significance, lesson, in a story or event; *(pl.)* principles of conduct, ethics; conduct, habits or outlook considered as right or wrong, *esp.* with regard to matters of sex. MORALLY, *adv.* in a m. fashion; according to morality; in effect. [L.].

MORALE [mo-rahl'], *n.* disposition, mental state, spirit, *esp.* of troops. [Fr.].

MORALIST [mo'ra-list], *n.* writer on ethics, one who moralizes. MORALISTIC [mo-ra-lis'tik], *adj.* teaching ethics.

MORALITY [mo-ra'li-ti], *n.* moral quality, ethics; quality of being moral, virtue; chastity; *(hist.)* form of early drama in which the characters personify virtues and vices. [L.].

MORALIZE [mo'ra-līz], *v.t. and i.* to draw the moral from, render moral; make moral reflections. [Fr.].

MORASS [mo-ras'], *n.* marsh or bog; *(fig.)* difficult position. [Du.].

MORATORIUM [mo-ra-taw'ri-um], *n.* period of authorized and legal delay in the payment of debts; decree sanctioning this; official agreement to delay the fulfilment of other engagements. [L.].

MORAVIAN (1) [mo-rā'vi-an], *adj.* pertaining to Moravia or to the Moravian religious sect. MORAVIAN (2), *n.* inhabitant of Moravia; member of an eighteenth-century Protestant sect holding doctrines derived from Huss.

MORBID [maw'bid], *adj.* connected with disease; diseased; unhealthy, unwholesome; depressed or depressing. [L.].

MORBIFIC [maw-bi'fik], *adj.* tending to cause disease. [L.].

MORDANT (1) [maw'dant], *adj.* biting, pungent; bitter, sarcastic; (of pain) burning; fixative. MORDANT (2), *n.* substance used to fix colours in materials; glue to make gold leaf adhere; acid used in etching to erode the pattern on the copperplate. MORDANCY, *n.* quality of being m. [OFr.].

MORE (1) [maw(r)], *adj.* greater in quantity, size, quality, degree etc.; additional, further. MORE (2), *n.* a greater quantity, amount, number etc.; something additional. MORE (3), *adv.* to a greater degree; again, additionally; moreover; *used also to form the comparative of many adjectives and adverbs;* **m. or less,** roughly, about. [OE.].

MORELLO [mo-re'lō], *n.* a bitter, dark-coloured cherry. [LL.].

MOREOVER [maw-rō'ver], *adv.* besides, in addition.

MORESQUE, MAURESQUE [maw-resk'], *adj.* in Moorish style. [It.].

MORGANATIC [maw-ga-na'tik], *adj.* **m. marriage,** legal marriage between a male member of a royal family and a woman of lower rank by which neither she nor her children can claim princely status nor right of succession. [MedL.].

MORGUE [mawg], *n.* building where corpses are displayed for identification, mortuary. [Fr.].

MORIBUND [mo'ri-bund], *adj.* in a dying state; in the last stages of decay. [L.].

MORMON [maw'mon], *n.* member of an American religious sect founded by Joseph Smith in 1830, originally professing and practising polygamy. ["Book of *Mormon,*" allegedly ancient book, claimed to have been discovered by Smith].

MORN [mawn], *n. (poet.)* morning; *(Scots)* tomorrow. [OE.].

MORNING (1) [maw'ning], *n.* the early part of the day from midnight to noon, and *esp.* from dawn to mid-day; *(fig.)* the beginning. MORNING (2), *adj.* pertaining to, suitable for, the m.; to be done in the m., **m. coat,** cut-away tail-coat worn on formal occasions during the day. MORNING-GLORY,

a climbing plant. MORNING-ROOM, breakfast room; sitting-room for use in the m. [ME.].

MORNING-STAR [maw-ning-stah(r)'], *n.* a star, *esp.* Venus, when seen before sunrise; *(fig.)* harbinger.

MOROCCO [mo-ro'kō], *n.* fine supple leather prepared from goatskin; soft, flexible, sheepskin imitation of this. [*Morocco,* Africa].

MORON [maw'ron], *n.* adult with an imperfectly developed brain; half-wit. [Gk.].

MOROSE [mo-rōs'], *adj.* sullen, surly. [L.].

MORPHIA [maw'fi-ah], *n.* narcotic alkaloid extracted from opium, used to alleviate pain. [Gk.].

MORPHINE [maw'fēn], *n.* morphia. MORPHINISM, *n.* morbid state brought on by overdoses of morphia; practice of taking morphia regularly. [Fr.].

MORPHINOMANIA [maw-fi-nō-mā'ni-ah], *n.* a craving for morphia. MORPHINOMANIAC, *n.* a morphia addict.

MORPHOLOGY [maw-fo'lō-ji], *n.* study of the form of plants and animals or of words and languages. [Gk.].

MORRIS [mo'ris], *n.* semi-dramatic country dance in which the dancers represent characters of the Robin Hood fable. MORRIS-DANCE, a m. [MOORISH].

MORRIS-TUBE [mo'ris-tyōōb], *n.* tube inserted into the barrel of a rifle to reduce its bore, for shooting practice on a short range. [R. *Morris,* inventor].

MORROW [mo'rō], *n.* the next day; *(archaic)* morning; period of time immediately ensuing after some particular event. [ME.].

MORSE (1) [maws], *n.* the walrus. [Finnish].

MORSE (2), *n.* method of signalling by telegraphy or the code employed in it. MORSE (3), *adj.* pertaining to telegraphy. [S. F. B. *Morse,* inventor].

MORSEL [maw'sel], *n.* tiny piece, fragment. [OFr.].

MORTAL (1) [maw'tal], *adj.* liable to death; deadly, causing death; pertaining to death; lasting till death; *(archaic)* long and tedious; *(archaic)* extreme. MORTAL (2), *n.* creature liable to die, *esp.* a human being. MORTALLY, *adv.* in m. fashion, fatally; *(coll.)* extremely. [L.].

MORTALITY [maw-ta'li-ti], *n.* state of being mortal; number of deaths, death-rate; the human race, as being mortal. [L.].

MORTAR (1) [maw'ter], *n.* mixture of sand, lime and water used to unite bricks or other building material; stout bowl-like vessel in which substances may be crushed with a pestle; short cannon of large bore for projecting shells etc. upwards at a high angle; smooth-bored tubular weapon for projecting light bombs. MORTAR (2), *v.t.* to bombard with mortars. [OE. from L.].

MORTAR-BOARD [maw'ter-bawd], *n.* small board on which bricklayers carry mortar; *(coll.)* academic cap.

MORTGAGE (1) [maw'gij], *n. (leg.)* the temporary making over of property by the owner as security for a loan, the property to be returned to him on the repayment of the loan upon the agreed terms; deed of such conveyance. MORTGAGE (2), *v.t.* to convey property under the terms of a m.; *(fig.)* pledge, lay under a debt or burden. MORTGAGEE [maw-gi-jē'], *n.* person to whom property is mortgaged. MORTGAGOR [maw-gi-jaw(r)'], *n.* person who grants property in a m. [OFr.].

MORTICE, see MORTISE.

MORTIFICATION [maw-ti-fi-kā'shn], *n.* act of mortifying; state of being mortified; that which mortifies; humiliation, shame; *(med.)* gangrene. [EcclesL.].

MORTIFY [maw'ti-fī], *v.t. and i.* to subject the body to spiritual discipline by acts of self-control, penance etc.; humiliate, shame and vex; *(med.)* gangrene. [EcclesL.].

MORTIFYING [maw'ti-fī-ing], *adj.* humiliating.

MORTISE (1), **MORTICE** [maw'tis], *n. (carp.)* slot or cavity cut into one piece of material, into which the tenon of another piece fits to form a joint; such a joint. MORTISE-LOCK, *n.* lock made to fit in a m. cut in the edge of a door. MORTISE (2), MORTICE, *v.t. (carp.)* to unite with a tenon and m. joint; make a m. in. [OFr.].

MORTMAIN [mawt'mān], *n. (leg.)* possession of property by a body which cannot alienate it. [OFr.].

MORTUARY (1) [maw'tyōō-a-ri], *n.* building in which bodies awaiting identification, an inquest etc. are placed. MORTUARY (2), *adj.* pertaining to death or burial; **m. chapel,** chapel in which bodies may be kept before burial. [L.].

MOSAIC (1) [mō-zā'ik], *n.* pattern or design made by

cementing together small pieces of coloured stone, glass or marble; (fig.) compilation of variegated fragments. MOSAIC (2), adj. pertaining to m. [LL.].

MOSAIC (3), adj. relating to Moses. [Moses, Exod. ii, 10].

MOSELLE [mō-zel'], n. a light German wine. [River Moselle].

MOSLEM (1), **MUSLIM** [moz'lem, mus'lim], n. a Mohammedan. MOSLEM (2), MUSLIM, adj. pertaining to Mohammedans or their faith. [Arab.].

MOSQUE [mosk], n. Mohammedan temple. [Fr. from Arab.].

MOSQUITO (1) [mos-kē'tō], n. any of several species of gnats, the females of which suck the blood of animals. MOSQUITO (2), adj. pertaining to, like, mosquitoes. MOSQUITO-CRAFT, small vessels of war intended for rapid movement; torpedo boats. MOSQUITO-NET, net used for protection against mosquitoes. [Span.].

MOSS [mos], n. (bot.) any cryptogamous plant of the group Musci, growing on marshy ground, rocks etc.; plant resembling these; bog, fen. MOSS-GROWN, overgrown with m. MOSS-ROSE, the cabbage rose. [OE.].

MOST (1) [mōst], adj. greatest in quantity, size or degree. MOST (2), n. the greatest in size, number, quantity or degree; at m., not more than; to make the m. of, to extract full advantage from. MOST (3), adv. in the greatest measure, to the highest degree; used also to form the superlative of many adjectives and adverbs. MOSTLY, adv. for the m. part. [OE.].

MOT [mō], n. a witticism. [Fr.].

MOTE (1) [mōt], n. tiny particle, esp. of dust seen in a beam of sunlight, spot, speck. [OE.].

MOTE (2), see MOOT (1).

MOTET [mō-tet'], n. piece of unaccompanied music for several voices. [Fr.].

MOTH [moth], n. any lepidopterous insect which is not a butterfly, esp. the clothes-moth, a nocturnal insect the larvae of which feed on cloth etc. MOTH-BALLS, balls of camphor used to keep moths away from clothes. [OE.].

MOTH-EATEN [moth'ē-ten], adj. (of cloth) damaged by the ravages of the clothes-moth; (fig.) dilapidated.

MOTHER (1) [muʹTHer], n. female parent; (fig.) origin, source; person acting as a female parent; **M. Superior**, head of a convent; **M. Carey's chicken**, the stormy petrel; **M. Carey's goose**, the great black fulmar. MOTHER (2), adj. native; parent; acting as a m.; **M. Church**, the church from which all others have arisen; church of the original parish; **M. country**, the country from which a colony has been founded; one's native land; **m. ship**, depot ship acting as base for a group of submarines, torpedo boats etc. MOTHER (3), v.t. to act as m. towards; adopt. [OE.].

MOTHERCRAFT [muʹTHer-krahft], n. art and science of rearing children.

MOTHERING (1) [muʹTHe-ring], n. an acting as a mother towards. MOTHERING (2), adj. that mothers; **M. Sunday**, fourth Sunday in Lent.

MOTHER-IN-LAW [muʹTHer-in-law], n. mother of one's spouse.

MOTHERLY [muʹTHer-li], adj. kind, tender and caring like a mother.

MOTHER-OF-PEARL [mu-THer-ov-purl'], n. the iridescent, hard lining of certain molluscan shells.

MOTHER TONGUE [muʹTHer-tung'], n. one's native language.

MOTHER WIT [mu-THer-wit'], n. common sense; natural wit.

MOTIF [mō-tēf'], n. a basic conception or feature characterizing an artistic production, esp. a recurring theme in a piece of music; ornament on a dress. [Fr.].

MOTION (1) [mō'shn], n. process of changing position or place; way in which this is carried out; change of position; gesture; bodily deportment; a working of the bowels; excrement; proposal made in a deliberative assembly etc.; (leg.) application to the court or its head to obtain an order or ruling on a matter affecting the action at issue. MOTION-PICTURES, cinema films. MOTION (2), v.t. and i. to beckon, make a significant gesture to; propose a m. [L.].

MOTIVATE [mō'ti-vāt], v.t. to provide a motive (for); investigate.

MOTIVE (1) [mō'tiv], adj. causing action or movement; relating to motive. MOTIVE (2), n. that which causes and influences an action; reason for doing

something; motif. MOTIVE (3), v.t. to motivate; cause to act in a particular way. [L.].

MOTIVITY [mō-ti'vi-ti], n. ability or capacity to produce motion.

MOTLEY (1) [mot'li], adj. of different colours; variegated; of divers kinds; ill-assorted. MOTLEY (2), n. variegated costume, as worn by a jester. [ME.].

MOTOR (1) [mō'ter], n. internal combustion engine; any contrivance productive of mechanical motion; motor-car, automobile; (anat.) muscle which moves some part of the body; nerve which stimulates such a muscle. MOTOR (2), adj. (anat.) causing movement; (anat.) (of a nerve) conveying an impulse which excites movement; driven by a m. [L.].

MOTOR-BANDIT [mō-ter-ban'dit], n. thief who uses a motor-car to effect a quick departure.

MOTOR-BICYCLE [mō-ter-bi'si-kl], n. motor-cycle.

MOTOR-BOAT [mō'ter-bōt], n. boat driven by an internal combustion engine.

MOTOR-BUS [mō'ter-bus], n. omnibus driven by an internal combustion engine.

MOTOR-CAR [mō'ter-kah(r)], n. four-wheeled vehicle propelled by an internal combustion engine.

MOTOR-CYCLE (1) [mō-ter-sī'kl], n. two-wheeled vehicle propelled by an internal combustion engine. MOTOR-CYCLE (2), v.t. and i. to traverse by m.; ride a m. MOTOR-CYCLIST, n. one who rides a m.

MOTOR-HORN [mō'ter-hawn], n. warning device on a motor vehicle.

MOTORING [mō'te-ring], n. act or habit of riding in a motor-car, esp. touring the countryside.

MOTORIZE [mō'te-rīz], v.t. (milit.) to equip with petrol-driven transport; equip with motors. [Fr., Germ.].

MOTOR-LORRY [mō'ter-lo-ri], n. lorry propelled by an internal combustion engine.

MOTORMAN [mō'ter-man], n. driver of a vehicle propelled by an electric motor, esp. a tram or train.

MOTOR-SPIRIT [mō'ter-spi-rit], n. petrol, alcohol or other similar fuel suitable for an internal combustion engine.

MOTOR VESSEL [mō'ter-ve-sel], n. large ship driven by motors.

MOTORWAY [mō'ter-wā], n. road specially built for fast motor traffic.

MOTORY [mō'te-ri], adj. producing or pertaining to motion.

MOTTLE (1) [mo'tl], v.t. to variegate with spots of different shades and colours. MOTTLE (2), n. spot or blotch; shading or pattern of such blotches. MOTTLED, adj. marked with spots of different shade or colour. [Uncert.].

MOTTO [mo'tō], n. the phrase associated with a crest or emblem; short pithy precept supposed to govern conduct, maxim; short phrase descriptive of that to which it is attached. [It.].

MOUCH, MOUCHER, see MOOCH, MOOCHER.

M(O)UFFLON [moo'flon], n. wild mountain sheep of southern Europe. [Fr.].

MOULD (1) [mōld], n. earth, soil, esp. fine friable soil. [OE.].

MOULD (2), n. furry, fungoid growth which appears on cloth, vegetable and animal substances etc. exposed to damp. [Uncert.].

MOULD (3), n. shaped and patterned cavity in which anything may be cast into its intended shape, matrix; something shaped in such a cavity; (fig.) embodiment, pattern; cast, shape, style. MOULD (4), v.t. to shape in a m. or with the fingers; produce (a required shape) out of a particular material; influence, control; fashion, base. [OFr. from L.].

MOULDER [mōl'der], v.i. to rot, decay or crumble with age or disuse. [MOULD (1).].

MOULDING [mōl'ding], n. act of one who moulds; that which has been moulded; way in which a thing is moulded; patterned or shaped strip of wood to ornament furniture, picture-frames etc.; (arch.) ornamental projection from a wall, wainscot etc.

MOULDWARP [mōld'wawp], n. mole (sense (3)). [ME.].

MOULDY [mōl'di], adj. covered with mould, decaying, musty; (slang) poor, disappointing. [MOULD (2).].

MOULT (1) [mōlt], v.t. and i. to shed, esp. feathers or hair, periodically. MOULT (2), n. state, period or action of moulting. [OE.].

MOUND [mownd], n. heap of earth, earthwork or barrow; small natural hillock. [Uncert.].

MOUNT (1) [mownt], n. mountain; hill; (palmistry) fleshy swelling on the palm below a finger. [OE. from L.].

MOUNT (2), v.t. and i. to climb, ascend; provide with

ōō is pronounced as in food; ŏŏ as in hood; th as in think; TH as in that; zh as in azure. ～ = related to.

a horse or horses; set in position in, or on, a mount; get on the back of a horse; provide the scenery for (a play); stuff animal skins etc.; rise, increase; **to m. guard**, to go on sentry-duty; **to m. guard over**, to watch, guard. MOUNT (3), *n.* a horse for riding; base on which a picture is mounted, often with a margin which remains when the whole is framed; piece of cardboard surrounding a picture within a frame; carriage or base for a gun; setting for a jewel; glass slide on which objects may be viewed under a microscope. [Fr.].

MOUNTAIN (1) [mown'ten], *n.* high natural eminence on the surface of the earth; (*fig.*) anything very large or high. MOUNTAIN (2), *adj.* connected with, resembling, a m. or mountains; found or used in the mountains. [OFr.].

MOUNTAIN-ASH [mown-ten-ash'], *n.* rowan tree.

MOUNTAIN DEW [mown-ten-dyōō'], *n.* Scotch whisky, *esp.* when illicitly distilled in the mountains of Scotland.

MOUNTAINEER (1) [mown-te-nēer'], *n.* one who lives among mountains; one skilled in climbing mountains. MOUNTAINEER (2), *v.i.* to climb mountains. MOUNTAINEERING, *n.* mountain-climbing.

MOUNTAINOUS [mown'te-nŏŏs], *adj.* with many mountains; rugged; huge, like a mountain in size.

MOUNTANT [mown'tant], *n.* paste or adhesive jelly for mounting photographs.

MOUNTEBANK [mown'ti-bangk], *n.* quack doctor who mounted a bench in market-places etc. to sell his wares; charlatan, impostor; clown. [It.].

MOUNTED [mown'tid], *adj.* on horseback; placed in position on, provided with, a mount; (of a horse) provided with a rider.

MOUNTING [mown'ting], *n.* act of one who mounts; that on which things are, or may be, mounted; way in which anything is mounted.

MOURN [mawn], *v.t. and i.* to feel or express grief; sorrow, lament the death of. [OE.].

MOURNER [maw'ner], *n.* one who mourns; one who goes to a funeral; paid attendant at a funeral.

MOURNFUL [mawn'fŏŏl], *adj.* causing sorrow; feeling sorrow or grief; expressing sorrow; sad.

MOURNING (1) [maw'ning], *n.* lamentation, grief; black clothes worn at a time of bereavement; period during which these are worn. MOURNING (2), *adj.* that mourns; expressive of grief. MOURNING-BAND, strip of black cloth worn on the sleeve in token of m. MOURNING-COACH, coach in which to attend a funeral.

MOUSE (1) (*pl.* **mice**) [mows], *n.* any small rodent of the genus *Mus*; (*fig.*) quiet, shy person. MOUSE-COLOUR, dark brownish-grey. MOUSE (2),*v.i.* to hunt for mice. MOUSER, *n.* cat which catches mice. [OE.].

MOUSSE [mŏŏs], *n.* dish made with whipped cream, variously flavoured. [Fr.].

MOUSTACHE [mŏŏs-tahsh'], *n.* hair grown on the upper lip. [It.].

MOUSY [mow'si], *adj.* overrun with mice; like a mouse in appearance or behaviour.

MOUTH (1) [mowth], *n.* the opening in the head of animals and humans, through which food is taken; the cavity behind the lips, containing the teeth, tongue etc.; any outlet or aperture as of a river, cave etc.; living creature to be fed; **to shut one's m.**, to be silent; **down in the m.**, dejected; **to make a m.**, to pout, grimace. MOUTH (2) [mowth], *v.t. and i.* to speak with affected pomposity and facial movement; rant; discipline a horse to the bit. [OE.].

MOUTH-ORGAN [mowth'aw-gan], *n.* small wind-instrument containing a series of small rectangular openings fitted with metal reeds from which different notes are produced when it is blown through.

MOUTHPIECE [mowth'pēs], *n.* that part of a pipe, tube or musical instrument to be inserted into the mouth; someone who or something which expresses the views of others on their behalf.

MOVABLE [mŏŏ'va-bl], *adj.* capable of being moved, variable in date, not fixed or stationary; (*Scots leg.*) personal (of estate, property etc.). MOVABLES, *n.*(*pl.*) things (*esp.* possessions) which may be moved, chattels, personal property.

MOVE (1) [mŏŏv], *v.t.* to change the position of; agitate, stir; set in motion; affect emotionally; influence; prevail on; propose; *v.i.* to be capable of changing its position; change position, shift; vibrate, oscillate; be propelled; change, develop; change one's place of residence; live (in specified social circles); **to m. in**, to settle in a new residence. MOVE (2), *n.* process of moving or of being moved; change to another residence; a prescribed or tactical movement

or act in a game or series of operations etc.; right or turn to move; **to get a m. on**, to hurry. [L.].

MOVEMENT [mŏŏv'ment], *n.* process of moving; change of place or position; action, activity; way in which anything or anyone moves; piece of mechanism, *esp.* that by which a watch works; a prescribed motion or evolution; (*mus.*) complete section of a long musical composition; a trend; widely shared body of opinion, *esp.* in favour of some change or plan; the people sharing this, considered collectively; organization to further such aims; (*pl.*) all that a person does in a given time.

MOVER [mŏŏ'ver], *n.* someone who or something which moves; proposer of a resolution; instigator.

MOVIE [mŏŏ'vi], *n.* (*slang, esp. U.S.*) (*pl.*) cinematograph pictures; cinema.

MOVING [mŏŏ'ving], *adj.* emotionally affecting, touching; that moves; **m. staircase**, escalator. MOVINGLY, *adv.* in a m. way.

MOW (1) [mō], *n.* sheaf or stack of corn, hay or other vegetable produce.

MOW (2), *n.* a grimace. MOW (3), *v.i.* to grimace. [Fr.].

MOW (4) (*pret.* **mowed**, *p.pt.* **mown**), *v.t. and i.* to cut down grass etc. with a scythe or machine; **to m. down**, to kill or fell indiscriminately in large numbers. [OE.].

MR. [mis'ter], abbreviation for MISTER.

MRS. [mi'siz], abbreviation for MISSIS.

MUCH (1) [much], *adj.* great in quantity or amount. MUCH (2), *n.* large amount, great deal. MUCH (3), *adv.* greatly, to a large degree or extent; by far; nearly, virtually; often, for long.

MUCHNESS [much'nes], *n.* (*coll.*) greatness in quantity or amount; **much of a m.**, almost alike.

MUCILAGE [myŏŏ'si-lij], *n.* viscous substance produced by steeping seeds or roots in water; gum; any bodily secretion acting as a lubricant. MUCILAGINOUS [myŏŏ-si-la'ji-nŏŏs], *adj.* pertaining to, producing, like, m., gummy, slimy. [L.].

MUCK (1) [muk], *n.* dung, manure; filth, dirt; (*coll.*) filthy rubbish, trash; **to make a m. of**, (*coll.*) to bungle, mess up; make dirty and untidy. MUCK-HEAP, heap of dung. MUCK (2), *v.t.* to manure with m.; (*coll.*) bungle, do badly or clumsily; **to m. about**, (*coll.*) loaf about idly; potter; play the fool; **to m. up**, (*coll.*) utterly to mismanage; ruin, upset; make untidy or dirty. MUCKER, *n.* (*coll.*) bad fall, cropper; incompetent muddler. [ME. ~OIcel.].

MUCKLE, see MICKLE.

MUCK-RAKE [muk'rāk], *n.* rake for collecting muck; (*fig.*) one searching for unsavoury facts or scandal.

MUCK-SWEAT [muk'swet], *n.* profuse perspiration.

MUCKY [mu'ki], *adj.* dirty, filthy; muddy; nasty; disgusting, obscene.

MUCOUS [myŏŏ'kŏŏs], *adj.* relating to, secreting, containing, like, mucus; viscous; **m. membrane**, membranous lining of various canals and cavities of the body secreting mucus. [L.].

MUCUS [myŏŏ'kus], *n.* viscid fluid secreted by the mucous membranes. [L.].

MUD [mud], *n.* soft, wet earth or soil; (*fig.*) something vile or contemptible; **m. bath**, bath of m. taken to cleanse the pores of the skin; **m. pack**, layer of fuller's earth applied to the skin to beautify it; **m. pie**, moulded cake of mud, *esp.* as made by children; **to sling m. at**, to level discreditable accusations or innuendoes at. [ME.~MLGerm.].

MUDDLE (1) [mu'dl], *v.t. and i.* to confuse, stupefy; bungle, put into a muddle; blunder along unmethodically. MUDDLE (2), *n.* complete mix-up, misunderstanding; state of confusion and disorder; bewildering tangle or perplexity. MUDDLE-HEADED, unable to think clearly, stupid. [~MDu.].

MUDDY (1) [mu'di], *adj.* covered with, containing mud, dirty; resembling mud in colour; drab; turbid, cloudy; muddled, confused. MUDDY (2), *v.t.* to make m.

MUDFISH [mud'fish], *n.* any of various fishes dwelling in the mud on the bed of streams etc.

MUDGUARD [mud'gahd], *n.* metal, plastic or wooden shield over the upper part of the wheel of a vehicle, to trap the mud thrown up as it rotates.

MUDLARK [mud'lahk], *n.* one who probes the mud round docks, in sewers etc., in the hope of finding something; one who plays in the mud; street urchin.

MUD-SLINGING [mud'sling-ing], *n.* abuse, slander.

MUEZZIN [mŏŏ-ez'zin], *n.* official attached to a mosque, whose business it is to summon Moslems to prayer. [Arab.].

MUFF (1) [muf], *n.* warm cylindrical covering, usually

The accent ' after a syllable = stress (u-pon'). The mark ⁻ over a vowel = length (ă in made; ŏ in bone).

of fur, into which the hands may be placed to keep them warm; similar covering for the feet; fabric cover fitting over the front of the radiator of a motor vehicle to prevent freezing in cold weather. [Du. from Fr.].

MUFF (2), *n.* clumsy, stupid person, duffer, *esp.* at games; blunder, miss, *esp.* in a game. MUFF (3), *v.t.* (*sport*) to bungle, miss badly. [Uncert.].

MUFFIN [mu'fin], *n.* flat, circular, spongy cake toasted, buttered and eaten hot. [Uncert.].

MUFFINEER [mu-fi-nëer'], *n.* covered dish for keeping toasted muffins hot; cruet for sprinkling salt on muffins.

MUFFLE [mu'fl], *v.t.* to wrap up so as to protect from the weather, or to conceal; deaden the sound of, render indistinct. [OFr.].

MUFFLER [muf'ler], *n.* scarf worn round the neck for warmth; (*U.S.*) silencer for the engine of a motor vehicle; felt pad interposed between the strings and hammers of a pianoforte by depressing a pedal.

MUFTI [muf'ti], *n.* expounder or doctor of Mohammedan law; plain clothes, civilian attire. [Arab.].

MUG (1) [mug], *n.* drinking vessel which does not taper to its base, fitted with a handle.

MUG (2), *n.* (*slang*) the face. [*Prec.*].

MUG (3), *n.* (*slang*) simpleton who is readily swindled; fool; duffer.

MUG (4) (*pres.pt.* mugging, *pret.* and *p.pt.* mugged), *v.i.* to m. up, (*slang*) to study intensively for examination purposes, cram. [Unkn.].

MUGGY [mug'i], *adj.* damp and close. [~OIcel.].

MUGWUMP [mug'wump], *n.* (*U.S. slang*) one who is outside party politics; superior person. [AmerInd.].

MULATTO [myōō-la'tō], *n.* child of a white and a negro. [Span.].

MULBERRY [mul'be-ri], *n.* a tree on whose leaves the silkworm feeds; fruit of this tree; colour of its berries, a deep reddish-purple. [ME.~MHGerm.].

MULCH (1) [mulch], *n.* mixture of decaying damp straw, leaves, manure etc., used to protect the roots of newly planted shrubs etc. MULCH (2), *v.t.* to spread m. round or on. [~ME.].

MULCT (1) [mulkt], *v.t.* to fine; deprive of. MULCT (2), *n.* monetary fine imposed for some offence; penalty. [L.].

MULE (1) [myōōl], *n.* offspring of a mare by a male ass; cross between a canary and another finch; a hybrid; machine for cotton-spinning; (*fig.*) stubborn, obstinate person. MULE-TRAIN, line of pack-mules. [OE. from L.].

MULE (2), *n.* low heelless slipper. [Fr.].

MULETEER [myōō-li-tëer'], *n.* driver of mules. [Fr.].

MULISH [myōō'lish], *adj.* like a mule, stubborn, obstinate.

MULL (1) [mul], *n.* (*Scots*) headland or promontory. [Gael.].

MULL (2), *v.t.* to heat, sweeten and season with spices (wine, beer etc.).

MULL (3), *v.t.* (*coll.*) to bungle, spoil; **to m. over,** (*U.S. coll.*) ponder over, cogitate. [Unkn.].

MULLA, MULLAH [mōō'lah], *n.* person versed in Mohammedan rites and laws; Mohammedan religious teacher; fanatical religious leader. [Pers. and Turk.].

MULLEIN [mu'lin], *n.* plant with rough leaves and yellow, mauve or white flowers, verbascum. [AFr.].

MULLET [mu'let], *n.* either of two varieties of seafish, the red m. or the grey m. [OFr. from L.].

MULLIGATAWNY [mu-li-ga-taw'ni], *n.* a thick, highly seasoned curry soup. [Tamil].

MULLION (1) [mul'yun], *n.* upright bar dividing the apertures of a window, *esp.* in Gothic windows. MULLION (2), *v.t.* to divide by mullions. [OFr.].

MULTANGULAR [mul-tang'gyōō-ler], *adj.* with many angles.

MULTI-, *pref.* many. [L.].

MULTIFARIOUS [mul-ti-fäer'i-ōōs], *adj.* many and varied. [LL.].

MULTIFORM [mul'ti-fawm], *adj.* possessing many forms or shapes. [LL.].

MULTILATERAL [mul-ti-la'te-ral], *adj.* many-sided.

MULTI-MILLIONAIRE [mul-ti-mil-yu-näer'], *n.* one who is several times a millionaire.

MULTINOMIAL (1) [mul-ti-nō'mi-al], *adj.* (*alg.*) containing three or more terms connected by plus or minus signs. MULTINOMIAL (2), *n.* (*alg.*) a m. expression. [MULTI and (BI)NOMIAL].

MULTIPAROUS [mul-ti'pa-rōōs], *adj.* producing many at a birth; pertaining to a woman who has borne more than one child. [MdL.].

MULTIPARTITE [mul-ti-pah'tīt], *adj.* split up into many parts. [L.].

MULTIPLE (1) [mul'ti-pl], *adj.* having many individual elements or components; containing or involving two or more; (*math.*) repeated; compound; **m. shop, store,** a retail organization with a chain of shops in different districts; one of such shops; **m. star,** group of stars appearing as one. MULTIPLE (2), *n.* (*math.*) a quantity or number which contains another an exact number of times; **common m.,** number which contains two or more different numbers exactly. [LL.].

MULTIPLEX [mul'ti-pleks], *adj.* manifold, multiple. [L.].

MULTIPLIABLE, MULTIPLICABLE [mul'ti-pli-a-bl, mul-ti-pli'ka-bl], *adj.* able to be multiplied.

MULTIPLICAND [mul-ti-pli-kand'], *n.* (*arith.*) the number to be multiplied by another. [L.].

MULTIPLICATION [mul-ti-pli-kā'shn], *n.* act of multiplying; state of being multiplied; (*arith.*) operation whereby any given number is multiplied. [L.].

MULTIPLICITY [mul-ti-pli'si-ti], *n.* quality of being multiple or numerous; a great number. [L.].

MULTIPLIER [mul'ti-pli-er], *n.* one who, or that which, multiplies; (*arith.*) the number by which another is multiplied; (*econ.*) the proportion of the increment of a consumer's income to the increased saving which results; (*elect.*) instrument for intensifying the sensitiveness of an electric meter.

MULTIPLY [mul'ti-pli], *v.t.* and *i.* to increase in number; (*math.*) add a number to itself a number of times governed by the multiplier; to breed. [L.].

MULTITUDE [mul'ti-tyōōd], *n.* quality of being numerous; large number; great crowd of people; **the m.,** the common people. [L.].

MULTITUDINOUS [mul-ti-tyōō'di-nōōs], *adj.* exceedingly numerous, manifold; having an innumerable variety of forms.

MULTIVALENT [mul-ti-vä'lent], *adj.* having more than one valency.

MULTUM [mul'tum], *n.* any of several compound preparations; **m. in parvo,** much contained in a small compass. [L.].

MUM (1) [mum], *n.* (*coll.*) mother. [MUMMY (1)].

MUM (2), *int.* hush, be silent; **mum's the word,** do not tell anyone. MUM (3), *adj.* (*coll.*) silent, dumb. MUM (4), *adv.* (*coll.*) silently. MUM (5) (*pres.pt.* MUMMING, *pret.* and *p.pt.* MUMMED), *v.i.* to act in dumb show. [Symbolic of closed lips].

MUMBLE (1) [mum'bl], *v.t.* and *i.* to speak or say indistinctly without moving the lips properly, mutter; chew or eat slowly and laboriously. MUMBLE (2), *n.* an indistinct articulation or sound. [MUM (2)].

MUMBO-JUMBO [mum'bō-jum-bō], *n.* grotesque negro idol worshipped by certain African tribes; (*fig.*) foolish fetish. [Unkn.].

MUMMER [mum'mer], *n.* masked actor in a dumb show; (*coll.*) actor. MUMMERY, *n.* performance given by mummers; grotesque and empty ceremonial or ritual. [OFr.].

MUMMIFY [mu'mi-fi], *v.t.* to make into a mummy; *v.i.* assume the appearance of a mummy. [Fr.].

MUMMING [mu'ming], *n.* masked acting in dumb show.

MUMMY (1) [mu'mi], *n.* (*childish*) mother. [MAMMY].

MUMMY (2), *n.* the dead body of a human being or animal embalmed and dried, *esp.* one preserved in this way by the ancient Egyptians. [Pers.].

MUMPS [mumps], *n.* (*pl.* treated as *grammatically sg.*) epidemic parotitis, an acute contagious disease characterized by swelling and inflammation of the salivary glands, *esp.* of the parotid gland.

MUNCH [munch], *v.t.* and *i.* to chew in a noisy and conspicuous fashion. [Echoic].

MUNDANE [mun'dān], *adj.* belonging to this world, worldly. MUNDANELY, *adv.* in m. fashion. [L.].

MUNGOOSE [mun'gōōs], *n.* see MONGOOSE.

MUNICIPAL [myōō-ni'si-pal], *adj.* pertaining to the local government of a city, town or borough; carried on or controlled by the governing body of a city, town or borough; internal, domestic. [L.].

MUNICIPALITY [myōō-ni-si-pa'li-ti], *n.* city, town, borough etc., governed by a mayor and corporation; its governing body.

MUNIFICENCE [myōō-ni'fi-sens], *n.* quality of being munificent.

MUNIFICENT [myōō-ni'fi-sent], *adj.* liberal, generous, bounteous. [L.].

MUNIMENTS [myōō'ni-ments], *n.*(*pl.*) title-deeds

ōō is pronounced as in *food*; ŏŏ as in *hood*; th as in *think*; TH as in *that*; zh as in *azure*. ~ = related to.

and other written records by which claims and rights are shown and maintained.

MUNITION (1) [myōō-ni'shn], *n. (usually pl.)* materials used for warfare, *esp.* ammunition, shells, bombs etc. MUNITION (2), *v.t.* to furnish with munitions. [L.].

MURAL (1) [myōō'ral], *adj.* pertaining to, resembling, a wall; placed, done, on a wall. MURAL (2), *n.* a painting on a wall. [L.].

MURDER (1) [mur'der], *n.* unlawful killing of a human being with premeditated malice; instance of this; wanton destruction of life. MURDER (2), *v.t.* to commit m. (upon); slay; *(fig.)* spoil by an atrocious rendering. [AFr.].

MURDERER [mur'de-rer], *n.* one who commits murder.

MURDEROUS [mur'de-rōōs], *adj.* guilty of, intent on, murder; attended with, intended to cause, murder; deadly, fatal; *(fig.)* atrocious.

MURE [myōōr], *v.t.* to wall up; imprison. [L.].

MUREX (*pl.* murices, murexes) [myōō'reks, myōō'ri-sēz], *n.* genus of marine whelk-like molluscs, some species of which produce a purple dye. [L.].

MURK, MIRK [murk], *n.* darkness, gloom. [OIcel.].

MURKY [mur'ki], *adj.* dark, obscure, gloomy; depressingly dirty.

MURMUR (1) [mur'mer], *n.* a gentle, indistinct, continuous, low-pitched sound; subdued hum of voices; muffled grumble or expression of discontent. MURMUR (2), *v.t. and i.* to make or utter a m.; grumble, complain in a subdued mutter; speak in a m. MUR-MURER, *n.* person who murmurs; grumbler. [L.].

MURMURING (1) [mur'me-ring], *n.* a murmur. MURMURING (2), *adj.* that murmurs. MURMURINGLY, *adv.* with a low continuous sound.

MURMUROUS [mur'me-rōōs], *adj.* murmuring, filled with murmurs.

MURPHY [mur'fi], *n. (coll.)* a potato. [*Murphy,* Irish name].

MURRAIN [mu'rin], *n.* infectious disease among cattle. [OFr.].

MURREY† [mu'ri], *adj. and n.* (of) a purplish-red colour, mulberry colour. [OFr.].

MUSCA (*pl.* muscae) [mus'kah, mus'kē], *n.* genus of dipterous insects, including the house-flies; **muscae volitantes,** *(med.)* specks floating in the eye. [L.].

MUSCADEL, see MUSCATEL.

MUSCADINE [mus'ka-dēn], *n.* muscatel wine; any of several musk-flavoured grapes. [Fr.].

MUSCAT [mus'kat], *n.* variety of musk-flavoured grape; vine from which it comes; muscatel wine. [Provenc.].

MUSCATEL, MUSCADEL [mus-ka-tel'], *n.* a rich, sweet wine; grapes which produce this; dessert raisin from these grapes. [OFr.].

MUSCLE (1) [mu'sl], *n.* membrane-lined band of elastic fibres, capable of contracting and relaxing to produce bodily movement; a part of the body consisting of these; *(fig.)* strength, physical power. MUSCLE-BOUND, having the muscles stiff from excessive development. MUSCLE (2), *v.i.* **to m. in on,** *(slang)* to force one's way into.

MUSCOVITE [mus'kō-vīt], *n. and adj. (archaic)* (a) Russian. [Russ.].

MUSCOVY-DUCK [mus'kō-vi-duk], *n.* a tropical American duck. [MUSK-DUCK].

MUSCULAR [mus'kyōō-ler], *adj.* pertaining to a muscle; consisting of, derived from, affecting the muscles; strong, with well-developed muscles. [L.].

MUSE (1) [myōōz], *n. (class. myth.)* any of nine sister goddesses, each of whom presided over one of the liberal arts; source of inspiration, *esp.* for poetry; poetry. [Gk.].

MUSE (2), *v.i.* to ponder, reflect deeply, be lost in thought; contemplate thoughtfully. MUSE (3), *n.* deep reverie, profound meditation. [OFr.].

MUSETTE [myōō-zet'], *n.* small bagpipe; soft pastoral tune fit to be played upon this; reed-stop on an organ. [Fr.].

MUSEUM [myōō-zē'um], *n.* institution in which specimens and objects of cultural, historical or scientific interest are housed and exhibited; the collection so housed; **m. piece,** an object fit to be displayed in a m.; *(coll.)* old-fashioned person. [Gk.].

MUSH [mush], *n.* thick porridge made from the boiled meal of maize; soft, slushy, spongy mass; *(fig.)* treacly sentiment; *(radio)* interference by high-power transmitting stations. [MASH (1)].

MUSHROOM (1) [mush'rōōm], *n.* any variety of edible fungus, *esp.* the species *Agaricus campestris;*

(fig.) person who or thing which has suddenly shot up into general notice; anything resembling a mushroom in shape or rapid growth. MUSHROOM (2), *adj.* like a m. in shape or in its sudden growth. [OFr.].

MUSHY [mu'shi], *adj.* consisting of, like, mush; mawkishly sentimental.

MUSIC [myōō'zik], *n.* art of producing a rhythmical sequence or combination of sounds in such a manner as to please the ear and appeal to the aesthetic sensibilities; example of this art; printed score of such a composition; *(fig.)* any pleasing sound or sounds; **to face the m.,** to answer for one's actions. [Gk.].

MUSICAL (1) [myōō'zi-kal], *adj.* belonging to, like, producing, of, music; performed to music; pleasing to the ear; fond of, skilled in performing or appreciating, music. MUSICAL (2), *n.* theatrical performance or film in which music is the main element. [MedL.].

MUSICAL-BOX [myōō'zi-kal-boks], *n.* box in which a clockwork mechanism produces a sequence of musical sounds.

MUSICAL COMEDY [myōō-zi-kal-ko'me-di], *n.* light form of musical dramatic entertainment.

MUSICALE [myōō-zi-kahl'], *n.* informal private recital or concert of music.

MUSICAL GLASSES [myōō-zi-kal-glah'sez], *n.(pl.)* set of glass vessels emitting musical notes when struck by a small hammer; glass harmonica.

MUSICALITY [myōō-zi-ka'li-ti], *n.* quality of being musical.

MUSIC-HALL [myōō'zik-hawl], *n.* theatre in which variety shows are given.

MUSICIAN [myōō-zi'shn], *n.* person skilled in the art of rendering, composing or appreciating music. MUSICIANLY, *adv.* worthy of a m., musical. [Fr.].

MUSICOLOGY [myōō-zi-ko'lo-ji], *n.* scientific study of music. [Gk.].

MUSIC PAPER [myōō'zik-pā-per], *n.* specially ruled paper for writing out music.

MUSK [musk], *n.* strong-scented secretion from the musk-deer, used in perfumes; the animal itself; scent as of musk; any of several plants with a musky odour. MUSK-DEER, the deer which secretes m. MUSK-DUCK, the Muscovy duck. [Pers.].

MUSKET [mus'ket], *n.* former muzzle-loading, smooth-bore, hand fire-arm. [It.].

MUSKETEER [mus-ke-tēer'], *n. (hist.)* soldier armed with a musket.

MUSKETRY [mus'ke-tri], *n.* use of small arms or rifles, rifle-shooting. [Fr.].

MUSK-MELON [musk'me-lon], *n.* the common melon.

MUSK-RAT [musk'rat], *n.* the musquash, a North American rodent allied to the beaver, and valued for its fur.

MUSK-ROSE [musk'rōz], *n.* rambling rose with a musky fragrance.

MUSKY [mus'ki], *adj.* having the fragrant odour of musk.

MUSLIM, see MOSLEM.

MUSLIN [muz'lin], *n.* fine, thin cotton fabric used for making dresses etc. [Fr. from It.].

MUSQUASH [mus'kwosh], *n.* the musk-rat; fur of this animal. [AmerInd.].

MUSSEL [mu'sel], *n.* a bivalve mollusc. [OE. from L.].

MUSSULMAN (*pl.* Mussulmans) [mu'sul-man], *n.* a Mohammedan. [Pers.].

MUST (1) [must], *n.* new wine from the fresh unfermented juice of grapes. [OE. from L.].

MUST (2), *adj.* (of elephants etc.) mad, in a state of frenzy. MUST (3), *n.* state of frenzy to which elephants over the age of about 21 are periodically subject. [Pers.].

MUST (4), *auxiliary v. used to express obligation, necessity, certainty or extreme likelihood and also for emphasis.*

MUSTACHIO [mus-tah'shi-ō], *n.* moustache. [It.].

MUSTANG [mus'tang], *n.* wild horse of the American prairies. [Span.].

MUSTARD [mus'terd], *n.* any of several plants of the genus *Sinapis;* spicy yellow powder from the ground seeds of these plants, used as a condiment and medicinally; *(coll.)* something or someone unusually keen; **m. and cress,** salad of cress and the leaves of white mustard. MUSTARD-GAS, heavy, persistent, irritant poison gas smelling of m. MUS-TARD-POT, small receptacle for holding m. mixed with water etc. [OFr.].

MUSTER (1) [mus'ter], *n.* an assembling of troops for review, numbering etc.; number of men present at this; roll of troops mustered; gathering, assembly; **to pass m.**, to be satisfactory. MUSTER-ROLL, register of troops or a ship's company. MUSTER (2), *v.t. and i.* to assemble, *esp.* for review, numbering etc.; number; **to m. up**, to summon, assemble. MUSTERER, *n.* (*Australian, N.Z. etc.*) one who musters sheep or cattle. [OFr. from L.].

MUSTER-MASTER [mus'ter-mahs-ter], *n.* the officer who keeps the muster-roll.

MUSTY [mus'ti], *adj.* mouldy, stale, fusty, antiquated. MUSTILY, *adv.* in m. fashion. [Uncert.].

MUTABLE [myōō'ta-bl], *adj.* changeable, unstable, susceptible of alteration. MUTABILITY [myōō-ta-bi'li-ti], *n.* quality of being m. [L.].

MUTAGE [myōō'tij], *n.* a process for arresting fermentation in the must of grapes. [Fr.].

MUTATE [myōō-tāt'], *v.t. and i.* to experience or bring about mutation, change. MUTATIVE [myōō-tā'tiv], *adj.* (*biol.*) tending to m. [L.].

MUTATION [myōō-tā'shn], *n.* a change, altering; (*biol.*) sudden change in the characteristics of the offspring, resulting in the formation of a new species; (*philol.*) change in the quality of a vowel due to the presence of a particular vowel in the following syllable. [L.].

MUTCH [much], *n.* a woman's linen or muslin cap. [MDu.].

MUTCHKIN [much'kin], *n.* a Scots liquid measure equivalent to three-quarters of an imperial pint.

MUTE (1) [myōōt], *adj.* dumb; silent; not expressed in speech, (*phon.*) (of a letter) not sounded; (of a consonant) produced with a stoppage of the airstream (*leg.*) refusing to plead. MUTE (2), *n.* dumb person; professional mourner; actor with a non-speaking part; (*phon.*) stopped consonant; (*mus.*) clip placed on the bridge of a stringed instrument to soften the tone; pad inserted in a wind instrument to deaden the sound. MUTE (3), *v.t.* (*mus.*) to soften the sound of by a m. [L.].

MUTILATE [myōō'ti-lāt], *v.t.* to maim, cut off or destroy the use of; render imperfect by removing some part. [L.].

MUTINEER (1) [myōō-ti-nēer'], *n.* one guilty of mutiny. MUTINEER (2), *v.t.* to mutiny. [Fr.].

MUTING [myōō'ting], *n.* the dung of birds.

MUTINOUS [myōō'ti-nōōs], *adj.* inclined to mutiny, guilty of mutiny, rebellious.

MUTINY (1) [myōō'ti-ni], *n.* insurrection against constituted authority, *esp.* the (wholesale) refusal of soldiers, sailors etc. to obey their commanders. MUTINY (2), *v.i.* to rise in m. [~Fr.].

MUTISM [myōō'tizm], *n.* state of being dumb; inability to speak or articulate audibly. [MUTE (1)].

MUTT [mut], *n.* (*U.S. slang*) incompetent fool. [MUTT(ON-HEAD)].

MUTTER (1) [mu'ter], *v.t. and i.* to speak or utter in a low indistinct voice, barely moving the lips, *esp.* to express resentment or dissatisfaction in this way; rumble faintly. MUTTER (2), *n.* subdued inarticulate utterance. [ME.].

MUTTON [mu'ton], *n.* edible flesh of sheep. MUTTON-FIST, large, brawny hand. MUTTON-HEAD, (*coll.*) thick-headed fool. MUTTONY, *adj.* like m. in taste or appearance. [Fr.].

MUTTON-BIRD [mu'ton-berd], *n.* the Antarctic petrel.

MUTUAL [myōō'tyōō-al], *adj.* reciprocal, interchanged, entertained by either or each for the other or others; common; joint, combined. MUTUALLY, *adv.* reciprocally, jointly. [L.].

MUTUALISM [myōō'tyōō-a-lizm], *n.* (*ethics*) theory that the members of a well-ordered society should be mutually dependent; (*biol.*) close connexion between two unlike organisms for their mutual benefit.

MUTULE [myōō'tyōōl], *n.* (*arch.*) a projecting block under the corona of the Doric cornice. [L.].

MUZZLE (1) [mu'zl], *n.* the projecting nose and mouth of an animal; guard of straps or wires fastened over this to prevent an animal, *esp.* a dog, from biting; the open end of a fire-arm from which the shot issues. MUZZLE-LOADER, fire-arm loaded through the m. MUZZLE (2), *v.t.* to fasten a m. over the snout of; gag, restrain from free comment. [MedL.].

MUZZY [mu'zi], *adj.* confused, muddle-headed; indistinct; befuddled with drink. [Uncert.].

MY [mi], *possessive adj.* belonging to me. [OE.].

MYALGIA [mi-al'ji-ah], *n.* stiffness and pain in the muscles. [Gk.].

MYALISM [mi'a-lizm], *n.* West Indian native witchcraft. [Native].

MYALL [mi'awl], *n.* any of the Australian varieties of

acacia, *esp. Acacia homalophylla*; the wood of these trees. [Native].

MYCETO-, MYCO-. *pref.* fungus. [Gk.].

MYCETOMA [mi-si-tō'mah], *n.* a destructive fungoid disease affecting the foot, and occasionally the hand. [Gk.].

MYCOLOGY [mi-ko'lo-ji], *n.* study of fungi. [Gk.].

MYCOSIS [mi-kō'sis], *n.* parasitic fungoid growth on or in the body. [Gk.].

MYELITIS [mi-e-li'tis], *n.* inflammation of the spinal cord. [Gk.].

MYO-, *pref.* muscle. [Gk.].

MYOCARDITIS [mi-ō-kah-di'tis], *n.* (*med.*) inflammation of the muscular structure of the heart. [Gk.].

MYOLOGY [mi-o'lo-ji], *n.* study of the muscles. [Gk.].

MYOMANCY [mi'ŏ-man-si], *n.* divination by the movements of mice. [Gk.].

MYOPE [mi'ōp], *n.* short-sighted person. MYOPIA [mi-ō'pi-ah], *n.* short-sightedness. [Gk.].

MYOPIC [mi-o'pik], *adj.* short-sighted; pertaining to, characteristic of, myopia.

MYOSITIS [mi-ō-si'tis], *n.* inflammation of the muscles. [Gk.].

MYRIA-, *pref.* countless, innumerable. [Gk.].

MYRIAD (1) [mi'ri-ad], *n.* ten thousand, multitude, countless number. MYRIAD (2), *adj.* innumerable, countless. [Gk.].

MYRIAPOD [mi'ri-a-pod], *n.* centipede or millipede. [Gk.].

MYRMIDON [mur'mi-don], *n.* ruthless retainer or executor of commands; **myrmidons of the law**, policemen, bailiffs etc. [Gk. *Murmidones*, fierce Thessalian followers of Achilles in the Trojan war].

MYRRH [mur], *n.* aromatic gum-resin obtained from several species of *Commiphora*. [OE. from Gk.].

MYRTLE [mur'tl], *n.* shrub of the genus *Myrtus*, *esp. Myrtus communis*, which bears white aromatic flowers. [OFr.].

MYSELF [mi-self'], *pron. used in apposition to "I" for emphasis or as the object of a reflexive verb in the first person.*

MYSTERIOUS [mis-tēer'i-ōōs], *adj.* full of mystery, strange, unaccountable, obscure.

MYSTERY (1) [mis'te-ri], *n.* baffling secret, something unaccountable or unaccounted for; secrecy, obscurity; (*pl.*) intricacies; medieval form of drama depicting religious scenes; (*antiq., pl.*) secret religious rites and ceremonies; (*eccles.*) religious doctrine or truth established by divine revelation; Christian sacramental rite. MYSTERY-SHIP, in the 1914-18 war, warship camouflaged to look like a trading vessel. [Gk.].

MYSTERY (2), *n.* † handicraft; (*archaic*) persons engaged in this; guild. [OFr.].

MYSTIC (1) [mis'tik], *adj.* pertaining to mysticism; pertaining to the ancient mysteries or to a religious mystery; allegorical, emblematical; occult; mysterious. MYSTIC (2), *n.* one who practises and believes in mysticism. [Gk.].

MYSTICAL [mis'ti-kal], *adj.* mystic.

MYSTICISM [mis'ti-sizm], *n.* attitude of belief which claims to establish direct communication and union with the Divine Spirit by ecstatic contemplation in which ultimate truths are divinely revealed.

MYSTIFICATION [mis-ti-fi-kā'shn], *n.* act of mystifying, state of being mystified, a cause of bewilderment.

MYSTIFY [mis'ti-fi], *v.t.* to bewilder, baffle; surround with mystery. [Fr.].

MYTH [mith], *n.* legend or traditional tale, often expressing primitive beliefs, and explaining natural and historical phenomena as due to the activities of supernatural beings; a widely believed fiction. [Gk.].

MYTHIC(AL) [mi'thik(-al)], *adj.* of the nature of, pertaining to, a myth; legendary.

MYTHO-, *pref.* myth. [Gk.].

MYTHOLOGICAL [mi-thō-lo'ji-kal, mi-thō-lo'ji-kal], *adj.* relating to mythology.

MYTHOLOGIST [mi-tho'lo-jist, mi-tho'lo-jist], *n.* one expert in mythology; writer of myths.

MYTHOLOGIZE [mi-tho'lō-jiz, mi-tho'lō-jiz], *v.t.* to turn into, explain by, a myth; *v.i.* to relate or make up myths.

MYTHOLOGY [mi-tho'lo-ji, mi-tho'lo-ji], *n.* body of myths native to a particular race, country or people; study of myths. [Gk.].

MYXOEDEMA [mik-sē-dē'mah], *n.* disease causing atrophy of the thyroid gland. [Gk.].

ōō is pronounced as in food; ŏŏ as in hood; th as in *think*; TH as in *that*; zh as in azure. ~ = related to.

N

N [en], fourteenth letter of the English alphabet; (*math.*) any unknown or unspecified power or quantity.

NAB (*pres.pt.* nabbing, *pret. and p.pt.* nabbed) [nab], *v.t.* (*slang*) to catch or seize suddenly, particularly during an illegal act, arrest. [~Swed.].

NABOB [nā′bob], *n.* an official under the Mogul emperors; † one of the Anglo-Indians who, under these emperors, became rich; a conspicuously rich man. [Hind.].

NACELLE [na-sel′], *n.* body of an aeroplane; car of an airship; outer casing of an aeroplane engine. [L.].

NACRE [nā′ker], *n.* the iridescent pearly part of shells, mother-of-pearl. NACREOUS, *adj.* consisting of, relating to, mother-of-pearl; having an iridescent lustre. [LL.].

NADIR [nā′dēer, nā′der], *n.* (*astron.*) a hypothetical point of the heavens diametrically opposite to the point overhead (or zenith); (*fig.*) the lowest point, most depressed stage. [Arab.].

NAEVUS (*pl.* naevi) [nē′vus, nē′vī], *n.* congenital mark on the skin, birthmark. [L.].

NAG (1) [nag], *n.* saddle-horse; inferior kind of horse used for hack work. [ME.].

NAG (2) (*pres.pt.* nagging, *pret. and p.pt.* nagged), *v.t. and i.* to worry by continuous scolding and complaining; find fault constantly. NAG (3), *n.* persistent scolding or complaining. [OIcel.].

NAIAD (*pl.* naiads, naiades) [nī′ad, nī′a-dēz], *n.* (*myth.*) freshwater nymph. [Gk.].

NAIL (1) [nāl], *n.* the horny substance growing on the outer side of the end of the human fingers and toes; claw or talon of an animal; small spiked length of metal with a flat head used for fastening two pieces of material together; similar piece of metal with a projecting head attached to boots to prevent slipping; **to hit the n. on the head,** to do or say exactly the right thing; **to pay on the n.,** to pay at once. NAIL (2), *v.t.* to fasten together or fix by means of nails; provide with nails, as boots; (*slang*) catch; (*fig.*) hold to a definite statement or line of action. NAILER, *n.* maker or user of nails. [OE.].

NAIL-BRUSH [nāl′brush], *n.* toilet brush for cleaning the fingernails.

NAIL-FILE [nāl′fīl], *n.* small file for manicure.

NAINSOOK [nān′sŏŏk], *n.* thick sort of plain cotton fabric formerly made in India. [Hind.].

NAIVE [nah-ēv′, nāv], *adj.* natural, artless, ingenuous; simple to the point of foolishness, childish, immature. NAIVELY, *adv.* in a n. manner, with unaffected simplicity. [Fr.].

NAIVETÉ, naïveté, [nah-ē′ve-tā], *n.* naivety. [Fr.].

NAIVETY [nah-ēv′ti, nā′vi-ti], *n.* unaffected manner, simplicity and ingenuousness.

NAKED [nā′kid], *adj.* having no clothes on, bare, nude; without the proper or accustomed covering; defenceless, unarmed; without ornament, plain; (*fig.*) unconcealed, evident, obvious. NAKEDLY, *adv.* in a n. condition, without covering; simply; evidently. [OE.].

NAMABLE, NAMEABLE [nā′ma-bl], *adj.* capable of being named.

NAMBY-PAMBY (1) [nam-bi-pam′bi], *adj.* lacking ordinary virility, childish, feeble, effeminate, sentimental. NAMBY-PAMBY (2), *n.* weak, effeminate person; writing of a stupid, trashy quality. [Invented to ridicule the poems of *Ambrose* Philips].

NAME (1) [nām], *n.* the word by which a person, place, object, idea, is known, means of designating an identity, appellation of an individual, group, or category; renown, fame; **to call someone names,** to insult, abuse; **n. day,** festival day of a saint from whom a person takes his name; **n. part,** the part in a play which gives it its name, title-rôle. NAME (2), *v.t.* to give a n. to, designate, call; distinguish, classify, mention by n.; nominate, appoint. [OE.].

NAMELESS [nām′les], *adj.* without a name; anonymous; unknown; unmentionable.

NAMELY [nām′li], *adv.* that is to say.

NAMEPLATE [nām′plāt], *n.* brass or other plate on a door etc., bearing the name of the occupant of the house or room.

NAMESAKE [nām′sāk], *n.* person having the same name as another. [NAME and SAKE].

NANCY [nan′si], *n.* (*coll.*) effeminate male, a homosexual. NANCY-BOY, effeminate youth, homosexual. [Girl's name].

NANKEEN [nan-kēn′], *n.* species of cloth, generally brownish-yellow in colour; (*pl.*) trousers of nankeen. [*Nanking*, town in China].

NANNY [na′ni], *n.* female goat; children's term for a nurse. [Girl's name *Anne, Nan*].

NAP (1) [nap], *n.* a game of cards; (*fig.*) **to go n. on,** to name as a certainty. [Abbreviation of *Napoleon*].

NAP (2), *n.* woolly or downy substance on the surface of cloth. [ME.].

NAP (3) (*pres.pt.* napping, *pret. and p.pt.* napped), *v.i.* to doze; to be caught napping, to be taken unawares. NAP (4), *n.* sort of fitful sleep or slumber, doze. [OE.].

NAP (5) (*pres.pt.* napping, *pret. and p.pt.* napped), *v.t.* (*racing*) to give a special recommendation that a certain horse will win a race.

NAPE [nāp], *n.* the back of the neck. [Uncert.].

NAPERY [nā′pe-ri], *n.* linen for domestic use, *esp.* at table. [LL.].

NAPHTHA [naf′thah], *n.* orig. a fluid, inflammable hydrocarbon drained from bitumen beds; now any of various inflammable hydrocarbons distilled from petroleum, coal-tar and shale oil. [Pers.].

NAPHTHALENE [naf′tha-lēn], *n.* (*chem.*) a white crystalline hydrocarbon obtained from the distillation of coal-tar used in the manufacture of dyes.

NAPKIN [nap′kin], *n.* cloth for wiping the hands while eating food; small cloth used for the toilet of a baby; **n. ring,** ring to hold a table n. [ME. from Fr.].

NAPOLEON [na-pō′li-on], *n.* the game of cards generally known as nap; French gold coin of the value of 20 francs. NAPOLEONIC [na-pō-li-o′nik], *adj.* of, resembling, pertaining to N.; dominating. [*Napoleon* I, French Emperor].

NAPOO [nah-pŏŏ′], *adj.* (*slang*) no good, hopeless. [Mispronunciation of Fr. *il n'y (en) a plus*, there is no more (of it)].

NAPPY [na′pi], *adj.* having a nap; covered with a good deal of nap, shaggy. [MDu.].

NARCISSISM [nah-si′sizm], *n.* (*psych.*) form of neurosis characterized by excessive self-admiration, *esp.* morbid admiration of one's own body; autosexuality. [*Next*].

NARCISSUS [nah-si′sus], *n.* genus of plants characterized by bulbous roots and flowers with yellow or white sepals round a corolla, comprising daffodils, jonquils; (*myth.*) handsome youth who fell in love with his own image reflected in water and was changed into the flower named after him. [Gk.].

NARCOTIC (1) [nah-ko′tik], *adj.* having the effect of inducing sleep or drowsiness, soothing. NARCOTIC (2), *n.* drug having the effect of inducing drowsiness or allaying pain. [Gk.].

NARCOTISM [nah′ko-tizm], *n.* the effect of a narcotic; state of stupefaction or drowsiness induced by narcotic poisoning.

NARCOTIZE [nah′ko-tīz], *v.t.* to make insensible by a drug; deaden.

NARD [nahd], *n.* a plant, the spikenard; odorous unguent prepared from it. Heb.].

NARK (1) [nahk], *n.* (*slang*) informer, police spy. NARK (2), *v.t.* to inform against someone. [Unkn.].

NARRATE [na-rāt′], *v.t.* to relate in a connected form past incidents or events; tell, recite or write, as a story. [~L.].

NARRATION [na-rā′shn], *n.* act of narrating; statement in words or writing, which is narrated. [L.].

NARRATIVE (1) [na′ra-tiv], *n.* account of an event and the incidents it is composed of, tale, story. NARRATIVE (2), *adj.* having the form of a n., giving a connected order to a series of recorded events; able to narrate.

NARRATOR [na-rā′ter], *n.* person who narrates,

esp. one who narrates intervening incidents in a play.
NARROW (1) [na´rō], *adj.* of small breadth in proportion to length, not wide or broad; limited, restricted at the sides for space; limited in outlook, bigoted; **n.** escape, escape made with minimum safety. NARROW (2), *n.* (*usu. pl.*) passage between two seas, lakes, mountains, which is n., strait. NARROW (3),*v.t. and i.* to reduce or lessen the width of, cause to become n.; become n.; contract. NARROWLY. *adv.* in a n. manner, closely; with little to spare. [OE.].
NARROW-MINDED [na-rō-mīn´dīd], *adj.* having a narrow mind, prejudiced, bigoted.
NARWHAL [nah´wal], *n.* the sea-unicorn, Arctic whale having a long tusk. [OIcel.].
NASAL (1) [nā´zal], *adj.* of, belonging to, relating to, the nose; (*phon.*) formed in such a way that the breath passes wholly or partly through the nose; characterized by the special quality imparted to sounds by articulation through the nose. NASAL (2), *n.* (*phon.*) a sound in the articulation of which some or all of the breath passes through the nose. [LL.].
NASCENT [nā´sent], *adj.* approaching the time of birth; beginning to exist or grow; springing up, beginning to appear. NASCENCY, *n.* process of being born; beginning of production, birth. [L.].
NASTURTIUM [na-stur´shum], *n.* (*bot.*) genus of plants which consists of fifty species of watercress; garden plant of the genus *Tropaeolum*. [L.].
NASTY [nah´sti], *adj.* having an offensive effect on the senses; very dirty; defiled; obscene; repellent, disagreeable; unpleasant; spiteful, malicious; threatening, dangerous; difficult, awkward. [Uncert.].
NATAL [nā´tal], *adj.* belonging to birth. [L.].
NATALITY [nā-ta´li-ti], *n.* birth rate.
NATATION [na-tā´shn], *n.* act or art of swimming.
NATATORIAL [nā-ta-taw´ri-al], *adj.* swimming, adapted to swimming.
NATATORY [nā´ta-te-ri], *adj.* enabling to swim; pertaining to swimming.
NATH(E)LESS † [nāth´les, nath´les], *adv.* nevertheless. [ME from OE.].
NATION [nā´shn], *n.* a considerable body of people sharing a common descent and a cultural tradition distinct enough to mark them as a recognizable unit, usually living together in one country, or in large groups, and so commonly forming a political and economic entity. [L.].
NATIONAL (1) [na´shn-al], *adj.* of, relating to, characteristic of, common to, a nation; having a general application or status throughout a nation; owned and controlled by the government of a people; popular, public, general; **n. anthem**, the song adopted by the state; **n. debt**, the total sum of money owed by the state; **n. service**, compulsory training in the armed forces. NATIONAL (2), *n.* citizen or subject of a state.
NATIONALISM [na´shn-a-lizm], *n.* state of being national; sense of national independence; upholding of the interests of one's country against competing interests.
NATIONALIST [na´shn-a-list], *n.* person who places the interests of his own country or racial group before all others; member of a political party whose principles and programmes are based on patriotism, as opposed to internationalism. NATIONALIST(IC) [na´shn-a-list(´ik)], *adj.* characteristic of nationalists.
NATIONALITY [na-shn-a´li-ti], *n.* official status of membership of a particular nation; national character; national attachment; nation.
NATIONALIZATION [na-shn-a-li-zā´shn], *n.* act or process of nationalizing.
NATIONALIZE [na´shn-a-liz], *v.t.* to make into a nation; transfer from private to state ownership.
NATIVE (1) [nā´tiv], *adj.* having a connexion by birth; of, belonging or relating to, one's birthplace; of, belonging or relating to, the people of a particular country; produced by nature, natural; conferred by birth, innate, not acquired; living or growing by nature in a particular place; indigenous; (*chem. and min.*) occurring naturally in an original state, not combined with another substance; found naturally, not artificially produced; **to go n.**, (of a white person) to go to live among a comparatively uncivilized people and adopt their ways. NATIVE (2), *n.* person born in a particular place or country; indigenous plant or animal; oyster raised in an artificial bed off the coast of England. [L.].
NATIVITY [na-ti´vi-ti], *n.* birth, coming into the

world; time, place, or manner of birth, particularly that of Jesus Christ; representation of the birth of Christ in an aesthetic medium; festival connected with Christ's birth; (*astrol.*) representation of the position of the heavenly bodies at the time of a person's birth, horoscope. [L.].
NATTER [na´ter], *v.i.* (*dial. and slang*) to grumble, nag; gossip, chatter.
NATTY [na´ti], *adj.* neat, trim, spruce. [Unkn.].
NATURAL (1) [na´tyōōr-al], *adj.* of, connected with, relating to, or arising from, nature or the external physical world; existing in an uncultivated state, not artificially produced, wild; characterized by or in accordance with the ordinary conditions of nature; ordinary, normal; true to nature, real, lifelike; possessed from birth, innate; without pretence or artifice, unaffected; habitual, familiar, characteristic of; arising out of human nature, acting according to the governing conditions of existence; born out of wedlock; (*mus.*) without sharps or flats; **n. history**, science of nature in all its organic aspects; **n. order**, a number of groups of genera having a base of similar characteristics; **n. philosophy**, science of physics; **n. science**, science dealing with all branches of the physical world; **n. selection**, Darwin's principle of the survival of the fittest. NATURAL (2), *n.* person born with an intelligence below normal, idiot; (*cards*) highest hand dealt to a player in the game of vingt-et-un, being a royalty and an ace; (*mus.*) white note on a pianoforte keyboard, note which is neither a sharp nor a flat, expressed thus ♮. [L.].
NATURALISM [na´tyōōr-a-lizm], *n.* state of living and social organization believed to result from the interdependence of nature and human instincts unmodified by reason or any form of conscious control; (*art*) mode of presentation characterized by close adherence to the forms of nature.
NATURALIST [na´tyōōr-a-list], *n.* student of the external forms of nature, particularly those of an organic character such as animals and plants, botanist, geologist, zoologist; believer in naturalism; artist who concentrates on naturalism as a means of expression; dealer in live pets; taxidermist.
NATURALISTIC [na-tyōōr-a-lis´tik], *adj.* having a close resemblance; pertaining to naturalism or natural history.
NATURALIZATION [na-tyōōr-a-li-zā´shn], *n.* act or process of naturalizing; act of investing an alien with the rights and privileges of a native.
NATURALIZE [na´tyōōr-a-liz], *v.t.* to confer on an alien the rights and privileges of a native; make native or natural; adapt to a different climate; acclimatize, adopt.
NATURALLY [na´tyōōr-a-li], *adv.* in a natural manner, unaffectedly; innately, according to nature; of course.
NATURE [nā´tyōōr], *n.* the complete power, composed of innumerable contributory processes, forces and agencies, which governs the character of all external phenomena and their production in terms of cause and effect; the universe; the material world and its geographical, botanical and zoological features; primitive state of social organization, characterized by purely instinctive reaction; state of a human being's instinctive, emotional and intellectual powers, person's disposition, character; sum total of properties and qualities of a thing having a recognizable effect; kind, sort. [L.].
NAUGHT (1) [nawt], *n.* (*archaic*) nothing. NAUGHT (2), *adj.* useless; worthless. [OE.].
NAUGHTY [naw´ti], *adj.* guilty of improper conduct, disobedient, perverse; mischievous, teasing. [Prec.].
NAUSEA [naw´si-ah], *n.* sensation of sickness; sickness of the stomach accompanied with a propensity to vomit; (*fig.*) loathing. [Gk.].
NAUSEATE [naw´si-āt], *v.t.* to cause a feeling of nausea or disgust; loathe or reject with disgust; affect with disgust. NAUSEATING, *adj.* that nauseates. [L.].
NAUSEOUS [naw´si-ŏŏs], *adj.* causing feelings of sickness, loathsome, disgusting.
NAUTCH [nawch], *n.* an Indian dance. [Skr.].
NAUTICAL [naw´ti-kal], *adj.* connected with, pertaining to, sea matters; **n. almanac**, book of tables and calculations for navigators and astronomers published years in advance; **n. mile**, sixtieth of a degree of longitude; 6,080 ft. [~Gk.].
NAUTILUS [naw´ti-lus], *n.* (*zool.*) small cuttlefish of the genus *Nautilus*, or of the genus *Argonauta*. [Gk.].
NAVAL [nā´val], *adj.* consisting of ships; connected

with, pertaining to, ships or to a navy; **n. brigade**, detachment of naval ratings or marines serving on land.

NAVE (1) [nāv], *n. (arch.)* middle or body of a church, extending from the chancel or choir to the principal entrance at the west end. [L.].

NAVE (2), *n.* centre of a wheel, hub. [OE.].

NAVEL [nā′vel], *n.* depression in the abdomen, marking the position where the umbilical cord is attached at birth; the centre; **n. orange**, species of seedless orange with a n.-like base. NAVEL-STRING, umbilical cord. [OE.].

NAVICERT [na′vi-sert], *n.* certificate granted by a British or allied consular authority to a neutral ship testifying that her cargo is not contraband of war. [NAVI(GATION) CERT(IFICATE)].

NAVIGABLE [na′vi-ga-bl], *adj.* capable of being navigated; able to be steered. [L.].

NAVIGATE [na′vi-gāt], *v.t. and i.* to voyage in ships; sail upon (the sea or a river); conduct (a vessel) on the sea or in the air according to a set course; **navigating officer**, *n.* officer on board ship or an aircraft responsible for the navigation. [L.].

NAVIGATION [na-vi-gā′shn], *n.* act or science of navigating, *esp.* the science of determining a course by astronomy, geometry etc.; progress or passage of ships or aircraft. [L.].

NAVIGATOR [na′vi-gā-ter], *n.* an expert in navigation; one who directs the course of a ship or aircraft. [L.].

NAVVY [na′vi], *n.* person employed at heavy, unskilled labour in the course of the construction of roads, railways and other engineering works. [Abbreviation of NAVIGATOR, † canal cutter].

NAVY [nā′vi], *n.* the total number of ships bearing armaments maintained by a state for its defence; fleet of armed ships; any fleet of ships; department run by the state to maintain its sea power. [L.].

NAVY BLUE (1) [nā-vi-blōō′], *n.* navy blue colour. NAVY BLUE (2), *adj.* of the dark blue typical of naval uniforms.

NAVY-CUT [nā-vi-kut′], *n.* cake tobacco cut into fine slices.

NAWAB [na-wahb′], *n.* hereditary title of a Mohammedan ruler in India corresponding to a rajah among Hindus; nabob. [Arab.].

NAY (1) [nā], *adv.* no; not only so, not this alone. NAY (2), *n. (archaic)* refusal, denial. [OScand.].

NAZARENE [na-za-rēn′], *n.* one of the early converts to Christianity; *(pl.)* early sect of Christians; **the N.**, Jesus Christ. [Gk.].

NAZARITE [na′za-rīt], *n.* Jewish man or woman consecrated to the service of God and bound to austerity of life which forbids him to marry, drink wine or cut his hair. [Heb.].

NAZE [nāz], *n.* cliff, headland. [OE.].

NAZI [naht′si], *n. and adj.* member of, pertaining to, the former National Socialist party in Germany. [Germ. *Na(tional So)zi(alist)*].

NEAP [nēp], *n.* tide at the beginning of the moon's second and fourth quarters when the high-water level reaches its lowest point. NEAPED, *adj. (naut.)* left aground between high tides; lacking sufficient depth of water for navigation. [OE.].

NEAPOLITAN [nē-a-po′il-tan], *n. and adj.* inhabitant of, connected with, pertaining to, Naples; **N. ice**, ice of different flavours and layers of colour. [Gk.].

NEAR (1) [nēer], *adj.* adjacent, neighbouring, close to; closely related, intimate; having a close correspondence in condition or quality; mean, miserly; referring to the left side of a vehicle which is normally driven towards the left of the road, and vice versa. NEAR (2), *adv.* within a short distance of, not far from. NEAR (3), *v.t. and i.* to draw n. to, approach. [OE.].

NEARBY [nēer-bi′], *adj.* adjacent, close at hand. NEAR BY (2), *adv.* close by, at hand.

NEAR EAST [nēer-ēst′], *n.* collective term for the Balkans and Asia Minor.

NEARLY [nēer′li], *adv.* not quite, almost; intimately; in a niggardly manner.

NEAR-SIGHTED [nēer-sī′tid], *adj.* short-sighted.

NEAT (1) [nēt], *n.* cattle, any bovine animal. [OE.].

NEAT (2), *adj.* simple and tidy in style of dress and appearance, trim; pure, unadulterated, without water; simple, clean and precise in arrangement; skilful, clever; to the point, apt. [OFr. from L.].

NEATH [nēth], *prep.* abbreviated form of BENEATH.

NEAT-HANDED [nēt-han′did], *adj.* skilful and quick with the hands, dexterous.

NEATHERD [nēt′herd], *n.* cowherd.

NEB [neb], *n. (Scots)* nose; beak; peak, tip. [OE.].

NEBULA *(pl.* **nebulae)** [ne′byŏō-lah, -lē], *n. (astron.)* faint luminous patch of misty matter in the sky; compact system of distant stars collectively having a luminous misty appearance; *(anat.)* white cloudy spot on the cornea of the eye. [L.].

NEBULAR [ne′byŏō-ler], *adj. (astron.)* relating to nebulae; **n. hypothesis**, theory which derived the stars and planets from condensations of nebulous matter.

NEBULOSITY [ne-byŏō-lo′si-ti], *n.* state of being cloudy or nebulous, cloudiness, vagueness. [Fr.].

NEBULOUS [ne′byŏō-lŏŏs], *adj. (astron.)* having the characteristics of a nebula, like a nebula; obscure; formless; *(fig.)* vague; hazy. [L.].

NECESSARY (1) [ne′se-sa-ri], *adj.* fulfilling an essential function, indispensable, needful; inevitably determined by nature or previous circumstances; compulsory. NECESSARY (2), *n.* that which has an essential place or purpose; *(pl.) (leg.)* things which are judged as essential accompaniments of living, NECESSARILY, *adv.* as an inevitable result; of, or by, necessity. [L.].

NECESSITARIAN (1) [ni-se-si-tāer′i-an], *n. (philos.)* advocate of the doctrine of necessity by which every event or experience is held to occur because of its being a link in a chain of cause and effect; a determinist. NECESSITARIAN (2), *adj.* relating to the doctrine of necessity. NECESSITARIANISM, *n. (philos.)* doctrine of necessity, or that which denies the freedom of the will.

NECESSITATE [ni-se′si-tāt], *v.t.* to render necessary or unavoidable, compel; imply as a logical consequence.

NECESSITOUS [ni-se′si-tŏŏs], *adj.* poor, needy.

NECESSITY [ni-se′si-ti], *n.* that which is necessary, particularly an action or decision to act rendered inevitable as a consequence of a particular set of circumstances; that which has an inevitable place or is an inevitable consequence; that which is essential or considered essential for the continuance of life; poverty, want; **of n.**, inevitably. [L.].

NECK (1) [nek], *n.* the part of the body connecting the head and trunk; anything having a similar form or function; an isthmus; *(slang)* insolence; **to get it in the n.**, *(slang)* to be severely reprimanded, punished or attacked; come off badly; **n. or nothing**, recklessly. STIFF-NECKED, obstinate. [OE.].

NECK (2), *v.i (U.S. slang)* to kiss and cuddle. [Germ.].

NECKBAND [nek′band], *n.* band at the top of a shirt fitting round the neck.

NECKCLOTH [nek′kloth], *n.* piece of cloth formerly worn by men round the neck.

NECKERCHIEF [ne′ker-chēf], *n.* kerchief for the neck, scarf.

NECKLACE [nek′lis], *n.* string of beads or other ornaments worn round the neck.

NECKLET [nek′let], *n.* thin necklace holding a locket or other ornament; fur necktie.

NECKWEAR [nek′wāer], *n.* men's collars, ties and scarves.

NECRO-, *pref.* dead. [Gk.].

NECROMANCY [nek′rō-man-si], *n.* divination by means of pretended communication with the spirits of the dead, black magic, sorcery. [Gk.].

NECROPOLIS [ne-kro′po-lis], *n.* cemetery. [Gk.].

NECROPSY [ne-krop′si], *n.* a post-mortem examination. [Gk.].

NECROSIS [ne-krō′sis], *n.* decay of tissue, dry gangrene, mortification in bone; a disease of plants. [Gk.].

NECROTIC [ne-kro′tik], *adj.* affected by, pertaining to, necrosis.

NECTAR [nek′tah(r)], *n. (myth)* drink of the Greek gods; any very sweet beverage; sweet secretion in flowers which is the source of honey. [Gk.].

NECTARINE [nek′ta-rēn], *n.* smooth-skinned variety of the peach.

NECTARY [nek′ta-ri], *n. (bot.)* honey gland of a flower.

NÉE, née [nā], *adj.* born as, *used to denote a married woman's maiden name.* [Fr.].

NEED (1) [nēd], *n.* state recognized for its serious deficiency in some quality, factor etc.; want, necessity, state which requires relief; indigence, poverty. NEED (2), *v.t. and i.* to be in n. of, want, lack, require urgently; be necessary, be obliged; be in want. [OE.].

NEEDFUL (1) [nēd′fŏŏl], *adj.* necessary, requisite.

The accent ′ after a syllable = stress (u-pon′). The mark ‾ over a vowel = length (ā in made; ō in bone).

NEEDFUL (2), *n.* (*coll.*) that which is needed, *esp.* money.

NEEDILY [nē'di-li], *adv.* necessitously.

NEEDLE (1) [nē'dl], *n.* small tool used for sewing, consisting of a thin, short piece of steel tapered off to a sharp point at one end, and with an eye or hole stamped out of the other, through which thread is drawn; slim length of rounded metal, bone etc. used in knitting; short, thin, pointed piece of steel, wood etc. for conveying to the diaphragm the vibrations of a gramophone record; magnetized strip of steel in a mariner's compass indicating the pole; hypodermic syringe; etching tool; tall sharp-peaked rock; long thin leaf of a fir or pine tree; anything in the form of a n.; **the n.**, (*U.S. slang*) nervous apprehension. NEEDLE-FISH, garfish. NEEDLE-LACE, lace made with a n. and not with a bobbin. NEEDLE-POINT, point-lace made with a n. NEEDLE (2), *v.t. and i.* to use a n. and thread, sew; pierce with a n.; form n.-shaped crystals. [OE.].

NEEDLE-BOOK, -CASE [nē'dl-book, -kās], *n.* book with leaves or pockets in which to keep needles.

NEEDLEFUL [nē'dl-fool], *n.* length of thread inserted into a needle and to be worked to a finish.

NEEDLESS [nēd'les], *adj.* not wanted, unnecessary.

NEEDLEWOMAN [nē'dl-woo-man], *n.* woman who sews, seamstress.

NEEDLEWORK [nē'dl-werk], *n.* work executed with a needle, sewing, embroidery.

NEEDS [nēdz], *adv.* necessarily, indispensably. [OE.].

NEEDY [nē'di], *adj.* necessitous, indigent, very poor.

NEEP [nēp], *n.* (*dial.*) turnip. [OE. from L.].

NE'ER [nāer], *adv.* contraction of NEVER.

NE'ER-DO-WELL [nāer'doo-wel], *n.* person who is never likely to do well, good-for-nothing fellow.

NEFARIOUS [ni-fāer'i-oos], *adj.* unlawful, impious, wicked, abominable. [L.].

NEGATE [ni-gāt'], *v.t.* to nullify; deny. [L.].

NEGATION [ni-gā'shn], *n.* act of negating, nullification, denial; declaration that something is not; (*philos.*) dialectical antithesis of a thesis. NEGATIONIST, *n.* person who believes in the necessity for the denial of ideas.

NEGATIVE (1) [ne'ga-tiv], *adj.* implying or expressing denial, refusal, prohibition; making no new or valuable contribution, not affirming anything; (*elect.*) derived from, relating to, the cathode or its function; (*math.*) of, or relating to, a minus quantity; (*phot.*) relating to, of the nature of, a negative. NEGATIVE (2), *n.* word expressing denial or prohibition, e.g. *no, not*; statement or proposition by which something is denied, opposite of an affirmative; (*elect.*) cathode plate or terminal in an electric circuit opposite to the positive; (*phot.*) chemically prepared glass plate or film bearing an image with the natural light and dark tones in a reversed relationship. NEGATIVE (3), *v.t.* to expose as logically false, disprove, prove to the contrary; reject by vote, veto; render ineffective, neutralize. NEGATIVELY, *adv.* in a n. manner; with or by a n.; without producing the expected result, making no valuable contribution. [L.].

NEGLECT (1) [ni-glekt'], *v.t.* to give no attention to, not to notice; leave uncared for, disregard, slight; omit to do on account of carelessness. NEGLECT (2), *n.* act of neglecting, lack of care or proper attention, negligence, indifference; state of being neglected, condition resulting from lack of care. [L.].

NEGLECTFUL [ni-glekt'fool], *adj.* negligent, accustomed to neglect, inattentive, heedless.

NEGLIGE(E), negligé(e) [ne'gli-zhā], *n.* loose, easy dress for informal wear, dressing-gown. [Fr.].

NEGLIGENCE [ne'gli-jens], *n.* behaviour due to inattention; condition due to such behaviour; neglect, carelessness. [L.].

NEGLIGENT [ne'gli-jent], *adj.* neglectful, careless, heedless.

NEGLIGIBLE [ne'gli-ji-bl], *adj.* that need not be noticed; of little value; not worth taking into account. [Fr.].

NEGOTIABLE [ni-gō'sha-bl], *adj.* able to be negotiated or transferred by assignment; transferable on endorsement by holder; able to provide a foothold or passage.

NEGOTIATE [ni-gō'shi-āt], *v.t. and i.* to arrange terms of business by means of discussion, conference and meetings, transact business, bargain; exchange a security for cash; cope with a complex section of a road or passage; participate in business transactions; discuss terms of peace. [L.].

NEGOTIATION [ni-gō-shi-ā'shn], *n.* act of negotiating, transacting of business; treating with another in

order to come to an agreement over specific terms. [L.].

NEGOTIATOR [ni-gō'shi-ā-ter], *n.* person who negotiates or treats with others. [L.].

NEGRESS [nē'gres], *n.* female negro.

NEGRILLO [ni-gri'lō], *n.* member of a race of pygmy negroes inhabiting Central Africa. [Span.].

NEGRITO [ni-grē'tō], *n.* member of an aboriginal race of Malaya and Polynesia, *esp.* the Philippines; member of the stock which embraces this race and the negrillos. [Span.].

NEGRO (1) (*pl.* **negroes**) [nē'grō], *n.* member of an African race having as physical characteristics a dark skin, woolly tightly-curled hair, thick lips and a flat nose; person having some negro blood. NEGRO (2), *adj.* relating to a n. or negroes. [Span. from L.].

NEGROHEAD [nē'grō-hed], *n.* tobacco mixed with molasses and pressed into cakes.

NEGUS (1) [nē'gus], *n.* Ethiopian title equivalent to king; Emperor of Ethiopia. [Amharic].

NEGUS (2), *n.* hot drink made of wine, water, sugar and sometimes nutmeg and lemon-juice. [Col. *Negus*, inventor].

NEIGH (1) [nā], *v.i.* to utter a cry, as a horse, whinny. NEIGH (2), *n.* cry of a horse; whinnying. [OE.].

NEIGHBOUR (1) [nā'ber], *n.* person who lives near or next door; person who is placed near; any member of a community regarded from the human aspects of love and friendship and social matters. NEIGHBOUR (2), *adj.* nearby, adjoining. NEIGHBOUR (3), *v.t. and i.* to be near to; act towards like a friendly n.; adjoin, border on. [OE.].

NEIGHBOURHOOD [nā'ber-hood], *n.* district or area surrounding or near to a specific point or place; place near, adjoining district; state of being near, proximity; inhabitants who live near each other, neighbours considered collectively.

NEIGHBOURING [nā'be-ring], *adj.* living or being near, adjacent.

NEIGHBOURLY (1) [nā'ber-li], *adj.* having the good qualities of a neighbour, kind, sociable, friendly. NEIGHBOURLY (2), *adv.* in the manner of a neighbour, with social civility. NEIGHBOURLINESS, *n.* quality of being n., sociability.

NEITHER [nī'ther], *pron. and conj.* not either.

NEKTON [nek'ton], *n.* (*biol.*) collective term for the various organisms which swim at the upper and middle levels of the ocean. [Gk.].

NELSON [nel'sun], *n.* a hold in wrestling in which one or both arms are brought under the opponent's arms from the back, and the hands press on his neck. [Proper name].

NEMATODES [ne'ma-tōdz], *n.*(*pl.*) (*zool.*) threadworms, entozoans with filiform elongated bodies. [Gk.].

NEMESIS [ne'mi-sis], *n.* (*myth.*) goddess of vengeance or retributive justice descending on those experiencing undeserved success; (*fig.*) fate bringing retribution. [Gk.].

NENUPHAR [ne'nyoo-fah(r)], *n.* (*bot.*) the white water-lily. [Pers.].

NEO-, *pref.* new; later; revived with modifications, based upon. [Gk.].

NEOLITHIC [nē-ō-li'thik], *adj.* relating to a primitive period of civilization characterized by implements of polished stone; the latest of the stone ages. [Gk.].

NEOLOGICAL [nē-ō-lo'ji-kal], *adj.* relating to neology; employing new words.

NEOLOGISM [nē-o'lo-jizm], *n.* word or expression which is new or of new significance; (*theol.*) new doctrine, particularly of a rationalistic nature. [Gk.].

NEOLOGY [nē-o'lo-ji], *n.* aptitude for inventing new words or giving new significance to old words, introduction of new words or new meanings; rationalistic views in theology. [Gk.].

NEON [nē'on], *n.* (*chem.*) the gaseous element denoted by Ne; **n. light,** type of light obtained by a silent electric discharge in n. gas; **n. sign,** display sign in n. lights. [Gk.].

NEOPHYTE [nē'ō-fit], *n.* (*eccles.*) new convert or proselyte; novice, tyro. [Gk.].

NEOPLASM [nē'ō-plazm], *n.* (*path.*) new and abnormal growth of tissue, *esp.* a tumour. [Gk.].

NEOPLASTIC [nē-ō-plas'tik], *adj.* (*med.*) characterized by, relating to, neoplasm, freshly formed.

NEOPLASTY [nē-ō-plas'ti], *n.* (*med.*) restoration by granulation.

NEOPLATONISM [nē-ō-plā'to-nizm], *n.* mixture of oriental and Platonic philosophy; philosophy of

---

Plotinus who lived in the third century. [NEO and PLATONISM].

NEOTERIC [nĕ-ō-te'rĭk], *adj.* new, recent in origin; new-fangled. [Gk.].

NEOZOIC [nĕ-ō-zō'ĭk], *adj.* (*geol.*) denoting the formations from the Trias up to the most recent time. [Gk.].

NEPENTHE [nĭ-pen'thĭ], *n.* drug which relieves pain, originally by inducing forgetfulness. [Gk.].

NEPHEW [ne'vyŏo], *n.* son of one's brother or sister. [Fr.].

NEPHOLOGY [ne-fo'lo-jĭ], *n.* study of clouds. [Gk.].

NEPHRITIC [ne-frĭ'tĭk], *adj.* (*med.*) pertaining to the kidneys, renal; affected with disease of the kidneys. [Gk.].

NEPHRITIS [ne-frī'tĭs], *n.* (*path.*) inflammation of the kidneys. [Gk.].

NEPHRO-, *pref.* relating to the kidneys. [Gk.].

NEPOTIC [ne-po'tĭk], *adj.* of the nature of, showing, nepotism.

NEPOTISM [nĕ'po'tizm], *n.* favouritism shown to relatives, particularly in filling government posts. [L.].

NEPTUNE [nep'tyŏon], *n.* (*myth.*) god of the sea; (*astron.*) large planet beyond Uranus. NEPTUNIST, *n.* person who adopted the Neptunian theory. [L.].

NEPTUNIAN (1) [nep-tyŏo'nĭ-an], *adj.* relating to the sea; formed by means of water; **N. theory,** theory which attempts to relate the formation of rocks and strata to particular activities of water. NEPTUNIAN (2), *n.* Neptunist.

NEREID [nĕer'ĭ-id], *n.* (*myth.*) sea-nymph; (*zool.*) marine annelid or worm. [~Gk.].

NERVE (1) [nurv], *n.* (*anat.*) any one of a complicated system of sensory and motor fibres which respond to stimuli, transmit sensation to the brain centre, or carry impulses to the muscles; state of mind under the control of a firm resolve, confidence, courage; (*coll.*) audacity, impertinence; (*pl.*) state of apprehension, irritability; (*bot.*) vein in a leaf; **war of nerves,** campaign of propaganda, rumour etc., designed to demoralize an enemy; **n. centre,** (*anat.*) junction of n. fibres, ganglion; (*fig.*) centre which controls the whole of an organization. NERVE (2), *v.t.* to impart strength, vigour or courage to, embolden. [L.].

NERVELESS [nurv'les], *adj.* having no strength, weak; having no nervous system, numb.

NERVOUS [nur'vŏos], *adj.* (*anat.*) relating to the nervous system; suffering from nerves; strong, vigorous; with nerves in an acutely sensitive condition, highly strung; timid, shyly apprehensive. NERVOUSLY, *adv.* in a n. manner; with strength or vigour; timidly. [L.].

NERVY [nur'vĭ], *adj.* having acutely sensitive nerves, nervous, jumpy, on edge.

NESCIENCE [ne'sĭ-ens], *n.* want of knowledge; ignorance. [L.].

NESCIENT [ne'sĭ-ent], *adj.* ignorant, unaware of; agnostic. [L.].

NESH [nesh], *adj.* (*dial.*) soft, delicate; tender. [OE.].

NESS [nes], *n.* promontory, headland. [OE.].

NEST (1) [nest], *n.* structure built by a bird out of such materials as twigs, moss etc., used as a bed or home in which eggs are laid and hatched; snug shelter; breeding ground, haunt; swarm, brood; number of boxes or tables constructed to fit into each other and fit into the largest of the series. NEST (2), *v.t.* and *i.* to put in a n.; build a n. and use it, as a bird. [OE.].

NEST-EGG [nest'eg], *n.* genuine or dummy egg left in the nest to induce the hen to lay or brood; something laid up as a beginning, small sum of money kept in reserve.

NESTLE [ne'sl], *v.t.* and *i.* to lie close and snug, as a bird in her nest; place, settle, in a close and snug position. [OE.].

NESTLING [nes(t)'ling], *n.* young bird from the nest, newly hatched and unable to fly.

NESTORIAN [nes-taw'rĭ-an], *n. and adj.* follower of, relating to the doctrine of, Nestorius, patriarch of Constantinople in A.D. 428, who maintained the co-existence, but not the union, of two natures in the person of Christ.

NET (1) [net], *n.* open-work fabric made of twine, cord etc. threads, which are knotted together at the points where the parallel horizontal threads cross the parallel vertical threads, the whole piece being used to catch fish, snare birds, protect fruits or a woman's hair etc.; oblong strip of such material used to divide a tennis-court or a table-tennis table;

the goal in certain games; **the nets,** (*cricket*) practice pitches guarded by nets to avoid the need for fielding. NET (2) (*pres.pt.* NETTING, *pret. and p.pt.* NETTED), *v.t. and i.* to catch or cover by means of a n.; set with nets; make a n.; (*sport*) send (the ball) into the n. [OE.].

NET (3), *adj.* neat, unadulterated; free from, or clear of, discount and all deductions or charges; not including packing etc. NET (4), *v.t.* to produce a n. profit. [Fr.].

NETBALL [net'bawl], *n.* outdoor game played with the hands in which the goals are nets shaped like a bag and hung from an iron loop at the top of a pole.

NETHER [ne'THer], *adj.* placed below, lower, opposed to upper; belonging to the regions below. NETHERMOST, *adj.* lowest. [OE.].

NETT [net], *adj.* without discount, net.

NETTING [ne'ting], *n.* strip, length or piece of net, network; the making of nets.

NETTLE (1) [ne'tl], *n.* plant covered with hair-like prickles, which sting severely. DEAD-NETTLE, a species of *Lamium.* NETTLE (2), *v.t.* to sting into a state of annoyance, irritate, vex, pique. [OE.].

NETTLE-RASH [ne'tl-rash], *n.* irritable eruption upon the skin, resembling a nettle sting.

NETWORK [net'werk], *n.* pattern of threads, wires etc. forming a net; anything resembling a net in form or pattern; inter-linked system of radio transmitting stations.

NEUM(E) [nyŏom], *n.* (*mus.*) group of notes sung to one syllable in plainsong. [Gk.].

NEURAL [nyŏo'ral], *adj.* relating to the nerves. [Gk.].

NEURALGIA [nyŏo-ral'jĭ-ah], *n.* (*med.*) pain occurring in paroxysms in a nerve situated across the forehead or behind the eyes. [Gk.].

NEURASTHENIA [nyŏo-ras-thĕ'nĭ-ah], *n.* state of nervous exhaustion. [Gk.].

NEURITIS [nyŏo-rī'tĭs], *n.* inflammation of a nerve. [Gk.].

NEURO-, *pref.* relating to the nervous system. [Gk.].

NEUROLOGIST [nyŏo-ro'lo-jist], *n.* an expert in neurology, nerve specialist.

NEUROLOGY [nyŏo-ro'lo-jĭ], *n.* study of the nerves, particularly in relation to their states of disturbance. [Gk.].

NEUROPATH [nyŏo'rō-path], *n.* (*med.*) person liable to nervous disorders. [Gk.].

NEUROPATHY [nyŏo-ro'pa-thĭ], *n.* any disease of the nerves.

NEUROSIS [nyŏo-rō'sis], *n.* (*med.*) a functional disorder of the nervous system; (*psych.*) state of nervous disorder attendant upon a type of personality inherently occupied with abnormal self-deceptions, such as obsession, hysteria etc. [Gk.].

NEUROTIC (1) [nyŏo-ro'tĭk], *adj.* relating to, affecting, the nerves; suffering from nervous disorder. NEUROTIC (2), *n.* person suffering from neurosis.

NEUTER (1) [nyŏo'ter], *adj.* having the recognized status of a non-participant in a dispute or war, impartial, neutral; (*bot., entom.*) having no sexual function, neither masculine nor feminine; (*gram.*) neither masculine nor feminine in gender. NEUTER (2), *n.* animal which is organically deprived of sexual function; person, group or nation which is recognized as standing apart in a contest or war; (*gram.*) noun, adjective or pronoun of the n. gender. [L.].

NEUTRAL (1) [nyŏo'tral], *adj.* remaining apart from either side engaged in a dispute or war, impartial; having no distinguishing marks or qualities; (of gears) disengaged, transmitting no power; (*bot., entom.*) having no organic function, asexual, of neuter gender; (*chem.*) neither acid nor alkaline. NEUTRAL (2), *n.* person, group or nation officially recognized as having the status of non-participant in a dispute or war; state of having the gears, particularly of a motor-car, disengaged. [L.].

NEUTRALIZE [nyŏo'tra-līz], *v.t.* to render neutral; render inert, inactive or of no effect.

NEUTRON [nyŏo'tron], *n.* (*phys.*) electrically neutral particle probably consisting of an electron and a proton.

NÉVÉ [ne'vā], *n.* granular snow which feeds a glacier. [Fr. from L.].

NEVER [ne'ver], *adv.* not ever, not at any time; in no degree, not under any condition. [OE.].

NEVERTHELESS [ne-ver-THe-les'], *adv.* none the less, in spite of that, notwithstanding.

NEW (1) [nyŏo], *adj.* of recent origin, having an

The accent ' after a syllable = stress (u-pon'). The mark ‾ over a vowel = length (ā in made; ō in bone).

existence for the first time, lately produced or invented; recently discovered or known, but of previous existence; recently made, bought or adopted; different and better, having a superior quality, original; modern, having a fresh application or significance; entering into the next phase of a recurrent cycle; unaccustomed, inexperienced; unfamiliar, strange; **N. Testament,** the latter of the two divisions of the Bible, containing the gospels and the other books of the new or Christian covenant. NEW (2), *adv.* freshly, recently. [OE.].

NEWCOMER [nyōo-ku'mer], *n.* one who has recently arrived; stranger.

NEWEL [nyōo'el], *n.* (*arch.*) upright post or central shaft supporting a spiral staircase; post at the foot or head of a staircase acting as a main support for the handrail. [OFr.].

NEWFANGLED [nyōo-fang'gld], *adj.* believed to be a muddle of modern complexities, formed with the affectation of novelty; fond of novelties. [ME.].

NEWFOUNDLAND [nyōo-fownd'land], *n.* variety of large dog of spaniel breed, originally from Newfoundland.

NEW-LAID [nyōo-lād'], *adj.* (of an egg) very fresh.

NEWLY [nyōo'li], *adv.* recently, lately, freshly, in a new way.

NEWMARKET [nyōo'mah-kit], *n.* a card-game. [*Newmarket* Races, Cambridgeshire].

NEWS [nyōoz], *n.* information, facts or a treatment of these, intelligence; a newspaper of this name; a broadcast of news; **N. Editor,** newspaper editor in charge of the presentation of it. NEWS-REEL, short film composed of shots of topical events.

NEWSAGENT [nyōoz'ā-jent], *n.* shopkeeper who sells newspapers and periodicals.

NEWSBOY [nyōoz'boi], *n.* boy who sells or delivers newspapers.

NEWSLETTER [nyōoz'le-ter], *n.* printed sheet or brochure circulating news.

NEWSPAPER [nyōoz'pā-per], *n.* printed paper issued daily or weekly containing news, editorials and advertisements, and usually embodying some group of interests or policy.

NEWSPRINT [nyōoz'print], *n.* paper used for printing newspapers.

NEWS-ROOM [nyōoz'rōom], *n.* room in a public or private institution for the reading of newspapers; room where incoming reports of news are edited.

NEWS-THEATRE [nyōoz'thē-a-ter], *n.* cinema showing a continuous programme of short news-reels, documentary films etc.

NEWSVENDOR [nyōoz'ven-der], *n.* seller of newspapers, newsagent, newsboy.

NEWT [nyōot], *n.* tailed amphibian of the genus *Triton.* [OE.].

NEW YEAR (1) [nyōo-yēer'], *n.* the first few days of a new year; **New Year's Day,** 1 January. NEW-YEAR (2), *adj.* pertaining to, given on the occasion of, N.

NEXT (1) [nekst], *adj.* nearest in place, adjoining, neighbouring, having a position immediately before or after a specific point; nearest in time or degree. NEXT (2), *adv.* in the most near position, point of time or degree.

NEXT-OF-KIN [nekst-ov-kin'], *n.* the nearest blood relative.

NEXUS [nek'sus], *n.* connecting link or principle; group with its units linked together. [L.].

NIB [nib], *n.* small pen; point of anything, particularly of a quill pen split in two; curved strip of steel or other metal tapering down to a split point and inserted into a penholder; (*slang*) smart person, "card." [~NEB].

NIBBLE (1) [ni'bl], *v.t. and i.* to eat by small bites or to take a nibble at. NIBBLE (2), *n.* act of nibbling; bite of the kind a fish makes; small bite made with the edge of the teeth; piece of food obtained in this way. [Uncert.].

NIBLICK [nib'lik], *n.* club with a broad, flat, round iron head and a face set obliquely, used for getting a ball out of a bunker or other hazard in golf. [Unkn.].

NICE [nīs], *adj.* dainty, refined, fastidious; precise, exact, requiring precision; discriminating; (*coll.*) agreeable, pleasant, attractive; kind, sociable. NICELY, *adv.* in a n. manner. NICENESS, *n.* quality of being n.; delicacy of perception; scrupulousness; precision; (*coll.*) agreeableness. [L.].

NICENE [ni-sēn'], *adj.* relating to, or coming from, Nicaea in Asia Minor, the meeting-place for the first important council of the Christian church; **N.**

Creed, declaration of faith drawn up at the Council of Nicaea in 325 A.D. [L.].

NICETY [ni'si-ti], *n.* capacity for delicate, exact perception; delicate handling or treatment; minute accuracy, precision, fastidiousness; **to a n.,** exactly, perfectly.

NICHE [nich], *n.* recess in a wall for a statue or other ornament; (*fig.*) position corresponding to the kind of ability a person has. [Fr.].

NICK (1) [nik], *n.* small, thin, shallow notch, slit or slot, by which a reckoning or point of time is marked; winning cast in a game of dice; **in the n. of time,** at the last possible moment. NICK (2), *v.t. and i.* to make a n. in; steal, pilfer; nip in. [Uncert.].

NICKEL (1) [ni'kel], *n.* (*min.*) hard metal of a silver-white colour used in steel manufacture, the chemical element denoted by Ni; (*U.S.*) five-cent piece. NICKEL (2), *v.t. and i.* (of firearms) to foul, become fouled, with n. from bullet-casings. [Germ.].

NICKNAME (1) [nik'nām], *n.* additional name given in derision or familiarity, usually of a descriptive nature. NICKNAME (2), *v.t.* to give a n. to. [Late ME.].

NICOTINE [ni-kŏ-tēn'], *n.* poisonous alkaloid obtained from tobacco. NICOTINISM, *n.* morbid condition caused by over-indulgence in tobacco. [J. *Nicot,* introducer of tobacco into France].

NIDIFY [ni'di-fī], *v.i.* to build a nest. [L.].

NIDUS [nī'dus], *n.* nest; (*med.*) place of incubation of a disease. [L.].

NIECE [nēs], *n.* daughter of one's brother or sister. [ME. from L.].

NIELLO (1) [ni-e'lō], *n.* black metallic composition applied to ornamental engraving on silver or gold; piece of metal inlaid with this. NIELLO (2), *v.t.* to inlay with n. [It.].

NIFTY [nif'ti], *adj.* (*U.S. slang*) admirable, smart; smelly. [Unkn.].

NIGELLA [ni-je'lah], *n.* (*bot.*) genus of annual plants including love-in-a-mist. [L.].

NIGGARD (1) [ni'gerd], *n.* avaricious person, miser. NIGGARD (2), *adj.* mean, stingy. [ME.].

NIGGARDLY (1) [ni'gerd-li], *adj.* avaricious, mean. NIGGARDLY (2), *adv.* in n. manner.

NIGGER [ni'ger], *n.* (*coll.*) negro; man of colour; **n. minstrel,** entertainer whose face is made up to resemble a negro's; **to work like a n.,** (*coll.*) to work as hard as a slave. NIGGER-BROWN, dark, chocolate shade of brown. [~Span., L.].

NIGGLE [ni'gl], *v.i.* to waste time in petty details, worry about trifles. [Uncert.].

NIGGLING [ni'gling], *adj.* fussy, finicking, petty, exhibiting a ridiculous care for details.

NIGH (1) [nī], *adj.* (*archaic*) close, near; closely allied. NIGH (2), *adv.* near to, in an adjacent place; nearly, almost. NIGHNESS, *n.* nearness. [OE.].

NIGHT [nīt], *n.* the dark period of the day between sunset and sunrise; period of darkness; death; (*fig.*) obscurity of understanding, adversity. NIGHT-BLINDNESS, inability to see after sunset, an affection of the eyes caused by strong light. NIGHT-CLOTHES, clothes worn in bed. NIGHT-LINE, fishing-line left baited and set to catch fish during the n. NIGHT-PIECE, (a painting of) a n. scene. NIGHT-SOIL, sewage contents of closets, removed and used as manure. NIGHT-WORK, work done at n. [OE.].

NIGHT-CAP [nīt'kap], *n.* cap worn in bed; drink at bedtime.

NIGHT-CLUB [nīt'klub], *n.* club for dancing and drinking at night; cabaret.

NIGHTDRESS [nīt'dres], *n.* full-length, loose garment for wearing in bed.

NIGHTGOWN [nīt'gown], *n.* nightdress.

NIGHT-HAWK [nīt'hawk], *n.* nightjar; person who works at night, particularly illegally.

NIGHTINGALE [nī'ting-gāl], *n.* European migratory bird outstanding for its sweet singing at night. [OE.].

NIGHTJAR [nīt'jah(r)], *n.* the goatsucker.

NIGHTLIGHT [nīt'līt], *n.* short, thick, slow-burning candle for burning in a bedroom at night.

NIGHTMARE [nīt'māer], *n.* †demon, incubus; bad dream of terrifying reality; dreadful experience or haunting fear; (*coll.*) person with an offensive face, habits or character. NIGHTMARISH, *adj.* like a n., nearly as frightening as a n. [OE.].

NIGHT-SCHOOL [nīt'skōol], *n.* institution which holds classes in the evening for the benefit of those employed in the daytime.

NIGHTSHADE [nīt'shād], *n.* (*bot.*) one of several

berry-bearing plants, of the genus *Solanum* or *Atropa Belladonna*. [OE.].

NIGHTSHIRT [nīt'shert], *n.* full-length shirt used as sleeping apparel by a man.

NIGHTWATCH [nīt'woch], *n.* guard or watch maintaining a look-out during the night; time of changing the watch at night; period of keeping watch during part of the night.

NIGRESCENT [ni-gre'sent], *adj.* growing black, approaching to blackness. [L.].

NIGRITUDE [nī'gri-tyōōd], *n.* blackness. [L.].

NIHILISM [nī'i-lizm], *n.* nothingness; (*philos.*) the destruction of existing beliefs or doctrines without making any attempt to establish the reality of phenomena; (*pol.*) system and principles of a Russian revolutionary party who aimed at the overthrow of Czarism and capitalism by terroristic means in order to establish a state of anarchy. [L.].

NIL [nil], *n.* nothing. [L.].

NILGAI [nil'gī], *n.* Indian antelope of bluish colour. [Hind.].

NIMBLE [nim'bl], *adj.* light and active in motion, moving with ease and celerity, agile; alert, quick-witted. NIMBLE-FINGERED, dexterous; expert at stealing. NIMBLE-WITTED, quick-witted. [ME.~OE.].

NIMBUS [nim'bus], *n.* rain-cloud; (*art*) disk of light portrayed round the heads of divinities, saints and sovereigns. [L.].

NIMROD [nim'rod], *n.* sportsman; mighty hunter. [Heb.].

NINCOMPOOP [ning'kum-pōōp], *n.* brainless booby, blockhead. [Unkn.].

NINE (1) [nīn], *n.* the cardinal number one more than eight; symbol representing this; **the N.**, the n. Muses; **dressed up to the nines**, wearing ultra-smart clothes. NINE (2), *adj.* one more than eight; **n. days' wonder**, short-lived piece of sensational scandal; **n. men's morris**, old English game resembling draughts. [OE.].

NINEFOLD [nīn'fōld], *adj.* nine times repeated, nine times as many.

NINEPINS [nīn'pinz], *n.* variety of skittles in which nine pieces of wood are set on end, and a ball rolled at them.

NINETEEN (1) [nīn-tēn'], *n.* the number nine and ten united. NINETEEN (2), *adj.* being n. in number.

NINETEENTH [nīn-tēnth'], *adj.* the ordinal of nineteen; being one of nineteen equal parts; **n. hole**, (*golf*) the club-house bar.

NINETIETH [nīn'ti-eth], *adj.* the ordinal of ninety; being one of ninety equal parts.

NINETY (1) [nīn'ti], *n.* the number consisting of nine times ten; **the nineties**, the last decade of a century, *esp.* the nineteenth. NINETY (2), *adj.* being ten times nine in number. [OE.].

NINNY [ni'ni], *n.* fool, simpleton. [Unkn.].

NINON [nī'no(ng)], *n.* a light silk fabric. [Fr.].

NINTH (1) [nīnth], *n.* one of nine equal parts; (*mus.*) interval which is a tone or semitone wider than an octave. NINTH (2), *adj.* the ordinal of nine; being one of nine equal parts. NINTHLY, *adv.* in the n. place.

NIOBIUM [nī-ō'bi-um], *n.* (*chem.*) metallic element denoted by Nb. [*Niobe*, heroine in Gk. mythology].

NIP (1) (*pres.pt.* nipping, *pret. and p.pt.* nipped) [nip], *v.t.* to pinch with the nails, fingers or teeth without drawing blood; cut or clip with a tool; check the growth of, as by a frost or sharp wind; (*coll.*) steal; catch in the act; (*fig.*) depress; *v.i.* to effect by means of nipping, pinching, biting; **to n. along**, to hurry; **to n. in**, to slip into place before another; **to n. in the bud**, to stop at the outset. NIP (2), *n.* sharp bite with the teeth or pinch with the fingers which does not break the skin; any action which has this effect; edge of cold or frost to the air or wind. [ME. ~Du.].

NIP (3) (*pres.pt.* nipping, *pret. and p.pt.* nipped), *v.t.* to sip, drink in small quantities. NIP (4), *n.* small drop of liquid, sip; (*Scots*) small measure of spirits. [Du.].

NIPPER [ni'per], *n.* one who, or that which, nips; front tooth of a horse; front claw of a lobster or crab; (*pl.*) small pincers; (*coll.*) small boy, urchin.

NIPPLE [ni'pl], *n.* teat of the human breast, *esp.* the female; anything similar in function or appearance; metal projection through which machinery is lubricated. [Unkn.].

NIPPON [nip'pon], *n.* Japan. [Jap.].

NIPPY [ni'pi], *adj.* cold; nimble, agile.

NIRVANA [ner-vah'nah], *n.* (*Buddhist philos.*) state

when all individual reactions are supposed to be extinguished and the spirit is sublimated by an affinity with the divine. [Skr.].

NISI [nī'sī], *adj.* (*leg.*) becoming valid unless sufficient cause to the contrary be shown before a certain date. [L.].

NISSEN HUT [ni-sen-hut'], *n.* (*prot.*) long portable hut, semi-circular in section. [Name of the inventor].

NIT [nit], *n.* egg of any small insect, such as a louse. [OE.].

NITRATE [nī'trāt], *n.* (*chem.*) a salt of nitric acid; saltpetre in its natural condition. [NITRE].

NITRE [nī'ter], *n.* (*chem.*) saltpetre; nitrate of potash; **cubic n.**, nitrate of soda. [Gk.].

NITRIC [nī'trik], *adj.* (*chem.*) relating to, impregnated with nitre; containing nitrogen in its higher valency; **n. acid**, a compound of hydrogen, oxygen and nitrogen, HNO_3.

NITRITE [nī'trīt], *n.* (*chem.*) a compound of nitrous acid with a base or an alcohol.

NITRO-, *pref.* made from, or including, nitrogen.

NITRO-BENZENE [ni-trō-ben'zēn], *n.* a combination of benzene and nitric acid having the flavour of the oil of bitter almonds, used in perfumery.

NITRO-CELLULOSE [nī-trō-se'lyōō-lōs], *n.* explosive product yielded by the action of nitric acid on cellulose; gun-cotton.

NITROGEN [nī'trō-jen], *n.* (*chem.*) a gaseous element denoted by N, composing a large percentage of the atmosphere. NITROGENIZE [ni-tro'je-nīz], *v.t.* to impregnate with, cause to combine with, n. NITROGENOUS (ni-tro'je-nŏŏs], *adj.* relating to or containing n. [Gk.].

NITRO-GLYCERIN(E) [nī-trō-gli'se-rin], *n.* (*chem.*) glycerol trinitrate, a highly explosive liquid used in the manufacture of dynamite.

NITROUS [nī'trŏŏs], *adj.* (*chem.*) relating to, containing, nitrogen in its lower valency; **n. oxide**, gas composed of oxygen and nitrogen, N_2O, laughing-gas. [L.].

NITWIT [nit'wit], *n.* (*slang*) person of no sense, fool. NITWITTED, *adj.* (*slang*) having no sense. [Germ.].

NIX (1) [niks], *n.* (*slang*) nil, nothing. NIX (2), *int.* (*slang*) take care, nothing doing as regards. [Germ.].

NIX (3), **NIXIE**, *n.* water-elf. [Germ.].

NIZAM [ni-zahm'], *n.* title of the ruler of Hyderabad. [Urdu].

NO (1) [nō], *adj.* not any, not one, none; hardly any; **n. go**, (*coll.*) useless; **n. wonder**, *int.* I do not wonder that. NO (2), *adv.* not at all, in n. respect. not in any degree, not any; not; **n. more**, neither. NO (3), *n.* a negative reply. [OE.].

NOB [nob], *n.* (*slang*) head, cranium; swell, nobleman, upper-class gentleman; (*cribbage*) the knave. [Uncert.].

NO-BALL [nō-bawl'], *n.* (*cricket*) ball so declared by the umpire at the moment of delivery because its method of delivery infringes the rules.

NOBBLE [no'bl], *v.t.* (*slang*) to render a horse unfit for a race either by injuring it or by drugging it; bribe a jockey for the same ends; obtain possession of dishonestly; cheat, swindle. NOBBLER, *n.* person who nobbles a horse.

NOBILIARY [nō-bi'li-a-ri], *adj.* belonging to the nobility.

NOBILITY [nō-bi'li-ti], *n.* quality of being noble, dignity of mind; distinction by birth, the rank of being noble; class of society whose members belong to families possessing a seat in the House of Lords, the peerage. [L.].

NOBLE (1) [nō'bl], *adj.* famous for high excellence, renowned for chivalry or virtuous deeds; having high ideals, possessing a selfless, courageous nature; expressed by a noble mind; stately, exalted; having a blood tie with a family of hereditary rank. NOBLE (2), *n.* person of high birth born into the class of the nobility, member of the peerage, nobleman; † old English gold coin. [L.].

NOBLEMAN [nō'bl-man], *n.* member of the nobility, peer.

NOBLESSE [nō-bles'], *n.* the nobility, persons of noble rank collectively; nobleness. [Fr.].

NOBODY [nō'bo-di], *n.* not any body, no one; person of no note. [NO and BODY].

NOCK [nok], *n.* notch, notch in an arrow; (*naut.*) weather corner of a gaff sail. [Uncert.].

NOCTI-, *pref.* of, by, or at night. [L.].

NOCTIVAGANT [nok-ti'va-gant], *adj.* wandering in the night. [L.].

NOCTURNAL [nok-tur'nal], *adj.* relating to or happening at night. [L.].

The accent ' after a syllable = stress (u-pon'). The mark ‾ over a vowel = length (ā in made; ō in bone).

NOCTURNE [nok'tern], *n.* (*art*) picture of a night scene; (*mus.*) piece of music inspired by or evoking reflections associated with night. [L.].

NOD (1) (*pres. pt.* **nodding,** *pret. and p.pt.* **nodded**) [nod], *v.t. and i.* to move the head quickly and sharply forward and downward as a curt form of greeting; make a short downward movement with the head as a sign of assent or as a form of greeting; be drowsy, let the head droop forward through drowsiness; (*fig.*) make a mistake through momentary inattention. **NOD** (2), *n.* quick, sharp inclination of the head expressing assent or a curt form of greeting; uncontrolled movement of the head as it drops forward through drowsiness; **on the n.,** (*U.S. slang*) on credit, on tick. [ME.].

NODAL [nō'dal], *adj.* relating or belonging to a node; **n. points,** centres of convergence. [~NODE].

NODDLE [nod'l], *n.* (*coll.*) the head. [Uncert.].

NODDY [nod'i], *n.* simpleton, fool; sea-fowl allied to the terns. [Unkn.].

NODE [nōd], *n.* point of intersection; protuberance or knot caused by a joining; (*bot.*) point on the stalk of a plant from which the leaf grows; (*astron.*) point where the orbit of a planet intercepts the ecliptic; (*math.*) point where a turning curve crosses itself; (*med.*) swelling of the tendons into a knot; (*phys.*) point of rest of a vibrating body. **NODICAL** [nō'di-kal], *adj.* (*astron.*) relating to nodes. **NODOSE** [nō-dōs'], *adj.* (*bot.*) having knots or swelling joints. **NODOSITY** [nō-do'si-ti], *n.* (*bot.*) knottiness. [L.].

NODULAR [no'dyōo-ler], *adj.* relating to a nodule or knot; possessing nodes.

NODULE [no'dyōol], *n.* small knot; rounded lump. **NODULATED, NODULOUS,** *adj.* having nodules. [L.].

NODUS [nō'dus], *n.* node; (*fig.*) point of difficulty. [L.].

NOEL [nō-el'], *n.* Christmas. [Fr. from L.].

NOETIC [nō-e'tik], *adj.* relating to reason, intellectual; originating in, or performed by, the intellect. [Gk.].

NOG (1) [nog], *n.* kind of strong ale; **egg n.,** drink consisting of a raw egg whipped up in a liquid, either milk or alcohol. [Unkn.].

NOG (2), *n.* wooden bolt or peg. [Unkn.].

NOGGIN [no'gin], *n.* small mug or wooden cup; measure of liquid, quartern, quarter of a pint. [Unkn.].

NOGGING [no'ging], *n.* brickwork or other filling in timber framing.

NOISE (1) [noiz], *n.* any sound having the quality of loudness or sharpness, or composed of a number of discordant tones; confused, disturbing and unpleasant sound, clamour, uproar, din; **big n.,** (*slang*) person in an influential position; person who considers himself of great importance. **NOISE** (2), *v.t.* to spread by rumour, cause to circulate by word of mouth. [Fr.].

NOISOME [noi'sum], *adj.* noxious to health, hurtful; disgusting, offensive. **NOISOMELY,** *adv.* in a n. manner, with a foetid smell. **NOISOMENESS,** *n.* quality of being n. [(AN)NOY and SOME].

NOISY [noi'zi], *adj.* making a noise, clamorous, rowdy; accompanied by noise.

NOMAD (1) [nō'mad], *adj.* wandering, belonging to a tribe of nomads. **NOMAD** (2), *n.* person who leads a wandering life, generally for pasture, in a country in a backward state of economic development. **NOMAD-ISM,** *n.* state of being nomadic; nomadic life. **NOMADIZE,** *v.i.* to wander with flocks and herds. [Gk.].

NOMADIC [nō-ma'dik], *adj.* wandering, roaming.

NO MAN'S LAND [nō'manz-land], *n.* land having no discoverable owner; contested area intervening between entrenched hostile forces.

NOM DE PLUME [nom-de-plōom'], *n.* name adopted by a writer to conceal his identity. [Fr.].

NOMENCLATOR [nō'men-klā-ter], *n.* person who gives names to things, inventor of new names. [L.].

NOMENCLATURE [nō'men-klā-tyōor, nō-men'kla-tyōor], *n.* system of names allotted to objects or ideas in scientific classification; terminology. [L.].

NOMINAL [no'mi-nal], *adj.* concerned with names; existing in name only, verbal, not actual; very light, very low in respect of amount. **NOMINALLY,** *adv.* to a n. degree; by name only. [L.].

NOMINALISM [no'mi-na-lizm], *n.* (*philos.*) doctrine that abstract names or terms are words only, having no existence in nature or any relationship with a corresponding reality. **NOMINALIST,** *n.* upholder of n.

NOMINATE [no'mi-nāt], *v.t.* to name or mention

by name as a candidate for office or election. [~L.].

NOMINATION [no-mi-nā'shn], *n.* act or power of nominating; state of being nominated; entry of a name as a competitor. [L.].

NOMINATIVE (1) [no'mi-na-tiv], *adj.* (*gram.*) belonging to the case of the subject of a sentence. **NOMINATIVE** (2), *n.* (*gram.*) the case of the subject of a sentence; any word in this case. [L.].

NOMINEE [no-mi-nē'], *n.* person named or appointed by another for an office; one on whose life an annuity depends. [~L.].

NON-, *pref.* used in compounds to denote negation, lack of, exclusion. [L.].

NONAGE [nō'nij], *n.* condition of not being of age, minority; state of being under twenty-one years of age. [OFr.].

NONAGENARIAN [nō-na-je-nāer'i-an], *n.* person over ninety and not yet a hundred years old. [~L.].

NONAGON [nō'na-gon], *n.* (*geom.*) a nine-angled figure. [L. and Gk.].

NONARY [nō'na-ri], *adj.* (*math.*) based on nine. [L.].

NON-BELLIGERENT [non-be-li'je-rent], *n. and adj.* (relating to) a state or party which, while remaining neutral, gives non-military aid to one side in a war.

NONCE [nons], *n.* the occasion, the time being. **NONCE-WORD,** word recorded only once. [ME.].

NONCHALANCE [non'sha-lans], *n.* state of being nonchalant, indifference; carelessness, coolness, absence of emotional response.

NONCHALANT [non'sha-lant], *adj.* exhibiting no response, indifferent; careless; cool, showing no feeling. [OFr.].

NON-CLAIM [non-klām'], *n.* (*leg.*) failure to make a claim within the legal time limit.

NON-COLLEGIATE [non-ko-lē'ji-at], *n. and adj.* (student at a university who is) not a member of a college.

NON-COMBATANT [non-kom'ba-tant], *adj. and n.* (pertaining to) a surgeon or chaplain or other person in the armed forces whose duty is other than to fight; (a) civilian.

NON-COMMISSIONED [non-ko-mi'shnd], *adj.* not holding a commission in the Army or Air Force, as all soldiers under the rank of second lieutenant.

NON-COMMITTAL [non-ko-mi'tal], *adj.* remaining neutral, not being committed or pledged.

NON-CONDUCTOR [non-kon-duk'ter], *n.* (*elect.*) substance which does not conduct electricity or heat.

NONCONFORMIST (1) [non-kon-faw'mist], *n.* person, other than a Roman Catholic, who does not conform to an established church. **NONCONFORMIST** (2), *adj.* of, or pertaining to, Nonconformists or Non-conformity; **N. conscience,** conscience governed by very narrow principles.

NONCONFORMITY [non-kon-faw'mi-ti], *n.* refusal to conform, *esp.* to the principles or practice of an established church; body of persons who refuse to conform.

NON-CONTENT [non-kon-tent'], *n.* (*pol.*) in the House of Lords, one who gives a negative vote.

NON-CONTRIBUTORY [non-kon-tri'byōo-ta-ri], *adj.* not based upon or requiring contributions.

NON-CO-OPERATION [non-kō-o-pe-rā'shn], *n.* abstinence from co-operation, *esp.* as an instrument of political policy.

NONDESCRIPT [non'di-skript], *n. and adj.* (person or thing) having no well-defined character; not easily classified; colourless, vague, indeterminate. [L.].

NONE (1) [nun], *pron.* not one, not any. **NONE** (2), *adv.* none at all, not any, by no account, in no way.

NON-EGO [non-e'gō], *n.* (*psych.*) the external or objective in perception or thought, all that is not the conscious self.

NONENTITY [no-nen'ti-ti], *n.* state of being non-existent, non-existence; thing not existing, or as good as not; person of no importance, a nobody.

NONES [nōnz], *n.(pl.)* † ninth day of the month before the Ides; one of the three divisions of the ancient Roman month; (*eccles.*) service formerly held at 3 p.m. [L.].

NONESUCH [nun'such], *n.* thing which has not its like, nonpareil.

NON-EXISTENCE [non-eg-zis'tens], *n.* state of being non-existent, the negation of being; thing which has no existence.

NON-FEASANCE [non-fē'zans], *n.* (*leg.*) failure to perform a legal duty.

NON-FERROUS [non-fe'rōos], *adj.* (*metal.*) containing no iron or allied metal.

NON-FLAM [non-flam'], *adj.* non-inflammable;

ōo is pronounced as in food; ŏŏ as in hood; th as in think; TH as in that; zh as in azure. ~ = related to.

(*cinema*) applying to films. [NON and (IN)FLAM-(MABLE)].

NON-INTERVENTION [non-in-ter-ven'shn], *n.* abstention from interfering, particularly as a political policy in connexion with war.

NONJUROR [non-jŏŏr'er], *n.* person who refused to take the oath of allegiance after the English Revolution of 1688.

NON-MORAL [non-mo'ral], *adj.* neither moral nor immoral, having nothing to do with morality.

NONPAREIL [non-pa-rel'], *n. and adj.* (person or object) without an equal, that which has no peer; (*typ.*) a type approximately six points in size. [Fr.].

NONPLUS (1) [non-plus'], *n.* state of perplexity; quandary. NONPLUS (2) (*pres.pt.* NONPLUSSING, *pret. and p.pt.* NONPLUSSED), *v.t.* to place in a baffling situation, puzzle, perplex. [L.].

NON-RESIDENT [non-re'zi-dent], *n. and adj.* (person) not residing permanently in a country; clergyman not living in the district in his charge.

NONSENSE [non'sens], *n.* an illogical or absurd statement, words or language which have no meaning; anything absurd.

NONSENSICAL [non-sen'si-kal], *adj.* full of nonsense, ridiculous, unmeaning.

NON SEQUITUR [non-se'kwi-ter], *n.* (*logic*) a conclusion which does not follow from the premises. [L.].

NON-SKID [non-skid'], *adj.* designed to prevent skidding.

NON-SMOKER [non-smō'ker], *n.* one who does not smoke; (*coll.*) railway compartment in which smoking is forbidden.

NON-STARTER [non-stah'ter], *n.* one who does not start; horse which, though entered for a race, does not appear at the starting-post.

NON-STOP (1) [non'stop], *adj.* without a break, particularly of a variety show with no intervals between turns. NON-STOP (2), *n.* an express train. NON-STOP (3), *adv.* without stopping.

NONSUCH [nun'such], *n.* nonpareil, nonesuch; (*bot.*) the wild plant, *Medicago lupulina.*

NONSUIT (1) [non-syŏŏt'], *n.* (*leg.*) judicial quashing of a law case owing to the default, neglect or non-appearance of the plaintiff. NONSUIT (2), *v.t.* (*leg.*) to record a n. against.

NON-UNION [non-yŏŏ'ni-on], *adj.* not belonging to a trade union.

NON USER [non-yŏŏ'zer], *n.* (*leg.*) neglect to take advantage of a right, by which it may lapse.

NOODLE (1) [nŏŏ'dl], *n.* (*slang*) simpleton. [Unkn.].

NOODLE (2), *n.* baked wheaten strip or ball served with soup etc. [Uncert.].

NOOK [nŏŏk], *n.* corner, narrow place formed by an angle; secluded place, recess. [ME.].

NOON (1) [nŏŏn], *n.* the middle of the day; twelve o'clock in the day; hour between midday and 1 p.m.; meridian height; (*fig.*) prime of power. NOON (2), *adj.* occurring at, relating to, n. [OE. from L.].

NOONDAY (1) [nŏŏn'dā], *n.* noon, midday. NOON-DAY (2), *adj.* occurring at, relating to, n.

NOONTIDE [nŏŏn'tid], *n.* midday.

NOOSE (1) [nŏŏs], *n.* running knot made with a rope which binds closer the more it is drawn, slip-knot. NOOSE (2), *v.t.* to catch in a n.; ensnare; lasso. [OFr.].

NOR [naw(r)], *conj. word correlative to* NEITHER, *used to deny the second of two alternatives*; (*at beginning of sentence*) and . . . not. [ME.].

NORDIC [naw'dik], *adj.* pertaining to or resembling the blond Germanic type of people found principally in Northern Europe. [Fr.].

NORFOLK JACKET [naw-fŏŏk-ja'kit], *n.* loose-fitting jacket, with a belt and pleated back and front.

NORLAND (1) [naw'land], *n.* the north country. NORLAND (2), *adj.* northern.

NORM [nawm], *n.* the acknowledged standard; typical form, type. [L.].

NORMAL (1) [naw'mal], *adj.* according to an accepted standard or type, regular, customary; having the usual value or degree; (*math.*) perpendicular; **n. school**, institution for training teachers. NORMAL (2), *n.* the customary standard; (*math.*) a perpendicular. [L.].

NORMALITY [naw-ma'li-ti], *n.* state of being normal, average degree or quality.

NORMAN (1) [naw'man], *n.* inhabitant of Normandy; member of a Scandinavian race which settled in Normandy in the 10th century; member or descendant of the branch of this race which, after

settling in France, conquered England in 1066. NORMAN (2), *adj.* pertaining to the Normans; (*arch.*) descriptive of a style of architecture fashionable in England during the 11th and 12th centuries, and derived from the French Romanesque. [OFr.].

NORN [nawn], *n.* one of the three fates of Norse mythology. [OIcel.].

NORROY [no'roi], *n.* the English King of Arms whose jurisdiction lies north of the Trent. [OFr.].

NORSE [naws], *adj. and n.* belonging to Scandinavia; the early Scandinavian language. NORSEMAN, *n.* a native of ancient Scandinavia, northman. [Du.].

NORTH (1) [nawth], *n.* one of the four cardinal points, in the Northern Hemisphere directly opposite the sun in the meridian; the region which lies to the right when the observer is facing due west; the part of a country lying northward of a defined point. NORTH (2), *adj.* lying at, or in the direction of, the n., towards the n.; coming from the n., opposite the south. NORTH (3), *adv.* northerly (2). [OE.].

NORTH-BOUND [nawth'bownd], *adj.* bound for the north, travelling northward.

NORTH-EAST (1) [nawth-ēst'], *n.* the point of the compass between the north and east, and equally distant from each; the district or direction lying between the north and the east. NORTH-EAST (2), *adj.* belonging to, situated between, coming from the n. NORTH-EASTER, *n.* north-easterly wind recognized for its coldness and strength.

NORTH-EASTERLY (1) [nawth-ēs'ter-li], *adj.* situated in, or coming from, the north-east. NORTH-EASTERLY (2), *adv.* towards the north-east, in a n. direction.

NORTHERLY (1) [naw'THer-li], *adj.* situated in, coming from, or moving towards, the north. NORTHERLY (2), *adv.* towards the north.

NORTHERN [naw'THern], *adj.* situated in, moving towards, or from, the north. NORTHERNER, *n.* person born in, or having the manners of, the north.

NORTHING [naw'thing], *n.* (*naut.*) the distance northward in relation to the last bearings taken.

NORTHMAN [nawth'man], *n.* inhabitant of the north of Europe, *esp.* of ancient Norway. [OE.].

NORTHWARD (1) [nawth'werd], *adj.* being towards the north. NORTHWARD (2), *adv.* in a northerly direction. NORTHWARDS, *adv.* towards the north. [OE.].

NORTH-WEST (1) [nawth-west'], *n.* the point of the compass exactly between north and west; the region indicated as lying between these two compass points. NORTH-WEST (2), *adj.* situated in, moving towards, coming from, facing, the n. NORTH-WESTER, *n.* a north-westerly wind rising to great strength.

NORTH-WESTERLY (1) [nawth-wes'ter-li], *adj.* towards, or coming from, the north-west. NORTH-WESTERLY (2), *adv.* in the direction of the north-west.

NOR'WESTER [naw-wes'ter], *n.* a sou'wester hat.

NOSE (1) [nōz], *n.* projecting part of the face placed between and below the eyes, the organ by means of which the sense of smell functions, and through which breathing is properly accomplished; keen sense of smell; ability for detection; fore-end of anything; nozzle, spout, prow etc.; **to lead by the n.,** to have in one's power; **to turn up one's n.,** to express dislike or contempt. NOSE (2), *v.t. and i.* to touch with the n., nuzzle; feel the way cautiously; **to n. out,** to detect by smelling, track; find out. [OE.].

NOSEBAG [nōz'bag], *n.* feeding-bag which can be tied to a horse's head.

NOSEBAND [nōz'band], *n.* nose-part of a bridle.

NOSE-DIVE (1) [nōz'dīv], *n.* a plunge head first towards the ground by an aircraft. NOSE-DIVE (2), *v.i.* to make a head-first descent towards the ground in an aircraft.

NOSEGAY [nōz'gā], *n.* bunch of sweet-scented flowers; small bouquet, usually of wild flowers.

NOSEPIECE [nōz'pēs], *n.* piece at the nose of a horse's bridle; the end of a microscope which carries the objectives; nozzle of a hose or pipe.

NOSE-RING [nōz'ring], *n.* ring worn by eastern women and savages as an ornament for the nose; ring passed through the nose of a bull etc., by which it is led.

NOSEY PARKER [nō-zi-pah'ker], *n.* prying, inquisitive person. [NOSY].

NO-SIDE [nō-sīd'], *n.* announcement by the referee which terminates a game of Rugby football.

NOSING [nō'zing], *n.* projecting rounded part of a moulding, as on the edge of a step.

NOSOLOGY [no-so'lo-ji], *n.* science of diseases; the

The accent ' after a syllable = stress (u-pon'). The mark ‾ over a vowel = length (ă in made; ō in bone).

defining, naming and grouping of diseases. [Gk.].

NOSOPHOBIA [no-so-fō′bi-ah], *n.* (*psych.*) fear of disease. [Gk.].

NOSTALGIA [nos-tal′ji-ah], *n.* morbid longing for the place of one's home or birth, homesickness. [Gk.].

NOSTRIL [nos′tril], *n.* aperture through the nose for the passage of air. [OE.].

NOSTRUM [nos′trum], *n.* quack medicine or prescription. [L.].

NOSY [nō′zi], *adj.* having a large nose; inquisitive; interfering. NOSINESS, *n.* inquisitiveness.

NOT [not], *adv. word expressing negation, denial or refusal, having various positions in various types of sentence.* [ME.].

NOTABILITY [nō-ta-bi′li-ti], *n.* quality of being notable; person of note.

NOTABLE (1) [nō′ta-bl], *adj.* worthy of notice, distinguished, remarkable; conspicuous. NOTABLE (2), *n.* a n. person. NOTABLY, *adv.* in a n. manner; especially, particularly.

NOTARY [nō′ta-ri], *n.* official whose profession is to attest and certify contracts of any kind such as deeds, protested bills of exchange etc.; in full **n. public.** NOTARIAL [nō-tāer′i-al], *adj.* relating to a n.; done or taken by a n. [L.].

NOTATION [nō-tā′shn], *n.* act or practice of recording anything by marks; system of figures and signs. NOTATIONAL, *adj.* of, pertaining or relating to, (a) n. [L.].

NOTCH (1) [noch], *n.* slot, slit, cut or nick made in wood or other material; nick at the feather end of an arrow to take the bow-string. NOTCH (2), *v.t. and i.* to make a n., score. [OFr.].

NOTE (1) [nōt], *n.* short record, memorandum; comment in writing, annotation; brief, informal letter; formal diplomatic communication; paper containing a written promise of payment, *esp.* by a bank; pre-eminence, repute; mark, sign or token conveying a specific meaning; (*mus.*) printed or written character or symbol indicating a particular sound; the sound itself thus indicated; any one of the keys on a pianoforte keyboard; a distinctive tone or tune; (*fig.*) quality, characteristic. NOTE (2), *v.t.* to make a n. of, set down in writing for future reference; observe, attend to; annotate; record the payment or non-payment of a bill of exchange. [L.].

NOTED [nō′tid], *adj.* well known by reputation, distinguished, famous.

NOTEPAPER [nōt′pā-per], *n.* small-sized writing paper for correspondence.

NOTEWORTHY [nōt′wer-THi], *adj.* worthy of note or observation, remarkable, distinctive.

NOTHING (1) [nu′thing], *n.* not anything, the total absence of anything, nought, a cipher; something of superficial importance, that which is negligible; that which has no grounds for comparison. NOTHING (2), *adv.* not at all, in no degree. [NO and THING].

NOTHINGNESS [nu′thing-nes], *n.* state of being nothing, non-existence; worthlessness.

NOTICE (1) [nō′tis], *n.* a sensory or mental observation, attention; indication of an intention or action, information, intelligence, warning, *esp.* of dismissal, leaving premises etc.; brief formal announcement, particularly one posted on a board; paragraph bearing information; critical appreciation of a book, play or film published in a paper or periodical, review. NOTICE (2), *v.t.* to observe, pay attention to, heed; make a remark on, refer to; publish a review on. [L.].

NOTICEABLE [nō′ti-sa-bl], *adj.* able to be noticed; worthy of notice, conspicuous, remarkable.

NOTIFIABLE [nō′ti-fī-a-bl], *adj.* (of a disease) required by law to be notified to the authorities.

NOTIFICATION [nō-ti-fi-kā′shn], *n.* act of notifying; means of notification; formal notice connected with public services; announcement.

NOTIFY [nō′ti-fī], *v.t.* to make known, give notice to, inform.

NOTION [nō′shn], *n.* experience or number of experiences reduced to a coherent abstract form by the mind; idea, conception, mental apprehension, opinion, inclination. [L.].

NOTIONAL [nō′shn-al], *adj.* relating to a notion; speculative, ideal, conveying an idea; imaginary. NOTIONALLY, *adv.* in an abstract or speculative manner.

NOTORIETY [nō-to-rī′i-ti], *n.* quality of being notorious.

NOTORIOUS [nō-taw′ri-ŏŏs], *adj.* well known in an

unfavourable capacity, known to disadvantage; manifest to all. [MedL.].

NO-TRUMPS [nō-trumps′], *n.* bid at bridge in which no suit is trumps. NO-TRUMPER, *n.* (*bridge*) hand which justifies a n. bid.

NOTWITHSTANDING (1) [not-wiTH-stan′ding], *adv.* although, nevertheless. NOTWITHSTANDING (2), *prep.* without hindrance or obstruction from, despite, in spite of. [~NOT and WITHSTAND].

NOUGAT [nōō′gah], *n.* confection of sugar, paste and almonds. [Fr. from L.].

NOUGHT [nawt], *n.* nothing, naught; a cipher, the figure or symbol 0. [OE.].

NOUMENON (*pl.* **noumena**) [nōō′me-non], *n.* (*philos.*) the object of intellectual, as opposed to sensory, perception; a thing, or the conception of a thing, as it is in itself or to pure thought; the real under the phenomenal. [Gk.].

NOUN [nown], *n.* (*gram.*) the name of anything, a substantive. [ME. from L.].

NOURISH [nu′rish], *v.t.* to feed, sustain by providing good food; encourage, entertain, cherish. [OFr. from L.].

NOURISHMENT [nu′rish-ment], *n.* that which nourishes, food, nutriment.

NOUS [nows], *n.* intelligent perception, common sense. [Gk.].

NOUVEAU-RICHE [nōō-vō-rēsh′], *n.* person of the lower classes whose ability to learn good manners does not equal his ability to make money, parvenu. [Fr.].

NOVEL (1) [no′vel], *adj.* new, unfamiliar, unusual. NOVEL (2), *n.* narrative in prose dealing with stories of character and incident representing and reflecting the social scene, romance, fantasy etc. [L.].

NOVELETTE [no-ve-let′], *n.* short novel. NOVELETTISH, *adj.* trivially sentimental, after the manner of many novelettes.

NOVELIST [no′ve-list], *n.* writer of novels.

NOVELTY [no′vel-ti], *n.* quality of being novel, newness; something new, product on the market for the first time; trivial, frippery knick-knack. [OFr.].

NOVEMBER [nō-vem′ber], *n.* eleventh month of the year. [L.].

NOVENA [nō-vē′nah], *n.* (*R.C. eccles.*) devotion lasting for a period of nine days, special form of intercession repeated on each of nine successive days. [LL.].

NOVENNIAL [nō-ve′ni-al], *adj.* recurring every ninth year. [L.].

NOVERCAL [nō-vur′kal], *adj.* pertaining to, like, a stepmother. [L.].

NOVICE [no′vis], *n.* one who is new in any business, beginner; one who has entered a religious house but has not yet taken the vows, probationer, convert. [L.].

NOVITIATE, NOVICIATE [nō-vi′shi-at], *n.* state or time of being a novice; time of probation before taking full religious vows; novice. [MedL.].

NOW (1) [now], *adv.* at the present time, at once, immediately; at the moment; in the circumstances. NOW (2), *conj.* since, seeing that, this being the case, after this, but. NOW (3), *n.* the present time. [OE.].

NOWADAYS [now′a-dāz], *adv.* in these days, at the present time.

NOWHERE [nō′wāer], *adv.* not anywhere, not in any place or state. [OE.].

NOWISE [nō′wiz], *adv.* by no means, not in any manner or degree. [NO and WISE].

NOXIOUS [nok′shŏŏs], *adj.* hurtful, corrupting, injurious. [L.].

NOZZLE [no′zl], *n.* projecting vent or mouthpiece; snout or nose. [*Dim.* of NOSE (1)].

NUANCE [nyŏŏ′ance], *n.* subtle, delicate difference or distinction. [Fr.].

NUB [nub], *n.* small lump. [*Var.* of KNOB].

NUBILE [nyŏŏ′bil], *adj.* (of a woman) marriageable, being of an age or condition to marry. [L.].

NUCIFORM [nyŏŏ′si-fawm], *adj.* having the shape of a nut. [L.].

NUCLEAR [nyŏŏ′kli-er], *adj.* of, or pertaining to, a nucleus; (*phys.*) *esp.* pertaining to the study of the structure of the atom; **n. fission,** approximately equipartite disintegration of the central core of an atom.

NUCLEATE (1) [nyŏŏ′kli-āt], *v.t. and i.* to form or cause to form into or about a nucleus. NUCLEATE (2), *adj.* possessing or formed into a nucleus.

NUCLEOLUS [nyŏŏ-klē′ō-lus, nyŏŏ-kli-ō′lus], *n.* small nucleus contained within another. [L.].

NUCLEUS (*pl.* **nuclei**) [nyŏŏ′kli-us], *n.* central core

ŏŏ is pronounced as in food; ŏŏ as in hood; th as in *think*; TH as in *that*; zh as in azure. ~ = related to.

or kernel about which matter gathers; beginning, starting-point; centre, essential, life-giving part of something; (*astron.*) centre of a sunspot; head of a comet; (*biol.*) essential, life-giving part of a cell or organism; (*phys.*) central unit of an atom. [L.].

NUDE (1) [nyōōd], *adj.* naked, bare, without covering or decoration; unclad; (*leg.*) not attested or recorded, void. **NUDE** (2), *n.* the human figure unclad, undraped; painting, sculpture etc. representing the human figure undraped; state of being unclad. [L.].

NUDGE (1) [nuj], *v.t.* to give a slight, sometimes furtive, push with the elbow so as to attract attention or give point to what one is saying or what is being said. **NUDGE** (2), *n.* slight push with the elbow. [Unkn.].

NUDISM [nyōō'dizm], *n.* practice of going naked.

NUDIST (1) [nyōō'dist], *n.* one who practises nudism. **NUDIST** (2), *adj.* pertaining to nudism; **n. camp,** open-air camp inhabited by nudists.

NUDITY [nyōō'di-ti], *n.* nakedness.

NUGATORY [nyōō'ga-te-ri], *adj.* valueless, trifling; ineffectual, invalid, futile. [L.].

NUGGET [nu'git], *n.* lump of metal, *esp.* of native gold. [Unkn.].

NUISANCE [nyōō'sans], *n.* that which causes damage, hindrance, injury or annoyance etc. [Fr.].

NULL [nul], *adj.* void, having no legal validity; ineffectual. [Fr. from L.].

NULLIFY [nu'li-fi], *v.t.* to cancel, render void. [L.].

NULLITY [nu'li-ti], *n.* condition of being void, cancelled or of no validity; nonentity. [Fr.].

NUMB (1) [num], *adj.* lacking the sense of touch; deadened, insensible. **NUMB** (2), *v.t.* to render n. [OE.].

NUMBER (1) [num'ber], *n.* total, sum, aggregate; the aggregate of a collection, group, series etc.; symbol for an arithmetical total; name of such a symbol; a total of abstract units; large quantity, large collection of units; something or somebody distinguished by a numerical symbol; a single issue of a periodical publication; one of a collection of poems, songs etc.; unit of an opera or oratorio; song or piece of music; (*gram.*) that quality in a word which is expressive of whether one, two or more than two are referred to; the form of the word denoting this; **numbers,** arithmetic; lines, verses; **in n.,** in quantity, considered numerically; **without, out of n.,** uncountable, very many; **one's n. is up,** one is finished, doomed. **NUMBER** (2), *v.t. and i.* to count, enumerate; be of a certain numerical quantity; divide, apportion; set in a numerical series; fix the n. of, end; **to n. among,** to include, comprise; **to n. with,** to be equal with numerically, reckon with. [Fr. from L.].

NUMBERLESS [num'ber-les], *adj.* too many to be counted.

NUMBER-PLATE [num'ber-plāt], *n.* metal plate bearing a number; plate on a motor-car bearing its index mark and number.

NUMERAL (1) [nyōō'me-ral], *adj.* pertaining to numbers, numbering, or numerical symbols. **NUMERAL** (2), *n.* symbol representing an arithmetical total; name of such a symbol. **NUMERALLY,** *adv.* by number. [LL.].

NUMERATION [nyōō-me-rā'shn], *n.* act or art of numbering; counting, calculation. [L.].

NUMERATOR [nyōō'me-rā-ter], *n.* (*arith.*) the term in a fraction denoting the number of units in the fraction; the figure or figures following the decimal point; one who counts, *esp.* a census-taker. [LL.].

NUMERICAL [nyōō-me'ri-kal], *adj.* pertaining to numbers, numeration etc.; expressed in numbers.

NUMEROUS [nyōō'me-rŏŏs], *adj.* consisting of a great number, containing many units.

NUMINOUS [nyōō'mi-nŏŏs], *adj.* divine; suggestive of divine power. [L.].

NUMISMATIC [nyōō-miz-ma'tik], *adj.* pertaining to coins, medals or coinage.

NUMISMATICS [nyōō-miz-ma'tiks], *n.*(*pl.*) science and study of coins and medals.

NUMISMATIST [nyōō-miz'ma-tist], *n.* one who studies coins, medals or coinage. [Fr.].

NUMISMATOLOGY [nyōō-miz-ma-to'lo-ji], *n.* numismatics. [L. and Gk.].

NUMMARY, NUMMULARY [nu'ma-ri, nu'myŏŏ-la-ri], *adj.* pertaining to coins and money, resembling a coin. [~L.].

NUMSKULL [num'skul], *n.* dunce, dolt. [NUMB (1) and SKULL].

NUN [nun], *n.* member of a religious order for women, inhabiting a convent, and living under vows of chastity etc.; (*zool.*) certain varieties of moths or birds; **nun's veiling,** delicate fabric of the sort used for nuns' veils. [OE.].

NUNCIO [nun'shi-ō], *n.* Papal ambassador. **NUNCIATURE** [nun'shi-a-tyōōr], *n.* dignity and tenure of the office of Papal N. [It.].

NUNCUPATIVE [nun'kyōō-pā-tiv], *adj.* conveyed by word of mouth, not by writing. [MedL.].

NUNNERY [nu'ne-ri], *n.* house for nuns, convent. [Fr.].

NUPHAR [nyōō'fah(r)], *n.* the yellow water-lily. [~NENUPHAR].

NUPTIAL [nup'shal], *adj.* pertaining to a marriage. [L.].

NUPTIALS [nup'shalz], *n.*(*pl.*) the wedding ceremony.

NURSE (1) [nurs], *n.* female attendant upon children; one who suckles children; person skilled to look after the sick; (*fig.*) that which fosters and protects. **NURSE** (2), *v.t. and i.* to suckle; carry (a child etc.) on the arms or support it in the lap; give skilled attention to (a sick person); cherish or foster; take care of, avoid waste of etc.; act as a nurse; **to n. the fire,** (*fig.*) to sit very close to the fire. [OFr. from L.].

NURSEMAID [nurs'mād], *n.* maid who looks after children.

NURSERY [nur'se-ri], *n.* room for children where they can play, keep their toys etc.; place for the rearing of young plants prior to their transplantation to the place where it is intended they shall reach maturity; (*fig.*) place where anything is trained and fostered; **n. school,** school for children under five.

NURSERYMAN [nur'se-ri-man], *n.* grower of plants for sale, one who keeps a nursery.

NURSING [nur'sing], *adj.* suckling a child.

NURSLING [nurs'ling], *n.* baby under the care of its nurse or mother; also (*fig.*). [NURSE].

NURTURE (1) [nur'tyōōr], *n.* food, nourishment; upbringing, training and education. **NURTURE** (2), *v.t.* to feed or nourish; rear, educate. [OFr. from LL.].

NUT (1) [nut], *n.* hard-shelled fruit of certain trees and plants the shell of which contains an edible kernel; the kernel of such fruit; small metal block pierced with a hole which is threaded with a female screw to screw on to a bolt; contrivance at the lower end of a violin bow by which the hairs may be tightened or relaxed; (*slang*) the head; (*slang*) young dandy; **tough n.,** very determined person, hard to be persuaded; **hard n. to crack,** very difficult problem; **can't do it for nuts,** (*coll.*) very bad at it; **to be (dead) nuts on,** (*coll.*) to be very fond of, very excited about; **to be off one's n.,** (*coll.*) to be mentally unbalanced, insane. **NUTS,** small lumps of coal; (*slang*) mad, eccentric; (*int.*) rubbish, tosh. **NUT** (2) [*pres.pt.* NUTTING, *pret. and p.pt.* NUTTED], *v.i.* to gather nuts. [OE.].

NUTATION [nyōō-tā'shn], *n.* drooping of the head; (*astron.*) slight oscillating movement of the earth's axis; slight bending of the stem of a plant. [L.].

NUT-BUTTER [nut-bu'ter], *n.* butter substitute made from the kernels of nuts.

NUTCRACKER (1) [nut'kra-ker], *n.* a European nut-eating bird. **NUT-CRACKERS,** *n.*(*pl.*) pincerlike instrument for cracking nuts. **NUT-CRACKER** (2), *adj.* (of the nose and chin) tending to meet.

NUTHATCH [nut'hach], *n.* a small bird which feeds upon nuts. [NUT (1) and ~HACK].

NUTMEG [nut'meg], *n.* aromatic fruit of a Malay tree, used as a spice in cooking. [NUT (1) and OFr.].

NUT-OIL [nut'oil], *n.* oil crushed from nuts, *esp.* the groundnut.

NUTRIA [nyōō'tri-ah], *n.* fur of the South American water rodent, the coypu. [Span.].

NUTRIENT (1) [nyōō'tri-ent], *adj.* nourishing. **NUTRIENT** (2), *n.* anything which nourishes. [L.].

NUTRIMENT [nyōō'tri-ment], *n.* that which nourishes; food, nourishment. [L.].

NUTRITION [nyōō-tri'shn], *n.* process by which a living organism feeds itself by assimilating to itself nourishing matter; food, nourishment.

NUTRITIOUS [nyōō-tri'shŏŏs], *adj.* nourishing, promoting growth. [L.].

NUTRITIVE [nyōō'tri-tiv], *adj.* nourishing; pertaining to nutrition.

NUTSHELL [nut'shel], *n.* hard case about the kernel of a nut; **in a n.,** briefly.

NUT-TREE [nut'trē], *n.* a nut-bearing tree, *esp.* the hazel.

NUTTY [nu'ti], *adj.* rich in nuts; having the flavour of nuts; (*slang*) smart, dandy-like; absurd, crazy.

NUTTINESS, *n.* the taste of nuts; flavour resembling this.

NUX VOMICA [nuks-vo'mi-kah], *n.* seed of the tree, *Strychnos,* containing strychnine; substance extracted from this and used for medicinal purposes. [L.].

NUZZLE [nu'zl], *v.t. and i.* to push or thrust with the nose. [~NOZZLE].

NYLGHAU [nil'gow], *n.* the nilgai. [Pers.].

NYLON [ni'lon], *n. (prot.)* a synthetic silk used to make fabrics and bristles; **nylons,** women's stockings made of n. yarn. [From *New York* and *London*].

NYMPH [nimf], *n. (classical myth.)* maiden deity

supposed to dwell in and be the spirit of wells, springs, woods, rivers etc.; *(poet.)* young woman; *(biol.)* pupa or chrysalis. [Gk.].

NYMPHOLEPSY [nim'fō-lep-si], *n.* state of frenzy produced by impassioned desire for something unattainable. NYMPHOLEPT, *n.* person suffering from n.; fanatic. [Gk.].

NYMPHOMANIA [nim-fō-mā'ni-ah], *n.* excessive and morbid sexual desire in women. NYMPHOMANIAC, *n. and adj.* (one) suffering from n. [NYMPH and MANIA].

NYSTAGMUS [nis-tag'mus], *n. (med.)* involuntary oscillation of the eyeball. [Gk.].

O (1) [ō], fourth vowel and fifteenth letter of the English alphabet; anything resembling the letter O in shape; the symbol for nought.

O (2), *int.* exclamation used in exhortation, invocation, appeal or solemn address.

O' (3), *prep.* short form of OF; in phrases like *four o'clock, tug-o'-war, man-o'-war* etc.

OAF [ōf], *n.* changeling; deformed child; lout; idiot. OAFISH, *adj.* stupid, clumsy, like an o. [OScand.].

OAK (1) [ōk], *n.* tree of the genus *Quercus;* **the Oaks,** race for three-year-old fillies, run at Epsom and named after an estate of Lord Derby. OAK (2), *adj.* of, made of, or pertaining to, o. [OE.].

OAK-APPLE [ōk'a-pl], *n.* excrescence produced on oaks by gall-flies; **O. Day,** 29 May, day of the restoration of Charles II.

OAKEN [ō'ken], *adj.* made of oak. [OE.].

OAK-GALL [ōk'gawl], *n.* oak-apple.

OAKLING [ōk'ling], *n.* young small oak.

OAKUM [ō'kum], *n.* fibre obtained by unpicking old ropes, used to caulk the seams of ships. [OE.].

OAR [aw(r)], *n.* long pole, one end of which is grasped by the hands and the other is shaped into a blade, for propelling a boat; oarsman; rowing boat; **pair (four) o.,** boat for two (four) rowers; **chained to the o.,** tied to a task; **to put one's o. in, to put in one's o.,** to meddle, interfere; **to rest on one's oars,** to slacken effort, content with what has been done; **to pull a good o.,** to row well; **to ship oars,** to take the oars aboard; **to unship oars,** to put them in position for rowing; **to toss oars,** to salute with raised oars. OARED, *adj.* having oars. [OE.].

OARAGE [aw'rij], *n. (poet.)* rowing; the number of oars in a boat.

OARSMAN [awz'man], *n.* man who rows with an oar.

OASIS *(pl.* oases) [ō-ā'sis, 'sēz], *n.* fertile place in a sandy desert; *(fig.)* relief after tedium; pleasant change amid unpleasant things. [Gk.].

OAST [ōst], *n.* kiln for drying hops. OAST-HOUSE, building which contains an oast-kiln.

OAT (1) [ōt], *n. (poet.)* pipe or other simple musical instrument made of an oat stalk. OAT (2), *adj.* oaten. [OE.].

OATCAKE [ōt'kāk], *n.* flat cake made of oatmeal.

OATEN [ō'ten], *n.* made of oats or oat straw.

OATH [ōth], *n.* sacred, solemn and binding promise; words expressing such a promise; blasphemous expletive, profanity; **on o., under o.,** (of a testimony) made after taking an official oath on the Bible to tell the truth; **to take the o.,** to swear formally to tell the truth, *esp.* in a court of law.

OATMEAL [ōt'mēl], *n.* meal ground from oats.

OATS [ōts], *n.* the cereal *Avena sativa,* or its grains, which are used as food; **wild o.,** *Avena fatua,* the uncultivated species; **to sow one's wild o.,** to indulge in dissipation as a young man; **to feel one's o.,** *(U.S. slang)* to feel important. [OE.].

OB-, *pref.* against, in the direction of, in the way of, harmful to, hostile to, down, across, over. [L.].

OBBLIGATO (1) [o-bli-gah'tō], *adj. (mus.)* necessary, intended to be played exactly as written. OBBLIGATO (2), *n.* second instrumental accompaniment to a song in addition to the first accompaniment. [It.].

OBDURACY [ob'dyōo-ra-si], *n.* stubbornness of character, sentiment or action.

OBDURATE [ob'dyōo-rat], *adj.* hardened in heart;

stubborn; obstinately impenitent, untouched by appeals to tender feeling.

OBEAH, OBI [ō-bē'ah, ō'bi], *n.* native West African magic; magic object, fetish. [Native].

OBEDIENCE [ō-bē'di-ens], *n.* submission to authority, to laws, rules and orders; condition of being obedient; *(eccles.)* fact of being obeyed, dominion, *esp.* such as is possessed by a church over its members. [L.].

OBEDIENT [ō-bē'di-ent], *adj.* submitting to command. [L.].

OBEDIENTIARY [ō-bē-di-en'sha-ri], *n.* member of a religious house who gives obedience to the authority of the Superior.

OBEISANCE [ō-bā'sans], *n.* low bow or curtsey. [OFr.].

OBELISK [o'be-lisk], *n.* four-sided stone pillar, tapering towards the top and crowned with a small pointed cone or pyramid; sign used in printed books, thus †. [Gk.].

OBELUS [o'bi-lus], *n.* mark used in manuscripts to suggest that the text is probably corrupt. [Gk.].

OBESE [ō-bēs'], *adj.* corpulent. [L.].

OBESITY [ō-bē'si-ti], *n.* state of being obese; corpulence. [Fr.].

OBEY [ō-bā'], *v.t. and i.* to execute the commands or wishes of; render obedience to; act in accordance with; be obedient. [L.].

OBFUSCATE [ob'fus-kāt], *v.t.* to obscure, render dark; bewilder. [L.].

OBI, see OBEAH.

OBITER [o'bi-ter], *adv.* incidentally; **o. dictum** *(pl.* **o. dicta),** *(leg.)* incidental remark by the judge not to be considered as part of his judgment; any incidental remark. [L.].

OBITUARY (1) [ō-bi'tyōo-a-ri], *n.* notice of a death in a newspaper, usually including a short account of the life and personality of the deceased; *(eccles.)* list of names of members of a religious community who have died. OBITUARY (2), *adj.* pertaining or relating to death. [MedL.].

OBJECT (1) [ob'jekt], *n.* something visible or tangible, a thing seen or touched, material thing; something mentally apprehensible; something which rouses emotion or excites attention; that on which desire is set and to which activity is directed, aim, purpose; *(gram.)* noun, pronoun, phrase or clause governed by a transitive verb; **o. ball,** ball in billiards at which a player takes aim when striking the cue ball; **no o.,** not important, not considered. OBJECT-FINDER, device for registering the position of any particular o. on a microscopic slide. OBJECT-GLASS, glass in a telescope or microscope which is nearest to the o. viewed and farthest from the eye of the viewer. OBJECT (2) [ob-jekt'], *v.t. and i.* to state or say as an objection; protest, oppose. OBJECTOR, *n.* one who objects, *esp.* on grounds of conscience. [L.].

OBJECTION [ob-jek'shn], *n.* statement, argument etc. put forward in disapproval of something; sense of disapproval and dislike; defect, flaw. [L.].

OBJECTIONABLE [ob-jek'shn-a-bl], *adj.* open to objection; offensive; undesirable, unpleasant.

OBJECTIVE (1) [ob-jek'tiv], *adj.* relating to objects; existing independently of the mind conceiving it; pertaining to the purpose of an action; *(gram.)* pertaining to a case other than the nominative; impartial, unprejudiced. OBJECTIVE (2), *n.* purpose towards which an action is directed; (milit.) position which is to be reached or attacked; (gram.) the o. case; object-glass; lens system of a camera.

OBJECTIVISM [ob-jek'ti-vizm], n. (philos.) theory that knowledge derived from sensuous perception possesses objective validity.

OBJECTLESS [ob'jekt-les], adj. lacking object; aimless, purposeless.

OBJECT-LESSON [ob'jekt-le-son], n. lesson in which the teacher has with him the object or a copy of it, with which to illustrate his remarks; piece of teaching by example, usually of a deserved misfortune which is considered as a warning to others.

OBJURE [ob-joor'], v.t. to charge under oath. OBJURATION [ob-joo-rā'shn], n. solemn swearing. [L.].

OBJURGATE [ob'jer-gāt], v.t. to reprove, chide. OBJURGATION [ob-jer-gā'shn], n. reproof, rebuke. OBJURGATORY [ob'jer-gā-te-ri, ob-jur'ga-te-ri], adj. conveying censure or reproof. [~L.].

OBLANCEOLATE [ob-lan'si-ō-lāt], adj. inversely lanceolate, tapering at the base.

OBLATE (1) [ob'lāt], n. dedicated person. [L.].

OBLATE (2) [o-blāt'], adj. (geom.) used of spheroid bodies which are flattened at the poles. [L.].

OBLATION [o-blā'shn], n. offering, pious gift; offering which forms part of an act of worship. OBLATIONAL, OBLATORY [o-blā'shn-al, ob'la-te-ri], pertaining to o. [L.].

OBLIGATE [ob'li-gāt], v.t. to place under obligation either legally or morally, compel. [L.].

OBLIGATION [ob-li-gā'shn], n. legal or moral constraint or compulsion; liability incurred by promise, oath or agreement; state of being indebted; moral debt arising from doing or receiving a kindness; necessity. [L.].

OBLIGATORY [o-bli'ga-te-ri], adj. morally or legally binding; compulsory.

OBLIGE [o-blij'], v.t. to cause to be indebted by a kindness; do a service or kindness to; constrain, compel. OBLIGEE [ob-li-jē'], n. person to whom another is under bond, whether legal or moral. OBLIGOR [ob-li-jaw(r)'], n. one who gives his bond. [Fr. from L.].

OBLIGING [o-bli'jing], adj. kind and courteous.

OBLIQUE [ō-blēk'], adj. aslant, neither vertical nor horizontal; indirect; allusive; (gram.) relating to a case other than the nominative; o. angle, angle other than a right angle. OBLIQUELY, adv. in an o. fashion. [L.].

OBLIQUITY [ō-bli'kwi-ti], n. obliqueness, indirectness; dishonesty or untruthfulness. [L.].

OBLITERATE [ob-li'te-rāt], v.t. to efface, wear out; cover up; render illegible. [L.].

OBLIVION [ob-li'vi-on], n. forgetfulness; state of being out of mind and forgotten. [L.].

OBLIVIOUS [ob-li'vi-ōōs], adj. forgetful, unaware. [L.].

OBLONG (1) [ob'long], adj. less broad than long. OBLONG (2), n. rectangular figure having two opposite and equal sides longer than the other two opposite and equal sides. [L.].

OBLOQUY [ob'lo-kwi], n. abusive language; reproachful, chiding or accusing utterance; state of being censured; disgrace. [LL.].

OBNOXIOUS [ob-nok'shi-ōōs], adj. odious, giving offence; hurtful.

OBOE [ō'bō], n. wooden wind-instrument; hautboy. OBOIST, n. o. player. [It.].

OBSCENE [ob-sēn'], adj. disgusting, immodest, lewd. OBSCENELY, adv. in an o. way. [L.].

OBSCENITY [ob-se'ni-ti], n. lewdness; indecent talk, action etc., immodesty. [L.].

OBSCURANT (1) [ob-skyoor'ant], n. a foe to enlightenment. OBSCURANT (2), adj. rendering obscure. OBSCURANTISM [ob-skyoor'an-tizm], n. principles of one who opposes enlightenment.

OBSCURANTIST (1) [ob-skyoor'an-tist], n. an obscurant. OBSCURANTIST (2), adj. of, or pertaining to, an o. or obscurantism.

OBSCURATION [ob-skyoor-ā'shn], n. act of darkening, or fact of being darkened.

OBSCURE (1) [ob-skyoor'], adj. lacking light, faintly lighted, dim, dark; gloomy; without clear outline, scarcely perceptible; (of sounds etc.) confused; indistinct; secret, retired, humble; puzzling, hard to understand. OBSCURE (2), v.t. to render o.; veil, hide, make only partly visible; render difficult to understand. [L.].

OBSCURITY [ob-skyoor'i-ti], n. state of being obscure, darkness; ambiguity; humble state. [L.].

OBSECRATE [ob'si-krāt], v.t. to implore, beseech. OBSECRATION [ob-si-krā'shn], n. supplication, entreaty. [L.].

OBSEQUIAL [ob-sē'kwi-al], adj. pertaining to obsequies.

OBSEQUIES [ob'si-kwiz], n.(pl.) funeral ceremonies; funeral. [OFr.].

OBSEQUIOUS [ob-sē'kwi-ōōs], adj. fawning and servile. [L.].

OBSERVABLE [ob-zur'va-bl], adj. noticeable; noteworthy.

OBSERVANCE [ob-zur'vans], n. act of observing; habit, custom; commemoration rite. [L.].

OBSERVANT (1) [ob-zur'vant], adj. strict in the keeping of commands; alert, vigilant. OBSERVANT (2), n. one of the branch of Franciscans called Friars O. [L.].

OBSERVATION (1) [ob-zer-vā'shn], n. act of observing; faculty or habit of observing; the watching and recording of phenomena etc.; a comment or critical remark; (pl.) facts collected as a result of observing; a collection of critical and deductive comments. OBSERVATION (2), adj. pertaining to, or used for, observing. OBSERVATIONAL, adj. pertaining to, or founded on, o. [L.].

OBSERVATORY [ob-zur'va-te-ri], n. place equipped for making observations, esp. astronomical.

OBSERVE [ob-zurv'], v.t. and i. to obey, keep, be observant of; watch attentively; remark, comment; take notice. [L.].

OBSERVER [ob-zur'ver], n. one who watches, observes or adheres to; Royal O. Corps, body of watchers who report the approach of enemy aircraft.

OBSESS [ob-ses'], v.t. to haunt; monopolize the thoughts of. [L.].

OBSESSION [ob-se'shn], n. intense mental preoccupation; fixed unshakable notion, monomania. [L.].

OBSIDIAN [ob-si'di-an], n. dark, vitreous volcanic rock, volcanic glass. [MdL.].

OBSOLESCENCE [ob-so-le'sens], n. process of passing into disuse.

OBSOLESCENT [ob-so-le'sent], adj. going out of use, becoming obsolete. [L.].

OBSOLETE [ob'so-lēt], adj. disused; old-fashioned. [L.].

OBSTACLE [ob'sta-kl], n. anything which hinders; impediment or barrier; o. race, race in which natural or artificial obstacles have to be surmounted. [L.].

OBSTETRIC(AL) [ob-ste'trik(-al)], adj. pertaining to, or used in, midwifery. [L.].

OBSTETRICIAN [ob-ste-tri'shan], n. one skilled in obstetrics.

OBSTETRICS [ob-ste'triks], n.(pl.) science of midwifery.

OBSTINACY [ob'sti-na-si], n. dogged resolution; unreasoning persistence in one's projects, opinions etc.; stubbornness.

OBSTINATE [ob'sti-nat], n. stubborn and pertinacious; pigheaded, intractable. [L.].

OBSTREPEROUS [ob-stre'pe-rōōs], adj. clamorous, noisy; turbulent and intractable. [L.].

OBSTRUCT [ob-strukt'], v.t. to make impassable; prevent from moving or passing; impede, get in the way of; oppose, thwart; oppose progress. OBSTRUCTER, n. one who obstructs. [L.].

OBSTRUCTION [ob-struk'shn], n. act of obstructing; hindrance or impediment; that which is or gets in the way. [L.].

OBSTRUCTIONISM [ob-struk'shn-izm], n. act or policy of putting obstacles in the way of progress or reform. OBSTRUCTIONIST, n. one who practises o.

OBSTRUCTIVE [ob-struk'tiv], adj. causing hindrance.

OBTAIN [ob-tān'], v.t. and i. to acquire, get possession of, receive; be prevalent; hold good, be valid. OBTAINABLE, adj. able to be obtained. [Fr. from L.].

OBTRUDE [ob-trōōd'], v.t. and i. to push forward, compel attention to (ideas etc.); intrude. [L.].

OBTRUSION [ob-trōō'zhn], n. act of thrusting upon or obtruding. [LL.].

OBTRUSIVE [ob-trōō'siv], adj. disposed to obtrude; pushing and intrusive.

OBTURATE [ob'tyoor-āt], v.t. to stop up; close the breech of a gun. OBTURATOR [ob'tyoor-ā-ter], n. device to prevent the escape of gas from a gun when it is fired; shutter of a camera; (anat.) a membrane in the thigh; (surg.) artificial plate used to cover a gap in the body, e.g. a cleft palate. [L.].

OBTUSE [ob-tyōōs'], adj. blunt, having no sharp

---

point; stupid, dull; **o. angle,** angle greater than a right angle and less than 180 deg.

OBVERSE (1) [ob′vers], *adj.* facing, turned towards, the person who is looking; (*bot.*) (of leaves) having the attached end narrower than the tip. OBVERSE (2), *n.* (*numis.*) side of a coin bearing the head; fact, idea etc., which is the complement of another. [L.].

OBVIATE [ob′vi-āt], *v.t.* to clear out of the way, get rid of, render unnecessary. [L.].

OBVIOUS [ob′vi-ŏos], *adj.* plainly apparent, easily perceived, impossible to mistake; too apparent, obtrusive; easily understandable, simple. [L.].

OCARINA [o-ka-rē′nah], *n.* small musical instrument, having a mouthpiece and finger-holes, in sound resembling a flute. [It.].

OCCASION (1) [o-kā′zhn], *n.* a point in time marked by a certain action or event; suitable moment; chance, opportunity; cause for action, an immediate provocation of events actually arising from older and deeper causes; **occasions,** lawful and necessary business; **on o.,** as and when time or circumstances demand; **to rise to the o.,** to be equal to the demands of the moment; **to take o. to,** to choose, in those circumstances or at that moment, to. OCCASION (2), *v.t.* to cause; provide opportunity for o. for. [L.].

OCCASIONAL [o-kā′zhn-al], *adj.* happening now and then, not frequently or continuously; occurring or appearing at long intervals; intended for or fitted to a special occasion. OCCASIONALLY, *adv.* now and then, from time to time.

OCCIDENT [ok′si-dent], *n.* the west generally; the western part of the world viewed from a European standpoint but including the west of Europe. [L.].

OCCIDENTAL [ok-si-den′tal], *adj.* western; pertaining to the occident. OCCIDENTALISM, *n.* civilization of the west. OCCIDENTALIST, *n.* student or admirer of western habits and ideas. OCCIDENTALIZE, *v.t.* to give western habits and ideas to.

OCCIPITAL [ok-si′pi-tal], *adj.* belonging to the occiput.

OCCIPUT [ok′si-put], *n.* back section of the head. [L.].

OCCLUDE [o-klŏod′], *v.t.* to shut in or shut out; (*chem.*) absorb. [L.].

OCCLUSION [o-klŏo′zhn], *n.* act of occluding or fact of having been occluded; (*phon.*) rapid momentary shutting of the vocal passage in speech; (*chem.*) absorption; (*anat.*) normal overlapping position of the upper teeth over the lower when the jaws are closed. [L.].

OCCULT (1) [o-kult′], *adj.* hidden, secret; magical, supernatural. OCCULT (2), *n.* the supernatural; that which lies beyond the normal; psychic experience. OCCULT (3), *v.t. and i.* to become hidden; (*astron.*) eclipse. [L.].

OCCULTATION [o-kul-tā′shn], *n.* (*astron.*) eclipse of one body by another. [L.].

OCCULTISM [o-kul′tizm], *n.* trust in, and study of, the supernatural; mysticism.

OCCUPANCY [o′kyŏo-pan-si], *n.* act of taking or retaining possession, residence in a place; (*leg.*) acquirement of right of possession of that which is owned by no one.

OCCUPANT [o′kyŏo-pant], *n.* he who occupies; one who inhabits a dwelling.

OCCUPATION [o-kyŏo-pā′shn], *n.* act of obtaining and retaining possession; temporary military possession of the territory of a defeated enemy; period of tenure of a property; tenure, residence; employment, trade. [L.].

OCCUPATIONAL [o-kyŏo-pā′shn-al], *adj.* relating to, occasioned by, an occupation or trade; **o. disease,** ailment brought about by the special conditions of specific work.

OCCUPIER [o′kyŏo-pī-er], *n.* one who occupies or dwells in; tenant.

OCCUPY [o′kyŏo-pī], *v.t.* to obtain and retain possession of; take and hold by military force; settle troops in (the territories of a defeated enemy) till peace terms are ratified; dwell in; fill with oneself (a chair etc.); hold, be regularly in, a particular place; consume time or attention of; busy oneself; **to be occupied with,** to be busy with. [Fr. from L.].

OCCUR (*pres.pt.* **occurring,** *pret. and p.pt.* **occurred**) [o-kur′], *v.i.* to happen; exist, arise; **to o. to,** to enter the mind of. [L.].

OCCURRENCE [o-ku′rens], *n.* event, that which occurs; act of occurring. [Fr.].

OCEAN (1) [ō′shn], *n.* the open sea; (*fig.*) large

quantity; **oceans of,** (*slang*) plenty and to spare of. OCEAN (2), *adj.* belonging to the o. OCEANIC [ō-shi-a′nik], *adj.* pertaining to, or coming from, the o. [Gk.].

OCEANID [ō-sē′a-nid], *n.* (*Gk. myth.*) ocean nymph; a marine mollusc. [Gk.].

OCEANOGRAPHIC(AL) [ō-shn-o-gra′fik(-al)], *adj.* pertaining to oceanography.

OCEANOGRAPHY [ō-shn-o′gra-fi], *n.* study of the ocean, its movements and its flora and fauna. [Gk.].

OCELOT [ō′si-lot], *n.* South American wild cat; tiger-cat. [Fr.].

OCHRE [ō′ker], *n.* clay-like oxide of iron used for making yellow or brown pigments; colouring made from these. OCHREOUS [ō′krē-ŏos], *adj.* resembling or consisting of o. [Gk.].

O′CLOCK [ō-klok′], *adv.* by or according to the clock. [Shortened from *of the clock*].

OCT-, OCTA-, OCTO-, *pref.* eight. [Gk.].

OCTACHORD [ok′ta-kawd], *n.* musical instrument which has eight strings; a diatonic octave. [Gk.].

OCTAD [ok′tad], *n.* a series of eight; (*chem.*) element which has the combining power of eight hydrogen atoms. [Gk.].

OCTAGON [ok′ta-gon], *n.* (*geom.*) an eight-sided and eight-angled polygon; (*arch.*) eight-sided building or room. OCTAGONAL [ok-ta′go-nal], *adj.* formed with eight sides and eight angles. [Gk.].

OCTAHEDRON (*pl.* **octahedra, octahedrons**) [ok-ta-hē′dron], *n.* solid figure having eight plane faces each of which, if the figure is regular, is an equilateral triangle. OCTAHEDRAL, *adj.* formed with eight plane faces; resembling an o.; consisting of octahedrons. [Gk.].

OCTANE [ok′tān], *n.* (*chem.*) a paraffin of the formula C_8H_{18}, used as a fuel for aeroplane engines. [OCT and (METH)ANE].

OCTANT [ok′tant], *n.* eighth part of the area of a circle; eighth part of the circumference of a circle; (*naut. and astron.*) device for taking angular measurements. [LL.].

OCTAVE [ok′tiv], *n.* (*eccles.*) the day falling a week after a festival; period between a festival and its octave; (*mus.*) note eight diatonic degrees above or below another note (counting both notes); scale contained by and including those two notes; chord consisting of two notes eight diatonic degrees apart (counting both notes); wine-cask holding 13½ gallons, an eighth of a pipe. [L.].

OCTAVO [ok-tā′vō], *n.* the size of a book or its pages when each page is one-eighth the size of the sheets from which it has been folded; book with pages of this size. [L.].

OCTENNIAL [ok-te′ni-al], *adj.* occurring once in eight years; lasting for eight years. [L.].

OCTET [ok′tet, ok-tet′], *n.* (*mus.*) composition with eight parts or voices; (*pros.*) eight lines of verse; the first eight lines of a sonnet. [OCT and (DU)ET].

OCTILLION [ok-til′yun], *n.* a million raised to the eighth power (1 followed by 48 ciphers). [Fr.].

OCTO-, see OCT-.

OCTOBER [ok-tō′ber], *n.* tenth month of the year. [L.].

OCTOCENTENARY [ok-tō-sen-tē′na-ri], *n.* eight-hundredth anniversary. [OCTO and CENTENARY].

OCTODECIMO [ok-tō-de′si-mō], *n.* book the sheets of which are folded into eighteen leaves; size of a page in such a book (often represented by 18mo). [L.].

OCTOGENARIAN (1) [ok-tō-je-näer′i-an], *adj.* eighty to ninety years old. OCTOGENARIAN (2), *n.* person over eighty but not yet ninety years of age. [L.].

OCTOPUS (*pl.* **octopodes** or **octopuses**) [ok′tō-pus], *n.* (*zool.*) group of cephalopod molluscs which have eight arms provided with suckers; (*fig.*) organization with influence and interests in many directions. [Gk.].

OCTOROON [ok-tō-rŏon′], *n.* child of a white person and a quadroon, person having one-eighth negro blood. [OCTO and (QUAD)ROON].

OCTOSYLLABLE [ok-tō-si′la-bl], *n.* word of eight syllables; (*pros.*) verse having eight syllables.

OCTUPLE (1) [ok′tyŏo-pl], *adj.* eightfold. OCTUPLE (2), *v.t.* to multiply by eight. [L.].

OCULAR (1) [o′kyŏo-ler], *adj.* pertaining to eyes or sight; visual; visible. OCULAR (2), *n.* eyepiece of an optical instrument. OCULARLY, *adv.* by the eye; by sight.

OCULIST [o′kyŏo-list], *n.* fully-qualified specialist in the treatment of the eye. [Fr.].

ŏo is pronounced as in *food*; ŏo as in *hood*; th as in *think*; ᴛʜ as in *that*; zh as in *azure*. ~ = related to.

ODALISQUE [ŏ′da-lisk], *n.* concubine or female slave in an eastern harem. [Turk.].

ODD (1) [od], *adj.* not yielding a whole number when divided by two; numbered by the series one, three, five etc.; not a pair; being surplus to the main amount; being left over and to spare; one of a pair left over; strange, not normal; occasional, not regular; of small importance. **ODD** (2), *n.* the thirteenth, and winning, trick where each side in the game of whist has scored six; (*golf*) next stroke played after each player has played an equal number of strokes. **ODDLY,** *adv.* in an o. fashion. **ODDNESS,** *n.* quality of being o. [OScand.].

ODDFELLOW [od′fe-lŏ], *n.* member of a mutual aid society so named.

ODDITY [o′di-ti], *n.* singular person or thing, misfit or curiosity; quality of being odd; singularity.

ODDMENT [od′ment], *n.* something left over; (*pl.*) odds and ends.

ODDS [odz], *n.*(*pl.*) things not equal; difference; balance of probability; that necessary to produce equality; (*betting*) ratio between the amount paid to make the bet and the amount payable if the bet is successful; **it makes no o.**, it does not matter; **against long o.**, against a heavy adverse chance; **to be at o. with,** to disagree with; **o. and ends,** remnants, things left over; **to lay the o.,** (*betting*) to offer to bet at such a price as will be favourable to the other party; **over the o.,** too much. **ODDS-ON,** on which o. are laid.

ODE [ōd], *n.* song in Greek drama, accompanied by music and dancing; lyric poem composed for some special occasion. [Fr.].

ODEON [ŏ′di-on, ŏ-dē′on], *n.* odeum. [Gk.].

ODEUM (*pl.* **odia**) [ŏ′dē-um, ŏ-dē′um], *n.* building for dramatic or musical entertainment in the ancient world; theatre, concert hall. [*Prec.*].

ODIOUS [ō′di-ŏŏs], *adj.* hateful, disgusting, repulsive. [L.].

ODIUM [ō′di-um], *n.* hatred or disgust; opprobrium. [L.].

ODOMETER [ŏ-do′mi-ter], *n.* device for measuring the mileage of a vehicle. [Gk.].

ODONT-, ODONTO-, *pref.* implying connexion with teeth. [Gk.].

ODONTOID [ŏ-don′toid], *adj.* (*anat.*) resembling a tooth. [Gk.].

ODONTOLOGY [ŏ-don-to′lo-ji], *n.* study of the teeth. [Gk.].

ODORIFEROUS [ŏ-de-ri′fe-rŏŏs], *adj.* diffusing a pleasant or unpleasant odour. **ODORIFEROUSLY,** *adv.* fragrantly. [L.].

ODOROUS [ŏ′de-rŏŏs], *adj.* fragrant, sweet-smelling; (*coll.*) smelly.

ODOUR [ō′der], *n.* smell, perfume, scent; (*fig.*) reputation; atmosphere, savour, suggestion of. [L.].

ODYSSEY [o′di-si], *n.* Homer's epic recounting the return of Odysseus from the siege of Troy; long and adventurous journey. [Gk.].

OECOLOGY, see ECOLOGY.

OECUMENICAL, see ECUMENICAL.

OECUMENICITY, see ECUMENICITY.

OEDEMA, EDEMA [ē-dē′mah], *n.* (*med.*) a localized dropsy.

OEDIPUS [ē′di-pus], *n.* (*Gk. myth.*) Theban king who solved the riddle of the Sphinx, and in ignorance married his mother; **O. complex,** (*psych.*) state in which a person shows excessive affection for the parent of the opposite sex. [Gk.].

O'ER [aw(r)], *prep.* (*poet.*) over. [OVER].

OESOPHAGUS, ESOPHAGUS [ē-so′fa-gus], *n.* (*anat.*) the gullet. [Gk.].

OESTRIN [ē′strin], *n.* a sex hormone secreted by women. [OESTRUM].

OESTRUM [ē′strum], *n.* an overpowering impulse; (of dogs) period during which the bitch will copulate; erotic frenzy, desire. [MedL.].

OESTRUS [ē′strus], *n.* gadfly; oestrum. [Gk.].

OF [ov], *prep.* expressing whence anything comes, its source or origin; indicating point of departure, distance from, measure, separation from; expressing the relationship between something and that of which it is made or consists; indicating cause or reason for; connecting an action (expressed by a noun) with the doer of the action; on or at in a temporal sense; during. [OE.].

OFF (1) [of], *adv.* not above or on; away from work or duty; expressing division, separation, avoidance or postponement, departure, distance between; expressing completion, after certain verbs, e.g. polish off, finish off etc.; **to knock o.,** to cease work, take a rest; **o. and on,** from time to time, now and then, at irregular intervals of time; **they're o.!** (*racing*) the race has started. OFF (2), *prep.* expressing removal from or place whence, reduction, distance away from; near to, at the side of. OFF (3), *adj.* not near or to hand; divided or removed from; unlucky, not full of business, dull; not fresh, stale; disappointing; **o. day,** dull or disappointing day when things do not go well. OFF-SIDE, side remote from the near side of a road-user; (*cricket*) side of the field to the right of a right-handed batsman as he faces the bowling. OFF (4), *n.* (*cricket*) the o.-side. [OF].

OFFAL [o′fal], *n.* refuse, rubbish; that which falls off or is cast away as waste; edible internal organs of an animal, liver, kidneys etc.; carrion. [OFF (1) and FALL (2)].

OFFENCE [o-fens′], *n.* breach of law, rule, custom etc.; wrongdoing, sin or crime; insult; sense of rebuff and annoyance felt by an insulted person; (*milit.*) attack, offensive. [L.].

OFFEND [o-fend′], *v.t. and i.* to do wrong, sin, commit a breach of law, order, custom or morality; disgust or displease; outrage or violate; annoy, insult; **to o. against,** to transgress (laws, morality etc.). OFFENDER, *n.* one who offends; criminal. [L.].

OFFENSIVE (1) [o-fen′siv], *adj.* giving offence, loathsome, repulsive; giving moral offence, indecent; insolent, insulting; suitable to attack with, provocative. OFFENSIVE (2), *n.* (*milit.*) attack; **to take the o.,** (*milit. and fig.*) to begin to attack before the enemy does so. [MedL.].

OFFER (1) [o′fer], *v.t. and i.* to bring or thrust forward, proffer, present; hold out towards; (of prayers, alms etc.) to give; arise, happen. OFFER (2), *n.* proposal; statement of willingness; bid in a business transaction; act of offering, presenting or proposing. [OE.].

OFFERING [o′fe-ring], *n.* something offered in worship; (*coll.*) gift. [OE.].

OFFERTORY [o′fer-te-ri], *n.* (*eccles.*) the placing of the bread and wine upon the altar ready for consecration; (*coll.*) the collecting and offering of alms at the Holy Communion service; piece of music played or sung at this point of the service; alms taken at a religious service. OFFERTORY-BOX, *n.* a box set up in a church for alms.

OFF-HAND (1) [of′hand], *adj.* extempore, unprepared; curt, aloof, unceremonious. OFFHAND (2), *adv.* in a casual, unprepared or o. fashion. [OFF (1) and HAND (1)].

OFF-HANDED [of-han′did], *adj.* casual, curt, offhand. OFF-HANDEDLY, *adv.* in a casual off-hand fashion.

OFFICE [o′fis], *n.* function, duty or service; position carrying with it certain definite functions and duties; a state department; room or set of rooms in which business is transacted, *esp.* business of a clerical or commercial nature; rite, ceremony or religious service; (*slang*) hint. OFFICES, rooms where the necessary work of a domestic establishment is carried on, e.g. kitchen etc. and also lavatories. OFFICE-BEARER, one who holds a special position or o. OFFICE-BOY, boy employed to perform odd jobs in an o. [OFr. from L.].

OFFICER (1) [o′fi-ser], *n.* one who holds an office; person in a recognized position of authority and responsibility and also of service and duty; holder of a commission in the navy, army or air force; master, captain or mate of a merchant-vessel; **police o.,** police constable; **o. at arms or of arms,** herald; **o. of the day,** officer in charge of the necessary arrangements and routines for a given number of troops on a particular day. OFFICER (2), *v.t.* to provide with officers; be in command of. [L.].

OFFICIAL (1) [o-fi′shal], *adj.* pertaining to an office; serving in a position of responsibility and authority; having authority, emanating from a person or persons in authority; formal, ceremonious; recognized as proper and lawful. OFFICIAL (2), *n.* person holding a position of responsibility and authority; servant of authority; officer; (*eccles.*) judge in an ecclesiastical court. OFFICIALLY, *adv.* in an o. way; with authority; formally, ceremoniously. [L.].

OFFICIALDOM [o-fi′shal-dum], *n.* officialism, bureaucracy; the typical point of view of officials; body of state officials, their habits and point of view.

OFFICIALESE [o-fi-sha-lēz′], *n.* (*coll.*) the kind of language characteristic of official letters and documents.

OFFICIALISM [o-fi′sha-lizm], *n.* official routine; over-insistence upon official regulations; red tape.

The accent ′ after a syllable = stress (u-pon′). The mark ¯ over a vowel = length (ā in made; ō in bone).

OFFICIANT [o-fi'shant]. *n.* priest who conducts a religious service, celebrant.

OFFICIATE [o-fi'shi-āt], *v.i.* to perform the duties of an office; (of a priest) perform a rite, lead a religious service. [MedL.].

OFFICINAL [o-fi'si-nal], *adj.* (of drugs, chemicals etc.) recognized in the pharmacopoeia; of medical utility; sold by chemists. [MedL.].

OFFICIOUS [o-fi'shŏos], *adj.* meddlesome, intruding with unwanted advice; presuming too much upon the authority of office; (*diplomacy*) informal, semi-official. [L.].

OFFING [o'fing], *n.* (*naut.*) the stretch of sea between the shore and the horizon visible from the shore; **in the o.**, (*naut.*) near shore; (*fig.*) to hand, near, likely to happen or to take action. [~OFF (1)].

OFF-LICENCE [of'lī-sens], *n.* licence permitting the sale of intoxicants for consumption away from the premises; shop or establishment to which one of these licences has been granted.

OFF-PRINT [of'print], *n.* a reprint in a self-contained pamphlet of an article from a periodical.

OFFSCOURING [of'skow-ring], *n.* refuse and dirt scoured off; rabble.

OFFSET (1) [of'set], *n.* that which grows away, springs or arises, from something else; (*arch.*) ledge produced when the part of a wall below a certain level is thicker than the part above; (*print.*) blurred impression of a wet and newly printed sheet which comes off on to the back of the sheet placed immediately above it; mode of printing by which the impression is taken from a rubber roller which has in turn taken the impression from an inked plate; (*naut.*) current flowing outwards from shore; (*surveying*) short line measured at right angles to the principal line in calculation of the area of an irregular figure or shape. OFFSET (2) (*pres.pt.* OFFSETTING, *pret. and p.pt.* OFFSET), *v.t.* to make an o. in building, printing or surveying; compensate for.

OFFSHOOT [of'shŏot], *n.* secondary growth or projection away from the main body, branch; collateral descendant.

OFFSHORE [of-shaw(r)'], *adj.* moving from the land; being some distance out to sea.

OFF-SIDE (1) [of'sīd], *n.* position on the off, off-side position. OFF-SIDE (2) [of-sīd'], *adj.* (*football* etc.) being in a particular position at which it is illegal by the rules of the game for a participant to take any part in the play. [OFF (1) and SIDE (1).].

OFFSPRING [of'spring], *n.* children, progeny; (*fig.*) result. [OE.].

OFF-WHITE [of-wīt'], *adj. and n.* (of) a colour which is very light but not pure white.

OFT [oft], *adv.* (*poet.*) often. [OE.].

OFTEN [of'(t)en], *adv.* frequently, repeatedly. [ME.].

OFTENTIMES [of'(t)en-tīmz], *adv.* (*archaic*) often.

OGEE [ō-jē'], *n.* S-shaped moulding, having a double curve; **o. arch**, (*arch.*) arch each side of which is shaped like an S. [*Var.* of OGIVE].

OG(H)AM (1) [o'gam], *n.* the ancient Irish alphabet. OG(H)AM (2), *adj.* pertaining to o. [OIr.].

OGIVE [ō'jiv], *n.* (*arch.*) pointed arch; diagonal rib of a vault. OGIVAL [ō-jī'val], *adj.* in the form of an o.; having ogives. [Fr.].

OGLE [ō'gl], *v.t. and i.* to cast amorous glances (at). OGLE (2), *n.* amorous glance. [LGerm.].

OGPU [ōg'pōo], *n.* (*coll.*) the G.P.U., former name of the Soviet Russian secret police, now the N.K.V.D.; (*fig.*) any similar body used as an instrument of oppression. [*Obedinennoe Gosudarstvennoe Politicheskoe Upravlenie,* United State Political Control].

OGRE [ō'ger], *n.* ugly giant or monster in fairy tales and folklore; (*fig.*) ugly or cruel person.

OGRESS [ō'gres], *n.* female monster, female ogre.

OH [ō], *int.* exclamation of surprise, rapture or pain.

OHM [ōm], *n.* unit of electrical resistance. OHMIC, *adj.* pertaining to ohms, measured in ohms. [G. S. *Ohm,* German scientist].

OIL (1) [oil], *n.* one of many fatty, inflammable substances, animal, vegetable and mineral, which remain fluid at moderate temperatures and are soluble in alcohol and ether but not in water; a painting done with oil-colours; **Holy O.**, consecrated o. used in Extreme Unction, at the coronation of a king etc.; **to strike o.**, to find a supply of mineral o.; (*fig.*) have very good luck; make a profitable discovery or invention; get rich quickly; **to pour o. on troubled waters**, to soothe a quarrel by sensible, tactful and

sympathetic remarks; **to throw o. on the flames**, to heighten ill-feeling by tactless or partisan speech of action; **to burn the midnight o.**, to read or work far into the night. OILS, oil-colours, oilskins. OIL (2), *v.t.* to lubricate, impregnate or smear with o.; **to o. someone's palm**, (*coll.*) to bribe someone; **to o. one's tongue**, to talk flatteringly; **to o. the wheels**, to help to produce smooth working and happy arrangements by tactful conduct or speech. [OFr. from L. from Gk.].

OIL-BATH [oil'bahth], *n.* receptacle containing oil in which substances may be gently warmed, or mechanism lubricated.

OIL-BOMB [oil'bom], *n.* incendiary bomb containing inflammable oil.

OIL-BOX [oil'boks], *n.* small box-like receptacle attached to the hub of a wheel and containing a supply of lubricating oil.

OILCAKE [oil'kāk], *n.* cattle fodder made by crushing oil-seeds.

OILCLOTH [oil'kloth], *n.* covering for a table or floor made of stout canvas coated with oil-paint; linoleum; American cloth.

OIL-COLOUR [oil'ku-ler], *n.* paint in which the pigments are mixed in oil.

OILED [oild], *adj.* having been treated with oil, lubricated; smooth-running, smooth-working; silent and efficient; **well o.**, (*slang*) drunk.

OILER [oi'ler], *n.* oil-can; man whose job it is on board ship to keep the ship's engine lubricated; ship engaged in and constructed for carrying oil.

OIL-FIELD [oil'fēld], *n.* tract of country having rich deposits of mineral oil.

OIL-GAUGE [oil'gāj], *n.* device for measuring the density of an oil; device to register the quantity of oil in a container.

OILINESS [oil'i-nes], *n.* condition of being oily; (*fig.*) a servile, obsequious manner.

OIL-MEAL [oil'mēl], *n.* linseed cake which has been ground.

OIL-PAINTING [oil'pān-ting], *n.* art of making pictures with oil-colours; picture in oils.

OIL-PAPER [oil'pā-per], *n.* paper which has been oiled so as to make it semi-transparent and water-proof.

OIL-SEED [oil'sēd], *n.* any seed from which oil can be extracted, as linseed or sunflower-seed.

OIL-SILK [oil-silk'], *n.* silk made waterproof with oil.

OILSKIN [oil'skin], *adj.* made of cloth oiled so as to be waterproof.

OILSTONE [oil'stōn], *n.* an oiled whetstone.

OIL-SUMP [oil'sump], *n.* oil-bath in which the crank of an engine moves.

OIL-TANKER [oil'tang-ker], *n.* ship, motor-truck or railway wagon specially built to carry oil in bulk.

OIL-WELL [oil'wel], *n.* well containing petroleum.

OILY [oi'li], *adj.* greasy, stained or damp with oil; having the consistency of oil; containing oil; (*fig.*) obsequious and flattering.

OINTMENT [oint'ment], *n.* fatty or oily compound for medicinal or cosmetic purposes. [OFr.].

OKAPI [ō-kah'pi], *n.* quadruped nearly related to the giraffe and found in West Africa. [Native].

O.K., OKAY (1) [ō-kā'], *adj.* (*coll., orig. U.S. slang*) all right, in order; agreed. O.K., OKAY (2), *n.* (*coll.*) approval, agreement, sanction; sign indicating this. O.K., OKAY (3), *v.t.* (*coll.*) to give approval of, sanction, pass. [Uncert.].

OKRA [ok'rah, ō'krah], *n.* African and American plant, the stem of which provides a fibre suitable for ropemaking, and the seeds a vegetable. [African].

OLD (1) [ōld], *adj.* aged, not young, elderly; of age; worn out with age, exhausted; belonging to past time, ancient; old-fashioned, no longer in use; having the wisdom and experience of previous practice, experienced; (*coll.*) dear, familiar, pleasant; **o. woman**, (*coll.*) fussy, fastidious person, *esp.* a fussy, elderly man; **O. World**, the known world before the discovery of America; **o. masters**, great painters of a previous age, usually the great exponents of Renaissance painting in Italy, Germany etc.; **o. master**, a work by one of these men, masterly painting of early date; **o. country**, mother-country from which colonial settlers have come, *esp.* England; **O. Glory**, the Stars and Stripes, U.S. national flag; **O. Style calendar**, the Julian calendar, now some thirteen days different from the one at present in general use; **O. Testament**, the former of the two great divisions of the Bible, containing Hebrew history, law, philosophy and poetry prior to the coming of Jesus Christ; **O. Nick**, (*coll.*) Satan, the

---

ōō is pronounced as in f*ōō*d; ŏŏ as in h*ŏŏ*d; th as in *th*ink; TH as in *th*at; zh as in azure. ~ = related to.

devil; **O. Man of the Mountains**, leader and founder of the sect of the Assassins; **O. Man of the Sea**, (from the story of Sindbad in the *Arabian Nights*) (*fig.*) person or thing from which one cannot get free; **O. Lady of Threadneedle Street**, Bank of England; **O. Year's Day**, last day of the year; **O. Age Pension**, state pension granted to old persons on account of their age. OLD (2), *n. o.* people as opposed to young people; anything o.; o. things in general; **of o.**, in times past. [O.E.].

OLDEN [ōl'den], *adj.* ancient, old, belonging to the past, antique.

OLD-FASHIONED [ōld-fa'shnd], *adj.* now out of fashion, not in the latest modern style; attached to old ways; (*coll.*) odd.

OLD MAN'S BEARD [ōld-manz-bēerd'], *n.* the wild plant, *Clematis vitalba*.

OLD-WORLD [ōld'werld], *adj.* antiquated, quaint, old-fashioned; pertaining to Europe, Africa and Asia.

OLEAGINOUS [ō-li-a'ji-nŏŏs], *adj.* greasy, oily, unctuous. [L.].

OLEANDER [ō-li-an'der], *n.* (*bot.*) evergreen rose-bay. [Fr.].

OLEASTER [ō-li-as'ter], *n.* (*bot.*) small tree native to Southern Europe which has yellow sweet-scented flowers and an olive-like fruit. [L.].

OLEO (1) [ō'li-ō], *n.* oleograph. [OLEO(GRAPH)].

OLEO- (2), *pref.* pertaining to oil. [L.].

OLEOGRAPH [ō'li-ō-grahf], *n.* lithograph imitating a painting in oils.

OLEOMARGARINE [ō-li-ō-mah'ja-rēn], *n.* butter-substitute made from animal and vegetable oil and milk.

OLFACTORY (1) [ol-fak'te-ri], *adj.* of, or pertaining to, the sense of smell or the act of smelling. OLFACTORY (2), *n.* (*physiol.*) an organ of smell. [L.].

OLIGARCH [o'li-gahk], *n.* leader or supporter of an oligarchy. [Gk.].

OLIGARCHY [o'li-gah-ki], *n.* government by a few; state controlled by a few people; small group of persons conducting the government of a state. OLIGARCHAL, OLIGARCHIC(AL), *adj.* pertaining to, of the nature of, ruled by, (an) o. [Gk.].

OLIGO-, *pref.* few, small. [Gk.].

OLIO [ō'li-ō], *n.* medley or miscellany; miscellaneous stew. [Span.].

OLIVE (1) [o'liv], *n.* (*bot.*) evergreen tree native to the Mediterranean countries; fruit of the cultivated olive tree; its wood; its leaves, *esp.* when wreathed into a coronet in token of victory; olive colour; (*cookery*) slices of veal or beef rolled and seasoned with onions, olives etc. OLIVE (2), *adj.* having the colour of the fruit of the o. at some stage of its maturing; sallow, pale yellow. OLIVE-GREEN, yellowish-green. OLIVACEOUS [o-li-vā'shŏŏs], *adj.* resembling an o.; o.-coloured, o.-green. [L.].

OLIVE-BRANCH [o'liv-brahnch], *n.* symbol of peace; child.

OLIVE OIL [o'liv-oil], *n.* oil extracted from olives, used for cooking, lubrication and lighting.

OLLA-PODRIDA [o-lah-po-drē'dah], *n.* stew of meat and vegetables; hotchpotch, miscellany. [Span.].

OLYMPIAD [ō-lim'pi-ad], *n.* space of four years reckoned from one celebration of the Olympic games to the next and used by ancient Greeks for purposes of chronology; one of the occasions on which modern Olympic Games, revived in 1896 and celebrated every four years, are held. [Gk.].

OLYMPIAN (1) [ō-lim'pi-an], *adj.* pertaining to Olympus, which, according to Greek mythology, was the mountain on which the gods lived; fit for a Greek god, magnificent; heavily condescending; Olympic. OLYMPIAN (2), *n.* one who lived on Olympus, a Greek god; stately person, like a Greek god.

OLYMPIC [ō-lim'pik], *adj.* pertaining to the plain of Olympia in Greece where, in classical times, the Olympic games were held; pertaining to a modern revival of this as an international sport and athletic meeting. [Gk.].

OMBRE [om'ber], *n.* an eighteenth-century card-game for three players. [Span.].

OMBRO-, *pref.* connected with rain. [Gk.].

OMEGA [ō'me-gah], *n.* the last letter of the Greek alphabet; **alpha and o.**, the beginning and end. [Gk.].

OMELET(TE) [om'let], *n.* (*cooking*) dish of eggs beaten up and fried. [Fr.].

OMEN [ō'men], *n.* portent of something to happen, either good or bad. [L.].

OMENTUM (*pl.* **omenta**) [ō-men'tum], *n.* (*anat.*) fold in the peritoneum connecting the intestines with the other viscera. OMENTAL, *adj.* relating to the o. [L.].

OMINOUS [o'mi-nŏŏs], *adj.* foreboding evil things; threatening. [L.].

OMISSION [ō-mi'shn], *n.* act of omitting, fact of having been omitted; something omitted. OMISSIVE, *adj.* omitting. [L.].

OMIT (*pres.pt.* **omitting**, *pret.* and *p.pt.* **omitted**) [ō-mit'], *v.t.* to leave out; neglect, fail to do. [L.].

OMNI-, *pref.* all. [L.].

OMNIBUS (1) (*pl.* **omnibuses**) [om'ni-bus], *n.* public vehicle for conveying passengers along a particular route or part of it, bus. OMNIBUS (2), *adj.* miscellaneous, including a variety of things, including everything; **o. book**, **o. volume**, one-volumed miscellany containing all sorts of literary specimens; single volume containing all or several of the works of an author. [L.].

OMNIDIRECTIONAL [om-ni-di-rek'shn-al], *adj.* (of a radio transmitting aerial) sending signals of equal strength in all directions.

OMNIPOTENCE [om-ni'pō-tens], *n.* unlimited power. [L.].

OMNIPOTENT [om-ni'pō-tent], *adj.* almighty, all-powerful; **the O.**, God.

OMNIPRESENCE [om-ni-pre'zens], *n.* presence at every moment in every place.

OMNIPRESENT [om-ni-pre'zent], *adj.* having the quality of omnipresence.

OMNISCIENCE [om-ni'shns], *n.* unlimited knowledge, knowledge of everything.

OMNISCIENT [om-ni'shnt], *adj.* all-knowing, possessing the quality of omniscience. [L.].

OMNIUM [om'ni-um], *n.* sum, sum total. [L.].

OMNIUM-GATHERUM [om-ni-um-ga'THe-rum], *n.* a very mixed collection. [*Prec.* and jocular Latinization of GATHERING].

OMNIVOROUS [om-ni've-rŏŏs], *adj.* able and willing to eat anything; eating both vegetable and animal matter; (*fig.*) eager, all-consuming. [L.].

ON (1) [on], *prep.* upon, above, resting upon, covering, supported by; *expressing place where*; *motion towards*; *expressing connexion with*; concerning, dealing with; *expressing state or manner*; *expressing time when*. ON (2), *adv.* not off, so as to rest upon or be in place; onwards, straight ahead, in the same direction as before; without stoppage or interruption, continually; at present in action or in being; **o. and o.**, uninterruptedly; **o. and off**, now and then, from time to time; **to be o.**, to be a member of (a committee, board etc.); to be willing; **and so o.**, continuing in the same way. ON (3), *adj.* (*cricket*) THE ON-SIDE, that part of the field which is to the left of a right-handed batsman as he faces the bowling. ON (4), *n.* (*cricket*) the o.-side. [O.E.].

ONAGER (*pl.* **onagri**, **onagers**) [o'na-jer, o'na-gri], *n.* (*zool.*) the Persian wild ass.

ONANISM [ō'na-nizm], *n.* self-abuse, masturbation. [*Onan*, Gen. xxxviii, 9].

ONCE (1) [wuns], *adv.* on one single occasion; in previous times, formerly; **o. upon a time**, in days gone by; **o. for all**, on one occasion and never again, for the last time; **not o.**, never; **o. in a way**, sometimes but rarely; **all at o.**, suddenly, unexpectedly; **at o.**, forthwith, immediately; **the o. over**, (*slang*) rapid preliminary inspection or inquiry; a superficial cleaning. ONCE (2), *conj.* as soon as. ONCE (3), *n.* one occasion. [O.E.].

ONCOMING (1) [on'ku-ming], *n.* approach, drawing near. ONCOMING (2), *adj.* approaching; (*slang*) affable, seeking acquaintance.

ONCOST [on'kost], *n.* overhead expenses; (*mining*) work paid by time.

ON DIT [aw(ng)-dē'], *n.* rumour. [Fr.].

ONE (1) [wun], *adj.* single, alone; pertaining to the number representing unity; first; being whole and undivided; having the quality of unity; *used to denote something which is contrasted with something else* (*denoted by* other); a certain. ONE (2), *n.* the first integer; symbol representing the first integer; a particular; a certain; **o. and all**, everyone; **to be at o.**, to be united, agreed. ONE (3), *indef. pron.* a certain thing or person; anyone; people generally; *referring to the speaker*. [O.E.].

ONE-EYED [wun-id'], *adj.* having one eye only; (*coll.*) poor, inferior, insignificant.

ONE-HORSE [wun-haws'], *adj.* drawn by, or constructed to be drawn by, one horse; (*coll.*) poor in quality, inferior.

ONEIRO-, *pref.* dream, pertaining to dreams. [Gk.].

The accent ' after a syllable = stress (u-pon'). The mark ‾ over a vowel = length (ā in made; ō in bone).

ONENESS [wun′nes], *n.* unity; condition of being at one and united.

ONEROUS [o′ne-rŏŏs], *adj.* heavy, burdensome; oppressive. ONEROUSLY, *adv.* heavily. [L.].

ONESELF [wun-self′], *reflex. form of indef. pron.* one, the person and ego of an individual.

ONE-SIDED [wun-sī′did], *adj.* arguing in favour of one side only; (of a game) in which one contestant or team is markedly superior to the other; unbalanced, unequal. ONE-SIDEDLY, *adv.* in a o. fashion, unfairly, unequally.

ONE-STEP (1) [wun′step], *n.* a simple ballroom dance. ONE-STEP (2), *v.i.* to dance the o.

ONE-TRACK [wun′trak], *adj.* running along only one track; (*fig.*) interested in one subject only, very restricted in outlook.

ONE-WAY [wun′wā], *adj.* (of a street) through which traffic may pass in one direction only; (of traffic) moving, allowed to move, in one direction only.

ONION [un′yun], *n.* (*bot.*) the plant *Allium Cepa*; its edible bulb, used as a vegetable and to provide flavouring; flaming o., form of rocket used against hostile aircraft. [Fr.].

ONLOOKER [on′lŏŏ-ker], *n.* spectator, one who looks on but does not join in.

ONLY (1) [ōn′li], *adj.* single, being the sole example of its kind; being of a certain, distinct category, outstanding in its kind. ONLY (2), *adv.* merely, exclusively; under such conditions that nothing else is possible; o. just, with no time, strength etc. to spare; a moment ago; o. too, very; if o., oh that! (expressing a strong desire). ONLY (3), *conj.* except that. [OE.].

ONOMA-, *pref.* name(s), pertaining to names. [Gk.].

ONOMATOPOEIA [o-no-ma-tō-pē′ah], *n.* principle of forming words by imitation of the sounds they signify or of sounds associated with their sense; (*rhet.*) use of words the sound of which seems to echo the sense of the passage. ONOMATOPOEIC, *adj.* relating to or displaying o.; imitative, echoic. [Gk.].

ONRUSH [on′rush], *n.* onset, attack; rapid, rushing approach or advance.

ONSET [on′set], *n.* violent attack, assault, charge.

ONSLAUGHT [on′slawt], *n.* furious assault or attack, charge. [OE.].

ONTO-, *pref.* being. [Gk.].

ONTOLOGICAL [on-to-lo′ji-kal], *adj.* pertaining to ontology. ONTOLOGICALLY, *adv.* by ontology.

ONTOLOGY [on-to′lo-ji], *n.* (*philos.*) metaphysical contemplation of the nature of being. [Gk.].

ONUS [ō′nus], *n.* burden, responsibility; o. probandi, (*leg.*) responsibility of producing proof of what one has asserted. [L.].

ONWARD (1) [on′werd], *adj.* advancing, going straight ahead in the direction already pursued; moving towards the goal. ONWARD (2), *adv.* to the front, in front, forwards. ONWARD (3), *int.* advance! [OE.].

ONWARDS [on′werdz], *adv. and int.* onward.

ONYX [o′niks], *n.* a variety of agate. [L.].

OO-, *pref.* egg. [Gk.].

OOF [ŏŏf], *n.* (*slang*) money. [Yiddish from Germ.].

OOLITE [ō′o-līt], *n.* a variety of limestone consisting of spherical granules; (*geol.*) series of rocks containing beds of o. OOLITIC [ō-o-li′tik], *adj.* composed of o.; (*geol.*) belonging to one of the o. formations. [Gk.].

OOLOGY [ō-o′lo-ji], *n.* study of birds' eggs. [Gk.].

OOZE (1) [ŏŏz], *n.* soft, slimy mud; sediment. [OE.].

OOZE (2), *n.* liquor used in tanning leather. OOZE (3), *v.t. and i.* to trickle slowly forth; drip; percolate; (*fig.*) diminish, fade away; exude, give off; to o. with, to exude. [OE.].

OOZY [ŏŏ′zi], *adj.* slimy and muddy.

OPACITY [o-pa′si-ti], *n.* quality of being opaque; darkness; obscurity of meaning; dulness of intellect. [L.].

OPAL [ō′pal], *n.* semi-transparent precious stone which flashes with rich colours as light plays upon it. [L.].

OPALESCENCE [ō-pa-le′sens], *n.* quality of gleaming with many colours like an opal.

OPALESCENT [ō-pa-le′sent], *adj.* having the quality of opalescence; iridescent.

OPALINE (1) [ō′pa-lēn], *adj.* resembling an opal. OPALINE (2), *n.* a semi-transparent, pearly glass.

OPAQUE [ō-pāk′], *adj.* not transmitting light; dark and obscure. [L.].

OPE [ōp], *v.t. and i.* (*poet.*) to open.

OPEN (1) [ō′pen], *adj.* not closed or shut, but allowing free passage; not enclosed by anything; not barred in any way; free from restrictions; available for all; accessible; not covered over; (of wounds etc.) not healed; unfolded, expanded; not defended; (of country) free from trees, bushes etc.; generous; frank; broad-minded; (of an offer) neither accepted nor withdrawn; (of a problem) still to be decided; not disguised, public, well known; (of a business agreement, bank account etc.) still in being; (of a shop) ready for customers; o. secret, so-called secret widely known; o. order, (*milit.*) extended formation; o. syllable, syllable ending in a vowel; o. consonant, consonant in the sounding of which the breath passage is never completely blocked; o. shop, business concern employing non-union workers as well as those belonging to a union; to keep o. house, to be ever ready to receive and entertain guests; with o. hand, generously; o. mind, unprejudiced point of view; o. letter, letter addressed to a particular person but intentionally published by the writer, usually for political reasons. OPEN (2), *n.* the o. air, countryside; to come into the o., (*fig.*) to be frank. OPEN (3), *v.t.* to unfasten; fling back (doors, windows etc.); remove bars and restrictions from; render exit and entrance possible; declare formally open; unfold, uncover; start, initiate; *v.i.* to expand; unfold; commence or recommence; become visible, begin to appear; to o. up, to explore; expand, become opened; begin business; to o. out, to stretch out, unfold, increase speed; to o. on to, to lead into, give access to. [OE.].

OPEN-AIR [ō-pen-āer′], *adj.* occurring out of doors; outdoor; delighting in out-of-door activities.

OPEN-ARMED [ō-pen-ahmd′], *adj.* cordial, welcoming.

OPEN-CAST [ō′pen-kahst], *adj.* (*mining*) requiring excavation on the surface only instead of deep shafts.

OPEN-EARED [ō-pen-ēerd′], *adj.* attentive, eager to hear whatever may be heard.

OPEN-EYED [ō-pen-īd′], *adj.* alert, vigilant; having wide eyes as with amazement etc.

OPEN-HANDED [ō-pen-han′did], *adj.* generous.

OPEN-HEARTED [ō-pen-hah′tid], *adj.* frank, magnanimous.

OPENING (1) [ō′pe-ning], *n.* gap, hole, breach; beginning; opportunity, chance to set out on a career; o. time, time when licensed houses open for the sale of alcoholic liquor. OPENING (2), *adj.* the first in order; initiatory.

OPENLY [ō′pen-li], *adv.* in an open manner, frankly publicly, without dissimulation.

OPEN-MINDED [ō-pen-mīn′did], *adj.* unprejudiced.

OPEN-MOUTHED [ō-pen-mowthd′], *adj. and adv.* greedy, greedily; agape with surprise or amazement.

OPEN-WORK (1) [ō′pen-werk], *n.* embroidery in which the material being embroidered is cut and pierced with holes; any tracery or lace-like pattern in wood, stone or metal. OPEN-WORK (2), *adj.* characterized by or adorned with o.

OPERA [o′pe-rah], *n.* play set to music in which the main part or all of the words are sung to an orchestral accompaniment; grand o., o. where everything is sung and the story is usually tragic. OPERA-BOUFFE [o-pe-rah-bŏŏf′], o. with a farcical plot. OPERA-CLOAK, cloak for formal evening wear. OPERA-GLASSES, binocular glasses for use in the theatre. OPERA-HAT, gibus. [Ital.].

OPERABLE [o′pe-ra-bl], *adj.* (*surg.*) capable of being operated upon.

OPERATE [o′pe-rāt], *v.t. and i.* to perform a certain function or task; work, manipulate; have a certain effect; perform a surgical operation.

OPERATIC [o-pe-ra′tik], *adj.* pertaining to opera.

OPERATING [o′pe-rā-ting], *adj.* connected with, used for, performing, an operation.

OPERATION [o-pe-rā′shn], *n.* act of operating; work, task; manipulation; act performed upon a living body by a surgeon, usually but not necessarily with instruments; mode of working; (*milit.*) a series of manoeuvres. OPERATIONAL, *adj.* connected with operations; (*milit.*) required for operations. OPERATIONALLY, *adv.* with regard to operations. [L.].

OPERATIVE (1) [o′pe-ra-tiv], *adj.* working, effective, capable of producing a certain effect; (*leg.*) valid. OPERATIVE (2), *n.* one who works, factory worker. OPERATIVELY, *adv.* effectively.

OPERATOR [o′pe-rā-ter], *n.* one who, or that which, operates a machine, *esp.* one who operates a radio transmitting set or telephone switchboard.

OPERCULUM (*pl.* opercula) [o-pur′kyŏŏ-lum], *n.*

(*zool.*) gill-cover of fishes; lid-like organ which closes down over the opening of the shell of some molluscs when they retreat into their shell; (*bot.*) lid-like structure which closes the fruits of certain plants. [L.].

OPERETTA [o-pe-re'tah], *n.* short light musical play. [It.].

OPHICLEIDE [o'fi-klīd], *n.* a brass wind-instrument. [Gk.].

OPHIDIA [o-fi'di-ah], *n.*(*pl.*) (*zool.*) group of reptiles including snakes. OPHIDIAN (1), *adj.* belonging or pertaining to the o. OPHIDIAN (2), *n.* one of the o. [~Gk.].

OPHIO-, *pref.* of snakes. [Gk.].

OPHIOLOGY [o-fi-o'lo-ji], *n.* study of snakes. [Gk.].

OPHTHALMIA [of-thal'mi-ah], *n.* inflammation of the eye.

OPHTHALMIC [of-thal'mik], *adj.* of, or concerning, the eyes. [L.].

OPHTHALMOLOGY [of-thal-mo'lo-ji], *n.* scientific study of the eye. [Gk.].

OPHTHALMOSCOPE [of-thal'mō-skōp], *n.* instrument having lenses for examining the interior of the eye. OPHTHALMOSCOPY [of-thal-mo'sko-pi], *n.* examination of the eye with an o.; skill in using an o. [Gk.].

OPIATE (1) [ō'pi-āt], *adj.* containing opium; soporific. OPIATE (2), *n.* a medicinal compound containing opium; soporific or narcotic; (*fig.*) something which causes drowsiness. OPIATE (3), *v.t.* to mix with opium; give an o. to; (*fig.*) make drowsy. [MedL.].

OPINE [ō-pīn'], *v.i.* to think; hold an opinion. [L.].

OPINION [o-pin'yun], *n.* what one thinks or believes to be true when definite knowledge is impossible; point of view; judgment, estimation. [L.].

OPINIONATED [o-pin'yu-nā-tid], *adj.* unduly obstinate in one's opinions.

OPINIONATIVE [o-pin'yu-na-tiv], *adj.* opinionated.

O-PIP [ō-pip'], *n.* (*milit.*) advanced position for observing the effect of artillery fire upon the enemy. [O for observation and *pip* (signallers' slang) P for post].

OPIUM [ō'pi-um], *n.* drug obtained from the seed capsules of the white poppy, used medicinally as a sedative and chewed as a narcotic, intoxicant or stimulant; **o. den**, place where o. can be bought and smoked. [L. from Gk.].

OPODELDOC [ō-pō-del'dok], *n.* kind of soap liniment.

OPOPANAX [ō-po'pa-naks], *n.* a gum-resin used in the making of perfumes. [Gk.].

OPOSSUM [ō-po'sum], *n.* small marsupial animal found in America; similar animal in Australia. [AmerInd.].

OPPIDAN [o'pi-dan], *n.* member of Eton College who boards outside the school buildings. [L.].

OPPONENT (1) [o-pō'nent], *adj.* antagonistic, opposed; (*anat.*) used of the muscles which cause the hand and fingers to open and shut; (*poet.*) opposite. OPPONENT (2), *n.* antagonist, adversary, rival. [L.].

OPPORTUNE [o'per-tyōōn], *adj.* seasonable; occurring at a suitable moment; well-timed. [L.].

OPPORTUNISM [o'per-tyōō-nizm], *n.* practice of changing one's intentions and point of view so as to profit by the circumstances of the moment. OPPORTUNIST, *n.* one who seizes upon opportunity, who habitually practises o.

OPPORTUNITY [o-per-tyōō'ni-ti], *n.* chance to do something; moment when events and circumstances are favourable to one's ambitions or intentions; chance to get on in the world. [Fr. from L.].

OPPOSABLE [o-pō'za-bl], *adj.* capable of being opposed.

OPPOSE [o-pōz'], *v.t. and i.* to resist, fight, argue, vote against; rival with, offer opposition to; set up as a rival; pursue a policy of resistance. OPPOSING, *adj.* acting against, inimical. [OFr.].

OPPOSITE (1) [o'po-zit], *adj.* facing, being in front of; being on the other side of a real or imaginary division; contrary, moving in the reverse direction; corresponding to; **o. number**, counterpart, one holding a corresponding position in another place. OPPOSITE (2), *n.* thing or person utterly different from another. [L.].

OPPOSITION (1) [o-pō-zi'shn], *n.* that which resists and is hostile; antagonism, hostility; (*parl.*) those Members of Parliament who consistently oppose the Government; the largest of those parties not in office; (*astron.*) position of two planets or stars when diametrically opposite. OPPOSITION (2), *adj.* pertaining to the parliamentary O. OPPOSITIONIST (1),

n. one who opposes, member of the O. OPPOSITIONIST (2), *adj.* befitting an Oppositionist, pertaining to the O., hostile, opposing. [L.].

OPPRESS [o-pres'], *v.t.* to crush down, treat with injustice and cruelty, deny freedom to; govern tyrannically; depress, dispirit; render sleepy and languid. [MedL.].

OPPRESSION [o-pre'shn], *n.* tyranny, harsh rule, denial of liberty; process of oppressing; physical languor; lassitude of spirit. [L.].

OPPRESSIVE [o-pre'siv], *adj.* tyrannical, harsh, burdensome; (of the weather and atmosphere) close, stifling; provoking languor of body or spirit.

OPPRESSOR [o-pre'ser], *n.* one who oppresses, tyrant.

OPPROBRIOUS [o-prō'bri-ŏŏs], *adj.* abusive and reproachful; scurrilous. [LL.].

OPPROBRIUM [o-prō'bri-um], *n.* contemptuous reproach; abuse; dishonour, disgrace. [L.].

OPSONIN [op'so-nin], *n.* (*med.*) substance obtainable from dead bacteria which, when injected into the blood-stream, strengthens the resistance of a person to that disease. OPSONIC [op-so'nik], *adj.* pertaining to o. [Gk.].

OPT [opt], *v.i.* to choose. [L.].

OPTANT [op'tant], *n.* one who is offered the right of choosing his nationality. [L.].

OPTATIVE (1) [op-tā'tiv], *adj.* (*gram.*) expressing desire in the mood of a verb. OPTATIVE (2), *n.* (*gram.*) the o. mood. [L.].

OPTIC (1) [op'tik], *adj.* pertaining to the eyes or sight. OPTIC (2), *n.* (*slang*) eye. [Gk.].

OPTICAL [op'ti-kal], *adj.* pertaining to the sight; ocular; **o. glass**, glass used for making lenses; **o. illusion**, illusion due to faulty interpretation of visual impression; trick to deceive the eyes. OPTICALLY, *adv.* according to the eye.

OPTICIAN [op-ti'shan], *n.* one who makes and sells optical instruments, *esp.* spectacles.

OPTICS [op'tiks], *n.*(*pl.*) science and study of light and vision.

OPTIME [op'ti-mi], *n.* Cambridge student who gains a second or third class in the mathematical tripos. [L.].

OPTIMISM [op'ti-mizm], *n.* disposition to look on the bright side of things; doctrine that all things work together for good; (*philos.*) doctrine of Leibnitz that this world is the very best possible world. [Fr.].

OPTIMIST [op'ti-mist], *n.* one who thinks that everything is for the best; one who believes in optimism.

OPTIMISTIC [op-ti-mis'tik], *adj.* having a cheerful, hopeful outlook; pertaining to optimism.

OPTIMUM (1) [op'ti-mum], *n.* the best. OPTIMUM (2), *adj.* best, most favourable. [L.].

OPTION [op'shn], *n.* right to choose; liberty of choice; commercial contract made on an initial part payment to sell or purchase something by a fixed date. [L.].

OPTIONAL [op'shn-al], *adj.* at choice; not compulsory. OPTIONALLY, *adv.* by choice.

OPTO-, *pref.* relating to the eyes or sight. [Gk.].

OPTOMETER [op-to'mi-ter], *n.* instrument for measuring range of vision and refractive power of the eye.

OPTOMETRY [op-to'mi-tri], *n.* measurement of eyesight. OPTOMETRIST, *n.* one who tests eyesight, *esp.* with regard to range of vision and refractive power.

OPULENCE [o'pyŏŏ-lens], *n.* wealth.

OPULENT [o'pyŏŏ-lent], *adj.* wealthy; abundant. OPULENTLY, *adv.* richly, profusely. [L.].

OPUS [o'pus, ō'pus], *n.* work, composition, *esp.* a musical composition; **magnum o.**, principal work of a writer, composer, scholar etc. [L.].

OPUSCULE [o-pus'kyŏŏl], *n.* a minor work. [L.].

OPUSCULUM [o-pus'kyŏŏ-lum], *n.* opuscule. [Prec.].

OR (1) [aw(r)], *n.* (*her.*) gold. [Fr. from L.].

OR (2), *conj.* used to express an alternative; used to connect a list of things from which choice is to be made. [ME.].

OR (3) (*archaic*), *conj.* before (in time); **o. ever**, before. [ME. from OE.].

ORACLE [o'ra-kl], *n.* declaration by an ancient Greek priest on behalf of the gods of what the future held; place where such statements were made; god supposed to inspire them; the answer itself; priest (or priestess) giving the answer; sanctuary in the Temple at Jerusalem where the Ark was kept; breastplate of the High Priest; divine revelation, the Scriptures;

The accent ' after a syllable = stress (u-pon'). The mark ⁻ over a vowel = length (ă in made; ō in bone).

a foretelling of the future; sure source of knowledge; wisdom of a person of much knowledge and experience; such a person; **to work the o.,** to obtain a favourable result by secret influence. [L.].

ORACULAR [o-ra′kyōō-ler], *adj.* pertaining to an oracle; ambiguous like the replies of the ancient Greek oracles; having the solemn manner or authority of an oracle; prophetic; full of wisdom and knowledge; claiming to possess infallible knowledge like an oracle.

ORAL [aw′ral], *adj.* spoken, not written; (*anat.*) pertaining to the mouth. [L.].

ORANGE (1) [o′rinj], *n.* evergreen tree grown in Southern Europe, the East and many other warm countries; fruit of this tree, a large berry with a thick yellow rind; the reddish-yellow colour of this rind. **Blenheim o., Cox's o.,** sorts of dessert apple. ORANGE-BLOSSOM, white flower of the o.-tree; ORANGE (2), *adj.* having the same colour as o. rind, o.-coloured. [OFr. from Arab.].

ORANGE (3), *n.* Protestant Unionist party in Ireland originally founded in support of the Protestant succession and William of Orange-Nassau.

ORANGEADE [o-rin-jād′], *n.* drink of sweetened and diluted orange juice. [ORANGE and (LEMON)ADE].

ORANGEMAN [*pl.* **Orangemen**] [o′rinj-man], *n.* member of the Orange party in Ireland. [ORANGE (3)].

ORANGERY [o′rin-je-ri], *n.* orange garden or hothouse, where orange-trees are grown. [Fr.].

ORANGE-STICK [o′rinj-stik], *n.* small stick of orange-wood for manicuring the nails.

ORANGE-TAWNY [o-rinj-taw′ni], *adj.* rich reddish-yellow colour.

ORANG-OUTANG, ORANG-UTAN [aw-rang-ōō-tang′], *n.* an anthropoid ape. [Malay].

ORATE [o-rāt′], *v.i.* (*coll.*) to make a speech. [*Next*].

ORATION [o-rā′shn], *n.* a formal discourse; (*gram.*) **direct o.,** direct speech; **indirect o.,** report of the substance of the words of another speaker. [L.].

ORATOR [o′ra-ter], *n.* one skilled in public speaking; person who makes speeches; **Public O.,** the official speaker of a university. [L.].

ORATORIAN (1) [or-ra-taw′ri-an], *adj.* pertaining to an oratory or to the Society of the Oratory. ORATORIAN (2), *n.* priest of an oratory; member of the Society of the Oratory.

ORATORICAL [o-ra-to′ri-kal], *adj.* rhetorical; in the manner of an orator; pertaining to an orator.

ORATORIO [o-ra-taw′ri-ō], *n.* quasi-dramatic and musical arrangement of a religious theme or story in which solo voices represent the characters and are supported by an orchestra and chorus, but which is performed without dramatic movement, scenery, costume etc. [It.].

ORATORY (1) [o′ra-te-ri], *n.* small chapel for private prayer; church of the Society of the Oratory, a R.C. society of secular priests; **Fathers of the O.,** members of this society. [L.].

ORATORY (2), *n.* art of the orator, art of speaking eloquently; rhetoric. [L.].

ORB (1) [awb], *n.* ball, globe, sphere; anything spherical in shape; small globe surmounted with a cross held by a monarch as symbol of sovereignty. ORB (2), *v.t.* (*poet.*) to encircle. ORBED, *adj.* round; shaped like an o.; encircled. [L.].

ORBICULAR [aw-bi′kyoo-ler], *adj.* having the form of an orb.

ORBIT [aw′bit], *n.* a circular track; (*astron.*) path of a heavenly body; (*opt.*) eye-socket; (*fig.*) track or path; way or habit of life; sphere of activity or influence. ORBITAL, *adj.* pertaining to an o.; (*opt.*) pertaining to the eye-socket. [L.].

ORCADIAN (1) [aw-kā′di-an], *adj.* pertaining to the Orkney Islands. ORCADIAN (2), *n.* inhabitant of the Orkney Islands. [L.].

ORCHARD [aw′cherd], *n.* enclosure where fruit-trees are cultivated. [OE.].

ORCHESTIC [aw-kes′tik], *adj.* pertaining to dancing. ORCHESTICS, *n.*(*pl.*) art of dancing.

ORCHESTRA [aw′kes-trah], *n.* space before the stage in an ancient Greek theatre where the chorus sang and danced; company of musicians playing various instruments, assembled for the performance of concerted musical works; place in front of the stage where such musicians sit; the instruments on which they play considered as an entity. ORCHESTRAL [aw-kes′tral], *adj.* pertaining to an o.; composed for, played by, resembling, an o. [L.].

ORCHESTRATE [aw′kes-trāt], *v.t.* to arrange or edit (a piece of music) for orchestral performance.

ORCHESTRATION [aw-kes-trā′shn], *n.* art of scoring a piece of music for performance by an o.

ORCHID [aw′kid], *n.* (*bot.*) plant of the family *Orchidaceae,* many varieties of which are remarkable for their vivid colouring and curious shapes. ORCHIDIST, *n.* student or collector of orchids. [Gk.].

ORCHIDACEOUS [aw-ki-dā′shōōs], *adj.* belonging to, relating to, orchids; (*coll.*) extravagantly luxurious.

ORCHIL, see ARCHIL.

ORCHIS [aw′kis], *n.* orchid, *esp.* of wild English varieties.

ORCHITIS [aw-ki′tis], *n.* (*med.*) inflammation of the testicles. [Gk.].

ORDAIN [aw-dān′], *v.t.* to enact, command, decree; (*eccles.*) consecrate to Holy Orders by the laying on of hands. [L.].

ORDEAL [aw-dēl′], *n.* (*hist.*) trial by testing, in which guilt or innocence was decided by the ability of the accused to walk through fire etc.; severe trial, exacting and unpleasant testing. [OE.].

ORDER (1) [aw′der], *n.* arrangement, relative position in place or time; logical sequence, systematic disposition in any sense, natural succession; (*milit.*) formation, ordering of ranks; discipline, state of being quietly obedient to authority; (of public meetings) orderly attention; custom and procedure; proper bodily functioning, health; the second broadest botanical and zoological classification; (*arch.*) a specified style; degree, rank, quality; social rank, economic status; society of monks, friars, nuns etc.; society of knights; the aggregate of members of certain bodies invested with special dignity by the sovereign; the collective whole of those performing certain spiritual and ecclesiastical functions; (*pl.*) office of a priest, deacon or (*R.C.*) subdeacon; (*eccles.*) the form of a ceremony; command, instruction; warrant to a banker instructing him to pay out money, written permit to go to a place or perform an action; instruction to a tradesman etc. to make or supply certain goods; **O. in Council,** command issued direct on behalf of the sovereign without special Act of Parliament; **o. of the day,** formal announcement, often an exhortation or commemorative statement, issued to troops by a commander; business of a legislative assembly; prevailing fashion; **in o.,** according to the rules laid down; sound, in good condition; **out of o.,** not working, defective; in violation of recognized procedure; **in o. to,** so as to (signifying intention). ORDER (2), *v.t.* to arrange in regular or proper series, bring in o.; arrange, ordain, decree; command, prescribe; give orders for something to be obtained or prepared; **to o. arms,** (*milit.*) to bring the rifle to a position with the butt on the ground and the barrel well in to the right side. ORDERING, *n.* o., disposition. [OFr.].

ORDERLY (1) [aw′der-li], *adj.* arranged in order, systematic, tidy; quiet, submissive to authority, well controlled; (*milit.*) concerned with carrying out general order on a specific day. ORDERLY (2), *n.* (*milit.*) soldier in attendance on a superior to carry his orders; hospital assistant.

ORDINAL (1) [aw′di-nal], *adj.* indicating position in a series. ORDINAL (2), *n.* an o. number; book prescribing the forms of ceremony of ordination and consecration. [L.].

ORDINANCE [aw′di-nans], *n.* public enactment, solemn and important order; ecclesiastical rite. [OFr.].

ORDINAND [aw-di-nand′], *n.* one who is awaiting ordination. [L.].

ORDINARY (1) [aw′di-na-ri], *adj.* according to general, regular, customary practice, normal, not remarkable; commonplace, dull, undistinguished. ORDINARY (2), *n.* officer having authority in his own right, cleric in his own sphere of office; (*her.*) a simple charge; **Lord O.,** (*Scots leg.*) judge of the Outer House of the Court of Sessions. ORDINARILY, *adv.* in o. fashion; usually. [L.].

ORDINATION [aw-di-nā′shn], *n.* act of ordaining; the conferring of Holy Orders. [L.].

ORDINEE [aw-di-nē′], *n.* one who is newly ordained.

ORDNANCE [awd′nans], *n.* artillery; military stores; **o. survey,** detailed geographical survey, originally made by the War Office. [ORDINANCE].

ORDURE [aw′dyoor], *n.* dung, filth. [Fr.].

ORE [aw(r)], *n.* impure, unrefined metal; rock from which metal may be extracted. [OE.].

OREAD [aw′ri-ad], *n.* (*myth.*) mountain nymph. [Gk.].

ORGAN [aw′gan], *n.* a part of the body performing

ōō is pronounced as in f*oo*d; ŏŏ as in h*oo*d; th as in *th*ink; TH as in *th*at; zh as in azure.   ~ = related to.

a function, instrument for exercising a function; medium for expressing opinion; large wind-instrument, consisting of a series of pipes supplied with air by bellows or fans, and having keyed manuals and pedals by means of which the wind is released; **o. loft**, elevated space or gallery where a large o. is situated. ORGAN-GRINDER, player of a barrel-organ. [L.].

ORGANDIE [aw′gan-di]. *n.* a transparent muslin. [Fr.].

ORGANIC [aw-ga′nik], *adj.* relating to, bound up with, affecting, springing from, the bodily organs; having organs specialized for the various functions of life; connected with organisms and their characteristics; fundamental to the nature of a thing; having a complete, organized unity; **o. chemistry**, the chemistry of the carbon compounds. ORGANIC-ALLY, *adv.* in o. fashion; fundamentally; through the bodily organs. [Gk.].

ORGANISM [aw′ga-nizm], *n.* (*biol.*) anything capable of reproducing its own kind; an independent unity having specialized parts performing the various functions necessary for the life of the whole.

ORGANIST [aw′ga-nist], *n.* player on the organ.

ORGANIZATION [aw-ga-ni-zā′shn], *n.* state of being organized, act or method of organizing; that which is organized, a systematic relation of specialized parts each performing some function of the whole; an association of persons organized to carry out a common purpose.

ORGANIZE [aw′ga-nīz], *v.t. and i.* to make organic; give organization to, group various parts into a systematic whole; arrange or rearrange a system or a body of people so as to make an efficient, co-ordinated whole; become an organization. ORGANIZER, *n.* one who organizes, one whose duty is to o. some undertaking into a systematic and effective working whole. [MedL.].

ORGANON [aw′ga-non], *n.* a system of philosophical scientific inquiry. [Gk.].

ORGANOTHERAPY [aw-ga-nō-the′ra-pi], *n.* medical treatment by organic extracts.

ORGASM [aw′gazm], *n.* the culminating excitement in the sexual act; violent paroxysm of excitement. [Gk.].

ORGIASTIC [aw-ji-as′tik], *adj.* relating to an orgy.

ORGY [aw′ji], *n.* † revels in honour of Dionysos; drunken debauch, noisy licentious revelry; excessive indulgence in any appetite or practice. [Gk.].

ORIEL [aw′ri-el], *n.* projecting or recessed window divided into bays and supported on corbels. [MedL.].

ORIENT (1) [aw′ri-ent], *n.* the East, Asia; a very lustrous pearl. ORIENT (2), *adj.* rising in the East; derived from the East; lustrous. ORIENT (3), *v.t.* to orientate. [L.].

ORIENTAL (1) [aw-ri-en′tal], *adj.* relating to the Eastern countries, to the Far East. ORIENTAL (2), *n.* a native of Asia, *esp.* of Further Asia. ORIENTALISM, *n.* the habits, outlook of Asiatics. ORIENTALIST, *n.* student of Asiatic culture. [L.].

ORIENTATE [aw′ri-en-tāt], *v.t. and i.* (*arch.*) to plan out a building so that the longest axis runs towards the east, plan a building to correspond with the points of the compass; place some object in definite relation to another; place a map so that its bearings correspond to those of one's position; (*reflex.*) take one's bearings; (*fig.*) align oneself, familiarize oneself with the implications of a subject or situation; turn towards the east; turn in a specified direction. [ORIENT (3)].

ORIENTATION [aw-ri-en-tā′shn], *n.* the relation of a body to the points of the compass; tendency, direction.

ORIFICE [o′ri-fis], *n.* the aperture of a tube, mouth of a thing, hole. [L.].

ORIFLAMME [o′ri-flam], *n.* ancient banner of the kings of France, the standard of St. Denis; a banner as an inspiring symbol. [L.].

ORIGAN [o′ri-gan], *n.* (*bot.*) wild marjoram. [Gk.].

ORIGIN [o′ri-jin], *n.* the source, beginning of anything; initial cause of a thing; ancestry, birth. [L.].

ORIGINAL (1) [o-ri′ji-nal], *adj.* relating to an origin, to the beginning of a thing; first-hand, made, written etc. for the first time; (of literature) saying something new, not suggested by anything else; (of persons) having ideas not derived from others, unconventional, inventive. ORIGINAL (2), *n.* the First Cause, originator, author of a thing; first pattern from which copies are made; genuine work of art as opposed to a copy; language in which a work was originally written. [L.].

ORIGINALITY [o-ri-ji-na′li-ti], *n.* state of being original; possession of ideas not derived from others, inventiveness; novelty; spontaneity; freshness of conception.

ORIGINATE [o-ri′ji-nāt], *v.t. and i.* to bring about, cause to exist, initiate; have origin (in), arise (from). ORIGINATION [o-ri-ji-nā′shn], *n.* act or process of originating or being originated. ORIGINATIVE [o-ri′ji-na-tiv], *adj.* having power to originate.

ORIOLE [aw′ri-ōl], *n.* passerine bird allied to the shrikes and wagtails. [L.].

ORION [o-rī′on], *n.* (*myth.*) hunter slain by Artemis; (*astron.*) southern constellation showing a group of seven bright stars. [Gk.].

ORISON [o′ri-zon], *n.* (*archaic*) a prayer. [OFr.].

ORMOLU [aw′mo-lōō], *n.* gilded bronze, lacquered brass; objects decorated with imitation gold; alloy of copper and zinc. [Fr.].

ORNAMENT (1) [aw′na-ment], *n.* decoration, embellishment; object of which the main function is to decorate a room, trinket; person, thing or quality bringing lustre to anything by virtue of his or its presence. ORNAMENT (2), *v.t. and i.* to decorate, provide with an o., serve as an o. to. [L.].

ORNAMENTAL [aw-na-men′tal], *adj.* serving as an ornament, decorative.

ORNAMENTATION [aw-na-men-tā′shn], *n.* decoration; act of ornamenting.

ORNATE [aw-nāt′], *adj.* richly adorned, elaborately decorated. [L.].

ORNITHO-, *pref.* relating to birds. [Gk.].

ORNITHOLOGY [aw-ni-tho′lo-ji], *n.* study of birds. ORNITHOLOGIST, *n.* student of o. [Gk.].

ORNITHORHYNCHUS [aw-ni-tho-ring′kus], *n.* Australian duck-billed mammal which lays eggs. [Gk.].

OROGRAPHY [aw-ro′gra-fi], *n.* scientific study of mountains. [Gk.].

OROTUND [o′rō-tund], *adj.* resonant, clear and loud; pompous. [L.].

ORPHAN (1) [aw′fan], *n.* child bereft of one or both (usually both) of its parents. ORPHAN (2), *adj.* bereft of parents. ORPHAN (3), *v.t.* to make an o. [Gk.].

ORPHANAGE [aw′fa-nij], *n.* state of being an orphan; institution for bringing up orphans.

ORPHEAN [aw-fē′an], *adj.* relating to Orpheus or his music. [L.].

ORPHIC [aw′fik], *adj.* relating to religious ceremonies connected with the Orpheus legend.

ORPHREY [aw′fri], *n.* embroidered border on an ecclesiastical vestment. [OFr.].

ORPIMENT [aw′pi-ment], *n.* yellow sulphide of arsenic. [OFr.].

ORPINE [aw′pin], *n.* (*bot.*) the purple-flowered stonecrop. [Fr.].

ORPINGTON [aw′ping-ton], *n.* breed of domestic fowl originating from *Orpington* in Kent.

ORRERY [o′re-ri], *n.* working model of the solar system. [Earl of *Orrery*, who first devised one].

ORRIS [o′ris], *n.* dried root of the Florentine iris, used in perfumery. [Gk.].

ORTHO-, *pref.* right, straight, true, upright. [Gk.].

ORTHOCHROMATIC [aw-thō-krō-ma′tik], *adj.* (*phot.*) giving true colour values.

ORTHOCLASE [aw′thō-klās], *n.* (*min.*) a monoclinic potash felspar. ORTHOCLASTIC [aw-thō-klas′tik], *adj.* (*min.*) of crystals etc. having the cleavages at right angles to each other. [Gk.].

ORTHODOX [aw′thō-doks], *adj.* right, correct in opinion or doctrine; right theologically; holding the opinions laid down by authority, conventional in belief; **O. Church**, the Greek Church, the Church in communion with the Patriarch of Constantinople. [Gk.].

ORTHODOXY [aw′thō-dok-si], *n.* state of being orthodox in theological or other opinion. [Gk.].

ORTHOEPY [aw′thō-e-pi], *n.* phonology, study of correct pronunciation. ORTHOEPIC(AL) [aw-thō-e′pik(-al)], *adj.* pertaining to o. ORTHOEPIST [aw-thō′e-pist], *n.* one skilled in, writer on, o. [Gk.].

ORTHOGENESIS [aw-thō-je′ni-sis], *n.* a consistent biological variation determined by inherent tendencies. [Gk.].

ORTHOGRAPHY [aw-tho′gra-fi], *n.* correct spelling; study of the spelling of a certain period; rules of spelling. [Gk.].

ORTHOPAEDIC [aw-thō-pē′dik], *adj.* (*med.*) of, pertaining to, or practising orthopaedics

---

The accent ′ after a syllable = stress (u-pon′). The mark ˉ over a vowel = length (ā in made; ō in bone).

ORTHOPAEDICS, ORTHOPAEDY [aw-thŏ-pē'diks, 'di], *n.* manipulative surgery for treating deformities of the bone. [Gk.].
ORTHOPHONY [aw-tho'fo-ni], *n.* correct speaking. ORTHOPHONIC [aw-thŏ-fo'nik], *adj.* pertaining to o.; reproducing sound accurately. [Gk.].
ORTHOPTERA [aw-thop'te-rah], *n.(pl.)* the straight-winged insects. ORTHOPTEROUS, *adj.* straight-winged; belonging to the o. [Gk.].
ORTHOPTIC [aw-thop'tik], *adj.* pertaining to the correction of defective sight. [Gk.].
ORTHOPTIST [aw-thop'tist], *n.* one who treats defects of sight by exercises of the eyes.
ORTOLAN [aw'tŏ-lan], *n.* (*ornith.*) the garden bunting. [It.].
OSCILLATE [o'si-lāt], *v.t. and i.* to swing, vibrate as a pendulum, move between two points; vacillate, waver between choices; (*elect.*) cause to swing to and fro; generate electro-magnetic waves; (*radio*) cause interference by radiating such waves. OSCILLATOR, *n.* apparatus generating electro-magnetic waves.
OSCILLATION [o-si-lā'shn], *n.* act or state of oscillating; vacillation. [L.].
OSCULATE [os'kyŏŏ-lāt], *v.t. and i.* to kiss; (*math.*) touch at more than one point. [L.].
OSCULATION [os-kyŏŏ-lā'shn], *n.* a kiss, kissing; (*math.*) contact at more than a single point, as of curves. [L.].
OSIER [ŏ'zi-er], *n.* willow used in basketwork. [Fr.].
OSMANLI [oz-man'li], *n. and adj.* Ottoman Turk; pertaining to the language and customs of these. [Sultan *Osman* I].
OSMIUM [oz'mi-um], *n.* (*chem.*) a rare metal, the heaviest element, denoted by Os. [Gk.].
OSMOSIS [oz-mŏ'sis], *n.* diffusion of fluids through a membrane or porous partition. OSMOTIC [oz-mo'tik], *adj.* relating to o. [Gk.].
OSMUNDA [oz-mun'dah], *n.* genus of six species of flowering ferns including the royal fern. [Fr.].
OSPREY [os'prā], *n.* the sea-eagle; egret's plume. [L.].
OSSEOUS [o'si-ŏŏs], *adj.* made of bones; bony, having a skeleton. [L.].
OSSICLE [o'si-kl], *n.* small bone, light bony structure. [L.].
OSSIFICATION [o-si-fi-kā'shn], *n.* process of ossifying; state of becoming ossified.
OSSIFY [o'si-fi], *v.t. and i.* to cause to become, turn into, bone; become changed into bony tissue; (of joints) become bony and immovable. [L.].
OSSUARY [o'syŏŏ-a-ri], *n.* charnel-house. [LL.].
OSTENSIBLE [os-ten'si-bl], *adj.* apparent, displayed, pretended, professed. OSTENSIBLY, *adv.* apparently, avowedly. [~L.].
OSTENTATION [os-ten-tā'shn], *n.* deliberate and pretentious show, vulgar display. [L.].
OSTENTATIOUS [os-ten-tā'shŏŏs], *adj.* indulging in, exhibiting, ostentation; intentionally obvious.
OSTENTION [os-ten'shn], *n.* (*eccles.*) exposure and adoration of the Host. [L.].
OSTEO-, *pref.* bone, bony, relating to bone.
OSTEOLOGY [os-ti-o'lo-ji], *n.* science or study of bones. OSTEOLOGIC(AL) [os-ti-o-lo'jik(-al)], *adj.* pertaining to o. [Gk.].
OSTEOPATH [os'ti-ŏ-path], *n.* one practising osteopathy.
OSTEOPATHY [os-ti-o'pa-thi], *n.* treatment of disease and deformity by manipulation and manipulative surgery. [Gk.].
OSTLER, HOSTLER [os'(t)ler], *n.* stableman at an inn. [ME.].
OSTRACISM [os'tra-sizm], *n.* in ancient Athens, banishment for ten years by the vote of a general plebiscite; social exclusion by one's fellows. [*Next*].
OSTRACIZE [os'tra-sīz], *v.t.* to banish by ostracism; exclude from society by common opinion. [Gk.].
OSTRICH [os'trich], *n.* large, flightless, long-legged African and Asiatic bird; (*fig.*) self-deluded person. [ME. from Gk.].
OTHER (1) [u'THer], *adj.* different, distinct from, not the same as, the thing referred to or pointed out; the second of two; additional to, besides this. OTHER (2), *pron.* a different, additional, person or thing. OTHER (3), *adv.* otherwise. [OE.].
OTHERWISE [u'THer-wīz], *adv.* in another fashion; in different circumstances; unless, if not; in other respects.
OTIOSE [ŏ'ti-ŏs], *adj.* lazy, slothful; futile, useless; superfluous. [L.].
OTITIS [ŏ-ti'tis], *n.* inflammation of the ear. [Gk.].
OTO-, *pref.* relating to the ear. [Gk.].

OTOLOGY [ŏ-to'lo-ji], *n.* study of the ear. OTOLOGIST, *n.* specialist in diseases of the ear. [Gk.].
OTTAR, see ATTAR.
OTTAVA-RIMA [o-tah-vah-rē'mah], *n.* stanza of eight lines, the first six rhyming alternately and the last two forming a rhymed couplet. [It.].
OTTER [o'ter], *n.* furry, aquatic, web-footed mammal; fishing device consisting of a heavy plank with bait attached. [OE.].
OTTO, see ATTAR.
OTTOMAN (1) [o'tŏ-man], *n. and adj.* a Turk; Turkish. OTTOMAN (2), *n.* padded backless settee of various types; settee whose seat contains a box. [*Osman*, first of the Osmanli Sultans].
OUBLIETTE [ŏŏ-bli-et'], *n.* dungeon whose only access is through a trap in the floor above. [Fr.].
OUGHT † (1) [awt], *n.* nought, cipher. [AUGHT].
OUGHT (2), *v. auxil. expressing duty, obligation, necessity; expressing probability.* [OE.].
OUIJA [wē'jah], *n.* planchette, a board lettered with the alphabet and used to receive spiritualist messages. [Fr. *oui* and Germ. *ja* yes].
OUNCE (1) [owns], *n.* unit of weight, being one-sixteenth of a pound avoirdupois, 480 grains troy, or one-twentieth of an Imperial pint; (*fig.*) very little. [ME. from L.].
OUNCE (2), *n.* Tibetan snow-leopard; any animal of the leopard family. [Fr.].
OUR [owr], *possessive adj.* belonging, relating to, connected with, us. [OE.].
OURS [owrz], *possessive pron.* belonging to us.
OURSELF [owr-self'], *pron. reflex. and emphatic form* of WE, used only regally or editorially. [ME.].
OURSELVES [owr-selvz'], *pron. reflex. and emphatic form* of WE. [ME.].
OUSEL, see OUZEL.
OUST [owst], *v.t.* to eject, turn out, dispossess from place or position. OUSTER, *n.* illegal dispossession. [OFr.].
OUT (1) [owt], *adv.* not in; with motion away from a point, position or concept (given or implied); from within such a point, position etc.; with remoteness from such a point, position, etc.; so as to vanish, to the final stage; so as to be evident to public notice; **o. of,** outside, beyond, because of, moved by, extracted from; (of animals) having as female parent; **o. on,** shame on; **o. with,** drive out; **all o.,** flat o., with all possible force or energy; **murder will o.,** (something hidden and discreditable) will always come to light; **to have it o.,** to settle a dispute. OUT (2), *adj.* outer; remote from; extinguished, having reached the final point; mistaken; evident; public; on strike; (*cricket*) dismissed by the decision of the umpire, and so not entitled to continue batting; (*boxing*) unable to rise within ten seconds; unconscious. OUT (3), *v.t.* to turn out, expel. [OE.].
OUT- (4), *pref. denoting almost all its adverbial meanings,* out, remote, excessive, superior. [OUT (1)].
OUT-AND-OUT [owt-and-owt'], *adj.* thorough, complete.
OUTBALANCE [owt-ba'lans], *v.t.* to outweigh.
OUTBOARD [owt'bawd], *adj.* on the outer side of a ship or boat.
OUTBOUND [owt'bownd], *adj.* outward bound, on the way out.
OUTBREAK [owt'brāk], *n.* sudden breaking out, bursting forth of anything (disease, war etc.).
OUTBUILDING [owt'bil-ding], *n.* subsidiary building detached from the main block.
OUTBURST [owt'berst], *n.* outbreak, *esp.* of passion etc. into speech.
OUTCAST [owt'kahst], *n.* one rejected and cast out by society etc.; vagabond.
OUTCLASS [owt-klahs'], *v.t.* to excel completely.
OUTCOME [owt'kum], *n.* result, upshot of a thing.
OUTCROP [owt'krop], *n.* (*geol.*) a formation of rock exposed at the surface.
OUTCRY [owt'kri], *n.* cry of indignation, alarm etc., general clamour of disapproval.
OUTDISTANCE [owt-dis'tans], *v.t.* to get in front of, get ahead of.
OUTDO (*pret.* **outdid,** *p.pt.* **outdone**) [owt-dŏŏ'], *v.t.* to excel in achievement, do better than.
OUTDOOR [owt-daw(r)'], *adj.* of the open air, not in a building.
OUTER (1) [ow'ter], *adj.* farther out, farther from the inside or centre; external; outside some intimacy, objective. OUTER (2), *n.* the ring of a circular target farthest from the bull.
OUTERMOST [ow'ter-mŏst], *adj.* farthest out.

ŏŏ is pronounced as in food; ŏŏ as in hood; th as in *think*; TH as in *that*; zh as in azure. ~ = related to.

OUTFACE [owt-fās'], *v.t.* to stare out, brazen out, successfully defy.

OUTFALL [owt'fawl], *n.* mouth of a river etc.

OUTFIELD [owt'fēld], *n.* (*cricket*) fieldsman placed farthest from the batsman; field separated from the main extent of a farm etc.

OUTFIT (1) [owt'fit], *n.* a person's complete clothes, equipment etc., for a specific task or situation; (*slang*) party of people and their equipment for some common venture, group of persons. OUTFIT (2), *v.t.* to fit out, equip.

OUTFLANK [owt-flangk'], *v.t.* to get round the side of an enemy and encompass one of his flanks; (*fig.*) outwit.

OUTFLOW [owt'flō], *n.* outfall; outpouring.

OUTGENERAL (*pres.pt.* outgeneralling, *pret. and p.pt.* outgeneralled) [owt-je'ne-ral], *v.t.* to out-manoeuvre, prove a better general than.

OUTGOING (1) [owt'gō-ing], *n.* (*sg. or pl.*) expenditure, outlay. OUTGOING (2), *adj.* going out, away; retiring.

OUTGROW (*pret.* outgrew, *p.pt.* outgrown) [owt-grō'], *v.t.* to grow too large or old for; grow beyond, lose (a taste or characteristic) with the passage of time.

OUTGROWTH [owt'grōth], *n.* the consequence of something, that which grows from a thing.

OUT-HEROD [owt-he'rod], *v.t.* to be more savage than (Herod).

OUTHOUSE [owt'hows], *n.* outbuilding, shed away from the house.

OUTING [ow'ting], *n.* excursion, brief holiday, short trip away from home.

OUTLANDER [owt'lan-der], *n.* an alien; non-Boer in the Transvaal. [Du.].

OUTLANDISH [owt-lan'dish], *adj.* oddly alien, barbarous.

OUTLAST [owt-lahst'], *v.t.* to last longer than; exceed in duration.

OUTLAW (1) [owt'law], *n.* one placed beyond the protection of the law by legal sentence; lawless person, vagabond. OUTLAW (2), *v.t.* to sentence to outlawry; expel from society. OUTLAWRY, *n.* legal declaration making someone an o.; state of being an o. [OScand.].

OUTLAY [owt'lā], *n.* expenditure, *esp.* money spent with the expectation of some definite return.

OUTLET [owt'let], *n.* passage outwards, orifice; means or chance of expression.

OUTLINE (1) [owt'līn], *n.* boundary line of a figure; apparent edge of an object, defining its shape, *esp.* the outer line of a drawing giving the plane shape of the whole; general features of a situation, theory, proposal etc., which give an impression of the whole without detail, short account of a thing giving the main points without particulars. OUTLINE (2), *v.t.* to draw an o. of, give an o. of, summarize.

OUTLIVE [owt-liv'], *v.t.* to live longer than.

OUTLOOK [owt'look], *n.* view seen from a place, prospect; (*fig.*) view of the future, future prospect suggested by present events; attitude of mind, way in which things are considered.

OUTLYING [owt'lī-ing], *adj.* lying at a distance, remote.

OUT-MANOEUVRE [owt-ma-noo'ver], *v.t.* to defeat by superiority in strategy or tactics.

OUTMODE [owt-mōd'], *v.t.* to put out of fashion.

OUTMOST [owt'mōst], *adj.* outermost.

OUTNUMBER [owt-num'ber], *v.t.* to exceed in number.

OUT-OF-DATE [owt-ov-dāt'], *adj.* obsolete, old-fashioned.

OUT-OF-DOOR [owt-ov-daw(r)'], *adj.* outdoor.

OUT-OF-THE-WAY [out-ov-the-wā'], *adj.* remote, isolated, difficult of approach; unusual.

OUTPACE [owt-pās'], *v.t.* to progress faster than.

OUT-PATIENT [owt'pā-shent], *n.* non-resident patient coming to hospital for treatment.

OUTPLAY [owt-plā'], *v.t.* to play markedly better than.

OUTPOST [owt'pōst], *n.* a detachment of troops holding a post at some distance from their main body; (*fig.*) place where some manner of life or culture exists far from its main home.

OUTPOURING [owt'pōr-ing], *n.* outburst, effusion of words and passionate feelings.

OUTPUT [owt'poot], *n.* quantity produced by a factory, instrument or person within a given time.

OUTRAGE (1) [owt'rāj], *n.* violent, disgusting and offensive act committed against person, property or public feeling; rape or sexual violence. OUTRAGE

(2), *v.t.* to rape, violate; commit an o. against the feelings of. [OFr.].

OUTRAGEOUS [owt-rā'jŏos], *adj.* of the nature of an outrage, flagrantly offensive, monstrous. [OFr.].

OUTRE, outré [ŏo'trā], *adj.* excessive, beyond good taste. [OFr.].

OUTRIDE (*pret.* outrode, *p.pt.* outridden) [owt-rīd'], *v.t.* to ride faster than.

OUTRIDER [owt'rī-der], *n.* mounted attendant riding before, behind or at the side of a carriage.

OUTRIGGER [owt'ri-ger], *n.* mast and tackle for lifting weights; rowlock projecting from a boat's side to give extra leverage, boat having such devices; projection from a carriage shaft for an extra trace.

OUTRIGHT (1) [owt'rīt], *adv.* frankly, brusquely, openly, immediately, all at once. OUTRIGHT (2), *adj.* downright, forthright.

OUTRUN (*pres.pt.* outrunning, *pret.* outran, *p.pt.* outrun) [owt-run'], *v.t.* to run or go faster than, exceed.

OUTSET [owt'set], *n.* beginning, start of a business, affair, series of events.

OUTSHINE (*pret. and p.pt.* outshone) [owt-shīn'], *v.t.* to excel in brilliance, make a better impression than.

OUTSIDE (1) [owt-sīd'], *n.* the external parts of a thing, position of what is not within. OUTSIDE (2) [owt'sīd], *adj.* on, related to, the outer part of a thing, external, not connected with a thing; extreme, reaching to the farthest extent; outdoor. OUTSIDE (3) [owt-sīd'], *adv.* on the exterior, outer side of, beyond, in the open air, not in a particular place. OUTSIDE (4) [owt-sīd'], *prep.* not inside, on the exterior of, not situated, contained or included in; except.

OUTSIDER [owt-sī'der], *n.* one who is unworthy of a place in good society; (*racing*) horse not considered to have any reasonable chance of success.

OUTSIZE [owt'sīz], *n. and adj.* (a size) larger than normal, *esp.* as applied to ready-made clothes intended for large or fat persons.

OUTSKIRTS [owt'skerts], *n.* the borders of a thing, outer fringes of a town, distant suburb.

OUTSPAN (*pres.pt.* outspanning, *pret. and p.pt.* outspanned) [owt-span'], *v.t.* to unyoke (beasts) from a wagon. [Du.].

OUTSPOKEN [owt-spō'ken], *adj.* forthright or straightforward in speech, frank.

OUTSTANDING [owt-stan'ding], *adj.* conspicuous, distinctive, remarkable; standing over, still unsettled or owing. OUTSTANDINGLY, *adv.* in an o. way.

OUTSTAY [owt-stā'], *v.t.* to exceed, stay longer than; **to o. one's welcome**, to stay so long that one is no longer welcome.

OUTSTRIP (*pres.pt.* outstripping, *pret. and p.pt.* outstripped) [owt-strip'], *v.t.* to leave behind by exceeding in pace; go faster or do better than.

OUTVOTE [owt-vōt'], *v.t.* to defeat by casting more votes.

OUTWALK [owt-wawk'], *v.t.* to walk faster or farther than.

OUTWARD (1) [owt'werd], *adj.* external, relating to the outside; material, visible; going outwards. OUTWARD (2), *adv.* outwards, towards the outside, away from. OUTWARDLY, *adv.* towards the outside; from the outside, externally. OUTWARDNESS, *n.* externality; objectivity. OUTWARDS, *adv.* towards the outside, from the inside, in a direction away from.

OUTWEAR (*pret.* outwore, *p.pt.* outworn) [owt-wāer'], *v.t.* to last longer than; wear out, exhaust.

OUTWEIGH [owt-wā'], *v.t.* to carry more weight, have more importance than.

OUTWIT (*pres.pt.* outwitting, *pret. and p.pt.* outwitted) [owt-wit'], *v.t.* to overreach or defeat by superior wit and tactics, deceive, get the better of by astuteness.

OUTWORK (1) [owt'werk], *n.* a fortification in advance of the main defences. OUTWORK (2), *n.* work done away from the factory etc.

OUZEL, OUSEL [ŏo'zel], *n.* one of several kinds of thrush. [O.E.].

OVA [ō'vah], *n. pl. of* OVUM.

OVAL (1) [ō'val], *adj.* elliptical, egg-shaped. OVAL (2), *n.* plane figure of o. shape. [L.].

OVARY [ō'va-ri], *n.* (*anat.*) reproductive organ in female animals producing the eggs for fertilization; (*bot.*) the part of the pistil containing the ovules. [L.].

OVATE [ō'vāt], *adj.* oval, egg-shaped. [L.].

OVATION [o-vā'shn], *n.* (*hist.*) a lesser Roman triumph; enthusiastic public greeting. [L.].

The accent ' after a syllable = stress (u-pon')   The mark ‾ over a vowel = length (ā in made; ō in bone).

OVEN [u'vn], *n.* enclosed receptacle for baking; small chemical kiln. [OE.].

OVER (1) [ō'ver], *adv.* above, across, towards and across, away and across; from one point, side, station to another; away from the perpendicular, upright, normal position; upwards, across and down; finished, gone, past; excessively, too much; everywhere, in every respect; in repetition. OVER (2), *n.* (*cricket*) series of six or eight balls delivered in succession from one end of the pitch by the same bowler before changing o.; (*pl.*) excess. OVER (3), *prep.* above, across, spanning, covering, towards and across; more than, superior to, lasting longer than. [OE.].

OVER- (4), *pref.* expressing superiority, situation or passage across or on top of, excess beyond the right or normal.

OVERACT [ō-ve-rakt'], *v.t. and i.* to act so as to make or be unnatural.

OVERALL [ō-ve-rawl'], *adj.* including all parts, general, total.

OVERALLS [ō've-rawlz], *n.(pl.)* loose garment worn over others for protection while engaged in manual work; officer's dress trousers.

OVERARM [ō've-rahm], *adj. and adv.* (*cricket, swimming, lawn tennis*), with the hand and arm raised above the shoulder.

OVERAWE [ō-ve-raw'], *v.t.* to browbeat, frighten into respectful submission.

OVERBALANCE [ō-ver-ba'lans], *v.t. and i.* to lose balance so as to fall over; upset the balance of a thing; exceed in weight or importance.

OVERBEAR (*pret.* **overbore**, *p.pt.* **overborne**) [ō-ver-bäer'], *v.t.* to dominate, impose one's will upon.

OVERBEARING [ō-ver-bäer'ing], *adj.* tending, endeavouring, to overbear; domineering, arrogant.

OVERBID (*pres.pt.* **overbidding**, *pret. and p.pt.* **overbid**) [ō-ver-bid'], *v.t.* to outbid; (*bridge*) overcall.

OVERBLOWN [ō-ver-blōn'], *adj.* past full bloom, blowzy.

OVERBOARD [ō'ver-bawd], *adv.* over the side of a ship into the sea; (*fig.*) cast aside, out of the way.

OVERBUILD [ō-ver-bild'], *v.t. and i.* to build over; build too much.

OVERBURDEN [ō-ver-bur'den], *v.t.* to burden too heavily.

OVERCALL [ō-ver-kawl'], *v.t. and i.* (*bridge*) to make a bid higher than; call more than one's cards justify.

OVERCAST (1) [ō'ver-kahst], *v.t.* to cast a gloom over; stitch over a seam to prevent unravelling. OVERCAST (2), *adj.* cloudy, gloomy.

OVERCHARGE (1) [ō-ver-chahj'], *v.t. and i.* to charge (a person) too high a price; charge too heavily with electricity, overload. OVERCHARGE (2) [ō'ver-chahj], *n.* an excessive charge.

OVERCOAT [ō'ver-kōt], *n.* coat worn over the rest of the garments, top-coat.

OVERCOME [ō-ver-kum'], *v.t.* to subdue, defeat, master, surmount.

OVERCROWD [ō-ver-krowd'], *v.t.* to crowd to excess, pack too close, force to live in insufficient space.

OVERDO (*pret.* **overdid**, *p.pt.* **overdone**) [ō-ver-dōō'], *v.t.* to over-emphasize, go too far, cook too long; **to o. things**, to tire oneself out by attempting too much.

OVERDOSE (1) [ō'ver-dōs], *n.* too great a dose. OVERDOSE (2), *v.t.* to administer an o. to.

OVERDRAFT [ō'ver-drahft], *n.* loan from a bank; such a debt incurred by withdrawing more than is at one's credit.

OVERDRAW (*pret.* **overdrew**, *p.pt.* **overdrawn**) [ō-ver-draw'], *v.t.* to exaggerate, strain; run up an overdraft on one's account.

OVERDRESS [ō-ver-dres'], *v.t. and i.* to dress too elaborately or formally.

OVERDRIVE (*pret.* **overdrove**, *p.pt.* **overdriven**) [ō-ver-driv'], *v.t.* to drive or work too hard.

OVERDUE [ō-ver-dyōō'], *adj.* behind its due time.

OVERESTIMATE (1) [ō-ve-res'ti-māt], *v.t. and i.* to make an overestimate of. OVERESTIMATE [ō-ve-res'ti-mat], *n.* exaggerated estimate, too great an expectation.

OVERFLOW (1) [ō-ver-flō'], *v.t. and i.* to flow over the edge of something; flood something by flowing over into it; be too much or too many for the available space; be abundant (with). OVERFLOW (2) [ō'ver-flō], *n.* that which overflows; outlet for overflowing; amount in excess of space etc.; **o. meeting**, secondary meeting held when the number of people

exceeds the capacity of the original place of meeting.

OVERGROW (*pret.* **overgrew**, *p.pt.* **overgrown**) [ō-ver-grō'], *v.t.* to grow over; outgrow. OVERGROWTH, *n.* excessive growth.

OVERHAND (1) [ō'ver-hand], *adj.* done with the hand above the shoulder. OVERHAND (2), *adv.* with the hand above the shoulder.

OVERHANG (*pret. and p.pt.* **overhung**) [ō-ver-hang'], *v.t. and i.* to hang out over, project over; (*fig.*) hang over threateningly, impend.

OVERHAUL (1) [ō-ver-hawl'], *v.t.* thoroughly to inspect and examine for faults (*esp.* machinery); overtake and pass, *esp.* at sea. OVERHAUL (2), [ō'ver-hawl], *n.* thorough examination and repairing.

OVERHEAD (1) [ō-ver-hed'], *adv.* above, above the head. OVERHEAD (2), *adj.* above the head, above; (of expenses) permanent, not related to price and wage fluctuations or to marketing. OVERHEADS, *n.* (*pl.*) o. expenses, such as rent, insurance and upkeep of premises.

OVERHEAR (*pret. and p.pt.* **overheard**) [ō-ver-hēer'], *v.t.* to hear what is meant for another, listen by stealth.

OVERISSUE [o-ve-ris'syōō], *v.t.* to issue too great a quantity of.

OVERJOYED [ō-ver-joid'], *adj.* extremely pleased.

OVERLAND (1) [ō-ver-land'], *adv.* by land, across land. OVERLAND (2) [ō'ver-land], *adj.* lying across country or o., travelling by land.

OVERLAP (*pres.pt.* **overlapping**, *pret. and p.pt.* **overlapped**) [ō-ver-lap'], *v.t. and i.* to lap over, project beyond the edge of something so as partly to cover it; (*fig.*) partly to correspond in subject or coincide in time.

OVERLAY (1) [*pret. and p.pt.* **overlaid**] [ō-ver-lā'], *v.t.* to coat, cover over heavily. OVERLAY (2) [ō'ver-lā], *n.* that which overlays, a covering.

OVERLEAF [ō-ver-lēf'], *adv.* on the next page.

OVERLIE (*pret.* **overlay**, *p.pt.* **overlain**) [ō-ver-lī'], to lie over, smother by lying upon.

OVERLOAD (1) [ō-ver-lōd'], *v.t.* to load too heavily. OVERLOAD (2) [ō'ver-lōd], *n.* excessive load or electric charge.

OVERLOOK [ō-ver-lōōk'], *v.t.* to look down on from a higher position; supervise, superintend; ignore through oversight; neglect; condone, excuse.

OVERLORD [ō'ver-lawd], *n.* a feudal superior.

OVERMANTEL [ō'ver-man-tel], *n.* mantelshelf.

OVERMUCH [ō-ver-much'], *adv.* too much.

OVERNICE [ō-ver-nīs'], *adj.* too refined or fastidious.

OVERNIGHT [ō-ver-nīt'], *adv.* on the previous night; through the night; in the coming night; suddenly, with great swiftness and unexpectedness.

OVERPLAY [ō-ver-plā'], *v.t.* **to o. one's hand**, to take risks unjustified by the strength of one's position.

OVERPLUS [ō'ver-plus], *n.* surplus, excess.

OVERPOWER [ō-ver-power'], *v.t.* to overcome, subdue, reduce to helplessness, vanquish.

OVERPRINT (1) [ō-ver-print'], *v.t.* to print too many copies of; provide with an overprint. OVERPRINT (2) [ō'ver-print], *n.* something printed on already printed material such as postage stamps.

OVERPROOF [ō-ver-prōōf'], *adj.* above alcoholic proof.

OVERRATE [ō-ver-rāt'], *v.t.* to rate too highly.

OVERREACH [ō-ver-rēch'], *v.t. and i.* to outwit, get the better of; (*reflex.*) defeat oneself by attempting too much subtlety; (of a horse) cut the hind leg against the front hoof in jumping.

OVERRIDE (*pret.* **overrode**, *p.pt.* **overridden**) [ō-ver-rid'], *v.t.* to ride down; ride to excess; (*fig.*) overrule, disregard.

OVERRULE [ō-ver-rōōl'], *v.t.* to set aside (a ruling), decide against; overcome the will of another.

OVERRUN (*pres.pt.* **overrunning**, *pret.* **overran**, *p.pt.* **overrun**) [ō-ver-run'], *v.t.* to spread over, infest, conquer by spreading far and wide in great number, exceed (a limit); (*typ.*) shift lines of type in making an adjustment.

OVERSEA(S) (1) [ō-ver-sē(z)'], *adj.* beyond, across the sea, foreign. OVERSEAS (2), *adv.* beyond, across the sea, abroad.

OVERSEE (*pret.* **oversaw**, *p.pt.* **overseen**) [ō-ver-sē'], *v.t.* to superintend.

OVERSEER [ō'ver-sēer], *n.* a superintendent.

OVERSELL (*pret. and p.pt.* **oversold**) [ō-ver-sel'], *v.t. and i.* to sell more of a thing than one possesses.

OVERSEW (*pret.* **oversewed**, *p.pt.* **oversewn**) [ō'ver-sō], *v.t.* to sew two edges together, passing the needle through from the same side in every stitch.

OVERSHADOW [ō-ver-sha'dō], *v.t.* to cover with

shade or shadow; put into the shade, make dim by contrast; cast gloom on, make depressed.

OVERSHOE [ō'ver-shoō], *n.* outer shoe worn for additional protection over bad going, golosh.

OVERSHOOT (*pret. and p.pt.* **overshot**) [ō-ver-shoōt'], *v.t.* to shoot above or beyond; **to o. the mark**, to exaggerate, overdo, go too far.

OVERSIGHT [ō'ver-sīt], *n.* lapse through carelessness, failure to observe something, error made through such a mistake.

OVERSLEEP (*pret. and p.pt.* **overslept**) [ō-ver-slēp'], *v.i.* to sleep beyond the proper time for waking.

OVERSPEND (*pret. and p.pt.* **overspent**) [ō-ver-spend'], *v.i.* to spend too much; *v.t.* to spend in excess of.

OVERSTATE [ō-ver-stāt], *v.t.* to state (a case) too strongly, exaggerate. OVERSTATEMENT, *n.* exaggeration.

OVERSTAY [ō-ver-stā'], *v.i.* to stay too long.

OVERSTEP (*pres.pt.* **overstepping**, *pret. and p.pt.* **overstepped**) [ō-ver-step'], *v.t.* to exceed, go beyond (proper bounds of behaviour).

OVERSTOCK [ō-ver-stok'], *v.t.* to stock with too many goods, furnish too great a supply of.

OVERSTRAIN (1) [ō-ver-strān'], *v.t.* to put too great a strain on. OVERSTRAIN (2), *n.* weakness, nervous disturbance, due to excessive mental or physical effort.

OVERSTRUNG [ō-ver-strung'], *adj.* too highly strung, having too sensitive nerves; (of a piano) having diagonally crossing strings.

OVERSUBSCRIBED [ō-ver-sub-skrībd'], *adj.* (of a loan or issue of shares) producing applications for more than the amount available.

OVERT [ō-vurt'], *adj.* obvious, done openly, apparent. OVERTLY, *adv.* in o. fashion. [OFr.].

OVERTAKE (*pret.* **overtook**, *p.pt.* **overtaken**) [ō-ver-tāk'], *v.t.* to catch up with, come suddenly upon, overcome.

OVERTAX [ō-ver-taks'], *v.t.* to tax (one's strength etc.) excessively.

OVERTHROW (1) (*pret.* **overthrew**, *p.pt.* **overthrown**) [ō-ver-thrō'], *v.t.* to throw down, overcome, defeat. OVERTHROW (2) [ō'ver-thrō], *n.* defeat, destruction; (*cricket*) fielded ball thrown past the wicket so that extra runs may be scored, run so made.

OVERTIME [ō'ver-tīm], *n.* time spent in work beyond the normal hours; extra wages, usually at a higher rate, received for such work.

OVERTONE (1) [ō'ver-tōn], *n.* a harmonic. OVERTONE (2) [ō-ver-tōn'], *v.t.* (*phot.*) to give too deep a tone to.

OVERTOP (*pres.pt.* **overtopping**, *pret. and p.pt.* **overtopped**) [ō-ver-top'], *v.t.* to exceed in height, rise over the top of.

OVERTURE [ō'ver-tyoōr], *n.* (*mus.*) orchestral prelude to a work, preliminary piece of music played before a performance; (*fig.*) preliminaries of a great event; (*pl.*) friendly approaches, formal tentative advances. [OFr.].

OVERTURN [ō-ver-turn'], *v.t. and i.* to upset, throw over; fall, tip over.

OVERWEENING [ō-ver-wē'ning], *adj.* presumptuously proud, arrogant, full of insolent conceit.

OVERWEIGHT [ō-ver-wāt'], *adj.* more in weight than the required or permissible amount.

OVERWHELM [ō-ver-welm'], *v.t.* to overpower by pouring upon, sweep over, master by extreme force or weight of numbers, abash, overcome.

OVERWORK (1) [ō-ver-wurk'], *v.t. and i.* to work a person or machine too hard; perform more work than one can stand. OVERWORK (2), *n.* excessive work, work too great for the system to endure.

OVERWROUGHT [ō-ver-rawt'], *adj.* overstrained, too much excited.

OVI- (1), *pref.* relating to an egg. [L.].

OVI- (2), *pref.* relating to sheep. [L.].

OVIDUCT [ō'vi-dukt], *n.* passage through which the egg passes from the ovary. [OVI (1) and DUCT].

OVIFORM [ō'vi-fawm], *adj.* egg-shaped. [OVI (1) and FORM].

OVINE [ō'vīn], *adj.* relating to sheep. [~OVI (2)].

OVIPAROUS [ō-vi'pa-roōs], *adj.* bringing forth young in eggs. [OVI (1) and L.].

OVO-, *pref.* egg. [L.].

OVOID [ō'void], *adj.* egg-shaped. [OVO and Gk.].

OVULE [ō'vyoōl], *n.* (*bot.*) unfertilized seed. [OVUM].

OVUM (*pl.* **ova**) [ō'vum], *n.* female germ cell in the ovary before fertilization. [L.].

OWE [ō], *v.t. and i.* to be indebted (to someone for something); be under an obligation to someone, have as a result of; be in debt; (*sport*) (of handicapped players) to have to concede (strokes or a score). [OE.].

OWING [ō'wing], *adj.* in the state of being a debt, not paid; **o. to**, as a result of, on account of. [*Prec.*].

OWL [owl], *n.* large-headed, hook-beaked, nocturnal bird of prey; (*fig.*) solemn, stupid, sleepy person. OWL-LIGHT, dusk. OWLISH, *adj.* foolish, sleepy as an o. [OE.].

OWLET, HOWLET [ow'let], *n.* young owl.

OWN (1) [ōn], *adj.* possessed by, related to, someone in the closest, most intimate degree; performed by a person for himself by his own skill and effort; **to hold one's o.**, to maintain one's position, hold one's ground against attack. OWN (2), *v.t.* to possess, have legal title to, acknowledge, admit as belonging to oneself, admit; confess to something. [OE.].

OWNER [ō'ner], *n.* one who owns, one with legal title. OWNERSHIP, *n.* condition or title of an o., period of being an o., régime of an o.

OX (*pl.* **oxen**) [oks], *n.* full-grown castrated male of domesticated cattle, used for meat (beef) and formerly, and still in some countries, as a draught animal; (*pl.*) cattle in general; (*fig.*) lumpish, patient, extremely strong person. [OE.].

OXALIC [ok-sa'lik], *adj.* relating to, derived from, oxalis; **o. acid**, poisonous acid used in dyeing and bleaching.

OXALIS [ok'sa-lis], *n.* (*bot.*) the wood-sorrel. [Gk.].

OXBOW [oks'bō], *n.* U-shaped yoke of a draught-ox; horseshoe bend in a river.

OXEN [ok'sen], *pl. of* ox. [OE.].

OX-EYE [oks'ī], *n.* the marguerite daisy.

OXFORD [oks'fawd], *n.* kind of shoe lacing up over the instep; **O. Group** religious movement founded by Dr. Buchman; **O. Movement**, Anglo-Catholic movement of Pusey and Newman. [University of *Oxford*].

OXIDATION [ok-si-dā'shn], *n.* process of oxidizing, state of being oxidized, process occurring when oxygen is combined with another element or radical.

OXIDE [ok'sīd], *n.* a compound of oxygen with a radical or another element. [Fr.].

OXIDIZATION [ok-si-dī-zā'shn], *n.* oxidation.

OXIDIZE [ok'si-dīz], *v.t. and i.* to make into an oxide, combine with oxygen or subject to an equivalent process; cover with oxide; become an oxide, become rusty through oxidation. OXIDIZING, *adj.* that tends to o.

OXLIP [oks'lip], *n.* the plant, *Primula elatior*. [OE.].

OXONIAN (1) [ok-sō'ni-an], *adj.* of, or pertaining to, Oxford. OXONIAN (2), *n.* a native of Oxford, member of the University of Oxford. [MedL.].

OXY-, *pref.* relating to oxygen or an oxide. [Gk.].

OXYACETYLENE [ok-si-a-se'ti-lēn], *adj.* of, or pertaining to, the welding and cutting processes employing acetylene gas burnt in a stream of oxygen. [OXY(GEN) and ACETYLENE].

OXYGEN [ok'si-jen], *n.* (*chem.*) the gaseous element denoted by O, a common colourless gas, essential to life, existing free in the atmosphere. [Gk.].

OXYGENATE [ok'si-je-nāt], *v.t.* to impregnate with oxygen. OXYGENATION [ok-si-je-nā'shn], *n.* act of oxygenating, state of being oxygenated.

OXYGENIZE [ok'si-je-nīz], *v.t.* to oxygenate.

OXYHYDROGEN [ok-si-hī'drō-jen], *adj.* of, or pertaining to, a flame of hydrogen burning in a stream of oxygen.

OXYMORON [ok-si-maw'ron], *n.* rhetorical figure in which diametrically opposite words and ideas are associated, e.g. bitter-sweet. [Gk.].

OXYTONE [ok'si-tōn], *adj.* uttered in a high tone; (*Gk. gram.*) having an acute accent on the last syllable. [Gk.].

OYER [oi'er], *n.* (*leg.*) Royal Commission to judges to try cases at Assize. [AFr.].

OYEZ [ō-yes'], *int.* call for attention by an usher or town-crier. [OFr.].

OYSTER [oi'ster], *n.* an edible bivalve marine mollusc; **as dumb as an o.**, completely uncommunicative; **the world is mine o.**, all is mine for the taking. OYSTER-BAR, bar where oysters and other shell-fish are served. OYSTER-BED, breeding ground for oysters. OYSTER-CATCHER, the wading-bird, the sea-pie. OYSTER-SHELL, shell of an o. [ME. from Gk.].

OZOCERITE, OZOKERIT(E) [ō-zō'se-rīt, ō-zō'ke-rit], *n.* wax-like mineral found in shale and used for making candles. [Gk.].

OZONE [ō'zōn], *n.* triatomic form of oxygen obtained by electric discharges in oxygen, so called from its smell; (*coll.*) the bracing smell of the seaside. [Gk.].

The accent ' after a syllable = stress (u-pon'). The mark ‾ over a vowel = length (ā in made; ō in bone).

P

P [pē], sixteenth letter of the English alphabet.
PA [pah], *n.* (*coll.*) father. [Shortened from PAPA].
PABULUM [pa'byōō-lum], *n.* food, fodder. [L.].
PACE (1) [pās], *n.* a single step in walking or running, space covered in such a step; speed of walking, speed of any (progressive) motion; mode of walking; running; manner of a horse's stepping; **to put (someone) through his paces,** to test (someone's) knowledge or ability in a routine of duties. PACE (2), *v.t. and i.* to take paces, walk with a regular step; help a runner by running beside him and setting a suitable speed, try out someone's (something's) speed; **to p. out,** to measure out (a length) by counting regular steps. PACER, *n.* pacemaker; horse which paces. [L.].
PACE (3) [pā'si], *prep.* notwithstanding, with deferential contradiction of. [L.].
PACEMAKER [pās'mā-ker], *n.* one who sets a runner's pace; leader in a race.
PACHYDERM [pa'ki-derm], *n.* a thick-skinned animal, hooved non-ruminant. PACHYDERMATOUS, [pa-ki-dur'ma-toōs], *adj.* thick-skinned, stolid, like a p. [Gk.].
PACIFIC [pa-si'fik], *adj.* peaceful, mild, desiring, promoting peace; pertaining to the Pacific Ocean.
PACIFICATION [pa-si-fi-kā'shn], *n.* act of pacifying, subduing resistance.
PACIFICATORY [pa-si'fi-kā-te-ri], *adj.* tending to pacify.
PACIFISM [pa'si-fizm], *n.* belief that violence, *esp.* military action as an instrument of policy, is evil; doctrine and policy of unilateral disarmament and non-resistance to aggression.
PACIFIST (1) [pa'si-fist], *n.* upholder of pacifism. PACIFIST (2), *adj.* relating to, advocating, in accordance with, pacifism.
PACIFY [pa'si-fi], *v.t.* to make peaceful, assuage (danger or hostility); appease; suppress hostility and opposition in a conquered country. [L.].
PACK (1) [pak], *n.* bundle of goods tied together for carriage on the back or by a beast of burden, haversack carried on the back; herd of animals hunting together; group, mob of persons; complete set of playing cards; packet of photographic film designed to be inserted flat into a camera; (*Rugby football*) that part of the team forming the scrum, the forwards; group of grouse; cold compress to reduce inflammation. PACK (2), *v.t.* to bundle together, fit, crowd together in a box etc. for storage or travel; get together (personal belongings) for travel; cram, cram together, fill tightly; (*med.*) wrap in a wet cloth to reduce inflammation; fill (an assembly, jury) with one's own supporters; *v.i.* to crowd together, gather one's goods together ready for travel; come together in a p.; **to p. off, send packing,** to send (a person) away; **to p. up,** (*slang*) to stop work, collapse, die. PACKER, *n.* one who, or that which, packs. [ME.].
PACKAGE [pa'kij], *n.* packed bundle, parcel.
PACKET [pa'kit], *n.* small package, parcel; packet-boat; (*slang*) large sum of money made or lost in business or gambling; **to catch a p.,** (*slang*) to receive a heavy blow, to be severely reprimanded or punished. PACKET-BOAT, vessel conveying mails under a government contract. [Fr.].
PACKHORSE [pak'haws], *n.* horse employed in carrying packs.
PACK-ICE [pak'īs], *n.* broken ice crushed together into heaps.
PACKING [pa'king], *n.* act of making packages or storing goods for travel; stuff used to pack round a delicate object for transport, or packed round pipes or machinery to prevent jarring or freezing. PACK-ING-CASE, wooden case in which goods are packed. PACKING-NEEDLE, strong needle for sewing up packages. PACKING-SHEET, coarse canvas for packing goods.
PACKMAN [pak'man], *n.* pedlar.
PACK-SADDLE [pak'sa-dl], *n.* saddle on which packs are laid.
PACKTHREAD [pak'thred], *n.* coarse strong thread for sewing up packages.
PACT [pakt], *n.* agreement made between two or more parties, covenant. [L.].

PAD (1) [pad], *n.* sound made by the foot of one who pads; (*archaic*) an easy-paced horse. PAD (2) (*pres.pt.* PADDING, *p.pt.* PADDED), *v.i* to trudge along on foot; (of an animal) move with a soft dull sound. [Du.].
PAD (3), *n.* something stuffed with soft material used to fill out, protect, prevent friction; stuffed legguard worn in cricket and other games; soft parts of an animal's paw, fleshy undersurface of a foot; a number of pieces of writing, blotting or drawing paper fastened one above the other in a block. PAD (4) (*pres.pt.* PADDING, *pret.* and *p.pt.* PADDED), *v.t.* to stuff out, cover with soft material, protect with a p.; (*fig.*) fill out a literary work with unnecessary verbiage so as to occupy more space. [Uncert.].
PADDING [pa'ding], *n.* stuffing material, stuff used to pad; literary verbiage to fill up space.
PADDLE (1) [pa'dl], *n.* short oar with broad, rounded blade, wielded with both hands without a rowlock, used in canoes; one of the boards of a paddlewheel. PADDLE (2), *v.t. and i.* to propel (a boat), move along by means of a p.; row without exerting full strength. [Unkn.].
PADDLE (3), *v.i.* to walk in shallow water, dabble the feet or hands in water. [Unkn.].
PADDLE-BOARD [pa'dl-bawd], *n.* one of the boards of a paddle-wheel.
PADDLE-STEAMER [pa'dl-stē-mer], *n.* steamship driven by paddle-wheel.
PADDLE-WHEEL [pa'dl-wēl], *n.* great wheel propelling a ship by means of boards fixed at right angles to its circumference.
PADDOCK (1) [pa'dok], *n.* toad. [ME.].
PADDOCK (2), *n.* small field for exercising horses; enclosure on a racecourse where the horses are assembled; (*Australian, N.Z. etc.*) any field. [OE.].
PADDY (1) [pa'di], *n.* fit of violent, childish temper; (*coll.*) Irishman. [Ir.].
PADDY (2), *n.* growing rice. [Malay].
PADLOCK (1) [pad'lok], *n.* detachable lock with hinged link to be fixed through a staple. PADLOCK (2), *v.t.* to fasten with a p. [Uncert.].
PADRE [pah'drā], *n.* military chaplain; (*coll.*) clergyman. [Portug.].
P(A)EAN [pē'an], *n.* hymn of thanksgiving sung to Apollo; song of joy and triumph. [Gk.].
PAEDEUTICS, PAIDEUTICS [pē-, pī-dyōō'tiks], *n.*(*pl.*) science of education. [Gk.].
P(A)EDO-, *pref.* relating to education or to children. [Gk.].
P(A)EDIATRIC [pē-di-at'rik], *adj.* pertaining to the treatment of children's diseases. [Gk.].
P(A)EDIATRICS [pē-di-at'riks], *n.*(*pl.*) science of treating children's diseases.
PAEONY, see PEONY.
PAGAN (1) [pā'gan], *n.* a heathen; (*fig.*) one without religion, morals or conventional taste. PAGAN (2), *adj.* relating to a p., his beliefs and barbarism; non-Christian. [L.].
PAGE (1) [pāj], *n.* youthful retainer of a prince or noble, youth of noble birth in attendance upon a lord; liveried boy servant employed as footman or messenger; male child attendant at a wedding. PAGE-BOY, a page. PAGE (2), *v.t.* to call out for a person through the rooms of a hotel etc. [OFr.].
PAGE (3), *n.* one side of a sheet of writing paper or leaf of a book. [Fr.].
PAGEANT [pa'jnt], *n.* splendid, colourful display of pomp and beauty; form of dramatics in which historical incidents are reconstructed by costumed players. [OFr.].
PAGEANTRY [pa'jn-tri], *n.* the display, pomp, colour of a pageant.
PAGINAL [pa'ji-nal], *adj.* relating to pages, in pages. [L.].
PAGINATE [pa'ji-nāt], *v.t.* to number the pages of a book in sequence. PAGINATION [pa-ji-nā'shn], *n.* act of paginating; numerical order of the pages of a book. [L.].
PAGODA [pa-gō'dah], *n.* Far-Eastern sacred tower built in a series of tapering storeys culminating in a slender pinnacle. [Portug.].
PAID [pād], *adj.* receiving pay for services. [PAY].
PAIL [pāl], *n.* bucket, conical open vessel for carrying

ōō is pronounced as in food; ŏŏ as in hood; th as in *think*; TH as in *that*; zh as in azure. ~ = related to.

liquid; quantity of liquid contained in this. **PAILFUL**, *n.* quantity of liquid a p. will contain. [O.E.].

PAIN (1) [pān], *n.* physical suffering, distressing sensation in a part of the body, smart, pang, ache etc.; mental suffering, grief; care, trouble; punishment, penalty; (*pl.*) trouble, conscientious care, careful and laborious effort. PAIN (2), *v.t.* to cause p. to, inflict suffering upon, distress. [OFr. from L.].

PAINFUL [pān'fŏŏl], *adj.* causing, inflicting pain; distressing, deplorably bad.

PAINSTAKING [pānz'tā-king], *adj.* taking pains, taking laborious care to accomplish a thing.

PAINT (1) [pānt], *v.t. and i.* to colour (a surface) by covering with paint; cover, smear (a surface) with liquid; make designs (on a surface) with coloured paint; colour (the face) with cosmetics; create a pictorial work of art with pigmented liquid; (*fig.*) describe, delineate vividly in speech or writing; *v.i.* to apply paint, practise the art of painting; use facial cosmetics; **to p. the town red**, to indulge in riotous horseplay and dissipation in public places. PAINT (2), *n.* a colouring substance, pigment mixed with water or other liquid to colour a surface; rouge, cosmetics; (*fig.*) superficial colouring, appearance. [OFr. from L.].

PAINTED LADY [pān-tid-lā'di], *n.* a handsome orange, black and white butterfly.

PAINTER (1) [pān'ter], *n.* one whose trade is painting, a house painter; painter of pictures.

PAINTER (2), *n.* rope mooring the bow of a boat; **to cut the p.**, to set oneself adrift. [ME.].

PAINTING [pān'ting], *n.* a painted picture, act of painting such a picture; act of painting generally; art or occupation of painting pictures.

PAIR (1) [pāer], *n.* two of a kind; two similar, corresponding or matching things; mated couple of persons or animals; couple in close association, two horses harnessed together; *applied to an object consisting of two corresponding parts working in conjunction.* PAIR (2), *v.t. and i.* to put, bring together, in pairs; come together in a p., mate; be absent from a parliamentary division together with a member of the hostile party, both agreeing to refrain from voting; **to p. off**, to mate, separate into couples. [ME. from L.].

PAL (1) [pal], *n.* (*slang*) friend. PAL (2) (*pres.pt.* PALLING, *pret. and p.pt.* PALLED), *v.i.* to become pals. [Romany].

PALA [pah'lah], *n.* South African antelope of the genus *Aepyceros.* [Native].

PALACE [pa'lis], *n.* residence of a prince, bishop or potentate; great and splendid mansion; (*coll.*) music-hall, dance hall. [OFr. from L.].

PALADIN [pa'la-din], *n.* one of Charlemagne's twelve peers; noble knight, chivalrous hero. [L.].

PALAEO-, *pref.* ancient, primitive. [Gk.].

PALAEOGRAPHY [pa-li-o'gra-fi], *n.* study of ancient writing and inscriptions. [Gk.].

PALAEOLITHIC [pa-li-ŏ-li'thik], *adj.* (*geol.*) relating to the Old Stone Age. [Gk.].

PALAEONTOLOGY [pa-li-on-to'lo-ji], *n.* study of fossils; science of extinct organisms. [Gk.].

PALAEOZOIC [pa-li-ŏ-zō'ik], *adj.* (*geol.*) of the second earliest geological era; containing the earliest forms of life. [Gk.].

PALAIS (DE DANCE) [pa'lā-(de-dah(ng)s)], *n.* dance hall. [Fr.].

PALANQUIN [pa-lan-kēn'], *n.* covered Oriental litter. [Portug.].

PALATABLE [pa'la-ta-bl], *adj.* pleasing to the taste, agreeable. [PALATE].

PALATAL (1) [pa'la-tal], *adj.* pertaining to the palate; (*phon.*) produced by contact of the tongue with the hard palate. PALATAL (2), *n.* (*phon.*) front consonant sounded by the hard palate and the tongue. PALATALIZE, *v.t.* (*phon.*) to make p. [Fr.].

PALATE [pa'lat], *n.* roof of the mouth; sense of taste, judgment of wines. [L.].

PALATIAL [pa-lā'shal], *adj.* like a palace; (of buildings, rooms) great and splendid. [PALACE].

PALATINE (1) [pa'la-tin], *adj.* pertaining to a lord who does homage to an overlord but is free within his own territory. PALATINATE [pa-la'ti-nāt], *n.* province of a Count P.; dominion of the Count P. of the Rhine. [L.].

PALATINE (2), *adj.* relating to the palate.

PALAVER (1) [pa-lah'ver], *n.* conference between African natives and Europeans; idle talk. PALAVER (2), *v.i.* to hold a p., chatter idly or fussily. [Portug. from L.].

PALE (1) [pāl], *n.* pointed stake used for a fence or

boundary; (*hist.*) district round Dublin in English control after the 12th century; (*her.*) vertical stripe, usually about one-third the width of the shield; **beyond the p.**, outside the limits of proper behaviour. [L.].

PALE (2), *adj.* whitish, pallid, without much colour; dim, faint. PALE (3), *v.i.* to become p., fade, become dim by comparison. PALELY, *adv.* dimly, wanly. [OFr. from L.].

PALEA [pā'li-ah], *n.* inner husk of a grass. [L.].

PALETTE [pa'let], *n.* small board on which an artist mixes his colours; range of colours in a painting. [Fr.].

PALFREY [pawl'fri], *n.* (*archaic*) saddle-horse. [OFr.].

PALI (1) [pah'li], *n.* the sacred Buddhist language. PALI (2), *adj.* of, in, or pertaining to, P. [Skr.].

PALIMPSEST [pa'limp-sest], *n.* parchment etc. on which two or more writings are found, one superimposed on another, the earlier having been imperfectly erased. [Gk.].

PALINDROME [pa'lin-drōm], *n.* word or series of words reading the same in either direction. [Gk.].

PALING [pā'ling], *n.* fence formed of a line of stakes planted close together. [PALE (1)].

PALINGENESIS [pa-lin-je'ni-sis], *n.* reincarnation; (*biol.*) reproduction of parental characteristics. [Gk.].

PALISADE (1) [pa-li-sād'], *n.* defensive barrier of stakes set close together, enclosure surrounded by such a fence; pointed stake. PALISADE (2), *v.t.* to surround with a p. [Fr.].

PALL (1) [pawl], *n.* dark velvet cloth draped over a coffin, any dark heavy covering, real or metaphorical; pallium; (*her.*) Y-shaped bearing on an escutcheon. [OE. from L.].

PALL (2), *v.i.* to become tedious or wearisome. [ME.].

PALLADIAN [pa-lā'di-an], *adj.* (*arch.*) in the style of Andrea *Palladio.*

PALLADIUM (1) [pa-lā'di-um], *n.* safeguard, protecting mascot. PALLADIUM (2), *n.* heavy, white metal resembling platinum; the chemical element Pd. [L.].

PALLBEARER [pawl'bāer-er], *n.* one of the attendants of the coffin at a funeral.

PALLET [pa'let], *n.* narrow straw mattress. [OFr.].

PALLIASSE [pa'li-as], *n.* straw mattress. [Fr.].

PALLIATE [pa'li-āt], *v.t.* to mitigate, alleviate, extenuate, soften. [L.].

PALLIATIVE [pa'li-a-tiv], *n. and adj.* (something) which tends to palliate. [Fr.].

PALLID [pa'lid], *adj.* wan, colourless, pale. [L.].

PALLIUM [pa'li-um], *n.* white Y-shaped vestment with four purple crosses, worn by the Pope and by archbishops of the R.C. Church. [L.].

PALL-MALL [pel'mel], *n.* obsolete game rather like croquet; court in which the game was played. [It.].

PALLOR [pa'ler], *n.* state of being pale, paleness of complexion. [L.].

PALM (1) [pahm], *n.* soft inner surface of the hand between wrist and fingers; breadth of a palm; **to oil a person's p.**, (*coll.*) to bribe a person. PALM (2), *v.t. and i.* to conceal in the p. of the hand, make disappear, substitute one thing for another by sleight of hand; **to p. off**, to pass off, foist on, by dexterous fraud or plausibility. PALMAR [pal'mer], *adj.* relating to, connected with, the p. of the hand. [L.].

PALM (3), *n.* (*bot.*) one of the family *Palmaceae*, whose many species have in common a branchless trunk surmounted by a tuft of foliage; branch of a palm as symbolizing victory or triumph; (*fig.*) victory, success. PALMACEOUS [pal-mā'shŏŏs], *adj.* of, pertaining or relating to, the p. family. PALMARY [pal'ma-ri], *adj.* relating to the p. of triumph; of great excellence. [OE. from L.].

PALMATE [pal'māt], *adj.* shaped like the palm of the hand; (*bot.*) (of leaves) having segments radiating from a centre. [L.].

PALMER [pah'mer], *n.* professional pilgrim who carried a palm leaf as a symbol of having been to the Holy Land.

PALMETTO [pal-me'to], *n.* (*bot.*) kind of small palm. [Span.].

PALMIPED [pal'mi-ped], *n. and adj.* (creature) having webbed feet.

PALMIST [pah'mist], *n.* one who practises palmistry.

PALMISTRY [pah'mis-tri], *n.* professed science or art of telling a person's past, future and character from lines on the hands.

PALM-OIL [pahm'oil], *n.* vegetable fat obtained

from the fruit of several species of palms; (slang) bribery.

PALM SUNDAY [pahm'sun-di], *n.* the last Sunday before Easter, kept in commemoration of Christ's triumphal entry into Jerusalem.

PALMY [pah'mi], *adj.* abounding in palm trees; (*fig.*) (of times and periods) flourishing, affluent.

PALPABLE [pal'pa-bl], *adj.* perceptible to the touch; (*fig.*) very evident, obvious, easily perceived. [L.].

PALPATE [pal'pāt], *v.t.* to examine by touch. [L.].

PALPITATE [pal'pi-tāt], *v.i.* to pulsate; (of the heart) beat irregularly. [L.].

PALPITATION [pal-pi-tā'shn], *n.* act, state or condition of palpitating; irregular action of the heart. [L.].

PALSY (1) [pawl'zi], *n.* paralysis, uncontrollable trembling of the limbs. PALSY (2), *v.t.* to make palsied, paralyse. PALSIED, *adj.* afflicted with p., surprised or terrified almost to p. [ME. from Gk.].

PALTER [pawl'ter], *v.i.* to potter about, trifle, shuffle, haggle, dither. [Swed.].

PALTRY [pawl'tri], *adj.* petty, trifling, worthless. [LGerm.].

PAMPAS [pam'pas], *n.(pl.)* the grassy plains of South America south of the Amazon; **p. grass**, a tall showy grass. [Peruvian].

PAMPER [pam'per], *v.t.* to cosset, treat with too much indulgence, feed too richly and plentifully. [Uncert.].

PAMPHLET [pam'flet], *n.* small, unbound, printed tract or treatise, *esp.* one dealing with current controversy. PAMPHLETEER [pam-fle-tēer'], *n.* writer of pamphlets. [OFr.].

PAN-, *pref.* embracing all, the whole of a thing. [Gk.].

PAN (1) [pan], *n.* Greek satyr deity of the countryside.

PAN (2), *n.* broad, flat vessel used in cooking, anything of similar shape, the quantity it contains; shallow depression in the ground. PAN (3) (*pres.pt.* PANNING, *pret. and p.pt.* PANNED), *v.t.* to wash auriferous earth to extract the gold; *v.i.* **to p. out,** to yield gold; (*fig.*) turn out well. [OE. from L.].

PAN (4), *n.* (*phot.*) panchromatic film. [PAN(CHROMATIC)].

PAN (5), *adj.* (*cinema*) PAN-SHOT, *n.* panoramic shot, continuous shot in which the camera moves to take a panorama of the scene. [PAN(ORAMIC)].

PANACEA [pa-na-sē'ah], *n.* universal cure, remedy for every ill. [Gk.].

PANACHE [pa-nash'], *n.* plume of a helmet; ostentatious display. [It.].

PANAMA [pa-na-mah'], *n.* hat made from fibre of the plant *Carludovica palmata*. [*Panama*, where the fibre is grown].

PAN-AMERICAN [pan-a-me'ri-kan], *adj.* embracing the whole of North and South America, usually excluding Canada. PAN-AMERICANISM, *n.* policy of drawing all countries of the Americas into a closer association. [PAN- and AMERICAN].

PANATROPE [pa'na-trōp], *n.* (*prot.*) electrical device for magnifying the sound of a gramophone record.

PANCAKE (1) [pan'kāk], *n.* thin cake of fried batter; (*aeron.*) flattened-out landing; **p. ice,** thin piece of floating ice. PANCAKE (2), *v.i.* (*aeron.*) to make a p. landing.

PANCHROMATIC [pan-krō-ma'tik], *adj.* (*phot.*) equally sensitive to all visible colours. [PAN- and CHROMATIC].

PANCREAS [pan'kri-as], *n.* (*anat.*) intestinal gland discharging digestive fluid into the duodenum; the sweetbread. [Gk.].

PANDA [pan'dah], *n.* Himalayan bear-cat; **giant p.,** large white bear with black markings. [Nepalese].

PANDEMIC [pan-de'mik], *adj.* (of disease) prevalent over a whole area or among a whole population. [Gk.].

PANDEMONIUM [pan-di-mō'ni-um], *n.* immense, demonic uproar, tumult and confusion. [Coined by Milton, from PAN- and DEMON].

PANDER (1) [pan'der], *n.* one who procures sexual gratification for another, pimp; one who provides the satisfaction of another's passions. PANDER (2), *v.i.* to act as p. to someone, play the p.; toady (to someone). [*Pandare* in Chaucer's *Troilus and Criseyde*].

PANDIT, see PUNDIT.

PANE [pān], *n.* single piece of glass in a division of a window; rectangular panel in a design. [ME. from L.].

PANEGYRIC [pa-ni-ji'rik], *n.* formal eulogy of a thing or person, laudatory oration, extravagant

praise. PANEGYRIC(AL), *adj.* eulogistic, of the nature of a p. [Gk.].

PANEL (1) [pa'nel], *n.* rectangular piece of wood or other material, forming part of a surface but slightly raised or depressed, and surrounded by a frame; piece of parchment; list, people on such a list; those liable for jury service; (formerly) those entitled to receive medical treatment under the Health Insurance Act; strip of material inserted into a body of different kind, colour or design. PANEL (2) (*pres.pt.* PANELLING, *pret. and p.pt.* PANELLED), *v.t.* to divide into panels, decorate with panels. PANELLING, *n.* panels, panelled wood. [ME. from L.].

PANG [pang], *n.* sudden strong spasm of physical or mental pain. [Uncert.].

PANHANDLE [pan'han-dl], *n.* straight projecting handle; narrow promontory. [PAN (2)].

PANHELLENIC [pan-he-lē'nik], *adj.* pertaining to all Greeks. [PAN- and HELLENIC].

PANIC (1) [pa'nik], *n.* sudden violent, senseless terror, *esp.* such terror spreading infectiously through a crowd, sudden general alarm and collapse of reason for no adequate motive. PANIC-STRICKEN, struck by p. PANIC (2), *adj.* impelled by p. PANIC (3), *v.t. and i.* to throw into a p., lose one's head, be seized with p. [Gk., PAN (1)].

PANICLE [pa'ni-kl], *n.* (*bot.*) an irregular flower-cluster. [L.].

PANNADE [pa-nād'], *n.* curvetting of a horse. [Fr.].

PANNE [pan], *n.* a soft cloth with a long nap. [Fr.].

PANNIER [pa'ni-er], *n.* one of a pair of wicker baskets carried by a beast of burden; framework of whalebone or bunched drapery for making a woman's dress appear full on the hips. [Fr. from L.].

PANNIKIN [pa'ni-kin], *n.* small tin mug or basin. [*Dim.* of PAN (2)].

PANOPLY [pa'nō-pli], *n.* complete armour; any kind of imposing array, *esp.* on important state occasions; (*fig.*) armour for spiritual contest. PANOPLIED, *adj.* fully armed. [Gk.].

PANORAMA [pa-no-rah'mah], *n.* realistic picture or series of pictures produced during the unrolling of a cylinder on the interior surface of which are represented all the objects of nature which are visible from any one point in all directions; an extensive view; series of scenes passing rapidly across the vision; (*fig.*) general survey of a subject. [Gk.].

PANPIPE [pan'pīp], *n.* (*mus.*) primitive wind-instrument made of reeds; mouth-organ. [PAN (1)].

PANSY (1) [pan'zi], *n.* a common wild and garden flower; heartsease; (*slang*) effeminate young man, sissy, male homosexual. PANSY (2), *adj.* (*slang*) effeminate. PANSY (3), *v. reflex.* (*slang*) to put on one's best clothes and smarten one's appearance. [AFr.].

PANT (1) [pant], *v.i.* to palpitate or throb; gasp for want of breath; (*fig.*) desire ardently, yearn. PANT (2), *n.* a palpitation of the heart; a gasping for want of breath; gasp. [OFr.].

PANT-, PANTA-, see PANTO-.

PANTALOON [pan-ta-lōon'], *n.* (in Italian comedy and pantomime) foolish old man who is the butt of the clown's jokes; (*pl.*) long, tight-fitting trousers fastened well above the ankle with ribbons; (*coll.*) trousers. [It.].

PANTECHNICON [pan-tek'ni-kon], *n.* large warehouse for storing furniture; furniture van. [Gk.].

PANTHEISM [pan'thi-izm], *n.* religious belief which identifies the universe with God. [PAN- and THEISM].

PANTHEON [pan'thi-on], *n.* temple dedicated to the worship of all the gods; building dedicated to the great men of a nation. [Gk.].

PANTHER [pan'ther], *n.* leopard; **American p.,** puma. [Gk.].

PANTILE [pan'tīl], *n.* roofing tile with two curves, one shallow and one deep. [PAN (2) and TILE].

PANTO-, PANT-, PANTA-, *pref.* all, universal. [Gk.].

PANTO [pan'tō], *n.* (*coll.*) pantomime.

PANTOGRAPH [pan'tō-grahf], *n.* instrument for copying, reducing or enlarging plans and drawings. [PANTO- and GRAPH].

PANTOMIME [pan'tō-mīm], *n.* representation in dumb show, in which the characters are Harlequin and Columbine, pantaloon and clown; a Christmas theatrical entertainment, generally a travesty of a fairy-tale; a representation in mute action. PANTOMIMIC [pan-tō-mi'mik], *adj.* of, or pertaining to, p. [Gk.].

PANTRY [pan'tri], *n.* small room for plate, glass and

ŌŌ is pronounced as in f*oo*d; ŏŏ as in h*oo*d; th as in *th*ink; TH as in *th*at; zh as in a*z*ure. ~ = related to.

china; room or cupboard in which provisions are kept. [MedL.].

PANTS [pants], *n.(pl.)* men's drawers; (*U.S.*) trousers; **to be caught with one's p. down**, to be taken at a disadvantage. [PANT(ALOON)S].

PANZER [pant'ser], *n.* former German armoured fighting vehicle. [Germ.].

PAP (1) [pap], *n.* nipple of the breast. PAP (2), *n.* soft food suitable for infants. [Echoic of infant's feeding].

PAPA [pa-pah'], *n.* former children's word for father. [Fr. from L.].

PAPACY [pā'pa-si], *n.* office of the Pope; papal authority; papal organization of the R.C. Church. [MedL.].

PAPAL [pā'pal], *adj.* proceeding from the Pope; pertaining to the Papacy. PAPALIST, *n.* one who favours the Papacy. [MedL.].

PAPAVERACEOUS [pa-pā-ve-rā'shŏŏs], *adj.* belonging to the poppy family; pertaining to poppies. [L.].

PAPAVEROUS [pa-pā've-rŏŏs], *adj.* pertaining to, or like, the poppy; soporific.

PAPAW [pa-paw'], *n.* a tropical tree; its orange-coloured fruit, used for pickles. [Carib.].

PAPER [pā'per], *n.* substance manufactured from pulped vegetable fibre or linen rags rolled into thin sheets and used as writing, printing, wrapping or cleaning material; newspaper; literary or scientific essay or lecture; set of questions to be answered by candidates in an examination; (*pl.*) documents, *esp.* legal or identity documents; **to commit to p.**, to write down; **on p.**, judging by written accounts; **to send in one's papers**, to resign; **p. money**, specially printed pieces of paper used officially as currency. PAPER (2), *adj.* made of p. PAPER (3), *v.t.* to line or cover with p.; hang p. on walls as a covering; **to p. up**, to fasten up any aperture by pasting p. over it; **to p. the house**, (*theatre slang*) to distribute free tickets liberally to ensure an audience. [OFr. from L.].

PAPER-CHASE [pā'per-chās], *n.* cross-country run following a trail of paper; hare-and-hounds.

PAPER-CLIP [pā'per-klip], *n.* device of springy metal for holding sheets of paper together.

PAPERHANGER [pā'per-hang-er], *n.* workman who hangs wallpaper.

PAPERKNIFE [pā'per-nif], *n.* knife or sharp instrument for cutting open the leaves of books or opening envelopes; thin blade for folding paper.

PAPERWEIGHT [pā'per-wāt], *n.* a weight to keep papers from being blown about.

PAPIER-MACHE, papier-mâché [pa-pyā-ma'shā], *n.* the pulp of paper shaped by pressure while moist and dried hard. [Fr.].

PAPILIONACEOUS [pa-pil-yo-nā'shŏŏs], *adj.* resembling the butterfly; having flowers like the wings of a butterfly.

PAPILLA (*pl.* **papillae**) [pa-pi'lah, 'lē], *n.* nipple of the breast; nipple-like projection in any part of the body or on a plant. PAPILLARY, PAPILLATE [pa'pi-la-ri, pa'pi-lāt], *adj.* pertaining to, or resembling, the nipple; covered with papillae. [L.].

PAPILLOSE [pa'pi-lōs], *adj.* covered with papillae; warty.

PAPIST [pā'pist], *n.* hostile term for a Roman Catholic. PAPISTIC(AL) [pa-pis'tik(-al)], *adj.* pertaining to popery or the R.C. Church.

PAPOOSE [pa-pōōs'], *n.* American Indian baby or small child. [AmerInd.].

PAPPUS [pa'pus], *n.* (*bot.*) tuft of down or soft hairs on the seeds of composite plants. PAPPOSE, PAPPOUS, *adj.* (*bot.*) having a p., downy. [Gk.].

PAPRIKA [pa'pri-kah], *n.* red pepper. [Hungarian].

PAPULE [pa'pyŏŏl], *n.* pimple. PAPULOSE, *adj.* covered with papules. [L.].

PAPYROLOGY [pa-pi-ro'lo-ji], *n.* study of ancient texts written on papyrus. [Gk.].

PAPYRUS [pa-pi'rus], *n.* an Egyptian sedge, from which the ancients made paper; scroll, document, written on papyrus. [L. from Gk.].

PAR (1) [pahr], *n.* equality of value or standing; (*comm.*) standard value of the currency of one country for purposes of exchange with that of another; (*golf*) number of strokes a scratch player should require for the course, generally at a higher standard than bogey; **above p.**, above face value; **at p.**, at the face value, *esp.* of stocks and shares; **below p.**, below face value; (*fig.*) not up to a normal state of mental or physical vigour. [L.].

PAR (2), *n.* (*coll.*) paragraph.

PARA- (1), *pref.* beside, beyond; contrary to. [Gk.].

PARA- (2), *pref.* defence, protection from. [It.].

PARABLE [pa'ra-bl], *n.* fable or short story containing some moral; short allegory. [Gk.].

PARABOLA [pa-ra'bo-lah], *n.* (*math.*) conic section obtained when cutting a cone by a plane parallel to its side. [Gk.].

PARABOLE [pa-ra'bo-li], *n.* (*rhet.*) metaphor; similitude, comparison. [Gk.].

PARABOLIC [pa-ra-bo'lik], *adj.* expressed by parable; metaphorical; pertaining to, shaped like, a parabola. PARABOLICAL, *adj.* expressed in parable form.

PARACHUTE (1) [pa'ra-shōōt], *n.* apparatus of an umbrella-like shape fastened to, or held by, a person leaping from an aeroplane, the density of the air causing it to open, so checking the speed of the descent; **p. troops**, soldiers trained to land by p. in order to attack an objective, or to reach a defensive position. PARACHUTE (2), *v.i.* to drop from an aircraft by p. PARACHUTIST, *n.* one who makes descents by p. [Fr.].

PARACLETE [pa'ra-klēt], *n.* comforter, advocate; the Holy Spirit. [Gk.].

PARADE (1) [pa-rād'], *n.* show, ostentation; military display, mustering and review of any organized body of people; ground on which a display is held; promenade, esplanade. PARADE (2), *v.t.* to make a display of; array in military order; *v.i.* to move in military array; walk about for show. [Fr.].

PARADIGM [pa'ra-dīm], *n.* example; model; (*gram.*) scheme of the inflexions of a verb or noun. [Gk.].

PARADISE [pa'ra-dīs], *n.* the Garden of Eden; heaven; any delightful place or state of perfect happiness; **bird of p.**, a passerine bird, native to New Guinea and remarkable for its beautiful plumage. [Gk.].

PARADOS [pa'ra-dos], *n.* (*milit.*) an artificial elevation behind a fortified place to secure it from attack from the rear; defensive rampart behind a trench. [Fr.].

PARADOX [pa'ra-doks], *n.* a proposition contrary to received opinion; proposition seemingly absurd, yet really true; anything which appears to contradict the seemingly sensible or possible; person whose characteristics seem to contradict each other. [Gk.].

PARADOXICAL [pa-ra-dok'si-kal], *adj.* having the nature of a paradox; not according to what might reasonably be expected.

PARADOXURE [pa-ra-dok'syŏŏr], *n.* (*zool.*) palm-civet or palm-cat. [Gk.].

PARAFFIN [pa'ra-fin], *n.* tasteless, inodorous fatty substance, derived from the distillation of wood or shale, or from petroleum; **p. oil**, refined petroleum; **p. wax**, solid p. [L.].

PARAGON [pa'ra-gon], *n.* model or pattern of perfection; nonpareil. [OFr.].

PARAGRAPH (1) [pa'ra-grahf], *n.* short passage in any writing consisting of one or several sentences relating to a particular point or aspect of a subject, generally distinguished by having the first line indented; short item of news or commentary in a newspaper; symbol ¶ used to indicate a new paragraph. PARAGRAPH (2), *v.t.* to divide into paragraphs. [Gk.].

PARAKEET, PARAQUET, PAROQUET, PARRAKEET [pa'ra-kēt, -ket], *n.* small variety of long-tailed parrot. [OFr.].

PARALDEHYDE [pa-ral'di-hīd], *n.* a strong sedative drug. [PARA (1) and ALDEHYDE].

PARALLAX [pa'ra-laks], *n.* apparent displacement of distant objects caused by shifting the point of view; (*astron.*) difference in the position of a heavenly body as seen from the earth's surface and from the centre of the earth or of the sun. PARALLACTIC [pa-ra-lak'tik], *adj.* pertaining to a p. [Gk.].

PARALLEL (1) [pa'ra-lel], *adj.* equidistant for any distance; in the same plane but never meeting; (*fig.*) resembling in essential particulars, similar, corresponding; **p. bars**, gymnastic apparatus consisting of two horizontal bars of equal height and length; **p. ruler**, mathematical instrument formed of two equal rulers connected by a pair of links; **in p.**, (*elect.*) with like poles connected together. PARALLEL (2), *n.* line which throughout its whole extent is equidistant from another line; person, thing or event closely resembling another; likeness, close comparison, counterpart; **p. of latitude**, one of the lines on a map or globe, p. to the equator and indicating degree of latitude as measured from the equator. PARALLEL (3), *v.t.* to place p.; compare, liken to; correspond, be equivalent; equal. [Gk.].

The accent ' after a syllable = stress (u-pon'). The mark ⁻ over a vowel = length (ā in made; ō in bone)

PARALLELOGRAM [pa-ra-le′lō-gram], *n.* (*geom.*) four-sided rectilinear figure with its opposite sides parallel. [Fr.].

PARALOGISM [pa-ra′lō-jizm], *n.* fallacious argument or syllogism. [Fr.].

PARALYSE [pa′ra-līz], *v.t.* to affect with paralysis; (*fig.*) destroy or weaken the power of mental or physical action; render impotent. [Fr.].

PARALYSIS [pa-ra′li-sis], *n.* (*anat.*) inability to contract a voluntary muscle; total or partial loss of sensation or motion in one or more parts of the body; palsy; (*fig.*) mental powerlessness; suspension of activity; impotence. [L.].

PARALYTIC (1) [pa-ra-li′tik], *adj.* pertaining to, affected by, paralysis. PARALYTIC (2), *n.* one affected with paralysis. [Gk.].

PARA-MILITARY [pa-ra-mi′li-ta-ri], *adj.* semi-military, subsidiary to the army. [PARA (1)].

PARAMOUNT [pa′ra-mownt], *adj.* of the highest rank or authority; supreme; pre-eminent. [AFr.].

PARAMOUR [pa′ra-mōōr], *n.* illicit lover of (either sex); mistress. [OFr.].

PARANOIA [pa-ra-noi′ah], *n.* (*path.*) chronic mental derangement characterized by delusions of grandeur or persecution. [Gk.].

PARANOIAC (1) [pa-ra-noi′ak], *adj.* of, pertaining to or resembling, paranoia or a paranoiac. PARANOIAC (2), *n.* one suffering from paranoia.

PARAPET [pa′ra-pet], *n.* low wall at the edge of a terrace, balcony etc., or at the side of a bridge; rampart in front of a trench; wall or elevation for protecting soldiers from an enemy's shot. [It.].

PARAPHERNALIA [pa-ra-fer-nā′li-ah], *n.* personal belongings; appendages; trappings; baggage. [L.].

PARAPHRASE (1) [pa′ra-frāz], *n.* a rendering of a text or passage in fuller and clearer terms; free translation. PARAPHRASE (2), *v.t.* to make a p. of, render in other words. PARAPHRASTIC [pa-ra-fras′tik], *adj.* of the nature of a p. [Gk.].

PARAQUET, see PARAKEET.

PARASITE [pa′ra-sīt], *n.* person who earns his welcome by flattery; hanger-on; sycophant; one who lives by the work of others; plant or animal which attaches itself to, and lives entirely upon, another. [Gk.].

PARASITIC(AL) [pa-ra-si′tik(-al)], *adj.* in the nature of a parasite; fawning to obtain favours; living on another.

PARASOL [pa′ra-sol], *n.* umbrella used as a shade from the sun. [PARA (2) and L.].

PARATHYROID [pa-ra-thī′roid], *adj* (*med.*) pertaining to the four ductless glands close to the thyroid gland. [PARA (1)].

PARATROOPS [pa′ra-trōōps], *n.*(*pl.*) troops trained to descend by parachute. [PARA(CHUTE) and TROOP (1)].

PARATYPHOID [pa-ra-tī′foid], *n.* (*path.*) infectious disease which, though resembling typhoid fever, is a distinct malady.

PARAVANE [pa′ra-vān], *n.* device for removing mines from the path of a ship. [PARA (2) and VANE].

PARBOIL [pah′boil], *v.t.* to half-boil; (*fig.*) cause to become unpleasantly warm. [OFr.].

PARBUCKLE (1) [pah′bu-kl], *n.* (*naut.*) rope for rolling bales and casks up a slope by looping it round them. PARBUCKLE (2), *v.t.* to roll a spar or package by looping it round with a p. [Fr.].

PARCEL (1) [pah′sel], *n.* part, portion, *esp.* of land; piece, section; small package. PARCEL (2) (*pres.pt.* PARCELLING, *pret. and p.pt.* PARCELLED), *v.t.* **to p. out,** to share, divide into parts; (*naut.*) cover a rope with strips of canvas; **to p. up,** (*coll.*) to wrap up, make into a p.

PARCEL-GILT [pah-sel-gilt′], *adj.* partly gilded. [PARCEL (1) and GILT].

PARCENER [pah′se-ner], *n.* a joint heir. PARCENARY, *n.* (*leg.*) co-heirship. [AFr.].

PARCH [pahch], *v.t.* to make very dry; shrivel with heat; dry to excess; *v.i.* to become excessively dry, be very thirsty. [Uncert.].

PARCHMENT [pahch′ment], *n.* skin of a sheep, goat or calf, dressed and rendered fit for writing on; document written on parchment; substance resembling parchment. [Fr. from L.].

PARD [pahd], *n.* leopard; panther. [Gk.].

PARDON (1) [pah′don], *n.* forgiveness, act of pardoning; the excusing of a fault or breach of manners; (*eccles.*) forgiveness of sins; (*leg.*) remission of the legal consequences of a crime. PARDON (2), *v.t.* to forgive; excuse a lapse in manners or a small fault; (*leg.*) grant a p. PARDONER, *n.* one who pardons;

(*eccles.*) † cleric licensed to sell or grant papal indulgences. [LL.].

PARE [pāer], *v.t.* to cut or shave off; trim; diminish little by little. [Fr.].

PAREGORIC [pa-ri-go′rik], *n.* medicine which deadens pain; a tincture of opium. [Gk.].

PARENCHYMA [pa-reng′ki-mah], *n.* (*anat.*) the tissue peculiar to the glandular organs of the body; soft, pulpy, cellular tissue; (*bot.*) pith of plants. [Gk.].

PARENT [pā′rent], *n.* father or mother; ancestor, forefather; protector, guardian; (*fig.*) origin, root. [OFr. from L.].

PARENTAGE [pā′ren-tij], *n.* extraction, birth, lineage. [Fr.].

PARENTAL [pa-ren′tal], *adj.* pertaining to a parent. PARENTALLY, *adv.* in a p. manner.

PARENTHESIS (*pl.* **parentheses**) [pa-ren′thi-sis], *n.* (*gram.*) clause inserted into a sentence, which is grammatically complete without it, for explanation or enlargement, and usually indicated thus ( ). [Gk.].

PARENTHETIC [pa-ren-the′tik], *adj.* pertaining to a parenthesis; introduced as a parenthesis.

PARGET (1) [pah′jet], *v.t.* to cover with plaster, rough-cast. PARGET (2), *n.* rough plaster laid upon walls and ceilings. [OFr.].

PARHELION (*pl.* **parhelia**) [pah-hē′li-on], *n.* spot of intensely bright light on the solar halo; mock sun. [Gk.].

PARIAH [pa′ri-ah], *n.* member of one of the lowest Indian castes; one without caste; (*fig.*) outcast, person (or animal) of a low or outcast class. [Tamil].

PARIAN (1) [pāer′i-an], *adj.* pertaining to the island of Paros, famed for its marble; resembling marble. PARIAN (2), *n.* a fine white clay used for porcelain and statuettes. [L.].

PARIETAL [pa-rī′e-tal], *adj.* pertaining to the wall of a cavity of the body; pertaining to the sides and upper part of the skull; (*bot.*) growing from the sides of hollow organs, *esp.* the ovary. [Fr.].

PARI-MUTUEL (*pl.* **paris-mutuels**) [pa-ri-myōō′-tyōō-el], *n.* betting-machine, totalisator, by means of which the winners share the money staked by the losers. [Fr.].

PARING [pāer′ing], *n.* that which is pared off; rind; a shaving.

PARISH [pa′rish], *n.* civil or ecclesiastical subdivision of a county; district assigned to a particular church; those living in such a district; **p. council,** body administering local affairs; **on the p.,** to be in receipt of Public Assistance. PARISH-PUMP, concerned with minor local affairs, limited in outlook. PARISH-REGISTER, register in which the christenings, marriages and deaths in a p. are recorded. [ME. from Gk.].

PARITY [pa′ri-ti], *n.* equality; equivalence; similarity, parallelism; (*comm.*) equivalence in another currency; standard rate of exchange. [L.].

PARK (1) [pahk], *n.* (*hist.*) enclosed tract of land preserved for hunting; ornamental piece of ground enclosed for public or private recreation; enclosure round a mansion; place in which motor-cars or other vehicles may be left for a stated period of time or indefinitely; (*milit.*) artillery encampment. PARK (2), *v.t.* to enclose, bring together in a p.; put vehicles in a space reserved for their special use; (*coll.*) put, place, leave. [OE.].

PARKA [pah′kah], *n.* fur jacket with a hood worn by Eskimos. [Eskimo].

PARKIN [pah′kin], *n.* kind of cake made with oatmeal, treacle and ginger. [Unkn.].

PARKY [pah′ki], *adj.* (*coll.*) chilly. [PARK (1)].

PARLANCE [pah′lans], *n.* speech, conversation; idiom. [AFr.].

PARLEY (1) [pah′li], *v.t.* (*coll.*) to talk fluently in a foreign language; *v.i.* to confer, or treat with, as an enemy. PARLEY (2), *n.* conference between opponents; discussion on a disputed point. [Fr.].

PARLIAMENT [pah′la-ment], *n.* a deliberative assembly; national assembly, or senate; the supreme legislature of Great Britain, consisting of the Lords and the Commons acting with the Sovereign. [OFr.].

PARLIAMENTARIAN [pah-la-men-taer′i-an], *n.* person skilled in the procedure of the English Parliament or other similar legislative bodies; adherent of Parliament in opposition to the King in the time of Charles I, Roundhead.

PARLIAMENTARY [pah-la-men′ta-ri], *adj.* pertaining to, enacted by, Parliament; **p. language,**

ōō is pronounced as in food; ŏŏ as in hood; th as in *think*; TH as in *that*; zh as in azure. ∼ = related to.

language such as is allowable in P., civil, concealing censure under a polite exterior.

PARLOUR [pah'ler], *n.* family sitting-room; large formally furnished room for public receptions as those of a mayor; **p. tricks**, elegant amusements and accomplishments. [OFr.].

PARLOURMAID [pah'ler-mād], *n.* woman servant who attends to the dining-room and answers the bell.

PARLOUS [pah'lŏŏs], *adj.* perilous; difficult; critical. [*Var.* of PERILOUS].

PARMESAN [pah'mi-zan], *n.* strong-tasting cheese used for cooking. [Fr. from *Parma*, Italy].

PARNASSIAN (1) [pah-na'si-an], *adj.* pertaining to Parnassus, mountain in Greece considered sacred to the Muses; devoted to poetry; pertaining to a school of French poetry in the second half of the nineteenth century. PARNASSIAN (2), *n.* member or follower of the P. school. [Gk.].

PAROCHIAL [pa-rŏ'ki-al], *adj.* pertaining to a parish; (*fig.*) narrow in range or interests. [LL.].

PAROCHIALISM [pa-rŏ'ki-a-lizm], *n.* approval of the parish as the unit of local government; narrowness of opinion; narrow provincialism.

PARODY (1) [pa'ro-di], *n.* burlesque imitation of a literary work or style; (*fig.*) feeble imitation, travesty. PARODY (2), *v.* to compose a p. on; ridicule; (*fig.*) travesty. [Gk.].

PAROLE [pa-rŏl'], *n.* word of honour; promise given by a prisoner when he has leave to depart from custody that he will report at the times agreed upon. [AFr. from L.].

PAROQUET, see PARAKEET.

PAROTID [pa-ro'tid], *adj.* pertaining to the parotis.

PAROTIS [pa-ro'tis], *n.* (*anat.*) salivary gland near the ear. PAROTITIS [pa-ro-tī'tis], *n.* inflammation of the p.; mumps. [Gk.].

PAROXYSM [pa'rok-sizm], *n.* a fit or exacerbation of any disease; any sudden violent spasm or action; outburst of emotion. PAROXYSMAL [pa-rok-siz'mal], *adj.* pertaining to, occurring in or occasioned by, a p. [Gk.].

PARQUET [pah'ki, pah'ket], *n.* wooden floor made of small rectangular pieces of wood laid on a base. PARQUETRY, *n.* inlaid woodwork flooring; p. flooring. [Fr.].

PARR [pah(r)], *n.* young salmon. [Unkn.].

PARRAKEET, see PARAKEET.

PARRICIDE (1) [pa'ri-sīd], *n.* murderer of a father or near relative; traitor to one's native land. PARRICIDE (2), *n.* act of murdering a father or near relative. [L.].

PARROT [pa'rot], *n.* one of an order of tropical birds with two toes in front and two behind and a hooked beak, remarkable for their beautiful colours and, in some cases, their power of imitating the human voice; (*fig.*) talkative or imitative person. [Fr.].

PARRY (1) [pa'ri], *v.t.* to ward off, turn aside. PARRY (2), *n.* action of parrying; in boxing, wrestling, fencing, the warding off of a blow or thrust. [Fr.].

PARSE [pahz], *v.t.* (*gram.*) to describe the form etc. of parts of speech (in a sentence) and their relations to each other. [L.].

PARSEE [pah-sē'], *n.* person of Persian descent and of the religion of Zoroaster, living in India. [Pers.].

PARSIMONIOUS [pah-si-mŏ'ni-ŏŏs], *adj.* very sparing in spending money, grudging, niggardly.

PARSIMONY [pah'si-mo-ni], *n.* extreme carefulness in expenditure; frugality; stinginess. [L.].

PARSLEY [pahs'li], *n.* green herb with crinkled leaves of a slight fragrance used in cookery; **cow p.**, wild chervil. [Gk.].

PARSNIP [pahs'nip], *n.* biennial umbelliferous plant with a succulent light-yellow root used as a vegetable. [ME.].

PARSON [pah'son], *n.* rector of a parish; vicar, clergyman, pastor; **p.'s nose**, the rump of a bird cooked for the table. [ME.].

PARSONAGE [pah'so-nij], *n.* residence of a parson; rectory, vicarage.

PART (1) [paht], *n.* portion, piece, fragment; a portion considered apart, slice; division, part contributing to the whole; a certain number but not all; ingredient; share; proportional quantity; essential constituent, duty; party, side, rôle, character; (*mus.*) one of the melodies in a harmony; (*pl.*) genitals; **p. of speech**, (*gram.*) a grammatical category, class of words according to function; **to play a p.**, to be insincere, conceal the real self; **man of parts**, man of power or talent; **in good p.**, favourably, good-naturedly. PART (2), *v.t.* to sever into two or more pieces; separate, divide into parts; break a friendship

or association of, cause to break asunder; *v.i.* to be separated; pursue a different path; fork; open up; **to p. with**, to give up, surrender. [L.].

PARTAKE (*pret.* **partook**, *p.pt.* **partaken**) [pah-tāk'], *v.t.* to have a part in, share; *v.i.* to take a part or share along with others. [PART and TAKE].

PARTERRE [pah-tâer'], *n.* system of flower-beds with intervening spaces to walk on. [Fr.].

PARTHENOGENESIS [pah-the-nŏ-je'ni-sis], *n.* (*biol.*) reproduction through the agency of unimpregnated ova or germs. [Gk.].

PARTHIAN [pah'thi-an], *n. and adj.* inhabitant of, pertaining to, Parthia, a former kingdom in northern Persia; **P. shot**, a telling remark spoken at parting.

PARTIAL [pah'shal], *adj.* biased in favour of one party or side; inclined to favour without reason; affecting a part only; **p. to**, having a liking for, prejudiced in favour of. [LL.].

PARTIALITY [pah-shi-a'li-ti], *n.* inclination to favour one party more than another; undue bias of mind; particular fondness.

PARTICIPANT [pah-ti'si-pant], *n.* one who participates; partaker. [L.].

PARTICIPATE [pah-ti'si-pāt], *v.t.* to partake, share in; *v.i.* to partake, have a part or share; share. PARTICIPATIVE, *adj.* capable of participating. [L.].

PARTICIPATION [pah-ti-si-pā'shn], *n.* action of participating; sharing in common with others. [L.].

PARTICIPIAL [pah-ti-si'pi-al], *adj.* having the nature and function of a participle; formed from a participle.

PARTICIPLE [pah'ti-si-pl], *n.* (*gram.*) word which has the nature partly of an adjective and partly of a verb; derivative of a verb with the function of an adjective; verbal adjective. [OFr.].

PARTICLE [pah'ti-kl], *n.* minute part or portion; smallest conceivable amount of anything; (*gram.*) minor part of speech which is not inflected or used alone; (*phys.*) smallest component part of matter. [L.].

PARTI-COLOURED [pah'ti-ku-lerd], *adj.* of two or more colours, variegated; (*fig.*) diversified, chequered. [PARTY and COLOURED].

PARTICULAR (1) [pah-ti'kyŏŏ-ler], *adj.* pertaining to a single person or thing; single, individual, special; detailed, exact; fastidious, difficult to please. PARTICULAR (2), *n.* a single instance; a distinct part, special detail. PARTICULARLY, *adv.* in a p. manner, especially; minutely, in detail. [L.].

PARTICULARISM [pah-ti'kyŏŏ-la-rizm], *n.* exclusive regard for oneself or one's party; (*theol.*) doctrine that redemption is the lot of a selected part only of the human race; (*pol.*) policy permitting each state in an empire or federation to act independently in certain matters of government. PARTICULARIST, *n.* advocate of p.

PARTICULARITY [pah-ti-kyŏŏ-la'ri-ti], *n.* quality of being particular; specification of particulars; a special detail; minuteness of detail. [Fr.].

PARTICULARIZE [pah-ti'kyŏŏ-la-rīz], *v.t.* to state or enumerate in detail; give particulars of, specify; *v.i.* to be attentive to details.

PARTING (1) [pah'ting], *n.* act of dividing; division, separation; leave-taking; division made in combing the hair from the forehead in two directions. PARTING (2), *adj.* given, or happening, at the time of departure or separation.

PARTISAN, PARTIZAN [pah-ti-zan'], *n.* an adherent to a party or faction; prejudiced adherent; guerrilla fighter outside the regular army organization. [It.].

PARTITION (1) [pah-ti'shn], *n.* act of dividing; division, separation; part separated from another; dividing wall. PARTITION (2), *v.t.* to divide into parts or shares. [L.].

PARTITIVE [pah'ti-tiv], *n. and adj.* (word) denoting a part of a whole.

PARTIZAN, see PARTISAN.

PARTNER (1) [paht'ner], *n.* one who shares with another; joint owner of stock or capital used in a business undertaking; one who dances with another; player on the same side; husband or wife. PARTNER (2), *v.t.* to become a p. with; be a p. of. (*Var.* of PARCENER].

PARTNERSHIP [paht'ner-ship], *n.* the association of persons for the purpose of business or ownership; sharing of interests in any undertaking. [Prec. and OE.].

PARTRIDGE [pah'trij], *n.* a game bird preserved in England for purposes of sport. [ME.].

PART-SINGING [paht'sing-ing], *n.* singing in which

The accent ' after a syllable = stress (u-pon'). The mark ‾ over a vowel = length (ā in made; ō in bone).

parts are taken by different voices to make harmony. **PART-SONG** [paht'song], *n.* song in which the parts are sung in harmony.

PARTURIENT [pah-tyōō'ri-ent], *adj.* about to bring forth young, travailing; (*fig.*) struggling to evolve ideas or forms. [L.].

PARTURITION [pah-tyōō-ri'shn], *n.* act of giving birth, labour, travail. [L.].

PARTY [pah'ti], *n.* number of persons united in opinion or design; one of two litigants; one concerned in an affair; a side; a distinct person; select company; social gathering; political faction; group of people pursuing a common activity; (*milit.*) small company of troops; (*coll.*) person; **p. politics**, political system in which the broad classes of opinion are represented by a small number of organized parties; **p. line**, telephone line shared by two or more subscribers; (*pol.*) policy laid down by the headquarters of a p. [Fr.].

PARTY-WALL [pah'ti-wawl], *n.* common wall dividing two tenements or other properties.

PARVENU [pah've-nyōō], *n.* person who has risen quickly from humble origin to a position of wealth or importance; upstart. [Fr.].

PAS [pah], *n.* a step in dancing; kind of dance; right of precedence. [Fr.].

PASCHAL [pas'kal], *adj.* pertaining to the Jewish Passover; of, or pertaining to, Easter.

PASHA [pah'shah, pa-shah'], *n.* Turkish title bestowed on officers of high rank. [Turk.].

PASQUE-FLOWER [pahsk'flower], *n.* a species of anemone which flowers about Easter. [OFr.].

PASQUINADE [pas-kwi-nād'], *n.* lampoon affixed to some public place. [It.].

PASS (1) [pahs], *v.t.* to move past, leave behind; leave unmentioned, omit; go from side to side, cross; approve; come up to the required standard; surpass; overshoot (a mark); outstrip; send, convey; make (a thing) go in a certain direction; utter, pronounce; emit; **to p. in review**, to contemplate, consider; **to p. by**, to go by, ignore; **to p. off**, (*fig.*) to put in a false light; **to p. over**, to overlook, forgive; **to p. through**, to travel across; (*fig.*) endure, experience; **to p. a dividend**, not to declare a dividend; *v.i.* to move from one place to another or from one state to another; move onward; be impelled onwards; go from one place to another, be transferred; be interchanged between two or more persons; elapse, glide by; go unchecked or uncensured; be adequate; be allowed or approved by a deliberative body; get through an examination successfully; take place, occur; make a pass in fencing or football etc.; refrain from playing or bidding at a hand of cards; **to p. away**, to die; **to p. for**, to be thought of as; **to p. out**, to become unconscious; die; successfully complete a course of training. PASS (2), *n.* act of passing; the satisfying of examiners in an examination; critical state of affairs; permission to pass; ticket authorizing the holder to travel on the railway or other means of transport; free ticket on the railway or to a theatre, concert etc.; threatening gesture; (*coll.*) an advance, approach; (*sport*) the transferring of the ball by a player to another on his own side; (*fencing*) lunge, thrust; **p. degree**, university degree gained by satisfying the examiners, without attaining the standard required for honours. PASS (3), *n.* passage; gap through mountains; (*milit.*) narrow pathway, usually in mountains, commanding the entrance to a country. [Fr.].

PASSABLE [pah'sa-bl], *adj.* able to be traversed or navigated; admissible; tolerable. PASSABLY, *adv.* in a p. manner, tolerably.

PASSAGE (1) [pa'sij], *n.* act of passing; transition; migratory flight of birds; lapse of time; journey, voyage; accommodation booked for a journey; sum paid for a journey; the passing into law of a bill; route, channel, pass; narrow corridor or hall; interchange of blows; (*fig.*) heated discussion; a certain specified part of a speech, book or musical composition. [Fr.].

PASS-BOOK [pahs'bŏŏk], *n.* book in which a bank customer's transactions are recorded.

PASSE, passé [pa'sā], *adj.* out-of-date, stale. [Fr.].

PASSENGER [pa'sin-jer], *n.* one who travels in some conveyance; (*fig.*) member of any crew, team or group who does not do his full share of work; **p. pigeon**, North American pigeon notable for its migratory habits. [OFr.].

PASSE-PARTOUT [pas-pah-tōō'], *n.* gummed paper strip for framing pictures; picture so framed. [Fr.].

PASSERINE [pa'se-rīn], *adj.* (*ornith.*) pertaining to perching birds or to the sparrow; of about the size of a sparrow. [L.].

PASSIM [pa'sim], *adv.* here and there; everywhere; in all parts (in reference to an author or book). [L.].

PASSING (1) [pah'sing], *n.* action of one who, or that which, passes; death; **p. bell**, bell tolled at the hour of a person's death. PASSING (2), *adj.* that passes; ephemeral; cursory. PASSING-NOTE, *n.* (*mus.*) note introduced between two harmonies to soften the interval. PASSING (3), *adv.* (*archaic*) surpassingly, exceedingly.

PASSION (1) [pa'shn], *n.* extreme suffering, *esp.* that of Christ; any strong, deep feeling or excitement, such as desire, joy, grief, love, hatred; a temper; eager desire; deep enthusiasm. PASSION (2), *adj.* and *i.* (*poet.*) to affect with, be affected by, p. [L.].

PASSIONATE [pa'shn-at], *adj.* easily moved to anger; moved or inspired by passion or strong emotion; intense, fervent. [MedL.].

PASSION-FLOWER [pa'shn-flower], *n.* flower of the genus *Passiflora*, adopted as the symbol of Christ's passion.

PASSION-PLAY [pa'shn-plā], *n.* a drama, medieval in origin, representing Christ's passion.

PASSION-SUNDAY [pa'shn-sun-dā], *n.* fifth Sunday in Lent.

PASSION-WEEK [pa'shn-wēk], *n.* (*eccles.*) week before Palm Sunday; (*coll.*) Holy Week, week in which Good Friday occurs.

PASSIVE (1) [pa'siv], *adj.* acted upon but not acting; offering no active resistance; inert; (*gram.*) that changes a verbal function so that the logical object of the action becomes the grammatical subject and suffers the action expressed by the verb; **p. resistance**, submission to punishment rather than comply with laws considered unjust. PASSIVE (2), *n.* (*gram.*) the p. voice. [L.].

PASSIVITY [pa-si'vi-ti], *n.* passiveness; inertia; submissiveness.

PASS-KEY [pahs'kē], *n.* key which will open any of a number of locks; master-key.

PASSMAN [pahs'man], *n.* one who takes a pass degree at a university.

PASSOVER [pah'sō-ver], *n.* feast of the Jews to commemorate the night in Egypt when the destroying angel passed over their homes. [Exodus xii. 27].

PASSPORT [pahs'pawt], *n.* document issued to a national by his government stating his identity, granting him the right to travel abroad and often requesting for him the protection of foreign governments; (*fig.*) those qualities whereby an individual gains entry into a certain social, business or political circle. [Fr.].

PASSWORD [pahs'werd], *n.* watchword; (*fig.*) secret of admission.

PAST (1) [pahst], *adj.* gone by, ended, spent, accomplished; (*gram.*) expressing actions which have gone by. PAST (2), *n.* time which has elapsed; things which happened in a time gone by; person's early life or life which has now gone by; doubtful or disreputable past life. PAST (3), *prep. and adv.* beyond in time or space; without power of. [PASS (1)].

PASTE (1) [pāst], *n.* a composition of a doughy consistency, whether of flour in baking or of clay in the arts; a cement, as flour and water boiled; fine glass compounded for artificial gems; soft edible compound made by beating various ingredients together as in meat or almond paste; **p. grain**, imitation morocco leather. PASTE (2), *v.t.* to fasten, stick, with p.; (*coll.*) beat or pound. [OFr.].

PASTEBOARD [pāst'bawd], *n.* thick, stiff paper board made by pasting sheets of paper together; wooden board on which dough is rolled in making pastry.

PASTEL [pas'tel], *n.* the plant woad; blue dye obtained from this; (*paint.*) dry flaky crayon made of pigments and gum-water; drawing made with such pigments; a soft colour. [Fr.].

PASTERN [pas'tern], *n.* that part of a horse's leg between the fetlock and the hoof; **p. joint**, joint in a horse's leg next to the hoof. [OFr.].

PASTEURISM [pah'ste-rizm], *n.* cure or prevention of disease by inoculation. [L. *Pasteur*, French bacteriologist].

PASTEURIZE [pah'ste-rīz], *v.t.* to kill germs (*esp.* in milk) by sterilizing with heat.

PASTICHE [pas-tēsh'], *n.* a literary, musical or pictorial composition made up of a number of parts from other works loosely connected together; work in another's style and manner. [Fr.].

PASTILLE [pas-tēl', pas'til], *n.* aromatic cone burnt

ōō is pronounced as in food; ŏŏ as in hood; th as in *think*; TH as in *that*; zh as in azure. ~ = related to.

for fumigating purposes; medicated lozenge; unit of measurement for X-ray dosage. [Fr.].

PASTIME [pahs'tim], *n.* recreation, amusement; game. [PASS (1) and TIME (1).].

PASTING [pās'ting], *n. (coll.)* a violent beating.

PAST-MASTER [pahst-mahs'ter], *n.* one who has held the office of master of a lodge, guild etc.; one who has long been an expert.

PASTOR [pah'ster], *n.* clergyman in charge of a congregation. [L.].

PASTORAL (1) [pah'ste-ral], *adj.* pertaining to shepherds or shepherd life; used for pasture; characteristic of pasture land; describing the loves of shepherds and shepherdesses in a conventionalized manner; relating to the pastor of a church; (*Australian etc.*) engaged in sheep-farming; **p. staff,** crosier; **p. theology,** study of the duties of spiritual pastors; **p. epistles,** epistles of Paul to Timothy and Titus. PASTORAL (2), *n.* poem on rural or shepherd life; letter addressed from a bishop to his diocese or from a minister to his congregation. [L.].

PASTORALE [pah-ste-rah'li], *n.* simple melody in a rustic style or on a rustic theme. [It.].

PASTORATE [pah'ste-rat], *n.* office or position of a pastor; body of pastors collectively. [MedL.].

PASTRY [pās'tri], *n.* food made of flour and fat kneaded to a dough, rolled and baked; pies, tarts etc. made of pastry. PASTRY-COOK, one whose occupation is to make p. [~PASTE].

PASTURE (1) [pah'styŏŏr], *n.* grass for grazing; land on which cattle or sheep feed. PASTURE (2), *v.t.* to feed on grass; *v.i.* to graze. PASTURAGE, *n.* action of pasturing; grazing; p.-land. [L.].

PASTY (1) [pas'ti], *n.* pie of meat or fruit enclosed in pastry and baked without a dish. PASTY (2) [pā'sti], *adj.* of a colour or consistency resembling paste; pale. [PASTE].

PAT (1) [pat], *n.* light quick slap of the hand; small sound made by striking lightly with something flat; small lump of butter shaped by patting. PAT (2) (*pres.pt.* PATTING, *pret. and p.pt.* PATTED), *v.t.* to touch or hit lightly with the hand or some flat surface; make a small sound when striking lightly; *v.i.* to carry out the action of patting; **to p. on the back,** to congratulate, express satisfaction with. PAT (3), *adv.* appositely, at the right moment, with precision. [Echoic].

PATCH (1) [pach], *n.* piece of any material sewn or stuck on to an article to repair or cover up a defect, *esp.* a piece of material sewn on a garment to repair a hole or strengthen a weak place; a piece of sheet rubber used to repair a hole in a pneumatic tyre etc.; small piece of black plaster formerly worn on the face to show up the beauty of the complexion; shield for an injured eye; small piece of land; part of an area different in colour or appearance from the whole extent; **not a p. on,** much inferior to; **bad p.,** spell of non-success, difficult situation. PATCH (2), *v.t.* to mend by sewing or fixing on pieces of material; repair clumsily; make up of pieces; **to p. up,** (*fig.*) to settle (a quarrel). [ME.].

PATCHOULI [pa-chōō'li], *n.* the odoriferous dried branches of an eastern plant; perfume produced from this. [Tamil].

PATCHWORK [pach'werk], *n.* work composed of pieces sewn together; jumble; surface divided into many small areas of different sizes.

PATCHY [pa'chi], *adj.* marked by patches, uneven. PATCHILY, *adv.* in patches.

PATE [pāt], *n.* head, crown of the head. [ME.].

PATE, paté [pa'tā], *n.* small pie; patty; **p. de foie gras,** goose-liver paste. [Fr.].

PATELLA (*pl.* patellae) [pa-te'lah], *n.* knee or knee-cap; (*zool.*) genus of mollusca including the limpet. PATELLAR, *adj.* pertaining to the knee-cap. [L.].

PATEN, PATIN(E) [pa'ten], *n.* plate or vessel on which the consecrated bread in the Eucharist is put. [L.].

PATENT (1) [pā'tent, pa'tent], *adj.* open, obvious, manifest; protected by a patent; (*coll.*) ingenious, well contrived; **letters p.,** a royal patent; **p. leather,** leather with a black varnished surface; **p. medicine,** ready-made proprietary medicine. PATENT (2), *n.* royal or official grant of privilege, as a title of nobility or the exclusive rights to property in a process or invention; document giving such rights; process or article so protected; (*coll.*) ingenious device; **p. office,** government office for the granting of patents; **p. rolls,** the records of patents. PATENT (3), *v.t.* to secure by p., take out a p. for. PATENTEE [pā-ten-tē'], *n.* one who has obtained a p. [L.].

PATERFAMILIAS [pā-ter-fa-mi'li-as], *n.* father of a family. [L.].

PATERNAL [pa-tur'nal], *adj.* of a father; fatherly; descended or derived from a father. PATERNALISM, *n.* quality or policy of being p.; benevolent despotism. [LL.].

PATERNITY [pa-tur'ni-ti], *n.* quality or condition of being a father; fatherhood; (*fig.*) source, origin. [L.].

PATERNOSTER [pā'ter-nos-ter], *n.* the Lord's Prayer; eleventh bead in a rosary. [L.].

PATH [pahth], *n.* a way trodden by the foot of man or beast; track for foot-passengers only at the side of the road, pavement; course along which anything proceeds, line of action. [OE.].

PATHAN [pa-tahn'], *n. and adj.* member of, pertaining to, the Afghan race of N.W. India. [Pushtu].

PATHETIC [pa-the'tik], *adj.* affecting the tender passions; causing pity, sympathy or sadness; full of pathos; **p. fallacy,** fallacy that nature has human feelings. [Gk.].

PATHFINDER [pahth'fīn-der], *n.* explorer; (*R.A.F.*) bomber pilot who locates and marks the target for following aircraft.

PATHO-, *pref.* concerning suffering or disease. [Gk.].

PATHOLOGICAL [pa-thŏ-lo'ji-kal], *adj.* pertaining to pathology; abnormal, diseased, morbid.

PATHOLOGIST [pa-tho'lŏ-jist], *n.* one skilled in pathology.

PATHOLOGY [pa-tho'lŏ-ji], *n.* study of disease. [Gk.].

PATHOS [pā'thos], *n.* deep emotion such as moves one to sympathy; literary quality which induces such feelings. [Gk.].

PATIENCE [pā'shens], *n.* calm endurance, resignation; perseverance in pursuit of an end; capacity for quietly awaiting an event or issue; game of cards played by one person. [L.].

PATIENT (1) [pā'shnt], *adj.* showing patience, sustaining pain, affliction or annoyance with calmness and fortitude; slow to anger; persistent, diligent in following out a long course of action. PATIENT (2), *n.* person under medical treatment. [L.].

PATIN(E), see PATEN.

PATINA [pa'ti-nah], *n.* green incrustation on bronze coins, works of art etc.; high polish acquired by old furniture and woodwork from long and constant polishing. [L.].

PATIO [pah'ti-ō], *n.* Spanish courtyard; open quadrangle enclosed by a large house. [Span.].

PATOIS [pa'twah], *n.* provincial form of speech; local dialect. [Fr.].

PATRIARCH [pā'tri-ahk], *n.* father or ruler of a family or tribe; one of the early fathers of the Hebrew race; bishop or metropolitan dignitary in the Eastern Church; venerable old man or chief; veteran of a class or profession. PATRIARCHISM, *n.* government by patriarchs. PATRIARCHY, *n.* primitive form of government in which the oldest man of the family or tribe is ruler; jurisdiction of a p. [L.].

PATRICIAN (1) [pa-tri'shan], *n.* in ancient Rome, nobleman of senatorial descent; nobleman, aristocrat. PATRICIAN (2), *adj.* pertaining to the old Roman nobility; noble, aristocratic. [L.].

PATRICIDE [pa'tri-sīd], *n.* parricide. [L.].

PATRIMONIAL [pa-tri-mŏ'ni-al], *adj.* pertaining to a patrimony; inherited from ancestors.

PATRIMONY [pa'tri-mo-ni], *n.* property inherited from a father or forebears; (*eccles.*) church estate or revenue. [L.].

PATRIOT [pa'tri-ot, pā'tri-ot], *n.* one who is devoted to his country.

PATRIOTIC [pa-tri-o'tik], *adj.* having the feelings of a patriot; actuated by patriotism.

PATRIOTISM [pa'tri-o-tizm], *n.* love for, loyalty to, one's own country.

PATRISTIC [pa-tris'tik], *adj.* pertaining to the fathers of the Christian Church; relating to the study of their writings. [Fr.].

PATROL (1) [pa-trōl'], *n.* act of going the rounds of a certain area by police, soldiers etc., for the purposes of guard; detachment of men appointed to perform this duty; unit of six Boy Scouts. PATROL (2) (*pres. pt.* PATROLLING, *pret and p.pt.* PATROLLED), *v.t. and i.* to go the rounds in a camp or garrison town; reconnoitre; march backwards and forwards in. [Fr.].

PATRON [pā'tron, pa'tron], *n.* one who stands to another in a paternal capacity; one who supports or protects a person or cause; regular customer or

---

The accent ' after a syllable = stress (u-pon'). The mark ‾ over a vowel = length (ā in made; ō in bone).

client; (eccles.) holder of an advowson; **p. saint**, saint constantly invoked as the particular protector of a person, place or cause. PATRONAL [pa-trō′nal, pa′tro-nal, pā′tro-nal], adj. performing the office of a p.; pertaining to a p. saint. [L.].

PATRONAGE [pa′tro-nij], n. support given by a patron; power to appoint to offices; condescension of manner in relations with another; (coll.) regular custom to a shopkeeper; (eccles.) right of appointing to a Church benefice.

PATRONIZE [pa′tro-nīz], v.t. to perform the functions of a patron to; give one's custom to; condescend to, assume airs of superiority over. PATRONIZING, adj. that patronizes, condescending.

PATRONYMIC [pa-tro-ni′mik], n. name derived from a father's or ancestor's name; family name. [Gk.].

PATTEN [pa′tn], n. clog shod with an iron ring. [MedL.].

PATTER (1) [pa′ter], v.t. to utter hurriedly and rapidly; v.i. to talk glibly, chatter. PATTER (2), n. professional talk of an entertainer; succession of words spoken or sung at a very rapid rate. [PATER (NOSTER)].

PATTER (3), v.t. to strike with a succession of quick light sounds; v.i. to move lightly and swiftly along with a patter of feet. PATTER (4), n. quick light sound as of rain falling. [PAT (1)].

PATTERN (1) [pa′tern], n. model to be copied; specimen or sample; anything cut or formed into a shape to be copied, esp. a shaped piece of wood from which a mould is to be made for casting metal; small piece of material used as a sample to assist a customer in a shop to choose the kind he requires; a design, esp. on carpets, wallpaper etc. PATTERN (2), v.t. to make in imitation of a model; draw a p. on. [OFr.].

PATTY [pa′ti], n. little pie; **p. pan**, pan to bake patties in. [Fr.].

PATULOUS [pa′tyoo-loos], adj. spreading, extending. [L.].

PAUCITY [paw′si-ti], n. fewness; smallness of number. [L.].

PAULINE [paw′līn], adj. pertaining to the Apostle Paul.

PAUNCH [pawnch], n. belly, abdomen; in ruminants, first and largest stomach; (coll.) protruding stomach in a man. [AFr.].

PAUPER [paw′per], n. person who, on account of his poverty, is dependent on public funds; one in very poor circumstances. [L.].

PAUPERIZE [paw′pe-rīz], v.t. to reduce to pauperism; make dependent on public relief.

PAUSE (1) [pawz], n. cessation or intermission in speaking or action; suspense; break in writing; (mus.) mark of cessation, rest, denoted by ⌢. PAUSE (2), v.i. to make a p.; stop; hesitate; linger, dwell (upon). [L.].

PAVANE [pa-vahn′], n. stately sixteenth-century dance in two-four time; music for this dance. [Fr.].

PAVE [pāv], v.t. to lay with stone or brick, so as to make a level surface for walking on; put a surface layer on a path or road; **to p. the way**, to prepare the way; (fig.) render easy the introduction of. [Fr. from L.].

PAVEMENT [pāv′ment], n. paved surface, esp. a paved footpath by the side of a road. [OFr.].

PAVILION (1) [pa-vil′yun], n. large tent; building or annex with a tent-shaped roof; club-house in a field devoted to outdoor games. PAVILION (2), v.t. to cover or shelter with, or as with, a p. or tent. [Fr.].

PAVING [pā′ving], n. upper surface of a road or path, usually of stone or brick.

PAVIO(U)R [pā′vi-er], n. one who paves.

PAW (1) [paw], n. foot of an animal having claws or nails; (coll.) hand. PAW (2), v.t. to scrape with the forefoot; touch, feel with the p.; (coll.) handle unnecessarily; v.i. (of a horse) to strike the ground repeatedly and restively with the fore-hoofs. [OFr.].

PAWKY [paw′ki], adj. shrewd, drolly artful. [Unkn.].

PAWL [pawl], n. catch which prevents recoil as it engages, the lever engaging a ratchet; short bar attached as a catch to a capstan. [PALE (1)].

PAWN (1) [pawn], n. piece or chessman of the lowest rank; agent used by another in effecting his own ends. [AFr.].

PAWN (2), n. a pledge; **in p.**, pledged; in the hands of a pawnbroker. PAWN-TICKET, voucher for anything pledged at a pawnshop. PAWN (3), v.t. to give or deposit in pledge to a pawnbroker; stake, risk.

PAWNEE, n. one who takes anything in p. PAWNER, n. one who pledges anything as security for the payment of borrowed money. [OFr.].

PAWNBROKER [pawn′brō-ker], n. one who lends money on interest on the security of personal property given over into his charge. [PAWN (2) and BROKER].

PAX [paks], int. (school slang) used to call a truce in games.

PAY (1) (pret. and p.pt. **paid**) [pā], v.t. to give to a person money or remuneration for services rendered; discharge a debt; give an agreed sum of money for goods received; render what is due; make profit for, recompense; give, render as a duty; v.i. to make payment, meet a debt; recompense for work; be profitable; **to p. away**, to spend; (naut.) let out (a line) gradually; **to p. back**, to give back, return tit for tat; **to p. off**, to settle a debt; discharge with wages paid; (naut.) (cause) (a ship) to fall to leeward; **to p. out**, to get one's own back on; (naut.) let out. PAY (2), n. money or remuneration for services rendered; wages, salary. [OFr.].

PAY (3) v.t. to coat with pitch or any watertight composition; render waterproof. [AFr. from L.].

PAYEE [pā-ē′], n. person to whom a sum of money is or will be paid.

PAY-LOAD [pā′lōd], n. (aeron.) weight of passengers or freight which an aircraft is capable of carrying.

PAYMASTER [pā′mahs-ter], n. man who regularly pays wages; officer in the navy or army whose duty it is to pay the officers and men; **P. General**, officer responsible for payments by the Treasury.

PAYMENT [pā′ment], n. act of paying; amount paid; (fig.) reward, recompense.

PAYNIM [pā′nim], n. a pagan, esp. a Moslem or Saracen. [OFr.].

PAY-SHEET [pā′shēt], n. list of names and wages of employees.

PEA [pē], n. leguminous climbing plant cultivated for its flowers or for its fruit-pods containing edible seeds. [OE.].

PEACE [pēs], n. freedom from disturbance or agitation; freedom from war or quarrel; treaty of peace between two nations; concord; rest; **to be at p.**, to become reconciled; to be dead; **to hold one's p.**, to be silent. [AFr. from L.].

PEACEABLE [pē′sa-bl], adj. disposed for peace, tranquil; at peace.

PEACEFUL [pēs′fool], adj. disposed to peace, pacific; characterized by peace, tranquil, calm.

PEACEMAKER [pēs′mā-ker], n. one who brings about peace or reconciliation where there was formerly war or disagreement.

PEACE-OFFERING [pēs′o-fe-ring], n. offering designed to bring about a reconciliation.

PEACH (1) [pēch], n. a rosaceous tree or its fruit; large edible fruit of a yellowy-pink colour with a downy skin and sweet pulpy flesh; (coll.) pretty young girl; anything excellent; **p. brandy**, kind of brandy flavoured with peaches; **p. Melba**, sweet of ice-cream and peaches. PEACH-COLOURED, deep soft pinky-cream like the blossom of a p. [ME. from L.].

PEACH (2), v.i. (slang) to turn informer; tell tales. [OFr.].

PEACOCK (1) [pē′kok], n. male bird of the genus Pavo, which has beautifully coloured plumage and a fan-shaped tail; vainglorious, strutting person. PEACOCK-BLUE, rich, blue colour like that of the plumage of a p.'s neck. PEACOCK (2), v.i. to strut vaingloriously about; give oneself airs; make a great display in dress. [OE. from L. and COCK].

PEAFOWL [pē′fowl], n. peacock or peahen.

PEA-GREEN [pē′grēn], n. light soft green colour as of fresh pea-pods.

PEAHEN [pē′hen], n. female of the peacock.

PEA-JACKET [pē′ja-kit], n. pilot coat or sailor's short overcoat. [Du.].

PEAK (1) [pēk], n. the top of anything terminating in a point, esp. the top of a hill or mountain; projecting piece in front of a cap; (naut.) narrow end of a hill at the bow; ship's hold in the bow; **p. load, period etc.**, load, period etc. when maximum effect is present. PEAK (2), v.t. to tilt upwards; (naut.) raise a yard obliquely to the mast. PEAKED, PEAKY (1), adj. with a p., pointed. [Var. of PIKE].

PEAK (3), v.i. to pine away, grow thin and pale. PEAKY (2), adj. thin and pale. [Uncert.].

PEAL (1) [pēl], n. set of bells or the changes rung on them; chime of bells; loud, reverberating sound.

PEAL (2), *v.i.* to ring out loudly and clearly; *v.t.* to cause to p. [~APPEAL].

PEAN, see PAEAN.

PEANUT [pē'nut], *n.* the plant *Arachis hypogaea*; oily nutritious seed of this plant.

PEAR [pāer], *n.* pear-tree; fleshy fruit of this tree. [OE. from L.].

PEARL (1) [purl], *n.* silvery-white, smooth and iridescent product of many bivalved molluscs, *esp.* the pearl-oyster; mother-of-pearl; something round and clear, like a dew-drop; anything very precious; *(typ.)* a small size of type; **p. button**, button made of mother-of-pearl. PEARL-BARLEY, barley reduced to small, round grains. PEARL-DIVER, man who dives for p.-oysters. PEARL-OYSTER, the oyster yielding pearls. PEARL (2), *v.t.* to set or adorn with pearls; decorate with p.-like drops; *v.i.* to fish for pearls; form into p.-like drops. PEARLED, *adj.* decorated with pearls; bespangled with p.-like drops. [Fr.].

PEARLIES [pur'liz], *n.(pl.)* *(coll.)* pearl buttons as worn for ornament on a costermonger's jacket; clothes bearing these adornments. [*Prec.*].

PEARLY [pur'li], *adj.* resembling a pearl in shape or texture; abounding with pearls; made of, adorned with, pearls; **p. king**, costermonger dressed in pearlies.

PEARMAIN [pāer'mān], *n.* smallish fairly soft apple ripening in August. [OFr.].

PEAR-TREE [pāer'trē], *n.* the tree *Pyrus communis*, or one of its cultivated varieties, bearing a soft edible fruit.

PEASANT [pe'zant], *n.* countryman, rustic labourer; countryman who owns and cultivates a small piece of land. PEASANTRY, *n.(pl.)* peasants as a class. [AFr.].

PEASE [pēs], *n.(pl.)* peas; **p. pudding**, split peas boiled and mashed. [OE.].

PEA-SHOOTER [pē'shoo-ter], *n.* narrow tube used by children to blow peas through as missiles; *(fig.)* inadequate weapon.

PEAT [pēt], *n.* fibrous brown substance formed in bogs or moors by partial carbonization of vegetable matter, and used as fuel. PEAT-BOG, moorland covered with p. PEAT-HAG, hole in the earth from which p. has been removed. PEAT-MOSS, peat-bog; any species of *Sphagnum* moss whose habitat is the peat-bog. [ME.].

PEBBLE [pe'bl], *n.* small rounded fragment of rock of any variety; a transparent rock crystal, *esp.* as used for lenses of spectacles; an agate. PEBBLED, *adj.* covered or heaped with pebbles; pebbly. [OE., ME.].

PECAN [pē'kan], *n.* species of hickory common in U.S.A.; nut or fruit of this tree. [Span.].

PECCABLE [pe'ka-bl], *adj.* capable of, with a tendency to, sin. PECCABILITY [pe-ka-bi'li-ti], *n.* tendency to sin. [MedL.].

PECCADILLO [pe-ka-di'lō], *n.* petty crime or fault; venial offence; an indiscretion. [Span. from L.].

PECCANT [pe'kant], *adj.* wrong, sinful; *(med.)* morbid. PECCANCY, *n.* sin, offence. [L.].

PECCARY [pe'ka-ri], *n.* *(zool.)* South American ungulate related to the swine. [SAmerInd.].

PECCAVI [pe-kā'vi, pe-kah'vi], *n.* confession of sin or error. [L.].

PECK (1) [pek], *n.* fourth part of a bushel or two gallons; *(coll.)* great deal, heap. [OFr.].

PECK (2), *v.t.* to strike with the beak; make a hole in by striking with the beak; pick up with the beak, pluck out by pecking; give a hasty and perfunctory kiss to; **to p. at**, to aim at with the beak; eat indifferently and without appetite. PECK (3), *n.* poke or bite made with the beak; hasty and perfunctory kiss. [*Var.* of PICK].

PECKER [pe'ker], *n.* one who, or that which, pecks; woodpecker; **to keep one's p. up**, *(coll.)* to keep up one's courage.

PECTIN [pek'tin], *n.* gelatinizing principle of certain fruits, such as apples and plums. [Gk.].

PECTINATE [pek'ti-nāt], *adj.* shaped like, having teeth like, a comb. [L.].

PECTORAL [pek'te-ral], *n.* ornamental breast-plate; pectoral fin. PECTORAL (2), *adj.* of, pertaining to, the breast, worn on the breast; *(med.)* good for diseases of the chest; **p. arch**, *(anat.)* the shoulder girdle. [L.].

PECTOSE [pek'tōs], *n.* substance related to cellulose and to pectin, found in fruit and vegetables. [PECT(IN)].

PECULATE [pe'kyoo-lāt], *v.i.* to appropriate to one's own use money or goods entrusted to one's care. PECULATOR, *n.* person who peculates; embezzler. [L.].

PECULATION [pe-kyoo-lā'shn], *n.* embezzlement, *esp.* of public money to one's own use.

PECULIAR [pi-kyoo'li-er], *adj.* characteristic of one person, individual; solely or specially belonging (to); singular, uncommon, queer. PECULIARLY, *adv.* in a p. manner, especially, unusually. [L.].

PECULIARITY [pi-kyoo-li-a'ri-ti], *n.* quality of being peculiar; a characteristic, distinguishing quality; eccentricity.

PECUNIARY [pi-kyoo'ni-a-ri], *adj.* relating to, consisting of, money; *(leg.)* having a money penalty. [L.].

PEDAGOGICS [pe-da-go'jiks, pe-da-go'giks], *n.(pl.)* science of pedagogy.

PEDAGOGUE [pe'da-gog], *n.* teacher of children or young people; schoolmaster; pedantic teacher. [Gk.].

PEDAGOGY [pe'da-go-gi, pe'da-go-ji], *n.* art or practice of teaching. [Gk.].

PEDAL (1) [pe'dal], *adj.* pertaining to a foot or feet. PEDAL (2), *n.* part of a machine or instrument worked by the foot; *(mus.)* one of the wooden keys of the organ keyboard worked by the feet; one of two or more levers on a piano or harp, which are worked by the foot, *esp.* the loud p. of a piano. PEDAL (3) *(pres. pt.* PEDALLING, *pret. and p.pt.* PEDALLED), *v.t. and i.* to work with a p.; bicycle. [Fr.].

PEDANT [pe'dant], *n.* person who makes a display of his learning; one who prides himself on his book-learning and meticulous observation of the letter, but is devoid of real taste or discrimination; one slavishly devoted to a system of rules. [Fr.].

PEDANTIC [pe-dan'tik], *adj.* given to, or characterized by, pedantry.

PEDANTRY [pe'dan-tri], *n.* vain ostentation of learning; slavish insistence on rules and forms.

PEDDLE [pe'dl], *v.t.* to sell small wares usually by travelling about the country; *v.i.* to trade as a pedlar. PEDDLING, *adj.* *(fig.)* small-minded; trifling. [~PEDLAR].

PEDESTAL [pe'des-tal], *n.* base of a column or statue; either of the two tiers of drawers supporting a kneehole writing-desk; **to put on a p.**, *(fig.)* to look up to, venerate. [Fr. from L.].

PEDESTRIAN (1) [pe-des'tri-an], *adj.* on foot, walking; representing a person on foot; *(fig.)* prosaic, commonplace. PEDESTRIAN (2), *n.* one who journeys on foot; **p. crossing**, marked crossing in the streets over which pedestrians have the prior right of way. [L.].

PEDI-, *pref.* relating to a foot or feet. [L.].

PEDICEL, PEDICLE [pe'di-sel, pe'di-kl], *n.* *(bot.)* stalk of each individual flower; *(zool.)* stem by which certain invertebrate animals attach themselves to an object. [MdL.].

PEDICULAR, PEDICULOUS [pe-di'kyoo-ler,-lōos], *adj.* lousy. [L.].

PEDICURE (1) [pe'di-kyoor], *n.* treatment of the feet, *esp.* the removal of corns etc. and the care of the toenails; chiropodist. PEDICURE (2), *v.t.* to practise p. upon (the feet). PEDICURIST, *n.* a p. [Fr.].

PEDIGREE (1) [pe'di-grē], *n.* genealogical table or family tree; genealogy, ancestry, descent. PEDIGREE (2), *adj.* (of an animal) having a known p. [Fr.].

PEDIMENT [pe'di-ment], *n.* *(arch.)* triangular structure over the portico of a Greek building; any structure resembling this in form. [Corruption of PYRAMID].

PEDLAR [ped'ler], *n.* travelling salesman who carries his pack from door to door. [ME.].

PEDO-, see PAEDO-.

PEDOLOGY [pe-do'lo-ji], *n.* scientific study of soils. PEDOLOGICAL [pe-do-lo'ji-kal], *adj.* pertaining to p. [Gk.].

PEDOMETER [pe-do'mi-ter], *n.* instrument which measures distances in walking. [PEDI and METER].

PEDUNCLE [pe'dung-kl], *n.* *(bot.)* stalk either of the flower or of the cluster; *(zool.)* stalk-like joining. [MdL.].

PEEK [pēk], *v.i.* to peep. [ME.].

PEEL (1) [pēl], *n.* small square fortress tower on the Scottish border. [OFr.].

PEEL (2), *v.t.* to strip off, remove, the skin, rind or outer coating of; *v.i.* to shed (its) peel, rind or covering; **to p. off**, to come off in strips or patches. PEEL (3), *n.* skin or rind of fruit; **candied p.**, rind of lemon, orange or citron preserved in sugar. PEELER (1), *n.* one who, or that which, peels. PEELING, *n.* that which is peeled off. [OE. from L.].

PEELER (2) [pē'ler], *n.* (*slang*) member of the 19th-century constabulary; policeman. [Sir Robert *Peel*, the founder].

PEEP (1) [pēp], *v.i.* to chirp or cry as young birds; cheep, squeak. PEEP (2), *n.* small, shrill cry of a young bird; cheep, chirp. [Echoic].

PEEP (3), *v.i.* to look through a restricted space; peer cautiously; take a hasty look; make a first tentative appearance; (*fig.*) be revealed unexpectedly through some small sign. PEEP (4), *n.* glimpse or hasty view; first tentative appearance. [~PEEK].

PEEPER [pē'per], *n.* bird, animal which peeps; young bird; (*coll.*) eye.

PEEP-SHOW [pēp'shō], *n.* well-lighted box in the side of which a magnifying glass is fixed through which are viewed pictures arranged within a small diorama; (*fig.*) a spectacle for the curious.

PEER (1) [pēer], *n.* person of equal rank or importance with another; one entitled to sit in the House of Lords by hereditary right or as a bishop or under rights granted for life; **temporal p.,** p. who is not a bishop; **spiritual p.,** bishop who has a seat in the House of Lords. [OFr. from L.].

PEER (2), *v.i.* to look carefully, narrowly, intently. [LGerm.].

PEERAGE [pēer'ij], *n.* peers collectively; rank of a peer; book with names and details of the families of peers.

PEERESS [pēer'es], *n.* consort of a peer; woman who holds a peerage in her own right.

PEERLESS [pēer'les], *adj.* having no equal; without peer.

PEEVISH [pē'vish], *adj.* querulous; hard to please; petulant, irritable. [ME.].

PEEWIT, PEWIT [pē'wit], *n.* the lapwing, the green plover; cry of this bird. [Imitative].

PEG (1) [peg], *n.* small wooden or metal pin used to fasten pieces of wood or metal together; split stick used to affix clothes to a line to dry; short projecting pin used as a support; a drink (from the measuring pegs inside tankards); **to take a person down a p.,** to humiliate him; **off the p.,** (of clothes) ready-made. PEG (2) (*pres.pt.* PEGGING, *pret. and p.pt.* PEGGED), *v.i.* to fasten, score, with pegs; (*econ.*) maintain a steady price for (stock etc.) by manipulation of the market; fix (wages, prices, exchange rates etc.) by regulation; **to p. away,** to work doggedly, **to p. down,** to secure by pegging to the ground; **to p. out,** to stake, mark out, with pegs; (*coll.*) die. [Du.].

PEGASUS [pe'ga-sus], *n.* (*Gk. myth.*) winged horse which with a stroke opened a spring in the ground whence the poets were fabled to have drawn their inspiration; the poetic muse; (*astron.*) a northern constellation; (*zool.*) genus of fishes with large pectoral fins. [Gk.].

PEG-TOP [peg'top], *n.* pear-shaped spinning-top; **p. trousers,** trousers wide at the hips and narrow at the ankles.

PEIGNOIR [pā'nwah(r)], *n.* woman's dressing jacket, dressing wrap. [Fr.].

PEJORATIVE [pē'je-ra-tiv], *adj.* disparaging; with a depreciatory meaning. [L.].

PEKIN(G)ESE [pē-ki-nēz'], *n.* a breed of Chinese pug-dogs. [*Pekin*, Chinese city].

PEKOE [pē'kō], *n.* a variety of black tea. [Chin.].

PELAGIC [pe-la'jik], *adj.* belonging to the deep sea. [Gk.].

PELARGONIUM [pe-lah-gō'ni-um], *n.* (*bot.*) genus of ornamental plants allied to the geranium. [Gk.].

PELERINE [pe'le-rēn], *n.* woman's mantle or cape; tippet. [Fr.].

PELF [pelf], *n.* money, wealth; money doubtfully acquired. [OFr.].

PELICAN [pe'li-kan], *n.* genus of birds allied to the storks, having a great bill with a large pouch. [Gk.].

PELISSE [pe-lēs'], *n.* woman's long, sleeved cloak; child's loose coat; cape or coat worn as part of a military uniform. [Fr.].

PELLAGRA [pe-la'grah, pe-lā'grah], *n.* eruptive skin disease caused by vitamin B2 deficiency. [It.].

PELLET [pe'lit], *n.* small ball of some soft substance as of medicine or food; pill; small shot. [Fr.].

PELLICLE [pe'li-kl], *n.* thin skin or crust; membrane; film. [L.].

PELL-MELL [pel'mel], *adv.* in disorder, confusedly. [Fr.].

PELLUCID [pe-lōō'sid], *adj.* allowing the passage of light; translucent; (*fig.*) clear, lucid. [L.].

PELMET [pel'met], *n.* narrow strip of material fixed over the tops of doors and windows to hide curtain fixtures. [Fr.].

PELOTA [pe-lō'tah], *n.* Spanish ball game resembling tennis in which the ball is struck from a wickerwork shield strapped to the arm. [Span.].

PELT (1) [pelt], *n.* skin or coat of an animal. [OFr.].

PELT (2), *v.t.* to strike with something thrown; throw something at; *v.i.* (of rain, hail) to pour down heavily, in full force. PELT (3), *n.* action of pelting; blow from something thrown; **at full p.,** rapidly. [ME.].

PELTATE [pel'tāt], *adj.* (*bot.*) shaped like a shield and bearing a stalk in the centre. [Gk.].

PELTRY [pel'tri], *n.* skins with the fur on, undressed skins. [AFr.].

PELVIC [pel'vik], *adj.* pertaining to the pelvis.

PELVIS [pel'vis], *n.* (*anat.*) hip-girdle at which the legs are joined to the body, the bones forming it being the sacrum and coccyx with a haunch bone on each side. [L.].

PEMMICAN [pe'mi-kan], *n.* lean meat dried, pounded and pressed with fat into cakes, for long journeys; (*U.S.*) a literary digest. [AmerInd.].

PEMPHIGUS [pem'fi-gus], *n.* (*path.*) a skin disease characterized by round or oval blisters. [Gk.].

PEN (1) [pen], *n.* small enclosure for animals. PEN (2) (*pres.pt.* PENNING, *pret. and p.pt.* PENNED), *v.t.* to shut in a p., coop up; confine. [OE.].

PEN (3), *n.* feather, quill; writing tool made formerly of a feather with the end of the shaft pointed, but now a metal nib fitted into a handle; (*fig.*) writing, profession of letters, literary style; **fountain p.,** p. with a storage tube for ink which runs on to the nib as required. PEN-AND-INK, written, or drawn, with p. and ink. PEN-NAME, nom de plume. PEN (4), *v.t.* to write with a p.; compose. [L.].

PENAL [pē'nal], *adj.* pertaining to legal punishment; making one liable to legal punishment; inflicted as legal punishment; **p. servitude,** formerly imprisonment for three years or more with hard labour; **p. settlement,** one for convicts. [Fr. from L.].

PENALIZE [pē'na-liz], *v.t.* to lay under a penalty, punish; handicap, put a penalty on.

PENALTY [pe'nal-ti], *n.* legal punishment; fine; loss or injury which results from wrongdoing; (*sport*) handicap, disadvantage imposed on one player or a side for breaking a rule of the game.

PENANCE [pe'nans], *n.* a sacrament of the Roman and Greek Churches involving contrition, confession and absolution; religious discipline undertaken as an earnest of repentance; (*fig.*) discomfort, misery, vexation. [OFr. from L.].

PENATES [pe-nā'tēz], *n.*(*pl.*) (*Rom. myth.*) guardian deities of the household, household gods; household possessions. [L.].

PENCE [pens], *n.*(*pl.*) pennies, *esp.* collectively, as a sum. [PENNY].

PENCHANT [pah(ng)'shah(ng)], *n.* inclination, liking, partiality. [Fr.].

PENCIL (1) [pen'sil], *n.* bar of blacklead or coloured chalk in a wooden or metal sheath; small brush used by painters for laying on colours; (*opt.*) collection of rays of light, rays of light meeting in a point. PENCIL-CASE, case or holder in which pencils are stored. PENCIL (2) (*pres.pt.* PENCILLING, *pret. and p.pt.* PENCILLED), *v.t.* to write, draw, mark with a p. PENCILLED, *adj.* painted, marked, drawn, written with or as with a p.; (*fig.*) finely marked. PENCILLING, *n.* painting, sketching; marking with fine, delicate lines. [OFr. from L.].

PENDANT (1), **PENDENT** [pen'dant, 'dent], *n.* anything hanging as an ornament, particularly on a chain or ribbon from the neck; hanging fitment for a lamp; (*arch.*) stone ornament depending from ceiling or roof; (*naut.*) pennant flown from the masthead. PENDENT, PENDANT (2) [pen'dent, 'dant], *adj.* hanging; overhanging, projecting. [Fr.].

PENDENCY [pen'den-si], *n.* state of being undecided.

PENDING [pen'ding], *adj. and prep.* not decided, awaiting decision; awaiting, until.

PENDULOUS [pen'dyōo-lōos], *adj.* hanging down loosely so as to swing; drooping.

PENDULUM [pen'dyōo-lum], *n.* weight suspended from a fixed point and free to swing rhythmically; **swing of the p.,** (*fig.*) movement of popular feeling or opinion away from its former loyalties to opposite ones and back again. [L.].

PENETRABLE [pe'ni-tra-bl], *adj.* able to be penetrated; (*fig.*) capable of being affected. [L.].

PENETRATE [pe'ni-trāt], *v.t.* to pass into the interior of; pierce; permeate; (*fig.*) see into, discern, reach by

---

ōō is pronounced as in food; ŏŏ as in hood; th as in *think*; TH as in *that*; zh as in azure. ~ = related to.

the intellect; *v.i.* to go through the action of penetrating. PENETRATING, *adj.* sharp, piercing, permeating; searching; piercing, shrill; (*fig.*) discerning, subtle. [L.].

PENETRATION [pe-ni-trā'shn], *n.* action of penetrating; state of being penetrated; intellectual acumen, insight, discernment; **peaceful p.,** method of spreading a doctrine by steady persistent dissemination of ideas rather than by force. [L.].

PENETRATIVE [pe'ni-tra-tiv], *adj.* having the power of penetrating.

PENGUIN [peng'gwin], *n.* sea bird having its wings developed into paddles; (*aeron.*) instructional aircraft of low power not intended for flight. [Uncert.].

PENICILLIN [pe-ni-si'lin], *n.* germ-killing substance derived from the bacterial mould *Penicillium notatum*.

PENINSULA [pe-nin'syŏŏ-lah], *n.* tract of land nearly surrounded by water; **the P.,** Spain and Portugal. [L.].

PENINSULAR [pe-nin'syŏŏ-ler], *adj.* like, in the form of, a peninsula; pertaining to a peninsula, *esp.* Spain and Portugal.

PENIS [pē'nis], *n.* male organ of copulation. [L.].

PENITENCE [pe'ni-tens], *n.* state of being penitent; feeling of contrition; repentance. [L.].

PENITENT (1) [pe'ni-tent], *adj.* contrite; repentant. PENITENT (2), *n.* repentant sinner; one who has made his confession to a priest and been admitted to penance. [L.].

PENITENTIAL (1) [pe-ni-ten'shal], *adj.* pertaining to penitence; expressing penitence. PENITENTIAL (2), *n.* book prescribing penances. [MedL.].

PENITENTIARY (1) [pe-ni-ten'sha-ri], *adj.* pertaining to penance; penitential. PENITENTIARY (2), *n.* Roman Catholic organ which deals with the punishment of serious ecclesiastical offences; house of correction; (*U.S.*) state prison. [MedL.].

PENKNIFE [pen'nīf], *n.* small folding pocket knife.

PENMAN [pen'man], *n.* man who teaches the art of handwriting, or who writes a good hand; author; forger.

PENNANT [pe'nant], *n.* small flag, pointed or swallow-tailed; long strip of bunting flown at the masthead of warships to show that they are in commission; streamer. [~PENNON and PENDANT].

PENNATE, see PINNATE.

PENNILESS [pe'ni-les], *adj.* not having a penny, poor, destitute.

PENNON [pe'non], *n.* small narrow flag, forked or swallow-tailed, attached to a lance so that, when the lance was held horizontally, the arms emblazoned on it appeared in their proper position. [OFr.].

PENNY (*pl.* **pence, pennies**) [pe'ni], *n.* British bronze coin worth one-twelfth of a shilling; **not to have a p.,** to be destitute; **a pretty p.,** a large sum of money; **to turn an honest p.,** to make a little money honestly. PENNY-A-LINER, one who writes for a journal for a small sum per line; reporter; journalist, *esp.* one who pads out his material so as to earn more for his work. PENNY-FARTHING, old-fashioned high bicycle with one large and one small wheel. PENNY-IN-THE-SLOT, denoting an automatic machine etc. operated by the insertion of a p. in the slot provided for the purpose. PENNY-POST, organization for the conveyance of letters at the charge of one p. introduced in 1840. [OE.].

PENNYROYAL [pe-ni-roi'al], *n.* (*bot.*) an aromatic plant yielding a medicinal oil. [ME. from OFr.].

PENNYWEIGHT [pe'ni-wāt], *n.* a troy weight of twenty-four grains.

PENNYWISE [pe-ni-wīz'], *adj.* saving small sums, foolishly niggardly; **p. and pound-foolish,** niggardly in small matters, extravagant in large ones.

PENNYWORT [pe'ni-wert], *n.* (*bot.*) a small herb growing in the crevices of rocks and walls; small herb growing in damp places. [PENNY and WORT].

PENOLOGY [pē-no'lo-ji], *n.* study of prison discipline and its bearing on the prevention of crime. [L. and Gk.].

PENSILE [pen'sīl], *adj.* hanging down, pendent. [L.].

PENSION (1) [pen'shn], *n.* periodical allowance in consideration of past services; periodic payment made to public servants or members of the fighting services or their dependants, or servants of certain business companies or individuals who have completed their term of service or have resigned office at the convenience of the state or business; **old age p.,** weekly pension paid by the state to old people. PENSION (2), *v.t.* to pay a p. to; **to p. off,** to cause or allow to retire from service with a p. [L.].

PENSION (3) [pah(ng)s'yaw(ng)], *n.* foreign boarding-house; **en p.,** paying a fixed inclusive rate for board and lodging. [Fr.].

PENSIONARY (1) [pen'shn-a-ri], *adj.* relating to a pension; maintained by a pension. PENSIONARY (2), *n.* pensioner.

PENSIONER [pen'shn-er], *n.* holder of a pension; dependant; Cambridge undergraduate living at his own expense; **Gentleman P.,** Gentleman-at-Arms, who attends upon the sovereign on state occasions; **Chelsea p.,** p. from the regular armed forces who is admitted to residence at Chelsea Hospital. [OFr.].

PENSIVE [pen'siv], *adj.* thoughtful; thoughtful with sadness; wistful. [Fr.].

PENSTEMON, see PENTSTEMON.

PENSTOCK [pen'stok], *n.* trough leading the water on to the waterwheel; sluice, flood-gate. [PEN (1) and STOCK].

PENT [pent], *adj.* shut up; cooped up. [*P.pt.* of PEN (2)].

PENTA-, PENT-, *pref.* five. [Gk.].

PENTACHORD [pen'ta-kawd], *n.* (*mus.*) five-stringed musical instrument; musical scale of five notes.

PENTACLE [pen'ta-kl], *n.* pentagram, formerly a five-pointed star, early symbol of the five virtues. [MedL.].

PENTAD [pen'tad], *n.* the number five; group of five things. [Gk.].

PENTAGON [pen'ta-gon], *n.* (*geom.*) plane figure with five sides and angles. [Gk.].

PENTAGRAM [pen'ta-gram], *n.* pentacle. [Gk.].

PENTAHEDRON [pen-ta-hē'dron], *n.* solid figure with five equal sides. PENTAHEDRAL, *adj.* having five faces, five equal sides. [Gk.].

PENTAMETER [pen-ta'mi-ter], *n.* (*pros.*) verse or line of poetry of five feet.

PENTATEUCH [pen'ta-tyōōk], *n.* the first five books in the Old Testament. [Gk.].

PENTATHLON [pen-tath'lon], *n.* athletic contest at the ancient Olympic games, now revived, in which each competitor takes part in five exercises. [Gk.].

PENTECOST [pen'ti-kost], *n.* solemn festival of the Jews held fifty days after the second day of the Passover; Whitsuntide, solemn feast of the Church in commemoration of the descent of the Holy Spirit. [Gk.].

PENTHOUSE [pent'hows], *n.* subsidiary structure such as a shed or porch attached to the wall of a main building; roof sloping away from the main building and forming a shelter; awning, canopy; (*U.S.*) dwelling-house on the roof of a skyscraper. [ME. from L.].

PENTILE, see PANTILE.

PENTSTEMON, PENSTEMON [pent-stē'mon], *n.* (*bot.*) genus of perennial herbaceous plants with bright flower-spikes. [Gk.].

PENULTIMATE (1) [pe-nul'ti-mat], *adj.* last but one, next to the last. PENULTIMATE (2), *n.* the last but one. [L.].

PENUMBRA [pe-num'brah], *n.* partly shaded region round the complete shadow of an opaque body; (*astron.*) shadow surrounding the deep shadow of the moon or earth during an eclipse; lighter border round the dark centre of a sunspot; (*paint.*) point of a picture or drawing where the light and shade are blended. [L.].

PENURIOUS [pe-nyŏŏr'i-ŏŏs], *adj.* poor, yielding little, scanty; slight, mean; niggardly. [L.].

PENURY [pe'nyŏŏ-ri], *n.* extreme poverty, want; destitution. [L.].

PEON [pē'on], *n.* (in India) foot soldier; policeman; (in Spanish America) day-labourer; bondman for debt. [Span.].

PEONY, PAEONY [pē'o-ni], *n.* plant with large red, pink or white flowers. [OFr. from Gk.].

PEOPLE (1) (*pl.* **peoples**) [pē'pl], *n.* body of persons forming a race, community, nation; (*pl. in sense*), populace; the masses; body of persons of a certain class, place, occupation; persons generally; kindred, relations, forebears; attendants, servants. PEOPLE (2), *v.t.* to stock with inhabitants; populate. [AFr. from L.].

PEPLUM [pe'plum], *n.* projecting appendage to a woman's jacket, cut so as to jut out from below the waist behind and over the hips. [L.].

PEPPER (1) [pe'per], *n.* a hot pungent condiment, the berry of *Piper nigrum*, used whole or ground to a powder; (*fig.*) fiery action, enthusiasm. PEPPER (2), *v.t.* to sprinkle with p.; (*fig.*) beat; pelt with shot or similar multiple missiles. [OE. from Gk.].

The accent ' after a syllable = stress (u-pon'). The mark ‾ over a vowel = length (ā in made; ō in bone).

PEPPERCORN [pe'per-kawn], *n.* berry of the pepper plant; **p. rent**, nominal rent for land or premises held on a long lease.

PEPPERMINT [pe'per-mint], *n.* pungent aromatic mint plant *Mentha piperita*; sweet flavoured with essence of peppermint. [PEPPER (1) and MINT (1)].

PEPPER-TREE [pe'per-trē], *n.* tropical South American tree which yields mastic.

PEPSIN [pep'sin], *n.* enzyme in the gastric juice of the stomach necessary in the digestive process for converting proteids into peptones; extract of this used medically to assist imperfect digestion. [Gk.].

PEPTIC (1) [pep'tik], *adj.* promoting digestion; able to digest; **p. glands**, glands secreting pepsin. PEPTIC (2), *n.* substance which promotes digestion. [Gk.].

PEPTONE [pep'tōn], *n.* substances formed in the stomach from proteids. [Gk.].

PER [pur], *prep.* by means of, by, through; for each. [*Next*].

PER-, *pref.* through, all over; thoroughly, completely; (*chem.*) containing the maximum amount of a substance. [L.].

PERADVENTURE [pe-rad-ven'tyoor], *n.* chance; *adv.* perhaps; perchance; by any chance.

PERAMBULATE [pe-ram'byoo-lāt], *v.t. and i.* to walk through or round, *esp.* in order to survey; walk round the boundaries of; walk about. [LL.].

PERAMBULATION [pe-ram-byoo-lā'shn], *n.* action of passing through; a travelling survey or inspection; survey or settling of boundaries.

PERAMBULATOR [pe-ram'byoo-lā-ter], *n.* one who perambulates; carriage for babies pushed by hand.

PER ANNUM [per-a'num], *adv.* by the year, yearly; annually. [L.].

PERCEIVE [per-sēv'], *v.t.* to apprehend by the senses; observe, discover, discern. [OFr. from L.].

PER CENT [per-sent'], *adv.* by the hundred; for or in every hundred. [L.].

PERCENTAGE [per-sen'tij], *n.* rate per hundred, interest paid on money per cent; proportion, part.

PERCEPT [pur'sept], *n.* (*philos.*) thing perceived. [L.].

PERCEPTIBLE [per-sep'ti-bl], *adj.* able to be perceived by the mind or the senses, appreciable. PERCEPTIBILITY [per-sep-ti-bi'li-ti], *n.* quality of being p. PERCEPTIBLY, *adv.* in a p. manner; to a p. degree or extent. [L.].

PERCEPTION [per-sep'shn], *n.* act or faculty of perceiving through the intellect or the senses; consciousness; intuition, insight; (*leg.*) collection, receiving. PERCEPTIONAL, *adj.* pertaining to, capable of, perceiving. [L.].

PERCEPTIVE [per-sep'tiv], *adj.* capable of perceiving; pertaining to perception; discerning, intelligent.

PERCH (1) [purch], *n.* an edible freshwater fish. [Fr. from Gk.].

PERCH (2), *n.* pole; roost-pole for fowls; measure of 5½ yd.; **square p.**, measure of 30½ sq. yd.; anything serving for a person, bird or animal to rest on, *esp.* if high up; (*fig.*) elevated, secure position. PERCH (3), *v.t.* to place on a p.; put down, fix, set in an inaccessible or insecure place; *v.i.* (of a bird) to alight or settle after flight; sit or balance oneself (on). [Fr. from L.].

PERCHERON [pur'she-ron], *n.* breed of draught-horses. [*La Perche*, France, where bred].

PERCIPIENCE [per-si'pi-ens], *n.* action of perceiving; state of being percipient.

PERCIPIENT (1) [per-si'pi-ent], *adj.* having the faculty of perceiving; having the power of perception. PERCIPIENT (2), *n.* p. person; one capable of receiving communications telepathically. [L.].

PERCOLATE [pur'ko-lāt], *v.t.* to cause to percolate; *v.i.* to ooze, drip, pass, filter through. [L.].

PERCLOSE [pur'klōz], *n.* enclosure; screen; railing enclosing a tomb. [ME.].

PERCOLATOR [pur'ko-lā-ter], *n.* filtering machine; coffee-pot in which the water percolates through the coffee.

PERCUSS [per-kus'], *v.t.* to strike forcibly; (*med.*) tap or strike firmly some part of the body for purpose of diagnosis. PERCUSSIVE, *adj.* pertaining to percussion, liable to detonate. [L.].

PERCUSSION [per-ku'shn], *n.* striking, collision; shock produced by collision of bodies; impression of sound on the ear; **p. bullet**, explosive bullet; **p. cap**, small copper cap containing fulminating powder; **p. lock**, gun-lock in which the p. cap is struck by a hammer; **p. instruments**, instruments played by striking, as drums. [L.].

PERDITION [per-di'shn], *n.* utter destruction; ruin;

utter loss of the soul or of happiness in a future state; damnation. [L.].

PEREGRINATE [pe'ri-gri-nāt], *v.i.* to travel; wander from place to place. [L.].

PEREGRINE † [pe'ri-grēn], *adj.* foreign, imported from abroad; **p. falcon**, blue falcon employed in hawking. [L.].

PEREMPTORY [pe'remp-te-ri], *adj.* excluding debate or expostulation; dictatorial; positive; (*leg.*) absolute, decisive. [L.].

PERENNIAL [pe-re'ni-al], *adj.* lasting, existing or continuing for a succession of years, permanent, continual; (*fig.*) remaining fresh through a succession of years; (of a topic or idea) recurring afresh regularly year by year; (*bot.*) remaining alive through a number of years. [L.].

PERFECT (1) [pur'fekt], *adj.* complete in all its parts; faultless, excellent; completely accurate, precise; of supreme moral excellence, righteous; thorough, utter; (*gram.*) of that tense which expresses completed action. PERFECT (2) [per-fekt'], *v.t.* to complete, bring to a state of perfection; instruct fully in some specific direction; (*print.*) print the second side of (a sheet of paper). PERFECTLY, *adv.* in a p. manner; completely, thoroughly. [L.].

PERFECTIBLE [per-fek'ti-bl], *adj.* capable of becoming perfect.

PERFECTION [per-fek'shn], *n.* state or quality of being perfect; act of making perfect; completeness, maturity, faultlessness; great proficiency in some accomplishment; **to p.**, completely, perfectly. PERFECTIONAL, *adj.* of the nature of p. PERFECTIONISM, *n.* system or doctrine of religious, moral or political p.; theory that man can attain moral p. [L.].

PERFERVID [per-fur'vid], *adj.* extremely fervid.

PERFIDIOUS [per-fi'di-oos], *adj.* faithless, false to a vow or trust, treacherous. [L.].

PERFIDY [pur'fi-di], *n.* breach of faith or allegiance, violation of trust reposed, treachery. [L.].

PERFORATE (1) [pur'fe-rāt], *v.t.* to bore through, pierce, make a hole or holes in; make a series of holes round the edge of, or a line of holes in, in order to assist tearing off; *v.i.* to penetrate. PERFORATE (2) [pur'fe-rat], *adj.* of a postage stamp, having perforations at the edges. PERFORATOR, *n.* perforating machine or tool. [L.].

PERFORATION [per-fe-rā'shn], *n.* act of perforating, state of being perforated; hole, line or border of small holes pierced close together to assist tearing or separation (as in a stamp).

PERFORCE [per-faws'], *adv.* of necessity. [OFr.].

PERFORM [per-fawm'], *v.t.* to accomplish, do, carry out, discharge; render, execute; *v.i.* to act, exhibit one's prowess, skill or talent before an audience; (of animals) give a display of tricks acquired after special training. [OFr.].

PERFORMANCE [per-faw'mans], *n.* act of performing, the carrying of anything into effect; execution or doing of anything; the action performed, feat; display of skill or ability, achievement; public rendering of a play or other form of entertainment.

PERFUME (1) [pur'fyoom], *n.* smell, odour, aroma; sweet smell, fragrance; scent, pleasant-smelling liquid sprinkled upon the clothes or person. PERFUME (2) [per-fyoom'], *v.t.* to scent, fill or impregnate with fragrant odours or with manufactured p. PERFUMER [per-fyoo'mer], *n.* maker or seller of perfumes. [OFr. from L.].

PERFUMERY [per-fyoo'me-ri], *n.* perfumes in general; establishment at which perfumes are made or sold; occupation or business of a perfumer.

PERFUNCTORY [per-fungk'te-ri], *adj.* done merely as a matter of form or as a duty which must be got through; careless, superficial, slight. [L.].

PERFUSE [per-fyooz'], *v.t.* to sprinkle, pour or spread over, suffuse, flood. [L.].

PERGOLA [pur'go-lah], *n.* long covered arbour, garden walk built over with a light wooden structure of intersecting laths along which climbing plants are trained. [L.].

PERHAPS [per-haps'], *adv.* possibly. [PER (2) and HAP].

PERI [pē'ri], *n.* (*Pers. myth.*) fairy being, originally considered as evil, but later as good and beautiful; (*fig.*) beauteous creature. [Pers.].

PERI-, *pref.* around, near, about. [Gk.].

PERIANTH [pe'ri-anth], *n.* (*bot.*) floral envelope, calyx and corolla. [Gk.].

PERICARDIAL [pe-ri-kah'di-al], *adj.* relating to, involving, connected with, the pericardium.

ōō is pronounced as in food; ŏŏ as in hood; th as in *think*; TH as in *that*; zh as in azure. ~ = related to.

PERICARDITIS [pe-ri-kah-di′tis], *n.* inflammation of the pericardium. [Gk.].

PERICARDIUM [pe-ri-kah′di-um], *n.* (*anat.*) membrane which surrounds the heart. [Gk.].

PERICARP [pe′ri-kahp], *n.* (*bot.*) seed-vessel of a plant, envelope in which the seed is enclosed. [Gk.].

PERICRANIUM [pe-ri-krā′ni-um], *n.* membrane surrounding the skull. [Gk.].

PERIGEE [pe′ri-jē], *n.* that point in the orbit of the moon, or a planet, which is nearest the earth. [Gk.].

PERIHELION [pe-ri-hē′li-on], *n.* the point in a planet's orbit when it is nearest the sun. [Gk.].

PERIKON [pe′ri-kon], *n.* (*radio*) zincite and bornite, in contact; **p. detector**, crystal detector made from this. [PERI(MORPH) and CON(TACT)].

PERIL (1) [pe′ril], *n.* danger, risk, exposure to injury, harm or destruction. PERIL (2) (*pres.pt.* PERILLING, *pret. and p.pt.* PERILLED), *v.t.* to expose to danger, imperil. [L.].

PERILOUS [pe′ri-loŏs], *adj.* dangerous, hazardous, fraught with peril.

PERIMETER [pe-ri′mi-ter], *n.* (*geom.*) line enclosing an area, or marking the limit of a closed figure, outline; length of this line; sight-testing instrument; enclosed area; **p. track**, road round the edge of an airfield. [Gk.].

PERIMORPH [pe′ri-mawf], *n.* a mineral surrounding another. [Gk.].

PERIOD (1) [pēer′i-od], *n.* portion of time marked by the recurrence of certain astronomical happenings, and used as a unit in reckoning time; any indefinite portion of time; specified portion of time; cycle, space of time in which a complete revolution of a recurring phenomenon is accomplished; time during a woman's menstrual cycle at which bleeding occurs; portion of time regarded as a separate unit or stage of history or individual development; (*gram.*) sentence, *esp.* one containing a number of clauses or phrases; (*pl.*) rhetorical passages in writing; pause at the end of a sentence, full stop marking this; (*phys.*) interval between repetition of vibrations or oscillations. PERIOD (2), *adj.* characteristic of, dealing with, a particular p. in history. [Gk.].

PERIODIC [pēer-i-o′dik], *adj.* recurring at (usually regular) intervals; pertaining to, written in, rhetorical periods; relating to the revolution of a heavenly body.

PERIODICAL (1) [pēer-i-o′di-kal], *adj.* periodic; published at regular intervals of more than a day. PERIODICAL (2), *n.* magazine or journal published periodically.

PERIODICITY [pēer-i-o-di′si-ti], *n.* quality of being periodic; frequency of recurrence or alternation.

PERIOSTEAL [pe-ri-os′ti-al], *adj.* pertaining to the periosteum, enveloping a bone.

PERIOSTEUM [pe-ri-os′ti-um], *n.* nervous vascular membrane which surrounds the bones of animals. [Gk.].

PERIOSTITIS [pe-ri-os-ti′tis], *n.* inflammation of the periosteum. [Gk.].

PERIPATETIC (1) [pe-ri-pa-te′tik], *adj.* pertaining to Aristotle or to his philosophy (from his custom of walking up and down when he taught); walking about, travelling round from place to place. PERIPATETIC (2), *n.* follower of Aristotle. [Gk.].

PERIPHERAL [pe-ri′fe-ral], *adj.* relating to, or constituting, a periphery; relating to the outskirts of a town, borders of a country.

PERIPHERY [pe-ri′fe-ri], *n.* circumference of a curvilinear figure, perimeter; external surface. [Gk.].

PERIPHRASIS (*pl.* **periphrases**) [pe-ri′fra-sis, -sēz], *n.* (*rhet.*) circumlocution, indirect method of expressing oneself; instance of this. PERIPHRASTIC [pe-ri-fras′tik], *adj.* using, speaking in, expressed by means of, p., circumlocutory. [Gk.].

PERISCOPE [pe′ri-skōp], *n.* optical instrument fitted with mirrors and lenses, and providing a reflected image of objects otherwise hidden from sight by an obstruction in the direct line of vision, an elaborate variety of this being used in submarines when submerged, to observe the position of objects on the surface of the water. PERISCOPIC [pe-ri-sko′pik], *adj.* pertaining to, seen through, a p.; increasing the width of the field of vision. [Gk.].

PERISH [pe′rish], *v.i.* to die, come to an end of existence, be destroyed; decay, become rotten; pass away. PERISHED, *adj.* (*coll.*) completely exhausted, almost dead, suffering physical distress because of cold, hunger etc. [ME. from OFr.].

PERISHABLE (1) [pe′ri-sha-bl], *adj.* liable to perish

or decay, easily destroyed. PERISHABLE (2), *n.* p. object or article.

PERISHING [pe′ri-shing], *adj.* deadly, intense, extreme; that perishes; (*coll.*) infernal, confounded. PERISHINGLY, *adv.* (*coll.*) extremely.

PERISTALSIS [pe-ri-stal′sis], *n.* (*physiol.*) wave-like motion of the intestines which carries food along the bowel. PERISTALTIC, *adj.* contracting in successive circles, as in p. [Gk.].

PERISTERONIC [pe-ri-ste-ro′nik], *adj.* relating to pigeons. [Gk.].

PERISTYLE [pe′ri-stīl], *n.* (*arch.*) series of columns round a building or square; enclosure surrounded by columns. [Gk.].

PERITONEAL [pe-ri-to-nē′al], *adj.* relating to the peritoneum.

PERITONEUM [pe-ri-to-nē′um], *n.* serous membrane lining the internal surface of the abdomen. [Gk.].

PERITONITIS [pe-ri-to-ni′tis], *n.* inflammation of the peritoneum. [Gk.].

PERIWIG [pe′ri-wig], *n.* wig, peruke. [Fr.].

PERIWINKLE (1) [pe′ri-wing-kl], *n.* genus of creeping evergreen plant with blue flowers. [OE. from L.].

PERIWINKLE (2), *n.* small univalve mollusc, having a snail-like shell and eaten as food. [~OE.].

PERJURE [pur′jer], *v. reflex.* to swear falsely, give false witness. PERJURED, *adj.* guilty of perjury.

PERJURY [pur′je-ri], *n.* crime of wilfully giving false evidence on oath, violation of a solemn promise or oath; false testimony. [L.].

PERK [purk], *v.i.* (usually with **up**) to hold up the head in a jaunty, self-confident manner; assume a lively, smart bearing; be saucy; cheer up, recover spirits, become perky. [Unkn.].

PERKY [pur′ki], *adj.* brisk, lively, jaunty; self-assertive.

PERMANENCE [pur′ma-nens], *n.* quality or state of being permanent; continuance in the same state or activity.

PERMANENCY [pur′ma-nen-si], *n.* quality of being permanent; something which is permanent; (*coll.*) security of tenure in employment.

PERMANENT [pur′ma-nent], *adj.* lasting, continuing without change, enduring indefinitely; **p. way**, railway lines and the bed on which they rest; **p. wave**, artificial wave produced in the hair by a special apparatus, and intended to last for a considerable time. [L.].

PERMANGANATE [per-mang′ga-nāt], *n.* (*chem.*) a salt of permanganic acid; **p. of potash**, purplish crystals which, when dissolved in water, form a strong disinfectant solution.

PERMANGANIC [per-mang-ga′nik], *adj.* (*chem.*) denoting an acid derived from manganese.

PERMEABLE [pur′mi-a-bl], *adj.* penetrable, able to be passed or diffused through; porous. [L.].

PERMEATE [pur′mi-āt], *v.t.* to pass through the pores and interstices, soak into, pervade, be diffused through; *v.i.* to diffuse itself. PERMEATION [per-mi-ā′shn], *n.* act of permeating; state of being permeated, diffusion. [L.].

PERMISSIBLE [per-mi′si-bl], *adj.* that may be permitted, allowable. [MedL.].

PERMISSION [per-mi′shn], *n.* leave, consent, liberty formally granted to do something. [L.].

PERMISSIVE [per-mi′siv], *adj.* allowing, granting permission; allowed, permitted. [L.].

PERMIT (1) (*pres.pt.* **permitting**, *pret. and p.pt.* **permitted**) [per-mit′], *v.t.* to allow, give leave or liberty to; tolerate, assent to; make possible; *v.i.* to allow, provide opportunity or means. PERMIT (2) [pur′mit], *n.* official document giving formal written permission to do something, warrant, licence. [L.].

PERMUTABLE [per-myōō′ta-bl], *adj.* that may be changed one for another, interchangeable. PERMUTABLY, *adv.* by exchange or interchange. [L.].

PERMUTATION [per-myōō-tā′shn], *n.* change, alteration; (*math.*) act of finding the different combinations or ways of arrangement of a given number of quantities; (*pl.*) all the different possible combinations or orders in which a given number of things may be arranged. [L.].

PERMUTE [per-myōōt′], *v.t.* (*math.*) to arrange in different ways, change the order of. [L.].

PERNICIOUS [per-ni′shŏs], *adj.* destructive, extremely harmful, tending to injure or destroy; **p. anaemia**, severe progressive form of anaemia. [L.].

PERNICKETY [per-ni′ke-ti], *adj.* fastidious, touchy,

---

cantankerous about small matters, fussy. [Unkn.].

PERORATE [pe'ro-rāt], *v.i.* to declaim at length; sum up and bring to an end a speech. [L.].

PERORATION [pe-ro-rā'shn], *n.* concluding part of a speech in which a general summing-up is made; oration, formal discourse. [L.].

PEROXIDE [pe-rok'sīd], *n.* (*chem.*) an oxide which contains more oxygen than a normal oxide; **p. of hydrogen**, fluid used for bleaching hair and as an antiseptic. [PER- and OXIDE].

PERPEND [per-pend'], *v.t. and i.* (*archaic*) to weigh in the mind, ponder (over). [L.].

PERPENDICULAR (1) [per-pen-di'kyōō-ler], *adj.* vertical, at right angles to the plane of the horizon; (*fig.*) extremely steep, (of a slope) sheer; (*geom.*) at right angles to a given line or surface; (*arch.*) applied to the late pointed Gothic style of English architecture. PERPENDICULAR (2), *n.* vertical position; instrument for finding the p. line from a certain point or level surface; plumb-line; (*geom.*) line at right angles to a given line or plane. [L.].

PERPETRATE [pur'pi-trāt], *v.t.* to perform, commit (something bad or wicked). PERPETRATION [per-pi-trā'shn], *n.* act of committing, *esp.* a crime or outrage. [L.].

PERPETUAL [per-pe'tyōō-al], *adj.* continuing for ever, never ceasing, continual; throughout the whole of one's life; acting or applicable for all time; continuing unbroken. [L.].

PERPETUATE [per-pe'tyōō-āt], *v.t.* to make perpetual; preserve from extinction or oblivion.

PERPETUITY [per-pi-tyōō'i-ti], *n.* quality of being perpetual, endless duration; that which is perpetual; a perpetual annuity; (*leg.*) quality of being inalienable for an indefinite period, or beyond the period permitted by law; estate limited in this way. [L.].

PERPLEX [per-pleks'], *v.t.* to puzzle, baffle, bewilder, harass with doubt; complicate, confuse.

PERPLEXITY [per-plek'si-ti], *n.* quality of being perplexed, bewilderment, confusion; doubt; that which is perplexing. [LL.].

PERQUISITE [pur'kwi-zit], *n.* anything obtained by one in employment beyond his or her ordinary salary, or occasionally in lieu of salary; anything claimed as a sole personal right or province. [L.].

PERRUQUE, see PERUKE.

PERRUQUIER [pe-rōō'ki-ā], *n.* maker of wigs. [Fr.].

PERRY [pe'ri], *n.* drink made rom the fermented juice of pears. [OFr.].

PERSECUTE [pur'si-kyōōt], *v.t.* to harass with unjust and cruel treatment, *esp.* on account of religious opinions; oppress continually with injurious attacks; worry, importune. [L.].

PERSECUTION [per-si-kyōō'shn], *n.* act of persecuting; state of being persecuted; continual oppression because of religious or other beliefs. [L.].

PERSECUTOR [pur'si-kyōō-ter], *n.* one who persecutes. [L.].

PERSEVERANCE [per-si-vēer'ans], *n.* persistence in anything undertaken, ability to persevere. [L.].

PERSEVERE [per-si-vēer'], *v.i.* to persist in anything undertaken, in spite of difficulties, rebuffs, failures etc. [L.].

PERSEVERING [per-si-vēer'ing], *adj.* steady in the pursuit of an object, full of perseverance. PERSEVERINGLY, *adv.* in a p. fashion.

PERSIFLAGE [pur'si-flahzh], *n.* light banter, mockingly frivolous treatment of a subject. [Fr.].

PERSIMMON [per-si'mon], *n.* the date-plum, fruit of a North American tree, a variety of ebony. [Native].

PERSIST [per-sist'], *v.i.* to continue steadfastly and obstinately in any course, belief etc., in spite of opposition; last, survive, remain. [L.].

PERSISTENCE [per-sis'tens], *n.* act or state of persisting; quality of being persistent; continuous survival.

PERSISTENCY [per-sis'ten-si], *n.* quality of being persistent; obstinacy in adhering to some opinion, purpose or action; pertinacity.

PERSISTENT [per-sis'tent], *adj.* persisting stubbornly in some action, purpose or belief; enduring, surviving unchanged, not easily got rid of; continual.

PERSON [pur'son], *n.* a human being in a general sense, as distinct from an animal or inanimate object; a particular human being; a distinct personality; the bodily form or appearance of a human being; the actual physical body itself; human being of importance; contemptuous term for a human being; (*theol.*) one of the three states of existence of

the Godhead; (*leg.*) human being or corporation regarded as having certain legal rights and duties; (*gram.*) one of three classes of pronouns considered in relation to a verb, namely oneself, the one spoken to, or the one spoken about; **in p.**, personally; **in the p. of**, in the character of. [L.].

PERSONABLE [pur'so-na-bl], *adj.* of good appearance, comely.

PERSONAGE [pur'so-nij], *n.* person, *esp.* one of distinction or eminence; one of the characters in a play. [OFr.].

PERSONAL [pur'so-nal], *adj.* pertaining to, characteristic of, a particular person; individual, private; carried on, done, in person; affecting or involving a person himself and not a representative; offensively directed against a particular person; pertaining to the external appearance or human bodily form; (*gram.*) denoting, referring to, one of the three persons; **p. property**, (*leg.*) movables, chattels, things belonging to a person as distinct from real estate in land or houses; **p. column**, part of a newspaper containing short advertisements or messages of a confidential or private nature. [L.].

PERSONALITY [per-so-na'li-ti], *n.* quality of being a person as distinct from a thing or animal, personal identity; an individual well known because of some particular idiosyncrasy, local character, celebrated person; qualities of mind and temperament constituting a particular person's character; quality of being personal or aimed at a particular person; (*pl.*) offensive personal remarks; **multiple p.**, (*psych.*) existence of more than one contrasting p. in an individual. [MedL.].

PERSONALLY [pur'so-na-li], *adv.* as a person; in person; oneself, individually; for my part.

PERSONALTY [pur'so-nal-ti], *n.* personal estate, personal goods, chattels and movables. [AFr.].

PERSONATE [pur'so-nāt], *v.t.* to act the part of, in a play; impersonate, pretend to be. [LL.].

PERSONIFICATION [per-so-ni-fi-kā'shn], *n.* representation as a person, embodiment in personal form; person regarded as embodying in himself an abstract quality, the exemplification of a quality.

PERSONIFY [per-so'ni-fi], *v.t.* to represent as a person or human being; exemplify in one's own person. [Fr.].

PERSONNEL [per-so-nel'], *n.* staff of persons employed, *esp.* in a public institution; body of men constituting an army, navy or air force. [Fr.].

PERSPECTIVE (1) [per-spek'tiv], *n.* art of representing objects in drawing on a plane surface so as to produce a realistic effect of relative position, distance etc.; view, vista; apparent relative position, distance and size of objects seen by the eye; (*math.*) science of the visual relations of objects; **in p.**, (*fig.*) in (its) true relation and significance. PERSPECTIVE (2), *adj.* pertaining to the art of p., in p. [MedL.].

PERSPEX [pur'speks], *n.* (*prot.*) tough transparent plastic substance much used for windscreens etc. instead of glass. [Trade name].

PERSPICACIOUS [per-spi-kā'shōōs], *adj.* shrewd, quick and acute in discernment, possessing a penetrating insight.

PERSPICACITY [per-spi-ka'si-ti], *n.* perspicaciousness, shrewdness, penetrating insight. [L.].

PERSPICUITY [per-spi-kyōō'i-ti], *n.* lucidity, freedom from obscurity. [L.].

PERSPICUOUS [per-spi'kyōō-ōōs], *adj.* clear, not obscure or ambiguous, plainly expressed. [L.].

PERSPIRATION [per-spi-rā'shn], *n.* act of perspiring; the moisture perspired, sweat.

PERSPIRE [per-spīer'], *v.t. and i.* to discharge moisture through the pores of the skin, sweat. PERSPIRATORY, *adj.* causing or concerned in the process of perspiration. [L.].

PERSUADE [per-swād'], *v.t.* to induce to believe something, convince by argument; cause or prevail upon (a person) to do a particular thing by appealing to his judgment, reason or feelings. [L.].

PERSUASIBLE [per-swā'zi-bl], *adj.* open to persuasion. [L.].

PERSUASION [per-swā'zhn], *n.* act of persuading; state of being persuaded; power of persuading; conviction, firm opinion; religious denomination or sect. [L.].

PERSUASIVE (1) [per-swā'siv, 'ziv], *adj.* having the power of persuading, tending to persuade. PERSUASIVE (2), *n.* inducement, incentive. [MedL.].

PERT [purt], *adj.* forward, saucy, impudent. [ME. from OFr.].

PERTAIN [per-tān'], *v.i.* to belong to, be connected

with; relate to, be concerned with; be appropriate to; **pertaining to,** connected or associated with, relating to. [OFr. from L.].

PERTINACIOUS [per-ti-nā'shōōs], *adj.* obstinate, perversely persistent, stubborn. [L.].

PERTINACITY [per-ti-na'si-ti], *n.* obstinate persistency, stubborn tenacity. [OFr.].

PERTINENCE, PERTINENCY [pur'ti-nens(-i)], *n.* relevancy, appositeness, quality of being pertinent.

PERTINENT [pur'ti-nent], *adj.* relevant, appropriate, to the point. [L.].

PERTURB [per-turb'], *v.t.* to upset, disturb, agitate, alarm. **PERTURBED,** *adj.* upset, apprehensive, restless. [L.].

PERTURBATION [per-ter-bā'shn], *n.* agitation of mind, disturbance, anxiety. [L.].

PERTUSSIS [per-tu'sis], *n.* whooping-cough. **PER-TUSSAL,** *adj.* relating to whooping-cough. [L.].

PERUKE, PERRUQUE [pe-rōōk'], *n.* artificial cap or head of hair, wig. [Fr.].

PERUSAL [pe-rōō'zal], *n.* act of reading through.

PERUSE [pe-rōōz'], *v.t.* to read through, *esp.* to read through closely or carefully. [PER- and USE].

PERUVIAN [pe-rōō'vi-an], *n. and adj.* a native of, pertaining to, Peru; **P. bark,** bark of several species of *Cinchona* used as medicine. [MdL.].

PERVADE [per-vād'], *v.t.* to permeate, spread or be diffused completely in, penetrate into every part of. **PERVADING,** *adj.* that fills, runs through, every part; universally felt. [L.].

PERVASION [per-vā'zhn], *n.* act of pervading; thorough diffusion. [L.].

PERVASIVE [per-vā'siv], *adj.* tending to pervade.

PERVERSE [per-vurs'], *adj.* deliberately persisting in what is wrong or wicked; wilfully obstinate, intractable; contrary, cantankerous, awkward; *(leg.)* contrary to the evidence or judge's direction. [L.].

PERVERSION [per-vur'shn], *n.* act of perverting; state of being perverted, *esp.* sexually perverted; distortion, misapplication. [L.].

PERVERSITY [per-vur'si-ti], *n.* perverseness, contrariness. [L.].

PERVERSIVE [per-vur'siv], *adj.* tending to pervert.

PERVERT (1) [per-vurt'], *v.t.* to turn from its proper purpose, use or meaning, misapply, misconstrue; corrupt, lead astray, distort, cause to be depraved; convert to a false religious belief. **PERVERT** (2), [pur'vert], *n.* one who has been perverted from truth to error, *esp.* in religious matters; one in whom natural desires and instincts are perverted. [L.].

PERVIOUS [pur'vi-ōōs], *adj.* allowing passage through, able to be penetrated, permeable; open to suggestion, persuasion or reason; *(biol.)* open. [L.].

PESETA [pe-sā'tah], *n.* Spanish silver coin corresponding to the franc or lira. [Span.].

PESO [pā'sō], *n.* former Spanish gold or silver coin; (now) S. American coin. [Span.].

PESSARY [pe'sa-ri], *n.* surgical appliance for supporting a prolapse of the uterus; vaginal suppository. [MedL.].

PESSIMISM [pe'si-mizm], *n.* tendency to look on the gloomy side of things; *(philos.)* doctrine that the universe is radically bad and evil. [L.].

PESSIMIST [pe'si-mist], *n.* one who expects things generally to turn out badly; one who believes in the doctrine of pessimism.

PESSIMISTIC [pe-si-mis'tik], *adj.* pertaining to, characterized by, pessimism; taking it for granted that everything will turn out badly.

PEST [pest], *n.* insect or other creature which destroys food or property or is otherwise harmful or troublesome; *(rare)* plague or epidemic disease; *(coll.)* troublesome, destructive thing or person; nuisance. [L.].

PESTER [pes'ter], *v.t.* to trouble, annoy, plague. [Fr.].

PESTIFEROUS [pes-ti'fe-rōōs], *adj.* pestilential, noxious or destructive to life or health; harmful to morals or to society, pernicious.

PESTILENCE [pes'ti-lens], *n.* any widespread infectious or contagious disease, *esp.* bubonic plague; *(fig.)* something morally injurious or noxious. [L.].

PESTILENT [pes'ti-lent], *adj.* injurious or destructive to life or health, deadly; harmful to morals or society, morally pernicious; *(coll.)* troublesome, annoying. [L.].

PESTILENTIAL [pes-ti-len'shal], *adj.* of the nature of, or producing, a pestilence; morally harmful or injurious; *(coll.)* extremely troublesome.

PESTLE (1) [pes'(t)l], *n.* club-shaped implement with a heavy rounded head, used for pounding substances

in a mortar. **PESTLE** (2), *v.t. and i.* to pound with a p. [OFr.].

PESTOLOGY [pes-to'lo-ji], *n.* study of pests. [PEST and Gk.].

PET (1) [pet], *n.* fit of peevishness, ill temper. [Uncert.].

PET (2), *n.* tame animal reared and kept as a companion or object to be pampered; favourite, darling. **PET** (3), *adj.* favourite; cherished as a p., often ironical. **PET** (4) *(pres.pt.* **PETTING,** *pret. and p.pt.* **PETTED),** *v.t.* to fondle, caress; treat as a p., spoil; *v.i. (coll.)* kiss and cuddle. [Uncert.].

PETAL [pe'tal], *n. (bot.)* a single distinct part of the corolla of a flower. **PETALINE, PETALOID,** *adj.* pertaining to a p.; like, in the form of, a p. [Gk.].

PETARD [pe-tahd'], *n.* explosive device, formerly used for breaking in gates or making breaches; firework cracker; **hoist with his own p.,** caught in his own trap. [Fr.].

PETER [pē'ter], *v.i.* **to p. out,** to give out gradually, become exhausted. [Uncert.].

PETERPENCE, PETER'S PENCE [pē-ter(z)-pens'], *n.(pl.)* voluntary donations given by Roman Catholics to the papal treasury. [St. *Peter*].

PETERSHAM [pē'ter-sham], *n.* strong kind of ribbed silk. [Lord *Petersham*].

PETIOLE [pe'ti-ōl], *n.* leaf-stalk. **PETIOLAR,** *adj.* like, pertaining to, a p. **PETIOLATE,** *adj.* having, growing upon, a leaf-stalk. **PETIOLULE,** *n.* small p. [L.].

PETITE [pe-tēt'], *adj.* (of a woman) small, trim and dainty. [Fr.].

PETITION (1) [pe-ti'shn], *n.* act of begging or humbly entreating; humble request, prayer or entreaty; formal written request to a superior, official body or person in authority to put right some wrong or grievance or grant a favour; *(leg.)* formal written application made to a court of law; **P. of Right,** *(hist.)* statement by the anti-Court party in parliament in the time of Charles I of certain demands; *(leg.)* mode of procedure to recover personal property or land which has come into the possession of the Crown. **PETITION** (2), *v.t.* to make a formal written request or application. **PETITIONARY,** *adj.* containing or making a p.; supplicatory. [L.].

PETITIONER [pe-ti'shn-er], *n.* one who petitions, *esp.* the plaintiff in a divorce suit.

PETREL [pet'rel], *n.* small sea-bird with long wings and black and greyish-white feathers; **stormy p.,** the smallest web-footed bird, known as Mother Carey's chicken; *(fig.)* person who brings disturbance and excitement wherever he goes. [Uncert.].

PETRIFACTION [pet-ri-fak'shn], *n.* process of petrifying; state of being petrified; anything petrified, incrustation; *(fig.)* amazement. [L.].

PETRIFY [pet'ri-fi], *v.t.* to convert into stone or into a stony substance, encrust with a mineral deposit; *(fig.)* deaden, make callous or obdurate; stupefy, dumbfound; *v.i.* to become changed into stone or a stony substance. [Fr.].

PETRO-, *pref.* rock, stone. [Gk.].

PETROL [pet'rol], *n.* a liquid hydrocarbon obtained by distillation from petroleum and forming an explosive gas when mixed with air, used in internal combustion engines. **PETROL-PUMP,** pumping machine for the supply of measured quantities of p. to motor vehicles. [*Next*].

PETROLEUM [pe-trō'li-um], *n.* a mineral oil consisting almost entirely of liquid hydrocarbons. [PETRO- and L.].

PETROLOGY [pe-tro'lo-ji], *n.* study of rocks and their structure. [Gk.].

PETTICOAT [pe'ti-kōt], *n.* underskirt worn by females; *(coll.)* woman. [PETTY and COAT (1)].

PETTIFOG [pe'ti-fog], *v.i.* to act as a pettifogger. **PETTIFOGGING,** *adj.* resorting to pettifoggery; paltry, contemptible.

PETTIFOGGER [pe'ti-fo-ger], *n.* inferior lawyer, one who indulges in disreputable trickery and other sharp practices. **PETTIFOGGERY,** *n.* disreputable legal trickery, quibbling. [PETTY, second element obscure].

PETTISH [pe'tish], *adj.* fretful, peevish, spoiled.

PETTITOES [pe'ti-tōz], *n.* pig's trotters, eaten as food. [Uncert.].

PETTY [pe'ti], *adj.* trivial, small in amount or importance; mean, contemptible, paltry; minor inferior, on a small scale; **p. cash,** miscellaneous small payments received or made; **p. larceny,** theft of articles or goods of comparatively small value; **p. officer,** officer in the navy of similar rank to a

---

The accent ′ after a syllable = stress (u-pon′). The mark ‾ over a vowel = length (ă in made; ō in bone).

non-commissioned officer in the army; **p. sessions**, court of law presided over by justices of the peace. [Fr.].

PETULANCE [pe'tyŏŏ-lans], *n.* peevishness, waywardness, fretful irritability. [L.].

PETULANT [pe'tyŏŏ-lant], *adj.* peevish, irritable, cross-grained. [L.].

PETUNIA [pe-tyŏŏ'ni-ah], *n.* genus of herbaceous plants allied to the nightshade, bearing white or purple flowers; a purple colour. [Fr. from Braz.].

PEW [pyŏŏ], *n.* long, fixed and partially enclosed bench with a back, on which the congregation sit in a place of worship; (*coll.*) seat, chair. [OFr.].

PEWIT, see PEEWIT.

PEWTER (1) [pyŏŏ'ter], *n.* alloy containing about four-fifths tin and one-fifth lead, with some variation and inclusion of other metals such as antimony, according to the hardness required; utensil made of this, a collection of pewter vessels or objects. PEWTER (2), *adj.* made of p. PEWTERER, *n.* one who makes utensils of p. [ME. from It.].

PFENNIG [pfe'nig], *n.* German copper coin, a hundredth of a mark. [Germ.].

PHAETON [fā'ton], *n.* light, open, four-wheeled carriage, usually drawn by two horses. [Gk. myth. *Phaeton*, who drove the chariot of the sun].

PHAGOCYTE [fa'gŏ-sīt], *n.* white blood corpuscle which destroys harmful bacteria in the system. [Gk.].

PHALANGEAL [fa-lan'ji-al], *adj.* like, pertaining to, a phalanx or phalanges.

PHALANGER [fa'lan-jer], *n.* genus of tree-living Australian marsupials. [Gk.].

PHALANGIOUS [fa-lan'ji-ŏŏs], *adj.* pertaining to *Phalangium*, genus of spiders with long thin legs.

PHALANX (*pl.* **phalanges, phalanxes**) [fa'lanks, fa-lan'jēz], *n.* (*Gk. antiq.*), compact body of infantry drawn up so closely as to form a solid wall or block; any body of troops or men in such close formation; band of people solidly united in a common purpose or cause; (*anat.*) one of the small bones forming the finger or toe. [Gk.].

PHALLIC [fa'lik], *adj.* pertaining to the phallus or its worship. [Gk.].

PHALLUS (*pl.* **phalli**) [fa'lus], *n.* a representation of the erected penis as a symbol of the procreative power of nature. [Gk.].

PHANEROGAM [fa'ne-rŏ-gam], *n.* (*bot.*) plant propagated by plainly visible flowers. PHANEROGAMOUS [fa-ne-ro'ga-mŏŏs], *adj.* having visible flowers. [Gk.].

PHANTASM [fan'tazm], *n.* fancy, illusion; image created by the fancy, figment of the imagination; spectre, apparition. [Gk.].

PHANTASMAGORIA [fan-taz-ma-gaw'ri-ah], *n.* series of optical illusions arranged for public display; array and procession of shadowy, rapidly moving figures, real or illusory. [Gk.].

PHANTASY, see FANTASY.

PHANTOM (1) [fan'tom], *n.* apparition, spectre; vision; optical illusion, delusion of the mind, hallucination. PHANTOM (2), *adj.* spectral, illusory, imaginary. [OFr.].

PHARAOH [fāer'ō], *n.* title borne by the kings of Ancient Egypt; **Pharaoh's serpent**, kind of firework melting in the form of a serpent.

PHARISAIC(AL) [fa-ri-sā'ik(-al)], *adj.* resembling the Pharisees, making a show of religion; self-righteous; formal, hypocritical.

PHARISAISM [fa'ri-sā-izm], *n.* principles, doctrines and conduct of the Pharisees; self-righteousness; hypocrisy.

PHARISEE [fa'ri-sē], *n.* member of a Jewish sect noted for their strict observance of traditional rites and ceremonies and their professed sanctity; one who attaches more importance to outward forms and ceremonies than to the inner meaning; one who is vainly conscious that he is holier than his fellows; hypocrite. [Gk. from Heb.].

PHARMACEUTICAL [fah-ma-syŏŏ'ti-kal], *adj.* pertaining to, occupied in, the preparation and dispensing of medicines; involving the use of medicines. [Gk.].

PHARMACEUTICS [fah-ma-syŏŏ'tiks], *n.(pl.)* science of the preparation and mixing of drugs to be taken as medicine.

PHARMACEUTIST [fah-ma-syŏŏ'tist], *n.* pharmacist.

PHARMACIST [fah'ma-sist], *n.* person skilled or occupied in the art of preparing medicinal drugs.

PHARMACOLOGY [fah-ma-ko'lo-ji], *n.* study of

the preparation and use of drugs as medicines. [Gk.].

PHARMACOPOEIA [fah-ma-kŏ-pē'ah], *n.* book of directions, published by authority, for the preparation, mixture and use of drugs as medicines; stock of drugs for medicinal use. [Gk.].

PHARMACOSIDERITE [fah-ma-kŏ-si'de-rīt], *n.* arsenate of iron. [Gk.].

PHARMACY [fah'ma-si], *n.* study or practice of preparing and dispensing medicinal drugs; a dispensary. [Gk.].

PHAROS [fāer'os], *n.* lighthouse; beacon. [From a lighthouse on the island of *Pharos* near Alexandria].

PHARYNGEAL [fa-rin'ji-al], *adj.* relating to the pharynx.

PHARYNGITIS [fa-rin-jī'tis], *n.* (*med.*) inflammation of the membrane of the pharynx. [Gk.].

PHARYNX [fa'ringks], *n.* muscular cavity at the back of the throat, lying between the mouth and the gullet. [Gk.].

PHASE [fāz], *n.* the amount of illuminated surface, of the moon or a planet, visible to the eye at a given time; aspect of a heavenly body at a given time; particular aspect, side, stage or state of a phenomenon which undergoes periodic change. [Gk.].

PHEASANT [fe'znt], *n.* a game-bird highly esteemed for the beauty of its plumage and the delicacy of its flesh; **pheasant's eye**, the plants *Adonis autumnalis* and *Narcissus poeticus*. [ME.].

PHENACETIN [fe-na'se-tin], *n.* a product of phenol used medicinally as an antipyretic. [PHENOL and ACETYL].

PHENOL [fē'nol], *n.* carbolic acid, a hydroxyl derivative of benzene, used as an antiseptic and disinfectant. [Gk.].

PHENOMENAL [fi-no'mi-nal], *adj.* pertaining to phenomena, of the nature of a phenomenon, perceptible to the senses; extraordinary, exceptional. PHENOMENALISM, *n.* system of philosophy which maintains that knowledge is limited to phenomena perceptible to the senses.

PHENOMENON (*pl.* **phenomena**) [fi-no'mi-non], *n.* anything which appears or is observed, that which is perceptible by the senses; extraordinary thing, something remarkable, marvel, wonder; (*coll.*) wizard, prodigy; (*philos.*) that which is directly perceived by the senses. [Gk.].

PHENYL [fē'nil], *n.* organic radical present in carbolic acid etc.

PHIAL [fī'al], *n.* small glass vessel or bottle in which liquids are kept. [Gk.].

PHILANDER [fi-lan'der], *v.i.* to flirt, play at making love, indulge in light-hearted love affairs without serious intentions. [Gk.].

PHILANTHROPIC(AL) [fi-lan-thro'pik(-al)], *adj.* pertaining to, practising, philanthropy.

PHILANTHROPIST [fi-lan'thro-pist], *n.* one filled with a love of mankind, who spends time, energy and money in helping others, person who makes large and frequent gifts to charity.

PHILANTHROPY [fi-lan'thro-pi], *n.* love of mankind, generosity in making charitable gifts. [Gk.].

PHILATELIST [fi-la'te-list], *n.* one who collects postage stamps.

PHILATELY [fi-la'te-li], *n.* study and collection of postage stamps. [Gk.].

PHILHARMONIC [fil-hah-mo'nik], *adj.* loving music. [PHILO and HARMONY].

PHILHELLENISM [fil-he'le-nizm], *n.* love of, admiration for, Greece and Greek civilization; support for Greece's efforts to secure independence from the Ottoman Empire. PHILHELLENIC [fil-he-lē'nik], *adj.* pertaining to p. or philhellenists. PHILHELLENIST, *n.* admirer of Greece; exponent of p.

PHILIBEG, see FILIBEG.

PHILIPPIC [fi-li'pik], *n.* one of four orations of Demosthenes against Philip of Macedon; Cicero's orations against Antony; any discourse full of acrimonious invective. [Gk.].

PHILISTINE (1) [fi'lis-tīn], *n.* member of a tribe of southern Palestine, who harassed the Israelites; inveterate enemy; blatantly prosperous, uncultured person oblivious of the arts, and solely concerned with his material welfare. PHILISTINE (2), *adj.* uncultured, boorish. PHILISTINISM [fi'lis-ti-nizm], *n.* outlook, tastes and modes of thinking of the uncultured p. [Gk.].

PHILO-, *pref.* loving, fond of. [Gk.].

PHILOLOGICAL [fi-lō-lo'ji-kal], *adj.* pertaining to, concerned with, in accordance with, philology.

PHILOLOGIST [fi-lo'lo-jist], *n.* student of philology.

PHILOLOGY [fi-lo'lo-ji], *n.* study of linguistic principles, study of languages, *esp.* their origin, structure and development. [Gk.].

PHILOMEL [fi'lō-mel], *n.* the nightingale. [Gk.].

PHILOPROGENITIVENESS [fi-lō-prō-je'ni-tiv-nes], *n.* love of producing offspring; fertility, tendency to produce many offspring. [PHILO- and L.].

PHILOSOPHER [fi-lo'sō-fer], *n.* one who studies, or is versed in, philosophy; one who adopts a philosophic attitude to life; **philosopher's stone,** imaginary substance formerly sought by alchemists as a means of converting baser metals into gold. [Gk.].

PHILOSOPHIC(AL) [fi-lo-sō'fik(-al)], *adj.* pertaining to philosophy; of the nature of, based on, like, philosophy; like a philosopher, wise; learned or versed in philosophy; behaving in a wise, reasonable manner; bearing misfortune resignedly.

PHILOSOPHIZE [fi-lo'sō-fiz], *v.t.* to deal with in a philosophical manner; *v.i.* to reason, speculate or theorize as a philosopher.

PHILOSOPHY [fi-lo'sō-fi], *n.* study of ultimate reality, an attempt to understand or explain the nature of phenomena or matter, of human action and conduct, or of consciousness, the mind and its reasoning; science dealing with the causes and principles of things; a particular philosophical system; a rationalized outlook on life, mental attitude influencing one's behaviour. [Gk.].

PHILTRE, PHILTER [fil'ter], *n.* love potion or charm. [Gk.].

PHLEBITIS [fle-bi'tis], *n.* (*path.*) inflammation of the lining or walls of a vein. [Gk.].

PHLEBOTOMY [fle-bo'tō-mi], *n.* practice of blood-letting as a remedy for certain diseases. PHLEBOTO-MIZE, *v.t.* to bleed by opening a vein; *v.i.* to let blood from a vein. [Gk.].

PHLEGM [flem], *n.* thick viscous fluid secreted by the mucous membrane of the throat and chest; (*fig.*) coolness, apathy, sluggishness. PHLEGMY [fle'mi], *adj.* pertaining to, resembling, p. [Gk.].

PHLEGMATIC [fleg-ma'tik], *adj.* sluggish, not easily stirred or excited, stolid.

PHLOGISTIC [flo-jis'tik], *adj.* (*chem.*) pertaining to, consisting of, resembling, phlogiston; (*med.*) inflammatory.

PHLOGISTON † [flō-jis'ton], *n.* supposed principle of inflammability present in all combustible substances, and separated by combustion. [Gk.].

PHLOX [floks], *n.* North American genus of herbaceous plants, with clusters of variously coloured flowers. [Gk.].

PHOBIA [fō'bi-ah], *n.* (*psych.*) a morbid fear, dislike or aversion. [Gk.].

PHOCA [fō'kah], *n.* the seal; any member of the seal or walrus family. PHOCAL, *adj.* relating to the seal or to the seal tribe. [Gk.].

PHOENIX [fē'niks], *n.* (*myth.*) fabulous Egyptian bird which was said to live for 500 years, at the end of which it burnt itself on a funeral pile, and rose again in the renewal of youth from the ashes. [Gk.].

PHON [fon], *n.* (*phys.*) unit of loudness used in measuring sound. [Gk.].

PHONE (1) [fōn], *n.* (*coll.*) telephone. PHONE (2), *v.t. and i.* to telephone. [(TELE)PHONE].

PHONETIC [fō-ne'tik], *adj.* pertaining to, representing, involving, dealing with, the sounds of speech and their articulation; **p. symbols,** method of spelling in which words would be spelt as they are pronounced, each letter or combination of letters always being used to represent the same sound.

PHONETICIAN [fō-ne-ti'shan], *n.* one who studies, or is versed in, phonetics.

PHONETICS [fō-ne'tiks], *n.(pl.)* that part of linguistic study dealing with the sounds of speech, their production, pronunciation and graphical representation by written characters.

PHONIC [fo'nik], *adj.* pertaining to sound, acoustic; pertaining to sounds of speech. [Gk.].

PHONO-, *pref.* voice, speech, vocal sound. [Gk.].

PHONOGRAM [fō'nō-gram], *n.* written sign or character representing a particular sound of speech; record, in the form of a cylinder, made by a phonograph. [Gk.].

PHONOGRAPH [fō'nō-grahf], *n.* instrument for recording and regulating sounds, in which a record was made upon a revolving cylinder coated with hard wax.

PHONOGRAPHY [fō-no'gra-fi], *n.* Pitman's system of shorthand; recording and reproduction of sounds by means of the phonograph. [Gk.].

PHONOLOGY [fō-no'lo-ji], *n.* study of the history and development of the sounds of speech; system of speech sounds in a particular language. [Gk.].

PHONOTYPE [fō'nō-tip], *n.* symbol or letter of a phonetic alphabet in type; a phonetic type.

PHOSGENE [foz'jēn], *n.* carbonyl chloride, a poisonous, non-persistent, lung-irritant, chemical gas used in warfare. [Gk.].

PHOSPHATE [fos'fāt], *n.* a salt of phosphoric acid, used largely as manure in agriculture.

PHOSPHIDE [fos'fīd], *n.* a combination of phosphorus and another element.

PHOSPHINE [fos'fēn], *n.* hydrogen phosphide, a spontaneously combustible gas believed to ignite the marsh-gas in will-o'-the-wisp.

PHOSPHITE [fos'fīt], *n.* a salt of phosphorous acid.

PHOSPHORATE [fos'fe-rāt], *v.t.* to combine with phosphorus, make phosphorescent.

PHOSPHORESCE [fos-fe-res'], *v.i.* to give out light without apparent combustion or heat, shine in the dark.

PHOSPHORESCENCE [fos-fe-re'sens], *n.* quality of being phosphorescent, emission of light without apparent combustion or heat; act or power of shining in the dark.

PHOSPHORESCENT [fos-fe-re'sent], *adj.* emitting a faint light or glow without apparent heat or combustion; shining in the dark.

PHOSPHORIC [fos-fo'rik], *adj.* pertaining to, containing, phosphorus in its higher valency state; phosphorescent.

PHOSPHOROUS [fos'fe-rōos], *adj.* containing phosphorus in its lower valency state.

PHOSPHORUS [fos'fe-rus], *n.* (*chem.*) the non-metallic element denoted by P., a yellowish wax-like inflammable substance appearing luminous in the dark, known also in non-luminous red and black forms. [Gk.].

PHOTO-, *pref.* light. [Gk.].

PHOTO [fō'tō], *n.* abbreviation of PHOTOGRAPH.

PHOTOCHEMISTRY [fō-tō-ke'mis-tri], *n.* study of chemical changes caused by the action of light.

PHOTOCHROMOTYPE [fō-tō-krō'mō-tip], *n.* printing in colours from photographic blocks.

PHOTOCHROMY [fō'tō-krō-mi], *n.* colour-photography; art of colouring photographs. [Gk.].

PHOTO-ELECTRIC CELL [fō-tō-i-lek-trik-sel'], *n.* cell whose electrical resistance varies according to the intensity of light to which it is exposed.

PHOTO-ENGRAVING [fō'tō-en-grā-ving], *n.* any photographic process for producing printing blocks.

PHOTO-FINISH [fō-tō-fi'nish], *n.* (*racing*) a race so closely contested that only a photograph of the finish can determine the winner.

PHOTOGENIC [fō-tō-je'nik, fō-tō-jē'nik], *adj.* producing light; applied to a subject which photographs well. [Gk.].

PHOTOGRAPH (1) [fō'tō-grahf], *n.* negative picture produced by the action of light on a film or glass plate sensitized with a chemically prepared emulsion, and developed and fixed thereon by chemical means; positive print on emulsified paper made from this. PHOTOGRAPH (2), *v.t.* to take a p. or photographs of; *v.i.* to take photographs, be a suitable subject for photography. [PHOTO and GRAPH].

PHOTOGRAPHIC [fō-tō-gra'fik], *adj.* pertaining to photography; resembling a photograph, faithfully recording or reproducing everything in the manner of a photograph.

PHOTOGRAPHY [fō-to'gra-fi], *n.* process of taking photographs. [Gk.].

PHOTOGRAVURE [fō-tō-gra-vyōōr'], *n.* photographic process by which printing plates are obtained, from which prints or engravings can be taken by intaglio printing. [PHOTO and Fr.].

PHOTOMETER [fō-to'mi-ter], *n.* instrument for measuring the intensity of light. PHOTOMETRIC(AL) [fō-tō-me'trik(-al)], *adj.* relating to a p. or to photometry. PHOTOMETRY [fō-to'mi-tri], *n.* measurement of light and its intensity. [Gk.].

PHOTON [fō'ton], *n.* a quantum of radiant energy.

PHOTOPHOBIA [fō-tō-fō'bi-ah], *n.* morbid hatred of light.

PHOTOSTAT (1) [fō'tō-stat], *n.* (*prot.*) apparatus for obtaining direct, facsimile, photographic reproductions of a manuscript, drawing or other document without the necessity of printing from a negative; a reproduction obtained in this way.

PHOTOSYNTHESIS [fō-tō-sin'the-sis], *n.* (*bot.*) process by which the chlorophyll in plants converts carbon dioxide into carbohydrates under the influence of light. [PHOTO and SYNTHESIS].

PHOTOTELEGRAPHY [fō-tō-te-le′gra-fi], *n.* telegraphic transmission of photographs and drawings.

PHOTOTYPE (1) [fō′tō-tip], *n.* a photographic impression of an engraving from which copies can be printed, process block. PHOTOTYPE (2), *v.t.* to make a p. of.

PHRASE (1) [frāz], *n.* group of words used to express a single idea and forming part of a sentence; group of words corresponding in function to a single part of speech; short idiomatic expression; short telling expression or catchword; (*mus.*) short passage considered as a unity in itself, yet forming part of a longer passage; **p. book**, book giving examples of the idioms and peculiar phrases of a language. PHRASE-MONGER, coiner or repeater of phrases and catchwords. PHRASE (2), *v.t.* to express in words or by a particular p., use a particular idiom or combination of words to express; divide into phrases. [Gk.].

PHRASEOGRAM [frā′zi-ō-gram], *n.* symbol representing a phrase, *esp.* in shorthand. [Gk.].

PHRASEOLOGY [frā-zi-o′lo-ji], *n.* manner of expression, diction, choice of words and phrases, *esp.* those characteristic of a period, person etc. [Gk.].

PHREN [fren], *n.* the intellectual principle, mind; diaphragm.

PHRENETIC [fre-ne′tik], *adj.* crazy, frantic. [Gk.].

PHRENIC [fre′nik], *adj.* (*anat.*) relating to the diaphragm. [Gk.].

PHRENOLOGICAL [fre-no-lo′ji-kal], *adj.* relating to phrenology.

PHRENOLOGY [fre-no′lo-ji], *n.* theory that the mental faculties and powers are connected with particular areas of action in the brain, and their development shown by the external undulations of the cranium; art of reading the bumps on a person's skull. [Gk.].

PHRYGIAN [fri′ji-an], *adj.* pertaining, belonging, to Phrygia; **P. bonnet**, cap worn by the French Revolutionaries as a symbol of liberty; **P. mode**, (*mus.*) one of the ancient Greek modes. [L.].

PHTHISICAL [ti′zi-kal], *adj.* of the nature of phthisis; suffering from phthisis. [Gk.].

PHTHISIS [thī′sis], *n.* pulmonary consumption, tuberculosis of the lungs. [Gk.].

PHYCOLOGY [fi-ko′lo-ji], *n.* study of the algae, or seaweeds. [Gk.].

PHYLACTERY [fi-lak′te-ri], *n.* small leather case containing strips of parchment inscribed with texts of Scripture, worn by the Jews at certain prayers as a reminder to observe the law; charm or amulet; (*fig.*) ostentatious profession of the outward forms of religion and righteousness; case or chest in which is enclosed a holy relic. [Gk.].

PHYLARCHY [fi′lah-ki], *n.* government of a tribe. [Gk.].

PHYLLO-, *pref.* leaf. [Gk.].

PHYLLOXERA [fi-lok-sēer′ah], *n.* genus of plant lice destroying the roots and leaves of the grapevine. [Gk.].

PHYSIC (1) [fi′zik], *n.* science or art of healing diseases, the medical profession; medicine, *esp.* a purge. PHYSIC (2), *v.t.* to treat with medicine, dose.

PHYSICAL [fi′zi-kal], *adj.* pertaining to, connected with, material things or phenomena perceived by the senses; pertaining to physics or the forces of nature, dealing with the natural features of the world; in accordance with the laws of nature, from the point of view of physics; bodily, connected with the body as opposed to the mind or soul. PHYSICALLY, *adv.* according to the laws of nature or physics; bodily, with regard to the body. [MedL.].

PHYSICIAN [fi-zi′shn], *n.* doctor of medicine, member of the medical profession, one whose profession it is to prescribe remedies in the form of medicines for the treatment of disease. [OFr.].

PHYSICIST [fi′zi-sist], *n.* student of physics; one who tries to explain everything on physical principles.

PHYSICS [fi′ziks], *n.* science dealing with the properties of matter and the effects of forces upon matter.

PHYSIO-, *pref.* nature. [Gk.].

PHYSIOGNOMY [fi-zi-o′no-mi], *n.* art of judging character from the features or general appearance of a person; the countenance, *esp.* the type of face, or habitual expression of the face; (*vulg.*) face; general external appearance of a region. PHYSIOGNOMIC [fi-zi-ō-no′mik], *adj.* pertaining to, skilled in, p.; pertaining to the face as a guide to character. PHYSIOGNOMIST [fi-zi-o′no-mist], *n.* one skilled in p.;

one who is able to read a person's character from his face. [Gk.].

PHYSIOGRAPHY [fi-zi-o′gra-fi], *n.* branch of geography dealing with the natural features of the surface of the earth, physical geography. [Gk.].

PHYSIOLOGICAL [fi-zi-o-lo′ji-kal], *adj.* relating to physiology.

PHYSIOLOGIST [fi-zi-o′lo-jist], *n.* student of physiology.

PHYSIOLOGY [fi-zi-o′lo-ji], *n.* science dealing with the constituent parts of living organisms and their functions. [Gk.].

PHYSIOTHERAPEUTIC [fi-zi-ō-the-ra-pyōō′tik], *adj.* pertaining to physiotherapy. [PHYSIO- and THERAPEUTIC].

PHYSIOTHERAPY [fi-zi-ō-the′ra-pi], *n.* curative treatment by physical means, such as massage, heat, light and electricity. [PHYSIO- and THERAPY].

PHYSIQUE [fi-zēk′], *n.* bodily structure or appearance, physical development, build. [Fr.].

PHYTOGEOGRAPHY [fi-tō-jē-og′ra-fi], *n.* study of the distribution of plants over the surface of the earth. [Gk.].

PI (1) [pī], *n.* (*math.*) the symbol π (Greek P) of the ratio of the circumference to the diameter of a circle.

PI (2), see PIE (3).

PI (3), *adj.* (*slang*) pious, sanctimonious.

PIA MATER [pi-ah-mā′ter], *n.* innermost of the three membranes in which the brain and spinal cord are enveloped. [MedL. translation from Arab.].

PIANISSIMO [pē-ah-ni′si-mō], *n., adj. and adv.* (*mus.*) (passage) (played) very softly. [It.].

PIANIST [pē′a-nist], *n.* one who plays the piano.

PIANO (1) [pya′nō], *n.* keyed musical instrument in which the notes are produced by the action of hammers, operated by the keyboard striking against wires tuned to a certain pitch; **grand p.**, large p. in which the strings are placed horizontally; **upright p.**, in which the strings are placed vertically; **p. accordian**, accordian in which the keys are arranged similarly to those of a p. PIANO (2) [pē-ah′nō], *n., adj. and adv.* (*mus.*) (passage) (played) softly. [It.].

PIANOFORTE [pya-nō-faw′ti], *n.* a piano. [It.].

PIANOLA [pē-a-nō′lah], *n.* (*prot.*) automatic piano operated by pedals.

PIASTRE [pi-ahs′ter], *n.* small Egyptian coin worth one hundredth of an Egyptian pound; coin of Syria and other Middle Eastern countries worth one hundredth of the local pound. [It.].

PIAT [pē′at], *n.* a type of anti-tank mortar. [Projector Infantry Anti-Tank].

PIAZZA [pē-ahd′zah], *n.* open square or market-place surrounded by buildings. [It.].

PIBROCH [pē′brokh], *n.* special kind of music played on the Highland bagpipe, usually a march or a dirge. [Gael.].

PICA [pī′kah], *n.* (*typ.*) standard size of type approximately six to the inch. [L.].

PICADOR [pi′ka-daw(r)], *n.* mounted rider in a bullfight, who infuriates the bull by pricking him with a lance. [Span.].

PICARESQUE [pi-ka-resk′], *adj.* (of literature) concerned with the exploits of rogues and adventurers. [Span.].

PICAROON [pi-ka-rōōn′], *n.* rogue, plunderer, pirate; pirate ship. [Span.].

PICCALILLI [pi-ka-li′li], *n.* kind of mixed pickle made with chopped vegetables, mustard and boiling vinegar. [Unkn.].

PICCANINNY [pi′ka-ni-ni], *n.* (*coll.*) negro baby; small child. [Span.].

PICCOLO [pi′ko-lō], *n.* small flute, with the notes an octave higher in pitch than the ordinary flute. [It.].

PICK (1) [pik], *n.* tool consisting of an iron bar with one end pointed and the other shaped like a chisel, with a wooden handle set at right angles to it, used for breaking up ground etc.; any sharp instrument used for picking. [PIKE (1)].

PICK (2), *v.t.* to break up with a pick; make or dig with a pick; pluck with the fingers so as to remove, gather; select; separate so as to pull apart; take up into the beak; (of a lock) open by an instrument other than a key; steal from; *v.i.* to steal; eat without appetite, nibble; **to p. on**, to select as an object of questioning, reproach etc.; **to p. out**, to select, distinguish, recognize; make colourful, set in relief or contrast; play hesitantly (a tune); **to p. up**, to take hold of, gather; receive more (passengers); meet with; obtain (a living); become acquainted with casually; acquire; (*radio*) succeed in receiving signals from;

see by means of a searchlight etc.; *v.i. (motoring)* to accelerate; *(elect.)* reach full voltage; *(coll.)* be better in health, more lively; **to p. a quarrel with,** deliberately to engage in acrimonious dispute with; **to p. holes in,** captiously to point out the flaws in; **to have a bone to p. with,** to have a cause of quarrel against. PICK (3), *n.* act of picking, right of selection; that which is chosen; best, choicest; *(print.)* dirt etc. collecting in the hollows of printing types. [~OE.].

PICKABACK [pi′ka-bak], *adv.* on the back of another in the manner of a pack carried on the shoulders. [PACK].

PICKAXE (1) [pi′kaks], *n.* pick for breaking up ground etc. PICKAXE (2), *v.t.* to strike with a p.; *v.i.* to use a p. [OFr.].

PICKET (1) [pi′kit], *n.* small sharp-pointed stake or peg; *(milit.)* small body of men selected as an outpost or for special duty; striker posted on guard outside a place of employment during a strike, to dissuade others from continuing at work. PICKET (2), *v.t.* to enclose or secure with pickets; post as a p.; patrol with pickets; *v.i.* to endeavour to dissuade persons from remaining at work by use of pickets; act as p. [Fr.].

PICKINGS [pi′kingz], *n.(pl.)* gleamings, scraps; petty objects obtained by theft.

PICKLE (1) [pi′kl], *n.* solution of salt and water or vinegar etc., in which foodstuffs are seasoned and preserved; *(pl.)* vegetables preserved in pickle and used as a condiment; acid solution used for scouring metals etc.; awkward situation, unfavourable plight; *(coll.)* mischievous child; scamp; **to have a rod in p. for,** to have punishment coming to. PICKLE (2), *v.t.* to preserve in p.; scour with p. PICKLED, *adj. (slang)* drunk. [MDu.].

PICK-ME-UP [pik′mē-up], *n.* stimulant, tonic.

PICKPOCKET [pik′po-kit], *n.* one who steals from the pocket of another.

PICKTHANK [pik′thank], *n.* informer; flatterer; one who continually curries favour.

PICK-UP [pik′up], *n. (radio)* broadcast received by a radio station from another, and in turn transmitted by this station to listeners; point in the route covered by a motor-bus etc. at which passengers may be picked up; electrical device fitted to a gramophone, by means of which a record may be heard through the loudspeaker of a radio set; *(motoring)* power of acceleration; recovery; *(slang)* casual female acquaintance.

PICNIC (1) [pik′nik], *n.* pleasurable outing in which an outdoor meal is eaten, the members of the party usually taking with them the food for this; *(coll.)* an easy matter; a good time. PICNIC (2) *(pres.pt.* PICNICKING, *pret.* and *p.pt.* PICNICKED), *v.i.* to take part in a p. [Fr.].

PICOT [pi-kō′], *n.* small loop of thread used as an edging. [Fr.].

PICOTEE [pi-ko-tē′], *n. (hort.)* carnation in which the edges are a darker colour than the main area of the petals. [Fr.].

PICRIC [pik′rik], *n. (chem.)* **p. acid,** yellow crystalline substance used in dyeing, making explosives and treating burns. [Gk.].

PICT [pikt], *n.* one of a race of people formerly dwelling in the north-east of Scotland.

PICTORIAL (1) [pik-taw′ri-al], *adj.* pertaining to, consisting of, illustrated by, pictures, picturesque, like a picture. PICTORIAL (2), *n.* illustrated journal. [L.].

PICTURE (1) [pik′tyoor], *n.* a painting, drawing or photograph; likeness; mental image or concept; a graphic description; cinematograph film; representation or embodiment (of an abstract quality or thing); *(pl.)* the cinema; *(coll.)* strikingly beautiful person, object or scene; **p. gallery,** building for the exhibition of pictures; **p. hat,** woman's wide-brimmed hat; **p. house, palace,** cinema; **in the p.,** prominent; informed. PICTUREGOER, one who frequents cinemas. PICTURE-WRITING, the use of pictures instead of written characters to express ideas, words etc. PICTURE (2), *v.t.* to represent in a p.; describe vividly; form a p. of in the mind, imagine. [L.].

PICTURESQUE [pik-tyoo-resk′], *adj.* like, suitable for, forming, a pleasing picture; vivid, graphic; original and interesting, colourful. [It.].

PIDDLE [pi′dl], *v.i. (archaic)* to trifle, dally; *(coll.)* make water. PIDDLING, *adj.* paltry, insignificant. [PUDDLE].

PIDGIN [pi′jin], *n. (coll.)* business, concern. PIDGIN-, PIGEON-ENGLISH, jargon or bastard form of English

used as a medium of communication between the natives of the Far East, *esp.* the Chinese, and the English. [Chin. corruption of BUSINESS].

PIE (1) [pi], *n.* crust baked with meat or fruit in or under it; *(coll.)* something easy; **to have a finger in the p.,** to be concerned or interested in some activity. [ME.].

PIE (2), *n.* magpie; variety of woodpecker. [OFr. from L.].

PIE (3), **PI,** *n. (print.)* a confused mixture of printing type; *(fig.)* medley, jumble. [Unkn.].

PIEBALD [pi′bawld], *adj.* marked with irregular patches of two different colours, one light and one dark; *(fig.)* motley. [PIE (2) and BALD].

PIECE (1) [pēs], *n.* a separate part or fragment; portion or fraction; some, an amount; a definite area of land; a single object, *esp.* when forming part of a set; firearm; coin; one of a set of draughts or chessmen; an individual specimen; a literary, musical or artistic composition; a definite quantity; sheet of paper; length of cloth or wallpaper; *(slang)* girl, woman; **p. of work,** a creation, production; **by the p.,** according to the quantity or amount; **a p.,** *(coll.)* each; **of a p.,** of the same kind; **p. of eight,** Spanish dollar; **to give a p. of one's mind,** to say exactly what one thinks about something; **p. goods,** *(pl.)* fabrics woven in standardized lengths. PIECE-WORK, work paid according to the amount done, not according to the time spent in doing it. PIECE (2), *v.t.* to join, mend, unite, *esp.* fasten together the threads in spinning; **to p. out,** to extend by the addition of a p. or pieces; **to p. together,** to fit together into a whole; **to p. up,** to patch. PIECER, *n.* one who pieces, *esp.* one employed in joining the threads in spinning. [LL.].

PIECE DE RESISTANCE, pièce de résistance [pyäs-de-rā-zēs-tah(ng)s′], *n.* chief item, principal feature, *esp.* of a meal. [Fr.].

PIECEMEAL (1) [pēs′mēl], *adv.* by pieces, bit by bit, a little at a time. PIECEMEAL (2), *adj.* made, done, p. [PIECE (1) and OE.].

PIED [pid], *adj.* marked with two contrasting colours, variegated. [PIE (2)].

PIER [pēer], *n.* column or mass of stone or brick for taking the thrust of an arch or the span of a bridge, or for supporting the roof of a building; supporting wall between windows and doors; mole or breakwater; jetty projecting into the sea, used as a landing-stage and as a promenade. PIER-GLASS, long narrow mirror, formerly set between windows. [LL.].

PIERCE [pēers], *v.t.* to penetrate, break through the surface and enter; thrust a pointed instrument into, make a hole in; be seen, heard or felt through; affect deeply, stab; *v.i.* to penetrate, make a hole. [OFr.] PIERCING [pēer′sing], *adj.* keen, sharp, penetrating with force.

PIERIAN [pi-ēer′i-an], *adj.* pertaining to Pieria or to the Muses. [L. *Pierius* pertaining to *Pieria,* mountain in Thrace, where the Muses were worshipped].

PIERRETTE [pēer-ret′], *n.* female pierrot. [Fr.].

PIERROT [pēer′ō], *n.* character in French pantomime; one of a group of entertainers dressed in loose-fitting white clothes. [Fr.].

PIETA [pyä′tah], *n.* representation of the Virgin Mary with the dead body of Jesus resting in her lap. [It.].

PIETISM [pi′e-tizm], *n.* religious devotion, piety; hypocritical cant, uncontrolled religious fervour.

PIETIST [pi′e-tist], *n.* one of a group of seventeenth-century Lutheran reformers who began a religious revival; one who attaches supreme importance **to** piety and to emotional religious fervour.

PIETY [pi′e-ti], *n.* godliness, devotion to God and faithful observance of religious principles and practices; respect for filial bonds and duties. [L.].

PIFFLE [pi′fl], *n.* nonsense, rubbish. [Uncert.].

PIG (1) [pig], *n.* swine or hog; member of a class of hoofed mammals with snouts; *(fig.)* greedy, ill-mannered, objectionable person; oblong mass of unforged metal; **to buy a p. in a poke,** to buy something without knowing how much it is really worth. PIG (2) *(pres.pt.* PIGGING, *pret.* and *p.pt.* PIGGED), *v.t. and i.* to bring forth pigs; crowd together like pigs; **to p.** it, to live like a p. [ME.].

PIGEON [pi′jin], *n.* wild or tame bird of the dove family; *(slang)* person easily swindled; **clay p.,** clay disk thrown up into the air from a trap, to be shot at; **p. post,** system of letter-carrying using homing pigeons. PIGEON-BREASTED, having a breast shaped like that of a p. PIGEON-HEARTED,

---

The accent ′ after a syllable = stress (u-pon′). The mark ‾ over a vowel = length (ā in made; ō in bone).

timid. PIGEON-HOUSE, -LOFT, dovecot. PIGEON-TOED, with turned-in toes. [OFr.].

PIGEON ENGLISH, see PIDGIN.

PIGEON-HOLE (1) [pi'jn-hōl], *n.* entrance in a dovecot; small recess or open compartment in a desk etc. for keeping documents etc. in order. PIGEON-HOLE (2), *v.t.* to file or put in a p.; put aside for future reference; classify, arrange under the proper headings.

PIGGERY [pi'ge-ri], *n.* enclosure where pigs are kept, pigsty; (*fig.*) untidy dwelling.

PIGHEADED [pig-he'did], *adj.* stupidly obstinate.

PIG-IRON [pig'īern], *n.* iron from a blast-furnace cast in ingots or pigs.

PIGLET [pig'let], *n.* young pig.

PIGMENT [pig'ment], *n.* dry colour powder for paint; paint; colouring matter, *esp.* the natural colouring matter of a plant or animal. [L.].

PIGMENTATION [pig-men-tā'shn], *n.* coloration due to the presence of pigment in the tissue.

PIGMY, see PYGMY.

PIGNORATE [pig'ne-rāt], *v.t.* to pledge, mortgage, give as security. [L.].

PIGNUT [pig'nut], *n.* the earth-nut.

PIGSKIN [pig'skin], *n.* leather made from the skin of the pig; (*slang*) the saddle.

PIGSTICKING [pig'sti-king], *n.* hunting the wild boar with a spear on horseback.

PIGSTY [pig'stī], *n.* pen in which pigs are kept; untidy room or dwelling.

PIGTAIL [pig'tāl], *n.* plait of hair worn hanging down the back; small roll of twisted tobacco.

PIKE (1) [pīk], *n.* weapon consisting of a long wooden shaft with a pointed flat steel head. [Fr.].

PIKE (2), *n.* large freshwater fish. [ME.].

PIKE (3), *n.* toll-bar or toll-gate; toll paid at such a gate; turnpike road. [(TURN)PIKE].

PIKELET [pīk'let], *n.* crumpet, muffin. [Wel.].

PIKESTAFF [pīk'stahf], *n.* shaft of a pike; **plain as a p.,** perfectly clear.

PILASTER [pi-las'ter], *n.* square pillar, projecting from the face of a wall. [MedL.].

PILAU, PILAW, PILAF(F) [pi-law', pe-lahf'], *n.* Oriental dish of rice boiled with fowl, meat or fish and flavoured with spices. [Pers., Turk.].

PILCH [pilch], *n.* infant's wrapper or drawers over the napkin. [OE. from L.].

PILCHARD [pil'cherd], *n.* small sea-fish of the herring family. [Unkn.].

PILE (1) [pīl], *n.* heap, mass or collection of objects stacked up in more or less orderly fashion; heaped-up mass of combustibles on which a corpse is burnt; large imposing building; (*slang*) large amount of money, fortune; **galvanic or voltaic p.,** (*elect.*) series of plates so arranged as to produce a current of electricity; **atomic p.,** (*phys.*) apparatus in which fissionable material generates energy. PILE (2), *v.t.* to form or arrange in a heap or p., stack up; **to p. up,** to accumulate, amass; **to p. on,** to intensify, add to. [L.].

PILE (3), *n.* pointed stake, large stake driven into the bed of a river or marshy ground as support for the foundations of a building etc.; iron or concrete pillar used for the same purpose. PILE (4), *v.t.* to drive piles into; support with piles. [OE. from L.].

PILE (5), *n.* nap on the surface of woven fabrics such as velvet, carpet etc. [L.].

PILE-DRIVER [pīl'drī-ver], *n.* machine for driving down piles; (*coll.*) powerful blow.

PILES [pīlz], *n.(pl.)* haemorrhoids, tumours formed by the dilatation of the veins of the lower rectum. [L.].

PILEWORT [pīl'wert], *n.* the lesser celandine.

PILFER [pil'fer], *v.t. and i.* to steal on a small scale, practise petty theft. [OFr.].

PILGRIM [pil'grim], *n.* (*poet., archaic*) traveller, wayfarer; one who makes a journey to a holy place or shrine from religious motives; **P. Fathers,** band of Puritans who sailed to North America and founded the colony of New Plymouth in 1620. [ME. from L.].

PILGRIMAGE [pil'gri-mij], *n.* journey to some holy place or shrine; visit to some place revered because of its associations; (*fig.*) journey of human life. [*Prec.*].

PILL [pil], *n.* medicinal substance in the form of a small ball or pellet to be swallowed whole; (*slang*) ball used for games; **bitter p.,** something unpleasant which must be suffered; **to gild the p.,** to make the unpleasant more palatable. [L.].

PILLAGE (1) [pi'lij], *n.* act of plundering or robbing; spoil, plunder taken from an enemy in war. PILLAGE

(2), *v.t.* to plunder, loot; take as spoil or booty. [Fr.].

PILLAR [pi'ler], *n.* single slender upright structure used as a support, or standing alone as a monument or ornament; anything resembling a pillar in shape or function; (*fig.*) prop, supporter, highly important member; foundation, principle or thing upon which something is based; **from p. to post,** from place to place. [ME.].

PILLAR-BOX [pi'ler-boks], *n.* hollow pillar provided with a slit near the top into which letters may be posted.

PILL-BOX [pil'boks], *n.* small round box in which pills are kept; (*milit.*) small concrete blockhouse or shelter resembling a pill-box in shape; hat of this shape.

PILLION [pil'yun], *n.* pad, seat or cushion behind the saddle for a second rider to ride on a horse; similar seat behind the driver on a motor-bicycle; **to ride p.,** to travel on this seat. [Ir.].

PILLORY (1) [pi'le-ri], *n.* wooden frame on posts, with movable boards and holes in them, through which the head and hands of an offender were put by way of punishment; (*fig.*) general ridicule and contempt. PILLORY (2), *v.t.* to punish with the pillory; expose to general abuse and public ridicule. [OFr.].

PILLOW (1) [pi'lō], *n.* cushion filled with feathers, down or other soft material, used as a support for the head when lying in bed; any object used for a similar purpose; pad. PILLOW-CASE, -SLIP, removable linen or cotton covering slipped over a p. PILLOW (2), *v.t.* to rest or lay on for support; serve as a p.; bolster up with pillows; *v.i.* to rest as on a pillow. [OE. from L.].

PILLWORT [pil'wert], *n.* plant of the genus *Pilularia*. [PILL and WORT].

PILOSE [pī'lōs], *adj.* hairy, covered with hair. [L.].

PILOT (1) [pī'lot], *n.* person who steers a ship, *esp.* one licensed to take charge of a vessel where navigation is difficult; (*aeron.*) person who navigates aircraft; guide, director of one's course. PILOT-BALLOON, balloon sent up to reveal the direction of the wind. PILOT-BOAT, boat used to take a p. to a vessel he has to navigate. PILOT-CLOTH, stout blue cloth used for greatcoats, as worn by pilots. PILOT-FISH, small fish allied to the horse-mackerel. PILOT-JACKET, pea-jacket. PILOT (2), *v.t.* to act as p., direct the course of, steer, navigate; also *fig.* PILOTAGE, *n.* act of piloting; pilot's fee. [It.].

PILOT LIGHT [pī'lot-līt], *n.* small gas-jet kept burning to ignite a geyser etc.; light used to illuminate the dial of a radio set etc., and to show that the current has been switched on.

PILOT OFFICER [pī'lot-o-fi-ser], *n.* officer of the Royal Air Force of equivalent rank to a second lieutenant in the Army.

PILOUS [pī'lŏŏs], *adj.* hairy, covered with or consisting of hair, like hair. [L.].

PILSENER [pils'ner], *n.* kind of lager beer. [*Pilsen,* Czechoslovakia, where made].

PILULE [pi'lyŏŏl], *n.* small pill. [L.].

PIMENTO [pi-men'tō], *n.* Jamaica pepper, allspice; tree from which this is obtained. [Span. from L.].

PIMP (1) [pimp], *n.* procurer. PIMP (2), *v.i.* to pander, act as p. [Uncert.].

PIMPERNEL [pim'per-nel], *n.* an annual plant bearing scarlet, blue or white flowers. [OFr.].

PIMPLE [pim'pl], *n.* small rounded inflamed pustule on the skin. [Unkn.].

PIN (1) [pin], *n.* short, thin, rigid, pointed piece of wire with a projecting head used for fastening or securing parts of garments, papers etc.; small round piece of metal or wood, usually pointed and used for fastening things together, as a peg or handle etc., peg, bolt; anything shaped like, or having the function of, a pin; (*pl.*) (*coll.*) legs; cask holding four-and-a-half gallons; **pins and needles,** tingling sensation in the limbs when coming to life again after numbness; **not to care two pins,** not to care at all. PIN (2) (*pres.pt.* PINNING, *pret. and p.pt.* PINNED), *v.t.* to fasten, attach with a p.; pierce with a p.; fasten, peg; hold fast so that one cannot move; enclose, impound; (*fig.*) place or stake entirely (of faith, hope etc.); **to p. down,** to bind to. [OE. from L.].

PINAFORE [pi'na-faw(r)], *n.* sleeveless overall or long apron worn over the dress. [PIN (2) and AFORE].

PINCE-NEZ [pa(ng)s-nā, pa(ng)s-nā'], *n.* pair of eyeglasses which clip on the nose with springs. [Fr.].

PINCERS [pin'serz], *n.* tool consisting of a pair of pivoted jaws which can be pressed together to grip

---

ōō is pronounced as in f*oo*d; ŏŏ as in h*oo*d; th as in *th*ink; TH as in *th*at; zh as in a*z*ure.   ~ = related to.

objects tightly, by means of two handles working as levers. [ME.].

PINCH (1) [pinch], *v.t.* to squeeze, nip, grip forcibly between the thumb and finger or between two hard objects, press painfully upon; distress, cause hardship and suffering, afflict so as to cause a drawn, shrunken appearance; (*slang*) steal; arrest; *v.i.* to press painfully upon some part of the skin; live frugally; **to p. back**, to nip off part of (a shoot). PINCH (2), *n.* a nip, squeeze, compression of a portion of the skin by means of the tip of the thumb and finger; as much as can be taken between thumb and finger, small amount; (*fig.*) distress, straits, restricting discomforting influence; **at a p.**, as a last resort, if need be. PINCHER, *n.* one who, or that which, pinches, (*pl.*) instrument for gripping tightly. [ONFr. from OFr.].

PINCHBECK (1) [pinch'bek], *n.* alloy of copper and zinc, used for cheap jewellery. PINCHBECK (2), *adj.* spurious, counterfeit. [C. *Pinchbeck*, the supposed inventor].

PINCUSHION [pin'kŏŏ-shn], *n.* small firm cushion in which to stick pins ready for use.

PINE (1) [pīn], *n.* genus of cone-bearing evergreen trees having clusters of their needle-shaped leaves; timber of this tree; pineapple. [OE. from L.].

PINE (2), *v.i.* to waste away through anxiety, longing or illness, languish; long (for) eagerly. [OE.].

PINEAL [pī'ni-al], *adj.* shaped like a pine-cone; **p. gland**, small cone-shaped body situated behind the third ventricle of the brain. [L.].

PINEAPPLE [pīn'a-pl], *n.* tropical plant yielding a fruit covered with a hard prickly rind, and like a pine-cone in shape; fruit of this plant; (*slang*) Mills bomb.

PINE-CONE [pīn'kōn], *n.* woody cone-shaped structure containing the seeds of the pine tree.

PIN-FEATHER [pin'fe-тher], *n.* small feather not fully formed.

PINFOLD [pin'fōld], *n.* pound, place in which stray cattle are confined. [OE.].

PING (1) [ping], *n.* sharp sudden ringing sound as of a bullet striking a hard surface. PING (2), *v.i.* to emit a p. [Echoic].

PING-PONG [ping'pong], *n.* (*coll.*) table-tennis. [Echoic].

PIN-HEAD [pin'hed], *n.* small, protruding head of a pin; anything resembling this.

PINION (1) [pin'yun], *n.* joint of a bird's wing farthest away from the body; one of the outer wingfeathers; (*poet.*) wing. PINION (2), *v.t.* to cut off the outermost joint of one wing of, prevent from flying, confine by binding the wings of; bind the arms of closely to the sides. [OFr.].

PINION (3), *n.* small cog-wheel or cogged axle whose teeth work in the teeth of a larger one. [~Fr.].

PINK (1) [pingk], *n.* plant of the genus *Dianthus*, yielding fragrant white, p. and crimson flowers; highest degree of excellence, height; pale-red colour; foxhunter's coat; (*coll.*) a mild socialist; **in the p.**, feeling perfectly healthy. PINK (2), *adj.* pale-red in colour; (*coll.*) mildly socialist. [Uncert.].

PINK (3), *v.t.* (of cloth, leather etc.) to pierce the edge of with small holes, figures etc., so as to form a decorative pattern, cut the edge in a zigzag to prevent fraying; stab, pierce, wound; *v.i.* (*motoring*) to work unevenly, causing a metallic knocking sound to be heard. [LGerm.].

PINK-EYE [pingk'ī], *n.* variety of potato; a contagious disease in horses; a form of conjunctivitis.

PIN-MONEY [pin'mu-ni], *n.* money received as gifts or wages by one who is not compelled to work for a living, and used to provide small personal luxuries etc.

PINNACE [pi'nas], *n.* warship's boat or small boat belonging to a larger vessel, and used for taking people to and from the shore. [Fr.].

PINNACLE (1) [pi'na-kl], *n.* slender turret, ornamental pointed top surmounting a roof, parapet or buttress; small peak; (*fig.*) highest point, culmination. PINNACLE (2), *v.t.* to ornament with pinnacles; set upon a p.; act as p. to. [LL.].

PINNATE(D), PENNATE [pi'nāt(-id)], *adj.* (*bot.*) branching like a feather; (*zool.*) arranged on each side of an axis in the manner of a feather. PINNATELY, *adv.* (*bot.*) in p. fashion.

PINPOINT (1) [pin'point], *n.* point of a pin; (*aeron.*) point on a map representing a target, droppingground etc. PINPOINT (2), *v.t.* (*aeron.*) to locate with the greatest precision.

PIN-PRICK (1) [pin'prik], *n.* tiny hole made by a pin;

(*fig.*) small thing causing irritation. PIN-PRICK (2), *v.t.* to afflict with constant minor irritations.

PIN-STRIPED [pin'strīpt], *adj.* bearing a series of narrow stripes no thicker than a pin.

PINT [pīnt], *n.* measure of capacity equal to an eighth of a gallon. [Fr.].

PIN-TABLE [pin'tā-bl], *n.* game of skill or chance in the form of a penny-in-the-slot machine, in which balls must pass pins stuck in a flat surface.

PIN-TAIL [pin'tāl], *n.* a sea-duck, the male of which has a pointed tail; pointed-tailed variety of goose.

PINTLE [pin'tl], *n.* vertical projecting pin, *esp.* one used as a pivot. [OE.].

PIN-TUCK [pin'tuk], *n.* small ornamental tuck.

PIONEER (1) [pī-o-nēer'], *n.* (*milit.*) *orig.* foot soldier who cleared obstructions and made a road ahead of an army; now, second-line soldier whose main duty is clearing and elementary construction behind the lines; one who takes the lead in anything, and prepares the way for others, one who explores new fields of activity or colonizes unknown lands, earliest exponent of something; **Royal P. Corps**, corps of the British Army employed to carry out road repairs, building etc. PIONEER (2), *v.t.* to lead the way in, initiate; *v.i.* to act as p., undertake p. work. [Fr.].

PIOUS [pī'ŏŏs], *adj.* devout, godly, sincere in and observant of one's religious duties; (*archaic*) having due respect and affection for one's parents and relatives; **p. fraud**, fraud practised under pretence of religion or some laudable object; **p. hope**, prediction based more on wish than on probability. [L.].

PIP (1) [pip], *n.* a disease in poultry; **the p.**, (*slang*) fit of depression, sense of boredom mingled with annoyance. [MDu. from LL.].

PIP (2), *n.* seed of an apple, orange or other similar fruit. [OFr.].

PIP (3), *n.* one of the spots on playing cards, dice or dominoes; (*coll.*) star worn by army officers as a mark of rank. [Uncert.].

PIP (4), *n.* short shrill note repeated as a time-signal in broadcasting, and in giving the precise time over the telephone. [Echoic].

PIP (5) (*pres.pt.* **pipping**, *pret.* and *p.pt.* **pipped**), *v.t.* (*slang*) to hit with a shot or other missile; defeat, thwart; blackball; fail; *v.i.* (*slang*) to fail in an examination; **to p. out**, (*coll.*) to die. [Uncert.].

PIPE (1) [pīp], *n.* musical wind-instrument in the form of a tube pierced with holes which are stopped by the fingers to produce different notes; boatswain's whistle; (*pl.*) bagpipes; sound made by a pipe, shrill call of a bird, thin voice of a child; short thin tube with a bowl at one end into which tobacco is packed; quantity contained in the bowl of a pipe; long cylindrical tube for conveying water, gas, steam etc.; each of the tubes in which the sound is produced in an organ; tubular channel in an animal body, *esp.* that by which air passes from the mouth to the lungs; measure of wine, a cask containing 105 imperial gallons. PIPE (2), *v.t.* to play (a tune) on a p.; call by means of a boatswain's whistle; ornament with piping; provide with pipes, lay pipes in; *v.i.* to play on a p.; speak in a shrill treble voice, whistle; (of a bird) utter shrill notes; **to p. up**, to begin to speak or p.; **to p. down**, (*slang*) to make less noise, make oneself heard less. [OE.].

PIPECLAY (1) [pīp'klā], *n.* fine, white, plastic clay used in making tobacco-pipes and for whitening leather and military equipment; (*fig.*) inordinate attention to details of dress in a regiment. PIPECLAY (2), *v.t.* to whiten with p.

PIPE-DREAM [pīp'drēm], *n.* wishful day-dream such as may be indulged in while smoking.

PIPE-LINE (1) [pīp'līn], *n.* line of pipes for conveying oil or water. PIPE-LINE (2), *v.t.* to transport by means of a p.

PIPE-OFFICE [pīp'o-fis], *n.* (*hist.*) ancient office in the Court of Exchequer, the duties of which are now merged with those of the Remembrancer.

PIPER [pī'per], *n.* one who plays upon the pipes, *esp.* the bagpipes; name given to several varieties of fish, *esp.* the gurnard; **to pay the p.**, to bear the cost of anything.

PIPETTE [pi-pet'], *n.* glass tube, swollen in the middle, used for transferring liquids in small quantities. [Fr.].

PIPING (1) [pī'ping], *n.* act of one who pipes; sound produced when playing a pipe; thin, treble voice, or song of a bird; group or arrangement of pipes for conveying water, gas etc.; ornamental trimming

---

The accent ' after a syllable = stress (u-pon'). The mark ⁻ over a vowel = length (ā in made; ō in bone).

resembling a pipe. PIPING (2), *adj.* shrill and thin, as of a pipe; **p. hot,** extremely hot.

PIPIT [pi'pit], *n.* a passerine bird, related to the wagtails. [Echoic].

PIPKIN [pip'kin], *n.* small earthenware pot or pan, used as a cooking utensil. [Unkn.].

PIPPIN [pi'pin], *n.* one of various kinds of dessert apples. [OFr.].

PIP-SQUEAK [pip'skwēk], *n.* (*slang*) small high-velocity shell; mean or paltry thing or person; two-stroke motor-cycle.

PIQUANCY [pē'kan-si], *n.* quality of being piquant, sharpness, pungency.

PIQUANT [pē'kant], *adj.* sharp, pungent, pleasantly biting to the taste; agreeably stimulating, whetting the appetite or curiosity. [Fr.].

PIQUE (1) [pēk], *v.t.* to offend, irritate, wound the pride of; stimulate, whet (curiosity etc.); *v. reflex.* have a good opinion of one's ability. PIQUE (2), *n.* petulant anger or resentful irritation arising from wounded feelings, huff. [Fr.].

PIQUE (3), *n.* (*piquet*) the scoring of thirty points before the opponent has opened his score. PIQUE (4), *v.t. and i.* (*piquet*) to score a p. against.

PIQUE, piqué [pē-kā'], *n.* stout ribbed cotton material patterned in the weaving. [Fr.].

PIQUET [pi-ket'], *n.* card-game for two players played with thirty-two cards. [Fr.].

PIRACY [pīer'a-si], *n.* occupation, act or crime of robbing on the high seas; act of a similar kind. [Gk.].

PIRATE (1) [pīer'at], *n.* person engaged in robbery upon the high seas; ship used by sea robbers or marauders; one who infringes the law of copyright; (*radio*) person operating a radio receiving or transmission set without a licence. PIRATE (2), *v.t.* to plunder, rob (a ship); publish or print (a book etc.) for profit without leave from the author or owner of the copyright. [Gk.].

PIRATICAL [pī-ra'ti-kal], *adj.* pertaining to a pirate, addicted to piracy.

PIROUETTE (1) [pi-rōo-et'], *n.* dancing step performed by spinning round on the tips of the toes. PIROUETTE (2), *v.i.* to perform a p. [Fr.].

PISCATORIAL [pis-ka-taw'ri-al], *adj.* relating to fishing.

PISCATORY [pis'ka-te-ri], *adj.* piscatorial.

PISCES [pi'sēz], *n.* (*pl.*) twelfth sign of the Zodiac, the Fishes. [L.].

PISCICULTURE [pi'si-kul-tyōor], *n.* artificial culture and rearing of fish. [L.].

PISCINA [pi-sē'nah], *n.* (*eccles.*) basin near the altar into which the priest empties the water used in the service. [L.].

PISCINE [pi'sin], *adj.* relating to fishes.

PISCIVOROUS [pi-si've-rōos], *adj.* living by, feeding on, fishes. [L.].

PISE, pisé [pē'zā], *n.* stiff earth or clay hardened between boards and left standing to form walls. [Fr.].

PISIFORM [pi'zi-fawm], *adj.* (*bot.*) having the form of a pea. [L.].

PISTACHIO [pis-tah'shi-ō], *n.* nut of *Pistacia vera*; pale-green colour of this nut. [Gk.].

PISTIL [pis'til], *n.* (*bot.*) female seed-bearing part of the flower. PISTILLARY [pis-ti'la-ri], *adj.* (*bot.*) relating to, growing on, the p. PISTILLATE, *adj.* (*bot.*) having a p. [L.].

PISTOL (1) [pis'tol], *n.* small fire-arm adapted for holding in one hand. PISTOL (2) (*pres.pt.* PISTOLLING, *pret. and p.pt.* PISTOLLED), *v.i.* to shoot with a p. [It.].

PISTON [pis'ton], *n.* (*mech.*) in a machine, a sliding circular plate or short cylinder, which is fitted into a cylinder and which by moving causes pressure or which pressure causes to move. PISTON-ROD rod connecting the p. with other parts of the machine; (*mus.*) valve of a wind-instrument. [L.].

PIT (1) [pit], *n.* deep hole in the earth; hole in the ground made for a purpose by artificial means; abyss; grave; arena for cock-fighting contests; rear section of an auditorium as distinct from the stalls; natural depression in the human or animal body, hollow; hole from which the underside of a motor-car can be inspected or overhauled; **the P.,** hell. PIT (2) (*pres.pt.* PITTING, *pret. and p.pt.* PITTED), *v.t.* to mark with hollows or small depressions; place, store or press into hollows; **to p. against,** to oppose to. [OE.].

PIT (3), *n.* a card-game.

PITAPAT (1) [pi'ta-pat], *adv.* with a series of light taps or beats quickly following one another, in a

flutter, with palpitation. PITAPAT (2), *n.* series of light, quick steps or taps. [Imitative].

PITCH (1) [pich], *n.* thick black substance obtained by boiling down tar, used in the manufacture of varnish and for preserving wood exposed to the weather. PITCH-BLACK, -DARK, *adj.* black, dark, as p. PITCH (2), *v.t.* to cover or smear with p. [OE. from L.].

PITCH (3), *v.t.* to throw, hurl, toss, particularly with a fork; throw headlong; throw at an objective; set up in a marked-out position, as a tent or stall; (*cricket*) set up the two wickets in readiness for a game; deliver a ball so that it falls at a particular point between the wickets; (*mus.*) arrange the tune in a specific key; *v.i.* to encamp, settle down; fall headlong; plunge and rock from head to stern, as a ship; **to p. into,** (*coll.*) to attack fast and furiously. PITCH (4), *n.* act of pitching or tossing; distance covered by an object which has been pitched; habitual place or station of a person or object; point of elevation or degree of height; degree, height, size, limit; angle or degree of inclination, measured rise of a slope; (*cricket*) prepared turf between the wickets; point where the ball delivered by the bowler hits the ground; (*mech.*) distance between the apices of two cogs on a wheel or saw; longitudinal distance travelled in one revolution of a screw, worm or propeller; (*mus.*) frequency of a note. [ME.].

PITCH-AND-TOSS [pich-and-tos'], *n.* game in which the person who pitches his coin nearest a mark is the first entitled to spin for the coins so thrown.

PITCHBLENDE [pich'blend], *n.* a black ore, an oxide of uranium yielding radium. [Germ.].

PITCHER (1) [pi'cher], *n.* large earthen jug for holding liquid, having two handles like ears. [MedL.].

PITCHER (2), *n.* person who pitches, particularly a player who delivers the ball at baseball; tool for making holes in the ground; paving stone.

PITCHER-PLANT [pi'cher-plahnt], *n.* American insectivorous plant with pitcher-shaped leaves.

PITCHFORK (1) [pich'fawk], *n.* long-handled fork having two curved prongs used in lifting and pitching hay or sheaves of grain. PITCHFORK (2), *v.t.* to throw with a p.; (*fig.*) thrust unceremoniously.

PITCH-PINE [pich'pīn], *n.* the Norwegian or red pine; the American tree *Pinus palustris.*

PITCHPIPE [pich'pīp], *n.* tuning pipe sounding the pitch for wind-instruments or for unaccompanied singers.

PITCHY [pi'chi], *adj.* resembling, or mixed with, pitch, black, dark.

PITEOUS [pi'ti-ōos], *adj.* that may excite pity, deserving compassion; lamentable, pitiful; paltry. [OFr.].

PITFALL [pit'fawl], *n.* pit slightly covered so that an animal may fall into it, concealed trap; (*fig.*) unseen danger.

PITH [pith], *n.* soft, spongy, organic tissue at the centre of plant stems; stringy parts and white underskin of an orange; marrow in the bones of an animal; spinal cord; (*fig.*) essential part, concentrated strength; importance, weight. [OE.].

PITHEAD [pit'hed], *n.* entrance to a coalpit; **p. price,** price of coal at the p.

PITHECOID [pi'thi-koid], *adj.* ape-like. [Gk.].

PITHY [pi'thi], *adj.* relating to, containing, or abounding with, pith; (*fig.*) concise, pointed, forcible.

PITIABLE [pi'ti-a-bl], *adj.* deserving pity, miserable; worthy of contempt.

PITIFUL [pi'ti-fool], *adj.* full of pity, compassionate; miserable; contemptible.

PITILESS [pi'ti-les], *adj.* feeling no pity, merciless, hard-hearted, ruthless.

PIT-PROP [pit'prop], *n.* (*mining*) prop of wood used as a temporary support for coal seams when undercut.

PITTANCE [pi'tans], *n.* small inadequate allowance; small portion. [ME.].

PITTITE [pi'tit], *n.* (*coll.*) frequenter of the pit in theatres.

PITUITARY [pi-tyōo'i-ta-ri], *adj.* secreting mucus; **p. gland,** endocrine gland at the base of the brain having a metabolic function. [L.].

PITUITRIN [pi-tyōo'i-trin], *adj.* hormone secreted by the pituitary gland.

PITY (1) [pi'ti], *n.* human emotion arising out of a capacity to feel with another, experiencing another's grief or misery, and promoting desire to provide help; compassion; a matter of regret. PITY (2), *v.t.* to feel p. for, commiserate with; (*fig.*) despise. [OFr.].

PITYRIASIS [pi ti-rī'a-sis], *n.* (*med.*) a chronic

ōo is pronounced as in food; ŏo as in hood; th as in think; TH as in that; zh as in azure. ~ = related to.

inflammation of the skin characterized by flaking. [Gk.].

PIVOT (1) [pi'vot], *n.* point on which something turns; (*milit.*) soldier at the flank round whom a company wheels. PIVOT (2), *v.i.* to turn as though on a p.; hinge, turn on a p. PIVOTAL, *adj.* relating to a p.; (*fig.*) of prime importance. [Fr.].

PIX, see PYX.

PIXY, PIXIE [pik'si], *n.* fairy, elf. [Swed.].

PIZZICATO [pit-si-kah'tō], *adv.* (*mus.*) with the finger-tips instead of the bow. [It.].

PLACABLE [pla'ka-bl], *adj.* able to be appeased, willing to forgive. [L.].

PLACARD (1) [pla'kahd], *n.* large-sized sheet of paper on which is written, printed or painted a notice for public display. PLACARD (2) [pla'kahd, pla-kahd'], *v.t.* to affix a p. to, provide with a p.; advertise by medium of a p. [OFr.].

PLACATE [pla-kāt'], *v.t.* to soothe out of anger or irritation, appease, pacify. PLACATION, *n.* appeasement, conciliation. PLACATORY, *adj.* tending to bring about placation. [L.].

PLACE (1) [plās], *n.* any part or specific area in space; a particular locality, definite social unit of habitation, village, town etc.; space occupied by one person, *esp.* at a table or in a vehicle, seat; residence, house; station in life, social class, position, in regard to one's associates; passage in a book; (in racing) position in the first three finishers. PLACE (2), *v.t.* to put or set in a particular p.; arrange for a commercial matter to be dealt with; fix; invest; put out at interest, lend; recognize; (in racing) judge a horse to finish in the first three. [ME. from Gk.].

PLACEBO [pla-sē'bō], *n.* (*eccles.*) introductory antiphon of the vespers for the dead; (*med.*) medicine having no real curative power other than psychological. [L.].

PLACE-KICK [plās'kik], *n.* (*Rugby football*) a kick at the ball taken by a player after a try has been scored, the ball being held over the mark by another player.

PLACENTA [pla-sen'tah], *n.* (*anat.*) protective tissue, discarded after birth, surrounding the foetus in the womb; (*bot.*) part of a plant feeding the ovules. [Gk.].

PLACER [plā'ser], *n.* an auriferous gravel. [L.].

PLACET [plā'set], *n.* affirmative vote given on a motion; **non p.**, negative vote. [L.].

PLACID [pla'sid], *adj.* having an unruffled disposition, gentle, quiet, serene.

PLACKET [pla'ket], *n.* slit where a skirt or petticoat is fastened. [Uncert.].

PLAGAL [plā'gal], *adj.* (*mus.*) ranging between the dominant and the octave. [Gk.].

PLAGE [plahzh], *n.* promenade beach at a fashionable seaside resort. [Fr.].

PLAGIARISM [plā'ji-a-rizm], *n.* act of plagiarizing; matter plagiarized; attempt to establish as one's own another person's literary work. [L.].

PLAGIARIST [plā'ji-a-rist], *n.* person who has plagiarized; copyist without acknowledgment.

PLAGIARIZE [plā'ji-a-rīz], *v.t.* to adopt and attempt to pass off as one's own the writings of another.

PLAGUE (1) [plāg], *n.* dreadful pestilence, fatal disease; terrible calamity; (*coll.*) any troublesome and persistent person or recurring situation; (*fig.*) superabundance. PLAGUE (2), *v.t.* to afflict with a p., infest with a sudden and widespread calamity; harass, be persistently troublesome to. PLAGUY, *adj.* troublesome, vexatious. [ME. from L.].

PLAGUE-SPOT [plāg'spot], *n.* spot on the flesh left by the plague; place or district harbouring disease; (*fig.*) haunt of evil-doers.

PLAICE [plās], *n.* an edible flatfish. [ME. from Gk.].

PLAID [plad], *n.* woollen garment of Scottish origin generally of a checked fabric, to wrap round the body; a tartan. [Uncert.].

PLAIN (1) [plān], *adj.* flat, smooth, level; having no ornament or pattern, simple; easy to perceive by the senses, distinctly visible, clearly heard; easy to understand; straightforward, unaffected, frank; blunt, ordinary-looking, having a somewhat ugly face. PLAIN (2), *adv.* clearly, distinctly. PLAIN (3), *n.* wide area of level land or open field. [L.].

PLAIN-DEALING (1) [plān-dē'ling], *n.* frankness in word and deed, particularly in commercial association. PLAIN-DEALING (2), *adj.* behaving with frankness and sincerity, honest.

PLAINSONG [plān'song], *n.* form of modal music consisting of a chant sung in unison, with the accents placed according to verbal emphasis, Gregorian chant.

PLAINT [plānt], *n.* lamentation, complaint; (*leg.*) complaint setting forth the cause of the action in a formal accusation. [L.].

PLAINTIFF [plān'tif], *n.* (*leg.*) person who sues another called the defendant. [OFr.].

PLAINTIVE [plān'tiv], *adj.* expressive of sorrow or sadness, mournful; harping on miseries. [OFr.].

PLAIT (1) [plat], *n.* combination of three or more interlaced strands forming a single length, particularly of hair, braid; fold of material creased at the bend, pleat. PLAIT (2), *v.t.* to interlace in the form of a p., braid; pleat. [ME. from L.].

PLAN (1) [plan], *n.* a drawing on a plane surface, proportionate design of a projected or completed structure or building; scheme; project set out on paper, proposed method of carrying it out. PLAN (2) (*pres.pt.* PLANNING, *pret. and p.pt.* PLANNED), *v.t.* to make a p., draw up plans of a projected scheme, showing all its details and the method of approach; work out a project in the head, scheme. [L.].

PLANCHETTE [plahn-shet'], *n.* small, thin board mounted on two wheels, with a pencil acting as a third support, which is supposed to respond without deliberate guidance to hands placed upon it, writing spiritualistic messages. [Fr.].

PLANE (1) [plān], *n.* tool used in smoothing wood. PLANE (2), *v.t.* to smooth, make level by means of a p. [LL.].

PLANE (3), *n.* tree of the genus *Platanus.* [Fr. from Gk.].

PLANE (4), *n.* aeroplane; wing of an aeroplane. PLANE (5), *v.i.* to glide through the air in an aeroplane with the engine switched off. [(AERO)PLANE].

PLANE (6), *n.* accurately flattened surface; stage, level, degree; **p. geometry**, manipulation of figures on a p. surface. PLANE (7), *adj.* having a perfectly flat surface. [L.].

PLANET [pla'net], *n.* celestial body which revolves in an orbit round the sun. [ME. from Gk.].

PLANETARIUM [pla-ne-tāer'i-um], *n.* model astronomical machine which represents the motions of the planets. [LL.].

PLANETARY [pla'ne-ta-ri], *adj.* of, relating to, consisting of or produced by, planets; having the characteristics of a planet, erratic or revolving. [L.].

PLANGENT [plan'jent], *adj.* beating with noise, as of a wave, resounding in great splashes of sound. [L.].

PLANI-, *pref.* level, flat. [L.].

PLANISH [pla'nish], *v.t.* to polish, smooth by hammering. [OFr.].

PLANK (1) [plangk], *n.* long strip of sawn timber usually not smaller than two inches thick by ten inches wide. PLANK (2), *v.t.* to cover, build a floor, with planks closely fitted in rows; (*slang*) **to p. down,** to put down in concrete form, particularly cash. [ME from LL.].

PLANKTON [plangk'ton], *n.*(*pl.*) (*biol.*) general word for organisms floating or drifting at various depths in seas and rivers. [Gk.].

PLANO-, *pref.* flat, level. [L.].

PLANT (1) [plahnt], *n.* any vegetable organism which can feed on substances collected from the soil and air; small green vegetable organism, as distinguished from a tree; total equipment of a factory; complete system of machinery. PLANT (2), *v.t.* to set in the soil as a necessary condition of intended growth; set out seeds, provide with plants; place in the ground to a depth which prevents toppling; place in position firmly; settle, particularly as colonizers; **to p. on,** (*slang*) to conceal on another's person or premises stolen or incriminating property. PLANT (3), *n.* (*slang*) swindle, put-up job. [OE. from L.].

PLANTAIN (1) [plan'tin], *n.* genus of wild plants with long broad leaves growing close to the ground. [ME. from L.].

PLANTAIN (2), *n.* tropical plant yielding a fruit very serviceable for food. [L.].

PLANTATION [plan-tā'shn], *n.* the place planted; group of planted trees; large cultivated estate; estate cultivated by slave labour for specific crops.

PLANTER [plahn'ter], *n.* person who plants; one who owns a plantation; settler.

PLANTIGRADE (1) [plan'ti-grād], *adj.* (*zool.*) walking on the sole of the foot. PLANTIGRADE (2), *n.* a p. animal. [L.].

PLAQUE [plak], *n.* disk or piece of metal, china etc., ornamented in relief. [Flem.].

PLASH (1) [plash], *n.* shallow puddle; splash; sound of

---

water when broken at the surface. PLASH (2), v./. to dabble in water; sprinkle with water or colour, splash. [OE., ME.].

PLASH (3), v.t. to bend (a branch) by half cutting through and interweaving it with others. PLASH (4), n. branch partly lopped and bound to others. [OFr. from L.].

PLASM [plazm], n. mould or matrix in which something is cast or formed; plasma; (biol.) the living matter forming a cell. [Gk.].

PLASMA [plaz'mah], n. variety of green, transparent quartz; colourless fluid from which is formed the organic lymph, and in which float the red corpuscles of the blood; plasm. PLASMATIC(AL) [plaz-ma'tik-(-al], adj. giving form; of, relating to, p. PLASMIC, adj. of, relating to, protoplasm or p. [Gk.].

PLASMODIUM [plaz-mō'di-um], n. mass of protoplasm; parasitic organism in the blood of sufferers from certain fevers. [Gk.].

PLASMOGEN [plaz'mō-jen], n. protoplasm. [Gk.].

PLASTER (1) [plahs'ter], n. mixture of lime, sand and water used for applying in coats to walls of houses; wad of fabric, cotton etc., treated with medicated liquids and applied externally to affected parts; adhesive tape for protecting wounds or broken skin; **p.-of-Paris**, a substance, finely ground, roasted gypsum, used in building and for surgical dressing. PLASTER (2), v.t. to smear or coat with p.; cover (a wound) with strips of adhesive tape; cover all over with a generous amount. [OE. from Gk.].

PLASTIC (1) [plas'tik], adj. having a consistency which allows manipulation by pressing, rolling etc.; capable of being shaped by pressure; capable of shaping or creating; (art) of, relating to, the art of modelling into solid, as distinct from graphic, form; connected with the media of clay, wood, metal etc.; (biol.) capable of metabolic change; (fig.) impressionable; (med.) relating to the art of grafting fresh organic tissue by surgical operation. PLASTIC (2), n. name sometimes applied to plastics. PLASTICITY [plas-ti'si-ti], n. quality of being p. [Gk.].

PLASTICINE [plas'ti-sēn], n. (prot.) proprietary brand of plastic material which does not harden, a substitute for modelling clay.

PLASTICS [plas'tiks], n. complex organic or semi-organic compounds which are plastic at some stage of their production and can be moulded and shaped by means of heat and pressure; the technique of using plastics.

PLASTID [plas'tid], n. (biol.) a living cell, unit of protoplasm.

PLASTRON [plas'tron], n. steel breastplate worn as armour; leather guard used in fencing to protect the chest; † ornamental front on a woman's dress; ventral part of the shells of chelonians. [Fr.].

PLAT (1) [plat], n. small plot of ground. [PLOT].

PLAT (2) (pres.pt. **platting**, pret. and p.pt. **platted**), v.t. to plait.

PLATE (1) [plāt], n. flat shallow domestic utensil, usually circular, for holding food at table; amount of food on a plate; helping; articles of domestic use, such as candlesticks, forks and spoons etc., plated with gold or silver; flat sheet of metal used as a support; thin sheet of copper or steel engraved with designs from which impressions are printed; impression from such a plate; oblong of metal engraved with the name of a person; thin piece of moulded material into which artificial teeth are fitted; (in horseracing) light shoe worn by racehorses; prize consisting of a piece of silver or gold plate set up for the winner of a race; race the winner of which must be sold for a minimum sum; (baseball) home base for the batting side; (phot.) sheet of sensitized glass acting as a negative; (radio) metal cylinder of a thermionic valve. PLATE (2), v.t. to cover or overlay with metal or precious metal plates; beat into thin plates. PLATER, n. one who plates metal; horse, usually of inferior quality, competing in selling races for a cup or p. [ME. from Gk.].

PLATE-ARMOUR [plāt'ah-mer], n. armour consisting of overlaid metal plates; very thick plates of metal used for protecting warships.

PLATEAU (pl. **plateaux, plateaus**) [pla'tō, pla-tō'], n. broad plain of elevated land. [Fr.].

PLATE-GLASS [plāt-glahs], n. high-class kind of glass cast so as to form thick plates, used for mirrors and shop-fronts.

PLATELAYER [plāt'lā-er], n. workman employed on a railroad to lay the rails and keep them in order.

PLATEMARK [plāt'mahk], n. legal mark indicative of various makes of plated ware and of the quality of a metal; mark on postage stamps which distinguishes the plate from which they are printed.

PLATEN [pla'ten], n. part of a printing-press upon which the impression is made; roller of a typewriter. [OFr.].

PLATFORM [plat'fawm], n. level place raised above the general level, as in an assembly hall or at a railway station; declared party scheme of action or policy, political programme; people seated on the platform at a meeting. [OFr.].

PLATING [plā'ting], n. process of covering something with a coating of metal; such a coating of metal.

PLATINIFEROUS [pla-ti-ni'fe-rōos], adj. bearing, yielding, platinum. [PLATINUM and L.].

PLATINOTYPE [pla'ti-nō-tīp], n. photographic printing process using platinum-black.

PLATINUM (1) [pla'ti-num], n. the rare metallic element Pt, grey-white in colour, very heavy and malleable. PLATINUM-BLACK, a modified form of p. consisting of a black powder. PLATINUM (2), adj. relating to, made of, resembling, p.; **p. blonde**, woman with hair of a natural or artificially dyed grey-gold colour. [Span.].

PLATITUDE [pla'ti-tyōod], n. vapidness, dulness; commonplace remark, obvious and over-used observation. PLATITUDINARIAN [pla-ti-tyōo-di-nǣr'i-an], n. person with a reputation for uttering platitudes. [Fr.].

PLATITUDINOUS [pla-ti-tyōo'di-nōos], adj. of, resembling, a platitude.

PLATONIC [pla-to'nik], adj. of, relating to, derived from, Plato or his teachings; descriptive of a relationship or love based on pure friendship and sympathy, with no tendency to experience physical passion. [Gk.].

PLATONISM [plā'to-nizm], n. philosophy or doctrines of Plato and his followers; a principle established by Plato. PLATONIST, n. follower of Plato.

PLATOON [pla-tōon'], n. subdivision of a company in a modern infantry battalion. [Fr.].

PLATTER [pla'ter], n. large shallow dish; wooden plate for bread. [ME. from OFr.].

PLATYPUS [pla'ti-pus], n. the duck-bill. [Gk.].

PLAUDIT [plaw'dit], n. praise bestowed; public expression of applause, particularly by clapping the hands. [L.].

PLAUSIBLE [plaw'zi-bl], adj. superficially worthy of approval, apparently reasonable, specious; having a persuasive but unsound quality of argument. [L.].

PLAY (1) [plā], v.t. to cause to move in a more or less defined direction; take part in a game; perform, carry out; introduce into a game, as a card; compete against; strike (a ball); act the part of on the stage; perform on (a musical instrument); in angling, tire the fish out; v.i. to undertake any kind of activity for the sake of amusement; gambol; trifle or toy (with); move about lightly and freely; move in accordance with a limited scope; **to p. down**, to make light of, minimize the importance of; **to p. off**, to use as a foil or contrast, display; **to p. on**, to continue to p.; (cricket) permit the ball to hit the stumps after it has touched the bat; **to p. up**, to act vigorously and commendably; make the most of; **to p. upon**, to deceive, endeavour to affect; **to p. the game**, to act fairly. PLAY (2), n. action or activity undertaken for the sake of the anticipated or consequent pleasure and relaxation, diversion, amusement; style or manner of playing; gambling; rapid movement; room, space for movement; amount or limit of space for or between connected mechanical parts; (fig.) unrestricted scope; literary composition designed for the stage, drama; stage performance. [OE., ME.].

PLAY-ACT [plā'akt], v.i. to pretend.

PLAYBILL [plā'bil], n. programme of a theatrical performance; printed advertisement of a play in the form of a handbill or poster.

PLAYBOY [plā'boi], n. man with no serious purpose in life who spends his whole time seeking amusement; entertaining fellow full of life and energy.

PLAYER [plā'er], n. person who plays; stage actor; musician; professional athlete, particularly a footballer or cricketer.

PLAYER-PIANO [plā-er-pya'nō], n. piano fitted with a mechanical apparatus which plays music from specially prepared rolls.

PLAYFELLOW [plā'fe-lō], n. companion of one's childhood amusements.

PLAYGOER [plā'gō-er], n. person who habitually goes to the theatre.

PLAYGROUND [plā'grownd], n. piece of ground

near to a school on which games are played; part of a public park fitted out for children.

PLAYHOUSE [plā′hows], *n.* theatre.

PLAYING-FIELD [plā′ing-fēld], *n.* field prepared and marked out for the playing of games.

PLAYLET [plā′let], *n.* short play.

PLAYMATE [plā′māt], *n.* playfellow.

PLAY-OFF [plā-of′], *n.* second game played between two players or teams after they have drawn a match.

PLAYPEN [plā′pen], *n.* portable framework of wood with railings, inside which a young child can be safely left to play.

PLAYTHING [plā′thing], *n.* something designed to be played with, toy.

PLAYWRIGHT [plā′rīt], *n.* writer of plays.

PLEA [plē], *n.* excuse, pretext; entreaty, urgent request; (*leg.*) defendant's allegation in answer to the plaintiff's case. [ME. from L.].

PLEACH [plēch], *v.t.* to interweave branches of trees or shrubs, plash. [ME.].

PLEAD [plēd], *v.t. and i.* to support by arguing on behalf of, e.g. another person's cause; allege in defence, put forward as an apology; entreat; (*leg.*) present an answer in a formal capacity to the declared accusation of a plaintiff. PLEADER, *n.* (*leg.*) one who pleads, advocate, barrister. [ME. from OFr.].

PLEADING [plē′ding], *n.* act of supporting by argument; (*leg.*) (*pl.*) case of both plaintiff and defendant in documentary form.

PLEASANT [plez′ant], *adj.* having a pleasing quality, agreeable to the mind and senses; having an amiable nature, affable; gay, enlivening. [OFr.].

PLEASANTRY [plez′zan-tri], *n.* merriment; lively talk; joke or humorous remark. [Fr.].

PLEASE [plēz], *v.t. and i.* to give pleasure to, render satisfied, behave so as to produce a sense of happy satisfaction; be a source of delight; choose, prefer, like; *used in imper. to accompany a request.* PLEASED, *adj.* experiencing happy satisfaction, gratified. [ME., OFr. from L.].

PLEASING [plē′zing], *adj.* gratifying to the senses or mind; agreeable, giving pleasure.

PLEASURABLE [plezh′e-ra-bl], *adj.* capable of affording pleasure, pleasing, enjoyable.

PLEASURE (1) [plezh′ōor], *n.* state of satisfaction with a basis of wellbeing and happiness due to the absence of pain or fear; experience producing an agreeable effect on the senses, enjoyment, delight; sensual satisfaction, gratification of the desires; arbitrary choice; source of satisfaction. PLEASURE-BOAT, boat owned or hired for p. PLEASURE-GROUND, recreation ground. PLEASURE-STEAMER, steamer which takes passengers for short excursion trips. PLEASURE-TRIP, excursion for p. PLEASURE (2),† *v.t.* to give p. to, gratify. [OFr.].

PLEAT (1) [plēt], *n.* double fold made in material and ironed flat. PLEAT (2), *v.t.* to make a p. in. [*Var.* of PLAIT].

PLEBEIAN (1) [pli-bē′an], *adj.* belonging to, originating in, the lower-classes; bad-mannered, common. PLEBEIAN (2), *n.* member of the lower classes; in ancient Rome, a member of a family who did not belong to the Patricians. [L.].

PLEBISCITE [ple′bi-sit, -sit], *n.* vote of a whole community expressed in a national ballot. [L.].

PLECTRUM [plek′trum], *n.* small splint or quill with which the ancients plucked the lyre; small flat thin piece of bone or flexible material used in playing a modern stringed instrument such as the banjo. [Gk.].

PLEDGE (1) [plej], *n.* something handed over as a security for the fulfilment of an obligation or contract, surety, token, something put in pawn in return for a money loan; promise, verbal bond of contract; a drinking to the health of another, toast. PLEDGE (2), *v.t.* to deposit or hand over as a security, put in p.; make a promise, place oneself under a binding engagement, particularly to abstain from drinking alcoholic liquor; drink a person's health. PLEDGEE, *n.* person to whom anything is pledged. [ME. from OFr.].

PLEIAD (*pl.* **pleiades, pleiads**) [plī′ad, plī′a-dēz, plī′adz], *n.* (*astron.*) one of a group of stars in the constellation Taurus. [Gk.].

PLEISTOCENE [plī′sto-sēn], *adj.* (*geol.*) pertaining to the series of rocks next above the Pliocene, the Glacial series. [Gk.].

PLENARY [plē′na-ri], *adj.* full, entire, complete; fully representative of all sections. [LL.].

PLENIPOTENTIARY (1) [ple-ni-pō-ten′sha-ri],

adj. possessing full powers of authority. PLENIPOTENTIARY (2), *n.* envoy or ambassador to a foreign state, furnished with full diplomatic powers to make decisions on behalf of his own state. [MedL.].

PLENITUDE [ple′ni-tyōod], *n.* state of being full, abundance, completeness. [L.].

PLENTEOUS [plen′ti-ōos], *adj.* plentiful, copious, sufficient for every purpose. [ME. from OFr.].

PLENTIFUL [plen′ti-fōol], *adj.* abundant, copious; available in large quantities.

PLENTY (1) [plen′ti], *n.* full supply, large quantity, abundance. PLENTY (2), *adv.* to an abundant degree, quite sufficient. [L.].

PLEONASM [plē′o-nazm], *n.* redundancy of words, repetitive style of expression. [Gk.].

PLEONASTIC [plē-o-nas′tik], *adj.* having the characteristic of a pleonasm, redundant in words. [Gk.].

PLETHORA [ple′the-rah], *n.* a superabundant quantity; (*med.*) excessive fulness of blood. PLETHORIC [ple-thaw′rik], *adj.* of, characterized by, p.; full-blooded. [Gk.].

PLEURA (*pl.* **pleurae**) [plōo′rah, ′rē], *n.* (*anat.*) thin membrane which encloses the lungs. [Gk.].

PLEURISY [plyōo′ri-si], *n.* (*path.*) inflammation of the pleura. PLEURITIC [plyōo-ri′tik], *adj.* of, relating to, affected with, p. [Gk.].

PLEURO-PNEUMONIA [plyōo-rō-nyōo-mō′ni-ah], *n.* inflammation of the pleura and the lungs at the same time.

PLEXUS [plek′sus], *n.* (*anat.*) a complicated junction of blood-vessels, nerves or fibres; (*fig.*) any involved structure of assembled units. [L.].

PLIABLE [plī′a-bl], *adj.* capable of being manipulated, flexible; (*fig.*) flexible in disposition, easily influenced. [Fr. from L.].

PLIANCY [plī′an-si], *n.* quality of being pliant; (*fig.*) readiness to be influenced.

PLIANT [plī′ant], *adj.* of a nature which permits of bending, flexible; (*fig.*) easily influenced, tractable. [Fr.].

PLIERS [plī′erz], *n.*(*pl.*) small pincers for seizing, bending or extracting nails and similar objects. [OFr.].

PLIGHT (1) [plīt], *n.* condition, state; sorry circumstances, predicament. [ME. from AFr. and OE.].

PLIGHT (2), *v.t.* to promise to marry, engage, pledge under formal conditions. [OE.].

PLIMSOLL-MARK [plim′sol-mahk], *n.* line painted on the sides of a vessel to indicate the loading capacity. [S. *Plimsoll*, sponsor of the system].

PLIMSOLLS [plim′solz], *n.*(*pl.*) canvas shoes with rubber soles. [*Prec.*].

PLINTH [plinth], *n.* (*arch.*) square-shaped, projecting part or base of a column, pedestal or wall; base for statuettes etc. [Gk.].

PLIOCENE [plī′ō-sēn], *adj.* (*geol.*) pertaining to the uppermost of the Tertiary rocks lying above the Miocene and below the Pleistocene. [Gk.].

PLOD (*pres.pt.* plodding, *pret. and p.pt.* plodded) [plod], *v.i.* to walk or travel steadily but laboriously; (*fig.*) work slowly but conscientiously. PLODDER, *n.* person who plods, steady slow worker. PLODDING, *adj.* steadily laborious, but slow; conscientious but not brilliant. [Uncert.].

PLONK [plongk], *n.* hollow report or sound. [Echoic].

PLOP (1) [plop], *n.* slightly resonant sound made by a solid body as it enters the water. PLOP (2) (*pres.pt.* PLOPPING, *pret. and p.pt.* PLOPPED) *v.i.* to fall into water with a p. [Echoic].

PLOT (1) [plot], *n.* a small extent of ground, particularly one used for growing vegetables or crops. PLOT (2) (*pres.pt.* PLOTTING, *pret. and p.pt.* PLOTTED), *v.t.* to divide into plots. [OE.].

PLOT (3), *n.* scheme worked out in elaborate secrecy to gain a specific end, conspiracy, intrigue; scheme, stratagem of a more harmless character; story of a book, play or film as embodied in the dialogue and actions of the characters. PLOT (4) (*pres.pt.* PLOTTING, *pret. and p.pt.* PLOTTED), to work out a scheme (usually illegal) in secrecy with some specific end in view, plan surreptitiously, intrigue; set down in a plan or diagram; participate in a p., conspire. [Fr.].

PLOUGH (1), **PLOW** [plow], *n.* agricultural implement used to drive furrows through the soil, cutting the sod up in preparation for sowing; **the P.,** (*astron.*) constellation showing the outline of a p.; (*slang*) examination failure. PLOUGH (2), *v.t. and i.* to turn up the soil with a p.; form by ploughing; work at ploughing; (*fig.*) drive a way (through); (*slang*) refuse to pass an examination candidate; fail in an

---

The accent ′ after a syllable = stress (u-pon′).   The mark ‾ over a vowel = length (ā in made; ō in bone).

examination; **to p. through.** (*fig.*) to work one's way through heavy or difficult reading matter. [OE., ME.].

PLOUGHBOY [plow'boi], *n.* boy who drives the plough; a rustic, yokel.

PLOUGHMAN [plow'man], *n.* man who ploughs or guides a plough.

PLOUGH-MONDAY [plow'mun-dā], *n.* the Monday after Epiphany.

PLOUGHSHARE [plow'shãer], *n.* pointed shoe of a plough which cuts the soil at the bottom of the furrow.

PLOVER [pluv'er], *n.* popular name for several species of birds frequenting low, moist ground; **green p.,** lapwing. [OFr.].

PLOW, see PLOUGH.

PLUCK (1) [pluk], *v.t. and i.* to extract, gather with a quick jerk, pull with sudden force, or with a twitch; strip feathers from; (*fig.*) fleece, swindle; (*slang*) reject in an examination; **to p. up courage,** to rouse one's spirits with an effort. PLUCK (2), *n.* act, or a single instance, of plucking, tug; that which is plucked out, *esp.* the heart, liver and lungs of an animal; (*fig.*) courage, spirit. [OE., ME.].

PLUCKY [pluk'i], *adj.* brave, spirited. [*Prec.*].

PLUG (1) [plug], *n.* something used to stop a hole, stopper, bung; cake of tobacco; piece of this; handle of a water-closet which causes the bowl to be flushed with water; (*elect.*) device for linking apparatus to a source of current, having metal projections which fit into conducting sockets. PLUG (2) (*pres.pt.* PLUGGING, *pret. and p.pt.* PLUGGED), *v.t. and i.* to stop up by means of a p., put a p. in; **to p. in,** (*elect.*) to connect to a circuit by means of a p.; (*slang*) plod, work continuously under difficulties; (*slang*) shoot with a bullet; (*slang*) bring to the fore by means of publicity, repeat or perform constantly (a song etc.) so as to catch the attention of the public. PLUG-IN, *adj.* (*elect.*) having a connexion made by an electric p. [Uncert.].

PLUM [plum], *n.* tree of the genus *Prunus*, or its fruit, which is round and has a juicy flesh sweet in flavour when ripe; raisin; (*fig., coll.*) anything good or choice, the best, the pick of its kind; **p. duff,** boiled suet pudding made of flour and raisins. PLUM-CAKE, large cake containing raisins. [OE. from Gk.].

PLUMAGE [plōō'mij], *n.* the feathers of a bird. [OFr.].

PLUMB (1) [plum], *n.* lump of lead or other weight attached to a line and used for taking soundings or measuring perpendiculars. PLUMB (2), *adj.* perpendicular, vertical, true. PLUMB (3), *adv.* perpendicularly, absolutely, exactly. PLUMB (4), *v.t.* to adjust or measure by means of a p.-line; test the perpendicular of; take the soundings of; (*fig.*) see or reach the bottom of, understand. [L.].

PLUMBAGO [plum-bā'gō], *n.* (*min.*) graphite, nearly pure carbon, used for pencils etc., and popularly called black lead; (*bot.*) plant with pale-blue flowers. PLUMBAGINOUS [plum-bā'ji-nōōs], *adj.* resembling, consisting of, the nature of, p. [L.].

PLUMBEOUS [plum'bi-ōōs], *adj.* consisting of, resembling, lead. [L.].

PLUMBER [plum'er], *n.* person who works in lead; person whose trade it is to fit and repair all kinds of metal piping and other apparatus connected with water supplies, drainage etc. [L.].

PLUMBIC [plum'bik], *adj.* (*chem.*) of, relating to, or containing lead; (*path.*) symptomatic of the presence of lead.

PLUMBING [plu'ming], *n.* art of working in lead; work of a plumber; system of pipes and fittings the installation of which is the business of a plumber.

PLUMB-LINE [plum'lin], *n.* device for testing perpendiculars, consisting of a cord with a plumb attached to it; perpendicular line.

PLUME (1) [plōōm], *n.* bird's feather, *esp.* a large or distinctive one; feather or group of feathers worn as an ornament; crest; tuft of hair. PLUME (2), *v.t.* to provide with plumes; clean or preen the feathers; adorn with feathers; *v. reflex.* (*fig.*) pride oneself on. [L.].

PLUMMET [plu'met], *n.* weight of lead or other heavy matter attached to a line for the purpose of testing depths and perpendiculars, plumb-line; small weight attached to a fishing-line to keep the float upright in the water. [ME. from OFr.].

PLUMMY [plu'mi], *adj.* of, or resembling, a plum or plums; (of a voice) sounding as if the speaker had a plum in the mouth.

PLUMOSE [plōō'mōs], *adj.* feathery.

PLUMP (1) [plump], *adj.* having a well-filled-out form, on the fat side. PLUMP (2), *v.t. and i.* to make p., fatten up; become p. [ME.].

PLUMP (3), *v.t. and i.* to cause to fall suddenly and heavily; fall or drop abruptly; **to p. for,** to express a decided preference for. PLUMP (4), *adj.* outright, downright. PLUMP (5), *adv.* suddenly, with a quick, heavy and resounding fall or plunge. PLUMP (6), *n.* act of plumping; fall of a solid body into water with a resounding noise, plop. [ME.].

PLUM-PUDDING [plum-pōō'ding], *n.* pudding containing raisins and currants and cooked by boiling or steaming; pudding containing plums.

PLUMULE, PLUMULA [plōō'myōōl, 'myōō-lah], *n.* (*bot.*) first growth of stem from a germinating seed. [L.].

PLUNDER (1) [plun'der], *v.t.* to seize property, possessions or money by violence, pillage; take by open force; rob, steal, embezzle. PLUNDER (2), *n.* act of plundering; booty, loot, profit. [Germ.].

PLUNGE (1) [plunj], *v.t. and i.* to thrust suddenly and forcibly downwards into water or any liquid, immerse; cause to enter into new and risky circumstances; dive with a rush into water or any liquid; move violently and dangerously downwards or forwards; (of a horse) throw all its weight suddenly and violently on its forefeet; gamble recklessly. PLUNGE (2), *n.* act of plunging, sudden propulsion of the body downwards; sudden act of immersion; sudden entry into a risky field of activity. PLUNGER. *n.* person who or animal which plunges; one who bets heavily; piston used as a forcer in pumps. [ME. from LL.].

PLUPERFECT [plōō'per-fekt], *adj.* (*gram.*) denoting an event which took place previous to another action which took place in the past. [L.].

PLURAL (1) [plōō'ral], *adj.* (*gram.*) denoting more than one, or more than two. PLURAL (2), *n.* (*gram.*) the form which expresses more than one. PLURALIZE, *v.t.* to make p. [L.].

PLURALISM [plōō'ra-lizm], *n.* state of being plural; system, *esp.* of ecclesiastical application, of holding more offices than one at a time; (*philos.*) theory that there are more first causes than one. PLURALIST, *n.* (*eccles.*) clergyman who holds more than one benefice at a time; (*philos.*) follower of pluralism.

PLURALITY [plōō-ra'li-ti], *n.* state of being plural; number of more than one; greater number; pluralism. [L.].

PLUS (1) [plus], *n.* symbol +, used as the sign of addition; extra quantity. PLUS (2), *adj.* having or including more, additional, extra. PLUS-FOURS, roomy knickerbockers having an extra few inches allowed to drop in a fold below the knee. [L.].

PLUSH [plush], *n.* species of shaggy cloth, generally with a velvety nap. [Fr.].

PLUTO [plōō'tō], *n.* (*myth.*) god of the nether world; (*astron.*) planet first observed in 1930. [Gk.].

PLUTOCRACY [plōō-to'kra-si], *n.* government by the wealthy. [Gk.].

PLUTOCRAT [plōō'tō-krat], *n.* person who is influential on account of his wealth. [*Prec.*].

PLUTO-DEMOCRACY [plōō-tō-di-mo'kra-si], *n.* country whose system of government combines elements of both plutocracy and democracy.

PLUTONIC [plōō-to'nik], *adj.* of, relating to, the kingdom of Pluto, infernal; dark; igneous; **P. rocks,** unstratified rocks such as granite, consolidated from a molten state at a great depth beneath the surface of the earth; **P. theory,** theory that the heat of the earth is responsible for geological phenomena.

PLUTONIUM [plōō-tō'ni-um], *n.* (*chem.*) rare radioactive element with properties similar to those of uranium. [PLUTO].

PLUVIAL [plōō'vi-al], *adj.* of, relating to, caused by, rain; rainy, humid; (*geol.*) due to rain. [L.].

PLUVIOMETER [plōō-vi-o'mi-ter], *n.* rain gauge. PLUVIOMETRIC(AL) [plōō-vi-ō-met'rik(-al), *adj.* pertaining to a p., or to the measurement of rainfall. [L. and METER].

PLY (1) [plī], *n.* fold, layer, thickness; strand, thread, twist, plait. [Fr. from L.].

PLY (2), *v.t. and i.* to work with diligently, use energetically; urge, solicit persistently; offer repeatedly; wait in a particular place or follow a particular route regularly, for business purposes; (*naut.*) make way against the wind. [Fr.].

PLYMOUTH BRETHREN [pli-mōōth-bre'THren], *n.* Christian sect of strict evangelical principles, founded at Plymouth about 1830.

PLYWOOD [pli'wood], *n.* wood made of three or

ōō is pronounced as in food; ŏŏ as in hood; th as in think; TH as in that; zh as in azure. ~ = related to.

more layers glued together under pressure with the grain of each layer set at right angles to that of the adjoining layer. [PLY (1)].

PNEUMATIC [nyōō-ma'tik], *adj.* of, relating to, consisting of, air or gases; inflated by air; moved by compressed air. [Gk.].

PNEUMATICS [nyōō-ma'tiks], *n.(pl.)* study of gases, *esp.* of the air.

PNEUMATO-, *pref.* of, relating to, driven by, air. [Gk.].

PNEUMOCOCCUS [nyōō-mō-ko'kus], *n. (path.)* micro-organism causing pneumonia. [Gk.].

PNEUMONIA [nyōō-mō'ni-ah], *n. (path.)* acute inflammation of the lungs. [Gk.].

PNEUMONIC [nyōō-mo'nik], *adj.* of, relating to, the lungs or to pneumonia.

PNEUMOTHORAX [nyōō-mō-thaw'raks], *n.* presence of air in the pleura, its artificial introduction in the treatment of disease. [Gk.].

POACH (1) [pōch], *v.t.* to cook eggs by breaking them into boiling water. [OFr.].

POACH (2), *v.t. and i.* to trespass on private property and steal game; *v.i.* to trespass on land in pursuit of game; *(tennis slang)* take one's partner's shots. [OFr.].

POACH (3), *v.t.* to stab or pierce, particularly by trampling, as cattle. [OFr.].

POCHARD [pō'cherd], *n.* a sea-duck. [Unkn.].

POCHETTE [po-shet'], *n.* woman's handbag in the form of a small pouch. [Fr.].

POCK [pok], *n.* pustule of smallpox. [OE., ME.].

POCKET (1) [po'kit], *n.* small bag sewn into one's clothing and used for carrying handkerchiefs, money etc.; any small bag, pouch, cavity or receptacle; one of six net bags forming part of a billiard table; section of air in which a partial vacuum has been created, eliminating the necessary lift for an aeroplane; measure, particularly of hops, in the form of a sack; small area surrounded by one of contrary characteristics; *(fig.)* one's financial resources. POCKET-BATTLESHIP, small battleship, unusually powerful for its size. POCKET-KNIFE, small clasp-knife for carrying in the p. POCKET (2), *v.t.* to pick up and place in one's p., particularly with a view to keeping for good; conceal in the p.; keep as profit. [ME. from OFr.].

POCKET-BOOK [po'kit-book], *n.* small folding case for carrying papers in the pocket; small notebook.

POCKET-BOROUGH [po-kit-bu'rer], *n.* parliamentary constituency before 1832 representation of which was controlled by a single person or small group.

POCKET-MONEY [po'kit-mu-ni], *n.* money for occasional expenses, small weekly allowance given by a parent to his child.

POCO [pō'kō], *adv. (mus.)* a little, rather. [It.].

POD (1) [pod], *n.* shell of a pea and other such leguminous plants which contains the seeds. POD (2) *(pres.pt.* PODDING, *pret. and p.pt.* PODDED), *v.i.* to produce pods, swell and grow because of the seeds ripening. [Unkn.].

PODAGRA [po-da'grah], *n.* gout in the foot. [Gk.].

PODGE [poj], *n.* person of short, fat figure. PODGY, *adj.* short and fat, dumpy. [Unkn.].

PODO-, *pref.* foot. [Gk.].

POEM [pō'im], *n.* literary composition expressing an imaginative or intensely felt experience or experiences, using language in a heightened form and often using rhyme, rhythm or metre; piece of poetry; anything which appears to possess some of the qualities of a poem. [Gk.].

POESY [pō'i-zi], *n.* art of composing poems; poetry; metrical composition. [Fr. from Gk.].

POET [pō'it], *n.* man who practises the art of poetry; one whose creative powers find their natural outlet in language raised to a fine pitch of quality and concentration of related thought and imagery; any person who has written a poem. [Gk.].

POETASTER [pō-e-tas'ter], *n.* writer of poor poems, petty poet. [POET and L.].

POETIC [pō-e'tik], *adj.* poetical; **p. justice,** triumph of good over evil; **p. licence,** permissible departure from exact regard for reality or from strict maintenance of the conventions of poetry. [Gk.].

POETICAL [pō-e'ti-kal], *adj.* of, relating to, poetry; suitable to poetry; expressed in poetry; having the qualities peculiar to poetry; characterized by imaginative and emotional power.

POETICS [pō-e'tiks], *n.(pl.)* study of the nature of poetry, particularly the treatise of Aristotle.

POETRY [pō'i-tri], *n.* art or work of poets; art of

raising all the capacities of language, rhythm, assonance and accent to a high degree of concentration in order to re-create an intense emotional and imaginative experience; any composition adopting the classical poetic conventions; any quality which has a recognizable emotional effect. [L.].

POGROM [po-grom'], *n.* act of systematic plunder and slaughter of a certain section of a population. [Russ.].

POIGNANCY [poi'nan-si], *n.* quality or state of being poignant.

POIGNANT [poi'nant], *adj.* sharply evoking the emotions of misery; keen, sharp; acutely painful. [OFr. from L.].

POIGNARD, see PONIARD.

POILU [pwah'lyōō], *n. (coll.)* French private soldier. [Fr.].

POINSETTIA [poin-se'ti-ah], *n. (bot.)* genus of Mexican plants with large red bracts. [J. R. Poinsett].

POINT (1) [point], *n.* sharp tip of a tapering end; mark, dot or full stop made by the sharp end of a piercing instrument, particularly a full stop or decimal dot; real or imaginary means of indicating position, spot or place without specific definition of characteristics; exact place or moment; a particular division, issue, item, detail; distinctive characteristic, capacity; degree; unit in counting the score in a game; gist of an argument or remark; sting of an epigram; small promontory; needle used by lace-makers; lace made by a needle; switch rail by which a train is transferred from one track to another; *(cricket)* position on the off-side of the field opposite the batsman and at right angles to a line drawn from wicket to wicket; *(math.)* that which has position but no magnitude; *(naut.)* one of the thirty-two dividing lines of the compass; *(typ.)* a unit of measurement; *(elect.)* pair of conducting plates connected to a wiring system and let into a wall to receive a plug connecting subsidiary apparatus; *(cross-country racing)* landmark serving as an objective; **p. to p.,** *n.* steeplechase. **p. of view,** mental basis or principle of an attitude; **at all points,** in full detail; **to stretch a p.,** to modify a demand; **what's the p.,** what's the use; **to make a p. of,** to take special care to; **p. steak,** corner cut from a rump steak; **dry p.,** an engraving tool; print taken from an engraved plate. POINT (2), *v.t.* to give a p. to by cutting or shaping, sharpen; add force to; direct by showing the way with the first finger or the hand, indicate by word or gesture; mark with points, stops or dots; fill in the joints with mortar using the p. of the trowel; *(mus.)* indicate pauses by points; *v.i.* (of dogs) to stand stock-still with the nose directed towards the game and the tail in a straight line with the back; **to p. at,** to direct a finger at as a means of indication; **to p. out,** **to p. to,** to call attention to, indicate. [Fr. from L.].

POINT-BLANK [point-blangk'], *adj.* aimed horizontally, direct, at close range; *(fig.)* outright. [Uncert.].

POINT-DUTY [point'dyōō-ti], *n.* duty of a policeman directing traffic at a particular point.

POINTED [poin'tid], *adj.* sharpened, having a point; aimed at someone or something; epigrammatic, incisive. POINTEDLY, *adv.* in a p. manner, suggestively.

POINTER [poin'ter], *n.* one who, that which, points; rod for pointing out details on a blackboard, screen etc.; hint, cue; breed of sporting dog, so called from its habit of indicating the position of game with its nose; small advertisement directing the reader's attention to a larger one.

POINTING [poin'ting], *n.* act of punctuating; act of trimming mortar placed between joints by means of the trowel point.

POINTLESS [point'les], *adj.* having no point; having no significance; ineffective, meaningless.

POINTSMAN [points'man], *n.* man who works or cares for the switches or points on a railway.

POISE (1) [poiz], *v.t. and i.* to maintain in a balanced state, maintain in a particular position; remain balanced; hover, as a bird. POISE (2), *n.* balanced distribution and support of the body's weight, equilibrium; regulating power, style of carrying oneself; balanced dignity of mind or body. [ME. from L.].

POISON (1) [poi'zn], *n.* any substance or liquid which when absorbed into the system destroys or injures the power of life; *(fig.)* any harmful social activity or influence; **p. gas,** injurious gas or vapour used for purposes of warfare. POISON (2), *v.t.* to kill

---

The accent ʹafter a syllable = stress (u-pon'). The mark ¯ over a vowel = length (ā in made; ō in bone).

or injure by p.; add p. to, infect with p.; (*fig.*) introduce an influence designed to corrupt, pervert. [ME. from L.].

POISONOUS [poi'zn-ŏŏs], *adj.* having the qualities or effect of poison; (*fig.*) corrupting; highly disagreeable.

POKE (1) [pōk], *v.t. and i.* to push or thrust against; thrust into with an instrument which is moved about; push forward; grope about; **p. bonnet,** bonnet with a rim projecting high over the forehead; **to p. fun at, to p. ridicule; to p. about,** (*slang*) to meddle, be inquisitive. POKE (2), *n.* a poking, thrust, dig, nudge. [ME.].

POKER [pō'ker], *n.* metal bar used in stirring a fire; card-game in which each player is dealt a hand of five cards which is compared to a specified order of value and betted on, the element of bluff being an important factor in the game. POKER-FACE, person whose face is inscrutable (as during a game of p.); countenance giving no sign of emotion. [Uncert.].

POKERWORK [pō'ker-werk], *n.* decoration of wood or leather by burning patterns into it with a heated point.

POKY [pō'ki], *adj.* cramped, confined, small in size.

POLAR [pō'ler], *adj.* of, relating to, belonging to, the North or South Pole; relating to a magnetic pole; possessing two opposed properties in a functioning relationship; diametrically opposed; **p. bear,** large white bear. [Gk.].

POLARIMETER [pō-la-ri'mi-ter], *n.* (*opt.*) instrument for measuring the degree of polarization of light. [Gk.].

POLARITY [pō-la'ri-ti], *n.* power of reacting and pointing to the Poles of the earth, which is peculiar to the magnetic needle; action by, or susceptibility to, magnetic influence; state of possessing two powers or properties in functional opposition.

POLARIZATION [pō-la-ri-zā'shn], *n.* act or process of polarizing, state of being polarized; **p. of light,** (*opt.*) modification of light waves by the action of certain media which transmit waves vibrating in one plane only; the obtaining of this result by reflection or any other method.

POLARIZE [pō'la-riz], *v.t.* to limit the vibration of light, heat or other electro-magnetic waves to one plane only; communicate polarity. POLARIZER, *n.* that which polarizes light or other electro-magnetic waves, *esp.* a device made for such use with microscopes.

POLDER [pol'der], *n.* reclaimed lowland below the level of the sea or a river which has been drained and cultivated and is protected by dykes. [Du.].

POLE (1) [pōl], *n.* long, relatively thin, and rounded piece of wood; such a piece used for propelling a punt, or for supporting a tent, flag-staff; measure of length of 5½ yd., rod or perch; square measure of 30½ sq. yd.; **up the p.,** (*slang*) silly, mad. POLE (2), *v.t. and i.* to propel by means of a p., punt; provide with poles. [OE. from L.].

POLE (3), *n.* (*astron.*) one of the two extremities of the earth's axis or of the celestial sphere; area round either the North or the South Pole; the pole-star; one of the two points in a magnetic body embodying the positive or negative power; (*elect.*) positive or negative terminal of a battery or accumulator, electrode; **magnetic p.,** either of the two points, near but not at the Poles of the earth, at which a magnetic needle dips vertically. [ME. from Gk.].

POLE-AXE [pōl'aks], *n.* slaughterer's axe having a hammer edge on the opposite side of the axe edge. [ME.].

POLECAT [pōl'kat], *n.* small fetid carnivore allied to the weasel. [ME.].

POLE-JUMP [pōl'jump], *n.* high jump in which the jumper uses a pole which he drops as he clears the bar.

POLEMIC (1) [po-le'mik], *adj.* polemical. POLEMIC (2), *n.* a disputant; controversy, dispute; (*pl.*) controversies on religious subjects. [Gk.].

POLEMICAL [po-le'mi-kal], *adj.* relating to, arising out of, a controversy, controversial, disputatious.

POLENTA [po-len'tah], *n.* porridge of semolina, maize etc. [It.].

POLE-STAR [pōl'stah(r)], *n.* the star which is nearly vertical to the pole of the earth; lodestar, guide; (*fig.*) fixed principle.

POLE-VAULT [pōl'vawlt], *n.* pole-jump.

POLICE (1) [po-lēs'], *n.* a civil force for the preservation of law and order. POLICE-CONSTABLE, policeman. POLICE (2), *v.t.* to maintain law and order by means of the p.; patrol by p.; (*fig.*) regulate. [LL.].

POLICE-COURT [po-lēs'kawt], *n.* court of summary jurisdiction presided over by a stipendiary magistrate.

POLICEMAN [po-lēs'man], *n.* member of a police force.

POLICE-STATION [po-lēs'stā-shn], *n.* building which a local branch of the police force uses as its headquarters.

POLICY (1) [po'li-si], *n.* writing or instrument by which a contract or indemnity is effected, *esp.* a document setting out an insurance contract. [Fr.].

POLICY (2), *n.* art or science of governing a nation; set of accepted principles and plans constituting a programme of political action; any single plan or measure adopted by a government or party in its management of public affairs; line of action laid down in theoretical form and directed towards personal ends; prudence, sagacity in the management of affairs. [Gk.].

POLIOMYELITIS [po-li-ō-mī-e-lī'tis], *n.* (*med.*) inflammation in the spinal cord, infantile paralysis. [Gk.].

POLISH (1) [po'lish], *v.t. and i.* to make smooth and glossy by rubbing; (*fig.*) make refined in manners; alter in style or form until considered in a state of perfection; become smooth, receive a gloss; **to p. off,** (*slang*) to finish summarily; murder. POLISH (2), *n.* glossiness, smoothness of surface effected by rubbing; substance which aids the process of polishing; (*fig.*) elegance, correctness of social manners; finish. [ME. from L.].

POLITE [po-līt'], *adj.* courteous and considerate in society, refined, well-mannered, well-bred. [L.].

POLITIC [po'li-tik], *adj.* of, relating to, the polity; constituting the state; astute, prudent; scheming; nicely adapted to a specific purpose; expedient; **body p.,** the people as a collective political body. [Gk.].

POLITICAL [po-li'ti-kal], *adj.* of, relating to, derived from, politics or the government of a state, its institutions, forms of administration and international relationships; concerned with politics; **p. economy,** study of the laws of national wealth as utilized by society in terms of raw materials, means of production and methods of distribution; **p. geography,** study of the earth according to its p. division. POLITICALLY, *adv.* in a p. or polite manner; with reference to politics.

POLITICIAN [po-li-ti'shn], *n.* person who assumes the status of an expert in the art of governing, person engaged in politics.

POLITICS [po'li-tiks], *n.(pl.)* science or art of governing; whole system of principles and forms of administration concerned with the theoretical and practical aspects of social organization; political affairs, management of party affairs.

POLITY [po'li-ti], *n.* form or constitution of civil government; constitution of a state; people organized into a state. [Gk.].

POLKA [pol'kah], *n.* lively dance in four-four time with a half-step in it; its appropriate music; **p. dot,** pattern of regularly spaced dots. [Uncert.].

POLL (1) [pol], *n.* parrot; abbreviated form of Polly, a girl's name. [*Var.* of MOLLY].

POLL (2) [pōl], *n.* † the head; register of voters; the voting at an election; place of voting; number of voters; unofficial estimate of public opinion based on the ascertained views of selected representative individuals. POLL (3), *v.t. and i.* to trim, lop the branches of (a tree); remove the horns of (cattle); cut even (the edges of paper); enter names on a register of votes; vote; receive (a certain number of) votes. POLLED, *adj.* lopped, cropped; without horns. [ME. from LGerm.].

POLLACK, POLLOCK [po'lak], *n.* a sea-fish allied to the whiting. [Unkn.].

POLLARD (1) [po'lerd], *n.* tree which has been polled; stag which has cast his horns; mixture of bran and meal as cattle feed. POLLARD (2), *v.t.* to lop the tops of (trees) so as to allow for a new growth, as in willows. [POLL (3)].

POLLEN [po'len], *n.* (*bot.*) fertilizing granules shed by the anther of a flower, the male element of flowering plants. [L.].

POLLINATE [po'li-nāt], *v.t.* (*bot.*) to fertilize with pollen. POLLINATION [po-li-nā'shn], *n.* (*bot.*) fertilization by conveyance of pollen from anther to stigma.

POLL-MAN [pōl'man], *n.* (*Cambridge University slang*) passman. [Uncert.].

POLLOCK, see POLLACK.

POLL-TAX [pōl'taks], *n.* capitation tax, tax levied on every person.

POLLUTE [po-lyōōt'], *v.t.* to defile or make unclean; (*fig.*) taint with guilt, profane, corrupt; violate. [L.].

POLLUTION [po-lyōō'shn], *n.* act of polluting; state of being polluted; defilement, corruption; (*med.*) involuntary discharge of semen. [L.].

POLO [pō'lō], *n.* game somewhat like hockey played on ponies. POLO-COLLAR, type of high collar which rolls down all round the neck, usually as part of a jersey. WATER-POLO, ball-game played in the water between two teams of swimmers. [Indian].

POLONAISE [po-lo-nāz'], *n.* woman's dress with a full boúce in Polish fashion; Polish air and dance in a dignified measure. [Fr.].

POLONIUM [po-lō'ni-um], *n.* radio-active element discovered by Pierre and Marie Curie. [MedL.].

POLONY [po-lō'ni], *n.* dry sausage of partly cooked meat. [*Bologna*, Italy].

POLTERGEIST [pol'ter-gīst], *n.* spirit reputed to be responsible for certain otherwise inexplicable violent movements of furniture and the like. [Germ.].

POLTROON [pol-trōōn'], *n.* arrant coward, dastard. [Fr.].

POLY-, *pref.* many, much. [Gk.].

POLYANDROUS [po-li-an'drŏŏs], *adj.* having many husbands; (*bot.*) having many stamens.

POLYANDRY [po-li-an'dri], *n.* practice of having more than one husband at a time. [Gk.].

POLYANTHUS [po-li-an'thus], *n.* (*bot.*) garden plant resembling the cowslip, but with larger flowers. [Gk.].

POLYCHROMATIC [po-li-krō-ma'tik], *adj.* many coloured. [POLY and CHROMATIC].

POLYCHROME (1) [po'li-krōm], *adj.* having many colours. POLYCHROME (2), *n.* vase painted in many colours. [Gk.].

POLYCYCLIC [po-li-sī'klik], *adj.* (*elect.*) having many cycles.

POLYGAMIST [po-li'ga-mist], *n.* person who practises or advocates polygamy.

POLYGAMOUS [po-li'ga-mŏŏs], *adj.* inclined to, or practising, polygamy. [Gk.].

POLYGAMY [po-li'ga-mi], *n.* practice of having more than one wife at a time.

POLYGLOT (1) [po'li-glot], *adj.* containing, written in, speaking, many languages. POLYGLOT (2), *n.* Bible in several languages; one who speaks many languages. [Gk.].

POLYGON [po'li-gon], *n.* (*geom.*) closed figure of many angles. [Gk.].

POLYHEDRON [po-li-hē'dron], *n.* (*geom.*) solid containing many sides or planes; (*opt.*) multiplying glass or lens, consisting of several plane surfaces arranged convexly. [Gk.].

POLYNOMIAL [po-li-nō'mi-al], *adj.* (*math.*) containing many terms or names.

POLYP [po'lip], *n.* (*zool.*) sea-anemone or any animal of the same class; (*path.*) polypus. [Gk.].

POLYPHASE [po'li-fāz], *adj.* (*elect.*) having three or more phases.

POLYPHONIC [po-li-fo'nik], *adj.* consisting of many voices; (*mus.*) consisting of two or more parts, each of which has an independent melody of its own, contrapuntal. [Gk.].

POLYPODY [po'li-pō-di], *n.* (*bot.*) fern of the genus *Polypodium* of which there are over five hundred species. [Gk.].

POLYPOID [po'li-poid], *adj.* resembling polyps. [Gk.].

POLYPOUS [po'li-pŏŏs], *adj.* of the nature of a polyp.

POLYPUS (*pl.* **polypi**) [po'li-pus], *n.* (*path.*) kind of tumour. [Gk.].

POLYSYLLABIC [po-li-si-la'bik], *adj.* consisting of several syllables, usually of three or more.

POLYSYLLABLE [po-li-si'la-bl], *n.* word of several syllables, usually of three or more.

POLYTECHNIC (1) [po-li-tek'nik], *adj.* of, relating to, teaching, the technique of many arts and sciences. POLYTECHNIC (2), *n.* school for technical instruction in many sciences and practical arts. [Gk.].

POLYTHEISM [po-li-thē'izm], *n.* worship of many gods. [POLY and THEISM].

POLYTHEIST [po-li-thē'ist], *n.* person who believes in a plurality of gods.

POLYZOA [po-li-zō'ah], *n.*(*pl.*) (*zool.*) group of invertebrate animals living in colonies, often resembling seaweeds or forming incrustations on stones

and plants. POLYZOON, *n.* an individual or species of p. [Gk.].

POM [pom], *n.* (*coll.*) Pomeranian dog.

POMACE [pu'mis], *n.* crushed pulp of apples used in making cider; any pulp from which oil has been pressed. [LL.].

POMACEOUS [po-mā'shŏŏs], *adj.* of, relating to, apples. [L.].

POMADE [po-mahd'], *n.* perfumed ointment for the hair. [It.].

POMANDER [po-man'der], *n.* perfumed ball of herbs and powder formerly used as preventive of infection. [OFr.].

POMATUM [po-mā'tum], *n.* pomade.

POMEGRANATE [pom'gra-nit], *n.* tree which produces a fruit with a thick rind and full of seeds; the fruit itself. [ME. from L.].

POMERANIAN (1) [po-me-rā'ni-an], *adj.* of, relating to, coming from, Pomerania in Prussia. POMERANIAN (2), *n.* P. dog, a breed derived from the Eskimo dog, but characterized by long soft hair and a thick ring of hair round the neck.

POMFRET [pum'fret], *n.* a sweet, round and flat in shape, made of liquorice. [*Pontefract*, Yorkshire].

POMICULTURE [pō'mi-kul-tyŏŏr], *n.* cultivation of fruit-trees. [L.].

POMMEL (1), **PUMMEL** [pu'mel], *n.* raised front part of a saddle; knob terminating the hilt of a sword. POMMEL (2), PUMMEL (pres.pt. POMMELLING, pret. and p.pt. POMMELLED), *v.t.* † to beat with the p. of a sword; give a beating to by punching. POMMELLING, *n.* a beating or bruising. [ME. from OFr.].

POMP [pomp], *n.* display of grandeur and splendour, pageantry; ostentation. [Gk.].

POMPADOUR [pom'pa-dŏŏr], *n.* style of hairdressing in which the hair is brushed back and upwards from the forehead. [Madame de *Pompadour*].

POMPOM [pom'pom], *n.* quick-firing automatic gun using small shells. [Imitative].

POMPON [pom'pon], *n.* (*milit.*) tuft ornament, round tuft on a soldier's headgear; coloured ball of wool, *esp.* on a clown's costume. [Fr.].

POMPOSITY [pom-po'si-ti], *n.* quality of being pompous, pompousness; ostentation.

POMPOSO [pom-pō'sō], *adv.* (*mus.*) majestically. [It.].

POMPOUS [pom'pŏŏs], *adj.* excessively dignified, arrogant and heavy in speech or bearing, displaying pomp or grandeur; ostentatious, self-important. [LL.].

PONCE [pons], *n.* (*coll.*) a souteneur.

PONCHO [pon'chō], *n.* woollen cloak formed out of a blanket, worn in South America, with a slit in the middle for the head to pass through. [Native].

POND [pond], *n.* small body of stagnant water forming in a natural hollow and fed by the rains or dew and not by a running stream; small lake. [ME.].

PONDER [pon'der], *v.t. and i.* to formulate in thought and weigh in the mind; think, cogitate. [ME. from L.].

PONDERABLE [pon'de-ra-bl], *adj.* capable of being pondered; able to be weighed. PONDERABILITY [pon-de-ra-bi'li-ti], *n.* state of being p.; heaviness.

PONDEROUS [pon'de-rŏŏs], *adj.* very heavy, weighty; forcible; clumsy. [L.].

PONDWEED [pond'wēd], *n.* plant of the genus *Potamogeton*.

PONE [pōn], *n.* Indian bread made of maize flour. [Uncert.].

PONGEE [pon'jē], *n.* soft kind of Chinese silk. [Uncert.].

PONIARD, POIGNARD (1) [po'nyahd], *n.* small dagger. PONIARD, POIGNARD (2), *v.t.* to stab with, or as with, a p. [Fr.].

PONTIFF [pon'tif], *n.* high priest; the Pope. [Fr.].

PONTIFICAL (1) [pon-ti'fi-kal], *adj.* of, relating to, issued by, a pontiff or bishop, *esp.* the Pope; pompous. PONTIFICAL (2), *n.* book of rites and ceremonies for bishops; (*pl.*) episcopal vestments. [L.].

PONTIFICATE (1) [pon-ti'fi-kāt], *n.* dignity or office of a pontiff; reign of a Pope. PONTIFICATE (2), *v.i.* to perform the functions of a pontiff; (*fig.*) speak with an air of pompous and dogmatic authority. [L.].

PONTOON (1) [pon-tōōn'], *n.* flat-bottomed boat or structure used for constructing temporary bridges; large lighter fitted with cranes; a card-game, vingt-et-un. PONTOON (2), *v.t. and i.* to form a bridge by means of pontoons; cross by means of such a

---

The accent ´after a syllable = stress (u-pon'). The mark ⁻ over a vowel = length (ă in made; ō in bone).

bridge. **PONTOON-BRIDGE**, bridge constructed on pontoons. [Fr.].

PONY [pō'ni], *n*. small horse of thirteen to fourteen hands high; (*slang*) bet of £25. [Scots from OFr.].

POODLE [pōō'dl], *n*. breed of dog with long curly hair often clipped to form affected designs. [LGerm.].

POOH-BAH, POOH BAH [pōō-bah], *n*. person holding several posts at once. [Character in Gilbert's *The Mikado*].

POOL (1) [pōōl], *n*. small sheet of water or liquid, puddle; specific area of a river or stream which is deeper than the main stream. [OE.].

POOL (2), *n*. stakes placed for in a number of card and gambling games; receptacle to hold these; form of gambling on the results of football matches; form of billiards in which each player takes a different coloured ball; (*comm*.) form of organization, amalgamating various firms and interests in order to eliminate competition. POOL (3), *v.t.* to form or put into a p.; establish a common fund. [Fr.].

POOP (1) [pōōp], *n*. raised deck in the stern of a ship. POOP (2), *v.t.* to strike or break over the p., as a wave. **POOPED**, *adj.* having a p.; struck on the p. [L.].

POOR (1) [pōōr], *adj.* having no wealth, necessitous, needy; pitiably mean and contemptible in character and strength; barren, unproductive; worth very little; worthy of pity; unlucky; lacking in good qualities, inferior, unhealthy. POOR (2), *n*. collective name for the class of people who have little money or possessions; **p. box,** box in a church for contributions for a parish's p.; fund to assist poor persons who appear in police courts. POOR-HOUSE, workhouse. POOR-LAWS, regulations for the state care and local support of the p. [ME. from L.].

POORLY (1) [pōōr'li], *adv.* without wealth; with little or no success; in a poor manner. POORLY (2), *adj.* somewhat ill, indisposed.

POOR-SPIRITED [pōōr-spi'ri-tid], *adj.* having little courage; cowardly; base.

POP (1) [pop], *n*. (*coll.*) popular concert. [POP(ULAR)].

POP (2), *n*. sudden sharp sound which is not loud and is very brief; (*coll.*) gingerbeer; a shot. POP (3) (*pres.pt.* POPPING, *pret. and p.pt.* POPPED), *v.t. and i.* to make, or cause to make, a p.; put in or down or take out with a quick, sudden movement; (*slang*) pawn; explode with a p.; **to p. the question,** to make a proposal of marriage; **to p. in,** to pay an unexpected and brief visit; **to p. off,** to leave quickly and unexpectedly; (*slang*) die. POP (4), *adv.* with the sound of a p.; suddenly so as to startle. [Imitative].

POPCORN [pop'kawn], *n*. parched maize eaten as confectionery when sugar-coated.

POPE [pōp], *n*. the Bishop of Rome, head of the R.C. Church; (*fig.*) one who believes his own judgments to be infallible; **P. Joan,** a card-game without the eight of diamonds. POPEDOM, *n*. office or dignity of the P.; jurisdiction of the P. [OE., ME. from Gk.].

POPE (2), *n*. parish priest of the Orthodox Church in Slav countries. [Russ.].

POPERY [pō'pe-ri], *n*. term describing the principles and power of Roman Catholicism and used by its enemies.

POPGUN [pop'gun], *n*. small toy gun worked by compressed air which fires a cork with a pop.

POPINJAY [po'pin-jā], *n*. parrot; effeminate overdressed youth, dandy, fop. [ME. from OFr.].

POPISH [pō'pish], *adj.* of, relating or belonging to, having some of the characteristics of, the Pope or popery.

POPLAR [pop'ler], *n*. tall tree with a relatively slender trunk of white, soft wood. [ME. from L.].

POPLIN [pop'lin], *n*. a fabric of silk and worsted wool. [Uncert.].

POPPET [po'pet], *n*. term of endearment for a child. [*Var.* of PUPPET].

POPPING-CREASE [po'ping-krēs], *n*. in cricket, crease marked in white chalk four feet from the stumps, within which is the batsman's ground.

POPPLE (1) [po'pl], *v.t.* to bubble; ripple. POPPLE (2), *n*. lively agitation of the surface of water. POPPLY, *adj.* (of water) broken, agitated, almost choppy. [ME.].

POPPY [po'pi], *n*. plant of the genus *Papaver*; **p. head,** seed-case of the p. [OE., ME.].

POPPYCOCK [po'pi-kok], *n*. (*slang, orig. U.S.*) nonsense, rubbish. [POPPY and COCK, shortened form of COCAINE].

POPULACE [po'pyōō-las], *n*. the common people considered collectively as a class; inhabitants of a city. [It. from L.].

POPULAR [po'pyōō-ler], *adj.* of, relating to, appealing to, the populace; admired or liked by many

people, favourite; easily comprehensible, plain; obvious, superficial; **p. government,** government according to a majority; **p. front,** movement advocating a coalition (government) of progressive political parties. [L.].

POPULARITY [po-pyōō-la'ri-ti], *n*. state of being popular or in favour with the people.

POPULARIZE [po'pyōō-la-rīz], *v.t.* to render popular or common; spread among people by using simple and attractive means.

POPULATE [po'pyōō-lāt], *v.t.* to furnish with inhabitants, provide with people. [LL.].

POPULATION [po-pyōō-lā'shn], *n*. act of populating; number of people in a country or place; inhabitants of a place considered collectively. [LL.].

POPULOUS [po'pyōō-lōōs], *adj.* full of inhabitants, abounding with people. [L.].

PORCATE [paw'kāt], *adj.* (*zool.*) formed in ridges. [L.].

PORCELAIN (1) [paw'se-lān], *n*. fine white semi-transparent earthenware; chinaware. PORCELAIN (2), *adj.* made of p. [It.].

PORCH [pawch], *n*. covered structure built round an entrance to a building. [L.].

PORCINE [paw'sīn], *adj.* of, relating to, resembling swine. [L.].

PORCUPINE [paw'kyōō-pīn], *n*. a rodent which is covered with protective quills. [ME. from OFr.].

PORE (1) [paw(r)], *n*. minute opening in the membranous surfaces of plants and animals by which fluids are exhaled or absorbed; small interstice between the molecules or particles of bodies. [Gk.].

PORE (2), *v.i.* **to p. over,** to study steadily and persistently with fixed attention. [ME.].

PORK [pawk], *n*. flesh of the pig, fresh or salted for eating; **p. butcher,** butcher who sells p. and sausages etc. made from p. PORKER, *n*. young pig; pig fattened for the table. PORKY, *adj.* resembling, containing, or tasting of, p.; (*coll.*) fat like a pig. [L.].

PORK PIE (1) [pawk-pī'], *n*. pie containing minced or chopped pork. PORK-PIE (2), *adj.* (of hats) shaped like a p., round and flat.

PORNOGRAPHY [paw-no'gra-fi], *n*. licentious painting or writing; literature which is deliberately obscene. PORNOGRAPHER, *n*. writer or seller of pornographic literature. [Gk.].

PORNOGRAPHIC [paw-no-gra'fik], *adj.* of, relating to, pornography; obscene.

POROSITY [paw-ro'si-ti], *n*. state of having pores or interstices. [*Next*].

POROUS [paw'rōōs], *adj.* having pores, or full of pores or interstices; capable of absorbing water.

PORPHYRY [paw'fi-ri], *n*. a rock, having a felspathic base, through which large crystals of a different colour are disseminated. PORPHYRITIC [paw-fi-ri'tik], *adj.* (*geol.*) of, relating to, resembling or containing, p. [Gk.].

PORPOISE [paw'pus], *n*. mammal of the dolphin family of the genus *Phocaena*, having a stubby snout. [OFr.].

PORRIDGE [po'rij], *n*. oatmeal or other meal boiled in water or milk as food. [POTTAGE].

PORRINGER [po'rin-jer], *n*. small dish for holding porridge.

PORT (1) [pawt], *n*. a heavy red wine. [*Oporto*, Portugal].

PORT (2), *n*. port-hole; hole in the hull of a man-of-war for a gun to shoot through; in machinery, hole for light and air or for steam, fuel and exhaust gases. [L.].

PORT (3), *n*. harbour for the protection and loading and unloading of ships; town provided with such; (*fig.*) place of refuge, shelter; **p. of entry,** p. providing customs facilities. [OE. from L.].

PORT (4), *v.t.* (*milit.*) to present (a rifle) for inspection. PORT (5), *n*. style of gait or bearing. [L.].

PORT (6), *n*. the left side of a ship viewed from the stern, larboard. PORT (7), *v.t.* to turn (the helm) so that a ship moves to the left.

PORTABLE [paw'ta-bl], *adj.* able to be carried about easily, movable; not bulky.

PORTAGE [paw'tij], *n*. act of carrying; price of carrying; stretch of land between watercourses over which a boat or canoe is carried. [Fr.].

PORTAL [paw'tal], *n*. gate, entrance or doorway, arched gateway; (*anat.*) passage leading to the liver; **p. vein,** large vein passing through this passage. [L.].

PORTECRAYON [pawt-krā'on], *n*. small metallic holder for a crayon. [Fr.].

PORTCULLIS [pawt-ku'lis], *n*. (*fort.*) powerful

grating held in position over a gateway and let down as a means of defence. [Fr.].

PORTEND [paw-tend'], *v.t.* to indicate some future event by signs, presage. [L.].

PORTENT [paw'tent], *n.* omen of evil, significant sign. [L.].

PORTENTOUS [paw-ten'tŏŏs], *adj.* having the power of a portent, ominous; monstrous; imposing; pompous. [*Prec.*].

PORTER (1) [paw'ter], *n.* doorkeeper or gatekeeper, *esp.* of an hotel or public institution. [L.].

PORTER (2), *n.* carrier of burdens; man employed at a railway station or elsewhere to handle passengers' luggage and to shift heavy loads; a dark brown beer. PORTERAGE, *n.* work of a p.; money paid to a p. [OFr.].

PORTERHOUSE [paw'ter-hows], *n.* † chop-house; **p. steak**, steak cut from between the sirloin and tenderloin.

PORTFIRE [pawt'fier], *n.* firework device used for igniting, *esp.* in mining operations. [Fr.].

PORTFOLIO [pawt-fō'li-ō], *n.* portable case for keeping papers, maps and drawings in; collection of papers connected with a state department; office of a minister of a state department. [It.].

PORT-HOLE [pawt'hōl], *n.* hole for ventilation in the side of a ship, scuttle; passage for steam.

PORTICO [paw'ti-kō], *n.* covered walk or entrance enclosed by columns. [It.].

PORTIERE, portière [paw-tyāer'], *n.* curtain hung over a doorway. [Fr.].

PORTION (1) [paw'shn], *n.* part, small share or division; part of an estate; a helping of food etc.). PORTION (2), *v.t.* to divide into shares; allot a certain amount, endow. [L.].

PORTLAND [pawt'land], *adj.* relating to the Isle of Portland; **P. cement**, a yellowish cement; **P. stone**, variety of oolite found in *Portland* in Dorset.

PORTLY [pawt'li], *adj.* corpulent. [PORT (5)].

PORTMANTEAU [pawt-man'tō], *n.* framed leather bag hinged at the middle for carrying clothes in. PORTMANTEAU-WORD, word which is a novel combination in form and meaning of two words or parts of two words. [Fr.].

PORTRAIT [paw'trit], *n.* representation of a person in paint or writing; picture of an individual.

PORTRAITURE [paw'tri-tyŏŏr], *n.* art of portrait painting; vivid delineation.

PORTRAY [paw-trā'], *v.t.* to paint or draw a likeness of; describe in words. PORTRAYAL, *n.* act of portraying; representation, delineation. [OFr.].

POSE (1) [pōz], *v.t. and i.* to place in a pose, arrange (the body) in a particular position, *esp.* to form a composition for a picture; set out as a problem; assume an unnatural attitude; give a false impression of oneself; take up a deliberately conceived position. POSE (2), *n.* position, posture adopted by the body; attitude of mind which is unnatural, pretence. [Fr. from L.].

POSE (3), *v.t.* to confuse by asking difficult questions, puzzle. [(OP)POSE].

POSER [pō'zer], *n.* one who poses; a puzzle.

POSEUR [pō-zur'], *n.* one who parades affected attitudes, exhibitionist. [Fr.].

POSH (1) [posh], *adj.* (*slang*) good, smart. POSH (2), *v.t. and i.* **to p. up**, to smarten up.

POSIT [po'sit], *v.t.* to postulate; lay down, affirm, or assume as a fact. [L.].

POSITION (1) [po-zi'shn], *n.* state of being placed; place or situation occupied by anything; state reached in the development of affairs; rank, social standing; job; pose. POSITION (2), *v.t.* to place in a particular p., assign a p. to; *v. reflex.* to take up a p. (chiefly in sport). POSITIONAL, *adj.* relating to p. [L.].

POSITIVE (1) [po'zi-tiv], *adj.* expressed explicitly, affirmed without qualification, definite, specific; unconditional; being absolutely convinced, without any mental reservation; dogmatic; existing in fact, actual, real; having definite characteristics; (*elect.*) state of electrical potential due to a deficiency in electrons; denoting a conventional current imagined to flow contrary to the movement of electrons; (*gram.*) expressing the simple state or degree; (*math.*) more than nought, plus; (*philos.*) of, related to, positivism. POSITIVE (2), *n.* that which is p.; (*elect.*) the p. pole, anode; print or film which is the reverse in tones to the negative. POSITIVELY, *adv.* in a p. manner. POSITIVENESS, *n.* state of being p. [L.].

POSITIVISM [po'zi-ti-vizm], *n.* (*philos.*) philosophy based on empirical investigation; dogmatism.

POSITIVIST, *n.* (*philos.*) advocate of p. POSITIVISTIC [po-zi-ti-vis'tik], *adj.* relating to p. [Fr.].

POSITRON [po'zi-tron], *n.* (*phys.*) a positive electron. [POSI(TIVE) (ELEC)TRON].

POSSE [po'si], *n.* a number of men. [L.].

POSSESS [po-zes'], *v.t.* to hold, own, occupy; have the power over, dominate. POSSESSED, *adj.* suffering from possession (by the Devil); in a frenzy. [L.].

POSSESSION [po-ze'shn], *n.* act of possessing; state of being possessed; ownership; that which is possessed, goods, property, territory controlled by a country outside of its own boundaries. [L.].

POSSESSIVE [po-ze'siv], *adj.* relating to, denoting, possession; **p. case**, (*gram.*) genitive case indicating possession. POSSESSIVELY, *adv.* in a p. manner. [L.].

POSSESSOR [po-ze'ser], *n.* one who possesses. POSSESSORY, *adj.* relating to possession; having possession. [L.].

POSSET [po'sit], *n.* milk curdled with wine or stout and spiced. [ME.].

POSSIBILITY [po-si-bi'li-ti], *n.* quality of being possible, power of existing or of happening; state of being possible; possible thing or event, chance; (*pl.*) potentialities. [L.].

POSSIBLE (1) [po'si-bl], *adj.* able to come about; that can be done; practicable; able to be considered, tolerable. POSSIBLE (2), *n.* (*coll.*) person with some chance of being selected, appointed etc. POSSIBLY, *adv.* according to events which may occur, perhaps. [L.].

POSSUM [po'sum], *n.* (*coll.*) opossum; **to play p.**, to sham death; sham disinterest or ignorance. [OPOSSUM].

POST (1) [pōst], *n.* upright stake set in the ground to serve as a support; **driven from pillar to p.**, driven from one place, extremity, to another. POST (2), *v.t.* to affix (a notice) to a p., *hence* to put up (a notice) for public reading, allot a duty to. [OE. from L.].

POST (3), *n.* position occupied by troops, air-raid wardens etc.; isolated position, outlying settlement; position, duty to which someone is assigned; employment, job; transmission and delivery of messages, letters and parcels; office, box, where letters are left for transmission; delivery of such letters; time of clearing a post-box; time taken in delivering letters by post; postman's round; **last p.**, military bugle-call sounded at tattoo and at funerals. GENERAL-POST, parlour game in which the players change places. POST (4), *v.t. and i.* to dispatch a letter; travel by stages (posts), travel in great haste; (*bookkeeping*) transfer to a ledger, bring (a ledger) up to date; keep (a person) well informed. POST-HASTE, as fast as possible. [Fr. from L.].

POST-, *pref.* after, later than; behind. [L.].

POSTAGE [pōs'tij], *n.* rate charged for postal conveyance; **p. stamp**, adhesive piece of paper used to prepay p. on letters etc.

POSTAL [pōs'tal], *adj.* relating to transmission by post; **p. order**, money order obtainable and cashable at a post office.

POST-BOX [pōst'boks], *n.* letter-box.

POSTBOY [pōst'boi], *n.* postilion.

POST-CAPTAIN [pōst'kap-tin], *n.* (*naut.*) formerly commander of a ship of more than twenty guns; now, a naval captain of substantive rank.

POSTCARD [pōst'kahd], *n.* card capable of bearing a message to be sent through the post.

POST-CHAISE [pōst'shāz], *n.* (*hist.*) four-wheeled, covered travelling carriage, changing its horses at each post.

POST-DATE [pōst-dāt'], *v.t.* to date a document, *esp.* a cheque, later than the time of writing.

POSTER [pōs'ter], *n.* one who posts notices; bill posted on walls etc. for advertisement and propaganda.

POSTE RESTANTE [pōst-res'tahnt], *n.* department of a post office at which letters are kept till called for. [Fr.].

POSTERIOR (1) [pos-tēer'i-er], *adj.* subsequent, succeeding; behind. POSTERIOR (2), *n.* the buttocks, rear of a thing.

POSTERITY [pos-te'ri-ti], *n.* descendants, children of a common forebear; future generations. [ME. from Fr.].

POSTERN [pos'tern], *n.* small door in the wall of a castle; back door. [OFr. from LL.].

POST-GRADUATE (1) [pōst-gra'dyŏŏ-at], *adj.* pertaining to university studies pursued after graduation. POST-GRADUATE (2), *n.* member of a university pursuing study after graduation.

POSTHUMOUS [pos'tyŏŏ-mŏŏs], *adj.* happening

after death; born after the father's death, received, awarded, after death. POSTHUMOUSLY, *adv.* after death. [L.].

POSTIL(L)ION [pos-til′yun], *n.* one riding on the foremost near horse of a carriage-team. [Fr. from L.].

POST-IMPRESSIONISM [pŏst-im-pre′shn-izm], *n.* an advanced form of impressionism.

POST-IMPRESSIONIST (1) [pŏst-im-pre′shn-ist], *n.* disciple or admirer of post-impressionism. POST-IMPRESSIONIST (2), *adj.* of, or pertaining to, post-impressionism or post-impressionists.

POSTING [pōs′ting], *n.* transference to a ledger; (*milit.*) sending to a different unit or duty.

POSTMAN [pōst′man], *n.* person who collects and delivers postal packages.

POSTMARK (1) [pōst′mahk], *n.* place, time and cancellation mark stamped on a letter etc. sent through the post. POSTMARK (2), *v.t.* to put a p. on.

POSTMASTER [pōst′mah-ster], *n.* head of a post office; foundation scholar at Merton College, Oxford. POSTMASTER-GENERAL, chief officer of the postal system.

POSTMERIDIAN [pŏst-me-ri′di-an], *adj.* afternoon, after the sun has passed the meridian.

POST-MORTEM (1) [pŏst-maw′tem], *adj.* done, happening to, the body after death. POST-MORTEM (2), *n.* official examination, autopsy of a dead body to ascertain the cause of death. [L.].

POSTNATAL [pŏst-nā′tal], *adj.* occurring after birth.

POSTNUPTIAL [pŏst-nup′shal], *adj.* occurring after marriage.

POST-OBIT (1) [post-ō′bit], *adj.* (*leg.*) effective, payable, after the death of a person. POST-OBIT (2), *n.* loan repayable only after the death of one to whom the borrower is heir. [L.].

POST OFFICE [pōst′o-fis], *n.* office for handling the dispatch and delivery of postal packages and communications; department of the state concerned with postal, telephone and telegraphic services.

POSTPONE [pōst-pōn′], *v.t.* to delay, defer to a later time. POSTPONER, *n.* one who postpones. [L.].

POSTPONEMENT [pōst-pōn′ment], *n.* act of postponing, length of time postponed.

POSTPRANDIAL [pōst-pran′di-al], *adj.* after dinner, lunch. [L.].

POSTRORSE [pŏst-raws′], *adj.* doubled back. [L.].

POSTSCRIPT [pōst′skript], *n.* note added to a completed letter, a written afterthought; talk at the end of a news broadcast. [L.].

POSTULANT [pos′tyŏo-lant], *n.* one who postulates; candidate for holy orders. [L.].

POSTULATE (1) [pos′tyŏo-lāt], *v.t.* to request, demand; assume as a basis of argument; (*eccles.*) nominate for a benefice. POSTULATE (2) [pos′tyŏo-lat], *n.* demand, request; assumption made as a basis, without proof. POSTULATION [pos-tyŏo-lā′shn], *n.* act of postulating, a p. [L.].

POSTURE (1) [pos′tyŏor], *n.* position, bearing of the body, *esp.* an attitude, pose consciously assumed; attitude of mind. POSTURE (2), *v.i.* to assume a p., adopt an affected attitude of mind or body. POSTURAL, *adj.* pertaining to p. [L.].

POST-WAR [pōst-waw(r)′], *adj.* after a war; **p. credit,** sum deducted from income tax during World War II, to be repayable after the war.

POSY [pō′zi], *n.* motto in verse, accompanying a gift; small bouquet of flowers. [POESY].

POT (1) [pot], *n.* rounded vessel for holding liquids; contents of a pot, *hence* (*pl.*) large amount; contents of the pool in certain card-games; (*coll.*) silver cup won as a trophy in athletic or other contests; deep hole containing water; (*coll.*) casual, rapid shot, usually from a short distance; vessel containing earth for growing flowers; [pŏ] (*coll.*), chamber-pot; **big p.,** (*slang*) important person; **to go to p.,** to be ruined. CHAMBER-POT, (*coll.*) bedroom utensil. JACK-POT, form of poker in which play cannot be opened unless one of the players holds a pair of jacks or better. POT (2) (*pres.pt.* POTTING, *pret. and p.pt.* POTTED), *v.t. and i.* to place in a p., *esp.* in order to keep or preserve, plant in a p.; (*billiards*) drive the red or the white into the pocket by striking with the cue ball; (*coll.*) shoot casually, take a p.-shot. [OE.].

POTABLE [pō′ta-bl], *adj.* drinkable. POTABILITY [pō-ta-bi′li-ti], *n.* fitness for drinking. [L.].

POTAGE, see POTTAGE.

POTASH [po′tash], *n.* potassium carbonate obtained from vegetable ashes, *hence* any compound of potassium; **caustic p.,** potassium hydroxide. [Du.].

POTASSIUM [po-ta′si-um], *n.* metallic alkaline element symbolized by K. [MdL.].

POTATION [po-tā′shn], *n.* a deep draught, act of taking such a draught. [L.].

POTATO (*pl.* **potatoes**) [pō-tā′tō], *n.* edible tuber of the plant *Solanum tuberosum*; the plant itself. [Native].

POT-BELLIED [pot-be′lid], *adj.* having a round prominent belly.

POTBOILER [pot′boi-ler], *n.* inferior literary or artistic work produced solely to obtain money.

POT-BOUND [pot′bownd], *adj.* (*hort.*) (of a plant) growing in a flowerpot too small for its roots.

POT-BOY [pot′boi], *n.* boy employed in a public-house.

POT(H)EEN [po-tĕn′], *n.* whisky made in an illicit still. [Ir.].

POTENCE, POTENCY [pō′tens(-i)], *n.* power, strength, *esp.* sexual vigour. [L.].

POTENT [pō′tent], *adj.* strong, effective, (of a man) sexually capable. POTENTLY, *adv.* in p. fashion. [L.].

POTENTATE [pō′ten-tāt], *n.* one exercising power, powerful ruler, prince. [L.].

POTENTIAL (1) [po-ten′shal], *adj.* having latent power, possessing inherent powers, capable of exerting power, energy; (*gram.*) expressing possibility. POTENTIAL (2), *n.* that which has latent power; capacity, potentiality; (*elect.*) electrical pressure, force compelling the flow of current from a higher-to a lower-powered pole of an apparatus. POTENTIALLY, *adv.* with respect to inherent power or capacity. [LL.].

POTENTIALITY [po-ten-shi-a′li-ti], *n.* inherent capacity, possibility of development.

POTHEEN, see POTEEN.

POTHER [po′Ther], *n.* noisy bother, fussy to-do. [Unkn.].

POT-HERB [pot′herb], *n.* herb used in cooking.

POT-HOLE [pot′hōl], *n.* (*geol.*) deep round hole in the earth; deep hole in a river bed; hole in a road surface.

POTHOOK [pot′hŏok], *n.* S-shaped hook on which pots are hung; S-shaped figure used in learning to write.

POTHOUSE [pot′hows], *n.* small, disreputable public-house.

POTION [pō′shn], *n.* draught of poison, drug or intoxicating liquid. [L.].

POTLUCK [pot-luk′], *n.* anything got haphazard on the spur of the moment; any food which happens to be available.

POTMAN [pot′man], *n.* employee in public-house who collects and cleans the glasses etc.

POT-POURRI [pō-pŏo′ri], *n.* mixture of dried herbs and rose or other flower petals kept in a jar for its perfume; musical medley. [Fr.].

POTSHERD [pot′sherd], *n.* fragment of broken pottery.

POT(T)AGE [po′tij], *n.* thick meat soup boiled with vegetables; **mess of p.,** something worthless. [Fr.].

POTTED [po′tid], *adj.* preserved in a pot; (*fig.*) applied to a condensed abstract of a whole subject. [OE.].

POTTER (1) [po′ter], *n.* maker of earthenware vessels. [OE.].

POTTER (2), *v.i.* to dawdle about, fuss feebly and incompetently, lounge. [ME.].

POTTERY [po′te-ri], *n.* earthenware; art of making earthenware; place where it is made.

POTTING [po′ting], *n.* act of making pots; act of placing in pots; act of taking pot-shots; **p. shed,** shed where plants are reared in pots for subsequent planting out.

POUCH (1) [powch], *n.* purse, small bag, *esp.* for carrying tobacco; one of the small pockets in military equipment for carrying cartridges; protuberant sac; pocket in which a marsupial carries its young; (*U.S.*) diplomatic bag. POUCH (2), *v.t.* to put in a p., hold in the cavity of the cheek, pocket. [ME.].

POUFFE [pŏof], *n.* circular stuffed cushion used as a seat. [Fr.].

POULT [pōlt], *n.* young pheasant or chicken. [ME.].

POULTERER [pōl′te-rer], *n.* dealer in poultry.

POULTICE (1) [pōl′tis], *n.* mass of hot, damp meal, bread etc., applied to sores or inflammation. POULTICE (2), *v.t.* to apply a p. to. [L.].

POULTRY [pōl′tri], *n.* domestic fowls used for food. [OFr.].

POUNCE (1) [powns], *n.* sudden downward swoop with intent to seize; front toe of a bird of prey's claws. POUNCE (2), *v.i.* to leap (upon), swoop (on)

ŏo is pronounced as in food; ŏo as in hood; th as in *think*; TH as in *that*; zh as in azure. ~ = related to.

suddenly in order to seize; intervene suddenly and fiercely; *(fig.)* **to p. on,** seize, detect rapidly. [Uncert.].

POUNCE (3), *n.* fine bone powder used to prepare vellum for writing or sprinkled on paper to prevent ink from spreading. POUNCE (4), *v.t.* to prepare paper with p. [Fr. from L.].

POUND (1) [pownd], *n.* unit of weight containing 16 ounces avoirdupois; 7,000 grains; monetary unit (£) containing, in England, 20 shillings or 240 pence; **p. troy,** standard for weighing precious metals and stones (12 ounces troy, 5,760 grains). [OE., L.].

POUND (2), *n.* walled enclosure for keeping strayed or distrained cattle; place for impounded objects. POUND (3), *v.t.* to place in a p., impound. [OE.].

POUND (4), *v.t. and i.* to hammer to powder, break up into small pieces; thump heavily, pummel, bombard heavily; walk, run, heavily and thumpingly. [OE.].

POUNDAGE [pown′dij], *n.* *(hist.)* 5-per-cent tax formerly levied on imported and exported goods; commission charged on the sale of distrained goods; commission charged on postal orders etc.

POUNDAL [pown′dal], *n.* the force which, acting for one second, will impart to a pound of matter a velocity of one foot per second. [Coined word].

POUR [paw(r)], *v.t. and i.* to cause to flow out in a stream, discharge copiously; dispense lavishly, shower upon; *(coll.)* rain heavily. POURER, *n.* that which pours. [ME.].

POURBOIRE [poor′bwah(r)], *n.* tip, gratuity. [Fr.].

POURPARLER [poor-pah′lā], *n.* a preliminary diplomatic conversation. [Fr.].

POUT (1) [powt], *v.t. and i.* to thrust the lips forward, assume a sulky expression. POUT (2), *n.* act of pouting; sulkiness. POUTER, *n.* one who pouts; pigeon with an excessively inflatable crop. [Unkn.].

POVERTY [po′ver-ti], *n.* state of being poor, of being deficient in any quality, indigence. POVERTY-STRICKEN, *adj.* afflicted with, displaying, p. [ME. from L.].

POWDER (1) [pow′der], *n.* fine particles produced by pulverizing a substance, *esp.* gunpowder; cosmetic powder applied to the skin; medicine in the form of powder. POWDER-BOX, box for cosmetic p. POWDER-FLASK, -HORN, flask in which gunpowder was carried. POWDER-MAGAZINE, magazine for storing explosives. POWDER (2), *v.t. and i.* to sprinkle, cover with p.; grind to p.; use p. on the hair, face etc. [ME., Fr. from L.].

POWDER-BLUE [pow-der-bloo′], *n. and adj.* (having the colour of) powdered smalt used as a pigment.

POWDER-MONKEY [pow′der-mung-ki], *n.* *(hist.)* boy who carried charges of powder from the ship's magazine to the guns.

POWDER-PUFF [pow′der-puf], *n.* pad or bunch of down for applying powder to the face or body.

POWDER-ROOM [pow′der-room], *n.* ladies' dressing-room.

POWDERY [pow′de-ri], *adj.* friable, resembling powder; covered with powder.

POWER (1) [powr], *n.* capacity for action, capacity for exerting force, doing work; influence, capacity for using the bodily organs; *(pl.)* physical vitality, bodily vigour; force exerted, the exercise of strength; capacity for, or exercise of, control, authority, rule, influence (over); person having influence or authority; a state and its government in respect of its effective military strength, *esp.* one of the great imperialist nations; *(pl.)* supernatural influences, deities, one of the Orders of Angels; *(leg.)* authority of action granted to another; *(math.)* product obtained by multiplying a quantity by itself; *(mech.)* energy doing work; *(opt.)* magnifying capacity of a lens; *(elect.)* current used to drive apparatus, as distinct from that used for lighting; **a p. of,** *(dial.)* a great number or amount of. POWER-DIVE, *(aeron.)* dive made with the engine working. POWER-DRIVEN, operated by a motor or engine, not by hand. POWER (2), *v.t.* to supply with p., provide (a vehicle, aircraft etc.) with an engine. [ME. from AFr.].

POWERFUL [powr′fool], *adj.* having power, capable of exerting great strength, having great authority, producing great energy, cogent. POWERFULLY, *adv.* with great power.

POWER-HOUSE [powr′hows], *n.* building or section of a building where electric power is produced.

POWERLESS [powr′les], *adj.* without power, helpless. POWERLESSLY, *adv.* in p. fashion.

POWER-LOOM [powr′loom], *n.* loom operated by mechanical power.

POWER-STATION [powr′stā-shn], *n.* power-house.

POW-WOW (1) [pow′wow], *n.* conference among North American Indians; a friendly discussion. POW-WOW (2), *v.i.* to hold a friendly and informal discussion. [NAmerInd.].

POX [poks], *n.* one of several diseases marked by pustular eruption on the skin, *esp.* syphilis. [*Pl.* of POCK].

PRACTICABLE [prak′ti-ka-bl], *adj.* feasible, possible of use or operation. PRACTICABILITY [prak-ti-ka-bi′li-ti], *n.* quality of being p., possibility.

PRACTICAL [prak′ti-kal], *adj.* concerned with, related to, action; workable; effective; soundly functional; (of persons) capable, sound, good at affairs, unimaginative, trained and experienced in a thing. PRACTICALITY, *n.* state of being p. PRACTICALLY, *adv.* in p. fashion; almost, virtually. [Gk.].

PRACTICE [prak′tis], *n.* the performance of a thing, action in accordance with a theory; habitual, customary action, regular performance, customary observance; repeated exercise of some kind in order to become skilled in its performance, time devoted to such training, the training itself; the exercise of a doctor's profession, his patients, the field of his activity (also applied to barristers, architects etc.); *(arith.)* a concise method of calculating; *(leg.)* procedure of a court of law. [*Next*].

PRACTISE [prak′tis], *v.t.* to carry out (a theory) in action; do as a custom or regular performance; constantly to perform some action, carry out (some activity) in order to become skilled in its exercise; follow a profession; *v.i.* to make an habitual practice, carry out an activity repeatedly in order to become skilled; follow the profession of medicine outside a hospital; play upon. PRACTISED, *adj.* skilled by practice. PRACTISING, *adj.* actively engaged in. [ME., OFr. from MedL.].

PRACTITIONER [prak-ti′shn-er], *n.* one who practises an art or profession, *esp.* a doctor. [OFr.].

PRAE-, *pref.* before, prior to. [L.].

PR(A)ETORIAN [prē-taw′ri-an], *adj.* *(Roman hist.)* relating to a praetor or Roman magistrate. [L.].

PRAGMATIC [prag-ma′tik], *adj.* *(hist.)* relating to affairs of state; pragmatical; relating to pragmatism. [Gk.].

PRAGMATICAL [prag-ma′ti-kal], *adj.* officious, dogmatic.

PRAGMATISM [prag′ma-tizm], *n.* *(philos.)* system which judges the truth of a conception by its concrete effects. PRAGMATIST, *n.* believer in p. [Gk.].

PRAIRIE [prāer′i], *n.* grassy plain, great tract of level grassland. PRAIRIE-DOG, rodent allied to the marmots. PRAIRIE-OYSTER, pick-me-up, usually containing raw egg and Worcester sauce. PRAIRIE-SQUIRREL, small burrowing American rodent. PRAIRIE-WOLF, coyote. [Fr. from L.].

PRAISE (1) [prāz], *v.t.* to express approval of, commend highly, glorify. PRAISE (2), *n.* act of praising; expression of commendation or approval; veneration of the Deity, worship. PRAISER, *n.* one who praises. [ME., OFr. from L.].

PRAISEWORTHY [prāz′wer-THi], *adj.* worthy of praise. PRAISEWORTHILY, *adv.* in p. fashion.

PRALINE [prah′lēn], *n.* sweetmeat of nut kernels roasted in boiling sugar. [Fr.].

PRANCE [prahns], *v.i.* (of a four-footed animal) to spring up on the hind legs, rear up; (of persons) strut, swagger about. PRANCING, *n.* act of prancing; swagger. [ME.].

PRANDIAL [pran′di-al], *n.* relating to luncheon or dinner. [L.].

PRANK (1) [prangk], *v.t. and i.* to deck out; dress oneself up. PRANK (2), *n.* irresponsible frolic, joking action, escapade. [Uncert.].

PRATE [prāt], *v.i.* to talk emptily, pretentiously and volubly, chatter sententiously. PRATING (1), *n.* stupid, idle, sententious talk. PRATING (2), *adj.* talking idly and dully. [ME. from OIcel.].

PRATIQUE [pra′tik, pra-tēk′], *n.* permission to communicate with the shore granted to a vessel showing a clean bill of health. [Fr.].

PRATTLE (1) [pra′tl], *v.i.* to chatter childishly, babble inconsequently. PRATTLE (2), *n.* childish chatter, aimless baby-talk. PRATTLER, *n.* one who prattles. [PRATE].

PRAWN (1) [prawn], *n.* an edible marine crustacean. PRAWN (2), *v.i.* to fish for prawns. [ME.].

PRAY [prā], *v.t. and i.* to beg for, entreat for; utter

The accent ′ after a syllable = stress (u-pon′). The mark ‾ over a vowel = length (ā in made; ō in bone).

prayers (for a thing), beg earnestly; address oneself to God. PRAYER (1) [prä′er], *n.* one who prays. [ME. from L.].

PRAYER (2) [präer], *n.* act of praying; supplication made to superior powers, earthly or supernatural, petition to God; words, form in which such petition or worship is made; fervent request or desire; **p. rug, wheel**, wheel or disk in which prayers are enclosed and rotated by Buddhists. PRAYER-BOOK, book containing set forms of p. for various occasions. PRAYER-MEETING, assembly for p. [ME., OFr. from L.].

PRAYERFUL [präer′fŏŏl], *adj.* devout, fervent in prayer. PRAYERFULLY, *adv.* in p. fashion. PRAYERFULNESS, *n.* state of being p.

PRAYING [prä′ing], *n.* act of making prayers.

PRE-, *pref.* before, in front of, prior to. [L.].

PREACH [prēch], *v.t. and i.* to proclaim the Gospel, teach the lessons of the Scriptures, utter moral exhortations, deliver a sermon; deliver (a discourse); (*slang*) give uncalled-for moral advice or instruction. [ME., OFr. from L.].

PREACHER [prē′cher], *n.* one who preaches, a minister of religion.

PREACHIFY [prē′chi-fī], *v.i.* to preach pratingly.

PREACHING (1) [prē′ching], *n.* act of preaching; sermon; mode of delivering a sermon. PREACHING, (2), *adj.* relating to p. or to a preacher.

PREACHMENT [prēch′ment], *n.* tedious sermon.

PREAMBLE (1) [prē-am′bl], *n.* preface, introductory statement, opening remarks of a speech. PREAMBLE (2), *v.i.* to make a p. [MedL. from L.].

PREBEND [pre′bend], *n.* endowment given to a church for the maintenance of one of the chapter; benefice in the gift of a chapter. PREBENDAL [pre-ben′dal], *adj.* relating to a p. [OFr. from MedL.].

PREBENDARY [pre′ben-da-ri], *n.* holder of a prebend. [MedL.].

PRECARIOUS [pri-käer′i-ŏŏs], *adj.* insecure, dependent on chance; held during the pleasure of another; risky. [L.].

PRECAST [prē-kahst′], *adj.* (of concrete) moulded in blocks before use in building.

PRECATORY [pre′ka-te-ri], *adj.* requesting, expressing a wish. [LL. from L.].

PRECAUTION [pri-kaw′shn], *n.* cautious foresight; provision made in advance, measures taken against a coming danger. PRECAUTIONARY, *adj.* relating to, by way of, p. [LL.].

PRECEDE [prē-sēd′], *v.t. and i.* to go, come, be before; be superior in rank to, take precedence over. [L.].

PRECEDENCE [pre′si-dens], *n.* act of preceding; right to a certain position (at functions etc.) by virtue of rank or office; position to which one is so entitled.

PRECEDENT [pre′si-dent], *n.* previous occurrence from which guidance and example may be drawn; (*leg.*) previous decision or ruling which may be cited in subsequent cases. PRECEDENTED, *adj.* based upon p. [L.].

PRECENTOR [prē-sen′ter], *n.* director of music and choir in a cathedral. PRECENTORSHIP, *n.* position or tenure of a p. [LL.].

PRECEPT [prē′sept], *n.* moral maxim, rule of conduct; (*leg.*) order for payment issued by local authority; election writ. PRECEPTIVE [prē-sep′tiv], *adj.* morally didactic. [L.].

PRECEPTOR [prē-sep′ter], *n.* teacher, tutor. PRECEPTORIAL [prē-sep-taw′ri-al], *adj.* relating to a p. [L.].

PRECEPTRESS [prē-sep′tres], *n.* female teacher.

PRECESSION [pri-se′shn], *n.* outward movement; **p. of the equinoxes**, (*astron.*) slow continuous shifting of the equinoctial points from east to west. [L.].

PRECINCT [prē′singkt], *n.* enclosure within the boundaries of a group of buildings (*esp. eccles.*); (*pl.*) environs of a town or building; American electoral division. [LL. from L.].

PRECIOSITY [pre-shi-o′si-ti], *n.* affectation of refinement. [OFr.].

PRECIOUS [pre′shŏŏs], *adj.* of great value or price; highly esteemed; over-refined and fastidious, (*coll.*) utter, complete (with hostile emphasis); *used elliptically as a noun*; **p. metals**, gold, silver, platinum; **p. stones**, ruby, diamond, sapphire, emerald etc. PRECIOUSLY, *adv.* in p. fashion. [ME., OFr. from L.].

PRECIPICE [pre′si-pis], *n.* sudden, sharp, deep

declivity; perpendicular face of rock; (*fig.*) dangerous situation. [Fr. from L.].

PRECIPITANCE, PRECIPITANCY [pri-si′pi-tans(-i)], *n.* state of being precipitate, rashness; swiftness.

PRECIPITANT [pri-si′pi-tant], *n.* (*chem.*) substance causing precipitation in a liquid. [L.].

PRECIPITANTLY [pri-si′pi-tant-li], *adv.* hastily, rashly, headlong.

PRECIPITATE (1) [pri-si′pi-tāt], *v.t. and i.* to hurl down from a height; hurry on, accentuate (a development); (*chem.*) cause matter held in solution in liquid to fall as a deposit; condense vapour to snow or water; be precipitated. PRECIPITATE (2) [pri-si′pi-tat], *adj.* violent, hasty. PRECIPITATE (3), *n.* (*chem. or meteor.*) something precipitated. PRECIPITATELY, *adv.* in p. fashion. PRECIPITATOR, *n.* that which precipitates; vessel for precipitation. [L.].

PRECIPITATION [pri-si-pi-tā′shn], *n.* impetuous, hasty action; (*chem.*) process of precipitating or being precipitated; that which has been precipitated. [L.].

PRECIPITOUS [pri-si′pi-tŏŏs], *adj.* very steep, of the nature of a precipice. PRECIPITOUSLY, *adv.* in p. fashion. [OFr.].

PRECIS, précis (1) [prä′sē], *n.* an abstract, short summary of the main features of a document. PRECIS (2), *v.t.* to make a p. of. [Fr.].

PRECISE [pri-sīs′], *adj.* clearly defined; punctilious, pedantically exact; carefully articulated. PRECISELY, *adv.* in p. fashion, exactly, unambiguously. PRECISENESS, *n.* state of being p. [Fr. from L.].

PRECISIAN [pri-si′zhn], *n.* formalist, precise observer of custom.

PRECISION [pri-si′zhn], *n.* exactness, preciseness, accuracy; **p. tools etc.**, tools capable of very exact work. [L.].

PRECLUDE [pri-klŏŏd′], *v.t.* to exclude, make impossible, rule out. [L.].

PRECOCIOUS [pri-kō′shŏŏs], *adj.* prematurely developed, either physically, mentally or morally. PRECOCIOUSLY, *adv.* in p. fashion. PRECOCIOUSNESS, *n.* condition of being p. [L.].

PRECOCITY [pri-ko′si-ti], *n.* precociousness. [Fr.].

PRECOGNITION [prē-kog-ni′shn], *n.* foreknowledge, previous cognition. [L.].

PRECONCEIVE [prē-kon-sēv′], *v.t.* to form (an opinion) beforehand.

PRECONCEPTION [prē-kon-sep′shn], *n.* judgment formed beforehand, prejudice.

PRECONCERT [prē-kon-surt′], *v.t.* to prearrange. PRECONCERTED, *adj.* previously planned and agreed.

PRECURSOR [pri-kur′ser], *n.* harbinger; predecessor. PRECURSORY, *adj.* introductory, preceding, announcing in advance. [L.].

PREDACIOUS [pri-dā′shŏŏs], *adj.* predatory, living by preying on others. [L.].

PREDATORY [pre′da-te-ri], *adj.* living by plunder and pillage, wandering in search of prey. [L.].

PREDECEASE (1) [prē-di-sēs′], *v.t.* to die before (another). PREDECEASE (2), *n.* death previous to another's.

PREDECESSOR [prē′di-se-ser], *n.* one who has preceded another in some rank, place or tenure. [ME. from L.].

PREDELLA [pri-de′lah], *n.* platform supporting an altar; raised ledge behind an altar; painting on the face of an altar-step. [It.].

PREDESTINARIAN (1) [prē-des-ti-näer′i-an], *n.* believer in predestination. PREDESTINARIAN (2), *adj.* relating to predestination.

PREDESTINATION [prē-des-ti-nā′shn], *n.* (*theol.*) belief that God has foreordained every action, and predestined every soul to hell or salvation. [MedL.].

PREDESTINE [prē-des′tin], *v.t.* to destine or decree beforehand.

PREDETERMINE [prē-di-tur′min], *v.t.* to predestine, decide, decree, settle in advance. [L.].

PREDIAL [prē′di-al], *adj.* (*leg.*) relating to landed property; pertaining to material objects. [MedL.].

PREDICABLE (1) [pre′di-ka-bl], *adj.* that may be predicated or affirmed. PREDICABLE (2), *n.* (*philos.*) general attribute. PREDICABILITY [pre-di-ka-bi′li-ti], *n.* quality of being p. [Fr. or L.].

PREDICAMENT [pri-di′ka-ment], *n.* difficult and puzzling situation; a predicable. [LL.].

PREDICANT [pre′di-kant], *adj.* relating to, devoted to, preaching. [L.].

PREDICATE (1) [pre′di-kāt], *v.t.* to assert; declare something (about a thing). PREDICATE (2) [pre′di-kat], *n.* that which is affirmed of a thing; (*gram.*) the

---

ŏŏ is pronounced as in food; ŏŏ as in hood; th as in think; TH as in that; zh as in azure.   ∼ = related to.

DSE—P*

words affirming things about the subject of a sentence. PREDICATION [pre-di-kā'shn], *n.* act of predicating; thing predicated; a p. [L.].

PREDICATIVE [pri-di'ka-tiv], *adj.* expressing predication. PREDICATIVELY, *adv.* (*gram.*) as a predicate. [L.].

PREDICT [pri-dikt'], *v.t.* to foretell, prophesy. PREDICTABLE, *adj.* able to be predicted. [L.].

PREDICTION [pri-dik'shn], *n.* act of predicting; that which is predicted. [L.].

PREDICTOR [pri-dik'ter], *n.* one who predicts; instrument enabling a gunner to predict the position of a moving aircraft. [L.].

PREDIGEST [prē-di-jest'], *v.t.* to digest artificially before consumption. PREDIGESTION, *n.* artificial digestion of a food before consumption.

PREDILECTION [prē-di-lek'shn], *n.* prepossession, partiality. [L.].

PREDISPOSE [prē-dis-pōz'], *v.t.* to incline beforehand (towards an attitude), make susceptible beforehand.

PREDISPOSITION [prē-dis-pō-zi'shn], *n.* state of being predisposed, attitude formed beforehand.

PREDOMINANCE [pri-do'mi-nans], *n.* state of being predominant; supremacy, ascendancy.

PREDOMINANT [pri-do'mi-nant], *adj.* most noticeable, prevailing, ascendant. PREDOMINANTLY, *adv.* in p. fashion.

PREDOMINATE [pri-do'mi-nāt], *v.i.* to be predominant, ascendant over; be the largest or most important element. PREDOMINATION [pri-do-mi-nā'shn], *n.* state or power of predominating; superiority, ascendancy.

PREDORSAL [prē-daw'sal], *adj.* before the back. [PRE and DORSAL].

PRE-ELECTION (1) [prē-i-lek'shn], *n.* election in advance. PRE-ELECTION (2), *adj.* (given, occurring) before an election.

PRE-EMINENCE [prē-e'mi-nens], *n.* state of being pre-eminent, superiority.

PRE-EMINENT [prē-e'mi-nent], *adj.* supremely eminent, surpassingly excellent. PRE-EMINENTLY, *adv.* in p. degree.

PRE-EMPTION [prē-emp'shn], *n.* (*leg.*) prior right to purchase goods. PRE-EMPTIVE, *adj.* by, relating to, p. PRE-EMPTIVE BID, (*bridge*) high bid intended to prevent further calling. [MedL.].

PREEN [prēn], *v.t.* (of birds) to clean (the feathers) with the beak; (*fig., reflex.*) (of persons) strut, show self-satisfaction. [ME.].

PRE-EXIST [prē-eg-zist'], *v.i.* to exist in a previous life. PRE-EXISTENCE, *n.* existence in a previous state, on a previous plane. PRE-EXISTENT, *adj.* existing previously.

PREFAB [prē-fab'], *n.* (*coll.*) prefabricated house.

PREFABRICATE [prē-fab'ri-kāt], *v.t.* to construct (buildings etc.) in shaped sections ready to be assembled.

PREFACE (1) [pre'fas], *n.* introductory and explanatory statement at the beginning of a book etc., initial part of a speech. PREFACE (2), *v.t.* to introduce by a p.; precede, introduce. [Fr. from L.].

PREFATORY [pre'fa-te-ri], *adj.* as, by way of, a preface. [L.].

PREFECT [prē'fekt], *n.* (*hist.*) Roman magistrate of high rank; public school monitor; administrative head of a department of France; head of the Paris police. PREFECTORIAL [prē-fek-taw'ri-al], *adj.* of, or pertaining to, a p. or his status or powers. [L.].

PREFECTURE [prē'fek-tyoor], *n.* jurisdiction, residence, office, or tenure of a prefect. [Fr.].

PREFER [pri-fur'], *v.t.* to like better than, wish rather than; bring forward, submit; promote. [L.].

PREFERABLE [pre'fe-ra-bl], *adj.* more to be desired, fit to be preferred. PREFERABLY, *adv.* in preference.

PREFERENCE [pre'fe-rens], *n.* act of preferring, feeling which inspires such action, thing so preferred, power of preferring; (*econ.*) special tariff discrimination in favour of a country; **p. share**, share entitled to first call on profits for its dividend payment. [MedL.].

PREFERENTIAL [pre-fe-ren'shal], *adj.* enjoying or giving a preference.

PREFERMENT [pri-fur'ment], *n.* act of preferring; promotion to a higher office, *esp.* in the Church.

PREFIGURE [prē-fi'ger], *v.t.* to represent what is to come. [MedL.].

PREFINE [prē-fīn'], *v.t.* to limit beforehand. [On the analogy of DEFINE].

PREFIX (1) [prē'fiks], *v.t.* to place before; put before as a prefix. PREFIX (2), *n.* word coming before other

words; (*gram.*) preceding particle forming part of a compounded word. [OFr.].

PREFLORATION [prē-flaw-rā'shn], *n.* (*bot.*) the arrangement of the floral envelopes before they expand. [Fr.].

PREGLACIAL [prē-glā'shal], *adj.* before the Pleistocene period.

PREGNANCY [preg'nan-si], *n.* state of being pregnant.

PREGNANT [preg'nant], *adj.* with child in the womb, having conceived; prolific; full of importance, matter or implication; (*gram.*) implying more than is directly expressed. PREGNANTLY, *adv.* in p. fashion. [L.].

PREHENSILE [prē-hen'sil], *adj.* capable of grasping and holding. PREHENSILITY [prē-hen-si'li-ti], *n.* quality of being p. [L.].

PREHENSION [prē-hen'shn], *n.* act of, capacity for, grasping, seizing; mental apprehension. [L.].

PREHISTORIC [prē-his-to'rik], *adj.* related to the periods before written records; (*coll.*) old, outmoded.

PREHISTORY [prē-his'te-ri], *n.* history of the ages before written records; prehistoric archaeology.

PREJUDGE [prē-juj'], *v.t.* to judge before examination, decide in advance of evidence.

PREJUDICE (1) [pre'joo-dis], *n.* a partial opinion, bias, prepossession; (*leg.*) harm, injury; **without** p., without detraction from, or abrogation of, any right or claim. PREJUDICE (2), *v.t.* to inspire with a p.; injure, detract from. PREJUDICED, *adj.* having a p., biased. [L.].

PREJUDICIAL [pre-joo-di'shal], *adj.* tending to prejudice; injurious to. PREJUDICIALLY, *adv.* in p. fashion.

PRELACY [pre'la-si], *n.* office of a prelate; the collective body of prelates; episcopacy. [MedL.].

PRELATE [pre'lat], *n.* ecclesiastical dignitary, *esp.* a bishop or archbishop. PRELATICAL [pre-la'ti-kal], *adj.* relating to prelates. [ME. from LL.].

PRELECT [prē-lekt'], *v.i.* to lecture, be a prelector. PRELECTION, *n.* public lecture. PRELECTOR, *n.* university lecturer. [L.].

PRELIMINARY (1) [pri-li'mi-na-ri], *adj.* prefatory, preceding the main action or business. PRELIMINARY (2), *n.* introductory measure, p. action, examination. [L.].

PRELUDE (1) [pre'lyood], *n.* a preliminary, that which precedes the main event; (*mus.*) opening movement, introducing the principal theme; piece of music resembling this. PRELUDE (2), *v.t. and i.* to introduce, foreshadow; serve as a p. [L.].

PREMATURE [pre'ma-tyoor], *adj.* before its time, earlier than is fitting, or usual; untimely; **p. birth**, birth occurring before gestation is complete. PREMATURELY, *adv.* before the proper time. [L.].

PREMEDITATE [prē-me'di-tāt], *v.t.* to think about, plan, contrive in advance. [L.].

PREMEDITATION [prē-me-di-tā'shn], *n.* act of premeditating, contrivance beforehand. [L.].

PREMIER (1) [pre'mi-er], *adj.* principal, foremost, first in importance or rank. PREMIER (2), *n.* Prime Minister. PREMIERSHIP, *n.* office of Prime Minister. [L.].

PREMIÈRE, première [pre-myäer'], *n.* first public performance of a dramatic entertainment, or of a film. [Fr.].

PREMISE (1), **PREMISS** [pre'mis], *n.* assumption on which an argument is based; (*log.*) one of the two propositions of a syllogism; (*leg.*) introductory part of a lease describing the property in question; (*pl.*) (**premises** *only*) building or part of a building, and any land going with it, occupied under a lease. PREMISE (2), *v.t.* to take as a p., assume. [OFr. from LL.].

PREMIUM [prē'mi-um], *n.* something paid over and above what is normally due, as a recompense for some special service or advantage; fee paid to join a business or be taught a profession; periodical payment on an insurance policy; amount by which the market value of shares exceeds their par value; (*fig., coll.*) a high value or advantage. [L.].

PREMOLAR [prē-mō'ler], *n.* a bicuspid tooth.

PREMONITION [prē-mo-ni'shn], *n.* forewarning; presentiment, irrational foreboding. [L.].

PREMONITORY [prē-mo'ni-te-ri], *adj.* forewarning. [L.].

PRE-NATAL [prē-nā'tal], *adj.* before birth.

PRENTICE [pren'tis], *n. and adj.* apprentice, relating to an apprentice. [APPRENTICE].

PREOCCUPATION [prē-o-kyoo-pā'shn], *n.* act of preoccupying, previous occupation; state of being mentally occupied with some matter, deeply thoughtful, oblivious of immediate events and surroundings.

PREOCCUPY [prē-o'kyōō-pi], *v.t.* to occupy in advance; engross, obsess, occupy the mind of to the ignoring of immediate surroundings or considerations. PREOCCUPIED, *adj.* in a state of mental preoccupation. [L.].

PREORDAIN [prē-aw-dān'], *v.t.* to determine in advance. [LL.].

PREPARATION [pre-pa-rā'shn], *n.* act of preparing, state of being prepared; act of, time spent in preparing school work; medicine, lotion etc. specially prepared for a specific purpose. [L.].

PREPARATORY [pri-pa'ra-te-ri], *adj.* preparing, introductory; (of schools) preparing for a public or high school; *adv.* **p. to,** before, by way of preparation for. [MedL.].

PREPARE [pri-pāer'], *v.t. and i.* to make ready or suitable; construct, put together, mix, cook etc. so as to be suitable for some use; equip; plan out; teach, train; learn; become ready, (of states) make military preparations. PREPAREDLY [pri-pāer'id-li], *adv.* in a state of preparedness, in a prepared manner. [L.].

PREPENSE [prē-pens'], *adj.* deliberate, previously planned. [Fr. from OFr.].

PREPONDERANCE [pri-pon'de-rans], *n.* state of being preponderant, the preponderant force.

PREPONDERANT [pri-pon'de-rant], *adj.* outweighing, more important. [L.].

PREPONDERATE [pri-pon'de-rāt], *v.i.* to outweigh, outnumber, predominate. [L.].

PREPOSITION [pre-po-zi'shn], *n.* (*gram.*) word placed before a noun or pronoun to express local, temporal, causal or other abstract relations. PREPOSITIONAL, *adj.* relating to, in the place of, introduced by, a p. [L.].

PREPOSSESS [prē-po-zes'], *v.t.* to influence, prejudice (usually favourably), make a good impression upon. PREPOSSESSING, *adj.* tending to p., attractive. PREPOSSESSION, *n.* state of being prepossessed; strong inclination.

PREPOSTEROUS [pri-pos'te-rōōs], *adj.* ridiculous, contrary to reason, absurd. [L.].

PREPOTENT [prē-pō'tent], *adj.* having superior power; (*biol.*) having prepotency. PREPOTENCY, *n.* state of being p.; (*biol.*) power of one parent to transmit its characteristics to offspring. [L.].

PRE-PREFERENCE [prē-pre'fe-rens], *n.* share ranking above a preference share.

PREPUCE [prē'pyōōs], *n.* foreskin.

PRE-RECORD [prē-ri-kawd'], *v.t.* to record (a programme for broadcasting) in advance.

PRE-RELEASE [prē-ri-lēs'], *n. and adj.* (of cinema films or shows) exhibited before the normal date of distribution.

PREREQUISITE (1) [prē-re'kwi-zit], *adj.* necessary beforehand. PREREQUISITE (2), *n.* essential preliminary. PREREQUISITE (3), *n.* essential preliminary condition, something required in advance.

PREROGATIVE [pri-ro'ga-tiv], *n.* a special, unlimited right, peculiar privilege attaching to some person, office or condition; right of exercising such privilege; the exercise itself; **Royal P.,** theoretical right of the sovereign to act without Parliament. [L.].

PRESAGE (1) [pres'ij], *n.* portent, omen, foreboding. PRESAGE (2) [pres'ij, pri-sāj'], *v.t.* to foretell, forebode. PRESAGEFUL [pri-sāj'fōōl], *adj.* warning, foreboding. [Fr. from L.].

PRESBYOPIA [prez-bi-ō'pi-ah], *n.* defective vision of old age, characterized by inability to focus near objects. [Gk.].

PRESBYTER [pres'bi-ter], *n.* church elder, in either the Early Christian, Episcopal or Presbyterian Churches. [Gk.].

PRESBYTERIAN (1) [pres-bi-tēer'i-an], *adj.* relating to church government by presbyters; **P. Church,** Christian sect which does not recognize an order of bishops, and is governed by presbyters. PRESBYTERIAN (2), *n.* member of the P. Church.

PRESBYTERY [pres'bi-te-ri], *n.* body of church elders; house of a R.C. parish priest; district court of the Presbyterian Church; that part of a cathedral or large church reserved for the clergy, the eastern end of the chancel. [OFr. from L.].

PRESCIENCE [prē'shi-ens, pre'si-ens], *n.* foreknowledge, foresight. [L.].

PRESCIENT [prē'shi-ent, pre'si-ent], *adj.* foreseeing, having foreknowledge. [L.].

PRESCIENTIFIC [prē-si-en-ti'fik], *adj.* dating from before the development of scientific method.

PRESCRIBE [pri-skrīb'], *v.t. and i.* to direct, ordain; (*med.*) recommend (a specific medicine or treatment); (*leg.*) claim by prescription; lay down rules. [L.].

PRESCRIPT [prē'skript], *n.* a decree. [L.].

PRESCRIPTION [pri-skrip'shn], *n.* act of prescribing; that which is prescribed; (*leg.*) uninterrupted possession for sufficient time to give legal title; right or title gained in this way; written recipe for the preparation of a medicine, the medicine itself. [L.].

PRESCRIPTIVE [pri-skrip'tiv], *adj.* owned, claimed, by prescription.

PRESELECTOR [prē-si-lek'ter], *n.* apparatus enabling the driver of a motor-car to select a fresh gear before changing; **p. gear,** gear embodying this principle.

PRESENCE [pre'zens], *n.* state of being present; state of being in the neighbourhood or sight of another, *esp.* of a sovereign or potentate; closeness, immanence, of something; the bearing of a person; feeling that something other than oneself is present, the mysterious something itself; **p. of mind,** mental quickness and control in novel or disturbing circumstances; **p. chamber,** royal audience chamber. [ME., L.].

PRESENT (1) [pre'zent], *adj.* being here, by, near, in one's presence, being in a specified place at a specified time; occurring, existing now (not in past or future); (*gram.*) belonging to the tense expressing action at this time. PRESENT (2), *n.* the p. time; p. tense; (*leg.*) (*pl.*) the document itself. [ME. from OFr.].

PRESENT (3), *n.* a gift. [OFr.].

PRESENT (4) [pri-zent'], *v.t.* to bring to the presence of, introduce, give directly to someone; introduce formally at court; exhibit publicly, bring (some performance or player) before the public; offer, display; nominate for a benefice; point (a weapon) at; bring (a rifle) to the ceremonial salute. PRESENT (5), *n.* (*milit.*) act of raising a weapon and pointing it towards someone; position of the weapon so held, vertical position of the rifle in the ceremonial salute. [L.].

PRESENTABLE [pri-zen'ta-bl], *adj.* fit for presentation; of pleasing external appearance; well-mannered.

PRESENTATION [pre-zen-tā'shn], *n.* act of presenting, mode of exposition, gift made as a mark of public esteem; right of presenting to a benefice; position in which a child is born; performance of a show or fashion in which it is produced. [L.].

PRESENTEE [pre-zen-tē'], *n.* one who is presented to a benefice.

PRESENTIMENT [pri-zen'ti-ment], *n.* foreboding, feeling of a future event (generally in unpleasant sense).

PRESENTLY [pre'zent-li], *adv.* † immediately; after a short time, soon, not immediately.

PRESENTMENT [pri-zent'ment], *n.* act or manner of presenting; (*eccles.*) formal statement or complaint before a court or visiting bishop; representation.

PRESERVATION [pre-zer-vā'shn], *n.* act of preserving, state of being preserved. [MedL.].

PRESERVATIVE (1) [pri-zur'va-tiv], *adj.* having the property of preserving. PRESERVATIVE (2), *n.* substance which preserves, *esp.* food. [MedL.].

PRESERVE (1) [pri-zurv'], *v.t.* to maintain, keep safe from harm or damage, treat so as to prevent decay; rear and protect (game) for hunting etc. PRESERVE (2), *n.* that which is preserved, *esp.* jam; game covert, river reserved for fishing; (*fig.*) anything regarded as a person's special right or interest. [LL.].

PRE-SHRINK [prē-shringk'], *v.t.* to shrink (cloth) before it is made into garments.

PRESIDE [pri-zīd'], *v.i.* to hold the place of authority at a meeting, be in the chair. [L.].

PRESIDENCY [pre'zi-den-si], *n.* office of president; tenure of such office; formerly, an administrative province in India. [MedL.].

PRESIDENT [pre'zi-dent], *n.* supreme officer of various kinds, *esp.* the elected head of a republic; official head and chairman of a society; head of certain colleges etc. [L.].

PRESIDENTIAL [pre-zi-den'shal], *adj.* relating to a president or his office. [MedL.].

PRESS (1) [pres], *v.t. and i.* to exert strong, steady force upon so as to crush or compress; squeeze, thrust (an object) against resistance; smooth (cloth) with a hot iron; crowd in upon, harry; urge strongly, urge acceptance of (a thing); oppress, exert pressure; **to p. on,** to hasten onwards. PRESS (2), *n.* act of pressing; that which presses, machine or device for

---

exerting pressure, closely compact crowd; cupboard, set of shelves; printing-press, process of printing, a publishing and printing establishment; newspapers, periodicals; **to have a good p.,** to receive favourable comment in newspapers. PRESS-CLIPPING, (*U.S.*) press-cutting. PRESS-CUTTING, extract cut from a newspaper or periodical. PRESS-GALLERY, place reserved for journalists in the House of Commons. [ME. from Fr.].

PRESS (3), *v.t.* to enlist forcibly for naval or military service; force (someone or something) into one's service. [OFr.].

PRESS-AGENT [pres'ā-jent], *n.* one professionally employed in furthering the interests of a person or organization through the medium of the Press.

PRESSGANG [pres'gang], *n.* formerly a party of men entitled to kidnap and press into naval or military service.

PRESSING [pre'sing], *adj.* insistent, importunate; urgent, demanding immediate attention.

PRESSMAN [pres'man], *n.* printing-machine minder; journalist.

PRESSMARK [pres'mahk], *n.* marking on a library book showing its place on the shelves.

PRESS STUD [pres'stud], *n.* fastener for clothing etc., consisting of a nipple gripped by a W-shaped spring.

PRESSURE [pre'sher], *n.* act of pressing, force exerted by pressing; (*fig.*) force and compulsion of business and circumstance; (*mech.*) force exerted by one body against another; (*phys.*) force exerted on its surroundings by a liquid, solid or gas; **p. point,** (*med.*) point at which the blood flows over a bony prominence near enough to the skin to be temporarily stopped by p.; **p. group,** association of persons with common interests able to exert (political) influence for their own ends. PRESSURE-COOKER, cooking utensil in which the food is cooked under steam-pressure in a sealed container. PRESSURE-GAUGE, instrument for registering on a suitably marked scale the p. exerted by a liquid or gas. PRESSURIZE, *v.t.* to treat (an aircraft cabin etc.) so that the air p. within remains constant irrespective of external conditions. [L.].

PRESTIDIGITATION [pres-ti-di-ji-tā'shn], *n.* conjuring, legerdemain. PRESTIDIGITATOR, *n.* conjurer. [Fr.].

PRESTIGE [pres-tēzh'], *n.* good opinion, influence due to a glorious or powerful reputation. [Fr.].

PRESTISSIMO [pres-ti'si-mō], *adv.* (*mus.*) very quickly. [It.].

PRESTO [pres'tō], *adv.* (*mus.*) quickly (also used as an exclamation by conjurers). [It.].

PRESUMABLE [pri-zyōo'ma-bl], *adj.* that may be presumed.

PRESUME [pri-zyōom'], *v.t. and i.* to assume, accept as true without evidence; assume more latitude than one legitimately possesses; be presumptuous, take too much for granted. [L.].

PRESUMPTION [pri-zump'shn], *n.* act or process of presuming, thing presumed; probability, reason for presuming; effrontery. [L.].

PRESUMPTIVE [pri-zump'tiv], *adj.* based on presumption, probable, likely; **heir p.,** one who is actually heir, but would cease to be so on the birth of a child in a more direct line of succession.

PRESUMPTUOUS [pri-zump'tyōo-ōos], *adj.* showing presumption and arrogance, insolently assuming. [LL.].

PRESUPPOSE [prē-su-pōz'], *v.t.* to assume in advance, require as a necessary preliminary. [Fr.].

PRESUPPOSITION [prē-su-po-zi'shn], *n.* act of presupposing; that which is presupposed. [MedL.].

PRETENCE [pri-tens'], *n.* act of pretending; thing pretended, pretension, false assumption of some attitude, fraud. [AFr.].

PRETEND [pri-tend'], *v.t. and i.* to feign, assume in order to deceive; put forward false claims; play at being, imagine oneself as, someone one is not. PRE-TENDED, *adj.* false, feigned. PRETENDEDLY, *adv.* in pretence, falsely. [ME from L.].

PRETENDER [pri-ten'der], *n.* one who pretends, *esp.* one who makes false claim to rank or position; claimant to a throne which is held by an opponent who does not admit the claim.

PRETENSION [pri-ten'shn], *n.* assertion, claim (*esp.* an arrogant one); attempt to appear superior to one's true worth. [MedL.].

PRETENTIOUS [pri-ten'shōos], *adj.* showing pretensions, ostentatious, attempting more than can be fulfilled. [Fr.].

PRETER-, *pref.* beyond, above, more than etc. [L.].

PRETERITE (1) [pre'te-rit], *adj.* (*gram.*) relating to the past definite tense. PRETERITE (2), *n.* (*gram.*) the past definite tense. [MdL.].

PRETERNATURAL [prē-ter-na'tyōo-ral], *adj.* supernatural. PRETERNATURALLY, *adv.* in p. fashion.

PRETEXT [prē'tekst], *n.* false reason, excuse for doing something, pretended motive. [Fr.].

PRETORIAN, see PRAETORIAN.

PRETTY (1) [pri'ti], *adj.* superficially but pleasantly attractive, pleasing without arousing any strong emotion, neat, clever in a minor fashion; (*in irony*) fine, grand; (*coll.*) of considerable quantity, of fair extent; dear. PRETTY-PRETTY, superficially and affectedly p., feebly charming. PRETTY (2), *n.* (*golf*) the fairway. PRETTY (3), *adv.* fairly, to a considerable extent; excessively, very. [OE.].

PREVAIL [pri-vāl'], *v.i.* to have advantage or victory over, be current, be habitual (with an understood triumph over something else); **to p. on,** to persuade, induce (someone) against his inclinations. PREVAIL-ING, *adj.* ruling, current, habitual; principal, most important. [ME. from L.].

PREVALENCE [pre'va-lens], *n.* state of being prevalent, extent to which a thing, belief etc. is prevalent.

PREVALENT [pre'va-lent], *adj.* prevailing, widely received, practised etc., current, general. [L.].

PREVARICATE [pri-va'ri-kāt], *v.i.* to avoid telling the truth, make an evasive answer, quibble. PRE-VARICATOR, *n.* one who prevaricates. [L.].

PREVARICATION [pri-va-ri-kā'shn], *n.* act of prevaricating; equivocation, verbal deception. [L.].

PREVENANCY [pre've-nan-si], *n.* courteous complaisance. [Fr.].

PREVENT [pri-vent'], *v.t.* † to precede; stop, hamper, check, thwart. PREVENTER, *n.* one who prevents; rope or stay taking the strain off another.

PREVENTATIVE (1) [pri-ven'ta-tiv], *adj.* preventive. PREVENTATIVE (2), *n.* that which prevents; medicine for preventing some disease.

PREVENTION [pri-ven'shn], *n.* act or process of preventing; that which prevents. [LL.].

PREVENTIVE (1) [pri-ven'tiv], *adj.* preventing, checking in advance, prophylactic. PREVENTIVE (2), *n.* a preventative.

PREVIEW [prē-vyōo'], *n.* inspection (of pictures etc.) before general exhibition.

PREVIOUS (1) [prē'vi-ōos], *adj.* preceding, prior, earlier; hasty, too early. PREVIOUS (2), *adv.* before (with *to*). PREVIOUSLY, *adv.* before. [L.].

PREY (1) [prā], *n.* animal hunted and devoured by another; (*fig.*) person who, thing which, becomes helpless victim of another person, or of circumstances; booty. PREY (2), *v.i.* to seize for p., devour; **to p. on,** (*fig.*) to rob, despoil, wear down, eat away. [ME., OFr. from L.].

PRICE (1) [pris], *n.* exchange value of an article, value received as recompense for goods, service or expenditure; marked value of goods offered for sale; recompense, value, worth; (*betting*) odds; **starting p.,** odds offered on a horse etc. at the last moment before the race begins. PRICE (2), *v.t.* to set a p. on, value; ask the p. of. [ME., OFr. from L.].

PRICELESS [pris'les], *adj.* beyond price, irreplaceable, enormously valuable; (*slang*) remarkably witty or amusing, utterly absurd.

PRICK (1) [prik], *v.t. and i.* to pierce, stab with a sharp, pointed object; make holes (in) by pricking, spur (a horse); wound by pricking; feel such a wound or pain, spur on, ride (a horse) vigorously; (of animal ears) stiffen in attention. PRICK (2), *n.* a sharp, pointed, slender piercing object, goad, thorn, discomfort; slight wound inflicted by a needle, thorn etc.; qualm; small mark or dot; **to kick against the pricks,** to rebel against the inevitable. PRICK-EARED, with erect, pricked-up ears. PRICKING, *n.* act of pricking; feeling as of being pricked. [OE.].

PRICKLE (1) [pri'kl], *n.* growth, process, of pricks or spines on the surface of a tree or plant; (*pl.*) spines of a hedgehog etc.; prickling sensation in the skin. PRICKLE (2), *v.t. and i.* to prick, feel prickly, have a pricking in the skin. [OE.].

PRICKLY [prik'li], *adj.* pricking, covered with prickles; causing a tingling in the skin as if being pricked. PRICKLY-HEAT, skin eruption caused by inflammation of the sweat glands. PRICKLY-PEAR, the cactus *Opuntia*, or its fruit.

PRIDE (1) [prid], *n.* feeling of self-esteem and self-satisfaction; proper awareness of what is fitting or due to one; arrogance; conceit; pleasure felt in the merits or achievements of something with which one has identified oneself; pomp; radiant beauty; troop

---

The accent ′ after a syllable = stress (u-pon′). The mark ‾ over a vowel = length (ā in made; ō in bone).

(of lions), flock (of peacocks). **PRIDE** (2), v. reflex. **to p. oneself on**, to take p. in, claim credit for. [OE. from L.].

PRIDIAN [pri'di-an], adj. relating to the previous day. [L.].

PRIEST [prēst], n. one whose office it is to perform sacred **rites** and **act** as intermediary between the people and God; Roman Catholic cleric; (eccles.) cleric below the rank of bishop and above that of deacon. **PRIEST-RIDDEN**, governed by, overrun by, priests. [OE. from Gk.].

PRIESTCRAFT [prēst'krahft], n. exercise of the priestly office; clerical policy directed towards political control.

PRIESTLY [prēst'li], adj. like, relating to, a priest or the priesthood.

PRIG (1) [prig], n. prim, conventional, conceited person, sure of his own morality. **PRIG** (2) (pres.pt. **PRIGGING**, pret. and p.pt. **PRIGGED**), v.t. to steal. **PRIGGERY**, n. fact or quality of being priggish. [Uncert.].

PRIGGISH [pri'gish], adj. having the characteristics and ideas of a prig.

PRIM [prim], adj. neatly conventional, easily shocked, over-restrained. [Uncert.].

PRIMACY [pri'ma-si], n. state of being first, pre-eminent; office of a primate. [MedL.].

PRIMA DONNA [prē-mah-do'nah], n. principal female singer in an opera. [It.].

PRIMAEVAL, see PRIMEVAL.

PRIMAL [pri'mal], adj. primary. [MedL.].

PRIMARY [pri'ma-ri], adj. first in time or importance, principal; original, elementary, rudimentary; (geol.) of the Palaeozoic strata or era; (elect.) producing current; **p. colours**, fundamental colours from whose mixture others are derived. **PRIMARILY**, adv. originally, chiefly, mainly. [L.].

PRIMATE [pri'mat], n. chief ecclesiastic in a prelatic national church; archbishop; **P. of all England**, Archbishop of Canterbury; **P. of England**, Archbishop of York. [LL.].

PRIMATES [pri-mā'tēz], n.(pl.) order of mammals which includes man, the anthropoid apes, the monkeys and the lemurs. [L.].

PRIME (1) [prim], adj. first in time, rank or importance; of the highest quality; initial, essential; **P. Minister**, chief minister of the Cabinet; **p. mover**, (mech.) initial source of motive power; **p. number**, (math.) number divisible only by one or itself. **PRIME** (2), n. best or earliest period of a thing, most vigorous period of a person's life; first of the day canonical hours; that which is p. **PRIME** (3), v.t. to charge, fill up (with), esp. a fire-arm with explosive, or a person with liquor or information; lay on a first coat of paint. **PRIMELY**, adv. excellently, healthily. [L.].

PRIMER [pri'mer, pri'mer], n. book of hours for the use of laymen; elementary text book; (print.) a size of type. [L.].

PRIM(A)EVAL [pri-mē'val], adj. belonging to the earliest times, prehistoric, ancient. [L.].

PRIMING [pri'ming], n. act of priming; powder etc. exploding a charge; first coat of paint.

PRIMIPAROUS [pri-mi'pa-rŏŏs], adj. bearing young for the first time. [L.].

PRIMITIVE [pri'mi-tiv], adj. related to the earliest stage of development; prehistoric; rude, original; uncivilized; (art) antecedent to the Renaissance. [L.].

PRIMOGENITURE [pri-mŏ-je'ni-tyŏŏr], n. (leg.) system by which the eldest son inherits the whole of his father's real estate. [MedL.].

PRIMORDIAL [pri-maw'di-al], adj. primary, existing from the beginning of time, first-created.

PRIMROSE [prim'rōz], n. a pale-yellow spring flower; the colour of this. [MedL.].

PRIMULA [pri'myŏŏ-lah], n. (bot.) genus including the primrose. [L.].

PRIMUS [pri'mus], n. eldest of several brothers; presiding bishop of the Scottish Episcopal Church; (prot.) type of oil-stove burning vaporized oil. [L.].

PRINCE [prins], n. ruler, potentate; male relation of the ruling monarch. [Fr. from L.].

PRINCELY [prins'li], adj. like, befitting, a prince; splendidly lavish.

PRINCESS [prin-ses'], n. female relation of a ruling monarch; wife of a prince; **p. dress**, woman's close-fitting one-piece gown. [ME. from OFr.].

PRINCIPAL (1) [prin'si-pal], adj. most important, first, highest in rank. **PRINCIPAL** (2), n. head of an institution, the p. person; capital sum on which

interest is paid; one of the chief parties in a transaction. [L.].

PRINCIPALITY [prin-si-pa'li-ti], n. territory of a reigning prince, power, reign of a prince; independent territorial unit less than a kingdom; † an order of angels. [MedL.].

PRINCIPLE [prin'si-pl], n. fundamental essence, first origin of a thing; basic truth from which deductions can be made; fundamental moral conviction, tenet, from which rules of conduct can be derived; constituent substance from which particular qualities can be derived. [L.].

PRINK [pringk], v.i. to dress showily, smarten; preen. [PRANK].

PRINT (1) [print], n. mark or impression on anything made by the pressure of another body; die designed for making such impressions, impression produced by a die, esp. lettering, printed matter; picture or representation reproduced from an engraved metal plate; (phot.) positive picture made from a negative; (textiles) fabric stamped with a pattern by means of dies; **in p.**, printed, published; still for sale as freshly printed; **out of p.**, (of books etc.) no longer obtainable except at second-hand. **PRINT** (2), v.t. and i. to mark by pressure, imprint, (fig.) leave a strong impression (on the mind, face etc.), reproduce words by stamping paper with inked type, cause to be so reproduced, publish in printed form, write so that each letter is separate, like a printed character; (phot.) obtain a positive of by exposing the negative to light; practise the art of a printer. [ME. from OFr.].

PRINTER [prin'ter], n. one who prints, esp. one who prints (books etc.) for publication.

PRINTING [prin'ting], n. art of the printer, style in which a thing is printed; the whole amount of books, pamphlets etc. printed at one time; handwriting in which every letter is written separately in capitals; typography. **PRINTING-FRAME**, (phot.) frame to hold negative and paper together for p. **PRINTING-INK**, ink used for p. **PRINTING-MACHINE**, mechanical p.-press. **PRINTING-PAPER**, paper used in p., esp. photographic sensitized paper. **PRINTING-PRESS**, machine for printing.

PRINTSELLER [print'se-ler], n. dealer in engravings and pictorial prints.

PRINT-WORKS [print'werks], n. factory for the mechanical printing of fabrics.

PRIOR (1) [pri'er], n. superior of a monastery, next in rank to an abbot. [ME. from L.].

PRIOR (2), adj. previous, antecedent, demanding first attention. [L.].

PRIORESS [pri'e-res], n. mother superior of a convent.

PRIORITY [pri-o'ri-ti], n. state of being prior, right to first consideration; degree of urgency; something accorded a (specified) degree of privilege. [Fr.].

PRIORY [pri'e-ri], n. monastic community governed by a prior. [ME. from MedL.].

PRISE, see PRIZE (5).

PRISM [prizm], n. (geom.) solid figure with similar, equal and parallel bases, and whose sides are parallelograms; (opt.) transparent body with parallel bases and rectangular sides used for refracting light. [Gk.].

PRISMATIC [priz-ma'tik], adj. of, employing, shaped like, a prism, refractive, capable of being refracted, iridescent; **p. colours**, colours in sunlight which may be separated by a prism.

PRISON (1) [pri'zn], n. place of confinement, esp. a building devoted to the confinement of those obnoxious to the government or to society; **p. breaking**, escape from p., esp. on a mass scale. **PRISON-HOUSE**, p. **PRISON** (2), to imprison. [OFr.].

PRISONER [pri'zn-er], n. one imprisoned, held in captivity, one detained or restricted. [OFr.].

PRISTINE [pris'tēn], adj. primitive, belonging to an early age; former; fresh, undiminished. [L.].

PRIVACY [pri'va-si, pri'va-si], n. state of being private; secrecy, freedom from observation.

PRIVATE (1) [pri'vat], adj. peculiar to an individual, not public, secluded, undisturbed; **p. parts**, sexual organs. **PRIVATE** (2), n. (milit.) soldier without command over others; (pl.) sexual organs. [L.].

PRIVATEER [pri-va-tēer'], n. (hist.) privately owned ship licensed to make war on behalf of its government; sailor in such a vessel.

PRIVATION [pri-vā'shn], n. hardship, destitution, absence of comfort. [L.].

PRIVATIVE [pri'va-tiv], adj. causing privation; (gram.) implying deprivation. [L.].

PRIVET [pri'vit], n. a shrub much used for garden hedges. [Uncert.].

PRIVILEGE (1) [pri'vi-lij], n. advantage or benefit

peculiar to a particular person or body, and not shared in by others; prerogative; that which confers a peculiar advantage. PRIVILEGE (2), *v.t.* to allow special advantages or immunities to. PRIVILEGED, *adj.* having a p., enjoying special immunity. [L.].

PRIVITY [priˈviti], *n.* private agreement with, or knowledge of, a thing. [OFr.].

PRIVY (1) [priˈvi], *adj.* knowing what is secret, private; **p. council,** advisory council appointed by the sovereign; **p. purse,** allowance for the sovereign's personal expenses. PRIVY (2), *n.* water-closet, latrine or any similar closet; (*leg.*) one having an interest in a lawsuit. [ME. from OFr.].

PRIZE (1) [priz], *n.* reward for merit or success; something won by chance; very valuable or envied acquisition. PRIZE (2), *adj.* won, awarded as a p.; (*coll.*) excellent, extreme, excessive. PRIZE (3), *v.t.* to esteem highly, hold valuable. [ME. from L.].

PRIZE (4), *n.* that which is captured in war, *esp.* a ship taken from the enemy; **p. court,** division of the Admiralty Court with jurisdiction over prizes; **p. money,** share in the value of prizes, formerly distributed to the capturing crew, and later to men with a certain length of service in the Royal Navy. [Fr.].

PRIZE (5), **PRISE,** *v.t.* to force (open) with a lever; (*fig.*) open, force out, by indirect pressure. [Fr.].

PRIZE-FIGHT [prizˈfit], *n.* boxing match for money.

PRIZEMAN [prizˈman], *n.* winner of a university prize.

PRO-, *pref.* for, in favour of, on behalf of, before (in place); *used to form many adjectival and some noun compounds signifying favouring, a partisan of, whatever is implied by the second element, as* pro-British, pro-Boer *etc.* [L.].

PROBABILITY [pro-ba-biˈli-ti], *n.* state of being probable, likelihood; the most probable of several alternatives. [L.].

PROBABLE [proˈba-bl], *adj.* likely, having more of the apparent evidence on its side. PROBABLY, *adv.* more likely than not. [L.].

PROBATE [proˈbat], *n.* official proof of wills, certified copy of a will so proved. [L.].

PROBATION [pro-baˈshn], *n.* a state of being under trial; (*leg.*) system by which a sentence is suspended on the condition that the offender reports every so often. PROBATIONARY, *adj.* relating to, under, p. [L.].

PROBATIONER [pro-baˈshn-er], *n.* novice in certain religious orders; nurse, teacher etc., in the early stages of training; offender dismissed under probation.

PROBE (1) [prob], *n.* (*med.*) instrument for probing into a wound; (*U.S.*) thorough investigation or inquiry. PROBE (2), *v.t.* to examine (a wound) by inserting an instrument into (it); (*fig.*) investigate thoroughly. [L.].

PROBITY [proˈbi-ti], *n.* proved integrity. [L.].

PROBLEM [probˈlem], *n.* something to be solved, question involving uncertainty or difficulty; (*geom.*) proposition to be solved. PROBLEM (2), *adj.* relating to, or containing, a p.; **p. play,** play whose theme is a moral or social p. [ME. from Gk.].

PROBLEMATICAL [prob-le-maˈti-kal], *adj.* questionable, relating to a problem.

PROBOSCIS [pro-boˈsis], *n.* a prolongation of the nose, as in the elephant; (*slang*) large nose. [Gk.].

PROCEDURE [pro-seˈdyŏr], *n.* technique, proper fashion in which to perform or proceed; way of acting, behaviour. [Fr.].

PROCEED [pro-sedˈ], *v.i.* to move (from or towards a place); make progress; begin to do or perform; behave in some fashion. PROCEEDS [proˈsedz], *n.(pl.)* money gained by an action or performance. [L.].

PROCEEDING [pro-seˈding], *n.* act of performing something, transaction, mode of doing; (*pl.*) mode, act of carrying out an action.

PROCESS (1) [proˈses], *n.* method of doing a thing, mode of doing in which each step proceeds out of that which precedes it, all the stages of a development regarded as a whole; a system of manufacture; (*leg.*) the whole course of court proceedings; (*anat.*) a bony protuberance; (*bot.*) a structure; **p. block,** (*print.*) printing block made by photography, or by some other means than simple engraving. PROCESS (2), *v.t.* to make a printing block of by photography; subject to a p. [L.].

PROCESS (3) [pro-sesˈ], *v.i.* (*coll.*) to walk in procession.

PROCESSION [pro-seˈshn], *n.* act of proceeding,

that which proceeds; a number of persons or things proceeding past a point, *esp.* if formally arranged. PROCESSIONAL, *n.* hymn sung during a religious p.; the book containing such hymns (in R.C. Church).[L.].

PROCLAIM [pro-klamˈ], *v.t.* to announce publicly, promulgate.

PROCLAMATION [pro-kla-maˈshn], *n.* official public announcement; act of proclaiming. [L.].

PROCLIVITY [pro-kliˈvi-ti], *n.* inclination. [L.].

PROCRASTINATE [pro-krasˈti-nat], *v.t. and i.* to postpone continually; delay. [L.].

PROCRASTINATION [pro-kras-ti-naˈshn], *n.* act of procrastinating. [L.].

PROCREATE [proˈkri-at], *v.t. and i.* to beget. PROCREATIVE, *adj.* able to, tending to, p. PROCREATOR, *n.* male parent. [L.].

PROCREATION [pro-kri-aˈshn], *n.* act of procreating. [L.].

PROCRUSTEAN [pro-krusˈti-an], *adj.* seeking to produce uniformity by violence. [*Procrustes,* legendary Greek robber who either stretched his victims or cut off their extremities to make them fit his bed].

PROCTOR [prokˈter], *n.* † agent who manages the affairs of, and represents, his employer; (*eccles.*) representative of a cathedral chapter or the clergy of a diocese at convocation; one of two disciplinary officials at Oxford and Cambridge; **Queen's P.,** representative of the Crown in probate and matrimonial causes with power to intervene to prevent collusion. [ME. from L.].

PROCURATION [pro-kyŏo-raˈshn], *n.* function of a procurator or agent acting on another's behalf; appointment of a procurator or proxy. [L.].

PROCURATOR [proˈkyŏo-ra-ter], *n.* official agent or proxy of another; (*eccles.*) agent in an ecclesiastical law-court. PROCURATOR-FISCAL, (*Scots leg.*) public prosecutor. PROCURATORIAL [pro-kyŏo-ra-tawˈri-al], *adj.* pertaining to the office of a p. [L.].

PROCURE [pro-kyŏorˈ], *v.t.* to obtain, acquire; cause, bring about; obtain (often objects of sexual satisfaction) for another. PROCURER, *n.* one who procures; pimp or pander. PROCURESS, *n.* bawd. [Fr. from L.].

PROD (*pres.pt.* **prodding,** *pret. and p.pt.* **prodded**) [prod], *v.t.* to poke with a stick, finger etc.; (*fig.*) urge or incite. [Uncert.].

PRODIGAL (1) [proˈdi-gal], *adj.* lavish, extravagant and wasteful; given to unnecessary expenditure. PRODIGAL (2), *n.* a spendthrift. [OFr. from L.].

PRODIGALITY [pro-di-gaˈli-ti], *n.* extravagance, wasteful expenditure. [Fr.].

PRODIGIOUS [pro-diˈjŏos], *adj.* monstrous, abnormal; amazing; of large dimensions. [L.].

PRODIGY [proˈdi-ji], *n.* amazing phenomenon, marvel; person of abnormal powers. [L.].

PRODUCE (1) [pro-dyŏosˈ], *v.t. and i.* to bring forth, yield; give rise to; make; present for inspection; (*geom.*) extend (a line); **to p. a play,** to arrange the stage presentation. PRODUCE (2) [proˈdyŏos], *n.* that which is produced either by the labour of man or by the action of nature; product. [L.].

PRODUCER [pro-dyŏoˈser], *n.* someone who or something which produces; one who produces a play; (*films*) one who directs or initiates the production of a film; **p. gas,** gas made by passing air and steam through glowing coke.

PRODUCT [proˈdukt], *n.* that which is produced, produce; result of labour or of natural growth or action; outcome, result; (*math.*) result of multiplying one number by another; (*chem.*) substance produced by chemical change or chemical action. [L.].

PRODUCTION [pro-dukˈshn], *n.* act of producing; manufacture, creation; act of producing a play; that which is produced, product; a play produced.

PRODUCTIVE [pro-dukˈtiv], *adj.* fertile, having the power to produce; giving results; causing; yielding wealth.

PROEM [proˈim], *n.* preface or prelude. [OFr., L. from Gk.].

PROFANATION [pro-fa-naˈshn], *n.* act of desecrating, the treating of sacred things with disrespect and irreverence. [Eccles.].

PROFANE (1) [pro-fanˈ], *adj.* not holy; secular, pertaining to the world; not connected with religious things, common; heathen; blasphemous. PROFANE (2), *v.t.* to desecrate, commit profanation in; vulgarize, treat with disrespect; use wrongly and dishonourably. [L.].

PROFANITY [pro-faˈni-ti], *n.* blasphemy, profane talk. [Eccles.].

PROFESS [pro-fesˈ], *v.t. and i.* to declare, affirm;

accept and practise as a religion; follow as a calling; teach in a professional capacity; pretend or feign; **to p. oneself**, to declare oneself to be. PROFESSED [pro-fest'], *adj.* openly declared and acknowledged; untruthfully declared. PROFESSEDLY [pro-fe'sid-li], *adj.* by open declaration, ostensibly, in accordance with, or according to, one's profession or statement. [L.].

PROFESSION [pro-fe'shn], *n.* confession or statement, either true or untrue; learned calling as distinct from a trade; members and practitioners of such a calling; act of taking religious vows before entering a religious order or community. [L.].

PROFESSIONAL (1) [pro-fe'shn-al], *adj.* belonging or pertaining to one of the learned callings; earning one's living as; trained in, so as to earn one's living by; characteristic of a profession; skilled. PROFESSIONAL (2), *n.* one engaged in a profession or calling so as to earn his or her livelihood by it; one who takes part in a game or sport as a regular occupation for profit.

PROFESSOR [pro-fe'ser], *n.* one who professes or believes in (a religious creed or doctrine); teacher holding a chair of a subject at a university; teacher. PROFESSORIAL [pro-fe-saw'ri-al], *adj.* pertaining to, or characteristic of, a p. PROFESSORSHIP, *n.* position of a p. [L.].

PROFFER (1) [pro'fer], *v.t.* to present, bring forward, for acceptance, propose or suggest; offer as a present. PROFFER (2), *n.* act of proffering; that which is proferred; offer or suggestion. [ME., OFr. from L.].

PROFICIENCY [pro-fi'shen-si], *n.* quality or state of being proficient.

PROFICIENT (1) [pro'fi'shent], *adj.* competent, skilled, trained. PROFICIENT (2), *n.* one who is p., an expert. [L.].

PROFILE [pro'fil, pro'fel], *n.* side view of a face; outline drawing, *esp.* of a side view, of a face; (*arch.*) outline drawing of a vertical section. [It.].

PROFIT (1) [pro'fit], *n.* advantage or gain produced by labour or endeavour; pecuniary gain produced by commercial activity; (*pl.*) pecuniary gain; **gross p.**, total pecuniary gain before the deduction of incidental and consequent costs; **net p.**, pecuniary gain when all costs have been deducted; **office of p.**, office, other than ministerial, under the Crown, which yields financial p. to the holder and which if accepted by a Member of Parliament necessitates resignation from his seat. PROFIT (2), *v.t. and i.* to benefit, yield p. to; be useful or of p. to; gain profits or advantage; make financial gains. [ME. from L.].

PROFITABLE [pro'fi-ta-bl], *adj.* being of use or benefit; yielding profit.

PROFITEER (1) [pro-fi-teer'], *n.* commercial opportunist who uses other people's necessity to make large and unjustifiable profits. PROFITEER (2), *v.i.* to make unduly large profits by taking advantage of the hardship or necessity of other people.

PROFLIGACY [pro'fli-ga-si], *n.* profligate living; condition or quality of being profligate.

PROFLIGATE (1) [pro'fli-gat], *adj.* dissolute and immoral; having no regard to morality and decency. PROFLIGATE (2), *n.* dissipated and depraved person.

PROFOUND [pro-fownd'], *adj.* having great depth, very deep; showing great intellectual power; not easily comprehended, but felt to be true; touching one's deepest feelings; (of a bow or curtsey) very low. [OFr. from L.].

PROFUNDITY [pro-fun'di-ti], *n.* state or quality of being profound; deep, abstruse thought; great abyss. [L.].

PROFUSE [pro-fyoos'], *adj.* liberal to the point of prodigality; abundant, copious. [L.].

PROFUSION [pro-fyoo'zhn], *n.* lavishness; extravagance; copious supply. [L.].

PROG (1) [prog], *n.* (*slang*) university proctor. PROG (2) (*pres.pt.* PROGGING, *pret. and p.pt.* PROGGED), *v.t.* (*slang*) to summon before a university proctor. [Jocular form of PROCTOR].

PROGENITOR [pro-je'ni-ter], *n.* forefather or ancestor.

PROGENITURE [pro-je'ni-tyoor], *n.* act of begetting; ancestry.

PROGENY [pro'je-ni], *n.* children, offspring or descendants. [L.].

PROGNATHIC, PROGNATHOUS [prog-na'-thik, prog'na-thoos], *adj.* having jaws which project.

PROGNOSIS [prog-no'sis], *n.* act of prognosticating. (*med.*) outlook, probable course, of a disease or malady. [Gk.].

PROGNOSTIC (1) [prog-nos'tik], *n.* omen, sign or symptom; an indication of the future. PROGNOSTIC (2), *adj.* foretelling. [MedL. from Gk.].

PROGNOSTICATE [prog-nos'ti-kāt], *v.t.* to foretell or foreshadow. PROGNOSTICATIVE, *adj.* predictive. PROGNOSTICATOR, *n.* one who predicts the future. [MedL.].

PROGNOSTICATION [prog-nos-ti-kā'shn], *n.* science of prognosticating; sign of the future, omen. [MedL.].

PROGRAM(ME) [pro'gram], *n.* sheet or pamphlet on which the necessary details of a concert, theatrical entertainment, sports meeting etc. are printed; at a ball, card on which the name of one's intended partner for each dance may be entered; entertainment provided at a theatre, concert etc.; statement of what is to be done, course of one's intended actions; statement of the policy a political party intends to pursue. [Fr. from L. from Gk.].

PROGRESS (1) [pro'gres], *n.* movement onward; movement from a starting-point and towards a goal; improvement, increase and expansion; official or state journey. PROGRESS (2) [pro-gres'], *v.i.* to move in a forward direction, move towards the intended goal; draw nearer to completion; improve, get on. [OFr. from L.].

PROGRESSION [pro-gre'shn], *n.* act of passing from one thing to the next, act of moving forward, *esp.* stage by stage; progress, improvement, a series, *esp.* one of significant arrangement; (*math.*) series of numbers each of which differs from the next by a constant law; (*mus.*) a passing from one chord to the next, succession of chords. [L.].

PROGRESSIVE (1) [pro-gre'siv], *adj.* moving forward by gradual and proper stages; growing better, developing, extending by stages; advocating political development and change, *esp.* of a social nature; (*med.*) (of a disease etc.) increasing in severity; **p. taxation**, taxation graded in proportion to the means of the taxpayers; **p. whist**, whist in which partners and opponents are changed after every game. PROGRESSIVE (2), *n.* member of a political party advocating reform. [Fr.].

PROHIBIT [pro-hi'bit], *v.t.* to forbid, oppose by law and authority; debar. [L.].

PROHIBITION [pro-hi-bi'shn], *n.* act of prohibiting, forbidding, *esp.* by lawful authority; the prohibiting by law of the manufacture, sale and consumption of alcoholic liquors. [L.].

PROHIBITIONIST (1) [pro-hi-bi'shn-ist], *n.* one who opposes the sale, consumption, and manufacture of alcoholic liquors. PROHIBITIONIST (2), *adj.* governed by a law forbidding the sale etc. of alcoholic liquors; advocating prohibition. [L.].

PROHIBITIVE [pro-hi'bi-tiv], *adj.* forbidding; preventing or tending to prevent; **p. price or cost**, price or cost so high as to render purchase impossible. [Fr.].

PROJECT (1) [pro-jekt'], *v.t. and i.* to throw, hurl; cast with deliberate aim, *esp.* of a beam of light; imagine, *esp.* what has not yet happened; form a mental picture of; cast (a picture) on a screen by means of a magic lantern or cinematograph; protrude; (*geom.*) represent a three-dimensional figure in a two-dimensional diagram. PROJECT (2) [pro'jekt], *n.* a plan or scheme. [L.].

PROJECTILE (1) [pro-jek'til], *adj.* hurling, projecting; intended to be hurled. PROJECTILE (2) [pro'jek-til, pro-jek'til], *n.* something intended to be thrown, missile; shell or bullet. [Fr.].

PROJECTION [pro-jek'shn], *n.* act of casting, hurling or projecting; act of casting the mind forward; act of jutting out, something which juts out; image or shadow which is projected; two-dimensional diagram of a three-dimensional figure; *esp.* one of the ways in which the world, or part of it, may be represented in a map; vivid mental image; (*geom.*) a representation on a line or plane of a figure not itself on that line or plane; (*psych.*) attribution to others of one's own motives and characteristics. PROJECTIONIST, *n.* operator of a cinema projector. [L.].

PROJECTOR [pro-jek'ter], *n.* someone who or something which projects; someone who forms projects; machine for projecting and focusing films etc. on a screen.

PROLAPSE (1) [pro-laps'], *v.i.* (*med.*) to fall from position. PROLAPSE (2) [pro'laps, pro'laps], *n.* (*med.*) act of falling out of position, *esp.* of the womb or rectum; condition of having so fallen. [L.].

PROLEGOMENA [pro-le-go'me-nah], *n.* (*pl.*) preliminary remarks; preface; prefatory treatise. [Gk.].

PROLEPSIS [pro-lep'sis], *n.* figure of speech by which

that which will occur is referred to as though it already has occurred. PROLEPTIC, *adj.* of, or pertaining to, p.; anticipatory. [Gk.].

PROLETARIAN (1) [prō-li-täer'i-an], *adj.* belonging to the lower classes; characteristic of the proletariat. PROLETARIAN (2), *n.* one of the proletariat. [L.].

PROLETARIAT(E) [prō-li-täer'i-at], *n.* the lower classes, masses, labourers. [Fr.].

PROLIFERATE [prō-li'fe-rat], *v.t. and i.* to reproduce by proliferation. PROLIFERATION [prō-li-fe-rā'shn], state of being proliferous; reproduction by division; development of new elementary parts. [Fr.].

PROLIFEROUS [prō-li'fe-rŏos], *adj.* pertaining to proliferation; reproducing or growing by proliferation. [MedL.].

PROLIFIC [prō-li'fik], *adj.* producing numerous offspring; fertile, fruitful; abundant; rich in. [MedL.].

PROLIX [prō'liks, prō-liks'], *adj.* lengthy, verbose. PROLIXITY [prō-lik'si-ti], *n.* condition or quality of being p.; verbosity. PROLIXLY [prō-liks'li], *adv.* in a p. style. [L.].

PROLOCUTOR [prō-lo'kyŏo-ter], *n.* chairman of the Lower House of Convocation and spokesman of that House in the Upper House. [L.].

PROLOGUE [prō'log], *n.* an introduction; prefatory section of a literary composition; short passage, usually in verse, introducing a play; (*fig.*) event which occurs before another and leads up to it. PROLOG(U)IZE [prō'lo-jīz, prō'lo-gīz], *v.i.* to make or deliver a p. [Gk.].

PROLONG [prō-long'], *v.t.* to make longer, extend; lengthen in time, protract. [OFr. from LL.].

PROLONGATION [prō-long-gā'shn], *n.* act of prolonging or state of having been prolonged.

PROM [prom], *n.* (*coll.*) promenade concert; a promenade.

PROMENADE (1) [pro-me-nahd'], *n.* short leisurely excursion, usually on foot; any place designed for promenading; **p. concert,** concert at which some of the audience stand or walk about the floor of the hall. PROMENADE (2), *v.t. and i.* to make a short excursion for pleasure and exercise; walk along with a leisurely air. PROMENADER, *n.* one who promenades. [Fr. from L.].

PROMETHEAN [pro-mē'thi-an], *adj.* (*Gk. myth.*) of, or pertaining to, *Prometheus*, Titan who stole fire from heaven for mankind.

PROMINENCE [pro'mi-nens], *n.* condition or quality of being prominent, protruding or notable; projecting point of land or rock, great crag.

PROMINENT [pro'mi-nent], *adj.* jutting out, projecting; distinguished, conspicuous; eminent, famous. PROMINENTLY, *adv.* in a p. fashion. [L.].

PROMISCUITY [pro-mis-kyŏo'i-ti], *n.* quality or condition of being promiscuous or indiscriminate.

PROMISCUOUS [pro-mis'kyŏo-ŏos], *adj.* composed of elements of various sorts; mingled indiscriminately; loose and indiscriminate in sexual relations. [L.].

PROMISE (1) [pro'mis], *n.* informal undertaking or guarantee about future conduct; probability of success or fulfilment; **to make a p.,** to give such an undertaking; **to break a p.,** to fail to keep a p.; **breach of p.,** failure to fulfil an engagement to marry. PROMISE (2), *v.t. and i.* to give an informal guarantee of one's future conduct; give an undertaking concerning; give a p. to; foreshadow; provide reasons for hope. PROMISE, *n.* (*leg.*) someone to whom a p. is made, or in whose favour a promissory note is made out. PROMISOR, *n.* (*leg.*) one who makes a p. [Fr. from L.].

PROMISING [pro'mi-sing], *adj.* likely to get on, succeed, improve; hopeful, encouraging.

PROMISSORY [pro'mi-se-ri], *adj.* of, or pertaining to, a promise; containing a promise; **p. note,** note promising over the promisor's signature to pay a sum of money, on demand, to a specified person. [MedL.].

PROMONTORY [pro'mon-te-ri], *n.* crag or cliff jutting out into the sea or other stretch of water; (*anat.*) protuberance on the body. [LL.].

PROMOTE [prō-mōt'], *v.t.* to forward, originate, propose, suggest and make the preliminary arrangements for; assist the growth or spread of; raise the rank of; evoke or incite; (*leg.*) start a (legal action). PROMOTER, *n.* one who promotes; one who originates or helps to organize; one who encourages; one who evokes or incites. [L.].

PROMOTION [prō-mō'shn], *n.* act of promoting; act of founding and fostering; act of advancing (someone) in rank; fact of having been advanced in rank, preferment. [ME. from L.].

PROMPT (1) [prompt], *adj.* ready, quick to act; quickly done; being to time, not late; **p. cash,** cash paid forthwith; **p. goods,** goods delivered forthwith. PROMPT (2), *adv.* promptly. PROMPT (3), *v.t.* to urge, incite, suggest; aid the memory of (*esp.* by suggesting words or phrases to a speaker); (*stage*) aid an actor's memory by whispering, from the wings, the line he has forgotten; act as a prompter. PROMPT (4), *n.* (*comm.*) time limit for payments; **p. note,** note fixing a time limit for payment; **p. side,** side of the stage to the left of an actor facing the audience. PROMPT (5), *n.* word or line supplied by a prompter. PROMPT-BOOK, (*stage*) copy of the play as prepared for the prompter's use. PROMPT-BOX, place where the prompter sits on the stage. [L.].

PROMPTER [promp'ter], *n.* someone who prompts; (*stage*) one whose job it is to follow the action of the play from the text and be ready to remedy any lapse of memory on the part of the actors.

PROMPTITUDE [promp'ti-tyōod], *n.* readiness, quickness, alertness; quality or condition of being to time. [Fr. from LL.].

PROMULGATE [pro'mul-gāt], *v.t.* to make public, proclaim (facts, decrees etc.); make, or endeavour to make, widely known. PROMULGATOR, *n.* one who promulgates. [L.].

PROMULGATION [pro-mul-gā'shn], *n.* act of promulgating; publication; declaration, public and official announcement. [L.].

PRONE [prōn], *adj.* lying prostrate with the face to the ground; liable, disposed. [L.].

PRONG [prong], *n.* forked tool used to move hay etc.; one of the projecting divisions of a fork; any spurlike projection on a larger body; any spur-like thing which may be used for prodding. [Uncert.].

PRONOMINAL [prō-no'mi-nal], *adj.* (*gram.*) of, or pertaining to, pronouns, resembling a pronoun in function.

PRONOUN [prō'nown], *n.* (*gram.*) word used in place of a noun or name.

PRONOUNCE [prō-nowns'], *v.t. and i.* to give solemn utterance to, say with emphasis; state; utter with the vocal organs, articulate; deliver one's opinion; **to p. against,** to give judgment against, oppose, vote against; **to p. for,** to give verbal support to, argue in favour of, vote for; **to p. on,** to give one's considered opinion about, *esp.* of an expert. PRONOUNCED [prō-nownst'], *adj.* emphatic, well defined. PRONOUNCEDLY [prō-nown'sed-li], *adv.* in a pronounced way, emphatically. [OFr. from L.].

PRONOUNCEMENT [prō-nowns'ment], *n.* act of pronouncing; solemn or formal declaration; considered statement of opinion.

PRONUNCIAMENTO [prō-nun-si-a-men'tō], *n.* manifesto, *esp.* Spanish political manifesto. [Span.].

PRONUNCIATION [prō-nun-si-ā'shn], *n.* act of pronouncing; way of pronouncing, *esp.* the generally received way of saying a word, phrase etc. [L.].

PROOF (1) [prŏof], *n.* act or process of proving a fact or showing it to be true; evidence demonstrating the truth of a statement, belief etc.; examination, test, trial; (*leg.*) attested evidence, *esp.* a written statement of what a witness is prepared to swear in court, or a written record of evidence given in court; (*engraving*) impression taken for the artist to correct; (*print.*) preliminary impression taken for the proofreader or author to correct. PROOF-READER, -READING, (*print.*) one who corrects, business of correcting, printers' proofs. PROOF (2), *adj.* capable of resisting penetration by some specified thing, impenetrable; (*fig.*) invulnerable to; (of liquors) containing a standard quantity of alcohol. PROOF (3), *v.t.* to render p. against, render waterproof, *esp.* of cloths. [ME., OFr. from L.].

PROP (1) [prop], *n.* stick or stage used as a support or partial support for a weight or body leaning upon it; anything which acts as a support; (*fig.*) moral support, source of financial or material aid, or of spiritual comfort etc. PROP (2) (*pres.pt.* PROPPING, *pret. and p.pt.* PROPPED), *v.t.* to act as a p. to; support; **to p. up,** to support as a p. [ME.].

PROP (3), *n.* (*school slang*) a proposition in geometry. [PROP(OSITION)].

PROP (4), *n.* (*stage*) necessary accessory to the performance of a stage play, property. [PROP(ERTY)].

PROPAGANDA [pro-pa-gan'dah], *n.* (*R.C.*) committee of cardinals in charge of foreign missions; any organization to propagate a set of ideas, facts or ideals; the ideas etc. propagated; books, broadcasts etc. used to propagate a set of ideas, ideals or facts; *often with derogatory sense,* deliberately misleading

---

The accent ' after a syllable = stress (u-pon'). The mark ‾ over a vowel = length (ā in made; ō in bone).

publicity. PROPAGANDIZE, v.t. and i. to disseminate p. to or among; spread p. [L.].

PROPAGANDIST [pro-pa-gan'dist], n. one who spreads propaganda; members of Propaganda in the R. C. Church. PROPAGANDISM, n. system or practice of disseminating propaganda.

PROPAGATE [pro'pa-gāt], v.t. and i. to breed, multiply by taking cuttings etc., disseminate, transmit; have offspring. PROPAGATOR, n. propagandist, one who propagates. [L.].

PROPAGATION [pro-pa-gā'shn], n. act of propagating, of producing offspring or spreading propaganda; act of spreading or transmitting. [L.].

PROPEL (pres.pt. **propelling**, pret. and p.pt. **propelled**) [prō-pel'], v.t. to cause to move forward; drive forward. [L.].

PROPELLER [prō-pe'ler], n. that which propels; screw of a ship, aeroplane etc.

PROPENSE [prō-pens'], adj. inclined to, biased towards, disposed to. [L.].

PROPENSITY [prō-pen'si-ti], n. bent of mind; disposition, inclination, natural tendency.

PROPER [pro'per], adj. belonging to, pertaining to or fitting for, oneself, one's own; special, distinctive, individual; suitable, appropriate, right; according to rule or custom, regular, normal; decent, chaste, modest; polite, prim; complete; thorough; (her.) depicted in natural colours; **p. noun**, (gram.) name denoting a particular place, person etc.; **p. fraction**, (arith.) fraction the numerator of which is less than the denominator, i.e. whose value is less than unity. PROPERLY, adv. in a p. way; correctly, according to rule or custom; decently. [Fr. from L.].

PROPERTY [pro'per-ti], n. a characteristic, attribute or quality proper to or inherent in anything; thing or things possessed, possessions; estate, land owned; (pl.) (stage) accessories of a stage play, costumes, furniture etc.; **personal p.**, movable p., goods, chattels; **real p.**, land owned; **p. owner**, one who owns p., esp. land, houses etc.; **p. man**, man who provides and looks after the properties in a stage production. [ME., OFr. from L.].

PROPHECY [pro'fi-si], n. power of prophesying; something prophesied, prediction. [OFr., LL. from Gk.].

PROPHESY [pro'fi-sī], v.t. and i. to make prophecies, foretell the future; give forewarning of.

PROPHET [pro'fit], n. human spokesman of a deity, esp. a teacher or leader inspired by God to declare His will; one of the great non-Christian and non-Judaic religious teachers; religious teacher claiming or credited with special inspiration; pioneer in any human venture; one who foretells the future; **Prophets**, the prophetical books of the Old Testament; **racing p.**, tipster. [LL. from Gk.].

PROPHETIC(AL) [pro-fe'tik(-al)], adj. of, or pertaining to, a prophet or prophecy; containing prophecy; foretelling. [LL. from Gk.].

PROPHYLACTIC (1) [pro-fi-lak'tik], adj. (med.) preventive. PROPHYLACTIC (2), n. (med.) preventive medicine or treatment. [Gk.].

PROPHYLAXIS [pro-fi-lak'sis], n. (med.) preventive medicine or treatment. [Gk.].

PROPINQUITY [prō-ping'kwi-ti], n. nearness in place, time, relationship etc. [OFr. from L.].

PROPITIATE [prō-pi'shi-āt], v.t. to conciliate, appease, win the favour of. PROPITIATOR, n. one who propitiates. [L.].

PROPITIATION [prō-pi-shi-ā'shn], n. act of propitiating; fact of having been propitiated; that with which reconcilement is purchased. [LL.].

PROPITIATORY [prō-pi'shi-ā-te-ri], adj. able, intended or serving, to propitiate.* [EcclesL.].

PROPITIOUS [prō-pi'shoos], adj. favourable, auspicious. [L.].

PROPOLIS [pro'po-lis], n. resinous substance which bees gather from tree-buds and use to fill the crevices of their hives. [Gk.].

PROPORTION (1) [pro-paw'shn], n. part or portion; comparative relation (in size, quantity, quality etc.); symmetry, balance; (math.) a relation of quantities in which, when the first number is divided by the second, the quotient is equal to that produced when the third is divided by the fourth; rule of three; (pl.) dimensions, shape, build; **out of all p.**, (fig.) unreasonable, outrageous; **in due p.**, with proper balance; (fig.) sensible, reasonable. PROPORTION (2), v.t. to render duly proportionate; share out in due p. [OFr. from L.].

PROPORTIONAL (1) [pro-paw'shn-al], adj. being in proportion; **p. representation**, electoral system

by which strength of representation is in ratio with the strength of political parties. PROPORTIONAL (2), n. (math.) a term in a proportion. [LL.].

PROPORTIONATE [pro-paw'shn-at], adj. proportional.

PROPORTIONED [pro-paw'shnd], adj. having proportions (of a specified kind); symmetrical, balanced, being to scale; evenly divided out.

PROPOSAL [prō-pō'zal], n. act of proposing; that which is proposed, plan, scheme; offer, offer of marriage.

PROPOSE [prō-pōz'], v.t. and i. to bring forward, proffer (a suggestion, plan etc.) for consideration; make a suggestion; present as a resolution (to a meeting, committee etc.); make an offer of marriage, plan, intend. PROPOSER, n. someone who proposes, esp. someone who moves a resolution at a committee, meeting etc. [Fr.].

PROPOSITION [pro-po-zi'shn], n. statement, plan or project; (log.) statement in which something is affirmed or denied of something; (math.) formal statement of a theorem or problem; (coll.) affair, problem, person; **tough p.**, (coll.) difficult job, difficult person to have dealings with. [L.].

PROPOUND [prō-pownd'], v.t. to set forth, explain. [~L.].

PROPRIETARY [prō-prī'e-ta-ri], adj. pertaining to a proprietor or proprietorship; (of goods) bearing a branded trade-mark. [L.].

PROPRIETOR [prō-prī'e-ter], n. owner. PROPRIETORIAL [prō-prī-e-taw'ri-al], adj. of, or pertaining to, ownership.

PROPRIETY [prō-prī'e-ti], n. appropriateness, suitability; accordance with standards of decency and respectability; decorum. [ME. from L.].

PROPS [props], n. (slang) property man in a theatre.

PROPULSION [prō-pul'shn], n. act of driving forward, or fact of being driven forward. PROPULSIVE, adj. driving forward. [Fr.].

PROPYLON [prō-pī'lon], n. gateway of an ancient Egyptian temple. [Gk.].

PRO RATA [prō-rä'tah], adj. and adv. phrase in proportion, proportionately. [L.].

PROROGUE [prō-rōg'], v.t. to adjourn the meeting of an assembly (esp. of Parliament) for an indefinite period, without dissolving it. PROROGATION [prō-rō-gā'shn], n. act of proroguing or fact of being prorogued. [L.].

PROSAIC(AL) [prō-zā'ik(-al)], adj. dull, unimaginative, commonplace. [MedL.].

PROS AND CONS [prōz-and-konz'], n.(pl.) points, reasons, for and against; advantages and drawbacks. [PRO and CON(TRA)].

PROSCENIUM (pl. **proscenia**) [prō-sē'ni-um], n. platform or stage of the classical theatre; in the modern theatre, space between the curtain and the orchestra, esp. the arch framing the stage. [L.].

PROSCRIBE [prō-skrīb'], v.t. to banish, outlaw; condemn or prohibit. [L.].

PROSCRIPTION [prō-skrip'shn], n. act of proscribing or fact of being proscribed. [L.].

PROSCRIPTIVE [prō-skrip'tiv], adj. pertaining to, concerned with, proscription; causing or demanding proscription.

PROSE (1) [prōz], n. unmetrical language of ordinary speech and writing; literature not written in verse; commonplace mode of expression; dull, tedious writing; passage set in examinations for unmetrical translation into another language. PROSE (2), adj. written as p.; prosaic, in p. PROSE (3), v.i. to talk or write in a dull, tedious fashion. [L.].

PROSECTOR [prō-sek'ter], n. person who prepares bodies for use in anatomical demonstrations or lectures. [L.].

PROSECUTE [pro'si-kyōōt], v.t. and i. to pursue, carry through to an end; take legal proceedings against; institute or conduct a prosecution. [L.].

PROSECUTION [pro-si-kyōō'shn], n. the following out (of a plan or ambition); (leg.) indictment or laying of information in court in order to put a person on trial; the taking of legal action against a person; person or persons (and their legal advisers) taking action against another person or persons. [L.].

PROSECUTOR [pro'si-kyōō-ter], n. one who prosecutes; one who institutes legal proceedings (against another person or persons); **public p.**, law officer of the state who conducts legal proceedings on behalf of the Crown. [L.].

PROSECUTRIX [pro'si-kyōō-triks], n. female prosecutor. [MdL.].

PROSELYTE [pro'si-līt], n. Gentile convert to

Judaism, any kind of convert. PROSELYTISM, *n.* condition of being or becoming a p.; act of proselytizing. [LL. from Gk.].

PROSIT [pro´zit], *int.* good luck! [German drinking toast from L.].

PROSODY [pro´so-di], *n.* art and theory of versification. PROSODIC(AL) [pro-so´dik(-al)], *adj.* pertaining to p. [L. from Gk.].

PROSPECT (1) [pros´pekt], *n.* condition of facing or being turned in a certain direction; view, wide expanse or range of sight; view presented to the mental eye, plan, outlook; probable trend of events; (*pl.*) expectation of advances in a career; (*mining*) plot or area giving good promise of mineral deposit; (*coll.*) likely customer. PROSPECT (2) [pro-spekt´], *v.t. and i.* to survey an area for signs of mineral deposits; survey for mineral deposits; (*fig.*) search (for something); (*fig.*) take stock of the prospects or outlook (of an enterprise). PROSPECTOR, *n.* one who prospects, *esp.* for minerals. [L.].

PROSPECTIVE [pro-spek´tiv], *adj.* having an eye on the future; pertaining to the probable trend of future events; looking forward; expected, future, to be. PROSPECTIVELY, *adv.* with reference to the future, in a p. fashion. [MedL.].

PROSPECTUS (*pl.* **prospectuses**) [pro-spek´tus], *n.* description of a forthcoming production or intended enterprise issued for advertisement; pamphlet describing an educational establishment.

PROSPER [pros´per], *v.t. and i.* to thrive, succeed; cause to thrive. [L.].

PROSPERITY [pro-spe´ri-ti], *n.* condition or quality of being prosperous.

PROSPEROUS [pros´pe-roos], *adj.* successful, fortunate, thriving; flourishing, profitable. [Fr.].

PROSTATE [pros´tāt], *n.* (*anat.*) gland accessory to the male generative organs in mammals. PROSTATIC [pro-sta´tik], *adj.* of, or pertaining to, the p. [MedL. from Gk.].

PROSTITUTE (1) [pros´ti-tyoot], *n.* woman who hires out her body for promiscuous sexual intercourse. PROSTITUTE (2), *v.t.* (of a woman) to sell (*reflex.* herself); employ for base and unworthy purpose, defile or corrupt. PROSTITUTOR, *n.* one who prostitutes. [L.].

PROSTITUTION [pro-sti-tyoo´shn], *n.* act of debasing or prostituting; fact of being or having been prostituted; practice of a woman who sells her body for promiscuous sexual intercourse; use of skill or talent for vile or unworthy ends. [L.].

PROSTRATE (1) [pros´trāt], *adj.* lying face down flat on the ground; (*fig.*) utterly vanquished; at the mercy of another without power to resist; physically exhausted; morally exhausted, spiritless. PROSTRATE (2) [pro-strāt´], *v.t.* to cast down flat on the ground; (*fig.*) exhaust; render weak and powerless; (*reflex.*) make a low and submissive bow; fall flat in worship. [L.].

PROSTRATION [pro-strā´shn], *n.* act of prostrating or fact of being prostrated; humiliation, abasement; exhaustion. [LL.].

PROSY [prō´zi], *adj.* written in a dull, wearisome, long-winded style; habitually talking in a dull tedious fashion. [PROSE].

PROTAGONIST [prō-ta´go-nist], *n.* first actor in a Greek drama; principal character in a play, story etc.; chief champion of a cause. [Gk.].

PROTEAN [prō´te-an], *adj.* readily appearing in different shapes; (*fig.*) versatile. [PROTEUS].

PROTECT [prō-tekt´], *v.t.* to defend from injury or assault; guard, keep safe and unhurt; tend the welfare of; (*political economy*) attempt to promote (a native industry) by laying a duty upon similar foreign products imported; (*comm.*) set aside a sum of money against the future payment of a bill. [L.].

PROTECTION [prō-tek´shn], *n.* act of protecting; state of being protected; defence, shelter; (*political economy*) policy which seeks to foster native industry by laying a duty on similar products from abroad. PROTECTIONISM, *n.* economic theory or policy of p. PROTECTIONIST, *n.* advocate of the economic policy of p.

PROTECTIVE [prō-tek´tiv], *adj.* affording protection; of, pertaining to, the economic theory of protection; **p. custody**, imprisonment of political opponents without trial on the pretext of providing for their safety; **p. foods**, foods containing (large quantities of) vitamins and similar substances necessary to health.

PROTECTOR [prō-tek´ter], *n.* someone who or something which protects; guardian; **Lord P.**, head of the state during the Cromwellian interregnum. [ME., OFr. from L.].

PROTECTORATE [prō-tek´te-rat], *n.* dignity and office of, or period of rule by, a regent or protector; government of a state by a greater power which claims a more advanced civilization, state so governed.

PROTEGE(E), protégé(e) [pro´te-zhā], *n.* male (female) person under guardianship or patronage. [Fr.].

PROTEID [prō´tēd], *n. and adj.* protein.

PROTEIN [prō´tēn], *n. and adj.* (*chem.*) one of, relating to, a class of compounds which are fundamental constituents of animal and vegetable matter and are of primary importance in foods. [Fr. from Gk.].

PROTEST (1) [prō-test´], *v.t. and i.* to make a solemn avowal; raise an objection; (*leg.*) declare formally in writing the non-acceptance or non-payment of (a bill of exchange duly presented); **to p. against**, to raise objections to. PROTEST (2) [prō´test], *n.* solemn assertion or avowal, protestation, expression of disapproval or dissent; the raising of an objection; (*leg.*) formal written statement that payment or acceptance of a bill duly presented has been refused; **to lodge** (**or make**) **a p.**, to give expression to an objection, p. formally; **under p.**, against one's will. [L.].

PROTESTANT (1) [pro´tes-tant], *n.* member of a Christian Church which by adherence to the principles of the Reformation holds itself distinct from the R.C. Church. PROTESTANT (2), *adj.* pertaining to, or supporting, the principles of Protestantism. PROTESTANTISM, *n.* principles of the Reformation and, in particular, severance from the Church of Rome. [Germ. and Fr. from L.].

PROTESTATION [pro-tes-tā´shn], *n.* affirmation or avowal. [LL.].

PROTEUS [prō´tyoos], *n.* (*class. myth.*) sea-god who could assume many different shapes; (*fig.*) person who easily changes his mind. [Gk.].

PROTO-, *pref.* first. [Gk.].

PROTOCOL (1) [prō´tō-kol], *n.* preliminary agreement in negotiations for a major treaty; formula opening or concluding a Papal Bull; on the Continent, diplomatic etiquette, department of the Ministry of Foreign Affairs concerned with this. PROTOCOL (2), *v.t. and i.* to make a p.; draw up in the form of a p. [OFr., MedL. from LateGk.].

PROTON [prō´ton], *n.* (*phys.*) a sub-atomic particle carrying a unit positive charge of electricity. [Gk.].

PROTOPLASM [prō´tō-plazm], *n.* complex semi-fluid substance which is essential in the composition of every living cell. PROTOPLASMIC [prō-tō-plaz´mik], *adj.* of, or pertaining to, p. [Germ. from Gk.].

PROTOTYPE [prō´tō-tīp], *n.* primary type of a series; pattern. [Gk.].

PROTOZOA [prō-tō-zō´ah], *n.*(*pl.*) (*zool.*) term used for all the simplest, unicellular forms of animal life. PROTOZOAN (1), *adj.* of, or pertaining to, the p. PROTOZOAN (2), *n.* any one of the p. [Gk.].

PROTRACT [prō-trakt´], *v.t.* to lengthen, *esp.* to cause to last longer; (*surveying*) draw to scale. PROTRACTED, *adj.* prolonged, made to last a long while. [L.].

PROTRACTION [prō-trak´shn], *n.* act of protracting, lengthening in duration; fact of being protracted; (*zool.*) act of thrusting out (an organ or limb); (*surveying*) act of making a scale plan of. [L.].

PROTRACTOR [prō-trak´ter], *n.* draughtsman's instrument for measuring angles; **p. muscle**, (*anat.*) muscle which causes a limb or organ to protract. [MedL.].

PROTRUDE [prō-trood´], *v.t. and i.* to project, jut out; cause to project, thrust out, extend. [L.].

PROTRUSION [prō-troo´zhn], *n.* act of protruding or fact of being protruded.

PROTRUSIVE [prō-troo´siv], *adj.* thrusting forward, causing to protrude; able to be protruded; obtrusive. PROTRUSIVELY, *adv.* in a p. fashion.

PROTUBERANCE [prō-tyoo´be-rans], *n.* state of being protuberant; lump, knob, projection.

PROTUBERANT [prō-tyoo´be-rant], *adj.* swelling or jutting out, bulging, prominent. [L.].

PROUD (1) [prowd], *adj.* having a sense of just and proper pride; having a feeling of undue satisfaction with oneself, arrogant; unwilling to lower one's dignity; arising from arrogance; haughty; giving cause for proper pride; splendid, gorgeous; eminent; **p. flesh**, granulated overgrowth of flesh round a healing wound. PROUD (2), *adv.* (*in coll. phrase*)

The accent ´ after a syllable = stress (u-pon´).   The mark ¯ over a vowel = length (ā in made; ō in bone).

to do (someone) p., to entertain (someone) splendidly; give great satisfaction. [OE.].

PROVE [proov], *v.t.* to test or try; test the worth or quality of; put to the test; demonstrate to be true; show to exist; (*reflex.*) give proof that (one) is, show (oneself) as; experience, suffer, get to know by experience; (*leg.*) establish the validity of; (*arith.*) test the accuracy of (a calculation); *v.i.* to turn out to be, be shown to be. [OFr. from L.].

PROVEN [pro̅'ven, proo̅'ven], (*archaic*) *p.pt. of* PROVE.

PROVENANCE [pro've-nans], *n.* origin, source. [Fr.].

PROVENDER [pro'ven-der], *n.* food, *esp.* a supply of food for horses. [OFr.].

PROVERB [pro'verb], *n.* short traditional phrase or sentence expressing some maxim of worldly wisdom or view borne out by experience; (*fig.*) familiar or notorious example; **Book of Proverbs**, book of the O.T. which is a collection of such maxims. [ME., Fr. from L.].

PROVERBIAL [pro-vur'bi-al], *adj.* of, pertaining to, or resembling, a proverb; (*fig.*) notorious, well known. PROVERBIALLY, *adv.* in a p. fashion, commonly, notoriously.

PROVIDE [pro-vid'], *v.t. and i.* to make provision; render available, supply; **to p. against**, to take steps to prevent, make provision in anticipation of; prohibit by law; **to p. for**, to supply at least the necessaries of life for; make provision against the future on behalf of, make allowance for, anticipate in one's preparations; render legally permissible; **to p. that**, to stipulate that; **to p. with**, to furnish, equip, with. PROVIDED, PROVIDING, *conj.* on condition (that). [L.].

PROVIDENCE [pro'vi-dens], *n.* quality of being provident; foresight; the benevolent personality of God. [L.].

PROVIDENT [pro'vi-dent], *adj.* having foresight, careful about the future, thrifty. PROVIDENTLY, *adv.* with foresight, frugality or careful attention to the future.

PROVIDENTIAL [pro-vi-den'shal], *adj.* as of the benevolence of God; opportune. PROVIDENTIALLY, *adv.* in a p. fashion.

PROVINCE [pro'vins], *n.* large tract of territory forming one unit in the administration of a great government; large piece of territory united by tradition, dialect etc.; territory under the ecclesiastical jurisdiction of an archbishop; (*fig.*) sphere of activity, learning, experience etc.; (*pl.*) those parts of any country which lie outside and away from the capital. [OFr. from L.].

PROVINCIAL (1) [pro-vin'shal], *adj.* of, or pertaining to, a province or the provinces; supposedly lacking in urban or metropolitan polish, countrified. PROVINCIAL (2), *n.* one who inhabits a province or the provinces. [L.].

PROVINCIALISM [pro-vin'sha-lizm], *n.* that outlook which puts the interests of a province before those of the whole country; outlook supposed to be that of a provincial; dialectal trick of speech; provincial habit or custom.

PROVISION (1) [pro-vi'zhn], *n.* action of providing, act of making arrangements for future circumstances; act of making available necessary supplies; anything, *esp.* a necessary thing, provided against the future; stipulation, proviso; (*pl.*) supply of necessary things, stock or store, *esp.* of food; necessary foodstuffs; **to make p. for**, to make arrangements for, provide for. PROVISION (2), *v.t.* to supply with provisions, *esp.* food. [L.].

PROVISIONAL [pro-vi'zhn-al], *adj.* having the nature of a temporary arrangement made to meet special circumstances, and intended to last only as long as these circumstances last; tentative, subject to revision.

PROVISO [pro-vi'zo], *n.* clause in a legal document or agreement controlling the validity of that document or agreement by stating those conditions under which it is operative; condition, stipulation. [MedL.].

PROVISORY [pro-vi'ze-ri], *adj.* provisional, temporary; controlled by a proviso.

PROVOCATION [pro-vo-ka'shn], *n.* act of provoking or being provoked; anything which provokes, instigates, annoys etc. [L.].

PROVOCATIVE [pro-vo'ka-tiv], *adj.* causing provocation, annoying, challenging. [LL.].

PROVOKE [pro-vok'], *v.t.* to call forth, bring about, induce, give rise to; stir up; annoy, exasperate; **to p. (someone) to**, to incite (someone) to, spur (someone)

on to. PROVOKER, *n.* someone who or something which provokes. PROVOKING, *adj.* annoying, irritating. [L.].

PROVOST [pro'vost], *n.* head of certain university colleges; officer of a Scottish burgh corresponding to a mayor in an English borough. [OE. from LL. from L.].

PROVOST-MARSHAL [pro-vo-mah'shal], *n.* head of the military police in a given place or with a given force; (in the navy) master-at-arms in a ship where a court-martial is in progress.

PROW [prow], *n.* foremost part of a ship or boat. [Fr. from L.].

PROWESS [prow'es], *n.* valour, courage, skill. [ME. from OFr.].

PROWL (1) [prowl], *v.i.* (of animals) to move about stealthily in search of prey; (of persons) walk about in a way resembling this; (*coll.*) walk or wander about. PROWL (2), *n.* act of prowling; **to go on the p.**, to p. [ME.].

PROXIMATE [prok'si-mat], *adj.* close, adjacent, next, in time or space; **p. cause**, immediate cause. [LL.].

PROXIME [prok'si-me], *adv.* next, nearest; **p. accessit**, (*used of*) the runner-up in a contest. [L.].

PROXIMITY [prok-si'mi-ti], *n.* condition or quality of being close, in space or time; affinity. [L.].

PROXIMO [prok'si-mo], *adv.* in the next month. [L.].

PROXY [prok'si], *n.* person acting as agent for another; authority, function or capacity of a person so acting; document authorizing a person to act thus. [ME., OFr. from MedL.].

PRUDE [prood], *n.* woman of affected or exaggerated modesty or propriety, *esp.* in sexual matters. [OFr.].

PRUDENCE [proo'dens], *n.* quality of being prudent; practice of discreet and politic conduct; circumspect outlook or actions, foresight, sagacity. [L.].

PRUDENT [proo'dent], *adj.* characterized by, or acting according to, discreet and politic principles; wise; cautious, circumspect, worldly wise. [L.].

PRUDENTIAL [proo-den'shal], *adj.* of, or pertaining to, prudence; characterized by prudence. [MedL.].

PRUDERY [proo'de-ri], *n.* affected or exaggerated propriety, point of view of a prude.

PRUDISH [proo'dish], *adj.* affectedly modest, characterized by prudery.

PRUNE (1) [proon], *n.* kind of dried plum; rich purple colour of this. [Fr., MedL., L. from Gk.].

PRUNE (2), *v.t.* (*hort.*) to cut off unnecessary growth on (trees or bushes); (*fig.*) cut down, lop off excrescences on. PRUNER, *n.* one who, or that which, prunes. PRUNING-HOOK, -KNIFE, *n.* knife with a curved blade used in pruning. [OFr.].

PRURIENCE, PRURIENCY [proo'ri-ens(-i)], *n.* state or quality of being prurient; morbid preoccupation with sex or obscenity.

PRURIENT [proo'ri-ent], *adj.* preoccupied with thoughts of sex or obscenity. [L.].

PRURIGO [proo-ri'go], *n.* (*med.*) a disease of the skin characterized by chronic itching. [L.].

PRURITUS [proo-ri'tus], *n.* (*med.*) an itching, *esp.* when not accompanied by eruption. [L.].

PRUSSIAN (1) [pru'shn], *adj.* of, or pertaining to, Prussia or the Prussians; **p. blue**, a deep blue colour, based on ferric ferro-cyanide. PRUSSIAN (2), *n.* inhabitant or native of Prussia. [MedL.].

PRUSSIC ACID [pru-sik-a'sid], *n.* hydrocyanic acid in an aqueous solution. [~PRUSSIAN BLUE].

PRY [pri], *v.i.* to peer into, spy on; **to p. into, to** search into, *esp.* impertinently. PRYING, *adj.* impertinently curious. [ME.].

PSALM [sahm], *n.* sacred song, hymn; one of the songs in the Book of Psalms (O.T.); (*pl.*) songs in the Book of Psalms as used in Christian worship. [L. from Gk.].

PSALMIST [sah'mist], *n.* writer of psalms; **the P.**, King David, traditionally associated with the Book of Psalms. [L.].

PSALMODY [sal'mo-di], *n.* art of singing psalms; collection of psalms and music for these. PSALMODIC, [sal-mo'dik], *adj.* of, or relating to, p. PSALMODIST, *n.* singer of psalms. [L. from Gk.].

PSALTER [sawl'ter], *n.* the Book of Psalms, *esp.* the version in the Book of Common Prayer; collection of psalms; special version of the Book of Psalms. [ME., OFr. from L.].

PSALTERY [sawl'te-ri], *n.* ancient stringed instrument, played by plucking the strings. [OFr.].

PSEUDO- [syoo'do], *pref.* false, sham. [Gk.].

PSEUDONYM [syoo'do-nim], *n.* assumed name;

---

esp. name assumed for the publication of literary works. PSEUDONYMITY [syōō-dō-ni'mi-ti], *n.* act of using, fact of being known under, a false name. PSEUDONYMOUS [syōō-do'ni-mŏŏs], *adj.* known under, bearing, a false name. [Gk.].

PSITTACOSIS [si-ta-kō'sis], *n.* (*path.*) a pneumonic disease among parrots **communicable to** human beings. [Gk.].

PSORIASIS [so-rī'a-sis], *n.* a severe but non-contagious skin disease. [Gk.].

PSYCHE [sī'ki], *n.* (*class. myth.*) young girl, beloved of Eros the god of love and representing immortality; the soul, principle of life in man; (*entom.*) genus of moths. [L. from Gk.].

PSYCHIATRIST [sī-kī'a-trist], *n.* doctor specializing in treatment of mental disease. [*Next*].

PSYCHIATRY [sī-kī'a-tri], *n.* cure of mental diseases. PSYCHIATRIC [sī-ki-at'rik], *adj.* of, or pertaining to, p. [Fr. from Gk.].

PSYCHIC (1) [sī'kik], *adj.* of, or pertaining to, the soul or mind; pertaining to the spirit world; susceptible to spirit influence. PSYCHIC (2), *n.* a medium in spiritualist investigation. PSYCHICAL [sī'ki-kal], *adj.* p., supernatural.

PSYCHO- [sī'kō], *pref.* **pertaining to the mind.** [Gk.].

PSYCHO-ANALYSIS [sī-kō-a-na'li-sis], *n.* investigation into mental processes based on the researches of Freud, Jung and others into the unconscious mind. PSYCHO-ANALYSE [sī-kō-a'na-līz], *v.t.* to subject to p. PSYCHO-ANALYST [sī-kō-a'na-list], *n.* one who practises p. [PSYCHO and ANALYSIS].

PSYCHOLOGICAL [sī-ko-lo'ji-kal], *adj.* of, or pertaining to, psychology; pertaining to the mind, mental; **p. moment,** momentum of a fact, idea, event or sensation upon the mind; (*coll.*) the precise moment when the greatest effect can be gained.

PSYCHOLOGIST [sī-ko'lo-jist], *n.* one who practises psychology.

PSYCHOLOGY [sī-ko'lo-ji], *n.* study of the mind, its nature, processes, habits etc.; (*pop.*) mental character, peculiarities of mind. [MdL. from Gk.].

PSYCHO-NEUROSIS [sī-kō-nyōō-rō'sis], *n.* mental disease. PSYCHO-NEUROTIC [sī-kō-nyōō-ro'tik], *n.* *and adj.* (one) suffering from p.; pertaining to p. [PSYCHO and NEUROSIS].

PSYCHOPATH [sī'kō-path], *n.* sufferer from a mental disease. PSYCHOPATHIC [sī-kō-pa'thik], *adj.* suffering from a mental disease or disorder; highly emotional; hysterical. [Gk.].

PSYCHO-PATHOLOGY [sī-kō-pa-tho'lo-ji], *n.* science and study of mental disorders.

PSYCHOPATHY [sī-ko'pa-thi], *n.* mental disorder; medical treatment by hypnotism. [Gk.].

PSYCHOPHYSICS [sī-kō-fi'ziks], *n.*(*pl.*) study of the relations between mind and body.

PSYCHOSIS [sī-kō'sis], *n.* mental disease or derangement which is not represented by any disorder or disease of the physical structure of the brain. [Gk.].

PSYCHOTHERAPEUTICS, PSYCHOTHERAPY [sī-kō-the-ra-pyōō'tiks, -the'ra-pi], *n.* treatment of illness or disease by hypnotism or psychoanalysis.

PSYCHOTIC [sī-ko'tik], *n.* *and adj.* (one) suffering from psychosis; pertaining to psychosis.

PTARMIGAN [tah'mi-gan], *n.* the white grouse of Northern Europe. [Gael.].

PTERO- [te'rō], *pref.* winged, connected with wings or feathers. [Gk.].

PTERODACTYL [te-rō-dak'til], *n.* an extinct winged reptile. [MdL. from Gk.].

PTOLEMAIC [to-le-mā'ik], *n. and adj.* (adherent) of, or pertaining to, Ptolemy (2nd century A.D.), an astronomer of Alexandria; of, or pertaining to, the Ptolemies, Greek dynasty ruling in Egypt from the death of Alexander the Great to Cleopatra.

PTOMAINE [tō'mān], *n.* any of several poisonous alkaloid substances formed by the putrefaction of proteins of animal origin; **p. poisoning,** poisoning caused by eating such matter; (*pop.*) food poisoning generally. [It. from Gk.].

PUBERTY [pyōō'ber-ti], *n.* age at which a member of either sex becomes capable of parenthood. [L.].

PUBESCENCE [pyōō-be'sens], *n.* state of reaching puberty; (*nat. hist.*) a down on the bodies of insects and on the leaves and stems of certain plants. PUBESCENT, *adj.* attaining puberty; (of plants and insects) covered with p. [L.].

PUBIC [pyōō'bik], *adj.* of, or pertaining to, the hair around the groin which appears at puberty, or to the part of the body where this grows. [L.].

PUBLIC (1) [pub'lik], *adj.* of, or pertaining to, the people as a whole; national, general, not private or personal; done on behalf of, concerning or involving, the people generally; generally known, available to all and sundry, well known, notorious, manifest; concerning, known to or serving the whole nation; concerning humanity, international; **P. Prosecutor,** (*leg.*) legal officer of the Crown who undertakes the prosecution of persons charged with grave offences; **p. nuisance,** (*leg.*) act, punishable by law, which is contrary to the interests of the community rather than of a private individual; (*coll.*) generally annoying or disturbing person; **p. notary (or notary p.),** official appointed to draw up and attest formal documents, such as deeds etc.; **p. enemy,** enemy to the community at large; **p. health,** health of the nation at large; **p. holiday,** statutory holiday enjoyed by everybody except the most essential trades and services; **p. ownership,** ownership by the nation or government, nationalization; **p. orator,** (in a university) orator appointed to deliver addresses on behalf of the whole university; **p. opinion,** attitude of the community generally; **p. benefactor,** person who benefits the community generally; **p. utility company,** privately owned firm operating p. services under government supervision; **p. relations officer,** official charged with presenting his department to the p. in the most favourable light. PUBLIC (2), *n.* the mass of persons making up a community or nation; that part of the community interested or likely to be interested in any particular idea, article or activity; (*coll.*) p.-house; **in p.,** openly. [ME. from L.].

PUBLICAN [pub'li-kan], *n.* (*Rom. hist.*) tax-gatherer; innkeeper.

PUBLICATION [pub-li-kā'shn], *n.* act of publishing or making public, act of proclaiming; act of issuing printed matter for sale to the general public; anything published, book, music etc. issued for sale to the public; proclamation or announcement; (*leg.*) act of making known to a third person or group of persons, *esp.* any libellous matter. [ME. from L.].

PUBLIC-HOUSE [pub-lik-hows'], *n.* inn or tavern, house where by licence alcoholic liquors may be sold and consumed.

PUBLICIST [pub'li-sist], *n.* authority on international law, art of government etc.; journalist concerning himself with current political topics and events.

PUBLICITY [pub-li'si-ti], *n.* quality or condition of being public; act or practice of advertising; advertisements. [Fr. from MedL.].

PUBLICIZE [pub'li-siz], *v.t.* to make known to the public; advertise.

PUBLIC SCHOOL [pub-lik-skōōl'], *n.* type of school, *esp.* in England, which prepares its scholars, often boarders, for the universities, the professions and higher government service; a school the headmaster of which is entitled to attend the Headmasters' Conference; state-controlled primary school in Scotland; (*U.S.*) state-controlled elementary or secondary school.

PUBLIC-SPIRITED [pub-lik-spi'ri-tid], *adj.* actuated by zeal for public welfare.

PUBLISH [pub'lish], *v.t.* to make public, announce, proclaim; issue (printed matter etc.) for sale to the general public; **to p. the banns of marriage,** to announce in the church of the parish where each is resident, the names of couples intending to marry; **to p. a will,** to execute a will before witnesses; **to p. a libel,** to communicate a libel to more than one person. [ME., OFr. from L.].

PUBLISHER [pub'li-sher], *n.* one who publishes, *esp.* a person or company engaged in the trade of issuing books, music and printed matter generally for sale to the general public.

PUCE [pyōōs], *n.* a purple-brown colour. [Fr. from L.].

PUCK (1) [puk], *n.* mischievous goblin, *esp.* Robin Goodfellow, mischievous sprite of rural legend, introduced by Shakespeare into *A Midsummer Night's Dream.* PUCKISH, *adj.* impish, suggestive of P. [OE.].

PUCK (2), *n.* flat rubber disk used in place of a ball in ice hockey. [Unkn.].

PUCKA, see PUKKA.

PUCKER (1) [pu'ker], *v.t. and i.* to knit into wrinkles, crease up; shrivel into wrinkles and creases. PUCKER (2), *n.* a wrinkle or crease. [Uncert.].

PUDDING [pŏŏ'ding], *n.* boiled or baked preparation of flour, suet, eggs or milk etc., to which either meat or fruit may be added; a batter; milk dish made with

---

The accent ' after a syllable = stress (u-pon'). The mark ⁻ over a vowel = length (ā in made; ō in bone).

rice, sago etc.; (fig.) anything resembling a pudding. PUDDING-FACED, having a large, fat, unintelligent face. [ME.].

PUDDLE (1) [pu'dl], n. small, shallow, dirty pool of water or other liquid; mixture of sand and clay with water to form a watertight base for a pool or lining for a canal. PUDDLE (2), v.t. and i. to dabble or paddle, esp. in dirty water; mix clay, water and sand for lining ponds or canals; stir molten iron so that what would otherwise have cooled into cast-iron becomes wrought-iron. [ME. from OE.].

PUDENCY [pyōō'den-si], n. sense of shame, modesty, bashfulness. [LL.].

PUDENDA (sg. **pudendum**) [pyōō-den'dah], n.(pl.) external genital organs, esp. of the female. [L.].

PUERILE [pyōō'e-rīl], adj. childish; trifling, of small account. [L.].

PUERILITY [pyōō-e-ri'li-ti], n. state of being puerile; something which is puerile.

PUERPERAL [pyōō-ur'pe-ral], adj. of, or pertaining to, childbirth; **p. fever**, fever arising from septic infection after confinement. [L.].

PUFF (1) [puf], v.t. and i. to emit a short, sharp blast; send forth puffs; breathe heavily and jerkily, pant; cause to be out of breath; emit, escape, in puffs; advertise or notice flatteringly; **to p. out**, to emit in puffs; render breathless, inflate, distend; extinguish by puffing; swell; come forth in puffs; **to p. away**, to drive off by puffing; emit a steady series of puffs; move away while puffing; **to p. up**, to distend, inflate; (fig.) make arrogant and elated; rise up in puffs. PUFF (2), n. action of puffing; short, quick blast of air, smoke, gas etc.; the sound accompanying puffing; (in clothes) puffed-up piece of material; fluffy ball of ribbons, hair or feathers; kind of light pastry or cake; flattering advertisement or notice in the Press etc.; **powder p.**, small ball or pad of swans' down or similar material for applying cosmetic powder. PUFF-PASTRY, a light, flaky pastry. PUFFER, n. someone who or something which puffs; (in childish talk) steam train or steam locomotive. [OE.].

PUFF-BALL [puf'bawl], n. a fungus, the rounded head of which when ripe will burst at a touch emitting spores in a cloud; feathery head on a dandelion when the blossom has died.

PUFFIN [pu'fin], n. a North Atlantic flightless seabird; coin formerly used on Lundy Island. [Uncert.].

PUFFY [pu'fi], adj. moving in puffs; exhausted, panting; swollen.

PUG (1) [pug], n. one of a breed of small, short-nosed dogs. PUG-DOG, p., small pet bulldog. PUG-NOSE, snub nose. [Unkn.].

PUG (2) (pres.pt. **pugging**, pret. and p.pt. **pugged**), v.t. to knead clay for bricks and pottery; pad (a wall, floor etc.) with sawdust etc., to make partially soundproof. PUG (3), n. clay kneaded for brick-making or pottery; sawdust and other material used for soundproofing. [Uncert.].

PUGILISM [pyōō'ji-lizm], n. art of boxing. [L.].

PUGILIST [pyōō'ji-list], n. boxer, prize-fighter. PUGILISTIC [pyōō-ji-lis'tik], adj. of, or pertaining to, pugilism. [L.].

PUGNACIOUS [pug-nā'shŏŏs], adj. quarrelsome, combative. [L.].

PUGNACITY [pug-na'si-ti], n. quality of being pugnacious; quarrelsomeness. [L.].

PUISNE (1) [pyōō'ni], adj. (leg.) subordinate, junior. PUISNE (2), n. a p. judge. [OFr.].

PUISSANCE [pyōō'i-sans, pwi'sans], n. (archaic) power, might, strength. [Fr.].

PUISSANT [pyōō'i-sant, pwi'sant], adj. (archaic) mighty, powerful. PUISSANTLY, adv. with might. [Fr.].

PUKE (1) [pyōōk], v.t. to vomit. PUKE (2), n. act of puking. [Echoic].

PUKKA, PUCKA [pu'kah], adj. (coll.) excellent, first-class; genuine; **p. sahib**, true gentleman. [Hind.].

PULCHRITUDE [pul'kri-tyōōd], n. beauty. [L.].

PULE [pyōōl], v.i. to whimper like a fretful baby. [Echoic].

PULL [pōōl], v.t. to exert such a force upon something as to cause it to move towards the point from which the force is exerted; draw, drag, haul; cause (an object) to change position by exerting a force which is always moving away from that object; extract; tug at, strain at; pluck; proceed and by so doing cause (an object) to follow after; propel by rowing; (fig.) attract; uproot (weeds etc.); (of a horse) strain constantly at the bit; (cricket) strike a ball, which has pitched straight or on the off-side, so as to propel it into the leg field; (golf) strike a ball hard over to the left; (print.) take an impression of; (racing) hold (a horse) back deliberately so as to prevent it from winning; (of a punch in boxing) strike with less force than is possible or expected; v.i. to tug, drag, haul; exert a drawing force towards the point from which the force is exerted; proceed by rowing; (of a pipe, cigar etc.) draw, admit of suction when sucked; smoke, draw at a pipe etc.; **to p. about**, to treat roughly and without ceremony; **to p. at**, to suck at (a pipe etc.); drink liquor from (a glass etc.); **to p. down**, to weaken in health; render more likely to fail in an examination or test; **to p. in**, to retract, withdraw; reduce, curtail; (of a belt) tighten; gain the help of; (thieves' slang) arrest; (motoring etc.) draw to the side of the road; **to p. in at**, to make a short stop at; **to p. off**, to be successful in, achieve; depart; row away; **to p. out**, v.t. to bring forth, extract, produce, extend, prolong; v.i. (of a train) move out of a station; **to p. round**, v.t. to render successful when failure appeared imminent; make well again; v.i. to recover from illness, imminent defeat etc.; **to p. through**, v.t. to help over danger or difficulty; v.i. to be successful despite difficulties, win through; **to p. together**, to co-operate; **to p. oneself together**, to recover one's energies, wits, regain one's self-control; **to p. up**, to stop, interrupt; rein in (a horse); cause someone to stop and think; v.i. to stop, pause; **to p. to pieces**, to tear in shreds, unravel; (fig.) criticize strongly and destructively; **to p. a face (or faces)**, to grimace; **to p. someone's leg**, to make someone the butt of a playful deception; **to p. a good oar**, to row well; **to p. one's weight**, to do all that could be expected of one; **to p. strings (or wires)**, to exert secret or backstairs influence. PULL (2), n. act of pulling; force exerted when pulling; influence, attraction; backstairs influence; (coll.) advantage; act of rowing; act of taking a draught of liquor; act of sucking at a pipe, cigar etc.; that which is pulled, handle or lever, esp. the handle of a beer-engine; amount of beer emitted at one movement of the handle of a beer-engine; (print.) rough proof or impression; (cricket) stroke which drives a ball, which has pitched on the off-side, over to the leg field; (riding, racing) tug of the bridle to check a horse, esp. when deliberately given to prevent a horse from winning; (golf) shot which drives the ball widely to the left; **p. at an oar**, short spell of rowing. [OE.].

PULLET [pŏŏl'let], n. young hen. [Fr.].

PULLEY [pŏŏl'li], n. wheel, grooved or otherwise, mounted on a shaft, generally for the transmission of power by means of an endless belt etc. [ME. from OFr.].

PULL-IN, PULL-UP [pŏŏl-in', -up'], n. (coll.) roadside café, esp. for truck-drivers.

PULLMAN [pŏŏl'man], n. car or sleeping-coach on a railway train. [G. M. Pullman, the designer].

PULL-ON [pŏŏl'on], adj. (of garments) designed to be simply pulled on, without fastenings.

PULLOVER [pŏŏl'ō-ver], n. woollen jersey, without fastenings, pulled on or off over the head.

PULL-THROUGH [pŏŏl'thrōō], n. (milit.) looped and weighted cord used for cleaning the bore of a rifle barrel.

PULLULATE [pu'lyōō-lāt], v.i. to sprout, spring up, multiply rapidly. PULLULATION [pu-lyōō-lā'shn], n. act of pullulating; numerous offspring. [L.].

PULMO-, pref. pertaining to the lungs. [L.].

PULMONARY [pul'mo-na-ri], adj. of, pertaining to, or affecting, the lungs. [L.].

PULMONATE [pul'mo-nāt], adj. equipped with lungs. [L.].

PULP (1) [pulp], n. soft fleshy matter like the soft interior of a gourd or fruit; soft formless mass reduced from fibrous matter by rubbing, crushing and boiling, as in the manufacture of paper from cloth or wood; anything of similar substance to this. PULP (2), v.t. to reduce to p., make pulpy. PULPER, n. machine for pulping. [L.].

PULPIT [pŏŏl'pit], n. raised box-like structure from which a sermon may be delivered or a service conducted. [OFr. from L.].

PULSATE [pul-sāt', pul'sāt], v.i. to throb, beat or move with a regular pulse. [L.].

PULSATION [pul-sā'shn], n. steady rhythmic beating or throbbing movement; steadily repeated pulse-like sound; one sound or movement in such a series of sounds or movements, esp. the variation of a pulsating electric current. [L.].

PULSE (1) [puls], n. rhythmical beating, throbbing.

ōō is pronounced as in food; ŏŏ as in hood; th as in think; TH as in that; zh as in azure. ~ = related to.

vibration or palpitation; one beat, throb etc., of a series rhythmically repeated; any movement regularly and frequently repeated; a single vibration or wave; (*anat.*) rhythmic beating or throbbing of the heart and blood stream, *esp.* as felt at the wrist, the rate of this pulsation; rhythmic stress of verse, music etc.; rhythm; (*fig.*) sensation of excitement, energy or vitality; **to feel (or take) someone's p.**, to feel or time the pulsations of the artery at the wrist; **to stir the p.**, to quicken to vitality and excitement. PULSE (2), *v.t. and i.* to beat or throb rhythmically, pulsate. [L.].

PULSE (3), *n.* seeds of leguminous plants grown for food as beans, lentils, peas etc. [ME., L. from Gk.].

PULVERIZE [pul've-rīz], *v.t. and i.* to reduce to fine powder, or dust; crumble away to dust; divide a liquid into tiny particles as in spray; (*fig.*) destroy, crush, criticize most adversely. [LL.].

PUMA [pyōo'mah], *n.* large South American feline quadruped, the cougar. [Peruvian].

PUMICE [pu'mis], *n.* light, porous, grey lava used to remove stains from the skin by scrubbing, pumicestone. PUMICE-STONE, p. in lump form. [ME.].

PUMMEL, see POMMEL.

PUMP (1) [pump], *n.* mechanical device for moving gases and liquids, consisting in its simplest form of a piston moving in a cylinder; anything resembling this in form, principle or function. PUMP (2), *v.t. and i.* to work a p.; move by means of a p.; move in a way resembling a p. or a person working a p.; (*fig.*) exhaust; extract information from by repeated questioning; instil laboriously; **to p. out,** to empty by using a p.; exhaust, fatigue; **to p. up,** to raise by means of a p.; inflate with a p.; **to p. ship,** (*coll.*) to make water. [ME.].

PUMP (3), *n.* light, low shoe worn by men for dancing or evening wear. [Unkn.].

PUMPERNICKEL [pōom'per-ni-kl], *n.* sweet, sticky, dark-coloured bread containing malt. [Germ.].

PUMPKIN [pump'kin], *n.* large tough-rinded fruit of the plant *Cucurbita pepo*; the plant itself. [Fr. from L.].

PUMP-ROOM [pump'rōom], *n.* building at a spa where the water is distributed for drinking.

PUN (1) [pun], *n.* a humorous use of words which have like sounds but different meanings. PUN (2) (*pres.pt.* PUNNING, *pret. and p.pt.* PUNNED), *v.i.* to make a p. on puns. [Unkn.].

PUNCH (1) [punsh], *n.* the crook-backed, harlequin-like hero of the puppet show *Punch and Judy*. [It.].

PUNCH (2), *n.* † short, thick animal; **Suffolk p.,** one of a sturdy breed of draught horses. [Uncert.].

PUNCH (3), *n.* drink consisting of a spirit diluted with milk or water, flavoured with lemon and spice and sweetened. PUNCH-BOWL, bowl for brewing or serving p.; (*fig.*) deep hollow in a hillside. [Uncert.].

PUNCH (4), *n.* instrument for piercing leather, wood etc., or for driving a nail right in below the surface of wood; small device containing a p. and used for piercing tickets on buses, trains etc. PUNCH (5), *v.t.* to pierce with a p. [ME., OFr.].

PUNCH (6), *v.t. and i.* to strike with a sharp hard blow using the clenched fist; deliver such a blow. PUNCH (7), *n.* sharp hard blow delivered with the clenched fist; (*coll.*) energy, wit, vivid personality etc. PUNCH-DRUNK, of a boxer, suffering from some sort of concussion as the result of continual punches, and giving the impression of being drunk. [ME.].

PUNCHINELLO [pun-chi-nel'lō], *n.* chief character in an Italian puppet-show; buffoon.

PUNCTILIO [pungk-ti'li-ō], *n.* a delicate point of conduct; precise and ceremonious behaviour; scrupulous attention to niceties of conduct. [Span.].

PUNCTILIOUS [pungk-ti'li-ōos], *adj.* scrupulous over even the smallest points of behaviour; scrupulous, very careful and precise.

PUNCTUAL [pungk'tyōo-al], *adj.* arriving exactly to time, prompt. [MedL.].

PUNCTUALITY [pungk-tyōo-a'li-ti], *n.* condition or quality of being punctual. [MedL.].

PUNCTUATE [pungk'tyōo-āt], *v.t.* to mark (a passage of writing) with commas, stops etc.; **to p. with,** to interrupt with, diversify with. PUNCTUATOR, *n.* one who punctuates or inserts punctuation. [MedL.].

PUNCTUATION [pungk-tyōo-ā'shn], *n.* act of punctuating, fact of being punctuated; systematic use of stops, commas, colons etc. in writing. [MedL.].

PUNCTURE (1) [pungk'tyōor], *n.* prick, perforation, *esp.* a cut or prick in a pneumatic tyre. PUNCTURE

(2), *v.t. and i.* to prick; receive a prick or perforation, *esp.* in a pneumatic tyre. [L.].

PUNDIT, PANDIT [pun'dit], *n.* a Hindu learned in the law, philosophy and religion of his race; an authority on any subject, learned person, *esp.* when referred to humorously; one who pretends to more learning than he has. [Hind.].

PUNGENCY [pun'jen-si], *n.* condition or quality of being pungent.

PUNGENT [pun'jent], *adj.* (*bot., zool.*) pricking, having prickles; affecting the senses of taste and smell strongly; sharp, acrid; (*fig.*) biting, caustic, acute (of intellect, wit etc.). [L.].

PUNIC [pyōo'nik], *adj.* of, or pertaining to, Carthage and the Carthaginians; **P. faith,** treachery. [L.].

PUNISH [pu'nish], *v.t.* to penalize for wrongdoing, chastise; inflict a penalty for; (*coll.*) treat roughly. [ME. from Fr. from L.].

PUNISHMENT [pu'nish-ment], *n.* act of punishing; fact of being punished; penalty inflicted for wrongdoing; (*coll.*) rough treatment. [OFr.].

PUNITIVE [pyōo'ni-tiv], *adj.* inflicting punishment.

PUNK [pungk], *n.* dry fungus which can be used for tinder, decayed wood; (*U.S. slang*) any worthless thing. [~SPUNK.]

PUNKA(H) [pung'kah], *n.* large fan for keeping a room cool in tropical countries. [Hind.].

PUNNET [pu'net], *n.* small shallow chip-basket used to hold fruit in small quantities. [Unkn.].

PUNSTER [pun'ster], *n.* one given to making puns.

PUNT (1) [punt], *n.* rectangular, flat-bottomed boat used on rivers and propelled with a pole. PUNT (2), *v.t. and i.* to propel a p.; carry in a p. [OE. from L.].

PUNT (3), *v.i.* (*football*) to drop the ball from the hands and kick it before it touches the ground. PUNT (4), *n.* (*football*) a volleying kick. [Unkn.].

PUNT (5), *v.i.* (*cards*) to lay a stake against the bank; (*racing*) back a horse heavily, bet. [Uncert.].

PUNTER [pun'ter], *n.* one who bets (habitually); one who uses a punt on a river.

PUNY [pyōo'ni], *adj.* small, weak, feeble. [Fr.].

PUP (1) [pup], *n.* very young dog, puppy; young seal; young otter; conceited young fellow; **in p.,** (of a bitch) pregnant; **to sell (someone) a p.,** to swindle. PUP (2) (*pres.pt.* PUPPING, *pret. and p.pt.* PUPPED), *v.i.* (of a bitch) to be delivered of pups. [PUP(PY)].

PUPA (1) (*pl.* **pupae**) [pyōo'pah], *n.* (*entom.*) insect at the chrysalis stage. PUPA (2), *adj.* of, pertaining to, a p. PUPATE, *v.i.* (*entom.*) to become a p. [L.].

PUPIL [pyōo'pil], *n.* person undergoing instruction by a teacher; (*leg.*) ward under the age of puberty; (*opt.*) opening in the iris through which light reaches the retina. PUPIL-TEACHER, young person who spends part of his time teaching in a school, while still undergoing training himself with a view to becoming a teacher. PUPIL(L)AGE, *n.* condition of being a p.; (*leg.*) minority. PUPIL(L)ARY, *adj.* having the status of a p. (in a university) until after taking the Master's degree; (*opt.*) pertaining to the p. [L.].

PUPPET [pu'pit], *n.* doll, *esp.* a small jointed figure worked by wires in a toy theatre or marionette-show, a marionette; (*fig.*) person of feeble will easily controlled by others and used for their ends; political figure ostensibly independent but in fact the tool of others; **p. state,** territory controlled by a government set up by a greater power and claiming to be independent but actually controlled by its originators. PUPPET-SHOW, play etc. performed by puppets. [ME., OFr. from L.].

PUPPY [pu'pi], *n.* pup, young dog; (*fig.*) conceited insolent youngster. [Fr.].

PURBLIND [pur'blīnd], *adj.* partly blind; (*fig.*) obtuse.

PURCHASE (1) [pur'chas], *v.t.* to buy, acquire in exchange for money; obtain in exchange for something else (often in *fig.* senses); (*naut.*) hoist with leverage or by pulleys etc.; (*leg.*) acquire other than by inheritance. PURCHASE (2), *n.* act of purchasing; something purchased; value reckoned in annual returns or profits; leverage, grip, pull; (*leg.*) acquisition of property other than by inheritance. [ME. from OFr.].

PURCHASER [pur'cha-ser], *n.* one who purchases; (*leg.*) one who has acquired property other than by inheritance.

PURDAH [pur'dah], *n.* curtain shutting the women's apartments in India; custom of secluding women in India. [Hind.].

PURE [pyōor], *adj.* clean, uncontaminated; unmixed, unadulterated; chaste; upright, disinterested; (of

---

The accent ′ after a syllable = stress (u-pon′). The mark ‾ over a vowel = length (ā in made; ō in bone).

mathematics etc.) **theoretical** as opposed to applied; (*coll.*) unmitigated. PURE-BRED, of unmixed breed. **PURELY**, *adv.* in a p. manner; innocently, chastely; merely, solely, absolutely. [ME., Fr. from L.].

PUREE, purée [pyōō'rā], *n.* any soft pulpy material, *esp.* a mashed foodstuff; soup made from such a foodstuff. [Fr.].

PURFLE (1) [pur'fl], *v.t.* (*arch.*) to ornament with crockets; embroider with a flowered border. PURFLE (2), *n.* embroidery at the edge of a cloth or garment; ornamentation on violins; (*arch.*) parapet etc. with crockets. [ME. from OFr.].

PURGATION [per-gā'shn], *n.* cleansing, purifying, *esp.* the purification of the soul from worldly sin while in purgatory; evacuation of the bowels by means of a purgative. [OFr. from L.].

PURGATIVE [pur'ga-tiv], *n. and adj.* (medicine) promoting the evacuation of the bowels; cleansing, purifying. [Fr. from LL.].

PURGATORY [pur'ga-te-ri], *n.* (*theol.*) condition of the souls of the departed who have died in the faith and in grace but still have to be cleansed from venial sins; place of this cleansing; (*loosely*) place or condition of torment or punishment. PURGATORIAL [per-ga-taw'ri-al], *adj.* expiatory; of, or pertaining to, p. [MedL.].

PURGE (1) [purj], *v.t.* to cleanse or purify; (*med.*) provoke an evacuation of the bowels; (*leg.*) clear (oneself) of a charge; (*pol.*) rid of undesirable elements by a purge. PURGE (2), *n.* act or process of purging, purgative; evacuation of the bowels; (*pol.*) wholesale and drastic removal of undesirable elements, often by forcible methods. PURGING (1), *n.* diarrhoea or dysentery. PURGING (2), *adj.* that purges. [ME., OFr. from L.].

PURIFICATION [pyōō-ri-fi-kā'shn], *n.* act of purifying, condition of being purified; **P. of the Blessed Virgin Mary**, feast of the Church kept on 2 February. [L.].

PURIFY [pyōō'ri-fi], *v.t.* to render pure, cleanse. PURIFICATORY, *adj.* having the power to p., tending to cleanse or p. [ME., Fr. from L.].

PURISM [pyōō'rizm], *n.* practice of laboured correctness in speech and writing.

PURIST [pyōō'rist], *n.* one who insists on and practises correctness in writing. PURISTIC [pyōō-ris'tik], *adj.* of, or pertaining to, purism.

PURITAN (1) [pyōō'ri-tan], *n.* member of the Church of England in the reign of Queen Elizabeth opposed to liturgical prayer and ceremonial; opponent of the Crown in the English Civil War; severe, austere person of ostentatious moral rectitude; extreme purist. PURITAN (2), *adj.* pertaining to, characteristic of, a P. or Puritans. PURITANIC(AL), *adj.* of, or pertaining to, Puritans or puritanism; insisting upon strict purity in any matter or practice. [~L.].

PURITY [pyōō'ri-ti], *n.* condition or quality of being pure; cleanliness, decency, chastity, continence; innocence; freedom from mixture, contamination or adulteration. [ME., OFr. from L.].

PURL (1) [purl], *n.* loop at the edge of lace or ribbon; (*knitting*) inverted stitch the use of which gives a ribbed appearance to the work. PURL (2), *v.i.* to put a looped edging to ribbon or lace; knit with a p. stitch. [Uncert.].

PURL (3), *v.i.* (of a brook) to flow with a gentle murmuring. PURL (4), *n.* quiet murmur of a brook. [Echoic].

PURLER [pur'ler], *n.* (*slang*) heavy fall, a cropper. [Unkn.].

PURLIEU [pur'lyōō], *n.* (*leg. hist.*) part of a forest marked off by perambulation; (*pl.*) outskirts, outlying or surrounding districts, *esp.* the poor and dingy parts of a town. [AFr. from OFr.].

PURLOIN [per-loin'], *v.t.* to steal. PURLOINER, *n.* one who filches. [ME., OFr.].

PURPLE (1) [pur'pl], *n.* secondary colour obtained by combining red and blue; purple clothing, *esp.* considered as the clothing of kings, emperors etc., hence, royal birth; **born in the p.**, born to royal, imperial or very exalted rank; **raised to the p.**, made a cardinal. PURPLE (2), *adj.* coloured with p. or (*esp. poet.*) crimson, blood-red.; **to go p. with rage**, to be furiously angry; **p. emperor**, a large butterfly. PURPLE (3), *v.t. and i.* to colour or dye with p.; turn p. [ME. from OFr. from L.].

PURPORT (1) [per-pawt', pur'pawt], *v.i.* to mean or signify, seem to mean or signify; imply, indicate. PURPORT (2) [pur'pawt], *n.* meaning, significance, import. [OFr. from L.].

PURPOSE (1) [pur'pus], *n.* aim, intention, design.

PURPOSE (2), *v.t. and i.* to intend, design. [ME., OFr. from L.].

PURPOSEFUL [pur'pus-fōōl], *adj.* resolute, firm of purpose; full of import, rich in significance.

PURPOSELY [pur'pus-li], *adv.* by design, intentionally, on purpose.

PURPOSIVE [pur'pu-siv], *adj.* done for a purpose; adapted to a specific purpose; signifying a purpose.

PURPURA [pur'pyōō-rah], *n.* (*path.*) a disease characterized by an eruption of purple patches on the skin, due to an ill condition of the blood; (*zool.*) genus of gastropods, including molluscs such as the murex from which a purple dye was formerly extracted. [L. from Gk.].

PURPUREAL [per-pyōō'ri-al], *adj.* (*poet.*) purple-coloured. [L.].

PURR (1) [pur], *n.* sound a cat makes when it is pleased or contented; any similar low humming sound, *esp.* that of the engine of a motor-car travelling smoothly and rapidly. PURR (2), *v.i.* to utter the low vibratory humming sound by which cats express content or satisfaction; (*fig.*) talk in a manner which suggests the contented purring of a cat; (of a motor-car) move rapidly and smoothly along with a low humming sound coming from the engine. [Echoic].

PURSE (1) [purs], *n.* small pouch for carrying money; cash; wealth; sum of money collected as a prize for a competition or contest; anything resembling a purse or pouch. PURSE-PROUD, *adj.* proud of one's wealth. PURSE (2), *v.t.* **to p. (up) one's lips or mouth**, to thrust out and wrinkle together one's lips. [OE. from LL.].

PURSER [pur'ser], *n.* (*naut.*) ship's officer who keeps the accounts, *esp.* on a passenger vessel; † paymaster in the navy.

PURSE-STRINGS [purs'stringz], *n.(pl.)* ends of a cord which closes the mouth of a pouch or purse; (*fig.*) control of funds; **to hold the p.**, to control expenditure.

PURSLANE [pur'slān], *n.* a salad herb. [OFr. from L.].

PURSUANCE [per-syōō'ans], *n.* act of pursuing or carrying out; performance, following out.

PURSUANT [per-syōō'ant], *adj.* (*with* to) done in consequence (of), conforming, being in accordance (with).

PURSUE [per-syōō'], *v.t. and i.* to follow in order to capture or kill or overtake, chase, hunt; accompany closely, dog; have as one's ambition; follow, practise, undertake and perform; continue, follow out, go on with. [ME., OFr. from L.].

PURSUIT [per-syōōt'], *n.* act of pursuing; a chase or hunt; act of seeking or searching; act of following up; that which one does or is engaged upon, profession, hobby etc. [AFr. from OFr.].

PURSUIVANT [pur'swi-vant], *n.* junior officer of the College of Heralds. [OFr.].

PURSY [pur'si], *adj.* short and stout; short-breathed. [ME., OFr.].

PURULENCE, PURULENCY [pyōō'rōō-lens(-i)], *n.* formation of pus; condition or quality of being purulent. [LL.].

PURULENT [pyōō'rōō-lent], *adj.* containing or discharging pus; putrid, septic. [L.].

PURVEY [per-vā'], *v.t. and i.* to provide, supply, procure; supply with, obtain supplies (food, equipment etc.) for. PURVEYANCE, *n.* act of purveying. [AFr. from L.].

PURVEYOR [per-vā'er], *n.* one who provides or purveys (*esp.* food, necessaries etc.), caterer. [ME.].

PURVIEW [pur'vyōō], *n.* clause limiting the scope or application of a statement, agreement etc.; range, scope, sphere. [OFr.].

PUS [pus], *n.* viscous matter produced in a wound, sore etc., by suppuration. [L.].

PUSEYISM [pyōō'zi-izm], *n.* name given by its opponents to the Oxford Movement in the Church of England. [Dr. *Pusey*, one of the leaders of the movement].

PUSH (1) [pōōsh], *v.t. and i.* to exert pressure against (an object) so as to cause it to move or tend to move away from the point from which the pressure is exerted; thrust, drive forward; jostle, shove; urge on (*esp. fig.*), press; advocate urgently for sale, use, promotion etc.; oppress, harass; (*pass.*) be hard pressed; thrust oneself forward, make oneself conspicuous; **to p. by**, to thrust oneself past; **to p. in**, (of a boat) to move to the shore; **to p. off**, (of a boat) to move from the shore; (*coll.*) depart; **to p. on**, to advance eagerly, *esp.* against difficulties; **to p. out**, (of a boat) to move away from shore; **to p. through**, to cause to be done by exerting force or influence. PUSH (2), *n.* action of pushing; a thrust or shove; (*milit.*) vigorous attack; vigorous attempt, determined effort to get something done; self-assertion; **to make a p.,** to make a vigorous and determined effort; **at a p.,** in an emergency, by special effort; **to get the p.,** (*slang*) to lose one's job, be dismissed. [ME. from Fr. from L.].

PUSH-BICYCLE [pŏosh'bī-si-kl], *n.* pedal-cycle.

PUSH-CART [pŏosh'kaht], *n.* cart or barrow small enough to be pushed by hand; small cart in which a baby can be pushed along.

PUSHER [pŏo'sher], *n.* someone who or something which pushes; ambitious self-assertive person; piece of cutlery used by babies to push food into a spoon; (*aeron. coll.*) aircraft having its propeller(s) behind the main lifting surface.

PUSHFUL [pŏosh'fŏol], *adj.* self-assertive, pushing.

PUSHING [pŏo'shing], *adj.* pressing forward in one's affairs, energetic, enterprising; self-assertive, officious.

PUSHTU, PUSHTOO [push'tŏo], *n.* the Afghan language. [Pers.].

PUSILLANIMITY [pyŏo-si-la-ni'mi-ti], *n.* quality of being pusillanimous, cowardice; timidity. [Eccles L.].

PUSILLANIMOUS [pyŏo-si-la'ni-mŏos], *adj.* cowardly, timid, feeble, mean-spirited. [EcclesL.].

PUSS [pŏos], *n.* (*coll.*) cat; hare; mischievous girl; **p. in the corner,** a nursery game; **p. moth,** a large woolly-bodied moth. [Uncert.].

PUSSY [pŏo'si], *n.* pet name for a cat; willow or hazel catkin. PUSSY-WILLOW, willow-tree bearing woolly catkins.

PUSTULAR [pus'tyŏo-ler], *adj.* resembling or displaying pustules. [MdL.].

PUSTULATE (1) [pus'tyŏo-lāt], *v.t. and i.* to shape into, take the shape of, pustules. PUSTULATE (2), *adj.* pustular. PUSTULATION [pus-tyŏo-lā'shn], *n.* formation of blisters or pustules. [LL.].

PUSTULE [pus'tyŏol], *n.* pimple containing pus. PUSTULOUS, *adj.* full of pustules. [L.].

PUT (1), see PUTT.

PUT (2) [pŏot], *v.t. and i.* to set, place, lay; (*fig.*) assign a value to in one's estimation; move (towards); (*fig.*) cause to be or come into (a certain mental or physical condition or set of circumstances); arrange, lay out, set down; affix, join; turn (in a particular direction); (*fig.*) apply the mind to; (of an idea, proposition etc.) lay before, explain; suggest, propose; state; **to p. about,** *v.i.* (*naut.*) to steer on a different course; *v.t.* to spread (a rumour) abroad; (*pass.*) worry, trouble; be worried; **to p. across,** (*slang*) to explain convincingly, expound (an idea etc.) successfully; **to p. it across,** (*slang*) to get the better of, impose upon; **to p. away,** (*fig.*) to store, save; kill; (*coll.*) eat or drink; **to p. back,** (*naut.*) to return; **to p. by,** to save, store; **to p. down,** (*fig.*) to repress, check; write; value, estimate; **to p. in,** to insert, interpose; **to p. in for,** to apply for; **to p. in at,** to make a short stay at; **to p. off,** (*fig.*) to delay, postpone, evade; dissuade from; discourage, abash, disconcert; **to p. on,** to simulate, affect; bring into action, (of a play) stage; add or increase; feel; **to p. out,** (*fig.*) to dislocate; extinguish; disturb, disconcert; **to p. over,** (*slang*) to be successful with (a plan, theatrical performance etc.); **to p. through,** (*coll.*) to do or cause to be done; subject or submit to; **to p. to,** to cause to follow (a career, occupation etc.); **to p. up,** to propose; offer, *esp.* for sale; provide food and lodging for; **a p.-up job,** (*slang*) something dishonestly pre-arranged; **to p. up at,** to lodge at; **to p. up to,** to tell to (do), incite; **to p. up with,** to tolerate; **to p. the weight,** (*athletics*) to raise a weight to the shoulder on the hand and fling it by suddenly straightening the arm forward; **to stay p.,** (*coll.*) to remain where one is. PUT (3), *n.* act of putting the weight. [OE.].

PUTATIVE [pyŏo'ta-tiv], *adj.* reputed, supposed. [Fr. from LL.].

PUTREFACTION [pyŏo-tri-fak'shn], *n.* process of becoming putrid; putrid matter.

PUTREFACTIVE [pyŏo-tri-fak'tiv], *adj.* of, pertaining to, or causing putrefaction. [Fr.].

PUTREFY [pyŏo'tri-fī], *v.t. and i.* to make putrid; become putrid. [L.].

PUTRESCENCE [pyŏo-tre'sens], *n.* condition of being putrescent; putrescent matter.

PUTRESCENT [pyŏo-tre'sent], *adj.* in the process of becoming putrid. [L.].

PUTRID [pyŏo'trid], *adj.* decayed and rotten (of organic bodies, *esp.* animal flesh); (*coll.*) unpleasant, very bad. [L.].

PUTRIDITY [pyŏo-tri'di-ti], *n.* state of being putrid; something putrid. [MedL.].

PUTSCH [pŏoch], *n.* attempt at revolution or coup d'état. [Germ.].

PUT(T) (1) [put], *v.t. and i.* (*golf*) to strike the ball with the putter; use a putter. PUT(T) (2), *n.* act of putting, stroke intended to hole the ball at golf. PUTTER, *n.* short club with a flat face used in golf for holing the ball when playing on a green. PUTTING-GREEN, *n.* (*golf*) closely mown green surrounding the hole, where putting is done; small green with several holes for practising short strokes. [*Var.* of PUT].

PUTTEE [pu'ti, pu-tē'], *n.* cloth legging which is wound round the leg in spiral fashion. [Hind.].

PUTTY (1) [pu'ti], *n.* fine lime and cement mixed with water, used by builders; a mixture of linseed oil and clay used by glaziers; polishing powder used by jewellers. PUTTY (2), *v.t.* to fix, fill, by means of p. [Fr.].

PUZZLE (1) [pu-zl], *v.t. and i.* to offer conditions, circumstances which are so complex that they confuse and bewilder, baffle, keep the solution or significance hidden from; **to p. out,** to solve after hard thinking. PUZZLE (2), *n.* something which puzzles; state of being puzzled, perplexity; problem, conundrum; contrivance which permits of an ingenious solution. [Unkn.].

PYAEMIA [pī-ē'mi-ah], *n.* blood-poisoning due to the absorption into the system of putrid matter and characterized by abscesses. PYAEMIC, *adj.* of, or like, p. [Gk.].

PYELITIS [pī-e-lī'tis], *n.* (*path.*) inflammation of the mucous membranes of the cavities of the kidneys. [Gk.].

PYGMY (1), **PIGMY** [pig'mi], *n.* person of stunted growth, dwarf. PYGMY (2), PIGMY, *adj.* very small, dwarfish. PYGMEAN, PIGMEAN [pig-mē'an], *adj.* relating to a p. or dwarf; very small. [Gk.].

PYJAMAS [pi-jah'mahz], *n.(pl.)* sleeping suit of jacket and trousers; loose trousers as worn by Moslems. PYJAMA, *adj.* of, pertaining to, p. [Pers.].

PYLON [pī'lon], *n.* gateway; tower erected as a landmark for aircraft; tower structure for overhead suspension of electric cables. [Gk.].

PYLORUS [pī-law'rus], *n.* (*anat.*) lower opening of the stomach, leading into the intestines. PYLORIC [pī-lo'rik], *adj.* (*anat.*) of, or relating to, the p. [Gk.].

PYORRHOEA [pī-o-rē'ah], *n.* (*path.*) a disease of the gums. [Gk.].

PYRAMID [pi'ra-mid], *n.* (*arch.*) Egyptian building with a square foundation, four sides each in the form of a triangle and rising to terminate in a point; anything in the shape of this; (*pl.*) form of billiards played with fifteen red balls. PYRAMIDAL [pi-ra'mi-dal], *adj.* relating to the pyramids. [Gk.].

PYRE [pīer], *n.* funeral pile of wood for burning a corpse. [Gk.].

PYREXIA [pī-rek'si-ah], *n.* (*med.*) febrile state, attack of fever; body temperature above normal. [Gk.].

PYRITES [pī-rī'tēz], *n.* a combination of sulphur with iron, copper, cobalt or nickel. [Gk.].

PYRO-, *pref.* produced or treated by fire or heat. [Gk.].

PYROMETER [pī-ro'mi-ter], *n.* instrument for measuring the expansion of bodies by heat; thermometer for measuring high degrees of temperature. [PYRO and METER].

PYROTECHNIC [pī-rō-tek'nik], *adj.* relating to fireworks or the art of making them.

PYROTECHNICS [pī-rō-tek'niks], *n.* art of making fireworks; a display of fireworks. [Gk.].

PYRRHIC [pi'rik], *adj.* typical of King *Pyrrhus,* who won a victory but only at an enormous cost of life. [Gk.].

PYTHAGOREAN (1) [pī-tha-go-rē'an], *adj.* relating to Pythagoras and his philosophic principles of a metaphysical nature. PYTHAGOREAN (2), *n.* follower of Pythagoras and his principles. [Gk.].

PYTHIAN (1) [pī'thi-an], *adj.* relating to Apollo's shrine at Delphi. PYTHIAN (2), *n.* priestess of Apollo who was believed to possess oracular powers. [Gk.].

PYTHON [pī'thon], *n.* (*zool.*) genus of large non-venomous serpents.

PYTHONESS [pī'tho-nes], *n.* priestess who gave oracular answers at Delphi; witch, sorceress. [L.].

PYX (1), **PIX** [piks], *n.* vessel used in the R.C. Church for holding the consecrated Host; case for sample coins at the Royal Mint. PYX (2), *v.t.* to test coins by a standard of fineness and weight. [Gk.].

The accent ' after a syllable = stress (u-pon').   The mark ‾ over a vowel = length (ā in made; ō in bone).

Q

Q [kyōō], seventeenth letter of the English alphabet.
QUA [kwā], adv. as being, in the capacity of. [L.].
QUACK (1) [kwak], n. ignorant person pretending to specialized knowledge, esp. in surgery and medical science, charlatan. QUACK (2), adj. made or prescribed by a q. doctor, bogus. [QUACKSALVER].
QUACK (3), n. cry or noise natural to a duck. QUACK (4), v.i. to make this noise; (fig.) chatter. [Imitative].
QUACKSALVER [kwak'sal-ver], n. (archaic) ignorant person claiming skill in medicines, travelling pedlar in ointments, medicines etc. of doubtful efficacy. [Du.].
QUAD (1) [kwod], n. (coll.) quadrangle.
QUAD (2), n. (coll.) quadrat.
QUAD (3). n. (coll.) quadruplet.
QUAD (4), see QUOD.
QUADRAGENARIAN (1) [kwod-ra-je-nāer'i-an], adj. aged forty to forty-nine. QUADRAGENARIAN (2), n. person in the forties. [L.].
QUADRAGESIMA [kwod-ra-je'si-mah], n. † Lent; **Q. Sunday**, first Sunday in Lent. QUADRAGESIMAL, adj. relating to, belonging to, used in, Lent. [L.].
QUADRANGLE [kwod'rang-gl], n. (geom.) plane figure with four angles and four sides; (arch.) rectangular court surrounded by buildings. QUADRANGULAR [kwod-rang'gyōō-ler], adj. (geom.) having four angles and four sides. [LL.].
QUADRANT [kwod'rant], n. (astron., naut.) instrument used in measuring angles and heights; (geom.) quarter of a circle or sphere. [L.].
QUADRAT [kwod'rat], n. (typ.) one of the pieces of metal used to space out short lines, usually called a quad; instrument employed for measuring altitudes. [Next].
QUADRATE (1) [kwo-drāt'], v.t. and i. to square up, make square; make correspond, conform. QUADRATE (2) [kwod'rāt], n. and adj. a square; square, particularly in bone formation. [L.].
QUADRATIC (1) [kwo-dra'tik], adj. of, resembling, relating to, a square; **q. equation**, (alg.) equation in which the unknown quantity is of the power of a square. QUADRATIC (2), n. a q. equation; (pl.) branch of algebra dealing with q. equations. [L.].
QUADRATURE [kwod'ra-tyōōr], n. (astron.) position of a heavenly body when measured as 90 deg. distant from another; (math.) expression of an area, esp. of a circle, in terms of an equivalent square. [L.].
QUADRENNIAL [kwo-dre'ni-al], adj. lasting, comprising, four years; occurring once in four years. [L.].
QUADRI-, pref. four. [L.].
QUADRILATERAL (1) [kwo-dri-la'te-ral], adj. having four sides. QUADRILATERAL (2), n. plane figure with four sides and angles. [QUADRI and LATERAL].
QUADRILLE [kwo-dril'], n. an old card-game played by four persons; a square dance for four or more couples; music for such a dance. [It.].
QUADRILLION [kwo-dril'yun], n. number produced by raising a million to the fourth power; (U.S.) a thousand multiplied by itself four times.
QUADRIPARTITE [kwo-dri-pah'tit], adj. (bot., zool.) divided into four parts; negotiated among four parties. [QUADRI and PARTITE].
QUADRISYLLABLE [kwo-dri-si'la-bl], n. word consisting of four syllables. QUADRISYLLABIC [kwo-dri-si-la'bik], adj. consisting of four syllables. [QUADRI and SYLLABLE].
QUADROON [kwo-droon'], n. offspring of a mulatto and a white. [Span.].
QUADRUPED [kwod'rōō-ped], n. (zool.) mammal with four feet. QUADRUPEDAL [kwod-rōō'pe-dal], adj. relating to a q. [L.].
QUADRUPLE (1) [kwod'rōō-pl, kwo-drōō'pl], adj. fourfold. QUADRUPLE (2) [kwo-drōō'pl'], v.t. to multiply by four. [L.].
QUADRUPLET [kwod'rōō-plet, kwo-drōō'plet], n. one of four children born at one birth; one of a set of four things, esp. mechanical parts working together. [QUADRU(PLE) and (TRI)PLET].
QUADRUPLICATE (1) [kwo-drōō'pli-kat], adj.

multiplied by four, reproduced in four copies. QUADRUPLICATE (2) [kwo-drōō'pli-kāt], v.t. to make fourfold, multiply by four. [L.].
QUAFF [kwof], v.t. and i. to drink, swallow in large draughts. [Unkn.].
QUAG [kwag], n. quagmire, bog. QUAGGY, adj. of the nature of, resembling, a q.; boggy. [Imitative].
QUAGGA [kwa'gah], n. South African quadruped allied to the wild ass and zebra. [Native].
QUAGMIRE [kwag'mïer], n. soft, wet ground which shakes or yields under the foot. [QUAG and MIRE].
QUAIL (1) [kwāl], n. a small game bird allied to the partridge. [OFr. from MedL.].
QUAIL (2), v.t. and i. to lose heart, be afraid, cower. [OE.].
QUAINT [kwānt], adj. unusual but not displeasing in form, fanciful; old-fashioned; eccentric, odd in character. [ME.].
QUAKE (1) [kwāk], v.i. to rock perceptibly but not violently from side to side, shiver, quiver, tremble, esp. with fear. QUAKE (2), n. a trembling, tremor; earthquake. [OE., ME.].
QUAKER [kwā'ker], n. person who quakes; member of the Society of Friends.
QUALIFICATION [kwo-li-fi-kā'shn], n. act of qualifying, modification; suitable acquirement and ability; fact of being qualified; legal or requisite power, restriction. [L.].
QUALIFY [kwo'li-fï], v.t. to give the requisite quality or accomplishments to, train for any employment or profession; limit or restrict by reservations, make conditional; moderate, ease, modify, regulate; v.i. to carry out a course of study and obtain the requisite professional qualifications; become competent. QUALIFICATORY [kwo'li-fi-kā-te-ri], adj. relating to qualification, modifying, restricting. QUALIFIED, adj. possessing the requisite qualifications, competent; modified. [L.].
QUALITATIVE [kwo'li-tā-tiv], adj. of, relating to, quality.
QUALITY [kwo'li-ti], n. the fundamental characteristic or sum of characteristics by which anything can be identified when compared with other things of a similar nature; attribute, characteristic; distinguishing degree of a particular power or property inherent in anything; disposition, nature; accomplishment; rank in the social scale; high rank; people of high rank; also used, esp. in trade, attrib., in sense of high quality. [ME. from L.].
QUALM [kwahm], n. faintness, sensation of nausea; (fig.) misgiving, scruple of conscience. [~OE.].
QUANDARY [kwon'da-ri], n. baffling situation capable of more than one solution, dilemma. [Uncert.].
QUANTITATIVE [kwon'ti-tā-tiv], adj. of, concerned with, relating to, quantity; estimable according to quantity. [LL.].
QUANTITIVE [kwon'ti-tiv], adj. quantitative.
QUANTITY [kwon'ti-ti], n. the property of anything which is measurable in terms of weight, size, bulk, extent; any specified amount or number; (math.) means of measurement; (mus.) relative duration of a tone; (pros.) length of a syllable; **bill of quantities**, working estimate of building job; **q. surveyor**, an expert in estimating costs of erecting a building. [ME. from LL.].
QUANTUM (pl. **quanta**) [kwon'tum], n. quantity, amount, sufficiency; (phys.) one of the units of uniform value (quanta) by which radiant energy is measured; **q. sufficit**, a sufficient amount; **q. theory**, (phys.) theory that radiant energy is emitted from bodies through space in the form of discrete quanta. [L.].
QUARANTINE (1) [kwo'ran-tēn], n. period during which a ship, passengers, crew and goods suspected of, or known to be, carrying infectious disease are kept in isolation and under medical observation; state of medical isolation. QUARANTINE (2), v.t. to put into q. [OFr.].
QUARREL (1) [kwo'rel], n. angry dispute or heated argument; reason for quarrelling; breach of friendship or love. QUARREL (2) (pres.pt. QUARRELLING, pret. and p.pt. QUARRELLED), v.i. to be a participant in

---

ōō is pronounced as in food; ŏŏ as in hood; th as in think; TH as in that; zh as in azure.   ~ = related to.

a q., argue heatedly, squabble; find fault; fall out, disagree. [ME. from L.].

QUARRELSOME [kwo'rel-sum], *adj.* inclined by temperament to quarrel; easily irritated, irascible.

QUARRY (1) [kwo'ri], *n.* animal hunted by man, hawk or hound; object of one's pursuit. [ME. from OFr.].

QUARRY (2), *n.* pit from which stone is cut, excavation worked above ground. QUARRY (3), *v.t.* to dig out of a q., excavate; *v.i.* to form a q. by digging; (*fig.*) seek out information at the source. QUARRYING, *n.* act or process of digging stones from a q. QUARRYMAN, *n.* worker at a q. [ME. from LL.].

QUART (1) [kwawt], *n.* a measure of liquid amounting to a quarter of a gallon; two pints; vessel of this content. [OFr.].

QUART (2) [kaht], *n.* four successive cards of the same suit in piquet; a position in fencing. [Fr.].

QUARTAN (1) [kwaw'tan], *adj.* occurring on every fourth day. QUARTAN (2), *n.* fever recurring every fourth day. [L.].

QUARTER (1) [kwaw'ter], *n.* a fourth part; fourth part of a cwt., 28 lb.; unit of wheat measurement, 8 bushels, 480 lb.; first or third of the moon's phases; any one of the four cardinal points of the compass; one of the four regions of the globe; a direction; a district of a town with particular characteristics; mercy to an enemy who has surrendered; legal division of the year when rent, rates and taxes fall due; one of the four divisions of an animal's carcase; (*pl.*) lodgings for troops, temporary barracks; post allotted to troops; (*her.*) one of the four divisions of a shield which has been divided crosswise; (*naut.*) direction about halfway between the beam and astern, on either side of a vessel; corresponding part of a ship's side; (*pl.*) posts in battle formation; section of an orange. QUARTER-PLATE, photographic plate, film or print measuring 4¼ in. by 3¼ in. QUARTER (2), *v.t. and i.* to divide or cut into quarters; provide troops with lodgings; be stationed in temporary lodgings. [L.].

QUARTER-BINDING [kwaw'ter-bïn-ding], *n.* style of bookbinding in which a special material (*e.g.* leather) covers the spine only.

QUARTER-DAY [kwaw'ter-dā], *n.* day when quarterly payments are made in England, 25 March, 24 June, 29 September and 25 December.

QUARTERDECK [kwaw'ter-dek], *n.* (*naut.*) formerly that part of the upper deck abaft the mainmast; after part of the promenade deck restricted to the use of officers.

QUARTERING [kwaw'te-ring], *n.* act of dividing into quarters; provision of billets for troops; (*her.*) division of a shield to include allied coats of arms.

QUARTERLY (1) [kwaw'ter-li], *adj.* recurring each quarter of the year; consisting of a fourth part. QUARTERLY (2), *n.* periodical published once every three months. QUARTERLY (3), *adv.* once every quarter of the year; (*her.*) arranged in diagonally opposite quarters.

QUARTERMASTER [kwaw'ter-mah-ster], *n.* (*milit.*) commissioned officer whose primary duty is to attend to the supply of provisions and equipment; (*naut.*) petty officer in charge of signals and ships' instruments; **q. general,** officer in charge of the stores and equipment of an army; **q. sergeant,** warrant officer assisting a q.

QUARTERN [kwaw'tern], *n.* a measure of liquid capacity, the fourth part of a pint or other measure, gill; 4-lb. loaf of bread. [ME. from OFr.].

QUARTER-SESSIONS [kwaw'ter-se-shnz], *n.* (*leg.*) court held every three months in each county or borough for the trial of criminal cases and general administrative purposes, and presided over by justices of the peace or a recorder.

QUARTERSTAFF [kwaw'ter-stahf], *n.* (*sport*) stout pole used for purposes of both attack and defence.

QUARTET(TE) [kwaw-tet'], *n.* a group of four; stanza in four lines; (*mus.*) composition for four performers; the four performers. [It.].

QUARTO [kwaw'tō], *n.* book with four leaves to each sheet; (*comm.*) size of paper about 9 in. by 12 in. produced when a sheet is folded into four leaves. [L.].

QUARTZ [kwawts], *n.* (*min.*) crystalline mineral silica, rock-crystal. [Germ.].

QUASH [kwosh], *v.t.* to crush, subdue; annul, make void. [ME. from L.].

QUASI [kwā'sī], *adv.* apparently, as if, as it were, in a sort. [L.].

QUASSIA [kwo'shah], *n.* the bitter ash, an American tropical tree, the wood of which yields a bitter principle used as a tonic and a garden insecticide. [*Quassi*, negro who discovered it].

QUATERCENTENARY [kwo-ter-sen-tĕ'na-ri], *n.* four-hundredth anniversary. [L.].

QUATERNARY (1) [kwo-tur'na-ri], *adj.* consisting of fours, by fours; (*geol.*) rocks above the Pliocene. QUATERNARY (2), *n.* number four; group of four. [L.].

QUATERNION [kwo-tur'ni-on], *n.* a set of four; (*pl.*) a method in mathematics.

QUATRAIN [kwo'trān], *n.* stanza of four lines, sometimes rhyming alternately. [Fr.].

QUATREFOIL [ka'tri-foil], *n.* (*arch.*) ornamental figure, being an opening in tracery divided by cusps into four leaves or petals; (*her.*) device in the same design on a shield. [OFr.].

QUATTROCENTO [kwa-trō-chen'tō], *n.* the fifteenth century in Italian art. QUATTROCENTISM, *n.* style of the q. [It.].

QUAVER (1) [kwā'ver], *v.i.* to talk, sing or play a musical instrument so that the sound or tone produced is affected by vibration or tremolo. QUAVER (2), *n.* sound or note, *esp.* one made by the voice, which is governed by a tremolo; (*mus.*) note held half the length of a crotchet. QUAVERY, *adj.* tremulous, shaky, as a quavery voice. [ME.].

QUAY [kē], *n.* pier, mole or wharf for loading and unloading vessels, landing place. QUAYAGE [kē'ij], *n.* q. dues. [ME. from OFr.].

QUEAN [kwēn], *n.* (*archaic*) worthless woman; saucy girl, hussy; (*Scots*) young woman. [OE., ME.].

QUEASY [kwē'zi], *adj.* affected with nausea, inclined to vomit; squeamish. QUEASILY, *adv.* in a q. manner. QUEASINESS, *n.* state of being q., nausea. [Uncert.].

QUEEN (1) [kwēn], *n.* woman who is sovereign in her own right, consort of a king; large, fertile female among certain kinds of insects; most revered or admired woman of a group or class; court-card or honour in value ranking between king and knave; piece in chess; **q. dowager,** widow of a king; **q. mother,** mother of a reigning monarch; **q. of the May,** girl chosen to preside over festivities held on May Day. **Queen's Bench, Counsel, Evidence,** see KING. QUEEN (2), *v.t. and i.* to make a q. of; rule over as a q.; **to q. it,** to play the q.; (*chess*) convert into a q. a pawn which has been moved up to the opponent's back-line. [OE.].

QUEENLY (1) [kwēn'li], *adj.* of, like or befitting a queen. QUEENLY (2), *adv.* in the manner of a queen; worthy of a queen, with dignity. [OE.].

QUEER (1) [kwēer], *adj.* out of the ordinary, odd, strange; unwell, indisposed; shady, questionable; a little mad; **q. street,** state of serious financial difficulty, state of being liable to prosecution. QUEER (2), *v.t.* (*slang*) **to q. someone's pitch,** to upset or disarrange someone's plans etc.

QUELL [kwel], *v.t.* to crush, subdue by force; allay. [OE., ME.].

QUENCH [kwensh], *v.t.* to put out, extinguish, repress; allay; destroy. [OE., ME.].

QUENELLE [ke-nel'], *n.* forcemeat ball. [Fr.].

QUERIST [kwēer'ist], *n.* inquirer, questioner.

QUERN [kwern], *n.* hand-mill for grinding corn. [OE.].

QUERULOUS [kwe'rŏŏ-lŏŏs], *adj.* complaining, peevish.

QUERY (1) [kwēer'i], *n.* question, inquiry, doubt put in the form of a question; question-mark. QUERY (2), *v.t.* to question or doubt something, mark (a written statement) as doubtful, require confirmation; put a question-mark after. [L.].

QUEST (1) [kwest], *n.* search, journey in search of; inquest. QUEST (2), *v.i.* to search, follow in search and pursuit. [OFr. from L.].

QUESTION (1) [kwes'tyun], *n.* request for information, remark demanding a reply, expression of doubt; problem, doubt, subject of debate; torture to extract information; matter, situation etc. with a general sense of doubt. QUESTION (2), *v.t. and i.* to interrogate, inquire of; doubt, dispute; ask questions. QUESTIONLESS, *adj.* unquestionable. [L.].

QUESTIONABLE [kwes'tyun-a-bl], *adj.* dubious, open to question; underhand, of doubtful honesty, shady.

QUESTION-MARK [kwes'tyun-mahk], *n.* punctuation mark (?) indicating that the foregoing words form a question.

QUESTIONNAIRE [kwes-tyun-āer'], *n.* series

The accent ′ after a syllable = stress (u-pon′).   The mark ‾ over a vowel = length (ā in made; ō in bone).

(usually written) of questions on a specific subject. [Fr.].

QUEUE (1) [kyōō], *n.* twisted pigtail tied with ribbon worn hanging down from the back of the head; long narrow line of people or vehicles waiting for admission to something or to perform some action. QUEUE (2), *v.i.* to line up, wait in a q. [Fr.].

QUIBBLE (1) [kwi'bl], *n.* trivial objection, distinction or equivocation, evasive, niggling objection; play on words. QUIBBLE (2), *v.i.* to use quibbles. [Uncert.].

QUICK (1) [kwik], *adj.* living; pregnant; swift, sudden; (*fig.*) swift of mind, lively of intellect, alert; happening in a short space of time, brief; (*coll.*) jumping to conclusions. QUICK (2), *n.* sensitive flesh, *esp.* that below the nails; centre of feeling and emotion; **the q.**, (*pl.*) living creatures in general; **to cut to the q.**, to hurt the feelings deeply. QUICK (3), *adv.* quickly, briefly. QUICKLY, *adv.* rapidly, with speed, in a short time. [OE.].

QUICKEN [kwi'ken], *v.t. and i.* to make live, give life to; stir into action; hasten; become alive or stimulated; (of a pregnant woman) have the foetus showing signs of life; move more rapidly. QUICK-ENER, *n.* that which quickens, invigorates, revives. QUICKENING, *adj.* reviving, invigorating. [ME.].

QUICKFIRER [kwik-fier'er], *n.* automatic, rapid-firing gun. QUICK-FIRING, *adj.* firing bullets in rapid succession.

QUICKLIME [kwik'līm], *n.* unslaked lime.

QUICK MARCH [kwik-mahch'], *n.* a march in quick time; (*imper.*) command to march in quick time.

QUICKSAND [kwik'sand], *n.* wet, loose, unstable sand, tending to engulf those walking on it; (also *fig.*).

QUICKSET [kwik'set], *adj.* formed of living, growing plants, *esp.* of hawthorn.

QUICKSILVER [kwik'sil-ver], *n.* mercury; (*fig.*) mercurial, unstable temperament.

QUICKSTEP [kwik'step], *n.* pace of the military quick march; dance in quick-time.

QUICK-TIME [kwik-tīm], *n.* 160 steps per minute, the speed of the military quick march; this speed of step used as a base for dance music.

QUID [kwid], *n.* piece of chewing tobacco. [*Var.* of CUD].

QUIDDITY [kwi'di-ti], *n.* fundamental essence of a thing; quibble, unnecessary subtlety. [MedL.].

QUIDNUNC [kwid'nungk], *n.* a gossip, idler. [L.].

QUIESCE [kwi-es'], *v.i.* to become still. [L.].

QUIESCENCE, QUIESCENCY [kwi-e'sens(-i)], *n.* state of being quiescent. [LL.].

QUIESCENT [kwi-e'sent], *adj.* quiet, still, passive, silent. QUIESCENTLY, *adv.* in q. fashion. [L.].

QUIET (1) [kwi'et], *n.* absence of noise, silence, rest, freedom from trouble, disturbance, activity; serenity, repose. QUIET (2), *adj.* free from noise, movement or disturbance; still, calm; unnoticed, undiscussed; peaceful, monotonous; unostentatious; silent. QUIET (3), *v.t. and i.* to cause to be q., pacify; become q., calm, die away, become abated. [L.].

QUIETEN [kwī'e-ten], *v.t. and i.* to make quiet, to quiet; become quiet.

QUIETISM [kwī'e-tizm], *n.* doctrine of passive mysticism and subordination of will; tranquillity of mind and spirit.

QUIETIST [kwī'e-tist], *n.* advocate, practiser, of quietism. QUIETISTIC [kwī-e-tis'tik], *adj.* pertaining to quietism.

QUIETUDE [kwī'e-tyōōd], *n.* quietness, tranquillity. [LL.].

QUIETUS [kwī-ē'tus], *n.* quittance, final discharge, *esp.* release from life. [L.].

QUIFF [kwif], *n.* curl or forelock over the forehead. [COIF].

QUILL (1) [kwil], *n.* large feather, hollow stem of such a feather, pen made from a feather; spine of a por-cupine; reed of a wooden wind-instrument, bobbin. QUILL (2), *v.t.* to pleat; wind (thread) round a bobbin. [Unkn.].

QUILT (1) [kwilt], *n.* coverlet made by stuffing some thick, woolly stuff between two layers of material, eiderdown. QUILT (2), *v.t.* to make into a q.; pad like a q. QUILTING, *n.* quilted stuff; act of making quilts.

QUINA [kē'nah, kwi'nah], *n.* quinine; cinchona bark yielding quinine. [Span.].

QUINARY [kwi'na-ri], *adj.* arranged in fives. [L.].

QUINCE [kwins], *n.* fruit of *Pyrus cydonia*, notable for its sharpness of flavour. [OFr. from Gk.].

QUINCENTENARY [kwin-sen-tē'na-ri], *adj. and n.* (relating to) a five-hundredth anniversary. [L.].

QUINCUNX [kwin'kungks], *n.* group of five

objects, four forming the corners of a square, the fifth as a centre, *esp.* shrubs, trees, so arranged. QUINCUNCIAL [kwin-kun'shal], *adj.* shaped like a q. [L.].

QUININE [kwi-nēn'], *n.* an alkaloid obtained from the bark of the cinchona; preparation of this used medicinally. [Span. from Peruvian].

QUINQUAGENARY [kwin-kwa-jē'na-ri], *adj. and n.* (relating to) a fiftieth anniversary; occurring every fifty years.

QUINQUAGESIMA [kwin-kwa-je'si-mah], *n.* the Sunday before Lent. [MedL.].

QUINQUE, *pref.* five. [L.].

QUINQUENNIAL [kwin-kwe'ni-al], *adj.* occurring every five years; lasting for five years. [L.].

QUINS [kwinz], *n.(pl.)* (*coll.*) set of quintuplets.

QUINSY [kwin'zi], *n.* inflammation and suppuration of the tonsils. [ME., MedL. from Gk.].

QUINTAIN [kwin'tān], *n.* (*hist.*) kind of tilting post. [MedL.].

QUINTAL, KENTLE [kwin'tl], *n.* measure of weight used in several parts of Europe, the French q. being equal to 100 kg. [OFr. from Arab.].

QUINTAN [kwin'tan], *adj.* occurring every five days, *esp.* of fevers. [L.].

QUINTESSENCE [kwin-te'sens], *n.* (*philos.*) the fifth, insubstantial, permeating element; hence, the fundamental essence of a thing, highest, most con-centrated, embodiment of a quality. QUINTESSEN-TIAL [kwin-ti-sen'shal], *adj.* of the nature of, relating to, q. [MedL.].

QUINTET [kwin-tet'], *n.* musical composition for five performers; five performers themselves. [Fr.].

QUINTILLION [kwin-til'yon], *n.* fifth power of a million. [L.].

QUINTUPLE [kwin'tyōō-pl, kwin-tyōō'pl], *adj.* fivefold. [Fr.].

QUINTUPLET [kwin'tyōō-plet, kwin-tyōō'plet], *n.* one of five children born at a single birth. [*Prec.*].

QUIP [kwip], *n.* jesting retort, witty remark, *esp.* if directed against anyone. [Uncert.].

QUIRE [kwier], *n.* twentieth of a ream of paper, twenty-four sheets. [OFr.].

QUIRINAL [kwi'ri-nal], *n.* former royal court of Italy; the Italian government. [L.].

QUIRK [kwurk], *n.* quibbling subterfuge; quip; oddity, twist, sudden turn; flourish. [Uncert.].

QUIRT [kwurt], *n.* a riding-whip. [Span.].

QUIT (1) (*pres.pt.* **quitting**, *pres. and p.pt.* **quitted**) [kwit], *v.t. and i.* to leave, depart from; throw in one's hand, give up a task. QUIT (2), *adj.* free (of), discharged (from). QUIT-CLAIM, deed of release. QUIT-RENT, rent in lieu of all other service. QUITTER, *n.* one who quits, *esp.* one who shows cowardice or lack of determination in difficulties. [ME. from OFr.].

QUITCH [kwich], *n.* couch-grass. [OE.].

QUITE [kwit], *adv.* utterly, wholly; fairly, largely, reasonably; (*as int.*) certainly. [QUIT].

QUITS [kwits], *n.* condition of being even with a person; **double or q.**, undertaking to repeat a wager so that the previous loser will lose double or be even.

QUITTANCE [kwi'tans], *n.* discharge from an obliga-tion, final recompense. [OFr.].

QUIVER (1) [kwi'ver], *n.* case for carrying arrows; **to have one's q. full**, to have a very large family. [AFr.].

QUIVER (2), *v.i.* to quake and tremble. QUIVER (3), *n.* act of quivering. [Imitative].

QUIXOTIC [kwik-zo'tik], *adj.* showing absurd chivalrousness. [Don *Quixote*, hero of a novel by Cervantes].

QUIZ (1) [kwiz], *v.t.* to banter, mock at jestingly. QUIZ (2), *n.* puzzle; inquiry, investigation by means of questions; contest in answering questions, *esp.* as a public entertainment; one who quizzes. QUIZZICAL, *adj.* fond of quizzing, faintly mocking, bantering. [Uncert.].

QUOAD [kwō'ad], *prep.* with respect to. [L.].

QUOD, QUAD [kwod], *n.* (*slang*) prison. [Uncert.].

QUOIN [koin], *n.* external angle of a wall; stone or brick forming this angle, corner-stone; (*print.*) wedge used for locking type; wedge used for various other purposes. [COIGN].

QUOIT [koit], *n.* ring to be pitched over a pin set in the ground; (*pl.*) game in which this is the object. [Uncert.].

QUONDAM [kwon'dam], *adj.* former. [L.].

QUORUM [kwaw'rum], *n.* the number of members sufficient to transact the business of a body. [L.].

QUOTA [kwō'tah], *n.* a proportionate share, *esp.*

ōō is pronounced as in food; ōō as in hood; th as in *think*, TH as in *that*; zh as in azure.   ~ = related to.

one allotted in advance; **the q.**, (*cinema*) the legally determined minimum proportion in which cinema exhibitors must use British films. [MedL.].

QUOTATION [kwŏ-tā′shn], *n.* act of quoting; that which is quoted, a previously written passage reproduced in a later work; price demanded for a proposed service; punctuation mark (‘) or (’) indicating matter quoted. [MedL.].

QUOTE (1) [kwŏt], *v.t. and i.* to repeat a passage which has already been written or uttered, cite; make a quotation, offer; perform the action of quoting; (*imper.*) (in dictation) begin a quotation.

QUOTE (2), *n.* (*print.*) quotation mark; (*vulg.*) **a** quotation. [MedL.].

QUOTH [kwŏth], *v.i.* (*poet. or sham archaic*) said. [OE.].

QUOTHA † [kwŏ′thah], *int.* said he. [QUOTH and HE].

QUOTIDIAN [kwŏ-ti′di-an], *adj.* occurring daily. [L.].

QUOTIENT [kwŏ′shent], *n.* the number of times **a** greater quantity contains a less. [L.].

QUOTIETY [kwŏ-ti′e-ti], *n.* the relation of an object to a number. [L.].

R

R [ah(r)], eighteenth letter of the alphabet; **the three R's**, reading, (w)riting and (a)rithmetic, as the basis of education.

RABBET (1) [ra′bit], *n.* groove cut lengthwise in the edge of a piece of wood to receive the edge of a board etc. RABBET (2), *v.t.* to join by a r. [OFr.].

RABBI [ra′bī], *n.* teacher of the Judaic law; Jewish minister of religion. RABBIN, *n.* a r. RABBINATE, *n.* office of a r. [Heb.].

RABBINIC(AL) [ra-bi′nik(-al)], *adj.* relating to the rabbis or to Jewish law and ritual; pertaining to, written in, the later Hebrew language. [Fr.].

RABBINISM [ra′bi-nizm], *n.* teaching of the rabbis; rabbinic idiom. RABBINIST, *n.* one who adheres to or studies the Talmud and the traditions of the rabbis.

RABBIT (1) [ra′bit], *n.* a burrowing rodent of the hare family; (*coll.*) cheap fur; (*fig.*) feeble person; bad performer at some game. RABBIT-PUNCH, a punch at the back of the neck. RABBIT-WARREN, mass of r. burrows; (*fig.*) place with a complicated system of rooms and passages, overcrowded warrenlike slum. RABBIT (2), *v.i.* to hunt rabbits. RABBITER, *n.* professional catcher of rabbits. [ME.].

RABBITRY [ra′bit-ri], *n.* enclosure for rabbits.

RABBLE [ra′bl], *n.* disorderly, tumultuous mob, *esp.* when consisting of the poorest and dirtiest sections of the population. [ME.].

RABELAISIAN [ra-be-lā′zi-an], *adj.* resembling the style and humour of Rabelais; (*coll.*) broadly obscene.

RABID [ra′bid], *adj.* afflicted with rabies, mad; (*fig.*) dangerously furious in some conviction, fanatically vehement. [L.].

RABIES [rā′bēz], *n.* hydrophobia, canine madness. [L.].

RACCOON, see RACOON.

RACE (1) [rās], *n.* division of mankind whose members share certain obvious physical characteristics distinguishing them from the other divisions; stock or breed of people; group of persons having a common peculiarity; characteristic flavour. [Fr.].

RACE (2), *n.* contest, competition in progression, in covering distance in the shortest possible time; (*pl.*) horse-races; swiftly moving stream of water; groove of a shuttle. RACE-CARD, card on which is printed the day's programme at a r.-meeting. RACE-MEETING, series of horse-races held at a special course and time. RACE (3), *v.t. and i.* to oppose in a r., enter (a horse etc.) for a r.; compete in a r.; move, progress rapidly in order to outdistance another; overtake; (*mech.*) move at too great speed owing to insufficient resistance; (*coll.*) attend race-meetings, gamble on horse races. [OScand.].

RACECOURSE [rās′kaws], *n.* track on which a horse-race is run.

RACE-GINGER [rās′jin-jer], *n.* ginger in the root, or not pulverized. [OFr.].

RACEME [ra-sēm′], *n.* (*bot.*) spike of regular stalked flowers springing from a common central stalk. RACEMOSE [ra′se-mōs], *adj.* growing in, resembling, a r. [L.].

RACER [rā′ser], *n.* one who, animal which, races; vehicle designed for racing; rail along which the platform of a heavy gun recoils.

RACHITIS [ra-kī′tis], *n.* rickets. RACHITIC [ra-ki′tik], *adj.* relating to, suffering from, r. [MedL.].

RACIAL [rā′shal], *adj.* pertaining to race.

RACIALISM [rā′sha-lizm], *n.* race sentiments, prejudices and loyalties; view that race is of primary importance. RACIALIST, *n.* exponent of r.

RACING [rā′sing], *n.* act of promoting, attending or gambling on horse-racing.

RACK (1) [rak], *n.* framework of bars for holding and containing something, *esp.* a receptacle for hay in a manger; small structure for holding or supporting garments, vessels etc.; (*mech.*) toothed bar fitting into the cogs of a wheel; instrument of torture consisting of a frame on which the victim was stretched until his limbs were dislocated. RACK (2), *v.t.* to place in a r.; torture upon the r., torment with pains as on the r.; (*fig.*) urge (one's brain) to think of something or solve some problem; oppress with demands. RACK-RENT, rent equal to the annual value of the property let. [ME.].

RACK (3), *n.* drifting cloud vapour; wreckage, state of being wrecked; **r. and ruin**, irrevocable ruin. [~Norw.].

RACK (4), *v.t.* to drain off wine from the lees. [Provenc.].

RACKET (1), **RACQUET** [ra′kit], *n.* bat made with catgut stretched taut across a frame, used in tennis and related games; (*pl.*) game related to tennis and fives, played in a four-walled court. [ME. from Arab.].

RACKET (2), *n.* confused, rowdy, clamorous noise; (*coll.*) business organization for making illegal or immoral profits, act of operating such a business; **to stand, face, the r.**, to meet the expense (of), face the consequences (of). RACKET (3), *v.i.* to behave rowdily; lead a life of stupid, noisy dissipation. RACKETY, *adj.* making a r.; dissipated.

RACKETEER (1) [ra-ki-tēer′], *n.* (*U.S. coll.*) one who operates a racket. RACKETEER (2), *v.i.* (*U.S. coll.*) to operate a racket. [RACKET (2)].

RACONTEUR [ra-kaw(ng)-tur′], *n.* one skilled in relating anecdotes. [Fr.].

RAC(C)OON [ra-kōōn′], *n.* a bushy-tailed arboreal carnivorous mammal. [AmerInd.].

RACQUET, see RACKET (1).

RACY [rā′si], *adj.* vigorously piquant, daring and entertaining; **r. of the soil**, conveying the true local atmosphere of a district. [RACE (1)].

RADAR [rā′dah(r)], *n.* radiolocation. [RA(DIO) D(ETECTION) A(ND) R(ANGING)].

RADDLE (1) [ra′dl], *n.* red ochre. RADDLE (2), *v.t.* to paint with r. or with rouge. [RUDDLE].

RADIAL [rā′di-al], *adj.* relating to a radius or to a ray; radiating, having radiations; relating to the radius bone of the forearm. [LL.].

RADIAN [rā′di-an], *n.* (*math.*) the angle subtended at the centre of a circle by an arc equal to its radius.

RADIANCE, RADIANCY [rā′di-ans(-i)], *n.* condition of being radiant; brightness.

RADIANT (1) [rā′di-ant], *adj.* emitting rays of light, shining brightly; (*fig.*) bright with pleasure, joy, health; (*phys.*) related to, transmitted by, radiation. RADIANT (2), *n.* piece of refractory material which may be heated to radiate heat from an electric fire or gas-fire. [L.].

RADIATE (1) [rā′di-āt], *v.t. and i.* to emit rays; issue in rays, spread in all directions equally; branch out; (*fig.*) penetrate, have effect all round; emit in, or as if in, rays; (*fig.*) spread all round. RADIATE (2), *adj.* radial, radiating, having rays. [L.].

RADIATION [rā-di-ā′shn], *n.* act of radiating, emission, transmission of heat etc. by rays; radio-activity; that which is radiated, diffusion from a centre. [L.].

RADIATOR [rā′di-ā-ter], *n.* that which radiates; device for heating by means of hot water or air in pipes; device for cooling the water heated in the cylinder-jacket of a petrol engine.

RADICAL [ra′di-kal], *adj.* relating to, reaching to, springing from, the root of a thing, original, funda-mental; (*pol.*) advocating complete change on leftist lines; (*math.*) relating to the root of a number; (*bot.*) relating to the root of a plant. RADICAL (2), *n.* (*chem.*) element or group passing unchanged from compound to compound; (*math.*) the root symbol; (*pol.*) one advocating complete change or holding r. views. RADICALLY, *adv.* in r. fashion; completely. [LL.].

RADICLE [ra′di-kl], *n.* (*bot.*) embryonic root; (*anat.*) beginning of a vein; (*chem.*) a radical. [L.].

RADIO-, *pref.* ray, radiation; connected with wireless telegraphy or telephony; radius. [L.].

RADIO (1) [rā′di-ō], *n.* wireless telegraphy or tele-phony; apparatus for receiving these; (*coll.*) pro-grammes transmitted by radio. RADIO (2), *v.t. and i.* to send (a message) by wireless telegraphy or telephony. [*Prec.*].

RADIO-ACTIVE [rā-di-ō-ak′tiv], *adj.* having the quality of spontaneously and continuously emitting electronic energy, as radium, thorium etc. RADIO-ACTIVITY [rā-di-ō-ak-ti′vi-ti], *n.* properties and qualities of r. substances.

RADIOGRAM (1) [rā′di-ō-gram], *n.* radio-telegram. [RADIO and (TELE)GRAM].

RADIOGRAM (2), *n.* radio-gramophone. [RADIO and GRAM(OPHONE)].

RADIO-GRAMOPHONE [rā-di-ō-gra′mō-fōn], *n.* apparatus combining a radio receiving set and a gramophone.

RADIOGRAPH [rā′di-ō-grahf], *n.* X-ray photograph. [RADIO and GRAPH].

RADIOGRAPHY [rā-di-o′gra-fi], *n.* science of taking a radiograph, of measuring and examining by means of a radiograph. [RADIO and Gk.].

RADIOLOCATION [rā-di-ō-lō-kā′shn], *n.* system by which the presence, position and distance of air-craft, icebergs etc. may be detected at night or in fog by means of electro-magnetic waves of very high frequency. [RADIO and LOCATION].

RADIOLOGIST [rā-di-o′lo-jist], *n.* one expert in radiology; person in charge of an X-ray machine.

RADIOLOGY [rā-di-o′lo-ji], *n.* science of radio-activity and X-rays. [RADIO and Gk.].

RADIOMETER [rā-di-o′mi-ter], *n.* instrument for measuring radiation. RADIOMETRY, *n.* measurement by r. [RADIO and METER].

RADIOSCOPE [rā′di-ō-skōp], *n.* instrument for detecting radio-activity or for examining the interior of opaque objects. RADIOSCOPY [rā-di-o′sko-pi], *n.* use of the r. [RADIO and Gk.].

RADIO SONDE [rā-di-ō-sond′], *n.* (*meteor.*) instru-ment for transmitting measurements of the atmo-sphere's temperature, pressure and humidity from high altitudes by radio to the ground. [RADIO and Fr.].

RADIO-TELEGRAPHY [rā-di-ō-te-le′gra-fi], *n.* radio (wireless) telegraphy.

RADIO-TELEPHONE [rā-di-ō-te′li-fōn], *n.* appara-tus for transmitting speech by radio.

RADIO-THERAPY [rā-di-ō-the′ra-pi], *n.* treatment of disease by radiation, either of rays or of radio-active substances.

RADISH [ra′dish], *n.* a pungent coarse-leaved plant. [OFr.].

RADIUM [rā′di-um], *n.* metallic element denoted by Ra, notable for its intense radio-activity. [RADIO].

RADIUS (*pl.* radii) [rā′di-us], *n.* (*geom.*) distance of a circle's circumference from its centre, hence, any-thing resembling a circle's radius, the spoke of a wheel; circular area centred on a specific point, distance in any direction from a centre; (*anat.*) the shorter of the bones in the forearm. [L.].

RADIX (*pl.* radices) [rā′diks], *n.* (*math.*) a number used as the basis of a system of numeration; number taken as a basis for calculations of percentage. [L.].

RADON [rā′don], *n.* inert, radio-active, gaseous element produced by the disintegration of radium, denoted by Rn. [RADIUM].

RAFFIA [ra′fi-ah], *n.* cuticle of the leaf of the Madagas-car palm *Raphia ruffia*, or of the Brazilian species, *R. taedigera*, both being used for tying up plants

and for making mats, baskets, hats etc. [Malagasy].

RAFFISH [ra′fish], *adj.* rakish, vulgarly dissipated. [RIFF-RAFF].

RAFFLE (1) [ra′fl], *n.* sale by lottery. RAFFLE (2), *v.t.* to sell by a r. [ME.].

RAFT (1) [rahft], *n.* flat structure of planks, logs etc., used as a conveyance over water; flat floating struc-ture used as a mooring or landing-place. RAFT (2), *v.t.* to convey by means of a r. [OScand.].

RAFTER [rahf′ter], *n.* sloping beam supporting the frame of a roof. [OE.].

RAG (1) [rag], *n.* torn, dirty, useless piece of cloth; (*pl.*) tattered, old, dirty garments; anything resemb-ling a rag; (*fig.*) (contemptuously) a newspaper. RAG-BAG, bag in which rags or odd pieces of dress materials are kept. RAG-PAPER, paper made from linen rags. [ME. from Swed.].

RAG (2), *n.* hard, rough stone, rough slate. [Unkn.].

RAG (3) (*pres.pt.* **ragging**, *pret. and p.pt.* **ragged**) *v.t. and i.* to persecute, taunt and ridicule, often with rowdy horseplay. RAG (4), *n.* rough, boisterous, good-humoured prank indulged in by a group of young people; rowdy practical joke; frolic among undergraduates. [Uncert.].

RAGAMUFFIN [ra′ga-mu-fin], *n.* ragged, disreput-able child, street urchin. [RAG (1) and MUFF (2)].

RAGE (1) [rāj], *n.* furious anger, fury of temper or of the elements, emotional frenzy; (*coll.*) temporary, unreasoned, fashionable craze. RAGE (2), *v.i.* to be in a r., inveigh furiously against; display furious passion and violence; (of elements and disease) be at the height of destructiveness. [Fr.].

RAGGED [ra′gid], *adj.* irregular in outline, (of cloth) torn into rags; unkempt, rough, jagged; irregular, not in regular form or time; **r. robin**, wild flower of the genus *Lychnis*; **r. school**, formerly, school for very poor children.

RAGING [rā′jing], *adj.* displaying rage and violence; violently tempestuous.

RAGLAN [rag′lan], *n.* informal type or style of over-coat with no shoulder seams. [Lord *Raglan*].

RAGOUT [ra-gōō′], *n.* highly seasoned dish of chopped meat and vegetables. [Fr.].

RAGSTONE [rag′stōn], *n.* (*min.*) dark-grey coarse sandstone. [RAG (2)].

RAG-TAG [rag′tag], *n.* (*usually*) **r. and bobtail**, the lowest orders of society, riff-raff.

RAGTIME [rag′tīm], *n.* form of syncopated music as in negro dances and songs; jazz.

RAGWORT [rag′wert], *n.* common weed with deeply indented leaves and clusters of yellow flowers. [RAG (1) and WORT].

RAID (1) [rād], *n.* sudden invasion, usually for destruc-tion or plunder; sudden descent on certain premises by the civil authorities; aerial bombardment. RAID (2), *v.t.* to make a r. into or upon; plunder, attack. [OE.].

RAIL (1) [rāl], *n.* any of various kinds of small birds, such as the corn-crake and moorhen. [OFr.].

RAIL (2), *n.* wooden or metal bar; wooden or iron fence formed of such bars; bar supported by brackets for hanging clothes etc. on; balustrade on a stair-case; one of the parallel steel lines forming the per-manent way for railway vehicles or trams; railway; (*pl.*) fence; railway stocks and shares; **r. motor**, petrol-driven vehicle running over the track of a steam-operated railway; **off the rails**, derailed; (*fig.*) gone astray in conduct or ideas, unhinged. RAIL (3), *v.t.* to furnish with rails; send by r.; **to r. in**, to fence in; **to r. off**, to shut off by rails or a fence. [OFr. from L.].

RAIL (4), *v.i.* **to r. against**, to utter reproaches against, revile bitterly. [Fr.].

RAILHEAD [rāl′hed], *n.* farthest point to which a railway penetrates.

RAILING (1) [rā′ling], *n.* fence of wooden or iron rails; rails in general; materials for rails. [RAIL (2)].

RAILING (2), *n.* bitter reproaches, expression of con-tempt or anger. RAILING (3), *adj.* uttering reproaches. [RAIL (4)].

RAILLERY [rā′le-ri], *n.* banter, persiflage. [Fr.].

RAILROAD [rāl′rōd], *n.* (*U.S.*) railway.

RAILWAY [rāl′wā], *n.* permanent way of steel rails on which trains are run; the whole system of lines, stations etc. used for this purpose. [RAIL (2) and WAY].

RAIMENT [rā′ment], *n.* clothing, clothes. [~OFr.].

RAIN (1) [rān], *n.* moisture of the atmosphere con-densed and falling as small drops of water; shower or storm of such drops; (*fig.*) fall or stream of small drops or particles; rapid succession or repetition of blows, bullets etc.). **RAIN-GAUGE**, instrument for measuring rainfall. **RAIN** (2), *v.i.* to fall as r., fall in rapid drops; send down r.; come in rapid succession like drops of r.; pour down (upon), shower; *v.t.* to give in great profusion, shower (upon); **to r. cats and dogs**, to r. heavily. [O.E.].

RAINBOW [rān'bō], *n.* arched bow showing the colours of the spectrum, formed in the sky opposite to the sun or moon by the refraction and reflection of light from raindrops. **RAINBOW-TINTED, -HUED**, *adj.* many-coloured. [O.E.].

RAINCOAT [rān'kōt], *n.* waterproof coat worn as a protection against rain.

RAINPROOF [rān'prōof], *adj.* and *n.* resisting rain; raincoat.

RAINY [rā'ni], *adj.* characterized by rain; showery; **r. day,** *(fig.)* time of need.

RAISE (1) [rāz], *v.t.* to cause to rise; lift; set upright; build; exalt, promote; increase the amount, value of; enhance; inspire, conjure up in the mind; stir up; bring into being, produce, rear; collect together, recruit; collect; levy; obtain possession of (money); **to r. Cain,** to create a violent disturbance; **to r. one's head,** to give evidence of one's independent existence; **to r. from the dead,** to bring to life again; **to r. a laugh,** to cause a laugh; **to r. a point,** to bring up a point for consideration; **to r. a siege, blockade, ban,** to withdraw from, remove; **to r. the wind,** *(slang)* to obtain a loan, gain possession of a sum of money. **RAISE** (2), *n.* (*U.S.*) a rise in wages. [OScand.].

RAISIN [rā'zin], *n.* kind of dried grape. [OFr.].

RAISON D'ETRE, raison d'être [rā-zaw(ng)-detr'], *n.* reason for existence, justification, explanation. [Fr.].

RAISONNE, raisonné [rā-zo'nā], *adj.* logical; systematic and descriptive. [Fr.].

RAJ [rahj], *n.* sovereignty, rule, dominion. [Hind.].

RAJA(H) [rah'jah], *n.* in India, title of a native king or prince, a chief. [Hind.].

RAJPUT [rahj'pōot], *n.* member of the Hindu military caste; substantial landowner. [Hind.].

RAKE (1) [rāk], *n.* agricultural or garden implement with a long handle attached to a horizontal bar of teeth or prongs for gathering together loose hay, leaves etc. or for smoothing the soil; similar farm implement drawn by horse or tractor; similar implement for drawing out the ashes from underneath a fireplace or furnace; instrument used by the croupier for drawing towards him the stakes won by the bank at a gaming-table. **RAKE** (2), *v.t.* to use a r. upon; gather together with a r.; smooth with a r.; collect, scrape together from every source; enfilade, sweep with fire lengthways; allow the eyes to travel along; *v.i.* to work with a r.; *(fig.)* ferret out; **to r. out,** to draw ashes from; *(fig.)* ferret out; **to r. up,** to bring to light, revive.

RAKE (3), *v.i.* to incline, lean from the perpendicular; incline as the upper parts of a ship's stem or stern beyond the line of the keel. **RAKE** (4), *n.* (*naut.*) projection of the upper parts of a ship at stern and stem beyond the keel; inclination (of a mast, theatre stage etc.) from the perpendicular. [Uncert.].

RAKE (5), *n.* dissolute, loose-living man, libertine. [Abbrev. of † *rakehell*].

RAKE-OFF [rāk'of], *n.* (*slang*) percentage or profit taken or abstracted by the intermediary in a transaction.

RAKISH (1) [rā'kish], *adj.* sloping backwards, set at an angle; (*naut.*) having the appearance of fast sailing and smartness; jaunty. [RAKE (4)].

RAKISH (2), *adj.* having the manners of a rake; given to a dissolute life. [RAKE (5)].

RALLENTANDO [ra-len-tahn'dō], *n., adj.* and *adv.* (*mus.*) (passage) (played) in increasingly slower time. [It.].

RALLY (1) [ra'li], *v.t.* to gather, collect together again; reassemble (disordered forces); rouse, revive for further effort; *v.i.* to come back to order after a repulse; recover strength; (*comm.*) (of shares, goods) command higher prices. **RALLY** (2), *n.* act of reassembling disordered troops after a repulse; recovery of strength; assembly; mass meeting; (*sport*) continuous interchange of strokes between opposing players in a game played with rackets. [Fr.].

RALLY (3), *v.t.* to banter, tease. [Fr.].

RAM (1) [ram], *n.* full-grown male sheep; (*astron.*) sign of the Zodiac and constellation of Aries; (*milit.*) engine formerly used for demolishing walls, battering-ram; (*nav.*) steel beak at the bow of a warship; (*eng.*)

hydraulic engine for raising weights; any of various devices for applying energy by pushing, thrusting. **RAM** (2) (*pres.pt.* RAMMING, *pret.* and *p.pt.* RAMMED), *v.t.* to drive with violence; crash into forcibly; butt like a r.; force in; beat; crush, cram; *(fig.)* assert something violently; **to r. down a person's throat,** to force into a reluctant mind. [O.E.].

RAMADAN, RAMAZAN [rah-mah-dahn', rah-mah-zahn'], *n.* ninth month of the Mohammedan year observed as a thirty days' fast between the hours of sunrise and sunset. [Arab.].

RAMBLE (1) [ram'bl], *v.i.* to wander about, roam; saunter about for pleasure; *(fig.)* wander in talk or writing; be delirious and babble inconsequentially; (*bot.*) grow in long slender shoots, trail. **RAMBLE** (2), *n.* a walk without a definite route, stroll; *(fig.)* discursive talk or book. **RAMBLER,** *n.* one who, or that which, rambles; climbing rose-tree. [Uncert.].

RAMBLING [ram'bling], *adj.* inclined to ramble; straggling, irregular; *(fig.)* desultory, disconnected, discursive.

RAMEKIN, RAMEQUIN [ra'me-kin], *n.* dish of cheese, eggs and breadcrumbs baked and served in a mould. [Fr.].

RAMIFICATION [ra-mi-fi-kā'shn], *n.* division into branches; branch; subdivision or single part of a complex structure; *(fig.)* a penetration into many directions.

RAMIFY [ra'mi-fī], *v.t.* to divide into branches; form into ramifications; *v.i.* to produce ramifications; be divided or subdivided. [L.].

RAMMER [ra'mer], *n.* one who, or that which, rams or drives in; tool for ramming; wooden instrument for beating down earth; machine for driving piles into place.

RAMP (1) [ramp], *v.t.* to make a ramp; *v.i.* to climb and spread luxuriantly as a plant; rage, storm violently. **RAMP** (2), *n.* slope; inclined plane connecting two different levels; slope of, or change of level in, a stair-rail or coping; slope connecting two different levels of a road; (*coll.*) rampage; (*slang*) swindle, fraud. [Fr.].

RAMPAGE (1) [ram-pāj'], *v.i.* to be on the rampage. **RAMPAGE** (2), *n.* violent behaviour, riot; **on the r.,** inclined to, indulging in, riotous behaviour. [Prec.].

RAMPAGEOUS [ram-pā'jŏŏs], *adj.* rowdy, noisy. [Prec.].

RAMPANCY [ram'pan-si], *n.* condition of being rampant.

RAMPANT [ram'pant], *adj.* rearing, standing with the forepaws in the air; (*her.*) of an animal, thus rearing; *(fig.)* angry, impatient; luxuriant in growth, spreading; rife, prevalent. [Fr.].

RAMPART [ram'paht], *n.* mound of earth raised for the defence of a place; that which defends and fortifies from assault; *(fig.)* protection, defence. [Fr.].

RAMROD [ram'rod], *n.* metal rod used for ramming home the charge in a muzzle-loaded gun; *(fig.)* person of stiff, uncompromising bearing.

RAMSHACKLE [ram'sha-kl], *adj.* loose and rickety as if liable to fall to pieces; makeshift; badly built. [Uncert.].

RAN [ran], *pret. of* RUN.

RANCH [rahnch], *n.* cattle farm, usually in America; large farm or estate. [SpanAmer.].

RANCID [ran'sid], *adj.* having the sour, stale smell of fats which have gone bad. [L.].

RANCOROUS [rang'ke-rŏŏs], *adj.* bitter, spiteful.

RANCOUR [rang'ker], *n.* deep-seated bitterness; smarting sense of injury; malignity; spite. [OFr.].

RANDAN [ran-dan'], *n.* rowing boat for three persons, one using a pair of sculls, stroke and bow using each an oar. [Unkn.].

RANDOM [ran'dom], *n.* **at r.,** aimlessly, without direction or thought. **RANDOM** (2), *adj.* done at hazard, aimlessly, without previous thought. [OFr.].

RANDY [ran'di], *adj.* (*coll.*) lustful; rowdy. [Uncert.].

RANEE, RANI [rah'nē], *n.* Hindu queen or princess; wife of a rajah. [Hind.].

RANG [rang], *pret. of* RING.

RANGE (1) [rānj], *n.* a row, collection, series; chain of mountains; space through which anything in motion carries, as the distance to which the projectile of a gun reaches, distance at which one can see or hear; extent, area; kitchen grate or cooking stove; *(fig.)* intellectual reach, capacity. **RANGE-FINDER,** optical instrument for ascertaining the distance of an object at one observation. **RANGE** (2), *v.t.* to place in a row, ranks or series; classify; get the r. of (with a gun etc.); traverse; *v.i.* to lie in a particular direction, extend; move at large; vary between two specified limits; (of guns) have a certain r.; (*fig.*) include in its intellectual grasp; **to r. oneself,** to put oneself in a certain group. RANGY, *adj.* lean and wiry. [OFr.].

RANGER [rān'jer], *n.* rover; officer appointed to patrol a royal park or forest; (*pl.*) body of troops used for scouting purposes, *esp.* those used to patrol frontiers or (*U.S.*) as commando troops.

RANI, see RANEE.

RANK (1) [rangk], *n.* a row, line of things or people; social class, order; eminence, high station; degree of worth; **to fall into r.,** to fall into an orderly arrangement; **to break ranks,** (*milit.*) to be thrown into confusion, to cease standing in ranks; **to take r.,** to enjoy precedence; **r. and file,** whole body of common soldiers, ordinary people; **other ranks,** (*milit.*) members of an armed force who are not commissioned officers. RANK (2), *v.t.* to place abreast or in line; dispose methodically; assign a r., class, position to; *v.i.* to take r., belong to a certain r., class, position; have validity. RANKING, *adj.* (*U.S.*) leading, taking precedence. [OFr.].

RANK (3), *adj.* luxuriant in growth; coarse, rampant; strong smelling, rancid; corrupt, loathsome. [OE.].

RANKER [rang'ker], *n.* one who disposes in ranks; common soldier; commissioned officer who has risen from the ranks.

RANKLE [rang'kl], *v.i.* to fester; be the cause of soreness or irritation; (*fig.*) be the cause of pain or ill-feeling. [OFr.].

RANSACK [ran'sak], *v.t.* to search, examine, thoroughly; turn everything upside down in searching; plunder. [OScand.].

RANSOM (1) [ran'sum], *n.* price paid for the redemption of a prisoner or slave or for goods captured by an enemy; release of a prisoner from the possession of an enemy or kidnapper in return for payment; price paid to procure the pardon of sins; (*theol.*) the sacrifice of Christ regarded as the price paid for the redemption of man; **to hold to r.,** to keep prisoner until r. is paid; **king's r.,** (*fig.*) very large sum. RANSOM (2), *v.t.* to redeem from captivity or bondage; exact r. from; (*theol.*) redeem from sin by sacrifice. [OFr.].

RANT (1) [rant], *v.i.* to rave in violent, empty declamation; talk on religious matters in a dramatic and extravagant manner. RANT (2), *n.* idle declamation, noisy, extravagant speech. RANTER, *n.* one who rants; (*coll.*) 19th-century Nonconformist preacher. [MDu.].

RANUNCULUS [ra-nung'kyŏŏ-lus], *n.* (*bot.*) genus of plants including the buttercup and crowfoot. [L.].

RAP (1) [rap], *n.* quick, smart blow or tap; knock on a door, table etc. RAP (2) (*pres.pt.* RAPPING, *pret. and p.pt.* RAPPED), *v.t. and i.* to strike with a r.; knock; **to r. out,** to express by rapping; utter sharply. [Echoic].

RAP (3), *n.* † counterfeit Irish halfpenny; something worthless; **not worth a r.,** valueless. [Uncert.].

RAPACIOUS [ra-pā'shŏŏs], *adj.* greedy, given to plunder; extortionate. [L.].

RAPACITY [ra-pa'si-ti], *n.* quality of being rapacious; greed of gain; avarice. [Fr.].

RAPE (1) [rāp], *v.t.* to seize and carry off by force; force (a woman) to sexual intercourse; ravish, violate. RAPE (2), *n.* a seizing and carrying off by force; act of raping; violation of a woman. [L.].

RAPE (3), *n.* plant of the genus *Brassica*, grown as food for sheep. RAPE-CAKE, cake made from the remains of rape-seed after the extraction of the oil. RAPE-SEED, seed of the r. from which colza oil is extracted. [L.].

RAPHAELESQUE [ra-fā-e-lesk'], *adj.* in the manner of the Italian painter *Raphael.* RAPHAELISM, *n.* principles of art introduced by *Raphael*; his method of painting.

RAPID (1) [ra'pid], *adj.* very quick, swift, steep. RAPID (2), *n.* (*usually in pl.*) that part of a river where the current flows very rapidly owing to a steep descent of the bed. [L.].

RAPIDITY [ra-pi'di-ti], *n.* state of being rapid; swiftness. [L.].

RAPIER [rā'pi-er], *n.* light sword with long narrow blade used only for thrusting; **r. thrust,** (*fig.*) a penetrating riposte. [Fr.].

RAPINE [ra'pin], *n.* act of plundering; pillage. [Fr.].

RAPPEE [ra-pē'], *n.* strong coarse kind of snuff. [Fr.].

RAPPORT [ra-paw(r)'], *n.* intimate relation; harmony; **to be in r. with,** to have close relations with;

be in communication with (a spirit) through a medium. [Fr.].

RAPPROCHEMENT [ra-prosh'mah(ng)], *n.* act of reconciling; re-establishing of cordial relations between individuals or nations. [Fr.].

RAPSCALLION [rap-ska'li-on], *n.* rascally vagabond, scamp. [RASCAL].

RAPT [rapt], *adj.* in an ecstasy; carried away, engrossed. [L.].

RAPTORIAL [rap-taw'ri-al], *adj.* predatory; belonging to the order *Raptores* of birds of prey, including the eagle, hawk etc. [L.].

RAPTURE [rap'tyōōr], *n.* ecstasy; extreme delight; **to go into raptures over,** to express extreme pleasure in or admiration for. [RAPT].

RAPTUROUS [rap'tyŏŏ-rŏŏs], *adj.* feeling, expressing, rapture; ecstatic.

RARA AVIS [răer-a-ā'vis or rah-rah-a'vis], *n.* unusual person or thing. [L.].

RARE (1) [răer], *adj.* nearly raw, underdone. [OE.].

RARE (2), *adj.* thinly scattered, not dense; rarefied, thin; infrequent, unusual, precious, excellent. RARELY, *adv.* seldom; exceptionally. [Fr.].

RAREBIT [răer'bit, ra'bit], *n.* **Welsh r.,** cooked cheese on toast. [~WELSH-RABBIT].

RAREE-SHOW [răer'ē-shō], *n.* peep-show carried in a box. [RARE and SHOW].

RAREFY [răer'i-fi], *v.t.* to make rare; make thin and porous or less dense; refine, render spiritual; *v.i.* to become rarefied. RAREFACTION [răer-i-fak'shn], *n.* act of rarefying; state of being rarefied. [Fr.].

RARITY [răer'i-ti], *n.* state of being rare; lack of density; infrequency, uncommonness; something rare. [L.].

RASCAL [rahs'kal], *n.* scoundrel, rogue; (*coll.*) fellow. [Fr.].

RASCALITY [rahs-ka'li-ti], *n.* rascally action or conduct; base fraud.

RASE, see RAZE.

RASH (1) [rash], *n.* an eruption of the skin. [OFr.].

RASH (2), *adj.* hasty in action or judgment; headstrong; imprudent. [ME.].

RASHER [ra'sher], *n.* thin slice of bacon or ham. [Uncert.].

RASP (1) [rahsp], *v.t. and i.* to file with a rasp; produce a harsh, grating sound; (*fig.*) irritate, exacerbate. RASP (2), *n.* coarse file; rough, grating sound. RASPING, *adj.* grating, harsh. [OFr.].

RASPBERRY (1) [rahs'be-ri], *n.* the plant *Rubus Idaeus*; fruit of this plant. RASPBERRY-VINEGAR, syrup made from raspberry-juice and vinegar. [Uncert.].

RASPBERRY (2), *n.* (*slang*) rasping sound made with the tongue and lower lip as a sign of contempt.

RASPER [rahs'per], *n.* large rasp or file; (*hunting*) high, difficult fence.

RAT (1) [rat], *n.* a small rodent, larger than a mouse; (*fig.*) cowardly treacherous person, one who deserts a place or cause when danger threatens; **water r.,** the water vole; **to smell a r.,** to be suspicious; **like a drowned rat,** wet to the skin. RAT-CATCHER, person employed in catching rats. RAT (2) (*pres.pt.* RATTING, *pret. and p.pt.* RATTED), *v.i.* to hunt rats; desert one's party or cause. [OE.].

RATABLE, RATEABLE [rā'ta-bl], *adj.* able to be set at a certain value or rate; liable to taxation; **r. value,** yearly sum at which a house or land is assessed for rates and taxes.

RATAFIA [ra-ta-fē'ah], *n.* liqueur distilled from fruits and flavoured with crushed kernels; biscuit similarly flavoured. [Fr.].

RATAPLAN [ra-ta-plan'], *n.* beat of a drum. [Fr.].

RATCH [rach], *n.* ratchet-wheel. [*Next*].

RATCHET [ra'chit], *n.* set of teeth on a bar or wheel, connected with a pawl, and so allowing the wheel to turn in only one direction. RATCHET-WHEEL, wheel equipped with a r. [Fr.].

RATE (1) [rāt], *n.* proportion or ratio by which an unvarying relation between two things different in kind is measured, as 30 miles an hour or 2d. per lb.; price fixed or stated; class based on estimated worth; municipal tax; (*nav.*) order or class of a ship; (*coll.*) speed. RATE (2), *v.t.* to value, fix the r. or grade of; assess for rating; (*nav.*) class (a vessel) according to its grade; *v.i.* to be classed in a certain grade or at a certain r. RATER, *n.* one of a certain r. [OFr.].

RATE (3), *v.t.* to scold, chide. [ME.].

RATEABLE, see RATABLE.

RATH(E) [rāth], *adj.* (*poet.*) coming early into flower; early ripening. [OE.].

RATHER [rah'THer], *adv.* sooner, preferably; more

properly, truly, accurately; slightly, somewhat; (*coll.*) certainly. [OE.].

RATIFICATION [ra-ti-fi-kā'shn], *n.* act of ratifying, confirming; sanction. [MedL.].

RATIFY [ra'ti-fi], *v.t.* to confirm, make valid; approve, sanction. RATIFIER, *n.* one who or that which ratifies. [Fr.].

RATING [rā'ting], *n.* act of valuing, assessing, fixing a rate; tonnage class or type of vessel; status in a ship's crew of an individual sailor; (*nav.*) member of a ship's crew, other than officers; rank, grade. [RATE (1)].

RATIO [rā'shi-ō], *n.* the fixed relation of one thing to another; proportion; (*math.*) relation of one quantity or magnitude of another expressed by their quotient. [L.].

RATIOCINATE [ra-ti-o'si-nāt, ra-shi-o'si-nāt], *v.i.* to reason; carry on a process of formal reasoning. RATIOCINATIVE, *adj.* characterized by ratiocination. [L.].

RATIOCINATION [ra-ti-o-si-nā'shn, ra-shi-o-si-nā'shn], *n.* process of reasoning; act of deducing consequences from given premises. [L.].

RATION (1) [ra'shn], *n.* fixed allowance of anything, *esp.* of provisions; (*pl.*) provisions; **r. book,** booklet containing coupons by which the permitted ration can be obtained; **short rations,** restricted provisions. RATION (2), *v.t.* to supply with rations; limit (people) to certain quantities of provisions; distribute (goods) by a fixed scale of allowances. [L.].

RATIONAL [ra'shn-al], *adj.* endowed with reason; pertaining to, having the faculty of, reason; intelligent; judicious; **r. quantity,** (*math.*) one expressed without a radical sign or by a whole number. [L.].

RATIONALE [ra-shn-ā'li], *n.* rational explanation; the principle of a matter. [L.].

RATIONALISM [ra'shn-a-lizm], *n.* (*theol.*) doctrine which claims to explain the universe by reason alone; (*philos.*) doctrine that reason is the sole source of knowledge; reliance on reason.

RATIONALIST (1) [ra'shn-a-list], *n.* believer in rationalism in philosophy or theology; one who is guided by reason. RATIONALIST (2), *adj.* pertaining to rationalists or rationalism.

RATIONALITY [ra-shn-a'li-ti], *n.* condition of being rational; reasonableness. [Fr.].

RATIONALIZATION [ra-shn-a-li-zā'shn], *n.* act of rationalizing; policy of reforming industry on a rational basis so as to avoid useless effort or cost.

RATIONALIZE [ra'shn-a-liz], *v.t.* to explain entirely by reason; apprehend rationally; explain away by means of reasoning; organize economically; (*math.*) clear from radical or irrational quantities; *v.i.* to rely solely or unduly on reason.

RATIONING [ra'shn-ing], *n.* system or practice of limiting the distribution of goods so that each individual receives only a fixed allocation.

RAT-TAIL(ED) [rat'tāl(d)], *adj.* narrow and tapering; (of a horse) having a thin hairless tail; (of a spoon) having a narrow tapering extension of the handle under the bowl.

RATTAN [ra-tan'], *n.* species of East Indian climbing plant; stem of this when peeled, used for walking-sticks etc.; walking-stick made of rattan. [Malay].

RAT-TAT [rat-tat], *n.* sound of a loud knocking at the door. [Echoic].

RATTEN [ra'ten], *v.t. and i.* to destroy or take away the tools or property of non-unionists during a labour dispute. [Uncert.].

RATTER [ra'ter], *n.* one who hunts rats; dog or ferret which hunts rats; man deserting his friends in a crisis.

RATTING [ra'ting], *n.* the catching and killing of rats; desertion of one's friends in a crisis.

RATTLE (1) [ra'tl], *v.t.* to cause to make a rattling sound; cause to move with much clattering; (*coll.*) disturb, agitate; **to r. off,** to complete briskly; *v.i.* to make a rattle; make a series of quick, clattering sounds; move quickly and with a rattling sound; speak briskly. RATTLE (2), *n.* a rapid succession of sharp clattering sounds; name of certain plants in which the seeds rattle in their capsules; sound produced by loose objects shaking against each other; intermittent sound produced by a loose door, window etc.; instrument or child's toy by which a clattering sound is made; noisy, empty talker. RATTLE-HEADED, -PATED, *adj.* shallow, empty-headed. RATTLER, *n.* one who, or that which, rattles; noisy person; rattlesnake; first-rate person or thing. [Echoic].

RATTLESNAKE [ra'tl-snāk], *n.* a venomous snake,

so called because of the noise that the loosely interlocking joints at the end of its tail make when shaken.

RATTLETRAP (1) [ra'tl-trap], *n.* shaky vehicle; rickety old bicycle or motor-car. RATTLETRAP (2), *adj.* rickety, shaky. [RATTLE (1) and TRAP (1)].

RATTLING [rat'ling], *adj.* making the sound of a rattle; quick, brisk; excellent; **r. good fellow,** fine fellow.

RAT-TRAP [rat'trap] *n.* trap for catching rats; toothed pedal on a bicycle.

RATTY [ra'ti], *adj.* infested with rats; (*slang*) angry, bad-tempered.

RAUCITY [raw'si-ti], *n.* roughness, hoarseness. [L.].

RAUCOUS [raw'koos], *adj.* rough, harsh, loud and coarse.

RAVAGE (1) [ra'vij], *n.* destruction by violence or decay; devastation; (*pl.*) effects of these. RAVAGE (2), *v.t.* to lay waste, plunder; ruin, destroy; *v.i.* to commit ravages. [Fr.].

RAVE [rāv], *v.i.* to wander in mind; speak incoherently or irrationally like a madman; (of a storm) howl, roar; **to r. about,** to speak very enthusiastically about. [OFr.].

RAVEL (1) [*pres.pt.* **ravelling**, *pret. and p.pt.* **ravelled**) [ra'vel], *v.t.* to unweave, untwist; make into a tangled mass; *v.i.* to fray out, become untwisted; **to r. out,** to disentangle. RAVEL (2), *n.* a tangled mass; (*fig.*) confusion. [MDu.].

RAVEN (1) [rā'ven], *n.* the largest of the crow family. RAVEN (2), *adj.* black like the r. [OScand.].

RAVEN (3) [ra'ven], *v.t.* to devour with eager greed; *v.i.* to plunder with rapacity; be ravenous. RAVENING, *adj.* voracious, eager for plunder. [OFr.].

RAVENOUS [ra've-noos], *adj.* furiously voracious, eager for gratification; famished; (*coll.*) very hungry. [*Prec.*].

RAVINE [ra-vēn'], *n.* long deep gully; narrow valley or gorge. [AFr.].

RAVISH [ra'vish], *v.t.* to carry away by violence; commit a rape upon; delight, fill with ecstasy. RAVISHING, *adj.* delightful, entrancing. [~OFr.].

RAW (1) [raw], *adj.* in the natural state, not cooked, prepared or treated; (of leather) untanned; (of silks, cottons, wools) not spun or twisted; (of spirits) undiluted; untrained, inexperienced; sore, having the skin rubbed off; cold and damp; (of manners or literature) crude; **r. deal,** (*slang*) unfair treatment. RAW-BONED, having little flesh on the bones; gaunt. RAW (2), *n.* a sore place; **on the r.,** in the most tender, sensitive place. [OE.].

RAY (1) [rā], *n.* any species of cartilaginous fishes of the genus *Raia,* such as the skates. [AFr.].

RAY (2), *n.* beam, shaft of light; a glimmering; also *fig.*; (*geom.*) radius; (*phys.*) line of radiant energy; (*bot.*) (*pl.*) outer whorl of a compound radiate flower; (*zool.*) any part of a radial arrangement as a spine in a fin. RAY (3), *v.t. and i.* to shine forth, issue in rays. [OFr.].

RAYON [rā'on], *n.* artificial silk. [Fr.].

RAZE, RASE [rāz], *v.t.* to erase, efface; completely destroy. [Fr.].

RAZOR [rā'zer], *n.* sharp instrument for shaving off hair; **to be on the razor's edge,** to be in acute difficulties, at a crisis. RAZOR-BACK, fin-backed whale; rorqual. RAZOR-FISH, shell-fish with a long narrow shell like the handle of a r. [OFr.].

RAZORBILL [rā'zer-bil], *n.* bird with a bill shaped like a r., *esp.* the auk.

RE-, *pref.* back; again; against. [L.].

RE (1) [rē], *n.* second note of the diatonic scale. [L.].

RE (2) [rē], *prep.* in the matter of, as regards, referring to. [L.].

REACH (1) [rēch], *v.t.* to stretch out, extend (usually with *out*); grasp or touch with outstretched arm; take (down or from) by extending the arm; pass, hand to; realize, achieve; arrive at; influence, affect; come into possession of or contact with; extend to, penetrate to, carry as far as; *v.i.* to stretch out an arm or leg; be extended so as to touch; extend, carry; **to r. after, for,** to aspire, strive after. REACH (2), *n.* act of reaching; power of touching or grasping by extending the arm or other limb; range of the arm; power of understanding; scope; possibility of being reached, *esp.* of being easily accessible; range of influence; distance over which something is perceptible; stretch of water on a river etc. [OE.].

REACH-ME-DOWN [rēch'mē-down], *n.* garment which is ready made; (*pl.*) trousers.

REACT [rē-akt'], *v.t.* to act over again; *v.i.* to act in response to a mental or physical stimulus; act or move in the opposite way (with *against*); act reciprocally on.

REACTION [rē-ak′shn], *n.* action in response or opposition to a mental or physical stimulus; reciprocal action; (*chem.*) action of one agent upon another or the effects of such action; opposite feeling or state induced as a result of a strong influence or continued force exerted on the mind or body, as collapse after prolonged strain; (*pol.*) suppression of reform or progress; (*radio*) energy produced by currents in an output circuit of a valve passed back to its grid.

REACTIONARY (1) [rē-ak′shn-a-ri], *adj.* involving or favouring reaction, opposed to reform or progress. REACTIONARY (2), *n.* one in favour of reaction, one adopting a policy of reaction in politics etc.

REACTIONIST [rē-ak′shn-ist], *n.* a reactionary.

REACTIVE [rē-ak′tiv], *adj.* having power to react, caused by reaction; reactionary.

READ (1) (*pret. and p.pt.* **read**) [rĕd, *pret. and p.pt.* red], *v.t.* to look at and make out the words and characters written, printed or engraved in a book, document etc.; be able to understand (works written in a foreign language); learn, acquire knowledge of by perusing; discover the answer to; interpret by contemplating or studying; (of an instrument) register; give as a reading, emendation or correction; understand, interpret; utter aloud (anything written); study (for a degree); (*parl.*) offer (a bill) for discussion and voting upon by a legislative assembly; correct (proofs of a MS.); *v.i.* to perform the act of reading; be able to read; utter aloud anything written; study by reading; stand written; produce a certain impression when read; **to r. for,** to study in order to be officially admitted to; **to r. into,** to assume that a particular meaning is implied in; **to r. of,** to learn by reading; **to r. up,** to increase one's knowledge of by reading; **to r. oneself in,** to enter into formal possession of a benefice in the Church of England by reading aloud in public the Thirty-nine Articles and the Declaration of Assent; **to r. between the lines,** to discover the real meaning or implication as distinct from what is expressed. READ (2), *n.* a perusal, reading, act of reading. READ (3) [red], *adj.* versed in a subject by reading. [OE.].

READABLE [rē′da-bl], *adj.* able to be read; (of handwriting) legible; pleasant and interesting to read.

READDRESS [rē-a-dres′], *v.t.* to redirect a letter or parcel to another address than that it already bears.

READER [rē′der], *n.* one who reads, *esp.* one fond of reading; one who reads lessons etc. in church; one employed in correcting proofs for the Press; university teacher usually ranking in status between professor and lecturer; one employed by publishers to give his opinion upon manuscripts submitted to them; reading-book.

READILY [re′di-li], *adv.* in a ready manner, promptly, willingly.

READINESS [re′di-nes], *n.* quality of being ready, preparedness; willingness; quickness.

READING (1) [rē′ding], *n.* act of one who reads; knowledge acquired from books; readable matter; public recital of selected passages of literature; presentation of a play in which the actors read the text; form of a word, words used or the way in which a passage reads in different copies or editions of a text; interpretation, rendering; figure registered by a barometer etc. when read; (*parl.*) formal presentation of a bill to the legislative body, and the succeeding stages it has to pass through before it can become an Act. READING-BOOK, book with passages for practice in r. READING-DESK, desk for supporting a book while being read, lectern. READING-LAMP, portable lamp with a shade, which directs the light on to the book when r. READING-ROOM, room in a club or public institution set apart for r. and writing. READING (2), *adj.* addicted to r.

READJUST [rē-a-just′], *v.t.* to adjust or put in order afresh. READJUSTMENT, *n.* a fresh adjustment.

READMIT (*pres.pt.* **readmitting,** *pret. and p.pt.* **readmitted**) [rē-ad-mit′], *v.t.* to admit anew. READMITTANCE, *n.* readmission.

READY (1) [re′di], *adj.* prepared, able to do something immediately, fit for immediate use; willing, inclined; liable to, on the point of; quick, dexterous; near at hand; **to make, get r.,** to prepare. READY (2), *n.* (*slang*) r. cash; **at the r.,** (of a fire-arm) held in readiness for immediate firing. [~OE.].

READY-MADE [re-di-mād′], *adj.* made ready for immediate use, *esp.* of clothes as opposed to those made to measure; not original; (of ideas, opinions etc.) fixed and produced on every available occasion.

READY MONEY (1) [re-di-mu′ni], *n.* hard cash, actual coin. READY-MONEY (2), *adj.* done or conducted by immediate payment in money.

READY RECKONER [re-di-re′ko-ner], *n.* book of tables for rapid arithmetical calculations.

REAFFOREST [rē-a-fo′rest], *v.t.* to plant with new trees in place of those cut down or destroyed. REAFFORESTATION [rē-a-fo-res-tā′shn], *n.* scientific replanting of trees in former forest areas now laid bare.

REAGENT [rē-ā′jent], *n.* that which reacts or sets up reaction; (*chem.*) substance employed in chemical analysis to detect the presence of another substance by setting up a reaction with this substance.

REAL (1) [rā-ahl′], *n.* small silver Spanish coin (2½d.), the fourth of a peseta. [Span.].

REAL (2) [rē′al], *adj.* actually being or existing; founded on fact; authentic, genuine (as opposed to artificial); sincere, undoubted; true; (of fictional characters) giving the impression of living; (*philos.*) existing in fact; (*leg.*) relating to or connected with things or property, *esp.* to lands and houses (as opposed to personal property); **r. estate,** freehold landed property, lands and houses etc.; **r. property,** lands and houses; **R. Presence,** the body and blood of Jesus Christ as believed to be actually present in the consecrated bread and wine of the Eucharist. REAL (3), *n.* that which is r. [LL.].

REALISM [rē′a-lizm], *n.* concentration upon actual fact or what is real, mental outlook which sees things as they actually are; principle in art and literature of representing life as it actually is; (*philos.*) doctrine that general terms are not abstractions but have a real existence; doctrine that external physical objects have a separate, real existence independent of the mind's perception and sensation of them.

REALIST [rē′a-list], *n.* one who supports the philosophical doctrine of realism; one who claims to see life as it actually is; disciple of realism in art or literature.

REALISTIC [rē-a-lis′tik], *adj.* pertaining to, characteristic of, the realists or realism; faithfully representing real life; actual; practical.

REALITY [rē-a′li-ti], *n.* state or quality of being real, actual existence; fact; the real nature of anything, the real thing; realistic quality. [MedL.].

REALIZATION [rē-a-li-zā′shn], *n.* act of forming a clear conception of or becoming fully aware in the mind of; the bringing into being or achievement; act of converting into cash.

REALIZE [rē′a-liz], *v.t.* to comprehend clearly, become fully conscious or aware of, make real, bring into existence as an accomplished fact; acquire, obtain, fetch by sale; convert into money or cash. [REAL (2)].

REALLY [rē′a-li], *adv.* actually, truly, in point of fact; mild exclamation of surprise or protest and for emphasis.

REALM [relm], *n.* kingdom, country or territory ruled over by a king or queen; sphere, province; (*bot., zool.*) primary division of the earth's surface from the point of view of distribution of plants and animals. [OFr.].

REALTY [rē′al-ti], (*leg.*) real property; real estate.

REAM [rēm], *n.* quantity of paper consisting usually of 20 quires or 480 sheets, but often consisting of 500 or 516 sheets to allow for wastage; (*fig.*) (*pl.*) great mass of writing or paper. [OFr.].

REAP [rēp], *v.t. and i.* to cut down (corn) with a sickle or reaping-machine; cut down the grain from; obtain by reaping; (*fig.*) receive as a reward or the fruits of some action or behaviour; (*fig.*) receive. REAPING-HOOK, sickle, tool used in reaping. [OE.].

REAPER [rē′per], *n.* one who reaps; machine for reaping.

REAPPEAR [rē-a-pēer′], *v.i.* to appear again, after having disappeared for a time. REAPPEARANCE, *n.* a fresh appearance.

REAR (1) [rēer], *n.* that which is behind; that part of an army, procession etc. which comes last in order, or which follows behind the rest; back part of anything; place or position behind; (*slang*) latrine; **in the r.,** behind the rest; from behind; **to bring up the r.,** to come at the end. REAR (2), *adj.* back, hind. [~ARREAR].

REAR (3), *v.t.* to raise, lift; breed, grow; nourish; *v.i.* to rise up on the hind legs. [OE.].

REAR-ADMIRAL [rēer-ad′mi-ral], *n.* rank in the British Navy between captain and vice-admiral.

REAR-GUARD [rēer′gahd], *n.* body of troops marching in the rear of an army, and protecting it from

---

ōō is pronounced as in food; ŏŏ as in hood; th as in think; TH as in that; zh as in azure. ~ = related to.

attacks from behind, *esp.* when retreating; **r. action**, engagement fought by the r. to assist and protect the retreat of the main body.

REARWARD (1) [rēer'werd], *n.* rear part or position. REARWARD (2), *adj. and adv.* in or towards the rear.

REASON (1) [rē'zon], *n.* that power of the mind by which we think, deduce conclusions or draw valid inferences from facts; sanity; logical motive or justification for saying or doing a particular thing; cause or series of circumstances etc. producing a particular result; that which is according to logic, common sense, logical argument, sensible thought or behaviour; **it stands to r.**, it is obvious or only to be expected; **to have neither rhyme nor r.**, to be sheer nonsense. REASON (2), *v.t.* to base on r.; persuade by reasoning (with *into* or *out of*); examine or discuss in a sensible manner; *v.i.* to exercise the faculty of r., think logically, make (sound) judgments; argue, debate, think. [OFr. from L.].

REASONABLE [rē'zo-na-bl], *adj.* fair, just, moderate; in accordance with reason; exercising reason, sensible, open to reason; endowed with reason, able to reason.

REASONING (1) [rē'zo-ning], *n.* exercise of the power of reason; method of argumentation. REASONING (2), *adj.* able to reason.

REASSEMBLE [rē-a-sem'bl], *v.t.* to put together again; gather together again; *v.i.* to come or collect together again.

REASSURANCE [rē-a-shōōr'ans], *n.* repeated or renewed assurance, restored confidence; second insurance against loss or damage.

REASSURE [rē-a-shōōr'], *v.t.* to dispel the doubts, fears, anxieties of etc., give fresh confidence to; insure a second time against loss or damage. REASSURING, *adj.* comforting, restoring courage and hope, renewing confidence.

REAUMUR, Réaumur [rā-ō-mur'], *adj.* relating to Réaumur or the thermometric scale he invented, in which the freezing-point is zero degrees and the boiling-point eighty degrees. [R. A. F. de *Réaumur*, French physicist.].

REAVE, REIVE (*pret. and p.pt.* **reft**) [rēv], *v.t. and i.* to plunder, seize unlawfully. [OE.].

REBATE [rē'bāt], *n.* deduction, discount from the full price; a repayment. [Fr.].

REBEL (1) [re'bel], *n.* one who defies legally established authority, *esp.* one who revolts against a lawful government; person who resists control or convention, insubordinate, untractable person. REBEL (2), *adj.* in revolt, rebellious; of, pertaining to, rebels. REBEL (3) (*pres.pt.* REBELLING, *pret. and p.pt.* REBELLED) [ri-bel'], *v.i.* to revolt, rise in arms and seek to overthrow the lawful government or ruler; feel repugnance, resist, react against. [Fr. from L.].

REBELLION [ri-bel'yun], *n.* armed insurrection against, or open resistance to, lawfully established authority, state of revolt; unconcealed resistance to some form of control. [L.].

REBELLIOUS [ri-bel'yōōs], *adj.* engaged in rebellion; insubordinate; characterized by rebellion; belonging to, connected with, rebels or rebellion.

REBORE (1) [rē-baw(r)'], *v.t.* to bore again; provide (the cylinder of an internal combustion engine) with a fresh bore. REBORE (2), *n.* act of reboring; process of being rebored.

REBOUND (1) [rē-bownd'], *v.i.* to bound back after striking some hard resisting surface; come back (upon); recoil. REBOUND (2) [rē'bownd], *n.* act or process of rebounding, resilience; (*fig.*) reaction of feeling. [OFr.].

REBOUND (3) [rē-bownd'], *adj.* provided with a new binding.

REBUFF (1) [ri-buf'], *n.* a sudden sharp check, snub, point-blank refusal to an offer or to advances; set-back to hopes of progress. REBUFF (2), *v.t.* to check, snub, repel severely. [OFr.].

REBUKE (1) [ri-byōōk'], *v.t.* to reprove, express disapproval of. REBUKE (2), *n.* reproof, reprimand, censure. REBUKINGLY, *adv.* by way of r. [AFr.].

REBUS [rē'bus], *n.* puzzle in which combinations of figures, pictures, letters etc. represent a word or phrase. [L.].

REBUT (*pres.pt.* **rebutting**, *pret. and p.pt.* **rebutted**) [ri-but'], *v.t.* to refute, disprove; (*leg.*) oppose, show to be false, by argument, plea or other counteracting proof. REBUTTAL, *n.* act of refuting; production of evidence in refutation of a previous statement made in a legal trial. REBUTTER, *n.* (*leg.*) reply of a defendant to a plaintiff's rejoinder. [AFr.].

RECALCITRANT [ri-kal'si-trant], *adj.* refractory,

refusing to submit to control or discipline. RECALCITRANCE, *n.* condition of being r., r. nature or conduct. [L.].

RECALL (1) [ri-kawl'], *v.t.* to call back, summon or order to return; remember; cause to remember; revive, restore; revoke, annul, rescind. RECALL (2), *n.* message, order or invitation to return; (*milit.*) signal to return to camp or to a certain place; reversal or annulment.

RECANT [ri-kant'], *v.t. and i.* to retract, renounce as being wrong, *esp.* applied to religious doctrines when formally repudiated in public. RECANTATION, [rē-kan-tā'shn], *n.* act of recanting, formal repudiation. [L.].

RECAPITULATE [rē-ka-pi'tyōō-lāt], *v.t.* to go over again briefly, by way of summary, the principal facts, points or arguments of. RECAPITULATORY, *adj.* repeating in a condensed form, summarizing. [L.].

RECAPITULATION [rē-ka-pi-tyōō-lā'shn], *n.* act of recapitulating; summary of the principal points. [L.].

RECAST (1) [rē-kahst'], *v.t.* to cast again, mould in a new form; plan again, reconstruct; (of a play) provide with a fresh cast; cause to play a different part. RECAST (2), *n.* act of recasting; state of being r.; that which is r.

RECEDE [ri-sēd'], *v.i.* to move backwards or to a more distant position; slope backwards; fade away into the background; retreat, suffer a decline, slump slightly. [L.].

RECEIPT (1) [ri-sēt'], *n.* act of receiving; fact of being received; amount received (*usually in pl.*); written acknowledgement of anything received, *esp.* of money received in payment, or of goods received; recipe. RECEIPT (2), *v.t.* to give a r. for, affix a r. to. [AFr.].

RECEIVE [ri-sēv'], *v.t.* to acquire, take as being offered, sent, due or dealt; accept; contain, harbour; support, take; admit to one's presence; welcome formally and individually as a guest; treat, welcome; acknowledge as true or valid; *v.i.* to accept, acquire; (*eccles.*) consume part of the consecrated elements; entertain visitors; (*tennis, fives etc.*) (stand ready to) return the service; **to r. the sacrament**, to partake of the consecrated elements in the Eucharist. RECEIVED, *adj.* generally recognized or admitted as true; standard, correct, generally accepted as proper. [AFr. from L.].

RECEIVER [ri-sē'ver], *n.* one who receives; (*leg.*) person appointed by law to receive money due, administer the property of a bankrupt, infant etc., or property of which the ownership is in dispute; person who receives stolen goods; that which receives, vessel to hold anything; earpiece of a telephone; apparatus which detects and rectifies electro-magnetic waves in a radio set; radio receiving set; **Official R.**, officer of the bankruptcy court who takes possession of the debtor's assets when the receiving order is made. RECEIVERSHIP, *n.* office, or term of office, of an Official R.

RECEIVING (1) [ri-sē'ving], *n.* act of one who receives; crime of receiving goods known to have been stolen. RECEIVING (2), *adj.* that receives, intended to receive; **r. order**, official order to appoint a person to administer an estate in bankruptcy.

RECENSION [ri-sen'shn], *n.* critical revision of a text; text so revised. [L.].

RECENT [rē'sent], *adj.* of late origin or occurrence, new, fresh. [L.].

RECEPTACLE [ri-sep'ta-kl], *n.* that which contains or receives anything, vessel, container; (*bot.*) apex of the peduncle; axis in certain forms of inflorescence; axis bearing the reproductive organs in ferns, mosses etc. [L.].

RECEPTION [ri-sep'shn], *n.* act of receiving, state of being received; formal and official welcoming of persons as guests; occasion for such a welcoming; manner of receiving or greeting anyone or anything; acceptance; process of absorption by the mind; **r. area**, district considered to be suitable for r. of evacuees in wartime; **r. order**, order for the detention of a lunatic in an asylum; **r. room**, room in which visitors may be received, distinct from bedrooms etc. RECEPTIONIST, *n.* one employed to receive people, *esp.* visitors or clients, and to book appointments. [L.].

RECEPTIVE [ri-sep'tiv], *adj.* able to receive, susceptible to ideas or impressions. [MedL.].

RECEPTOR [ri-sep'ter], *n.* (*psych.*) (*usually attrib.*)

organ of sense which receives impressions. [L.].

RECESS (1) [ri-ses'], *n.* cessation from work, suspension of business, *esp.* of Parliament or of a court of law; (*U.S.*) vacation; place of retirement; secluded spot; hollowed space, alcove or part set back in a wall; indentation in a coastline. RECESS (2), *v.t.* to make a r. in; set in a r. RECESSION, *n.* act of withdrawing from a place; act of receding; (*econ.*) a slackening of trade and industry. [L.].

RECESSIONAL (1) [ri-se'shn-al], *adj.* pertaining to a recession of choir and clergy after a service; pertaining to a recess of Parliament. RECESSIONAL (2), *n.* hymn sung during the recession of choir and clergy.

RECESSIVE [ri-se'siv], *adj.* receding, tending to recede; (*biol.*) (of a characteristic) tending to be replaced in the offspring by the dominant trait of the other parent.

RECHARGE [rē-chahj'], *v.t. and i.* to reload.

RECHAUFFE, réchauffé [rā-shō'fā], *n.* rehash. [Fr.].

RECHERCHE, recherché [re-shāer'shā], *adj.* choice, rare, carefully chosen. [Fr.].

RECIDIVIST [ri-si'di-vist], *n.* an habitual and incorrigible criminal, one who continually relapses into crime. RECIDIVISM, *n.* habitual indulgence in, or relapse into, crime. [Fr.].

RECIPE [re'si-pi], *n.* list of ingredients and quantities to be used, with instructions for their preparation into a food or drink; remedy, means of acquiring and maintaining. [L.].

RECIPIENT (1) [ri-si'pi-ent], *adj.* receiving, receptive. RECIPIENT (2), *n.* one who receives. [L.].

RECIPROCAL (1) [ri-si'pro-kal], *adj.* shared or experienced equally by each of two parties for the other, mutual, felt or done in return for some similar thing received; complementary, (*gram.*) inversely equivalent or corresponding; (*gram.*) expressing mutual relationship; (*gram.*) reflexive; (*log.*) mutually convertible; **r. ratio**, (*math.*) ratio between the reciprocals of two quantities. RECIPROCAL (2), *n.* that which is complementary, counterpart; (*math.*) result of dividing unity by a given number or quantity, the r. of 8 being ⅛. RECIPROCALITY [ri-si-pro-ka'li-ti], *n.* state or property of being r. [L.].

RECIPROCATE [ri-si'pro-kāt], *v.t.* to give and take, exchange mutually; cause to move backwards and forwards in a straight line; (*math.*) determine the reciprocal to; *v.i.* (of a piston or machinery) alternate, move backwards and forwards in a straight line; make a similar gesture, act reciprocally; (*math.*) change by reciprocation. RECIPROCATING, *adj.* moving alternately backwards and forwards along a straight line. [~L.].

RECIPROCATION [ri-si-pro-kā'shn], *n.* act of reciprocating, reciprocal interchange of acts, mutual exchange; motion backwards and forwards along a straight line. [L.].

RECIPROCITY [re-si-pro'si-ti], *n.* state of being reciprocal; mutual giving and taking between two parties, equal rights and benefits which are mutually granted, *esp.* in trading and commercial relations.

RECITAL [ri-si'tal], *n.* act of reciting; that which is recited, account, rehearsal or enumeration of a number of things, happenings etc., narrative, tale; musical performance by a single vocal or instrumental artist, or devoted to the works of a single composer or a single period; (*leg.*) formal statement of facts in a legal or official document, the part containing this.

RECITATION [re-si-tā'shn], *n.* act of reciting; the speaking in public of a composition or extract previously learnt by heart; passage or composition chosen to be recited. [L.].

RECITATIVE (1) [re-si-ta-tēv'], *n.* kind of declamatory singing in opera or oratorio, as a means of expressing narrative and dialogue musically; passages sung in this way. RECITATIVE (2) [re'si-ta-tiv], *adj.* of the nature of, in the form of, r. [It.].

RECITE [ri-sit'], *v.t.* to repeat aloud from memory; relate, give a verbal account of; (*leg.*) state in a deed or document; *v.i.* to repeat aloud in public pieces of poetry or prose previously learnt by heart. RECITER, *n.* one who recites; narrator; book containing selections for recitation. [L.].

RECK [rek], *v.t. and i.* (*poet.*) to care, be concerned about; be aware of; (*impers.*) concern, trouble. [OE.].

RECKLESS [rek'les], *adj.* not caring at all, without consideration. [OE.].

RECKON [re'kon], *v.t.* to count up, calculate; include, class; regard, judge; think; *v.i.* to calculate, count; guess, suppose; **to r. on**, to rely on, count on; **to r. with**, to have to deal with, take into account.

RECKONER, *n.* one who reckons; book of calculations; ready reckoner.

RECKONING [re'ko-ning], *n.* act of one who reckons; act of counting or calculating; statement of accounts or charges, bill; (*naut.*) calculation of a ship's position from the account of the ship's course and progress in a log-book, or observation of the sun or stars; **day of r.**, day on which all accounts must be paid, settling day; Judgment Day.

RECLAIM [ri-klām'], *v.t.* to claim back; reform; recover from the sea or from being waste land. [OFr.].

RECLAMATION [re-kla-mā'shn], *n.* act of bringing back from error or wrongdoing; act of bringing waste land under cultivation; act of protesting. [L.].

RECLAME, réclame [rā-klahm'], *n.* notoriety and the art of achieving it, self-publicity. [Fr.].

RECLINE [ri-klin'], *v.i.* to lie down, rest leaning back upon something. [L.].

RECLUSE [ri-klōōs'], *n.* one who lives in seclusion; hermit or monk who confines himself to a cell. [Fr.].

RECOGNITION [re-kog-ni'shn], *n.* act of recognizing; state of being recognized; acknowledgment as being lawful, valid or authentic; notice, appreciation; fact of identifying a person or thing as being a particular person or thing, or as being the same as someone or something previously known; formal admission of a new status of a country or state. [L.].

RECOGNIZANCE [ri-kog'ni-zans, ri-ko'ni-zans], *n.* (*leg.*) obligation, entered into before a court of record, to keep some guarantee, as to appear before the court on a certain date, keep the peace, pay a debt etc. in default of which a sum of money is to be forfeited; sum of money to be thus forfeited [OFr.].

RECOGNIZE [re'kog-niz], *v.t.* to perceive by the senses as being a particular person or thing previously known; give sign of recognition of by greeting etc.; admit as lawful, valid or authentic; accept as being true or as a fact; appreciate or acknowledge in some tangible way; acknowledge formally as possessing a certain status or rank. [L.].

RECOIL (1) [ri-koil'], *v.i.* to fall or draw back, retreat; stagger back; rebound, spring back; (of a gun) kick; shrink from; **to r. from**, to feel disgust and loathing at; **to r. on**, to affect the one responsible. RECOIL (2), *n.* act of rebounding or springing back, *esp.* the rebound of a gun when fired; a shrinking away from. [OFr.].

RECOLLECT [re-ko-lekt'], *v.t.* to remember, call to mind again. RECOLLECTIVE, *adj.* having the power of recollecting, that recollects. [*Next*].

RE-COLLECT [rē-ko-lekt'], *v.t.* to collect again, gather together again, rally. [L.].

RECOLLECTION [re-ko-lek'shn], *n.* act of recollecting; memory; that which is recollected.

RECOMMEND [re-ko-mend'], *v.t.* to commend to favour, speak favourably of, as suitable for a certain use or for a particular position; entrust to the care or keeping of another; counsel, advise. RECOMMENDATORY, *adj.* that recommends, serving to recommend. [MedL.].

RECOMMENDATION [re-ko-men-dā'shn], *n.* act of recommending; that which recommends; qualifications serving to recommend a person to the favour of another; letter or document requesting a favourable or kind reception for a person.

RECOMMIT [*pres.pt.* recommitting, *pret. and p.pt.* recommitted) [rē-ko-mit'], *v.t.* to commit again; (*parl.*) refer (a bill) again to committee. RECOMMITTAL, *n.* second commitment; (*parl.*) a referring back of a bill to a committee.

RECOMPENSE (1) [re'kom-pens], *v.t.* to requite, repay; compensate for some wrong, loss or injury undergone. RECOMPENSE (2), *n.* that which is given or done in order to r., reward, compensation, reparation. [LL.].

RECONCILABLE [re'kon-si-la-bl], *adj.* able to be reconciled.

RECONCILE [re'kon-sil], *v.t.* (often followed by *to* or *with*) to restore to friendship, cause to be friends (after a quarrel or estrangement); make compatible with; settle, adjust; (*v. reflex.*) acquiesce in. [L.].

RECONCILIATION [re-kon-si-li-ā'shn], *n.* act of reconciling persons at variance or things which seem to be opposed; state of being reconciled.

RECONDITE [re'kon-dīt, ri-kon'dīt], *adj.* abstruse; profound; dealing in abstruse matters. [L.].

RECONDITION [rē-kon-di'shn], *v.t.* to put into fresh condition, renovate, refit, repair.

ōō is pronounced as in food; ŏŏ as in hood; th as in *think*; TH as in *that*; zh as in azure. ~ = related to.

RECONNAISSANCE [ri-ko'ni-sans], *n.* act of reconnoitring; (*milit.*) detailed investigation of a region in order to find out its general characteristics and resources, the strength, position and movements of the enemy etc.; a survey preliminary to practical or scientific operations. [Fr.].

RECONNOITRE [re-ko-noi'ter], *v.t.* to examine, explore, survey by way of reconnaissance; view, inspect; *v.i.* to make a reconnaissance. [OFr.].

RECONSIDER [rē-kon-si'der], *v.t.* to consider again with a view to changing or modifying.

RECONSTITUTE [rē-kon'sti-tyōōt], *v.t.* to constitute afresh; reconstruct, reform. RECONSTITUTION [rē-kon-sti-tyōō'shn], *n.* act of constituting afresh.

RECONSTRUCT [rē-kon-strukt'], *v.t.* to construct again; rebuild, *esp.* to build up into what one supposes is the original form. RECONSTRUCTION, *n.* act of constructing again; that which is reconstructed.

RECORD (1) [ri-kawd'], *v.t.* to register, keep a record of, set down in writing; preserve in a permanent fashion; make a gramophone record of; to give (a vote, record); *v.i.* to make gramophone records. RECORD (2) [re'kawd], *n.* official note of any fact, copy of any writing, or authentic account of any proceeding or event, preserved in writing; an authentic representation of something past; circular disk which, when played on a gramophone or similar instrument, reproduces musical and other sounds; unique phenomenon or feat, best performance of the kind yet accomplished; (*leg.*) written statements or pleadings of parties in a litigation, written copy of the evidence and judgment of a lawsuit; (*fig.*) known facts of a person's ability or character as determined by previous actions; **on r.,** known, *esp.* from documentary evidence; **off the r.,** (*coll.*) in confidence, not to be put on the r. [OFr.].

RECORDER [ri-kaw'der], *n.* one who records in writing, judge presiding at the court of Quarter-Sessions of a borough or city; that which records, apparatus or instrument for recording sounds or signals; ancient form of flute.

RECORDING (1) [ri-kaw'ding], *n.* a record. RECORDING (2), *adj.* registering, that records.

RECOUNT (1) [rē'kownt], *n.* a second count. RECOUNT (2) [rē-kownt'], *v.t.* to count over again.

RECOUNT (3) [ri-kownt'], *v.t.* to narrate, recite, relate in detail. [AFr.].

RECOUP [ri-kōōp'], *v.t.* to compensate, make good, indemnify. [Fr.].

RECOURSE [ri-kaws'], *n.* resorting to a person, thing or action for help or assistance. [Fr.].

RE-COVER [rē-ku'ver], *v.t.* to provide with a new cover.

RECOVER [ri-ku'ver], *v.t.* to get back, regain; make good, retrieve; reclaim; (*leg.*) get possession of again by judgment, obtain by way of compensation; (*reflex.*) regain one's balance, composure etc.; *v.i.* to regain health after sickness or injury; win back a former position or state; (*comm.*) (of shares etc.) improve after a drop; (*leg.*) succeed in a lawsuit involving a claim; (*fencing*) resume a defensive position after attacking. [OFr.].

RECOVERY [ri-ku've-ri], *n.* act of recovering; the regaining of what has been lost or taken away; restoration to health or to a former position; (*leg.*) the obtaining of something by a judgment in one's favour in a court of law. [AFr.].

RECREANT (1) [re'kri-ant], *adj.* cowardly, craven; apostate, false to one's faith or duty. RECREANT (2), *n.* coward; one who is false to his duty or principles. RECREANCY, *n.* cowardly yielding. [OFr.].

RE-CREATE [rē-kri-āt'], *v.t.* to create or form afresh. RE-CREATION [rē-kri-ā'shn], *n.* a forming anew; fresh creation.

RECREATE [re'kri-āt], *v.t. and i.* to refresh.

RECREATION [re-kri-ā'shn], *n.* refreshment of the body and mind after toil by taking part in some form of pleasurable voluntary activity; act of refreshing the mind and body in this way; amusement, entertainment, sport etc.; **r. ground,** playground, enclosed space set apart for outdoor games. [L.].

RECREATIVE [re'kri-ā-tiv], *adj.* providing recreation, tending to divert and refresh.

RECREMENT [re'kri-ment], *n.* superfluous matter separated from what is useful, dross, refuse, scum; (*physiol.*) waste products of the body, excretion; a fluid given out from the blood and later absorbed into it again. [L.].

RECRIMINATION [ri-kri-mi-nā'shn], *n.* the replying to one accusation with another, counter-charge to an accusation. RECRIMINATIVE, RECRIMINATORY [ri-kri'mi-na-tiv, ri-kri'mi-nā-te-ri], *adj.* employing, of the nature of, consisting of, r. [~MedL.].

RECRUDESCE [rē-krōō-des'], *v.i.* to recur. RECRUDESCENT, *adj.* breaking out afresh with renewed activity. [L.].

RECRUDESCENCE [rē-krōō-de'sens], *n.* a fresh outbreak, renewed activity, act or state of breaking out again (of a disease, epidemic etc.).

RECRUIT (1) [ri-krōōt'], *n.* newly enlisted person in the navy, army, air force, police force etc.; (*fig.*) one who has recently joined a movement, organization etc. RECRUIT (2), *v.t.* to seek or enlist reinforcements of (persons) for the navy, army, air force etc.; supply (a regiment etc.) with new men; restore, revive (health, strength etc.); *v.i.* to seek or enlist recruits or new members; (*rare*) recover health. [Fr.].

RECTAL [rek'tal], *adj.* of, or pertaining to, the rectum. RECTALLY, *adv.* through the rectum.

RECTANGLE [rek'tang-gl], *n.* plane, four-sided figure whose interior angles are right angles. [LL.].

RECTANGULAR [rek-tang'gyōō-ler], *adj.* right-angled; having the shape of a rectangle.

RECTIFICATION [rek-ti-fi-kā'shn], *n.* act of rectifying or putting right; a correction; (*chem.*) refinement or purification by repeated distillation; (*elect.*) conversion of an alternating current into a direct current. [L.].

RECTIFIER [rek'ti-fī-er], *n.* one who, or that which, rectifies; one who refines spirits by repeated distillations, apparatus used in this process; (*elect.*) apparatus or valve for transforming an alternating current into a direct current.

RECTIFY [rek'ti-fī], *v.t.* to put right, correct; remedy, reform; refine by repeated distillation; adjust, set right (an instrument etc.); (*elect.*) transform (an alternating current) into a direct current. RECTIFIED, *adj.* put right; re-distilled, purified (of spirit). [LL.].

RECTILINEAL [rek-ti-li'ni-al], *adj.* rectilinear.

RECTILINEAR [rek-ti-li'ni-er], *adj.* in a straight line, bounded by straight lines. [LL.].

RECTITUDE [rek'ti-tyōōd], *n.* rightness of principle or conduct, uprightness, integrity. [L.].

RECTO [rek'tō], *n.* right-hand page of an open book; front, as opposed to the back, of a page. [L.].

RECTOR [rek'ter], *n.* (*eccles.*) priest holding a parish benefice who has the right to its great tithes; head of a continental university; head of various English and Scottish colleges and similar institutions; **Lord R.,** in Scottish universities, president of the University Court, elected by the students. [L.].

RECTORY [rek'te-ri], *n.* benefice of which the holder is a rector; house in which the rector of a parish lives. [MedL.].

RECTUM [rek'tum], *n.* the final bottom section of the large intestine. [L.].

RECUMBENCY [ri-kum'ben-si], *n.* state of being recumbent, reclining position.

RECUMBENT [ri-kum'bent], *adj.* reclining, reposing, lying down.

RECUPERATE [ri-kyōō'pe-rāt], *v.t.* to restore to health; *v.i.* to recover health and strength; recover from monetary losses. RECUPERATIVE, *adj.* that recuperates or tends to r., having the power to r.

RECUPERATION [ri-kyōō-pe-rā'shn], *n.* recovery, *esp.* of health.

RECUR (*pres.pt.* **recurring**, *pret. and p.pt.* **recurred**) [ri-kur'], *v.i.* to repeat itself; return to the mind; refer back, return; (*math.*) be repeated indefinitely. RECURRING, *adj.* returning, *esp.* periodically, occurring again repeatedly; (*math.*) repeated indefinitely. [L.].

RECURRENCE [ri-ku'rens], *n.* act of recurring, return, repeated occurrence; resort, recourse.

RECURRENT [ri-ku'rent], *adj.* returning, *esp.* from time to time, occurring again or repeatedly.

RECUSANCY [re'kyōō-zan-si], *n.* refusal to attend the Church of England for public religious worship (*esp.* applied to Roman Catholics); refusal to obey authority.

RECUSANT (1) [re'kyōō-zant], *n.* one who refuses to attend the Established Church for public religious worship, applied *esp.* to Roman Catholics in the 17th century; one who refuses to obey authority. RECUSANT (2), *adj.* refusing to conform to state authority, *esp.* in religious matters. [L.].

RED (1) [red], *adj.* being of the primary colour red; inflamed, bloodshot; ruddy; (*pol.*) pertaining or belonging to the Communist Party or extreme left wing; **r. admiral,** a brightly coloured butterfly;

The accent ′ after a syllable = stress (u-pon′). The mark ‾ over a vowel = length (ā in made; ō in bone).

r. rag, anything which arouses anger; r. ribbon, ribbon which denotes membership of the Order of the Bath or the Legion of Honour; r. spider, a harvest mite; to paint the town r., to indulge in drunken riotous behaviour; to see r., to become violently angry. RED-BLOODED, (*fig.*) vigorous, lusty. RED-HEAD, *n.* person with r. hair. RED (2), *n.* a primary colour of long wavelength forming one of the extremes of the visible spectrum; various objects of this colour, the r. ball at billiards, the r. colour in roulette; a Communist, leftist; in the r., (*slang*) overdrawn at a bank. [OE.].

REDACT [ri-dakt′], *v.t.* to arrange or reduce to a form suitable for publication, edit. REDACTOR, *n.* editor. [L.].

REDACTION [ri-dak′shn], *n.* act of editing or arranging in a form suitable for publication; edition.

REDBREAST [red′brest], *n.* the European robin.

REDCAP [red′kap], *n.* goldfinch; goblin; (*coll.*) military policeman; (*U.S. coll.*) railway porter.

RED CROSS [red-kros′], *n.* the Geneva cross, badge of the ambulance and hospital service organized under the Geneva Convention; a society organized in accordance with the Geneva Convention, 1864, to provide an ambulance and hospital service for those wounded in war; a red cross on a white background, the national emblem of England.

RED CURRANT [red-ku′rant], *n.* the currant *Ribes rubrum*; fruit of this plant.

RED DEER [red-dēer′], *n.* species of brown-coloured deer, the largest native British deer.

REDDEN [re′den], *v.t.* to make red; *v.i.* to grow or become red; blush.

REDE † (1) [rēd], *v.t.* to counsel, advise; guess. REDE † (2), *n.* counsel, advice; scheme, plan; tale, proverb. [OE.].

REDEEM [ri-dēm′], *v.t.* to purchase back; free (a mortgaged thing), obtain again by paying the stipulated sum; regain or recover by diligence and effort; fulfil; make atonement for; compensate for; ransom, set free; (*theol.*) deliver from the bondage of sin and its penalties. [L.].

REDEEMER [ri-dē′mer], *n.* one who redeems or ransoms; the Saviour, Jesus Christ.

REDEMPTION [ri-demp′shn], *n.* a buying back; release or restoration of mortgaged or pledged property; the clearing off of a debt by payment of a lump sum; ransom, deliverance of slaves by making a payment; act of delivering from evil ways; (*theol.*) deliverance of sinners from the penalty and bondage of sin; act of freeing or recovery of anything; atonement for wrong done; that which redeems: **beyond r.**, without hope of recovery or reformation. RE-DEMPTIVE, *adj.* pertaining to r., that redeems. [L.].

RED ENSIGN [red-en′sīn, -′sin], *n.* flag of the British merchant service.

RED FLAG [red-flag′], *n.* signal of danger; symbol of revolution and of communism; name of a song sung by political parties of the left.

RED-HANDED [red-han′did], *adj.* in the very act of doing something wrong.

RED HEAT [red-hēt′], *n.* state or temperature at which a thing is red hot.

RED HERRING [red-he′ring], *n.* herring cured and made red by smoking; (*fig.*) point, topic or thing introduced to divert attention from the real matter at issue, and set people on a false trail.

RED HOT [red-hot′], *adj.* heated to redness; (*slang*) fresh and of a sensational nature; (of dance music) highly syncopated, and full of elaborate rhythm and solo passages for various instruments; r. poker, a garden plant resembling this.

RED INDIAN [red-in′di-an], *n.* one of, a descendant of, the aboriginal inhabitants of North America.

REDINTEGRATE [re-din′ti-grāt], *v.t.* to make whole again, restore to a unified or perfect state. REDINTEGRATION [re-din-ti-grā′shn], *n.* renovation, restoration to a whole or sound state, renewal. [L.].

REDIRECT [rē-di-rekt′], *v.t.* to readdress; direct afresh. REDIRECTION [rē-di-rek′shn], *n.* a fresh direction; act of readdressing.

REDISTRIBUTE [rē-dis-tri′byōōt], *v.t.* to distribute again or in a fresh way. REDISTRIBUTION [rē-dis-tri-byōō′shn], *n.* a fresh or different distribution; (*parl.*) rearrangement of the size and limits of parliamentary constituencies.

RED LAMP [red-lamp′], *n.* (sign of) a brothel.

RED LEAD [red-led′], *n.* the red oxide of lead, P_3bO_4, used as a pigment.

RED-LETTER [red-le′ter], *adj.* marked by a red letter, as a principal saint's day or church festival in a

calendar; a r. day, principal saint's day or church festival; (*fig.*) an auspicious, memorable day.

RED LIGHT [red-līt′], *n.* a light shining through red glass; danger signal; (sign of) a brothel; r. district, brothel quarter of a town.

RED MULLET [red-mu′let], *n.* an edible sea-fish whose flesh has a reddish tinge.

RED OCHRE [red-ō′ker], *n.* ruddle, a substance used as a colouring pigment.

REDOLENCE [re′dō-lens], *n.* sweetness of scent, fragrance, perfume. [OFr.].

REDOLENT [re′dō-lent], *adj.* diffusing a pleasant scent, sweet-smelling, fragrant; (*fig.*) r. of, suggesting the presence of, reminiscent of. [L.].

REDOUBLE [rē-du′bl], *v.t.* to double again, increase to approximately twice as much (penalties at cards) as a double; renew; *v.i.* to become twice as much; become greater; (*bridge*) double a bid already doubled.

REDOUBT [ri-dowt′], *n.* (*fort.*) small temporary fort or field-work. [Fr.].

REDOUBTABLE [ri-dow′ta-bl], *adj.* formidable, to be feared. [Fr.].

REDOUND [ri-downd′], *v.i.* to conduce, contribute as a result; recoil, react (upon). [L.].

REDPOLL [red′pōl], *n.* one of three species of linnets with red heads; one of a breed of red-haired hornless cattle.

RE-DRESS [rē-dres′], *v.t.* to dress again or in different clothes; put fresh dressings on.

REDRESS (1) [ri-dres′], *v.t.* to set right, remedy, rectify; adjust (balance of); compensate, obtain reparation for (a person). REDRESS (2), *n.* act of redressing; reparation, compensation for a loss or injury. [Fr.].

REDSHANK [red′shangk], *n.* the sandpiper.

REDSKIN [red′skin], *n.* North American Indian.

REDSTART [red′staht], *n.* a migratory warbler allied to the thrush. [OE.].

RED TAPE [red-tāp′], *n.* pink tape used in tying up official documents; (*fig.*) excessive attention to the formality of official routine, often resulting in unnecessary delay; official rules and methods of procedure which must be complied with.

REDUCE [ri-dyōōs′], *v.t.* to diminish, make smaller or fewer; lower in rank or position; bring into some unpleasant condition; weaken, impair; bring into a simpler form, break down or convert into a different form; bring into classes or under rules; subdue, bring into subjection; (*surg.*) restore to its original position (a fracture etc.); (*arith.*) change from one denominator into a lower; *v.i.* to get rid of superfluous fat, slim; **reduced circumstances,** comparative poverty; to r. to the ranks, (*milit.*) to degrade an officer or non-commissioned officer for misconduct to the rank of private soldier. REDUCER, *n.* one who, or that which, reduces; (*phot.*) substance used to r. the contrast or density of negatives; something which reduces weight. [L.].

REDUCTION [ri-duk′shn], *n.* act of reducing; state of being reduced; shortening, lessening; subjugation; conversion into a different or simpler form; (*arith.*) changing numbers from one denominator into a lower or from a different denominator into a common denominator; (*surg.*) replacement of a displaced part. [L.].

REDUNDANCE, REDUNDANCY [ri-dun′dans- (-i)], *n.* state or quality of being redundant; that which is redundant, superfluity. [L.].

REDUNDANT [ri-dun′dant], *adj.* superfluous, excessive, unnecessary; prolix; copious, plentiful. [L.].

REDUPLICATE [ri-dyōō′pli-kāt], *v.t.* to redouble, repeat; (*gram.*) form (a tense) by repeating the initial syllable or letter; *v.i.* to undergo reduplication. REDUPLICATION [ri-dyōō-pli-kā′shn], *n.* act of reduplicating; that which is produced by reduplicating; (*gram.*) repetition of the first syllable to form a new tense etc.; example of this. REDUPLICATIVE [ri-dyōō′pli-ka-tiv], *adj.* that reduplicates or tends to r.; (*gram.*) formed by reduplication. [L.].

REDWOOD [red′wōōd], *n.* name for trees producing red timber, *esp.* trees of the genus *Sequoia,* which grow to a great height; red timber.

RE-ECHO [rē-e′kō], *v.i.* to echo back, reverberate.

REED (1) [rēd], *n.* an aquatic grass with a long jointed stem, growing along banks of lakes, rivers etc.; single straight stem of one of these plants; (*poet.*) arrow; musical pipe made from the stem of a reed; (*mus.*) thin slip of reed cane or metal in the mouthpiece of certain wind-instruments and vibrated by a column

---

ōō is pronounced as in food; ŏŏ as in hood; th as in think; TH as in that; zh as in azure. ~ = related to.

of air from the mouth of the player, similar device in an organ pipe or bagpipe; musical wind-instrument of this type; (*arch.*) one of a series of mouldings like a group of reeds laid side by side; (*fig.*) pastoral poetry; **broken r.**, person who fails to give support when needed. REED-BUNTING, a waterside bird. REED-MACE, the cat's-tail, erroneously called the bulrush, having a tall stem with a club-shaped cluster of small brownish flowers. REED-PIPE, organ pipe fitted with a r.; musical pipe made of a r. REED-WARBLER, -WREN, a bird, *Acrocephalus streperus*. REED (2), *v.t.* to thatch with r.; ornament with r. moulding; (*mus.*) fit reeds to. REEDY, *adj.* abounding in reeds; (of a pipe) made of reeds; long and slender; thin and rough in tone like a r. [OE.].

REEF (1) [rēf], *n.* (*naut.*) one of the horizontal portions of a sail which may be taken in to lessen the amount of sail. REEF (2), *v.t.* to reduce the area of (a sail) by folding or rolling up a part; (*fig.*) shorten or draw up. [~OScand.].

REEF (3), *n.* ridge or shelf of rocks, shingle or sand lying at or near the surface of the water; mineral lode or vein. [Du.].

REEFER [rē'fer], *n.* short, thick, double-breasted coat as worn by sailors. [REEF (2)].

REEF-KNOT [rēf'not], *n.* knot used for tying reefs. [REEF (1)].

REEK (1) [rēk], *n.* smoke, vapour; strong unpleasant smell, stench. REEK (2), *v.i.* to emit smoke or vapour, steam, smoke with heat or perspiration; emit a strong disagreeable smell, stink; (*fig.*) be blatantly and offensively filled (with). REEKING, REEKY, *adj.* smoking, steaming, emitting vapour; giving off strong and unpleasant odours. [OE.].

REEL (1) [rēl], *n.* rotatory framework on which thread or silk is wound after being spun; bobbin on which thread or silk is wound ready for use; amount wound on a reel; flattened cylinder on which a length of cinema film is wound; length of film wound on a reel; cylindrical drum on which cable, wire etc. is wound; small cylindrical winch attached to a fishing-rod, for winding the line in or out; **off the r.**, without stopping, in uninterrupted succession. REEL (2), *v.t.* to wind upon a r.; **to r. off,** to rattle off, utter quickly and without stopping; unwind from a r. [OE.].

REEL (3), *n.* lively Scottish square dance in which the couples describe a number of figure eights; music to which this is danced. [Gael.].

REEL (4), *v.i.* to stagger and lurch from side to side; sway and totter under the effects of a blow; be shaken, tremble under some powerful force or shock; whirl round, be in a giddy whirl; (of the mind, brain) lose its equilibrium under some powerful shock or feeling of dizziness. [Uncert.].

RE-ENTER [rē-en'ter], *v.t.* to enter again; (*leg.*) resume possession of (leased property) upon the failure of the lessee to observe the conditions of tenure; *v.i.* to enter again; (*leg.*) resume possession. RE-ENTRY, *n.* act of entering again; (*leg.*) act of resuming possession of leased property.

REEVE (1) [rēv], *n.* (*hist.*) chief magistrate of a district; (*mining*) foreman. [OE.].

REEVE (2) (*pret.* reeved, rove, *p.pt.* reeved, rove, roven), *v.t.* (*naut.*) to pass the end of (a rope) through a hole in a bolt, block etc.; pass the end of a rope through a hole; secure (a rope) in this way. [Du.].

RE-EXPORT (1) [rē-eks-pawt'], *v.t.* to export again; export what has been imported. RE-EXPORT (2) [rē-eks'pawt], *n.* commodity or goods re-exported.

REFECTORY [ri-fek'te-ri], *n.* room where meals are taken, *esp.* in a monastery, college etc. [MedL.].

REFER (*pres.pt.* referring, *pret.* and *p.pt.* referred) [ri-fur'], *v.t.* to attribute, assign; pass on, seek for information or further consideration, submit for decision; **to r. to,** to have recourse to, appeal to; allude to, indicate; relate to, be concerned with; **to r. back,** to defer a decision on a meeting until after consultation with the bodies from which delegates receive their mandates. [L.].

REFEREE (1) [re-fe-rē'], *n.* one to whom something is referred, *esp.* an arbitrator; (*games*) umpire or person in charge of a football match, boxing contest etc. REFEREE (2), *v.t.* and *i.* to act as r. for (a sporting contest).

REFERENCE [re'fe-rens], *n.* act of referring to another person for decision; act of referring to for information; a note as to the source of some particular information mentioned or allusion made; allusion; connexion, relation; person who may be referred to, and who will furnish information as to one's ability, personal character etc. if required; testimonial,

written statement by some responsible person as to the character and abilities of another person; **book of r.,** book to be referred to for some specific information, and not intended to be read straight through; **r. library,** library in which specialized books may be consulted, but from which books are not normally borrowed; **with r. to,** concerning, in regard to. CROSS-REFERENCE, r. in a work to another page or section in that work.

REFERENDUM [re-fe-ren'dum], *n.* the referring of parliamentary or constitutional issues to the general vote of the electorate. [L.].

REFINE [ri-fīn'], *v.t.* to purify, free from impurities, make finer in quality; make polished and cultured, remove traces of coarseness or roughness; *v.i.* to become purified, finer in quality or more polished in manner; affect nicety or subtlety in speech or argument. REFINER, *n.* one who refines, *esp.* one whose occupation is refining; apparatus used in refining.

REFINED [ri-fīnd'], *adj.* made finer in quality, freed from impurities; polished, elegant, cultured.

REFINEMENT [ri-fīn'ment], *n.* act of refining; state or quality of being refined; polish and elegance in manner and speech; example of this; a subtlety something brought to a more perfect or elaborate form.

REFINERY [ri-fī'ne-ri], *n.* place or apparatus for refining substances.

REFIT (1) (*pres.pt.* refitting, *pret.* and *p.pt.* refitted) [rē-fit'], *v.t.* to fit out or prepare again, furnish with fresh equipment and supplies, repair; fit on again; *v.i.* to undergo refitment; take on fresh supplies or equipment. REFIT (2) [rē'fit], REFITMENT, *n.* a fitting out afresh, *esp.* of a ship.

REFLECT [ri-flekt'], *v.t.* to throw back, cause to rebound; give back an image of, mirror; shed, bring upon; (*fig.*) record, express faithfully; *v.i.* to throw back light, heat or sound waves; give back an image or picture of an object facing it; **to r. on,** upon, to ponder over, consider carefully; bring into discredit or reproach; disparage, cast doubt on. REFLECTOR, *n.* that which reflects, a hard polished surface reflecting light, heat, sound or electromagnetic waves, *esp.* in a particular direction. [L.].

REFLECTION, REFLEXION [ri-flek'shn], *n.* act or process of reflecting; that which is reflected, *esp.* an image reflected in a polished surface or mirror; thoughtful consideration, profound thought; (*pl.*) thoughts arising, remarks made, after thinking something over; reproach, censure; intended or implied disparagement; that which casts discredit upon someone. [L.].

REFLECTIVE [ri-flek'tiv], *adj.* that reflects; thoughtful, meditative; exercising reflection; (*gram.*) reflexive.

REFLEX (1) [rē'fleks], *n.* that which is reflected or brought about by reflection, reflection in a polished surface; (*fig.*) a visible expression of some essential feature or fact; (*physiol.*) reflex action, involuntary movement caused by this. REFLEX (2), *adj.* directed back; produced in reaction; **r. action,** involuntary action of a muscle or other organ caused by an impulse or stimulus. [L.].

REFLEXION, see REFLECTION.

REFLEXIVE (1) [ri-flek'siv], *adj.* of the nature of a reflex; (*gram.*) referring back to the subject of a sentence; in which the object of an action is the same as the subject of a verb. REFLEXIVE (2), *n.* a r. verb or pronoun.

REFLUX [rē'fluks], *n.* a flowing back; backward course, ebbing.

RE-FORM (1) [rē-fawm'], *v.t.* to form or arrange again; *v.i.* to assume a new formation; come into formation again.

REFORM (1) [ri-fawm'], *v.t.* to change for the better, improve, amend; cause to lead a better life; *v.i.* to give up one's vices and lead a better life, improve one's conduct. REFORM (2), *n.* a changing for the better, improvement, alleged removal of an abuse or injustice, *esp.* social or political; abandonment of evil ways; **R. Acts,** political measures passed to obtain a wider distribution of the franchise. REFORM-ATIVE, *adj.* that reforms or is intended to r. [L.].

RE-FORMATION [rē-faw-mā'shn], *n.* the forming or arranging again, a fresh formation.

REFORMATION [re-faw-mā'shn], *n.* act of reforming; state of being reformed; change for the better, correction of faults; **the R.,** religious revolt in the 16th century against the R.C. Church and Papacy. [L.].

REFORMATORY (1) [ri-faw'ma-te-ri], *adj.* tending

The accent ´ after a syllable = stress (u-pon´)　　The mark ‾ over a vowel = length (ā in made; ō in bone).

to, intended to, reform. **REFORMATORY** (2), *n.* (formerly) institution to which juvenile criminals were sent to be reformed.

REFORMED [ri-fawmd'], *adj.* that has undergone reform, improved; **R. Church,** the Protestant Church.

REFORMER [ri-faw'mer], *n.* one who reforms; advocate of social or political reform; supporter of the Reform Bill of 1832; one who took a prominent part in the Reformation.

REFRACT [ri-frakt'], *v.t.* to bend (light, heat or sound rays) at an angle as in refraction. **REFRACTING,** *adj.* causing refraction; provided with a device to r. rays; **refracting angle,** angle made by two faces of a prism; **refracting telescope,** telescope in which an object-glass bends the rays of light to bring them into focus. **REFRACTOR,** *n.* that which refracts; refracting telescope. [L.].

REFRACTION [ri-frak'shn], *n.* act of refracting, the bending at an angle, or change of direction, which light, heat or sound waves undergo as they pass from one medium into another of a different density; **angle of r.,** angle made by a ray of light and a line perpendicular to the surface of the medium through which it is passing. **REFRACTIONAL,** *adj.* (*opt.*) of, or pertaining to, or caused by, r.; refractive. [L.].

REFRACTIVE [ri-frak'tiv], *adj.* that refracts, refracting; pertaining to, caused by, refraction.

REFRACTORY [ri-frak'te-ri], *adj.* perverse, stubborn in opposition or disobedience, obstinate; (of a disease) not responding to treatment; heat-resisting, hard to fuse. [L.].

REFRAIN (1) [ri-frān'], *n.* line or verse regularly repeated at intervals, *esp.* at the end of each stanza of a poem or song. [OFr.].

REFRAIN (2), *v.i.* to forbear, abstain (usually with *from*). [L.].

REFRANGIBLE [ri-fran'ji-bl], *adj.* that may be refracted. [L.].

REFRESH [ri-fresh'], *v.t.* to make fresh again; give new strength to; cool and revive; (*fig.*) stimulate, jog (the memory); *v. reflex.* to recover one's strength and freshness by taking food, drink, sleep etc.; *v.i.* to take in refreshment. [OFr.].

REFRESHER [ri-fre'sher], *n.* one who, or that which, refreshes; (*coll.*) refreshing drink; (*leg.*) additional daily fee paid to a barrister; **r. course,** course of instruction to bring up to date the knowledge of people already qualified in a particular subject.

REFRESHING [ri-fre'shing], *adj.* cooling and reviving, giving new strength and vigour; stimulating; attractive in its unexpectedness.

REFRESHMENT [ri-fresh'ment], *n.* act of refreshing; state of being refreshed, new life and vigour; that which refreshes; (*pl.*) food and drink, *esp.* a light and informal meal; (*coll.*) drink. [OFr.].

REFRIGERANT (1) [ri-fri'je-rant], *adj.* cooling, reducing fever. **REFRIGERANT** (2), *n.* medicine which reduces fever; cooling drink; substance used in freezing something. [L.].

REFRIGERATE [ri-fri'je-rāt], *v.t.* to make cool, freeze; chill by putting into a refrigerator in order to preserve; make into ice; *v.i.* become cold, freeze. **REFRIGERATION** [ri-fri-je-rā'shn], *n.* act of refrigerating; state of being cooled or frozen; preservation of food by keeping in cold storage. [L.].

REFRIGERATOR [ri-fri'je-rā-ter], *n.* ice-chest or chamber into which food may be put into cold storage to be preserved; anything which refrigerates, a refrigerating machine.

REFT [reft], *p.pt. of* † **REAVE;** bereft, deprived.

REFUGE [re'fyōōj], *n.* shelter, protection from danger or distress; place affording such protection; place of safety for hiding; portion of pavement in the middle of a broad and busy road for the convenience of pedestrians; expedient adopted as a means of escaping trouble or retribution. [L.].

REFUGEE [re-fyōō-jē'], *n.* one who flees for shelter to a place of refuge, *esp.* to a foreign country, for political reasons or in times of persecution. [Fr.].

REFULGENCE [ri-ful'jens], *n.* flood of light, splendour, brightness. [L.].

REFULGENT [ri-ful'jent], *adj.* gleaming, shining brightly, radiant, dazzling. [L.].

REFUND (1) [rē-fund'], *v.t.* to repay, give back, return (money paid); *v.i.* to make repayment. **REFUND** (2) [rē'fund], *n.* money paid back, repayment. [L.].

REFURBISH [rē-fur'bish], *v.t.* to restore to its former new condition.

REFUSAL [ri-fyōō'zal], *n.* act of refusing, denial or rejection of anything demanded or offered; choice of taking or refusing.

RE-FUSE [rē-fyōōz'], *v.t.* to fuse again.

REFUSE (1) [ri-fyōōz'], *v.t. and i.* to deny or decline (a request, command); decline to accept (an offer); (*cards*) be unable to follow suit in; (of a horse) jib at, make no attempt to clear. **REFUSE** (2) [re'fyōōs], *n.* that which is discarded as useless or worthless, waste matter, garbage; scum, dregs of (society, a class). **REFUSE** (3) [re'fyōōs], *adj.* discarded as useless or worthless. [Fr. from L.].

REFUTATION [re-fyōō-tā'shn], *n.* act of refuting; that which refutes or disproves. [L.].

REFUTE [ri-fyōōt'], *v.t.* to prove (a person) to be wrong; prove (an argument) to be false. [L.].

REGAIN [rē-gān'], *v.t.* to recover possession of; win again; reach again. [OFr.].

REGAL [rē'gal], *adj.* of, or belonging to, a king, royal; worthy of a king, splendidly magnificent. [L.].

REGALE [ri-gāl'[, *v.t.* to entertain, feast sumptuously; delight, give pleasure to; *v.i.* to feast. [Fr.].

REGALIA [ri-gā'li-ah], *n.* (*hist.*) rights and prerogatives of a king; emblems or insignia of royalty; symbols or ornaments of certain societies and orders of knighthood. [L.].

REGALITY [rē-ga'li-ti], *n.* royalty, sovereignty, kingly rule; (*pl.*) royal rights or privileges.

REGARD (1) [ri-gahd'], *v.t.* to look, gaze at; contemplate, view in the mind; value, esteem; consider, think; pay attention to, heed, observe; concern; **as regards,** with reference to. **REGARD** (2), *n.* look, gaze, *esp.* of a particular significance; esteem, respect; heed, attention, concern; (*pl.*) expressions of kindly feeling towards a particular person; **with r. to,** with reference to. [Fr.].

REGARDFUL [ri-gahd'fōōl], *adj.* taking notice, attentive, heedful, respectful.

REGARDING [ri-gah'ding], *prep.* concerning, with reference to.

REGARDLESS [ri-gahd'les], *adj.* heedless, unobservant, unmindful; (*coll.*) taking no account of cost.

REGATTA [ri-ga'tah], *n.* race-meeting for yachts, rowing boats and other water craft. [It.].

REGENCY (1) [rē'jen-si], *n.* government by a regent, or by a body of men having similar powers; office or jurisdiction of a regent; period during which a country is governed by a regent, *esp.* the Regency of the Prince Regent, later George IV, in England. **REGENCY** (2), *adj.* of, pertaining to, the styles of architecture, dress etc. current during the R. of George IV.

REGENERATE (1) [rē-je'ne-rāt], *v.t.* to generate or produce again, re-create; cause to experience spiritual rebirth, reform spiritually; revive and raise to greater heights; (*path.*) form again; *v.i.* to be born again spiritually; reform. **REGENERATE** (2) [rē-je'ne-rat], *adj.* having experienced spiritual rebirth; reformed, improved. **REGENERACY,** *n.* state of being r. **REGENERATOR,** *n.* one who, or that which, regenerates; fuel-saving device fitted to a furnace. [L.].

REGENERATION [rē-je-ne-rā'shn], *n.* act or process of regenerating; state of being regenerated; spiritual rebirth; (*path.*) formation of fresh tissue; (*radio*) reaction.

REGENERATIVE [rē-je'ne-ra-tiv], *adj.* reproducing, renewing, having the power to regenerate; using the device of a regenerator.

REGENT (1) [rē'jent], *n.* one who rules or governs for another, one who rules over a kingdom in the minority, absence or disability of a monarch. **REGENT** (2), *adj.* acting as r. [Fr.].

REGICIDE [re'ji-sīd], *n.* one who kills a king; crime of killing a king; **the Regicides,** those who tried and ordered the execution of Charles I. **REGICIDAL** [re-ji-sī'dal], *adj.* pertaining to, disposed to, r. [L.].

RÉGIME, régime [rā-zhēm'], *n.* mode or system of government, order, social and political administration; mode of living, course of treatment to ensure sound health. [Fr.].

REGIMEN [re'ji-men], *n.* (*gram.*) the governing of one word by another, relation of a word to the word it governs; (*med.*) regulation of diet, exercise etc. to ensure better health. [L.].

REGIMENT (1) [re'ji-ment], *n.* body of troops or an infantry unit, on a territorial basis, consisting of a varying number of battalions; cavalry unit; general term for artillery as a whole; (*coll.*) a vast number; (*archaic*) government. **REGIMENT** (2), *v.t.* to form

---

into a r. or regiments; organize into a trained, disciplined body or ordered system. [L.].

REGIMENTAL [re-ji-men'tal], *adj.* relating to a regiment. REGIMENTALS, *n.(pl.)* distinguishing uniform worn by the soldiers of particular regiments.

REGIMENTATION [re-ji-men-tā'shn], *n.* division into regiments; organization into an ordered system or trained, disciplined body; officious management.

REGINA [re-ji'nah], *n.* queen; official designation of a reigning female monarch. [L.].

REGION [rē'jn], *n.* tract, area of land, sea or space of indefinite, but usually considerable, extent; a part of the body; *(fig.)* sphere, realm. REGIONAL, *adj.* pertaining to a r. or particular district, occurring in a particular part; provincial. [L.].

REGISTER (1) [re'jis-ter], *n.* official written record of events, names and addresses etc., *esp.* a record of births, marriages and deaths kept by a registrar; book in which this is kept; apparatus for regulating the admission of air or heat; mechanical device for recording something; *(mus.)* range, compass; range of notes which can be sung without change of voice; slider in an organ; organ stop; **parliamentary, municipal r.**, list of persons eligible to vote at elections. REGISTER (2), *v.t.* to record or enter in a r.; record automatically; insure against damage in postal transit or non-delivery, by payment of an extra fee; adjust; record and fix indelibly (in the memory); *(cinema)* express (some particular emotion) on the countenance; *v.i* to sign one's name in a r.; report for registration, *esp.* for national service; make an impression. REGISTER-OFFICE, office for purposes of registration, or in which a public r. is kept; registry-office. [MedL.].

REGISTRAR [re-jis-trah(r)'], *n.* official keeper of records or of a register; **R. General,** official appointed to superintend registration of any kind, *esp.* of births, marriages and deaths in England and Wales.

REGISTRATION [re-jis-trā'shn], *n.* act of registering or entering in a register; entry in a register.

REGISTRY [re'jis-tri], *n.* act of recording in a register; place where a register is kept. REGISTRY-OFFICE, office at which a registrar performs civil marriages; office at which the registrar keeps a register of the births, marriages and deaths within his district; office for supplying domestic servants.

REGIUS [rē'ji-us], *adj.* royal; **R. Professor,** holder of a professorship of royal foundation. [L.].

REGNAL [reg'nal], *adj.* relating to a reign; **r. year,** a year counted from the date of accession of a sovereign. [L.].

REGNANT [reg'nant], *adj.* reigning, ruling; predominant, prevalent. [L.].

REGRESS (1) [rē'gres], *n.* a going back, return; retrogression. REGRESS (2) [ri-gres'], *v.i.* to move backwards. REGRESSION [ri-gre'shn], *n.* act of going back, return; relapse to a former worse state; *(math.)* the turning back of a curve. REGRESSIVE [ri-gre'siv], *adj.* moving backward, relapsing to a former inferior condition. [L.].

REGRET (1) *(pres.pt.* **regretting,** *pret. and p.pt.* **regretted)** [ri-gret'], *v.t.* to feel sorrow at, grieve at, deplore; remember with regret. REGRET (2), *n.* sorrow, grief at some unpleasant event, usually involving loss; remorse, discomfort of mind upon reflecting on something which has been done or left undone, or which has happened. [Fr.].

REGRETFUL [ri-gret'fool], *adj.* full of regret.

REGULAR (1) [re'gyōō-ler], *adj.* following some rule or plan, symmetrical, even, orderly; habitual, constant, not varying, never failing to do some action, and (often with the implication of) at a set time, recurring at set times; conforming to custom or precedent, in accordance with what is deemed normal or correct; ordered, steady; proper, fully qualified; (of an army) permanent; (eccles.) bound by the rule of a religious order; *(gram.)* formed in accordance with a uniform pattern; *(geom.)* with the sides and angles equal; (of a solid) having exactly corresponding faces; *(coll.)* complete, thorough, typical; **r. troops,** troops of a standing or permanent army. REGULAR (2), *n.* member of a religious order bound by a rule; soldier who is a member of the permanent army. REGULARLY, *adv.* in a r. manner; at r. intervals, without fail; with regularity, constantly; *(coll.)* completely. [L.].

REGULARITY [re-gyōō-la'ri-ti], *n.* quality of being regular; uniformity, symmetry; recurrence at fixed intervals; orderliness; conformity to rule or precedent; steadiness in pursuing a course.

REGULARIZE [re'gyōō-la-riz], *v.t.* to make regular.

REGULATE [re'gyōō-lāt], *v.t.* to govern by rule, subject to rule; adjust so that it functions accurately; adjust to a particular standard or rate, control. [~L.].

REGULATION (1) [re-gyōō-lā'shn], *n.* act of regulating; state of being regulated; a prescribed rule or order to be complied with. REGULATION (2), *adj.* in accordance with, prescribed or fixed by, r.

REGULATOR [re'gyōō-lā-ter], *n.* one who regulates; mechanical device for controlling the working of a machine, or the flow, pressure or force of air, steam, gas etc.; lever for regulating the movement of a watch or clock.

REGURGITATE [rē-gur'ji-tāt], *v.t.* to throw or pour back, vomit out or eject from (the stomach or other receptacle); *v.i.* to be poured back or ejected, as from the stomach. REGURGITATION [rē-gur-ji-tā'shn], *n.* act of pouring or flowing back, or of being cast out again; backward flow of blood to the heart or food to the mouth. [MedL.].

REHABILITATE [rē-ha-bi'li-tāt], *v.t.* to restore to a former capacity or position, reinstate; re-establish in favour again, restore to esteem or good repute. [L.].

REHABILITATION [rē-ha-bi-li-tā'shn], *n.* act of reinstating in a former rank or capacity; restoration to former rights, or to favour and good repute; resettlement of discharged servicemen in civilian life.

REHASH (1) [rē-hash'], *v.t.* to hash up again, offer again in a slightly modified form or new guise. REHASH (2) [rē'hash], *n.* a serving up anew in a different form.

REHEARSAL [ri-hur'sal], *n.* act of rehearsing; performance or recital in private in preparation for future public performance.

REHEARSE [ri-hurs'], *v.t.* to repeat, recount, enumerate; go through repeatedly or practise in private in preparation for future public performance; *v.i.* to have a rehearsal. [OFr.].

REICH [rīkh], *n.* the German State; **Third R.,** Germany while under National Socialist rule. [Germ.].

REICHSTAG [rīkhs'tahg], *n.* formerly one of the houses of the supreme legislature of Germany. [Germ.].

REIGN (1) [rān], *n.* rule, supreme power of a sovereign, royal authority; period during which a monarch reigns; sway, dominion; predominance. REIGN (2), *v.i.* to rule as a monarch; hold sway; prevail. [OFr. from L.].

REIMBURSE [rē-im-burs'], *v.t.* to refund; pay back to.

REIMPORT [rē-im-pawt'], *v.t.* to import back again (what has been exported), *esp.* in a manufactured form.

REIN (1) [rān], *n.* long leather strap fastened to each side of the bit or bridle of a horse, by which the horse is controlled (often in *pl.*); *(fig.)* anything which curbs, controls or guides; **to give r. to,** to indulge; **to keep a tight r. on,** to keep under rigid control. REIN (2), *v.t.* to provide with a r.; hold in or check with a r. (often with *in*); *(fig.)* restrain, curb. [OFr.].

REINCARNATE (1) [rē-in-kah'nāt], *v.t. and i.* to re-embody, appear again in bodily form. REINCARNATE (2) [rē-in-kah'nat], *adj.* born again in another body.

REINCARNATION [rē-in-kah-nā'shn], *n.* re-embodiment; return of the soul to earth after death, in a fresh bodily form.

REINDEER *(pl.* reindeer) [rān'dēer], *n.* species of deer found in N. Europe and Asia, having large branching antlers, and used for drawing sledges and for milking; **r. moss,** lichen on which the r. feeds in winter. [OScand.].

REINFORCE [rē-in-faws'], *v.t.* to strengthen by additional men or supplies; increase the numbers of in order to strengthen; strengthen by additional support, thickness etc.; add to the strength of, backup; **reinforced concrete,** concrete strengthened by having steel bars or netting embedded in it.

REINFORCEMENT [rē-in-faws'ment], *n.* act of reinforcing; that which reinforces; *(pl.)* (*milit.*) fresh troops or supplies to reinforce an army etc.

REINS (1), see REIN (1).

REINS (2) [rānz], *n.* (*pl.*) (*archaic*) the kidneys; loins; lower part of the back. [OFr. from L.].

REINSTATE [rē-in-stāt'], *v.t.* to restore to a former state or position. REINSTATEMENT, *n.* act of re-instating, state of being reinstated.

REINSURANCE [rē-in-shōōr'ans], *n.* transfer of the risks of insurance to others by an insurer to insure himself against possible loss on a policy which he has issued.

REINSURE [rĕ-in-shoōr'], *v.i.* (of an insurance company or agent) to safeguard oneself against possible loss on a policy of insurance issued by insuring again with a different insurer.

REINVEST [rĕ-in-vest'], *v.t.* to restore to, endow again (with); invest (money) again. REINVESTMENT, *n.* act of investing money anew.

REITERATE [rĕ-i'te-rāt], *v.t.* to repeat again and again. REITERATIVE, *adj.* characterized by repetition. [L.].

REJECT (1) [ri-jekt'], *v.t.* to throw away, discard, as being worthless or unsatisfactory; decline to accept; refuse to grant or recognize; (of the stomach) refuse to assimilate. REJECT (2) [rĕ'jekt], *n.* that which has been rejected. [L.].

REJECTION [ri-jek'shn], *n.* act of rejecting; refusal to accept or grant. [L.].

REJOICE [ri-jois'], *v.t.* to gladden, make joyful; *v.i.* to be joyful, make merry; be delighted. [ME. from OFr.].

REJOICING [ri-joi'sing], *n.* a feeling of joy, expression of gladness or exultation, occasion or subject for joy (often *pl.*).

REJOIN (1) [rĕ-join'], *v.t.* to join together again; meet again, become reunited with; *v.i.* to come together again.

REJOIN (2), *v.i.* to reply to an answer; (*leg.*) (of a defendant) answer to the plaintiff's replication. [Fr.].

REJOINDER [ri-join'der], *n.* a reply to an answer; answer; (*leg.*) defendant's answer to the plaintiff's replication. [Fr.].

REJUVENATE [rĕ-joō've-nāt], *v.t.* to make young and active again; *v.i.* to become young and fresh again. REJUVENATION [rĕ-joō-ve-nā'shn], *n.* act of rejuvenating; state of being rejuvenated. REJUVENATOR, *n.* person who or thing which rejuvenates. [L.].

REJUVENESCENCE [rē-joō-ve-ne'sens], *n.* renewal of youth; state of becoming young again; (*biol.*) formation of new cells to replace older ones. REJUVENESCENT, *adj.* growing young again. [LL.].

REKINDLE [rĕ-kin'dl], *v.t.* to kindle again; inflame or rouse anew; *v.i.* to be rekindled, blaze up again.

RELAPSE (1) [ri-laps'], *v.i.* to fall back to a former worse state, fall back into error or evil ways; fall back into a worse state of health, become worse; (of shares and stocks) depreciate. RELAPSE (2), *n.* a falling back to a former bad state or worse condition. [L.].

RELATE [ri-lāt'], *v.t.* to tell, narrate; show the connexion between; *v.i.* to have reference to; **to r. to,** to be in relation, show connexion with; (*pass.*) belong to the same family as, be connected by blood, marriage or fundamental traits to. RELATED, *adj.* connected by birth or marriage; allied, standing in some relation to each other. [L.].

RELATION [ri-lā'shn], *n.* that which, or one who, is related; kinship, connexion by birth or marriage; one belonging to the same family as another, kinsman or kinswoman, relative; way in which things or persons are related, the connexion; (*pl.*) mutual intercourse and dealings, esp. the manner in which these are carried out; act of telling or relating, narrative. [L.].

RELATIONSHIP [ri-lā'shn-ship], *n.* state of being related by kindred, affinity or other alliance; way in which things are related; connexion.

RELATIVE (1) [re'la-tiv], *adj.* considered in relation to, or with respect to, something else, comparative, not absolute, having or implying a relation to something else; referring, belonging; possessing mutual relationship; (*gram.*) relating to a previous word, sentence or clause. RELATIVE (2), *n.* person related to another by blood or marriage, kinsman or kinswoman; (*gram.*) word which relates to, and stands in place of, an antecedent word, clause or sentence. [L.].

RELATIVITY [re-la-ti'vi-ti], *n.* state or quality of being relative; (*phys.*) a mathematical theory of the universe, put forward by Einstein, that all measurements are relative, since there are no absolute standards of comparison.

RELAX [ri-laks'], *v.t.* to loosen, slacken, make less tense or rigid; make less strict or severe, lessen the force of, ease; relieve from constipation; enervate, make languid; *v.i.* to slacken, become less tense, excited or firm, become limp and at rest; become less severe or strict; slacken in zeal and intensity;

relaxed throat, form of sore throat. RELAXING *adj.* enervating. [L.].

RELAXATION [rĕ-lak-sā'shn], *n.* act of relaxing; state of being relaxed; abatement of tension, attention or application; recreation, amusement, diversion from work.

RELAY (1) [rĕ'lā], *n.* fresh shift of workers to relieve those who have worked a certain length of time; fresh supply of hounds for hunting, or horses in travelling, to take the place of those tired; (*elect.*) device by which a circuit of relatively weak current is able to control a circuit of high current; (*radio*) broadcast in which the programme is sent to a broadcasting station from which it is re-diffused to listeners; **r. station,** (*radio*) broadcasting station transmitting programmes received by telephone line from another station. RELAY-RACE, race between teams of which each member runs a portion of the distance to be covered, and hands over a baton, as he completes his lap, to the next member, who may not start until he has received it. RELAY (2) [rĕ-lā'], *v.t.* (*teleg.* or *radio*) to receive from a transmitting apparatus or broadcasting station, and then re-broadcast to listeners; replace by relays. [OFr.].

RELEASE (1) [ri-lēs'], *v.t.* to set free, liberate, (from restraint, captivity, pain, trouble etc.); discharge; (*leg.*) give up, surrender, transfer; permit to be exhibited, published or offered for sale for the first time or by a certain date. RELEASE (2), *n.* discharge from an obligation; liberation from pain, trouble etc., or from confinement or captivity; act of releasing or discharging; act of allowing a thing to be exhibited, published or offered for sale on a particular date; that which is exhibited, published etc. in this way; catch by which some part of machinery is released; (*leg.*) formal written discharge of a debt or obligation; transfer of ownership of an estate, right etc.; document in which this is set forth. [OFr. from L.].

RELEGATE [re'li-gāt], *v.t.* to consign to an inferior rank, status or less important place; transfer for carrying out, refer for decision; (*sport*) (chiefly Association football) cause to play in a lower division for the next season at least, as a penalty for finishing the season at the foot of the final table of precedence. [L.].

RELENT [ri-lent'], *v.i.* to soften in temper, become less severe in intention, yield to entreaty. [OFr.].

RELENTLESS [ri-lent'les], *adj.* unmoved by pity; unrelenting, merciless, inflexible, inexorable.

RELEVANCE, RELEVANCY [re'li-vans(-i)], *n.* state or quality of being relevant, pertinence.

RELEVANT [re'li-vant], *adj.* pertinent, applicable, concerned with the matter in hand.

RELIABILITY [ri-lī-a-bi'li-ti], *n.* quality of being reliable; **r. trials,** long-distance trials for motor vehicles to test their r. rather than their speed.

RELIABLE [ri-lī'a-bl], *adj.* that may be relied on or trusted, trustworthy, dependable.

RELIANCE [ri-lī'ans], *n.* act of relying, confidence, trust, dependence.

RELIANT [ri-lī'ant], *adj.* confident, trusting.

RELIC [re'lik], *n.* a memorial of some holy person, usually a part of the body or a personal possession, kept and regarded with reverence; fragment left over from the past, object, custom, belief etc. surviving into a period when it is outmoded, any valued token of the past; (*poet. usually pl.*) remains of a dead person. [L.].

RELICT [re'likt], *n.* widow. [L.].

RELIEF (1) [ri-lēf'], *n.* condition of being relieved; alleviation of pain, distress etc.; that which affords such alleviation; help, assistance; the raising of a siege of a town, castle etc.; official grant of money to relieve poverty or want; anything providing a change from that which has become tedious or monotonous; release from a duty or office, or from a spell of duty; person or persons who so relieve one; (*leg.*) exemption, remission. [OFr.].

RELIEF (2), *n.* mode of carving in which the figures stand out from the background; amount by which the figures stand out; example of such relief; (*fig.*) sharpness or distinctness provided by contrast, contrast; **r. map,** map in which the contour of the country is imitated in three dimensions, or suggested by shading or hatching on the surface of the map. [It.].

RELIEVE [ri-lēv'], *v.t.* to lessen, alleviate, mitigate; free, help, succour; deprive; break the monotony of; **to r. one's feelings,** to give expression to one's feelings; **to r. oneself,** to evacuate the bowels;

oō is pronounced as in food; oō as in hood; th as in think; TH as in that; zh as in azure. ∼ = related to.

DSE—Q*

relieving officer, officer who administers relief to the poor in a given district. [L.].

RELIEVO [ri-lē'vō], *n.* relief; **alto r.,** high relief; **basso r.,** low relief. [It.].

RELIGION [ri-li'jn], *n.* belief in a supernatural power or powers, belief in a god or gods, *esp.* such as entails acts of worship on the part of the believer; system of philosophical, theological and ethical tenets and theories depending upon a belief in a deity or deities; the Christian religion; monastic life; (*fig.*) object of great devotion. [L.].

RELIGIOSE [ri-li'ji-ōs], *adj.* excessively or morbidly religious. **RELIGIOSITY** [ri-li-ji-o'si-ti], *n.* state of being r.

RELIGIOUS (1) [ri-li'jōs], *adj.* pertaining to religion; believing in a religion, pious, godly; connected with a monastery or convent; (*fig.*) exact, scrupulous, conscientious. **RELIGIOUS (2),** *n.* one bound by r. vows, *esp.* to a monastic order. **RELIGIOUSLY,** *adv.* in a r. way, piously; scrupulously. [L.].

RELINQUISH [ri-ling'kwish], *v.t.* to resign, let go one's hold on; surrender; cease from. [Fr. from L.].

RELIQUARY [re-li'kwa-ri], *n.* casket or shrine where a sacred relic is kept. [MedL.].

RELISH (1) [re'lish], *n* taste or smell, flavour, *esp.* an appetizing flavour; spice or condiment added to food to make it more appetizing; stimulating, spicy quality; keenness or zest for anything. **RELISH (2),** *v.t. and i.* to make appetizing, impart a r. to; eat with pleasure, enjoy in the eating; (*fig.*) enjoy, be eager for; contain a hint or suspicion of. [OFr.].

RELIVE [rē-liv'], *v.t. and i.* to live through again, revive; live again.

RELUCTANCE [ri-luk'tans], *n.* quality or state of being reluctant.

RELUCTANT [ri-luk'tant], *adj.* unwilling, expressing disinclination. [L.].

RELUME [rē-lyōōm'], *v.t.* (*poet.*) to rekindle; make bright. [RE and (IL)LUME].

RELY [ri-lī'], *v.i.* to trust (in), depend (on). [OFr.].

REMAIN [ri-mān'], *v.i.* to be left over; survive, persist; stay in the same place or condition, continue to be. [OFr. from L.].

REMAINDER (1) [ri-mān'der], *n.* that which is left over; residue, remnant. **REMAINDER (2),** *v.t.* to offer (a book) for sale as a r. at a reduced price. [OFr.].

REMAINS [ri-mānz'], *n.(pl.)* persons or things left over, survivors; relics; works of an author not yet published at his death; a corpse. [~REMAIN].

REMAND (1) [ri-mahnd'], *v.t.* to send back; order a charged person to be recommitted to prison pending the discovery or examination of further evidence. **REMAND (2),** *n.* act of remanding. [OFr.].

REMANET [re'ma-net], *n.* something left over; (*leg.*) a case postponed to another sitting; (*parl.*) a bill left over to another session. [L.].

REMARK (1) [ri-mahk'], *v.t. and i.* to observe or notice; perceive; say or write by way of comment. **REMARK (2),** *n.* act of remarking; a comment spoken or written. [Fr.].

REMARKABLE [ri-mah'ka-bl], *adj.* worthy of notice; extraordinary, striking.

REMEDIAL [ri-mē'di-al], *adj.* providing a remedy; intended for a remedy, curative. [L.].

REMEDY (1) [re'mi-di], *n.* that which heals or cures, a treatment or medicine; that which counteracts an evil, trouble etc.; reparation, legal redress. **REMEDY (2),** *v.t.* to put right, improve, provide a r. for. [L.].

REMEMBER [ri-mem'ber], *v.t. and i.* to call to mind, bear in mind; recall; have the faculty of memory; present with a gift, tip; **to r. someone to somebody else,** to convey the regards of one to the other. [OFr.].

REMEMBRANCE [ri-mem'brans], *n.* act of remembering; state of being remembered; faculty of memory; souvenir; (*pl.*) kindly greetings. [OFr.].

REMEMBRANCER [ri-mem'bran-ser], *n.* person who or thing which serves to remind; **the King's R.,** officer of the Supreme Court representing the Exchequer, who collects debts on behalf of the Crown; **the City R.,** legal officer of the City of London Corporation who represents its interests on Parliamentary committees etc. [AFr.].

REMIND [ri-mīnd'], *v.t.* to cause to remember.

REMINDER [ri-mīn'der], *n.* anything which reminds.

REMINISCE [re-mi-nis'], *v.i.* (*coll.*) to indulge in reminiscence. [*Next*].

REMINISCENCE [re-mi-ni'sens], *n.* act and faculty of remembering; recollection; something remembered, anecdote of some remembered event; something which causes one to remember something else,

usually by similarity or echo; (*pl.*) book of reminiscences. [Fr.].

REMINISCENT [re-mi-ni'sent], *adj.* serving to recall; dwelling on and telling reminiscences.

REMISS [ri-mis'], *adj.* careless, negligent. [L.].

REMISSIBLE [ri-mi'si-bl], *adj.* able to be remitted or forgiven.

REMISSION [ri-mi'shn], *n.* act of remitting; pardon, forgiveness; condition of being pardoned; act of yielding or giving up (something); abatement. [OFr.].

REMISSIVE [ri-mi'siv], *adj.* remitting, causing or permitting remission.

REMIT [ri-mit'], *v.t. and i.* to abstain from exacting; cause to diminish, abate; send (money); (*leg.*) direct (a case) to a lower court; refer a case for authoritative decision. **REMITTER,** *n.* one who remits money to another. [L.].

REMITTANCE [ri-mi'tans], *n.* act of sending money; money sent as a payment or allowance etc. **REMITTANCE-MAN,** one living abroad on an allowance from home.

REMITTENT [ri-mi'tent], *adj.* abating from time to time.

REMNANT [rem'nant], *n.* thing or collection of things or persons left over; (*pl.*) short pieces of fabric left over after the main pieces have been used or sold. [OFr.].

REMONSTRANCE [ri-mon'strans], *n.* act of remonstrating; a protest. [OFr.].

REMONSTRANT (1) [ri-mon'strant], *adj.* expostulating. **REMONSTRANT (2),** *n.* one who remonstrates.

REMONSTRATE [ri-mon'strāt], *v.i.* to expostulate, make formal protestation. [~MedL.].

REMORSE [ri-maws'], *n.* strong sense of regret for a sin or wrong committed or duty left undone, repentance, scruple, compunction; **without r.,** unscrupulously, callously. [OFr.].

REMORSELESS [ri-maws'les], *adj.* having no pity, relentless, showing no compunction.

REMOTE [ri-mōt'], *adj.* distant, far removed; far off, sequestered; having only a slight connexion (with), unlikely; (of ideas etc.) vague; **r. control,** manipulation of apparatus from a point some distance away; device making this possible. [L.].

REMOUNT (1) [rē-mownt'], *v.t. and i.* to ascend, climb again; provide with fresh horses; provide (a picture) with another mount; mount (a horse) again. **REMOUNT (2)** [rē'mownt], *n.* (*milit.*) horse to replace one put out of action; a supply of such horses.

REMOVABLE [ri-mōō'va-bl], *adj.* able to be removed.

REMOVAL [ri-mōō'val], *n.* act of removing; act of transferring effects from one house to another; act of abolishing, getting rid of.

REMOVE (1) [ri-mōōv'], *v.t.* to take, carry, move away; get rid of, abolish; clean off; relieve (a person) of his office or post; dismiss; *v.i.* to change one's residence. **REMOVE (2),** *n.* distance that one thing is from another, a natural step or degree of that distance; degree of relationship; (in schools) form between the upper fourth and lower fifth. [L.].

REMOVER [ri-mōō'ver], *n.* one who removes, *esp.* a person who employs vans and men to remove furniture from one house to another.

REMUNERATE [ri-myōō'ne-rāt], *v.t.* to pay, give reward to; recompense. [L.].

REMUNERATION [ri-myōō-ne-rā'shn], *n.* act of remunerating; payment, wages.

REMUNERATIVE [ri-myōō'ne-ra-tiv], *adj.* yielding remuneration, profitable.

RENAISSANCE [re-nā'sans], *n.* rebirth; revival; **the R.,** the fifteenth-century European revival of interest in classical (*esp.* ancient Greek) culture. [Fr.].

RENAL [rē'nal], *adj.* pertaining or adjacent to the kidneys. [L.].

RENASCENCE [re-na'sens], *n.* state of being renascent; rebirth; the Renaissance.

RENASCENT [re-na'sent], *adj.* renewing, reviving, rejuvenating. [L.].

RENCONTRE [ra(ng)-kaw(ng)tr'], *n.* an encounter, unexpected meeting. [Fr.].

REND (*pret. and p.pt.* **rent**) [rend], *v.t. and i.* to tear in pieces; split, shatter; be torn. [OE.].

RENDER [ren'der], *v.t.* to give in return, pay back; give, tender, perform, do a service to; cause to be, make; reproduce, represent; translate, interpret; melt (fat) in order to clarify it, *esp.* **to r. down.** [LL.].

RENDERING [ren'de-ring], *n.* act of one who renders; version, translation; representation, delineation.

The accent ´ after a syllable = stress (u-pon´). The mark ¯ over a vowel = length (ā in made; ō in bone).

RENDEZVOUS (1) [ra(ng)'dā-vōō], *n.* place appointed for a meeting. RENDEZVOUS (2), *v.i.* to meet at a r. [Fr.].

RENDITION [ren-di'shn], *n.* version, translation; rendering. [LL.].

RENEGADE (1) [re'ni-gād], *n.* one who abjures his faith, apostate, deserter. RENEGADE (2), *adj.* pertaining to a r.; deserting. [MedL.].

RENEW [ri-nyōō'], *v.t.* to make as good as new again, renovate; give fresh energy to, revitalize; recommence, resume; repeat, reiterate; revive; grant again, prolong.

RENEWAL [ri-nyōō'al], *n.* act of renewing; state of being renewed; restoration, revival; regeneration.

RENNET [re'nit], *n.* substance prepared from the inner membrane of a calf's stomach, and used for curdling milk. [ME.].

RENOUNCE [ri-nowns'], *v.t. and i.* to announce formally the giving up of a right or claim, disown, reject; forsake, cast off, give up participating in. [OFr. from L.].

RENOVATE [re'nō-vāt], *v.t.* to make as good as new by repairing, restore to its former state, do up. [L.].

RENOVATION [re-nō-vā'shn], *n.* act of renewing, state of being renewed.

RENOWN [ri-nown'], *n.* fact or condition of being widely celebrated; celebrity, fame. RENOWNED, *adj.* famous, celebrated.

RENT (1) [rent], *n.* slit or hole in material due to a tear, opening produced by rending or violent separation. [REND].

RENT (2), *pret. and p.pt. of* REND.

RENT (3), *n.* payment made by a tenant to a landlord whose house or lands he occupies over a stipulated period; payment made for temporary use. RENT-CHARGE, *r.* from land payable by settlement to a nominee other than the landlord. RENT-FREE, (occupied) without payment of r. RENT-ROLL, account of rents or income drawn up by a landlord or his agents. RENT (4), *v.t. and i.* to occupy as a tenant certain rooms, lands or tenements for an agreed payment; lease, let, hire out on specified terms; be leased or rented. RENTER, *n.* one who pays rent; wholesale dealer in cinematograph films. [OFr.].

RENTAL [ren'tal], *n.* the amount of the rent. [L.].

RENTIER [rah(ng)'ti-ā, ren'ti-er], *n.* person whose income is derived from interest on investments. [Fr.].

RENUNCIATION [ri-nun-si-ā'shn], *n.* act of renouncing; repudiation. RENUNCIATIVE, RENUNCIATORY [ri-nun'si-a-tiv, -te-ri], *adj.* characterized by, having the nature of, r. [L.].

REORGANIZE [rē-aw'ga-nīz], *v.t.* to organize anew, change the system of organization of.

REP (1), **REPP** [rep], *n.* fabric with a ribbed or corded texture. REP (2), *adj.* made of r. [Fr.].

REP (3), *n.* (*school slang*) repetition, recitation.

REP (4), *n.* (*coll.*) a repertory theatre or company.

REPAID [rē-pād'], *pret. and p.pt. of* REPAY.

REPAINT (1) [rē-pānt'], *v.t.* to paint again, give a fresh coat of paint to. REPAINT (2) [rē'pānt], *n.* golf-ball which has been furbished and painted again for further use.

REPAIR (1) [ri-pāer'], *v.t.* to restore to a sound or proper state, mend; put right, make amends for, remedy. REPAIR (2), *n.* act of restoring to a sound condition; work performed on any object in order to restore it to a satisfactory state; relative degree to which a thing requires repairing, state of soundness; **under r.,** being repaired; **in good r.,** in a sound and satisfactory state. [OFr. from L.].

REPAIR (3), *v.i.* to go, betake oneself, resort. [OFr.].

REPARABLE [re'pa-ra-bl], *adj.* able to be mended or recovered.

REPARATION [re-pa-rā'shn], *n.* act of putting right or repairing; amends, compensation for injury, damage or loss; restitution; (*pl.*) compensation exacted from a defeated country for damage done in war. [L.].

REPARTEE [re-pah-tē'], *n.* ready and witty reply, smart retort; lively, clever retorts. [Fr.].

REPAST [ri-pahst'], *n.* meal, a quantity of food and drink taken on one occasion. [OFr.].

REPATRIATE [rē-pat'ri-āt], *v.t.* to send (someone) back to his native land. REPATRIATE [rē-pat'ri-at], *n.* one who has been repatriated.

REPAY (*pret. and p.pt.* **repaid**) [rē-pā'], *v.t. and i.* to pay back, refund; recompense, reward; give back in return; make repayment. [OFr.].

REPAYMENT [rē-pā'ment], *n.* act of paying back, requital, reimbursement; the money repaid.

REPEAL (1) [ri-pēl'], *v.t.* to revoke, annul, cancel (law, judicial sentence etc.). REPEAL (2), *n.* act of repealing, abrogation. [AFr.].

REPEAT (1) [ri-pēt'], *v.t.* to say again; recite by heart; spread abroad, circulate; do again, cause to happen again; *v.i.* to strike the last hour or part of the hour again (of a clock etc.); recur; (of food) rise and be tasted again. REPEAT (2), *n.* act of repeating, repetition; pattern which repeats itself; (*mus.*) passage which is to be repeated, sign on the score indicating this. REPEATING, *adj.* regurgitating; reproducing; saying or doing something again; able to be fired several times without reloading. [L.].

REPEATED [ri-pē'tid], *adj.* done again, recurring, continual. REPEATEDLY, *adv.* with repetition; again and again; continually.

REPEATER [ri-pē'ter], *n.* one who, or that which, repeats; watch which strikes again the hours and parts of hours, on the compression of a spring; fire-arm which may be discharged a number of times without being reloaded; (*teleg.*) automatic transmitting instrument.

REPEL (*pres.pt.* **repelling**, *pret. and p.pt.* **repelled**) [ri-pel'], *v.t.* to drive back, repulse; reject, refuse; resist; inspire with abhorrence or distaste, cause to shrink from. [L.].

REPELLENT [ri-pe'lent], *adj.* that repels; loathsome, provoking disgust or aversion.

REPENT [ri-pent'], *v.t.* to feel sorrow or regret at, and resolve to make amends for, feel contrite about; *v.i.* to be sorry, feel regret for something done. [Fr.].

REPENTANCE [ri-pen'tans], *n.* penitence, contrition; regret or grief at what has been wrongfully done or said, with a resolve to make amends.

REPENTANT [ri-pen'tant], *adj.* penitent, regretful for past conduct; expressing repentance.

REPERCUSSION [rē-per-ku'shn], *n.* recoil, rebound; reverberation, echo; (*fig.*) (*usually pl.*) events arising as an indirect result of some action. REPERCUSSIVE, *adj.* producing repercussions, of the nature of a r. [PERCUSSION].

REPERTOIRE [re'per-twah(r)], *n.* repertory; stocks of pieces or tricks readily at command. [Fr.].

REPERTORY [re'per-te-ri], *n.* storehouse, repository; repertoire; **r. theatre,** theatre in which a succession of plays is performed, usually by a permanent company, for short runs, rather than a single play for a long run. [L.].

REPETITION [re-pe-ti'shn], *n.* act of doing or uttering again; that which is done or said again; copy or reproduction in a slightly varying form; art of reciting that which has been learnt by heart; (*mus.*) rapid repeating of a note, harmony or interval. [L.].

REPETITIVE [ri-pe'ti-tiv], *adj.* repeating, containing repetition.

REPINE [ri-pīn'], *v.i.* to be discontented, complain, grumble. [PINE (2).]

REPLACE [ri-plās'], *v.t.* to put back into its original position; restore to a former position; supersede; fill the place of; find a substitute for.

REPLACEMENT [rē-plās'ment], *n.* act of replacing; state of being replaced; article which replaces another; spare part.

REPLAY (1) [rē-plā'], *v.t.* to play again (as a gramophone record); (*sport*) play a match again as the previous match has been abandoned or, in a knock-out competition, has ended in a draw. REPLAY (2) [rē'plā], *n.* (*sport*) a match replayed.

REPLENISH [ri-ple'nish], *v.t.* to fill up again, obtain a fresh supply of, restock. [~OFr.].

REPLENISHMENT [ri-ple'nish-ment], *n.* act of filling up again; state of being replenished.

REPLETE [ri-plēt'], *adj.* completely filled, crammed full; thoroughly equipped, abundantly provided. [L.].

REPLETION [ri-plē'shn], *n.* act of eating or drinking to capacity; state of being completely full.

REPLICA [re'pli-kah], *n.* copy of a work of art, *esp.* one by the author of the original; facsimile. [It.].

REPLICATION [re-pli-kā'shn], *n.* (*leg.*) plaintiff's reply to the defendant's plea; copy. [L.].

REPLY (1) [ri-plī'], *v.t.* to return by way of answer; *v.i.* to answer, say, write or do something in response to something said, written or done; (*leg.*) answer a defendant's plea. REPLY (2), *n.* that which is said, written or done in answer to something, response, rejoinder; (*leg.*) plaintiff's answer to a defendant's plea. [OFr.].

REPORT (1) [ri-pawt'], *v.t.* to give an account of,

relate; communicate, convey as a message; write an account of for publication in a newspaper or journal; write down word for word or in condensed form (a speech etc.) for publication in the Press; announce officially, issue a formal statement after making an investigation; give a periodical account of to some authority; complain about to a higher authority; *(parl.)* announce the end of the Committee stage of (a bill); *v.i.* to make a report; present oneself for duty or questioning, or to comply with an order; act as a press reporter. REPORT (2), *n.* rumour, gossip; statement of facts obtained as a result of an investigation or in reply to an inquiry, *esp.* the official statement issued by a person or commission appointed to investigate some particular matter; periodical account of a pupil's progress and conduct at school, issued by his teachers; written account of some event or proceedings, *esp.* of speeches made on such an occasion; loud sudden noise, noise of an explosion; *(leg.)* formal account of a case together with the legal arguments used, and the decisions made; **r. stage,** *(parl.)* end of the Committee stage of a bill, after the second and before the third reading. REPORTAGE [re'paw-tahzh], *n.* written r. on current events as seen by the writer. REPORTING, *n.* act of making a r., occupation or art of a newspaper reporter. [OFr. from L.].

REPORTER [ri-paw'ter], *n.* one who reports, *esp.* one employed to write the official legal reports of law cases; one whose occupation is to write accounts of events, proceedings, speeches etc., and to gather news in general, for publication in newspapers.

REPOSE (1) [ri-pōz'], *v.t. and i.* to rest, lay at rest; *v.i.* to lie at rest; be supported (on). REPOSE (2), *n.* rest, cessation of activity; complete relaxation; stillness, peace, tranquillity; composure; restful harmony of colour and treatment in a work of art. REPOSEFUL, *adj.* inducing r. [Fr., LL.].

REPOSE (3), *v.t.* to set or place (in). REPOSAL, *n.* act of reposing (trust, confidence etc.). [L.].

REPOSITORY [ri-po'zi-te-ri], *n.* place or receptacle where things are deposited for preservation or safety, store, warehouse; copious source, storehouse; one to whom secrets, confidences etc. are or may be entrusted. [L.].

REPOUSSÉ, repoussé [re-pōō'sā], *adj.* set in relief or embossed by hammering, or punching from behind, and afterwards by chasing. [Fr.].

REPP, see REP.

REPREHEND [re-pri-hend'], *v.t.* censure, reprove, rebuke. [L.].

REPREHENSIBLE [re-pri-hen'si-bl], *adj.* deserving reproof, blameworthy. [Prec.].

REPREHENSION [re-pri-hen'shn], *n.* act of reprehending, censure, blame, reproof.

RE-PRESENT [rē-pri-zent'], *v.t.* to present anew.

REPRESENT [re-pri-zent'], *v.t.* to depict, portray; describe as, make out to be; show clearly, point out; signify, mean; typify, stand for; exhibit, exemplify; correspond to; act on behalf of, or as agent for; be a Member of Parliament, or be the elected deputy for, on a legislative council; play the part of in a play; *(reflex.)* claim to be. [L.].

REPRESENTATION [re-pri-zen-tā'shn], *n.* act of representing; that which represents; a delineation, likeness, picture or pictorial account; reproduction invisible or concrete form (of abstract conceptions); reproduction by acting on the stage; statement intended to convey a point of view; expression of remonstrance with a statement of attitude, protest; act of representing a body of voters on an assembly appointed by election; state of being represented in this way. [L.].

REPRESENTATIVE (1) [re-pri-zen'ta-tiv], *adj.* describing or symbolizing; typical, stock; representing, or acting on behalf of, others, *esp.* in a governing or legislative capacity; conducted by elected delegates or deputies; **r. peers,** those Scottish and Irish peers elected to sit in the House of Lords. REPRESENTATIVE (2), *n.* one who, or that which, represents someone or something else; agent, delegate, deputy; one who represents a body of electors in a legislative assembly; embodiment, type, specimen; *(leg.)* one who stands in the place of another.

REPRESS (1) [rē-pres'], *v.t.* to press once more.

REPRESS (2) [ri-pres'], *v.t.* to put down, crush, suppress; check, curb; *(psych.)* shut out from the conscious mind and force into the subconscious (instinctive tendencies, fears etc.). [L.].

REPRESSION [ri-pre'shn], *n.* act of repressing; state of being repressed; suppression, restraint; *(psych.)*

a shutting out of fears, instinctive tendencies etc. from the conscious mind, from which they are driven into the subconscious.

REPRESSIVE [ri-pre'siv], *adj.* tending to subdue or restrain.

REPRIEVE (1) [ri-prēv'], *v.t.* to suspend or delay the execution of a sentence, *esp.* the death sentence, upon; grant a respite to. REPRIEVE (2), *n.* act of reprieving; suspension or postponement of the execution of a criminal's sentence, *esp.* by remission of a death sentence; official document authorizing this; respite, temporary relief or release. [~ME.].

REPRIMAND (1) [re'pri-mahnd], *n.* severe reproof, rebuke or censure, *esp.* when administered officially. REPRIMAND (2), *v.t.* to reprove, censure severely, *esp.* to rebuke publicly and officially. [Fr.].

REPRINT (1) [rē-print'], *v.t.* to print again, publish a fresh impression or new edition of. REPRINT (2) [rē'print], *n.* new impression of a printed work, without alterations, from a previous edition.

REPRISAL [ri-prī'zal], *n.* (usually pl.) counteraction taken by a person attacked against the attacker; retaliatory measures taken by one state against another. [OFr.].

REPROACH (1) [ri-prōch'], *v.t.* to rebuke, censure, upbraid. REPROACH (2), *n.* rebuke, censure tinged with sorrow and disgust; shame or disgrace; anything bringing shame and discredit on one. [OFr.].

REPROACHFUL [ri-prōch'fool], *adj.* expressing or containing reproach, upbraiding.

REPROBATE (1) [re'prō-bāt], *v.t.* to condemn, disapprove of wholeheartedly; *(theol.)* reject or exclude from salvation. REPROBATE (2), *adj.* damned by God, lost to salvation; unprincipled, abandoned, sinful. REPROBATE (3), *n.* worthless person, abandoned to sin and lacking in honourable principles; *(coll.)* rascal. [L.].

REPROBATION [re-prō-bā'shn], *n.* act of reprobating; state of being abandoned to eternal destruction, *esp.* by divine decree; severe censure. [L.].

REPRODUCE [rē-prō-dyōōs'], *v.t.* to propagate, procreate; produce again, cause to grow afresh; make a copy of; imitate; bring back again, repeat exactly; publish, present; *v.i.* to propagate one's species. REPRODUCER, *n.* one who, or that which, reproduces; device for reproducing sounds.

REPRODUCTION [rē-prō-duk'shn], *n.* act or process of reproducing, *esp.* the process by which fresh members of the same species are generated, or fresh organisms produced by parent organisms; something reproduced, a copy.

REPRODUCTIVE [rē-prō-duk'tiv], *adj.* concerned with, relating to, employed in, reproduction; that reproduces or tends to reproduce.

REPROOF (1) [rē-prōōf'], *v.t.* to make waterproof once more.

REPROOF (2) [ri-prōōf'], *n.* censure, rebuke, scolding; an expression of this. [OFr.].

REPROVE [ri-prōōv'], *v.t.* to blame, censure, scold, reprimand.

REPTILE (1) [rep'til], *n.* a creeping animal moving on its belly or on very short legs, *esp.* *(zool.)* a class of cold-blooded, crawling vertebrates covered with plates or scales; *(fig.)* insignificant, base, sly, creature. REPTILE (2), *adj.* crawling, like a r.; *(fig.)* grovelling, mean. [LL.].

REPTILIAN [rep-ti'li-an], *adj.* pertaining to, resembling, reptiles. REPTILIAN (2), *n.* a reptile.

REPUBLIC [ri-pub'lik], *n.* form of government in which the supreme ruling power is vested in representatives elected by the people; state or country having this form of government, the head of the state being elected by popular vote. [L.].

REPUBLICAN (1) [ri-pub'li-kan], *adj.* relating to, by means of, according to, a republic; in the spirit of, in favour of, a republic; of, or pertaining to, the Republicans. REPUBLICAN (2), *n.* one who favours a r. form of government; member of the R. Party in the U.S.A. REPUBLICANISM, *n.* system of government; attachment to a r. form of government; principles of a r. government.

REPUDIATE [ri-pyōō'di-āt], *v.t.* to disown, deny responsibility for or connexion with; refuse to recognize or admit, reject; refuse to acknowledge, disclaim (a debt or liability); *(hist.)* divorce (a wife). [L.].

REPUDIATION [ri-pyōō-di-ā'shn], *n.* disclaiming of a responsibility or obligation; refusal to acknowledge and discharge a debt. [L.].

REPUGNANCE [ri-pug'nans], *n.* aversion, scornful distaste, violent dislike; incompatibility. [L.].

REPUGNANT [ri-pug'nant], *adj.* distasteful, highly unpleasant, offensive; hostile; contrary. [L.].

REPULSE (1) [ri-puls'], *v.t.* to repel, drive back; rebuff, reject. REPULSE (2), *n.* act of repelling or driving back; state of being repelled; set-back; rebuff, refusal. [L.].

REPULSION [ri-pul'shn], *n.* act of repelling; dislike, aversion; (*phys.*) tendency of bodies to be driven farther apart from one another. [LL.].

REPULSIVE [ri-pul'siv], *adj.* arousing abhorrence, loathsome, disgusting; forbidding, repellent, unattractive; (*phys.*) exhibiting repulsion. [Fr.].

REPUTABLE [re'pyŏŏ-ta-bl], *adj.* being in good repute; held in esteem; honourable.

REPUTATION [re-pyŏŏ-tā'shn], *n.* esteem or regard in which a person or thing is commonly held, character according to public report; popular opinion of a person or thing, *esp.* as having some particular attribute; good name; honour, renown. [L.].

REPUTE (1) [ri-pyŏŏt'], *v.t.* (*pass.*) to be generally considered as (being). REPUTE (2), *n.* esteem, reputation, general public opinion of a person or thing; good reputation, honour. REPUTED, *adj.* generally regarded or accepted; supposed, ostensible; renowned. REPUTEDLY, *adv.* by r. [L.].

REQUEST (1) [ri-kwest'], *n.* expression of a desire or need for something, entreaty; that which is asked for; demand; **in r.**, eagerly sought after. REQUEST (2), *v.t.* to ask for, express a desire for, seek; ask. [OFr.].

REQUIEM [re'kwi-em], *n.* (*R. C.*) a mass for the dead; musical setting of the words of this; dirge or poem recited or sung upon the death of a person. [L.].

REQUIRE [ri-kwier'], *v.t.* to need, want; order, command; demand as by right or authority, claim; request, call for. [L.].

REQUIREMENT [ri-kwier'ment], *n.* (*usually pl.*) that which is required, need, demand, want; that which must be conformed to, condition, stipulation. [L.].

REQUISITE (1) [re'kwi-zit], *adj.* needed, necessary; essential for some purpose or occasion. REQUISITE (2), *n.* that which is necessary for something, something indispensable for a particular purpose or occasion. [L.].

REQUISITION (1) [re-kwi-zi'shn], *n.* forma ldemand or request for something, made as of right, *esp.* an official application, made by authority, that something shall be done or provided for military purposes; state of being put into service or active use; requirement, condition. REQUISITION (2), *v.t.* to commandeer, require to be done or provided for military purposes; make a r. upon; call into service. [L.].

REQUITAL [ri-kwi'tal], *n.* act of requiting, action repaying or in return for a previous action; retaliation; recompense, reward.

REQUITE [ri-kwit'], *v.t.* to repay, do or give back in return; avenge; reward; punish (a person); recompense (a person). [RE and ~QUIT].

REREDOS [rēer'e-dos], *n.* screen, usually decorated with ornamental carving, at the back of the altar in a church; screen in front of the choir. [AFr. from OFr.].

RESCIND [ri-sind'], *v.t.* to annul; revoke; abrogate, repeal. [L.].

RESCISSION [ri-si'zhn], *n.* act of rescinding. [L.].

RESCRIPT [rē'skript], *n.* written official answer made by the Pope in reply to some question submitted to him; official edict or decree, issued by a ruler. [L.].

RESCUE (1) [res'kyŏŏ], *v.t.* to set free from confinement, danger, harmful influences or any hazardous plight; extricate from a difficulty; recover by force. RESCUE (2), *n.* deliverance from danger, captivity or other harmful plight; **to come to the r.**, to provide necessary assistance; **r. squad,** squad of people organized to r. persons trapped in débris after an air-raid. [AFr.].

RESEARCH (1) [ri-surch'], *n.* investigation in order to discover some particular fact or facts about someone or something, *esp.* methodical and original study of some subject by trained investigators, in order to add to existing knowledge of, or to furnish new ideas upon, that subject. RESEARCH (2), *v.i.* to engage in r. [OFr.].

RESEDA [re-sē'dah], *n.* (*bot.*) genus of plants including mignonette; [re'ze-dah] light greenish colour. [L.].

RESEMBLANCE [ri-zem'blans], *n.* state of being like, likeness, similarity of appearance or any other aspect. [AFr.].

RESEMBLE [ri-zem'bl], *v.t.* to be like, possess certain attributes in common with. [OFr.].

RESENT [ri-zent'], *v.t.* to object to strongly as a personal offence or source of annoyance, feel angry and aggrieved at. [Fr.].

RESENTFUL [ri-zent'fŏŏl], *adj.* filled with resentment; inclined to harbour grievances.

RESENTMENT [ri-zent'ment], *n.* feeling of soreness or aggrievedness aroused by a sense of personal injury or affront; grievance, ill-will. [~Fr.].

RESERVATION [re-zer-vā'shn], *n.* act of reserving; that which is reserved; an exception or limitation expressed or mentally resolved; act of reserving some right or privilege for oneself; (*eccles.*) act of keeping for some purpose some part of the consecrated elements after the celebration of the Eucharist; tract of land set apart for the sole use of certain native tribes or for any other special purpose; (*leg.*) retention of a right or interest in property conveyed or leased to another; (*U.S.*) accommodation reserved; **mental r.,** the withholding in the mind of something which, if expressed, would alter a statement. [LL.].

RESERVE (1) [ri-zurv'], *v.t.* to keep back for future use, keep as a spare supply; set aside for the use of a particular person or persons; order in advance; set apart; postpone; (*leg.*) retain (rights or interest) in property which is conveyed; (*eccles.*) set aside (part of the consecrated elements) for use for some particular purpose; declare exempt from military service on grounds of national expediency. RESERVE (2), *n.* that which is reserved for some reason; limitation or exception; the withholding of whole-hearted approval or acceptance; lowest price at which a thing may be sold at an auction; restraint, aloofness, avoidance of undue familiarity or exuberance; stretch of country enclosed for some particular use; that which is kept back for future use, spare supply; (*milit.*) (*pl.*) armed forces kept back from action to give later support when needed; (*milit.*) branch of the fighting forces consisting of trained and experienced men whose services are now only required in the event of war or special emergency; (*sport*) player or athlete selected to take the place of a member of a team if required; (*pl., sport*) second best team of a club; (*comm.*) capital held in readiness to meet ordinary or likely demands; **gold r.,** sufficient quantity of gold kept to cover the issue of paper money; **without r.,** unrestrictedly; **in r.,** in readiness for possible future use. [L.].

RESERVED [ri-zurvd'], *adj.* aloof, reticent, shy, avoiding undue familiarity; kept apart for someone, booked in advance; **R. List,** list of naval officers no longer in active service, but who could be called upon in the event of war or emergency; **r. occupation,** occupation in which workers are exempt from national service.

RESERVIST [ri-zur'vist], *n.* member of the reserve forces.

RESERVOIR [re'zer-vwah(r)], *n.* large receptacle built or adapted to collect and store water for the use of the inhabitants of a town, city etc.; that part of an apparatus or implement in which liquid is stored; receptacle in an animal or plant in which fluid is contained; store, supply. [Fr.].

RESET (1) (*pres.pt.* **resetting,** *pret. and p.pt.* **reset**) [rē-set'], *v.t.* to set again; put a fresh edge upon; replant; (*typ.*) set up again. RESET (2), *n.* (*typ.*) act of resetting; piece of printing which has been r.

RESHUFFLE (1) [rē-shu'fl], *v.t.* to shuffle afresh; rearrange. RESHUFFLE (2), *n.* a fresh shuffle; rearrangement of positions.

RESIDE [ri-zid'], *v.i.* to live (in or at) permanently or for a length of time, dwell (in or at); (of power etc.) rest (in); be present, inhere; live at some official residence for the discharge of official duties. [L.].

RESIDENCE [re'zi-dens], *n.* act of residing in a place; act of residing in a specified place for the discharge of some duty; dwelling place, abode; time during which one resides in a place; imposing type of house. [LL.].

RESIDENCY [re'zi-den-si], *n.* formerly, the official residence of the representative of the British Government at the court of an Indian prince.

RESIDENT (1) [re'zi-dent], *adj.* residing; living at a particular place in order to satisfy some condition or discharge some duty; present, inherent. RESIDENT (2), *n.* one who lives more or less permanently in a place; formerly, a political agent or representative of the Viceroy and British Government at the court of an Indian prince.

RESIDENTIARY (1) [re-zi-den'sha-ri], *adj.* necessitating official residence; having to live at an official residence; resident. RESIDENTIARY (2), *n.* (*eccles.*)

---

an ecclesiastic, *esp.* a canon who has to live in an official residence for a certain period of time.

RESIDUAL [ri-zi'dyōō-al], *adj.* outstanding, remaining, left as a residue; (*math.*) left after subtraction; (*phys.*) left unexplained. [L.].

RESIDUARY [ri-zi'dyōō-a-ri], *adj.* remaining, left over; in the form of a residue; (*leg.*) relating to the residue of an estate; **r. legatee,** person to whom is bequeathed the residue of an estate.

RESIDUE [re'zi-dyōō], *n.* remainder, rest, that which is left over after something has been taken away; (*chem.*) residuum; (*leg.*) that which remains of an estate after all debts, charges upon it, and special legacies have been deducted. [Fr.].

RESIDUUM (*pl.* **residua**) [ri-zi'dyōō-um], *n.* remainder; (*chem.*) that which is left after a process of separation, combustion, evaporation etc., waste product or deposit; (*leg.*) residue. [L.].

RESIGN [ri-zin'], *v.t.* to give up, relinquish; withdraw, abandon; *v.i.* to give up an office or position; *v. reflex.* to yield, submit, hand oneself over (to), accept with equanimity. [L.].

RESIGNATION [re-zig-nā'shn], *n.* act of resigning; expression of one's intention to resign; submission with equanimity to the will of Providence, reconcilement to one's fate. [MedL.].

RESIGNED [ri-zind'], *adj.* submissive, patiently accepting, reconciled. **RESIGNEDLY** [ri-zi'ned-li], *adv.* with resignation.

RESILIENCE, RESILIENCY [ri-zi'li-ens(-i)], *n.* elasticity, quality of returning to its original shape and position after stretching or compression; act of springing back; recoil from anything; power of recovering from a shock etc. [L.].

RESILIENT [ri-zi'li-ent], *adj.* elastic, springing back to its original position or shape; (*fig.*) readily recovering from depression.

RESIN (1) [re'zin], *n.* gum-like secretion of plants, *esp.* firs and pines. **RESIN** (2), *v.t.* to treat or rub with r. [L.].

RESIST [ri-zist'], *v.t.* to obstruct, act in opposition to, strive against; withstand the force of without giving way; be proof against, be unaffected by; oppose, stand firm against; refuse to succumb to; *v.i.* to offer resistance. **RESISTANT,** *adj.* resisting, offering opposition. [L.].

RESISTANCE [ri-zis'tans], *n.* act of resisting; opposition, hindrance; power of resisting, antagonism; ability to be unaffected by a specified influence; (*phys.*) tendency of any form of matter to oppose force exerted by, or pressure of, another body upon it; (*phys.*) non-conductivity; (*elect.*) degree of opposition offered by an electric circuit to the passage of an electric current; apparatus designed to resist the passage of an electric current; in the Second World War, armed opposition by citizens of occupied countries; an organized movement with this object; **passive r.,** any form of protest in which no active opposition is offered; **line of least r.,** easiest course to follow; **r. box,** (*elect.*) box fitted with resistances. **RESISTANCE-COIL,** (*elect.*) coil of wire placed in an electric circuit to increase its r. [Fr.].

RESISTIVE [ri-zis'tiv], *adj.* having the power, tending, to resist.

RESOLUTE [re'zō-lyōōt], *adj.* firm, determined, unwavering in purpose.

RESOLUTION [re-zō-lyōō'shn], *n.* act of resolving or splitting up into its component parts, analysis; state of being so resolved; solution; formal statement of opinion passed by, or decision made at, a meeting or public assembly; proposal offered to such a meeting for consideration; fixed intention or determination to perform some specific course of action; resoluteness; conversion to something else; (*pros.*) the using of two short syllables for one long one; (*med.*) disappearance of inflammation without discharge of matter; (*mus.*) the moving from a discord to a concord to complete the harmony. [L.].

RESOLVE (1) [ri-zolv'], *v.t.* to split up into its constituent elements; break up (a complex idea or problem) into simple parts or aspects; clear up, settle; explain; (*pass.*) be determined; (*med.*) remove without suppuration; *v.i.* to determine, decide; (*mus.*) pass from a discord to a concord to complete the harmony; *v. reflex.* to be reduced. **RESOLVE** (2), *n.* determination, firm intention; firmness of purpose. [L.].

RESOLVED [ri-zolvd'], *adj.* determined in purpose, resolute.

RESONANCE [re'zō-nans], *n.* vibration set up in a body in sympathy with another body already

vibrating; sound set up by such sympathetic vibration; sonority. [L.].

RESONANT [re'zo-nant], *adj.* sonorous, resounding, ringing; setting up resonance.

RESORBENT [ri-saw'bent], *adj.* absorbing again; taking in once more. [L.].

RESORT (1) [ri-zawt'], *v.i.* to have recourse to, use as a means of accomplishing some purpose; proceed, go regularly. **RESORT** (2), *n.* act of resorting to, recourse; act of visiting frequently; expedient, means to accomplish something, thing or person to which one has recourse; place which one regularly visits, place frequented, *esp.* for a specific purpose or by a particular type of people. [OFr.].

RESOUND [ri-zownd'], *v.t.* to re-echo, send back; (*fig.*) proclaim, spread abroad, celebrate; *v.i.* to reverberate, ring with a particular sound; echo, sound loudly and continually; (*fig.*) be celebrated, be proclaimed far and wide.

RESOURCE [ri-saws'], *n.* expedient, shift, resort, source of aid or support; source of distraction or recreation; ingenuity, skill in devising ways and means of accomplishing something; (*pl.*) stock, means of supplying requirements; money or property, means of support. [Fr.].

RESOURCEFUL [ri-saws'fōōl], *adj.* clever at devising ways and means of dealing with or accomplishing anything.

RESPECT (1) [ri-spekt'], *n.* esteem or appreciation; suitable deference; attention, consideration; due regard; a particular aspect or detail; regard, reference; (*pl.*) greetings, kind regards; **to pay one's respects to,** to visit in order to express one's goodwill towards; **in r. of, with r. to,** concerning. **RESPECT** (2), *v.t.* to pay due heed to, appreciate fully; regard with deference, honour, esteem; show consideration for, observe. [L.].

RESPECTABILITY [ri-spek-ta-bi'li-ti], *n.* quality of being respectable; person who is accounted respectable; conduct considered proper by those claiming to be respectable; (*coll.*) slavish adherence to a conventional social creed of conduct.

RESPECTABLE [ri-spek'ta-bl], *adj.* worthy of, held in, respect; decent, honest, well-behaved; adhering to the conventional social creed of conduct; suitable, proper, presentable; reasonably good, above the average.

RESPECTFUL [ri-spekt'fōōl], *adj.* showing respect, deferential.

RESPECTING [ri-spek'ting], *prep.* concerning, in regard to, with reference to.

RESPECTIVE [ri-spek'tiv], *adj.* of each one compared with each of the others mentioned, relative; several, individual, separate. **RESPECTIVELY,** *adv.* as relating to each, referring to each individually.

RESPIRATION [re-spi-rā'shn], *n.* act of breathing; a single breath.

RESPIRATOR [re'spi-rā-ter], *n.* apparatus for protecting the lungs from the inspiration of smoke, fumes, gases or cold air; gas-mask.

RESPIRE [ri-spier'], *v.t.* to exhale; breathe out; *v.i.* to breathe; inhale air into the lungs and exhale it; take a respite. [L.].

RESPITE (1) [re'spit, re'spit], *n.* temporary intermission of labour, pain or danger, interval of rest; pause, suspension of the execution of a criminal; prolongation of time for the payment of a debt. **RESPITE** (2) [re-spit'], *v.t.* to relieve by an interval of rest; postpone; reprieve. [OFr.].

RESPLENDENCE, RESPLENDENCY [ri-splen'dens(-i)], *n.* brilliant lustre; vivid brightness; splendour. [LL.].

RESPLENDENT [ri-splen'dent], *adj.* very bright; shining with brilliant lustre; (*coll.*) very fine. [~L.].

RESPOND [ri-spond'], *v.i.* to reply; answer; reply to a letter; be responsive. [L.].

RESPONDENT (1) [ri-spon'dent], *adj.* that responds to a demand or expectation. **RESPONDENT** (2), *n.* (*leg.*) person who answers to a suit at law, *esp.* one for divorce; defendant.

RESPONSE [ri-spons'], *n.* reply; reaction to stimulus; (*eccles.*) answer of the congregation to the priest; (*R. C. Church*) kind of anthem sung after a lesson at matins. [L.].

RESPONSIBILITY [ri-spon-si-bi'li-ti], *n.* state of being responsible; what one is responsible for; obligation; trust; duty.

RESPONSIBLE [ri-spon'si-bl], *adj.* answerable; liable to account; able to discharge an obligation; trustworthy; rational; involving responsibility.

RESPONSIONS [ri-spon'shnz], *n.(pl.)* entrance

The accent ´ after a syllable = stress (u-pon´).   The mark ‾ over a vowel = length (ā in made; ō in bone).

examination at Oxford University for students for the B.A. degree.

RESPONSIVE [ri-spon'siv], *adj.* responding; answering; reacting easily to stimulus; sensitive.

RESPONSORY [ri-spon'se-ri], *n.* an anthem sung during a church service after the lesson. [LL.].

REST (1) [rest], *n.* cessation from motion or action; repose; quiet, sleep; peace; place of quiet or repose; death, the grave; that on or in which anything rests; short pause; (*mus.*) interval of time, during which there is an intermission of the voice or sound. REST-CURE, treatment for nervous illnesses, in which the patient is kept completely quiet. REST (2), *v.t.* to place; quiet; allow to r.; lay in r.; *v.i.* to cease from action or motion; be quiet; repose; sleep; be dead; lean; stand (on); rely. [OE.].

REST (3), *v.t.* to remain. REST (4), *n.* the remainder; what is left. [Fr.].

RESTATE [rē-stāt'], *v.t.* to state a second or subsequent time. RESTATEMENT, *n.* act of stating a thing for a second time or in a different manner.

RESTAURANT [res'te-rant, res'te-ro(ng)], *n.* establishment for the provision of food and drink; superior eating-house. [Fr.].

RESTAURATEUR [res-taw-rah-tur'], *n.* one who keeps a restaurant. [Fr.].

RESTFUL [rest'fool], *adj.* affording rest, quiet; reposeful; soothing.

RESTHARROW [rest'ha-rō], *n.* (*bot.*) a shrub, any one of the various species of the genus *Ononis*. [ARREST and HARROW (1)].

RESTING-PLACE [res'ting-plās], *n.* place where a person or thing may rest or remain; the grave.

RESTITUTION [re-sti-tyōō'shn], *n.* act of restoring some right of which a person has been unjustly deprived; compensation. [L.].

RESTIVE [res'tiv], *adj.* unwilling to be driven; stubborn; restless or impatient under restraint; inclined to jib.

RESTLESS [rest'les], *adj.* continually moving; sleepless; uneasy; not satisfied to remain at rest; turbulent; unsettled; without tranquillity.

RESTORATION [re-staw-rā'shn], *n.* act of restoring; renewal; recovery; (*hist.*) return to the English throne of Charles II in 1660; reconstruction or model of an extinct animal, ruined building etc. [L.].

RESTORATIVE (1) [ri-staw'ra-tiv], *adj.* capable of giving fresh strength. RESTORATIVE (2), *n.* medicine or food for restoring strength. [OFr.].

RESTORE [ri-staw(r)'], *v.t.* to bring back to a former condition; repair; heal; rebuild; revive; recover; give back; replace. [L.].

RESTRAIN [ri-strān'], *v.t.* to hold back or check; repress; hinder; restrict; hold under restraint. RESTRAINING, *adj.* curbing; checking. [OFr.].

RESTRAINT [ri-strānt'], *n.* act of restraining; abridgment of liberty; that which restrains; check; curb. [OFr.].

RESTRICT [ri-strikt'], *v.t.* to limit; confine; restrain within bounds; impose legal limitations upon. RESTRICTED, *adj.* under a legal limitation; confined, restrained; **r. area,** area in which the speed limit for motor vehicles is r., usually to 30 m.p.h. [L.].

RESTRICTION [ri-strik'shn], *n.* action of restricting; limitation, restraint; law or regulation restricting some activity. [L.].

RESTRICTIVE [ri-strik'tiv], *adj.* having the quality of limiting; imposing restrictions.

RESULT (1) [ri-zult'], *v.i.* to follow as a consequence; issue. RESULT (2), *n.* consequence; conclusion; effect; outcome; (*math.*) answer following a process of calculation. [L.].

RESULTANT (1) [ri-zul'tant], *adj.* resulting; following as a result. RESULTANT (2), *n.* the outcome of something; (*phys.*) the force which is the combined effect of two or more forces acting in various directions.

RESUME [ri-zyōōm'], *v.t.* to take back; begin, take up, again; continue once more. [L.].

RESUME, résumé [re'zyōō-mā], *n.* a summing-up; condensed statement; précis. [Fr.].

RESUMPTION [ri-zump'shn], *n.* action of resuming. RESUMPTIVE, *adj.* resuming; taking back or again. [L.].

RESURGENT [ri-sur'jent], *adj.* rising again; reviving. [L.].

RESURRECT [re-ze-rekt'], *v.t.* to restore to life; raise again from the dead; bring into use again something previously discarded or hidden away.

RESURRECTION [re-ze-rek'shn], *n.* a rising again; resuscitation; **the R.,** Christ's rising from the grave;

the rising of man from death on the Day of Judgment. [L.].

RESURRECTIONIST [re-ze-rek'shn-ist], *n.* (*hist.*) one who exhumed and stole dead bodies for dissection; body-snatcher.

RESUSCITATE [ri-su'si-tāt], *v.t.* to revivify; revive; recover from apparent death; resurrect; *v.i.* to revive. [L.].

RESUSCITATION [ri-su-si-tā'shn], *n.* action of reviving from a state of apparent death; state of being resuscitated.

RETAIL (1) [rē'tāl], *n.* sale of commodities in small quantities to the consumer. RETAIL (2), *adj.* pertaining to the sale of goods by r. or to the goods thus sold. RETAIL (3), *adv.* by r. RETAIL (4) [rē-tāl'], *v.t.* to sell in small quantities; sell direct to the consumer goods bought wholesale; (*fig.*) tell to many, repeat.

RETAIN [ri-tān'], *v.t.* to hold or keep in possession; remember; detain; keep back; keep in pay; engage by prepayment. [OFr. from L.].

RETAINER [ri-tā'ner], *n.* one who, or that which, retains; attendant; servant; dependant; (*leg.*) fee paid to engage a barrister, retaining fee; fee paid to any adviser, contributor etc. to secure his services; retention by legal right.

RETAINING [ri-tā'ning], *adj.* keeping in possession; engaging by a fee; **r. fee,** fee paid in advance to a barrister to accept a brief; fee paid to an adviser for an option on his services; **r. wall,** wall to prevent a bank of earth from collapsing.

RETAKE (1) (*pret.* **retook**, *p.pt.* **retaken**) [rē-tāk'], *v.t.* to take again; recapture. RETAKE (2) [rē'tāk], *n.* (*cinema*) the photographing of a scene a second time; the section of film thus made.

RETALIATE [ri-ta'li-āt], *v.t.* to return like for like; requite; *v.i.* to practise reprisals; pay back injury for injury. RETALIATIVE, RETALIATORY, *adj.* pertaining to retaliation; returning like for like. [LL.].

RETALIATION [ri-ta-li-ā'shn], *n.* act of returning like for like; requital of evil, reprisals.

RETARD [ri-tahd'], *v.t.* to diminish the speed of; hamper; delay. [L.].

RETARDATION [rē-tah-dā'shn], *n.* action of retarding; delay; (*phys.*) rate of loss of velocity.

RETCH [rēch], *v.i.* to try hard to vomit; strain, as in vomiting. [OE.].

RETENTION [ri-ten'shn], *n.* action of retaining; power of retaining; esp. ideas in the mind. [OFr.].

RETENTIVE [ri-ten'tiv], *adj.* having the power to retain in the memory; not forgetful. [OFr.].

RETICENCE [re'ti-sens], *n.* reserve in speech, esp. about one's own affairs; uncommunicativeness. [L.].

RETICENT [re'ti-sent], *adj.* reserved in speech; taciturn; uncommunicative.

RETICULAR [re-ti'kyōō-ler], *adj.* having the form of, resembling, network; formed with interstices.

RETICULATE [re-ti'kyōō-lāt], *adj.* reticulated.

RETICULATED [re-ti'kyōō-lā-tid], *adj.* netted; resembling network; **r. work,** kind of masonry formed of small square stones or bricks placed lozenge-wise. RETICULATION [re-ti-kyōō-lā'shn], *n.* condition of being reticulated; network. [L.].

RETICULE [re'ti-kyōōl], *n.* lady's small handbag formerly of network. [L.].

RETINA [re'ti-nah], *n.* an expansion of the optic nerve in the eye, which receives the impressions of light giving rise to vision. [L.].

RETINUE [re'ti-nyōō], *n.* train of attendants of a distinguished personage, suite. [OFr.].

RETIRE [ri-tier'], *v.i.* to go from company or from a public place into privacy; give up one's occupation or office; withdraw; go to bed; retreat; recede; *v.t.* to cause to resign; withdraw from publicity; (*comm.*) take up and pay a bill when due. RETIRING, *adj.* reserved; not forward or obtrusive; given on retirement from work. [Fr.].

RETIRED [ri-tierd'], *adj.* secluded from society; quiet; private; gone into retirement; **r. list,** list of officers who have r. from service; **to put on the r. list,** to send into retirement from active life.

RETIREMENT [ri-tier'ment], *n.* act of retiring, withdrawing from society or public life; state of being retired; retired abode; privacy; act of going to bed.

RETORT (1) [ri-tawt'], *n.* glass or earthenware vessel with a long curved neck, for the purpose of distillation; iron or steel vessel in which coal is heated to produce gas. [L.].

RETORT (2), *v.t. and i.* to reply in answer to a question

ōō is pronounced as in *food*; ŏŏ as in *hood*; th as in *think*; ŧн as in *that*; zh as in *azure*. ~ = related to.

or argument; answer sharply. RETORT (3), *n.* a ready reply; sharp counter-statement. [L.].

RETOUCH [rē-tuch´], *v.t.* to touch again; improve by touching up here and there.

RETRACE [rē-trās´], *v.t.* to go over once more; trace back; renew the outline of, as a drawing; return by the same way.

RETRACT (1) [ri-trakt´], *v.t.* to draw back; withdraw (in physical senses); (*phon.*) articulate with the tongue further back. RETRACTILE, *adj.* able to be retracted. RETRACTIVE, *adj.* causing to r.; retracting. [L.].

RETRACT (2), *v.t.* to withdraw, recall; recant; *v.i.* to withdraw (one's words). RETRACTATION [rē-trak-tā´-shn], *n.* withdrawal (of words or opinions), recantation. [L.].

RETRACTION [ri-trak´shn], *n.* act of drawing back; act of withdrawing. [L.].

RETREAT (1) [ri-trēt´], *v.i.* to retire from any position or place; withdraw to seclusion or safety; retire from an enemy; abandon one's position in an argument. RETREAT (2), *n.* act of retiring; retirement or seclusion; place of retirement or of safety; short retirement for quiet meditation into a religious institution; the retiring of an army from the face of an enemy or from an advanced position; signal for retiring to quarters or from an engagement. [OFr.].

RETRENCH [ri-trensh´], *v.t.* to pare away; lessen; curtail; *v.i.* to cut down expenses, economize. RETRENCHMENT, *n.* act of removing what is superfluous; reduction of expenditure. [L.].

RETRIBUTION [re-tri-byōō´shn], *n.* suitable requital for good, or *esp.* evil; reward or punishment, just requital; distribution of rewards and punishments at the Judgment Day. RETRIBUTIVE, RETRIBUTORY [ri-tri´byōō-tiv, -te-ri], *adj.* involving, pertaining to, r. [L.].

RETRIEVE [ri-trēv´], *v.t.* to find again; restore; rescue; (of dogs) to fetch game which has been shot. RETRIEVAL, *n.* act of retrieving. [OFr.].

RETRIEVER [ri-trē´ver], *n.* one who, or that which, retrieves; dog trained to fetch game which has been shot; dog of a breed especially fitted for this.

RETRO-, *pref.* back, backwards; in return. [L.].

RETROACTIVE [re-trō-ak´tiv], *adj.* working backwards; affecting what is past; retrospective.

RETROGRADE (1) [re´trō-grād], *adj.* going or moving backwards; going from a civilized to a less civilized condition; (*astron.*) apparently moving backwards, and contrary to the succession of the signs of the Zodiac; declining, deteriorating. RETROGRADE (2), *v.i.* to move backwards; deteriorate. [L.].

RETROGRESS [re-trō-gres´], *v.i.* to deteriorate; move backwards. RETROGRESSION [re-trō-gre´shn], *n.* act of going backwards; deterioration. RETROGRESSIVE, *adj.* going or moving backwards; declining in excellence. [L.].

RETROSPECT [re´trō-spekt], *n.* a looking back on things past; review in the memory. RETROSPECTION [re-trō-spek´shn], *n.* act or faculty of looking back on things past. [L.].

RETROSPECTIVE [re-trō-spek´tiv], *adj.* pertaining to the past; looking back to the past; applying to, based on, the past.

RETROUSSE, retroussé [re-trōō´sā], *adj.* (of the nose) turned up, tip-tilted. [Fr.].

RETROVERSION [re-trō-vur´shn], *n.* act of turning or bending back; a turning or falling backwards. [~L.].

RETURN (1) [ri-turn´], *v.i.* to come back, go back to the same place, condition, state; answer; revert; recur; *v.t.* to bring or send back; repay; give back in recompense; yield; give back in reply; give in an official account; elect. RETURNING-OFFICER, presiding officer at a municipal or parliamentary election. RETURN (2), *n.* act of going back; act of giving back; a periodical coming back; periodical renewal; official report; profit of business; dividends on capital invested; repayment; restitution; ticket on a public conveyance entitling the holder to a journey to the destination and back again; (*pl.*) unsold articles, *esp.* newspapers, returned to the wholesaler; (*pl.*) a mild light tobacco. [OFr.].

REUNION [rē-yōō´ni-on], *n.* act of reuniting; union formed anew after separation; a meeting or gathering of friends or associates.

REV [rev], *v.t. and i.* (usually with *up*) (of an engine) to increase the number of revolutions per minute (of). [REV(OLUTION)].

REVEAL [ri-vēl´], *v.t.* to disclose to view; make known, divulge; (of God) make known (by divine power or agency). REVEALED, *adj.* made known, declared; **revealed religion,** religion taught by divine revelation or supernatural agency. [L.].

REVEILLE [re-va´li], *n.* (*milit.*) bugle-call sounded to rouse sleeping men. [Fr.].

REVEL (1) (*pres.pt.* **revelling,** *pret. and p.pt.* **revelled**) [re´vel], *v.t. and i.* to carouse, make merry riotously; **to r. in,** to take delight in, indulge in without restraint. REVEL (2), *n.* carousal, noisy merrymaking; (*pl.*) prearranged entertainment, including pageantry, singing, dancing etc.; **Master of the Revels,** official responsible for court entertainments. [OFr.].

REVELATION [re-ve-lā´shn], *n.* act of revealing; that which is revealed; disclosure (of something hitherto secret); (*coll.*) event, fact or experience which opens a wider field of knowledge or understanding; (*religion*) declaration of the mystery of God to man by divine power; **R. of St. John the Divine,** the Apocalypse, the last book of the Bible. REVELATIONIST, *n.* one who accepts divine r.; **the Revelationist,** St. John the Divine, traditional author of the Apocalypse. [L.].

REVELLER [re´ve-ler], *n.* one who revels; habitual and riotous merrymaker.

REVELRY [re´vel-ri], *n.* noisy festivity, revels.

REVENANT [re´ve-nah(ng)], *n.* person returned after a long absence; one risen from the dead, ghost. [Fr.].

REVENGE (1) [ri-venj´], *v.t. and i.* to avenge, requite for (an injury), exact vengeance for; **to be revenged,** to take vengeance; **to r. oneself (up)on,** to inflict vengeance on, repay with evil for evil. REVENGE (2), *n.* act of taking vengeance on; malicious desire to do this; a return game. [OFr.].

REVENUE [re´ve-nyōō], *n.* income, profits, *esp.* the total income of the state; **Inland R.,** the r. to the state from taxes, duties etc.; **the R.,** government department concerned with the collecting of taxes and duties; **r. officer,** customs official. [OFr.].

REVER, see REVERS.

REVERBERATE [ri-vur´be-rāt], *v.t. and i.* to cause to re-echo or resound; (*fig.*) reflect; resound; be reflected. REVERBERANT, *adj.* resounding. REVERBERATIVE, REVERBERATORY, *adj.* reverberating, pertaining to reverberation. [L.].

REVERBERATION [ri-ver-be-rā´shn], *n.* act of reverberating; a re-echoing sound.

REVERE [ri-vēer´], *v.t.* to regard with profound veneration, respect greatly. [L.].

REVERENCE (1) [re´ve-rens], *n.* feeling of profound admiration or respect, veneration; deep bow or other action expressive of respect; person to whom such respect is or should be paid, *esp.* used formerly in England and still in Ireland as a title of address to a cleric. REVERENCE (2), *v.t.* to regard with loving respect and veneration, revere. [L.].

REVEREND [re´ve-rend], *adj.* worthy of reverence; as a title of address to a clergyman (in writing shortened to *Rev.*).

REVERENT [re´ve-rent], *adj.* moved by a feeling of reverence; exhibiting such a manner as befits nearness or reference to sacred things. [L.].

REVERENTIAL [re-ve-ren´shal], *adj.* pertaining to, or proceeding from, reverence.

REVERIE [re´ve-ri], *n.* daydream, mood of pensive abstraction in which one becomes temporarily oblivious of one's surroundings; piece of music intended to express such a mood. [Fr.].

REVER(S) [ri-vēer(z)´], *n.* (*often as pl.*) lapel or any similar part of the edge of a garment which turns back so as to show the inner surface. [Fr.].

REVERSAL [ri-vur´sal], *n.* act of reversing; a change or overthrowing, a defeat, check.

REVERSE (1) [ri-vurs´], *v.t.* to turn upside down or completely round, turn over or backwards, turn in a contrary direction; cause to move backwards or to work in a backward direction; cause to be contrary to the normal or present state; cancel, revoke; *v.i.* to proceed in a direction opposite to that usually followed, move backwards; **to r. arms,** to hold a rifle etc. with the barrel pointing to the ground. REVERSE (2), *adj.* turned completely round or backward, contrary, having an opposite direction; **r. gear,** gear by which the direction of motion imparted by an engine is reversed. REVERSE (3), *n.* a complete change round in the course of events, contrary turn of affairs; misfortune, set-back; the opposite, the contrary; the back surface, underside; back of a leaf of paper etc.; design on the face of a coin, medal etc.,

---

The accent ´ after a syllable = stress (u-pon´). The mark ‾ over a vowel = length (ā in made; ō in bone).

opposite the head; a r. gear; (milit.) defeat; (sport) set-back, defeat. [L.].

REVERSED [ri-vurst'], adj. turned round, backwards or upside down; changed to the contrary; annulled, cancelled.

REVERSION [ri-vur'shn], n. (leg.) return of an estate to the grantor, lessor, or to his heirs upon the termination of the grant or lease; estate granted in this way, esp. one to be transferred to a specified person on the death of the person to whom it was granted; right of succession to an estate or thing; sum of money due upon the death of an insured person; act of reverting to a former thing or state; act of turning round or upside down; (biol.) atavism. REVERSIONARY, adj. (leg.) pertaining to, issuing from, a r.; by way of r. [L.].

REVERSO [ri-vur'sō]. n. left-hand page in a book. [It.].

REVERT [ri-vurt'], v.i. to return again to a former state or time, go back (to); (leg.) return to the original possessor, lessor or grantor or to his heirs upon the expiry of the lease or grant; return to the original topic or subject under discussion. [L.].

REVIEW (1) [ri-vyōō'], n. retrospective survey or summary, detailed résumé of a situation etc.; critical notice or consideration; written consideration of the merits and demerits of a recent publication or performance; periodical containing articles and essays on various topics; (leg.) consideration by a higher court of the decisions of an inferior court; formal official inspection by an eminent person, esp. of troops etc. REVIEW (2), v.t. to consider in retrospect; examine critically, consider carefully; write a press r. of; inspect formally and officially; (leg.) examine (findings of an inferior court) for acceptance or modification; v.i. to write reviews. [OFr.].

REVIEWER [ri-vyōō'er], n. one who reviews, esp. a writer of reviews of books, plays, films etc.

REVILE [ri-vīl'], v.t. to curse, shower abuse upon; v.i. to indulge in abuse, curse and swear. REVILEMENT, n. abuse and reproach. [OFr.].

REVISE (1) [ri-vīz'], v.t. to go through or examine again in detail for purposes of correction or amendment; study afresh in order to become better acquainted with for examination purposes; v.i. to be engaged in revision. REVISE (2), n. (print.) proof-sheet taken after the first correction. REVISORY, adj. pertaining to, by way of, revision, having power to r. [L.].

REVISION [ri-vi'zhn], n. act of revising, detailed examination again for purposes of correction, study of something again for purposes of examination; that which is revised. [L.].

REVISIONIST [ri-vi'zhn-ist], adj. and n. (one) advocating revision of anything, as a treaty or the Bible. REVISIONISM, n. the policy of revisionists.

REVIVAL [ri-vī'val], n. act of reviving, state of being revived, recall or return to activity, re-awakening of interest in something formerly neglected; process of bringing back into use or fashion again (something formerly current); evangelical campaign seeking to bring about a recall to religion; **r. of learning**, the Renaissance.

REVIVALISM [ri-vī'va-lizm], n. recall to religion by means of evangelical campaigns.

REVIVALIST (1) [ri-vī'va-list], n. one who promotes and takes part in revivals of religion. REVIVALIST (2), adj. pertaining to, of the nature of, a religious revival.

REVIVE [ri-vīv'], v.t. to bring to life again; rouse from depression, exhaustion etc., refresh, renew; bring into fashion or use again, cause to flourish again, re-awaken; produce again (a play which has not been produced for some time); (chem.) restore to its natural state; v.i. to recover life or consciousness; recover, be renewed; flourish again, return to use or favour; (chem.) recover its natural state. [L.].

REVIVIFY [rē-vi'vi-fī], v.t. to recall to life, reanimate; give new life or vigour to. REVIVIFICATION [rē-vi-vi-fi-kā'shn], n. restoration of life and vigour. [L.].

REVOCABLE [re'vo-ka-bl], adj. capable of being revoked.

REVOCATION [re-vo-kā'shn], n. act of revoking; state of being revoked; (leg.) repeal, annulment of a decree, edict etc. [L.].

REVOKE (1) [ri-vōk'], v.t. to rescind, repeal, annul; v.i. (cards) fail to play a card of the suit led, when able to do so. REVOKE (2), n. (cards) failure to follow suit when able to do so. [L.].

REVOLT (1) [ri-vōlt'], v.i. to rise against and seek to overthrow established authority, rebel, refuse to obey the governing body; fill with disgust and

repugnance, nauseate, repel. REVOLT (2), n. widespread insurrection, wholesale rising against the governing body, open resistance to authority. [Fr.].

REVOLTING [ri-vōl'ting], adj. disgusting, nauseating, filling with repugnance.

REVOLUTION [re-vo-lyōō'shn], n. rotation, circular motion of a body on its axis so that each part periodically returns to the same point or position; movement of a body round a centre to form a closed curve; a single complete turning round an axis, centre or central body; period of time taken to complete such a movement; regular periodic return of some phenomenon, a cycle; overthrow (often violent) of an existing political system or established authority, and its replacement by a new form of government; complete and violent change in attitude, belief, theories and methods of working. REVOLUTIONIST, n. a revolutionary. [L.].

REVOLUTIONARY (1) [re-vo-lyōō'shn-a-ri], adj. pertaining to, tending towards, in favour of, of the nature of, producing or engaged in, political revolution; causing, tending to produce, of the nature of, a revolution in theory, belief or practice. REVOLUTIONARY (2), n. one in favour of, or engaged in, revolution.

REVOLUTIONIZE [re-vo-lyōō'shn-īz], v.t. to effect radical changes in, alter drastically, produce a revolution in existing theory and practice.

REVOLVE [ri-volv'], v.t. to cause to revolve, rotate; turn over in the mind; v.i. to rotate about an axis; move in a circular course round a centre or central object; recur in regular periodic succession. [L.].

REVOLVER [ri-vol'ver], n. pistol fitted with a revolving cylinder containing several chambers for cartridges, and thus able to be fired several times without reloading.

REVUE [ri-vyōō'], n. spectacular musical variety entertainment, consisting of a number of disconnected scenes, in the form of sketches, songs and dances. [Fr.].

REVULSION [ri-vul'shn], n. abrupt and complete change in the opposite direction, recoil or reaction against something. [L.].

REWARD (1) [ri-wawd'], n. something received in return for something done, recompense, requital for good or evil; money payment offered to the finder of lost articles, to a person giving information leading to the arrest of a criminal, etc. REWARD (2), v.t. to recompense, requite; give a r. to, pay back for merit or services specially rendered. [AFr.].

REXINE [rek'sēn], n. (prot.) kind of artificial leather used in upholstery.

RHADAMANTHINE [ra-da-man'thīn], adj. rigorous, inflexible and scrupulously just. [Rhadamanthus, in Gk. myth. one of the judges of the dead].

RHAPSODIC [rap-so'dik], adj. pertaining to, in the style of, a rhapsody.

RHAPSODICAL [rap-so'di-kal], adj. pertaining to, of the nature of, a rhapsody; rambling, unrestrained and effusive.

RHAPSODIST [rap'so-dist], n. one who writes, or indulges in, rhapsodies.

RHAPSODY [rap'so-di], n. ancient Greek epic poem; rambling literary or musical composition expressing an unrestrained, passionate outburst of feeling; (pl.) wild transports of joy and delight. [Gk.].

RHENISH (1) [re'nish], adj. pertaining to, obtained from, the Rhine or the Rhine valley. RHENISH (2), n. wine from the Rhine or Rhine valley. [MHigh-Germ., AFr.].

RHEO-, pref. current, esp. electric current. [Gk.].

RHETORIC [re'te-rik], n. art of oratory, art of speaking with eloquence and persuasiveness; art of prose composition and style; florid, artificial manner of writing or speaking. [Gk.].

RHETORICAL [ri-to'ri-kal], adj. pertaining to rhetoric, oratorical; given to empty rhetoric; bombastic, ornate, florid (of style); **r. question**, question put merely for the sake of emphasis or effect, to which no answer is expected or needed.

RHETORICIAN [re-te-ri'shn], n. one skilled in the art of rhetoric, consummate orator; one who indulges in empty rhetoric.

RHEUMATIC (1) [rōō-ma'tik], adj. pertaining to, due to, afflicted with, rheumatism. RHEUMATIC (2), n. person afflicted with rheumatism; (coll.) (pl.) rheumatic pains.

RHEUMATISM [rōō'ma-tizm], n. disease characterized by a painful affliction of the muscles and

---

ōō is pronounced as in food; ŏŏ as in hood; th as in think; TH as in that; zh as in azure. ~ = related to.

joints, which become swollen, stiff and inflamed. [Gk.].

RHEUMATOID [rōō'ma-toid], *adj.* resembling rheumatism; **r. arthritis**, disease indicated by the wasting of the joint-surfaces, thickening of the parts around the joint, and distortion due to muscular contraction. [Gk.].

RHEUMY [rōō'mi], *adj.* (*archaic*) full of rheum or watery matter; causing catarrh.

RHINESTONE [rin'stōn], *n.* a sort of rock crystal; imitation diamond.

RHINO-, *pref.* nose. [Gk.].

RHINOCEROS [ri-no'se-rōs], *n.* large mammal with a thick hide creased into folds, and with one or two horns rising from the nose. [Gk.].

RHIZO-, *pref.* root. [Gk.].

RHODIUM [rō'di-um], *n.* silvery-white metallic element resembling platinum, denoted by Ro. [Gk.].

RHODODENDRON [rō-dō-den'dron], *n.* an ericaceous genus of ornamental evergreen shrubs and trees, with beautiful flowers. [Gk.].

RHODOMONTADE see RODOMONTADE.

RHOMB [rom], *n.* rhombus. RHOMBIC, *adj.* in the shape of, resembling, a rhombus. [Gk.].

RHOMBOID (1) [rom'boid], *adj.* resembling a rhombus in shape; in the form of a rhomb. RHOMBOID (2), *n.* parallelogram with only its opposite sides equal. [Gk.].

RHOMBUS [rom'bus], *n.* oblique-angled equilateral parallelogram; one of a genus of flatfish including turbot and brill. [RHOMB.]

RHUBARB [rōō'bahb], *n.* genus of large-leaved plants with thick fleshy stems or leaf-stalks; leaf-stalks of certain varieties of this, cooked and eaten as food; roots of several varieties of this used medicinally as a purgative. [MedL. from L.].

RHUMB [rum], *n.* one of the points of the compass; angle of 11 deg. 15 min. opposite the arc joining two consecutive points of the compass.

R(H)UMBA [rōōm'bah, rum'bah], *n.* ballroom dance based on Caribbean folk-dances.

RHYME (1), **RIME** [rīm], *n.* correspondence of sound in the terminating words or syllables of two or more lines of verse; word or syllable which corresponds in sound to another; verse in which the terminating words or syllables of the lines correspond in sound; poetry; poem; **feminine r.**, r. in which the two final syllables of the line r.; **masculine r.**, r. in which only the final syllables r.; **without r. or reason**, without sense. RHYME (2), *v.t.* to put into r.; use as a r.; *v.i.* to form a r.; compose verses in r. [OFr. from Gk.].

RHYTHM [riTHm], *n.* periodic variation or regular alternation of strong and weak or weaker stress, regular recurrence of emphasis or accent according to a particular pattern; example of this, scheme in which the emphasis or stress occurs according to a set pattern; regular periodic recurrence or cycle of events, phenomena etc.; symmetry in some form of activity or operation. [Gk.].

RHYTHMIC(AL) [riTH'mik(-al)], *adj.* characterized by, exhibiting, rhythm; according to, in, a rhythm.

RIB (1) [rib], *n.* one of the curved side bones of vertebrate animals, extending from the spine and serving to enclose the thorax; long, narrow strip raised to form a ridge-like protuberance in anything; (*arch.*) supporting arch of a vault; projecting moulding on the interior of a vaulted roof, groin; one of the curved vertical pieces forming part of the framework of a ship; one of the curved members supporting a bridge; one of the stiff wire strips supporting the cover of an umbrella; one of the curved pieces of wood forming the body of a lute or the sides of a violin; raised row of stitches or woven threads in knitted or other fabrics; (*bot.*) main vein of a leaf; **floating r.**, r. which is not fastened to the breast-bone. RIB (2) (*pres.pt.* RIBBING, *pret. and p.pt.* RIBBED), *v.t.* to furnish with ribs, form into r.-like projections; (*U.S. and Canadian slang*) to tease. RIBBED, *adj.* furnished with ribs; narrowly ridged. RIBBING, *n.* series of ribs; act of marking or furnishing with ribs. [OE.].

RIBALD [ri'bawld], *adj.* scurrilous, obscene, lewd, coarse. [OFr.].

RIBAND [ri'band], *n.* ribbon. [OFr.].

RIBBON (1) [ri'bon], *n.* narrow strip of silk, satin or similar material; a length of this worn as a head-band; short strip of ribbon by which a cross or medal is suspended, or which forms a badge of knighthood or mark of other high honour; narrow strip, anything

like a ribbon in shape; (*pl.*) (*coll.*) driving reins; **r. building etc.**, building etc. (*esp.* of houses' in long strips at the side of main roads. RIBBON (2), *v.t.* to adorn with ribbons. [OFr.].

RIBES [ri'bēz], *n.* genus of the saxifrage family which includes the red currant, black currant and goose-berry. [MedL.].

RICE [rīs], *n.* a cereal plant, the seeds of which are extensively used as food. RICE-PAPER, fine paper prepared in China from the pith of a tree; an edible paper used for packing sweetmeats. [OFr.].

RICH (1) [rich], *adj.* abounding in money and possessions; wealthy; blessed (with); fertile; abundant in valuable materials or qualities; splendid; costly; sumptuous; abounding in a variety of delicious or nourishing foods; (of food) heavy, *usually* fatty, and hard to digest; (of colour and sound) deep, strong, intense; (*coll.*) very amusing. RICH (2), *n.* the wealthy. RICHES [ri'chiz], *n.(pl.)* possession of land, goods, money in abundance; wealth; plenty. [OFr.].

RICK (1) [rik], *n.* a stack of grain, hay or peas. [OE.].

RICK (2), *n.* a strain or wrench, usually in the back. [Uncert.].

RICKETS [ri'kits], *n.* (*path.*) disease of young children characterized by softening of the bones which causes deformity, particularly in the legs. RICKETY, *adj.* having r.; weak, unhealthy; shaky, unstable. [Unkn.].

RICKSHAW [rik'shaw], *n.* a light man-drawn carriage; a jinricksha. [Jap.].

RICOCHET [ri'kō-shā], *n.* the rebounding of a projectile when it strikes the ground or other solid object. RICOCHET (2), *v.t.* to induce to rebound; *v.i.* to glance off, rebound; skim. [Fr.].

RID (*pret. and p.pt.* rid) [rid], *v.t.* to free; drive away; clear from, disencumber; **to get r. of**, to free oneself from.

RIDDANCE [ri'dans], *n.* act of getting rid; condition of being rid; **a good r.**, a welcome freedom from some nuisance. [OScand.].

RIDDEN [ri'den], *p.pt. of* RIDE.

RIDDLE (1) [ri'dl], *n.* enigmatic proposition or puzzle; anything ambiguous or puzzling; person or thing difficult to understand. RIDDLE (2), *v.t. and i.* to propound, solve, a r.; speak in riddles. [OE.].

RIDDLE (3), *n.* large coarse-meshed sieve. RIDDLE (4), *v.t.* to sift with a r.; make many holes in, perforate (with bullets etc.). [OE.].

RIDE (1) (*pret.* rode, *p.pt.* ridden) [rīd], *v.t.* to sit on, be carried by; be held up by; **to r. down**, to overtake on horseback, knock down and trample underfoot; **to r. to death**, to kill by riding too hard; (*fig.*) make tiresome by constant repetition; **to r. the storm**, to weather the storm; *v.i.* to be borne along on a horse or bicycle or in a vehicle; practise riding habitually; sit upon someone's back and be carried; float; move, be supported; **to r. easy**, (of a ship) to be at anchor without a great strain on her cables; **to r. hard**, to r. at full speed; (*naut.*) pitch violently; **to r. for a fall**, to r. or behave recklessly or arrogantly; **to r. up**, to work out of position, climb upward. RIDE (2), *n.* act of riding; journey on horseback, on a bicycle or in a vehicle; track for riding. [OE.].

RIDER [rī'der], *n.* one who rides; addition made to a verdict; additional clause; (*geom.*) further development of a geometrical proposition; (*mech.*) part of a machine placed above and working upon another part.

RIDGE (1) [rij], *n.* top, crest, rim of any long narrow elevation; long, narrow range of hills or mountains; long crest; edge of the coping where the two sloping sides of a roof meet; raised rim or edge between two grooves. RIDGE (2), *v.t.* to form a r.; wrinkle; *v.i.* to form into ridges, extend in ridges. [OE.].

RIDGEWAY [rij'wā], *n.* path or road along the ridge of a hill or downs.

RIDICULE (1) [ri'di-kyōōl], *n.* contemptuous laughter; mockery, derision. RIDICULE (2), *v.t.* to treat with derision; expose to contempt; make fun of. [L.].

RIDICULOUS [ri-di'kyōō-lŏs], *adj.* arousing ridicule; absurd, laughable. [L.].

RIDING (1) [rī'ding], *n.* one of the three administrative divisions of Yorkshire; a district. [OScand.].

RIDING (2), *n.* action of one who rides, *esp.* one travelling on horseback; track for riding. RIDING-HABIT, costume worn by women for horse-riding. RIDING-HOOD, large hood worn when r.; this as an outdoor costume in bad weather. RIDING-LIGHT, light carried in a ship's rigging while she is anchored. RIDING-MASTER, teacher of the art of horsemanship.

RIFE [rif], *adj.* prevalent; everywhere flourishing; abundant; luxuriant to excess. [OE.].

RIFF-RAFF [rif'raf], *n.* the rabble, scum of society; worthless or disreputable people. [OFr.].

RIFLE (1) [ri'fl], *v.t.* to seize and bear away by force; ransack; rob; cut spiral grooves in (*esp.*) the barrel of a rifle or gun. RIFLE (2), *n.* fire-arm with its barrel spirally grooved, fired from the shoulder; (*pl.*) infantry armed with rifles. RIFLE-RANGE, place used for the practice of shooting with the r.; distance which a r.-shot carries. RIFLE-SHOT, shot fired with a r.; distance which the shot covers; one who is a good shot with a r. RIFLING, *n.* process of making the spiral grooves in the barrel of a gun; the grooves themselves.

RIFLEMAN [ri'fl-man], *n.* man, usually a soldier, armed with a rifle; member of a rifle brigade.

RIFT [rift], *n.* opening, cleft, fissure; **r. in the lute**, unfavourable circumstance which disturbs harmonious relations. [OScand.].

RIG (1) [rig], *v.t. and i.* to dress, put on; (*naut.*) fit with tackle, rigging; **to r. out**, to provide with clothes; **to r. up**, to construct; improvise, contrive. RIG (2), *n.* style and number of masts of a ship; dress, outfit. RIGGER, *n.* man who rigs ships or aircraft; (*mech.*) cylindrical pulley or drum. [OScand.].

RIG (3), *v.t.* to manipulate, influence dishonestly or secretly. [Unkn].

RIGADOON [ri-ga-doon'], *n.* a brisk, lively dance for two people. [Fr.].

RIGGING [ri'ging], *n.* (*naut.*) tackle; ropes which support the masts and set and work the sails of a ship.

RIGHT (1) [rit], *adj.* most convenient, most likely to achieve a desired end; correct; well performed; dexterous; most direct; opposite to the left side; just, fit, proper, equitable; sound, healthy; rectangular; (*pol.*) conservative; **r. angle**, (*geom.*) angle of 90 deg.; **r. side**, the side made to be seen; **r. as rain**, perfectly r., absolutely sound and healthy; **to put r.**, to repair (a machine), settle (a disagreement or difficulty), cure (an illness). RIGHT (2), *adv.* in a straight line; rightly, justly, correctly; thoroughly, very; quite; precisely, absolutely; towards, on to, the r.; **r. and left**, everywhere, on every side; RIGHT (3), *n.* that which is true, correct, accurate; that which is in conformity with truth and justice; rectitude, justice; propriety; just claim; legal title; prerogative; privilege; property; the side (of the body or any object) opposed to the left; **the r.**, a conservative party or group, or that section of a party most conservative in its principles; **by r. of**, held, enjoyed, as a consequence of; **in one's own r.**, independently, without reference to others. RIGHT (4), *v.t.* to put in its original position, set upright; do justice, correct, redress, improve; **to r. oneself**, to recover one's balance; (*fig.*) vindicate one's conduct. RIGHTER, *n.* one who settles or sets. [OE.].

RIGHTABOUT (1) [ri-ta-bowt'], *n.* the opposite direction; **to the r.**, facing the other way; **to send to the r.**, to dismiss peremptorily. RIGHTABOUT (2), *adj.* reverse, having a reverse movement. RIGHTABOUT (3), *adv.* to the r.

RIGHTEOUS [ri'tyoos], *adj.* characterized by justice, equity, virtue; virtuous, upright, just; justifiable. [OE.].

RIGHTFUL [rit'fool], *adj.* disposed to do right; in conformity with what is right; having a lawful claim.

RIGHT-HAND [rit-hand'], *adj.* on or to the right hand; clockwise; (*fig.*) indispensable.

RIGHT-HANDED [rit-han'did], *adj.* using the right hand more easily than the left; constructed for the use of the right hand; clockwise.

RIGHT-MINDED [rit-min'did], *adj.* just, moral, well-disposed.

RIGHT OF WAY [rit-ov-wā'], *n.* legal right to pass through another's property; public path through private property.

RIGHT WING [rit-wing'], *adj. and n.* (*pol.*) (pertaining to) the most conservative elements in a state or party. RIGHT WINGER, *n.* (*pol.*) member of the r.

RIGID [ri'jid], *adj.* stiff, not pliant; immobile; (*fig.*) unyielding, severe; fixed, inflexible, stiff. [L.].

RIGIDITY [ri-ji'di-ti], *n.* quality of being rigid; stiffness; want of adaptability.

RIGMAROLE [rig'ma-rōl], *n.* rambling, incoherent discourse; confused story. [ME.].

RIGOR [ri'gaw(r)], *n.* a sudden chill, *esp.* when accompanied by fits of shivering as in some fevers; **r.**

mortis, stiffness of the muscles which sets in a few hours after death. [L.].

RIGOROUS [ri'ge-roos], *adj.* stern, inflexible, uncompromising, thorough; inclement, harsh.

RIGOUR [ri'ger], *n.* severity, austerity; relentlessness, strictness, thoroughness; inclemency.

RILE [ril], *v.t.* (*U.S. and dial.*) to stir up, make muddy; (*fig.*) stir up, make angry, exacerbate. [ME.].

RILL [ril], *n.* small brook, rivulet. [Germ.].

RIM (1) [rim], *n.* border or margin; raised margin or edge; verge of the horizon; outer part of a wheel on which the tyre fits. RIM (2) (*pres.pt.* RIMMING, *pret. and p.pt.* RIMMED), *v.t.* to put a r. on, form a r. round. [OE.].

RIME (1) [rim], *n.* hoar frost. RIME (2), *v.t.* to cover with r. [OE.].

RIME (3), see RHYME.

RIMMON [ri'mon], *n.* heathen god of the Syrians; **to bow down in the house of R.**, to conform to principles one does not really accept. [2 Kings v, 18].

RIND [rind], *n.* outer coating of a fruit which may be peeled off; peel, bark; hard, outer coating of cheese or bacon. [ME.].

RINDERPEST [rin'der-pest], *n.* a malignant and contagious cattle plague. [Germ.].

RING (1) [ring], *n.* a circle or anything in the form of a circular line or hoop; circular course or area; circular object with a hollow centre; hoop of gold, silver or other metal, sometimes ornamented with jewels and worn on the finger or some other part of the body; group standing together or around; enclosed space for boxing or prize-fighting; betting enclosure; (*collect.*) bookmakers generally; boxing generally; (*comm.*) group of firms in a particular industry combining for private gain. RING-FINGER, third finger of the left hand. RING-MASTER, one directing the performance in a circus arena. RING-STAND, small branched stand for hanging finger-rings upon. RING (2), *v.t.* to encircle; fit with a r. or rings; make circular grooves in (the bark of a tree trunk); *v.i.* to rise in rings or a spiral. [OE.].

RING (3) (*pret.* **rang**, *p.pt.* **rung**), *v.t.* to cause to sound with a clear resonant note, particularly by striking a metallic body; sound by means of bells; *v.i.* to produce a clear, resonant note; resound; reverberate; practise the art of ringing bells; **to r. true** (**false**), to produce sound characteristic of a genuine (false) article; (*fig.*) be sincere, genuine (untruthful); **to r. the changes**, to pass from one theme to another and back again; **to r. the knell of**, to signify the ruin or downfall of; **to r. down the curtain**, to give the sign for lowering the curtain at the end of a play; **to r. in**, to celebrate by ringing bells; **to r. off**, to conclude a telephone call; **to r. up**, to give the signal for raising; get into telephone communication with. RING (4), *n.* sound produced when anything metallic is struck; any clear, ringing sound; a reverberation; sound made by a bell; peal of bells harmonically tuned; (*fig.*) convincing sound, character. [OE.].

RING-DOVE [ring'duv], *n.* the wood-pigeon.

RINGER [ring'er], *n.* one who rings; bell-ringer; arrangement for making bells ring; quoit thrown on to the peg.

RINGING (1) [ring'ing], *n.* act of one who rings; ringing sound. RINGING (2), *adj.* clear, reverberating, resonant.

RINGLEADER [ring'lē-der], *n.* leader of an association, *esp.* when it is engaged in some mischievous or illegal enterprise.

RINGLET [ring'let], *n.* little ring; little curl; fairyring; butterfly of the wall brown family.

RINGWORM [ring'werm], *n.* a contagious fungus, usually affecting the scalp, giving rise to a circular eruption in small vesicles with a reddish base.

RINK (1) [ringk], *n.* space on the ice measured off for curling; sheet of artificial ice for skating on; place in which people skate on roller skates; smooth, hard surface, *esp.* prepared for roller skating; building in which skating takes place; (*sport*) team of players, *esp.* in bowls or curling; division of a bowling green on which a single game is played. RINK (2), *v.i.* to skate on a r. [ME.].

RINSE (1) [rins], *v.t.* to cleanse with clean water; cleanse with repeated applications of water after the first washing; **to r. out**, to cleanse (a utensil, clothes, the mouth) by the repeated application of clean water or other cleansing liquid. RINSE (2), *n.* act of rinsing; liquid used for rinsing purposes. [Fr.].

RIOT (1) [ri'ot], *n.* violent disturbance of the public

---

oo is pronounced as in food; oo as in hood; th as in *th*ink, TH as in *th*at; zh as in azure. ~ = related to.

peace by three or more persons; tumultuous uprising; uproar; noisy festivity; (*coll.*) anything received with great popular enthusiasm; (*fig.*) abundance, profusion; **to read the R. Act**, to read during a r. a proclamation ordering the dispersal of riotous gatherings; (*coll.*) utter a warning against people behaving in an unruly way; **to run r.**, to behave or move about without restraint; grow luxuriantly. RIOT (2), *v.i.* to take part in a r.; raise an uproar; run to excess in indulgence; revel. [OFr.].

RIOTOUS [rī'o-tŏŏs], *adj.* characterized by rioting; marked by excessive revelry; dissolute; extravagant; unrestrained; luxuriant, abundant. [OFr.].

RIP (1) [rip], *n.* worn-out horse; worthless fellow, rake. [~REP (2)].

RIP (2), *v.t.* to cut or tear open or asunder; unstitch; *v.i.* to slash vigorously; tear asunder; move with great speed; rush in a headlong course; **to r. asunder, open, up,** to cut or tear apart, or in pieces, in a violent manner; **to r. off,** to tear off with a violent movement. RIP (3), *n.* a tear, long slash. [OScand.].

RIPARIAN [ri-pãer'i-an], *adj.* pertaining to the banks of a river; (*bot., zool.*) growing on, living in or near, the banks of a river; **r. rights,** rights of the owner of the banks of a river. [L.].

RIP-CORD [rip'kawd], *n.* cord attached to a parachute for opening it if the normal device fails; a cord operating an emergency device to allow rapid escape of gas from a balloon.

RIPE [rīp], *adj.* brought to perfection in growth; mature; having fully developed, matured; ready, prepared, finished. [OE.].

RIPEN [rī'pen], *v.t.* to make ripe, mature; bring to maturity or perfection; *v.i.* to grow ripe, attain maturity.

RIPOSTE [ri-post'], *n.* (*fencing*) lightning-like return lunge; counter-stroke; (*fig.*) quick repartee. [Fr.].

RIPPLE (1) [ri'pl], *v.t.* to cause to r., undulate lightly; curl, undulate as with ripples; *v.i.* to move in wavelets, be gently ruffled; sound like ripples in water. RIPPLE (2), *n.* slight fretting of the surface of water, little undulation or wave; slight movement or mark suggestive of a r. on water; light swish as of rippling water. RIPPLE-CLOTH, woollen or cotton material with a r.-like surface. RIPPLE-MARK, slight undulation on the surface of a sea-beach, left by the receding waves; (*geol.*) similar undulation on the surface of rocks. [Uncert.].

RISE (1) (*pret.* **rose,** *p.pt.* **risen**) [rīz], *v.i.* to get up from a recumbent position; come to a standing position; get out of bed; ascend, go from a lower to a higher level; revolt, rebel; end a session; increase in power and volume, swell; grow louder; be raised; appear above the horizon; increase in force; get on in the world; appear, stir; originate; be roused; be raised above; **the curtain rises,** (*fig.*) the play begins, the situation develops; **to r. to a bait,** to be gulled into action by a false hope of reward; **to r. to it,** to respond to a certain stimulus, allow (oneself) to be teased. RISE (2), *n.* upward motion, ascent, elevation; advance in rank, honour, fame; upward slope; origin, source, process of developing; increase in amount, value, degree; **to take its r. in,** to originate in; **to take a r. out of,** (*coll.*) to make fun of, get the better of, tease. RISER, *n.* person who or thing which rises; vertical part of a step in a stairway. [OE.].

RISIBLE [ri'zi-bl], *adj.* concerned with the faculty of laughing; capable of exhibiting laughter; laughable. RISIBILITY [ri-zi-bi'li-ti], *n.* tendency to laugh. [LL.].

RISING (1) [rī'zing], *n.* action of that which rises; a getting up; resurrection; rebellion, revolt; act of closing a session; the coming (of the sun or moon) above the horizon; a swelling; advance in importance. RISING (2), *adj.* ascending, having an upward slope; mounting; growing in strength, intensity, volume; increasing in wealth, power or distinction; approaching any given age, amount or size; **R. Sun,** Japanese national emblem, Japan.

RISK (1) [risk], *n.* hazard of danger; chance of injury, loss; exposure to danger; (*comm.*) chances of financial loss. RISK (2), *v.t.* to expose to the possibility of injury, loss; venture, dare, face the possibility of. [Fr.].

RISQUÉ, risqué [rē'skä, ri'skä], *adj.* bordering on indecency or immorality. [Fr.].

RISSOLE [ri'sōl], *n.* fried ball of minced meat or fish mixed with breadcrumbs etc. [Fr.].

RITE [rīt], *n.* a ceremonial usage in religious worship or in other observances; (*fig.*) formal observance, rigid and solemnly performed habit. [L.].

RITUAL (1) [ri'tyŏŏ-al], *adj.* pertaining to, consisting of, rites. RITUAL (2), *n.* the body of religious rites and observances; manner of performing religious or other services; formal and traditional ceremony; book of rites. [L.].

RITUALISM [ri'tyŏŏ-a-lizm], *n.* system of ritual or prescribed forms and ceremonies of religious worship; observance of these; more than usual respect for, and observance of, ritual.

RITUALIST [ri'tyŏŏ-a-list], *n.* man skilled in ritual; one who attaches great importance to ritual in the church, or to formal ceremony in general.

RIVAL (1) [rī'val], *n.* one who competes with another in any pursuit; an equal. RIVAL (2), *adj.* rivalling; competing; having the same claims. RIVAL (3), *v.t.* to stand in competition with; strive to equal or excel; emulate; equal. [L.].

RIVALRY [rī'val-ri], *n.* act of being a rival; competition; emulation; similarity or equality in status.

RIVE (*pret.* **rived,** *p.pt.* **rived, riven**) [rīv], *v.t.* to rend, tear, split; *v.i.* to be rent. [OScand.].

RIVEN [ri'ven], *adj.* torn, split. [*P.pt.* of RIVE].

RIVER [ri'ver], *n.* big stream of water following a natural course into the sea, a lake or another river; abundant flow or flood. RIVER-BASIN, land drained by a r. RIVER-BED, trough in which a r. runs. RIVER-HORSE, hippopotamus. [OFr.].

RIVET (1) [ri'vit], *n.* headed metal pin or bolt on which a second head is formed when it is in position. RIVET (2), *v.t.* to fasten with rivets; make firm; (*fig.*) attract, fix (the attention). RIVETER, *n.* one who, or a machine which, rivets. [OFr.].

RIVIERE, rivière [ri'vi-āer], *n.* necklace of diamonds or other precious stones, usually made up of particular strings fastened together. [Fr.].

RIVULET [ri'vyŏŏ-let], *n.* a little river.

ROACH [rōch], *n.* small freshwater fish. [OFr.].

ROAD [rōd], *n.* the highway; public, metalled way for travelling; way; place where ships may ride at anchor; **r. sense,** skill in driving vehicles on the r. ROAD-BOOK, book with maps of roads, distances etc. ROAD-HOG, (*coll.*) reckless and inconsiderate driver. ROAD-MAP, map in which the roads are shown and classified according to grade. ROAD-METAL, broken stones used in constructing or repairing roads. [OE.].

ROAD-HOUSE [rōd'hows], *n.* large restaurant or hotel situated in the country on a main road.

ROADMAN [rōd'man], *n.* man who works on the roads, building or keeping them in repair.

ROADSTEAD [rōd'sted], *n.* place near, but outside, a harbour, where ships may ride at anchor.

ROADSTER [rōd'ster], *n.* horse or vehicle for use on long journeys by road.

ROADWAY [rōd'wā], *n.* the highway; that part of a road used by vehicles.

ROAM [rōm], *v.t.* to wander over; *v.i.* to wander, travel haphazardly.

ROAN (1) [rōn], *n.* soft sheepskin leather used in binding books. [*Rouen*, France].

ROAN (2), *adj.* of a ground colour with white or grey intermixed. ROAN (3), *n.* a r. horse. [OFr.].

ROAR (1) [raw(r)], *v.i.* to cry with a loud, deep sound; bellow. ROAR (2), *n.* loud, deep cry of an animal; cry of pain; any sudden cry; any loud, deep sound resembling this. ROARER, *n.* one who, or that which, roars; broken-winded horse. [OE.].

ROARING (1) [raw'ring], *n.* sound made by anything which roars; disease of a horse's windpipe which renders the breathing audible. ROARING (2), *adj.* noisy, boisterous, disorderly; brisk, active.

ROAST (1) [rōst], *v.t.* to cook by simple exposure to heat in an oven or before a fire; heat thus; parch by exposure to heat; (*coll.*) reprimand severely; *v.i.* to become exceedingly hot; (*metal.*) dissipate the volatile parts of ore by heat. ROAST (2), *n.* something roasted, *esp.* a joint of beef. ROASTING-JACK, *n.* contrivance for turning a spit. [OFr.].

ROB [rob], *v.t.* to steal from (someone), often with violence; plunder; withhold forcibly what is due. [OFr.].

ROBBERY [ro'be-ri], *n.* act of robbing; unlawful taking of another person's goods by force; unfair exaction.

ROBE (1) [rōb], *n.* long, loose, outer garment; ceremonial garment; elegant frock; any covering serving to drape the figure; a drapery. ROBE (2), *v.t.* to put a r. on (someone), dress with a r.; array; cover; *v.i.* to dress oneself in robes. [OFr.].

ROBIN [ro'bin], *n.* small brown singing-bird with a red breast. ROBIN-REDBREAST, the r. [OFr.].

ROBOT [rō'bot], *n.* automaton with some of the powers of man; person whose activities are merely mechanical. [Mechanical man in Capek's play *R.U.R.* (Rossum's Universal Robots) from Czech *robotnik* serf].

ROB-ROY [rob-roi'], *n.* light canoe paddled by a double-bladed paddle. [*Rob Roy*, pseudonym of its inventor, John MacGregor].

ROBUST [rō-bust'], *adj.* possessing great strength and vigour; sound, healthy. [L.].

ROC [rok], *n.* fabulous eastern bird of immense size and strength. [Arab.].

ROCAMBOLE [ro'kam-bōl], *n.* a form of wild garlic, *Allium Scorodoprasum*. [Fr.].

ROCHET [ro'chet], *n.* long, white, linen vestment worn by bishops. [OFr.].

ROCK (1) [rok], *n.* the solid mineral matter of the earth's crust; cliff, crag, boulder; projecting crag or stone above or close to the surface of the sea; hard kind of boiled sugar sweetmeat; (*fig.*) source of danger; **on the rocks**, wrecked on rocks; (*fig.*) in financial straits; **r. crystal**, the finest transparent quartz; **r. dove**, pigeon, wild pigeon inhabiting rocks and caves. ROCK-GARDEN, large rockery or garden where Alpine and r. plants grow. ROCK-BUN, -CAKE, small currant bun with a rough, hard outside. ROCK-GARDEN, large rockery or garden where Alpine and r. plants grow. ROCK-ROSE, plant of the genus *Cistus* or *Helianthemum*. ROCK-SALT, mineral sodium chloride found in lumps. ROCK-WORK, stones fixed in mortar in imitation of rough r.; rockery; natural wall of r. [OFr.].

ROCK (2), *v.t.* to make to swing backwards and forwards; lull a child to sleep by moving it backwards and forwards in a cradle; *v.i.* to sway, move suddenly and violently. ROCK (3), *n.* act of rocking. [OE.].

ROCK-BOTTOM (1) [rok-bo'tom], *n.* the solid rocky bed of the ocean; lowest level to which prices and the like descend. ROCK-BOTTOM (2), *adj.* down to the living rock, to the very bottom; the very lowest.

ROCKER [ro'ker], *n.* one who, or that which, rocks or causes to rock; curved piece of wood on which a cradle or chair rocks; skate with a curved blade; (*slang*) **off his r.**, crazy.

ROCKERY [ro'ke-ri], *n.* artificial, rock-strewn bank on which, in a garden, rock plants grow.

ROCKET (1) [ro'kit], *n.* firework which, when lighted, shoots through the air and serves for display purposes, to give a signal or to carry a life-line; such a projectile used as a lethal weapon. ROCKET (2), *v.t.* to fire rockets at something; *v.i.* to fly straight upwards; rush swiftly and noisily like a r.; (*fig.*) (of prices etc.) rise rapidly. [Fr.].

ROCKING [ro'king], *adj.* moving backwards and forwards or from side to side; unsteady, shaky. ROCKING-CHAIR, *n.* chair mounted on rockers. ROCKING-HORSE, *n.* toy wooden horse mounted on rockers. ROCKING-STONE, *n.* great boulder which can be made to rock to and fro.

ROCOCO [ro-kō'kō], *n.* a florid form of architectural ornamentation; style in furniture and decoration fashionable in the reigns of Louis XIV and Louis XV. [Fr.].

ROD [rod], *n.* long twig; wand; instrument of punishment; slender, tapering cane or stick, used by anglers to carry the line; slender metal bar; measure of 5¼ yd. [OE.].

RODE [rōd], *pret. of* RIDE.

RODENT (1) [rō'dent], *adj.* of the order of those vertebrates which have chisel-edged incisor teeth; gnawing. RODENT (2), *n.* a r. animal. [L.].

RODEO [rō-dā'ō], *n.* round-up of cattle on an American ranch; display of skill in such rounding-up, often made for entertainment. [Span.].

R(H)ODOMONTADE (1) [ro-dō-mon-tād'], *n.* bluster, bombast, vain boasting. R(H)ODOMONTADE (2), *adj.* boastful, bombastic. [*Rodomonte*, personage in Ariosto's *Orlando Furioso*].

ROE (1) [rō], *n.* a small kind of deer.

ROE (2), *n.* a mass of fish eggs. [OIcel.].

ROEBUCK [rō'buk], *n.* the male of the roe-deer.

ROGATION [rō-gā'shn], *n.* (*hist.*) submission of a Roman law to the people for approval, or the law so approved; (*eccles.*) (*pl.*) a litany; **R. Days**, the three days before Ascension Day; **R. Week**, week in which the R. Days fall. [L.].

ROGER [ro'jer], *n.* a man's name; **Jolly R.**, the pirates' flag; **Sir R. de Coverley**, an English country dance. [Fr.].

ROGUE [rōg], *n.* wandering beggar; dishonest person; (*hort.*) plant not of true strain; **r. elephant**, elephant

living apart from the herd and usually savage. [Uncert.].

ROGUERY [rō'ge-ri], *n.* knavish tricks; cheating; mischievousness.

ROGUISH [rō'gish], *adj.* like a rogue; waggish.

ROISTER [roi'ster], *v.i.* to act boisterously; swagger. [OFr.].

ROLAND [rō'land], *n.* courageous person who is a match for another; **R. for an Oliver**, apt repartee. [*Roland*, nephew of Charlemagne, who, with his comrade Oliver, accomplished many brave deeds].

ROLE, rôle [rōl], *n.* part played by an actor; part a person plays in life or in any set of events. [Fr.].

ROLL (1) [rōl], *n.* quantity of material wrapped so as to form a cylinder; long strip of papyrus, parchment or paper written upon and rolled up instead of being bound in leaves; official document; official register; list of names; small loaf; **Master of the Rolls**, one of the four ex-officio judges of the Court of Appeal. ROLL-CALL, the calling over of a list of names to ascertain who is present. ROLL (2), *v.t.* to revolve along; cause something to move forward by rotating it; wrap round and round; spread out or level something with a roller; sound (the consonant *r*) with a trill; utter (sounds) resonantly; *v.i.* to move on by revolving; move, as waves; turn over and over; (of land) undulate; form into a ball; sway from side to side; waddle or swagger along; (of thunder, drums etc.) reverberate, re-echo with deep and closely succeeding sounds; **to r. off**, to print or duplicate on a rotary machine; **to r. on**, (of time) to pass; **to r. up**, (*slang*) to arrive, appear; overwhelm; **to be rolling in money**, (*coll.*) to be extremely rich. ROLL-ON, kind of elastic girdle worn by women which is put on by rolling. ROLL (3), *n.* action of rolling; a swaying movement; the swaying of a ship from side to side; rapid series of beats on a drum; any reverberating sound. ROLLED, *adj.* plated by rolling; **rolled gold**, thin film of gold rolled over another metal so as to cover it. [OFr.].

ROLLER [rō'ler], *n.* that which turns on its own axis; any cylinder for rolling; (*pl.*) long heavy waves; **r. bandage**, long surgical bandage; **r. skate**, skate to which four wheels have been fitted in place of a runner; **r. towel**, endless towel suspended round a r.

ROLLICK [ro'lik], *v.i.* to behave in a sportive manner. ROLLICKING, *adj.* careless and gay. [Uncert.].

ROLLING [rō'ling], *adj.* used for rolling; moving along by turning round and round; running on wheels; undulating; **r. stone**, (*fig.*) wanderer, good-for-nothing. ROLLING-MILL, *n.* a machine in which ingots of metal are rolled into rods and strips. ROLLING-PIN, *n.* round bar of wood or glass with which dough is flattened for baking. ROLLING-STOCK, *n.* locomotives, wagons, carriages etc., used on a railway.

ROLY-POLY [rō'li-pō-li], *n.* suet pudding spread out, covered with jam etc., rolled up and boiled; short, plump person. [ROLL (1) and POLL (1)].

ROMAIC (1) [rō-mā'ik], *n.* language spoken in modern Greece. ROMAIC (2), *adj.* pertaining to R. [Gk.].

ROMAN (1) [rō'man], *adj.* pertaining to, derived from, Rome or the ancient Roman Republic or Empire; of, pertaining to, the Latin Church whose centre is Rome; **R. alphabet**, form of alphabet used by the Romans, and still used over all Western Europe and America; **R. candle**, kind of firework; **R. Catholic**, member of the Catholic Church of which the Pope is head; **R. numerals**, capital letters (I, IV etc.) used as numerals; **R. type**, (*print.*) ordinary upright type (like this) as distinct from black letter or italic types. ROMAN (2), *n.* citizen of ancient R. or of Rome; R. Catholic; (*print.*) R. type. [*Rome*, Italy].

ROMANCE (1) [rō-mans'], *n.* the group of languages developed from Latin; tale of chivalry, often in verse; fictitious story or novel; extravagant story; (*pop.*) love story; imaginative character or quality. ROMANCE (2), *adj.* in, of, or pertaining to, R. languages. ROMANCE (3), *v.i.* to tell fictitious stories; exaggerate, give a highly coloured account of events. ROMANCER, *n.* person who romances; writer of romances; one who tells far-fetched stories, liar. [OFr.].

ROMANESQUE (1) [rō-ma-nesk'], *adj.* pertaining to, resembling, a sub-Roman round-arched style of architecture of which the Norman style is a particular school. ROMANESQUE (2), *n.* this style of architecture.

ROMANIC [rō-ma'nik], *adj.* pertaining to the Romance languages; derived from Latin. [L.].

ROMANIST [rō'ma-nist], *n.* member of the Church of Rome; student of Roman antiquities or law.

ōō is pronounced as in f*ood*; ŏŏ as in h*ood*; th as in *th*ink; TH as in *th*at; zh as in azure.   ∼ = related to.

ROMANISM, *n.* doctrine and organization of the R.C. Church.

ROMANSCH [rō-mahnsh'], *n.* a Rhaeto-Romanic dialect spoken in the Engadine. [LL.].

ROMANTIC (1) [rō-man'tik], *adj.* pertaining to romance; based on romances; remote from everyday life, heroic, extravagant, wild, unreal, sentimental; (*art*) strange or picturesque in episode or style; allowing form to be dominated by atmosphere and mood; emotional and unregulated as distinct from classical. ROMANTIC (2), *n.* a r. writer, painter etc.; one of a school or tradition of r. poets. [Fr.].

ROMANTICISM [rō-man'ti-sizm], *n.* quality of being romantic; (*art*) anti-classical movement in late eighteenth- and early nineteenth-century art and literature towards a more subjective and emotional treatment. ROMANTICIST, *n.* adherent of r.; artist of the romantic school.

ROMANY [rō'ma-ni], *n.* a gipsy; the gipsy language. [Gipsy].

ROME [rōm], *n.* city in Italy; the Roman Republic and Empire; the Roman Church. [L.].

ROMP (1) [romp], *v.i.* to play boisterously, noisily and energetically; **to r. home,** (*coll.*) to win with ease. ROMP (2), *n.* person, *esp.* a girl, who plays roughly or noisily; noisy game. ROMPERS, *n.*(*pl.*) overall with leg openings for a child just beginning to crawl or walk. [~RAMP (1)].

RONDEAU [ron'dō], *n.* type of verse consisting of ten or thirteen lines with only two rhymes and a refrain; kind of jig which ends with the first strain repeated. [Fr.].

RONDEL [ron'del], *n.* verse form similar to, but earlier than, the rondeau, having fourteen lines with two rhymes and a refrain. [Fr.].

RONDO [ron'dō], *n.* (*mus.*) musical piece, in which return is repeatedly made to the first theme; rondeau. [It.].

RONEO (1) [rō'ni-ō], *n.* (*prot.*) instrument for duplicating typescript. RONEO (2), *v.t.* to duplicate on a r.; *v.i.* to use a r.

ROOD [rōōd], *n.* crucifix, *esp.* one placed above the entrance to the chancel with supporting figures of St. Mary and St. John; the cross; measure of one-fourth of an acre in extent. ROOD-SCREEN, screen separating the nave from the choir in a church. [OE.].

ROOF (1) [rōōf], *n.* covering of the top of a building; anything resembling this, e.g. the top of a car, coach or other vehicle; **r. of the mouth,** palate. ROOF-SPOTTER, (*coll.*) one who keeps watch on the r. of a building for the approach of hostile aircraft. ROOF-TREE, main horizontal beam of the r.; (*fig.*) the house or family. ROOF (2), *v.t.* to cover with a r.; shelter. ROOFING, *n.* covering with a r.; materials used for this purpose. [OE.].

ROOK (1) [rōōk], *n.* one of the chess pieces, a castle. [OFr. from Pers.].

ROOK (2), *n.* large, black bird, having a raucous cry and building its nest in colonies high in the trees; crow; (*fig.*) cheat. ROOK (3), *v.t.* (*coll.*) to cheat; charge an excessive price to. [OE.].

ROOM (1) [rōō'm], *n.* space, area; enclosed portion of a house or building, apartment; the people in a room, the assembled company; opportunity, scope. ROOM (2), *v.i.* to share a r., lodge (with). [OE.].

ROOMY [rōō'mi], *adj.* having ample room or space; capacious.

ROOST (1) [rōōst], *n.* pole where fowls perch at night; group of roosting fowls. ROOST (2), *v.i.* to perch on a pole, sleep as fowls; (*fig.*) rest, lodge. ROOSTER, *n.* cock. [OE.].

ROOT (1) [rōōt], *n.* that part of a plant which grows downwards and draws nourishment from the soil; that which resembles a r. in position or function; fundamental cause or source of anything; (*math.*) the quantity which, multiplied by itself, produces a given quantity or a particular series; (*philol.*) basic element of a word; **to take r.,** to become fixed or established. ROOT (2), *v.t.* to fix by the r., plant deeply; (*fig.*) impress deeply, ineradicably on the mind; *v.i.* to fix its r., be firmly established; put out roots; **to r. up, out,** to tear up, eradicate, destroy completely. ROOTLET, *n.* small branch of a r.; radicle. [OE.].

ROOT (3), *v.t. and i.* to dig (up), *esp.* with the snout; (*U.S. coll.*) cheer (for) (a team etc.). [OE.].

ROOTED [rōō'tid], *adj.* having roots; firmly fixed; (*fig.*) deep, well-grounded; deep-seated.

ROPE (1) [rōp], *n.* cord of some thickness formed of twisted strands often made of hemp; row or number of things strung together; **to give a person r.,** to give him wide freedom in the hope that he will make a mistake; **to know the ropes,** to be among the initiated. ROPE-DANCER, one who performs difficult feats while standing or walking on a r. stretched at some height above the ground. ROPE-LADDER, ladder made of r. ROPE-WALK, long, narrow, covered alley where ropes are made. ROPE (2), *v.t.* to tie, lash or join together with a r.; **to r. in,** (*coll.*) to bring (a person) into some enterprise; *v.i.* (*mountaineering*) to link oneself to another member of the party by a length of r.; (of viscid matter) be drawn out like r., become ropy. [OE.].

ROPY [rō'pi], *adj.* like a rope; stringy; **viscous;** adhesive.

ROQUEFORT [rok'faw(r)], *n.* kind of cheese of the milk of goats and sheep, made in *Roquefort*, France.

ROQUELAURE [ro'ke-law(r)], *n.* a cloak, buttoning from top to bottom, and worn mainly in the eighteenth century. [Duke of *Roquelaure*].

ROQUET [rō'ki], *v.t.* in croquet, to strike another player's ball in playing one's own. [~CROQUET (1)].

RORQUAL [rawr'kwal], *n.* whale with a dorsal fin. [Fr. from OScand.].

ROSACEOUS [rō-zā'shōōs], *adj.* rose-like; (*bot.*) belonging to the natural order *Rosaceae*. [L.].

ROSARY [rō'za-ri], *n.* rose garden; string of beads for counting prayers. [L.].

ROSE (1) [rōz], *pret. of* RISE.

ROSE (2), *n.* any of various wild or cultivated plants or their flowers of the genus *Rosa*; pink colour resembling that of certain roses; perforated nozzle; (*fig.*) beautiful woman; rosette; **under the r.,** secretly. ROSE-BAY, species of willow herb; oleander; rhododendron. ROSE-DIAMOND, diamond cut into twenty-four triangular surfaces. ROSE-LEAF, leaf or petal of a r. ROSE-NOBLE, old English gold coin. ROSE-QUARTZ, variety of rose-red quartz. ROSE-TREE, a r. plant, *esp.* one grafted on to a standard. ROSE-WATER, water tinctured with roses and used as a perfume. ROSE-WINDOW, round window in the form of a fully opened r. [OE. from L.].

ROSEATE [rō'zi-at], *adj.* rosy; like a rose in colour or form; full of roses; (*fig.*) hopeful. [L.].

ROSEBUD [rōz'bud], *n.* bud of the rose; (*fig.*) attractive girl.

ROSE-COLOUR [rōz'ku-ler], *n.* a deep rich pink colour, as of certain roses; (*fig.*) optimism.

ROSEMARY [rōz'ma-ri], *n.* fragrant evergreen shrub yielding an aromatic oil. [L.].

ROSEOLA [rō-zē'ō-lah], *n.* (*path.*) rash of red spots on the skin occurring in measles, German measles and similar diseases. [MdL.].

ROSERY [rō'ze-ri], *n.* rose garden.

ROSETTE [rō-zet'], *n.* imitation of a rose made of ribbons; (*arch.*) stone ornament in the form of a rose. [Fr.].

ROSEWOOD [rōz'wōōd], *n.* fragrant wood growing in tropical countries and used largely for furniture.

ROSICRUCIAN (1) [rō-zi-krōō'shn], *n.* one of a fraternity who in the fifteenth century affected an intimate acquaintance with the secrets of nature and pretended to possess occult powers. ROSICRUCIAN (2), *adj.* of, pertaining, or relating to Rosicrucians or their practices. [C. *Rosenkreuz*, its supposed founder].

ROSIN [ro'zin], *n.* resin, *esp.* the solid residue after oil of turpentine has been distilled from crude turpentine. ROSIN (2), *v.t.* to rub or smear with r., as a violin bow. [~RESIN].

ROSTER [ros'ter], *n.* a prescribed order regulating the rotation in which individuals, companies and regiments are to be called on duty. [Du.].

ROSTRAL [ros'tral], *adj.* furnished with, or pertaining to, a rostrum or beak. [L.].

ROSTRATE [ros'trāt], *adj.* rostral; beak-like. [L.].

ROSTRUM [ros'trum], *n.* beak or bill of a bird; beak or head of a ship; platform from which a speaker addresses his audience; pulpit. [L.].

ROSY [rō'zi], *adj.* resembling a rose; of a deep pink colour; of a bright, healthy colour in complexion; flushing; (*fig.*) bright, promising, favourable.

ROT (1) [rot], *v.t. and i.* to (cause to) decay; decompose; develop the rot; grow ill and wasted, deteriorate with confinement or inactivity; (*slang*) joke, make fun of. ROT (2), *n.* putrefaction; rubbish; a fatal distemper incident to sheep; (*fig.*) deterioration; (*slang*) nonsense. [OScand.].

ROTA [rō'tah], *n.* list determining the order of services; roster. [L.].

ROTARY [rō'ta-ri], *adj.* moving round on an axis like

a wheel; acting in rotation; **R. Club,** international business and professional men's organization for the promotion of good relations locally and internationally. ROTARIAN [rō-tāer'i-an], *n.* man who is a member of a R. Club. [LL.].

ROTATE [rō-tāt'], *v.t. and i.* to revolve round a centre or axis; go by rotation. ROTATIVE, *adj.* rotating, turning, as a wheel; of, or pertaining to, rotation. [L.].

ROTATION [rō-tā'shn], *n.* act of turning about an axis; regular succession. [L.].

ROTATOR [rō-tā'ter], *n.* that which produces or has rotatory action; (*anat.*) muscle which has this function. ROTATORY [rō'ta-te-ri, rō-tā'te-ri], *adj.* pertaining to rotation; turning about an axis like a wheel; following in succession. [L.].

ROTE [rōt], *n.* † repetition; **by r.,** by a mere mechanical repetition without attention to the underlying meaning or principles; by heart. [Uncert.].

ROTOGRAPH [rō'to-grahf], *n.* photostat made on part of a roll of paper. [L. and Gk.].

ROTOGRAVURE [rō-tō-gra-vyōōr'], *n.* printing by photogravure on a rotary press. [L. and (PHOTO)-GRAVURE].

ROTOR [rō'ter], *n.* machine driven by the wind acting on fans working in lofty funnels; any revolving part, *esp.* an electric coil capable of rotation; one of the revolving horizontal blades of a helicopter. [RO(TA)TOR].

ROTTEN [ro'ten], *adj.* decayed, putrid; unsound; (*fig.*) corrupt, unsound; (*slang*) unpleasant, beastly. [ROT].

ROTUND [rō-tund'], *adj.* round in form; (of a person) short and plump. [L.].

ROTUNDA [rō-tun'dah], *n.* a building circular in plan both within and without, roofed with a dome. [L.].

ROUBLE [rōō'bl], *n.* a silver coin, the Russian monetary unit. [Russ.].

ROUE, roué [rōō'ā], *n.* dissipated man; rake; debauchee; profligate. [Fr.].

ROUGE (1) [rōōzh], *n.* red cosmetic for reddening the lips and cheeks; red powder used for polishing plate. ROUGE (2), *v.t.* to apply r. to. ROUGE-ET-NOIR [rōōzh-ā-nwah(r)'], *n.* gambling card-game, so called because of red and black markings on the table where the players place their stakes. [Fr.].

ROUGH (1) [ruf], *adj.* not smooth or even; not polished; abounding with stones or stumps; rugged; stormy; harsh; grating to the ear; shaggy; rugged in temper or manners; uncouth; difficult; incomplete; **r. diamond,** uncut diamond; (*fig.*) uncouth but worthy fellow; **r. house,** a free fight. ROUGH-DRIED, (of clothes) dried but not ironed or pressed. ROUGH-RIDER, *n.* one who breaks in horses; one who rides unbroken horses. ROUGH (2), *adv.* (*coll.*) in a rude or harsh way; **to cut up r.,** (*slang*) to get angry. ROUGH (3), *n.* ground which has an uneven surface; the unpleasant, difficult side of anything; hardship; rowdy, turbulent person; (*golf*) uneven ground off the greens and fairway; **in the r.,** in an unfinished state. ROUGH (4), *v.t.* to make r., ruffle; **to r. it,** to live hardly and without the usual comforts of life; **to r. out,** to sketch in outline, prepare a r. draft of. ROUGHLY, *adv.* in a r. manner; brusquely; approximately, in a general way. [OE.].

ROUGHAGE [ru'fij], *n.* that which is discarded as rough; food which stimulates the excretive processes by its bulk.

ROUGH-AND-READY [ruf-and-re'di], *adj.* hastily finished without much care; unpolished but effective.

ROUGH-AND-TUMBLE [ruf-and-tum'bl], *n.* (*coll.*) a disorderly struggle.

ROUGH-CAST [ruf'kahst], *n.* plaster mixed with small pebbles for coating the outsides of brick houses; (*fig.*) something imperfectly contrived.

ROUGH-HEW [ruf-hyōō'], *v.t.* to hew roughly; give a preliminary rough shape to. ROUGH-HEWN, *adj.* coarsely hewn into shape; (*fig.*) rugged, unpolished.

ROUGHSHOD [ruf'shod], *adj.* shod with shoes of which the nail-heads project; **to ride r. over,** to flout.

ROULADE [rōō-lahd'], *n.* (*mus.*) in singing, a run of short notes. [Fr.].

ROULEAU [rōō-lō'], *n.* little roll of coins neatly wrapped in paper; roll; piping or trimming in the form of a tight roll. [Fr.].

ROULETTE [rōō-let'], *n.* game of chance employing a revolving disk and ball; wheeled instrument for making a dotted line or series of punctures.

ROULETTED, *adj.* of postage stamps etc., prepared for separation by means of a r. [Fr.].

ROUND (1) [rownd], *adj.* having every part of the surface at an equal distance from the centre; having the form of a circle, sphere, ball or cylinder; plump, well-rounded; having a curved form; approximately calculated; positive; candid or plain in speech; **r. dance,** dance in which the dancers are ranged in a circle; **r. game,** game, *esp.* at cards, in which an indefinite number of players can take part each on his own account; **r. number,** number which ends with a cipher. ROUND-HAND, *n.* bold, well-rounded style of penmanship. ROUND-ROBIN, *n.* petition with signatures arranged in a ring. ROUND-SHOT, *n.*(*pl.*) spherical cannon balls. ROUND (2), *adv.* on all sides, circularly, not in a direct line; from one side or party to another. ROUND (3), *prep.* with circular movement or encirclement about. ROUND (4), *n.* that which is r., e.g. a circle or sphere; that which goes or passes r., a passage r.; series of events or duties coming back to the beginning again; walk of surveillance, beat; daily series of visits; **period** between intervals in a boxing-match; **full slice** of bread; rung of a ladder; (*milit.*) general discharge of firearms in which each soldier fires once; ammunition for firing once; (*mus.*) short composition in three or more parts, each starting at the beginning. ROUND (5), *v.t.* to make r.; make circular, spherical, cylindrical; encircle; move r. or about; make full, smooth-flowing; *v.i.* to grow or become r.; become complete, full; develop into the full type; **to r. off,** to finish, put the final touch to; **to r. on,** to turn suddenly upon, attack with words, scold; **to r. up,** to collect together. ROUNDLY, *adv.* in a r. manner; in a downright, outspoken fashion. [OFr. from L.].

ROUNDABOUT (1) [rown'da-bowt], *n.* merry-go-round; circular enclosure at crossroads around which all traffic must pass in one direction. ROUNDABOUT (2), *adj.* indirect; not straightforward. ROUND-ABOUT (3), *prep.* around and about.

ROUNDARM [rown'dahm], *n.* (*cricket*) former style of bowling in which the arm turned at shoulder level.

ROUNDEL [rown'del], *n.* a round figure; (*poet.*) roundelay. [OFr.].

ROUNDELAY [rown'de-lā], *n.* simple song with refrain. [OFr.].

ROUNDERS [rown'derz], *n.*(*pl.*) game played with a ball and a short stick in which the players try to make a round of a number of bases after striking the ball.

ROUNDHEAD [rownd'hed], *n.* nickname given to the Puritans by the Cavaliers in the Civil War from their close-cropped hair.

ROUNDHOUSE [rownd'hows], *n.* (in a ship) lavatory for the use of officers; (in a windmill) room built round the supporting post of a post mill.

ROUND-TABLE [rownd-tā'bl], *adj.* (of a conference) held among powers or parties having equal status in the deliberations.

ROUND TRIP [rownd'trip], *n.* journey to one's destination, and back by a different route; **r. ticket,** return ticket.

ROUND-UP [rownd'up], *n.* the herding of cattle or other animals into large groups to brand them, pick out the young etc.; any forcible collecting together of a group of people; a collection of (written) material on a given subject, résumé.

ROUP [rōōp], *n.* disease among poultry. [Unkn.].

ROUSE [rowz], *v.t.* to startle (game) and cause it to rise; wake up, stir, agitate; *v.i.* to awake. [Uncert.].

ROUT (1) [rowt], *n.* clamorous multitude; † evening party; (*leg.*) assembly and attempt of three or more people to avenge some common wrong; defeat and confused flight of an army. ROUT (2), *v.t.* to defeat heavily, put to flight in confusion. [OFr.].

ROUT (3), *v.t. and i.* to dig up with the snout (of swine); root up; drive (a person out of bed, the house etc.). [∼ROOT (3)].

ROUTE (1) [rōōt, (*milit.*) rowt], *n.* way, course travelled; itinerary; (*milit.*) order to change quarters; **en r.,** during the journey, on the way. ROUTE-MARCH, long military march in column. ROUTE (2) (*pres.pt.* ROUTEING, *pret. and p.pt.* ROUTED) [rōōt], *v.t.* to plan the course of, send or direct by a particular r.

ROUTINE [rōō-tēn'], *n.* round or course of duties regularly or frequently returning; fixed habit of proceeding; organization. [Fr.].

ROUX [rōō], *n.* a preparation of butter and flour used to thicken soups and gravies. [Fr.].

ROVE [rōv], *v.i.* to wander about at large; roam; (*fig.*)

(of the attention, eye etc.), move restlessly. ROVING (1), *n.* act of wandering or rambling. ROVING (2), *adj.* that roves; **roving commission**, commission which leaves the person to whom it is entrusted full liberty to travel or do what seems best fitted to execute the commission. [*Next*].

ROVER [rō'ver], *n.* one who roves; senior grade of boy scout; one who leads a roving life, *esp.* at sea; pirate. [MDu.].

ROW (1) [rō], *n.* series of persons or things arranged in a line; line, rank, file. [OE.].

ROW (2), *v.t. and i.* to propel or move along the surface of water by oars or sculls; transport by rowing; **to r. out**, to exhaust by rowing. ROW (3), *n.* a trip in a rowing boat. [OE.].

ROW (4) [row], *n.* noisy disturbance; riot; quarrel. ROW (5), *v.t. and i.* (*coll.*) to quarrel with, upbraid noisily; quarrel, brawl. [~ROWDY].

ROWAN [rō'an], *n.* the mountain ash tree; berry of this tree. [Norw.].

ROWDY (1) [row'di], *adj.* noisy, causing a noisy disturbance; unruly. ROWDY (2), *n.* a r. fellow. [Uncert.].

ROWEL [row'el], *n.* the sharply spiked wheel of a spur. [OFr.].

ROWLOCK [ru'luk, ro'luk], *n.* part of a boat's gunwale, or the crutch, which provides a fulcrum for an oar. [OE.].

ROYAL (1) [roi'al], *adj.* pertaining to a sovereign or to the Crown, regal; noble; generous. ROYAL (2), *n.* a large size of paper; stag with twelve or more tines; (*naut.*) sail immediately above the topgallant; (in vingt-et-un) ace with a court-card of the same suit. ROYAL-MAST, (*naut.*) mast immediately above the topgallant. ROYALLY, *adv.* in a r. manner; magnificently and with dignity. [OFr. from L.].

ROYALIST [roi'a-list], *n.* supporter of a king or queen, line of kings or queens, or kingly government, *esp.* in the reigns of Charles I and II; adherent of their house.

ROYALTY [roi'al-ti], *n.* character, state, office or person of a king or queen; one of a royal family; proprietary rights of part profit; payment to an author of a part of the price of each copy sold, or to a writer of plays for each performance, or to a proprietor of a patent for each specified number of articles sold under it. [OFr.].

RUB (1) (*pres.pt.* **rubbing**, *pret. and p.pt.* **rubbed**) [rub], *v.t.* to apply friction to the surface of; wipe, polish, scour; massage; *v.i.* to move (along) with pressure; chafe; **to r. along**, (*coll.*) to get along fairly well; **to r. down**, to clean by rubbing, r. (the body) briskly with a towel, or as massage; **to r. off**, to clean off by rubbing; **to r. out**, to erase; **to r. up**, to cause to shine by rubbing; (*coll.*) to revise; **to r. up the wrong way**, to irritate. RUB (2), *n.* act of rubbing; friction; something which makes motion or progress difficult or painful; difficulty; obstruction; gibe. RUBBING, *n.* reproduction of a raised or incised design by means of rubbing superimposed paper with chalk etc.; friction; act of one who rubs. RUB-DOWN, *n.* act of rubbing the body vigorously with a towel; massage. [ME.].

RUBATO [rōō-bah'tō], *n.* (*mus.*) varied tempo employed for purposes of expression. [It.].

RUBBER [ru'ber], *n.* one who, or that which, rubs; instrument or thing used in rubbing or cleaning; whetstone; coarse file; at cards and other games, series of games or hands, ended when one side has won most of them; elastic material, sometimes called indiarubber, made from the coagulated latex of certain trees; (*pl.*) overshoes made of r. RUB-BERIZE, *v.t.* to coat with r. [RUB (1)].

RUBBISH [ru'bish], *n.* fragments of buildings or any structure, débris; waste matter; anything useless; (*coll.*) nonsense. RUBBISHING, RUBBISHY, *adj.* pertaining to r.; worthless. [Uncert.].

RUBBLE [ru'bl], *n.* rough undressed stones; old building materials used again; débris left by the destruction of a building etc.; (*geol.*) mass of rock-fragments often found beneath alluvium. RUBBLY, *adj.* containing r. [Uncert.].

RUBELLA [rōō-be'lah], *n.* (*path.*) German measles. [L.].

RUBEOLA [rōō-bē'o-lah], *n.* (*path.*) German measles. RUBEROID [ru'be-roid], *n.* (*prot.*) a bituminized felt for roofing etc. [RUBBER and Gk.].

RUBICUND [rōō'bi-kund], *adj.* inclined to redness; ruddy; red-faced. RUBICUNDITY [rōō-bi-kun'di-ti], *n.* condition of being r. [L.].

RUBRIC [rōō'brik], *n.* writing in red ink, pencil etc.;

heading to a paragraph in a prayer-book, legal code etc., *esp.* when printed or written in red; instruction contained in such a heading. RUBRICAL, *adj.* marked with red; pertaining to a r. or rubrics. RUBRICATE, *v.t.* to write, decorate, or print in red letters. [Fr. from L.].

RUBY (1) [rōō'bi], *n.* precious stone of a carmine-red colour; anything red; redness; (*print.*) a small-sized type. RUBY (2), *adj.* red like the r. [OFr.].

RUCHE [rōōsh], *n.* pleated frilling; ruffle. [Fr.].

RUCK (1) [ruk], *n.* wrinkle, ridge, *esp.* in material. RUCK (2), *v.t. and i.* to wrinkle, crease; pucker or gather into small folds. [OIcel.].

RUCK (3), *n.* heap; crowd; throng; the losing horses which come in a group behind the winners of a race. [ME.].

RUCKLE [ru'kl], *v.t.* to ruck, wrinkle, crease. [Norw.].

RUCKSACK [rōōk'sak], *n.* knapsack carried on the back by straps round the shoulders. [Germ.].

RUCTION [ruk'shn], *n.* (*usually pl.*) (*coll.*) uproar, disturbance, row. [Uncert.].

RUDD [rud], *n.* a freshwater fish with red fins. [OE.].

RUDDER [ru'der], *n.* vertical plate at the stern of a ship or aeroplane by which it is steered; that which guides or governs the course of anything; tail-feathers of a bird. [OE.].

RUDDLE (1), **RADDLE** [ru'dl], *n.* red ochre used for marking sheep. RUDDLE (2), RADDLE, *v.t.* to mark or dye with r. [OE.].

RUDDY [ru'di], *adj.* of a bright red colour; fresh-complexioned; (*low slang*) great, offensive, unmitigated. [OE.].

RUDE [rōōd], *adj.* rough, rustic, uncouth; unlettered; untaught; boorish, ill-mannered, discourteous; (of health) robust. [OE. from L.].

RUDIMENT [rōō'di-ment], *n.* a thing in its first stages, preliminary step; unformed, embryonic thing; (*pl.*) preliminary stages of a subject, foundations or elementary first principles. [L.].

RUE (1) [rōō], *n.* a strong-smelling evergreen plant. [Fr.].

RUE (2), *v.t.* to lament, repent; fill with remorse; *v.i.* to repent, regret. RUE (3), *n.* (*archaic*) sorrow, remorse, pity. [OE.].

RUEFUL [rōō'fōol], *adj.* remorseful, regretful, doleful.

RUFF (1) [ruf], *n.* pleated linen collar worn standing out horizontally round the neck; something puckered or pleated; bird allied to the sandpipers; species of pigeon. [Uncert.].

RUFF (2), *n.* act of trumping; old game of cards from which whist is derived. RUFF (3), *v.t. and i.* to trump at cards. [OFr.].

RUFF (4), *n.* a small freshwater fish of the perch family. [ROUGH (1)].

RUFFIAN [ru'fi-an], *n.* low and violent fellow; desperate character. [OFr.].

RUFFLE (1) [ru'fl], *v.t.* to disorder, disturb something smooth or even; agitate; furnish with ruffles; *v.i.* to stir, flutter, grow rough. RUFFLE (2), *n.* strip of fine cloth, lace etc., pleated and attached to some border of a garment; small ruffs worn round the wrist or neck; disturbance. [Uncert.].

RUFFLE (3), *n.* subdued roll on the drums. [Echoic.].

RUFOUS [rōō'fōos], *adj.* of a red-brown colour. [L.].

RUG [rug], *n.* large piece of woollen cloth, used as a wrap or coverlet for the feet or on a bed; mat of wool, fur etc. for the floor. [Scand.].

RUGATE [rōō'gāt], *adj.* wrinkled. [L.].

RUGBY [rug'bi], *n.* a type of football in which the ball may be handled, first played at *Rugby* school. RUGBEIAN [rug-bē'an], *n.* past or present pupil of R. School.

RUGGED [ru'gid], *adj.* rough, rocky, craggy; strong and rough; (of features) strongly marked; (of character) strong and without superficial refinement. [RUG].

RUIN (1) [rōō'in], *n.* destruction, overthrow; that which is destroyed or overthrown; physical or moral deterioration or destruction; (*pl.*) remains of anything decayed or partly demolished, *esp.* a building. RUIN (2), *v.t.* to demolish, destroy, overthrow, spoil; impoverish; destroy morally. RUINATION [rōō-i-nā'-shn], *n.* act or means of ruining; that which is ruined. [OFr. from L.].

RUINOUS [rōō'i-nōos], *adj.* fallen into ruins; bringing to ruin; disastrous; (*coll.*) exorbitant.

RULE (1) [rōōl], *n.* established principle regulating conduct or the running of institutions etc.; government, regulation; custom, habit; routine; accepted regulation in a game; instrument for drawing and

measuring lines; (*gram.*) established form of construction in a particular class of words or in syntax; (*math.*) determinate method for performing any operation and producing certain results; **r. of three**, (*math.*) the rule of proportion; (*leg.*) order made by a court of justice for regulating a certain case in question; **r. of the road**, rules prescribed in the Highway Code; **r. of thumb**, system worked out by practical experience; **slide r.**, ruler divided into scales and having slides for facilitating calculation. RULE (2), *v.t.* to govern, manage, regulate; settle as by r.; determine; mark (lines) with a r., mark with regularly spaced lines made with a r.; *v.i.* to have power or command; (*comm.*) stand or maintain a certain level; **to r. the roost**, (*coll.*) to be master of the situation. [L.].
RULER [rōō′ler], *n.* one who rules; instrument of wood etc. for ruling lines and for measuring, a rule.
RULING (1) [rōō′ling], *n.* regulation, authoritative decision. RULING (2), *adj.* that rules; dominating, predominant; prevailing, current.
RUM (1) [rum], *n.* spirituous liquor distilled from sugar cane. [Uncert.].
RUM (2), *adj.* (*slang*) odd, queer. [Uncert.].
RUMBA (1) [rum′bah], *n.* ballroom dance based on Caribbean folk-dances. RUMBA (2), *v.i.* to dance the r.
RUMBLE (1) [rum′bl], *v.i.* to make a low, dull, continuous sound by rolling along heavily; *v.t.* (*slang*) to understand, see through. RUMBLE (2), *n.* low, dull, continuous sound; back part of a carriage used for an extra seat or for luggage; dickey. [ME.].
RUMBLING (1) [rum′bling], *n.* rumbling sound. RUMBLING (2), *adj.* that rumbles.
RUMINANT (1) [rōō′mi-nant], *n.* animal which, like the cow, chews the cud. RUMINANT (2), *adj.* chewing the cud; (*fig.*) thoughtful. [~L.].
RUMINATE [rōō′mi-nāt], *v.i.* to chew the cud; (*fig.*) consider deeply, turn thoughts over in the mind. RUMINATIVE, *adj.* meditative. [L.].
RUMMAGE (1) [ru′mij], *n.* action of rummaging; things brought to light by rummaging; lumber. RUMMAGE (2), *v.t.* to ransack; find in rummaging; *v.i.* to tumble things about indiscriminately in searching. [OFr.].
RUMMER [ru′mer], *n.* kind of deep glass or cup; glass spoon or stirrer. [Du.].
RUMMY [ru′mi], *n.* American card-game for two or more players. [Unkn.].
RUMOUR (1) [rōō′mer], *n.* hearsay, gossip; popular report; current story not based on definite facts. RUMOUR (2), *v.t. usually pass.* **to be rumoured**, to be circulated as a r. [L.].
RUMP [rump], *n.* hindquarters; buttocks; **r. steak**, cut of beefsteak from near the animal's r. [ME.].
RUMPLE [rum′pl], *v.t.* to crease up, crumple. [MDu.].
RUN (1) [run], *pres.pt.* **running**, *pret.* **ran**, *p.pt.* **run** [run], *v.t.* to drive, force; cause to run; manage, operate; fuse, cast; incur; venture; thrust; draw; discharge; smuggle; *v.i.* to pass swiftly over the ground on the legs, or in a vehicle; sail; rush violently; spread, extend; slide; move quickly; work, turn round (of machinery); contend in a rôle or competition; flee; discharge matter; continue in operation; (*fig.*) pursue in thought; **to r. across**, to meet accidentally; **to r. after**, to pursue, pester; **to r. at**, to attack; **to r. up against**, **r. into**, to collide with; meet by chance; **to r. down**, to r. over, cause to sink; (*fig.*) depreciate; **to r. on**, to go on, talk endlessly; **to r. out of**, to come to an end of; **to r. over**, to overflow; knock down and move over in a vehicle; (*fig.*) cast the eye rapidly over; **to r. riot**, to behave in a disorderly manner; (of plants) grow in riotous profusion; **to r. through**, to look, read, quickly over; waste, spend; **to r. up**, to incur; **also ran**, was in the contest but not placed, also of a person only moderately successful; **to r. in**, (*mech.*) to use at moderate speed when new; (*slang*) arrest. RUNBACK, space behind the base-line at each end of a tennis court. RUN (2), *n.* action of running on foot or in a vehicle; swift movement of a vehicle; voyage, journey; slope for a vehicle to r. down; successful course; continuous flow (of); period of some length; a rush, eager call on; stretch of land used for animals or fowls; hole caused by a dropped or torn stitch in knitted materials, ladder; ordinary type, average; (*cricket*) point scored by, act of, running successfully from one wicket to the other; (*comm.*) uncommon pressure on a bank for payment; (*mus.*) rapid series of notes for the voice or instrument; **in the long r.**, in the end, as a whole; **on the r.**, in flight, running

away; **to have a r. for one's money**, to get fun or benefit out of one's efforts or expenditure; **to have the r. of**, to be free to go anywhere in. [OE.].
RUNABOUT [ru′na-bowt], *n.* a gadabout; light motor-car.
RUNAGATE † [ru′na-gāt], *n.* deserter, fugitive, apostate. [~RENEGADE].
RUNAWAY (1) [ru′na-wā], *n.* one who, that which, has run away; fugitive; horse which has bolted. RUNAWAY (2), *adj.* having run away, bolted; **r. marriage**, elopement; **r. victory**, (*sport*) a win by an overwhelming margin.
RUNE [rōōn], *n.* one of the characters of the early alphabet in use among the ancient Germanic peoples; character, mark, supposed to have magical powers; poem, song, *esp.* Finnish. RUNIC (1), *adj.* of, or pertaining to, runes. RUNIC (2), *n.* thick lettering used for display work. [OE.].
RUNG (1) [rung], *p.pt. of* RING.
RUNG (2), *n.* step of a ladder; cross rail on chair legs. [OE.].
RUNLET [run′let], *n.* little stream, runnel.
RUNNEL [ru′nel], *n.* small stream; gutter. [OE.].
RUNNER [ru′ner], *n.* one who, that which, runs; racer; messenger; shoot from which roots grow; name for certain climbing plants; blade of a skate or sledge; long strip of carpet, or of cloth for covering furniture; horse which runs in a race; **rum r.**, smuggler of dutiable drink; **Bow Street r.**, (*hist.*) London policeman. RUNNER-UP, the second in a race, competition or application for a post.
RUNNING (1) [ru′ning], *n.* act of moving with speed; racing; that which runs or flows; discharge; **in the r.**, having a fair chance of success; **to make the r.**, to set the standard or pace; **r. board**, footboard on a locomotive; footboard for use as a step on either side of a motor-car. RUNNING (2), *adj.* that runs; flowing; continuous; discharging; **r. commentary**, succession of comments accompanying any event; **r. fire**, continuous rain of shots; **r. title**, title in a book which reappears at the top of every (other) page.
RUNT [runt], *n.* variety of pigeon; small thick-set ox; person or animal stunted in growth. [Unkn.].
RUNWAY [run′wā], *n.* path or track; (sloping) track prepared for the transfer of vehicles from their parking place; prepared track from which aircraft take off.
RUPEE [rōō-pē′], *n.* silver coin, the Indian monetary unit. [Hind.].
RUPTURE (1) [rup′tyoor], *n.* action of breaking or bursting; state of being broken or violently parted; quarrel, breach of friendship; (*med.*) hernia. RUPTURE (2), *v.t.* to burst; (*path.*) produce a hernia in; *v.i.* to suffer a breach or disruption. [L.].
RURAL [rōō′ral], *adj.* pertaining to the countryside; agricultural; **r. dean**, see DEAN.
RURIDECANAL [rōō-ri-de-kā′nal], *adj.* pertaining to a rural dean or his office.
RURITANIAN [rōō-ri-tā′ni-an], *adj.* of, pertaining to, or resembling, *Ruritania*, a fictitious Balkan kingdom used as the setting for modern romances of adventure. [A. Hope's *The Prisoner of Zenda*].
RUSE [rōōz], *n.* trick, stratagem. [Fr.].
RUSH (1) [rush], *n.* aquatic plant with a very pliant stem, used when dry for basket-making etc. RUSH-CANDLE, taper made from the pith of a r. dipped in tallow. RUSH-MAT, mat made of woven rushes. RUSHLIGHT, *n.* light of a r. candle; (*fig.*) mere glimmer of light. [OE.].
RUSH (2), *v.t.* to cause to travel or act rapidly; get over by going at high speed; take by storm; perform with great haste; *v.i.* to press forward with vigour; flow rapidly; blow strongly; enter impetuously; come rapidly into the mind or on to the lips. RUSH (3), *n.* a moving forward in a burst of speed and energy; a run; sudden outburst, gush; great bustle and activity; **gold r.**, sudden hurried dash by large numbers of people to newly found gold fields. RUSH (4), *adj.* (*coll.*) very urgent, done in great haste; characterized by large crowds. [OFr.].
RUSK [rusk], *n.* kind of light, crusty biscuit or sweetened bread crisply baked throughout. [Span.].
RUSSET (1) [ru′sit], *n.* red-brown colour; coarse homespun cloth; kind of apple with a coarse reddish-brown skin. RUSSET (2), *adj.* reddish-brown; of r. material. [L.].
RUSSIA LEATHER [ru-sha-le′THer], *n.* fine dyed leather impregnated with oil distilled from birch bark.
RUSSO-, *pref.* pertaining to Russia or the Russians.

RUST (1) [rust], *n.* red incrustation on iron, caused by its oxygenation under exposure to air and moisture; anything like rust; a disease of plants, resembling rust in its manifestation; (*fig.*) mental dullness. RUST (2), *v.t.* to cause to contract r.; (*fig.*) cause to degenerate, lose skill or dexterity; *v.i.* to contract r.; grow rusty; (*fig.*) degenerate mentally, grow stale; lose one's skill. [OE.].

RUSTIC (1) [rus′tik], *adj.* of, or pertaining to, the country; living in the country; rural; unpolished, uncouth; plain, simple, artless; (of woodwork) made of rough branches fastened together; (*arch.*) with a rough surface and deeply indented joints. [L.].

RUSTICATE [rus′ti-kāt], *v.t.* to compel to live in the country; banish for a time from a university as a punishment; *v.i.* to dwell in the country. [L.].

RUSTLE (1) [ru′sl], *v.t.* to make to rustle; (*U.S. slang*) steal; *v.i.* to make a rustle; move with the sound of rustling clothes. RUSTLE (2), *n.* soft crisp sound caused by the surfaces of dry yet pliable things rubbing together; **to r. up.** (*slang*) collect, produce. RUSTLER, *n.* person who or thing which rustles; (*U.S slang*) cattle- or horse-thief. [Echoic].

RUSTY [rus′ti], *adj.* covered with rust; affected by rust; (*fig.*) out of practice; brownish-red; **to cut up r.**, (*slang*) to become difficult, cross.

RUT (1) [rut], *n.* sexual heat of a male animal, particularly the deer. [OFr. from L.].

RUT (2), *n.* groove or depression made by wheels; well-worn groove; (*fig.*) settled habits. [Uncert.].

RUTH † [rōōth], *n.* pity, compassion. [OE.].

RUTHENIUM [rōō-thē′ni-um], *n.* a metallic element of the platinum group, denoted by Ru. [MedL.].

RUTHLESS [rōōth′les], *adj.* without pity, cruel.

RYE [rī], *n.* grain obtained from the *Secale cereale*; flour obtained from this grain; (*U.S. and Canadian*) rye whisky; **r. whisky**, whisky distilled from r. RYE-GRASS, grass of the genus *Lolium*. [OE.].

S

S [es], nineteenth letter of the English alphabet.

SABAOTH [sa′bā-ŏth, sa-bā′oth], *n.*(*pl.*) armies, hosts (*only in phr.* **Lord of S.**). [Heb.].

SABBATARIAN (1) [sa-ba-tāer′i-an], *adj.* of, or pertaining to, sabbatarians or sabbatarianism. SABBATARIAN (2), *n.* one who observes the seventh day of the week as the sabbath; rigid observer of the sabbath; one who considers that Sunday should be observed as strictly as the Jewish sabbath. [L.].

SABBATH [sa′bath], *n.* a day of the week set apart for rest and divine worship; a time of rest; Sunday. [Heb.].

SABBATIC(AL) [sa-ba′tik(-al)], *adj.* pertaining to, or resembling, the sabbath; **s. year**, in the Jewish economy, every seventh year, during which the lands were to lie fallow; hence, name given to the one year's vacation in every seven awarded to teachers in certain universities.

SABLE (1) [sā′bl], *n.* small carnivore of the weasel family; fur of this animal. SABLE (2), *n.* black colour; (*pl.*) black clothes, *esp.* those worn in mourning; paint-brush of sable hairs. SABLE (3), *adj.* black, dark; made of the dark brown fur of the s.; (*her.*) black. [OFr. from Russ.].

SABOT [sa′bō], *n.* wooden shoe worn by the French and Belgian peasantry. [Fr.].

SABOTAGE (1) [sa′bo-tahzh], *n.* deliberate damage to machinery, tools, plant or property; other forms of deliberate injury to business by enemies or malcontents. SABOTAGE (2), *v.t.* to wreck deliberately. [Fr.].

SABOTEUR [sa-bo-tur′], *n.* one who performs an act or acts of sabotage. [Fr.].

SABRE [sā′ber], *n.* heavy curved cavalry sword. SABRE-TOOTHED, with long, curved, canine teeth. SABRETACHE [sa′ber-tash], *n.* leather case hung from the sword belt of a cavalry officer. [Fr. from Germ.].

SAC [sak], *n.* (*biol.*) small bag or receptacle. [L.].

SACBUT. see SACKBUT.

SACCHAR-, SACCHARO-, *pref.* containing, with other things, sugar; sweet like sugar. [MedL.].

SACCHARIN(E) (1) [sa′ka-rin], *n.* chemical compound of extreme sweetness obtained from coal-tar; a small tablet containing this. SACCHARINE (2), *adj.* pertaining to sugar; sweet; (*fig.*) over-sweet, sugary. [*Prec.*].

SACCHARO-. see SACCHAR-.

SACERDOTAL [sa-ser-dō′tal], *adj.* pertaining to priests; given to undue regard for priests or the priesthood. SACERDOTALISM, *n.* a priestly system; undue regard for the priesthood or the power of priests. [L.].

SACHET [sa′shā], *n.* small bag of soft material for holding handkerchiefs or lavender. [Fr.].

SACK (1) [sak], *n.* large bag of coarse material for holding flour, potatoes, coal etc.; the quantity of goods contained in a sack; (*coll.*) loose shapeless dress or coat; **the s.,** (*coll.*) (notice of) dismissal from employment. SACK (2), *v.t.* to put in a s.; (*coll.*) give notice of dismissal from employment. SACKING, *n.* coarse cloth used for making sacks and as wrapping material for heavy packages. [OE.].

SACK (3), *n.* plunder or pillage of a captured town or village by troops; looting, pillage. SACK (4), *v.t.* to plunder (a captured town etc.); loot. [Fr.].

SACK (5), *n.* dry white Spanish wine much drunk during the sixteenth century. [Fr.].

SAC(K)BUT [sak′but], *n.* obsolete wind-instrument resembling a trombone; Babylonian harp. [Uncert.].

SACKCLOTH [sak′kloth], *n.* cloth of which sacks are made; coarse cloth formerly worn in expression of mourning, distress or penitence.

SACRAL [sā′kral], *adj.* (*anat.*) of, or pertaining to, the sacrum. [MdL.].

SACRAMENT [sa′kra-ment], *n.* ceremonial observance in the Christian Church, *esp.* one instituted as an outward and visible sign of an inward and spiritual grace; the Lord's Supper; Baptism. SACRAMENTAL [sa-kra-men′tal], *adj.* pertaining to a s., very sacred. SACRAMENTALISM, *n.* excessive observance of sacraments. [Fr.].

SACRED [sā′kred], *adj.* holy, consecrated, inviolable; consecrated to a religious purpose; hallowed by association; held in very dear regard. [L.].

SACRIFICE (1) [sa′kri-fīs], *n.* the making of an offering to a god, primarily of a slaughtered animal, later of any possession; thing sacrificed; victim; one who destroys himself or sinks his own desires for the benefit of another; sale at a loss; (*theol.*) the offering of Christ of his life to expiate the sins of men; the Eucharistic celebration. SACRIFICE (2), *v.t.* to offer to a divinity upon an altar; surrender; abandon. SACRIFICIAL [sa-kri-fi′shal], *adj.* of, or pertaining to, s. [OFr.].

SACRILEGE [sa′kri-lij], *n.* sin of profaning sacred things; alienation to a common purpose of what has been consecrated; breaking into a church and stealing from it. SACRILEGIOUS [sa-kri-li′jŏŏs], *adj.* violating sacred things; polluted with s.; profane; irreverent. [L.].

SACRING [sā′kring], *n.* (*R.C.*) consecration of the Eucharistic elements at Mass; **s. bell**, bell rung at the elevation of the Host in the Eucharist. [ME.].

SACRIST, SACRISTAN [sa′krist(-an)], *n.* keeper of the sacristy; church official who has charge of the sacred vessels and vestments; a sexton. [OFr., MedL.].

SACRISTY [sa′kris-ti], *n.* room in a church where the sacred utensils and vestments are kept. [MedL.].

SACROSANCT [sa′krō-sangkt], *adj.* sacred, inviolable. [L.].

SACRUM [sā′krum], *n.* (*anat.*) triangular bone at the base of the vertebral column joining with the haunch bones to form the pelvis. [L.].

SAD [sad], *adj.* sorrowful, grieved; melancholy; deplorable; heavy, not fully risen (of bread, cake etc.); sober coloured. [OE.].

SADDLE (1) [sa′dl], *n.* seat on a horse's back or on a cycle or similar machine for the rider to sit on;

something like a saddle; ridge on a high hill resembling a saddle; **in the s.,** on horseback; (*fig.*) in control, in office. SADDLE-BOW, curved fore-part of a s. SADDLE (2), *v.t.* to place a s. on; (*fig.*) place a burden or responsibility upon. SADDLEBAG, *n.* one of a pair of bags joined by straps and slung across a horse's back behind the s.; fabric for making saddlebags for camels and also formerly for upholstering chairs; bicycle tool-bag. [OE.].

SADDLEBACK [sa'dl-bak], *n.* the great black-backed gull; the harp-seal; saddle of a hill; large breed of pig, black with a white mark across the back. SADDLEBACKED, *adj.* having the back shaped like a saddle.

SADDLER [sad'ler], *n.* one who makes or sells saddles and horse furniture.

SADDUCEE [sa'dyōō-sē], *n.* member of a party among the Jews in the time of Christ, who held by the written word to the exclusion of tradition, and denied the doctrine of immortality or the separate existence of the spirit; (*fig.*) self-righteous materialist. [LL.].

SADISM [sā'dizm, sah'dizm], *n.* form of sexual perversion of which cruelty is a characteristic feature; pleasure arising from inflicting or watching cruelty. [Marquis de *Sade*].

SAFARI [sa-fah'ri], *n.* hunting expedition. [Swahili, from Arab.].

SAFE (1) [sāf], *adj.* secure; free from danger, hurt, injury or damage; (*fig.*) reliable, predictable. SAFE-CONDUCT, *n.* convoy, guard or passport ensuring a s. passage. SAFE-KEEPING, *n.* action of preserving in safety from injury or escape. SAFE (2), *n.* strong cupboard, usually of steel, and fitted with locks, for storing valuables; cupboard for storing food, *esp.* meat and milk; **s. deposit,** institution which contains strong-rooms and safes to be let separately. [Fr. from L.].

SAFEGUARD (1) [sāf'gahd], *n.* one who or that which guards safely; defence; protective convoy. SAFEGUARD (2), *v.t.* to guard; protect, look after; (*comm*) impose tariffs on goods (entering a country) so as to protect home industry.

SAFETY [sāf'ti], *n.* freedom from danger, hurt, injury or loss; close custody; security; **s. catch,** attachment to mechanism to prevent accidents if something goes wrong, *esp.* a device to prevent the accidental discharge of a firearm; **s. curtain,** fireproof curtain which can be lowered to cut off the stage premises from the auditorium; **s. glass,** glass which does not splinter dangerously when broken; **s. zone,** refuge for pedestrians. SAFETY-LAMP, miner's lamp, so constructed as to give light without danger of firing explosive gases. SAFETY-MATCH, match which ignites only by being rubbed on a specially prepared surface. SAFETY-PIN, pin shaped like a brooch and with a guarded point. SAFETY-RAZOR, razor with a detachable blade, fitted with a guard to minimize risk of laceration during shaving. SAFETY-VALVE, valve fitted to any container or system of pipes holding liquids or gases under pressure, which opens automatically when the pressure is excessive; (*fig.*) outlet for suppressed feelings which prevents a dangerous outburst. [Fr.].

SAFFRON [sa'fron], *n.* a bulbous plant; bright orange colouring and flavouring matter obtained from this; bright orange-yellow colour. [Arab.].

SAG (1) (*pres.pt.* **sagging,** *pret.* and *p.pt.* **sagged**) [sag], *v.i.* to yield; incline from an upright position for want of support; sink down; go limp, flaccid; (*fig.*) droop, become depressed; (*comm.*) drop in price. SAG (2), *n.* fact of sagging. [~Norw.].

SAGA [sah'gah], *n.* old heroic Scandinavian story; ancient composition dealing with the history and mythology of the northern European races; chronicle of a family. [OIcel.].

SAGACIOUS [sa-gā'shŏŏs], *adj.* wise, discerning, acute; having shrewd practical insight. [L.].

SAGACITY [sa-ga'si-ti], *n.* quality of being sagacious.

SAGE (1) [sāj], *n.* a savoury herb much used in cooking. [OFr. from L.].

SAGE (2), *adj.* wise, venerable, sagacious. SAGE (3), *n.* wise man; venerable old man of tried wisdom.

SAGITTARIUS [sa-ji-tāer'i-us], *n.* (*astron.*) ninth sign of the Zodiac, the Archer. [L.].

SAGO [sā'gō], *n.* starch food obtained from the pith of several palms native to Malaya. [Malay].

SAHARA [sa-hah'rah], *n.* great North African desert; (*fig.*) any dry and barren place. [Arab.].

SAHIB [sah'ib], *n.* courtesy title formerly given to any gentleman of rank in India by the Indians; English

gentleman in India; **pukka s.,** genuinely English gentleman of the former ruling classes in India. [Arab.].

SAID [sed], *pret.* and *p.pt.* of SAY. [OE.].

SAIL (1) [sāl], *n.* spread of canvas for receiving the impulse of the wind by which a sailing ship is driven; ship or other vessel; excursion in some vessel; object spread out like a s. to catch the wind, as one of the revolving arms on a windmill; **to take the wind out of the sails of,** to destroy the confidence of; **under s.,** under way; **to set s.,** to begin the journey; **to shorten s.,** to reduce the extent of s.; **to strike s.,** to lower the sails suddenly. SAIL-LOFT, place where sails are cut and made. SAIL-NEEDLE, large needle with a triangular tapering point. SAIL-YARD, yard or spar on which sails are stretched. SAIL (2), *v.t.* to pass over in a ship; navigate; *v.i.* to be driven along by the action of wind upon sails; go by water; glide through the air; move smoothly along; walk with smooth dignity; **to s. near the wind,** to steer a sailing ship as near into the wind as possible to maintain way on her; (*fig.*) carry on any undertaking approaching dangerously near the border-line of safety or honesty. SAILER, *n.* sailing ship with reference to her speed or manner of sailing. [OE.].

SAILCLOTH [sāl'kloth], *n.* strong canvas used for making sails.

SAILING [sā'ling], *n.* act of sailing; act or art of navigating; act of moving by means of sails; departure of a ship on her journey; act of moving smoothly through the air or on the ground. SAILING-MASTER, officer who superintends the details of navigating the ship.

SAILOR [sā'ler], *n.* seaman, mariner; one of the crew of a ship; **bad (good) s.,** one who travels with (without) discomfort on board ship. [SAIL (2)].

SAILPLANE [sāl'plān], *n.* a glider.

SAINFOIN [sān'foin], *n.* a leguminous plant largely cultivated for fodder. [Fr.].

SAINT (1) [sānt], *n.* holy man or woman; one of the blessed dead in Paradise; person eminent for piety and virtue; (*R.C.*) one canonized by the Church; **saint's day,** Church festival in commemoration of some particular s. SAINT (2), *v.t.* to canonize; give the name of s. to. SAINTED, *adj.* canonized, holy. [OFr. from L.].

ST. BERNARD [snt-bur'nahd], *n.* breed of mastiffs kept by the monks of the hospice of *St. Bernard* in Switzerland to help in the rescue of travellers exposed to danger on the mountains.

ST. JOHN'S WORT [snt-jonz-wurt'], *n.* a low-growing plant with yellow flowers.

ST. VITUS'S DANCE [snt-vi-tus-dahns'], *n.* chorea.

SAKE [sāk], *n.* account; end; purpose; regard; **for the s. of,** on account of, because of, out of regard for, in the interests of. [OE.].

SAKER [sā'ker], *n.* the hawk, *Falco sacer.* [Arab.].

SAL [sal], *n.* (*chem.*) salt or salts; **s. ammoniac,** hydrochloride of ammonia; **s. volatile,** an aromatic solution of carbonate of ammonia. [L.].

SALAAM (1) [sa-lahm'], *n.* ceremonious oriental salutation; obeisance. SALAAM (2), *v.i.* to make a s. [Arab.].

SALACIOUS [sa-lā'shŏŏs], *adj.* lewd, lustful; dealing with lewd matters. [L.].

SALACITY [sa-la'si-ti], *n.* condition of being salacious. [L.].

SALAD [sa'lad], *n.* dish of various mixtures of prepared vegetables, raw or cooked, served cold and flavoured with a dressing of mixed oil, vinegar and mustard; lettuce as the main ingredient of a salad; **s. days,** immaturity, raw youth. [Portug.].

SALAMANDER [sa'la-man-der], *n.* (*zool.*) tailed amphibian allied to the newts, one species of which was fabled to be able to live in fire. [Gk.].

SALAMI [sa-lah'mi], *n.* Italian variety of sausage, highly seasoned. [It.].

SALARY [sa'la-ri], *n.* fixed payment made at regular intervals, as per year, quarter or month, to a person in a clerical or administrative position in business etc., as distinct from a wage paid for manual labour; stipend. [L.].

SALE [sāl], *n.* act of selling; transfer of goods, produce or possession from the owner, manufacturer or retailer to the consumer or purchaser at a price agreed by both parties; period during which the goods of a retail shop are offered to the public at reduced prices; auction; **s. of work,** charitable function at which goods made or presented by helpers are sold. SALE-PRICE, specially reduced price of an article at a general s. SALE-ROOM, room in which goods are sold by auction or tender. SALES-RESISTANCE, reluctance of potential buyers to be overcome by salesmanship, or to buy at exorbitant prices. [OE.].

SALESMAN, SALESWOMAN (*pl.* **salesmen, -women**) [sālz′man, ′wŏo-man], *n.* man, woman, who sells merchandise. SALESMANSHIP, *n.* technique of inducing people to buy goods.

SALIC [să′lik], *adj.* relating to the Salian Franks; **s. law,** French law alleged to exclude women from succeeding to the crown. [LL.].

SALICIN [să′li-sĭn], *n.* (*chem.*) bitter principle obtained from certain species of willow. [L.].

SALICYLIC [sa-li-si′lik], *adj.* relating to, obtained from, salicin; **s. acid,** medicinal acid originally derived from salicin.

SALIENCE, SALIENCY [sā′li-ens(-i)], *n.* state of being salient; prominent feature.

SALIENT (1) [sā′li-ent], *adj.* projecting, jutting outward; (*fig.*) conspicuous. SALIENT (2), *n.* prominent or projecting angle in a line, particularly a line of troops in advance of the main line. [L.].

SALINE (1) [sā′lĭn], *adj.* containing salt; tasting of salt; of the nature of a salt. SALINE (2), *n.* deposit of salt; salt-spring; effervescing aperient. [∼SAL.]

SALIVA [sa-lī′vah], *n.* fluid secreted by the salivary glands, which moistens the mouth and promotes the digestion of food, spittle. SALIVATE [să′li-vāt], *v.t.* and *i.* to cause to produce an excessive secretion and discharge of s.; secrete s. to an abnormal extent. [L.].

SALIX [sā′liks], *n.* (*bot.*) the numerous genus of willows and osiers. [L.].

SALLOW (1) [sa′lō], *n.* a willow identified by its broad leaves. [OE.].

SALLOW (2), *adj.* having a complexion of a pale, sickly, yellow colour. [OE.].

SALLY (1) [sa′li], *n.* sudden flash of wit, witty piece of bantering; (*milit.*) sudden attack by troops from a besieged position in order to harry the enemy. SALLY (2), *v.i.* to set out on an excursion; (*milit.*) make a s.; **s. forth,** to go out hopefully.

SALLY LUNN [sa-li-lun′], *n.* kind of light tea-cake. [*Sally Lunn*, of Bath].

SALMI [sal′mē], *n.* partly roasted game stewed with wine and condiments. [Fr.].

SALMON [sa′mon], *n.* species of large fish with firm, pink flesh, which makes a journey from the sea up difficult rivers and streams to its spawning ground; light-pink colour resembling that of a s.; **rock s.,** name in the fish trade for the large blenny fish. SALMON-TROUT, a sea-trout sometimes sold as s. [L.].

SALON [sa-law(ng)′], *n.* drawing-room used for receptions in a private house; circle of friends, *esp.* artistic; exhibition of pictures. [Fr.].

SALOON [sa-lŏon′], *n.* large reception-room; any large room used for various forms of public entertainment; largest cabin in a passenger steamer; large room in a liner or aircraft; first-class accommodation in a liner; luxurious railway carriage not divided into compartments; motor-car with a closed-in body; more comfortable and expensive bar in a public-house. [*Prec.*].

SALOPIAN [sa-lō′pi-an], *n.* and *adj.* a native of, pertaining to, Shropshire; past or present member of Shrewsbury school. [*Salop*, name for Shropshire from AFr.].

SALSIFY [sal′si-fi], *n.* a composite plant cultivated for its root which is eaten as a vegetable. [Uncert.].

SALT (1) [sawlt], *n.* substance found in crystalline form and in solution, which is prepared for various domestic and industrial uses, known by chemists as sodium chloride; sailor; salt-cellar; (*chem.*) a compound resulting from the union of an acid with a base; (*fig.*) piquancy, characteristic flavour; wit; (*med.*) (*pl.*) various popular brands of purgative, as Epsom, Glauber's etc.; **with a grain of s.,** with reserve; **not worth his s.,** (*coll.*) worthless. SALT-CELLAR, small domestic utensil for holding the table s.; (*coll.*) deep hollow at the base of the neck above the collar-bones. SALT-MARSH, land sometimes covered with grass, which is invaded by the overflow of salt water. SALT-PAN, basin or pit where s. is obtained from brine by evaporation. SALT (2), *adj.* having the flavour of s.; impregnated with s.; growing among s.; salacious. SALT-JUNK, dry s. beef; SALT (3), *v.t.* to sprinkle or season with s.; preserve by impregnating with s.; (*coll.*) create a false deposit of precious metal in; falsify credits or profits in. SALTER, *n.* one who salts; dealer in s. [OE.].

SALTATION [sal-tā′shn], *n.* a leaping or jumping. [L.].

SALTATORY [sal′ta-te-ri], *adj.* leaping or dancing; (*biol.*) not regular in development. [L.].

SALTING [sawl′ting], *n.* salt-water marsh; process of applying salt to the preservation of animal and vegetable substances for food.

SALTIRE [sal′tēer], *n.* (*her.*) diagonal cross; St. Andrew's cross, in the form of an X. [LL.].

SALTPETRE [sawlt-pē′ter], *n.* nitre; nitrate of potash. SALTPETROUS, *adj.* relating to s.; of the nature of s.; impregnated with s. [LL.].

SALUBRIOUS [sa-lŏo′bri-ŏos], *adj.* (of climate, situation etc.) favourable to health; healthful. [L.].

SALUKI [sa-lŏo′ki], *n.* breed of very fast dogs with long legs, sharp nose, fine silky coat, and a flowing tail, used in Persia for hunting gazelles. [Arab.].

SALUTARY [sa′lyŏo-ta-ri], *adj.* wholesome, promoting health; having a moral effect for good. [L.].

SALUTATION [sa-lyŏo-tā′shn], *n.* act or style of saluting or paying respect; words or gestures expressive of a greeting. [L.].

SALUTE (1) [sa-lŏot′], *n.* act of saluting; greeting in one of various forms, kiss, a firing of a number of guns as a ritual of honour, act of dipping flags; (*fencing*) formal crossing of swords or foils; (*milit.*) disciplinary gesture of respect made by a member of the armed forces to a superior officer. SALUTE (2), *v.t.* to greet or welcome in a conventional mode of address, make a salutation to; make a conventional gesture to as an act of respect, bow to, kiss the hand of, touch the hat to, dip the colours, fire guns in honour of. [L.].

SALVAGE (1) [sal′vij], *n.* the saving of a derelict ship by another vessel; compensation allowed by law for the saving of a ship or goods from loss at sea; cargo or ship which is so saved; act of saving; waste specially collected to be re-used for manufacture. SALVAGE (2), *v.t.* to save from total loss; recover (property etc.) from effects of fire, flood etc. [L.].

SALVARSAN [sal′vah-san], *n.* arsenical compound used as a cure for syphilis. [L.].

SALVATION [sal-vā′shn], *n.* act of saving, particularly from sin or from habitual immorality; deliverance, redemption; person who, or that which, saves; rescue from danger which might have proved mortal; **S. Army,** an organization acting on Christian principles and engaged in missionary and rescue work. [LL.].

SALVE (1) [salv, sahv], *n.* kind of adhesive composition; ointment with curative powers applied to wounds and sores; help; remedy. SALVE (2), *v.t.* to soothe, heal by means of a s. [OE.].

SALVE (3), *v.t.* to save, salvage. SALVOR, *n.* one who saves a ship or goods from destruction at sea or by fire. [SALVAGE].

SALVER [sal′ver], *n.* tray on which something is presented. [Span.].

SALVIA [sal′vi-ah], *n.* (*bot.*) genus of herbs allied to sage. [L.].

SALVO (1) [sal′vō], *n.* exception, reservation; (*leg.*) conditional clause. [L.].

SALVO (2), *n.* volley of guns discharged in salute; broadside. [L.].

SAMARITAN (1) [sa-ma′ri-tan], *n.* the language or an inhabitant of Samaria; charitable person like the man in the parable, Luke x, 33. SAMARITAN (2), *adj.* relating to the people or language of Samaria. [L.].

SAM BROWNE [sam-brown′], *n.* leather belt worn as part of the uniform of officers in the British Army. [General Sir *Samuel Browne*].

SAME [sām], *adj.* identical; having reciprocal possession of points of comparison, not different; of the identical kind, sort or degree, exactly similar, mentioned before; unchanged, being no different in condition. [OE.].

SAMITE † [sā′mĭt], *n.* fabric of silk woven with gold thread. [L. from Gk.].

SAMOVAR [sa′mō-vah(r)], *n.* Russian copper tea-urn kept hot by heated air. [Russ.].

SAMOYED [sa-mŏ′yed], *n.* member of a Mongol race in the extreme north of Asia; their breed of dog. [Russ.].

SAMPAN [sam′pan], *n.* Chinese river boat. [Chin.].

SAMPHIRE [sam′fier], *n.* (*bot.*) umbelliferous plant usually found on cliffs by the sea. [ME. from OFr.].

SAMPLE (1) [sahm′pl], *n.* single part, portion or specimen representing the characteristics and qualities of the whole, *esp.* a single example of a quantity of mass-produced products. SAMPLE (2), *v.t.* to take a s. of a

---

The accent ′ after a syllable = stress (u-pon′). The mark ‾ over a vowe l= length (ă in made; ō in bone).

group or series, test the quality by means of a specimen; examine the standard of by tasting or sipping. **SAMPLER,** *n.* a pattern of work, specimen of embroidery or needlework; one who samples. [EXAMPLE].

SAMURAI [sa′mōō-ri], *n.* formerly a Japanese gentleman of the military class under the old feudal system. [Jap.].

SANATIVE [sa′na-tiv], *adj.* sanatory, having the power to heal, tending to heal. [LL.].

SANATORIUM (*pl.* **sanatoria**) [sa-na-taw′ri-um], *n.* establishment for the treatment of tuberculosis or other diseases; health resort; hospital of a school. [L.].

SANATORY [sa′na-te-ri], *adj.* curative, conducive to health.

SANCTIFY [sangk′ti-fi], *v.t.* to make holy, hallow, consecrate; purify from sin; justify, sanction as holy. [L.].

SANCTIMONIOUS [sangk-ti-mō′ni-ōōs], *adj.* assuming the outward appearance of sanctity, hypocritically pious.

SANCTION (1) [sangk′shn], *n.* ratification of a subordinate's act by a superior authority, consent to a specific action; acknowledged acceptance of general conduct; justification; (*leg.*) penalty which gives weight to the power of a law and its observance. SANCTION (2), *v.t.* to ratify, allow; give s. to. [L.].

SANCTITY [sangk′ti-ti], *n.* state of being sacred or holy, saintliness, sacredness; solemnity. [L.].

SANCTUARY [sangk′tyōō-a-ri], *n.* sacred place, holy shrine; consecrated building; most holy part of a church or temple; altar place in a church; asylum for fugitives, place of refuge, formerly sanctioned by ecclesiastical authority; territory set apart for the protection and preservation of wild animals or birds; (*fig.*) place of private holiness. [L.].

SANCTUM (*pl.* **sancta**) [sangk′tum], *n.* sacred place; private study; **s. sanctorum,** the Holy of Holies in a tabernacle. [L.].

SANCTUS [sangk′tus], *n.* hymn sung in the Communion Service beginning "Holy, holy, holy;" **S. bell,** bell rung when the S. is sung. [L.].

SAND (1) [sand], *n.* mass of minute grains of disintegrated rock accumulating on seashores or river beds, or in deserts etc.; (*pl.*) stretch of s.; (*fig.*) moments of time; (*slang*) grit, courage. SAND-BANK, sandy shoal. SAND-BAR, bank of S. formed across the mouth of a river. SAND-DUNE, ridge of drifted s. SAND-EEL, small elongated fish which buries itself in the s. SAND-FLY, stinging fly occurring in hot, sandy countries. SAND-MARTIN, species of martin nesting in s. pits and s.-banks. SAND-STORM, storm in which clouds of fine s. are blown about, *esp.* in the desert. SAND (2), *v.t.* to sprinkle or cover with s.; mix with s. [OE.].

SANDAL [san′dal], *n.* kind of open-worked shoe consisting of a sole fastened to the foot by straps. SANDALLED, *adj.* wearing sandals; like sandals. [Gk.].

SANDALWOOD [san′dal-wōōd], *n.* close-grained fragrant wood of an East Indian tree. [Skr.].

SANDBAG (1) [sand′bag], *n.* canvas bag filled with sand, used in fortification etc. SANDBAG (2) (*pres.pt.* SANDBAGGING, *pret.* and *p.pt.* SANDBAGGED), *v.t.* to hit over the head with a s., so as to render unconscious; protect with sandbags.

SANDBOY [sand′boi], *n.* **as happy as a s.,** as happy as a carefree boy. [Uncert.].

SANDGLASS [sand′glahs], *n.* glass apparatus pinched in at the middle to form a bottleneck through which sand from the upper chamber trickles into the lower, emptying itself in an exactly measured time.

SANDPAPER (1) [sand′pā-per], *n.* paper covered with a gritty substance for smoothing and polishing wood. SANDPAPER (2), *v.t.* to smooth or polish with s.

SANDPIPER [sand′pī-per], *n.* one of several species of small plover.

SANDSHOE [sand′shōō], *n.* light shoe of canvas with a rubber sole for wear on a sandy beach.

SANDSTONE [sand′stōn], *n.* (*geol.*) stone or rock composed chiefly of consolidated sand.

SANDWICH (1) [sand′wich], *n.* two pieces of bread spread with butter or some substitute and with a slice of meat, jam etc. between them; sponge cake in this form with jam spread in the middle; **s. board,** one of a pair of boards on which advertisements are displayed, carried on the back and chest by perambulating sandwichmen. SANDWICHMAN, man employed to parade in the streets with s. boards hanging over his shoulders. SANDWICH (2), *v.t.* to insert, interpose, squeeze. [John, Earl of *Sandwich*].

SANE [sān], *adj.* of a balanced emotional and rational nature, sound in mind; sound in opinion; reasonable, sober in judgment, sensible. [L.].

SANG [sang], *pret. of* SING. [OE.].

SANGFROID [sah(ng)-frwah′], *n.* freedom from excitement or nervousness, presence of mind in awkward or dangerous circumstances. [Fr.].

SANGUINARY [sang′gwi-na-ri], *adj.* attended with much bloodshed; bloodthirsty by nature; bloody. [L.].

SANGUINE [sang′gwin], *adj.* blood-red; courageous, confident, optimistic. [L.].

SANGUINEOUS [sang-gwi′ni-ōōs], *adj.* abounding with blood; sanguine; blood-red. [L.].

SANHEDRIM [sa′ni-drim], *n.* great council of justice of the ancient Jews. [Heb.].

SANITARY [sa′ni-ta-ri], *adj.* relating to health or hygienic principles and conditions, designed to promote health, hygienic; clean, disinfected; having proper drainage; **s. inspector,** official employed to make regular inspections of local drainage and plumbing systems. SANITARY-TOWEL, *n.* absorbent pad used by women for personal hygiene during menstruation. SANITARIAN [sa-ni-tāer′i-an], *n.* advocate of s. reforms or reforms in sanitation. [L.].

SANITATION [sa-ni-tā′shn], *n.* sanitary science and its application; drainage. [*Prec.*].

SANITY [sa′ni-ti], *n.* state of being sane. [L.].

SANK [sangk], *pret. of* SINK. [OE.].

SANSCULOTTE [sah(ng)-kōō-lot′], *n.* (*hist.*) contemptuous term for the mob during the French Revolution. [Fr.].

SANSERIF [san-se′rif], *n.* a type fount designed without serifs, as that in which the headwords of this dictionary are set. [Fr. *sans* without and SERIF].

SANSKRIT (1) [san′skrit], *n.* the ancient sacred language of the Hindus. SANSKRIT (2), *adj.* relating to, written in, S. [Skr.].

SANTA CLAUS [san′tah-klawz], *n.* legendary figure who dispenses presents at Christmas time, *esp.* to children; Father Christmas. [Du. *Sante Klaus* St. Nicholas].

SAP (1) [sap], *n.* circulating juice of plants; vital fluid; (*fig.*) vitality, vigour. SAP-WOOD, external part of wood, newly formed under the bark. SAP-LESS, *n.* destitute of s., dry. [OE.].

SAP (2), *n.* (*milit.*) trench providing head protection; (*slang*) fool, dupe. SAP (3) (*pres.pt.* SAPPING, *pret.* and *p.pt.* SAPPED), *v.t.* and *i.* (*milit.*) to attack by means of a s., undermine, dig a s.; weaken by draining away vital energy or by tapping the source of strength, devitalize. [OFr.].

SAPIENCE [sā′pi-ens], *n.* wisdom; (when used ironically) an affectation of wisdom. [L.].

SAPIENT [sā′pi-ent], *adj.* sagacious, wise; would-be wise. [L.].

SAPLING [sap′ling], *n.* young tree; (*fig.*) an adolescent youth.

SAPONACEOUS [sa-po-nā′shōōs], *adj.* resembling or having the qualities of soap; (*fig.*) oily. [L.].

SAPONIFY [sa-po′ni-fi], *v.t.* to convert into soap. [~Fr.].

SAPPER [sa′per], *n.* one who saps, undermines; (*milit.*) equivalent rank to that of private in the Royal Engineers; (*milit. coll.*) officer in the Royal Engineers. [SAP (3)].

SAPPHIC (1) [sa′fik], *adj.* derived from, relating to, Sappho, who used a form of verse consisting of three five-beat lines followed by a short fourth line. SAPPHIC, *n.* poetic stanza or poem in the S. form. [Gk.].

SAPPHIRE (1) [sa′fier], *n.* precious stone of an intense translucent blue; a deep, bright blue. SAPPHIRE (2), *adj.* relating to, made of, s. or sapphires; having the colour of a s. [Gk.].

SAPRO-, *pref.* decaying, rotten, putrid. [Gk.].

SAPROPHYTE [sa′prō-fit], *n.* (*bot.*) plant which lives on decaying vegetable matter. [Gk.].

SARABAND [sa′ra-band], *n.* Spanish slow dance; short piece of music composed in three-four time having the second beat accented. [Span.].

SARACEN [sa′ra-sen], *n.* a Mohammedan, *esp.* in the Middle Ages, an enemy of the Crusaders. [Gk.].

SARCASM [sah′kazm], *n.* bitter jibe, taunt; remark uttered with scorn or contempt; the utterance of such remarks; satirical mockery. [Gk.].

SARCASTIC [sah-kas′tik], *adj.* embodying sarcasm, bitterly satirical or ironical; prone to sarcasm; having a nature which delights in sarcasm. [Gk.].

SARCENET, see SARSENET.

SARCO-, *pref.* flesh. [Gk.].

SARCOMA [sah-kō′mah], *n.* (*path.*) cancerous tumour of the connective cells. [Gk.].

ōō is pronounced as in foo*d*; ŏŏ as in hoo*d*; th as in *th*ink; TH as in *th*at; zh as in azure.   ~ = related to.

SARCOPHAGUS (*pl.* **sarcophagi**) [sah-ko'fa-gus], *n.* variety of stone, credited with the power of disintegrating flesh, of which the ancient Greeks made coffins; (*archae.*) large, carved coffin found in Egypt. [Gk.].

SARD [sahd], *n.* (*min.*) variety of semi-precious hard quartz of a blood-red colour. [Gk.].

SARDINE [sah-dēn'], *n.* young of the pilchard, abundant in the Mediterranean and Bay of Biscay, and exported preserved in oil. [Fr.].

SARDONIC [sah-do'nik], *adj.* expressive of irony or of cynicism; having a nature governed by a cynical frame of mind; malicious, bitter. [Late Gk.].

SARDONYX [sah'do-niks], *n.* (*min.*) semi-precious stone, being a banded variety of sard. [Gk.].

SARI [sah'rē], *n.* Hindu woman's robe worn wound round the body. [Hind.].

SARONG [sah-rong'], *n.* knee-length garment worn wrapper-wise by natives of the East Indies. [Malay].

SARSAPARILLA [sahr-sa-pa-ri'lah], *n.* tropical American species of smilax, with a medicinal root. [Span.].

SARSENET, SARCENET [sah'se-net], *n.* a fine thin woven silk. [OFr. from LL.].

SARTORIAL [sah-taw'ri-al], *adj.* of, relating to, a tailor or tailoring. [L.].

SASH (1) [sash], *n.* scarf worn for ornament or military decoration round the waist or over the shoulder. [Arab.].

SASH (2), *n.* frame of a window into which the panes of glass are fitted; **s. cord** (**line**), rope by which a vertically moving s. is hung in a window frame. SASH-FASTENER, metal fitment for keeping a s. window firmly closed. [Fr.].

SASSAFRAS [sa'sa-fras], *n.* a North American tree, from the wood and bark of which a medicinal tonic is obtained. [Span.].

SASSENACH [sa'se-nakh], *n.* Scots name for an Englishman; lowlander. [Gael.].

SAT [sat], *pret. and p.pt. of* SIT. [OE.].

SATAN [sā'tan], *n.* devil or prince of darkness, *esp.* as regarded as the spiritual enemy of mankind. SATANIC [sa-ta'nik], *adj.* relating to S.; having the qualities of S.; fiendish, devilish, extremely malicious, wicked or self-centred. SATANISM [sā'ta-nizm], *n.* devil worship as a travesty of Christianity by inversion; deliberate wickedness; the evil disposition of S. [Heb.].

SATCHEL [sa'chel], *n.* small sack or bag, slung from the shoulder, for books, papers etc., particularly as used by schoolchildren. [OFr.].

SATE [sāt], *v.t.* to satisfy the appetite of; glut, surfeit. [L.].

SATEEN [sa-tēn'], *n.* cotton imitation of satin. [~SATIN].

SATELLITE [sa'te-līt], *n.* (*astron.*) a moon; small body attendant on a planet; (*fig.*) obsequious attendant, hanger-on; **s. state**, state which obediently follows a policy desired by a larger power; **s. town**, smaller town at a short distance from, and depending upon, a larger one. [L.].

SATIATE (1) [sā'shi-āt], *v.t.* to satisfy fully; satisfy beyond the natural capacity, surfeit. SATIATE (2) [sā'shi-at], *adj.* having experienced more than enough; surfeited. [~L.].

SATIETY [sa-tī'i-ti], *n.* state of full satisfaction or of gratification beyond desire. [L.].

SATIN (1) [sa'tin], *n.* glossy silk fabric of a thick close texture with a smooth shining surface. SATIN (2), *adj.* made of s.; having some or all of the characteristics of s.; **s. stitch**, embroidery stitch which gives a glossy surface; **s. walnut**, wood of the sweet gum tree, much prized for furniture. SATINET(TE), *n.* thin kind of s., glossy cloth woven with cotton and silk in imitation of s. [Fr.].

SATINWOOD [sa'tin-wood], *n.* lemon-coloured wood of an East Indian or a tropical American tree, of a mottled grain, used in cabinet work.

SATIRE [sa'tīer], *n.* denunciation of vices, folly or abuses of any kind by means of sarcasm, irony, derision etc.; literary composition of this kind, *esp.* when in verse; lampoon; (*fig.*) circumstance or thing which has the effect of making some person or thing ridiculous. SATIRIST [sa'ti-rist], *n.* person who satirizes or writes s. SATIRIZE, *v.t.* to represent satirically; censure or ridicule with severity. [L.].

SATISFACTION [sa-tis-fak'shn], *n.* state of being satisfied, act of satisfying, that which satisfies; content, gratification; reparation, amends; payment. [L.].

SATISFACTORY [sa-tis-fak'te-ri], *adj.* meeting one's

requirements or desires, satisfying one's sense of fitness; giving satisfaction, supplying one's demands, pleasing, suitable, good; (*theol.*) making amends, atoning. [~L.].

SATISFY [sa'tis-fī], *v.t.* to provide with means which render the mind, the emotions or the body contented; gratify; provide enough for, supply fully; meet one's requirements, pay so as to make complete amends to; discharge a debt; free from doubt, convince; *v.i.* to come up to standard; give satisfaction. [L.].

SATRAP [sā'trap], *n.* governor of a province in ancient Persia, ruling it with the power of an absolute monarch; lesser tyrant. [Gk.].

SATURATE [sa'tyoo-rāt], *v.t.* to soak, add as much to as can be absorbed, cause to absorb so much moisture that it can contain no more; (*chem.*) dissolve in or combine with to the maximum; bomb so heavily as to overwhelm all defences and destroy utterly; (*fig.*) steep (in facts etc.). SATURATION [sa-tyoo-rā'shn], *n.* act of saturating; state of being saturated; impregnation of one body with another till the receiving body can contain no more; **s. bombing**, bombing so heavy as to destroy every part of a target area. [L.].

SATURDAY [sa'ter-dā], *n.* seventh day of the week. [OE. from L.].

SATURN [sa'tern], *n.* (*astron.*) one of the major planets, being the second largest; (*myth.*) ancient Roman god of agriculture. SATURNALIA [sa-ter-nā'li-ah], *n.*(*pl.*) annual feast of S. SATURNALIAN, *adj.* relating to the Saturnalia; loose, dissolute, sportive. SATURNIAN [sa-tur'ni-an], *adj.* (*myth.*) relating to S. whose reign was called the Golden age; happy, distinguished for purity and simplicity. [L.].

SATURNINE [sa'ter-nīn], *adj.* supposed to be under the influence of the planet Saturn; dull, heavy, phlegmatic; dark in visage, glowering.

SATYR [sa'ter], *n.* (*myth.*) sylvan deity, represented as part man and part goat, believed to be addicted to promiscuous loving; lecher. SATYRIC [sa-ti'rik], *adj.* relating to satyrs. [Gk.].

SAUCE (1) [saws], *n.* a preparation taken with meat, fish, sweets etc., to enhance the flavour; (*coll.*) cheek, impudence. SAUCE-BOAT, small deep dish to hold s. for use at table. SAUCE-BOX, saucy, impudent fellow. SAUCE (2), *v.t.* to season with s.; (*coll.*) be impudent or impertinent to. [L.].

SAUCEPAN [saws'pan], *n.* cooking pot, with a handle, used for boiling, stew-pan.

SAUCER [saw'ser], *n.* shallow circular dish, in which a cup is set. [OFr.].

SAUCY [saw'si], *adj.* of a cheeky nature, impudent, rude; expressive of impudence; (*slang*) smart, gay. [SAUCE].

SAUERKRAUT [sow'er-krowt], *n.* chopped cabbage pressed in layers with salt between till it ferments. [Germ.].

SAUNTER (1) [sawn'ter], *v.i.* to walk in a leisurely aimless way, stroll, wander idly. SAUNTER (2), *n.* a sauntering, stroll. [Unkn.].

SAURIAN (1) [saw'ri-an], *adj.* belonging to, resembling, a reptile. SAURIAN (2), *n.* reptile of the lizard group. [Gk.].

SAUSAGE [so'sij], *n.* roll of seasoned, finely chopped meat etc., packed in a skin. SAUSAGE-MEAT, meat and bread etc., minced up together and seasoned. SAUSAGE-ROLL, small oblong pastry filled with sausage-meat and lightly baked. [OFr. from L.].

SAUTÉ, sauté [sō'tā], *adj.* fried quickly and lightly in fat. [Fr.].

SAUTERNE [sō-tãern'], *n.* a sweet white wine. [Fr.].

SAVAGE (1) [sa'vij], *adj.* primitive, uncivilized, cruel, wild; of, relating to, inhabited by, a savage; fierce, untamed; barbarous, merciless, brutal; (*coll.*) furiously angry. SAVAGE (2), *n.* human being born into a social group whose members are at a primitive stage of development; person whose nature is predominantly fierce, cruel and instinctive; bad-mannered person. SAVAGE (3), *v.t.* to handle savagely; (of horses) harm viciously by suddenly turning wild. [OFr. from L.].

SAVANNA(H) [sa-va'nah], *n.* grass-covered treeless plain, prairie. [Span.].

SAVANT [sa'vant], *n.* an expert in one or more branches of learning; scientist. [Fr.].

SAVE (1) [sāv], *v.t.* to extricate from a dangerous situation, lead to safety, rescue; preserve or store for future use, hoard; eliminate (inconvenience), act so as to dispense with, avoid (a disadvantage), set free from the influence of evil or sin; *v.i.* to hoard, economize. SAVE (2), *n.* (*sport*) act of saving a goal, run, ball, point or otherwise preventing an opponent from scoring an advantage. SAVE (3), *prep.* except; **s. that**, *conj.* except that. [OFr. from L.].

SAVELOY [sa've-loi], *n.* highly seasoned dried sausage. [It.].

SAVING (1) [sā'ving], *n.* act of saving; that which is saved, an economy; (*pl.*) money accumulated by thrift. SAVINGS-BANK, bank in which small sums are deposited at low interest. SAVING (2), *adj.* of a thrifty disposition, frugal; (of a quality) exempting from censure; excepting, involving a condition or reservation. SAVING (3), *prep.* excepting, with the exception of.

SAVIOUR [sā'vyŏr], *n.* person who saves or delivers from danger; **The S.**, Jesus Christ, as the Redeemer of mankind. [OFr. from LL.].

SAVORY [sā've-ri], *n.* an aromatic pot-herb. [Fr.].

SAVOUR (1) [sā'ver], *n.* taste or flavour discerned by the palate; (*archaic*) fragrance; (*fig.*) distinctive quality; spice, sharpness, zest; hint, smack. SAVOUR (2), *v.t. and i.* to appreciate a flavour, relish; possess a distinctive characteristic affecting one of the senses, particularly the sense of taste; (*fig.*) appreciate; embody a slight suggestion (of), hint. [OFr.].

SAVOURY (1) [sā'vŏo-ri], *adj.* pleasing to the smell or taste, seasoned and salted; pleasant; (*fig.*) clean, attractive, reputable. SAVOURY (2), *n.* a light dish, usually seasoned or salted.

SAVOY [sa-voi'], *n.* curly-leafed cabbage cultivated for winter use. [*Savoie*, France].

SAVOYARD [sa-voi'ahd], *n.* member of the original casts of the Gilbert and Sullivan operas at the *Savoy* theatre.

SAW (1) [saw], *n.* tool made in various forms, consisting of a steel blade with a serrated edge, used for cutting. SAW (2) (*p.pt.* SAWN), *v.t. and i.* to cut by means of a s.; form by means of a s.; use, work with, a s. SAW-MILL, *n.* mill or works for sawing timber. SAW-PIT, *n.* pit over which timber is sawn by two men. [OE.].

SAW (3), *n.* traditional saying or maxim. [OE., ME.].

SAW (4), *pret. of* SEE. [OE.].

SAWBILL [saw'bil], *n.* the goosander.

SAWDUST [saw'dust], *n.* dust or fragments of wood caused by the sawing of wood.

SAWFISH [saw'fish], *n.* fish whose upper jaw is prolonged into a flattened snout set with horizontal spines or teeth.

SAWYER [saw'yer], *n.* person who saws timber into planks.

SAXE [saks], *adj.* made in Saxony; of a light bright blue in colour. [Germ.].

SAXHORN [saks'hawn], *n.* brass musical instrument, resembling the trumpet. [J. A. *Sax*, inventor].

SAXIFRAGE [sak'si-frāg], *n.* (*bot.*) plant growing among rocks, any of the 200 species of *Saxifraga*. [L.].

SAXON (1) [sak'son], *n.* member of a race of people who inhabited part of the northern coast of Germany and conquered Britain during the fifth and sixth centuries with the aid of the Angles and Jutes; language of these tribes. SAXON (2), *adj.* relating to the Saxons or their country and language. [LL.].

SAXOPHONE [sak'sō-fōn], *n.* brass musical instrument with plated keys and a reed and clarinet mouthpiece. [*Sax*, inventor, and Gk.].

SAY (1) (*pret. and p.pt.* **said**) [sā], *v.t.* to utter in the form of words, express by means of words, speak; repeat by heart, recite; allege, report; *v.i.* to assert, express an opinion in words. SAY (2), *n.* that which is said, one's opinion, a speech. SAYING, *n.* something said; expression; proverb, maxim. [OE., ME.].

SCAB (1) [skab], *n.* dry crust formed over a healed-up sore or wound; rough incrustation formed by congealed pus; a disease of potatoes etc.; (*slang*) worker who works when a strike has been declared. SCAB (2) (*pres.pt.* SCABBING, *pret. and p.pt.* SCABBED), *v.i.* to form a s.; (*slang*) follow the line of action taken by a s. [OScand.].

SCABBARD [ska'bahd], *n.* sheath of a sword, dagger or bayonet. [OFr.].

SCABIES [skā'bēz], *n.* the itch, a troublesome contagious skin disease. [L.].

SCABIOUS [skā'bi-ŏos], *n.* any of the species of *Scabiosa*, plants with blue or purple flowers. [Prec.].

SCABROUS [skab'rŏos], *adj.* (*bot.*, *zool.*) bristly;

rough; having sharp points; (*fig.*) indecent. [LL.].

SCAFFOLD (1) [ska'fold], *n.* temporary structure of poles and boards roped together, or of jointed metal struts, providing support to workmen erecting or renovating a building; raised platform on which criminals are executed; place of execution; gallows. SCAFFOLD (2), *v.t.* to furnish or surround with a s. SCAFFOLDING, *n.* temporary structure for support in an elevated place; frame; materials such as poles, boards, planks etc. for scaffolds. [OFr.].

SCALAR [skā'lah(r)], *n.* (*math.*) a quantity having magnitude but not direction. [L.].

SCALD (1) [skawld], *n.* ancient Scandinavian poet. [OScand.].

SCALD (2), *v.t.* to injure (the skin or flesh) by contact with boiling water or steam; heat (milk etc.) till it nearly reaches boiling point; sterilize by means of boiling water. SCALD (3), *n.* injury to the tissues caused by the heat of boiling liquid or steam. [LL.].

SCALE (1) [skāl], *n.* one of the two plates, pans or bowls of a balance; (*pl.*) weighing-machine; Libra, a sign of the Zodiac. SCALE (2), *v.t.* to weigh (so much). [OFr.].

SCALE (3), *n.* one of the many thin plates of horny substance grown by fishes and reptiles as a protective covering; anything resembling in flaky thinness the scales of a fish, particularly flakes of crust, rust or skin; any of the minute feather-like particles which cover the wings of butterflies and moths; film which forms over the pupil of the eye; (*fig.*) any blinding covering. SCALE (4), *v.t. and i.* to pare off a surface, scrape roughness or scales from; cause scales to form; peel or flake off in scales. [Prec.].

SCALE (5), *n.* ladder, series of steps; system of classification consisting of a graded range of specified standards, system of proportional reproduction of an original, representation in terms of a mathematical ratio; set of marks graded at equal distances as on a ruler; (*math.*) system of numerical notation based on a specified constant; (*mus.*) sounds graded in succession so as to form a gamut of regular notes. SCALE (6), *v.t.* to climb up by means of a ladder; climb over the top of (some obstruction or height); set in proportion, design or regulate according to a ratio; **to s. down**, to reduce. [L.].

SCALENE (1) [skā'lēn], *adj.* (*geom.*) having unequal sides; set obliquely. SCALENE (2), *n.* triangle having all its sides and angles unequal. [Gk.].

SCALLION [ska'li-on], *n.* a kind of onion. [ONFr. from L.].

SCALLOP (1), **SCOLLOP** [sko'lop], *n.* escallop, a bivalvular marine mollusc having a fan-shaped shell with a corrugated surface; scallop shell as the badge of a pilgrim in the Middle Ages; (*pl.*) series of convex curves at the edge of a garment, piece of cloth etc. SCALLOP (2), *v.t.* to cook in a s. shell; edge a piece of material etc. in the wavy line of a s. shell. [OFr.].

SCALLYWAG [ska'li-wag], *n.* scapegrace, scamp. [Unkn.].

SCALP (1) [skalp], *n.* hairy skin of the head; this skin, or part of it, with the hair on, torn off as a trophy by Red Indians. SCALP (2), *v.t.* to remove the s. of with a knife. [OIcel.].

SCALPEL [skal'pel], *n.* dissecting knife used in anatomical and surgical operations. [L.].

SCAMMONY [ska'mo-ni], *n.* (*bot.*) the plant *Convolvulus Scammonia*; inspissated gum run from the plant, used in medicine as a cathartic. [Gk.].

SCAMP (1) [skamp], *v.t.* to do a job of work leaving it in an unfinished state, work on so as to leave a poor, ragged, slipshod finish; skimp. SCAMP (2), *n.* lazy rogue, one who lives on his wits; lovable rascal; mischievous boy. [Uncert.].

SCAMPER (1) [skam'per], *v.i.* to run off in flight with a ragged action due to haste; run about aimlessly, gaily as children, romp. SCAMPER (2), *n.* rapid, ragged run or canter, hasty departure, scurry. [OFr.].

SCAN [skan], *v.t. and i.* to examine critically, scrutinize; speak (verse) accenting the correct beats and giving them their full rhythmic value; analyse verse into its metrical elements; be written according to the rules of scansion; (*television*) resolve the image of (an object) into its components of light and shade. [L.].

SCANDAL [skan'dal], *n.* outrageous gossip; allegations of disgraceful or immoral conduct on the part of others calculated to injure their reputations; outraged feelings caused by such talk or conduct; malicious rumour; (*leg.*) defamation of character.

SCANDALMONGER, *n.* person who delights in talking or inventing s. [Gk.].

SCANDALIZE [skan'da-līz], *v.t.* to offend or shock by some immoral or unconventional action; disgrace. [Gk.].

SCANDALOUS [skan'da-lōos], *adj.* having the effect of scandal, giving offence; disgraceful to reputation, defamatory; giving cause for scandal.

SCANSION [skan'shn], *n.* process of scanning; the metrical base of verse. [L.].

SCANT (1) [skant], *adj.* few in number; small, not plentiful; insufficient, deficient; grudging, unsatisfying. SCANT (2), *v.t. and i.* to stint. [OIcel.].

SCANTLING [skant'ling], *n.* small amount or portion; specific proportion or dimension in building a timber frame. [OFr.].

SCANTY [skan'ti], *adj.* scarcely sufficient in amount or extent; narrow, small; not ample, sparing. [SCANT (1)].

SCAPEGOAT [skāp'gōt], *n.* in Hebraic ritual, goat let loose in the wilderness symbolically bearing all the sins of the people; person who is made to suffer for another's mistakes or offences. [ESCAPE and GOAT].

SCAPEGRACE [skāp'grās], *n.* graceless, good-for-nothing fellow, rogue, rascal. [ESCAPE and GRACE].

SCAPULA [ska'pyōo-lah], *n. (anat.)* shoulder-blade. SCAPULAR (1), *adj.* relating to the s. SCAPULAR (2), SCAPULARY, *n. (eccles.)* monastic vestment consisting of two narrow pieces of stuff hung over the shoulders by means of straps. [LL.].

SCAR (1) [skah(r)], *n.* mark left on the body by a wound or sore; blemish; groove or chip along the surface of a piece of inorganic matter. SCAR (2) (*pres.pt.* SCARRING, *pret. and p.pt.* SCARRED), *v.t.* to mark with a s. [Gk.].

SCAR (3), *n.* steep rock; isolated crag. [OIcel.].

SCARAB [ska'rab], *n.* black-winged beetle of a genus living on dung, revered by the ancient Egyptians as a symbol of long life and creation; gem with a representation of this beetle engraved upon it originally worn by the Egyptians as an amulet. [L.].

SCARAMOUCH [ska'ra-mōosh], *n.* clown in old Italian comedy, representing a cowardly braggart; rascal and braggart. [It.].

SCARCE (1) [skāers], *adj.* not plentiful, deficient, insufficient; rare. SCARCE (2), *adv.* scarcely. SCARCELY, *adv.* barely; only just; with difficulty. [OFr.].

SCARCITY [skāer'si-ti], *n.* quality of being scarce, deficiency, dearth. [AFr.].

SCARE (1) [skāer], *v.t.* to strike with sudden and uncontrollable terror, terrify; keep in a state of apprehension by threatening danger; **to s. away**, to frighten away. SCARE (2), *n.* state of being scared, particularly one experienced collectively, panic; state of alarm caused by unfounded rumours. SCAREMONGER, *n.* person who spreads news calculated to cause the listeners to panic. [ME.].

SCARECROW [skāer'krō], *n.* dummy device set up to frighten crows or other birds from crops; a needless terror; guy, object of ridicule.

SCARF (1) (*pl.* **scarfs** or **scarves**) [skahf, skahvz], *n.* covering worn about the shoulders; light neckerchief or necktie; length of warm material or knitted wool to be wound round the throat. [ONFr.].

SCARF (2), *n. (carp.)* special form of joint keeping two ends of timber firmly clamped together. SCARF (3), *v.t. (carp.)* to fasten by means of a s. [Swed.].

SCARIFY [skāer'i-fī], *v.t. (surg.)* to scratch or cut the skin so as to draw blood; break up the soil; (*fig.*) criticize bitterly, wound. SCARIFIER, *n.* person who scarifies; instrument so used; (*agric.*) implement for breaking up the soil. [LL.].

SCARLATINA [skah-la-tē'nah], *n.* scarlet fever. [It.].

SCARLET (1) [skah'let], *n.* brilliant, bright red colour with a hint of yellow in it; cloth of this colour worn by the military and clergy. SCARLET (2), *adj.* having a s. colour; (*fig.*) sinful; **s. fever**, infectious disease characterized by the presence of a red rash, inflammation of the tonsils, and a peeling off of the skin in the later stages; **s. runner**, edible variety of climbing bean with a s. flower. [OFr.].

SCARP (1) [skahp], *n.* steep face of a mountain, escarpment. SCARP (2), *v.t.* to cut so as to leave a steep slope. [It.].

SCATHE (1), **SCATH** [skāTH], *n. (archaic)* damage, injury. SCATHE (2), *v.t.* to injure. [OIcel.].

SCATHING [skā'THing], *adj.* withering in its effect, bitterly severe in censure. [Prec.].

SCATTER (1) [ska'ter], *v.t. and i.* to throw loosely about in various directions, fling indiscriminately around; disperse, cause to be dispersed or dissipated. SCATTER (2), *n.* dispersal, art or result of scattering; something scattered, a sprinkling. SCATTERING, *n.* action of one who scatters; sparse amount or quantity; (*phys.*) dispersal of rays or fine particles. [OE.].

SCATTER-BRAIN [ska'ter-brān], *n.* person who is temperamentally unable to concentrate, careless, unreliable person.

SCAVENGER [ska'vin-jer], *n.* person employed as a street cleaner; bird or animal feeding on carrion and refuse; device for exhausting gases from a combustion-engine cylinder. SCAVENGE, *v.t. and i.* to scour the streets for refuse; act as a s. [~OFr.].

SCENARIO [shā-nah'ri-ō], *n.* plan of a play, giving the order of the scenes and a synopsis of the story; detailed exposition of the theme of a film in terms of the practical conventions of the medium. [It.].

SCENE [sēn], *n.* place where any event occurs; picture of a locality; any remarkable sight viewed as a whole; stage fitted up with a backcloth or background depicting suitable scenery and containing the necessary "props" (properties) for the production of a play; locality representing the background of a literary work of art; one of the short divisions of a play, a subdivision of an act, usually brought to an end by the lowering of the curtain; incident, episode, particularly one marked by an emotional outburst; **behind the scenes**, part of a theatre stage invisible to the audience; (*fig.*) (relating to) circumstances not known to the public. [Gk.].

SCENERY [sē'ne-ri], *n.* the general appearance of a natural view in terms of the related disposition of its larger features, landscape; painted representation of a scene for the stage. [Prec.].

SCENIC [sē'nik, se'nik], *adj.* of, relating to, the stage, dramatic, theatrical; **s. railway**, miniature railway running on a small-gauge track, carrying passengers for amusement through artificial scenery, switch-back. [Gk.].

SCENT (1) [sent], *v.t.* to become aware of by means of the sense of smell; sense; sprinkle or spray with perfume. SCENT (2), *n.* that which stimulates the sense of smell, odour; a manufactured distillation of essence having an agreeable fragrance; perfume; the odour which lingers in an animal's tracks and is perceptible to other animals; flair for a particular activity; sense of smell; **on the s.**, (of animals) on the track as perceived by the sense of smell; (*fig.*) proceeding in the right direction when on a quest. [L.].

SCEPTIC [skep'tik], *n.* person whose attitude of mind causes him to doubt a dogmatic or given statement of fact; person with a critical temperament who refuses to acknowledge or yield to emotional dominion; person who doubts the validity or the divine origins of religious principles; (*philos.*) thinker who believes the evidence of the senses to be an untrustworthy guide to absolute truth. SCEPTIC(AL), *adj.* being temperamentally inclined to doubt; suspicious; (*philos.*) adopting an attitude of mind which refuses to admit without absolute proof the certainty of doctrines or principles; denying the truth of revelation. [Gk.].

SCEPTICISM [skep'ti-sizm], *n.* attitude of mind of a sceptic; (*philos.*) sceptics' principles; observance of the principle of guarding against belief; doctrine which expresses doubt in the reliability of the senses as guides to the transcendental. [Prec.].

SCEPTRE [sep'ter], *n.* royal mace of ornamental gold carried by a monarch as an emblem of authority. [Gk.].

SCHADENFREUDE [shah'dn-froi-de], *n. (psych.)* malicious pleasure at another's discomfort. [Germ.].

SCHEDULE (1) [she'dyōōl], *n.* inventory, list or catalogue, particularly one giving details under heads of a programme of work to be carried out to time; time-table. SCHEDULE (2), *v.t.* to draw up in the form of a s.; enter in a s.; settle the time for an event to take place. [L.].

SCHEME (1) [skēm], *n.* an arrangement of activities or data drawn up in accordance with a definite plan, systematic order for future steps or events; any project laid out in broad outline; suspicious plan, plot. SCHEME (2), *v.t. and i.* to work on a plan, formulate a s.; work out a s. in secret, intrigue; form a plan, design. [Gk.].

SCHERZO [skāer'tsō], *n.* playful movement in a musical composition; section of a sonata or symphony scored and played in such a style. [It.].

The accent ′ after a syllable = stress (u-pon′). The mark ‾ over a vowel = length (ā in made; ō in bone).

SCHIEDAM [skhě'dahm], *n.* Hollands gin, schnapps. [*Schiedam*, Dutch town].

SCHIPPERKE [ski'per-ki, shi'per-ki], *n.* Belgian breed of dog, smooth-haired and tailless, allied to the Pomeranian. [Du.].

SCHISM [sizm], *n.* division or separation, *esp.* in religion; deliberate split in the ranks of an organized society; (*eccles.*) sin of causing schism. SCHISMATIC [siz-ma'tik], *n.* person who separates from an established church or religious faith on the ground of disagreement on principles. SCHISMATIC(AL), *adj.* relating to, connected with, tending to, or implying, s.; disruptive. [OFr. from Gk.].

SCHIZOMYCETES [ski-zō-mi-sē'tēz], *n.(pl.)* (*biol.*) the lowest forms of life which multiply by division; bacteria. [Gk.].

SCHIZOPHRENIA [ski-zō-frē'ni-ah], *n.* (*psych.*) a form of hallucinatory insanity characterized by disassociation of different aspects of the personality. [Gk.].

SCHNAPPER [shna'per], *n.* edible sea-fish found in Australian and New Zealand waters. [Germ.].

SCHNAPPS [shnaps], *n.* schiedam, a variety of Hollands gin. [Germ.].

SCHNAUZER [shnowt'ser], *n.* breed of German house-dog resembling a short-haired terrier.

SCHNITZEL [shnit'zel], *n.* a fried veal cutlet, *esp.* as prepared in Vienna. [Germ.].

SCHOLAR [sko'ler], *n.* man of learning; an expert in a branch of knowledge, undergraduate who by virtue of an examination belongs to the foundation of a college, and is entitled to a grant so that he can pursue his studies; pupil. SCHOLARLY, *adj.* erudite, learned; characteristic of a s. SCHOLARSHIP, *n.* capacity for, or acknowledged status attained in, detailed and thorough knowledge; erudition, high standard of specialized learning; annual allowance granted to a s. to permit a continued pursuit of studies. [LL.].

SCHOLASTIC [sko-las'tik], *adj.* relating to a scholar; relating to the schoolmen; characterized or produced by erudition; scholarly; too subtle, pedantic; **s. profession,** the teaching profession. SCHOLASTICISM, *n.* s. philosophy or learning which kept strictly to the principles of Aristotle; adherence to the subtleties of the schools. [Gk.].

SCHOLIAST [skō'li-ast], *n.* ancient commentator on Greek or Latin classics; writer of explanatory notes in texts. [Gk.].

SCHOOL (1) [skōōl], *n.* shoal of whales, porpoises etc. [Du.].

SCHOOL (2), *n.* institution which provides a systematic method of teaching the young, educational establishment; the pupils of a school considered as a whole or as belonging to one of various grades; the school buildings and grounds; time devoted to attendance in the classrooms; institution for research by adults; group of disciples acknowledging the authority and principles of a master; the body of learning, principles and style established by a master or leader; opinions held by a substantial body of people; university faculty offering a degree to a successful student; (*pl.*) final examination for a degree at Oxford University; **grammar s.,** *orig.* a school at which Latin was taught, now, a secondary s.; **high s.,** secondary s.; **of the old s.,** old-fashioned; **S. Board,** committee formerly elected by local ratepayers to provide and administer elementary education in the district. SCHOOL-BOOK, text-book for use in schools. SCHOOL-HOUSE, house containing classrooms for the use of a s.; residence of the principal of a s. adjoining it. SCHOOL (3), *v.t.* to educate, instruct; train a horse in jumping; (*reflex.*) submit to discipline. SCHOOLING, *n.* instruction in s., education, tuition; a reproof, reprimand. [OE. from Gk.].

SCHOOLFELLOW [skōōl'fe-lō], *n.* one of a number of boys or girls educated at the same school at the same time.

SCHOOLMAN (*pl.* **schoolmen**) [skōōl'man], *n.* man of the Middle Ages expert in the niceties of academical disputation, or of school philosophy or divinity.

SCHOOLMARM [skōōl'mahm], *n.* (*coll.*) schoolmistress, particularly of a priggish, prudish type. [SCHOOL and MA'AM].

SCHOOLMASTER [skōōl'mah'ster], *n.* man who presides over, or teaches in, a school.

SCHOOLMISTRESS [skōōl'mis-tres], *n.* woman following the teaching profession.

SCHOOLROOM [skōōl'rōōm], *n.* room in a school; room in a building where children study.

SCHOONER [skōō'ner], *n.* fore-and-aft rigged sailing vessel fitted with two or more masts; measure of beer, reputed to contain 14 ounces. [Uncert.].

SCHOTTISCHE [sho-tēsh'], *n.* German round dance resembling a polka; music for this dance in two-four time. [Germ.].

SCIATIC [si-a'tik], *adj.* relating to or affecting the hip. [Gk.].

SCIATICA [si-a'ti-kah], *n.* neuralgia in the sciatic nerve. [MedL.].

SCIENCE [si'ens], *n.* the accumulation and organization of knowledge acquired by means of tested methods of observation and systematized with a view to the formulation of general laws or hypotheses to account for natural phenomena or their behaviour; any branch of knowledge so organized; **applied s.,** knowledge adapted for material or functional use, as in industry. SCIENTIAL [si-en'shal], *adj.* relating to, producing, s. [L.].

SCIENTIFIC [si-en-ti'fik], *adj.* pertaining, relating, to science; employed in science; according to science, arranged or performed in a systematic manner with regard to the greatest degree of accuracy; precise, exact; expert, highly trained, skilled in applying principles. [MedL.].

SCIENTIST [si'en-tist], *n.* person trained in science; authority on scientific matters; man of science.

SCILICET [si'li-set], *adv.* to wit, namely, viz. [L.].

SCILLA [si'lah], *n.* (*bot.*) genus of bulbous plants including the squills and the wild bluebell. [Gk.].

SCIMITAR [si'mi-tah(r)], *n.* short curved oriental sword with a single cutting edge. [It.].

SCINTILLA [sin-ti'lah], *n.* a gleam, spark; (*fig.*) a trace. [L.].

SCINTILLATE [sin'ti-lāt], *v.i.* to emit sparks, sparkle; gleam, glitter; (*fig.*) shine in company, particularly by wit or brilliance of conversation. SCINTILLATION [sin-ti-lā'shn], *n.* act of sparkling or twinkling; twinkling of the stars. [L.].

SCIOLISM [si'o-lizm], *n.* pretentious wisdom, superficial knowledge. [L.].

SCION [si'on], *n.* slip, young shoot or twig for grafting; young branch or offshoot of a family, descendant.

SCISSORS [si'zerz], *n.(pl.)* small cutting tool, consisting of two blades each having a looped handle crossing the other and fixed at a pivot, the cutting being performed by the two blades being worked against each other. SCISSOR, *v.t.* to cut or clip with scissors. SCISSOR-BILL, *n.* a sea-bird, the shearwater. [OFr.].

SCLERO-, *pref.* hard, dry. [Gk.].

SCLEROSIS [skle-rō'sis], *n.* (*path.*) a hardening of the tissues. [Gk.].

SCLEROTIC (1) [skle-ro'tik], *adj.* hard and dry, indurated; affected by sclerosis. SCLEROTIC (2), *n.* the firm white outer coat of the eye. [Gk.].

SCOFF (1) [skof], *n.* (*slang*) anything to eat; act of eating greedily. SCOFF (2), *v.t.* (*slang*) to eat greedily or quickly. [Du.].

SCOFF (3), *n.* an expression of scorn or derision, gibe; object of contempt, butt for ridicule. SCOFF (4), *v.i.* **to s. at,** to deride, ridicule, scorn; show scorn or contempt for; exhibit a lack of respect for. [~OIcel.].

SCOLD (1) [skōld], *n.* nagging woman who uses abusive language. SCOLD (2), *v.t. and i.* to reprimand, rate; reprove loudly; rail loudly. [OIcel.].

SCOLLOP, see SCALLOP.

SCONCE (1) [skons], *n.* the tube of a candlestick for holding the candle; hanging or projecting candlestick fitted with a reflector; headpiece, the head. [OFr.].

SCONCE (2), *n.* at Oxford University, a pot of beer exacted by undergraduates dining in hall as a penalty from any of their number who offends against convention. SCONCE (3), *v.t.* at Oxford, to impose a fine of a s. upon. [Unkn.].

SCONE [skön, skon], *n.* a plain unsweetened cake of wheat or barley flour, baked on a girdle or in an oven. [~LGerm.].

SCOOP (1) [skōōp], *n.* ladle with a shallow bowl used for baling up liquid or shovelling loose-grained substances like wheat or sugar; act of using a scoop; (*slang*) profitable piece of good luck; exclusive item of news for newspaper publication, profitable transaction made suddenly at the expense of one's competitors. SCOOP (2), *v.t.* to ladle, shovel, bale out by means of a s.; hollow out, excavate; (*slang*) get away with, clear, win; obtain suddenly at the expense of competitors; (*esp. journalism*) score over. [LGerm., Du.].

SCOOT [skōōt], *v.i.* (*slang*) to hurry off, move quickly. SCOOTER, *n.* kind of low bicycle with a

ōō is pronounced as n *food*; ŏŏ as in *hood*; th as in *think*; TH as in *that*; zh as in azure. ∼ = related to.

DSE—R

narrow short board, used as a foot-rest, and a steering-rod. [Uncert.].

SCOPE [skōp], *n.* range, area, field for mental or physical activity; room; (*naut.*) a cable-length. [Gk.].

SCORBUTIC [skaw-byōō'tik], *adj.* pertaining to, affected by, scurvy. [Fr.].

SCORCH (1) [skawch], *v.t.* to burn superficially; affect painfully with heat so as to injure and discolour the skin or surface; (*slang*) ride at top speed; *v.i.* to be parched, become scorched. SCORCH (2), *n.* a burn made by scorching; (*slang*) a ride at high speed; **scorched earth**, territory abandoned by a combatant after being rendered useless to the attacking force. [OFr. from L.].

SCORE (1) [skaw(r)], *n.* notch, cut or mark leaving an indelible groove; such a mark used on a tally; a reckoning, account, bill of expenses; (*sport*) number of points, runs etc. gained by a player or side; advantage over another; point made at a rival's expense; (*mus.*) copy of a composition giving the parts on separate staves; **a s.**, twenty, *esp.* as a unit of reckoning (*pl.* **score**). SCORE (2), *v.t.* to mark or record by means of scores or notches; mark with pen lines, hatch; make a s. in games; enter as an item in an account; (*mus.*) arrange in separate staves, orchestrate; *v.i.* to reap an advantage; **to s. off,** to make runs from, triumph at the expense of. [OE. from OIcel.].

SCORN (1) [skawn], *n.* state of mental superiority taking satisfaction in refusing to see value in another's acts or opinions, contemptuous attitude of mind; derision; object of contempt. SCORN (2), *v.t.* to feel or express s. for, hold in contempt, treat disdainfully; consider unworthy, beneath one. [OFr.].

SCORNFUL [skawn'fŏŏl], *adj.* expressing, or full of, scorn; disdainful, contemptuous.

SCORPIO [skaw'pi-ō], *n.* scorpion; the Scorpion, eighth sign of the Zodiac. [L.].

SCORPION [skaw'pi-on], *n.* arachnid having two claws like a lobster and a six-jointed tail ending in a sting; whip armed with points like a scorpion's tail; eighth sign of the Zodiac; (*fig.*) painful scourge. [Prec.].

SCOT [skot], *n.* (*hist.*) a tax; **s. and lot,** parish payments assessed according to means. SCOT-FREE, free from payment, untaxed; unhurt, safe; let off punishment. [OIcel.].

SCOTCH (1) [skoch], *adj.* Scottish; **S. barley,** barley with its husk removed; **S. broth,** mutton broth containing pearl-barley; **S. fir,** pine, the Scots pine; **S. mist,** fine drizzle mixed with mist; **S. terrier,** breed of terrier with short stubby legs, rough coat and short tail; **S. woodcock,** scrambled egg on toast with anchovies on top. SCOTCH (2), *n.* (*coll.*) whisky distilled in Scotland.

SCOTCH (3), *n.* slight cut or shallow incision, notch, particularly one in the ground. SCOTCH (4), *v.t.* to make a s., score; kill or maim mortally; suppress brutally; stop. [Uncert.].

SCOTCH (5), *n.* wedge set against a wheel etc. to prevent movement. SCOTCH (6), *v.t.* to wedge (a wheel etc.) so as to prevent movement; (*fig.*) frustrate, block. [Uncert.].

SCOTCHMAN (*pl.* **Scotchmen**) [skoch'man], *n.* Scotsman; tall crane for lifting girders.

SCOTS [skots], *adj.* relating to, connected with, Scotland, its people or language; **S. pine,** the common pine tree, found in northern Europe. [ME.].

SCOTTICISM [sko'ti-sizm], *n.* a Scots idiom, word or phrase.

SCOTTISH [sko'tish], *adj.* connected with, belonging to, Scotland or its people.

SCOUNDREL [skown'drel], *n.* vicious and dangerous member of society, blackguard, villain. [Uncert.].

SCOUR (1) [skowr], *v.t.* and *i.* to clean by continual hard rubbing; cleanse by rubbing with something rough of surface such as sand; clean by flushing with water; purge violently, as the intestines of cattle; get rid of dirt by scouring. SCOUR (2), *n.* a cleaning or clearing; swift deep current which washes away anything in its path; diarrhoea in cattle. [L.].

SCOUR (3), *v.t.* and *i.* to range over; search through thoroughly; run about in search of something. [Uncert.].

SCOURGE (1) [skurj], *n.* instrument for flogging, whip; (*fig.*) person who is the instrument of drastic punishment; evil pest or plague of drastic persistence. SCOURGE (2), *v.t.* to flog thoroughly, whip; afflict persistently and drastically. [ME. from L.].

SCOUT (1) [skowt], *n.* person or service unit dispatched ahead of the main body to observe enemy movements; male college servant at Oxford University; dart thrown outside the board when aiming for a final double; **Boy S.**, member of an organization for boys encouraging open-air life and social responsibility; **A.A.** or **R.A.C. s.**, man employed by the Automobile Association or Royal Automobile Club to patrol the roads and render assistance to members. SCOUT (2), *v.i.* to act as a s., reconnoitre. [OFr.].

SCOUT (3), *v.t.* to sneer at, treat with scorn. [OIcel.].

SCOWL (1) [skowl], *v.i.* to look angry or sullen, assume a scowl. SCOWL (2), *n.* a facial expression indicating anger or displeasure, characterized by the eyebrows drawn together and a puckered forehead; angry frown. [ME.].

SCRABBLE [skra'bl], *v.i.* to make irregular unmeaning marks, scribble; scrape haphazardly so as to cover a surface with irregular marks. [Du.].

SCRAG (1) [skrag], *n.* any thin or lean object or person; bony part of a sheep's neck. SCRAG (2) (*pres.pt.* SCRAGGING, *pret.* and *p.pt.* SCRAGGED), *v.t.* (*slang*) to screw or twist the neck of; make a pretence of throttling; (*Rugby football*) tackle round the neck. [Norw.].

SCRAGGY [skra'gi], *adj.* lean and bony in appearance, skinny. [Prec.].

SCRAMBLE (1) [skram'bl], *v.t.* and *i.* to mix together; (*cookery*) beat up eggs with butter etc., and cook; proceed or climb by means of a scramble; hurry across rough ground affording a poor foothold; (*teleg., teleph.*) make (a message or conversation) unintelligible to the ordinary listener by changing frequency so that sounds are confused. SCRAMBLE (2), *n.* act of scrambling; a method of movement, particularly climbing over rough ground using both arms and legs, a clamber; a friendly struggle for something. SCRAMBLER, *n.* one who scrambles; (*teleg., teleph.*) device for scrambling messages. SCRAMBLING, *adj.* scuffling, straggling. [Uncert.].

SCRAN [skran], *n.* (*coll.*) food, *esp.* of a makeshift kind. [Unkn.].

SCRAP (1) [skrap], *n.* small piece, broken or torn oddment; very small portion of food; refuse, piece of waste metal; fight, scuffle; **not to care a s.**, to be quite indifferent. SCRAP-HEAP, pile of refuse; (*fig.*) anonymity; oblivion. SCRAP (2) (*pres.pt.* SCRAPPING, *pret.* and *p.pt.* SCRAPPED), *v.t.* and *i.* to throw away or clear out as useless, discard, destroy; fight. SCRAPBOOK, *n.* book of blank sheets on which press-cuttings or pictures are pasted. [OIcel.].

SCRAPE (1) [skrāp], *v.t.* and *i.* to clean or make smooth a surface by rubbing it with a sharp-edged instrument; scratch or abrade by sliding along a hard or rough surface; gather together slowly and laboriously in the form of bits and pieces, odds and ends; produce a sharp, harsh sound by drawing one surface across another; play (a string instrument) badly; save money laboriously; **to s. acquaintance with,** to get to know (someone) slightly; get to know (someone) by dubious methods; **to s. a living by,** to make a bare living by means of; **to s. through,** to manage to escape from a difficult situation; pass by a narrow margin, particularly an examination; **to bow and s.**, to behave obsequiously. SCRAPE (2), *n.* act of scraping; a scoring mark, scratch; a smearing, thin layer; sound of scraping; awkward situation due to one's bad behaviour, a difficulty. [~OE.].

SCRAPPY [skra'pi], *adj.* consisting of bits and pieces; fragmentary; having no logical sequence. [SCRAP (1)].

SCRATCH (1) [skrach], *v.t.* and *i.* to break into a surface, particularly the skin, leaving a slight mark, tear with a sharp point or with the fingernails; rub slightly to and fro as a remedy for itching; excavate with the claws or fingernails; use the fingernails or claws to fight with, rub with or scrape with; withdraw an entry in a race or contest; **s. my back and I'll s. yours,** let us indulge in mutual admiration; **to s. out,** to delete, erase. SCRATCH (2), *n.* act of scratching; mark made by scratching, superficial wound, slit in the skin; scraping, fidgety sound made by scratching; official mark from which a race is started; mark which divides two boxers before the match; top of the handicap, par, zero; **to play (start) from s.**, to play (start) without handicap; **to come up to s.**, (*fig.*) to meet requirements, be on form. SCRATCH-RACE, race in which all competitors start from the s. mark. SCRATCH-WIG, wig only partially covering the head. SCRATCH (3), *adj.* composed of members drawn from sources of different standards,

---

The accent ′ after a syllable = stress (u-pon′).   The mark ‾ over a vowel = length (ā in made; ō in bone).

hastily formed into a group or team; receiving no handicap. SCRATCHER, *n.* one who, or that which, scratches; (*zool.*) bird which scratches for food. [Uncert.].

SCRATCHY [skra'chi], *adj.* that is scratched on the surface; making a noise resembling scratching; itchy, irritating; (*coll.*) ill-tempered; mixed (of a collection of players).

SCRAWL (1) [skrawl], *v.t. and i.* to write hastily and in poor handwriting; write badly; move a pencil or pen haphazardly on a surface or paper etc. SCRAWL (2), *n.* piece of hasty bad handwriting; poor piece of drawing or literature. [Uncert.].

SCRAWNY [skraw'ni], *adj.* gaunt and lean, raw-boned. [Norw.].

SCREAM (1) [skrēm], *v.i.* to utter a scream; utter a sudden harsh, piercing cry. SCREAM (2), *n.* a sudden, loud, shrill cry as an expression of intense pain or terror, a shriek; (*slang*) an object of intense mirth. SCREAMER, *n.* person who screams; tropical American bird allied to the geese. [OIcel.].

SCREE [skrē], *n.* steep slope covered with small loose stones; a collection of insecure stones at the foot of a cliff. [OIcel.].

SCREECH (1) [skrēch], *v.i.* to utter harsh piercing sounds disagreeable to the ear, shriek. SCREECH (2), *n.* a short, loud scream, shrill, piercing cry. SCREECH-OWL, owl which utters a harsh, disagreeable cry; popular name for the barn-owl or the tawny owl. [*Var.* of SHRIEK].

SCREED [skrēd], *n.* long reprimand or list of grievances; lengthy, somewhat boring epistle. [*Var.* of SHRED].

SCREEN (1) [skrēn], *n.* device to provide shelter or protection, *esp.* a piece of furniture consisting of a light covered framework used to shut off draughts; device fitted to a motor-car for protecting driver and passengers from the wind; partition in church separating the choir from the nave; large sheet or other smooth surface upon which cinematograph or magic-lantern pictures are projected; framework of white wooden boards placed in the cricket field on the boundary behind the bowler's arm; coarse sieve; (*elect.*) device in the form of a sheet of metal to protect a circuit from being affected by stray magnetic fields; (*phot.*) mesh device for breaking up a photograph into small dots for reproduction by means of a half-tone block. SCREEN (2), *v.t.* to give protection and shelter to by means of a s.; act as a shield between a person and moral or physical danger; pass through a sieve, sift; scrutinize, check (persons) in order to identify any who may be untrustworthy etc.; project on to a s.; convert into a film; **to s. off,** to shut off. SCREEN(ED)-GRID, *adj.* (*radio*) descriptive of a four-electrode thermionic valve built with one grid screening another. SCREENING, *n.* act of one who, that which, screens; (*elect.*) device consisting of a metal s. for preventing one electric circuit carrying an alternating current from affecting another adjacent to it; material which has been screened. [~OFr.].

SCREW (1) [skrōō], *n.* mechanical device for joining two pieces of wood or metal together, consisting of a cylindrical shaft of metal with a spiral groove cut round its surface and a head at the end opposite the point provided with a straight groove by means of which the shaft can be turned or undone; one of several principles of mechanical power, being a more complex development of the inclined plane; action of screwing; screw-propeller; that which is screwed up or is in the form of a twisted length, *esp.* a half-ounce of tobacco; miser; (*slang*) salary, wages; prison warder; worn-out horse; **to have a s. loose,** to be slightly mentally deficient; SCREW-PROPELLER, a modification of the s., consisting of two or more vanes set obliquely in a boss, and used for propelling ships or aircraft. SCREW-THREAD, ridge formed by the groove on a s. SCREW (2), *v.t. and i.* to fasten or tighten by means of a s.; twist round and round as far as possible in one direction; twist, distort; press, squeeze, extract; function as a s.; **to have one's head screwed on the right way,** to have plenty of common sense. [ME. from OFr.].

SCREWDRIVER [skrōō'drī-ver], *n.* tool with a blunt-edged shaft for turning screws.

SCRIBBLE (1) [skri'bl], *v.t. and i.* to write hastily so that the letters are badly formed; compose too hastily for any concern with style; form a series of inconsequential marks; write or compose carelessly. SCRIBBLE (2), *n.* handwriting written hastily and indistinctly; writing composed too carelessly or hastily to be of value. SCRIBBLER, *n.* one who

scribbles; careless writer; author of inferior compositions. [MedL.].

SCRIBE [skrīb], *n.* author who earns his living by his pen; formerly, writer who lived by copying manuscripts; (*hist.*) Jewish lawyer expert in ecclesiastical law. [L.].

SCRIMMAGE, SCRUMMAGE [skri'mij], *n.* close, confused struggle; (*Rugby football*) the formation of two opposing sets of forwards when packed tightly head to head; a scrum. [*Var.* of SKIRMISH].

SCRIMP (1) [skrimp], *adj.* reduced stinted. SCRIMP (2), *v.t.* to reduce, shorten or stint. [~OE.].

SCRIP (1) [skrip], *n.* (*archaic*) small bag or leather wallet. [LL.].

SCRIP (2), *n.* brief piece of writing, certificate or schedule; (*comm.*) provisional certificate of stock or of shares in a joint-stock company. [*Next*].

SCRIPT [skript], *n.* characters or letters written in the style of a sanserif type fount; handwriting as distinct from print or typewriting; manuscript; typescript; text of a play etc.; set of written answers to an examination paper. [OFr.].

SCRIPTURE [skrip'tyoor], *n.* any manuscript of holy writings, the Bible, the Old and New Testaments; what is written in Scripture, particularly any single text. [L.].

SCRIVENER [skri've-ner], *n.* (*hist.*) law-stationer; person who drafted legal contracts etc.; money-broker; person whose business was to place money received on deposit at interest. [LL.].

SCROFULA [skro'fyoo-lah], *n.* (*path.*) formation and deposition of tubercle in the lymphatic glands; king's evil. [L.].

SCROLL [skrōl], *n.* roll of paper or parchment; writing in the form of a roll, ribbon carrying a motto in armorial bearings; (*arch.*) spiral ornament of the Ionic period. [ME. from OFr.].

SCROTUM [skrō'tum], *n.* (*anat.*) the bag of skin which contains the testicles. [L.].

SCROUNGE [skrownj], *v.t. and i.* (*slang*) to help oneself to things with possible intent to keep them. [Unkn.].

SCRUB (1) [skrub], *n.* underwood, stunted dwarf trees and bushes; (*U.S. slang*) athlete not a member of the first team. [*Var.* of SHRUB].

SCRUB (2) (*pres.pt.* scrubbing, *pret. and p.pt.* scrubbed), *v.t. and i.* to clean by rubbing hard with a brush, clean by vigorous rubbing with something rough. SCRUB (3), *n.* act of scrubbing. SCRUBBER, *n.* one who or that which scrubs; charwoman; apparatus for cleaning gas by a process of spraying.

SCRUBBY [skru'bi], *adj.* small and mean, stunted in growth, dwarf; dirty and untidy in appearance. [SCRUB (1)].

SCRUFF [skruf], *n.* the skin on the back of the neck. SCRUFFY, *adj.* scurfy; (*coll.*) having a disreputable appearance. [OE.].

SCRUM (1) [skrum], *n.* scrimmage. SCRUM-HALF, (*Rugby football*) the half-back who puts the ball into the s. SCRUM (2) (*pres.pt.* SCRUMMING, *pret. and p.pt.* SCRUMMED), *v.i.* to form a s.; **to s. down,** to form a scrimmage. [SCRUM(MAGE)].

SCRUMMAGE, see SCRIMMAGE.

SCRUNCH (1) [skrunsh], *v.t. and i.* to crunch, crush; make a sound of being crushed. SCRUNCH (2), *n.* act or sound of scrunching. SCRUNCHY, *adj.* crisp and brittle. [Imitative].

SCRUPLE (1) [skrōō'pl], *n.* a measurement of weight, twenty grains, the third part of a drachm; very small quantity; hesitation, *esp.* from conscientious motives, doubt arising from difficulty in judging the ethics of one's action, a nice point in morals. SCRUPLE (2), *v.t. and i.* to have scruples, hesitate for ethical reasons. [L.].

SCRUPULOUS [skrōō'pyoo-loos], *adj.* careful over the ethics of one's conduct, having scruples; taking strict care over details and accuracy, exact, strict. [L.].

SCRUTATOR [skrōō-tā'ter], *n.* one who scrutinizes or examines; examiner. [L.].

SCRUTINEER [skrōō-ti-nēer'], *n.* one who scrutinizes or examines, *esp.* ballot papers.

SCRUTINIZE [skrōō'ti-nīz], *v.t.* to search closely; examine minutely or critically.

SCRUTINY [skrōō'ti-ni], *n.* close search; minute critical examination; examination of the votes given at an election after the demand for a recount. [L.].

SCRYING [skrī'ing], *n.* a perceiving, *esp.* by crystal-gazing; descrying. [*Var.* of DESCRYING].

SCUD (1) (*pres.pt.* scudding, *pret. and p.pt.* SCUDDED) [skud], *v.i.* to move rapidly along on a level driven by the wind, glide swiftly and smoothly propelled by the wind. SCUD (2), *n.* act of scudding; swift running, gliding movement given impetus by a strong wind, mass of loose rain-laden clouds driven along by the winds. [Uncert.].

SCUFF [skuf], *v.t.* to scrape on the ground, *esp.* the feet.

SCUFFLE (1) [sku'fl], *v.i.* to struggle, wrestle in catch-as-catch-can form; engage in a short bout of nondescript grappling and tussling. SCUFFLE (2), *n.* struggle for mastery with close grappling; confused fight; brief hand-to-hand tussle. [~Swed.].

SCUFFLE (3), *v.t.* to hoe, turn over with a scuffler. SCUFFLER, *n.* agricultural implement for turning over the surface of the ground between the rows of a crop. [~Du.].

SCULL (1) [skul], *n.* light one-handed oar; action of sculling. SCULL (2), *v.t. and i.* to row (a boat) by means of a s.; use a s. in rowing.

SCULLERY [sku'le-ri], *n.* room adjoining the kitchen in which dishes are washed and other rough household work is carried out. [MedL.].

SCULLION [sku'li-on], *n.* (*archaic*) boy employed in washing up, dish-washer. [OFr.].

SCULPIN [skul'pin], *n.* a fish of the North Atlantic, the dragonet. [Uncert.].

SCULPTOR [skulp'ter], *n.* person who practises the art of sculpture. [L.].

SCULPTURE (1) [skulp'tyŏŏr], *n.* art of using three-dimensional material by cutting, chiselling or carving it into masses with compositional value so as to reproduce a natural object or an emotional experience about such an object; art of modelling in plastic material such as clay; any work of art created in wood, stone, metal, clay etc. SCULPTURE (2), *v.t. and i.* to work at or produce a s. of; decorate with pieces of s.; practise the art of representation by means of pieces of s. [L.].

SCUM (1) [skum], *n.* froth bearing the impurities which rise to the surface of liquor in boiling or fermentation; refuse; the throw-outs, leavings; that which is vile and worthless. SCUM (2) (*pres.pt.* SCUMMING, *pret. and p.pt.* SCUMMED), *v.t.* to skim off the s. from. [~Dan.].

SCUMBLE [skum'bl], *v.t.* to rub over with a semi-opaque colour; diffuse as an outline in painting. SCUMBLING, *n.* in oil-painting, process of thinly rubbing semi-opaque colours over others, to soften the effect, *esp.* of sharp outlines. [Uncert.].

SCUNNER (1) [sku'ner], *v.t. and i.* (*Scots and northern dial.*) to disgust, feel disgusted. SCUNNER (2), *n.* strong dislike, disgust. [Unkn].

SCUPPER (1) [sku'per], *n.* (*naut.*) channel, cut through the sides of a ship, for draining the sea water or swab water from off the deck. SCUPPER (2), *v.t.* (*naut.*) to cut holes for emergency draining in a ship's side; throw a ship on its side; (*slang*) wreck, ruin; massacre. [~OFr.].

SCURF [skurf], *n.* small dry bits of skin which flake off a scalp in bad condition, dandruff; dry miliary scab formed on the skin; anything adhering to the surface. [OIcel.].

SCURRILITY [sku-ri'li-ti], *n.* quality of being scurrilous, that which is scurrilous; low vulgar abuse. [L.].

SCURRILOUS [sku'ri-lŏŏs], *adj.* characterized by coarse invective, using the low and indecent language of the vulgar; containing indecency or low abuse; foul, abusive; coarsely opprobrious or jocular. [~L.].

SCURRY (1) [sku'ri], *v.i.* to run with rapid scampering steps, scuttle. SCURRY (2), *n.* hasty running movement, a scamper; short race between horses or boats. [Uncert.].

SCURVY (1) [skur'vi], *adj.* suffering from scurvy; mean, contemptible, shabby. SCURVY (2), *n.* a disease due to the lack of fresh fruit and vegetables. [~SCURF].

SCUT [skut], *n.* short tail of a hare or rabbit. [Uncert.].

SCUTCHEON [sku'chn], *n.* escutcheon; plate for an inscription; ornamental plate protecting a keyhole. [ESCUTCHEON].

SCUTTLE (1) [sku'tl], *n.* broad shallow basket; metal receptacle for holding coals. [OE. from L.].

SCUTTLE (2), *n.* small opening with a hinged cover in a wall or roof, trap-door; (*naut.*) opening in a deck protected by a cover, small hatchway. SCUTTLE (3), *v.t.* to sink a ship by making holes in its hull. [Span.].

SCUTTLE (4), *v.i.* to run off in a hasty scurrying manner, bolt. SCUTTLE (5), *n.* quick pace with short

steps; hasty flight with a scurrying movement. [~SCUD].

SCYTHE (1) [sīth], *n.* agricultural implement with a long, curving blade, sharp on the inner edge, for mowing grass and cutting grain. SCYTHE (2), *v.t. and i.* to cut with a s.; handle a s. for mowing. [OE.].

SEA [sē], *n.* the body of salt water covering the major part of the earth's surface, the ocean; any particular part of this water, *esp.* if partly enclosed or defined by land; large expanse of salt water; wave, billow of water; (*fig.*) great expanse, vast, overwhelming mass, of anything; **at s.**, (*naut.*) on the sea aboard ship; (*fig.*) lost, confused; **S. Lord,** naval member of the Board of Admiralty. SEA-ANCHOR, a floating anchor to check drifting. SEA-ANEMONE, marine polyp of the order *Actinaria.* SEA-CALF, the common seal. SEA-CAPTAIN, captain of a s.-going vessel. SEA-DOG, hardened sailor; seal. SEA-ELEPHANT, the great Atlantic seal. SEA-FRONT, marine parade of a seaside town. SEA-GOD, Poseidon, Neptune, an ocean deity. SEA-GOING, travelling across the open s. SEA-GREEN, the bluish-green colour of shallow water; of this colour. SEA-GULL, s.-bird of the *Laridae.* SEA-HORSE, a warm-water fish remarkable for its horse-like head. SEA-LAWYER, argumentative amateur lawyer, one who is forever standing out for the real or imaginary rights of himself and others. SEA-LEGS, ability to keep steady on a moving ship. SEA-LETTER, passport issued to a neutral ship in time of war, stating the nature of its cargo. SEA-LEVEL, the mean tidal level. SEA-LION, a species of large seal. SEA-MARK, beacon or mark to guide a ship approaching land. SEA-MEW, the common gull. SEA-MILE, the geographical mile of 6,080 feet used at s. SEA-PIE, the oyster catcher; boiled meat pie commonly eaten by seamen. SEA-PIECE, seascape. SEA-PINK, pink-and-white flowered s. plant, thrift. SEA-ROOM, space enough for a ship to sail without danger of collision or grounding. SEA-SERPENT, fabulous monster of enormous size and fantastic shape, reported to have been observed at s. on numerous occasions. SEA-SHELL, shell of a marine mollusc. SEA-SWALLOW, tern; stormy petrel. SEA-URCHIN, animal with a prickly spherical shell, living at the bottom of the s. SEA-WALL, wall against the encroachment of the s. SEA-WAY, forward progress of a ship. [OE.].

SEABOARD [sē'bawrd], *n.* the sea-coast, land adjoining the sea.

SEAFARER [sē'fāer-er], *n.* seaman, mariner; one who travels by sea.

SEAFARING (1) [sē'fāer-ing], *n.* act of travelling by sea; occupation of a sailor. SEAFARING (2), *adj.* habitually travelling by sea; earning one's livelihood as a sailor.

SEAKALE [sē'kāl], *n.* edible colewort.

SEAL (1) [sēl], *n.* amphibious marine mammal with flippers or webbed feet. SEAL (2), *v.i.* to hunt seals. [OE.].

SEAL (3), *n.* device stamped on wax or similar material by an engraved die, and attached to documents etc. to prove their authenticity; the die itself, or anything used as a die; (*fig.*) a sure sign of genuineness; something securing secrecy, undertaking of silence or discretion; that which closes. SEAL (4), *v.t.* to stamp, mark, validate with a s.; secure with a s., utterly shut up and secure from any access; set aside as certain, or already performed; confirm, ratify. SEALING-WAX, *n.* substance of resin and shellac which becomes plastic when heated, used in sealing documents etc. [AFr.].

SEALYHAM [sē'li-(h)am], *n.* breed of white terrier with short legs. [*Sealyham,* Pembrokeshire].

SEAM (1) [sēm], *n.* join where two pieces of material are sewn together; junction where two boards are caulked together; suture; line of a scar; (*geol.*) vein, thin layer, between two thicker strata. SEAM (2), *v.t.* to join with a s., mark as if with a s. [OE.].

SEAMAN (*pl.* **seamen**) [sē'man, 'men], *n.* sailor; (*nav.*) sailor below the rank of officer. [OE.].

SEAMSTRESS [sem'stres], *n.* woman who sews, professional needlewoman. [OE.].

SEAMY [sē'mi], *adj.* showing the rough underside of a seam; relating to the unattractive underworld of a thing; **the s. side,** the sordid aspect.

SEANCE, séance [sā'ah(ng)s], *n.* meeting of a society, *esp.* a gathering of spiritualists in order to communicate with the spirits of the dead. [Fr.].

SEAPLANE [sē'plān], *n.* aeroplane fitted with floats so that it can alight on or take off from the sea.

SEAPORT [sē'pawt], *n.* town with a harbour for sea-going ships.

SEAR (1), see SERE.

SEAR (2) [sēer], *v.t.* to shrivel up, cause to wither; scorch, cauterize; make faded; (of feelings etc.) make hard or calloused. [OE.].

SEARCH (1) [surch], *v.t. and i.* to examine thoroughly in order to discover, go through, ransack a thing for this purpose; examine carefully the garments and body of a person in order to find something; scrutinize, read through carefully, in order to find something; penetrate searchingly, probe; seek, inquire, pursue; **s. me,** (*coll.*) I am at a loss. SEARCH (2), *n.* act of searching or seeking; the actual inquiry, going about in which the seeking is carried out; pursuit, quest of a thing. SEARCH-PARTY, group of people organized to s. for someone missing. SEARCH-WARRANT, magistrate's warrant giving authority to enter and search private premises. SEARCHER, *n.* one who, or that which, searches, *esp.* one employed to s. passengers and baggage at a Customs. SEARCHING, *adj.* thorough, penetrating; illuminating weaknesses. [OFr.].

SEARCHLIGHT [surch'lit], *n.* lamp producing a powerful beam of light directed upon distant objects, *esp.* used at sea and against aircraft.

SEASCAPE [sē'skāp], *n.* picture giving a view of the sea. [SEA and (LAND)SCAPE].

SEASHORE [sē'shaw(r)], *n.* sea-coast, land bordering the sea between high and low water.

SEASON (1) [sē'zon], *n.* a division of the year distinguished by the altitude of the noonday sun above the horizon, temperature, weather and the growth of plants; part of the year dedicated to certain processes or human activities, time of the year when certain creatures are hunted, or fit to be eaten; the suitable time for anything; **the S.,** early summer, when London's upper-class social life is at its most active. SEASON (2), *v.t.* to render mature or fit for some use by exposure to some process or climate; acclimatize, accustom; spice (food); add zest to something. SEASONAL, *adj.* occurring only at certain seasons. SEASONED, *adj.* accustomed or hardened to certain conditions; spiced. SEASONER, *n.* that which seasons. SEASONING, *n.* spice, condiments, that which is used to s. food. [OFr. from L.].

SEASONABLE [sē'zo-na-bl], *adj.* appropriate, suitable to a particular season.

SEAT (1) [sēt], *n.* that which is sat upon; that which is made to be sat upon; space in which one may sit down; the part of a chair etc. which directly supports the body; the buttocks, the part of the trousers etc. covering the buttocks; sitting accommodation for a specific time, place and occasion; membership of a body, symbolized by the right to sit in a certain place, *esp.* membership of Parliament, of the Bench; the location of a thing, permanent situation of a central authority, principal residence of a dignitary, family, *esp.* a great country house; fashion in which one sits on a horse. SEAT (2), *v.t.* to place on or in a s.; accommodate in seats, be able to afford seats for; put a s. in a chair or garment. SEATING, *n.* provision of seats, accommodation in seats. [OScand.].

SEAWORTHY [sē'wer-THi], *adj.* (of ships) fit to go to sea.

SEBACEOUS [se-bā'shŏŏs], *adj.* fatty, containing or secreting fat. [L.].

SECANT (1) [sē'kant], *adj.* (*geom.*) cutting, intersecting. SECANT (2), *n.* (*geom.*) an intersecting line; (*trigonometry*) the ratio of the hypotenuse of a right-angled triangle to an adjacent side, viewed as a function of the angle (or its supplement) which these subtend. [L.].

SECATEURS [se-ka-turz'], *n.*(*pl.*) pair of clippers operated with one hand, used to prune shrubs etc. [Fr.].

SECEDE [si-sēd'], *v.i.* to withdraw voluntarily from membership of a group, *esp.* in a political or religious sense. [L.].

SECESSION [si-se'shn], *n.* act of seceding. [L.].

SECLUDE [si-klōōd'], *v.t.* to shut up apart, keep away from others. SECLUDED, *adj.* separated from others, solitary, quiet and undisturbed. [L.].

SECLUSION [si-klōō'zhn], *n.* state of being secluded, act of secluding, retired privacy. [MedL.].

SECOND (1) [se'kond], *adj.* the ordinal of two; next to, following closest after, the first in space, time, position, value, dignity or importance; exactly resembling another, being a counterpart; **s. chamber,** upper house of a bicameral legislature; **s. childhood,** weakening of the faculties in old age; **s. cousin,** child of a parent's cousin; **s. nature,** behaviour so habitual as to be almost instinctive; **s. sight,** supposed ability to foresee events. SECOND-BEST, one who, that which, is next in quality to the best; distinctly inferior person or thing. SECOND-CLASS, of the class next to the first. SECOND (2), *n.* the sixtieth part of a minute (of time or of an angle); (*coll.*) a very short period of time; a supporter in a duel, who manages the preliminary arrangements on behalf of his principal; one who attends to the needs of a boxer between rounds; a s.-class degree; the competitor in a contest who comes nearest to the winner; (*motoring*) s. gear of a motor engine; (*mus.*) the interval between two tones of the diatonic scale. SECOND (3), *v.t.* to support someone, act as his s. in a duel or boxing-match etc.; (*parl.*) support a motion immediately after the proposer; [se-kond'], withdraw (an officer) from the active list of a regiment in order to employ (him) specially on other service; transfer temporarily from a usual post to some special duty. SECOND (4), *adv.* in the s. place. [L.].

SECONDARY [se'kon-da-ri], *adj.* second in order, importance, dignity, urgency etc., second in time or order of development; inferior; (*astron.*) revolving round a primary planet; (*biol.*) applied to differences between the sexes not directly connected with generation; (*geol.*) pertaining to the strata between the palaeozoic and tertiary, mesozoic; **s. school,** school giving instruction to pupils who have completed the primary stage of their education. [L.].

SECOND-HAND (1) [se'kond-hand], *n.* the hand of a clock or watch marking the seconds. SECOND-HAND (2) [se-kond-hand'], *adj.* already used, not new; (of ideas etc.) derived, not original.

SECOND-RATE [se-kond-rāt'], *adj.* not first-class, of inferior quality, mediocre.

SECRECY [sē'kre-si], *n.* state of being secret, state of being concealed, condition of concealment or occurrence without general knowledge or awareness; secretiveness.

SECRET (1) [sē'kret], *adj.* hidden from sight and knowledge, designed for concealment; done in secret; (of documents) not to be divulged except to authorized persons; clandestine; remote and hidden; secretive; mysterious, inscrutable; **s. service,** a state organization engaged in espionage and counter-espionage of various kinds. SECRET (2), *n.* that which is s., something known to a very small number of people who have undertaken not to reveal it; the truth of something mysterious and obscure, the hidden meaning of a thing, the unknown means by which something wonderful was performed; a mystery. [L.].

SECRETAIRE [se-kre-tāer'], *n.* bureau, writing-desk. [Fr.].

SECRETARIAT [se-kri-tāer'i-at], *n.* body of officials carrying out the secretarial functions of a great organization. [Fr.].

SECRETARY [se'kri-ta-ri], *n.* person employed to manage the correspondence, written records etc. of an organization or person; one employed to assist a person in the organizational and routine part of his business or intellectual work; principal assistant to a minister or ambassador, head of a department of state (nominally responsible to the Sovereign); the second responsible official of a department. SECRETARY-BIRD, an African bird, having pen-like feathers at the back of the head. SECRETARIAL [se-kri-tāer'i-al], *adj.* relating to a s. or to the functions of a s. [MedL.].

SECRETE [si-krēt'], *v.t.* to conceal in a secret place; (*physiol.*) extract from the system and give out as a secretion. SECRETORY [si-krē'te-ri], *adj.* relating to, causing, secretion. [L.].

SECRETION [si-krē'shn], *n.* act of secreting; (*physiol.*) biological process whereby extractions from the blood or sap are either discharged as waste or elaborated into functional substances. [L.].

SECRETIVE [si-krē'tiv], *adj.* tending to conceal one's thoughts and actions, over-reticent.

SECT [sekt], *n.* body of persons with certain religious or philosophical views, *esp.* such a group which has seceded from one of the great churches. SECTARY, *n.* a sectarian. [OFr. from L.].

SECTARIAN [sek-taer'i-an], *n. and adj.* (one who or that which is) characteristic of, peculiar to, a sect, narrowly exclusive; supporting a sect (usually in disparagement), tending to destroy the unity of some broad body of opinion; member of a sect. [Prec.].

SECTION (1) [sek'shn], *n.* act or process of cutting or dividing; thing cut off, severed portion, slice cut off across the whole of an object, a representative cutting of an object; a separate part of a thing, separate part made to be joined to other parts, a subdivision of something written; (*zool.*) a natural subdivision of a genus; (*milit.*) one of the subdivisions of a platoon, troop or battery; (*geom.*) the intersection of a solid by a plane, a representation of an object as if cut through by a plane, the subdivision mark §. SECTION (2), *v.i.* to divide into sections. SECTIONALISM, *n.* preoccupation with the interests of a s. as distinct from those of the whole community. [L.].

SECTOR [sek'ter], *n.* astronomical or mathematical measuring instrument; (*geom.*) part of a circle contained between two of its radii; (*milit.*) part of a front or position, *esp.* as a scene of military operations. [L.].

SECULAR [se'kyōō-ler], *adj.* continuing over a very long period; relating to this world, temporal, material, not ecclesiastical; (*R.C.*) not bound by monastic vows. SECULARISM, *n.* theory of the separation of church from state; theory of morality divorced from religion. SECULARIZE [se'kyōō-la-rīz], *v.t.* to make s., transfer from church to state, make temporal; (*R.C.*) absolve from monastic vows. [L.].

SECURE (1) [si-kyōōr], *adj.* safe, free from danger, care or anxiety, undisturbed; stable, fast, firmly held and retained; certain, firmly fixed. SECURE (2), *v.t.* to make s., make safe against danger or loss; make fast, hold firmly, safely; (*milit.*) hold (a rifle) muzzle down with breech under the armpit; make certain; (*leg.*) confirm possession of by deed or will; get hold of, obtain sure possession of; guarantee by security. [L.].

SECURITY [si-kyōō'ri-ti], *n.* state of being secure; safety; feeling of being secure; defence, protection; something of value deposited as pledge for the repayment of a loan etc., person who guarantees a loan; (*pl.*) bonds, shares etc.; **s. officer**, (*milit.*) officer charged with ensuring the secrecy of forthcoming operations, or the safety of the forces in general, by guarding against espionage etc.; **s. police**, military police. [L.].

SEDAN [si-dan'], *n.* portable covered chair carried by means of poles projecting before and behind; (*U.S.*) closed motor-car accommodating five or more persons. [*Sedan*, France].

SEDATE [si-dāt'], *adj.* calmly staid, tranquil, composedly quiet and self-possessed. [L.].

SEDATIVE (1) [se'da-tiv], *adj.* calming, soothing, having the effect of reducing mental and bodily excitement or agitation. SEDATIVE (2), *n.* drug or medicine producing a s. effect. [Fr.].

SEDENTARY [se'den-ta-ri], *adj.* sitting still; tending to keep or be inactive, immobile; (of occupations) involving no bodily activity; (of animals) not migratory. [L.].

SEDERUNT [se-dēer'unt], *n.* session of a court or assembly.

SEDGE [sej], *n.* a coarse, perennial, tufted grass-like plant. SEDGE-WARBLER, a brown-and-white bird. [OE.].

SEDILIA [se-di'li-ah], *n.*(*pl.*) three seats for the clergy recessed in the wall of a church behind the altar rail. [L.].

SEDIMENT [se'di-ment], *n.* solid matter which settles to the bottom of a liquid, the dregs of wine. SEDIMENTARY [se-di-men'ta-ri], *adj.* formed of, relating to, containing, s.; (*geol.*) formed or deposited by the action of water. [L.].

SEDITION [si-di'shn], *n.* unlawful action or propaganda directed against the state or its authority; an offence against the government not amounting to treason. [L.].

SEDITIOUS [si-di'shōōs], *adj.* relating to, of the nature of, inciting to, guilty of, tending to produce, sedition. [L.].

SEDUCE [si-dyōōs'], *v.t.* to entice away or persuade (almost invariably in sense of leading away from good to evil) to debauch, to sexual surrender; to corrupt. [L.].

SEDUCTION [si-duk'shn], *n.* act of seducing, *esp.* sexually; that which seduces, means of seducing. [L.].

SEDUCTIVE [si-duk'tiv], *adj.* tending to seduce, attractive, enticing, offering seductions.

SEDULITY [si-dyōō'li-ti], *n.* state of being sedulous; diligence, application. [L.].

SEDULOUS [se'dyōō-lōōs], *adj.* assiduous, carefully eager, persistently attentive. [L.].

SEE (1) [sē], *n.* diocese of a bishop or an archbishop. [OFr. from L.].

SEE (2) (*pret.* **saw**, *p.pt.* **seen**), *v.t.* to perceive visually, obtain an impression of through the eyes; understand, grasp mentally; experience, observe, encounter; perceive emotionally or mystically; witness, examine, attend (some visual spectacle), witness (a play); meet, interview (a person) officially; *v.i.* to have sight, have the capacity of apprehending visually; possess intellectual perception, understand; inquire, investigate; take care that; consider, deliberate; **to s. about**, to attend to, inquire into; **to s. after**, to look after; **to s. off**, to attend the departure of; **to s. out**, to s. the end of; **to s. through**, to perceive the deception of; **to s. (something) through**, to go through with something. [OE.].

SEED (1) [sēd], *n.* the fertilized germ of a plant which can develop into a new plant of the same kind; (*coll.*) seeds used in sowing; semen in men or animals, posterity; the source of a thing, germ of an idea; **to run to s.**, to form s., (*fig.*) lose one's energy and initiative. SEED-BED, earth prepared to receive s. SEED-CAKE, cake flavoured with caraway seeds. SEED-LEAF, cotyledon. SEED-PEARL, a diminutive pearl. SEED-TIME, season for sowing. SEED-VESSEL, pericarp. SEED (2), *v.t.* to plant with s.; remove seeds from; sort out; (*sport, esp. tennis*) separate (players of high quality or of a particular nationality) from the mass of competitors and manipulate the draw so that they do not meet until the later rounds. [OE.].

SEEDLING [sēd'ling], *n.* young plant grown from seed.

SEEDSMAN [sēdz'man], *n.* dealer in garden seeds and requisites.

SEEDY [sē'di], *adj.* full of seeds; (*coll.*) slightly unwell; shabby.

SEEING [sē'ing], *conj.* since; in view of the fact (that).

SEEK (*pret. and p.pt.* **sought**) [sēk], *v.t. and i.* to look for, search out, search to obtain, strive to achieve, pursue; inquire after; **to s. to**, to attempt to. SEEKER, *n.* one who seeks. [OE.].

SEEM [sēm], *v.i.* to appear to be, be apparently. SEEMING (1), *n.* external appearance; the immediate impression given. SEEMING (2), *adj.* apparent, outward, ostensible. [OScand.].

SEEMLY [sēm'li], *adj.* proper, suitable; decent, fitting, decorous. [OScand.].

SEEN (1) [sēn], *p.pt.* of SEE (2). SEEN (2), *adj.* (*archaic*) versed (in). [~SEE (2)].

SEEP [sēp], *v.i.* to ooze (through), percolate. SEEPAGE, *n.* liquid which has seeped through. [OE.].

SEER [sēer], *n.* one who sees visions; prophet.

SEERSUCKER [sēer'su-ker], *n.* light fabric of striped linen or cotton. [Pers.].

SEE-SAW (1) [sē'saw], *n.* plank balanced on a central fulcrum, so that the minimum of downward pressure on one side elevates the other; children's game in which a child sits at each end alternately raising and depressing the plank. SEE-SAW (2), *adj.* moving like a s. SEE-SAW (3), *v.i.* to ride on, move like, a s. [Imitative].

SEETHE [sēTH], *v.t. and i.* to cook by boiling; soften by steeping; boil up, swirl and bubble; be violently stirred and agitated. [OE.].

SEGMENT (1) [seg'ment], *n.* part into which a body may be divided, separable sections; (*geom.*) portion cut from a figure by a line or plane. SEGMENT (2), *v.t. and i.* to divide into segments; split up into segments. SEGMENTAL, SEGMENTARY [seg-men'tal, seg'men-ta-ri], *adj.* relating to, containing, divided into, segments. SEGMENTATION [seg-men-tā'shn], *n.* division into segments; (*biol.*) cellular formation by cleavage. [L.].

SEGNO [se'nyō], *n.* (*mus.*) mark denoting repetition. [It.].

SEGREGATE [seg'ri-gāt], *v.t. and i.* to separate, put apart from the main body, isolate; become separated, separate oneself from the main body. SEGREGATION [seg-ri-gā'shn], *n.* act or process of segregating; state, condition, position of being segregated. [L.].

SEIDLITZ POWDER [sed'lits-pow-der], *n.* saline aperient in the form of two powders. [*Seidlitz*, Bohemia].

SEIGNEUR [sā'nyer], *n.* (*hist.*) feudal lord; **the Grand S.**, Sultan of Turkey. SEIGNEURIAL [[sā-nyur'i-al], *adj.* held by feudal tenure; relating to a s. [OFr.].

SEINE [sān], *n.* large fishing-net suspended vertically in the water by means of floats on one edge and weights on the other. [Fr.].

SEISIN, see SEIZIN.

SEISMIC [siz'mik], *adj.* relating to, caused by, an earthquake. [Gk.].

SEISMO-, *pref.* relating to earthquakes.

SEISMOGRAPH [siz'mō-grahf], *n.* instrument for measuring and recording earthquakes. [SEISMO and GRAPH].

SEISMOLOGY [siz-mo'lo-ji], *n.* science treating of earthquakes. [Gk.].

SEISMOMETER [siz-mo'mi-ter], *n.* instrument for measuring the direction and intensity of earthquakes. [SEISMO and METER].

SEISMOSCOPE [siz'mō-skōp], *n.* simple seismometer. [Gk.].

SEIZE [sēz], *v.t. and i.* (*leg.*) to put in possession of, take possession of; grasp, take hold of suddenly and forcibly; grab, clutch with the hand; (*fig.*) grasp, take advantage of, immediately understand; (*naut.*) lash together with pieces of cord; adhere, become stuck (*esp.* **to s. up**). [OFr.].

SEIZIN, SEISIN [sē'zin], *n.* (*leg.*) act of taking possession of land; land so taken. [OFr.].

SEIZURE [sē'zhŏŏr], *n.* act of seizing; (*med.*) fit, stroke, sudden paroxysm of illness.

SELAH [sē'lah], *n.* Hebrew word of uncertain meaning found at the end of verses in the Psalms.

SELDOM [sel'dom], *adv.* not often, rarely. [OE.].

SELECT (1) [si-lekt'], *adj.* picked out from a number, chosen from others, *esp.* on account of merit or for a specific purpose; carefully chosen; **s. committee**, committee appointed from all parties in Parliament to inquire into a specific matter. SELECT (2), *v.t.* to pick out, choose out of a number of others, choose for **a** specific purpose. SELECTED, *adj.* carefully picked out (with the implication of being the best). SELECTOR, *n.* one who, or that which, selects or chooses; (*radio*) device for eliminating certain wavelengths. [L.].

SELECTION [si-lek'shn], *n.* act of selecting, thing selected; a number of things from which choice can be made, representative specimens extracted from a large number; a number of isolated passages selected from an author's works; **natural s.**, Darwinian biological theory of the survival of the fittest. [L.].

SELECTIVE [si-lek'tiv], *adj.* tending to select; choosing representative examples; (*radio*) of, or pertaining to, a set or system of tuning which will separate transmissions on neighbouring wavelengths. SELECTIVITY [se-lek-ti'vi-ti], *n.* (*radio*) ability of a tuning system to separate transmissions on adjoining wavebands.

SELENIUM [se-lē'ni-um], *n.* non-metallic element denoted by Se, somewhat resembling sulphur. [Gk.].

SELENOGRAPHY [se-le-no'gra-fi], *n.* scientific description of the moon. [Gk.].

SELENOLOGY [se-le-no'lo-ji], *n.* study of the moon. [Gk.].

SELENOTROPIC [se-lē-nō-tro'pik], *adj.* (*bot.*) turning to face the moon. [Gk.].

SELF (*pl.* **selves**) [self], *n.* the individual being, identity, personality, interests; the fundamental, essential character of a person; one's own person. [OE.].

SELF-, *pref. indicating the agent or the object of an action or condition.* SELF-ABUSE, masturbation. SELF-ACTING, automatic. SELF-ADJUSTING, automatically adjusting itself. SELF-ASSERTION, insistence on one's claims, pushing oneself forward. SELF-BINDER, reaping machine which automatically binds the sheaves, device for automatically clipping papers together. SELF-COLOURED, of only one colour, of the natural colour. SELF-COMMAND, self-control. SELF-CONCEIT, good opinion of oneself. SELF-CONSCIOUS, acutely aware of one's own personality, shy. SELF-CONTAINED, reticent, self-sufficient; (of flats etc.) having all offices etc. within its own boundaries. SELF-DECEPTION, process of deceiving oneself, state of being so deceived, instance of this. SELF-DENIAL, ascetism. SELF-DETERMINATION, act of deciding for oneself, *esp.* on political independence. SELF-EDUCATED, educated without external assistance. SELF-EDUCATOR, form of publication designed for home study without a teacher. SELF-EVIDENT, obvious, evident or (a thing's) own merits. SELF-EXCITING, (*elect.*) (of a dynamo) that excites its own field. SELF-EXISTENT, existing independently. SELF-EXPLANATORY, explaining itself without external assistance. SELF-FEEDING, automatically supplying itself (with fuel etc.). SELF-FERTILE, (*bot.*) fertilizing

itself by its own pollen. SELF-GOVERNING, governed by its own representatives and without external assistance or supervision. SELF-GOVERNMENT, government of a people by its own representatives. SELF-IMPORTANT, full of a sense of one's own importance. SELF-INDUCTION, (*elect.*) production in a circuit of a current induced by variation of current in the same circuit. SELF-INTEREST, one's personal interest or profit. SELF-MADE, owing one's position entirely to one's own efforts. SELF-OPINIONATED, aggressively convinced of one's own rightness. SELF-PORTRAIT, portrait by an artist of himself. SELF-POSSESSED, unperturbed, with confidence in one's own abilities. SELF-RAISING, containing substances such as bicarbonate of soda which, when heated, evolve gas; containing a substitute for yeast. SELF-RELIANT, self-possessed. SELF-REPRESSION, repression of one's own desires, opinions. SELF-RESTRAINT, restraint imposed by oneself on one's actions or desires. SELF-RIGHTEOUS, convinced of one's own virtue. SELF-SACRIFICE, sacrifice of oneself or one's own interests. SELF-SEEKING, seeking one's own advantage. SELF-SOWN, (*bot.*) sown by itself without external agency. SELF-STARTER, electrical starter of a car etc. SELF-STYLED, called by oneself, but without authorization. SELF-SUFFICIENT, requiring no aid or companionship from others; economically s.-supporting. SELF-TAUGHT, s.-educated. SELF-WILLED, s.-opinionated, obstinate. SELF-WINDING, (of clocks etc.) winding automatically.

SELFISH [sel'fish], *adj.* solely influenced by one's own interests, preoccupied by considerations of personal benefit.

SELFLESS [self'les], *adj.* unselfish.

SELFSAME [self'sām], *adj.* the very same.

SELL (1) (*pret. and p.pt.* **sold**) [sel], *v.t.* to barter, transfer to another in return for a valuable consideration, obtain a price in exchange for; deal in, have for sale; help to sell; betray for material gain; (*pass.*) be tricked, swindled; live by selling; (of commodities) attract purchasers; **to s. off**, to s. cheaply for quick disposal; **to s. out**, to s. so as to exhaust the supply; betray cause or companions and retire with a profit; **to s. up**, to s. the goods of (a debtor) to pay (his) creditors. SELL (2), *n.* (*coll.*) that which deceives expectation, a swindle. [OE.].

SELTZER [selt'ser], *n.* an aerated mineral water. [*Selters*, Germany].

SELVAGE, see SELVEDGE.

SELVEDGE, SELVAGE [sel'vij], *n.* edge of a cloth woven to prevent ravelling. [~MDu.].

SELVES [selvz], *pron., pl.* of SELF.

SEMANTIC [se-man'tik], *adj.* of, or relating to, meaning. SEMANTICS, *n.* scientific study of the meanings of words and the development of these. [Gk.].

SEMAPHORE (1) [se'ma-faw(r)], *n.* signalling device consisting of two movable arms worked by levers; alphabet used in such signalling; act of sending messages by such or similar means. SEMAPHORE (2), *v.t. and i.* to send messages by s. [Gk.].

SEMBLANCE [sem'blans], *n.* seeming, likeness, appearance. [Fr.].

SEMEN [sē'men], *n.* sperm-bearing fluid of male mammals. [L.].

SEMESTER [se-mes'ter], *n.* (*U.S.*) period, university term, of six months. [Germ. from L.].

SEMI-, *pref.* half; partly, to some extent. SEMI-DETACHED, (of houses) pertaining to either of two houses which together form a single detached building. SEMI-FINAL (1), *n.* last match but one in a competition. SEMI-FINAL (2), *n.* penultimate. SEMI-FINALIST, *n.* competitor in a semi-final. SEMI-OFFICIAL, *adj.* not formally official, but carrying some authority. SEMI-SOLID, *adj.* half liquid. [L.].

SEMIBREVE [se'mi-brēv], *n.* (*mus.*) a note of half a breve, note equal in length to four crochets.

SEMICIRCLE [se'mi-ser-kl], *n.* half circle; group of persons, things, arranged in a half circle.

SEMICOLON [se-mi-kō'lon], *n.* the punctuation mark (;) intermediate in force between a comma and a colon.

SEMINAL [se'mi-nal], *adj.* relating to, or containing semen; relating to seed or sowing; primary; fruitful. [L.].

SEMINAR [se'mi-nah(r)], *n.* discussion class for senior students of a subject. [Germ. from L.].

SEMINARY [se'mi-na-ri], *n.* school, college, training college for R.C. priests. [L.].

SEMINATION [se-mi-nā'shn], *n.* act of sowing or

ŏŏ is pronounced as in food; ŏŏ as in hood; th as in *think*; TH as in *that*; zh as in azure.   ~ = related to.

impregnating; dissemination; (*bot.*) process of seeding. [L.].

SEMIQUAVER [se'mi-kwā-ver], *n.* (*mus.*) a note of the length of half a quaver.

SEMITE [sē'mīt], *n.* one belonging to an Asiatic racial group which includes Jews, Arabs, Babylonians, Assyrians etc. [~Heb.].

SEMITONE [se'mi-tōn], *n.* (*mus.*) a half tone.

SEMIVOWEL [se'mi-vow-el], *n.* a sound having the characteristics of both vowel and consonant.

SEMOLINA [se-mō-lē'nah], *n.* coarsely ground meal of wheat, used in making macaroni. [It.].

SEMPITERNAL [sem-pi-tur'nal], *adj.* everlasting.

SEMPSTRESS [semp'stres], *n.* seamstress.

SENATE [se'nat], *n.* deliberative assembly of elders; the administrative and legislative council of ancient Rome, the Upper House in the parliamentary system of many countries; the academic governing body of various universities. [L.].

SENATOR [se'na-ter], *n.* member of a senate. [L.].

SEND (*pret. and p.pt.* sent) [send], *v.t.* to cause to go, be dispatched to some other place; have conveyed, compel to go away from the place where the speaker is, discharge; launch upon (schooling); elect, appoint; propel (something) in some direction; bestow on; cause to become, drive, compel to be; *v.i.* to s., dispatch a message to someone; **to s. after,** to s. a message after one who has gone; **to s. away,** to dismiss; **to s. to Coventry,** to ostracize; **to s. down,** to expel from a university; remit; **to s. for,** to summon to come to a place; **to s. forth,** to emit, discharge; bear fruit; **to s. home,** to expel; deliver (a blow) effectively; cause to retire from service; **to s. in,** to s. for consideration to a particular person; **to s. on,** to dispatch in advance; **to s. out,** to dispatch, s. on some mission; **to s. packing, about** (one's) **business,** to dismiss. [OE.].

SENESCENT [se-ne'sent], *adj.* growing old. [L.].

SENESCHAL [se'ne-shal], *n.* steward of a great medieval household. [OFr.].

SENILE [sē'nīl], *adj.* characteristic of old age; mentally and physically decayed with age. SENILITY [se-ni'li-ti], *n.* weakness of old age. [L.].

SENIOR (1) [sē'ni-er], *adj.* older than another, more advanced in rank than another, of a higher educational standard; **S. Service,** the Royal Navy. SENIOR (2), *n.* elder or superior person; more advanced student. [L.].

SENNA [se'nah], *n.* shrub of the genus *Cassia,* which bears flat pods; aperient made from these pods. [Arab.].

SENOR (-A), (-ITA), señor, (-a), (-ita) [se'nyaw(r), (-ah), se-nyaw-rē'tah], *n.* Spanish form of address corresponding to Mr. (Mrs.), (Miss).

SENSATION [sen-sā'shn], *n.* sensual perception, nervous impression produced by the stimulus of a sense organ; feeling; profound emotional excitement produced by some event, the event or news itself. [L.].

SENSATIONAL [sen-sā'shn-al], *adj.* tending to produce a sensation, astonishing and exciting in the highest degree. SENSATIONALISM, *n.* theory that physical sensation is the only source of knowledge; that style of writing or journalism intended to provoke a violent and exciting emotional effect of a crude sort. SENSATIONALIST, *n.* believer in the theory of sensationalism; one who propagates sensations. [*Prec.*].

SENSE (1) [sens], *n.* faculty of perceiving through the stimulation of bodily organs; any one of these bodily means of perception; perception by the bodily organs; the reason, cognitive faculty, judgment, the lowest form of understanding; (*coll.*) that attitude of mind which is able to carry on material transactions; the intellectual meaning of a thing, general meaning of a thing as perceived by the intelligence; understanding of the behaviour appropriate to a specified place or situation. SENSE (2), *v.t.* to perceive intuitively but not directly through the senses or intelligence. [L.].

SENSIBILITY [sen-si-bi'li-ti], *n.* capacity of sensation, power of responding to stimuli; delicacy of aesthetic or emotional response, sensitiveness of perception; that part of a person which feels moral, emotional and spiritual refinements. [LL.].

SENSIBLE [sen'si-bl], *adj.* capable of stimulating or being perceived by the senses; having command of the senses, having the capacity of comprehending realities and causal relations, reasonable, undisturbed by emotions, according to commonsense, judicious; understanding, conscious, aware. SENSIBLY, *adv.*

in s. fashion, to an extent sufficient to be perceived by the senses. [L.].

SENSITIVE [sen'si-tiv], *adj.* highly perceptive of sensations, very sensible of sensory stimulation, tender, easily pained or hurt; easily stirred emotionally, easily distressed; refined, highly perceptive of emotional atmosphere; delicately adjusted, easily disturbed by outside factors; responding easily to physical stimuli. SENSITIVE-PLANT, *n.* (*bot.*) plant of the genus *Mimosa,* so called from the drooping of its leaves when touched. [Fr.].

SENSITIVITY [sen-si-ti'vi-ti], *n.* state of being sensitive, *esp.* chemically or emotionally, or in connexion with delicate instruments.

SENSITIZE [sen'si-tīz], *v.t.* (*phot.*) to render sensitive to light; (*med.*) render sensitive to foreign protein or other substances.

SENSORIUM [sen-saw'ri-um], *n.* the grey matter of the brain; the nervous system as a whole.

SENSORY [sen'se-ri], *adj.* of, or relating to, the senses or sensation, or sensation-bearing ganglia.

SENSUAL [sen'syoo-al], *adj.* relating to, perceived by, the senses; relating to the sexual passions and their gratification, or the carnal pleasures generally; licentious. SENSUALIST, *n.* one preoccupied with s. pleasures, licentious person. [LL.].

SENSUOUS [sen'syoo-oos], *adj.* relating to, appealing to, the semi-aesthetic senses.

SENTENCE (1) [sen'tens], *n.* (*gram.*) a conventionally grammatical arrangement of words coherently expressing a single identifiable thought; (*leg.*) statement of the penalty imposed by a criminal court; period of imprisonment; the penalty itself; a judgment. SENTENCE (2), *v.t.* (*leg.*) to pass s. upon.

SENTENTIOUS [sen-ten'shoos], *adj.* prone to expressing worthless opinions in a pompous fashion; (of statements) ponderously trite. [L.].

SENTIENT [sen'shent], *adj.* perceiving by the senses, having the capacity of feeling, living and thinking. [L.].

SENTIMENT [sen'ti-ment], *n.* feeling expressed intellectually; an expressed opinion; banal aphorism; that which is intended to appeal to the weaker emotions, sentimentality. [LL.].

SENTIMENTAL [sen-ti-men'tal], *adj.* relating to, arising from, feeling rather than reason; mawkish, weakly emotional over some foolish object. [*Prec.*].

SENTINEL [sen'ti-nel], *n.* one who stands guard, sentry. [OFr.].

SENTRY [sen'tri], *n.* armed guard posted to give warning of hostile approach. SENTRY-BOX, s.'s shelter. SENTRY-GO, duty of a s., his march up and down his beat. [OFr.].

SEPAL [se'pal], *n.* (*bot.*) leaf of a flower's calyx. [Fr.].

SEPARABLE [se'pa-ra-bl], *adj.* able to be separated.

SEPARATE (1) [se'pa-rāt], *v.t. and i.* to disunite, make separate; estrange, cause disagreement; divide, come between, keep separate from; sift, discriminate; go apart, leave each other's company, cease to cohabit, secede. SEPARATE (2) [se'pa-rat], *adj.* not joined, divided, disconnected, distinct, isolated, having distinctive functions, not related. SEPARATISM, *n.* policy based upon the desire of certain groups to obtain independence from larger organizations to which they belong. SEPARATIST (1), *n.* one who wishes to secede from the main body of a church or policy. SEPARATIST (2), *adj.* of or pertaining to separatism or separatists. SEPARATIVE, SEPARATORY, *adj.* tending to s.; with the purpose of separating. SEPARATOR, *n.* one who separates; machine for separating substances, *esp.* cream from milk. [L.].

SEPARATION [se-pa-rā'shn], *n.* act of separating, state of being separate; formal or informal arrangement by which a married couple cease to cohabit; **s. allowance,** allowance received by the wife or other dependent of someone on active service. [L.].

SEPIA [sē'pi-ah], *n.* a coloured secretion of the cuttlefish; pigment made from this; dark-brown colour of this pigment. [Gk.].

SEPOY [sē'poi], *n.* European-trained Indian soldier. [Hind.].

SEPSIS [sep'sis], *n.* putrefaction, infection of the blood. [Gk.].

SEPT [sept], *n.* Irish clan; branch of a Highland clan or family. [OFr.].

SEPT-, *pref.* seven, containing, relating to, connected with, seven. [L.].

SEPTEMBER [sep-tem'ber], *n.* ninth (in the Roman calendar the seventh) month of the year. [L.].

The accent ' after a syllable = stress (u-pon'). The mark ⁻ over a vowel = length (ā in made; ō in bone).

SEPTENARY [sep-te′na-ri], *adj.* consisting of seven. [L.].

SEPTENNIAL [sep-te′ni-al], *adj.* happening every seven years, lasting seven years. SEPTENNIALLY, *adv.* every seven years. [L.].

SEPTET [sep-tet′], *n.* (*mus.*) composition for seven performers; group of seven performers.

SEPTIC [sep′tik], *adj.* relating to sepsis; poisoned, putrefied. [Gk.].

SEPTICAEMIA [sep-ti-se′mi-ah], *n.* blood-poisoning. [Gk.].

SEPTUAGENARIAN [sep-tyōo-a-je-naer′i-an], *adj. and n.* seventy years old; person aged between seventy and eighty years. [L.].

SEPTUAGESIMA [sep-tyōo-a-je′si-mah], *n.* third Sunday before Lent. [L.].

SEPTUAGINT [sep′tyōo-a-jint], *n.* Hellenistic version of the Old Testament. [L.].

SEPTUM (*pl.* **septa**) [sep′tum], *n.* a membrane dividing two bodily cavities. [L.].

SEPTUPLE [sep′tyōo-pl], *adj.* sevenfold. [L.].

SEPULCHRAL [si-pul′kral], *adj.* like, relating to, a sepulchre, dismal, funereal. [L.].

SEPULCHRE (1) [se′pul-ker], *n.* tomb cut out of rock, vault, building etc. for the interment of the dead; **whited s.**, hypocrite. SEPULCHRE (2), *v.t.* to bury in a tomb. [L.].

SEPULTURE [se′pul-tyōor], *n.* act, process or mode of burying the dead. [L.].

SEQUACIOUS [si-kwā′shōos], *adj.* following, attending; docile; consistent, logically following. [L.].

SEQUEL [se′kwel], *n.* that which follows and is related to something preceding it, the outcome, continuation of a thing after it is apparently completed; literary work continuing one which preceded it; result, consequence. [L.].

SEQUENCE [se′kwens], *n.* the order of a series of events, series of events leading out of each other or occurring in succession; series of cards in uninterrupted order of value; (*mus.*) succession of graduate tones; (*films*) a continuous action ended by a dissolve, the equivalent of a theatrical scene. [LL.].

SEQUENT [se′kwent], *adj.* following, consequent. SEQUENTIAL [si-kwen′shal], *adj.* following, consequential.

SEQUESTER [si-kwes′ter], *v.t. and reflex.* (*leg.*) to take possession of for a definite purpose and time, confiscate; withdraw from society; sequestrate. SEQUESTERED, *adj.* retired, in seclusion.

SEQUESTRATE [si-kwes′trāt], *v.t. and i.* (*leg.*) to take (a person's property) and hold it against the satisfaction of claims; confiscate. SEQUESTRATION [se-kwes-trā′shn], *n.* act or process of sequestrating. SEQUESTRATOR [se′kwes-trā-ter], *n.* one who sequestrates property, one holding sequestered property. [LL.].

SEQUIN [se′kwin], *n.* medieval Italian gold coin; ornamental circular spangle. [Arab.].

SERAC, sérac [sā′rak], *n.* pinnacle of glacial ice. [Fr.].

SERAGLIO [se-rah′lyō], *n.* old palace of the Sultans of Turkey; harem; concubines of an oriental ruler. [It.].

SERAPH (*pl.* **seraphim**) [se′raf], *n.* angel of the highest order, having six wings. SERAPHIC [se-ra′fik], *adj.* relating to a s.; angelic, holy. [Heb.].

SERE, SEAR (1) [sēer], *adj.* withered, shrivelled. [OE.].

SERENADE (1) [se-re-nād′], *n.* music played at night in the open air, *esp.* under a loved one's window; (*mus.*) piece composed to be performed in the open air. SERENADE (2), *v.t. and i.* to play, sing a s. to; perform a s. [Fr.].

SERENE [si-rēn′], *adj.* calm, peaceful, smooth, tranquil, unclouded; (*coll.*) safe; also used as a royal title. [L.].

SERENITY [si-re′ni-ti], *n.* undisturbed tranquillity. [L.].

SERF [surf], *n.* (*hist.*) peasant bound to his lord's land; (*coll.*) oppressed wage-slave, person degraded by virtual servitude. [L.].

SERGE [surj], *n.* twilled woollen stuff used in making heavy garments. [L.].

SERGEANT, SERJEANT [sah′jant], *n.* (*milit.*) non-commissioned officer next above a corporal; police officer next above a constable; any one of various court officials. SERGEANT-MAJOR, warrant officer of various functions and appointments. [OFr.].

SERIAL (1) [sēer′i-al], *adj.* relating to, arranged in, a series; (of literary works) appearing at intervals in instalments; **s. rights**, rights of publishing instalments of a work in a journal. SERIAL (2), *n.* a work, film etc. published or exhibited in a succession of instalments. SERIALIZE, *v.t.* to publish as a s. [~SERIES].

SERIATIM [sēer-i-ā′tim], *adv.* in regular series, point by point. [MedL.].

SERICEOUS [se-ri′shōos], *adj.* resembling, relating to silk. [Gk.].

SERICULTURE [sēer′i-kul-tyōor], *n.* the cultivation of silkworms. [L.].

SERIES (*pl.* **series**) [sēer′ez], *n.* a number of things arranged in some graded order, number of things standing in some successive relation; number of books published successively with a common format; (*math.*) succession of terms in accordance with a common law, sequence, progressive gradation. [L.].

SERIF [se′rif], *n.* one of the flourishes and decorative lines on letters in most printing types. [Uncert.].

SERIOUS [sēer′i-ōos], *adj.* sober, thoughtful, occupied with, interested in, grave or important matters; not marked by levity; said, done, or intended in earnest; dangerous, critical, requiring earnest attention; thorough, careful. [LL.].

SERJEANT, see SERGEANT. SERJEANT-AT-ARMS, officer in charge of the mace in the House of Commons. SERJEANT-AT-LAW, member of a former order of barristers.

SERMON [sur′mon], *n.* moral, doctrinal and religious address delivered during a church service; (*coll.*) moralizing lecture of reproach for some evil behaviour. SERMONIZE, *v.i.* to harangue, moralize. [OFr.].

SEROLOGY [sēer-o′lo-ji], *n.* study of serums. [SERUM and Gk.].

SEROUS [sēer′ōos], *adj.* resembling, secreting, serum.

SERPENT [sur′pent], *n.* snake; (*fig.*) treacherous, smooth-tongued tempter, the Devil; (*mus.*) wood-wind instrument with a long curved tube. [L.].

SERPENTINE (1) [sur′pen-tin], *adj.* sinuous like a serpent, meandering; (*fig.*) treacherously subtle. SERPENTINE (2), *n.* (*geol.*) a highly polishable dull green mineral.

SERRATE(D) [se-rāt′(-id)], *adj.* with a notched edge. SERRATION [se-rā′shn], *n.* state of being serrated; notched edge like that of a saw. [L.].

SERRIED [se′rid], *adj.* packed compactly together, *esp.* of troops in close formation. [Fr.].

SERUM (*pl.* **sera, serums**) [sēer′um], *n.* watery fluid remaining after the coagulation of the blood; such a fluid as prepared for use in inoculation. [L.].

SERVAL [sur′val], *n.* a ring-tailed African wild cat. [Native].

SERVANT [sur′vant], *n.* one who serves, person in the service of another, one employed to wait upon another's bodily or domestic requirements, devoted adherent of anything, that which aids any purpose or person. [OFr.].

SERVE (1) [surv], *v.t.* to aid, help, tend, work for, be servant to (a person or thing), wait upon, supply the needs of, present food to (a person); fulfil (a purpose); do what is required; (*eccles.*) assist a priest at Mass; undergo (a prison sentence) (usually **to s. time**); operate (a machine), load and work a gun; (of male animals) mate with; (*tennis etc.*) strike the ball to begin a rally; (*leg.*) deliver (a summons or notice of a legal process to a person); **to s. a person right**, to give a person what he deserves; *v.i.* to be, or to perform the duties of, a servant or slave, perform duties in the armed forces, perform an office; suffice, be adequate, be suitable for a specific purpose; **to s. as**, to perform the functions of. SERVE (2), *n.* act of serving, a turn to s. at a game. SERVER, *n.* one who serves; one serving at Mass; implement for serving food. [L.].

SERVICE (1) [sur′vis], *n.* act, process or occupation of serving, by which a person is served; employment, *esp.* as a domestic servant; period of employment in one of the services; an official administrative department, department for providing a public utility; a regularly-plying means of transport; (*pl.*) armed forces of a government; (*eccles.*) formal performances of religious worship or ritual; attention given to a customer; maintenance of machinery in good order; way in which, means by which, food is served, set of implements and dishes for eating food; (*leg.*) serving of a process or summons; (*tennis*) striking of the ball to begin play; **active s.**, s. in the armed forces involving actual military operations; **Senior S.**, the Royal Navy. SERVICE-BOOK, book

ōo is pronounced as in food; ŏŏ as in hood; th as in think; TH as in that; zh as in azure.   ~ = related to.

DSE—R*

containing an order of religious s. SERVICE-FLAT, flat where the rent covers domestic s. SERVICE-LINE, line across a tennis court, between which and the net the ball must fall in s. SERVICE (2), adj. pertaining or belonging to one of the armed forces. EX-SERVICE, discharged from one of the armed forces. SERVICE (3), v.t. to provide s. for (machinery etc.). [OFr. from L.].

SERVICEABLE [sur'vi-sa-bl], adj. fit for use, useful rather than decorative.

SERVIETTE [ser-vi-et'], n. table napkin. [Fr.].

SERVILE [sur'vil], adj. relating to slaves or slavery; in the condition of a slave; fawning, cringing slavishly. [L.].

SERVILITY [ser-vi'li-ti], n. state or quality of being servile.

SERVING-MAID, -MAN [sur'ving-mād, -man], n. female, male, domestic servant.

SERVITOR [sur'vi-ter], n. one who serves another, esp. in a personal capacity; (hist.) Oxford undergraduate who received free lodging and partial board. [L.].

SERVITUDE [sur'vi-tyōōd], n. slavery, complete subjection; **penal s.**, formerly imprisonment with hard labour for three years or more (abolished 1948). [L.].

SESAME [se'sa-mi], n. an East Indian herb; **open s.!** magic invocation by which, in Arabian legend, Ali Baba opened the robbers' cave; (fig.) that which facilitates entry or approach. [OFr. from Gk.].

SESQUI-, pref. one and one-half more. [L.].

SESQUIPEDALIAN [ses-kwi-pe-dā'li-an], adj. containing a foot and a half; (of speech) many-syllabled, long-worded. [L.].

SESSILE [se'sil], adj. (bot.) attached directly to the main stem. [L.].

SESSION [se'shn], n. a formal sitting, meeting, of a body or assembly, time occupied by such a sitting, period for which an assembly remains sitting without dissolution; a university year; (pl.) meetings of certain judicial courts; (coll.) a period continuously occupied by some business or discussion. [L.].

SESTET [ses-tet'], n. sextet; last six lines of the Italian sonnet. [L.].

SET (1) (pres.pt. **setting**, pret. and p.pt. **set**) [set], v.t. to take and put in a certain position in relation to something else, put facing, direct towards, a certain direction; fix (a jewel etc.) in a metal holder, adjust (machinery) to a certain purpose, prepare (a device) for some future action, get (a thing) ready, prepare for something to follow; (typ.) arrange (type) for printing; put (eggs) under a bird to be hatched; cause to stiffen, esp. solidify (a liquid); have an influence on (the mind); appoint some duty for, direct to some action or task; compose music for (words); fix (the hair) in waves; v.i. (astron.) to pass below the horizon; (of liquids) become solidified; become rigid and determined; **to s. about,** to begin, undertake; **to s. about a person,** to attack a person; **to s. aside,** to disregard; **to s. back,** to hinder the progress of; **to s. down,** to record, write down; **to s. in,** to become increasingly present; **to s. off,** to explode, cause to begin; begin a journey; enhance the appearance of; **to s. on,** to urge on; **to s. out,** to arrange, give an exposition of; begin a journey; **to s. to,** to act vigorously, begin vigorous effort; **to s. up,** to establish in good style, establish oneself in some profession, found. SET-BACK, rebuff; discouraging experience. SET-OFF, that which enhances a thing; compensation of a gain against a loss; (leg.) settlement of a debt by a counterclaim by the debtor. SET-PIECE, a performance elaborately prepared in advance, large pictorial firework display on a framework. SET-SQUARE, flat, right-angled, triangular drawing instrument. SET-TO, fracas, fight or violent dispute. SET-UP, (coll.) organization, arrangement, disposition of elements. SET (2), n. group of individual objects bearing a natural or planned relationship to each other, and together making up a complete series or whole; outfit, piece of equipment composed of various parts; the way in which a thing is placed in relation to something else, angle at which a thing rests; a general inclination in a certain direction, mental or physical; a drift, determined inclination; group of persons having some intent in common; number of eggs hatched at one time; (lawn tennis) the game's principal scoring unit, gained by the first side to win six or more games with a clear lead of two; (films, theatre) the complete scenery or setting for a part of the action; (films) the part of the studio in

which acting is taking place; act of setting; an adjustment of the hair. SET (3), adj. rigid, fixed (esp. of facial expression), determined in some course; established, prescribed. SETTING, n. act of setting, manner or material in which a thing is s.; process of solidifying; surroundings or environment of a thing. [OE.].

SETT [set], n. block of wood or stone used in street-paving. [SET (1)].

SETTEE [se-tē'], n. upholstered sofa with back and arms, capable of holding two or more persons. [Uncert.].

SETTER [se'ter], n. one who, or that which, sets; one of several kinds of game-dog.

SETTLE (1) [se'tl], n. long, high-backed seat. [OE.].

SETTLE (2), v.t. to set and place securely in, establish (people) as inhabitants, provide (a place) with inhabitants, establish (a person) in a place or situation; make calm, decide; make up one's mind about, bring to a conclusion, finally to dispose of; pay (a debt); (coll.) deal firmly with; v.i. to go to a place as an inhabitant, establish oneself in a place or occupation; become stable, decided; come to rest, subside; (of sediment) sink to the bottom; **to s. down,** to adapt oneself to a new mode of life; **to s. on,** (leg.) to endow with; **to s. up,** to pay all one's outstanding debts; **to s. with,** to make a settlement with; deal with finally. SETTLER, n. one who settles, esp. one settling in an undeveloped country. SETTLING, n. act of making settled, result of such action; act of subsiding. [ME.].

SETTLEMENT [se'tl-ment], n. act of settling, state of being settled; group of settlers, place in which they have settled, esp. a township of settlers; (leg.) formal conveyance of property, property so conveyed.

SEVEN (1) [se'ven], n. the number between six and eight, numeral representing this. SEVEN (2), adj. of the number 7. SEVEN-FOLD, adj. repeated s. times; with s. folds; s. times as much or as many. [OE.].

SEVENTEEN (1) [se-ven-tēn'], n. the number equalling seven plus ten. SEVENTEEN (2), adj. of the number s. [OE.].

SEVENTEENTH [se-ven-tēnth'], n. and adj. the ordinal of seventeen; (being) one of seventeen equal parts.

SEVENTH [se'venth], n. and adj. the ordinal of seven; (being) one of seven equal parts; **s. heaven,** the ultimate height of bliss. SEVENTHLY, adv. in the s. place.

SEVENTIETH [se'ven-ti eth], n. and adj. the ordinal of seventy; (being) one of seventy equal parts.

SEVENTY (1) [se'ven-ti], n. the number equalling seven times ten. SEVENTY (2), adj. seven times ten. [OE.].

SEVER [se'ver], v.t. to divide by cutting, separate from, cut in two; (fig.) estrange, divide (from). [OFr. from L.].

SEVERAL [se've-ral], adj. separate, distinct, various; a few, more than two but not a great many; (leg.) able to be treated separately. SEVERALLY, adv. separately, individually. [AFr.].

SEVERANCE [se've-rans], n. act of severing, state of being severed. [OFr.].

SEVERE [si-vēer'], adj. strict, stern, rigorous, exacting; grave, austere; violent, excessive, intense. [L.].

SEVERITY [si-ve'ri-ti], n. act or state of being severe. [L.].

SEVILLE [se-vil'], n. name of a city in Spain used to denote a type of bitter orange.

SEW (pret. **sewed**, p.pt. **sewed**, **sewn**) [sō], v.t. and i. to fasten together by drawing thread, make by stitching; stitch, work with needle and thread. [OE.].

SEWAGE [syōō'ij], n. waste matter carried through sewers; **s. farm,** place outside a town where s. is rendered innocuous.

SEWER [syōō'er], n. main drain, underground conduit for removing excreta and waste from a town. SEWERAGE, n. system of drains and sewers in a town, disposal of waste by means of sewage. [OFr.].

SEWING [sō'ing], n. craft of stitching; needlework.

SEX [seks], n. distinguishing physiological characteristics of male and female, one of these two groups as a whole; everything relating to these organic differences and the various emotions and ideas associated with them. SEX-APPEAL, the attribute or power which excites sexual desire in the opposite s. SEXED, adj. having sexual desires or capacity developed to a specified degree. SEXLESS, *adj.* lacking sexual passions or characteristics. SEXY, *adj.* exploiting or flaunting s. [L.].

SEX-. *pref.* six, pertaining to six. [L.].

SEXAGENARIAN [sek-sa-je-nāer'i-an], *adj. and n.* sixty years old; person aged between sixty and seventy years. [L.].

SEXAGESIMA [sek-sa-je'si-mah], *n.* second Sunday before Lent. [L.].

SEXCENTENARY [seks-sen-tē'na-ri], *n.* a six-hundredth anniversary.

SEXENNIAL [sek-se'ni-al], *adj.* happening every six years, lasting six years. [L.].

SEXTANT [seks'tant], *n.* instrument for determining position by finding latitude and longitude; (*math.*) sixth part of a circle. [L.].

SEXTET [seks-tet'], *n.* (*mus.*) composition for six performers; group of six performers. [L.].

SEXTO [seks'tō], *n.* (*typ.*) book made up of sheets folded into six. [L.].

SEXTON [seks'ton], *n.* man employed to dig graves and tend church and churchyard. [~SACRISTAN].

SEXTUPLE [seks'tyōō-pl], *adj.* sixfold.

SEXUAL [sek'syōō-al], *adj.* relating to, connected with, arising from, preoccupied by or tending to, sex, its characteristics or the emotions it arouses. [L.].

SFORZANDO [sfawt-zahn'dō], *adv.* (*mus.*) emphatically, with force. [It.].

SHABBY [sha'bi], *adj.* ragged, wearing threadbare; squalid, drab; mean, despicable. [~OE.].

SHACK [shak], *n.* roughly built hut, cabin. [Unkn.].

SHACKLE (1) [sha'kl], *n.* horseshoe-shaped link closed by a bolt or pin across the ends; chain joined to the wrist- or ankle-rings of a prisoner, fetter; (*fig.*) a restraint, that which binds. SHACKLE (2), *v.t.* to bind with a s., restrict, fetter. [OE.].

SHAD [shad], *n.* edible marine fish related to the herring. [OE.].

SHADDOCK [sha'dok], *n.* grapefruit, tree bearing this fruit. [Captain *Shaddock*, who introduced it to the West Indies].

SHADE (1) [shād], *n.* darkness caused by the intervention of something before a source of light, area shielded from the direct rays of the sun, that which provides protection from direct light; darkening in a pictorial representation to represent a suppression of light; very slight difference in colour or brightness, or in any quantity or quality, the faintest tinge of some feeling; ghost, memory of one dead; **in the s.,** (*fig.*) overshadowed, outdone, by another. SHADE (2), *v.t. and i.* to cast s. on, shield from the light, indicate gradations of light on a drawing etc.; **to s. away,** to fade slowly into difference; **to s. into,** to change gradually into. SHADING, *n.* darkening in a drawing to indicate differences of light; act of giving s. [OE.].

SHADOW (1) [sha'dō], *n.* patch of shade produced on a surface by the intervention of an object between it and a source of light, *esp.* such a shade as falls in the shape of the object which produces it; space from which light is cut off by the presence of an object; (*fig.*) that which casts a shade, gloom; insubstantial copy, feeble reflection, of someone or something; the slightest degree, a shade; person following another as closely as his s., *esp.* someone following and spying on another; a warning of coming ill; **s. boxing,** practice boxing against an imaginary opponent; **s. cabinet,** (*pol.*) draft list of members of a cabinet made before the party concerned is in office; **s. factory,** factory prepared for use only in the event of the destruction by war etc. of another. SHADOW (2), *v.t.* to throw a s. upon, throw into the shade; shade (a drawing); outline, foretell; follow and spy upon. [OE.].

SHADOWY [sha'dō-i], *adj.* shady; full of shadows; mysterious; insubstantial.

SHADY [shā'di], *adj.* shaded, giving shade, in the shade; (*coll.*) underhand, of dubious reputation, probably dishonest.

SHAFT [shahft], *n.* stem, stock of an arrow or spear, haft of various implements; anything long, straight and slim in proportion to its length, bar, stalk, part of a column between base and capital, narrow beam of light, narrow, vertical opening leading down to a mine; (*pl.*) two parallel poles between which a horse is harnessed to pull a vehicle. [OE.].

SHAG [shag], *n.* rough, untidy mass of hair; a coarse tobacco; small crested cormorant. [OE.].

SHAGGED [sha'gid], *adj.* shaggy; (*coll.*) tired out.

SHAGGY [sha'gi], *adj.* rough, unkempt, with long, thick, untidy hair.

SHAGREEN [sha-grēn'], *n.* rough, untanned leather

made from horse-hide, with an artificially granulated surface; skin of various sharks which resembles this. [Pers.].

SHAH [shah], *n.* the king of Persia. [Pers.].

SHAKE (1) (*pret.* **shook,** *p.pt.* **shaken**) [shāk], *v.t.* to move a thing quickly backwards and forwards, hold in the hand and move (suddenly); cause to vibrate rapidly; weaken the stability of, render less firm; (*fig.*) disturb, upset, weaken; **to s. hands,** to grasp another's hand in greeting or farewell; *v.i.* to vibrate, move rapidly back and forth, tremble, shiver with fear or excitement; **to s. down,** to settle down on an impromptu bed; **to s. off,** to get rid of for good; **to s. up,** to mix by shaking; shock and disturb severely. SHAKE (2), *n.* act of shaking, single movement of shaking, negative gesture of the head; a drink made by shaking two or more ingredients together; (*mus.*) trill; (*coll.*) very short time. SHAKEDOWN, *n.* makeshift bed. SHAKEN, *adj.* perturbed, upset by some experience. SHAKER, *n.* one who, or that which, shakes; member of a religious sect in the U.S. whose devotions are accompanied by a form of dancing; container for mixing drinks by shaking. [OE.].

SHAKO [sha-kō'], *n.* peaked, partly conical, flat-topped military headgear. [Hungarian].

SHAKY [shā'ki], *adj.* easily shaken, unstable, flimsy; tottering, feeble in bodily movements; (*fig.*) uncertain, vague, unreliable.

SHALE [shāl], *n.* laminated clay-rock; **s. oil,** oil obtained by distillation of bituminous s. [Germ.].

SHALL (*pret.* **should**) [shal], *v. auxil, expressing future intention, obligation, or compulsion.* [OE.].

SHALLOT [sha-lot'], *n.* a small species of onion. [OFr.].

SHALLOW (1) [sha'lō], *adj.* not deep; (*fig.*) lacking depth, intensity; having few original ideas, superficial. SHALLOW (2), *n. a s.* place. SHALLOW (3), *v.i.* (of water) gradually to become s. SHALLOWS, *n.(pl.)* tract of s. water, shoals. [ME.].

SHAM (1) (*pres.pt.* **shamming,** *pret. and p.pt.* **shammed**) [sham], *v.t. and i.* to feign, simulate; pretend, affect (to be). SHAM (2), *n.* that which is spurious, a counterfeit, fake; assumption of some quality or attribute not really possessed, deception, fraud. SHAM (3), *adj.* bogus, not genuine, spurious. [~SHAME].

SHAMBLE (1) [sham'bl], *v.i.* to shuffle, walk in clumsy and ungainly fashion. SHAMBLE (2), *n.* a shambling walk, clumsy, shuffling gait. [ODu.].

SHAMBLES [sham'blz], *n.* butcher's stall, slaughter-house, place of blood and slaughter, bloody massacre. [OE. from L.].

SHAME (1) [shām], *n.* strong emotion of regret, self-disgust, or embarrassment, feeling of guilt, feeling of offended modesty; disgrace, dishonour; a cause of ignominy, embarrassment or disgust; (*coll.*) unfairness, exceptionally bad luck. SHAME (2), *v.t.* to bring s. upon, make feel ashamed, disgrace; coerce by making feel ashamed. [OE.].

SHAMEFACED [shām'fāst], *adj.* bashful, shy; showing shame at some ill-conduct, sheepish. [OE.].

SHAMEFUL [shām'fōōl], *adj.* that which shames, disgraceful, outrageous, disgusting.

SHAMELESS [shām'les], *adj.* without shame, immodest, brazen, impudent.

SHAMMY [sha'mi], *n.* chamois leather. [~CHAMOIS].

SHAMPOO (1) [sham-pōō'], *v.t.* to wash the hair with a shampoo, or under a spray of water. SHAMPOO (2), *n.* act of shampooing; soap etc. used for shampooing the hair. [Hind.].

SHAMROCK [sham'rok], *n.* the white clover; this or any of several similar plants used as the Irish national emblem. [Ir.].

SHANDY [shan'di], *n.* (*coll.*) shandygaff.

SHANDYGAFF [shan'di-gaf], *n.* drink consisting of beer and gingerbeer or lemonade. [Unkn.].

SHANGHAI [shang-hī'], *v.t.* to drug or stun (a man) and put him aboard an outgoing ship as a sailor. [*Shanghai*, Chinese port].

SHANK [shangk], *n.* shin of a man or certain animals; (*pl.*) (*coll.*) the legs; haft of an instrument, part of a tool between handle and working end. [OE.].

SHANTUNG [shan-tung'], *n.* silk from the Chinese province of *Shantung*.

SHANTY (1) [shan'ti], *n.* sailor's song, *esp.* one sung while heaving at ropes etc. [Fr.].

SHANTY (2), *n.* lean-to shed, shack, small hut. [Uncert.].

SHAPE (1) [shāp], *n.* the external form, two- or three-dimensional outline of a thing; something having a

---

ōō is pronounced as in f*oo*d; ŏŏ as in h*oo*d; th as in *th*ink; TH as in *th*at; zh as in azure. ~ = related to.

form, something of which only the outlines can be distinguished; (fig.) orderly plan or conception; practical expression of some conception; mould for shaping something; that which is shaped in a mould; **to be in good s.**, to be in good spirits and physical condition. SHAPE (2), v.t. and i. to give s. to, mould; assume a s., become formed, ordered; develop; **to s. up to**, to approach in a boxing attitude; (fig.) assert oneself. [OE.].

SHAPELESS [shăp'les], adj. without shape, with an indistinguishable outline, unsymmetrical.

SHAPELY [shāp'li], adj. well shaped, well proportioned (esp. of the female body).

SHARD, SHERD [shahd, shurd], n. fragment of pottery; hard wing-case of a beetle. [OE.].

SHARE (1) [shāer], n. a portion of something held in common allocated to one of the possessors, portion of a thing obtained by any one party by division, part obtained from, borne in, anything in which others also participate; part-ownership of a business undertaking, one of the equal parts into which is divided the invested capital of a joint-stock company; (pl.) stock. SHARE-LIST, list showing the current prices of joint-stock shares. SHARE-PUSHER, one who peddles shares in dubious joint-stock companies. SHARE (2), v.t. and i. to give out shares in a thing, divide a thing with others, participate with in the possession of a thing; have a s., take part in. [OE.].

SHARE (3), n. ploughshare. [OE.].

SHAREHOLDER [shāer'hōl-der], n. one holding shares in a joint-stock company.

SHARK [shahk], n. one of a group of voracious seafishes; (fig.) predatory rogue. [Uncert.].

SHARP (1) [shahp], adj. keen, having a cutting edge, piercing, able to divide or penetrate substances; pointed, acute, steep; shrill; distinctly outlined; sour, bitter, astringent; swift, sudden; quick, clever, alert; (mus.) raised a semitone in pitch, too high in pitch; brusque. SHARP-SET, hungry, eager. SHARP (2), n. (mus.) a s. note, the symbol for this, one of the black keys on a piano; sharper, swindler. SHARP (3), adv. punctually, exactly. SHARP (4), v.t. (coll.) swindle, cheat. SHARPER, n. swindler, trickster, esp. at cards. [OE.].

SHARPEN [shah'pen], v.t. and i. to make sharp, whet, make quick or ready; become sharp. SHARPENER, n. one who, or that which, sharpens, esp. a contrivance for sharpening pencils.

SHARPSHOOTER [shahp'shoo-ter], n. (milit.) sniper, skilled marksman, lightly-equipped skirmisher. SHARPSHOOTING, n. sniping, rapid accurate shooting at the enemy by a carefully located marksman.

SHATTER [sha'ter], v.t. and i. to break into fragments, smash to pieces; (fig.) destroy quickly and utterly; jar upon.

SHAVE (1) (pret. **shaved**, p.pt. **shaved, shaven**) [shāv], v.t. and i. to cut, scrape hair from the body with a razor, esp. to remove hair from the face; cut, pare, thin slices from a surface; graze very slightly; perform the action of shaving the face. SHAVE (2), n. act of shaving, state of the face after having been shaved; a shaving; very narrow escape, the barest contact with something; tool for paring wood. SHAVER, n. one who, or that which, shaves; (coll.) young boy. SHAVING, n. act of removing hair from the body with a razor; thin slice of wood or metal. [OE.].

SHAWL [shawl], n. piece of material for loosely covering the head and (usually) shoulders. [Pers.].

SHAWM [shawm], n. a double-reed instrument, forerunner of the oboe. [OFr. from Gk.].

SHAY [shā], n. a chaise. [~CHAISE.].

SHE [shē], pron. 3rd person sg. fem. nom. case. [ME.].

SHEAF (pl. **sheaves**) [shēf, shēvz], n. bundle of reaped grain tied together in a stack; number of arrows sufficient to fill the quiver; bundle of papers or banknotes. [OE.].

SHEALING, SHIELING [shē'ling], n. small shepherd's or fisherman's hut or croft. [~Norw.].

SHEAR (1) (pret. **sheared, shore**, p.pt. **sheared, shorn**) [shēer], v.t. and i. to cut with shears, cut off at a stroke, cut off (the hair); remove (fleece) with the shears; alter in shape under stress. SHEAR-LEGS, crane-like device for raising heavy weights. SHEAR (2), n. rupture or distortion in any material caused by forces acting in opposite directions but not in the same straight line. SHEARER, n. one who shears sheep. SHEARING, n. act of clipping wool from sheep with shears; (pl.) wool so cut off. SHEARS, n.(pl.) large

scissor-like cutting tool consisting of two blades with handles, bolted together at a point on each between the blade and the handle and pivoting about that point so that the action of bringing the handles together closes the blades and causes them to cut. [OE.].

SHEARWATER [shēer'waw-ter], n. sea-bird of the genus Puffinus.

SHEATH [shēth], n. close-fitting case or covering used to encase a sharp tool or weapon when it is not being used; scabbard of a sword; any similar covering or envelope, esp. in the anatomy of animals, birds, fish etc., or in the structure of plants; a form of contraceptive. [OE.].

SHEATHE [shēth], v.t. to place or replace in a sheath; cover with a protecting case or envelope. SHEATHED, adj. fitted in a sheath, protected by a close outer covering. SHEATHING, n. act of placing in a sheath; anything which envelops closely. [Prec.].

SHEAVE (1) [shēv], n. grooved pulley-wheel over which a rope passes. [Uncert.].

SHEAVE (2), v.t. to gather into sheaves. [~SHEAF].

SHED (1) [shed], n. hut or outhouse used for storage or as a temporary shelter; lean-to. [~SHADE.].

SHED (2) [(pres.pt. **shedding**, pret. and p.pt. **shed**), v.t. to let fall, abandon, divest oneself of; let flow, pour forth, diffuse; cause to flow; **to s. the blood of**, to slay. SHED (3), n. parting in the wool of a sheep made so that the skin may be reached and treated medicinally; (in weaving) parting of the threads of the warp on the loom so that the shuttle may pass between. SHEDDING, n. act of casting off, pouring forth or causing to pour forth; that which is s.; division or parting. [OE.].

SHEEN [shēn], n. gloss, lustre. [OE.].

SHEEP (pl. **sheep**) [shēp], n. ungulate ruminant mammal of the genus Ovis, valuable for its woolly coat and edible flesh; leather made from the skin of a sheep; (fig.) member(s) of a religious congregation; (coll.) timid person lacking in initiative; **black s.**, rogue; **sheep's eyes**, amorous glances; **lost s.**, person who has strayed from upright habits or who has left a community to which he previously belonged; **the s. and the goats**, the good and the bad; **s. run**, (orig. Australian) large farm devoted exclusively to the raising of s.; sheepwalk; **s.'s head**, head of a s.; dull-witted person; **s. wash**, lotion used to clean s. of vermin. SHEEP-DIP, strong disinfectant insecticide in which s. are immersed to free them of vermin; concreted trench in which s. are plunged in this liquid. SHEEP-SHEARING, process of shearing s.; time of year when s. are sheared; rural feast held at this time. SHEEP-TICK, a parasitic insect troublesome to s. SHEEP-WALK, tract of s. pasture. [OE.].

SHEEPCOTE [shēp'kōt], n. a sheepfold.

SHEEPFOLD [shēp'fōld], n. enclosure for sheep.

SHEEPISH [shē'pish], adj shy, bashful; silly.

SHEEPSHANK [shēp'shangk], n. leg of a sheep; (naut.) knot made in a rope so as to shorten it without cutting it.

SHEEPSKIN [shēp'skin], n. skin of a sheep; parchment or leather made from it; rug or coat made from the skin of a sheep with the wool still on.

SHEER (1) [shēer], adj. unmixed; absolute, mere, downright; precipitous; (of fabric) transparent, very thin, diaphanous. SHEER (2), adv. absolutely, utterly; precipitously, straight down without a break. [~OScand.].

SHEER (3), v.i. (naut.) to turn aside; **to s. off**, (coll.) to depart, leave. SHEER (4), n. (naut.) deviation in the course of a ship; upward slope towards the bow or stern of a ship. [Du.].

SHEER-HULK [shēer'hulk], n. hulk of a dismantled ship equipped with cranes and shear-legs for removing heavy cargoes from other ships in port. [SHEAR (1) and HULK].

SHEER-LEGS, see SHEAR-LEGS.

SHEET (1) [shēt], n. rectangular piece of linen or of some cotton mixture, used as bed-clothing; piece of paper; thin expanse of any material; expanse resembling a sheet in appearance; **blank s.**, unbiased mind ready to receive impressions; **clean s.**, unbroken record of good conduct; **news s.**, small newspaper; **winding s.**, shroud. SHEET-COPPER, -IRON, -LEAD, -METAL, copper, iron, lead, metal in s. form. SHEET-MUSIC, music published on unbound sheets. SHEET (2), n. (naut.) chain or cable fixed to the lower part of a sail to control its tension; **three sheets in the wind**, (coll.) very inebriated. SHEET (3), v.t. to provide a s. or sheets for; cover with a s. SHEETING, n. cloth suitable for use as sheets on a bed; any material

---

The accent ′ after a syllable = stress (u-pon′).   The mark ‾ over a vowel = length (ă in made; ō in bone).

in s. form; lining or surface covering of timber; act of making into, act of covering with, sheets. [OE.].

SHEET-ANCHOR [shēt'ang-ker], *n.* (*naut.*) large anchor for use in emergency; (*fig.*) last hope, mainstay in difficulty. [Uncert.].

SHEIK(H) [shēk, shākh], *n.* head of a tribe or family in Arab and Moslem lands; head of an Arab village. [Arab.].

SHEKEL [she'kel], *n.* an old Hebrew measure of weight; old Hebrew coin; (*pl.*) (*slang*) cash, money. [Heb.].

SHEKINAH [ske-kī'nah], *n.* symbolical radiancy or similar manifestation of the presence of God. [Heb.].

SHELDRAKE [shel'drāk], *n.* a wild sea-duck. [ME.].

SHELDUCK [shel'duk], *n.* female of the sheldrake.

SHELF (*pl.* **shelves**) [shelf, shelvz], *n.* narrow flat projection in a cupboard or on a wall where articles may be stood for storing or ornament; ledge on the face of a cliff; flat bank or reef beneath the surface of a river or of the sea. [OE.].

SHELL (1) [shel], *n.* hard outer covering, husk; hard protective outer coat of many fish, crustaceans, molluscs, reptiles, animals, insects and vegetable growths; outer casing of anything, *esp.* when emptied of its contents; tortoiseshell; the outer ear; rough coffin; framework, *esp.* of a building; outer appearance; very light boat for racing; (*milit.*) heavy explosive, metal projectile, often filled with shrapnel, gases etc., fitted with a fuse and fired from guns; (*fig.*) **to retire into one's s.**, to become extremely reserved of manner in company; **to come out of one's s.**, to cease to be reserved. SHELL-EGG, an egg in its s., as distinct from one dried and powdered. SHELL (2), *v.t. and i.* to remove the s., pod, husk etc., from, peel; (*milit.*) bombard with shells; cast off one's s.; **to s. out**, to make a due or demanded payment. [OE.].

SHELLAC (1) [she-lak'], *n.* lac melted, strained and made into thin layers and used to make varnishes etc. SHELLAC (2), *v.t.* to cover with a coating of s. [SHELL (1) and LAC (1)].

SHELLBACK [shel'bak], *n.* (*slang*) old mariner.

SHELL-FISH [shel'fish], *n.* edible crustacean or mollusc having a hard external shell.

SHELLSHOCK (1) [shel'shok], *n.* nervous derangement caused by the patient's having suffered the nearby explosion of a shell. SHELLSHOCK (2), *v.t.* to affect with s.

SHELTER (1) [shel'ter], *n.* state of protection and safety from hurt or danger; that which provides such protection; place of refuge; small erection built as a refuge from danger, cold etc.; strongly protected place intended to be safe against air-raids; **s. marshal**, person appointed to supervise a public air-raid s. SHELTER (2), *v.t. and i.* to give s. to, protect morally or physically; take under one's care; give lodging and entertainment to, *esp.* a benighted or distressed stranger; seek or take s. [Uncert., perhaps OE.].

SHELTIE, SHELTY [shel'ti], *n.* (*Scots*) any small pony, *esp.* a Shetland pony. [~ONorw.].

SHELVE (1) [shelv], *v.t.* to put on a shelf; fit with shelves; cease to use; put out of the way or on one side; get rid of. [SHELVES, *pl.* of SHELF].

SHELVE (2), *v.i.* to slope gently. SHELVING, *adj.* gently sloping. [Uncert.].

SHEPHERD (1) [she'perd], *n.* man who tends sheep; pastor, minister or priest; **the good S.**, Jesus Christ; **s.'s pie**, cottage pie; **s.'s plaid**, woollen fabric with a black-and-white check pattern; any cloth with a similar pattern. SHEPHERD (2), *v.t.* to care for, look after; guide, conduct. [OE.].

SHERATON (1) [she'ra-ton], *n.* piece of furniture in the mode of *Sheraton*, 18th-century cabinet-maker; that mode itself. SHERATON (2), *adj.* in the style of furniture popularized by S.

SHERBET [shur'bet], *n.* oriental drink of sweetened fruit juices, cooled with snow; effervescent beverage made by adding water to a powder containing bicarbonate of soda and tartaric acid, sweetened and flavoured in various ways. [Pers.].

SHERD, see SHARD.

SHERIFF [she'rif], *n.* an honorary official in counties and some cities of the United Kingdom performing certain mainly judicial functions; (*Scots leg.*) judge who presides over the Sheriff Court; (*U.S.*) elected county official responsible for keeping the peace and performing certain judicial functions. [OE.].

SHERRY [she'ri], *n.* a fortified brown wine from southern Spain. SHERRY-COBBLER, drink made of

iced sherry, lemon and sugar. [*Jerez de la Frontera*, Spanish town].

SHEW, see SHOW (1).

SHEWBREAD, see SHOWBREAD.

SHIBBOLETH [shi'bo-leth], *n.* (*O.T.*) word used as a means of distinguishing between Gileadites and Ephraimites; any single tenet, formula or doctrine; arbitrary test of conformity to any given creed. [Heb.].

SHIELD (1) [shēld], *n.* piece of protective armour formerly carried on the left arm in battle; (*fig.*) any source of protection or defence; a defensive covering; object having the conventional shape of a shield, usually triangular with curving sides tapering to the bottom point; sports trophy in this shape; escutcheon. SHIELD (2), *v.t.* to protect, shelter. [~OE.].

SHIELING, see SHEALING.

SHIFT (1) [shift], *v.t. and i.* to remove, rearrange, cause to move; get rid of, transfer; make a move; (of wind) veer, change; depart; be unstable; manage somehow; **to s. for oneself**, to manage one's affairs and face one's difficulties without assistance. SHIFT-KEY, on a typewriter, device to change the position of the platen relative to the keys in order to type capitals etc. SHIFT (2), *n.* a change in position, rearrangement; variation in direction of advance; change of habit, work, mood, rank etc.; a trick or expediency, revised plan or method; group of labourers working in relays with similar groups at the same piece of work; number of hours spent at the job by any such group; † woman's undergarment; (*agric.*) rotation of crops; **to make a s.**, to adopt an expedient; (*coll.*) depart; **to get a s. on**, (*coll.*) to make a start; begin to speed things up; **to make s. with**, to make do, manage with; **to make s. to**, to set about to (do something) despite difficulties; **last s.**, final resource. SHIFTER, *n.* shifty, unreliable person; one who shifts scenery in a theatre. SHIFTING, *adj.* moving, uncertain, variable; adjustable. [OE.].

SHIFTLESS [shift'les], *adj.* displaying no resource.

SHIFTY [shif'ti], *adj.* cunning and resourceful, unreliable, deceitful.

SHILLELAGH [shi-lā'lah], *n.* tough oaken cudgel. [*Shillelagh*, Irish village.].

SHILLING [shi'ling], *n.* silver coin worth twelve pence, one-twentieth of a pound. [OE.].

SHILLY-SHALLY (1) [shi'li-sha-li], *n.* unnecessary delay; hesitation and lack of decision. SHILLY-SHALLY (2), *v.i.* to vacillate. [~*Shall I? Shall I?*].

SHIMMER (1) [shi'mer], *v.i.* to emit or reflect a quivering light; glitter or gleam in an uncertain way. SHIMMER (2), *n.* a trembling, glinting light; gleam. [OE.].

SHIN (1) [shin], *n.* front of the leg bone from knee to ankle; (*coll.*) leg. SHIN (2), *v.t. and i.* to hit on the s.; **to s. up**, to climb. [OE.].

SHINDY [shin'di], *n.* (*slang*) disturbance, row, quarrel. [~HEB.].

SHINE (1) (*pret. and p.pt.* **shone**) [shīn], *v.t. and i.* to glow with light either by emitting it or by reflecting it; be bright and full of lustre; have a fresh appearance of vigour and alertness; be intellectually brilliant, be eminent; excel; polish, render glossy; **to s. at**, to excel at; **to s. out**, to become suddenly bright; be conspicuous. SHINE (2), *n.* glossiness, polish; **to take the s. out of**, to take the excellence from. SHINER, *n.* (*coll.*) new coin. [OE.].

SHINE (3), *n. U.S.* (*coll.*) **to take a s. to**, to take a liking to. [Uncert.].

SHINGLE (1) [shing'gl], *n.* loose pebbles often found in banks on the seashore. [Uncert.].

SHINGLE (2), *n.* small rectangular piece of wood having a greater thickness at one of its edges than at the edge opposite, used for roofing; mode of hairdressing for women. SHINGLE (3), *v.t.* to roof over with shingles; cut (a woman's hair) short and in such a way that it tapers down to the nape of the neck. [ME. from L.].

SHINGLES [shing'glz], *n.(pl.)* disease causing an eruption on the skin above the affected nerve, often encircling the middle of the body. [~L.].

SHINTO [shin'tō], *n.* the original religion of Japan, which inculcates ancestor- and hero-worship; adherent of Shinto. [Jap.].

SHINY [shī'ni], *adj.* bright, glossy.

SHIP (1) [ship], *n.* large ocean-going vessel; crew of a ship; any vessel of transport not necessarily seagoing, as an aeroplane, airship, etc.; **s. of the desert**, camel; **when my s. comes home**, when wealth comes my way; **to take s.**, to embark.

SHIP-BREAKER, one who purchases old ships and breaks them up for the materials. SHIP-BROKER, broker who obtains cargoes for or insurance on ships. SHIP-CANAL, canal big enough for sea-going vessels. SHIP-CHANDLER, one who supplies small necessary stores for a s. SHIP (2) (*pres.pt.* SHIPPING, *pret. and p.pt.* SHIPPED), *v.t. and i.* to transport by s.; put on board a s. for transport; accept (sailors) as crew; (of seamen) enter into an engagement to work aboard s.; **to s. off**, to send away, transport. SHIPPER, *n.* one who sends goods by s. [O.E.].

SHIPMASTER [ship'mah-ster], *n.* captain of a merchant vessel.

SHIPMATE [ship'māt], *n.* sailor who serves with another in the same ship.

SHIPMENT [ship'ment], *n.* act of taking or placing aboard ship for overseas transport; shipload, consignment.

SHIPPEN, SHIPPON [shi'pen], *n.* cowhouse. [O.E.].

SHIPPING [shi'ping], *n.* trade or business of overseas commerce by ship; group of ships; ships in general. SHIPPING-MASTER, official witness of the agreement between captain and crew.

SHIPPON, see SHIPPEN.

SHIPSHAPE [ship'shāp], *adj.* in good trim, as tidy as on board ship.

SHIPWRECK (1) [ship'rek], *n.* loss of or extensive damage to a ship at sea; broken hulk of a ship so damaged, *esp.* when left stranded on a shoal or reef; *(fig.)* any disaster ruinous to an ambition or enterprise. SHIPWRECK (2), *v.t.* to cause (someone) to suffer s.; *(fig.)* ruin (plans, hopes etc.); *pass.* suffer s.

SHIPWRIGHT [ship'rīt], *n.* skilled person or company engaged in the building of ships.

SHIPYARD [ship'yahd], *n.* yard where ships are built.

SHIRE (1) [shīer], *n.* former name for an English, Welsh or Scottish county; second element in the names of most of these counties; **The Shires**, the fox-hunting counties of the Midlands. SHIRE-HORSE, one of a heavily built English breed of draught horses. SHIRE (2), *n.* a shire-horse. [O.E.].

SHIRK [shurk], *v.t. and i.* to evade, avoid, *esp.* duty, danger, difficulty etc. [*Var.* of SHARK (2)].

SHIRR [shur], *n.* pucker or gathering. SHIRRED, *adj.* gathered, ornamented with shirrs. [Uncert.].

SHIRT [shurt], *n.* loose, sleeved undergarment worn by men; any loose garment resembling this; plain blouse for women; **in one's shirt-sleeves**, without one's jacket; **to put one's s. on**, *(fig.)* to back with everything one possesses, give one's fullest support to; **to have one's s. out**, *(slang)* to be in a bad temper; **to get someone's s. up**, to annoy to the point of ill temper; **not to have a s. to one's back**, *(fig.)* to lack even the necessities of life. SHIRT-FRONT, stiffened front of a s. SHIRT-WAIST, (*U.S.*) woman's blouse. SHIRTING, *n.* material for making shirts. SHIRTY, *adj.* (*slang*) angry, peevish. [O.E.].

SHIVER (1) [shi'ver], *v.i.* to quiver and quake, as with cold, fear etc. SHIVER (2), *n.* tremor; trembling of one's body when cold or excited etc.; **the shivers**, repeated attacks of shivering; nervous revulsion; horrified fear. [M.E.].

SHIVER (3), *n.* fragment, splinter or flake. SHIVER (4), *v.t. and i.* to break into fragments; **s. my timbers**, an expression of surprise or protest. [M.E.].

SHOAL (1) [shōl], *n.* large massed group of individuals, school or bank of fish; **shoals of**, (*coll.*) plenty of. SHOAL (2), *v.i.* to move or swim in a s. or shoals. [O.E.].

SHOAL (3), *adj.* shallow. SHOAL (4), *n.* shallow place in a river or the sea, such as is caused by a deposit of sand; *(fig.)* pitfall, danger. SHOAL (5), *v.i.* (of a river or sea) become shallow. [*Var.* of SHALLOW (2)].

SHOCK (1) [shok], *n.* sudden violent impact or jolting producing a disturbance or overthrow of stability; sharp impact of opposing forces, violent onset between two opposing bodies of troops, earthquake; strong emotional excitement or reaction due to some unexpected or violent circumstances; collapse of the nervous system due to some violent or sudden experience; such an experience itself; physical and nervous disturbance due to the passage of an electric current through an animal body. SHOCK-ABSORBER, device attached to the springs of a vehicle to even out the vibrations set up while the vehicle is in motion. SHOCK-PROOF, proof against electric shocks or violent impact; *(fig.)* inured to emotional disturbance. SHOCK (2), *adj.* employing, employed for, or associated with, violent physical action;

s. tactics, tactics of violent onslaught in overwhelming force; **s. troops**, troops used for such tactics. SHOCK (3), *v.t. and i.* to cause to suffer a s.; cause to oscillate by a violent impact; overwhelm with a sudden and violent emotion, cause great surprise to; give grave offence to the moral opinion of. SHOCKER, *n.* sensational novelette with a strong story, usually of crime and horror. [Fr.].

SHOCK (4), *n.* a heap of twelve corn sheaves. [M.E.].

SHOCK (5), *n.* a mass of unkempt hair. SHOCK (6), *adj.* having the nature of a s. of hair. SHOCK-HEADED, having a shaggy, luxuriant head of hair. [Uncert.].

SHOCKING [sho'king], *adj.* causing repugnance, scandalous, revolting; of poor quality.

SHOD [shod], *pret. and p.pt.* of SHOE (2).

SHODDY (1) [sho'di], *n.* coarse fabric made of worn-out woollen cloth unwoven, combed out and rewoven; fibre from which this is made; *(fig.)* cheap article made in imitation of something more valuable. SHODDY (2), *adj.* made of s.; (of material objects) cheap, inferior in quality; (of conduct) mean.

SHOE (1) [shōō], *n.* a covering for the foot, usually of leather, distinguished from a boot in that it does not cover the ankle; crescent-shaped strip of metal nailed to the underside of a horse's hoof; anything resembling a shoe in shape; holder for a brake block, brake block; **to wait for a dead man's shoes**, to wait for someone to die in the hope of obtaining his position; **to die in one's shoes**, to die at work; **another pair of shoes**, a different set of circumstances; **to stand in another man's shoes**, to enjoy the same fortune as someone else; succeed to another man's honours, authority, difficulties etc.; **to step into someone's shoes**, to succeed to someone's position; **to shake in one's shoes**, *(fig.)* to be apprehensive, nervous; **to feel where the s. pinches**, to have experienced grief etc. and so be in a position to sympathize with others. SHOE-HORN, curved blade which, when placed in the back of the s., enables the foot to slip into it more easily. SHOE-LEATHER, leather for making shoes. SHOE (2) (*pret. and p.pt.* SHOD), *v.t.* to furnish (a horse) with shoes; furnish (a stick etc.) with a ferrule; fit a wheel with an iron tyre. [O.E.].

SHOEBLACK [shōō'blak], *n.* one who cleans boots and shoes for a living; black preparation for cleaning shoes.

SHOGUN [shō'gōōn], *n.* former Japanese military chief of great power. [Jap.].

SHONE [shon], *pret. and p.pt.* of SHINE (1).

SHOO (1) [shōō], *int.* begone! SHOO (2), *n.* cry intended to frighten intruders, *esp.* animals or birds. SHOO (3), *v.t.* to make a s.; **to s. away**, to frighten off. [Imitative].

SHOOK [shōōk], *pret.* of SHAKE (1).

SHOOT (1) (*pret. and p.pt.* shot) [shōōt], *v.t.* to hurl, throw or propel swiftly and suddenly forward; dart out, send forth in flashes; project (a missile); discharge (a gun, rifle etc.); fasten (a bolt); wound or kill with an arrow or bullet; traverse rapidly by sliding down, pass over (rapids etc.) in a boat; *v.i.* to move rapidly, flash forth; (of a pain) stab; discharge a fire-arm; practise the sport of shooting at game; *(football etc.)* aim a shot at the goal; *(cricket)* (of the ball) leave the ground with increased speed at the first bounce, travel along the ground after first touching it; **to s. up**, to rise suddenly up; grow very rapidly; fire at persons with the intent to kill or injure them; **to s. about**, to dart hither and thither; **to s. ahead**, to outdistance competitors; **to s. down**, to kill with fire-arms, massacre; **to s. off**, to depart suddenly; deflect suddenly from a previous line of advance; **to s. home**, to hit the mark; make a penetrating observation; **to s. beside the mark**, *(fig.)* to miss the point; **to s. a line**, (*slang*) to boast; **to s. the moon**, to remove by night from a rented dwelling to avoid paying the rent; **to s. one's** (*last*) **bolt**, to exhaust one's capabilities; **to s. a scene**, to film a scene. SHOOT (2), *n.* a sprout just appearing above the ground, new growth on a plant; chute; shooting party; land over which game may be shot. SHOOTER, *n.* one who shoots; (*cricket*) ball which keeps low and does not bounce. [O.E.].

SHOOTING [shōō'ting], *n.* action of one who, or that which, shoots; pursuit of game with fire-arms; land over which game may be shot. SHOOTING-BOX, small house with good s. land round it. SHOOTING-GALLERY, miniature shooting-range. SHOOTING-RANGE, place for practice at s. SHOOTING-STAR, star like a meteor which flashes across the sky.

SHOOTING-STICK, walking-stick convertible into a seat.

SHOP (1) [shop], *n.* room or building where retail trade is conducted; workshop; (*slang*) any building; **to talk s.**, to discuss one's business; **all over the s.**, in great disorder; **to set up s.**, to commence a retail business; **to shut (up) s.**, to close (one's business); (*fig.*) desist from some activity; **closed s.**, see CLOSED. SHOP-ASSISTANT, -BOY, -GIRL, salesman (or woman), boy, girl, working in a retail s. SHOP-SOILED, *adj.* faded, soiled or damaged as a result of being displayed or handled. SHOP-STEWARD, trades union official in a workshop. SHOP-WALKER, one who walks about a large s. to guide customers and see that the assistants attend to them properly. SHOP (2), *v.t.* (*slang*) to cause to be put in prison by informing; *v.i.* to visit shops to make purchases. SHOPKEEPER, *n.* proprietor of a retail s. SHOPLIFTER, SHOPLIFTING, *n.* one who steals, act of stealing, from a s. when it is open. SHOPPER, *n.* one who visits shops to make purchases. SHOPPING, *n.* act of making purchases in a s.; goods purchased at a s. [O.E.].

SHORE (1) [shaw(r)], *n.* that part of the land immediately adjacent to the sea or to a lake, estuary or large river; (*rhetorical*) land in general; **on s.**, ashore, on the land; moving towards the land; **in s.**, (*naut.*) near to the s. SHORELESS, *adj.* having no s. or coast; boundless. [ME.].

SHORE (2), *n.* large, heavy supporting prop. SHORE (3), *v.t.* to support with shores. [ME.].

SHORELING [shaw'ling], *n.* a newly-shorn sheep.

SHORN [shawn], *p.pt. of* SHEAR (1).

SHORT (1) [shawt], *adj.* of no great length or extension; of no great height; brief in duration; concise, curt; of reduced amount, not up to standard; scarce; inadequately supplied; (*coll.*) inadequately supplied with money; almost exhausted; (*comm.*) (of a bill etc.) maturing at an early date; (of pastry) crumbly; (*pros.*) not long, unstressed; **s. ball**, (*cricket*) ball bowled so as to pitch further than usual from the wicket; **s. commons**, low rations; **s. cut**, a route taking less time than a more orthodox one; **s. head**, the amount, less than the length of its head, by which a racehorse or greyhound reaches the winning-post ahead of the next horse or greyhound; (*fig.*) (*coll.*) a bare margin; **s. list**, list of selected candidates from which a final choice is to be made; **s. measure**, less than the stated quantity; **s. shrift**, brusque attention; **s. story**, piece of fiction dealing with a small and compact theme, much shorter than a novel; **s. wave**, (*radio*) a wavelength below 100 metres; **s. weight**, less than the stated amount according to weight; **to make s. work of**, to consume, perform etc. rapidly; **nothing s. of**, quite, truly. SHORT-DATED, (*comm.*) maturing early. SHORT-HANDED, understaffed. SHORT-LEG, (*cricket*) position close in on the leg-side; the man fielding there. SHORT-LIST, (*coll.*) to place (a candidate) on a s. list. SHORT-LIVED, not surviving for long. SHORT-RIB, a false rib. SHORT-SEA, a choppy sea. SHORT-SLIP, (*cricket*) position in the slips close in to the wicket; the man fielding there. SHORT-SUITED, (*cards*) having a relatively small number of cards of a particular suit. SHORT-TEMPERED, irritable, easily annoyed. SHORT-TERM, having in view only a s. period. SHORT-WAISTED, (of persons) not long in the waist; (of clothes) cut so as to give the impression of a s. waist. SHORT-WINDED, subject to shortness of breath. SHORT (2), *n.* anything which is s., s. things or persons in general; a s. film; (*elect.*) a s. circuit; (*pl.*) s. trousers ending just above the knees; **the long and the s. of it**, the net result; **for s.**, by way of abbreviation. SHORT (3), *adv.* in a s. manner, shortly; abruptly; **s. of**, except; **to fall s.**, to be inadequate; **to fall s. of**, not to come up to the standard of; **to cut (someone) s.**, to interrupt in speech; **to run s.**, to approach exhaustion; **to stop s.**, to come to, cause to come to, a sudden cessation; **to stop s. of (something)**, to do everything else except . . . . SHORT (4), *v.t.* (*elect.*) to cause a s. circuit; *v.i.* to become s.-circuited. SHORTLY, *adv.* soon; briefly; curtly. [O.E.].

SHORTAGE [shaw'tij], *n.* lack, deficiency; extent of this.

SHORTBREAD, SHORTCAKE [shawt'bred, 'kāk], *n.* brittle kind of cake made of flour, sugar and butter.

SHORT CIRCUIT (1) [shawt-sur'kit], *n.* a path, other than that intended, taken by an electric current; closed electric circuit offering negligible resistance to the passage of a current. SHORT-CIRCUIT (2), *v.t. and i.* to cause (an electric current)

to take a s.; (*fig*) adopt briefer methods for in place of orthodox procedure.

SHORTCOMING [shawt'ku-ming], *n.* deficiency, failure to meet a required standard; an imperfection; a foible.

SHORTEN [shaw'ten], *v.t. and i.* to reduce in extent, in length or time; abbreviate, cut down; become shorter; dress (a child) in shorter clothes.

SHORTHAND [shawt'hand], *n.* system of rapid writing based on the substitution of symbols or contractions for sounds, words or phrases; stenography.

SHORTHORN [shawt'hawn], *n.* a breed of cattle with short horns.

SHORTS, see SHORT (2).

SHORT SIGHT [shawt-sīt'], *n.* defect of vision by which distant objects are seen less clearly, and near objects more clearly, than is normal. SHORT-SIGHTED, *adj.* suffering from s. sight; myopic; (*fig.*) lacking in imagination, unable to anticipate future circumstances.

SHOT (1) [shot], *n.* missile suitable to be projected from a gun, rifle, pistol etc.; one of the small leaden pellets fired from a sporting gun, a quantity of these; sound or act of shooting with a fire-arm; attempt to hit with some sort of missile; a stroke at a game, *esp.* billiards, cricket, tennis or football; (*coll.*) an injected dose of a drug; (*mining*) a charge of explosive for blasting; explosion of this; one who shoots; (*cinema*) the photographing of a scene in a film; scene so photographed; **dead s.**, man who never misses; **in s.**, in range of fire; **out of s.**, out of range of fire; **s. in the dark**, random attempt; **to have a s. at**, to make an attempt; **s. in the locker**, reserve of ability, ready cash; **like a s.**, very rapidly; with alacrity; **not by a long s.**, (*coll.*) by no means, not at all; **big s.**, (*U.S. coll.*) important person. POT-SHOT, easy s. that could not possibly miss; a bird in flight. SHOT-PROOF, impenetrable by s. SHOT-TOWER, tower in which molten lead is dropped from the top through a sieve so that it falls in round pellets at the bottom. SHOT (2), *n.* contribution, share of payment; **to pay one's s.**, to pay one's share of the expenses. [O.E.].

SHOT (3), *adj.* fashioned so that the colour changes according to the angle from which viewed; (*fig.*) commingled. SHOT (4), *pret. and p.pt. of* SHOOT (1).

SHOTGUN [shot'gun], *n.* sporting gun which discharges shot, fowling-piece.

SHOULD [shood], *pret. of* SHALL, *expressing probability, intention and obligation, and used in forming the conditional mood.* [O.E.].

SHOULDER (1) [shōl'der], *n.* either of the two projections on the body of an animal below or behind the neck from which depend the arms or forelegs; (*butchering*) upper part of an animal's foreleg; anything resembling a s.; **to put one's s. to the wheel**, to make a vigorous effort; **s. to s.**, united, together; **to give the cold s. to**, to act unsocially towards, avoid. SHOULDER-BELT, belt which passes over one s., baldrick. SHOULDER-BLADE, -BONE, one of the two large flat triangular bones of the s.; the scapula. SHOULDER-KNOT, knot of ribbon or lace worn on the s. in certain uniforms. SHOULDER-STRAP, length of leather or other material attached to a bag etc. for carrying it over the s.; (*milit.*) small strap extending from the base of the collar to the point of the s. in officers' uniforms and bearing the badge of rank; tape or ribbon supporting garments from the s. SHOULDER (2), *v.t.* to place on the shoulders ready to carry; (*fig.*) undertake; push, make a path for oneself by pushing, with the s. [O.E.].

SHOUT (1) [showt], *n.* loud vocal utterance, outcry; sudden cry. SHOUT (2), *v.t. and i.* to emit a s., call; speak in a very loud voice, bawl; utter very loudly; **to s. down**, to drown someone else's words by speaking more loudly; **to s. at**, to demand attention. [ME.].

SHOVE (1) [shuv], *v.t. and i.* to push or jostle roughly; (*coll.*) put or place; **to s. off**, to push away from the shore in a boat; (*coll.*) depart. SHOVE-HALFPENNY, *n.* the game of shovel-board. SHOVE (2), *n.* action of shoving. [O.E.].

SHOVEL (1) [shu'vel], *n.* spade-like implement used to move loose hard material; any similar implement. SHOVEL (2), *adj.* resembling, pertaining to, a s.; **s. hat**, flat clerical hat. SHOVEL (3) (*pres.pt.* SHOVEL-LING, *pret. and p.pt.* SHOVELLED), *v.t. and i.* to use a s., move with a s.; **to s. in**, to collect quickly, gain rapid possession of. SHOVELLER, *n.* one who shovels; a broad-billed freshwater duck. [O.E.].

SHOVEL-BOARD, SHUFFLE-BOARD [shu'vel-bawd], *n.* game played by sliding coins along a marked board; board on which this is played; similar game played on the deck of a ship with disks moved by cues across chalk-marked divisions.

SHOW (1), **SHEW** (*pret.* showed, shewed, *p.pt.* shown, showed, shewn) [shō], *v.t. and i.* to present to view, allow to be seen; exhibit; offer proof of, explain; guide to; be or become visible; **to s. off,** to display, *esp.* in an extravagant manner; **to s. out,** to guide to the exit; **to s. up,** to reveal, *esp.* that which has been wrongly hidden; expose the character of; hand in (work); (*coll.*) appear; **to s.** (someone) **the door,** to give a broad hint to leave; **to s. one's hand,** to reveal one's intentions; **to s. fight,** to display an inclination to fight, resist. SHOW (2), *n.* display or exhibition; something displayed or exhibited; spectacle, object of interest; anything presenting itself to the view; (*slang*) any institution or organization; theatrical performance; pomp, worthless ceremony; false appearance, pretence; sign, trace, appearance; **s. of hands,** vote taken by raising hands. SHOW-BILL, broadsheet advertisement, play-bill. SHOW-CASE, case containing articles for exhibition. SHOW-GIRL, actress engaged rather for her beauty than for histrionic ability. SHOW-PLACE, place much resorted to by tourists because of its visual attractions. SHOW (3), *adj.* (*coll.*) fit for display, excellent; **s. piece,** piece of work fit for exhibition. SHOWING, *n.* act of presenting to view; one in a series of identical cinema programmes. [OE.].

SHOWBREAD, SHEWBREAD [shō'bred], *n.* (*hist.*) twelve loaves placed by a Jewish priest on the golden table in the sanctuary as an offering to God.

SHOWDOWN [shō'down], *n.* (*cards*) the laying down of everybody's cards on the table; deliberate disclosure of their intentions by the conflicting parties in a dispute; open conflict; exposure.

SHOWER (1) [shower], *n.* light or brief fall of rain, snow, hail etc.; a sprinkling; massed and copious flood or discharge of missiles, liquids, dust or falling objects of any kind; a rapid succession of things arriving; s.-bath. SHOWER-BATH, bath in which water is sprinkled in a s. from above. SHOWER (2), *v.t. and i.* to discharge in a s.; arrive in a s.; bestow copiously and constantly. [OE.].

SHOWMAN [shō'man], *n.* exhibitor of a show; one skilled in making an impression on his audience.

SHOWMANSHIP, *n.* skill as a showman.

SHOWN [shōn], *p.pt. of* SHOW (1).

SHOWROOM [shō'room], *n.* room where wares are exhibited for sale.

SHOWY [shō'i], *adj.* pretentious, ostentatious, gaudy.

SHRANK [shrangk], *pret. of* SHRINK.

SHRAPNEL [shrap'nel], *n.* shell which explodes and scatters pieces of metal and bullets in all directions; the pieces so scattered. [General *Shrapnel,* its inventor].

SHRED (1) [shred], *n.* small fragment, strip torn or cut off; (*fig.*) particle, fragment. SHRED (2) (*pret.* SHREDDED, *p.pt.* SHREDDED, SHRED), *v.t. and i.* to tear or cut into shreds; flake, break up into shreds. [OE.].

SHREW [shrōō], *n.* nagging, ill-tempered woman; shrew-mouse. SHREW-MOUSE (*pl.* SHREW-MICE), small insectivore resembling a mouse in appearance. [OE.].

SHREWD [shrōōd], *adj.* sharp-witted, cunning, sagacious. [ME.].

SHREWISH [shrōō'ish], *adj.* of, or like, a shrew; ill-tempered.

SHRIEK (1) [shrēk], *v.t. and i.* to utter a sudden, shrill, piercing cry, scream; utter in shrieking tones; **to s. with laughter,** to laugh with loud and uncontrolled mirth; laugh hysterically. SHRIEK (2), *n.* sudden shrill and piercing cry of alarm, pain or laughter; shrill sound. [ME.].

SHRIEVALTY [shrē'val-ti], *n.* office, dignity or jurisdiction of a sheriff. [~SHERIFF].

SHRIFT [shrift], *n.* confession and absolution; **short s.,** (*fig.*) brief, inadequate attention, curt treatment. [OE.].

SHRIKE [shrīk], *n.* bird of the genus *Lanius.* [OScand.].

SHRILL (1) [shril], *adj.* (of a sound) high-pitched, sharp and penetrating; (*fig.*) complaining and insistent. SHRILL (2), *v.t. and i.* to utter a s. cry; make a s. sound. [ME.].

SHRIMP (1) [shrimp], *n.* small crustacean with a long tail found about the English coast and used for food; (*fig.*) a little person, any little thing; pale pink

colour like that of a boiled shrimp. SHRIMP (2), *v.i.* to go fishing for shrimps. [ME.].

SHRINE (1) [shrīn], *n.* ornamental casket containing holy objects, relics etc.; tomb of a martyr or saint; holy place; object of pilgrimage; any place or object rendered precious by its associations. SHRINE (2), *v.t.* to enshrine. [OE. from L.].

SHRINK (*pret.* shrank, *p.pt.* shrunk) [shringk], *v.t. and i.* to become less in size; cause to become smaller; cower; **to s. away,** to diminish gradually; **to s.** (away), (back) **from,** to draw back from, withdraw from. SHRINKAGE, *n.* contraction in bulk or area; act of shrinking. [OE.].

SHRIVE (*pret.* shrove, *p.pt.* shriven) [shrīv], *v.t.* to hear the confession of and give absolution to. [OE.].

SHRIVEL [shri'vel], *v.t. and i.* to wrinkle up, shrink; cause to contract and wrinkle. [Unkn.].

SHROUD (1) [shrowd], *n.* burial cloth, winding-sheet; (*fig.*) anything which envelops, covers or conceals; (*pl.*) (*naut.*) set of stays connecting the masthead with the bulwarks of a ship, ship's rigging. SHROUD (2), *v.t.* to wrap in a s.; (*fig.*) cover up, conceal. [OE.].

SHROVE-TIDE [shrōv'tīd], *n.* the four days before Ash Wednesday. SHROVE TUESDAY, *n.* the last day of S., the day before Ash Wednesday. [~SHRIVE].

SHRUB (1) [shrub], *n.* low, tree-like plant or bush. [ME.].

SHRUB (2), *n.* drink of fruit juice, usually lemon juice, mixed with sugar and rum. [Arab.].

SHRUBBERY [shru'be-ri], *n.* plantation of shrubs.

SHRUG (1) [shrug], *v.t.* (of the shoulders) to raise or hunch up a little to express doubt, indifference or disapproval. SHRUG (2), *n.* act of shrugging the shoulders. [Unkn.].

SHRUNK [shrungk], *p.pt. of* SHRINK. SHRUNKEN, *adj.* shrivelled, contracted, withered.

SHUCK [shuk], *n.* husk, pod; (*pl.*) (*U.S.*) nonsense ! [Unkn.].

SHUDDER (1) [shu'der], *v.i.* to tremble violently; shake with disgust, terror or excessive chill etc.; (*fig.*) shake or vibrate spasmodically. SHUDDER (2), *n.* intense trembling expressing disgust, terror or cold; spasmodic vibration. [ME.].

SHUFFLE (1) [shu'fl], *v.t. and i.* to walk scraping the feet on the ground without lifting them; fidget in one's seat; move (something) about in a purposeless fashion; mix playing cards before a game; mix promiscuously and incongruously; act or speak evasively; **to s. off,** to depart with a shuffling walk; wriggle out of; **to s. out of,** to avoid by devious means. SHUFFLE-BOARD, see SHOVEL-BOARD. SHUFFLE (2), *n.* action of shuffling; act of mixing playing cards etc.; act of shuffling the feet; act of fidgeting in one's chair; a step in dancing; a trick, lie. SHUFFLER, *n.* one who shuffles; trickster. SHUFFLINGLY, *adv.* evasively, slyly. [LGerm.].

SHUN [shun], *v.t.* to avoid, have nothing to do with. [OE.].

SHUNT (1) [shunt], *v.t. and i.* to divert, switch off on to another track, turn (rolling-stock) on a railway from one track to another; provide an alternative track for (an electric current); (*coll.*) push aside, shelve; **to s. off,** (*coll.*) to depart or cause to depart. SHUNT (2), *n.* act of shunting or being shunted; alternative circuit for an electric current; switch by which an electric current may be diverted over such a circuit. SHUNTER, *n.* person employed in shunting on a railway. [Unkn.].

SHUT (1) (*pres.pt.* shutting, *pret. and p.pt.* shut) [shut], *v.t.* (of a door, gate, window, lid etc.) to close; place in such a position that it blocks the aperture which it commands; cover with a lid; (of a drawer) thrust home so that the interior is not accessible; (of an aperture etc.) block with something; fold up; encase with an outer covering; lock up; bring to an end; *v.i.* to close of its own accord; be capable of being closed; **to s. off,** to cut off, separate from; **to s. down,** to close by a downward movement; bring to an end, close down (a business etc.); **to s. out,** to keep outside by shutting, exclude; hide from view; **to s. up,** to s. completely, lock up (a building), fold up into a closed position; store in a closed receptacle; confine in close quarters; seal, close permanently; (*coll.*) cease speaking; **to s. one's eyes to,** to ignore, refuse to consider; **to s. one's mouth,** to keep silent; **to s. someone else's mouth,** to compel silence. SHUT (2), *adj.* closed; **to be s. of,** to be rid of. [OE.].

SHUTTER (1) [shu'ter], *n.* something which shuts; hinged outer covering of wood for a window; (*phot.*) small movable screen in a camera which makes the exposure. SHUTTER (2), *v.t.* to fit or close with a s.

SHUTTLE (1) [shu'tl], *n.* (*weaving*) small instrument which carries the weft thread and is shot to and fro between the warp in a loom; sliding thread-holder which carries the under-thread in a sewing-machine; **s. train**, train running up and down a short branch line; **s. service**, service operating to and fro on one line. SHUTTLE (2), *v.i.* to move backwards and forwards like a s. [OE.].

SHUTTLECOCK [shu'tl-kok], *n.* ball of cork fitted with evenly spaced feathers, used in the game of badminton.

SHY (1) [shī], *adj.* timid, nervous, self-conscious. SHY (2), *v.i.* (of a horse) to swerve nervously aside; **to s. at,** (of a horse) to swerve nervously away from; (of persons) be unwilling to face or do (something), have scruples about. SHY (3), *n.* (of a horse) act of shying. SHYER, *n.* horse given to shying. [OE.].

SHY (4), *v.t. and i.* (*coll.*) to throw. SHY (5) (*pl.* SHIES), *n.* (*coll.*) a throw; (*coll.*) an attempt. [Unkn.].

SI [sē], *n.* (*mus.*) in the sol-fa system the seventh note of the diatonic scale, called also te. [Invented].

SIAMESE (1) [sī-a-mēz'], *adj.* pertaining to Siam; **S. cat,** breed of cat from S.; **S. twins,** twins born imperfectly separated. SIAMESE (2), *n.* inhabitant, language, of Siam.

SIBILANCE [sī'bi-lans], *n.* condition or quality of being sibilant.

SIBILANT (1) [sī'bi-lant], *adj.* hissing; uttered with a hissing sound. SIBILANT (2), *n.* a hissing sound; (*phon.*) sound produced by the rapid passage of air between the raised tip of the tongue and the upper teeth or the alveolar ridge. SIBILATE, *v.t.* to utter with a hiss, make a hissing sound. [L.].

SIC [sik], *adv.* thus (usually printed in brackets after a word or phrase quoted which is, or looks as if it is, a mistake). [L.].

SICK (1) [sik], *adj.* in bad health, suffering from a disease or illness, ill; vomiting, tending to vomit; (*coll.*) disgusted, exasperated, disappointed, weary; **s. at heart,** dejected; **s. for,** longing for; **to be s.,** to vomit; be ill; **to look s.,** (*coll.*) to have a look of disgust, annoyance etc.; **s. benefit,** allowance made to a worker or member of a benefit club when s.; **s. quarters,** infirmary in a barracks or camp; **s. room,** room where a person is lying ill. SICK-BAY, (*naut.*) that part of a ship reserved for s. persons. SICK-BED, bed on which a s. person is lying. SICK-LEAVE, leave granted for medical reasons. SICK-LIST, list of s. persons' names. SICK-PARADE, formal attendance of service personnel for medical attention. SICK (2), *n.(pl.)* s. persons. SICKISH, *adj.* inclined to be s. or sickened. [OE.].

SICKEN [si'ken], *v.t. and i.* to become ill; show signs that one has an illness coming on; nauseate, cause to vomit; cause a sense of disgust or nausea; **to s. of,** to grow weary of. SICKENER, *n.* something causing disgust. SICKENING, *adj.* disgusting, nauseating; (*coll.*) annoying. [*Prec.*].

SICKLE [si'kl], *n.* small reaping-hook. [OE.].

SICKLY [sik'li], *adj.* inclined to be ill, inclined to vomit; constantly ailing; having the appearance of being unwell, pale; (*fig.*) feeble; provoking a sense of nausea; mawkish.

SIDE (1) [sīd], *n.* a surface or boundary not at the front or back; lateral part or substance of anything; material forming the external surface of an object; either surface of a leaf or sheet of anything; space or volume etc. lying to the right or left of a division; (of the human body) that part of the body between either hip and the ribs above it; line of descent by one parent; one of two opposing parties or points of view; slope of a hill or mountain; bank of a river, lake or sea; (*fig.*) way of approach, point of view; (*coll.*) arrogant or patronizing manner; (*billiards*) sideways rotation of the cue-ball in addition to its forward rotation; **to put (something) on one s.,** to shelve, refuse to deal with, something; **to put on s.,** to behave in a pretentious manner; **to take sides,** to go into dispute, divide into factions; **to take sides with,** to join the party of (in a dispute); **on all sides, on every s.,** everywhere; **from every s.,** from every direction; **s. by s.,** together, unitedly; **on the s.,** as a s. line (often involving the idea of secrecy or dishonesty). ON-SIDE, (*football*) in such a position in relation to opposing players on the field as not to transgress the laws of the game, not off-s.; (*cricket*) the leg-side. SIDE-DISH, extra course in a meal. SIDE-DRUM, small drum. SIDE-KICK, (*U.S. slang*) assistant, (junior) partner. SIDE-ON, *adj. and adv.* with one s. striking

something. SIDE-SCREEN, detachable curtain for the s. of an open motor-car. SIDE-SPLITTING, so funny as to make the sides ache with laughter. SIDE-TABLE, table placed at the s. SIDE-VIEW, view from one s. SIDE (2), *adj.* pertaining to, belonging to, fitting, a s.; **s. line,** subsidiary activity or interest. SIDE (3), *v.t.* to s. with, take the part of in a dispute. [OE.].

SIDEBAND [sīd'band], *n.* (*radio*) group of waves slightly higher or slightly lower in frequency than the wavelength of a transmitter.

SIDEBOARD [sīd'bawd], *n.* piece of dining-room furniture consisting essentially of a shelf and cupboard; board exhibiting destination, advertisements etc. on the side of a vehicle; (*pl.*) (*coll.*) short side whiskers.

SIDECAR [sīd'kah(r)], *n.* small carriage attached at the side to a motor-cycle; kind of cocktail.

SIDELIGHT [sīd'līt], *n.* light from the side; small light on the side of a vehicle; (*fig.*) information obtained by approaching a subject from an unusual or special angle.

SIDELING (1) [sīd'ling], *adj.* (*archaic*) moving sideways; sloping. SIDELING (2), *adv.* sideways, obliquely.

SIDELONG [sīd'long], *adj.* aimed or moving in a sideways direction.

SIDEREAL [sī-dēer'i-al], *adj.* pertaining to, or concerned with, the stars; measured by the stars. [L.].

SIDE-SADDLE (1) [sīd'sa-dl], *n.* saddle for women on which they sit with both feet on the same side of the horse. SIDE-SADDLE (2), *adv.* on a s.

SIDESHOW [sīd'shō], *n.* subordinate exhibition or display; (*coll.*) any subsidiary or subordinate matter.

SIDESLIP (1) [sīd'slip], *n.* a skid to one side. SIDE-SLIP (2), *v.i.* to skid sideways; (of an aeroplane) slip sideways towards the inside of a turn.

SIDESMAN (*pl.* sidesmen) [sīdz'man], *n.* assistant to a churchwarden.

SIDESTEP (1) [sīd'step], *n.* a step to the side. SIDE-STEP (2), *v.t. and i.* to make a s., avoid by making a s.

SIDESTROKE [sīd'strōk], *n.* a stroke in swimming made when swimming on the side.

SIDETRACK (1) [sīd'trak], *n.* a track at the side. SIDETRACK (2), *v.t.* to divert; cause to converse about something other than intended.

SIDEWALK [sīd'wawk], *n.* path at the side; (*U.S.*) pavement.

SIDEWAYS [sīd'wāz], *adv.* towards one side and neither forwards nor backwards, laterally.

SIDEWHISKERS [sīd'wis-kerz], *n.(pl.)* whiskers on the face between the temples and the jaws.

SIDING [sī'ding], *n.* track at the side of the main line of a railway where rolling-stock may be shunted.

SIDLE [sī'dl], *v.i.* to walk sideways, walk in a shy, nervous manner. [~SIDE].

SIEGE [sēj], *n.* (*milit.*) the surrounding of a town, castle or fortified place by a hostile force with a view to its capture; condition of besieging or being besieged; **to lay s. to,** to besiege; **to raise a s.,** to cease in an attempt to take a city, castle etc. by s.; **to stand s.,** to be besieged. SIEGE-TRAIN, equipment necessary to conduct a s. [OFr.].

SIENNA [si-e'nah], *n.* a ferruginous earth pigment; the colour produced by it, a rich brown. [*Siena*, Italy, where found].

SIERRA [si-āer'rah], *n.* a jagged mountain range. [Span.].

SIESTA [si-es'tah], *n.* a sleep taken in warm countries during the hot early afternoon. [Span.].

SIEVE (1) [siv], *n.* wire mesh stretched over a frame through which a broken substance may be shaken to separate the larger from the smaller pieces; any similar device; (*fig.*) someone incapable of keeping a secret; **head like a s.,** bad memory. SIEVE (2), *v.t.* to sift in a s. [OE.].

SIFT [sift], *v.t.* to shake through a sieve or sprinkler; pass through anything as if through a sieve; examine very critically. [OE.].

SIGH (1) [sī], *v.t. and i.* to make a sigh; utter with a sigh; utter a sound like a sigh; **to s. for,** to long for; grieve over. SIGH (2), *n.* a long, slow intaking and exhaling of breath, expressive of weariness or sorrow; sound accompanying this; any similar sound. [ME. from OE.].

SIGHT (1) [sīt], *n.* faculty of the eye to see, act or power of seeing; vision; glimpse, view; presentation of something to the view; range of vision; (*fig.*) point of view, judgment; something seen, something worth seeing, something unusually conspicuous; any

---

ōō is pronounced as in food; ŏŏ as in hood; th as in *th*ink; TH as in *th*at; zh as in azure. ~ = related to.

device helping to direct the vision, small projection on the barrel of a gun to aid the user to get the weapon in line with the target; (*dial.*) great amount; (*coll.*) a comic figure; **long s.**, power of long-ranged vision; **short or near s.**, see SHORT S.; **second s.**, faculty of supernatural vision; **in one's s.**, in one's opinion; **the sights**, places of note which every visitor should see; **at s., on s., at first s.**, as soon as seen; according to first impressions; **to keep s. of**, to keep in view; (*fig.*) keep in mind; **to keep in s.**, to remain visible; have constantly in mind; **to lose s. of**, to be no longer able to see; forget. SIGHT-READER, -READING, one who can read, faculty of reading (music, shorthand etc.), at s. SIGHT-SEEING, -SEER, act of travelling, one who travels about to see **sights**. SIGHT (2), *v.t.* to see; approach near to (so as to see); look at through a telescope etc.; equip (a gun, **rifle** etc.) with sights; aim a gun or rifle by means of the sight(s) on it; aim a gun or rifle at, using the **sight(s)** on it. SIGHTED, *adj.* equipped with sight(s); trained on a target; enjoying the faculty of s. SIGHTER, *n.* (*shooting*) preliminary shot at a target to help in estimating aim. [O.E.].

SIGN (1) [sīn], *n.* that by which something is shown or represented; token; nod or gesture indicative of a wish or command; miracle; evidence or proof; something hung out for notice; a visible representation; mark of distinction; signpost; symptom, indication; symbol; constellation occupying one of the twelve divisions of the Zodiac; (*math.*) mark indicative of operation; (*mus.*) a character. SIGN-BOARD, board on which a man announces his name, or that of his house or trade. SIGN-MANUAL, signature appended to a document, *esp.* by a sovereign or important state official. SIGN (2), *v.t.* to mark by means of a s.; put one's signature to; signify; indicate by a s.; *v.i.* to make a signal; **to s. on**, to write one's signature, register in a new employment. [Fr. from L.].

SIGNAL (1) [sig'nal], *n.* a sign; sign agreed upon as denoting some special thing; device for distant communication; notice giving information or warning, semaphore used on railways to show whether or not the track is free; message; transmission which is received. SIGNAL-BOOK, book which gives a list of signals and their meanings. SIGNAL-BOX, hut from which railway signals are worked. SIGNAL-GUN, gun firing a s. SIGNAL-POST, post on which signals are shown. SIGNAL (2), *adj.* singular, remarkable; pertaining to signals. SIGNAL (3) (*pres.pt.* SIGNALLING, *pret. and p.pt.* SIGNALLED), *v.t.* to announce by s.; make signals; *v.i.* to communicate by signalling. SIGNALLY, *adv.* in a remarkable way, extraordinarily. SIGNALMAN (*pl.* SIGNALMEN), *n.* man who works signals, usually on a railway. [Fr.].

SIGNALIZE [sig'na-līz], *v.t.* to mark out as signal, noteworthy or eminent.

SIGNATORY (1) [sig'na-te-ri], *n.* one who signs a document, *esp.* as representing a state. SIGNATORY (2), *adj.* that is a s. [L.].

SIGNATURE [sig'na-tyŏŏr], *n.* sign, stamp or mark impressed; sign-manual; name of a person written by himself; sign which shows the key in music; (*print.*) letter or figure by which the sheets are distinguished and their order designated; the sheet so distinguished; **s. tune**, tune introducing certain regularly appearing stage artists, turns, shows etc., or certain series in broadcasting. [Fr.].

SIGNET [sig'net], *n.* small seal; **writer to the s.**, Scottish law officer acting as attorney in the Court of Session. SIGNET-RING, finger ring bearing an embossed seal. [Fr.].

SIGNIFICANCE [sig-ni'fi-kans], *n.* meaning, import, implication; action of signifying. [OFr.].

SIGNIFICANCY [sig-ni'fi-kan-si], *n.* quality of being significant.

SIGNIFICANT [sig-ni'fi-kant], *adj.* full of meaning; important; expressive of something; indicative of some important reality. [L.].

SIGNIFICATION [sig-ni-fi-kā'shn], *n.* action of signifying; that which is signified; particular and specific meaning.

SIGNIFICATIVE [sig-ni'fi-ka-tiv], *adj.* betokening or representing by an external sign; having a signification; serving to indicate something. [LL.].

SIGNIFY [sig'ni-fī], *v.t.* to represent by sign or symbol; make known by words or signs; declare; import; matter; *v.i.* to be of significance. [Fr.].

SIGNOR(-A), (-INA) [sē-nyawr'(-ah), sē-nyaw-rē'nah], *n.* Italian form of address corresponding to Mr. (Mrs.), (Miss).

SIGNPOST (1) [sīn'pōst], *n.* post to which a sign is

fastened, *esp.* one at a crossroads giving directions; (*fig.*) mark, indication. SIGNPOST (2), *v.t.* to provide (roads) with signposts.

SIKH [sēk], *n.* member of a religion which is a monotheistic and casteless adaptation of Hinduism. [Hind.].

SILENCE (1) [sī'lens], *n.* complete absence of sound; absolute quiet; abstinence from speech or noise; secrecy; absence of mention; oblivion; **S. !** a demand for s. SILENCE (2), *v.t.* to induce or enforce s. on; suppress the noise of; cause to stop speaking, overcome in argument; repress; (*milit.*) cause to cease firing; affix a silencer to (a gun). SILENCER, *n.* appliance for reducing the sound of the escaping gases in motor engines or for silencing the report of a gun. [OFr. from L.].

SILENT [sī'lent], *adj.* absolutely quiet; speechless; still, calm; (*phon.*) (of a letter) not sounded. [L.].

SILHOUETTE (1) [si-lŏŏ-et'], *n.* portrait made by drawing the outline only of a face or figure and filling in the rest with black; profile; aspect of any opaque object when seen outlined against a strong light; **in s.**, in outline. SILHOUETTE (2), *v.t.* to make a s.; throw up in relief against a light background. [M. de *Silhouette*, French politician].

SILICA [si'li-kah], *n.* silicon dioxide, a substance which enters into the composition of most earthy minerals. SILICEOUS [si-li'shŏŏs], *adj.* flinty; pertaining to s. [~L.].

SILICO-, *pref.* containing, in combination with, silica or silicon.

SILICON [si'li-kon], *n.* non-metallic chemical element denoted by Si, abundant in nature. [L.].

SILICOSIS [si-li-kō'sis], *n.* (*path.*) an affection of the lungs caused by inhalation of gritty particles. [SILICA and Gk.].

SILK (1) [silk], *n.* fine lustrous thread produced by the pupae of several moths of the genus *Bombyx*; cloth made of silk; a Queen's Counsel; (*pl.*) garments of silk; **artificial s.**, silky material made chemically from cellulose; **to take s.**, to become a Queen's Counsel. SILK (2), *adj.* silken, made of s. SILKEN, *adj.* like s.; made of s.; of a silky texture; smooth and soft. [O.E. from Gk.].

SILKY [sil'ki], *adj.* made of silk; like silk; silken; smooth and soft. SILKILY, *adv.* (of speech) smoothly, ingratiatingly.

SILKWORM [silk'werm], *n.* caterpillar of the moth which produces silk.

SILL [sil], *n.* the wood, metal or stone which forms the lower horizontal part of the frame of a window or door. [O.E.].

SILLABUB, SYLLABUB [si'la-bub], *n.* liquor made by mixing wine or cider with milk and sugar to form a soft curd. [Uncert.].

SILLY [si'li], *adj.* foolish, weak in intellect, unintelligent, frivolous, trivial, tiresome; † innocent, helpless; (*cricket*) (of fieldsmen or their positions) abnormally close to the bat. [O.E.].

SILO [sī'lō], *n.* airtight pit or kind of tall barn in which grain, green fodder etc. is stored. [Span.].

SILT (1) [silt], *n.* a deposit in water of mud or sand. SILT (2), *v.t. and i.* to obstruct, choke up with s.; **to s. up**, to become blocked up with s.; **to s. through**, to trickle through an obstruction of s. [ME.].

SILURIAN [si-lyŏŏ'ri-an], *adj.* (*geol.*) of the Palaeozoic rocks lying next below the Devonian. [L.].

SILVAN, SYLVAN [sil'van], *adj.* wooded, pertaining to woods, trees. [L.].

SILVER (1) [sil'ver], *n.* metallic element denoted by Ag; precious metal of a brilliant white colour; coin made of s.; money; articles made of or plated with s.; anything resembling s. in colour or lustre; **s. gilt**, s. or s.-plate with a coating of gold. SILVER-LEAF, s. beaten into thin leaves. SILVER-PLATE, article or articles coated with s.; electroplate. SILVER (2), *adj.* made of s.; looking like s. in colour or lustre; bright; of a soft grey colour; melodious, dulcet; eloquent; **s. age**, (in cultural history) period which follows after the finest, the golden age; **s. paper**, very thin sheets of tinfoil etc., used for wrapping purposes. SILVER-FISH, silvery-coloured insect of the genus *Lepisma*. SILVER-FOX, the black fox, distinguished by its rich fur and white tips to its hairs. **s. sand**, fine white sand; **the s. screen**, the cinema; **s. wedding**, twenty-fifth anniversary of one's wedding. SILVER-POINT, process of drawing with a pencil tipped with s.; the pencil itself; the drawing produced. SILVER-SIDE, topside of beef suitable for salting. SILVER-WEED, a wayside perennial plant. SILVER (3), *v.t.* to cover with s.;

The accent ' after a syllable = stress (u-pon'). The mark ‾ over a vowel = length (ā in made; ō in bone).

give the appearance of **s. to.** SILVERING, *n.* plating of s.; anything used for making like s. [OE.].

SILVERSMITH [sil'ver-smith], *n.* workman or dealer in silver.

SIMIAN (1) [si'mi-an], *adj.* pertaining to the anthropoid apes; ape-like in appearance. SIMIAN (2), *n.* a s. ape. [L.].

SIMILAR [si'mi-ler], *adj.* like, resembling; having the same form, appearance or nature; (*math.*) having all corresponding angles equal. [L.].

SIMILARITY [si-mi-la'ri-ti], *n.* condition of being similar.

SIMILE [si'mi-li], *n.* similitude; (*rhet.*) figure of speech in which one thing is compared with another. [L.].

SIMILITUDE [si-mi'li-tyōōd], *n.* likeness, resemblance, similar appearance. [L.].

SIMMER (1) [si'mer], *v.t. and i.* to boil gently; (*coll.*) be in a state of suppressed excitement; **to s. down.** (*coll.*) to grow calmer. SIMMER (2), *n.* a gentle boil. [Echoic].

SIMNEL [sim'nel], *n.* rich cake eaten on Mothering Sunday, the fourth in Lent. [OFr.].

SIMONIAC [si-mō'ni-ak], *n.* one who is guilty of simony.

SIMONY [si'mo-ni], *n.* crime of buying or selling holy orders or church preferment. [*Simon Magus*, Acts viii, 18].

SIMOOM [si-mōōm'], *n.* a hot, arid, suffocating wind, which blows in Africa, Arabia etc. from the interior deserts. [Arab.].

SIMPER (1) [sim'per], *v.i.* to smile in an insincere and affected manner; smirk. SIMPER (2), *n.* a silly affected smile; a smirk. [Uncert.].

SIMPLE (1) [sim'pl], *adj.* consisting of one thing; uncompounded; pure; not complex; artless, unaffected; unadorned; straightforward; unlearned; unsophisticated; weak in intellect; **pure and s.** absolute. SIMPLE-HEARTED, sincere; unsophisticated. SIMPLE-MINDED, artless, undesigning; ingenuous. SIMPLE (2), *n.* (*archaic*) a herbal medicine. [Fr. from L.].

SIMPLETON [sim'pl-ton], *n.* foolish person.

SIMPLICITY [sim-pli'si-ti], *n.* state or quality of being simple.

SIMPLIFY [sim'pli-fi], *v.t.* to make simple; (*math.*) reduce to its simplest terms. [Fr.].

SIMPLY [sim'pli], *adv.* in a simple manner; without ostentation or affectation; without adornment; unequivocally; absolutely; by itself, merely.

SIMULACRUM (*pl.* **simulacra, simulacrums**) [si-myōō-lā'krum], *n.* a representation; mere form or shadow of a reality; a sham. [L.].

SIMULATE [si'myōō-lāt], *v.t.* to feign; counterfeit; assume the mere appearance of without the reality; *v.i.* to pretend. SIMULATION [si-myōō-lā'shn], *n.* act of simulating; assumption of a false appearance or character. [L.].

SIMULTANEOUS [si-mōōl-tā'ni-ōōs], *adj.* existing or taking place at the same time. [LL.].

SIN (1) [sin], *n.* an offence against the divine law; iniquity; violation of the moral code; depravity; immorality; wrongdoing; an offence; (*coll.*) a shame, pity; **original s.,** s. inherited from Adam after the Fall; inherited tendency to evil; **to live in s.,** to cohabit without being married. SIN (2), *v.i.* to commit s., offend. [OE.].

SINCE (1) [sins], *adv.* from that time, after that time; from then till now, in the interval; ago. SINCE (2), *prep.* after, from that time. SINCE (3), *conj.* because; inasmuch as; from the time when. [~OE.].

SINCERE [sin-sēer'], *adj.* genuine; pure; not simulated; true, heartfelt. [L.].

SINCERITY [sin-se'ri-ti], *n.* quality of being sincere; honesty of mind and intention. [L.].

SINE [sin], *n.* (*math.*) the ratio of the line opposite a given angle to the hypotenuse of a right-angled triangle containing that angle. [L.].

SINE-, *pref.* without. [L.].

SINECURE [si'ni-kyōōr], *n.* ecclesiastical benefice entailing no cure of souls; office with a salary but no work. [L.].

SINEW [si'nyōō], *n.* that which unites a muscle to a bone; tendon; (*pl.*) muscles; (*fig.*) strength, essential motive power, necessary material. SINEWY, *adj.* consisting of sinews; strong; well-braced with sinews; (*fig.*) vigorous. [OE.].

SING (*pret.* **sang,** *p.pt.* **sung**) [sing], *v.t.* to articulate with musical inflections of voice; give praises to, tell of, in verse; **to s. to sleep,** to put to sleep by singing; **to s. out,** (*coll.*) to call out; (*fig.*) **to s. another (different) tune,** to speak or act in a quite different

manner; *v.i.* to utter sweet or melodious sounds; make a small shrill or humming sound; relate in poetry; produce a ringing, murmuring sound; reverberate. [OE.].

SINGE (1) [sinj], *v.t.* to burn the surface of slightly; burn superficially. SINGE (2), *n.* a burning of the surface; a scorch. [OE.].

SINGER [sing'er], *n.* one who, or that which, sings; professional vocal artist.

SIN(G)HALESE, CINGALESE [sing-ga-lēz'], *n.* a native of Ceylon; language of Ceylon. [Skr.].

SINGLE (1) [sing'gl], *adj.* separate; consisting of one only; not complex; sole; individual; not married; not double; direct and honest. SINGLE-BREASTED, *adj.* (of a garment) having only one thickness of cloth over the breast, not overlapping. SINGLE-ENTRY, (*comm.*) entry of a transaction into one account only of the ledger. SINGLE-HANDED, having no one to help; working alone and unassisted. SINGLE-HEARTED, devoted to one thing; sincere. SINGLE-MINDED, having one purpose; s.-hearted. SINGLE (2), *n.* (*sport*) game in which there is only one player on each side; (*pl.*) set of contests between s. players. SINGLE (3), *v.t.* to separate; select; choose; cause to stand (out). SINGLY, *adv.* individually; alone; by oneself; in a s.-minded manner. [OFr. from L.].

SINGLESTICK [sing'gl-stik], *n.* stick about the length of a sword used for sword exercise. [SINGLE (1)].

SINGLET [sing'glet], *n.* undervest not buttoning in front; vest. [SINGLE (1)].

SINGLETON [sing'gl-ton], *n.* the only one of a suit in a hand at cards; a solitary entry in a competition. [SINGLE (1)].

SINGSONG (1) [sing'song], *n.* jolly, informal concert; monotonous tone of voice. SINGSONG (2), *adj.* having a monotonous droning sound; having no modulations; drawling.

SINGULAR [sing'gyōō-ler], *adj.* relating to one person or thing; not common; peculiar; unique; outstanding; **s. number,** (*gram.*) the number denoting one person or thing. SINGULARLY, *adv.* in a s. manner; peculiarly; strangely; specially. [L.].

SINGULARITY [sing-gyōō-la'ri-ti], *n.* quality of being singular; peculiarity; uncommon character or form; oddity. [L.].

SINISTER [si'nis-ter], *adj.* of evil import; mysteriously evil, threatening; ominous; base or underhand; on the left hand. [L.].

SINK (1) (*pret.* **sank, sunk,** *p.pt.* **sunk**) [singk], *v.t.* to cause to sink; immerse in a fluid; make by digging, excavation, boring; degrade; reduce, diminish; suppress, conceal; *v.i.* to fall towards the bottom; subside; fall gradually; become lower; settle to a level; decline; (*fig.*) fall lower in social position or standard of behaviour. SINK (2), *n.* a drain to carry off filthy water; basin of stone, metal or wood in which rough washing is done, esp. in a kitchen. SINKER, *n.* plummet; weight fixed on something to s. it; **hook, line and s.,** completely. SINKING (1), *n.* excavation of shafts and wells. SINKING (2), *adj.* falling, subsiding; **sinking feeling,** (*coll.*) heavy sensation in the pit of the stomach caused by hunger or fear; **sinking fund,** fund set aside by a government or company for the reduction of debts or other liabilities. [OE.].

SINNER [si'ner], *n.* one who sins; offender, criminal; morally guilty person.

SINN FEIN [shin-fān'], *n.* political party in Ireland which worked for the complete political independence of Ireland. [Ir.].

SINO-, *pref.* Chinese. [Gk.].

SINOLOGY [si-no'lo-ji], *n.* study of Chinese culture, history, religion and art. SINOLOGICAL [si-no-lo'ji-kal], *adj.* pertaining to s. SINOLOGIST, SINOLOGUE [si-no'lo-jist, si'no-log], *n.* one versed in Chinese culture. [L.].

SINTER [sin'ter], *n.* a siliceous or calcareous deposit of mineral springs. [Germ.].

SINUOSITY [si-nyōō-o'si-ti], *n.* quality of curving in and out; series of bends, turns or windings. [Fr.].

SINUOUS [si'nyōō-ōōs], *adj.* bending in and out; winding; undulating; supple. [Fr.].

SINUS [si'nus], *n.* curve, bend; cavity usually in a bone or other tissue of the body; (*path.*) a suppurating place, usually in the passages of the nose or ear. SINUSITIS [si-nu-si'tis], *n.* (*path.*) inflammation of the nasal s. [L.].

SIOUX [sōō], *n.* (one of) a nation of American Indians of the Dakotan group; its language. [Fr.].

SIP (1) [sip], *v.t.* to take into the mouth by the lips in very small quantities; take very small drinks of; (*fig.*)

taste; *v.i.* to take in small tastes. SIP (2), *n.* the taking of liquid with the lips; small drink of liquid; small taste of something. [O.E.].

SIPHON (1), **SYPHON** [sī'fon], *n.* bent tube or pipe, having one end lower than the other, used for drawing off fluids by atmospheric pressure; bottle containing aerated water which is forced out through a tap by pressure of dissolved carbonic acid gas. SIPHON (2), SYPHON, *v.t.* to draw (off) by the action of a s. [Gk.].

SIPPET [si'pit], *n.* small piece of bread, fried or toasted, served as a garnish with mince, soup etc. [~SOP].

SIR [sur], *n.* title of honour used of a knight or baronet; word of respect used formerly in addressing a man of superior station, and now more generally. [O.Fr.].

SIRDAR [sur'dah(r)], *n.* commander-in-chief of the Egyptian Army; leader, chieftain. [Pers.].

SIRE (1) [sīer], *n.* father; title used in addressing the King; male parent; progenitor; ancestor. SIRE (2), *v.t.* to beget (*esp.* of horses). [O.Fr. from L.].

SIREN, SYREN [sī'ren], *n.* (*Gk. myth.*) one of a class of sea nymphs who used to lure passing sailors to ruin by the fascination of their music; woman dangerous because of her enticing arts; steam-whistle; hooter used to sound an air-raid warning; (*zool.*) a genus of tailed amphibians. [L. from Gk.].

SIRIUS [si'ri-us], *n.* (*astron.*) a bright star of the first magnitude, also called the dog-star. [L.].

SIRLOIN [sur'loin], *n.* upper part of the loin of beef. [O.Fr.].

SIROCCO [si-ro'kō], *n.* hot southerly wind from the Libyan deserts. [It.].

SIRRAH [si'rah], *n.* (*archaic*) mode of address used to a male, and implying contempt. [~SIR].

SIRUP, see SYRUP.

SISAL [sī'sal], *n.* a fibre plant, used for making rope. [*Sisal*, Yucatan].

SISTER [sis'ter], *n.* a female of the same parentage; one who acts like a sister; one of the same kind; nun; nurse in charge of a hospital ward. [OScand.].

SISTERHOOD [sis'ter-hood], *n.* a community of sisters; society of women joined in one faith or order; the relationship of a sister.

SISTER-IN-LAW [sis'ter-in-law], *n.* sister of a husband or wife; wife of a brother.

SISYPHEAN [si-si-fē'an], *adj.* (*Gk. myth.*) pertaining to Sisyphus, who was condemned in the underworld endlessly to roll up a hill a great stone which always rolled down again at once; **S. labour, task,** endless and ineffective labour. [Gk.].

SIT (1) (*pres.pt.* **sitting,** *pret. and p.pt.* **sat**) [sit], *v.t.* to rest upon the haunches, rest upon a seat; rest; remain, abide; have a seat or position; be placed; cover eggs for hatching; hold a session; hold a seat in Parliament; weigh heavily (upon); remain seated upon; **to s. down,** to place oneself on a seat; settle down; **to s. in,** (*coll.*) look after a child at home while the parents go out; **to s. on,** (*coll.*) snub; **to s. out,** to remain seated and endure; **to s. out a dance,** to refrain from joining in; **to s. under,** to listen to, receive instruction from; **to s. up,** to refrain from going to bed; (*coll.*) pay attention, be on the alert; **to s. pretty,** (*slang*) to be in a very advantageous position. SIT-DOWN, *adj.* describing a strike in which workers refuse to work but remain in occupation of the factory etc. SIT (2), *n.* the way in which something sits, is fixed or hangs; a certain time taken up in sitting. SITTER, *n.* person who sits, *esp.* to an artist; bird which incubates; easy target; one employed to s. in a house where there is a child or an elderly person, so that those usually in charge can go out. [O.E.].

SITE (1) [sīt], *n.* situation; local position; ground plot for building. SITE (2), *v.t.* to locate; find the position of. SITING, *n.* condition of being sited, planned situation or location; act of planning sites. [AFr.].

SITTING (1) [si'ting], *n.* action of one who sits; session; business meeting; time during which one sits; time during which one sits for a portrait; seat in a church; clutch of eggs for incubation. SITTING-ROOM, room for s. in; reception room; drawing room. SITTING (2), *adj.* being in the position of one who, or that which, sits.

SITUATE (1) [si'tyōō-āt], *v.t.* to place, locate; provide a site for; place in a particular set of circumstances. SITUATE (2) [si'tyōō-at], *adj.* situated. [MedL.].

SITUATION [si-tyōō-ā'shn], *n.* position; state; condition; place; office; employment; job. [Fr.].

SIX (1) [siks], *n.* the cardinal number next after five, numeral representing this. SIX (2), *adj.* of the

number s. SIX-FOOTER, *n.* person or thing s. feet in length or height. SIX-SHOOTER, *n.* revolver which can fire s. shots with one loading. SIXFOLD, *adj.* s. times or things together; s. times as much or many. [O.E.].

SIXPENCE [siks'pens], *n.* silver coin of the value of six pennies; the value of s.

SIXTEEN (1) [siks-tēn'], *n.* the cardinal number after fifteen and before seventeen; six and ten. SIXTEEN (2), *adj.* of the number s.

SIXTEENTH (siks-tēnth'], *n. and adj.* the ordinal of sixteen; (being) one of sixteen equal parts; (*mus.*) semi-quaver; interval of two octaves and a second. [~O.E.].

SIXTH [siksth], *n. and adj.* the ordinal of six; (being) one of six equal parts; (*mus.*) interval of six notes; chord of two notes so separated; **s. sense,** supposed instinctive perception not dependent on any of the five senses.

SIXTIETH [siks'ti-eth], *n. and adj.* the ordinal of sixty; (being) one of sixty equal parts.

SIXTY (1) [siks'ti], *n.* the number equalling six times ten. SIXTY (2), *adj.* six times ten. [O.E.].

SIZAR [sī'zer], *n.* (*hist.*) undergraduate at Cambridge and Dublin of a corresponding grade with the servitor at Oxford. [*Next*].

SIZE (1) [sīz], *n.* bulk; magnitude; dimensions; settled quantity or allowance, *esp.* of food and drink, made to sizars at Cambridge; standard dimension of gloves, shoes, hats etc. SIZE (2), *v.t.* to put in order according to s.; make of a certain dimension; *v.i.* to order food or drink from the buttery (at Cambridge University); **to s. up,** to form an estimate of. SIZABLE, *adj.* of some s.; of a considerable s. [O.Fr.].

SIZE (3), *n.* liquid glue. SIZE (4), *v.t.* to prepare or cover with s. [Uncert.].

SIZZLE [si'zl], *v.i.* to emit a spluttering noise in process of frying. [Echoic].

SJAMBOK [syam'bok], *n.* whip made of rhinoceros hide. [Afrik.].

SKALD † [skald], *n.* poet in ancient Scandinavia.

SKATE (1) [skāt], *n.* a large flatfish. [OIcel.].

SKATE (2), *n.* kind of frame strapped on to the foot and furnished with a steel blade for gliding over the ice; **roller s.,** s. with wheels for travelling on any smooth surface. SKATE (3), *v.i.* to slide along on skates; **to s. on thin ice,** (*fig.*) to venture into a dangerous or awkward situation. [Du.].

SKEAN-DHU [skē'an-dyōō, skēn-dōō'], *n.* Highlander's dirk, usually carried stuck into the top of the stocking. [Gael.].

SKEIN [skān], *n.* a measure of thread, yarn or silk; coil or loose knot into which this is wound; **tangled s.,** (*fig.*) confused affair. [O.Fr.].

SKELETAL [ske'li-tal], *adj.* (*biol.*) of, pertaining to, of the nature of, a skeleton.

SKELETON [ske'li-ton], *n.* the bones of an animal body in their natural arrangement, separated from the flesh; supporting parts of an animal whether vertebrate or invertebrate; general supporting framework of anything; outline; very thin, emaciated person; **s. staff,** the smallest possible number of workers essential to the performance of a task. SKELETON-KEY, thin light key capable of opening many locks; master-key. [Gk.].

SKEP [skep], *n.* light wicker basket; amount of goods which may be carried in such a basket; straw bee-hive. [OIcel.].

SKERRY [ske'ri], *n.* small rocky island; reef. [OIcel.].

SKETCH (1) [skech], *n.* outline or general delineation of something; first rough draft; descriptive essay or newspaper article; slight character play in one act; (*coll.*) absurdly dressed person. SKETCH-BOOK, book for sketching in. SKETCH (2), *v.t.* to delineate the outline or general figure of; make a first draft of; plan by outlining the principal ideas of; write out the preliminary basic details of; *v.i.* to make sketches. [Du. from Gk.].

SKETCHY [ske'chi], *adj.* drawn in outline; rough, unfinished, inadequate.

SKEW [skyōō], *adj.* slanting; oblique; **on the s.,** aslant. [~AFr.].

SKEWBALD [skyōō'bawld], *adj.* (of a horse) marked with patches of white, brown or red.

SKEWER (1) [skyōō'er], *n.* pin of wood or metal for keeping a joint of meat in shape. SKEWER (2), *v.t.* to fasten with skewers. [~Norw.].

SKI (1) [shē, skē], *n.* long, flat, wooden runner with an upcurved front used for moving quickly over snow. SKI (2), *v.i.* to go on skis. [Norw. from OScand.].

SKID (1) [skid], *n.* curving timber to preserve a ship's side from injury; drag to check the wheel of a wagon when descending a hill; brake; piece of timber to keep one object from resting on another; runner on some aircraft; sideslip by a motor-car or bicycle. SKID (2), *v.i.* to sideslip with a car or bicycle. [OScand.].

SKIFF [skif], *n.* light sculling boat; any light, small boat. [OFr.].

SKILFUL [skil'fŏŏl], *adj.* showing skill; well versed in any occupation; dexterous; expert.

SKILL [skil], *n.* familiar knowledge of any art, united with dexterity in the practice of it; expertness in execution; proficiency. **SKILLED**, *adj.* having or demanding s. [OIcel.].

SKILLET [skil'lit], *n.* small, long-handled metal vessel, used for boiling or heating. [OFr.].

SKILLY [skil'li], *n.* watery oatmeal gruel formerly used as food for paupers and convicts. [Uncert.].

SKIM [skim], *v.t.* to take the scum off; take off (matter) floating on the surface; brush the surface of lightly; scan superficially; *v.i.* pass over lightly; glide over the surface; hurry over superficially. SKIM-MILK, *n.* milk from which the cream has been skimmed. SKIMMER, *n.* one who, or that which, skims; scoop used for skimming milk; bird of the genus *Rhynchops*. [~OIcel.].

SKIMP [skimp], *v.t.* to stint; use insufficient material; give a poor amount of; *v.i.* to be mean, parsimonious. [Uncert.].

SKIMPY [skim'pi], *adj.* scanty; meagre; having insufficient material.

SKIN (1) [skin], *n.* natural outer covering of an animal; hide; outer covering; rind of a fruit; s. receptacle for wine or water; **to have a thick (thin) s.,** to be insensitive (sensitive); **by the s. of the teeth,** narrowly. SKIN (2), *v.t.* to strip off the s. or hide of; flay; graze the s. of; peel; cover with, or as with, s.; (*coll.*) punish severely; swindle; *v.i.* to be covered with s.; **to s. over,** to have a s. growing over; **to keep one's eyes skinned,** to be on the look-out. [OScand.].

SKINFLINT [skin'flint], *n.* grasping person; miser.

SKINNER [ski'ner], *n.* one who sells skins, furrier.

SKINNY [ski'ni], *adj.* having much skin; very thin; tough and fibrous; (*coll.*) mean, parsimonious.

SKIP (1) [skip], *v.t.* to leave out, pass hastily over; *v.i.* to leap; jump over a rope repeatedly in play; frisk, frolic; read quickly leaving out passages; (*coll.*) run away hastily. SKIP (2), *n.* small leap, bound, spring. SKIPPING-ROPE, *n.* rope for skipping with. [ME.].

SKIP (3), *n.* basket or bucket used in mines. [~SKEP].

SKIP (4), *n.* captain of a bowling or curling team or rink. SKIP (5), *v.t.* to captain (a bowling or curling team). [SKIP(PER)].

SKIPPER (1) [ski'per], *n.* captain of a ship; (*coll.*) captain of a side. SKIPPER (2), *v.t.* to captain, *esp.* a sporting side. [MDu.].

SKIRL (1) [skurl], *v.i.* to emit a shrill sound like the note of the bagpipes. SKIRL (2), *n.* shrill sound; sound of the bagpipes. [~Norw.].

SKIRMISH (1) [skur'mish], *n.* irregular engagement in which small numbers are engaged; contest; (*fig.*) argument, brief contest of wits. SKIRMISH (2), *v.i.* to fight irregularly, in scattered parties; fight in extended order; have a s. [OFr.].

SKIRT (1) [skurt], *n.* the lower and loose part of a coat or other garment; border; margin; woman's garment fitted in at the waist and falling over the legs; diaphragm or midriff in animals; (*slang*) woman. SKIRT (2), *v.t.* to run, pass along the edge, margin of; border; *v.i.* to be on the border; live near the extremity. SKIRTING, *n.* border; lower edge of a dado; material for women's skirts. [OIcel.].

SKIT (1) [skit], *v.t.* to ridicule; write a s. upon; *v.i.* to make satirical fun of. SKIT (2), *n.* lampoon, caricature, light humorous sketch. [Uncert.].

SKITTISH [ski'tish], *adj.* easily frightened, nervous; volatile; unsuitably frolicsome or gay. [Uncert.].

SKITTLES [ski'tlz], *n.*(*pl.*) set of ninepins; game played with these. [Dan.].

SKIVVY [ski'vi], *n.* (*slang*) domestic servant in a house, usually a "general." [Uncert.].

SKUA [skyŏŏ'ah], *n.* a pirate gull. [OIcel.].

SKULK [skulk], *v.i.* to lurk in corners; hide furtively; sneak about; malinger. [~Norw.].

SKULL [skul], *n.* bony structure which encloses the brain in man and certain animals; human skull as a symbol of mortality; **s. and crossbones,** pirate's symbol. SKULL-CAP, cap fitting closely to the head. [ME.].

SKUNK [skungk], *n.* species of American carnivore which defends itself by the ejection of offensively foetid matter, and whose fur when dressed is known as Alaska-sable; (*fig.*) mean, low type of person. [NAmerInd.].

SKY (1) [ski], *n.* aerial region which surrounds the earth; the apparent vault of heaven; the heavens; (*fig.*) prospect, situation. SKY-BLUE, *adj.* of a blue colour like that of a clear summer s. SKY-HIGH, *adj.* very high. SKY-PILOT, (*slang*) clergyman. SKY (2), *v.t.* to hit or throw high into the air; place something in a high position, *esp.* to hang a picture in an unflatteringly high place at an exhibition. [OIcel.].

SKYLARK (1) [ski'lahk], *n.* the common lark, which mounts and sings as it flies. SKYLARK (2), *v.i.* to romp about, play roughly.

SKYLIGHT [ski'lit], *n.* window built in the roof of a building or room.

SKYLINE [ski'lin], *n.* horizon; outline of anything against the sky.

SKYROCKET [ski'ro-kit], *n.* rocket which rises high into the air and then explodes.

SKYSAIL [ski'sl], *n.* (*naut.*) square-sail immediately above a royal.

SKYSCRAPER [ski'skrā-per], *n.* very high building with many storeys.

SLAB [slab], *n.* thin flat piece of marble or other stone; outside piece taken from timber in sawing it into planks; (*coll.*) large thick slice of bread or cake. [OFr.].

SLACK (1) [slak], *adj.* not tense, tight, taut; loose, sagging; careless, indifferent; inefficient, shipshod; not prosperous; having little work; **s. water,** point at high or low tide when the water is not visibly moving either way. SLACK (2), *n.* the part of a rope which hangs loose; loose part; motionless state of water at high or low tide; dull season in trade; small coal; (*pl.*) loose trousers worn by persons of either sex for leisure or work. SLACK (3), *v.t.* to slacken; *v.i.* to become s.; (*coll.*) be remiss, idle, careless; **to s. off,** to stop working hard. SLACKER, *n.* lazy person, one who slacks. SLACKLY, *adv.* in a s. manner; not tightly; negligently. [OE.].

SLACKEN [sla'ken], *v.t.* to lessen the tension of; relax; mitigate; cause to become slower; abate; deprive of cohesion; moderate; *v.i.* to become less tense; be remiss; lose cohesion; abate; become slower, less energetic. [~SLACK].

SLAG [slag], *n.* vitrified cinders; refuse left after the smelting of a metal; volcanic ashes. [~Swed.].

SLAIN [slān], *p.pt. of* SLAY. [OE.].

SLAKE [slāk], *v.t.* to quench; extinguish; mix with water; *v.i.* to become mixed with water; go out; become extinct; abate; (*fig.*) moderate, assuage. [OE.].

SLAM (1) [slam], *v.t. and i.* to shut with violence; bang; throw noisily; (*bridge*) win all or all but one of the tricks. SLAM (2), *n.* violent shutting of a door; noise so produced; (*whist or bridge*) the winning of all or all but one of the tricks; **grand s.,** (*bridge*) the winning of thirteen tricks; **little, small, s.,** the winning of twelve tricks. [~Swed.].

SLANDER (1) [slahn'der], *n.* a malicious report uttered to damage a person's character; defamation. SLANDER (2), *v.t.* to defame; injure by maliciously uttering a false report; traduce. [AFr.].

SLANDEROUS [slahn'de-rŏŏs], *adj.* containing, uttering, implying, slander; calumnious.

SLANG (1) [slang], *n.* language of a particularly informal or familiar kind, felt to be hardly admissible even in more serious colloquial use; a conversational expression of an irregular but not necessarily vulgar type; **back s.,** thieves' s. in which words are pronounced approximately as if spelt backwards; **rhyming s.,** cockney s. in which a word is represented by a word or phrase which rhymes with it. SLANG (2), *v.t.* to abuse; scold in a violent and abusive fashion. [Uncert.].

SLANT (1) [slahnt], *v.t.* to turn from a direct line, give an oblique direction to; *v.i.* to slope; incline away from the straight. SLANT (2), *n.* slope; inclined plane; oblique reflection; **s. on,** (*coll.*) angle of approach to, useful information concerning. SLANT (3), *adj.* slanting. [ME.].

SLAP (1) [slap], *n.* a blow with the open hand or something flat; (*fig.*) nasty snub. SLAP-BANG, (*coll.*) violently, noisily. SLAP-UP, (*slang*) first-rate; sumptuous. SLAP (2), *v.t.* to give a s. to; strike with the open hand; **to s. down,** (*coll.*) to throw rudely or carelessly down. SLAPPING, *adj.* large; well built; strapping. [Echoic].

SLAPDASH [slap'dash], *adj.* rash, careless, slipshod.

ŏŏ is pronounced as in food; ŏŏ as in hood; th as in *th*ink; TH as in *th*at; zh as in azure.   ~ = related to.

SLAPJACK [slap′jak], *n.* kind of pancake baked on a grid.

SLAPSTICK (1) [slap′stik], *n.* wooden wand of two flat boards fastened together so as to make a noisy slap when shaken; knockabout comedy, farce. SLAPSTICK (2), *adj.* relating to, consisting of, rough knockabout farce.

SLASH (1) [slash], *v.t.* to cut by striking violently; cut gashes in; lash; (*fig.*) criticize savagely; *v.i.* to strike violently with an edged weapon; lay about one with blows. SLASH (2), *n.* a long cut; cut made at random; large slit formerly made in garments in order to show a bright-coloured lining. SLASHING, *adj.* severe, violent. [OFr.].

SLAT [slat], *n.* thin wooden strip such as a blind-lath or a bed-lath; narrow piece of timber, used to fasten together larger pieces; thin slab of stone used for roofing instead of a slate. [OFr.].

SLATE (1) [slāt], *n.* hard, blue-black or purple shaly rock which splits easily into thin plates; piece of this squared up and used as a section of roof tiling; oblong piece of this set in a frame and used for chalking words or diagrams on; the colour of slate, dark blue-grey; **s. club,** voluntary society of members who subscribe a small sum each week, with a view to a share-out. SLATE-PENCIL, pencil made of s. powder compressed into a thin stick, used for writing on s. SLATE (2), *adj.* made of, consisting of, s.; having the colour of s. SLATE (3), *v.t.* to cover with a s. roofing; (*coll.*) criticize harshly; reprimand severely. SLATER, *n.* one who shapes or fixes slates. SLATING, *n.* act of covering with slates; a covering of slates; material for slating; (*coll.*) harsh criticizm. [ME.].

SLATTERN [sla′tern], *n.* woman who is careless over her dress, or untidy, slut. [Unkn.].

SLAUGHTER (1) [slaw′ter], *n.* act of slaughtering; condition or fact of having been slaughtered, indiscriminate dealing out of death on a large scale as in battle; the butchering of animals. SLAUGHTER (2), *v.t.* to kill indiscriminately and savagely; massacre; butcher animals for their meat. SLAUGHTERER, *n.* one employed to s. cattle; slayer. SLAUGHTER-HOUSE, *n.* shed where beasts are killed for the market. SLAUGHTERMAN, *n.* man employed to s. cattle. SLAUGHTEROUS, *adj.* feeling roused to be destructive, murderous. [ME. ~OIcel.].

SLAV [slahv], *n.* member of a race inhabiting Eastern Europe. [Uncert., perhaps ~OSlav.].

SLAVE (1) [slāv], *n.* person whose conditions of living are imposed by the will of another, one who is legally recognized as being the property of and under the absolute control of an owner; serf; (*coll.*) one who is compelled to spend his life working hard for someone else's profit, drudge; one who is dominated in his actions by psychological weaknesses. SLAVE-DRIVER, person in charge of slaves who keeps them at their work; person who overworks subordinates. SLAVE-DRIVING, bullying methods of a s.-driver. SLAVE (2), *adj.* of, relating to, dealing with, a s. or slaves; composed of slaves. SLAVE (3), *v.i.* to work under conditions resembling a slave's, drudge. SLAVER (1), *n.* ship employed in s. traffic; person who trades in slaves. [~SLAV].

SLAVER (2) [sla′ver], *v.t. and i.* to smear or cover with saliva; dribble at the mouth, slobber; (*fig.*) address mawkishly. SLAVER (3), *n.* act of salivating; saliva dribbling from the mouth; (*coll.*) mawkish drivel. [OIcel.].

SLAVERY [slā′ve-ri], *n.* condition of life of a slave; system of society which permits of slave ownership; excessive hard work, drudgery. [~MDu.].

SLAVEY [slā′vi], *n.* (*slang*) servant girl who does the dirtiest jobs of work in a house.

SLAVISH [slā′vish], *adj.* relating to or like slaves; servile, mean; laborious; mechanical.

SLAVONIC [sla-vo′nik], *adj.* of, or relating to, the Slavs or their languages.

SLAY (*pret.* **slew**, *p.pt.* **slain**) [slā], *v.t.* to put to death with a weapon or by violence, kill, destroy. [OE.].

SLED (1) [sled], *n.* sleigh, sledge. SLED (2) (*pres.pt.* SLEDDING, *pret. and p.pt.* SLEDDED), *v.t. and i.* to travel or transport by means of a s.

SLEDGE (1) [slej], *n.* large heavy type of hammer wielded with both hands. SLEDGE-HAMMER, a s.; **sledge-hammer blows,** violent, heavy blows. [OE.].

SLEDGE (2), *n.* means of transport over ice or snow, consisting of a low framework of wood fitted with metal runners, sled, sleigh. SLEDGE (3), *v.t. and i.* to transport by means of a s.; travel on a s. [MDu.].

SLEEK (1) [slēk], *adj.* having a smooth, glossy surface or appearance, not rough; smooth in manners, oily. SLEEK (2), *v.t.* to smooth, make s. [OIcel.].

SLEEP (1) [slēp], *n.* state of temporary unconsciousness, recurring naturally in human beings every twenty-four hours; the time such a state lasts; (*fig.*) mental apathy or lethargy; **last s.,** death. SLEEP (2) (*pret. and p.pt.* SLEPT), *v.i.* to experience s.; be in a state of inactivity, be lethargic; become numb and without feeling; spin round at high speed, as a top, the movement being imperceptible; be dead. [OE.].

SLEEPER [slē′per], *n.* person who sleeps; one of the stout oblong pieces of timber used on a permanent way to support railway lines; railway coach designed to accommodate passengers who wish to sleep during a night journey; single compartment in such a carriage.

SLEEPING (1) [slē′ping], *n.* state of being asleep; instance of this. SLEEPING-BAG, warm bag, usually waterproofed, used by Service personnel and others sleeping in tents or in the open air. SLEEPING-CAR, railway coach fitted with s. accommodation. SLEEPING-DRAUGHT, medicine which induces sleep, opiate. SLEEPING-SICKNESS, disease spread by a species of tsetse-fly, the characteristic symptom being a deep sleep which usually ends in death; sleepy sickness. SLEEPING (2), *adj.* taking rest; **s. partner,** director of a firm who draws a salary but has no specific duties.

SLEEPLESS [slēp′les], *adj.* marked by the absence of sleep, wakeful; alert, ever watchful; restless, perpetually agitated.

SLEEPY [slē′pi], *adj.* requiring, overcome by, sleep; drowsy, inclined to sleep; tending to induce sleep, not stimulating; characterized by relative inactivity; dull; lazy; over-ripe; **s. sickness,** disease caused by a virus, and resulting in lethargy and mental deterioration.

SLEET (1) [slēt], *n.* fine snow mingled with rain, rain frozen to smaller grains of softer consistency than hail. SLEET (2), *v.i.* (*impers.*) to shower down s. [ME.].

SLEEVE (1) [slēv], *n.* that part of a garment which covers the arm; mechanism consisting of a tube enclosing a smaller tube; any tubular outer covering; **to have up one's s.,** to keep in secret reserve; **to laugh up (in) one's s.,** to laugh at another unobserved, gloat slyly over another's discomfiture. SLEEVE-LINK, two studs joined by a link, cuff-link. SLEEVE (2), *v.t.* to provide with sleeves. SLEEVED, *adj.* designed or provided with sleeves. [OE.].

SLEIGH (1) [slā], *n.* carriage on runners for use on snow; sledge or sled. SLEIGH-BELL, small, jingling bell hanging on a s. or its harness. SLEIGH (2), *v.t. and i.* to travel by means of a s.; use a s. as a vehicle. [Du.].

SLEIGHT [slīt], *n.* dexterous trick, deceptive device; illusion created by manipulation; **s. of hand,** tricks performed by a skilful conjurer. [ME. from OIcel.].

SLENDER [slen′der], *adj.* small in width compared with length, thin, slim; small in the waist; slight, inconsiderable; feeble; weak; inadequate, scanty. [ME.].

SLEPT [slept], *pret. and p.pt. of* SLEEP. [OE.].

SLEUTH (1) [slōōth], *n.* track of an animal; animal or person who follows a track; bloodhound; (*coll.*) detective. SLEUTH-HOUND, hound trained to track a man by scent; (*coll.*) man expert in detection. SLEUTH (2), *v.t.* to follow, track; (*coll.*) act as a detective.

SLEW (1) [slōō], *pret. of* SLAY. [ME.].

SLEW (2), **SLUE,** *v.t.* to swing round or askew. [Uncert.].

SLICE (1) [slīs], *n.* thin, broad piece cut off something, piece cut out of a whole; share, portion; flat implement used in cooking; broad, flat knife with which fish is served; (*sport*) stroke in which with a right-handed player the ball veers to the right of the line of flight; **s. of life,** typical specimen of life in a play or story. SLICE (2), *v.t. and i.* to cut up in slices, divide into thin portions by cutting; cause to slide off sharply; (*sport*) make a s. [OFr.].

SLICK (1) [slik], *adj.* smooth, sleek; clever, smart, deft. SLICK (2), *adv.* effectually, cleverly, easily done; head-on. [ME.].

SLID [slid], *pret. and p.pt. of* SLIDE. [OE.].

SLIDE (1) (*pret. and p.pt.* **slid**) [slīd], *v.t. and i.* to cause to slide, thrust along a slippery surface, make glide; put into position with an oblique movement; move smoothly along a polished surface, slip along; work easily in a specified groove; move into position

---

The accent ′ after a syllable = stress (u-pon′). The mark ⁻ over a vowel = length (ā in made; ō in bone).

obliquely or unobserved; pass silently; (*fig.*) undergo imperceptible change from one state to another; treat superficially, pass (over) lightly or too facilely. SLIDE (2), *n.* act of sliding; stretch of smooth, slippery surface, particularly of ice or snow; highly polished incline providing a means of transport; sliding seat; small piece of glass used as a base for objects put under a microscope; piece of glass on which scenes or designs are drawn or printed, and which is slid into a magic lantern or cinema projector; landslip; hair grip in the form of a clip; (*mus.*) a grace of two semitones; rapid chromatic run on an instrument; slider. [OE.].

SLIDE-RULE, SLIDING-RULE [slīd'rōol], *n.* ruler fitted with a sliding attachment by means of which certain mathematical calculations are simplified.

SLIDING SCALE [slī-ding-skāl'], *n.* scale of duties, wages or charges which is modified in terms of current market prices or similar factors.

SLIDING SEAT [slī-ding-sēt'], *n.* seat on a rowing boat which slides on runners with the swing of the body.

SLIGHT (1) [slīt], *adj.* having a physical constitution or frame which is not strong; slender of limb, slim; delicate, fragile in appearance; having little effect, making little difference, not severe; inconsiderable, not deep; insignificant, superficial, trivial. SLIGHT (2), *v.t.* to treat with contempt, insult. SLIGHT (3), *n.* gesture with a social significance of disrespect, breach of convention, insult. [ME.].

SLILY, see SLYLY.

SLIM (1) [slim], *adj.* having a natural tendency not to put on flesh; small-boned; slender; of small diameter; weak, slight; (*slang*) astute, crafty. SLIM (2) (*pres.pt.* SLIMMING, *pret.* and *p.pt.* SLIMMED), *v.t.* and *i.* to make s.; reduce one's weight. SLIMNESS, *n.* quality of being s., slenderness; (*slang*) cunning. [~Du.].

SLIME (1) [slīm], *n.* liquid mud in a greasy or sticky condition, viscous mud; bitumen; viscous secretion; any viscous substance; a mould belonging to the *Mycetozoa*. SLIME (2), *v.t.* to cover or smear with s. [OE.].

SLIMY [slī'mi], *adj.* resembling, consisting of, smeared with, slime; sticky, filthy, viscous; (*fig.*) offensively ingratiating.

SLING (1) [sling], *n.* primitive weapon consisting of a strip of looped leather with a pad in the centre from which a pebble is hurled; a throw made by means of a sling; loop used as a support, *esp.* one placed round the neck to hold up an injured arm. SLING (2) (*pret.* and *p.pt.* SLUNG), *v.t.* to throw by means of a s.; hurl from the hand by swinging the arm; lift by means of a loop; suspend in a s. or in a swinging position; (*coll.*) **to s. out,** to throw out bodily; **s. your hook!** (*slang*) go away! [OE.].

SLING (3), *n.* (*U.S.*) iced drink consisting of equal parts of rum, gin or other spirit, and water sweetened. [Uncert.].

SLINK (*pret.* and *p.pt.* **slunk**) [slingk], *v.t.* and *i.* to move in a stealthy or furtive way; (of animals) give birth prematurely; miscarry. SLINKY, *adj.* (*coll.*) (of persons) lithe and slim; (of garments) close-fitting. [OE.].

SLIP (1) [slip], *n.* shoot or twig cut from a stock or plant for grafting or transplanting; young boy or girl, adolescent; young sole; blank microscope slide; leash securing a dog, particularly a greyhound; escape by subterfuge; loose undergarment, the modern equivalent of a petticoat; outer covering for a pillow or bolster; narrow strip of material, *esp.* a small piece of paper; galley-proof in the form of a long piece of paper with the type printed in a column on one side of the paper; (*pl.*) short bathing drawers or trunks worn by men round the loins. [MDu.].

SLIP (2) (*pres.pt.* **slipping,** *pret.* and *p.pt.* **slipped**), *v.t.* to cause to move into a specific position quietly and easily; slide; place in position quietly and furtively; cause to make a slip, omit; escape from, evade, unseen or by subterfuge; let loose, release; (of animals) give premature birth to, miscarry; (*coll.*) pass, give; *v.i.* to move along a smooth surface, slide; progress swiftly and easily; move accidently out of an accustomed position; make a false step owing to an uneven or slippery surface, stumble, trip over; fall unexpectedly out of one's hand; escape unseen; make a mistake, do the wrong thing by accident; pass rapidly; **to s. up,** (*coll.*) to make a mistake. SLIP-COACH, railway carriage which can be detached from a train while in motion. SLIP-KNOT, knot which slips along the rope on which it is made, making a loop which can be tightened or loosened by a pull.

SLIP-ON, (garment) able to be put on easily, with few fastenings. SLIP-OVER, light sleeveless sweater. SLIP-UP, (*coll.*) mistake. SLIP (3), *n.* act of slipping; accidental movement of the foot caused by a slippery or uneven surface, a stumble; accidental movement out of an accustomed position; error, slight mistake; slope from which a vessel is launched, slipway; a failure to grip (clutch or pulley) or engage (gears); (*cricket*) offside fielder whose position is behind the popping crease; (*aeron.*) sideslip; **propeller s.,** difference between the actual and theoretical headway made by a propeller; **s. of the tongue,** something said which was not intended; **to give someone the s.,** to escape from someone. SLIPPY, *adj.* (*coll.*) slippery, lively, quick. [MDu.].

SLIPPER [sli'per], *n.* loose shoe easily slipped on; light, smart shoe worn by ladies; man who releases coursing greyhounds. SLIPPERED, *adj.* wearing slippers; **slippered ease,** comfort of the sort accompanying the wearing of slippers.

SLIPPERY [sli'pe-ri], *adj.* not affording a firm footing, causing to slip, skid or slide by reason of smoothness or greasiness of surface, unreliable, changeable; (*fig.*) crafty in conduct. [OE.].

SLIPSHOD [slip'shod], *adj.* originally descriptive of a person wearing shoes down at heel; careless, slovenly and inaccurate.

SLIPSLOP (1) [slip'slop], *n.* poor quality liquor; a feeble composition; anything weak or trivial. SLIP-SLOP (2), *adj.* weak, feeble; lacking quality or substance; trashy. [SLIP (2) and SLOP (2).]

SLIPSTREAM [slip'strēm], *n.* (*aeron.*) backwash from a propeller.

SLIPWAY [slip'wā], *n.* slope for launching a vessel from a dock or shipyard; slope for transferring seaplanes to the water.

SLIT (1) (*pres.pt.* **slitting,** *pret.* and *p.pt.* **slit**) [slit], *v.t.* and *i.* to cut into two strips, split, make a clean cut lengthwise; make an incision; be slit. SLIT (2), *n.* long, narrow incision, clean cut; an opening of small width; **s. trench,** narrow trench giving protection against enemy fire or bombs. [OE.].

SLITHER (1) [sli'THer], *v.i.* to slip or slide along a slippery surface; slide about, particularly on wet ground. SLITHER (2), *n.* act of slithering. SLITHERY, *adj.* slippery; deceitful. [OE.].

SLIVER (1) [sli'ver, slī'ver], *n.* long, thin piece split, cut or chipped off a mass; strand of loose fibres ready for spinning. SLIVER (2), *v.t.* and *i.* to split or cut a s. off a mass, reduce to slivers; cut into slivers. [~OE.].

SLOBBER (1) [slo'ber], *v.t.* and *i.* to smear with saliva; run at the mouth with saliva, dribble; (*fig.*) fuss sentimentally. SLOBBER (2), *n.* act of slobbering; saliva. SLOBBERER, *n.* one who slobbers, gushes sentimentally. [ME.].

SLOE [slō], *n.* small wild plum of bluish-black colour and bitter flavour, the fruit of the blackthorn. SLOE-GIN, gin in which sloes have been steeped. [OE.].

SLOG (1) (*pres.pt.* **slogging,** *pret.* and *p.pt.* **slogged**) [slog], *v.t.* and *i.* to hit hard, make a powerful but rather wild stroke at (a ball), swipe; work hard by a series of strong laborious efforts, plod. SLOG (2), *n.* act of slogging; a violent hit at a ball, swipe. SLOGGER, *n.* person who slogs; hard reckless hitter; hard worker. [Uncert.].

SLOGAN [slō'gan], *n.* battle-cry or gathering cry of a Highland clan; phrase giving pithy expression to a principle, and used to stimulate public response; catch phrase for advertising purposes. [Gael.].

SLOOP [slōōp], *n.* small single-masted vessel, rigged fore and aft; type of small warship. [Du.].

SLOP (1) [slop], *n.*(*pl.*) loose-fitting clothes, overall; sailor's equipment. SLOP-SELLER, shopkeeper who sells ready-made clothes; sailor's outfitter. SLOP-SHOP, (*coll.*) shop where ready-made clothes are sold. [Oicel.].

SLOP (2), *n.* act of slopping; pool of spilt water or liquid; (*pl.*) washing-up water, waste liquid; food in liquid form easily digestible by invalids. SLOP-BASIN, bowl for containing the dregs of teacups. SLOP (3) (*pres.pt.* SLOPPING, *pret.* and *p.pt.* SLOPPED), *v.t.* and *i.* to cause to brim over, spill; be spilt. [~OE.].

SLOPE (1) [slōp], *n.* direction or position inclined away from a flat or upright plane, real or imaginary; plane inclining downwards, declivity; measurement of ascent or descent using ground level as a base; (*milit.*) position of a rifle when held sloping across the shoulder. SLOPE (2), *v.t.* and *i.* to cause to take up a sloping position, place obliquely, cause to slant;

take or lie in an oblique direction or position, possess a surface slanting upwards; (*slang*) make off. SLOPING, *adj.* slanting, oblique, inclining or inclined from a horizontal or upright plane. [ME.].

SLOPPY [slo'pi], *adj.* saturated and immersed in water or other liquid; wet; muddy; careless, untidy, floppy; weak, flabby; (*fig.*) sentimental.

SLOT (1) [slot], *n.* track of a deer, spoor. [OFr.].

SLOT (2), *n.* a slit, narrow opening designed to contain a smaller object, groove; broad, flat wooden bar to hold larger pieces together. SLOT-MACHINE, machine which automatically delivers goods after its mechanism has been set in motion by a coin inserted in a s. SLOT (3) (*pres.pt.* SLOTTING, *pret. and p.pt.* SLOTTED), *v.t.* to make a s. in. [Uncert.].

SLOTH [slōth], *n.* absence of desire for exertion, mental and physical apathy, lethargy; American mammal of arboreal habits and characterized by a slow, lumbering gait on the ground. SLOTH-BEAR, a long-clawed Indian bear. [OE.].

SLOTHFUL [slōth'fool], *adj.* indolent by nature, lazy, sluggish.

SLOUCH (1) [slowch], *n.* shuffling gait, ungainly bearing; clumsy person; slouch-hat. SLOUCH-HAT, soft felt hat with a turned-down brim. SLOUCH (2), *v.t. and i.* to cause to hang down, make stoop; allow one's body to move or rest in a s., carry oneself with a s. SLOUCHING, *adj.* characterized by a s.; hanging down; walking with a s. [Uncert.].

SLOUGH (1) [slow], *n.* muddy swamp, bog. [OE.].

SLOUGH (2) [sluf], *n.* skin, *esp.* that of a snake, which has been cast off; dead tissue shed by a healed-up wound. SLOUGH (3), *v.t. and i.* to cast off, shed; discard a dead skin, as a snake. [ME.].

SLOVEN [slu'ven], *n.* person careless of dress or cleanliness; dirty lazy person; slattern. [ME.].

SLOVENLY (1) [slu'ven-li], *adj.* habitually untidy, negligent of dress or neatness; disorderly. SLOVENLY (2), *adv.* in the manner of a sloven, carelessly, untidily. [SLOVEN.]

SLOW (1) [slō], *adj.* taking a long time to travel a relatively short distance, to come to an end or to take effect, not rapid, not quick in motion; sluggish, not alert, inactive; not punctual, late; in a condition which necessitates a lower rate of progress than normal; tedious, boring. SLOW-COACH, *n.* dull person, laggard. SLOW-MOTION, *adj.* (*cinema*) having the action slowed down below normal rate. SLOW (2), *adv.* slowly. SLOW (3), *v.t. and i.* to cause to move more slowly, retard; become s. [OE.].

SLOW-WORM [slō'werm], *n.* the limbless lizard, the blindworm. [OE.].

SLUD [slud], *n.* soft muddy rock made by washing ore. [ME.].

SLUDGE [sluj], *n.* layer of slushy snow; thick, soft mud; wet refuse. [ME.].

SLUE, see SLEW (2).

SLUG (1) [slug], *n.* sluggard; air-breathing mollusc in which the shell is rudimentary or absent. [ME.].

SLUG (2), *n.* piece of metal used as crudely formed shot to fire from a gun; (*coll.*) bullet, *esp.* of an air-gun; (*typ.*) metal casting of a line of type; prefix to a cabled message; (*pl.*) (*mining*) heavy pieces of crude ore. [Uncert.].

SLUG (3) (*pres.pt.* slugging, *pret. and p.pt.* slugged), *v.t.* (*slang*) to hit so as to knock unconscious. [*Var.* of SLOG].

SLUGGARD (1) [slu'gerd], *n.* person habitually lazy, idler. SLUGGARD (2), *adj.* lazy, idle. [~ME.].

SLUGGISH [slu'gish], *adj.* reluctant to move, indolent; slow, inert, inactive; slightly unhealthy, not toned up.

SLUICE (1) [slōōs], *n.* artificial vent for stream or river water, fitted with an adjustable gate for the control of the volume of water, flood-gate; trough used in gold-mining in which earth is washed away from gold dust by a stream of water; a quick wash. SLUICE-GATE, gate sliding in grooves, permitting of an adjustable aperture controlling the volume of water allowed to flow through. SLUICE (2), *v.t. and i.* to provide with sluices; flood with water for washing purposes; wash quickly; flow freely. [OFr.].

SLUM (1) [slum], *n.* squalid quarter of a town or city, or a street in such a quarter, characterized by insanitary, dilapidated and overcrowded houses; also *pl.* SLUM-CLEARANCE, (scheme for) demolishing s. areas and building in their place; new sanitary houses with adequate amenities. SLUM (2) (*pres.pt.* SLUMMING, *pret. and p.pt.* SLUMMED), *v.i.* to visit a s. for the purpose of sight-seeing, or to give charity. [Uncert.].

SLUMBER (1) [slum'ber], *v.i.* to sleep lightly, doze; be

in a dormant or inactive state. SLUMBER (2), *n.* sleep, rest, repose. SLUMB(E)ROUS, *adj.* tending to induce sleep, soporific, drowsy, sleepy. [ME.].

SLUMMOCKY [slu'mo-ki], *adj.* slovenly. [Unkn.].

SLUMP (1) [slump], *v.i.* to fall suddenly in value or esteem; collapse in confidence; fall heavily and awkwardly, plump down. SLUMP (2), *n.* sudden decline in value or reputation, *esp.* a sudden fall in price level or demand; a financial depression. [Uncert.].

SLUNG [slung], *pret. and p.pt.* of SLING. [OE.].

SLUNK [slungk], *pret. and p.pt.* of SLINK. [OE.].

SLUR (1) (*pres.pt.* slurring, *pret. and p.pt.* slurred) [slur], *v.t. and i.* to run syllables together in pronunciation so as to be indistinct; (*mus.*) play or sing a passage so that the notes slide by degrees one into another; **to s. over,** to pass over superficially; disguise or conceal (a fault). SLUR (2), *n.* act of slurring; insult, stain on a reputation, or a suggestion of such an insult; (*mus.*) carelessly or deliberately played passage in which the notes are made to slide one into the other; the symbol ⌣ or ⌢. [ME.].

SLUSH [slush], *n.* sludge, soft watery mud; melted snow and mud; a soft greasy mixture; (*fig.*) sentimental trash, *esp.* in the form of literature. [*Var.* of SLUDGE.]

SLUT [slut], *n.* slovenly woman; name of contempt for a disreputable woman. [ME. ~OIcel.].

SLY [slī], *adj.* artful, meanly cunning, crafty; underhand; quietly humorous, playful. SLY-BOOTS, (*coll.*) sly, cunning person, rascal. [ME. from OIcel.].

SLYPE [slīp], *n.* covered passage between two walls, *esp.* the covered passage from a cathedral or monastery to any adjoining building. [Uncert.].

SMACK (1) [smak], *n.* small fishing boat with a single mast rigged fore and aft; small coaster, yawl. [Du.].

SMACK (2), *n.* a distinctive flavour, characteristic taste; trace of a substance imparting such a flavour; hint, trace. SMACK (3), *v.i.* to have a characteristic taste, savour; possess a suggestion (of), hold a hint (of). [OE.].

SMACK (4), *v.t. and i.* to press (the lips) together and then part them sharply so as to produce a quick, slapping sound; strike with the flat palm of the hand, slap; make a sharp loud noise as of hands clapped together, crack, as a whip. SMACK (5), *n.* sharp, loud sound like the crack of a whip or the clap of a hand against flesh; slap, blow with an open hand held flat; loud kiss; **s. in the eye,** (*coll.*) distinct rebuff; **to have a s. at,** to make an attempt at. [Du.].

SMALL (1) [smawl], *adj.* comparatively little in size, height, bulk or stature, of slight extent, not large, less than normal size; being few in number; slender, slim; of little importance, insignificant; trivial; mean, narrow-minded; below average standard; **s. arms,** s. hand fire-arms such as rifles and revolvers; **s. beer,** weak thin beer; (*fig.*) anything insignificant; **s. hours,** hours after midnight and before dawn; **s. talk,** light, social conversation. SMALL-CLOTHES, *n.* † knee-breeches; underpants. SMALL-COAL, *n.* coals broken up into s. pieces. SMALL-FRY, *n.* tiny young fish; people or objects of little value or importance. SMALL-MINDED, *adj.* having a mind occupied with insignificant details; narrow-minded. SMALL-SWORD, *n.* light duelling sword, rapier. SMALL (2), *n.* slim or small part of anything, *esp.* the middle of the back just above the buttocks and beneath the shoulder-blades. SMALLS, *n.(pl.)* entrance examinations to the University of Oxford; Responsions; (*coll.*) ladies' underwear. [OE.].

SMALLHOLDING [smawl-hōl'ding], *n.* small strip of land leased by a county council to a local tenant for the cultivation of vegetable produce; a holding markedly smaller than a normal farm.

SMALLPOX [smawl'poks], *n.* a contagious and infectious fever, attended by eruptions which leave small round scars pitted in the skin.

SMALT [smawlt], *n.* a dark blue pigment; glass of a fine deep blue made out of this. [It.].

SMARM [smahm], *v.t. and i.* (*coll.*) to smooth down the hair with hair-cream etc.; behave in an ingratiating manner. [Dial.].

SMART (1) [smaht], *v.i.* to experience a sensation of sharp pain superficially diffused over an area, feel a hurt as though on raw flesh; suffer from emotional distress real but not deep, be resentful. SMART (2), *adj.* causing a sharp but superficial pain, mental or physical; severe, energetic; rapid, alert; capable, efficient; quick to seize an opportunity of personal advancement; quick-witted, witty, vivacious; neat in appearance, sprucely dressed; fashionable. SMART-ALEC(K), n. (coll.) person who fancies himself as clever. SMART-MONEY, n. compensation; (milit.) money paid as compensation for wounds received on active service. SMART (3), n. a sharp pain which is diffused superficially; emotional suffering, resentment, the after-effects of distress. SMARTLY, adv. in a s. manner; keenly; rapidly, briskly; efficiently; vigorously; sprucely, neatly.

SMARTEN [smah'ten], v.t. to make smart, impart a neat, spruce appearance to.

SMASH (1) [smash], v.t. and i. to break beyond repair, dash to pieces, crush into little pieces; hit hard; bring destruction to, esp. to make bankrupt; come into violent collision with; be destroyed. SMASH (2), n. act of smashing, violent breaking beyond repair; the sound of such an act; result of being involved in such a situation; s. and grab raid, raid by a thief who smashes a shop window and grabs the valuables displayed. SMASH-UP, catastrophic collision. SMASHER, n. one who smashes; something having a decisive effect; remarkable person or thing. [Uncert.].

SMATTERING [sma'te-ring], n. slight superficial knowledge (of a subject). [ME.].

SMEAR (1) [smeer], v.t. and i. to mark with a smear, put a mark or layer of grease or dirt upon, make blotchy, daub, soil; spread a crude layer of grease on; blur by rubbing; produce a smear; (orig. U.S.) circulate a smear about. SMEAR (2), n. act of smearing; rough layer of greasy, dirty substance, mark, blotch, stain; (orig. U.S.) scandalous rumour. [OE.].

SMELL (1) [smel], n. faculty of smelling, sense dependent for sensations on the stimulation of the olfactory nerve in the nose; that which is experienced by means of this sense, a scent; stench, stink. SMELL (2) (pret. and p.pt. SMELT), v.t. and i. to experience through the sense faculty provided by the nose; emit an odour; exercise the sense of s.; (coll.) appear dishonest or otherwise suspect; to s. of, to be permeated with; to s. a rat, (coll.) to be suspicious; to s. out, to track, discover. [ME.].

SMELLING [sme'ling], n. sense or act by which odours are experienced. SMELLING-BOTTLE, bottle containing s.-salts. SMELLING-SALTS, perfumed ammonium carbonate etc., used to revive a person feeling faint or giddy.

SMELT (1) [smelt], n. small edible fish of the salmon family. [OE.].

SMELT (2), pret. and p.pt. of SMELL (2).

SMELT (3), v.t. to heat (ore) so as to extract metal. SMELTER, n. one who smelts ore. [~Norw.].

SMEW [smyōō], n. small migratory sea duck. [Uncert.].

SMIFT [smift], n. fuse used in blasting. [Unkn.].

SMILAX [smī'laks], n. (bot.) a numerous genus of liliaceous plants. [Gk.].

SMILE (1) [smīl], v.t. and i. to indicate by means of a smile; express pleasure, approval or happiness by a smile; allow the face to break slowly into a mild expression of joy. SMILE (2), n. act of smiling; facial expression as a response to a pleasurable experience, marked by a slight lifting of corners of the mouth and a brightening of the eyes, a look indicating pleasure or happiness. [ME. ~Dan.].

SMIRCH (1) [smurch], v.t. to blur or stain, soil, smear; depreciate, disparage. SMIRCH (2), n. act of smirching; a blot, stain, smear. [Uncert.].

SMIRK (1) [smurk], v.i. to wear an unpleasant expression on the face, half smile, half sneer. SMIRK (2), n. self-satisfied smile; silly smile, simper. [OE.].

SMITE (pret. **smote**, p.pt. **smitten**) [smīt], v.t. and i. (archaic and poet.) to strike hard; give a blow calculated to kill; descend on with a tremendous impact, affect the senses violently, afflict; strike or affect with passion. [OE.].

SMITH [smith], n. one who forges with the hammer; worker in molten or heated metals. SMITHERY, n. business of a s.; workshop of a s. SMITHY, n. workshop of a s., forge of a blacksmith. [OE.].

SMITHEREENS [smi-THe-rēnz'], n.(pl.) (coll.) little pieces, small fragments. [Ir.].

SMITTEN [smi'ten], p.pt. of SMITE. [OE.].

SMOCK (1) [smok], n. † chemise; loose-fitting overall of linen, smock-frock; child's romping frock. SMOCK-FROCK, coarse linen frock, reaching to the knees, formerly worn by farm-labourers over other clothes. SMOCK (2), v.t. to clothe with a s.; adorn with smocking. SMOCKING, n. pleating closely in the form of a honeycomb. [OE.].

SMOG [smog], n. mixture of smoke and fog such as

often hangs over industrial cities. [SM(OKE) and (F)OG].

SMOKE (1) [smōk], n. finely divided particles given off by burning matter and held in suspension in the air, cloud of vapour, steam or fumes; act of smoking a pipe, cigarette or cigar; cigarette, cigar; s. gas, one of various kinds of heavy fumes used as poison gas. SMOKE-BLACK, sooty substance obtained from the s. of burning oil; lampblack. SMOKE-BOMB, n. (milit.) bomb which throws out a s.-screen. SMOKE-DRIED, adj. dried in s., cured. SMOKE-SCREEN, n. (milit.) dense cloud of s. raised for concealing movements from the enemy; (fig.) barrage of words intended to confuse or conceal motive. SMOKE (2), v.t. and i. to subject to s., cure, as meat or fish; make taste of s.; fumigate; emit, eject s., give off fumes; indulge in the practice of inhaling and exhaling tobacco s. from a cigarette, cigar or pipe. SMOKESTACK, n. tall chimney of a factory, funnel. [OE.].

SMOKER [smō'ker], n. worker at a process of drying tobacco; one who smokes tobacco; concert at which smoking is permitted, informal show; railway carriage where smoking is permitted.

SMOKING (1) [smō'king], n. act of emitting smoke; process of curing by smoke; practice of inhaling and emitting tobacco fumes. SMOKING (2), adj. emitting or discharging smoke; where smoking is allowed.

SMOOTH (1) [smōōTH], adj. having an even, regular surface, free from roughness, polished, level; not broken up, calm, unruffled; flowing gently and easily, having an even movement of rhythm; having a fine texture; having suave manners, bland. SMOOTH-BORE, n. gun with a barrel which has not been rifled. SMOOTH-FACED, adj. clean-shaven, having a mild, soft look; (fig.) plausible. SMOOTH-TONGUED, adj. conciliatory in speech, plausible; flattering. SMOOTH (2), n. anything s., esp. a pleasant experience unaccompanied by discomfort; act of making s. SMOOTH (3), SMOOTHE, v.t. and i. to make s., clear away ruffles, lumps or rucks; remove obstructions, make easy in progress; calm, soothe; become s.; to s. down, to become (make) less disordered. [OE.].

SMOOTHE, see SMOOTH (3).

SMOOTHING [smōō'THing], adj. designed for making smooth; having the power to smooth.

SMOTE [smōt], pret. of SMITE. [OE.].

SMOTHER (1) [smu'THer], n. act of smothering; suffocating cloud of smoke or dust. SMOTHER (2), v.t. and i. to envelop so as to stifle or suffocate, block up the passage of air so as to cause choking; kill by suffocation; suppress, conceal; be suffocated, feel stifled. [ME.].

SMOULDER (1) [smōl'der], n. act of smouldering; that which smoulders. SMOULDER (2), v.i. to burn away slowly; burn or exist in a stifled state; exist in a powerful latent but suppressed condition. [ME.].

SMUDGE (1) [smuj], v.t. and i. to smear a smut across, make a dirty mark on, make dirty with marks of a blurred character. SMUDGE (2), n. smeared smut, black stain, smear, dirty, blurred mark. [Uncert.].

SMUG [smug], adj. maintaining an attitude of prudish self-satisfaction, complacent in appearance; prim. [~Du.].

SMUGGLE [smu'gl], v.t. and i. to take (goods) into or out of a country with intent to evade customs duties; give illegal transport over a frontier. SMUGGLING, n. act of a smuggler; practice of importing or exporting prohibited goods or other goods with the intent of evading customs duties or other official control. [LGerm.].

SMUGGLER [smug'ler], n. one who smuggles; vessel employed in carrying contraband.

SMUT (1) (pres.pt. **smutting**, pret. and p.pt. **smutted**) [smut], v.t. and i. to make or be made dirty with smut, stain with grains of soot or coal-dust, cover with particles of dirt. SMUT (2), n. particle of coal-dust or soot, spot of dirt; mark or stain made by such a particle; parasitic fungus on grass cereals characterized by a mass of black spots; obscenity. [~Swed.].

SMUTCH (1) [smuch], n. a smut, smudge. SMUTCH (2), v.t. to blacken with smoke, soot or coal, to smut or smudge. [Var. of SMUDGE].

SMUTTY [smu'ti], adj. marked, soiled with smut; tainted with mildew; obscene.

SNACK [snak], n. light meal eaten to save time. SNACK-BAR, small shop or counter, esp. in the bar of a public-house, where light refreshments are on sale. [Uncert.].

SNAFFLE (1) [sna'fl], n. a bit for a horse made of two linked bars, lighter and less severe than one with a curb. SNAFFLE (2), *v.t.* to place a s. on (a horse); (*slang*) steal, pilfer. [Du.].

SNAG (1) [snag], *n.* projecting piece of broken branch, root or tree-stump, *esp.* one sticking up from a river bed and forming a danger to boats; (*fig.*) unexpected difficulty, source of trouble or obstruction. SNAG (2) (*pres.pt.* SNAGGING, *pret.* and *p.pt.* SNAGGED), *v.t.* and *i.* to collide with a s.; lop off the projecting parts of trees, remove snags; catch (a fabric etc.) on some projection. SNAGGY, SNAGGED, *adj.* having the characteristics of a s.; full of snags; knotty. [OIcel.].

SNAIL [snāl]. *n.* one of a species of slimy, slow-creeping, air-breathing univalve molluscs; slow-moving person; spiral cam. [OE.].

SNAKE (1) [snāk], *n.* (*zool.*) member of the order *Ophidia*, having the characteristics of a reptile, limbless, long, tubular form, covered with small scales, which drags its length by muscular convulsion along the ground; (*fig.*) cunning, malevolent person; **s. in the grass,** hidden danger; deceitful enemy. SNAKE-CHARMER, one who gives a performance with snakes and charms them into obedience by various means; **s.'s head,** a bulbous plant of Arabia; a British plant, the fritillary. SNAKE (2), *v.i.* to move in the manner of a s., wend one's way smoothly and quickly. SNAKEWISE, *adv.* moving like a s.; in the manner of a s. [OE.].

SNAKESTONE [snāk'stōn], *n.* crinoidal limestone containing the fossilized stems of sea-lilies which resemble snakes; it is alleged to be a charm against snake bites.

SNAKY [snā'ki], *adj.* relating to, or resembling, a snake; serpentine, winding; sly, insinuating, deceitful; infested with snakes.

SNAP (1) (*pres.pt.* snapping, *pret.* and *p.pt.* snapped) [snap], *v.t.* to break suddenly and sharply; cause to make a cracking sound, crack; strike suddenly so as to make a sharp report; catch at suddenly bringing the teeth together sharply, bite; bring together, fasten with a click; take a snapshot of; (*cricket*) catch smartly a ball coming quickly off the bat; **to s. up,** to seize eagerly; *v.i.* to break sharply in two, come apart suddenly making a sharp sound; bring the teeth together sharply; speak sharply and irritably; bring together with a click, shut suddenly so as to make a sharp report; (*U.S.*) move briskly; **to s. out of it,** (*slang*) to get quickly out (of an attitude or mood); **to s. a person's head off,** to interrupt rudely with the purpose of reprimanding; **to s. one's fingers at,** to show one's contempt for. SNAP (2), *n.* act of snapping; sound which snapping teeth make; quick, sudden bite; sudden breaking; cracking sound made by such an act; clasp which snaps to when used as a fastening; sudden spell of cold weather; conciseness of expression; small cake or biscuit of gingerbread; game of cards in which the word "s." is used; (*phot.*) instantaneous photograph taken by an amateur. SNAP (3), *adj.* unexpected, done by surprise, quickly accomplished. SNAP-DIVISION, -VOTE, *n.* division, vote, called for suddenly. SNAP-JUDGMENT, *n.* opinion or decision formed or taken rapidly. SNAPPER, *n.* one who snaps; the alligator-terrapin. [MLGerm.].

SNAPDRAGON [snap'dra-gon], *n.* (*bot.*) the herbaceous plant *Antirrhinum*; game played at Christmas of snatching raisins out of burning brandy.

SNAPHANCE [snap'hans], *n.* old-fashioned gun or pistol with a spring lock. [Du.].

SNAPPISH [sna'pish], *adj.* inclined to snap, eager to bite; curt in reply; inclined to speak angrily or sharply.

SNAPPY [sna'pi], *adj.* abrupt, curt, irritable, in manner or speech; efficient, lively; (*coll.*) neat in appearance, smart; (of weather) brisk, sharp; **to make it s.,** (*coll.*) to be quick about it.

SNAPSHOT (1) [snap'shot], *n.* shot without a deliberate aim; (*phot.*) instantaneous exposure made with a hand camera, *esp.* informally. SNAPSHOT (2) (*pres.pt.* SNAPSHOTTING, *pret.* and *p.pt.* SNAPSHOTTED), *v.t.* and *i.* to take a s. of. [SNAP (3) and SHOT].

SNARE (1) [snār], *n.* contrivance such as a noose, pit or trap for catching birds or animals; that which has the power to entangle. SNARE (2), *v.t.* to catch by means of a s.; entangle, entrap. [OIcel.].

SNARKY [snah'ki], *adj.* (*coll.*) short of temper, irritable; unpleasant.

SNARL (1) [snahl], *v.i.* to show the teeth and growl when roused to vicious anger; speak savagely or surlily. SNARL (2), *n.* act of snarling; vicious growling sound made when snarling. [~MDu.].

SNARL (3), *n.* entanglement, complication difficult to unravel. [~SNARE].

SNATCH (1) [snach], *v.t.* and *i.* to seize hastily and vigorously; catch up in the hand firmly and swiftly, grasp, grab; take without permission; remove by sudden force; seize suddenly with the hand; attempt to seize vigorously. SNATCH (2), *n.* act of snatching, hasty vigorous effort to seize; a grab; short spell of exertion or sleep; fragment, small portion; snack. SNATCHY, *adj.* bitty, scrappy. [ME.].

SNEAK (1) [snēk], *v.t.* to steal, pilfer; *v.i.* to move quickly and furtively, keep close to cover while stealing away, crouch while slinking away so as to escape observation; (*slang*) tell of another's punishable activities; **s. thief,** *n.* petty pilferer. SNEAK (2), *n.* mean fellow; (*slang*) person who tells tales, informer; (*cricket*) ball which keeps low to the ground. SNEAKING, *adj.* acting like a s.; furtive; servile; engaged in telling tales; small, private. [Uncert.].

SNEER (1) [snēer], *v.t.* and *i.* to express by means of a sneer; assume a mocking smile indicating contempt; make contemptuous mocking remarks, disparage by means of a sneer. SNEER (2), *n.* act of sneering; facial expression characterized by a superior smile indicating contempt, look of disdain; verbal expression of contempt, gibe. [ME.].

SNEEZE (1) [snēz], *v.i.* to make an involuntary response to an irritant affecting the inner mucous membrane of the nose by blowing air loudly and violently through the nose in an effort to be rid of the irritant; **not to be sneezed at,** having values or advantages worth considering. SNEEZE (2), *n.* act of sneezing; sound made by this. [OE.].

SNICK (1) [snik], *v.t.* to mark with a small notch, nick; (*cricket*) touch slightly with the edge of the bat so that the ball is scarcely deflected from its course. SNICK (2), *n.* act of snicking; nick cut in a piece of wood, notch; (*cricket*) slight touch of the ball with the edge of the bat. [Unkn.].

SNICKER (1) [sni'ker], *v.i.* to snigger. SNICKER (2), *n.* a snigger. [Imitative].

SNIFF (1) [snif], *v.t.* and *i.* to breathe in through the nose; inhale, draw in with the breath, particularly so as to experience a scent; obtain a sensation of scent or smell by means of a sniff; draw in air swiftly and shortly through the nose so as to make a brief, thin noise; act in this way as an expression of disapproval, or to restrain flow of tears or mucus from the nose. SNIFF (2), *n.* act of sniffing; sound made by this; that which is sniffed. SNIFFY, *adj.* (*coll.*) off-hand, contemptuous, expressing a sense of superiority in a slightly insulting fashion; smelly, malodorous. [~Dan.].

SNIFTER [snif'ter], *n.* (*slang*) a short strong drink. [Uncert.].

SNIGGER (1) [sni'ger], *v.i.* to laugh with half-suppressed catches of voice, keep up a continual nervous high-pitched laugh, giggle. SNIGGER (2), *n.* act of sniggering. [Uncert.].

SNIGGLE [sni'gl], *v.i.* to fish for eels by dropping the bait into their holes; to snare fish.

SNIP (1) (*pres.pt.* snipping, *pret.* and *p.pt.* snipped) [snip], *v.t.* to cut by means of a short, quick clip or series of clips, clip with scissors or shears. SNIP (2), *n.* act of snipping; single, quick cut made with scissors or shears; (*coll.*) tailor; small piece snipped off; certainty; bargain. SNIPPER, *n.* one who snips or clips. [~LGerm.].

SNIPE (1) [snip], *n.* a marshland bird with brown mottled plumage and a long straight bill. SNIPE (2), *v.t.* and *i.* to shoot from an ambush; kill by such means; shoot at enemy troops one by one as an expert marksman from a concealed position. [OIcel.].

SNIPPET [sni'pit], *n.* small part or share, clipping, small snip.

SNITCH [snich], *v.i.* (*slang*) to inform, turn informer; pilfer; catch (salmon etc.) by means of a noose. [Unkn.].

SNIVEL (1) (*pres.pt.* snivelling, *pret.* and *p.pt.* snivelled) [sni'vel], *v.i.* to run at the nose with mucus so as to sniff continually, snuffle; complain of misery in a whimpering way. SNIVEL (2), *n.* act of snivelling; whining, whimpering expression of misery. [OE.].

SNOB [snob], *n.* one who pretentiously assumes a superior social status, social climber who continually boasts of important connexions; (*dial.*) cobbler. [Unkn.].

SNOOD (1) [snood], *n.* band or net with which the

hair is tied up; short length of gut to which a fish-hook is bound. SNOOD (2), v.t. to dress with a s. [O.E.].

SNOOK [snŏŏk], n. derisive gesture made by opening out the fingers and placing the thumb at the tip of the nose. [Unkn.].

SNOOKER [snŏŏ′ker], n. game played on a billiard table with six variously coloured balls, a triangle of fifteen red balls and one white cue-ball. SNOOKER′S POOL, s. [Unkn.].

SNOOP [snŏŏp], v.i. (coll.) to investigate stealthily, pry inquisitively, esp. into other people's affairs. SNOOPER, n. (coll.) one who snoops, esp. a government agent armed with authority to enter and search private property without notice. [Du.].

SNOOTY [snŏŏ′ti], adj. (slang) haughty, affectedly superior. [Uncert.].

SNOOZE (1) [snŏŏz], v.i. to indulge in a short sleep, doze. SNOOZE (2), n. short sleep or nap. [Uncert.].

SNORE (1) [snaw(r)], v.i. to breathe noisily, as though snorting, while asleep. SNORE (2), n. act of snoring, hoarse, nasal breathing in sleep, the sound made by this. [ME.].

SNORT (1) [snawt], v.i. to force air violently through the nostrils. SNORT (2), n. act of snorting; the sound made by this. SNORTER, n. person who or animal which snorts; abusive letter etc.; strong wind; difficult problem; (slang) snifter. SNORTY, adj. (coll.) angry, annoyed. [ME.].

SNOT [snot], n. (vulg.) mucus discharged from the nose. SNOTTY (1), adj. dribbling with mucus; (coll.) angry, short-tempered. SNOTTY (2), n. (nav. slang) midshipman. [ME.].

SNOUT [snowt], n. projecting nose or muzzle of a beast; nozzle of a pipe; anything which projects from a mass, as a cliff; (coll.) human being's nose. [ME.].

SNOW (1) [snō], n. moisture in the atmosphere frozen into light, fluffy crystals or flakes which float to the earth; a fall of this to the ground; (slang) cocaine in powder form. SNOW-BLINDNESS, amblyopia due to continual exposure of the eyes to the glare from 's. SNOW-CAPPED, crowned with s. SNOW-LEOPARD, the ounce. SNOW-LINE, the lower limit of perpetual s. SNOW-PLOUGH, implement for clearing away s. from roads and railways. SNOW-SPECTACLES, spectacles fitted with tinted lenses to take away the dazzle of s. SNOW (2), v.t. and i. to cause to shower down like s.; fall from the sky as s.; descend in the form of s.; **snowed under**, overwhelmed; **snowed up**, prevented from moving by a heavy fall of s. [O.E.].

SNOWBALL (1) [snō′bawl], n. round ball of snow, pressed or rolled together by the hands into a compact mass; (coll.) white-haired negro; scheme, petition etc. which increases in size as it progresses; **s. tree**, the guelder rose. SNOWBALL (2), v.t. and i. to pelt with snowballs; hurl snowballs; (fig.) grow continually larger like a rolled s.

SNOWBOUND [snō′bownd], adj. snowed up, unable to move because of a heavy fall of snow.

SNOWDRIFT [snō′drift], n. snow driven by the wind into a bank, heap or pile.

SNOWDROP [snō′drop], n. (bot.) a bulbous plant bearing a white flower of a delicate cup form which appears in early spring.

SNOWFIELD [snō′fēld], n. permanent expanse of snow common to cold regions.

SNOWFLAKE [snō′flāk], n. flake of snow in the form of a mass of frozen crystals matted together; the snow bunting, an Arctic bird.

SNOWSHOE [snō′shŏŏ], n. shoe in the form of a racket to prevent the feet from sinking into the snow; one of a pair of skis.

SNOWY [snō′i], adj. covered with snow; abounding in snow; pure white, pure, unblemished like snow.

SNUB (1) (pres.pt. **snubbing**, pret. and p.pt. **snubbed**) [snub], v.t. to check by means of a contemptuous cutting remark, reprove by a pose of indifference. SNUB (2), n. act of snubbing, a rebuke; **s. nose**. SNUB (3), adj. short and turned up at the end (esp. of a nose). [Icel.].

SNUFF (1) [snuf], n. charred wick of a candle left by the flame as it burns its way downward. SNUFF (2), v.t. and i. to clip off the wick or s. of a candle. SNUFFERS, n.(pl.) instrument in the form of a pair of scissors for trimming the wick of a candle. [ME.].

SNUFF (3), v.t. and i. to take in through the nose, inhale snuff; sniff, snort. SNUFF (4), n. pinch of powdered tobacco or drug to be sniffed up the nose; **(not) up to s.**, adj. (not) sharp, knowing, adequate.

SNUFF-BOX, small ornamental box or tin for carrying s. about the person. [MDu.].

SNUFFLE (1) [snu′fl], v.i. to sniff weakly through a dribbling nose; breathe or speak through the nose when obstructed. SNUFFLE (2), n. act of snuffling; sound of a s. [Du.].

SNUG (1) [snug], adj. made to fit or lie close together and tidily; so designed or arranged as to be small, compact and cosy, warm, sheltered. SNUG (2), n. small and comfortable place, esp. a small private bar in a public-house. SNUG (3), v.t. and i. to make s.; make oneself comfortable and cosy, snuggle. SNUGGERY, n. small cosy room, a s. [Unkn.].

SNUGGLE [snu′gl], v.t. and i. to enfold so as to warm, cuddle; lie close for comfort and warmth.

SO (1) [sō], adv. in such a manner, in this way, in that way; to that extent, to such a degree; in the same way, in like manner; for that reason, therefore; too, as well; more or less; in such a way; **s. much for**, that dismisses; **and s. on**, etcetera. SO-CALLED, adj. so named, having certain pretensions to being. SO-SO, in a not particularly noteworthy manner or condition. SO (2), pron. **s. and s.**, person whose name is understood; (slang) person to whom an abusive name is given by implication. SO (3), conj. therefore; in order that; in such a way; **s. long as**, providing that, on condition that. [O.E.].

SOAK (1) [sōk], v.t. and i. to immerse in liquid so as to be thoroughly impregnated, steep until saturated; wet thoroughly, drench; lie immersed in a liquid; (coll.) drink (alcohol) immoderately and habitually; (slang) tax or charge excessively; **to s. through**, to percolate through. SOAK (2), n. act of soaking; condition of being soaked; (coll.) drenching shower of rain, period of such weather; habitual drinker. SOAKAGE, n. liquid which has soaked in; (elect.) residual charge in a cable or capacitor. SOAKING, adj. having the power to wet thoroughly; thoroughly wet. [O.E.].

SOAP (1) [sōp], n. substance made of animal or vegetable fats mixed with an alkaline base, used for cleansing and washing when dissolved in water. SOAP-BOILER, s. manufacturer; pan used for boiling s. SOAP-BOX, box for holding s.; (fig.) a temporary platform for a street-corner speaker. SOAP-BUBBLE, bubble of air formed by a film of soapy water. SOAP-SUDS, (pl.) water impregnated with s. so as to form a mass of lather. SOAP (2), v.t. and i. to clean or wash by means of s. and water; use s. and water for washing purposes; (fig.) flatter. [O.E.].

SOAPSTONE [sōp′stōn], n. a soft, cloudy stone, talc or steatite; French chalk.

SOAPY [sō′pi], adj. resembling soap; having the qualities of soap; soft and smooth; covered with, containing soap; (coll.) unctuous.

SOAR [saw(r)], v.i. to ascend to a great height in the air, rise high; (fig.) rise to a high pitch of imagination, thought or feeling.

SOB (1) (pres.pt. **sobbing**, pret. and p.pt. **sobbed**) [sob], v.t. and i. to express by sobs; utter a sob or a series of sobs; produce a sound or sounds which resemble a sob. SOB (2), n. act of sobbing; sound made by such an act; involuntary convulsion deep in the throat or chest, violent catch in the breath due to extreme misery. [ME.].

SOBER (1) [sō′ber], adj. not under the influence of alcohol, not drunk; temperate, of abstemious habits; having a temperament which does not indulge in extremes of passion or judgment; not fanciful; having a subdued tone or colour scheme. SOBER-MINDED, cool of judgment, having a disposition which is habitually s., temperate and calm. SOBER (2), v.t. and i. to make s.; become s. SOBERLY, adv. to a s. degree, in a s. manner. SOBERSIDES, n. (coll.) very serious and sedate person. [L.].

SOBOLIFEROUS [so-bō-li′fe-rŏŏs], adj. (bot.) bearing suckers. [L.].

SOBRIETY [sō-brī′i-ti], n. state of being sober, habitual moderation. [L.].

SO(U)BRIQUET [sō′bri-kā], n. nickname; assumed name. [Fr.].

SOCCER [so′ker], n. (coll.) variety of football played under the laws of the Football Association. [(AS)-SOC(IATION)].

SOCIABILITY [sō-sha-bi′li-ti], n. quality of being sociable, disposition to associate and converse with others; the practice of friendly intercourse.

SOCIABLE (1) [sō′sha-bl], adj. ready to be friendly, prepared to associate with other people for the sake of their company, willing to strike up an acquaintance. SOCIABLE (2), n. (U.S. coll.) informal party

---

ŏŏ is pronounced as in food; ŏŏ as in hood; th as in think; TH as in that; zh as in azure. ~ = related to.

without dancing or alcoholic drinks; (*hist.*) four-wheel carriage with two opposite seats each for two passengers; tricycle for two [L.].

SOCIAL (1) [sō′shal], *adj.* relating to, concerned with, man in society; living in a form of society characterized by mutual interdependence; relating to, consisting of, forms of conduct the organization of which has human sanction; disposed to be friendly, fond of convivial intercourse; formed for the purpose of uniting in groups seeking diversion or sports; (*biol.*) gregarious; **s. democrat**, socialist who believes in parliamentary government and free elections; **s. security**, national insurance against unemployment, old age, sickness etc. SOCIAL (2), *n.* meeting or party for talk and gossip, a sociable. SOCIALITY [sō-shi-a′li-ti], *n.* conventional socialness. SOCIALIZE, *v.t.* to render s.; govern according to the principles of socialism; nationalize. [L.].

SOCIALISM [sō′sha-lizm], *n.* the political theory which advocates nationalization of the means of production, distribution and exchange.

SOCIALIST (1) [sō′sha-list], *n.* advocate of socialism, member of a socialist party. SOCIALIST (2), *adj.* relating to a s. or his beliefs; composed of socialists, under the control of socialists. SOCIALISTIC [sō-sha-lis′tik], *adj.* relating to socialism; tending to be influenced by socialism.

SOCIETY (1) [sō-sī′i-ti], *n.* form of human association in which men and women live in organized communities accepting a norm of behaviour which finds its expression in authorized regulations concerned with the ownership of the wealth and the control of the individuals' activities; any people considered collectively from the aspect of their laws and customs; any particular class of human beings the nature of whose work places them in a specific category; class of society regarded as setting a high standard of manners and fashion, the upper class; human association, the company of a human being or group; an association of persons for the promotion or protection of some common object or interest. SOCIETY (2), *adj.* relating to, consisting of, formed by, members of the upper class of s. [L.].

SOCINIAN [sō-si′ni-an], *n. and adj.* believer in, relating to, influenced by, the principles of Socinus, a sixteenth-century theologian who denied the atonement.

SOCIOLOGY [sō-si-o′lo-ji], *n.* scientific study of the nature of human society and the laws which govern its development. SOCIOLOGICAL [sō-si-o-lo′ji-kal], *adj.* relating to s. SOCIOLOGIST [sō-si-o′lo-jist], *n.* an expert in s. [SOCIAL and Gk.].

SOCK (1) [sok], *n.* stocking with a short leg covering the foot, ankle and the lower half of the calf; detachable sole inserted into a shoe; † shoe worn by actors in ancient Greek comedy; **to pull up one's socks**, (*coll.*) to prepare oneself for a big effort; **to put a s. in it**, (*coll.*) to subdue the noise one is making. [OE.].

SOCK (2), *v.t.* (*slang*) to fling at; hit, punch. SOCK (3), *n.* (*slang*) a blow. [Unkn.].

SOCKET (1) [so′kit], *n.* cavity into which something fits, and which permits of movement. SOCKET (2), *v.t.* to fit with a s.; set in a s. [OFr.].

SOCRATIC [sō-kra′tik], *adj.* relating to Socrates, to his manner of teaching by question and answer, or to his philosophy.

SOD (1) [sod], *n.* soil covered with grass and compact with its roots; piece of turf cut in a square or oblong. [~MDu.].

SOD (2), *n.* (*low*) obscene term of abuse implying sodomitic habits. [SOD(OMITE)].

SODA [sō′dah], *n.* a compound of sodium; **washing s.**, carbonate of sodium used for household washing; **s. fountain**, shop or counter equipped to sell ice-cream, fruit and aerated drinks. SODA-WATER, weak solution of s.; water charged with carbonic acid gas under pressure, so that it effervesces when the pressure is released. [It.].

SODALITY [sō-da′li-ti], *n.* fellowship or fraternity, a brotherhood. [L.].

SODDEN (1) [so′den], *adj.* † *p.pt.* of SEETHE; saturated, soaked; heavy and dull with alcohol. SODDEN (2), *v.t. and i.* to make s.; become soaked. [OE.].

SODIUM [sō′di-um], *n.* a soft metallic element denoted by Na. [SODA].

SODOMITE [so′do-mīt], *n.* inhabitant of Sodom; person guilty of sodomy. [Gk.].

SODOMY [so′do-mi], *n.* sexual connexion between males. [*Sodom*, Gen. xix].

SOFA [sō′fah], *n.* kind of long stuffed seat or couch,

which is sometimes fitted with back and arms. [Arab.].

SOFT (1) [soft], *adj.* responding to manipulation, easily pressed or squeezed, not hard, of a yielding consistency; smooth to the touch; not rough or harsh; having a tender, impressionable nature; merciful, gentle, delicate; not strong, effeminate; lenient, humane; not vivid, subdued; having a blurred outline; not loud, low of tone; (of water) readily forming a lather; (of drinks) non-alcoholic; **s. goods**, (*pl.*) drapery, linen; **s. pedal** (1), pedal on a piano which softens the tone when depressed; **s. soap** (1), viscid soap made from potash lye; (*coll.*) (*fig.*) ingratiating flattery. SOFT-HEARTED, *adj.* gentle, compassionate. SOFT-PEDAL (2), *v.t.* (*coll.*) (*fig.*) to under-emphasize, keep in the background; tone down. SOFT-SOAP (2), *v.t.* (*coll.*) (*fig.*) to flatter or humour ingratiatingly. SOFT (2), *adv.* in a s. manner, gently. SOFT (3), *int.* be careful, be still, quiet. SOFTY, *n.* (*coll.*) coward or weakling. [OE.].

SOFTEN [so′fn], *v.t. and i.* to make soft; become soft. SOFTENING, *n.* act of making or becoming softer; the blending of colours harmoniously; (*med.*) a decrease of the consistency of a tissue.

SOFTWOOD [soft′wood], *n.* the timber of coniferous trees; a conifer.

SOGGY [so′gi], *adj.* wet through; soaked with water; boggy, marshy; sloppy, heavy. [Uncert.].

SOIGNE, soigné [swun′yā], *adj.* well-groomed. [Fr.].

SOIL (1) [soil], *n.* upper layer of the earth's crust in which plants are nourished; country, land. [AFr. ~L.].

SOIL (2), *v.t. and i.* to make or become dirty; (*fig.*) stain, tarnish. SOIL (3), *n.* a stain, mark which soils; dirt; manure; sewage. [OFr.].

SOIREE, soirée [swah′rā], *n.* social entertainment or party in the evening. [Fr.].

SOJOURN (1) [so′jern, su′jern], *v.i.* to stay, dwell for a time. SOJOURN (2), *n.* a temporary stay [OFr.].

SOL (1) [sol], *n.* the sun (personified). [L.].

SOL (2), *n.* (*mus.*) fifth note in the diatonic sol-fa scale. [L.].

SOLA [sō′lah], *n.* an East Indian plant; pith of this used for sun-helmets. [Hind.].

SOLACE (1) [so′las], *n.* comfort, consolation, relief in grief or disappointment. SOLACE (2), *v.t. and i.* to offer s. to, comfort, cheer. [OFr.].

SOLAN-GOOSE [sō′lan-goos], *n.* gannet. [OIcel.].

SOLANUM [sō-lā′num], *n.* large genus of plants including the nightshades, the potato etc. [L.].

SOLAR [sō′ler], *adj.* pertaining to, coming from, due to, by means of, the sun; measured or determined by the sun; **s. plexus**, a network of nerves in the abdomen behind the stomach; **s. system**, the planets and other heavenly bodies which revolve round the sun. SOLARIZE, *v.t. and i.* to over-expose to the sun's rays; (*phot.*) reverse the negative and positive parts of a film or print. [L.].

SOLATIUM (*pl.* **solatia**) [sō-lā′shi-um], *n.* compensation for injury or loss; monetary consolation. [L.].

SOLD [sōld], *pret. and p.pt.* of SELL.

SOLDER (1) [sōl′der], *n.* easily fusible alloy used for cementing metals together. SOLDER (2), *v.t.* to unite or cement with s. [OFr.].

SOLDIER (1) [sōl′dyer], *n.* one who is a member of an army and undergoing a special training for war; private soldier as distinct from an officer; man distinguished for his military achievements. SOLDIER-CRAB, the hermit crab. SOLDIER (2), *v.i.* to serve as a s. SOLDIERING, *n.* the activities or profession of a s. SOLDIERLIKE, SOLDIERLY, *adj.* having the appearance of a s., straight-backed, brisk and efficient in action; having the mental and emotional qualities of a s., brave, loyal. [OFr.].

SOLE (1) [sōl], *n.* underside of the foot between the toes and the arch of the instep; the part of a shoe, boot etc. on which this rests; lower or bottom part. SOLE (2), *v.t.* to provide with a (new) s. [OFr.].

SOLE (3), *n.* an edible marine flatfish. [L.].

SOLE (4), *adj.* only, single, alone, being or acting without another; exclusive; (*leg.*) unmarried. SOLELY, *adv.* singly, alone; to the extent of one reason or person. [L.].

SOLECISM [so′li-sizm], *n.* grammatical mistake, incorrect usage in speech; an impropriety, a violation of the social conventions. SOLECISTIC(AL) [so-li-sis′tik(-al)], *adj.* of the nature of, constituting, a s. [L. from Gk.].

SOLEMN [so′lem], *adj.* characterized by a serious and

formal series of acts performed at a slow pace, as at a religious ceremony, worthy of being approached or participated in reverently; grave, important, serious; impressive in dignity of mien; not smiling; affectedly serious. [L.].

SOLEMNITY [so-lem′ni-ti], *n.* condition or quality of being solemn; ceremonial formality; impressiveness, serious dignity suitable to an important, particularly a religious, occasion. [L.].

SOLEMNIZE [so′lem-nīz], *v.t.* to celebrate with rites, perform with due solemnity as proper to ritual ceremonies; make solemn, render grave and reverential.

SOL-FA (1) [sol-fah′], *n.* (*mus.*) system of spoken syllables designating the notes of the diatonic scale. SOL-FA (2), *v.i.* to sing the notes of a scale in terms of the syllabic system, do, re, mi, fa, sol, la, si (te) [SOL and FA].

SOLICIT [so-li′sit], *v.t. and i.* to ask, beg for, petition earnestly; make an immoral request, accost; be engaged in solicitation. SOLICITATION [so-li-si-tā′-shn], *n.* act of soliciting, earnest request, persistent invitation. [L.].

SOLICITOR [so-li′si-ter], *n.* person who solicits; (*leg.*) legal practitioner who, being an expert in the theory and practice of law, conducts suits at law on behalf of others in the lower courts; legal adviser, legal practitioner other than a barrister. SOLICITOR-GENERAL, second in rank of the law officers of the Crown, junior to the Attorney-General. [OFr.].

SOLICITOUS [so-li′si-toōs], *adj.* particularly careful, anxious; very concerned; making anxious inquiries. [L.].

SOLICITUDE [so-li′si-tyoōd], *n.* state of being solicitous, concern, anxiety. [L.].

SOLID (1) [so′lid], *adj.* retaining its form under moderate pressure; having a dense consistency, not fluid, firm; substantial; completely filled, not hollow; strong, sound, reliable; genuine; characterized by fact, valid; grave, profound; unanimous in opinion; (*math.*) existing in, referring to, three dimensions. SOLID (2), *adv.* without exception, unanimously. SOLID (3), *n.* that which is s.; (*pl.*) food which is s. (in contrast to slops); (*geom.*) any three-dimensional figure; (*phys.*) a s. body. [L.].

SOLIDARITY [so-li-da′ri-ti], *n.* unanimity of opinion and resultant action. [Fr.].

SOLIDIFY [so-li′di-fī], *v.t. and i.* to make solid; become solid.

SOLIDITY [so-li′di-ti], *n.* quality of being solid, firmness, compactness; moral firmness; validity. [L.].

SOLILOQUY [so-li′lō-kwi], *n.* talking aloud to oneself; speech spoken by a character in a play expressing private thoughts out of hearing of other characters; such a speech in its written or printed form; monologue. SOLILOQUIZE, *v.i.* to speak in the form of a s., talk to oneself. [L.].

SOLITAIRE [so-li-tāer′], *n.* a single precious stone, *esp.* a diamond, worn as a piece of jewellery; game played on the same principle as draughts but using a round board fitted with small pits to hold pegs or marbles; a card-game for one, patience. [Fr.].

SOLITARY (1) [so′li-ta-ri], *adj.* being or living by oneself, living apart from others, being unaccompanied, alone, lonely; not frequented by people, remote, not inhabited; desolate, deserted; single, sole. SOLITARY (2), *n.* one who lives in solitude, hermit, recluse.

SOLITUDE [so′li-tyoōd], *n.* state of being solitary; place barely affected by human activity, desert. [L.].

SOLO (1) [so′lō], (*pl.* **solos, soli**) [so′lō], *n.* (*mus.*) tune or air to be played or sung by a single instrument or voice; card-game based on the principle of whist, particularly a call in this made by a player who undertakes to make five tricks. SOLO (2), *adj.* performed alone. SOLO (3), *adv.* by oneself. SOLOIST, *n.* performer of a s. [It.].

SOLOMON [so′lo-mon], *n.* **S.'s seal,** six-pointed star formed by interlacing two triangles; (*bot.*) perennial herb with flowers the shape of bells hanging on curving stems. [*Solomon,* king of Israel].

SO-LONG [sō-long′], *int.* (*coll.*) good-bye, au revoir.

SOLSTICE [sol′stis], *n.* the points on the ecliptic which mark the earth's position at the sun's extreme limit of distance north or south of the equator. SOLSTITIAL [sol-sti′shal], *adj.* relating to the s.; occurring at a s. [L.].

SOLUBLE [so′lyoō-bl], *adj.* capable of being dissolved in a fluid, capable of solution. [L.].

SOLUS [sō′lus], *adj.* by oneself, alone. [L.].

SOLUTION [so-lyoō′shn], *n.* act or process of separating out the component parts of any body; act or process of dissolving a solid in a fluid so that the various elements are absorbed; a liquid containing something dissolved; an adhesive preparation of rubber used in mending tires; act or process of solving a problem, puzzle or mystery; the answer to a problem; method for discovering this; an explanation, particularly of a difficulty or doubt. [L.].

SOLVE [solv], *v.t.* to explain by finding the correct relationship of the parts, provide the right answer to, clear up, resolve; remove the cause of difficulty in. [L.].

SOLVENCY [sol′ven-si], *n.* condition of being solvent; ability to pay all debts.

SOLVENT (1) [sol′vent], *adj.* having the power of dissolving; having enough money or wealth to pay all debts. SOLVENT (2), *n.* a substance which has the power of dissolving specific substances; that which explains or modifies.

SOMBRE [som′ber], *adj.* presenting a dark and dismal scene, overcast; gloomy; covered with shadow; having a low tone of colour, subdued; expressing melancholy or depression of spirits, dejected. [Span.].

SOMBRERO [som-brāer′ō], *n.* type of broad-brimmed soft felt hat. [Span.].

SOME (1) [sum], *adj.* a quantity, number, person or thing which is not given a specific definition; approximately, more or less; one or other; (*slang*) fine, great. SOME (2), *pron.* an unspecified number of people or objects. [OE.].

SOMEBODY [sum′bo-di], *n.* a person unknown or uncertain; person not identified; person of importance or influence.

SOMEHOW [sum′how], *adv.* in some way, in one way or other not yet known; by some means left unspecified.

SOMEONE [sum′wun], *pron.* some person.

SOMERSAULT (1) [su′mer-sawlt], *n.* leap in the air in which a person turns heels over head before landing on his feet again. SOMERSAULT (2), *v.i.* to turn a s. [OFr.].

SOMETHING (1) [sum′thing], *n.* that which is indicated but left undefined as to characteristics; anything unspecified or indefinite; that which is important; **s. of,** characterized by the possession of (certain features or qualities) but undefined as to degree. SOMETHING (2), *adv.* to some extent or degree; in some degree; **s. like,** having a vague resemblance; approximately, nearly; fine, excellent.

SOMETIME [sum′tīm], *adv.* at some time left unspecified; at one time or other hereafter; formerly.

SOMETIMES [sum′tīmz], *adv.* at times; at intervals; at one time; occasionally; now and then.

SOMEWHAT [sum′wot], *adv.* in some degree or quantity, rather, to some extent, slightly.

SOMEWHERE [sum′wāer], *adv.* in some place unknown or not specified; in one place or another.

SOMNAMBULISM [som-nam′byoō-lizm], *n.* practice of walking and performing actions of various kinds in sleep, sleep-walking. SOMNAMBULIST, *n.* person who walks in sleep; person who is subject to s. SOMNAMBULISTIC (som-nam-byoō-lis′tik), *adj.* relating to s.; having a tendency to s. [L.].

SOMNI-, *pref.* inducing, inclined to, affected by, sleep. [L.].

SOMNIFEROUS [som-ni′fe-roōs], *adj.* causing or inducing sleep, soporific. [L.].

SOMNOLENCE [som′no-lens], *n.* a physical and mental condition characterized by drowsiness and a tendency to fall asleep, condition of being half awake and half asleep. [L.].

SOMNOLENT [som′no-lent], *adj.* tending to fall asleep, sleepy, drowsy; inclined to induce sleep. [L.].

SON [sun], *n.* a male child in relation to his parent or parents; form of address used by an old man to a young; term of affection; male member of a country, or of any group or activity which commands an emotional loyalty, as a church, school etc. [OE.].

SONANT (1) [sō′nant], *adj.* articulated by means of a sound; (*phon.*) voiced. SONANT (2), *n.* (*phon.*) a voiced speech sound. [L.].

SONATA [so-nah′tah], *n.* form of musical composition for one or more instruments written in three or four movements. [It.].

SONATINA [so-na-tē′nah], *n.* short and simplified form of sonata. [It.].

SONG [song], *n.* series of modulated sounds produced

---

oō is pronounced as in food; ŏŏ as in hood; th as in *think*; TH as in *that*; zh as in azure. ~ = related to.

by a human being or bird by means of the vocal chords in the throat; a musical composition, composed as a setting to a lyric; a singing of such a composition; such a composition in manuscript form; lyric poem; poetry in general; the notes of birds; (*slang*) a mere trifle, practically nothing; **to make a s. about,** to make a fuss about. SONG-THRUSH, the common thrush. [OE.].

SONGSTER [song'ster], *n.* person who is continually singing; bird which sings. [OE.].

SONIC [so'nik], *adj.* pertaining to sound, using the properties of sound. [L.].

SON-IN-LAW [sun'in-law], *n.* a daughter's husband.

SONNET [so'nit], *n.* decasyllabic or dodecasyllabic poem of fourteen lines, with limited rhyming scheme and a single theme. SONNETEER, *n.* composer of sonnets. [It.].

SONORITY [so-no'ri-ti], *n.* quality of being sonorous.

SONOROUS [so-naw'rŏŏs], *adj.* resonant in quality of sound; emitting a deep, loud sound when struck; yielding sound; high-sounding; rhetorical. [L.].

SONSY [son'si], *adj.* (*Scots*) buxom, handsome. [Gael.].

SOON [sŏŏn], *adv.* in a short time; before the anticipated time, early; without delay, willingly; **as s. as,** at the exact moment that, directly, immediately. SOONER, rather. [OE.].

SOOT (1) [sŏŏt], *n.* a black substance, mostly carbon, deposited in chimneys by fuel during imperfect combustion. SOOT (2), *v.t.* to cover or stain with s. SOOTING, *n.* deposit of carbon on a sparking plug. [OE.].

SOOTH † [sŏŏth], *n.* a true fact, truth, reality. [OE.].

SOOTHE [sŏŏth], *v.t.* to cause to become less disturbed emotionally, pacify, calm; mitigate, allay. [OE.].

SOOTHSAYER [sŏŏth'sā-er], *n.* person who predicts the future, prophet, fortune-teller. [ME.].

SOOTY [sŏŏ'ti], *adj.* consisting of, affected by, soot; relating to, resembling, soot; covered, stained, with soot.

SOP (1) [sop], *n.* food such as bread etc., soaked in liquid such as milk or soup; anything soaked through with liquid; (*fig.*) small concession. SOP (2) (*pres.pt.* SOPPING, *pret.* and *p.pt.* SOPPED), *v.t.* to soak in an edible thick liquid such as soup; soak, drench; **to s. up,** to remove (water etc.) by means of an absorbent substance. SOPPING, *adj.* (*coll.*) very wet; **sopping wet,** soaked with water. SOPPY, *adj.* resembling a s.; saturated, very wet; (*coll.*) sloppy, feeble, foolishly sentimental; **to be soppy on,** to be infatuated with. [OE.].

SOPHISM [so'fizm], *n.* an ingenious but fallacious argument, specious line of reasoning. [Gk.].

SOPHIST [so'fist], *n.* person expert in putting forward plausible but fallacious arguments, specious arguer, unscrupulous propagandist; formerly, member of a class of professional teachers in ancient Greece. SOPHISTIC(AL) [so-fis'tik(-al)], *adj.* relating to a s. or his type of argument; containing sophistry, plausible but specious. [Gk.].

SOPHISTICATE [so-fis'ti-kāt], *v.t.* and *i.* to make sophistical; make impure, corrupt; cause to become artificial or affected in conduct; be sophistical. SOPHISTICATED, *adj.* affected, artificial, in behaviour; possessing a smartness of social attitude; worldly wise. [LL.].

SOPHISTICATION [so-fis-ti-kā'shn], *n.* state of being sophisticated; act of one who is sophisticated; process of making impure or corrupt sophistically.

SOPHISTRY [so'fis-tri], *n.* art or method of a sophist; specious reasoning. [OFr.].

SOPORIFIC (1) [sŏ-, so-po-ri'fik], *adj.* causing or tending to induce sleep. SOPORIFIC (2), *n.* medicine or drug which induces sleep. [L.].

SOPRANO (1) (*pl.* sopranos, soprani) [sŏ-prah'nŏ], *n.* music for one with a singing range which reaches the higher notes accessible to a human being or for the treble voice of a boy; person possessed of such a singing range; the part in a composition written for treble voices. SOPRANO (2), *adj.* with the musical range of a s.; written for a s. [It.].

SORB [sawb], *n.* the service-tree or its fruit. [L.].

SORCERER [saw'se-rer], *n.* one who practises sorcery, magician, wizard. [LL.].

SORCERY [saw'se-ri], *n.* art of magic, control of reality or divination by the help of evil spirits, or the power of commanding them; witchcraft. [OFr.].

SORDID [saw'did], *adj.* naturally associated with filth, dirty, squalid; given an existence by ignoble

methods or motives, contemptible; base-minded, mean, low. [L.].

SORE (1) [saw(r)], *adj.* painful when touched or rubbed; susceptible of pain, tender, affected with inflammation; hurt, upset emotionally through an experience of grief, insult, resentment or anger; † severe, intense. SORE (2), *n.* a morbid condition of the skin caused by injury or disease, ulcer, boil. SORE (3), *adv.* † severely, grievously. SORELY, *adv.* to a s. extent, in a s. manner; severely, greatly. SORENESS, *n.* quality of being s.; painfulness, tenderness; resentment, rancour. [OE.].

SORGHUM [saw'gum], *n.* (*bot.*) genus of tall, cereal grasses, including the Indian millet. [It.].

SOROPTIMIST [so-rop'ti-mist], *n.* member of a women's Rotary Club. [L. and OPTIMIST].

SORREL (1) [so'rel], *n.* a wild herb with sour leaves; **wood s.,** plant with small pinkish-white flowers and trefoil leaves. [OFr.].

SORREL (2), *adj.* of a reddish-brown colour. SORREL (3), *n.* horse of a red-brown colour. [OFr.].

SORROW (1) [so'rŏ], *n.* state of mind governed by prolonged misery and grief due to a sense of one's own or another's loss, affliction, deep unhappiness; regret for error or sin committed, contrition. SORROW (2), *v.i.* to feel or express s., grieve; mourn.

SORROWFUL [so'rŏ-fŏŏl], *adj.* full of sorrow; miserable, sad; producing sorrow; accompanied with sorrow.

SORRY [so'ri], *adj.* feeling grief, sorrow, regretting, contrite; *a term of apology;* inferior in quality; mean; ridiculous. [OE.].

SORT (1) [sawt], *n.* a group composed of individual members, objects, persons etc. having certain qualities in common, a class, kind, category; a class not precisely defined; degree, quality, condition, manner; **s. of,** (*coll.*) something like or in the category of; more or less, approximately; **good s.,** generous, likeable person; **out of sorts,** unwell, but not seriously ill; **of sorts,** of a kind. SORT (2), *v.t.* and *i.* to separate into sorts, classes or categories, classify, put in order; arrange postal matter for delivery; † agree. [L.].

SORTIE [saw'ti], *n.* sudden raid made by a body of troops from a besieged place on the enemy; sally, expedition. [Fr.].

S.O.S. [es-ō-es'], *n.* letters in the Morse code used in an appeal for rescue at sea; broadcast appeal for a relative or friend of a patient dangerously ill; urgent appeal.

SO-SO [sŏ'sŏ], *adj. and adv.* (*coll.*) of mediocre quality; not characterized by excellence; indifferent(ly).

SOSTENUTO [sos-te-nŏŏ'tŏ], *adv.* (*mus.*) with a sustained touch or utterance; with the notes held. [It.].

SOT (1) [sot], *n.* dull, drunken and befuddled fool; habitual drunkard with his brain sodden by drink. SOT (2) (*pres.pt.* SOTTING, *pret.* and *p.pt.* SOTTED), *v.t.* and *i.* (*archaic*) to make stupid by filling with drink; drink till fuddled in the brain. [ME.].

SOTTISH [so'tish], *adj.* being in the state of a sot; given to drinking; fuddled with drink.

SOTTO-VOCE [so-tō-vō'chā], *adv.* by means of a whisper, in an undertone. [It.].

SOU [sŏŏ], *n.* French copper coin, worth five centimes. [Fr.].

SOUBRETTE [sŏŏ-bret'], *n.* waiting-maid in a play; actress playing the part of a coquettish, pert character in comedy. [OFr.].

SOUBRIQUET, see SOBRIQUET.

SOUCHONG [sŏŏ'chong], *n.* kind of black tea from China, of fine quality. [Chin.].

SOUFFLE, soufflé [sŏŏ'flā], *n.* dish of sweet or savoury, made light by being mixed with the beaten whites of eggs and then baked. [Fr.].

SOUFFLE [sŏŏ'fl], *n.* (*med.*) soft, blowing sound made by the lungs. [Fr.].

SOUGH (1) [suf, sow], *n.* sound of low moaning, or of continuous sighing, such as the wind makes as it blows through the branches and leaves of trees. SOUGH (2), *v.i.* to make a sound like the wind sighing. [OE.].

SOUGHT [sawt], *pret. and p.pt. of* SEEK; searched for. [OE.].

SOUL [sŏl], *n.* the capacity for emotional or spiritual experience conditioning the functioning of conscience, feeling and rationality which is considered the core of a person's individuality, and credited by religious thought with the potentiality of eternal existence; the vital principle or power which maintains a person in the realm of life; the side of a man's nature sustained by the higher, nobler emotions and motives; a person when considered as animated by one of the nobler virtues; person who provides life and enthusiasm; spirit believed to have left the body of its owner, and departed elsewhere; a single person, one human being. [O.E.].

SOULFUL [sōl'fŏŏl], *adj.* full of power to stir the nobler emotions, emotional; yearningly sentimental.

SOULLESS [sōl'les], *adj.* having no soul; without nobleness of mind; destitute of human virtues; cruel, merciless; selfish, mean.

SOUND (1) [sownd], *n.* narrow passage of water as between a mainland and an island; shallow sea or strait forming the means of communication between two seas; inlet of the sea; air-bladder of a fish. [O.E.].

SOUND (2), *n.* that which is heard, a vibratory disturbance in the air which affects the eardrum and stimulates the sense of hearing, impression received by means of the hearing known to be characteristic of a certain cause; auditory impression made by the power of speech; noise, report; **s. locator,** instrument for detecting the presence and course of aircraft or submarines by the s. of their engines; **s. wave,** one of a regular series of disturbances in the air which affect the auditory nerves. SOUND-BOX, box containing the stylus and diaphragm of a gramophone. SOUND-FILM, (*cinema*) cinematograph film with synchronized sound effects, speech etc. SOUND-PROOF, having the structure and properties to shut out s. SOUND-SCREEN, (*cinema*) cinema screen specially adapted for s. projection. SOUND-TRACK, (*cinema*) narrow margin on a celluloid film on which synchronized s. is recorded. SOUND (3), *v.t. and i.* to cause a s., cause to make a noise; express by the voice; signal by means of a particular s.; celebrate, announce by sounds; make a s. or noise; make an impression of a particular quality on the ear; make a s. characteristic of a certain condition or event; seem, appear. SOUNDER (1), *n.* telegraphic instrument for signalling by means of s. [OFr. from L.].

SOUND (4), *n.* anatomical instrument used by a surgeon for probing. SOUND (5), *v.t. and i.* to measure the depth of (water); attempt to ascertain (opinion or feeling which has not been expressed); (*fig.*) learn by experience; (*med.*) test, examine, by means of a s.; (*meteor.*) examine scientifically by sending up balloons. [Fr.].

SOUND (6), *adj.* in a properly co-ordinated condition, entire, whole, unbroken; in good physical condition, perfect, healthy; hearty; solid; valid, right, logical, sagacious; complete, thorough; efficient, effective; strongly equipped with specific qualities; stout, lusty; reliable, unimpaired. SOUND (7), *adv.* to a whole degree; healthily. SOUNDNESS, *n.* quality of being s. [O.E.].

SOUNDER (2), *n.* herd of wild swine; a young boar. [O.E.].

SOUNDING (1) [sown'ding], *n.* act or process of measuring a depth of water; measurement obtained by this process; place submitted to such a process.

SOUNDING (2), *n.* act or power of making a s. or sounds. SOUNDING-BOARD, contrivance suspended over a pulpit to amplify the sound of a preacher's voice; any appliance which helps to increase the resonance of a sound. SOUNDING (3), *adj.* full of sound, sonorous; making a noise; providing more noise than significance.

SOUP [sŏŏp], *n.* food in the form of water or gravy impregnated with meat or vegetables which have been boiled in it and strained off; **in the s.,** (*slang*) in trouble. SOUP-KITCHEN, public establishment supplying s. gratuitously to the poor. SOUP-PLATE, plate with a deeper bowl than usual in which s. is served. SOUP-TICKET, ticket entitling the bearer to obtain free s. from a public kitchen.

SOUPCON [sŏŏp'saw(ng)], *n.* a suggestion, trace, taste. [Fr.].

SOUR (1) [sowr], *adj.* having a quality which is recognizable by tasting as sharp or bitter, acidulous in flavour, astringent; curdled, rancid, as milk; disagreeable, acrimonious; impoverished, as soil. SOUR (2), *n.* that which is s.; a drink made by mixing spirits, lemon juice etc. SOUR (3), *v.t. and i.* to turn s., cause to become rancid; make miserable and bitter in feelings, make peevish; become acidulous. SOURLY, *adv.* in a s. manner; to a s. degree; with acidity; discontentedly, peevishly. SOURNESS, *n.* quality of being s., acidity, tartness, asperity. [O.E.].

SOURCE [saws], *n.* place of a spring or fountain from which a stream of water flows; first cause, original, starting-point of something; original work providing material for successors. SOURCE-BOOK, collection of original documents recording historical material. [Fr.].

SOUSAPHONE [sŏŏ'za-fōn], *n.* large bass wind-instrument with a very wide mouth much used in jazz bands. [J. P. *Sousa,* American composer].

SOUSE (1) [sows], *v.t.* to pickle, keep saturated in pickle; soak with water, drench; duck in water. SOUSE (2), *n.* something kept steeped in pickle; downpour of water or rain water; a ducking in water; (*U.S.*) drunkard. SOUSE (3), *adv.* with a plunge, with a swoop. SOUSED, *adj.* (*coll.*) drunk, tipsy. [OFr.].

SOUTANE [sŏŏ-tahn'], *n.* black robe worn by R.C. priests, cassock; wearer of such a robe. [Fr. from LL.].

SOUTENEUR [sŏŏ-te-nur'], *n.* man who lives on a prostitute's earnings. [Fr.].

SOUTH (1) [sowth], *n.* the cardinal point of the compass opposite to the north; imaginary point facing an observer standing north of the equator and looking towards the sun at noon; southern hemisphere; area or district spoken of collectively as lying s. of a certain point or line. SOUTH (2), *adj.* situated in a territory or district in the s., southern; facing the s.; coming from, obtained from, grown, found in, the s. SOUTH (3), *adv.* towards the s. SOUTH (4), *v.i.* to move in a southerly direction. [O.E.].

SOUTH-EAST (1) [sowth-ēst'], *n.* point of the compass midway between the south and the east; region or district in this direction. SOUTH-EAST (2), *adj. and adv.* situated in, facing, (moving) towards, the s.; coming from the s. SOUTH-EASTER, *n.* south-easterly wind or gale.

SOUTHERLY [su'ᴛʜer-li], *adj. and adv.* towards the south; lying in, coming from, the south.

SOUTHERN [su'ᴛʜern], *adj.* situated in, belonging to, the south; lying towards the south; coming from, characteristic of, the south; operating in the south. [O.E.].

SOUTHERNWOOD [su'ᴛʜern-wŏŏd], *n.* (*bot.*) an aromatic plant, allied to wormwood.

SOUTHING [sow'ᴛʜing], *n.* tendency or motion to the south; course or distance south by drifting from a given course.

SOUTHRON [suᴛʜ'ron], *n. and adj.* (*Scots archaic*) inhabitant of a southern district. [~SOUTHERN].

SOUTHWARD(S) (1) [sowth'werd(z)], *adj.* directed towards the south. SOUTHWARD(S) (2), *adv.* in a southerly direction.

SOUTH-WEST (1) [sowth-west'], *n.* point of the compass midway between the south and the west; region or district in this direction. SOUTH-WEST (2), *adj. and adv.* situated in, facing, or coming from the s. SOUTH-WESTER, *n.* south-westerly wind or gale; sou'wester.

SOUVENIR [sŏŏ've-nēer], *n.* small object kept as a reminder, keepsake. [Fr.].

SOU'WESTER [sow-wes'ter], *n.* strong wind blowing from the south-west; sailor's waterproof hat enveloping the head and with a flap protecting the back of the neck. [SOUTH-WESTER].

SOVEREIGN (1) [so've-rin], *n.* person acknowledged as possessing a status entitling him (or her) to supreme rule, monarch, king (queen), emperor (empress); British gold coin worth originally twenty shillings. SOVEREIGN (2), *adj.* possessing the status of supreme dominion, paramount, supreme; powerfully efficient or effective; excellent. [OFr.].

SOVEREIGNTY [so've-rin-ti], *n.* state of holding supreme power; supreme dominion; authority of a supreme ruler; absolute and independent power claimed by a state within its boundaries; rule over other states. [OFr.].

SOVIET (1) [so'vi-et], *n.* the functioning unit of national or local administration in the U.S.S.R. SOVIET (2), *adj.* governed by soviets. SOVIETIZE, *v.t.* to bring under government by soviets; incorporate in the political system of the U.S.S.R. [Russ.].

SOW (1) [sow], *n.* adult female pig. SOW-THISTLE, thistle of the genus *Sonchus.*

SOW (2) (*pret.* sowed, *p.pt.* sowed, sown) [sō], *v.t. and i.* to cast seed on the ground, plant with seed; (*fig.*) disseminate, inculcate; perform the act of sowing. SOWN, *adj.* (of seed or plants) placed in the ground, *esp.* deliberately as distinct from wild growth; (of land) having seed planted in it. [O.E.].

SOYA BEAN [soi'a-bēn], *n.* the edible bean of *Glycine Soja.* [Du. from Jap.].

SOZZLE [so'zl], *v.t.* to make drunkenly confused and muddle-headed; splash, slop. [Uncert.].

ŏŏ is pronounced as in food; ŏŏ as in hood; th as in *think*; ᴛʜ as in *that*; zh as in azure. ~ = related to.

SPA [spah], *n.* health-resort with a mineral spring. [*Spa*, Belgium].

SPACE (1) [spās], *n.* extension between objects, area, the extension supposed to contain the universe, distance separating objects, period of time; (*typ.*) blank interval between words, available room for matter in a journal; (*mus.*) interval between the lines of a score; **to work on s.,** (*journalism*) to be paid according to the amount of work printed. SPACE-TIME, in Einstein's theory of relativity, the continuum formed by the addition of time to the three dimensions of s. SPACE (2), *v.t.* to arrange (objects) in regard to the spaces between them; **to s. out,** to place at intervals, place (objects) so that they are separated by a considerable s. [OFr. from L.].

SPACIOUS [spā'shŏŏs], *adj.* affording ample space, extensive; (*fig.*) broad and unrestricted. [L.].

SPADE [spād], *n.* a digging implement, any flat-bladed implement resembling this; black suit of playing cards resembling this; **to call a s. a s.,** to speak plainly and bluntly. SPADE-WORK, the laborious routine work of a project. [OE.].

SPAGHETTI [spa-get'ti], *n.* Italian preparation of wheat like small macaroni. [It.].

SPAHI [spah'hē], *n.* formerly a Turkish, now an Algerian, cavalryman. [Pers.].

SPAKE † [spāk], *pret. of* SPEAK. [ME.].

SPAN (1) [span], *n.* distance between the tips of the thumb and little finger when the hand is fully extended, nine inches; short distance or period, the full period, duration, of anything; measurement of an aeroplane between the wing-tips; space between the abutments or supports of an arch; team of oxen or draught horses. SPAN-ROOF, roof sloping on both sides from a common ridge. SPAN (2) (*pres.pt.* SPANNING, *pret. and p.pt.* SPANNED), *v.t.* to measure by stretching thumb and fingers; stretch across, or from side to side; cross over, extend over a period, carry over. [OE.].

SPANDREL [span'drel], *n.* triangular space between the shoulder and frame of an arch. [~EXPAND].

SPANGLE (1) [spang'gl], *n.* tiny disk of bright metal attached to a dress etc. as an ornament. SPANGLE (2), *v.t.* to set (as) with spangles. [ME. from OE.].

SPANIEL [span'yel], *n.* breed of dogs notable for their silky hair and drooping ears. [OFr.].

SPANISH [spa'nish], *adj. and n.* relating to, coming from, Spain; language of Spain; **S. chestnut,** the edible chestnut; **S. fly,** the small beetle *Cantharides*; **S. grass,** esparto grass. [ME.].

SPANK (1) [spangk], *v.t. and i.* to strike on or near the buttocks with the open hand or some flat object; perform the action of spanking; **to s. along,** to move at a brisk pace. SPANK (2), *n.* a blow (usually on the buttocks) with the flat of the hand. SPANKER, *n.* that which, one who, spanks; horse with a spirited action; (*naut.*) aftermost sail of a ship; (*coll.*) good stroke, excellent action or object. SPANKING (1), *n.* a beating with a flat object. SPANKING (2), *adj.* brisk; striking. [~Dan.].

SPANNER [spa'ner], *n.* tool for turning nuts, wrench.

SPAR (1) [spah(r)], *n.* pole supporting sails or tackle; long piece of timber; one of the main beams of an aircraft wing. [ME.].

SPAR (2), *n.* a crystalline mineral. [OE.].

SPAR (3), *v.i.* to box, *esp.* to practise boxing without endeavouring to injure one's opponent, make the motions of striking without actually doing so; (of cocks) fight. SPAR (4), *n.* act of sparring, sparring-match. [OFr.].

SPARE (1) [spāer], *v.t. and i.* to be meagre, refrain from using or performing, withhold, dispense with; *hence*, remit from use, show mercy, abstain from imposing one's power against a person or thing, save from injury or punishment, abstain from injuring or destroying. SPARE (2), *adj.* meagre, lean, scanty; left over, available as desired, extra, additional, ready for use as a replacement; (*of time*) not occupied by any necessity, available for leisure or other than essential business; **s. room,** guest room. SPARE-RIB, part of the ribs of a bacon pig. SPARE (3), *n.* a s. part, an extra available as replacement. SPARING, *adj.* frugal. SPARINGLY, *adv.* in sparing fashion. [OE.].

SPARK (1) [spahk], *n.* minute incandescent particle thrown off by a body in a state of combustion, tiny flash of fire or light; (*fig.*) the germ of animation, smallest trace of life or intelligence; flash accompanying electric discharge, ignition of an internal combustion engine. SPARK (2), *v.i.* to give out sparks; (of an engine) fire, have the ignition working;

spark(ing) plug, device in an internal combustion engine through which the electric current ignites the explosive gas in the cylinder. [OE.].

SPARK (3), *n.* lively, dashing young fellow. SPARK (4), *v.i.* to play the gallant. [OScand.].

SPARKLE (1) [spah'kl], *n.* scintillation, rapid glitter, vivacity, witty brilliance. SPARKLE (2), *v.i.* to give out sparks of light, glitter, coruscate, effervesce; show gaiety and brilliance. SPARKLER, *n.* that which sparkles; (*slang*) a diamond. [ME.].

SPARKLET [spahk'let], *n.* small sparkle; (*prot.*) cartridge containing carbonic-acid for charging soda-water siphons.

SPARKLING [spahk'ling], *adj.* giving off sparkles, flashing, scintillating, brilliantly witty, gay and polished.

SPARRING [spah'ring], *n.* practice boxing in which the opponents are not supposed to strike serious blows, motions of striking without actually hitting, movement of the fists in preparation for a blow; **s. partner,** person with whom a boxer practises during training. [SPAR (3)].

SPARROW [spa'rō], *n.* small bird of the genus *Passer*, allied to the finches. SPARROW-HAWK, small species of short-winged hawk. [OE.].

SPARSE [spahs], *adj.* growing thinly, not abundant, scarce. [L.].

SPARTAN [spah'tan], *n. and adj.* a native of, pertaining to, Sparta, in ancient Greece; courageous and enduring, austerely hardy.

SPASM [spazm], *n.* brief, violent, involuntary muscular contraction, sudden violent physical or mental reaction; sudden, strong but brief burst of energy. [Gk.].

SPASMODIC [spaz-mo'dik], *adj.* occurring in, relating to, spasms; violent but infrequent, intermittent.

SPASTIC [spas'tik], *adj.* (*med.*) spasmodic, afflicted with spasms.

SPAT (1) [spat], *n.* spawn of an oyster. [~SPIT].

SPAT (2), *n.* short gaiter for the upper part of the shoe. [SPAT(TERDASH)].

SPAT (3), *pret. and p.pt. of* SPIT.

SPATCHCOCK [spach'kok], *n.* a bird cooked immediately after killing. [Uncert.].

SPATE [spāt], *n.* sudden flood, *esp.* of a river after rain. [ME.].

SPATIAL [spā'shl], *adj.* relating to space. [L.].

SPATTER (1) [spa'ter], *v.t. and i.* to sprinkle with drops of liquid, splash, befoul; smirch; splash, fall in drops. SPATTER (2), *n.* a light splash. SPATTER-DASHES, *n.*(*pl.*) leggings worn as protection against mud and splashing. [~Frisian].

SPATULA [spa'tyŏŏ-lah], *n.* broad-bladed implement used for spreading paint or plaster; (*med.*) instrument used for holding down the tongue. SPATULATE, *adj.* (*bot.*) shaped like a s.; elliptical. [L.].

SPAVIN [spa'vin], *n.* morbid swelling in the hock-joint of a horse. SPAVINED, *adj.* affected with s.; (*fig.*) lame, crippled. [OFr.].

SPAWN (1) [spawn], *v.t. and i.* (of fish etc.) to deposit eggs; produce spawn, give birth to; supply with mushroom spawn; (*slang*) generate copiously. SPAWN (2), *n.* eggs of fish, frogs etc.; mycelium of mushrooms; (*slang*) children, offspring. [ME. from OFr.].

SPAY [spā], *v.t.* to sterilize by removing the ovary. [OFr.].

SPEAK (*pret.* **spoke,** *p.pt.* **spoken**) [spēk], *v.t. and i.* to utter words without musical modulation, make sounds, declare, address an audience, convey a meaning, say, express in words, make oneself understood in; (of an organ-pipe, trumpet etc.) sound (a note); **to s. for,** to urge on behalf of; **to s. of,** to talk about; **to s. out,** to s. clearly and unrestrainedly; **to s. up,** to s. distinctly. [OE.].

SPEAKEASY [spē'kē-zi], *n.* (*U.S.*) formerly a bar where illicit liquor was sold. [SPEAK and U.S. *easy* softly].

SPEAKER [spē'ker], *n.* one who speaks, one who addresses a meeting, the officer presiding in certain parliamentary assemblies, notably the House of Commons; loud-speaker.

SPEAKING [spē'king], *adj.* articulate; **on s. terms,** on good enough terms to exchange passing greetings; **s. likeness,** lifelike portrait. SPEAKING-TUBE, tube for s., carried through partitions etc.

SPEAR (1) [spēer], *n.* throwing or thrusting weapon, having a sharp-pointed head set on a shaft; anything resembling this; man armed with a spear. SPEAR (2), *v.t.* to pierce with a spear, impale with a spike.

The accent ′ after a syllable = stress (u-pon′).   The mark ‾ over a vowel = length (ā in m**a**de; ō in b**o**ne).

SPEARHEAD [spēer'hed], *n.* metal head of a spear; (*fig.*) forces in the van of an attack.

SPEARMINT [spēer'mint], *n.* aromatic garden mint.

SPECIAL (1) [spe'shl], *adj.* of a particular sort, intended for a particular circumstance, distinguished by a peculiar characteristic; detailed, not general; individual, for one person or purpose in particular; (*coll.*) especially good, out-of-the-ordinary, for a particular occasion; **s. pleading**, (*leg.*) pleading designed to meet the s. conditions of the case at issue; (*coll.*) specious argument, unfair attempt to bias a verdict. SPECIAL (2), *n.* anything prepared or designed for a s. purpose; s. edition of a newspaper; voluntary constable enrolled for a s. emergency. [OFr. from L.].

SPECIALIST [spe'sha-list], *n.* one who specializes in or has special knowledge of a certain subject, *esp.* a branch of medicine.

SPECIALITY [spe-shi-a'li-ti], *n.* study, knowledge, occupation in which a person is especially skilled, or to which he gives his main attention; something in the supply of which a trader specializes; quality of being special. [L.].

SPECIALIZE [spe'sha-līz], *v.t. and i.* to be a specialist, devote one's abilities and inquiry to a special subject or to some specific branch of accomplishment; (*biol.*) develop special functions or characteristics; qualify, make specific.

SPECIALTY [spe'shl-ti], *n.* a speciality; special point; (*leg.*) contract under seal. [OFr.].

SPECIE [spē'shē], *n.* coin, as distinct from paper money. [L.].

SPECIES (*pl.* **species**) [spē'shiz], *n.* (*biol.*) a classified set of living organisms, referable to one type, and distinguishable from any other members of its genus by constant, well-marked, inherited characteristics; kind, sort; (*theol.*) sensory appearance of the consecrated elements. [L.].

SPECIFIC (1) [spe-si'fik], *adj.* of a distinct kind, of a certain definite sort; explicit, precise, definite and therefore limited in meaning; relating to a species. SPECIFIC (2), *n.* a medicine for a s. purpose.

SPECIFICATION [spe-si-fi-kā'shn], *n.* act of specifying, a detailed description, *esp.* of a projected work; a detailed enumeration. [MedL.].

SPECIFY [spe'si-fī], *v.t.* to particularize, state specifically, enumerate in detail, indicate precisely. [MedL.].

SPECIMEN [spe'si-men], *n.* a representative example of a class or division, typical instance of a whole, sample, *esp.* when labelled, classified and preserved for study, a characteristic example; (*coll.*) peculiar individual. [L.].

SPECIOUS [spē'shŏŏs], *adj.* outwardly pleasing but deceptive; superficially good or plausible. [L.].

SPECK (1) [spek], *n.* small spot or mark, minute object, mark which is only just visible. SPECK (2), *v.t. and i.* to mark with specks; become so marked. [OE.].

SPECKLE (1) [spe'kl], *n.* small mark of different colour on a surface, a pattern of such markings. SPECKLE (2), *v.t. and i.* to mark, become marked, with speckles. [*Prec.*].

SPECS [speks], *n.(pl.)* (*coll.*) spectacles.

SPECTACLE [spek'ta-kl], *n.* something looked at, something displayed for inspection; an elaborate display; something remarkable, something arousing pity or contempt; (*pl.*) lenses, supported by a frame, worn to strengthen or correct faults in the vision, eye-glasses. [L.].

SPECTACULAR [spek-ta'kyŏŏ-ler], *adj.* relating to a spectacle, flamboyant, showy; amazing.

SPECTATOR [spek-tā'ter], *n.* one who watches, observer, one who witnesses a spectacle. SPECTATORIAL [spek-ta-taw'ri-al], *adj.* of a looker-on or an eye-witness. [L.].

SPECTRAL [spek'tral], *adj.* of or relating to a spectre or the spectrum.

SPECTRE [spek'ter], *n.* ghost, apparition, spirit appearing in visible form; (*fig.*) terrifying but insubstantial danger. [L.].

SPECTRO-, *pref.* relating to the spectrum. [L.].

SPECTROSCOPE [spek'trō-skōp], *n.* instrument for analysing a spectrum by means of prisms or a diffraction grating. SPECTROSCOPIC [spek-trō-sko'pik], *adj.* of, pertaining to, by means of, the s. SPECTROSCOPY [spek-tro'sko-pi], *n.* study of the spectrum. [SPECTRO and Gk.].

SPECTRUM (*pl.* **spectra**) [spek'trum], *n.* the component colours or wavelengths of light emitted by a given source; the colours displayed in order by means of a prism, raindrops etc., or a spectroscope; the colours of the rainbow; image retained by the retina after the removal of the stimulus which produces it. [L.].

SPECULATE [spe'kyŏŏ-lāt], *v.i.* to form theories, wonder about, cogitate; invest, *esp.* in stocks and shares. SPECULATOR, *n.* one who speculates, stock-market investor. [L.].

SPECULATION [spe-kyŏŏ-lā'shn], *n.* act of speculating, theory formed by speculating, unconfirmed conjecture; a gamble, investment without security, investing on the stock-market. [L.].

SPECULATIVE [spe'kyŏŏ-la-tiv], *adj.* based on, given to, speculation; risky, of the nature of a gamble.

SPECULUM (*pl.* **specula, speculums**), *n.* mirror, *esp.* of a telescope; (*med.*) instrument for dilating a cavity so that the interior may be seen. [L.].

SPED [sped], *pret. and p.pt. of* SPEED.

SPEECH [spēch], *n.* faculty of expressing meaning orally; a language; a particular form, tone or manner of speaking, a public address. SPEECH-DAY, annual celebration at a school, when prizes are handed out and a visitor delivers an address. SPEECH-READER, one who can understand s. by observing the lip-movements. [OE.].

SPEECHIFY [spē'chi-fī], *v.i.* to make a long, silly speech, make speeches too frequently.

SPEECHLESS [spēch'les], *adj.* dumb, silent, temporarily prevented from speaking by some strong emotion.

SPEED (1) [spēd], *n.* rapid movement, swiftness; velocity, rate of movement whether rapid or not. SPEED-BOAT, fast motor-boat. SPEED-COP, (*U.S. coll.*) policeman whose duty it is to enforce the s. limit. SPEED (2) (*pret. and p.pt.* SPED), *v.t. and i.* to move rapidly, hasten; (*motoring*) drive fast; make progress; help, wish success to, cause to move rapidly. SPEED-UP, † cause to prosper; **to s. up,** to increase (the) s. (of); (*coll.*) increase in s. SPEEDER, *n.* one who, that which, speeds; device for regulating s. SPEEDWAY, *n.* a race-track for mechanically propelled vehicles, *esp.* for motor-cycles.

SPEEDOMETER [spē-do'mi-ter], *n.* device for measuring and indicating the speed of a vehicle.

SPEEDWELL [spēd'wel], *n.* (*bot.*) herbaceous plant or shrub of the genus *Veronica*.

SPEEDY [spē'di], *adj.* swift, rapid of movement; prompt, quick.

SPELL (1) [spel], *n.* short period, *esp.* one coming or recurring in rotation, brief space of time; short turn of activity; (*dial. and Australian*) a rest. [~OE.].

SPELL (2), *n.* magical charm, compelling incantation; (*fig.*) very powerful attraction or influence. SPELL (3) (*pret. and p.pt.* SPELLED, SPELT), *v.t. and i.* to write or recite in succession the letters constituting a word; (of the letters) make a sensible word; (*fig.*) result in, mean as inevitable consequence; *v.i.* to be able to put the letters of a word in the right order; **to s. out,** to utter a word letter by letter; decipher with difficulty. [OE.].

SPELLBINDER [spel'bīn-der], *n.* orator who can hold his audience spellbound; (ironically) facile and plausible orator.

SPELLBOUND [spel'bownd], *adj.* fascinated, entranced as if by a spell.

SPELLING [spe'ling], *n.* orthography. SPELLING-BEE, a s. game. SPELLING-BOOK, book for teaching s.

SPELT [spelt], *pret. and p.pt. of* SPELL.

SPELTER [spel'ter], *n.* zinc; a soldering alloy. [LGerm.].

SPENCER [spen'ser], *n.* short woollen jacket. [Earl *Spencer*].

SPEND (*pret. and p.pt.* **spent**) [spend], *v.t. and i.* to give, part with, in payment, exchange money for goods, services etc.; expend, use up strength, resources, consume; pay out money. SPENDER, *n.* one who spends freely. [OE.].

SPENDTHRIFT [spend'thrift], *n.* wasteful, thriftless, extravagant person.

SPENSERIAN [spen-sēer'i-an], *adj.* of or resembling Edmund *Spenser* or his poetry; **S. stanza,** form of stanza used by Spenser in *The Faerie Queene.*

SPENT [spent], *adj. pret. and p.pt. of* SPEND; exhausted, wholly consumed.

SPERM (1) [spurm], *n.* (*also pl.*) fertilizing germs in the male animal. SPERMATIC [sper-ma'tik], *adj.* relating to; or secreting, s. [Gk.].

SPERM (2), *n.* sperm-whale; spermaceti. SPERM-OIL, oil obtained from the s.-whale. [SPERM(ACETI)].

SPERMACETI [sper-ma-se'ti], *n.* wax-like substance

ŏŏ is pronounced as in f*oo*d; ŏŏ as in h*oo*d; th as in *th*ink; TH as in *th*at; zh as in azure. ~ = related to.

DSE—S

obtained from the head of the sperm-whale, and used for making candles and preparing certain ointments. [Gk.].

SPERMATO-, *pref.* relating to sperm. [Gk.].

SPERMATOZOA [sper-ma-tŏ-zō'ah], *pl. of Next.*

SPERMATOZOON (*pl.* **spermatozoa**) [sper-ma-tŏ-zō'on], *n.* germ cell in the semen of male animals. [SPERMATO- and Gk.].

SPERM-WHALE [sperm'wāl], *n.* the whale from which spermaceti is obtained.

SPEW, SPUE [spyōō], *v.t. and i.* to vomit. [OE.].

SPHAGNUM (*pl.* **sphagna, sphagnums**) [sfag'num], *n.* peat-moss, bogmoss. [Gk.].

SPHERE [sfēer], *n.* a solid figure, every point on whose surface is equidistant from the centre, globe, ball; one of the spherical, hollow bodies in which the stars, planets etc. were formerly held to subsist; (*fig.*) scope, extent, region of a thing, circle in which a person moves. SPHERICAL, *adj.* of, relating to, resembling, a s. [Gk.].

SPHEROID [sfēer'oid], *n.* slightly flattened sphere, *esp.* when produced by the revolution of an ellipse. [Gk.].

SPHINCTER [sfingk'ter], *n.* muscular ring closing a bodily orifice. [Gk.].

SPHINX [sfingks], *n.* fabulous monster having human features and a lion's body, noted for its habit of asking insoluble riddles; (*fig.*) inscrutable person; the colossal sphinx of Gizeh. [Gk.].

SPICE (1) [spīs], *n.* aromatic tropical product used in flavouring, *esp.* the more pungent of such preparations; (*fig.*) that which flavours, gives taste to a thing. SPICE (2), *v.t.* to flavour with s. [OFr. from L.].

SPICK-AND-SPAN [spik-and-span'], *adj.* smart, spruce. [Uncert.].

SPICY [spī'si], *adj.* flavoured with spice; (*coll.*) piquantly indecent.

SPIDER [spī'der], *n.* member of the order *Arachnida*, having eight legs and a capacity for spinning webs to catch prey. [OE.].

SPIFFING [spi'fing], *adj.* (*slang, now rare*) excellent, splendid. [Uncert.].

SPIF(F)LICATE [spif'li-kāt], *v.t.* (*slang, now rare*) to squash utterly, disconcert, crush. [Unkn.].

SPIGOT [spi'got], *n.* vent-peg of a cask; (*eng.*) projecting flange or pin which enables one machined surface to be accurately located on another which has corresponding holes. [ME.].

SPIKE (1) [spīk], *n.* sharp-pointed, tapering rod or projection, *esp.* of metal and intended as a protection; (*bot.*) small sessile flowers about an axis, ear of corn. SPIKE (2), *v.t.* to pierce with a s., provide with spikes; put a cannon out of action by driving a s. into the match hole; (*fig.*) thwart (a plan). SPIKELET, *n.* small s., *esp.* in the inflorescence of grasses. [OScand. and L.].

SPIKENARD [spīk'nahd], *n.* (*bot.*) aromatic herb related to valerian, ointment prepared from this plant. [L.].

SPILL (1) [spil], *n.* splinter of wood or twist of paper used for lighting fires or tobacco. [OE.].

SPILL (2) (*pret. and p.pt.* **spilt, spilled**), *v.t. and i.* to fall, tip out of something, *esp.* liquid from a vessel; upset, splash out, allow to fall out and waste; **to s. the beans,** (*coll.*) to divulge a secret, *esp.* unintentionally. SPILL (3), *n.* a fall, upset, tumble. [OE.].

SPILLIKIN [spi'li-kin], *n.* splinter of wood or ivory used in spillikins; (*pl.*) game in which the players have to extract a spillikin without disturbing the others.

SPILT [spilt], *pret. and p.pt. of* SPILL.

SPIN (1) (*pret.* **span, spun,** *p.pt.* **spun**) *v.t. and i.* to draw and twist yarn etc. into thread; make rotate rapidly, whirl round; (*fig.*) devise subtly; perform the act or practice of spinning yarn; rotate, revolve; **to s. a yarn,** (*coll.*) to tell a story. SPIN (2), *n.* act of spinning; rotation; short but rapid journey in a vehicle, or by bicycle, taken for pleasure; (*aeron.*) spinning dive. [OE.].

SPINACH [spi'nij], *n.* an edible plant; **s. beet,** beet whose leaves are cooked and eaten like s. [Arab.].

SPINAL [spī'nal], *adj.* of, or pertaining to, the spine; **s. column,** vertebral column or backbone; **s. cord,** elongated part of the cerebro-spinal axis contained within the s. column. [LL.].

SPINDLE (1) [spin'dl], *n.* thin rod on which is wound the thread of a distaff; steel rod in a spinning machine by which yarn is spun and wound; shaft on which something rotates. SPINDLE-SHANKS, *n.* person with long, thin legs. SPINDLE-SHAPED, *adj.* slender,

attenuated. SPINDLE-SIDE, *n.* the mother's side. SPINDLE-TREE, *n.* shrub of the genus *Euonymus.* SPINDLE (2), *v.i.* (of plants) to grow into (excessively) slender stalks. SPINDLY, *adj.* excessively slender. [OE.].

SPINDRIFT [spin'drift], *n.* wind-blown foam and spray. [~SPOONDRIFT].

SPINE [spīn], *n.* (*anat.*) bony column running from head to pelvis in vertebrates, backbone; any stiff, pointed structure, quill, spike, thorn; the part of the back of a book which protects the sewing of the sheets. SPINELESS, *adj.* without a s.; (*fig.*) lacking in courage and determination. SPINY, *adj.* covered with, full of, spines. [L.].

SPINEL [spi'nel], *n.* crystalline mineral; **s. ruby,** scarlet gem resembling the true ruby. [OFr.].

SPINET [spi'net, spi-net'], *n.* small keyboard musical instrument from which developed the harpsichord. [It.].

SPINNAKER [spi'na-ker], *n.* (*naut.*) triangular sail carried opposite the mainsail when running before the wind. [Uncert.].

SPINN(E)Y [spi'ni], *n.* small copse. [OFr.].

SPINNING [spi'ning], *n.* business, practice or technique of spinning into thread. SPINNING-JENNY, machine for s. many threads simultaneously. SPINNING-MILL, factory for s. SPINNING-WHEEL, primitive s. machine, usually worked by a treadle.

SPINNY, see SPINNEY.

SPINOUS [spi'nŏŏs], *adj.* spiny, thorny.

SPINSTER [spin'ster], *n.* unmarried woman, *esp.* if elderly. [ME.].

SPIRACLE [spi'ra-kl], *n.* respiratory orifice; blow-hole of a whale. [L.].

SPIRAEA [spi-rē'ah], *n.* numerous genus of rosaceous plants, including the meadowsweet. [Gk.].

SPIRAL (1) [spi'ral], *adj.* in a curve revolving regularly away from a fixed central point; in a curve revolving at a constant distance from a centre, but on a continually shifting plane. SPIRAL (2), *n.* s. curve; objects arranged in a s. SPIRAL (3), *v.i.* to revolve in, form, a s. [L.].

SPIRANT (1) [spi'rant], *n.* consonant made by partial constriction of the air passage, fricative consonant. SPIRANT (2), *adj.* pronounced as a s. [L.].

SPIRE [spier], *n.* tower tapering to a point; anything resembling this. [OE.].

SPIRIT (1) [spi'rit], *n.* the animating, non-material, divine element in man which gives life and reason, soul, intelligent principle; will and intelligence divorced from a body, an immaterial being possessing conation, cognition or both; ghost, spectre; pervading influence, feeling which prevails in any particular circumstances; personal qualities which cannot, apparently, be directly related to the body, *esp.* courage, pride, vivacity; the fundamental principle, true meaning, of a thing; alcohol, a volatile, inflammable liquid; (*pl.*) alcoholic liquor produced by distillation; **spirits of salts,** commercial hydrochloric acid. SPIRIT-LAMP, lamp burning methylated s. SPIRIT-LEVEL, instrument for ascertaining the true horizontal by means of a bubble of air in a tube of s. SPIRIT-RAPPING, a variety of psychic phenomena in which the spirits of the dead are held to manifest their presence by rapping on material or immaterial objects. SPIRIT (2), *v.t.* to inspirit; **to s. away** or **off,** to take away, make to disappear as if by magic. [L.].

SPIRITED [spi'ri-tid], *adj.* full of spirit, vigour and vitality; full of courage and independence.

SPIRITUAL (1) [spi'ri-tyŏŏ-al], *adj.* consisting of, relating to, the spirit; relating to the soul, pertaining to religion and its principles, not materialist; inspired by moral or religious motives, not preoccupied with material things. SPIRITUAL (2), *n.* American-negro hymn characterized by simple words and sometimes by a syncopated rhythm. [L.].

SPIRITUALISM [spi'ri-tyŏŏ-a-lizm], *n.* belief that the spirits of the dead retain all the interests they possessed in life, and are able and willing to communicate with the living, *esp.* through a medium; the numerous practices based upon this belief. SPIRITUALIST, *n.* believer in s.

SPIRITUALITY [spi-ri-tyŏŏ-a'li-ti], *n.* state or quality of being spiritual. [LL.].

SPIRITUALIZE [spi'ri-tyŏŏ-a-līz], *v.t.* to make spiritual, refine; bring into closer relationship with religion.

SPIRITUEL(LE) [spē-ri-tyŏŏ-el'], *adj.* displaying great refinement and delicacy. [Fr.].

SPIRITUOSITY [spi-ri-tyŏŏ-o'si-ti], *n.* state or quality of containing distilled alcohol.

SPIRITUOUS [spi′ri-tyŏŏ-ŏŏs], *adj.* containing distilled alcohol.

SPIRT (1) [spurt], *v.t. and i.* to issue out in a small vigorous jet. SPIRT (2), *n.* sudden, small, vigorous jet of flame, fluid etc. [O.E.].

SPIT (1) [spit], *n.* long, thin, pointed spike or rod, *esp.* such a metal rod impaling meat for roasting; narrow point of low land running out into the sea. SPIT (2), *v.t.* to pierce with a s. [O.E.].

SPIT (3) (*pres.pt.* **spitting,** *pret. and p.pt.* **spat, spit†**), *v.t. and i.* to eject saliva from the mouth; throw out (liquid) in small drops; eject anything violently from the mouth. SPIT (4), *n.* act of spitting, mass of saliva so ejected from the mouth; splutter (of rain), slight fall of liquid; **the s. of,** the exact likeness of (a person). [O.E.].

SPITE (1) [spit], *n.* malevolence, vicious petty hostility; cause of such a feeling. SPITE (2), *v.t.* to injure, annoy through s., behave spitefully towards. [~DESPITE].

SPITEFUL [spit′fŏŏl], *adj.* malevolent, full of spite towards.

SPITFIRE [spit′fīer], *n.* hasty, vicious, ill-tempered person, *esp.* a woman of this kind.

SPITTLE [spi′tl], *n.* ejected saliva. [~O.E.].

SPITTOON [spi-tŏŏn′], *n.* receptacle into which saliva may be ejected.

SPIV [spiv], *n.* (*coll.*) one who lives precariously within the law by selling dubiously-acquired goods. [Reverse of letters V.I.P.S. for Very Important Persons].

SPLASH (1) [splash], *v.t. and i.* to cause (liquid) to scatter, fly about in drops; stain, wet a surface by scattering some liquid; perform with an accompaniment of splashing; (of liquid) be scattered, be dashed about, *esp.* as a result of being struck or violently shaken; make a bold display of (news etc.) in a newspaper. SPLASH (2), *n.* act of splashing; noise of splashing; small quantity of liquid flung on a surface by splashing, or squirted from a siphon; patch of bright colour or light; **to make a s.,** (*coll.*) to cut a dash, indulge in reckless expenditure. SPLASH-BOARD, a guard in front of a vehicle to prevent the occupants being splashed with mud; mudguard. [Echoic].

SPLAY (1) [splā], *v.t. and i.* to dislocate (a joint), spread out at an angle; (*arch.*) slope at an angle. SPLAY (2), *n.* (*arch.*) outward slope of the sill or sides of a window or door opening; degree of inclination of this; similar outward slope of a vessel. SPLAY (3), *adj.* sloping, spreading out at an angle. SPLAY-FOOT, flat, outward-turned foot. [ME.].

SPLEEN [splēn], *n.* ductless gland situated near the stomach, formerly held to be the seat of ill-humour and melancholy; dejection, ill-tempered despondency. SPLEENFUL, SPLEENY, *adj.* spleenish. [Gk.].

SPLENDENT [splen′dent], *adj.* shining, resplendent. [L.].

SPLENDID [splen′did], *adj.* gorgeous, magnificent in appearance, dazzling, rich and impressive to the eye; illustrious, brilliant, glorious; (*coll.*) excellent, admirable. [L.].

SPLENDOUR [splen′der], *n.* gorgeous and radiant brilliance of appearance, magnificence, rich and splendid panoply; pre-eminence, glory. [L.].

SPLENETIC [sple-ne′tik], *adj.* relating to the spleen; suffering from spleen, ill-tempered, melancholy. [LL.].

SPLENIC [splē′nik], *adj.* belonging to the spleen. [Gk.].

SPLICE (1) [splīs], *v.t.* to join (ropes) by interweaving the strands, join (timbers) by overlapping or fitting, and binding; (*slang*) join in marriage; **to s. the mainbrace,** to serve out an allowance of spirits in the Navy. SPLICE (2), *n.* a join in a rope made by intertwining the strands; join of wood by overlapping and binding; **to sit on the s.,** (*cricket slang*) to stonewall. [MDu.].

SPLINT (1) [splint], *n.* strip of wood tied to a broken limb to keep the ends of bone in position; strip of split wood used in basket making; bony tumour on the metacarpal bones of a horse. SPLINT (2), *v.t.* to fix with a s. [~Swed.].

SPLINTER (1) [splin′ter], *n.* small, hard, sharp fragment of anything, roughly broken off from the main body, *esp.* a sliver of wood or a fragment of a projectile or bomb; **s. party,** small group which detaches itself from a main part. SPLINTER-PROOF, *adj.* proof against bomb or shell splinters, though not against direct impact. SPLINTER (2), *v.t. and i.* to split, smash, shatter into small pointed fragments; break into sharp, pointed fragments under a blow or heavy pressure. SPLINTERLESS, *adj.* (of glass) made so as not to s. if broken. SPLINTERY, *adj.* tending to s. [MDu.].

SPLIT (1) (*pret. and p.pt.* **split**) [split], *v.t. and i.* to divide into two or more parts by fissure through the whole body, *esp.* as the result of pressure or impact, come apart along continuous lines through an entire mass; (*fig.*) become disunited, divide up into parties; cause to divide, separate; share out with others. SPLIT-PEAS(E), *n.*(*pl.*) husked peas s. SPLIT-RING, *n.* ring consisting of two turns of a spiral pressed together so as to look as if it were s. SPLIT (2), *n.* process or act of splitting; result of splitting; fissure, cleft produced by splitting; (*fig.*) division, difference of opinion leading to divergence; a fifty-fifty division, division according to any proportions; roll or bun s. and filled with jam and whipped cream; bottle of soda-water half the normal size; (*pl.*) acrobatic contortion in which the legs are opened to the fullest extent so that they form a straight line at right angles to the trunk. [MDu.].

SPLODGE [sploj], *n.* splotch.

SPLOTCH [sploch], *n.* smear, blotch, irregular patch. [~O.E.].

SPLURGE [splurj], *n.* (*coll.*) pretentious show or talk. [Symbolic].

SPLUTTER (1) [splu′ter], *n.* noise as of spluttering; act of spluttering. SPLUTTER (2), *v.t. and i.* to spit, sputter out saliva, speak as if one were so doing. [Echoic].

SPODE [spōd], *n.* kind of chinaware. [*J. Spode,* the potter].

SPOIL (1) [spoil], *n.* goods captured by violence, booty; earth dug up in excavating; (*fig.*) profits, prizes won by contest. SPOIL (2), *v.t. and i.* to plunder, take s. from; injure (a thing), *esp.* to impair its outward appearance; (*fig.*) detract from the pleasure or merit of; (of persons) injure the character by excessive indulgence; become spoiled, deteriorate, lose value. SPOIL-SPORT, *n.* person who, by untimely self-righteousness, spoils the pleasure of other people. [L.].

SPOKE (1) [spōk], *n.* bar joining the hub and rim of a wheel; rung of a ladder; handle projecting from the rim of a ship's steering wheel. [O.E.].

SPOKE (2), *pret. of* SPEAK.

SPOKEN [spō′ken], *p.pt. of* SPEAK.

SPOKESHAVE [spōk′shāv], *n.* blade set in the middle of a rod, used in planing the curves of spokes etc.

SPOKESMAN (*pl.* **spokesmen**) [spōks′man], *n.* person who speaks on behalf of others, *esp.* authoritatively for a government etc.

SPOLIATION [spō-li-ā′shn], *n.* act of plundering or despoiling. [L.].

SPONDAIC [spon-dā′ik], *adj.* consisting of or relating to a spondee or spondees.

SPONDEE [spon′dē], *n.* (*pros.*) poetic foot of two long syllables. [Gk.].

SPONDYLE [spon′dil], *n.* one of the vertebrae. SPONDYLITIS [spon-di-lī′tis], *n.* inflammation of the vertebrae. [Gk.].

SPONGE (1) [spunj], *n.* a marine creature notable for its fibrous skeleton; skeleton of this creature used in cleaning because of its absorbent qualities; sponger; **to throw up the s.,** to admit defeat, give in; **s. cake,** very light plain sweet cake. SPONGE-CLOTH, fabric with an open texture resembling the surface of a fine s. SPONGE (2), *v.t. and i.* to wipe with a s.; dive for sponges; act the sponger; **to s. on,** to live as the parasite of. SPONGER, *n.* parasitical hanger-on. [Gk.].

SPONGING-HOUSE [spun′jing-hows], *n.* (*hist.*) bailiff's house in which debtors were formerly kept before being consigned to prison. [Prec.].

SPONGY [spun′ji], *adj.* like a sponge, yielding, absorbent, soggy.

SPONSOR (1) [spon′ser], *n.* one who makes an agreement, accepts responsibility for another, one vouching for another; godparent. SPONSOR (2), *v.t.* to act as s. for; promote, lend countenance to; (*U.S.*) finance (on the radio) an entertainment programme for advertising purposes. [L.].

SPONTANEITY [spon-ta-nē′i-ti], *n.* state of being spontaneous; spontaneous action.

SPONTANEOUS [spon-tā′ni-ŏŏs], *adj.* self-generated, occurring from purely internal causes, without the intervention of any outside force; of one's own free will, voluntary; happening without any apparent cause. [L.].

SPOOF (1) [spŏŏf], *n. and adj.* a joking deception,

---

hoax; bogus, hoaxing. SPOOF (2), *v.t.* to deceive, hoax (a person). [Invented].

SPOOK [spook], *n.* (*coll.*) a supernatural apparition. [Du.].

SPOOL [spool], *n.* bar on which thread is wound; reel of cotton; bar on the reel of a fishing-rod; cylinder on which photographic film is wound. [MDu.].

SPOON (1) [spoon], *n.* implement having a long handle supporting a shallow bowl, used for raising, stirring or drinking liquids; a wooden-headed golf club. SPOON-BAIT, *n.* bait in the form of a s., used by anglers. SPOONBILL, *n.* a wading bird. SPOON-FEED, *v.t.* to feed by means of a s.; instruct in an elementary way so as to give the recipient no scope for original thought. SPOON (2), *v.t.* to lift, convey with a s.; (*golf*) strike with the s.; scoop up or along as if with a s. [OE.].

SPOON (3), *v.i.* (*coll.*) to make love in a sentimental fashion. SPOON(EY), *adj.* stupidly, awkwardly amorous. [Uncert.].

SPOONDRIFT [spoon'drift], *n.* spindrift. [Uncert.].

SPOONERISM [spoo'ne-rizm], *n.* accidental transposition of syllables in adjoining words, *esp.* when the effect is humorous. [Dr. *Spooner*, formerly Warden of New College, Oxford].

SPOOR [spoor], *n.* the trail of an animal. [Du.].

SPORADIC [spo-ra'dik], *adj.* occurring at irregular intervals. [Gk.].

SPORE [spaw(r)], *n.* (*biol.*) one of the minute bodies, formed in flowerless plants after fertilization, from which the new plant develops. [Gk.].

SPORRAN [spo'ran], *n.* Highlander's pouch worn hanging down in front of the kilt. [Gael.].

SPORT (1) [spawt], *n.* activity engaged in as recreation, *esp.* when engaged in by several persons in planned, friendly competition, athletics; fun, pleasure, an amusing occurrence; object of sport, plaything; (*biol.*) a spontaneous deviation from normal type; (*pl.*) meeting for athletic contests; (*coll.*) good fellow, sportsman. SPORT (2), *v.t.* and *i.* to disport oneself; wear for display; **to s. one's oak**, (*University coll.*) to lock one's outer door. SPORTS COAT, JACKET, *n.* kind of loose jacket, usually of tweed, suitable for quite informal occasions. [~DISPORT].

SPORTING (1) [spaw'ting], *n.* organized sports in general, *esp.* horse-racing and field sports; (*biol.*) spontaneous deviation from the normal. SPORTING (2), *adj.* devoted to sports, *esp.* field sports, sportsmanlike; **s. chance**, a possibility having a risk, but with a reasonable likelihood of success.

SPORTIVE [spaw'tiv], *adj.* playful, frolicsome.

SPORTSMAN (*pl.* **sportsmen**) [spawts'man], *n.* one indulging in athletic activities; good fellow, fair, honourable, manly person. SPORTSMANLIKE, *adj.* like or befitting a s., chivalrous, fair-minded.

SPORTY [spaw'ti], *adj.* willing to take a risk; adventurous.

SPOT (1) [spot], *n.* a small marking, patch of different colour on a surface, stain, pimple on the skin; blemish; a specific place, *esp.* one of very small extent; (*billiards*) place on the table from which balls are played at the commencement of the game; black mark on one white ball to distinguish it from the other; (*coll.*) small quantity of drink or food; **s. cash**, payment on delivery; **on the s.**, at once, there and then; (*U.S. slang*) in imminent danger from one's enemies, called to account; **in a (tough) s.**, (*U.S.*) in difficulties. SPOT (2) (*pres.pt.* SPOTTING, *pret.* and *p.pt.* SPOTTED), *v.t.* and *i.* to stain, mark with spots; see, catch sight of, detect; become marked or spotted. SPOTTER, *n.* one who spots; one who keeps a look-out, *esp.* for impending attack from enemy aircraft. [ME.].

SPOTLESS [spot'les], *adj.* without blemish.

SPOTLIGHT (1) [spot'lit], *n.* light which is capable of being directed on to a particular spot, *esp.* on a stage; that which draws attention to a particular person or happening. SPOTLIGHT (2), *v.t.* to illuminate with a s.; (*coll.*) draw special attention to.

SPOTTED [spot'tid], *pret.* and *p.pt.* of SPOT; **s. dog**, (*coll.*) Dalmatian dog; rolled suet pudding containing currants.

SPOUSE [spowz], *n.* husband or wife. [OFr.].

SPOUT (1) [spowt], *n.* narrow projection at the orifice of a vessel, serving to direct the flow of its contents, moulded projection conveying rain water from a roof; the blow-hole of a whale; violent gush, jet of water; **down the s.**, (*slang*) lost, ruined irretrievably; **up the s.**, (*slang*) in pawn. SPOUT (2), *v.t.* and *i.* to gush forth in a strong jet; (*fig.*) orate copiously;

pour, spurt out in a stream; declaim copiously. [ME.].

SPRAIN (1) [spran], *v.t.* to strain, twist the muscles or ligaments of so as to produce painful and incapacitating inflammation. SPRAIN (2), *n.* a twist of the muscles or ligaments, leading to painful inflammation. [OFr.].

SPRANG [sprang], *pret. of* SPRING.

SPRAT [sprat], *n.* a small sea-fish. [OE.].

SPRAWL (1) [sprawl], *v.i.* to sit or recline with the limbs loosely and casually splayed out, lie or sit in an attitude of ungainly relaxation; (*fig.*) spread out or over widely and in ugly disorder. SPRAWL (2), *n.* act, position, of sprawling.

SPRAY (1) [spra], *n.* a flowering branch, design representing or imitating such a branch. [ME.].

SPRAY (2), *n.* spume, fine particles of liquid squirted through the air; wind-blown particles of sea water; mechanical device for producing a s., atomizer. SPRAY (3), *v.t.* and *i.* to scatter in s., dampen, disinfect with a s.; become s. [LGerm.].

SPREAD (1) [spred], *v.t.* and *i.* to make to cover a larger surface by reducing in height and increasing in length or breadth, *esp.* to do so by pressing out (a substance); smear (butter etc.); cover with (butter etc.); disseminate, cause to be diffused; circulate, proclaim widely; (*reflex.*) indulge in self-assertion, be assertively profuse; extend over a larger surface; open out (as wings); be diffused; **to s. out**, to unfold, be unfolded. SPREAD (2), *n.* act of spreading, condition or extent of being s.; process of diffusion, increasing extension of anything; (*coll.*) great feast, table provided with a large amount of food; a relish of soft consistency for spreading on bread; (*advertising*) a display occupying two facing pages; range, extent. [OE.].

SPREAD-EAGLE (1) [spred-e'gl], *n.* (*her.*) an eagle displayed; bird split open for broiling. SPREAD-EAGLE (2), *adj.* (*U.S.*) bombastically patriotic (from the spread-eagle emblem of the U.S.A.). SPREAD-EAGLE (3), *v.t.* to tie up, stretch out, with the arms and legs spread out to the fullest extent.

SPREADOVER [spre'do-ver], *n. and adj.* (relating to) a system by which the weekly quota of working hours may be made up in spells greater (or less) than the average daily amount; extension, range over a period of time. [SPREAD (1) and OVER (3)].

SPREE [spre], *n.* bout of drinking and debauchery; holiday prank, lark. [Ir.].

SPRIG [sprig], *n.* small branching twig, spray; headless nail; off-shoot, young man. [ME.].

SPRIGHT [sprit], *n.* sprite. [SPRITE].

SPRIGHTLY [sprit'li], *adj.* lively, bright, vivacious, gay.

SPRING (1) (*pret.* **sprang**, *p.pt.* **sprung**) [spring], *v.t.* and *i.* to leap upwards or forwards by contraction and release of the muscles, or by the release from pressure of an elastic substance; bound swiftly and suddenly in any direction, *esp.* on to something; move very rapidly; (*fig.*) come very rapidly into some position; gush up (as water) from a source, arise from, come into existence, emerge; (of timber) become warped, begin leaking; cause to move, recoil, rapidly; set off, cause to happen rapidly, announce unexpectedly; (of wood) cause to split, warp; provide with springs. SPRING (2), *n.* act of springing, capacity of so doing, distance sprung, resilience; any body (*esp.* bent metal) tending to return to its original shape or position after distortion by pressure; quality of recoil and bounce possessed by such an object; (*fig.*) mental resilience; that which springs from anything, *esp.* a stream of water rising from the ground; time of annual vegetable rebirth, period between winter and summer; source, origin or initiating force of anything; (*arch.*) starting-point of a curve. SPRING-BACK, (of) a loose-leaf book cover holding the pages by means of a s. SPRING-BALANCE, instrument measuring weights by means of a s. SPRING-BOARD, resilient plank used to give impetus for diving. SPRING-GUN, gun set to go off by the action of trespassers stumbling on it. SPRING-CLEAN, *v.t.* and *i.* to clean (a house) thoroughly, *esp.* in the springtime. [OE.].

SPRINGAL [spring'al], *n.* † a medieval military engine. [OFr.].

SPRINGBOK [spring'bok], *n.* an African antelope; (*coll.*) a South African, *esp.* a member of a representative sporting team. [Du.].

SPRINGE [sprinj], *n.* (*archaic*) snare for catching birds and small game. [~SPRING (2)].

SPRINGER [spring'er], *n.* one who, or that which,

springs; kind of spaniel; (arch.) lowest part of the curve of an arch.

SPRING-TIDE [spring'tīd], n. the great tide occurring at new and full moon; (poet.) springtime.

SPRINKLE (1) [spring'kl], v.t. and i. to scatter, strew in small drops or particles; fall in small particles. SPRINKLE (2), n. a light scattering of liquid or solid particles. SPRINKLER, n. that which sprinkles, esp. a device for fighting fires. SPRINKLING, n. a few drops, a few scattered objects. [ME.].

SPRINT (1) [sprint], v.i. to run at full speed for a short distance. SPRINT (2), n. a short dash, short burst of running at full speed. [~OIcel.].

SPRIT [sprit], n. (naut.) spar extending from a mast diagonally upwards. [ME.].

SPRITE [sprīt], n. elf, fairy. [Var. of SPIRIT].

SPROCKET [spro'kit], n. (arch.) triangular piece of wood used in strengthening wooden frames; (eng.) projection on a gear-wheel to engage with a chain; wheel with such toothed projections on its periphery. [Unkn.].

SPROUT (1) [sprowt], v.t. and i. to put forth buds, shoots etc.; begin to grow; grow up rapidly; give forth as by growth. SPROUT (2), n. young shoot; (pl.) young colewort, Brussels sprouts. [OE.].

SPRUCE (1) [sprōōs], n. coniferous tree related to the pine. [ME. Spruce, Prussia].

SPRUCE (2), adj. neat, spry, dapper. SPRUCE (3), v.t. to make s. [~Prec.].

SPRUE (1) [sprōō], n. tropical disease characterized by enteritis and ulceration of the mouth. [Du.].

SPRUE (2), n. an inferior quality of asparagus. [Unkn.].

SPRUNG [sprung], p.pt. of SPRING. [OE.].

SPRY [sprī], adj. brisk, nimble, mentally active, sharp. [Uncert.].

SPUD [spud], n. small spade; (slang) potato. [ME.].

SPUE, see SPEW.

SPUME [spyōōm], n. foam, froth. [L.].

SPUN [spun], pret. and p.pt. of SPIN. SPUN-OUT, adj. made lengthy. SPUN-YARN, n. rope made of several twisted strands. [OE.].

SPUNK [spungk], n. touchwood; (coll.) courage, spirit. [Unkn.].

SPUR (1) [spur], n. spike or pricking device worn on the heel to goad on a horse; any sharp, pointed projection resembling this, esp. the horny spike on the leg of a cock; (fig.) incitement, goad to endeavour; **to win one's spurs**, to receive knighthood; attain honour in any profession; **on the s. of the moment**, impulsively, without reflection. SPUR (2), v.t. and i. to goad, urge on with a s., equip with spurs; use spurs, ride fast and furiously; **to s. on**, to encourage vigorously. [OE.].

SPURGE [spurj], n. plant of the genus Euphorbia. [OFr.].

SPURIOUS [spyōō'ri-ōōs], adj. counterfeit, not genuine. [L.].

SPURN [spurn], v.t. to thrust at, strike, with the foot drive away rudely and scornfully, reject with disdain. [OE.].

SPURT (1) [spurt], v.t. and i. to give out a gush of liquid; gush out in a sudden violent jet; make a brief but violent increase of speed in running, or of effort in any contest. SPURT (2), n. sudden gush of fluid, flame etc.; sudden dash of speed. [OE.].

SPUTNIK (1) [spu'ter], v.t. and i. to make a sound of spitting and spluttering, speak with such a sound. SPUTTER (2), n. act, noise, of sputtering. [Du.].

SPUTNIK (1) [spoot'nik], n. artificial earth satellite sent up into space by rocket. [Russ.].

SPUTUM [spyōō'tum], n. matter which is coughed up and spat out. [L.].

SPY (1) [spī], n. one practising espionage, or keeping another under secret observation, one engaged in discovering what is intended to be secret. SPY (2), v.t. and i. to seek to discover secrets, esp. of a national or military character on behalf of another country; espy, observe; **to s. on**, to watch secretly the movements of. SPY-GLASS, n. small telescope. SPY-HOLE, n. inconspicuous hole for observation. [OFr.].

SQUAB (1) [skwob], n. nestling pigeon; sofa; squab person. SQUAB-PIE, pigeon-pie; meat-and-apple pie. SQUAB (2), adj. short, squat and plump. [~Swed.].

SQUABBLE (1) [skwo'bl], n. a petty, undignified, noisy quarrel. SQUABBLE (2), v.i. to engage in a s. [~Swed.].

SQUAD [skwod], n. small military detachment, esp. a small detachment engaged in drill or physical exercise; (fig.) small, loosely organized group. [It.].

SQUADRON [skwod'run], n. body of cavalry,

usually of about 200 men; group of warships under the command of a flag-officer; group of military aeroplanes, varying in number according to type. SQUADRON-LEADER, rank in the R.A.F. equivalent to that of major in the Army. [It.].

SQUALID [skwo'lid], adj. dirty, sordid and dingy, mean and poverty-stricken; base, unworthy. [L.].

SQUALL (1) [skwawl], v.t. and i. to utter a squall, sound loudly and inharmoniously; utter with a squall. SQUALL (2), n. briefly violent storm of wind; (fig.) trouble, brief quarrel; a loud, harsh and inharmonious cry. [~OIcel.].

SQUALOR [skwo'ler], n. state of being sordid, dirty and depressing poverty. [L.].

SQUAMOUS [skwā'mōōs], adj. scaly; covered with scales. [L.].

SQUANDER [skwon'der], v.t. to spend lavishly and wastefully, dissipate, expend foolishly. [Uncert.].

SQUARE (1) [skwāer], adj. in the shape or figure of a square, resembling a square, (of persons) short and broad, (of shoulders) straight, not hunched forward; (math.) relating to a square; on even terms, with liabilities settled, level; (coll.) honest, straightforward; **all s.**, with level scores; **to get s. with**, to be revenged on, get even with. SQUARE (2), n. plane rectangular figure with four equal sides, anything in the shape of a s.; open space in a town, esp. when containing a garden in the centre; (math.) the product of a quantity multiplied by itself; (geom.) instrument for determining right angles; troops drawn up in a defensive s. formation; **on the s.**, honest, on the level; **s. measure**, the s. of a lineal measure; system of measures of area. SQUARE-RIGGED, (naut.) with horizontal yards at right angles to the keel. SQUARE-ROOT, (math.) a number's base or root which, when multiplied by itself, produces that number. SQUARE-SAIL, four-cornered sail supported on a yard across the mast. SQUARE (3), adv. so as to form a right angle; honestly. SQUARE (4), v.t. and i. to make s. or right-angled; (math.) multiply a quantity by itself; (of the shoulders etc.) draw back and up, straighten; adapt, reconcile an idea (with a fact); (coll.) bribe, persuade to connive at some illicit action; be in agreement (with), harmonize (with); **to s. up**, to adopt a fighting attitude; settle debts. SQUARELY, adv. so as to form a s., at right angles; in s. fashion; directly facing; plainly, without ambiguity; honestly. [OFr. from L.].

SQUASH (1) [skwosh], v.t. and i. to pack, squeeze together so as to crush, press into pulp; (fig.) silence and disconcert; become crushed, pressed to pulp. SQUASH (2), n. a close packing together, great crowding; state of being reduced to pulp; drink made from crushed fruits; s.-rackets. SQUASH-RACKETS, variety of rackets played by two persons with a soft ball. [ME.].

SQUASH (3), n. thick, fleshy fruit eaten as a staple by American Indians; gourd, marrow. [NAmer-Ind.].

SQUAT (1) [skwot], v.i. to sit back on the heels, crouch with the legs drawn up to the body; settle on land or in vacant buildings without right or permission; occupy unenclosed and unclaimed land as a settler. SQUAT (2), adj. short and thick, stumpy. SQUATTER, n. one who squats; one who settles on land or in vacant buildings without permission; one who settles on government land in the colonies, with a view to eventual ownership; (Australian) sheepfarmer on a large scale. [ME.].

SQUAW [skwaw], n. American Indian married woman. [NAmerInd.].

SQUAWK (1) [skwawk], v.i. to utter a squawk; (slang) betray a criminal undertaking. SQUAWK (2), n. short, harsh cry, as of an inharmonious bird, esp. a cry of pain or complaint. [Imitative].

SQUEAK (1) [skwēk], v.i. to utter a squeak; (slang) inform on a criminal. SQUEAK (2), n. weak, thin, piercing cry, esp. of excitement or pain, cry made by a mouse; **narrow s.**, close escape. SQUEAKER, n. one who, or that which, squeaks; (slang) informer. [Echoic].

SQUEAL (1) [skwēl], v.i. to utter a squeal; (slang) betray a person or undertaking. SQUEAL (2), n. shrill, prolonged, high-pitched cry of pain or excitement. [ME.].

SQUEAMISH [skwē'mish], adj. fastidious, easily nauseated, over-scrupulous. [ME.].

SQUEEGEE [skwē'jē], n. strip of rubber used as a broom on wet surfaces; similar implement or a rubber roller used for pressing wet photographic prints on to glazing plates; squeezer. [~SQUEEZE].

ōō is pronounced as in food; ŏŏ as in hood; th as in think; TH as in that; zh as in azure. ~ = related to.

SQUEEZE (1) [skwēz], *v.t. and i.* to press, compress slowly but firmly; extract moisture by pressure; (*fig.*) constrain by persuasion or threat; pack, press in tightly; (*bridge*) play a suit in which one's opponent is short, so as to force the discard of a valuable card; take an impression on a plastic surface; get through or into by squeezing. **SQUEEZE** (2), *n.* act of squeezing, state of being squeezed, a crowding together; impression taken by pressure, on a soft surface. **SQUEEZING**, *n.* act of compression; that which is extracted by pressure. [O.E.].

SQUELCH (1) [skwelch], *v.i.* to make a splashing, smacking sound as of watery suction; walk through mud and produce this sound. **SQUELCH** (2), *n.* sound of squelching. [Imitative].

SQUIB [skwib], *n.* small exploding firework; ephemeral lampoon. [Uncert.].

SQUID [skwid], *n.* long-tentacled cuttle-fish; artificial bait imitating this. [Uncert.].

SQUIFFY [skwi'fi], *adj.* (*coll.*) slightly intoxicated. [Unkn.].

SQUILL [skwil], *n.* genus of plants related to the lily, used in medicine. [OFr.].

SQUINT (1) [skwint], *v.i.* to look, gaze in a squinting fashion; peer obliquely. **SQUINT** (2), *n.* condition of the eyes in which both cannot look in the same direction at the same time; oblique look; narrow observation hole through a wall. **SQUINT-EYED**, *adj.* squinting. **SQUINTING**, *adj.* tending to s. [ME.].

SQUIRE (1) [skwier], *n.* body-servant of a medieval knight; country landowner; gallant. **SQUIRE** (2), *v.t.* to attend, escort (a lady). **SQUIREARCHY**, *n.* (*coll.*) country gentlemen as a body, *esp.* as a ruling class. **SQUIREEN**, *n.* petty squire. [~ESQUIRE].

SQUIRM [skwurm], *v.t. and i.* to wriggle, writhe the body; feel humiliated. [Uncert.].

SQUIRREL [skwi'rel], *n.* rodent of the genus *Sciurus.* [OFr.].

SQUIRT (1) [skwurt], *v.t. and i.* to emit, spray with, a jet of liquid. **SQUIRT** (2), *n.* a spurt of liquid; instrument for producing this; (*coll.*) insignificant fellow. [~LGerm.].

SQUITCH [skwich], *n.* couch-grass. [~QUITCH].

STAB (1) [stab], *n.* sudden, fierce thrust with a sharp instrument; (*coll.*) sudden, treacherous attack; **a s. at**, (*coll.*) an attempt at. **STAB** (2) (*pres.pt.* STABBING, *pret.* and *p.pt.* STABBED), *v.t. and i.* to pierce, wound with a s.; jab at with a sharp instrument. [~Swed.].

STABILITY [sta-bi'li-ti], *n.* state of being stable. [L.].

STABILIZE [stā'bi-līz], *v.t.* to make stable, steady, confirm. **STABILIZER**, *n.* one who, or that which, stabilizes; (*aeron.*) device for keeping an aircraft in equilibrium. [~L.].

STABLE (1) [stā'bl], *adj.* steady, in equilibrium, firm, well-founded, consistent; (*chem.*) resisting decomposition. [L.].

STABLE (2), *n.* building for keeping horses; group of racehorses under one trainer or one ownership. **STABLE** (3), *v.t.* to put in a s. **STABLEBOY**, **STABLE-MAN**, *n.* boy, man, who looks after horses in a s. **STABLING**, *n.* accommodation for horses in stables. [L.].

STACCATO [sta-kah'tō], *adv.* (*mus.*) with notes played abruptly and distinctly. [It.].

STACK (1) [stak], *n.* a regular pile of hay; orderly heap; funnel of a ship or engine; cluster of chimneys; tall chimney. **STACK** (2), *v.t.* to arrange in a s. [OIcel.].

STADHOLDER [staht'hŏl-der], *n.* (*hist.*) head of the former Dutch Republic. [Germ.].

STADIUM (*pl.* **stadia**) [stā'di-um], *n.* ancient Greek unit of length; track for athletics; sports arena. [Gk.].

STAFF (1) (*pl.* **staffs, staves**) [stahf], *n.* long, slender rod, pole, wand of authority, support; group of persons working under a single direction to perform some organizational function, military or civil; the five parallel lines on which music is written; **s. notation**, musical notation on staves; **s. officer**, officer attached to a military general s. **STAFF** (2), *v.t.* to furnish with a s. of officials, teachers etc. [OE.].

STAG [stag], *n.* the male red deer; (*comm. slang*) one who buys newly-issued shares with a view to immediate resale at a profit; **s. party**, an all-male party. **STAG-BEETLE**, beetle which has projecting antler-like mandibles in the male. [~OIcel.].

STAGE (1) [stāj], *n.* platform, raised scaffolding; that part of a theatre on which the play is performed; acting as a profession; the theatre, the drama; scene of an action; halting place; distance between

stopping places on a road-transport service; section or division of a process; period of development; **s. door**, door by which performers enter the theatre; **s. fright**, nervous disability or fear when appearing before audiences. **STAGE-COACH**, horse-drawn coach, with regular route and stopping places. **STAGE-MANAGE**, to arrange so as to produce an intended effect. **STAGE-MANAGER**, person responsible for the general arrangements for a s. performance. **STAGE-STRUCK**, *adj.* keenly desirous of entering the theatrical profession. **STAGE-WHISPER**, loud whisper meant to be heard by other people, as by the audience in a theatre. **STAGE** (2), *v.t.* to present on the s., arrange for dramatic effect; *v.i.* to travel by stages. **STAGE-CRAFT**, *n.* skill in theatrical production, writing or presentation. **STAGER**, *n.* one who stages; **old stager**, experienced person. [OFr.].

STAGGER (1) [sta'ger], *v.t. and i.* to walk unsteadily; cause to be unsteady, disconcert; set (trenches etc.) inclined at alternate angles; (of holidays, working hours etc.) arrange so as not all to coincide. **STAGGER** (2), *n.* a staggering movement. **STAGGERS**, *n.* horse and cattle disease of which staggering and reeling are symptoms. [MDu.].

STAGHOUND [stag'hownd], *n.* hound trained for hunting stags.

STAGING [stā'jing], *n.* temporary structure of scaffolding and boards; platform, stage; the setting and presentation of a theatrical production; **s. post**, (*esp.* of aerodromes) place where passengers and goods may wait temporarily or be transhipped.

STAGNANCY [stag'nan-si], *n.* condition of being stagnant.

STAGNANT [stag'nant], *adj.* (of water) not flowing, foul through remaining undisturbed; inactive, sluggish. [L.].

STAGNATE [stag-nāt'], *v.i.* to be or become stagnant. **STAGNATION**, *n.* state of being stagnant.

STAGY [stā'ji], *adj.* crudely theatrical.

STAID [stād], *adj.* sedate, sober. **STAIDLY**, *adv.* in a s. way. [~STAY (3)].

STAIN (1) [stān], *v.t. and i.* to discolour, blemish, mar; colour with dark pigment; become blemished; tend to become discoloured. **STAIN** (2), *n.* mark, blot, discoloration; a dark colouring matter; moral blemish. **STAINLESS**, *adj.* without s.; unblemished; that will not become stained. [OFr.].

STAIR [stār], *n.* one of a series of steps; the steps for ascending a building. **STAIR-CARPET**, long, narrow carpet for stairs. **STAIR-HEAD**, top of a staircase. **STAIR-ROD**, rod for securing in place a s.-carpet. **STAIRCASE**, **STAIRWAY**, *n.* flight of stairs. [ME.].

STAKE (1) [stāk], *n.* pointed wooden pole, such a pole to which people were tied to be burnt to death; that which is risked in a wager. **STAKE-HOLDER**, one holding the stakes in a wager or other transaction. **STAKE** (2), *v.t.* to mark with a s.; wager.

STALACTITE [sta'lak-tīt], *n.* tapering, calcareous deposit hanging from the roofs of caverns. [Gk.].

STALAGMITE [sta'lag-mīt], *n.* tapering, calcareous deposit rising from the floor of a cavern. [Gk.].

STALE (1) [stāl], *n.* urine of cattle and horses. [Du.].

STALE (2), *adj.* not fresh, having lost, through the passage of time, some original quality, *esp.* (of food) dry, beginning to decay, having lost its flavour and nutritional value, having lost vigour or interest, tedious. [ME.].

STALEMATE (1) [stāl-māt'], *n.* position in chess in which a player cannot move without bringing his king into check, a draw; (*fig.*) deadlock. **STALEMATE** (2), *v.t.* to bring to a s. [AFr. and MATE (2)].

STALK (1) [stawk], *n.* stem of a plant, anything resembling a stem, long, slender support, thin shaft. [ME.].

STALK (2), *v.t. and i.* to walk with a long, stiff, angular stride, walk with lofty dignity; (*fig.*) progress with silent and terrible irresistibility; practice the stalking of game; walk after (game), pursue (enemies) silently and remorselessly, pursue without being observed. **STALK** (3), *n.* stalking gait; act of stalking game. **STALKED**, *adj.* having a s. **STALKING**, *n.* practice of hunting or pursuing game, *esp.* silently, stealthily. **STALKING-HORSE**, horse used as a cover in stalking game; (*fig.*) pretence, feigned motive. [ME.].

STALL (1) [stawl], *n.* compartment of a stable or cattle-house; recessed seat in the choir of a church; small booth, covered stand for selling goods in public open places, markets etc.; sheath for protecting an injured finger or toe; *pl.* seats nearest the stage on the ground floor of a theatre; (*fig.*) best and most comfortable situation for viewing anything. STALL (2), *v.t. and i.* to place in a s.; (of engines) (cause to) stop working owing to inadequate application of power; (of aeroplanes) go out of control through lack of flying speed; play for time, deliberately delay, avoid a direct issue; **to s. off**, to put off, keep from coming to definite settlement. [OE.].

STALLION [stal'yun], *n.* uncastrated male horse. [OFr.].

STALWART (1) [stawl'wert], *adj.* physically strong, big and muscular; (*fig.*) strong in support of a cause. STALWART (2), *n.* unshakable supporter of a cause. [OE.].

STAMEN [stā'men], *n.* (*bot.*) pollen-bearing organ of a flower. [L.].

STAMINA [sta'mi-nah], *n.* capacity for physical endurance, constitutional vigour; (*fig.*) mental toughness and stability. [L.].

STAMINAL [sta'mi-nal], *adj.* relating to stamens; pertaining to, imparting, stamina.

STAMMER (1) [sta'mer], *v.t. and i.* to speak with a stammer, suffer from a defect of speech marked by involuntary repetitions of a syllable or sound; utter with a stammer. STAMMER (2), *n.* act of stammering, a hesitation in speech. [OE.].

STAMP (1) [stamp], *v.t. and i.* to strike downwards with the foot, walk heavily; mark by striking with an engraved block or indiarubber stamp, affix a stamp to, make a lasting impression on; **to s. out**, to extirpate utterly. STAMP (2), *n.* act of striking downwards with the foot; instrument for making impressions by a heavy, usually downward, blow on a softer substance; small hand instrument for making impressions on paper etc. by means of a moulded indiarubber surface which is inked; impression so made, *esp.* the imprint made by an engraved block; imprint certifying the validity of a document, quality of goods etc., *esp.* a label fixed to postal packages as evidence of the charge required for delivery having been paid, embossed mark stamped on a document as a receipt of legal payment; (*fig.*) evident mark of a quality, character. STAMP-COLLECTOR, philatelist. STAMP-DUTY, tax on certain legal transactions. [OFr.].

STAMPEDE (1) [stam-pēd'], *n.* sudden, tumultuous rush, usually inspired by panic, *esp.* such a rush by a herd of cattle. STAMPEDE (2), *v.t. and i.* to cause to s.; run in s. [Span.].

STANCE [stans], *n.* attitude in which one stands, position previous to striking the ball in golf or cricket. [Fr.].

STANCH, STANCHNESS, see STAUNCH, STAUNCHNESS.

STANCHION [stan'shn], *n.* upright bar serving as a support. [OFr.].

STAND (1) (*pret. and p.pt.* stood) [stand], *v.t. and i.* to be at rest in an unsupported upright position; hold one's ground, endure; buy something (usually an alcoholic drink) for (a person); make to be in an upright unsupported position; act in the capacity of; **to s. back**, to move away from, stay in the rear; **to s. by**, to support, stay with; await developments; **to s. down**, (*milit.*) to go off duty, cease to s. to; release (a force) from active duty while retaining it in being; withdraw from a contest; **to s. for**, to represent, signify; (*coll.*) tolerate; **to s. in**, (*coll.*) to act as a substitute; **to s. to**, (*milit.*) to assemble ready and equipped to execute orders; **to s. off**, to be distant; dismiss (an employee) temporarily; **to s. up**, to s. on one's feet; **to s. up to**, to oppose, refuse to submit to; **to s. up for**, to defend; **to s. with**, to support. STAND-BY, *n.* person or thing to be relied upon, *esp.* in an emergency. STAND-IN, *n.* substitute; person who deputizes for a cinema actor or actress in the preliminary arrangements for a scene. STAND-OFF, *adj.* (*Rugby football*) (of one of the two half-backs) standing at some distance from the scrum. STAND-OFFISH, *adj.* uncompanionable from a consciousness of superiority. STAND-PIPE, vertical pipe, *esp.* one connected with a water-main, provided with a tap. STAND-UP, *adj.* (*coll.*) (of conflicts) violently and unashamedly contested; (of a meal) taken while standing. STAND (2), *n.* act of standing, of stopping, of taking up a position; position taken up, place, position, beyond which one will not retreat; firm opposition to attack, prolonged resistance at a particular point; (*cricket*) prolonged period without loss of a wicket; place where one may s. or, more usually, sit to watch a sports contest or other outdoor entertainment, raised platform for spectators; station where cabs or public vehicles may wait; place on which something may be put, small

structure for supporting ornaments etc.; (*coll.*) halt made in a theatrical tour in order to give a performance; (*U.S.*) witness-box in a court of justice. [OE.].

STANDARD (1) [stan'derd], *n.* military ensign, device, elevated on a pole and used as a symbol or rallying point; upright pole, *esp.* one carrying a lamp, wires etc.; (*hort.*) plant having a firm and tall stem; a quantity taken as an absolute, with which other quantities may be compared, a certain amount, level, of quantity, quality or behaviour used as a measuring rod for others of the same kind, criterion, general means of judgment; average degree of a thing to which the rest of the kind are expected to conform; 1,980 board feet of timber. STANDARD-BEARER, one who carries a military standard. STANDARD-LAMP, lamp on a tall movable stand. STANDARD (2), *adj.* of, or according to, a given s.; accepted; usual. [MedL.].

STANDARDIZE [stan'der-dīz], *v.t.* to make conformable to a standard, level out irregularities in and bring into a uniform pattern.

STANDING (1) [stan'ding], *n.* status. STANDING (2), *adj.* established, on a permanent footing; (of armies) permanently in being and under arms; that is always in effect, regular; s. up. [STAND (1)].

STANDPOINT [stand'point], *n.* viewpoint, moral or intellectual position.

STANDSTILL (1) [stand'stil], *n.* a complete stoppage. STANDSTILL (2), *adj.* marked by, providing for, a cessation of movement or avoidance of change.

STANK [stangk], *pret. of* STINK.

STANZA [stan'zah], *n.* (*pros.*) a number of lines of verse forming a composite unit, and often linked together by various arrangements of rhyme and metre. [It.].

STAPLE (1) [stā'pl], *n.* place fixed for a market, market; chief product of a place; essential raw materials; the length of fibre in wool, also in cotton, flax etc.; U-shaped pointed metal rod driven into wood etc. to form a receptacle for hooks, latches etc.; wire contrivance for fastening papers together; (*fig.*) high quality. STAPLE (2), *adj.* fixed by agreement or tradition, established; chief (of products and raw materials), principal, basic. STAPLE (3), *v.t.* to sort out different qualities of wool, thread, flax etc.; fasten with a s. STAPLER, *n.* one who grades wool etc.; instrument for stapling papers. [OE.].

STAR (1) [stah(r)], *n.* a luminous fixed heavenly body; (*fig., astrol.*) such a body as supposed to control a person's life; regular pointed figure resembling a heavenly body radiating flashes of light; (*print.*) asterisk; white patch on a horse's forehead; leading actor or actress, *esp.* in films; S. of Bethlehem, (*bot.*) plant of the genus *Ornithogalum*; S. of Jerusalem, (*bot.*) salsify; S. of the Sea, (*bot.*) the plant *Aster Tripolium*; Stars and Stripes, national flag of the U.S.A.; S. Chamber, important court of criminal justice of Tudor and early Stuart times; s. turn, principal item in a programme. STAR-GAZING, astrology; (*fig.*) absent-mindedness. STAR-SHELL, shell which bursts in flight and sheds a bright light around. STAR-SPANGLED BANNER, U.S. national flag; national hymn of the U.S.A. STAR (2) (*pres.pt.* STARRING, *pret. and p.pt.* STARRED), *v.t. and i.* to adorn with stars, mark with an asterisk to call special attention to; shine like a s.; take a leading rôle in a dramatic representation; give a leading rôle to, have in the leading rôle(s), exhibit in the most conspicuous position. [OE.].

STARBOARD (1) [stah'berd, stah'bawd], *n.* right side of a ship when looking forward. STARBOARD (2), *adj.* pertaining to, or lying on, the s. [STEER (2) and BOARD (1)].

STARCH (1) [stahch], *n.* a granular carbohydrate found in plant cells and used in laundering stiff white linen etc. STARCH (2), *v.t.* to stiffen with s.

STARCHY [stah'chi], *adj.* pertaining to, or containing, starch; (*fig.*) stiff in manner and bearing.

STARE (1) [stāer], *v.t. and i.* to look fixedly with wide-open eyes, affect someone with such a look; **to s. one in the face**, to be right in front of one's eyes. STARE (2), *n.* a fixed look with wide-open eyes. [OE.].

STARFISH [stah'fish], *n.* a flat star-shaped echinoderm.

STARING (1) [stāer'ing], *n.* action of one who stares. STARING (2), *adj.* looking with a stare; (of colours etc.) unpleasantly obtrusive.

STARK (1) [stahk], *adj.* stiff, rigid; absolute, complete; s.-naked. STARK (2), *adv.* absolutely, completely.

STARLIGHT [stah'līt], *n.* light emitted by the stars.

STARLIKE [stah'lik], *adj.* resembling a star; bright; shining; radiated.

STARLING [stah'ling], *n.* a passerine bird with black glossy plumage. [OE.].

STARRED [stahd], *adj.* studded with stars; influenced in fortune by the stars; playing the part of the star or chief actor or actress.

STARRY [stah'ri], *adj.* abounding or adorned with stars; made up of stars; shining like stars; resembling stars.

START (1) [staht], *v.t.* to alarm; startle; rouse suddenly from concealment; move suddenly from its place; begin; cause to begin; set going, set in motion; raise; invent; dislocate; *v.i.* to move suddenly and spasmodically; make a sudden involuntary movement of the body; shrink, wince; move suddenly aside; move out of place; begin, commence; **to s. in**, (*coll.*) to begin; **to s. out**, to set forth, intend; **to s. up,** to spring up; put (an engine) into motion. START (2), *n.* a sudden movement or twitch from alarm; little shock; a spring; a darting; act of setting out or beginning; place where a race begins; **by fits and starts,** spasmodically. STARTER, *n.* one who, or that which, starts; dog which rouses game. SELF-STARTER, *n.* electric motor for starting the engine of a motor-car. STARTING-POINT, *n.* point of departure. STARTING-POST, *n.* barrier or line from which competitors begin a race. [OE.].

STARTLE [stah'tl], *v.t. and i.* to feel sudden alarm; alarm. STARTLING, *adj.* suddenly impressing with fear or surprise; (of dress, colour etc.) vivid, arresting. [OE.].

STARVATION [stah-vā'shn], *n.* act of starving, or state of being starved; (*fig.*) condition of having too little nourishment for the mind.

STARVE [stahv], *v.i.* to perish of hunger; suffer extreme hunger or want; (*Scots and northern dial.*) perish of cold; *v.t.* to deprive of food and nourishment. [OE.].

STARVELING (1) [stahv'ling], *n.* animal or plant thin and weak from want of food. STARVELING (2), *adj.* hungry; ill-fed; pining.

STARWORT [stah'wert], *n.* plant of the genus. *Stellaria*; **water s.,** plant of the genus *Callitriche*.

STASIS [stā'sis], *n.* (*med.*) stagnation of the blood or of other fluid; constipation. [Gk.].

STATE (1) [stāt], *n.* condition; rank; quality; pomp; dignity; grandeur; a body politic; the whole body of people united under one ruler or government; (*pl.*) a legislative body; **s. paper,** document concerned with the political interests or government of a s. STATE-HOUSE, house of legislature of a s. STATE-PRISON, public prison; prison for offenders against the s. STATE (2), *adj.* of or pertaining to the s.; ceremonial. STATE-CARRIAGE, -COACH, *n.* official carriage for ceremonial occasions. STATE-ROOM, *n.* magnificent room in a palace or great house; private cabin on board a ship; (*U.S.*) apartment in a railway sleeping-car. STATE (3), *v.t.* to give a reasoned statement of; express the particulars of; set down; say, tell. STATELESS, *adj.* without a s., having no nationality; without ceremonial. [OFr. from L.].

STATECRAFT [stāt'krahft], *n.* statesmanship; art of politics or government.

STATED [stā'tid], *adj.* settled; established; regular; related, told as a fact. STATEDLY, *adv.* at certain s. times, regularly; allegedly.

STATELY [stāt'li], *adj.* characterized by dignity and loftiness; magnificent; elevated in sentiment; imposing. [STATE(1)].

STATEMENT [stāt'ment], *n.* act of stating; that which is stated; account, announcement or recital; opinion, judgment; (*comm.*) a setting out of the financial affairs of some business or institution; an account in detail. [STATE (3)].

STATES-GENERAL [stāts-je'ne-ral], *n.* (in France before the Revolution) the assembly of the three legislative orders of the kingdom, the clergy, nobles and commons. [Fr.].

STATESMAN (*pl.* statesmen) [stāts'man], *n.* man engaged in affairs of government; able legislator with foresight and exceptional abilities.

STATIC (1) [sta'tik], *adj.* stationary; standing still; immovable; pertaining to bodies at rest or in equilibrium. STATIC (2), *n.* (*elect.*) atmospheric discharges of electricity, *esp.* as audible on a radio receiver. STATICS, *n.(pl.)* that branch of mechanics which deals with the forces which keep bodies at rest or in equilibrium. [Gk.].

STATION (1) [stā'shn], *n.* spot or place where a person or thing stands; post assigned; office; situation; position; place assigned for the rendezvous of troops; employment; occupation; rank; condition of life; railway depot; district police office; Australian stock farm; **Stations of the Cross,** (*R.C.*) fourteen pictures of scenes from the Passion painted on the walls of churches. STATION-MASTER, official in charge of a railway s. STATION (2), *v.t.* to place; appoint to the occupation of a place, post or office; (*milit.*) assign to a certain s. [L.].

STATIONARY [stā'shn-a-ri], *adj.* motionless; fixed; not moving, progressively or regressively; not appearing to move; not advancing; not improving; operating in one fixed position. [L.].

STATIONER [stā'shn-er], *n.* tradesman who sells all kinds of writing materials. STATIONERY, *n.* writing materials. [MedL.].

STATISTIC(AL) [sta-tis'tik(-al)], *adj.* of, or pertaining to, statistics.

STATISTICS [sta-tis'tiks], *n.(pl.)* branch of political science dealing with the collection and arrangement of the numerical facts respecting the state of a people, their economy, health, wealth etc.; science which treats of these subjects; systematic collection and examination of numerical facts. STATIST, STATISTICIAN [stā-tist, sta-tis-ti'shn], *n.* one versed in s.; statistical expert. [~L.].

STATUARY [sta'tyōō-a-ri], *n.* sculptor; art of carving statues; statues and sculptured work collectively. [L.].

STATUE [sta'tyōō], *n.* a representation, usually of a human or animal figure, in some solid material as stone, marble, bronze, wood; sculptured cast or moulded figure in the round. [OFr. from L.].

STATUESQUE [sta-tyōō-esk'], *adj.* in the style or manner of a statue; having the repose and dignity of a statue.

STATURE [sta'tyōōr], *n.* the natural height of the body; mental proportions. [Fr.].

STATUS [stā'tus], *n.* standing; condition; relative position in society; (*leg.*) legal position; **s. quo,** the existing condition, state, previous position. [L.].

STATUTE [sta'tyōōt], *n.* enactment by the legislative body of a state; written law; Act of Parliament; act of a corporation or of its founder, intended as a permanent rule or law. STATUTORY [sta'tyōō-te-ri], *adj.* pertaining to, enacted by a s.; depending on a s. for its authority. [OFr.].

STAUNCH (1), **STANCH** [stawnsh, stahnsh], *adj.* trustworthy, loyal, firm. [OFr.].

STAUNCH (2), **STANCH** [stawnsh, stahnsh], *v.t.* to stop or stop partially a flow (*esp.* of blood). [OFr. from L.].

STAUROLITE [staw'rō-līt], *n.* (*min.*) mineral made up of silicate of aluminium, magnesium and iron, crystallized in prisms, often in the shape of a cross. [Fr.].

STAVE (1) [stāv], *n.* one of the side timbers of a cask; rung of a ladder; staff; stanza, verse of a song; (*mus.*) set of lines and spaces on which music is written, staff. STAVE (2) (*pret. and p.pt.* STAVED, STOVE, *esp. naut.*), *v.t.* to break a hole in; burst; push as with a staff; **to s. off,** to delay, defer, ward off. [OE.].

STAY (1) [stā], *n.* a support, prop, buttress; (*naut.*) fore-and-aft rope supports of masts and spars; (*fig.*) (moral) support, comfort. STAY-LACE, thin cord for lacing corsets. STAY (2), *v.t.* hold up, prop, by means of a s.; satisfy. STAYS, *n.(pl.)* corset. STAYSAIL, *n.* (*naut.*) triangular sail stretched out on a s. [OE.].

STAY (3), *v.t.* to hold back; stop, delay, obstruct progress of; endure; *v.i.* to remain, put off one's departure; reside temporarily. STAY-IN, *adj.* referring to a strike in which the employees remain at their posts but do not work. STAY (4), *n.* time of remaining in one place; period of residence; halt; (*fig.*) restraint, curb. [OFr.].

STEAD [sted], *n.* place, position; **to stand in good s.,** to render useful service to. [OE.].

STEADFAST [sted'fahst], *adj.* firm, constant, unwavering. [OE.].

STEADING [ste'ding], *n.* (*Scots and northern dial.*) central buildings of a farm, with or without the farmhouse.

STEADY (1) [ste'di], *adj.* firm in standing or position; fixed; constant in mind, purpose or pursuit; not changeable; unwavering; uniform. STEADY (2), *v.t.* to make or hold s.; *v.i.* to become s. [ME.].

STEAK [stāk], *n.* thick slice of meat or fish; thick piece of beef from the rump or fillet. [OIcel.].

STEAL (*pret.* stole, *p.pt.* stolen) [stēl], *v.t.* to take or carry away feloniously the personal goods of another; withdraw or convey clandestinely; gain by address or by gradual imperceptible means; *v.i.* to move secretly or stealthily: **to s. a march on,** to gain an advantage over by surprise. [OE.].

STEALTH [stelth], *n.* clandestine or underhand procedure. [∼STEAL].

STEALTHY [stel'thi], *adj.* of stealth; secret; furtive; clandestine.

STEAM (1) [stēm], *n.* vapour obtained by heating water to boiling point; mist formed by vapour when condensing; any exhalation. STEAM-ENGINE, engine driven by the expansion of s. STEAM-LAUNCH, -TUG, -VESSEL, -YACHT, launch, tug, vessel, yacht driven by s.-power. STEAM-ROLLER, s.-engine provided with a heavy roller, used to level road surfaces; (*fig.*) irresistible power. STEAM-WHISTLE, pipe attached to the boiler of a s.-engine, through which s. is discharged, causing a loud, shrill whistle. STEAM (2), *v.t.* to expose to s.; clean, cook by s.; *v.i.* to rise or pass off in s.; send off a visible vapour; move by s.; open (a sealed envelope) by holding it over s. [OE.].

STEAMBOAT [stēm'bōt], *n.* boat propelled through the water by power supplied from steam.

STEAMER [stē'mer], *n.* ship propelled by steam-power; cooking vessel in which food is steamed; fire-engine worked by steam; **s. lane,** a regular route used by steamers.

STEAMY [stē'mi], *adj.* vaporous; covered with, giving off, steam; hot and misty.

STEARIN [stē'a-rin], *n.* the chief constituent of solid fats. [Gk.].

STEAT(O)-, *pref.* fat, fatty. [Gk.].

STEATITE [stē'a-tīt], *n.* soapstone, amorphous talc.

STEED [stēd], *n.* (*poet.*) horse. [OE.].

STEEL (1) [stēl], *n.* iron containing a small percentage of carbon; any instrument of s.; a weapon of war; spike of s. used for sharpening knives; (*fig.*) extreme hardness; obduracy. STEEL (2), *adj.* made of s.; having the qualities of s.; hard and bright; **s. engraving,** engraving on s. plates; **s. wool,** s. cut into a mass of thread-like shavings, used for cleaning kitchen utensils etc. STEEL (3), *v.t.* to cover with s.; sharpen on a s.; harden; (*fig.*) render obdurate, hard. [OE.].

STEELY [stē'li], *adj.* having the qualities of steel; hard and bright; (*fig.*) hard, relentless.

STEELYARD [stēl'yahd], *n.* lever balance with arms of unequal length, the weight being suspended from the long, and the thing to be weighed from the short, arm. [Uncert.].

STEEP (1) [stēp], *adj.* ascending or descending at a high gradient; precipitous; having an abrupt slope; (*coll.*) almost unbelievable; too expensive. [OE.].

STEEP (2), *v.t.* to soak in liquid; (*fig.*) imbue, dye deeply. STEEP (3), *n.* action of steeping; liquor used in steeping. [OIcel.].

STEEPEN [stē'pen], *v.t.* to render steep; *v.i.* to become steep.

STEEPLE [stē'pl], *n.* high tapering structure surmounting a building, and often ending in a spire; church spire. STEEPLEJACK, *n.* man who builds or repairs steeples and tall chimneys. [ME.].

STEEPLECHASE [stē'pl-chās], *n.* cross-country horse race with jumps, originally towards a church steeple as a landmark; cross-country race on foot across natural or artificial obstacles.

STEER (1) [stēer], *n.* young ox or bullock up to four years old. [OE.].

STEER (2), *v.t.* to direct the course of a ship, vehicle or anything moving along; direct; guide; *v.i.* to direct and govern a ship in its course; sail; be governed; conduct oneself; take or pursue a course or way; **to s. clear of,** to keep out of the way of. [OE.].

STEERAGE [stēer'ij], *n.* act of steering; effect of a rudder on a ship; that part of a ship from which she is steered; quarters in a ship of the passengers travelling at the cheapest fares; regulation; management. STEERAGE-WAY, (*naut.*) movement at a sufficient speed for effective steering.

STEERING (1) [stēering], *n.* action of one who steers; apparatus for steering; **s. committee,** committee appointed to arrange and manage the programme of a conference etc. STEERING-GEAR, apparatus used in s. STEERING-WHEEL, wheel which controls s.-gear. STEERING (2), *adj.* having the function of guiding, which steers.

STEERSMAN [stēerz'man], *n.* one who steers; helmsman.

STEINBOK [stīn'bok], *n.* an antelope indigenous to South Africa; the Alpine ibex. [Germ.].

STELLAR [ste'lah(r)], *adj.* pertaining to stars; astral; starry; of or full of stars; set with stars. [LL.].

STEM (1) [stem], *n.* ascending axis of a plant; peduncle of a flower; stalk; stock of a family; branch of a family; stem-like structure as on a wine-glass; narrow part of a tobacco pipe, including the mouthpiece; (*naut.*) prow of a ship; post to which the two sides of a ship are united at the fore end. STEM (2) (*pres.pt.* **stemming,** *pret. and p.pt.* **stemmed**), *v.t.* (of a vessel, swimmer etc.) to face, make headway against (a tide, current etc.); *v.i.* to derive, originate (from). [OE.].

STEM (3), *v.t.* to obstruct, hold back. [ME.].

STENCH [stensh], *n.* offensive smell; stink. [OE.].

STENCIL (1) [sten'sil], *n.* piece of thin metal or other substance perforated with holes which form a design through which colour or ink may be applied to a surface beneath; design made on the surface beneath by using the s.; such a device used to reproduce typescript. STENCIL (2), *v.t.* to make a copy of by use of a s. [∼OFr.].

STEN GUN [sten'gun], *n.* a form of simple submachine gun. [*S. T.* designers' initials and *En*field].

STENO-, *pref.* narrow, constricted. [Gk.].

STENOGRAPHER [ste-no'gra-fer], *n.* shorthand writer.

STENOGRAPHY [ste-no'gra-fi], *n.* art of writing rapidly by using abbreviations. [Gk.].

STENOSIS [ste-nō'sis], *n.* (*path.*) stricture of an aperture. [Gk.].

STENTORIAN [sten-taw'ri-an], *adj.* (of the voice) loud, powerful. [Gk. *Stentor,* herald in the Trojan War].

STEP (1) (*pres.pt.* **stepping,** *pret. and p.pt.* **stepped**) [step], *v.t.* to set (the foot); (*naut.*) put (a mast) in place; **to s. aside,** (*fig.*) to give place; **to s. out,** to increase the pace, walk quickly; (*fig.*) adventure; **to s. on it,** (*coll.*) to go very quickly, hurry; **to s. up,** to increase the rate of; (*elect.*) increase the voltage; arrange as in steps; *v.i.* to advance or recede by a movement of the foot; go; walk. STEP-INS, *n.*(*pl.*) underwear, shoes etc., which can be put on without the use of buttons or fasteners. STEP (2), *n.* footfall; pace; space between the feet in walking or running; tread of a stair; small space; gradation; degree, stage in progression; footstep; gait; proceeding; action; rung of a ladder; (*naut.*) that on which the foot of a mast rests. STEP-LADDER, ladder with flat treads and a hinged support, opening at an angle for use and standing alone. [OE.].

STEP-, *pref.* related by the second marriage of one parent. [OE.].

STEPBROTHER [step'bru-THer], *n.* brother who is the son of one's stepfather or stepmother by a former marriage.

STEPDAUGHTER [step'daw-ter], *n.* daughter of a husband or wife by a former wife or husband.

STEPFATHER [step'fah-THer], *n.* a mother's second or subsequent husband.

STEPHANOTIS [ste-fa-nō'tis], *n.* (*bot.*) genus of tropical plants with scented flowers. [Gk.].

STEPMOTHER [step'mu-THer], *n.* a father's wife by a later marriage.

STEPPE [step], *n.* expanse of uncultivated, arid, treeless plains in the south-east of Europe and the south-west of Asia. [Russ.].

STEPPING-STONE [ste'ping-stōn], *n.* stone to keep the feet above the water or dirt in walking; (*fig.*) means of progress, aid in one's advancement.

STEPSISTER [step'sis-ter], *n.* stepmother's or stepfather's daughter by a previous marriage.

STEPSON [step'sun], *n.* son of a husband or wife by a previous marriage.

STEREO (1) [ste'ri-ō], *n.* (*coll.*) a stereotype.

STEREO- (2), *pref.* firm. [Gk.].

STEREOGRAPHY [ste-ri-o'gra-fi], *n.* art of delineating solid bodies on a plane. [Gk.].

STEREOSCOPE [ste'ri-ō-skōp], *n.* optical instrument through which two pictures of the same object appear as one, and cause it to stand out in solid form as though real. [Gk.].

STEREOTYPE (1) [ste'ri-ō-tīp], *n.* (*print.*) metallic plate cast from a mould taken from a page of movable type. STEREOTYPE (2), *v.t.* to cast, print in s.; (*fig.*) fix in one style irrevocably. [STEREO- and TYPE].

STERILE [ste'rīl], *adj.* barren; unfruitful; producing little or no crop; producing no young; barren of ideas or sentiment; free from septic germs; free from living bacteria. [L.].

STERILITY [ste-ri'li-ti], *n.* barrenness; unfruitfulness; barrenness of ideas or sentiments.

STERILIZE [ste'ri-līz], *v.t.* to render barren; exhaust

ōō is pronounced as in *food*; ŏŏ as in *hood*; th as in *think*; TH as in *that*; zh as in *azure*.   ∼ = related to.

DSE—S*

of fertility; **destroy bacteria in**; spray or wash with an antiseptic.

STERLING (1) [stur'ling], *n.* the money of Great Britain as distinguished from that of other countries; **s. area,** those parts of the world where British money is the standard. STERLING (2), *adj.* of standard worth; genuine; pure; of excellent quality; according to the British monetary standard; (*fig.*) having fine dependable moral qualities. [ME.].

STERN (1) [sturn], *n.* rear part of a ship or aeroplane; hinder part. STERN-SHEETS, that part of a boat between the s. and the aftmost seat of the rowers. [OIcel.].

STERN (2), *adj.* severe in expression; austere; severe in manner and morals; harsh; rigidly steadfast; unrelenting. [OE.].

STERNUM (*pl.* **sterna, sternums**) [stur'num], *n.* the breastbone, the bone which forms the front of the human chest from the neck to the stomach and to which the upper ribs are joined. [Gk.].

STERTOROUS [stur'te-roos], *adj.* snoring; emitting a sound like snoring. [~L.].

STET [stet], *v.t.* (*print.*) instruction written on the margin of a proof to intimate to the printer that something which has been deleted is to stand; *v.imp.* let it stand. [L.].

STETHOSCOPE [ste'thŏ-skōp], *n.* instrument for distinguishing sounds within the body, particularly those connected with the heart and lungs. [Gk.].

STETSON [stet'sn], *n.* broad-brimmed felt hat. [*Stetson,* original maker].

STEVEDORE [stē'vi-daw(r)], *n.* one whose occupation is to stow goods in a ship's hold; loader or unloader of vessels. [Span.].

STEW (1) [styŏō], *n.* fish-pond, *esp.* one serving as a store for fish shortly to be used; brothel. [OFr.].

STEW (2), *v.t.* to cook (meat or fruit) slowly in a small quantity of liquid; *v.i.* to be boiled in a slow, gentle manner; **to s. in one's own juice,** to cope with one's own difficulties. STEW (3), *n.* dish of stewed meat and vegetables; (*slang*) state of agitation; **Irish s., s.** of mutton and vegetables. [OFr.].

STEWARD [styŏō'erd], *n.* man who manages the concerns of a large estate or a great family; an officer of state; officer in a college who provides the food and superintends the concerns of the kitchen; **head** of that department in a ship which supplies food or refreshment; waiter on board ship; person in charge of a race-meeting; one who assists in running a public meeting. STEWARDSHIP, *n.* office, work of a s.; management, administration. [OE.].

STICK (1) [stik], *n.* small shoot or branch cut off a tree; long slender piece of wood or other material; slender piece; staff; printer's tool for composing type with; a thrust with a pointed instrument which penetrates the body, stab; group of bombs released at one time from an aeroplane; (*coll.*) stiff uninteresting person; **in a cleft s.,** on the horns of a dilemma; **to get hold of the wrong end of the s.,** to misunderstand. STICK (2), *v.t.* to fasten to a s. or provide with sticks as a support. [OE.].

STICK (3) (*pret. and p.pt.* **stuck**), *v.t.* to pierce; thrust a pointed instrument into; stab; kill by piercing; thrust; fasten, cause to adhere by means of an adhesive such as gum; fix in; set with something pointed; (*coll.*) endure, put up with; *v.i.* to remain with the point thrust in; adhere; cling fast to; stop; be impeded; hesitate; be embarrassed; **to s. out,** to project; to resist; **to s. in one's throat,** (*fig.*) to be very distasteful, hard to accept; **to s. out for,** to insist upon having; **to s. up for,** to defend, champion; **to s. to one's guns,** to defend one's own position or opinions. STICK-IN-THE-MUD, *n. and adj.* (one who is) lacking in initiative, unprogressive, dull, sluggish. STICK-JAW, *n.* (*coll.*) food, toffee etc. which is sticky and difficult to chew. [ME.].

STICKLE [sti'kl], *v.i.* to take part with one side or other; insist on the observance of every trifle; contend obstinately. STICKLER, *n.* obstinate contender about trivialities; **a s. for,** one who is punctilious about. [ME.].

STICKLEBACK [sti'kl-bak], *n.* a little nest-building fish with a spiny back. [OE.].

STICKY [sti'ki], *adj.* having a tendency to stick to surfaces; glutinous; having adhesive properties; (*coll.*) having many scruples, difficult, over-punctilious; **s. end,** (*slang*) unpleasant, violent death.

STIFF [stif], *adj.* not easily bent; rigid; firm, not fluid; strong; violent; stubborn; constrained; formal; difficult; (*coll.*) exorbitant, excessive; **s. neck,** rheumatic affection of the muscles of the neck; **s. 'un,**

(*slang*) corpse. STIFF-NECKED, (*fig.*) stubborn; haughty; extremely punctilious. STIFF (2), *n.* (*slang*) corpse; **big s.,** (*slang*) blockhead. [OE.].

STIFFEN [sti'fen], *v.t.* to render stiff, rigid; make less pliable; (*fig.*) make more determined; *v.i.* to become stiff, thicker, less yielding; (*fig.*) assume a cold and formal manner; become less amenable and friendly. STIFFENER, *n.* something which makes stiff, or causes stiffening; (*slang*) a drink as a stimulant, *esp.* in an emergency.

STIFLE (1) [stī'fl], *n.* joint in a horse's hind leg; a disease affecting this joint. [~STIFF].

STIFLE (2), *v.t. and i.* to suffocate; choke; stop the breath temporarily; extinguish; deaden; put down; smother; suppress. [OIcel.].

STIGMA (*pl.* **stigmata, stigmas**) [stig'mah], *n.* mark made with a burning iron; brand; any mark of infamy; moral spot on or imputation attaching to character; (*bot.*) receptive organ for the pollen grains; (*pl.*) (*eccles.*) marks as of five wounds corresponding to those of Christ, sometimes alleged to appear miraculously on the bodies of saints and martyrs. [Gk.].

STIGMATIZE [stig'ma-tīz], *v.t.* to cause to bear a stigma; brand; hold up to disgrace; discredit irrevocably.

STILE [stīl], *n.* step or set of steps or any similar device for ascending and descending over a fence or wall; (*arch.*) upright piece in framing or panelling. [OE.].

STILETTO [sti-le'tō], *n.* small dagger having a round blade; pointed instrument for making eyelet holes. [It.].

STILL (1) [stil], *n.* apparatus used in distilling. STILL-ROOM, room where distilling is done; household storeroom for jams, pickles etc.; room in a hotel etc. where alcoholic drinks are handled. [~L.].

STILL (2), *adj.* without movement; motionless; quiet; silent; tranquil; without a sparkle. STILL-BIRTH, *n.* birth of a s.-born child. STILL-BORN, *adj.* born dead; abortive. STILL-LIFE, *n.* (*paint.*) picture portraying immobile objects, *esp.* such as flowers, fruit, dead game. STILL (3), *n.* a s. (as opposed to a moving) picture. STILL (4), *adv.* to this time, even now; nevertheless, notwithstanding; even more, yet. STILL (5), *v.t.* to make s.; quieten, soothe; render (pain) less acute. [OE.].

STILT (1) [stilt], *n.* a support of wood with a rest for the foot used in walking over rough ground; a long-legged plover. STILT (2), *v.t.* to raise on stilts; elevate unnaturally. STILTED, *adj.* affected, bombastic, unnatural; **stilted arch,** (*arch.*) arch springing not directly from the impost but from the horizontal courses of stone above it. [~MDu.].

STILTON [stil'ton], *n.* kind of rich soft cheese. [*Stilton,* Huntingdonshire].

STIMULANT (1) [sti'myŏō-lant], *adj.* having the power to stimulate. STIMULANT (2), *n.* a drink which stimulates; alcoholic drink; (*fig.*) anything which stimulates to thought or action.

STIMULATE [sti'myŏō-lāt], *v.t.* to excite to action or more vigorous exertion; produce a sudden increase of vital energy in; stir to thought. STIMULATIVE, *adj.* having the power of stimulating. [L.].

STIMULATION [sti-myŏō-lā'shn], *n.* act of goading or exciting; sudden increase of vital energy; mental inspiration.

STIMULUS (*pl.* **stimuli**) [sti'myŏō-lus], *n.* something which stimulates; stimulant; goad; exciter to thought or action. [L.].

STING (1) (*pret. and p.pt.* **stung**) [sting], *v.t.* (of insects etc.) to pierce with a sting; pain acutely; (*slang*) get money out of; (*fig.*) occasion sharp mental pain to; *v.i.* to inflict a sting; feel a sting or stinging sensation. STING (2), *n.* sharp, poisonous organ with which certain creatures and plants are armed for their defence; the thrust of a s. into the flesh; anything which gives acute pain; the point of an epigram; that wherein lies the principal pain or which constitutes the chief terror. STING-RAY, a sea-fish having a long tail which is armed with spines.

STINGY [stin'ji], *adj.* mean, niggardly; parsimonious. [OE.].

STINK (1) (*pret.* **stank, stunk†,** *p.pt.* **stunk**) [stingk], *v.i.* to emit a strong unpleasant odour; (*fig.*) be offensive to good taste; (*slang*) be of very poor quality. STINK (2), *n.* extremely unpleasant and strong odour; stench; (*slang*) scandal, commotion. STINK-BOMB, bomb emitting an offensive odour when it is let off. STINKER, *n.* one who, or that which, stinks; (*slang*) highly unpleasant person or thing. STINKING, *adj.* giving off an offensive smell, *esp.* of animals and plants when caused by natural secretions. [OE.].

STINT (1) [stint], *v.t* to restrict unduly the amount of; be stingy with, grudging of. STINT (2), *n.* limit; restraint; (*esp.* mining) an allotted amount of work; **without s.,** ungrudgingly, without limit. STINTED, *adj.* limited to a certain insufficient quantity. [OE.].

STIPEND [sti'pend], *n.* annual payment for services rendered; salary, *esp.* of a clergyman. [L.].

STIPENDIARY (1) [sti-pen'di-a-ri], *adj.* involving salary in return for services; **s. magistrate,** paid magistrate in the service of the state. STIPENDIARY (2), *n.* a s. magistrate. [L.].

STIPPLE [sti'pl], *v.t.* to paint or engrave by means of dots in place of lines. STIPPLING, *n.* drawing, painting or engraving by means of minute dots instead of lines. [Du.].

STIPTIC, see STYPTIC.

STIPULATE [sti'pyōō-lāt], *v.t.* to insist upon, demand as a condition; *v.i.* to make an agreement; contract; settle terms. [~L.].

STIPULATION [sti-pyōō-lā'shn], *n.* action of stipulating; contract or bargain.

STIR (1) [stur], *v.t.* to put in motion, *esp.* to move in a circular direction; rouse, agitate, excite; *v.i.* to move oneself; be in a state of movement; move from one position to another; **to s. up,** to mix; (*fig.*) agitate, arouse. STIR (2), *n.* disturbance; movement; agitation of mind; (*slang*) prison. STIRRING, *adj.* active; rousing; thrilling; moving. [OE.].

STIRRUP [sti'rup], *n.* hoop or ring for the foot, suspended from a strap, to enable a rider to mount or sit steadily on horseback. STIRRUP-CUP, parting drink taken on horseback immediately before departure. STIRRUP-LEATHER, strap of leather for supporting a s. STIRRUP-PUMP, type of pump used for spraying water, and held in position by inserting the foot in its support. [OE.].

STITCH (1) [stich], *n.* the complete action of a needle and thread when sewing; single turn of the thread round the needle in knitting or crochet; method of doing a stitch; sharp stabbing pain in the side. STITCH (2), *v.t.* to sew; unite with stitches; embroider; *v.i.* to practise needlework. STITCHERY, *n.* art of stitching; needlework. STITCHING, *n.* act of stitching; work done by sewing. [OE.].

STITCHWORT [stich'wert], *n.* any species of *Stellaria*, the genus which includes the chickweeds. [OE.].

STIVE [stiv], *v.t.* and *i.* to stew, be stewed. [OFr.].

STOAT [stōt], *n.* the ermine, related to the weasel. [ME.].

STOCK (1) [stok], *n.* stem of a tree or other plant; post; dull, stupid person; frame of a rifle; neckcloth; an original progenitor; lineage; family; fund; capital; merchandise unsold; a share of the subscribed capital of a public trading company or of the public debt; a store, provision; goods on hand; domestic animals or beasts belonging to a farm; (*bot.*) plant of the genus *Matthiola*; (*pl.*) frame in which the legs of criminals were confined; frame on which a ship rests while building; the public funds; **stocks and stones,** inanimate things; **to take s.,** to make an inventory of s. or goods in hand; (*fig.*) estimate resources, appraise. STOCK-BOOK, ledger in which s. is entered. STOCK-BREEDER, one who breeds animals. STOCK-DOVE, the wild pigeon. STOCK-FISH, fish, such as cod or ling, dried in the sun without salt. STOCK-IN-TRADE, s. for carrying on one's business; assets, material or mental, to facilitate the carrying on of one's business. STOCK-JOBBER, member of the S. Exchange who buys and sells shares for brokers. STOCK-JOBBING, the buying and selling of stocks and shares for brokers. STOCK-RIDER, (*Australian*) mounted stockman. STOCK-MARKET, the S. Exchange; market in stocks and shares. STOCK-STILL, *adj.* as still as a post; motionless. STOCK-TAKING, periodical taking s. of business goods or properties in hand. STOCK-WHIP, short-handled whip with a long thong used in herding cattle. STOCK (2), *adj.* kept in s.; (*fig.*) conventional, stereotyped, average. STOCK (3), *v.t.* to store for sale or use; supply; fill; lay up in store; pack; equip with domestic animals; plant land. STOCKIST, *n.* one who keeps certain goods in s. [OE.].

STOCKADE (1) [sto-kād'], *n.* palisaded defence; line of posts or stakes set up as a fence or barrier; enclosure for cattle. STOCKADE (2), *v.t.* to fortify by means of a s. [Fr.].

STOCKBROKER [stok'brō-ker], *n.* broker engaged in the purchase and sale of stocks and shares on behalf of his clients.

STOCK EXCHANGE [stok'eks-chānj], *n.* corporate body of stockbrokers forming and controlling an official market for stocks and shares; building where their business is carried on.

STOCKHOLDER [stok'hōld-er], *n.* one who holds stock in the public funds or a public company.

STOCKINETTE [sto-ki-net'], *n.* knitted fabric of silk, wool or cotton material. [~STOCKING].

STOCKING [sto'king], *n.* close-fitting knitted or woven covering for the leg and foot. STOCKINGED, *adj.* clothed in, wearing, stockings; **in one's stockinged feet,** wearing stockings but no shoes. [~STOCK (1)].

STOCKMAN [stok'man], *n.* (*Australian*) man in charge of farm-stock; herdsman.

STOCKPOT [stok'pot], *n.* vessel in which bones, meat etc., which are to be the basis of soup, are stewed and kept.

STOCKY [sto'ki], *adj.* short and thickset; of a stumpy build.

STOCKYARD [stok'yahd], *n.* yard or enclosure where cattle are herded.

STODGE [stoj], *n.* stodgy food; literary material etc. resembling this.

STODGY [sto'ji], *adj.* dull and heavy; (*fig.*) tedious and heavy, lacking inspiration. [Uncert.].

STOEP, STOOP [stōōp], *n.* verandah of a Dutch South African house. [Afrik.].

STOIC [stō'ik], *n.* disciple of the Greek philosopher Zeno, who taught that men should subdue all passion, conform to reason and accept the inevitable; one who keeps all emotions within strict control; person with calm fortitude. STOICISM [stō'i-sizm], *n.* opinions and maxims of the Stoics; indifference to pleasure or pain; calm fortitude. [Gk.].

STOKE [stōk], *v.t.* and *i.* to shovel (fuel) into a furnace; **to s. up,** (*slang*) to fortify (oneself) with a good meal. STOKEHOLD, *n.* that part of a ship's hold containing the boilers. STOKEHOLE, *n.* hole through which a furnace is stoked. [~Next].

STOKER [stō'ker], *n.* man employed to stoke a furnace. [Du.].

STOLE (1) [stōl], *pret.* of STEAL.

STOLE (2), *n.* band of silk reaching from the neck to below the waist, worn over both shoulders by priests and bishops and over the left shoulder only by deacons; long narrow fur necklet. [L.].

STOLEN [stō'len], *p.pt.* of STEAL.

STOLID [sto'lid], *adj.* impassive, slow, heavy, without animation or vivacity. [L.].

STOLIDITY [sto-li'di-ti], *n.* quality of being stolid.

STOMACH (1) [stu'mak], *n.* membranous receptacle below the liver and diaphragm, the principal organ of digestion; inclination. STOMACH-PUMP, small medical syringe for drawing liquids from the s., or for injecting them. STOMACH (2), *v.t.* to retain in the s.; endure, tolerate. STOMACHIC (stu-ma'kik), *adj.* pertaining to the s.; strengthening to the s.; stimulating the action of the s. [OFr. from Gk.].

STOMACHER [stu'ma-ker, stu'ma-cher], *n.* ornamental covering for the breast, part of women's dress in the sixteenth century.

STONE (1) [stōn], *n.* small fragment of rock; gem or precious jewel; anything made of stone; calculous concretion in the kidneys or bladder; fourteen pounds; a weight varying in different trades; monument; (*fig.*) insensibility; hard-heartedness. STONE-BLIND, *adj.* absolutely blind. STONE-DEAD, *adj.* absolutely dead. STONE-DEAF, *adj.* completely deaf. STONE-FRUIT, fruit whose seeds are covered with a hard shell embedded in pulp, as a plum. STONE-MASON, man who works in building s. STONE-PINE, umbrella-shaped coniferous tree of the Mediterranean coastal region. STONE'S-CAST, -THROW, distance a s. may be thrown; **within a s.'s-throw,** within a very short distance. STONE (2), *adj.* made of s.; (*fig.*) hard, unyielding; unfeeling. STONE (3), *v.t.* to throw stones at; injure or kill by throwing stones at; line or pave with s.; take the stones from (fruit). [OE.].

STONECHAT [stōn'chat], *n.* a small European bird. [STONE (1) and CHAT].

STONECROP [stōn'krop], *n.* succulent native plant of the genus *Sedum*.

STONEHATCH [stōn'hach], *n.* the ringed plover.

STONEWALL [stōn-wawl'], *v.i.* (*cricket*) to block balls persistently; defend oneself doggedly; obstruct business.

STONEWORK [stōn'werk], *n.* masonry.

STONY [stō'ni], *adj.* made of, resembling, stone;

---

abounding in stones; petrifying; hard; (fig.) obdurate, unrelenting; (slang) penniless. STONY-BROKE, (coll.) penniless. STONY-HEARTED, hard-hearted; cold and relentless.

STOOD [stŏŏd], pret. and p.pt. of STAND.

STOOGE (1) [stōōj], n. (U.S. slang) a dupe, one who performs humble but necessary tasks to assist another. STOOGE (2), v.i. (slang) to act as a s.; wander aimlessly. [Uncert.].

STOOK (1) [stŏŏk], n. group of sheaves of grain piled against each other. STOOK (2), v.t. to build up in stooks for drying and gathering. [ME.].

STOOL [stŏŏl], n. seat without a back; little form with three or four legs as a seat for one person; seat used in evacuating the bowels; an evacuation; (hort.) sucker. STOOL-BALL, early form of cricket in which the wicket was a s. and the bat held in one hand. STOOL-PIGEON, apparatus with a wooden pigeon attached, used as a decoy in pigeon-shooting; (fig.) decoy, informer. [OE.].

STOOP (1) [stŏŏp], v.t. to bow down; cause to incline down; v.i. to bend down or incline the body; hold oneself in a round-shouldered position; condescend; lower one's dignity by an unworthy act. STOOP (2), n. action or posture of stooping; round-shouldered position. [OE.].

STOOP (3), see STOEP.

STOP (1) (pres.pt. **stopping**, pret. and p.pt. **stopped**) [stop], v.t. to close by filling or obstructing; obstruct; cause to come to a standstill; check or withhold; impede; repress; restrain; intercept; regulate sounds; punctuate; v.i. to fill (a tooth); forbid transmission of (a message); (coll.) remain for a while; halt; cease to go forward; discontinue; **to s. up,** to obstruct, clog. STOP-COCK, n. tap or valve for regulating flow. STOP-GAP, n. a substitute in an emergency; temporary expedient. STOP-PRESS, n. late news printed in a special place in a newspaper. STOP-WATCH, n. chronograph; watch which can be started or stopped at any moment so as to measure the exact time taken by some action. STOP (2), n. cessation of progressive motion; obstruction; repression; interruption; obstacle; indicator or place at which a public vehicle stops for the convenience of passengers; point or mark in writing for regulating the necessary pauses; (mus.) apparatus by which the sounds of musical instruments are regulated; diaphragm in a camera; act of supplying the stops; instruction to s. STOPPING, n. something which stops or fills; the filling of a tooth; (mus.) act of using a s. or pressing a string. [OE.].

STOPPAGE [sto'pij], n. act of arresting progress or motion; condition of being stopped; deduction from pay.

STOPPER (1) [sto'per], n. one who, or a thing which, stops; that which closes or fills an opening in a vessel, esp. a bottle; **put the s. on,** v.t. (fig.) repress, cause to cease. STOPPER (2), v.t. to shut or secure with a s.

STORAGE [staw'rij], n. a placing in store; safe keeping of goods in a warehouse; price for keeping goods in a store; system of storing electricity in accumulators; **cold s.,** the keeping of food or furs in refrigerating chambers.

STORE (1) [staw(r)], n. a stock laid up for supply; abundance; quantity accumulated; warehouse, storage place; shop; (pl.) (milit.) arms, ammunition, provisions and clothing. STORE (2), v.t. to fill; supply; hoard; reserve; stow away for safe keeping; warehouse; afford storage space for. STORES, n. large modern shop with many departments; department s. [OFr.].

STOREHOUSE [staw'hows], n. room or building in which goods are stored; repository, warehouse; (fig.) of the mind, place stored well with knowledge.

STOR(E)Y [staw'ri], n. one floor of a building; set of rooms on one floor.

STORIED [staw'rid], adj. painted with pictures which tell a story; celebrated in history or legend.

STORK [stawk], n. large, long-beaked, long-legged wading bird. [OE.].

STORM (1) [stawm], n. (meteor.) violent commotion in the atmosphere, generally widespread and destructive; tempest; assault on a fortified place; violent civil commotion; insurrection; clamour; tumult; violence; emotional upheaval; **to take by s.,** to take by a sudden assault; (fig.) get possession of instantaneously. STORM-COCK, the missel-thrush. STORM-CONE, large canvas cone, part of a s.-signal. STORM-LANTERN, oil lantern with the flame protected from the wind. STORM-SIGNAL, an arrangement of a hollow drum of canvas and a hollow cone of canvas,

used as a signal to indicate the approach of a s. STORM-TOSSED, adj. suffering from violent storms; (fig.) agitated by passion. STORM-TROOPER, member of the former National Socialist brown-shirt organization in Germany. STORM (2), v.t. to assault, take by s.; v.i. to raise a tempest; blow with violence; give way to violent emotion. [OE.].

STORMY [staw'mi], adj. tempestuous; accompanied or agitated with furious winds; boisterous; violent; agitated with passion; **s. petrel,** the small sea-bird Mother Carey's chicken.

STORTHING [staw'ting], n. the Norwegian parliament. [OScand.].

STORY (1) [staw'ri], n. oral narration or written narrative of a series of facts or events; history; petty tale; a fiction; a falsehood; anecdote. STORY-BOOK, book of stories or short tales; a romance. STORY-TELLER, person who tells stories; novelist; (coll.) liar. STORY-TELLING, practice of telling stories; (coll.) lying. [AFr. from L.].

STORY (2), see STOREY.

STOUP [stŏŏp], n. flagon; basin for holy water. [~OIcel.].

STOUT (1) [stowt], adj. strong, lusty, thickset; bold, intrepid, resolute; fat, corpulent. STOUT-HEARTED, endowed with a brave heart; courageous, intrepid. STOUT (2), n. dark strong drink resembling porter. [OFr.].

STOVE (1) [stōv], n. apparatus enclosing a fire for heating or cooking. STOVE-PIPE, iron pipe to carry off the smoke of a s.; † cylindrical hat. STOVE (2), v.t. to heat by means of a s.; fumigate. [OE.].

STOVE (3), pret. and p.pt. of STAVE (2).

STOW [stō], v.t. to place; put in a suitable place or position; lay up; pack; **s. it,** (slang) be quiet. [OE.].

STOWAGE [stō'ij], n. act of stowing; state of being stowed; room for stowing goods; money paid for stowing things.

STOWAWAY [stō'a-wā], n. one who hides in a ship in order to secure a free passage.

STRABISMUS [stra-biz'mus], n. non-coincidence of the optic axes of the eyes upon an object; squinting; cast in the eye. [~Gk.].

STRAD [strad], n. (coll.) a Stradivarius.

STRADDLE (1) [stra'dl], v.t. to bestride; v.i. to stand or walk with the legs far apart; (nav. gunnery) make shells fall on both sides of (a target) without hitting it; (fig.) vacillate. STRADDLE (2), n. act of straddling; distance between legs astraddle. [Uncert.].

STRADIVARIUS [stra-di-vah'ri-us], n. violin or similar stringed instrument made by Antonio Stradivari. [Stradivarius, Latin form of Stradivari].

STRAFE (1) [strahf], v.t. to put up a heavy concentration of fire against. STRAFE (2), n. concentrated artillery or aerial bombardment. [Germ.].

STRAGGLE [stra'gl], v.i. to wander from the direct course or way; rove; wander at large without any definite direction or object; ramble; shoot too far in growth; be dispersed; fall behind the main body. STRAGGLING, adj. wandering, rambling; scattered; separated from the main place or group; (of hair) in untidy wisps; (of handwriting) unformed and feeble. [Uncert.].

STRAIGHT (1) [strāt], adj. direct; not deviating or crooked; upright; honest; reliable; fair and truthful; frank; undiluted. STRAIGHT (2), adv. in a s. line; in a forthright manner; directly; without ambiguity; without diluting; **s. away,** at once, straightway. [OE.].

STRAIGHTEN [strā'ten], v.t. and i. to make straight; change from a crooked to a straight form.

STRAIGHTFORWARD [strāt-faw'werd], adj. proceeding in a straight course; upright; open; frank; simple.

STRAIGHTWAY [strāt'wā], adv. (archaic) immediately; straight away.

STRAIN (1) [strān], n. racial descent, breed, lineage; descendants, race; inherited tendency; class of people, animals or things linked by common characteristics. [OE.].

STRAIN (2), v.t. to stretch violently; draw with force; injure by stretching; tax to the utmost strength; filter; tighten; force; constrain; v.i. to make a great effort; be filtered. STRAIN (3), n. action or result of straining or stretching; reach; stretch, muscular effort; passage of music or poetry or its characteristic style and content. [OFr. from L.].

STRAIT (1) [strāt], adj. narrow; strict, rigorous, difficult. STRAIT-JACKET, -WAISTCOAT, n. garment to restrain the arms of a dangerous lunatic. STRAIT-LACED, strict in manners or morals. STRAIT (2), n.

The accent ′ after a syllable = stress (u-pon′). The mark ˉ over a vowel = length (ā in made; ō in bone).

narrow passage in the sea between two portions of land; (pl.) distress, difficulty; straitened means. [AFr.].

STRAITEN [strā'ten], v.t. to make narrow; contract; confine; make tense or tight; distress; press with poverty or other necessity; embarrass by want of sufficient room.

STRAND (1) [strand], n. beach, shore. STRAND (2), v.t. to cause to be driven ashore; run aground. STRANDED, adj. aground; abandoned, left helpless or without resources. [OE.].

STRAND (3), n. one twisted thread in yarn or rope; tress of hair. STRAND (4), v.t. to twist strands together to make rope etc. [OFr.].

STRANGE [strānj], adj. foreign; belonging to others; not before known, heard or seen; wonderful; odd, unusual; unfamiliar; inexperienced. [OFr. from L.].

STRANGER [strān'jer], n. person who belongs to another town or country; one unknown or unacquainted; guest, visitor; (leg.) one not party or privy to any act. [OFr.].

STRANGLE [strang'gl], v.t. to destroy the life of by stopping respiration; hinder from birth or appearance; suppress, stifle. [OFr.].

STRANGLEWEED [strang'gl-wēd], n. the dodder.

STRANGULATE [strang'gyōō-lāt], v.t. to stop the circulation by compression; strangle. STRANGULATION [strang-gyōō-lā'shn], n. action of strangling; hysterical constriction of the throat; compression of the intestines in hernia.

STRAP (1) [strap], n. long narrow strip of cloth or leather; iron plate for connecting two or more timbers; (milit.) shoulder-strap; (coll.) corporal punishment. STRAP-HANGER, standing passenger steadying himself by holding on to a s. affixed to the side or roof of a vehicle. STRAP (2) (pres.pt. STRAPPING, pret. and p.pt. STRAPPED), v.t. to fasten, tie up, bind with a s.; beat with a s. as a punishment; v.i. to be capable of fastening with a s. STRAPPING (1), n. material used for straps; adhesive plaster. STRAPPING (2), adj. tall, lusty. [OE.].

STRAPPADO [stra-pah'dō], n. old form of torture or military punishment by drawing up a person to a height by a rope and letting him fall with a jerk to the length of the rope. [It.].

STRATAGEM [stra'ta-jem], n. an artifice, esp. in war; plan, scheme or trick for deceiving an enemy or obtaining an advantage. [OFr. from Gk.].

STRATEGIC(AL) [stra-tē'jik(-al)], adj. based on, of or resembling, strategy.

STRATEGY [stra'ti-ji], n. generalship; science or art of combining and employing military resources, or of manoeuvring an army; direction of the operations of war; (fig.) clever manoeuvring. [Gk.].

STRATH [strath], n. wide open valley through which a river runs. [Gael.].

STRATHSPEY [strath-spā'], n. lively Scottish dance; music for this. [Strathspey, Scotland].

STRATIFY [strah'ti-fī], v.t. and i. to form into a layer or layers, as rocks in the earth; deposit in strata.

STRATOSPHERE [strah'tō-sfēer], n. upper part of the atmosphere where the temperature no longer falls with an increase in height. [Next and SPHERE].

STRATUM (pl. strata) [strā'tum, strah'tum], n. bed or layer of rock occurring in a series in the crust of the earth; bed or layer artificially made; (fig.) social level or class. [L.].

STRATUS (pl. strati) [strā'tus, strah'tus], n. a cloud form, so called from its being spread over the dome of the sky in horizontal layers. [L.].

STRAW [straw], n. a stalk of certain species of grass, grain etc.; mass of such stalks cut and thrashed; anything proverbially worthless; **man of s.,** imaginary or fictitious person, unreliable or financially unsound person. [OE.].

STRAWBERRY [straw'be-ri], n. any one of the species of the genus Fragaria; its fruit; **crushed s.,** soft pinky colour resembling that of strawberries when crushed. STRAWBERRY-LEAF, trifoliate leaf of the s. plant; this forming the decoration of the coronet of a duke, marquis or earl; symbol of ducal rank. [OE.].

STRAY (1) [strā], v.i. to wander, move away or aside (from); deviate; roam; (fig.) deviate from the course of strict virtue; of one's thoughts, wander in a desultory fashion. STRAY (2), n. any domestic animal which has left an enclosure, and wanders at large or is lost; lost or forlorn child; waif; (fig.) one who wanders from the path of duty or rectitude. STRAY (3), adj. having strayed; scattered, found here and there irregularly; of a bullet, casual. [OFr.].

STREAK (1) [strēk], n. line or stripe of a different colour from the ground; stripe flash of lightning; (fig.) strain, small endowment; **s. of luck,** run of luck. STREAK (2), v.t. to form streaks in; stripe; variegate with streaks; v.i. (coll.) to flash swiftly. STREAKED, adj. marked or variegated with stripes of a different colour, shade, substance or texture; (of lightning) swiftly flashing, forked. [OE.].

STREAKY [strē'ki], adj. having streaks, esp. of fat and lean meat.

STREAM (1) [strēm], n. current of water or other fluid; river, brook or rivulet; current of air or of light; current; drift; act of streaming; (fig.) continuously moving crowd or series of objects; general flow of events or opinions. STREAM (2), v.t. to cause to pour out in a s.; v.i. to flow; move or run in a continuous current; issue in a s.; move continuously; run with liquid; float out. STREAMLET, n. little s. [OE.].

STREAMER [strē'mer], n. long narrow banner; pennant; long strip of paper used for party decorations etc.; beam or ray of light shooting up from the horizon.

STREAMLINE (1) [strēm'līn], n. gracefully curved shape which presents no projecting portions to offer resistance to air or water. STREAMLINE (2), v.t. to shape so as to offer the minimum of resistance to air or water.

STREET [strēt], n. paved road in a city or town, lined with and including houses; a Roman road; **not in the same s. with,** (coll.) greatly inferior to; **streets ahead of,** far ahead of; **up one's s.,** (slang) in one's line of business; **on the streets,** being a prostitute; **s. sweeper,** scavenger; **s. walker,** prostitute. [OE. from L.].

STRENGTH [strength], n. quality of being strong; active muscular power of an animal body; firmness; toughness; power or vigour of any kind; support; mental activity and power; intensity; force of writing, nervous diction; vividness; legal force; natural force; amount of force, military or naval; vehemence; **on the s. of,** because of, relying on. [OE.].

STRENGTHEN [streng'then], v.t. to make strong; add strength to; confirm, animate; cause to increase in power or security; v.i. to grow strong or stronger.

STRENUOUS [stre'nyōō-ōōs], adj. eagerly pressing or urgent; zealous; ardent; needing effort; persistent, energetic. [L.].

STREPITANT [stre'pi-tant], adj. loud, noisy.

STREPTOCOCCUS (pl. **streptococci**) [strep-tō-ko'kus], n. (path.) a type of bacillus which occurs arranged in chains. [Gk.].

STREPTOMYCIN [strep-tō-mī'sin], n. (med.) a drug obtained from the fungus Streptomyces grisens, which destroys the bacilli of certain diseases.

STRESS (1) [stres], n. force; urgency; intense pressure; importance; that which bears most weight; violence; strain; emphasis; accent. STRESS (2), v.t. to subject to strain; lay s. on; emphasize. [OFr.].

STRETCH (1) [strech], v.t. to draw out to greater length or breadth; spread; expand; reach; strain towards; exaggerate; v.i. to be drawn out in length or breadth; be extended; free one's limbs from the stiffness of sleep; **to s. one's legs,** to go for a brisk walk. STRETCH (2), n. extension in length or breadth; reach; effort; strain; straining; utmost extent of meaning; utmost reach of power; extent of space, reach; distance travelled on one tack; course; direction; period of time; (slang) period of time in prison. STRETCHY, adj. liable to s. [OE.].

STRETCHER [stre'cher], n. person who or thing which stretches; brick or stone laid lengthwise in the surface of a wall; piece of timber in building; narrow piece of plank placed across a boat for the rower to set his feet against; frame or litter for carrying sick or wounded; an expanding device.

STREW (pret. **strewed,** p.pt. **strewed, strewn**) [strōō], v.t. to scatter; spread here and there; sprinkle loosely; cover by being scattered.

STRIAE [strī'ē], n.(pl.) small channels, grooves or threadlike lines; (arch.) fillets between the flutes of columns. STRIATE(D), adj. marked with narrow lines or grooves; channelled; streaked. [L.].

STRICKEN [stri'ken], adj. struck down; afflicted. [Old p.pt. of STRIKE (1)].

STRICKLE [stri'kl], n. rod used to strike grain to a level with the measure; hone for whetting scythes. [OE.].

STRICT [strikt], adj. precise, exact, accurate, definite, restricted, severe. [L.].

STRICTURE [strik'tyŏor], n. severe criticism;

censure; (*path.*) a morbid contraction of any passage of the body. [L.].

STRIDE (1) (*pret.* **strode**, *p.pt.* (*rare*) **stridden**) [strid], *v.t.* to cross over with one long step; bestride; *v.i.* to walk with long steps; straddle. STRIDE (2), *n.* a long step; wide stretch of the legs; **to take in one's s.**, to accomplish without extra effort in the ordinary pursuit of one's affairs. [OE.].

STRIDENCY [strī'den-si], *n.* fact or quality of being strident.

STRIDENT [strī'dent], *adj.* harsh; loud and raucous.

STRIDULATE [stri'dyōō-lāt], *v.i.* to make a harsh grating noise like a cricket.

STRIDULOUS [stri'dyōō-lŏŏs], *adj.* making a harsh creaking sound.

STRIFE [strīf], *n.* contention for superiority; competition; struggle for victory; dissension, discord. [OFr.].

STRIKE (1) (*pret. and p.pt.* **struck**) [strīk], *v.t.* to hit, deal a blow to; dash against; stab with a blow; reach, arrive at; come upon; sound by percussion; make by stamping; cause to light; take down (one's flag); dismantle (a camp); fill (with an emotion); take up (an attitude); impinge on (the mind); occur to (the mind); *v.i.* to deliver blows; collide; direct one's course; take part in a s.; **to s. at**, to aim a blow at; **to s. in**, to break in; **to s. off**, to cancel; cut off, remove from (a register etc.); **to s. out**, to hit out; make a bold stroke in swimming or in an enterprise; cancel; **to s. up**, to begin; **to s. work**, to cease work and enter upon a s.; **to s. oil**, to discover a deposit of mineral oil; (*fig.*) encounter good fortune. STRIKE (2), *n.* act of workmen combining in a refusal to work; attack by aircraft launched from a carrier; (*geol.*) direction of the outcrop of a stratum; **lucky s.**, a lucky find. [OE.].

STRIKER [strī'ker], *n.* person who or thing which strikes. STRIKER-OUT, (*tennis*) player who receives the ball when served.

STRIKING [strī'king], *adj.* affecting with strong emotions; surprising; forcible; impressive; effective, smart; that strikes the hours etc.

STRING (1) [string], *n.* small rope, line or cord used for fastening or tying anything; a ribbon; a line of things; gut or wire cord of a musical instrument; any wire; a fibre; nerve or tendon; line or cord of a bow; a series of things; (*pl.*) instruments of the violin class, in an orchestra or band; **first, second s.,** (*athletics*) first and second men chosen for a representative team; **to have on a s.,** to have at one's mercy, deceive. STRING-BAND, band made up of players of stringed instruments. STRING-BEANS, French beans. STRING-MAN, (*coll.*) assistant, *esp.* one who collects information for a newspaper correspondent. STRING (2), *v.t.* to furnish with a s. or strings; thread on a s.; render taut; **to s. out**, *v.t.* to prolong; *v.i.* to extend singly over some distance. STRINGED, *adj.* (of instruments) having strings as the source of sound. STRINGER, *n.* maker of strings; horizontal timber or bar serving as a support. [OE.].

STRINGENCY [strin'jen-si], *n.* condition of being stringent; strictness.

STRINGENT [strin'jent], *adj.* strictly enforceable; strict; severe; rigid. [L.].

STRINGY [string'i], *adj.* consisting of strings or small threads; ropy, viscid; fibrous.

STRIP (1) (*pres.pt.* **stripping**, *pret. and p.pt.* **stripped**) [strip], *v.t. and i.* to pull or tear off; take away the covering of; skin, deprive; divest; pillage; remove the long loose hair of (a dog); take off all one's clothes. STRIP-POKER, *n.* form of poker in which the loser of each hand must remove a garment. STRIP-TEASE, *n.* form of music-hall entertainment in which the performer removes her garments one at a time. STRIP (2), *n.* long narrow piece or band; edge or border; shred. [OE.].

STRIPE (1) [strip], *n.* a line or strip of material of a different colour or texture from the ground; chevron marking rank; strip attached to something of a different colour; (*archaic*) stroke made with a lash or stick. STRIPE (2), *v.t.* to make stripes on; mark with a s. or stripes. STRIPED, *adj.* having stripes of different colours. [MDu.].

STRIPLING [strip'ling], *n.* youth just passing from boyhood to manhood; growing lad. [~STRIP (2)].

STRIVE (*pret.* **strove**, *p.pt.* **striven**) [strīv], *v.i.* to make efforts; endeavour with earnestness; labour hard; struggle; fight, contend. [OFr.].

STRODE [strōd], *pret. of* STRIDE.

STROKE (1) [strōk], *n.* a blow; the striking of one body against another; hostile blow or attack; sudden attack of disease or affliction; seizure of apoplexy or paralysis; a calamity; the sound of a clock; touch of a pencil; touch; masterly effort; effort suddenly or unexpectedly produced; a series of operations; a dash in writing or printing; a line; working length of a rod; complete movement either way of a piston etc.; travel or throw of a valve; oarsman nearest the stern of the boat and the one who sets the rowing pace; sweep of an oar; a movement of the limbs in swimming, any of several methods of combining these movements into a regular pattern. STROKE-OAR, oar nearest the stern. STROKE (2), *v.t.* to rub gently with the hand; soothe; rub gently in one direction; make smooth; pull s.-oar and so set the rate of rowing. [OE.].

STROLL (1) [strōl], *v.i.* to ramble idly or leisurely; saunter. STROLL (2), *n.* a saunter; quiet, leisurely walk. STROLLER, *n.* one who strolls; itinerant actor. STROLLING, *adj.* moving leisurely from place to place; itinerant. [Unkn.].

STROMA [strō'mah], *n.* (*anat.*) groundwork of a tissue, organ or cell. [Gk.].

STRONG [strong], *adj.* well; having physical power; vigorous; firm; having ability to bear or endure; fortified; powerful; violent; forcible; sound; cogent; affecting a sense forcibly; bright; full of spirit; intoxicating; having great force of character or intellect; **s. waters**, alcoholic drink, spirits. STRONG-BOX, *n.* metal box, fitted with s. locks, used for storing valuables. STRONG-MINDED, *adj.* resolute, determined. STRONG-POINT, *n.* (*milit.*) strongly fortified place. STRONG-ROOM, *n.* s. fireproof room in which valuables are stored. [OE.].

STRONGHOLD [strong'hōld], *n.* strongly fortified place, fortress; place of security; (*fig.*) s. centre of some opinion or movement.

STROP (1) [strop], *n.* strip of leather used for sharpening a razor; (*naut.*) band of leather or rope used for suspending a block. STROP (2), *v.t.* to sharpen on a s.; (*naut.*) provide with a s. [OE.].

STROPHE [strō'fi], *n.* in classical Greek drama, the part sung by the chorus when moving to the left; in Greek poetry, the first member of a poem; stanza. [Gk.].

STROVE [strōv], *pret. of* STRIVE.

STRUCK [struk], *pret. and p.pt. of* STRIKE.

STRUCTURAL [struk'tyōō-ral], *adj.* of, or pertaining to, structure.

STRUCTURE [struk'tyōōr], *n.* manner of building; form; make; construction; a building of any kind, *esp.* one of considerable size; edifice; arrangement of the elements or parts of anything; texture; manner of organization. [L.].

STRUGGLE (1) [strug'l], *v.i.* to use great bodily or mental efforts to attain an end; strive; contend; fight. STRUGGLE (2), *n.* strenuous effort to obtain an object or to avoid an evil; contest; contention; contortions of extreme distress. [ME.].

STRUM [strum], *v.t. and i.* to play badly and noisily on a stringed instrument. [Phonic].

STRUMPET [strum'pit], *n.* prostitute. [Uncert.].

STRUNG [strung], *pret. and p.pt. of* STRING.

STRUT (1) [strut], *n.* piece of timber obliquely placed to support a rafter; a support. [~Dan.].

STRUT (2) (*pres.pt.* **strutting**, *pret. and p.pt.* **strutted**), *v.i.* to walk in a stiff, haughty, self-important manner; walk with affected dignity or pomposity. STRUT (3), *n.* lofty proud step or walk with the head erect; stiff and unnatural affectation of dignity in walking. [OE.].

STRUTH, STREWTH [strōōth], *int.* (*vulg.*) expressing amazement. [Abbrev. of *God's truth*].

STRYCHNINE [strik'nēn], *n.* a poisonous alkaloid, in minute quantities usually as a medicine, usually obtained from the seeds of *Strychnos Nux-vomica*. [~Gk.].

STUB (1) [stub], *n.* stump of a tree after the tree has been cut down; a nail broken off; short end of a pencil or cigarette when the main part has been used or consumed. STUB (2) (*pres.pt.* **STUBBING**, *pret. and p.pt.* **STUBBED**), *v.t.* to grub up by the roots; extirpate; rid of roots; strike (the toe) violently against an object; **to s. out**, to extinguish (a cigarette) by pressing the lighted end against a hard surface. [OE.].

STUBBLE [stu'bl], *n.* short hard stalks of the corn left standing in the ground when the crop has been cut; growth of beard resembling this. STUBBLY, *adj.* pertaining to, resembling, s.; hard, short and bristling. [OFr.].

STUBBORN [stu'bern], *adj.* obstinate; self-willed; difficult to move either mentally or physically; fixed in opinion; obstinately resisting force of any kind. [ME.].

STUBBY [stu'bi], *adj.* of the nature of a stub; short and stocky; short and thick.

STUCCO (1) [stu'kō], *n.* fine plaster used as a coating for walls or for interior decorations; work made of s. STUCCO (2), *v.t.* and *i.* to plaster; overlay (a surface) with s. [It.].

STUCK [stuk], *pret. and p.pt. of* STICK. STUCK-UP, conceited; affecting an air of consequence.

STUD (1) [stud], *n.* ornamental knob; double-headed shirt-button; small piece of timber or joist for supporting the main timbers; large flat-topped metal nail, one of several used to mark out lines in the streets. STUD (2) (*pres.pt.* STUDDING, *pret. and p.pt.* STUDDED), *v.t.* to adorn with studs; set with detached objects or ornaments; adorn, set thickly with small shining objects. [OE.].

STUD (3), *n.* a number of pedigree horses, cattle, dogs or other animals kept for breeding or any special purpose. STUD-BOOK, book in which the pedigree and history of thoroughbred animals are recorded. STUD-FARM, farm for breeding horses. STUD-GROOM, groom at a s.-farm, *esp.* a head groom. STUD-HORSE, horse kept for the purpose of breeding. [OE.].

STUDENT [styōō'dent], *n.* person engaged in study; pupil at a technical school or college; man devoted to books; one who studies or examines something in an intensive way; fellow of Christ Church, Oxford. STUDENTSHIP, *n.* state of being a s.; a scholarship; a fellowship at Christ Church. [L.].

STUDIED [stu'did], *adj.* carefully considered; deliberate; elaborate-mannered.

STUDIO [styōō'di-ō], *n.* room designed for an artist's workroom or for a photographer to take portraits in; room used for broadcasting or making films or gramophone records; (*pl.*) premises in which cinema films are made. [It. from L.].

STUDIOUS [styōō'di-ōōs], *adj.* devoted to the acquisition of knowledge from books; contemplative; diligent to find or effect something; attentive; zealous; favourable to study. [L.].

STUDY (1) [stu'di], *n.* application of mind to books or to any subject for the purpose of acquiring knowledge or skill; thoughtful attention; meditation; any branch of learning which is studied; a subject of attention; room devoted to study or literary employment; work undertaken for improvement in an art; artist's or musician's sketch for aid in the composition of a larger work, or as an exercise in technique. STUDY (2), *v.t.* to apply the mind to; consider attentively; *v.i.* to fix the mind intently upon a subject; apply the mind to books; learn systematically; endeavour diligently. [OFr. from L.].

STUFF (1) [stuf], *n.* a mass of matter or collection of substances; the matter of which anything is formed; that which fills anything; elemental part; textile material, *esp.* woollen; worthless matter; (*coll.*) **to do one's s.**, to perform one's part in an entertainment or demonstration; **s. and nonsense!** expression of contemptuous incredulity. STUFF (2), *v.t.* and *i.* to fill with stuffing; thrust vigorously (into a limited space); (*coll.*) eat to excess; **to s. up**, to choke with s.; (*coll.*) deceive. STUFFING, *n.* material used for filling something; filling of savoury herbs etc. used in cooking; taxidermy; (*slang*) spirit, courage. [OFr.].

STUFFY [stu'fi], *adj.* close, airless, badly ventilated; (*coll.*) fussy, narrow-minded.

STULTIFY [stul'ti-fī], *v.t.* to render worthless, make of no avail; cause to seem foolish or inconsistent. [LL.].

STUMBLE (1) [stum'bl], *v.i.* to trip up, take a false step in walking, fall over some obstruction; fall into crime or error; (*in speech*) hesitate, become confused; **to s. at**, to hesitate over, boggle at; **to s. (up)on**, to come across by chance. STUMBLE (2), *n.* action of stumbling; a slip, trip, partial fall, moral lapse. STUMBLING-BLOCK, *n.* a cause of stumbling; difficulty; obstacle. [ME.].

STUMER [styōō'mer], *n.* (*slang*) counterfeit coin or note; racehorse deliberately held back from winning; fraudulent race; something worthless. [Unkn.].

STUMP (1) [stump], *n.* part of a tree remaining in the earth after the trunk is cut down; part of a limb or other body remaining after the rest is amputated or destroyed; remnant; (*cricket*) one of the upright sticks of a wicket; **to draw stumps**, to end play for the day; (*slang*) leg. STUMP-ORATOR, one who harangues a mob from any tree s. or other out-of-door place of vantage; one who goes about appealing to the passions of the mob. STUMP (2), *v.t.* to lop; travel

round making speeches; (*cricket*) dismiss (a batsman) for being out of his ground, by dislodging a bail with the ball or the hand containing the ball; (*coll.*) puzzle, defeat; *v.i.* to walk heavily; **to s. up**, (*coll.*) to pay up, fork out. STUMPER, *n.* wicket-keeper in cricket. [OIcel.].

STUN (*pres.pt.* **stunning**, *pret. and p.pt.* **stunned**) [stun], *v.t.* to make senseless by a blow; blunt or stupefy the hearing of; make dizzy by loud and mingled sound; amaze; (*slang*) captivate. STUNNER, *n.* person who or thing which stuns; (*slang*) fine sight, handsome person or thing. STUNNING, *adj.* producing a stunned condition; (*slang*) splendid, delightful. [OE.].

STUNG [stung], *pret. and p.pt. of* STING.

STUNK [stungk], *pret.* (*now rare*) *and p.pt. of* STINK.

STUNSAIL [stun'sl], *n.* (*naut.*) a studding-sail. [~STUDDING-SAIL.]

STUNT (1) [stunt], *n.* feat of skill; performance; newspaper sensation or agitation; any trick or course of action for gaining notoriety. STUNT (2), *v.i.* to perform a s. or stunts. [U.S. slang from Germ.].

STUNT (3), *v.t.* to hinder the growth of; dwarf. STUNTED, *adj.* undersized; dwarfed; retarded in development of body or mind. [OE.].

STUPE [styōōp], *n.* flannel or other soft material dipped in hot water or medicaments and applied as a fomentation to a wound or sore.

STUPEFACTION [styōō-pi-fak'shn], *n.* action of rendering stupid; amazement; stupefied state; dullness.

STUPEFY [styōō'pi-fī], *v.t.* to make stupid; deprive of sensibility; amaze; deaden, render incapable of intelligent action. [L.].

STUPENDOUS [styōō-pen'dōōs], *adj.* amazing, wonderful, extraordinary. [L.].

STUPID (1) [styōō'pid], *adj.* having one's faculties dulled; dull-witted, unintelligent, foolish. STUPID (2), *n.* (*coll.*) a s. person.

STUPIDITY [styōō-pi'di-ti], *n.* condition or quality of being stupid; dullness of wit. [L.].

STUPOR [styōō'per], *n.* state of torpor or coma when the senses and faculties are numbed; slowness of wit caused by amazement. [L.].

STURDY [stur'di], *adj.* strong, hardy, robust and vigorous; unshakable; well-founded. [OFr.].

STURGEON [stur'jn], *n.* large fish found about the coasts and in the rivers of countries bordering on the North Atlantic and Mediterranean, valued as the source of caviare and isinglass. [OFr.].

STUTTER (1) [stu'ter], *v.t. and i.* to speak with involuntary hesitations, stammer; utter with involuntary hesitations. STUTTER (2), *n.* defective mode of speech of one who stutters; recurring reports of machine-gun fire. STUTTERING (1), *n.* involuntary hesitation in speaking. STUTTERING (2), *adj.* spoken with, characterized by, a s. [~ME.].

STY (1) (*pl.* **sties**) [stī], *n.* pen where pigs are kept. STY (2), *v.t.* to keep or put in a s. [OE.].

STY (3), *n.* small sore on the eyelid. [~OE.].

STYGIAN [sti'ji-an], *adj.* (*class. myth.*) pertaining to, or typical of, the infernal river, Styx. [L. from Gk.].

STYLE (1) [stīl], *n.* mode of expression in writing; characteristic features of syntax and diction in a piece of writing; characteristic manner of expression of a writer or group of writers or which was commonly used at one period; fine writing, characteristics of fine writing; general formal characteristics in any fine art; mode of conduct and behaviour, *esp.* polite behaviour practised by cultured persons; fashion, *esp.* in dress; deportment; distinction of conduct and bearing; mode of living or taste of a person; sort, kind; correct mode of address, full title; mode of reckoning, *esp.* of date; **in s.**, grandly, expensively; (*class. antiq.*) small instrument for writing on wax etc.; any similar modern device, as for writing on wax paper; gnomon of a sundial; (*bot.*) narrow extension of the ovary, occurring in some plants, which supports the stigma; (*zool., entom.*) small, pointed, bristle-like process. STYLE (2), *v.t.* to address with full titles, give a title to. STYLIZE, *v.t.* to bring into line with one s., conventionalize. [OFr. from L.].

STYLISH [stī'lish], *adj.* fashionable, smart, showy. [Prec.].

STYLIST [stī'list], *n.* writer who exercises great care in matters of style; writer noted for his style. STYLISTIC [stī-lis'tik], *adj.* of, or pertaining to, literary style.

STYLO [stī'lō], *n. short form of* STYLOGRAPH.

STYLOGRAPH [stī'lō-grahf], *n.* variety of fountain

pen with a pointed and undivided nib. STYLO-GRAPHIC [sti-lō-gra'fik], *adj.* like, or pertaining to, a s. [STYLE (1) and Gk.].

STYMIE (1) [sti'mi], *n.* (*golf*) situation in which the striker finds that his opponent's ball lies between his own and the hole. STYMIE (2), *v.t.* (*golf*) to embarrass (one's opponent) by leaving one's ball directly between his and the hole; (of the ball) lie between the hole and the striker's ball; also *fig.* [Unkn.].

STYPTIC (1), **STIPTIC** [stip'tik], *adj.* (*med.*) able to check bleeding. STYPTIC (2), STIPTIC, *n.* (*med.*) substance which checks bleeding. [Gk.].

STYX [stiks], *n.* (*class. myth.*) river of the underworld over which Charon ferried the souls of the dead; **to cross the S.**, to die. [Gk.].

SUASION [swā'zhn], *n.* persuasion. [L.].

SUASIVE [swā'siv], *adj.* having or exercising the power to persuade.

SUAVE [swäv], *adj.* bland, urbane, courteous, smooth-mannered; (of wine) smooth to the palate. [L.].

SUAVITY [swa'vi-ti], *n.* quality of being suave.

SUB (1) [sub], *n.* (*coll.*) subaltern; sub-editor; subscription.

SUB (2), *prep.* **s. judice,** still under consideration; **s. rosa,** in secret. [L.].

SUB- (3), *pref.* below, under; almost, towards, about. [L.].

SUBADAR [sōō'ba-dah(r)], *n.* formerly a native officer in command of a company in an Indian regiment. [Hind.].

SUBAGENCY [su-bā'jen-si], *n.* organization, office or function of a sub-agent.

SUB-AGENT [sub-ā'jent], *n.* agent employed by another.

SUBALPINE [su-bal'pīn], *adj.* (*bot., zool.*) of, pertaining to, inhabiting, regions immediately below the Alpine.

SUBALTERN [su'bal-tern], *n.* (*milit.*) any commissioned officer beneath the rank of captain. [Fr.].

SUBAQUEOUS [su-bā'kwi-ŏŏs], *adj.* being, formed, under water; intended for use under water.

SUBARCTIC [su-bahk'tik], *adj.* pertaining to the region next to the Arctic.

SUBCLASS [sub'klahs], *n.* subsection of a class.

SUBCOMMITTEE [sub'ko-mi-ti], *n.* section of a committee appointed by the main body to deal with some specified minor or subsidiary matter.

SUBCONSCIOUS (1) [sub-kon'shŏŏs], *adj.* being within the range of consciousness but outside the range of clear mental perception. SUBCONSCIOUS (2), *n.* the s. mind.

SUBCONTINENT [sub-kon'ti-nent], *n.* mass of land large enough to be reasonably thought of as a continent but not actually classed as one of the five great continents.

SUBCONTRACT (1) [sub-kon'trakt], *n.* contract which is subordinate or subsidiary to another or performed by one contractor for another. SUBCONTRACT (2) [sub-kon-trakt'], *v.i.* to enter or make a s.

SUBCOSTAL [sub-cos'tal], *adj.* (*anat.*) lying below or beneath the ribs.

SUBCUTANEOUS [sub-kyōō-tā'ni-ŏŏs], *adj.* situated beneath the skin.

SUBDIVIDE [sub-di-vid'], *v.t. and i.* to divide up parts; become part of a part.

SUBDIVISION [sub-di-vi'zhn], *n.* act of subdividing, condition of being subdivided; part or section produced by subdivision.

SUBDOMINANT [sub-do'mi-nant], *n.* (*mus.*) fourth note of the diatonic scale, note below the dominant, the tonic fa. [SUB and DOMINANT (1)].

SUBDUAL [sub-dyōō'al], *n.* act of subduing, condition of being subdued.

SUBDUE [sub-dyōō'], *v.t.* to overcome, conquer, *esp.* by force; lessen in force or intensity. SUBDUED, *adj.* overcome, repressed, diminished in force or intensity. [OFr. from L.].

SUB-EDIT [sub-e'dit], *v.t.* to act as an editorial assistant of. SUB-EDITOR, *n.* an editorial assistant.

SUBFUSC (1) [sub-fusk'], *adj.* of a dark or sober hue. SUBFUSC (2), *n. s.* colour; clothing of this colour. [L.].

SUBHEADING [sub-he'ding], *n.* heading or title of a subsection of an essay, article, treatise etc.

SUB-HUMAN [sub-hyōō'man], *adj.* not quite human.

SUBJACENT [sub-jā'sent], *adj.* lying beneath; lying directly underneath. [L.].

SUBJECT (1) [sub'jekt], *adj.* being under authority; **s. to,** dependent on; liable, tending to; under the authority of. SUBJECT (2), *adv.* **s. to,** provided, conditionally upon. SUBJECT (3), *n.* person under the authority of a king or ruler; person or thing undergoing a given process or action, one suffering from a stated malady, one who is the object of medical, pathological or psychological investigation; topic, theme or matter of a literary composition; object or material subjected to scientific, critical consideration; theme or matter of studious investigation or dissertation; (*mus.*) principal musical phrase upon which a composition or part of a composition is founded, theme; (*gram.*) nominative phrase or word of a sentence, that part of a sentence about which something is predicated; (*philos.*) the actuality of anything contrasted with whatever is attributive to it; the thinking mind or self; **s. matter,** theme, topic or substance of a literary product. SUBJECT (4) [sub-jekt'], *v.t.* to place under authority, subdue; **to s. to,** to cause to suffer, undergo; expose, lay open to (a process, experience, experiment). [L.].

SUBJECTION [sub-jek'shn], *n.* condition of being subject, act of subjecting. [L.].

SUBJECTIVE (1) [sub-jek'tiv], *adj.* (*gram.*) pertaining to the subject of a sentence; (*philos.*) arising from the mind without the aid or influence of anything external to the mind; personal. SUBJECTIVE (2), *n.* (*gram.*) the case of the subject, nominative case. [L.].

SUBJECTIVISM [sub-jek'ti-vizm], *n.* (*philos.*) doctrine that all knowledge arises from subjective experience only.

SUBJECTIVITY [sub-jek-ti'vi-ti], *n.* subjectiveness; doctrine that religious belief should be based upon subjective experience.

SUBJOIN [sub-join'], *v.t.* to make (an addition) to what has been already stated. [OFr. from L.].

SUBJUGATE [sub'jōō-gāt], *v.t.* to subdue, place under control or authority. [L.].

SUBJUNCTIVE (1) [sub-jungk'tiv], *adj.* (*gram.*) subjoined; **s. mood,** mood of the verb expressing a wish, command, condition, contingency, possibility. SUBJUNCTIVE (2), *n.* (*gram.*) the s. mood.

SUBLEASE (1) [sub'lēs], *n.* lease granted by one who is himself a tenant of the property leased. SUBLEASE (2) [sub-lēs'], *v.t.* to grant a s. of.

SUBLESSEE [sub-le-sē'], *n.* one holding a sublease.

SUBLESSOR [sub-le-saw(r)'], *n.* one who subleases.

SUBLET (*pres.pt.* subletting, *pret. and p.pt.* sublet) [sub-let'], *v.t.* to let that which one holds oneself as a tenant.

SUB-LIEUTENANT [sub-lef-te'nant], *n.* naval officer immediately lower in rank than a lieutenant.

SUBLIMATE (1) [sub'li-māt], *v.t.* (*chem.*) to purify by vaporizing and solidifying again; (*fig.*) refine; (*psych.*) transform, apply to other (usually more exalted) ends. SUBLIMATE (2), *n.* (*chem.*) substance which has been sublimated. SUBLIMATION [sub-li-mā'shn], *n.* act of sublimating, condition of being sublimated; that which is sublimated. [L.].

SUBLIME (1) [sub-lim'], *adj.* lofty, noble, grand, impressive; (*fig.*) haughty; (*coll.*) extreme. SUBLIME (2), *n.* quality of being s.; anything evincing the qualities of sublimity. SUBLIME (3), *v.t.* to sublimate, refine. [L.].

SUBLIMITY [sub-li'mi-ti], *n.* quality of being sublime.

SUBLIMINAL [sub-li'mi-nal], *adj.* (*psych.*) within the range of consciousness but beyond that of perception or attention. [SUB- and L.].

SUBLUNARY [sub-lōō'na-ri], *adj.* lying beneath the moon; earthly, terrestrial.

SUB-MACHINE-GUN [sub-ma-shēn'gun], *n.* type of light and simple machine-gun.

SUB-MAN [sub'man], *n.* man of poor physique or low intellect.

SUBMARINE (1) [sub-ma-rēn'], *adj.* living or capable of travelling beneath the surface of the sea. SUBMARINE (2) [sub'ma-rēn], *n.* vessel which can travel beneath the surface of the water.

SUBMERGE [sub-murj'], *v.t. and i.* to cause to go beneath the surface of water, cover with a liquid; go below the surface of the water. SUBMERGENCE, *n.* act of submerging; condition of being submerged.

SUBMERSE [sub-murs'], *v.t.* to make to sink under the water. SUBMERSED, *adj.* (*bot.*) growing under water. SUBMERSION, *n.* act of submersing; condition of being submersed. [L.].

SUBMISSION [sub-mi'shn], *n.* act of submitting; condition of being submitted; spirit of humble acquiescence, surrender; that which is submitted. [L.].

SUBMISSIVE [sub-mi'siv], *adj.* characterized by

submission, ready to submit, humble, resigned, acquiescing.

SUBMIT [pres.pt. **submitting**, pret. and p.pt. **submitted**) [sub-mit'], v.t. and i. to yield, surrender; proffer for consideration, urge or put forward; **to s. to**, to acknowledge as superior, yield to, admit the authority of. [L.].

SUBORDINACY [su-baw'di-na-si], n. condition of being subordinate.

SUBORDINATE (1) [su-baw'di-nat], adj. inferior in rank, importance etc.; dependent, subsidiary; **s. clause**, (gram.) clause which qualifies and modifies the principal clause in a sentence. SUBORDINATE (2), n. one who is s., an inferior. SUBORDINATE (3) [su-baw'di-nāt], v.t. to give an inferior position to; make dependent or s. [SUB- and L.].

SUBORDINATION [su-baw-di-nā'shn], n. condition of being subordinate; act of subordinating.

SUBORN [su-bawn'], v.t. to entice (a person) to commit a crime by bribery or other illegal means. [L.].

SUBORNATION [su-baw-nā'shn], n. act of suborning; condition of being suborned.

SUBPOENA (1) [sub-pē'nah], n. (leg.) writ by which a person is summoned to court under penalty for non-appearance. SUBPOENA (2) (pret. and p.pt. SUBPOENAED), v.t. to issue a s. to. [L.].

SUBPOLAR [sub-pō'lah(r)], adj. (astron.) beneath the celestial pole; verging on polar.

SUBSCRIBE [sub-skrīb'], v.t. and i. to sign one's name to; (fig.) give one's assent or approval; contribute, esp. at regular intervals; **to s. to**, to buy regularly (a service, newspaper etc.); agree with (opinions etc.). [L.].

SUBSCRIPTION [sub-skrip'shn], n. act of subscribing, condition of being subscribed; that which is subscribed. [L.].

SUBSECTION [sub'sek-shn], n. a section of something which is itself only a section.

SUBSEQUENCE [sub'si-kwens], n. condition of being subsequent.

SUBSEQUENT [sub'si-kwent], adj. occurring at a later point of time, following; consequent, resulting. SUBSEQUENTLY, adv. later.

SUBSERVE [sub-surv'], v.t. to aid, serve, fulfil. [L.].

SUBSERVIENT [sub-sur'vi-ent], adj. serving, promoting, esp. in a subordinate capacity; obsequious. [L.].

SUBSIDE [sub-sīd'], v.i. to collapse, (esp. of the ground) fall in, sink down; slacken, diminish, weaken. [L.].

SUBSIDENCE, SUBSIDENCY [sub'si-dens(-), sub-sī'dens(-i)], n. fact or process of subsiding.

SUBSIDIARY (1) [sub-si'di-a-ri], adj. aiding or promoting in a secondary capacity, auxiliary; having the nature of, or pertaining to, a subsidy; **s. company**, company of which most of the shares are held by a larger firm. SUBSIDIARY (2), n. person or thing acting in an ancillary capacity. [L.].

SUBSIDIZE [sub'si-dīz], v.t. to pay a subsidy to.

SUBSIDY [sub'si-di], n. grant made from public funds in support of a commercial or similar undertaking; (hist.) grant made by Parliament to the Sovereign. [L.].

SUBSIST [sub-sist'], v.t. and i. to exist in reality; continue in existence.

SUBSISTENCE [sub-sis'tens], n. act of subsisting; things necessary to maintain life, that on which one subsists, livelihood; **s. money**, an allowance for maintenance. [LL.].

SUBSOIL [sub'soil], n. the layer of soil which lies immediately beneath the top layer.

SUB-SPECIES [sub'spē-shēz], n. an intermediate between a species and a variety.

SUBSTANCE [sub'stans], n. the essence of a thing, the essential nature, quality or reality of a thing; that of which something is composed or consists; matter; solid matter, body; the meaning or purport of a book, essay, speech, argument etc.; the essential part or character of a thing; wealth, possessions, resources. [L.].

SUBSTANTIAL [sub-stan'shal], adj. pertaining to substance; having the character of substance, solid, real, firm; (of a meal etc.) satisfying; concerning substance or purport; important, remarkable, considerable; wealthy. [L.].

SUBSTANTIALITY [sub-stan-shi-a'li-ti], n. condition of being substantial.

SUBSTANTIATE [sub-stan'shi-āt], v.t. to make real, give substance to; prove to be true, establish. [L.].

SUBSTANTIATION [sub-stan-shi-ā'shn], n. act of substantiating; condition of being substantiated.

SUBSTANTIVAL [sub-stan-tī'val], adj. pertaining to, or serving as, a substantive.

SUBSTANTIVE (1) [sub'stan-tiv], adj. having a distinct and real being; (gram.) expressing existence; **noun s.**, (gram.) word denoting a specific thing, idea etc.; **s. rank**, (milit.) one's actual paid rank. SUBSTANTIVE (2), n. a noun s. [L.].

SUBSTITUTE (1) [sub'sti-tyōōt], n. person or thing employed in place of, or acting instead of, another. SUBSTITUTE (2), v.t. and i. to put or employ instead of another; act as a substitute. [L.].

SUBSTITUTION [sub-sti-tyōō'shn], n. act of substituting; condition of being substituted.

SUBSTRATUM (pl. **substrata**) [sub-strā'tum], n. an underlying stratum.

SUBTENANT [sub'te-nant], n. tenant holding property from one who himself holds it only as a tenant.

SUBTEND [sub-tend'], v.t. (geom.) to extend under, be opposite to. [L.].

SUBTER-, pref. beneath; somewhat. [L.].

SUBTERFUGE [sub'ter-fyōoj], adj. an artifice, subtle concealment of real conduct or motive, means of evading discovery. [L.].

SUBTERRANEAN [sub-te-rā'ni-an], adj. underground.

SUBTILIZATION [su-ti-li-zā'shn], n. act of subtilizing; state of being subtilized.

SUBTILIZE [su'ti-līz], v.t. and i. to refine, make subtle; make subtle distinctions, argue subtly.

SUB-TITLE (1) [sub'tī-tl], n. secondary, explanatory title of a book; caption in a film. SUB-TITLE (2), v.t. to provide with a s. or sub-titles.

SUBTLE [su'tl], adj. intellectually penetrating, with a delicate and accomplished critical sense; able to devise complex schemes and perceive delicate distinctions; almost indefinable, highly refined, delicate.

SUBTLETY [su'tl-ti], n. quality of being subtle; that which is subtle, subtle device or argument. [L.].

SUBTONIC [sub-to'nik], n. (mus.) seventh note of the diatonic scale, the tonic te.

SUBTRACT [sub-trakt'], v.t. to take away (a part) from a quantity; (math.) find the difference between two numbers. [L.].

SUBTROPIC(AL) [sub-tro'pik(-al)], adj. slightly less than tropical.

SUBURB [su'berb], n. part of a town lying beyond its walls; residential area lying on the outskirts of a city. SUBURBIA, n. areas occupied by the suburbs of a large city; body of opinion and prejudices typical of the inhabitants of these areas. [L.].

SUBURBAN [su-bur'ban], adj. relating to, dwelling in, a suburb; (fig.) pettily conventional, narrow-minded. SUBURBANIZE, v.t. to turn into, make like, a suburb.

SUBVENTION [sub-ven'shn], n. act of supporting; subsidy. [L.].

SUBVERSION [sub-vur'shn], n. act of subverting; state of being subverted. [L.].

SUBVERT [sub-vurt'], v.t. to overthrow, esp. by means of subtle propaganda; undermine the loyalty of, esp. of the armed forces of a government. [L.].

SUBWAY [sub'wā], n. underground pathway, esp. a passage beneath busy crossings or railway lines; (U.S.) tube railway.

SUCCEED [suk-sēd'], v.t. to follow in order immediately after; replace, come immediately after; v.i. to follow immediately after, fill an office in place of a deceased person; achieve an object; bring to a satisfactory end what is attempted; be prosperous. [Fr.].

SUCCENTOR [suk-sen'ter], n. a precentor's deputy; leading bass voice in a choir. [LL.].

SUCCESS [suk-ses'], n. achievement of a desired aim, prosperous conclusion of what is attempted. [L.].

SUCCESSFUL [suk-ses'fool], adj. characterized by success, prosperous, brought to a satisfactory conclusion.

SUCCESSION [suk-se'shn], n. that which succeeds; series of things or events following upon one another in time or place; act of succeeding; lineage; (mus.) successive notes in a melody; **Apostolic S.**, the spiritual power transmitted from St. Peter and the Apostles through successive generations of bishops; **s. state**, state newly formed from part of the territory and population of an earlier and larger one. SUCCESSIONAL, adj. following in a regular order. [L.].

SUCCESSIVE [suk-se'siv], adj. following or coming

by succession or in order, consecutive. **SUCCES-SIVELY**, *adv.* in s. manner or order.
SUCCESSOR [suk-se'ser], *n.* one who succeeds; one who takes over the office or rank previously held by another. [L.].
SUCCINCT [suk-singkt'], *adj.* compressed into small space; concise, short. [L.].
SUCCORY [su'ke-ri], *n.* chicory. [~CHICORY].
SUCCOTASH [su'kŏ-tash], *n.* green maize and beans boiled together. [AmerInd.].
SUCCOUR (1) [su'ker], *v.t. and i.* to give or bring succour to; relieve distress and want. **SUCCOUR** (2), *n.* help, relief from trouble or distress; one who, or that which, brings such help. [OFr. from L.].
SUCCULENCE [su'kyŏŏ-lens], *n.* juiciness.
SUCCULENT [su'kyŏŏ-lent], *adj.* juicy (*esp.* of food). [L.].
SUCCUMB [su-kum'], *v.i.* to submit, fall, yield; die. [L.].
SUCH (1) [such], *adj.* of that kind, similar, same, like. **SUCH** (2), *pron.* s. a person or thing; the same; it, them; **s. and s.**, certain, particular but unspecified. [OE.].
SUCK (1) [suk], *v.t. and i.* to draw in by means of a suck or series of sucks; take milk from the breast; imbibe, draw into the mouth; absorb; draw or hold to by exhausting the air; **to s. in**, (*coll.*) to cheat or deceive. **SUCK** (2), *n.* act of drawing in through the mouth by the muscular action of the lips and the inspiration of the lungs; what is drawn in in this manner; milk drawn from the breast, pap. **SUCKING**, *adj.* at the breast, fed by the mother's milk; (*fig.*) very young. [OE.].
SUCKER [su'ker], *n.* one who, or that which, sucks or draws or holds by a suck; piston or plunger of a pump; (*bot.*) a shoot from the roots or lower part of the stem of a plant; (*U.S.*) gullible person.
SUCKLE [su'kl], *v.t.* to feed at the breast. **SUCKLER, SUCKLING**, *n.* child or animal being still fed at the breast.
SUCTION [suk'shn], *n.* action of sucking; process of drawing a liquid or gas into a vessel in which a partial vacuum is created by withdrawing the air; similar process by which one thing is made to adhere to another by withdrawing the air between them. **SUCTION-PIPE**, inlet pipe at the lower end of a pump. **SUCTION-PUMP**, pump for lifting water and other liquids to a higher level by raising a piston in a cylinder in order to create a vacuum into which the liquid is forced by atmospheric pressure. [~L.].
SUCTORIAL [suk-taw'ri-al], *adj.* having the power to suck or adhere by suction.
SUDDEN (1) [su'den], *adj.* occurring without warning or notice; happening unexpectedly; unexpected. **SUDDEN** (2), *n.* **of a s., on a s.,** unexpectedly. [OFr.].
SUDORIFIC (1) [syŏŏ-de-ri'fik], *adj.* producing sweating. **SUDORIFIC** (2), *n.* medicine to induce sweating. [L.].
SUDS [sudz], *n.*(*pl.*) frothy, bubbly formation on the surface of water in which soap has been dissolved and agitated. [OE.].
SUE (*pres.pt.* **suing**, *pret. and p.pt.* **sued**) [syŏŏ], *v.t. and i.* (*leg.*) to take proceedings in a court of law to obtain justice; prosecute; beg, petition.
SUEDE, suède [swād], *n.* soft, pliable, unglazed leather. [Fr.].
SUET [sŏŏ'it], *n.* hard animal fat taken from the loins etc.; **s. pudding**, (boiled) pudding in which one of the chief ingredients is s. [OFr.].
SUFFER [su'fer], *v.t. and i.* to feel and endure physical or mental anguish and distress; endure, undergo; allow (often unwillingly). **SUFFERING** (1), *n.* the bearing of pain and distress; pain and anguish. **SUFFERING** (2), *adj.* bearing pain and distress. [L.].
SUFFERANCE [su'fe-rans], *n.* the bearing of pain or distress; consent implied by the absence of directions to the contrary; **on s.,** tolerated but unwelcome. [L.].
SUFFICE [su-fis'], *v.t. and i.* to be enough; be satisfied; satisfy. [OFr.].
SUFFICIENCY [su-fi'shen-si], *n.* state of being sufficient or adequate; competence, self-confidence; adequate resources.
SUFFICIENT [su-fi'shent], *adj.* enough, adequate, satisfying the needs adequately. [L.].
SUFFIX (1) [su'fiks], *n.* particle or element added to the end of a word, *esp.* to form a new grammatical or sense development of the original word. **SUFFIX** (2), *v.t.* to form or add as a s. [L.].
SUFFOCATE [su'fŏ-kāt], *v.t. and i.* to take away or lose life by stopping respiration. [~L.].

SUFFOCATION [su-fŏ-kā'shn], *n.* act of suffocating; state of being suffocated; **to s.,** so as to s.
SUFFRAGAN [su'fra-gan], *n.* (*eccles.*) assistant to a diocesan bishop or to an archbishop. [MedL.].
SUFFRAGE [su'frij], *n.* a vote; the right to vote. **SUFFRAGIST**, *n.* one who supports s. for women. [L.].
SUFFRAGETTE [su-fra-jet'], *n.* woman who agitated for female suffrage.
SUFFUSE [su-fyŏŏz'], *v.t.* to flood over, cover. [~L.].
SUFFUSION [su-fyŏŏ'zhn], *n.* that which suffuses; state of being suffused. [L.].
SUGAR (1) [shŏŏ'ger], *n.* a sweet crystalline substance extracted from various plants and used extensively in cooking; (*fig.*) gross flattery; (*coll.*) attractive young female; **s. candy**, sweetmeat of clear crystallized s.; **s. cane**, a grass from whose stem s. is extracted. **SUGAR-BASIN**, bowl for holding s. at table. **SUGAR-BEET**, a plant from whose root s. is extracted. **SUGAR-DADDY**, (*slang*) old man who provides meals and entertainments for young women. **SUGAR-LOAF**, cone-shaped mass of refined s. **SUGAR-PLUM**, sweetmeat made of s. **SUGAR** (2), *v.t.* to sweeten with s.; (*fig.*) make agreeable. **SUGARY**, *adj.* sweet; sickly sweet. [OFr. from Arab.].
SUGGEST [su-jest'], *v.t.* to call up (an idea), *esp.* by association; propose (a plan), propound (a theory); imply. **SUGGESTER**, *n.* one who suggests. [L.].
SUGGESTIBLE [su-jes'ti-bl], *adj.* capable of being influenced by suggestion. **SUGGESTIBILITY** [su-jes-ti-bi'li-ti], *n.* capacity for receiving suggestions.
SUGGESTION [su-jes'chn], *n.* that which is suggested; act of suggesting; an implication; indecent proposal.
SUGGESTIVE [su-jes'tiv], *adj.* tending to suggest; having an indecent implication.
SUICIDAL [syŏŏ-i-si'dal], *adj.* tending to, relating to, suicide.
SUICIDE [syŏŏ'i-sīd], *n.* act of self-destruction, physical or metaphorical; one who destroys himself. [~L.].
SUIT (1) [syŏŏt], *n.* act of suing, judicial action, request; act of seeking a woman's hand in marriage; set of clothes made of the same stuff; one of the four sets of playing cards. **SUIT** (2), *v.t. and i.* to be satisfactory to, harmonious with, appropriate for; agree with; match; be agreeable. **SUITING**, *n.* s. of clothes; material for making clothes. [OFr.].
SUITABLE [syŏŏ'ta-bl], *adj.* tending to suit, appropriate, proper, fitting.
SUITE [swēt], *n.* retinue; set of apartments; matching furniture for one room; (*mus.*) series of dances or loosely related pieces; attendants, followers etc. of a person of importance. [OFr.].
SUITOR [syŏŏ'ter], *n.* one who makes a suit, *esp.* for a woman's hand in marriage.
SULK (1) [sulk], *v.i.* to be silently sullen. **SULK** (2), *n.* a sulky mood (often in *pl.*). [Uncert.].
SULKY (1) [sul'ki], *adj.* showing silent ill temper, sullen, obstinately morose. **SULKY** (2), *n.* light carriage holding one person only. [~OE.].
SULLAGE [su'lij], *n.* scum on molten metal. [~SULLY].
SULLEN [su'len], *adj.* sombrely sulky, obstinately silent and ill-tempered, lowering. [OFr.].
SULLY [su'li], *v.t.* to stain, soil, tarnish. [OE.].
SULPH(O)-, *pref.* relating to, containing, sulphur. [~L.].
SULPHANILAMIDE [sul-fa-ni'la-mīd], *n.* (*chem.*) one of the group of sulphonamides employed to combat certain diseases caused by *coccos* bacteria. [SULPH(UR), ANIL(INE) and AMIDE].
SULPHATE [sul'fāt], *n.* a salt of sulphuric acid, containing four atoms of oxygen.
SULPHIDE [sul'fīd], *n.* a compound of sulphur with some other element.
SULPHITE [sul'fīt], *n.* a salt of sulphurous acid, containing three atoms of oxygen.
SULPHONAMIDE [sul-fo'na-mīd], *n.* (*chem.*) the amide of a sulphonic acid; any of a group of drugs of this composition used against bacteria.
SULPHONIC [sul-fo'nik, sul-fŏ'nik], *adj.* (*chem.*) containing the group SO_2OH.
SULPHUR [sul'fer], *n.* chemical element denoted by s, light yellow in colour, inflammable, brittle, insoluble in water. **SULPHURETTED**, *adj.* in combination with s. **SULPHURIZE**, *v.t.* to cause to combine with s. [~L.].
SULPHUREOUS [sul-fyŏŏ'ri-ŏŏs], *adj.* like, relating to, sulphur. [L.].
SULPHURIC [sul-fyŏŏ'rik], *adj.* relating to, derived

from, containing, sulphur; **s. acid,** oil of vitriol, the corrosive acid H_2SO_4.

SULPHUROUS [sul-fy$\overline{oo}$'r$\overline{oo}$s], (*chem.*) *adj.* containing, resembling, sulphur, *esp.* in its lower valency; (*fig.*) [sul'fy$\overline{oo}$-r$\overline{oo}$s, sul'fe-r$\overline{oo}$s], devilish, connected with hell, dangerously passionate.

SULTAN [sul'tan], *n.* former emperor of the Ottomans, a Moslem ruling prince; (*bot.*) plant of the genus *Centaurea*. [Arab.].

SULTANA [sul-tah'nah], *n.* chief consort of a sultan; variety of seedless raisin. [It.].

SULTRY [sul'tri], *adj.* oppressively warm and damp, thundery; (*fig.*) angry, lurid, threatening. [~SWELTER].

SUM (1) [sum], *n.* the total quantity of a thing, the product of numerical addition, the totality of related things or ideas; a quantity of money; mathematical problem dealing with addition, subtraction, multiplication or division. SUM (2) (*pres. pt.* SUMMING, *pret. and p.pt.* SUMMED) (*usually* **s. up**), *v.t.* to add up, total; review arguments on either side in order to facilitate judgment. [L.].

SUMACH [s$\overline{oo}$'mak, sh$\overline{oo}$'mak], *n.* a shrub, the leaves of which are used medicinally and in dyeing. [Arab.].

SUMMARIZE [su'ma-r$\overline{i}$z], *v.t.* to make a summary of, abstract and state concisely the principal features of.

SUMMARY (1) [su'ma-ri], *adj.* concise, brief and to the point, with the minimum of formality. SUMMARY (2), *n.* epitome, brief, concise abstract of a statement etc., giving the principal points or heads of argument, précis. [L.].

SUMMATION [su-m$\overline{a}$'shn], *n.* act of summing up, or forming a grand total. [Fr.].

SUMMER (1) [su'mer], *n.* annual season of the greatest heat, months between spring and autumn; (*fig.*) flourishing period, a year of age. SUMMER-HOUSE, ornamental, open-sided garden shelter for sitting in. SUMMER-TIME, the s.; system by which clocks are put on one hour in the s. months. SUMMER (2), *adj.* of, in, relating to, the s. months. SUMMER (3), *v.i.* to spend the s. [OE.].

SUMMER (4), *n.* (*arch.*) stone supporting an arch, a cross-piece, supported on two uprights, and upholding a structure above it. SUMMERING, *n.* stone bedding of a vault. [Fr.].

SUMMING-UP [su-ming-up'], *n.* (*leg.*) the judge's summary and criticism of the evidence leading to his direction to the jury.

SUMMIT [su'mit], *n.* topmost point of a thing, *esp.* of a hill or material height. SUMMIT-LEVEL, highest level reached by a railway or road. [Fr.].

SUMMON [su'mon], *v.t.* to command to be present, imperatively call to a place or to perform a duty; (*leg.*) serve with a court summons. [OFr. from L.].

SUMMONS (1) (*pl.* **summonses**) [su'monz], *n.* a command to attend, *esp.* a legal notice to appear in court. SUMMONS (2), *v.t.* (*leg.*) to call to a court of law as witness or defendant. [OFr.].

SUMP [sump], *n.* pool of water at the bottom of an excavation; pit for receiving freshly fused metal; oil-container of a motor. [~SWAMP].

SUMPTER [sump'ter], *n.* (*archaic*) packhorse. [OFr.].

SUMPTUARY [sump'ty$\overline{oo}$-a-ri], *adj.* relating to expenditure.

SUMPTUOSITY [sump-ty$\overline{oo}$-o'si-ti], *n.* extravagance. [L.].

SUMPTUOUS [sump'ty$\overline{oo}$-$\overline{oo}$s], *adj.* lavish, costly, luxurious, expensively magnificent. [L.].

SUN (1) [sun], *n.* the heavenly body around which the planetary system revolves, rays of this heavenly body; any similar star having revolving planets; (*fig.*) centre of attraction, magnificent patron; **s. treatment,** exposure to artificial ultra-violet rays. SUN-BATH, exposure of the body to the s. SUN-BATHE, *v.i.* to take a s.-bath. SUN-BLIND, blind suitable for keeping out the s. SUN-BONNET, bonnet protecting the face from the s. SUN-GLASSES, glasses worn to protect the eyes from the glare of the s. SUN-GOD, the s. regarded as a deity. SUN-HAT, hat to protect the head from the s. SUN-HELMET, broad-brimmed helmet worn as a protection from the tropical sun, topee. SUN-LOUNGE, -PARLOUR, lounge designed to admit the maximum of sunshine. SUN-PROOF, *adj.* impervious or resistant to sunshine. SUN-RAY, a ray of the s. SUN-SPOT, dark, fluctuating spot on the s. SUN-TRAP, locality or site which appears to attract the s.'s rays. SUN (*U.S.*) sunrise. SUN-WORSHIP, worship of the s. as a deity. SUN (2) (*pres.pt* SUNNING, *pret. and p.pt.* SUNNED), *v.t.* to expose to the s.'s rays; (*reflex.*) bask in the s. [OE.].

SUNBEAM [sun'b$\overline{e}$m], *n.* a ray of the sun.

SUNBIRD [sun'berd], *n.* tropical, long-beaked bird, of the *Nectariniidae.*

SUNBURN (1) (*pret. and p.pt.* **sunburnt, sunburned**) [sun'bern], *v.t.* to burn, tan, by exposure to the sun; *v.i.* to become burnt or tanned by the sun. SUNBURN (2), *n.* darkening or peeling of the skin from exposure to the sun.

SUNBURST [sun'berst], *n.* a burst of sunshine; gem arranged in the form of the sun with its rays.

SUNCLAD [sun'klad], *adj.* shining in the sun's rays.

SUNDAE [sun'd$\overline{a}$], *n.* ice-cream served with fruits in syrup. [SUNDAY].

SUNDAY [sun'd$\overline{a}$], *n.* first day of the week. SUNDAY-SCHOOL, school for religious instruction held on S. [OE.].

SUNDER [sun'der], *v.t. and i.* to sever; come apart. [OE.].

SUNDEW [sun'dy$\overline{oo}$], *n.* plant of the genus *Drosera.*

SUNDIAL [sun'd$\overline{i}$-al], *n.* device for indicating the hour of the day by means of a shadow thrown by the sun upon a marked plane.

SUNDOWN [sun'down], *n.* sunset. SUNDOWNER, *n.* (*Australian*) a tramp, *esp.* one who arrives at s. to obtain shelter for the night; (*coll.*) alcoholic drink taken in the evening.

SUNDRIES [sun'driz], *n.(pl.)* miscellaneous articles or items not listed separately; (*cricket*) (*Australian*) extras.

SUNDRY [sun'dri], *adj.* various, unspecified. [OE.].

SUNFISH [sun'fish], *n.* a species of the genus *Orthagoriscus;* the opah, *Lampris luna;* the basking shark, *Selache maxima.*

SUNFLOWER [sun'flow-er], *n.* a tall yellow-flowered plant.

SUNK [sungk], *pret. and p.pt. of* SINK. [OE.].

SUNKEN [sung'ken], *adj.* having been sunk, lying at the bottom of water; fallen in, hollow, cavernous. [Old *p.pt. of* SINK.].

SUNLIGHT [sun'lit], *n.* light of the sun; **s. lamp,** ultra-violet lamp providing a substitute for s.

SUNNY [su'ni], *adj.* exposed to, warmed by, the sun; shining, unclouded; (*fig.*) cheerful, bright.

SUNRISE [sun'r$\overline{i}$z], *n.* dawn, the time when the sun rises above the horizon; phenomenon of the first appearance of the sun above the horizon daily.

SUNSET [sun'set], *n.* the time, process, spectacle, of the sun's descent below the horizon.

SUNSHADE [sun'sh$\overline{a}$d], *n.* light umbrella for protection against the sun, parasol; shield for the eyes against sunlight.

SUNSHINE [sun'sh$\overline{i}$n], *n.* the direct light of the sun, as warming and brightening the earth; (*fig.*) radiant happiness; **s. roof,** car roof which can be slid open.

SUNSTROKE [sun'str$\overline{o}$k], *n.* feverish collapse caused by exposure to intense, burning sunlight.

SUNWISE [sun'w$\overline{i}$z], *adj. and adv.* in the direction of the sun's motion.

SUP (1) (*pres.pt.* **supping,** *pret. and p.pt.* **supped**) [sup], *v.t. and i.* to eat supper; sip; take liquid in small mouthfuls. SUP (2), *n.* small mouthful of liquid. [OE.].

SUPER (1) [s$\overline{oo}$'per], *n.* (*coll.*) a supernumerary; a film extra.

SUPER (2), *adj.* (*coll.*) requiring superlatives to describe; (when referring to square measure) superficial.

SUPER- (3), *pref.* above in position, superior to, exceeding the normal. [L.].

SUPERABLE [s$\overline{oo}$'pe-ra-bl], *adj.* able to be surmounted.

SUPERABUNDANCE [s$\overline{oo}$-pe-ra-bun'dans], *n.* extraordinary abundance.

SUPERABUNDANT [s$\overline{oo}$-pe-ra-bun'dant], *adj.* excessively abounding.

SUPERADD [s$\overline{oo}$-pe-rad'], *v.t.* to add in addition.

SUPERANNUATE [s$\overline{oo}$-pe-ra'ny$\overline{oo}$-$\overline{a}$t], *v.t.* to retire on grounds of excessive age. SUPERANNUATED, *adj.* retired on grounds of age; worn out, antiquated, obsolete. [~L.].

SUPERANNUATION [s$\overline{oo}$-pe-ra-ny$\overline{oo}$-$\overline{a}$'shn], *n.* act of superannuating; state of being superannuated; pension or payment enjoyed as of right on being superannuated.

SUPERB [sy$\overline{oo}$-purb'], *adj.* supremely excellent, splendid, magnificent. [L.].

SUPERCARGO [s$\overline{oo}$'per-kah-g$\overline{o}$], *n.* person travelling in a ship to take charge of the cargo.

SUPERCHARGE [s$\overline{oo}$-per-chahj'], *v.t.* to surcharge; (*her.*) place one bearing over another; provide with a

---

$\overline{oo}$ is pronounced as in *food*; $\overline{oo}$ as in *hood*; th as in *think*; TH as in *that*; zh as in *azure*. ~ = related to.

supercharger. SUPERCHARGER, *n. (eng.)* mechanically driven fan used to increase the pressure of the petrol mixture in an induction system.

SUPERCILIARY [sŏŏ-per-sĭ'li-a-ri], *adj.* situated or being above the eyebrow. [L.].

SUPERCILIOUS [sŏŏ-per-sĭ'li-ŏŏs], *adj.* disdainful, contemptuous, nonchalantly haughty. [L.].

SUPERCONSCIOUS [sŏŏ-per-kon'shŏŏs], *adj. (psych.)* transcending the human consciousness.

SUPERCOOL [sŏŏ-per-kŏŏl'], *v.t.* to cool below freezing-point without solidifying.

SUPERCRESCENCE [sŏŏ-per-kre'sens], *n.* a growth upon something which is already growing. [SUPER- and L.].

SUPEREMINENT [sŏŏ-pe-re'mi-nent], *adj.* surpassingly eminent.

SUPEREROGATION [sŏŏ-pe-re-ro-gā'shn], *n.* performance of more than duty requires; **works of s.,** *(R.C.)* those good deeds supposed to have been performed by saints, over and above what is required for their own salvation, the merit of which is held to be transferable to others in need of indulgence. SUPEREROGATORY [sŏŏ-pe-re-ro'ga-te-ri], *adj.* done in s. [MedL.].

SUPER-FATTED [sŏŏ-per-fa'tid], *adj.* of soap, made with a larger proportion of fat than usual.

SUPERFICIAL [sŏŏ-per-fi'shal], *adj.* relating only to the surface of a thing; not profound.

SUPERFICIES [sŏŏ-per-fi'shi-ēz], *n.* the outer surface of a thing. [L.].

SUPERFINE [sŏŏ'per-fīn], *adj.* especially fine.

SUPERFLUITY [sŏŏ-per-flŏŏ'i-ti], *n.* a quantity which is superfluous; state of being superfluous.

SUPERFLUOUS [sŏŏ-pur'flŏŏ-ŏŏs], *adj.* having, or which is, more than is required; unwanted, useless.

SUPERHEAT [sŏŏ-per-hēt'], *v.t.* to heat (vapour) above the boiling-point of water. SUPERHEATER, *n.* apparatus for superheating steam.

SUPER-HETERODYNE [sŏŏ-per-he'te-rō-dīn], *n.* a supersonic heterodyne.

SUPERHUMAN [sŏŏ-per-hyŏŏ'man], *adj.* having more than human attributes.

SUPERIMPOSE [sŏŏ-pe-rim-pōz'], *v.t.* to place above something.

SUPERINCUMBENT [sŏŏ-pe-rin-kum'bent], *adj.* lying or resting on something else.

SUPERINDUCE [sŏŏ-pe-rin-dyŏŏs'], *v.t.* to bring about in addition.

SUPERINTEND [sŏŏ-pe-rin-tend'], *v.t.* to oversee, control and direct. SUPERINTENDENCE, SUPERINTENDENCY, *n.* act of superintending; supervision; management. [L.].

SUPERINTENDENT [sŏŏ-pe-rin-ten'dent], *n.* one who superintends, *esp.* one specially appointed for the purpose; police rank next above that of chief inspector.

SUPERIOR (1) [sŏŏ-pēer'i-er], *adj.* above or higher, in a physical, moral, social, intellectual or qualitative sense; in greater number; of good quality or attainment, without any direct comparison; above in position; supercilious, disdainful, patronizing; **s. to,** unaffected by. SUPERIOR (2), *n.* one who is above another in any respect; ruler of a religious house. [L.].

SUPERIORITY [sŏŏ-pēer-i-o'ri-ti], *n.* state or fact of being superior.

SUPERLATIVE (1) [sŏŏ-pur'la-tiv], *adj.* of extreme excellence; *(gram.)* of the highest degree. SUPERLATIVE (2), *n. (gram.)* the s. degree; a s. adjective. [L.].

SUPERLUNARY [sŏŏ-per-lŏŏ'na-ri], *adj.* being above the moon; not sublunary or of this world.

SUPERMAN [sŏŏ'per-man], *n.* a man of extraordinary attributes.

SUPERMUNDANE [sŏŏ-per-mun'dān], *adj.* above the earthly.

SUPERNAL [sŏŏ-pur'nal], *adj.* celestial. [L.].

SUPERNATIONAL [sŏŏ-per-na'shn-al], *adj.* above nationality.

SUPERNATURAL [sŏŏ-per-na'tyŏŏ-ral], *adj.* above obedience to natural laws, unbounded by matter.

SUPERNORMAL [sŏŏ-per-naw'mal], *adj.* above the normal, not obeying normal laws.

SUPERNUMERARY (1) [sŏŏ-per-nyŏŏ'me-ra-ri], *adj.* exceeding the normal or necessary number. SUPERNUMERARY (2), *n.* person in excess of the normal or proper complement of a group.

SUPERPHOSPHATE [sŏŏ-per-fos'fāt], *n.* an acid phosphate, *esp.* **s. of lime,** used as a fertilizer.

SUPERPOSE [sŏŏ-per-pōz'], *v.t.* to place above.

SUPERPOSITION [sŏŏ-per-pō-zi'shn], *n.* state of being, act of placing, above or on top.

SUPERSCRIBE [sŏŏ'per-skrīb], *v.t.* to write above or on the upper side of.

SUPERSCRIPTION [sŏŏ-per-skrip'shn], *n.* inscription above or on a thing; act of superscribing. [L.].

SUPERSEDE [sŏŏ-per-sēd'], *v.t.* to take the place of. [L.].

SUPERSENSITIVE [sŏŏ-per-sen'si-tiv], *adj.* excessively sensitive.

SUPERSESSION [sŏŏ-per-se'shn], *n.* act of superseding; state of being superseded.

SUPERSONIC [sŏŏ-per-so'nik], *adj. (phys.)* of, or pertaining to, frequencies or oscillations higher than those of sound and so inaudible to man; (of speed) faster than the rate at which sound travels; **s. heterodyne,** radio circuit in which a heterodyne of supersonic frequency is set up between the incoming signals and a local oscillator. SUPERSONICS, *n.(pl.) (phys.)* study of the properties and applications of frequencies higher than that of sound. [L.].

SUPERSTITION [sŏŏ-per-sti'shn], *n.* that which is believed in face of reason and common sense, *esp.* irrational belief in the supernatural; condition of mind which holds superstitions. [L.].

SUPERSTITIOUS [sŏŏ-per-sti'shŏŏs], *adj.* relating to, believing in, superstitions. [L.].

SUPERSTRUCTURE [sŏŏ'per-struk-tyŏŏr], *n.* structure built above or on top of another.

SUPERTAX [sŏŏ'per-taks], *n.* additional income tax for large incomes.

SUPERTONIC [sŏŏ-per-to'nik], *n. (mus.)* the note next above the keynote.

SUPERVENE [sŏŏ-per-vēn'], *v.i.* to come in addition; come in consequence of, while being in nature different from, the cause. SUPERVENIENT, *adj.* coming in addition. [L.].

SUPERVENTION [sŏŏ-per-ven'shn], *n.* act of supervening.

SUPERVISE [sŏŏ'per-vīz], *v.t. and i.* to oversee; superintend; act as supervisor. [L.].

SUPERVISION [sŏŏ-per-vi'zhn], *n.* act of supervising; superintendence. [MedL.].

SUPINE (1) [sŏŏ'pīn], *adj.* lying face upward; *(fig.)* wholly inactive. SUPINE (2), *n.* Latin verbal noun formed upon the past participle stem.

SUPPER [su'per], *n.* the last meal of the day. [OFr.].

SUPPLANT [su-plahnt'], *v.t.* to displace and take the place of, usurp the place of. SUPPLANTATION [su-plahn-tā'shn], *n.* act of supplanting. [L.].

SUPPLE [su'pl], *adj.* smoothly pliant, flexible; docile, subtly compliant, adaptable. [L.].

SUPPLEMENT (1) [sup'pli-ment], *n.* that which is in addition, *esp.* an additional part of a publication giving more detailed treatment to some specific subject; *(geom.)* amount by which an angle is less than two right angles; an additional charge. SUPPLEMENT (2), *v.i.* to bring in addition to, supply with additional help. SUPPLEMENTAL, SUPPLEMENTARY, *adj.* serving as a s., additional. [L.].

SUPPLIANT (1) [su'pli-ant], *adj.* supplicating; beseeching humbly. SUPPLIANT (2), *n.* one who supplicates. [Fr.].

SUPPLICANT [su'pli-kant], *n.* one who supplicates. [L.].

SUPPLICATE [su'pli-kāt], *v.t. and i.* to beg humbly and beseechingly, earnestly to request a favour; make a humble request to. [L.].

SUPPLICATION [su-pli-kā'shn], *n.* act of supplicating, thing supplicated. [L.].

SUPPLY (1) [su-plī'], *v.t.* to provide (with) that which will satisfy a need, *esp.* to provide regularly with necessaries; satisfy (a need). SUPPLY (2), *n.* that which is supplied; the whole stock of necessary goods in hand at any time; the total available quantity of a commodity. [L.].

SUPPORT (1) [su-pawt'], *v.t.* to bear up, prevent from falling, sustain; *(fig.)* provide sustenance for, be responsible for the maintenance of; endure; help, back up, be of assistance to. SUPPORT (2), *n.* that which supports, prop, stay; moral encouragement; one who maintains dependants. [L.].

SUPPORTABLE [su-pawt'a-bl], *adj.* able to be supported; endurable.

SUPPORTER [su-pawt'er], *n.* one who supports, *esp.* one who supports a cause; *(her.)* one of two figures standing at the side of a coat of arms.

SUPPOSE [su-pōz'], *v.t.* to imagine, assume on grounds of probability, but without absolute conviction; require as a general, but not invariable,

---

concomitant; expect; (*pass.*) be required as a matter of law, duty etc. (to do something). SUPPOSEDLY [su-pō'zed-li], *adv.* as one supposes or is given to s. [Fr.].

SUPPOSITION [su-po-zi'shn], *n.* that which is supposed, assumption, opinion held without definite evidence; act of supposing. SUPPOSITIONAL, *adj.* relating to, based on, s.

SUPPOSITITIOUS [su-po-zi-ti'shŏŏs], *adj* fraudulently substituted, spurious. [L.].

SUPPOSITORY [su-po'zi-te-ri], *n.* a body introduced into the rectum or vagina for medical purposes. [L.].

SUPPRESS [su-pres'], *v.t.* to press down, crush; prevent from expression, forbid or stifle publication of; subdue by force, repress; ban. SUPPRESSIVE, *adj.* tending to s.; subduing; concealing. [~L.].

SUPPRESSION [su-pre'shn], *n.* act of suppressing; state of being suppressed.

SUPPRESSOR [su-pre'ser], *n.* one who, that which, suppresses; (*elect.*) device fitted to electrical apparatus to prevent interference with neighbouring radio installations; (*radio*) device for suppressing outside interference.

SUPPURATE [su'pyŏŏ-rāt], *v.i.* to generate, discharge, pus; come to a head. SUPPURATIVE, *adj.* relating to or producing suppuration. [L.].

SUPPURATION [su-pyŏŏ-rā'shn], *n.* the generation of pus.

SUPRA-, *pref.* above; transcending; before. [L.].

SUPREMACY [sŏŏ-pre'ma-si], *n.* state or power of being supreme. [OFr.].

SUPREME [sŏŏ-prēm'], *adj.* holding absolute power; greater, in some respect, than all others. [L.].

SUR-, *pref.* beyond; above; in addition. [OFr. from L.].

SURCEASE (1) [ser-sēs'], *v.t.* (*archaic*) to cease, leave off. SURCEASE (2), *n.* (*archaic*) cessation. [OFr.].

SURCHARGE (1) [ser-chahj'], *v.t.* to charge to excess, charge in addition; overprint with a different value. SURCHARGE (2) [sur'chahj], *n.* a charge over and above another, or more than is usual; an imprint on the face of a postage stamp giving it a postal value other than that at which it was issued; excessive charge.

SURCLE [sur'kl], *n.* twig, small shoot. [L.].

SURCOAT [sur'kōt], *n.* (*hist.*) coat worn over armour; loose outer coat, overcoat.

SURD [surd], *n.* (*math.*) a quantity not exactly expressible in figures, irrational number. [L.].

SURE (1) [shŏŏr], *adj.* dependable, certainly reliable, certain, secure, wholly confident. SURE-FOOTED, unlikely to stumble. SURE (2), *int.* (*U.S.*) certainly, yes. SURELY, *adv.* safely, securely, certainly, almost certainly. [OFr. from L.].

SURETY [shŏŏr'i-ti], *n.* person responsible for the behaviour of another, person standing monetary security for a defendant's appearance in court, sum guaranteed in default of appearance; sureness. SURETYSHIP, *n.* state of being s.; obligation of a person to answer for another. [L.].

SURF (1) [surf], *n.* the foamy water of breaking waves, *esp.* waves breaking on a shelving shore. SURF-BATHING, bathing in s. SURF-BOARD, specially designed board for riding on the s. SURF-BOAT, boat for use in s. [Uncert.].

SURFACE (1) [sur'fis], *n.* the outer area of a thing; a two-dimensional limit; the outside, superficial appearance of anything; the top of a mass of liquid; the works of a mine above ground. SURFACE (2), *adj.* of, pertaining to, travelling on, the s. or outside part; (of mails) not sent by air. SURFACE (3), *v.t.* to treat, polish a s.; skim on, or come to, the s. of water. SURFACEMAN, *n.* worker maintaining the condition of a railway track. [OFr.].

SURFEIT (1) [sur'fit], *n.* over-indulgence, excessive quantity of anything, *esp.* of food. SURFEIT (2), *v.t.* to satiate by excess. [OFr.].

SURGE (1) [surj], *n.* a billowing heave, vast heaving movement of a whole surface; the sea; noise of the sea; sudden oscillation in an electric current. SURGE (2), *v.i.* to billow powerfully over a whole surface, move tumultuously like the waves of the sea; move with a s. [L.].

SURGEON [sur'jon], *n.* one practising surgery. SURGEONCY, *n.* office or post of s. in the Navy, Army or Air Force. [ME. ~CHIRURGEON].

SURGERY [sur'je-ri], *n.* medical treatment by manual operation; dispensary of a doctor. [ME.].

SURGICAL [sur'ji-kal], *adj.* pertaining to surgeons or surgery; done by means of, employed in surgery.

SURLY [sur'li], *adj.* sullenly ill-tempered and morose. [Uncert.].

SURMISE (1) [sur'mīz, ser-mīz'], *v.t.* to conjecture, make a surmise. SURMISE (2), *n.* a reasonable guess, conjecture backed by some evidence. [OFr.].

SURMOUNT [ser-mownt'], *v.t.* to overcome; get on top of. [OFr.].

SURNAME (1) [sur'nām], *n.* a family name, originally a nickname. SURNAME (2), *v.t.* to give a s. to. [~Fr.].

SURPASS [ser-pahs'], *v.t.* and *i.* to exceed or excel in quality or achievement. SURPASSING, *adj.* excelling. SURPASSINGLY, *adv.* so as to s. [OFr.].

SURPLICE [sur'plis], *n.* white vestment worn *esp.* by officiating clergy. [OFr.].

SURPLUS (1) (*pl.* **surpluses**) [sur'plus], *n.* a quantity above what is necessary; amount by which receipts exceed expenditure. SURPLUS (2), *adj.* exceeding what is necessary; **s. value**, amount by which price exceeds cost of production, and so provides profit. [MedL.].

SURPRISE (1) [ser-prīz'], *n.* occurrence of the unexpected; emotional shock produced by such occurrence; a taking advantage over someone by unexpected action, *esp.* in military sense; (*coll.*) an unexpected pleasure. SURPRISE (2), *v.t.* to shock emotionally by the unexpected, astonish; attack, overcome by an unanticipated assault.

SURREALISM [sur-rē'a-lizm], *n.* a form of art which claims to express the subconscious mind. [Fr.].

SURREALIST (1) [sur-rē'a-list], *n.* exponent or admirer of surrealism. SURREALIST (2), *adj.* of, resembling or pertaining to, surrealism or surrealists.

SURRENDER (1) [su-ren'der], *v.t.* and *i.* to submit to an opponent after defeat, give way to compulsion; relinquish under pressure, yield; give up (an insurance policy) upon repayment of part of the premiums. SURRENDER (2), *n.* act of surrendering. SURRENDEREE [su-ren-de-rē'], *n.* (*leg.*) person to whom a thing is surrendered, or a point conceded. SURRENDERER, *n.* one who surrenders. SURRENDEROR, *n.* (*leg.*) one who surrenders an estate to the holder of the reversion. [OFr.].

SURREPTITIOUS [su-rep-ti'shŏŏs], *adj.* performed or obtained secretly, *esp.* in dishonest fashion. [L.].

SURROGATE [su'rō-gāt], *n.* a substitute; deputy of a bishop. [L.].

SURROUND (1) [su-rownd'], *v.t.* to encircle, encompass; (*milit.*) occupy all lines of a force's advance or retreat; be present on every side of. SURROUND (2), *n.* that which surrounds, *esp.* the bare floor or linoleum around a carpet. SURROUNDINGS, *n.(pl.)* environment. SURROUNDING, *adj.* encompassing, everywhere adjacent. [OFr.].

SURTAX (1) [sur'taks], *n.* additional tax on incomes exceeding a certain figure. SURTAX (2), *v.t.* to impose a s. on.

SURTOUT [ser-tŏŏ'], *n.* (*hist.*) kind of frock-coat. [Fr.].

SURVEILLANCE [ser-vā'lans], *n.* close observation over a person's activities. [Fr.].

SURVEY (1) [ser-vā'], *v.t.* to take a general view of an area or situation; conduct a geographical and geometrical examination of a tract of country. SURVEY (2) [sur'vā], *n.* a broad, general consideration of a whole situation or field of circumstances; act, process, methods or result of inspecting and recording the physical, geological and geographical characteristics of a tract of land. [OFr.].

SURVEYOR [ser-vā'er], *n.* one skilled in surveying and measuring land; one who surveys.

SURVIVAL [ser-vī'val], *n.* state of surviving; anything which survives the rest of its kind.

SURVIVE [ser-vīv'], *v.t.* and *i.* to outlive, endure longer than another; live beyond a certain period; remain alive after what might have been a fatal disaster, continue to exist. [L.].

SURVIVOR [ser-vī'ver], *n.* one who survives. SURVIVORSHIP, *n.* state of being a s.; (*leg.*) rights of the surviving holder of a joint property.

SUSCEPTIBILITY [su-sep-ti-bi'li-ti], *n.* quality or state of being susceptible.

SUSCEPTIBLE [su-sep'ti-bl], *adj.* capable (of); liable (to); emotionally sensitive, easily influenced by the feelings, readily overcome by sexual attraction. [MedL.].

SUSCEPTIVE [su-sep'tiv], *adj.* susceptible; receptive of emotional stimuli. [MedL.].

SUSPECT (1) [sus-pekt'], *v.t.* to be inclined to believe in the existence of (a thing) without having definite

---

ŏŏ is pronounced as in *food*; ŏŏ as in *hood*; th as in *think*; TH as in *that*; zh as in *azure*. ~ = related to.

proof; distrust, disbelieve in (a thing) without
adequate evidence for so doing; consider (a person)
probably guilty without possessing certain knowledge; mistrust. SUSPECT (2) [sus'pekt], n. suspected person. SUSPECT (3) [sus'pekt], adj. under
suspicion, suspected. SUSPECTED [sus-pek'tid], adj.
under suspicion; imagined without proof. [L.].

SUSPEND [sus-pend'], v.t. to hang from above;
hold up, cause to remain in suspense; cause (an
activity) temporarily to cease, deprive from office for
a period or pending a final decision. [L.].

SUSPENDER [sus-pen'der], n. one who, or that
which, suspends; device for holding up stockings or
socks on the leg. SUSPENDER-BELT, belt worn by
women round the waist to support suspenders.

SUSPENSE [sus-pens'], n. state of being suspended;
state of anxiety while awaiting news of an important
decision. SUSPENSIVE, adj. able to suspend; liable
to be suspended; in s. SUSPENSORY, adj. supporting,
relating to suspension.

SUSPENSION [sus-pen'shn], n. act of suspending;
condition of being suspended; **s. bridge**, bridge in
which the roadway is suspended by chains or cables
from piers or towers.

SUSPICION [sus-pi'shn], n. act or state of suspecting; a feeling of unproved mistrust; the smallest
possible trace of a thing, a faint indication of something without definite proof of its presence. [L.].

SUSPICIOUS [sus-pi'shŏos], adj. feeling suspicion;
giving rise to, inviting, suspicion. [L.].

SUSPIRE [sus-pier'], v.i. to sigh. SUSPIRATION,
[sus-pi-rā'shn], n. act of sighing or drawing a long,
deep breath, a sigh. [L.].

SUSTAIN [sus-tān'], v.t. to hold up, take the weight
of, keep from falling; support; approve, uphold as
correct, support as just; support, endure; prolong,
maintain; keep alive, nourish. [L.].

SUSTENANCE [sus'ti-nans], n. that which supports
life; nourishment, food. [LL.].

SUSURRATION [syŏo-su-rā'shn], n. a whispering,
murmurous rustling, a hissing sound. [L.].

SUTTEE [su-tē', su'tē], n. Hindu widow who sacrifices herself on the funeral pyre of her husband;
ritual of self-immolation. [Skr.].

SUTURE [syŏo'tyŏor], n. (anat.) the joining of
bones or parts of a skull by means of an interlocking
serrated seam; (bot.) line or seam formed by a joining;
(surg.) act or process of stitching a wound; line or
seam so formed; stitching material used in such an
operation. SUTURE (2), v.t. to join, close, by a s.
SUTURAL, adj. (bot.) relating to a s. or seam; occurring
near a s. [L.].

SUZERAIN [syŏo'ze-rān], n. a supreme authority
in feudal times, lord or superior, paramount ruler.
[OFr.].

SVELTE [svelt], adj. slender, supple of figure, graceful.
[Fr.].

SWAB (1) [swob], n. mop for cleaning up spilt liquid,
esp. on decks; (surg.) absorbent pad; (med.) specimen
taken with a swab for bacteriological examination;
(slang) dirty fellow. SWAB (2) (pres.pt. SWABBING,
pret. and p.pt. SWABBED), v.t. to clean up, wash, wipe,
sweep by means of a s. [Du.].

SWADDLE [swo'dl], v.t. to wrap up warmly in several
layers of garments, pieces of cloth or bandage,
swathe. SWADDLING-CLOTHES †, n.(pl.) bands or
clothes wrapped closely round a baby. [~OE.].

SWAG [swag], n. (arch.) ornamental hanging wreath;
(slang) booty, plunder, stolen goods; (Australian)
bundle carried on the back by a traveller in the back
country, or by a tramp. SWAG-BELLIED, having a
pendulous belly. [Unkn.].

SWAGGER (1) swa'ger], v.i. to show one's sense of
superiority by defiantly strutting about, be insolent
in manner, boastful in speech. SWAGGER-CANE, n.
soldier's short walking stick. SWAGGER-COAT, n.
woman's loose-fitting three-quarter-length coat.
SWAGGER (2), n. act of swaggering; boastfulness of
manner, exaggerated self-conceit manifested in a
jaunty gait, dashing talk or unconventional behaviour. SWAGGER (3), adj. swaggering, smart,
extremely fashionable. [Uncert.].

SWAIN [swān], n. young man, rustic; (archaic)
agricultural labourer; lover in pastoral poetry,
admiring youth. [OScand.].

SWALLOW (1) [swo'lō], n. a passerine bird characterized by a forked tailed. SWALLOW-DIVE, n., v.t. and
i. (swimming) dive from a height with arms outstretched sideways. SWALLOW-TAIL, anything forked
like a s.'s tail; a kind of butterfly; dress coat.
SWALLOW-TAILED, adj. having a forked tail, having a

form with two points formed either by a split at one
end or by a piece cut out of one end in the shape of a
V, forked, dove-tailed. [OE.].

SWALLOW (2), v.t. and i. to pass (food etc.) from
the mouth through the passage of the throat into the
stomach, eat or drink; cause the muscles of the
throat to act as when something is being swallowed;
(fig.) feign indifference to, tolerate; believe implicitly,
accept as true; **to s. up**, to absorb, exhaust, use up;
consume, waste; engulf; envelop; **to s. (one's)
words**, to recant. SWALLOW (3), n. act of swallowing; throat, gullet; amount swallowed in one mouthful; capacity for eating or drinking, voracity. [OE.].

SWAM [swam], pret. of SWIM. [OE.].

SWAMP (1) [swomp], n. tract of low-lying ground
softened and saturated by water to a considerable
depth; bog, marsh, morass. SWAMP (2), v.t. to overwhelm with water, cover, saturate with water, inundate; (fig.) overwhelm with something. [~Du.].

SWAN [swon], n. a large bird characterized by
webbed feet, a long graceful neck, red bill and black
legs, the plumage being usually white; **S. of Avon**,
Shakespeare. SWAN-NECK, (having) a curve resembling a s.'s neck. SWAN'S-DOWN, soft under-plumage
of a s. SWAN-SONG, death-rattle in the throat of a s.,
transformed by popular imagination into a song;
(fig.) last work produced by an artist before death.
SWAN-UPPING, annual marking of swans on their
beaks for identification purposes. SWANNERY, n.
place where swans congregate to nest. [OE.].

SWANEE-WHISTLE [swo-ni-wi'sl], n. musical
instrument of simple design consisting of a single
hollow tube fitted with a sliding valve. [Suwannee
River, U.S.A.].

SWANK (1) [swangk], v.t. (slang) to show off, act in an
ostentatious manner so as to demonstrate one's
superiority, put on side, swagger. SWANK (2), n.
behaviour of a person who swanks; brag, swagger.
[Unkn.].

SWAP (1), **SWOP** (pres.pt. **swapping**, pret. and p.pt.
swapped) [swop], v.t. and i. (coll.) to exchange after a
bargain, barter. SWAP (2), SWOP, n. (coll.) act of
swapping; any object which is swapped. [~OE.].

SWARD [swawd], n. stretch of ground covered with
short green grass, turf. [OE.].

SWARE † [swäer], pret. of SWEAR (1). [ME.].

SWARM (1) [swawm], n. large number of bees
gathered in an active, compact cluster, esp. when
they quit a parent hive escorting a queen to build a
fresh home; multitude of people on the move seen as a
collective whole, throng; large number. SWARM (2),
v.t. and i. to cover with a s.; gather in great number in
the form of a s., congregate, throng, collect in one
place as a moving crowd. [OE.].

SWARM (3), v.t. and i. to climb (up) anything steep or
almost perpendicular, clinging very close. [Unkn.].

SWART(H) [swawt(h)], adj. swarthy. [OE.].

SWARTHY [swaw'THi], adj. having a dark complexion, being of dark hue, sunburnt.

SWASH (1) [swosh], n. the sound of splashing water;
a heavy blow, esp. on something soft; the rush of
water up a beach following the breaking of a wave.
SWASH (2), v.t. and i. to dash, splash against; move
about clashing, splashing etc., like swirling water.
SWASHY, adj. sloppy, squashy. [Imitative].

SWASH (3), adj. (turning) inclined obliquely; (typ.)
having flourishes. [Unkn.].

SWASHBUCKLER [swosh'buk-ler], n. swaggering
belligerent adventurer, bully or braggart. [SWASH
(2) and BUCKLER].

SWASTIKA [swos'ti-kah], n. fylfot; right-angled
cross with four equal arms, each having an extension
at right angles; primitive sun-symbol; badge of the
Nazi party, of the German Third Reich. [Skr.].

SWAT (1) (pres.pt. **swatting**, pret. and p.pt. **swatted**)
[swot], v.t. to strike sharply with the flat of the hand;
hit with a swat. SWAT (2), n. implement for swatting;
blow with a s. [U.S.].

SWATH [swawth, swoth], n. amount of grass cut by
a scythe at a single sweep; space cleared by a scythe
with one sweep. [OE.].

SWATHE (1) [swāth], n. bandage, wrapping; swath.
SWATHE (2), v.t. to wrap, bind with a bandage.
[OE.].

SWAY (1) [swā], v.t. and i. to cause to move slowly
from side to side, make incline; control the movement
or action of a person, group or body by reason of
authority; persuade, cause to swing into line; sway
slowly to the side, incline, lean; rule, govern. SWAY
(2), n. act of swaying, movement of that which
sways; weight or power which causes something to

sway; governing influence, authority, dominion, rule. [OScand.].

SWEAR (1) (*pret.* **swore**, *p.pt.* **sworn**) [swãer], *v.t. and i.* to utter as a solemn promise, declare on oath; cause to take an oath; utter a solemn promise; speak profane oaths, curse, blaspheme; **to s. by**, to invoke as a solemn witness; (*coll.*) express confidence in; **to s. in**, to administer an oath of office to, install under oath; **to s. off**, to promise to renounce. SWEAR (2), *n.* act of swearing, oath; a series of hearty oaths. SWEARING, *n.* act of affirming on oath; habit or practice of blaspheming, profanity. [OE.].

SWEAT (1) (*pret. and p.pt.* **sweated**, † **sweat**) [swet], *v.t. and i.* to exude in the manner of sweat; cause to sweat; wear down by friction; force to work hard for long hours at starvation wages; exude sweat, perspire; exude moisture in the manner of sweat; work hard, drudge; (*slang*) suffer; weld; **to s. out**, to get rid of by means of sweating. SWEAT (2), *n.* moisture exuded through the pores of the skin, perspiration; moisture condensed on the surface of any substance; emotional or physical state of excitation which causes s. to be exuded; process of sweating; (*coll.*) laborious work, drudgery, heavy manual labour; **cold s.**, state of fear, funk; **old s.**, old soldier. SWEAT-BAND, lining round the inside edge of a man's hat, usually of leather. SWEAT-DUCT, (*anat.*) small channel conveying the secretion of a s. gland to the surface of the skin. SWEATED, *adj.* produced by sweating; employed at starvation wages; done by underpaid workers. [OE.].

SWEATER [swe'ter], *n.* one who, or that which, causes to sweat; employer at starvation wages; thick jersey worn as a protection against cold after exercise.

SWEATY [swe'ti], *adj.* covered with or moist with sweat; consisting of sweat; smelling of stale sweat; laborious.

SWEDE [swed], *n.* a native of Sweden; the Swedish turnip, whose vegetable root is edible. [MLGerm.].

SWEEP (1) (*pret. and p.pt.* **swept**) [swep], *v.t.* to remove (dirt or dust) by means of a broom, clean by brushing, remove by vigorous action, carry, brush, drive away; cause to disappear, obliterate with a comprehensive, wide-flung movement; clear with a swift, decisive movement; *v.i.* to pass over a broad surface swiftly and comprehensively, cross with a vigorous driving movement; move with a stately bearing, walk with pomp; stretch, extend in a wide curve; move with a long reach; engage in cleaning with a broom; pass the fingers over the strings of a musical instrument. SWEEP (2), *n.* act of sweeping; scope, range, of a movement or stroke, usually of a semi-circular nature; gesture which covers a wide area; forward movement with a steady power covering a wide area; comprehensive range or grasp of a subject; person whose business it is to s. chimneys; crossing-sweeper; scamp, blackguard; curved carriage drive; long oar; sail of a windmill; piece of timber functioning on a fulcrum; long, gradual curve; beam-compass; (*coll.*) sweepstake; incursion by fighter planes across a considerable area; **to make a clean s. of**, to get rid of, abolish. SWEEPING, *adj.* having a wide range; comprehending a great deal or a great many; having small regard for details or facts. SWEEPINGS, *n.*(*pl.*) things, rubbish, collected by sweeping, refuse. [OScand.].

SWEEPSTAKE(S) [swep'stāk(s)], *n.* form of gambling in which each participant pays a specified sum for a ticket entitling him to a chance to draw a competitor in a race or other competition, the prize money for the successful ticket(s) being paid out of the common fund provided by the losers.

SWEET (1) [swet], *adj.* having the flavour of honey or sugar, stimulating the palate to experience one of the primary sensations of taste, not bitter, sour or salt; seasoned with sugar; agreeable, pleasing to any of the senses, delightful; pleasant to the body, restful; fragrant; melodious; soft; having a nature free from viciousness, tender, gentle, kind; (*coll.*) pretty, likeable, charming; **to be s. on**, (*coll.*) to be in love with; **s. potato**, creeper plant having an edible root s. in flavour; **s. william**, plant having small pink-and-white flowers forming in a cluster. SWEET-CHESTNUT, *n.* the common Spanish chestnut, with an edible nut. SWEET-CORN, *n.* variety of maize having a s. taste, and used, *esp.* in the U.S., as a vegetable. SWEET-OIL, *n.* salad oil, olive oil. SWEET-PEA, *n.* leguminous plant with flowers which have a very s. fragrance. SWEET-STUFF, *n.* sweets, sweetmeats. SWEET (2), *n.* any substance which tastes s.; single piece of confectionery, sweetmeat made of various forms of sugar and ingredients in various mixtures; a course, eaten at a meal after the main dish, which is sweetened; term of affection. SWEETLY, *adv.* in a s. manner; easily, freely. [OE.].

SWEETBREAD [swet'bred], *n.* pancreas, or thymus gland, of an animal prepared as food.

SWEETBRIER, SWEETBRIAR [swet'brī-er], *n.* species of rose, a shrubby plant whose leaves have a delicate fragrance.

SWEETEN [swe'ten], *v.t. and i.* to make sweet, season with sugar or honey; make more agreeable or enjoyable or less painful, soften; become sweet. SWEETENER, *n.* one who, or that which, sweetens; (*slang*) tip, bribe. SWEETENING, *n.* act of making sweet; substance or ingredient which sweetens.

SWEETHEART [swet'haht], *n.* a lover, darling.

SWEETIE, SWEETY [swe'ti], *n.* (*coll.*) sweetheart, lover, *esp.* a woman; (*coll.*) piece of confectionery.

SWEETING [swe'ting], *n.* a sweet apple; † sweetheart.

SWEETMEAT [swet'met], *n.* a confection of sugar, a sweet; fruit preserved with sugar.

SWELL (1) (*pret.* **swelled**, *p.pt.* **swollen, swelled**) [swel], *v.t.* to cause to swell; increase in size, bulk, dimension or volume; increase, augment; make bigger in arrogance, puff out with pride; *v.i.* to grow larger, expand as by dilation or inflation; be inflated, blown out, bloated; be abnormally extended by inflammation; bulge out, be extended in a curve; experience a sensation of strength or power due to accumulating emotion; increase in arrogance; rise in a curved protuberance. SWELLED-HEADED, (*coll.*) vain; **swelled head**, (*coll.*) vanity, conceit. SWELL (2), *n.* act or process of swelling; increase in volume, magnitude or bulk; a single, gradual undulation of land; continual undulating motion of the sea which does not break up the surface into waves; (*coll.*) rich person, notable for smart clothes; important person; (*mus.*) a crescendo; device in an organ to produce a crescendo. SWELL (3), *adj.* (*coll.*) smart, fashionable; first-rate, high-class. SWELL-MOB, *n.* (*slang*) class of well-dressed thieves or pickpockets. SWELL-MOBSMAN, *n.* (*slang*) well-dressed pickpocket. [OE.].

SWELLING (1) [swe'ling], *n.* that which swells or is swollen; a natural prominence, undulation of the earth; a swollen part of the body, boil, tumour. SWELLING (2), *adj.* marked by a s.; having a bulging shape, protruding; becoming fuller, rising higher; growing louder; (*fig.*) (of style) pompous, inflated.

SWELTER [swel'ter], *v.i.* to be overcome with heat, be affected by extreme heat, perspire freely. [OE.].

SWEPT [swept], *pret. and p.pt. of* SWEEP. [ME.].

SWERVE (1) [swurv], *v.t. and i.* to cause to deviate; deviate in a curving line of progress from a set course, diverge from a straight line, move suddenly to one side of a line of progression; suffer a lapse in moral conduct or duty. SWERVE (2), *n.* act of swerving, a curving deviation from a course, divergence from a straight line, *esp.* one followed by a ball in mid-air. [OE.].

SWIFT (1) [swift], *n.* a species of bird resembling a swallow, having long, pointed wings and a short forked tail. [Next].

SWIFT (2), *adj.* having the power to move at a fast pace, capable of rapid propulsion, rapid, quick; acting promptly, following quickly in succession. SWIFT (3), *adv.* swiftly. [OE.].

SWIG (1) [swig], *n.* draught of liquor, *esp.* of an alcoholic drink, a gulp; drink lasting as long as the breath can be held. SWIG (2) (*pres.pt.* SWIGGING, *pret. and p.pt.* SWIGGED), *v.t. and i.* to drink in large draughts; take in big gulps; drink. [Unkn.].

SWILL (1) [swil], *v.t. and i.* to wash out and clean with a generous amount of water, rinse; drink in great gulps, in large quantities. SWILL (2), *n.* act of swilling; copious draught of liquor; food refuse soaked in water for pigs and poultry, hogwash. SWILLER, *n.* one who drinks excessively. SWILLINGS, *n.*(*pl.*) refuse for pigs, hogwash. [OE.]. SWILL (3), *n.* a shallow basket. [Unkn.].

SWIM (1) (*pres.pt.* **swimming**, *pret.* **swam**, *p.pt.* **swum**) [swim], *v.t. and i.* to make swim; cross by swimming; compete against as a swimmer; move through water using the extremities and limbs or fins as a means of propulsion, float on or in water; glide smoothly; be flooded, overflow; be giddy, reel. SWIM (2), *n.* act of swimming; time spent in swimming; part of a river usually frequented by fish, fisherman's pitch; **in the s.**, in the know, fashionable. SWIMMER, *n.* person who swims; animal or bird which naturally indulges in swimming. SWIMMINGLY, *adv.*

ᴏᴏ is pronounced as in food; ᴏᴏ as in hood; th as in think; ᴛʜ as in that; zh as in azure. **~ =** related to.

easily, smoothly; without obstruction; prosperously. SWIMMY, *adj.* giddy. [OE.].

SWIMMING (1) [swi'ming], *n.* act or art of moving in water by means of the limbs; dizziness, giddiness. SWIMMING-BELT, rubber belt used to support on the water a person learning to swim.

SWINDLE (1) [swin'dl], *v.t. and i.* to cheat and defraud grossly; carry on transactions for gain by means of gross misrepresentations which have a deceptive appearance of honesty and legality. SWINDLE (2), *n.* act of swindling; deliberate deception for gain under the guise of honesty; illegal transaction carried on under a legal guise, deliberately framed to defraud; object which is actually worthless in relation to the claims made for it. [Germ.].

SWINE (*pl.* swine) [swin], *n.* a pig; term of abuse; **s. fever,** a disease affecting pigs. SWINERY, *n.* pig farm; pigsty. [OE.].

SWINEHERD [swin'herd], *n.* man who attends to swine, keeper of pigs.

SWING (1) (*pret. and p.pt.* swung) [swing], *v.t.* to cause to swing, make move backwards and forwards or from side to side; hold suspended so that a free movement from side to side is permitted, dangle; wave, brandish; rock on a swing; cause to move on a pivot; cause to move rapidly in a semi-circular motion; *v.i.* to go or move from side to side like anything weighty suspended in space; move backwards and forwards, sway; vibrate, oscillate; move in relation to a pivot; move backwards and forwards on a swing; walk or run with a rhythmic rolling gait; **to s. for,** (*slang*) to be hanged for; **to s. the lead,** to tell lies as an excuse to escape work; **to s. it,** to play (music) with a s.; **s. bridge,** bridge which may be moved by swinging on a pivot. SWING-BOAT, *n.* boatshaped seat providing a pleasure s. in a fair-ground. SWING (2), *n.* act of swinging, a movement from side to side, motion to and fro; distance traversed by such a motion, range of that which swings; the mode of a person's walk, a free gait with a slight roll of the body from the hips from side to side; unhindered movement, freedom in a specific action; beat, rhythm, extempore jazz music; apparatus to s. on, *esp.* a loop of rope with a seat attached, which is fastened to a height, on which one sits and is swung backwards and forwards; **in full s.,** at full pressure, with all units functioning; **to make up on the swings what is lost on the roundabouts,** to compensate losses by profits from other sources. [OE.].

SWINGE [swinj], *v.t.* (*archaic*) to hit hard, beat soundly; chastise. SWING(E)ING, *adj.* (*coll. and archaic*) very large. [OE.].

SWINGLE (1) [swing'gl], *n.* operation of swingling; wooden instrument for beating out the fibre from flax, flat part of a flail which falls on the grain in threshing. SWINGLE-TREE, pivoted crossbar to which a horse's traces are attached. SWINGLE (2), *v.t.* to thrash flax so as to free the fibre from the wood pulp. [OE.].

SWINISH [swi'nish], *adj.* having the character of, befitting, or like, swine; gross, greedy, coarse.

SWIPE (1) [swip], *n.* strong blow or hit made without taking accurate aim, given with the arm swinging, or with a bat or similar implement. SWIPE (2), *v.t. and i.* to hit hard in a somewhat uncontrolled manner; aim a strong, but rather wild, blow, *esp.* in cricket; (*slang*) steal, *esp.* by snatching. SWIPES, *n.(pl.)* weak, washy beer; waste beer. [OE.].

SWIRL (1) [swurl], *n.* eddying motion of water, movement of water in a circular, convoluted manner; twist or curl. SWIRL (2), *v.t. and i.* to cause to revolve, whirl; move in a circular, convoluted form, move in revolving currents of water. [OIcel.].

SWISH (1) [swish], *n.* rapid movement with something flexible which makes a whistling, hissing noise as it cuts through the air; sound made by such a movement; short-handled broom. SWISH (2), *v.t. and i.* to move through the air so as to make a hissing or whistling sound; flog, thrash; pass through the air with a swift cutting movement. SWISH (3), *adj.* (*slang*) smart, fashionable, fine. [Echoic].

SWITCH (1) [swich], *n.* slender, flexible branch, twig or shoot; device consisting of a short section of railway line moving on a pivot axis for diverting railway traffic from one line to another; apparatus for making and breaking an electric circuit; **musical s.,** series of extracts from various works linked together at points of resemblance and played as a whole. SWITCH (2), *v.t. and i.* to lash or thrash with a s.; move with a quiet swing, swish; transfer, divert, shunt by means of a railway s.; make or break an

electric circuit by operating a s.; be transferred, diverted, shunted to another railway line; transfer, convert. SWITCH-OVER, *n.* transference, conversion, change from one activity to another. SWITCHMAN, *n.* man who works railway switches by hand, pointsman. [~LGerm.].

SWITCHBACK [swich'bak], *n.* elevated railway, in amusement parks, on an undulating track which imparts an impetus to the carriages.

SWITCHBOARD [swich'bawd], *n.* board or plate fitted with electric switches which are connected to a number of circuits, *esp.* for telephonic purposes.

SWIVEL (1) [swi'vel], *n.* link which turns on a pivot; anything which turns on a pivot. SWIVEL-EYE, (*coll.*) eye which rolls in its socket, squint eye. SWIVEL (2) (*pres.pt.* SWIVELLING, *pret. and p.pt.* SWIVELLED), *v.t. and i.* to cause to move on a s.; move round in a socket or staple. [~OE.].

SWIZZLE-STICK [swi'zl-stik], *n.* stick or whisk for stirring drinks. [Unkn.].

SWOLLEN [swõ'len], *p.pt. of* SWELL; dilated. SWOLLEN-HEADED, swelled-headed.

SWOON (1) [swoon], *v.i.* to experience loss of consciousness and physical control preceded by a reeling giddiness, faint. SWOON (2), *n.* act of swooning; fainting fit. [OE.].

SWOOP (1) [swoop], *v.i.* to descend with a sudden sweeping movement which surprises by its rapidity in order to seize, pounce, as a bird of prey. SWOOP (2), *n.* act of swooping, sudden approach with a sweeping movement as though from above, like a bird of prey. [OE.].

SWOP, see SWAP.

SWORD [sawd], *n.* weapon consisting of a sharp-edged blade tapering to a point at one end, and furnished with a hilt at the other; (*fig.*) military power, warfare; **at the point of the s.,** under a threat of death; **to cross swords,** to engage in hostilities. SWORD-DANCE, Highland dance over two swords, laid crosswise, performed with intricate steps without touching them. SWORD-KNOT, strong ribbon or thong tied to the hilt of a s., acting as a safety device round the wrist. SWORD-STICK, walking-stick which acts also as a sheath for a thin s. [OE.].

SWORDBILL [sawd'bil], *n.* South American humming-bird with a long, sharp beak.

SWORDFISH [sawd'fish], *n.* large sea-fish characterized by a prolongation of the upper jaw, which is serrated and sharp like a sword.

SWORDSMAN [sawdz'man], *n.* expert fencer; soldier, fighting man.

SWORE [swaw(r)], *pret. of* SWEAR. [OE.].

SWORN [swawn], *adj. and p.pt. of* SWEAR; bound by an oath; **s. enemies,** bitter enemies; **s. friends,** close or intimate friends. [OE.].

SWOT (1) [swot], *n.* (*slang*) person who swots; term of contempt used by adolescent athletes for scholars; brain work, *esp.* the concentrated memorizing of facts in preparation for an examination. SWOT (2) (*pres.pt.* SWOTTING, *pret. and p.pt.* SWOTTED), *v.i.* (*slang*) to apply oneself assiduously to study, work hard at memorizing facts for examinations. [*Var.* of SWEAT].

SWUM [swum], *p.pt. of* SWIM. [OE.].

SWUNG [swung], *pret. and p.pt. of* SWING. [OE.].

SYBARITE [si'ba-rit], *n. and adj.* (one) having wealth enough to indulge continually a liking for luxury; luxurious. [Gk., inhabitant of *Sybaris,* formerly noted for luxuriousness].

SYCAMORE, SYCOMORE [si'ka-maw(r)], *n.* species of large maple; species of fig-tree common in Egypt. [Gk.].

SYCHNOCARPOUS [sik-nõ-kah'poos], *adj.* (*bot.*) bearing fruit many times without perishing, perennial. [Gk.].

SYCOPHANT [si'kõ-fant], *n.* person whose social relationships are based on a deliberate appeal to the vanity of his associates, person who gains the support or friendship of another by means of servile flattery, parasite, toady. [Gk.].

SYLLABIC [si-la'bik], *adj.* relating to a syllable or syllables; consisting of, or based on, a syllable or syllables. [L.].

SYLLABIFY [si-la'bi-fi], *v.t.* to form into syllables, pronounce in separate syllables. [L.].

SYLLABLE [si'la-bl], *n.* speech sound or group of speech sounds consisting of a single vowel, with or without a consonant or consonants, forming a word or part of a word, and pronounced as a complete unit; the group of symbols or letters giving graphic

---

The accent ' after a syllable = stress (u-pon'). The mark ‾ over a vowel = length (ā in made; õ in bone).

representation to such a sound; an utterance. SYLLABICATION [si-la-bi-kā'shn], *n.* act of forming into syllables. [Gk.].

SYLLABUB, see SILLABUB.

SYLLABUS (*pl.* syllabi, syllabuses), [si'la-bus], *n.* summary of a subject or outline of a course of studies consisting of heads denoting the main aspects to be covered; (*eccles.*) in the R. C. Church, list of erroneous beliefs condemned by the Church. [~Gk.].

SYLLEPSIS (*pl.* syllepses) [si-lep'sis], *n.* (*gram.*) figure of speech in which one word in a sentence is made to govern two others, one of them in a different or transferred sense. SYLLEPTIC(AL), *adj.* of the nature of, relating to, or implying, s. [Gk.].

SYLLOGISM [si'lo-jizm], *n.* (*log.*) form of rational argument consisting of three elements, the major and minor premises and the conclusion which follows from the first two, e.g. all men are mortal, John is a man, therefore John is mortal. SYLLOGIZE [si'lo-jīz], *v.i.* to reason by s. [Gk.].

SYLPH [silf], *n.* imaginary spirit like a woman, believed to consist of, and live in, the element of air, and to be light, quick in movement; slim woman; woman, *esp.* a young girl, with a graceful figure. SYLPH-LIKE, *adj.* slender. SYLPHID, *n.* small s. [Gk.].

SYLVAN, see SILVAN.

SYLVICULTURE [sil'vi-kul-tyoor], *n.* cultivation of trees, forestry. [L. and CULTURE].

SYM-, *pref.* together. [Gk.].

SYMBIOSIS [sim-bī-ō'sis], *n.* (*biol.*) union of two differently constituted organisms dependent for existence on each other. [Gk.].

SYMBOL [sim'bol], *n.* concrete or graphic representation of one element or aspect of reality; image or emblem standing for something else as a substitute able to evoke the emotional stimulus of the original by resemblance or suggestion of its qualities and properties; graphic sign, letter, figure signifying a sound or mathematical quantity or operation. [Gk.].

SYMBOLIC(AL) [sim-bo'lik(-al)], *adj.* relating to, serving as, a symbol, representative.

SYMBOLISM [sim'bo-lizm], *n.* process or practice of taking a fact, object or incident as a symbol of a larger or deeper source of experience; representation by means of symbols; system of symbols accepted as representing certain events and ideas; science of symbols; (*art*) use of revealed symbols in a poem or painting for the emotive, mystic power they are believed to embody.

SYMBOLIST [sim'bo-list], *n.* one who uses symbols; artist or poet of the nineteenth-century school of symbolism in France.

SYMBOLIZE [sim'bo-līz], *v.t.* to represent as a symbol, typify. SYMBOLIZATION [sim-bo-lī-zā'shn], *n.* process or act of symbolizing; representation of properties. [Gk.].

SYMMETRIC(AL) [si-me'trik(-al)], *adj.* governed by symmetry; having one half in an exact relationship of size, measurement, shape and proportion to the other half; having balanced proportions, harmonious in design, having proportionate dimensions.

SYMMETRY [si'mi-tri], *n.* precise correspondence of opposite sides in terms of shape, proportions and dimensions; regularity of form, balanced relation of proportionate parts, harmony of structural parts.

SYMPATHETIC [sim-pa-the'tik], *adj.* relating to, expressing, feeling, sympathy; reacting with mutual emotions; affected by the feelings of others, compassionate, produced by sympathy; inducing sympathy, congenial; acting in unison as the effect of a cause; **s. ink,** ink which is invisible on the paper until subjected to heat.

SYMPATHIZE [sim'pa-thīz], *v.i.* to feel or express sympathy; share an emotional experience with another without being subjected to the same causes, have an affinity.

SYMPATHY [sim'pa-thi], *n.* capacity of being susceptible to the feelings of others; compassion; correspondence of feelings experienced by two persons in relation to a third realm of experience, sensitive interaction of complementary temperaments; capacity to share the emotions of another without being subjected to the direct cause of the emotions; (*phys.*) tendency to react or unite, accordance of state or motion; (*med.*) tendency of an organ to react as a result of a condition in another organ or part. [Gk.].

SYMPHONIC [sim-fo'nik], *adj.* relating to, in the form of, resembling, a symphony; **s. poem,** (*mus.*)

composition for full orchestra, loosely resembling a symphony, but lacking divisions, and usually of an impressionistic character.

SYMPHONY [sim'fo-ni], *n.* (*mus.*) composition, usually in three or four movements, the first in sonata form, designed for an orchestra; overture or prelude; a harmony of sound or colour. [Gk.].

SYMPODIA [sim-pō'di-ah], *n.* malformation in which the lower limbs are united. [SYM- and Gk.].

SYMPOSIUM (*pl.* symposia) [sim-pō'zi-um], *n.* in ancient Greece, a feast abundantly supplied with drink, and usually accompanied by music; a gathering of philosophers; collection of opinions, often in the form of essays, of different thinkers on a specific subject. [Gk.].

SYMPTOM [simp'tom], *n.* abnormal change of condition indicating the existence of a hidden causative change, sign, evidence of organic alteration; (*path.*) change in physical or mental condition, recognized as abnormal, and accepted as evidence of the existence of disease. SYMPTOMATOLOGY [simp-to-ma-to'-lo-ji], *n.* science of the symptoms indicating disease. [Gk.].

SYMPTOMATIC [simp-to-ma'tik], *adj.* relating to, having the nature of, a symptom, indicative, evident.

SYN-, *pref.* with, together. [Gk.].

SYNAGOGUE [si'na-gog], *n.* congregation of Jews for religious purposes; place set aside for such a meeting, Jewish place of worship. [Gk.].

SYNCHRONISM [sing'kro-nizm], *n.* state of being synchronous; arrangement of events in a relation of simultaneousness; concurrence of timing relating one set of events to another which runs parallel to it. SYNCHRONISTIC [sing-kro-nis'tik], *adj.* marked by s., synchronous.

SYNCHRONIZE [sing'kro-nīz], *v.t. and i.* to cause to occur at the same time, to make coincide; regulate so as to keep time together; occur or exist simultaneously; effect a relationship in timing between two parallel sets of events; (*cinema*) fit a silent film with sound effects; cause sound effects selected as relevant to a film or part of a film to coincide with the film's action. SYNCHRONIZATION [sing-kro-nī-zā'shn], *n.* fact or process of being synchronized; concurrence of events in time. [Gk.].

SYNCHRONOUS [sing'kro-nŏŏs], *adj.* occurring at the same time, simultaneous; (*cinema*) fitted with sound. [Gk.].

SYNCHROTON [sing'krō-ton], *n.* (*phys.*) apparatus for accelerating electrons or nuclear particles to very high speeds. [SYNCHRO(NIZE) and (ELEC)TRON].

SYNCOPATE [sing'kō-pāt], *v.t. and i.* to compose or play (a piece of music) so that the beats of the anticipated regular rhythm are for the most part omitted and the accents placed on the off-beat or half-beat, give a jazzy lilt to; compose or play with syncopation; (*gram.*) shorten by leaving out a syllable. [L.].

SYNCOPE [sing'ko-pi], *n.* fainting fit, swoon. [Gk.].

SYNDIC [sin'dik], *n.* an administrative official, *esp.* one having the powers of a magistrate, in various European countries; (in Cambridge University) member of a special committee of the Senate. [Gk.].

SYNDICALISM [sin'di-ka-lizm], *n.* theory which advocates the control of political and economic power by organizations of producers. [Fr.].

SYNDICATE (1) [sin'di-kat], *n.* group of business men each of whom puts a certain sum of money into a commercial project, *esp.* in the initial stages of the formation of a limited liability company; body of syndics, senate, council. SYNDICATE (2) [sin'di-kāt], *v.t.* to form into a s.; publish simultaneously in a number of newspapers.

SYNDROME [sin'drŏm], *n.* (*med.*) the combination of several symptoms in disease. [Gk.].

SYNECDOCHE [si-nek'do-ki], *n.* (*rhet.*) figure of speech by which a whole stands for a part or a part for the whole. [Gk.].

SYNOD [si'nod], *n.* (*eccles.*) a council of the clergy, *esp.* of Presbyterians who are delegates from their presbyteries; assembly, convention. SYNODAL, *adj.* relating to a s. SYNODIC(AL) [si-no'dik(-al)], *adj.* relating to, sanctioned by, a s.; (*astron.*) relating to the conjunction of two heavenly bodies. [Gk.].

SYNONYM [si'no-nim], *n.* word having the same meaning as another; word having the same general sense as another but possessing particular implications. SYNONYMITY, SYNONYMY [si-no'ni-mi], *n.* condition or quality of expressing the same meaning by different words. [Gk.].

SYNONYMOUS [si-no'ni-mŏŏs], *adj.* having the

nature of a synonym, having the same general sense, identical in meaning.

SYNOPSIS (*pl.* **synopses**) [si-nop'sis], *n.* statement in summary form giving a brief account of a whole by means of a selection from the main parts or heads, outline. [Gk.].

SYNOPTIC(AL) [si-nop'tik(-al)], *adj.* having the characteristics of a synopsis, relating to a synopsis; **s. gospels,** (*N.T.*) gospels of Matthew, Mark and Luke, which give a similar general view of the life of Christ. SYNOPTICALLY, *adv.* in a s. manner, by means of an outline. SYNOPTIC, SYNOPTIST, *n.* one of the writers of the s. gospels. [Gk.].

SYNOVIA [si-nō'vi-ah], *n.* (*anat.*) fluid resembling the white of egg, secreted into the cavities of joints as a natural lubricant. SYNOVIAL, *adj.* relating to, affected by, s. [SYN and L.].

SYNOVITIS [si-nō-vi'tis], *n.* (*path.*) inflammation of the synovial membrane. [*Prec.* and Gk.].

SYNTACTICAL [sin-tak'ti-kal], *adj.* relating to syntax; according to the rules of syntax.

SYNTAX [sin'taks], *n.* (*gram.*) arrangement and mutual relationship of words in a sentence; rules dealing with the order of words in a sentence established by accepted usage. [Gk.].

SYNTHESIS (*pl.* **syntheses**) [sin'the-sis], *n.* (*chem.*) process of building up substances into compounds; (*philos.*) process of testing and working with simple propositions until out of a complex series a final conclusion is deduced; final stage in a thought-process which follows the thesis and antithesis and embodies the best elements of these two; the opposite of analysis; (*surg.*) reunion of dissected parts. SYNTHESIZE, *v.t.* to make a s. of, introduce as part of a s., unite in a s., combine into a whole; make artificially. [Gk.].

SYNTHETIC(AL) [sin-the'tik(-al)], *adj.* pertaining or relating to synthesis; consisting in synthesis or composition; (*chem.*) artificially manufactured as a compound; (*coll.*) bogus. SYNTHETIZE [sin'the-tiz], *v.t.* to synthesize. [Gk.].

SYNTONIC [sin-to'nik], *adj.* (*radio*) tuned to the same wavelength. SYNTONIZE [sin'to-niz], *v.t.* (*radio*) to tune (a radio set). SYNTONY [sin'to-ni], *n.* (*radio*) correspondence of frequencies of a radio receiving set and transmitter. [Gk.].

SYPHILIS [si'fi-lis], *n.* a venereal disease caused by a

parasite, and characterized by skin affections and, finally, paralysis. SYPHILIZATION [si-fi-li-zā'shn], *n.* state of being infected by s.; process of inoculating against s. [From the title of a poem published in 1530 by G. Fracastoro].

SYPHON, see SIPHON.

SYREN, see SIREN.

SYRIAC (1) [si'ri-ak], *adj.* relating to, written in, coming from, Syria or Syriac. SYRIAC (2), *n.* language of Syria, *esp.* the ancient dialect of Aramaic. [Gk.].

SYRINGA [si-ring'gah], *n.* (*bot.*) genus of plants containing the lilac; (*pop.*) the mock-orange, with scented white flowers. [Gk.].

SYRINGE (1) [si'rinj], *n.* instrument in the form of a cylinder fitted with a piston or rubber bulb by means of which liquid is drawn in by suction and ejected by pressure through a nozzle; **hypodermic s.,** s. fitted with a sharp needle for forcing injections under the skin. SYRINGE (2), *v.t.* to spray with water or other liquid by means of a s. [Gk.].

SYRINX [si'ringks], *n.* wind-instrument consisting of a set of hollow tubes, panpipe. [Gk.].

SYRUP, SIRUP [si'rup], *n.* a solution of water and sugar; liquid extracted from the sugar cane. [OFr. from Arab.].

SYSTALTIC [sis-tal'tik], *adj.* contracting, as in the case of the muscular contraction of the heart.

SYSTEM [sis'tem], *n.* group of units, objects, ideas or phenomena, functioning in association as a whole; body of related principles, classificatory scheme, plan of categories listed in a possible working relationship; method of procedure worked out in accordance with an accepted set of principles; the human body as a functioning whole, the constitution. [Gk.].

SYSTEMATIC [sis-te-ma'tik], *adj.* relating to, consisting of, based on, a system, functioning according to plan.

SYSTEMATIZE [sis'te-ma-tiz], *v.t.* to reduce to system or regular method, build up into a system.

SYSTOLE [sis'to-li], *n.* (*anat., physiol.*) regular muscular contraction of the heart and arteries (alternating with diastole) which pumps the blood outward into circulation. SYSTOLIC [sis-to'lik], *adj.* (*anat., physiol.*) relating to s. or contraction. [Gk.].

SYSTYLE [sis'til], *n.* (*arch.*) the placing of columns the distance of two diameters apart from each other; a building having columns so spaced. [Gk.].

T

T [tē], twentieth letter of the alphabet; **to a T,** exactly; **to cross one's t's,** to be precise in attention to details.

TA [tah], *int.* (*coll.*) thank you! [Childish].

TAAL [tahl], *n.* Dutch dialect spoken in South Africa, Afrikaans. [Du.].

TAB (1) [tab], *n.* tongue of a shoe; end of a bootlace or shoelace; tag, flap, strip of material sewn on as a distinctive mark; (*slang*) check, record; **to keep a t. on,** to keep a check on. TAB (2) [*pres.pt.* TABBING, *pret. and p.pt.* TABBED], to provide with a t. [Unkn.].

TABARD [ta'bahd], *n.* military tunic or mantle reaching below the loins, sleeveless, but open at the sides, and worn over armour by knights of the feudal era; coat of a herald. [OFr.].

TABARET [ta'ba-ret], *n.* strong fabric of satin-striped silk, used for furniture upholstery. [Uncert.].

TABBY [ta'bi], *n.* kind of watered silk with a coarse texture; cat which has a coat mainly light brown or grey in colour but marked with darker patches or stripes, a brindled cat, *esp.* a female cat; woman who gossips spitefully; mixture of lime and gravel which hardens as concrete. [Span. from Arab.].

TABERNACLE (1) [ta'ber-na-kl], *n.* temporary shelter, *esp.* one used by the nomad Israelites in which to worship; place or house of worship; niche for a saint's statue; (*eccles.*) figured chest kept on the altar of a R.C. church to contain the consecrated elements of the Eucharist; (*fig.*) the human body as a temporary receptacle for the spirit. TABERNACLE-WORK, (*arch.*) decorative carvings in the form of canopies. TABERNACLE (2), *v.t.* to provide with a t.

TABERNACULAR [ta-ber-na'kyōō-lah(r)], *adj.* relating to a t.; (*arch.*) formed with delicate tracery; latticed. [L.].

TABES [tā'bēz], *n.* (*path.*) a wasting away of the body, emaciation; locomotor ataxy. TABESCENT [ta-be'sent], *adj.* having a tendency to waste away, emaciated. [~L.].

TABETIC [ta-be'tik], *n. and adj.* (*path.*) (person) suffering from tabes.

TABLE (1) [tā'bl], *n.* piece of furniture consisting of a flat surface on supports or legs to a height convenient to a person sitting on a chair to eat or work on; any flat surface; group of people sitting at a table; food prepared for a meal, meals; flat slab of wood, stone or metal, *esp.* one bearing an inscription, a tablet; inscription on such a tablet; list of facts, synopsis, index; (*arch.*) a rectangular, ornamental unit; (*math.*) system of numbers learnt by heart to facilitate calculations; **at t.,** at meals; **the Round T.,** order of knights said to have been instituted by King Arthur; **to turn the tables on,** to reverse the advantage of. TABLE-BOOK, small book containing the mathematical tables of multiplication and weights and measures. TABLE-CUT, *adj.* of a diamond etc. cut with a broad rectangular flat surface. TABLE-MONEY, allowance granted to general and flag-officers in the Army and Navy for official hospitality. TABLE-TALK, conversation of the trivial, gossipy kind spoken at t. or meals. TABLE-TENNIS, a form of indoor tennis played with a small celluloid ball and wooden bats on a t. TABLE-TURNING, act or process of causing a t. to move, professedly by spiritualistic agency. TABLE (2), *v.t.* to

---

The accent´ after a syllable = stress (u-pon´). The mark ‾ over a vowel = length (ā in made; ō in bone).

form into, or place upon, a t.; write a list of, or add to a t.; submit for discussion. [L.].

TABLEAU [tab'lō], *n.* a representation, picture; picture or composition represented by a group of posed persons. [Fr.].

TABLECLOTH [tā'bl-kloth], *n.* cloth for covering a table.

TABLE D'HOTE, table d'hôte, [tahbl-dōt'], *n. and adj.* (restaurant meal) costing a fixed price, and composed of a number of courses chosen by the management. [Fr.].

TABLELAND [tā'bl-land], *n.* stretch of elevated flat land, plateau.

TABLESPOON [tā'bl-spōōn], *n.* large spoon for the table. TABLESPOONFUL, *n.* amount a t. can hold; half a fluid ounce.

TABLET (1) [tab'let], *n.* monument in the form of a flat slab of wood, metal or stone bearing an inscription fixed to a wall; something flat on which to write, a note-pad; medicine or sweetmeat in a flat round form. TABLET (2), *v.t.* to provide with a t. [MedL.].

TABLOID [tab'loid], *n.* (*prot.*) small round medicinal lozenge, tablet; newspaper which provides news in a simple, concentrated and usually sensational form. [TABLE and Gk.].

TABOO (1) [ta-bōō'], *adj.* banned, prohibited by convention, forbidden by the custom of society. TABOO (2), *n.* a prohibition of using or touching an object or person based on religion or magic; ban or prohibition sanctioned by social convention. TABOO (3) (*pret. and p.pt.* TABOOED), *v.t.* to prohibit, ban, forbid. [Polynesian].

TABOR [tā'ber], *n.* small drum used to provide a rhythmic accompaniment to a pipe. [OFr. from Arab.].

TABOURET [ta'bōō-ret], *n.* small four-legged seat without arms or back, low stool. [OFr.].

TABULAR [ta'byōō-ler], *adj.* arranged in the form of a table; included in a list; having a flat surface. TABULARIZE, *v.t.* to tabulate. [~L.].

TABULATE [ta'byōō-lāt], *v.t.* to arrange in tables or synopses; provide with a flat surface; operate a tabulator. [L.].

TACIT [ta'sit], *adj.* implied, not expressed directly, understood even though left unspoken; silent. [L.].

TACITURN [ta'si-tern], *adj.* naturally inclined to speak little or to remain silent, not talkative. [L.].

TACK (1) [tak], *n.* short nail with a broad head; long loose stitch in needlework making a temporary fastening; (*naut.*) course of a ship running in an oblique direction to the wind; side of a ship receiving the wind; rope for fastening the fore corner at the bottom of a sail; corner of the sail fastened by such a rope; shift of direction due to a swing over of the sails calculated to obtain the full benefit of the wind; (*fig.*) course of action; (*slang*) food in a semi-liquid state; contemptuous term for food of any kind; **t. room,** part of a stable where saddles etc. are kept. TACK (2), *v.t. and i.* to fasten or attach by means of a t. or tacks; stitch together with long loose stitches in a temporary way; attach, append; (*naut.*) cause a sailing vessel to shift its direction by putting the sails in a position to obtain the full benefit of the wind; chop and change a line of action. TACKING, *n.* act or process of changing a ship's course; temporary loose stitching. TACKY, *adj.* slightly adhesive, sticky. [AFr.].

TACKLE (1) [ta'kl], *n.* simple mechanism for moving heavy weights, *esp.* a system of ropes and pulleys; any manipulative apparatus or set of instruments, gear, equipment; (*football*) an attempt to rob an opponent of the ball. TACKLE (2), *v.t.* to manipulate by means of t.; (*fig.*) grapple with, deal with, undertake, attempt to solve; (football) attempt to rob (an opponent) of the ball. TACKLING, *n.* (*football*) act of tackling an opponent. [ME.].

TACT [takt], *n.* ability to respond to a person or situation so that the least offence is given, faculty to foresee awkward effects of speech or action and thus lessen social friction, discretion, ingenuity which provides extempore forms of expression calculated to lessen the shock of unpalatable truth. [L.].

TACTFUL [takt'fool], *adj.* possessing tact.

TACTIC(S) [tak'tik(s)], *n.* (*usually pl.*) art or science of manoeuvring forces in battle according to established principles; mode of operation; art of handling a situation adroitly. TACTICIAN [tak-ti'shn], *n.* one expert in t. [Gk.].

TACTILE [tak'til], *adj.* affecting, relating to, the sense of touch; tangible. TACTILITY [tak-ti'li-ti], *n.*

condition of being t.; tangibleness; perceptibility to touch. [L.].

TACTLESS [takt'les], *adj.* characterized by absence of tact, destitute of tact.

TACTUAL [tak'tyōō-al], *adj.* relating to touch; consisting in, or derived from, touch.

TADPOLE [tad'pōl], *n.* frog, toad etc. in its first state after leaving the egg, with a long tail and external gills. [ME.].

TA'EN [tān], *p.pt. contracted poetical and dialectal form of* TAKEN.

TAFFETA [ta'fi-tah], *n.* fabric of fine silk having a lustrous texture. [Pers.].

TAFFRAIL [taf'rl], *n.* handrail placed round a ship's stern. [Du.].

TAFFY [ta'fi], *n.* (*coll.*) Welshman. [Wel.].

TAG (1) [tag], *n.* that which is tacked on; supplementary piece attached to the end or edge of something; loop at the back of a boot; metal clip fastened round the tip of a piece of string or bootlace; piece of torn material hanging loose; actor's catchword, cue; short refrain of a poem or song; cliché quotation; game of pursuit played by children. TAG-RAG, lowest class of people, riff-raff. TAG (2) (*pres.pt.* TAGGING, *pret. and p.pt.* TAGGED), *v.t.* to provide with a t.; tack on, append; join together (verses). [~Swed.].

TAI, THAI [tī], *n.(pl.)* race of people inhabiting the Indo-Chinese peninsula; the Siamese. TAIC [tah'ik], *adj. and n.* pertaining to, the language of, the T. [Chin.].

TAIL (1) [tāl], *n.* part of the backbone in vertebrates which extends beyond the trunk and which is usually long and flexible; projecting feathers at the posterior extremity of a bird; finny extremity of a fish; any object which has the characteristics of an animal's t., any trailing length, appendage; lowest or hindermost part of anything; **to have the t. between the legs,** to be disheartened; **to turn t.,** to retreat in flight; (*pl.*) side of a coin on the reverse of the head; (*coll.*) t.-coat; **tails up,** cheerful. TAIL-BOARD, movable board at the back of a cart. TAIL-COAT, coat with long tails for formal occasions. TAIL-END, extreme end. TAIL-FLOAT, (*aeron.*) landing float at the rear of a seaplane. TAIL-LIGHT, red light attached to the rear of a vehicle as a warning to following traffic. TAIL-PIECE, (*mus.*) piece of ebony designed to take the strings of an instrument; (*print.*) ornamental design at the end of a chapter or of a book; closing remark or quotation. TAIL-RACE, stream of water which runs below the mill-wheel. TAIL-SKID, (*aeron.*) sturdy metal support at the rear of a plane which acts as a stabilizer when taxi-ing. TAIL-SPIN, (*aeron.*) kind of spinning dive; also (*fig.*). TAIL (2), *v.t. and i.* to provide with a t.; deprive of a t., *esp.* to cut off a stem or stalk; track closely, trail; **to t. away,** to fade away; straggle; **to t. off,** to fall behind, deteriorate. TAILED, *adj.* possessing a t. [OE.].

TAIL (3), *n.* limitation; **estate in t.,** (*leg.*) estate limited to a particular line of descendants. [OFr.].

TAILOR (1) [tā'ler], *n.* person who is expert in making outer clothes for wear by cutting, sewing and fitting the cloth; retailer who sells men's suits. TAILOR-BIRD, Asiatic bird which sews together leaves with silk and fibres by means of its bill in order to make a nest. TAILOR-MADE, made by a t. who gives personal attention to the fittings, *esp.* of women's costumes cut in a man's style. TAILOR (2), *v.t. and i.* to work as a t., make in the manner of a t.; provide (a person) with t.-made clothes. [OFr.].

TAINT (1) [tānt], *n.* tincture or trace of decay, infection, corruption; pollution, contamination; moral blemish, stain on a reputation. TAINT (2), *v.t. and i.* to impregnate with something which corrupts or pollutes, infect with decay, make putrid; become putrid, be affected by decaying matter. [Fr.].

TAKE (1) (*pret.* took, *p.pt.* taken) [tāk], *v.t.* to carry away in the hands, get hold of and remove bodily, seize; transfer into one's keeping; catch, trap, make prisoner; earn, win in cash; grasp mentally, understand; gain possession of and use, adopt as one's own, undertake, engage in as an occupation; swallow, inhale; choose, select; endure, withstand; experience, assume in the mind; perform, carry out (an action); test, ascertain, estimate; record, write down; photograph; rent, engage, hire; *v.i.* to be effective, work according to plan; please, have a good reception; photograph; **to t. after,** to have a facial or other resemblance to; **to t. away,** to remove, deduct; deprive of; **to t. back,** to retract; withdraw; **to t. care,** to be cautious, beware; **to t. care of,** to be in charge of; **to t. down,** to remove by lifting down, transfer to a lower level; pull down, allow to fall down; write down; **to t. for**, to judge, consider; **to t. for a ride**, (slang) to fool; (U.S.) kidnap and kill; **to t. for granted**, to assume; **to t. hold**, to grasp; gain influence over; **to t. in**, to enclose, encompass; comprise; impose upon, deceive; give a place to, admit, give comfort or welcome to; grasp intellectually; **to t. off**, to doff; mimic, imitate; subtract; (of an aircraft) become airborne; **to t. on**, to undertake; employ, hire; challenge; (coll.) exhibit distress; **to t. oneself off**, to depart, withdraw; **to t. out**, to extract; obtain (a licence, policy, shares etc.); accompany out of doors, escort, entertain; **to t. over**, to assume control of; **to t. place**, to happen, occur; **to t. to**, to feel an attraction, have an affinity for; **to t. to heart**, to feel sorrow, deeply; **to t. up**, to raise, lift; underwrite; engross, absorb; occupy, fill; engage in; pick up; resume; arrest; **to t. up with**, to become associated with; **to t. upon oneself**, to assume responsibility for; **t. it from me**, believe me; **to t. the chair**, to act as chairman; **to t. it out of**, to get one's own back on, exhaust. TAKE-IN, (coll.) swindle. TAKE-OFF, n. act of taking off; the rising of an aircraft from the ground or sea into the air; the manner in which the feet and body etc. are disposed in the act of jumping; parody. TAKE (2), n. amount taken, received or caught; (cinema) the photographing of a single scene; (print.) compositor's share of text to be set up; section of a press message. TAKER, n. one who takes or receives; one who catches; one who accepts the odds laid in betting. [OScand.].

TAKEN [tā'ken], p.pt. of TAKE. [ME.].

TAKING (1) [tā'king], n. act of one who takes, process of gaining a required effect; seizure, capture; (pl.) earnings, cash receipts; (coll.) mental distress. TAKING (2), adj. attractive, fetching.

TALC [talk], n. (min.) a hydrated silicate of magnesium, used as a fine dusting powder; laminated steatite; (pop.) mica. TALCOSE, TALCOUS, adj. relating to, containing or composed of, t. [Arab.].

TALCUM [tal'kum], n. French chalk, powdered talc.

TALE [tāl], n. narrative of a series of events, real or imaginary, story; account of an incident; legend; report, rumour; anecdote; **to tell tales**, to inform. TALE-BEARER, one who tells tales with malicious intent. TALE-BEARING, act or practice of telling tales with mischievous intent. [OE.].

TALENT [ta'lent], n. natural aptitude for a specific form of activity, congenital faculty of a creative nature, a particular ability, skill; formerly, a standard weight or money unit, its value differing in various historical periods. TALENTED, adj. possessing talents; having natural ability or skill. [Gk.].

TALISMAN (pl. talismans) [ta'liz-man], n. small object superstitiously considered to possess a protective or lucky influence over the owner, amulet, charm. [Gk.].

TALK (1) [tawk], v.t. and i. to express in words, speak; engage in social intercourse by means of speech; disclose information; **to t. at**, to address obliquely, harangue; **to t. big**, to boast; **to t. down**, to silence by loud or continual talking; **to t. down to**, to address in condescendingly simple language; **to t. of**, to discuss; relate, tell; **to t. over**, to discuss; persuade; **to t. round**, to evade the real issue of; argue into agreement; **to t. to**, to scold. TALK (2), n. act of talking, social intercourse by means of speech, mutual discussion, conversation; the subject of a discussion; short informal lecture; rumour, gossip. SMALL-TALK, trivial conversation. TALKIES, n.(pl.) (coll.) cinematograph pictures synchronized with sound. TALKY-TALKY, n. (coll.) trivial or worthless t. [ME.].

TALKATIVE [taw'ka-tiv], adj. fond of talking, given to much talking.

TALKING (1) [taw'king], n. act of speaking, of expressing in words. TALKING-POINT, topic on which one can enlarge in order to sell goods or to persuade a waverer to come to a definite decision. TALKING-TO, scolding. TALKING (2), adj. having the power of speech, able to t.; given to talking, loquacious; expressive.

TALL (1) [tawl], adj. above the average in height, relatively high in stature; having an extended height; big; (coll.) almost incredible, extravagant. TALL (2), adv. (slang) boastfully. [Uncert.].

TALLBOY [tawl'boi], n. high chest of drawers.

TALLOW [ta'lō], n. animal fat melted down, used for candles or lubrication. TALLOW-CHANDLER, person who manufactures and sells t. candles. TALLOW-FACED, adj. having a pale, bloodless com-plexion. TALLOW (2), adj. made of t. TALLOW (3), v.t. to grease with t.

TALLY (1) [ta'li], n. piece of wood bearing notches corresponding to those on a similar piece of wood, thus forming a check or account of an amount, number or reckoning; duplicated account, ticket, label, tag etc. TALLY-MAN, person who keeps or sells goods for a tally-shop. TALLY-SHOP, shop where accounts are kept by means of a t., payments being made on an instalment system. TALLY (2), v.t. and i. to record by means of a t., reckon, mark with equal notches; agree, correspond, esp. in number. [OFr.].

TALLY-HO (1) [ta-li-hō'], n. huntsman's call on sighting a fox. TALLY-HO (2), v.i. to utter a t. [Fr.].

TALMUD [tal'mud], n. the fundamental code of the Jewish civil and canonical law. [Heb.].

TALON [ta'lon], n. claw of a bird of prey. [Fr.].

TAMARIND [ta'ma-rind], n. a tropical leguminous tree which bears yellow flowers. [Arab. and Hind.].

TAMARISK [ta'ma-risk], n. an ornamental evergreen tree or shrub; any of the sixty-four species of Tamarix. [L.].

TAMBOUR [tam'boor], n. small drum, tambourine; bass drum; frame on which embroidery is done; (arch.) round stone like a drum forming part of a column. [Arab.].

TAMBOURINE [tam-boo-rēn'], n. light, shallow drum with a single head and tinkling disks of metal attached to the sides, used for beating out a rhythm as an accompaniment to a dance. [Fr.].

TAME (1) [tām], adj. made or disciplined to be responsive to authority, esp. to human control; having a nature freed of savagery; subdued, submissive; domesticated; passive; insipid, dull. TAME (2), v.t. to make t., accustom to human command and influence, domesticate, make obedient; subdue, curb. [OE.].

TAMIL (1) [tah'mil], n. a Dravidian language spoken in Southern India and Northern Ceylon; one whose native tongue is Tamil. TAMIL (2), adj. of, or pertaining to, T. or the Tamils. [Native].

TAMIS [ta'mi], n. a worsted cloth used for straining sauces; a strainer made of t. [Fr.].

TAMMANY [ta'ma-ni], n. originally a charitable society in New York, now the central organization of the Democratic Party with its headquarters in Tammany Hall.

TAMMY [ta'mi], n. (coll.) tam-o'-shanter. [Next].

TAM-O'-SHANTER [tam-o-shan'ter], n. broad flat cap or bonnet of knitted wool. [Tam o' Shanter, in the poem by Robert Burns].

TAMP [tamp], v.t. to stop up, with a plug of clay, a hole bored in a rock for blasting. TAMPING, n. act of filling up a hole in a rock for the purpose of blasting it; plug used in such a process. [Uncert.].

TAMPER [tam'per], v.i. **to t. with**, to interfere, meddle with; corrupt. [Var. of TEMPER].

TAMPION, see TOMPION.

TAMPON [tam'pon], n. (surg.) plug for stopping bleeding. [OFr.].

TAN (1) [tan], n. a tone of brown imparted to the skin by the sun; colour of tan, a golden- or nut-brown; bark bruised and used in the process of tanning; discarded bark from which tannic acid has been extracted. TAN (2), adj. having the colour of t.; golden-brown. TAN (3) (pres.pt. TANNING, pret. and p.pt. TANNED), v.t. and i. to convert (leather) by steeping in tannic acid; make brown; (slang) beat, thrash; become brown in complexion from exposure to the sun's rays. [Fr.].

TANDEM (1) [tan'dem], n. carriage with two horses harnessed one behind the other; bicycle made for two, with the seats one behind the other. TANDEM (2), adj. and adv. made for two people who sit one behind the other; (placed or accommodating) one behind or after another. [L.].

TANG (1) [tang], n. a strong flavour usually of an astringent nature; penetrating smell; prolongation of a blade which fits into the hilt or handle. TANG (2), v.t. to provide with a spike, fit into a handle or shaft. [OIcel.].

TANG (3), v.t. and i. to clash together; clang; cause to ring loudly; ring loudly with a metallic sound. TANG (4), n. a harsh, clanging sound. [Imitative].

TANGENT (1) [tan'jent], n. meeting at a point without intersecting. TANGENT (2), n. a junction at a point without intersection; (geom.) straight line which touches a curve without cutting t; **to go off at a t.**, (fig.) to wander from the point, to forsake the subject (of discussion) for a related one. TANGENTIAL [tan-jen′shal], *adj.* relating to, or in the direction of, a t. [L.].

TANGERINE [tan-je-rēn′], *n.* a native of Tangier; species of small, scented orange.

TANGIBLE [tan′ji-bl], *adj.* capable of being touched, experienced through the sense of touch, material, concrete; (*fig.*) definite, clear in outline, not vague in form; not visionary. [LL.].

TANGLE (1) [tang′gl], *v.t. and i.* to form into a tangle; become tangled. **TANGLE** (2), *n.* disorderly knot of threads, mass of interwoven strands hard to disengage; state of confusion. [~Dan.].

TANGO (1) [tang′gō], *n.* an Argentine dance; French version of this dance. **TANGO** (2), *v.i.* to dance the t. [SpanAmer.].

TANK (1) [tangk], *n.* large receptacle, usually rectangular and made of metal, for storing water, oil or gas, a cistern, basin, reservoir; chamber in a locomotive for storing water; (*milit.*) heavily armoured tracked vehicle mounted with guns and used in attack. **TANK-ENGINE**, small type of locomotive requiring no fuel tender. **TANK** (2), *v.i.* **to t. up**, to fill the t. of a car or engine with fuel. **TANKAGE**, *n.* (space for) storage of water or fuel in tanks; the cost of this. [Portug.].

TANKARD [tang′kerd], *n.* vessel for containing drink, usually made of metal and with a capacity of half a pint or a pint. [OFr.].

TANKER [tang′ker], *n.* ship or truck built for transporting liquids, *esp.* petroleum, in bulk.

TANNER [ta′ner], *n.* one whose craft is to tan hides.

TANNERY [ta′ne-ri], *n.* workshop used for tanning; process of tanning.

TANNIC [ta′nik], *adj.* relating to, or derived from, tannin; **t. acid**, a white soluble astringent solid obtained from oak-galls, used in making leather, ink etc.; any of a number of other astringent vegetable substances, of various origins.

TANNIN [ta′nin], *n.* any of a group of astringent vegetable substances capable of tanning hides etc., *esp.* that obtained from oak-galls; tannic acid.

TANSY [tan′zi], *n.* (*bot.*) a bitter aromatic plant bearing clusters of rayless yellow flowers. [OFr.].

TANTALIZE [tan′ta-līz], *v.t.* to raise to a pitch of frustrated expectation by exhibiting that which fulfils a desire but keeping it out of reach, torment deliberately by continually retracting a proffered promise. [TANTALUS].

TANTALUM [tan′ta-lum], *n.* metallic element denoted by Ta, used in making lamp filaments. [*Next*].

TANTALUS [tan′ta-lus], *n.* decanter stand with a special locking device; genus of storks, the wood-ibis. [Gk. *Tantalos*, King of Phrygia.].

TANTAMOUNT [tan′ta-mownt], *adj.* equal, equivalent, in value or signification, having a similar effect. [AFr.].

TANTIVY (1) [tan-ti′vi], *adv.* (*archaic*) with great speed. **TANTIVY** (2), *n.* a hunting cry; flourish on a hunting-horn. **TANTIVY** (3), *adj.* swift, pelting. [Imitative].

TANTRUM [tan′trum], *n.* outburst of ill temper. [Unkn.].

TAOISM [tah′ō-izm], *n.* religion of China founded on principles traditionally established by Lao-tze. [Chin.].

TAP (1) [tap], *n.* safety device consisting of a short piece of piping fitted with a control screw which stops up or releases the flow of a liquid held in storage; tool for cutting the thread of an internal screw; tap-room; special beer or liquor stored in a vat or cask; **on t.**, stored in a cask ready to hand; (*slang*) always available. **TAP-ROOM**, bar in a public-house in which casks of beer are stored and where cheaper drinks are served. **TAP-ROOT**, straight enlarged root tapering towards the base. **TAP** (2) (*pres.pt.* TAPPING, *pret. and p.pt.* TAPPED), *v.t.* to fit with a t.; draw (liquor) from a cask fitted with a t., broach; penetrate in order to make use of available resources; (*slang*) extract money from; draw accumulated fluid from the body; (*elect.*) to connect an external conductor to some part of an existing circuit; **to t. a line**, to listen secretly to another's conversation over a telephone. **TAPPING**, *n.* (*surg.*) operation of draining accumulated fluid from the body. [OE.].

TAP (3) (*pres.pt.* tapping, *pret. and p.pt.* tapped), *v.t. and i.* to hit by means of a tap, strike lightly and quickly, touch, making a brief impact; insert a tapping in; knock lightly, give a series of taps, rap. **TAP** (4), *n.* light blow, contact with a small area for

the shortest possible time; sound made by such an impact; (*milit.*) lights-out signal. **TAP-DANCE** (1), *n.* dance accompanied by syncopated music to which heel and toe are tapped in rhythm. **TAP-DANCE** (2), *v.i.* to perform a tap-dance. [OFr.].

TAPE (1) [tāp], *n.* narrow strip of material, usually of cotton fabric or silk, used for fastening; roll or strip of paper on which are recorded messages transmitted by an electrical telegraphic system; **red t.**, dilatoriness and enslavement to routine arising from traditional usage and bureaucratic outlook. **TAPE-MACHINE**, instrument which receives and records on a paper t. messages transmitted by an electrical telegraphic system. **TAPE-MEASURE**, t. marked with a measure of length, used in dressmaking. **TAPE** (2), *v.t.* to fasten by means of t.; measure; **to have (someone, something) taped**, (*slang*) to understand (someone, something) completely. [OE.].

TAPER (1) [tā′per], *n.* thin wax candle; small light. **TAPER** (2), *adj.* having a long shape gradually narrowing to a point at one end. **TAPER** (3), *v.t. and i.* to cause to t.; narrow gradually to a point at one end; **to t. off**, (*fig.*) to decrease gradually. **TAPERING**, *adj.* becoming gradually smaller at one end, narrowing in one direction down to a point. [OE.].

TAPESTRY [ta′pes-tri], *n.* hand-woven fabric of linen, wool, silk etc., into which are worked designs, patterns, pictures, by means of coloured thread, the whole piece being used for adorning walls etc.; piece of textile in imitation of this, manufactured by machinery. **TAPESTRIED**, *adj.* hung with t. [OFr.].

TAPEWORM [tāp′werm], *n.* ribbon-shaped worm parasitic in the intestines.

TAPIOCA [ta-pi-ō′kah], *n.* grains from the root of the cassava; **t. pudding**, pudding made from t. baked in milk. [Braz.].

TAPIR [tā′per, ta′pēer], *n.* one of a genus of ungulates allied to the rhinoceros. [Braz.].

TAPIS [ta′pē], *n.* the cover of a council table; **(up)on the t.**, under consideration. [Fr.].

TAPPET [ta′pit], *n.* projecting arm or lever of a machine transmitting movement to another part. [TAP (3)].

TAPSTER [tap′ster], *n.* man employed to draw ale or other liquor, barman. [OE.].

TAR (1) [tah(r)], *n.* thick, black, sticky liquid with a resinous smell, obtained by the destructive distillation of wood or coal, used in the preparation of road surfaces, antiseptics and preservatives; **touch of the t. brush**, physical attribute denoting negro antecedents. **TAR** (2) (*pres.pt.* TARRING, *pret. and p.pt.* TARRED), *v.t.* to coat or smear with t.; **to t. with the same brush**, to give the same characteristics to. [OE.].

TAR (3), *n.* (*coll.*) sailor. [TAR(PAULIN)].

TARANTELLA [ta-ran-te′lah], *n.* vigorous Neapolitan dance; music in 6-8 time adapted to this dance. [It.].

TARANTULA [ta-ran′tyōō-lah], *n.* large venomous spider of Southern Europe and elsewhere. [MedL.].

TARAXACUM [ta-rak′sa-kum], *n.* (*bot.*) genus of plants including the dandelion. [MedL.].

TARBOOSH [tah-bōōsh′], *n.* brimless cap of felt, fez; basic support of the turban. [Arab.].

TARDY [tah′di], *adj.* slow to act, dilatory, sluggish; given to delaying, late in performance, action or arrival, behind time. [L.].

TARE (1) [tāer], *n.* weed which grows in cornfields, a vetch. [ME.].

TARE (2), *n.* difference between gross and net weight, weight of a container and packing; unladen weight of a goods vehicle; (*comm.*) allowance on dutiable goods for weight of packing. **TARE** (3), *v.t.* to calculate in respect of t. [Arab.].

TARGE [tahj], *n.* (*archaic*) small shield. [OFr.].

TARGET [tah′get], *n.* shield or buckler of a small kind; mark to aim at, *esp.* a board bearing a series of concentric circles with the smallest one in the centre known as a bull; the objective of an air-raid; (*fig.*) aim, objective, *esp.* a fixed quantity to be produced; **t. area**, area in which a t. stands. [OFr.].

TARIFF (1) [ta′rif], *n.* list of goods or articles chargeable for duty on import or export; list of items or services with their respective cost, *esp.* the price list of a hotel. **TARIFF-WALL**, means of checking imports by setting high duties payable on foreign goods. **TARIFF** (2), *v.t.* to draw up, list, in the form of a t. [Arab.].

TARLATAN [tah′la-tan], *n.* kind of muslin with an open-work texture. [Fr.].

TARMAC [tah′mak], *n.* (*prot.*) road material of tar

and macadam; aerodrome runway of this material. [TAR (1) and MAC(ADAM)].

TARN [tahn], *n.* small lake on a mountain side or moor. [~OIcel.].

TARNISH (1) [tah′nish], *v.t. and i.* to cause to become dull of surface by exposure to heat, air or damp, spoil by affecting the lustre of, sully; become tarnished; (*fig.*) detract from the purity of. TARNISH (2), *n.* film of colour forming on a metallic surface when exposed to the action of heat or damp; (*fig.*) a dulling or tainting of qualities, blemish. [Fr.].

TAROT [tah′rō], *n.* pack of seventy-eight playing cards, used *esp.* in fortune-telling; game played with these. [It.].

TARPAULIN [tah-paw′lin], *n.* canvas treated with a coating of tar to render it waterproof. [TAR (1) and PALL (1)].

TARPON [tah′pon], *n.* the large jew-fish, of the herring family. [Uncert.].

TARRAGON [ta′ra-gon], *n.* (*bot.*) an aromatic herb; **t. vinegar**, vinegar flavoured with t. [MedL. from Gk.].

TARRAGONA [ta-ra-gō′nah], *n.* a kind of Spanish red wine. [*Tarragona*, Spain].

TARRY (1) [ta′ri], *adj.* resembling tar, having some of the characteristics of tar; covered with tar.

TARRY (2) [ta′ri], *v.t. and i.* † to wait for; (*archaic*) be slow in coming; linger; remain in a place. [OE.].

TARSAL [tah′sal], *adj.* relating to the tarsus.

TARSUS (*pl.* **tarsi**) [tah′sus], *n.* the part of the foot to which the leg is articulated, consisting of the ankle, heel and instep; a joint of the foot in insects. [Gk.].

TART (1) [taht], *n.* dish consisting of a layer of pastry covered with fruit or jam, which may be of sandwich form by the addition of a top layer of pastry, the whole being baked and eaten hot or cold as a sweet; small variety of this eaten as cake. [OFr.].

TART (2), *adj.* sharp to the taste, acid, sour; (*fig.*) having an ungenerous, caustic manner, severe. TARTLY, *adv.* in a t. manner; severely. [OE.].

TARTAN (1) [tah′tan], *n.* woollen fabric with a pattern of stripes crossing each other at right angles, the various patterns being distinctive of particular Highland clans. TARTAN (2), *adj.* made of t. [Unkn.].

TARTAR (1) [tah′ter], *n.* hard crust of tartrate of potassium forming on the sides of a cask in which fermentation of wine has taken place; deposit of calcium phosphate accreting on the teeth; **t. emetic**, compound consisting of tartaric acid combined with oxide of antimony and potassium; **cream of t.**, substance obtained by boiling and filtering t., added to baking-powder, and used medicinally etc. [Fr.].

TARTAR (2), **TATAR**, *n.* a native of the former Tartary, east of the Caspian Sea; member of one of the branches of the Ural-Altaic family, comprising Turks, Cossacks etc.; (*fig.*) (*always* **Tartar**) person of irritable, intractable or violent disposition. TARTAR (3), TATAR, *adj.* of, relating to, the Tartars. TARTARIAN [tah-tāer′i-an], *adj.* relating to Tartary. [Pers.].

TARTARUS [tah′ta-rus], *n.* (*myth.*) the deepest, darkest wastes below the surface of the earth; the infernal regions, hell. [Gk.].

TARTRATE [tah′trāt], *n.* (*chem.*) a salt of tartaric acid.

TARTUFFE [tah-tōōf′], *n.* religious hypocrite. [*Tartuffe*, character in Molière's play of that name].

TASK (1) [tahsk], *n.* a specific piece of work or study imposed by another, *esp.* such as is likely to prove troublesome; any job of work involving laborious effort. TASK-FORCE, (*U.S.*) a force dispatched to carry out a specific naval or military undertaking; commando. TASK (2), *v.t.* to impose a t. on; provide a severe test of, tax. [L.].

TASKMASTER [tahsk′mah-ster], *n.* person authorized to impose a task; an authority which demands unremitting effort.

TASSEL (1) [ta′sel], *n.* knot of threads or cords with a bunched fringe hanging from it, forming a decorative pendant for dress or furniture; anything like a tassel, as a catkin or hanging blossom. TASSEL (2) (*pres.pt.* TASSELLING, *pret. and p.pt.* TASSELLED), *v.t.* to decorate with tassels. [MedL.].

TASTE (1) [tāst], *v.t. and i.* to experience, perceive, sense by means of the tongue and palate, test for characteristic flavour; try by eating a small portion or by sipping, sample; participate in, experience; exercise the sense of taste; possess a characteristic flavour. TASTE (2), *n.* act of tasting; sense by which

flavours are distinguished by means of the tongue and palate; sensation experienced by this sense; the distinctive flavour of anything; that which is tasted; appreciation of material providing aesthetic or intellectual experience, critical discernment of the artistic; a liking, preference; sample; small portion. TAST(E)ABLE, *adj.* able to be tasted. TASTER, *n.* person employed to t. food or liquor; sample specimen; that which contains a sample; a publisher's reader. [OFr.].

TASTEFUL [tāst′fŏŏl], *adj.* possessed of, showing, good taste; (*rare*) characterized by a pleasant flavour.

TASTELESS [tāst′les], *adj.* characterized by absence of taste, insipid; showing no good taste.

TASTY [tās′ti], *adj.* characterized by an agreeable flavour, pleasant to the taste, esp. savoury.

TAT (*pres.pt.* **tatting**, *pret. and p.pt.* **tatted**) [tat], *v.t.* to make a coarse lace with thickish threads. [Unkn.].

TATAR, see TARTAR.

TATLER [tat′ler], *n.* tattler.

TATTER (1) [ta′ter], *n.* that which is torn or torn off, shred, rag. TATTER (2), *v.t.* to tear into rags. TATTERED, *adj.* dressed in rags; torn up into strips. [OIcel.].

TATTING [ta′ting], *n.* lace woven out of coarse, strong threads by a small hand-shuttle; process of weaving it. [Unkn.].

TATTLE (1) [ta′tl], *v.t. and i.* to talk superficially about; gossip. TATTLE (2), *n.* superficial conversation, chatter, gossip. TATTLING, *adj.* given to chatting. [~LGerm.].

TATTOO (1) [ta-tōō′], *n.* military pageant of spectacular scenes presented usually at night; signal by drum or bugle calling soldiers into barracks for the night; continuous rapping like a drum roll. TATTOO (2) (*pret. and p.pt.* TATTOOED), *v.i.* to beat or sound a t. [Du.].

TATTOO (3), *n.* indelible pictorial design on the body made by punctures into which coloured pigments are inserted. TATTOO (4) (*pret. and p.pt.* TATTOOED), *v.t.* to decorate with tattoo. [Tahiti].

TATTY [ta′ti], *adj.* tangled, matted; scrappy. [AHind.].

TAU [taw, tow], *n.* the Greek letter T; moth, beetle or fly marked with the shape of this letter. [Gk.~Heb.].

TAUGHT [tawt], *pret. and p.pt.* of TEACH. [OE.].

TAUNT (1) [tawnt], *n.* a remark calculated to wound another's pride, penetrating sarcasm, sneer, gibe. TAUNT (2), *v.t.* to wound the pride of, with sneering gibes, reproach with remarks expressing contempt. [OFr.].

TAURINE [taw′rin], *n.* having the appearance of, relating to, a bull or bull-fighting. [L.].

TAURUS [taw′rus], *n.* the bull, the second sign of the Zodiac; (*astrol.*) constellation which includes the Pleiades. [Gk.].

TAUT [tawt], *adj.* stretched tight; secure, firmly connected. [~OE.].

TAUTEN [taw′ten], *v.t. and i.* to pull tight, make taut; grow taut.

TAUTO-, *pref.* the same. [Gk.].

TAUTOLOGICAL [taw-tō-lo′ji-kal], *adj.* relating to, having the characteristics of, tautology.

TAUTOLOGY [taw-to′lo-ji], *n.* repetition of an idea, previously expressed, in different words, redundancy. TAUTOLOGIZE, *v.i.* to repeat the same idea in different words. [Gk.].

TAVERN [ta′vern], *n.* house licensed to carry on a retail trade in alcoholic drinks, inn, public-house. [Fr. from L.].

TAW [taw], *n.* a special variegated marble; game at marbles; line toed by marble players. [Unkn.].

TAWDRY [taw′dri], *adj.* cheap, gaudy, flashy in substance and appearance, decorated with cheap jewellery or ornaments. [*St. Audrey* on whose day a fair was held annually].

TAWNY [taw′ni], *adj.* golden or bronzed in colour, coloured with a rich yellow-brown, sunburnt. [ME. from OFr.].

TAX (1) [taks], *v.t.* to subject to a system of assessment, compel to pay a specific sum of money as a contribution to national expenditure; burden, subject to exacting demands; (*leg.*) assess (the costs of a suit); **to t. with**, to bring an accusation against. TAX (2), *n.* a means of levying money from the public for national purposes by assessing marketable goods, property or income; heavy burden, exorbitant demand. [L.].

TAXATION [tak-sā′shn], *n.* act of taxing; system of

---

taxes; total sum of money raised either from an individual or from the whole nation.

TAXI (1) [tak'si], *n*. light, low-horse-powered motor-car hired by passengers, the mileage being measured by a taximeter; any motor-car for passenger hire. TAXI-RANK, official park where taxis wait for fares. TAXI (2) (*pres.pt.* TAXYING, *pret. and p.pt.* TAXIED), *v.i.* to go by t.; (*aeron.*) run along the ground before taking off or after landing. [TAXI(METER)].

TAXICAB [tak'si-kab], *n*. taxi.

TAXIDERMY [tak'si-der-mi], *n*. craft of preserving and stuffing the skins of dead animals and birds so as to present them in a lifelike form. [Gk.].

TAXIMETER [tak-si'mi-ter], *n*. instrument which registers automatically on a dial the mileage of a taxi and the fare to be charged to the passenger.

TE [tē], *n*. seventh note in the tonic-solfa scale, si. [Invented].

TEA (1) [tē], *n*. dried leaves of the tea-plant; drink made by infusing these in boiling water; meal taken in the afternoon or early evening. TEA-CADDY, box or container for holding t. TEA-CAKE, large round scone, usually toasted, buttered and eaten at t. TEA-CANISTER, tea caddy. TEA-CHEST, large box lined with metal foil, suitable for the transport of t. TEA-CLOTH, small tablecloth used at t.-time; small cloth for drying washed crockery. TEA-COSY, thick cover for keeping a teapot warm. TEA-FIGHT, (*coll.*) t.-party. TEA-GARDEN, garden or estate where t. is cultivated; garden where afternoon t. is served to the public. TEA-LEAF, leaf of the t.-plant; one of the fragments of the dried leaf used for making t. TEA-PARTY, party held in the afternoon at which t. is served. TEA-PLANT. (*bot.*) evergreen shrub, *Lycium chinense*. (*bot.*) a variety of light yellow rose. TEA-SERVICE, -SET, set of crockery for use at t.-time. TEA-SHOP, shop where teas are sold. TEA-THINGS, (*pl.*) crockery and utensils used at t.; t.-service. TEA-TRAY, small tray from which t. may be served. TEA-URN, large container in which water is boiled for t. TEA-WAGGON, small trolley for wheeling tea-things round a drawing-room. TEA (2), *v.i.* (*coll.*) to take t. [Chin.].

TEACH (*pret. and p.pt.* taught) [tēch], *v.t. and i.* to lay facts, details, examples, methods, before, with the aim of impressing the memory, transfer knowledge to, *esp.* by means of a systematic series of studies, instruct, develop the intelligence or abilities of; counsel, advise. TEACHING, *n*. act or profession of instructing; instruction. [OE.].

TEACHER [tē'cher], *n*. one who teaches or instructs; schoolmaster or schoolmistress.

TEAK [tēk], *n*. tree of the genus *Tectona*, notable for the hardness of its wood. [Malay].

TEAL [tēl], *n*. a small wild duck. [ME.].

TEAM (1) [tēm], *n*. a pair, or more, of domesticated animals in draught harness; group of which each member takes a part in a particular form of work or play, number of players constituting a side. TEAM-WORK, work done by a t.; work attempted or achieved by co-operative effort. TEAM (2), *v.t.* to harness or work together as a t. TEAMSTER, *n*. one who drives a t. [OE.].

TEAR (1) [tēer], *n*. small drop of clear moisture secreted by the lachrymal gland in the eye, stimulated by emotion, *esp.* sorrow, and by physical suffering; small drop of anything, *esp.* pear-shaped, resembling a t.; **crocodile tears**, grief which is not genuine. TEAR-DROP, a single t. dropping from the eye. TEAR-DUCT, (*anat.*) passage leading from the lachrymal gland to the nasal orifice. TEAR-GAS, type of poison gas which affects the lachrymal glands, and induces a flow of tears. [OE.].

TEAR (2) (*pret.* tore, *p.pt.* torn) [tāer], *v.t. and i.* to make a crude long division in by a violent pull, divide violently into separate parts, split into two pieces each being left with jagged edges; lacerate; shatter, destroy; remove, pull or drag away by violence so as to leave rough and ragged edges at the breaking points; disturb violently; experience tearing; move, run, hastily and excitedly, rush; **to t. away**, to rush off; **to t. down**, to hurry impetuously along; **to t. from**, to deprive by force; **to t. oneself away**, to leave with reluctance; **torn between**, reacting equally to two claims on one's allegiance. TEAR (3), *n*. a split or rent; action of tearing. TEAR-ING, *adj.* (*coll.*) tremendous, violent. [OE.].

TEASE (1) [tēz], *v.t.* to comb out (a matted surface or mass), *esp.* by brushing with a teasel; annoy, irritate, by persistent impertinence or mockery, pester, worry. TEASE (2), *n*. person who likes teasing

others. TEASER, *n*. one who teases; difficult problem. [OE.].

TEASEL (1), **TEAZLE** [tē'zl], *n*. (*bot.*) a plant with a head of hooked prickles set firmly together; head of this plant adapted as a brush for raising the nap of cloth. TEASEL (2), TEAZLE, *v.t.* to brush with a t. [OE.].

TEAT [tēt], *n*. the small projecting part of the breast, nipple; rubber nipple of a child's feeding bottle.

TECHNIC [tek'nik], *n*. technique; (*pl.*) the technical side of any subject, *esp.* of the arts. [Gk.].

TECHNICAL [tek'ni-kal], *adj.* relating to, made according to, technique; accurately descriptive; from the aspect of technique.

TECHNICALITY [tek-ni-ka'li-ti], *n*. state of being technical; a particular item peculiar to a special branch of knowledge; a detail of formal procedure.

TECHNICIAN [tek-ni'shn], *n*. a technical expert.

TECHNICOLOR [tek-ni-ku-ler], *n*. (*prot.*) a process for photographing cinema films in colour. [TECHNI-(CAL) and COLO(U)R].

TECHNIQUE [tek-nēk'], *n*. knowledge of established theory and practice connected with some activity; skill based on systematic application of accepted principles; method in execution. [Fr. from Gk.].

TECHNOCRACY [tek-nok'ra-si], *n*. control of industry by skilled technicians. [Gk.].

TECHNOLOGY [tek-no'lo-ji], *n*. science of the mechanical and industrial arts. [Gk.].

TED (*pres.pt.* tedding, *pret. and p.pt.* tedded) [ted], *v.t.* to spread (new-mown grass) for drying. TEDDER, *n*. one who teds; agricultural machine for tedding grass. [OIcel.].

TEDDY BEAR [te-di-bāer'], *n*. children's toy bear made of yellowish-brown plush; **t. overcoat**, kind of loose overcoat made of material resembling that used for teddy bears. [~*Teddy* (Theodore) Roosevelt, U.S. President and big-game hunter].

TE DEUM [tē-dē'um], *n*. hymn sung on occasions of thanksgiving. [L. *Te Deum* "Thee, O God," the first words of the hymn].

TEDIOUS [tē'di-ŏŏs], *adj.* producing boredom, exhausting and boring by reason of length, monotonously dull.

TEDIUM [tē'di-um], *n*. state of being tedious, wearisomeness. [L.].

TEE (1) [tē], *n*. the letter T; anything of this shape. TEE (2), *adj.* having the shape of a T.

TEE (3), *n*. small pile of sand or support of rubber, wood etc., on which a golf ball is placed for the drive; teeing ground where it is permissible to use such a support; mark at quoits or curling. TEE-BOY, box containing sand on the teeing ground. TEE (4), *v.t.* to place on a t; **to t. up**, to lay on a slightly elevated piece of ground; (*fig., coll.*) get ready; **teeing ground**, flat piece of ground which marks the beginning of a hole on a golf course. [Unkn.].

TEEM (1) [tēm], *v.t. and i.* to pour out, rain heavily, gush, discharge. [OIcel.].

TEEM (2), *v.t. and i.* to produce; produce in abundance; be full, abound (with); be prolific. TEEMFUL, *adj.* characterized by teeming; prolific, brimful. TEEM-ING, *adj.* fertile, fruitful. [OE.].

TEENAGER [tē'nā-jer], *n*. person in his or her teens.

TEENS [tēnz], *n.(pl.)* period of adolescence between thirteen and twenty years of age.

TEETH [tēth], *n.pl. of* TOOTH.

TEETHE [tēth], *v.i.* to have the teeth erupting through the gums. TEETHING, *n*. process by which the teeth of a baby gradually pierce the gums. [ME.].

TEETOTAL [tē-tō'tal], *adj.* relating to, adhering to, teetotalism; non-alcoholic. TEETOTALISM, *n*. theory and practice of total abstinence from all intoxicating drink. [Reduplication of the initial t of TOTAL].

TEETOTUM [tē-tō'tum], *n*. type of top with numbers marked on the sides, one side being marked with a T standing for *totum*, "all" (of the stake).

TEG [teg], *n*. young sheep which has never been shorn. [Uncert.].

TEGUMENT [te'gyŏŏ-ment], *n*. a natural covering of an organism; skin, integument. [L.].

TE-HEE [tē-hē'], *n*. high, silly sound made in laughing. [Echoic].

TELE-, *pref.* afar, at a distance. [Gk.].

TELE-ARCHICS [te-li-ah'kiks], *n.(pl.)* remote control (of aircraft) by radio. [Gk.].

TELEGRAM [te'li-gram], *n*. telegraphic message.

TELEGRAPH (1) [te'li-grahf], *n*. apparatus consisting

of two instruments, a transmitter and receiver, between which an electric circuit is made and broken in a form of code conveying a message over a distance; any device by which a message is signalled. TELEGRAPH (2), *v.t. and i.* to send by t.; transmit by t.; signal. TELEGRAPHIST [te-le'gra-fist], *n.* t. operator. [TELE and GRAPH].

TELEGRAPHIC [te-li-gra'fik], *adj.* relating to the telegraph; communicated by telegraph; concise in form of verbal expression.

TELEGRAPHY [te-le'gra-fi], *n.* the system of telegraphic communication.

TELEKINESIS [te-li-ki-nē'sis], *n.* (*psychics*) movement or change of physical state caused in a body by a force or agent not in contact with it. [TELE and Gk.].

TELEMARK [te'li-mahk], *n.* a kind of turn in skiing. [*Telemark*, Norway].

TELEMETER [te'li-mē-ter], *n.* electrical instrument for recording phenomena taking place at a distance, effects of which are conveyed to it by radio waves. [TELE and METER].

TELEOLOGICAL [te-li-ō-lo'ji-kal], *adj.* of, or relating to, teleology.

TELEOLOGY [te-li-o'lo-ji], *n.* doctrine that each of the parts of nature is designed to fulfil a particular end, *esp.* as being so designed by God. [Gk.].

TELEPATHIC [te-li-pa'thik], *adj.* of, pertaining to, or resembling, telepathy.

TELEPATHY [te-le'pa-thi], *n.* transmitting of thoughts from one person to another without any apparent means, thought-transference. [TELE and Gk.].

TELEPHONE (1) [te'li-fōn], *n.* electrical instrument for transmitting conversation over a distance, *esp.* a single unit consisting of a mouthpiece, earpiece and stand. TELEPHONE (2), *v.t. and i.* to transmit, converse, by means of a t. TELEPHONIST [te-le'fo-nist], *n.* person employed to operate a t. or t. switchboard. [TELE and Gk.].

TELEPHONIC [te-li-fo'nik], *adj.* transmitted by, relating to, the telephone.

TELEPHONY [te-le'fo-ni], *n.* process and system of sending messages by telephone.

TELEPHOTE [te'li-fōt], *n.* instrument for transmitting pictures by electricity. [TELE and Gk.].

TELEPHOTO [te-li-fō'tō], *n. and adj.* (*coll.*) telephotograph, telephotographic. [TELEPHOTO-(GRAPHIC)].

TELEPHOTOGRAPH [te-li-fō'tō-grahf], *n.* photograph received and recorded by telephote; photograph of a distant object made with a telephotographic lens.

TELEPHOTOGRAPHIC [te-li-fō-tō-gra'fik], *adj.* of, pertaining to, or based on a system of lenses by which very distant objects can be photographed.

TELEPHOTOGRAPHY [te-li-fo-to'gra-fi], *n.* transmission of photographs by telephote; photography with a telephotographic lens.

TELEPRINTER [te-li-prin'ter], *n.* form of typewriter operated electrically from a distance. TELEPRINT, *v.t. and i.* to send a message by t.; operate a t. [TELE and PRINTER].

TELESCOPE (1) [te'li-skōp], *n.* optical instrument consisting of an arrangement of lenses to make a viewed object appear nearer. TELESCOPE (2), *v.t. and i.* to cause to pack, *esp.* by force, into a small space by fitting the parts one inside another, as the sections of a collapsible t.; fit one into another by pressure. [TELE and Gk.].

TELESCOPIC [te-li-sko'pik], *adj.* relating to a telescope; seen only by means of a telescope; having sections which fit one in another.

TELESEME [te'li-sēm], *n.* an electric apparatus for obtaining service in hotels etc. by registering signals on an indicator. [TELE and Gk.].

TELETYPE [te'li-tīp], *n. and v.t. and i.* electric telegraph which prints automatically; to send by t. [TELE and TYPE (1)].

TELEVISE [te'li-vīz], *v.t.* to transmit by television.

TELEVISION [te-li-vi'zhn], *n.* process and system of transmitting images of moving or still objects or scenes, and simultaneously receiving them at a distant point, by radio or by wire linkage. [TELE and VISION].

TELEVISOR [te'li-vī-zer], *n.* apparatus for transmitting or reproducing images by television.

TELL (*pret. and p.pt.* told) [tel], *v.t. and i.* to communicate orally, express in words; narrate; inform by word of mouth, disclose; report, admit, explain; command; distinguish, disclose; indicate, teach; † count; reveal a secret; have a distinct effect; **to t. on,**

to inform against; weary, exhaust; **to t. off,** (*coll.*) to reprimand; **all told,** everything being counted, altogether. TELLING, *adj.* having a great effect. TELLINGLY, *adv.* effectively. [OE.].

TELLER [te'ler], *n.* one who tells; narrator; bank clerk who pays out money; one who counts votes.

TELLTALE (1) [tel'tāl], *n.* person who does not keep to himself the confidences given by another, sneak, gossip; mechanical or electrical indicator. TELLTALE (2), *adj.* tending to reveal what is secret.

TELPHER (1) [tel'fer], *n.* truck travelling along a cable. TELPHER (2), *adj.* pertaining to transport worked by overhead cable; **t. line,** overhead cable carrying trucks. TELPHERAGE, *n.* transport by means of a t. line. [TEL and Gk.].

TEMERARIOUS [te-me-rāer'i-ōos], *adj.* rash, headstrong, reckless. [L.].

TEMERITY [ti-me'ri-ti], *n.* extreme boldness, rashness, audacity. [L.].

TEMPER (1) [tem'per], *v.t. and i.* to moderate the properties of (something) by admixture of something else of neutral or opposite qualities; produce a desired consistency in (clay) by kneading with water; make (a metal) hard and elastic by suddenly cooling it from a great temperature and then reheating it; possess or be capable of attaining a desired consistency or quality. TEMPER (2), *n.* balance, calmness or composure of the emotions and feelings; quality or state of mind; a passing mood; anger, annoyance; irritation; condition of a material (a combination of elasticity and hardness produced by tempering. TEMPERED, *adj.* moderate; adjusted in constitution by tempering or admixture. [OE.].

TEMPERA [tem'pe-rah], *n.* painting medium in which no oil is used; distemper, such as is used in frescoes. [It.].

TEMPERAMENT [tem'pe-ra-ment], *n.* mental, moral and emotional constitution, natural disposition; a violent, passionate nature; (*mus.*) the slightly inaccurate adjustment of the intervals on a keyboard instrument which makes it possible to play it harmoniously in all keys. [L.].

TEMPERAMENTAL [tem-pe-ra-men'tal], *adj.* pertaining to temperament; having a violent, passionate, unstable disposition.

TEMPERANCE [tem'pe-rans], *n.* condition or quality of being temperate; moderation; self-control; *esp.* moderation in the use of alcoholic or intoxicant drinks; **t. hotel,** hotel where alcoholic liquor cannot be bought. [OFr. from L.].

TEMPERATE [tem'pe-rat], *adj.* equable, moderate; not given to excess, self-controlled; (of climate) showing neither extreme cold nor extreme heat.

TEMPERATURE [tem'pe-ra-tyōōr], *n.* condition or degree of heat or cold; warmth or lack of it in a living organism; excessive heat of the blood, feverishness; **to take someone's t.,** to measure the t. of the blood by a clinical thermometer; **to have a t.,** to be feverish. [L.].

TEMPEST [tem'pest], *n.* rough violent weather, a storm; (*fig.*) anything resembling this, a violent, noisy upheaval of some sort. TEMPEST-TOST, tossed and beaten by tempests, weather-beaten. [L.].

TEMPESTUOUS [tem-pes'tyōō-ōos], *adj.* very stormy, turbulent, resembling a tempest; (*fig.*) agitated, excited.

TEMPLAR [tem'pler], *n.* member of a religious military order founded early in the twelfth century to protect the Holy Sepulchre; student of law, *esp.* one occupying chambers in the Temple, London; one of an order of Freemasons. [LL.].

TEMPLATE, see TEMPLET.

TEMPLE (1) [tem'pl], *n.* building used to worship in; sacred religious building, shrine, church; **the T.,** sacred building at Jerusalem which was the centre of Hebrew worship of Jehovah; the two Inns of Court (the *Inner* and *Middle Temples*) in London, standing on a site formerly held by the Knights Templars. [OE. from L.].

TEMPLE (2), *n.* one of the flattened parts of the head on each side of the forehead. [OFr. ~L.].

TEMPLET, TEMPLATE [tem'plet], *n.* (*building*) flat horizontal piece of wood laid under the end of a girder, beam etc. to distribute the weight; thin wooden or metal plate used as a guide by stone-, metal- or wood-workers. [Unkn.].

TEMPO [tem'pō], *n.* (*mus.*) time or speed of movement. [It.].

TEMPORAL (1) [tem'pe-ral], *adj.* of, pertaining or adjacent to, the temples.

TEMPORAL (2), *adj.* existing under the condition of,

controlled or limited by, pertaining to, time; of or pertaining to time as the essential and limiting condition of human life, pertaining to life in this world, earthly, transient, worldly; pertaining to worldly and civil affairs as contrasted with things spiritual and ecclesiastical; (gram.) pertaining to tense. [L.].

TEMPORALITY [tem-pe-ra'li-ti], n. worldly possessions; (pl.) material possessions of the Church. [LL.].

TEMPORARY [tem'pe-ra-ri], adj. lasting for a limited time only, transient, not permanent.

TEMPORIZE [tem'pe-riz], v.i. to avoid or delay by hesitation and evasion the taking of a definite or irrevocable decision, in order to gain time. TEMPORIZATION [tem-pe-ri-zā'shn], n. action of temporizing. [Fr.].

TEMPT [tempt], v.t. to incite, entice; urge, solicit, persuade to do wrong; persuade; allure, attract; test.

TEMPTATION [temp-tā'shn], n. action of tempting; condition of being tempted; something which tempts.

TEMPTER [temp'ter], n, one who tempts or entices to evil; **the T.**, the Devil.

TEMPTING [temp'ting], adj. attractive, enticing, alluring.

TEN (1) [ten], n. the numeral one more than nine; symbol for this. TEN (2), adj. twice five, one more than nine; **t. times as**, (coll.) much more, much better etc. [OE.].

TENABLE [te'na-bl, tĕ'na-bl], adj. able to be held; sensible, logical; able to be defended. [Fr.].

TENACIOUS [te-nā'shŏŏs], adj. holding fast, retentive; tough; (of the mind) retentive; obstinate, determined. [~L.].

TENACITY [te-na'si-ti], n. obstinacy, resolution, retentiveness; quality of being tenacious. [L.].

TENANCY [te'nan-si], n. a holding or tenure of property in the position of tenant; property held by a tenant.

TENANT (1) [te'nant], n. (leg.) person holding real estate for a terminable period; person holding property by payment of rent; (poet.) inhabitant. TENANT (2), v.t. to hold or inhabit as a t. TENANTABLE, adj. able to be held by, fit for, a t. TENANTED, adj. held by a t. or tenants; inhabited. TENANTRY, n. tenants regarded collectively. [Fr.].

TENCH [tench], a freshwater fish. [OFr.].

TEND (1) [tend], v.t. to look after, protect, provide with necessaries etc.; (naut.) stand near to, ready to manipulate or control (something). TENDANCE, n. act of tending or caring for. [~ATTEND].

TEND (2), v.i. to move or be moved in a certain direction; be biased or inclined in a certain way; **to t. to**, to be liable to result in, be prone to. [Fr. from L.].

TENDENCY [ten'den-si], n. bias, bent, inclination.

TENDENTIOUS, TENDENCIOUS [ten-den'shŏŏs], adj. biased, written or spoken with a special motive. [Germ.].

TENDER (1) [ten'der], n. one who tends or looks after, attendant; ship operating under orders from the captain of another; railway truck which immediately follows a locomotive, and carries coal and water-supplies.

TENDER (2), v.t. and i. to offer to pay (an amount due) or make (a payment) in satisfaction of a claim; offer, present (thanks, apologies etc.); **to t. for**, to make an offer to contract for (a specified piece of work) at a stated price. TENDER (3), n. an offer to carry out a specified piece of work at a stated price; money offered to wipe out a debt; **legal t.**, currency legally recognized as fit and acceptable for the payment of debt. [AFr.].

TENDER (4), adj. soft, delicate, fragile, not strong or firm; (of food) succulent, soft; not robust, delicate, weak in health or constitution, not able to stand exposure, easily hurt or injured; immature, having the delicacy of youth; gentle, not strong or vivid, soft; loving, affectionate; kind, considerate; easily pained, painful when touched; morally scrupulous. [OFr. from L.].

TENDERFOOT [ten'der-fŏŏt], n. new arrival in a colonial settlement; novice; lowest rank of Boy Scout.

TENDER-HEARTED [ten-der-hah'tid], adj. gentle, compassionate.

TENDERLOIN [ten'der-loin], n. (U.S.) (coll.) part of any city largely devoted to amusements; undercut of sirloin. [TENDER (4) and LOIN].

TENDON [ten'don], n. (anat.) strong tissue which connects a muscle to a bone or some other part. TENDINOUS, adj. pertaining to or like a t.; sinewy. [OFr.].

TENDRIL [ten'dril], n. small, string-like organ in climbing plants which projects from the stem and winds itself round anything it touches so as to hold the plant up. [Fr.].

TENEBRAE [te'ni-brē], n.(pl.) (R.C.) offices of Matins and Lauds for the Thursday and Saturday of Holy Week, recited in each case on the previous day. [L.].

TENEBROSE, TENEBROUS [te'ni-brōs, -brŏŏs]. adj. dark and gloomy. [L.].

TENEMENT [te'ni-ment], n. (leg.) property held by a tenant, anything held by tenure; a dwelling; one set of rooms in a large building where each set is occupied by a different family; (poet.) dwelling place. [L.].

TENET [te'net], n. any strongly held opinion, principle, dogma or doctrine. [L.].

TENFOLD [ten'fōld], adj. and adv. ten times more, ten times as many or as much. [OE.].

TENNER [te'ner], n. (coll.) a ten-pound note.

TENNIS [te'nis], n. ball game played in a prepared court divided by a net across which the players (two or four in number) hit the ball to and fro either with their hands or with rackets; lawn tennis; **t. ball**, ball used when playing t.; **t. elbow**, inflammation of the elbow due to strain at lawn t. TENNIS-COURT, prepared court or grass patch where t. is played. [ME.].

TENON (1) [te'non], n. (carp.) a projection from a piece of wood shaped to fit into a mortise or slot in another piece of wood so as to join the two pieces together. TENON (2), v.t. (carp.) to cut a t. in. [OFr.].

TENOR (1) [te'ner], n. the import, general meaning of, a writing or utterance; career, course; (mus.) a high pitch of adult male voice, above bass but below alto; line of notes to be sung by this voice in any composition; person who sings with such a voice; violin with a similar pitch, viola. TENOR (2), adj. (mus.) pertaining to the voice, pitch or part of a t. [L.].

TENSE (1) [tens], n. (gram.) any of the parts of a verb implying the time (past, present, future etc.) or the nature (i.e. whether continuous or not) of the action expressed by the verb; quality imparted to a verb by such inflexion or root vowel variation. [OFr. from L.].

TENSE (2), adj. stretched tight, strained, taut; overwrought but held in restraint, expectant, keyed up; **t. vowel**, (phon.) vowel uttered with the tongue held in a firm, taut position. TENSE (3), v.t. to make t., brace up; (phon.) make (a vowel) t. [L.].

TENSIBLE [ten'si-bl], adj. tensile.

TENSILE [ten'sīl], adj. able to be stretched.

TENSION (1) [ten'shn], n. act of stretching; state of being stretched; emotional stress. TENSION (2), v.t. to tighten, make taut. [L.].

TENSIVE [ten'siv], adj. producing tension, straining, pulling, stretching. [Fr.].

TENT (1) [tent], n. portable shelter made of canvas stretched over a pole or poles and held firm by ropes pegged into the ground; any fabric covering resembling this; device for controlling the content of the air breathed by persons suffering from certain diseases. TENT-BED, bed with a canopy over it; small collapsible bed for use in a t. TENT-PEG, wooden or metal peg to which the guys of a t. are fastened. TENT-PEGGING, cavalry exercise in which when the horse is at the gallop the rider picks up a peg, fixed firmly in the ground, on the end of a lance. TENT (2), v.t. and i. to camp in a t.; cover with tents. TENTAGE, n. tents collectively. TENTED, adj. covered with tents; living in tents. [L.].

TENT (3), n. a sweet red Spanish wine, often used at the Eucharist. [Span.].

TENTACLE [ten'ta-kl], n. slender, flexible limb possessed by some lower forms of animal life, used for gripping or grasping or as a means of moving along. [L.].

TENTATIVE [ten'ta-tiv], adj. provisional, experimental, offered merely as a suggestion or experiment. [MedL.].

TENTER [ten'ter], n. frame over which cloth is stretched so as to prevent its shrinking while drying. [OFr.].

TENTERHOOK [ten'ter-hŏŏk], n. hook on a tenter; **on tenterhooks**, keyed up, expectant, anxious, nervous.

TENTH (1) [tenth], adj. the ordinal of ten; being one

ōō is pronounced as in food; ŏŏ as in hood; th as in think; ᴛʜ as in that; zh as in azure. ~ = related to.

of ten equal parts. TENTH (2), *n.* the one after the ninth; one of ten equal parts.

TENUITY [te-nyōō'i-ti], *n.* condition of being tenuous; slenderness; thinness. [L.].

TENUOUS [te'nyōō-ŏos], *adj.* slender, thin, fine; rarefied; subtle; flimsy, weak.

TENURE [te'nyŏor], *n.* act of holding property; right to possess property; action or fact of holding an office; conditions on which property or office is held. [OFr.].

TENUTO [te-nōō'tō], *adj.* (*mus.*) of a note, given or to be given its full time value; sustained. [It.].

TEPID [te'pid], *adj.* lukewarm, warmish. [L.].

TEPIDITY [te-pi'di-ti], *n.* moderate warmth.

TERATOLOGY [te-ra-to'lo-ji], *n.* scientific study of freaks and monstrosities in animals and vegetables. [Gk.].

TERCE, see TIERCE.

TERCEL, TIERCEL [tur'sel], *n.* male falcon. [Fr.].

TERCENTENARY (1) [ter-sen-tē'na-ri], *adj.* pertaining to a period of three hundred years or to a t. TERCENTENARY (2), *n.* three hundredth anniversary of an event, celebrations connected therewith.

TERCET, TIERCET [tur'set], *n.* (*pros.*) a triplet; (*mus.*) a triplet; a third. [Fr.].

TEREBENE [te'ri-bēn], *n.* oil of turpentine treated with sulphuric acid to make a disinfectant.

TEREBINTH [te'ri-binth], *n.* a Mediterranean turpentine tree. TEREBINTHINE [te-ri-bin'thin], *adj.* pertaining to or like turpentine. [Gk.].

TEREDO (*pl.* teredines, teredos) [te-rē'dō], *n.* mollusc which bores into the submerged wood of ships. [Gk.].

TERGIVERSATE [tur'ji-ver-sāt], *v.i.* to act in an evasive manner, shift one's point of view. [~L.].

TERM (1) [turm], *n.* limit to a period of time, *esp.* a day fixed by which rent must be paid; limited period of time, *esp.* one during which an agreement, contract, right etc. is valid; fixed number of consecutive weeks in which instruction is given at universities and schools, and the law courts are open for the hearing of cases; one of a set of special and precise names used in the study or science of anything, in an art, profession etc.; (*log.*) one of the parts of a proposition; (*geom.*) point, line or surface which forms a limit or boundary; completion of the period of pregnancy; (*pl.*) stated provisos of an agreement, contract etc.; (*pl.*) money demanded as payment; (*pl.*) conditions of friendship, personal relations; (*pl.*) style, phraseology, mode of expression; terms of reference, statement or set of terms defining the scope of an investigation by a person or group of persons. TERM (2), *v.t.* to give a t. to, name, designate. [OFr. from L.].

TERMAGANT (1) [tur'ma-gant], *n.* boisterous, brawling, turbulent woman, so called from a supposed Mohammedan deity represented in morality plays as a boisterous person. TERMAGANT (2), *adj.* boisterous. [OFr.].

TERMES (*pl.* termites) [tur'mēz, tur'mi-tēz], *n.* group of destructive boring insects including the white ant. [LL.].

TERMINABLE [tur'mi-na-bl], *adj.* limitable, able to be terminated.

TERMINAL (1) [tur'mi-nal], *adj.* pertaining to, situated at, a limit or end; concluding, final; lasting for the duration of a term; occurring every term; pertaining to a university or school term. TERMINAL (2), *n.* (*elect.*) each of the ends of a circuit; metal device for attaching these to a switch, plug etc.; railway terminus. TERMINALLY, *adv.* at the end; once a term; at regular fixed intervals. [L.].

TERMINATE [tur'mi-nāt], *v.t. and i.* to limit or bound; bring to an end; finish or cause to finish; be at the end of; come to an end. TERMINATIVE, *adj.* serving to t. or determine. TERMINATIVELY, *adv.* absolutely; in a terminative way; bringing to a conclusion. [L.].

TERMINATION [ter-mi-nā'shn], *n.* act of terminating; condition of being terminated; end or conclusion (in time or space); that which is at the end, extremity; (*gram.*) final part of a word, suffix or inflexion.

TERMINATOR [tur'mi-nā-ter], *n.* someone who or something which terminates; (*astron.*) separating line between the illuminated and unilluminated parts of a planet. [LL.].

TERMINER [tur'mi-ner], *n.* oyer and t., (*leg.*) Royal Commission granted to judges to hear cases on circuit. [Fr.].

TERMINOLOGICAL [ter-mi-no-lo'ji-kal], *adj.* pertaining to terminology; t. inexactitude, a lie.

TERMINOLOGY [ter-mi-no'lo-ji], *n.* technical terms; system of technical terms pertaining to a particular art, trade, profession etc. [L. and Gk.].

TERMINUS (*pl.* termini) [tur'mi-nus], *n.* limit, end, extremity, goal; end of a railway line, tram-route, bus-route etc., station or depot at such a place; t. ad quem, point beyond which an argument cannot or is not intended to go; t. a quo, starting point of an argument.

TERMITE [tur'mīt], *n.* one of a group of destructive insects commonly called white ants, having the communal habits of ants. TERMITARY, *n.* (*zool.*) a nest of white ants or termites. [TERMES].

TERN (1) [turn], *n.* one of a group of small gull-like birds. [~OIcel.].

TERN (2), *n.* a group of three. [L.].

TERNARY [tur'na-ri], *adj.* arranged in groups of three, triple, threefold; pertaining to such an arrangement.

TERNION [tur'ni-on], *n.* a group of three. [L.].

TERPSICHOREAN [terp-si-ko-rē'an], *adj.* pertaining to dancing. [Gk. *Terpsichore*, muse of dancing].

TERRA [te'rah], *n.* t. firma, dry land as contrasted with the sea; t. incognita, unknown, unexplored country. [L.].

TERRACE (1) [te'ras], *n.* raised level bank or mound, usually longer than broad, often employed as an ornament in landscape gardening; row of non-detached houses along a street. TERRACE (2), *v.t.* to make into a t.; form (sloping ground) into a series of level-topped banks; ornament with a t., add a t. to. [OFr.].

TERRACOTTA [te-ra-ko'tah], *n.* a brownish-red pottery. [It.].

TERRAIN [te-rān'], *n.* tract of land, *esp.* (*milit.*) with reference to configuration, surface conditions and other features affecting operations; region. [Fr.].

TERRAPIN [te'ra-pin], *n.* any one of a number of edible turtles found about the Atlantic coasts and estuaries of North America. [AmerInd.].

TERRAQUEOUS [te-rā'kwi-ŏos], *adj.* consisting of land and water. [L.].

TERRAZZO [te-rat'sō], *n.* (*prot.*) kind of polished concrete used for building and paving. [It.].

TERRENE [te-rēn'], *adj.* pertaining to the earth, mundane, terrestrial. [L.].

TERRESTRIAL (1) [te-res'tri-all], *adj.* pertaining to the earth, mundane, earthly; resembling the earth in its ball-like shape; living on land. TERRESTRIAL (2), *n.* inhabitant of the earth. [OFr.].

TERRIBLE [te'ri-bl], *adj.* evoking horror, fear, awe; monstrous, horrible; (*coll.*) extreme, excessive; very bad, ill-done, disappointing. [L.].

TERRIER (1) [te'ri-er], *n.* dog of one of several breeds of small dogs commonly kept as pets, and used in hunting burrowing animals because of their habit of pursuing the animal right into its burrow. [Fr.].

TERRIER (2), *n.* (*slang*) territorial soldier. [TERRITORIAL].

TERRIFIC [te-ri'fik], *adj.* dreadful, huge, vast, violent, evoking terror by hugeness or violence. [L.].

TERRIFY [te'ri-fī], *v.t.* to frighten, alarm, overwhelm with terror. [L.].

TERRINE [te'rēn], *n.* earthenware vessel in which some special delicacy is kept. [Fr.].

TERRITORIAL (1) [te-ri-taw'ri-al], *adj.* pertaining to territory, to a special territory or region; (*milit.*) pertaining to a voluntary force grouped according to certain divisions of the country. TERRITORIAL (2), *n.* soldier in the T. Army.

TERRITORY [te'ri-te-ri], *n.* large region or tract of land; single governmental division of a country; dependent state, not entirely self-governing; area traversed by a commercial traveller. [L.].

TERROR [te'rer], *n.* state of extreme fear; extreme, abject fear; person or thing evoking such fear; (*coll.*) troublesome person, *esp.* a mischievous child.

TERRORISM [te're-rizm], *n.* policy of terror and intimidation, government or administration founded upon such a policy.

TERRORIST [te're-rist], *n. and adj.* (characteristic of, pertaining to) a political fanatic or member of a party of such persons carrying out or proposing to carry out a policy based on terror and intimidation.

TERRORIZE [te're-rīz], *v.t.* to fill with terror, coerce or intimidate; rule by intimidation.

TERRY (1) [te'ri], *n.* the uncut loop of a pile fabric. TERRY (2), *adj.* having a pile of uncut loops.

TERSE [turs], *adj.* brief, concise; (of persons) abrupt almost to rudeness. [L.].

TERTIAN (1) [tur'shn], *adj.* (*med.*) recurring every

third day. TERTIAN (2), *n.* (*med.*) a t. malady. [L.].

TERTIARY [tur'sha-ri], *adj.* third in order of time, importance etc.; (*geol.*) pertaining to that geological era which followed the mesozoic. [~L.].

TERTIUM QUID [ter-shi-um-kwid'], *n.* something which is intermediate, a compromising alternative, third suggestion; possibility etc. [L.].

TERTIUS [tur'shi-us], *adj.* third. [L.].

TESSELLATE [te'se-lāt], *v.t.* to cover or pave with small stones as in mosaic work. TESSELLATION [te-se-lā'shn], *n.* mosaic work, paving of small stones as in mosaics. [L.].

TESSERA (*pl.* tesserae) [te'se-rah], *n.* one of a number of small cubes of glass, stone or marble used in mosaic. [Gk.].

TEST (1) [test], *n.* container in a furnace used for refining precious metals; means or method of proving the quality of something, examination, critical survey; (*chem.*) analysis of a substance; short written examination less important than and usually in preparation for a vital or authoritative examination; special fact or circumstance which serves to bring out the true character or work of a person or thing by trying their qualities to the utmost; (*hist.*) oath taken under the Test Act (passed 1672, repealed 1828); **t. case**, (*leg.*) suit at law the ruling in which fixes a precedent; set of circumstances which are likely to provide proof or disproof of something; **t. (match)**, (*cricket*) one of a series of matches played between sides representing their countries, TEST-TUBE, (*chem.*) cylindrical phial or vessel of glass, open at the top, rounded and closed at the bottom, used in chemical experiments. TEST (2), *v.t.* to try, prove, put to the t., submit (a person or thing) to trial with a view to ascertaining the nature and strength of his, her or its qualities; (*chem.*) analyse. [OFr. from L.].

TEST (3), *n.* (*zool.*) hard shell of molluscs and other invertebrates. [L.].

TESTACEA [tes-tā'shah], *n.*(*pl.*) (*zool.*) creatures with a hard outer shell. TESTACEAN, *n.* and *adj.* (*zool.*) one of the t.; having a shell, pertaining to t. [L.].

TESTACEOUS [tes-tā'shŏŏs], *adj.* pertaining to shells; shelly; of the colour of unglazed pottery; (*zool.*) having a shell.

TESTACY [tes'ta-si], *n.* (*leg.*) condition of being testate.

TESTAMENT [tes'ta-ment], *n.* a declaration; either of the two major sections of the Bible, regarded as covenants of God with Man, called the *Old* and *New Testaments*; (*coll.*) the New Testament; **last will and t.**, a person's will, the document in which he expresses his wishes as to the disposal of his property after death. TESTAMENTARY [tes-ta-men'ta-ri], *adj.* pertaining to a will or wills; bequeathed by or appointed in a will. [L.].

TESTATE (1) [tes'tāt], *adj.* (*leg.*) leaving a valid will at death. TESTATE (2), *n.* (*leg.*) person who dies t. [L.].

TESTATOR [tes-tā'ter], *n.* (*leg.*) one who makes a will or dies testate; man so doing or so dying.

TESTATRIX [tes-tā'triks], *n.* woman who makes a will or dies testate.

TESTER (1) [tes'ter], *n.* person who or thing which tests.

TESTER (2), *n.* canopy over a four-poster bed. [ME.].

TESTER (3), *n.* (*hist.*) shilling of Henry VIII. [OFr.].

TESTICLE [tes'ti-kl], *n.* one of the male sperm-secreting glands in mammals. [L.].

TESTIFY [tes'ti-fī], *v.t.* and *i.* to give evidence; (*leg.*) give sworn evidence or testimony; provide or be evidence of. [L.].

TESTIMONIAL [tes-ti-mŏ'ni-al], *n.* written statement by some responsible person as to the character and abilities of another person; gift or presentation of some kind made in token of gratitude, admiration, esteem etc.

TESTIMONY [tes'ti-mo-ni], *n.* evidence given, either written or spoken; that which serves to prove or give evidence of; (*pl.*) the Scriptures. [L.].

TESTIS (*pl.* testes) [tes'tis, 'tēz], *n.* (*anat.*) testicle. [L.].

TESTUDINAL [tes-tyŏŏ'di-nal], *adj.* pertaining to, resembling, tortoises.

TESTUDINARIOUS [tes-tyŏŏ-di-nāer'i-ŏŏs], *adj.* mottled like tortoiseshell.

TESTUDINEOUS [tes-tyŏŏ-di'ni-ŏŏs], *adj.* resembling the shell, or the slow pace, of a tortoise. [L.].

TESTUDO [tes-tyŏŏ'dŏ], *n.* (*Rom. antiq.*) shield-like engine under cover of which attackers could advance close to the walls of a besieged city or fortress; (*zool.*) land-tortoise. [L.].

TESTY [tes'ti], *adj.* peevish, easily annoyed, irritable. [AFr.].

TETANIC [te-ta'nik], *adj.* (*med.*) of, or pertaining to, tetanus; producing tetanus.

TETANUS [te'ta-nus], *n.* (*path.*) disease of which the principal sympton is contraction and spasms of the muscles. [Gk.].

TETCHY [te'chi], *adj.* testy, peevish, touchy. [Uncert.].

TÊTE-A-TÊTE, tête-à-tête (1) [tāt-ah-tāt'], *adj.* and *adv.* confidentially, privately, between two people, with one other person. TÊTE-A-TÊTE (2), *n.* a private confidential chat. [Fr.].

TETHER (1) [te'тнer], *n.* rope used to tie an animal to a post or stake and yet allow a moderate amount of freedom and movement; **to be at the end of one's t.**, to be at the end of one's resources. TETHER (2), *v.t.* to fasten (an animal) with a t.; (*fig.*) fix, fasten, deprive of freedom. [OScand.].

TETRA-, *pref.* fourfold, containing four parts, consisting of four. [Gk.].

TETRACHORD [te'tra-kawd], *n.* (*mus.*) a series of four successive tones.

TETRAD [te'trad], *n.* set or group of four; (*mus.*) chord made up of four notes; (*biol.*) group of four cells. [Gk.].

TETRAGON [te'tra-gon], *n.* (*geom.*) closed geometrical figure with four sides. TETRAGONAL [te-tra'go-nal], relating to a t.; having four angles; (*zool., bot.*) used to describe anything which is quadrangular in section. [Gk.].

TETRAHEDRON (*pl.* tetrahedra, tetrahedrons) [te-tra-hē'dron], *n.* (*geom.*) three-dimensional figure contained in four sides. TETRAHEDRAL, *adj.* possessing four sides, quadrilateral; (of a three-dimensional figure) enclosed in four plane surfaces. [Gk.].

TETRALOGY [te-tra'lo-ji], *n.* a related series of four dramas on the same theme or developments of it. [Gk.].

TETRAMETER [te-tra'mi-ter], *n.* (*pros.*) line of verse containing four metrical sections.

TETRAPOD (1) [te'tra-pod], *adj.* having four feet. TETRAPOD (2), *n.* (*zool., entom.*) four-footed creature. [Gk.].

TETRARCH [tě'trahk], *n.* (*Rom. hist.*) governor of a fourth part of a province; any governor over a small territory. [Gk.].

TETRASYLLABLE [te-tra-si'la-bl], *n.* word containing four syllables.

TETRODE [te'trŏd], *n.* (*elect.*) thermionic valve having four electrodes. [TETR(A) and (ELECTR)ODE].

TETTER [te'ter], *n.* a skin disease such as eczema etc. [OE.].

TEUTONIC (1) [tyŏŏ-to'nik], *adj.* pertaining to the Germanic race or to Germanic languages, *esp.* to primitive Germanic. TEUTONIC (2), *n.* the primitive Germanic language.

TEXT [tekst], *n.* the wording of written or printed matter; the written or printed words of which a literary work is composed; the words and phrases originally used by an author as distinct from a later paraphrase, translation or amended version; the main body of a literary or academic work as distinct from notes and prefaces and other supplementary matter; quotation, phrase or sentence from the Bible, *esp.* one used as the basis or starting-point for a sermon or lecture, such a phrase or sentence quoted as authority for an assertion, argument etc.; any phrase, proverb, quotation etc. used to give authority to a writer's or speaker's remarks; theme or subject of a discourse, discussion, literary work etc.; **t. book**, informative book on a given subject for use by students etc., treatise or compendious summary of knowledge on a given subject. [L.].

TEXTILE (1) [teks'tīl], *adj.* pertaining to weaving; woven. TEXTILE (2), *n.* woven stuff or material, fabric. [L.].

TEXTUAL [teks'tyŏŏ-al], *adj.* connected with, pertaining to, a text or texts; (of a translation) word for word. TEXTUALLY, *adv.* in accordance with a text; from consideration of the text or t. problems; verbatim.

TEXTURE [teks'tyŏŏr], *n.* anything made by weaving; manner of weaving or character of a woven fabric; constitution, character or structure of anything considered with special regard to its real or supposed constituents. [L.].

THAI, see TAI.

THALAMUS [tha'la-mus], *n.* (*anat.*) a part of the

brain in which a nerve is rooted, that part from which the optic nerve comes. [Gk.].

THALER [tah′ler], *n.* obsolete German coin roughly equivalent to a shilling. [Germ.].

THALIA [tha-lī′ah], *n.* (*class. myth.*) the Muse of pastoral and comic poetry. THALIAN, *adj.* relating to T.; comic. [Gk.].

THALLIUM [tha′li-um], *n.* (*chem.*) the rare metallic element denoted by Tl. [Gk.].

THALLOPHYTE [tha′lō-fīt], *n.* (*bot.*) a plant of the lowest order of plants, containing those in which stem and leaf are not distinct, and which have no true root, such as algae, fungi and lichens. [Gk.].

THALLUS [tha′lus], *n.* (*bot.*) plant structure which has no true root, and in which the stem and leaf are not distinct, as in a lichen etc. [Gk.].

THAN [THan], *conj. and prep.* used to express inequality *after a comparative.* [OE.].

THANE, THEGN [thān], *n.* (*hist.*) member of the Anglo-Saxon nobility. [OE.].

THANK [thangk], *v.t.* to express one's gratitude to (someone) in speech or writing; (*fig.*) be indebted to; **t. you,** I am grateful to you. [OE.].

THANKFUL [thangk′fŏŏl], *adj.* grateful; having a proper sense of kindness received or service rendered; expressing or uttering thanks.

THANKLESS [thangk′les], *adj.* (of a person) unthankful; ungrateful; (of an action etc.) not arousing or likely to arouse gratitude in others.

THANKS [thangks], *n.(pl.)* gratitude, an expression of gratitude; (*coll.*) thank you; **t. to,** owing to, because of. [OE.].

THANKSGIVING [thangks′gi-ving], *n.* act of rendering thanks or expressing gratitude; liturgical formula expressing thanks; special church service to return thanks to God; **T. Day,** (*U.S.*) day on which thanks are given to God for the harvest and other blessings, usually the last Thursday in November.

THAT (1) (*pl.* **those**) [THat], *dem. pron. expressing a person or thing pointed out, a person, thing, idea just referred to, a statement, command or wish just expressed, a phrase just used etc.*; **after t.,** when those things had happened; **by t.,** by that time; **with t.,** thereupon; **t. is,** in other words; **like t.,** thus, after that fashion; **take t.,** receive this blow; **and all t.,** and so on and so forth; **t.'s t.,** that is all over. THAT (2) (*pl.* THOSE), *dem. adj. used to emphasize or indicate the person or thing referred to; used before the name of a person or thing to express disapproval;* **t. once,** on the indicated occasion only. THAT (3), *dem. adv.* (*coll.*) to such a degree, to t. extent; very, greatly. THAT (4), *rel. pron.* the person, persons, thing or things which; (*adverbially*) on which, at which, in which. THAT (5), *conj. used to introduce a subordinate noun clause; used to introduce an exclamatory clause; used to introduce a clause expressing purpose, desire, result; used to introduce a subordinate clause expressing a fact from which the fact expressed in the principal clause might be deduced or upon which it is or might be consequent.* [OE.].

THATCH (1) [thach], *n.* roof for a house or cottage or covering for the top of a rick, made of reed and straw pegged tightly down; (*fig.*) thick shaggy head of hair. THATCH (2), *v.t.* to cover with t. THATCHING, *n.* act of covering with t.; materials used to make a t. [OE.].

THAUMATO [thaw′ma-tō], *pref.* pertaining to a wonder, marvel, miracle, magical trick etc. [Gk.].

THAUMATURGE [thaw′ma-terj], *n.* magician, miracle-worker, wonder-worker; (*fig.*) conjurer.

THAUMATURGY [thaw′ma-ter-ji], *n.* act of performing miracles, magic, conjuring. [Gk.].

THAW (1) [thaw], *v.t. and i.* to cause (something which is frozen solid) to melt and become liquid by the application of heat; (of snow, ice) melt under the influence of heat. THAW (2), *n.* process by which ice, snow, frost etc. liquefy when the temperature rises; instance of this; **silver t.,** frost coming immediately after a t. [OE.].

THE (1) [THē (stressed), THe, THi (before vowels)], *def. art. used before a noun to denote that a particular one of a series, group, variety etc. is referred to; used before nouns denoting things of which only one exists or is known or when one particular example is of special importance and commonly referred to (natural phenomena, geographical phenomena, famous events, movements etc.); used before names indicating a group or before the name of one specimen of a group taken as typical of the whole; used before titles; used before adjectives used as nouns; used in phrases of measurement to express proportion; used emphatically before a*

noun to denote that the thing referred to is unique or outstanding. THE (2), *adv.* by so much (usually followed by a *comp. adj.*) [ME.].

THEATRE [thē′a-ter], *n.* building consisting of a large hall with seats for spectators facing a stage or platform where dramatic performances are given; hall or room similarly arranged where lectures are delivered; place where a connected series of events occur; body of dramatic writers; the theatrical art and profession generally; dramatic effect; **operating t.,** room in a hospital where operations are performed; **t. of war,** place where military operations are conducted, usually one of a number in which fighting is simultaneous. [Gk.].

THEATRICAL [thē-at′ri-kal], *adj.* pertaining to a theatre or representation; showy, unreal, artificial, merely impressive. THEATRICALS, *n.(pl.)* the hobby of amateur dramatics.

THE DANSANT, thé dansant [tā-dah(ng)′sah(ng)], *n.* afternoon tea accompanied by dancing. [Fr.].

THEE [THē], *pers. pron. 2nd pers. sing. objective case of* THOU. [OE.].

THEFT [theft], *n.* act of stealing. [OE.].

THEGN, see THANE.

THEINE [thē′ēn], *n.* (*chem.*) an alkaloid contained in tea, and identical with caffeine.

THEIR [THāer], *possessive adj.* belonging to them.

THEIRS [THāerz], *possessive pron.* belonging to them.

THEISM [thē′izm], *n.* belief in the existence of God as a deity who makes Himself known by divine revelation. [~Gk.].

THEIST [thē′ist], *n.* believer in theism.

THEM [THem], *pron. objective case of* THEY. [OScand.].

THEMATIC [thē-ma′tik], *adj.* (*mus.*) pertaining to themes; (*gram.*) pertaining to the stem of a word. [Gk.].

THEME [thēm], *n.* a subject of writing, thought, conversation, argument etc.; (*mus.*) the melodic subject or main melody or figure of composition; (*gram.*) the section of a word to which suffixes and inflexions are added; **t. song,** song which recurs several times in the course of a musical play, film or revue. [Gk.].

THEMSELVES [Them-selvz′], *pron. pl. emphatic or reflex. form of* THEM.

THEN (1) [THen], *adv.* at some specified time in either the past or future; immediately after, next; at a later date; **now t.,** (*coll.*) phrase introducing a *warning or threat, or initiating another stage in a conversation.* THEN (2), *adj.* existing at that time. THEN (3), *conj.* in that case; moreover, also. [OE.].

THENCE [THens], *adv.* from that place or time; from that cause; from that point in the argument etc., therefore. [ME.].

THENCEFORTH [THens-fawth′], *adv.* from that time onwards.

THENCEFORWARD [THens-faw′werd], *adv.* from that time forward.

THEO-, *pref.* pertaining to God or to gods. [Gk.].

THEOBROMINE [thē-o-brō′mēn], *n.* (*chem.*) the volatile alkaloid found in the seeds of the cacao tree. [~Gk.].

THEOCRACY [thē-ok′ra-si], *n.* government by priests claiming authority from God. [Gk.].

THEODOLITE [thē-o′dō-līt], *n.* instrument by which a surveyor measures angles. [Unkn.].

THEOLOGIAN [thē-ō-lō′ji-an], *n.* one learned in theology.

THEOLOGICAL [thē-ō-lo′ji-kal], *adj.* relating or pertaining to theology.

THEOLOGIZE [thē-o′lo-jīz], *v.t. and i.* to render theological; speculate in, or discourse on, theology.

THEOLOGY [thē-o′lo-ji], *n.* the systematic study of the nature of God or of religion; a specific theological theory or system. [Gk.].

THEOREM [thē′o-rem], *n.* (*math.*) general statement or proposition which requires proof. [Gk.].

THEORETIC(AL) [thē-o-re′tik(-al)], *adj.* pertaining to theory; in accordance with theory as contrasted with practical experience or knowledge, speculative. [Gk.].

THEORIST [thē′o-rist], *n.* one who speculates or forms theories; person who upholds a certain theory; one learned in the theory of a certain subject.

THEORIZE [thē′o-rīz], *v.t. and i.* to form a theory or theories; speculate concerning; base one's arguments upon unpractical or speculative grounds.

THEORY [thē′o-ri], *n.* a speculative system based upon and offering an explanation of observed facts or phenomena; the underlying laws and principles of a science, art, craft etc., as contrasted with practical or technical knowledge of it; a systematized statement of these laws or principles; speculation, mental view or imagination; (*coll.*) a notion, fad or fancy; **in t.**, in accordance with theoretical knowledge, though not necessarily with practical experience as well. [Gk.].

THEOSOPHIC(AL) [thē-ō-so'fik(-al)], *adj.* pertaining to theosophy.

THEOSOPHIST [thē-o'so-fist], *n.* one who believes in theosophy.

THEOSOPHY [thē-o'so-fi], *n.* a recent mystical and speculative religious system which claims to attain a profound knowledge and insight by establishing a close and direct relationship between the individual soul and the deity; any speculative system of religious thought claiming a knowledge of nature through mystical contemplation and knowledge of the deity. [Late Gk.].

THERAPEUTIC(AL) [the-ra-pyōō'tik(-al)], *adj.* relating to the art of healing and the treatment of disease.

THERAPEUTICS [the-ra-pyōō'tiks], *n.(pl.)* art of healing and curing diseases; that branch of medical science concerned with this.

THERAPY [the'ra-pi], *n.* (*med.*) treatment intended to cure.

THERE (1) [THāer], *adv.* in that place or towards that place (always referring to a locality other than that in which the speaker is); (*fig.*) at that point in an argument, discussion, speculation, story etc.; *used as an impersonal pronoun as the subject of a verb* (*usually the verb to be*) *and at the beginning of a sentence*; **to be all t.**, to be sane, be very sharp witted; **to get t.**, to attain one's ambition; **t. you are,** I told you so; **t. you go,** you are doing it again. THERE (2), *int.* **there, there,** *used in soothing a child*; **t. now,** I told you it would happen; **that's better,** isn't it? [O.E.].

THEREABOUT(S) [THāer'a-bowt(s)], *adv.* in that vicinity, near that place; (*fig.*) approximately that number, degree or quantity.

THEREAFTER [THāer-ahf'ter], *adv.* after that, on subsequent occasions; in accordance with that.

THEREAT [THāer-at'], *adv.* at that place or time; in consequence of that, immediately after that.

THEREBY [THāer-bī'], *adv.* near that place; by that means.

THEREFORE [THaer'faw(r)], *adv.* on that account, for that reason; consequently. [ME.].

THEREIN [THāer-in'], *adv.* in that place; **in or within** that.

THEREINAFTER [THāer-in-ahf'ter], *adv.* **in all** which follows (in another document).

THEREOF [THāer-ov'], *adv.* (*archaic*) of that, of those.

THEREON [THāer-on'], *adv.* on that, on this; after that, as a result of that.

THERETO [THāer-tōō'], *adv.* to that; moreover, in addition.

THERETOFORE [THāer-tōō-faw(r)'], *adv.* (*archaic*) previously, up to that time.

THEREUNDER [THāer-un'der], *adv.* under that.

THEREUPON [THāer-u-pon'], *adv.* upon that; on account of that; straightway, immediately.

THEREWITH [THāer-wiTH'], *adv.* together **with** that; immediately following that, straightway.

THERM [thurm], *n.* (*phys.*) the amount of heat required to raise one gramme of water at its maximum density by one degree centigrade; unit of heating value used in measuring coal-gas, and equal to 100,000 British thermal units. [Gk.].

THERMAL [thur'mal], *adj.* pertaining to heat; hot, warm; **British t. unit,** the amount of heat required to raise one pound of water at maximum density by one degree Fahrenheit.

THERMIC [thur'mik], *adj.* thermal.

THERMION [thur'mi-on], *n.* (*elect.*) an electron emitted by a heated body. [Gk.].

THERMIONIC [ther-mi-o'nik], *adj.* (*elect.*) relating to thermionics; **t. valve,** vacuum-tube used in radio engineering, containing at least two cathodes, one of which is a heated filament; **t. emission,** the stream of electrons emitted by the heated filament in a t. valve.

THERMIONICS [ther-mi-o'niks], *n.(pl.)* (*elect.*) science which deals with the emission of electrons from a heated body.

THERMIT(E) [thur'mit, 'mīt], *n.* a mixture of very finely granulated aluminium with the oxide of some other metal (usually iron) which, when ignited, burns at a very high temperature. [Germ.].

THERMO-, *pref.* pertaining to heat. [Gk.].

THERMODYNAMICS [ther-mō-dī-na'miks], *n.(pl.)* science which deals with the relationship between

thermal energy (heat) and mechanical energy, and the conversion of one into the other.

THERMO-ELECTRIC(AL) [ther-mō-i-lek'trik(-al)], *adj.* relating to thermo-electricity.

THERMO-ELECTRICITY [ther-mō-i-lek-tri'si-ti], *n.* electricity developed by the action of heat at the junction of two different metals.

THERMOGENESIS [ther-mō-je'ni-sis], *n.* generation of heat in an animal body.

THERMOMETER [ther-mo'mi-ter], *n.* instrument by which temperature is measured. [THERMO and METER].

THERMOMETRIC(AL) [ther-mō-me'trik(-al)], *adj.* pertaining to or measured by means of a thermometer.

THERMOS FLASK [thur'mos-flahsk], *n.* (*prot.*) flask of which the sides are a double wall enclosing a vacuum, and which is used to keep liquids at a constant temperature. [~THERMO and FLASK].

THERMO-SIPHON [ther-mō-sī'fon], *n.* a siphon for inducing the movement of water through the cooling system in the engine of a motor-car. [THERMO and SIPHON].

THERMOSTAT [thur'mō-stat], *n.* instrument which regulates temperature automatically. [THERMO and Gk.].

THERMOSTATICS [ther-mō-sta'tiks], *n.(pl.)* science and theory dealing with the equilibrium of heat.

THERMOTHERAPY [ther-mō-the'ra-pi], *n.* cure of disease by heat.

THESAURUS (*pl.* **thesauri**) [thi-saw'rus], *n.* a collection of any sort, anthology, lexicon etc. [Gk.].

THESE [THēz], *dem. pron. and adj. pl.* of THIS.

THESIS (*pl.* **theses**) [thē'sis], *n.* (*pros.*) usually, the unstressed part of a foot in classical or modern verse, contrasted with the arsis; *orig.* the stressed part indicated by the lowering of hand or foot in beating time; a theory or proposition stated or presented for proof or as a subject for discussion; an academic dissertation on a fixed theme presented by a candidate for a university degree, and usually expected to embody the results of original research. [Gk.].

THESPIAN [thes'pi-an], *adj. and n.* pertaining to acting and the drama; an actor. [Gk. *Thespis,* traditional founder of the drama].

THETA [thē'tah], *n.* the letter θ in the Greek alphabet corresponding to *th.* [Gk.].

THEWS [thyōōz], *n.(pl.)* muscle, sinew, bodily strength, mental or moral strength. [O.E.].

THEY [THā], *pron.* 3rd *person pl. common gender, nom.* those (people or things), those already referred to; (*coll.*) *indefinite pron.* people. [OScand.].

THICK (1) [thik], *adj.* of considerable size between opposite surfaces; (of fluids) having considerable density, muddy, sluggish; (of a group of objects) placed closely together, crowded; very frequently repeated; (of the voice) harsh and confused, not clear; (of the intellect) dull-witted; (*coll.*) very intimate; **a bit t.,** (*coll.*) scarcely tolerable; **t. head,** headache. THICK-SKINNED, having a t. skin; (*fig.*) (of persons) insensitive, not easily touched by common emotions, *esp.* insensitive to taunts and abuse. THICK (2), *n.* the thickest place in anything; **to be in the t. of it,** to be in the press of battle surrounded with difficulties, or in the midst of difficult or exacting work; **lay it on t.,** apply (it) excessively, make much of it to an inordinate degree. [ME.].

THICKEN [thi'ken], *v.t. and i.* to make thick or become thick. THICKENING, *n.* process of making or becoming thick; that part of an object which grows thicker than the rest; that which serves to make a liquid more dense.

THICKET [thi'kit], *n.* a small wood, *esp.* one with dense undergrowth. [O.E.].

THICKHEAD [thik'hed], *n.* (*coll.*) dull-witted person.

THICKSET [thik'set], *adj.* arranged densely and closely together; (of persons etc.) short and broad, of solid build, sturdy.

THIEF (*pl.* **thieves**) [thēf, thēvz], *n.* one who commits robbery; fault in the wick of a candle. [O.E.].

THIEVE [thēv], *v.t. and i.* to commit theft; steal. [O.E.].

THIEVISH [thē'vish], *adj.* of, as addicted to, stealing; resembling a thief.

THIGH [thi], *n.* that part of the human leg between the knee and the trunk; corresponding part of the leg in apes and birds; corresponding part of the hind legs of quadrupeds; t.-bone. THIGH-BONE, bone of the t., the femur. [O.E.].

THIMBLE [thim'bl], *n.* small cap fitted over the middle finger of the right hand when sewing; any similar article used in playing mechanical instruments. [OE.].

THIMBLERIG (1) [thim'bl-rig], *n.* cheating game in which the operator rapidly shifts a pea or other small object from under one of three inverted thimbles or cups. THIMBLERIG (2), *v.t. and i.* to swindle at t.; cheat or swindle. [THIMBLE and RIG (3).].

THIN (1) [thin], *adj.* not thick, used of an object having a small distance between opposite surfaces; (of a person or animal) not fat or plump, bony, emaciated; sparsely arranged; (of liquids) having a low density; (of soup and other liquid foods) containing very little or no solids in suspension; (of an argument etc.) being of no great account, easily refuted or improved upon, lacking in thought; **a t. time,** (*slang*) a miserable experience. THIN-SKINNED, having a t. skin; unduly sensitive, easily offended. THIN (2), *v.t. and i.* to make t. or become t. or thinner; **to t. out,** to make or become more sparse. THINLY, *adv.* in a t. fashion; sparsely, sparingly. THINNER, *n.* one who, that which, thins; *esp.* a substance used to reduce the consistency of paint. THINNISH, *adj.* somewhat t. [OE.].

THINE [thin], *possessive pron. and adj. 2nd person sing.* (*archaic*) of THEE. [OE.].

THING [thing], *n.* an animate or inanimate object, made of a material stuff or substance, and forming an entity in itself; any conception of the mind, idea, fact, thought, subject of conversation etc.; *applied familiarly or colloquially to persons*; a circumstance or fact; (*coll.*) that which is suitable, the state of affairs generally, trade, business, the matter in hand; (usually *pl.*) personal belongings, baggage, parcels, clothes etc.; **to make a good t.** (out) of, (*coll.*) to render very profitable; **for one t.,** as one consideration; **it's just the t.!** (*coll.*) it's exactly what we want!; **not to feel quite the t.,** (*coll.*) to feel rather unwell; **no such t.!** (*coll.*) certainly not, by no means! **to know a t. or two,** (*coll.*) to be well informed; to be knowing, artful; **quite the t.,** (*coll.*) (sarcastically) to the manner born; **not quite the t.,** (*coll.*) not suitable, not in good taste. [OE.].

THINK [thingk], *v.t. and i.* to exercise the reasoning or contemplative faculties; reason within the mind, meditate or reflect; be of an opinion, believe without certainly knowing; consider to be (such and such); expect, surmise; bring oneself into a certain state by too much thought, or by anticipating in the mind the circumstances of that state; **to t. of,** to call to mind, hit upon in the mind; remember, reflect upon; be of an opinion about; **to t. about,** to occupy one's thoughts with, reflect upon, consider, remember, reason about in the mind; **to t. better of,** to change one's intention concerning; **not to t. of** (doing something), to have no intention of (doing something); **not to t. much of** (someone or something), to have a low opinion of (someone or something); **to t. out,** to work out mentally; **to t. up,** (*coll.*) to concoct, invent; **to t. over,** to consider carefully; reconsider; **I don't t.!** (*coll.*) emphatic negative used to cancel a statement ironically put in the affirmative; **to t. nothing of,** to hold in low esteem. THINKER, *n.* one who thinks; philosopher, man of intellect. [OE.].

THINKABLE [thingk'a-bl], *adj.* able to be thought of or conceived.

THINKING (1) [thing'king], *n.* act of exercising the reasoning and contemplative faculties. THINKING (2), *adj.* given to thought, thoughtful, capable of thought and reason.

THIRD (1) [thurd], *adj.* the ordinal of three; being one of three equal parts or divisions; **t. degree,** rough handling by the police of a suspected person to obtain information or a confession; **T. International,** the international, world-wide communist party organization aiming at world revolution on communistic lines, officially dissolved in 1943; **t. man,** (*cricket*) fielder on the off-side between slip and point; **t. party,** (*leg.*) a party other than the two principals involved in a case; **t.-party risks,** liability of the holder of an insurance policy with regard to persons or parties not specifically referred to in the policy. THIRD-RATE, (*coll.*) of poor quality. THIRD (2), *n.* that thing or person etc. in a series coming next after the second; one of three equal parts; (*mus.*) interval of three consecutive degrees of the scale; (*motoring*) t. gear of a motor engine. [OE.].

THIRST (1) [thurst], *n.* desire to drink, painful sensation caused by lack of drink; (*fig.*) any powerful craving, as for knowledge, adventure etc.; extreme dryness of the soil. THIRST (2), *v.i.* to experience thirst; lack drink; **to t. for** (or **after**), to have a great desire or craving for. [OE.].

THIRSTY [thurs'ti], *adj.* suffering from thirst, desiring drink; parched, lacking moisture, causing thirst. [OE.].

THIRTEEN (1) [ther-tēn'], *n.* one more than twelve. THIRTEEN (2), *adj.* amounting to one more than twelve. [OE.].

THIRTEENTH (1) [ther-tēnth'], *adj.* the ordinal of thirteen; being one of thirteen equal parts. THIRTEENTH (2), *n.* the next after the twelfth; one of thirteen equal parts or divisions. [OE.].

THIRTIETH (1) [thur'ti-eth], *adj.* the ordinal of thirty; being one of thirty equal parts. THIRTIETH (2), *n.* person or thing in a series who or which follows next after the twenty-ninth; one of thirty equal parts or divisions.

THIRTY (1) [thur'ti], *n.* the cardinal number, three times ten; the symbol for this; (*pl.*) fourth decade of any century; fourth decade of a person's life. THIRTY (2), *adj.* amounting to three times ten. THIRTYFOLD (1), *adj.* amounting to three times ten. THIRTYFOLD (2), *adv.* thirty times. [OE.].

THIS (1) [this], *dem. pron. used to refer to a person or thing actually near or that which was last referred to, spoken or thought, or that which will be next referred to or spoken*; **all t.,** these things considered collectively; **like t.,** in this manner; **for all t.,** despite these considerations. THIS (2), *dem. adj. referring to the one nearest to hand, last referred to etc.; used with expressions referring to periods of time, e.g. year, morning, week etc., and meaning the current one; frequently used in contrast with* THAT. THIS (3), *adv.* **t. much,** so much and no more. [OE.].

THISTLE [this'l], *n.* (*bot.*) one of various prickly plants of the genus *Carduus*; the national emblem of Scotland; **Order of the T.,** a Scottish order of knights (K.T., Knight of the T.). THISTLY, *adj.* overgrown with thistles; prickly like a t. [OE.].

THISTLE-DOWN [this'l-down], *n.* the long hairs on the seed of thistles, by means of which the seeds are carried along in the air.

THITHER (1) [thi'ther], *adv.* to that place; towards that place, in that direction. THITHER (2), *adj.* lying on the other side, away from the speaker, beyond. [OE.].

THOLE (1), **THOWL** [thōl], *n.* peg in the gunwale of a rowing boat against which the oar is pulled, rowlock. THOLE-PIN, a t. [OE.].

THOLE (2), *v.t.* to endure, tolerate. [OE.].

THONG [thong], *n.* strip of leather used as a strap or lash. [OE.].

THORAX [thaw'raks], *n.* (*anat., zool.*) in a mammal, that part of the body between the neck and abdomen, including ribs, breasts and lungs etc.; similar part in the lower vertebrates, fish, birds etc.; in insects, middle segment of the body. [Gk.].

THORIUM [thaw'ri-um], *n.* (*chem.*) rare metallic element denoted by the symbol Th. [~Swed.].

THORN [thawn], *n.* spike, spine or prickle on the twigs and branches of some trees and bushes; plant bearing these, *esp.* the hawthorn; one of the Old English symbols for the sound now represented by *th*; (*fig.*) any nuisance, worry or irritating disability; **t. in one's side,** nuisance or annoyance; **t. in the flesh,** secret worry, trouble, ailment or disability. THORN-APPLE, a weed with prickly fruits. [OE.].

THORNBACK [thawn'bak], *n.* the common ray or skate.

THOROUGH † (1) [thu'ru], *prep.* through; THOROUGH-BASS, *n.* (*mus.*) notation in which the chords intended for the bass part are indicated by figures; theory and practice of harmony. THOROUGH (2), *adj.* complete, perfect, entire, downright. [OE.].

THOROUGHBRED (1) [thu'ru-bred], *adj.* (of animals) being of pure breed; (*esp.* of horses) having ancestors which for a considerable number of generations back are recorded in the stud-book; (of human beings) being of aristocratic birth and showing the characteristics of such birth. THOROUGHBRED (2), *n.* a t. creature or plant, *esp.* a horse.

THOROUGHFARE [thu'ru-fäer], *n.* a way through, open road.

THOROUGHGOING [thu-ru-gō'ing], *adj.* going the full length, uncompromising.

THOROUGHPACED [thu-ru-pāst'], *adj.* complete, downright, thorough.

THORP(E) † [thawp], *n.* small village, hamlet (usually in place-names). [ODan.].

THOSE [thōz], *dem. pron. and adj. pl.* of THAT.

THOU [thow], *pron. 2nd person sing. nom.* of the

The accent ′ after a syllable = stress (u-pon′). The mark ¯ over a vowel = length (ā in made; ō in bone).

THOUGH

577

THRONG

personal pronoun now employed chiefly in dial., poet. and liturgical language. [OE.].

THOUGH [thō], *conj. and adv.* despite that, notwithstanding that; nevertheless; **as t.**, as if; **even t.**, even if. [OScand.].

THOUGHT (1) [thawt], *n.* act of thinking, process of thinking; capacity to think; result of thinking, *esp.* a short and sometimes epigrammatical statement of an idea or conception; intellectual outlook, body of ideas and opinions; reasoned and logical ideas; reflection, consideration, care; opinion, point of view; *(coll.)* small amount or degree; **to have thoughts of**, to have some intention of; **to take t. for**, to consider take into account. THOUGHT-READING, power of knowing other people's thoughts by telepathy. THOUGHT-TRANSFERENCE, telepathy. THOUGHT-WAVE, hypothetical wave of t. travelling between two minds. THOUGHT (2), *pret. and p.pt. of* THINK. [OE.].

THOUGHTFUL [thawt'fŏŏl], *adj.* full of thought; pensive, much given to thinking; kind, considerate.

THOUGHTLESS [thawt'les], *adj.* careless, stupid, inconsiderate.

THOUSAND (1) [thow'zand], *n.* the number obtained when 100 is multiplied by 10; *(coll.) (pl.)* an immense, uncountable number; **one in a t.**, very good, with scarcely an equal or rival. THOUSAND (2), *adj.* ten times one hundred; *(coll.)* very many, indefinite in number. THOUSANDFOLD, *adj. and adv.* multiplied a thousand times. [OE.].

THOUSANDTH (1) [thow'zandth], *adj.* the ordinal of a thousand; being one of a thousand equal parts. THOUSANDTH (2), *n.* one of a thousand equal parts or divisions.

THOWL, see THOLE (1).

THRALDOM [thrawl'dum], *n.* slavery; bondage, condition of a thrall.

THRALL [thrawl], *n.* **slave or serf**; slavery, bondage. [OScand.].

THRASH [thrash], *v.t. and i.* to beat severely, flog; separate the grain of (cereal) from the husks and straw by beating; beat at a game; **to t. out**, to discuss (a problem) very thoroughly; **to t. about**, (as of a swimmer) to move the limbs as if flogging something. THRASHER, *n.* person who or thing which thrashes; implement for thrashing corn; the fox-shark. [OE.].

THRASHING-FLOOR, -MACHINE, -MILL, see THRESHING-FLOOR, -MACHINE, -MILL.

THRASONICAL [thra-so'ni-kal], *adj.* boastful, bragging. [*Thraso*, bragging Greek soldier in Terence's *Eunuchus*].

THRAWN [thrawn], *adj.* (Scots) twisted; *(fig.)* perverse, cross-grained. [THROWN].

THREAD (1) [thred], *n.* slender cord made of fibres (e.g. of silk, wool, cotton etc.) and used in sewing; slender, cylindrical filament; spiral groove of a screw or of a bolt; connexion in a series of thoughts, ideas, events in a narrative etc.; **to hang by a t.**, to be in a precarious situation. THREAD (2), *v.t.* to put (a t.) into the eye of (a needle); place on a t., string up; **to t. one's way**, to make one's way with care and caution. THREADER, *n.* person who or thing which threads; machine which cuts the t. on a screw. [OE.].

THREADBARE [thred'bãer], *adj.* (of a fabric) having the nap so worn down that the thread is visible; (of persons) shabbily dressed in old, worn clothes; *(fig.)* hackneyed, familiar.

THREADWORM [thred'werm], *n.* tiny parasitic worm infesting the human intestine.

THREAT [thret], *n.* menacing statement of intention to hurt, punish or damage; circumstance or circumstances which indicate the probability of an undesirable occurrence. [OE.].

THREATEN [thre'ten], *v.t. and i.* to utter a threat or threats to; utter threats; offer an appearance suggesting that some undesirable event will occur; seem likely to happen. THREATENING, *adj.* foreboding, menacing, portentous.

THREE (1) [thrē], *n.* number which is one more than two; the symbol representing this. THREE (2), *adj.* one more than two. THREE-DECKER, *n.* old-fashioned sailing ship with t. decks; old-fashioned pulpit with t. tiers; novel in t. volumes; sandwich with two layers of filling. THREE-FIGURE, requiring t. figures to express, between a hundred and a thousand. THREE-HANDED, having t. hands; suitable for t. hands or t. players. THREE-LEGGED RACE, *n.* race for pairs of competitors in which the right leg of one competitor in a pair is tied to the left leg of the other. THREE-PLY, (of a thread) with t. strands; (of wood) consisting of t. layers.

THREEFOLD, *adj. and adv.* triple, multiplied by t.; t. times. [OE.].

THREE-QUARTER (1) [thrē-kwaw'ter], *adj.* being equivalent to or consisting of three of four equal parts of a whole. THREE-QUARTER (2), *n.* (Rugby football) one whose playing position is between the half-backs and the full-back, (pl.) the sum of three out of four equal parts, the greater part of something.

THREESCORE [thrē-skaw(r)'], *n.* thrice twenty sixty.

THREESOME [thrē'sum], *n.* (golf) game for three persons.

THRENODY [thrē'no-di], *n.* dirge or lament, funeral chant. THRENODIST [thrē'no-dist], *n.* writer or singer of a t. [Gk.].

THRESH [thresh], *v.t.* to beat (corn) so as to separate the grain from the chaff. THRESHER, *n.* person who or machine which threshes. THRESHING-FLOOR, THRASHING-FLOOR, *n.* area where corn is threshed. THRESHING-MACHINE, THRASHING-MACHINE, *n.* machine for threshing corn. THRESHING-MILL, THRASHING-MILL, *n.* a threshing-machine, *esp.* when stationary. [*Var. of* THRASH].

THRESHOLD [thre'shold], *n.* wooden beam or stone lying immediately under a door; entrance to a room, building etc.; *(fig.)* a beginning; **t. of consciousness**, (psych.) borderline of consciousness. [OE.].

THREW [thrōō], *pret. of* THROW (1). [OE.].

THRICE [thris], *adv.* three times; in a threefold measure. THRICE-BLESSED, very greatly blessed. [ME.].

THRIFT [thrift], *n.* frugality and economical management; (bot.) the sea-pink. [OScand.].

THRIFTLESS [thrift'les], *adj.* extravagant and wasteful.

THRIFTY [thrif'ti], *adj.* frugal, thriving by frugality, given to steady saving.

THRILL (1) [thril], *v.t. and i.* to provoke to deep emotional excitement, stir, rouse the emotions of; feel great enthusiasm, be deeply stirred in the emotions; vibrate. THRILL (2), *n.* the feeling one has when one's emotions are deeply stirred or great enthusiasm is aroused; glow of enthusiasm or excitement; *(coll.)* exciting event or circumstance, *esp.* in a story or film. THRILLER, *n.* that which provokes thrills; sensational novel or film, *esp.* a story of murder and detection. [OE.].

THRILLING [thri'ling], *adj.* stirring, rousing, exciting, provoking thrills; (of a voice) clear, ringing.

THRIVE (*pret.* **throve, thrived,** *p.pt.* **thriven, thrived**) [thrīv], *v.i.* (of persons) to prosper, grow vigorously, become steadily better off, get on in one's profession or calling; (of plants, animals etc.) increase and flourish; (of ideas, ideologies etc.) spread, gain more and more adherents. [OScand.].

THRIVING [thrī'ving], *adj.* steadily increasing in prosperity; increasing or multiplying in numbers; progressing and developing notably in any way.

THRO' [thrōō], *adv.* through. [THRO(UGH) (2)].

THROAT [thrōt], *n.* (anat.) passage in the neck connecting the mouth and nose with the stomach and lungs, gullet, windpipe; front of the neck; *(fig.)* any similar narrow passage; **to thrust (or ram) (something) down (a person's) t.**, to preach to a person about or force him to accept (something), even against his will. [OE.].

THROATY [thrō'ti], *adj.* (of the voice) harsh and guttural.

THROB (1) [throb], *v.i.* to beat, pulsate or palpitate, to do this rapidly. THROB (2), *n.* one of a succession of vibrations, a pulsation or beat, pulse. [ME.].

THROE [thrō], *n.* a burst of violent pain, great momentary anguish or agony; *(pl.)* series of such experiences; **to be in the throes of**, to be busily battling with the difficulties and problems of. [OScand.].

THROMBOSIS [throm-bō'sis], *n.* (med.) stoppage in the blood stream by the formation of a clot. [Gk.].

THROMBUS [throm'bus], *n.* (med.) a clot in the blood stream.

THRONE (1) [thrōn], *n.* chair of state, *esp.* of a king, bishop or archbishop; (theol.) an order of angels; *(fig.)* power and authority of a king; the monarchy; the sovereign himself. THRONE (2), *v.t.* to place on a t., enthrone; pay great respect and veneration to. [Gk.].

THRONG (1) [throng], *n.* a great closely-packed crowd of people, multitude. THRONG (2), *v.t. and i.* to crowd round, press upon in a crowd; gather together in a crowd; fill with multitudes of people; come in great numbers or in a crowd. [OE.].

ōō is pronounced as in food; ŏŏ as in hood; th as in think; TH as in that; zh as in azure. ~ = related to.

THROSTLE [thro'sl], *n.* the common song-thrush or mavis; kind of spinning machine for wool, cotton etc. [OE.].

THROTTLE (1) [thro'tl], *v.t.* to choke by squeezing the throat or windpipe; kill by this method; (*fig.*) check, suppress; **to t. down**, to reduce the power (and so the speed) of an engine by partly closing the t. THROTTLE (2), *n.* throat or neck; anything resembling this, *esp.* the valve in an engine regulating the supply of gas, steam etc., or the lever controlling this. [ME.].

THROUGH (1) [throo], *prep.* from end to end of; in the midst of; across; during; by means of. THROUGH (2), *adv.* from end to end of, from start to finish, right to the very end, completely; **t. and t.**, entirely, completely; **to be t. with**, to refuse to have any further dealings with. THROUGH (3), *adj.* going, stretching, from end to end, unobstructed; (of a train or other vehicle) travelling the entire journey, so that the passengers do not have to change; doing the whole journey without a break. [OE.].

THROUGHOUT (1) [throo-owt'], *prep.* through each and every part of; (of time) lasting from the beginning to the end of a given period. THROUGHOUT (2), *adv.* through each and every part, section, detail or particular of. [OE.].

THROVE [throv], *pret.* of THRIVE. [ME.].

THROW (1) [*pret.* **threw**, *p.pt.* **thrown**] [thro], *v.t. and i.* to propel through the air, fling, hurl; cause to fly from the hand by a jerk of the arm; shoot, project, give forth, give away, utter etc.; cause to fall, prostrate; place hurriedly in position, *esp.* of obstacles, impediments opposing troops etc.; (*U.S.*) lose deliberately (a game etc.); **to t. about**, to toss in several or various directions, scatter; **to t. back**, to revert to an hereditary type; **to t. in**, to give with other things an extra unspecified and not bargained for; (cricket) (of a fielder) return the ball from the field to the wicket-keeper or bowler; **to t. off**, to get rid of (illness etc.); (of clothes) take off hurriedly; dispense with, discard; disconcert, put off; utter, give forth; **to t. (oneself) on (or upon)**, to trust oneself to; **to t. open**, to cause to open suddenly (a door, window etc.); permit general access to; **to t. out**, to emit, cast forth; reject; utter, say; **to t. over (or overboard)**, to reject, refuse, discountenance; **to t. up**, to cast upwards; give up, cease to do or be interested in; (*coll.*) vomit; **to t. in one's hand, t. up the sponge**, to give in; **to t. oneself into**, to engage in with all one's strength and enthusiasm; **to t. a fit**, (*coll.*) to have a fit; **to t. a party**, (*slang*) to give a party. THROW-OFF, *n.* beginning of a hunt. THROW-OUT, *n.* (*coll.*) person who or thing which has been rejected. THROW (2), *n.* act of throwing; the motions, immediate effects, of something thrown; distance or degree of displacement; (*geol.*) direction of displacement of strata in a fault; (*dice, skittles, darts etc.*) a score. THROWER, *n.* person who or thing which throws; one who twists silk. [OE.].

THROWAWAY [thro'a-wā], *n.* (*coll.*) small advertisement, circular, handbill.

THROWBACK [thro'bak], *n.* member of a family reverting in some way to an ancestral type.

THROWN [thron], *p.pt.* of THROW. [OE.].

THRUM (1) [thrum], *n.* any one of the ends of the warp remaining on the loom after the web is cut off; fringe formed thus; any tassel or fringe or loose end of thread. THRUM (2), *v.t.* to give a fringe to. [OE.].

THRUM (3), *v.t. and i.* to strum; play a musical instrument carelessly or noisily, strum upon. [~OIcel.].

THRUSH (1) [thrush], *n.* any one of several varieties of song-birds of the genus *Turdus*. [OE.].

THRUSH (2), *n.* disease which most commonly affects the throats and mouths of children. [Uncert.].

THRUST (1) [thrust], *v.t.* to push vigorously with a sharp jerk, make a stab with, jerk or push forward; make a series of stabs; **to t. oneself forward**, to cause oneself deliberately to be noticed, make oneself conspicuous. THRUST (2), *n.* action of thrusting, stabbing, pushing violently; a steady pushing or pressure; (*eng.*) forward-moving power of an engine, propeller etc.; (*arch. etc.*) stress; (*geol.*) displacement of strata by lateral pressure; **cut and t.**, exchange of blows in a duel or fight; (*fig.*) rapid exchange of witty remarks. THRUSTER, *n.* one who thrusts; person who rides too close to the hounds in a hunt; (*coll.*) one (in business etc.) who is not over-scrupulous in his determination to succeed.

THRUSTING (1) [thrus'ting], *n.* act of pushing suddenly and violently, of stabbing or making a

thrust. THRUSTING (2), *adj.* thrustful, self-assertive, *esp.* used of a member of a hunt who rides too close to the hounds.

THUD (1) [thud], *n.* dull, heavy sound produced by a blow, collision or fall. THUD (2), *v.i.* to fall on to, collide with or strike something with a t. [OE.].

THUG [thug], *n.* one of a gang of robbers and assassins in northern India who were suppressed in the first half of the 19th century; murderer, ruffianly thief; gangster. THUGGEE, THUGGISM, *n.* assassination by strangling as committed by Indian thugs. THUGGERY, *n.* ruffianism. [Hind.].

THULE [thyoo'li], *n.* the northernmost territory known to the ancients; **ultima T.**, (*fig.*) the extreme limits of anything, lying almost beyond the borders of knowledge or experience. [L. from Gk.].

THUMB (1) [thum], *n.* the short innermost digit of the human hand which is opposable to the other fingers; corresponding digit on the hands or feet of animals; compartment in a glove which covers this digit; **to be under somebody's t.**, to be dominated by someone; **rule of t.**, an empirical method or process. THUMB-INDEX, system of reference consisting of a series of labelled indentations in the side of a book marking where each section commences. THUMB-NAIL, sheath or covering for the t. THUMB-SCREW, instrument of torture by means of which the victim's thumbs were slowly crushed; screw with winged tap which can be turned by the finger and t. THUMB (2), *v.t.* to touch with the t., make t.-marks upon; (referring to a book) use very much and soil with t.-marks. THUMBED [thumd], *adj.* possessing thumbs; soiled with t.-marks. [OE.].

THUMP (1) [thump], *v.t. and i.* to strike with a blow producing a dull, heavy sound; give a heavy blow to, strike with a series of heavy blows; fall with a dull, heavy sound; make such a sound. THUMP (2), *n.* dull sound produced by an impact or blow; blow producing such a sound. THUMPER, *n.* person who or thing which thumps; (*coll.*) anything excessive or remarkable, *esp.* an exaggerated lie. THUMPING, *adj.* (*coll.*) excessive, very big. [Echoic].

THUNDER (1) [thun'der], *n.* the sound which follows a flash of lighting; any similar sound; (*fig.*) anger, wrath; **to steal a person's t.**, to anticipate and do what he intended and so rob him of applause or the advantage of novelty. THUNDER-STORM, storm of t. and lighting, usually accompanied by heavy rain. THUNDER (2), *v.i.* to roar with t.; utter a loud t.-like noise; speak with great wrath; move very noisily or with a noise like t. THUNDERING (1), *adj.* roaring with t.; speaking in loud angry tones. THUNDERING (2), *adv.* (*coll.*) exceedingly. [OE.].

THUNDERBOLT [thun'der-bōlt], *n.* a flash of lightning striking the ground or an object on the ground; solid body which is supposed to fall from the heavens in a flash of lightning; (*coll.*) a great surprise.

THUNDERCLAP [thun'der-klap], *n.* one peal of thunder.

THUNDEROUS [thun'der-oos], *adj.* thundery, as loud as, resembling, thunder; also *fig.*

THUNDERSTRUCK [thun'der-struk], *adj.* (*fig.*) amazed, astonished beyond measure.

THURIBLE [thyoo'ri-bl], *n.* censer. [L.].

THURSDAY [thurz'dā], *n.* fifth day in the week; **Maundy T.**, fifth day of Holy Week, the day before Good Friday. [OE.].

THUS [THus], *adv.* in this manner; in the following manner or way; to this specified degree; **t. far**, so far. [OE.].

THWACK (1) [thwak], *v.t.* to beat sharply, give a sharp blow or series of blows to. THWACK (2), *n.* sharp, vigorous blow, *esp.* such as may be given with a staff or stick. [Echoic].

THWART (1)† [thwawrt], *adv. and prep.* athwart. THWART-SHIPS, (*naut.*) from one side to the other of a boat or ship. THWART (2), *v.t.* to oppose, cross, hinder, balk, take successful action against. THWART (3), *n.* seat in a rowing boat. [OScand.].

THY [THī], *possessive adj.* of, pertaining to, or belonging to, thee. [OE.].

THYME [tim], *n.* (*bot.*) any of various plants of the genus *Thymus*, *esp.* the garden thyme. [L.].

THYMOL [ti'mol], *n.* a preparation from oil of thyme used medicinally, *esp.* as an antiseptic.

THYMUS (*pl.* thymi) [thī'mus], *n.* (*anat.*) a ductless gland, occurring in the lower part of the neck in vertebrates, and which in human beings disperses before or during puberty. [Gk.].

THYROID (1) [thī'roid], *adj.* (*anat.*) pertaining to the

The accent ′ after a syllable = stress (u-pon′). The mark ‾ over a vowel = length (ā in made; ō in bone)

t. cartilage or gland; **t. cartilage**, large cartilage in the throat commonly called the Adam's apple; **t. gland**, ductless gland in the neck of vertebrates. THYROID (2), *n.* (*anat.*) the t. cartilage or the t. gland. [~Gk.].

THYSELF [thī-self'], *pron. emphatic and reflex. form of* THY.

TIARA [ti-ah'rah], *n.* jewelled coronet or head-dress very high at the front and very low at the back now usually worn only by women; any similar head-dress; the Papal crown. [Gk.].

TIBIA [ti'bi-ah], *n.* (*anat.*) the bone in the front of the leg reaching from the knee to the ankle, the shin-bone. [L.].

TIC [tik], *n.* a nervous facial twitching. TIC-DOULOUREUX [tik-do-lo-rōō'], twitching of the face accompanied with a neuralgic pain. [Fr.].

TICK (1) [tik], *n.* any one of several small blood-sucking creatures parasitic on men and animals. [ME.].

TICK (2), *n.* (*slang*) credit. [TICK(ET) (1)].

TICK (3), *n.* linen or cotton cover of a pillow, mattress. [ME.].

TICK (4), *n.* light tapping sound such as is made by a watch or clock; symbol resembling a V with an elongated upward stroke, used to indicate approval or correctness; **on the t.**, punctually. TICK (5), *v.t. and i.* to make a sound like a t.; mark with a t.; **to t. off**, (*slang*) to rebuke sharply; **to t. over**, (of a motor) to run gently with the gears not engaged. TICKER, *n.* (*slang*) clock or watch; telegraphic tape-machine. [Uncert.].

TICKET (1) [ti'kit], *n.* receipt made of paper or light cardboard which is proof that the holder has paid for or is otherwise entitled to enjoy a certain privilege, such as to attend a specified entertainment, be carried on a specified public vehicle to a specified place etc.; any similar small document, printed card or label; the **t.**, (*slang*) the done thing, just what is wanted; **t. of leave**, document giving a prisoner a certain restricted or conditional liberty before the expiry of his full sentence. TICKET-DAY, day before settlement day on the Stock Exchange. TICKET (2), *v.t.* to put a t. on to. [Fr.].

TICKING [ti'king], *n.* cloth for making mattresses.

TICKLE (1) [ti'kl], *v.t. and i.* to caress lightly a part of the body till the nerves become irritated, causing spasms or laughter; (of a part of the body) itch or otherwise feel that this is being done; (*fig.*) give pleasure to. TICKLE (2), *n.* act or sensation of tickling. TICKLER, *n.* one who tickles; stick with a bunch of feathers or strips of paper at the end, used at a fair etc.; (*fig.*) puzzle or difficulty. TICKLING, *n.* titillation. [Uncert.].

TICKLISH [tik'lish], *adj.* very sensitive to tickling; (of persons or tasks) difficult to handle.

TIC(K)-TAC(K) [tik'tak], *n.* (*racing jargon*) system of signs and gestures used among bookmakers to signal changes in betting prices; **t. man**, bookmaker's assistant who signals such information. [Imitative].

TIDAL [ti'dal], *adj.* pertaining to or affected by tides.

TIDBIT, see TIT-BIT.

TIDDLER [tid'ler], *n.* stickleback; any very small fish; (*coll.*) small child. [Unkn.].

TIDDL(E)Y (1) [tid'li], *adj.* (*slang*) slightly intoxicated; (*naval slang*) smart. TIDDL(E)Y (2) †, *n.* (*slang*) a drink, *esp.* alcoholic. [Unkn.].

TIDDLEYWINKS [tid'li-wingks], *n.* children's game in which small counters are nipped at the edge with larger ones and so made to spring up in the air, the object being for each player to get by this means as many counters as possible into a wooden cup. [Uncert.].

TIDE (1) [tid], *n.* the ebb and flow of the sea; (*fig.*) movement, tendency; † season, *esp.* in the phrase **time and t.**, and in certain compounds, e.g. Eastertide. TIDE-WATER, (*U.S.*) water moved by tides; tidal water. TIDE (2), *v.t. and i.* **to t. over**, to struggle through, manage to get through; help to deal with and overcome; (*naut.*) drift with the t. [OE.].

TIDEWAY [tid'wā], *n.* channel in which tidal waters flow; tidal currents in such a channel.

TIDINGS [ti'dingz], *n.(pl.)* news, information. [OE.].

TIDY (1) [ti'di], *adj.* arranged in good order, neat; fond of keeping things in good order; (*coll.*) moderately large. TIDY (2), *n.* box, bag, or other receptacle for odds and ends. TIDY (3), *v.t.* to make t.; **to t. up**, to make t.; put things in order. [~TIDE (1)].

TIE (1) [ti], *n.* strip of cloth worn round the collar and

knotted in front; small fur worn round the neck; emotional or moral bond or obligation; anything which curbs one's freedom; that result in a sporting event in which two competitors or opposing teams obtain equal scores, reach the winning-post at the same moment etc.; an eliminating competition between several competitors or teams; (*mus.*) small curve printed between notes of identical pitch, the second of which is not intended to be played though the first is to be sustained for the value of both; (*arch., carp. etc.*) support, link etc., to make firmer the essential pieces of a structure. TIE-BEAM, (*arch.*) beam which connects two principal rafters at the bottom. TIE (2) (*pres.pt.* TYING, *pret. and p.pt.* TIED), *v.t. and i.* to fasten or connect with rope, string etc., make a knot in; hamper, rob of liberty; (*carp., arch. etc.*) provide with a t. or support; do equally well with a rival in a game, competition, examination etc.; **to t. down**, to fix firmly down with cord; hamper, limit the scope of; **to t. up**, to bind into a firm parcel or bundle etc.; restrict, corner, limit the freedom, the free use, of; bind or enwrap. TIED HOUSE, *n.* public-house owned by or under contract to a brewer whose liquors alone may be sold there. [OE.].

TIER [tēer], *n.* one of a series of horizontal rows arranged one over the other. [OFr.].

TIERCE, TERCE [tēers], *n.* (*eccles.*) the third canonical hour or the service said then; a position in fencing; cask which will hold forty-two gallons of wine. [Fr.].

TIERCEL, see TERCEL.

TIERCET, see TERCET.

TIERS ETAT, tiers état [tyäerz-ā-tah'], *n.* that one of the three sections of the old French legislative body which represented the commons; the common people generally. [Fr.].

TIFF (1) [tif], *n.* trifling quarrel. TIFF (2), *v.i.* to be in a peevish mood. [Uncert.].

TIFFANY [ti'fa-ni], *n.* sort of gauze or thin silk. [OFr. from LL.].

TIFFIN [ti'fin], *n.* lunch among English people in the East. [Uncert.].

TIG [tig], *n.* a children's game of pursuit, tag. [ME.].

TIGER [ti'ger], *n.* fierce carnivorous feline of Asia, whose fur is yellow and marked with black stripes; very cruel person; (*hist.*) male servant, *esp.* a pageboy; vigorous and skilful opponent, *esp.* at tennis or golf; (*U.S. coll.*) extra cheer after the usual three. TIGER-CAT, the South American margay, or any other wild cat like a t. in colouring. TIGER-LILY, the tall, bright orange lily. TIGER-MOTH, any of several varieties of large spotted English moths. TIGER-SHARK, name given to several fierce sharks. TIGER-WOOD, wood streaked with black and brown, used in cabinet making. [L.].

TIGHT (1) [tit], *adj.* tied fast, firmly secured and bound taut; cramped, closely packed, compact; close fitting; (of a flask, cask, vessel) not leaking or admitting liquids; (of money) hard to come by, scarce; (of persons) ungenerous, given to driving hard bargains; (of a situation or circumstance) presenting grave difficulties, dangerous; (*slang*) drunk. TIGHT-ROPE, stretched rope for acrobatic performances. TIGHT (2), *adv.* tightly, securely; **to sit t.**, to be unshakable in the opinion or position one has taken up; stay where one is. TIGHTS, *n.(pl.)* close-fitting breeches; hose reaching to the waist, worn by stage performers etc. [ME.].

TIGHTEN [ti'ten], *v.t. and i.* to make or become tight or tighter; **to t. up**, to make stricter.

TIGRINE [ti'grin], *adj.* pertaining to or like a tiger.

TIKE, TYKE [tik], *n.* mongrel cur; rustic boor; Yorkshireman. [OScand.].

TILBURY [til'be-ri], *n.* light two-wheeled horse carriage of the early 19th century. [*Tilbury* the inventor].

TILDE [tild'(-i)], *n.* (*typ.*) curved mark or slur over a letter (~). [Span.].

TILE (1) [til], *n.* thin, flat clay brick glazed or unglazed; (*coll.*) hat, *esp.* a top hat. TILE (2), *v.t.* to roof or line with tiles. TILER, *n.* man who makes roofs of tiles; doorkeeper at a masonic ceremony. [OE.].

TILL (1) [til], *n.* cash-box with a drawer, used in a shop. [Uncert.].

TILL (2), *v.t.* to plough and sow. [OE.].

TILL (3), *prep.* up to the time of. TILL (4), *conj.* up to the time when. [OScand.].

TILLAGE [ti'lij], *n.* practice of tilling; agriculture.

TILLER (1) [ti'ler], *n.* person who tills. [TILL (2)].

ōō is pronounced as in f*oo*d; ŏŏ as in h*oo*d; th as in *th*ink; TH as in *th*at; zh as in a*z*ure. ~ = related to.

TILLER (2), *n.* (*naut.*) lever by means of which the steersman operates a rudder. [~Du.].

TILT (1) [tilt], *v.t. and i.* to move or cause to move into a sloping position. TILT (2), *n.* action of tilting; condition or degree of being tilted; **full t.**, at top speed. [ME.].

TILT (3), *v.i.* to charge on horseback with a lance; **to t. at**, to charge with a lance; (*fig.*) make an attack on, *esp.* in a speech. TILT-YARD, (*hist.*) place for tilting or jousting. TILTER, *n.* one who jousts. [ME.].

TILT (4), *n.* canvas hood on a wagon, market stall etc. [ME.].

TILTH [tilth], *n.* cultivation of the land; soil so cultivated.

TILTING [til'ting], *n.* act of one who tilts; state of being tilted.

TIMBALE [tam-bahl'], *n.* (*cookery*) small pie of minced fish, fowl or meat, with a crust. [Fr.].

TIMBER (1) [tim'ber], *n.* wood, *esp.* wood cut from a tree and ready for use. TIMBER-YARD, yard where t. is sold or stored. TIMBER (2), *v.t.* to provide t. for, equip with wooden supports. TIMBERED, *adj.* made wholly or partly of wood; wooded. TIMBERMAN, *n.* man who fells trees for t. TIMBERTOES, *n.* (*coll.*) wooden-legged man. [OE.].

TIMBRE [tam'ber, ta(ng)br], *n.* (*mus.*) the individual quality in the sound of a voice or instrument. [Fr.].

TIMBREL [tim'brel], *n.* tambourine. [~TIMBRE].

TIME (1) [tim], *n.* the idea of past, present and future; the limited duration of the material world contrasted with the eternity of spiritual things; a particular portion of this, a period; a particular point in this, a moment; a system of measuring this; an occasion, the moment at which an event occurs or is repeated, period in which an event occurs; (*mus.*) ratio of regularly unstressed beats to regularly stressed beats in a composition; (*pl.*) period, era, age; **in t., on t., to t.**, punctually, not late; **behind t.**, late; **in good t.**, punctually and with time to spare; **at times**, sometimes, occasionally; **in no t.**, very quickly; **at all times**, always, constantly; **t. and (t.) again**, repeatedly; **from t. to t.**, every now and then; **at the same t.**, nevertheless, all the same, moreover; **for the t. being**, meanwhile, for a little while to come; **what t.**, (*poet.*) while, at which moment; **to take one's t.**, to be unhurried; **to have a good t.**, to enjoy oneself; **to work against t.**, to have almost more to do than there is t. to do it in; **to pass the t. of day with**, to salute with formal greetings; **to do t.**, to suffer imprisonment; **to keep good t.**, (of a clock, watch etc.) to register the t. steadily and accurately; **to beat t.**, to conduct an instrumental or choral performance by means of a wand; **to mark t.**, to raise the feet alternately as if marching, but without moving backward or forward; (*fig.*) put off or delay; **t. bomb**, bomb designed to explode at a pre-arranged t.; **t. fuse**, fuse designed to detonate a charge after a fixed t. TIME-HONOURED, *adj.* respected for many years, ancient. TIME-LAG, interval of time between one event and another connected with it; delay. TIME-SHEET, paper on which is recorded the time of an employee's arrival at and departure from work. TIME-SIGNAL, signal marking the t., *esp.* one broadcast by radio. TIME-SWITCH, (*elect.*) switch automatically operated at a pre-arranged time. TIME-TABLE, book, sheet or pamphlet containing a list of times at which certain events are due to happen (*esp.* the arrival and departure of trains etc.) or at which certain tasks have to be done; schedule. TIME-WORK, work paid for by the hour and not by the piece. TIME-WORN, *adj.* worn by time; decayed. TIME (2), *v.t.* to do or say in season or opportunely; measure the duration of; record the instant of; adjust the happening of. TIMER, *n.* device for timing the spark in an internal combustion engine; a device for measuring short periods of time. [OE.].

TIMEKEEPER [tim'kē-per], *n.* one who keeps a record of how long employees spend at their work; one who observes the time taken in races, boxing rounds and other sports; clock.

TIMELESS [tim'les], *adj.* eternal, not measured by time.

TIMELY (1) [tim'li], *adj.* seasonable, opportune. TIMELY (2), *adv.* opportunely.

TIMEPIECE [tim'pēs], *n.* clock.

TIMESERVER [tim'ser-ver], *n.* person who always does and says the most expedient thing without regard to dignity or principles. TIMESERVING (1),

n. action of a t. TIMESERVING (2), *adj.* obsequious, always careful to do what is expedient.

TIMID [ti'mid], *adj.* fearful, shy, nervous. [L.].

TIMIDITY [ti-mi'di-ti], *n.* state of being timid; fearfulness; want of courage or boldness to face danger; habitual cowardice.

TIMING [ti'ming], *n.* the opportune arrangement of events; adjustment of the spark of an internal combustion engine so that the fuel ignites at the right moment.

TIMOROUS [ti'me-roŏs], *adj.* full of fear; timid, apprehensive.

TIMOTHY [ti'mo-thi], *n.* the cat's-tail grass.

TIN (1) [tin], *n.* the metallic element denoted by Sn; a silvery-white, very malleable metal; thin plate of iron covered with tin; canister; box made of sheets of tin; (*slang*) money; **t. hat**, steel helmet worn by soldiers etc.; **to put the t. hat on**, to put an end to, spoil completely. TIN (2), *v.t.* to coat, cover with t.; preserve in an airtight t. can or box. TINMAN, *n.* man who makes tinplate vessels; dealer in tinware. TINNED, *adj.* coated with t.; preserved in tinned cans or boxes; (*slang*) (of music etc.) recorded. TINNING, *n.* craft of covering or lining something with melted t. or with tinfoil; process, business, of preserving food and packing it in canisters. TINNY, *adj.* rich in t.; similar to t.; (of a sound) thin and metallic. [OE.].

TINCTORIAL [tingk-taw'ri-al], *adj.* connected with colour; used for dyeing.

TINCTURE (1) [tingk'tyŏor], *n.* tinge or hue; slight superadded taste or quality; the finer and more volatile parts of a substance, separated by a solvent; a solution in alcohol; (*her.*) term applied to metals, colours and tints used for the field of an emblazoned shield. TINCTURE (2), *v.t.* to tinge, impregnate; imbue to a slight degree. [L.].

TINDER [tin'der], *n.* anything inflammable used for catching fire from a spark, *esp.* prepared linen impregnated with saltpetre; (*fig.*) inflammable material or ideas. TINDER-BOX †, box where t. and the materials for striking a light are kept. [OE.].

TINE [tin], *n.* tooth or spike of a fork, harrow etc.; prong; branch of an antler. [OE.].

TINEA [ti'ni-ah], *n.* (*path.*) contagious skin disease of several varieties, including ringworm; genus of clothes moths. [L.].

TINFOIL [tin'foil], *n.* alloy of lead and tin reduced to a thin leaf, much used for wrapping.

TING (1) [ting], *v.t. and i.* to ring; sound a bell. TING (2), *n.* a single, short, sharp ringing made on a metallic object. [Echoic].

TINGE (1) [tinj], *v.t.* to tint, colour, stain; impregnate with something foreign; alter slightly the colour, taste or character by something added; (*fig.*) colour slightly the mind, opinions. TINGE (2), *n.* a slight degree of some colour, taste or quality; tincture; hue. [L.].

TINGLE (1) [ting'gl], *v.t.* to cause to feel a sharp thrilling sensation; *v.i.* to feel a sharp stinging sensation; feel a sharp thrilling pain; smart; vibrate. TINGLE (2), *n.* sensation of tingling. TINGLING, *n.* a thrilling sensation; a vibrating. [~TING (1)].

TINK [tingk], *n.* ringing sound made by striking metal or glass lightly with a hard object. [Echoic].

TINKER (1) [ting'ker], *n.* one who repairs pots and pans and other household utensils; (*Scots and northern dial.*) gipsy; (*fig.*) unskilful repairer; botcher; bungler; **not to care a t.'s cuss, damn etc.**, not to care at all. TINKER (2), *v.t.* to mend like a t.; *v.i.* to work at tinkering; **to t. with**, to play about with and try to improve, construct, repair amateurishly. [ME.].

TINKLE (1) [ting'kl], *v.t.* to cause to clink or make sharp, light metallic sounds; *v.i.* to make a series of sharp, light metallic sounds. TINKLE (2), *n.* action or sound of tinkling. TINKLING, *n.* a tinkle. [ME.].

TINPLATE [tin'plāt], *n.* thin sheet-iron coated with tin.

TIN-POT [tin'pot], *adj.* gimcrack, made of odds and ends, worthless.

TINSEL (1) [tin'sel], *n.* something very, but merely, shining and gaudy; thin, shiny metal for theatrical use; (*fig.*) anything showy but worthless. TINSEL (2), *adj.* made of t.; gaudy; (*fig.*) showy but of no real value, meretricious. TINSEL (3), *v.t.* to cover, decorate with t. [Fr.].

TINSMITH [tin'smith], *n.* worker in tin or maker of tinplate.

TINT (1) [tint], *n.* hue; shade; colour; surface hue as distinct from groundwork; tinge. TINT (2), *v.t.* to

tinge; give a faint colouring to; stain the surface of. TINTER, *n.* person who tints; map-colourer. [∼L.].
TINTACK [tin′tak], *n.* short nail of tinned iron.
TINTINNABULATION [tin-ti-na-byōō-lā′shn], *n.* a tinkling of bells; sound resembling this. [∼L.].
TINWARE [tin′wāer], *n.* goods made of tinplate.
TINY [tī′ni], *adj.* very small; little; minute. [Unkn.].
TIP (1) [tip], *n.* the small pointed extremity of anything; gentle hit; suggestion; piece of inside information; small present given as a recognition of services to a servant or an inferior; place where refuse is dumped. TIP (2) (*pres.pt.* TIPPING, *pret. and p.pt.* TIPPED), *v.t.* to form a point to; cover the top or end of; lower one end of; cant; hit gently; hint; tell; give a gratuity to; empty out; turn out of a vehicle; *v.i.* to tilt; **to t. (someone) the wink,** to give information; **to t. a winner,** to give an indication of the horse likely to win a race; **to t. up,** to fall backwards, give up one's money; **to t. over,** to overturn; **to t. out,** to upset, throw out; **to t. off,** (*coll.*) to give a warning to, inform privately. TIP-OFF, *n.* (*slang*) a private warning or hint. TIP-CART, *n.* cart in which the body can be tilted up from the frame so as to empty out a load from the back. [ME.].
TIP-AND-RUN (1) [tip-and-run′], *n.* form of cricket where a run must be attempted from every ball. TIP-AND-RUN (2), *adj.* pertaining to a form of attack in which the hitting of the objective is less important than a safe getaway.
TIPCAT [tip′kat], *n.* game in which a spindle-shaped piece of wood is hit into the air and then knocked forward with a stick.
TIPPET [ti′pit], *n.* long narrow kind of cape for the shoulders, fastened round the neck, small cape of cloth, silk or fur. [ME.].
TIPPLE (1) [ti′pl], *v.i.* to drink spirituous liquors frequently. TIPPLE (2), *n.* (*coll.*) liquor. [∼Norw.].
TIPSTAFF [tip′stahf], *n.* † staff tipped with metal; officer of the law who took into custody any person committed to prison by the High Court.
TIPSTER [tip′ster], *n.* one who gives tips and inside information in racing and other sports.
TIPSY [tip′si], *adj.* almost drunk. TIPSY-CAKE, *n.* pudding consisting of a sponge cake soaked in sherry, with custard, cream and blanched almonds. [∼TIP (2)].
TIPTOE (1) [tip′tō], *n.* the tips of the toes considered collectively, *esp. in phr.* **on t.; on t.,** (*fig.*) warily, eagerly, excitedly. TIPTOE (2), *adv.* on t. TIPTOE (3), *v.i.* to walk on the tips of the toes; (*fig.*) walk carefully, warily.
TIP-TOP [tip-top′], *adj.* first-rate; the best imaginable; superlative.
TIRADE [ti-rād′], *n.* outburst of words; declamatory speech of invective or abuse. [Fr.].
TIRE (1), **TYRE** [tier], *n.* band or hoop usually of iron to bind the felloes of wooden wheels; solid or pneumatic tire, the casing of a pneumatic tire; **solid t.,** solid band of rubber which encircles the rims of wheels; **pneumatic t.,** rubber tube to be inflated with air, and its rubber casing, for encircling the rim of a wheel; † apparel, trappings. TIRE (2) †, *v.t.* to attire, dress. [∼ATTIRE (1)].
TIRE (3), *v.t.* to exhaust the strength of by toil or labour; weary or fatigue; bore; *v.i.* to grow weary; be fatigued; be bored; **to t. out,** to exhaust completely. [ME.].
TIRESOME [tier′sum], *adj.* exhausting the strength; wearisome; fatiguing; exhausting the patience; tedious.
TIRO, TYRO [tier′ō], *n.* novice, amateur. [L.].
TISSUE [ti′syōō], *n.* structure formed of cells and cell products; fabric interwoven with gold or silver or with figured colours; connected series; web. TISSUE-PAPER, very thin gauze-like paper used for wrapping.
TIT (1) [tit], *n.* titmouse, small bird of the genus *Parus.* [OScand.].
TIT (2), *n.* **t. for tat,** a return for something received; injury for an injury. [Unkn.].
TITAN [tī′tan], *n.* (*myth.*) one of a race of gigantic beings, representing the primitive powers of Nature, with seeming reluctance submissive to the world order which established itself in the hands of Zeus; a strong nature vainly battling with fate; person of magnificent powers; anything very powerful. TITANIC [tī-ta′nik], *adj.* huge; pertaining to the Titans; gigantic. [Gk.].
TITANIUM [tī-tā′ni-um], *n.* metallic element somewhat resembling silicon, denoted by Ti. [∼TITAN].
TIT-BIT, TIDBIT [tit′bit], *n.* small dainty piece; appetizing morsel; piquant item of gossip.

TITHE (1) [tīth], *n.* the tenth part of anything; tenth part of the increase annually arising from the profits of land and stock, formerly allotted to the clergy; a very small part. TITHE-BARN, barn where the grain for the t. was stored. TITHE (2), *v.t.* to put a t. upon. [OE.].
TITHING [tī′THing], *n.* (*hist.*) old Saxon territorial unit consisting of ten householders, who were sureties or free pledges to each other; township. [OE.].
TITIAN [ti′shan], *adj.* resembling the works of Titian, *esp.* in colouring; of a rich auburn. [*Titian,* Italian painter].
TITILLATE [ti′ti-lāt], *v.t.* to tickle; tempt the palate; stimulate pleasantly the appetite or the mind. [∼L.].
TITIVATE [ti′ti-vāt], *v.t.* to dress up; bedeck; *v.i.* to make oneself look smart. [Unkn.].
TITLARK [tit′lahk], *n.* a bird, the meadow pipit.
TITLE (1) [tī′tl], *n.* inscription put over something, *esp.* that one in the beginning of a book, denoting the subject of the work; an appellation of dignity, distinction or pre-eminence; name; appellation; right; that which constitutes a just right to exclusive possession; instrument which is evidence of a right; title-deed; (*eccles. law*) agreement by which a beneficiary holds a benefice; (*publishing*) a book. TITLE-DEED, document in evidence of ownership of real property. TITLE-PAGE, page at the front of a book giving the subject and the author's name. TITLE-ROLE, character in a book or play from which its t. is taken. TITLE (2), *v.t.* to give a name or t. to; write a t. on. TITLED, *adj.* having a t., *esp.* one denoting nobility. [OFr. from L.].
TITMOUSE (*pl.* titmice) [tit′mows], *n.* a tit, any one of the small active perching birds of the genus *Parus.*
TITRATE [ti-trāt′], *v.t.* (*chem.*) to subject to volumetric analysis. TITRATION [ti-trā′shn], *n.* (*chem.*) volumetric analysis. [Fr.].
TITTER (1) [ti′ter], *v.i.* to utter a subdued laugh; snigger, giggle. TITTER (2), *n.* a snigger; subdued laugh; giggle. [Echoic].
TITTLE [ti′tl], *n.* small particle; jot; iota. [ME.].
TITTLE-TATTLE (1) [ti′tl-ta-tl], *n.* small talk; gossip. TITTLE-TATTLE (2), *v.i.* to gossip; indulge in idle chatter. [TATTLE].
TITTUP [ti′tup], *v.i.* to behave in a gay light-hearted way; step gaily; prance about, *esp.* of a horse. [∼L.].
TITULAR (1) [ti′tyōō-ler], *adj.* of, or pertaining to, a title; holding the title; having the title only, nominal. TITULAR (2), *n.* person invested with the title of an office without performing the duties attached to it. [∼L.].
TO (1) [tōō], *prep.* denoting motion towards a place, purpose, object, or thing; denoting extent, degree or end; in comparison with; denoting addition, junction or union; denoting opposition or contrast; denoting the indirect object, that is the person or thing indirectly affected by the action or state described in a verb; preceding the simple verb as sign of the infinitive. TO (2), *adv.* forward, on; denoting motion towards a junction, union, closing; **t. and fro,** backwards and forwards. [OE.].
TOAD [tōd], *n.* an amphibian somewhat resembling the frog in form, but thicker and clumsier. TOAD-IN-THE-HOLE, savoury dish of sausage or other meat cooked in batter. [OE.].
TOADFLAX [tōd′flaks], *n.* common European plant of the genus *Linaria.*
TOADSTOOL [tōd′stōōl], *n.* an inedible fungus somewhat like a mushroom.
TOADY (1) [tō′di], *n.* a fawning obsequious parasite; sycophant. TOADY (2), *v.i.* to behave like a t.; **to t. to,** to fawn upon and seek for personal motives to obtain the favour of. [TOAD].
TOAST (1) [tōst], *n.* bread browned before a fire; act of drinking to the health, honour or prosperity of a person, institution or enterprise; person or thing so honoured; † woman who is a favourite object of such healths. TOAST-MASTER, announcer of the toasts at a dinner or other formal occasion. TOAST-RACK, small rack of metal, china etc., for serving t. at table. TOAST (2), *v.t.* to make crisp and brown by exposure to heat; warm before a fire to a comfortable heat; *v.i.* to become so warmed. TOAST (3), *v.t.* to propose or honour a t. to; *v.i.* to drink a t. TOASTER, *n.* person who toasts; apparatus for toasting bread. [OFr.].
TOBACCO [to-ba′kō], *n.* any of the forty species of the genus *Nicotiana,* the leaves of which when

dried are used for smoking and chewing, and in snuff. [Span.].

TOBACCONIST [to-ba'ko-nist], *n.* retailer of tobacco.

TOBOGGAN (1) [to-bo'gan], *n.* light sledge for sliding down a slope. TOBOGGAN (2), *v.i.* to ride, coast down a hill, on a t. [AmerInd.].

TOBY [tō'bi], *n.* mug in the shape of a stout man wearing a three-cornered hat; name of the dog in a Punch-and-Judy show. [Personal name *Tobias*].

TOCCATA [to-kah'tah], *n.* (*mus.*) prelude designed to display the executant's touch and technique. [It.].

TOCSIN [tok'sin], *n.* alarm-bell or the ringing of it to sound an alarm. [Fr.].

TODAY (1) [tōō-dā'], *adv.* on this day; at the present time; now. TODAY (2), *n.* the present day; this very day. [OE.].

TODDLE (1) [to'dl], *v.i.* to walk with little, tottering, uncertain, childish steps; (*coll.*) walk easily along; depart, walk away. TODDLE (2), *n.* act of toddling. [~TOTTER].

TODDY [to'di], *n.* a juice drawn from a palm-tree; mixture of whisky with hot water and sugar; punch. [~Hind.].

TO-DO [tōō-dōō'], *n.* ado; disturbance; stir.

TOE (1) [tō], *n.* a digit of the foot, corresponding to a finger of the hand; forepart of the hoof of a horse or of any other hoofed animal; forepart of a boot, shoe or stocking which covers the toes; projecting portion of an object resembling the human toe; **to tread on a person's toes**, (*fig.*) to hurt a person's feelings. TOE (2), *v.t.* to fit with a t.; place the t. of the foot on (a given point); **to t. the line**, (*fig.*) to obey orders. TOECAP, *n.* extra piece over the t. of a boot or shoe. [OE.].

TOFF [tof], *n.* (*slang*) well-dressed man; swell; gentleman. [Unkn.].

TOFFEE [to'fi], *n.* sweetmeat made of syrup, butter, sugar etc., boiled together and flavoured; **not for t.**, not at all. [Uncert.].

TOGA [tō'gah], *n.* (*Rom. antiq.*) outer garment of a Roman citizen in peace, long, broad and flowing, and consisting of a single piece of stuff. [L.].

TOGETHER [tōō-geTHer'], *adv.* in company, in or into union; in or into contest; in the same place or time, uninterruptedly; in concert, simultaneously; **t. with**, in union with, accompanied by. [OE.].

TOGGLE [to'gl], *n.* (*naut.*) small wooden pin which tapers at both ends. [Uncert.].

TOGS [togz], *n.*(*pl.*) (*slang*) clothes. [Uncert.].

TOIL (1) [toil], *v.i.* to exert great strength of body or mind in labour; labour; work; walk painfully and with great effort. TOIL (2), *n.* labour with oppressive pain and fatigue; drudgery; strenuous effort over a long period. [OFr.].

TOIL (3), see TOILS.

TOILET [toi'let], *n.* operation of dressing; costume, finished effect of performing the toilet; lavatory. TOILET-COVER, cover for a dressing-table. TOILET-GLASS, mirror on a dressing-table. TOILET-PAPER, paper for wiping the anus after defecation. TOILET-POWDER, talcum powder used after shaving etc. TOILET-TABLE, dressing-table. [Fr.].

TOILETTE [twah-let'], *n.* toilet; a particular costume, usually of an elaborate kind. [Fr.].

TOILS [toilz], *n.*(*pl.*) net, snare, web; **in the t.**, entrapped; fascinated; in the clutches of someone. [Fr.].

TOILSOME [toil'sum], *adj.* necessitating toil; laborious; wearisome.

TOKAY [tō-kā'], *n.* a rich, aromatic wine made at *Tokay* in Hungary.

TOKEN [tō'ken], *n.* something intended to represent another thing or event; sign; mark; memorial of friendship; piece of money not coined by authority but current by sufferance; **t. payment**, small payment made for form's sake. [OE.].

TOLBOOTH, see TOLL-BOOTH.

TOLD [tōld], *pret. and p.pt. of* TELL. [OE.].

TOLERABLE [to'le-ra-bl], *adj.* able to be endured; fairly good. [L.].

TOLERANCE [to'le-rans], *n.* power or act of tolerating; disposition to tolerate; forbearance; permissible variation. [L.].

TOLERANT [to'le-rant], *adj.* disposed to tolerate; permitting, favouring toleration; broad-minded; forbearing.

TOLERATE [to'le-rāt], *v.t.* to suffer to be or be done without prohibition or hindrance; allow or permit negatively by not preventing; exercise forbearance

towards; endure. TOLERATION, *n.* action or state of tolerating; forbearance. [~L.].

TOLL (1) [tōl], *n.* a tax; sum to be paid for the right to pass along a certain road or bridge; telephone call for a place too distant to be connected directly through the local exchange but nearer than points which require the long-distance "trunk" system. TOLL-BAR, bar, beam or gate to stop boats on a canal, or vehicles on a road, until t. is paid. TOLL-BOOTH, place where goods were weighed to ascertain the duties of t.; (*Scots*) town prison. TOLL-BRIDGE, bridge where t. must be paid for passing over it. [OE.].

TOLL (2), *v.t.* to cause a bell to sound with notes slowly repeated in regular time; a mournful ringing; *v.i.* to sound as a bell. TOLL (3), *n.* deep sound of the tolling of a bell. [Uncert.].

TOLLY [to'li], *n.* (*slang*) candle. [~TALLOW].

TOLUENE [to'lyōō-ēn], *n.* methyl benzene.

TOM [tom], *n.* tom-cat.

TOMAHAWK (1) [to'ma-hawk], *n.* light Indian war and hunting hatchet. TOMAHAWK (2), *v.t.* to cut or slay with a t. [AmerInd.].

TOMALLY [to-ma'li], *n.* the part of lobster flesh which turns green with boiling. [~TOURMALINE].

TOMATO [tō-mah'tō], *n.* a South American plant, having an edible reddish-yellow pulpy fruit. [Span. from Mexican].

TOMB [tōōm], *n.* a grave; sepulchre; monument erected over a grave in memory of the dead; (*fig.*) death. [OFr.].

TOMBOLA [tom-bō'lah], *n.* a form of lottery. [It.].

TOMBOY [tom'boi], *n.* a strong and romping girl. [*Tom* from *Thomas*].

TOMBSTONE [tōōm'stōn], *n.* stone set over a grave and usually inscribed with the name and particulars of the dead person; monument.

TOM-CAT [tom-kat'], *n.* male cat. [Hypocoristic form of *Thomas*].

TOME [tōm], *n.* book; large volume. [Fr.].

TOMFOOL [tom-fōōl'], *n.* great fool; silly trifler.

TOMMY [to'mi], *n.* (*coll.*) private soldier in the British Army, so called from *Thomas* Atkins, the name given as an example in the filling up of papers on enlistment; (*slang*) bread, provisions. TOMMY-ROT, (*slang*) nonsense.

TOMMY-GUN [to'mi-gun], *n.* sub-machine gun with a short barrel. [*Thompson*, the maker].

TOMNODDY [tom-no'di], *n.* (*slang*) dolt, foolish fellow; **Lord T.**, self-important person. [*Tom* from *Thomas* and NODDY].

TOMORROW (1) [tōō-mo'rō], *adv.* on the day after today. TOMORROW (2), *n.* the day which comes after today.

TOMPION [tom'pi-on], *n.* stopper inserted in the mouth of a gun; inking pad used in lithography. [~TAMPON].

TOMTIT [tom-tit'], *n.* the blue titmouse.

TOMTOM [tom'tom], *n.* primitive drum used by the Hindus; drum of the African races. [Hind.].

TON [tun], *n.* a weight of 20 cwt. or 2,240 lb.; **metric t.**, 1000 kg., 2,204·6 lb.; **short t.**, 2,000 lb.; (*fig.*) a very heavy weight; (*pl.*) a great quantity. [~TUN].

TONAL [tō'nal], *adj.* of, or pertaining to, tone. TONALITY [tō-na'li-ti], *n.* tones collectively; (*mus.*) general quality of the pitch or tone; relation of notes in conformity with a musical scale.

TONE (1) [tōn], *n.* sound or a modification of sound; a particular inflexion of the voice adapted to express emotion or passion; prevailing atmosphere, spirit; a shade, colour, tinge; (*mus.*) an interval of sound; the usual quality of sound of an instrument; (*med.*) that state of body in which the animal functions are healthy; (*paint.*) the harmonious relation of the colours of a picture in light and shade; **t. poem,** (*mus.*) short descriptive piece of music. TONE-ARM, tube which supports the sound-box of a gramophone, and acts as a connexion between the diaphragm and the horn. TONE-DEAF, *adj.* incapable of distinguishing between sounds of different pitch. TONE-SYLLABLE, accented syllable. TONE (2), *v.t.* to give t. to; (*phot.*) modify the colour of by immersion in a bath; *v.i.* to blend agreeably as to colour; **to t. down**, to make the sound or colour of less strong; (*fig.*) modify, pacify, subdue; **to t. up**, to make the sound, colour stronger; (*fig.*) strengthen, give more vitality to. TONED, *adj.* with a t. [Gk.].

TONELESS [tōn'les], *adj.* without tone; (of a voice) lifeless, dull; unmusical.

TONGS [tongz], *n.*(*pl.*) implement consisting of two bars joined by a pivot or united by a spring, used for handling and lifting, **particularly burning fuel and hot metals.** [OE.].

TONGUE (1) [tung], *n.* **the organ of taste in animals**, and more especially of speech in man; speech; power of utterance; fluency of speech; mode of speaking a language; word or words; language of a race or nation; point, as of a buckle; projecting point of land; projection along an edge to fit a groove; the taper part of something; thin strip of leather which fits underneath the lace-holes in boots and shoes; **to give t.**, to utter loudly, bark; **to hold one's t.**, to be silent. TONGUE-GRAFTING, (*hort.*) inserting the end of a scion in a special manner. TONGUE-TIED, *adj.* having an impediment in the speech; unable to speak freely; awkwardly silent. TONGUE-TWISTER, series of words difficult to articulate quickly. TONGUE (2), *v.t.* to scold; modify with the t. the sound of when playing a flute etc.; *v.i.* to use the t. in modifying sound. [OE.].

TONIC (1) [to'nik], *adj.* increasing the strength, tone, *esp.* of the animal system; obviating the effects of debility, and restoring healthy functions; stimulating; inspiriting; **t. sol-fa**, style of notation in music which, dispensing with the staff, its lines and spaces, indicates the notes by letters, and time and accent by dashes and colons; **t. spasm**, (*med.*) continuous spasmodic contraction. TONIC (2), *n.* something which stimulates the mind or body; (*med.*) medicine which gives tone and vigour of nerve and muscle; (*mus.*) keynote; (*mus.*) sound produced by a vocal string in a given degree of tension. TONICITY [tō-ni'si-ti], *n.* elasticity or contractility of the muscular fibres; (*mus.*) musical tone. [Gk.].

TONIGHT (1) [too-nit'], *adv.* on this night; on the night of today. TONIGHT (2), *n.* this night; the night after the present day.

TONNAGE [tu'nij], *n.* nominal capacity of a ship; cubical content or burden which a ship can carry in tons; duty or impost on ships, estimated formerly per ton, now according to bulk. [OFr.].

TONSIL [ton'sil], *n.* (*anat.*) one of two lymphoid glands in the throat or fauces. [L.].

TONSILLITIS [ton-si-li'tis], *n.* **inflammation of the** tonsils. [~TONSIL and Gk.].

TONSORIAL [ton-saw'ri-al], *adj.* of, or pertaining to, a barber or to shaving. [L.].

TONSURE (1) [ton'syoor], *n.* action of clipping the hair or of shaving the head; state of being shorn, as a sign of dedication to the ministry or initiation into holy orders; shaven bald part on the head of a priest or monk. TONSURE (2), *v.t.* to shave the head of. [L.].

TONTINE [ton'tin], *n.* loan on which annuities are paid instead of interest, each annuity increasing as the number of the subscribers diminishes by death, until the last to survive receives as much as all of them had at first shared among them. [*Tonti*, Italian banker].

TOO [too], *adv.* excessively; over; more than enough; very; in addition; moreover. [OE.].

TOOK [took], *pret. of* TAKE. [OE.].

TOOL (1) [tool], *n.* implement, instrument, apparatus used for performing some operation either by hand or by machinery; implement used in bookbinding; (*fig.*) equipment for study; person used as a mere instrument by another. TOOL (2), *v.t.* to shape, mark with a t.; *v.i.* (*coll.*) to drive oneself along in a smooth, brisk way; **to t. up**, to equip (a factory) with machine-tools. TOOLING, *n.* workmanship performed with a t.; marks made on the binding of a book with the t. [OE.].

TOOT (1) [toot], *v.t. and i.* to sound a horn, *esp.* a motor-car horn; hoot; make a noise like the sounding of a horn. TOOT (2), *n.* the sounding of a horn. [Echoic].

TOOTH (1) (*pl.* teeth) [tooth], *n.* one of the hard ivory-like instruments growing in the jaws of human beings and animals, used to masticate food; one of a series of wood or metal objects resembling teeth; prong of a comb; **to cast in the teeth**, to reproach with, blame; **in the teeth of**, in the face of, in spite of; **to be armed to the teeth**, to be thoroughly armed; **to show the teeth**, to grow dangerous, threatening; **to set the teeth on edge**, to irritate greatly, anger; to cause an unpleasant sensation by grating or screeching sounds etc.; **by the skin of the teeth**, narrowly, only just; **sweet t.**, liking for sweet things. TOOTH-ORNAMENT, (*arch.*) decoration consisting of a close succession of small four-leaved flowers projecting forward to a central point. TOOTH-PASTE, -POWDER, paste, powder, for cleaning the teeth. TOOTH-PICK, instrument for cleaning the teeth of food lodged between them. TOOTH (2), *v.t.* to provide with teeth, indent; *v.i.* to interlock. [OE.].

TOOTHACHE [too'thāk], *n.* an ache in the nerves of the teeth or in the gums.

TOOTHSOME [tooth'sum], *adj.* appetizing, palatable.

TOOTLE (1) [too'tl], *v.t. and i.* to toot gently; play the flute or flageolet gently. TOOTLE (2), *n.* sound made in tootling. [~TOOT].

TOP (1) [top], *n.* the highest part of anything; summit; surface; upper side; highest place or person or degree or rank; hair on the crown of the head; head of a plant or the part above the ground; uppermost division of a fishing-rod; (*naut.*) sort of platform surrounding the head of the lower mast, and projecting on all sides, serving to extend the shrouds. TOP (2), *adj.* relating to the t.; nearest to, at, the t.; principal; first, primary; best; **t. gear**, highest gear in motoring etc., giving the greatest road speed. TOP-COAT, *n.* overcoat. TOP-DRESSING, *n.* dressing of manure laid on the surface of land; final coat of paint or other material in decorating. TOP-HOLE, (*slang*) splendid, fine. TOP (3) (*pres.pt.* TOPPING, *pret. and p.pt.* TOPPED), *v.t.* to cover on the t.; cap; rise above; excel, surpass; crop the surface of; **to t. up**, to restore the level of liquid in (*e.g.* an accumulator), refill; *v.i.* to rise aloft; predominate, be eminent, excel. [OE.].

TOP (4), *n.* wooden or metal toy in the shape of an inverted pear which children play with by spinning it on its point; **old t.**, (*slang*) old fellow; **to sleep like a t.**, to sleep very soundly. [OE.].

TOP-, see TOPO-.

TOPAZ [tō'paz], *n.* one of the gems, generally yellowish, occurring in rhombic prisms, a silicate of aluminium with fluorine. [Gk.].

TOP-BOOT [top-boot'], *n.* one of a pair of riding-boots extending nearly to the knee with a broad top of light-coloured leather representing the lining which used to be shown when the upper part of the boot was turned down.

TOPE (1) [top], *n.* species of small shark, otherwise known as the dogfish. [Unkn.].

TOPE (2), *v.i.* to drink strong or spirituous liquors frequently and to excess. [Fr.].

TOPEE, TOPI [tō-pē'], *n.* pith helmet worn as a protection against the sun. [Hind.].

TOPER [tō'per], *n.* person who drinks to excess; drunkard.

TOPGALLANT [tu-ga'lant, top-ga'lant], *adj.* (*naut.*) above the top or second mast and below the royal; highest; elevated; splendid; **t. mast, sail**, mast, sail, above the topmast. [TOP (2) and GALLANT (1)].

TOP HAT [top-hat'], *n.* high cylindrical hat worn by men with formal morning and evening dress or with certain uniforms.

TOP-HEAVY [top-he'vi], *adj.* having the top or upper part too heavy for the lower; unstable.

TOPI, see TOPEE.

TOPIARY [tō'pi-a-ri], *n.* art of cutting trees and shrubs into shapes, *esp.* in order to represent birds or animals; garden of trees thus cut. [L.].

TOPIC [to'pik], *n.* a general statement useful in developing an argument; a general truth; the subject of conversation or writing; any subject which is discussed or spoken of at the moment. [Gk.].

TOPICAL [to'pi-kal], *adj.* pertaining to a subject of current interest.

TOP-KNOT [top'not], *n.* knot or bow worn on top of the head; tuft of hair on top of the head.

TOPMAST [top'mahst], *n.* (*naut.*) mast next above that which rises from the deck, and below the topgallant; **t. head**, that part of the t. above the crosstrees or, in fore-and-aft rigged vessels, the part above the topsail-halyard block.

TOPO-, TOP-, *pref.* place. [Gk.].

TOPOGRAPHIC(AL) [to-pō-gra'fik(-al)], *adj.* pertaining to topography.

TOPOGRAPHY [to-po'gra-fi], *n.* art of giving a detailed accurate account of a particular place; such an account when given. [TOPO- and Gk.].

TOPPER [to'per], *n.* (*slang*) man's tall silk hat; good sort, thoroughly likeable person.

TOPPING (1) [to'ping], *n.* a top; the cutting off of the top; the top cut off; (*naut.*) act of pulling one extremity of a yard higher than the other. TOPPING (2), *adj.* very high; overhanging; (*slang*) first-rate, splendid, fine.

TOPPLE [to'pl], *v.t.* to throw down; *v.i.* to fall from

---

oo is pronounced as in food; oo as in hood; th as in *think*; TH as in *that*; zh as in azure. ~ = related to.

being top-heavy; fall forward; pitch or tumble down; (fig.) fall from a great but unstable eminence. [~TOP (2)].

TOPSAIL [top'sl], n. (naut.) sail carried on the topmast which, in square-rigged vessels, is usually divided into the upper and lower topsails.

TOPSIDE [top'sīd], n. the upper portion; that part of a vessel's hull above the waterline; joint of beef cut from between the leg and the aitch-bone.

TOPSY-TURVY [top-si-tur'vi], adj. upside down; muddled.

TOQUE [tōk], n. small, close-fitting brimless hat worn by women. [Fr.].

TOR [taw(r)], n. high pointed hill or rock. [OE.].

TORCH [tawch], n. lighted stick carried in the hand; flambeau; portable electric battery lamp; (fig.) something which lights up a mental darkness. TORCH-DANCE, dance in which each dancer carries a t. aloft. TORCH-LILY, a garden plant, the red-hot poker. [OFr.].

TORCHON [taw'shon], n. bobbin lace of geometrical pattern; strong rough paper used for water-colours. [Fr.].

TORE [taw(r)], pret. of TEAR. [OE.].

TOREADOR [to'ri-a-daw(r)], n. bull-fighter fighting on horseback. [Span.].

TORERO [to-rāer'ō], n. bull-fighter fighting on foot. [Span.].

TORIC [taw'rik], adj. pertaining to, like, a torus; (opt.) (of a lens) having one surface curved as a segment of a torus.

TORMENT (1) [taw'ment], n. extreme pain or anguish, bodily or mental; that which causes pain or misery. TORMENT (2) [taw-ment'], v.t. to put to extreme pain or anguish, bodily or mental; distress; harass; tease, irritate. TORMENTOR, n. person who torments; (agric.) a form of harrow. [L.].

TORMENTIL [taw'men-til], n. (bot.) a herb whose root is used as an astringent in medicine and tanning. [Fr.].

TORN [tawn], p.pt. of TEAR. [OE.].

TORNADO [taw-nā'dō], n. local tropical thunderstorm; hurricane; whirling tempest; (fig.) outburst of noise, cheering etc. [~Span.].

TORPEDO (1) (pl. **torpedoes**) [taw-pē'dō], n. self-driven cigar-shaped submarine weapon charged with an explosive, designed for blowing up shipping; same kind of weapon discharged by aircraft; **t. boat**, small swift boat armed with torpedoes; **t. boat destroyer**, small warship of high speed originally designed to oppose t. boats but which has now largely superseded them; **t. net**, net hung round a ship as a protection against torpedoes; **t. tube**, steel tube through which torpedoes are fired; **t. fish**, the electric ray. TORPEDO (2) (pres.pt. TORPEDOING, pret. and p.pt. TORPEDOED), v.t. to hit with a t., destroy by a t. [L.].

TORPID (1) [taw'pid], adj. having lost the power of exertion; benumbed; destitute of sensibility; inactive; dull; sluggish. TORPID (2), n. clinker-built eightoared boat used in the Hilary term races at Oxford; (pl.) the Hilary term races at Oxford. [L.].

TORPIDITY [taw-pi'di-ti], n. state of being torpid; insensibility; inactivity or stupidity.

TORPOR [taw'per], n. numbness; inactivity; loss of motion; dulness; laziness; mental sluggishness. [L.].

TORQUE [tawk], n. collar of twisted wires or of chain worn by the Gauls and Ancient Britons; collar; (eng.) moment of a rotating or twisting force. TORQUATED [taw-kwā'tid], adj. having a collar or ring round the neck; formed as a torque. [L.].

TORRENT [to'rent], n. violent rushing stream; stream suddenly rising and running rapidly downwards; strong current; (fig.) flow, gush of words. [Fr.].

TORRID [to'rid], adj. parched; dried with the heat of the sun; violently hot; burning or parching; **t. zone**, zone between the tropics, in which the heat is very great. [L.].

TORSION [taw'shn], n. action of twisting; (mech.) force with which a wire or rod when twisted tends to return to its original state; (surg.) the stopping of a haemorrhage by twisting the ends of the blood-vessels; **t. balance**, apparatus for estimating very minute forces by the action of a twisted thread or wire. [~L.].

TORSO (pl. **torsos**) [taw'sō], n. trunk of the body; trunk of a statue deprived of head and limbs. [It.].

TORT [tawt], n. (leg.) wrong or injury to person or property remediable by a civil action for damages.

TORTIOUS [taw'shŏos], adj. (leg.) of the nature of, pertaining to, a t.; wrongful. [AFr.].

TORTILLA [taw-tē'lyah], n. thin flat cake made of soaked maize, baked on an iron plate. [Span.].

TORTOISE [taw'tŏs], n. land or freshwater chelonian reptile from the shell of which protrude the head and tail and the twisted legs (whence its name). [Fr.].

TORTUOUS [taw'tyŏo-oos], adj. twisted, wreathed; winding; crooked, not straightforward; disingenuous. [AFr.].

TORTURE (1) [taw'tyŏŏr], n. extreme pain; anguish of body or mind; torment; acute pain inflicted judicially, often for the sake of extorting confession. TORTURE (2), v.t. to inflict mental or physical t. upon; torment; punish in a painful and cruel manner; distort, drag out of natural shape. [Fr.].

TORUS (pl. **tori**) [taw'rus], n. (arch.) large convex moulding employed in the bases of columns; (bot.) the floral receptacle, growing point of the pistil; (geom.) a solid ring. [L.].

TORY [taw'ri], n. name sometimes applied to a Conservative in English politics. [Orig. an Irish robber, applied to supporters of James II by his Whig opponents].

TOSS (1) [tos], v.t. to throw with the hand; fling upwards; throw up with a quick, sharp movement; cause to rise up and down violently; agitate; (fig.) agitate violently, disturb the mind; v.i. to fling; be in violent commotion; be agitated; be tossed about; spin a coin to decide a course of action. TOSS-POT, (slang) habitual drinker, toper. TOSS (2), n. a throwing upward or with a jerk; act of tossing; a throwing up of the head; a particular manner of raising the head with a jerk; act of spinning a coin; **to take a t.**, to fall, have a disappointment. TOSS-UP, n. resort to the spin of a coin; an uncertain issue. [Uncert.].

TOST [tost], (poet.) p.pt. of TOSS.

TOT (1) [tot], n. very little child; small quantity of anything; dram. [Uncert.].

TOT (2), n. the total in addition. TOT (3), v.t. to add (up). [TOT(AL)].

TOTAL (1) [tō'tal], adj. entire, whole, complete; **t. war**, war involving civilians equally with combatants. TOTAL (2), n. the whole; the full amount; result of an addition. TOTAL (3), v.t. and i. to add up the whole; arrive at the total; add up to; constitute, take together. [L.].

TOTALISATOR, TOTALIZATOR [tō'ta-lī-zāter], n. automatic betting machine, where the winnings equal all the money staked less a percentage for expenses.

TOTALITARIAN [tō-ta-li-tāer'i-an], adj. of a state or polity, having only one political party, esp. when subject to the domination of a single individual who claims to represent the general will. [~TOTAL (1)].

TOTALITY [tō-ta'li-ti], n. the whole sum or amount; everything; the whole; total eclipse.

TOTE (1) [tōt], n. (coll.) totalisator.

TOTE (2), v.t. (U.S.) to carry, lift. [Uncert.].

TOTEM [tō'tem], n. animal, plant or other natural object between which and himself a member of an uncivilized race believes some occult relationship to exist so that he takes it as his hereditary emblem; the representation of this object as a badge, mark or emblem; **t. pole**, column, usually of wood, bearing a representation of a t. [Uncert.].

TOTTER (1) [to'ter], v.i. to walk along with hesitating shaky steps; shake so as to be in danger of falling; stagger; (fig.) be on the verge of ruin; be in process of decay. TOTTER (2), n. action of tottering; an uncertain hesitating walk. [ME.].

TOUCAN [tōō'kan, tōō-kahn'], n. one of a family of tropical American birds, remarkable for the size of their bright-coloured bills. [Portug.].

TOUCH (1) [tuch], v.t. to come into contact with; perceive by the sense of feeling; come to; reach; concern; handle slightly; meddle with; affect; impress; move; soften; delineate slightly; strike; v.i. to be in contact; be in a state of junction; **to t. at**, to call at (a port); **to t. down**, (Rugby football) to touch the ball on the ground within a specified area behind the goal-posts; **to t. for**, (slang) to (attempt to) borrow from; **to t. on**, to treat of slightly in discourse; **to t. up**, to repair; put finishing touches to, as a painting; enhance the colour of (the complexion); wound a person's feelings by sarcasm. TOUCH-AND-GO, (something) risky, capable of eventuating one way or the other. TOUCH-ME-NOT, a plant, the pods of which explode when touched. TOUCH (2), n. contact; junction of two bodies at the surface

---

The accent ' after a syllable = stress (u-pon'). The mark ˉ over a vowel = length (ā in made; ŏ in bone).

so that there is no space between them; sense of feeling; act of touching; test; tried qualities; characteristic manner; single act of a pencil or brush; act of the hand on a musical instrument; a stroke; slight amount; mild attack; (*football*, *hockey*) ground beyond the side lines lying between the extended goal lines. TOUCH-LINE, (*football etc.*) one of the boundary lines at the side of the field. TOUCH-PAPER, paper impregnated with saltpetre which causes it to burn slowly. TOUCH-TYPIST, person who can type without seeing the keyboard of the typewriter. TOUCHED, *adj.* (*slang*) not quite sane; unbalanced. TOUCHER, *n.* one who, or that which, touches; (*bowls*) ball which strikes the jack. [OFr.].

TOUCHING (1) [tu'ching], *adj.* affecting, pathetic. TOUCHING (2), *prep.* concerning, as regards.

TOUCHSTONE [tuch'stōn], *n.* a black variety of flinty slate used for ascertaining the purity of gold and silver by the streak traced on it; (*fig.*) something taken as a test or criterion.

TOUCHWOOD [tuch'wŏŏd], *n.* wood tinder; decayed wood used as a match for catching up fire from a spark.

TOUCHY [tu'chi], *adj.* peevish, irritable; oversensitive; apt to fire up.

TOUGH (1) [tuf], *adj.* flexible without being brittle; strong and flexible; firm; not easily broken; able to endure hardship; vigorous; powerful and hardy; sinewy and hard to chew; difficult, involving much labour; (*slang*) difficult to manage, violent; hard, unfortunate. TOUGH (2), *n.* *a.* *t.* person, reprobate, criminal.

TOUGHEN [tu'fen], *v.t.* to render tough; *v.i.* to grow tough.

TOUPEE, TOUPET [tōō'pā], *n.* little tuft; front of false hair; false curl. [Fr.].

TOUR (1) [tōōr], *n.* a journey in a circuit; spell of duty; journey from place to place for pleasure or business; ramble; **t. de force**, feat of skill or power. TOUR (2), *v.t.* to visit while touring; *v.i.* to make a t.; travel. TOURER, *n.* open car for touring.

TOURIST (1) [tōōr'ist], *n.* one who goes on a tour, travelling from place to place for pleasure. TOURIST (2), *adj.* pertaining to, suitable for, tourists. TOURISM, *n.* practice of touring; the t. traffic.

TOURMALINE [tōōr'ma-lēn], *n.* a mineral occurring in prisms, used in polarizing light, the finer kinds being much valued by jewellers. [Fr.].

TOURNAMENT [tōōr'na-ment], *n.* in medieval times, a contest between mounted knights armed with lances; joust; competition for a sports championship, *esp.* in tennis, chess, bridge and croquet. [OFr.].

TOURNEY [tōōr'ni], *n.* medieval tournament; joust. [OFr.].

TOURNIQUET [tōōr'ni-kā], *n.* surgical apparatus or bandage, which is tightened or relaxed by twisting, used to check haemorrhages. [Fr.].

TOUSLE [tow'zl], *v.t.* to put into disorder, make untidy; rumple, make dishevelled. [~TUSSLE (1)].

TOUT (1) [towt], *v.i.* to try to get custom by canvassing, usually in an importunate manner; go canvassing for custom; go about trying to pick up and sell rumours and bits of information about the chances of horses in races. TOUT (2), *n.* one who endeavours by canvassing to obtain custom; racing tipster. TOUTER, *n.* a t. [~TOOT (1)].

TOW (1) [tō], *n.* the coarser fibres of flax and hemp used for ropemaking. [OE.].

TOW (2), *v.t.* to pull along by means of a rope (*esp.* of a boat or broken-down vehicle). TOW-ROPE, *n.* rope used during towing operations. TOW (3), *n.* action of towing; **in t.**, being towed; (*coll.*) hanging on; following in attendance. TOWAGE, *n.* act of towing, price paid for this. [OE.].

TOWARD (1) [tō'erd], *adj.* (*archaic*) ready to do or learn, apt; about to happen, impending. TOWARDLY, *adj.* (*archaic*) auspicious, promising; propitious. [OE.].

TOWARD (2), **TOWARDS** [tōō-wawd(z)'], *prep.* in the direction of; in relation to; with respect to; round about; near. [OE.].

TOWEL (1) [tow'el], *n.* a cloth of absorbent material for wiping the person after washing; **to throw in the t.**, to admit defeat. TOWEL-HORSE, stand with bars for hanging towels on. TOWEL (2), *v.t.* to dry or rub down with a t. TOWELLING, *n.* absorbent cotton or linen material from which towels are made. [OFr.].

TOWER (1) [tow'er], *n.* a building, usually either square or circular, of considerable elevation, and generally flat on top; citadel; fortress; high flight;

elevation; (*fig.*) **t. of strength**, someone to be relied on absolutely. TOWER (2), *v.i.* to rise up like a t.; rear itself; **to t. over**, to exceed in stature or mental power. TOWERING, *adj.* very high; lofty; (*fig.*) violent. [OFr.].

TOWN [town], *n.* a collection, of indefinite extent, of houses, larger than a village, *esp.* one with a regular market and inferior to a city; city; the inhabitants collectively of a town or city; the metropolis or its inhabitants; the West End of London; **t. house**, house in t., as distinct from a country house. TOWN CRIER, t. functionary whose duty it is to proclaim official and other notices by shouting them in the streets. TOWN-PLANNING, science and practice of preparing plans for the building or reconstruction of towns so as to preserve amenities while providing for housing and industrial needs. [OE.].

TOWN CLERK [town-klahk'], *n.* official who keeps the records, and helps in the administration, of a municipal borough.

TOWN COUNCIL [town-kown'sil], *n.* the elected body for purposes of local government of a town.

TOWNEE [tow-nē'], *n.* inhabitant of a university town (as distinct from the undergraduates). [TOWN].

TOWN HALL [town-hawl'], *n.* public building used for council meetings and other business of a town.

TOWNSHIP [town'ship], *n.* district having municipal privileges.

TOWPATH [tō'pahth], *n.* path along a canal or riverside on which the barge horses walk.

TOXAEMIA [tok-sē'mi-ah], *n.* blood-poisoning. [TOX(ICO-) and Gk.].

TOXIC [tok'sik], *adj.* poisonous; caused by poisoning.

TOXICO-, TOXIC-, *pref.* pertaining to poison. [Gk.].

TOXICOLOGY [tok-si-ko'lo-ji], *n.* study of poisons, their nature, action and antidotes. TOXICOLOGIST [tok-si-ko'lo-jist], *n.* person versed in t. [TOXICO- and Gk.].

TOXIN [tok'sin], *n.* an organic poisonous substance. [~TOXIC].

TOXOPHILITE [tok-so'fi-līt], *n. and adj.* one who practices archery; pertaining to archers and archery. [Gk.].

TOY (1) [toi], *n.* child's plaything; amusing trifle; anything used as or considered suitable for a plaything; **t. dog**, lapdog. TOY (2), *v.i.* to trifle; play; dally amorously. [~Du.].

TRACE (1) [trās], *n.* strap or chain fastened at one end to the collar of a horse's harness and at the other to the vehicle to be drawn. TRACE-HORSE, draughthorse pulling in front of another between the shafts. [OFr.].

TRACE (2), *v.t.* to draw or delineate with marks, copy through transparent paper or film; follow by footsteps or tracks; follow with exactness; walk over; traverse; find; discover as a result of a process of thought. TRACE (3), *n.* mark left by anything passing, footprint; track; vestige; remains; a small quantity. [Fr.].

TRACER [trā'ser], *n.* person who traces; tracer-bullet. TRACER-BULLET, flaming bullet which leaves a trail of smoke or flame behind it.

TRACERY [trā'se-ri], *n.* a delicate pattern of lines; (*arch.*) ornamental stonework in the upper part of a Gothic window.

TRACHEA, (*pl.* **tracheae**) [tra-kē'ah], *n.* (*anat.*) the windpipe; (*bot.*) one of the spiral vessels in leaves; (*zool.*) breathing tube of an insect.

TRACHEO-, *pref.* neck, throat. [TRACHEA].

TRACHEOTOMY [tra-ki-o'to-mi], *n.* operation of making an incision in the windpipe. [TRACHEO- and Gk.].

TRACHOMA [tra-kō'mah], *n.* a disease manifested by a granular condition of the mucous lining of the eyelids. [Gk.].

TRACING [trā'sing], *n.* a course; regular track or path; process of making a copy of some drawing through a transparent sheet; the copy thus made. TRACING-PAPER, thin transparent paper used for tracing drawings and engravings.

TRACK (1) [trak], *n.* mark left by something which has passed along; mark or impression left by the foot; road; beaten path; a running course; (*mech.*) distance which separates pairs of wheels of a vehicle transversely; treaded metal belt enclosing the wheels (of a tank etc.) instead of tyres; **on the t. of**, following, in hot pursuit of; **off the t.**, off the scent, following the wrong course of action; **the beaten t.**, the conventional way; **to conceal one's tracks**, to

---

ōō is pronounced as in *food*; ŏŏ as in *hood*; th as in *think*; TH as in *that*; zh as in *azure*.   ~ = related to.

hide one's projects or affairs; **to make tracks for.**
(*coll.*) to make towards. TRACK (2), *v.t.* to follow
when guided by a t. or footsteps; trail; (*mech.*)
to t. up, to measure and adjust to the right width the
transverse distance between a pair of a vehicle's
wheels; *v.i.* to move in a t TRACKED, *adj.* (of
vehicles) having caterpillar tracks instead of ordinary
wheels. [OFr.].

TRACT (1) [trakt], *n.* wide expanse of land, water or
sky; a wide area; an extent; (*anat.*) a system in the
body (as all the digestive organs). [L.].

TRACT (2), *n.* tractate; short treatise usually of a
political or religious character. [~TRACTATE].

TRACTABLE [trak′ta-bl], *adj.* able to be led, taught
or managed without difficulty; docile; manageable.
[L.].

TRACTARIAN [trak-tăer′i-an], *n. and adj.* founder
of, or believer in, Tractarianism; of or pertaining to
Tractarianism. TRACTARIANISM, *n.* system of
principles advocated in *Tracts for the Times*, published at Oxford between 1833 and 1841, which led a
reaction against rationalism and formalism; the
Oxford Movement.

TRACTATE [trak′tāt], *n.* treatise; tract. [L.].

TRACTION [trak′shn], *n.* action of drawing or state
of being drawn, *esp.* along a plane against friction;
attraction; **t. engine,** locomotive for drawing a load
along the highway. [L.].

TRACTIVE [trak′tiv], *adj.* having the power necessary to drag an object along a surface; pulling.

TRACTOR [trak′ter], *n.* that which draws, **or is**
employed for traction; vehicle with an internal
combustion engine for drawing ploughs etc.

TRADE (1) [trād], *n.* act or business of exchanging
commodities; buying and selling; commerce; the
business which a person has learned; occupation,
particularly manual or mercantile employment;
men engaged in the same occupation; **the trades,**
the t.-winds; **t. mark,** exclusive device adopted by a
manufacturer, and affixed to his goods as a sign that
they are made by him; **t. name,** name used in
trading; **t. price,** wholesale price. TRADE-BOARD,
committee of employers, employees and experts
appointed by the Board of T. to fix wages and conditions of work in specified industries. TRADE (2),
adj. at t. prices. TRADE (3),
adv. at t. prices. TRADE (4), *v.t.* to sell or exchange
in commerce; *v.i.* to buy and sell; traffic; carry on
commerce as a business; **to t. in,** to give (an old
article) as part payment for something new; **to t.
upon,** to take advantage of. [MLow Germ.].

TRADER [trā′der], *n.* one engaged in trade or commerce; vessel employed in trading.

TRADE(S) UNION [trād(z)′yōō-ni-un], *n.* combination of the workmen in a particular trade or group of
trades for mutual support. TRADE-UNIONISM, *n.*
system employed by the trade unions; principle of
organized association of the employees in a particular
industry.

TRADE-WIND [trād′wind], *n.* a wind blowing continuously from the N.E. between 7 deg. and 29 deg.
north of the equator, or from the S.E. between 3 deg.
and 20 deg. south of the equator.

TRADING (1) [trā′ding], *n.* the carrying on of trade;
commerce, trade. TRADING (2), *adj.* concerned with
carrying on commerce.

TRADITION [tra-di′shn], *n.* the handing down of
opinions, doctrines or customs from ancestors to
posterity, from the past to the present, by oral communication; an opinion, doctrine or custom thus
handed down; principles or accumulated experiences
of earlier generations handed on to others. [L.].

TRADITIONAL [tra-di′shn-al], *adj.* delivered orally
from father to son; transmitted from age to age;
customary; according to tradition. TRADITIONAL-
ISM, *n.* deference to the authority of tradition.

TRADUCE [tra-dyōōs′], *v.t.* to misrepresent wilfully
and abuse; calumniate; defame; vilify. TRADUCE-
MENT, *n.* act of traducing; slander, calumny. [L.].

TRAFFIC (1) [tra′fik], *n.* a moving, transferring to and
fro; commerce; trade; amount of transport performed by an undertaking; intercourse; vehicles in
motion. TRAFFIC-LIGHTS, automatic electric lights
serving as t. signals at crossroads. TRAFFIC (2),
(*pres.pt.* TRAFFICKING, *pret. and p.pt.* TRAFFICKED),
v.t. to exchange in t.; *v.i.* to trade; buy and sell wares;
have dealings, *esp.* of an illicit nature. TRAFFICATOR,
n. direction-indicator affixed to motor vehicles.
[Fr.].

TRAGACANTH, DRACANTH [tra′ga-kanth], *n.*
a kind of gum used in medicine. [Gk.].

TRAGEDIAN [tra-jĕ′di-an], *n.* dramatist who writes
tragedy; tragic actor.

TRAGEDY [tra′je-di], *n.* play or story dealing with the
sufferings of human beings, and ending in disaster;
calamity in real life, sorrowful and disastrous event or
series of events. [OFr. from Gk.].

TRAGIC(AL) [tra′jik(-al), *adj.* of the nature or
character of tragedy; calamitous; expressive of
tragedy or sorrow; disastrous.

TRAGICOMEDY [tra-ji-ko′me-di], *n.* drama in
which both tragic and comic scenes occur.

TRAGULINE [tra′gyōō-lin], *adj.* goat-like.

TRAIL (1) [trāl], *v.t.* to hunt by the track; draw along
the ground; carry, as arms, in a horizontal position,
muzzle foremost; drill, exercise; tread down grass by walking
through it; *v.i.* to be drawn out in length; (of plants)
run along or climb; straggle, be extended along;
(*coll.*) walk slowly and wearily along. TRAIL (2), *n.*
mark or track left by something which has passed;
track followed by a hunter; scent or spoor left by the
animal pursued; anything drawn to length; (*milit.*)
end of an artillery carriage, upon which the carriage
slides when unlimbered. TRAIL-NET, drag-net;
trawl. [OFr.].

TRAILER [trā′ler], *n.* person who or thing which
trails; vehicle towed behind another; advance
selection from a film.

TRAIN (1) [trān], *v.t.* to educate; rear and instruct;
teach and form by practice; drill, exercise; discipline;
break, reduce to docility; teach to perform certain
tricks; subject to proper diet and exercise for the
performance of some act of physical skill or endurance; (*hort.*) form to a desired shape by twisting or
pruning; *v.i.* to practise; subject oneself to rigorous
diet and exercise so as to arrive at fine physical
condition for some athletic contest or other feat.
TRAIN (2), *n.* something drawn along behind; trailing
extension of a dress; tail of a bird; retinue; series of
actions or objects; procession; line of gunpowder to
lead fire to a charge; line of vehicles on a railway;
all the apparatus and implements of war; **t. of artillery,** any number of guns accompanying an army;
in t., in order, in course of preparation. TRAIN-
BEARER, attendant who holds up the t. of the gown or
robe of a lady or high official personage on occasions
of ceremony. TRAIN-MILE, mile run by a t., the basic
unit of railway calculations. TRAIN-SICKNESS,
nausea caused by the motion of a railway t. TRAIN
(3), *v.i.* to travel by railway. [OFr.].

TRAINEE [trā-nē′], *n.* one who is being trained; one
qualified to a limited degree by special short training
instead of apprenticeship.

TRAINER [trā′ner], *n.* person who trains men and
women for athletics or horses for racing.

TRAINING [trā′ning], *n.* act of acquiring the necessary qualifications for the performance of some
career, occupation or feat of physical skill or endurance; condition of being so trained. TRAINING-
COLLEGE, college for training school-teachers.
TRAINING-SHIP, ship in which boys are trained to be
sailors.

TRAIN-OIL [trān′oil], *n.* oil obtained from the
blubber or fat of whales by boiling. [MDu.].

TRAIPSE, TRAPES [trāps], *v.i.* to wander aimlessly
about; (*coll.*) trudge. [~OFr.].

TRAIT [trā, trāt], *n.* a touch; distinguishing feature,
characteristic.

TRAITOR [trā′ter], *n.* one guilty of treason; one who,
in breach of trust, delivers his country to its enemy;
one who betrays his trust. [OFr.].

TRAITOROUS [trā′te-rŏŏs], *adj.* like a traitor,
guilty of treason; treacherous; perfidious.

TRAJECTORY [tra-jek′te-ri], *n.* the curve of a projectile fired through the air. [L.].

TRAM (1) [tram], *n.* public vehicle propelled by
electricity, steam or horse-power, along rails laid in
the streets; truck used underground for conveyance
of coal. TRAM-CAR, a t. TRAM-LINE, tramway, t.
rail. TRAM (2), *v.i.* to travel by t. [Uncert.].

TRAMMEL (1) [tra′mel], *n.* long net for catching
birds or fishes; that which trammels; hindrance,
impediment; carpenter's instrument for drawing
ellipses; beam-compass. TRAMMEL (2), *v.t.* to
catch; encumber with trammels; (*fig.*) restrict,
shackle. [Fr.].

TRAMONTANE [tra-mon′tān], *n. and adj.* (person)
living beyond the mountains; transalpine; foreign;
barbarous. [It.].

TRAMP (1) [tramp], *v.t. and i.* to walk heavily along;
plod; go for a long walk; travel as a tramp. TRAMP
(2), *n.* vagabond who tramps the roads; long walk;

sound of heavy feet walking or marching; cargo boat; shoulder of a spade. [ME.].

TRAMPLE (1) [tram'pl], *v.t.* to tread under foot; crush; knock down and crush by treading on; (*fig.*) bully, oppress; *v.i.* to commit the action of trampling. **TRAMPLE** (2), *n.* action of trampling; treading under foot. [ME.].

TRAMWAY [tram'wā], *n.* system of rails for trams; the whole system of trams and rails.

TRANCE [trahns], *n.* (*med.*) morbid bodily condition resembling sleep wherein all conscious functions are suspended; catalepsy; mystic rapture during which the soul is felt to be in direct communion with the divine ecstasy. [OFr.].

TRANQUIL [trang'kwil], *adj.* quiet; reposeful; restful; calm, peaceful. [L.].

TRANQUILLITY [trang-kwi'li-ti], *n.* condition of being tranquil.

TRANQUILLIZE [trang'kwi-liz], *v.t.* to calm; quieten; *v.i.* to become tranquil; sink into quietness.

TRANS-, *pref.* over, across, beyond; through. [L.].

TRANSACT [tran-sakt'], *v.t.* to do; perform; manage; *v.i.* to arrange matters; negotiate. **TRANSACTOR,** *n.* person who transacts any business. [L.].

TRANSACTION [tran-sak'shn], *n.* the doing or performing of any business; management of an affair; that which is performed; affair; (*pl.*) reports of the proceedings of a learned society.

TRANSALPINE [tran-sal'pin], *adj.* living, situated, beyond the Alps from Rome.

TRANSATLANTIC [tran-sat-lan'tik], *adj.* living, existing, beyond the Atlantic; crossing the Atlantic.

TRANSCEND [tran-send'], *v.t.* to rise higher; be greater; exceed; surpass. [L.].

TRANSCENDENT [tran-sen'dent], *adj.* surpassing all others; supreme; (*theol.*) beyond human limitations; divine.

TRANSCENDENTAL [tran-sen-den'tal], *adj.* (*philos.*) transcending; transcending the ordinary range of perception or conception. **TRANSCENDENTALISM,** *n.* system of philosophy which seeks the fundamental form of thought and perception not empirically but intuitively.

TRANSCRIBE [tran-skrib'], *v.t.* to copy; write down; write over again; reproduce from hieroglyphics or another alphabet; arrange (for the piano etc.). [L.].

TRANSCRIPT [tran'skript], *n.* that which is transcribed; a copy of a document.

TRANSCRIPTION [tran-skrip'shn], *n.* action of transcribing; the thing transcribed.

TRANSEPT [tran'sept], *n.* the transverse portion, crossing at right angles before the chancel, of a cruciform church. [~L.].

TRANSFER (1) (*pres.pt.* **transferring,** *pret. and p.pt.* **transferred**) [trans-fur'], *v.t.* to convey or remove from one place or person to another; make over; convey, as a right; produce by impression; print a design, picture, from one surface to another; *v.i.* to change from one place to another. **TRANSFER** (2) [trans'fer], *n.* that which is transferred; removal or conveyance of a person or thing from one place or person to another; picture, design or pattern which is so drawn that it can be transferred to another surface usually by some form of pressure or the application of heat; conveyance of a right or title; (*milit.*) soldier moved from one company to another. **TRANSFER-PAPER,** specially prepared paper for transferring drawings or printed matter to a printing surface. **TRANSFEREE** [trans-fe-rē'], *n.* person to whom a legal t. is made. **TRANSFERRER, TRANSFEROR** (trans-fur'er, 'aw(r)], *n.* person who transfers, in the legal sense. [L.].

TRANSFERENCE [trans'fe-rens], *n.* action of transferring.

TRANSFIGURATION [trans-fi-gyōō-rā'shn], *n.* change of form; the supernatural change in the personal appearance of Christ on the Mount; feast on 6 August in commemoration of this. [L.].

TRANSFIGURE [trans-fi'ger], *v.t.* to change the outward form or appearance so as to glorify it; transform. [Fr.].

TRANSFIX [trans-fiks'], *v.t.* to pierce through, as with a pointed weapon; (*fig.*) amaze, petrify. [L.].

TRANSFORM [trans-fawm'], *v.t.* to change the form, shape or appearance of; change substantially and make seem entirely different; change the nature of spiritually; (*alg.*) change (an equation) into another of a different form but of equal value; *v.i.* to be changed in form. **TRANSFORMATIVE,** able to or having a tendency to t. [L.].

TRANSFORMATION [trans-faw-mā'shn], *n.* action

or operation of transforming; metamorphosis; transmutation; change of heart in a man; an arrangement of false hair; partial wig; **t. scene,** elaborate set of scenery on the stage in which changes take place in view of the audience.

TRANSFORMER [trans-faw'mer], *n.* person who or thing which transforms; (*elect.*) instrument which changes the voltage of a current, transfers oscillations from one circuit to another, or converts direct current into alternating current.

TRANSFUSE [trans-fyōōz'], *v.t.* to put out of one vessel into another; transfer, as blood, from one animal to another; cause to be instilled; imbue. [L.].

TRANSFUSION [trans-fyōō'zhn], *n.* action or process of transfusing; act of transferring the blood of one animal into another; transmission, transference.

TRANSGRESS [trans-gres'], *v.t.* to pass beyond any limit; overstep the bounds of; offend against; break or violate in law; *v.i.* offend by violating a law or ignoring a convention. **TRANSGRESSIVE,** *adj.* liable to t. [Fr.].

TRANSGRESSION [trans-gre'shn], *n.* action of transgressing; violation of a law; offence; crime.

TRANSHIP, TRANS-SHIP [tran-ship'], *v.t. and i.* to transfer passengers or cargo from one ship or mode of conveyance to another; betake oneself from one ship to another for a continuation of the journey.

TRANSIENT (1) [tran'zi-ent], *adj.* passing quickly away; ephemeral; fleeting. **TRANSIENT** (2), *n.* one who is passing through; (*phys.*) surge of sound or electrical energy which rises or falls with sudden intensity. [L.].

TRANSIRE [tran-zīer'ē], *n.* (*leg.*) custom-house warrant for allowing goods to pass. [~L.].

TRANSIT [tran'sit, tran'zit], *n.* a passing over or through; conveyance; (*astron.*) the passing of an inferior planet across the sun's disk, or of satellites across the face of a planet; the passing of a heavenly body across the meridian of a place. [L.].

TRANSITION [tran-si'zhn, tran-zi'shn], *n.* a gradual passage from one place or state to another; change; a passing from one subject to another; the passing from Norman to Early English architecture.

TRANSITIVE [tran'si-tiv, trahn'si-tiv], *adj.* capable of passing from one person or thing to another; (*gram.*) expressive of an action passing from a subject to a direct object. [LL.].

TRANSITORY [tran'si-te-ri], *adj.* fleeting; ephemeral. [L.].

TRANSLATE [trans-lāt'], *v.t.* to remove from one place to another; convey to heaven without death; turn written or spoken words from one language into another; change, transform from thought into action; *v.i.* to be translatable. [LL.].

TRANSLATION [trans-lā'shn], *n.* action or result of translating; act of translating into another language; that which has been translated, an interpretation, version; (*phys.*) motion free from rotation. [L.].

TRANSLITERATE [trans-li'te-rāt], *v.t.* to write (the words of one language) in the corresponding characters of another. [TRANS- and L.].

TRANSLUCENCE, TRANSLUCENCY [trans-lōō'sens(-i)], *n.* condition of transmitting rays of light; transparency.

TRANSLUCENT [trans-lōō'sent], *adj.* transmitting rays of light, but not completely transparent. [L.].

TRANSLUNAR(Y) [trans-lōō'ner(-i)], *adj.* beyond the moon; far distant; beyond human sight.

TRANSMIGRATE [trans-mi-grāt'], *v.i.* to remove or migrate; pass from one country into another; (of the soul) transfer at death from one body to another about to be born. **TRANSMIGRATORY** [trans-mi'grate-ri], *adj.* of, or pertaining to, transmigration; passing from one place, body or state to another.

TRANSMIGRATION [trans-mi-grā'shn], *n.* action of transmigrating; the passing of a thing into another state or condition; the passing of the soul after death into another body.

TRANSMISSIBLE [trans-mi-si-bl], *adj.* able to be transmitted.

TRANSMISSION [trans-mi'shn], *n.* act of transmitting; conveyance through any body as light through glass; conveyance through a medium; state of being transmitted; that which is transmitted. [L.].

TRANSMIT [trans-mit'], *v.t.* to send from one person or place to another; suffer to pass through; hand down from one generation to another; communicate, pass on; *v.t. and i.* to send by radio. [L.].

TRANSMITTER [trans-mi'ter], *n.* person who or

---

thing which transmits; (*teleg.*) apparatus for sending out a message over the wires; (*radio*) apparatus which transmits radio waves through the air.

TRANSMOGRIFY [trans-mog'ri-fī], *v.t.* (*coll.*) to transform; bring about an absolute change in the nature or look of.

TRANSMUTATION [trans-myōō-tā'shn], *n.* act of transmuting, or condition of being transmuted, as the baser metals into gold, according to the alchemists.

TRANSMUTE [trans-myōōt'], *v.t.* to change from one nature, substance or form into another; (*alchemy*) change a base metal into gold or silver; transform. [L.].

TRANSOM [tran'sum], *n.* beam of timber extended across the sternpost of a ship to strengthen the after part and give it proper form; crossbar; horizontal mullion or crossbar in a window, or a lintel over a door; (*U.S.*) transom-window; (*pl.*) pieces of wood which join together the cheeks of gun-carriages. TRANSOM-WINDOW, window divided into two by a t.; window over a t. [L.].

TRANSPARENCY [trans-pãer'en-si, trans-pa'ren-si], *n.* state of being transparent; picture on semi-transparent material seen by light passing through it from behind.

TRANSPARENT [trans-pãer'ent, trans-pa'rent], *adj.* having the property of transmitting rays of light so as not to hide the view of objects behind; pervious to light; clear; (*fig.*) obvious, ingenuous, without duplicity. [MedL.].

TRANSPIRE [trans-pīer'], *v.t.* to emit through the excretories of the skin; send off in vapour; *v.i.* to be emitted through the excretories of the skin; exhale; become public; (*pop.*) happen, turn out. [L.].

TRANSPLANT [trans-plahnt'], *v.t.* to take up and plant in another place; remove; move away from one district and set up with a home in another. [L.].

TRANSPONTINE [trans-pon'tīn], *adj.* across the bridge; on the south side of the Thames. [TRANS- and L.].

TRANSPORT (1) [trans-pawt'], *v.t.* to carry or convey from one place to another; (*hist.*) banish as a criminal; (*fig.*) carry away by violence of passion; ravish with pleasure. TRANSPORT (2) [trans'pawt], *n.* transportation; conveyance; ship used for transporting troops and munitions of war; conveyances required by an army; (*fig., esp. pl.*) rapture, ecstasy. TRANSPORTER, *n.* one who, or that which, transports; travelling crane for moving goods from one place to another. [L.].

TRANSPORTATION [trans-paw-tā'shn], *n.* act of transporting or of being transported; (*U.S.*) means of transport.

TRANSPOSE [trans-pōz'], *v.t. and i.* to transfer; interchange; (*alg.*) add to or subtract from each of the expressions of an equation one or more of the terms of one expression; (*mus.*) alter the key of; be capable of transposition. [Fr.].

TRANSPOSITION [trans-pŏ-zi'shn], *n.* action of transferring; transference; interchange.

TRANSUBSTANTIATE [tran-sub-stan'shi-āt], *v.t.* to transform into another substance.

TRANSUBSTANTIATION [tran-sub-stan-shi-ā'-shn], *n.* change of substance; (*theol.*) doctrine of the conversion of substance, *esp.* the conversion of the bread and wine in the Eucharist into the body and blood of Christ. [MedL.].

TRANSUDE [tran-syōōd'], *v.i.* to pass through the pores or interstices of texture, as perspiration or other fluid. [TRANS- and L.].

TRANSVALUATION [trans-va-lyōō-ā'shn], *n.* change of values; revaluation.

TRANSVERSAL (1) [trans-vur'sal], *adj.* transverse; running, lying transverse. TRANSVERSAL (2), *n.* (*geom.*) a straight or curved line which traverses or intersects a system of other lines.

TRANSVERSE (1) [trans'vers], *adj.* lying across; lying in a crosswise direction. TRANSVERSE (2), *n.* something lying in a t. position; (*geom.*) the long axis of an ellipse. [L.].

TRAP (1) [trap], *n.* contrivance which shuts suddenly or with a spring, used for snaring animals; ambush; stratagem; device used in the game of trap and ball; contrivance to stop foul air escaping from a drain; light carriage with two wheels, drawn by one horse; box from which a greyhound is released at the start of a race; **t. and ball**, game in which a ball is jerked up on a t., and then hit. TRAP-DOOR, hinged door in a floor or roof opening and shutting like a valve. TRAP-SHOOTING, shooting at pigeons released from boxes or at clay disks, imitation birds, thrown from a catapult.

TRAP (2) (*pres.pt.* **TRAPPING**, *pret. and p.pt.* **TRAPPED**), *v.t.* to catch in a t.; ensnare; take, capture, by means of a trick; make a t. for a drain; *v.i.* to set a t. for game or fur-bearing animals; (*fig.*) lay a t. [OE.].

TRAP (3), *n.* (*geol.*) one of various dark-coloured metamorphic rocks. [Swed.].

TRAPES, see TRAIPSE.

TRAPEZE [tra-pēz'], *n.* trapezium; swinging horizontal bar for the exhibition of feats in gymnastics and acrobatic performances. [Fr. from Gk.].

TRAPEZIUM (*pl.* **trapezia**) [tra-pē'zi-um], *n.* (*geom.*) plane figure contained within four straight lines, only two of which are parallel; (*anat.*) a bone of the carpus. [Gk.].

TRAPEZOID [tra'pē-zoid], *n.* plane figure of four unequal sides none of which is parallel to another; (*anat.*) a bone in the wrist, the second of the distal row of the carpus. [Late Gk.].

TRAPPER [tra'per], *n.* man whose occupation it is to entrap wild animals, usually for furs.

TRAPPINGS [tra'pingz], *n.*(*pl.*) horse's harness, *esp.* such as is used on important occasions; (*fig.*) ceremonial dress or uniform. [~TRAPS].

TRAPPIST [tra'pist], *n.* monk of the Cistercian religious order as reformed in the 17th century by the Abbé de Rancé at the monastery of La Trappe.

TRAPS [traps], *n.*(*pl.*) (*coll.*) clothes; personal possessions. [~ME.].

TRASH [trash], *n.* rubbish; any waste or worthless matter, a worthless person; cheap, shoddy goods; poor rubbishy reading matter, music etc; **white t.**, the destitute whites of the southern states of America. [Uncert.].

TRAUMA [traw'mah], *n.* (*med.*) a bodily injury occasioned by violence; (*psych.*) a psychological injury. [Gk.].

TRAVAIL (1) [tra'vāl], *v.i.* to labour with pain; toil; suffer the pangs of childbirth. TRAVAIL (2), *n.* pains, labour of childbirth. [Fr.].

TRAVEL (1) (*pres. pt.* **travelling**, *pret. and p.pt.* **travelled**) [tra'vel], *v.t.* to traverse, journey over; *v.i.* to go; move along or from place to place; make a tour, visit places; (*mech.*) make a certain movement; (*comm.*) go from place to place in search of business orders, follow the occupation of a commercial traveller. TRAVEL (2), *n.* action or practice of journeying, *esp.* abroad; journey; motion, movement; (*pl.*) journey; tour; book describing this. TRAVEL-BUREAU, office at which a traveller may obtain information and make all his arrangements for t. TRAVELLED, *adj.* having travelled extensively. [OFr.].

TRAVELLER [tra've-ler], *n.* person who travels, *esp.* one who travels to secure orders for goods; **t.'s cheque**, cheque payable at any branch or by any agent of the bank which issues it, and convenient for tourists; **t.'s joy**, (*bot.*) old man's beard, a climbing plant with starry white flowers.

TRAVELOGUE [tra've-log], *n.* (*coll.*) article or talking film on travel and touring. [TRAVEL and Gk.].

TRAVERSE (1) [tra'vers], *v.t.* to lay in a cross direction; pass, cross, journey over or through; thwart, obstruct; survey carefully; turn and point in any direction; plane across the grain; (*leg.*) deny what the opposite party has alleged; *v.i.* to turn, as on a pivot; move round; swivel; in fencing, use the posture or motions of opposition. TRAVERSE (2), *n.* anything laid or built across; something which thwarts, crosses or obstructs; a turning; (*fort.*) parapet made across the covert-way to prevent its being enfiladed; (*mountaineering*) horizontal crossing of a face; (*arch.*) gallery or loft of communication in any large building; (*leg.*) denial of what the opposite party has advanced in any stage of the pleadings; (*naut.*) tack when beating to windward. TRAVERSE-TABLE, apparatus in the form of a travelling platform for shifting railway vehicles from one set of rails to another alongside it; (*naut.*) table of difference of latitude and departure. [Fr.].

TRAVERTINE [tra'ver-tēn], *n.* massive calcium carbonate deposited by water and forming a soft rock used for architectural ornamentation.

TRAVESTY (1) [tra'ves-ti], *n.* the representation of a serious work in a burlesque style; parody; complete caricature; a perversion. TRAVESTY (2), *v.t.* to parody; burlesque; make a mock of; render ridiculous. [Fr.].

TRAWL (1) [trawl], *n.* drag-net held open by a frame near the bottom of the sea; long buoyed fishing-line from which short lines hang. TRAWL (2), *v.t.* to draw (a net) along after a vessel; *v.i.* to fish by dragging a

---

The accent ' after a syllable = stress (u-pon'). The mark ˉ over a vowel = length (ā in made; ō in bone).

net along the bottom of the sea. TRAWLER, *n.* one who trawls; type of vessel employed for trawling. [OFr.].

TRAY [trā], *n.* flat object with a rim, made of wood, metal, china etc., used for carrying table appointments, food or letters; salver; object resembling the domestic tray, and used for other purposes. [OFr.].

TREACHEROUS [tre′che-rŏŏs], *adj.* violating allegiance or plighted faith; traitorous to king and country; untrustworthy; deceptive; unreliable; dangerous. [OFr.].

TREACHERY [tre′che-ri], *n.* breaking of faith or allegiance; perfidy; deceitful behaviour; treason.

TREACLE [trē′cl], *n.* molasses; a viscid dark-coloured sugar syrup; a saccharine fluid consisting of the inspissated juices of certain vegetables; (*coll.*) flattery; insincere amiability. TREACLY, *adj.* like t.; thick and sticky; (*fig.*) over-sweet, nauseatingly amiable. [OFr. from Gk.].

TREAD (1) (*pret.* **trod**, *p.pt.* **trodden, trod**) [tred], *v.t.* to step, walk on; press, trample, under the feet; crush, oppress; traverse; measure out by walking; work a treadle; (of cock birds) copulate with (a hen); *v.i.* to walk, step, go. TREAD (2), *n.* a step; manner of walking, gait; footstep; that on which one steps or is intended to step, e.g. on a stair; that which presses the ground when one steps, the sole of a shoe; that part of a tyre which presses upon the ground. [OE.].

TREADLE, TREDDLE [tre′dl], *n.* part of a machine worked by the foot so as to turn a crank. [OE.].

TREADMILL [tred′mil], *n.* mill turned by persons treading on steps upon the periphery of a wheel, formerly worked by convicts as part of their punishment; (*fig.*) any trying occupation characterized by sameness and monotony.

TREASON [trē′zn], *n.* betrayal of trust; treachery; offence of trying to betray the state or to subvert the government of the state to which the offender owes allegiance; **high t.**, t. which immediately affects the monarchy. [AFr.].

TREASURE (1) [tre′zhŏŏr], *n.* money or valuables accumulated and stored; something much valued; money; great abundance; (*coll.*) invaluable person; **t. house**, place where treasures and stores are kept. TREASURE-TROVE, any valuables, bullion and the like, found hidden, the owner of which is not known. TREASURE (2), *v.t.* to hoard as t.; value highly; retain in the mind. [OFr.].

TREASURER [tre′zhŏŏ-rer], *n.* one who has the care of funds or of a treasury; officer who receives and takes charge of the money of the public or of private companies, corporations or societies. [OFr.].

TREASURY [tre′zhŏŏ-ri], *n.* that department of government which has charge of the finances; repository; small encyclopedia or anthology; **t. bench**, the first row of seats on the Speaker's right in the House of Commons, occupied by cabinet ministers; **T. bill**, form of short-term loan issued by the T. to the highest bidders.

TREAT (1) [trēt], *v.t.* to behave or act towards; handle, deal with in a particular way; negotiate; manage; combat (a disease) by the use of remedies; seek to cure (a person); discourse on in speech or writing; entertain; bear the expenses for; *v.i.* to discourse; discuss terms; deal. TREAT (2), *n.* an exceptional entertainment or pleasure which affords great satisfaction; such an entertainment planned for pleasure; (*slang*) funny person or amusing incident. TREATER, *n.* one who discourses on a subject; negotiator; one who gives a t. [OFr.].

TREATISE [trē′tiz], *n.* written discourse in which a particular subject is fully or scientifically treated; monograph. [AFr.].

TREATMENT [trēt′ment], *n.* act or way of treating; management; manipulation; good or bad behaviour toward; manner of applying remedies; (*med.*) mode of dealing with a disease.

TREATY [trē′ti], *n.* a discussion of differences; a formal agreement, league or contract between states.

TREBLE (1) [tre′bl], *adj.* threefold; of, pertaining to, the third part in music, the boys' voices; hence, the highest part; shrill, sharp, (of a voice) unbroken. TREBLE (2), *n.* the highest of the parts in singing or playing; one who sings in the t. or plays a t. instrument. TREBLE (3), *v.t.* to make threefold; *v.i.* to become threefold. [OFr.].

TRECENTO [trā-chen′tō], *n.* the 14th century, *esp.* as a period in Italian art and literature. [It.].

TREDDLE, see TREADLE.

TREE (1) [trē], *n.* a plant larger than a shrub, and

having a single trunk; anything like a t., consisting of a stem and branches; piece of wood; the Cross; **genealogical t.**, family pedigree, diagram showing lines of descent; **up a t.**, (*coll.*) in difficulties. TREE-CREEPER, a small bird which preys on insects found on trees. TREE-FERN, large tropical and Australasian fern with a hole like a t. TREE (2), *v.t.* to drive to, or into, a t.; *v.i.* to take to a t. for a refuge. [OE.].

TREFOIL [trē′foil, tre′foil], *n.* a plant having leaves of three leaflets, such as clover; (*arch.*) ornament resembling three-leaved clover. [OFr. from L.].

TREK (1) [trek], *v.i.* to travel by ox-wagon; migrate; journey. TREK (2), *n.* a journey by ox-wagon; migration; journey. [Afrik.].

TRELLIS (1) [tre′lis], *n.* structure of lattice work for supporting plants. TRELLIS-WORK, small bars nailed across each other, as used for verandas and summer-houses. TRELLIS (2), *v.t.* to fit with a t. [OFr.].

TREMATODE [tre′ma-tōd], *n.* (*zool.*) a parasitic worm; fluke-worm. [Gk.].

TREMBLE (1) [trem′bl], *v.i.* to shake involuntarily as with fear, cold or weakness; shake; quiver; flutter; (*fig.*) feel intense anxiety, be agitated. TREMBLE (2), *n.* act of trembling, a shudder; (*mus.*) a shake. TREMBLER, *n.* person who trembles; electric device which trembles as it makes and breaks a circuit. [Fr.].

TREMENDOUS [tri-men′dŏŏs], *adj.* formidable; gigantic; overpowering; (*coll.*) very great, astonishing. TREMENDOUSLY, *adv.* in a manner to cause awe or astonishment; (*coll.*) very, extremely. [L.].

TREMOLO [tre′mō-lō], *n.* a shake or trembling of the voice, an imitation of this by an organ; tremulous delivery. [It.].

TREMOR [tre′mer], *n.* sudden access of trembling, shivering or quivering; a tremble; earthquake. [OFr.].

TREMULANT (1) [tre′myŏŏ-lant], *adj.* tremulous, quivering. TREMULANT (2), *n.* stop on an organ.

TREMULOUS [tre′myŏŏ-lŏŏs], *adj.* affected with tremors, trembling, uneven; fearful, nervous. [L.].

TRENCH (1) [trench], *v.t.* to cut or dig a channel in for water; furrow; dig; *v.i.* to encroach; make a trench in warfare. TRENCH (2), *n.* long narrow ditch cut or dug in the earth; (*fort.*) such a ditch cut deep into the ground as cover for soldiers; (*pl.*) military front so fortified; fighting in general; **t. mortar**, short-range mortar for work in trenches; **t. plough**, kind of plough for deep ploughing. TRENCH-COAT, belted waterproof coat of the kind worn by soldiers in trenches. TRENCH-FEVER, form of fever carried by lice during the First World War. TRENCHING, *n.* the digging of a t. or trenches; thorough form of digging over a garden. [OFr.].

TRENCHANCY [tren′chan-si], *n.* quality of being trenchant; sharpness of speech.

TRENCHANT [tren′chant], *adj.* cutting, sharp; severe, brief and telling in speech, caustic. [OFr.].

TRENCHER [tren′cher], *n.* wooden plate on which to cut meat at table; bread-platter; food. TRENCHER-MAN, *n.* one who eats from a t.; **good t.**, one with a hearty appetite. [OFr.].

TREND (1) [trend], *v.i.* to move or incline in a particular direction; take a course; drift. TREND (2), *n.* inclination or tendency; the general course of a speech etc. [~OE.].

TREPAN (1) [tri-pan′], *n.* circular saw for removing a piece of bone from the skull. TREPAN (2) (*pres.pt.* TREPANNING, *pret. and p.pt.* TREPANNED), *v.t.* (*surg.*) to operate on with a t. [Gk.].

TREPAN (3), *v.t.* to ensnare, entrap, lure. [Unkn.].

TREPANG [tre-pang′], *n.* the sea-slug. [Malay].

TREPHINE (1) [tre-fīn′, tre-fēn′], *n.* (*surg.*) improved trepan with a centre-pin, by which it is adjusted and set to work. TREPHINE (2), *v.t.* (*surg.*) to operate on with a t. [Fr.].

TREPIDATION [tre-pi-dā′shn], *n.* state of alarm and anxiety; nervousness; quaking or shivering of the limbs. [L.].

TRESPASS (1) [tres′pas], *v.i.* to enter unlawfully on the land of another; intrude, encroach (upon); sin, transgress, offend; **to t. on a person's time**, to take up a person's time. TRESPASS (2), *n.* act of trespassing; harm caused thereby; transgression; sin. [OFr.].

TRESS [tres], *n.* long strand or curl of hair; (*pl.*) the hair of the head. TRESSED, *adj.* having tresses; coiled up. [OFr.].

TRESTLE [tre′sl], *n.* two braced legs and a horizontal bar forming a movable frame for a temporary table; similar framework for supporting anything. [OFr.].

ŏŏ is pronounced as in food; ŏŏ as in hood; th as in *think*; TH as in *that*; zh as in azure. ~ = related to.

TREWS [trōōz], *n.(pl.)* tartan trousers as worn by Highland regiments. [Gael.].

TREY [trā], *n.* the three at cards or dice. [OFr.].

TRI-, *pref.* three, threefold. [Gk.].

TRIABLE [trī′a-bl], *adj.* able to be tried or tested; liable to trial; requiring to be tried.

TRIAD [trī′ad], *n.* a set of three persons or things; union of three elements; (*chem.*) an element, each atom of which, in combining, is equal to three atoms of hydrogen; (*mus.*) chord consisting of a note sounded along with its third and fifth; poem with a triple structure. [Gk.].

TRIAL [trī′al], *n.* an attempt; examination by test; experience; suffering; temptation; annoyance, irritation; (*leg.*) judicial examination in a court of law subsequent to a charge; **on t.**, on approbation; **t. run**, short run in a vehicle to test its efficiency; **t. marriage**, temporary union for the purpose of seeing whether the two parties are compatible; **method of t. and error**, way of arriving at the best method by testing several. [AFr.].

TRIANGLE [trī′ang-gl], *n.* figure bounded by three lines, and containing three angles; steel percussion instrument in music, bent into the form of an open triangle; **eternal t.**, (*fig.*) dramatic situation in which the mutual relations of one woman and two men, or one man and two women, are involved. [L.].

TRIANGULAR [trī-ang′gyōō-ler], *adj.* having a **t.** form; involving three sides, persons or groups.

TRIANGULATE [trī-ang′gyōō-lāt], *v.i.* to measure by triangulation. TRIANGULATION [trī-ang-gyōō-lā′shn], *n.* employment of a series of triangles in a trigonometrical survey.

TRIAS [trī′as], *n.* (*geol.*) the lowest group of Secondary rocks. [Gk.].

TRIBAL [trī′bal], *adj.* of, or pertaining to, a tribe. TRIBALISM, *n.* government by tribes; the characteristics of a tribe.

TRIBE [trīb], *n.* a social grouping of individuals descending usually from the same progenitor, and kept distinct; a division or distinct class of a people; a number of plants or animals having common qualities; a division; a nation of savages; a number of persons of any character or profession, in contempt. [L.].

TRIBULATION [tri-byōō-lā′shn], *n.* great distress; affliction. [L.].

TRIBUNAL [tri-byōō′nal], *n.* court of justice; board set up to adjudicate upon certain claims. [L.].

TRIBUNE (1) [trī′byōōn], *n.* ancient Roman military or civil official chosen by the people to defend their privileges; popular leader. [L.].

TRIBUNE (2), *n.* platform for a magistrate's official chair; bishop's throne in a R.C. basilican church; elevated place from which speeches are delivered. [Fr.].

TRIBUTARY (1) [trī′byōō-ta-ri], *adj.* paying tribute; paid in tribute; contributing supplies; subsidiary. TRIBUTARY (2), *n.* one paying a tribute; secondary river running into the main stream.

TRIBUTE [trī′byōōt], *n.* sum of money paid by one nation or group to another as a result of conquest or for defence services; periodical sum paid by a subject to the government or king; (*fig.*) admiration, grateful sentiments expressed by one person for another. [L.].

TRICAR [trī′kah(r)], *n.* three-wheeled motor-car.

TRICE (1) [trīs], *n.* moment of time; instant. [Unkn.].

TRICE (2), *v.t.* to hoist up (a sail) and make secure by means of a small rope. [MDu.].

TRICEPS [trī′seps], *n.* the three-headed extensor muscle of the forearm. [L.].

TRICHINOSIS, TRICHINIASIS [tri-ki-nō′sis, tri-ki-nī′a-sis], *n.* (*path.*) a disease in either man or animal due to the presence of minute nematoid parasitic worms in the body. [Gk.].

TRICHO-, (*pref.*) hair, of the hair. [Gk.].

TRICHOLOGY [tri-ko′lo-ji], *n.* study of the hair and its diseases; a treatise on hair. [Gk.].

TRICHOTOMY [tri-ko′to-mi], *n.* division into three parts. [Gk.].

TRICHROMATIC [trī-krō-ma′tik], *adj.* pertaining to three different colours. [Gk.].

TRICK (1) [trik], *n.* arrangement or device for the purpose of deception; fraudulent contrivance; a deception; illusion; legerdemain; sly prank; a peculiarity of manner, idiosyncrasy, curious habit; a round of cards; (*naut.*) steersman's spell of duty; **to do the t.**, (*coll.*) to achieve the desired end; **dirty t.**, mean or treacherous action. TRICK (2), *v.t.* to cheat, deceive;

v.i. to practise fraud and treachery; **to t. out, to** bedeck, dress up. [ONFr.].

TRICKERY [tri′ke-ri], *n.* cheating; artifice; roguery. [OFr.].

TRICKLE (1) [tri′kl], *v.t.* to make to trickle; *v.i.* to flow in a small gentle stream. TRICKLE (2), *n.* a thin stream; small flow; **t. charger**, (*elect.*) device which charges storage batteries slowly. [Uncert.].

TRICKSOME [trik′sum], *adj.* full of tricks; sportive.

TRICKSTER [trik′ster], *n.* one who practises trickery; rogue; cheat.

TRICKSY [trik′si], *adj.* (*coll.*) given to tricks; playful; pretty, fine.

TRICKY [tri′ki], *adj.* full of tricks; not very straightforward, rather difficult.

TRICOLOUR [trī′ku-ler], *n.* a national flag of three colours, *esp.* that of France. [Fr.].

TRICORN (1) [trī′kawn], *adj.* having three horns, points or corners. TRICORN (2), *n.* a t. hat. [L.].

TRICOT [trī′kō], *n.* knitting; special style of coarse knitting; jersey or other garment made of this kind of knitting. [Fr.].

TRICYCLE [trī′si-kl], *n.* three-wheeled cycle.

TRIDENT [trī′dent], *n.* form of sceptre or spear with three prongs, represented in the hands of Neptune, as god of the sea, and used as a symbol of maritime power. [L.].

TRIENNIAL [trī-e′ni-al], *adj.* of three years' duration; occurring every three years. [L.].

TRIENNIUM [trī-e′ni-um], *n.* period of three years; something recurring every third year. [L.].

TRIFLE (1) [trī′fl], *n.* thing of very little value or importance; sponge cake soaked in custard, and covered with whipped cream. TRIFLE (2), *v.i.* to act or talk with levity; indulge in light amusements; play (with); hurt the feelings of another with thoughtless levity. [OFr.].

TRIFLING [trī′fling], *adj.* of small value or importance; insignificant.

TRIFOLIATE [trī-fō′li-at], *adj.* bearing three leaves; (*bot.*) arranged in groups of three. [L.].

TRIFOLIUM [trī-fō′li-um], *n.* trefoil; clover. [L.].

TRIFORIUM (*pl.* **triforia**) [tri-faw′ri-um], *n.* (*arch.*) arcaded gallery built below a clerestory over the arches of the nave or transept of a church. [L.].

TRIG [trig], *n.* a sprag for a wheel. [Uncert.].

TRIGAMY [tri′ga-mi], *n.* condition of having three husbands or wives at the same time. [Gk.].

TRIGGER [tri′ger], *n.* the catch of a fire-arm, which, if pulled, looses the lock; similar catch in other mechanism. [~Du.].

TRIGLYPH [trī′glif], *n.* three-grooved ornamental tablet in the Doric frieze, repeated at equal intervals. [Gk.].

TRIGONOMETRIC(AL) [tri-go-nō-me′trik(-al)], *adj.* pertaining to trigonometry.

TRIGONOMETRY [tri-go-no′me-tri], *n.* (*math.*) science of measuring the sides and angles of triangles and their functions. [Gk.].

TRIKE [trik], *n.* (*coll.*) tricycle.

TRILATERAL [trī-la′te-ral], *adj.* with three sides.

TRILBY [tril′bi], *n.* a certain shape of soft felt hat. [*Trilby* by George Du Maurier].

TRILINGUAL [trī-ling′gwal], *adj.* written in, speaking, three languages. [L.].

TRILL (1) [tril], *n.* a quaver; a shake on two adjacent notes in singing or playing; the vibratory notes in a bird's song; a warble; (*phon.*) sound produced by the vibration of the tongue. TRILL (2), *v.t. and i.* to utter with a t.; sing or play with a quavering or tremulous quality; quaver. [Fr.].

TRILLION [tril′yun], *n.* the product of a million involved to the third power, and expressed by a unit with eighteen zeros; in America, a million times a million, that is, a unit and twelve zeros. [TRI- and (MI)LLION].

TRILOGY [tri′lo-ji], *n.* group of three related literary or dramatic compositions. [Gk.].

TRIM (1) (*pres.pt.* **trimming**, *pret. and p.pt.* **trimmed**) [trim], *v.t.* to put in order, make neat; clip; adjust the burning of (a lamp); adjust the sails of (a boat) or the equilibrium of (an aircraft); ornament (a garment etc.); adjust the relationship of (two or more radio circuits); *v.i.* to modify one's behaviour to secure advantage from changing circumstances. TRIM (2), *adj.* neat; in good order. TRIM (3), *n.* good or neat condition; order. [OE.].

TRIMETER [tri′mi-ter], *n.* a verse of three measures, sometimes of three feet, but in iambic, trochaic or anapaestic metre of three dipodies. [Gk.].

TRIMMER [tri′mer], *n.* one who trims; device for

The accent ′ after a syllable = stress (u-pon′). The mark ¯ over a vowel = length (ā in made; ō in bone).

trimming a radio circuit; (fig.) **opportunist; a fishing float.**
TRIMMING [tri'ming], *n.* the **trimmed** edge of a fabric; unessential ornaments.
TRINITARIAN [tri-ni-tăer'i-an], *n.* believer in Trinitarianism. TRINITARIANISM, *n.* doctrine of the Trinity.
TRINITROTOLUENE, -TOLUOL [trī-nī-trō-to'lyoo-ēn, -to'lyoo-ol], *n.* a high explosive, often called T.N.T., obtained by the action of nitric acid on toluene.
TRINITY [tri'ni-ti], *n.* a unity consisting of three parts; group of three things or persons closely connected; (*theol.*) the indivisible unity of Father, Son and Holy Ghost. [L.].
TRINKET [tring'kit], *n.* small ornament, worthless little jewel. [ME.].
TRINOMIAL [trī-nō'mi-al], *adj.* having three algebraic terms; (*nat. hist.*) (of nomenclature) having three terms to describe genus, species and variety. [TRI- and (BI)NOMIAL].
TRIO [trē'ō], *n.* musical composition for three performers; group of three persons, *esp.* musical performers. [It.].
TRIODE [tri'ōd], *n.* (*radio*) three-electrode valve. [TRI- and Gk.].
TRIOLET [tri'ō-let], *n.* stanza of eight lines, the first, third, fourth, fifth and seventh lines having a common rhyme, the second, sixth and eighth lines rhyming together, the fourth and seventh lines identical with the first, the eighth identical with the second. [Fr.].
TRIP (1) [pres.pt. tripping, *pret. and p.pt.* **tripped**] [TRIP], *v.t. and i.* to make to fall by sudden interference with the feet; catch out in a falsehood or error; loose (an anchor) by means of a cable; operate a mechanism by releasing a catch; move with short, light, rapid steps; stumble through catching one's foot against a thing; (*fig.*) commit an error, betray oneself. TRIP-WIRE, *n.* wire set so as to t. an approaching enemy and operate a booby-trap. TRIP (2), *n.* short journey, excursion, pleasure-voyage; act of tripping or stumbling; deliberate tripping of another by interposing one's foot. [OFr.].
TRIPARTITE [trī-pah'tīt], *adj.* divided into three parts; having three corresponding parts; pertaining to three parties. TRIPARTITION [trī-pah-ti'shn], *n.* division by three or into three. [L.].
TRIPE [trīp], *n.* stomach of a ruminant animal, *esp.* the ox, used as food; (*coll.*) nonsense, literary rubbish. [Fr.].
TRIPHIBIOUS [trī-fi'bi-ŏŏs], *adj.* concerning, inhabiting, land, sea and air. [TRI- and (AM)PHIBIOUS].
TRIPHTHONG [trif'thong], *n.* group of three vowels in one compound sound. [TRI- and (DI)PHTHONG].
TRIPLE (1) [tri'pl], *adj.* threefold. TRIPLE-HEADED, having three heads. TRIPLE (2), *v.t. and i.* to multiply threefold. [L.].
TRIPLET [tri'plet], *n.* one of three children born of a single gestation; group of three successive rhyming lines.
TRIPLEX [tri'pleks], *adj.* threefold; (*mus.*) in triple (time); **T. glass,** (*prot.*) three-ply amalgam of glass and micaceous substance. [L.].
TRIPLICATE (1) [tri'pli-kat], *adj.* threefold; in three copies. TRIPLICATE (2), *n.* one of three copies; **in t., so as to provide three copies.** TRIPLICATE (3) [tri'pli-kāt], *v.t.* to treble. [L.].
TRIPOD [tri'pod], *n.* stool, vessel, supported on three legs; a support with three legs. [Gk.].
TRIPOS [tri'pos], *n.* honours examination at Cambridge. [Gk.].
TRIPPER [tri'per], *n.* one who trips; (*coll.*) holiday excursionist, tourist.
TRIPPING [tri'ping], *adj.* walking nimbly; (of words) coming nimbly off the tongue.
TRIPTYCH [trip'tik], *n.* picture or design on three panels, those at the side hinging on that in the centre. [Gk.].
TRIPTYQUE [trip'tēk], *n.* customs permit for the temporary importation of a motor-car into a particular country. [Fr.].
TRIREME [tri'rēm], *n.* warship of the classical period, having its oars arranged in three banks. [L.].
TRISECT [tri-sekt'], *v.t.* to divide into three equal parts. [TRI- and L.].
TRISKELE [tris'kēl], *n.* device of three radiating spokes, *esp.* the three-legged device of the Isle of Man. [Gk.].
TRISTE [trēst], *adj.* melancholy; (*coll.*) unfortunate. [Fr.].
TRISYLLABLE [tri-si'la-bl], *n.* word of three syllables.

TRITE [trīt], *adj.* commonplace, pettily platitudinous, stale with use, hackneyed. TRITELY, *adv.* in a t. manner. [L.].
TRITOMA [trī-tō'mah], *n.* (*bot.*) the torch lily or red-hot poker. [Gk.].
TRITON [tri'ton], *n.* (*myth.*) son of Poseidon and Amphitrite; a sea-demigod. [Gk.].
TRITURATE [tri'tyŏŏ-rāt], *v.t.* to grind to powder, pulverize. [L.].
TRIUMPH (1) [tri'umf], *n.* state of triumphing; a great, complete and glorious victory, great success; feeling of exaltation of a victory; (*Rom. hist.*) processional entry into Rome of a general at the head of his army, granted by the senate in honour of an important victory. TRIUMPH (2), *v.i.* to be gloriously victorious or successful; exult in victory; **to t. over,** to overcome; exult over. [L.].
TRIUMPHANT [trī-um'fant], *adj.* triumphing; victorious; exultant. [L.].
TRIUMVIR (*pl.* **triumvirs, triumviri**) [trī-um'ver], *n.* one of three co-rulers; (*Rom. hist.*) member of one of the triple coalitions which ruled Rome in the last days of the Republic. [L.].
TRIUNE [tri'yŏŏn], *adj.* three in one. TRIUNITY [trī-yŏŏ'ni-ti], *n.* trinity. [TRI- and L.].
TRIVALENT [tri-vā'lent], *adj.* combining with three univalent atoms. [TRI- and L.].
TRIVET [tri'vit], *n.* tripod stand for a vessel placed over a fire. [Uncert.].
TRIVIAL [tri'vi-al], *adj.* of little importance, slight. [L.].
TRIVIALITY [tri-vi-a'li-ti], *n.* a trivial matter; state of being trivial.
TROCHAIC [trō-kā'ik], *adj.* consisting of trochees.
TROCHEE [trō'kē], *n.* (*pros.*) foot consisting of a long and a short syllable or a stressed followed by an unstressed syllable. [Gk.].
TROD [trod], *pret. and p.pt.* of TREAD.
TRODDEN [tro'den], *p.pt.* of TREAD.
TROGLODYTE [trog'lō-dīt], *n.* cave dweller, *esp.* in contempt. [Gk.].
TROJAN [trō'jan], *n. and adj.* inhabitant of, pertaining to, ancient Troy; (*fig.*) highly energetic, vigorous and enduring worker. [L.].
TROLL (1) [trōl], *n.* (*myth.*) amphibious giant; **dwarf** troglodyte. [OScand.].
TROLL (2), *v.t. and i.* to sing carelessly and cheerfully; fish with a trailed bait. [OFr.].
TROLLEY, TROLLY [tro'li], *n.* four-wheeled truck running on rails; any light wheeled structure, *esp.* for pushing; grooved pulley running along an electrified overhead cable from which it receives current to drive a vehicle. TROLLEY-BUS, bus propelled by electricity supplied from a t. TROLLEY-POLE, overhead arm, carrying the **t.,** of an electric tramcar or bus. [Uncert.].
TROLLOP [tro'lop], *n.* blowsy and disreputable female. [~TROLL].
TROMBONE [trom'bōn], *n.* trumpet-like brass wind-instrument, whose notes are controlled by a sliding tube or valves. [It.].
TROOP (1) [trŏŏp], *n.* band, group; small body of cavalry; (*pl.*) soldiers, military force. TROOP-CARRIER, aeroplane or truck designed for the transport of troops. TROOP (2), *v.t. and i.* to move in large groups; transport troops; **to t. the colour,** to parade the regimental standard ceremonially. [LL.].
TROOPER [trŏŏ'per]. *n.* cavalryman; **to swear like a t.,** to swear profusely and hard.
TROPE [trōp], *n.* an expression used metaphorically or figuratively. [Gk.].
TROPHY [trō'fi], *n.* spoil taken from a conquered enemy as a symbol of victory, *esp.* the pile of enemy arms set up on a battlefield by the victorious party; prize awarded for a sporting contest. [Gk.].
TROPIC (1) [trō'pik], *n.* latitude at which the sun is directly overhead at noon at the December solstice **(t. of Capricorn)** or at the June solstice **(t. of Cancer)**; (*pl.*) torrid zone between these two latitudes. TROPIC (2), *adj.* tropical. [Gk.].
TROPICAL [tro'pi-kal], *adj.* of, or relating to, the tropics; excessively hot.
TROT (1) [trot], *v.t. and i.* (of a horse etc.) to move at a pace between walking and galloping; (of a person) run with brief, brisk steps; make (a horse) trot; **to t. out,** to bring out (as if of interest) commonplace old sentiments etc. TROT (2), *n.* act, pace, of trotting. TROTTER, *n.* one who trots; horse specially trained for trotting; pig's foot; (*coll.*) foot. [ME.].
TROTH [trōth], *n.* fidelity; sworn word. [OE.].
TROUBADOUR [trŏŏ'ba-daw(r)], *n.* medieval

(chiefly Provençal) wandering singer and amorous poet. [Provenc.].

TROUBLE (1) [tru'bl], *n.* inconvenience, laborious difficulty; care, pains; state of disturbance or affliction; a disease, persistent ailment; state of being mentally disturbed, worry. TROUBLE (2), *v.t. and i.* to stir, disturb, set into movement; agitate, worry, annoy; cause inconvenience to, bother; be anxious, feel agitated; take care, pay attention. [Fr. ~L.].

TROUBLESOME [tru'bl-sum], *adj.* causing trouble or inconvenience, unruly.

TROUBLOUS [trub'loos], *adj.* troubled, disturbed, turbulent.

TROUGH [trof], *n.* long, open vessel holding the water and food of domestic animals; depression between two waves. [OE.].

TROUNCE [trowns], *v.t.* to beat severely, thoroughly defeat. [~Fr.].

TROUPE [troop], *n.* company of players or performers. TROUPER, *n.* member of a theatrical t. [Fr.].

TROUSERS [trow'zers], *n.(pl.)* garment for the lower part of the body, consisting of two tubular coverings for the legs, joining at the groin; long drawers. TROUSER, *adj.* relating to t. [Fr.].

TROUSSEAU [troo'sō], *n.* the clothes and personal necessaries with which a bride is provided at her marriage. [Fr.].

TROUT [trowt], *n.* any fish of the genus *Salmo*; small spotted freshwater fish of this genus; (*slang*) pig-headed fool. [ME.].

TROW [trō, trow], *v.i.* (*archaic*) to believe, assume. [OE.].

TROWEL [trowl], *n.* small, hollow-bladed implement used for scooping earth in gardening; flat, diamond-shaped implement used for spreading mortar. [~L.].

TROY WEIGHT [troi'wāt], *n.* a weight of 480 grains to the ounce and 12 ounces to the pound by which gold, silver and precious stones are weighed. [*Troyes*, France].

TRUANCY [troo'an-si], *n.* act of playing truant.

TRUANT (1) [troo'ant], *n.* person who remains away from his duty for a personal whim, *esp.* a child who absents himself from school. TRUANT (2), *adj.* being, relating to, a t. [OFr.].

TRUCE [troos], *n.* agreement between combatants to suspend hostilities temporarily without settling the cause at issue. [ME.].

TRUCK (1) [truk], *n.* light wagon for carrying goods; open railway wagon; lorry. TRUCK (2), *v.t. and i.* to transport by t. [L.].

TRUCK (3), *v.t. and i.* to exchange, barter; bargain, have dealings with. TRUCK (4), *n.* trade; commerce; payment in kind; (*coll.*) dealings (with). [Fr.].

TRUCKLE (1) [truk'l], *n.* small wheel or castor; truckle-bed. TRUCKLE-BED, bed which runs on wheels and may be pushed under another. TRUCKLE (2), *v.i.* to submit, yield obsequiously; *v.t.* to trundle. [Gk.].

TRUCULENT [tru'kyoo-lent], *adj.* ferociously insolent, bullyingly violent.

TRUDGE (1) [truj], *v.i.* to walk with laborious determination, tramp along wearily. TRUDGE (2), *n.* a laborious tramp. [Uncert.].

TRUDGEN [truj'en], *n.* style of hand-over-hand swimming. [*Trudgen*, who popularized the stroke].

TRUE (1) [troo], *adj.* conforming to fact and reality, not false or fictitious; faithful, loyal, honest; rightful, proper, accurate, without variation; **t. love**, faithful and exclusive love; the object so loved; the plant *Paris quadrifolia.* TRUE-BLUE, of inflexible honesty and steadfastness. TRUE-BORN, legitimate; t. to type. TRUE-BRED, thoroughbred. TRUE (2), *adv.* truly; accurately; without deviation. TRUE (3), *v.t.* to make accurate, plumb, level; adjust exactly. [OE.].

TRUFFLE [tru'fl], *n.* a fleshy underground fungus, much esteemed in cookery. [Fr.].

TRUG [trug], *n.* hod for mortar; shallow gardening basket made of wood. [Uncert.].

TRUISM [troo'izm], *n.* an obvious and hackneyed truth, platitude.

TRUMP (1) [trump], *n.* (*archaic and poet.*) trumpet. [ME.].

TRUMP (2), *n.* (*card-games*) card of the suit which, for the time being, ranks above the other three suits. TRUMP (3), *v.t.* to play a t. on (a card of another suit); play a t. on the card of; **to t. up**, to fabricate, invent, falsely allege an accusation or excuse. [~TRIUMPH].

TRUMPERY [trum'pe-ri], *adj.* worthless, trashy, silly and useless. [Fr.].

TRUMPET (1) [trum'pit], *n.* brass wind-instrument,

straight or slightly curved and with a widened outer end, giving a high, powerful note; the sound of a trumpet; something which proclaims loudly; something shaped like a trumpet. TRUMPET-MAJOR, leading trumpeter in a cavalry regiment. TRUMPET (2), *v.t. and i.* to sound on a t., proclaim; make a sound like that of a t. [Fr.].

TRUMPETER [trum'pi-ter], *n.* one who sounds a trumpet; the swan *Cygnus buccinator.*

TRUNCAL [trung'kal], *adj.* relating to the trunk.

TRUNCATE (1) [trung-kāt'], *v.t.* to slice off a projecting angle or edge so as to leave a plain face; cut down, cut short. TRUNCATE (2), [trung'kāt], *adj.* truncated. [L.].

TRUNCHEON (1) [trun'shn], *n.* short rounded club, used as a wand of office or as a weapon. TRUNCHEON (2), *v.t.* to beat with a t. [OFr.].

TRUNDLE (1) [trun'dl], *n.* castor, small wheel. TRUNDLE (2), *v.t. and i.* to roll, wheel along heavily; move along on, or as if on, wheels; (*coll.*) (*cricket*) to bowl. [~OE.].

TRUNK [trungk], *n.* main body of a tree; torso; large case or box used to carry travellers' effects; long flexible proboscis; **t. road**, main long-distance road providing communication between important centres. TRUNK-CALL, long-distance telephone call. TRUNK-HOSE, (*pl.*) short, wide breeches, formerly worn, which were gathered in above or just below the knee. TRUNKS, *n.(pl.)* short light drawers worn by swimmers, athletes etc.; † t.-hose. [L.].

TRUNNION [trun'yun], *n.* one of the two supporting pivots of a cannon etc. [Fr.].

TRUSS (1) [trus], *v.t.* to bind up into, or as if into, a truss; fasten (the carcase of a bird) closely together ready for cooking. TRUSS (2), *n.* bundle of hay or straw tied at the ends; surgical device for supporting organs affected by rupture; framework of girders used to support a roof etc. [OFr.].

TRUST (1) [trust], *n.* belief in, reliance on, anything, unquestioning faith in the reliability of a person; something with which a person is entrusted; (*leg.*) a holding of property for the benefit of another; legal form and framework of such nominal ownership; committee of persons administering a fund for the benefit of others; business ring to pursue a common interest. TRUST (2), *v.t.* to have implicit faith in the reliability of (a person or thing); hope almost to belief; entrust. [ME.].

TRUSTEE [trus-tē'], *n.* one holding property in trust. TRUSTEESHIP, *n.* office of t.; administration of colonial territory by more advanced states under the authority of an international body, with the object of safeguarding the interests of the inhabitants.

TRUSTWORTHY [trust'wer-THi], *adj.* worthy of trust or confidence.

TRUSTY [trus'ti], *adj.* that may be safely trusted; faithful.

TRUTH [trooth], *n.* that which is true, *esp.* as contrasted with something false, that which is real. [OE.].

TRY (1) [trī], *v.t. and i.* to put to trial, test, judge (a person) in a court of law; put a severe strain on; irritate; experiment with; attempt, make an endeavour. TRY (2), *n.* an attempt, endeavour; (*Rugby football*) the scoring of three points when the ball is touched down by a player behind his opponents' goal-line; the three points thus scored. TRY-ON, venture or act performed to test the reactions of other persons or parties. TRY-OUT, preliminary test, trial, or performance. TRYING, *adj.* irritating; putting a strain on. [ME.].

TRYPANOSOME [tri'pa-nō-sōm], *n.* parasitic protozoan which causes sleeping-sickness. [~Gk.].

TRYPSIN [trip'sin], *n.* digestive ferment secreted in the pancreas. [~Gk.].

TRYSAIL [trī'sāl], *n.* fore-and-aft sail without a boom.

TRYST (1) [trist, trīst], *n.* assignation, romantic rendezvous. TRYST (2), *v.i.* to engage to meet; set as a rendezvous. [ME.].

TSAR, TSAREVITCH, TSAREVNA, TSARINA, see CZAR, CZAREVITCH, CZAREVNA, CZARINA.

TSETSE, TZETZE [tse'tsi], *n.* an African fly, a carrier of various diseases to human beings and animals. [Native].

T-SQUARE [tē'skwāer], *n.* drawing instrument shaped like a T.

TUB (1) [tub], *n.* round wooden vessel, usually for containing water; clumsy boat; (*coll.*) bath. TUB-THUMPER, (*coll.*) noisy and extravagant preacher or public speaker. TUB (2) (*pres.pt.* TUBBING, *pret. and p.pt.* TUBBED), *v.t. and i.* to give a bath to; take a bath; line (the sides of a shaft) with watertight material. [OFr.].

TUBA [tyoo'bah], *n.* valved brass wind-instrument of very low pitch. [L.].

TUBBY [tu'bi], *adj.* round, short and fat.

TUBE [tyoob], *n.* hollow cylinder, pipe; underground railway running through metal tubes; (**inner**) **t.**, inflatable rubber **t.** which holds the air in a pneumatic tire. [L.].

TUBER [tyoo'ber], *n.* (*bot.*) enlarged underground stem of a plant, containing buds. [L.].

TUBERCLE [tyoo'ber-kl], *n.* small protuberance; small morbid growth on a bodily organ; tuberculosis. TUBERCLED, TUBERCULATE [tyoo'ber-kld, tyoo-bur'kyoo-lat], *adj.* having small knobs or tubercles. [L.].

TUBERCULAR [tyoo-bur'kyoo-ler], *adj.* having tubercles; suffering from tuberculosis.

TUBERCULIN [tyoo-bur'kyoo-lin], *n.* a solution of the culture of the tubercle bacillus.

TUBERCULOSIS [tyoo-ber-kyoo-lo'sis], *n.* infectious disease marked by the growth of tubercles in the tissues; consumption.

TUBEROSE [tyoo'be-roz, tyoob'roz], *n.* a perfumed white garden plant.

TUCK (1) [tuk], *v.t. and i.* to make compact by stuffing or thrusting in; shorten by sewing up into a fold; **to t. up or in**, to secure the bedclothes of by thrusting the edges beneath the mattress; **to t. in**, (*coll.*) to eat largely and rapidly. TUCK (2), *n.* a fold sewn into cloth; (*coll.*) food, delicacies. TUCK-BOX, wooden box used by schoolboys for their t. TUCK-IN, (*slang*) hearty meal. TUCK-SHOP, sweetstuff and pastry shop at a school. [ME.].

TUCKER [tu'ker], *n.* band of cloth, lace etc., formerly worn by women at the top of the bodice; frill round the neck; (*Australian coll.*) food; **one's best bib and t.**, one's smartest clothes.

TUCKET [tu'kit], *n.* (*archaic*) flourish of trumpets. [It.].

TUDOR [tyoo'der], *adj.* relating to, in the style of, 16th-century England. [*Tudor* Dynasty].

TUESDAY [tyooz'dā], *n.* third day of the week. [OE.].

TUFA [too'fah], *n.* massive mineral deposit of crystalline calcium carbonate; travertine. [It. from L.].

TUFF [tuf], *n.* light porous rock of volcanic ashes cemented together; any similar rock. [Fr. from L.].

TUFT [tuft], *n.* loose clump of stalks, hairs etc. joined at the base, cluster of grasses. TUFT-HUNTER, one who seeks the company of the rich and important. [ME.].

TUG (1) (*pres.pt.* **tugging,** *pret. and p.pt.* **tugged**) [tug], *v.t. and i.* to pull strongly and spasmodically, jerk violently at; heave violently. TUG (2), *n.* sudden violent jerk or heave; vessel used for towing. TUG-OF-WAR, athletic contest in which two teams t. at opposite ends of a rope, until one party is dragged across a central mark. [ME.].

TUITION [tyoo-i'shn], *n.* act of teaching; that which is taught. [L.].

TULIP [tyoo'lip], *n.* a brightly coloured liliaceous plant. TULIP-TREE, a North American flowering tree. [~Turk.].

TULLE [tyool], *n.* kind of fine silk net or muslin. [*Tulle,* France].

TUMBLE (1) [tum'bl], *v.t. and i.* to stumble and fall, fall over headlong, collapse utterly; turn somersaults; throw over, rumple; **to t. to,** to comprehend, realize, see the point. TUMBLE (2), *n.* act of tumbling. TUMBLING, *adj.* acrobatic clowning. [~OE.].

TUMBLEDOWN [tum'bl-down], *adj.* dilapidated.

TUMBLER [tum'bler], *n.* one who tumbles; clown; kind of pigeon; cylindrical drinking glass; catch of a lock. TUMBLERFUL, *n.* as much as a t. will hold (usually half a pint).

TUMBREL, TUMBRIL [tum'bril], *n.* dung-cart; wagon in which the condemned were taken to the guillotine during the French Revolution. [Fr.].

TUMESCENCE [tyoo-me'sens], *n.* tumour; act of swelling.

TUMESCENT [tyoo-me'sent], *adj.* swelling. [L.].

TUMID [tyoo'mid], *adj.* swollen; congested; pompous. [L.].

TUMOUR [tyoo'mer], *n.* bodily swelling due to abnormal cell-growth; abnormal protuberance. [L.].

TUMULAR [tyoo'myoo-ler], *adj.* relating to, shaped like, a tumulus.

TUMULT [tyoo'mult], *n.* violent, confused uproar; public commotion; (*fig.*) confusion of mind. [L.].

TUMULTUOUS [tyoo-mul'tyoo-oos], *adj.* in a tumult; furiously disordered.

TUMULUS (*pl.* **tumuli**) [tyoo'myoo-lus], *n.* barrow; prehistoric burial-mound. [L.].

TUN [tun], *n.* great cask or vat for storing liquor; a measure of two pipes of wine. [OE.].

TUNA [too'nah], *n.* the tunny of the Pacific coast of North America. [Span.].

TUNDRA [tun'drah], *n.* a treeless waste supporting grasses and lichens in sub-arctic regions, *esp.* in North Russia. [Russ.].

TUNE (1) [tyoon], *n.* a melody; series of musical notes arranged harmoniously; correctness of pitch of a musical note; **in t.,** in agreement, in harmony, in accordance. TUNE (2), *v.t.* to put in t., adjust (musical instruments) so that their notes are true; adjust (a motor etc.) to its best performance; **to t. in,** *v.t. and i.* to adjust (a radio set) to receive a certain station; **to t. up,** (of an orchestra) to test and adjust the instruments before a musical performance. [OFr.].

TUNELESS [tyoon'les], *adj.* unmelodious.

TUNER [tyoo'ner], *n.* one who tunes musical instruments; (*radio*) an arrangement of oscillatory circuits which may be adjusted for the reception of desired signals.

TUNGSTEN [tung'sten], *n.* metallic element denoted by W, used for electric filaments; wolfram; **t. steel,** an alloy of steel and t. [Swed.].

TUNIC [tyoo'nik], *n.* loose garment covering the trunk; short, close-fitting coat of a soldier's, policeman's etc. uniform. [L.].

TUNING [tyoo'ning], *n.* act of putting an instrument into tune; adjustment of a radio set to a given wavelength. TUNING-FORK, fork-like instrument for setting the note in t. TUNING-HAMMER, instrument for t. pianos.

TUNNEL (1) [tu'nel], *n.* underground passage, *esp.* if cylindrical and artificial. TUNNEL (2) (*pres.pt.* TUNNELLING, *pret. and p.pt.* TUNNELLED), *v.i.* to make a t. [OFr.].

TUNNY [tu'ni], *n.* a fish of the mackerel family, sometimes of very great size. [Gk.].

TUP [tup], *n.* a ram. [ME.].

TURBAN [tur'ban], *n.* Eastern head-dress consisting of a long strip of fabric wound about a small cap or the head itself. [~Turk.].

TURBID [tur'bid], *adj.* thickly confused, disturbed; opaque with sediment. [L.].

TURBINE [tur'bin], *n.* rotating wheel driven by water, steam or gas, and used as a prime mover. [~L.].

TURBIT [tur'bit], *n.* a ruffled and crested pigeon. [Uncert.].

TURBO-JET [ter-bo-jet'], *adj.* (of an engine) providing propulsive power by an exhaust-gas turbine and an exhaust jet in combination.

TURBO-PROP [ter-bo-prop'], *n.* a turbine which drives an aircraft propeller.

TURBOT [tur'but], *n.* a large, flat, edible fish. [Fr.].

TURBULENCE [tur'byoo-lens], *n.* state of being turbulent; unruliness, lawless disturbance.

TURBULENT [tur'byoo-lent], *adj.* unruly, tumultuous, violently agitated; (*meteor.*) (of wind) eddying, unsteady. [L.].

TUREEN [tyoo-rēn'], *n.* deep, oval vessel for serving soup and vegetables. [Fr.].

TURF (1) (*pl.* **turves**) [turf], *n.* conglomeration of earth and vegetable mould forming the surface layer of the ground; grass-sward; peat; piece cut from the grassy surface of the ground; **the t.,** horse-racing. TURF-ACCOUNTANT, bookmaker. TURF (2), *v.t.* to overlay, cover, with t.; **to t. out,** (*slang*) to expel roughly or unceremoniously. TURFITE, *n.* (*slang*) race-goer. [OE.].

TURFING [tur'fing], *n.* act of covering with turf. TURFING-IRON, implement for paring off turf. TURFING-SPADE, tool for undercutting turf when marked out by the plough.

TURGESCENCE, TURGESCENCY [ter-je'sens-(i)], *n.* state of being swollen; act of swelling; bombast, pomposity.

TURGESCENT [ter-je'sent], *adj.* swelling, in a state of turgescence. [L.].

TURGID [tur'jid], *adj.* swollen, distended, tumid, inflated, tortuously bombastic. [L.].

TURK [turk], *n.* member of the Turkish race, an Ottoman; (*coll.*) young rascal. [It.].

TURKEY [tur'ki], *n.* large bird of the genus *Meleagris*, originally American, traditionally eaten on Christmas Day; **to talk t.,** to get down to business, talk business; **T. carpet,** kind of brightly coloured woollen carpet of the type exported from T. TURKEY-BUZZARD, the South American vulture. TURKEY-RED, a fine, fast red dye. [*Turkey*, where supposed to have originated].

TURKISH [tur'kish], *adj.* of, relating to, Turkey, its inhabitants or language; **T. bath**, originally, a steam bath; now, a steam bath followed by cold douches, massage etc.; **T. delight**, sweetmeat made of gelatine and sugar, originally T.

TURMERIC [tur'me-rik], *n.* an aromatic plant. [Fr.].

TURMOIL [tur'moil], *n.* tumultuous confusion, noisy agitation. [Unkn.].

TURN (1) [turn], *v.t. and i.* to cause to change direction, divert from an intended course; reverse, make to face in an opposite direction; cause to revolve, spin round; shape on a lathe; (*fig.*) present in polished fashion; transform, cause to assume some specified form; sicken, shock; direct; (*milit.*) get behind (an enemy's line of battle); take a new direction, *esp.* at right angles to the previous one; face about to a reverse direction; spin round, revolve; become, be transformed; (of food) go bad, become sour; direct the attention (towards), incline (towards); **to t. away**, to rebuff; **to t. back**, to make to return; return; give way; **to t. down**, to reject, refuse; **to t. in**, to hand in; go to bed; **to t. out**, to eject; fit out; become; eventuate; (*milit.*) summon to parade, come to parade; **to t. over**, to hand over; **to t. to**, to set to work; **to t. up**, to appear, arrive; (*U.S. slang*) reveal; discover espionage; **to t. upon**, to attack (an associate) unexpectedly. TURN (2), *n.* act of turning, motion made in turning, condition of having turned; a change, alteration in the condition of a person or thing; a deflection of 90 deg.; regularly recurring chance or compulsion to perform some task; rightful opportunity; short spell of exercise; short theatrical performance included among others; sudden shock; peculiar ability; action done to another; **to serve a t.**, to meet a particular need; **done to a t.**, cooked to perfection. [OFr.].

TURNCOAT [turn'kōt], *n.* traitor, one who changes his principles to suit his convenience.

TURNCOCK [turn'kok], *n.* one who turns water on and off from the main.

TURNER [tur'ner], *n.* one working on a lathe. TURNERY, *n.* craft of working with a lathe; things worked with a lathe; place where turning is done. [Fr.].

TURNING [tur'ning], *n.* road leading off another; place at which a road branches off; practice of working wood etc. on a lathe. TURNING-POINT, crux of a matter; decisive instant at which the course of events changes.

TURNIP [tur'nip], *n.* edible (root of the) plant *Brassica campestris, var. Rapa*. [~OE.].

TURNKEY [turn'kē], *n.* warder in a prison.

TURN-OUT [turn'owt], *n.* act of turning out; state of being turned out; (*milit.*) state of a soldier's uniform and equipage; equipage.

TURNOVER [turn'nō-ver], *n.* cake of folded pastry; the money, as distinct from the profits, taken by a business; that which is turned over.

TURNPIKE [turn'pik], *n.* toll-gate, *esp.* when worked by a pivot; **t. road**, road on which turnpikes or toll-gates were established by law.

TURN-ROUND [turn'rownd], *n.* operation of making a ship ready for a return voyage from a port of destination.

TURNSPIT [turn'spit], *n.* person who turned a spit; breed of dog formerly employed to turn spits.

TURNSTILE [turn'stil], *n.* small turnpike stopping the passage of cattle and vehicles but allowing pedestrians to pass; revolving gate for checking the admission of spectators.

TURNTABLE [turn'tā-bl], *n.* large revolving platform for turning locomotives in a different direction; revolving platform on a gramophone.

TURPENTINE [tur'pen-tin], *n.* oily secretion of pine trees. TURPENTINE-TREE, the terebinth. [~Gk.].

TURPITUDE [tur'pi-tyōōd], *n.* moral baseness. [L.].

TURQUOISE (1) [tur'koiz, 'kwoiz, 'kwahz], *n.* greenish-blue semi-precious stone. TURQUOISE (2), *adj.* of the colour of a t. [Fr.].

TURRET [tu'rit], *n.* small tower, usually one of a series comprising fortifications; armoured rotating gun-emplacement on a warship; similar fitment on a tank or aeroplane. [Fr.].

TURTLE [tur'tl], *n.* marine tortoise; any species of the

Chelonidae, esp. Chelone mydas, the green turtle largely used for soup at banquets; **to turn t.**, to capsize. TURTLESHELL, *n.* tortoiseshell. [Uncert.].

TURTLE-DOVE [tur'tl-duv], *n.* the pigeon *Turtur communis*; (*coll.*) ostentatiously affectionate lover. [L. and DOVE].

TURVES [turvz], *n. pl. of* TURF.

TUSCAN [tus'kan], *adj.* pertaining to Tuscany; **T. order**, the simplest of the five classic orders of architecture.

TUSK [tusk], *n.* long tooth projecting from the closed mouth, as in the elephant, walrus etc.; (*coll.*) tooth. TUSKY, *adj.* furnished with tusks. [OE.].

TUSSLE (1) [tu'sl], *v.i.* to wrestle, struggle; take part in a t. TUSSLE (2), *n.* a vigorous, rough, clumsy struggle; wrestle. [Uncert.].

TUSSOCK [tu'sok], *n.* thick clump of grass. [Uncert.].

TUSSORE [tu'saw(r)], *n.* a coarse silk from the cocoons of the wild Bengal silkworm. [Hind.].

TUTELAGE [tyōō'ti-lij], *n.* state of being guided and instructed; guardianship. [~L.].

TUTELARY [tyōō'ti-la-ri], *adj.* protecting; instructing.

TUTOR (1) [tyōō'ter], *n.* one who instructs; private teacher; (in universities) college teacher who arranges and supervises the work of his students. TUTOR (2), *v.t.* to teach, be a t. to. TUTORAGE, *n.* the charge and instruction of a pupil. [L.].

TUTORIAL (1) [tyōō-taw'ri-al], *adj.* pertaining to a tutor. TUTORIAL (2), *n.* a session with a tutor.

TUTTI [tōōt'ti], *n.* (*mus.*) direction that all the performers play in concert; passage so played. [It.].

TUTTI-FRUTTI [tōōt-ti-frōōt'ti], *n.* fruit salad; compote of preserved fruits. [It.].

TUXEDO [tuk-zē'dō], *n.* (*U.S.*) dinner-jacket. [*Tuxedo* Park near New York].

TWADDLE (1) [two'dl], *n.* silly and ridiculous talk. TWADDLE (2), *v.t. and i.* to talk t.

TWAIN (1) [twān], *adj.* in two parts. TWAIN (2), *n.* (*poet.*) two. [OE.].

TWANG (1) [twang], *n.* sharp, ringing sound produced by the rapid vibration of a taut string; nasal tone of speech. TWANG (2), *v.t. and i.* to cause to produce a t.; utter a twanging sound. [Echoic].

TWEAK (1) [twēk], *v.t.* to give a t. to. TWEAK (2), *n.* sudden sharp nip or pinch. [ME.].

TWEE [twē], *adj.* (*slang*) self-consciously engaging, quaint or whimsical. [Childish corruption of SWEET].

TWEED (1) [twēd], *n.* woollen cloth woven from different coloured yarns. TWEED (2), *adj.* made of t. [River *Tweed* in Scotland, in the district where it is manufactured].

TWEEN [twēn], *prep.* (*poet. and naut.*) between.

TWEEZERS [twē'zerz], *n.*(*pl.*) small pincers for taking hold of small or delicate objects. [~Fr.].

TWELFTH [twelfth], *n. and adj.* the ordinal of twelve; (being) one of twelve equal parts; the twelfth day etc., *esp.* 12 August when grouse shooting begins. TWELFTH-NIGHT, Epiphany eve. [OE.].

TWELVE [twelv], *n. and adj.* (of) one more than eleven; a dozen. TWELVEMONTH, *n.* a year. [OE.].

TWENTIETH [twen'ti-eth], *n. and adj.* the ordinal of twenty; (being) one of twenty equal parts. [OE.].

TWENTY [twen'ti], *n. and adj.* (of) twice ten; a score. [OE.].

TWENTY-FIVE [twen-ti-fiv'], *n.* (*Rugby football and hockey*) line across the field t. yards from the goal-line; area between this and the goal-line. [OE.].

TWICE [twis], *adv.* two times. [ME.].

TWIDDLE [twi'dl], *v.t.* to spin round in the fingers, twist and play idly with. [OScand.].

TWIG (1) [twig], *n.* a shoot from the branch of a tree. [OE.].

TWIG (2), *v.t.* (*coll.*) to grasp mentally, comprehend. [Ir.].

TWILIGHT [twi'lit], *n.* the half-light immediately after sunset or before dawn; (*fig.*) uncertain view, obscurity of understanding; **t. sleep**, partial narcosis induced by certain drugs to lessen the pain of childbirth. [ME.].

TWILIT [twi'lit], *adj.* dimly lit as if by twilight.

TWILL [twil], *n.* a fabric woven into parallel ribs. [OE.].

TWIN (1) [twin], *n.* one of a pair of persons or animals born at the same birth; one of an exactly identical pair. TWIN (2), *adj.* being a t.; being one of an identical pair. TWIN-BORN, born at the same birth. [OE.].

TWINE (1) [twin], *n.* strong cord made of twisted

---

strands, *esp.* of hemp-strands. TWINE (2), *v.t. and i.* to twist, wind, round about. [OE.].

TWINGE [twinj], *n.* sudden spasm of pain; sudden sharp pinch; mental qualm. [OE.].

TWINKLE (1) [twing'kl], *v.i.* to emit a t.; give out an intermittent winking light; laugh with the eyes; move rapidly to and fro. TWINKLE (2), *n.* intermittent, winking light; sudden gleam; momentary flash of amusement in the eyes; the shortest possible space of time. TWINKLING, *n.* the briefest of moments. [OE.].

TWIRL (1) [twurl], *v.t. and i.* to make a thing whirl on its own axis; whirl round. TWIRL (2), *n.* that which twirls or is twirled; act of twirling. [~OE.].

TWIST (1) [twist], *v.t. and i.* to twine, plait together, turn, bend, divert out of normal position, distort by turning; deviate from the normal, turn deviously, writhe; (*fig.*) behave dishonestly; (*slang*) swindle. TWIST (2), *n.* something twined together, mass of plaited threads; lump of coarse tobacco; act of twisting; tortuous deviation; (*fig.*) streak of abnormality. TWISTER, *n.* that which twists; (*slang*) untrustworthy person; swindler. [ME.].

TWIT [twit], *v.t.* to reproach in half-humorous, half-nagging fashion; taunt. [OE.].

TWITCH (1) [twich], *v.t. and i.* to jerk with a sudden nervous movement; give or display a muscular t. TWITCH (2), *n.* sudden, brief, uncontrollable muscular movement, *esp.* of the facial muscles. [ME.].

TWITCH-GRASS [twich'grahs], *n.* couch-grass. [QUITCH].

TWITTER (1) [twi'ter], *v.i.* to utter high, rapid chattering sounds, as birds; be in a state of feeble excitement. TWITTER (2), *n.* the rapid, shrill chattering of birds; **all of a t., in a t.,** in a condition of nervous fluttering excitement.

TWO [too], *n. and adj.* (of) the number between one and three. TWO-EDGED, having both edges sharp; (*fig.*) ambiguous, having t. opposite effects. TWO-FACED, having t. faces; double-dealing. [OE.].

TWOFOLD [too'fold], *adj. and adv.* double; doubly.

TWOSOME [too'sum], *n.* game (usually golf) played by two players. [TWO and OE.].

TYCOON [ti-koon'], *n.* shogun; (*coll.*) high authority.

TYKE, see TIKE.

TYMPANUM (*pl.* tympana) [tim'pa-num], *n.* drum, kettledrum, tambourine etc.; (*anat.*) membrane of the ear; (*arch.*) face of a pediment. TYMPANIC [tim-pa'nik], *adj.* like a drum; pertaining to the t. [L. from Gk.].

TYNWALD [tin'wawld], *n.* the parliament of the Isle of Man. [OScand.].

TYPE (1) [tip], *n.* the image, symbol, representation of a thing; model of a thing; kind, variety, general class, of a thing; representative member of a class or kind, or representative possessor of a quality; pieces of wood or metal with carved or moulded impressions of letters or characters used in printing. TYPE-SETTER, person or machine setting t. for printing. TYPE (2), *v.t. and i.* to typify; write with a typewriter; be, or become, typical; be able to use a typewriter; (*med.*) classify (blood for transfusion). [Gk.].

TYPESCRIPT [tip'skript], *n.* typewritten document.

TYPEWRITER [tip'ri-ter], *n.* small machine for writing with printed characters, by striking lettered keys so that the corresponding symbols are impressed on the paper. TYPEWRITTEN, *adj.* written with a t.

TYPHOID (1) [ti'foid], *adj.* resembling, related to, typhus; infectious disease resembling typhus. TYPHOID (2), *n.* t. fever. [TYPHUS and Gk.].

TYPHOON [ti-foon'], *n.* cyclone in the China Sea; hurricane. TYPHONIC [ti-fo'nik], *adj.* pertaining to a t. [Uncert.].

TYPHUS [ti'fus], *n.* contagious spotted fever, usually carried by parasites. TYPHOUS, *adj.* of, or relating to, t. [Gk.].

TYPICAL [ti'pi-kal], *adj.* true to type; wholly representative of its kind.

TYPIFY [ti'pi-fi], *v.t.* to exemplify.

TYPOGRAPHY [ti-po'gra-fi], *n.* art of printing; choice and arrangement of type on a printed page. TYPOGRAPHER, *n.* printer, *esp.* one skilled in the artistic arrangement of printed matter. TYPO-GRAPHIC(AL) [ti-po-gra'fik(-al)], *adj.* pertaining to t.; emblematic.

TYPOLOGY [ti-po'lo-ji], *n.* study of symbols, *esp.* in the Scriptures; theory that the Old Testament foretells and prefigures the New; (*archae.*) classification of remains according to type. TYPOLOGICAL [ti-po-lo'ji-kal], *adj.* pertaining to t.

TYRANNICAL [ti-ra'ni-kal], *adj.* befitting, characterizing, relating to a tyrant or to his tyrannies.

TYRANNICIDE [ti-ra'ni-sid], *n.* assassination of a tyrant; slayer of a tyrant.

TYRANNIZE [ti'ra-niz], *v.i.* to play the tyrant, behave tyrannically, domineer (over).

TYRANNOUS [ti'ra-noos], *adj.* tyrannical.

TYRANNY [ti'ra-ni], *n.* rule, conduct, of a tyrant; state governed by a tyrant.

TYRANT [ti'rant], *n.* (*hist.*) absolute ruler seizing and maintaining power by violence or the threat of it; cruel despot; non-hereditary absolute ruler; harsh, oppressive, despotic person. [Gk.].

TYRE, see TIRE (1).

TYRIAN [ti'ri-an], *adj.* relating to Tyre; of a rich purple colour.

TYRO, see TIRO.

TYRRHENE, TYRRHENIAN [ti-ren'(i-an)], *n. and adj.* (an) Etruscan. [L.].

TZETZE, see TSETSE.

TZIGANE [tsi-gahn'], *n.* Hungarian gipsy. [Magyar].

U

U [yoo], *n.* twenty-first letter of the English alphabet.

UBIQUITOUS [yoo-bi'kwi-toos], *adj.* existing everywhere at the same time. [~L.].

UBIQUITY [yoo-bi'kwi-ti], *n.* condition of being ubiquitous; omnipresence.

U-BOAT [yoo'bot], *n.* submarine in the German Navy. [Germ.].

UDDER [u'der], *n.* external glandular organ in certain female animals, secreting milk. [OE.].

UGH, *int.* sound resembling a suppressed cough, expressing great disgust.

UGLY [ug'li], *adj.* utterly lacking in beauty; hideous to behold, repulsive; (*fig.*) morally loathsome or vile; menacing, dreadful, suggesting unpleasant things to come; **u. customer,** person dangerous as an opponent. [OIcel.].

UHLAN [oo'lahn], *n.* cavalryman in the armies of some central European countries. [Polish].

UITLANDER [oit'lan-der], *n.* (*South Africa*) foreigner. [Du.].

UKASE [yoo-kās'], *n.* a command or decree. [Russ.].

UKULELE [yoo-ku-lā'li], *n.* (*mus.*) small, soft-toned, four-stringed instrument originating in Hawaii, and used in dance bands. [Hawaiian].

ULCER [ul'ser], *n.* open sore which discharges pus; (*fig.*) source of moral corruption. ULCERED, *adj.* having an u. or ulcers. ULCEROUS, *adj.* like an u.; ulcerated; morally corrupting. [L.].

ULCERATE [ul'se-rāt], *v.t. and i.* to cause to break out in ulcers; break out in ulcers; (*fig.*) cause moral corruption in. ULCERATION (ul-se-rā'shn], *n.* state of being or process of becoming ulcerated. ULCERATIVE [ul'se-rā-tiv], *adj.* causing ulcers; affected with ulcers.

ULLAGE [u'lij], *n.* difference between the amount of liquor actually in a container and its full capacity. [OFr.].

ULNA (*pl.* ulnae) [ul'nah], *n.* (*anat.*) inner bone of the arm between the wrist and elbow; corresponding bone in animals. ULNAR, *adj.* (*anat.*) pertaining to the u. [L.].

ULSTER [ul'ster], *n.* long, loose, heavy overcoat. [*Ulster,* Ireland].

ULT [ult], *adj.* short for ULTIMO.

ULTERIOR [ul-teer'i-er], *adj.* remote, further;

u. motive, (*coll.*) unavowed and often discreditable reason or purpose. [L.].

ULTIMATE [ul'ti-mat], *adj.* last, final; furthest, most remote; fundamental, basic. **ULTIMATELY,** *adv.* in the end, finally. [LL.].

ULTIMATUM (*pl.* **ultimata or ultimatums**) [ul-ti-mā'tum], *n.* final statement of views and intentions, *esp.* a statement by one of two parties in a negotiation expressing that party's final terms, and usually accompanied by a threat that, if these are not accepted by a specified time, peaceful negotiations will be at an end. [L.].

ULTIMO [ul'ti-mō], *adv.* (*comm.*) in the month immediately before this. [L.].

ULTRA (1) [ul'trah], *adj.* extreme, *esp.* professing extreme opinions. **ULTRA** (2), *n.* person of extreme opinions.

ULTRA-, *pref.* extreme, or lying beyond. [L.].

ULTRAMARINE (1) [ul-tra-ma-rēn'], *adj.* lying overseas; being of a brilliant blue colour. **ULTRAMARINE** (2), *n.* u. blue.

ULTRA MICROSCOPE [ul-tra-mīk'rō-skōp], *n.* microscope permitting observation of objects too small for examination by visible light, but resolvable by ultra violet rays.

ULTRAMONTANE (1) [ul-tra-mon'tān], *adj.* living on the other side of a mountain range, *esp.* on the other side of the Alps from France; (*fig.*) upholding the most extreme claims of Papal authority. **ULTRAMONTANE** (2), *n.* one who lives on the other side of the Alps; (*fig.*) supporter of extreme Papal claims. **ULTRAMONTANISM,** *n.* principles advocated by an u.

ULTRA-SHORT [ul-tra-shawt'], *adj.* (of radio waves) having a wavelength of approximately one to fifteen metres.

ULTRA-SONIC [ul-tra-so'nik], *adj.* (*phys.*) pertaining to sound waves of a frequency above the range of audible waves.

ULTRA-VIOLET [ul-tra-vī'ō-let], *adj.* (*phys.*) pertaining to those rays which lie between the X-rays and the violet rays of the visible spectrum.

ULTRA VIRES [ul-tra-vī'rēz], *adj. and adv.* (*leg.*) (lying) beyond the scope of authority. [L.].

ULULATE [yōō'lyōō-lāt], *v.i.* to hoot or howl; lament. **ULULATION** [yōō-lyōō-lā'shn], *n.* act or sound of ululating. [~L.].

UMBEL [um'bel], *n.* (*bot.*) head of blossom all the stalks of which rise from a single point, and form a more or less flat head. **UMBELLAR,** *adj.* (*bot.*) having the shape of an u. **UMBELLATE,** *adj.* bearing umbels; umbellar. [L.].

UMBELLIFEROUS [um-be-li'fe-rōōs], *adj.* (*bot.*) having umbels. [MedL.].

UMBER (1) [um'ber], *n.* brownish-yellow pigment which assumes a reddish quality if burnt. **UMBER** (2), *adj.* having a dark brown colour. **UMBER** (3), *v.t.* to paint with an u. colour. [OFr. from L.].

UMBILICAL [um-bi'li-kal], *adj.* (*anat.*) pertaining to the navel; resembling a navel. [MedL.].

UMBILICUS (*pl.* **umbilici**) [um-bi-lī'kus], *n.* (*anat.*) navel; anything resembling this. [L.].

UMBLE-PIE, see HUMBLE-PIE.

UMBRA [um'brah], *n.* (*astron.*) the complete darkness or shadow in an eclipse. **UMBRAL,** *adj.* (*astron.*) pertaining to an u. [L.].

UMBRAGE [um'brij], *n.* resentment, annoyance; (*poet.*) shade, shadow; **to take u.,** to be annoyed. **UMBRAGEOUS** [um-brā'jōōs], *adj.* shady or shaded; disposed to suspicion or resentment. [Fr.].

UMBRELLA [um-bre'lah], *n.* portable shelter from the rain etc., consisting of a shallow ribbed dome of silk or other cloth, supported on a central stick, folded about it when not in use; parasol; large canopy used in oriental ceremonies. It.].

UMLAUT [ōōm'lowt], *n.* sound change in most Germanic and various other languages by which a following vowel (*esp.* i) modifies the vowel in the syllable which precedes. [Germ.].

UMPIRE (1) [um'pier], *n.* arbitrator; (*sport*) one appointed to judge the fairness of the play and give necessary decisions; (*leg.*) third party who gives a decision when arbitrators cannot come to agreement. **UMPIRE** (2), *v.t. and i.* to act as u. (in). [OFr.].

UN- (1), *pref. used before adjectives, adverbs and nouns to express negation.* **UN-** (2), *pref. used before verbs to express negation, separation or reversal.* [OE.].

UNABATED [un-a-bā'tid], *adj.* not in any way checked or repressed, in full force.

UNACCOMPANIED [un-a-kum'pa-nid], *adj.* having no companions; (*mus.*) (of a song etc.) not rendered with an instrumental accompaniment.

UNACCOMPLISHED [un-a-komp'lisht], *adj.* not finished or completed; having no accomplishments.

UNACCOUNTABLE [un-a-kown'ta-bl], *adj.* that cannot be explained or accounted for.

UNACCUSTOMED [un-a-kus'tumd], *adj.* not accustomed, unused; unusual.

UNACQUIRED [un-a-kwierd'], *adj.* not obtained; innate.

UNADAPTABLE [un-a-dap'ta-bl], *adj.* impossible to adapt; not amenable.

UNADMITTED [un-ad-mi'tid], *adj.* not allowed to enter; not permitted; not acknowledged or confessed.

UNADORNED [un-a-dawnd'], *adj.* plain, without adornment.

UNADULTERATED [un-a-dul'te-rā-tid], *adj.* genuine, pure, not adulterated.

UNAFFECTED [un-a-fek'tid], *adj.* not affected; plain, natural, without affectation, sincere.

UNAFRAID [un-a-frād'], *adj.* bold, daring, undismayed.

UNAIDED [un-ā'did], *adj.* unassisted, not helped.

UNALIENABLE [un-ā'li-e-na-bl], *adj.* not able to be alienated or transferred. **UNALIENATED,** *adj.* not alienated; not diverted (from a purpose).

UNALLOYED [un-a-loid'], *adj.* pure, unmixed; (of happy emotions) unspoiled.

UNANIMITY [yōō-na-ni'mi-ti], *n.* condition or fact of being unanimous.

UNANIMOUS [yōō-na'ni-mōōs], *adj.* (of persons) agreed, undivided in opinion; (of resolution, opinion) held by all, agreed to by everyone. **UNANIMOUSLY,** *adv.* with unanimity.

UNANSWERABLE [un-ahn'se-ra-bl], *adj.* not answerable, that cannot be refuted. **UNANSWERABLY,** *adv.* beyond refutation, in an u. way.

UNAPPEALABLE [un-a-pē'la-bl], *adj.* (*leg.*) (of a decision or sentence) that cannot be appealed against; (of a case) incapable of being contested in a higher court.

UNAPPETIZING [un-a'pi-tī-zing], *adj.* not appetizing or attractive.

UNAPPRECIATED [un-a-prē'shi-ā-tid], *adj.* not adequately valued.

UNAPPREHENSIVE [un-a-pri-hen'siv], *adj.* not afraid or suspecting; not quick to apprehend mentally.

UNAPPROACHABLE [un-a-prō'cha-bl], *adj.* that cannot be approached; inaccessible, aloof.

UNAPPROPRIATED [un-a-prō'pri-ā-tid], *adj.* not appropriated; (of money) not earmarked for any particular purpose.

UNAPT [un-apt'], *adj.* not apt, unsuitable; lacking skill and readiness, slow.

UNARGUABLE [un-ah'gyōō-a-bl], *adj.* not able to be supported by argument; not open to legitimate argument; beyond argument.

UNARM [un-ahm'], *v.t. and i.* to disarm; put aside one's arms. **UNARMED,** *adj.* not having or using arms; (*zool., bot.*) not having scales or prickles.

UNASHAMED [un-a-shāmd'], *adj.* not ashamed, brazen.

UNASKED [un-ahskt'], *adj.* not invited; not sought or asked for.

UNASSUMING [un-a-syōō'ming], *adj.* not forward, modest.

UNASSURED [un-a-shōōrd'] *adj.* not assured; not insured.

UNATTACHED [un-a-tacht'], *adj.* not attached; (*milit.*) not connected with any particular regiment.

UNAVAILING [un-a-vā'ling], *adj.* ineffective, having no result, vain.

UNAVOWED [un-a-vowd'], *adj.* not confessed, unacknowledged.

UNAWAKENED [un-a-wā'kend], *adj.* still sleeping; (*fig.*) latent, not aware.

UNAWARE (1) [un-a-wäer'], *adj.* uninformed (of), having no knowledge (of), unsuspicious (of). **UNAWARE** (2), *adv.* unawares.

UNAWARES [un-a-wäerz'], *adv.* unexpectedly, unknowingly, innocently, without full knowledge.

UNBALANCED [un-ba'lanst], *adj.* not balanced; unsteady, unreliable, temperamental; insane; (of financial accounts) not showing an equal sum on both debit and credit side; *esp.* showing a deficit.

UNBAR [un-bah(r)'], *v.t.* to remove the bar from, unlock, open.

UNBEARABLE [un-bäer'a-bl], *adj.* that cannot be borne, intolerable. **UNBEARABLY,** *adv.* intolerably.

UNBECOMING [un-bi-ku'ming], *adj.* not suitable or appropriate; indecorous.

UNBELIEF [un-bi-lēf'], *n.* lack of faith, disbelief.

The accent ' after a syllable = stress (u-pon'). The mark ⁻ over a vowel = length (ā in made; ō in bone).

UNBELIEVER [un-bi-lē'ver], *n.* one who does not believe; a pagan; atheist. **UNBELIEVING**, *adj.* refusing or unable to believe, sceptical.

UNBEND (*pret. and p.pt.* **unbent**) [un-bend'], *v.t. and i.* to bend from a curved to a straight position; (*fig.*) cease to be aloof or arrogant, and become gracious and sociable.

UNBENDING [un-ben'ding], *adj.* rigid, not bendable; determined, unrelenting, inflexible.

UNBENT [un-bent'], *pret. and p.pt. of* UNBEND.

UNBIDDEN [un-bi'den], *adj.* uninvited.

UNBIND (*pret. and p.pt.* **unbound**) [un-bind'], *v.t.* to take the binding from, undo; release.

UNBLEMISHED [un-ble'misht], *adj.* not blemished; (*fig.*) free from blame or reproach.

UNBLOWN [un-blōn'], *adj.* (of a plant) having its buds still closed; (of a bugle etc.) not sounded; (of a person) not winded with running or exercise.

UNBLUSHING [un-blu'shing], *adj.* brazen, shameless, impudent. **UNBLUSHINGLY**, *adv.* in an u. fashion.

UNBOLT [un-bōlt'], *v.t.* to release the bolt of, open or unfasten by so doing. **UNBOLTED**, *adj.* not locked with a bolt, open, openable.

UNBOSOM [un-boo'zom], *v. reflex.* to confess one's trouble or worry.

UNBOUNDED [un-bown'did], *adj.* having no limit; boundless, unlimited, infinite.

UNBOWED [un-bowd'], *adj.* not bowed or bent; unsubdued, unconquered.

UNBRACE [un-brās'], *v.t. and i.* to loosen, untie; relax, rest.

UNBREATHED (1) [un-brēтнd'], *adj.* undivulged. **UNBREATHED** (2), *adj.* out of breath.

UNBREECH [un-brēch'], *v.t.* to take the breeches from; (*milit.*) unlock the breech of (a cannon). **UNBREECHED**, *adj.* not yet wearing trousers; deprived of trousers.

UNBRIDLED [un-bri'dld], *adj.* not bridled; unrestrained, licentious, violent.

UNBRITISH [un-bri'tish], *adj.* uncharacteristic, unworthy, of the British.

UNBROKEN [un-brō'ken], *adj.* not broken; whole, unshattered; continuous; (of land) unploughed; (of a horse) unbacked, not broken; (of a record) not bettered.

UNBROTHERLY [un-braтнer-li], *adj.* not according with what is expected of a brother, unfeeling.

UNBURDEN, UNBURTHEN [un-bur'den, 'then], *v.t.* to relieve of a load or burden; (*fig.*) relieve (one's mind) by confessing one's worry or trouble.

UNBURTHEN, See UNBURDEN.

UNBUSINESSLIKE [un-biz'nes-līk], *adj.* inefficient, muddled, not businesslike.

UNBUTTON [un-bu'ton], *v.t. and i.* to undo the buttons of; relax.

UNCAGE [un-kāj'], *v.t.* to liberate from a cage; (*fig.*) free, release.

UNCALCULATED [un-kal'kyoo-lā-tid], *adj.* not arrived at by calculation; undetermined, indefinite; (*fig.*) accidental, unintentional.

UNCALLED [un-kawld'], *adj.* not called. **UNCALLED-FOR**, unnecessary; unprovoked.

UNCANNY [un-ka'ni], *adj.* weird, mysterious.

UNCANONICAL [un-ka-no'ni-kal], *adj.* not canonical; outside the canon of Holy Scripture.

UNCARED [un-kāerd'], *adj.* UNCARED-FOR, not loved or looked after.

UNCEASING [un-sē'sing], *adj.* not ceasing, uninterrupted, incessant.

UNCEREMONIOUS [un-se-ri-mō'ni-oos], *adj.* lacking ceremony, curt, rude, abrupt.

UNCERTAIN [un-sur'tan], *adj.* not certain, doubtful, undecided; not reliable, fickle; precarious.

UNCERTAINTY [un-sur'tan-ti], *n.* state or quality of being uncertain; dubiousness; want of certainty or precision; vagueness, variableness.

UNCHAIN [un-chān'], *v.t.* to remove chains or fetters from; (*fig.*) free, release, liberate.

UNCHANCY [un-chahn'si], *adj.* ill-omened; illtimed; awkward.

UNCHANGING [un-chān'jing], *adj.* suffering or liable to suffer no alteration.

UNCHARACTERISTIC [un-ka-rak-te-ris'tik], *adj.* not characteristic or typical.

UNCHARITABLE [un-cha'ri-ta-bl], *adj.* not generous in giving; not in accordance with Christian charity or goodwill.

UNCHARTED [un-chah'tid], *adj.* not shown on a chart, unexplored, unknown.

UNCHASTE [un-chāst'], *adj.* not chaste, lewd; incontinent. **UNCHASTELY**, *adv.* in an u. manner.

UNCHASTITY [un-chas'ti-ti], *n.* quality of being unchaste, incontinence, lewdness.

UNCHEQUERED [un-che'kerd], *adj.* not varied, not eventful.

UNCIAL (1) [un'shal], *adj.* in, of or having majuscule letters of the type found in early manuscripts. UNCIAL (2), *n.* an u. character. [MedL.].

UNCIRCUMCISED [un-sur'kum-sīzd], *adj.* not circumcised; pagan; **the u.** (*N.T.*) the Gentiles. UNCIRCUMCISION [un-ser-kum-si'zhn], *n.* state of being u., paganism.

UNCIVIL [un-si'vil], *adj.* not polite or civil, rude, illmannered. UNCIVILLY, *adv.* in an u. fashion.

UNCLE [ung'kl], *n.* brother of one's mother or father, or the husband of an aunt; (*slang*) pawnbroker; **U. Sam,** a symbol of the U.S.A. [OFr.].

UNCLEAN [un-klēn'], *adj.* not clean, foul; unchaste; not ceremonially clean.

UNCLEANLY (1) [un-klen'li], *adj.* unclean, *esp.* of a person with dirty habits. UNCLEANLY (2) [un-klēn'li], *adv.* in an unclean manner.

UNCLOAK [un-klōk'], *v.t. and i.* to take off a cloak from; (*fig.*) reveal; remove one's cloak.

UNCLOUDED [un-klow'did], *adj.* free from clouds; (*fig.*) not spoiled in any way.

UNCO (1) [ung'kō], *adj.* (*Scots*) strange, marvellous. UNCO (2), *adv.* very, unusually, extremely; **the u. guid,** self-righteous moralists. UNCO (3), *n.* unknown person or strange object; unusual happening or event. [Scots *var.* of UNCOUTH].

UNCOMFORTABLE [un-kum'fer-ta-bl], *adj.* affording no comfort; not comfortable or at ease.

UNCOMMERCIAL [un-ko-mur'shal], *adj.* not commercial; not carrying on commerce; not seeking profit; not conforming to commercial standards.

UNCOMMITTED [un-ko-mi'tid], *adj.* not done or committed; not bound by any pledge or promise.

UNCOMMON (1) [un-ko'mon], *adj.* not common, scarce, unusual. UNCOMMON (2), *adv.* (*dial.*) very. UNCOMMONLY, *adv.* in an u. degree; not frequently.

UNCOMPLAINING [un-kom-plā'ning], *adj.* not disposed to complain, patient.

UNCOMPLIMENTARY [un-kom-pli-men'ta-ri], *adj.* not complimentary, uncivil.

UNCOMPROMISING [un-kom'pro-mī-zing], *adj.* not admitting of compromise; not yielding to compromise; firm, unyielding.

UNCONCERN [un-kon-surn'], *n.* lack of concern or anxiety. UNCONCERNED [un-kon-surnd'], *adj.* not anxious; having no interest or part (in); indifferent, unmoved.

UNCONDITIONAL [un-kon-di'shn-al], *adj.* absolute, not limited by any condition.

UNCONDITIONED [un-kon-di'shnd], *adj.* unconditional; not in a good state or condition; (*psych.*) inherent, instinctive.

UNCONFIRMED [un-kon-furmd'], *adj.* not confirmed, attested or corroborated; not having received Confirmation.

UNCONFORMABLE [un-kon-faw'ma-bl], *adj.* not conforming, inconsistent; (*geol.*) not parallel.

UNCONGENIAL [un-kon-jē'ni-al], *adj.* not congenial, not in sympathy; repellent.

UNCONSCIONABLE [un-kon'shn-a-bl], *adj.* unscrupulous, excessive, unfair.

UNCONSCIOUS (1) [un-kon'shoos], *adj.* not conscious; not perceiving, unaware; unintentional, involuntary; (*psych.*) unknown to the person who or personality which possesses (it), subconscious. UNCONSCIOUS (2), *n.* (*psych.*) the u. mind.

UNCONSTITUTIONAL [un-kon-sti-tyoo'shn-al], *adj.* contrary to the constitution.

UNCONSTRAINED [un-kon-strānd'], *adj.* free from constraint; voluntary; unembarrassed and at ease.

UNCONTROLLED [un-kon-trōld'], *adj.* free from restraint; not subject to government control.

UNCONVENTIONAL [un-kon-ven'shn-al], *adj.* not according to the usual customs, free from convention.

UNCONVERTED [un-kon-vur'tid], *adj.* not converted; unchanged in opinion or faith; not Christianized; (*Rugby football*) (of a try) not converted into a goal.

UNCOUPLE [un-ku'pl], *v.t.* to disengage, disconnect.

UNCOUTH [un-kōōth'], *adj.* awkward, clumsy. [OE.].

UNCOVENANTED [un-ku'vi-nan-tid], *adj.* not promised or agreed to.

UNCOVER [un-ku'ver], *v.t. and i.* to remove the

---

cover from, make bare, expose; (archaic) take off one's hat.

UNCREATED [un-kri-ā'tid], adj. not produced by creation, spontaneous, eternal; non-existent, unborn, unmade.

UNCRITICAL [un-kri'ti-kal], adj. not critical, not willing or able to criticize; not according to strict standards of criticism; undiscriminating.

UNCROWNED [un-krownd'], adj. not crowned; **u. king**, person whose popularity or power is such as to invest him with unchallengeable authority.

UNCTION [ungk'shn], n. act of smearing with oil or grease; oil or grease so used; (fig.) anything which soothes; (fig.) great fervour or sincerity of manner, esp. religious fervour; affectation of this; ceremonial anointing, esp. of a king; **Extreme u.**, the sacrament administered to the dying of anointing with holy oil. [L.].

UNCTUOUS [ungk'tyōō-ōōs], adj. greasy; resembling oil or grease; (fig.) professing an insincere earnestness, sympathy or enthusiasm. [MedL.].

UNCULTIVATED [un-kul'ti-vā-tid], adj. (of land) not tilled; (fig.) uncivilized, unrefined; not developed or fostered.

UNCUT [un-kut'], adj. (of books) having the margins untrimmed; not having the pages cut open; (of gems) not cut and polished.

UNDAUNTED [un-dawn'tid], adj. bold, undismayed, intrepid.

UNDECIDED [un-di-sī'did], adj. not decided; not certain in one's own mind; vacillating, irresolute; vague, uncertain.

UNDECLARED [un-di-klâerd'], adj. not declared; (of imported goods) not shown to the customs officers.

UNDEDICATED [un-de'di-kā-tid], adj. not dedicated; not consecrated; (of a book) not inscribed to anyone; (of a road) maintained privately.

UNDEMONSTRATIVE [un-di-mon'stra-tiv], adj. not given to a display of feeling, taciturn, reserved.

UNDENOMINATIONAL [un-di-no-mi-na'shn-al], adj. making no distinction between one denomination and another; belonging to no denomination.

UNDER (1) [un'der], adj. inferior, subordinate. UNDER (2), adv. in an inferior or lower position or condition. UNDER (3), prep. below, on a lower level or in a lower position than, beneath the surface of; in the power of, during the reign of; according to; beneath; beneath the cover of; **u. cover**, in a protected position; **u. arms**, equipped with military arms and ready for warfare. [OE.].

UNDER-, pref. subsidiary; insufficiently; lower.

UNDERACT [un-de-rakt'], v.t. and i. to act with insufficient vitality.

UNDERARM (1) [un'de-rahm], adj. (tennis, cricket etc.) with the arm kept below the shoulder. UNDERARM (2), adv. in u. fashion.

UNDERBID [un-der-bid'], v.t. and i. to bid less than; (bridge) bid low so as to suggest that one's hand is weaker than is actually the case.

UNDERCARRIAGE [un'der-ka-rij], n. the landing wheels of an aircraft and their supports.

UNDERCLOTHES [un'der-klōTHz], n.(pl.) underclothing.

UNDERCLOTHING [un'der-klō-THing], n. garments worn near or next to the skin and beneath other garments.

UNDERCOAT [un'der-kōt], n. a coat worn under another, a shorter growth of hair on a furred animal; a first coat of paint.

UNDERCOVER [un-der-ku'ver], adj. secret, underground.

UNDERCROFT [un'der-kroft], n. crypt; any similar vaulted subterranean chamber.

UNDERCURRENT [un'der-ku-rent], n. current running below the surface of water; unseen influence or feeling among a group of people.

UNDERCUT (pret. and p.pt. undercut) [un-der-kut'], v.t. to cut beneath or at a lower level; sell at a cheaper rate than; (golf) strike (the ball) so as to prevent its running very far when it touches the ground again. UNDERCUT (2) [un'der-kut], n. the tender part of a sirloin of beef.

UNDERDOG [un'der-dog], n. person who is always at the mercy of circumstances or of other people.

UNDERDRESS [un-der-dres'], v.i. to wear insufficient clothing (for the climate etc.); dress meanly or too plainly.

UNDERESTIMATE (1) [un-de-res'ti-mät], v.t. to put too low a value on; value too lightly. UNDERESTIMATE (2) [un-de-res'ti-mat], n. an undervaluing, an

estimate which is too low. UNDERESTIMATION, n. an undervaluing.

UNDERGARMENT [un'der-gah-ment], n. any garment worn near or next to the skin and beneath other garments.

UNDERGO (pret. underwent, p.pt. undergone) [un-der-gō'], v.t. to suffer, endure, be subjected to.

UNDERGRAD [un-der-grad'], n. (coll.) undergraduate.

UNDERGRADUATE [un-der-gra'dyōō-at], n. student at a university who has not yet taken a degree.

UNDERGRADUETTE [un-der-gra-dyōō-et'], n. (coll.) woman undergraduate.

UNDERGROUND (1) [un'der-grownd], adj. situated beneath the earth's surface, subterranean; (fig.) secret. UNDERGROUND (2), n. an u. railway; an u. association. UNDERGROUND (3), adv. beneath the surface of the earth; (fig.) in secret.

UNDERGROWTH [un'der-grōth], n. shrubs and small trees in a wood.

UNDERHAND [un'der-hand], adj. secret, sly, mean. UNDERHANDED, adj. u., clandestine; short of employees or assistants.

UNDERHUNG [un-der-hung'], adj. (of the lower jaw) projecting further than the upper jaw; having a lower jaw so formed.

UNDERLAY (1) (pret. and p.pt. underlaid) [un-der-lā'], v.t. to lay beneath; (print.) raise by laying something beneath. UNDERLAY (2) [un'der-lā], n. (print.) material used to u. type; thick felt laid beneath a carpet; cloth laid under a mattress.

UNDERLIE (pret. underlay, p.pt. underlain) [un-der-lī'], v.t. to lie beneath; (fig.) be implicit in, be the basis of.

UNDERLINE (1) [un-der-līn'], v.t. to mark (a word or words) in a book or manuscript with a line underneath; (fig.) emphasize. UNDERLINE (2), n. a mark which underlines.

UNDERLINEN [un'der-li-nen], n. underwear.

UNDERLING [un'der-ling], n. inferior person at the beck and call of another.

UNDERMAN [un-der-man'], v.t. to provide with insufficient workers or helpers. UNDERMANNED, adj. (of a ship, factory etc.) having too few hands.

UNDERMINE [un-der-mīn'], v.t. to excavate the earth from beneath; (fig.) weaken or attack by indirect means.

UNDERNEATH (1) [un-der-nēth'], adv. under, beneath, below; in a situation directly below. UNDERNEATH (2), prep. beneath, below. UNDERNEATH (3), adj. situated beneath or u. UNDERNEATH (4), n. that part or surface of anything which is situated lowest or beneath the rest. [OE.].

UNDERPIN [un-der-pin'], v.t. to provide a temporary supporting structure for, while existing foundations are repaired or replaced. UNDERPINNING, n. act of one who underpins; material used to u.

UNDERPLAY [un-der-plā'], v.t. to underact; (at cards) deliberately to lose a trick when strategically profitable to do so.

UNDERPLOT [un'der-plot], n. a secondary theme in a story or play.

UNDER-PROOF [un-der-prōōf'], adj. having less alcohol than proof spirit.

UNDERQUOTE [un-der-kwōt'], v.t. to offer goods at a lower price than.

UNDERRATE [un-der-rāt'], v.t. to estimate or value too low.

UNDERRUN (pret. underran, p.pt. underrun) [un-der-run'], v.t. to pass beneath; examine by passing through the hand.

UNDERSCORE [un-der-skaw(r)'], v.t. to underline.

UNDER-SECRETARY [un-der-se'kre-ta-ri], n. assistant secretary; **Parliamentary U.**, Member of Parliament assisting a minister who holds a portfolio; **Permanent U.**, member of the Civil Service who is the head of a state department.

UNDERSELL (pret. and p.pt. undersold) [un-der-sel'], v.t. to sell at a lower price than.

UNDERSET (1) [un-der-set'], v.t. to support from beneath by masonry or other work. UNDERSET (2), n. (naut.) current low down in the water running opposite to the main current.

UNDERSHOT [un-der-shot'], adj. (of a water-mill) driven by a stream of water which passes under and not over the wheel.

UNDERSLUNG [un-der-slung'], adj. (of a road vehicle) with the spring suspension below axle level.

UNDERSTAND (pret. and p.pt. understood) [un-der-stand'], v.t. and i. to perceive in one's mind

the meaning (of); be able to interpret; perceive what is meant; possess intelligence; believe, be informed, have reason to believe; supply in one's mind something beside what is actually expressed; **to u. each other, one another,** to know and respect each other's views.
UNDERSTANDING (1) [un-der-stan'ding], *n.* the faculty of the mind by which it discerns and apprehends; act of comprehending or apprehending; intelligence, discernment; knowledge; agreement of thought and feeling between two persons; a tacit agreement; **on the u. that,** provided that. UNDERSTANDING (2), *adj.* knowing; sympathetic.
UNDERSTATE [un-der-stāt'], *v.t.* to state with deliberate moderation and with an avoidance of emphasis so as ostensibly to minimize the importance of what is stated. UNDERSTATEMENT, *n.* statement which ostensibly minimizes the gravity or importance of what is discussed.
UNDERSTOOD, *pret. and p.pt. of* UNDERSTAND.
UNDERSTUDY (1) [un'der-stu-di], *v.t.* to learn the part or work of so as to be able to perform it if required. UNDERSTUDY (2), *n.* one who studies an actor's part so as to be able to take his place if required; a substitute.
UNDERTAKE *(pret.* **undertook,** *p.pt.* **undertaken)** [un-der-tāk'], *v.t. and i.* to take in hand, set about (to); promise or contract (to); take upon one's self (some business etc.); [un'der-tāk] *(coll.)* engage in business as an undertaker. UNDERTAKING, *n.* any task or business undertaken; profession or business of an undertaker.
UNDERTAKER [un'der-tā-ker], *n.* one whose trade is to manage funerals; one who undertakes a project.
UNDERTONE [un'der-tōn], *n.* a quiet tone or voice; *(fig.)* tone or element implied in but subordinate to a theme, statement etc.; very faint tone.
UNDERTOOK, *pret. of* UNDERTAKE.
UNDERTOW [un'der-tō], *n.* an underset.
UNDERWEAR [un'der-wāer], *n.* undergarments.
UNDERWENT, *pret. of* UNDERGO.
UNDERWING [un'der-wing], *n.* wing lying under another; *(entom.)* either of the two posterior wings of a four-winged insect; moth of the genus *Catocala.*
UNDERWORK [un-der-wurk'], *v.t. and i.* to fail to obtain sufficient work from; do less work than one is paid or expected to do; do work for a lower price than.
UNDERWORLD [un'der-werld], *n.* the world of crime and immorality; *(fig.)* the world of the dead.
UNDERWRITE [un-der-rīt'], *v.t. and i.* to write underneath; insure *(esp.* shipping) against risk; contract to purchase all shares of an issue not taken up by the public. UNDERWRITING, *n.* practice of an underwriter.
UNDERWRITER [un'der-rī-ter], *n.* one who insures *(esp.* shipping); one who underwrites an issue of shares.
UNDESCENDED [un-di-sen'did], *adj.* that has not descended; **u. testicle,** a testicle which has failed to descend into the scrotum.
UNDESIGNED [un-di-zīnd'], *adj.* not planned or designed; *(fig.)* not intended, not deliberate.
UNDESIGNING [un-di-zī'ning], *adj.* not scheming, having no guile.
UNDESIRABLE (1) [un-di-zīer'a-bl], *adj.* not to be wished for, disagreeable, disreputable. UNDESIRABLE (2), *n.* unwanted, troublesome person.
UNDEVELOPED [un-di-ve'lopt], *adj.* not developed; not worked out fully; not exploited for building purposes, still rural.
UNDEVIATING [un-dē'vi-ā-ting], *adj.* not departing from a given way, principle or purpose; steady.
UNDID, *pret. of* UNDO.
UNDINE [un'dēn, ōōn-dēn'], *n.* a water-nymph. [MdL.].
UNDIPLOMATIC [un-dip-lō-ma'tik], *adj.* not conforming to diplomatic usages; lacking tact.
UNDISCIPLINED [un-di'si-plind], *adj.* not subject to regular and systematic training and instruction, untrained in military discipline; lacking in self-control; raw; disobedient.
UNDISCRIMINATING [un-dis-kri'mi-nā-ting], *adj.* not discriminating, lacking discrimination.
UNDISGUISED [un-dis-gīzd'], *adj.* not disguised; open, candid; deliberately calculated.
UNDISPUTED [un-dis-pyōō'tid], *adj.* not called in doubt; not disputed; sole.
UNDISTRACTED [un-dis-trak'tid], *adj.* not distracted; able to give full and undivided attention to one thing.
UNDISTRIBUTED [un-dis-tri'byōō-tid], *adj.* not

distributed, concentrated in one place; **u. middle,** *(logic)* the middle term of a syllogism where the term is not made universally applicable.
UNDO *(pres.* 3rd *person sg.* **undoes,** *pret.* **undid,** *p.pt.* **undone)** [un-dōō'], *v.t.* to cancel out (what has been done); untie or unfasten; ruin. UNDOING, *n.* act by which something is undone; cause of a person's ruin.
UNDOMESTICATED [un-dō-mes'ti-kā-tid], *adj.* (of animals) not trained to live with or be used by human beings; (of men and women) having little love or aptitude for home life or for domestic work.
UNDONE [un-dun'], *adj.* unfastened; not performed; ruined. *[p.pt. of* UNDO].
UNDOUBTED [un-dow'tid], *adj.* not doubted, certain, indubitable. UNDOUBTEDLY, *adv.* beyond doubt, certainly.
UNDOUBTING [un-dow'ting], *adj.* not doubting, trustful, believing.
UNDREAMED, UNDREAMT [un-drēmd', un-dremt'], *adj.* not thought of or imagined.
UNDRESS (1) [un-dres'], *v.t. and i.* to remove the clothes from; take one's clothes off. UNDRESS (2), *n.* informal attire. UNDRESSED, *adj.* not dressed, naked; (of game) not paunched or skinned; (of wounds etc.) not treated and bandaged.
UNDUE [un-dyōō'], *adj.* excessive, unreasonable, unseemly.
UNDULANT [un'dyōō-lant], *adj.* undulating.
UNDULATE [un'dyōō-lāt], *v.i.* to be shaped in a series of alternate ridges and troughs. UNDULATING, *adj.* rising and falling in alternate troughs and ridges. UNDULATORY, *adj.* wavy, undulating. [~L.].
UNDULATION [un-dyōō-lā'shn], *n.* a wave, a rising or falling movement; a vibratory motion.
UNDYING [un-dī'ing], *adj.* immortal; having no end or conclusion, unceasing.
UNEARNED [un-urnd'], *adj.* not gained directly by labour; **u. increment,** increase in the value of property which has not been brought about by the owner.
UNEARTH [un-urth'], *v.t.* to exhume; drive an animal out of its burrow; *(fig.)* find in some obscure place.
UNEARTHLY [un-urth'li], *adj.* not earthly or natural; weird, strange; *(coll.)* unaccustomed.
UNEASY [un-ē'zi], *adj.* feeling some physical discomfort or pain; restless; disturbed; anxious or worried; not graceful, awkward, embarrassed.
UNECONOMIC [un-ē-ko-no'mik], *adj.* not according to economic principles; wasteful, lavish.
UNELASTIC [un-i-las'tik], *adj.* not elastic; *(fig.)* admitting no variation or variety.
UNEMPLOYED (1) [un-em-ploid'], *adj.* not occupied, not busy; not in use; not having a regular job. UNEMPLOYED (2), *n.* the aggregate of persons out of work at any given time.
UNENCUMBERED, UNINCUMBERED [un-en-(-in)-kum'berd], *adj.* not encumbered; free from debt or mortgage.
UNENDING [un-en'ding], *adj.* not ending, eternal; continual. UNENDINGLY, *adv.* in an u. fashion, interminably; *(fig.)* to exasperating length.
UN-ENGLISH [un-ing'glish], *adj.* not according with the customs, preferences or habits of thought of English people.
UNEQUAL [un-ē'kwal], *adj.* not equal; not of the same length, size etc.; disproportioned; ill-matched; not uniform in quality; **u. to,** not adequate or sufficient for; incapable of performing.
UNEQUIVOCAL [un-i-kwi'vō-kal], *adj.* not equivocal, not ambiguous; clear.
UNERRING [un-ur'ing], *adj.* committing no mistake; incapable of error; sure, unfailing.
UNETHICAL [un-e'thi-kal], *adj.* not honest, morally questionable.
UNEVEN [un-ē'ven], *adj.* (of a surface) not smooth; rough and broken; not constant in quality, rhythm etc.; uncertain, not to be counted on; of a number, not exactly divisible by two, odd.
UNEXAMPLED [un-eg-zahm'pld], *adj.* having no parallel or example; unique.
UNEXCELLED [un-ek-seld'], *adj.* not surpassed.
UNEXCEPTIONABLE [un-ek-sep'shn-a-bl], *adj.* not liable to any exception or objection, irreproachable.
UNEXCEPTIONAL [un-ek-sep'shn-al], *adj.* unexceptionable; not subject to exceptions; not unusual or extraordinary.
UNEXECUTED [un-ek'si-kyōō-tid], *adj.* not performed; *(leg.)* not formally attested and signed.

UNEXPECTED [un-eks-pek'tid], *adj.* not expected, sudden. UNEXPECTEDLY, *adv.* in an u. fashion.

UNEXPOSED [un-eks-pōzd'], *adj.* sheltered, protected; not denounced; (*phot.*) not yet exposed.

UNEXPURGATED [un-eks'per-gā-tid], *adj.* not expurgated, published or retold in full.

UNFADING [un-fā'ding], *adj.* not fading or liable to fade.

UNFAILING [un-fā'ling], *adj.* not likely to fail, not failing; sure and certain, trustworthy.

UNFAIR [un-fāer'], *adj.* not according to fair play; unjust. UNFAIRLY, *adv.* in an u. fashion.

UNFAITHFUL [un-fāth'fōōl], *adj.* not observant of promises, allegiance or duty; treacherous; adulterous; not performing proper duty; unbelieving; not accurate. UNFAITHFULLY, *adv.* in an u. way.

UNFAMILIAR [un-fa-mi'li-ah(r)], *adj.* not familiar, not known; not versed in. UNFAMILIARITY [un-fa-mi-li-a'ri-ti], *n.* lack of familiarity.

UNFATHERLY [un-fah'THer-li], *adj.* not befitting a father.

UNFATHOMABLE [un-fa'THo-ma-bl], *adj.* incapable of being sounded or fathomed; (*fig.*) obscure or difficult to understand.

UNFAVOURABLE [un-fā'vŏŏr-a-bl], *adj.* not favourable or favouring; adverse; unlucky, unpropitious.

UNFEELING [un-fē'ling], *adj.* lacking feelings, merciless, callous. UNFEELINGLY, *adv.* in an u. way.

UNFEIGNED [un-fānd'], *adj.* not feigned or affected, true, genuine.

UNFEMININE [un-fe'mi-nin], *adj.* unlike or unfitting for a woman.

UNFETTER [un-fe'ter], *v.t.* to free from fetters; (*fig.*) make free. UNFETTERED, *adj.* not bound in fetters; (*fig.*) free, uncontrolled, unrestrained.

UNFINISHED [un-fi'nisht], *adj.* not completed or concluded; not exhibiting the highest workmanship, rough, unskilled, clumsy.

UNFIT (1) [un-fit'], *adj.* faulty, incapable, not in a fit state (to); not fitted or suited (to). UNFIT (2), *v.t.* to make u. (for), incapable (of).

UNFITTED [un-fi'tid], *adj.* not supplied with or lacking fittings; not fixed into place; made unfit (for) or incapable of.

UNFITTING [un-fi'ting], *adj.* not suitable; unseemly.

UNFIX [un-fiks'], *v.t.* to release from a fixed state or position. UNFIXED, *adj.* not yet fixed; released from a fixed state or position; (*coll.*) not determined upon.

UNFLAGGING [un-fla'ging], *adj.* constant, persevering, unremitting, unwavering.

UNFLATTERING [un-fla'te-ring], *adj.* not flattering or falsely pleasing; not pleasing to pride or vanity.

UNFLEDGED [un-flejd'], *adj.* not yet covered with feathers; (*fig.*) immature.

UNFLINCHING [un-flin'shing], *adj.* resolute, not flinching; steadfast amid dangers.

UNFOLD [un-fōld'], *v.t. and i.* to open from a folded state; expand; (*fig.*) reveal (something hitherto unknown); tell (a tale) stage by stage; (of a narrative) be set forth stage by stage.

UNFORCED [un-fawst'], *adj.* not forced, easy, natural, unconstrained, fluent.

UNFORGETTABLE [un-faw-ge'ta-bl], *adj.* that cannot be forgotten; striking, memorable.

UNFORGIVING [un-faw-gi'ving], *adj.* not disposed to forgive, relentless, unmerciful.

UNFORMED [un-fawmd'], *adj.* not yet shaped or given a form, not yet brought into actuality; (of thoughts) vague, nebulous, imperfectly conceived; untrained, undisciplined.

UNFORTUNATE (1) [un-faw'tyŏŏ-nat], *adj.* not fortunate or lucky; wretched, miserable, dogged with ill-luck; unpropitious; unsuccessful. UNFORTUNATE (2), *n.* an u. person. UNFORTUNATELY, *adv.* in an u. fashion, by mischance, regrettably.

UNFOUNDED [un-fown'did], *adj.* not based on fact, fictitious.

UNFREQUENTED [un-frē-kwen'tid], *adj.* not much visited, solitary.

UNFROCK [un-frok'], *v.t.* to turn out of the priesthood.

UNFRUITFUL [un-frŏŏt'fŏŏl], *adj.* not bearing fruit; barren; unprofitable.

UNFURL [un-furl'], *v.t. and i.* to unroll (a flag) at the mast; (of a flag) become opened or spread out.

UNFURNISHED [un-fur'nisht], *adj.* containing no furniture; not supplied.

UNGAINLY [un-gān'li], *adj.* clumsy; uncouth.

UNGALLANT [un-ga'lant], *adj.* not gallant, discourteous. UNGALLANTLY, *adv.* in an u. fashion.

UNGENEROUS [un-je'ne-rŏŏs], *adj.* not generous or liberal; mean, dishonourable.

UNGENTLE [un-jen'tl], *adj.* rough, not tender.

UNGENTLEMANLY [un-jen'tl-man-li], *adj.* vulgar; unfitting, unbecoming a gentleman.

UNGIFTED [un-gif'tid], *adj.* not talented.

UNGIRD (*pret. and p.pt.* ungirded, ungirt), [un-gurd'], *v.t.* to take the girdle from; take off by undoing one's girdle. UNGIRT, *adj.* not girdled; unprepared.

UNGLOVED [un-gluvd'], *adj.* not covered with a glove or gloves.

UNGODLY [un-god'li], *adj.* wicked, impious; having no thought or fear of God; (*coll.*) appalling.

UNGOVERNABLE [un-gu'ver-na-bl], *adj.* incapable of being governed; uncontrollable.

UNGOVERNED [un-gu'vernd], *adj.* having no rule or governance; unbridled, licentious.

UNGRACIOUS [un-grā'shŏŏs], *adj.* unkind, discourteous, rude.

UNGRAMMATICAL [un-gra-ma'ti-kal], *adj.* not in accordance with the rules of grammar.

UNGRATEFUL [un-grāt'fŏŏl], *adj.* wanting gratitude, unthankful; unprofitable, unpleasant.

UNGRATIFIED [un-gra'ti-fīd], *adj.* not indulged, not satisfied.

UNGROUNDED [un-grown'did], *adj.* (of a statement etc.) having no foundation, without reason or support.

UNGRUDGING [un-gru'jing], *adj.* giving without stint or envy. UNGRUDGINGLY, *adv.* in an u. fashion.

UNGUARDED [un-gah'did], *adj.* having no guard or protection, uncircumspect, incautious.

UNGUENT [ung'gwent], *n.* an ointment. [L.].

UNGULATE (1) [ung'gyŏŏ-lāt], *adj.* (*zool.*) having hoofs, belonging to that group of mammals having hoofs. UNGULATE (2), *n.* a mammal which has hoofs.

UNHALLOWED [un-ha'lōd], *adj.* not consecrated; desecrated; profane, wicked.

UNHAND [un-hand'], *v.t.* to let go from one's grip.

UNHANDSOME [un-hand'sum], *adj.* not handsome; ungenerous, uncivil.

UNHANDY [un-han'di], *adj.* not dexterous, clumsy; out of the way. UNHANDILY, *adv.* clumsily.

UNHANG [un-hang'], *v.t.* to remove the ornaments or hangings from; release from a hanging position.

UNHAPPY [un-ha'pi], *adj.* not happy, wretched, miserable; unfortunate, ill-timed, tactless. UNHAPPILY, *adv.* unfortunately; wretchedly.

UNHARNESS [un-hah'nes], *v.t.* to remove the trappings or harness from.

UNHASP [un-hahsp'], *v.t.* to unfasten by loosening the hasp of.

UNHATCHED [un-hacht'], *adj.* still in the egg; (*fig.*) not matured or revealed.

UNHEALTHFUL [un-helth'fŏŏl], *adj.* unwholesome, unhealthy.

UNHEALTHY [un-hel'thi], *adj.* not healthy, diseased, unwholesome; (*slang*) dangerous.

UNHEARD [un-hurd'], *adj.* not heard. UNHEARD-OF, outrageous, unprecedented.

UNHEEDING [un-hē'ding], *adj.* careless, negligent, inattentive. UNHEEDINGLY, *adv.* in an u. fashion.

UNHELPFUL [un-help'fŏŏl], *adj.* affording no aid, not helpful. UNHELPFULLY, *adv.* in an u. fashion.

UNHERALDED [un-he'ral-did], *adj.* not announced or proclaimed.

UNHESITATING [un-he'zi-tā-ting], *adj.* prompt, brisk. UNHESITATINGLY, *adv.* without hesitation, promptly.

UNHINGE [un-hinj'], *v.t.* to remove from the hinges; make (the mind) unbalanced.

UNHISTORIC(AL) [un-his-to'rik(-al)], *adj.* not found in history; not having actually happened; mythical. UNHISTORICALLY, *adv.* in an u. way.

UNHITCH [un-hich'], *v.t.* to undo, unfasten, separate.

UNHOLY [un-hō'li], *adj.* not holy or hallowed; wicked; (*coll.*) very bad.

UNHOPED [un-hōpt'], *adj.* not likely, not expected.

UNHOPEFUL [un-hōp'fŏŏl], *adj.* not hopeful, hopeless.

UNHORSE [un-haws'], *v.t.* to cause to fall from horseback.

UNHURRIED [un-hu'rid], *adj.* not hurried; deliberate.

UNI-, *pref.* having only one. [~L.].

UNIAT(E) [yŏŏ'ni-at], *n.* member of an Eastern church acknowledging the Papal authority. [Russ.].

UNICELLULAR [yŏŏ-ni-sel'yŏŏ-ler], *adj.* consisting of, comprising, one cell.

UNICORN [yŏŏ'ni-kawn], *n.* legendary horse-like

creature depicted with a single horn in its brow and a lion's or horse's tail. [LL.].

UNIFICATION [yōō-ni-fi-kā'shn], n. act of unifying, fact or condition of being unified.

UNIFORM (1) [yōō'ni-fawm], adj. constant, unvarying; pertaining to a u. UNIFORM (2), n. a distinctive official or regulation dress, worn by all the members of a military force, civilian body, school, sports club etc. [L.].

UNIFORMITY [yōō-ni-faw'mi-ti], n. condition of being uniform.

UNIFY [yōō'ni-fī], v.t. to make into a single whole; make uniform.

UNILATERAL [yōō-ni-la'te-ral], adj. having only one side; pertaining to only one party in an agreement. UNILATERALLY, adv. with respect to, on the part of, one side only; without regard to the interests or rights of other parties.

UNIMPASSIONED [un-im-pa'shnd], adj. not actuated by passion, dispassionate.

UNIMPEACHABLE [un-im-pē'cha-bl], adj. incapable of being impeached; irreproachable, faultless, blameless. UNIMPEACHABILITY, UNIMPEACHABLENESS [un-im-pē-cha-bi'li-ti, un-im-pē'cha-bl-nes], n. quality of being u. UNIMPEACHABLY, adv. in u. fashion.

UNIMPORTANT [un-im-paw'tant], adj. not important, insignificant, immaterial.

UNIMPOSING [un-im-pō'zing], adj. not commanding respect by outward appearance, not imposing.

UNIMPRESSED [un-im-prest'], adj. not impressed or attracted.

UNIMPRESSIVE [un-im-pre'siv], adj. not impressive or commanding.

UNINFLUENCED [un-in'flōō-enst], adj. not actuated or persuaded by outside influences.

UNINFORMED [un-in-fawmd'], adj. not having knowledge or information; ignorant.

UNINQUIRING [un-in-kwier'ing], adj. not curious, not disposed to inquire.

UNINSPIRED [un-in-spierd'], adj. not inspired; lacking inspiration.

UNINSTRUCTED [un-in-struk'tid], adj. not taught or instructed, not furnished with instructions.

UNINTELLIGENT [un-in-te'li-jent], adj. not gifted with understanding; stupid, foolish, dull.

UNINTELLIGIBLE [un-in-te'li-ji-bl], adj. incapable of being understood; incomprehensible; confused.

UNINTENTIONAL [un-in-ten'shn-al], adj. unintended. UNINTENTIONALLY, adv. in u. fashion.

UNINTERESTING [un-in'te-res-ting], adj. not exciting interest.

UNINTERRUPTED [un-in-te-rup'tid], adj. not interrupted, incessant.

UNINVITING [un-in-vī'ting], adj. not attractive or inviting.

UNION [yōō'ni-un], n. action of joining together or uniting; condition of being joined together or united; the unit or unity resulting from a juncture or association of two or more things; a political league or combination; act of joining two persons in marriage, the married state; formerly, the incorporation of several parishes under a Board of Guardians for the administration of Poor Law relief; the workhouse; the unity of two or more nations in a political entity; an association of non-professional workers, a trade union; device for connecting together two pipes etc.; **U. flag,** flag of the United Kingdom of Great Britain and Northern Ireland; **U. Jack,** U. flag when flown at a ship's bow; (pop.) the U. flag. [L.].

UNIONISM [yōō'ni-u-nizm], n. (hist.) policy of centralized imperial government with regard to the British Empire as contrasted with the policy of self-governing dominions; this principle applied in particular to Ireland in the Home Rule controversy.

UNIONIST [yōō'ni-u-nist], n. (hist.) supporter of the trade union movement; supporter of imperial unionism, esp. one opposing Irish Home Rule.

UNIPAROUS [yōō-ni'pa-rŏŏs], adj. (bot.) having only one axis; (zool.) producing only one at a birth. [UNI and L.].

UNIPARTITE [yōō-ni-pah'tīt], adj. containing only one part, not subdivided.

UNIPOLAR [yōō-ni-pō'ler], adj. having only a single pole.

UNIQUE [yōō-nēk'], adj. alone in its kind or class, unequalled, resembling nothing else.

UNISEXUAL [yōō-ni-sek'syōō-al], adj. of one sex only.

UNISON [yōō'ni-son, yōō'ni-zon], n. agreeable concord of sound; (mus.) identical pitch; (fig.) concord, agreement; **in u.,** (mus.) so as to be identical in pitch;

(fig.) in agreement. UNISONAL, UNISONANT, UNISONOUS [yōō-ni'so-nal, -nant, -nŏŏs], adj. in u. [L.].

UNIT [yōō'nit], n. that which is an entity in itself; a convenient subdivision, as of an army; a standard of measurement; the numeral one; (elect.) the commercial standard of current consumption, one kilowatt-hour; (fig.) a single object, person; abstract u., the number one. [UNIT(Y)].

UNITARIAN (1) [yōō-ni-tāer'i-an], n. member of a religious sect professing itself Christian but denying the Deity of Christ and the doctrine of the Trinity. UNITARIAN (2), adj. of, or pertaining to, Unitarians or the tenets of Unitarianism. UNITARIANISM, n. the religious system of Unitarians.

UNITARY [yōō'ni-ta-ri], adj. relating to a unit or units; undivided.

UNITE [yōō-nīt'], v.t. and i. to bring into union, join together into one body; form, combine into, one whole; form or be a connecting link between; join by or in marriage; become or be capable of being linked, joined together or combined; enter into association, amalgamate; agree, come to agreement; (of a fractured bone) mend. UNITER, n. someone who or something which links or joins. UNITIVE [yōō'ni-tiv], adj. causing to u. [~L.].

UNITED [yōō-nī'tid], adj. joined together, linked, associated, esp. in political organization or in affections or principles etc.; (of an action) undertaken by various bodies or persons jointly; **U. Nations,** an association of nations, based upon those victorious in the war of 1939-45, with the object of preserving world peace.

UNITY [yōō'ni-ti], n. quality or condition of being a unit or being united, oneness; state or quality of agreeing in principles, sentiments, purposes etc., concord, agreement; the number one; (leg.) a joint tenancy; **the three unities,** (drama) u. of plot or story, of place and of time. [L.].

UNIVALENT [yōō-ni-vā'lent], adj. (chem.) able to replace one atom of hydrogen. [UNI and L.].

UNIVALVE [yōō'ni-valv], n. and adj. (mollusc) having a single valve.

UNIVERSAL (1) [yōō-ni-vur'sal], adj. pertaining to the universe; widespread, general; generally applicable, generally used or usable; **u. joint,** swivelled pivot or other mechanical device permitting movement in every direction. UNIVERSAL (2), n. (logic) a u. proposition; a general idea. UNIVERSALITY [yōō-ni-ver-sa'li-ti], n. condition of being u. UNIVERSALIZE, v.t. to render u. UNIVERSALLY, adv. in a u. fashion; everywhere and always. [L.].

UNIVERSE [yōō'ni-vers], n. the whole of creation; the heavenly bodies and space; space; (coll.) the earth and all it contains. [L.].

UNIVERSITY [yōō-ni-vur'si-ti], n. institution consisting of one or more colleges, where students are educated in higher branches of learning, where research is conducted, and by which degrees are awarded; the corporate body of persons employed by, educated at or connected with, such an institution; any group of persons or team representing such an institution. [L.].

UNIVOCAL (1) [yōō-ni'vō-kal], adj. having a single meaning, unambiguous. UNIVOCAL (2), n. a u. word. UNIVOCALLY, adv. in a u. fashion. [LL.].

UNJAUNDICED [un-jawn'dist], adj. not jealous, impartial.

UNJUST [un-just'], adj. contrary to, not actuated by, justice; unfair, inequitable, prejudiced.

UNKEMPT [un-kempt'], adj. uncombed; slovenly, untidy. [UN and OE.].

UNKIND [un-kīnd'], adj. not kind; inconsiderate, harsh. UNKINDNESS, n. unkindliness. UNKINDLY, adj. unkind, inconsiderate, malignant; (adv.) in an u. fashion.

UNKNOWN [un-nōn'], adj. not known, unexplored, not experienced, lying beyond knowledge.

UNLADE (pret unladed, p.pt. unladen, unladed) [un-lād'], v.t. to unload.

UNLADEN [un-lā'den], adj. not burdened or loaded.

UNLASH [un-lash'], v.t. (of lashings) to undo; unfasten and remove the lashings from.

UNLAWFUL [un-law'fŏŏl], adj. contrary to the law. UNLAWFULLY, adv. illegally.

UNLEARN [un-lurn'], v.t. to forget purposely (what has been learned). UNLEARNED (1), UNLEARNT [un-lurnd', -lurnt'], adj. not learned.

UNLEARNED (2) [un-lur'nid], adj. ignorant, illiterate. UNLEARNEDLY, adv. in an u. way.

UNLEARNT, pret. and p.pt. of UNLEARN (1).

UNLEASH [un-lēsh'], v.t. to free from a leash; (fig.)

---

let loose. UNLEASHED, *adj.* let loose from the leash; (*fig.*) unconstrained, unchecked.

UNLEAVENED [un-le'vend], *adj.* made without yeast.

UNLESS [un-les'], *conj.* if . . . not; supposing that . . . not; except, save. [ME.].

UNLETTERED [un-le'terd], *adj.* unlearned, illiterate.

UNLIKE (1) [un-līk'], *adj.* dissimilar. UNLIKE (2), *prep.* bearing no resemblance to, not according to the character of.

UNLIKELY [un-līk'li], *adj.* not likely; not promising success; *adv.* improbably.

UNLIMITED [un-li'mi-tid], *adj.* without limit or restriction, without constraint or condition.

UNLOAD [un-lōd'], *v.t.* to take a load from; discharge (a load); remove the charge from (a gun); (of shares etc.) sell out.

UNLOOKED-FOR [un-lŏŏkt'faw(r)], *adj.* unexpected.

UNLOOSE [un-lōōs'], *v.t.* to make loose, free.

UNLOVELY [un-luv'li], *adj.* ugly, not lovely.

UNLOVING [un-lu'ving], *adj.* not loving, cold.

UNLUCKY [un-lu'ki], *adj.* experiencing constant bad luck; badly timed, tactless; ill-omened.

UNMADE (1) [un-mād'], *adj.* not made, not fashioned, formed or shaped.

UNMADE (2), *pret. and p.pt. of* UNMAKE.

UNMAIDENLY [un-mā'den-li], *adj.* not seemly for a maiden.

UNMAKE (*pret. and p.pt.* unmade) [un-māk'], *v.t.* to destroy (something made); cancel, annul.

UNMAN [un-man'], *v.t.* to take away the courage and manly qualities of; take the men or crew from; emasculate.

UNMANAGEABLE [un-ma'ni-ja-bl], *adj.* incapable of being managed; not easily governed or directed; out of hand.

UNMANLY [un-man'li], *adj.* effeminate, unworthy of a man.

UNMANNERLY [un-ma'ner-li], *adj.* ill-bred, uncivil.

UNMARRIAGEABLE [un-ma'ri-ja-bl], *adj.* too young to be married, unfit for marriage.

UNMASK [un-mahsk'], *v.t. and i.* to strip the mask from; (*fig.*) reveal or expose; take off one's own mask; (*fig.*) appear in one's true character, cease dissimulating.

UNMASTERED [un-mah'sterd], *adj.* not subdued or conquered; not thoroughly learnt.

UNMEANING [un-mē'ning], *adj.* having no sense, meaningless. UNMEANINGLY, *adv.* in u. fashion.

UNMEASURED [un-me'zherd], *adj.* limitless, unstinted; immoderate, ill-considered.

UNMECHANICAL [un-mi-ka'ni-kal], *adj.* not mechanical, not depending on mechanics; with no talent for mechanics.

UNMEET [un-mēt'], *adj.* (*archaic*) not fitted (for).

UNMELODIOUS [un-me-lō'di-ŏŏs], *adj.* not melodious or tuneful.

UNMELTED [un-mel'tid], *adj.* not melted; (*fig.*) unappeased, unsoftened.

UNMENTIONABLE [un-men'shn-a-bl], *adj.* that cannot be spoken of. UNMENTIONABLES, (*pl.*) (*obsolete coll.*) trousers.

UNMERCIFUL [un-mur'si-fŏŏl], *adj.* cruel, hardhearted, showing no mercy.

UNMETHODICAL [un-me-tho'di-kal], *adj.* lacking plan or method.

UNMETRICAL [un-met'ri-kal], *adj.* not written in metre; not in accordance with the laws of prosody.

UNMINDED [un-mīn'ded], *adj.* not intending (to); unnoticed; untended.

UNMINDFUL [un-mīnd'fŏŏl], *adj.* not heedful; forgetful. UNMINDFULLY, *adv.* in an u. fashion.

UNMITIGATED [un-mi'ti-gā-tid], *adj.* not mitigated; downright; out-and-out.

UNMIXED [un-mikst'], *adj.* not mixed; (*fig.*) unqualified.

UNMORAL [un-mo'ral], *adj.* not moral; not involving moral principles, standards.

UNMOTHERLY [un-mu'THer-li], *adj.* unworthy of, unlike, lacking the characteristics of, a mother.

UNMOVED [un-mŏŏvd'], *adj.* not moved; not emotionally affected; still resolute, unshaken.

UNMOVING [un-mŏŏ'ving], *adj.* motionless; not exciting emotion.

UNMUFFLE [un-mu'fl], *v.t. and i.* to take a muffler from (the face); take the muffling from (a drum).

UNMURMURING [un-mur'me-ring], *adj.* not murmuring, not complaining, long-suffering.

UNMUSICAL [un-myŏŏ'zi-kal], *adj.* not musical, harsh-sounding; having no ear for or skill in music.

UNMUZZLE [un-mu'zl], *v.t.* **to** remove the muzzle from; allow free speech to.

UNNAMABLE [un-nā'ma-bl], *adj.* not to be named; unmentionable. UNNAMED, *adj.* not having a name; not mentioned; unspecified.

UNNATURAL [un-na'tyŏŏ-ral], *adj.* not natural, contrary to the laws of nature, supernatural, monstrous; contrary to human nature, vile; contrary to the usual course of events, unusual, not to be expected. UNNATURALLY, *adv.* in an u. way.

UNNECESSARY [un-ne'se-sa-ri], *adj.* not necessary. UNNECESSARILY, *adv.* in an u. way, needlessly.

UNNEIGHBOURLY [un-nā'ber-li], *adj.* unworthy of a neighbour, not friendly.

UNNERVE [un-nurv'], *v.t.* to cause to lose courage, shake the nerve of.

UNNUMBERED [un-num'berd], *adj.* innumerable; not distinguished by numbers.

UNOBTRUSIVE [un-ob-trŏŏ'siv], *adj.* retiring, diffident. UNOBTRUSIVELY, *adv.* in an u. fashion.

UNOCCUPIED [un-o'kyŏŏ-pīd], *adj.* (of a person) not busy; (of a house) having no occupant; (of territory) not under military occupation.

UNOFFENDING [un-o-fen'ding], *adj.* not causing offence, inoffensive, meek.

UNOFFICIAL [un-o-fi'shal], *adj.* not official; (of information) not officially confirmed or vouched for.

UNORGANIZED [un-aw'ga-nīzd], *adj.* not organized; (*biol.*) not having an organic structure.

UNORTHODOX [un-aw'tho-doks], *adj.* not orthodox. UNORTHODOXY, *n.* quality of being u.

UNOSTENTATIOUS [un-os-ten-tā'shŏŏs], *adj.* not ostentatious, modest, not showy.

UNPACK [un-pak'], *v.t. and i.* to remove from a case, box or package; empty; remove clothing and other belongings from cases etc.

UNPALATABLE [un-pa'la-ta-bl], *adj.* not palatable; disagreeable, offensive to the mind.

UNPARALLELED [un-pa'ra-leld], *adj.* unequalled, unmatched.

UNPARLIAMENTARY [un-pah-li-men'ta-ri], *adj.* not according to parliamentary usage; rude.

UNPATRIOTIC [un-pat-ri-o'tik], *adj.* not patriotic.

UNPEOPLED [un-pē'pld], *adj.* lacking people.

UNPHILOSOPHICAL [un-fi-lō-so'fi-kal], *adj.* not conforming to philosophical principles or method.

UNPICK [un-pik'], *v.t.* to undo the stitches of by picking, unfasten (stitches) by picking. UNPICKED, *adj.* not chosen.

UNPIN [un-pin'], *v.t.* to undo (something fastened with a pin or pins).

UNPLACED [un-plāst'], *adj.* not placed; not in the first three in a race or similar competition.

UNPLANNED [un-pland'], *adj.* not planned, accidental, haphazard.

UNPLAYABLE [un-plā'a-bl], *adj.* incapable of being struck or played successfully.

UNPLEASANT [un-ple'zant], *adj.* not pleasant. UNPLEASANTLY, *adv.* in an u. manner. UNPLEASANTNESS, *n.* condition of being u.; bad feeling, a misunderstanding.

UNPLUMBED [un-plumd'], *adj.* unfathomed.

UNPOPULAR [un-po'pyŏŏ-ler], *adj.* not popular. UNPOPULARITY, [un-po-pyŏŏ-la'ri-ti], *n.* state or quality of being u.

UNPRACTISED [un-prak'tist], *adj.* not skilled; not tried out, not done.

UNPRESENTABLE [un-pri-zen'ta-bl], *adj.* not fit to be presented or exhibited in society.

UNPRESUMING [un-pri-zyŏŏ'ming], *adj.* modest, not presuming.

UNPRETENTIOUS [un-pri-ten'shŏŏs], *adj.* modest, not pretentious.

UNPRINCIPLED [un-prin'si-pld], *adj.* adhering to no principles, unscrupulous.

UNPROFESSIONAL [un-prō-fe'shn-al], *adj.* not conforming to professional usages and standards.

UNPROVED [un-prŏŏvd'], *adj.* lacking proof; untried.

UNQUALIFIED [un-kwo'li-fīd], *adj.* not qualified; lacking professional diplomas etc.

UNQUENCHABLE [un-kwen'cha-bl], *adj.* that cannot be quenched, inextinguishable.

UNQUESTIONABLE [un-kwes'chn-a-bl], *adj.* not to be questioned, absolutely certain. UNQUESTIONABLY, *adv.* in u. fashion.

UNQUIET [un-kwī'et], *adj.* not quiet, restless, uneasy.

UNQUOTE [un-kwōt'], *v.t. imper.* (*U.S.*) (in dictation) end quotation. UNQUOTABLE [un-kwō'ta-bl].

The accent ' after a syllable = stress (u-pon'). The mark ¯ over a vowel = length (ā in made; ō in bone).

adj. unfit for quotation; not to be quoted. **UNQUOTED**, *adj.* not repeated or quoted.
UNRAVEL [un-ra'vel], *v.t.* to disentangle or extricate; *(fig.)* work out the solution of (a complex problem). **UNRAVELLED**, *adj.* disentangled, unknitted, frayed. **UNRAVELMENT**, *n.* act of unravelling, fact of being unravelled.
UNREAD [un-red'], *adj.* not read; illiterate.
UNREADABLE [un-rē'da-bl], *adj.* not legible; not fit to read; impossible or practically impossible to read.
UNREADY [un-re'di], *adj.* not prepared; not alert.
UNREASON [un-rē'zon], *n.* want of reason, folly.
UNREASONABLE [un-rē'zo-na-bl], *adj.* not reasonable, irrational.
UNRECTIFIED [un-rek'ti-fid], *adj.* not rectified; *(chem.)* not distilled again, not refined.
UNREEL [un-rēl'], *v.t.* to wind from a reel.
UNREFINED [un-ri-find'], *adj.* not refined, coarse.
UNREFLECTING [un-ri-flek'ting], *adj.* not acting as a reflector; not thinking; thoughtless.
UNREGULATED [un-re'gyōō-lā'tid], *adj.* not regulated, disciplined or controlled.
UNREHEARSED [un-ri-hurst'], *adj.* not rehearsed; not intended to occur.
UNREIN [un-rān'], *v.t.* to cease holding back with the rein, loose from the rein. **UNREINED**, *adj.* not checked by the rein; *(fig.)* uncontrolled.
UNRELENTING [un-ri-len'ting], *adj.* not relenting, merciless.
UNRELIEVED [un-ri-lēvd'], *adj.* not relieved, not eased or helped, not rescued; not diversified.
UNREMARKABLE [un-ri-mah'ka-bl], *adj.* not remarkable. **UNREMARKED**, *adj.* not noticed.
UNREMITTING [un-ri-mi'ting], *adj.* not remitting, persistent. **UNREMITTINGLY**, *adv.* continuously, in u. fashion.
UNREQUITED [un-ri-kwi'tid], *adj.* not recompensed or reciprocated.
UNRESERVED [un-ri-zurvd'], *adj.* not reserved; very frank of speech; not booked or engaged. **UNRESERVEDLY** [un-ri-zur'vid-li], *adv.* openly, frankly; without reservation.
UNRESOLVED [un-ri-zolvd'], *adj.* hesitant, undecided; not analysed; not solved.
UNREST [un-rest'], *n.* turbulence, agitation; anxiousness, worry.
UNRESTING [un-res'ting], *adj.* not resting, restless, tireless.
UNRESTRICTED [un-ri-strik'tid], *adj.* not restricted, unlimited.
UNRHETORICAL [un-ri-to'ri-kal], *adj.* not rhetorical; plain, straightforward.
UNRHYTHMICAL [un-riTH'mi-kal], *adj.* lacking rhythm; conforming to no rhythmic pattern.
UNRIDDLE [un-ri'dl], *v.t.* to solve the puzzle or mystery of.
UNRIGHTEOUS [un-ri'tyōōs], *adj.* not godly or righteous; unjust, iniquitous, wicked.
UNRIP [un-rip'], *v.t.* to tear undone.
UNRIVALLED [un-ri'vald], *adj.* without a rival, unequalled, incomparable.
UNROBE [un-rōb'], *v.t. and i.* to remove robes or clothing from; undress.
UNROLL [un-rōl'], *v.t. and i.* to open (something which has been rolled up); unfold from a rolled-up position.
UNROYAL [un-roi'al], *adj.* unworthy of a king.
UNRUFFLED [un-ru'fld], *adj.* not ruffled; calm.
UNRULED [un-rōōld'], *adj.* ungoverned; (of paper) not having printed lines.
UNRULY [un-rōō'li], *adj.* disobedient, ungovernable.
UNSALTED [un-sawl'tid], *adj.* fresh, not salted.
UNSANCTIONED [un-sangk'shnd], *adj.* not allowed, approved or authorized.
UNSATISFYING [un-sa'tis-fi-ing], *adj.* not giving satisfaction; not satisfying the appetite.
UNSAVOURY [un-sā've-ri], *adj.* not savoury; *(fig.)* disreputable, unpleasant, immoral.
UNSAY (*pret. and p.pt.* **unsaid**) [un-sā'], *v.t.* to cancel or recall (what has been said).
UNSCATHED [un-skāTHd'], *adj.* undamaged, unharmed.
UNSCHOLARLY [un-sko'ler-li], *adj.* not befitting a scholar or the work of a scholar.
UNSCHOOLED [un-skōōld'], *adj.* undisciplined, untrained, lacking experience.
UNSCRAMBLE [un-skram'bl], *v.t.* to decipher (a scrambled message).
UNSCRATCHED [un-skracht'], *adj.* not scratched, unhurt, unscathed.
UNSCREENED [un-skrēnd'], *adj.* not covered with a

screen; not sifted; not having been subjected to investigation for security purposes.
UNSCREW [un-skrōō'], *v.t. and i.* to take (a screw etc.) out by twisting (it); take the screws out of; become unscrewed; be capable of being unscrewed.
UNSCRIPTED [un-skrip'tid], *adj.* (of a discussion, lecture etc.) not read from a script, spontaneous.
UNSCRUPULOUS [un-skrōō'pyōō-loos], *adj.* having no scruples, stopping at nothing.
UNSEAL [un-sēl'], *v.t.* to break, remove the seal of, open (something sealed). **UNSEALED**, *adj.* not fastened with a seal.
UNSEARCHABLE [un-sur'cha-bl], *adj.* that cannot be found by searching; hidden, inscrutable.
UNSEASONABLE [un-sē'zo-na-bl], *adj.* not seasonable; untimely.
UNSEAT [un-sēt'], *v.t.* to remove from or rob of a seat; throw (a rider) from the saddle; *(parl.)* deprive (a member) of his right to sit in the House of Commons or other elective body. **UNSEATED**, *adj.* lacking somewhere to sit, standing up; deprived of a seat in Parliament; (of a chair) having the seat missing.
UNSECONDED [un-se'kon-did], *adj.* having no second or seconder, unsupported.
UNSECTARIAN [un-sek-tāer'i-an], *adj.* not sectarian, not conforming to any particular sect.
UNSEEING [un-sē'ing], *adj.* blind, not seeing.
UNSEEMLY [un-sēm'li], *adj.* not seemly, indecent.
UNSEEN (1) [un-sēn'], *adj.* not seen; spiritual; (of a passage for translation) not previously known or prepared. **UNSEEN** (2), *n.* **the u.**, the divine or spiritual world; the hereafter; **an u.**, a passage (of a text) for translation not previously prepared.
UNSELFISH [un-sel'fish], *adj.* not selfish, charitable, generous, altruistic.
UNSENTIMENTAL [un-sen-ti-men'tal], *adj.* not trading on sentiment; not given to sentimental ideas or emotions.
UNSERVICEABLE [un-sur'vi-sa-bl], *adj.* not fit for use or service.
UNSETTLE [un-se'tl], *v.t.* to disturb, disarrange, upset. **UNSETTLED**, *adj.* not settled, disturbed, unstable; not paid; not finally determined upon; *(leg.)* not controlled by a settlement. **UNSETTLING**, *adj.* disquieting, disturbing.
UNSEX [un-seks'], *v.t.* to deprive of those qualities characteristic of the sex of. **UNSEXED**, *adj.* (of chicks etc.) not separated according to sex; having become sexually impotent.
UNSHACKLE [un-sha'kl], *v.t.* to unfetter; *(fig.)* liberate.
UNSHADED [un-shā'did], *adj.* not shady; (of a drawing) without shading; (of a light etc.) not having a shade.
UNSHADOWED [un-sha'dōd], *adj.* not dark or shadowed; *(fig.)* not sad or gloomy.
UNSHAKABLE [un-shā'ka-bl], *adj.* not to be shaken, changed or upset; resolute. **UNSHAKEN**, *adj.* not shaken, resolute, determined.
UNSHAPELY [un-shāp'li], *adj.* ill-shapen, ugly.
UNSHAVEN [un-shā'ven], *adj.* not shaven; bearded.
UNSHEATHE [un-shēTH'], *v.t.* to draw out of the sheath.
UNSHELTERED [un-shel'terd], *adj.* not sheltered, not protected.
UNSHINGLED [un-shing'gld], *adj.* not covered with shingles; (of hair) not cut short in a shingle.
UNSHIP [un-ship'], *v.t.* to disembark or discharge (from a ship); *(naut.)* remove (a mast, oars etc.) from position.
UNSHRINKING [un-shring'king], *adj.* not shrinking or hesitating.
UNSIFTED [un-sif'tid], *adj.* not sifted in a sieve; *(fig.)* not closely examined.
UNSIGHT [un-sit'], *v.t.* to obstruct the view of. **UNSIGHTED**, *adj.* not yet seen or within view; (of a gun) lacking sights.
UNSIGHTLY [un-sit'li], *adj.* ugly, displeasing to the eye.
UNSINKABLE [un-sing'ka-bl], *adj.* designed to keep afloat in all circumstances.
UNSISTERLY [un-sis'ter-li], *adj.* not befitting a sister.
UNSKILFUL [un-skil'fool], *adj.* lacking skill, clumsy, not expert.
UNSLAKED [un-slākt'], *adj.* (of lime) not watered; (of thirst) unquenched, not eased.
UNSLEEPING [un-slē'ping], *adj.* not sleeping, having abundant energy, constantly diligent.
UNSLING (*pret. and p.pt.* **unslung**) [un-sling'], *v.t.*

ōō is pronounced as in food; ŏŏ as in hood; th as in *think*; TH as in *that*; zh as in azure. ~ = related to.

DSE—U

to take down (something slung up); (*naut.*) take from the slings.

UNSLUMBERING [un-slum'be-ring], *adj.* not slumbering, wakeful, tireless.

UNSOCIABLE [un-sō'sha-bl], *adj.* not sociable.

UNSOCIAL [un-sō'shal], *adj.* not social; not suitable for society; lacking community sense.

UNSOLDIERLY [un-sōl'jer-li], *adj.* unworthy of a soldier.

UNSOLVABLE [un-sol'va-bl], *adj.* inexplicable, incapable of being solved. UNSOLVED, *adj.* not solved or explained.

UNSOUGHT [un-sawt'], *adj.* not sought, not asked for.

UNSOUND [un-sownd'], *adj.* not sound, rotten, defective; not reasoned, erroneous; not authoritative.

UNSOUNDED [un-sown'did], *adj.* unfathomed.

UNSPARING [un-spâer'ing], *adj.* not sparing or stinting, liberal; not merciful.

UNSPEAKABLE [un-spē'ka-bl], *adj.* too wonderful to be spoken of or expressed; too bad for description.

UNSPENT [un-spent'], *adj.* not spent, drained or exhausted.

UNSPIRITUAL [un-spi'ri-tyōō-al], *adj.* not spiritual. UNSPIRITUALITY [un-spi-ri-tyōō-a'li-ti], *n.* quality of being u.

UNSPORTING [un-spaw'ting], *adj.* (*coll.*) not fair or sportsmanlike.

UNSPORTSMANLIKE [un-spawts'man-līk], *adj.* not like, not worthy of, a sportsman.

UNSPOTTED [un-spo'tid], *adj.* not spotted, unsoiled; (*fig.*) blameless, untainted.

UNSTABLE [un-stā'bl], *adj.* not stable or steady; (*fig.*) irresolute, inconstant.

UNSTAINED [un-stānd'], *adj.* not stained; (*fig.*) not dishonoured.

UNSTEADY [un-ste'di], *adj.* not firm and steady; unreliable, inconstant, not morally balanced.

UNSTICK [un-stik'], *v.t.* to undo (what is stuck); separate (things stuck together).

UNSTINTING [un-stin'ting], *adj.* ungrudging.

UNSTIRRED [un-sturd'], *adj.* not stirred; (*fig.*) not emotionally moved.

UNSTOP [un-stop'], *v.t.* to clear of obstruction; remove the stopper from. UNSTOPPED, *adj.* not stopped or blocked up.

UNSTRAINED [un-strānd'], *adj.* not strained, not constrained or forced, natural; not passed through a filter.

UNSTRAP [un-strap'], *v.t.* to loosen or remove the strap of.

UNSTRING [un-string'], *v.t.* to loosen or take away the string of; take (jewels etc.) off a string.

UNSTRUNG [un-strung'], *adj.* not strung; (*fig.*) emotionally or nervously unstable.

UNSTUCK [un-stuk'], *adj.* not stuck together; **to come u.**, to come to grief, fail, break down.

UNSTUDIED [un-stu'did], *adj.* not studied; natural.

UNSUBMISSIVE [un-sub-mi'siv], *adj.* not submissive or obedient; refusing to recognize authority.

UNSUBSTANTIAL [un-sub-stan'shal], *adj.* having little or no substance, flimsy; unreal, dreamlike, spiritual.

UNSUBSTANTIATED [un-sub-stan'shi-ā-tid], *adj.* unconfirmed, unsupported by evidence.

UNSUITED [un-syōo'tid], *adj.* not suited; having no cards of a particular suit.

UNSUNG [un-sung'], *adj.* not sung; not lauded in verse.

UNSUPPORTED [un-su-paw'tid], *adj.* not having, receiving support.

UNSUSPECTING [un-sus-pek'ting], *adj.* not suspicious.

UNSUSPICIOUS [un-sus-pi'shōos], *adj.* free from suspicion, not causing suspicion.

UNSWAYED [un-swād'], *adj.* not influenced or biased.

UNSWERVING [un-swur'ving], *adj.* not deviating; (*fig.*) resolute, determined.

UNSYMPATHETIC [un-sim-pa-the'tik], *adj.* showing no feeling or sympathy.

UNSYSTEMATIC [un-sis-te-ma'tik], *adj.* not according to system.

UNTACK [un-tak'], *v.t.* to undo (something lightly sewn together).

UNTANGLE [un-tang'gl], *v.t.* to unravel, disentangle.

UNTAUGHT [un-tawt'], *adj.* not instructed or taught.

UNTEACH (*pret. and p.pt.* **untaught**) [un-tēch'], *v.t.* to teach the reverse of (what has been previously

taught). UNTEACHABLE, *adj.* that cannot be taught.

UNTENABLE [un-te'na-bl, un-tē'na-bl], *adj.* not defensible, not tenable.

UNTENDED [un-ten'did], *adj.* not tended; neglected.

UNTETHER [un-te'THer], *v.t.* to release from a tether; (*fig.*) liberate.

UNTHANKED [un-thangkt'], *adj.* having received no thanks.

UNTHINKABLE [un-thing'ka-bl], *adj.* unexpected, improbable, outrageous; not to be thought of.

UNTHINKING [un-thing'king], *adj.* not thinking, inconsiderate.

UNTHOUGHTFUL [un-thawt'fōōl], *adj.* not thoughtful; lacking in consideration for others.

UNTHREAD [un-thred'], *v.t.* to remove the threads from; disentangle; take off a thread or string; (*fig.*) solve (a complicated problem).

UNTHRIFTY [un-thrif'ti], *adj.* not thrifty, prodigal, lavish.

UNTIL (1) [un-til'], *prep.* up to the time of, till. UNTIL (2), *conj.* up to the time at which, till. [OScand.].

UNTIMELY (1) [un-tīm'li], *adj.* premature; inopportune. UNTIMELY (2), *adv.* prematurely, at an inopportune moment.

UNTIRING [un-tīer'ing], *adj.* not flagging, indefatigable.

UNTO [un'tōō], *prep.* (*archaic*) to, towards. [ME.].

UNTOLD [un-tōld'], *adj.* not told or revealed; not counted; uncountable.

UNTOUCHABLE (1) [un-tu'cha-bl], *adj.* not fit to be touched. UNTOUCHABLE (2), *n.* a Hindu without caste. UNTOUCHED, *adj.* not touched; not affected; not equalled.

UNTOWARD [un-tō'erd, un-tōō-wawd'], *adj.* (*archaic*) perverse, refractory; troublesome, inconvenient.

UNTRAMMELLED [un-tra'meld], *adj.* not shackled or hindered.

UNTRAVELLED [un-tra'veld], *adj.* not visited by travellers; not experienced in foreign travel.

UNTRIED [un-trīd'], *adj.* not tasted or experienced; not tested; not having been put on trial in a law court.

UNTRODDEN [un-tro'den], *adj.* not trodden; secluded, unfrequented.

UNTROUBLED [un-tru'bld], *adj.* not troubled by care or sorrow; calm.

UNTRUE [un-trōō'], *adj.* not true; contrary to fact; disloyal. UNTRULY, *adv.* in an u. fashion.

UNTRUTH [un-trōōth'], *n.* falsehood, want of veracity, quality of being untrue; a lie.

UNTUCK [un-tuk'], *v.t.* to loosen what is tucked up; remove the tucks from.

UNTUNEFUL [un-tyōōn'fōōl], *adj.* not tuneful, tuneless.

UNTUTORED [un-tyōō'terd], *adj.* uneducated, untaught; uncouth.

UNTWINE [un-twīn'], *v.t.* and *i.* to untwist (something twined up); come untwisted.

UNTWIST [un-twist'], *v.t.* and *i.* to undo (something twisted up); disentangle; come untangled or untwisted.

UNUSED (1) [un-yōōzd'], *adj.* not used, never having been used. UNUSED (2) [un-yōōst'], *adj.* not accustomed to.

UNUSUAL [un-yōō'zhōo-al], *adj.* not usual; strange, odd, remarkable. UNUSUALLY, *adv.* in an u. manner; not in the usual way; to an u. extent.

UNUTTERABLE [un-u'te-ra-bl], *adj.* indescribable; (*coll.*) utter, absolute.

UNVARNISHED [un-vah'nisht], *adj.* not varnished; unadorned, simple.

UNVEIL [un-vāl'], *v.t.* and *i.* to take the veil from, uncover; inaugurate (a monument etc.) ceremonially; (*fig.*) reveal, make public; throw off one's disguise; lift one's veil.

UNVENTILATED [un-ven'ti-lā-tid], *adj.* not at all, badly, ventilated.

UNVERSED [un-vurst'], *adj.* not skilled or versed; without extensive knowledge.

UNVOICED [un-voist'], *adj.* not spoken; (*phon.*) uttered without vibration of the vocal chords.

UNWANTED [un-won'tid], *adj.* not wanted, superfluous.

UNWARRANTABLE [un-wo'ran-ta-bl], *adj.* not defensible or justifiable. UNWARRANTED, *adj.* not authorized; not justified or fitting.

UNWARY [un-wāer'i], *adj.* not vigilant or wary.

UNWASHED [un-wosht'], *adj.* not washed; not touched by water; **the great u.**, the mob.

The accent ' after a syllable = stress (u-pon'). The mark ⁻ over a vowel = length (ā in made; ō in bone).

UNWATERED [un-waw'terd], *adj.* not watered or irrigated.

UNWAVERING [un-wā've-ring], *adj.* not wavering or hesitant.

UNWEARYING [un-wēer'i-ing], *adj.* untiring, indefatigable.

UNWED, UNWEDDED [un-wed'(-ed)], *adj.* not married.

UNWELL [un-wel'], *adj.* suffering from ill-health, not well.

UNWEPT [un-wept'], *adj.* not lamented.

UNWIELDY [un-wēl'di], *adj.* clumsy, unmanageable.

UNWILLING [un-wil'ling], *adj.* not willing, reluctant.

UNWIND (*pret. and p.pt.* **unwound**) [un-wīnd'], *v.t. and i.* to undo (that which is wound up), unravel, straighten out; become unwound.

UNWINKING [un-wing'king], *adj.* not winking; unceasingly vigilant.

UNWISDOM [un-wiz'dom], *n.* folly.

UNWITHERED [un-wi'THerd], *adj.* not withered; still fresh and vigorous.

UNWITNESSED [un-wit'nest], *adj.* not seen or attested by a witness.

UNWITTINGLY [un-wi'ting-li], *adv.* in ignorance, unconsciously.

UNWONTED [un-wŏn'tid], *adj.* unusual.

UNWORKABLE [un-wur'ka-bl], *adj.* not practicable.

UNWORTHY [un-wur'THi], *adj.* not worthy, unbecoming, not suitable.

UNWOUND [un-wownd'], *pret. and p.pt.* of UNWIND.

UNWRITTEN [un-ri'ten], *adj.* not written down, not marked with writing; **u. law,** the justification pleaded for murder done to require one's honour.

UNWRUNG [un-rung'], *adj.* not wrung, not touched by tender feeling.

UNYIELDING [un-yēl'ding], *adj.* resolute, obstinate.

UNYOKE [un-yōk'], *v.t.* to remove the yoke from; (*fig.*) make free from some bond or bondage.

UP (1) [up], *adv.* expressing transition to, or existence upon, a higher level; expressing growth, development, elevation (physical, moral, social etc.); expressing increase of value, power, importance, speed etc.; expressing the ideas of being laid aside after use, disuse, inactivity etc.; expressing motion towards or existence in the north; expressing the idea of being out of bed; **u. with or to,** level with, (*fig.*) equal to; **to be u. to** (**something**), to be doing (something), *esp.* in a secret way; **to be u. against it,** to have serious difficulties; **what's u.?** (*coll.*) what's happening?; **it's all u.,** (*coll.*) it's finished, nothing more can be done, we are beaten etc.; **it's u. to** (**someone**), (*coll.*) it is (someone's) responsibility; **u. and down,** alternately raised and lowered, or rising and descending; to and fro; hither and thither; here and there; all over; **to be on the u. and u.,** to be progressing. UP (2), *prep.* expressing movement towards or existence on a higher level; (*fig.*) expressing increasing importance, worth, power etc.; along the course of, *esp.* against the current. UP (3), *adj.* moving upwards; (*fig.*) increasing, developing, improving; travelling towards an important city, *esp.* London; **u. and coming,** (*coll.*) progressive, promising. UP (4), *n.* a movement or thrust upwards; **to have an u. and a downer,** (*coll.*) to skirmish; **ups and downs,** rises and falls, changes of fortune. UP (5) (*pres.pt.* UPPING, *pret. and p.pt.* UPPED), *v.t.* to drive u. (swans) for marking; *v.i.* to **u. and,** to begin to. [OE.].

UP-, *pref.* in an upward direction or position. [UP (1)].

UPAS [yōō'pas], *n.* a poisonous tree supposed to exist in Java; a Javanese tree, Antiaris toxicaria; the poisonous sap of this tree; (*fig.*) any source of corruption. [Malay].

UPBRAID [up-brād'], *v.t.* to chide, reproach, reprove. UPBRAIDING (1), *n.* a chiding, reproof. UPBRAIDING (2), *adj.* chiding, reproachful.

UPBRINGING [up'bring-ing], *n.* training and education of a child.

UPCAST (1) [up'kahst], *n.* that which is cast up; ventilation shaft in a mine. UPCAST (2), *adj.* cast upwards.

UP-COUNTRY (1) [up-kun'tri], *n.* the interior part of a country. UP-COUNTRY (2), *adj.* relating to the interior of a country.

UP-END [up-end'], *v.t.* to put or throw up on end.

UP-GRADE (1) [up'grād], *n.* **on the u.,** improving. UP-GRADE (2), [up-grād'], *v.t.* to raise the grade or status of.

UPHEAVAL [up-hē'val], *n.* act of upheaving;

earthquake or any similar eruption; sudden unexpected trouble or disturbance in normal conditions.

UPHEAVE [up-hēv'], *v.t.* to heave or raise up.

UPHELD [up-held'], *pret. and p.pt.* of UPHOLD.

UPHILL (1) [up'hil], *adj.* ascending, leading upwards; (*fig.*) difficult, laborious. UPHILL (2), [up-hil'], *adv.* towards the top of a hill.

UPHOLD (*pret. and p.pt.* **upheld**) [up-hōld'], *v.t.* to sustain or support; agree with, encourage, give approval to. UPHOLDER, *n.* supporter.

UPHOLSTER [up-hōl'ster], *v.t.* to provide (a room) with furniture and ornaments; stuff or cover (a chair etc.). [UPHOLD].

UPHOLSTERY [up-hōl'ste-ri], *n.* household furniture; the covers, springs and stuffing of chairs etc.; trade of an upholsterer. [Prec.].

UPKEEP [up'kēp], *n.* maintenance; cost of maintenance.

UPLAND (1) [up'land], *n.* (often pl.) higher land on the slopes of hills and mountains above the valleys. UPLAND (2), *adj.* pertaining to the uplands.

UPLIFT (1) [up-lift'], *v.t.* to hold or raise; (*fig.*) cheer or edify. UPLIFT (2) [up'lift], *n.* upheaval; act of uplifting; (*coll.*) moral edification and profit.

UPMOST [up'mōst], *adj.* highest, uppermost.

UPON [u-pon'], *prep.* expressing the idea of a state of contact with the upper surface of anything; on. [UP (2) and ON].

UPPER (1) [u'per], *adj.* lying or placed above; higher in esteem or rank; greater in power or dignity; **to have the u. hand,** to be in a position of power and ascendancy (over); **U. House,** House of Lords; **the u. ten,** (*coll.*) the aristocracy. UPPER-CUT, *n.* (*boxing*) blow delivered with an upward swing. UPPER (2), *n.* that part of a shoe or boot other than the heel and sole; (**down**) **on one's uppers,** (*slang*) destitute.

UPPERMOST (1) [u'per-mōst], *adj.* highest; (*fig.*) dominant. UPPERMOST (2), *adv.* in an u. position, on top.

UPPISH [u'pish], *adj.* (*coll.*) arrogant, self-assertive, impudent, snobbish.

UPRAISE [up-rāz'], *v.t.* to raise up.

UPRIGHT (1) [up'rit], *adj.* vertical; (*fig.*) honest, honourable, just; **u. piano,** piano which has vertical and not horizontal strings. UPRIGHT (2), *n.* a vertical post or support in a structure; u. piano. UPRIGHTLY, *adv.* in an u. fashion. [OE.].

UPRISE (*pret.* **uprose,** *p.pt.* **uprisen**) [up-rīz'] *v.i* to ascend; stand up. UPRISING, *n.* act of rising up; act of getting up from bed; insurrection, revolt.

UPROAR [up'raw(r)], *n.* great tumult and clamour; noisy disturbance.

UPROARIOUS [up-raw'ri-ōōs], *adj.* very noisy and violent; boisterous, rowdy.

UPROOT [up-rōōt'], *v.t.* to tear up by the roots; (*fig.*) exterminate.

UPROSE [up-rōz'], *pret.* of UPRISE.

UPRUSH [up'rush], *n.* a sudden rushing upwards or into consciousness.

UPSET (1) (*pret. and p.pt.* **upset**) [up-set'], *v.t. and i.* to cause to capsize; throw down; dislocate, throw out, disturb; make ill; cause mental distress to; capsize, be overthrown. UPSET (2) [up'set], *n.* a capsizing or overturning; any trouble or disturbance; (*coll.*) a quarrel.

UPSHOT [up'shot], *n.* final issue, result, conclusion.

UPSIDE [up'sid], *n.* the upper surface of anything; that line or section of a railway track on which trains run towards an important city, *esp.* London; **u. down,** with the upper side below.

UP-STAGE (1) [up-stāj'], *adv.* at, or towards, the back of the stage; i.e. away from the audience. UP-STAGE (2), *adj.* (*slang*) uppish.

UPSTAIRS (1) [up-stāerz'], *adv.* in or towards the upper rooms of a house. UPSTAIRS (2), UPSTAIR [up'stāer(z)], *adj.* of, or pertaining to, storeys above the ground floor. UPSTAIRS (3) [up-stāerz'], *n.* the upper rooms of a house.

UPSTANDING [up-stan'ding], *adj.* (of a man etc.) straight-backed, well-built.

UPSTART (1) [up'staht], *n.* a parvenu, person who by sudden access of wealth or success is raised from insignificance to importance or from a low rank of society to a high one. UPSTART (2), *adj.* suddenly raised from insignificance to importance or from comparative poverty to wealth.

UPSTREAM [up-strēm'], *adj. and adv.* (travelling) towards the source, against the current.

UPSTROKE [up'strōk], *n.* stroke made with an upward movement as in writing.

UPSURGE [up'serj], *n.* an upward surge.

ōō is pronounced as in food; ŏŏ as in hood; th as in think; TH as in that; zh as in azure. ~ = related to

UPTAKE [up'tāk], *n.* perception.

UPTURN [up-turn'], *v.i.* to overturn, turn up, throw into disorder.

UPWARD (1) [up'werd], *adj.* moving, caused to move, aimed towards, a higher position, ascending, pointing away from the earth. UPWARDS, UPWARD (2), *adv.* into or towards a higher level, away from the earth. [OE.].

URAEMIA [yoo-rē'mi-ah], *n.* (*path.*) unhealthy state arising in the body when the kidneys fail to cleanse the blood of certain impurities. [Gk.].

URANIA [yoo-rā'ni-ah], *n.* (*class. myth.*) the Muse of astronomy. URANIAN, *adj.* pertaining to non-sexual, spiritual or homosexual love. [~Gk.].

URANIUM [yoo-rā'ni-um], *n.* metallic element denoted by the symbol U. [The planet *Uranus*].

URANUS [yoo-rā'nus], *n.* (*Gk. myth.*) father of Cronus; (*astron.*) the major planet between Saturn and Neptune.

URBAN [ur'ban], *adj.* pertaining to a town or city. [L.].

URBANE [er-bān'], *adj.* civil, refined. [L.].

URBANITY [er-ba'ni-ti], *n.* civility or courtesy, refinement of speech and manner. [L.].

URBANIZE [ur'ba-nīz], *v.t.* to impart the qualities and conditions of a town or city to, make urban.

URCHIN [ur'chin], *n.* (*dial.*) hedgehog; mischievous child. [ME. from OFr.].

URDU (1) [oor-doo'], *n.* a form of Hindustani. URDU (2), *adj.* in, or pertaining to, U. [Hind.].

UREA [yoo-rē'ah], *n.* (*chem.*) crystalline compound found in urine. [~URINE].

URETER [yoo-rē'ter], *n.* (*anat.*) duct conveying urine to the bladder. [Gk.].

URETHRA [yoo-rē'thrah], *n.* (*anat.*) passage by which urine passes out of the bladder. [Gk.].

URGE [urj], *v.t.* to drive, compel to advance; exhort, advise vigorously; call attention to, vigorously and persistently. URGE (2), *n.* a powerful incentive, impulse. URGER, *n.* one who urges. URGING, *adj.* importunate, pressing. [L.].

URGENCY [ur'jen-si], *n.* quality of being urgent; great stress or necessity; persistent demand, importunity.

URGENT [ur'jent], *adj.* insistent, importunate; very important, on no account to be overlooked or delayed.

URIC [yoo'rik], *adj.* pertaining to urine; **u. acid**, an acid which forms a small proportion of the urine of a mammal but a large proportion of the urine of reptiles and birds.

URINAL [yoo'ri-nal, yoo-rī'nal], *n.* vessel into which urine is passed; public convenience for urinating. [L.].

URINARY [yoo'ri-na-ri], *adj.* connected with urine.

URINATE [yoo'ri-nāt], *v.i.* to discharge urine. [~L.].

URINE [yoo'rin], *n.* liquid excrement secreted by the kidneys into the bladder and discharged from the body by the urethra. URINOUS, *adj.* (*anat., chem.*) resembling, pertaining to, derived from, u. [L.].

URN [urn], *n.* large vessel, circular at the base, usually having a circular lip and a narrow neck; large metal container, with a lid and a tap, in which water or other liquids may be heated. [L.].

URSINE [ur'sīn], *adj.* relating to or resembling bears. [L.].

URSULINE (1) [ur'syoo-līn], *n.* member of an order of nuns founded in the 16th century. URSULINE (2), *adj.* of, or relating to, the Ursulines. [St. *Ursula*].

URTICARIA [er-ti-kāer'i-ah], *n.* nettle-rash.

US [us], *pron. objective case* of WE. [OE.].

USABLE [yoo'za-bl], *adj.* able to be used.

USAGE [yoo'sij], *n.* manner of use, *esp.* of a word; established custom or habit. [OFr.].

USANCE [yoo'zans], *n.* habit, usage; usual period allowed for the payment of foreign exchange bills. [OFr.].

USE [yoos], *n.* act of using; ability or right to use; a reason for doing or using; condition or quality of being useful; something usually done, a habit or custom; (*eccles.*) form of ceremony, liturgy; (*leg.*) profit derived from a trust or tenancy; **to make u. of,** to use; **to have no u. for,** (*coll.*) to dislike. USE (2) [yooz], *v.t. and i.* to employ as an instrument; manipulate, operate; utilize, employ or avail oneself of in a task or activity; cause to operate or have effect; employ so much that none is left, consume; take as an ingredient; utter (words, phrases etc.); treat, handle in a certain way, adopt a specified attitude or conduct towards; be wont (to); be accustomed to

have or possess; **to u. up, to exhaust the supply of.** [OFr. from L.].

USEFUL [yoos'fool], *adj.* handy, advantageous to use; helpful.

USELESS [yoos'les], *adj.* not useful, unserviceable.

USER (1) [yoo'zer], *n.* one who uses (something). USER (2), *n.* (*leg.*) use or tenure of property and the title to it which can be made out in virtue of such use when long continued. [OFr. from L.].

USHER (1) [u'sher], *n.* officer at any large public gathering who sees to it that only those entitled to enter do so, and guides them to their places; officer in a ceremony who precedes an important person; formerly, a junior master in a boarding-school. USHER (2), *v.t.* to perform the duties of an u. for, direct (someone) to his or her place, or announce his arrival; **to u. in,** to come as a prelude to, be the first intimation of. USHERSHIP, *n.* office and function of an u. [OFr. from L.].

USHERETTE [u-she-ret'], *n.* female attendant who shows people to their seats in a cinema, etc. [USHER (1)].

USQUEBAUGH † [us'kwi-baw], *n.* whiskey. [Ir.].

USUAL [yoo'zhoo-al], *adj.* customary; frequently done, normal, common; commonplace. USUALLY, *adv.* in accordance with habit or custom, habitually, normally.

USUFRUCT [yoo'zhoo-frukt], *n.* (*leg.*) right of temporary possession of what is another's on condition that such possession causes no damage to it. USUFRUCTUARY (1) [yoo-zhoo-fruk'tyoo-a-ri], *n.* (*leg.*) person enjoying u. USUFRUCTUARY (2), *adj.* relating to u. [L.].

USURER [yoo'zhoor-er], *n.* one who makes his living by lending out money at very high interest. [LL.].

USURIOUS [yoo-zhoor'i-oos], *adj.* pertaining to, or making a practice of, usury.

USURP [yoo-zurp'], *v.t.* to take wrongful possession of.

USURPATION [yoo-zer-pā'shn], *n.* act of usurping, fact of having been usurped. [L.].

USURPER [yoo-zur'per], *n.* one who usurps, one who has wrongfully seized the crown.

USURY [yoo'zhoo-ri], *n.* business of making loans at very high rates of interest; interest and profit on this. [L.].

UTENSIL [yoo-ten'sil], *n.* any vessel or receptacle employed for culinary or domestic purposes. [OFr.].

UTERINE [yoo'te-rin], *adj.* having the same mother but not the same father; (*med.*) connected with the uterus. [LL.].

UTERUS (*pl.* **uteri**) [yoo'te-rus], *n.* (*med.*) the womb.

UTILITARIAN (1) [yoo-ti-li-tāer'i-an], *n.* believer in utilitarianism. UTILITARIAN (2), *adj.* pertaining to utilitarianism; practical. UTILITARIANISM, *n.* doctrine of Jeremy Bentham based on the ideas that to provide the greatest possible happiness for the greatest possible number is the highest ideal, and that utility is the soundest criterion.

UTILITY [yoo-ti'li-ti], *n.* quality of being useful. [L.].

UTILIZE [yoo'ti-līz], *v.t.* to make useful or profitable. UTILIZABLE, *adj.* able to be utilized. [Fr.].

UTMOST (1) [ut'mōst], *adj.* lying farthest away from the centre; (*fig.*) most extreme, greatest, fullest, most. UTMOST (2), *n.* the fullest extent, the greatest measure, that which implies the most or greatest possible. [OE.].

UTOPIA [yoo-tō'pi-ah], *n.* fictitious island which Sir Thomas More describes as possessing a perfect political, religious, legal and economic system; an ideal state. UTOPIAN (1), *adj.* pertaining to an ideal state or U.; unpractically optimistic, *esp.* in social theory or planning. UTOPIAN (2), *n.* dweller in U. [Coined by Sir T. More from Gk.].

UTRICLE [yoo'tri-kl], *n.* (*anat., bot.*) bag-like structure, a hollow in the inner ear. UTRICULAR [yoo-tri'kyoo-ler], *adj.* pertaining to a u. [L.].

UTTER (1) [u'ter], *adj.* absolute, without qualification; total; definite, unconditional. UTTERLY, *adv.* fully, completely, totally. [OE.].

UTTER (2), *v.t.* to speak, pronounce, give forth with the voice; put into circulation. [Uncert.].

UTTERMOST (1) [u'ter-mōst], *adj.* farthest from the centre; greatest, strongest possible, utmost. UTTERMOST (2), *n.* the greatest extent, highest measure or degree etc. [ME.].

UVULA (*pl.* **uvulae**) [yoo'vyoo-lah], *n.* (*anat.*) soft, pendent extension at the back of the palate. UVULAR, *adj.* relating to the u.; (*phon.*) spoken with the u. [L.].

UXORIOUS [uk-zaw'ri-oos], *adj.* very devoted to one's wife, *esp.* to a foolish degree. [L.].

---

e accent ′ after a syllable = stress (u-pon′).   The mark ‾ over a vowel = length (ā in made; ō in bone).

V

V [vē], twenty-second letter of the English alphabet; symbol of victory; **v. sign,** sign made by raising two fingers or thumb and forefinger to form a V.

VAC [vak], *coll. abbreviation for* VACATION.

VACANCY [vā'kan-si], *n.* state of being vacant; condition of being unoccupied; an unoccupied post, position or employment. [L.].

VACANT [vā'kant], *adj.* empty, unoccupied; (*fig.*) empty-headed, unintelligent, inane; having no tenant. [L.].

VACATE [va-kāt'], *v.t. and i.* to make vacant, leave unoccupied; go away (from a place or position). [~L.].

VACATION [va-kā'shn], *n.* act of vacating; formal holiday period from a school, university or court of law. [L.].

VACCINATE [vak'si-nāt], *v.t.* to inoculate with vaccine. VACCINATOR, *n.* one who vaccinates. [Fr.].

VACCINATION [vak-si-nā'shn], *n.* inoculation with vaccine. VACCINATIONIST, *n.* advocate of (compulsory) v.

VACCINE [vak'sēn], *n.* virus of cow-pox, obtained in lymph, and used for inoculation against smallpox; any similar virus. [L.].

VACCINIA [vak-si'ni-ah], *n.* cow-pox. [MedL.].

VACILLATE [va'si-lāt], *v.i.* to sway unsteadily; hesitate, show indecision. VACILLATING, *adj.* wavering. [~L.].

VACILLATION [va-si-lā'shn], *n.* act, state of vacillating; mental hesitancy. [L.].

VACUITY [va-kyōō'i-ti], *n.* emptiness; mental vacancy. [L.].

VACUOUS [va'kyōō-ōōs], *adj.* empty; mentally vacant. [L.].

VACUUM [va'kyōō-um], *n.* space containing no matter of any kind whatsoever; space from which the air has been removed. VACUUM-CLEANER, cleaning tool which removes dust etc. by suction. VACUUM-FLASK, evacuated, double-walled glass container with silvered interior surface, designed to keep substances at a constant temperature. VACUUM-TUBE, evacuated electrical-discharge tube with two or more electrodes. [L.].

VADE-MECUM [vā-di-mē'kum], *n.* manual or handbook for ready reference. [L.].

VAGABOND (1) [va'ga-bond], *adj.* vagrant, wandering. VAGABOND (2), *n.* wandering rogue, tramp, person of no fixed residence or means of support. VAGABONDIZE [va'ga-bon-dīz], *v.i.* to wander like a v. [L.].

VAGARY [va-gāer'i, vā'ge-ri], *n.* irrational impulse; whim. [~L.].

VAGINA (*pl.* **vaginae**) [va-jī'nah], *n.* passage from the uterus to the external orifice in the female mammal; (*bot.*) the sheath in grasses. VAGINAL, *adj.* resembling, relating to, of, a sheath or the v.; in the form of a sheath. [L.].

VAGRANCY [vā'gran-si], *n.* state of being or living as a vagrant.

VAGRANT (1) [vā'grant], *adj.* wandering as a tramp; like, relating to, a vagrant. VAGRANT (2), *n.* a tramp, person wandering about the countryside without means of support. [ME.].

VAGUE [vāg], *adj.* undefined, not distinct, uncertain; mentally unprecise. [Fr.].

VAIN [vān], *adj.* empty, useless, fruitless; conceited; **in v.,** idly, to no effect. VAINLY, *adv.* in v.; foolishly; conceitedly. [L.].

VAINGLORIOUS [vān-glaw'ri-ōōs], *adj.* ostentatiously boastful.

VAINGLORY [vān'glaw-ri], *n.* ostentatious vanity; empty pride; boastfulness. [ME.].

VALANCE [va'lans], *n.* drapery hanging down from a window-shelf, the framework of a bed or an open cupboard etc. [ME.].

VALE (1) [vāl], *n.* valley. [L.].

VALE (2) [vā'li], *n.* a farewell salutation. [L.].

VALEDICTION [va-li-dik'shn], *n.* a farewell; a bidding farewell. [L.].

VALEDICTORY [va-li-dik'te-ri], *adj.* relating to, of the nature of, a valediction.

VALENCIENNES [va-lah(ng)-si-en', va-len-sēnz'], *n.* kind of lace made at *Valenciennes* in France.

VALENCY [vā'len-si], *n.* the combining potentialities of a chemical substance, measured by comparison with those of hydrogen. [L.].

VALENTINE [va'len-tīn], *n.* greeting-card, usually of an amorous nature, sent on St. Valentine's Day, 14 February.

VALERIAN [va-lēer'i-an], *n.* perennial plant of the genus *Valeriana,* the medicinal root of *Valeriana officinalis.* [MedL.].

VALET (1) [va'let, va'li, va'lā], *n.* male personal servant. VALET (2) [va'let], *v.t. and i.* to care for, or repair (clothes) in the manner of a v.; act as a v. (to). [OFr.].

VALETUDINARIAN [va-li-tyōō-di-nāer'i-an], *n. and adj.* (relating to) one who is perpetually sickly; preoccupied with one's own diseases. [L.].

VALHALLA [val-ha'lah], *n.* (*Old Norse myth.*) Odin's Hall in the abode of the gods, where heroes slain in battle go. [OIcel.].

VALIANT [val'yant], *adj.* brave, showing valour; requiring great courage to perform. [OFr.].

VALID [va'lid], *adj.* effectively true, based on good reason; effective, available; (*leg.*) having legal force, maintainable in a court of law. [L.].

VALIDATE [va'li-dāt], *v.t.* to make valid; maintain the validity of. [~MedL.].

VALIDITY [va-li'di-ti], *n.* quality of being valid; legal force. [MedL.].

VALISE [va-lēs'], *n.* rolled travelling-bag carried slung to a horse's saddle; any large travelling-bag. [Fr.].

VALKYR(I)E [val'kēr, val'ki-ri], *n.* (*myth.*) one of the twelve Norse goddesses who chose those to be killed in battle, and carried them to Valhalla. VALKYRIAN [val-ki'ri-an], *adj.* pertaining to the Valkyries. [OIcel.].

VALLEY [va'li], *n.* narrow tract of low-lying land between more or less parallel ridges of higher ground; low-lying river-basin. [L.].

VALOROUS [va'le-rōōs], *adj.* valiant; calling for valour. [MedL.].

VALOUR [va'ler], *n.* extreme, active, courage, usually in warfare. [L.].

VALSE (1) [vahls], *n.* a waltz. VALSE (2), *v.i.* to waltz. [Fr.].

VALUABLE (1) [va'lyōō-a-bl], *adj.* having material worth, being of value; highly useful; estimable. VALUABLE (2), *n.* that which is of value; a costly personal possession or trinket.

VALUATION [va-lyōō-ā'shn], *n.* act of valuing; the estimated monetary worth of a thing; estimation.

VALUE (1) [va'lyōō], *n.* worth, importance, monetary price; desirability; quality; exact force (of a word or syllable). VALUE (2), *v.t.* to place a v. on; estimate the worth or monetary price of; prize. VALUED, *adj.* regarded as valuable. VALUELESS, *adj.* of no v.; worthless. [OFr.].

VALUTA [va-lyōō'tah], *n.* a currency of standard value. [It.].

VALVE [valv], *n.* an aperture and its covering, regarded as a control over entrance and exit, *esp.* when operated automatically; door, opening; leaf of a folding door; (*elect.*) vacuum-tube used to control the direction and strength of electric currents; (*biol.*) a mollusc shell, one of the leaves of a mollusc shell. [L.].

VALVULAR [val'vyōō-ler], *adj.* containing, relating to, a valve, *esp.* of the heart.

VAMOOSE [va-mōōs'], *v.i.* to go away rapidly; (*slang*) decamp. [Span.].

VAMP (1) [vamp], *n.* woman who seeks to attract men. VAMP (2), *v.t.* to seek to attract (a man) sexually. [~VAMPIRE].

VAMP (3), *n.* front portion of a shoe; patch on a shoe; improvised musical accompaniment. VAMP (4), *v.t. and i.* to patch (a shoe); do up (old material) to look like new; improvise a musical accompaniment. [OFr.].

VAMPIRE [vam'pīer], *n.* malignant spirit of a dead person supposed to bring the body out of its grave to suck the blood of the living; (fig.) unscrupulous extortioner; **v. bat,** a blood-sucking bat. VAM-PIRISM, *n.* belief in vampires; behaviour of a v. [Fr.].

VAN (1) [van], *n.* vanguard, *esp.* the front of an army in line of battle. [~VANGUARD].

VAN (2), *n.* covered cart or truck. [~CARAVAN].

VAN (3), *n.* (lawn tennis coll.) vantage.

VANADIUM [va-nā'di-um], *n.* metallic element denoted by V; **v. steel,** steel alloyed with v. [~OIcel.].

VANDAL [van'dal], *n.* one who destroys or spoils natural beauties or works of art, out of carelessness or deliberate spite. VANDALIC, VANDALISTIC [van-da'lik, van-da-lis'tik], *adj.* relating to a v. or the Vandals. VANDALISM, *n.* behaviour, spirit, of the Vandals; wanton destruction of beautiful things. [L. *Vandali,* Germanic race notorious for their destructive violence].

VANDYKE [van-dīk'], *n.* elaborately bordered lace collar; picture painted by Van Dyck; **v. beard,** a close-cut, pointed beard; **v. brown,** a rich brown pigment. [Van Dyck, Flemish painter].

VANE [vān], *n.* weathercock; one of the wings of a windmill or propeller. [OE.].

VANGUARD [van'gahd], *n.* advance guard. [Fr.].

VANILLA [va-ni'lah], *n.* tropical American plant from the pods of one species of which a flavouring substance is extracted; the flavouring itself. [~Span.].

VANISH [va'nish], *v.i.* to disappear suddenly and completely. VANISHING, *adj.* disappearing; **vanishing cream,** skin-cream which is absorbed soon after application. [~OFr.].

VANITY [va'ni-ti], *n.* uselessness, emptiness, worthlessness; conceit, self-pride; **v. bag,** small handbag for cosmetics etc. [L.].

VANNING [va'ning], *n.* winnowing, *esp.* the act of separating ore by shaking in a shovel.

VANQUISH [vang'kwish], *v.t.* to conquer; defeat completely. VANQUISHABLE, *adj.* that may be vanquished. [OFr. from L.].

VANTAGE [vahn'tij], *n.* state of having advantage in combat; place which overlooks another; (tennis) next point after deuce. VANTAGE-GROUND, a commanding or advantageous position, *esp.* in military operations. [~ADVANTAGE].

VAPID [va'pid], *adj.* flat, lifeless, stupidly insipid, empty-headed. [L.].

VAPORIZE [vā'pe-rīz], *v.t. and i.* to convert into vapour; become vapour. VAPORIZATION [vā-pe-rī-zā'shn], *n.* process of vaporizing; the formation of vapour. VAPORIZER, *n.* apparatus for converting substances into vapour or fine spray.

VAPOROUS [vā'pe-roōs], *adj.* like, consisting of or filled with, vapour.

VAPOUR (1) [vā'per], *n.* moisture suspended visibly in the air; the gas of a substance; (fig.) an empty imagining; (pl.) (archaic) hysterical fainting fits. VAPOUR-BATH, immersion of one's body in hot v.; place where this is done. VAPOUR (2), *v.i.* to spout windy nonsense. VAPOURER, *n.* a moth, the male of which has a distinctive quivering flight; (coll.) windy, pretentious talker. VAPOURING, *n.* windy, pretentious talk. VAPOURINGLY, *adv.* in a pretentiously windy fashion. VAPOURY, *adj.* full of vapours; (archaic) hypochondriac. [L.].

VAREC [va'rek], *n.* kelp. [Fr.].

VARIABLE (1) [vāer'i-a-bl], *adj.* able, liable, to vary; (math.) indeterminate. VARIABLE (2), *n.* an indeterminate number. [L.].

VARIANCE [vāer'i-ans], *n.* difference of opinion; an observed variation between two similar objects; discrepancy; discord between persons. [L.].

VARIANT (1) [vāer'i-ant], *adj.* varying, different from type. VARIANT (2), *n.* that which is v. [L.].

VARIATION [vāer-i-ā'shn], *n.* act or process of varying, a partial modification of qualities or form; state or form or quality consequent upon change, alteration; degree of change; (astron.) change in orbit, *esp.* of the moon in relation to the sun; (biol.) organic deviation from a norm; (naut.) declination of a magnetic needle from true North; (mus.) development and elaboration of a theme. VARIATIONAL, *adj.* of, or pertaining to, (biological) v. or variations. [OFr.].

VARICOSE [va'ri-kōs], *adj.* of, or affected by, abnormal swellings of the veins. [L.].

VARIED [vāer'id], *adj.* having variety, characterized by changes. [VARY].

VARIEGATE [vāer'i-gāt], *v.t.* to make parti-coloured.

VARIEGATED, *adj.* having various colours on one surface, parti-coloured. [~LL.].

VARIETY [va-rī'i-ti], *n.* state or quality characterized by many facets, aspects and diverse units, antonym of monotony; group of diverse elements or objects; something with distinguishing characteristics, one of a kind; an entertainment in the theatre composed of various short turns, vaudeville; (biol., bot.) subgroup distinguished from other members of a species only by various unimportant characteristic features. [L.].

VARIOLA [va-rī'ō-lah], *n.* (med.) smallpox. VARIOLAR, *adj.* (med.) relating to smallpox. [L.].

VARIOMETER [vāer-i-o'mi-ter], *n.* (radio) a variable inductance for adjusting a receiving set to different wavelengths. [VARIOUS and METER].

VARIORUM [vāer-i-aw'rum], *adj.* annotated by various experts. [L.].

VARIOUS [vāer'i-ōos], *adj.* characterized by diversity, different, varied; many, numerous, *esp.* unlike, of different kinds. VARIOUSLY, *adv.* by v. means. [L.].

VARLET † [vah'let], *n.* a page, knight's groom; rascal, low-class fellow. [OFr.].

VARMINT [vah'mint], *n.* (dial.) rascal. [~VERMIN].

VARNISH (1) [vah'nish], *n.* resinous, oily substance applied to surfaces to impart a protective gloss; (fig.) appearance of worth designed to conceal faults and flaws. VARNISH (2), *v.t.* to cover with v.; (fig.) hide defects by using brilliant externals or superficialities. [OFr.].

VARSITY [yah'si-ti], *n.* (coll.) university.

VARY [vāer'i], *v.t. and i.* to change, alter, modify, diversify; become different in condition or quality. [L.].

VASCULAR [vas'kyō-ler], *adj.* (biol., bot.) relating to or possessing a circulatory system. [~L.].

VASE [vahz], *n.* vessel used for holding liquid or as an ornament in the house. [L.].

VASELINE [va'se-lēn], *n.* (prot.) proprietary name for a preparation of petroleum jelly. [Germ. and L.].

VASSAL [va'sal], *n.* person kept in a state of subjection, slave; † tenant who has sworn fealty and homage to a feudal lord in return for a holding of land. VASSALAGE, *n.* subjection, servitude. [OFr. from MedL.].

VAST [vahst], *adj.* characterized by enormous size, height, breadth, bulk or by a great number; extremely important. VASTLY, *adv.* to a v. extent; extremely. [L.].

VAT [vat], *n.* large tub or storing vessel for liquids, *esp.* spirituous liquors. [OE.].

VATICAN [va'ti-kan], *n.* the Papal residence and an independent state within the boundaries of Rome ruled over by the Pope as a temporal sovereign. VATICANISM, *n.* theory of Papal infallibility, ultramontanism. VATICANIST, *n.* believer in Vaticanism. [L.].

VATICINATE [va-ti'si-nāt], *v.t. and i.* to prophesy. [L.].

VAUDEVILLE [vō'de-vil], *n.* mixed entertainment in a theatre, variety. [Fr.].

VAULT (1) [vawlt], *n.* an arched roof; chamber formed by the arched foundations of a building; strongly guarded and protected room used for the storage of money, valuables and bonds; underground cave; repository for the dead. VAULT (2), *v.t.* to equip with a v. VAULTAGE, *n.* space in a v. VAULTED, *adj.* built in the form of a v. VAULTY, *adj.* resembling a v. [LL.].

VAULT (3), *v.t. and i.* to leap by using one hand and arm as a support or by means of a pole. VAULT (4), *n.* act of vaulting. VAULTER, *n.* one who vaults. [OFr.].

VAUNT (1) [vawnt], *n.* a boast, ostentatious display. VAUNT (2), *v.t. and i.* to boast, flaunt. [OFr.].

V-BOMB [vē'bom], *n.* any of various robot projectiles, *esp.* a flying bomb or a rocket, employed by the Germans in the Second World War as "retaliation weapons." [Germ.].

VEAL [vēl], *n.* flesh of a calf prepared for eating. [OFr.].

VEDA [vā'dah], *n.* a collection of writings stating the fundamentals of Brahminism. VEDIC, *adj.* of or from the V. [Skr.].

VEER (1) [vēer], *v.t. and i.* (of wind) to change direction gradually; (of a ship) change course; (cause to) deviate from a course; (fig.) change one's opinions; vary. VEERING, *n.* process of shifting in the wind.

VEER (2), *v.t.* (naut.) to slacken and let run, pay out. [MDu.].

VEGETABLE (1) [ve'ji-ta-bl], *adj.* relating to,

composed of, derived from, plants or vegetables. **VEGETABLE** (2), *n.* a plant; (any part of) a plant cultivated as food. [LL.].

VEGETAL [ve'ji-tal], *adj.* relating to, resembling, a vegetable; (*physiol.*) relating to functional development. [L.].

VEGETARIAN (1) [ve-ji-tãer'i-an], *n.* person who lives on a vegetable diet or a diet excluding flesh. **VEGETARIAN** (2), *adj.* consisting of vegetables, made for a v.; relating to the principles of a v.

VEGETATE [ve'ji-tãt], *v.i.* to pass a passive existence like a plant. [~L.].

VEGETATION [ve-ji-tã'shn], *n.* process of vegetating; vegetable growth. [LL.].

VEGETATIVE [ve'ji-ta-tiv], *adj.* able to grow; (*fig.*) passive in mode of life. [MedL.].

VEHEMENCE [vē'i-mens], *n.* condition of being vehement or violent; urgency, ardour. [LL.].

VEHEMENT [vē'i-ment], *adj.* full of power, functioning forcefully, violent, ardent, urgent, passionate. [L.].

VEHICLE [vē'i-kl], *n.* any means of conveyance on wheels designed for the transport of persons or goods; a means or medium of communication; (*painting*) a medium for paint. **VEHICULAR**, **VEHICULATORY** [vē-hi'kyōō-lah(r), vē-hi-kyōō-la'te-ri], *adj.* of, relating to or resembling, a v. or vehicles. [L.].

VEIL (1) [vãl], *n.* piece of open-work or semi-transparent fabric offering partial concealment; decorative covering for a woman's face; (*fig.*) that which obscures; **to take the v.**, to enter a convent. **VEIL** (2), *v.t.* to cover with a v.; obscure. **VEILING**, *n.* material used for veils. [OFr.].

VEIN (1) [vãn], *n.* one of the main tubular channels of the circulatory system by which blood passes back to the heart and lungs; a blood-vessel in general; that which looks like a vein; (*bot.*) rib in a leaf; (*fig.*) distinctive trait, underlying quality characteristic of a person's temperament; mood, style; (*geol.*) seam of a mineral or minerals running through a rock; streak different in quality from surrounding matter. **VEIN** (2), *v.t.* to introduce veins into, mark with streaks like a v. **VEINED**, *adj.* having veins. **VEINING**, *n.* delicate form of needlework on muslin; veinlike marks, ornament or structure. **VEINLESS**, *adj.* without veins. **VEINOUS**, *adj.* relating to veins. **VEINY**, *adj.* full of veins. [OFr. from L.].

VELDT [felt], *n.* large stretch of wild open country in South Africa. [Du.].

VELETA [ve-lē'tah], *n.* kind of ballroom dance based on the waltz. [Invented].

VELLUM [ve'lum], *n.* skin, *esp.* of calves, specially prepared for use as writing material or bookbinding; a text written on this. [OFr.].

VELOCIPEDE † [ve-lo'si-pēd], *n.* (*hist.*) kind of wheeled vehicle propelled by the feet of the passenger, *esp.* an early form of bicycle. [L.].

VELOCITY [ve-lo'si-ti], *n.* rate of motion, speed, swiftness. [L.].

VELOUR (1) [ve-lōōr'], *n.* a heavy, velvet-like material; hat of this material. **VELOUR** (2), *adj.* made of v. [OFr.].

VELVET (1) [vel'vit], *n.* a heavy textile of silk, with sometimes a mixture of cotton, woven with a fine, soft nap on one side; **to be on v.**, to be in rich circumstances, fortunately situated; **v. glove**, apparent gentleness masking power. **VELVET** (2), *adj.* made of v. [OFr.].

VELVETEEN [vel-vi-tēn'], *n.* imitation velvet made with cotton.

VENAL [vē'nal], *adj.* impure of motive; open to bribery, mercenary. **VENALITY** [vē-na'li-ti], *n.* condition of being v., corruption. [L.].

VEND [vend], *v.t.* to sell. [L.].

VENDEE [ven-dē'], *n.* (*leg.*) recipient of an article sold. [*Prec.*].

VENDETTA [ven-de'tah], *n.* blood feud, *esp.* between Corsican families; (*fig.*) feud. [It.].

VENDOR [ven'der], *n.* person who offers for sale; (*leg.*) person who sells real estate. [VEND].

VENEER (1) [ve-nēer'], *v.t.* to apply a veneer to; (*fig.*) make appear superior to actual quality. **VENEER** (2), *n.* thin layer of expensive wood laid over furniture of cheaper material; (*fig.*) a characteristic or form concealing basic inferiority. **VENEERING**, *n.* process or craft of treating with a v.; product of such craft. [~Fr.].

VENERABLE [ve'ne-ra-bl], *adj.* worthy of respect, reverence or honour, *esp.* by virtue of age or religious associations. [L.].

VENERATE [ve'ne-rãt], *v.t.* to possess deep feelings of respect for, reverence; worship. [~L.].

VENERATION [ve-ne-rã'shn], *n.* act of venerating; profound respect. [L.].

VENEREAL [ve-nēer'i-al], *adj.* of, relating to, communicable by, sexual intercourse. [~L.].

VENETIAN (1) [ve-nē'shn], *n.* a native of Venice. **VENETIAN** (2), *adj.* made in, coming from or relating to, Venice; **V. blind**, window blind made of wooden slats. [MedL.].

VENGEANCE [ven'jans], *n.* act of exacting a painful retribution for having been wronged or harmed; **with a v.**, with very great thoroughness and energy. [OFr.].

VENGEFUL [venj'fōol], *adj.* governed by desire to revenge.

VENIABLE [vē'ni-a-bl], *adj.* not serious; pardonable.

VENIAL [vē'ni-al], *adj.* pardonable; not deserving of punishment. [L.].

VENISON [ven'zn], *n.* flesh of deer prepared for eating. [OFr.].

VENITE [ve-ni'ti], *n.* the ninety-fifth psalm. [L.].

VENOM [ve'num], *n.* poisonous secretion of snakes and insects transmitted in their sting; any poison; (*fig.*) vindictiveness, malice; harm. [OFr. from L.].

VENOMOUS [ve'nu-mōos], *adj.* poisonous; (*fig.*) malicious.

VENOUS [vē'nōos], *adj.* (*bot.*) characterized by veins; (*anat., physiol.*) pertaining to, contained in, the veins. [L.].

VENT (1) [vent], *n.* small opening which allows the escape of air, gas or liquid; hole, passage, outlet; act or process of an escape through such a means, emission, egress. **VENT** (2), *v.t. and i.* to allow to escape through a v.; release from a repressed state. [OFr. from L.].

VENT (3), *n.* a slit at the back of a coat. [Fr.].

VENTILATE [ven'ti-lãt], *v.t.* to provide with a free circulation of fresh air; fit with a ventilating system; (*fig.*) submit to free discussion, make public. [~L.].

VENTILATION [ven-ti-lã'shn], *n.* act or process of ventilating; system for ventilating. [L.].

VENTILATOR [ven'ti-lã-ter], *n.* apparatus for providing ventilation. [L.].

VENTRAL [ven'tral], *adj.* of, relating to, coming from, the belly. [L.].

VENTRICLE [ven'tri-kl], *n.* (*anat.*) small cavity, *esp.* one of the two cardiac chambers. [L.].

VENTRILOQUISM [ven-tri'lō-kwizm], *n.* art of disguising the voice so as to create an illusion of separate identity at a distance. **VENTRILOQUIST**, *n.* an expert in v. **VENTRILOQUIZE**, *v.t. and i.* to utter as a ventriloquist. [L.].

VENTURE (1) [ven'tyōor], *n.* undertaking, expedition or enterprise involving incalculable or definitely risky factors, a speculation in commerce; **at a v.**, at random, haphazardly. **VENTURE** (2), *v.t.* to expose to incalculable or dangerous elements, risk; presume (to express); *v.i.* to dare, run a risk. [OFr.].

VENTURESOME [ven'tyōor-sum], *adj.* daring, bold, taking risks; involving risk or hazard.

VENTUROUS [ven'tyōor-ōos], *adj.* venturesome.

VENUE [ve'nyōō], *n.* meeting place; (*leg.*) place to which a jury is summoned. [Fr.].

VENUS (*pl.* **Venuses**) [vē'nus], *n.* (*astron.*) the evening star, the major planet whose orbit is between the Earth and Mercury; (*myth.*) the goddess of love and beauty; (*coll.*) beautiful woman. [L.].

VERACIOUS [ve-rã'shōos], *adj.* given to telling the truth; relying on or reflecting truth. [~L.].

VERACITY [ve-ra'si-ti], *n.* habitual observance of truth, truthfulness.

VERANDA(H) [ve-ran'dah], *n.* covered-in space built alongside the wall of a house to which it gives access; ground-floor balcony. [Span.].

VERB [vurb], *n.* (*gram.*) part of speech which affirms mode of existence, or what a thing is or does, or how it reacts to external stimuli. [L.].

VERBAL [vur'bal], *adj.* relating to, consisting of, words; limited to words; literal, word for word; (*pop.*) not written, oral; (*gram.*) relating to, derived from, a verb. **VERBALLY**, *adv.* in v. form; (*pop.*) orally. [LL.].

VERBATIM [ver-bã'tim], *adj. and adv.* word for word. [L.].

VERBENA [ver-bē'nah], *n.* (*bot.*) genus of plants comprising the vervains. [L.].

VERBERATION [ver-be-rã'shn], *n.* act of beating so as to cause noise. [L.].

VERBIAGE [vur'bi-ij], *n.* use of superfluous words, verbosity. [Fr.].

ōō is pronounced as in food; ŏŏ as in hood; th as in *think*; TH as in *that*; zh as in azure.   ~ = related to.

VERBOSE [ver-bōs'], *adj.* characterized by super-fluous words, talkative; loquacious, prolix. [L.].
VERBOSITY [ver-bo'si-ti], *n.* quality or condition of being verbose.
VERDANCY [vur'dan-si], *n.* quality of being green; *(fig.)* immaturity, innocence. [*Next*].
VERDANT [vur'dant], *adj.* green, like new grass; covered with vegetation; *(fig.)* immature; innocent. VERDANTLY, *adv.* with verdancy. [L.].
VERD-ANTIQUE [verd-an-tēk'], *n.* green incrustation due to prolonged action of air, *esp.* on bronze; marble mottled with green. [Fr.].
VERDERER † [vur'de-rer], *n.* a forester. [AFr.].
VERDICT [vur'dikt], *n.* (*leg.*) jury's decision in any tried cause; judgment, decision, opinion. [OFr. from L.].
VERDIGRIS [vur'di-grēs], *n.* green incrustation forming on copper exposed to air; (*chem.*) acetate of copper used in manufacturing pigment or dyes. [OFr.].
VERDITER [vur'di-ter], *n.* pigment of copper carbonate of blue or green. [OFr.].
VERDURE [vur'dyōor], *n.* green vegetation, new grass. [Fr.].
VERGE (1) [vurj], *n.* margin, edge, brink; (*leg.*) extent of jurisdiction of the King's Court. VERGE (2), *v.i.* to move or incline in a specific direction; **to v. on**, *(fig.)* to tend towards, approach the condition of. [L.].
VERGER [vur'jer], *n.* ecclesiastical official bearing a mace before higher church functionaries; church official. [OFr.].
VERIFIABLE [ve'ri-fī-a-bl], *adj.* capable of being verified.
VERIFICATION [ve-ri-fi-kā'shn], *n.* act of verifying; process of proving authentic.
VERIFY [ve'ri-fī], *v.t.* to prove authentic, show to be true, confirm. [L.].
VERILY [ve'ri-li], *adv.* (*archaic*) truly, really. [VERY].
VERISIMILITUDE [ve-ri-si-mi'li-tyōōd], *n.* appear-ance of truth, probability. [L.].
VERITABLE [ve'ri-ta-bl], *adj.* true, actual. [OFr.].
VERITY [ve'ri-ti], *n.* quality of being true; assertion or proposition to be taken as true. [L.!.
VERJUICE [vur'jōōs], *n.* sour liquid obtained from unripe grapes or crab-apples. [OFr.].
VERMEIL (1) [vur'mil], *adj.* (*poet.*) bright red in colour. VERMEIL (2), *n.* bright red, as a garnet.
VERMI-, *pref.* worm. [L.].
VERMICELLI [ver-mi-se'li, ver-mi-che'li], *n.* thin macaroni. [It.].
VERMICIDE [vur'mi-sīd], *n.* preparation for destroy-ing worms; (*med.*) medicine for killing internal worms. [VERMI- and L.].
VERMIFORM [vur'mi-fawm], *adj.* having the form of a worm or worms. [VERMI- and FORM].
VERMIFUGE [vur'mi-fyōōj], *n.* (*med.*) substance for purging the body of worms. VERMIFUGAL [ver-mi-fyōō'gal], *adj.* relating to, composed of v. [VERMI- and L.].
VERMILION (1) [ver-mil'yun], *n.* brilliant red pig-ment composed chiefly of red sulphide of mercury; the colour of this. VERMILION (2), *adj.* having the colour of or made of v. [OFr.].
VERMIN [vur'min], *n.* animals harmful to game or domestically destructive; insects which thrive in dirty conditions; *(fig.)* people contemptible for parasitism or filth. VERMINOUS, *adj.* infested by, resembling, caused by, v.; filthy, disgusting. [L.].
VERMOUTH [vāer'mōōt, vur'mōōth], *n.* aromatic liquor made from white wine flavoured with worm-wood. [Fr. from OHGerm.].
VERNACULAR (1) [ver-na'kyōō-ler], *adj.* spoken by the people native to a locality; written in dialect. VERNACULAR (2), *n.* the language native to a country or part of a country; language of the common people. [~L.].
VERNAL [vur'nal], *adj.* belonging to, appearing in, resembling, the spring; fresh; **v. equinox**, the equinox occurring in March. [L.].
VERNIER [vur'ni-er], *n.* graduated sliding-scale for calculating subdivisions in measuring etc.; supple-mentary device to provide a fine adjustment. [P. *Vernier*, the French inventor].
VERONAL [ve'ro-nal], *n.* (*prot.*) a soporific drug. [Germ.].
VERONICA [ve-ro'ni-kah], *n.* (*bot.*) a numerous genus of plants including the speedwell. [St. *Veronica*].
VERSATILE [vur'sa-tīl], *adj.* having many gifts or talents with a facility to turn quickly from one to another. [L.].

VERSATILITY [ver-sa-ti'li-ti], *n.* quality of being versatile; aptness at many subjects or tasks.
VERSE [vurs], *n.* a line of words whose metrical or numerical accents are arranged according to the rules of prosody; the technical basis for poetry; a number of such lines considered as a unit of poetic form; stanza of a poem, piece of poetry; matter written in metre but lacking poetic quality; **free v.**, vers libre. [L.].
VERSED [vurst], *adj.* having an extensive knowledge of; skilled, trained. [MdL.].
VERSICLE [vur'si-kl], *n.* short verse, *esp.* one intoned in church. [L.].
VERSIFICATION [ver-si-fi-kā'shn], *n.* act or art of composing verse. [L.].
VERSIFY [vur'si-fī], *v.t. and i.* to put into the form of verse; compose metrical but unpoetical works. [L.].
VERSION [vur'shn], *n.* a translation from one lan-guage into another; a particular arrangement of some-thing expressed in an artistic medium; a definite account, description or statement of facts. [L.].
VERS LIBRE [vāer-lēbr'], *n.* free verse, verse com-posed in free rhythm not subject to metrical rules. [Fr.].
VERSO [vur'sō], *n.* left-hand page; reverse side of a coin or folio. [L.].
VERSUS [vur'sus], *prep.* against. [L.].
VERTEBRA (*pl.* **vertebrae**) [vur'ti-brah], *n.* (*anat.*) a spinal joint; (*pl.*) the backbone. VERTEBRAL, *adj.* of, relating to, placed by or coming from, the spine. [L.].
VERTEBRATE (1) [vur'ti-brāt], *adj.* having a back-bone. VERTEBRATE (2), *n.* animal with a backbone. [L.].
VERTEX (*pl.* **vertices**) [vur'teks], *n.* the highest point; (*anat.*) crown of the head; (*astron.*) zenith; (*geom.*) angle opposite a given side of a figure; **v. of a curve**, point where the diameter meets the curve. [L.].
VERTICAL [vur'ti-kal], *adj.* relating to, placed at, the vertex; pointing to the zenith, placed in a position or moving in a direction at right angles to the surface of the earth; perpendicular, upright. [~*Prec.*].
VERTIGINOUS [ver-ti'ji-nŏŏs], *adj.* whirling; suffering from, inducing, vertigo. [*Next*].
VERTIGO [vur'ti-gō, ver-tī'gō], *n.* giddiness, faint-ness, *esp.* when due to disturbance of balance etc. [L.].
VERTU, see VIRTU.
VERVAIN [vur'vān], *n.* plant of the genus *Verbena*, *esp. Verbena officinalis*, formerly prized for its medicinal properties. [~L.].
VERVE [vurv], *n.* imaginative dash, aesthetic gusto, quality producing a tasteful flourish, liveliness. [Fr.].
VERY (1) [ve'ri], *adj.* true, veritable; requisite. VERY (2), *adv.* in a great degree, to a great extent; abso-lutely. [OFr. from L.].
VERY LIGHT [ve'ri-līt], *n.* kind of flare, fired from a pistol, for signalling or temporary illumination. [*Very*, inventor].
VESICLE [ve'si-kl], *n.* little bladder; blister. [L.].
VESPER [ves'per], *n.* the evening star; (*pl.*) (*eccles.*) evensong. VESPERTINE, *n.* pertaining to or occurring in the evening. [L.].
VESSEL [ve'sel], *n.* hollow utensil, *esp.* for containing liquids; ship; (*anat., zool., bot.*) tube or duct; (*fig.*) a person, *esp.* when regarded as possessing some special quality. [OFr. from L.].
VEST (1) [vest], *n.* garment worn round the torso, *esp.* next to the skin; (*coll.*) waistcoat. VEST-POCKET, *adj.* small enough to be carried in the pocket of a waist-coat. VEST (2), *v.t.* to clothe with, invest; endow. VESTED, *adj.* invested, clothed (with), endowed; established and hard to displace. VESTING, *n.* act of legally endowing, or establishing in possession. [L.].
VESTA [ves'tah], *n.* (*myth.*) Roman goddess of the household; kind of match. [L.].
VESTAL [ves'tal], *adj.* relating, consecrated, to Vesta; holy, chaste, virginal. [L.].
VESTIBULE [ves'ti-byōōl], *n.* porch, entrance hall, of a building. [L.].
VESTIGE [ves'tij], *n.* trace, sign, remnant. [L.].
VESTMENT [vest'ment], *n.* garment, *esp.* a cere-monial garment. [L.].
VESTRY [ves'tri], *n.* part of a church where the vest-ments are kept and donned; general assembly of the ratepayers of a parish. VESTRYMAN, *n.* member of a v. [L.].
VESTURE [ves'tyōor], *n.* clothing. [OFr.].

VET (1) [vet], *n.* (*coll.*) veterinary surgeon. **VET** (2) (*pres.pt.* VETTING, *pret. and p.pt.* VETTED), *v.t.* (*coll.*) to examine medically; (*fig.*) revise, check critically. [VET(ERINARY)].

VETCH, FITCH [vech, fich], *n.* a common leguminous plant. [OFr. from L.].

VETERAN (1) [ve'te-ran], *n.* experienced person; old soldier. **VETERAN** (2), *adj.* experienced in a service. [L.].

VETERINARY [ve'te-ri-na-ri], *adj.* relating to the study and treatment of sickness in animals. [L.].

VETO (1) [vē'tō], *n.* an absolute prohibition, *esp.* a constitutional right so to prohibit. **VETO** (2), *v.t.* to prohibit absolutely. [L.].

VEX [veks], *v.i.* to irritate, annoy, stir to mild anger; harass. **VEXED**, *adj.* bitterly contested; causing much vexation. [L.].

VEXATION [vek-sā'shn], *n.* act of vexing; condition of being vexed. [L.].

VEXATIOUS [vek-sā'shŏŏs], *adj.* vexing, tending to vex; (*leg.*) done or brought in order to vex or harass. [L.].

VIA [vī'ah], *prep.* by way of. [L.].

VIABLE [vī'a-bl], *adj.* capable of remaining alive in a particular environment. [Fr.].

VIADUCT [vī'a-dukt], *n.* bridge in the form of a series of arches, crossing a road or ravine, *esp.* if bearing a railway. [L.].

VIAL [vī'al], *n.* small vessel; small bottle containing drugs etc. [OFr. from Gk.].

VIANDS [vī'andz], *n.*(*pl.*) food, cooked meat. [Fr.].

VIATICUM [vī-a'ti-kum], *n.* (*R.C.*) communion administered to one on the point of death. [L.].

VIBRANT [vī'brant], *adj.* vibrating, resonant. [L.].

VIBRATE [vī-brāt'], *v.t. and i.* to quiver rapidly, oscillate; swing on an axis; cause to quiver. VIBRA-TOR, *n.* that which vibrates; instrument having a vibratory action; vibrating reed in an organ. [L.].

VIBRATION [vī-brā'shn], *n.* state of vibrating, extent to which a thing vibrates; oscillation. [L.].

VIBRATO [vī-brah'tō], *n.* (*mus.*) tremulousness. [It.].

VICAR [vī'ker], *n.* deputy; incumbent of a parish who is not entitled to great tithes. VICAR-GENERAL, (*R.C.*) assistant, usually the chancellor, to a bishop or archbishop in ecclesiastical trials etc.; principal deputy of a bishop. VICARIAL [vī-, vī-kāer'i-al], *adj.* relating to a v.; vicarious. [L.].

VICARAGE [vī'ka-rij], *n.* official residence of a vicar.

VICARIOUS [vī-, vī-kāer'i-ŏŏs], *adj.* relating to a vicar; serving as a substitute; performed on behalf of another. [L.].

VICE (1) [vīs], *n.* moral weakness, *esp.* when translated into action, immoral behaviour; defect. [L.].

VICE (2), *n.* mechanical device for gripping an object, tool for holding tightly by pressure on either side; **hand v.**, small v. fitted with a handle. [OFr. from L.].

VICE (3) [vī'si], *prep.* in the place of. [L.].

VICE-, *pref.* in place of, acting on behalf of (another). [L.].

VICE-ADMIRAL [vīs-ad'mi-ral], *n.* one next in rank below a full admiral.

VICE-CHANCELLOR [vīs-chahn'se-ler], *n.* one next in rank below a chancellor; official in charge of the administration of an English university.

VICE-PRESIDENT [vīs-pre'zi-dent], *n.* deputy of a president; subsidiary president.

VICE-CONSUL [vīs-kon'sul], *n.* subordinate consul.

VICEGERENT [vīs-je'rent], *n.* deputy entrusted with full powers. [VICE- and L.].

VICEREGAL [vīs-rē'gal], *adj.* pertaining to a viceroy.

VICE-REGENT [vīs-rē'jent], *n.* deputy of a regent.

VICEREINE [vīs'rān], *n.* wife or consort of a viceroy. [VICE- and Fr.].

VICEROY [vīs'roi], *n.* deputy ruling a country in the name of his sovereign. [VICE- and Fr.].

VICE VERSA [vī-si-vur'sah], *adv.* with the roles or relationships interchanged; conversely. [L.].

VICINITY [vi-si'ni-ti], *n.* neighbourhood; state of being near. [L.].

VICIOUS [vī'shŏŏs], *adj.* performing, tending to or relating to, vice; malevolent; (*coll.*) (of a dog etc.) dangerous; **v. circle**, argument which begs the question; reciprocal aggravation. [AFr.].

VICISSITUDE [vī-si'si-tyŏŏd], *n.* alteration in affairs, *esp.* one of several changes of fortune. [L.].

VICTIM [vik'tim], *n.* living creature offered as a religious sacrifice; person or animal sacrificed for the sake of another; person suffering through the action of another, or of some natural agency, or through some uncontrollable quality in himself. [L.].

VICTIMIZE [vik'ti-mīz], *v.t.* to make into a victim; cause to suffer for one's own ends; penalize. [*Prec.*].

VICTOR [vik'ter], *n.* conqueror. [L.].

VICTORIA [vik-taw'ri-ah], *n.* light, two-seater, horse-drawn carriage, with a driver's box and a hood. [Queen *Victoria*].

VICTORIAN (1) [vik-taw'ri-an], *adj.* relating to Queen Victoria, her reign and the manners etc. of her period; old-fashioned, prudish. VICTORIAN (2), *n.* person living in the reign of Queen Victoria. [Queen *Victoria*].

VICTORIOUS [vik-taw'ri-ŏŏs], *adj.* having gained the victory; relating to victory. [L.].

VICTORY [vik'te-ri], *n.* conquest gained over another, *esp.* a conquest made by battle; success gained over anything. [L.].

VICTUAL [vi'tal], *v.t.* to supply with provisions. VICTUALLER, *n.* one who victuals; innkeeper. [L.].

VICTUALS [vi'talz], *n.*(*pl.*) food. [L.].

VIDE [vī'di], *v. imper.* look at, refer to. [L.].

VIDELICET [vi-dē'li-set], *adv.* namely. [L.].

VIDEO [vi'di-ō], *n.* (*U.S.*) television. [L.].

VIE [vī], *v.i.* to strive, compete. [OFr.].

VIEW (1) [vyŏŏ], *n.* act of seeing; that which is seen; a natural prospect; the extent or amount of a thing which can be seen; clarity with which a thing is seen; opinion, considered impression. VIEW-FINDER, (*phot.*) attachment through which the object or scene to be photographed is sighted. VIEW (2), *v.t.* to look at, observe, inspect, examine; consider, regard, contemplate. VIEWER, *n.* one who views or examines; apparatus to assist viewing; one who watches television broadcasts. VIEWLESS, *adj.* without a v.; from which no prospect is visible; invisible. [OFr.].

VIEWPOINT [vyŏŏ'point], *n.* point of view; vantage point for observation.

VIGIL [vi'jil], *n.* state of being awake, action of watching; night spent in voluntary wakefulness for religious reasons. [L.].

VIGILANCE [vi'ji-lans], *n.* state of being vigilant; **v. committee**, committee to keep order in unsettled country, or to watch and report on the moral behaviour of a local population. [L.].

VIGILANT [vi'ji-lant], *adj.* keenly watchful; suspiciously on guard; unsleepingly alert. [L.].

VIGILANTE [vi-ji-lan'ti], *n.* member of a vigilance committee. [Span.].

VIGNETTE (1) [vin-yet'], *n.* small ornamental engraving at the head or foot of a page; inset book illustration; picture whose edges merge into the background; short word-picture. VIGNETTE (2), *v.t.* to convert into a v. [Fr.].

VIGOROUS [vi'ge-rŏŏs], *adj.* possessing, displaying, vigour; potent; forceful; in full possession of the physical powers. [L.].

VIGOUR [vi'ger], *n.* physical strength, potency, animal energy, vitality, force. [OFr. from L.].

VIKING [vī'king, vī'king], *n.* Norse sea-rover. [OScand.].

VILAYET [vi-lah'yet], *n.* Turkish province. [Turk.].

VILE [vīl], *adj.* base, depraved, worthless, morally filthy. [L.].

VILIFY [vi'li-fī], *v.t.* to slander, speak ill of, represent as vile. [L.].

VILLA [vi'lah], *n.* large country house in its own estate, *esp.* in Italy; (*coll.*) small suburban house. VILLADOM, *n.* suburbia. [L.].

VILLAGE [vi'lij], *n.* small community in a rural district; collection of houses etc. less than a town. VILLAGERY, *n.* villages in one district. [OFr.].

VILLAIN [vi'lan], *n.* wicked person, actively vicious and depraved person, thorough scoundrel.

VILLAINY [vi'la-ni], *n.* act, behaviour, of a v.; wicked piece of work. [OFr. from LL.].

VILLAINOUS [vi'la-nŏŏs], *adj.* wicked, having the qualities of a villain; ill-done, wholly bad.

VILLANAGE, see VILLENAGE.

VILLANELLE [vi-la-nel'], *n.* elaborate form of poem of nineteen lines rhyming on two sounds. [Fr.].

VILLEIN [vi'lan], *n.* (*hist.*) medieval serf bound to the soil. VILLENAGE, VILLANAGE, *n.* position or state of being a v. [~VILLAIN].

VIM [vim], *n.* (*coll.*) vigorous energy. [L.].

VINAIGRETTE [vi-nā-gret'], *n.* metal smelling-box or bottle, usually containing a sponge soaked in vinegar. [Fr.].

VINDICABLE [vin'di-ka-bl], *adj.* capable of being vindicated. [LL.].

VINDICATE [vin'di-kāt], *v.t.* to validate, justify, prove just or correct, defend successfully. [~L.].

ŏŏ is pronounced as in food; ŏŏ as in hood; th as in *th*ink; TH as in *th*at; zh as in azure.   ～ = related to.

VINDICATION [vin-di-kā′shn], *n.* act of vindicating; fact or circumstance which vindicates.

VINDICTIVE [vin-dik′tiv], *adj.* revengeful. [L.].

VINE [vīn], *n.* a climbing plant which bears grapes; any creeping stem resembling this. VINERY, *n.* glasshouse for the cultivation of vines. [L.].

VINEGAR [vi′ni-ger], *n.* acid liquid used as a condiment, made originally from fermented wine. [OFr.].

VINEYARD [vin′yerd], *n.* a plantation of grapevines.

VINGT-ET-UN [va(ng)t-ā-ur(ng)′], *n.* card-game in which the object is to get cards whose pips add up to twenty-one, also called pontoon. [Fr.].

VINICULTURE [vī′ni-kul-tyōōr], *n.* cultivation of vines.

VIN-ORDINAIRE [va(ng)-aw-di-nāer′], *n.* cheap draught wine supplied in French restaurants. [Fr.].

VINOUS [vī′nŏŏs], *adj.* like, relating to, characteristic of, wine; drunk with wine. [L.].

VINTAGE (1) [vin′tij], *n.* grape gathering, the time of grape gathering; wine (especially of good quality) made from the grapes of a specific year. VINTAGE (2), *adj.* (*coll.*) of good quality, of a particular v. VINTAGE (3), *v.t.* to gather (grapes) for wine; make wine. VINTAGER, *n.* one who gathers the v. grapes. [OFr.].

VINTNER [vint′ner], *n.* wine merchant. [OFr.].

VIOL †[vī′ol], *n.* a stringed musical instrument with flat back and fretted finger-board, a forerunner of the modern violin; the viola da gamba. [Fr.]

VIOLA (1) [vi-ō′lah], *n.* tenor violin. VIOLA DA GAMBA, the bass viol, corresponding with the modern violoncello. [It.]

VIOLA (2) [vī′ō-lah], *n.* (*bot.*) a numerous genus of flowering plants, including the pansy. [L.].

VIOLATE [vī′ō-lāt], *v.t.* to treat with violence; break rudely into a forbidden place, blaspheme against; rape. [∼L.].

VIOLATION [vī-ō-lā′shn], *n.* act of violating; state of being violated. [L.].

VIOLENCE [vī′ō-lens], *n.* vigorously forceful action; vehement energy; brutal force, violation, unlawfully vigorous action; assault. [L.].

VIOLENT [vī′ō-lent], *adj.* using, displaying violence; with great strength and vigour; impetuously forcible; very rough. [L.].

VIOLET (1) [vī′ō-let], *n.* mauve or white flower of the genus *Viola*; bluish-purple colour characteristic of this flower. VIOLET (2), *adj.* bluish-purple; coloured like the v. [Fr.].

VIOLIN [vī-ō-lin′], *n.* stringed musical instrument played with a bow; fiddle. [It.].

VIOLINIST [vī-ō-li′nist], *n.* one who plays the violin.

VIOLIST [vī′ō-list, vī-ō′list], *n.* one who plays the viola or viol.

VIOLONCELLO [vī-, vē-o-lon-che′lō], *n.* bass instrument similar in shape and principle to the violin. [It.].

VIPER [vī′per], *n.* a poisonous snake, the adder; (*fig.*) malicious or treacherous person. VIPERINE, *adj.* like a v.; relating to vipers. VIPEROUS, *adj.* having the qualities of a v.; evil, poisonous. [L.].

VIRAGO [vi-rā′gō], *n.* a violent, fierce, vixenish woman. [L.].

VIRESCENT [vi-re′sent], *adj.* turning, beginning to be, green. VIRESCENCE, *n.* state of being v. [L.].

VIRGIN (1) [vur′jin], *n.* woman without carnal knowledge of a man; person who has never had sexual experience; **the V.**, the V. Mary; the constellation Virgo. VIRGIN (2), *adj.* chaste; untouched; relating to, characteristic of, a v. VIRGINHOOD, *n.* state of being a v. [OFr. from L.].

VIRGINAL (1) [vur′ji-nal], *n.* (*often pl.*) small musical instrument of the 16th and 17th centuries played by means of a keyboard; *also* **a pair of virginals.** [*Next*].

VIRGINAL (2), *adj.* virgin; relating to a virgin. [L.].

VIRGINIA [ver-ji′ni-ah], *n.* an American tobacco grown in V.; **V. creeper,** (*bot.*) a climbing plant. [The *Virgin* Queen, Elizabeth I].

VIRGINITY [ver-ji′ni-ti], *n.* the physical and moral state of being a virgin; maidenhood, the maidenhead. [L.].

VIRGO [vur′gō], *n.* a constellation between Leo and Libra, the Virgin; sixth sign of the Zodiac. [L.].

VIRILE [vi′ril], *adj.* relating to virility, sexually potent; male; strong and vigorous. [L.].

VIRILITY [vi-ri′li-ti], *n.* potency; masculinity; male vigour. [L.].

VIRTU, VERTU [ver′-, vair′tyōō], *n.* love of the aesthetically exquisite; a combination of rarity, antiquity and artistic merit. [It.].

VIRTUAL [vur′tyōō-al], *adj.* to all intents and purposes. VIRTUALLY, *adv.* in effect, practically. [Fr.].

VIRTUE [vur′tyōō], *n.* quality of being morally good and upright; any particular moral excellence; the inward power or merit of a thing; the moral and psychological strength of a person; sexual continence, chastity; the quality of a thing by which it produces effects; **by v. of,** through, because of, by the power or authority of. [OFr. from L.].

VIRTUOSITY [ver-tyōō-o′si-ti], *n.* great practical skill in a fine art. [*Next*].

VIRTUOSO (*pl.* **virtuosi**) [ver-tyōō-ō′sō], *n.* one highly skilled and knowledgeable in a fine art. [It.].

VIRTUOUS [vur′tyōō-ŏŏs], *adj.* practising moral virtues; chaste. [L.].

VIRULENCE [vi′ryōō-lens], *n.* quality of being virulent.

VIRULENT [vi′ryōō-lent], *adj.* highly poisonous; bitterly malignant. [L.].

VIRUS [vīer′us], *n.* poison; (*path.*) a noxious substance, capable of passing through a porcelain filter, giving rise to infectious diseases. [L.].

VISA (1) [vē′zah], *n.* endorsement on a passport permitting the holder to enter certain territories. VISA (2), *v.t.* to stamp a v. on (a passport).

VISAGE [vi′zij], *n.* the human face, countenance, expression of a face. [Fr.].

VIS-A-VIS (1) [vēz-ah-vē′], *n.* person opposite another; opposite number. VIS-A-VIS (2), *adv.* face to face, opposite each other. VIS-A-VIS (3), *prep.* in relation to, in comparison with. [Fr.].

VISCERA [vi′se-rah], *n.*(*pl.*) the intestines and other internal organs including liver, lungs, heart etc. [L.].

VISCID [vi′sid], *adj.* slimy and sticky. [L.].

VISCOSE [vis′kōs], *n.* a viscous solution of cellulose used in making artificial silk. [∼L.].

VISCOSITY [vis-ko′si-ti], *n.* state of being viscous; (*phys.*) internal friction of fluids. [OFr. from L.].

VISCOUNT [vī′kownt], *n.* rank of nobility next above a baron; eldest son of an earl. VISCOUNTCY, VISCOUNTSHIP, VISCOUNTY, *n.* rank and position of a v. [OFr.].

VISCOUS [vis′kŏŏs], *adj.* slimily glutinous. [L.].

VISE, visé [vē′zā], *n. and v.t.* (*U.S.*) (a) visa. [Fr.].

VISIBILITY [vi-zi-bi′li-ti], *n.* state of the atmosphere in relation to the clarity with which objects are visible; state or quality of being visible.

VISIBLE [vi′zi-bl], *adj.* able to be seen; apparent to the eye. VISIBLY, *adv.* perceptibly to the eye. [L.].

VISIGOTHS [vi′zi-goths], *n.*(*pl.*) (*hist.*) branch of the Gothic invaders who settled in South Western Europe. [LL.].

VISION [vi′zhn], *n.* quality by which one perceives with the eyes; that which is so perceived; power of sight; imaginative perception; intuition; that which is clearly visualized without sensory aid; a supernatural appearance. VISIONAL, *adj.* pertaining to a v. [L.].

VISIONARY (1) [vi′zhn-a-ri], *adj.* relating to a vision; subsisting only in impracticable imagination; wildly idealistic, immune from the ordinary realities. VISIONARY (2), *n.* one who experiences visions; idealistic dreamer.

VISIT (1) [vi′zit], *v.t. and i.* to make a call on; go to see for a special reason; inspect; make visits. VISIT (2), *n.* act of visiting; temporary stay in a place; brief call; inspection. VISITANT, *n.* one who visits. [L.].

VISITATION [vi-zi-tā′shn], *n.* act of visiting; special visit of inspection by a superior; message or messenger of God, *esp.* in the form of a natural catastrophe; visit which the visited find unpleasant. [L.].

VISITATORIAL [vi-zi-ta-tawr′ri-al], *adj.* relating to an official visit or visitor.

VISITING (1) [vi′zi-ting], *n.* act of paying a visit; **v. card,** small rectangle of pasteboard on which one's name etc. is printed, left as an indication that one has paid a call. VISITING (2), *adj.* authorized to inspect.

VISITOR [vi′zi-ter], *n.* one who visits; official who pays visits of inspection; patron; one who takes up a temporary sojourn in a place. [Fr.].

VISOR, VIZOR [vi′zer], *n.* movable front piece of a helmet covering the face. [AFr.].

VISTA [vis′tah], *n.* prospect down an avenue; mental prospect surveying a long period of time or a long series of events. [It.].

VISUAL [vi′zhyōō-al], *adj.* relating to the sight; perceived by the eyes. [L.].

The accent ′ after a syllable = stress (u-pon′).   The mark ⁻ over a vowel = length (ā in made; ō in bone).

VISUALIZE [vi'zhyōō-a-līz], *v.t. and i.* to imagine visually; picture.

VITAL [vī'tal], *adj.* having life, relating to life; actively alive and vigorous; all-important, urgent, essential. VITALLY, *adv.* so as to be v.; essentially. [L.].

VITALISM [vī'ta-lizm], *n.* a theory based upon the belief in a vital principle. VITALIST, *n.* one who believes in v.

VITALITY [vī-ta'li-ti], *n.* vital force and vigour. [L.].

VITALIZE [vī'ta-līz], *v.t.* to impart life to; animate; make vital and vigorous.

VITALS [vī'talz], *n.(pl.)* the essential organs. [VITAL].

VITAMIN [vī'ta-min, vi'ta-min], *n.* one of several chemical substances found in certain foods, and essential to life and health. VITAMINIZE, *v.t.* to add vitamins to. [~L.].

VITIATE [vī'shi-āt], *v.t.* to impair, render ineffective; sully; weaken or destroy the effect of. [~L.].

VITICULTURE [vī'ti-kul-tyōōr], *n.* culture of the grape-vine. [L. and CULTURE].

VITREOUS [vī'tri-ŏos], *adj.* relating to, resembling, consisting of, glass. [L.].

VITRESCENCE [vi-tre'sens], *n.* quality of being glassy. [L.].

VITRIFACTION, VITRIFICATION [vi-tri-fak'-shn, vi-tri-fi-kā'shn], *n.* act, process or operation of converting into glass by heat; state of being vitrified. [L.].

VITRIFY [vī'tri-fī], *v.t. and i.* to convert into glass by subjecting to heat and fusion; become glass in form. VITRIFIABLE, *adj.* capable of being vitrified. VITRIFIED, *adj.* converted into glass. [Fr.].

VITRIOL [vī'tri-ol], *n.* (*chem.*) (a salt of) sulphuric acid; **blue v.**, copper sulphate; **green v.**, ferrous sulphate; **oil of v.**, sulphuric acid. VITRIOLIC [vi-tri-o'lik], *adj.* relating to, containing, having the qualities of, v.; obtained from v.; (*fig.*) violently penetrative, biting. VITRIOLIZE [vi'tri-ō-līz], *v.t.* to treat with, or change into, v. [L.].

VITUPERATE [vī-tyōō'pe-rāt], *v.t.* to blame abusively, scold violently. [~L.].

VITUPERATION [vī-tyōō-pe-rā'shn], *n.* act of vituperating, blame, abuse.

VITUPERATIVE [vī-tyōō'pe-ra-tiv], *adj.* having a scolding nature, uttering or containing abuse. VITUPERATIVELY, *adv.* in a v. manner. [VITUPERATE].

VIVA [vī'vah], *n.* (*coll.*) viva voce examination. [VIVA (VOCE)].

VIVACE [vi-vah'chã], *adv.* (*mus.*) in a lively manner. [It.].

VIVACIOUS [vi-vā'shŏos], *adj.* having animated manners and a natural liveliness in society; having great vitality. [~L.].

VIVACITY [vi-va'si-ti], *n.* an inherent quality of temperament characterized by an animated and energetic style of expression in speech and carriage, high spirits. [L.].

VIVARIUM (*pl.* **vivaria**) [vī-vāer'i-um], *n.* place for keeping live animals under natural conditions. [L.].

VIVA VOCE (1) [vi-vah-vō'si], *adv.* orally. VIVA VOCE (2), *adj.* oral. VIVA VOCE (3), *n.* (*coll.*) an oral examination. [L.].

VIVID [vi'vid], *adj.* having form, colour or characteristics brought out strongly, having an intense brilliance; reproducing in brilliant, lifelike images or form; painted in bright colours. VIVIDLY, *adv.* in a v. manner; (of a narrative) realistically. [L.].

VIVIFICATION [vi-vi-fi-kā'shn], *n.* act of vivifying, restoration. [L.].

VIVIFY [vī'vi-fī], *v.t.* to endue with life, revive, quicken. [Fr.].

VIVIPAROUS [vī-, vi-vi'pa-rŏos], *adj.* giving birth to young in a living state, as opposed to *oviparous.* [L.].

VIVISECT [vi-vi-sekt'], *v.t. and i.* to practise vivisection. [L.].

VIVISECTION [vi-vi-sek'shn], *n.* technique or act of operating or experimenting on live creatures for scientific purposes. VIVISECTIONIST, *n.* one who practises or advocates v. [L.].

VIXEN [vik'sen], *n.* female fox; maliciously quarrelsome woman, shrew. [OE.].

VIXENISH [vik'se-nish], *adj.* like a vixen.

VIZ [viz], *adv.* that is; namely. [~VIDELICET].

VIZARD [vi'zerd], *n.* (*archaic*) mask. [~VISOR].

VIZIER [vi-zēer'], *n.* administrative official of high rank in Mohammedan countries, *esp.* Turkey; † **Grand V.**, Turkish Prime Minister. [~Arab.].

VIZOR, see VISOR.

VLACH [vlakh], *n. and adj.* member of, pertaining to, a Romance-speaking people of Rumanian origin now in various parts of south-eastern Europe. [Serbian].

VOCABLE [vō'ka-bl], *n.* word, term. [L.].

VOCABULARY [vō-ka'byōō-la-ri], *n.* glossary of lingual or technical terms, *esp.* as appended to a text; the total number of words at the command of a person, extent of language. [~Prec.].

VOCAL [vō'kal], *adj.* relating to, produced by, expressed by, the voice; resembling the sound of a voice or voices; having found a means of expression; noisy; **v. cords,** the two membranes in the larynx, at the opening of the glottis, which vibrate to produce vocal sounds; convert into a vowel. VOCALIZATION for the voice; accompanied or unaccompanied singing. [L.].

VOCALISM [vō'ka-lizm], *n.* use of the voice; the specific vowel sounds of a word or language.

VOCALIST [vō'ka-list], *n.* singer, *esp.* a professional singer.

VOCALITY [vō-ka'li-ti], *n.* quality of being vocal; state of being a vowel.

VOCALIZE [vō'ka-līz], *v.t. and i.* to adapt into a form suitable for the voice; make vocal; sing vowel sounds; convert into a vowel. VOCALIZATION [vō-ka-lī-zā'shn], *n.* act of vocalizing; technique of singing with clear articulation.

VOCATION [vō-kā'shn], *n.* calling; natural talent for a particular profession; the adopted profession governing one's life; trade, occupation; (*theol.*) call, believed to be of divine origin, to a religious mission. VOCATIONAL, *adj.* pertaining to, engaged in, suitable for, a v. [L.].

VOCATIVE (1) [vo'ka-tiv], *adj.* (*gram.*) forming the case of personal address. VOCATIVE (2), *n.* (*gram.*) case used to denote address to a person. [~L.].

VOCIFERANT [vō-si'fe-rant], *adj.* clamorous. VOCIFERANCE, *n.* state of clamour; clamorousness. [~L.].

VOCIFERATE [vō-si'fe-rāt], *v.t. and i.* to utter loudly; shout, cry; yell, bawl. [~L.].

VOCIFERATION [vō-si-fe-rā'shn], *n.* violent outcry, exclamation, clamour. [L.].

VOCIFEROUS [vō-si'fe-rŏos], *adj.* making a vigorous use of the voice, clamorous; turbulent or noisy. [~L.].

VODKA [vod'kah], *n.* intoxicating spirit drunk principally in Russia, distilled from rye or potatoes. [Russ.].

VOGUE [vōg], *n.* fashion prevailing at any particular time, temporary craze; popularity. [Fr.].

VOICE (1) [vois], *n.* sound expressed by means of the mouth and human larynx; any sound given utterance by breath acting upon the vocal cords, *esp.* words or song; power of speech; any medium of self-expression, speaker, vote; precept, command; (*gram.*) aspect of a verb indicating the relation between the subject and predicate; the form indicating this; **to give v.**, to give utterance, bay. VOICE (2), *v.t.* to express; express by articulation; act as a medium of expression for. VOICED, *adj.* possessing a v.; uttered with the v.; (*phon.*) uttered with vibration of the vocal cords. [OFr. from L.].

VOICELESS [vois'les], *adj.* having no voice or vote; (*phon.*) uttered without vibration of the vocal cords.

VOID (1) [void], *adj.* empty of all concrete matter, unoccupied, vacant, untenanted; destitute, devoid of; legally invalidated, nullified. VOID (2), *n.* a large, empty space of indeterminate dimensions, vacuum; space between the stars; (*fig.*) a spiritual or emotional deficiency. VOID (3), *v.t.* to leave, quit; get rid of, evacuate; (*leg.*) nullify, render ineffective. VOIDABLE, *adj.* (*leg.*) able to be annulled or made v.; able to be discharged. VOIDING, *n.* act of emptying; discharged matter; that which is voided, ejected. [OFr. from LL.].

VOILE [voil, vwahl], *n.* light, semi-transparent, cotton material used for women's and children's clothing and light furnishings. [Fr.].

VOLATILE [vo'la-til], *adj.* subject to quick evaporation; (*fig.*) responding quickly and with fickleness to different emotional stimuli, full of a gay, capricious life. [L.].

VOLATILIZE [vo-la'ti-līz], *v.t.* to render volatile; cause to evaporate. VOLATILIZABLE, *adj.* able to be volatilized.

VOL-AU-VENT [vol-ō-vah(ng)'], *n.* small pasty filled with mince. [Fr.].

VOLCANIC [vol-ka'nik], *adj.* relating to, produced

by, a volcano or its action; (*fig.*) subject to violent outbursts. [*Next*].

VOLCANO [vol-kā'nō], *n.* mountain or hill of ashes and lava which have accumulated round a vent in the earth's crust through which they have been discharged in a molten state. [It. from L.].

VOLE [vōl], *n.* a rodent resembling a rat; **field v.**, field mouse. [Uncert.].

VOLITION [vō-li'shn], *n.* act of willing; faculty or power of determining choice or forming a purpose. [MedL.].

VOLKSLIED [folks'lēt], *n.* folksong. [Germ.].

VOLLEY (1) [vo'li], *n.* a discharge of a number of projectiles more or less simultaneously; in games, the hitting of the ball by the receiving player before it touches the ground; (*fig.*) a vigorous series. VOLLEY (2), *v.t. and i.* to let fly or fire in the form of a v.; discharge a v.; in games, receive and hit (the ball) before it touches the ground. [Fr.].

VOLPLANE (1) [vōl'plān], *n.* gliding descent of an aeroplane with engines shut off. VOLPLANE (2), *v.t. and i.* to (cause to) descend without engine power. [Fr.].

VOLT [vōlt], *n.* the unit of electromotive force or pressure. [*Volta*, Italian scientist].

VOLTAGE [vōl'tij], *n.* measurement in volts; electrical pressure measured in volts.

VOLTAIC [vol-tā'ik], *adj.* relating to Alessandro *Volta*, discoverer of voltaism; relating to, consisting of, electrical energy.

VOLTAISM [vol'tā-izm], *n.* production of an electric current by chemical action between metals immersed in liquids; galvanism. [*Volta*, the discoverer.].

VOLTAMETER [vol-ta'mi-ter], *n.* (*elect.*) instrument for measuring a quantity of current electricity by the decomposition of an electrolyte. [*Volta*, discover of voltaism, and METER].

VOLTMETER [vōlt'mē-ter], *n.* instrument for measuring voltage. [VOLT and METER].

VOLUBILITY [vo-lyōō-bi'li-ti], *n.* power of being voluble, excessive fluency of speech.

VOLUBLE [vo'lyōō-bl], *adj.* having a natural gift for quick and continuous speech; overwhelming in speech. [L.].

VOLUME [vo'lyōōm], *n.* a book, complete in itself or one of a number completing a whole work; compass, dimensions, capacity; amount of solid mass, body of material; (*mus.*) loudness. VOLUME-CONTROL, (*radio*) the variable resistance on a radio set which diminishes or increases the v. of sound. VOLUMETRIC [vo-lyōō-met'rik], *adj.* relating to measurement by means of standard units of v. [L.].

VOLUMINOUS [vo-lyōō'mi-nōōs], *adj.* containing many volumes; of a size sufficient to occupy many volumes, copious, vast, extensive. [L.].

VOLUNTARY (1) [vo'lun-ta-ri], *adj.* acting from reasons not immediately governed or influenced by others, acting willingly and freely; done without compulsion, performed deliberately and freely; supported by charity; **v. hospital etc.,** hospital etc. supported by v. contributions. VOLUNTARY (2), *n.* solo, sometimes of an extempore nature, played on a church organ. [L.].

VOLUNTEER (1) [vo-lun-tēer'], *n.* person who voluntarily offers to serve in some capacity, *esp.* military. VOLUNTEER (2), *adj.* composed of volunteers; pertaining to, characteristic of, a v., spontaneous; (of a plant) springing up casually. VOLUNTEER (3), *v.t. and i.* to offer out of one's own free will; offer oneself as a v., *esp.* for military purposes. [L.].

VOLUPTUARY [vo-lup'tyōō-a-ri], *n.* person who habitually seeks voluptuous experiences, sensualist; debauchee. [LL.].

VOLUPTUOUS [vo-lup'tyōō-ōōs], *adj.* having an abnormal appetite for sensual or sexual experiences, fond of luxury or refined lechery; inducing, suggesting, sensual pleasure or sexual excitement. [~L.].

VOLUTE [vo-lyōōt'], *n.* (*arch.*) spiral scroll characteristic of the Ionic capital; (*zool.*) a mollusc having a spiral shell. [L.].

VOMIT (1) [vo'mit], *v.t. and i.* to eject from the stomach into the mouth; discharge in a mass; be rid involuntarily of the contents of the stomach, be sick. VOMIT (2), *n.* swallowed food and gastric juices discharged from the stomach into the mouth; act of being sick. [L.].

VOODOO [vōō'dōō], *n.* primitive form of religion or witchcraft practised by the negroes of Haiti and elsewhere in the West Indies and America. [Native].

VORACIOUS [vo-rā'shōōs], *adj.* having a powerful

undiscriminating appetite, greedy from hunger, having an apparently insatiable appetite; (*fig.*) all-consuming. VORACITY, *n.* state of being v. [~L.].

VORTEX [vaw'teks], *n.* violent whirlpool; whirling movement of the air, whirlwind; (*fig.*) overwhelming set of circumstances into which human society is uncontrollably drawn. [L.].

VORTICAL [vaw'ti-kal], *adj.* having the characteristics of a vortex, whirling. [*Prec.*].

VOTARY [vō'ta-ri], *n.* person who has taken vows dedicating his whole life to a god, an institution or a particular aim; practical worker for an ideal; devotee. [~L.].

VOTE (1) [vōt], *n.* means of giving expression to one's preference or opinion concerning a resolution, motion or choice of representative by one of various methods such as a ballot-paper or show of hands; the opinion of a person recorded officially in this way. VOTE (2), *v.t. and i.* to express by means of a v.; consider, estimate; propose; elect by suffrage; establish by v.; give judgment by means of a v. [L.].

VOTER [vō'ter], *n.* person who is legally entitled to vote; one who records a vote. [*Prec.*].

VOTIVE [vō'tiv], *adj.* offered in accordance with a vow. [L.].

VOUCH [vowch], *v.t.* to offer by way of official evidence, warrant; offer proof; **to v. for,** to affirm the truth of, bear witness to, guarantee. [OFr. from L.].

VOUCHER [vow'cher], *n.* person who vouches; ticket which acts as a substitute for money; statement or document confirming the truth or fact of certain events etc. [*Prec.*].

VOUCHSAFE [vowch-sāf'], *v.t.* to permit with condescension. [ME.].

VOW (1) [vow], *n.* solemn promise, usually made in the name of a god, pledge. VOW (2), *v.t. and i.* to assert in the form and spirit of a v.; consecrate by a v., devote, dedicate; declare. [OFr. from L.].

VOWEL (1) [vow'el], *n.* (*phon.*) sound produced in speaking by allowing an air-stream to pass uninterruptedly through the vocal cords and mouth; characters or letters indicating this as *a, e, i, o, u.* VOWEL (2), *adj.* of or relating to a v. [L.].

VOYAGE (1) [voi'ij], *n.* journey by water over a comparatively long distance, *esp.* between countries. VOYAGE (2), *v.i.* to undertake a v., travel by water. [OFr.].

VOYAGEUR [vwi-ah-zhur'], *n.* Canadian timber-worker. [Fr.].

VULCAN [vul'kan], *n.* (*myth.*) the god of fire, who specialized in the working of metals. [L.].

VULCANITE [vul'ka-nit], *n.* solid substance made of rubber mixed with a larger proportion of sulphur. [*Prec.*].

VULCANIZE [vul'ka-nīz], *v.t.* to subject (rubber) to heat, and add a high percentage of sulphur so as to produce a rigid, durable substance; join (pieces of rubber) together by means of heat. [VULCAN].

VULGAR (1) [vul'ger], *adj.* ignorant of or disregarding the accepted conventions of polite society; **v. tongue,** the vernacular; **v. fraction,** a fraction expressed as a numerator above a denominator. VULGAR (2), *n.* those who are v. [L.].

VULGARIAN [vul-gãer'i-an], *n.* vulgar person.

VULGARISM [vul'ga-rizm], *n.* an example of vulgarity, *esp.* in speech; crude grammatical error.

VULGARITY [vul-ga'ri-ti], *n.* quality of being vulgar; crudity of manners or language; an expression of bad taste and insensitivity.

VULGARIZE [vul'ga-rīz], *v.t.* to render vulgar.

VULGATE (1) [vul'gat], *n.* version of the Scriptures in Latin made during the fourth century A.D. VULGATE (2), *adj.* relating to the v. [~L.].

VULNERABLE [vul'ne-ra-bl], *adj.* able to be wounded; susceptible to, liable to, injury; (*fig.*) open to criticism; (*contract bridge*) having won one game towards winning a rubber. [L.].

VULPINE [vul'pīn], *adj.* relating to, having the characteristics of, foxes; cunning, crafty. [L.].

VULTURE [vul'tyŏŏr], *n.* large bird of prey living chiefly on carrion; (*fig.*) person who lives by preying on others. VULTURINE, *adj.* of or relating to the v.; having the characteristics of the v.; rapacious. [OFr.].

VULVA [vul'vah], *n.* (*anat.*) orifice, *esp.* the opening of the female genitals; the external female genitals. [L.].

VYING (1) [vī'ing], *n.* act of competing. VYING (2) *adj.* striving for superiority. [VIE].

The accent ′ after a syllable = stress (u-pon′).   The mark ‾ over a vowel = length (ā in m*a*de; ō in b*o*ne).

W [du'bl-yōō], twenty-third lettter of the English alphabet; **W.C.**, water-closet, lavatory.

WAAC [wak], *n.* (*coll.*) member of the *W*omen's *A*rmy *A*uxiliary *C*orps during the First World War.

WAAF [waf], *n.* (*coll.*) member of the *W*omen's *A*uxiliary *A*ir *F*orce in the Second World War of 1939-45.

WAD (1) [wod], *n.* a small amount of soft, tightly packed fibres or grasses etc., used to supplement packing, parcelling or bandages, pad, plug; thick pile of bank-notes. WAD (2) (*pres.pt.* WADDING, *pret. and p.pt.* WADDED), *v.t.* to form into a w.; apply to as a w. WADDED, *adj.* formed into a w. or mass; packed tightly by means of a w. [Uncert.].

WADDING [wo'ding], *n.* a soft material, *esp.* of cotton-wool, used as padding or absorbent; material out of which wads for guns are manufactured. [*Prec.*].

WADDLE (1) [wo'dl], *v.i.* to walk in an ungainly style characterized by short steps and a rolling from side to side; move with the gait of a duck. WADDLE (2), *n.* act of waddling. [Unkn.].

WADE (1) [wād], *v.t. and i.* to cross by wading; walk through water which reaches to a level above the ankles; (*fig.*) work (through an almost impenetrable mass of dull material); **to w. in,** to proceed to enter into, participate with vigour. WADE (2), *n.* act of wading. [OE.].

WADER [wā'der], *n.* one who wades; angler's long waterproof boot; bird characterized by wading habits. [*Prec.*].

WADI [wo'di], *n.* in Arab countries, a deep water-course in which water flows only during the rainy season. [Arab.].

WAE (1) [wā], *n.* (*Scots*) woe. WAE (2), *adj.* (*Scots*) woeful, sad. [OE.].

WAFER (1) [wā'fer], *n.* piece of very thin biscuit, flaky layer of baked flour; that characterized by extreme thinness; round piece of very thin bread used for Holy Communion; red seal in the form of a circular piece of gummed paper. WAFER (2), *v.t.* to form into a w.; seal with a w. [OFr.].

WAFFLE (1) [wo'fl], *n.* batter cake baked in an iron mould. [Du.].

WAFFLE (2), *v.t. and i.* (*coll.*) to talk vague nonsense; utter vaguely and nonsensically. [~OE.].

WAFT (1) [woft], *v.t. and i.* to cause to move in a light buoyant manner, carry on an eddying, jerky stream of air or water; drift or float in the air. WAFT (2), *n.* act of wafting; that which moves by wafting; flag at half-mast. WAFTAGE, *n.* buoyant conveyance. [Uncert.].

WAG (1) (*pres.pt.* **wagging,** *pret. and p.pt.* **wagged)** [wag], *v.t. and i.* to move up and down or to and fro with one end fixed; shake, vibrate. WAG (2), *n.* act of wagging. WAG (3), *n.* humorist, person with a characteristic sense of fun, one with a fund of humorous stories and a comic turn of phrase. [~OE.].

WAGE (1) [wāj], *n.* a rate of payment for work, usually on a weekly basis; (*pl.*) money paid at regular intervals for work done. WAGE (2), *v.t.* to undertake, carry on, organize; bet, wager. [ONFr.].

WAGER (1) [wā'jer], *n.* agreement to stake money or its equivalent on the result of a future event or a question to be settled, a bet. WAGER (2), *v.t. and i.* to gamble, bet; make a w. [ONFr.].

WAGGERY [wa'ge-ri], *n.* the humour, jokes and tricks of a wag, impish humour.

WAGGISH [wa'gish], *adj.* resembling the humour of a wag, done from waggery; merry, comic. [WAG (3)].

WAGGLE (1) [wa'gl], *v.t. and i.* (*coll.*) to move from side to side, shake up and down, *esp.* of the human body. WAGGLE (2), *n.* act of waggling. WAGGLY, *adj.* (*coll.*) that waggles. [~WAG (1)].

WAGGON, WAGGONER, WAGGONET, see WAGON, WAGONER, WAGONETTE.

WAG(G)ON [wa'gon], *n.* sturdy flat-bedded vehicle on four wheels used for carrying heavy loads. WAG(G)ONER, *n.* one who drives and loads a w. [Du.].

WAGONETTE, WAGGONET [wa-go-net'], *n.* open four-wheeled passenger carriage with the back seats facing each other in pairs. [*Prec.*].

WAGON LIT [vah-gaw(ng)-lē'], *n.* sleeping-car attached to a train. [Fr.].

WAGTAIL [wag'tāl], *n.* a small bird, named from the wagging of its long tail.

WAIF [wāf], *n.* person without home, money, food or job, *esp.* a child; (*leg.*) piece of lost property. [OScand.].

WAIL (1) [wāl], *v.t. and i.* to lament; make a prolonged high cry or sound which rises and then falls in pitch and intensity, expressive of deep sorrow or pain; mourn, sigh loudly. WAIL (2), *n.* act of wailing; high, continuous sound which rises and then falls in pitch and intensity, a plaintive cry. WAILER, *n.* one who wails. WAILFUL, *adj.* expressive of a state of sorrow, mournful. [~OScand.].

WAIN [wān], *n.* (*archaic*) wagon; **The, Charles's, W.,** (*astron.*) the group of stars also called the Great Bear. [OE.].

WAINSCOT (1) [wānz'kot], *n.* wooden panelling at the base of a wall. WAINSCOT (2), *v.t.* to furnish with a w. WAINSCOTING, *n.* material for a w.; a skirting of wood round the base of a wall. [Du.].

WAINWRIGHT [wān'rit], *n.* wagonmaker.

WAIST (1) [wāst], *n.* narrowest part of the trunk between the hips and lowest ribs; the part of a garment designed to fit round this; narrow middle part of various objects, as a shoe, violin etc.; middle part of the upper deck of a ship. WAIST-CLOTH, strip of cloth worn round the w. and crutch. WAIST (2), *v.t.* to make narrow at the w., as a dress. [ME.].

WAISTBAND [wāst'band], *n.* band or upper part of trousers or of a skirt, which fits to the waist.

WAISTCOAT [wāst'kōt], *n.* short sleeveless garment for men fitting closely round the waist and chest, opening at the front, and worn beneath a jacket.

WAIT (1) [wāt], *v.t. and i.* to watch for; remain in expectancy; pass the time before an expected event, stay, remain until a certain thing happens; attend at table to serve food and drink; **to w. for,** to defer taking another course until; **to w. on,** to serve as a waiter to; keep in close attendance on; call on. WAIT (2), *n.* act or period of waiting. [OFr.].

WAIT (3), *n.* member of a group singing Christmas carols outside houses and collecting money. [ONFr.].

WAITER [wā'ter], *n.* one who waits; male servant in attendance in a public dining-room. [WAIT (1)].

WAITING (1) [wā'ting], *n.* act of staying, attendance; work of a waiter; **in w.,** in attendance. WAITING-LIST, list of names of people waiting their turn for a vacancy falling due etc. WAITING (2), *adj.* serving. WAITING-MAID, -WOMAN, *n.* female servant who attends at table.

WAITRESS [wā'tres], *n.* woman employed to serve customers at table in a hotel, restaurant or café.

WAIVE [wāv], *v.t.* to defer temporarily; relinquish, not to insist on or claim. WAIVER, *n.* (*leg.*) act of consenting to w. a right or claim; document expressing this. [~OE.].

WAKE (1) [wāk], *n.* the smooth swirling track of water left behind a moving ship; **in the w. of,** behind, after. [OIcel.].

WAKE (2) (*pret.* **woke, waked,** *p.pt.* **waked, woke, woken),** *v.t.* to cause to pass from a state of sleep, rouse from sleep; stimulate to a state of consciousness; cause to stir, make active, excite; *v.i.* to become awake, be or remain in a conscious state, have the senses and mind functioning; stir the mind into activity, attain a state of quick realization and mental alertness; excite out of a state of lethargy. WAKE (3), *n.* annual vigil or commemoration service of a church dedication; the watching over a corpse by mourners during the night before the funeral; party held during this ritual; festivity and fair held in the north of England annually. WAKE (4), *v.i.* to participate in a w. [OE.].

WAKEFUL [wāk'fool], *adj.* not sleeping; unable to sleep; watchful, vigilant. [*Prec.*].

WAKEN [wā'ken], *v.t. and i.* to stir into conscious activity; excite to action or motion by breaking a state of sleep; wake, break out of a state of sleep or unconsciousness. [O.E.].

WAKING [wā'king], *n.* period of being awake; **w. hours,** hours when one is awake. [WAKE (2)].

WALE (1) [wāl], *n.* ridge raised on the flesh by a blow or lash etc., weal; ridge raised in a fabric. WALE (2), *v.t.* to raise wales on. [O.E.].

WALK (1) [wawk], *v.t. and i.* to proceed by placing one foot alternately before the other, there being always one foot in contact with the ground; make to proceed by walking; accompany at walking pace; proceed, go on foot; cover (a distance) on foot; **to w. away with,** to win easily; **to w. off with,** to steal; **to w. out,** to leave a factory or shop as a form of strike; **to w. out with,** to court; **to w. over,** to win with ease or by opponent's absence. WALK-OUT, strike of workers who quit their work. WALK-OVER, victory easily gained; contest in which there is only one competitor. WALK-UP, (*slang*) introductory matter. WALK (2), *n.* act or action of walking; manner of walking, gait; distance covered during a time spent in walking; journey, route; place specially laid out for walking in, promenade, shaded avenue; course of life, occupation; social sphere or class; speed of progress by walking, *esp.* of a horse. WALK-ABLE, *adj.* able to be walked. [O.E.].

WALKER [waw'ker], *n.* one who walks; person who walks or trains young hounds. [*Prec.*].

WALKIE-TALKIE [waw-ki-taw'ki], *n.* (*coll.*) portable radio-telephone apparatus.

WALKING [waw'king], *n.* act of moving on the feet by alternate steps at a slow pace. WALKING-STICK, stick or cane used when out walking either as a means of support or for display.

WALL (1) [wawl], *n.* structure of stone, brick etc., usually more extended in height than thickness, acting as a means of defence, partition or privacy for private property; one side of a building; anything acting as a partition; anything of an extended apparently solid nature. WALL-GAME, football game peculiar to Eton College. WALL (2), *v.t.* to enclose with a w. WALLED, *adj.* enclosed by a w. [O.E.].

WALLABY [wo'la-bi], *n.* Australian marsupial allied to the kangaroo; (*coll.*) an Australian. [Native].

WALLAH [wo'lah], *n.* Indian employee; (*coll.*) person, fellow, *esp.* one connected with a specialized job, a specialist. [Hindī].

WALLET [wo'lit], *n.* small pocket-book for holding banknotes or correspondence; brief-case; † pilgrim's knapsack. [ME.].

WALL-EYE [wawl'ī], *n.* affliction of the eye in which the iris turns a whitish colour. WALL-EYED, *adj.* afflicted by w. [~Icel.].

WALLFLOWER [wawl'flow-er], *n.* (*bot.*) a fragrant cruciferous plant; (*coll.*) girl who sits beside a dance floor waiting for a partner.

WALLOP (1) [wo'lop], *v.t. and i.* to beat, punch, hit; boil. WALLOP (2), *n.* act of walloping, blow, punch; (*slang*) beer. WALLOPING, *adj.* (*slang*) huge. [~GALLOP].

WALLOW (1) [wo'lō], *v.i.* to roll with sensual pleasure in (filthy) water or mire; (*fig.*) take pleasure in moral irregularities; **to w. in money,** riches, to be very rich. WALLOW (2), *n.* act of wallowing; place where animals w. WALLOWER, *n.* one who wallows; wheel which works the trundle head in a mill. [O.E.].

WALLPAPER [wawl'pā-per], *n.* paper, usually coloured or patterned, pasted in strips on the interior walls of a room as a form of decoration.

WALNUT [wawl'nut], *n.* a tree, *Juglans regia*, the timber being used for cabinet work; edible nut of this tree with a crinkly kernel. [O.E.].

WALPURGIS-NIGHT [vahl-pŏŏr'gis-nīt], *n.* witches' festival supposed to be held on the eve of 1 May, *esp.* on the German Brocken. [St. *Walpurga*].

WALRUS [wawl'rus], *n.* large carnivore, allied to the seals, having a tusk on either side of the mouth, living in the Arctic Ocean. [Du.].

WALTZ (1) [wawls], *n.* dance for two partners, based on three-four or three-two time, and characterized by long sweeping steps governing a series of turns; music for accompanying such a dance. WALTZ (2), *v.t. and i.* to hold so as to w.; dance a w.; move with a waltzing motion. [Germ.].

WALTZING (1) [wawl'sing], *n.* act of dancing a waltz. WALTZING (2), *adj.* that waltzes; **w. mice,** breed of mice which spin round rapidly at intervals.

WAMPUM [won'pum], *n.* strings of beads made from coloured shells, used by the American Indians as money. [NAmerInd.].

WAN [won], *adj.* pale, pallid. WANLY, *adv.* in a pale fashion. [O.E.].

WAND [wond], *n.* small stick, usually smooth and slender, rod; staff of authority; rod used by conjurers; baton used by orchestral conductors. [~OIcel.].

WANDER [won'der], *v.i.* to proceed by a vague route; travel in a leisurely manner and not keeping to a direct route, ramble, roam; fail to keep to the point in discussion; lose control of the mind, be delirious in thought. WANDER-PLUG, *n.* (*radio*) plug which can be connected to various points. [O.E.].

WANDERER [won'de-rer], *n.* one who wanders, *esp.* by habit; person who deviates from duty. [*Prec.*].

WANDERING (1) [won'de-ring], *n.* act of one who wanders; extensive travelling, peregrination; delirious rambling of the mind. WANDERING (2), *adj.* travelling aimlessly, roaming, rambling; **W. Jew,** Jew in legend condemned to eternal w. till Christ's return on earth.

WANDERLUST [won'der-lust], *n.* urge to travel. [Germ.].

WANE (1) [wān], *v.i.* to diminish, lessen, decrease, *esp.* of the illuminated section of the moon visible from the earth. WANE (2), *n.* act of waning; diminution of lunar illumination; decline; **on the w.,** declining. [O.E.].

WANGLE (1) [wang'gl], *v.t. and i.* (*slang*) to arrange by manipulation which is clever to the point of trickery. WANGLE (2), *n.* (*slang*) act or instance of wangling, fraudulent manipulation. [Uncert.].

WANT (1) [wont], *v.t. and i.* to need, require for one's health's sake, be destitute of necessaries; be deficient in quality; wish to possess, have a use for; desire; be deficient, be lacking; fail, fall short. WANT (2), *n.* condition of having an inadequate amount, insufficiency, deficiency, *esp.* of the necessary means of life and comfort, need, poverty, frustration of one's wishes and requirements. WANTING, *adj.* lacking, absent; deficient, without essentials; (*coll.*) weakminded. [OIcel.].

WANTON (1) [won'tn], *adj.* lacking moral discipline, characterized by licentious conduct; uncontrollable, irresponsible; capricious; extravagant; arbitrary. WANTON (2), *n.* person who is w., *esp.* a woman of dissolute or flirtatious habits, harlot. WANTON (3), *v.i.* to behave in a w. manner; act or grow without restraint; disport oneself, frolic; play with licentious intentions, flirt. [ME.].

WAPITI [wo'pi-ti], *n.* American stag, the elk. [NAmerInd.].

WAR (1) [waw(r)], *n.* hostilities undertaken on a large scale between tribes, parties or nations involving the killing of men; the military profession; science and tactics of warfare; contest of enemies; **civil w.,** open conflict between armies of opposing factions fighting for control of state power within a nation; **holy w.,** w. undertaken in religious interests, crusade; **ideological w.,** w. prosecuted for the sake of a political or social idea, principle; **in the wars,** suffering from injury; **w. to the knife,** bitter and ruthless warfare, *esp.* as between individuals; **sinews of w.,** money and materials necessary to make w.; **w. bonds,** government securities issued to finance a w.; **w. bride,** woman married in wartime, *esp.* to a member of an allied or a Commonwealth nation; **W. Office,** British department of State concerned with the administration of the Army and with military affairs; **w. widow,** woman whose husband has been killed in w.; **w. work,** any work connected with the prosecution of a w. WAR-CRY, formal cry, shout, cheer or slogan used as a stimulant before battle. WAR-DANCE, ritual dance performed by savages before battle. WAR-HEAD, fully charged explosive head of a torpedo, rocket-bomb etc. WAR-HORSE, cavalry horse, charger; (*fig.*) w. veteran. WAR-LORD, military leader who glories in warfare. WAR-PAINT, pigment daubed on the face and other parts of the body by savages and North American Indians on going to w.; *also fig.* WAR-SONG, song inciting to w.; *esp.* one accompanying the w.-dance before battle. WAR-WHOOP, full-throated yell raised in charging an enemy; w.-cry. WAR (2) (*pres.pt.* WARRING, *pret.* and *p.pt.* WARRED), *v.i.* to carry on a w., fight till death or defeat. [OFr.].

WARATAH [wah'ra-tah], *n.* (*bot.*) an Australian plant, *Telopea speciosissima*, with scarlet flowers. [Native].

WARBLE (1) [wawr'bl], *v.t. and i.* to sing with a tremolo in the voice, give voice to quavering trills, as a bird; sing. WARBLE (2), *n.* act or sound of that which warbles. WARBLING (1), *n.* a w., trill.

WARBLING (2), *adj.* having the ability to w., singing in warbles. [OFr.].

WARBLER [waw'bler], *n.* person who warbles; small song-bird of a subfamily of the thrushes. [*Prec.*].

WARD (1) [wawd], *n.* act of guarding, a defence position in fencing; room for persons held in custody or under protection, *esp.* one in a prison or hospital; state of being kept under guard, custody, confinement; child under the protection of a guardian, minor; an administrative division of a borough; the characteristic part of a particular lock. WARD-MOTE, assembly held in a city or borough w. WARD (2), *v.t.* to act in the capacity of a guardian for; protect, defend. [OE.].

WARDEN [waw'den], *n.* status carrying authority of administration over certain areas; guard, warder; head of certain Oxford colleges; one appointed for general duties among the civil population during air-raids. [ONFr.].

WARDER [waw'der], *n.* guard over a ward, prison-guard, jailer. [GUARD (2)].

WARDROBE [wawd'rōb], *n.* large cupboard or piece of furniture where clothes are kept, outfit of clothes; **w. dealer**, dealer in old clothes. WARDROBE-TRUNK, elaborately fitted trunk which, when stood on end, serves as a w. [~OFr.].

WARDROOM [wawd'room], *n.* messroom of the senior officers of a warship. [WARD (1)].

WARDSHIP [wawd'ship], *n.* status of being a guardian; state of being under the protection of a guardian. [WARD (1)].

WARE (1) [wāer], *n.* article for sale; manufactured articles, *esp.* earthenware; (*pl.*) products for sale, commodities, merchandise. [OE.].

WARE (2), *adj.* aware, wary. WARE (3), *v.t.* (*coll.*) to beware of. WARE (4), *int.* beware ! look out ! [OE.].

WAREHOUSE (1) [wāer'hows], *n.* large building fitted for storing goods in bulk as a distributing centre to retail traders; storehouse. WAREHOUSE (2), *v.t.* to place in a w. WAREHOUSING, *n.* act or system of storing in a w., *esp.* in bonded warehouses where goods are not subject to excise duty until put into retail circulation.

WARFARE [waw'fāer], *n.* the waging of war; condition of being engaged in war; military service.

WARILY [wāer'i-li], *adv.* in a wary fashion.

WARLIKE [waw'līk], *adj.* having a natural propensity for war; relating to war; resembling war; characterized by military factors, martial.

WARLOCK [waw'lok], *n.* (*archaic*) magician, wizard. [OE.].

WARM (1) [wawm], *adj.* emitting a degree of heat sufficient to be appreciated but not so extreme as to burn or scorch, not hot, characterized by a mild degree of heat, not cold; (*fig.*) possessing enthusiasm, ardent, zealous; heated in response, angry, impassioned; affectionate; rich in tone, reddish in colour; (*old-fashioned coll.*) well-to-do; **getting w.**, getting nearer, *esp.* to a concealed mark or object in a child's game. WARM-BLOODED, having w. blood, as mammals and birds; quick in emotional response. WARM-HEARTED, having or showing quick sensitivity of affection, cordial. WARM (2), *v.t.* and *i.* to impart a degree of heat to, make w.; excite, make deeply interested in, arouse enthusiasm of; become w. by absorbing heat; **to w. up**, to heat again; grow warm; become more enthusiastic. WARM (3), *n.* act of warming; **British w.**, overcoat worn by British Army officers. WARMLY, *adv.* in a w. manner; to a w. degree; ardently, cordially. [OE.].

WARMING-PAN [waw'ming-pan], *n.* enclosed metal pan with a long handle, filled with ignited coals, formerly used for warming beds.

WARMONGER [waw'mung-ger], *n.* one who encourages warfare. WARMONGERING, *n.* the activities of a w.

WARMTH [wawmth], *n.* quality of heat retained or emitted, mild degree of heat; state of excitement or impassioned ardour, zeal; vehemence; glow of colour, usually reddish in tone; (*coll.*) mild anger. [WARM].

WARN [wawn], *v.t.* to inform in advance of approaching or possible danger, advise caution; advise care against a failure in performing a duty; admonish; indicate by a sign. [OE.].

WARNING (1) [waw'ning], *n.* act of a person who warns, caution against danger; means of being warned, previous notice; notice to quit. WARNING (2), *adj.* that warns. [*Prec.*].

WARP (1) [wawp], *v.t. and i.* to put out of shape, change in shape, *esp.* by twisting, turning or bending;

turn from truth, change in purity, pervert; (*naut.*) tow by a rope attached to a buoy etc.; become twisted out of shape by extremes of temperature. WARP (2), *n.* the threads in a fabric which cross the loom lengthwise at right angles to the woof; mud deposited by tides, and regarded as a land fertilizer; (*naut.*) rope used for towing. WARPED, *adj.* twisted or bent by warping; perverted. WARPING, *n.* arrangement of the w.; fertilization of land by allowing floods to deposit mud; (*naut.*) use of a w. line. [OE.].

WARPATH [waw'pahth], *n.* route followed by American Indians on a marauding expedition; **on the w.**, militant.

WARRANT (1) [wo'rant], *n.* an official means of authorization, in documentary form; commission transferring authority to the bearer; writ of arrest; that which is of a status commanding authority, proof, sanction; **dividend w.**, document entitling payment of dividend; **w. officer**, officer next in rank below a commissioned officer, and acting under a w. WARRANT (2), *v.t.* to support or sanction in an official or semi-official capacity, guarantee by implying power to provide proof, authorize; justify; stand by (a statement). WARRANTED, *adj.* authorized; justified; guaranteed. WARRANTEE [wo-ran-tē'], *n.* (*leg.*) person to whom something is granted by w. WARRANTER, *n.* person who guarantees a contract or engagement; official who issues a w. [OFr.].

WARRANTABLE [wo'ran-ta-bl], *adj.* able to be authorized by warrant; justifiable; **w. stag**, stag when six years old.

WARRANTY [wo'ran-ti], *n.* authorization, guarantee, security; (*leg.*) manufacturer's assurance that goods are up to standard. [WARRANT (1)].

WARREN [wo'ren], *n.* breeding ground for rabbits, riddled with burrows; also *fig.* [ME. from ONFr.].

WARRIOR [wo'ri-er], *n.* professional soldier; man engaged in military life; soldier who has achieved distinction. [ONFr.].

WARSHIP [waw'ship], *n.* man-of-war; naval vessel fitted with a full quota of armaments.

WART [wawt], *n.* tough knot of cells appearing chiefly on the hands; protuberance on trees. WART-HOG, an African ungulate allied to the swine. WARTY, *adj.* covered with, full of, of the nature of, warts. [OE.].

WARY [wāer'i], *adj.* cautious of danger; alert, on guard against potential enemies; circumspect. [WARE (2)].

WAS [woz], *1st and 3rd person pret. sg. of* BE. [OE.].

WASH (1) [wosh], *v.t.* to cleanse by soaking, rubbing and scrubbing in water, usually with the help of soap; cover with water which ebbs and flows, bathe, dash against, as the sea; purify of sin; move by means of current or drift; give a thin metal coating, or a thin coat of paint, to; *v.i.* to clean oneself with soap and water; come through a process of washing unchanged; contact by ebbing and flowing; **to w. down**, to cleanse quickly but not too thoroughly by means of a large quantity of water; **to w. off**, to take off by means of water; **to w. out**, to soak in water, rinse and squeeze so as to clean; (*coll.*) cancel; **to w. up**, to cleanse crockery etc. in water; **won't w.**, (*slang*) is unconvincing; **to w. one's hands of**, to refuse responsibility for, break connexions with; **washed out**, tired out, pale in complexion. WASH-BASIN, basin usually fitted with running water, for washing in. WASH-BOWL, bowl for washing in. WASH-HOUSE, house or room in which clothes are washed, laundry. WASH-LEATHER, a soft leather, like chamois, made from sheepskin. WASH-OUT, damage caused by flood; a washing out; (*coll.*) a failure. WASH-STAND, small table on which a w.-basin and toilet requisites are kept. WASH-TUB, tub in which clothes are washed; (*coll.*) bath-tub. WASH (2), *n.* act of washing, *esp.* of dirty clothes; articles of clothing ready to be washed; deposits left by the ebb and flow of water, alluvial mud, a marsh; lotion for cosmetic or hygienic purposes; dirty water, *esp.* that in which food has been cooked, thrown away, usually to pigs; shallows of a river, *esp.* at the mouth; current of water left behind a moving ship or the blades of oars; sound of waves as they ebb and flow over shingle or sand; a weak liquid for drinking, *esp.* weak tea; thin layer of water infused with a little pigment used by a water-colourist; thin plating of metal. WASH-BOARD, board with a ribbed or corrugated surface as an aid for scrubbing dirty clothes in a w.-tub. WASHABLE, *adj.* able to be washed. [OE.].

WASHER [wo'sher], *n.* one who or that which washes;

washing-machine; round piece of metal or other material perforated in the centre and placed between the head of a bolt etc. and the surface against which it is tightened, **or between working parts to absorb friction.**

WASHHAND-BASIN [wosh'hand-bā-sin], *n.* bowl on a wash-stand in which to wash the hands and face.

WASHING (1) [wo'shing], *n.* act of cleansing with water; the clothes dispatched to the laundry to be washed at one time. WASHING-SODA, hydrous sodium carbonate used for cleaning purposes. WASHING-UP, operation of w. dirty crockery after a meal; crockery so washed. WASHING (2), *adj.* that can be washed. WASHING-FROCK, woman's dress made of light, washable material.

WASHY [wo'shi], *adj.* consisting mostly of water, weak; not firm or hardy; vapid; lacking colourfulness. WASHILY, *adv.* in a w. manner; to a w. degree.

WASP [wosp], *n.* a winged insect characterized by a thin petiole at the waist and alternate markings of black and yellow on the body, and with a sting concealed in the abdomen; **w. waist,** exaggeratedly narrow waist. [OE.].

WASPISH [wos'pish], *adj.* like a wasp; bad-tempered; irascible.

WASSAIL (1) [wo'sl, wo'sāl], *n.* (*archaic*) festive occasion, *esp.* one accompanied by hard drinking; spiced ale formerly drunk on such an occasion. WASSAIL-BOWL, vessel containing ale during a festival. WASSAIL (2), *v.i.* to participate in a carousal. WASSAILER, *n.* participator at a w., reveller, drunkard. [ME.].

WAST [wost], (*poet.*) *2nd person pret. sg. of* BE. [OE.].

WASTAGE [wās'tij], *n.* amount lost by waste; waste.

WASTE (1) [wāst], *adj.* made barren, converted into a barren tract; untouched by human habitation, deserted, desolate; rejected as worthless, superfluous. WASTE-PAPER BASKET, basket for discarded papers. WASTE (2), *n.* territory untouched by human habitation, desolate tract of land, barren wilderness; act of wasting, extravagance; rejected matter, refuse. WASTE-PIPE, pipe for conveying off w. water or sewerage. WASTE (3), *v.t. and i.* to cause to diminish by unnecessary extravagance, squander, lose by neglect; **to w. away,** to become emaciated, lose strength by gradual loss; (*leg.*) lessen in value by neglect. WASTING, *adj.* diminishing by consuming of substance or strength. [ONFr.].

WASTEFUL [wāst'fŏŏl], *adj.* causing waste, extravagant, prodigal; expending unnecessarily that which is valuable; destructive, ruinous.

WASTER [wās'ter], *n.* one who squanders money or property; a ne'er-do-well; animal losing condition or failing to fatten; article damaged in process of being manufactured. [WASTE (3)].

WASTREL [wās'trel], *n.* person who wastes his time and money, a ne'er-do-well.

WATCH (1) [woch], *n.* act of watching; period in which sleep is abstained from, vigil; maintenance of a strict and systematic scrutiny, observation of a person's movements; person or body of men whose duty it is to keep guard, watchman; period of the night when a specific guard is on duty; (*naut.*) period allotted for one section of a crew to be on deck; small portable mechanism for registering the time, timepiece; **W. Committee,** committee of a local governing body concerned with police services. WATCH-CASE, outer case of a w. WATCH-DOG, dog trained to guard premises. WATCH-FIRE, fire used by the guard at night. WATCH-GLASS, piece of glass for covering the face of a w. WATCH-GUARD, chain or strap attached to a w.; metal grid covering the glass of a w. WATCH-MAKER, person whose occupation is to make or repair watches. WATCH-NIGHT, religious service held towards midnight on New Year's Eve. WATCH-TOWER, tower giving a commanding view over the countryside, and manned by a sentry. WATCH (2), *v.t.* to maintain a close observation on, *esp.* with intent to protect, to guard; tend; remain in expectancy of; note carefully; maintain a strict scrutiny over; *v.i.* to keep awake with intent to guard against dangers, keep on the alert; act as a sentry, keep guard; look with attention, observe; take care of an invalid, keep vigil. [OE.].

WATCHFUL [woch'fŏŏl], *adj.* on the alert, vigilant, attentive.

WATCHMAN [woch'man], *n.* sentinel; man who guards offices or buildings at night; (*hist.*) night policeman.

WATCHWORD [woch'werd], *n.* word or phrase by which friends recognize each other in battle; password; slogan.

WATER (1) [waw'ter], *n.* liquid compound consisting of two parts of hydrogen to one of oxygen; any large body of water accumulated under natural conditions, lake, river; any serum or secretion in the body; urine; **in deep w., in hot w.,** in trouble; **in low w.,** nearing insolvency; **like a fish out of w.,** out of one's element; **to hold w.,** (*fig.*) to hang together, be logical; stand up to investigation; **to keep one's head above w.,** to keep out of danger, keep solvent; **to make w.,** to urinate; (*naut.*) leak; **of the first w.,** first-class; **w. cure,** hydropathy. WATER-BED, rubber mattress containing w. WATER-BISCUIT, unsweetened type of biscuit made with w. and flour. WATER-BOTTLE, bottle or similar container for w., *esp.* as carried by troops on the march or in the field. WATER-BUFFALO, the domesticated Indian buffalo. WATER-BUTT, large cask in which rain-water gathers. WATER-CARRIER, one who carries w. for sale in hot countries; (*astron.*) the constellation Aquarius, a sign of the Zodiac. WATER-CART, cart bearing a tank of w. for spraying roads and gutters. WATER-CHUTE, sloping board along which w. flows, *esp* one used by bathers as a means of sliding into the w. WATER-CLOSET, lavatory flushed by a w. system. WATER-COLOUR, pigment mixed with w., painting painted in this medium. WATER-COLOURIST, person who paints in w.-colours. WATER-COOLED, fitted with a cooling system of circulating w. WATER-DIVINER, person who detects the presence of subterranean w. by means of a dowsing rod. WATER-FOWL, (*pl.*) birds which frequent the w. WATER-GAUGE, instrument for registering the quantity of w. in a container and the rate of flow through a pipe etc. WATER-GLASS, a silicate of soda or potash, soluble in hot water and impervious to the air. WATER-GOD, deity supposed to control the element of w.; Neptune or Poseidon. WATER-HAMMER, sound which w. in a pipe or cylinder makes when its flow is suddenly stopped. WATER-HEN, the moorhen. WATER-ICE, iced sweet made principally of frozen w. and essence of fruits. WATER-LEVEL, level formed by the surface of still w.; instrument in which w. is employed for ascertaining levels. WATER-LILY, aquatic plant with floating leaves and large flowers, growing in ponds. WATER-LINE, level of the w. on a ship's hull, dock-side etc.; mark indicating this; line corresponding to the maximum permitted draught of a fully laden ship. WATER-MAIN, one of the large pipes carrying a (public) w.-supply. WATER-MEADOW, meadow irrigated by an adjoining stream. WATER-MELON, the plant and edible fruit *Citrullus vulgaris.* WATER-MILL, mill turned by w. WATER-POLO, ball game played in w. by two teams of swimmers with rules of play derived from those of football. WATER-POWER, power derived from the action of w. WATER-RAT, species of vole which can take to the w. WATER-RATE, charge set by the appropriate authority for the supply of w. WATER-SOFTENER, device fitted to a w.-supply to remove hardness or chalky elements from the w. WATER-SPANIEL, breed of spaniel trained for duck-shooting. WATER-SUPPLY, system of pipes drawing on a river, lake or reservoir for supplies of w. to be distributed to consumers. WATER-TOWER, tower supporting a tank of w. to obtain the necessary pressure for a w.-supply. WATER-WAGON, watering-cart; **on the w.-wagon,** abstaining from alcoholic drinks. WATER-WAGTAIL, the pied wagtail. WATER-WAVE, wave produced in the hair by setting it with w. WATER-WHEEL, wheel operated by the pressure of running w. WATER-WINGS, (*pl.*) safety device, consisting of a pair of inflatable bladders, worn by persons learning to swim. WATER (2), *v.t.* to apply w. to, sprinkle, irrigate, supply with w.; dilute by adding w.; render wavy in surface; issue new stocks or shares without adding to (the capital of a company etc.); *v.i.* to imbibe w.; secrete w., shed in the form of moisture; **to w. down,** to make weaker; **to make one's mouth w.,** to stimulate one's expectation of pleasure. WATERED, *adj.* supplied with w.; made wavy and shiny of surface; diluted. [OE.].

WATERBORNE [waw'ter-bawn], *adj.* disseminated or borne by water, *esp.* of disease spread by water; (of troops etc.) carried in ships or other vessels.

WATERCOURSE [waw'ter-kaws], *n.* stream of water; passage for water.

WATERCRESS [waw'ter-kres], *n.* (*bot.*) small creeping plant growing in watery places.

WATERFALL [waw'ter-fawl], *n.* perpendicular

The accent ' after a syllable = stress (u-pon'). The mark ¯ over a vowel = length (ā in made; ō in bone).

descent of river or stream, cascade, cataract; place where this occurs.

WATERINESS [waw'te-ri-nes], *n.* quality or condition of being watery.

WATERING [waw'te-ring], *n.* act of sprinkling or supplying with water; process by which a wavy surface is imparted to a fabric; **w. place.** pool or part of a river bank where animals are accustomed to drink; town by the seaside; town where medicinal waters are taken. WATERING-TROUGH, trough containing water for cattle and horses to drink.

WATERLOGGED [waw'ter-logd], *adj.* saturated to a point when floating is no longer possible; (*naut.*) lying like a log on the water, the hold being flooded.

WATERLOO [waw-ter-loo'], *n.* battle in which Napoleon suffered final defeat; **to meet one's W.,** to suffer defeat after a long run of success. [*Waterloo,* Belgium].

WATERMAN [waw'ter-man], *n.* man employed to look after boats, boatman; ferryman. WATERMANSHIP, *n.* art of controlling a rowing-boat; oarsmanship.

WATERMARK [waw'ter-mahk], *n.* mark or limit showing the highest level of a flood; mark indicating the rise and fall of the tide; distinguishing mark worked into the texture of paper during manufacture.

WATERPROOF (1) [waw'ter-proof], *adj.* impervious to water. WATERPROOF (2), *n.* cloth or coat which has been made proof against water. WATERPROOF (3), *v.t.* to treat with a preparation so as to render w.

WATERSHED [waw'ter-shed], *n.* ridge dividing river basins.

WATERSIDE (1) [waw'ter-sīd], *n.* land forming the edge of a stretch of water. WATERSIDE (2), *adj.* pertaining to, situated on, working at, the water's edge, *esp.* docks. WATERSIDER, *n.* labourer working at docks.

WATERSPOUT [waw'ter-spowt], *n.* whirling column of water spun from a cloud to the sea or lake by a whirlwind.

WATERTIGHT [waw'ter-tīt], *adj.* adapted in such a way as to retain, or not to admit, water.

WATERWAY [waw'ter-wā], *n.* navigable river; canal; (*naut.*) deck channel for draining water to the scuppers.

WATERWORKS [waw'ter-werks], *n.(pl.)* headquarters of a local water-supply; (*slang*) organs discharging urine; **to turn on the w.,** to burst into tears.

WATERY [waw'te-ri], *adj.* containing an amount of water, *esp.* to a disadvantageous extent, saturated, sodden; resembling water; weak, insipid; misty, rainy.

WATT [wot], *n.* the unit of electrical power. WATT-HOUR, amount of work done by one w. in one hour. WATTAGE, *n.* electrical energy measured in watts; amount of energy which an electrical circuit etc. is designed to carry. [James *Watt,* inventor].

WATTLE (1) [wo'tl], *n.* hurdle made by twisting flexible twigs across a frame; lobe of flesh growing at the neck of poultry or fish. WATTLE (2), *v.t.* to make with wattles; bind with twigs; plait. WATTLED, *adj.* bound, plaited, with twigs. [OE.].

WAVE (1) [wāv], *v.t. and i.* to cause to undulate, raise a series of curving ridges in a surface; manipulate with a series of up and down movements, brandish; raise and flourish the hand as a signal; move in the air from side to side, sway; undulate; grow or be trained in a series of curves, as the hair; flourish the hand as a signal. WAVE (2), *n.* a ridge of water travelling across the surface of the sea, ocean swell, billow, undulation on the surface of any body of water; a rippling irregularity of any surface or mass, as of silk, hair; (*fig.*) strong emotional movement stirring a body of people; one of several groups of troops, aircraft etc., making a series of attacks; (*phys.*) a periodic motion, the transmission of periodic motions through a continuous medium; (*radio*) periodic disturbance in the ether set up by electrical oscillations radiated by a conductor. WAVE-BAND, (*radio*) a group of wavelengths between determined limits. WAVE-LIKE, *adj.* having the characteristics of a w., undulating. WAVED, *adj.* possessing or given the form of a series of waves. [OE.].

WAVELENGTH [wāv'length], *n.* distance between the peaks of two successive waves; (*radio*) the length of electro-magnetic wave (adopted by a transmitting station).

WAVELET [wāv'let], *n.* little wave, ripple.

WAVEMETER [wāv'mē-ter], *n.* apparatus for registering or measuring electrical wavelengths.

WAVER [wā'ver], *v.i.* to play or move uncertainly

to and fro, fluctuate; be unsettled in opinion; vacillate, hesitate; totter. WAVERER, *n.* person who wavers; irresolute person. [~OIcel.].

WAVY [wā'vi], *adj.* characterized by an undulating surface; full of waves; susceptible to the movement of the breeze; (*bot.*) undulating in form.

WAX (1) [waks], *n.* firm, yellow, plastic substance, malleable when warm, which bees secrete for the building of cells; yellow substance secreted by the ear; substance prepared out of fats and oils from which candles are made; a secretion of certain plants; beeswax with which cobblers smear their thread; similar substance extracted from mineral oils. WAX-CLOTH, floor-cloth for polishing. WAX-DOLL, doll with its head modelled out of w. and hardened. WAX-LIGHT, taper made of w. WAX-MYRTLE, the candleberry, an American shrub. WAX-PAPER, type of paper treated with w. WAX (2), *v.t.* to smear with w., apply w. to. WAXEN, *adj.* made of w.; having the appearance or properties of w. [OE.].

WAX (3), *n.* (*schoolboy slang*) a temper, rage. [Uncert.].

WAX (4), *v.i.* to increase in size, as the moon; pass from one state to another, become. [OE.].

WAXBILL [waks'bil], *n.* weaver bird of the genus *Estrelda.*

WAXWING [waks'wing], *n.* bird with quills tipped with a substance like red sealing-wax.

WAXWORK [waks'werk], *n.* effigy in wax; modelling in wax; (*pl.*) collection of such effigies open to the public.

WAXY (1) [wak'si], *adj.* containing, resembling wax; having one or more of the characteristics of wax. [WAX (1)].

WAXY (2), *adj.* (*slang*) angry. [WAX (3)].

WAY [wā], *n.* direction or line of progress from one place to another, road, street, avenue, path; the route taken; course of a journey; distance travelled; a direction followed or faced; (*naut.*) motion through the water, speed, momentum; drift; manner, means or method of accomplishing something, technique of tackling a job of work, plan of action, mode of procedure; a characteristic manner, custom or habit; range, sphere; a characteristic; **by w. of,** as a means of; **by the w.,** incidentally; **to give w.,** to yield, retreat; **to go out of one's w.,** to give oneself trouble on behalf of another; **in the family w.,** pregnant; **out of the w.,** not easily accessible; extraordinary; **to pave the w.,** to settle the initial stages; **to put in the w. of,** to provide with an opportunity of; **under w.,** (*naut.*) moving under its own power, travelling; **right of w.,** right of traversing; **ways and means,** method, devices. WAY-BILL, record of passengers or goods. [OE.].

WAYFARER [wā'fāer-er], *n.* traveller, *esp.* on foot. WAYFARING, *adj.* travelling.

WAYLAY (*pret.* and *p.pt.* **waylaid**) [wā-lā'], *v.t.* to seize or accost by lying in wait for; ambush.

WAYSIDE (1) [wā'sīd], *n.* edge of a road; roadside. WAYSIDE (2), *adj.* found by, or growing on, the w.

WAYWARD [wā'werd], *adj.* temperamentally inclined to disregard others; perverse; wilful.

WE [wē], *pron. 1st person pl.* of I; *also formerly used by royalty.* [OE.].

WEAK [wēk], *adj.* lacking in muscular power, deficient in physical strength; puny, feeble; having insufficient power of resistance; unable to withstand pressure or weight; offering little resistance; defenceless, frail, delicate in constitution; irresolute, indecisive; lacking strong ingredients; deficient in alcoholic content; insipid, diluted. WEAK-HEADED, mentally w. WEAK-HEARTED, having little courage. WEAK-KNEED, (*fig.*) having no strength or force of mind. WEAK-MINDED, mentally deficient. WEAK-SIGHTED, having w. eyesight. WEAK-SPIRITED, timid; lacking in moral or emotional drive. WEAKLY (1), *adj.* not strong of constitution; delicate in health. WEAKLY (2), *adv.* in a w. manner. WEAKNESS, *n.* quality of being w.; absence of muscular power; irresolution; unhealthiness; a defect, failing; a rather unjustified or unreasonable liking (for). [ME.].

WEAKEN [wē'ken], *v.t. and i.* to make weaker, cause to diminish in vigour or powers of endurance; lessen in the capacity to withstand weight or pressure; make less convincing; grow weaker, become weakly; become less certain.

WEAKLING [wēk'ling], *n.* physically weak person or animal; habitually irresolute person, one with little ability.

WEAL (1) [wēl], *n.* healthy or flourishing condition; welfare; happiness, well-being. [OE.].

WEAL (2), *n.* mark or long reddish bruise left by a stripe or lash; wale. [OE.].

WEALD [wēld], *n.* open tract of country, *esp.* that occupying the area between the N. and S. Downs. WEALDEN, *adj.* (*geol.*) relating to, found in, formations of Lower Cretaceous age. [~OE.].

WEALTH [welth], *n.* sum total of a nation's or person's resources, money and property; state of prosperity accompanied by an amount of material riches far above the average, affluence; abundance, inordinate amount. [ME.].

WEALTHY [wel'thi], *adj.* owning wealth, rich, having large possessions; opulent; affluent.

WEAN (1) [wēn, wān], *n.* (*Scots*) child. [Scots].

WEAN (2) [wēn], *v.t.* to deprive (a child) gradually of milk from the breast, giving other food as a substitute; (*fig.*) attract from one interest towards another. WEANLING, *n.* infant or young of a mammal newly weaned. [OE.].

WEAPON [we'pn], *n.* any instrument of offence or defence fitted for the killing or wounding of enemies; also *fig.* [OE.].

WEAR (1) (*pret.* **wore**, *p.pt.* **worn**) [wāer], *v.t.* to reduce gradually by friction or usage, cause to diminish owing to the action of functioning parts one upon the other, make inroads into (a solid) by constant rubbing; waste, exhaust, weary; carry on the body as clothing or ornament; possess on one's person; give expression to, exhibit; (*coll.*) tolerate, endure; *v.i.* to endure, last, withstand severe usage; **to w. away**, to cause to disappear, consume; pass out of existence gradually; **to w. down**, to lessen by constant rubbing; break down; **to w. off**, to disappear through constant use or friction; **to w. out**, to cause to become thin by constant usage; exhaust; lose substance by attrition; **to w. the breeches**, to rule the roost, assume command. WEAR (2), *n.* act of wearing; clothes worn, *esp.* in a collective sense; act of being used, usage; process of being impaired in value or quality by persistent use; **w. and tear**, damage to an object attendant upon regular use. WEARABLE, *adj.* fit or able to be worn. WEARER, *n.* one who wears; that which wastes or diminishes. WEARING (1), *n.* action of wearing. WEARING (2), *adj.* denoting what is worn; characterized by power to exhaust. [OE.].

WEAR (3) (*pret. and p.pt.* **wore**), *v.t. and i.* (*naut.*) to turn (a ship's head) away from the wind, veer. [*Var.* of VEER (1)].

WEARILESS [wēer'i-les], *adj.* unaffected by exhausting conditions; continual.

WEARISOME [wēer'i-sum], *adj.* causing weariness; tedious.

WEARY (1) [wēer'i], *adj.* sapped of strength by working in exhausting conditions, tired; causing fatigue; boring, tedious. WEARY (2), *v.t. and i.* to make w.; exhaust the interest of a person by persistence; become w. [OE.].

WEASEL [wē'zl], *n.* a small carnivore, allied to the stoat. [OE.].

WEATHER (1) [we'ther], *n.* the atmospheric conditions existing at a particular time over a particular area; **under the w.**, (*coll.*) not feeling well, depressed. WEATHER-BEATEN, affected by the w., *esp.* in complexion; seasoned. WEATHER-BOARD, board forming part of the outside wall of a wooden building; board set over a window to keep out rain; (*naut.*) side of a ship facing the wind. WEATHER-BOARDING, lengths of wood so tapered at one longitudinal edge as to permit of their being overlapped when secured. WEATHER-BOUND, unable to move because of bad w. WEATHER-EYE, watchful eye. WEATHER-FORECAST, scientific prediction of future w. WEATHER-GLASS, barometer. WEATHER-PROOF, adapted to withstand rough w. WEATHER-PROPHET, person who forecasts w. conditions. WEATHER-STAINED, discoloured by exposure to w. WEATHER-VANE, weathercock. WEATHER-WISE, knowledgeable in w. lore. WEATHER (2), *v.t. and i.* to expose to atmospheric conditions; wear by the action of the elements; survive, bear up against; (*naut.*) sail to the windward of; suffer damage from the w. WEATHERED, *adj.* (*arch.*) designed as a protection against rain; (*geol.*) affected by exposure. [OE.].

WEATHERCOCK [we'ther-kok], *n.* device usually in the form of a metal plate shaped like a cock, placed on the top of a building, flagpole etc., to indicate the direction of the wind; (*fig.*) fickle person.

WEAVE (1) (*pret.* **wove**, *p.pt.* **woven**) [wēv], *v.t. and i.* to make into a piece of material by interlacing threads in close texture on a loom, intertwine, plait;

arrange in a series of insertions; practise weaving; in boxing, to make weaving motions with the gloves and body; (*aeron.*) fly with a weaving motion; (*fig.*) put into narrative form; move drunkenly. WEAVE (2), *n.* basic pattern of a fabric dependent on the method of weaving. WEAVING, *n.* act or craft of one who weaves. [OE.].

WEAZEN, WEAZENED, see WIZEN, WIZENED.

WEB (1) [web], *n.* piece of woven material, *esp.* one or open mesh like a net; delicate fly-trap of interlinked threads spun by a spider, cobweb; (*fig.*) a complicated system of organization; membrane between the toes of an aquatic bird; the part of a girder connecting the upper flange to the lower; large reel of the paper on which newspapers are printed; thin metal plate acting as a partition or means of connexion in machinery; **w. of deceit**, elaborate tissue of lies. WEB (2) (*pres.pt.* **webbing**, *pret. and p.pt.* **webbed**), *v.t.* to form into a w. WEBBED, *adj.* (*ornith. and physiol.*) having the digits connected by a w. WEBBY, *adj.* like a w., webbed. [OE.].

WEBBING [we'bing], *n.* strong narrow fabric for supporting upholstery etc.

WED (*pres.pt.* **wedding**, *pret. and p.pt.* **wedded**, **wed**) [wed], *v.t. and i.* to take a woman for wife or a man for husband, marry; participate in a marriage ceremony with another; (*fig.*) unite, combine; be married. WEDDED, *adj.* married; (*fig.*) closely attached. [OE.].

WEDDING [we'ding], *n.* religious or civil ceremony in which a man and woman are joined in marriage. WEDDING-BREAKFAST, party for friends and relations of bride and bridegroom held after the w. ceremony. WEDDING-RING, ring given at the marriage ceremony by the bridegroom to the bride as a symbol of the bond.

WEDGE (1) [wej], *n.* piece of wood or metal shaped down to a thin edge at one end, and designed to be driven into a mass so as to split it, or to act as a support by insertion next to something which requires a rigid fixture; any mass shaped like a w.; **thin end of the w.**, apparently insignificant incident likely to have undesired consequences. WEDGE-HEEL, denoting a type of shoe in which the heel, in the shape of a w., is prolonged under the arch. WEDGE (2), *v.t. and i.* to make rigid by means of a w.; split by driving a w. into; hold fast as if by an inserted w. [OE.].

WEDGWOOD [wej'wood], *n.* a kind of pottery. [J. *Wedgwood*, famous potter].

WEDLOCK [wed'lok], *n.* status of a married couple, matrimony. [OE.].

WEDNESDAY [wenz'dā], *n.* fourth day of the week. [OE.].

WEE (1) [wē], *n.* (*Scots*) a little while. WEE (2), *adj.* (*esp. Scots*) tiny, very small. [ME. from OE.].

WEED (1) [wēd], *n.* any plant whose growth interferes with other cultivated plants, *esp.* one hardy, prolific and bearing little blossom; (*slang*) cheap cigar; weedy fellow; **the w.**, tobacco. WEED (2), *v.t. and i.* to clear of weeds by uprooting them; purge of obstructive elements; remove weeds; **to w. out**, to remove by selection. WEEDER, *n.* one who weeds; garden tool for uprooting weeds; chemical w.-killer. [OE.].

WEED (3), *n.* mourning dress; (*pl.*) sombre clothes and veil worn by a widow. [OE.].

WEEDY [wē'di], *adj.* consisting of weeds; invaded by weeds; lanky and underdeveloped.

WEEK [wēk], *n.* division of time consisting of seven successive days, *esp.* the period beginning on a Sunday and ending with the following Saturday; (*coll.*) the period from a Monday morning to the following Friday night or Saturday noon, as distinct from the week-end; **Holy W.**, week before Easter w. [OE.].

WEEKDAY (1) [wēk'dā], *n.* any day of the week except Sunday. WEEK-DAY (2), *adj.* occurring on a w.

WEEK-END (1) [wēk-end'], *n.* period lasting from Friday night to Monday morning, the whole of Saturday and Sunday, or from Saturday noon till Sunday night; holiday or visit covering this period. WEEK-END (2), *adj.* occurring at the w. WEEK-END (3), *v.i.* to take a holiday over a w.

WEEKLY (1) [wēk'li], *adj.* occurring, published, regularly each week. WEEKLY (2), *n.* periodical published w. WEEKLY (3), *adv.* once a week.

WEEN † [wēn], *v.t.* (*poet.*) to think, opine; imagine; believe, expect. [OE.].

WEEP (1) (*pret. and p.pt.* **wept**) [wēp], *v.t. and i.* to shed tears; lament, bemoan; fill the eyes to overflowing with tears as an expression of grief or nervous reaction; cry; secrete moisture. WEEP (2), *n.* act or period of weeping. WEEPER, *n.* one who weeps; long crepe hat-band formerly worn by a mourner; broad white cuff formerly worn by widows; (*pl.*) (*slang*) side-whiskers. [O.E.].

WEEPING (1) [wē′ping], *n.* action of a person who weeps; lamentation. WEEPING (2), *adj.* secreting moisture in drops; (of trees) drooping.

WEEVIL [wē′vil], *n.* long-snouted, destructive beetle. WEEVILY, *adj.* infested with weevils. [O.E.].

WEFT [weft], *n.* the threads interwoven with the warp from selvedge to selvedge to form a piece of material or fabric. [O.E.].

WEIGH (1) [wā], *v.t.* to ascertain, record, the weight of, *esp.* by a mechanical balance; equal the weight of, test by means of a balance; subject to a process of reconsideration, ponder over, *esp.* with a view to forming a conclusion; raise, as an anchor; *v.i.* to possess significance, have importance; **to w. down**, to cause to bend, oppress; **to w. in**, to test the specific weight of a jockey before a race; check the weight of a boxer or aircraft passenger and luggage; (*fig.*) plunge in; **to w. out**, to allot measured portions of; test the specific weight of a jockey after a race; **to w. up**, to form an opinion of; **to w. upon**, to depress; **to w. one's words**, to consider carefully what one has to say. WEIGH (2), *n.* act of weighing; bulk weighed. WEIGHER, *n.* one who weighs; supervisor of official weighing-machines. [O.E.].

WEIGHBRIDGE [wā′brij], *n.* apparatus for weighing laden carts.

WEIGHT (1) [wāt], *n.* amount of heaviness characterizing a mass or object as registered by a pair of scales, measure of the gravitation of a body towards the centre of the earth; piece of metal of specific heaviness for ascertaining by balance the heaviness of a body, quantity or object; standard system of measuring degrees of heaviness; object with the function of keeping something held down; heavy load, burden; set of circumstances or facts which by its importance has an oppressive influence; significance, influence, importance. WEIGHT (2), *v.t.* to equip with weights, render heavy by adding weights, load. [M.E.].

WEIGHTY [wā′ti], *adj.* possessing an appreciable weight, distinctly heavy, ponderous; exerting considerable influence in argument, possessing significant or important characteristics, convincing.

WEIR [wēer], *n.* dam formed across a river or stream; trap for fish consisting of stakes placed across a stream. [O.E.].

WEIRD (1) [wēerd], *n.* (*Scots*) fate. WEIRD (2), *adj.* relating to, derived from, fate; strange, queer, uncanny; (*slang*) eccentric, odd. [O.E.].

WELCH, see WELSH.

WELCOME (1) [wel′kum], *adj.* given a hospitable reception, received with gladness; accepted as promoting happiness or as supplying a want, gratifying; greeted as opportune; offered as gratuitous; **w. to**, at liberty to. WELCOME (2), *n.* act of making w.; occasion of hospitable reception. WELCOME (3), *v.t.* to offer a w. to, greet hospitably; accept with pleasure. [O.I.cel., O.E.].

WELD (1) [weld], *n.* (*bot.*) a plant used by dyers for the yellow colour it yields, dyer's weed. [M.E.].

WELD (2), *v.t. and i.* to join (metal) by hammering or pressure when subjected to heat; unite closely and firmly; undergo a process of welding. WELD (3), *n.* act of welding; join made by welding. [~O.E.].

WELFARE [wel′fāer], *n.* general level of existence from the point of view of comfort, health and wealth; prosperity, satisfactory standard of living, *esp.* for a society or community; **w. worker**, paid person in a factory, local government area etc., who looks after the health and general circumstances of employees or local inhabitants. WELFARE-CENTRE, institution for amelioration of local conditions, *esp.* in connexion with children, expectant mothers and unemployed. [O.E.].

WELKIN [wel′kin], *n.* (*archaic*) the sky. [~O.E.].

WELL (1) [wel], *n.* place where the water of a subterranean stream is accessible, *esp.* a shaft hollowed out of the earth which has access at the bottom to an underground spring; any narrow, deep excavation in the earth; any deep enclosed space; compartment in a fishing-smack or trawler to hold the catch; central space in a building, *esp.* in a court room; space provided in a building for a staircase or lift; (*naut.*) space round a ship's pump. WELL-DECK, lower deck not covered by upper decks. WELL-HEAD, source of a spring. WELL-HOLE, open space in the middle of a building designed to accommodate a flight of stairs.

WELL-HOUSE, structure built over a w. WELL-SPRING, a natural source of water-supply. WELL-WATER, water which flows into and is drawn from a w. WELL (2), *v.i.* to issue out in a bubbling stream, gush forth, gain exit. [O.E.].

WELL (3), *adv.* to a satisfactory degree, in a proper manner; correctly, rightly; in a skilful manner, expertly; efficiently, thoroughly; to a suitable degree; in a manner worthy of praise; to a convenient extent; **as w.**, as an extra, besides; **as w. as**, together with; **just as w.**, at least as good. WELL-APPOINTED, satisfactorily equipped. WELL-BALANCED, set in a satisfactory and accurate balance; having good proportions. WELL-BEING, sound state of health or prosperity. WELL-BORN, born into a distinguished family. WELL-BRED, possessing hereditary qualities of a high standard; w.-mannered. WELL-CONNECTED, having relatives of good family. WELL-DISPOSED, friendly. WELL-DOING, the doing of good deeds. WELL-EDUCATED, that indicates a good education; (of a person) having had a good education, cultured. WELL-FAVOURED, pleasing to the eye; having handsome features. WELL-FOUNDED, based on sound reasons, authentic. WELL-INTENTIONED, meaning w. even though failing to achieve the desired end. WELL-KNIT, having a compact physique. WELL-KNOWN, widely known. WELL-MARKED, w. differentiated, pronounced. WELL-MEANING, of good intentions. WELL-MEANT, showing kindly intentions. WELL-OFF, having ample means. WELL-OILED, (*slang*) w. primed with alcohol, but not drunk. WELL-PROPORTIONED, having fine proportions, *esp.* in physique. WELL-READ, having an extensive and discriminating knowledge of good literature. WELL-SET(-UP), *adj.* of a compact build, having a firm physique. WELL-SPOKEN, aptly spoken; having an accent and diction free from uncouthness. WELL-TO-DO, w.-off, fairly wealthy. WELL-TRIED, proven. WELL-TRODDEN, much trodden or frequented; conventional. WELL-WORN, threadbare; trite. WELL (4), *adj.* possessing good health, physically fit; advantageous, favourable, suitable; advisable; good. WELL (5), *n.* what is judged good. WELL (6), *int.* expressing surprise or resignation, or implying a question. [O.E.].

WELLINGTONIA [we-ling-tō′ni-ah], *n.* a tall coniferous tree. [*Next*].

WELLINGTONS [we′ling-tonz], *n.*(*pl.*) boots (of rubber) made in one piece and reaching to just below the knee. [Duke of *Wellington*].

WELLWISHER [wel′wi-sher], *n.* non-active supporter, friend.

WELSH (1), **WELCH** [welsh], *adj.* of, relating to, characteristic of, coming from, made in, Wales; in or of Welsh or the Welsh. WELSH (2), *n.* the native Celtic language of Wales; **the W.**, (*pl.*) native inhabitants of Wales; **W. harp**, harp with three rows of strings; **W. rarebit, rabbit**, toasted cheese. [O.E.].

WELSH (3), *v.i.* to decamp from a racecourse, as a bookmaker, without paying winnings to backers. WELSHER, *n.* bookmaker who welshes. [Unkn.].

WELT (1) [welt], *n.* form of reinforcement for a hem or border; thin strip of leather by which the sole of a shoe or boot is attached to the uppers; mark on the body raised by a lash, scar, weal; (*coll.*) a blow, smack. WELT (2), *v.t.* to fit with a w. WELTED, *adj.* fitted with a w. WELTING, *n.* process of equipping with a w.; material for making welts; the w. itself. [M.E.].

WELTER (1) [wel′ter], *adj.* extra heavy; (in boxing) weighing between 135 and 147 lb.; (in horse-racing) riding well above average weight. WELTER-WEIGHT, boxer with a weight between light-weight and middle-weight, from 135 to 147 lb.; in racing, any extra heavy weight. [Uncert.].

WELTER (2), *v.i.* to slip and roll about uncontrollably in a w., wallow. WELTER (3), *n.* a confused mass. [~O.E.].

WEN [wen], *n.* cyst, *esp.* on the head. [O.E.].

WENCH (1) [wensh], *n.* (*coll.*) young woman. WENCH (2), *v.i.* to indulge in promiscuous sexual relations. [M.E.].

WEND (1) [wend], *n.* member of a Slavic race who occupied the north-east of Germany. [Germ.].

WEND (2), *v.i.* † to wander; **to w. one's way**, to follow one's road. [O.E.].

WENT [went], *pret.* of GO.

WEPT [wept], *pret. and p.pt.* of WEEP.

WERE [wur, wāer], *pret. pl.*, *pl.* and *1st* and *3rd person sg. subj.* of BE. [O.E.].

WEREWOLF [wēer′woolf, wur′woolf], *n.* person

ŏŏ is pronounced as in *food*; ŏŏ as in *hood*; th as in *think*; TH as in *that*; zh as in *azure*.   ~ = related to.

fabled to change into a wolf; person with the voracious nature of a wolf. [O.E.].

WERT [wurt], (*poet.*) *2nd person sg. pret ind. and subj. of* BE.

WEST (1) [west], *n.* the cardinal point of the compass marked by the setting of the sun at the equinox; area of a country or of the globe situated in this direction in relation to a particular viewpoint. WEST (2), *adj.* relating to, coming from, facing, the w.; **the W. End**, fashionable quarter of London. WEST-END, relating to, proper to, frequenting, the W. End of London. WEST (3), *adv.* towards the w.; **to go w.**, (*coll.*) to die; be lost; be rendered useless. [O.E.].

WESTERING [wes'te-ring], *adj.* travelling towards the west. [M.E.].

WESTERLY [wes'ter-li], *adj. and adv.* relating to, situated in, the west; arriving from the west; moving towards the west; in the general direction of the west.

WESTERN (1) [wes'tern], *adj.* relating to, situated in, moving towards, coming from, the west; **W. Church**, the Latin Church. WESTERN (2), *n.* (*slang*) cowboy film or book. WESTERNER, *n.* a native of the west; inhabitant of the west, *esp.* in U.S.A. WESTERNISM, (*U.S.*) a w. idiom. WESTERNIZE, *v.t.* to convert to w. manners or modes of thought. [O.E.].

WESTING [wes'ting], *n.* (*naut.*) course or drift of a boat westward.

WESTWARD (1) [west'werd], *adj. and adv.* western, towards the west. WESTWARD (2), *n.* westerly direction or quarter.

WET (1) [wet], *adj.* drenched with, covered with, containing, water or other liquid; marked by a downpour of rain, by persistent rainfall; (*coll.*) anti-prohibitionist; (*slang*) characterless; **w. blanket**, blanket soaked in water in order to put a fire out; (*fig.*) gloomy or depressing person or event; **w. bob**, (*Eton slang*) boy who rows. WET-DOCK, dock in which vessels are maintained afloat. WET-NURSE (1), nurse who suckles another's child. WET-NURSE (2), to act as w.-nurse to; (*fig.*) tend with special care. WET (2), *n.* water, moisture; (*slang*) characterless person. WET (3) (*pres.pt.* WETTING, *pret. and p.pt.* WET, WETTED), *v.t.* to make w., drench; (*coll.*) seal (a bargain) with a drink. WETNESS, *n.* quality or state of being w. WETTISH, *adj.* rather w. [O.E.].

WETHER [we'THer], *n.* castrated ram. [O.E.].

WHACK (1) [wak], *v.t. and i.* to hit so that the blow resounds; thwack. WHACK (2), *n.* a resounding blow, thwack. WHACKER, *n.* (*slang*) huge one; a particularly audacious lie. WHACKING (1), *n.* a beating. WHACKING (2), *adj.* (*slang*) huge. [Echoic].

WHALE (1) [wāl], *n.* large marine mammal characterized by its size, which is often longer than 60 ft., and by a large caudal fin, and hunted commercially in the Arctic and Antarctic regions; (*slang*) anything big. WHALE-BACK, cargo steamer with upper works designed like the back of a w.; mound or hill shaped like the back of a w. WHALE-BOAT, long boat designed and equipped for whaling. WHALE-FISHERY, area where whales are caught; industry of fishing for whales. WHALE-MEAT, edible flesh of the w. WHALE (2), *v.i.* to hunt whales. WHALER, *n.* ship equipped for w.-fishery; seaman employed in whaling. [O.E.].

WHALING (1) [wā'ling], *n.* industry of catching whales. WHALING-GUN, apparatus by which the harpoon is fired from a whaler. WHALING-MASTER, officer in charge of a whaler. WHALING (2), *adj.* related to, concerned with, the business of whale-fishery.

WHANG (1) [wang], *n.* leather thong; resounding noise made when this strikes something. WHANG (2), *v.t.* to thrash, *esp.* with a leather strap. [Echoic].

WHARF (1) (*pl.* **wharves**) [wawf, wawvz], *n.* landing stage where ships are loaded and unloaded. WHARF (2), *v.t. and i.* to anchor alongside a w. WHARFAGE, *n.* payment for accommodation at a w.; the accommodation itself. WHARFING, *n.* a collection of wharves; materials for building or supporting wharves. WHARFINGER [waw'fin-jer], *n.* owner or superintendent of a w. [O.E.].

WHAT [wot], *pron.* who or which (of several alternatives); (*rel.*) that which (of several alternatives); how much; (*interrog.*) which (of several alternatives); how much. [O.E.].

WHATE'ER [wo-tāer'], *pron.* (*poet.*) whatever.

WHATEVER (1) [wo-te'ver], *pron.* regardless of anything, one thing or another, all that, all manner of things. WHATEVER (2), *adj.* no matter what.

WHATNOT [wot'not], *n.* piece of furniture for

displaying or storing ornamental odds and ends.
WHATSO'ER [wot-so-āer'], *pron.* (*poet.*) whatsoever.

WHATSOEVER [wot-sō-e'ver], *pron.* whatever.

WHAUP [w(h)awp], *n.* (*Scots*) the curlew. [Echoic].

WHEAL [wēl], *n.* pustule; weal. [M.E.].

WHEAT [wēt], *n.* a plant cultivated for its edible seed which is ground into flour. WHEAT-EAR, spike of w. WHEATEN, *adj.* made of wheat. [O.E.].

WHEATEAR [wē'tēer], *n.* a small bird, allied to the stonechat. [O.E.].

WHEEDLE [wē'dl], *v.t. and i.* to persuade to one's own ends by fawning or flattery, coax, cajole; **to w. out of**, to obtain from by flattery. [Uncert.].

WHEEL (1) [wēl], *n.* circular piece of any hard material capable of revolving round its centre; such an article of various constructions revolving in a vertical plane on an axle, supporting a vehicle or other load, or transmitting the power of the axle on which it is mounted; any apparatus designed on the principle of this; a single turn of a wheel; any movement which takes in a wide arc; (*naut.*) steering mechanism; **to break on the w.**, (*hist.*) to bind to the rim of a large w. and maim by breaking all the bones in the body; also (*fig.*); **to put a spoke in someone's w.**, to obstruct someone's plan or purpose; **to put one's shoulder to the w.**, to give aid in a task; **wheels within wheels**, a complicated series of interdependent agents. WHEEL-CHAIR, chair fitted with wheels, *esp.* for use of an invalid. WHEEL-HOUSE, (*naut.*) structure protecting the w. of a ship. WHEEL (2), *v.t. and i.* to cause to be conveyed by a vehicle fitted with wheels; cause to move on wheels by pushing, pulling etc.; manoeuvre (a body of troops) so that one end of a line keeps its ground and the other swings round in a wide arc; revolve on an axis; change direction so that one end of a line swings round in a wide semicircle; turn on a pivot so as to face another direction; (of birds etc.) fly in a wide arc. WHEELED, *adj.* fitted with a w. or wheels. WHEELER, *n.* wheelwright; one who, or that which, runs on wheels. [O.E.].

WHEELBARROW [wēl'ba-rō], *n.* small sturdy barrow with deep sides set on a more or less triangular frame of which the apex at the front is declined, and fitted with a small single wheel.

WHEELBASE [wēl'bās], *n.* distance between front and back axles.

WHEELWRIGHT [wēl'rīt], *n.* craftsman who makes wheels.

WHEEZE (1) [wēz], *v.i.* to breathe hard, making an audible whistling sound in the chest or at the back of the throat. WHEEZE (2), *n.* breathing accompanied by an involuntary whistling or thin-sounding noise in the chest or at the back of the throat; (*slang*) idea, plan, *esp.* for a joke. [O.E.].

WHEEZY [wē'zi], *adj.* afflicted with wheezing; sounding like one who wheezes.

WHEFT [weft], *n.* a signaller's flag. [*Var.* of WAFT].

WHELK [welk], *n.* an edible gastropod. [O.E.].

WHELP (1) [welp], *n.* the young of a bitch, puppy; lion cub; (*coll.*) contemptuous term for a young man. WHELP (2), *v.t. and i.* to give birth (to offspring) as a bitch. [O.E.].

WHEN (1) [wen], *adv. and conj.* which period, at what time, on what date; in what situation; at the time, on the day; at any time, whenever; even though. WHEN (2), *rel. pron.* on the occasion which; at which time. [O.E.].

WHENCE (1) [wens], *adv.* from where, from what place. WHENCE (2), *conj.* as a result of which. [M.E.].

WHENCESOEVER [wens-sō-e'ver], *adv. and conj.* (*poet.*) from whatever place or source.

WHENEVER [we-ne'ver], *adv. and conj.* at whatever time or occasion.

WHENSOEVER [wen-sō-e'ver], *adv. and conj.* whenever.

WHERE (1) [wāer], *adv. and conj.* to what place, at which place; in what particular; at the point at which. WHERE (2), *rel. pron.* from, to, at, which region, place etc.; the point at or on which. [O.E.].

WHEREABOUTS (1) [wāer-a-bowts'], *adv.* in which spot, place, area, position etc. WHEREABOUTS (2), [wāer'a-bowts], *n.* the place, situation, area. [WHERE (1) and ABOUT].

WHEREAS [wāer-az'], *rel. adv., conj.* but, from an opposite viewpoint, on the other hand, on the contrary, when in fact, since it is established that.

WHEREAT [wāer-at'], *adv.* at which.

WHEREBY [wāer-bī'], *adv.* by which; by what.

WHEREFORE (1) [wāer'faw(r)], *adv.* why, for what

reason, on what account; for that reason. WHERE-FORE (2), *n.* reason.

WHEREIN [wäer-in'], *adv.* into which; in respect of which; where.

WHEREOF [wäer-ov'], *adv.* of which.

WHEREON [wäer-on'], *adv.* on which.

WHERESOEVER [waer-sō-e'ver], *adv. and conj.* in whatever place, wherever.

WHERETO [wäer-tōō'], *adv.* to which; to what; to what end, for what.

WHEREUNDER [wäer-un'der], *adv.* under which.

WHEREUNTO [wäer-un'tōō], *adv.* whereto.

WHEREUPON [wäer-u-pon'], *adv.* upon which; at which point.

WHEREVER [wäer-e'ver], *adv. and conj.* at whatever place, in any part, position etc.

WHEREWITH [wäer-wiTH'], *adv* with which; with what.

WHEREWITHAL (1) [wäer'wi-THawl], *adv.* (*archaic*) wherewith. WHEREWITHAL (2), *n.* the means, the money necessary.

WHERRY [we'ri], *n.* rowing boat with seats for from six to eight passengers; large sailing barge. [Uncert.].

WHET (1) (*pres.pt.* **whetting**, *pret. and p.pt.* **whetted**) [wet], *v.t.* to rub on the surface of a flat stone so as to put a sharp edge on, sharpen, strop; stimulate. WHET (2), *n.* act of whetting; appetizer. [OE.].

WHETHER † (1) [we'THer], *pron.* which of two. WHETHER (2), *conj. indicating alternatives of choice, and often followed by* or; **w. or no,** no matter if. [OE.].

WHETSTONE [wet'stōn], *n.* any hard stone on which tools are sharpened by whetting.

WHEW (1) [whyōō], *int. expressing surprise or relief;* a forcing out of the breath accompanied by half a gasp and half a whistling sound. WHEW (2), *v.i.* to emit a w. [Echoic].

WHEY [wā], *n.* the thin watery part of milk which remains after removing the curds. WHEYISH, *adj.* containing or resembling w.; having the qualities of w. [OE.].

WHICH (1) [wich], *adj.* which, in interrogation; what person or object; of what sort, type, group. WHICH (2), *pron.* what one, thing, person etc., in interrogation; (*rel.*) that object or series of objects. [OE.].

WHICHEVER (1) [wi-che'ver], *adj.* that, any that. WHICHEVER (2), *pron.* either one or the other; which one.

WHICHSOEVER [wich-sō-e'ver], *pron.* whichever.

WHIFF (1) [wif], *n.* slight amount of air inhaled by a single sniff; puff or stream of air slightly tainted with a bad smell; brief contact with a smell; sculling boat fitted with outriggers for one rower; (*coll.*) small, cheap cigar. WHIFF (2), *v.i.* to possess a slight smell, give off a tainted odour. WHIFFY, *adj.* pervaded with whiffs; (*slang*) slightly smelly. [Echoic].

WHIFFING [wi'fing], *n.* technique of fishing with a handline for mackerel.

WHIFFLE (1) [wi'fl], *v.t. and i.* to cause to drift or float away haphazardly by gusts; blow in intermittent gusts or puffs, veer; drift with opinion. WHIFFLE (2), *n.* act of whiffling. WHIFFLER, *n.* one who vacillates, trifler. [Uncert.].

WHIG (1) [wig], *n.* (*hist.*) member or supporter of a political party originating with the Scottish Covenanters of the seventeenth century, and later becoming the Liberal Party. WHIG (2), *adj.* relating to the Whigs. WHIGGERY, *n.* theories and practice, *esp.* corrupt practices, of the Whigs. [Uncert.].

WHILE (1) [wīl], *n.* a time, the trouble or expense spent on something. WHILE (2), *adv. and conj.* as long as, during the same time that; in which case; although. WHILE (3), *v.t.* to cause (time) to pass (away) in pleasant but unimportant occupations. WHILES, *adv.* (*Scots*) (*coll.*) sometimes. [OE.].

WHILOM [wī'lom], *adv. and adj.* (*archaic*) previously, formerly; once; in ancient times; former. [OE.].

WHILST [wīlst], *conj.* while.

WHIM [wim], *n.* idea, fancy, which has no deep emotional or mental roots, a sudden desire, capricious wish. [~OScand.].

WHIMPER (1) [wim'per], *v.t. and i.* to cry in the form of low sobs and intermittent whining out of self-commiseration or the after-effects of pain; utter as one who whimpers. WHIMPER (2), *n.* act or period of whimpering. [Echoic].

WHIMSICAL [wim'zi-kal], *adj.* full of whimsy, temperamentally inclined to whimsy, expressing a quaint, fanciful capriciousness; freakish, eccentric. [*Next*].

WHIMSY [wim'zi], *n.* expression, idea, fanciful to the pitch of fantasy, caprice, whim. [WHIM].

WHIN [win], *n.* gorse; a plant of the genus *Ulex.* [~Norw.].

WHINBERRY [win'be-ri], *n.* whortleberry. [OE.].

WHINCHAT [win'chat], *n.* a small singing-bird, allied to the stonechat. [WHIN and CHAT].

WHINE (1) [wīn], *v.t. and i.* to express with a whine; give expression to sounds or verbal complaints while weeping and talking through the nose like a hurt child, complain fretfully like a child. WHINE (2), *n.* act of whining, noise made by a complaining, querulous cry; weepy, fawning complaint or request. [OE.].

WHINNY (1) [wi'ni], *v.i.* to make a noise, as a horse, by blowing air through the nose. WHINNY (2), *n.* noise made by a horse when it blows air through its nostrils. [Echoic].

WHINSTONE [win'stōn], *n.* kind of sandstone. [Uncert.].

WHIP (1) [wip], *n.* flexible thong, lash or plaited cord, fastened to a handle, and used for beating or thrashing; lash administered by this instrument; driver of a carriage; member of Parliament who organizes the attendance of his party members at divisions; summons sent out by this member; **w. hand,** position of advantage and control, upper hand. WHIP-LASH, lash of a w. WHIP-ROUND, spontaneously organized collection of voluntary contributions for some charity. WHIP-TOP, whipping-top. WHIP (2) (*pres.pt.* WHIPPING, *pret. and p.pt.* WHIPPED), *v.t.* to strike, hit, lash with a w., administer punishment by means of a w., thrash, flog; beat out by subjecting to a series of lashes; conquer, vanquish; beat into a froth; sew together (the bases of a fold in a material forming a ridge); *v.i.* to act quickly, make a movement in a flash; **to w. from,** to snatch away from; **to w. in,** to keep (hounds) from straying from a pack; **to w. off,** to lift off quickly; hurry away with a sudden movement; **to w. out,** to draw out quickly; speak suddenly in a decisive tone of voice; **to w. round,** to pivot suddenly; **to w. up,** to beat into a froth; pick up suddenly; stimulate quickly. [ME.].

WHIP (3), *n.* white pennant adorned with the cross of St. George flown by commissioned ships of the British Navy. [WHIP (1)].

WHIPCORD [wip'kawd], *n.* strong, closely twisted string out of which lashes are made for whips; strong woollen material woven in a ribbed pattern.

WHIPPER [wi'per], *n.* one who whips; officer detailed to inflict a legal whipping; (*naut.*) ship's hand stacking coal in a ship's hold. WHIPPER-IN, assistant who keeps hounds to the course of a hunt; competitor who finish last in a race.

WHIPPER-SNAPPER [wi'per-sna-per], *n.* small but cheeky boy; unimportant but presumptuous person. [Uncert.].

WHIPPET [wi'pit], *n.* small crossbred greyhound trained for speed; (*milit.*) light tank built for speed. [Uncert.].

WHIPPING [wi'ping], *n.* act of punishing with a whip; punishment administered by a whip; state of being whipped; severe defeat; close-coiled binding of cord to act as a support. WHIPPING-BOY, (*hist.*) boy educated along with an important personage for whose faults he had to take punishment; (*fig.*) one who has to take the blame for another's fault. WHIPPING-POST, (*hist.*) post to which offenders were tied when undergoing a w. by authority. WHIPPING-TOP, top spun by being whipped.

WHIR(R) (1), **WHUR** (*pres.pt.* **whirring,** *pret. and p.pt.* **whirred**) [wur], *v.t. and i.* to rotate rapidly so as to set up an audible vibration; make a humming sound by whirling round rapidly. WHIR(R) (2), WHUR, *n.* sound made by anything revolving rapidly. [~Dan.].

WHIRL (1) [wurl], *v.t. and i.* to spin round rapidly as on a pivot, gyrate; hurry off. WHIRL (2), *n.* act or condition of whirling, rapid rotation; (*fig.*) confused bustle, dizzy excitement. [OIcel.].

WHIRLIGIG [wur'li-gig], *n.* toy turned on a pivot, roundabout; something which whirls; a whirling, revolution. WHIRLIGIG BEETLE, *n.* a small water beetle. [WHIRL (1) and GIG].

WHIRLPOOL [wurl'pōōl], *n.* violent current of water eddying round in a circle, vortex.

WHIRLWIND [wurl'wind], *n.* atmospheric phenomenon consisting of a body of air, revolving violently and made visible by dust drawn into it by suction.

ōō is pronounced as in f*oo*d; ŏŏ as in h*oo*d; th as in *th*ink; TH as in *th*at; zh as in azure.   ∼ = related to.

WHIRR, see WHIR.

WHISHT, see WHIST (2).

WHISK (1) [wisk], *v.t. and i.* to remove by sweeping smartly away; swing, flip, toss; mix up thoroughly by beating as with a whisk; **to w. out,** to leave rapidly, (re)move nimbly. WHISK (2), *n.* act of whisking; small bunch of straw, stiff hairs etc., gathered to form a light brush; small culinary utensil for beating eggs. [OScand.].

WHISKER [wis'ker], *n.* one of the prominent hairs growing on the face, *esp.* of a man; bristle characteristic of the upper lip of the feline species; (*pl.*) cultivated growth of hair on the cheeks. [*Prec.*].

WHISKEY [wis'ki], *n.* whisky distilled in Ireland.

WHISKY [wis'ki], *n.* spirituous drink distilled, originally and chiefly in Scotland, from malted barley. [Gael.].

WHISPER (1) [wis'per], *v.t. and i.* to talk in a low sibilant voice without using the vocal cords; (*fig.*) intrigue, make mischief by rumour; give expression to an indistinct hissing or murmuring sound; give utterance to in a whisper, communicate secretly by means of a whisper. WHISPER (2), *n.* act of whispering; speech uttered with a low sibilant voice; subdued hissing sound with no definite articulation; (*fig.*) suggestion, hint. [OE.].

WHISPERING (1) [wis'pe-ring], *n.* act of one who whispers; that which is whispered. WHISPERING (2), *adj.* characterized by utterance in whispers; **w. campaign,** campaign of furtive rumour-spreading.

WHIST (1) [wist], *n.* game of cards for four players competing in pairs. [*Var.* of WHISK (1)].

WHIST (2), **WHISHT,** *int.* be silent, hush. [Echoic].

WHISTLE (1) [wi'sl], *n.* simple form of musical wind-instrument played by finger-stops; thin, high-pitched sound produced by this, or by forcing air through pursed-up lips with the tip of the tongue resting at the back of the front bottom teeth; any shrill, piercing sound; small instrument or pipe designed to make such a sound when blown; (*slang*) the throat. WHISTLE (2), *v.t. and i.* to give utterance to a high, shrill note or noise by forcing the breath out through pursed-up lips; make the noise natural to a bird; play on a w., blow a w.; give vent to a tune by forcing the breath through the teeth and lips; cause a high-pitched vibration of the air by moving (something) swiftly through it; produce, *esp.* as music, by whistling; call by whistling. [OE.].

WHIT (1) [wit], *n.* the minutest fraction, a jot. [OE.].

WHIT (2), *adj.* of, pertaining to, occurring at Whitsun. [WHIT(SUN)].

WHITE (1) [wit], *adj.* having the colour of driven snow; reflecting the colours of the spectrum as a light characterized by no predominating colour; not dark; pale in colour; deprived of colour; bloodless; pure; free from marks or spots; (*fig.*) good, pure in heart, honest; (of Russians in the 1917 revolution) anti-communist; **w. ant,** destructive tropical insect, termite; **w. elephant,** the grey elephant held in holy awe by the Siamese, and not trained for work; (*fig.*) costly but useless possession; **w. ensign,** flag of the Royal Navy and the Royal Yacht Squadron; **w. feather,** symbol of cowardice; **W. Friar,** Carmelite monk; **w. heat,** degree of heat at which a metal becomes w.; (*fig.*) mental or emotional state in which the faculties function at an unusual intensity; **w. horse,** ridge of foam at the summit of a wave; **W. House,** official residence of the President of U.S.A. used (*fig.*) to signify the office itself; **W. Lady,** cocktail of gin and lemon juice; **w. man,** member of the w.-skinned races of Europe; honourable and upright man; **w. man's burden,** responsibility of the w. races for civilizing the world; **w. meat,** flesh of poultry, veal etc.; **w. metal,** alloy of zinc etc. used by silversmiths; **w. paper,** book or pamphlet issued by the British Government on a specific matter of national interest, and bound in w. paper; **w. slave,** young (w.)girl seduced or forced and exported into prostitution. WHITE-COLLAR, descriptive of the class of workers, mostly clerks, who wear starched w. collars, or of the work they do. WHITE-LIVERED, cowardly. WHITE (2), *n.* colour or paint which is w.; that which is w.; person who is w., that is, of fair complexion as distinct from a negro or Oriental; **w. of egg,** the albumen in which the yolk is suspended in the shell; **w. of the eye,** the part of the eyeball round the iris; (*pl.*) leucorrhoea. WHITELY, *adv.* to a degree of whiteness. [OE.].

WHITEBAIT [wit'bāt], *n.* small fry of herrings and sprats and other small edible fishes.

WHITEBEARD [wit'bēerd], *n.* old man.

WHITEHALL [wit-hawl'], *n.* (*fig.*) the British Government; bureaucracy. [WHITEHALL, a street in London where many Government offices are housed].

WHITEHEART [wit'haht], *n.* cherry with cream-coloured flesh.

WHITEN [wi'ten], *v.t. and i.* to give a coating of white to, make white; bleach; grow white.

WHITETHORN [wit'thawn], *n.* hawthorn.

WHITETHROAT [wit'thrōt], *n.* a species of warbler characterized by a white-feathered throat.

WHITEWASH (1) [wit'wosh], *n.* a wash containing lime for whitening walls. WHITEWASH (2), *v.t.* to paint over with w.; (*fig.*) cause to appear virtuous.

WHITHER [wi'THer], *adv.* to what place; in which way; to what point or degree. [OE.].

WHITING [wi'ting], *n.* prepared chalk; an edible sea fish.

WHITISH [wi'tish], *adj.* light in colour, almost white.

WHITLOW [wit'lō], *n.* swollen tumour affecting the tips of the fingers. [ME.].

WHITSUN (1) [wit'sun], *n.* the week beginning with Whit Sunday, Whitsuntide. WHITSUN (2), *adj.* relating to, occurring at, W. [ME.].

WHIT SUNDAY [wit-sun'dā], *n.* seventh Sunday after Easter, marking a Church festival in commemoration of the descent of the Holy Spirit on the day of Pentecost. [ME.].

WHITSUNTIDE [wit'sun-tīd], *n.* the week following Whit Sunday; the Whit Sunday week-end.

WHITTLE [wi'tl], *v.t. and i.* to cut down by thin slivers, slice small strips from (a stick, piece of wood) with a knife, *esp.* so as to leave bare of bark; make thin by shaving off slices; (*fig.*) cause to diminish by a process of gradual subtraction. [ME.].

WHIZZ (1) [wiz], *v.i.* to make a hissing, whirring sound like an arrow or ball forcing its way through the air. WHIZZ (2), *n.* the hissing, whirring sound made by passage of a projectile through the air. WHIZZ-BANG, (*milit. slang*) high-velocity shell preceded by a whizzing noise before exploding; (*schoolboy slang*) exploding firework. [Echoic].

WHO [hōō], *rel. and interrog. pron.* that person; which person; **W.'s W.,** title of a book issued annually giving brief biographies of prominent living persons; similar compilation in a special field. [OE.].

WHOA [wō], *int.* (to horses) stop !

WHOEVER [hōō-e'ver], *rel. and interrog. pron.* whatever person, any one.

WHOLE (1) [hōl], *adj.* possessing the parts in a completed aggregate, having an established entity, entire, unbroken, not impaired or defective; † sound in health. WHOLE-HOGGER, (*coll.*) one who goes or advocates going the w. hog. WHOLE (2), *n.* anything in its entirety; the complete entity of a thing in terms of all its parts and qualities, the total number, the complete amount. WHOLENESS, *n.* state of being w., totality. [OE.].

WHOLEHEARTED [hōl-hah'tid], *adj.* giving of the utmost of one's deepest emotions, sincere.

WHOLEMEAL (1) [hōl'mēl], *n.* flour which contains the milled husk and kernel of the cereal. WHOLE-MEAL (2), *adj.* made of w.

WHOLESALE (1) [hōl'sāl], *n.* the sale of goods in large quantities, carried out *esp.* by the manufacturer or his agent doing business with retailers. WHOLE-SALE (2), *adj.* relating to, trading in, goods sold in gross; consisting of commodities sold by w. WHOLESALE (3), *adv.* on a w. basis; in large amounts; indiscriminately.

WHOLESOME [hōl'sum], *adj.* having natural food values, good for maintaining the body in health; having a salutary effect on the mind or morals. [OE.].

WHOLLY [hōl'li], *adv.* entirely, completely; unconditionally.

WHOM [hōōm], *n. rel. and interrog. pron. objective case of* WHO.

WHOMSOEVER (*archaic*) [hōōm-sō-e'ver], *rel. and interrog. pron. objective case of* WHOSOEVER.

WHOOP (1) [hōōp], *v.i.* to give vent to high spirits by shouting at the top of one's voice, yell. WHOOP (2), *n.* loud shout uttered in high spirits. [Echoic].

WHOOPEE [wōō'pē, wōō-pē'], *n.* a half-yell, half-scream of delight; **to make w.,** (*slang*) to participate in a wild, noisy party; go on a spree. [*Prec.*].

WHOOPING-COUGH, HOOPING COUGH [hōō'ping-kof], *n.* an ailment, especially infectious to children, notable for bouts of violent coughing accompanied by a characteristic whooping sound.

The accent ' after a syllable = stress (u-pon'). The mark ⁻ over a vowel = length (ā in made; ō in bone).

WHOP (1) [wop], *v.t.* to hit; defeat, *esp.* in fisticuffs. WHOP (2), *n.* sudden fall, flop. WHOPPER, *n.* (*slang*) something abnormally big, *esp.* a monstrous lie. WHOPPING, *adj.* (*coll.*) huge. [ME.].

WHORE (1) [haw(r)'], *n.* woman who hires her body to men for sexual use; woman who breaks the social code of sexual morality, harlot. WHORE (2), *v.i.* to associate with whores. WHOREDOM †, *n.* condition of behaving as a w.; (*O.T.*) idolatry. WHOREMONGER, *n.* man who consorts with whores. WHORING, *n.* fornication; the frequenting of whores; prostitution. [OE.].

WHORL [wurl, worl], *n.* the form taken by a spiral twist; (*bot.*) ring of leaves or petals round a stem; (*zool.*) coil of a spiral shell. [ME.].

WHORT, WHURT [wurt], *n.* (*dial.*) whortleberry.

WHORTLEBERRY, HURTLEBERRY [wur'tl-be-ri, hur'tl-be-ri], *n.* bilberry; purple fruit of this shrub. [Uncert.].

WHOSE [hōōz], *rel. and interrog. pron. possessive or genitive case of* WHO *or* WHICH.

WHOSESOEVER † [hōōz-sō-e'ver], *rel. and interrog. pron. possessive case of* WHOSOEVER.

WHOSO † [hōō'sō], *rel. and interrog. pron.* whosoever.

WHOSOEVER † [hōō-sō-e'ver], *rel. and interrog. pron.* any person whatever, whoever.

WHUR, see WHIR.

WHURT, see WHORT.

WHY (1) [wī], *adv.* for what cause or reason (in a relative or interrogative clause). WHY (2), *n.* the reason for a thing; **the w.(s) and wherefore(s)**, the precise reason(s) for a certain action or thing. [OE.].

WICK [wik], *n.* length of twisted or plaited cotton or other fibres set in the middle of a candle or in a vessel containing oil, paraffin or petrol, for the purpose of conducting the fuel to the flame. [OE.].

WICKED [wi'kid], *adj.* breaking the laws of God and man which embody the accepted principles of good thoughts and conduct; by nature or deliberation following a line of social conduct considered fundamentally vicious, abhorrent and evil; sinful, immoral; (*coll.*) malicious, roguish. [ME.].

WICKER (1) [wi'ker], *n.* osier; flexible branch or twig. WICKER (2), *adj.* made of wickers arranged in a plaited open-work. WICKERWORK, *n.* basketwork made from plaited wickers. [MSwed.].

WICKET [wi'kit], *n.* small door built into a larger door or gate; (*cricket*) set of three stumps surmounted by a pair of bails, to be defended by a batsman; the pitch; a batsman's innings. WICKET-KEEPER, (*cricket*) fielder who stands immediately behind the batsman's w. [AFr.].

WIDDERSHINS, see WITHERSHINS.

WIDE (1) [wīd], *adj.* covering a relatively extensive range from side to side, broad; covering a large space, extending over a large area, spacious; occurring some distance from the centre, badly directed; remote, distant; all-embracing, general; **w. boy**, *n.* (*orig. U.S. slang*), spiv; one who lives on his wits at the expense of strangers; one who is wide awake, *esp.* a costermonger. WIDE (2), *adv.* to a large, or to the fullest, extent; at a distance; to an inaccurate degree; **w. of**, far from. WIDE (3), *n.* (*cricket*) ball bowled out of a reasonable reach of the batsman; run counted as a penalty against the side of the bowler of such a ball; **to the w.**, to the w. world, utterly. WIDELY, *adv.* with considerable extension; to a great distance; so as to cover a considerable area. [OE.].

WIDEAWAKE (1) [wī-da-wāk'], *adj.* having the eyes wide open and the mind on the alert; being on the look-out for danger. WIDEAWAKE (2), [wī'da-wāk], *n.* type of soft, low-crowned, wide-brimmed felt hat.

WIDEN [wī'den], *v.t. and i.* to make wide or wider, extend in breadth; grow wide or wider; enlarge, increase in width.

WIDESPREAD [wīd'spred], *adj.* covering a great distance or area.

WIDGEON [wi'jn], *n.* a migratory wild duck.

WIDOW (1) [wi'dō], *n.* woman whose husband is dead and who has not married again; **grass w.**, woman whose husband has been obliged to leave her temporarily; **w.'s peak**, triangular growth of hair over the forehead. WIDOW (2), *v.t.* to make a w. [OE.].

WIDOWER [wi'dō-er], *n.* man whose wife has died. [Prec.].

WIDTH [width], *n.* distance from one side to the other, wideness; also (*fig.*). [WIDE].

WIELD [wēld], *v.t.* to grasp by the hand and have under control, manipulate as one in command,

handle. WIELDER, *n.* one who wields. WIELDY, *adj.* manageable, easily handled. [~OE.].

WIFE (*pl.* **wives**) [wīf], *n.* woman joined to a man by marriage; married woman; (*archaic*) woman. [OE.].

WIG [wig], *n.* false set of hair as a covering for the head, designed to give the impression of a natural head of hair; highly artificial head-dress of hair fashionable in the 17th and 18th centuries; head-covering of a judge etc. WIGGED, *adj.* adorned with a w. [(PERI)WIG].

WIGGING [wi'ging], *n.* (*slang*) a scolding. [Uncert.].

WIGGLE (1) [wi'gl], *v.t. and i.* to make a contorted, twisted movement with the limbs; waggle, wriggle. WIGGLE (2), *n.* act of wiggling, a squirm, twist. [*Var.* of WAGGLE].

WIGHT † [wīt], *n.* person; poor wretch, fool. [OE.].

WIGWAM [wig'wom], *n.* portable tent of the North American Indians; Indian hut. [NAmerInd.].

WILD (1) [wīld], *adj.* roving at will according to primitive instincts, not tamed by man; seeded by nature; left uninhabited by man, savage, uncivilized; characterized by a state of violent disorder, tempestuous; extremely untidy; emotionally disturbed; mad with anger, furious; irregular in social behaviour, wanton; crazy, frantic, frenzied; ill-considered; **w. duck**, the mallard; **w. fowl**, (*pl.*) w. birds, game. WILD (2), *adv.* to a w. degree. WILD (3), *n.* territory not occupied by man, impenetrable area of the earth. WILDISH, *adj.* somewhat w. [OE.].

WILD CAT [wīld-kat'], *n.* the British wild cat, *Felis sylvestris.* WILD CAT, *adj.* reckless, hysterical.

WILDEBEEST [vil'de-bāst], *n.* the gnu. [Afrik.].

WILDERNESS [wil'der-nes], *n.* vast tract of country remaining uninhabited and uncultivated, often because of the impenetrable nature of its geographical features; any enormous area of desolation; any area in which the flora and fauna are allowed to run wild; (*fig.*) desolate, uninviting place; **in the w.**, (*politics*) out of office. [ME.].

WILDFIRE [wīld'fīr], *n.* lightning without thunder, called also summer lightning; inflammable substance used by the ancient Greeks in warfare, Greek fire; fire out of control.

WILD GOOSE [wīld-gōōs'], *n.* wild bird of the goose family; **w. chase**, vain search, stupid undertaking.

WILDING [wīl'ding], *n.* wild plant, *esp.* one growing from and among cultivated plants.

WILE (1) [wīl], *n.* a trick, stratagem or ruse. WILE (2), *v.t.* to trick, beguile, entice. [OE.].

WILFUL [wil'fool], *adj.* self will d, perverse, stubborn; done intentionally, premeditated. [WILL (1)].

WILL (1) [wil], *n.* that power o the mind by which we consciously desire and endeavour to carry out our intentions; intention, determining faculty, mental control; purpose; individual choice, determination or volition; legal testament in which a person declares how he wishes his property to be bestowed or used after his death; (*archaic*) fleshly desire. WILL-POWER, energy of the w., determination. WILL (2), *v.t. and i.* to desire, intend, exercise the w. (as to); control by w.-power; be willing or desirous; bequeath. [OE.].

WILL (3) (*pret.* **would**) [wil, wood], *v. auxil.* expressing future tense; expressing custom or habit; expressing intention as to the future; expressing choice in certain circumstances. [OE.].

WILLIES [wi'liz], *n.(pl.)* (*slang*) a feeling of nervous apprehension, the creeps.

WILLING [wi'ling], *adj.* desiring, wishing (to); eager (to); gladly and voluntarily done. WILLINGLY, *adv.* in a w. fashion. [WILL].

WILL-O'-THE-WISP [wil-o-the-wisp'], *n.* luminous marsh-gas, *Ignis fatuus*; (*fig.*) person or thing whose whereabouts are always uncertain. [*Will*, personal name, and WISP].

WILLOW (1) [wi'lō], *n.* any tree or plant of the genus *Salix*; (*cricket*) (*coll.*) a bat. WILLOW (2), *adj.* like or made of w. WILLOW-HERB, any species of the plant genus *Epilobium.* WILLOW-PATTERN, oriental pattern in blue, common on English crockery from the 18th century onwards. WILLOWY, *adj.* graceful like a w., drooping. [OE.].

WILLY NILLY [wi-li-ni'li], *adv.* willingly or unwillingly, inevitably. [WILL HE and ME. *nill he*, he does not wish].

WILT (1) [wilt], *v.t. and i.* (of plants) to (cause to) become limp and drooping. [Uncert.].

WILT (2), *2nd person sg. pres. of* WILL (3).

WILY [wī'li], *adj.* using wiles to accomplish a purpose, cunning. [WILE (1)].

WIMPLE [wim'pl], *n.* piece of linen folded across the

forehead and down each side of the face, worn by women in the Middle Ages and still by nuns. [OE.].

WIN (2) (*pres.pt.* **winning**, *pret. and p.pt.* **won**) [win], *v.t. and i.* to achieve or gain in competition with others or despite rivalry or opposition; obtain, attain or reach by effort; be victorious or successful in; be victorious; **to w. over**, to persuade; **to w. through**, (*U.S.*) **out**, to overcome a succession of difficulties; **to w. hands down**, (*coll.*) to obtain an easy victory. WIN (2), *n.* fact of having won, victory; act of winning. [OE.].

WINCE (1) [wins], *v.i.* to make a nervous involuntary movement in pain or fear. WINCE (2), *n.* act of wincing. [ME.].

WINCEY [win'si], *n.* cloth made of wool and cotton. WINCEYETTE [win-si-et'], *n.* stuff made in imitation of real w. [Uncert.].

WINCH [winsh], *n.* windlass, crank or pulley. [Late OE.].

WINCHESTER (1) [win'ches-ter], *n.* a standard of measure for capacity formerly kept at Winchester; a large bottle used in chemistry laboratories.

WINCHESTER (2), *n.* type of breech-loading rifle. [*Winchester*, Mass., U.S.A., where made].

WIND (1) [wind, *poet. sometimes* wind], *n.* air set in motion by atmospheric conditions; similar movement of air caused mechanically; the breath and lungs; flatulence; wordy talk meaning little or nothing; (*mus.*) wind-instruments; (*fig.*) rumour; **to be in the w.**, to be under consideration and likely to be done; **to get w. of**, to hear a hint or rumour concerning; **to raise the w.**, to raise money when hard pressed for it; **to sail near or close to the w.**, to take a matter to the very limits of decency and honesty; **to go like the w.**, to go very fast; **to cast to the winds**, to discard, leave deliberately out of account; **second w.**, steady breath which comes to a runner in a long race after the first breathlessness; also (*fig.*). WIND-EGG, egg with a soft shell. WIND-GALL, soft tumour on a horse's fetlock. WIND-GAUGE, device by which the strength of the w. is measured. WIND-INSTRUMENT, (*mus.*) instrument sounded by breath or pumped air. WIND-SOCK, large tube of fabric hung on a mast at an aerodrome to show w. direction. WIND (2), *v.t. and i.* to make breathless; regain a steady breath after breathlessness; [wind] (*pret. and p.pt. often* WOUND), blow (a bugle, horn or similiar w.-instrument); sound a call on; (*hunting*) get the scent of. [OE.].

WIND (3) (*pret. and p.pt.* **wound**) [wind], *v.t. and i.* to travel or lie along a crooked course, bending this way and that; twist like a spiral; revolve or turn in successive revolutions; raise by turning a winch or windlass; form (string, wool etc.) into a compact lump by twining it evenly together; wrap round or embrace with; **to w. up**, to twine or coil (string etc.) into a tight spiral; to set a spiral spring, *esp.* of clock-work; (*fig.*) bring to emotional tension; conclude (proceedings etc.); dissolve (a commercial firm); **to w. round (something)**, to twist and twine about it; **to w. one's way**, (often *fig.*) to pursue one's course with care; **to w. round one's little finger**, to influence completely. WIND (4), *n.* act of winding; a single revolution, a bend or curve. [OE.].

WINDAGE [win'dij], *n.* deflection by the wind of a projectile from the course it would take if there were no wind; the amount of this and allowance made for it; difference in diameter between the bore of a gun and the shell or bullet etc. used in it.

WINDBAG [wind'bag], *n.* a wordy talker.

WINDFALL [wind'fawl], *n.* fruit blown down before maturity; (*fig.*) unexpected piece of good luck, legacy.

WINDFLOWER [wind'flow-er], *n.* anemone.

WINDHOVER [wind'ho-ver], *n.* kestrel.

WINDILY [win'di-li], *adv.* in a windy fashion.

WINDINESS [win'di-nes], *n.* quality of being windy.

WINDING (1) [win'ding], *n.* course or action of something which winds; a curve, twist, turn. WIND-ING-SHEET, shroud. WINDING (2), *adj.* twisting this way and that, turning in a spiral course.

WINDJAMMER [wind'ja-mer], *n.* large sailing vessel; (*coll.*) type of lumber jacket. [WIND (1) and JAM (2)].

WINDLASS (1) [wind'las], *n.* hoisting device containing a horizontal roller which, when turned, winds a rope about itself. WINDLASS (2), *v.t.* to raise with a w. [ME.].

WINDMILL [wind'mil], *n.* mill driven by the wind; any similar wind-driven device.

WINDOW [win'dō], *n.* gap or space in a wall of a building to admit the light, often glazed so as to be adjustable for ventilation; anything resembling this. WINDOW-BOX, box in front of a w. for growing plants in. WINDOW-DRESSING, the displaying of goods in a shop w.; (*fig.*) display intended to conceal shortcomings. WINDOW-SHOPPING, habit of looking much at the goods in shop windows without making purchases. WINDOWED, *adj.* furnished with windows. [OIcel.].

WINDPIPE [wind'pīp], *n.* (*anat.*) the trachea, the passage from lungs to mouth.

WINDSCREEN [wind'skrēn], *n.* glass or transparent plastic screen in front of the driver's seat in an automobile etc.

WINDSOR [wind'zer], *n.* trade name denoting certain types of manufactured goods; **w. chair**, chair with the back formed of upright wooden rods; **w. soap**, a brown or white unperfumed soap. [*Windsor*, the town in Berkshire].

WIND-UP (1) [wind'up], *n.* conclusion.

WIND-UP (2) [wind'up], *n.* (*slang*) panic, alarm; **to get, have, put, the w.**, to become, be, cause to be, alarmed. [~*to have the wind up one's trousers* as an euphemism for *to shake with fright*].

WINDWARD (1) [wind'werd, win'derd], *n.* side or direction from which the wind blows. WINDWARD (2), *adj.* lying on the side exposed to the wind.

WINDY [win'di], *adj.* having the wind constantly blowing; exposed to the wind; (of a speech or speaker) verbose; (*coll.*) scared, nervous, flatulent; (*slang*) angry.

WINE (1) [win], *n.* fermented juice of the grape or other fruits; a rich red colour. WINE-COOLER, receptacle for cooling w. with ice. WINE-GLASS, glass for drinking w. WINE-GLASSFUL, amount of liquid a w.-glass will hold. WINE-PRESS, place where grapes are crushed in making w. WINE-VAULT, WINE-CELLAR, (underground) shop where drinks are sold. WINE (2), *v.t. and i.* to toast; drink w. WINELESS, *adj.* lacking w. [OE.].

WINEBIBBER [win'bi-ber], *n.* (*archaic*) person who drinks wine excessively.

WINEGROWER [win'grō-wer], *n.* one who grows grapes for wine.

WINESAP [win'sap], *n.* North American variety of dark red apple with a vinous aroma and flavour.

WINESKIN [win'skin], *n.* wine bottle made of skin.

WING (1) [wing], *n.* one of the limbs of flight of a bird or other creature; anything resembling this as on an aeroplane etc.; lateral extension of a house or other building; (*usually pl.*) side parts of a stage not visible to the audience; section of an army in the field protecting the flank of the main body; group of three R.A.F. squadrons; (*pl.*) badge worn by a pilot of the R.A.F. irrespective of rank; motor-car mudguard; (*hockey, football*) player on either extreme of the forward or three-quarter line. WING-HALF, left or right half-back in Association football. WING-CASE, -SHEATH, hard sheath covering the wings of some insects. WING-SPAN, distance from the tip of one w. to the tip of the other. WING (2), *v.t. and i.* to propel quickly, set in motion or flight; provide with wings; wound in the wing; (*fig.*) injure in the leg or arm; fly on wings; soar. WINGLET, *n.* little w. WINGY, *adj.* having wings. [OIcel.].

WING-COMMANDER [wing'ku-mahn-der], *n.* officer of the R.A.F. equivalent in rank to a lieutenant-colonel in the Army.

WINK (1) [wingk], *v.t. and i.* to close and open one or both eyes very quickly; move (the eyelid) in this way; (of the eyelids) perform this action; **to w. at**, to make a sign to by winking; overlook deliberately, connive at. WINK (2), *n.* action of winking; **to tip the w. to**, (*slang*) to give a hint to. [OE.].

WINKING [wing'king], *n.* action of one who winks; **as easy as w.**, very easy.

WINKLE (1) [wing'kl], *n.* small shell-fish, periwinkle. WINKLE (2), *v.t.* **to w. out**, to extract gradually by force, prise out, **as w.** from its shell. [(PERI)-WINKLE (2)].

WINNER [wi'ner], *n.* one who wins; (*coll.*) something sure to win or bring victory.

WINNING (1) [wi'ning], *n.* act of winning. WIN-NING-POST, post erected to mark the finishing line of a racecourse. WINNING (2), *adj.* victorious; (of a stroke or shot in a game) finally giving victory to one side; charming, winsome. WINNINGLY, *adv.* in a w. way. WINNINGS, *n.(pl.)* profits, *esp.* of gambling.

WINNOW [wi'nō], *v.t.* to separate (corn) into husks and grain by fanning it or directing an air current upon it in some way; (*fig.*) discern between what is

---

The accent ' after a syllable = stress (u-pon'). The mark ‾ over a vowel = length (ā in made; ō in bone).

good and bad in, separating one from the other. [OE.].

WINSOME [win'sum], *adj.* charming, attractive. [OE.].

WINTER (1) [win'ter], *n.* cold season between autumn and spring, astronomically considered to begin on 22 December, and to end on 20 March; sometimes used instead of year in reckoning a person's age. WINTER (2), *adj.* typical of, coming during, customary in, ripening in, w.; **w. quarters,** *(pl.)* military base used in w.; any habitation occupied in w.; **w. sports,** *(pl.)* games or athletic excercises taking place on snow and ice in w., *esp.* in Switzerland. WINTER-CHERRY, name given to various plants of the family *Solanaceae, esp. Alkekengi,* a hardy perennial. WINTER-GARDEN, large hothouse or conservatory with flowers, shrubs etc. WINTER-WEIGHT, (of under-clothing) sufficiently thick to be worn in w. WINTER (3), *v.i.* to spend the w. [OE.].

WINTERBERRY [win'ter-be-ri], *n.* the black alder.
WINTERGREEN [win'ter-grēn], *n.* an evergreen shrub from which an oil is obtained.

WINTRY [win'tri], *adj.* cold and stormy; bleak; *(fig.)* unfriendly, unkind.

WINY [wī'ni], *adj.* having the flavour or qualities of wine.

WIPE (1) [wīp], *v.t.* to rub smoothly and gently with a cloth or other article so as to make dry or clean; **to w. away, off, up,** to clean away by wiping; **to w. out,** to clean by wiping; clean away by wiping; *(fig.)* cancel; exterminate, destroy; **to w. the floor (or ground) with,** to inflict a complete defeat on. WIPE (2), *n.* action of wiping; *(slang)* blow. WIPE-OUT, *(radio)* phenomenon by which a louder or nearby transmission blots out reception of a weaker or more distant one on an adjacent wavelength. WIPER, *n.* person who or thing which wipes; that with which one wipes. [OE.].

WIRE (1) [wīer], *n.* fine thread of metal, sometimes single, sometimes made of woven or twisted filaments like cord; *(coll.)* telegram; **to pull wires,** to exert a secret influence. WIRE-DANCER, -WALKER, one who performs or dances on a stretched w. WIRE-EDGE, easily blunted edge of a knife which has been too finely sharpened. WIRE-ENTANGLEMENT, *(milit.)* protective fence of barbed w. twisted to and fro over a line of upright posts. WIRE-GAUZE, gauze made of w. WIRE-HAIRED, having stiff, short hair, as the coats of some terriers. WIRE-NETTING, w. mesh used in fencing. WIRE-ROPE, rope made of w. WIRE-WOVE, (of paper) of a certain fine quality made in a w.-gauze frame. WIRE (2), *v.t. and i.* to fasten with or provide with w.; fix wires for (an electrical device); *(coll.)* send by telegraph; communicate with by telegraph; **to w. in (to),** to begin vigorously; WIRING, *n.* wires or system of wires of an electrical device. [OE.].

WIREDRAWN [wīer'drawn], *adj.* drawn out to a great fineness; excessively subtle.

WIRELESS (1) [wīer'les], *adj.* having no wires, per-taining to radio or any system of radio broadcasting. WIRELESS (2), *n.* radio; any process or system by which messages can be transmitted by electric waves in the ether without communicating wires; instru-ment for receiving such communications; pro-grammes provided by a broadcasting station. WIRELESS-CABIN, room or cabin of a w.-operator. WIRELESS-OPERATOR, person responsible for receiving and transmitting radio messages, *esp.* on board ship. WIRELESS-STATION, place where radio messages may be received or broadcast. WIRELESS (3), *v.t. and i.* to transmit by radio.

WIREPULLER [wīer'pŏŏ-ler], *n.* one who tries to achieve his ends by using personal or secret influence.
WIREWORM [wīer'werm], *n.* larva of the click-beetle, so called from its appearance.

WIRY [wīer'i], *adj.* like wire; (of a man) strong and sinewy but not heavily built.

WISDOM [wiz'dom], *n.* condition of being wise; knowledge and point of view of one who is wise. WISDOM-TOOTH, back molar in the human mouth, which does not appear till the late teens or early twenties. [OE.].

WISE (1) [wīz], *n.* manner, way. [OE.].

WISE (2), *adj.* possessing or exhibiting the qualities of clear thinking, careful judgment, tact and under-standing; prudent, foreseeing; possessing know-ledge; **to be none the wiser,** to be no better informed; **to put (someone) w. to** (on, about), *(U.S. slang)* to inform, give hints, of; **to be (or get) w. to,** to be (or become) informed about or aware of;

w. guy, *(U.S. slang)* fellow who pretends to know everything. [OE.].

WISEACRE [wī'zā-ker], *n.* one who pretends to be very wise, often without cause. [MDu.].

WISECRACK (1) [wīz'krak], *n.* *(U.S. slang)* witti-cism, joke, smart retort. WISECRACK (2), *v.i.* *(U.S. slang)* to utter a w. or wisecracks.

WISH (1) [wish], *v.t. and i.* to desire, long for; desire that; express a desire in words; desire (someone else) to have; **to w. for,** to desire to possess, experience etc. WISH (2), *n.* act of wishing; longing or desire, verbal expression of this; thing longed for. [OE.].

WISHBONE [wish'bōn], *n.* forked bone in a bird's breast. [WISH (2) and BONE (1)].

WISHFUL [wish'fŏŏl], *adj.* anxious, longing, desirous; **w. thinking,** thinking conditioned more by one's wishes than by the actual facts or by reason.

WISHING-CAP [wī'shing-kap], *n.* magic cap whose wearer finds his wishes fulfilled.

WISH-WASH [wish'wosh], *n.* *(coll.)* a very weak drink; nonsense. WISHY-WASHY, *adj.* weak and watery; indeterminate, irresolute. [WASH (2)].

WISP [wisp], *n.* thin strand of anything; small tuft or bunch; flock of snipe. WISPY, *adj.* resembling a w. or wisps. [OE.].

WIST † [wist], *v.t. and i.* to know. [OE.].

WISTARIA [wis-tāer'i-ah], *n.* genus of blue-flowered climbing plants. [Prof. C. *Wistar*].

WISTFUL [wist'fŏŏl], *adj.* longing, yearning, *esp.* in a sad, unhopeful way. [Uncert.].

WIT (1) [wit], *n.* the mind, mental vigour and agility; ability to observe humorous connexions and similari-ties between one thing and another, and to express them in a neat, memorable way; person able to do this; *(pl.)* one's faculties. [OE.].

WIT (2), *v.t. and i.* *(hist.)* now only in the phrase, **to w.,** that is, namely. [OE.].

WITCH (1) [wich], *n.* woman supposed by the super-stitious to have supernatural power and knowledge, sorceress; any ill-looking, hard-hearted old woman, hag; a flatfish; *(fig.)* fascinating woman. WITCH-DOCTOR, tribal medicine-man. WITCH-HUNT, form-erly, a search for women believed to be witches; *(fig.)* persecution of people of unorthodox views. WITCH (2), *v.t.* to cast a spell over like a w. [OE.].

WITCHCRAFT [wich'krahft], *n.* supernatural power and craft of a witch; magic practices.

WITCH-ELM, see WYCH-ELM.

WITCHERY [wī'che-ri], *n.* magic, witchcraft; *(fig.)* fascination.

WITCH-HAZEL, see WYCH-HAZEL.

WITCHING [wī'ching], *adj.* enchanting, potent with magic; suitable for the practice of witchcraft; *(fig.)* fascinating.

WITENAGEMOT [wi-te-nah-ge-mōt'], *n.* *(hist.)* Anglo-Saxon deliberative assembly. [OE.].

WITH (1) [with], *prep. expressing alliance, agreement, companionship, communication or physical propin-quity; expressing opposition, contrast, proportion, equality etc.; expressing separation or disagreement; introducing an attribute or possession or the manner, instrument or cause of an action; expressing similarity of direction or simultaneity.* [OE.].

WITH (2), see WITHE.

WITH-, *pref. expressing opposition and separation.* [OE.].

WITHAL (1) [wi-thawl'], *adv.* *(archaic)* in addition. WITHAL † (2), *prep.* (used at the end of a phrase or sentence) with. [ME.].

WITHDRAW (*pret.* **withdrew,** *p.pt.* **withdrawn**) [with-draw'], *v.t. and i.* to pull back, remove or bring back (what has been advanced or thrust forward); retract (what one has said); come back after having gone forward, retreat, go away; retire; cancel one's statement, promise. WITHDRAWING-ROOM, *n.* *(archaic)* drawing-room.

WITHE, WITH [with, with, with], *n.* long slender, tough, flexible twig or shoot. [OE.].

WITHER [wi'ther], *v.t. and i.* (of flowers etc.) to fade, shrivel up, wilt; *(fig.)* diminish, grow weaker; *(lit. and fig.)* cause to wilt and shrivel; *(fig.)* confuse, embarrass (a person), WITHERED, *adj.* faded and dry; *(fig.)* shrunk, wrinkled, withered. WITHERING, *adj.* causing to w.; *(fig.)* embarrassing, scornful, hostile. [~weather (2)].

WITHERS [wi'therz], *n.* front of a horse's shoulder next to the neck. [OE.].

WITHERSHINS, WIDDERSHINS [wi'ther-shinz, wi'der-shinz], *adv.* anti-clockwise. [MLGerm.].

WITHHOLD (*pret.* and *p.pt.* **withheld,** *p.pt.* † **with-holden**) [with-hōld'], *v.t.* to check, keep back,

---

ŏŏ is pronounced as in *food*; ŏŏ as in *hood*; th as in *think*, TH as in *that*; zh as in azure. ∼ = related to.

restrain; keep unused; retain in one's possession. refuse to grant. [OE.].

WITHIN (1) [wi-ᴛʜɪɴ'], *adv.* on the inside, internally; inside a specific space or area; indoors, inside one's house; in the mind or spirit; (*stage, archaic*) offstage, in the wings. **WITHIN** (2), *prep.* in the interior or inside of, inside; not beyond the range or limit of, not beyond the power or resources of; in not more than (a given time); not farther than (a given distance). **WITHIN** (3), *n.* the inside, interior. [OE.].

WITHOUT (1) [wi-ᴛʜout'], *adv.* on the outside, externally; (*archaic*) out of doors, outside the house. **WITHOUT** (2), *prep.* lacking, not having; not helped by, not using; not accompanied by; (*archaic*) outside, beyond. **WITHOUT** (3), *n.* the outside. [OE.].

WITHSTAND (*pret. and p.pt.* **withstood**) [wɪᴛʜstand'], *v.t.* to oppose; be capable of enduring or keeping out. [OE.].

WITHY [wɪ'ᴛʜi], *n.* a sort of willow. [OE.].

WITLESS [wit'les], *adj.* having no wits, dull, stupid, wanting thought.

WITLING † [wit'ling], *n.* person of slight intelligence or understanding.

WITNESS (1) [wit'nes], *n.* evidence, testimony, manifestation; person or thing providing evidence; (*leg.*) person present at the signing of a document, who appends his or her name in testimony of this; one who gives evidence in a court of law. **WITNESS BOX**, place in a court of law where witnesses stand to give evidence. **WITNESS** (2), *v.t. and i.* to offer proof or testimony (of); be present at and aware of, see; append one's name, seal or mark to (a document) in declaration that one has seen it legally signed. [OE.].

WITTED [wi'tid], *adj.* (*usu.* in compounds) having wits.

WITTICISM [wi'ti-sizm], *n.* witty remark, clever retort. [WITT(Y) and (CRIT)ICISM].

WITTING [wi'ting], *adj.* conscious or intended. **WITTINGLY**, *adv.* intentionally. [WIT (2)].

WITTY [wi'ti], *adj.* exhibiting or possessing wit, ingenious. [OE.].

WIVERN, WYVERN [wī'vern], *n.* legendary and heraldic winged beast with a dragon's head and two legs. [ONFr.].

WIVES [wīvz], *n. pl. of* **WIFE**.

WIZARD (1) [wi'zerd], *n.* man supposed to have magic power; person who can do things and influence others as if by magic. **WIZARD** (2), *adj.* (*slang*) remarkable, clever. [ME.].

WIZARDRY [wi'zerd-ri], *n.* arts of a wizard; personal charm.

WIZEN(ED), WEAZEN(ED) [wi'zen(d), wē'zen(d)] *adj.* shrivelled. [~OE.].

WOAD [wōd], *n.* the plant *Isatis tinctoria*; blue dye yielded by this. [OE.].

WOBBLE, WABBLE (1) [wo'bl], *v.i.* to sway to and fro with instability, be unstable or shaky; (*fig.*) be hesitant or vacillating. **WOBBLE, WABBLE** (2), *n.* act of wobbling, instability. [~MHighGerm.].

WOE (1) [wō], *n.* grief, sorrow, affliction. **WOE** (2), *int.* alas! [OE.].

WOEBEGONE [wō'bi-gon], *adj.* sorrowful, of miserable appearance. [ME.].

WOEFUL [wō'fōl], *adj.* wretched, sorrowful, mournful.

WOKE [wōk], *pret. and p.pt. of* **WAKE** (2). [OE.].

WOKEN [wō'ken], *p.pt. of* **WAKE** (2).

WOLD [wōld], *n.* uncultivated, unwooded land, *esp.* a moor in a limestone district; (*pl.*) downs. [OE.].

WOLF (1) (*pl.* **wolves**) [wōolf, wōolvz], *n.* the carnivore *Canis lupus*; any animal of the same genus; (*fig.*) person who is greedy like a w.; (*slang*) man with lecherous tendencies; rasping sound in a violin etc.; **to cry w.**, to give a false alarm. **WOLF-CUB**, young w.; junior Boy Scout. **WOLF-DOG**, any large dog kept for hunting, or protection against, wolves; animal which is a cross between w. and dog. **WOLF'S-BANE**, any of various plants of the genus *Aconitum*. **WOLF-SPIDER**, tarantula; spider which leaps on its prey. **WOLF** (2), *v.t.* to eat quickly and greedily. [OE.].

WOLFHOUND [wōolf'hownd], *n.* large type of dog first bred to hunt wolves.

WOLFISH [wōol'fish], *adj.* like a wolf, fierce and greedy; ravenous; voracious.

WOLFRAM [wōol'ram], *n.* (*min.*) ore of tungsten; tungsten. [Germ.].

WOLFSKIN [wōolf'skin], *n.* skin of a wolf, *esp.* when prepared as a rug etc.

WOLVERENE, WOLVERINE [wōol've-rēn], *n.*

a North American carnivore; this animal's skin. [~WOLF (1)].

WOMAN (*pl.* **women**) [wōo'man, wi'min], *n.* adult person of the female sex; women generally; essential character of a woman; lady-in-waiting. [OE.].

WOMANHOOD [wōo'man-hōod], *n.* state of being a woman; essential characteristics of women.

WOMANISH [wōo'ma-nish], *adj.* effeminate; old w., fussy about trifles.

WOMANIZE [wōo'ma-nīz], *v.t. and i.* to make effeminate; (*coll.*) have casual sexual intercourse with women.

WOMANKIND [wōo'man-kīnd], *n.* women in general.

WOMANLY [wōo'man-li], *adj.* like a woman, characteristic of a woman.

WOMB [wōom], *n.* uterus, female organ of conception and prenatal development in mammals; any hollow cave or cavity; matrix. [OE.].

WOMBAT [wom'bat], *n.* a nocturnal burrowing marsupial, native to Australia. [Native].

WOMEN [wi'min], *n. pl. of* **WOMAN**.

WOMENFOLK [wi'min-fōk], *n.*(*pl.*) womankind.

WOMENKIND [wi'min-kīnd], *n.*(*pl.*) womankind.

WON [wun], *pret. and p.pt. of* **WIN** (1).

WONDER (1) [wun'der], *n.* person who or thing which excites great admiration or astonishment, prodigy; marvellous deed, miracle; strangeness, beauty, prodigious or marvellous quality; emotion of mingled admiration, awe and astonishment; (*coll.*) a sensation, person who does sensational things. **WONDER-STRUCK**, overwhelmed with w., awe-struck. **WONDER** (2), *v.i.* to experience an emotion of almost doubting admiration or surprise; be amazed; be amazed (at); desire to be told or get to know. [OE.].

WONDERFUL [wun'der-fōl], *adj.* exciting wonder and amazement, marvellous, surpassingly beautiful, miraculous; (*coll.*) very good.

WONDERING [wun'de-ring], *adj.* feeling wonder, amazed, almost doubting; expressing wonder.

WONDERLAND [wun'der-land], *n.* land or place of wonders.

WONDERMENT [wun'der-ment], *n.* emotion of wonder; bemused fascination.

WONDERWORKER [wun'der-wer-ker], *n.* one who works wonders.

WONDROUS (1) [wun'drōos], *adj.* wonderful. **WONDROUS**† (2), *adv.* wonderfully.

WONKY [wong'ki], *adj.* (*slang*) wobbly, unstable; (of a machine etc.) working badly; hesitant, doubtful; not very well, in poor health. [~Germ.].

WONT (1) [wōnt], *adj.* accustomed. **WONT** (2), *n.* habit. **WONTED**, *adj.* accustomed, usual. **WONTLESS** †, *adj.* unusual. [ME.].

WON'T [wōnt], *v.auxil.* (*coll.*) will not. [ME.].

WOO [wōo], *v.t.* to court, seek to marry, make love to; endeavour to get or attain to. [OE.].

WOOD [wōod], *n.* large group of trees, small forest; the substance of the trunk and branches of a tree; timber; (*sport*) a ball used in bowls; a shot at bowls; (*mus.*) wood-wind instruments of an orchestra; wine- or beer-barrel; **w. ash(es)**, (*pl.*) ashes left by burnt w. **WOOD-ALCOHOL**, methyl alcohol obtained by distillation of wood. **WOOD-ANEMONE**, uncultivated anemone growing under trees. **WOOD-BLOCK**, block of engraved w. for printing a design; block of w. used for paving roads. **WOOD-CARVING**, a carving done in w.; art process of carving in w. **WOOD-ENGRAVING**, art or process of engraving on w. **WOOD-FIBRE**, fibre contained in w.; fibre made from w. **WOOD-NOTES**, (*pl.*) bird's song; (*poet.*) simple, unartificial poetry. **WOOD-NYMPH**, (*myth.*) nymph living in a forest; kind of humming-bird; moth of the genus *Eudryas*. **WOOD-PIGEON**, the ring-dove, a wild pigeon. **WOOD-PULP**, pulp made from w. and used to manufacture inferior paper. **WOOD-SORREL**, a small herb with trifoliate leaves. **WOOD-WIND**, (pertaining to) that section of an orchestra in which wind-instruments generally made of w. are played. **WOODED**, *adj.* covered with trees. [OE.].

WOODBINE, WOODBIND [wōod'bīn(d)], *n.* wild honeysuckle. [OE.].

WOODCHUCK [wōod'chuk], *n.* an American marmot. [NAmerInd.].

WOODCOCK [wōod'kok], *n.* a migratory bird allied to the sandpiper.

WOODCRAFT [wōod'krahft], *n.* knowledge of how to live in, or travel through, forests.

WOODCUT [wōod'kut], *n.* engraving on, or a print

made from, a wood-block. WOODCUTTER, *n.* one who engraves wood-blocks; one who fells trees.

WOODEN [wŏŏ'den], *adj.* made of wood; (*coll.*) clumsy; stiff, dull, stupid. WOODEN-HEAD, dullard. WOODENLY, *adv.* in a stiff, w. manner.

WOODINESS [wŏŏ'di-nes], *n.* condition or quality of being woody.

WOODLAND (1) [wŏŏd'land] *n.* wooded tract of land. WOODLAND (2), *adj.* pertaining to woods.

WOODLOUSE [wŏŏd'lows], *n.* small insect of the genus *Oniscus.*

WOODMAN [wŏŏd'man], *n.* one who fells, or looks after, trees.

WOODPECKER [wŏŏd'pe-ker], *n.* any variety of bird of the family *Picidae.*

WOODSHED [wŏŏd'shed], *n.* shed for storing timber.

WOODSMAN [wŏŏdz'man], *n.* one who lives in a wood; forester.

WOODWORK [wŏŏd'werk], *n.* any structure or part of a structure made of wood; carpentry.

WOODY [wŏŏ'di], *adj.* wooded; made of wood; resembling wood.

WOOER [wŏŏ'er], *n.* one who woos.

WOOF [wŏŏf], *n.* threads which run at right angles to the warp; weft. [OE.].

WOOING (1) [wŏŏ'ing], *n.* courtship, action of a wooer. WOOING (2), *adj.* intending to persuade or court.

WOOL [wŏŏl], *n.* soft hair of a sheep or other animal; thread or yarn made from this; fabric made of such threads; any substance resembling these; (*slang*) hair, *esp.* the curly hair of a negro; **keep your w. on!**, (*slang*) don't get angry; **to lose one's w.,** (*slang*) to grow angry; **to pull the w. over one's eyes,** to trick or deceive one; **dyed in the w.,** (of a colour) imparted to the w. before it is spun; (*fig.*) out and out, absolute. WOOL-CLASSING, grading of w. according to quality. WOOL-FAT, -OIL, lanolin. WOOL-GATHERING, absentmindedness, dreaminess. WOOL-GROWER, one who breeds sheep for their w. WOOL-PACK, bag or bale of w.; large canvas sack for w. WOOL-SALE, auction sale of w. WOOL-SHED, large shed in which sheep are shorn and w. is baled and stored. WOOL-SORTER, one who sorts w. WOOL-SORTER'S DISEASE, anthrax. WOOL-WORK, embroidery done with w. [OE.].

WOOLLEN [wŏŏ'len], *adj.* made of wool. WOOLLENS, *n.*(*pl.*) w. articles.

WOOLLY (1) [wŏŏ'li], *adj.* made of wool; looking or feeling like wool; (*fig.*) not precise, vague, muddled. WOOLLY-BEAR, large hairy caterpillar of the tiger moth. WOOLLY (2), *n.* woollen garment, sweater or jersey. WOOLLINESS, *n.* condition of being w.

WOOLSACK [wŏŏl'sak], *n.* bale of wool; large square cushion, stuffed with wool, on which the Lord Chancellor sits in the House of Lords; office and dignity of Lord Chancellor.

WOOLSTAPLE [wŏŏl'stā-pl], *n.* wool market. WOOLSTAPLER, *n.* one who deals in wool.

WOP [wop], *n.* (*U.S. slang*) person from South Europe, *esp.* an Italian. [Unkn.].

WORD (1) [wurd], *n.* a unit of spoken or written language, by itself denoting a thing, idea, action, quality, qualification or relationship, but not fully significant until associated with other words in a phrase or sentence; the written or printed symbol or symbols representing this; (*theol.*) Second Person of the Trinity; the Scriptures; the gospel; that which is said, speech, utterance; password; brief conversation; news, information, rumour; promise; asseveration not supported by proof but intended to be taken as made in good faith; plea or recommendation on behalf of a third party; (*pl.*) verses set to music; a speech, remarks; **the last w.,** (*coll.*) the limit; the most modern of its kind; **to have a w. (with),** to hold a short conversation (with); **to have words (with),** to quarrel (with); **to say a few words,** to make a short speech; **to be as good as one's w.,** to act up to one's promise; **w. for w.,** literally, exactly. WORD-BOOK, vocabulary, lexicon. WORD-PAINTING, -PICTURE, vivid description in words. WORD-PERFECT, *adj.* (of memorized text or instructions) absolutely correct. WORD-PLAY, puns; witty repartee. WORD-SPLITTING, unduly precise or subtle use of words. WORD-SQUARE, group of words of equal length so chosen that they may be printed one above the other in the form of a square and read both vertically and horizontally. WORD (2), *v.t.* to express verbally. WORDAGE, *n.* total number of words in a text. WORDED, *adj.* expressed verbally.

WORDING, *n.* act of expressing in words; phrases or style in which something is expressed. WORDLESS, *adj.* unable to speak, lacking words. [OE.].

WORDY [wur'di], *adj.* verbal, using words; verbose, containing too many words; wont to use too many words.

WORE [waw(r)], *pret. of* WEAR (1). [Late ME.].

WORK (1) [wurk], *n.* mental or physical action carried out with a serious object in view, labour of mind or body, *esp.* such action regularly performed to earn a living; results of any given activity or action of any kind; material instruments necessary for such action, *esp.* needlework; product of any such activity, *esp.* when of a skilled or artistic nature; task or duty which must be done; (*phys.*) energy expended in raising a given weight to a given height, or an equivalent of this; (*pl.*) moving part or driving mechanism of an instrument or machine; excavations, buildings, large architectural structures etc., *esp.* of a military nature or such as are of benefit to the whole community; factory; (*theol.*) actions done in accordance with one's religious convictions and as an expression of them; **to be out of w.,** to be unemployed, have no regular means of living; **to set to w.,** to give w. to; to set about doing something; **to go (or set) to w.,** to start w.; **to have one's w. cut out,** to be hard pressed; **to make short w. of,** to deal with, overcome, consume, quickly and easily; **to give (one) the works,** (*U.S. slang*) to kill, ill-treat, deal energetically with. WORK-BAG, -BASKET, -BOX, bag, basket, box for holding needlework and things used in needlework. WORK-FELLOW, -MATE, one working in company with another. WORK-PEOPLE, manual workers. WORK-SHY, not eager to w., lazy. WORK-TABLE, table conveniently arranged and fitted for needlework. WORK (2), *v.t.* to make to do w., supervise the w. of; cause to act or operate; shape by pressing or hammering; perform or achieve, do; do w. connected with, make profitable; dig, till, plough; *v.i.* to do w.; operate or act in the way intended, be successful; have effect, produce results; progress laboriously (through or over), penetrate slowly, spread gradually (through); change position or state by successive small motions; ferment; be regularly employed; **to w. at,** to devote one's effort and attention to; **to w. in,** to mix in; **to w. in with,** to fit, be capable of adjustment, with; **to w. on (or upon),** to do w. in connexion with; exercise influence upon; **to w. out,** to solve by calculation, compute; be able to be solved, come to a solution; be computed or estimated; carry to a logical conclusion; **to w. up,** to increase or develop; produce or rouse; make excited; **to w. it,** (*coll.*) to arrange matters. WORK-OUT, (*coll.*) period of training or practice, *esp.* for boxing. [OE.].

WORKABLE [wur'ka-bl], *adj.* able to be worked; practicable.

WORKADAY [wur'ka-dā], *adj.* pertaining to week-days or workdays; ordinary, prosaic. [ON.].

WORKDAY [wurk'dā], *n.* day on which most people work.

WORKER [wur'ker], *n.* one who works, *esp.* for wages; neuter bee, ant etc.

WORKHOUSE [wurk'hows], *n.* formerly, a public institution maintained under the Poor Law for the support of paupers.

WORKING (1) [wur'king], *n.* manner or process of work or action, the way something is done or in which a system or instrument operates; (*min.*) section of the excavation where work is in progress. WORKING-DAY, the number of hours in any day during which one regularly works; day on which work is done or should be done. WORKING-OUT, development and elaboration of any concept or theme, series of resulting events from any one cause etc. WORKING (2), *adj.* engaged in work, moving, operating; employed on work for wages; used for, connected with, work; necessary for work, business or operations in hand; adapted for immediate needs, makeshift, practical; **w. class** (1), wage-earning section of the community as distinct from salaried and professional workers and those desiring profit from trade etc.; labourers in general; **w. class** (2), of, pertaining to, characteristic of the w. class; **w. man,** (*pop.*) man engaged in manual labour, labourer; member of the w. class.

WORKMAN (*pl.* **workmen**) [wurk'man], *n.* one who does work, person considered in respect of his work, manual labourer.

WORKMANLIKE [wurk'man-līk], *adj.* done in a skilful way as by a good workman.

WORKMANLY (1) [wurk′man-li], *adj.* workman-like; having the appearance of a workman. WORK-MANLY (2), *adv.* in a workmanlike manner.

WORKMANSHIP [wurk′man-ship], *n.* skill of a workman; skill and craft employed on making anything; something made, *esp.* by manual labour.

WORKSHOP [wurk′shop], *n.* place where work, *esp.* manual work, is done.

WORLD [wurld], *n.* the universe, *esp.* the earth and the visible heavens; the earth; planet resembling, or imagined to resemble, the earth; the earth and all creatures on it; the human race, society; life, terrestrial existence, this life; state of existence; a department of terrestrial life and the creatures representing it considered as a unit; sphere of interest and activity; a number of associated interests and activities and the persons concerned therein, considered as a group; range of experience and activity of any single person; ordinary affairs of life; material, temporal activities and those persons who are more concerned with these than with things spiritual; secular life and its temptations; an era in the history of the human race, stage in civilization; a great number of anything, vast amount or extent; **the next w.**, the life after death; **w. without end**, eternally, for ever and ever; **the New W.**, the Americas, the Western Hemisphere; **the Old W.**, the Eastern Hemisphere, including Europe, Asia and Africa; **man (or woman) of the w.**, one not ignorant of the ways and habits of mankind, skilful in business and social adjustments; **for all the w. like, as if**, closely resembling, very much as if; **to think the w. of, a w. and all of**, to hold in very high esteem. WORLD-LANGUAGE, a language used or intended to be used universally, one artificially devised for such use. WORLD-OLD, of great antiquity. WORLD-POWER, state or nation of major importance, having w.-wide influence and interests. WORLD-WEARY, tired of this w. WORLD-WIDE, spread into every part of the w. [O.E.].

WORLDLING [wurld′ling], *n.* one who thinks mainly of worldly things.

WORLDLY [wurld′li], *adj.* pertaining to the world, to this life or the business of human society; mundane, not spiritual, secular; concerned with earthly pleasure and profit. WORLDLY-MINDED, devoted to earthly pleasures and profit. WORLDLY-WISE, possessing that philosophy and knowledge which is directed towards w. pleasure and profit; knowledgeable in the ways of the world.

WORM (1) [wurm], *n.* invertebrate crawling creature without legs; earthworm, any similar creature; (*fig.*) grovelling, obsequious, mean person; groove of a screw; spiral pipe in a still or furnace. WORM-CAST, little heap of earth left by a w. WORM-EATEN, eaten into by w.-like insects; (*fig.*) so old as to be useless. WORM-HOLE, hole made by a w. or w.-like larva. WORM-POWDER, powder for expelling parasitic worms from the intestines. WORM (2), *v.t.* to bore, insinuate; treat for intestinal worms; **to w. oneself into**, to enter by insinuating or cautious means; **to w. one's way through**, to penetrate, pass through with great difficulty; **to w. (information) out of**, to obtain (information) from by insinuating and round-about methods. [O.E.].

WORMWOOD [wurm′wood], *n.* a plant notable for its bitter flavour. [~O.E.].

WORN [wawn], *adj.* damaged by continued or protracted use; (of a person's face or hands) marked with toil, tired-looking. WORN-OUT, rendered useless by continuous service; (*fig.*) tired, exhausted. [*P.pt.* of WEAR (1)].

WORRIED [wu′rid], *adj.* harassed with troubles and worries.

WORRIT (1) [wu′rit], *v.t. and i.* (*dial.*) to worry. WORRIT (2), *n.* (*dial.*) worry. [WORRY].

WORRY (1) [wu′ri], *v.t. and i.* (of a dog) to tease, shake in the teeth; annoy, irritate, pester, *esp.* with a request or question; make anxious, distress; feel anxiety, ponder over some problem or trouble. WORRY (2), *n.* act of worrying or teasing; state of being worried; anything which causes one to be worried. WORRIER, *n.* one who habitually worries. WORRYING, *adj.* harassing, full of worries. [O.E.].

WORSE (1) [wurs], *adj.* to a greater extent, or in a greater measure, bad; less good, less satisfactory, less pleasing (than); not so well as before; **to be none the w. for**, to have received no injury on account of. WORSE (2), *n.* that which is w.; a w. state. WORSE (3), *adv.* to a w. degree, in a w. fashion. [O.E.].

WORSEN [wur′sen], *v.t. and i.* to make worse; grow worse. WORSENING, *n.* act of growing worse; aggravation.

WORSHIP (1) [wur′ship], *n.* praise and adoration offered to a deity, *esp.* to God; veneration, admiration; divine service; **His W.**, title of a mayor; **Your W.**, used in addressing a magistrate. WORSHIP (2), *v.t. and i.* to offer w. to (a deity); love almost to excess; perform an act of w. WORSHIPPER, *n.* one who offers w.; one attending divine service. [O.E.].

WORSHIPFUL [wur′ship-fool], *adj.* deserving to be honoured, *esp.* as a title of mayors, etc.

WORST (1) [wurst], *adj.* bad in the greatest measure or to the greatest extent. WORST (2), *n.* that which is w., most unlucky or disastrous; state of being w. WORST (3), *adv.* in the w. way. WORST (4), *v.t.* to overcome, outplay. [O.E.].

WORSTED (1) [woos′ted], *n.* a high-quality woollen yarn. WORSTED (2), *adj.* made of w. [*Worstead*, Norfolk, where first made].

WORT [wurt], *n.* a plant; infusion of malt before it has fermented. [O.E.].

WORTH (1) [wurth], *adj.* possessing a stated value, valued at; having possessions amounting to; profitable; **for all one is w.**, to the utmost of one's powers; **to be w. while**, to be profitable, not useless; **to be w. it**, (*coll.*) to be profitable, to justify possession, action. WORTH-WHILE, w. the trouble of doing, profitable, of some value. WORTH (2), *n.* value or price; excellence, admirable qualities; the quantity obtainable for a given price. [O.E.].

WORTH (3), *v.t.* (*archaic, poet.*) in the phrase **woe w.** (with the object following); to happen, befall. [O.E.].

WORTHLESS [wurth′les], *adj.* of no material value; of low principles and character.

WORTHY (1) [wur′THi], *adj.* of sound principles, honourable, respectable; meritorious; **w. of**, deserving, meriting. WORTHY (2), *n.* excellent person, *esp.* one of importance; a notability. *esp.* local. [M.E.].

WOT † [wot], *v.i.* to know. [O.E.].

WOULD [wood], *pret. of* WILL (3). WOULD-BE, desiring or pretending to be but not having succeeded.

WOUND (1) [woond], *n.* a hurt to an animal body by which the skin is pierced or ripped; mark on the skin from such a hurt; any similar hurt and the mark resulting, though not inflicted on an animal body; (*fig.*) pain caused to a person's feelings. WOUND (2), *v.t.* to hurt as with a w.; (*fig.*) cause mental or emotional distress to. WOUNDING, *n.* a w., act of one who wounds. [O.E.].

WOUND (3) [wownd], *pret. and p.pt. of* WIND (3). [O.E.].

WOVE (1), *pret. of* WEAVE. [M.E.].

WOVE (2) [wov], *adj.* **w. paper**, fine variety of paper, made on a wire-gauze frame. [*Var. of* WOVEN].

WOVEN (1), *p.pt. of* WEAVE. WOVEN (2), *adj.* manufactured by a process of weaving. [M.E.].

WOW [wow], *n.* (*slang*) good fun, remarkably successful person or affair.

WRACK [rak], *n.* state of ruin; disaster; seaweed etc. washed ashore. [M.E.].

WRAITH [rāth], *n.* ghost or apparition, *esp.* one which appears as an omen of death; (*fig.*) very thin, ill-looking person. [Unkn.].

WRANGLE (1) [rang′gl], *v.i.* to argue or quarrel in a noisy, angry fashion. WRANGLE (2), *n.* heated argument. [M.E.].

WRANGLER [rang′gler], *n.* one who wrangles; (at Cambridge University) one who is placed in the first class of Part II of the Mathematical Tripos; **senior w.**, title formerly given to one who was top of the list for first-class honours in mathematics in any one year at Cambridge University.

WRAP (1) [rap], *v.t.* to enclose or enfold (in an outer covering); (*fig.*) hide or mask; **to w. up**, to enfold in an outer covering; conceal in verbose language; put on or wear plenty of warm clothing; **to w. (something) round (something else)**, to fold the one about the other. WRAP (2), *n.* large scarf or other cloth to keep the body warm; cloak. BATH-WRAP, large towel, kind of dressing-gown made of towelling. WRAPPING, *n.* that which is used to w. something else in. [M.E.].

WRAPPER [ra′per], *n.* person who or thing which wraps; something used as an envelope or outer covering; a wrap or scarf.

WRATH [rawth], *n.* great and violent anger. WRATHY, *adj.* (*coll.*) wrathful. [~O.E.].

WRATHFUL [rawth′fool], *adj.* very angry. [*Prec.*].

WREAK [rēk], *v.t.* to inflict or execute. [OE.].

WREATH [rēth, *pl.* rēTHz], *n.* circlet of twigs, leaves and flowers given as a token of remembrance at a funeral; coronet of leaves symbolizing victory; garland of flowers, leaves etc., often artificial, worn by women and girls as an adornment on festal occasions; twisting wisp of vapour etc. WREATHY, *adj.* twisted like a w. [OE.].

WREATHE [rēTH], *v.t. and i.* to twist or twine; wrap or coil round; encircle with a wreath; move in a twining, coiling way. [*Prec.*].

WRECK (1) [rek], *n.* destruction of, or grave damage done to, a ship by storm, rocks etc.; abandoned ship cast upon the shore; disaster at sea ending in such damage to a vessel; any event of ruin or destruction; ruins left by such an event; (*fig.*) complete overthrow of plans and ambitions; person whose state suggests collapse or ruin. WRECK (2), *v.t. and i.* to bring (*esp.* a ship) to ruin and disaster; be wrecked or ruined. WRECKAGE, *n.* condition of being wrecked; act of wrecking; remains of a wrecked ship; fragments left over after any great disaster. WRECKER, *n.* one who deliberately causes a shipwreck in order to plunder the wreckage; one who deliberately causes ruin or destruction. [AFr.].

WREN (1) [ren], *n.* genus of small passerine birds. [OE.].

WREN (2), *n.* (*coll.*) member of the *W*omen's *R*oyal Naval Service.

WRENCH (1) [rensh], *v.t.* to give a wrench to; interpret in a false or distorting manner. WRENCH (2), *n.* sharp sudden screwing pull; tool for screwing nuts on or off; twist or jerk which injures a muscle or tendon; (*fig.*) emotional pain felt at parting with something familiar. [OE.].

WREST [rest], *v.t.* to pull out by wrenching or tugging vigorously; get by toil and effort; (of meanings of words) twist, misinterpret. [OE.].

WRESTLE (1) [re'sl], *v.t. and i.* to fight with another person by engaging him in a grip and trying to throw him down; fight in this way; fight in this way according to certain accepted rules as an athletic exercise; earn one's living by this sort of fighting; **to w. with,** to struggle with in this way; (*fig.*) labour in the mind with. WRESTLE (2), *n.* act of wrestling; contest between two wrestlers; (*fig.*) struggle. WRESTLER, *n.* one who wrestles; one who earns a living by wrestling. WRESTLING, *n.* sport in which wrestlers engage, skill of a trained or professional wrestler. [OE.].

WRETCH [rech], *n.* one afflicted by poverty or other misery; person miserably unhappy; contemptible person, mean rascal. [OE.].

WRETCHED [re'chid], *adj.* unfortunate, miserable, unhappy, desperately poor or distressed; having no good qualities, lacking all or any comfort or decency, squalid, utterly undesirable; of very poor quality, contemptible, worthless. [*Prec.*].

WRIGGLE (1) [ri'gl], *v.t. and i.* to twist about to and fro, writhe or squirm; (*fig.*) endeavour to avoid the main issue; cause to wriggle, make twist about; **to w. out of,** to get out of by wriggling; cleverly to avoid committing oneself, evade, on a vital point of discussion. WRIGGLE (2), *n.* act of wriggling, writhing or squirming movement. WRIGGLER, *n.* person who or thing which wriggles; one who evades or tries to evade something. [~LGerm.].

WRIGHT [rit], *n.* (*archaic and dial. except in compounds*) maker, fashioner of things, *esp.* ships, wheels, carts and plays. [OE.].

WRING (1) (*pret. and p.pt.* **wrung**) [ring], *v.t.* to squeeze by twisting very tightly; grasp and squeeze; (*fig.*) (of an appeal to the feelings) penetrate, hurt with poignancy; get (out of) by wringing. WRING (2), *n.* act of one who wrings; similar accomplishment by a machine. WRINGER, *n.* that which wrings; device for partly drying wet fabrics by squeezing them between rollers. WRINGING, *adj.* in the phrase **wringing wet,** so wet that water could easily be wrung out. [OE.].

WRINKLE (1) [ring'kl], *n.* small crease or furrow, *esp.* on the face; clever trick, hint. WRINKLE (2), *v.t. and i.* to make or become wrinkly; **to w. up,** to contract so that the surface becomes puckered; contract and become wrinkly. [OE.].

WRIST (1) [rist], *n.* narrow joint between the hand and arm in human beings; any similar joint in other animals; lower end of a sleeve. WRIST-WATCH, watch worn on the w., and attached by a strap or bracelet. WRIST (2), WRISTY, *adj.* (*cricket and other games*) done by suppleness of the w. [OE.].

WRISTBAND [rist'band], *n.* cuff of a shirt or other garment.

WRISTLET (1) [rist'let], *n.* bracelet or strap for the wrist. WRISTLET (2), *adj.* fastened by a w.

WRIT (1) [rit], *n.* (*leg.*) document containing royal instructions or instructions issued, *esp.* under royal authority; † something written; **Holy W.,** the Bible. [OE.].

WRIT † (2), *pret. and p.pt. of* WRITE.

WRITE (*pret.* **wrote,** *p.pt.* **written**) [rit], *v.t. and i.* to mark paper etc. with symbols, letters, words etc.; produce literary works; communicate by letter; set down on paper etc.; set down and publish in a book; cover with words, symbols etc.; draw up, complete, in writing; **to w. down,** to set down in written characters; describe with less than the truth; reduce in value, simplify to excess; **to w. off,** to liquidate, cancel; **to w. for,** to send for by letter; **to w. up,** to describe in detail, give a glowing account of; bring up to date; **to w. out,** to copy out in a clear, fair hand. WRITE-UP, (*coll.*) written account of something, *esp.* journalistic and in favourable terms. [OE.].

WRITER [ri'ter], *n.* one who writes, *esp.* one who writes books, essays etc.; (*nav.*) clerk; **w. to the signet,** (*Scots leg.*) solicitor; **w.'s cramp,** cramp in the hand produced by a long spell of writing. WRITERSHIP, *n.* position of a clerk or writer.

WRITHE (1) [riTH], *v.t. and i.* to twist and turn this way and that; cause to do this. WRITHE (2), *n.* movement or part of the movement of one who writhes. [OE.].

WRITING [ri'ting], *n.* action of a writer, art of penmanship; the characters and their style in any written document; document or inscription; act of setting down in literary form, authorship. WRITING-BOOK, book of blank or ruled pages for w. in; book containing w. exercises. WRITING-CASE, receptacle for pens, ink, paper etc. WRITING-DESK, desk or box for w. at. WRITING-INK, ink for use with a pen but not with type. WRITING-PAPER, paper which is properly glazed for w. upon. WRITING-TABLE, table suitably shaped and fitted for use as a desk.

WRITTEN [ri'ten], *adj.* expressed in writing; penned, as opposed to printed or typed. [*P.pt. of* WRITE].

WRONG (1) [rong], *adj.* not right, not just and good, sinful, vicious; inaccurate, not true; not well ordered; not as was intended; **w. end of the stick,** false impression; **w. side,** that side of a fabric etc. which is turned inward and not intended to be seen; **to be on the w. side of,** to have incurred the hostility of; **w. 'un,** (*coll.*) person of criminal tendencies. WRONG-HEADED, obstinately mistaken, stubborn, deliberately perverse. WRONG (2), *adv.* wrongly; **to go w.,** to break down, cease to operate, turn out badly. WRONG (3), *n.* that which is w.; injustice, unkindness, vicious act (against somebody); evil, wickedness; **to do w.,** to commit sin. WRONG (4), *v.t.* to do violence or w. to, act unjustly or unkindly to; accuse falsely. [OE.].

WRONGDOER [rong-dōo'er], *n.* one who does what is wrong, sinner.

WRONGFUL [rong'fōol], *adj.* wicked, unfair, mistaken; (*leg.*) adversely affecting another's rights.

WROTE [rōt], *pret. of* WRITE. [OE.].

WROTH † [rōth, roth], *adj.* very angry. [OE.].

WROUGHT (1) [rawt], *archaic pret. and p.pt. of* WORK. WROUGHT (2), *adj.* fashioned by beating, and not in a mould. WROUGHT-IRON, *adj.* made of w. iron. [OE.].

WRUNG [rung], *pret. and p.pt. of* WRING (1). [OE.].

WRY [ri], *adj.* twisted or contorted; **w. face,** face for the moment wrinkled up to express disapproval or discomfort. WRY-NECKED, having a deformed or stiff neck. [ME.].

WRYNECK [ri'nek], *n.* a bird, the *Iynx torquilla*; a bent neck. [*Prec.*].

WYANDOTTE [wi'an-dot], *n.* breed of U.S. poultry of medium size. [*W*yandotte tribe of Red Indians].

WYCH-, WITCH-ELM [wich'elm], *n.* a variety of elm. [OE. and ELM].

WYCH-, WITCH-HAZEL [wich'hā-zel], *n.* a North American shrub yielding an astringent extract. [OE. and HAZEL].

WYKEHAMIST (1) [wi'ka-mist], *n.* present or former pupil of Winchester College. WYKEHAMIST (2), *adj.* of, or pertaining to, Winchester or Wykehamists. [William of *W*ykeham, founder].

WYND [wind], *n.* (*Scots*) narrow walled alley. [~OE.].

WYVERN, see WIVERN.

ōō is pronounced as in f*oo*d; ŏŏ as in h*oo*d; th as in *think*; TH as in *that*; zh as in azure. ~ = related to.

X [eks], twenty-fourth letter of the English alphabet; symbol for ten in Roman figures; an unknown quantity in mathematics; anything unknown.

XANTIPPE [zan-ti′pi], *n.* bad-tempered woman, shrew. [*Xantippe*, wife of Socrates].

XEBEC, ZEBEC(K) [zē′bek], *n.* small Mediterranean sailing vessel. [Span.].

XENO- [ze′nō], *pref.* pertaining to things outside, to foreigners or to hospitality.

XENOMANIA [ze-nō-mā′ni-ah], *n.* excessive admiration for foreign people and things. [XENO and MANIA].

XENON [ze′non], *n.* (*chem.*) the inert gaseous element denoted by Xe. [Gk.].

XENOPHOBE [ze′no-fōb], *n. and adj.* (person) hating foreigners. [XENO and Gk.].

XENOPHOBIA [ze-nō-fō′bi-ah], *n.* hatred of foreigners or things foreign. [XENO and PHOBIA].

XMAS, *written abbreviation of* CHRISTMAS.

X-RAY (1) [eks-rā′], *adj.* pertaining to, made by, x-rays. X-RAY (2), *v.t.* to examine, photograph or treat by means of x-rays.

X-RAYS [eks-rāz′], *n.(pl.)* rays, called also Röntgen rays, which are found in the spectrum beyond the ultra-violet and which can penetrate matter opaque to light-rays.

XYL(O)-, *pref.* pertaining to wood. [Gk.].

XYLOCARP [zi′lō-kahp], *n.* fruit which is hard and woody; tree which bears such fruit. [XYLO- and Gk.].

XYLONITE [zi′lō-nit], *n.* celluloid. [~Gk.].

XYLOPHONE [zi′lō-fōn], *n.* musical instrument consisting of a series of wooden bars, each sounding a different note when struck. XYLOPHONIST [zi-lo′fonist, zi′lō-fō-nist], *n.* player of the x. [XYLO and Gk.].

Y [wi], twenty-fifth letter of the English alphabet; anything resembling this in shape.

YACCA-WOOD [ya′ka-wood], *n.* wood of a small West Indian tree. [Native].

YACHT (1) [yot], *n.* light sailing vessel; private vessel for sport or pleasure. YACHT-CLUB, club of persons interested in yachting. YACHT (2), *v.i.* to sail a y. YACHTING, *n.* craft of sailing a y.; practice of sailing a y. for pleasure or racing. [Du.].

YACHTSMAN [yots′man], *n.* one who sails a yacht.

YAH, *int. expressing defiance, contempt.*

YAHOO [yah-hōō′], *n.* member of an imaginary race of creatures, resembling human beings in form, but filthy and animal-like in habits, described in Swift's *Gulliver's Travels*; human being resembling this. [Coined by Swift].

YAHWEH [yah′vā], *n.* deity of the Jews, Jehovah. [Heb.].

YAK [yak], *n.* long-haired bovine animal found in Central Asia. [Tibetan].

YAM [yam], *n.* plant of the tropical genus *Dioscorea*; edible tuber of any such plant. [African].

YANK (1) [yangk], *n. and adj.* (*slang*) Yankee.

YANK (2), *v.t. and i.* (*coll.*) to give a yank or tug to, pull. YANK (3), *n.* (*coll.*) sharp pull or tug. [Unkn.].

YANKEE (1) [yang′ki], *n.* American living in New England, *esp.* of the stock of original settlers, or in the northern states generally; an American. YANKEE (2), *adj.* American. YANKEEFIED, *adj.* made to resemble the corresponding thing in the U.S.; having acquired the characteristics of a Y. YANKEEISM, *n.* a Y. habit or mannerism; U.S. customs in general. [Uncert.].

YAOURT, YOGH(O)URT [yah′awt, yo′gōort, yō′gōort], *n.* a Near Eastern preparation of fermented milk. [Turk.].

YAP (1) [yap], *v.i.* to utter yaps; (*coll., slang*) chatter. YAP (2), *n.* quick excited bark from a dog. [Echoic].

YAPOCK [ya′pok], *n.* water opossum found in South America. [R. *Oyapok* in Brazil].

YAPON [yaw′pon], *n.* North American evergreen from the leaves of which a tea can be brewed which acts as a purgative. [Native].

YAPP [yap], *n.* manner of bookbinding in limp leather so that the edges of the cover project beyond the leaves. [*Yapp*, bookseller].

YARBOROUGH [yah′bu-rer], *n.* hand of cards containing nothing higher than nine. [Earl of *Yarborough*, who betted against the occurrence of so poor a hand].

YARD (1) [yahd], *n.* a length measure of three feet; this length of anything; (in a sailing ship) subsidiary pole fastened at an angle to the mast and carrying the sails. YARD-ARM, (*naut.*) either half of a y. as measured from the mast. YARD-MEASURE, stick a y. long with lesser measurements marked on it. YARD-STICK, y.-measure; (*fig.*) a basis of comparison. YARDAGE (1), *n.* number of yards anything measures, *esp.* the aggregate of textile production; payment by the y. for hewing coal. [OE.].

YARD (2), *n.* enclosure, often paved, near a house or farm; any similar enclosed space; space adjoining industrial buildings or plant, or for assembling and distributing goods trains etc.; **the Y.**, Scotland Y., the London Metropolitan Police headquarters. YARDAGE (2), *n.* right to put cattle in a stockyard; cost of this. YARDMAN, *n.* one who works in a (railway) y. YARDMASTER, *n.* official in charge of a (railway) y. [OE.].

YARN (1) [yahn], *n.* woven fibre for cloth, rope etc.; (*coll.*) story, anecdote, *esp.* an exaggerated tale; comfortable talk or chat. YARN (2), *v.i.* (*coll.*) to tell stories, talk in a friendly and informal fashion. [OE.].

YARROW [ya′rō], *n.* the plant *Achillea millefolium*, otherwise called milfoil. [OE.].

YARWHELP [yah′welp], *n.* name given in the Provinces to both the bar-tailed godwit and the black-tailed godwit. [Uncert.].

YASHMAK [yahsh′mahk], *n.* veil covering the face from beneath the eyes down, as worn by Mohammedan women. [Arab.].

YATE [yāt], *n.* name given to two varieties of Australian gum-tree. [Native].

YAW (1) [yaw], *v.i.* (*naut., aeron.*) to follow an uncertain, wavering course. YAW (2), *n.* (*naut.*) action of yawing. [~OIcel.].

YAWL [yawl], *n.* small sailing ship equipped with a mainmast and a jigger and built like a cutter; small rowing boat, ship's boat. [Du.].

YAWN (1) [yawn], *v.i.* to open the mouth wide and breathe in and out as when sleepy; gape wide open. YAWN (2), *n.* act of yawning. [~OE.].

YAWP [yawp], *v.i.* (*U.S. and dial.*) to cry out, yelp; talk noisy nonsense. [Echoic].

YAWS [yawz], *n.* contagious tropical disease caused by a protozoan parasite. [Uncert.].

YE † (1) [yē], *pron.* 2nd person pl. *of* YOU. [OE.].

YE † (2) [THē, yē], *def. art.* (*pseudo-archaic*) the. [Initial *y* is a misreading of a similarly shaped letter formerly used for *th*].

YEA [yā], *int.* (*archaic*) yes. [OE.].

YEAR [yēer], *n.* that length of time in which the earth travels once round the sun, reckoned as 365 days, but more accurately 365¼ days; space of 365 or 366 days; **leap y.**, y. of 366 days occurring as every fourth y.;

a y. and a day, (legal) formula to make certain that a whole y. elapses; **y. by y.,** every y.; **y. in and y. out,** y. after y. successively, with monotonous regularity and seeming endlessness; **full of years,** (bibl., archaic) very old. YEAR-BOOK, reference book issued in a revised edition each y. YEARLONG, adj. lasting a full y. [O.E.].

YEARLING (1) [yēer'ling], n. animal (esp. a race-horse) in its second year. YEARLING (2), adj. being one year old.

YEARLY (1) [yēer'li], adj. annual. YEARLY (2), adv. year by year, annually.

YEARN [yurn], v.i. to desire greatly; **to y. for,** to feel a deep love or longing for. [O.E.].

YEARNING (1) [yur'ning], n. desire or longing. YEARNING (2), adj. desirous, expressing desire. [Prec.].

YEAST [yēst], n. pungent yellow fungus organism which, when mingled with sugary fluid, causes fermentation; the same substance when it has been dried for preservation. YEASTY, adj. pertaining to, like, y.; (fig.) frothy, verbose, restless, pointless. [O.E.].

YELL (1) [yel], v.t. and i. to scream, cry, howl very loudly; laugh very loudly; say loudly and excitedly. YELL (2), n. noise made when someone yells. YELLING, n. act of uttering a y.; loud outcry. [O.E.].

YELLOW (1) [ye'lō], adj. having the colour of butter, gold etc.; belonging to a Mongolian race; (U.S. slang) cowardly, mean; **y. fever,** an infectious tropical fever marked by jaundice; **y. jack,** y. fever; **y. press,** highly sensational news publications, and the organizations behind them. YELLOW-EARTH, a clay pigment producing a y. colour. YELLOW-HAMMER, a y.-feathered bird. YELLOW (2), n. one of the primary colours, which, in combination with blue, makes green, or with red, orange; pigment giving this colour; (fig.) yolk of an egg. YELLOWISH, YELLOWY, adj. somewhat y. [O.E.].

YELP (1) [yelp], n. short, high-pitched bark. YELP (2), v.i. to give out a y. YELPER, n. one who yelps. [O.E.].

YEN (1) [yen], n. Japanese coin worth, at par, a little more than two shillings. [Jap.].

YEN (2), n. (U.S. slang) an urge or desire. [Unkn.].

YEOMAN (pl. **yeomen**) [yō'man, 'men], n. (hist.) superior attendant in a royal or lordly household; small freeholder or farmer; member of a mounted force of men of this rank; **Yeomen of the Guard,** royal bodyguard now stationed at the Tower of London; **y. service,** invaluable aid. YEOMANLY, adj. befitting a y. [ME.].

YEOMANRY [yō'man-ri], n. (milit.) volunteer cavalry force formerly recruited from the class of small farmers; yeomen and small landholders in general.

YEP [yep], int. (U.S. vulg.) yes. [~YES].

YERCUM [yur'kum], n. a shrub found in the East Indies, the bark of which is used to make a fibre; this fibre. [Tamil].

YES [yes], int. expressing agreement or affirmation; used interrogatively, expressing a desire for further information. YES-MAN, (U.S. slang) docile, characterless fellow who never dares to disagree. [O.E.].

YESTER [yes'ter], pref. (archaic) relating to yesterday; preceding, last before this. [O.E.].

YESTERDAY (1) [yes'ter-dā], adv. on the day before this one. YESTERDAY (2), n. the day before this one. [O.E.].

YESTREEN [yes-trēn'] adv. and n. (archaic) yesterday evening. [MScots].

YET (1) [yet], adv. until and including this moment, still; at this moment and for some time into the future; .... **nor y.,** and not even, and not so much as; **as y.,** up to the present, so far. YET (2), conj. moreover, in addition, nevertheless. [O.E.].

YEW (1) [yōō], n. an evergreen conifer; the wood of this tree. YEW (2), adj. made of y. wood. [O.E.].

Y-GUN [wī'gun], n. (nav.) gun with two barrels set at an angle. [Y and GUN].

YID [yid], n. (slang) a Jew. [Next].

YIDDISH (1) [yi'dish], n. Judaized form of German written in Hebrew characters and containing a considerable Slavonic element. YIDDISH (2), adj. pertaining to or in Y. [Germ.].

YIELD (1) [yēld], v.t. and i. to produce, give forth, generate (implying profitable production); surrender, give up willingly; provide produce or profit; surrender, admit defeat; move, withdraw, bend back under physical pressure. YIELD (2), n. profit, produce, crop. [O.E.].

YIELDING [yēl'ding], adj. compliant, submissive, ready to surrender; pliant, flexible.

YODEL (1) [yō'del], v.t. and i. to sing in alternately natural and falsetto pitch in the Tyrolean manner. YODEL (2), n. any musical phrase sung in alternate natural and falsetto pitch. [Germ.].

YOGA [yō'gah], n. meditative Hindu philosophy which aims at uniting the individual soul with the universal spirit. [Hind.].

YOGHOURT, see YAOURT.

YOGI [yō'gi], n. Hindu who practises yoga. [Hind.].

YO-HEAVE-HO [yō-hēv-hō'], int. (naut.) shout of sailors working a capstan.

YOHO [yō-hō'], int. (naut.) shout of sailors working a capstan; also used to attract attention.

YOICKS [yoiks], int. hunting cry. [Unkn.].

YOKE (1) [yōk], n. wooden crosspiece put over the shoulders of cattle used for draught; anything like this; that part of a garment which fits the shoulders; pair of oxen harnessed together for ploughing; (fig.) authority, rule, obligation, tyranny. YOKE-FELLOW, companion in toil. YOKE (2), v.t. to harness with a y.; (fig.) join in the same bond or servitude. [O.E.].

YOKEL [yō'kel], n. a rustic. [Uncert.].

YOLK (1) [yōk], n. yellow middle part of an egg. YOLKY (1), adj. like y. [O.E.].

YOLK (2), n. oily secretion which keeps the wool of the sheep soft, lanolin. YOLKY (2), adj. greasy with y. [O.E.].

YON (1) [yon], adj. that over there. YON (2), adv. over yonder. [O.E.].

YONDER (1) [yon'der], adj. situated over there. YONDER (2), adv. over there. [ME.].

YONKER, see YOUNKER.

YORE [yaw(r)], n. times past; **days of y.,** bygone times. [O.E.].

YORK [yawk], n. name of the county town of Yorkshire used to designate certain goods produced there, as **Y. ham, Y. paving** etc. YORKIST, n. (hist.) supporter of the House of Y. during the Wars of the Roses. [ON.].

YORKER [yaw'ker], n. (cricket) ball pitching just under the bat. [Unkn.].

YORKSHIRE [yawk'sher], adj. belonging to Yorkshire; **Y. pudding,** light savoury batter pudding; **to come the Y. on,** (coll.) to dupe, hoax.

YOU [yōō], pron. 2nd person sg. and pl.; also used indef. anyone. [O.E.].

YOUNG (1) [yung], adj. having lived for a short while, being comparatively recently born; not yet in middle age; of or pertaining to children and adolescents; energetic, youthful; (fig.) recent, recently begun; lacking knowledge or experience. YOUNG (2), n. y. people in general, children, offspring. YOUNGISH, adj. rather y. [O.E.].

YOUNGLING [yung'ling], n. (archaic) young creature, child.

YOUNGSTER [yung'ster], n. lad, child, boy.

YO(U)NKER [yung'ker], n. (coll.) young man. [MDu.].

YOUR [yōor, yaw(r)], possessive adj. belonging to or connected with you; (used indefinitely) such a one as would be commonly imagined. [O.E.].

YOURS [yōorz, yawz], pron. possessive 2nd person sg. and pl. belonging or pertaining to you.

YOURSELF (pl. **yourselves**) [yaw-self', -selvz'], pron. reflex. and emphatic form of YOU.

YOUTH [yōōth], n. condition of being young; period when a person is young, that is, between childhood and manhood or womanhood; period of early manhood or womanhood; young person, esp. a young man; strength, activity, vigour; young men and women; **Y. Hostel,** country hostel for the use of young persons on tour. [O.E.].

YOUTHFUL [yōōth'fool], adj. young; having the qualities of youth. [O.E.].

YOWL (1) [yowl], v.i. (of various creatures) to utter a wailing cry. YOWL (2), n. cry of an animal which is yowling. [ME.].

YO-YO [yō'yō], n. toy consisting of a grooved disk spinning up and down a length of string.

YTTRIA [it'ri-ah], n. (chem.) a white oxide of yttrium.

YTTRIFEROUS [it-ri'fe-rōos], adj. (chem.) containing yttrium.

YTTRIUM [it'ri-um], n. (chem.) a rare metallic element denoted by Yt. [Ytterby in Sweden].

YUCCA [yu'kah], n. genus of American shrubs which belong to the lily family. [Native].

YULE [yōōl], n. the festival and festivities of Christmas. YULE-LOG, large log of wood burnt at Christmas. YULETIDE, n. Christmas time. [IOcel.].

ōō is pronounced as in food; ŏŏ as in hood; th as in think; TH as in that; zh as in azure. ~ = related to.

Z

Z [zed], twenty-sixth and last letter of the English alphabet.

ZANY [zā'ni], *n*. idiot, fool; (*hist*.) comic actor who appeared with the principal comedian and imitated him. ZANYISM, *n*. state of being a z., comic tricks of a z. [It.].

ZARATHUSTRIAN [zah-rah-thŏŏs'tri-an], *adj. and n*. Zoroastrian. [*Zarathustra*, founder of Zoroastrianism].

ZEAL [zēl], *n*. unflagging and uncompromising enthusiasm, ardour. [Gk.].

ZEALOT [ze'lot], *n*. fanatic, over-enthusiastic supporter. ZEALOTRY, *n*. conduct of a z. [Gk.].

ZEALOUS [ze'lŏŏs], *adj*. actuated by, expressing zeal. [MedL.].

ZEBEC(K), see XEBEC.

ZEBRA [zeb'rah], *n*. striped South African ungulate quadruped. [Congolese].

ZEBU [zē'bŏŏ], *n*. humped ox found in Asia, and domesticated. [Tibetan].

ZED [zed], *n*. the letter Z. [Gk.].

ZEITGEIST [tsīt'gīst], *n*. the characteristic spirit of an age. [Germ.].

ZELOSO [se-lō'sō], *adj*. (*mus*.) with fervour. [It.].

ZEMINDAR, ZAMINDAR [ze-mēn'dah(r)], *n*. in Northern India, a tenant who pays rent for his land direct to the government. [Pers.].

ZEND [zend], *n*. an ancient Aryan language, a form of Old Persian.

ZEND-AVESTA [zend-ah-ves'tah], *n*. the sacred scriptures of the Parsees. [Pers.].

ZENITH [ze'nith], *n*. that point in the heavens vertically above any point on the earth; (*fig*.) highest point (of achievement, excitement, growth etc.), peak, apex. [Fr. from Arab.].

ZEPHYR [ze'fer], *n*. the west wind; any warm and gentle breeze. [Gk.].

ZEPPELIN [ze'pe-lin], *n*. large German dirigible balloon. [Count *Zeppelin* the inventor].

ZERO [zēer'ō], *n*. nought, nothing; the Arabic figure 0; (*arith*.) that amount of which any increase is positive (or plus) and any decrease negative (or minus); that point on a thermometric scale immediately preceding the minimum recognized degree of heat; similar point on any other scale; (*fig*.) lowest point, state of being nothing; **z. hour**, time at which an attack is to start. [It. from Arab.].

ZEST [zest], *n*. appetizing flavour, piquancy; (*fig*.) eagerness, enthusiasm. [OFr.].

ZETA (1) [zē'tah], *n*. sixth letter of the Greek alphabet. [Gk.]. ZETA (2), experimental device for obtaining great heat by the fusion of hydrogen atoms. [Zero Energy Thermonuclear Assembly].

ZEUGMA [zyŏŏg'mah], *n*. grammatical figure by which a word is made to agree with, or to apply to, two substantives when strictly it should agree with, or be applied to, only one of them. [Gk.].

ZEUS [zyŏŏs], *n*. the supreme deity of Ancient Greek mythology. [Gk.].

ZIGZAG (1) [zig'zag], *n*. a crooked line turning from side to side with sharp angles. ZIGZAG (2), *adj*. resembling a z. ZIGZAG (3), *adv*. in the manner, along the course, of a z. ZIGZAG (4) (*pres.pt*. ZIGZAGGING, *pret. and p.pt*. ZIGZAGGED), *v.t. and i*. to pursue the course of a z.; shape like a z.; decorate with zigzags. [Germ.].

ZINC (1) [zingk], *n*. white metallic element denoted by Zn. ZINC (2), *adj*. made of z. ZINC (3), *v.t.* to give a coat of z. to. [Germ.].

ZINCO-, *pref*. pertaining to zinc.

ZINCOGRAPHY [zing-ko'gra-fi], *n*. technique of printing from zinc plates. ZINCOGRAPH [zing'kografi], *n*. picture made by z. [ZINCO and Gk.].

ZINNIA [zi'ni-ah], *n*. (*bot*.) annual composite garden plant with brightly coloured flowers. [J. G. *Zinn*, German botanist].

ZION [zi'on], *n*. a hill in Jerusalem; (*fig*.) city o Jerusalem; Judaism; Christianity; paradise; Nonconformist chapel. ZIONISM, *n*. movement which established a Jewish National State of Israel. [Eccles. L. from Heb.].

ZIP (1) [zip], *n*. a rippling or whizzing noise; z.-fastener;

(*coll*.) vigour, energy; liveliness, quickness. ZIP-FASTENER, joining device consisting of a row of small metal teeth along each of the edges to be joined, which are interlocked by pulling them through a Y-shaped metal rider and unlocked by pulling the rider the other way. ZIP (2), *v.t.* to fasten with a z-fastener. ZIPPER, *n*. z.-fastener. ZIPPY, *adj*. (*coll*.) lively, energetic. [Echoic].

ZIRCON [zur'kon], *n*. (*min*.) native crystalline silicate of zirconium. [Pers.].

ZIRCONIUM [zer-kō'ni-um], *n*. metallic element Zr. obtained from zircon.

ZITHER [zi'THER], *n*. (*mus*.) instrument with horizontal strings over a sounding-board, played by plucking. ZITHERIST, *n*. performer on a z. [Germ.].

ZODIAC [zō'di-ak], *n*. (*astrol*.) section of the heavens in which the orbits of the chief celestial bodies lie, and which is divided into twelve sections called, and represented by, signs. [Gk.].

ZOETROPE [zō'i-trōp], *n*. cylinder with vertical slits in it through which a revolving roller, painted with successive and slightly different representations of a figure in motion, can be seen. [Gk.].

ZOLLVEREIN [tsol'fe-rīn], *n*. an economic agreement between a group of nations by which they raise no tariffs against each other and have a uniform rate against other powers. [Germ.].

ZONAL [zō'nal], *adj*. relating to zones, divided into zones.

ZONE (1) [zōn], *n*. † girdle; part of the surface of a sphere in the form of a belt; one of the five climatic divisions of the earth, torrid, north and south temperate, and north and south frigid. ZONE (2), *v.t.* to divide into, mark with, zones; restrict the distribution of (goods) to certain zones of a country. ZONING, *n*. act of dividing (a country etc.) into zones for purposes of manufacture, building, transport etc. [Gk.].

ZOO [zŏŏ], *n*. a collection of animals in confinement for exhibition and study. [ZOO(LOGICAL) Gardens].

ZOO-, *pref*. pertaining to animals. [Gk.].

ZOOLOGICAL [zō-o-lo'ji-kal], *adj*. relating to zoology.

ZOOLOGY [zō-o'lo-ji], *n*. science which is concerned with the form, structure, habits etc., of animals. ZOOLOGIST, *n*. student of z. [Gk.].

ZOOM [zŏŏm], *v.t. and i*. to cause (an aeroplane) to mount sharply and quickly; pursue such a course in an aeroplane; emit a noise like an aeroplane doing this; (*fig*.) be a great success, sell quickly and at a high price etc. [Echoic].

ZOOPHYTE [zō'ō-fīt], *n*. animal which resembles a plant in appearance. [Gk.].

ZOROASTRIAN (1) [zo-rō-as'tri-an], *adj*. relating to *Zoroaster* and the religion he founded. ZOROASTRIAN (2), *n*. follower of Zoroaster, founder of the Parsee religion. ZOROASTRIANISM, *n*. religion of Zoroaster.

ZOUAVE [zŏŏ'ahv], *n*. French light infantryman belonging to a regiment at one time recruited in Algeria, and formerly wearing an eastern uniform. [Fr.].

ZOUNDS [zowndz], *int*. (*archaic*) a mild expletive. [Short for *God's wounds*].

ZULU [zŏŏ'lŏŏ], *n. and adj*. a member of, pertaining to, certain native South African tribes of Bantu stock; their language. [Native].

ZYGO- [zī'gō], *pref*. yoke-shaped, going in twos. [Gk.].

ZYGOTE [zī'gōt], *n*. (*biol*.) the cell arising when two cells conjugate in reproduction. [Gk.].

ZYMOLOGY [zī-mo'lo-ji], *n*. study of ferments and fermentation. [Gk.].

ZYMOSIS [zī-mō'sis], *n*. fermentation; action of germs or a disease regarded as akin to fermentation. [Gk.].

ZYMOTIC [zī-mo'tik], *adj*. relating to diseases when regarded as similar to fermentation in their development. [Gk.].

ZYMURGY [zī'mer-ji], *n*. chemistry of brewing, distilling and wine-making, the commercial branch of zymology. [Gk.].

The accent ' after a syllable = stress (u-pon'). The mark ‾ over a vowel = length (ā in made; ō in bone).